Ethn   ue

Volu 2

Maps and Indexes

To the Fourteenth Edition of the Ethnologue
Barbara F. Grimes, Editor

For Reference

Not to be taken from this re

SIL International
Dallas, Texas

Maps by

Irene Tucker, Bernard Wafukho, Matt Benjamin
Global Mapping International

Graphic Artist

Francisco Afanador

Previous editions

First edition	1951
Second edition	1951
Third edition	1952
Fourth edition	1953
Fifth edition	1958
Sixth edition	1965
Seventh edition	1969
Eighth edition	1974
Ninth edition	1978
Tenth edition	1984
Eleventh edition	1988
Twelfth edition	1992
Thirteenth edition	1996
Fourteenth edition	2000

ISBN 1–55671–106–9 (Set)
ISBN 1–55671–103–4 (Volume 1)
ISBN 1–55671–104–2 (Volume 2)
ISBN 1–55671–105–0 (CD)

Additional copies of *Ethnologue Vol 2: Maps and Indexes*, plus the Ethnologue *Vol 1: Languages of the World* may be obtained from

SIL International
International Academic Bookstore
7500 West Camp Wisdom Road
Dallas, Texas 75236-5699 USA

Voice	(972) 708–7404
Fax	(972) 708–7363
Internet	academic_books@sil.org
Web	http//www.sil.org

TABLE OF CONTENTS

Introduction v

Maps 1
   World map 2
   Africa maps 5
   Americas maps 61
   Asia maps 103
   Europe maps 151
   Pacific maps 165

Names Index 189

Family Index 583
   Afro-Asiatic (372) 585
   Alacalufan (2) 592
   Algic (40) 592
   Altaic (65) 593
   Amto-Musan (2) 594
   Andamanese (13) 594
   Arauan (8) 594
   Araucanian (2) 594
   Arawakan (60) 594
   Artificial Language (3) 595
   Arutani-Sape (2) 595
   Australian (258) 595
   Austro-Asiatic (168) 600
   Austronesian (1262) 604
   Aymaran (3) 630
   Barbacoan (7) 630
   Basque (3) 631
   Bayono-Awbono (2) 631
   Caddoan (5) 631
   Cahuapanan (2) 631
   Carib (29) 631
   Chapacura-Wanham (5) 632
   Chibchan (2) 632
   Chimakuan (1) 632
   Choco (10) 632
   Chon (2) 632
   Chukotko-Kamchatkan (5) 632
   Chumach (7) 632
   Coahuiltecan (1) 633
   Creole (81) 633
   Deaf sign language (114) 634
   Dravidian (75) 636
   East Bird's Head (3) 637
   East Papuan (36) 637
   Eskimo-Aleut (11) 638
   Geelvink Bay (33) 638
   Gulf (4) 639
   Hmong-Mien (32) 639
   Hokan (28) 640
   Huavean (4) 640
   Indo-European (443) 641
   Iroquoian (10) 649
   Japanese (12) 649
   Jivaroan (4) 650

Katukinan (3) 650
Keres (2) 650
Khoisan (29) 650
Kiowa Tanoan (6) 650
Kwomtari-Baibai (6) 651
Language Isolate (28) 651
Left May (7) 651
Lower Mamberamo (2) 651
Lule-Vilela (1) 651
Macro-Ge (32) 651
Maku (6) 652
Mascoian (5) 652
Mataco-Guaicuru (11) 652
Mayan (69) 653
Misumalpan (4) 654
Mixe-Zoque (16) 654
Mixed Languages (8) 654
Mosetenan (1) 654
Mura (1) 654
Muskogean (6) 655
Na-Dene (47) 655
Nambiquaran (5) 656
Niger-Congo (1489) 656
Nilo-Saharan (199) 687
North Caucasian (34) 691
Oto-Manguean (172) 692
Paezan (1) 695
Panoan (30) 695
Peba-Yaguan (2) 695
Penutian (33) 695
Pidgin (17) 696
Quechuan (46) 696
Salishan (27) 697
Salivan (2) 698
Sepik-Ramu (104) 698
Sign language (2) 700
Sino-Tibetan (365) 700
Siouan (17) 707
Sko (7) 707
South Caucasian (5) 708
Subtiaba-Tlapanec (4) 708
Tacanan (6) 708
Tai-Kadai (70) 708
Tarascan (2) 709
Torricelli (48) 709
Totonacan (11) 709
Trans-New Guinea (552) 710
Tucanoan (25) 721
Tupi (70) 722
Unclassified (96) 723
Uralic (38) 725
Uru-Chipaya (2) 725
Uto-Aztecan (62) 725
Wakashan (5) 727
West Papuan (26) 727
Witotoan (6) 727
Yanomam (4) 728

Yenisei Ostyak (2) 728
Yukaghir (2) 728
Yuki (2) 728
Zamucoan (2) 728

Zaparoan (7) 728

Bibliography **729**

Introduction

Maps. The maps were created using software from Global Mapping International (GMI). Geography data is from Global Ministry Mapping System 1997. Language locations data is from World Language Mapping System 1997. The representation of international and language boundaries is not necessarily authoritative. No political statement is intended by any language or international boundaries placed on any map. Permission to reproduce these maps in any print, electronic, or other medium must be obtained in writing from SIL International.

The producers of the maps wish to acknowledge the help of many people in the revision process for the maps in this volume. These include the staff at GMI, Jan Tissing, Marco Evenhuis, Claude Buchli, Jarmo Hupli, Jerry Edmonson, Georges P. Carillet, Nigel Statham, Roger Blench, and Clive H. Beaumont. We also wish to thank the many people within SIL who have corrected and commented on the work as it has progressed through many stages.

Language Name Index. This is a computer-produced index of 41,806 entries to the names that are associated with the 6,809 languages listed in *Ethnologue, Volume 1: Languages of the World*, Fourteenth Edition, 2000. It identifies all the language names and their alternates, and all the dialect names and their alternates. For each language it gives its main name, its three-letter Language Identification Code, the country with which the language is most centrally identified, and other countries where it is spoken. For alternate names and dialect names it gives the main language name they go with, and its Language Identification Code.

We have followed our sources in using conventional symbols for 'click' sounds, such as /, //, !, and ", used to write Khoisan languages and a few others in southern Africa. The Semitic pharyngeal commonly called <*ain* or <*ayin* is represented inconsistently, but when it is given it is represented with < in both the Language Name Index and the Language Family Index.

Language Family Index. This is a computer produced index to the language families that are associated with the languages listed in *Ethnologue, Volume 1: Languages of the World*, Fourteenth Edition, 2000. For each language it gives the main name, its three-letter Language Identification Code, the country with which the language is most centrally identified, and the language family under which it is currently classified, from the most comprehensive grouping down to the smallest. From this listing the reader can go directly to the main entry in the *Ethnologue* itself, which in turn points to entries for the same language in other countries if there are any.

As in volume 1 of the *Ethnologue*, the criterion for listing speech varieties separately is low intelligibility, as far as that can be ascertained. Some scholars prefer to keep dialect chains and networks unbroken; it is more consistent with what we now know about such configurations, however, to partition them into optimal clusters within which intelligibility is high and between which intelligibility is low (J. Grimes 1989, 1995). Volume 1 of the *Ethnologue* lists speech varieties that show high intelligibility with some central variety as dialects within a single entry; the dialects do not appear in this language family index.

The classification scheme used here is largely that of the Oxford University Press *International Encyclopedia of Linguistics*, William O. Bright, editor in chief, which appeared in 1992. As the co-editors for Language Identification, we worked closely with Bright, Bernard Comrie, and the other editors to achieve a reasonable representation for the *Encyclopedia* of what is known about language families of the world. The classification information in the present edition still reflects the scheme followed in the *Encyclopedia* fairly closely, but incorporates some more recent classifications. The *Ethnologue* goes into greater low level detail than the *Encyclopedia* for some groupings.

For Austronesian languages, the *Comparative Austronesian Dictionary*, 1995, Darrell Tryon, editor, is also followed. For Afro-Asiatic languages, Omotic tentatively replaces West Cushitic and stands as a separate branch of Afro-Asiatic. Changes in other language groupings have also been entered as more recent comparative studies have become available.

We are well aware that few classifications are airtight, and that there are good arguments for other groupings. Where the information is available, we give priority to classifications based on shared structural and lexical innovations, as opposed to lexicostatistical, purely typological, or impressionistic subgroupings.

What is presented here represents the current state of our data base, not a claim to definitiveness. This should pose no problem for specialists engaged in the study of the languages concerned, though we must beg them to recognize that to include all possible proposals for classification (including their own), or to present a history of classifications, would change this from a simple reference to a very different kind of work. At the same time, we look forward to examining the arguments for what we hope will be more firmly grounded classifications with a view to future editions.

In the area of remote comparisons we adopt a conservative stance, as is appropriate in a publication that focuses more on the branches of trees than on the roots. Not only do we omit proposals such as proto-Human and Nostratic and Amerind, but we have even kept Baltic and Slavic separate at the highest level within Indo-European, simply because the evidence at that level does not appear as clear-cut as does the evidence for other groupings at about the same level of remoteness.

Several nongenetic categories are presented along with the genetic groupings for want of a better way to fit them into the index: creole languages, pidgins, mixed languages, language isolates, languages that remain unclassified, deaf sign languages, and other sign languages. There are also language isolates and unclassified languages listed within genetic groupings.

As better information has become available, we have shifted some language names from where they were in earlier editions of the *Ethnologue*. Some speech varieties that had been listed as dialects under a single language are now treated as separate entries because of low intelligibility or incompatible social attitudes, and some varieties that had been listed as separate languages are now combined because of high intelligibility. Others have been merged because of earlier confusion of language names with people names and geographic names. Usually the reason for changing a main name has to do with information about which name speakers of the language itself prefer; names imposed by outsiders seem to be all too often less than complimentary.

Each page of this index begins with the highest grouping name to which the first language on that page belongs, followed by the entire tree from more inclusive to least inclusive groupings. Grouping names that are duplicates of the name on the line above are represented by a hyphen (-) in order to highlight the branching and in general make things easier to find. After each grouping name there is a count of the number of distinct language entries listed under that node.

The first language listed in a subgroup follows the subgrouping name and a colon on the same line, thereby conserving about thirty pages' worth of trees. The languages within a subgroup are listed in alphabetical order. So are the subgroupings within a larger grouping. This is not the general practice of comparative linguists, who often use ordering to show either geographic topology or degrees of closeness in a way that a family tree as such does not convey well; but for a general index like this one, alphabetic ordering is essential for finding things.

Maps

Cartographers:

Irene Tucker
Matt Benjamin
Bernard Wafukho

LANGUAGES OF THE WORLD

EACH DOT REPRESENTS THE PRIMARY LOCATION
OF A LIVING LANGUAGE LISTED IN THE ETHNOLOGUE

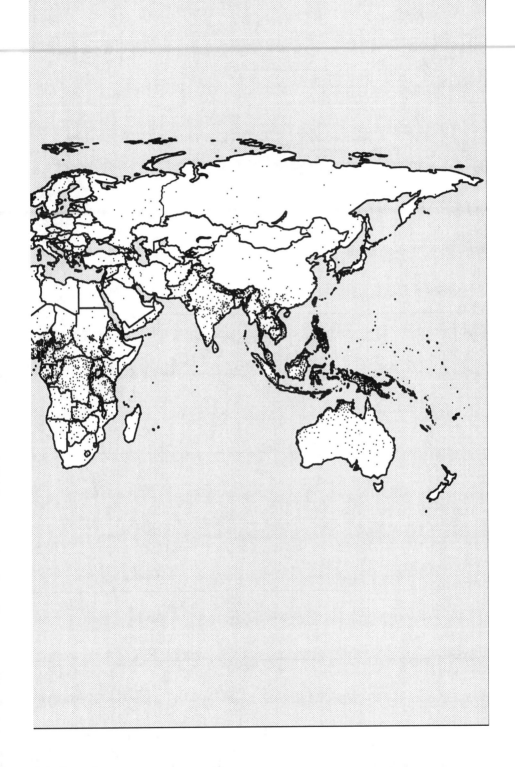

Africa Maps

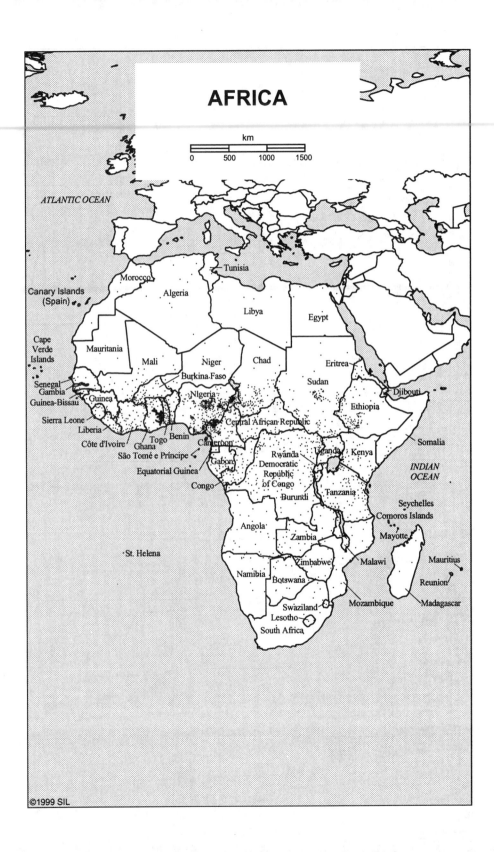

AFRICA

km

0   500   1000   1500

ATLANTIC OCEAN

Morocco

Canary Islands
(Spain)

Algeria

Tunisia

Libya

Egypt

Cape
Verde
Islands

Mauritania

Mali

Niger

Chad

Eritrea

Burkina·Faso

Sudan

Djibouti

Senegal

Gambia

Guinea-Bissau

Guinea

Nigeria

Ethiopia

Sierra Leone

Liberia

Central African Republic

Somalia

Côte d'Ivoire

Togo

Benin

Ghana

São Tomé e Príncipe

Cameroon

Rwanda

Uganda

Kenya

Equatorial Guinea

Gabon

Democratic
Republic
of Congo

INDIAN
OCEAN

Congo

Burundi

Tanzania

Seychelles

Comoros Islands

Angola

Zambia

Mayotte

St. Helena

Zimbabwe

Malawi

Mauritius

Namibia

Botswana

Reunion

Mozambique

Madagascar

Swaziland

Lesotho

South Africa

Maps

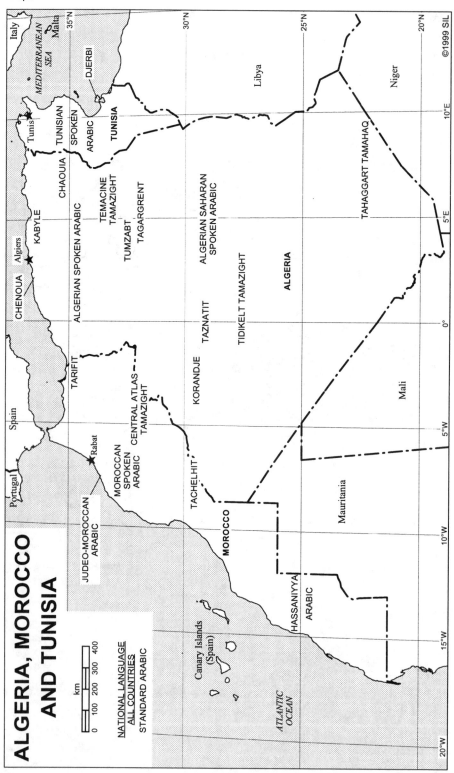

8

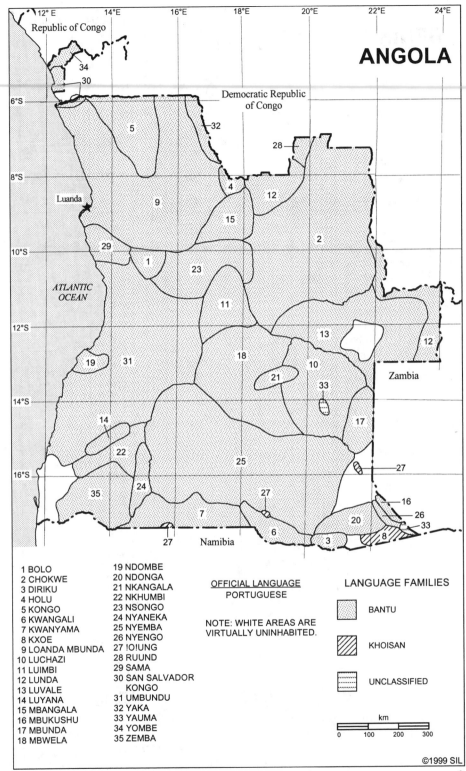

Africa

ANGOLA

Republic of Congo

Democratic Republic
of Congo

Luanda

ATLANTIC
OCEAN

Zambia

Namibia

1 BOLO
2 CHOKWE
3 DIRIKU
4 HOLU
5 KONGO
6 KWANGALI
7 KWANYAMA
8 KXOE
9 LOANDA MBUNDA
10 LUCHAZI
11 LUIMBI
12 LUNDA
13 LUVALE
14 LUYANA
15 MBANGALA
16 MBUKUSHU
17 MBUNDA
18 MBWELA

19 NDOMBE
20 NDONGA
21 NKANGALA
22 NKHUMBI
23 NSONGO
24 NYANEKA
25 NYEMBA
26 NYENGO
27 !O!UNG
28 RUUND
29 SAMA
30 SAN SALVADOR
    KONGO
31 UMBUNDU
32 YAKA
33 YAUMA
34 YOMBE
35 ZEMBA

OFFICIAL LANGUAGE
PORTUGUESE

NOTE: WHITE AREAS ARE
VIRTUALLY UNINHABITED.

LANGUAGE FAMILIES

BANTU

KHOISAN

UNCLASSIFIED

km
0   100   200   300

©1999 SIL

9

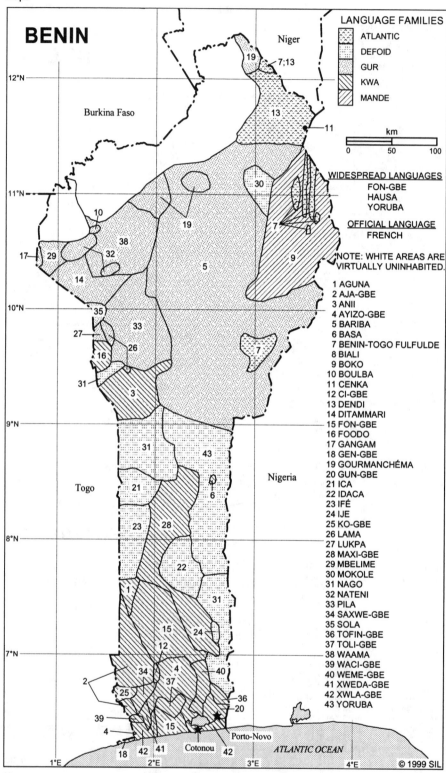

BENIN

LANGUAGE FAMILIES
ATLANTIC
DEFOID
GUR
KWA
MANDE

WIDESPREAD LANGUAGES
FON-GBE
HAUSA
YORUBA

OFFICIAL LANGUAGE
FRENCH

NOTE: WHITE AREAS ARE VIRTUALLY UNINHABITED.

1 AGUNA
2 AJA-GBE
3 ANII
4 AYIZO-GBE
5 BARIBA
6 BASA
7 BENIN-TOGO FULFULDE
8 BIALI
9 BOKO
10 BOULBA
11 CENKA
12 CI-GBE
13 DENDI
14 DITAMMARI
15 FON-GBE
16 FOODO
17 GANGAM
18 GEN-GBE
19 GOURMANCHÉMA
20 GUN-GBE
21 ICA
22 IDACA
23 IFÉ
24 IJE
25 KO-GBE
26 LAMA
27 LUKPA
28 MAXI-GBE
29 MBELIME
30 MOKOLE
31 NAGO
32 NATENI
33 PILA
34 SAXWE-GBE
35 SOLA
36 TOFIN-GBE
37 TOLI-GBE
38 WAAMA
39 WACI-GBE
40 WEME-GBE
41 XWEDA-GBE
42 XWLA-GBE
43 YORUBA

Niger
Burkina Faso
Togo
Nigeria
ATLANTIC OCEAN
Porto-Novo
Cotonou

km
0   50   100

© 1999 SIL

Africa

BOTSWANA

Angola

Zambia

Namibia

Zimbabwe

KXOE
//GANA
MBUKUSHU   /ANDA
YEYI   KXOE
HERERO
JU/'HOAN
=KX'AU//'EIN

SUBIYA

SHUA

GANÁDI
DETI
HIETSHWARE

KALANGA

NARO
//GANA   SHUA   BIRWA
/GWI
HIETSHWARE   TSWAPONG
TSWANA
=/HUA

KGALAGADI   Gaborone
!XÓÕ   South Africa

NAMA
AFRIKAANS

OFFICIAL LANGUAGE
ENGLISH

NATIONAL LANGUAGE
TSWANA

LANGUAGE FAMILIES

BANTU	KHOISAN
BIRWA	/ANDA
HERERO	DETI
KALANGA	GANÁDI
KGALAGADI	//GANA
MBUKUSHU	/GWI
SUBIYA	HIETSHWARE
TSWANA	=/HUA
TSWAPONG	JU/'HOAN
YEYI	=KX'AU//'EIN
	KXOE
	NAMA
	NARO
INDO-EUROPEAN	!XÓÕ
AFRIKAANS	SHUA

km

0   100   200   300   400

©1999 SIL

11

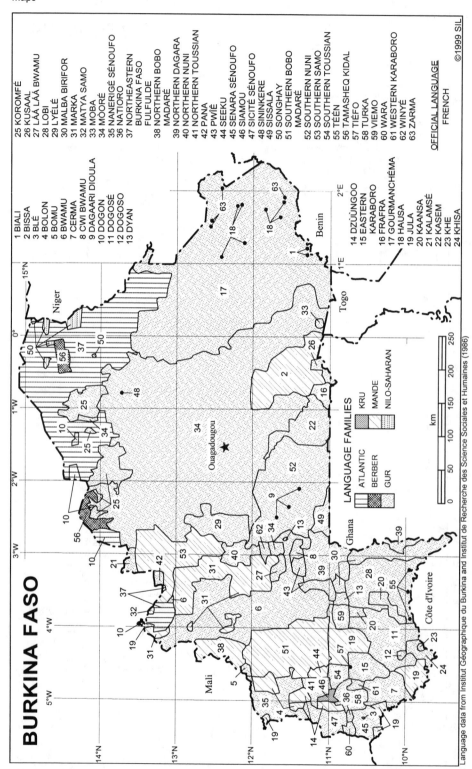

BURKINA FASO

LANGUAGE FAMILIES

| ATLANTIC | BERBER | KRU |
| GUR | MANDE | NILO-SAHARAN |

km

0   50   100   150   200   250

1 BIALI
2 BISSA
3 BLÉ
4 BOLON
5 BOMU
6 BWAMU
7 CERMA
8 CWI BWAMU
9 DAGAARI DIOULA
10 DOGON
11 DOGOSÉ
12 DOGOSO
13 DYAN

14 DZÙUNGOO
15 EASTERN KARABORO
16 FRAFRA
17 GOURMANCHÉMA
18 HAUSA
19 JULA
20 KAANSA
21 KALAMSÉ
22 KASEM
23 KHE
24 KHISA

25 KOROMFÉ
26 KUSAAL
27 LÁÁ LÁÁ BWAMU
28 LOBI
29 LYÉLÉ
30 MALBA BIRIFOR
31 MARKA
32 MATYA SAMO
33 MOBA
34 MÒORÉ
35 NANERIGÉ SÉNOUFO
36 NATIORO
37 NORTHEASTERN BURKINA FASO FULFULDE
38 NORTHERN BOBO MADARÉ
39 NORTHERN DAGARA
40 NORTHERN NUNI
41 NORTHERN TOUSSIAN
42 PANA
43 PWĨĚ
44 SEEKU
45 SENARA SÉNOUFO
46 SIAMOU
47 SICITÉ SÉNOUFO
48 SININKERE
49 SISSALA
50 SONGHAY
51 SOUTHERN BOBO MADARÉ
52 SOUTHERN NUNI
53 SOUTHERN SAMO
54 SOUTHERN TOUSSIAN
55 TEÉN
56 TAMASHEQ KIDAL
57 TIÉFO
58 TURKA
59 VIEMO
60 WARA
61 WESTERN KARABORO
62 WINYÉ
63 ZARMA

OFFICIAL LANGUAGE
FRENCH

©1999 SIL

Language data from Institut Géographique du Burkina and Institut de Recherche des Science Sociales et Humaines (1986)

CAMEROON LEGEND

ABO	210	BYEP	258	KANO-KATSINA-		META'	166	NZANYI	53
ADAMAWA		CAKA	180	BORORRO		MFUMTE	111	OBLO	87
FULFULDE	32	CAMEROON		FULFULDE	4	MINA	57	OKU	145
AFADE	6	MAMBILA	108	KARANG	95	MISSONG	129	OSATU	178
AGHEM	135	CENTRAL		KARE	94	MMAALA	235	OSO	139
AKOOSE	207	KANURI	12	KEMEZUNG	123	MMEN	138	PAM	89
AKUM	134	CUNG	126	KENDEM	195	MOFU-GUDUR	37	PANA	100
AMBELE	191	CUVOK	38	KENSWEI NSEI	150	MOKPWE	212	PAPE	78
ATONG	187	DABA	56	KENYANG	196	MOM JANGO	70	PARKWA	14
AWING	170	DAMA	85	KERA	62	MONO	84	PEERE	92
BABA	146	DENYA	188	KOL	254	MPADE	3	PELASLA	16
BABANKI	143	DII	90	KOLBILA	76	MPIEMO	264	PEVÉ	83
BAFANJI	153	DIMBONG	225	KOM	141	MPONGMPONG		PINYIN	168
BAFAW-		DOYAYO	80	KOMA	71		263	POL	261
BALONG	204	DUALA	211	KOONZIME	253	MSER	8	PSIKYE	46
BAFIA	240	DUGWOR	26	KOROP	199	MUNDANG	59	SAA	77
BAFUT	173	DUUPA	79	KOSKIN	127	MUNDANI	164	SAMBA LEKO	74
BAKA	252	DZODINKA	114	KUO	68	MUNGAKA	157	SHARWA	51
BAKOKO	216	EJAGHAM	197	KUTEP	131	MUNGONG	125	SHUWA ARABIC	2
BAKOLE	202	ELIP	234	KWA'	220	MUSEY	63	SO	255
BAKUNDU-		EMAN	186	KWAJA	112	MUSGU	33	SOUTH FALI	66
BALUE	206	ESIMBI	179	KWAKUM	259	MUYANG	30	SOUTH GIZIGA	35
BALDAMU	31	ETON	233	KWANJA	106	NAGUMI	82	SUGA	102
BALUNDU-		EVANT	184	LA'BI	97	NAKI	130	TIBEA	241
BIMA	201	EWONDO	242	LAGWAN	9	NCANE	120	TIGON	
BAMALI	151	FANG	249	LAMNSO'	117	NDAI	88	MBEMBE	115
BAMBALANG	152	FE'FE'	208	LETI	237	NDAKTUP	113	TIKAR	243
BAMBILI	142	FUNGOM	140	LIMBUM	116	NDA'NDA'	221	TIV	181
BAMENYAM	155	GADUWA	21	LONGTO	75	NDEMLI	219	TO	98
BAMUN	160	GAVAR	45	MADA	29	NDOOLA	93	TSUVAN	55
BAMUNKA	148	GEMZEK	22	MAFA	18	NGAMAMBO	167	TUKI	239
BANA	49	GEY	67	MAJERA	11	NGAMBAY	86	TUNEN	223
BANGANDU	265	GHOMÁLÁ'	159	MAKAA	251	NGEMBA	171	TUOTOMB	226
BANGOLAN	149	GIDAR	58	MALGBE	5	NGIE	194	TUPURI	60
BAROMBI	205	GIMME	73	MALIMBA	217	NGIEMBOON	161	TWENDI	107
BASAA	218	GIMNIME	72	MAMBAI	64	NGISHE	174	USAGHADE	200
BASSOSSI	198	GLAVDA	17	MANTA	189	NGOMBA	158	VEMGO-	
BATA	69	GUDE	52	MASANA	61	NGOMBALE	169	MABAS	42
BATANGA	245	GUDUF	40	MASLAM	7	NGONG	81	VENGO	144
BATI	232	GVOKO	39	MATAL	19	NGUMBA	246	VUTE	244
BEBE	122	GYELE	247	MBE'	109	NGWE	163	WANDALA	13
BEBELE	256	HDI	41	MBEDAM	36	NGWO	175	WAWA	103
BEBIL	257	HIJUK	231	MBO	209	NIMBARI	65	WEH	137
BEEZEN	133	HYA	47	MBONGA	260	NJEN	165	WUMBOKO	203
BEFANG	176	ICEVE-MACI	183	MBUKO	27	NOMAANDE	227	WUSHI	147
BEKWEL	266	IPULO	185	MBULE	228	NOONE	118	WUZLAM	15
BITARE	104	ISU(ISU)	136	MBUM	91	NORTH FALI	54	YAMBA	110
BOKYI	190	ISU(SZV)	214	MEDUMBA	222	NORTH GIZIGA	25	YAMBETA	224
BOMWALI	267	IYIVE	182	MEFELE	43	NORTH MOFU	23	YANGBEN	230
BU	128	JIMI	50	MENGAKA	156	NORTHWEST		YASA	248
BUBIA	213	JINA	10	MELOKWO	28	GBAYA	101	YEMBA	162
BUDUMA	1	JUKUN		MENDANKWE	172	NSARI	121	YUKUBEN	132
BULU	250	TAKUM	124	MENGISA	238	NUBACA	229	ZIZILIVAKAN	48
BUM	119	KAKO	262	MENKA	192	NUGUNU	236	ZULGWA	20
BUSAM	193	KAMKAM	105	MEREY	24	NYONG	154	ZUMAYA	34
BUWAL	44			MESAKA	177	NZAKAMBAY	99		

Maps

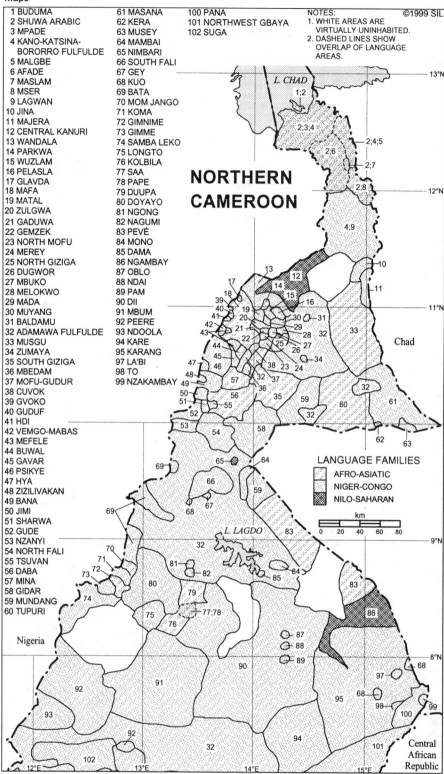

1 BUDUMA
2 SHUWA ARABIC
3 MPADE
4 KANO-KATSINA-
   BORORRO FULFULDE
5 MALGBE
6 AFADE
7 MASLAM
8 MSER
9 LAGWAN
10 JINA
11 MAJERA
12 CENTRAL KANURI
13 WANDALA
14 PARKWA
15 WUZLAM
16 PELASLA
17 GLAVDA
18 MAFA
19 MATAL
20 ZULGWA
21 GADUWA
22 GEMZEK
23 NORTH MOFU
24 MEREY
25 NORTH GIZIGA
26 DUGWOR
27 MBUKO
28 MELOKWO
29 MADA
30 MUYANG
31 BALDAMU
32 ADAMAWA FULFULDE
33 MUSGU
34 ZUMAYA
35 SOUTH GIZIGA
36 MBEDAM
37 MOFU-GUDUR
38 CUVOK
39 GVOKO
40 GUDUF
41 HDI
42 VEMGO-MABAS
43 MEFELE
44 BUWAL
45 GAVAR
46 PSIKYE
47 HYA
48 ZIZILIVAKAN
49 BANA
50 JIMI
51 SHARWA
52 GUDE
53 NZANYI
54 NORTH FALI
55 TSUVAN
56 DABA
57 MINA
58 GIDAR
59 MUNDANG
60 TUPURI

61 MASANA
62 KERA
63 MUSEY
64 MAMBAI
65 NIMBARI
66 SOUTH FALI
67 GEY
68 KUO
69 BATA
70 MOM JANGO
71 KOMA
72 GIMNIME
73 GIMME
74 SAMBA LEKO
75 LONGTO
76 KOLBILA
77 SAA
78 PAPE
79 DUUPA
80 DOYAYO
81 NGONG
82 NAGUMI
83 PEVÉ
84 MONO
85 DAMA
86 NGAMBAY
87 OBLO
88 NDAI
89 PAM
90 DII
91 MBUM
92 PEERE
93 NDOOLA
94 KARE
95 KARANG
97 LA'BI
98 TO
99 NZAKAMBAY

100 PANA
101 NORTHWEST GBAYA
102 SUGA

NOTES:
1. WHITE AREAS ARE
   VIRTUALLY UNINHABITED.
2. DASHED LINES SHOW
   OVERLAP OF LANGUAGE
   AREAS.

©1999 SIL

L. CHAD

NORTHERN
CAMEROON

13°N

12°N

11°N

Chad

LANGUAGE FAMILIES

AFRO-ASIATIC

NIGER-CONGO

NILO-SAHARAN

km
0   20   40   60   80

L. LAGDO

9°N

Nigeria

8°N

Central
African
Republic

12°E   13°E   14°E   15°E

14

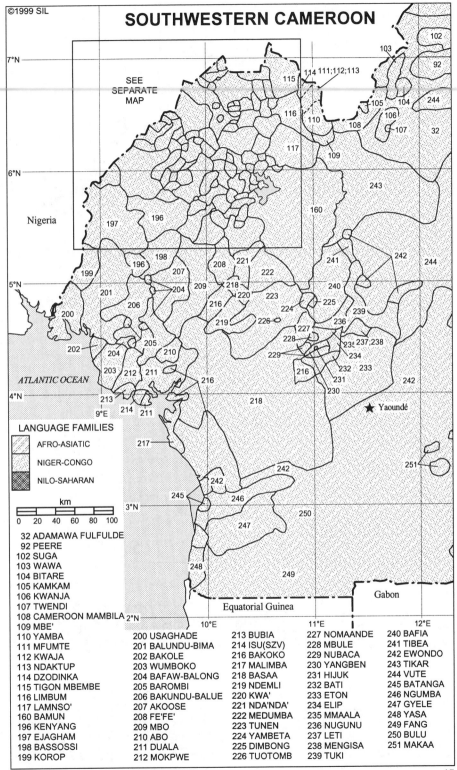

SOUTHWESTERN CAMEROON

©1999 SIL

Africa

LANGUAGE FAMILIES

- AFRO-ASIATIC
- NIGER-CONGO
- NILO-SAHARAN

km
0 20 40 60 80 100

SEE SEPARATE MAP

Nigeria

ATLANTIC OCEAN

Equatorial Guinea

Gabon

Yaoundé

32 ADAMAWA FULFULDE
92 PEERE
102 SUGA
103 WAWA
104 BITARE
105 KAMKAM
106 KWANJA
107 TWENDI
108 CAMEROON MAMBILA
109 MBE'
110 YAMBA
111 MFUMTE
112 KWAJA
113 NDAKTUP
114 DZODINKA
115 TIGON MBEMBE
116 LIMBUM
117 LAMNSO'
160 BAMUN
196 KENYANG
197 EJAGHAM
198 BASSOSSI
199 KOROP

200 USAGHADE
201 BALUNDU-BIMA
202 BAKOLE
203 WUMBOKO
204 BAFAW-BALONG
205 BAROMBI
206 BAKUNDU-BALUE
207 AKOOSE
208 FE'FE'
209 MBO
210 ABO
211 DUALA
212 MOKPWE

213 BUBIA
214 ISU(SZV)
216 BAKOKO
217 MALIMBA
218 BASAA
219 NDEMLI
220 KWA'
221 NDA'NDA'
222 MEDUMBA
223 TUNEN
224 YAMBETA
225 DIMBONG
226 TUOTOMB

227 NOMAANDE
228 MBULE
229 NUBACA
230 YANGBEN
231 HIJUK
232 BATI
233 ETON
234 ELIP
235 MMAALA
236 NUGUNU
237 LETI
238 MENGISA
239 TUKI

240 BAFIA
241 TIBEA
242 EWONDO
243 TIKAR
244 VUTE
245 BATANGA
246 NGUMBA
247 GYELE
248 YASA
249 FANG
250 BULU
251 MAKAA

15

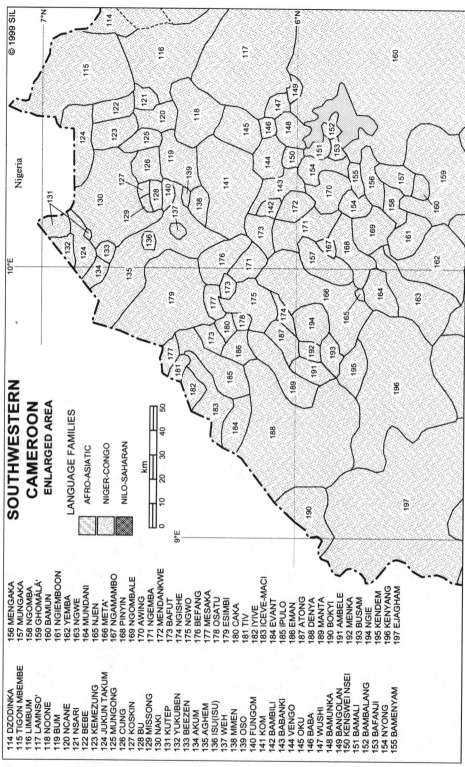

© 1999 SIL

SOUTHWESTERN CAMEROON
ENLARGED AREA

LANGUAGE FAMILIES

AFRO-ASIATIC

NIGER-CONGO

NILO-SAHARAN

km

0 10 20 30 40 50

Nigeria

7°N
6°N
10°E
9°E

114 DZODINKA	156 MENGAKA
115 TIGON MBEMBE	157 MUNGAKA
116 LIMBUM	158 NGOMBA
117 LAMNSO'	159 GHOMÁLÁ'
118 NOONE	160 BAMUN
119 BUM	161 NGIEMBOON
120 NCANE	162 YEMBA
121 NSARI	163 NGWE
122 BEBE	164 MUNDANI
123 KEMEZUNG	165 NJEN
124 JUKUN TAKUM	166 META'
125 MUNGONG	167 NGAMAMBO
126 CUNG	168 PINYIN
127 KOSKIN	169 NGOMBALE
128 BU	170 AWING
129 MISSONG	171 NGEMBA
130 NAKI	172 MENDANKWE
131 KUTEP	173 BAFUT
132 YUKUBEN	174 NGISHE
133 BEEZEN	175 NGWO
134 AKUM	176 BEFANG
135 AGHEM	177 MESAKA
136 ISU(ISU)	178 OSATU
137 WEH	179 ESIMBI
138 MMEN	180 CAKA
139 OSO	181 TIV
140 FUNGOM	182 IYIVE
141 KOM	183 ICEVE-MACI
142 BAMBILI	184 EVANT
143 BABANKI	185 IPULO
144 VENGO	186 EMAN
145 OKU	187 ATONG
146 BABA	188 DENYA
147 WUSHI	189 MANTA
148 BAMUNKA	190 BOKYI
149 BANGOLAN	191 AMBELE
150 KENSWEI NSEI	192 MENKA
151 BAMALI	193 BUSAM
152 BAMBALANG	194 NGIE
153 BAFANJI	195 KENDEM
154 NYONG	196 KENYANG
155 BAMENYAM	197 EJAGHAM

16

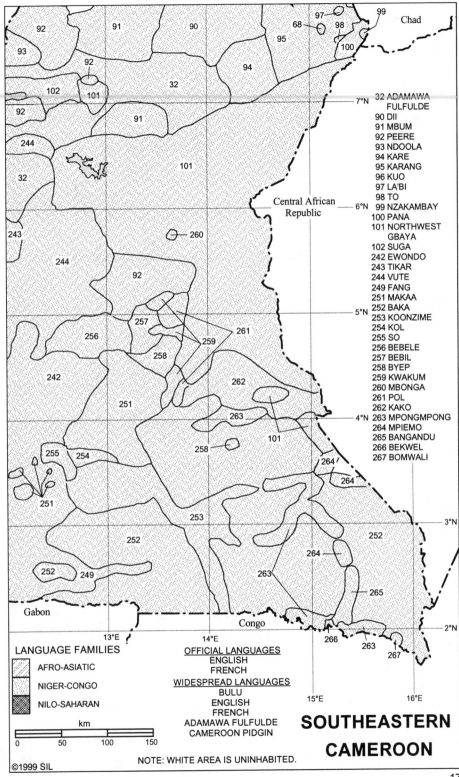

32 ADAMAWA
   FULFULDE
90 DII
91 MBUM
92 PEERE
93 NDOOLA
94 KARE
95 KARANG
96 KUO
97 LA'BI
98 TO
99 NZAKAMBAY
100 PANA
101 NORTHWEST
    GBAYA
102 SUGA
242 EWONDO
243 TIKAR
244 VUTE
249 FANG
251 MAKAA
252 BAKA
253 KOONZIME
254 KOL
255 SO
256 BEBELE
257 BEBIL
258 BYEP
259 KWAKUM
260 MBONGA
261 POL
262 KAKO
263 MPONGMPONG
264 MPIEMO
265 BANGANDU
266 BEKWEL
267 BOMWALI

Chad

Central African
Republic

Gabon

Congo

LANGUAGE FAMILIES

- AFRO-ASIATIC
- NIGER-CONGO
- NILO-SAHARAN

km

0   50   100   150

©1999 SIL

OFFICIAL LANGUAGES
ENGLISH
FRENCH
WIDESPREAD LANGUAGES
BULU
ENGLISH
FRENCH
ADAMAWA FULFULDE
CAMEROON PIDGIN

NOTE: WHITE AREA IS UNINHABITED.

SOUTHEASTERN
CAMEROON

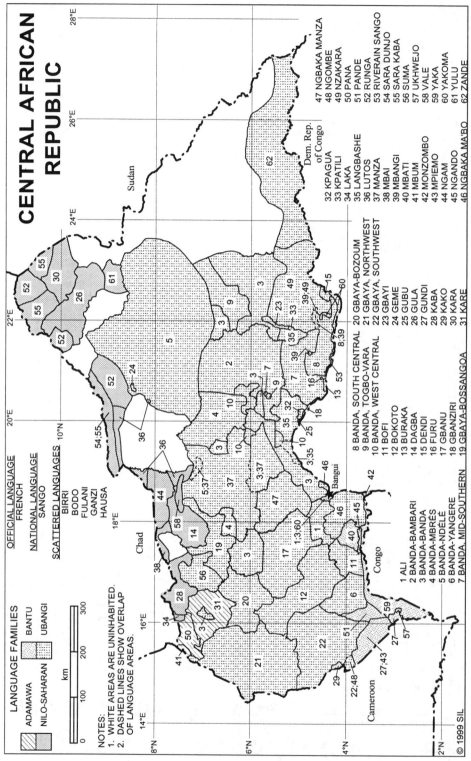

CENTRAL AFRICAN REPUBLIC

LANGUAGE FAMILIES

ADAMAWA   BANTU

NILO-SAHARAN   UBANGI

OFFICIAL LANGUAGE
FRENCH

NATIONAL LANGUAGE
SANGO

SCATTERED LANGUAGES
BIRRI
BODO
FULANI
GANZI
HAUSA

NOTES:
1. WHITE AREAS ARE UNINHABITED.
2. DASHED LINES SHOW OVERLAP
   OF LANGUAGE AREAS.

km
0   100   200   300

1 ALI
2 BANDA-BAMBARI
3 BANDA-BANDA
4 BANDA-MBRÈS
5 BANDA-NDÉLÉ
6 BANDA-YANGERE
7 BANDA, MID-SOUTHERN
8 BANDA, SOUTH CENTRAL
9 BANDA, TOGBO-VARA
10 BANDA, WEST CENTRAL
11 BOFI
12 BOKOTO
13 BURAKA
14 DAGBA
15 DENDI
16 FURU
17 GBANU
18 GBANZIRI
19 GBAYA-BOSSANGOA
20 GBAYA-BOZOUM
21 GBAYA, NORTHWEST
22 GBAYA, SOUTHWEST
23 GBAYI
24 GEME
25 GUBU
26 GULA
27 GUNDI
28 KABA
29 KAKO
30 KARA
31 KARE
32 KPAGUA
33 KPATILI
34 LAKA
35 LANGBASHE
36 LUTOS
37 MANZA
38 MBAI
39 MBANGI
40 MBATI
41 MBUM
42 MONZOMBO
43 MPIEMO
44 NGAM
45 NGANDO
46 NGBAKA MA'BO
47 NGBAKA MANZA
48 NGOMBE
49 NZAKARA
50 PANA
51 PANDE
52 RUNGA
53 RIVERAIN SANGO
54 SARA DUNJO
55 SARA KABA
56 SUMA
57 UKHWEJO
58 VALE
59 YAKA
60 YAKOMA
61 YULU
62 ZANDE

Chad

Cameroon

Congo

Sudan

Dem. Rep.
of Congo

Bangui

© 1999 SIL

18

CHAD

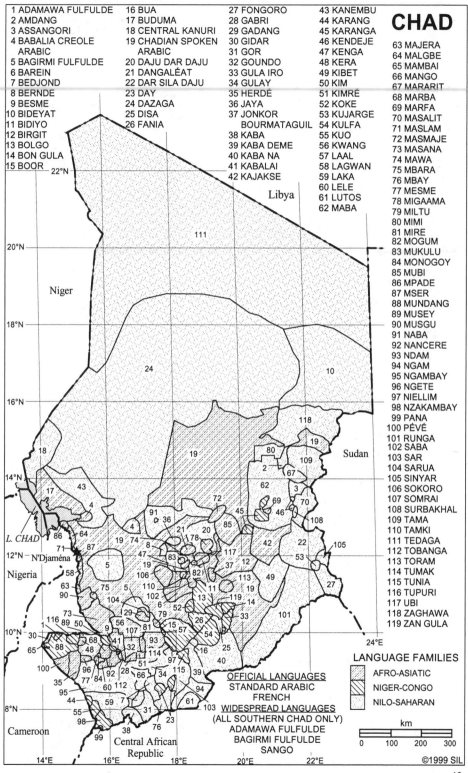

1 ADAMAWA FULFULDE	16 BUA	27 FONGORO	43 KANEMBU
2 AMDANG	17 BUDUMA	28 GABRI	44 KARANG
3 ASSANGORI	18 CENTRAL KANURI	29 GADANG	45 KARANGA
4 BABALIA CREOLE	19 CHADIAN SPOKEN	30 GIDAR	46 KENDEJE
ARABIC	ARABIC	31 GOR	47 KENGA
5 BAGIRMI FULFULDE	20 DAJU DAR DAJU	32 GOUNDO	48 KERA
6 BAREIN	21 DANGALÉAT	33 GULA IRO	49 KIBET
7 BEDJOND	22 DAR SILA DAJU	34 GULAY	50 KIM
8 BERNDE	23 DAY	35 HERDÉ	51 KIMRÉ
9 BESME	24 DAZAGA	36 JAYA	52 KOKE
10 BIDEYAT	25 DISA	37 JONKOR	53 KUJARGE
11 BIDIYO	26 FANIA	BOURMATAGUIL	54 KULFA
12 BIRGIT		38 KABA	55 KUO
13 BOLGO		39 KABA DEME	56 KWANG
14 BON GULA		40 KABA NA	57 LAAL
15 BOOR		41 KABALAI	58 LAGWAN
		42 KAJAKSE	59 LAKA
			60 LELE
			61 LUTOS
			62 MABA

63 MAJERA
64 MALGBE
65 MAMBAI
66 MANGO
67 MARARIT
68 MARBA
69 MARFA
70 MASALIT
71 MASLAM
72 MASMAJE
73 MASANA
74 MAWA
75 MBARA
76 MBAY
77 MESME
78 MIGAAMA
79 MILTU
80 MIMI
81 MIRE
82 MOGUM
83 MUKULU
84 MONOGOY
85 MUBI
86 MPADE
87 MSER
88 MUNDANG
89 MUSEY
90 MUSGU
91 NABA
92 NANCERE
93 NDAM
94 NGAM
95 NGAMBAY
96 NGETE
97 NIELLIM
98 NZAKAMBAY
99 PANA
100 PÉVÉ
101 RUNGA
102 SABA
103 SAR
104 SARUA
105 SINYAR
106 SOKORO
107 SOMRAI
108 SURBAKHAL
109 TAMA
110 TAMKI
111 TEDAGA
112 TOBANGA
113 TORAM
114 TUMAK
115 TUNIA
116 TUPURI
117 UBI
118 ZAGHAWA
119 ZAN GULA

OFFICIAL LANGUAGES
STANDARD ARABIC
FRENCH
WIDESPREAD LANGUAGES
(ALL SOUTHERN CHAD ONLY)
ADAMAWA FULFULDE
BAGIRMI FULFULDE
SANGO

LANGUAGE FAMILIES
AFRO-ASIATIC
NIGER-CONGO
NILO-SAHARAN

km
0 100 200 300

©1999 SIL

19

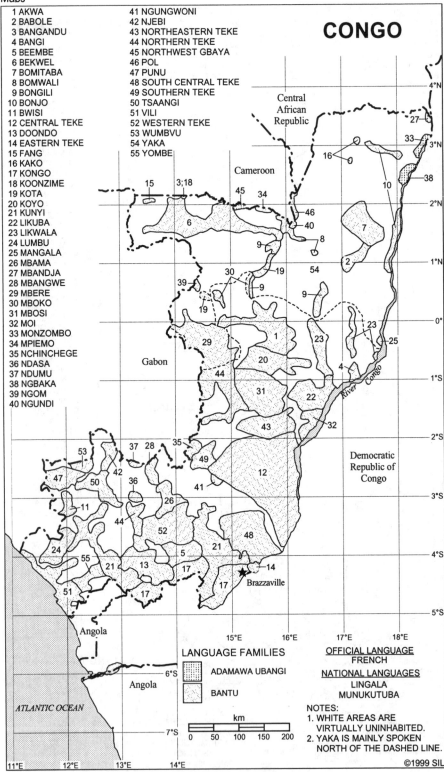

CONGO

1 AKWA
2 BABOLE
3 BANGANDU
4 BANGI
5 BEEMBE
6 BEKWEL
7 BOMITABA
8 BOMWALI
9 BONGILI
10 BONJO
11 BWISI
12 CENTRAL TEKE
13 DOONDO
14 EASTERN TEKE
15 FANG
16 KAKO
17 KONGO
18 KOONZIME
19 KOTA
20 KOYO
21 KUNYI
22 LIKUBA
23 LIKWALA
24 LUMBU
25 MANGALA
26 MBAMA
27 MBANDJA
28 MBANGWE
29 MBERE
30 MBOKO
31 MBOSI
32 MOI
33 MONZOMBO
34 MPIEMO
35 NCHINCHEGE
36 NDASA
37 NDUMU
38 NGBAKA
39 NGOM
40 NGUNDI
41 NGUNGWONI
42 NJEBI
43 NORTHEASTERN TEKE
44 NORTHERN TEKE
45 NORTHWEST GBAYA
46 POL
47 PUNU
48 SOUTH CENTRAL TEKE
49 SOUTHERN TEKE
50 TSAANGI
51 VILI
52 WESTERN TEKE
53 WUMBVU
54 YAKA
55 YOMBE

Central African Republic

Cameroon

Gabon

Democratic Republic of Congo

Brazzaville

Angola

Angola

ATLANTIC OCEAN

LANGUAGE FAMILIES

ADAMAWA UBANGI

BANTU

OFFICIAL LANGUAGE
FRENCH

NATIONAL LANGUAGES
LINGALA
MUNUKUTUBA

NOTES:
1. WHITE AREAS ARE
   VIRTUALLY UNINHABITED.
2. YAKA IS MAINLY SPOKEN
   NORTH OF THE DASHED LINE.

km
0   50   100   150   200

River Congo

©1999 SIL

20

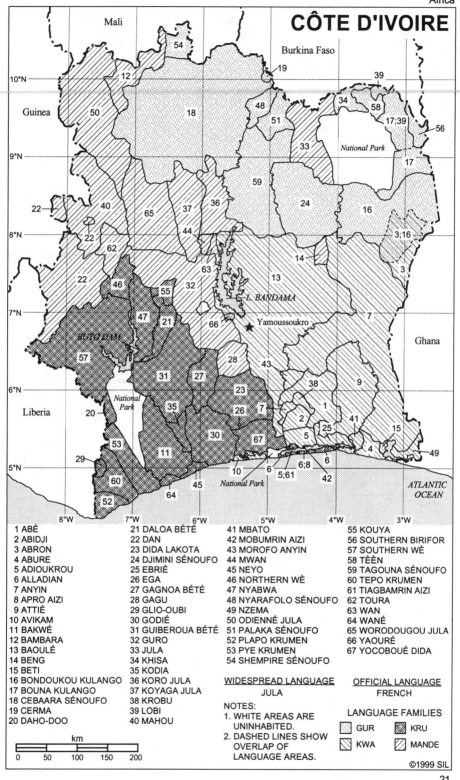

CÔTE D'IVOIRE

Mali

Burkina Faso

Guinea

National Park

Ghana

Liberia

L. BANDAMA

Yamoussoukro

BUYO DAM

National Park

National Park

ATLANTIC OCEAN

1 ABÉ	21 DALOA BÉTÉ	41 MBATO	55 KOUYA
2 ABIDJI	22 DAN	42 MOBUMRIN AIZI	56 SOUTHERN BIRIFOR
3 ABRON	23 DIDA LAKOTA	43 MOROFO ANYIN	57 SOUTHERN WÈ
4 ABURE	24 DJIMINI SÉNOUFO	44 MWAN	58 TÈÈN
5 ADIOUKROU	25 EBRIÉ	45 NEYO	59 TAGOUNA SÉNOUFO
6 ALLADIAN	26 EGA	46 NORTHERN WÈ	60 TEPO KRUMEN
7 ANYIN	27 GAGNOA BÉTÉ	47 NYABWA	61 TIAGBAMRIN AIZI
8 APRO AIZI	28 GAGU	48 NYARAFOLO SÉNOUFO	62 TOURA
9 ATTIÉ	29 GLIO-OUBI	49 NZEMA	63 WAN
10 AVIKAM	30 GODIÉ	50 ODIENNÉ JULA	64 WANÉ
11 BAKWÉ	31 GUIBEROUA BÉTÉ	51 PALAKA SÉNOUFO	65 WORODOUGOU JULA
12 BAMBARA	32 GURO	52 PLAPO KRUMEN	66 YAOURÉ
13 BAOULÉ	33 JULA	53 PYE KRUMEN	67 YOCOBOUÉ DIDA
14 BENG	34 KHISA	54 SHEMPIRE SÉNOUFO	
15 BETI	35 KODIA		
16 BONDOUKOU KULANGO	36 KORO JULA	WIDESPREAD LANGUAGE	OFFICIAL LANGUAGE
17 BOUNA KULANGO	37 KOYAGA JULA	JULA	FRENCH
18 CEBAARA SÉNOUFO	38 KROBU		
19 CERMA	39 LOBI	NOTES:	
20 DAHO-DOO	40 MAHOU	1. WHITE AREAS ARE	LANGUAGE FAMILIES

NOTES:
1. WHITE AREAS ARE UNINHABITED.
2. DASHED LINES SHOW OVERLAP OF LANGUAGE AREAS.

LANGUAGE FAMILIES

GUR   KRU
KWA   MANDE

km
0   50   100   150   200

©1999 SIL

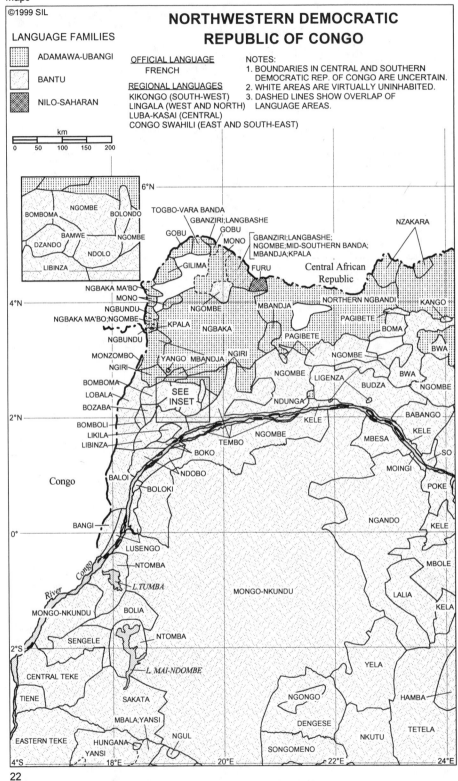

©1999 SIL

NORTHWESTERN DEMOCRATIC
REPUBLIC OF CONGO

LANGUAGE FAMILIES

ADAMAWA-UBANGI

BANTU

NILO-SAHARAN

OFFICIAL LANGUAGE
FRENCH

REGIONAL LANGUAGES
KIKONGO (SOUTH-WEST)
LINGALA (WEST AND NORTH)
LUBA-KASAI (CENTRAL)
CONGO SWAHILI (EAST AND SOUTH-EAST)

NOTES:
1. BOUNDARIES IN CENTRAL AND SOUTHERN
   DEMOCRATIC REP. OF CONGO ARE UNCERTAIN.
2. WHITE AREAS ARE VIRTUALLY UNINHABITED.
3. DASHED LINES SHOW OVERLAP OF
   LANGUAGE AREAS.

km

0   50   100   150   200

6°N

BOMBOMA   NGOMBE   BOLONDO
        BAMWE   NGOMBE
DZANDO   NDOLO
    LIBINZA

TOGBO-VARA BANDA
    GBANZIRI;LANGBASHE
GOBU   GOBU
        MONO
            FURU

GBANZIRI;LANGBASHE;
NGOMBE;MID-SOUTHERN BANDA;
MBANDJA;KPALA

NZAKARA

Central African
Republic

GILIMA

NGBAKA MA'BO
    MONO
NGBUNDU
NGBAKA MA'BO;NGOMBE
    KPALA   NGBAKA
    NGBUNDU

NGOMBE   MBANDJA   NORTHERN NGBANDI   KANGO

4°N

PAGIBETE   BOMA

MONZOMBO
    NGIRI
        YANGO MBANDJA   NGIRI
                PAGIBETE

BWA

BOMBOMA
LOBALA
BOZABA

SEE
INSET

NGOMBE

NGIRI

NGOMBE   LIGENZA   BWA

BUDZA   NGOMBE

2°N

BOMBOLI
LIKILA
LIBINZA

NDUNGA
    KELE

TEMBO   NGOMBE

BABANGO

KELE

MBESA   SO

BOKO

MOINGI

BALOI   NDOBO
    BOLOKI

POKE

Congo

BANGI

0°

NGANDO   KELE

LUSENGO
    NTOMBA

MBOLE

L.TUMBA

MONGO-NKUNDU

LALIA

MONGO-NKUNDU   BOLIA

KELA

SENGELE   NTOMBA

2°S

L. MAI-NDOMBE

YELA

CENTRAL TEKE

TIENE   SAKATA

NGONGO   HAMBA

MBALA;YANSI

DENGESE   TETELA

EASTERN TEKE   HUNGANA   NGUL
        YANSI

NKUTU

SONGOMENO

4°S   18°E   20°E   22°E   24°E

Congo

River

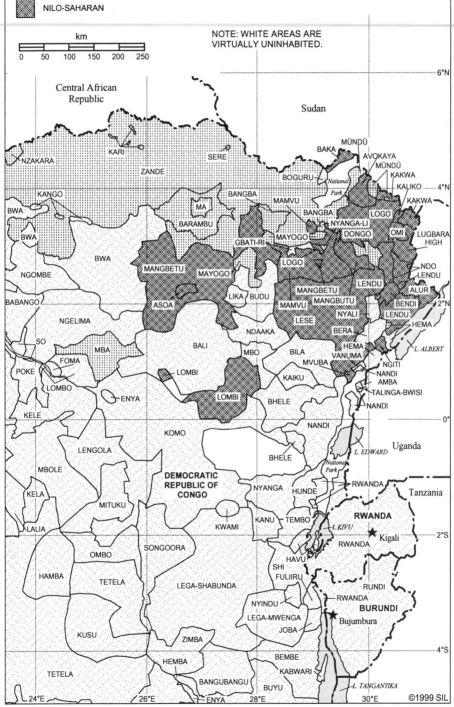

NORTHEASTERN DEMOCRATIC REPUBLIC OF CONGO, RWANDA AND BURUNDI

LANGUAGE FAMILIES

ADAMAWA-UBANGI

BANTU

NILO-SAHARAN

NOTE: WHITE AREAS ARE VIRTUALLY UNINHABITED.

km
0   50   100   150   200   250

Central African Republic

Sudan

6°N

NZAKARA

KARI

SERE

ZANDE

BAKA

MÜNDÜ

AVOKAYA

MÜNDÜ

KAKWA

BOGURU

National Park

KALIKO

KAKWA

4°N

KANGO

BWA

BWA

MA

BARAMBU

BANGBA

BANGBA

MAMVU

NYANGA-LI

LOGO

DONGO

OMI

LUGBARA HIGH

GBATI-RI

MAYOGO

BWA

NGOMBE

MANGBETU

MAYOGO

LOGO

LENDU

NDO LENDU

ALUR

BABANGO

ASOA

LIKA

BUDU

MANGBETU

MAMVU

MANGBUTU

NYALI

BENDI

LENDU

2°N

NGELIMA

LESE

BERA

HEMA

SO

MBA

BALI

NDAAKA

MBO

BILA

HEMA

VANUMA

L. ALBERT

FOMA

MVUBA

NGITI

POKE

LOMBI

KAIKU

NANDI

AMBA

LOMBO

ENYA

LOMBI

BHELE

TALINGA-BWISI

NANDI

KELE

NANDI

0°

KOMO

BHELE

NANDI

L. EDWARD

Uganda

LENGOLA

National Park

RWANDA

MBOLE

DEMOCRATIC REPUBLIC OF CONGO

NYANGA

HUNDE

RWANDA

Tanzania

KELA

MITUKU

TEMBO

L. KIVU

RWANDA

Kigali

2°S

LALIA

KWAMI

KANU

RWANDA

OMBO

SONGOORA

HAVU

SHI

FULIIRU

HAMBA

TETELA

LEGA-SHABUNDA

RUNDI

RWANDA

NYINDU

KUSU

LEGA-MWENGA

JOBA

BURUNDI

Bujumbura

ZIMBA

HEMBA

BEMBE

KABWARI

TETELA

BANGUBANGU

BUYU

L. TANGANYIKA

©1999 SIL

24°E   26°E   ENYA   28°E   30°E

4°S

Congo
Congo
NTOMBA
MBOLE
L. TUMBA
MONGO-NKUNDU
LALIA
BOLIA
MONGO-NKUNDU
NGANDO
KELA
River
SENGELE
NTOMBA
2°S
L. MAI-NDOMBE
CENTRAL TEKE
NGONGO
YELA
TIENE
SAKATA
HAMBA
DENGESE
HUNGANA
NGUL
EASTERN TEKE
YANSI
SONGOMENO
NKUTU
TETELA
4°S
MBALA;YANSI
MFINU
YANSI
DING
LUNA
LONZO
BUSHOONG
BINJI
PELENDE
SONGO
MPUONO
LELE
MBALA
SUKU
KWESE
KWESE
YANSI
SONGE
TETELA
KWESE;MBALA
WONGO
PHENDE
SALAMPASU
BINJI
6°S
SUKU
SONDE
LUBA-KASAI
KETE;LUBA-KASAI
SAMBA
SONGE
KETE
CHOKWE
LWALU
KANYOK
YAKA
LUBA-KASAI
LUNDA
SALAMPASU
HOLU
Angola
8°S
16°E
18°E
20°E
KANYOK;KETE;RUUND
RUUND
LUBA-SHABA
CHOKWE;RUUND
CHOKWE
LUNDA;RUUND
CHOKWE;LUNDA
CHOKWE
LUNDA
CHOKWE;LUNDA
12°S
22°E
24°E

WESTERN DEMOCRATIC REPUBLIC OF CONGO
(at same scale)
14°E
EASTERN TEKE
4°S
Kinshasa
Congo
Angola
10°S
YOMBE
KONGO;SAN SALVADOR KONGO
6°S
Angola

LANGUAGE FAMILIES

ADAMAWA-UBANGI

BANTU

NILO-SAHARAN

SOUTHWESTERN DEMOCRATIC

REPUBLIC OF CONGO

km

0   100   200   300

©1999 SIL

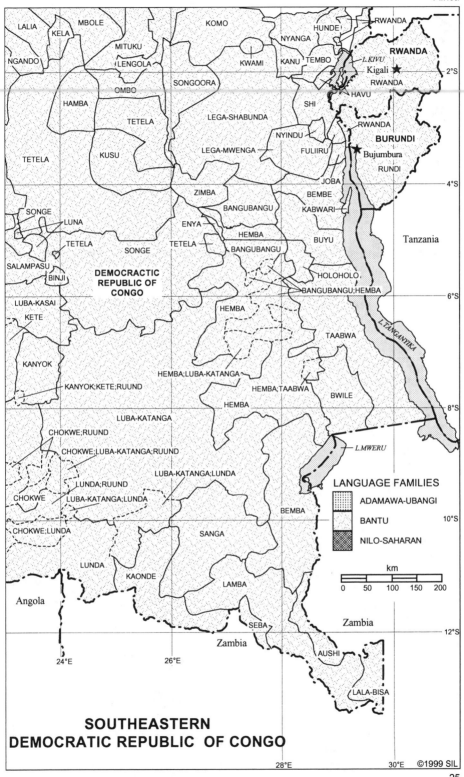

SOUTHEASTERN
DEMOCRATIC REPUBLIC OF CONGO

©1999 SIL

25

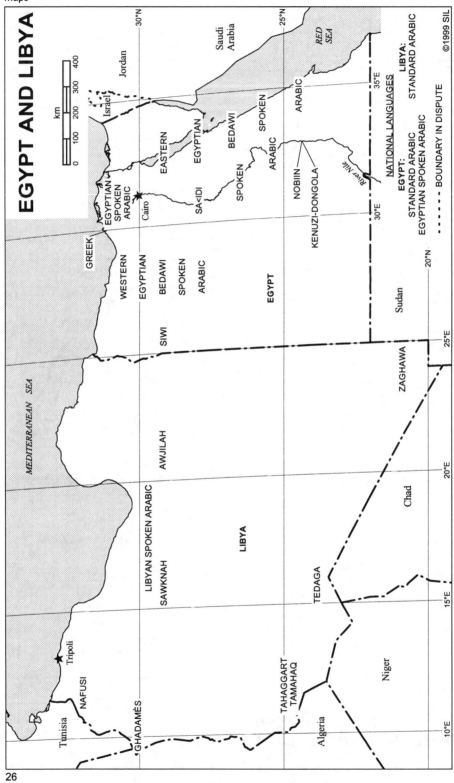

EGYPT AND LIBYA

km
0 100 200 300 400

MEDITERRANEAN SEA

Jordan
Israel
Saudi Arabia
RED SEA

GREEK
EGYPTIAN SPOKEN ARABIC
Cairo
WESTERN EGYPTIAN BEDAWI SPOKEN ARABIC
EASTERN EGYPTIAN BEDAWI SPOKEN ARABIC
SA<IDI SPOKEN ARABIC
SPOKEN ARABIC
ARABIC

SIWI

AWJILAH

LIBYAN SPOKEN ARABIC
SAWKNAH

NAFUSI
Tripoli
GHADAMÈS
Tunisia

TAHAGGART TAMAHAQ
TEDAGA

EGYPT

LIBYA

NOBIIN
KENUZI-DONGOLA
River Nile

Sudan

ZAGHAWA

Chad

Niger

Algeria

NATIONAL LANGUAGES

EGYPT:
STANDARD ARABIC
EGYPTIAN SPOKEN ARABIC

LIBYA:
STANDARD ARABIC

········ BOUNDARY IN DISPUTE

©1999 SIL

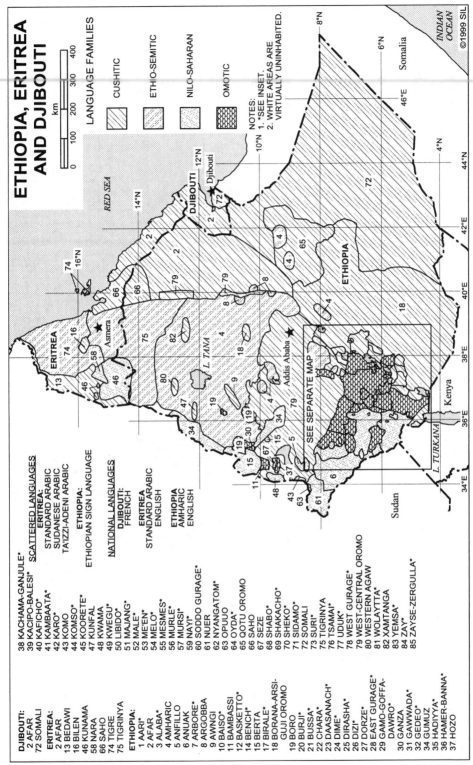

ETHIOPIA, ERITREA AND DJIBOUTI

©1999 SIL

LANGUAGE FAMILIES

- CUSHITIC
- ETHIO-SEMITIC
- NILO-SAHARAN
- OMOTIC

NOTES:
1. *SEE INSET.
2. WHITE AREAS ARE VIRTUALLY UNINHABITED.

km
0 100 200 300 400

DJIBOUTI:
2 AFAR
72 SOMALI

ERITREA:
2 AFAR
13 BEDAWI
16 BILEN
46 KUNAMA
58 NARA
66 SAHO
74 TIGRE
75 TIGRINYA

ETHIOPIA:
1 AARI*
2 AFAR
3 ALABA*
4 AMHARIC
5 ANFILLO
6 ANUAK
7 ARBORE*
8 ARGOBBA*
9 AWNGI
10 BAISO*
11 BAMBASSI
12 BASKETTO*
14 BENCH*
15 BERTA
17 BIRALE*
18 BORANA-ARSI-
GUJI OROMO
19 BORO
20 BURJI*
21 BUSSA*
22 CHARA*
23 DAASANACH*
24 DIME*
25 DIRASHA*
26 DIZI*
27 DORZE*
28 EAST GURAGE*
29 GAMO-GOFFA-
DAWRO*
30 GANZA
31 GAWWADA*
32 GEDEO*
34 GUMUZ
35 HADIYYA*
36 HAMER-BANNA*
37 HOZO

38 KACHAMA-GANJULE*
39 KACIPO-BALESI*
40 KAFICHO*
41 KAMBAATA*
42 KARO*
43 KOMO
44 KOMSO*
45 KOORETE*
47 KUNFAL
48 KWAMA
49 KWEGU*
50 LIBIDO*
51 MAJANG*
52 MALE*
53 ME'EN*
54 MELO*
55 MESMES*
56 MURLE*
57 MURSI*
59 NAYI*
60 SODDO GURAGE*
61 NUER
62 NYANGATOM*
63 OPUUO
64 OYDA*
65 QOTU OROMO
66 SAHO
67 SEZE
68 SHABO*
69 SHAKACHO*
70 SHEKO*
71 SIDAMO*
72 SOMALI
73 SURI*
75 TIGRINYA
76 TSAMAI*
77 UDUK*
78 WEST GURAGE*
79 WEST-CENTRAL OROMO
80 WESTERN AGAW
81 WOLAYTTA*
82 XAMTANGA
83 YEMSA*
84 ZAY*
85 ZAYSE-ZERGULLA*

SCATTERED LANGUAGES
ERITREA:
STANDARD ARABIC
SUDANESE ARABIC
TA'IZZI-ADENI ARABIC

ETHIOPIA:
ETHIOPIAN SIGN LANGUAGE

NATIONAL LANGUAGES
DJIBOUTI:
FRENCH

ERITREA:
STANDARD ARABIC
ENGLISH

ETHIOPIA:
AMHARIC
ENGLISH

RED SEA

INDIAN OCEAN

Somalia

ETHIOPIA

Kenya

Sudan

L. TANA

L. TURKANA

Djibouti

Asmera

Addis Ababa

SEE SEPARATE MAP

DJIBOUTI

ERITREA

27

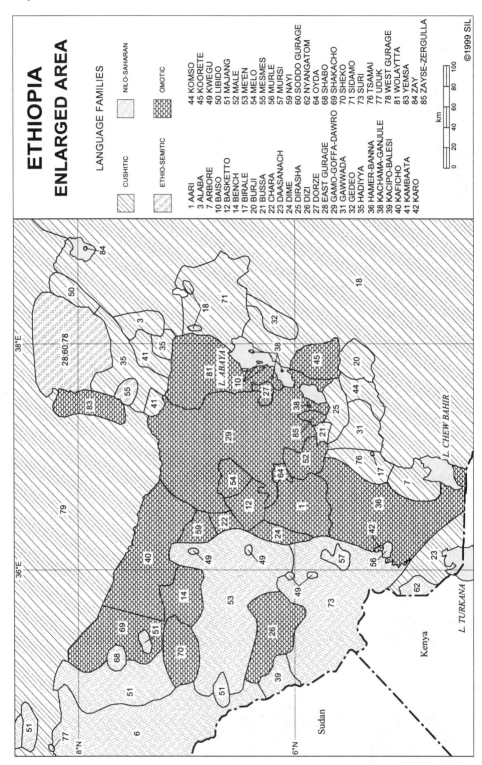

ETHIOPIA
ENLARGED AREA

LANGUAGE FAMILIES

CUSHITIC

NILO-SAHARAN

ETHIO-SEMITIC

OMOTIC

1 AARI
3 ALABA
7 ARBORE
10 BAISO
12 BASKETTO
14 BENCH
17 BIRALE
20 BURJI
21 BUSSA
22 CHARA
23 DAASANACH
24 DIME
25 DIRASHA
26 DIZI
27 DORZE
28 EAST GURAGE
29 GAMO-GOFFA-DAWRO
31 GAWWADA
32 GEDEO
35 HADIYYA
36 HAMER-BANNA
38 KACHAMA-GANJULE
39 KACIPO-BALESI
40 KAFICHO
41 KAMBAATA
42 KARO

44 KOMSO
45 KOORETE
49 KWEGU
50 LIBIDO
51 MAJANG
52 MALE
53 ME'EN
54 MELO
55 MESMES
56 MURLE
57 MURSI
59 NAYI
60 SODDO GURAGE
62 NYANGATOM
64 OYDA
68 SHABO
69 SHAKACHO
70 SHEKO
71 SIDAMO
73 SURI
76 TSAMAI
77 UDUK
78 WEST GURAGE
81 WOLAYTTA
83 YEMSA
84 ZAY
85 ZAYSE-ZERGULLA

©1999 SIL

km

0   20   40   60   80   100

GABON, EQUATORIAL GUINEA AND SÃO TOMÉ E PRÍNCIPE

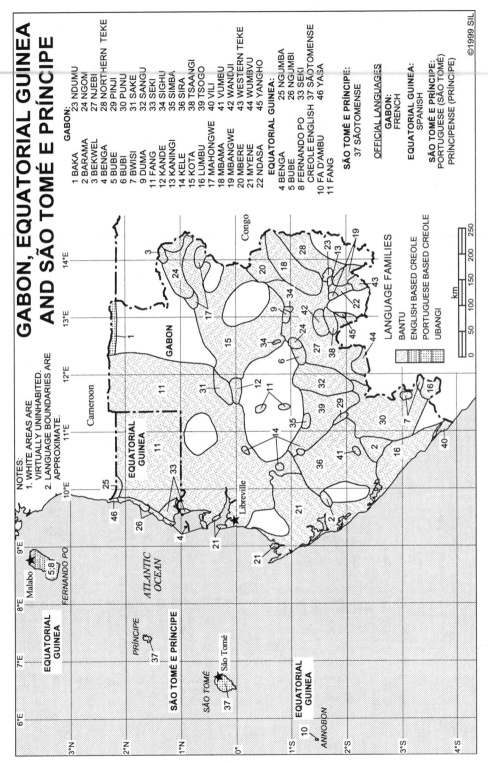

NOTES:
1. WHITE AREAS ARE VIRTUALLY UNINHABITED.
2. LANGUAGE BOUNDARIES ARE APPROXIMATE.

©1999 SIL

GABON:

1 BAKA	23 NDUMU
2 BARAMA	24 NGOM
3 BEKWEL	27 NJEBI
4 BENGA	28 NORTHERN TEKE
5 BUBE	29 PINJI
6 BUBI	30 PUNU
7 BWISI	31 SAKE
9 DUMA	32 SANGU
11 FANG	33 SEKI
12 KANDE	34 SIGHU
13 KANINGI	35 SIMBA
14 KELE	36 SIRA
15 KOTA	38 TSAANGI
16 LUMBU	39 TSOGO
17 MAHONGWE	40 VILI
18 MBAMA	41 VUMBU
19 MBANGWE	42 WANDJI
20 MBERE	43 WESTERN TEKE
21 MYENE	44 WUMBVU
22 NDASA	45 YANGHO

EQUATORIAL GUINEA:

4 BENGA	25 NGUMBA
5 BUBE	26 NGUMBI
8 FERNANDO PO	33 SEKI
10 FA D'AMBU	37 SÃOTOMENSE
11 FANG	46 YASA
	CREOLE ENGLISH

SÃO TOMÉ E PRÍNCIPE:
37 SÃOTOMENSE

<u>OFFICIAL LANGUAGES</u>

GABON:
FRENCH

EQUATORIAL GUINEA:
SPANISH

SÃO TOMÉ E PRÍNCIPE:
PORTUGUESE (SÃO TOMÉ)
PRÍNCIPENSE (PRÍNCIPE)

LANGUAGE FAMILIES

BANTU
ENGLISH BASED CREOLE
PORTUGUESE BASED CREOLE
UBANGI

km
0   50 100 150 200 250

EQUATORIAL GUINEA

FERNANDO PO

Malabo

PRÍNCIPE
37

SÃO TOMÉ E PRÍNCIPE

SÃO TOMÉ
37
São Tomé

EQUATORIAL GUINEA
10
ANNOBON

ATLANTIC OCEAN

Cameroon

EQUATORIAL GUINEA

GABON

Libreville

Congo

Maps

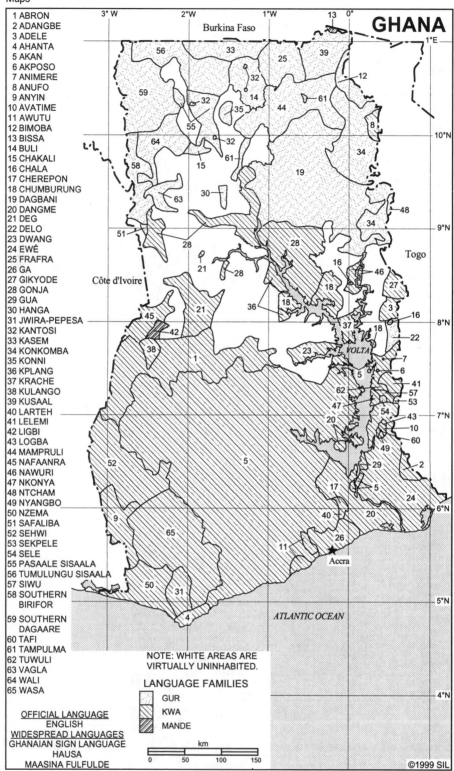

1 ABRON
2 ADANGBE
3 ADELE
4 AHANTA
5 AKAN
6 AKPOSO
7 ANIMERE
8 ANUFO
9 ANYIN
10 AVATIME
11 AWUTU
12 BIMOBA
13 BISSA
14 BULI
15 CHAKALI
16 CHALA
17 CHEREPON
18 CHUMBURUNG
19 DAGBANI
20 DANGME
21 DEG
22 DELO
23 DWANG
24 EWÉ
25 FRAFRA
26 GA
27 GIKYODE
28 GONJA
29 GUA
30 HANGA
31 JWIRA-PEPESA
32 KANTOSI
33 KASEM
34 KONKOMBA
35 KONNI
36 KPLANG
37 KRACHE
38 KULANGO
39 KUSAAL
40 LARTEH
41 LELEMI
42 LIGBI
43 LOGBA
44 MAMPRULI
45 NAFAANRA
46 NAWURI
47 NKONYA
48 NTCHAM
49 NYANGBO
50 NZEMA
51 SAFALIBA
52 SEHWI
53 SEKPELE
54 SELE
55 PASAALE SISAALA
56 TUMULUNGU SISAALA
57 SIWU
58 SOUTHERN
   BIRIFOR
59 SOUTHERN
   DAGAARE
60 TAFI
61 TAMPULMA
62 TUWULI
63 VAGLA
64 WALI
65 WASA

OFFICIAL LANGUAGE
ENGLISH
WIDESPREAD LANGUAGES
GHANAIAN SIGN LANGUAGE
HAUSA
MAASINA FULFULDE

GHANA

Burkina Faso

Côte d'Ivoire

Togo

Accra

ATLANTIC OCEAN

NOTE: WHITE AREAS ARE
VIRTUALLY UNINHABITED.

LANGUAGE FAMILIES

GUR
KWA
MANDE

km
0   50   100   150

©1999 SIL

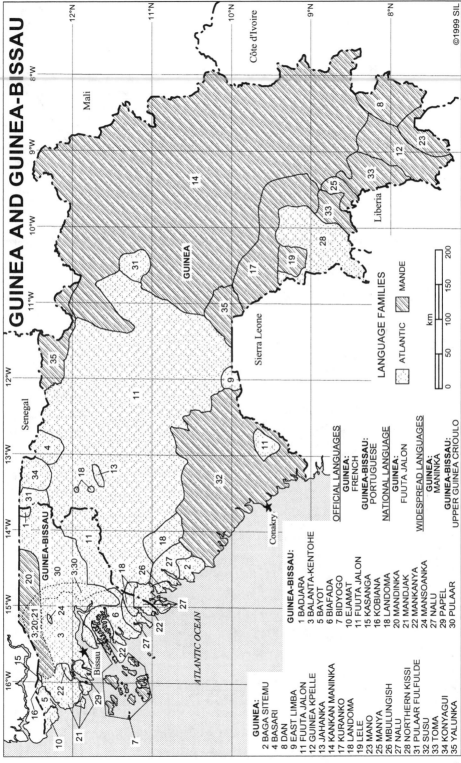

GUINEA AND GUINEA-BISSAU

Africa

©1999 SIL

LANGUAGE FAMILIES

ATLANTIC

MANDE

km
0   50   100   150   200

OFFICIAL LANGUAGES
GUINEA:
FRENCH
GUINEA-BISSAU:
PORTUGUESE

NATIONAL LANGUAGE
GUINEA:
FUUTA JALON

WIDESPREAD LANGUAGES
GUINEA:
MANINKA
GUINEA-BISSAU:
UPPER GUINEA CRIOULO

GUINEA:
2 BAGA SITEMU
4 BASARI
8 DAN
9 EAST LIMBA
11 FUUTA JALON
12 GUINEA KPELLE
13 JAHANKA
14 KANKAN MANINKA
17 KURANKO
18 LANDOMA
19 LELE
23 MANO
25 MANYA
26 MBULUNGISH
27 NALU
28 NORTHERN KISSI
31 PULAAR FULFULDE
32 SUSU
33 TOMA
34 KONYAGUI
35 YALUNKA

GUINEA-BISSAU:
1 BADJARA
3 BALANTA-KENTOHE
5 BAYOT
6 BIAFADA
7 BIDYOGO
10 EJAMAT
11 FUUTA JALON
15 KASANGA
16 KOBIANA
18 LANDOMA
20 MANDINKA
21 MANDJAK
22 MANKANYA
24 MANSOANKA
27 NALU
29 PAPEL
30 PULAAR

GUINEA

GUINEA-BISSAU

Senegal

Mali

Côte d'Ivoire

Liberia

Sierra Leone

ATLANTIC OCEAN

Bissau

Conakry

Maps

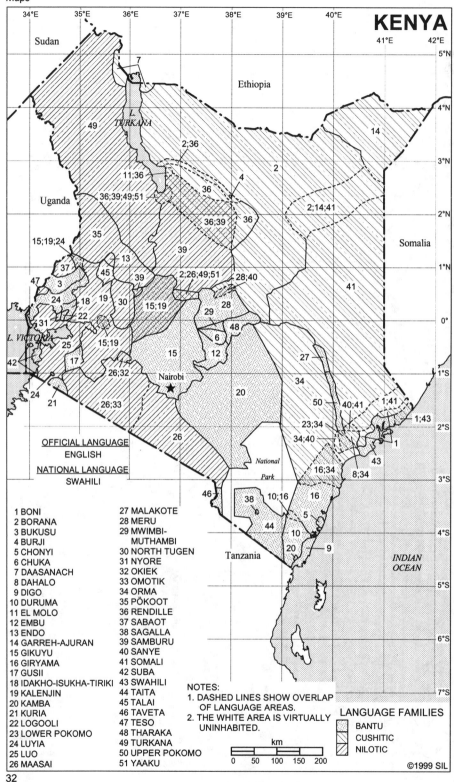

KENYA

OFFICIAL LANGUAGE
ENGLISH

NATIONAL LANGUAGE
SWAHILI

1 BONI
2 BORANA
3 BUKUSU
4 BURJI
5 CHONYI
6 CHUKA
7 DAASANACH
8 DAHALO
9 DIGO
10 DURUMA
11 EL MOLO
12 EMBU
13 ENDO
14 GARREH-AJURAN
15 GIKUYU
16 GIRYAMA
17 GUSII
18 IDAKHO-ISUKHA-TIRIKI
19 KALENJIN
20 KAMBA
21 KURIA
22 LOGOOLI
23 LOWER POKOMO
24 LUYIA
25 LUO
26 MAASAI

27 MALAKOTE
28 MERU
29 MWIMBI-
   MUTHAMBI
30 NORTH TUGEN
31 NYORE
32 OKIEK
33 OMOTIK
34 ORMA
35 PÖKOOT
36 RENDILLE
37 SABAOT
38 SAGALLA
39 SAMBURU
40 SANYE
41 SOMALI
42 SUBA
43 SWAHILI
44 TAITA
45 TALAI
46 TAVETA
47 TESO
48 THARAKA
49 TURKANA
50 UPPER POKOMO
51 YAAKU

NOTES:
1. DASHED LINES SHOW OVERLAP
   OF LANGUAGE AREAS.
2. THE WHITE AREA IS VIRTUALLY
   UNINHABITED.

LANGUAGE FAMILIES
BANTU
CUSHITIC
NILOTIC

km
0   50   100   150   200

©1999 SIL

32

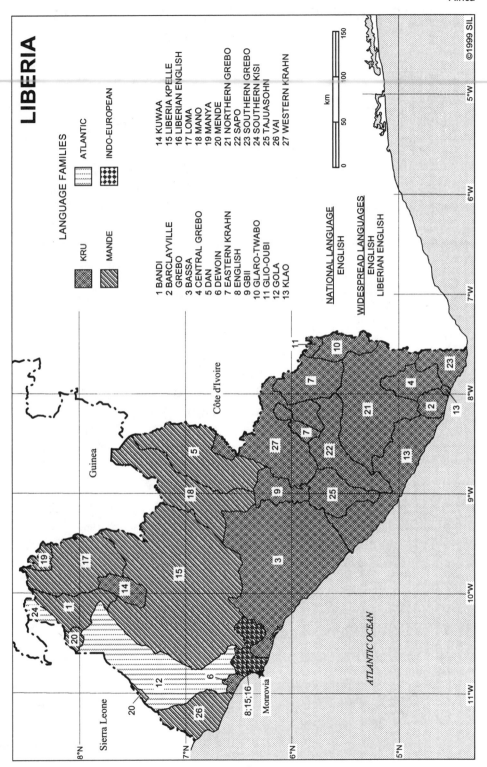

LIBERIA

Africa

LANGUAGE FAMILIES

KRU

MANDE

ATLANTIC

INDO-EUROPEAN

1 BANDI
2 BARCLAYVILLE GREBO
3 BASSA
4 CENTRAL GREBO
5 DAN
6 DEWOIN
7 EASTERN KRAHN
8 ENGLISH
9 GBII
10 GLARO-TWABO
11 GLIO-OUBI
12 GOLA
13 KLAO
14 KUWAA
15 LIBERIA KPELLE
16 LIBERIAN ENGLISH
17 LOMA
18 MANO
19 MANYA
20 MENDE
21 NORTHERN GREBO
22 SAPO
23 SOUTHERN GREBO
24 SOUTHERN KISI
25 TAJUASOHN
26 VAI
27 WESTERN KRAHN

NATIONAL LANGUAGE
ENGLISH

WIDESPREAD LANGUAGES
ENGLISH
LIBERIAN ENGLISH

km

0   50   100   150

©1999 SIL

Guinea

Côte d'Ivoire

Sierra Leone

Monrovia

ATLANTIC OCEAN

33

MADAGASCAR, COMOROS ISLANDS, MAURITIUS, MAYOTTE AND REUNION

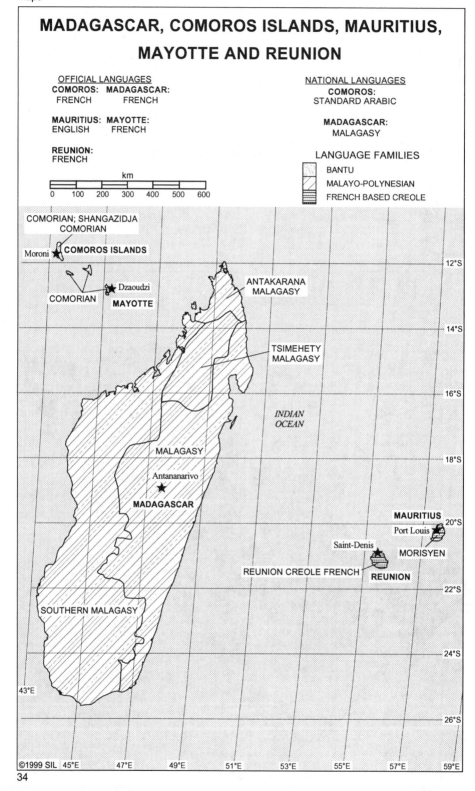

OFFICIAL LANGUAGES

COMOROS: **MADAGASCAR:**
FRENCH FRENCH

MAURITIUS: **MAYOTTE:**
ENGLISH FRENCH

REUNION:
FRENCH

NATIONAL LANGUAGES
COMOROS:
STANDARD ARABIC

MADAGASCAR:
MALAGASY

LANGUAGE FAMILIES

BANTU
MALAYO-POLYNESIAN
FRENCH BASED CREOLE

km
0 100 200 300 400 500 600

COMORIAN; SHANGAZIDJA
COMORIAN

Moroni ★ **COMOROS ISLANDS**

COMORIAN ★ Dzaoudzi

MAYOTTE

ANTAKARANA
MALAGASY

TSIMEHETY
MALAGASY

INDIAN OCEAN

MALAGASY

Antananarivo ★

MADAGASCAR

MAURITIUS
Port Louis
MORISYEN

Saint-Denis
REUNION CREOLE FRENCH **REUNION**

SOUTHERN MALAGASY

12°S
14°S
16°S
18°S
20°S
22°S
24°S
26°S

43°E

©1999 SIL 45°E 47°E 49°E 51°E 53°E 55°E 57°E 59°E

MALAWI

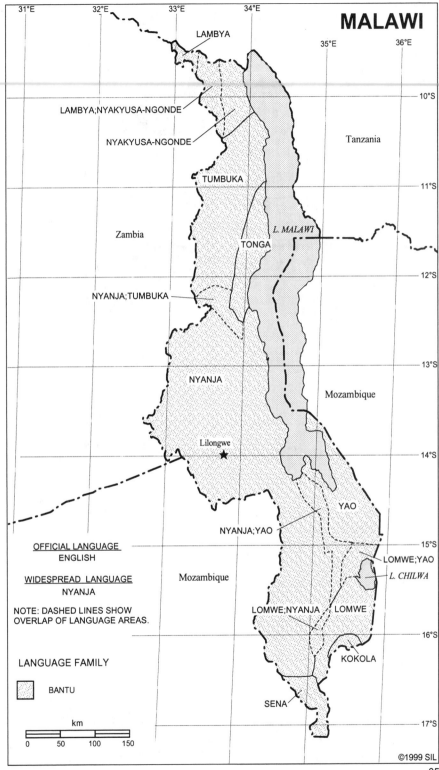

LAMBYA

LAMBYA;NYAKYUSA-NGONDE

NYAKYUSA-NGONDE

Tanzania

TUMBUKA

Zambia

L. MALAWI

TONGA

NYANJA;TUMBUKA

NYANJA

Mozambique

Lilongwe

YAO

NYANJA;YAO

OFFICIAL LANGUAGE
ENGLISH

LOMWE;YAO

L. CHILWA

WIDESPREAD LANGUAGE
NYANJA

Mozambique

NOTE: DASHED LINES SHOW
OVERLAP OF LANGUAGE AREAS.

LOMWE;NYANJA   LOMWE

LANGUAGE FAMILY

KOKOLA

BANTU

SENA

km

0   50   100   150

©1999 SIL

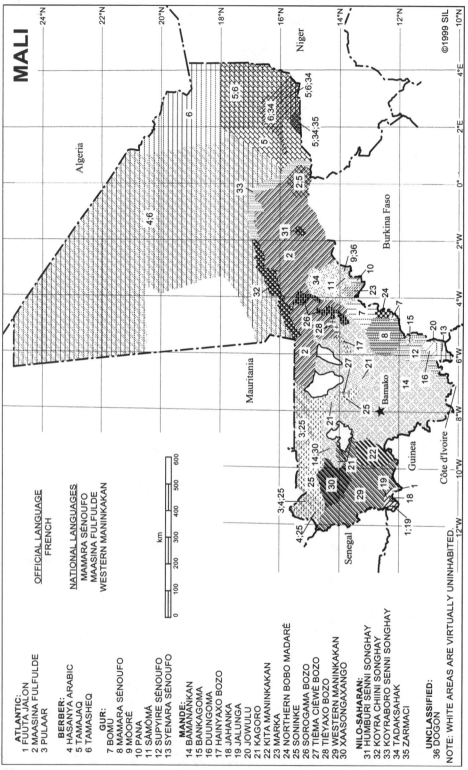

MALI

©1999 SIL

ATLANTIC:
1 FUUTA JALON
2 MAASINA FULFULDE
3 PULAAR

BERBER:
4 HASANYA ARABIC
5 TAMAJAQ
6 TAMASHEQ

GUR:
7 BOMU
8 MAMARA SÉNOUFO
9 MÒORÉ
10 PANA
11 SÀMÒMÀ
12 SUPYIRE SÉNOUFO
13 SYENARA SÉNOUFO

MANDE:
14 BAMANANKAN
15 BANKAGOMA
16 DUUNGOMA
17 HAINYAXO BOZO
18 JAHANKA
19 JALUNGA
20 JOWULU
21 KAGORO
22 KITA MANINKAKAN
23 MARKA
24 NORTHERN BOBO MADARÉ
25 SONINKE
26 SOROGAMA BOZO
27 TIÉMA CIÉWÉ BOZO
28 TIÉYAXO BOZO
29 WESTERN MANINKAKAN
30 XAASONGAXANGO

NILO-SAHARAN:
31 HUMBURI SENNI SONGHAY
32 KOYRA CHIINI SONGHAY
33 KOYRABORO SENNI SONGHAY
34 TADAKSAHAK
35 ZARMACI

UNCLASSIFIED:
36 DOGON

OFFICIAL LANGUAGE
FRENCH

NATIONAL LANGUAGES
MAMARA SÉNOUFO
MAASINA FULFULDE
WESTERN MANINKAKAN

km
0   100   200   300   400   500   600

NOTE: WHITE AREAS ARE VIRTUALLY UNINHABITED.

Algeria

Niger

Burkina Faso

Mauritania

Bamako

Guinea

Côte d'Ivoire

Senegal

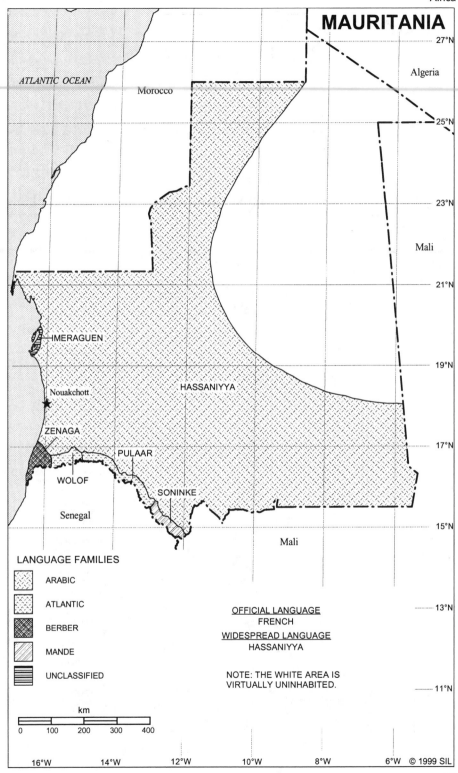

MAURITANIA

ATLANTIC OCEAN

Morocco

Algeria

Mali

IMERAGUEN

Nouakchott

HASSANIYYA

ZENAGA

PULAAR

WOLOF

SONINKE

Senegal

Mali

LANGUAGE FAMILIES

- ARABIC
- ATLANTIC
- BERBER
- MANDE
- UNCLASSIFIED

OFFICIAL LANGUAGE
FRENCH

WIDESPREAD LANGUAGE
HASSANIYYA

NOTE: THE WHITE AREA IS
VIRTUALLY UNINHABITED.

km

0   100   200   300   400

16°W   14°W   12°W   10°W   8°W   6°W   © 1999 SIL

27°N
25°N
23°N
21°N
19°N
17°N
15°N
13°N
11°N

MOZAMBIQUE

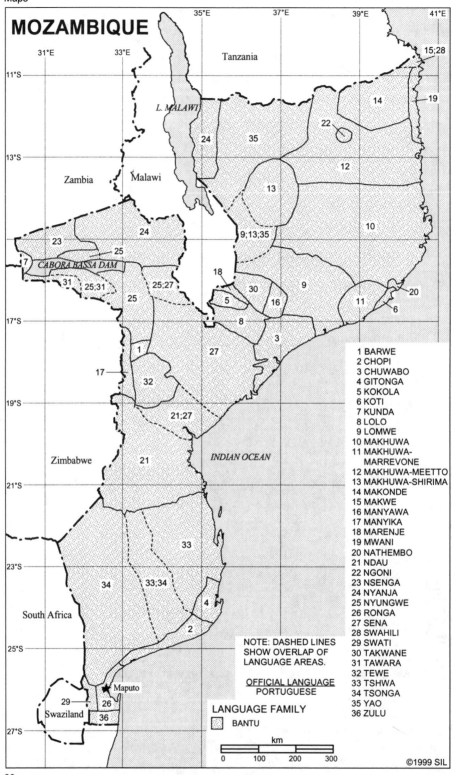

31°E   33°E   35°E   37°E   39°E   41°E

Tanzania

15;28

11°S

L. MALAWI

14

19

22

24   35

12

13°S

Zambia   Malawi

13

24

9;13;35

10

23

25

7   CABORA BASSA DAM

31

18

30   9

25;31   25;27

5   16   11   20

25

8   6

17°S

3

1

27

17

32

19°S

21;27

Zimbabwe   21

INDIAN OCEAN

21°S

33

23°S

34   33;34

4

South Africa

2

25°S

NOTE: DASHED LINES
SHOW OVERLAP OF
LANGUAGE AREAS.

OFFICIAL LANGUAGE
PORTUGUESE

29
26
Swaziland   36

Maputo

LANGUAGE FAMILY
BANTU

27°S

1 BARWE
2 CHOPI
3 CHUWABO
4 GITONGA
5 KOKOLA
6 KOTI
7 KUNDA
8 LOLO
9 LOMWE
10 MAKHUWA
11 MAKHUWA-
    MARREVONE
12 MAKHUWA-MEETTO
13 MAKHUWA-SHIRIMA
14 MAKONDE
15 MAKWE
16 MANYAWA
17 MANYIKA
18 MARENJE
19 MWANI
20 NATHEMBO
21 NDAU
22 NGONI
23 NSENGA
24 NYANJA
25 NYUNGWE
26 RONGA
27 SENA
28 SWAHILI
29 SWATI
30 TAKWANE
31 TAWARA
32 TEWE
33 TSHWA
34 TSONGA
35 YAO
36 ZULU

km

0   100   200   300

©1999 SIL

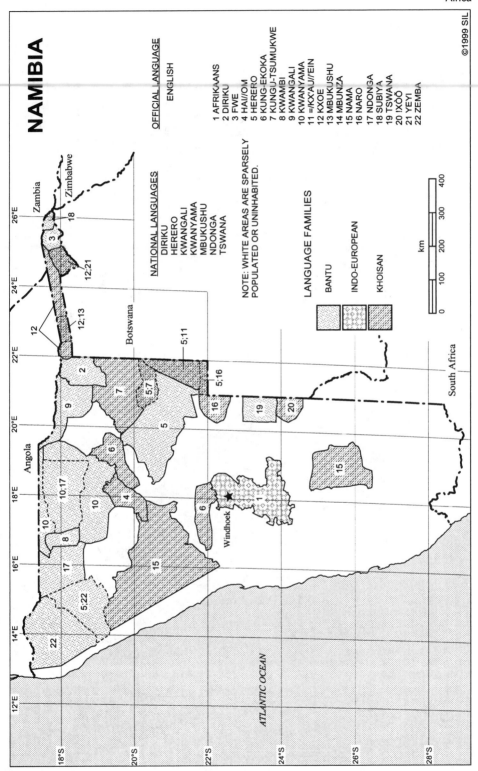

NAMIBIA

©1999 SIL

OFFICIAL LANGUAGE

ENGLISH

1 AFRIKAANS
2 DIRIKU
3 FWE
4 HAI//OM
5 HERERO
6 KUNG-EKOKA
7 KUNGU-TSUMUKWE
8 KWAMBI
9 KWANGALI
10 KWANYAMA
11 =/KX'AU//'EIN
12 KXOE
13 MBUKUSHU
14 MBUNZA
15 NAMA
16 NARO
17 NDONGA
18 SUBIYA
19 TSWANA
20 !XÓO
21 YEYI
22 ZEMBA

NATIONAL LANGUAGES
DIRIKU
HERERO
KWANGALI
KWANYAMA
MBUKUSHU
NDONGA
TSWANA

NOTE: WHITE AREAS ARE SPARSELY
POPULATED OR UNINHABITED.

LANGUAGE FAMILIES

BANTU

INDO-EUROPEAN

KHOISAN

km

0   100   200   300   400

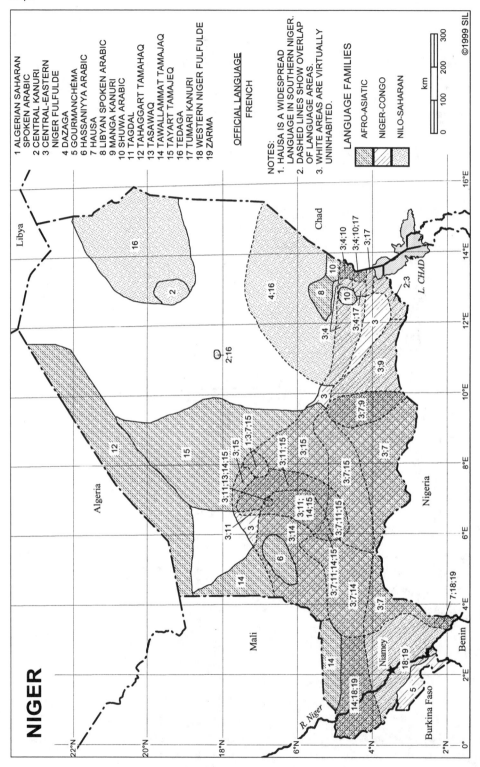

NIGER

1 ALGERIAN SAHARAN SPOKEN ARABIC
2 CENTRAL KANURI
3 CENTRAL-EASTERN NIGER FULFULDE
4 DAZAGA
5 GOURMANCHÉMA
6 HASSANIYYA ARABIC
7 HAUSA
8 LIBYAN SPOKEN ARABIC
9 MANGA KANURI
10 SHUWA ARABIC
11 TAGDAL
12 TAHAGGART TAMAHAQ
13 TASAWAQ
14 TAWALLAMMAT TAMAJAQ
15 TAYART TAMAJEQ
16 TEDAGA
17 TUMARI KANURI
18 WESTERN NIGER FULFULDE
19 ZARMA

OFFICIAL LANGUAGE
FRENCH

NOTES:
1. HAUSA IS A WIDESPREAD LANGUAGE IN SOUTHERN NIGER.
2. DASHED LINES SHOW OVERLAP OF LANGUAGE AREAS.
3. WHITE AREAS ARE VIRTUALLY UNINHABITED.

LANGUAGE FAMILIES
AFRO-ASIATIC
NIGER-CONGO
NILO-SAHARAN

©1999 SIL

km
0 100 200 300

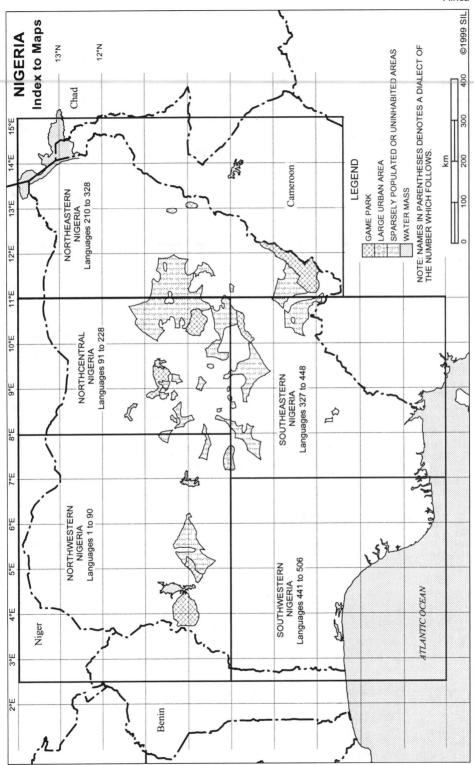

NIGERIA
Index to Maps

Africa

©1999 SIL

Niger

Benin

Chad

Cameroon

ATLANTIC OCEAN

NORTHWESTERN
NIGERIA
Languages 1 to 90

NORTHCENTRAL
NIGERIA
Languages 91 to 228

NORTHEASTERN
NIGERIA
Languages 210 to 328

SOUTHWESTERN
NIGERIA
Languages 441 to 506

SOUTHEASTERN
NIGERIA
Languages 327 to 448

LEGEND

GAME PARK
LARGE URBAN AREA
SPARSELY POPULATED OR UNINHABITED AREAS
WATER MASS

NOTE: NAMES IN PARENTHESES DENOTES A DIALECT OF
THE NUMBER WHICH FOLLOWS.

km
0   100   200   300   400

2°E   3°E   4°E   5°E   6°E   7°E   8°E   9°E   10°E   11°E   12°E   13°E   14°E   15°E

12°N

13°N

ABANYOM	386	BOLE	194	EFAI	422	GWAMHI-		JU	167
(ABAWA)(41)	42	BO-RUKUL	348	EFIK	419	WURI	12	JUKUN	
ABON	329	BU	134	EFUTOP	395	GWANDARA	52	TAKUM	354
ABUA	137	(BUJI)(110)	119	(EGBEMA)		(GWOROK)(69)	66	KAAN	258
ADUGE	464	BUKWEN	337	(503)	485	GYEM	104	KADARA	72
AFADE	276	BUMAJI	362	EGGON	350	(HANDA)(302)	304	(KAFANCHAN)	
AGATU	46	BURAK	224	EHUEUN	472	HASHA	131	(69)	67
AGOI	396	BURA-PABIR	268	EJAGHAM	412	HAUSA	11	KAG-FER-JIIR-	
AGWAGWUNE		BURE	197	EKAJUK	374	HOLMA	300	KOOR-ROR-	
	401	BURU	330	EKI	417	HUBA	297	US-ZUKSUN	13
ÀHÀN	469	BUSA	3	(EKIN)(412)	418	HUNGWORO	22	KAGOMA	57
AKE	351	CAKFEM-		EKIT	426	HUN-SAARE	15	KAIVI	84
AKPA	379	MUSHERE	140	EKPEYE	489	HWANA	267	KAKANDA	40
AKPES	468	CARA	111	ELEME	443	IBANI	413	KALABARI	495
ALAGO	50	(CENTRAL		ELOYI	47	IBIBIO	434	KAM	341
ALEGE	367	IDOMA)		EMAI-IULEHA-		IBILO	471	KAMANTAN	71
AMBO	331	(381)	380	ORA	477	IBINO	423	KAMI	37
AMO	92	CENTRAL		ENGENNI	488	(IBUNU)(110)	107	KAMO	230
ANAANG	435	KANURI	188	ENWAN	421	IBUORO	407	KANINGDON-	
ÁNCÁ	320	CENTÚÚM	233	EPIE	490	ICEVE-MACI	360	NINDEM	64
ARIGIDI	467	CHE	117	ERUWA	502	IDERE	433	KANUFI	63
ARUM-TESU	136	CIBAK	292	ESAN	451	IDOMA	381	KAPYA	356
ASHE	62	CINDA-REGI-		ETEBI	428	IDON	73	KAREKARE	191
ASU	23	TIYAL	20	ETKYWAN	338	IDUN	55	KARIYA	182
(ATAKAR)(69)	65	CISHINGINI	6	ETULO	353	IGALA	45	KHANA	436
ATEN	122	CIWOGAI	178	(ETUNO)(43)	458	IGBO	448	KHOLOK	220
ATSAM	114	C'LELA	14	EVANT	361	IGEDE	378	KINUKU	83
AWAK	229	COMO KARIM		FALI	295	IGUTA	118	KIONG	415
AYERE	466		210	FAM	339	IKA	450	KIR-BALAR	166
AYU	127	CORI	59	FIRAN	123	IKO	424	KIRIKE	441
BAAN	442	CROSS RIVER		FUM	321	IKPESHI	454	KOENOEM	146
BAANGI	17	MBEMBE	394	FUNGWA	28	IKU-GORA-		KOFA	305
BACAMA	256	DABA	294	FYAM	155	ANKWA	77	KOFYAR	347
BADE	190	DADIYA	235	FYER	153	IKULU	76	KOHUMONO	397
BAKPINKA	414	DASS	161	GAA	248	IKWERE	446	(KOLO)(498)	501
BALI	244	DAZA	202	GA'ANDA	266	ILUE	420	KOMA	310
BANGWINJI	226	DEFAKA	437	GADE	54	IRIGWE	116	KONA	240
(BANKAL)(205)	162	DEGEMA	494	GALAMBU	203	ISEKIRI	505	KONO	86
BARIBA	2	DENDI	9	GBAGYI	32	ISOKO	483	KORA IJA	34
BASA	44	DENO	195	GBARI	36	ITO	432	KORO ZUBA	35
BASA-		DERA	263	GBIRI-NIRAGU	91	ITU MBON		KPAN	340
GURMANA	30	DGHWEDE	282	GEJI	171	UZO	408	KPASAM	245
BATA	301	DIBO	38	GERA	198	IVBIE NORTH-		KUBI	196
BATU	328	DIJIM-BWILIM	232	GERUMA	175	OKPELA-		KUDU-CAMO	186
BAUCHI	27	DIRI	184	GHOTUO	478	ARHE	457	KUGAMA	252
BEELE	201	DOKA	74	GIIWO	199	IYAYU	475	KUGBO	497
BEGBERE-		DOKO-		GLAVDA	279	IYIVE	358	KUKELE	375
EJAR	61	UYANGA	404	GOEMAI	345	IZERE	120	KULERE	143
BEKWARRA	370	DONG	249	GOKANA	439	IZI-EZAA-IKWO-		KULUNG	217
BENA	303	DUGUZA	241	GUDE	296	MGBO	383	KUMBA	251
(BENDEGHE)		DUHWA	128	(GUDUF)(280)	265	IZON	503	KUPA	39
(412)	390	DULBU	168	GUDUF-GAVA	280	IZORA	99	KURAMA	78
BEROM	121	DUNGU	87	GUN-GBE	506	JANJI	112	KUSHI	223
BETE-BENDI	365	DUWAI	189	GUPA-ABAWA	41	JARA	269	KUTEP	355
BILE	243	DZA	242	(GURA)(91)	102	JARAWA	205	KUTTO	270
BINA	81	EASTERN		GURMANA	31	JERE	110	KUTURMI	75
BISENI	484	ACIPA	18	GURUNTUM-		JIBU	313	KWA	238
BITARE	332	EBIRA	43	MBAARU	204	JIMI	176	KWAAMI	200
BOGA	298	EBUGHU	429	(GUSU)(110)	108	JIRU	342	KWAK	322
BOGHOM	206	(ECHE)(471)	447	GVOKO	284	JJU	70	(KWONCI)	
BOKYI	389	EDO	479	GWA	106	JORTO	346	(221)	219

KYAK	236	(MUNGA LEELAN)	
LABIR	173	(239)	215
LAKA	213	MVANIP	325
LALA-ROBA	262	MWAGHAVUL	
LAMANG	281		124
LAME	97	NANDU TARI	132
LAMJA-DENGSA-		NDE-NSELE-	
TOLA	311	NTA	387
LARU	5	NDOE	388
LEGBO	399	NDOOLA	314
LEMORO	93	NDUNDA	324
LERE	95	NGAMO	193
LIJIYI	51	NGAS	151
LIMBUM	318	NGGWAHYI	293
LOKAA	400	NGIZIM	192
LONGUDA	260	NIGERIA	
LOO	222	MAMBILA	317
LOPA	4	NIGERIAN	
LUBILA	411	FULFULDE	172
LURI	164	NINGYE	126
MAAKA	272	(NIRAGU)(91)	80
MADA	53	NKARI	409
(MADAKA)		NKEM-NKUM	373
(27)	26	NKOROO	438
MAFA	283	NKUKOLI	403
MAK	216	NNAM	385
MALA	89	(NORTH ETUNG)	
MAMA	349	(412)	391
MANGAS	165	NORTHWEST	
MARGHI		GBAYA	343
CENTRAL	291	NUMANA-NUNKU-	
MASHI	336	GWANTU-	
MBE	368	NUMBU	133
MBOI	302	NUNGU	125
MBONGNO	326	NUPE-NUPE-	
MBULA-BWAZZA		TAKO	24
	257	NYAM	218
MBURKU	179	NYONG	250
MINGANG DOSO		NZANYI	299
	239	OBANLIKU	364
MINI	496	OBOLO	427
MISHIP	144	OBULOM	444
MIYA	181	ODUAL	500
MOM JANGO	308	ODUT	416
(MOMI)(308)	306	OGBAH	486
MONTOL	147	OGBIA	498
MOO	237	OGBOGOLO	492
MUMUYE	253	OGBRONUAGUM	
MUNDAT	130		445

OKOBO	431	(SHOLIO)(69)	68
OKODIA	487	SHOO-MINDA-	
OKO-ENI-		NYE	211
OSAYEN	461	SHUWA-	
OKPAMHERI	470	ZAMANI	275
OKPE	476	(SI)(101)	96
OKPE-IDESA-		SIRI	180
AKUKU	459	SOMYEWE	315
OLOMA	452	(SOUTH ETUNG)	
OLULUMO		(412)	392
IKOM	393	(SOUTH IDOMA)	
ORING	377	(381)	382
ORO	430	SOUTHEAST	
ORUMA	491	IJO	499
OSOSO	460	SUKUR	288
OTANK	359	SURUBU	79
PA'A	185	(TAKAYA)	
PAI	150	(95)	101
PERO	225	TAL	149
PITI	113	TALA	169
PIYA-		TAMBAS	152
KWONCI	221	TANGALE	228
POLCI	163	TANJIJILI	33
PONGU	25	TAROK	209
PSIKYE	289	TEDAGA	273
PUTAI	290	TEME	246
PUTUKWAM	369	TERA	271
PYAPUN	145	THA	214
RESHE	7	TIGON	
(ROBA)(262)	264	MBEMBE	333
RON	142	TITA	344
(RUHU)(97)	100	TIV	49
RUMA	90	(TIYAL)(20)	19
SAMBA DAKA	312	TORO	135
SAMBA LEKO	309	TSO	234
SANGA	109	TULA	231
SASARU-ENWAN-		TUMI	88
IGWE	455	TYAP	69
SAYA	157	UBAGHARA	402
SHA	129	UBANG	363
SHALL-		UDA	425
ZWALL	158	UHAMI	474
SHAMANG	60	UKAAN	465
SHAMA-		UKPE-	
SAMBUGA	21	BAYOBIRI	366
SHANGA	8	UKPET-	
SHAU	103	EHOM	405
SHENI	94	UKUE	473
SHIKI	174	UKWA	406

UKWUANI-ABOH-			
NDONI	482		
ULUKWUMI	449		
UMON	410		
UNEME	453		
URHOBO	481		
UVBIE	504		
UZEKWE	376		
VAGHAT-			
YA-BIJIM-			
LEGERI	156		
VEMGO-			
MABAS	286		
(VISIK)(286)	287		
VITI	323		
VONO	85		
VORO	259		
VUTE	316		
WAJA	261		
WAKA	247		
WANDALA	278		
WANNU	352		
WAPAN	208		
WARJI	183		
(WAYAM-			
RUBU)(27)	29		
WESTERN			
ACIPA	16		
WOM	307		
XEDI	285		
YACE	371		
YALA	372		
YAMBA	319		
YANGKAM	207		
YEKHEE	456		
YENDANG	255		
YESKWA	56		
YIWOM	148		
YORUBA	1		
(YOTI)(255)	254		
YUKUBEN	357		
ZANGWAL	170		
ZARI	159		
ZARMA	10		
ZEEM	160		
ZHIRE	58		
ZIRIYA	98		
ZIZILIVAKAN	277		
ZUMBUN	177		

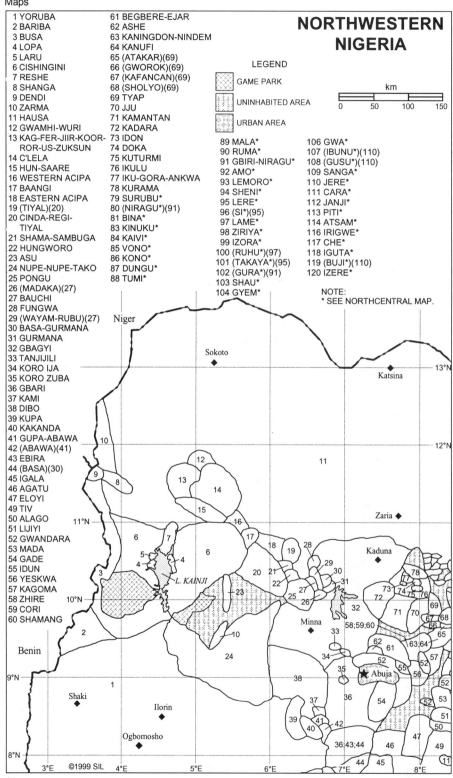

NORTHWESTERN NIGERIA

1 YORUBA
2 BARIBA
3 BUSA
4 LOPA
5 LARU
6 CISHINGINI
7 RESHE
8 SHANGA
9 DENDI
10 ZARMA
11 HAUSA
12 GWAMHI-WURI
13 KAG-FER-JIIR-KOOR-ROR-US-ZUKSUN
14 C'LELA
15 HUN-SAARE
16 WESTERN ACIPA
17 BAANGI
18 EASTERN ACIPA
19 (TIYAL)(20)
20 CINDA-REGI-TIYAL
21 SHAMA-SAMBUGA
22 HUNGWORO
23 ASU
24 NUPE-NUPE-TAKO
25 PONGU
26 (MADAKA)(27)
27 BAUCHI
28 FUNGWA
29 (WAYAM-RUBU)(27)
30 BASA-GURMANA
31 GURMANA
32 GBAGYI
33 TANJIJILI
34 KORO IJA
35 KORO ZUBA
36 GBARI
37 KAMI
38 DIBO
39 KUPA
40 KAKANDA
41 GUPA-ABAWA
42 (ABAWA)(41)
43 EBIRA
44 (BASA)(30)
45 IGALA
46 AGATU
47 ELOYI
49 TIV
50 ALAGO
51 LIJIYI
52 GWANDARA
53 MADA
54 GADE
55 IDUN
56 YESKWA
57 KAGOMA
58 ZHIRE
59 CORI
60 SHAMANG

61 BEGBERE-EJAR
62 ASHE
63 KANINGDON-NINDEM
64 KANUFI
65 (ATAKAR)(69)
66 (GWOROK)(69)
67 (KAFANCAN)(69)
68 (SHOLYO)(69)
69 TYAP
70 JJU
71 KAMANTAN
72 KADARA
73 IDON
74 DOKA
75 KUTURMI
76 IKULU
77 IKU-GORA-ANKWA
78 KURAMA
79 SURUBU*
80 (NIRAGU*)(91)
81 BINA*
83 KINUKU*
84 KAIVI*
85 VONO*
86 KONO*
87 DUNGU*
88 TUMI*

89 MALA*
90 RUMA*
91 GBIRI-NIRAGU*
92 AMO*
93 LEMORO*
94 SHENI*
95 LERE*
96 (SI*)(95)
97 LAME*
98 ZIRIYA*
99 IZORA*
100 (RUHU*)(97)
101 (TAKAYA*)(95)
102 (GURA*)(91)
103 SHAU*
104 GYEM*

106 GWA*
107 (IBUNU*)(110)
108 (GUSU*)(110)
109 SANGA*
110 JERE*
111 CARA*
112 JANJI*
113 PITI*
114 ATSAM*
116 IRIGWE*
117 CHE*
118 IGUTA*
119 (BUJI*)(110)
120 IZERE*

LEGEND

GAME PARK

UNINHABITED AREA

URBAN AREA

km
0   50   100   150

NOTE:
* SEE NORTHCENTRAL MAP.

©1999 SIL

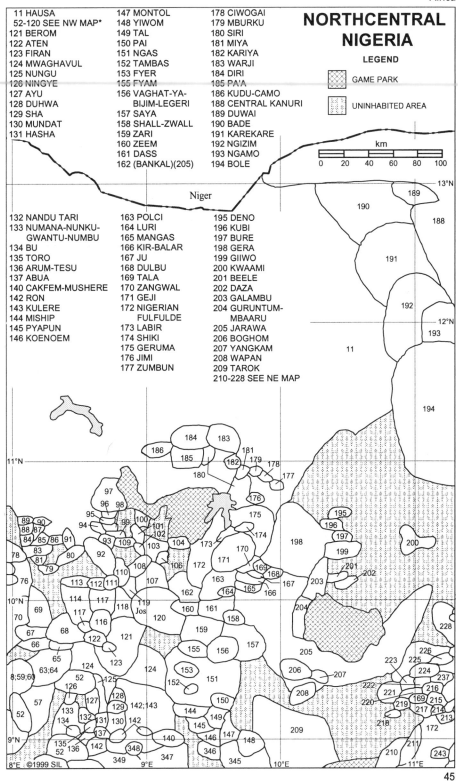

NORTHCENTRAL NIGERIA

LEGEND

GAME PARK

UNINHABITED AREA

km

0 20 40 60 80 100

11 HAUSA
52-120 SEE NW MAP*
121 BEROM
122 ATEN
123 FIRAN
124 MWAGHAVUL
125 NUNGU
126 NINGYE
127 AYU
128 DUHWA
129 SHA
130 MUNDAT
131 HASHA

147 MONTOL
148 YIWOM
149 TAL
150 PAI
151 NGAS
152 TAMBAS
153 FYER
155 FYAM
156 VAGHAT-YA-
     BIJIM-LEGERI
157 SAYA
158 SHALL-ZWALL
159 ZARI
160 ZEEM
161 DASS
162 (BANKAL)(205)

178 CIWOGAI
179 MBURKU
180 SIRI
181 MIYA
182 KARIYA
183 WARJI
184 DIRI
185 PA'A
186 KUDU-CAMO
188 CENTRAL KANURI
189 DUWAI
190 BADE
191 KAREKARE
192 NGIZIM
193 NGAMO
194 BOLE

Niger

132 NANDU TARI
133 NUMANA-NUNKU-
     GWANTU-NUMBU
134 BU
135 TORO
136 ARUM-TESU
137 ABUA
140 CAKFEM-MUSHERE
142 RON
143 KULERE
144 MISHIP
145 PYAPUN
146 KOENOEM

163 POLCI
164 LURI
165 MANGAS
166 KIR-BALAR
167 JU
168 DULBU
169 TALA
170 ZANGWAL
171 GEJI
172 NIGERIAN
     FULFULDE
173 LABIR
174 SHIKI
175 GERUMA
176 JIMI
177 ZUMBUN

195 DENO
196 KUBI
197 BURE
198 GERA
199 GIIWO
200 KWAAMI
201 BEELE
202 DAZA
203 GALAMBU
204 GURUNTUM-
     MBAARU
205 JARAWA
206 BOGHOM
207 YANGKAM
208 WAPAN
209 TAROK
210-228 SEE NE MAP

©1999 SIL

45

Maps

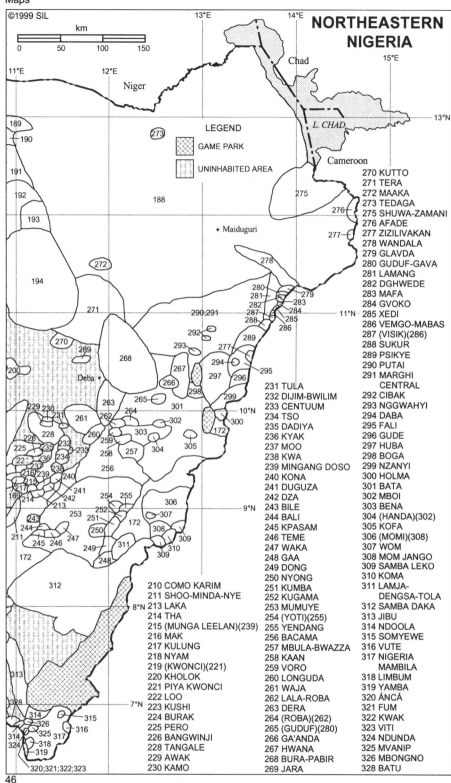

©1999 SIL

NORTHEASTERN NIGERIA

km

0   50   100   150

11°E   12°E   13°E   14°E   15°E

Niger

Chad

Cameroon

L. CHAD

13°N

Maiduguri

Deba

11°N

10°N

9°N

8°N

7°N

LEGEND

GAME PARK

UNINHABITED AREA

189
190
191
192
193
194
188
273
272
271
270
269
268
200
267
266
265
264
263
262
261
260
259
258
257
256
255
254
253
252
251
250
249
248
247
246
245
244
243
242
241
240
239
238
237
236
235
234
233
232
231
230
229
228
227
226
225
224
223
222
221
220
219
218
217
216
215
214
213
212
211
210
169
301
300
302
303
304
305
306
307
308
309
310
311
312
313
314
315
316
317
318
319
320
321
322
323
324
325
326
328
297
298
299
296
295
294
293
292
291
290
289
288
287
286
285
284
283
282
281
280
279
278
277
276
275
172

210 COMO KARIM
211 SHOO-MINDA-NYE
213 LAKA
214 THA
215 (MUNGA LEELAN)(239)
216 MAK
217 KULUNG
218 NYAM
219 (KWONCI)(221)
220 KHOLOK
221 PIYA KWONCI
222 LOO
223 KUSHI
224 BURAK
225 PERO
226 BANGWINJI
228 TANGALE
229 AWAK
230 KAMO

231 TULA
232 DIJIM-BWILIM
233 CENTUUM
234 TSO
235 DADIYA
236 KYAK
237 MOO
238 KWA
239 MINGANG DOSO
240 KONA
241 DUGUZA
242 DZA
243 BILE
244 BALI
245 KPASAM
246 TEME
247 WAKA
248 GAA
249 DONG
250 NYONG
251 KUMBA
252 KUGAMA
253 MUMUYE
254 (YOTI)(255)
255 YENDANG
256 BACAMA
257 MBULA-BWAZZA
258 KAAN
259 VORO
260 LONGUDA
261 WAJA
262 LALA-ROBA
263 DERA
264 (ROBA)(262)
265 (GUDUF)(280)
266 GA'ANDA
267 HWANA
268 BURA-PABIR
269 JARA

270 KUTTO
271 TERA
272 MAAKA
273 TEDAGA
275 SHUWA-ZAMANI
276 AFADE
277 ZIZILIVAKAN
278 WANDALA
279 GLAVDA
280 GUDUF-GAVA
281 LAMANG
282 DGHWEDE
283 MAFA
284 GVOKO
285 XEDI
286 VEMGO-MABAS
287 (VISIK)(286)
288 SUKUR
289 PSIKYE
290 PUTAI
291 MARGHI
     CENTRAL
292 CIBAK
293 NGGWAHYI
294 DABA
295 FALI
296 GUDE
297 HUBA
298 BOGA
299 NZANYI
300 HOLMA
301 BATA
302 MBOI
303 BENA
304 (HANDA)(302)
305 KOFA
306 (MOMI)(308)
307 WOM
308 MOM JANGO
309 SAMBA LEKO
310 KOMA
311 LAMJA-
     DENGSA-TOLA
312 SAMBA DAKA
313 JIBU
314 NDOOLA
315 SOMYEWE
316 VUTE
317 NIGERIA
     MAMBILA
318 LIMBUM
319 YAMBA
320 ÁNCÁ
321 FUM
322 KWAK
323 VITI
324 NDUNDA
325 MVANIP
326 MBONGNO
328 BATU

46

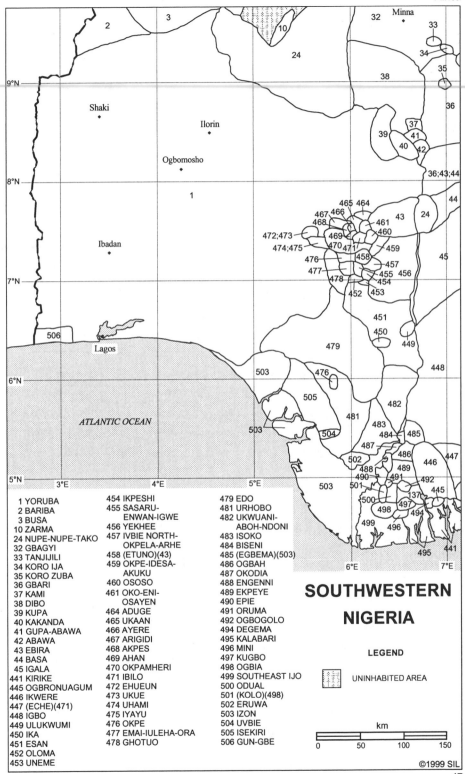

Africa

Minna

32

33

34

35

36

9°N

Shaki

Ilorin

Ogbomosho

37
41
40 42

39

38

36;43;44

8°N

1

44

465 464
467 466
468 461
460
43 24

472;473 469
474;475 470 471 459

476 458 457
477 455 456
478 454
452 453

45

451

450
449

Ibadan

7°N

506

Lagos

479

448

503

476

6°N

505

ATLANTIC OCEAN

481 482

483
484 485

503

504

487

486
446 447

502

488 489

490 491 492

5°N
3°E   4°E   5°E

503 501

500 137 445

498 497 494

499 496

495

441

6°E   7°E

SOUTHWESTERN

NIGERIA

LEGEND

UNINHABITED AREA

km

0   50   100   150

©1999 SIL

1 YORUBA
2 BARIBA
3 BUSA
10 ZARMA
24 NUPE-NUPE-TAKO
32 GBAGYI
33 TANJIJILI
34 KORO IJA
35 KORO ZUBA
36 GBARI
37 KAMI
38 DIBO
39 KUPA
40 KAKANDA
41 GUPA-ABAWA
42 ABAWA
43 EBIRA
44 BASA
45 IGALA
441 KIRIKE
445 OGBRONUAGUM
446 IKWERE
447 (ECHE)(471)
448 IGBO
449 ULUKWUMI
450 IKA
451 ESAN
452 OLOMA
453 UNEME

454 IKPESHI
455 SASARU-
    ENWAN-IGWE
456 YEKHEE
457 IVBIE NORTH-
    OKPELA-ARHE
458 (ETUNO)(43)
459 OKPE-IDESA-
    AKUKU
460 OSOSO
461 OKO-ENI-
    OSAYEN
464 ADUGE
465 UKAAN
466 AYERE
467 ARIGIDI
468 AKPES
469 AHAN
470 OKPAMHERI
471 IBILO
472 EHUEUN
473 UKUE
474 UHAMI
475 IYAYU
476 OKPE
477 EMAI-IULEHA-ORA
478 GHOTUO

479 EDO
481 URHOBO
482 UKWUANI-
    ABOH-NDONI
483 ISOKO
484 BISENI
485 (EGBEMA)(503)
486 OGBAH
487 OKODIA
488 ENGENNI
489 EKPEYE
490 EPIE
491 ORUMA
492 OGBOGOLO
494 DEGEMA
495 KALABARI
496 MINI
497 KUGBO
498 OGBIA
499 SOUTHEAST IJO
500 ODUAL
501 (KOLO)(498)
502 ERUWA
503 IZON
504 UVBIE
505 ISEKIRI
506 GUN-GBE

Maps

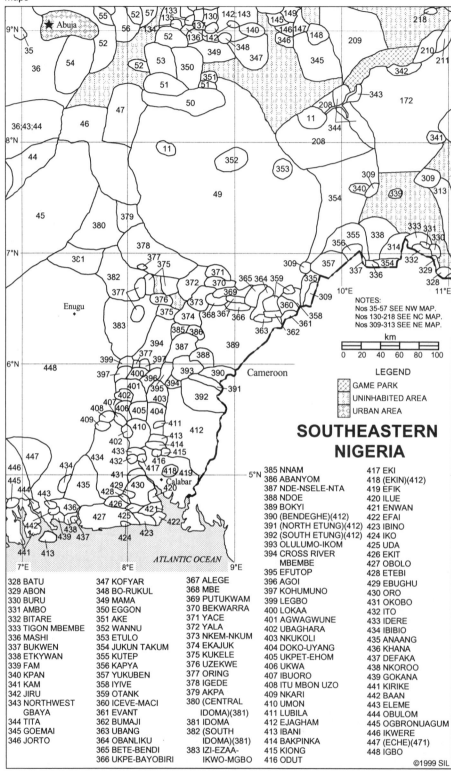

SOUTHEASTERN NIGERIA

NOTES:
Nos 35-57 SEE NW MAP.
Nos 130-218 SEE NC MAP.
Nos 309-313 SEE NE MAP.

LEGEND
GAME PARK
UNINHABITED AREA
URBAN AREA

385 NNAM
386 ABANYOM
387 NDE-NSELE-NTA
388 NDOE
389 BOKYI
390 (BENDEGHE)(412)
391 (NORTH ETUNG)(412)
392 (SOUTH ETUNG)(412)
393 OLULUMO-IKOM
394 CROSS RIVER
    MBEMBE
395 EFUTOP
396 AGOI
397 KOHUMUNO
399 LEGBO
400 LOKAA
401 AGWAGWUNE
402 UBAGHARA
403 NKUKOLI
404 DOKO-UYANG
405 UKPET-EHOM
406 UKWA
407 IBUORO
408 ITU MBON UZO
409 NKARI
410 UMON
411 LUBILA
412 EJAGHAM
413 IBANI
414 BAKPINKA
415 KIONG
416 ODUT

417 EKI
418 (EKIN)(412)
419 EFIK
420 ILUE
421 ENWAN
422 EFAI
423 IBINO
424 IKO
425 UDA
426 EKIT
427 OBOLO
428 ETEBI
429 EBUGHU
430 ORO
431 OKOBO
432 ITO
433 IDERE
434 IBIBIO
435 ANAANG
436 KHANA
437 DEFAKA
438 NKOROO
439 GOKANA
441 KIRIKE
442 BAAN
443 ELEME
444 OBULOM
445 OGBRONUAGUM
446 IKWERE
447 (ECHE)(471)
448 IGBO

328 BATU
329 ABON
330 BURU
331 AMBO
332 BITARE
333 TIGON MBEMBE
336 MASHI
337 BUKWEN
338 ETKYWAN
339 FAM
340 KPAN
341 KAM
342 JIRU
343 NORTHWEST
    GBAYA
344 TITA
345 GOEMAI
346 JORTO

347 KOFYAR
348 BO-RUKUL
349 MAMA
350 EGGON
351 AKE
352 WANNU
353 ETULO
354 JUKUN TAKUM
355 KUTEP
356 KAPYA
357 YUKUBEN
358 IYIVE
359 OTANK
360 ICEVE-MACI
361 EVANT
362 BUMAJI
363 UBANG
364 OBANLIKU
365 BETE-BENDI
366 UKPE-BAYOBIRI

367 ALEGE
368 MBE
369 PUTUKWAM
370 BEKWARRA
371 YACE
372 YALA
373 NKEM-NKUM
374 EKAJUK
375 KUKELE
376 UZEKWE
377 ORING
378 IGEDE
379 AKPA
380 (CENTRAL
    IDOMA)(381)
381 IDOMA
382 (SOUTH
    IDOMA)(381)
383 IZI-EZAA-
    IKWO-MGBO

©1999 SIL

48

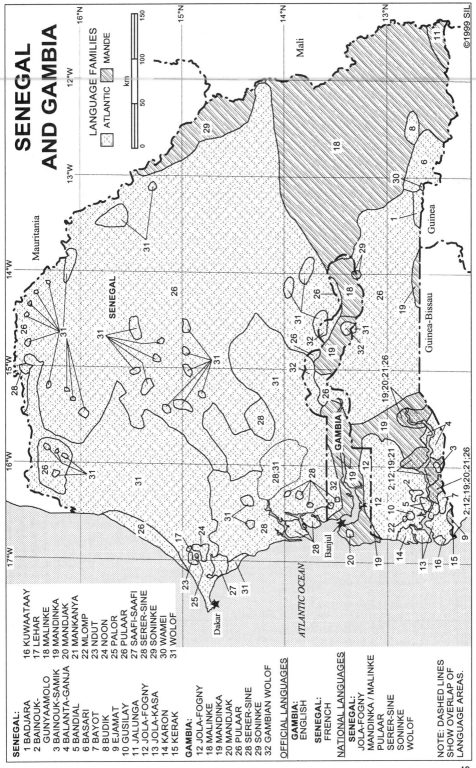

SENEGAL AND GAMBIA

Africa

©1999 SIL

LANGUAGE FAMILIES

ATLANTIC   MANDE

km
0   50   100   150

SENEGAL:

1 BADJARA	16 KUWAATAAY
2 BAINOUK-	17 LEHAR
GUNYAAMOLO	18 MALINKE
3 BAINOUK-SAMIK	19 MANDINKA
4 BALANTA-GANJA	20 MANDJAK
5 BANDIAL	21 MANKANYA
6 BASARI	22 MLOMP
7 BAYOT	23 NDUT
8 BUDIK	24 NOON
9 EJAMAT	25 PALOR
10 GUSILAY	26 PULAAR
11 JALUNGA	27 SAAFI-SAAFI
12 JOLA-FOGNY	28 SERER-SINE
13 JOLA-KASA	29 SONINKE
14 KARON	30 WAMEI
15 KERAK	31 WOLOF

GAMBIA:

12 JOLA-FOGNY	28 SERER-SINE
18 MALINKE	29 SONINKE
19 MANDINKA	32 GAMBIAN WOLOF
20 MANDJAK	
26 PULAAR	

OFFICIAL LANGUAGES

GAMBIA:
ENGLISH

SENEGAL:
FRENCH

NATIONAL LANGUAGES

SENEGAL:
JOLA-FOGNY
MANDINKA / MALINKE
PULAAR
SERER-SINE
SONINKE
WOLOF

NOTE: DASHED LINES
SHOW OVERLAP OF
LANGUAGE AREAS.

49

SIERRA LEONE

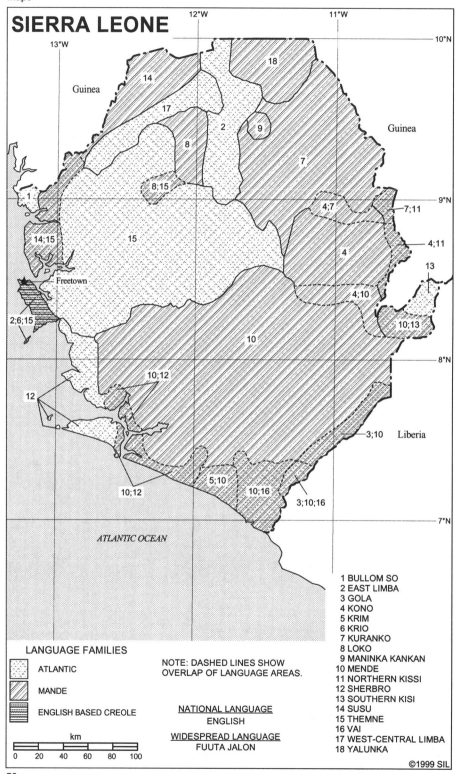

LANGUAGE FAMILIES

- ATLANTIC
- MANDE
- ENGLISH BASED CREOLE

km
0   20   40   60   80   100

NOTE: DASHED LINES SHOW
OVERLAP OF LANGUAGE AREAS.

NATIONAL LANGUAGE
ENGLISH

WIDESPREAD LANGUAGE
FUUTA JALON

1 BULLOM SO
2 EAST LIMBA
3 GOLA
4 KONO
5 KRIM
6 KRIO
7 KURANKO
8 LOKO
9 MANINKA KANKAN
10 MENDE
11 NORTHERN KISSI
12 SHERBRO
13 SOUTHERN KISI
14 SUSU
15 THEMNE
16 VAI
17 WEST-CENTRAL LIMBA
18 YALUNKA

©1999 SIL

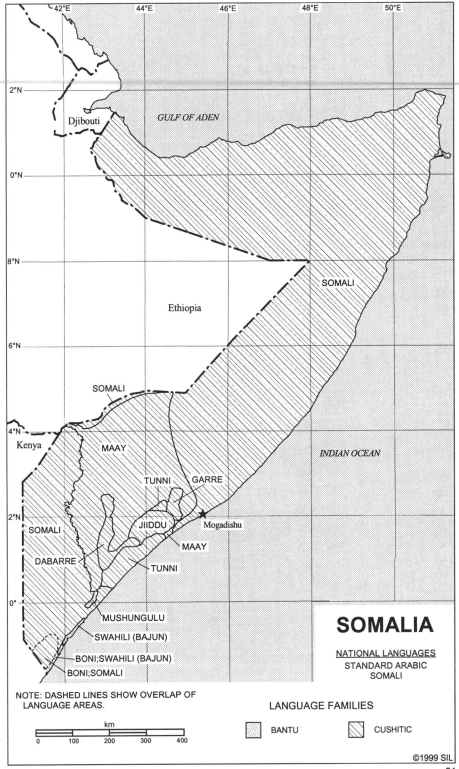

SOMALIA

NATIONAL LANGUAGES
STANDARD ARABIC
SOMALI

NOTE: DASHED LINES SHOW OVERLAP OF
LANGUAGE AREAS.

LANGUAGE FAMILIES

BANTU   CUSHITIC

km
0   100   200   300   400

©1999 SIL

Maps

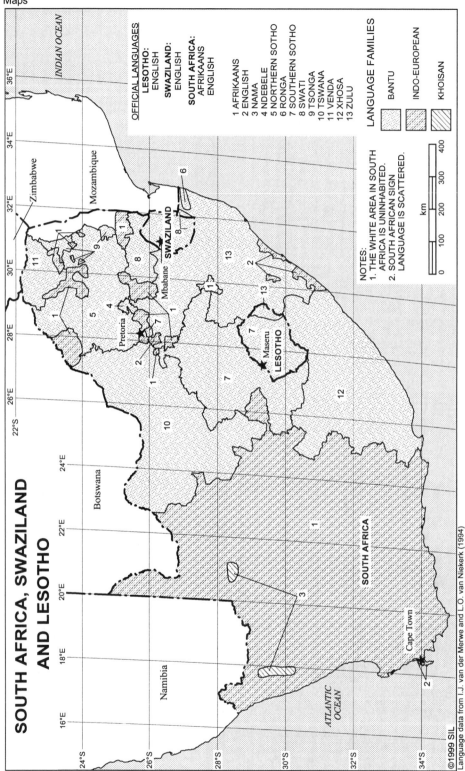

SOUTH AFRICA, SWAZILAND AND LESOTHO

OFFICIAL LANGUAGES
LESOTHO:
ENGLISH
SWAZILAND:
ENGLISH
SOUTH AFRICA:
AFRIKAANS
ENGLISH

1 AFRIKAANS
2 ENGLISH
3 NAMA
4 NDEBELE
5 NORTHERN SOTHO
6 RONGA
7 SOUTHERN SOTHO
8 SWATI
9 TSONGA
10 TSWANA
11 VENDA
12 XHOSA
13 ZULU

LANGUAGE FAMILIES

BANTU

INDO-EUROPEAN

KHOISAN

NOTES:
1. THE WHITE AREA IN SOUTH
AFRICA IS UNINHABITED.
2. SOUTH AFRICAN SIGN
LANGUAGE IS SCATTERED.

km
0 100 200 300 400

©1999 SIL

Language data from I.J. van der Merwe and L.O. van Niekerk (1994)

52

SUDAN

28°E 30°E 32°E 34°E 36°E 38°E

23°N

22°E 24°E 26°E Egypt

Libya

RED SEA

21°N

NOBIIN

BEDAWI

19°N

KENUZI-DONGOLA

Chad

TIGRÉ

17°N

Al-Khartoum

Eritrea

ZAGHAWA

15°N

MIDOB

SUNGOR

13°N

FUR

SINYAR DAJU DAR FUR SEE SEPARATE MAP

DAJU DAR SILA

GAAM
AKA

11°N

MOLO
BURUN
JUMJUM

YULU MASALIT

UDUK

Ethiopia

NORTHWESTERN DINKA SHILLUK MABAAN

GULA INDRI NJALGULGULE

KOMO

9°N

AJA THURI

SOUTHWESTERN DINKA NUER OPUUO

GBAYA

FEROGE BANDA, WEST CENTRAL

BANDA-NDÉLÉ LUWO

BANDA-BANDA BAI

BANDA-MBRÉS BONGO ANUAK

BANDA, MID-SOUTHERN BELANDA BOR SOUTHEASTERN DINKA KACIPO-BALESI

7°N

BANDA, TOGBO-VARA SOUTH CENTRAL DINKA MURLE

BELI MURLE

BELANDA VIRI REEL SURI

MO'DA NYAMUSA-MOLO

Central African
Republic

JUR MODO MANDARI

MOROKODO PÄRI TENNET

MORU LULUBO TOPOSA

ZANDE AVOKAYA LOPPIT LONGARIM

5°N

BAKA

BARI LOKOYA

Democratic Republic
of
Congo

MÜNDÜ KAKWA MA'DI OTUHO DONGOTONO

LANGO DIDINGA

KELIKO ACHOLI L. TURKANA

3°N

Uganda

Kenya

53

SUDAN - ENLARGED AREA

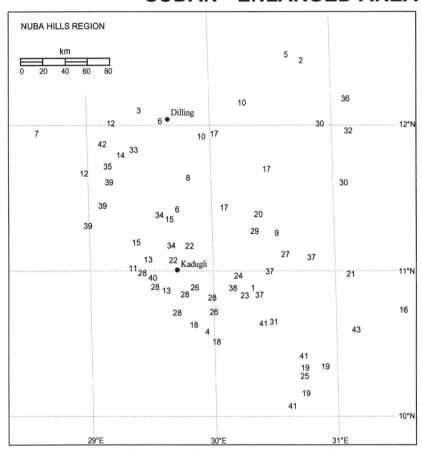

NUBA HILLS REGION

km

| 0 | 20 | 40 | 60 | 80 |

1 ACHERON	22 LOGORIK
2 AFITTI	23 LUMUN
3 AMA	24 MORO
4 DAGIK	25 NDING
5 DAIR	26 NGILE
6 DILLING	27 OTORO
7 EL HUGEIRAT	28 SHATT
8 GHULFAN	29 SHWAI
9 HEIBAN	30 TAGOI
10 KADARU	31 TALODI
11 KANGA	32 TEGALI
12 KARKO	33 TEMEIN
13 KATCHA- KADUGLI-MIRI	34 TESE
14 KATLA	35 TIMA
15 KEIGA	36 TINGAL
16 KO	37 TIRA
17 KOALIB	38 TOCHO
18 KRONGO	39 TULISHI
19 LAFOFA	40 TUMMA
20 LARO	41 TUMTUM
21 LOGOL	42 WALI
	43 WARNANG

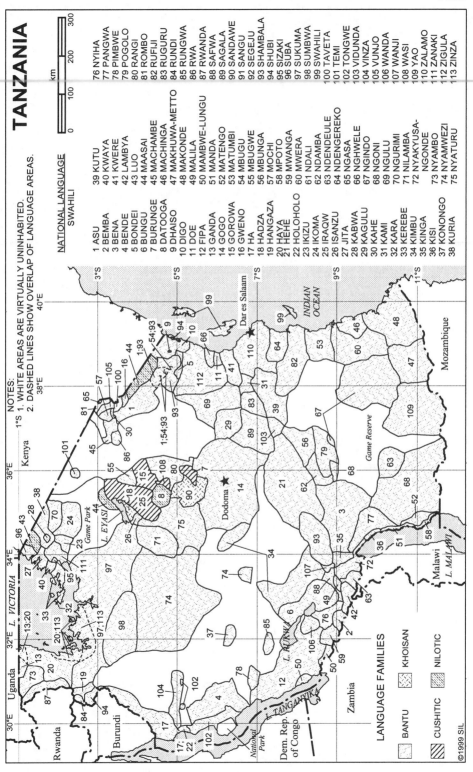

TANZANIA

NATIONAL LANGUAGE
SWAHILI

1 ASU
2 BEMBA
3 BENA
4 BENDE
5 BONDEI
6 BUNGU
7 BURUNGE
8 DATOOGA
9 DHAISO
10 DIGO
11 DOE
12 FIPA
13 GANDA
14 GOGO
15 GOROWA
16 GWENO
17 HA
18 HADZA
19 HANGAZA
20 HAYA
21 HEHE
22 HOLOHOLO
23 IKIZU
24 IKOMA
25 IRAQW
26 ISANZU
27 JITA
28 KABWA
29 KAGULU
30 KAHE
31 KAMI
32 KARA
33 KEREBE
34 KIMBU
35 KINGA
36 KISI
37 KONONGO
38 KURIA

39 KUTU
40 KWAYA
41 KWERE
42 LAMBYA
43 LUO
44 MAASAI
45 MACHAMBE
46 MACHINGA
47 MAKHUWA-METTO
48 MAKONDE
49 MALILA
50 MAMBWE-LUNGU
51 MANDA
52 MATENGO
53 MATUMBI
54 MBUGU
55 MBUGWE
56 MBUNGA
57 MOCHI
58 MPOTO
59 MWANGA
60 MWERA
61 NDALI
62 NDAMBA
63 NDENDEULE
64 NDENGEREKO
65 NGASA
66 NGHWELE
67 NGINDO
68 NGONI
69 NGULU
70 NGURIMI
71 NILAMBA
72 NYAKYUSA-NGONDE
73 NYAMBO
74 NYAMWEZI
75 NYATURU

76 NYIHA
77 PANGWA
78 PIMBWE
79 POGOLO
80 RANGI
81 ROMBO
82 RUFIJI
83 RUGURU
84 RUNDI
85 RUNGWA
86 RWA
87 RWANDA
88 SAFWA
89 SAGALA
90 SANDAWE
91 SANGU
92 SEGEJU
93 SHAMBALA
94 SHUBI
95 SIZAKI
96 SUBA
97 SUKUMA
98 SUMBWA
99 SWAHILI
100 TAVETA
101 TEMI
102 TONGWE
103 VIDUNDA
104 VINZA
105 VUNJO
106 WANDA
107 WANJI
108 WASI
109 YAO
110 ZALAMO
111 ZANAKI
112 ZIGULA
113 ZINZA

NOTES:
1. WHITE AREAS ARE VIRTUALLY UNINHABITED.
2. DASHED LINES SHOW OVERLAP OF LANGUAGE AREAS.

LANGUAGE FAMILIES

BANTU

KHOISAN

CUSHITIC

NILOTIC

©1999 SIL

Maps

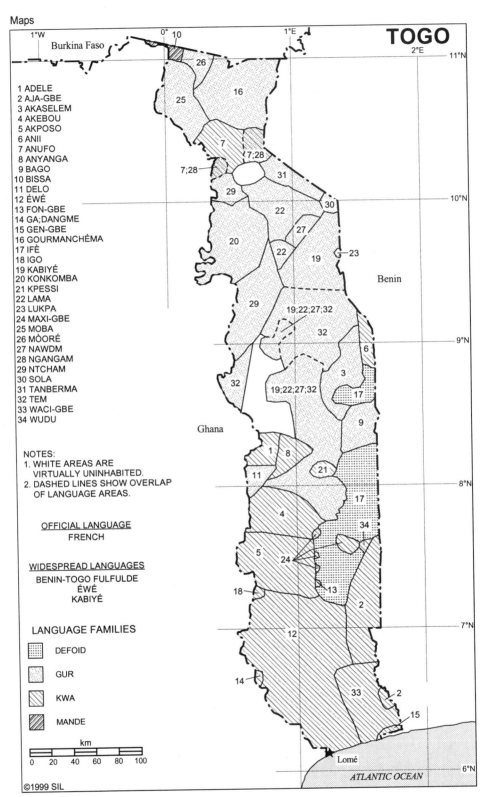

TOGO

1 ADELE
2 AJA-GBE
3 AKASELEM
4 AKEBOU
5 AKPOSO
6 ANII
7 ANUFO
8 ANYANGA
9 BAGO
10 BISSA
11 DELO
12 ÉWÉ
13 FON-GBE
14 GA;DANGME
15 GEN-GBE
16 GOURMANCHÉMA
17 IFÈ
18 IGO
19 KABIYÉ
20 KONKOMBA
21 KPESSI
22 LAMA
23 LUKPA
24 MAXI-GBE
25 MOBA
26 MÒORÉ
27 NAWDM
28 NGANGAM
29 NTCHAM
30 SOLA
31 TANBERMA
32 TEM
33 WACI-GBE
34 WUDU

NOTES:
1. WHITE AREAS ARE
   VIRTUALLY UNINHABITED.
2. DASHED LINES SHOW OVERLAP
   OF LANGUAGE AREAS.

OFFICIAL LANGUAGE
FRENCH

WIDESPREAD LANGUAGES
BENIN-TOGO FULFULDE
ÉWÉ
KABIYÉ

LANGUAGE FAMILIES

DEFOID

GUR

KWA

MANDE

km

0   20   40   60   80   100

©1999 SIL

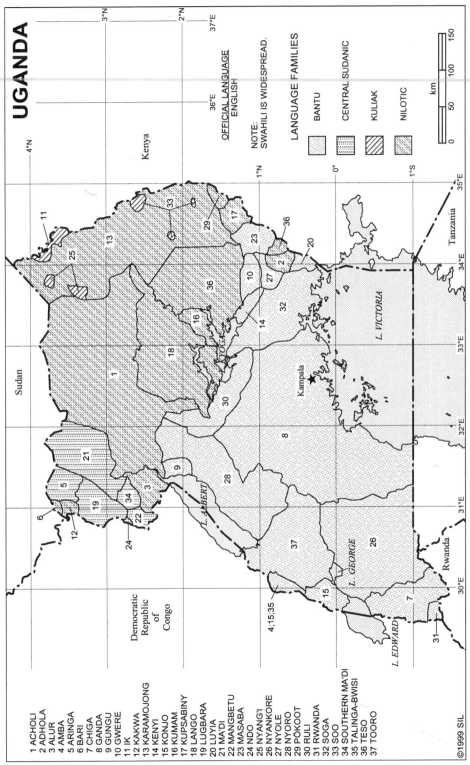

UGANDA

Africa

OFFICIAL LANGUAGE
ENGLISH

NOTE:
SWAHILI IS WIDESPREAD.

LANGUAGE FAMILIES

BANTU

CENTRAL SUDANIC

KULIAK

NILOTIC

km
0   50   100   150

Kenya

Sudan

Democratic
Republic
of
Congo

Tanzania

Rwanda

L. VICTORIA

L. ALBERT

L. GEORGE

L. EDWARD

Kampala

1 ACHOLI
2 ADHOLA
3 ALUR
4 AMBA
5 ARINGA
6 BARI
7 CHIGA
8 GANDA
9 GUNGU
10 GWERE
11 IK
12 KAKWA
13 KARAMOJONG
14 KENYI
15 KONJO
16 KUMAM
17 KUPSABINY
18 LANGO
19 LUGBARA
20 LUYIA
21 MA'DI
22 MANGBETU
23 MASABA
24 NDO
25 NYANG'I
26 NYANKORE
27 NYOLE
28 NYORO
29 PÖKOOT
30 RULI
31 RWANDA
32 SOGA
33 SOO
34 SOUTHERN MA'DI
35 TALINGA-BWISI
36 TESO
37 TOORO

©1999 SIL

57

Maps

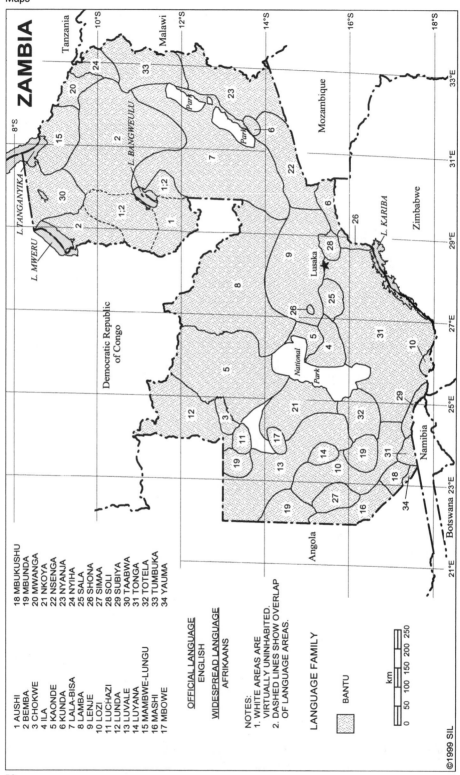

ZAMBIA

1 AUSHI
2 BEMBA
3 CHOKWE
4 ILA
5 KAONDE
6 KUNDA
7 LALA-BISA
8 LAMBA
9 LENJE
10 LOZI
11 LUCHAZI
12 LUNDA
13 LUVALE
14 LUYANA
15 MAMBWE-LUNGU
16 MASHI
17 MBOWE

18 MBUKUSHU
19 MBUNDA
20 MWANGA
21 NKOYA
22 NSENGA
23 NYANJA
24 NYIHA
25 SALA
26 SHONA
27 SIMAA
28 SOLI
29 SUBIYA
30 TAABWA
31 TONGA
32 TOTELA
33 TUMBUKA
34 YAUMA

OFFICIAL LANGUAGE
ENGLISH

WIDESPREAD LANGUAGE
AFRIKAANS

NOTES:
1. WHITE AREAS ARE
VIRTUALLY UNINHABITED.
2. DASHED LINES SHOW OVERLAP
OF LANGUAGE AREAS.

LANGUAGE FAMILY

BANTU

km
0 50 100 150 200 250

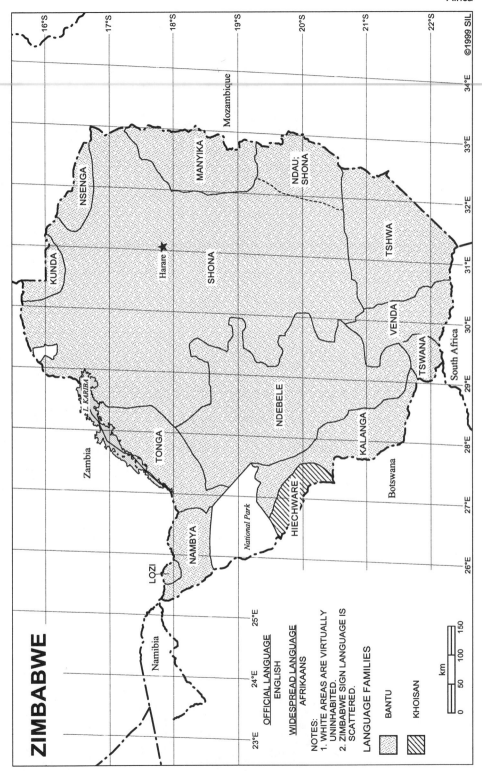

ZIMBABWE

Africa

©1999 SIL

Mozambique

NSENGA

MANYIKA

NDAU;
SHONA

KUNDA

Harare

SHONA

TSHWA

VENDA

Zambia

KARIBA

TONGA

NDEBELE

TSWANA

South Africa

KALANGA

Botswana

National Park

HIECHWARE

NAMBYA

LOZI

Namibia

OFFICIAL LANGUAGE
ENGLISH

WIDESPREAD LANGUAGE
AFRIKAANS

NOTES:
1. WHITE AREAS ARE VIRTUALLY
UNINHABITED.
2. ZIMBABWE SIGN LANGUAGE IS
SCATTERED.

LANGUAGE FAMILIES

BANTU

KHOISAN

km

0   50   100   150

Americas Maps

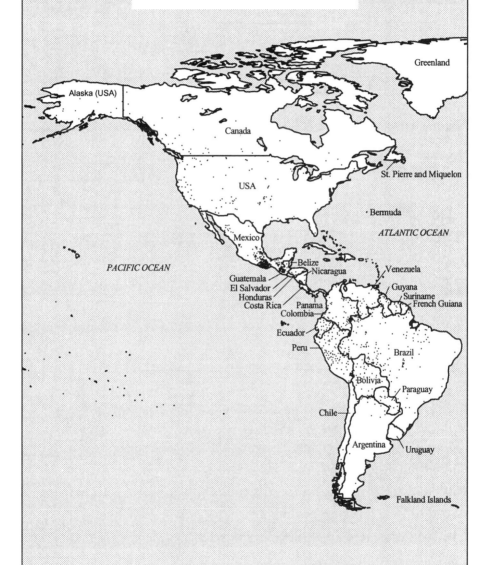

THE AMERICAS

km

0   2000   4000   6000

Greenland

Alaska (USA)

Canada

USA

St. Pierre and Miquelon

· Bermuda

ATLANTIC OCEAN

Mexico

PACIFIC OCEAN

Belize
Nicaragua
Guatemala
El Salvador
Honduras
Costa Rica   Panama
Colombia

Venezuela

Guyana
Suriname
French Guiana

Ecuador

Peru

Brazil

Bolivia

Paraguay

Chile

Argentina   Uruguay

Falkland Islands

©1999 SIL

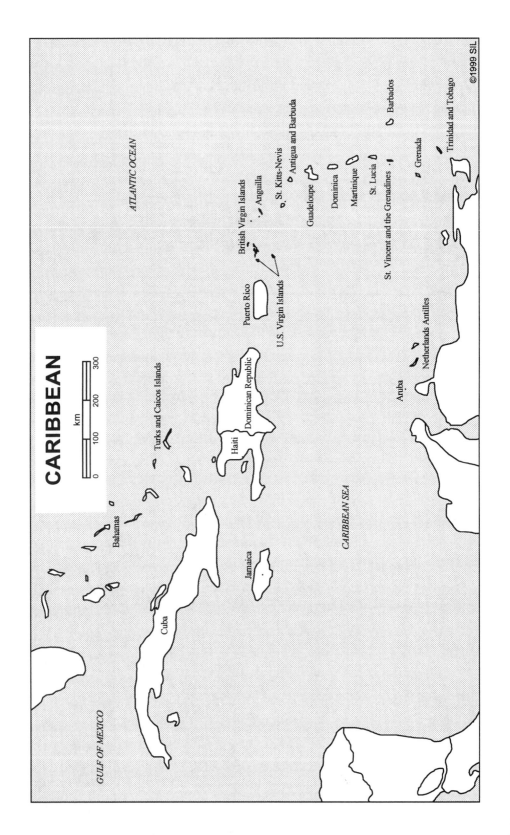

CARIBBEAN

km

0 100 200 300

©1999 SIL

GULF OF MEXICO

ATLANTIC OCEAN

CARIBBEAN SEA

Cuba

Jamaica

Bahamas

Turks and Caicos Islands

Haiti

Dominican Republic

Puerto Rico

U.S. Virgin Islands

British Virgin Islands

Anguilla

St. Kitts-Nevis

Antigua and Barbuda

Guadeloupe

Dominica

Martinique

St. Lucia

St. Vincent and the Grenadines

Barbados

Grenada

Trinidad and Tobago

Aruba

Netherlands Antilles

ARGENTINA AND CHILE

NATIONAL LANGUAGES
SPANISH

LANGUAGE FAMILIES

- ALACALUFAN
- ARAUCANIAN
- AUSTRONESIAN
- AYMARAN
- CHON
- TUPI
- LULE-VILELA
- MATACO-GUAICURU
- QUECHUAN

NOTE: DASHED LINES SHOW
OVERLAP OF LANGUAGE AREAS.

©1999 SIL

Map labels:

CHILEAN QUECHUA
CENTRAL AYMARA
PILAGÁ
TOBA
MBYÁ GUARANÍ
VILELA
KAIWÁ
CHILE
SANTIAGO DEL ESTERO QUICHUA
MOCOVÍ
Paraná River
Uruguay
Santiago
Buenos Aires
ARGENTINA
MAPUDUNGUN
HUILLICHE
MAPUDUNGUN
TEHUELCHE
PACIFIC OCEAN
ATLANTIC OCEAN
QAWASQAR

Inset (66°W – 62°W, 22°S – 24°S):

Bolivia
Paraguay
Argentina

1 SOUTH BOLIVIAN QUECHUA
2 NORTHWEST JUJUY QUECHUA
3 WICHÍ LHAMTÉS NOCTEN
4 CHULUPÍ
5 IYOJWA'JA CHOROTE
6 IYO'WUJWA CHOROTE
7 TAPIETÉ
8 WICHÍ LHAMTÉS GÜISNAY
9 WESTERN ARGENTINE GUARANÍ
10 WICHÍ LHAMTÉS VEJOZ

CHILE - EASTER ISLAND

RAPA NUI

27°S
109°W

km
0   200   400   600

Peru
Bolivia
Paraguay
Brazil
SEE INSET

65

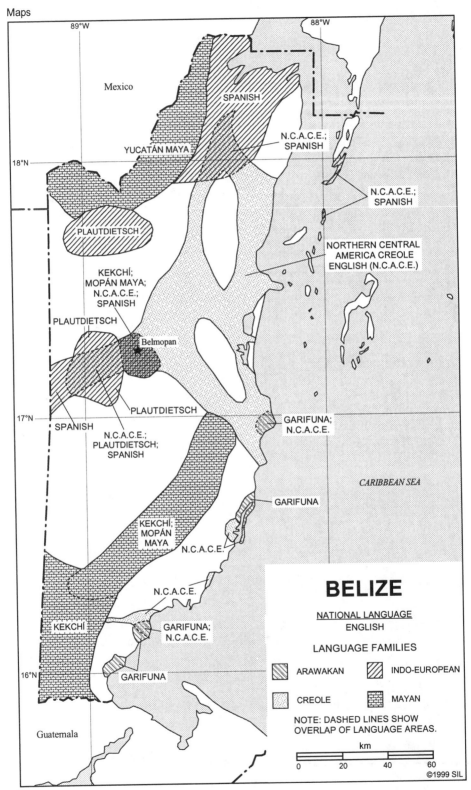

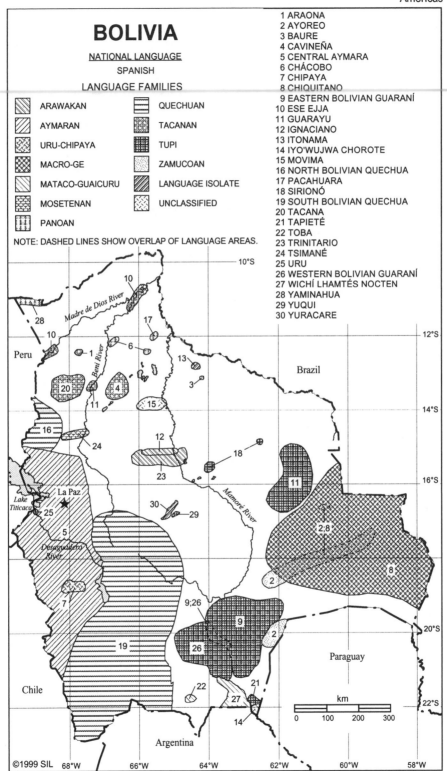

BOLIVIA

NATIONAL LANGUAGE

SPANISH

LANGUAGE FAMILIES

ARAWAKAN

AYMARAN

URU-CHIPAYA

MACRO-GE

MATACO-GUAICURU

MOSETENAN

PANOAN

QUECHUAN

TACANAN

TUPI

ZAMUCOAN

LANGUAGE ISOLATE

UNCLASSIFIED

NOTE: DASHED LINES SHOW OVERLAP OF LANGUAGE AREAS.

1 ARAONA
2 AYOREO
3 BAURE
4 CAVINEÑA
5 CENTRAL AYMARA
6 CHÁCOBO
7 CHIPAYA
8 CHIQUITANO
9 EASTERN BOLIVIAN GUARANÍ
10 ESE EJJA
11 GUARAYU
12 IGNACIANO
13 ITONAMA
14 IYO'WUJWA CHOROTE
15 MOVIMA
16 NORTH BOLIVIAN QUECHUA
17 PACAHUARA
18 SIRIONÓ
19 SOUTH BOLIVIAN QUECHUA
20 TACANA
21 TAPIETÉ
22 TOBA
23 TRINITARIO
24 TSIMANÉ
25 URU
26 WESTERN BOLIVIAN GUARANÍ
27 WICHÍ LHAMTÉS NOCTEN
28 YAMINAHUA
29 YUQUI
30 YURACARE

Peru

Madre de Dios River

Beni River

Brazil

Lake Titicaca

La Paz

Desaguadero River

Mamoré River

Chile

Paraguay

km

0   100   200   300

Argentina

©1999 SIL

10°S

12°S

14°S

16°S

20°S

22°S

68°W   66°W   64°W   62°W   60°W   58°W

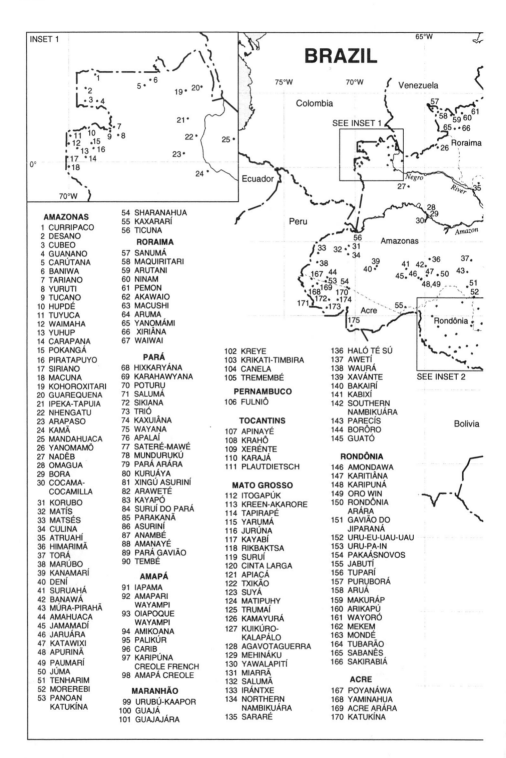

INSET 1

BRAZIL

65°W

75°W 70°W Venezuela

Colombia

SEE INSET 1

Ecuador

Peru

Amazonas

Roraima

Negro River

Acre

Rondônia

SEE INSET 2

Bolívia

AMAZONAS
1 CURRIPACO
2 DESANO
3 CUBEO
4 GUANANO
5 CARÚTANA
6 BANIWA
7 TARIANO
8 YURUTI
9 TUCANO
10 HUPDÉ
11 TUYUCA
12 WAIMAHA
13 YUHUP
14 CARAPANA
15 POKANGÁ
16 PIRATAPUYO
17 SIRIANO
18 MACUNA
19 KOHOROXITARI
20 GUAREQUENA
21 IPEKA-TAPUIA
22 NHENGATU
23 ARAPASO
24 KAMÃ
25 MANDAHUACA
26 YANOMAMÖ
27 NADÉB
28 OMAGUA
29 BORA
30 COCAMA-
   COCAMILLA
31 KORUBO
32 MATÍS
33 MATSÉS
34 CULINA
35 ATRUAHÍ
36 HIMARIMÃ
37 TORÁ
38 MARÚBO
39 KANAMARÍ
40 DENÍ
41 SURUAHÁ
42 BANAWÁ
43 MÚRA-PIRAHÃ
44 AMAHUACA
45 JAMAMADÍ
46 JARUÁRA
47 KATAWIXI
48 APURINÃ
49 PAUMARÍ
50 JÚMA
51 TENHARIM
52 MOREREBI
53 PANOAN
   KATUKÍNA

54 SHARANAHUA
55 KAXARARÍ
56 TICUNA
RORAIMA
57 SANUMÁ
58 MAQUIRITARI
59 ARUTANI
60 NINAM
61 PEMON
62 AKAWAIO
63 MACUSHI
64 ARUMA
65 YANOMÁMI
66 XIRIÃNA
67 WAIWAI

PARÁ
68 HIXKARYÁNA
69 KARAHAWYANA
70 POTURU
71 SALUMÁ
72 SIKIANA
73 TRIÓ
74 KAXUIÂNA
75 WAYANA
76 APALAÍ
77 SATERÉ-MAWÉ
78 MUNDURUKÚ
79 PARÁ ARÁRA
80 KURUÁYA
81 XINGÚ ASURINÍ
82 ARAWETÉ
83 KAYAPÓ
84 SURUÍ DO PARÁ
85 PARAKANÃ
86 ASURINÍ
87 ANAMBÉ
88 AMANAYÉ
89 PARÁ GAVIÃO
90 TEMBÉ

AMAPÁ
91 IAPAMA
92 AMAPARI
   WAYAMPI
93 OIAPOQUE
   WAYAMPI
94 AMIKOANA
95 PALIKÚR
96 CARIB
97 KARIPÚNA
   CREOLE FRENCH
98 AMAPÁ CREOLE

MARANHÃO
99 URUBÚ-KAAPOR
100 GUAJÁ
101 GUAJAJÁRA

102 KREYE
103 KRIKATI-TIMBIRA
104 CANELA
105 TREMEMBÉ

PERNAMBUCO
106 FULNIÔ

TOCANTINS
107 APINAYÉ
108 KRAHÔ
109 XERÉNTE
110 KARAJÁ
111 PLAUTDIETSCH

MATO GROSSO
112 ITOGAPÚK
113 KREEN-AKARORE
114 TAPIRAPÉ
115 YARUMÁ
116 JURÚNA
117 KAYABÍ
118 RIKBAKTSA
119 SURUÍ
120 CINTA LARGA
121 APIACÁ
122 TXIKÃO
123 SUYÁ
124 MATIPUHY
125 TRUMAÍ
126 KAMAYURÁ
127 KUIKÚRO-
   KALAPÁLO
128 AGAVOTAGUERRA
129 MEHINÁKU
130 YAWALAPITÍ
131 MIARRÃ
132 SALUMÃ
133 IRÁNTXE
134 NORTHERN
   NAMBIKUÁRA
135 SARARÉ

136 HALÓ TÉ SÚ
137 AWETÍ
138 WAURÁ
139 XAVÁNTE
140 BAKAIRÍ
141 KABIXÍ
142 SOUTHERN
   NAMBIKUÁRA
143 PARECÍS
144 BORÔRO
145 GUATÓ

RONDÔNIA
146 AMONDAWA
147 KARITIÂNA
148 KARIPUNÁ
149 ORO WIN
150 RONDÔNIA
   ARÁRA
151 GAVIÃO DO
   JIPARANÁ
152 URU-EU-UAU-UAU
153 URU-PA-IN
154 PAKAÁSNOVOS
155 JABUTÍ
156 TUPARÍ
157 PURUBORÁ
158 ARUÁ
159 MAKURÁP
160 ARIKAPÚ
161 WAYORÓ
162 MEKEM
163 MONDÉ
164 TUBARÃO
165 SABANÊS
166 SAKIRABIÁ

ACRE
167 POYANÁWA
168 YAMINAHUA
169 ACRE ARÁRA
170 KATUKÍNA

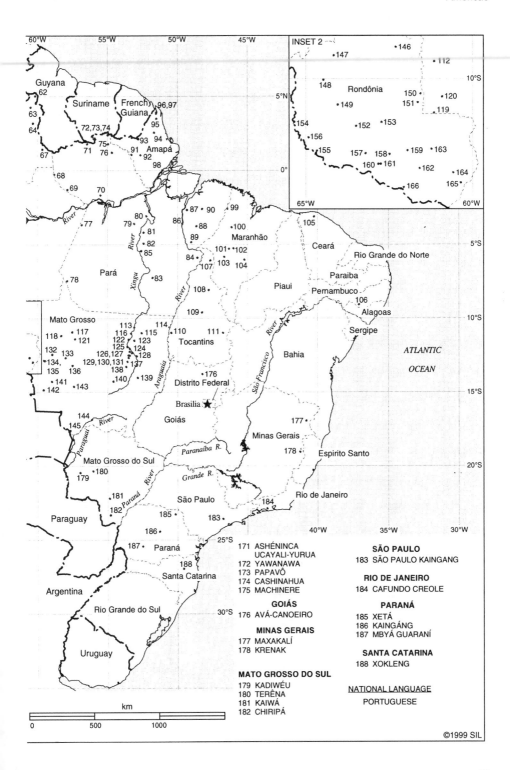

60°W 55°W 50°W 45°W

INSET 2

•146
•147
•112
10°S

Guyana
62
63
64
Suriname
72,73,74
67
71
76•
French
Guiana
96,97
95
93 94
91 Amapá
92
98
75

68
69
70

148
Rondônia
5°N
•149
150•
151•
•120
•119
154
•152 •153
•156
0°
155
157• 158•
160 •• 161
•159 •163
•162
•164
166
165•
65°W
60°W

•87 • 90 • 99
80
77
79•
86
•88
•100
105
•81
89
Maranhão
•82
85
84•
101• •102
•107 103 104
Ceará
Rio Grande do Norte
5°S

78
Pará
•83
108•
109•
Piaui
Paraiba
Pernambuco
•106
Alagoas
10°S

Mato Grosso
118•
•117
•121
113 114
116 •115 •110 111•
122 •123
125 124
126,127 •128
132 133
•134,
135 136
129,130,131•137
138•
•140 •139
•141
•142 •143
144
145
River
•80

Tocantins
Bahia
Sergipe
ATLANTIC
OCEAN

•176
Distrito Federal
Brasilia ★
Goiás
177•
Minas Gerais
178 •
Espirito Santo
15°S
20°S

Paraguai River
Mato Grosso do Sul
•180
179
•181
182
185•
São Paulo
186•
187•
Paraná
188
Santa Catarina
Paranaíba R.
Grande R.
184
Rio de Janeiro
183•
25°S
40°W 35°W 30°W

Argentina
Rio Grande do Sul
Uruguay
30°S

171 ASHÉNINCA
     UCAYALI-YURUA
172 YAWANAWA
173 PAPAVÔ
174 CASHINAHUA
175 MACHINERE

GOIÁS
176 AVÁ-CANOEIRO

MINAS GERAIS
177 MAXAKALÍ
178 KRENAK

MATO GROSSO DO SUL
179 KADIWÉU
180 TERÊNA
181 KAIWÁ
182 CHIRIPÁ

SÃO PAULO
183 SÃO PAULO KAINGANG

RIO DE JANEIRO
184 CAFUNDO CREOLE

PARANÁ
185 XETÁ
186 KAINGÁNG
187 MBYÁ GUARANÍ

SANTA CATARINA
188 XOKLENG

NATIONAL LANGUAGE
PORTUGUESE

km
0   500   1000

©1999 SIL

WESTERN CANADA

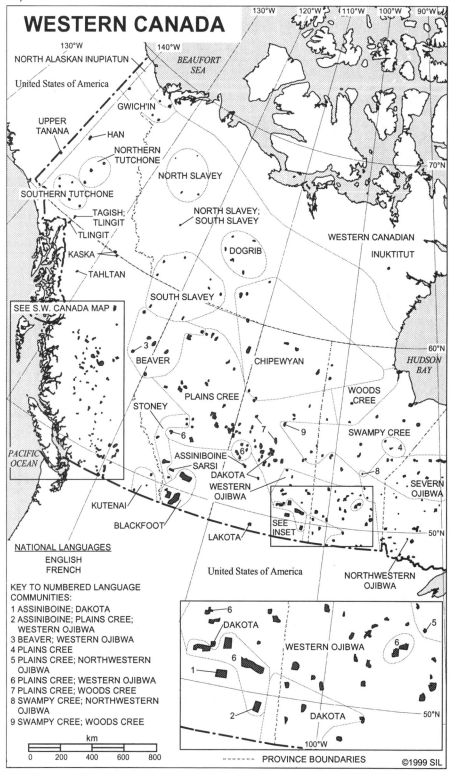

NORTH ALASKAN INUPIATUN

United States of America

GWICH'IN

UPPER TANANA — HAN

NORTHERN TUTCHONE

SOUTHERN TUTCHONE

TAGISH; TLINGIT

TLINGIT

KASKA

TAHLTAN

SEE S.W. CANADA MAP

BEAUFORT SEA

NORTH SLAVEY

NORTH SLAVEY; SOUTH SLAVEY

DOGRIB

SOUTH SLAVEY

3

BEAVER

CHIPEWYAN

PLAINS CREE

STONEY

6

7

9

ASSINIBOINE
SARSI
DAKOTA
WESTERN OJIBWA

KUTENAI

BLACKFOOT

LAKOTA

WESTERN CANADIAN INUKTITUT

HUDSON BAY

WOODS CREE

SWAMPY CREE

4

8

SEVERN OJIBWA

SEE INSET

PACIFIC OCEAN

NATIONAL LANGUAGES
ENGLISH
FRENCH

United States of America

NORTHWESTERN OJIBWA

KEY TO NUMBERED LANGUAGE COMMUNITIES:
1 ASSINIBOINE; DAKOTA
2 ASSINIBOINE; PLAINS CREE; WESTERN OJIBWA
3 BEAVER; WESTERN OJIBWA
4 PLAINS CREE
5 PLAINS CREE; NORTHWESTERN OJIBWA
6 PLAINS CREE; WESTERN OJIBWA
7 PLAINS CREE; WOODS CREE
8 SWAMPY CREE; NORTHWESTERN OJIBWA
9 SWAMPY CREE; WOODS CREE

6

DAKOTA

WESTERN OJIBWA

6

5

6

1

2

DAKOTA

km

0   200   400   600   800

- - - - - - PROVINCE BOUNDARIES   ©1999 SIL

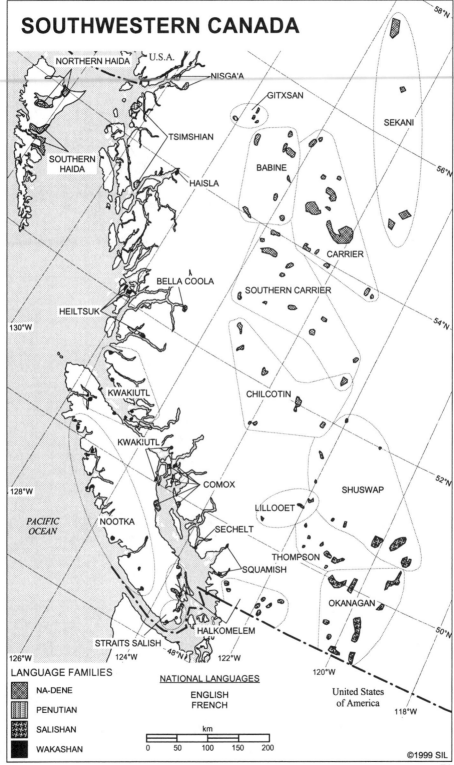

SOUTHWESTERN CANADA

58°N

NORTHERN HAIDA   U.S.A.

NISGA'A

GITXSAN

SEKANI

TSIMSHIAN

SOUTHERN HAIDA

BABINE

56°N

HAISLA

CARRIER

BELLA COOLA

SOUTHERN CARRIER

HEILTSUK

54°N

130°W

KWAKIUTL

CHILCOTIN

KWAKIUTL

COMOX

SHUSWAP

52°N

128°W

LILLOOET

PACIFIC OCEAN

NOOTKA

SECHELT

THOMPSON

SQUAMISH

OKANAGAN

50°N

HALKOMELEM

STRAITS SALISH   48°N

126°W   124°W   122°W   120°W

118°W

United States of America

LANGUAGE FAMILIES

NATIONAL LANGUAGES

ENGLISH
FRENCH

- NA-DENE
- PENUTIAN
- SALISHAN
- WAKASHAN

km

0   50   100   150   200

©1999 SIL

71

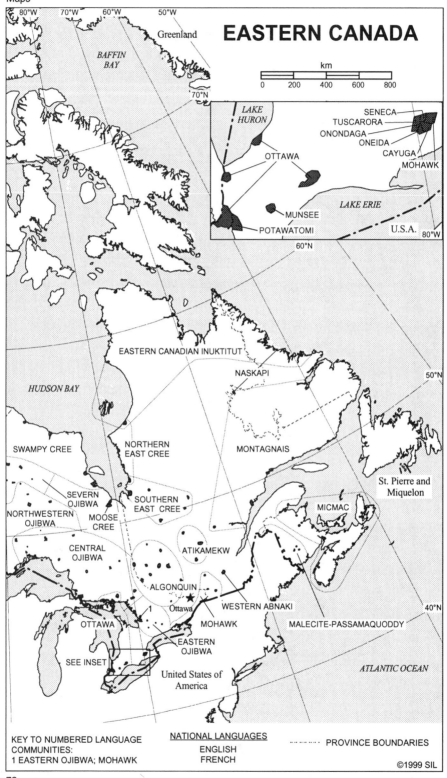

EASTERN CANADA

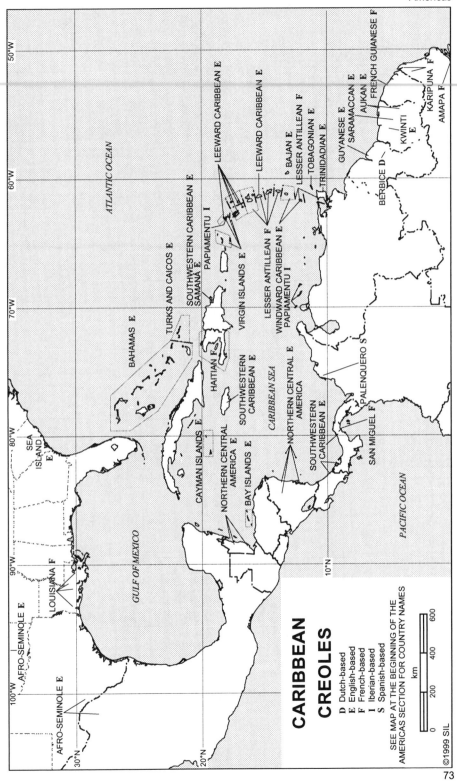

CARIBBEAN CREOLES

D Dutch-based
E English-based
F French-based
I Iberian-based
S Spanish-based

SEE MAP AT THE BEGINNING OF THE
AMERICAS SECTION FOR COUNTRY NAMES

km

0   200   400   600

©1999 SIL

AFRO-SEMINOLE E

LOUISIANA F

SEA ISLAND E

GULF OF MEXICO

BAHAMAS E

TURKS AND CAICOS E

SOUTHWESTERN CARIBBEAN E
SAMANÁ E
PAPIAMENTU I

LEEWARD CARIBBEAN E

LEEWARD CARIBBEAN E

BAJAN E
LESSER ANTILLEAN F
TOBAGONIAN E
TRINIDADIAN E

ATLANTIC OCEAN

GUYANESE E
SARAMACCAN E
AUKAN E

KWINTI E

BERBICE D

FRENCH GUIANESE F

KARIPUNA F

AMAPÁ F

CAYMAN ISLANDS E

HAITIAN F

VIRGIN ISLANDS E

LESSER ANTILLEAN F
WINDWARD CARIBBEAN E
PAPIAMENTU I

CARIBBEAN SEA

NORTHERN CENTRAL
AMERICA E

SOUTHWESTERN
CARIBBEAN E

BAY ISLANDS E

NORTHERN CENTRAL E
AMERICA

SOUTHWESTERN
CARIBBEAN E

SAN MIGUEL F

PALENQUERO S

PACIFIC OCEAN

AFRO-SEMINOLE E

73

Maps

COLOMBIA

NATIONAL LANGUAGE
SPANISH

NOTE: DASHED LINES SHOW
OVERLAP OF LANGUAGE AREAS.

km
0 50 100 150 200

LANGUAGE FAMILIES

ARAWAKAN   CHOCO   QUECHUAN   WITOTOAN

BARBACOAN   CREOLE   SALIVAN   LANGUAGE ISOLATE

CARIB   MAKU   TUCANOAN   UNCLASSIFIED

CHIBCHAN   PAEZAN   TUPI

©1999 SIL

COLOMBIA ENLARGED AREA

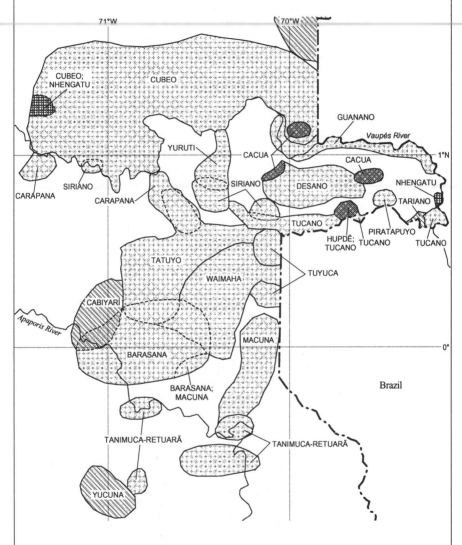

NOTE: DASHED LINES SHOW OVERLAP OF LANGUAGE AREAS.

LANGUAGE FAMILIES

 ARAWAKAN

 MAKU

 TUCANOAN

 TUPI

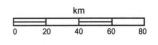

©1999 SIL

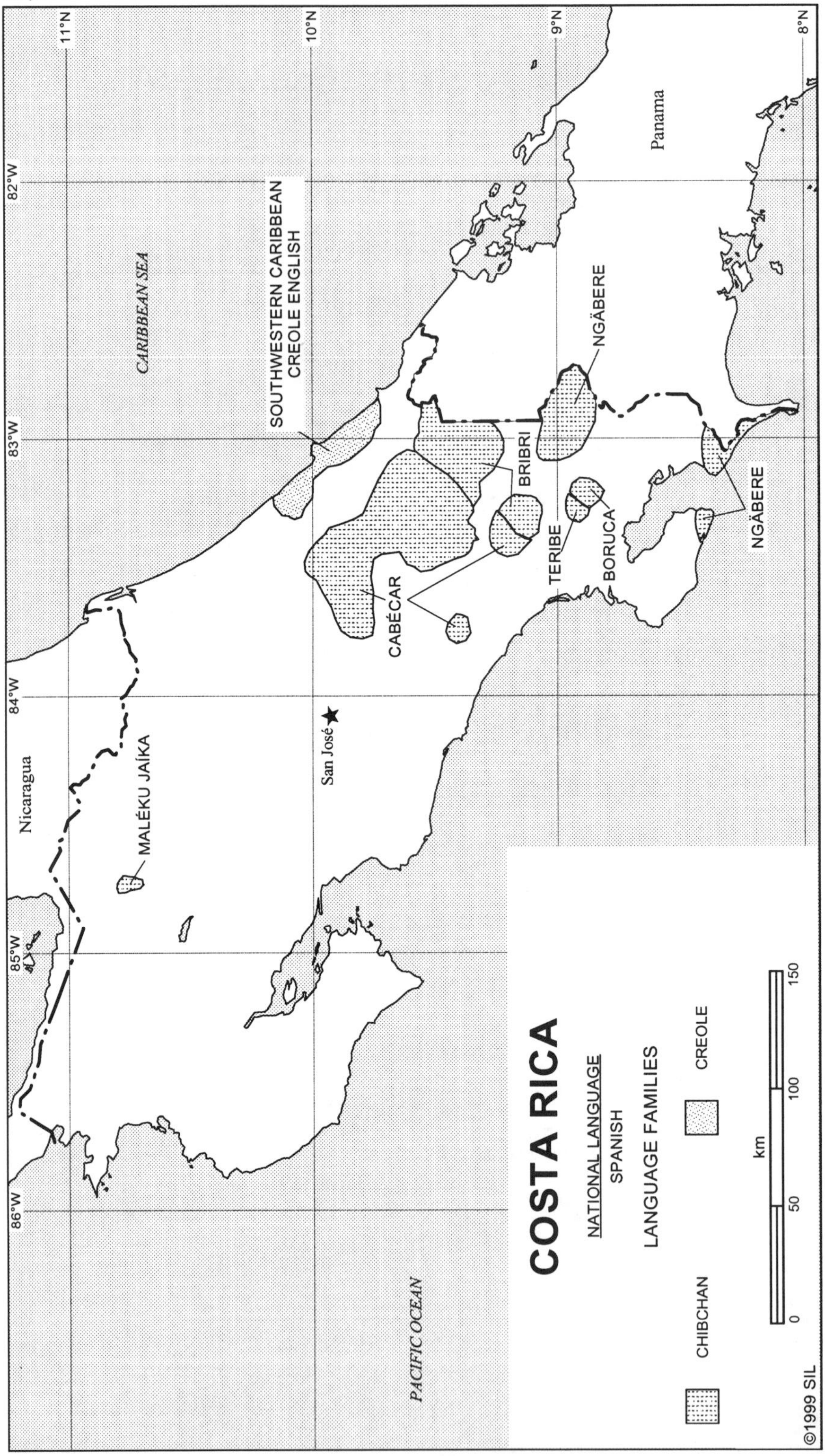

COSTA RICA
NATIONAL LANGUAGE
SPANISH
LANGUAGE FAMILIES
CHIBCHAN
CREOLE
km
0
50
100
150
©1999 SIL
CARIBBEAN SEA
PACIFIC OCEAN
Nicaragua
Panama
San José
MALÉKU JAÍKA
SOUTHWESTERN CARIBBEAN CREOLE ENGLISH
CABÉCAR
BRIBRI
TERIBE
BORUCA
NGÄBERE
NGÄBERE
11°N
10°N
9°N
8°N
82°W
83°W
84°W
85°W
86°W

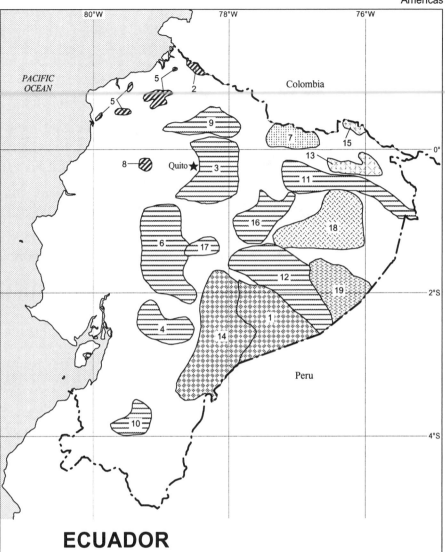

PACIFIC
OCEAN

Colombia

Quito ★

Peru

ECUADOR

<u>NATIONAL LANGUAGE</u>
SPANISH

LANGUAGE FAMILIES

 BARBACOAN

 CHIBCHAN

 JIVAROAN

 QUECHUAN

TUCANOAN

ZAPAROAN

UNCLASSIFIED

1 ACHUAR-SHIWIAR
2 AWA-CUAIQUER
3 CALDERÓN HIGHLAND QUICHUA
4 CAÑAR HIGHLAND QUICHUA
5 CHACHI
6 CHIMBORAZO HIGHLAND QUICHUA
7 COFÁN
8 COLORADO
9 IMBABURA HIGHLAND QUICHUA
10 LOJA HIGHLAND QUICHUA
11 NAPO LOWLAND QUICHUA
12 NORTHERN PASTAZA QUICHUA
13 SECOYA
14 SHUAR
15 SIONA
16 TENA LOWLAND QUICHUA
17 TUNGURAHUA HIGHLAND QUICHUA
18 WAORANI
19 ZÁPARO

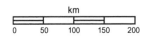

km

0   50   100   150   200

©1999 SIL

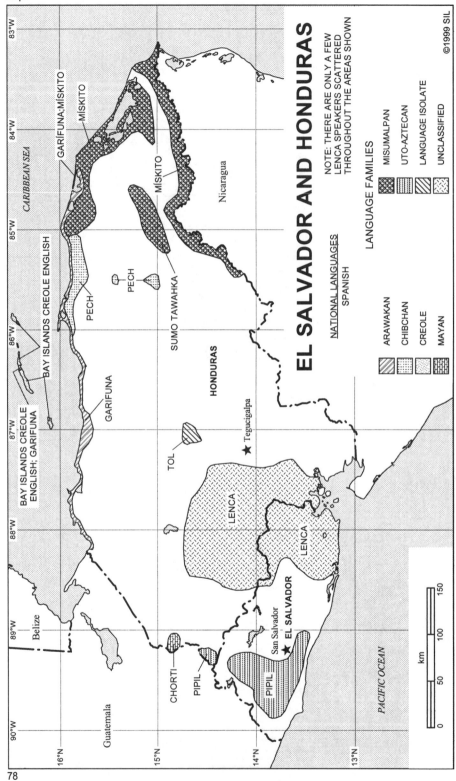

EL SALVADOR AND HONDURAS

NOTE: THERE ARE ONLY A FEW
LENCA SPEAKERS SCATTERED
THROUGHOUT THE AREAS SHOWN

©1999 SIL

NATIONAL LANGUAGES
SPANISH

LANGUAGE FAMILIES

ARAWAKAN
CHIBCHAN
CREOLE
MAYAN

MISUMALPAN
UTO-AZTECAN
LANGUAGE ISOLATE
UNCLASSIFIED

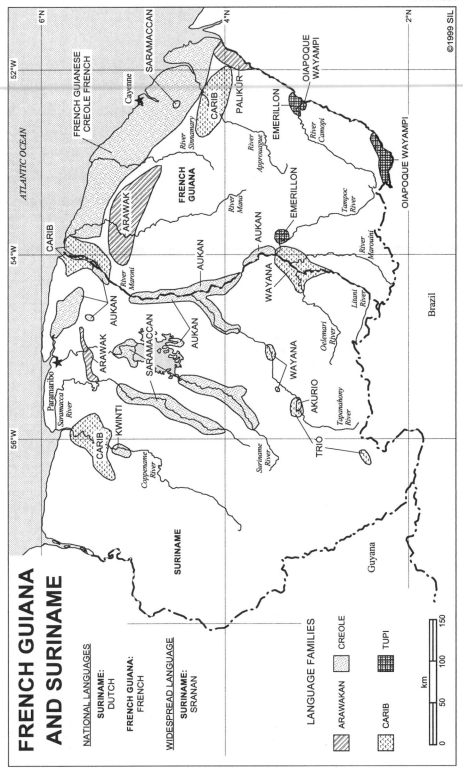

FRENCH GUIANA AND SURINAME

©1999 SIL

NATIONAL LANGUAGES
  SURINAME: DUTCH
  FRENCH GUIANA: FRENCH

WIDESPREAD LANGUAGE
  SURINAME: SRANAN

LANGUAGE FAMILIES

ARAWAKAN

CREOLE

CARIB

TUPI

km
0   50   100   150

ATLANTIC OCEAN

FRENCH GUIANESE CREOLE FRENCH

SARAMACCAN

Cayenne

CARIB

PALIKUR

EMERILLON

OIAPOQUE WAYAMPI

ARAWAK

FRENCH GUIANA

River Sinnamary

River Approuague

River Camopi

EMERILLON

River Mana

AUKAN

Tampoc River

OIAPOQUE WAYAMPI

CARIB

AUKAN

River Maroni

AUKAN

River Marouini

WAYANA

AUKAN

ARAWAK

SARAMACCAN

AUKAN

Litani River

WAYANA

Oelemari River

Brazil

Paramaribo

Saramacca River

KWINTI

AKURIO

Tapanahony River

CARIB

TRIÓ

Coppename River

Suriname River

SURINAME

Guyana

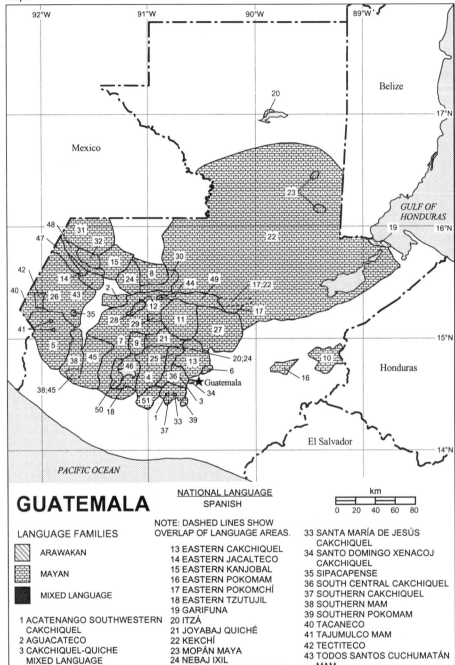

GUATEMALA

<u>NATIONAL LANGUAGE</u>
SPANISH

NOTE: DASHED LINES SHOW
OVERLAP OF LANGUAGE AREAS.

km
0   20   40   60   80

LANGUAGE FAMILIES

ARAWAKAN

MAYAN

MIXED LANGUAGE

1 ACATENANGO SOUTHWESTERN
  CAKCHIQUEL
2 AGUACATECO
3 CAKCHIQUEL-QUICHE
  MIXED LANGUAGE
4 CENTRAL CAKCHIQUEL
5 CENTRAL MAM
6 CENTRAL POKOMAM
7 CENTRAL QUICHÉ
8 CHAJUL IXIL
9 CHICHICASTENANGO
  EASTERN QUICHÉ
10 CHORTÍ
11 CUBULCO ACHÍ
12 CUNÉN QUICHÉ

13 EASTERN CAKCHIQUEL
14 EASTERN JACALTECO
15 EASTERN KANJOBAL
16 EASTERN POKOMAM
17 EASTERN POKOMCHÍ
18 EASTERN TZUTUJIL
19 GARIFUNA
20 ITZÁ
21 JOYABAJ QUICHÉ
22 KEKCHÍ
23 MOPÁN MAYA
24 NEBAJ IXIL
25 NORTHERN CAKCHIQUEL
26 NORTHERN MAM
27 RABINAL ACHÍ
28 SACAPULTECO
29 SAN ANDRÉS QUICHÉ
30 SAN JUAN COTZAL IXIL
31 SAN MATEO IXTATÁN
  CHUJ
32 SAN SEBASTIÁN COATÁN
  CHUJ

33 SANTA MARÍA DE JESÚS
  CAKCHIQUEL
34 SANTO DOMINGO XENACOJ
  CAKCHIQUEL
35 SIPACAPENSE
36 SOUTH CENTRAL CAKCHIQUEL
37 SOUTHERN CAKCHIQUEL
38 SOUTHERN MAM
39 SOUTHERN POKOMAM
40 TACANECO
41 TAJUMULCO MAM
42 TECTITECO
43 TODOS SANTOS CUCHUMATÁN
  MAM
44 USPANTECO
45 WEST CENTRAL QUICHÉ
46 WESTERN CAKCHIQUEL
47 WESTERN JACALTECO
48 WESTERN KANJOBAL
49 WESTERN POKOMCHÍ
50 WESTERN TZUTUJIL
51 YEPOCAPA SOUTHWESTERN
  CAKCHIQUEL

©1999 SIL

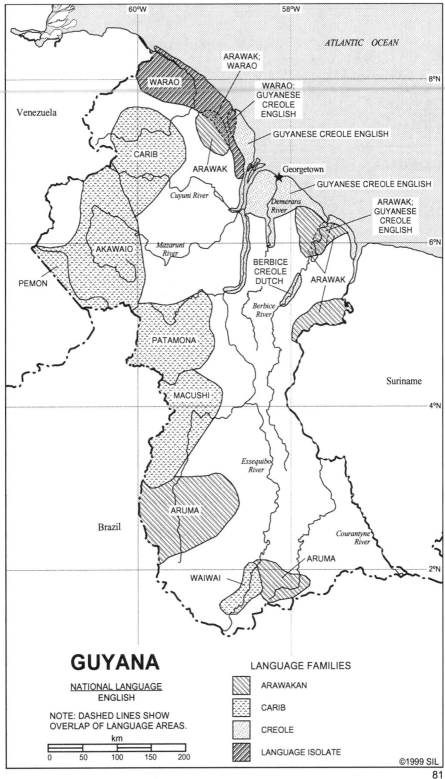

GUYANA

<u>NATIONAL LANGUAGE</u>
ENGLISH

NOTE: DASHED LINES SHOW
OVERLAP OF LANGUAGE AREAS.

km

| 0 | 50 | 100 | 150 | 200 |

LANGUAGE FAMILIES

ARAWAKAN

CARIB

CREOLE

LANGUAGE ISOLATE

©1999 SIL

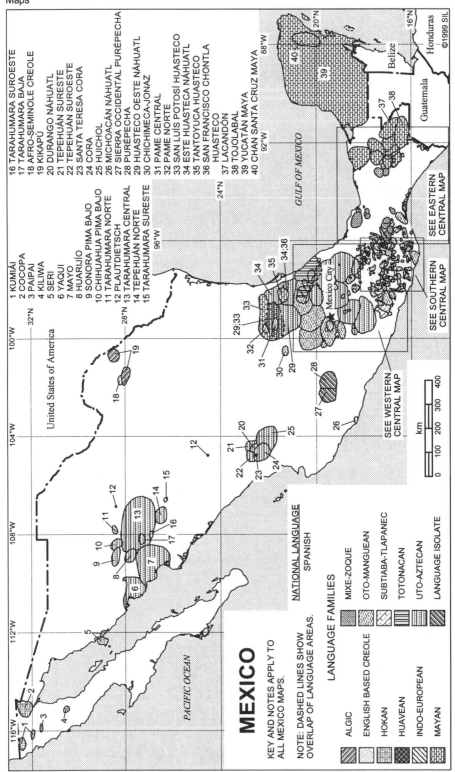

MEXICO

KEY AND NOTES APPLY TO
ALL MEXICO MAPS.

NOTE: DASHED LINES SHOW
OVERLAP OF LANGUAGE AREAS.

NATIONAL LANGUAGE
SPANISH

LANGUAGE FAMILIES

ALGIC

ENGLISH BASED CREOLE

HOKAN

HUAVEAN

INDO-EUROPEAN

MAYAN

MIXE-ZOQUE

OTO-MANGUEAN

SUBTIABA-TLAPANEC

TOTONACAN

UTO-AZTECAN

LANGUAGE ISOLATE

1 KUMIÁI
2 COCOPA
3 PAIPAI
4 KILIWA
5 SERI
6 YAQUI
7 MAYO
8 HUARIJÍO
9 SONORA PIMA BAJO
10 CHIHUAHUA PIMA BAJO
11 TARAHUMARA NORTE
12 PLAUTDIETSCH
13 TARAHUMARA CENTRAL
14 TEPEHUÁN NORTE
15 TARAHUMARA SURESTE
16 TARAHUMARA SUROESTE
17 TARAHUMARA BAJA
18 AFRO-SEMINOLE CREOLE
19 KIKAPÚ
20 DURANGO NÁHUATL
21 TEPEHUÁN SURESTE
22 TEPEHUÁN SUROESTE
23 SANTA TERESA CORA
24 CORA
25 HUICHOL
26 MICHOACÁN NÁHUATL
27 SIERRA OCCIDENTAL PURÉPECHA
28 PURÉPECHA
29 HUASTECO OESTE NÁHUATL
30 CHICHIMECA-JONAZ
31 PAME CENTRAL
32 PAME NORTE
33 SAN LUIS POTOSÍ HUASTECO
34 ESTE HUASTECA NÁHUATL
35 TANTOYUCA HUASTECO
36 SAN FRANCISCO CHONTLA HUASTECO
37 LACANDÓN
38 TOJOLABAL
39 YUCATÁN MAYA
40 CHAN SANTA CRUZ MAYA

PACIFIC OCEAN

United States of America

GULF OF MEXICO

Mexico City

SEE WESTERN
CENTRAL MAP

SEE SOUTHERN
CENTRAL MAP

SEE EASTERN
CENTRAL MAP

Belize

Guatemala

Honduras

©1999 SIL

km
0 100 200 300 400

AFRO-SEMINOLE CREOLE	18	MAZAHUA CENTRAL	71
AMUZGO, GUERRERO	84	MAZAHUA, MICHOACÁN	70
AMUZGO, IPALAPA	86	MAZATECO, AYAUTLA	171
AMUZGO, SAN PEDRO AMUZGOS	87	MAZATECO, CHIQUIHUITLÁN	184
CHATINO, NOPALA	280	MAZATECO, HUAUTLA	109
CHATINO, SIERRA OCCIDENTAL	274	MAZATECO, IXCATLÁN	110
CHATINO, SIERRA ORIENTAL	273	MAZATECO, JALAPA DE DÍAZ	111
CHATINO, TATALTEPEC	277	MAZATECO, MAZATLÁN	168
CHATINO, ZACATEPEC	279	MAZATECO, SAN JERÓNIMO TECÓATL	100
CHATINO, ZENZONTEPEC	240	MAZATECO, SOYALTEPEC	112
CHICHIMECA-JONAZ	30	MIXE, COATLÁN	154
CHINANTECO, CHILTEPEC	175	MIXE, ISTMO	152
CHINANTECO, COMALTEPEC	179	MIXE, JUQUILA	155
CHINANTECO, LALANA	120	MIXE, MAZATLÁN	153
CHINANTECO, LEALAO	122	MIXE, QUETZALTEPEC	124
CHINANTECO, OJITLÁN	113	MIXE, TLAHUITOLTEPEC	210
CHINANTECO, OZUMACÍN	177	MIXE, TOTONTEPEC	123
CHINANTECO, PALANTLA	176	MIXTECO, ALACATLATZALA	90
CHINANTECO, QUIOTEPEC	182	MIXTECO, ALCOZAUCA	91
CHINANTECO, SOCHIAPAN	181	MIXTECO, AMOLTEPEC	241
CHINANTECO, TEPETOTUTLA	180	MIXTECO, APASCO Y APOALA	186
CHINANTECO, TEPINAPA	119	MIXTECO, ATATLÁHUCA	234
CHINANTECO, TLACOATZINTEPEC	173	MIXTECO, AYUTLA	80
CHINANTECO, USILA	174	MIXTECO, CACALOXTEPEC	189
CHINANTECO, VALLE NACIONAL	178	MIXTECO, CHAYUCO	275
CHOCHOTECO	187	MIXTECO, CHAZUMBA	95
CH'OL, TILA	131	MIXTECO, CHIGMACATITLÁN	64
CH'OL, TUMBALÁ	132	MIXTECO, COATZOSPAN	170
CHONTAL DE OAXACA, COSTA	166	MIXTECO, CUYAMECALCO	169
CHONTAL DE OAXACA, SIERRA	164	MIXTECO, DIUXI-TILANTONGO	226
CHONTAL, TABASCO	128	MIXTECO, HUITEPEC	246
CHUJ, SAN MATEO IXTATÁN	138	MIXTECO, ITUNDUJIA	238
COCOPA	2	MIXTECO, IXTAYUTLA	239
CORA	24	MIXTECO, JAMILTEPEC	276
CORA, SANTA TERESA	23	MIXTECO, JUXTLAHUACA	229
CUICATECO, TEPEUXILA	183	MIXTECO, JUXTLAHUACA OESTE	88
CUICATECO, TEUTILA	172	MIXTECO, MAGDALENA PEÑASCO	195
HUARIJÍO	8	MIXTECO, METLATONOC	89
HUASTECO, SAN FRANCISCO CHONTLA	36	MIXTECO, MITLATONGO	198
HUASTECO, SAN LUÍS POTOSÍ	33	MIXTECO, MIXTEPEC	192
HUASTECO, TANTOYUCA	35	MIXTECO, NOCHIXTLÁN SURESTE	200
HUAVE, SAN DIONISIO DEL MAR	159	MIXTECO, OAXACA NOROESTE	190
HUAVE, SAN FRANCISCO DEL MAR	160	MIXTECO, OCOTEPEC	232
HUAVE, SAN MATEO DEL MAR	162	MIXTECO, PEÑOLES	223
HUAVE, SANTA MARÍA DEL MAR	161	MIXTECO, PINOTEPA NACIONAL	85
HUICHOL	25	MIXTECO, PUEBLA SUR	98
IXCATECO	185	MIXTECO, SAN JUAN COLORADO	237
JACALTECO, WESTERN	144	MIXTECO, SAN JUAN TEITA	227
KANJOBAL, WESTERN	137	MIXTECO, SAN MIGUEL EL GRANDE	235
KIKAPÚ	19	MIXTECO, SAN MIGUEL PIEDRAS	224
KILIWA	4	MIXTECO, SANTA MARÍA ZACATEPEC	236
KUMIÁI	1	MIXTECO, SILACAYOAPAN	92
LACANDÓN	37	MIXTECO, SINDIHUI	245
MAM, NORTHERN	142	MIXTECO, SINICAHUA	194
MAM, TODOS SANTOS CUCHUMATÁN	139	MIXTECO, SOYALTEPEC	188
MATLATZINCA, ATZINGO	74	MIXTECO, TACAHUA	242
MATLATZINCA, SAN FRANCISCO DE LOS RANCHOS	73	MIXTECO, TAMAZOLA	199
		MIXTECO, TEZOATLÁN	191
MAYA, CHAN SANTA CRUZ	40	MIXTECO, TIDAÁ	197
MAYA, YUCATÁN	39	MIXTECO, TIJALTEPEC	244
MAYO	7	MIXTECO, TLAXIACO NORTE	193

MIXTECO, TLAXIACO, SUROESTE	233	PURÉPECHA, SIERRA OCCIDENTAL	27
MIXTECO, TUTUTEPEC	278	SERI	5
MIXTECO, YOLOXOCHITL	81	TACANECO	141
MIXTECO, YOSONDÚA	243	TARAHUMARA BAJA	17
MIXTECO, YUCUAÑE	196	TARAHUMARA CENTRAL	13
MIXTECO, YUTANDUCHI	225	TARAHUMARA NORTE	11
MOCHO	143	TARAHUMARA SURESTE	15
NÁHUATL CENTRAL	62	TARAHUMARA SUROESTE	16
NÁHUATL, COATEPEC	76	TECTITECO	140
NÁHUATL, DURANGO	20	TEPEHUA, HUEHUETLA	46
NÁHUATL, GUERRERO	77	TEPEHUA, PISA FLORES	51
NÁHUATL, HUASTECA, ESTE	34	TEPEHUA, TLACHICHILCO	50
NÁHUATL, HUASTECO OESTE	29	TEPEHUÁN NORTE	14
NÁHUATL, HUAXCALECA	106	TEPEHUÁN SURESTE	21
NÁHUATL, ISTMO-COSOLEACAQUE	126	TEPEHUÁN SUROESTE	22
NÁHUATL, ISTMO-MECAYAPAN	115	TLAPANECO, ACATEPEC	78
NÁHUATL, ISTMO-PAJAPAN	114	TLAPANECO, AZOYÚ	82
NÁHUATL, IXHUATLANCILLO	107	TLAPANECO, MALINALTEPEC	79
NÁHUATL, MICHOACÁN	26	TOJOLABAL	38
NÁHUATL, MORELOS	65	TOTONACA, COYUTLA	55
NÁHUATL, OAXACA NORTE	99	TOTONACA, FILOMENO MATA-	
NÁHUATL, OMETEPEC	83	COAHUITLÁN	56
NÁHUATL, ORIZABA	108	TOTONACA, OZUMATLÁN	45
NÁHUATL, PUEBLA CENTRAL	63	TOTONACA, PAPANTLA	54
NÁHUATL, PUEBLA NORTE	43	TOTONACA, PATLA-CHICONTLA	53
NÁHUATL, PUEBLA SURESTE	101	TOTONACA, SIERRA	57
NÁHUATL, PUEBLA, SIERRA	59	TOTONACA, XICOTEPEC DE JUÁREZ	52
NÁHUATL, SANTA MARÍA LA ALTA	103	TOTONACA, YECUATLA	58
NÁHUATL, TEMASCALTEPEC	72	TRIQUE, CHICAHUAXTLA	228
NÁHUATL, TENANGO	44	TRIQUE, COPALA	231
NÁHUATL, TETELCINGO	66	TRIQUE, SAN MARTÍN ITUNYOSO	230
NÁHUATL, TLALITZLIPA	60	TZELTAL, BACHAJÓN	134
NÁHUATL, TLAMACAZAPA	75	TZELTAL, OXCHUC	135
OTOMÍ, ESTADO DE MÉXICO	69	TZOTZIL, CHAMULA	146
OTOMÍ, IXTENCO	61	TZOTZIL, CH'ENALHÓ	133
OTOMÍ, MEZQUITAL	42	TZOTZIL, HUIXTÁN	136
OTOMÍ, NORTHWESTERN	41	TZOTZIL, SAN ANDRÉS LARRAINZAR	148
OTOMÍ, SIERRA ORIENTAL	49	TZOTZIL, VENUSTIANO CARRANZA	145
OTOMÍ, TEMOAYA	68	TZOTZIL, ZINACANTÁN	147
OTOMÍ, TENANGO	47	YAQUI	6
OTOMÍ, TEXCATEPEC	48	ZAPOTECO, ALBARRADAS	211
OTOMÍ, TILAPA	67	ZAPOTECO, ALOÁPAM	201
PAIPAI	3	ZAPOTECO, AMATLÁN	270
PAME CENTRAL	31	ZAPOTECO, ASUNCIÓN MIXTEPEC	221
PAME NORTE	32	ZAPOTECO, AYOQUESCO	252
PIMA BAJO, CHIHUAHUA	10	ZAPOTECO, CAJONOS	213
PIMA BAJO, SONORA	9	ZAPOTECO, CHICHICAPAN	257
PLAUTDIETSCH	12	ZAPOTECO, CHOAPAN	121
POPOLOCA, COYOTEPEC	96	ZAPOTECO, COATECAS ALTAS	253
POPOLOCA, MEZONTLA	97	ZAPOTECO, COATLÁN	281
POPOLOCA, SAN FELIPE OTLALTEPEC	94	ZAPOTECO, EL ALTO	222
POPOLOCA, SAN JUAN ATZINGO	102	ZAPOTECO, ELOTEPEC	247
POPOLOCA, SAN LUÍS TEMALACAYUCA	104	ZAPOTECO, GUEVEA DE HUMBOLDT	157
POPOLOCA, SAN MARCOS		ZAPOTECO, GÜILÁ	258
TLALCOYALCO	105	ZAPOTECO, ISTMO	158
POPOLOCA, SANTA INÉS AHUATEMPAN	93	ZAPOTECO, IXTLÁN SURESTE	216
POPOLUCA, OLUTA	117	ZAPOTECO, JUÁREZ, SIERRA	203
POPOLUCA, SAYULA	118	ZAPOTECO, LACHIGUIRI	163
POPOLUCA, SIERRA	116	ZAPOTECO, LACHIRIOAG	207
POPOLUCA, TEXISTEPEC	125	ZAPOTECO, LOXICHA	283
PURÉPECHA	28	ZAPOTECO, MAZALTEPEC	217

ZAPOTECO, MIAHUATLÁN CENTRAL	271	ZAPOTECO, TABAA	215
ZAPOTECO, MITLA	259	ZAPOTECO, TEJALAPAN	218
ZAPOTECO, MIXTEPEC	261	ZAPOTECO, TEXMELUCAN	250
ZAPOTECO, OCOTLÁN OESTE	255	ZAPOTECO, TILQUIAPAN	256
ZAPOTECO, OZOLOTEPEC	268	ZAPOTECO, TLACOLULITA	165
ZAPOTECO, PETAPA	151	ZAPOTECO, TOTOMACHAPAN	249
ZAPOTECO, QUIAVICUZAS	156	ZAPOTECO, XADANI	265
ZAPOTECO, QUIOQUITANI Y QUIERÍ	262	ZAPOTECO, XANAGUÍA	266
ZAPOTECO, RINCÓN	205	ZAPOTECO, YALÁLAG	209
ZAPOTECO, RINCÓN SUR	204	ZAPOTECO, YARENI	202
ZAPOTECO, SAN AGUSTÍN MIXTEPEC	269	ZAPOTECO, YATEE	206
ZAPOTECO, SAN BALTÁZAR LOXICHA	282	ZAPOTECO, YATZACHI	208
ZAPOTECO, SAN JUAN GUELAVÍA	220	ZAPOTECO, YAUTEPEC	167
ZAPOTECO, SAN PEDRO QUIATONI	260	ZAPOTECO, ZAACHILA	219
ZAPOTECO, SAN VICENTE COATLÁN	272	ZAPOTECO, ZANIZA	248
ZAPOTECO, SANTA CATARINA		ZAPOTECO, ZOOGOCHO	214
ALBARRADAS	212	ZOQUE, CHIMALAPA	150
ZAPOTECO, SANTA INÉS YATZECHI	254	ZOQUE, COPAINALÁ	149
ZAPOTECO, SANTA MARÍA QUIEGOLANI	263	ZOQUE, FRANCISCO LEÓN	130
ZAPOTECO, SANTIAGO LAPAGUÍA	264	ZOQUE, RAYÓN	129
ZAPOTECO, SANTIAGO XANICA	267	ZOQUE, TABASCO	127
ZAPOTECO, SOLA DE VEGA ESTE	251		

Maps

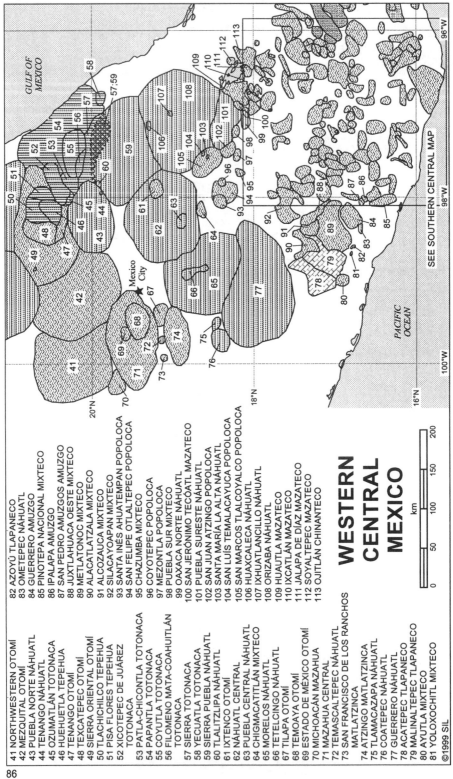

GULF OF MEXICO

PACIFIC OCEAN

SEE SOUTHERN CENTRAL MAP

Mexico City

WESTERN CENTRAL MEXICO

km

0   50   100   150   200

41 NORTHWESTERN OTOMÍ
42 MEZQUITAL OTOMÍ
43 PUEBLA NORTE NÁHUATL
44 TENANGO NÁHUATL
45 OZUMATLÁN TOTONACA
46 HUEHUETLA TEPEHUA
47 TENANGO OTOMÍ
48 TEXCATEPEC OTOMÍ
49 SIERRA ORIENTAL OTOMÍ
50 TLACHICHILCO TEPEHUA
51 PISA FLORES TEPEHUA
52 XICOTEPEC DE JUÁREZ
    TOTONACA
53 PATLA-CHICONTLA TOTONACA
54 PAPANTLA TOTONACA
55 COYUTLA TOTONACA
56 FILOMENO MATA-COAHUITLÁN
    TOTONACA
57 SIERRA TOTONACA
58 YECUATLA TOTONACA
59 SIERRA PUEBLA NÁHUATL
60 TLALITZLIPA NÁHUATL
61 IXTENCO OTOMÍ
62 NÁHUATL CENTRAL
63 PUEBLA CENTRAL NÁHUATL
64 CHIGMACATITLÁN MIXTECO
65 MORELOS NÁHUATL
66 TETELCINGO NÁHUATL
67 TILAPA OTOMÍ
68 TEMOAYA OTOMÍ
69 ESTADO DE MÉXICO OTOMÍ
70 MICHOACÁN MAZAHUA
71 MAZAHUA CENTRAL
72 TEMASCALTEPEC NÁHUATL
73 SAN FRANCISCO DE LOS RANCHOS
    MATLATZINCA
74 ATZINGO MATLATZINCA
75 TLAMACAZAPA NÁHUATL
76 COATEPEC NÁHUATL
77 GUERRERO NÁHUATL
78 ACATEPEC TLAPANECO
79 MALINALTEPEC TLAPANECO
80 AYUTLA MIXTECO
81 YOLOXOCHITL MIXTECO

82 AZOYÚ TLAPANECO
83 OMETEPEC NÁHUATL
84 GUERRERO AMUZGO
85 PINOTEPA NACIONAL MIXTECO
86 IPALAPA AMUZGO
87 SAN PEDRO AMUZGOS AMUZGO
88 JUXTLAHUACA OESTE MIXTECO
89 METLATONOC MIXTECO
90 ALACATLATZALA MIXTECO
91 ALCOZAUCA MIXTECO
92 SILACAYOAPAN MIXTECO
93 SANTA INÉS AHUATEMPAN POPOLOCA
94 SAN FELIPE OTLALTEPEC POPOLOCA
95 CHAZUMBA MIXTECO
96 COYOTEPEC POPOLOCA
97 MEZONTLA POPOLOCA
98 PUEBLA SUR MIXTECO
99 OAXACA NORTE NÁHUATL
100 SAN JERÓNIMO TECÓATL MAZATECO
101 PUEBLA SURESTE NÁHUATL
102 SAN JUAN ATZINGO POPOLOCA
103 SANTA MARÍA LA ALTA NÁHUATL
104 SAN LUIS TEMALACAYUCA POPOLOCA
105 SAN MARCOS TLALCOYALCO POPOLOCA
106 HUAXCALECA NÁHUATL
107 IXHUATLANCILLO NÁHUATL
108 ORIZABA NÁHUATL
109 HUAUTLA MAZATECO
110 IXCATLÁN MAZATECO
111 JALAPA DE DÍAZ MAZATECO
112 SOYALTEPEC MAZATECO
113 OJITLÁN CHINANTECO

©1999 SIL

86

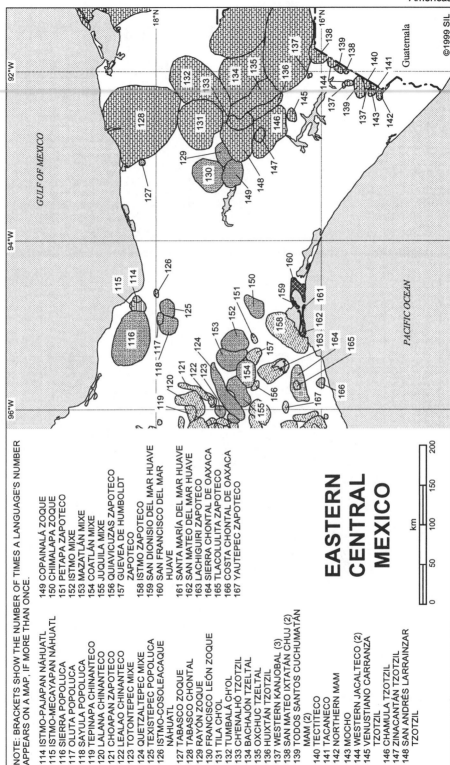

©1999 SIL

GULF OF MEXICO

PACIFIC OCEAN

Guatemala

NOTE: BRACKETS SHOW THE NUMBER OF TIMES A LANGUAGE'S NUMBER APPEARS ON A MAP, IF MORE THAN ONCE.

114 ISTMO-PAJAPAN NÁHUATL
115 ISTMO-MECAYAPAN NÁHUATL
116 SIERRA POPOLUCA
117 OLUTA POPOLUCA
118 SAYULA POPOLUCA
119 TEPINAPA CHINANTECO
120 LALANA CHINANTECO
121 CHOAPAN ZAPOTECO
122 LEALAO CHINANTECO
123 TOTONTEPEC MIXE
124 QUETZALTEPEC MIXE
125 TEXISTEPEC POPOLUCA
126 ISTMO-COSOLEACAQUE NÁHUATL
127 TABASCO ZOQUE
128 TABASCO CHONTAL
129 RAYÓN ZOQUE
130 FRANCISCO LEÓN ZOQUE
131 TILA CH'OL
132 TUMBALÁ CH'OL
133 CHENALHÓ TZOTZIL
134 BACHAJÓN TZELTAL
135 OXCHUC TZELTAL
136 HUIXTÁN TZOTZIL
137 WESTERN KANJOBAL (3)
138 SAN MATEO IXTATÁN CHUJ (2)
139 TODOS SANTOS CUCHUMATÁN MAM (2)
140 TECTITECO
141 TACANECO
142 NORTHERN MAM
143 MOCHO
144 WESTERN JACALTECO (2)
145 VENUSTIANO CARRANZA TZOTZIL
146 CHAMULA TZOTZIL
147 ZINACANTÁN TZOTZIL
148 SAN ANDRÉS LARRAINZAR TZOTZIL

149 COPAINALÁ ZOQUE
150 CHIMALAPA ZOQUE
151 PETAPA ZAPOTECO
152 ISTMO MIXE
153 MAZATLÁN MIXE
154 COATLÁN MIXE
155 JUQUILA MIXE
156 QUIAVICUZAS ZAPOTECO
157 GUEVEA DE HUMBOLDT ZAPOTECO
158 ISTMO ZAPOTECO
159 SAN DIONISIO DEL MAR HUAVE
160 SAN FRANCISCO DEL MAR HUAVE
161 SANTA MARÍA DEL MAR HUAVE
162 SAN MATEO DEL MAR HUAVE
163 LACHIGUIRI ZAPOTECO
164 SIERRA CHONTAL DE OAXACA
165 TLACOLULITA ZAPOTECO
166 COSTA CHONTAL DE OAXACA
167 YAUTEPEC ZAPOTECO

EASTERN CENTRAL MEXICO

km

0   50   100   150   200

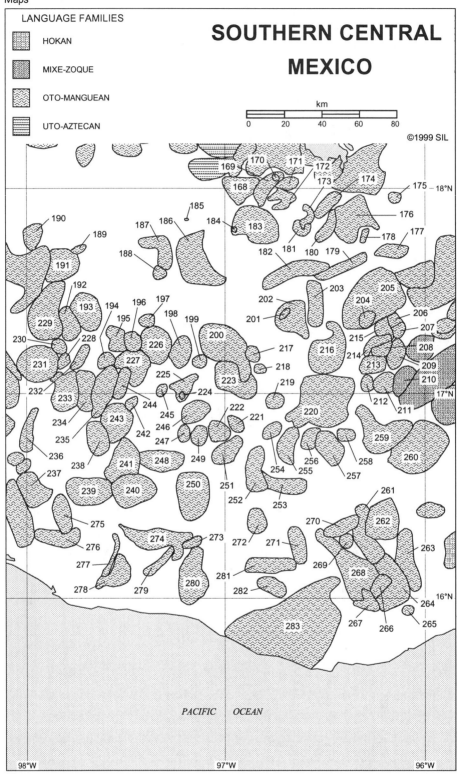

SOUTHERN CENTRAL
MEXICO

LANGUAGE FAMILIES

HOKAN

MIXE-ZOQUE

OTO-MANGUEAN

UTO-AZTECAN

km

0   20   40   60   80

©1999 SIL

PACIFIC   OCEAN

98°W   97°W   96°W

18°N

17°N

16°N

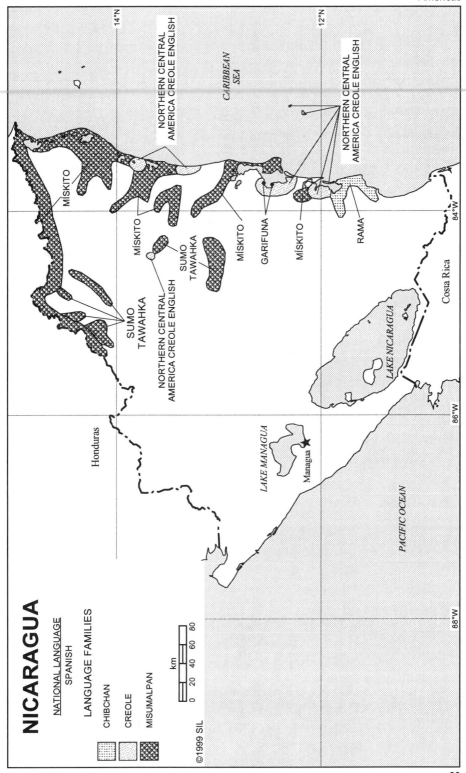

NICARAGUA

NATIONAL LANGUAGE
SPANISH

LANGUAGE FAMILIES

CHIBCHAN

CREOLE

MISUMALPAN

km
0 20 40 60 80

©1999 SIL

MISKITO

NORTHERN CENTRAL
AMERICA CREOLE ENGLISH

MISKITO

SUMO
TAWAHKA

NORTHERN CENTRAL
AMERICA CREOLE ENGLISH

SUMO
TAWAHKA

MISKITO

MISKITO

GARIFUNA

NORTHERN CENTRAL
AMERICA CREOLE ENGLISH

NORTHERN CENTRAL
AMERICA CREOLE ENGLISH

MISKITO

RAMA

SUMO
TAWAHKA

CARIBBEAN
SEA

Honduras

LAKE MANAGUA

Managua

LAKE NICARAGUA

Costa Rica

PACIFIC OCEAN

14°N

12°N

84°W

86°W

88°W

89

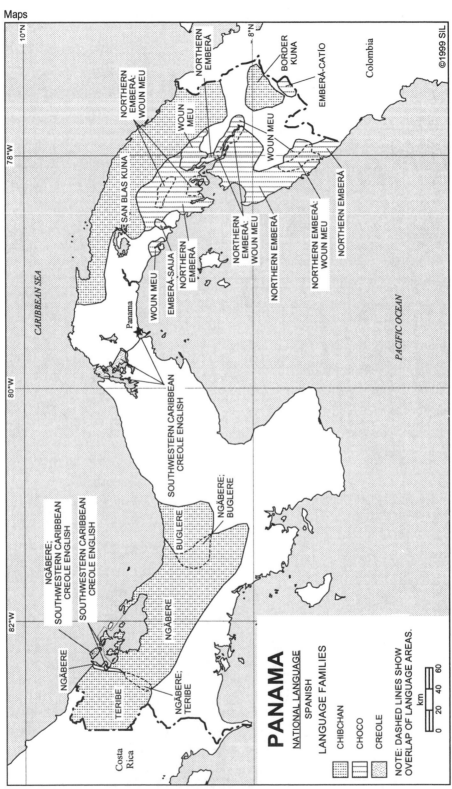

PANAMA

NATIONAL LANGUAGE
SPANISH

LANGUAGE FAMILIES

CHIBCHAN

CHOCO

CREOLE

NOTE: DASHED LINES SHOW
OVERLAP OF LANGUAGE AREAS.

km
0 20 40 60

©1999 SIL

CARIBBEAN SEA

PACIFIC OCEAN

Costa Rica

Colombia

Panama

10°N

8°N

78°W

80°W

82°W

NGÄBERE;
SOUTHWESTERN CARIBBEAN
CREOLE ENGLISH

SOUTHWESTERN CARIBBEAN
CREOLE ENGLISH

NGÄBERE

TERIBE

NGÄBERE;
TERIBE

NGÄBERE

BUGLERE

NGÄBERE;
BUGLERE

SOUTHWESTERN CARIBBEAN
CREOLE ENGLISH

SAN BLAS KUNA

WOUN MEU

EMBERA-SAIJA

NORTHERN
EMBERA

NORTHERN EMBERÁ:
WOUN MEU

WOUN
MEU

NORTHERN
EMBERÁ:
WOUN MEU

NORTHERN EMBERÁ

NORTHERN EMBERÁ

WOUN MEU

NORTHERN EMBERÁ:
WOUN MEU

NORTHERN EMBERÁ

NORTHERN
EMBERÁ

BORDER
KUNA

EMBERA-CATÍO

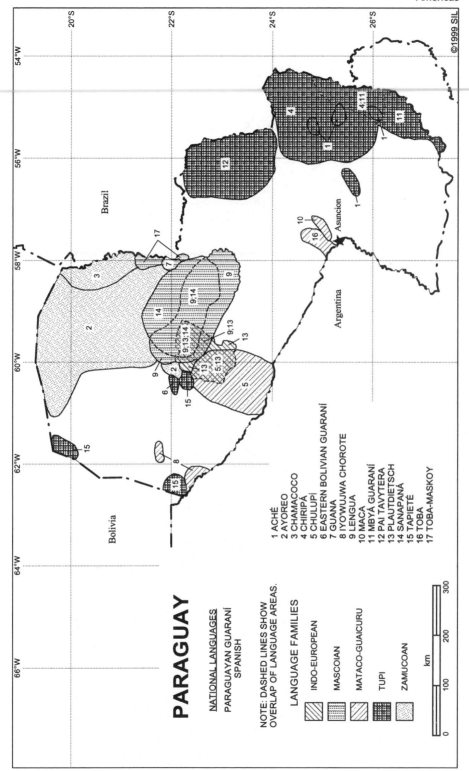

PARAGUAY

<u>NATIONAL LANGUAGES</u>
PARAGUAYAN GUARANÍ
SPANISH

NOTE: DASHED LINES SHOW
OVERLAP OF LANGUAGE AREAS.

LANGUAGE FAMILIES

INDO-EUROPEAN

MASCOIAN

MATACO-GUAICURU

TUPI

ZAMUCOAN

1 ACHÉ
2 AYOREO
3 CHAMACOCO
4 CHIRIPÁ
5 CHULUPÍ
6 EASTERN BOLIVIAN GUARANÍ
7 GUANA
8 ÍYO'WUJWA CHOROTE
9 LENGUA
10 MACA
11 MBYÁ GUARANÍ
12 PAI TAVYTERA
13 PLAUTDIETSCH
14 SANAPANÁ
15 TAPIETÉ
16 TOBA
17 TOBA-MASKOY

km

0   100   200   300

©1999 SIL

Brazil

Bolivia

Argentina

Asuncion

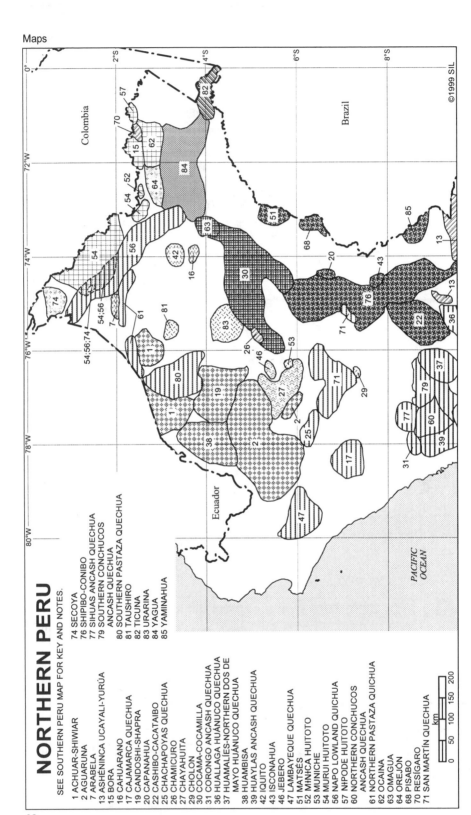

Maps

NORTHERN PERU

SEE SOUTHERN PERU MAP FOR KEY AND NOTES.

1 ACHUAR-SHIWIAR
2 AGUARUNA
7 ARABELA
13 ASHÉNINCA UCAYALI-YURÚA
15 BORA
16 CAHUARANO
17 CAJAMARCA QUECHUA
19 CANDOSHI-SHAPRA
20 CAPANAHUA
22 CASHIBO-CACATAIBO
25 CHACHAPOYAS QUECHUA
26 CHAMICURO
27 CHAYAHUITA
29 CHOLON
30 COCAMA-COCAMILLA
31 CORONGO ANCASH QUECHUA
36 HUALLAGA HUÁNUCO QUECHUA
37 HUAMALÍES-NORTHERN DOS DE
    MAYO HUÁNUCO QUECHUA
38 HUAMBISA
39 HUAYLAS ANCASH QUECHUA
42 IQUITO
43 ISCONAHUA
46 JEBERO
47 LAMBAYEQUE QUECHUA
51 MATSÉS
52 MIN+CA HUITOTO
53 MUNICHE
54 MURUI HUITOTO
56 NAPO LOWLAND QUICHUA
57 N+PODE HUITOTO
60 NORTHERN CONCHUCOS
    ANCASH QUECHUA
61 NORTHERN PASTAZA QUICHUA
62 OCAINA
63 OMAGUA
64 OREJÓN
68 PISABO
70 RESÍGARO
71 SAN MARTÍN QUECHUA

74 SECOYA
76 SHIPIBO-CONIBO
77 SIHUAS ANCASH QUECHUA
79 SOUTHERN CONCHUCOS
    ANCASH QUECHUA
80 SOUTHERN PASTAZA QUECHUA
81 TAUSHIRO
82 TICUNA
83 URARINA
84 YAGUA
85 YAMINAHUA

0 50 100 150 200
        km

©1999 SIL

92

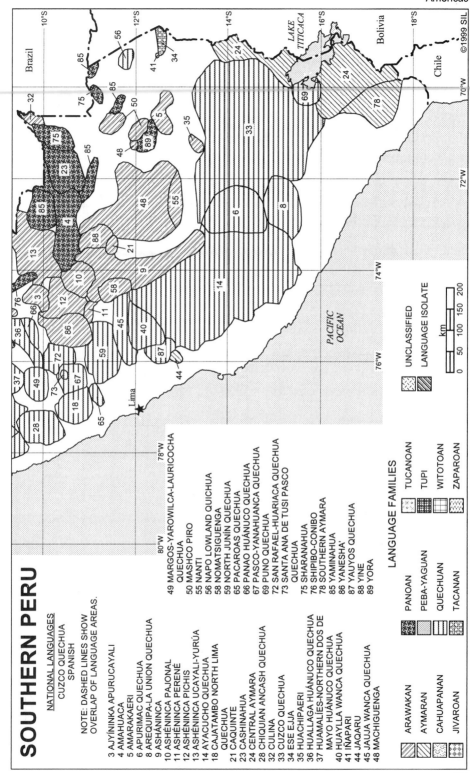

SOUTHERN PERU

NATIONAL LANGUAGES
CUZCO QUECHUA
SPANISH

NOTE: DASHED LINES SHOW
OVERLAP OF LANGUAGE AREAS.

3 AJYÍNINKA APURUCAYALI
4 AMAHUACA
5 AMARAKAERI
6 APURIMAC QUECHUA
8 AREQUIPA-LA UNION QUECHUA
9 ASHÁNINCA
10 ASHÉNINCA PAJONAL
11 ASHÉNINCA PERENÉ
12 ASHÉNINCA PICHIS
13 ASHÉNINCA UCAYALI-YURÚA
14 AYACUCHO QUECHUA
18 CAJATAMBO NORTH LIMA
   QUECHUA
21 CAQUINTE
23 CASHINAHUA
24 CENTRAL AYMARA
28 CHIQUIAN ANCASH QUECHUA
32 CULINA
33 CUZCO QUECHUA
34 ESE EJJA
35 HUACHIPAERI
36 HUALLAGA HUÁNUCO QUECHUA
37 HUAMALÍES-NORTHERN DOS DE
   MAYO HUÁNUCO QUECHUA
40 HUAYLLA WANCA QUECHUA
41 IÑAPARI
44 JAQARU
45 JAUJA WANCA QUECHUA
48 MACHIGUENGA
49 MARGOS-YAROWILCA-LAURICOCHA
   QUECHUA
50 MASHCO PIRO
55 NANTI
56 NAPO LOWLAND QUICHUA
58 NOMATSIGUENGA
59 NORTH JUNIN QUECHUA
65 PACAROAS QUECHUA
66 PANAO HUÁNUCO QUECHUA
67 PASCO-YANAHUANCA QUECHUA
69 PUNO QUECHUA
72 SAN RAFAEL-HUARIACA QUECHUA
73 SANTA ANA DE TUSI PASCO
   QUECHUA
75 SHARANAHUA
76 SHIPIBO-CONIBO
78 SOUTHERN AYMARA
85 YAMINAHUA
86 YANESHA'
87 YAUYOS QUECHUA
88 YINE
89 YORA

LANGUAGE FAMILIES

ARAWAKAN
AYMARAN
CAHUAPANAN
JIVAROAN

PANOAN
PEBA-YAGUAN
QUECHUAN
TACANAN

TUCANOAN
TUPI
WITOTOAN
ZAPAROAN

UNCLASSIFIED
LANGUAGE ISOLATE

km
0 50 100 150 200

Brazil

Bolivia

Chile

LAKE
TITICACA

PACIFIC
OCEAN

Lima

©1999 SIL

93

Maps

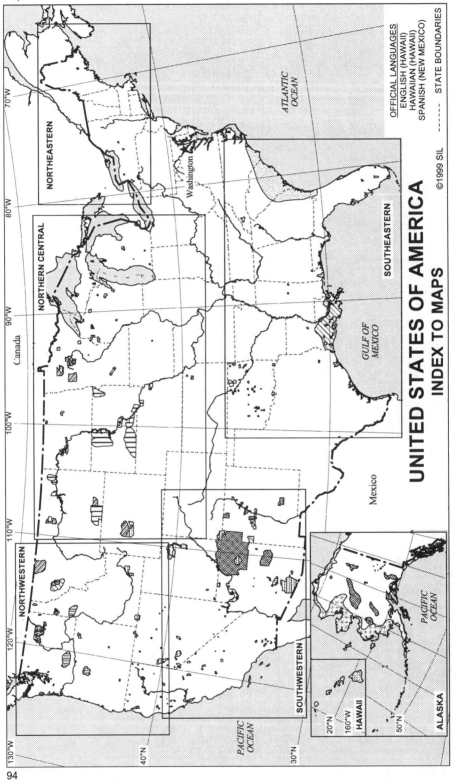

UNITED STATES OF AMERICA
INDEX TO MAPS

NORTHEASTERN

NORTHERN CENTRAL

SOUTHEASTERN

NORTHWESTERN

SOUTHWESTERN

HAWAII

ALASKA

Washington

Canada

Mexico

ATLANTIC OCEAN

GULF OF MEXICO

PACIFIC OCEAN

PACIFIC OCEAN

OFFICIAL LANGUAGES
ENGLISH (HAWAII)
HAWAIIAN (HAWAII)
SPANISH (NEW MEXICO)
– – – – – STATE BOUNDARIES

©1999 SIL

70°W
80°W
90°W
100°W
110°W
120°W
130°W

40°N
30°N

20°N
160°W

50°N

94

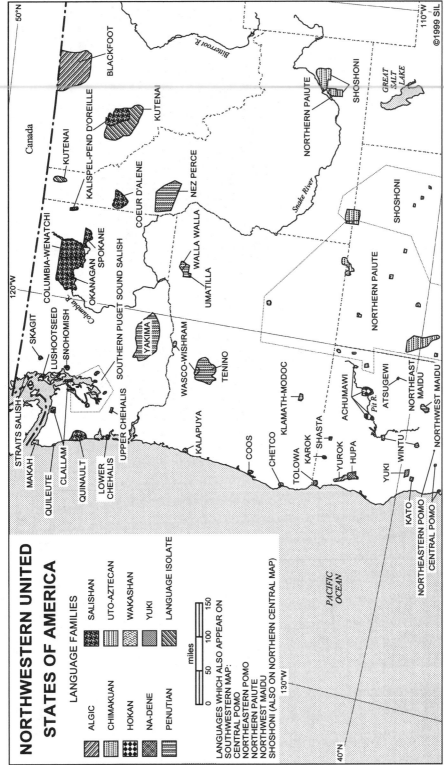

NORTHWESTERN UNITED STATES OF AMERICA

©1999 SIL

LANGUAGE FAMILIES

- ALGIC
- CHIMAKUAN
- HOKAN
- NA-DENE
- PENUTIAN
- SALISHAN
- UTO-AZTECAN
- WAKASHAN
- YUKI
- LANGUAGE ISOLATE

miles

0   50   100   150

LANGUAGES WHICH ALSO APPEAR ON SOUTHWESTERN MAP:
CENTRAL POMO
NORTHEASTERN POMO
NORTHERN PAIUTE
NORTHWEST MAIDU
SHOSHONI (ALSO ON NORTHERN CENTRAL MAP)

BLACKFOOT

KUTENAI

KALISPEL-PEND D'OREILLE

KUTENAI

Canada

Bitterroot R.

NORTHERN PAIUTE

SHOSHONI

GREAT SALT LAKE

COEUR D'ALENE

NEZ PERCE

Snake River

SHOSHONI

COLUMBIA-WENATCHI

OKANAGAN   SPOKANE

SKAGIT

LUSHOOTSEED

SNOHOMISH

SOUTHERN PUGET SOUND SALISH

Columbia

WALLA WALLA

UMATILLA

NORTHERN PAIUTE

STRAITS SALISH

MAKAH

QUILEUTE

CLALLAM

QUINAULT

LOWER CHEHALIS

UPPER CHEHALIS

YAKIMA

WASCO-WISHRAM

TENINO

KALAPUYA

COOS

CHETCO

KLAMATH-MODOC

SHASTA

TOLOWA

KAROK

YUROK

HUPA

ACHUMAWI

Pit R.

ATSUGEWI

NORTHEAST MAIDU

NORTHWEST MAIDU

WINTU

YUKI

KATO

NORTHEASTERN POMO

CENTRAL POMO

PACIFIC OCEAN

50°N

120°W

130°W

40°N

110°W

95

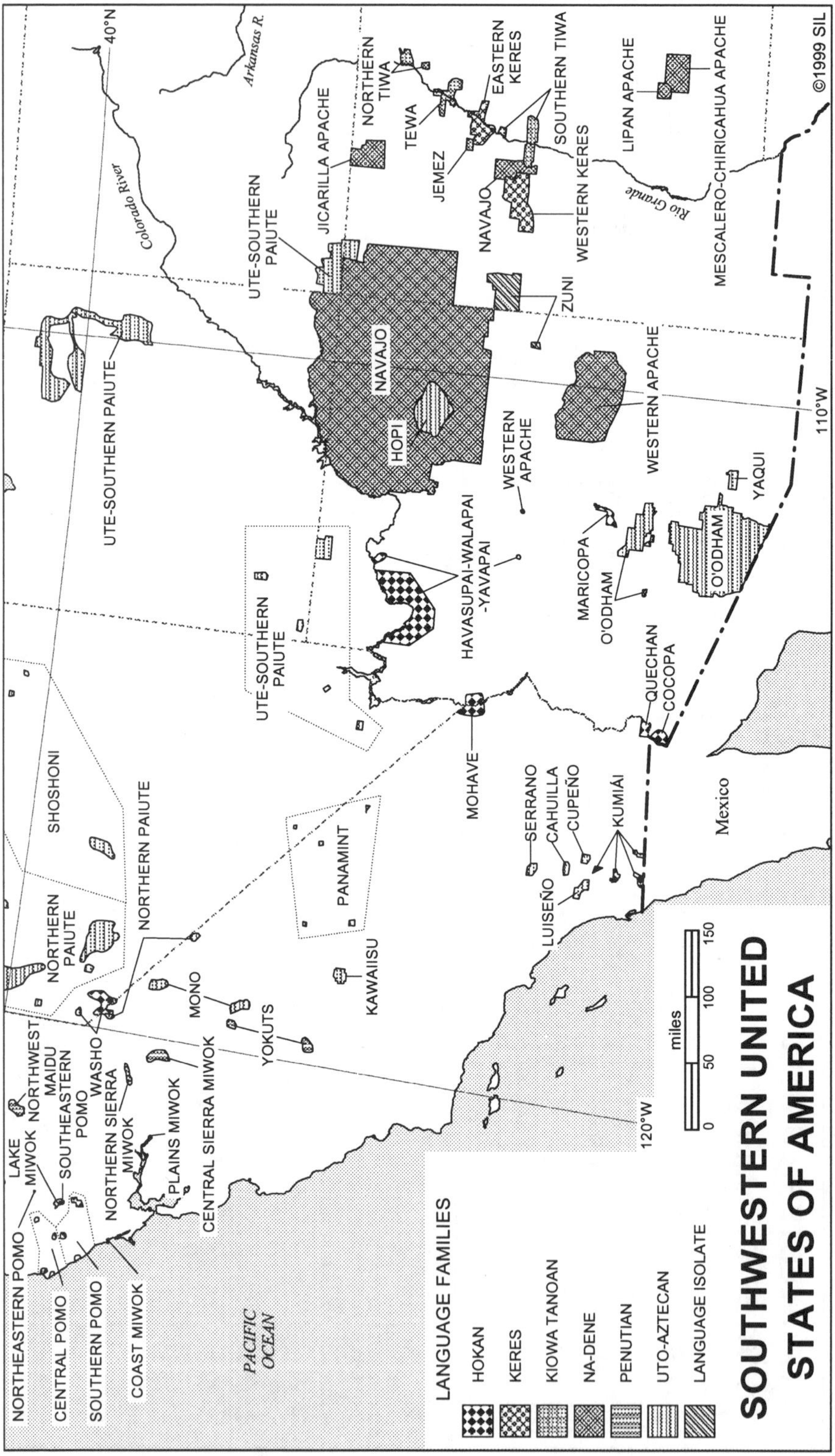

SOUTHWESTERN UNITED STATES OF AMERICA
LANGUAGE FAMILIES
HOKAN
KERES
KIOWA TANOAN
NA-DENE
PENUTIAN
UTO-AZTECAN
LANGUAGE ISOLATE
miles
0
50
100
150
©1999 SIL
40°N
120°W
110°W
PACIFIC OCEAN
Mexico
Colorado River
Arkansas R.
Rio Grande
NORTHEASTERN POMO
CENTRAL POMO
SOUTHERN POMO
COAST MIWOK
LAKE MIWOK
SOUTHEASTERN POMO
NORTHWEST MAIDU
WASHO
NORTHERN SIERRA MIWOK
PLAINS MIWOK
CENTRAL SIERRA MIWOK
YOKUTS
MONO
NORTHERN PAIUTE
NORTHERN PAIUTE
SHOSHONI
KAWAIISU
PANAMINT
LUISEÑO
SERRANO
CAHUILLA
CUPEÑO
KUMIÁI
MOHAVE
QUECHAN
COCOPA
UTE-SOUTHERN PAIUTE
UTE-SOUTHERN PAIUTE
UTE-SOUTHERN PAIUTE
HAVASUPAI-WALAPAI -YAVAPAI
MARICOPA
O'ODHAM
O'ODHAM
YAQUI
WESTERN APACHE
WESTERN APACHE
HOPI
NAVAJO
ZUNI
JICARILLA APACHE
NAVAJO
WESTERN KERES
JEMEZ
TEWA
NORTHERN TIWA
EASTERN KERES
SOUTHERN TIWA
LIPAN APACHE
MESCALERO-CHIRICAHUA APACHE

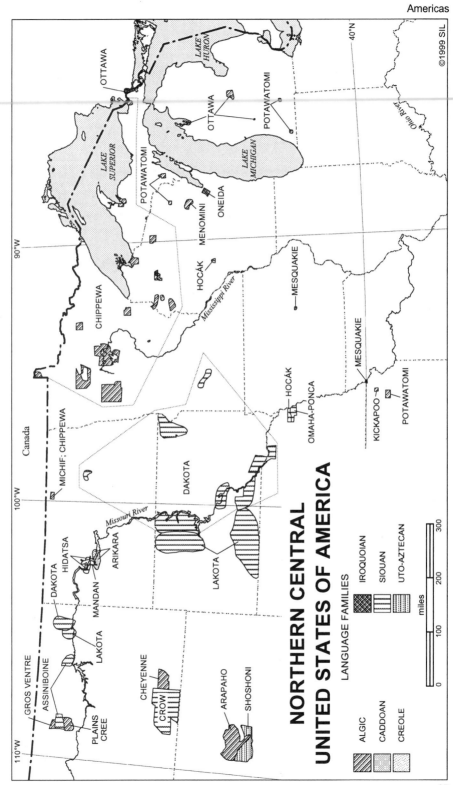

NORTHERN CENTRAL
UNITED STATES OF AMERICA

LANGUAGE FAMILIES

ALGIC

CADDOAN

CREOLE

IROQUOIAN

SIOUAN

UTO-AZTECAN

miles

0   100   200   300

©1999 SIL

97

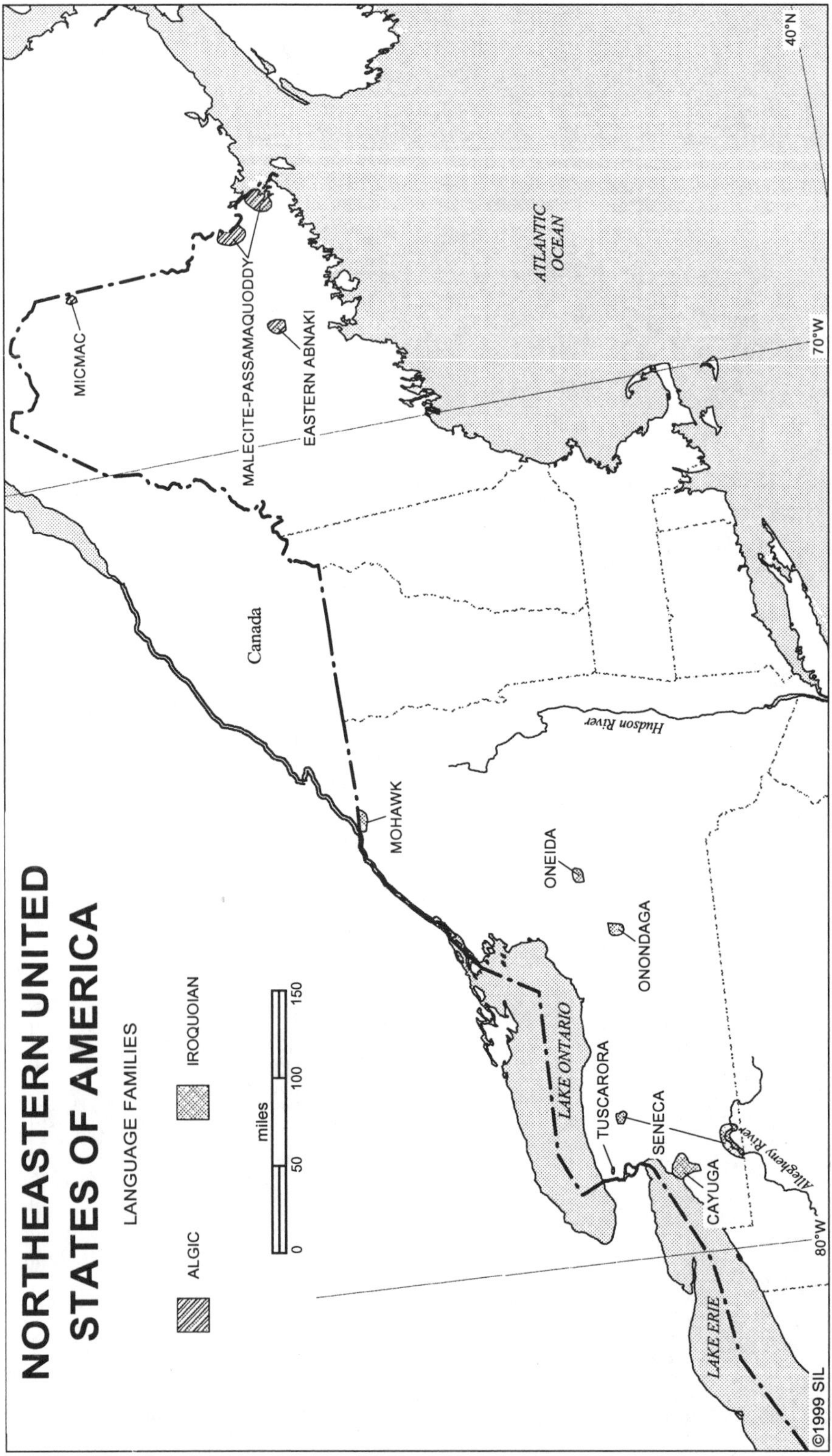

NORTHEASTERN UNITED STATES OF AMERICA

LANGUAGE FAMILIES

ALGIC

IROQUOIAN

miles

0   50   100   150

MICMAC

MALECITE-PASSAMAQUODDY

EASTERN ABNAKI

ATLANTIC OCEAN

40°N

70°W

Canada

Hudson River

MOHAWK

ONEIDA

ONONDAGA

LAKE ONTARIO

TUSCARORA

SENECA

CAYUGA

Allegheny River

80°W

LAKE ERIE

©1999 SIL

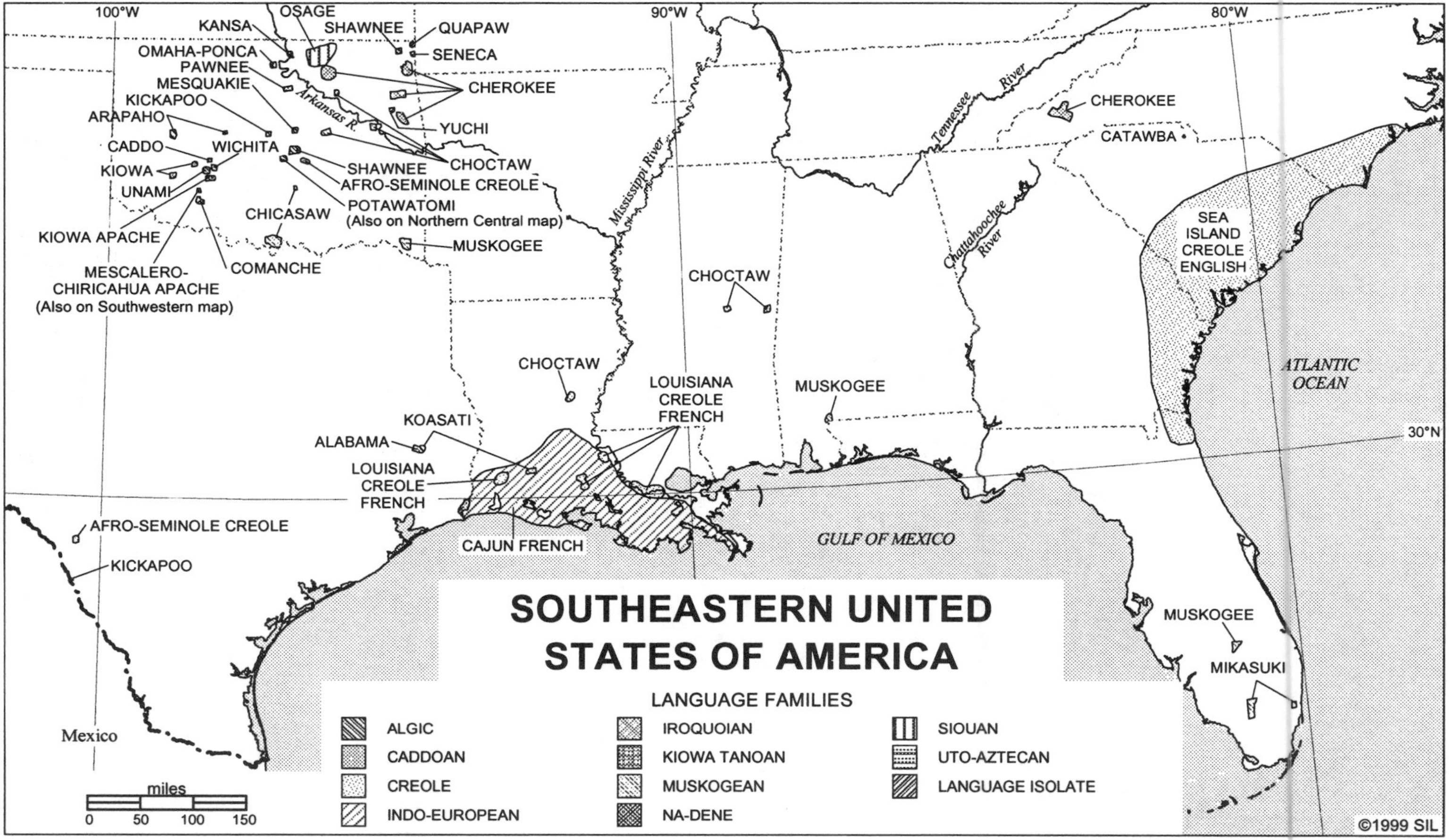

©1999 SIL

SOUTHEASTERN UNITED STATES OF AMERICA

ATLANTIC OCEAN

SEA ISLAND CREOLE ENGLISH

MIKASUKI

MUSKOGEE

CHEROKEE

CATAWBA

Chattahoochee River

Tennessee River

GULF OF MEXICO

MUSKOGEE

CHOCTAW

LOUISIANA CREOLE FRENCH

CAJUN FRENCH

CHOCTAW

Mississippi River

CHOCTAW

MUSKOGEE

QUAPAW

SENECA

CHEROKEE

YUCHI

SHAWNEE

CHOCTAW

AFRO-SEMINOLE CREOLE

POTAWATOMI
(Also on Northern Central map)

KOASATI

ALABAMA

LOUISIANA CREOLE FRENCH

OSAGE

KANSA

OMAHA-PONCA

PAWNEE

MESQUAKIE

KICKAPOO

ARAPAHO

CADDO

KIOWA

UNAMI

KIOWA APACHE

MESCALERO-CHIRICAHUA APACHE
(Also on Southwestern map)

SHAWNEE

Arkansas R.

WICHITA

CHICASAW

COMANCHE

AFRO-SEMINOLE CREOLE

KICKAPOO

Mexico

LANGUAGE FAMILIES

ALGIC	IROQUOIAN	SIOUAN
CADDOAN	KIOWA TANOAN	UTO-AZTECAN
CREOLE	MUSKOGEAN	LANGUAGE ISOLATE
INDO-EUROPEAN	NA-DENE	

miles

0   50   100   150

30°N

80°W

90°W

100°W

99

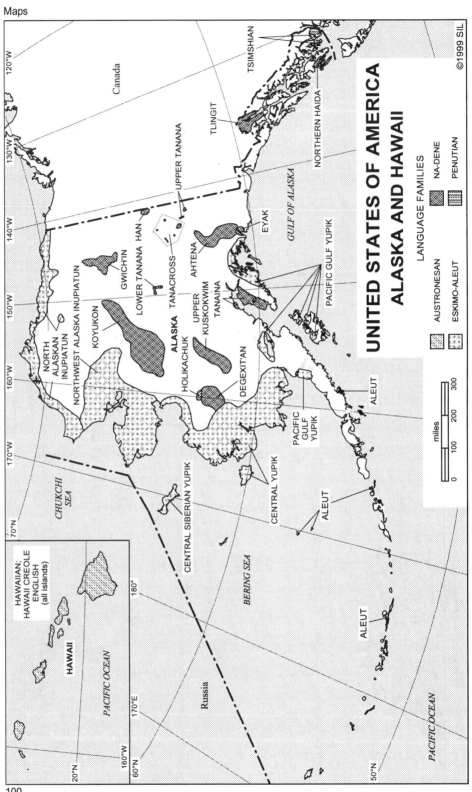

UNITED STATES OF AMERICA
ALASKA AND HAWAII

LANGUAGE FAMILIES

AUSTRONESAN

ESKIMO-ALEUT

NA-DENE

PENUTIAN

©1999 SIL

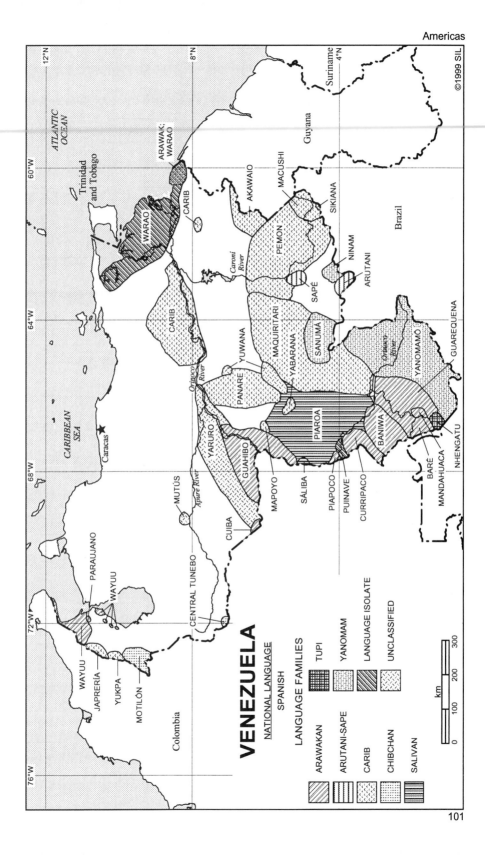

©1999 SIL

VENEZUELA

NATIONAL LANGUAGE

SPANISH

LANGUAGE FAMILIES

ARAWAKAN	TUPI
ARUTANI-SAPE	YANOMAM
CARIB	LANGUAGE ISOLATE
CHIBCHAN	UNCLASSIFIED
SALIVAN	

km

0 100 200 300

Asia Maps

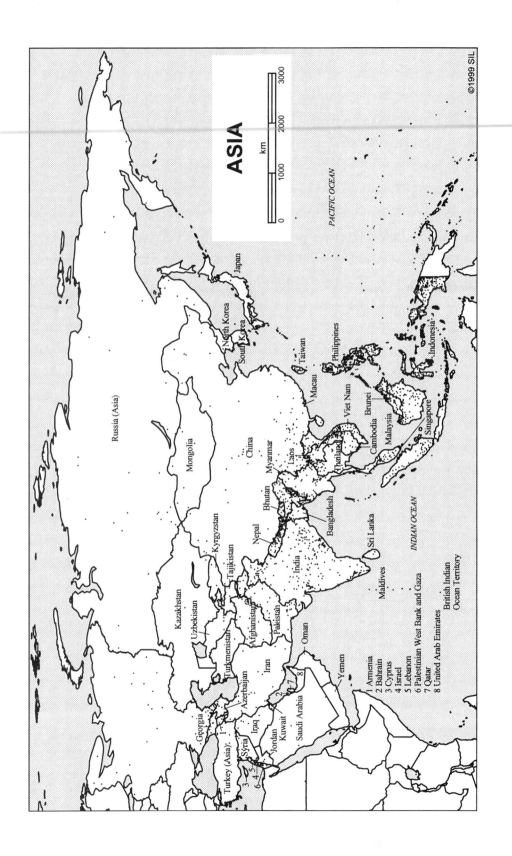

ASIA

km

0 1000 2000 3000

©1999 SIL

PACIFIC OCEAN

Russia (Asia)

Japan

North Korea
South Korea

Mongolia

China

Taiwan
Macau

Philippines

Indonesia

Kazakhstan

Kyrgyzstan

Tajikistan

Uzbekistan

Turkmenistan

Afghanistan

Pakistan

Nepal

Bhutan

Myanmar

Laos

Viet Nam

Thailand

Cambodia

Brunei

Malaysia

Singapore

Bangladesh

India

Sri Lanka

Maldives

INDIAN OCEAN

British Indian
Ocean Territory

Georgia

Azerbaijan

Iran

Oman

Yemen

Turkey (Asia):

Syria

Iraq

Jordan
Kuwait

Saudi Arabia

1 Armenia
2 Bahrain
3 Cyprus
4 Israel
5 Lebanon
6 Palestinian West Bank and Gaza
7 Qatar
8 United Arab Emirates

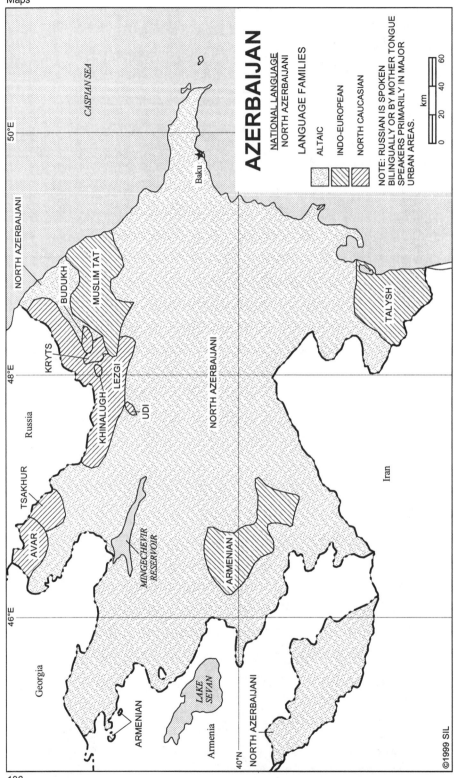

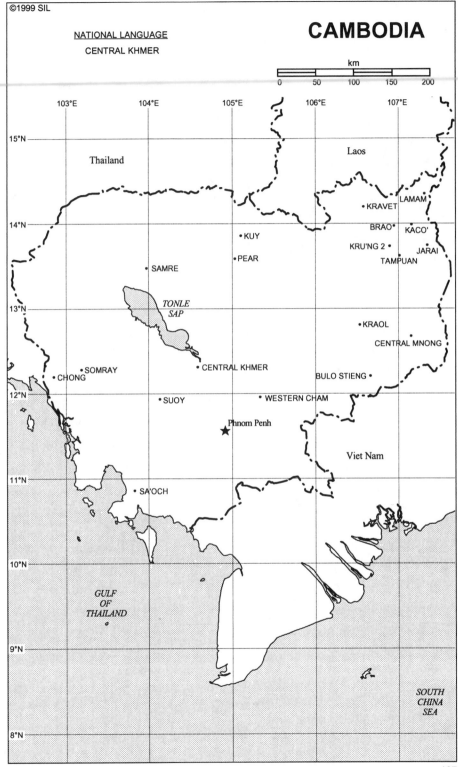

©1999 SIL

NATIONAL LANGUAGE
CENTRAL KHMER

CAMBODIA

km

0   50   100   150   200

Thailand

Laos

LAMAM

• KRAVET

BRAO•   KACO'

• KUY

KRU'NG 2 •   JARAI

•PEAR   TAMPUAN

• SAMRE

TONLE SAP

• KRAOL

CENTRAL MNONG

•SOMRAY   • CENTRAL KHMER

•CHONG

BULO STIENG •

• SUOY   • WESTERN CHAM

Phnom Penh
★

Viet Nam

• SA'OCH

GULF OF THAILAND

SOUTH CHINA SEA

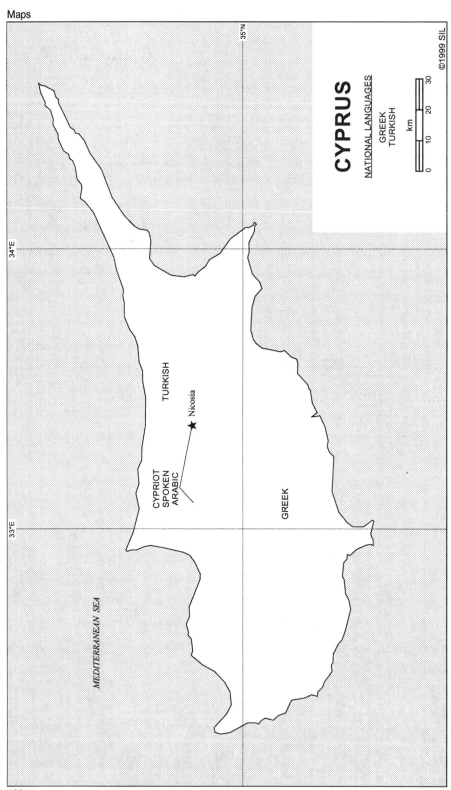

CYPRUS

NATIONAL LANGUAGES

GREEK
TURKISH

km

0   10   20   30

©1999 SIL

TURKISH

★ Nicosia

CYPRIOT
SPOKEN
ARABIC

GREEK

MEDITERRANEAN SEA

34°E

33°E

35°N

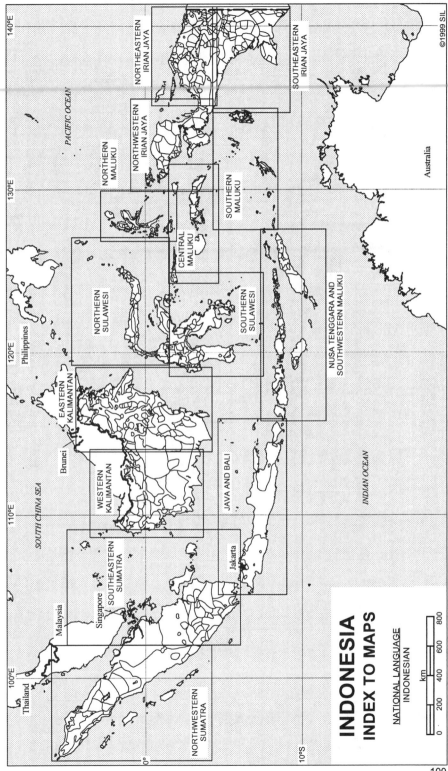

INDONESIA
INDEX TO MAPS

NATIONAL LANGUAGE
INDONESIAN

km

0   200   400   600   800

NORTHEASTERN IRIAN JAYA

SOUTHEASTERN IRIAN JAYA

NORTHWESTERN IRIAN JAYA

NORTHERN MALUKU

SOUTHERN MALUKU

CENTRAL MALUKU

NORTHERN SULAWESI

SOUTHERN SULAWESI

NUSA TENGGARA AND SOUTHWESTERN MALUKU

EASTERN KALIMANTAN

WESTERN KALIMANTAN

JAVA AND BALI

SOUTHEASTERN SUMATRA

NORTHWESTERN SUMATRA

Jakarta

Singapore

Malaysia

Brunei

Philippines

Thailand

Australia

PACIFIC OCEAN

SOUTH CHINA SEA

INDIAN OCEAN

©1999 SIL

140°E

130°E

120°E

110°E

100°E

0°

10°S

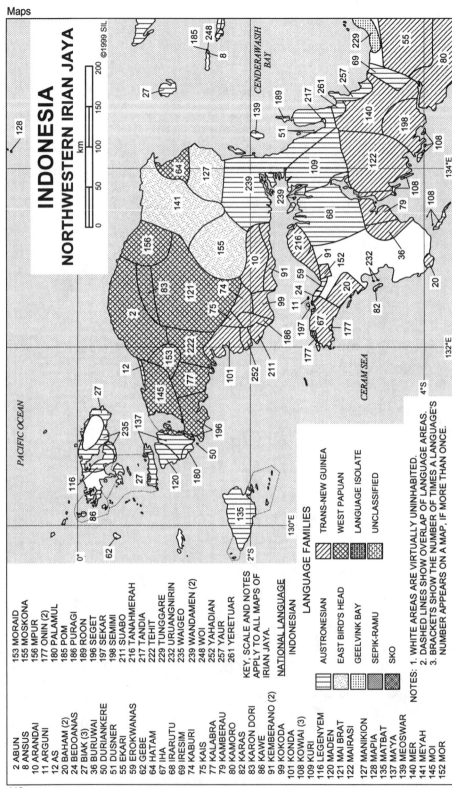

INDONESIA
NORTHWESTERN IRIAN JAYA

©1999 SIL

km

0 50 100 150 200

PACIFIC OCEAN

CENDERAWASIH BAY

CERAM SEA

130°E 132°E 134°E

0°

2°S

4°S

2 ABUN
8 ANSUS
10 ARANDAI
11 ARGUNI
12 AS
20 BAHAM (2)
24 BEDOANAS
27 BIAK (3)
36 BURUWAI
50 DURIANKERE
51 DUSNER
55 EKARI
59 EROKWANAS
62 GEBE
64 HATAM
67 IHA
68 IRARUTU
69 IRESIM
74 KABURI
75 KAIS
77 KALABRA
79 KAMBERAU
80 KAMORO
82 KARAS
83 KARON DORI
86 KAWE
91 KEMBERANO (2)
99 KOKODA
101 KONDA
108 KOWIAI (3)
109 KURI
116 LEGENYEM
120 MADEN
121 MAI BRAT
122 MAIRASI
127 MANIKION
128 MAPIA
135 MATBAT
137 MA'YA
139 MEOSWAR
140 MER
141 MEYAH
145 MOI
152 MOR

153 MORAID
155 MOSKONA
156 MPUR
177 ONIN (2)
180 PALAMUL
185 POM
186 PURAGI
189 ROON
196 SEGET
197 SEKAR
198 SEMIMI
211 SUABO
216 TANAHMERAH
217 TANDIA
222 TEHIT
229 TUNGGARE
232 URUANGNIRIN
235 WAIGEO
239 WANDAMEN (2)
248 WOI
252 YAHADIAN
257 YAUR
261 YERETUAR

KEY, SCALE AND NOTES
APPLY TO ALL MAPS OF
IRIAN JAYA.

NATIONAL LANGUAGE
INDONESIAN

LANGUAGE FAMILIES

AUSTRONESIAN		TRANS-NEW GUINEA
EAST BIRD'S HEAD		WEST PAPUAN
GEELVINK BAY		LANGUAGE ISOLATE
SEPIK-RAMU		UNCLASSIFIED
SKO		

NOTES: 1. WHITE AREAS ARE VIRTUALLY UNINHABITED.
2. DASHED LINES SHOW OVERLAP OF LANGUAGE AREAS.
3. BRACKETS SHOW THE NUMBER OF TIMES A LANGUAGE'S
   NUMBER APPEARS ON A MAP, IF MORE THAN ONCE.

INDONESIA
NORTHEASTERN IRIAN JAYA

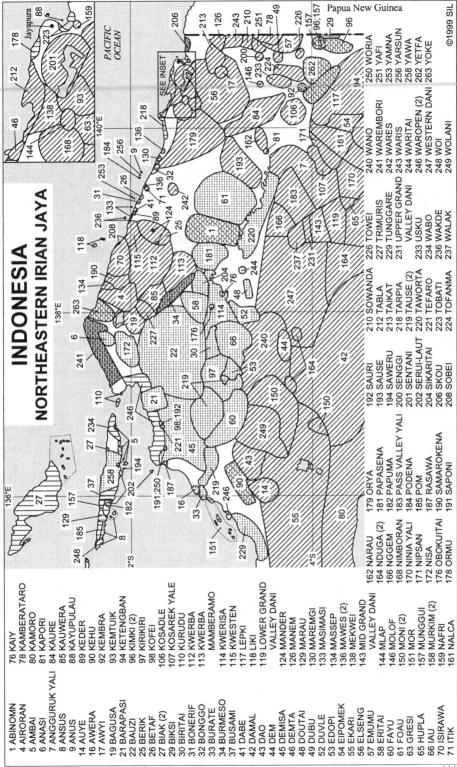

©1999 SIL

Papua New Guinea

PACIFIC OCEAN

1 ABINOMN	76 KAIY	162 NARAU	240 WANO
4 AIRORAN	78 KAMBERATARO	164 NDUGA (2)	241 WAREMBORI
5 AMBAI	80 KAMORO	166 NGGEM	242 WARES
6 ANASI	81 KAPORI	168 NIMBORAN	243 WARIS
7 ANGGURUK YALI	84 KAURE	170 NINIA YALI	244 WARITAI
8 ANSUS	85 KAUWERA	171 NIPSAN	246 WAROPEN (2)
9 ANUS	88 KAYUPULAU	172 NISA	247 WESTERN DANI
14 AUYE	89 KEDER	176 OBOKUITAI	248 WOI
16 AWERA	90 KEHU	178 ORMU	249 WOLANI
17 AWYI	92 KEMBRA	179 ORYA	250 WORIA
19 BAGUSA	93 KEMTUIK	181 PAPASENA	251 YAFI
21 BARAPASI	94 KETENGBAN	182 PAPUMA	253 YAMNA
22 BAUZI	96 KIMKI (2)	183 PASS VALLEY YALI	256 YARSUN
25 BERIK	97 KIRIKIRI	184 PODENA	258 YAWA
26 BETAF	98 KOFEI	185 POM	262 YETFA
27 BIAK (2)	106 KOSADLE	187 RASAWA	263 YOKE
29 BIKSI	107 KOSAREK YALE	190 SAMAROKENA	
30 BIRITAI	110 KURUDU	191 SAPONI	
31 BONERIF	112 KWERBA	192 SAURI	
32 BONGGO	113 KWERBA MAMBERAMO	193 SAUSE	
33 BURATE	114 KWERISA	194 SAWERU	
34 BURMESO	115 KWESTEN	200 SENGGI	
37 BUSAMI	117 LEPKI	201 SENTANI	
41 DABE	118 LIKI	202 SERUI-LAUT	
42 DAMAL	119 LOWER GRAND VALLEY DANI	204 SIKARITAI	
43 DAO	124 MANDER	206 SKOU	
44 DEM	126 MANEM	208 SOBEI	
45 DEMISA	129 MARAU	210 SOWANDA	
46 DEMTA	130 MAREMGI	212 TABLA	
48 DOUTAI	133 MASIMASI	213 TAIKAT	
49 DUBU	134 MASSEP	218 TARPIA	
52 DUVLE	136 MAWES (2)	219 TAUSE (2)	
53 EDOPI	138 MEKWEI	220 TAWORTA	
54 EIPOMEK	143 MID GRAND VALLEY DANI	221 TEFARO	
55 EKARI	144 MLAP	223 TOBATI	
56 ELSENG	146 MOLOF	224 TOFANMA	
57 EMUMU	150 MONI (2)	226 TOWEI	
58 ERITAI	151 MOR	227 TRIMURIS	
60 FAYU	157 MUNGGUI	229 TUNGGARE	
61 FOAU	158 MURKIM (2)	231 UPPER GRAND VALLEY DANI	
63 GRESI	159 NAFRI	233 USKU	
65 HUPLA	161 NALCA	234 WABO	
66 IAU		236 WAKDE	
70 ISIRAWA		237 WALAK	
71 ITIK			

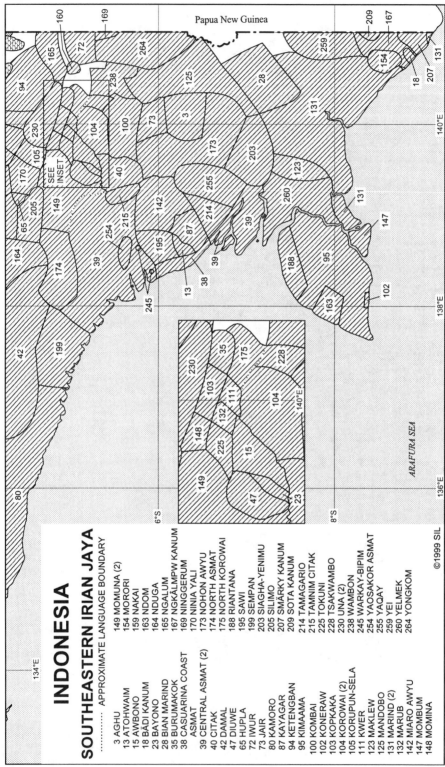

Maps

INDONESIA
SOUTHEASTERN IRIAN JAYA
········· APPROXIMATE LANGUAGE BOUNDARY

3 AGHU
13 ATOHWAIM
15 AWBONO
18 BÄDI KANUM
23 BAYONO
28 BIAN MARIND
35 BURUMAKOK
38 CASUARINA COAST
   ASMAT
39 CENTRAL ASMAT (2)
40 CITAK
42 DAMAL
47 DIUWE
65 HUPLA
72 IWUR
73 JAIR
80 KAMORO
87 KAYAGAR
94 KETENGBAN
95 KIMAAMA
100 KOMBAI
102 KONERAW
103 KOPKAKA
104 KOROWAI (2)
105 KORUPUN-SELA
111 KWER
123 MAKLEW
125 MANDOBO
131 MARIND (2)
132 MARUB
142 MIARO AWYU
147 MOMBUM
148 MOMINA

149 MOMUNA (2)
154 MORORI
159 NAKAI
163 NDOM
164 NDUGA
165 NGALUM
167 NGKÂLMPW KANUM
169 NINGGERUM
170 NINIA YALI
173 NOHON AWYU
174 NORTH ASMAT
175 NORTH KOROWAI
188 RIANTANA
195 SAWI
199 SEMPAN
203 SIAGHA-YENIMU
205 SILIMO
207 SMÄRKY KANUM
209 SOTA KANUM
214 TAMAGARIO
215 TAMNIM CITAK
225 TOKUNI
228 TSAKWAMBO
230 UNA (2)
238 WAMBON
245 WARKAY-BIPIM
254 YAOSAKOR ASMAT
255 YAQAY
259 YEI
260 YELMEK
264 YONGKOM

©1999 SIL

Papua New Guinea

ARAFURA SEA

112

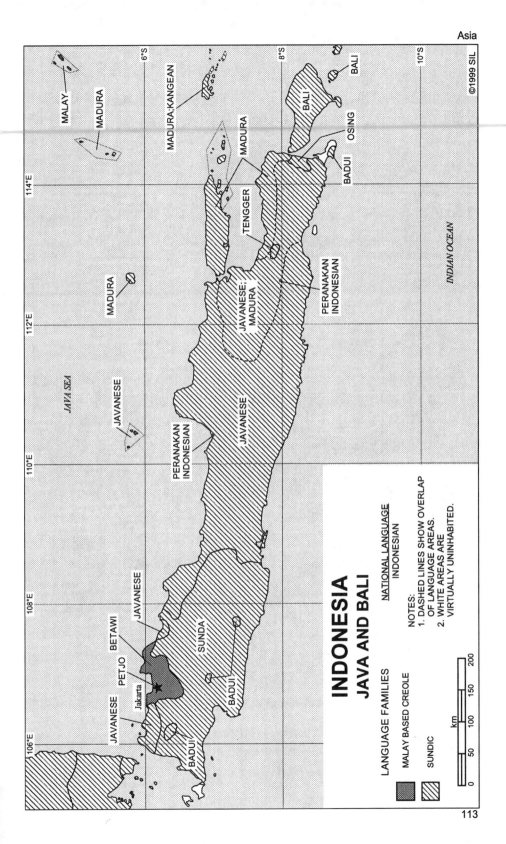

INDONESIA
JAVA AND BALI

LANGUAGE FAMILIES

MALAY BASED CREOLE

SUNDIC

NATIONAL LANGUAGE
INDONESIAN

NOTES:
1. DASHED LINES SHOW OVERLAP
   OF LANGUAGE AREAS.
2. WHITE AREAS ARE
   VIRTUALLY UNINHABITED.

km
0 50 100 150 200

©1999 SIL

INDIAN OCEAN

JAVA SEA

MALAY
MADURA
MADURA;KANGEAN
MADURA
TENGGER
JAVANESE;
MADURA
PERANAKAN
INDONESIAN
BALI
BADUI   OSING
MADURA
JAVANESE
PERANAKAN
INDONESIAN
JAVANESE
PERANAKAN
INDONESIAN
JAVANESE
BETAWI
PETJO
JAVANESE
Jakarta
SUNDA
BADUI
BADUI
BALI

6°S
8°S
10°S

106°E   108°E   110°E   112°E   114°E

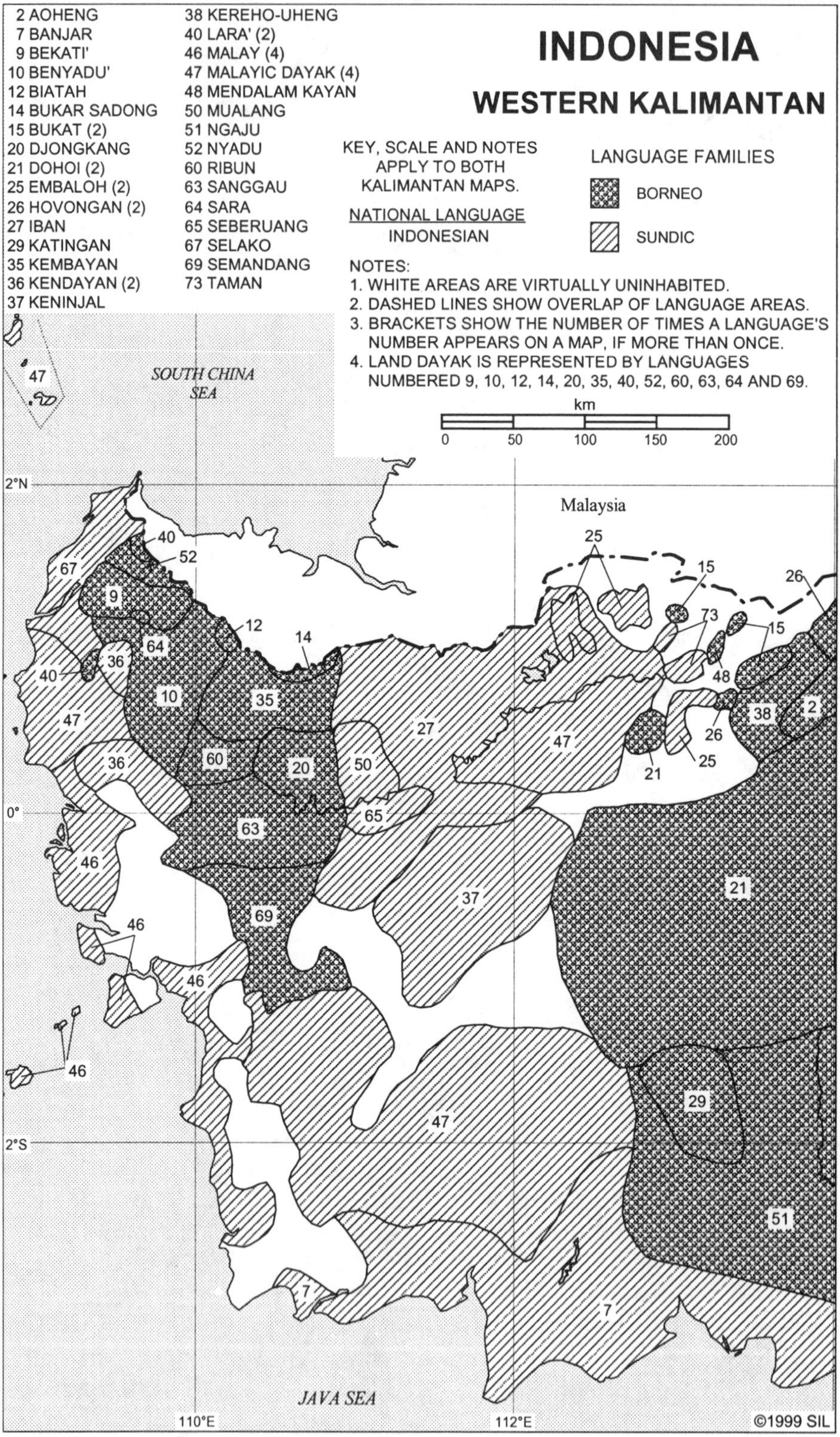

2 AOHENG
7 BANJAR
9 BEKATI'
10 BENYADU'
12 BIATAH
14 BUKAR SADONG
15 BUKAT (2)
20 DJONGKANG
21 DOHOI (2)
25 EMBALOH (2)
26 HOVONGAN (2)
27 IBAN
29 KATINGAN
35 KEMBAYAN
36 KENDAYAN (2)
37 KENINJAL

38 KEREHO-UHENG
40 LARA' (2)
46 MALAY (4)
47 MALAYIC DAYAK (4)
48 MENDALAM KAYAN
50 MUALANG
51 NGAJU
52 NYADU
60 RIBUN
63 SANGGAU
64 SARA
65 SEBERUANG
67 SELAKO
69 SEMANDANG
73 TAMAN

INDONESIA

WESTERN KALIMANTAN

KEY, SCALE AND NOTES
APPLY TO BOTH
KALIMANTAN MAPS.

NATIONAL LANGUAGE
INDONESIAN

LANGUAGE FAMILIES

BORNEO

SUNDIC

NOTES:
1. WHITE AREAS ARE VIRTUALLY UNINHABITED.
2. DASHED LINES SHOW OVERLAP OF LANGUAGE AREAS.
3. BRACKETS SHOW THE NUMBER OF TIMES A LANGUAGE'S
   NUMBER APPEARS ON A MAP, IF MORE THAN ONCE.
4. LAND DAYAK IS REPRESENTED BY LANGUAGES
   NUMBERED 9, 10, 12, 14, 20, 35, 40, 52, 60, 63, 64 AND 69.

km

0   50   100   150   200

SOUTH CHINA
SEA

Malaysia

JAVA SEA

2°N

0°

2°S

110°E   112°E

©1999 SIL

114

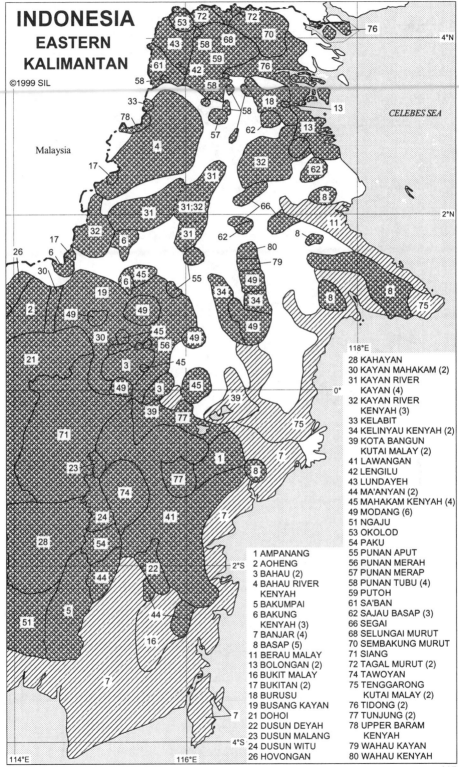

INDONESIA
EASTERN
KALIMANTAN

©1999 SIL

Malaysia

CELEBES SEA

4°N

2°N

0°

2°S

4°S

118°E

28 KAHAYAN
30 KAYAN MAHAKAM (2)
31 KAYAN RIVER
   KAYAN (4)
32 KAYAN RIVER
   KENYAH (3)
33 KELABIT
34 KELINYAU KENYAH (2)
39 KOTA BANGUN
   KUTAI MALAY (2)
41 LAWANGAN
42 LENGILU
43 LUNDAYEH
44 MA'ANYAN (2)
45 MAHAKAM KENYAH (4)
49 MODANG (6)
51 NGAJU
53 OKOLOD
54 PAKU
55 PUNAN APUT
56 PUNAN MERAH
57 PUNAN MERAP
58 PUNAN TUBU (4)
59 PUTOH
61 SA'BAN
62 SAJAU BASAP (3)
66 SEGAI
68 SELUNGAI MURUT
70 SEMBAKUNG MURUT
71 SIANG
72 TAGAL MURUT (2)
74 TAWOYAN
75 TENGGARONG
   KUTAI MALAY (2)
76 TIDONG (2)
77 TUNJUNG (2)
78 UPPER BARAM
   KENYAH
79 WAHAU KAYAN
80 WAHAU KENYAH

1 AMPANANG
2 AOHENG
3 BAHAU (2)
4 BAHAU RIVER
  KENYAH
5 BAKUMPAI
6 BAKUNG
  KENYAH (3)
7 BANJAR (4)
8 BASAP (5)
11 BERAU MALAY
13 BOLONGAN (2)
16 BUKIT MALAY
17 BUKITAN (2)
18 BURUSU
19 BUSANG KAYAN
21 DOHOI
22 DUSUN DEYAH
23 DUSUN MALANG
24 DUSUN WITU
26 HOVONGAN

114°E

116°E

115

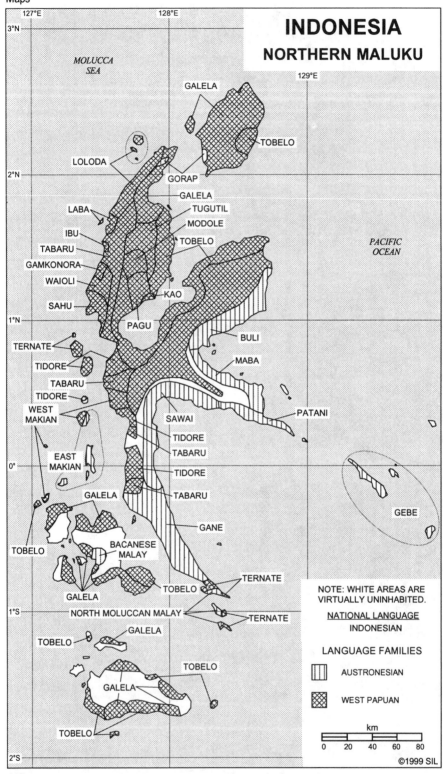

INDONESIA
NORTHERN MALUKU

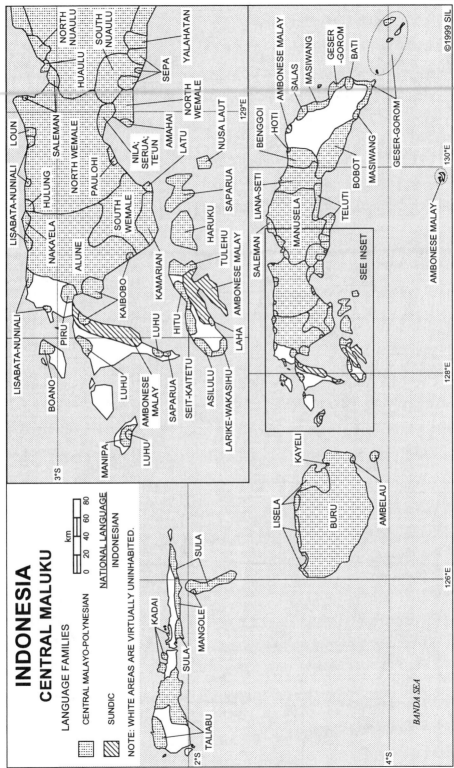

INDONESIA
CENTRAL MALUKU

LANGUAGE FAMILIES

CENTRAL MALAYO-POLYNESIAN

SUNDIC

NOTE: WHITE AREAS ARE VIRTUALLY UNINHABITED.

NATIONAL LANGUAGE
INDONESIAN

km
0   20   40   60   80

©1999 SIL

Maps

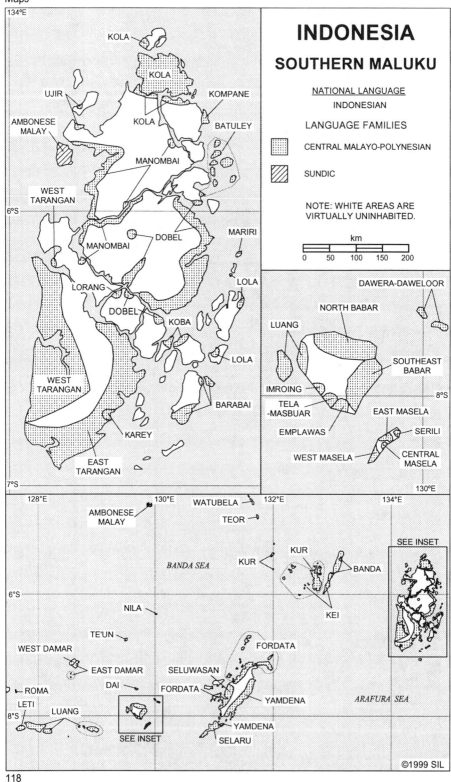

INDONESIA
SOUTHERN MALUKU

NATIONAL LANGUAGE
INDONESIAN

LANGUAGE FAMILIES

CENTRAL MALAYO-POLYNESIAN

SUNDIC

NOTE: WHITE AREAS ARE
VIRTUALLY UNINHABITED.

km
0   50   100   150   200

©1999 SIL

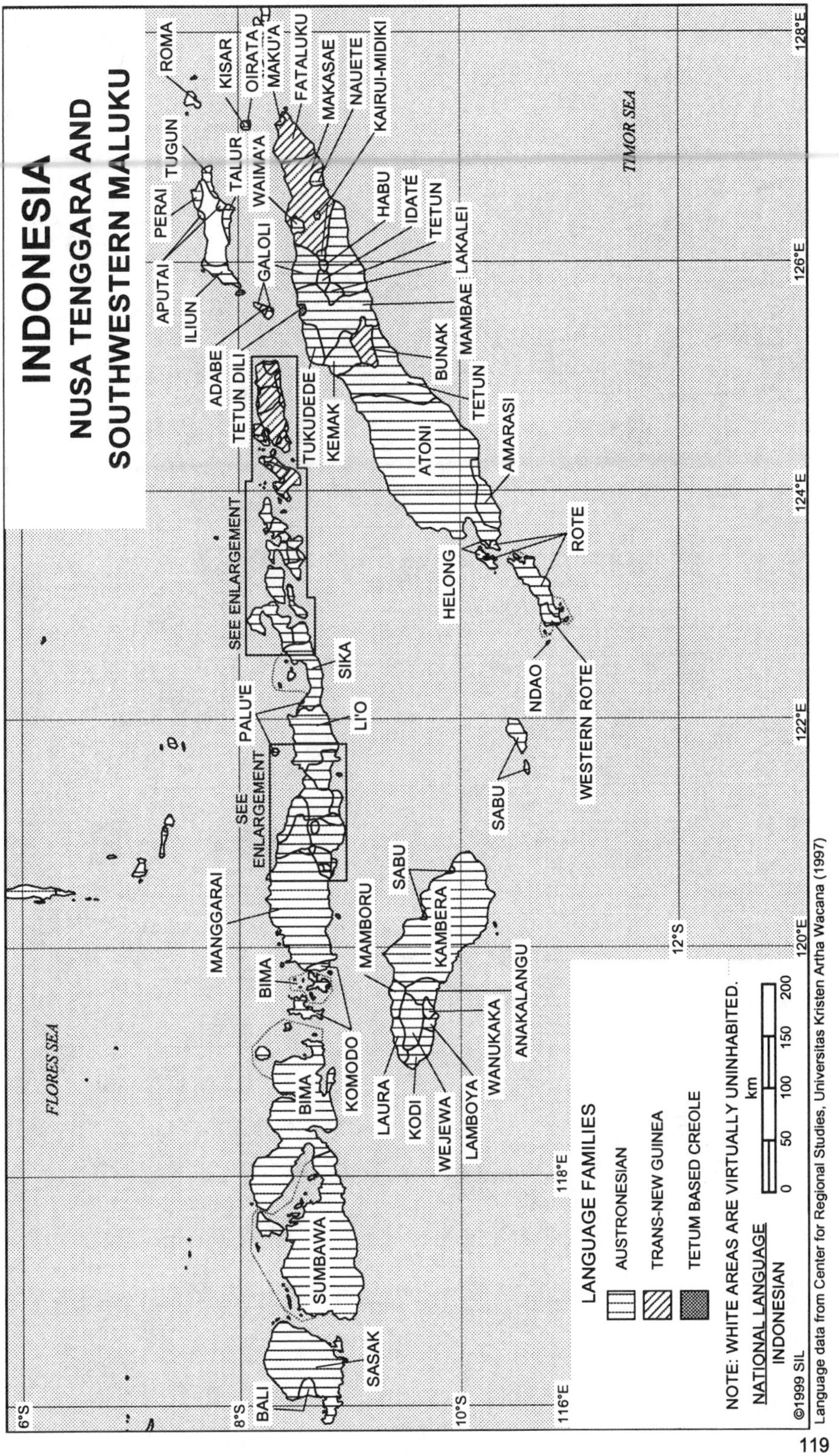

INDONESIA
NUSA TENGGARA AND SOUTHWESTERN MALUKU

Asia

FLORES SEA

TIMOR SEA

LANGUAGE FAMILIES

AUSTRONESIAN

TRANS-NEW GUINEA

TETUM BASED CREOLE

NOTE: WHITE AREAS ARE VIRTUALLY UNINHABITED.

NATIONAL LANGUAGE
INDONESIAN

km
0   50   100   150   200

©1999 SIL

Language data from Center for Regional Studies, Universitas Kristen Artha Wacana (1997)

ROMA
KISAR
OIRATA
MAKU'A
FATALUKU
MAKASAE
NAUETE
KAIRUI-MIDIKI
TUGUN
PERAI
TUGUN
TALUR
WAIMA'A
HABU
IDATÉ
TETUN
APUTAI
ILIUN
GALOLI
MAMBAE
LAKALEI
ADABE
TETUN DILI
TUKUDEDE
KEMAK
BUNAK
ATONI
TETUN
AMARASI
SEE ENLARGEMENT
HELONG
ROTE
WESTERN ROTE
NDAO
SABU
SIKA
LI'O
PALU'E
SEE ENLARGEMENT
MANGGARAI
BIMA
KOMODO
BIMA
SASAK
SUMBAWA
BALI
MAMBORU
SABU
KAMBERA
LAURA
KODI
WEJEWA
LAMBOYA
WANUKAKA
ANAKALANGU

116°E   118°E   120°E   122°E   124°E   126°E   128°E

6°S
8°S
10°S
12°S

119

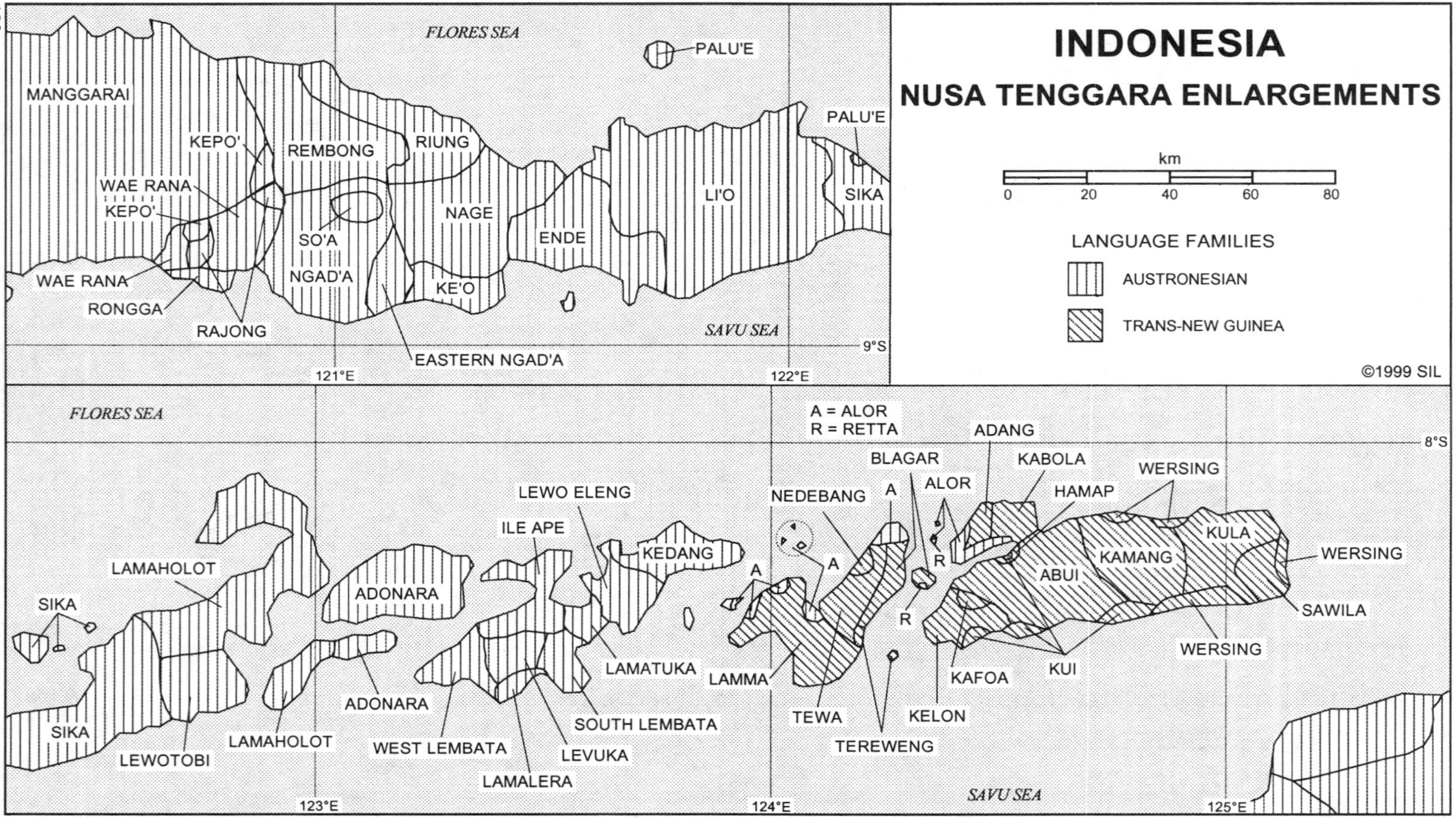

Maps

INDONESIA
NUSA TENGGARA ENLARGEMENTS

©1999 SIL

LANGUAGE FAMILIES

AUSTRONESIAN

TRANS-NEW GUINEA

Language data from Center for Regional Studies, Universitas Kristen Artha Wacana (1997)

120

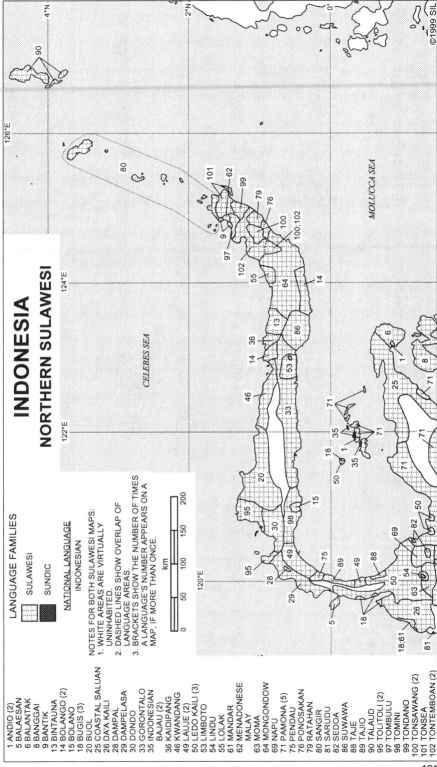

INDONESIA
NORTHERN SULAWESI

LANGUAGE FAMILIES

SULAWESI

SUNDIC

NATIONAL LANGUAGE

INDONESIAN

NOTES FOR BOTH SULAWESI MAPS:
1. WHITE AREAS ARE VIRTUALLY UNINHABITED.
2. DASHED LINES SHOW OVERLAP OF LANGUAGE AREAS.
3. BRACKETS SHOW THE NUMBER OF TIMES A LANGUAGE'S NUMBER APPEARS ON A MAP, IF MORE THAN ONCE.

km

0   50   100   150   200

1 ANDIO (2)
5 BALAESAN
6 BALANTAK
8 BANGGAI
9 BANTIK
13 BINTAUNA
14 BOLANGO (2)
15 BOLANO
18 BUGIS (3)
20 BUOL
25 COASTAL SALUAN
26 DA'A KAILI
28 DAMPAL
29 DAMPELASA
30 DONDO
33 GORONTALO
35 INDONESIAN
   BAJAU (2)
36 KAIDIPANG
46 KWANDANG
49 LAUJE (2)
50 LEDO KAILI (3)
53 LIMBOTO
54 LINDU
55 LOLAK
61 MANDAR
62 MENADONESE
   MALAY
63 MOMA
64 MONGONDOW
69 NAPU
71 PAMONA (5)
75 PENDAU
76 PONOSAKAN
79 RATAHAN
80 SANGIR
81 SARUDU
82 SEDOA
86 SUWAWA
88 TAJE
89 TAJIO
90 TALAUD
95 TOLITOLI (2)
97 TOMBULU
98 TOMINI
99 TONDANO
100 TONSAWANG (2)
101 TONSEA
102 TONTEMBOAN (2)

CELEBES SEA

MOLUCCA SEA

©1999 SIL

121

Maps

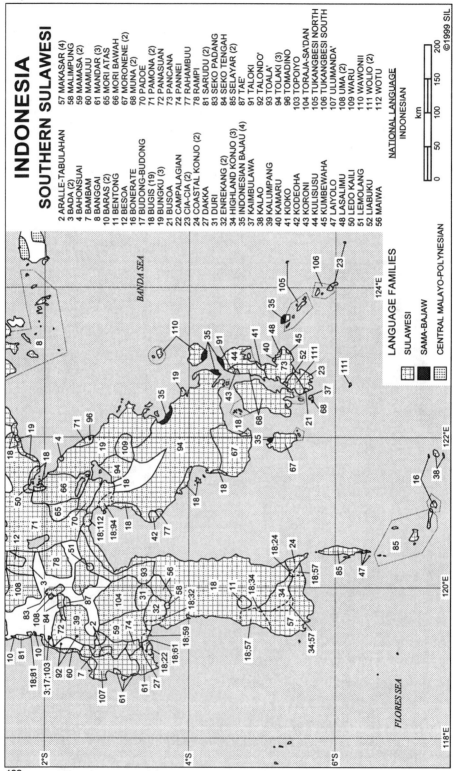

122

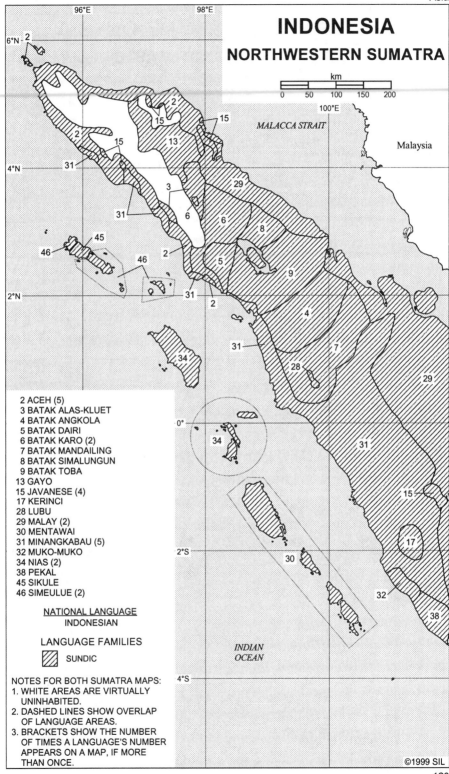

INDONESIA
NORTHWESTERN SUMATRA

km
0   50   100 150 200

MALACCA STRAIT

Malaysia

2 ACEH (5)
3 BATAK ALAS-KLUET
4 BATAK ANGKOLA
5 BATAK DAIRI
6 BATAK KARO (2)
7 BATAK MANDAILING
8 BATAK SIMALUNGUN
9 BATAK TOBA
13 GAYO
15 JAVANESE (4)
17 KERINCI
28 LUBU
29 MALAY (2)
30 MENTAWAI
31 MINANGKABAU (5)
32 MUKO-MUKO
34 NIAS (2)
38 PEKAL
45 SIKULE
46 SIMEULUE (2)

NATIONAL LANGUAGE
INDONESIAN

LANGUAGE FAMILIES

SUNDIC

NOTES FOR BOTH SUMATRA MAPS:
1. WHITE AREAS ARE VIRTUALLY
   UNINHABITED.
2. DASHED LINES SHOW OVERLAP
   OF LANGUAGE AREAS.
3. BRACKETS SHOW THE NUMBER
   OF TIMES A LANGUAGE'S NUMBER
   APPEARS ON A MAP, IF MORE
   THAN ONCE.

*INDIAN
OCEAN*

©1999 SIL

Maps

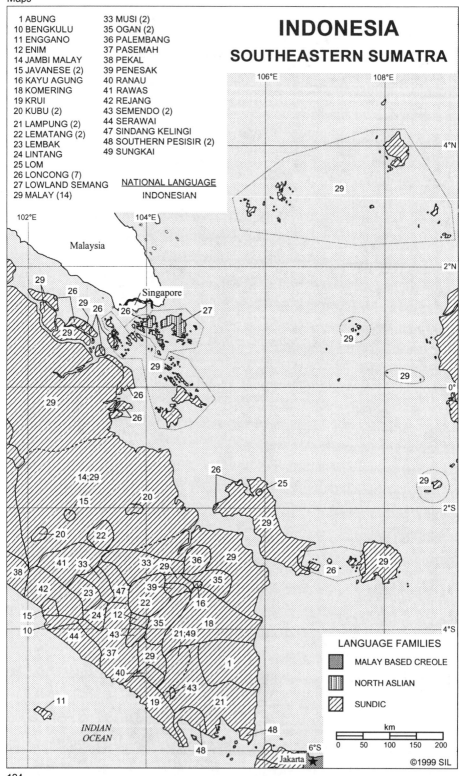

1 ABUNG
10 BENGKULU
11 ENGGANO
12 ENIM
14 JAMBI MALAY
15 JAVANESE (2)
16 KAYU AGUNG
18 KOMERING
19 KRUI
20 KUBU (2)

21 LAMPUNG (2)
22 LEMATANG (2)
23 LEMBAK
24 LINTANG
25 LOM
26 LONCONG (7)
27 LOWLAND SEMANG
29 MALAY (14)

33 MUSI (2)
35 OGAN (2)
36 PALEMBANG
37 PASEMAH
38 PEKAL
39 PENESAK
40 RANAU
41 RAWAS
42 REJANG
43 SEMENDO (2)
44 SERAWAI
47 SINDANG KELINGI
48 SOUTHERN PESISIR (2)
49 SUNGKAI

NATIONAL LANGUAGE
INDONESIAN

INDONESIA
SOUTHEASTERN SUMATRA

LANGUAGE FAMILIES

▓ MALAY BASED CREOLE

▥ NORTH ASLIAN

▨ SUNDIC

km

0   50   100   150   200

©1999 SIL

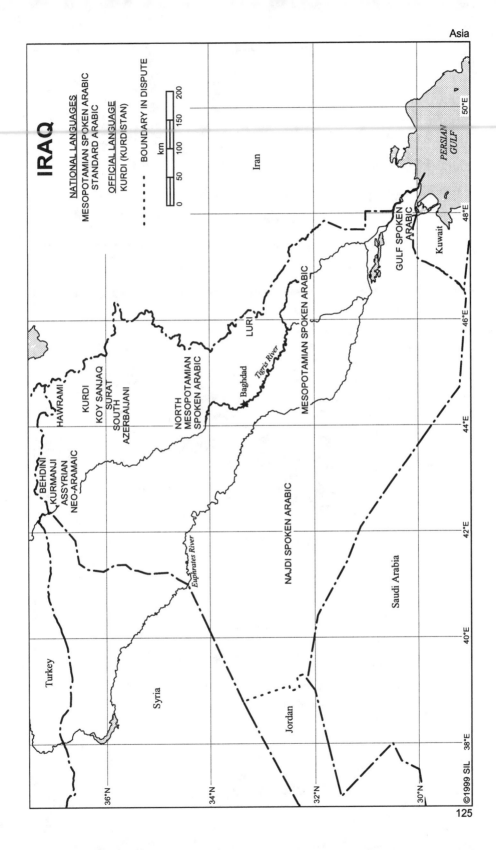

IRAQ

NATIONAL LANGUAGES
MESOPOTAMIAN SPOKEN ARABIC
STANDARD ARABIC

OFFICIAL LANGUAGE
KURDI (KURDISTAN)

· · · · · · · BOUNDARY IN DISPUTE

km
0   50   100   150   200

©1999 SIL

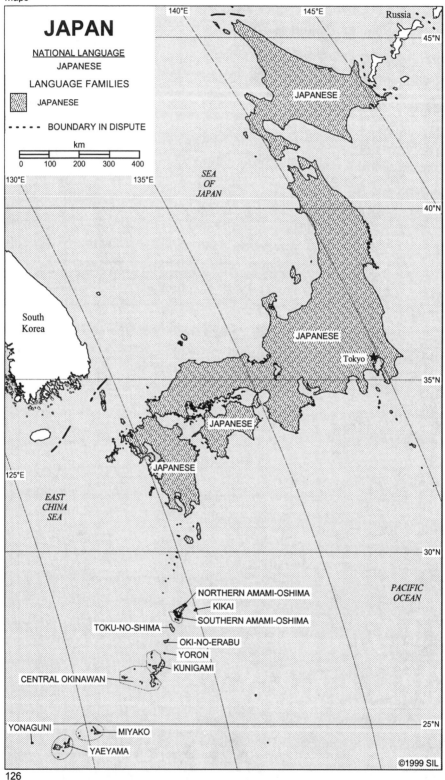

JAPAN

<u>NATIONAL LANGUAGE</u>
JAPANESE

LANGUAGE FAMILIES

JAPANESE

- - - - BOUNDARY IN DISPUTE

km

0   100   200   300   400

140°E

145°E

Russia

45°N

JAPANESE

SEA
OF
JAPAN

130°E

135°E

40°N

South
Korea

JAPANESE

JAPANESE

Tokyo

35°N

JAPANESE

125°E

JAPANESE

EAST
CHINA
SEA

30°N

PACIFIC
OCEAN

NORTHERN AMAMI-OSHIMA

KIKAI

TOKU-NO-SHIMA

SOUTHERN AMAMI-OSHIMA

OKI-NO-ERABU

YORON

KUNIGAMI

CENTRAL OKINAWAN

25°N

YONAGUNI

MIYAKO

YAEYAMA

©1999 SIL

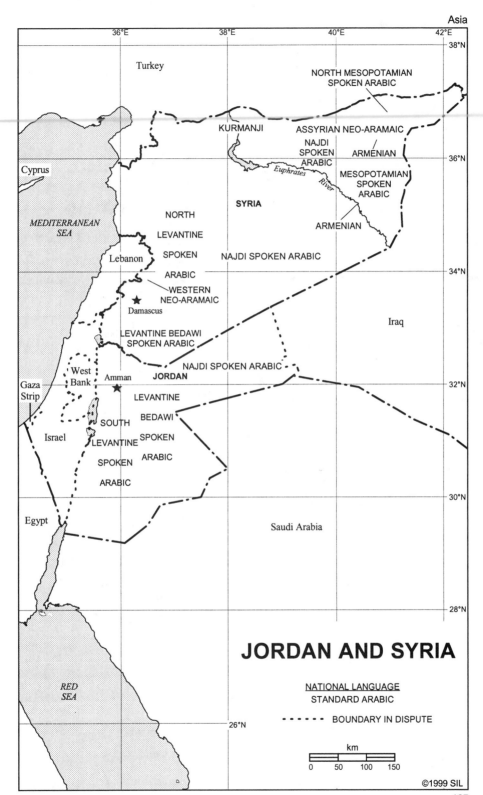

JORDAN AND SYRIA

<u>NATIONAL LANGUAGE</u>
STANDARD ARABIC

• • • • • BOUNDARY IN DISPUTE

km

0   50   100   150

©1999 SIL

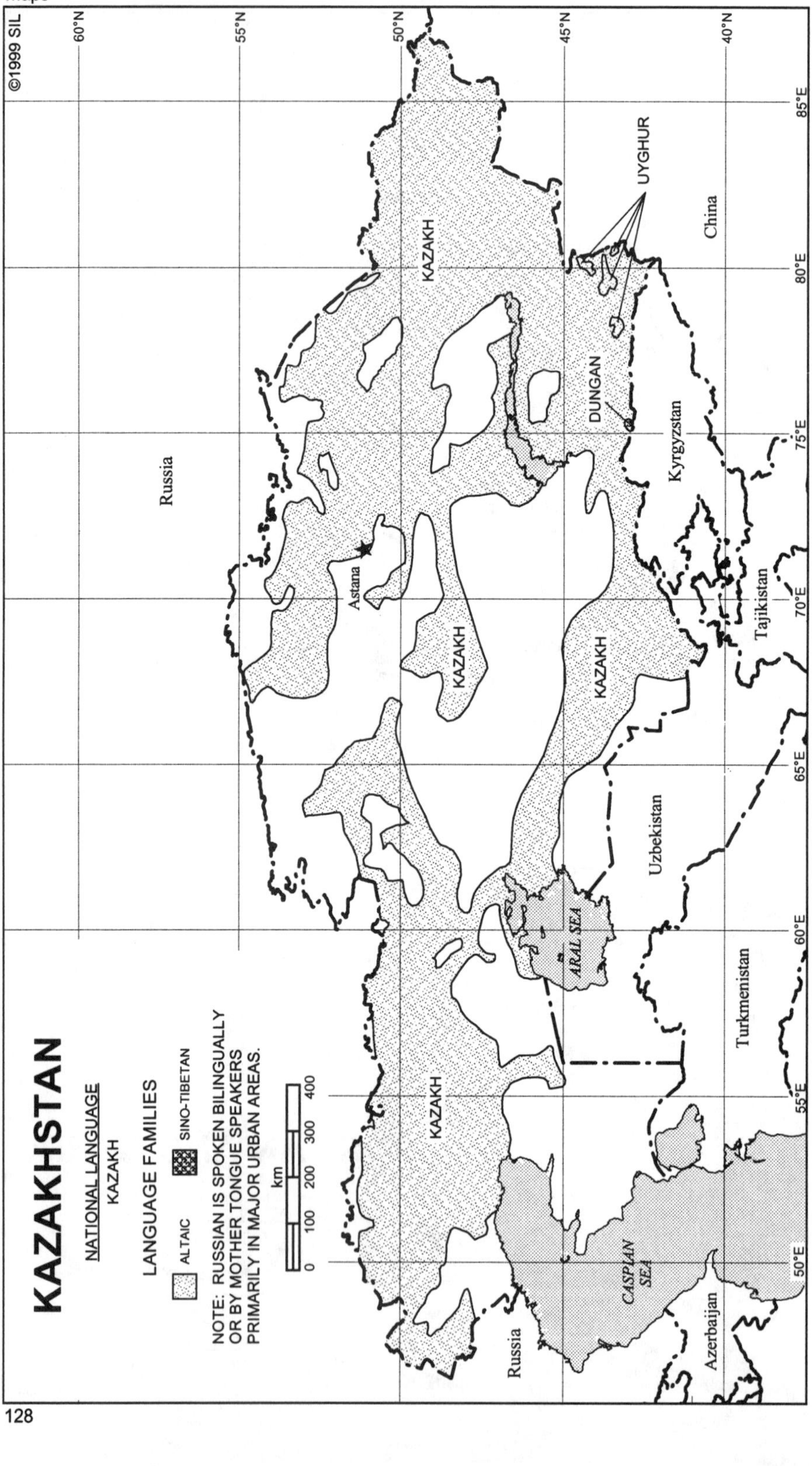

KAZAKHSTAN
NATIONAL LANGUAGE
KAZAKH
LANGUAGE FAMILIES
ALTAIC
SINO-TIBETAN
NOTE: RUSSIAN IS SPOKEN BILINGUALLY OR BY MOTHER TONGUE SPEAKERS PRIMARILY IN MAJOR URBAN AREAS.
km
0 100 200 300 400
©1999 SIL
60°N
55°N
50°N
45°N
40°N
50°E
55°E
60°E
65°E
70°E
75°E
80°E
85°E
Russia
Russia
KAZAKH
KAZAKH
KAZAKH
KAZAKH
Astana
UYGHUR
DUNGAN
China
Kyrgyzstan
Tajikistan
Uzbekistan
Turkmenistan
Azerbaijan
ARAL SEA
CASPIAN SEA

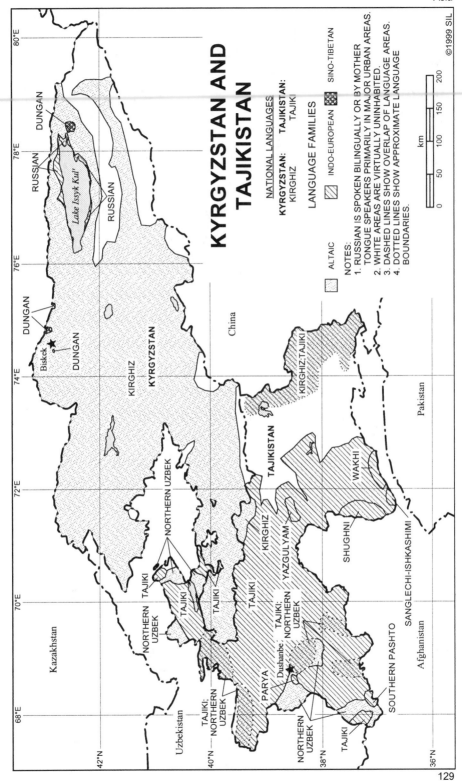

KYRGYZSTAN AND TAJIKISTAN

NATIONAL LANGUAGES

KYRGYZSTAN: **TAJIKISTAN:**
KIRGHIZ TAJIKI

LANGUAGE FAMILIES

INDO-EUROPEAN   SINO-TIBETAN

ALTAIC

NOTES:
1. RUSSIAN IS SPOKEN BILINGUALLY OR BY MOTHER
   TONGUE SPEAKERS PRIMARILY IN MAJOR URBAN AREAS.
2. WHITE AREAS ARE VIRTUALLY UNINHABITED.
3. DASHED LINES SHOW OVERLAP OF LANGUAGE AREAS.
4. DOTTED LINES SHOW APPROXIMATE LANGUAGE
   BOUNDARIES.

km

0   50   100   150   200

Kazakhstan

Uzbekistan

DUNGAN

RUSSIAN

RUSSIAN

DUNGAN

Lake Issyk Kul'

DUNGAN

DUNGAN

Biskek

DUNGAN

KIRGHIZ

KYRGYZSTAN

China

NORTHERN UZBEK

NORTHERN
TAJIKI

TAJIKI

NORTHERN
UZBEK

TAJIKI

TAJIKI

TAJIKI

KIRGHIZ

NORTHERN
YAZGULYAM

TAJIKI;
NORTHERN
UZBEK

KIRGHIZ;TAJIKI

TAJIKISTAN

WAKHI

SHUGHNI

SANGLECHI-ISHKASHIMI

TAJIKI;
NORTHERN
UZBEK

PARYA   Dushanbe

NORTHERN
UZBEK

TAJIKI

SOUTHERN PASHTO

Afghanistan

Pakistan

129

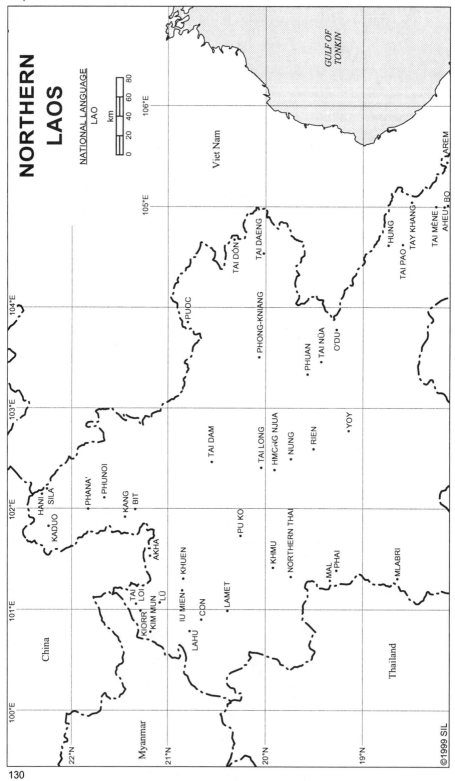

NORTHERN
LAOS

NATIONAL LANGUAGE
LAO

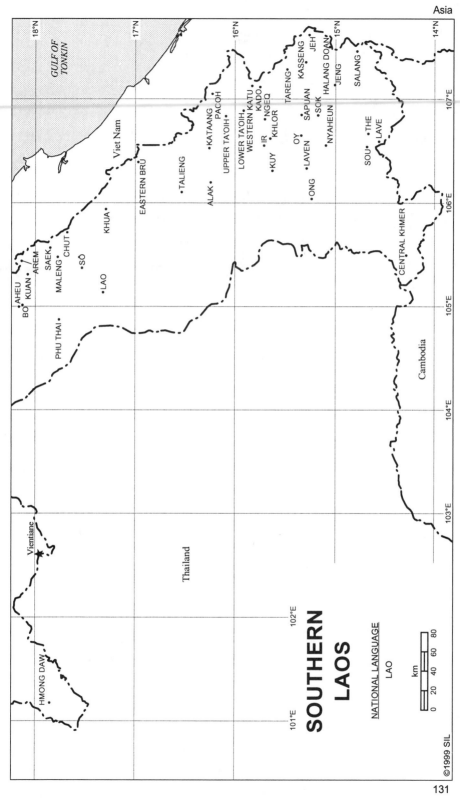

Asia

GULF OF
TONKIN

Viet Nam

EASTERN BRŪ

•TALIENG

ALAK•

•KATAANG

UPPER TA'OIH•

LOWER TA'OIH•
WESTERN KATU•
•IR   •KADO
•KUY •NGEQ
      •KHLOR

PACOH

TARENG•

KASSENG

•OY
•LAVEN

•ONG

SAPUAN•
        •SOK
•NYAHEUN

JEH•

HALANG DOAN•

JENG•

SALANG•

SOU• •THE
      •LAVE

CENTRAL KHMER

Cambodia

KHUA•

•LAO

•SŌ

CHUT•

MALENG•
SAEK•

AREM•
KUAN•
BO•
AHEU•

PHU THAI•

Vientiane
★

Thailand

HMONG DAW•

SOUTHERN
LAOS

NATIONAL LANGUAGE
LAO

km

0 20 40 60 80

©1999 SIL

131

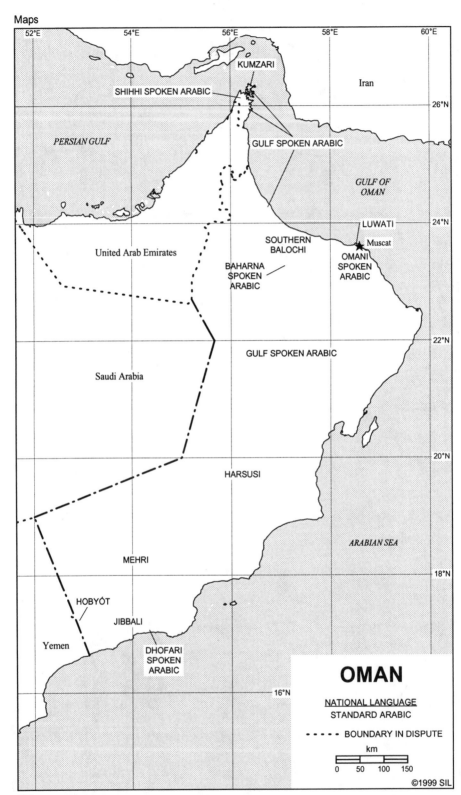

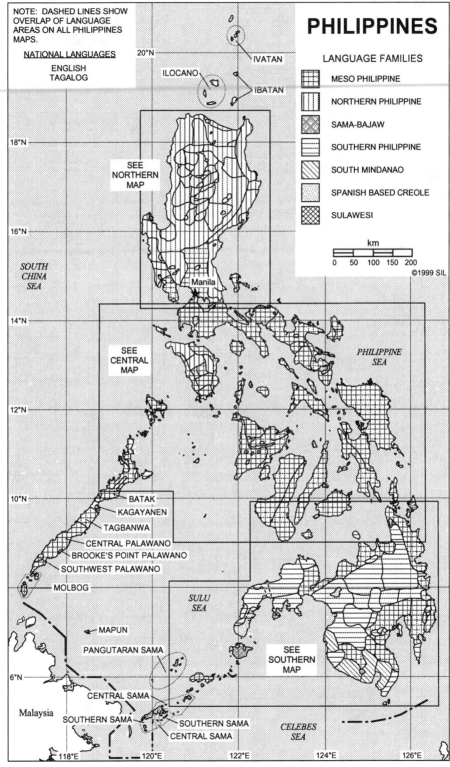

PHILIPPINES

NOTE: DASHED LINES SHOW OVERLAP OF LANGUAGE AREAS ON ALL PHILIPPINES MAPS.

NATIONAL LANGUAGES
ENGLISH
TAGALOG

LANGUAGE FAMILIES

MESO PHILIPPINE

NORTHERN PHILIPPINE

SAMA-BAJAW

SOUTHERN PHILIPPINE

SOUTH MINDANAO

SPANISH BASED CREOLE

SULAWESI

km
0 50 100 150 200

©1999 SIL

IVATAN

ILOCANO

IBATAN

SEE NORTHERN MAP

SOUTH CHINA SEA

Manila

PHILIPPINE SEA

SEE CENTRAL MAP

BATAK
KAGAYANEN
TAGBANWA
CENTRAL PALAWANO
BROOKE'S POINT PALAWANO
SOUTHWEST PALAWANO
MOLBOG

SULU SEA

MAPUN

PANGUTARAN SAMA

SEE SOUTHERN MAP

CENTRAL SAMA

SOUTHERN SAMA

SOUTHERN SAMA

CENTRAL SAMA

Malaysia

CELEBES SEA

133

Maps

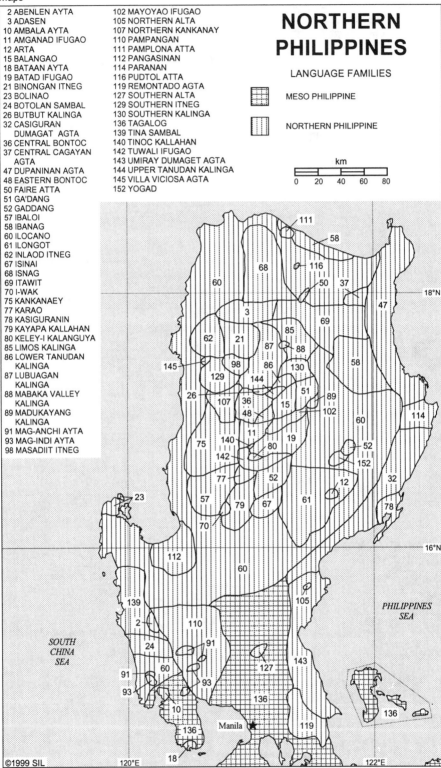

2 ABENLEN AYTA
3 ADASEN
10 AMBALA AYTA
11 AMGANAD IFUGAO
12 ARTA
15 BALANGAO
18 BATAAN AYTA
19 BATAD IFUGAO
21 BINONGAN ITNEG
23 BOLINAO
24 BOTOLAN SAMBAL
26 BUTBUT KALINGA
32 CASIGURAN
   DUMAGAT AGTA
36 CENTRAL BONTOC
37 CENTRAL CAGAYAN
   AGTA
47 DUPANINAN AGTA
48 EASTERN BONTOC
50 FAIRE ATTA
51 GA'DANG
52 GADDANG
57 IBALOI
58 IBANAG
60 ILOCANO
61 ILONGOT
62 INLAOD ITNEG
67 ISINAI
68 ISNAG
69 ITAWIT
70 I-WAK
75 KANKANAEY
77 KARAO
78 KASIGURANIN
79 KAYAPA KALLAHAN
80 KELEY-I KALANGUYA
85 LIMOS KALINGA
86 LOWER TANUDAN
   KALINGA
87 LUBUAGAN
   KALINGA
88 MABAKA VALLEY
   KALINGA
89 MADUKAYANG
   KALINGA
91 MAG-ANCHI AYTA
93 MAG-INDI AYTA
98 MASADIIT ITNEG

102 MAYOYAO IFUGAO
105 NORTHERN ALTA
107 NORTHERN KANKANAY
110 PAMPANGAN
111 PAMPLONA ATTA
112 PANGASINAN
114 PARANAN
116 PUDTOL ATTA
119 REMONTADO AGTA
127 SOUTHERN ALTA
129 SOUTHERN ITNEG
130 SOUTHERN KALINGA
136 TAGALOG
139 TINA SAMBAL
140 TINOC KALLAHAN
142 TUWALI IFUGAO
143 UMIRAY DUMAGET AGTA
144 UPPER TANUDAN KALINGA
145 VILLA VICIOSA AGTA
152 YOGAD

NORTHERN PHILIPPINES

LANGUAGE FAMILIES

MESO PHILIPPINE

NORTHERN PHILIPPINE

km

0   20   40   60   80

18°N

16°N

PHILIPPINES
SEA

SOUTH
CHINA
SEA

Manila

©1999 SIL

120°E

122°E

134

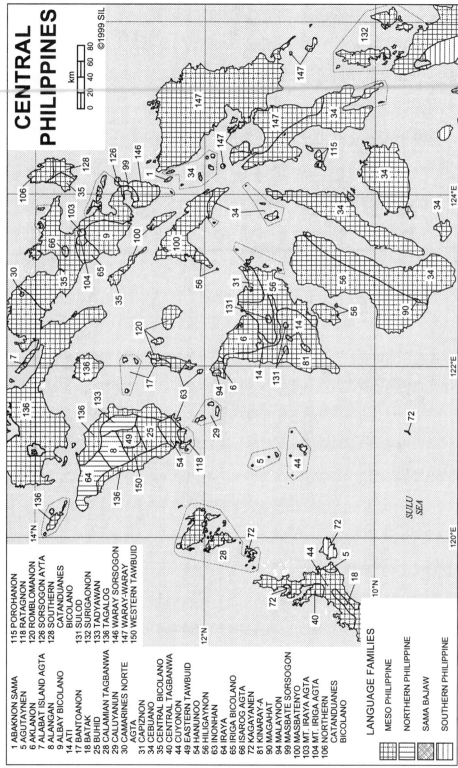

CENTRAL
PHILIPPINES

km

0 20 40 60 80

©1999 SIL

1 ABAKNON SAMA
5 AGUTAYNEN
6 AKLANON
7 ALABAT ISLAND AGTA
8 ALANGAN
9 ALBAY BICOLANO
14 ATI
17 BANTOANON
18 BATAK
25 BUHID
28 CALAMIAN TAGBANWA
29 CALUYANUN
30 CAMARINES NORTE
   AGTA
31 CAPIZNON
34 CEBUANO
35 CENTRAL BICOLANO
40 CENTRAL TAGBANWA
44 CUYONON
49 EASTERN TAWBUID
54 HANUNOO
56 HILIGAYNON
63 INONHAN
64 IRAYA
65 IRIGA BICOLANO
66 ISAROG AGTA
72 KAGAYANEN
81 KINARAY-A
90 MAGAHAT
94 MALAYNON
99 MASBATE SORSOGON
100 MASBATENYO
103 MT. IRAYA AGTA
104 MT. IRIGA AGTA
106 NORTHERN
    CATANDUANES
    BICOLANO

115 POROHANON
118 RATAGNON
120 ROMBLOMANON
126 SORSOGON AYTA
128 SOUTHERN
    CATANDUANES
    BICOLANO
131 SULOD
132 SURIGAONON
133 TADYAWAN
136 TAGALOG
146 WARAY SORSOGON
147 WARAY-WARAY
150 WESTERN TAWBUID

LANGUAGE FAMILIES

MESO PHILIPPINE

NORTHERN PHILIPPINE

SAMA BAJAW

SOUTHERN PHILIPPINE

SULU
SEA

135

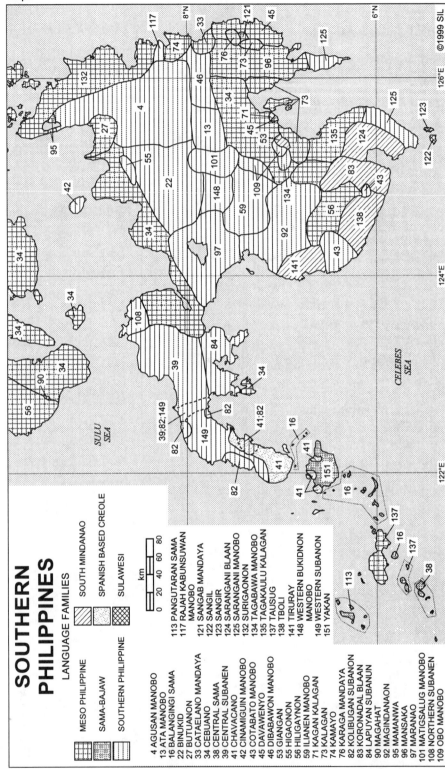

SOUTHERN PHILIPPINES

LANGUAGE FAMILIES

▨	MESO PHILIPPINE
▨	SAMA-BAJAW
▥	SOUTHERN PHILIPPINE
▨	SOUTH MINDANAO
▨	SPANISH BASED CREOLE
▨	SULAWESI

km

0 20 40 60 80

4 AGUSAN MANOBO
13 ATA MANOBO
16 BALANGINGI SAMA
22 BINUKID
27 BUTUANON
33 CATAELANO MANDAYA
34 CEBUANO
38 CENTRAL SAMA
39 CENTRAL SUBANEN
41 CHAVACANO
42 CINAMIGUIN MANOBO
43 COTABATO MANOBO
45 DAVAWENYO
46 DIBABAWON MANOBO
53 GIANGAN
55 HIGAONON
56 HILIGAYNON
59 ILIANEN MANOBO
71 KAGAN KALAGAN
73 KALAGAN
74 KAMAYO
76 KARAGA MANDAYA
82 KOLIBUGAN SUBANON
83 KORONADAL BLAAN
84 LAPUYAN SUBANUN
90 MAGAHAT
92 MAGINDANAON
95 MAMANWA
96 MANSAKA
97 MARANAO
101 MATIGSALUG MANOBO
108 NORTHERN SUBANEN
109 OBO MANOBO

113 PANGUTARAN SAMA
117 RAJAH KABUNSUWAN MANOBO
121 SANGAB MANDAYA
122 SANGIL
123 SANGIR
124 SARANGANI BLAAN
125 SARANGANI MANOBO
132 SURIGAONON
134 TAGABAWA MANOBO
135 TAGAKAULU KALAGAN
137 TAUSUG
138 TBOLI
141 TIRURAY
148 WESTERN BUKIDNON MANOBO
149 WESTERN SUBANON
151 YAKAN

SULU SEA

CELEBES SEA

©1999 SIL

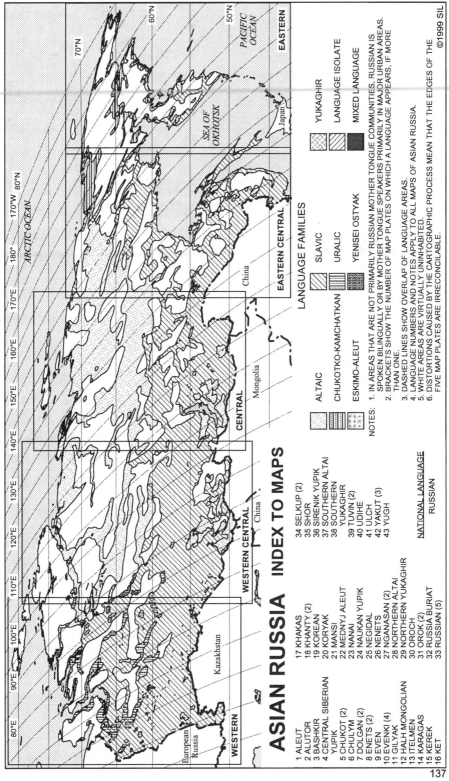

ASIAN RUSSIA   INDEX TO MAPS

1 ALEUT
2 ALUTOR
3 BASHKIR
4 CENTRAL SIBERIAN YUPIK
5 CHUKOT (2)
6 CHULYM
7 DOLGAN (2)
8 ENETS (2)
9 EVEN
10 EVENKI (4)
11 GILYAK
12 HALH MONGOLIAN
13 ITELMEN
14 KARAGAS
15 KEREK
16 KET

17 KHAKAS
18 KHANTY (2)
19 KOREAN
20 KORYAK
21 MANSI
22 MEDNYJ ALEUT
23 NANAI
24 NAUKAN YUPIK
25 NEGIDAL
26 NENETS
27 NGANASAN (2)
28 NORTHERN ALTAI
29 NORTHERN YUKAGHIR
30 OROCH
31 OROK (2)
32 RUSSIA BURIAT
33 RUSSIAN (5)

34 SELKUP (2)
35 SHOR
36 SIRENIK YUPIK
37 SOUTHERN ALTAI
38 SOUTHERN YUKAGHIR
39 TUVIN (2)
40 UDIHE
41 ULCH
42 YAKUT (3)
43 YUGH

NATIONAL LANGUAGE
RUSSIAN

LANGUAGE FAMILIES

ALTAIC

CHUKOTKO-KAMCHATKAN

ESKIMO-ALEUT

SLAVIC

URALIC

YENISEI OSTYAK

YUKAGHIR

LANGUAGE ISOLATE

MIXED LANGUAGE

NOTES:

1. IN AREAS THAT ARE NOT PRIMARILY RUSSIAN MOTHER TONGUE COMMUNITIES, RUSSIAN IS SPOKEN BILINGUALLY OR BY MOTHER TONGUE SPEAKERS PRIMARILY IN MAJOR URBAN AREAS.

2. BRACKETS SHOW THE NUMBER OF MAP PLATES ON WHICH A LANGUAGE APPEARS, IF MORE THAN ONE.

3. DASHED LINES SHOW OVERLAP OF LANGUAGE AREAS.

4. LANGUAGE NUMBERS AND NOTES APPLY TO ALL MAPS OF ASIAN RUSSIA.

5. WHITE AREAS ARE VIRTUALLY UNINHABITED.

6. DISTORTIONS CAUSED BY THE CARTOGRAPHIC PROCESS MEAN THAT THE EDGES OF THE FIVE MAP PLATES ARE IRRECONCILABLE.

©1999 SIL

Maps

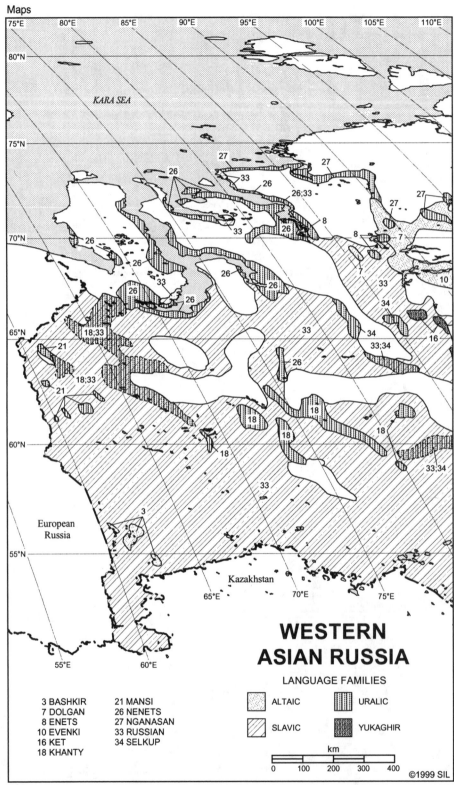

KARA SEA

European
Russia

Kazakhstan

WESTERN
ASIAN RUSSIA

LANGUAGE FAMILIES

3 BASHKIR
7 DOLGAN
8 ENETS
10 EVENKI
16 KET
18 KHANTY

21 MANSI
26 NENETS
27 NGANASAN
33 RUSSIAN
34 SELKUP

ALTAIC

SLAVIC

URALIC

YUKAGHIR

km

0   100   200   300   400

©1999 SIL

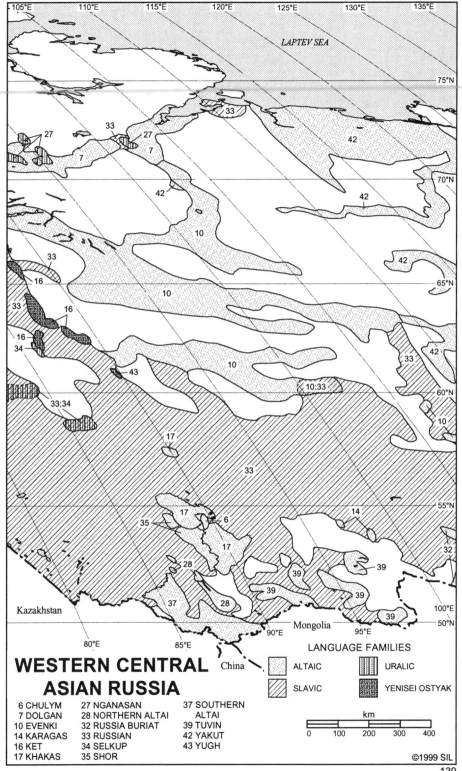

LAPTEV SEA

Kazakhstan

Mongolia

China

WESTERN CENTRAL
ASIAN RUSSIA

LANGUAGE FAMILIES

ALTAIC		URALIC	
SLAVIC		YENISEI OSTYAK	

km

| 0 | 100 | 200 | 300 | 400 |

6 CHULYM	27 NGANASAN	37 SOUTHERN
7 DOLGAN	28 NORTHERN ALTAI	ALTAI
10 EVENKI	32 RUSSIA BURIAT	39 TUVIN
14 KARAGAS	33 RUSSIAN	42 YAKUT
16 KET	34 SELKUP	43 YUGH
17 KHAKAS	35 SHOR	

©1999 SIL

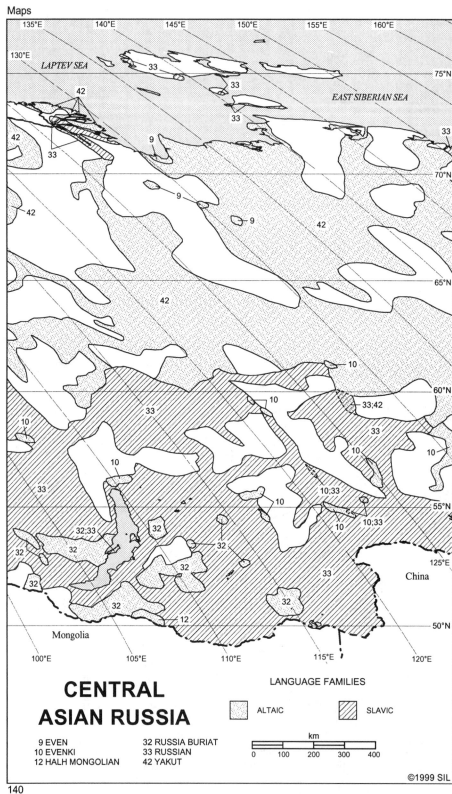

CENTRAL
ASIAN RUSSIA

LANGUAGE FAMILIES

9 EVEN
10 EVENKI
12 HALH MONGOLIAN

32 RUSSIA BURIAT
33 RUSSIAN
42 YAKUT

ALTAIC

SLAVIC

km

0   100   200   300   400

©1999 SIL

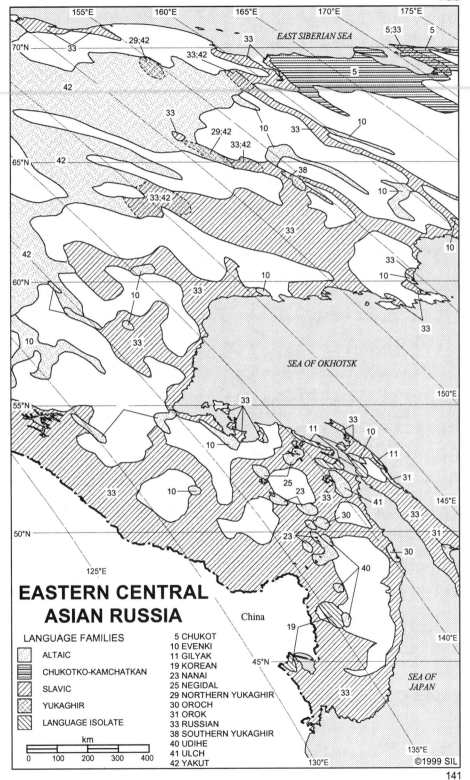

EASTERN CENTRAL ASIAN RUSSIA

China

SEA OF JAPAN

SEA OF OKHOTSK

EAST SIBERIAN SEA

LANGUAGE FAMILIES

ALTAIC

CHUKOTKO-KAMCHATKAN

SLAVIC

YUKAGHIR

LANGUAGE ISOLATE

km

| 0 | 100 | 200 | 300 | 400 |

5 CHUKOT
10 EVENKI
11 GILYAK
19 KOREAN
23 NANAI
25 NEGIDAL
29 NORTHERN YUKAGHIR
30 OROCH
31 OROK
33 RUSSIAN
38 SOUTHERN YUKAGHIR
40 UDIHE
41 ULCH
42 YAKUT

©1999 SIL

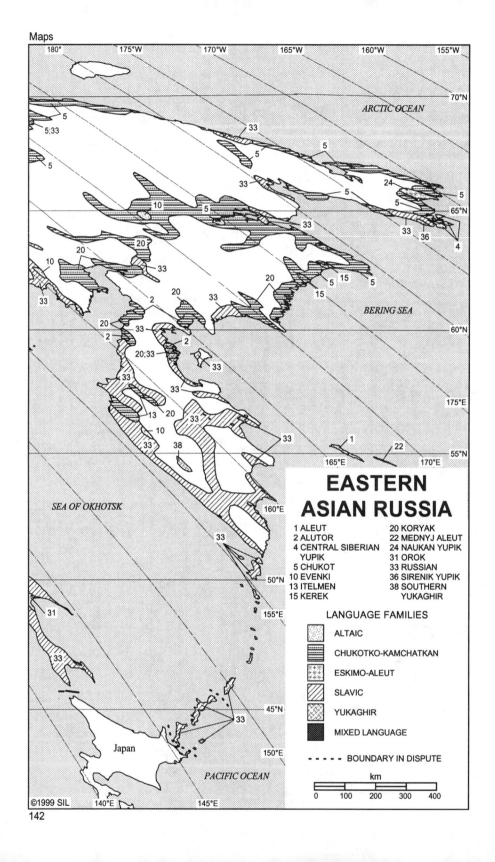

EASTERN
ASIAN RUSSIA

1 ALEUT
2 ALUTOR
4 CENTRAL SIBERIAN
YUPIK
5 CHUKOT
10 EVENKI
13 ITELMEN
15 KEREK

20 KORYAK
22 MEDNYJ ALEUT
24 NAUKAN YUPIK
31 OROK
33 RUSSIAN
36 SIRENIK YUPIK
38 SOUTHERN
YUKAGHIR

LANGUAGE FAMILIES

ALTAIC

CHUKOTKO-KAMCHATKAN

ESKIMO-ALEUT

SLAVIC

YUKAGHIR

MIXED LANGUAGE

- - - - BOUNDARY IN DISPUTE

km
0   100   200   300   400

©1999 SIL

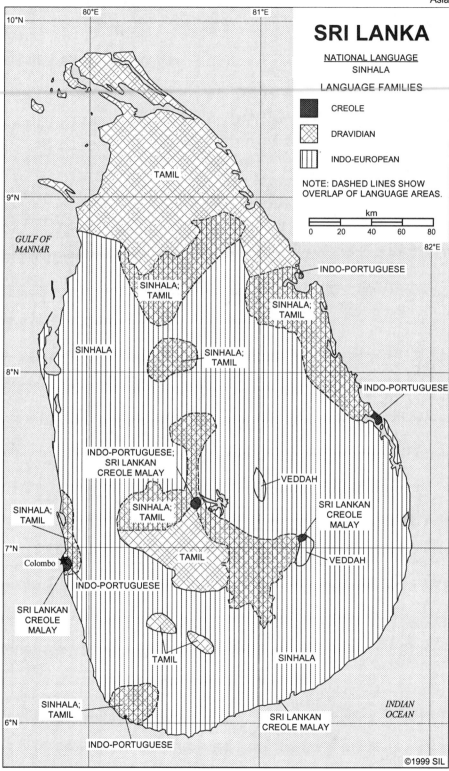

SRI LANKA

NATIONAL LANGUAGE
SINHALA

LANGUAGE FAMILIES

- CREOLE
- DRAVIDIAN
- INDO-EUROPEAN

NOTE: DASHED LINES SHOW
OVERLAP OF LANGUAGE AREAS.

km
0   20   40   60   80

GULF OF
MANNAR

TAMIL

INDO-PORTUGUESE

SINHALA;
TAMIL

SINHALA;
TAMIL

SINHALA

SINHALA;
TAMIL

INDO-PORTUGUESE

INDO-PORTUGUESE;
SRI LANKAN
CREOLE MALAY

VEDDAH

SINHALA;
TAMIL

SINHALA;
TAMIL

SRI LANKAN
CREOLE
MALAY

SINHALA;
TAMIL

TAMIL

Colombo

VEDDAH

INDO-PORTUGUESE

SRI LANKAN
CREOLE
MALAY

TAMIL

SINHALA

SINHALA;
TAMIL

INDIAN
OCEAN

SRI LANKAN
CREOLE MALAY

INDO-PORTUGUESE

©1999 SIL

143

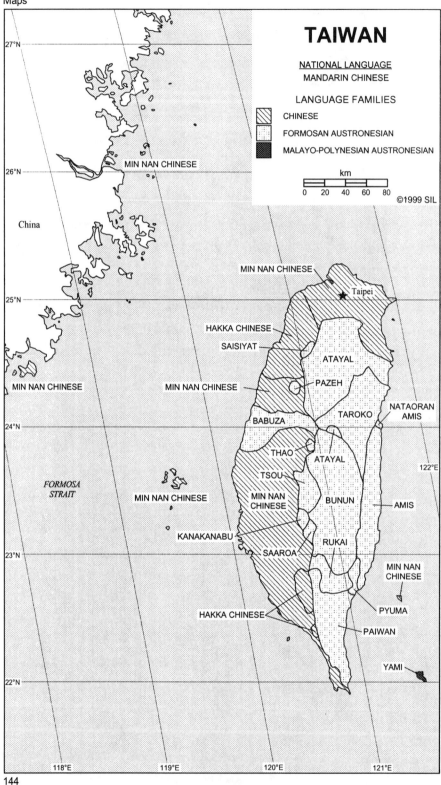

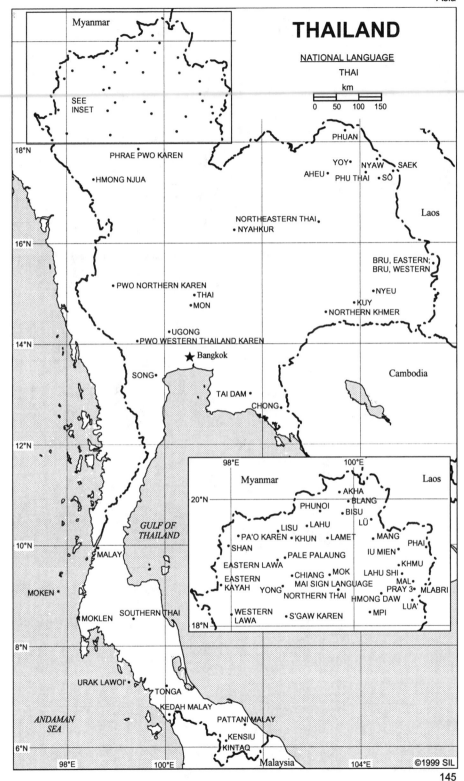

THAILAND

NATIONAL LANGUAGE

THAI

Myanmar

SEE
INSET

km

0   50   100   150

PHUAN

18°N   PHRAE PWO KAREN

YOY•   NYAW   SAEK
AHEU• PHU THAI •SO

•HMONG NJUA

Laos

NORTHEASTERN THAI•
• NYAHKUR

16°N

BRU, EASTERN;
BRU, WESTERN

• PWO NORTHERN KAREN
• THAI   •NYEU
•MON   •KUY
        •NORTHERN KHMER

•UGONG
14°N   •PWO WESTERN THAILAND KAREN

★ Bangkok

Cambodia

SONG•

TAI DAM •

CHONG•

12°N

98°E   100°E
Myanmar   Laos

• AKHA
20°N   • BLANG
PHUNOI   •BISU
LISU • LAHU   LÜ•
GULF OF   •PA'O KAREN •KHUN •LAMET   •MANG
10°N   THAILAND   •SHAN   PHAI•
MALAY   •PALE PALAUNG   IU MIEN•
EASTERN LAWA   •KHMU
EASTERN   •CHIANG •MOK LAHU SHI•
KAYAH YONG• MAI SIGN LANGUAGE   MAL•
MOKEN •   NORTHERN THAI HMONG DAW PRAY 3• MLABRI
WESTERN   LUA'
•MOKLEN   SOUTHERN THAI   LAWA •S'GAW KAREN   •MPI
18°N
8°N

URAK LAWOI' •
TONGA
KEDAH MALAY

ANDAMAN   PATTANI MALAY
SEA
•KENSIU
KINTAQ
6°N
98°E   100°E   Malaysia   104°E   ©1999 SIL

Maps

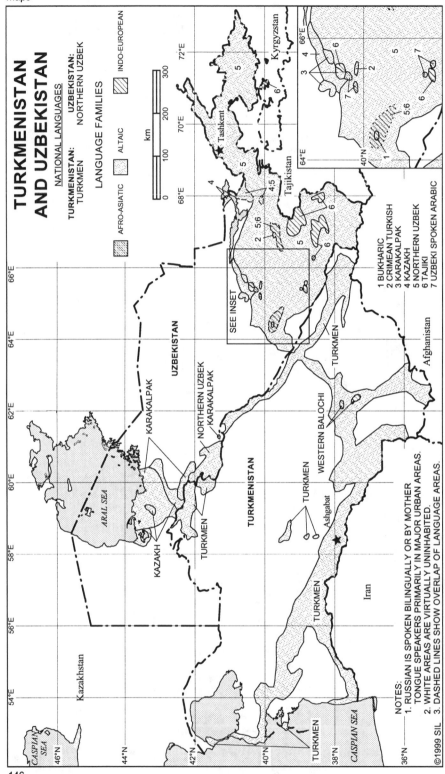

TURKMENISTAN
AND UZBEKISTAN

NATIONAL LANGUAGES

TURKMENISTAN:
TURKMEN

UZBEKISTAN:
NORTHERN UZBEK

LANGUAGE FAMILIES

AFRO-ASIATIC

ALTAIC

INDO-EUROPEAN

1 BUKHARIC
2 CRIMEAN TURKISH
3 KARAKALPAK
4 KAZAKH
5 NORTHERN UZBEK
6 TAJIKI
7 UZBEKI SPOKEN ARABIC

NOTES:
1. RUSSIAN IS SPOKEN BILINGUALLY OR BY MOTHER
TONGUE SPEAKERS PRIMARILY IN MAJOR URBAN AREAS.
2. WHITE AREAS ARE VIRTUALLY UNINHABITED.
3. DASHED LINES SHOW OVERLAP OF LANGUAGE AREAS.

©1999 SIL

146

NORTHERN
VIET NAM

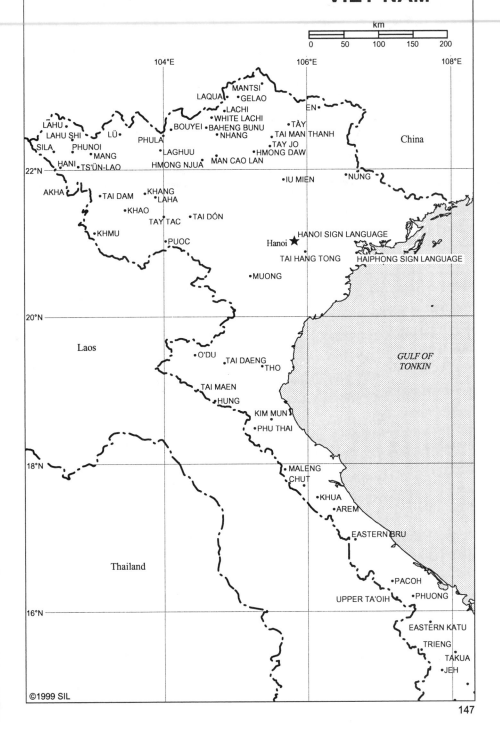

©1999 SIL

© 1999 SIL

NATIONAL LANGUAGE
VIETNAMESE

SOUTHERN
VIET NAM

km

0   50   100   150   200

Thailand

Laos

• PACOH
• PHUONG
UPPER TA'OIH
16°N
EASTERN KATU
TRIENG • TAKUA
• JEH • CUA
HALANG DOAN
KATUA • • KAYONG
• SEDANG • HRE
RENGAO • MONOM
HALANG TODRAH
• ROMAM
• BRAO
14°N
• JARAI
• BAHNAR

• HAROI

• RADE

Cambodia
CENTRAL MNONG
EASTERN MNONG
NORTHERN ROGLAI •
• SOUTHERN MNONG
12°N
• BULO STIENG
• BUDEH STIENG
WESTERN CHAM • KOHO
• MAA • CHRU • CACGIA
ROGLAI
SOUTHERN ROGLAI •
EASTERN CHAM
• CHRAU
• HO CHI MINH CITY SIGN LANGUAGE
• CENTRAL KHMER

SOUTH
CHINA
SEA

10°N

104°E   106°E   108°E

Asia

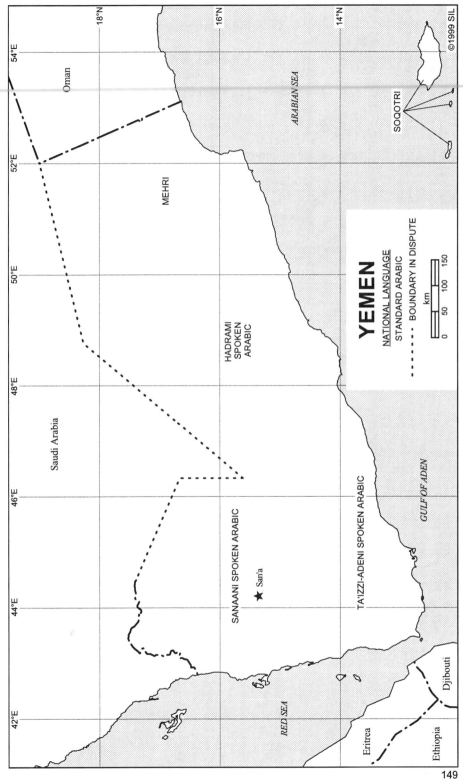

©1999 SIL

YEMEN

NATILNAL LANGUAGE
STANDARD ARABIC
······ BOUNDARY IN DISPUTE

km
0   50   100   150

SOQOTRI

MEHRI

HADRAMI
SPOKEN
ARABIC

SANAANI SPOKEN ARABIC
★ San'a

TA'IZZI-ADENI SPOKEN ARABIC

Saudi Arabia

Oman

ARABIAN SEA

GULF OF ADEN

RED SEA

Eritrea

Ethiopia

Djibouti

18°N
16°N
14°N
42°E   44°E   46°E   48°E   50°E   52°E   54°E

149

Europe Maps

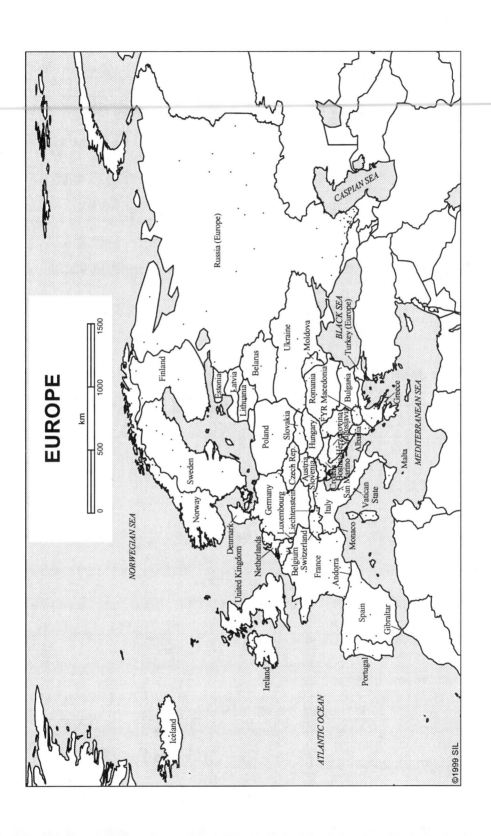

EUROPE

km

0   500   1000   1500

NORWEGIAN SEA

ATLANTIC OCEAN

Iceland

Ireland

United Kingdom

Norway

Sweden

Finland

Denmark

Netherlands

Germany

Belgium

Luxembourg

Switzerland

Liechtenstein

France

Andorra

Monaco

Spain

Portugal

Gibraltar

Italy

San Marino

Vatican State

Malta

MEDITERRANEAN SEA

Austria

Slovenia

Croatia

Bosnia-Herzegovina

Yugoslavia

Albania

FYR Macedonia

Czech Rep.

Slovakia

Poland

Hungary

Romania

Bulgaria

Greece

Moldova

Ukraine

Belarus

Lithuania

Latvia

Estonia

Russia (Europe)

BLACK SEA

Turkey (Europe)

CASPIAN SEA

©1999 SIL

Maps

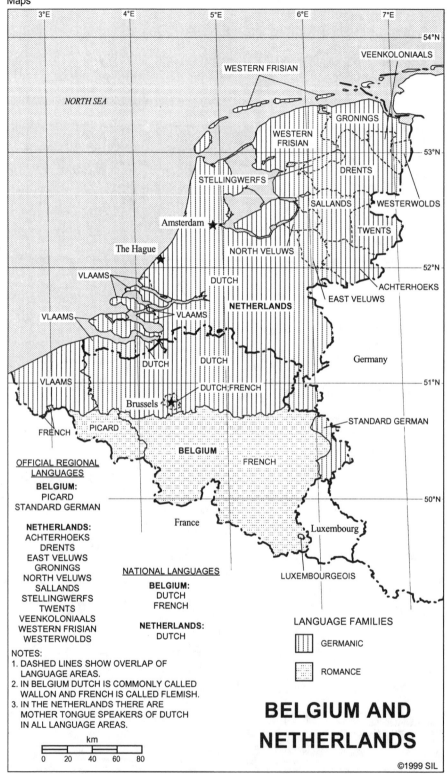

OFFICIAL REGIONAL
LANGUAGES

BELGIUM:
PICARD
STANDARD GERMAN

NETHERLANDS:
ACHTERHOEKS
DRENTS
EAST VELUWS
GRONINGS
NORTH VELUWS
SALLANDS
STELLINGWERFS
TWENTS
VEENKOLONIAALS
WESTERN FRISIAN
WESTERWOLDS

NATIONAL LANGUAGES
BELGIUM:
DUTCH
FRENCH

NETHERLANDS:
DUTCH

NOTES:
1. DASHED LINES SHOW OVERLAP OF
   LANGUAGE AREAS.
2. IN BELGIUM DUTCH IS COMMONLY CALLED
   WALLON AND FRENCH IS CALLED FLEMISH.
3. IN THE NETHERLANDS THERE ARE
   MOTHER TONGUE SPEAKERS OF DUTCH
   IN ALL LANGUAGE AREAS.

LANGUAGE FAMILIES

GERMANIC

ROMANCE

**BELGIUM AND
NETHERLANDS**

©1999 SIL

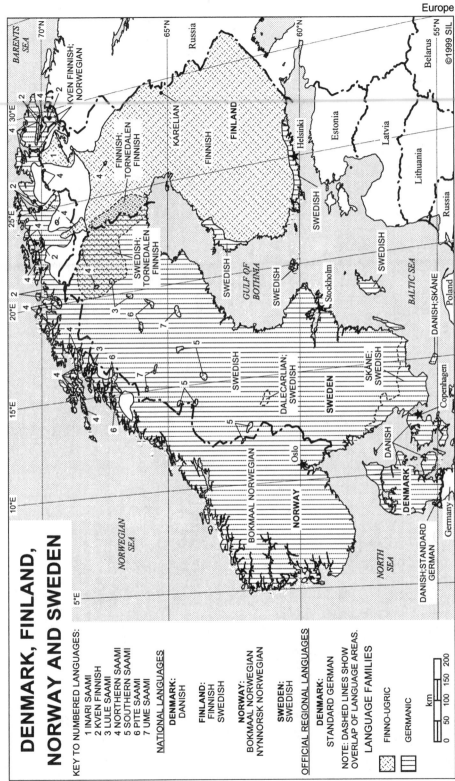

DENMARK, FINLAND, NORWAY AND SWEDEN

KEY TO NUMBERED LANGUAGES:

1 INARI SAAMI
2 KVEN FINNISH
3 LULE SAAMI
4 NORTHERN SAAMI
5 SOUTHERN SAAMI
6 PITE SAAMI
7 UME SAAMI

NATIONAL LANGUAGES

DENMARK:
DANISH

FINLAND:
FINNISH
SWEDISH

NORWAY:
BOKMAAL NORWEGIAN
NYNNORSK NORWEGIAN

SWEDEN:
SWEDISH

OFFICIAL REGIONAL LANGUAGES

DENMARK:
STANDARD GERMAN

NOTE: DASHED LINES SHOW
OVERLAP OF LANGUAGE AREAS.

LANGUAGE FAMILIES

FINNO-UGRIC

GERMANIC

km
0 50 100 150 200

©1999 SIL

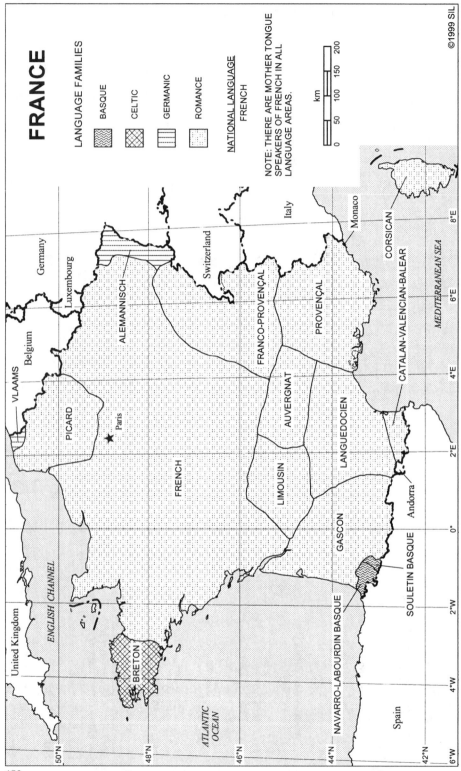

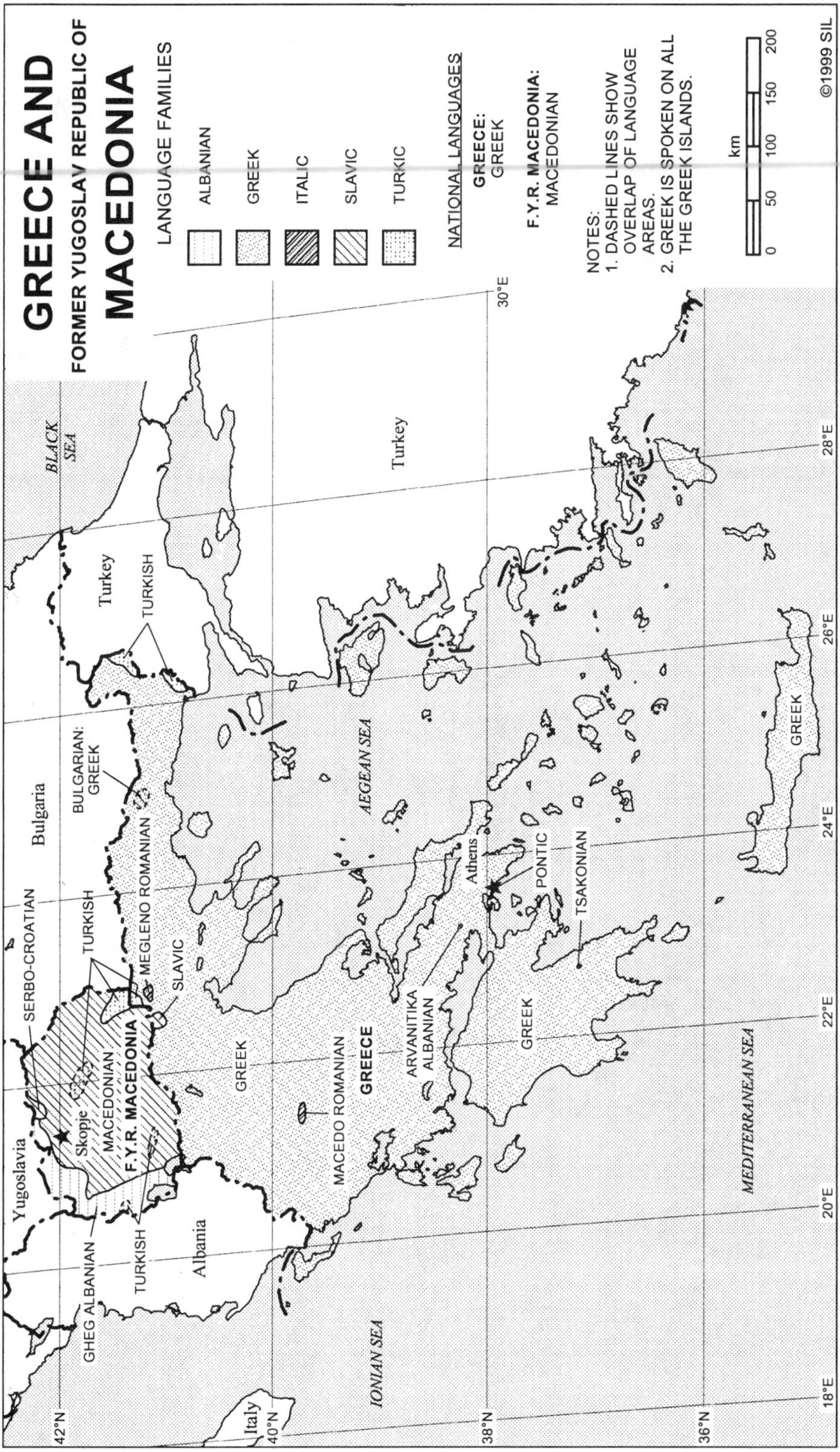

GREECE AND
FORMER YUGOSLAV REPUBLIC OF
MACEDONIA

LANGUAGE FAMILIES

- ALBANIAN
- GREEK
- ITALIC
- SLAVIC
- TURKIC

NATIONAL LANGUAGES

GREECE:
GREEK

F.Y.R. MACEDONIA:
MACEDONIAN

NOTES:
1. DASHED LINES SHOW OVERLAP OF LANGUAGE AREAS.
2. GREEK IS SPOKEN ON ALL THE GREEK ISLANDS.

km

0   50   100   150   200

©1999 SIL

BLACK SEA

Turkey

TURKISH

BULGARIAN:
GREEK

Bulgaria

SERBO-CROATIAN

TURKISH

MEGLENO ROMANIAN

SLAVIC

Yugoslavia

Skopje

MACEDONIAN
F.Y.R. MACEDONIA

TURKISH

GHEG ALBANIAN

TURKISH

Albania

Italy

IONIAN SEA

GREEK

MACEDO ROMANIAN

GREECE

ARVANITIKA
ALBANIAN

GREEK

AEGEAN SEA

Athens

PONTIC

TSAKONIAN

MEDITERRANEAN SEA

GREEK

Turkey

42°N

40°N

38°N

36°N

18°E   20°E   22°E   24°E   26°E   28°E   30°E

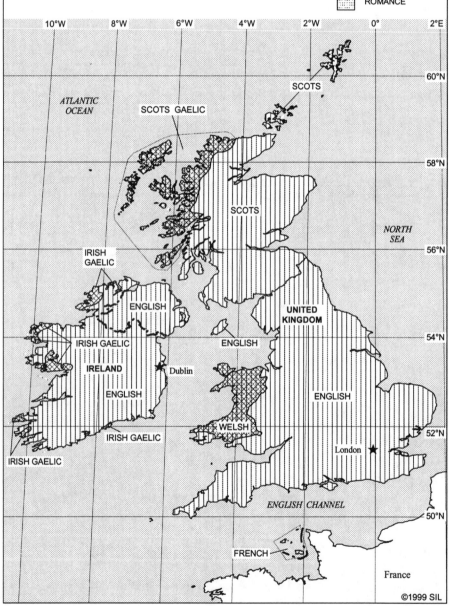

IRELAND AND UNITED KINGDOM

NOTE:
THERE ARE MOTHER TONGUE SPEAKERS
OF ENGLISH IN ALL LANGUAGE AREAS.

NATIONAL LANGUAGES

IRELAND: **UNITED KINGDOM:**
ENGLISH ENGLISH
IRISH GAELIC WELSH

OFFICIAL LANGUAGE
FRENCH (CHANNEL ISLANDS)

LANGUAGE FAMILIES

CELTIC

GERMANIC

ROMANCE

miles
0 20 40 60 80

10°W 8°W 6°W 4°W 2°W 0° 2°E

60°N
58°N
56°N
54°N
52°N
50°N

ATLANTIC
OCEAN

SCOTS

SCOTS GAELIC

SCOTS

NORTH
SEA

IRISH
GAELIC

ENGLISH

IRISH GAELIC

ENGLISH

UNITED
KINGDOM

IRELAND Dublin

ENGLISH

IRISH GAELIC

ENGLISH

WELSH

London

IRISH GAELIC

ENGLISH CHANNEL

FRENCH

France

©1999 SIL

158

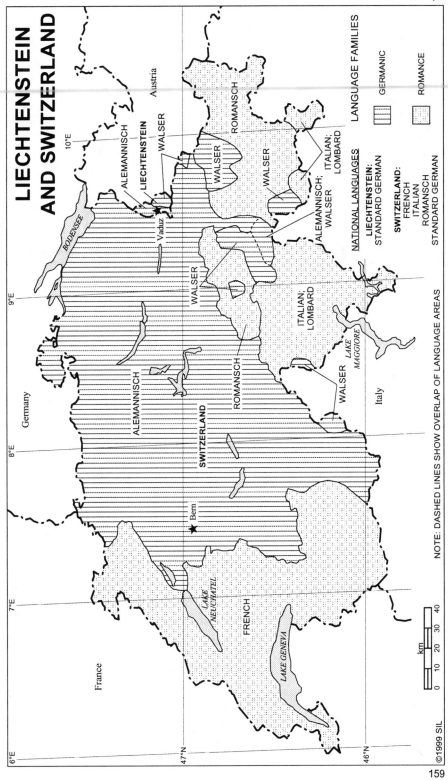

LIECHTENSTEIN AND SWITZERLAND

LANGUAGE FAMILIES

GERMANIC

ROMANCE

NATIONAL LANGUAGES

LIECHTENSTEIN:
STANDARD GERMAN

SWITZERLAND:
FRENCH
ITALIAN
ROMANSCH
STANDARD GERMAN

NOTE: DASHED LINES SHOW OVERLAP OF LANGUAGE AREAS

©1999 SIL

Germany

France

Austria

Italy

ALEMANNISCH

LIECHTENSTEIN

WALSER

Vaduz

ROMANSCH

WALSER

WALSER

WALSER

ITALIAN; LOMBARD

ALEMANNISCH; WALSER

WALSER

ALEMANNISCH

SWITZERLAND

ROMANSCH

ITALIAN; LOMBARD

WALSER

Bern

BODENSEE

LAKE NEUCHATEL

FRENCH

LAKE GENEVA

LAKE MAGGIORE

km
0 10 20 30 40

6°E   7°E   8°E   9°E   10°E

47°N

46°N

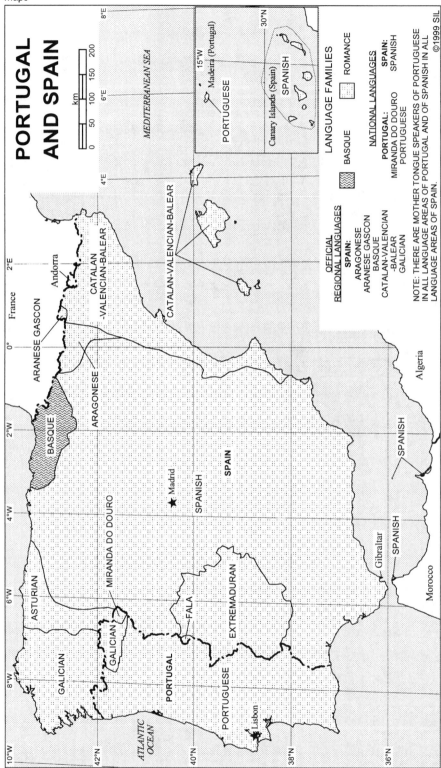

PORTUGAL AND SPAIN

LANGUAGE FAMILIES

ROMANCE

BASQUE

NATIONAL LANGUAGES

PORTUGAL:
MIRANDA DO DOURO
PORTUGUESE

SPAIN:
SPANISH

OFFICIAL
REGIONAL LANGUAGES
SPAIN:
ARAGONESE
ARANESE GASCON
BASQUE
CATALAN-VALENCIAN
-BALEAR
GALICIAN

NOTE: THERE ARE MOTHER TONGUE SPEAKERS OF PORTUGUESE
IN ALL LANGUAGE AREAS OF PORTUGAL AND OF SPANISH IN ALL
LANGUAGE AREAS OF SPAIN.

©1999 SIL

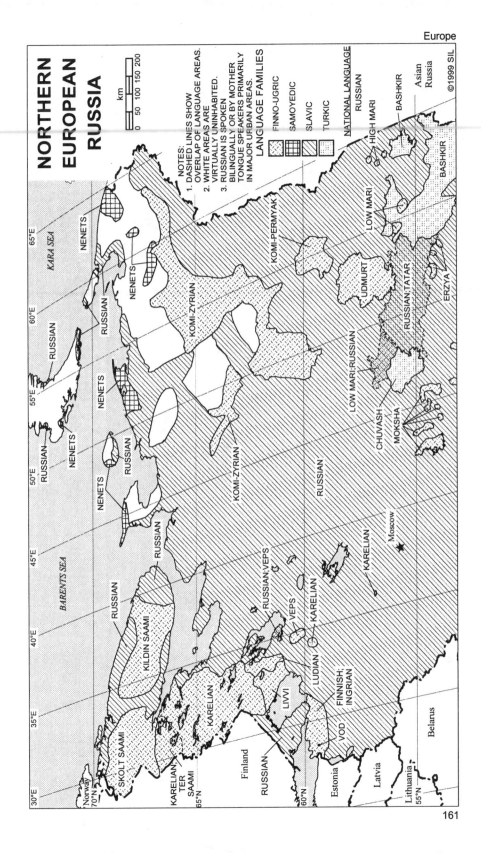

NORTHERN EUROPEAN RUSSIA

km
0 50 100 150 200

NOTES:
1. DASHED LINES SHOW OVERLAP OF LANGUAGE AREAS.
2. WHITE AREAS ARE VIRTUALLY UNINHABITED.
3. RUSSIAN IS SPOKEN BILINGUALLY OR BY MOTHER TONGUE SPEAKERS PRIMARILY IN MAJOR URBAN AREAS.

LANGUAGE FAMILIES

FINNO-UGRIC
SAMOYEDIC
SLAVIC
TURKIC

NATIONAL LANGUAGE
RUSSIAN

Asian Russia

©1999 SIL

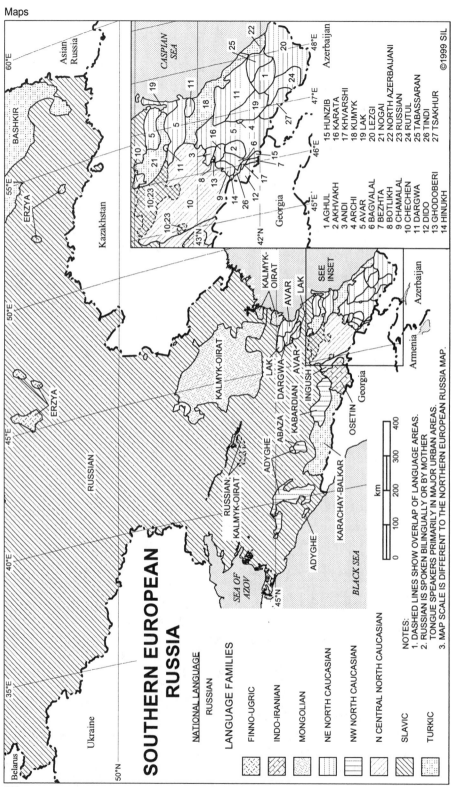

SOUTHERN EUROPEAN
RUSSIA

NATIONAL LANGUAGE

RUSSIAN

LANGUAGE FAMILIES

FINNO-UGRIC

INDO-IRANIAN

MONGOLIAN

NE NORTH CAUCASIAN

NW NORTH CAUCASIAN

N CENTRAL NORTH CAUCASIAN

SLAVIC

TURKIC

NOTES:
1. DASHED LINES SHOW OVERLAP OF LANGUAGE AREAS.
2. RUSSIAN IS SPOKEN BILINGUALLY OR BY MOTHER
   TONGUE SPEAKERS PRIMARILY IN MAJOR URBAN AREAS.
3. MAP SCALE IS DIFFERENT TO THE NORTHERN EUROPEAN RUSSIA MAP.

1 AGHUL
2 AKHVAKH
3 ANDI
4 ARCHI
5 AVAR
6 BAGVALAL
7 BEZHTA
8 BOTLIKH
9 CHAMALAL
10 CHECHEN
11 DARGWA
12 DIDO
13 GHODOBERI
14 HINUKH
15 HUNZIB
16 KARATA
17 KHVARSHI
18 KUMYK
19 LAK
20 LEZGI
21 NOGAI
22 NORTH AZERBAIJANI
23 RUSSIAN
24 RUTUL
25 TABASSARAN
26 TINDI
27 TSAKHUR

©1999 SIL

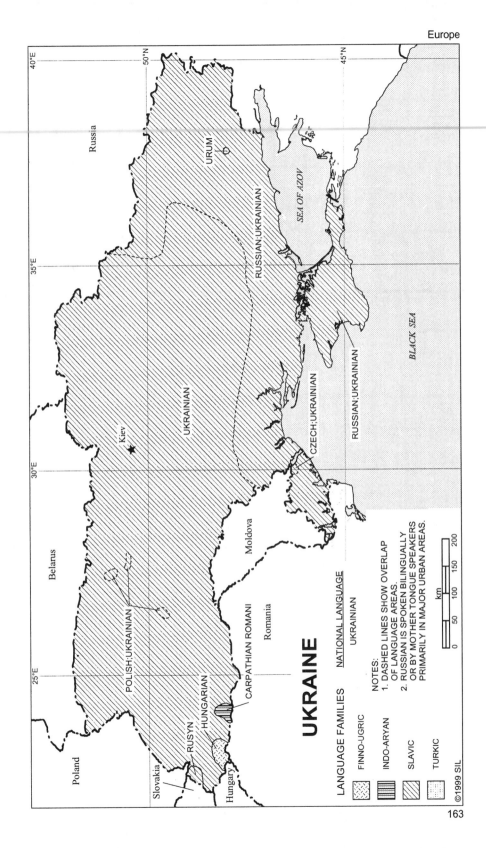

UKRAINE

LANGUAGE FAMILIES

FINNO-UGRIC

INDO-ARYAN

SLAVIC

TURKIC

NATIONAL LANGUAGE

UKRAINIAN

NOTES:
1. DASHED LINES SHOW OVERLAP
   OF LANGUAGE AREAS.
2. RUSSIAN IS SPOKEN BILINGUALLY
   OR BY MOTHER TONGUE SPEAKERS
   PRIMARILY IN MAJOR URBAN AREAS.

©1999 SIL

The Pacific Maps

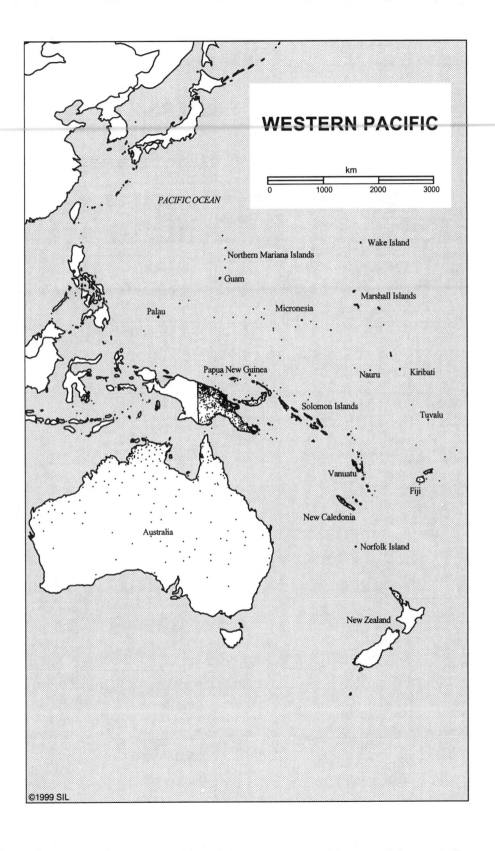

WESTERN PACIFIC

km

0   1000   2000   3000

PACIFIC OCEAN

• Wake Island

Northern Mariana Islands

• Guam

Marshall Islands

Palau

Micronesia

Papua New Guinea

Nauru   • Kiribati

Solomon Islands

Tuvalu

Vanuatu

Fiji

New Caledonia

• Norfolk Island

Australia

New Zealand

©1999 SIL

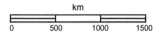

EASTERN PACIFIC

km
0   500   1000   1500

Midway Islands

Hawaiian Islands (USA)

PACIFIC OCEAN

Kiribati

Tokelau

Western Samoa

Cook Islands

Wallis and Futuna

American Samoa

French Polynesia

Niue

Tonga

Pitcairn

Easter Island
(Chile)

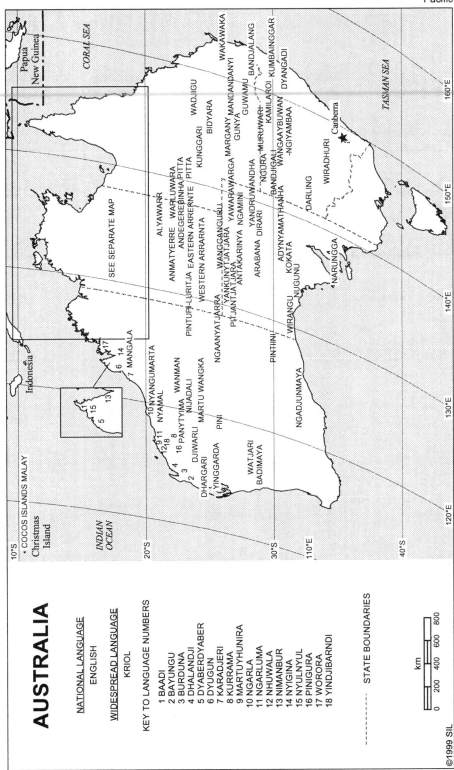

AUSTRALIA

NATIONAL LANGUAGE
ENGLISH

WIDESPREAD LANGUAGE
KRIOL

KEY TO LANGUAGE NUMBERS

1 BAADI
2 BAYUNGU
3 BURDUNA
4 DHALANDJI
5 DYABERDYABER
6 DYUGUN
7 KARADJERI
8 KURRAMA
9 MARTUYHUNIRA
10 NGARLA
11 NGARLUMA
12 NHUWALA
13 NIMANBUR
14 NYIGINA
15 NYULNYUL
16 PINIGURA
17 WORORA
18 YINDJIBARNDI

--------- STATE BOUNDARIES

km

0   200 400 600 800

© 1999 SIL

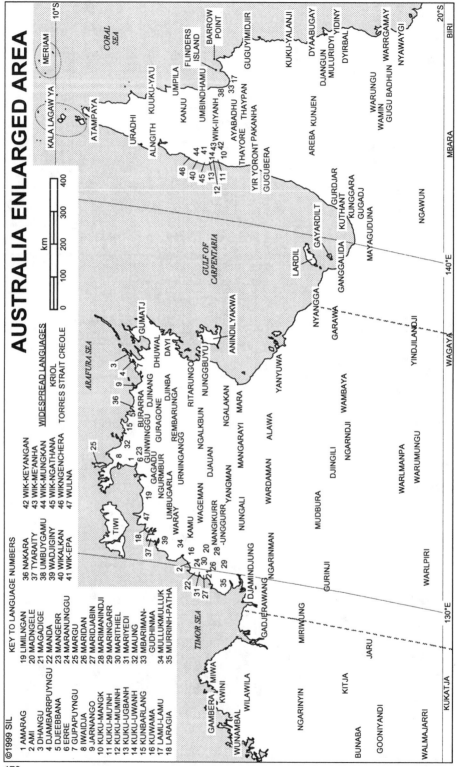

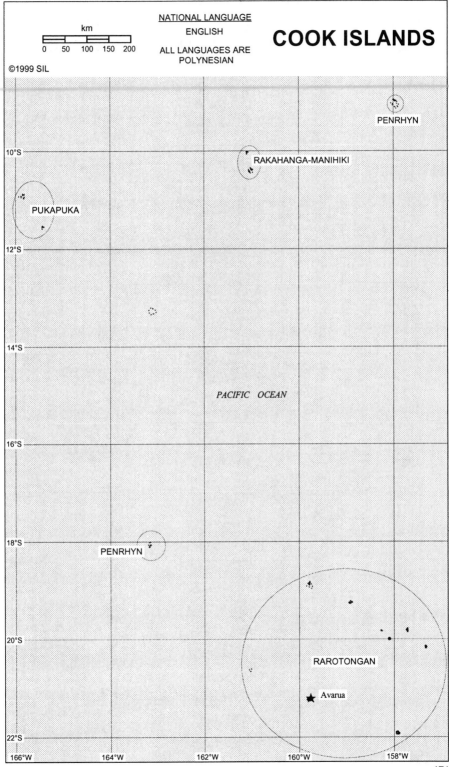

COOK ISLANDS

NATIONAL LANGUAGE
ENGLISH

ALL LANGUAGES ARE
POLYNESIAN

km

0   50   100   150   200

©1999 SIL

PENRHYN

10°S

RAKAHANGA-MANIHIKI

PUKAPUKA

12°S

14°S

PACIFIC OCEAN

16°S

18°S

PENRHYN

20°S

RAROTONGAN

★ Avarua

22°S

166°W   164°W   162°W   160°W   158°W

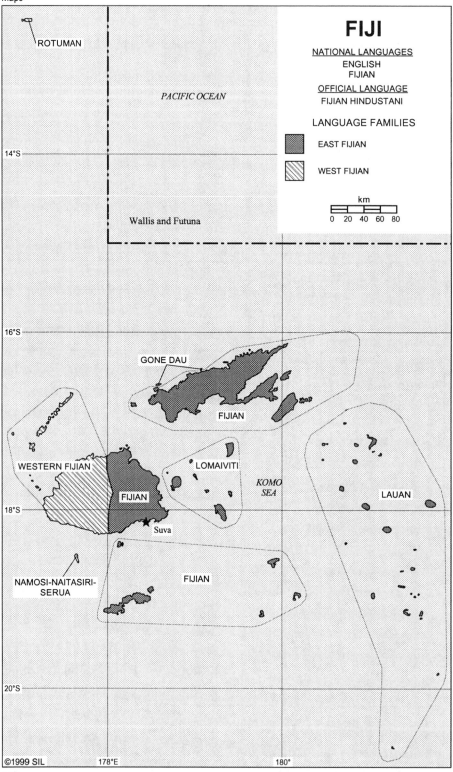

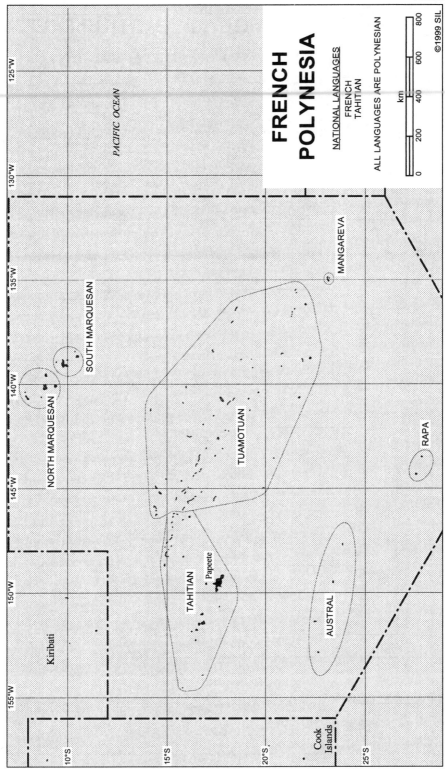

FRENCH
POLYNESIA

<u>NATIONAL LANGUAGES</u>
FRENCH
TAHITIAN

ALL LANGUAGES ARE POLYNESIAN

©1999 SIL

km

0   200   400   600   800

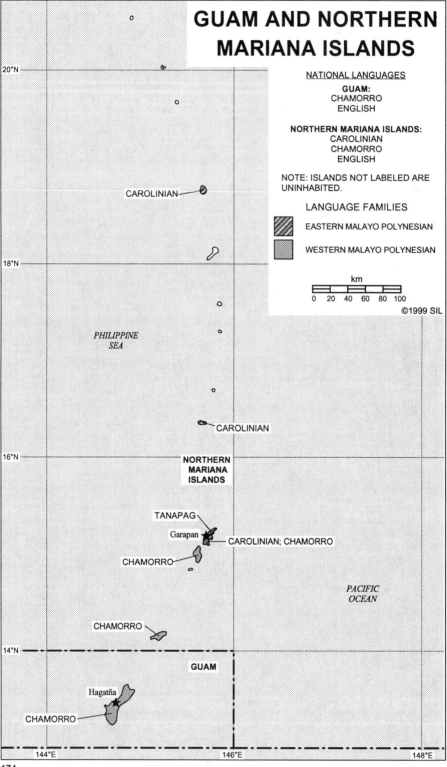

GUAM AND NORTHERN MARIANA ISLANDS

NATIONAL LANGUAGES

GUAM:
CHAMORRO
ENGLISH

NORTHERN MARIANA ISLANDS:
CAROLINIAN
CHAMORRO
ENGLISH

NOTE: ISLANDS NOT LABELED ARE UNINHABITED.

LANGUAGE FAMILIES

EASTERN MALAYO POLYNESIAN

WESTERN MALAYO POLYNESIAN

km

0   20   40   60   80   100

©1999 SIL

CAROLINIAN

20°N

18°N

PHILIPPINE
SEA

CAROLINIAN

16°N

NORTHERN
MARIANA
ISLANDS

TANAPAG

Garapan   CAROLINIAN; CHAMORRO

CHAMORRO

PACIFIC
OCEAN

CHAMORRO

14°N

GUAM

Hagåtña

CHAMORRO

144°E   146°E   148°E

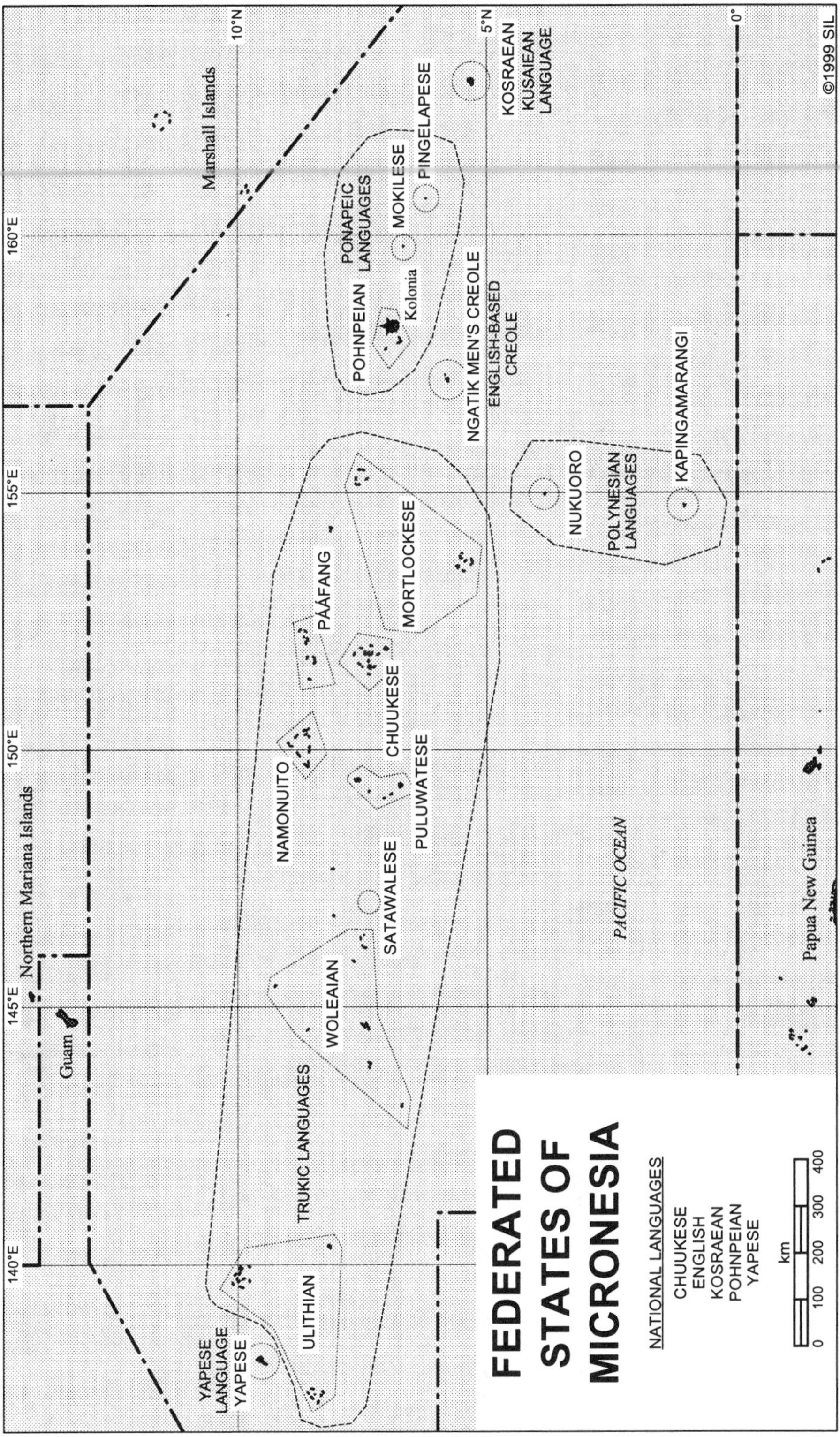

©1999 SIL

10°N

5°N

Marshall Islands

160°E

KOSRAEAN
KUSAIEAN
LANGUAGE

PINGELAPESE

MOKILESE

PONAPEIC
LANGUAGES

POHNPEIAN

Kolonia

NGATIK MEN'S CREOLE
ENGLISH-BASED
CREOLE

0°

155°E

NUKUORO

POLYNESIAN
LANGUAGES

KAPINGAMARANGI

PAÁFANG

MORTLOCKESE

NAMONUITO

CHUUKESE

PULUWATESE

SATAWALESE

PACIFIC OCEAN

150°E

WOLEAIAN

Northern Mariana Islands

Guam

145°E

TRUKIC LANGUAGES

Papua New Guinea

140°E

YAPESE
LANGUAGE
YAPESE

ULITHIAN

FEDERATED
STATES OF
MICRONESIA

NATIONAL LANGUAGES
CHUUKESE
ENGLISH
KOSRAEAN
POHNPEIAN
YAPESE

km

0   100   200   300   400

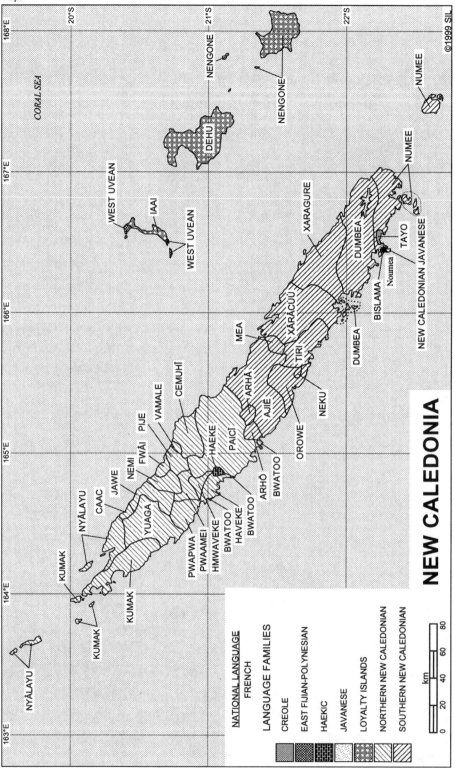

NEW CALEDONIA

NATIONAL LANGUAGE
FRENCH

LANGUAGE FAMILIES
CREOLE
EAST FIJIAN-POLYNESIAN
HAEKIC
JAVANESE
LOYALTY ISLANDS
NORTHERN NEW CALEDONIAN
SOUTHERN NEW CALEDONIAN

©1999 SIL

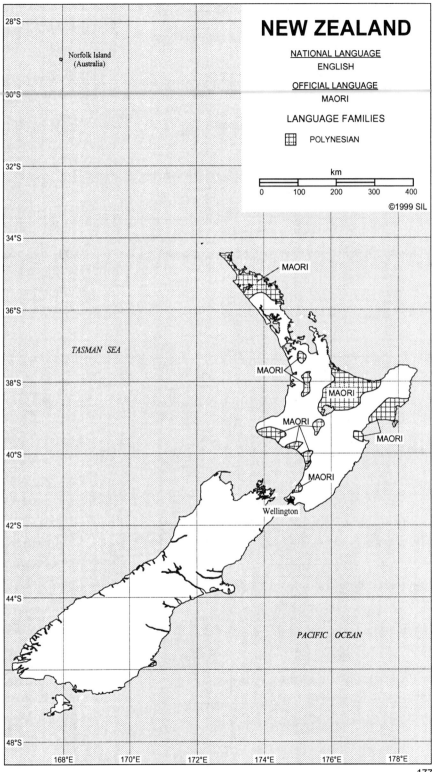

NEW ZEALAND

NATIONAL LANGUAGE
ENGLISH

OFFICIAL LANGUAGE
MAORI

LANGUAGE FAMILIES

POLYNESIAN

km

0   100   200   300   400

©1999 SIL

Norfolk Island
(Australia)

MAORI

TASMAN SEA

MAORI

MAORI

MAORI

MAORI

MAORI

MAORI

Wellington

PACIFIC OCEAN

Maps

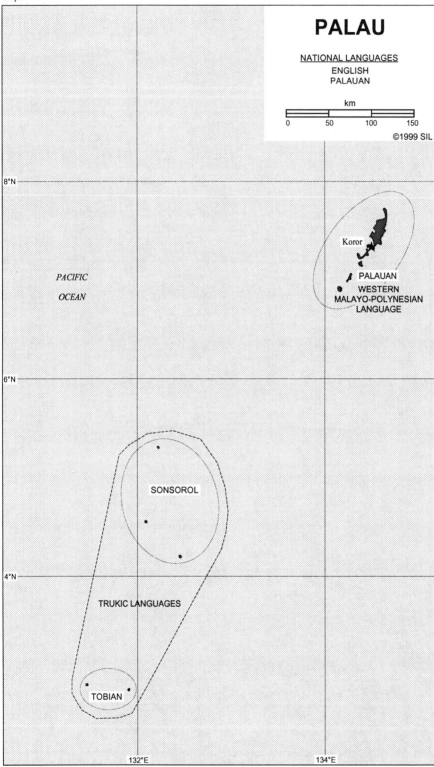

PALAU

<u>NATIONAL LANGUAGES</u>
ENGLISH
PALAUAN

km

| 0 | 50 | 100 | 150 |

©1999 SIL

8°N

PACIFIC

OCEAN

Koror

PALAUAN
WESTERN
MALAYO-POLYNESIAN
LANGUAGE

6°N

SONSOROL

4°N

TRUKIC LANGUAGES

TOBIAN

132°E

134°E

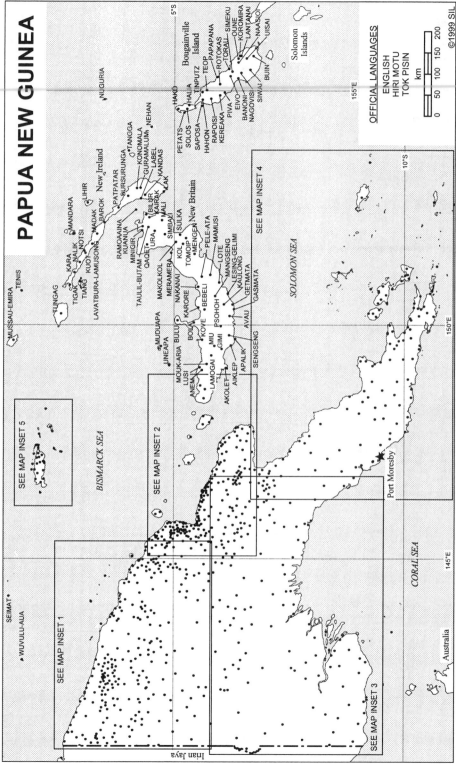

Pacific

PAPUA NEW GUINEA

©1999 SIL

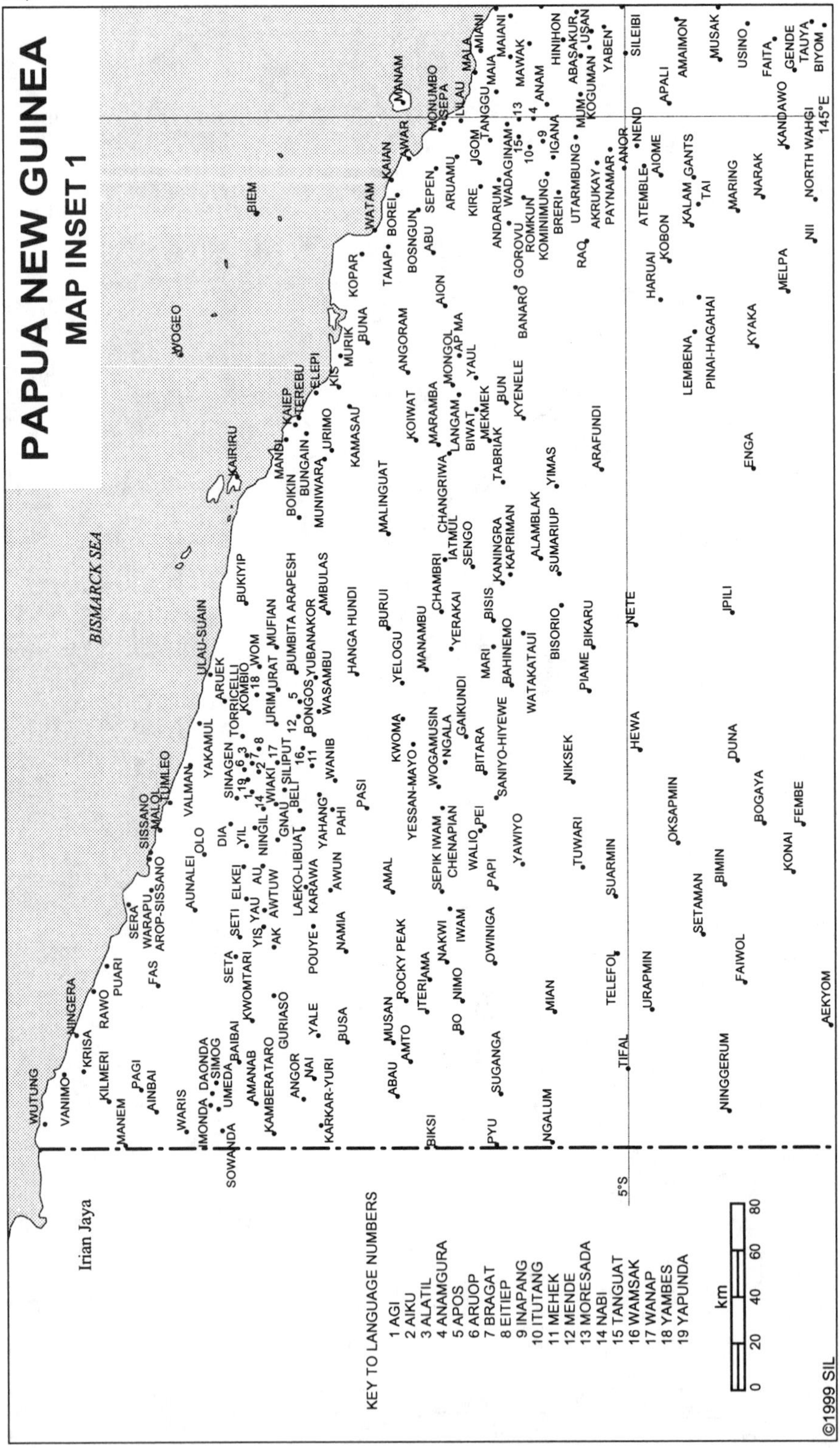

PAPUA NEW GUINEA
MAP INSET 1
BISMARCK SEA
Irian Jaya
5°S
145°E
KEY TO LANGUAGE NUMBERS
1 AGI
2 AIKU
3 ALATIL
4 ANAMGURA
5 APOS
6 ARUOP
7 BRAGAT
8 EITIEP
9 INAPANG
10 ITUTANG
11 MEHEK
12 MENDE
13 MORESADA
14 NABI
15 TANGUAT
16 WAMSAK
17 WANAP
18 YAMBES
19 YAPUNDA
km
0 20 40 60 80
©1999 SIL
WUTUNG
VANIMO
KRISA
NINGERA
RAWO
PUARI
KILMERI
MANEM
PAGI
AINBAI
FAS
SERA
WARAPU
AROP-SISSANO
SISSANO
MALOL
TUMLEO
VALMAN
YAKAMUL
ULAU-SUAIN
WOGEO
KAIRIRU
BIEM
WARIS
MONDA
DAONDA
SIMOG
UMEDA
SOWANDA
BAIBAI
AMANAB
KAMBERATARO
KWOMTARI
SETA
SETI
ELKEI
AUNALEI
OLO
DIA
YIL
AU
YIS
YAU
AK
AWTUW
NINGIL
WIAKI
SINAGEN
TORRICELLI
ARUEK
KOMBIO
WOM
URIM
URAT
MUFIAN
BUKIYIP
BUMBITA ARAPESH
YUBANAKOR
AMBULAS
WASAMBU
BONGOS
SILIPUT
BELI
GNAU
LAEKO-LIBUAT
KARAWA
YAHANG
PAHI
WANIB
GURIASO
ANGOR
NAI
YALE
POUYE
KARKAR-YURI
BUSA
NAMIA
AWUN
PASI
HANGA HUNDI
BOIKIN
BUNGAIN
MUNIWARA
MANDI
KAIEP
TEREBU
ELEPI
URIMO
KIS
MURIK
BUNA
KOPAR
KAMASAU
WATAM
KAIAN
AWAR
MANAM
BOREI
TAIAP
BOSNGUN
ABU
SEPEN
MONUMBO
SEPA
LILAU
MALA
MIANI
MAIANI
MAIA
MAWAK
TANGGU
JGOM
ARUAMU
KIRE
ANDARUM
WADAGINAM
GOROVU
ROMKUN
KOMINIMUNG
BRERI
IGANA
ANAM
HINIHON
ABASAKUR
USAN
KOGUMAN
MUM
YABEN
UTARMBUNG
AKRUKAY
PAYNAMAR
RAO
ANOR
NEND
SILEIBI
AIOME
ATEMBLE
APALI
AMAIMON
MUSAK
USINO
FAITA
GENDE
TAUYA
BIYOM
KANDAWO
NORTH WAHGI
NII
NARAK
MARING
KALAM
GANTS
TAI
KOBON
HARUAI
MELPA
PINAI-HAGAHAI
LEMBENA
KYAKA
ENGA
AION
ANGORAM
BANARO
MONGOL
AP MA
YAUL
KOIWAT
MARAMBA
LANGAM
BIWAT
MEKMEK
BUN
KYENELE
TABRIAK
MALINGUAT
CHANGRIWA
IATMUL
SENGO
CHAMBRI
YERAKAI
KANINGRA
KAPRIMAN
ALAMBLAK
SUMARIUP
YIMAS
ARAFUNDI
BURUI
YELOGU
MANAMBU
GAIKUNDI
BISIS
MARI
BAHINEMO
WATAKATAUI
BISORIO
BIKARU
PIAME
NETE
KWOMA
WOGAMUSIN
NGALA
YESSAN-MAYO
SEPIK IWAM
CHENAPIAN
WALIO
PEI
BITARA
SANIYO-HIYEWE
YAWIYO
PAPI
OWINIGA
NAKWI
IWAM
AMAL
ROCKY PEAK
ITERI
AMA
NIMO
BO
MUSAN
AMTO
ABAU
BIKSI
SUGANGA
PYU
NGALUM
MIAN
TELEFOL
TIFAL
URAPMIN
SUARMIN
TUWARI
NIKSEK
HEWA
OKSAPMIN
SETAMAN
BIMIN
FAIWOL
NINGGERUM
AEKYOM
KONAI
BOGAYA
FEMBE
DUNA
IPILI

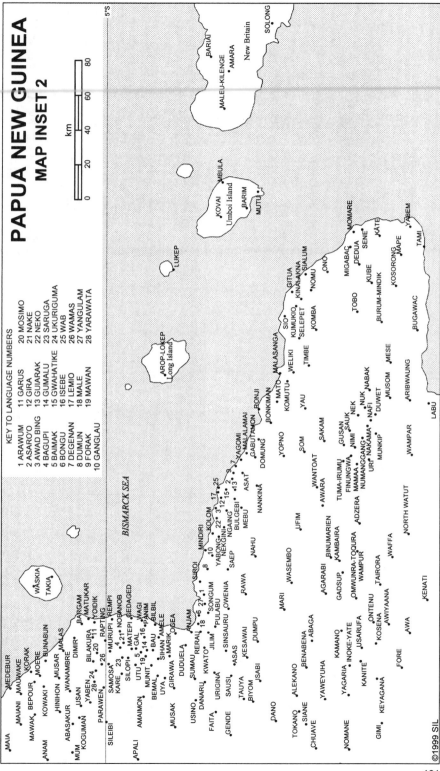

PAPUA NEW GUINEA
MAP INSET 2

KEY TO LANGUAGE NUMBERS

1 ARAWUM	11 GARUS	20 MOSIMO
2 ASARO'O	12 GIRA	21 NAKE
3 AWAD BING	13 GUIARAK	22 NEKO
4 BAGUPI	14 GUMALU	23 SARUGA
5 BAIMAK	15 GWAHATIKE	24 UKURIGUMA
6 BONGU	16 ISEBE	25 WAB
7 DEGENAN	17 LEMIO	26 WAMAS
8 DUMUN	18 MALE	27 YANGULAM
9 FORAK	19 MAWAN	28 YARAWATA
10 GANGLAU		

Pacific

BISMARCK SEA

km
0 20 40 60 80

©1999 SIL

181

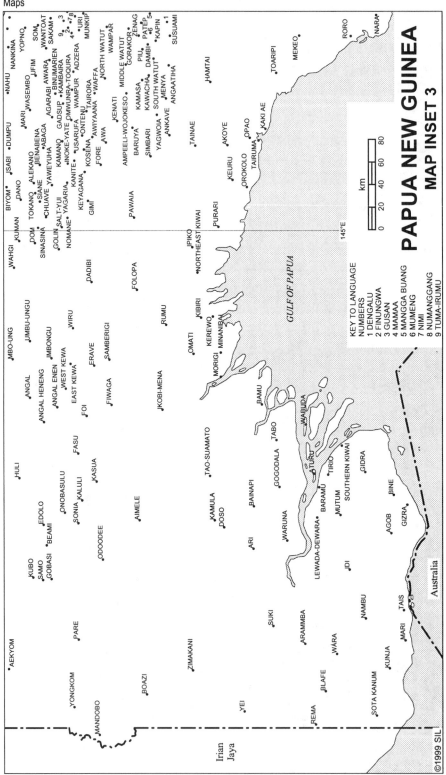

PAPUA NEW GUINEA
MAP INSET 3

KEY TO LANGUAGE
NUMBERS
1 DENGALU
2 FINUNGWA
3 GUSAN
4 MAMAA
5 MANGGA BUANG
6 MUMENG
7 NIMI
8 NUMANGGANG
9 TUMA-IRUMU

km
0   20   40   60   80

GULF OF PAPUA

145°E

Australia

Irian
Jaya

©1999 SIL

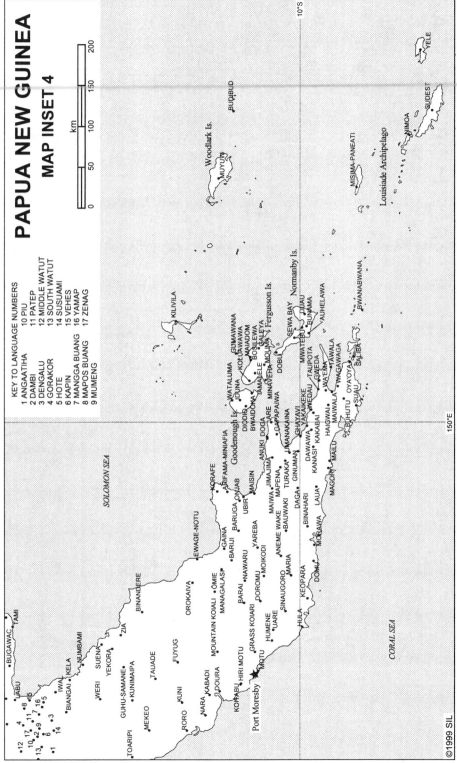

PAPUA NEW GUINEA
MAP INSET 4

km
0 50 100 150 200

KEY TO LANGUAGE NUMBERS

1 ANGAATIHA	10 PIU
2 DAMBI	11 PATEP
3 DENGALU	12 MIDDLE WATUT
4 GORAKOR	13 SOUTH WATUT
5 HOTE	14 SUSUAMI
6 KAPIN	15 VEHES
7 MANGGA BUANG	16 YAMAP
8 MAPOS BUANG	17 ZENAG
9 MUMENG	

10°S

150°E

SOLOMON SEA

CORAL SEA

Port Moresby

©1999 SIL

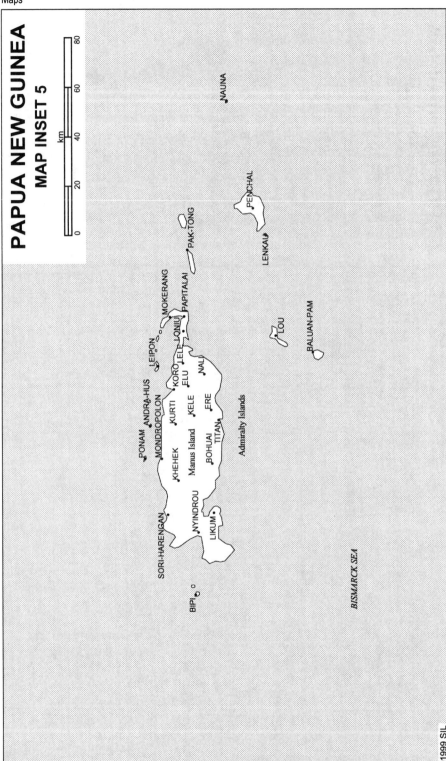

PAPUA NEW GUINEA
MAP INSET 5

km

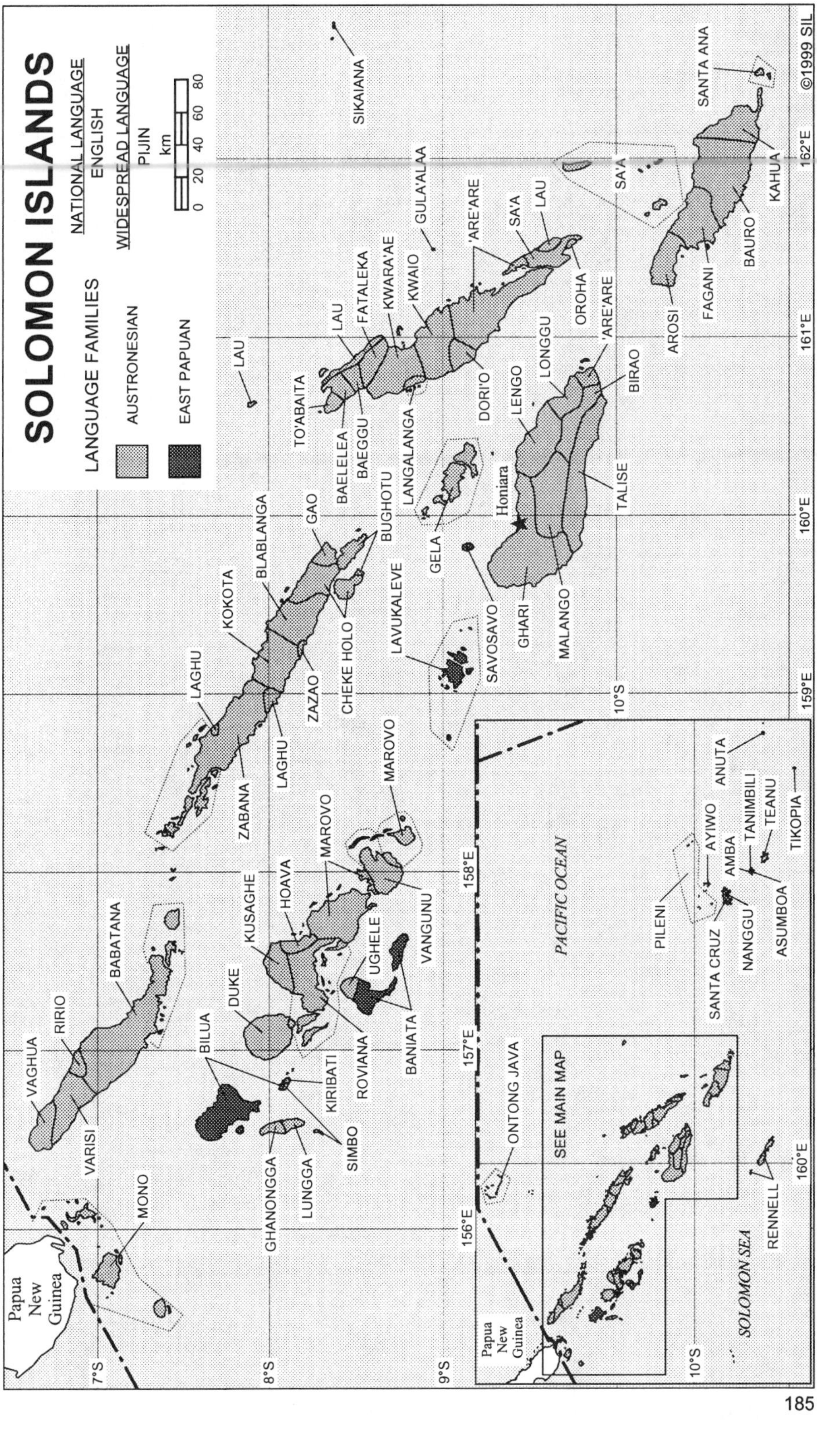

SOLOMON ISLANDS
NATIONAL LANGUAGE
ENGLISH
WIDESPREAD LANGUAGE
PIJIN
LANGUAGE FAMILIES
AUSTRONESIAN
EAST PAPUAN
km
0 20 40 60 80
©1999 SIL
Papua New Guinea
7°S
8°S
9°S
10°S
156°E
157°E
158°E
159°E
160°E
161°E
162°E
MONO
VAGHUA
RIRIO
BABATANA
VARISI
BILUA
DUKE
GHANONGGA
LUNGGA
SIMBO
KIRIBATI
ROVIANA
KUSAGHE
HOAVA
MAROVO
UGHELE
BANIATA
VANGUNU
LAGHU
ZABANA
KOKOTA
BLABLANGA
ZAZAO
CHEKE HOLO
GAO
BUGHOTU
LAVUKALEVE
SAVOSAVO
GELA
Honiara
GHARI
MALANGO
TALISE
LENGO
LONGGU
BIRAO
'ARE'ARE
LANGALANGA
TO'ABAITA
BAELELEA
BAEGGU
LAU
FATALEKA
KWARA'AE
KWAIO
DORI'O
GULA'ALAA
SA'A
OROHA
SIKAIANA
AROSI
FAGANI
BAURO
KAHUA
SANTA ANA
ONTONG JAVA
SEE MAIN MAP
PACIFIC OCEAN
PILENI
SANTA CRUZ
AYIWO
AMBA
NANGGU
ASUMBOA
TANIMBILI
TEANU
ANUTA
TIKOPIA
RENNELL
SOLOMON SEA

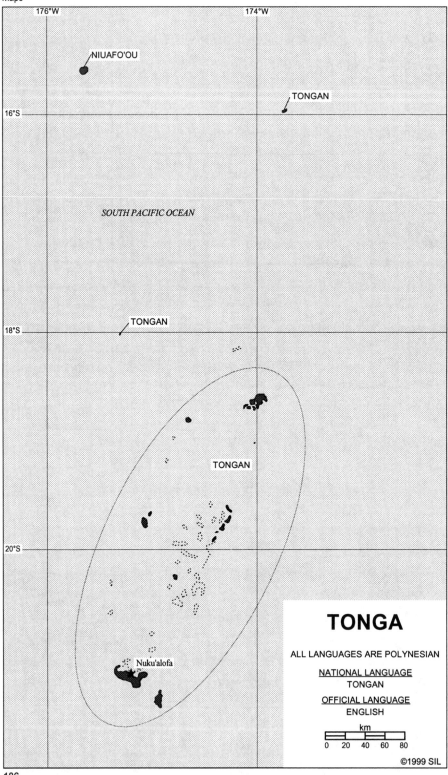

NIUAFO'OU

TONGAN

16°S

SOUTH PACIFIC OCEAN

TONGAN

18°S

TONGAN

20°S

Nuku'alofa

TONGA

ALL LANGUAGES ARE POLYNESIAN

NATIONAL LANGUAGE
TONGAN

OFFICIAL LANGUAGE
ENGLISH

km

0   20   40   60   80

©1999 SIL

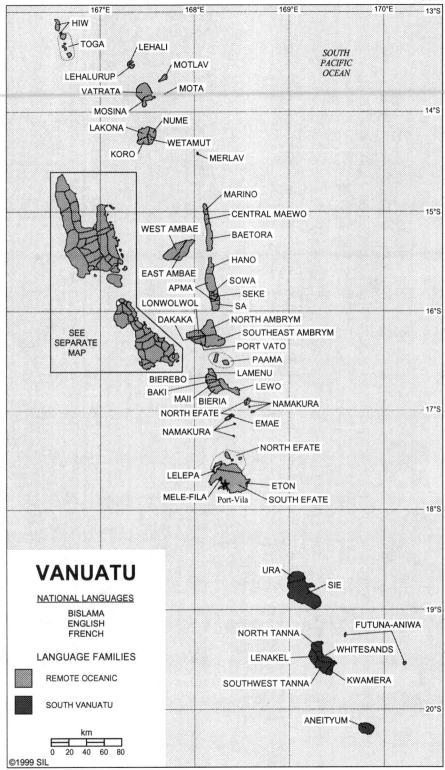

VANUATU

NATIONAL LANGUAGES

BISLAMA
ENGLISH
FRENCH

LANGUAGE FAMILIES

REMOTE OCEANIC

SOUTH VANUATU

km
0 20 40 60 80

©1999 SIL

Maps

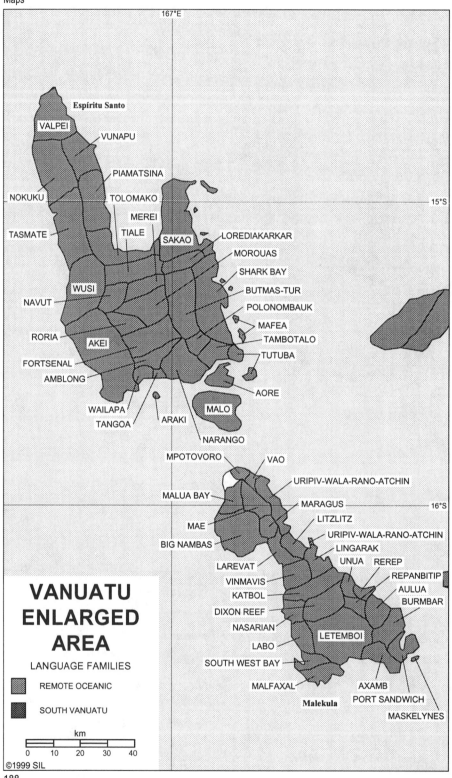

VANUATU
ENLARGED
AREA

LANGUAGE FAMILIES

REMOTE OCEANIC

SOUTH VANUATU

km

0   10   20   30   40

©1999 SIL

Language Name Index

Editors

Joseph E. Grimes
Barbara F. Grimes

A' ANANIN alt for GROS VENTRE [ATS]
A FALA DE XÁLIMA alt for FALA [FAX]
A FALA DO XÃLIMA alt for FALA [FAX]
A NDEN alt for ABUN [KGR]
A'A SAMA alt for SAMA dial of SAMA, SOUTHERN [SIT]
AACHTERHOEKS alt for ACHTERHOEKS [ACT]
AAGE alt for ESIMBI [AGS]
AAIMASA alt for AIMARA dial of KUNAMA [KUM]
AAL MURRAH alt for SOUTH ANJDI dial of ARABIC, NAJDI SPOKEN [ARS]
AALAWA dial of RAMOAAINA [RAI]
AALAWAA alt for AALAWA dial of RAMOAAINA [RAI]
AALEIRA alt for LARO [LRO]
A'ARA alt for CHEKE HOLO [MRN]
AARAI alt for AARI [AIZ]
AARI [AIZ] lang, Ethiopia
AARIYA [AAR] lang, India
AASÁX [AAS] lang, Tanzania
/AAYE alt for //'AIYE dial of SHUA [SHG]
ABA alt for AMBA [UTP]
ABA alt for SHOR [CJS]
ABÁ alt for AVÁ-CANOEIRO [AVV]
ABAALI alt for BALI [BCN]
ABAANGI alt for GWAMHI dial of GWAMHI-WURI [BGA]
ABABDA dial of BEDAWI [BEI]
ABACA alt for ABAKA dial of ILONGOT [ILK]
ABACAMA alt for BACAMA [BAM]
ABACHA alt for BASA [BZW]
ABADEKH alt for ABADZEX dial of ADYGHE [ADY]
ABADHI alt for AWADHI [AWD]
ABADI alt for AWADHI [AWD]
ABADI alt for TSUVADI [TVD]
ABADZEG alt for ABADZEX dial of ADYGHE [ADY]
ABADZEX dial of ADYGHE [ADY]
ABAGA [ABG] lang, Papua New Guinea
ABAI dial of PUTOH [PUT]
ABAI SUNGAI [ABF] lang, Malaysia (Sabah)
ABAK dial of ANAANG [ANW]
ABAKA dial of ILONGOT [ILK]
ABAKAN alt for KPAN [KPK]
ABAKAN TATAR alt for KHAKAS [KJH]
ABAKAY SPANISH alt for DAVAWENYO ZAMBOANGUENYO dial of CHAVACANO [CBK]
ABAKNON alt for SAMA, ABAKNON [ABX]
ABAKOUM alt for KWAKUM [KWU]
ABAKPA alt for SOUTHERN EJAGHAM dial of EJAGHAM [ETU]
ABAKUM alt for KWAKUM [KWU]
ABAKWARIGA alt for HAUSA [HUA]
ABALETTI dial of YELE [YLE]
ABAM dial of GIDRA [GDR]
ABANE alt for BANIVA [BVV]
ABANGBA alt for BANGBA [BBE]
ABANLIKU alt for OBANLIKU [BZY]
ABANYAI alt for NYAI dial of KALANGA [KCK]
ABANYOM [ABM] lang, Nigeria
ABANYUM alt for ABANYOM [ABM]
ABARAMBO alt for BARAMBU [BRM]

ABASAKUR [ABW] lang, Papua New Guinea
ABATHWA alt for //XEGWI [XEG]
ABATONGA alt for TONGA dial of NDAU [NDC]
ABATSA alt for BASA [BZW]
ABAU [AAU] lang, Papua New Guinea
ABAW alt for ABO [ABB]
ABAWA dial of GUPA-ABAWA [GPA]
ABAYONGO dial of AGWAGWUNE [YAY]
ABAZA [ABQ] lang, Russia (Europe); also in Germany, Turkey (Asia), USA
ABAZIN alt for ABAZA [ABQ]
ABAZINTSY alt for ABAZA [ABQ]
ABBÉ alt for ABÉ [ABA]
ABBEY alt for ABÉ [ABA]
ABBEY-VE dial of ABE [ABA]
ABBRUZZESI dial of ROMANI, SINTE [RMO]
<ABD AL-KURI dial of SOQOTRI [SQT]
ABDAL alt for AINU [AIB]
ABDEDAL alt for GAGADU [GBU]
ABE dial of ANYIN [ANY]
ABÉ [ABA] lang, Côte d'Ivoire
ABEDJU-AZAKI dial of LUGBARA [LUG]
ÀBÉÉLÉ alt for BEELE [BXQ]
ABEFANG alt for BEFANG dial of BEFANG [BBY]
ABELAM alt for AMBULAS [ABT]
ABENAKI alt for ABNAKI, WESTERN [ABE]
ABENAQUI alt for ABNAKI, WESTERN [ABE]
ABENDAGO alt for YALI, PASS VALLEY [YAC]
ABENG dial of GARO [GRT]
A'BENG dial of GARO [GRT]
A'BENGYA alt for A'BENG dial of GARO [GRT]
ABENLEN alt for AYTA, ABENLEN [ABP]
ABEWA alt for ASU [AUM]
ABGUE dial of BIRGIT [BTF]
ABI alt for ABÉ [ABA]
ABIA alt for ANEME WAKE [ABY]
ABIDDUL alt for GAGADU [GBU]
ABIDJI [ABI] lang, Côte d'Ivoire
ABIE alt for ANEME WAKE [ABY]
ABIEM dial of DINKA, SOUTHWESTERN [DIK]
ABIGAR alt for EASTERN NUER dial of NUER [NUS]
ABIGAR dial of NUER [NUS]
ABIGIRA alt for ABISHIRA [ASH]
ABIJI alt for ABIDJI [ABI]
ABILIANG dial of DINKA, NORTHEASTERN [DIP]
ABINI dial of AGWAGWUNE [YAY]
ABINOMN [BSA] lang, Indonesia (Irian Jaya)
ABINSI alt for WANNU [JUB]
ABIQUIRA alt for ABISHIRA [ASH]
ABIRA alt for PANARE [PBH]
ABIRI alt for ABINI dial of AGWAGWUNE [YAY]
ABIRI alt for MARARIT [MGB]
ABISHIRA [ASH] lang, Peru
ABISI alt for PITI [PCN]
ABIYI alt for MARARIT [MGB]
ABKAR dial of MABA [MDE]
ABKHAZ [ABK] lang, Georgia; also in Turkey (Asia), Ukraine
ABLEG-SALEGSEG dial of KALINGA, LUBUAGAN [KNB]
ABNAKI, EASTERN [AAQ] lang, USA

ABNAKI, WESTERN [ABE] lang, Canada
ABO [ABB] lang, Cameroon
ABO alt for MULAM [MLM]
ABO dial of BOKYI [BKY]
ABÕ alt for ABON [ABO]
ABOH dial of UKWUANI-ABOH-NDONI [UKW]
ABOHI alt for AWADHI [AWD]
ABON [ABO] lang, Nigeria
ABONG alt for ABON [ABO]
ABONWA alt for ABURE [ABU]
ABOR alt for ADI [ADI]
ABOR alt for LUOBA, BOGA'ER [ADI]
ABORIGINAL ENGLISH dial of ENGLISH [ENG]
ABORLAN TAGBANWA alt for TAGBANWA [TBW]
ABORO alt for BEROM [BOM]
'ABOTEE alt for VUTE [VUT]
ABOU CHARIB dial of MARARIT [MGB]
ABOURÉ alt for ABURE [ABU]
ABRA-DE-ILOG dial of IRAYA [IRY]
ABRI alt for KOALIB [KIB]
ABRON [ABR] lang, Ghana; also in Côte d'Ivoire
ABRUZZESE dial of ITALIAN [ITN]
ABSHERON dial of TAT, MUSLIM [TTT]
ABU [ADO] lang, Papua New Guinea
ABU alt for ABO dial of BOKYI [BKY]
ABU alt for BU dial of BU [JID]
ABU SHARIB alt for ABOU CHARIB dial of MARARIT
  [MGB]
ABU SHARIN alt for ABOU CHARIB dial of MARARIT
  [MGB]
ABU SINUN dial of KANGA [KCP]
ABUA [ABN] lang, Nigeria
ABUAN alt for ABUA [ABN]
ABUI [ABZ] lang, Indonesia (Nusa Tenggara)
ABUJHMADIA alt for ABUJMARIA [ABJ]
ABUJHMARIA alt for ABUJMARIA [ABJ]
ABUJMAR MARIA alt for ABUJMARIA [ABJ]
ABUJMARIA [ABJ] lang, India
ABUJMARIYA alt for ABUJMARIA [ABJ]
ABUKEIA alt for AVOKAYA [AVU]
ABUL alt for HEIBAN [HEB]
ABULAS alt for AMBULAS [ABT]
ABULDUGU dial of BURUN [BDI]
ABULE alt for ABURE [ABU]
ABULOMA alt for OBULOM [OBU]
ABUN [KGR] lang, Indonesia (Irian Jaya)
ABUN JE dial of ABUN [KGR]
ABUN JI dial of ABUN [KGR]
ABUN TAT dial of ABUN [KGR]
ABUNG [ABL] lang, Indonesia (Sumatra)
ABURE [ABU] lang, Côte d'Ivoire
ABURLIN NEGRITO alt for AYTA, ABENLEN [ABP]
ABUYA alt for AGEER dial of DINKA, NORTH-
  EASTERN [DIP]
'ABWETEE alt for VUTE [VUT]
ABXAZO alt for ABKHAZ [ABK]
ABYSSINIAN alt for AMHARIC [AMH]
ABZHUI dial of ABKHAZ [ABK]
ACADIAN alt for FRENCH, CAJUN [FRC]
ACADIAN dial of FRENCH [FRN]
ACADIEN alt for ACADIAN dial of FRENCH [FRN]

ACAHUAYO alt for AKAWAIO [ARB]
ACANG alt for ACHANG [ACN]
ACATEC alt for KANJOBAL, WESTERN [KNJ]
ACATECO alt for KANJOBAL, WESTERN [KNJ]
ACATEPEC dial of TLAPANECO, ACATEPEC
  [TPX]
ACATLÁN MIXTECO alt for MIXTECO, PUEBLA
  SUR [MIT]
ACAWAYO alt for AKAWAIO [ARB]
ACCHAMI dial of NEPALI [NEP]
ACCRA alt for GA [GAC]
ACEH [ATJ] lang, Indonesia (Sumatra)
ACEWAIO alt for AKAWAIO [ARB]
ACGACHEMEM alt for JUANEÑO dial of LUISENO
  [LUI]
ACHAGUA [ACA] lang, Colombia
ACHANG [ACN] lang, China; also in Myanmar
ACH'ANG alt for ACHANG [ACN]
ACHANTI alt for ASANTE dial of AKAN [TWS]
ACHARIAN alt for ADZHAR dial of GEORGIAN
  [GEO]
ACHAWA alt for YAO [YAO]
ACHE alt for ACHÉ [GUQ]
ACHE alt for ASHE [AHS]
ACHÉ [GUQ] lang, Paraguay
ACHEHNESE alt for ACEH [ATJ]
ACHERO alt for BANGDALE dial of NACHERING
  [NCD]
ACHERON [ACZ] lang, Sudan
ACHÍ, CUBULCO [ACC] lang, Guatemala
ACHÍ, RABINAL [ACR] lang, Guatemala
A'CHICK dial of GARO [GRT]
A'CHIK alt for A'CHICK dial of GARO [GRT]
ACHIK dial of GARO [GRT]
ACHINESE alt for ACEH [ATJ]
ACHIPA alt for ACIPA, EASTERN [AWA]
ACHIPA alt for ACIPA, WESTERN [AWC]
ACHLO alt for IGO [AHL]
ACHOLI [ACO] lang, Uganda; also in Sudan
ACHOMAWI alt for ACHUMAWI [ACH]
ACHPAR dial of AGAW, WESTERN [QIM]
ACHTERHOEK alt for ACHTERHOEKS [ACT]
ACHTERHOEKS [ACT] lang, Netherlands
ACHUAL alt for ACHUAR-SHIWIAR [ACU]
ACHUALE alt for ACHUAR-SHIWIAR [ACU]
ACHUAR alt for ACHUAR-SHIWIAR [ACU]
ACHUARA alt for ACHUAR-SHIWIAR [ACU]
ACHUAR-SHIWIAR [ACU] lang, Peru; also in
  Ecuador
ACHUMAWI [ACH] lang, USA
ACHUNG alt for ACHANG [ACN]
ACI alt for ZAIWA [ATB]
ACI dial of APALI [ENA]
ACILOWE alt for LOMWE [NGL]
ACIPA, EASTERN [AWA] lang, Nigeria
ACIPA, WESTERN [AWC] lang, Nigeria
ACIPANCI alt for ACIPA, EASTERN [AWA]
ACIPANCI alt for ACIPA, WESTERN [AWC]
ACIRA alt for ADZERA [AZR]
ACOLI alt for ACHOLI [ACO]
ACOMA dial of KERES, WESTERN [KJQ]

ACOOLI alt for ACHOLI [ACO]
ACRA alt for GA [GAC]
ACROÁ [ACS] lang, Brazil
ACULO alt for DEG [MZW]
ACYE alt for LASHI [LSI]
AC'YE alt for LASHI [LSI]
ADA alt for KUTURMI [KHJ]
ADA dial of DANGME [DGM]
ADABE [ADB] lang, Timor Lorosae
ADAL alt for AFAR [AFR]
ADAMAWA FULANI alt for FULFULDE, ADAMAWA
    [FUB]
ADAMOROBE SIGN LANGUAGE [ADS] lang,
    Ghana
ADAN alt for ADANGBE [ADQ]
ADANG [ADN] lang, Indonesia (Nusa Tenggara)
ADANG dial of LUNDAYEH [LND]
ADANGBE [ADQ] lang, Ghana; also in Togo
ADANGME alt for DANGME [DGM]
ADANTONWI alt for ADANGBE [ADQ]
ADAP [ADP] lang, Bhutan
ADARA alt for KADARA [KAD]
ADARAWA dial of HAUSA [HUA]
ADARE alt for HARARI [HAR]
ADARINNYA alt for HARARI [HAR]
ADARU dial of CARUTANA [CRU]
ADASEN [TIU] lang, Philippines
ADASEN ITNEG alt for ADASEN [TIU]
ADDASEN alt for ADASEN [TIU]
ADDASEN TINGUIAN alt for ADASEN [TIU]
ADDO alt for EDO [EDO]
ADE BHASHA alt for ARE [AAG]
ADEA alt for HADIYYA [HDY]
ADEEYAH alt for BUBE [BVB]
ADEKA alt for MADAKA dial of BAUCHI [BSF]
ADELE [ADE] lang, Togo; also in Ghana
<ADEN dial of ARABIC, JUDEO-YEMENI [JYE]
ADENI dial of ARABIC, TAIZZI-ADENI SPOKEN
    [ACQ]
ADERAWA dial of HAUSA [HUA]
ADERE alt for DZODINKA [ADD]
ADERE alt for HARARI [HAR]
ADERINYA alt for HARARI [HAR]
ADEWADA dial of MARIA [MRR]
ADGAWAN dial of MANOBO, AGUSAN [MSM]
A-DHAM alt for ADHAM dial of RADE [RAD]
ADHAM dial of RADE [RAD]
ADHIANG alt for TUIC dial of DINKA,
    SOUTHWESTERN [DIK]
ADHO-ADHOM alt for DJANGUN [DJF]
ADHOLA [ADH] lang, Uganda
ADI [ADI] lang, India; also in China
ADI alt for LUOBA, BOGA'ER [ADI]
ADI dial of KOWIAI [KWH]
ADI DRAVIDA dial of TAMIL [TCV]
ADIANGOK alt for BISOO dial of BAKOKO [BKH]
ADI-BOKAR alt for LUOBA, BOGA'ER [ADI]
ADIBOM dial of ODUAL [ODU]
ADIE dial of BAKOKO [BKH]
ADIHUP alt for HATAM [HAD]
ADIHUP dial of HATAM [HAD]

ADIJA alt for BUBE [BVB]
ADIKIMMU SUKUR alt for SUKUR [SUK]
ADILABAD alt for NIRMAL dial of GONDI,
    SOUTHERN [GGO]
ADIM dial of AGWAGWUNE [YAY]
ADIOUKROU [ADJ] lang, Côte d'Ivoire
ADIRI alt for DZODINKA [ADD]
ADIVASI ORIYA dial of ORIYA, ADIVASI [ORT]
ADIVASI WAGDI dial of WAGDI [WBR]
ADIWASI GIRASIA alt for GARASIA, ADIWASI
    [GAS]
ADIWASI GUJARATI alt for GARASIA, ADIWASI
    [GAS]
ADIWASI ORIYA alt for ORIYA, ADIVASI [ORT]
ADIYA alt for HADIYYA [HDY]
ADIYA alt for RAVULA [YEA]
ADIYAN alt for RAVULA [YEA]
ADIYE alt for HADIYYA [HDY]
ADJA alt for AJA [AJA]
ADJA alt for AJA-GBE [AJG]
ADJABDURAH dial of NARUNGGA [NNR]
ADJAHDURAH alt for ADJABDURAH dial of
    NARUNGGA [NNR]
ADJER alt for AZER dial of SONINKE [SNN]
ADJIGA alt for AJIGU dial of AVOKAYA [AVU]
ADJIO alt for TAJIO [TDJ]
ADJORA alt for ABU [ADO]
ADJORIA alt for ABU [ADO]
ADJUKRU alt for ADIOUKROU [ADJ]
ADJUMANI dial of MADI [MHI]
ADJUMBA alt for AJUMBA dial of MYENE [MYE]
ADKIBBA alt for MURLE [MUR]
ADKURI dial of HALBI [HLB]
ADLAI alt for ROGLAI, NORTHERN [ROG]
AD'N'AMADANA alt for ADYNYAMATHANHA
    [ADT]
ADO dial of KAILI, LEDO [LEW]
ADOMA dial of CLELA [DRI]
ADONA alt for RER BARE [RER]
ADONARA [ADA] lang, Indonesia (Nusa Tenggara)
ADONG alt for IDUN [LDB]
ADONG alt for RUNGU dial of MAMBWE-LUNGU
    [MGR]
ADOR alt for CIEC dial of DINKA, SOUTH CENTRAL
    [DIB]
ADORA alt for AIRORAN [AIR]
ADOUMA alt for DUMA [DMA]
ADOWEN alt for DJAUAN [DJN]
ADOYO dial of ANUAK [ANU]
ADSAWA alt for YAO [YAO]
ADSOA alt for YAO [YAO]
ADU dial of TABARU [TBY]
ADUGE [ADU] lang, Nigeria
ADULU alt for ATURU [AUP]
ADUMA alt for DUMA [DMA]
ADUN dial of MBEMBE, CROSS RIVER [MFN]
ADYAKTYE alt for KAKANDA [KKA]
ADYGEI alt for ADYGHE [ADY]
ADYGEY alt for ADYGHE [ADY]
ADYGHE [ADY] lang, Russia (Europe); also in
    Australia, Egypt, France, Germany, Iraq, Israel,

Jordan, Macedonia, Netherlands, Syria, Turkey (Asia), USA
ADYNYAMATHANHA [ADT] lang, Australia
ADYOUKROU alt for ADIOUKROU [ADJ]
ADYUKRU alt for ADIOUKROU [ADJ]
ADYUMBA alt for AJUMBA dial of MYENE [MYE]
ADZERA [AZR] lang, Papua New Guinea
ADZERMA alt for ZARMA [DJE]
ADZERMA alt for ZARMACI [DJE]
ADZHAR dial of GEORGIAN [GEO]
ADZU BALAKA alt for ASSAKA dial of CAKA [CKX]
ADZU BATANGA alt for BATANGA dial of CAKA [CKX]
A'E alt for REMPI [RMP]
AEJAUROH alt for SAWI [SAW]
AEKA dial of BINANDERE [BHG]
AEKA dial of OROKAIVA [ORK]
AEKE alt for HAEKE [AEK]
'AEKE alt for HAEKE [AEK]
AEKYOM [AWI] lang, Papua New Guinea
AER [AEQ] lang, Pakistan
AERORAN alt for AIRORAN [AIR]
AETA NEGRITO alt for SAMBAL, BOTOLAN [SBL]
AFA alt for PA'A [AFA]
AFA dial of ARIGIDI [AKK]
AFADA alt for AFADE [AAL]
AFADE [AAL] lang, Nigeria; also in Cameroon
AFADEH alt for AFADE [AAL]
AFAKANI alt for DEFAKA [AFN]
AFAN MAO alt for KWAMA [KMQ]
AFAN OROMO alt for OROMO, BORANA-ARSI-GUJI [GAX]
AFANCI alt for PA'A [AFA]
AFANGO alt for BEROM [BOM]
AFAO alt for ELOYI [AFO]
AFAR [AFR] lang, Ethiopia; also in Djibouti, Eritrea
<AFAR AF alt for AFAR [AFR]
AFARAF alt for AFAR [AFR]
AF-ASHRAAF dial of SOMALI [SOM]
AFATIME alt for AVATIME [AVA]
AFAWA alt for PA'A [AFA]
AF-BAJUUN alt for BAJUNI dial of SWAHILI [SWA]
AF-BOON alt for BOON [BNL]
AF-CHIMWIINI alt for MWINI dial of SWAHILI [SWA]
AF-DABARRE alt for DABARRE [DBR]
AFENMAI alt for YEKHEE [ETS]
AFERIKE alt for AFRIKE dial of PUTUKWAM [AFE]
AFFA alt for AFA dial of ARIGIDI [AKK]
AFFADE alt for AFADE [AAL]
AFFINIAM dial of BANDIAL [BQJ]
AFFITTI alt for AFITTI [AFT]
AF-GARRE alt for GARRE [GEX]
AFGHAN alt for PASHTO, NORTHERN [PBU]
AFGHAN alt for PASHTO, SOUTHERN [PBT]
AFGHAN FARSI alt for DARI dial of FARSI, EASTERN [PRS]
AFGHANA-YI NASFURUSH alt for PARYA [PAQ]
AFGHANA-YI SIYARUI alt for PARYA [PAQ]
AF-HELLEDI dial of MAAY [QMA]
AFIKPO dial of IGBO [IGR]
AF-IROOLE alt for IROOLE dial of DABARRE [DBR]

AFITTI [AFT] lang, Sudan
AFIZARE alt for IZERE [FIZ]
AFIZAREK alt for IZERE [FIZ]
AF-JIIDDU alt for JIIDDU [JII]
AFKABIYE alt for GUDUF [GDF]
AFKABIYE alt for GUDUF-GAVA [GDF]
AF-KARETI alt for KOMSO [KXC]
AF-MAAY alt for MAAY [QMA]
AF-MAAY TIRI alt for MAAY [QMA]
AF-MAXAAD TIRI alt for SOMALI [SOM]
AF-MAY alt for MAAY [QMA]
AF-MAYMAY alt for MAAY [QMA]
AFO alt for BAFAW dial of BAFAW-BALONG [BWT]
AFO alt for ELOYI [AFO]
AFORE dial of MANAGALASI [MCQ]
AFORO alt for KALAM [KMH]
AFRIKAANS [AFK] lang, South Africa; also in Australia, Botswana, Canada, Lesotho, Malawi, Namibia, New Zealand, Zambia, Zimbabwe
AFRIKE dial of PUTUKWAM [AFE]
AFRO-GUYANESE CREOLE dial of GUYANESE CREOLE ENGLISH [GYN]
AFRO-SEMINOL CRIOLLO alt for AFRO-SEMINOLE CREOLE [AFS]
AFRO-SEMINOLE alt for AFRO-SEMINOLE CREOLE [AFS]
AFRO-SEMINOLE CREOLE [AFS] lang, USA; also in Mexico
AFSAR alt for AFSHARI dial of AZERBAIJANI, SOUTH [AZB]
AFSHAR alt for AFSHARI dial of AZERBAIJANI, SOUTH [AZB]
AFSHARI dial of AZERBAIJANI, SOUTH [AZB]
AF-SOOMAALI alt for SOMALI [SOM]
AF-TUNNI alt for TUNNI [TQQ]
AFU alt for ELOYI [AFO]
AFUGHE alt for BUFE dial of BAFUT [BFD]
AFUNATAM alt for NTA dial of NDE-NSELE-NTA [NDD]
AFUNGWA alt for FUNGWA [ULA]
AFUSARE alt for IZERE [FIZ]
AGA alt for KANURI, CENTRAL [KPH]
AGA dial of BURIAT, CHINA [BXU]
AGA dial of BURIAT, MONGOLIA [BXM]
AGA BEREHO alt for BARIJI [BJC]
AGACHEMEM alt for JUANEÑO dial of LUISENO [LUI]
AGADEZ alt for AIR dial of TAMAJEQ, TAYART [THZ]
AGALA alt for FEMBE [AGL]
AGAM dial of MINANGKABAU [MPU]
AGAMORU alt for AJIGU dial of AVOKAYA [AVU]
AGAR alt for DINKA, SOUTH CENTRAL [DIB]
AGAR dial of DINKA, SOUTH CENTRAL [DIB]
AGARABE alt for AGARABI [AGD]
AGARABI [AGD] lang, Papua New Guinea
AGARAR alt for ANGAL HENENG [AKH]
AGARI alt for GBIRI dial of GBIRI-NIRAGU [GRH]
AGARI alt for GURA dial of LAME [BMA]
AGARIYA [AGI] lang, India
AGATU [AGC] lang, Nigeria

AGAU alt for AWNGI [AWN]
AGAU alt for NOGAU dial of JUHOAN [KTZ]
AGAUNSHE dial of TSIKIMBA [KDL]
AGAUSHI alt for TSIKIMBA [KDL]
AGAVOTAGUERRA [AVO] lang, Brazil
AGAVOTOKUENG alt for AGAVOTAGUERRA
    [AVO]
AGAVOTOQUENG alt for AGAVOTAGUERRA
    [AVO]
AGAW alt for AWNGI [AWN]
AGAW, WESTERN [QIM] lang, Ethiopia; also in
    Eritrea
AGAWINYA alt for XAMTANGA [XAN]
AGBARAGBA alt for EFUTOP [OFU]
AGBARHO dial of URHOBO [URH]
AGBAWI alt for KWANGE dial of GBARI [GBY]
AGBIRI alt for GBIRI dial of GBIRI-NIRAGU [GRH]
AGBIRI alt for GURA dial of LAME [BMA]
AGBO alt for LEGBO [AGB]
AGE alt for ESIMBI [AGS]
AGEER dial of DINKA, NORTHEASTERN [DIP]
AGEIR alt for AGEER dial of DINKA, NORTH-
    EASTERN [DIP]
AGER alt for AGEER dial of DINKA, NORTH-
    EASTERN [DIP]
AGERE alt for BEGBERE-EJAR [BQV]
AGERLEP alt for AIKLEP [MWG]
AGEW alt for AWNGI [AWN]
AGHARIA alt for AGARIYA [AGI]
AGHEM [AGQ] lang, Cameroon
AGHU [AHH] lang, Indonesia (Irian Jaya)
AGHU THARNGGALU [GGR] lang, Australia
AGHUL [AGX] lang, Russia (Europe); also in
    Azerbaijan
AGHULSHUY alt for AGHUL [AGX]
AGI [AIF] lang, Papua New Guinea
AGI dial of MORU [MGD]
AGIBA alt for MURLE [MUR]
AGIRYAMA alt for GIRYAMA [NYF]
AGIYAN alt for AGTA, CAMARINES NORTE [ABD]
AGNAGAN alt for ANYANGA [AYG]
AGNANG alt for DENYA [ANV]
AGNI alt for ANYIN [ANY]
AGO alt for IGO [AHL]
AGOB [KIT] lang, Papua New Guinea
AGOB dial of AGOB [KIT]
AGOI [IBM] lang, Nigeria
AGOLOK alt for KAGORO dial of TYAP [KCG]
AGOMA alt for KAGOMA [KDM]
AGOMES alt for HERMIT [LLF]
AGONA dial of AKAN [TWS]
AGORIA alt for AGARIYA [AGI]
AGOTIME alt for ADANGBE [ADQ]
AGOUISIRI alt for ABISHIRA [ASH]
AGOW alt for AWNGI [AWN]
AGRAB dial of BIRGIT [BTF]
AGTA, ALABAT ISLAND [DUL] lang, Philippines
AGTA, CAMARINES NORTE [ABD] lang, Philippines
AGTA, CASIGURAN DUMAGAT [DGC] lang,
    Philippines
AGTA, CENTRAL CAGAYAN [AGT] lang, Philippines

AGTA, DICAMAY [DUY] lang, Philippines
AGTA, DUPANINAN [DUO] lang, Philippines
AGTA, ISAROG [AGK] lang, Philippines
AGTA, MT. IRAYA [ATL] lang, Philippines
AGTA, MT. IRIGA [AGZ] lang, Philippines
AGTA, REMONTADO [AGV] lang, Philippines
AGTA, UMIRAY DUMAGET [DUE] lang, Philippines
AGTA, VILLA VICIOSA [DYG] lang, Philippines
AGU dial of RAWANG [RAW]
AGUA alt for OMAGUA [OMG]
AGUACATEC alt for AGUACATECO [AGU]
AGUACATECO [AGU] lang, Guatemala
AGUAJUN alt for AGUARUNA [AGR]
AGUALINDA GUAHIBO alt for MACAGUÁN [MBN]
AGUANO [AGA] lang, Peru
AGUANU alt for AGUANO [AGA]
AGUARICO dial of COFAN [CON]
AGUARUNA [AGR] lang, Peru
AGUAS BLANCAS alt for TUNEBO, WESTERN
    [TNB]
AGUFI dial of FAGANI [FAF]
AGUL alt for AGHUL [AGX]
AGUL dial of AGHUL [AGX]
AGULIS dial of ARMENIAN [ARM]
AGULY alt for AGHUL [AGX]
AGUNA [AUG] lang, Benin
AGUNACO alt for AGUNA [AUG]
AGUOK dial of DINKA, SOUTHWESTERN [DIK]
AGURO alt for KAGORO dial of TYAP [KCG]
AGUSAN alt for MANOBO, AGUSAN [MSM]
AGUTAYNEN [AGN] lang, Philippines
AGUTAYNO alt for AGUTAYNEN [AGN]
AGUTAYNON alt for AGUTAYNEN [AGN]
AGVALI-RICHAGANIK-TSUMADA-URUKH alt
    for GAKVARI dial of CHAMALAL [CJI]
AGWAGUNA alt for AGWAGWUNE [YAY]
AGWAGWUNE [YAY] lang, Nigeria
AGWAGWUNE dial of AGWAGWUNE [YAY]
AGWAMIN [AWG] lang, Australia
AGWARA KAMBARI alt for CISHINGINI [ASG]
AGWATASHI dial of ALAGO [ALA]
AGWOK alt for AGUOK dial of DINKA, SOUTH-
    WESTERN [DIK]
AGWOLOK alt for KAGORO dial of TYAP [KCG]
AGWOT alt for KAGORO dial of TYAP [KCG]
AHAAN alt for ÀHÀN [AHN]
AHAFO dial of AKAN [TWS]
AHAGGAREN alt for HOGGAR dial of TAMAHAQ,
    TAHAGGART [THV]
AHAHNELIN alt for GROS VENTRE [ATS]
AHAMB alt for AXAMB [AHB]
ÀHÀN [AHN] lang, Nigeria
AHANTA [AHA] lang, Ghana
AHASA alt for AKASSA dial of IJO, SOUTHEAST
    [IJO]
AHCHAN alt for ACHANG [ACN]
AHE [AHE] lang, Indonesia (Kalimantan)
AHE alt for GROS VENTRE [ATS]
AHE DAYAK alt for AHE [AHE]
AHEAVE dial of KEURU [QQK]
AHEIMA dial of NGILE [MAS]

AHERI dial of GONDI, SOUTHERN [GGO]
AHEU [THM] lang, Thailand; also in Laos
AHI alt for AXI dial of YI, SOUTHEASTERN [YIE]
AHIRANI [AHR] lang, India
AHIRI alt for AHIRANI [AHR]
AHIRI dial of BHILI [BHB]
AHIZI alt for AIZI, APROUMU [AHP]
AHIZI alt for AIZI, MOBUMRIN [AHM]
AHIZI alt for AIZI, TIAGBAMRIN [AHI]
AHKA alt for AKHA [AKA]
AHKKIL alt for SAAMI, AKKALA [SIA]
AHLÕ alt for IGO [AHL]
AHLON alt for IGO [AHL]
AHLON-BOGO alt for IGO [AHL]
A-HMAO alt for HMONG, NORTHEASTERN DIAN
[HMD]
AHMEDABAD GAMADIA alt for GAMADIA dial of
GUJARATI [GJR]
AHO alt for ELOYI [AFO]
AHOLIO alt for SHOLIO dial of TYAP [KCG]
AHOM [AHO] lang, India
AHONLAN alt for IGO [AHL]
AHTENA [AHT] lang, USA
AHTIAGO alt for BOBOT [BTY]
AHTNA alt for AHTENA [AHT]
AHUAJUN alt for AGUARUNA [AGR]
AHUATEMPAN POPOLOCA alt for POPOLOCA,
SANTA INÉS AHUATEMPAN [PCA]
AHUS alt for ANDRA-HUS [ANX]
AHUWA alt for ABAZA [ABQ]
AHVAZ alt for AHWAZ dial of MANDAIC [MID]
AHWAZ dial of MANDAIC [MID]
A'I alt for COFÁN [CON]
AI NAN alt for MAONAN [MMD]
AI SUI alt for SUI [SWI]
AI'ALU dial of MOLIMA [MOX]
AIBONDENI dial of WANDAMEN [WAD]
AICA alt for JAUARI dial of YANOMAMI [WCA]
AI-CHAM [AIH] lang, China
AIDUMA alt for KOWIAI [KWH]
//AI//E alt for NARO [NHR]
//AI//EN alt for NARO [NHR]
AIEWOMBA dial of AMPEELI-WOJOKESO [APZ]
AIGA alt for AEKA dial of BINANDERE [BHG]
AIGANG alt for KEIGA [KEC]
AIGANG alt for KEIGA dial of KEIGA [KEC]
AIGON dial of PSOHOH [BCL]
AIGUAVIVAN alt for NORTHWESTERN
CATALAN dial of CATALAN-VALENCIAN-
BALEAR [CLN]
AIKANÃ alt for TUBARÃO [TBA]
AIKE alt for AKE [AIK]
AIKI alt for RUNGA [ROU]
AIKLEP [MWG] lang, Papua New Guinea
AIKOA dial of MORI ATAS [MZQ]
AIKOLI alt for KAFOA [KPU]
AIKU [MZF] lang, Papua New Guinea
AIKWAKAI alt for SIKARITAI [TTY]
//AIKWE alt for NARO [NHR]
/AIKWE alt for NARO [NHR]
AILI GAILI alt for HINDUSTANI, CARIBBEAN [HNS]

AILI GAILI alt for SARNAMI HINDUSTANI dial of
HINDUSTANI, CARIBBEAN [HNS]
AIMAQ [AIQ] lang, Afghanistan; also in Iran, Tajikistan
AIMARA dial of KUNAMA [KUM]
AIMELE [AIL] lang, Papua New Guinea
AIMOL [AIM] lang, India
AIMOLI dial of ADANG [ADN]
AINBAI [AIC] lang, Papua New Guinea
AINE KURUBA dial of KANNADA [KJV]
AINI alt for AINU [AIB]
AINI alt for AKHA [AKA]
AINU [AIB] lang, China
AINU [AIN] lang, Japan; also in Russia (Asia)
AINU ITAK alt for AINU [AIN]
AIOME [AKI] lang, Papua New Guinea
AION [AEW] lang, Papua New Guinea
AIPKI alt for KIMKI [SBT]
AIR dial of TAMAJEQ, TAYART [THZ]
AIR MATA dial of MALAY, KUPANG [MKN]
AIR TABUN alt for KETUNGAU dial of IBAN [IBA]
AIRD HILLS dial of KIBIRI [PRM]
AIRIMAN alt for NGARINMAN [NBJ]
AIRMADIDI dial of TONSEA [TXS]
AIRMATI alt for KWERBA [KWE]
AIRORAN [AIR] lang, Indonesia (Irian Jaya)
AIRYM dial of AZERBAIJANI, NORTH [AZE]
/AIS alt for /XAISE dial of SHUA [SHG]
//AISAN alt for NARO [NHR]
AISO alt for KAIS [KZM]
AISORSKI alt for ASSYRIAN NEO-ARAMAIC [AII]
AISSUARI alt for AIZUARE dial of OMAGUA [OMG]
AITA alt for ROTOKAS [ROO]
AITON [AIO] lang, India
AITONIA alt for AITON [AIO]
AITUTAKI dial of RAROTONGAN [RRT]
AIWANAT dial of YUPIK, CENTRAL SIBERIAN [ESS]
AIWIN alt for AEKYOM [AWI]
AIYANGAR dial of TAMIL [TCV]
AIYAR dial of TAMIL [TCV]
//'AIYE dial of SHUA [SHG]
AIZI, APROUMU [AHP] lang, Côte d'Ivoire
AIZI, MOBUMRIN [AHM] lang, Côte d'Ivoire
AIZI, TIAGBAMRIN [AHI] lang, Côte d'Ivoire
AIZUARE dial of OMAGUA [OMG]
AÏWO alt for AYIWO [NFL]
AJA [AJA] lang, Sudan
AJA alt for AJA-GBE [AJG]
AJA alt for AJAWA [AJW]
AJACHEMA alt for JUANEÑO dial of LUISENO [LUI]
AJACHEMEM alt for JUANEÑO dial of LUISENO
[LUI]
AJA-GBE [AJG] lang, Benin; also in Togo
AJAGUA alt for ACHAGUA [ACA]
AJAK alt for CIEC dial of DINKA, SOUTH CENTRAL
[DIB]
AJAK alt for PALIET dial of DINKA, SOUTH-
WESTERN [DIK]
AJAM dial of ASMAT, CENTRAL [AST]
AJAMARU alt for MAI BRAT [AYZ]
AJANCI alt for AJAWA [AJW]
AJANJI alt for JANJI [JNI]

AJAU alt for AWYU, NOHON [AWJ]
AJAWA [AJW] lang, Nigeria
AJAWA alt for YAO [YAO]
AJE dial of ARIGIDI [AKK]
AJEKA dial of OROKAIVA [ORK]
AJER alt for AZER dial of SONINKE [SNN]
AJI alt for ZAIWA [ATB]
AJI dial of MALAY [MLI]
AJIBBA alt for MURLE [MUR]
AJIĚ [AJI] lang, New Caledonia
AJIGU dial of AVOKAYA [AVU]
AJIRI OF HAZARA dial of GUJARI [GJU]
AJIW dial of MPUR [AKC]
AJJA alt for AJA [AJA]
AJJER alt for HOGGAR dial of TAMAHAQ,
    TAHAGGART [THV]
<AJMAAN alt for CENTRAL NAJDI dial of ARABIC,
    NAJDI SPOKEN [ARS]
'AJNABI alt for LINGUA FRANCA [PML]
AJO alt for MAJANG [MPE]
AJOKOOT alt for MARGU [MHG]
AJOMANG alt for TALODI [TLO]
AJONG DIT alt for ABIEM dial of DINKA, SOUTH-
    WESTERN [DIK]
AJONG THI alt for ABIEM dial of DINKA, SOUTH-
    WESTERN [DIK]
AJUGU alt for AJIGU dial of AVOKAYA [AVU]
AJUH dial of LAWANGAN [LBX]
AJUJURE alt for ARÁRA, PARÁ [AAP]
AJUKRU alt for ADIOUKROU [ADJ]
AJUMBA dial of MYENE [MYE]
AJURAN dial of GARREH-AJURAN [GGH]
AJURE alt for KAJURU dial of KADARA [KAD]
AJURÚ alt for WAYORÓ [WYR]
AJUURAAN alt for AJURAN dial of GARREH-
    AJURAN [GGH]
AJYÉNINKA alt for AJYÍNINKA APURUCAYALI [CPC]
AJYÍNINKA APURUCAYALI [CPC] lang, Peru
AK [AKQ] lang, Papua New Guinea
AK alt for WHITE NOGAI dial of NOGAI [NOG]
AKA [SOH] lang, Sudan
AKA alt for AKHA [AKA]
AKA alt for ASOA [ASV]
AKA alt for HRUSO [HRU]
AKA alt for YAKA [AXK]
AK'A alt for AKHA [AKA]
AKA LEL dial of NISI [DAP]
AKAB alt for KALLAHAN, KAYAPA [KAK]
AKABAFA dial of MANAGALASI [MCQ]
AKA-BEA [ACE] lang, India
AKA-BEADA alt for AKA-BEA [ACE]
AKA-BO [AKM] lang, India
AKA-CARI [ACI] lang, India
AKA-JERU [AKJ] lang, India
AKAJO alt for EKAJUK [EKA]
AKAJUK alt for EKAJUK [EKA]
AKA-KEDE [AKX] lang, India
AKA-KOL [AKY] lang, India
AKA-KORA [ACK] lang, India
AKALAK alt for KATLA [KCR]
AKAN [TWS] lang, Ghana

AKANDA alt for KAKANDA [KKA]
AKANDE alt for KULERE [KUL]
AKANDI alt for KULERE [KUL]
AKANI dial of NANAI [GLD]
AKANY KOK alt for ABIEM dial of DINKA, SOUTH-
    WESTERN [DIK]
AKAPLASS alt for ABURE [ABU]
AKARA alt for AKERRE dial of ARRARNTA,
    WESTERN [ARE]
AKARA alt for TOPOSA [TOQ]
AKAR-BALE [ACL] lang, India
AKASELE alt for AKASELEM [AKS]
AKASELEM [AKS] lang, Togo
AKASSA dial of IJO, SOUTHEAST [IJO]
AKAWAI alt for AKAWAIO [ARB]
AKAWAIO [ARB] lang, Guyana; also in Brazil,
    Venezuela
AKAYON alt for KIONG [KKM]
AKE [AIK] lang, Nigeria
AKEBOU [KEU] lang, Togo
AKEBU alt for AKEBOU [KEU]
AKEI [TSR] lang, Vanuatu
AKELE alt for KÉLÉ [KEB]
AKELE alt for KILI [KEB]
AKER alt for ALIAP dial of DINKA, SOUTH
    CENTRAL [DIB]
AKERN JOK alt for ABIEM dial of DINKA, SOUTH-
    WESTERN [DIK]
AKERRE dial of ARRARNTA, WESTERN [ARE]
AKEWARA alt for SURUÍ DO PARÁ [MDZ]
AKEWERE alt for SURUÍ DO PARÁ [MDZ]
AKHA [AKA] lang, Myanmar; also in China, Laos,
    Thailand, Viet Nam
'AKHOE [AKE] lang, Namibia; also in Angola
AKHTY dial of LEZGI [LEZ]
AKHVAKH [AKV] lang, Russia (Europe)
AKI alt for BANGGAI [BGZ]
AKI alt for NGORO dial of TUKI [BAG]
AKI dial of APALI [ENA]
AKIAPMIN alt for SUARMIN [SEO]
"AKIDO" pejorative alt for TOLAKI [LBW]
AKIE alt for ATTIÉ [ATI]
AKIEK alt for OKIEK [OKI]
AKIMBA alt for TSIKIMBA [KDL]
AKIMEL O'ODHAM dial of OODHAM [PAP]
AKIT dial of KERINCI [KVR]
AKIUM alt for AEKYOM [AWI]
AKIUM-PARE alt for PARE [PPT]
AKIURU alt for LAMOGAI [LMG]
AKJUET alt for PALIOUPINY dial of DINKA, SOUTH-
    WESTERN [DIK]
AKKHUSHA alt for AKUSHA dial of DARGWA
    [DAR]
AKKIN dial of CHECHEN [CJC]
AKLAN alt for AKLANON [AKL]
AKLANO alt for AKLANON [AKL]
AKLANON [AKL] lang, Philippines
AKLANON-BISAYAN alt for AKLANON [AKL]
AKN dial of ARMENIAN [ARM]
AKO alt for BORORRO dial of FULFULDE, KANO-
    KATSINA-BORORRO [FUV]

AKO alt for BORORRO dial of FULFULDE, NIGERIAN [FUV]
AKO dial of AKHA [AKA]
AKO dial of BADA [BHZ]
AKO dial of EKPEYE [EKP]
AKOERIO alt for AKURIO [AKO]
AKOINKAKE alt for AKOYE [MIW]
AKOIYANG alt for KIONG [KKM]
AKOKOLEMU alt for KUMAM [KDI]
AKOLET [AKT] lang, Papua New Guinea
AKOLI alt for ACHOLI [ACO]
AKONO dial of YORUBA [YOR]
AKONTO alt for MBEMBE, TIGON [NZA]
AKOON alt for ABILIANG dial of DINKA, NORTH-EASTERN [DIP]
AKOOSE [BSS] lang, Cameroon
AKOSI alt for AKOOSE [BSS]
AKOTI alt for KOTI [EKO]
AKOYE [MIW] lang, Papua New Guinea
AKOYI alt for AKOYE [MIW]
AKPA [AKF] lang, Nigeria
AKPAFU dial of SIWU [AKP]
AKPAFU-LOLOBI alt for SIWU [AKP]
AKPANZHI alt for DONGA dial of JUKUN TAKUM [JBU]
AKPANZHI alt for DONGA dial of KPAN [KPK]
AKPARABONG alt for EKPARABONG dial of NDOE [NBB]
AKPE alt for ANII [BLO]
AKPES [IBE] lang, Nigeria
AKPES alt for AKUNNU dial of AKPES [IBE]
AKPESE alt for KPELLE, GUINEA [GKP]
AKPET alt for UKPET dial of UKPET-EHOM [AKD]
AKPET-EHOM alt for UKPET-EHOM [AKD]
AKPO-MGBU-TOLU dial of IKWERE [IKW]
AKPOSO [KPO] lang, Togo; also in Ghana
AKPOSSO alt for AKPOSO [KPO]
AKPOTO alt for IDOMA CENTRAL dial of IDOMA [IDO]
AKPWAKUM alt for KWAKUM [KWU]
AKRUKAY [AFI] lang, Papua New Guinea
AKSANA alt for AKSANÁS dial of QAWASQAR [ALC]
AKSANÁS dial of QAWASQAR [ALC]
AKU alt for LI'O [LJL]
AKU alt for MODELE dial of BEFANG [BBY]
AKU dial of KRIO [KRI]
AKUAPEM dial of AKAN [TWS]
AKUAPIM alt for AKUAPEM dial of AKAN [TWS]
AKUÊN alt for XAVÁNTE [XAV]
AKUKU dial of OKPE-IDESA-AKUKU [OKP]
AKULE alt for POLI dial of YENDANG [YEN]
AKULIYO alt for AKURIO [AKO]
AKUM [AKU] lang, Cameroon; also in Nigeria
AKUM alt for BAGANGU dial of NGEMBA [NGE]
AKUM alt for KUMAM [KDI]
"AKUNAKUNA" pejorative alt for AGWAGWUNE [YAY]
AKUNNU dial of AKPES [IBE]
AKURAKURA alt for AGWAGWUNE [YAY]
AKURI alt for AKURIO [AKO]

AKURIJO alt for AKURIO [AKO]
AKURIO [AKO] lang, Suriname
AKURIYO alt for AKURIO [AKO]
AKURMI alt for KURAMA [KRH]
AKURUMI alt for KURAMA [KRH]
AKUSHA dial of DARGWA [DAR]
AKUWAGEL alt for BELI [BEY]
AKWA [AKW] lang, Congo
AKWA dial of PONGU [PON]
AKWA'ALA alt for PAIPAI [PPI]
AKWANG alt for PALIOUPINY dial of DINKA, SOUTHWESTERN [DIK]
AKWANTO alt for MBEMBE, TIGON [NZA]
AKWAPEM TWI alt for AKUAPEM dial of AKAN [TWS]
AKWAPI alt for AKUAPEM dial of AKAN [TWS]
AKWAYA alt for ASURINÍ [ASU]
AKWAYA MOTOM alt for OLITI dial of ICEVE-MACI [BEC]
AKWEN alt for XAVÁNTE [XAV]
AKWETO alt for NSARI [ASJ]
AKWEYA alt for AKPA [AKF]
AKWUN alt for NORTH KOMBIO dial of KOMBIO [KOK]
AKYAB alt for ROHINGA dial of CHITTAGONIAN [CIT]
AKYE alt for AKE [AIK]
AKYE alt for ATTIÉ [ATI]
AKYEM BOSOME dial of AKAN [TWS]
AL ARABIYA alt for ARABIC, STANDARD [ABV]
AL FUS-HA alt for ARABIC, STANDARD [ABV]
ALA alt for ASHE [AHS]
ALA alt for WALI [WLX]
A-LA CONG alt for ALAKONG dial of BAHNAR [BDQ]
'ALA'ALA alt for NARA [NRZ]
ALABA [ALB] lang, Ethiopia
ALABAMA [AKZ] lang, USA
ALABAT ISLAND DUMAGAT alt for AGTA, ALABAT ISLAND [DUL]
ALACALUF alt for QAWASQAR [ALC]
ALACALUFE alt for QAWASQAR [ALC]
ALACATLATZALA MIXTEC alt for MIXTECO, ALACATLATZALA [MIM]
ALADA alt for GUN-GBE [GUW]
ALADA dial of GUN-GBE [GUW]
ALADA-GBE alt for ALADA dial of GUN-GBE [GUW]
ALADA-GBE alt for GUN-GBE [GUW]
ALAG-BAKO dial of IRAYA [IRY]
ALAGO [ALA] lang, Nigeria
ALAGWA alt for WASI [WBJ]
ALAGWASE alt for WASI [WBJ]
ALAI alt for AMAL [AAD]
ALAK [ALK] lang, Laos
ALAKAMAN dial of ABUI [ABZ]
ALAKAMAT alt for HUAULU [HUD]
ALAKI alt for LEKI dial of LURI [LRI]
ALAKONG dial of BAHNAR [BDQ]
ALALAO alt for PADOE [PDO]
ALAM alt for MALA [PED]

ALAMA alt for QUICHUA, PASTAZÁ, NORTHERN [QLB]
ALAMATU alt for MBUTU dial of NGEMBA [NGE]
ALAMBLAK [AMP] lang, Papua New Guinea
ALAND ISLANDS SWEDISH dial of SWEDISH [SWD]
ALANGAN [ALJ] lang, Philippines
ALANGO dial of SIANE [SNP]
ALANGUA dial of ANYIN [ANY]
ALANTE alt for BALANTA-GANJA [BJT]
ALANTE alt for BALANTA-KENTOHE [BLE]
ALAR dial of BURIAT, RUSSIA [MNB]
ALAS dial of BATAK ALAS-KLUET [BTZ]
ALASAI dial of PASHAYI, NORTHWEST [GLH]
ALAS-KLUET BATAK alt for BATAK ALAS-KLUET [BTZ]
ALATENING dial of NGEMBA [NGE]
ALATESU dial of NAMBIKUARA, SOUTHERN [NAB]
ALATIL [ALX] lang, Papua New Guinea
ALATINING alt for ALATENING dial of NGEMBA [NGE]
ALAUAGAT alt for BRAGAT [AOF]
ALAWA [ALH] lang, Australia
ALAWA alt for AALAWA dial of RAMOAAINA [RAI]
ALAWA alt for WASI [WBJ]
ALBANIAN, ARBËRESHË [AAE] lang, Italy
ALBANIAN, ARVANITIKA [AAT] lang, Greece
ALBANIAN, GHEG [ALS] lang, Yugoslavia; also in Albania, Bulgaria, Macedonia, Romania, Slovenia, USA
ALBANIAN, TOSK [ALN] lang, Albania; also in Belgium, Canada, Egypt, Germany, Sweden, Turkey (Europe), Ukraine, USA
ALBANY RIVER OJIBWA dial of OJIBWA, NORTH-WESTERN [OJB]
ALBARRADAS ZAPOTEC alt for ZAPOTECO, ALBARRADAS [ZAS]
ALBURZ dial of KURMANJI [KUR]
ALCANTARANON dial of INONHAN [LOC]
ALDAN TIMPTON dial of EVENKI [EVN]
ALE alt for NAKE [NBK]
ALEALUM alt for MALAYALAM [MJS]
ALEGE [ALF] lang, Nigeria
ALEGI alt for ALEGE [ALF]
ALEKANO [GAH] lang, Papua New Guinea
ALEMÁN COLONEIRO alt for GERMAN, COLONIA TOVAR [GCT]
ALEMANNIC alt for ALEMANNISCH [GSW]
ALEMANNISCH [GSW] lang, Switzerland; also in Austria, France, Germany, Liechtenstein
ALENG alt for MON [MNW]
ALEPA dial of SINAUGORO [SNC]
ALEUT [ALW] lang, USA; also in Russia (Asia)
ALEUT alt for YUPIK, PACIFIC GULF [EMS]
ALEVICA alt for KIRMANJKI [QKV]
ALFENDIO alt for ARAFUNDI [ARF]
ALFOLD dial of HUNGARIAN [HNG]
ALGERIAN alt for ARABIC, ALGERIAN SPOKEN [ARQ]
ALGERIAN SIGN LANGUAGE [ASP] lang, Algeria

ALGHERESE dial of CATALAN-VALENCIAN-BALEAR [CLN]
ALGIERS dial of ARABIC, ALGERIAN SPOKEN [ARQ]
ALGONKIN alt for ALGONQUIN [ALG]
ALGONQUIN [ALG] lang, Canada
AL-HASAA dial of ARABIC, GULF SPOKEN [AFB]
ALI [AIY] lang, CAR
ALI alt for YAKAMUL [YKM]
ALI dial of YAKAMUL [YKM]
ALIAB alt for ALIAP dial of DINKA, SOUTH CENTRAL [DIB]
ALIAP dial of DINKA, SOUTH CENTRAL [DIB]
ALIBAMU alt for ALABAMA [AKZ]
ALIFOKPA dial of YACE [EKR]
ALIKI alt for BIRITAI [BQQ]
ALIKI alt for ERITAI [BAD]
ALIKI alt for OBOKUITAI [AFZ]
ALILE dial of PARAUJANO [PBG]
ALINGA alt for ELING dial of TUNEN [BAZ]
ALINGAR dial of PASHAYI, SOUTHEAST [DRA]
ALIS alt for TOMÁS-ALIS dial of QUECHUA, YAUYOS [QUX]
ALIS I RUN alt for BOKKOS dial of RON [CLA]
ALITTA alt for SIDRAP dial of BUGIS [BPR]
ALIUTOR alt for ALUTOR [ALR]
ALJAMIA alt for LINGUA FRANCA [PML]
ALJAWARA alt for ALYAWARR [ALY]
ALKALI alt for BAISO [BSW]
ALKANSEA alt for QUAPAW [QUA]
ALLAABA alt for ALABA [ALB]
ALLADIAN [ALD] lang, Côte d'Ivoire
ALLADYAN alt for ALLADIAN [ALD]
ALLAGIA alt for ALLADIAN [ALD]
ALLAGIAN alt for ALLADIAN [ALD]
ALLAGIR dial of OSETIN [OSE]
ALLANG dial of LARIKE-WAKASIHU [ALO]
ALLAR [ALL] lang, India
ALLAR alt for GADABA, OLLAR, POTTANGI [GDB]
ALMATSON alt for SHOMBA dial of NGEMBA [NGE]
ALMOMOLOYA NÁHUATL alt for NÁHUATL, TEMASCALTEPEC [NHV]
ALNGITH [AID] lang, Australia
ALO alt for ALU dial of MONO [MTE]
ALOA dial of KWANG [KVI]
ALOÁPAM ZAPOTEC alt for ZAPOTECO, ALOÁPAM [ZAQ]
ALOCOCAUCA MIXTEC alt for MIXTECO, ALCOZAUCA [QMX]
ALOEKOE alt for ALUKU dial of AUKAN [DJK]
ALOMA alt for AROMA dial of KEOPARA [KHZ]
ALOMWE alt for LOMWE [NGL]
ALONG alt for ELUNG dial of AKOOSE [BSS]
ALOR [AOL] lang, Indonesia (Nusa Tenggara)
ALOR alt for ADANG [ADN]
ALOR dial of DINKA, NORTHWESTERN [DIW]
ALORESE alt for ALOR [AOL]
ALORO alt for ALUR [ALZ]
ALOWIEMINO alt for ITERI [ITR]
ALPIN alt for GAVOT dial of PROVENCAL [PRV]
ALPINE LOMBARD dial of LOMBARD [LMO]

AL-QASIIM alt for CENTRAL NAJDI dial of ARABIC, NAJDI SPOKEN [ARS]
ALQOSH dial of CHALDEAN NEO-ARAMAIC [CLD]
ALSACIEN alt for ALSATIAN dial of ALEMANNISCH [GSW]
ALSATIAN dial of ALEMANNISCH [GSW]
ALSEA [AES] lang, USA
ALSÉYA alt for ALSEA [AES]
AL-SHIHUH alt for ARABIC, SHIHHI SPOKEN [SSH]
ALTA, NORTHERN [AQN] lang, Philippines
ALTA, SOUTHERN [AGY] lang, Philippines
ALTAI alt for ALTAI, SOUTHERN [ALT]
ALTAI PROPER dial of ALTAI, SOUTHERN [ALT]
ALTAI, NORTHERN [ATV] lang, Russia (Asia)
ALTAI, SOUTHERN [ALT] lang, Russia (Asia)
ALTAI-KIZHI alt for ALTAI PROPER dial of ALTAI, SOUTHERN [ALT]
ALTAJ KIZI alt for ALTAI PROPER dial of ALTAI, SOUTHERN [ALT]
ALTO BAYANO alt for BAYANO dial of KUNA, SAN BLAS [CUK]
ALTO NAVARRO MERIDIONAL dial of BASQUE [BSQ]
ALTO NAVARRO SEPTENTRIONAL dial of BASQUE [BSQ]
ALTOARAGONÉS alt for ARAGONESE [AXX]
ALU alt for DIA [DIA]
ALU alt for MONO [MTE]
ALU dial of MONO [MTE]
ALU KURUMBA NONSTANDARD KANNADA alt for KURUMBA, ALU [QKA]
ALUA alt for ALUR [ALZ]
ALUKU dial of AUKAN [DJK]
ALUKUYANA alt for WAYANA [WAY]
ALULU alt for ALUR [ALZ]
ALUMBIS dial of TAGAL MURUT [MVV]
ALUMU alt for ARUM-TESU [AAB]
ALUNE [ALP] lang, Indonesia (Maluku)
ALUR [ALZ] lang, DCR; also in Uganda
ALURU dial of LUGBARA [LUG]
ALUTIIQ alt for YUPIK, PACIFIC GULF [EMS]
ALUTOR [ALR] lang, Russia (Asia)
ALUTORSKIJ dial of ALUTOR [ALR]
ALUU dial of IKWERE [IKW]
ALVIR dial of ALVIRI-VIDARI [AVD]
ALVIRI alt for ALVIR dial of ALVIRI-VIDARI [AVD]
ALVIRI-VIDARI [AVD] lang, Iran
ALYAWARR [ALY] lang, Australia
ALYAWARRA alt for ALYAWARR [ALY]
ALYAWARRE alt for ALYAWARR [ALY]
ALYK dial of KRYTS [KRY]
ALYUTOR alt for ALUTOR [ALR]
AMA [AMM] lang, Papua New Guinea
AMA [NYI] lang, Sudan
AMAARRO alt for KOORETE [KQY]
AMABI alt for AMFOAN-FATULE'U-AMABI dial of ATONI [TMR]
AMABUSMANA alt for //XEGWI [XEG]
AMACACORE alt for IQUITO [IQU]
AMADI alt for MA [MSJ]
AMADIYA dial of LISHANA DENI [LSD]

AMAGE alt for YANESHA' [AME]
AMAGUACO alt for AMAHUACA [AMC]
AMAGUES alt for YANESHA' [AME]
AMAHAI [AMQ] lang, Indonesia (Maluku)
AMAHEI alt for AMAHAI [AMQ]
AMAHUACA [AMC] lang, Peru; also in Brazil
AMAIMON [ALI] lang, Papua New Guinea
AMAIZUHO dial of DANO [ASO]
AMAJE alt for YANESHA' [AME]
AMAJO alt for YANESHA' [AME]
AMAKERE alt for MAKERE dial of MANGBETU [MDJ]
AMAL [AAD] lang, Papua New Guinea
AMALA alt for MALA [RUY]
AMALE alt for AMELE [AMI]
AMAM alt for BAMBASSI [MYF]
AMAM alt for KWAMA [KMQ]
AMAMI-OSHIMA, NORTHERN [RYN] lang, Japan
AMAMI-OSHIMA, SOUTHERN [AMS] lang, Japan
AMAMPA alt for SHERBRO [BUN]
AMAN alt for AMANAVIL dial of EMAN [EMN]
AMANA alt for AMANAVIL dial of EMAN [EMN]
AMANA dial of MANINKA, KANKAN [MNI]
AMANAB [AMN] lang, Papua New Guinea
AMANAGE alt for AMANAYÉ [AMA]
AMANAJÉ alt for AMANAYÉ [AMA]
AMANATUN alt for AMANUBAN-AMANATUN dial of ATONI [TMR]
AMANAVIL dial of EMAN [EMN]
AMANAYÉ [AMA] lang, Brazil
AMANDA-AFI dial of BATU [BTU]
AMANGBETU alt for MANGBETU [MDJ]
AMANI alt for AMANAVIL dial of EMAN [EMN]
AMANKGQWIGQWI alt for //XEGWI [XEG]
AMANUBAN alt for AMANUBAN-AMANATUN dial of ATONI [TMR]
AMANUBAN-AMANATUN dial of ATONI [TMR]
AMANUBANG alt for AMANUBAN-AMANATUN dial of ATONI [TMR]
AMANYÉ alt for AMANAYÉ [AMA]
AMAPÁ CREOLE [AMD] lang, Brazil
AMAR alt for HAMER-BANNA [AMF]
AMAR TITA alt for NINZAM [NIN]
AMARA [AIE] lang, Papua New Guinea
AMARA dial of BEDAWI [BEI]
AMARACAIRE alt for AMARAKAERI [AMR]
AMARAG [AMG] lang, Australia
AMARAKAERI [AMR] lang, Peru
AMARAKAIRE alt for AMARAKAERI [AMR]
AMARASI [AAZ] lang, Indonesia (Nusa Tenggara)
AMARASI BARAT dial of AMARASI [AAZ]
AMARASI TIMUR dial of AMARASI [AAZ]
AMARCOCCHE alt for HAMER-BANNA [AMF]
AMARI dial of ADZERA [AZR]
AMARIBA dial of ARUMA [WAP]
AMARIGNA alt for AMHARIC [AMH]
AMARINYA alt for AMHARIC [AMH]
AMARRO alt for KOORETE [KQY]
AMARUWA dial of CUIBA [CUI]
AMASI alt for MANTA [MYG]
AMASSI alt for MANTA [MYG]

AMAT DARAT alt for CITAK [TXT]
AMATENANGO DEL VALLE dial of TZELTAL,
BACHAJON [TZB]
AMATLÁN ZAPOTEC alt for ZAPOTECO,
AMATLÁN [ZPO]
AMAWACA alt for AMAHUACA [AMC]
AMAWAKA alt for AMAHUACA [AMC]
AMAWÁKA alt for AMAHUACA [AMC]
AMAYO dial of EMAN [EMN]
AMAZIGH alt for TAMAJAQ, TAWALLAMMAT [TTQ]
AMAZIGH alt for TAMAJEQ, TAYART [THZ]
AMAZONAS alt for QUECHUA, CHACHAPOYAS
[QUK]
"AMAZONAS MACUSA" pejorative alt for
CARABAYO [CBY]
AMBA [RWM] lang, Uganda; also in DCR
AMBA [UTP] lang, Solomon Islands
AMBABIKO alt for MODELE dial of BEFANG [BBY]
AMBAE, EAST [OMB] lang, Vanuatu
AMBAE, WEST [NND] lang, Vanuatu
AMBAI [AMK] lang, Indonesia (Irian Jaya)
AMBAI dial of AMBAI [AMK]
AMBAI-MENAWI alt for AMBAI [AMK]
AMBALA AGTA alt for AYTA, AMBALA [ABC]
AMBALA SAMBAL alt for AYTA, AMBALA [ABC]
AMBALI alt for BALI dial of TEKE, EASTERN [TEK]
AMBANDI alt for PIYA-KWONCI [PIY]
AMBAQUISTA alt for MBAKA dial of MBUNDU,
LOANDA [MLO]
AMBARI alt for AMPEELI-WOJOKESO [APZ]
AMBASI dial of BINANDERE [BHG]
AMBAWANG dial of KENDAYAN [KNX]
AMBEDE alt for MBERE [MDT]
AMBELAU [AMV] lang, Indonesia (Maluku)
AMBELE [AEL] lang, Cameroon
AM'BENG alt for A'BENG dial of GARO [GRT]
AMBENO alt for AMBENU dial of ATONI [TMR]
AMBENU dial of ATONI [TMR]
AMBER alt for WAIGEO [WGO]
AMBER dial of WAIGEO [WGO]
AMBERBAKEN alt for MPUR [AKC]
AMBERI alt for WAIGEO [WGO]
AMBLAU alt for AMBELAU [AMV]
AMBLONG [ALM] lang, Vanuatu
AMBO [AMB] lang, Nigeria
AMBO alt for NDONGA [NDG]
AMBO dial of LALA-BISA [LEB]
AMBODHI alt for AWADHI [AWD]
AMBODI alt for DEHVALI dial of VASAVI [VAS]
AMBONESE alt for MALAY, AMBONESE [ABS]
AMBO-PASCO QUECHUA alt for QUECHUA, SAN
RAFAEL-HUARIACA [QEG]
AMBRYM, NORTH [MMG] lang, Vanuatu
AMBRYM, SOUTHEAST [TVK] lang, Vanuatu
AMBUAL dial of KENINGAU MURUT [KXI]
AMBUELA alt for MBWELA [MFU]
AMBUELLA alt for MBWELA [MFU]
AMBUL alt for APALIK [PLI]
AMBULAS [ABT] lang, Papua New Guinea
AMBULE alt for CHOURASE [TSU]
AMBUMI dial of WANDAMEN [WAD]

AMCHAUKE alt for AMCHOKE dial of BANTAWA
[BAP]
AMCHOKE dial of BANTAWA [BAP]
AMDANG [AMJ] lang, Chad
AMDO [ADX] lang, China
AME alt for AMI [AMY]
AMEGI alt for BISENI [IJE]
AMELE [AMI] lang, Papua New Guinea
AMENFI dial of WASA [WSS]
AMENGI dial of MAMVU [MDI]
AMENGUACA alt for AMAHUACA [AMC]
AMER alt for HAMER-BANNA [AMF]
AMERAX [AEX] lang, USA
AMERICAN SIGN LANGUAGE [ASE] lang, USA;
also in Canada, Guatemala
AMERICAN SPANISH dial of SPANISH [SPN]
AMERIDISH alt for YINGLISH [YIB]
AMESLAN alt for AMERICAN SIGN LANGUAGE
[ASE]
AMEUHAQUE alt for AMAHUACA [AMC]
AMFOAN alt for AMFOAN-FATULE'U-AMABI dial
of ATONI [TMR]
AMFOAN-FATULE'U-AMABI dial of ATONI [TMR]
AMFUANG alt for AMFOAN-FATULE'U-AMABI
dial of ATONI [TMR]
AMGANAD alt for IFUGAO, AMGANAD [IFA]
AMHARIC [AMH] lang, Ethiopia; also in Egypt,
Israel, Sweden
AMI [AMY] lang, Australia
AMI alt for AMIS [ALV]
AMIA alt for AMIS [ALV]
AMIANGBA alt for BARAMBU [BRM]
AMIANGBWA alt for BARAMBU [BRM]
AMIENOIS dial of PICARD [PCD]
AMIJANGAL alt for AMI [AMY]
AMIKOANA [AKN] lang, Brazil
AMINA alt for GA [GAC]
AMINI alt for NAI [BIO]
AMIOL alt for TUIC dial of DINKA, SOUTH-
WESTERN [DIK]
AMIS [ALV] lang, Taiwan
AMIS, NATAORAN [AIS] lang, Taiwan
AMISH PENNSYLVANIA GERMAN dial of
GERMAN, PENNSYLVANIA [PDC]
/AMKWE dial of NARO [NHR]
AMMAR alt for HAMER-BANNA [AMF]
AMNIAPÉ alt for KANOÉ [KXO]
AMO [AMO] lang, Nigeria
AMOISHE alt for YANESHA' [AME]
AMOK alt for MOK [MQT]
AMOLTEPEC MIXTEC alt for MIXTECO,
AMOLTEPEC [MBZ]
AMON alt for AMO [AMO]
AMON alt for UMON [UMM]
AMONDAWA [ADW] lang, Brazil
AMONG alt for AMO [AMO]
AMONO alt for MONO [MNH]
AMORUA alt for AMARUWA dial of CUIBA [CUI]
AMORUA dial of GUAHIBO [GUH]
AMOTA dial of MARIA [MDS]
AMOU OBLOU dial of AKPOSO [KPO]

AMOY alt for FUKIENESE dial of CHINESE, MIN NAN [CFR]

AMOY alt for HOKKIEN dial of CHINESE, MIN NAN [CFR]

AMOY alt for XIAMEN dial of CHINESE, MIN NAN [CFR]

AMOY dial of CHINESE, MIN NAN [CFR]

AMPALE alt for AMPEELI-WOJOKESO [APZ]

AMPANANG [APG] lang, Indonesia (Kalimantan)

AMPAS alt for MOLOF [MSL]

AMPEELI-WOJOKESO [APZ] lang, Papua New Guinea

AMPELE alt for AMPEELI-WOJOKESO [APZ]

AMPEYI alt for NUPE CENTRAL dial of NUPE-NUPE TAKO [NUP]

AMPEZZANO dial of LADIN [LLD]

AMPIBABO alt for LAUJE [LAW]

AMPIKA alt for BOLE [BOL]

AMRAVATI dial of GONDI, NORTHERN [GON]

AMRI dial of MIKIR [MJW]

AMRI KARBI alt for AMRI dial of MIKIR [MJW]

AMTO [AMT] lang, Papua New Guinea

AMTO dial of AMTO [AMT]

AMTUL alt for TAL [TAL]

AMU dial of SWAHILI [SWA]

AMUBRE-KATSI dial of BRIBRI [BZD]

AMUEIXA alt for YANESHA' [AME]

AMUESE alt for YANESHA' [AME]

AMUESHA alt for YANESHA' [AME]

AMUETAMO alt for YANESHA' [AME]

AMUGEN dial of ONO [ONS]

AMUN dial of PIVA [TGI]

AMUNDAVA alt for AMONDAWA [ADW]

AMUNDAWA alt for AMONDAWA [ADW]

AMUNG alt for DAMAL [UHN]

AMUNG dial of DAMAL [UHN]

AMUNG KAL alt for DAMAL [UHN]

AMUNGME alt for DAMAL [UHN]

AMUR dial of GILYAK [NIV]

AMURAG alt for AMARAG [AMG]

AMURU dial of BORO [BWO]

AMUTOURA alt for SAISIYAT [SAI]

AMUY alt for DAMAL [UHN]

AMUZGO alt for AMUZGO, SAN PEDRO AMUZGOS [AZG]

AMUZGO DE SAN PEDRO AMUZGOS alt for AMUZGO, SAN PEDRO AMUZGOS [AZG]

AMUZGO, GUERRERO [AMU] lang, Mexico

AMUZGO, IPALAPA [AZM] lang, Mexico

AMUZGO, SAN PEDRO AMUZGOS [AZG] lang, Mexico

AMWI [AML] lang, India

ÀMZÍRÍV alt for ZIZILIVAKAN [ZIZ]

ANA alt for IFÈ [IFE]

ANAANG [ANW] lang, Nigeria

ANABEZE alt for BUJI dial of JERE [JER]

ANAFEJANZI alt for JANJI [JNI]

ANAGO alt for IFÈ [IFE]

ANAGUTA alt for IGUTA [NAR]

ANA-IFE alt for IFÈ [IFE]

ANA-IFÈ alt for IFÈ [IFE]

ANAKALANG alt for ANAKALANGU [AKG]

ANAKALANGU [AKG] lang, Indonesia (Nusa Tenggara)

ANAKOLA alt for BATAK ANGKOLA [AKB]

ANAKTUVIK PASS INUPIATUN dial of INUPIATUN, NORTH ALASKAN [ESI]

ANAL [ANM] lang, India; also in Myanmar

ANAM [PDA] lang, Papua New Guinea

ANAMAGI alt for TORRICELLI [TEI]

ANAMBÉ [AAN] lang, Brazil

ANAMGURA [IMI] lang, Papua New Guinea

ANANA alt for GUANANO [GVC]

ANANDJOOBI alt for ANANJUBI dial of ANII [BLO]

ANANG alt for ANAANG [ANW]

ANANJUBI dial of ANII [BLO]

ANAPIA alt for OMAGUA [OMG]

ANAR alt for SAAMI, INARI [LPI]

ANARYA dial of BHILI [BHB]

ANASI [BPO] lang, Indonesia (Irian Jaya)

ANATOLIAN alt for TURKISH [TRK]

ANATOLIAN CLUSTER dial of ARABIC, MESOPOTAMIAN SPOKEN [ACM]

ANATRI dial of CHUVASH [CJU]

ANAULI dial of TURKMEN [TCK]

ANAWLA alt for GAMADIA dial of GUJARATI [GJR]

ÁNCÁ [ACB] lang, Nigeria

ANCALONG KUTAI dial of MALAY, TENGGARONG KUTAI [VKT]

ANCHA (INCHA) alt for NINZAM [NIN]

ANCHAN alt for ACHANG [ACN]

ANCHIX dial of KARATA [KPT]

ANCIENT ETHIOPIC alt for GEEZ [GEE]

ANCIENT SYRIAC alt for SYRIAC [SYC]

ANCUX dial of AVAR [AVR]

/ANDA [HNH] lang, Botswana

ANDAGARINYA alt for ANTAKARINYA [ANT]

ANDAHUAYLAS dial of QUECHUA, AYACUCHO [QUY]

ANDAKI alt for ANDAQUI [ANA]

ANDALAL-GXDATL dial of AVAR [AVR]

ANDALI alt for ANGWE dial of MANGBUTU [MDK]

ANDALUSIAN dial of SPANISH [SPN]

ANDANG alt for AMDANG [AMJ]

ANDANGTI alt for AMDANG [AMJ]

ANDAQUI [ANA] lang, Colombia

ANDARUM [AOD] lang, Papua New Guinea

ANDASA alt for NDASA [NDA]

ANDASTE alt for SUSQUEHANNOCK [SQN]

ANDEGEREBINHA [ADG] lang, Australia

ANDELALE dial of UMBU-UNGU [UMB]

ANDH [ANR] lang, India

ANDHA alt for ANDH [ANR]

ANDHI alt for ANDH [ANR]

ANDHRA alt for TELUGU [TCW]

ANDHRA PRADESH LAMANI dial of LAMBADI [LMN]

ANDI [ANI] lang, Russia (Europe)

ANDIAN alt for MANDAR [MHN]

ANDII alt for ANDI [ANI]

ANDILJANGWA alt for ANINDILYAKWA [AOI]

ANDILYAUGWA alt for ANINDILYAKWA [AOI]

ANDINAI dial of MANGBUTU [MDK]
ANDIO [BZB] lang, Indonesia (Sulawesi)
ANDIO'O alt for ANDIO [BZB]
ANDIRA alt for SATERÉ-MAWÉ [MAV]
ANDIY alt for ANDI [ANI]
ANDOA [ANB] lang, Peru
ANDOKE alt for ANDOQUE [ANO]
ANDONE alt for OBOLO [ANN]
ANDONI alt for OBOLO [ANN]
ANDONNI alt for OBOLO [ANN]
ANDOQUE [ANO] lang, Colombia
ANDRA-HUS [ANX] lang, Papua New Guinea
ANDRI dial of MORU [MGD]
ANDRO dial of KADO [KDV]
ANDUO alt for AMDO [ADX]
ANEGOROM alt for RIBINA dial of JERE [JER]
ANEI alt for ABIEM dial of DINKA, SOUTH-
    WESTERN [DIK]
ANEITEUM alt for ANEITYUM [ATY]
ANEITEUMESE alt for ANEITYUM [ATY]
ANEITYUM [ATY] lang, Vanuatu
ANEJ alt for GULE [GLE]
ANEJOM alt for ANEITYUM [ATY]
/ANEKWE dial of NARO [NHR]
ANEM [ANZ] lang, Papua New Guinea
ANEME WAKE [ABY] lang, Papua New Guinea
ANEMORO alt for LEMORO [LDJ]
ANEP alt for BALEP dial of NDOE [NBB]
ANESU alt for XÂRÂCÙÙ [ANE]
ANEWA alt for ANIWA dial of FUTUNA-ANIWA [FUT]
ANFILLO [MYO] lang, Ethiopia
ANGA alt for ANGIKA [ANP]
ANGA alt for HANGA [HAG]
ANGAATAHA alt for ANGAATIHA [AGM]
ANGAATIHA [AGM] lang, Papua New Guinea
ANGAATIYA alt for ANGAATIHA [AGM]
ANGAITE dial of SANAPANA [SAP]
ANGAL [AGE] lang, Papua New Guinea
ANGAL ENEN [AOE] lang, Papua New Guinea
ANGAL HENENG [AKH] lang, Papua New Guinea
ANGAMIS alt for NAGA, ANGAMI [NJM]
ANGAN alt for KAMANTAN [KCI]
ANGANIWAI alt for KAHUA [AGW]
ANGANIWEI alt for KAHUA [AGW]
ANGAS alt for NGAS [ANC]
ANGATAHA alt for ANGAATIHA [AGM]
ANGATE alt for ANGAITE dial of SANAPANA [SAP]
ANGAUA alt for NEND [ANH]
ANGAVE alt for ANKAVE [AAK]
ANGBA alt for NGELIMA [AGH]
ANGEL ALBINO CORZO dial of TZOTZIL, HUIXTAN
    [TZU]
ANGEVIN dial of FRENCH [FRN]
ANGGOR alt for ANGOR [AGG]
ANGGURUK alt for YALI, ANGGURUK [YLI]
ANGIE alt for NGIE [NGJ]
ANGIKA [ANP] lang, India
ANGIKAR alt for ANGIKA [ANP]
ANGKA alt for HRUSO [HRU]
ANGKAE alt for HRUSO [HRU]
ANGKOLA alt for BATAK ANGKOLA [AKB]

ANGLAT AGTA dial of AGTA, UMIRAY DUMAGET
    [DUE]
ANGLIT alt for ENGLISH [ENG]
ANGLO dial of EWE [EWE]
ANGLOROMANI [RME] lang, United Kingdom; also
    in Australia, South Africa, USA
ANGOCHE alt for KOTI [EKO]
ANGOLAR [AOA] lang, São Tomé e Príncipe
ANGOLE dial of KUSAAL [KUS]
ANGOM alt for NGOM [NRA]
ANGOMERRY alt for NGENKIWUMERRI dial of
    NANGIKURRUNGGURR [NAM]
ANGONI alt for NGONI [NGU]
ANGOR [AGG] lang, Papua New Guinea
ANGORAM [AOG] lang, Papua New Guinea
ANGOTERO alt for SECOYA [SEY]
ANGOTERO dial of SECOYA [SEY]
ANGOXE alt for KOTI [EKO]
ANGOYA alt for AKOYE [MIW]
ANGPHANG dial of NAGA, KONYAK [NBE]
ANGUILLAN CREOLE ENGLISH dial of LEEWARD
    CARIBBEAN CREOLE ENGLISH [AIG]
ANGWE dial of BATU [BTU]
ANGWE dial of MANGBUTU [MDK]
ANHAQUI dial of BIDYOGO [BJG]
ANHIL dial of TUROYO [SYR]
//ANI alt for /ANDA [HNH]
//ANI dial of KXOE [XUU]
ANIBAU alt for GUSU dial of JERE [JER]
ANIGIBI alt for ARIGIBI dial of KIWAI, NORTHEAST
    [KIW]
ANII [BLO] lang, Benin; also in Togo
//ANI-KHOE alt for BUGA-KXOE dial of KXOE [XUU]
[[ANIKXOE alt for BUGA-KXOE dial of KXOE [XUU]
ANIMERE [ANF] lang, Ghana
ANINDILYAKWA [AOI] lang, Australia
ANINI-Y dial of KINARAY-A [KRJ]
ANIOCHA dial of IGBO [IGR]
ANIR dial of TANGGA [TGG]
ANIRAGO alt for NIRAGU dial of GBIRI-NIRAGU
    [GRH]
ANIULA alt for YANYUWA [JAO]
ANIWA dial of FUTUNA-ANIWA [FUT]
ANJAM [BOJ] lang, Papua New Guinea
ANJIE alt for AJIË [AJI]
ANJIMATANA alt for ADYNYAMATHANHA [ADT]
ANJIWATANA alt for ADYNYAMATHANHA [ADT]
ANJOUAN alt for SHINDZWANI dial of COMORIAN
    [SWB]
ANJOUAN alt for SHINZWANI dial of COMORIAN
    [SWB]
ANJUSKI dial of UDIHE [UDE]
ANKAI dial of ANKAVE [AAK]
ANKAVE [AAK] lang, Papua New Guinea
ANKIYAKMIN dial of FAIWOL [FAI]
ANKOBER dial of ARGOBBA [AGJ]
ANKPA dial of IGALA [IGL]
ANKULU alt for IKULU [IKU]
ANKWAI alt for GOEMAI [ANK]
ANKWE alt for GOEMAI [ANK]
ANKWEI alt for GOEMAI [ANK]

ANLO alt for IGO [AHL]
ANLOUR dial of KUY [KDT]
ANMATJIRRA alt for ANMATYERRE [AMX]
ANMATYERRE [AMX] lang, Australia
ANNA alt for BIDEYAT [BIH]
ANNABERG alt for RAO [RAO]
ANNAMESE alt for VIETNAMESE [VIE]
ANNAMITE FRENCH alt for TAY BOI [TAS]
ANNANG alt for ANAANG [ANW]
ANNOBONENSE alt for FA D'AMBU [FAB]
ANNOBONÉS alt for FA D'AMBU [FAB]
ANNOBONESE alt for FA D'AMBU [FAB]
ANO dial of ANYIN [ANY]
ANODÖUB alt for NADËB [MBJ]
ANOONG alt for NUNG [NUN]
ANOR [ANJ] lang, Papua New Guinea
ANORUBUNA alt for RIBINA dial of JERE [JER]
ANOSANGOBARI alt for GUSU dial of JERE [JER]
ANOWURU alt for LEMORO [LDJ]
ANPIKA alt for FIKA dial of BOLE [BOL]
ANSAKARA alt for NZAKARA [NZK]
ANSERMA [ANS] lang, Colombia
ANSERNA alt for ANSERMA [ANS]
ANSHUENKUAN NYARONG alt for ATUENCE [ATF]
ANSITA alt for OPUUO [LGN]
ANSOTANO alt for WESTERN ARAGONESE dial of ARAGONESE [AXX]
ANSUS [AND] lang, Indonesia (Irian Jaya)
ANTA alt for MANTA [MYG]
ANTABAMBA dial of QUECHUA, AREQUIPA-LA UNION [QAR]
ANTAIFASY alt for TAIFASY dial of MALAGASY [MEX]
ANTAIMANAMBONDRO alt for TAIMANAMBONDRO dial of MALAGASY [MEX]
ANTAIMORO alt for TAIMORO dial of MALAGASY [MEX]
ANTAISAKA alt for TAISAKA dial of MALAGASY [MEX]
ANTAIVA alt for BEZANOZANO dial of MALAGASY [MEX]
ANTAKARINYA [ANT] lang, Australia
ANTALAOTRA alt for BUSHI [BUC]
ANTAMBAHOAKA alt for TAMBAHOAKA dial of MALAGASY [MEX]
ANTANALA alt for TANALA dial of MALAGASY [MEX]
ANTANDROY 1 dial of MALAGASY [MEX]
ANTANDROY 2 dial of MALAGASY [MEX]
ANTANKA alt for BEZANOZANO dial of MALAGASY [MEX]
ANTANKARANA alt for MALAGASY, ANTANKARANA [XMV]
ANTANOSY alt for TANOSY dial of MALAGASY [MEX]
ANTARBEDI alt for BRAJ BHASHA [BFS]
ANTARBEDI dial of BRAJ BHASHA [BFS]
ANTARVEDI alt for BRAJ BHASHA [BFS]
ANTIGUAN CREOLE ENGLISH dial of LEEWARD CARIBBEAN CREOLE ENGLISH [AIG]

ANTIPOLO IFUGAO alt for KALANGUYA, KELEY-I [IFY]
ANTIQUEÑO alt for KINARAY-A [KRJ]
ANTRA dial of KUY [KDT]
ANTSUKH alt for ANCUX dial of AVAR [AVR]
ANU [ANL] lang, Myanmar
ANU alt for NUNG [NUN]
ANU dial of GUA [GWX]
ANUAK [ANU] lang, Sudan; also in Ethiopia
ANUFO [CKO] lang, Ghana; also in Benin, Togo
ANUKI [AUI] lang, Papua New Guinea
ANULA alt for YANYUWA [JAO]
ANUM alt for ANU dial of GUA [GWX]
ANUM-BOSO alt for GUA [GWX]
ANUNG alt for NUNG [NUN]
ANUPE alt for NUPE CENTRAL dial of NUPE-NUPE TAKO [NUP]
ANUPECWAYI alt for NUPE CENTRAL dial of NUPE-NUPE TAKO [NUP]
ANUPERI alt for NUPE CENTRAL dial of NUPE-NUPE TAKO [NUP]
ANUS [AUQ] lang, Indonesia (Irian Jaya)
ANUTA [AUD] lang, Solomon Islands
ANWAIN alt for ESAN [ISH]
ANYAH alt for DENYA [ANV]
ANYAMA dial of OGBIA [OGB]
ANYAN alt for DENYA [ANV]
ANYANG alt for DENYA [ANV]
ANYANG dial of NGEMBA [NGE]
ANYANGA [AYG] lang, Togo
ANYAR alt for AKUM [AKU]
ANYARAN alt for UKAAN [KCF]
ANYEP alt for BALEP dial of NDOE [NBB]
ANYI alt for ANYIN [ANY]
ANYIMA alt for LENYIMA [LDG]
ANYIMERE alt for ANIMERE [ANF]
ANYIN [ANY] lang, Côte d'Ivoire; also in Ghana
ANYIN, MOROFO [MTB] lang, Côte d'Ivoire
ANYO alt for NAGA, MELURI [NLM]
ANYUAK alt for ANUAK [ANU]
ANYUGBA dial of IGALA [IGL]
ANYULA alt for YANYUWA [JAO]
ANYWA alt for ANUAK [ANU]
ANYWAK alt for ANUAK [ANU]
ANYX dial of LEZGI [LEZ]
AO alt for NAGA, AO [NJO]
AO TÁ dial of MUONG [MTQ]
AO YAO alt for BIAO MIN dial of BIAO-JIAO MIEN [BJE]
AOAQUI alt for ARUTANI [ATX]
AOBA alt for AMBAE, EAST [OMB]
AOHENG [PNI] lang, Indonesia (Kalimantan)
AOLA dial of LENGO [LGR]
AOLUGUYA dial of EVENKI [EVN]
AOMIE alt for ÖMIE [AOM]
AONA alt for ONA [ONA]
AONIKEN alt for TEHUELCHE [TEH]
AORE [AOR] lang, Vanuatu
AORR alt for NAGA, AO [NJO]
AOSHEDD alt for NAGA, KHIAMNIUNGAN [NKY]
A'OU dial of GELAO [KKF]

AOUDJILA alt for AWJILAH [AUJ]
AOUEI alt for KUY [KDT]
AOWIN dial of ANYIN [ANY]
AP MA [KBX] lang, Papua New Guinea
AP MA BOTIN alt for AP MA [KBX]
APA alt for APATANI [APT]
APA dial of KPAN [KPK]
APABHRAMSA alt for MAITHILI [MKP]
APACHE, JICARILLA [APJ] lang, USA
APACHE, KIOWA [APK] lang, USA
APACHE, LIPAN [APL] lang, USA
APACHE, MESCALERO-CHIRICAHUA [APM] lang,
   USA
APACHE, WESTERN [APW] lang, USA
APAE'AA alt for SA'A [APB]
APAGIBETE alt for PAGIBETE [PAG]
APAGIBETI alt for PAGIBETE [PAG]
APAHAPSILI dial of YALI, PASS VALLEY [YAC]
APAKABETI alt for PAGIBETE [PAG]
APAKIBETI alt for PAGIBETE [PAG]
APAL alt for APALI [ENA]
APALAÍ [APA] lang, Brazil
APALAKIRI alt for KUIKÚRO-KALAPÁLO [KUI]
APALAQUIRI alt for KUIKÚRO-KALAPÁLO [KUI]
APALAY alt for APALAÍ [APA]
APALI [ENA] lang, Papua New Guinea
APALIK [PLI] lang, Papua New Guinea
APAMBIA alt for PAMBIA [PAM]
APANHECRA alt for APANJEKRA dial of CANELA
   [RAM]
APANI dial of IKWERE [IKW]
APANIEKRA alt for APANJEKRA dial of CANELA
   [RAM]
APANJEKRA dial of CANELA [RAM]
APAPOCUVA dial of CHIRIPA [NHD]
APARAI alt for APALAÍ [APA]
APASCO MIXTEC alt for MIXTECO, APASCO Y
   APOALA [MIP]
APATANI [APT] lang, India
APBHRAMSA alt for MAITHILI [MKP]
APEKU alt for BONGOS [BXY]
APEKU dial of BONGOS [BXY]
API alt for LAMPUNG [LJP]
APIACÁ [API] lang, Brazil
APIAKÁ alt for APIACÁ [API]
APIAKE alt for APIACÁ [API]
APIAPUM dial of MBEMBE, CROSS RIVER [MFN]
APINAGÉ alt for APINAYÉ [APN]
APINAJÉ alt for APINAYÉ [APN]
APINAYÉ [APN] lang, Brazil
APINDJE alt for PINJI [PIC]
APINDJI alt for PINJI [PIC]
APINJI alt for PINJI [PIC]
APMA [APP] lang, Vanuatu
APMISIBIL dial of NGALUM [SZB]
AP-NE-AP dial of TORRES STRAIT CREOLE [TCS]
APOALA MIXTEC alt for MIXTECO, APASCO Y
   APOALA [MIP]
APOI dial of IZON [IJC]
APOKINSKIJ dial of KORYAK [KPY]
APOLO dial of QUECHUA, NORTH BOLIVIAN [QUL]

APONTE INGA dial of INGA [INB]
APOS [APO] lang, Papua New Guinea
APOWASI dial of BITARA [BIT]
APPA alt for TAROK [YER]
APPENZEL dial of ALEMANNISCH [GSW]
APPOLO alt for NZEMA [NZE]
APROU alt for AIZI, APROUMU [AHP]
APROUMU alt for AIZI, APROUMU [AHP]
APRWE alt for AIZI, APROUMU [AHP]
APSAALOOKE alt for CROW [CRO]
A-PUCIKWAR [APQ] lang, India
APUK dial of DINKA, SOUTHWESTERN [DIK]
APUKIN alt for APOKINSKIJ dial of KORYAK
   [KPY]
APUOTH alt for ABIEM dial of DINKA, SOUTH-
   WESTERN [DIK]
APURAHUANO alt for TAGBANWA [TBW]
APURI dial of BLAGAR [BEU]
APURÍ dial of QUECHUA, YAUYOS [QUX]
APURIMAC alt for ANTABAMBA dial of QUECHUA,
   AREQUIPA-LA UNION [QAR]
APURINÃ [APU] lang, Brazil
APURUCAYALI CAMPA alt for AJYÍNINKA
   APURUCAYALI [CPC]
APUT alt for PUNAN APUT [PUD]
APUTAI [APX] lang, Indonesia (Maluku)
APWOTH alt for ABIEM dial of DINKA, SOUTH-
   WESTERN [DIK]
APYTARE alt for CHIRIPÁ [NHD]
AQUA alt for SOUTHERN EJAGHAM dial of
   EJAGHAM [ETU]
ARA alt for AARI [AIZ]
ARA alt for ARHÂ [ARN]
ARA alt for KONJO PESISIR dial of KONJO,
   COASTAL [KJC]
ARA alt for WÁRA [TCI]
ARABANA [ARD] lang, Australia
ARABE CHOA alt for ARABIC, CHADIAN SPOKEN
   [SHU]
ARABE CHOA alt for ARABIC, SHUWA [SHU]
ARABELA [ARL] lang, Peru
ARABI alt for ARABIC, JUDEO-IRAQI [YHD]
ARABIC, ALGERIAN SAHARAN SPOKEN [AAO]
   lang, Algeria; also in Niger
ARABIC, ALGERIAN SPOKEN [ARQ] lang,
   Algeria; also in Belgium, France, Germany,
   Netherlands, St. Pierre and Miquelon
ARABIC, BABALIA CREOLE [BBZ] lang, Chad
ARABIC, BAHARNA SPOKEN [AFH] lang, Bahrain;
   also in Oman
ARABIC, CHADIAN SPOKEN [SHU] lang, Chad;
   also in Cameroon, CAR, Niger, Nigeria
ARABIC, CYPRIOT SPOKEN [ACY] lang,
   Cyprus
ARABIC, DHOFARI SPOKEN [ADF] lang, Oman
ARABIC, EASTERN EGYPTIAN BEDAWI SPOKEN
   [AVL] lang, Egypt; also in Israel, Jordan,
   Palestinian West Bank and Gaza, Syria
ARABIC, EGYPTIAN SPOKEN [ARZ] lang, Egypt;
   also in Iraq, Israel, Jordan, Kuwait, Libya, Saudi
   Arabia, UAE, Yemen

ARABIC, GULF SPOKEN [AFB] lang, Iraq; also in Bahrain, Iran, Kuwait, Oman, Qatar, Saudi Arabia, UAE, Yemen

ARABIC, HADRAMI SPOKEN [AYH] lang, Yemen; also in Eritrea, Kenya

ARABIC, HASANYA [MEY] lang, Mauritania; also in Algeria, Mali, Morocco, Niger, Senegal

ARABIC, HASSANIYYA [MEY] lang, Mauritania; also in Algeria, Mali, Morocco, Niger, Senegal

ARABIC, HIJAZI SPOKEN [ACW] lang, Saudi Arabia; also in Eritrea

ARABIC, JUDEO-IRAQI [YHD] lang, Israel; also in India, Iraq, United Kingdom

ARABIC, JUDEO-MOROCCAN [AJU] lang, Israel; also in Canada, France, Morocco

ARABIC, JUDEO-TRIPOLITANIAN [YUD] lang, Israel; also in Italy

ARABIC, JUDEO-TUNISIAN [AJT] lang, Israel; also in France, Italy, Spain, Tunisia, USA

ARABIC, JUDEO-YEMENI [JYE] lang, Israel; also in Yemen

ARABIC, LEVANTINE BEDAWI SPOKEN [AVL] lang, Egypt; also in Israel, Jordan, Palestinian West Bank and Gaza, Syria

ARABIC, LIBYAN SPOKEN [AYL] lang, Libya; also in Egypt, Niger

ARABIC, MESOPOTAMIAN SPOKEN [ACM] lang, Iraq; also in Iran, Jordan, Syria, Turkey (Asia)

ARABIC, MOROCCAN SPOKEN [ARY] lang, Morocco; also in Belgium, Egypt, France, Germany, Gibraltar, Netherlands, United Kingdom

ARABIC, NAJDI SPOKEN [ARS] lang, Saudi Arabia; also in Canada, Iraq, Jordan, Kuwait, Syria, USA

ARABIC, NORTH LEVANTINE SPOKEN [APC] lang, Syria; also in Antigua and Barbuda, Argentina, Belize, Cyprus, Dominican Republic, French Guiana, Israel, Jamaica, Lebanon, Mali, Puerto Rico, Suriname, Trinidad and Tobago, Turkey (Asia)

ARABIC, NORTH MESOPOTAMIAN SPOKEN [AYP] lang, Iraq; also in Jordan, Syria, Turkey (Asia)

ARABIC, OMANI SPOKEN [ACX] lang, Oman; also in Kenya, Tanzania, UAE

ARABIC, SA<IDI SPOKEN [AEC] lang, Egypt

ARABIC, SANAANI SPOKEN [AYN] lang, Yemen

ARABIC, SHIHHI SPOKEN [SSH] lang, UAE; also in Oman

ARABIC, SHUWA [SHU] lang, Chad; also in Cameroon, CAR, Niger, Nigeria

ARABIC, SOUTH LEVANTINE SPOKEN [AJP] lang, Jordan; also in Argentina, Egypt, Israel, Kuwait, Palestinian West Bank and Gaza, Puerto Rico, Syria

ARABIC, STANDARD [ABV] lang, Saudi Arabia; also in Algeria, Bahrain, Chad, Comoros Islands, Egypt, Eritrea, Iraq, Israel, Jordan, Kuwait, Lebanon, Libya, Morocco, Oman, Palestinian West Bank and Gaza, Qatar, Somalia, Sudan, Syria, Tanzania, Tunisia, UAE, Yemen

ARABIC, SUDANESE CREOLE [PGA] lang, Sudan

ARABIC, SUDANESE SPOKEN [APD] lang, Sudan; also in Egypt, Eritrea, Ethiopia, Saudi Arabia

ARABIC, TA'IZZI-ADENI [ACQ] lang, Yemen; also in Djibouti, Eritrea, Kenya, United Kingdom

ARABIC, TA'IZZI-ADENI SPOKEN [ACQ] lang, Yemen; also in Djibouti, Eritrea, Kenya, United Kingdom

ARABIC, TAJIKI SPOKEN [ABH] lang, Tajikistan; also in Afghanistan, Uzbekistan

ARABIC, TUNISIAN SPOKEN [AEB] lang, Tunisia; also in Belgium, France, Germany, Netherlands

ARABIC, UZBEKI SPOKEN [AUZ] lang, Uzbekistan

ARABIC, WESTERN EGYPTIAN BEDAWI SPOKEN [AYL] lang, Libya; also in Egypt, Niger

ARABIZED HEBREW alt for ORIENTAL HEBREW dial of HEBREW [HBR]

ARABKIR dial of ARMENIAN [ARM]

ARAB-SWAHILI alt for SWAHILI [SWA]

ARADHIN dial of CHALDEAN NEO-ARAMAIC [CLD]

ARADIGI alt for RATAGNON [BTN]

ARAFUNDI [ARF] lang, Papua New Guinea

ARAGO alt for ALAGO [ALA]

ARAGOIERAZ alt for ARAGONESE [AXX]

ARAGONÉS alt for ARAGONESE [AXX]

ARAGONESE [AXX] lang, Spain

ARAGONESE dial of SPANISH [SPN]

ARAGU alt for ALAGO [ALA]

ARAGURE alt for XARAGURE [ARG]

'ARAGURE alt for XARAGURE [ARG]

ARAKANESE [MHV] lang, Myanmar; also in Bangladesh, India

ARAKI [AKR] lang, Vanuatu

ARAKI dial of FARSI, WESTERN [PES]

ARALLE dial of ARALLE-TABULAHAN [ATQ]

ARALLE-TABULAHAN [ATQ] lang, Indonesia (Sulawesi)

ARAMA alt for SOUTH WAIBUK dial of HARUAI [TMD]

ARAMANIK [AAM] lang, Tanzania

ARAMBA alt for ARAMMBA [STK]

ARAMIA RIVER dial of TABO [KNV]

'ARAMIT alt for HULAULÁ [HUY]

<ARAMIT alt for HULAULÁ [HUY]

ARAMMBA [STK] lang, Papua New Guinea

ARAMO alt for PINAI-HAGAHAI [PNN]

ARANADAN [AAF] lang, India

ARANDA alt for ARRARNTA, WESTERN [ARE]

ARANDAI [JBJ] lang, Indonesia (Irian Jaya)

ARANDAI alt for DOMBANO dial of ARANDAI [JBJ]

ARANDUI alt for GAWAR-BATI [GWT]

ARANÉS alt for GASCON, ARANESE [GSC]

ARANESE alt for GASCON, ARANESE [GSC]

ARANESE dial of GASCON [GSC]

ARANESE OCCITAN alt for GASCON, ARANESE [GSC]

ARANGKA'A dial of TALAUD [TLD]

ARAONA [ARO] lang, Bolivia

ARÁP dial of JARAI [JRA]

ARAPAÇO alt for ARAPASO [ARJ]

ARAPAHO [ARP] lang, USA

ARAPASO [ARJ] lang, Brazil
ARAPESH, BUMBITA [AON] lang, Papua New
  Guinea
ARAPIUM alt for SATERÉ-MAWÉ [MAV]
ARARA alt for JÚMA [JUA]
ARARA dial of CARUTANA [CRU]
ARARA DO AMAZONAS alt for CARÚTANA [CRU]
ARARA DO BEIRADÃO alt for ARÁRA, MATO
  GROSSO [AXG]
ARÁRA DO JIPARANÁ alt for ARÁRA, RONDÔNIA
  [ARR]
ARARA DO RIO BRANCO alt for ARÁRA, MATO
  GROSSO [AXG]
ARÁRA, ACRE [AXA] lang, Brazil
ARÁRA, MATO GROSSO [AXG] lang, Brazil
ARÁRA, PARÁ [AAP] lang, Brazil
ARÁRA, RONDÔNIA [ARR] lang, Brazil
ARARAPINA dial of KATUKINA, PANOAN [KNT]
ARARA-SHAWANAWA dial of KATUKINA, PANOAN
  [KNT]
ARARAWA dial of KATUKINA, PANOAN [KNT]
ARASAIRI dial of HUACHIPAERI [HUG]
ARASPASO alt for ARAPASO [ARJ]
"ARAUCANO" pejorative alt for MAPUDUNGUN
  [ARU]
ARAUCANO alt for MAPUDUNGUN [ARU]
ARAUINE alt for AWETÍ [AWE]
ARAUITE alt for AWETÍ [AWE]
ARAVA dial of TAMIL [TCV]
ARAVIA dial of HAHON [HAH]
ARAWÁ alt for ARUA [ARA]
ARAWAK [ARW] lang, Suriname; also in French
  Guiana, Guyana, Venezuela
ARAWE alt for SOLONG [AAW]
ARAWETÉ [AWT] lang, Brazil
ARAWUM [AWM] lang, Papua New Guinea
ARAY alt for ARE [AAG]
ARAYANS alt for MALARYAN [MJQ]
ARBANASI dial of ALBANIAN, TOSK [ALN]
ARBËRESHË alt for ALBANIAN, ARBËRESHË
  [AAE]
ARBERICHTE alt for ALBANIAN, ARVANITIKA
  [AAT]
ARBILI dial of KURDI [KDB]
ARBILI NEO-ARAMAIC alt for LISHANID NOSHAN
  [AIJ]
ARBOR alt for ADI [ADI]
ARBORA alt for ARBORE [ARV]
ARBORE [ARV] lang, Ethiopia
ARBORENSE dial of SARDINIAN, CAMPIDANESE
  [SRO]
ARCHI [ARC] lang, Russia (Europe)
ARCHIN alt for ARCHI [ARC]
ARCHINTSY alt for ARCHI [ARC]
ARCHUALDA alt for ADYNYAMATHANHA [ADT]
ARCTIC RED RIVER dial of GWICHIN [KUC]
ARCTIC VILLAGE GWICH'IN dial of GWICHIN [KUC]
ARDAIÂNI dial of KURDI [KDB]
ARDERI alt for DZODINKA [ADD]
ARDIDO alt for LAREDO dial of DZA [JEN]
ARE [AAG] lang, India

ARE [MWC] lang, Papua New Guinea
ARÉ alt for XETÁ [XET]
'ARE'ARE [ALU] lang, Solomon Islands
'ARE'ARE dial of AREARE [ALU]
AREARE alt for 'ARE'ARE [ALU]
AREBA [AEA] lang, Australia
ARECUNA dial of PEMON [AOC]
AREGEREK alt for MUSAR [MMI]
AREGWE alt for IRIGWE [IRI]
AREKUNA alt for ARECUNA dial of PEMON [AOC]
A-REM alt for AREM [AEM]
AREM [AEM] lang, Viet Nam; also in Laos
ARENG alt for CHIN, KHUMI [CKM]
AREQUENA alt for GUAREQUENA [GAE]
AREQUIPA QUECHUA alt for QUECHUA,
  AREQUIPA-LA UNION [QAR]
ARET dial of PASHAYI, NORTHEAST [AEE]
AREWA dial of HAUSA [HUA]
ARGENTINE SIGN LANGUAGE [AED] lang,
  Argentina
ARGO alt for ALAGO [ALA]
ARGOBBA [AGJ] lang, Ethiopia
ARGOENI alt for ARGUNI [AGF]
ARGUNI [AGF] lang, Indonesia (Irian Jaya)
ARGUNI BAY alt for IRARUTU [IRH]
ARHÂ [ARN] lang, New Caledonia
ARHE dial of IVBIE NORTH-OKPELA-ARHE [ATG]
ARHÖ [AOK] lang, New Caledonia
ARHUACO alt for ICA [ARH]
ARI [AAC] lang, Papua New Guinea
ARI alt for AARI [AIZ]
ARI alt for ERRE [ERR]
ARIA alt for RAPANGKAKA dial of PAMONA [BCX]
ARIA alt for SOUTHERN UMA dial of UMA [PPK]
ARIA-MOUK alt for MOUK-ARIA [MWH]
ARIANA alt for OMAGUA [OMG]
ARIANGULU alt for SANYE [SSN]
ARIAWIAI alt for ARUAMU [MSY]
ARIBWATSA [LAZ] lang, Papua New Guinea
ARIBWAUNG [YLU] lang, Papua New Guinea
ARIBWAUNGG alt for ARIBWAUNG [YLU]
ARICAPÚ alt for ARIKAPÚ [ARK]
ARICUNA alt for ARECUNA dial of PEMON [AOC]
ARIÉGEOIS dial of GASCON [GSC]
ARIFAMA dial of ARIFAMA-MINIAFIA [AAI]
ARIFAMA-MINIAFIA [AAI] lang, Papua New Guinea
ARIGIBI dial of KIWAI, NORTHEAST [KIW]
ARIGIDI [AKK] lang, Nigeria
ARIGIDÍ dial of ARIGIDI [AKK]
ARIHINI alt for BARÉ [BAE]
ARIHINI alt for MANDAHUACA [MHT]
ARIKAPÚ [ARK] lang, Brazil
ARIKARA [ARI] lang, USA
ARIKAREE alt for ARIKARA [ARI]
ARIKARI alt for ARIKARA [ARI]
ARIKARIS alt for ARIKARA [ARI]
ARIKUN dial of HOANYA [HON]
ARIMA alt for WANIB [AUK]
ARINGA [LUC] lang, Uganda
ARINUA alt for WANIB [AUK]
ARINWA alt for WANIB [AUK]

ARIOM dial of BIAK [BHW]
ARIPAKTSA alt for RIKBAKTSA [ART]
ARISEACHI TARAHUMARA alt for TARAHUMARA NORTE [THH]
ARKANSAS alt for QUAPAW [QUA]
ARLENG ALAM alt for MIKIR [MJW]
ARLIJA dial of ROMANI, BALKAN [RMN]
ARMA [AOH] lang, Colombia
ARMAN dial of EVEN [EVE]
ARMANSKI alt for ARMENIAN [ARM]
ARMENIAN [ARM] lang, Armenia; also in Azerbaijan, Bulgaria, Canada, Cyprus, Egypt, Estonia, France, Georgia, Greece, Honduras, Hungary, India, Iran, Iraq, Israel, Jordan, Kazakhstan, Kyrgyzstan, Lebanon, Palestinian West Bank and Gaza, Russia (Europe), Syria, Tajikistan, Turkey (Europe), Turkmenistan, Ukraine, USA, Uzbekistan
ARMENIAN BOSA alt for LOMAVREN [RMI]
ARMENIAN BOSHA alt for LOMAVREN [RMI]
ARMENIAN SIGN LANGUAGE [AEN] lang, Armenia
ARMINA alt for ROMANIAN, MACEDO [RUP]
ARMJANSKI alt for ARMENIAN [ARM]
ARMJANSKI YAZYK alt for ARMENIAN [ARM]
ARMOPA alt for BONGGO [BPG]
ARNAIS alt for GASCON, ARANESE [GSC]
ARNAUT alt for ALBANIAN, TOSK [ALN]
ARNEBUAB BISA alt for LOMAVREN [RMI]
ARNIYA alt for KHOWAR [KHW]
ARO alt for AARI [AIZ]
ARO alt for ARHÖ [AOK]
AROGBO dial of IZON [IJC]
AROI dial of HAROI [HRO]
AROKWA alt for ERUWA [ERH]
AROMA alt for ADOMA dial of CLELA [DRI]
AROMA dial of KEOPARA [KHZ]
AROMANIAN alt for ROMANIAN, MACEDO [RUP]
AROMUNIAN alt for ROMANIAN, MACEDO [RUP]
ARONA alt for AROMA dial of KEOPARA [KHZ]
AROP alt for AROP-SISSANO [APS]
AROP dial of AROP-LOKEP [APR]
AROP-LOKEP [APR] lang, Papua New Guinea
AROP-SISSANO [APS] lang, Papua New Guinea
AROSARIO alt for MALAYO [MBP]
AROSI [AIA] lang, Solomon Islands
AROSI dial of AROSI [AIA]
AROVE alt for SOLONG [AAW]
AROWAK alt for ARAWAK [ARW]
ARRAPAHOE alt for ARAPAHO [ARP]
ARRARNTA, WESTERN [ARE] lang, Australia
ARRERNTE, EASTERN [AER] lang, Australia
ARREY alt for ARE [AAG]
ARRINGEU alt for PONGU [PON]
ARSARIO alt for MALAYO [MBP]
ARSI dial of OROMO, BORANA-ARSI-GUJI [GAX]
ARSO alt for TAIKAT [AOS]
ARTA [ATZ] lang, Philippines
ARTHARE alt for ATHPARIYA [APH]
ARTHARE alt for DUNGMALI [RAA]
ARTHARE-KHESANG alt for ATHPARIYA [APH]
ARTHARE-KHESANG alt for DUNGMALI [RAA]
ARTOIS dial of PICARD [PCD]

ARTON alt for HÉRTEVIN PROPER dial of HERTEVIN [HRT]
ARTU EHTREMEÑU alt for NORTHERN EXTREMADURAN dial of EXTREMADURAN [EXT]
ARTVIN dial of ARMENIAN [ARM]
ARTWIN alt for ARTVIN dial of ARMENIAN [ARM]
ARU alt for ALATIL [ALX]
ARU alt for JAQARU [JQR]
ARUA [ARA] lang, Brazil
ARUA dial of LUGBARA [LUG]
ARUÁ [ARX] lang, Brazil
ARUACHI alt for ARUÁSHI dial of ARUA [ARX]
ARUACO alt for ICA [ARH]
ARUAMU [MSY] lang, Papua New Guinea
ARUÁSHI dial of ARUA [ARX]
ARUBA ENGLISH dial of ENGLISH [ENG]
ARUEK [AUR] lang, Papua New Guinea
ARUFE alt for NAMBU [NCM]
ARUGHAUNYA dial of ODUAL [ODU]
ARUI alt for SERUI-LAUT [SEU]
ARUM dial of ARUM-TESU [AAB]
ARUMA [WAP] lang, Guyana; also in Brazil
ARUMAKA dial of KULA [TPG]
ARUMANIAN alt for ROMANIAN, MACEDO [RUP]
ARUMBI dial of LESE [LES]
ARUM-CESU alt for ARUM-TESU [AAB]
ARUM-CHESSU alt for ARUM-TESU [AAB]
ARUM-TESU [AAB] lang, Nigeria
ARUMUN alt for ROMANIAN, MACEDO [RUP]
ARUNDUM alt for RUNDUM dial of TAGAL MURUT [MVV]
ARUNG alt for NAGA, ZEME [NZM]
ARUNTA alt for ARRARNTA, WESTERN [ARE]
ARUNTA alt for ARRERNTE, EASTERN [AER]
ARUOP [LSR] lang, Papua New Guinea
ARUPAI dial of MARITSAUA [MSP]
ARUSA dial of MAASAI [MET]
ARUSHA alt for ARUSA dial of MAASAI [MET]
ARUSHA dial of MAASAI [MET]
ARUSI alt for ARSI dial of OROMO, BORANA-ARSI- GUJI [GAX]
ARUSKUSH-DAQQUSHCHU dial of TAT, MUSLIM [TTT]
ARUSSI alt for ARSI dial of OROMO, BORANA-ARSI-GUJI [GAX]
ARUTANI [ATX] lang, Brazil; also in Venezuela
ARVANITIC alt for ALBANIAN, ARVANITIKA [AAT]
ARVANITIKA alt for ALBANIAN, ARVANITIKA [AAT]
ARWALA dial of TUGUN [TZN]
ARWUR alt for WARAY [WRZ]
ARYA alt for ARE [AAG]
ARZEU dial of TARIFIT [RIF]
AS [ASZ] lang, Indonesia (Irian Jaya)
ASA dial of IRAQW [IRK]
ASÁ alt for AASÁX [AAS]
ASAHYUE alt for SEHWI [SFW]
ASAK alt for AASÁX [AAS]
ASAK alt for KADO [KDV]
ASAKE alt for SAKE [SAG]
ASAMBE alt for ASSAMESE [ASM]

ASAMI alt for ASSAMESE [ASM]
ASAMIYA alt for ASSAMESE [ASM]
ASANDE alt for ZANDE [ZAN]
ASANGA alt for GUSU dial of JERE [JER]
ASANGA alt for SANGA [SGA]
ASANTE dial of AKAN [TWS]
ASANTI alt for ASANTE dial of AKAN [TWS]
ASAPA dial of OMIE [AOM]
ASARO alt for DANO [ASO]
ASARO'O [MTV] lang, Papua New Guinea
ASAS [ASD] lang, Papua New Guinea
ASAT [ASX] lang, Papua New Guinea
ASAX alt for AASÁX [AAS]
ASBALMIN dial of TIFAL [TIF]
ASCHINGINI alt for CISHINGINI [ASG]
ASE dial of AKPES [IBE]
ASEBI dial of PONGU [PON]
ASEN dial of AKAN [TWS]
ASENGSENG alt for SENGSENG [SSZ]
ASENTO dial of GUN-GBE [GUW]
ASER alt for AZER dial of SONINKE [SNN]
ASERA dial of TOLAKI [LBW]
ASHAGANNA alt for CISHINGINI [ASG]
ASHÁNINCA [CNI] lang, Peru
ASHANTE TWI alt for ASANTE dial of AKAN [TWS]
ASHE [AHS] lang, Nigeria
ASHEN dial of TSIKIMBA [KDL]
ASHÉNINCA alt for ASHÉNINCA PICHIS [CPU]
ASHÉNINCA APURUCAYALI alt for AJYÍNINKA
    APURUCAYALI [CPC]
ASHÉNINCA PAJONAL [CJO] lang, Peru
ASHÉNINCA PERENÉ [CPP] lang, Peru
ASHÉNINCA PICHIS [CPU] lang, Peru
ASHÉNINCA UCAYALI-YURUA [CPB] lang, Peru;
    also in Brazil
ASHÉNINCA UCAYALI-YURÚA [CPB] lang, Peru;
    also in Brazil
ASHINGINI alt for CISHINGINI [ASG]
ASHINGINI alt for TSISHINGINI [KAM]
ASHKARAUA dial of ABAZA [ABQ]
ASHKHARIK dial of ARMENIAN [ARM]
ASHKUN [ASK] lang, Afghanistan
ASHKUND alt for ASHKUN [ASK]
ASHKUNI alt for ASHKUN [ASK]
ASHLUSHLAY alt for CHULUPÍ [CAG]
ASHO alt for CHIN, ASHO [CSH]
ASHOLIO alt for SHOLIO dial of TYAP [KCG]
ASHRAAF alt for AF-ASHRAAF dial of SOMALI
    [SOM]
ASHREE alt for ASURI [ASR]
ASHRETI dial of PHALURA [PHL]
ASHTIANI [ATN] lang, Iran
ASHTIKULIN dial of LAK [LBE]
ASHU alt for CHIN, ASHO [CSH]
ASHUKU dial of MBEMBE, TIGON [NZA]
ASHURUVERI dial of ASHKUN [ASK]
ASHUWA alt for ABAZA [ABQ]
ASI alt for WASI [WBJ]
ASIAN SWAHILI alt for CUTCHI-SWAHILI [CCL]
ASIANARA alt for BURUWAI [ASI]
ASIAORO dial of MAILU [MGU]

ASIATIC ESKIMO alt for YUPIK, CENTRAL
    SIBERIAN [ESS]
ASIENARA alt for BURUWAI [ASI]
ASIFABAD dial of KOLAMI, SOUTHEASTERN [NIT]
ASIGA alt for LEYIGHA [AYI]
ASILULU [ASL] lang, Indonesia (Maluku)
ASILULU dial of ASILULU [ASL]
ASIQ alt for BANTOANON [BNO]
ASKOTI dial of KUMAUNI [KFY]
ASL alt for AMERICAN SIGN LANGUAGE [ASE]
ASMAT DARAT alt for CITAK, TAMNIM [TML]
ASMAT, CASUARINA COAST [ASC] lang, Indonesia
    (Irian Jaya)
ASMAT, CENTRAL [AST] lang, Indonesia (Irian Jaya)
ASMAT, NORTH [NKS] lang, Indonesia (Irian Jaya)
ASMAT, YAOSAKOR [ASY] lang, Indonesia (Irian
    Jaya)
ASOA [ASV] lang, DCR
ASOBSE alt for BASSOSSI [BSI]
ASOLIO alt for SHOLIO dial of TYAP [KCG]
ASOM alt for AZOM dial of POL [PMM]
ASOM alt for COMO KARIM [CFG]
ASONG alt for ASSANGORI [SUN]
ASONG dial of AKHA [AKA]
ASONGA dial of NGUMBI [NUI]
ASONGA dial of YASA [YKO]
ASONGORI alt for SUNGOR [SUN]
ASPROMONTE dial of GREEK [GRK]
ASSAGORI alt for SUNGOR [SUN]
ASSAIKIO dial of ALAGO [ALA]
ASSAKA dial of CAKA [CKX]
ASSAM KHAMTI dial of KHAMTI [KHT]
ASSAMESE [ASM] lang, India; also in Bangladesh,
    Bhutan
ASSANGORI [SUN] lang, Chad; also in Sudan
ASSEM dial of JAGOI [SNE]
ASSIGA alt for LEYIGHA [AYI]
ASSINIBOIN alt for ASSINIBOINE [ASB]
ASSINIBOINE [ASB] lang, Canada; also in USA
ASSOUNGOR alt for ASSANGORI [SUN]
ASSUMBO alt for IPULO [ASS]
ASSUR alt for ASURI [ASR]
ASSURINÍ alt for ASURINÍ [ASU]
ASSURINÍ DO TOCANTINS alt for ASURINÍ [ASU]
ASSYRIAN alt for ASSYRIAN NEO-ARAMAIC [AII]
ASSYRIAN NEO-ARAMAIC [AII] lang, Iraq; also in
    Armenia, Australia, Austria, Azerbaijan, Belgium,
    Brazil, Canada, Cyprus, France, Georgia,
    Germany, Greece, Iran, Italy, Lebanon,
    Netherlands, New Zealand, Russia (Europe),
    Sweden, Switzerland, Syria, Turkey (Asia),
    United Kingdom, USA
ASSYRIANCI alt for ASSYRIAN NEO-ARAMAIC
    [AII]
ASSYRISKI alt for ASSYRIAN NEO-ARAMAIC [AII]
ASTARA dial of TALYSH [TLY]
ASTIANI alt for ASHTIANI [ATN]
ASTOR alt for ASTORI dial of SHINA [SCL]
ASTORI dial of SHINA [SCL]
ASTRACHAN alt for ASTRAKHAN dial of
    ARMENIAN [ARM]

ASTRAKHAN dial of ARMENIAN [ARM]
ASTURIAN [AUB] lang, Spain; also in Portugal
ASTURIAN-LEONESE alt for ASTURIAN [AUB]
ASTURIANU alt for ASTURIAN [AUB]
ASTUR-LEONESE alt for ASTURIAN [AUB]
ASU [ASA] lang, Tanzania
ASU [AUM] lang, Nigeria
ASUA alt for ASOA [ASV]
ASUAE alt for ASOA [ASV]
ASUATI alt for ASOA [ASV]
ASUMBO alt for IPULO [ASS]
ASUMBO alt for IYIVE [UIV]
ASUMBOA [AUA] lang, Solomon Islands
ASUMBUA alt for ASUMBOA [AUA]
ASUMUO alt for ASUMBOA [AUA]
ASUNCIÓN MIXTEPEC ZAPOTEC alt for
    ZAPOTECO, ASUNCIÓN MIXTEPEC [ZOO]
ASUNCIÓN TLACOLULITA ZAPOTECO alt for
    ZAPOTECO, TLACOLULITA [ZPK]
ASUNGORE alt for ASSANGORI [SUN]
ASUNGORE alt for SUNGOR [SUN]
ASURA alt for ASURI [ASR]
ASURI [ASR] lang, India
ASURINÍ [ASU] lang, Brazil
ASURINÍ, XINGÚ [ASN] lang, Brazil
ASWANIK alt for SONINKE [SNN]
ATA [ATM] lang, Philippines
ATA dial of PELE-ATA [ATA]
ATA OF DAVAO alt for MANOBO, ATA [ATD]
ATABA dial of OBOLO [ANN]
ATACAMEÑO alt for KUNZA [KUZ]
ATAIYAL alt for ATAYAL [TAY]
ATAK alt for JIRU [JRR]
ATAKAPA [ALE] lang, USA
ATAKAR alt for ATAKAT dial of TYAP [KCG]
ATAKAT dial of TYAP [KCG]
ATAKORA FULFULDE dial of FULFULDE, BENIN-
    TOGO [FUE]
ATALA dial of DEGEMA [DEG]
ATAM alt for HATAM [HAD]
ATAM alt for NTA dial of NDE-NSELE-NTA [NDD]
ATA-MAN alt for MAGAHAT [MTW]
ATAMANU alt for YALAHATAN [JAL]
ATAMPAYA [AMZ] lang, Australia
ATAO MANOBO alt for MANOBO, ATA [ATD]
ATARIPOE dial of MALO [MLA]
ATATLÁHUCA MIXTEC alt for MIXTECO,
    ATATLÁHUCA [MIB]
ATAURA alt for ADABE [ADB]
ATAURO alt for ADABE [ADB]
ATAURU alt for ADABE [ADB]
ATAYAL [TAY] lang, Taiwan
ATCHE alt for ATTIÉ [ATI]
ATCHIN dial of URIPIV-WALA-RANO-ATCHIN [UPV]
ATE alt for ARHE dial of IVBIE NORTH-OKPELA-
    ARHE [ATG]
ATE alt for GARUS [GYB]
ATEMBLE [ATE] lang, Papua New Guinea
ATEMPLE alt for ATEMBLE [ATE]
ATEMPLE-APRIS alt for ATEMBLE [ATE]
ATEN [GAN] lang, Nigeria

ATEPEC ZAPOTECO alt for ZAPOTECO, JUÁREZ,
    SIERRA [ZAA]
ATESINO dial of LADIN [LLD]
ATESO alt for TESO [TEO]
ATHAPRE alt for ATHPARIYA [APH]
ATHOC dial of DINKA, SOUTHEASTERN [DIN]
ATHOIC alt for ATHOC dial of DINKA, SOUTH-
    EASTERN [DIN]
ATHPAGARI alt for BELHARIYA [BYW]
ATHPAHARIYA alt for BELHARIYA [BYW]
ATHPARE alt for ATHPARIYA [APH]
ATHPARE alt for BELHARIYA [BYW]
ATHPARIYA [APH] lang, Nepal
ATHPARIYA alt for BELHARIYA [BYW]
ATHU alt for ASU [ASA]
ATI [ATK] lang, Philippines
ATI alt for BIRITAI [BQQ]
ATI alt for BUTMAS-TUR [BNR]
ATI alt for KINARAY-A [KRJ]
ATI alt for KUTEP [KUB]
ATI alt for OBOKUITAI [AFZ]
ATIAHU alt for BOBOT [BTY]
ATICHERAK alt for KACHICHERE dial of TYAP
    [KCG]
ATICUM alt for UAMUÉ [UAM]
ATIE alt for ATTIÉ [ATI]
ATIHKAMEKW alt for ATIKAMEKW [TET]
ATIKAMEK alt for ATIKAMEKW [TET]
ATIKAMEKW [TET] lang, Canada
ATIKUM alt for UAMUÉ [UAM]
ATIMELANG dial of ABUI [ABZ]
ATINA dial of LAZ [LZZ]
ATINGGOLA alt for BOLANGO [BLD]
ATIRI alt for NOMATSIGUENGA [NOT]
ATISA dial of EPIE [EPI]
ATISSA alt for ATISA dial of EPIE [EPI]
ATITLÁN MIXE dial of MIXE, QUETZALTEPEC
    [MVE]
ATIU dial of RAROTONGAN [RRT]
ATJEH alt for ACEH [ATJ]
ATJEHNESE alt for ACEH [ATJ]
ATKA alt for WESTERN ALEUT dial of ALEUT
    [ALW]
ATKAN alt for BERINGOV dial of ALEUT [ALW]
ATKAN alt for WESTERN ALEUT dial of ALEUT
    [ALW]
ATLACOMULCO-TEMASCALCINGO dial of
    MAZAHUA CENTRAL [MAZ]
ATNA alt for AHTENA [AHT]
ATNEBAR alt for TANIMBAR KEI dial of KEI
    [KEI]
ATO MAJANG alt for MAJANG [MPE]
ATO MAJANGER-ONK alt for MAJANG [MPE]
ATOC alt for ATHOC dial of DINKA, SOUTH-
    EASTERN [DIN]
ATOHWAIM [AQM] lang, Indonesia (Irian Jaya)
ATOKTOU alt for MALUAL dial of DINKA, SOUTH-
    WESTERN [DIK]
ATONG [ATO] lang, Cameroon
A'TONG [AOT] lang, India
ATONGA alt for TONGA dial of NDAU [NDC]

ATONI [TMR] lang, Indonesia (Nusa Tenggara)
ATORADA dial of ARUMA [WAP]
ATORAI alt for ATORADA dial of ARUMA [WAP]
ATORI alt for KAIS [KZM]
ATOR'TI alt for ATORADA dial of ARUMA [WAP]
ATRATO alt for EMBERÁ, NORTHERN [EMP]
ATROAHY alt for ATRUAHÍ [ATR]
ATROAÍ alt for ATRUAHÍ [ATR]
ATROARÍ alt for ATRUAHÍ [ATR]
ATROWARI alt for ATRUAHÍ [ATR]
ATRUAHI dial of ATRUAHÍ [ATR]
ATRUAHÍ [ATR] lang, Brazil
ATRUSH dial of LISHANA DENI [LSD]
ATSAHUACA [ATC] lang, Peru
ATSAM [CCH] lang, Nigeria
ATSAM alt for AI-CHAM [AIH]
ATSANG alt for ACHANG [ACN]
ATSANG-BANGWA alt for YEMBA [BAN]
ATSCHOLI alt for ACHOLI [ACO]
ATSE alt for XIAO HUA MIAO dial of HMONG NJUA [BLU]
ATSHE alt for ATTIÉ [ATI]
ATSHI alt for ZAIWA [ATB]
ATSI alt for ZAIWA [ATB]
ATSILIMA dial of ROTOKAS [ROO]
ATSI-MARU alt for ZAIWA [ATB]
ATSINA alt for GROS VENTRE [ATS]
ATSIRI alt for ASHÉNINCA PAJONAL [CJO]
ATSUGEWI [ATW] lang, USA
ATTA, FAIRE [ATH] lang, Philippines
ATTA, PAMPLONA [ATT] lang, Philippines
ATTA, PUDTOL [ATP] lang, Philippines
ATTAKA alt for ATAKAT dial of TYAP [KCG]
ATTAKAR alt for ATAKAT dial of TYAP [KCG]
ATTAYAL alt for ATAYAL [TAY]
ATTE alt for ARHE dial of IVBIE NORTH-OKPELA-ARHE [ATG]
ATTIÉ [ATI] lang, Côte d'Ivoire
ATTIKAMEK alt for ATIKAMEKW [TET]
ATTIMEWK alt for ATIKAMEKW [TET]
ATTO alt for GIANGAN [BGI]
ATTOCK HINDKO dial of HINDKO, SOUTHERN [HIN]
ATTOCK-HARIPUR HINDKO alt for ATTOCK HINDKO dial of HINDKO, SOUTHERN [HIN]
ATTUAN alt for MEDNYJ ALEUT [MUD]
ATTUAN alt for WESTERN ALEUT dial of ALEUT [ALW]
ATUENCE [ATF] lang, China
ATUENTSE alt for ATUENCE [ATF]
ATUI alt for LESING-GELIMI [LET]
ATUMFUOR dial of LIGBI [LIG]
ATUMFUOR-KASA alt for ATUMFUOR dial of LIGBI [LIG]
ATUOT alt for REEL [ATU]
ATURA alt for ATURU [AUP]
ATURU [AUP] lang, Papua New Guinea
ATWOT alt for REEL [ATU]
ATYAP alt for KATAB dial of TYAP [KCG]
ATZERA alt for ADZERA [AZR]
ATZI alt for ZAIWA [ATB]

ATZINGO POPOLOCA alt for POPOLOCA, SAN JUAN ATZINGO [POE]
ATZINTECO alt for MATLATZINCA, ATZINGO [OCU]
AU [AVT] lang, Papua New Guinea
AU alt for IMBONGU [IMO]
AU TÁ alt for AO TÁ dial of MUONG [MTQ]
AUA alt for IMBONGU [IMO]
AUA dial of PILENI [PIV]
AUA dial of WUVULU-AUA [WUV]
AUAKE alt for ARUTANI [ATX]
AUAQUÉ alt for ARUTANI [ATX]
AUARIS dial of SANUMA [SAM]
AUA-VIWULU alt for WUVULU-AUA [WUV]
"AUCA" pejorative alt for WAORANI [AUC]
AUCHI dial of YEKHEE [ETS]
//AU//EI alt for 'AKHOE [AKE]
//AU//EI alt for ‡KX'AU//'EIN [AUE]
//AU//EI' alt for 'AKHOE [AKE]
//AU//EN alt for 'AKHOE [AKE]
/AU-//EN alt for 'AKHOE [AKE]
AUEN alt for 'AKHOE [AKE]
AUEN alt for ‡KX'AU//'EIN [AUE]
AUETO alt for AWETÍ [AWE]
AUGA alt for UKAAN [KCF]
AUGA dial of UKAAN [KCF]
AUGILA alt for AWJILAH [AUJ]
AUGU alt for ANGAL HENENG [AKH]
AUGU dial of ANGAL HENENG [AKH]
'AUHELAWA [KUD] lang, Papua New Guinea
AUIA-TARAUWI dial of KARKAR-YURI [YUJ]
AUISHIRI alt for ABISHIRA [ASH]
AUISHIRI alt for WAORANI [AUC]
AUITI alt for AWETÍ [AWE]
AUJILA alt for AWJILAH [AUJ]
AUKA alt for LOSA dial of NAKANAI [NAK]
AUKAANS alt for AUKAN [DJK]
AUKAN [DJK] lang, Suriname; also in French Guiana
AUKAN dial of AUKAN [DJK]
AUKSHTAICHIAI alt for AUKSHTAITISH dial of LITHUANIAN [LIT]
AUKSHTAITISH dial of LITHUANIAN [LIT]
AUKSTAITISKAI alt for AUKSHTAITISH dial of LITHUANIAN [LIT]
AUKWE alt for 'AKHOE [AKE]
//AUKWE alt for 'AKHOE [AKE]
/AUKWE alt for 'AKHOE [AKE]
AULUA [AUL] lang, Vanuatu
AULUA BAY alt for AULUA [AUL]
AUMENEFA dial of BAUZI [PAU]
AUNA alt for TSIKIMBA [KDL]
AUNALEI [AUN] lang, Papua New Guinea
AUNGE alt for NAASIOI [NAS]
/AUNI alt for AUNI dial of XOO [NMN]
/'AUNI dial of NU [NGH]
AUNI dial of XOO [NMN]
AUNUS alt for LIVVI [OLO]
/AUO alt for AUNI dial of XOO [NMN]
AURA alt for WAURÁ [WAU]
AURÃ alt for PURUBORÁ [PUR]
AURAMA alt for PAWAIA [PWA]
AURAMA dial of PAWAIA [PWA]

AURAMOT alt for URA [URO]
AUREI dial of FOLOPA [PPO]
AUSHI [AUH] lang, Zambia; also in DCR
AUSHIRI [AUS] lang, Peru
AUSLAN alt for AUSTRALIAN SIGN LANGUAGE
    [ASF]
AUSSA dial of AFAR [AFR]
AUSTRAL [AUT] lang, French Polynesia
AUSTRALIAN ABORIGINES SIGN LANGUAGE
    [ASW] lang, Australia
AUSTRALIAN SIGN LANGUAGE [ASF] lang,
    Australia
AUSTRALIAN STANDARD ENGLISH dial of
    ENGLISH [ENG]
AUSTRIAN SIGN LANGUAGE [ASQ] lang, Austria
AUSTRO-HUNGARIAN SIGN LANGUAGE alt for
    AUSTRIAN SIGN LANGUAGE [ASQ]
AUSTRONESIAN HIRI MOTU dial of MOTU, HIRI
    [POM]
AUTU alt for AWTUW [KMN]
AUVERGNAT [AUV] lang, France
AUVERNE alt for AUVERGNAT [AUV]
AUVERNHAS alt for AUVERGNAT [AUV]
AUWAKA dial of ANEME WAKE [ABY]
AUWE [SMF] lang, Papua New Guinea
AUWJE alt for AUYE [AUU]
AUX alt for AKKIN dial of CHECHEN [CJC]
AUXIRA alt for AUSHIRI [AUS]
AUYAKAWA alt for AUYOKAWA [AUO]
AUYANA alt for AWIYAANA [AUY]
AUYE [AUU] lang, Indonesia (Irian Jaya)
AUYOKAWA [AUO] lang, Nigeria
AUYU alt for AWYU, NOHON [AWJ]
AVA alt for CHIRIPÁ [NHD]
AVA alt for PAI TAVYTERA [PTA]
AVÁ alt for AVÁ-CANOEIRO [AVV]
AVA GUARANÍ alt for CHIRIPÁ [NHD]
AVÁ-CANOEIRO [AVV] lang, Brazil
AVADHI alt for AWADHI [AWD]
AVADI alt for TSUVADI [TVD]
AVALAN dial of BASQUE [BSQ]
AVAM dial of NGANASAN [NIO]
AVAND alt for EVANT [BZZ]
AVANDE alt for EVANT [BZZ]
AVAÑE'E alt for GUARANÍ, PARAGUAYAN [GUG]
AVANI alt for BANIVA [BVV]
AVANKI alt for EVENKI [EVN]
AVANKIL alt for EVENKI [EVN]
AVAR [AVR] lang, Russia (Europe); also in
    Azerbaijan, Kazakhstan, Turkey (Asia)
AVARE alt for AVARI dial of NDO [NDP]
AVARI dial of NDO [NDP]
AVARO alt for AVAR [AVR]
AVASÖ dial of BABATANA [BAQ]
AVATIME [AVA] lang, Ghana
AVAU [AVB] lang, Papua New Guinea
AVAUSHI alt for AUSHI [AUH]
AVEKE alt for HAVEKE [AVE]
'AVEKE alt for HAVEKE [AVE]
AVEKOM alt for AVIKAM [AVI]
AVERE alt for AVARI dial of NDO [NDP]

AVERI dial of MANAGALASI [MCQ]
AVESTA alt for AVESTAN [AVS]
AVESTAN [AVS] lang, Iran
AVIANWU dial of YEKHEE [ETS]
AVIARA dial of ISOKO [ISO]
AVIELE dial of YEKHEE [ETS]
AVIKAM [AVI] lang, Côte d'Ivoire
AVINOMEN alt for ABINOMN [BSA]
AVIO alt for AWYU, NOHON [AWJ]
AVIRITU alt for AVARI dial of NDO [NDP]
AVIRXIRI alt for ABISHIRA [ASH]
AVOKAYA [AVU] lang, DCR; also in Sudan
AVOKAYA PUR dial of AVOKAYA [AVU]
AVREAS alt for VURES dial of MOSINA [MSN]
AVUKAYA alt for AVOKAYA [AVU]
AVUNATARI dial of MALO [MLA]
AWA [AWB] lang, Papua New Guinea
AWA alt for AWA-CUAIQUER [KWI]
AWA alt for BUSUU [BJU]
AWA alt for CHIN, KHUMI [CKM]
AWA alt for IMBONGU [IMO]
AWA alt for VO [WBM]
AWA GUAJÁ alt for GUAJÁ [GUJ]
AWA PIT alt for AWA-CUAIQUER [KWI]
<AWAAZIM alt for CENTRAL NAJDI dial of ARABIC,
    NAJDI SPOKEN [ARS]
AWABAGAL alt for AWABAKAL [AWK]
AWABAKAL [AWK] lang, Australia
AWA-CUAIQUER [KWI] lang, Colombia; also in
    Ecuador
AWAD BING [BCU] lang, Papua New Guinea
AWADHI [AWD] lang, India; also in Nepal
AWAIAMA alt for AWAYAMA dial of TAWALA [TBO]
AWAIYA alt for YALAHATAN [JAL]
AWAK [AWO] lang, Nigeria
AWAKE alt for ARUTANI [ATX]
AWAKÉ alt for ARUTANI [ATX]
AWALAMA alt for AWAYAMA dial of TAWALA [TBO]
AWALE dial of DIODIO [DDI]
AWAN dial of DINKA, SOUTHWESTERN [DIK]
AWANA alt for AVÁ-CANOEIRO [AVV]
AWANO alt for AGUANO [AGA]
AWAR [AYA] lang, Papua New Guinea
AWAR dial of AWAR [AYA]
AWARA [AWX] lang, Papua New Guinea
AWARAI alt for WARAY [WRZ]
AWARRA alt for WARAY [WRZ]
AWATÉ alt for ASURINÍ, XINGÚ [ASN]
AWAU alt for AVAU [AVB]
AWAWAR alt for AWNGI [AWN]
AWAYAMA dial of TAWALA [TBO]
AWBONO [AWH] lang, Indonesia (Irian Jaya)
AWE alt for BIDEYAT [BIH]
AWE dial of PENGO [PEG]
A'WE alt for XAVÁNTE [XAV]
A'WE dial of GARO [GRT]
AWEER alt for BONI [BOB]
AWEERA alt for BONI [BOB]
AWEGE dial of PONGU [PON]
AWEIKOMA alt for XOKLENG [XOK]
AWEMBAK dial of MONI [MNZ]

AWEMBIAK alt for AWEMBAK dial of MONI [MNZ]
AWERA [AWR] lang, Indonesia (Irian Jaya)
AWETÍ [AWE] lang, Brazil
AWETÖ alt for AWETÍ [AWE]
AWI alt for AWING [AZO]
AWI alt for AWNGI [AWN]
AWIAKA alt for AUYOKAWA [AUO]
AWIN alt for AEKYOM [AWI]
AWING [AZO] lang, Cameroon
AWIT dial of TALAUD [TLD]
AWIYA alt for AWNGI [AWN]
AWIYAANA [AUY] lang, Papua New Guinea
AWJE alt for AWYI [AUW]
AWJI alt for AWYI [AUW]
AWJILAH [AUJ] lang, Libya
AWJU alt for AWYU, NOHON [AWJ]
AWKA alt for OKA dial of IGBO [IGR]
AWNGI [AWN] lang, Ethiopia
AWOK alt for AWAK [AWO]
AWON alt for AWUN [AWW]
AWORI dial of YORUBA [YOR]
AWORO dial of YORUBA [YOR]
AWO-SUMAKUYU alt for ULUMANDA' [ULM]
AWTUW [KMN] lang, Papua New Guinea
AWU dial of YI, SOUTHEASTERN [YIE]
AWUN [AWW] lang, Papua New Guinea
AWUNA alt for AGUNA [AUG]
AWUNA dial of EWE [EWE]
AWUTU [AFU] lang, Ghana
AWUTU dial of AWUTU [AFU]
AWYA alt for AWYU, NOHON [AWJ]
AWYE alt for AWYI [AUW]
AWYI [AUW] lang, Indonesia (Irian Jaya)
AWYU alt for JAIR [YIR]
AWYU, MIARO [PSA] lang, Indonesia (Irian Jaya)
AWYU, NOHON [AWJ] lang, Indonesia (Irian Jaya)
AXAMB [AHB] lang, Vanuatu
AXE alt for ACHÉ [GUQ]
AXHEBO dial of YI, SOUTHEASTERN [YIE]
AXI dial of YI, SOUTHEASTERN [YIE]
AXLUSLAY alt for CHULUPÍ [CAG]
AXVAX alt for AKHVAKH [AKV]
AYA alt for AYU [AYU]
AYABADHU [AYD] lang, Australia
AYAM alt for AJAM dial of ASMAT, CENTRAL [AST]
AYAMARU alt for MAI BRAT [AYZ]
AYAN alt for BASARI [BSC]
AYANE alt for BANIVA [BVV]
AYANGAN IFUGAO dial of IFUGAO, BATAD [IFB]
AYAN-MAYA dial of EVENKI [EVN]
AYAO alt for YAO [YAO]
AYAPANEC alt for ZOQUE, TABASCO [ZOQ]
AYAT alt for PALIOUPINY dial of DINKA, SOUTH-
    WESTERN [DIK]
AYAWA alt for YAO [YAO]
AYAYA alt for GUAJÁ [GUJ]
AYERBENSE alt for SOUTHERN ARAGONESE
    dial of ARAGONESE [AXX]
AYERE [AYE] lang, Nigeria
AYI [AYX] lang, China

AYIGA alt for LEYIGHA [AYI]
AYIGHA alt for LEYIGHA [AYI]
AYIKIBEN alt for YUKUBEN [YBL]
AYIWO [NFL] lang, Solomon Islands
AYIZO alt for AYIZO-GBE [AYB]
AYIZO-GBE [AYB] lang, Benin
AYKI alt for RUNGA [ROU]
AYKINDANG alt for RUNGA [ROU]
AYMALLAL alt for SODDO dial of GURAGE, SODDO
    [GRU]
AYMARA, CENTRAL [AYM] lang, Bolivia; also in
    Argentina, Chile, Peru
AYMARA, SOUTHERN [AYC] lang, Peru
AYMASA alt for AIMARA dial of KUNAMA [KUM]
AYMELLEL alt for SODDO dial of GURAGE, SODDO
    [GRU]
AYNALLU dial of AZERBAIJANI, SOUTH [AZB]
AYNU alt for AINU [AIB]
AYO alt for MULAM [MLM]
AYO alt for YAO [YAO]
AYOM alt for AIOME [AKI]
AYORÉ alt for AYOREO [AYO]
AYOREO [AYO] lang, Paraguay; also in Bolivia
AYOTZINTEPEC dial of CHINANTECO, OZUMACIN
    [CHZ]
AYT WAZITEN dial of GHADAMES [GHA]
AYTA ABENLEN SAMBAL alt for AYTA, ABENLEN
    [ABP]
AYTA, ABENLEN [ABP] lang, Philippines
AYTA, AMBALA [ABC] lang, Philippines
AYTA, BATAAN [AYT] lang, Philippines
AYTA, MAG-ANCHI [SGB] lang, Philippines
AYTA, MAG-INDI [BLX] lang, Philippines
AYTA, SORSOGON [AYS] lang, Philippines
AYTA, TAYABAS [AYY] lang, Philippines
AYU [AYU] lang, Nigeria
AYUN dial of JOLA-KASA [CSK]
AYURÚ alt for WAYORÓ [WYR]
AYUTLA MIXTEC alt for MIXTECO, AYUTLA [MIY]
AYZO alt for AYIZO-GBE [AYB]
AZA alt for AZZAGA dial of DAZAGA [DAK]
AZA dial of TEDAGA [TUQ]
AZAGHVANA alt for DGHWEDE [DGH]
AZANDE alt for ZANDE [ZAN]
AZÁNGARO-HUANGÁSCAR-CHOCOS dial of
    QUECHUA, YAUYOS [QUX]
AZANGORI alt for SUNGOR [SUN]
AZANGURI alt for ASSANGORI [SUN]
AZAO alt for ABU [ADO]
AZARGI alt for HAZARAGI [HAZ]
AZBINAWA alt for TAMAJAQ, TAWALLAMMAT
    [TTQ]
AZELLE alt for JERE dial of JERE [JER]
AZER dial of SONINKE [SNN]
AZERA alt for ADZERA [AZR]
AZERA dial of ADZERA [AZR]
AZERBAIJAN alt for AZERBAIJANI, NORTH [AZE]
AZERBAIJANI, NORTH [AZE] lang, Azerbaijan;
    also in Armenia, Estonia, Georgia, Kazakhstan,
    Kyrgyzstan, Russia (Asia), Turkmenistan,
    Uzbekistan

AZERBAIJANI, SOUTH [AZB] lang, Iran; also in Afghanistan, Azerbaijan, Iraq, Jordan, Syria, Turkey (Asia), USA
AZERBAYDZHANI alt for AZERBAIJANI, NORTH [AZE]
AZERI alt for AZERBAIJANI, SOUTH [AZB]
AZERI TURK alt for AZERBAIJANI, NORTH [AZE]
AZHIGA dial of PONGU [PON]
AZI alt for ZAIWA [ATB]
AZIANA alt for KENATI [GAT]
AZOM dial of POL [PMM]
AZONYU dial of NAGA, RENGMA [NRE]
AZORA alt for IZORA [CBO]
AZUMEINA alt for MARBA [MPG]
'AZUMEINA alt for MARBA [MPG]
AZUMU alt for KURAMA [KRH]
AZZA alt for AZZAGA dial of DAZAGA [DAK]
AZZAGA dial of DAZAGA [DAK]
BA alt for AKA-BO [AKM]
BA alt for AMO [AMO]
'BA alt for BUA [BUB]
BA MALI alt for BAH MALEI dial of KENYAH, SEBOB [SIB]
BA PAI [BPN] lang, China
BAA alt for KWA [KWB]
BA'Ä-LOLEH dial of ROTE [ROT]
BAADA alt for KUNAMA [KUM]
BAADEN alt for KUNAMA [KUM]
BAADI [BCJ] lang, Australia
BAADU dial of AFAR [AFR]
BA'ADU dial of AFAR [AFR]
BA<ADU alt for BAADU dial of AFAR [AFR]
BAAGANDJI alt for BAGUNDJI dial of DARLING [DRL]
BAAGANDJI alt for DARLING [DRL]
BAAGATO alt for BAGETO dial of MPONGMPONG [MGG]
BAAGATO dial of BANGANDU [BGF]
BAALE alt for BALESI dial of KACIPO-BALESI [KOE]
BAALI alt for BALI [BCP]
BA'AMANG dial of NGAJU [NIJ]
BAAN [BVJ] lang, Nigeria
BAANGI [BQX] lang, Nigeria
BAANGINGI' alt for SAMA, BALANGINGI [SSE]
BAAN-OGOI alt for BAAN [BVJ]
BAARAVI alt for CENTRAL VANUA LEVU dial of FIJIAN [FJI]
BAARAVI alt for NUCLEAR WESTERN FIJIAN dial of FIJIAN, WESTERN [WYY]
BAATE alt for IFÈ [IFE]
BAATI alt for BATI dial of BWA [BWW]
BAATO BALOI alt for BALOI [BIZ]
BAATOMBU alt for BARIBA [BBA]
BAATONU alt for BARIBA [BBA]
BAATONUN alt for BARIBA [BBA]
BAATONUN-KWARA alt for BARIBA [BBA]
BAAZA alt for KUNAMA [KUM]
BAAZAYN alt for KUNAMA [KUM]
BAAZEN alt for KUNAMA [KUM]
BABA [BBW] lang, Cameroon
BABA alt for MALAY, BABA [BAL]

BABA dial of GALOLI [GAL]
BABA INDONESIAN alt for INDONESIAN, PERANAKAN [PEA]
BABADJI alt for BEBA' dial of BAFUT [BFD]
BABADJOU dial of NGOMBALE [NLA]
BABAGA dial of KEOPARA [KHZ]
BABAGARUPU dial of SINAUGORO [SNC]
BABAL alt for LASSA dial of MARGHI CENTRAL [MAR]
BABALIA alt for ARABIC, BABALIA CREOLE [BBZ]
BABALIA alt for BERAKOU [BXV]
BABALIYA alt for ARABIC, BABALIA CREOLE [BBZ]
BA'BAN alt for ABON [ABO]
BABANGO [BBM] lang, DCR
BABANKI [BBK] lang, Cameroon
BABAR, NORTH [BCD] lang, Indonesia (Maluku)
BABAR, SOUTHEAST [VBB] lang, Indonesia (Maluku)
BABASI alt for BATOMO dial of MESAKA [IYO]
BABATA alt for UBAE dial of NAKANAI [NAK]
BABATANA [BAQ] lang, Solomon Islands
BABATANA dial of BABATANA [BAQ]
BABA'ZHI alt for BEBA' dial of BAFUT [BFD]
BABESSI alt for WUSHI [BSE]
BABETE dial of NGOMBA [NNO]
BABINE [BCR] lang, Canada
BABINE CARRIER alt for BABINE [BCR]
"BABINGA" pejorative alt for YAKA [AXK]
BABINGA alt for BAKA [BKC]
BABINGA alt for GYELE [GYI]
BABINGA alt for YAKA [AXK]
BABINSK alt for SAAMI, AKKALA [SIA]
BABIR alt for BURA-PABIR [BUR]
BABIRUWA alt for ERITAI [BAD]
BABLE alt for CENTRAL ASTURIAN dial of ASTURIAN [AUB]
BABOK alt for BOK dial of MANDJAK [MFV]
BABOLE [BVX] lang, Congo
BABON dial of NYINDROU [LID]
BABONG dial of BAKAKA [BQZ]
BABOUTE alt for VUTE [VUT]
BABRI alt for BAURIA [BGE]
BABRUA alt for ERITAI [BAD]
BABRUWA alt for ERITAI [BAD]
BA-BUCHE alt for GAMO dial of GAMO-NINGI [BTE]
BABUE alt for BALUE dial of BAKUNDU-BALUE [BDU]
BABUNGO alt for VENGO [BAV]
BABUR alt for BURA-PABIR [BUR]
BABURIWA alt for ERITAI [BAD]
BABUSA alt for BABUZA [BZG]
BABUTE alt for VUTE [VUT]
BABUYAN alt for BATAK [BTK]
BABUYAN alt for IBATAN [IVB]
BABUZA [BZG] lang, Taiwan
BABWA alt for KWA' dial of KWA [BKO]
BABYLONIAN TALMUDIC ARAMAIC [BYA] lang, Israel
BAC alt for BATS [BBL]
BACA alt for NUBACA [BAF]
BACA dial of SWATI [SWZ]

BACADIN dial of AVAR [AVR]
BACAIRÍ alt for BAKAIRÍ [BKQ]
BACAMA [BAM] lang, Nigeria
BACAN alt for MALAY, BACANESE [BTJ]
BACAVÈS alt for CATALAN-VALENCIAN-BALEAR [CLN]
BACENGA alt for TOCENGA dial of TUKI [BAG]
BACENGA alt for TUKI [BAG]
BACEVE alt for BACHEVE dial of ICEVE-MACI [BEC]
BACHA alt for KWEGU [YID]
BACHADI dial of MALVI [MUP]
BACHAMA alt for BACAMA [BAM]
BACHE alt for CHE [RUK]
BACHEVE alt for ICEVE-MACI [BEC]
BACHEVE alt for ICHEVE dial of ICEVE-MACI [BEC]
BACHEVE dial of ICEVE-MACI [BEC]
BACHIT-GASHISH dial of BEROM [BOM]
BACO alt for BAKO dial of AARI [AIZ]
BADA [BAU] lang, Nigeria
BADA [BHZ] lang, Indonesia (Sulawesi)
BÁDA alt for CACUA [CBV]
BADA alt for KUNAMA [KUM]
BADA dial of BADA [BHZ]
BADA' alt for BADA [BHZ]
BADÄ BA'A alt for BA'Ä-LOLEH dial of ROTE [ROT]
BADAG alt for BADAGA [BFQ]
BADAGA [BFQ] lang, India
BADAGU alt for BADAGA [BFQ]
BADAK alt for BAURIA [BGE]
BADAKHSHI alt for FARSI, EASTERN [PRS]
BADANCHI alt for BADA [BAU]
BADANG alt for MADANG [MQD]
BADARA alt for BADJARA [PBP]
BADARA DUGURI dial of DUGURI [DBM]
BADAWA alt for BADA [BAU]
BADE [BDE] lang, Nigeria
BADE-KADO alt for SOUTHERN BADE dial of BADE [BDE]
BADEN alt for KUNAMA [KUM]
BADERWALI alt for BHADRAWAHI [BHD]
BADESHI [BDZ] lang, Pakistan
BADHANI dial of GARHWALI [GBM]
BADI alt for BAADI [BCJ]
BADIAN alt for BADJARA [PBP]
BADIE alt for GBADI dial of BETE, GAGNOA [BTG]
BADIMAYA [BIA] lang, Australia
BADIN dial of SINDHI BHIL [SBN]
BADIOTTO dial of LADIN [LLD]
BADITTU alt for KOORETE [KQY]
BADJANDE alt for ZANDE [ZAN]
BADJARA [PBP] lang, Guinea; also in Guinea-Bissau, Senegal
BADJARANKE alt for BADJARA [PBP]
BADJAVA alt for NGAD'A [NXG]
BADJAW alt for BAJAU, INDONESIAN [BDL]
BADJIA dial of EWONDO [EWO]
BADJIRI dial of NGURA [NBX]
BADJO alt for BAJAU, INDONESIAN [BDL]
BADJOUE alt for BADWE'E dial of KOONZIME [NJE]

BADJOUE dial of KOONZIME [NJE]
BADONJUNGA alt for NGADJUNMAYA [NJU]
BADOU alt for LITIME dial of AKPOSO [KPO]
BADOUMA alt for DUMA [DMA]
BADROHI alt for BHADRAWAHI [BHD]
BADUGA alt for BADAGA [BFQ]
BADUGU alt for BADAGA [BFQ]
BADUI [BAC] lang, Indonesia (Java and Bali)
BADUNG alt for LOWLAND BALI dial of BALI [BZC]
BADWE'E dial of KOONZIME [NJE]
BADYARA alt for BADJARA [PBP]
BADYARANKE alt for BADJARA [PBP]
BADZUMBO alt for IPULO [ASS]
BA'E alt for MANG [MGA]
BAEAULA alt for WAGAWAGA [WGW]
BAEAULA alt for WAGAWAGA dial of WAGAWAGA [WGW]
BAEBUNTA alt for LEMOLANG [LEY]
BAEGGU [BVD] lang, Solomon Islands
BAEGU alt for BAEGGU [BVD]
BAEGWA alt for ZIMAKANI [ZIK]
BAELE alt for BIDEYAT [BIH]
BAELELEA [BVC] lang, Solomon Islands
BAETORA [BTR] lang, Vanuatu
BAFANG alt for FA' dial of FE'FE' [FMP]
BAFANG alt for FE'FE' [FMP]
BAFANGI alt for BAFANJI [BFJ]
BAFANIO alt for WEST BAFWANGADA dial of BUDU [BUU]
BAFANJI [BFJ] lang, Cameroon
BAFANYI alt for BAFANJI [BFJ]
BAFATÁ CREOLE dial of CRIOULO, UPPER GUINEA [POV]
BAFAW dial of BAFAW-BALONG [BWT]
BAFAW-BALONG [BWT] lang, Cameroon
BAFEUK dial of EWONDO [EWO]
BAFFINLAND "ESKIMO" pejorative name for dial of INUKTITUT, EASTERN CANADIAN [ESB]
BAFIA [KSF] lang, Cameroon
BAFMEN alt for MMEN [BFM]
BAFMENG alt for MMEN [BFM]
BAFO alt for BAFAW dial of BAFAW-BALONG [BWT]
BAFOU alt for YEMBA [BAN]
BAFOUMENG alt for MMEN [BFM]
BAFOWU alt for BAFAW dial of BAFAW-BALONG [BWT]
BAFRENG alt for NKWEN dial of MENDANKWE [MFD]
BAFUCHU alt for NGAMAMBO [NBV]
BAFUMEN alt for MMEN [BFM]
BAFUN dial of BAKAKA [BQZ]
BAFUT [BFD] lang, Cameroon
BAFUT alt for BUFE dial of BAFUT [BFD]
BAFWAKOYI dial of BUDU [BUU]
BAFWANDAKA dial of BALI [BCP]
BAG LACHI alt for LIPUTE dial of LACHI [LBT]
BAGA BINARI [BCG] lang, Guinea
BAGA FORÉ alt for MBULUNGISH [MBV]
BAGA KAKISSA alt for BAGA SOBANÉ [BSV]
BAGA KALOUM [BQF] lang, Guinea
BAGA KOGA [BGO] lang, Guinea

BAGA MANDURI [BMD] lang, Guinea
BAGA MBOTENI [BGM] lang, Guinea
BAGA MONSON alt for MBULUNGISH [MBV]
BAGA SITEMU [BSP] lang, Guinea
BAGA SOBANÉ [BSV] lang, Guinea
BAGADJI alt for KUUKU-YA'U [QKL]
BAGAHAK alt for BEGAK dial of IDAAN [DBJ]
BAGAM dial of MENGAKA [XMG]
BAGANDJI alt for BAGUNDJI dial of DARLING
  [DRL]
BAGANDO alt for BANGANDU [BGF]
BAGANDO-NGOMBE alt for NGOMBE [NMJ]
BAGANDOU alt for NGANDO [NGD]
BAGANGTE alt for MEDUMBA [BYV]
BAGANGU dial of NGEMBA [NGE]
BAGARI alt for BAGRI [BGQ]
BAGASIN alt for GIRAWA [BBR]
BAGDI dial of HARYANVI [BGC]
BAGELA alt for BHAGIRA dial of LOGO [LOG]
BAGELKHANDI alt for BAGHELI [BFY]
BAGERO alt for FURU [FUU]
BAGETO dial of MPONGMPONG [MGG]
BAGHATI alt for LOWER MAHASU PAHARI dial
  of PAHARI, MAHASU [BFZ]
BAGHDADI ARABIC alt for ARABIC,
  MESOPOTAMIAN SPOKEN [ACM]
BAGHELI [BFY] lang, India; also in Nepal
BAGHELI dial of AWADHI [AWD]
BAGHI alt for KAREN, BWE [BWE]
BAGHIRMI alt for BAGIRMI [BMI]
BAGHIRMI PEUL alt for FULFULDE, BAGIRMI [FUI]
BAGHLIANI alt for LOWER MAHASU PAHARI dial
  of PAHARI, MAHASU [BFZ]
BAGIELE alt for GYELE [GYI]
BAGILI alt for GBAGIRI dial of GBANU [GBV]
BAGIRA alt for BWEEN dial of FALI [FLI]
BAGIRMI [BMI] lang, Chad; also in Nigeria
BAGIRMI FULA alt for FULFULDE, BAGIRMI [FUI]
BAGIRO alt for FURU [FUU]
BAGLANI alt for NAHARI dial of BHILI [BHB]
BAGLUNG dial of NEWARI [NEW]
BAGNOUN alt for BAINOUK-GUNYAAMOLO [BCZ]
BAGNOUN alt for BAINOUK-GUNYUÑO [BAB]
BAGO [BQG] lang, Togo
BAGO S'AAMAKK-ULO alt for TSAMAI [TSB]
BAGOBO alt for GIANGAN [BGI]
BAGOBO alt for MANOBO, OBO [OBO]
BAGRI [BGQ] lang, India; also in Pakistan
BAGRI LOHAR alt for LOHAR, GADE [GDA]
BAGRIA alt for BAGRI [BGQ]
BAGRIMMA alt for BAGIRMI [BMI]
BAGRIS alt for BAGRI [BGQ]
BAGROTE alt for GILGITI dial of SHINA [SCL]
BAGU alt for MIWA [VMI]
BAGUERO alt for FURU [FUU]
BAGUILI alt for GBAGIRI dial of GBANU [GBV]
BAGUIRME alt for BAGIRMI [BMI]
BAGUIRMI alt for BAGIRMI [BMI]
BAGUIRO alt for FURU [FUU]
BAGULAL alt for BAGVALAL [KVA]
BAGUNDJI dial of DARLING [DRL]

BAGUPI [BPI] lang, Papua New Guinea
BAGUSA [BQB] lang, Indonesia (Irian Jaya)
BAGVALAL [KVA] lang, Russia (Europe)
BAGVALIN alt for BAGVALAL [KVA]
BAGWA dial of ZIMAKANI [ZIK]
BAGWA ZIMAKANI alt for ZIMAKANI [ZIK]
BAGWAMA alt for KURAMA [KRH]
BAGWAMA alt for RUMA [RUZ]
BAGYELE alt for GYELE [GYI]
BAH MALEI dial of KENYAH, SEBOB [SIB]
BAHAM [BDW] lang, Indonesia (Irian Jaya)
BAHAM alt for GHOMÁLÁ' CENTRAL dial of
  GHOMALA [BBJ]
BAHAMAS CREOLE ENGLISH [BAH] lang,
  Bahamas; also in USA
BAHAMIAN CREOLE ENGLISH alt for BAHAMAS
  CREOLE ENGLISH [BAH]
BAHAMIAN DIALECT alt for BAHAMAS CREOLE
  ENGLISH [BAH]
BAHANGA-LA alt for BANGGARLA [BJB]
BAHARLU dial of AZERBAIJANI, SOUTH [AZB]
BAHARNA alt for ARABIC, BAHARNA SPOKEN
  [AFH]
BAHARNAH alt for ARABIC, BAHARNA SPOKEN
  [AFH]
BAHASA ASLI alt for HUAULU [HUD]
BAHASA GERAGAU alt for MALACCAN CREOLE
  PORTUGUESE [MCM]
BAHASA INDONESIA alt for INDONESIAN [INZ]
BAHASA MALAY alt for MALAY [MLI]
BAHASA MALAYSIA alt for MALAY [MLI]
BAHASA MALAYSIA KOD TANGAN alt for
  MALAYSIAN SIGN LANGUAGE [XML]
BAHASA MALAYU alt for MALAY [MLI]
BAHASA MELAYU alt for MALAY [MLI]
BAHASA SERANI alt for MALACCAN CREOLE
  PORTUGUESE [MCM]
BAHAU [BHV] lang, Indonesia (Kalimantan)
BAHAU RIVER KENYA alt for KENYAH, BAHAU
  RIVER [BWV]
BAHAWALPURI alt for SARAIKI [SKR]
BAHAWALPURI dial of SARAIKI [SKR]
BÂHDINÂNI alt for KURMANJI [KUR]
BAHDINI alt for BEHDINI [BDF]
BAHE dial of RAJBANGSI [RJB]
BAHELIA alt for PARDHI [PCL]
BAHENEMO alt for BAHINEMO [BJH]
BAHENG alt for BUNU, BAHENG [PHA]
BAHENGMAI alt for BUNU, BAHENG [PHA]
BAHGRI alt for BAGRI [BGQ]
BA-HI alt for PAHI dial of PACOH [PAC]
BAHI alt for BHADRAWAHI [BHD]
BAHINEMO [BJH] lang, Papua New Guinea
BAHING [RAR] lang, Nepal
BAHING LO alt for BAHING [RAR]
BAHNAR [BDQ] lang, Viet Nam; also in USA
BAHNAR BONOM dial of BAHNAR [BDQ]
BAHNAR CHAM alt for HAROI [HRO]
BAHNAR-RENGAO dial of RENGAO [REN]
BAHONSUAI [BSU] lang, Indonesia (Sulawesi)
BAHRAIN dial of TORWALI [TRW]

BAHRAINI GULF ARABIC dial of ARABIC, GULF SPOKEN [AFB]

BAHRAINI SHI'ITE ARABIC alt for ARABIC, BAHARNA SPOKEN [AFH]

BAHRI GIRINTI dial of BELI [BLM]

BAHU EHTREMEÑU alt for SOUTHERN EXTREMADURAN dial of EXTREMADURAN [EXT]

BAHULI alt for HULI dial of FALI [FLI]

BAHUMONO alt for KOHUMONO [BCS]

BAI [BDJ] lang, Sudan

BAI [PIQ] lang, China

BAI alt for BALONG dial of BAFAW-BALONG [BWT]

BAI alt for DUMUN [DUI]

BAI dial of SAKATA [SAT]

BAI MA alt for BAIMA [BQH]

BAI MIAO alt for HMONG DAW [MWW]

BAIAP alt for DAKAKA [BPA]

BAIBAI [BBF] lang, Papua New Guinea

BAIBARA dial of MAILU [MGU]

BAICIT alt for KENDAYAN [KNX]

BAIGA alt for BAIGANI dial of CHHATTISGARHI [HNE]

BAIGANA alt for MACUNA [MYY]

BAIGANI dial of CHHATTISGARHI [HNE]

BAIGO alt for BAYGO [BYG]

BAIHONG dial of HONI [HOW]

BAIHUA alt for CHINESE, YUE [YUH]

BAIKENU alt for AMBENU dial of ATONI [TMR]

BAILALA alt for OROKOLO [ORO]

BAILKO alt for NIJADALI [NAD]

BAIMA [BQH] lang, China

BAIMAK [BMX] lang, Papua New Guinea

BAIMAK alt for GAL [GAP]

BAINAPI [PIK] lang, Papua New Guinea

BAING alt for BAHING [RAR]

BAINGE RAI alt for BAHING [RAR]

BAINING alt for QAQET [BYX]

BAINOUK-GUNYAAMOLO [BCZ] lang, Senegal; also in Gambia

BAINOUK-GUNYUÑO [BAB] lang, Guinea-Bissau

BAINOUK-SAMIK [BCB] lang, Senegal

BAINUK alt for BAINOUK-GUNYAAMOLO [BCZ]

BAINUK alt for BAINOUK-GUNYUÑO [BAB]

BAIONG alt for BAYUNGU [BXJ]

BAIOT alt for BAYOT [BDA]

BAIOTE alt for BAYOT [BDA]

BAIRIN alt for JO-UDA dial of MONGOLIAN, PERIPHERAL [MVF]

BAIRISCH alt for BAVARIAN [BAR]

BAISH ARANÉS dial of GASCON, ARANESE [GSC]

BAISHA-YUANMEN alt for BENDI dial of HLAI [LIC]

BAISO [BSW] lang, Ethiopia

BAISWARI alt for AWADHI [AWD]

BAITADI dial of NEPALI [NEP]

BAITE dial of CHIN, THADO [TCZ]

BAITSI dial of SIWAI [SIW]

BAIUNG alt for BAYUNGU [BXJ]

BAIYER alt for KYAKA [KYC]

BAJALANI alt for BAJELAN [BJM]

BAJAMA alt for GOLA dial of MUMUYE [MUL]

BAJAN [BJS] lang, Barbados

BAJAO alt for BAJAU, INDONESIAN [BDL]

BAJAT dial of KUBU [KVB]

BAJAU ASLI alt for BAJAU SEMPORNA dial of SAMA, SOUTHERN [SIT]

BAJAU BANARAN dial of SAMA, SOUTHERN [SIT]

BAJAU BUKIT alt for PAPAR [DPP]

BAJAU DARAT dial of SAMA, SOUTHERN [SIT]

BAJAU KAGAYAN alt for MAPUN [SJM]

BAJAU LAUT dial of SAMA, SOUTHERN [SIT]

BAJAU SEMPORNA dial of SAMA, SOUTHERN [SIT]

BAJAU, INDONESIAN [BDL] lang, Indonesia (Sulawesi)

BAJAU, WEST COAST [BDR] lang, Malaysia (Sabah)

BAJAVA alt for NGAD'A [NXG]

BAJAWA alt for NGAD'A [NXG]

BAJAWA dial of NGADA [NXG]

BAJELAN [BJM] lang, Iraq

BAJELE alt for GYELE [GYI]

BAJELI alt for GYELE [GYI]

BAJHANGI dial of NEPALI [NEP]

BÀJII dial of SENOUFO, MAMARA [MYK]

BAJO alt for BAJAU, INDONESIAN [BDL]

BAJO NAVARRO OCCIDENTAL alt for WESTERN LOW NAVARRESE dial of BASQUE, NAVARRO-LABOURDIN [BQE]

BAJO NAVARRO ORIENTAL alt for EASTERN LOW NAVARRESE dial of BASQUE, NAVARRO-LABOURDIN [BQE]

BAJPURI alt for BHOJPURI [BHJ]

BAJUN alt for BAJUNI dial of SWAHILI [SWA]

BAJUNGU alt for BAYUNGU [BXJ]

BAJUNI dial of SWAHILI [SWA]

BAJURA alt for BAJURALI dial of NEPALI [NEP]

BAJURALI dial of NEPALI [NEP]

BAJUTA dial of DATOOGA [TCC]

BAJWE'E alt for BADWE'E dial of KOONZIME [NJE]

BAJWO dial of DENYA [ANV]

BAKA [BDH] lang, Sudan; also in DCR

BAKA [BKC] lang, Cameroon; also in Gabon

BAKAA alt for KALANGA [KCK]

BAKAIRÍ [BKQ] lang, Brazil

BAKAKA [BQZ] lang, Cameroon

BAKAKA dial of BAKAKA [BQZ]

BAKALANG dial of BLAGAR [BEU]

BAKANIKE alt for KANINGI [KZO]

BAKATAN alt for BUKITAN [BKN]

BAKATIQ alt for BEKATI' [BAT]

BAKAWALI dial of KASHMIRI [KSH]

BAKE dial of BERTA [WTI]

BAKEDI alt for TESO [TEO]

BAKELE alt for KUKELE [KEZ]

BAKEM dial of BASAA [BAA]

BAKH<A dial of WESTERN NEO-ARAMAIC [AMW]

BAKHA dial of KARANGA [KTH]

BAKHA dial of MABA [MDE]

BAKHAT alt for BAKHA dial of KARANGA [KTH]

BAKHTIARI dial of LURI [LRI]

BAKI [BKI] lang, Vanuatu
BAKI alt for TUKI [BAG]
BAKI dial of KWAKUM [KWU]
BAKIDI alt for TESO [TEO]
BAKITAN alt for BUKITAN [BKN]
BAKJO alt for BADJIA dial of EWONDO [EWO]
BAKO alt for GYELE [GYI]
BAKO dial of AARI [AIZ]
BAKO dial of NGWO [NGN]
BAKOA alt for KWA' [BKO]
BAKOI dial of LAWANGAN [LBX]
BAKOKAN alt for JULA, WORODOUGOU [JUD]
BAKOKO [BKH] lang, Cameroon
BAKOLA alt for GYELE [GYI]
BAKOLE [KME] lang, Cameroon
BAKOLLE alt for BAKOLE [KME]
BAKOMBE alt for KOMBE dial of TUKI [BAG]
BAKONG alt for KENYAH, BAKUNG [BOC]
BAKONG alt for WONGO [WON]
BAKONI dial of KENYANG [KEN]
BAKOROKA alt for KWADI [KWZ]
BAKOSSI alt for AKOOSE [BSS]
BAKOTA alt for MBAMA [MBM]
BAKOTI alt for SANGAMESVARI dial of KONKANI
   [KNK]
BAKOUA alt for KWA' dial of KWA [BKO]
BAKOVI alt for BOLA [BNP]
BAKPINKA [BBS] lang, Nigeria
BAKPWE alt for MOKPWE [BRI]
BAKSA alt for SIRAIYA [FOS]
BAKSAN dial of KABARDIAN [KAB]
BAKTAPUR dial of NEWARI [NEW]
BAKU dial of AZERBAIJANI, NORTH [AZE]
BAKUELE alt for GYELE [GYI]
BAKULI alt for KULUNG [BBU]
BAKULU alt for KULUNG [BBU]
BAKULUNG alt for KULUNG [BBU]
BAKUM alt for KWAKUM [KWU]
BAKUMPAI [BKR] lang, Indonesia (Kalimantan)
BAKUMPAI dial of BAKUMPAI [BKR]
BAKUMPAI dial of MALAY [MLI]
BAKUN dial of LOLODA [LOL]
BAKUNDU dial of BAKUNDU-BALUE [BDU]
BAKUNDU-BALUE [BDU] lang, Cameroon
BAKUNDUMU dial of BALI [BCP]
BAKUNG alt for KENYAH, BAKUNG [BOC]
BAKUNG KENYA alt for KENYAH, BAKUNG [BOC]
BAKUN-KIBUNGAN dial of KANKANAEY [KNE]
BAKURUT alt for AMIS [ALV]
BAKUTU alt for KUTU dial of MONGO-NKUNDU
   [MOM]
BAKWA alt for KWA' [BKO]
BAKWÉ [BAK] lang, Côte d'Ivoire
BAKWEDI alt for MOKPWE [BRI]
BAKWELE alt for BEKWEL [BKW]
BAKWELE alt for MOKPWE [BRI]
BAKWERI alt for MOKPWE [BRI]
BAKWIL alt for BEKWEL [BKW]
BALA dial of MEOHANG, WESTERN [RAF]
BALAABE alt for YUKUBEN [YBL]
BALAABEN alt for YUKUBEN [YBL]

BALABAN alt for TADYAWAN [TDY]
BALAESAN [BLS] lang, Indonesia (Sulawesi)
BALAESANG alt for BALAESAN [BLS]
BALAFI alt for LA'FI dial of FEFE [FMP]
BALAGNINI alt for SAMA, BALANGINGI [SSE]
BALAHAIM alt for ISEBE [IGO]
BALAISANG alt for BALAESAN [BLS]
BALAIT dial of LUNDAYEH [LND]
BALAIT JATI alt for BELAIT [BEG]
BALAKEO dial of BENGGOI [BGY]
BALAKHANI dial of TAT, MUSLIM [TTT]
BALALI alt for BALA dial of MEOHANG, WESTERN
   [RAF]
BALAMATA alt for PALUMATA [PMC]
BALAMBU alt for BARAMBU [BRM]
BALAMULA dial of LEWADA-DEWARA [LWD]
BALANDA alt for BALANTA-GANJA [BJT]
BALANDA alt for BALANTA-KENTOHE [BLE]
BALANGAO [BLW] lang, Philippines
BALANGAO BONTOC alt for BALANGAO [BLW]
BALANGAW alt for BALANGAO [BLW]
BALANGINGI dial of SAMA, BALANGINGI [SSE]
BALANGINGI BAJAU alt for SAMA, BALANGINGI
   [SSE]
BALANIAN alt for SAMA, BALANGINGI [SSE]
BALANINI alt for SAMA, BALANGINGI [SSE]
BALANIPA dial of MANDAR [MHN]
BALANT alt for BALANTA-GANJA [BJT]
BALANT alt for BALANTA-KENTOHE [BLE]
BALANTA alt for BALANTA-KENTOHE [BLE]
BALANTA-GANJA [BJT] lang, Senegal
BALANTAK [BLZ] lang, Indonesia (Sulawesi)
BALANTA-KENTOHE [BLE] lang, Guinea-Bissau;
   also in Gambia
BALANTE alt for BALANTA-GANJA [BJT]
BALANTE alt for BALANTA-KENTOHE [BLE]
BALANTIAN alt for NYADU [NXJ]
BALANTIANG alt for NYADU [NXJ]
BALAR dial of KIR-BALAR [KKR]
BALATCHI dial of NGIEMBOON [NNH]
BALAU [BUG] lang, Malaysia (Sarawak)
BALA'U alt for BALAU [BUG]
BALAWAIA dial of SINAUGORO [SNC]
BALBALASANG dial of KALINGA, LUBUAGAN
   [KNB]
BALDA alt for MATAL [MFH]
BALDAM alt for BAYMUNA dial of MISKITO [MIQ]
BALDAMU [BDN] lang, Cameroon
BALE alt for AKAR-BALE [ACL]
BALE alt for BALESI dial of KACIPO-BALESI [KOE]
BALE alt for LENDU [LED]
BALE alt for SELE [SNW]
BALEAR alt for BALEARIC dial of CATALAN-
   VALENCIAN-BALEAR [CLN]
BALEARIC dial of CATALAN-VALENCIAN-BALEAR
   [CLN]
BALEGETE alt for EVANT [BZZ]
BALEN alt for BILEN [BYN]
BALENDRU alt for LENDU [LED]
BALENGUE alt for MOLENGUE [BXC]
BALEP dial of NDOE [NBB]

BALER NEGRITO alt for ALTA, NORTHERN [AQN]
BALESE alt for LESE [LES]
BALESI dial of KACIPO-BALESI [KOE]
BALETHA alt for LENDU [LED]
BALGARSKI alt for BULGARIAN [BLG]
BALGU alt for NIJADALI [NAD]
BALI [BCN] lang, Nigeria
BALI [BCP] lang, DCR
BALI [BZC] lang, Indonesia (Java and Bali)
BALI alt for BALI NYONGA dial of MUNGAKA [MHK]
BALI alt for MUNGAKA [MHK]
BALI alt for UNEAPA [BBN]
BALI dial of TEKE, EASTERN [TEK]
"BALI AGA" pejorative alt for HIGHLAND BALI dial of BALI [BZC]
BALI HOLMA alt for HOLMA [HOD]
BALI NYONGA dial of MUNGAKA [MHK]
BALI SIGN LANGUAGE [BQY] lang, Indonesia (Java and Bali)
'BALI'BA dial of MORU [MGD]
BALIEM VALLEY DANI alt for DANI, MID GRAND VALLEY [DNT]
BALIET alt for PALIET dial of DINKA, SOUTH-WESTERN [DIK]
BALIF dial of MUFIAN [AOJ]
BALIGNINI alt for SAMA, BALANGINGI [SSE]
BALIKPAPAN dial of MALAY [MLI]
BALIN alt for JO-UDA dial of MONGOLIAN, PERIPHERAL [MVF]
BALINESE alt for BALI [BZC]
BALINGIAN dial of MELANAU [MEL]
BALIWON alt for GA'DANG [GDG]
BALKAN GAGAUZ TURKISH [BGX] lang, Turkey (Europe); also in Greece, Macedonia
BALKAN TURKIC alt for BALKAN GAGAUZ TURKISH [BGX]
BALKAR dial of KARACHAY-BALKAR [KRC]
BALKAR-TSALAKAN alt for BALXAR-CALAKAN dial of LAK [LBE]
BALKE (CIBALKE) alt for BARWE [BWG]
BALKH ARABIC dial of ARABIC, TAJIKI SPOKEN [ABH]
BALKHU-SISNERI dial of JERUNG [JEE]
BAL-LA alt for RATHAWI [RTW]
BALLANTE alt for BALANTA-GANJA [BJT]
BALLANTE alt for BALANTA-KENTOHE [BLE]
BALLO-KAI-POMO alt for POMO, CENTRAL [POO]
BALO [BQO] lang, Cameroon
'BALO alt for KPASAM [PBN]
BALOBO alt for LIKILA [LIE]
BALOBO alt for LOBO dial of MABAALE [MMZ]
BALOCHI alt for BALOCHI, EASTERN [BGP]
BALOCHI, EASTERN [BGP] lang, Pakistan; also in India
BALOCHI, SOUTHERN [BCC] lang, Pakistan; also in Iran, Oman, UAE
BALOCHI, WESTERN [BGN] lang, Pakistan; also in Afghanistan, Iran, Tajikistan, Turkmenistan
BALOCI alt for BALOCHI, EASTERN [BGP]
BALOCI alt for BALOCHI, SOUTHERN [BCC]

BALOCI alt for BALOCHI, WESTERN [BGN]
BALOGA alt for AYTA, MAG-INDI [BLX]
BALOI [BIZ] lang, DCR
BALOKI alt for BOLOKI [BKT]
BALOM dial of BAFIA [KSF]
BALON alt for BALONG dial of BAFAW-BALONG [BWT]
BALONDO dial of BAKAKA [BQZ]
BALONG dial of BAFAW-BALONG [BWT]
BALOUM alt for GHOMÁLÁ' [BBJ]
BALOUMBOU alt for LUMBU [LUP]
BALSAPUERTINO alt for CHAYAHUITA [CBT]
BALTAP alt for MONTOL [MTL]
BALTAP-LALIN dial of MONTOL [MTL]
BALTI [BFT] lang, Pakistan; also in India
BALTISTANI alt for BALTI [BFT]
BALUAN dial of BALUAN-PAM [BLQ]
BALUAN-PAM [BLQ] lang, Papua New Guinea
BALUCHI alt for BALOCHI, EASTERN [BGP]
BALUCHI alt for BALOCHI, SOUTHERN [BCC]
BALUCHI alt for BALOCHI, WESTERN [BGN]
BALUCI alt for BALOCHI, EASTERN [BGP]
BALUCI alt for BALOCHI, SOUTHERN [BCC]
BALUCI alt for BALOCHI, WESTERN [BGN]
BALUD alt for BLAAN, SARANGANI [BIS]
BALUE dial of BAKUNDU-BALUE [BDU]
BALUGA alt for ALTA, SOUTHERN [AGY]
BALUNDU dial of BALUNDU-BIMA [NGO]
BALUNDU-BIMA [NGO] lang, Cameroon
BALUNG alt for BALONG dial of BAFAW-BALONG [BWT]
BALUNGADA alt for NEDEBANG [NEC]
BALUOMBILA dial of POKE [POF]
BALURBI dial of DJINANG [DJI]
BALWA alt for AKAR-BALE [ACL]
BALXAR-CALAKAN dial of LAK [LBE]
BALYGU alt for NIJADALI [NAD]
BAM alt for BIEM [BMC]
BAM dial of WANTOAT [WNC]
BAMA alt for BURMESE [BMS]
BAMA alt for NAGUMI [NGV]
BAMACHAKA alt for BURMESE [BMS]
BAMAKO SIGN LANGUAGE [BOG] lang, Mali
BAMALI [BBQ] lang, Cameroon
BAMANA alt for BAMBARA [BRA]
BAMANAKAN alt for BAMANANKAN [BRA]
BAMANAKAN alt for BAMBARA [BRA]
BAMANANKAN [BRA] lang, Mali; also in Burkina Faso, Côte d'Ivoire, Gambia, Guinea, Mauritania, Senegal
BAMANYEKA alt for MANYIKA [MXC]
BAMASSA alt for BOMASSA [BME]
BAMBAA alt for HUKUMINA [HUW]
BAMBAAMA alt for MBAMA [MBM]
BAMBADION-DOGOSO alt for DOGOSO [DGS]
BAMBADION-DOKHOSIÉ alt for DOGOSO [DGS]
BAMBADION-KHESO alt for KHE [KQG]
BAMBALA alt for BURJI [BJI]
BAMBALANG [BMO] lang, Cameroon
BAMBAM [PTU] lang, Indonesia (Sulawesi)
BAMBANG dial of BAMBAM [PTU]

BAMBARA [BRA] lang, Mali; also in Burkina Faso, Côte d'Ivoire, Gambia, Guinea, Mauritania, Senegal
BAMBARA alt for BAMANANKAN [BRA]
BAMBARA alt for MBARU dial of LAME [BMA]
BAMBARO alt for MBARU dial of LAME [BMA]
BAMBASSI [MYF] lang, Ethiopia
BAMBASSI dial of BAMBASSI [MYF]
BAMBEIRO alt for MBAMBA dial of MBUNDU, LOANDA [MLO]
BAMBELE alt for MBERE dial of TUKI [BAG]
"BAMBENGA" pejorative alt for YAKA [AXK]
BAMBENZELE dial of YAKA [AXK]
BAMBESHI alt for BAMBASSI [MYF]
BAMBILI [BAW] lang, Cameroon
BAMBILI dial of BAMBILI [BAW]
BAMBO alt for AMBO dial of LALA-BISA [LEB]
BAMBOKO alt for WUMBOKO [BQM]
BAMBOLANG alt for BAMBALANG [BMO]
BAMBOMA alt for BOMA dial of TEKE, CENTRAL [TEC]
BAMBOMA alt for BOO dial of TEKE, CENTRAL [TEC]
BAMBOUTE alt for VUTE [VUT]
BAMBUBA alt for MVUBA [MXH]
BAMBUI alt for BAMBILI [BAW]
BAMBUI dial of BAMBILI [BAW]
BAMBUKA alt for KYAK [BKA]
BAMBUKU alt for WUMBOKO [BQM]
BAMBULUWE alt for AWING [AZO]
BAMBUR alt for KULUNG [BBU]
BAMBURO alt for MBARU dial of LAME [BMA]
BA-MBUTU alt for GAMO dial of GAMO-NINGI [BTE]
BAMBUTU alt for MBUTU dial of NGEMBA [NGE]
BAMBUTUKU alt for VANUMA [VAU]
BAMECHOM alt for SHOMBA dial of NGEMBA [NGE]
BAMEKON alt for KOM [BKM]
BAMENDA alt for MENDANKWE dial of MENDANKWE [MFD]
BAMENDJIN alt for BAMENDJING dial of MENGAKA [XMG]
BAMENDJINDA dial of NGOMBA [NNO]
BAMENDJING dial of MENGAKA [XMG]
BAMENDJO dial of NGOMBA [NNO]
BAMENJOU alt for NGEMBA dial of GHOMALA [BBJ]
BAMENKOMBIT alt for BAMUKUMBIT [BQT]
BAMENKOUMBIT alt for BAMUKUMBIT [BQT]
BAMENKUMBO dial of NGOMBA [NNO]
BAMENYAM [BCE] lang, Cameroon
BAMENYAN alt for BAMENYAM [BCE]
BAMESSING alt for KENSWEI NSEI [NDB]
BAMESSINGUE dial of NGOMBALE [NLA]
BAMESSO dial of NGOMBA [NNO]
BAMETA alt for META' [MGO]
BAMETA alt for MENEMO dial of META [MGO]
BAMETE alt for BABETE dial of NGOMBA [NNO]
BAMILEKE-BANDJOUN alt for GHOMÁLÁ' [BBJ]
BAMILEKE-FE'FE' alt for FE'FE' [FMP]
BAMILEKE-KWA alt for KWA' [BKO]

BAMILEKE-MEDUMBA alt for MEDUMBA [BYV]
BAMILEKE-MENGAKA alt for MENGAKA [XMG]
BAMILEKE-NDA'NDA' alt for NDA'NDA' [NNZ]
BAMILEKE-NGOMBA alt for NGOMBA [NNO]
BAMILEKE-NGOMBALE alt for NGOMBALE [NLA]
BAMILEKE-NGWE alt for NGWE [NWE]
BAMILEKE-NGYEMBOON alt for NGIEMBOON [NNH]
BAMILEKE-YEMBA alt for YEMBA [BAN]
BAMINGE alt for NGIE [NGJ]
BAMITABA alt for BOMITABA [ZMX]
BAMONGO alt for BUSHOONG [BUF]
BAMOTA alt for MAGOBINENG dial of KATE [KMG]
BAMOUKOUMBIT alt for BAMUKUMBIT [BQT]
BAMOUM alt for BAMUN [BAX]
BAMOUN alt for BAMUN [BAX]
BAMOUNGONG dial of NGIEMBOON [NNH]
BAMU [BCF] lang, Papua New Guinea
BAMU KIWAI alt for BAMU [BCF]
BAMUKUMBIT [BQT] lang, Cameroon
BAMUM alt for BAMUN [BAX]
BAMUMBO dial of MUNDANI [MUN]
BAMUMBU alt for BAMUMBO dial of MUNDANI [MUN]
BAMUN [BAX] lang, Cameroon
BAMUNDUM 1 alt for MBREREWI dial of NGEMBA [NGE]
BAMUNDUM 2 alt for ANYANG dial of NGEMBA [NGE]
BAMUNKA [NDO] lang, Cameroon
BAMUNKUM alt for BAMUKUMBIT [BQT]
BAMUNKUN alt for BAMUNKA [NDO]
BAMUSSO alt for BAKOLE [KME]
BAMVELE alt for BEBELE [BEB]
BAMVELE alt for MBERE dial of TUKI [BAG]
BAMVELE dial of EWONDO [EWO]
BAMVUBA alt for MVUBA [MXH]
BAMWE [BMG] lang, DCR
BAMYILI CREOLE dial of KRIOL [ROP]
BAN KHOR SIGN LANGUAGE [BLA] lang, Thailand
BAN YAO alt for IU MIEN [IUM]
BANA [BCW] lang, Cameroon
BANA alt for BAHNAR [BDQ]
BANA alt for HAMER-BANNA [AMF]
BANA alt for IMBANA dial of MUNDANG [MUA]
BANA alt for NEE dial of FE'FE' [FMP]
BANA dial of UMA [PPK]
BANA' alt for PHANA' [PHN]
BANABAN dial of KIRIBATI [GLB]
BANADAN alt for SAMA, BALANGINGI [SSE]
BANAG alt for PANANG [PCR]
BANAGERE alt for MESAKA [IYO]
BANAI dial of KOCH [KDQ]
BANAKA alt for BANO'O dial of BATANGA [BNM]
BANALA dial of KENGA [KYQ]
BANAMA dial of KENGA [KYQ]
BANAN BAY alt for BURMBAR [VRT]
"BANANA" pejorative alt for MASANA [MCN]
BANANA' dial of MALAYIC DAYAK [XDY]
BANANG alt for PANANG [PCR]
BANANNA alt for MUSEY [MSE]

BANANNA HO alt for MUSEY [MSE]
BANANNA HO HO alt for MUSEY [MSE]
BANAO ITNEG dial of KALINGA, LUBUAGAN [KNB]
BANAPARI dial of BAGHELI [BFY]
BANAPHARI dial of BUNDELI [BNS]
BANAR alt for BANARO [BYZ]
BANAR alt for MAIA [SKS]
BANARA alt for BANARO [BYZ]
BANARA alt for MAIANI [TNH]
BANARA alt for MALA [PED]
BANARO [BYZ] lang, Papua New Guinea
BANAT dial of ROMANIAN [RUM]
BANAUÁ alt for BANAWÁ [BNH]
BANAUE IFUGAO dial of IFUGAO, AMGANAD [IFA]
BANAULE alt for BEBELI [BEK]
BANAVA alt for UNDE dial of KAILI, DAA [KZF]
BANAVÁ alt for BANAWÁ [BNH]
BANAWA alt for UNDE dial of KAILI, DAA [KZF]
BANAWÁ [BNH] lang, Brazil
BANCHAPAI dial of MURIA, WESTERN [MUT]
BANDA [BND] lang, Indonesia (Maluku)
BANDA alt for LIGBI [LIG]
BANDA alt for NAFAANRA [NFR]
BANDA alt for NORTHERN CHUMBURUNG dial
  of CHUMBURUNG [NCU]
BANDA alt for SHOO dial of SHOO-MINDA-NYE
  [BCV]
BANDA ACEH dial of ACEH [ATJ]
BANDA CENTRAL SUD alt for BANDA, MID-
  SOUTHERN [BJO]
BANDA DE BRIA alt for BEREYA dial of BANDA-
  BANDA [BPD]
BANDA OF BAMBARI alt for BANDA-BAMBARI [LIY]
BANDA OF BRIA alt for BEREYA dial of BANDA-
  BANDA [BPD]
BANDA OF MBRÉS alt for BANDA-MBRÈS [BQK]
BANDA OF MBRÈS alt for BANDA-MBRÈS [BQK]
BANDA OF NDÉLÉ alt for BANDA-NDÉLÉ [BFL]
BANDA, MID-SOUTHERN [BJO] lang, CAR; also
  in DCR, Sudan
BANDA, SOUTH CENTRAL [LNL] lang, CAR;
  also in DCR
BANDA, TOGBO-VARA [TOR] lang, DCR; also in
  CAR, Sudan
BANDA, WEST CENTRAL [BBP] lang, CAR; also
  in Sudan
BANDA-BAMBARI [LIY] lang, CAR
BANDA-BANDA [BPD] lang, CAR; also in Sudan
BANDA-BANDA dial of BANDA-BANDA [BPD]
BANDA-KPAYA dial of BANDA-NDELE [BFL]
BANDA-MBRE alt for BANDA-MBRÈS [BQK]
BANDA-MBRÈS [BQK] lang, CAR; also in Sudan
BANDA-NDÉLÉ [BFL] lang, CAR; also in Sudan
BANDA-NDÉLÉ dial of BANDA-NDELE [BFL]
BANDANGAO alt for NGAO dial of BANDA-NDELE
  [BFL]
BANDAS alt for DURR-BARAZA dial of DASS [DOT]
BANDAWA alt for SHOO dial of SHOO-MINDA-NYE
  [BCV]
BANDA-YANGERE [YAJ] lang, CAR
BANDE alt for BANDI [GBA]

BANDE alt for BUDIK [TNR]
BANDE alt for MANGKUNGE dial of NGEMBA [NGE]
BANDE' alt for MANGKUNGE dial of NGEMBA
  [NGE]
BANDEM alt for NDEMLI [NML]
BANDENG alt for MANGKUNGE dial of NGEMBA
  [NGE]
BANDENG alt for NDE dial of MUNGAKA [MHK]
BANDI [GBA] lang, Liberia; also in Guinea
BANDIAL [BQJ] lang, Senegal
BANDINANI alt for BEHDINI [BDF]
BANDJA-BABOUNTOU alt for NJEE-POANTU dial
  of FE'FE' [FMP]
BANDJALANG [BDY] lang, Australia
BANDJARESE alt for BANJAR [BJN]
BANDJELANG alt for BANDJALANG [BDY]
BANDJIGALI [BJD] lang, Australia
BANDJIMA alt for PANYTYIMA [PNW]
BANDJOUN alt for GHOMÁLÁ' [BBJ]
BANDJOUN alt for GHOMÁLÁ' CENTRAL dial of
  GHOMÁLÁ' [BBJ]
BANDOBO dial of TIKAR [TIK]
BANDOUGOU dial of SIAMOU [SIF]
BANDOUMOU alt for NDUMU [NMD]
BANDU dial of THAI, NORTHERN [NOD]
BANDZABI alt for NJEBI [NZB]
BANDZHOGI alt for CHIN, ZOTUNG [CZT]
BANE dial of EWONDO [EWO]
BANEKA dial of BAKAKA [BQZ]
BANEN alt for TUNEN [BAZ]
BANEND alt for TUNEN [BAZ]
BANENGE dial of BAHING [RAR]
BANFORA-SIENENA dial of CERMA [GOT]
BANG alt for MAMBILA, CAMEROON [MYA]
BANG alt for MAMBILA, NIGERIA [MZK]
BANG dial of MFUMTE [NFU]
BANGA alt for GWAMHI dial of GWAMHI-WURI
  [BGA]
BANGA alt for RUKAI [DRU]
BANGA dial of KABA NA [KWV]
BANGA dial of MBOI [MOI]
BANGA-BHASA alt for BENGALI [BNG]
BANGAD dial of KALINGA, SOUTHERN [KSC]
BANGALA [BXG] lang, DCR
BANGALA alt for BANGGARLA [BJB]
BANGALA alt for BENGALI [BNG]
BANGALA alt for LAMBADI [LMN]
BANGALA alt for MBANGALA [MXG]
BANGALAM alt for OLAM dial of MURLE [MUR]
BANGALEMA alt for NGELIMA [AGH]
BANGALORE-MADRAS SIGN LANGUAGE dial
  of INDIAN SIGN LANGUAGE [INS]
BANGAN alt for NGAM dial of FEFE [FMP]
BANGANCI alt for GWAMHI dial of GWAMHI-WURI
  [BGA]
BANGANDO alt for BANGANDU [BGF]
BANGANDO-NGOMBE alt for NGOMBE [NMJ]
BANGANDOU alt for NGANDO [NGD]
BANGANDU [BGF] lang, Cameroon; also in Congo
BANGANG dial of MUNDANI [MUN]
BANGANGTE alt for MEDUMBA [BYV]

BANGANTU alt for BAGETO dial of MPONGMPONG [MGG]
BANGANTU alt for BANGANDU [BGF]
BANGARU alt for HARYANVI [BGC]
BANGARU PROPER dial of HARYANVI [BGC]
BANGASSOGO dial of SAMO, MAYA [SYM]
BANGAWA alt for GWAMHI dial of GWAMHI-WURI [BGA]
BANGAY alt for BONGGI [BDG]
BANGBA [BBE] lang, DCR
BANGBA LWO alt for CHAUDANGSI [CDN]
BANGBINDA alt for NGBINDA [NBD]
BANGDALE alt for NACHERING [NCD]
BANGDALE dial of NACHERING [NCD]
BANGDEL TÛM alt for NACHERING [NCD]
BANGDILE alt for NACHERING [NCD]
BANGELA alt for LIKILA [LIE]
BANGELIMA alt for NGELIMA [AGH]
BANGER alt for HARYANVI [BGC]
BANGGAI [BGZ] lang, Indonesia (Sulawesi)
BANGGALA alt for BANGGARLA [BJB]
BANGGARLA [BJB] lang, Australia
BANGGI alt for BONGGI [BDG]
BANGGI dial of BAJAU, WEST COAST [BDR]
BANGGI DUSUN alt for BONGGI [BDG]
BANG-GO dial of TUPURI [TUI]
BANGI [BNI] lang, DCR; also in CAR, Congo
BANGINDA dial of GBAYA, NORTHWEST [GYA]
BANGINGI SAMA alt for SAMA, BALANGINGI [SSE]
BANGJINGE alt for BANGWINJI [BSJ]
BANGKA dial of MALAY [MLI]
BANGKALAN dial of MADURA [MHJ]
BANGKALON alt for BANGKALAN dial of MADURA [MHJ]
BANGLA alt for BENGALI [BNG]
BANGLA dial of SAMBA LEKO [NDI]
BANGLA-BHASA alt for BENGALI [BNG]
BANG-LING dial of TUPURI [TUI]
BANGLORI alt for KANNADA [KJV]
BANGNI alt for NISI [DAP]
BANGO alt for NUBACA [BAF]
BANGOBANGO alt for BANGUBANGU [BNX]
BANGOLAN [BGJ] lang, Cameroon
BANGOM alt for NGOM [NRA]
BANGOMO alt for NGOM [NRA]
BANGON alt for BUHID [BKU]
BANGON alt for TAWBUID, EASTERN [BNJ]
BANGOUL dial of DAY [DAI]
BANGRI alt for HARYANVI [BGC]
BANGRI dial of BAGIRMI [BMI]
BANGRU alt for HARYANVI [BGC]
BANGRU alt for LEVAI dial of HRUSO [HRU]
BANGRU dial of KOMA [KMY]
BANGUBANGU [BNX] lang, DCR
BANGUBANGU dial of BANGUBANGU [BNX]
BANGUI dial of BEFANG [BBY]
BANGUNJI alt for BANGWINJI [BSJ]
BANGWA alt for SONGWA dial of NGEMBA [NGE]
BANGWA alt for YEMBA [BAN]
BANGWE alt for BANGUI dial of BEFANG [BBY]
BANGWE alt for SENA BANGWE dial of SENA [SEH]

BANG-WERE dial of TUPURI [TUI]
BANGWI alt for BANGUI dial of BEFANG [BBY]
BANGWINJI [BSJ] lang, Nigeria
BANHUM alt for BAINOUK-GUNYAAMOLO [BCZ]
BANHUM alt for BAINOUK-GUNYUÑO [BAB]
BANI KHAALID alt for NORTH NAJDI dial of ARABIC, NAJDI SPOKEN [ARS]
BANIATA [BNT] lang, Solomon Islands
BANIBA alt for BANIWA [BAI]
BANINGE alt for NGIE [NGJ]
BANIUA DO IÇANA alt for BANIWA [BAI]
BANIVA [BVV] lang, Venezuela
BANIVA alt for BANIWA [BAI]
BANIVA dial of BANIVA [BVV]
BANIWA [BAI] lang, Brazil; also in Venezuela
BANJA alt for NGAMAMBO [NBV]
BANJAAL alt for BANDIAL [BQJ]
BANJANGI alt for KENYANG [KEN]
BANJAR [BJN] lang, Indonesia (Kalimantan); also in Malaysia (Sabah)
BANJAR MALAY alt for BANJAR [BJN]
BANJARA alt for LAMBADI [LMN]
BANJARESE alt for BANJAR [BJN]
BANJARI alt for LAMBADI [LMN]
BANJIMA alt for PANYTYIMA [PNW]
BANJIRAM alt for NYA CERIYA dial of LONGUDA [LNU]
BANJOGI alt for CHIN, ZOTUNG [CZT]
BANJONG alt for NJONG dial of NGEMBA [NGE]
BANJORI alt for LAMBADI [LMN]
BANJOUN-BAHAM alt for GHOMÁLÁ' [BBJ]
BANJUN alt for GHOMÁLÁ' [BBJ]
BANJUR alt for KETUNGAU dial of IBAN [IBA]
BANJURI alt for LAMBADI [LMN]
BANKA alt for BANKAGOMA [BXW]
BANKA alt for NKA' dial of FE'FE' [FMP]
BANKAGOMA [BXW] lang, Mali
BANKAL dial of JARAWA [JAR]
BANKALA alt for BANKAL dial of JARAWA [JAR]
BANKASA dial of DOGON [DOG]
BANKON dial of ABO [ABB]
BANKOTI alt for KONKANI [KNK]
BANKOTI alt for SANGAMESVARI dial of KONKANI [KNK]
BANKUTU alt for NKUTU [NKW]
BANLOL dial of MAYA [SLZ]
BANNA alt for HAMER-BANNA [AMF]
BANNOCHI alt for BANNUCHI dial of PASHTO, CENTRAL [PST]
BANNOCK dial of PAIUTE, NORTHERN [PAO]
BANNU alt for BANNUCHI dial of PASHTO, CENTRAL [PST]
BANNUCHI dial of PASHTO, CENTRAL [PST]
BANOHO alt for BATANGA [BNM]
BANOKO alt for BANO'O dial of BATANGA [BNM]
BANONI [BCM] lang, Papua New Guinea
BANOO alt for BANO'O dial of BATANGA [BNM]
BANOO alt for BATANGA [BNM]
BANO'O alt for BATANGA [BNM]
BANO'O dial of BATANGA [BNM]
BANPARA NAGA alt for NAGA, WANCHO [NNP]

BANSAW alt for LAMNSO' [NSO]
BANSBALI dial of CHAMBEALI [CDH]
BANSO alt for LAMNSO' [NSO]
BANSO' alt for LAMNSO' [NSO]
BANSYARI dial of CHAMBEALI [CDH]
BANTA alt for MANTA [MYG]
BANTA dial of THEMNE [TEJ]
BANTABA alt for BANTAWA [BAP]
BANTAENG dial of KONJO, COASTAL [KJC]
BANTAKPA alt for MANTA [MYG]
BANTALANG alt for RUKAI [DRU]
BANTAR dial of MAITHILI [MKP]
BANTAURANG alt for RUKAI [DRU]
BANTAWA [BAP] lang, Nepal
BANTAWA DUM alt for BANTAWA [BAP]
BANTAWA RAI alt for BANTAWA [BAP]
BANTAWA YONG alt for BANTAWA [BAP]
BANTAWA YÜNG alt for BANTAWA [BAP]
BANTAYAN dial of HILIGAYNON [HIL]
BANTEN dial of JAVANESE [JAN]
BANTEN dial of SUNDA [SUO]
BANTI dial of MUNDANI [MUN]
BANTIAN dial of LAWANGAN [LBX]
BANTIK [BNQ] lang, Indonesia (Sulawesi)
BANTOANON [BNO] lang, Philippines
BANTON alt for BANTOANON [BNO]
BANTUANON alt for BANTOANON [BNO]
BANU alt for GBANU [GBV]
BANUWANG dial of LAWANGAN [LBX]
BANYA dial of NGWO [NGN]
BANYAI alt for NYAI dial of KALANGA [KCK]
BANYANG alt for KENYANG [KEN]
BANYANGI alt for KENYANG [KEN]
BANYOK dial of SIBU [SDX]
BANYUK alt for BAINOUK-GUNYAAMOLO [BCZ]
BANYUK alt for BAINOUK-GUNYUÑO [BAB]
BANYUM alt for BAINOUK-GUNYAAMOLO [BCZ]
BANYUM alt for BAINOUK-GUNYUÑO [BAB]
BANYUN alt for BAINOUK-GUNYAAMOLO [BCZ]
BANYUN alt for BAINOUK-GUNYUÑO [BAB]
BANYUNG alt for BAINOUK-GUNYAAMOLO
    [BCZ]
BANYUNG alt for BAINOUK-GUNYUÑO [BAB]
BANYUQ alt for LONG BANYUQ dial of KAYAN,
    MURIK [MXR]
BANYUWANGI alt for OSING [OSI]
BANZA dial of MABAALE [MMZ]
BANZIRI alt for GBANZIRI [GBG]
BANZ-NONDUGL dial of WAHGI, NORTH [WHG]
BAO dial of PSOHOH [BCL]
BAO'AN alt for BONAN [PEH]
BAOJING dial of TUJIA, NORTHERN [TJI]
BAOKAN alt for BAUKAN dial of BAUKAN [BNB]
BAOL dial of WOLOF [WOL]
BAONAN alt for BONAN [PEH]
BAORI alt for BAURIA [BGE]
BAORI dial of BHILI [BHB]
BAORIAS alt for BAGRI [BGQ]
BAOULÉ [BCI] lang, Côte d'Ivoire
BAPA alt for BABA [BBW]
BAPAI dial of YAQAY [JAQ]

BAPAKUM alt for BABA [BBW]
BAPE alt for DIMBONG [DII]
BAPE dial of BAFIA [KSF]
BAPINYI alt for PINYIN dial of PINYIN [PNY]
BAPO dial of KRUMEN, TEPO [TED]
BAPU alt for ANASI [BPO]
BAPUKU dial of BATANGA [BNM]
BAPUU alt for BAPUKU dial of BATANGA [BNM]
BAR alt for ANUAK [ANU]
"BARÁ" pejorative alt for WAIMAHA [BAO]
BARA alt for BODO [BRX]
BARA alt for GHERA [GHR]
BARÁ alt for POKANGÁ [POK]
BARA dial of BOLE [BOL]
BARA dial of FOLOPA [PPO]
BARA dial of MALAGASY [MEX]
BARA SONA alt for POKANGÁ [POK]
BARAA alt for LIKES-UTSIA dial of MANDJAK
    [MFV]
BARAAMU [BRD] lang, Nepal
BARAAN alt for BLAAN, KORONADAL [BIK]
BARABAIG alt for BARABAYIIGA dial of DATOOGA
    [TCC]
BARABAIK alt for BARABAYIIGA dial of DATOOGA
    [TCC]
BARABARA dial of BUNAMA [BDD]
BARA-BARE alt for BA'AMANG dial of NGAJU [NIJ]
BARABAYIIGA dial of DATOOGA [TCC]
BARABO dial of ANYIN [ANY]
BARA-DIA alt for KAPUAS dial of NGAJU [NIJ]
BARAGAON alt for BARAGAUNLE [BON]
BARAGAUN alt for BARAGAUNLE [BON]
BARAGAUNLE [BON] lang, Nepal
BARAGE dial of DHATKI [MKI]
BARAGUYU dial of MAASAI [MET]
BARAHUWI dial of BALOCHI, SOUTHERN [BCC]
BARAI [BCA] lang, Papua New Guinea
BARAÏN alt for BAREIN [BVA]
BARAIN alt for BARANI dial of FULFULDE,
    NORTH- EASTERN BURKINA FASO [FUH]
BARA-JIDA alt for BAKUMPAI [BKR]
BARAKA dial of BISSA [BIB]
BARAKAI [BAJ] lang, Indonesia (Maluku)
BARAKAI dial of BARAKAI [BAJ]
BARAKE dial of DOMARI [RMT]
BARAKI alt for ORMURI [ORU]
BARAKS alt for ORMURI [ORU]
"BARAKWENA" "BARAKWENGO" pejorative alt
    for KXOE [XUU]
BARALA alt for BARALAKA dial of MAHOU [MXX]
BARALAKA dial of MAHOU [MXX]
BARAM alt for BARAAMU [BRD]
BARAM dial of POLCI [POL]
BARAM DUTSE alt for DIR dial of POLCI [POL]
BARAM KAJAN alt for KAYAN, BARAM [KYS]
BARAMA [BBG] lang, Gabon
BARAMBO alt for BARAMBU [BRM]
BARAMBU [BRM] lang, DCR
BARAMU [BMZ] lang, Papua New Guinea
BARANCI alt for BANKAL dial of JARAWA
    [JAR]

223

BARANG alt for BARAM dial of POLCI [POL]
BARANGAN alt for TAWBUID, EASTERN [BNJ]
BARANG-BARANG alt for LAIYOLO [LJI]
BARANG-BARANG dial of LAIYOLO [LJI]
BARANI dial of FULFULDE, NORTHEASTERN
  BURKINA FASO [FUH]
BARANIIRE alt for BARANI dial of FULFULDE,
  NORTHEASTERN BURKINA FASO [FUH]
BARAOG alt for PARAUK [PRK]
BARAPASI [BRP] lang, Indonesia (Irian Jaya)
BARAS [BRS] lang, Indonesia (Sulawesi)
BARAS dial of TAGBANWA, CALAMIAN [TBK]
BARASANA [BSN] lang, Colombia
BARASANO alt for POKANGÁ [POK]
BARASANO alt for WAIMAHA [BAO]
BARAT dial of ORYA [URY]
BARAU dial of KEMBERANO [BZP]
BARAUANA alt for BARÉ [BAE]
BARAUNA alt for BARÉ [BAE]
BARAWA alt for DASS [DOT]
"BARAWAHING" pejorative alt for ABUI [ABZ]
BARAWANA alt for BARÉ [BAE]
BARBA alt for BARIBA [BBA]
BARBACOAS [BPB] lang, Colombia
BARBADIAN CREOLE ENGLISH alt for BAJAN
  [BJS]
BARBADOS alt for UMOTÍNA [UMO]
BARBAIG alt for BARABAYIIGA dial of DATOOGA
  [TCC]
BARBALIN alt for BAGVALAL [KVA]
BARBAREÑO [BOI] lang, USA
BARBARI alt for AIMAQ [AIQ]
BARBARICINO dial of SARDINIAN, LOGUDORESE
  [SRD]
BARBUDA CREOLE ENGLISH dial of LEEWARD
  CARIBBEAN CREOLE ENGLISH [AIG]
BARBURR alt for BURA-PABIR [BUR]
BARD alt for BAADI [BCJ]
BARDESKARI dial of KONKANI, GOANESE [GOM]
BARDI alt for BAADI [BCJ]
BARDI dial of BAADI [BCJ]
BARDOJUNGA alt for NGADJUNMAYA [NJU]
BARE alt for AGARABI [AGD]
BARE alt for BWAZZA dial of MBULA-BWAZZA
  [MBU]
BARÉ [BAE] lang, Venezuela
"BAREA" pejorative alt for NARA [NRB]
BAREDJI alt for BAREJI dial of GAINA [GCN]
BAREE alt for PAMONA [BCX]
BARE'E alt for PAMONA [BCX]
BARE'E alt for PAMONA dial of PAMONA [BCX]
BARE'E alt for TOBAU dial of PAMONA [BCX]
BAREI dial of MAITHILI [MKP]
BAREIN [BVA] lang, Chad
BAREJI dial of BARUGA [BBB]
BAREJI dial of GAINA [GCN]
BAREKE dial of VANGUNU [MPR]
BAREKO dial of MBO [MBO]
BAREL alt for BARELI [BGD]
BAREL dial of BHILI [BHB]
BARELI [BGD] lang, India

BARELI alt for BARLI dial of BARELI [BGD]
BARELI PAURI dial of BARELI [BGD]
BAREM alt for BREM [BUQ]
BARERA alt for BURARRA [BVR]
BARESHE alt for RESHE [RES]
BARGA alt for MABAAN [MFZ]
BARGAM [MLP] lang, Papua New Guinea
BARGANCHI alt for BARIBA [BBA]
BARGAWA alt for BARIBA [BBA]
BARGISTA alt for ORMURI [ORU]
BARGU alt for BARIBA [BBA]
BARGU dial of BURIAT, CHINA [BXU]
BARGU BURIAT alt for BURIAT, CHINA [BXU]
BARGUZIN dial of BURIAT, RUSSIA [MNB]
BARHAMU alt for BARAAMU [BRD]
BARI [BFA] lang, Sudan; also in Uganda
BARI alt for BAI [BDJ]
BARI alt for MOTILÓN [MOT]
BARÍ alt for MOTILÓN [MOT]
BARI alt for NIMBARI [NMR]
BARI dial of LOGO [LOG]
BARI KAKWA alt for KAKWA [KEO]
"BARIA" pejorative alt for NARA [NRB]
BARIA alt for MBELALA dial of PAMONA [BCX]
BARIAI [BCH] lang, Papua New Guinea
BARIBA [BBA] lang, Benin; also in Nigeria
"BARIBARI" pejorative alt for KANURI, CENTRAL
  [KPH]
BARIJI [BJC] lang, Papua New Guinea
BARIK dial of BENGALI [BNG]
BARIKANCHI [BXO] lang, Nigeria
BARI-LOGO alt for BARI dial of LOGO [LOG]
BARIM [BBV] lang, Papua New Guinea
BARIO dial of KELABIT [KZI]
BARITI alt for BARI dial of LOGO [LOG]
BARKA alt for BAGA BINARI [BCG]
BARKA alt for BAGA KOGA [BGO]
BARKA alt for BAGA MANDURI [BMD]
BARKA alt for BAGA SITEMU [BSP]
BARKA alt for BAGA SOBANÉ [BSV]
BARKA dial of BISSA [BIB]
BARKA dial of KUNAMA [KUM]
BARKE alt for MBURKU [BBT]
BARKLY KRIOL dial of KRIOL [ROP]
BARKO alt for MBURKU [BBT]
BARKOUNDOUBA dial of FULFULDE, NORTH-
  EASTERN BURKINA FASO [FUH]
BARLAVENTO dial of KABUVERDIANU [KEA]
BARLI dial of BARELI [BGD]
BARLIG dial of BONTOC, EASTERN [BKB]
BARMA alt for BAGIRMI [BMI]
BARMA alt for ZUL dial of POLCI [POL]
BARMELI dial of MAITHILI [MKP]
BÄRNDÜTSCH alt for BERN dial of ALEMANNISCH
  [GSW]
BAROK [BJK] lang, Papua New Guinea
BAROK dial of BAROK [BJK]
BAROKE alt for PARAUK [PRK]
BAROMBI [BBI] lang, Cameroon
BARONDO alt for BALUNDU dial of BALUNDU-
  BIMA [NGO]

BARONGAGUNAY dial of AGTA, DUPANINAN [DUO]
BAROPASI alt for BARAPASI [BRP]
BAROTAC VIEJO NAGPANA dial of ATI [ATK]
BARPAK dial of GHALE, SOUTHERN [GHE]
BARRAWA dial of KURANKO [KHA]
BARROW POINT [BPT] lang, Australia
BARRU dial of BUGIS [BPR]
BARTA alt for BERTA [WTI]
BARTANG alt for BARTANGI dial of SHUGHNI [SGH]
BARTANGI dial of SHUGHNI [SGH]
BARTILLE dial of CHALDEAN NEO-ARAMAIC [CLD]
BARU alt for BRU, WESTERN [BRV]
BARUA alt for BARUYA [BYR]
BARUA alt for ERITAI [BAD]
BARUBA alt for BARIBA [BBA]
BARUE alt for ABUI [ABZ]
BARUE alt for BALUE dial of BAKUNDU-BALUE [BDU]
BARUGA [BBB] lang, Papua New Guinea
BARUGA alt for MADO dial of BARUGA [BBB]
BARUGA dial of BARUGA [BBB]
BARUH dial of ACEH [ATJ]
BARUN alt for BURUN [BDI]
BARUP dial of MAMBILA, NIGERIA [MZK]
BARUYA [BYR] lang, Papua New Guinea
BARUYA dial of BARUYA [BYR]
BARWAANI alt for MWINI dial of SWAHILI [SWA]
BARWE [BWG] lang, Mozambique
"BARYA" pejorative alt for NARA [NRB]
BAS SORABE alt for SORBIAN, LOWER [WEE]
BASA [BQA] lang, Benin
BASA [BZW] lang, Nigeria
BASA alt for BASAA [BAA]
BASA dial of NGWO [NGN]
BASA KUPANG dial of MALAY [MLI]
BASA KUTA alt for BASA-GUMNA [BSL]
BASA MATHURA alt for MADURA [MHJ]
BASAA [BAA] lang, Cameroon
BASA-BENUE alt for BASA [BZW]
BASA-GUMNA [BSL] lang, Nigeria
BASA-GURMANA [BUJ] lang, Nigeria
BASAI alt for BASAY [BYQ]
BASA-KADUNA alt for BASA-GUMNA [BSL]
BASANG dial of OBANLIKU [BZY]
BASANGA alt for DOKO-UYANGA [UYA]
BASAP [BDB] lang, Indonesia (Kalimantan)
BASAR alt for NTCHAM [BUD]
BASARE alt for NTCHAM [BUD]
BASARI [BSC] lang, Senegal; also in Guinea, Guinea-Bissau
BASARI alt for NTCHAM [BUD]
BASARI DU BANDEMBA alt for BUDIK [TNR]
BAS-AUVERGNAT dial of AUVERGNAT [AUV]
BASAY [BYQ] lang, Taiwan
BASAYA alt for BISAYA, BRUNEI [BSB]
BASAYA alt for BISAYA, SABAH [BSY]
BASCO IVATAN dial of IVATAN [IVV]
BASECA alt for ANII [BLO]
BASEL dial of ALEMANNISCH [GSW]

BASESE dial of YAKA [AXK]
BASHALDO alt for ROMANI, CARPATHIAN [RMC]
BASHAMMA alt for BACAMA [BAM]
BASHAR alt for YANGKAM [BSX]
BASHARAWA alt for YANGKAM [BSX]
BASHGAADI dial of BALOCHI, SOUTHERN [BCC]
BASHGALI alt for KATI [BSH]
BASHGHARIK alt for KALAMI [GWC]
BASHILELE alt for LELE [LEL]
BASHIRI alt for YANGKAM [BSX]
BASHKARDI [BSG] lang, Iran
BASHKARIK alt for KALAMI [GWC]
BASHKIR [BXK] lang, Russia (Europe); also in Kazakhstan, Kyrgyzstan, Tajikistan, Turkmenistan, Ukraine, Uzbekistan
BASHO dial of DENYA [ANV]
BASHUA alt for BASUA dial of BOKYI [BKY]
BASIC ZULU alt for FANAGOLO [FAO]
BASILA alt for ANII [BLO]
BASILAKI alt for BOHILAI dial of TAWALA [TBO]
BASILI alt for SERE [SWF]
BASILICATAN alt for NORTHERN CALABRESE-LUCANO dial of NAPOLETANO-CALABRESE [NPL]
BASIMA dial of GALEYA [GAR]
BASING alt for MOKEN [MWT]
BASINYARI dial of NUNI, SOUTHERN [NNW]
BASIQ dial of ROMBLOMANON [ROL]
BASIRI alt for SERE [SWF]
BASKATTA alt for BASKETTO [BST]
BAS-KENYANG alt for LOWER KENYANG dial of KENYANG [KEN]
BASKETO alt for BASKETTO [BST]
BASKETTO [BST] lang, Ethiopia
BAS-LANGUEDOCIEN dial of LANGUEDOCIEN [LNC]
BAS-LIMOUSIN dial of LIMOUSIN [LMS]
"BASO" pejorative alt for ABINOMN [BSA]
BASOO alt for BAKOKO [BKH]
BASOO BA DIE alt for ADIE dial of BAKOKO [BKH]
BASOO BA LIKOL alt for BISOO dial of BAKOKO [BKH]
BASOO D'EDEA alt for ADIE dial of BAKOKO [BKH]
BASOSI alt for BASSOSSI [BSI]
BASOSSI alt for BASSOSSI [BSI]
BASQUE [BSQ] lang, Spain; also in Australia, Costa Rica, Mexico, Philippines, USA
BASQUE CALO dial of CALO [RMR]
BASQUE, NAVARRO-LABOURDIN [BQE] lang, France
BASQUE, SOULETIN [BSZ] lang, France
BASQUORT alt for BASHKIR [BXK]
BASRIA alt for BAURIA [BGE]
BASSA [BAS] lang, Liberia; also in Sierra Leone
BASSA alt for BASA dial of NGWO [NGN]
BASSA alt for BASAA [BAA]
BASSA dial of DWANG [NNU]
BASSA NGE alt for NUPE TAKO dial of NUPE-NUPE TAKO [NUP]
BASSA-KADUNA alt for BASA-GUMNA [BSL]
"BASSA-KOMO" pejorative alt for BASA [BZW]

BASSA-KONTAGORA [BSR] lang, Nigeria
"BASSA-KWOMU" pejorative alt for BASA [BZW]
BASSAR alt for NTCHAM [BUD]
BASSARI alt for BASARI [BSC]
BASSARI alt for NTCHAM [BUD]
BASSEIN dial of KAREN, PWO WESTERN [PWO]
BASSEIN PWO KAREN alt for KAREN, PWO
    WESTERN [PWO]
BASSERI dial of FARSI, WESTERN [PES]
BASSILA alt for ANII [BLO]
BASSING alt for BAMESSINGUE dial of NGOMBALE
    [NLA]
BASSO alt for BABADJOU dial of NGOMBALE
    [NLA]
BASSO alt for BISOO dial of BAKOKO [BKH]
BASSO dial of BASAA [BAA]
BASSOSSI [BSI] lang, Cameroon
BASTARI alt for HALBI [HLB]
BASTARI dial of HALBI [HLB]
BASTI alt for NORTHERN STANDARD BHOJPURI
    dial of BHOJPURI [BHJ]
BASTIA alt for NORTHERN CORSICAN dial of
    CORSICAN [COI]
BASTURIA alt for BHATRI [BGW]
BASUA dial of BOKYI [BKY]
BASURUDO dial of EMBERA-SAIJA [SJA]
BASWO alt for WULA dial of BOKYI [BKY]
BAT alt for BADA [BAU]
BATA [BTA] lang, Nigeria; also in Cameroon
BATAAN dial of TAGALOG [TGL]
BATAAN AYTA alt for AYTA, BATAAN [AYT]
BATAAN SAMBAL alt for AYTA, BATAAN [AYT]
BATAD alt for IFUGAO, BATAD [IFB]
BATAD IFUGAO dial of IFUGAO, BATAD [IFB]
BATADJI alt for BEBA' dial of BAFUT [BFD]
BATAK [BTK] lang, Philippines
BATAK ALAS-KLUET [BTZ] lang, Indonesia
    (Sumatra)
BATAK ANGKOLA [AKB] lang, Indonesia (Sumatra)
BATAK DAIRI [BTD] lang, Indonesia (Sumatra)
BATAK KARO [BTX] lang, Indonesia (Sumatra)
BATAK MANDAILING [BTM] lang, Indonesia
    (Sumatra)
BATAK SIMALUNGUN [BTS] lang, Indonesia
    (Sumatra)
BATAK TOBA [BBC] lang, Indonesia (Sumatra)
BATA-NDEEWE alt for NDEEWE dial of BATA [BTA]
BATANG LUPAR dial of IBAN [IBA]
BATANGA [BNM] lang, Equatorial Guinea; also in
    Cameroon
BATANGA dial of BATANGA [BNM]
BATANGA dial of CAKA [CKX]
BATANGA-BAKOKO alt for DOTANGA dial of
    BALUNDU-BIMA [NGO]
BATANGAN alt for BUHID [BKU]
BATANGAN alt for TAWBUID, EASTERN [BNJ]
BATANGAS dial of TAGALOG [TGL]
BATANTA ISLAND dial of MAYA [SLZ]
BATAVI alt for BETAWI [BEW]
BATAWI alt for BETAWI [BEW]
BATAXAN alt for BUTEHA dial of DAUR [DTA]

BATCHAM dial of NGIEMBOON [NNH]
BATCHENGA alt for TUKI [BAG]
BATEG alt for BATEK [BTQ]
BATEK [BTQ] lang, Malaysia (Peninsular)
BATEK DE' dial of BATEK [BTQ]
BATEK IGA dial of BATEK [BTQ]
BATEK NONG dial of BATEK [BTQ]
BATEK TEH dial of JEHAI [JHI]
BATEK TEQ dial of BATEK [BTQ]
BATEM-DA-KAI-EE alt for KATO [KTW]
BATEQ alt for BATEK [BTQ]
BATERA KOHISTANI alt for BATERI [BTV]
BATERAWAL alt for BATERI [BTV]
BATERAWAL KOHISTANI alt for BATERI [BTV]
BATERI [BTV] lang, Pakistan; also in India
BATERI KOHISTANI alt for BATERI [BTV]
BATHA alt for LENDU [LED]
BATHA dial of ARABIC, CHADIAN SPOKEN [SHU]
BAT-HARI alt for BATHARI dial of MEHRI [MHR]
BATHARI dial of MEHRI [MHR]
BATHI dial of PANJABI, EASTERN [PNJ]
BATI [BTC] lang, Cameroon
BATI [BVT] lang, Indonesia (Maluku)
BATI alt for TI dial of MUNGAKA [MHK]
BATI dial of BWA [BWW]
BATI BA NGONG alt for BATI [BTC]
BATI DE BROUSSE alt for BATI [BTC]
BATIBO alt for META' [MGO]
BATIBO alt for MOGHAMO dial of META [MGO]
BATICOLA dial of GUARANI, MBYA [GUN]
BATIE alt for GHOMÁLÁ' [BBJ]
BATIN alt for SUKU BATIN [SBV]
BATIWAI dial of NAMOSI-NAITASIRI-SERUA [BWB]
BATJAN alt for MALAY, BACANESE [BTJ]
BATLUX dial of AVAR [AVR]
BATOK alt for BATEK [BTQ]
BATOKA alt for TONGA dial of NDAU [NDC]
BATOMO dial of MESAKA [IYO]
BATONGA alt for TONGA dial of NDAU [NDC]
BATONGTOU dial of MEDUMBA [BYV]
BATONNUM alt for BARIBA [BBA]
BATONU alt for BARIBA [BBA]
BATS [BBL] lang, Georgia
BATSANGUI alt for TSAANGI [TSA]
BATSAW alt for BATS [BBL]
BATSBI alt for BATS [BBL]
BATSBIITSY alt for BATS [BBL]
BATSI alt for BATS [BBL]
BATSINGO alt for TSINGA dial of TUKI [BAG]
BATTA alt for BATA [BTA]
BATTA alt for BATAK MANDAILING [BTM]
BATTA alt for BATAK TOBA [BBC]
BATU [BTU] lang, Nigeria
BATU alt for NIAS [NIP]
BATU dial of NIAS [NIP]
BATU BELAH alt for BATU BLA dial of BERAWAN
    [LOD]
BATU BLA dial of BERAWAN [LOD]
BATU MERAH dial of LUHU [LCQ]
BATU SANGKAR-PARIANGAN dial of
    MINANGKABAU [MPU]

BATUAN alt for SIBUGUEY dial of SAMA,
    BALANGINGI [SSE]
BATUI dial of PAMONA [BCX]
BATULEY [BAY] lang, Indonesia (Maluku)
BATULOLONG dial of KUI [KVD]
BATWA alt for //XEGWI [XEG]
BAU [BBD] lang, Papua New Guinea
BAU dial of FIJIAN [FJI]
BAUAN alt for BAU dial of FIJIAN [FJI]
BAUBAU alt for WOLIO [WLO]
BAUCHI [BSF] lang, Nigeria
BAUCI alt for BAUCHI [BSF]
BAUDI alt for BAUZI [PAU]
BAUDJI alt for BAUZI [PAU]
BAUDÓ alt for EMBERÁ-BAUDÓ [BDC]
BAUDZI alt for BAUZI [PAU]
BAU-JAGOI alt for JAGOI [SNE]
BAUKAN [BNB] lang, Malaysia (Sabah)
BAUKAN dial of BAUKAN [BNB]
BAUKAN MURUT alt for BAUKAN [BNB]
BAULE alt for BAOULÉ [BCI]
BAULE dial of TULA [TUL]
BAUMAA alt for SOUTHEAST VANUA LEVU dial
    of FIJIAN [FJI]
BAUNGSHE alt for CHIN, HAKA [CNH]
BAURE [BRG] lang, Bolivia
BAURI alt for BAUZI [PAU]
BAURIA [BGE] lang, India
BAURO [BXA] lang, Solomon Islands
BAURO dial of BAURO [BXA]
BAUSHI alt for BAUCHI [BSF]
BAUTAHARI alt for BATHARI dial of MEHRI [MHR]
BAUTZEN dial of SORBIAN, UPPER [WEN]
BAUWAKI [BWK] lang, Papua New Guinea
BAUZI [PAU] lang, Indonesia (Irian Jaya)
BAVARAMA alt for BARAMA [BBG]
BAVARIAN [BAR] lang, Austria; also in Czech
    Republic, Germany, Hungary, Italy
BAVARIAN AUSTRIAN alt for BAVARIAN [BAR]
BAVARIAN-AUSTRIAN alt for BAVARIAN [BAR]
BAVRI alt for VAGHRI [VGR]
BAWAKI alt for BAUWAKI [BWK]
BAWANDJI alt for WANDJI [WDD]
BAWANG alt for HORPA [ERO]
BAWARI alt for BAURIA [BGE]
BAWARIA alt for BAURIA [BGE]
BAWEAN dial of MADURA [MHJ]
BAWERA alt for BURARRA [BVR]
BAWM alt for CHIN, BAWM [BGR]
BAWN alt for CHIN, BAWM [BGR]
BAWNG alt for CHIN, BAWM [BGR]
BAWO alt for BAKUNDU dial of BAKUNDU-BALUE
    [BDU]
BAWOM alt for ABILIANG dial of DINKA, NORTH-
    EASTERN [DIP]
BAWRI alt for BAGRI [BGQ]
BAWU dial of LAWANGAN [LBX]
BAWULE alt for BAOULÉ [BCI]
BAWULI alt for TUWILI [BOV]
BAX<A alt for BAKH<A dial of WESTERN NEO-
    ARAMAIC [AMW]

BAXA alt for BAKHA dial of KARANGA [KTH]
BAXOJE alt for IOWA dial of IOWA-OTO [IOW]
BAY dial of ENETS [ENE]
BAY ISLANDS CREOLE ENGLISH [BYH] lang,
    Honduras
BAY OF PLENTY dial of MAORI [MBF]
BAYA alt for GBAYA, NORTHWEST [GYA]
BAYAG dial of ISNAG [ISD]
BAYAKA alt for BEKA dial of YAKA [AXK]
BAYAKA alt for YAKPA dial of BANDA, MID-
    SOUTHERN [BJO]
BAYALI [BJY] lang, Australia
BAYANGI alt for KENYANG [KEN]
BAYANO dial of KUNA, SAN BLAS [CUK]
BAYASH dial of ROMANIAN [RUM]
BAYASH ROMANIAN dial of ROMANIAN [RUM]
BAYAT dial of AZERBAIJANI, SOUTH [AZB]
BÂYAZIDI dial of KURMANJI [KUR]
BAYERISCH alt for BAVARIAN [BAR]
BAYGO [BYG] lang, Sudan
BAYI alt for BALONG dial of BAFAW-BALONG
    [BWT]
BAYING alt for BAHING [RAR]
BAYINO alt for ABAYONGO dial of AGWAGWUNE
    [YAY]
BAYIT dial of KALMYK-OIRAT [KGZ]
BAYMUNA dial of MISKITO [MIQ]
BAYMUNANA alt for BAYMUNA dial of MISKITO
    [MIQ]
"BAYNAWA" pejorative alt for GIDAR [GID]
BAYNAWA alt for GIDAR [GID]
BAYNINAN dial of KALANGUYA, KELEY-I [IFY]
BAYO alt for BAJAU, INDONESIAN [BDL]
BAYO dial of BERNDE [BDO]
BAYOBIRI dial of UKPE-BAYOBIRI [UKP]
BAYOMBE alt for YOMBE [YOM]
BAYONG alt for NDEMLI [NML]
BAYONGHO alt for YANGHO [YNH]
BAYONO [BYL] lang, Indonesia (Irian Jaya)
BAYONO alt for ABAYONGO dial of AGWAGWUNE
    [YAY]
BAYOT [BDA] lang, Senegal; also in Gambia,
    Guinea-Bissau
BAYOTE alt for BAYOT [BDA]
BAYOTTE alt for BAYOT [BDA]
BAYSO alt for BAISO [BSW]
BAYUNG alt for BAHING [RAR]
BAYUNG LO alt for BAHING [RAR]
BAYUNGU [BXJ] lang, Australia
BAYYU dial of BONTOC, CENTRAL [BNC]
BAZA alt for BANA [BCW]
BAZA alt for KUNAMA [KUM]
BAZA alt for NGBANDI, NORTHERN [NGB]
BAZAAR MALAY alt for MALAY, SABAH [MSI]
BAZAAR MALAY alt for MELAYU PASAR dial of
    MALAY [MLI]
BAZAAR MALAY dial of MALAY [MLI]
BAZEN alt for KUNAMA [KUM]
BAZENDA alt for ZANDE [ZAN]
BAZEZURU alt for ZEZURU dial of SHONA [SHD]
BAZHI alt for BEBA' dial of BAFUT [BFD]

BAZIGAR [BFR] lang, India
BAZUZURA alt for ZEZURU dial of SHONA [SHD]
BAZZA alt for DAKWA dial of KAMWE [HIG]
BBADHA alt for LENDU [LED]
BBALEDHA alt for LENDU [LED]
BBATE dial of MBAY [MYB]
BE alt for DENO [DBB]
BÊ alt for LINGAO [ONB]
BEA alt for AKA-BEA [ACE]
BEA alt for MAMBILA, CAMEROON [MYA]
BEADA alt for AKA-BEA [ACE]
BEAFADA alt for BIAFADA [BIF]
BEAMI [BEO] lang, Papua New Guinea
BEARLAKE dial of SLAVEY, NORTH [SCS]
BÉARNAIS dial of GASCON [GSC]
BEAUFORT dial of DUSUN, CENTRAL [DTP]
BEAUFORT MURUT dial of TIMUGON MURUT
    [TIH]
BEAVER [BEA] lang, Canada
BEBA' dial of BAFUT [BFD]
BEBA-BEFANG alt for BEFANG [BBY]
BEBA-BEFANG alt for BEFANG dial of BEFANG
    [BBY]
BEBADJI alt for BEBA' dial of BAFUT [BFD]
BEBAROE alt for YAMBA [YAM]
BEBAYAGA alt for BAKA [BKC]
BEBAYAKA alt for BAKA [BKC]
BEBE [BZV] lang, Cameroon
BEBELE [BEB] lang, Cameroon
BEBELI [BEK] lang, Papua New Guinea
BEBENDE alt for BEBENT dial of MAKAA [MCP]
BEBENT dial of MAKAA [MCP]
BEBI dial of OBANLIKU [BZY]
BEBIL [BXP] lang, Cameroon
BÉBOTE dial of BEDJOND [MAP]
BECHATI dial of MUNDANI [MUN]
BECHERE alt for BACHEVE dial of ICEVE-MACI
    [BEC]
BECHERE alt for ICEVE-MACI [BEC]
BECHEVE alt for BACHEVE dial of ICEVE-MACI
    [BEC]
BECHEVE alt for ICEVE-MACI [BEC]
BECHITIN alt for BEZHTA [KAP]
BEDA alt for VEDDAH [VED]
BE:DA dial of ARABIC, JUDEO-YEMENI [JYE]
BEDAMINI alt for BEAMI [BEO]
BEDAMUNI alt for BEAMI [BEO]
BEDANGA dial of SOKORO [SOK]
BEDAUYE alt for BEDAWI [BEI]
BEDAWI [BEI] lang, Sudan; also in Egypt, Eritrea
BEDAWI alt for ARABIC, EASTERN EGYPTIAN
    BEDAWI SPOKEN [AVL]
BEDAWI alt for ARABIC, GULF SPOKEN [AFB]
BEDAWI alt for ARABIC, LEVANTINE BEDAWI
    SPOKEN [AVL]
BEDAWI alt for ARABIC, NAJDI SPOKEN [ARS]
BEDAWI alt for ARABIC, SOUTH LEVANTINE
    SPOKEN [AJP]
BEDAWI alt for ARABIC, WESTERN EGYPTIAN
    BEDAWI SPOKEN [AYL]
BEDÀWIE alt for BEDAWI [BEI]

BEDAWIYE alt for BEDAWI [BEI]
BEDAWYE alt for BEDAWI [BEI]
BEDDA alt for VEDDAH [VED]
BEDDE alt for BADE [BDE]
BEDE alt for BADE [BDE]
BÉDÉGUÉ dial of MBAY [MYB]
BEDERE alt for ADELE [ADE]
BEDFOLA alt for BIAFADA [BIF]
BEDIA alt for KUDMALI [KYW]
BEDIA alt for PANCHPARGANIA [TDB]
BEDIK alt for BUDIK [TNR]
BEDIONDO alt for BEDJOND [MAP]
BEDIONDO MBAI alt for BEDJOND [MAP]
BEDJA alt for BEDAWI [BEI]
BEDJOND [MAP] lang, Chad
BEDJOND dial of BEDJOND [MAP]
BÉDJONDE alt for BEDJOND [MAP]
BEDJONDO alt for BEDJOND [MAP]
BÉDJOU dial of MBAY [MYB]
BEDOANAS [BED] lang, Indonesia (Irian Jaya)
BEDUANDA dial of TEMUAN [TMW]
BEDWI alt for BEDAWI [BEI]
BEDYA alt for BEDAWI [BEI]
BEEGE dial of MUSGU [MUG]
BEEKE [BKF] lang, DCR
BEEKURU alt for MODELE dial of BEFANG [BBY]
BEELE [BXQ] lang, Nigeria
BEEMBE [BEJ] lang, Congo
BEEMBE alt for BEMBE [BMB]
BEER alt for AGEER dial of DINKA, NORTH-
    EASTERN [DIP]
BEETJUANS alt for TSWANA [TSW]
BEEZEN [BNZ] lang, Cameroon
BEFANG [BBY] lang, Cameroon
BEFANG dial of BEFANG [BBY]
BEFE alt for BAFUT [BFD]
BEFI alt for KENSWEI NSEI [NDB]
BEFON alt for NDE dial of NDE-NSELE-NTA [NDD]
BEFUN alt for ABANYOM [ABM]
BEGA alt for BAIGANI dial of CHHATTISGARHI
    [HNE]
BEGA alt for GUMUZ [GUK]
BEGAHAK alt for BEGAK dial of IDAAN [DBJ]
BEGAK dial of IDAAN [DBJ]
BEGASIN alt for GIRAWA [BBR]
BEGBERE-EJAR [BQV] lang, Nigeria
BEGBUNGBA alt for BAKPINKA [BBS]
BEGE alt for NJALGULGULE [NJL]
BEGESIN alt for GIRAWA [BBR]
BEGI alt for NJALGULGULE [NJL]
BEGI-MAO alt for HOZO [HOZ]
BEGINCI dial of SEMANDANG [SDM]
BEGI-NIBUM alt for NIGII dial of YAMBETA [YAT]
BEGO alt for BAYGO [BYG]
BEGUA alt for BAGWA dial of ZIMAKANI [ZIK]
BEHDINI [BDF] lang, Iraq; also in Germany
BEHE dial of DAYAK, LAND [DYK]
BEHERE dial of KOI [KKT]
BEHEVE alt for BACHEVE dial of ICEVE-MACI
    [BEC]
BEHIE alt for NUGUNU [YAS]

BEHLI alt for BELI [BLM]
BEHOA alt for BESOA [BEP]
BEHRAN alt for THAYORE [THD]
BEIÇO DE PAU dial of SUYA [SUY]
BEIFANG FANGYAN alt for CHINESE, MANDARIN [CHN]
BEIGO alt for BAYGO [BYG]
BEIK alt for MERGUESE dial of BURMESE [BMS]
BEILI alt for BELI [BLM]
BEILLA dial of KOMO [KOM]
BEIR alt for MURLE [MUR]
BEIRA dial of PORTUGUESE [POR]
BEIRUT dial of DOMARI [RMT]
BEJA alt for BEDAWI [BEI]
BEJAMSE alt for SOUTHERN CHUMBURUNG dial of CHUMBURUNG [NCU]
BEK alt for PAK dial of VATRATA [VLR]
BEKA alt for YAKA [AXK]
BEKÁ alt for YAKA [AXK]
BEKA dial of YAKA [AXK]
BEKATI' [BAT] lang, Indonesia (Kalimantan)
BEKE alt for BEEKE [BKF]
BEKE alt for DAJU, DAR FUR [DAJ]
BEKE alt for NUGUNU [YAS]
BEKENI dial of BALI [BCP]
BEKETAN alt for BUKITAN [BKN]
BEKIAU alt for BISAYA, BRUNEI [BSB]
BEKIAU alt for BISAYA, SARAWAK [BSD]
BEKO alt for BAYGO [BYG]
BEKO alt for NJALGULGULE [NJL]
BEKOE alt for GYELE [GYI]
BEKOL alt for KOL [BIW]
BEKOMBO alt for EKOMBE dial of BAKUNDU-BALUE [BDU]
BEKOOSE alt for AKOOSE [BSS]
BEKPAK alt for BAFIA [KSF]
BEKUNDE alt for BAKUNDU dial of BAKUNDU-BALUE [BDU]
BEKWA' alt for KWA' dial of KWA [BKO]
BEKWARRA [BKV] lang, Nigeria
BEKWEL [BKW] lang, Congo; also in Cameroon, Gabon
BEKWIE alt for BEKWEL [BKW]
BEKWIL alt for BEKWEL [BKW]
BEKWIRI alt for MOKPWE [BRI]
BEKWORRA alt for BEKWARRA [BKV]
BEL alt for GEDAGED [GDD]
BELA [BEQ] lang, China
BELA alt for MBELALA dial of PAMONA [BCX]
BELAGAR alt for BLAGAR [BEU]
BELAIT [BEG] lang, Brunei
BELALA alt for MBELALA dial of PAMONA [BCX]
BELANA alt for BELANDA dial of TEMUAN [TMW]
BELANAS alt for BELANDA dial of TEMUAN [TMW]
BELANA'U alt for MELANAU [MEL]
BELANDA alt for BELANDA VIRI [BVI]
BELANDA dial of TEMUAN [TMW]
BELANDA BOR [BXB] lang, Sudan
BELANDA VIRI [BVI] lang, Sudan
BELANDAS alt for BELANDA dial of TEMUAN [TMW]
BELANI alt for LOHAR, GADE [GDA]

BELANTE alt for BALANTA-GANJA [BJT]
BELANTE alt for BALANTA-KENTOHE [BLE]
BELANYA dial of TUMMA [TBQ]
BELARUSAN [RUW] lang, Belarus; also in Azerbaijan, Canada, Estonia, Kazakhstan, Kyrgyzstan, Latvia, Lithuania, Moldova, Poland, Russia (Europe), Tajikistan, Turkmenistan, Ukraine, USA, Uzbekistan
BELARUSIAN alt for BELARUSAN [RUW]
BELAUAN alt for PALAUAN [PLU]
BELAYAN dial of KAYAN, BUSANG [BFG]
BELE alt for BEELE [BXQ]
BELE dial of FALI, SOUTH [FAL]
BELEBELE dial of IDUNA [VIV]
BELEDUGU dial of BAMANANKAN [BRA]
BELEGETE alt for EVANT [BZZ]
BELEN alt for BILEN [BYN]
BELENI alt for BILEN [BYN]
BELEP dial of NYALAYU [YLY]
BELEPA alt for KEURU [QQK]
BELFAST dial of ENGLISH [ENG]
BELGIAN PICARD alt for PICARD [PCD]
BELGIAN SIGN LANGUAGE [BVS] lang, Belgium
BELHARE alt for BELHARIYA [BYW]
BELHARIYA [BYW] lang, Nepal
BELI [BEY] lang, Papua New Guinea
BELI [BLM] lang, Sudan
BELI alt for BEBELI [BEK]
'BELI alt for BELI [BLM]
BELIBI alt for ELIP [EKM]
BELIDE dial of MALAY [MLI]
BELIP alt for ELIP [EKM]
BELITUNG dial of MALAY [MLI]
BELIZE CREOLE ENGLISH dial of NORTHERN CENTRAL AMERICA CREOLE ENGLISH [BZI]
BELLA BELLA dial of HEILTSUK [HEI]
BELLA COOLA [BEL] lang, Canada
BELLARI [BRW] lang, India
BELLARI dial of TULU [TCY]
BELLAWA alt for BEELE [BXQ]
BELLE alt for KUWAA [BLH]
BELLEH alt for KUWAA [BLH]
BELLONA alt for MUNGIKI dial of RENNELL [MNV]
BELLONESE alt for MUNGIKI dial of RENNELL [MNV]
BELO alt for TETUN [TTM]
BELOH alt for KARAU dial of LAWANGAN [LBX]
BELOM alt for LOM [MFB]
BELORUSSIAN alt for BELARUSAN [RUW]
BELSETÁN alt for CENTRAL ARAGONESE dial of ARAGONESE [AXX]
BELTIR dial of KHAKAS [KJH]
BELU alt for TETUN [TTM]
BELU SELATAN alt for SOUTHERN TETUN dial of TETUN [TTM]
BELU UTARA alt for NORTHERN TETUN dial of TETUN [TTM]
BELUBAA alt for BILBA-DIU-LELENUK dial of ROTE [ROT]
BELUBN alt for KENSIU [KNS]
BELUDJI dial of DOMARI [RMT]

BEMAL [BMH] lang, Papua New Guinea
BEMAR dial of NGAMBAY [SBA]
BEMBA [BEM] lang, Zambia; also in Botswana, DCR, Malawi, Tanzania
BEMBA [BMY] lang, DCR
BEMBALA alt for BURJI [BJI]
BEMBE [BMB] lang, DCR; also in Tanzania
BEMBE alt for BEEMBE [BEJ]
BEMBE dial of MABAALE [MMZ]
BEMBI alt for FAS [FAS]
BEMBI alt for PAGI [PGI]
BEMILI dial of BALI [BCP]
BEMINA alt for BEBENT dial of MAKAA [MCP]
BÉMOUR dial of LAKA [LAM]
BEN alt for BENG [NHB]
BEN alt for MOBA [MFQ]
BENA [BEZ] lang, Tanzania
BENA [YUN] lang, Nigeria
BENA alt for BENABENA [BEF]
BENA alt for VORO [VOR]
BENAADIR dial of SOMALI [SOM]
BENABENA [BEF] lang, Papua New Guinea
BENAFFARERA alt for EASTERN LOW NAVARRESE dial of BASQUE, NAVARRO-LABOURDIN [BQE]
BENARSI alt for WESTERN STANDARD BHOJPURI dial of BHOJPURI [BHJ]
BENASQUÉS alt for EASTERN ARAGONESE dial of ARAGONESE [AXX]
BENAULE alt for BEBELI [BEK]
BENBAKANJAMATA alt for ADYNYAMATHANHA [ADT]
BENCH [BCQ] lang, Ethiopia
BENCH dial of BENCH [BCQ]
BENCHO alt for BENCH dial of BENCH [BCQ]
BENCOOLEN alt for BENGKULU [BKE]
BENDE [BDP] lang, Tanzania
BENDE alt for ISLANDER CREOLE ENGLISH dial of NORTHERN CENTRAL AMERICA CREOLE ENGLISH [BZI]
BENDI [BCT] lang, DCR
BENDI dial of BETE-BENDI [BTT]
BENDI dial of HLAI [LIC]
BENDI LOLO alt for LAQUA [LAQ]
BENE dial of BULU [BUM]
BENEHES dial of MODANG [MXD]
BENERAF alt for BONERIF [BNV]
BENESHO alt for BENCH dial of BENCH [BCQ]
BENG [NHB] lang, Côte d'Ivoire
BENGA [BEN] lang, Equatorial Guinea; also in Gabon
BENGALI [BNG] lang, Bangladesh; also in India, Malawi, Nepal, Saudi Arabia, Singapore, UAE, United Kingdom, USA
BENGE dial of BOBO MADARE, NORTHERN [BBO]
BENGE dial of BOBO MADARE, SOUTHERN [BWQ]
BENGE dial of BWA [BWW]
BENGGAULU dial of UMA [PPK]
BENGGOI [BGY] lang, Indonesia (Maluku)
BENGGOI dial of BENGGOI [BGY]
BENGKULU [BKE] lang, Indonesia (Sumatra)
BENGNI-BOGA'ER alt for LUOBA, BOGA'ER [ADI]

BENGOI alt for BENGGOI [BGY]
BENGUET-IGOROT alt for IBALOI [IBL]
BENI IZNASSEN alt for IZNACEN dial of TARIFIT [RIF]
BENI IZNASSEN dial of TARIFIT [RIF]
"BENI SHANGUL" pejorative alt for BERTA [WTI]
BENI SHANGUL alt for BERTA [WTI]
BENI SHEKO dial of KELO [TSN]
BENI-AMIR dial of BEDAWI [BEI]
BENIN alt for EDO [EDO]
BENIN PIDGIN dial of PIDGIN, NIGERIAN [PCM]
BENKONJO alt for UKHWEJO [UKH]
BENKULAN alt for BENGKULU [BKE]
BENOYE dial of NGAMBAY [SBA]
BENTENAN alt for RATAHAN [RTH]
BENTIAN alt for BANTIAN dial of LAWANGAN [LBX]
BENTOENI alt for WANDAMEN [WAD]
BENTONG [BNU] lang, Indonesia (Sulawesi)
BENTUNI alt for WANDAMEN [WAD]
BENUA alt for TEMUAN [TMW]
BENUA dial of LAWANGAN [LBX]
BENYADU' [BYD] lang, Indonesia (Kalimantan)
BENYI alt for MMAALA [MMU]
BENZA dial of LIGENZA [LGZ]
BENZING alt for MENGAKA [XMG]
BEO dial of NGELIMA [AGH]
BEO dial of TALAUD [TLD]
BEOTHUC alt for BEOTHUK [BUE]
BEOTHUK [BUE] lang, Canada
BEPOUR [BIE] lang, Papua New Guinea
BERA [BRF] lang, DCR
BERA dial of KAKO [KKJ]
BERAD dial of TELUGU [TCW]
BERAKOU [BXV] lang, Chad
BERANG alt for GUGUBERA [KKP]
BERANG dial of DAYAK, LAND [DYK]
BERAR MARATHI alt for VARHADI-NAGPURI [VAH]
BERARI alt for VARHADI-NAGPURI [VAH]
BERAU alt for MALAY, BERAU [BVE]
BERAU dial of BASAP [BDB]
BERAUR alt for KALABRA [KZZ]
BERAWAN [LOD] lang, Malaysia (Sarawak)
BERBA alt for BARIBA [BBA]
BERBA alt for BIALI [BEH]
BERBERI alt for AIMAQ [AIQ]
BERBICE CREOLE DUTCH [BRC] lang, Guyana
BERBOU dial of TSO [LDP]
BERDAMA alt for NAMA [NAQ]
BERE alt for BWAZZA dial of MBULA-BWAZZA [MBU]
BEREGADOUGOU-TOUMOUSSENI dial of TURKA [TUZ]
BEREINA dial of RORO [RRO]
BEREMBUN dial of TEMUAN [TMW]
BERENS RIVER OJIBWA dial of OJIBWA, NORTH-WESTERN [OJB]
BEREYA dial of BANDA-BANDA [BPD]
BERGAMASCO dial of LOMBARD [LMO]
BERGDAMARA alt for NAMA [NAQ]
BERGIT alt for BIRGIT [BTF]

BERGOTÉS alt for CENTRAL ARAGONESE dial of ARAGONESE [AXX]
BERGUID alt for BIRGIT [BTF]
BERI alt for BARI [BFA]
BERI alt for BIDEYAT [BIH]
BERI alt for CHEWONG [CWG]
BERI alt for ZAGHAWA [ZAG]
BERI alt for ZANDE [ZAN]
BERIA alt for BIDEYAT [BIH]
BERIA alt for ZAGHAWA [ZAG]
BERI-AA alt for ZAGHAWA [ZAG]
BERI-AA alt for ZANDE [ZAN]
"BERIBERI" pejorative alt for KANURI, CENTRAL [KPH]
BERIBERI alt for KANURI, CENTRAL [KPH]
BERICK alt for BERIK [BER]
BERIK [BER] lang, Indonesia (Irian Jaya)
BERIN alt for JUMJUM [JUM]
BERING alt for BERINGOV dial of ALEUT [ALW]
BERING STRAIT INUPIATUN alt for KING ISLAND INUPIATUN dial of INUPIATUN, NORTHWEST ALASKA [ESK]
BERINGOV dial of ALEUT [ALW]
BERKA alt for BARKA dial of KUNAMA [KUM]
BERMEJO VEJOZ dial of WICHI LHAMTES VEJOZ [MAD]
BERMUDAN ENGLISH dial of ENGLISH [ENG]
BERN dial of ALEMANNISCH [GSW]
BERNDE [BDO] lang, Chad
BERO alt for OWINIGA [OWI]
BERO dial of MESME [ZIM]
BEROM [BOM] lang, Nigeria
BERONK alt for CENTRAL KANUM dial of KANUM, SOTA [KRZ]
BERREMBEEL alt for WIRADHURI [WRH]
BERRI alt for ZAGHAWA [ZAG]
BERRI alt for ZANDE [ZAN]
BERRICHON dial of FRENCH [FRN]
BERRIK alt for BERIK [BER]
BERRINGEN alt for MARITHIEL [MFR]
BERTA [WTI] lang, Ethiopia; also in Sudan
BERTHA alt for BERTA [WTI]
BERTI [BYT] lang, Sudan
BERUM alt for BEROM [BOM]
BESALI dial of MUNDANI [MUN]
BESAYA alt for BISAYA, BRUNEI [BSB]
BESAYA alt for BISAYA, SABAH [BSY]
BESEKI alt for SEKI [SYI]
BESEMA alt for BACAMA [BAM]
BESEMAH alt for PASEMAH [PSE]
BESEMBO dial of KAKO [KKJ]
BESEME alt for BESME [BES]
BESEMME alt for BESME [BES]
BESEP dial of BYEP [MKK]
BESHA alt for BESEP dial of BYEP [MKK]
BESHADA alt for HAMER-BANNA [AMF]
BESI alt for MOGHAMO dial of META [MGO]
BESI alt for PASI [PSI]
BESISI [MHE] lang, Malaysia (Peninsular)
BESLENEI alt for KABARDIAN [KAB]
BESLENEI dial of KABARDIAN [KAB]

BESLENEJ alt for BESLENEI dial of KABARDIAN [KAB]
BESLERI alt for MINA [HNA]
BESLERI dial of MINA [HNA]
BESME [BES] lang, Chad
BESOA [BEP] lang, Indonesia (Sulawesi)
BETA dial of DAYAK, LAND [DYK]
BETAF [BFE] lang, Indonesia (Irian Jaya)
BÉTANURE dial of LISHANA DENI [LSD]
BETAU dial of SEMAI [SEA]
BETAWI [BEW] lang, Indonesia (Java and Bali)
BETAWI MALAY alt for BETAWI [BEW]
BETAYA alt for TUCANO [TUO]
BETE [BYF] lang, Nigeria
BETE alt for BATA [BTA]
BETE alt for BIETE [BIU]
BETE dial of BETE-BENDI [BTT]
BÉTÉ, DALOA [BEV] lang, Côte d'Ivoire
BÉTÉ, GAGNOA [BTG] lang, Côte d'Ivoire
BÉTÉ, GUIBEROUA [BET] lang, Côte d'Ivoire
BETE-BENDI [BTT] lang, Nigeria
BETEF alt for ITIK [ITX]
BETEN dial of KWAKUM [KWU]
BETHEL YUPIK alt for KUSKOKWIM "ESKIMO" dial of YUPIK, CENTRAL [ESU]
BETHEN alt for BETEN dial of KWAKUM [KWU]
BETHUCK alt for BEOTHUK [BUE]
BETHUK alt for BEOTHUK [BUE]
BETI [BTB] lang, Cameroon
BETI [EOT] lang, Côte d'Ivoire
BETI dial of EWONDO [EWO]
BETISE' dial of BESISI [MHE]
BETISEK alt for BETISE' dial of BESISI [MHE]
BETOYA alt for TUCANO [TUO]
BETSILEO dial of MALAGASY [MEX]
BETSIMISARAKA dial of MALAGASY [MEX]
BETSINGA alt for TUKI [BAG]
BETTA KURUMBA NONSTANDARD TAMIL alt for KURUMBA, BETTA [QKB]
BETTE alt for BETE dial of BETE-BENDI [BTT]
BETTE-BENDI alt for BETE-BENDI [BTT]
BETUL dial of GONDI, NORTHERN [GON]
BETZINGA alt for TUKI [BAG]
BEU dial of WE SOUTHERN [GXX]
BEWANI alt for WESTERN PAGI dial of PAGI [PGI]
BEWIL alt for BEBENT dial of MAKAA [MCP]
BEXITA alt for BEZHTA [KAP]
BEYGO alt for BAYGO [BYG]
BEYIDZOLO dial of ETON [ETO]
BEZANOZANO dial of MALAGASY [MEX]
BEZHEDUKH dial of ADYGHE [ADY]
BEZHEHUX-TEMIRGOI alt for BEZHEDUKH dial of ADYGHE [ADY]
BEZHETA alt for BEZHTA [KAP]
BEZHITA alt for BEZHTA [KAP]
BEZHTA [KAP] lang, Russia (Europe)
BEZHTA dial of BEZHTA [KAP]
BEZHTI alt for BEZHTA [KAP]
BEZSHAGH dial of ABAZA [ABQ]
BGHAI KAREN alt for KAREN, BWE [BWE]
BGU alt for BONGGO [BPG]

BHABARI OF RAMPUR dial of KUMAUNI [KFY]
BHADAURI dial of BUNDELI [BNS]
BHADERBHAI JAMU alt for BHADRAWAHI [BHD]
BHADERWALI PAHARI alt for BHADRAWAHI [BHD]
BHADRAVA alt for BHADRAWAHI [BHD]
BHADRAWAHI [BHD] lang, India
BHADRI alt for BHADRAWAHI [BHD]
BHAGIRA dial of LOGO [LOG]
BHAGORIA alt for BHILI [BHB]
BHAIPEI alt for VAIPHEI [VAP]
BHAKHA alt for KANAUJI [BJJ]
BHALAY [BHX] lang, India
BHALESI dial of BHADRAWAHI [BHD]
BHALU dial of SANGPANG [RAV]
BHAMAM alt for CHAM, EASTERN [CJM]
BHAMANI alt for BHAMANI MARIA dial of MARIA
    [MRR]
BHAMANI MARIA dial of MARIA [MRR]
BHAMRAGARH dial of GONDI, SOUTHERN [GGO]
BHANDARA dial of GONDI, NORTHERN [GON]
BHANDARI dial of KONKANI [KNK]
BHAR alt for BHARIA [BHA]
BHARAT alt for BHARIA [BHA]
BHARIA [BHA] lang, India
BHARMAURI dial of GADDI [GBK]
BHARMAURI BHADI alt for GADDI [GBK]
BHATBALI dial of DOGRI-KANGRI [DOJ]
BHATEALI alt for BHATTIYALI [BHT]
BHATIA dial of SINDHI [SND]
BHATIALI PAHARI alt for BHATTIYALI [BHT]
BHATIARI dial of BENGALI [BNG]
BHATIYALI alt for BHATTIYALI [BHT]
BHATNERI alt for BHATYIANA dial of PANJABI,
    EASTERN [PNJ]
BHATOLA [BTL] lang, India
BHATRA alt for BHATRI [BGW]
BHATRI [BGW] lang, India
BHATRI dial of ORIYA [ORY]
BHATTI alt for BHATYIANA dial of PANJABI,
    EASTERN [PNJ]
BHATTIANI dial of GARHWALI [GBM]
BHATTIYALI [BHT] lang, India
BHATTRA alt for BHATRI [BGW]
BHATTRI alt for BHATRI [BGW]
BHATYIANA dial of PANJABI, EASTERN [PNJ]
BHAWALPURI alt for BAHAWALPURI dial of
    SARAIKI [SKR]
BHAWNAGARI alt for KATHIYAWADI dial of
    GUJARATI [GJR]
BHAYA [BHE] lang, Pakistan
BHELE [PER] lang, DCR
BHIÉT alt for BIAT dial of MNONG, CENTRAL [MNC]
BHIL alt for BHILI [BHB]
BHILALA alt for BHILALI [BHI]
BHILALI [BHI] lang, India
BHILBARI alt for BHILI [BHB]
BHILBOLI alt for BHILI [BHB]
BHILI [BHB] lang, India
BHILI alt for WAGDI [WBR]
BHILKI alt for SANSI [SSI]
BHILLA alt for BHILI [BHB]

BHILODI alt for BHILORI [BQI]
BHILODI dial of BHILORI [BQI]
BHILORI [BQI] lang, India
BHIM dial of BHILI [BHB]
BHOI MYNRI dial of MIKIR [MJW]
BHOI-KHASI dial of KHASI [KHI]
BHOJAPURI alt for BHOJPURI [BHJ]
BHOJPURI [BHJ] lang, India; also in Mauritius,
    Nepal
BHOJPURI THARU dial of BHOJPURI [BHJ]
BHOKHA alt for TIBETAN [TIC]
BHONDA BHASHA alt for BONDO [BFW]
BHOO dial of YAOURE [YRE]
BHORIA alt for BAURIA [BGE]
BHOTEA OF UPPER KINNAURI alt for KINNAURI,
    BHOTI [NES]
BHOTI GURUNG alt for BARAGAUNLE [BON]
BHOTI OF BALTISTAN alt for BALTI [BFT]
BHOTIA alt for TIBETAN [TIC]
BHOTIA OF BALTISTAN alt for BALTI [BFT]
BHOTIA OF BHUTAN alt for DZONGKHA [DZO]
BHOTIA OF DUKPA alt for DZONGKHA [DZO]
BHOTIA OF LAHUL alt for TINANI [LBF]
BHOTTADA alt for BHATRI [BGW]
BHOTTARA alt for BHATRI [BGW]
BHOTTE alt for GHALE, KUTANG [GHT]
BHOYARI dial of MALVI [MUP]
BHOZPURI alt for BHOJPURI [BHJ]
BHRAMU alt for BARAAMU [BRD]
BHUANI dial of NIMADI [NOE]
BHUBALIYA LOHAR alt for LOHAR, GADE [GDA]
BHUBHI alt for BUBI [BUW]
BHUGELKHUD alt for BAGHELI [BFY]
BHUJEL KHAM dial of KHAM, NISI [KIF]
BHUKSA dial of BRAJ BHASHA [BFS]
BHULIA dial of CHHATTISGARHI [HNE]
BHUMIA alt for BAIGANI dial of CHHATTISGARHI
    [HNE]
BHUMIA alt for BHARIA [BHA]
BHUMIJ dial of MUNDARI [MUW]
BHUMIJ MUNDA alt for BHUMIJ dial of MUNDARI
    [MUW]
BHUMIJ THAR alt for BHUMIJ dial of MUNDARI
    [MUW]
BHUMIYA alt for BHARIA [BHA]
BHUMJIYA alt for BHUNJIA [BHU]
BHUMTAM alt for BUMTHANGKHA [KJZ]
BHUNJIA [BHU] lang, India
BHUNJIYA alt for BHUNJIA [BHU]
BHUTANESE alt for DZONGKHA [DZO]
BIA alt for GUHU-SAMANE [GHS]
BIABO dial of GREBO, GBOLOO [GEC]
BIADA alt for AKA-BEA [ACE]
BIADJU alt for NGAJU [NIJ]
BIAFADA [BIF] lang, Guinea-Bissau
BIAFAR alt for BIAFADA [BIF]
BIAI dial of KRAHN, WESTERN [KRW]
BIAK [BHW] lang, Indonesia (Irian Jaya)
BIAKA alt for NAI [BIO]
BIAK-NUMFOR alt for BIAK [BHW]
BIAKPAN dial of UBAGHARA [BYC]

BIAKSI alt for BIKSI [BDX]
BIALI [BEH] lang, Benin; also in Burkina Faso
BIAMI alt for PIAME [PIN]
BIAN alt for MARIND, BIAN [BPV]
BIANDA alt for BIYANDA dial of GBAYA, SOUTH-
WEST [MDO]
BIANGAI [BIG] lang, Papua New Guinea
BIANGWALA dial of LAMMA [LEV]
BIANJIIDA dial of DATOOGA [TCC]
BIAO CHAO alt for BIAO-JIAO MIEN [BJE]
BIAO MIEN [BMT] lang, China
BIAO MIEN alt for BIAO MIN dial of BIAO-JIAO MIEN
[BJE]
BIAO MIN dial of BIAO-JIAO MIEN [BJE]
BIAO MON alt for BIAO MIEN [BMT]
BIAO-JIAO MIEN [BJE] lang, China
BIAOMAN alt for BIAO MIEN [BMT]
BIAOMIN alt for BIAO MIN dial of BIAO-JIAO MIEN
[BJE]
BIAPIM alt for WASEMBO [GSP]
BIARNESE alt for BÉARNAIS dial of GASCON [GSC]
BIARU-WARIA dial of WERI [WER]
BIAT dial of MNONG, CENTRAL [MNC]
BIATAH [BTH] lang, Malaysia (Sarawak); also in
Indonesia (Kalimantan)
BIATE alt for BIETE [BIU]
BIBA alt for BEBA' dial of BAFUT [BFD]
BIBAALI alt for BALI [BCN]
BIBA-BIFANG alt for BEFANG [BBY]
BIBAYA alt for BAKA [BKC]
BIBENG dial of BASAA [BAA]
BIBLING alt for AMARA [AIE]
BIBO alt for GOBASI dial of GOBASI [GOI]
BIBOKI alt for BIBOKI-INSANA dial of ATONI [TMR]
BIBOKI-INSANA dial of ATONI [TMR]
BIBOT alt for BOTO dial of ZARI [ZAZ]
BICEK alt for BASAA [BAA]
BICHELAMAR alt for BISLAMA [BCY]
BICOLANO, ALBAY [BHK] lang, Philippines
BICOLANO, CENTRAL [BKL] lang, Philippines
BICOLANO, IRIGA [BTO] lang, Philippines
BICOLANO, NORTHERN CATANDUANES [CTS]
lang, Philippines
BICOLANO, SOUTHERN CATANDUANES [BLN]
lang, Philippines
BICOLI alt for MABA [MQA]
BIDA alt for MANKON dial of NGEMBA [NGE]
BIDA-BIDA alt for PITTA PITTA [PIT]
BIDAYAH alt for BUKAR BIDAYUH dial of BUKAR
SADONG [SDO]
BIDAYUH alt for BUKAR BIDAYUH dial of BUKAR
SADONG [SDO]
BIDEYAT [BIH] lang, Chad
BIDEYU alt for BIATAH [BTH]
BIDHABIDHA alt for PITTA PITTA [PIT]
BIDIKILI alt for BUDIGRI dial of GBANU [GBV]
BIDIO alt for BIDIYO [BID]
'BIDIO alt for BIDIYO [BID]
BIDIRE alt for ADELE [ADE]
BIDIYA alt for BIDIYO [BID]
BIDIYO [BID] lang, Chad

'BIDIYO alt for BIDIYO [BID]
BIDIYO-WAANA alt for BIDIYO [BID]
BIDJARA dial of NGURA [NBX]
BIDJIR dial of KENGA [KYQ]
BIDJOUKI alt for BIDJUKI dial of MPIEMO [MCX]
BIDJUKI dial of MPIEMO [MCX]
BIDOR dial of SEMAI [SEA]
BIDUANDA alt for BEDUANDA dial of TEMUAN
[TMW]
BIDYARA [BYM] lang, Australia
BIDYO alt for BIDIYO [BID]
BIDYOGO [BJG] lang, Guinea-Bissau
BIDYOLA alt for BIAFADA [BIF]
BIELORUSSIAN alt for BELARUSAN [RUW]
BIEM [BMC] lang, Papua New Guinea
BIEREBO [BNK] lang, Vanuatu
BIERI alt for BIALI [BEH]
BIERI alt for BIERIA [BRJ]
BIERIA [BRJ] lang, Vanuatu
BIERIA dial of BIERIA [BRJ]
BIETE [BIU] lang, India
BIFANG alt for BEFANG [BBY]
BIFANG alt for BEFANG dial of BEFANG [BBY]
BIG BAY alt for TOLOMAKO [TLM]
BIG BOLGO alt for BOLGO KUBAR dial of BOLGO
[BVO]
BIG FLOWERY MIAO alt for HMONG, NORTH-
EASTERN DIAN [HMD]
BIG SEPIK alt for IATMUL [IAN]
BIG WOODS FRENCH dial of FRENCH, CAJUN
[FRC]
BIGA alt for MATBAT [XMT]
BIGA alt for SOBEI [SOB]
BIGAWGUNO dial of BIDIYO [BID]
BI-GIMU alt for JIMI [JMI]
BIGOLA alt for BADJARA [PBP]
BIH dial of RADE [RAD]
BIHAK dial of SEMANDANG [SDM]
BIHAR HO alt for HO [HOC]
BIHARI alt for BHOJPURI [BHJ]
BIHARI alt for MAGAHI [MQM]
BIHARI alt for MAITHILI [MKP]
BIHI dial of GHALE, KUTANG [GHT]
BIHOR alt for BIRHOR [BIY]
BIIJIANG dial of BAI [PIQ]
BIIRA alt for FULFULDE, ADAMAWA [FUB]
BIISA alt for BISA dial of LALA-BISA [LEB]
BIISHAH alt for CENTRAL NAJDI dial of ARABIC,
NAJDI SPOKEN [ARS]
BIJAGO alt for BIDYOGO [BJG]
BIJAPUR dial of KANNADA [KJV]
BIJAPURI dial of DECCAN [DCC]
BIJBHASHA alt for BRAJ BHASHA [BFS]
BIJBRI alt for GARRUSI dial of KURDI [KDB]
BIJIANG-LANPING alt for BIIJIANG dial of BAI [PIQ]
BIJIL NEO-ARAMAIC [BJF] lang, Israel
BIJIM dial of VAGHAT-YA-BIJIM-LEGERI [BIJ]
BIJOBE alt for SOLA [SOY]
BIJOGO alt for BIDYOGO [BJG]
BIJORI [BIX] lang, India
BIJOUGOT alt for BIDYOGO [BJG]

BIJUGA alt for BIDYOGO [BJG]
BIK alt for JUDEO-TAT [TAT]
BIKAKA dial of UKHWEJO [UKH]
BIKANERI dial of MARWARI [MKD]
BIKARU [BIC] lang, Papua New Guinea
BIKARU alt for PIKARU dial of BISORIO [BIR]
BIKELE dial of KOL [BIW]
BIKELE-BIKAY alt for KOL [BIW]
BIKELE-BIKENG alt for KOL [BIW]
BIKEN alt for BEBENT dial of MAKAA [MCP]
BIKENG dial of KOL [BIW]
BIKENU alt for AMBENU dial of ATONI [TMR]
BIKIN dial of UDIHE [UDE]
BIKOL alt for BICOLANO, CENTRAL [BKL]
BIKOL SORSOGON alt for SORSOGON, WARAY
[SRV]
BIKOM alt for KOM [BKM]
BIKSHI alt for BIKSIT dial of LORUNG, NORTHERN
[LBR]
BIKSI [BDX] lang, Indonesia (Irian Jaya); also in
Papua New Guinea
BIKSIT dial of LORUNG, NORTHERN [LBR]
BIKUAB alt for BIATAH [BTH]
BIKYA [BYB] lang, Cameroon
BIKYEK alt for BASAA [BAA]
BIL dial of SEMAI [SEA]
BILA [BIP] lang, DCR
BILA dial of TSONGA [TSO]
BILAAN alt for BLAAN, SARANGANI [BIS]
BILADABA alt for PIRLATAPA [BXI]
BILAKURA [BQL] lang, Papua New Guinea
BILALA dial of NABA [MNE]
BILANES alt for BLAAN, KORONADAL [BIK]
BILASPURI [KFS] lang, India
BILASPURI PAHARI alt for BILASPURI [KFS]
BILAYN alt for BILEN [BYN]
BILBA alt for BILBA-DIU-LELENUK dial of ROTE
[ROT]
BILBA-DIU-LELENUK dial of ROTE [ROT]
BILBIL [BRZ] lang, Papua New Guinea
BILE [BIL] lang, Nigeria
BILEIN alt for BILEN [BYN]
BILEKI dial of NAKANAI [NAK]
BILEMBO-MANGO dial of LEGA-MWENGA [LGM]
BILEN [BYN] lang, Eritrea
BILENO alt for BILEN [BYN]
BILI alt for BHELE [PER]
BILI alt for BILE [BIL]
BILI dial of MONO [MNH]
BILIAU alt for AWAD BING [BCU]
BILIAU dial of AWAD BING [BCU]
BILIBIL alt for BILBIL [BRZ]
BILICHI dial of KAREN, PAKU [KPP]
BILIN alt for BILEN [BYN]
BILINARA dial of NGARINMAN [NBJ]
BILIRI dial of TANGALE [TAN]
BILKIRE FULANI dial of FULFULDE, ADAMAWA
[FUB]
BILKIRI alt for BILKIRE FULANI dial of
FULFULDE, ADAMAWA [FUB]
BILLANCHI alt for BILE [BIL]

BILLE alt for BILE [BIL]
BILMA dial of KANURI, CENTRAL [KPH]
BILOXI [BLL] lang, USA
BILTINE alt for AMDANG [AMJ]
BILTINE alt for BATHA dial of ARABIC, CHADIAN
SPOKEN [SHU]
BILTUM alt for BURUSHASKI [BSK]
BILUA [BLB] lang, Solomon Islands
BILUR [BXF] lang, Papua New Guinea
BIMA [BHP] lang, Indonesia (Nusa Tenggara)
BIMA dial of BALUNDU-BIMA [NGO]
BIMA dial of BIMA [BHP]
BIMANESE alt for BIMA [BHP]
BIMBAAN alt for MBAAN dial of TRINGGUS [TRX]
BIMBIA alt for ISU [SZV]
BIME dial of KETENGBAN [KIN]
BIMIN [BHL] lang, Papua New Guinea
BIMOBA [BIM] lang, Ghana
BIMU alt for MPIEMO [MCX]
BINA [BMN] lang, Papua New Guinea
BINA [BYJ] lang, Nigeria
BINADAN alt for SAMA, BALANGINGI [SSE]
BINAHARI [BXZ] lang, Papua New Guinea
BINAMARIR alt for BINUMARIEN [BJR]
BINANDERE [BHG] lang, Papua New Guinea
BINANDERE dial of BINANDERE [BHG]
BINARI alt for BAGA BINARI [BCG]
BINATANG dial of BASAP [BDB]
BINATANGAN alt for TAWBUID, EASTERN [BNJ]
BINAWA alt for BINA [BYJ]
BINBARNJA alt for ADYNYAMATHANHA [ADT]
BINBINGA dial of WAMBAYA [WMB]
BINDAFUM alt for BESEP dial of BYEP [MKK]
BINDDIBU alt for PINTUPI-LURITJA [PIU]
BINDI alt for NGITI [NIY]
BINDJI alt for BINJI [BIN]
BINE [ORM] lang, Papua New Guinea
BING alt for AWAD BING [BCU]
BINGA alt for YAKA [AXK]
BINGA dial of YULU [YUL]
BINGKOKAK alt for MEKONGGA dial of TOLAKI
[LBW]
BINGKOLU alt for BENGGAULU dial of UMA [PPK]
BINI alt for BUNU dial of YORUBA [YOR]
BINI alt for EDO [EDO]
BINI alt for PINI [PII]
BINI dial of ANYIN [ANY]
BINIGURA alt for PINIGURA [PNV]
BINISAYA alt for CEBUANO [CEB]
BINISAYA alt for WARAY-WARAY [WRY]
BINJA alt for SONGOORA [SOD]
BINJA dial of NGOMBE [NGC]
BINJA dial of ZIMBA [ZMB]
BINJARA alt for MULURIDYI [VMU]
BINJHIA alt for BIJORI [BIX]
BINJHWARI dial of CHHATTISGARHI [HNE]
BINJI [BIN] lang, DCR
BINLI dial of HANUNOO [HNN]
BINNA alt for BENA [YUN]
BINOKID alt for BINUKID [BKD]
BINONGKO dial of TUKANGBESI SOUTH [BHQ]

BINTA' alt for BEAUFORT MURUT dial of TIMUGON
MURUT [TIH]
BINTAUNA [BNE] lang, Indonesia (Sulawesi)
BINTUCUA alt for ICA [ARH]
BINTUHAN alt for KAUR [VKK]
BINTUK alt for ICA [ARH]
BÍNTUKUA alt for ICA [ARH]
BINTULU [BNY] lang, Malaysia (Sarawak)
BINTUNI alt for WANDAMEN [WAD]
BINTUNI dial of WANDAMEN [WAD]
BINUANG alt for PATTAE' dial of MAMASA
[MQJ]
BINUANG-PAKI-BATETANGA-ANTEAPI alt for
PATTAE' dial of MAMASA [MQJ]
BINUKID [BKD] lang, Philippines
BINUKID MANOBO alt for BINUKID [BKD]
BINUMARIA alt for BINUMARIEN [BJR]
BINUMARIEN [BJR] lang, Papua New Guinea
BINZA alt for BINJA dial of NGOMBE [NGC]
BINZABI alt for NJEBI [NZB]
BIO alt for BIYO [BYO]
BIO alt for BIYO dial of AARI [AIZ]
BIONAH alt for SERMAH dial of DAYAK, LAND
[DYK]
BIONG alt for BAYUNGU [BXJ]
"BIOTU" pejorative alt for ISOKO [ISO]
BIOTU alt for URHOBO [URH]
BIPI [BIQ] lang, Papua New Guinea
BIPIM alt for WARKAY-BIPIM [BGV]
BIPIM AS-SO alt for WARKAY-BIPIM [BGV]
BIQUENO alt for AMBENU dial of ATONI [TMR]
BIRA alt for KONJO PESISIR dial of KONJO,
COASTAL [KJC]
BIRA alt for KOTO dial of EBIRA [IGB]
BIRAAN alt for BLAAN, KORONADAL [BIK]
BIRAHUI alt for BRAHUI [BRH]
BIRALE [BXE] lang, Ethiopia
BIRAO [BRR] lang, Solomon Islands
BIRAR alt for BILUR [BXF]
BIRAR dial of NANAI [GLD]
BIRARIE dial of BARAI [BCA]
BIRATAK alt for SAU dial of DAYAK, LAND [DYK]
BIRELLE alt for BIRALE [BXE]
BIRGID alt for BIRGIT [BTF]
BIRGID alt for BIRKED [BRK]
BIRGIT [BTF] lang, Chad
BIRGUID alt for BIRKED [BRK]
BIRHAR alt for BIRHOR [BIY]
BIRHOR [BIY] lang, India
BIRHOR alt for KURUX [KVN]
BIRHORE alt for BIRHOR [BIY]
BIRI [BZR] lang, Australia
BIRI alt for BELANDA VIRI [BVI]
BIRI alt for BIRRI [BVQ]
BIRI alt for KOTO dial of EBIRA [IGB]
BIRI alt for LOKATHAN dial of TESO [TEO]
BIRIFO alt for BIRIFOR, MALBA [BFO]
BIRIFO alt for BIRIFOR, SOUTHERN [BIV]
BIRIFOR dial of BIRIFOR, MALBA [BFO]
BIRIFOR, MALBA [BFO] lang, Burkina Faso; also
in Côte d'Ivoire

BIRIFOR, SOUTHERN [BIV] lang, Ghana; also in
Côte d'Ivoire
BIRIJIA alt for BIJORI [BIX]
BIRIR alt for NORTHERN KALASHA dial of
KALASHA [KLS]
BIRITAI [BQQ] lang, Indonesia (Irian Jaya)
BIRIWA-SAROKO-KALANTUBA-SUNKO alt for
SOUTHERN LIMBA dial of LIMBA, EAST [LMA]
BIRJANDI dial of KURMANJI [KUR]
BIRJIA alt for BIJORI [BIX]
BIRJIA alt for BRIJIA dial of ASURI [ASR]
BIRKAI dial of KAREKARE [KAI]
BIRKED [BRK] lang, Sudan
BIRKIT alt for BIRKED [BRK]
BIRMINGHAM dial of ENGLISH [ENG]
BIRMUN alt for BEREMBUN dial of TEMUAN [TMW]
BIRNI alt for PINI [PII]
BIROM alt for BEROM [BOM]
BIRQED alt for BIRKED [BRK]
BIRRI [BVQ] lang, CAR
BIRSA alt for BATA [BTA]
BIRWA [BRL] lang, Botswana; also in South Africa
BISA alt for BISSA [BIB]
BISA dial of LALA-BISA [LEB]
BISÃ alt for BUSA [BQP]
BISAA alt for BASAA [BAA]
BISAIA alt for BISAYA, BRUNEI [BSB]
BISAIA alt for BISAYA, SABAH [BSY]
BISARIAB alt for BISHARIN dial of BEDAWI [BEI]
BISARIN alt for BISHARIN dial of BEDAWI [BEI]
BISAYÃ alt for BUSA [BQP]
BISAYA BUKIT alt for BISAYA, BRUNEI [BSB]
BISAYA BUKIT alt for BISAYA, SARAWAK [BSD]
BISAYA, BRUNEI [BSB] lang, Brunei
BISAYA, SABAH [BSY] lang, Malaysia (Sabah)
BISAYA, SARAWAK [BSD] lang, Malaysia (Sarawak)
BISAYAH alt for BISAYA, BRUNEI [BSB]
BISAYAH alt for BISAYA, SABAH [BSY]
BISAYAH alt for BISAYA, SARAWAK [BSD]
BISAYAN alt for CEBUANO [CEB]
BISCAYAN dial of BASQUE [BSQ]
BISENI [IJE] lang, Nigeria
BISHARIN dial of BEDAWI [BEI]
BISHIRI dial of OBANLIKU [BZY]
BISHNUPRIA MANIPURI alt for BISHNUPRIYA
[BPY]
BISHNUPRIYA [BPY] lang, India; also in Bangladesh
BISHNUPURIYA alt for BISHNUPRIYA [BPY]
BISHUO [BWH] lang, Cameroon
BISI alt for PITI [PCN]
BISIACCO dial of VENETIAN [VEC]
BISINGAI alt for SINGGE dial of JAGOI [SNE]
BISIO alt for KWASIO dial of NGUMBA [NMG]
BISIS [BNW] lang, Papua New Guinea
BISITAANG alt for STANG dial of BIATAH [BTH]
BISIWO alt for KWASIO dial of NGUMBA [NMG]
BISLAMA [BCY] lang, Vanuatu; also in New
Caledonia
BISNA PURIYA alt for BISHNUPRIYA [BPY]
BISON HORN MARIA alt for MARIA, DANDAMI
[DAQ]

BISOO dial of BAKOKO [BKH]
BISORIO [BIR] lang, Papua New Guinea
BISSA [BIB] lang, Burkina Faso; also in Côte d'Ivoire, Ghana, Togo
BISSAU-BOLAMA CREOLE dial of CRIOULO, UPPER GUINEA [POV]
BISSAULA dial of KPAN [KPK]
BISSIO alt for KWASIO dial of NGUMBA [NMG]
BISU [BII] lang, China; also in Thailand
BISU dial of OBANLIKU [BZY]
BIT [BGK] lang, Laos; also in China
BITAAMA alt for BITAMA dial of KUNAMA [KUM]
BITAAPUL dial of NTCHAM [BUD]
BITAMA dial of KUNAMA [KUM]
BITARA [BIT] lang, Papua New Guinea
BITARE [BRE] lang, Nigeria; also in Cameroon
BITHARA alt for BIDYARA [BYM]
BITI alt for NDE-GBITE [NED]
BITI dial of MOROKODO [MGC]
BITIEKU dial of DENYA [ANV]
BITINKOORE dial of FULFULDE, WESTERN NIGER [FUH]
BITJARA alt for BIDYARA [BYM]
BITJOLI alt for MABA [MQA]
BITONGA alt for GITONGA [TOH]
BITUI dial of NDAKTUP [NCP]
BITWI alt for BITUI dial of NDAKTUP [NCP]
BIWANGAN dial of MAGINDANAON [MDH]
BIWAT [BWM] lang, Papua New Guinea
BIYALI alt for BAYALI [BYJ]
BIYAM alt for BISHUO [BWH]
BIYAN alt for BASARI [BSC]
BIYANDA dial of GBAYA, SOUTHWEST [MDO]
BIYO [BYO] lang, China
BIYO dial of AARI [AIZ]
BIYOBE alt for SOLA [SOY]
BIYOM [BPM] lang, Papua New Guinea
BIYORI alt for PHALURA [PHL]
BIYUE alt for BIYO [BYO]
BIZA-LALA alt for LALA-BISA [LEB]
BJERB alt for BIALI [BEH]
BJERI alt for BIALI [BEH]
BLAAN, KORONADAL [BIK] lang, Philippines
BLAAN, SARANGANI [BIS] lang, Philippines
BLABLANGA [BLP] lang, Solomon Islands
BLACK AMERICAN SIGN LANGUAGE dial of AMERICAN SIGN LANGUAGE [ASE]
BLACK BAGA alt for MBULUNGISH [MBV]
BLACK BOBO alt for BOBO MADARÉ, NORTHERN [BBO]
BLACK BOBO alt for BOBO MADARÉ, SOUTHERN [BWQ]
BLACK BOLON dial of BOLON [BOF]
BLACK BUSHMAN alt for KXOE [XUU]
BLACK CARIB alt for GARIFUNA [CAB]
BLACK DOGOSE alt for DOGOSO [DGS]
BLACK ENGLISH dial of ENGLISH [ENG]
BLACK KAREN alt for KAREN, PA'O [BLK]
BLACK KAREN alt for RIANG [RIL]
BLACK KHOANY dial of PHUNOI [PHO]

BLACK KONJO alt for TANA TOA dial of KONJO, COASTAL [KJC]
BLACK LACHI alt for LIPUTIÕ dial of LACHI [LBT]
BLACK LAHU alt for NA dial of LAHU [LAH]
BLACK LISU alt for LIPO [TKL]
BLACK MIAO alt for HMONG, EASTERN QIANDONG [HMQ]
BLACK MIAO alt for HMONG, NORTHERN QIANDONG [HEA]
BLACK MIAO alt for HMONG, SOUTHERN QIANDONG [HMS]
BLACK NOGAI dial of NOGAI [NOG]
BLACK RIANG alt for YINCHIA [YIN]
BLACK SEMINOLE alt for AFRO-SEMINOLE CREOLE [AFS]
BLACK TAI alt for TAI DAM [BLT]
BLACK YANG alt for RIANG [RIL]
BLACKFEET alt for BLACKFOOT [BLC]
BLACKFOOT [BLC] lang, Canada; also in USA
BLAFE [IND] lang, Papua New Guinea
BLAGAR [BEU] lang, Indonesia (Nusa Tenggara)
BLANCHE BAY alt for KUANUA [KSD]
BLANDA alt for BELANDA dial of TEMUAN [TMW]
BLANG [BLR] lang, China; also in Myanmar, Thailand
BLE alt for MAMBILA, CAMEROON [MYA]
BLÉ [BXL] lang, Burkina Faso
BLEKINGSKA dial of SKANE [SCY]
BLI alt for HLAI [LIC]
BLIP alt for FJAALIB dial of BALANTA-GANJA [BJT]
BLISS dial of JOLA-KASA [CSK]
BLIT dial of MANOBO, COTABATO [MTA]
BLITI alt for LEMBAK BLITI dial of LEMBAK [LIW]
BLO dial of RADE [RAD]
BLOOD dial of BLACKFOOT [BLC]
BLOWO dial of DAN [DAF]
BLUE MEO alt for HMONG NJUA [BLU]
BLUE MIAO alt for HMONG NJUA [BLU]
BLUE MIAO alt for TAK MIAO dial of HMONG NJUA [BLU]
BLUEFIELDS CREOLE ENGLISH alt for MÍSKITO COAST CREOLE ENGLISH dial of NORTHERN CENTRAL AMERICA CREOLE ENGLISH [BZI]
BO [BGL] lang, Laos
BO [BPW] lang, Papua New Guinea
BO alt for ABO [ABB]
BO alt for AKA-BO [AKM]
BO alt for BOLON [BOF]
BO dial of BO-RUKUL [MAE]
BÖ dial of MANINKA, KANKAN [MNI]
BO RIVER VAN KIEU alt for PACOH [PAC]
BOA alt for BUA [BUB]
BOA alt for BWA [BWW]
BOADJI alt for BOAZI [KVG]
BOAN alt for BONAN [PEH]
BOANA alt for NUMANGGANG [NOP]
BOANAI alt for GHAYAVI [BMK]
BOANAKI alt for GHAYAVI [BMK]
BOANO [BZN] lang, Indonesia (Maluku)
BOANO alt for BOLANO [BZL]
BOAR alt for GBAYA KARA dial of GBAYA, NORTH-WEST [GYA]

BOAZI [KVG] lang, Papua New Guinea
BOBA alt for BOMBOMA [BWS]
BOBANGI alt for BANGI [BNI]
BOBAR dial of JARAWA [JAR]
BOBASAN dial of GAYO [GYO]
BOBE alt for BUBE [BVB]
BOBE alt for BUBIA [BBX]
BOBEA alt for BUBIA [BBX]
BOBILI dial of POL [PMM]
BOBILIS alt for BEBIL [BXP]
BOBO alt for BOBO MADARÉ, NORTHERN [BBO]
BOBO alt for BOBO MADARÉ, SOUTHERN [BWQ]
BOBO DA alt for BOBO MADARÉ, NORTHERN
    [BBO]
BOBO DIOULA alt for ZARA dial of BOBO MADARÉ,
    SOUTHERN [BWQ]
BOBO FI alt for BOBO MADARÉ, NORTHERN
    [BBO]
BOBO FI alt for BOBO MADARÉ, SOUTHERN
    [BWQ]
BOBO FING alt for BOBO MADARÉ, NORTHERN
    [BBO]
BOBO FING alt for BOBO MADARÉ, SOUTHERN
    [BWQ]
BOBO JULA alt for ZARA dial of BOBO MADARÉ,
    SOUTHERN [BWQ]
BOBO MADARÉ, NORTHERN [BBO] lang, Burkina
    Faso; also in Mali
BOBO MADARÉ, SOUTHERN [BWQ] lang, Burkina
    Faso
BOBO OULE alt for BOMU [BMQ]
BOBO WULE alt for BOMU [BMQ]
BOBONAZA alt for QUICHUA, PASTAZA,
    NORTHERN [QLB]
BOBONAZA QUICHUA alt for QUICHUA, PASTAZA,
    NORTHERN [QLB]
"BOBONGKO" pejorative alt for ANDIO [BZB]
BOBOT [BTY] lang, Indonesia (Maluku)
BOBOTA alt for BUGLERE [SAB]
BOCHA dial of MANYIKA [MXC]
BOCOTA alt for BUGLERE [SAB]
BODEGA dial of MIWOK, COAST [CSI]
BODELE dial of YASA [YKO]
BODHO dial of THURI [THU]
BODI alt for BODO [BRX]
BODI dial of MEEN [MYM]
BODIMAN dial of DUALA [DOU]
BODIN dial of ATTIE [ATI]
BODO [BOY] lang, CAR
BODO [BRX] lang, India; also in Nepal
BODO alt for BUDU [BUU]
BODO alt for GOR [GQR]
BODO alt for NAGA PIDGIN [NAG]
BODO dial of GOR [GQR]
BODO dial of MPADE [MPI]
BODO PARAJA alt for BODO PARJA [BDV]
BODO PARJA [BDV] lang, India
BODOE dial of GBAYA, NORTHWEST [GYA]
BODOMO alt for MBODOMO dial of GBAYA,
    SOUTHWEST [MDO]
BODOR alt for BESME [BES]

BODORO alt for KPATOGO dial of KAANSA [GNA]
BODOUGOUKA dial of JULA, ODIENNE [JOD]
BOD-SKAD alt for KINNAURI, BHOTI [NES]
BODZANGA alt for NGANDO [NGD]
BOËNG dial of TOBELO [TLB]
BOE alt for BORÔRO [BOR]
BOE dial of DEG [MZW]
BOEGINEESCHE alt for BUGIS [BPR]
BOEGINEZEN alt for BUGIS [BPR]
BOENGA KO MUZOK alt for YAMBA [YAM]
BOEROE alt for BURU [MHS]
BOETONEEZEN alt for CIA-CIA [CIA]
BOEWE alt for OROWE [BPK]
BOFFI alt for BOFI [BFF]
BOFI [BFF] lang, CAR
BOFON alt for ABANYOM [ABM]
BOFOTA alt for BUGLERE [SAB]
BOGA [BOD] lang, Nigeria
BOGA alt for BUGA-KXOE dial of KXOE [XUU]
BOGADJIM alt for ANJAM [BOJ]
BOGA'ER alt for LUOBA, BOGA'ER [ADI]
BOGA'ER LUOBA alt for ADI [ADI]
BOGA'ER LUOBA alt for BOKAR dial of ADI [ADI]
BOGAIA alt for BOGAYA [BOQ]
BOGAJIM alt for ANJAM [BOJ]
BOGANA alt for BINA [BYJ]
BOGANDÉ dial of FULFULDE, NORTHEASTERN
    BURKINA FASO [FUH]
BOGATI alt for ANJAM [BOJ]
BOGAYA [BOQ] lang, Papua New Guinea
BOGGANGER alt for BANDJALANG [BDY]
BOGGHOM alt for BOGHOM [BUX]
BOGHOM [BUX] lang, Nigeria
BOGHOROM alt for BOGHOM [BUX]
BOGIJIAB alt for AKA-BEA [ACE]
BOGNAK-ASUNGORUNG alt for ASSANGORI
    [SUN]
BOGO alt for BILEN [BYN]
BOGODO alt for BOKOTO [BDT]
BOGOMIL alt for PALITYAN dial of BULGARIAN
    [BLG]
BOGON alt for ABULDUGU dial of BURUN [BDI]
BOGONGO dial of PANDE [BKJ]
BOGOR dial of SUNDA [SUO]
BOGOS alt for BILEN [BYN]
BOGOTA alt for BUGLERE [SAB]
BOGOTO alt for BOKOTO [BDT]
BOGU alt for BONGGO [BPG]
BOGUE alt for ESIMBI [AGS]
BOGUNG alt for BARIBA [BBA]
BOGURU [BQU] lang, Sudan; also in DCR
BOGURU dial of BOGURU [BQU]
BOGYEL alt for GYELE [GYI]
BOGYELI alt for GYELE [GYI]
BOH dial of KENYAH, MAHAKAM [XKM]
BOH BAKUNG dial of KENYAH, BAKUNG [BOC]
BOHAAN dial of BURIAT, RUSSIA [MNB]
BOHAIRIC dial of COPTIC [COP]
BOHEMIAN alt for CZECH [CZC]
BOHENA dial of DANO [ASO]
BOHILAI dial of TAWALA [TBO]

BOHIRA'I alt for BOHILAI dial of TAWALA [TBO]
BOHOLANO dial of CEBUANO [CEB]
BOHOM alt for BOGHOM [BUX]
BOHTAN alt for SHIRNAK-CHIZRE dial of
  CHALDEAN NEO-ARAMAIC [CLD]
BOHTAN NEO-ARAMAIC [BHN] lang, Georgia;
  also in Russia (Asia)
BOHTÂNI alt for JEZIRE dial of KURMANJI [KUR]
BOHUAI [RAK] lang, Papua New Guinea
BOHUAI dial of BOHUAI [RAK]
BOHUAI-TULU alt for BOHUAI [RAK]
BOHUTU alt for BUHUTU [BXH]
BO-I alt for BOUYEI [PCC]
BOI alt for YA dial of VAGHAT-YA-BIJIM-LEGERI
  [BIJ]
BOI BI dial of MUONG [MTQ]
BOI GADABA alt for GADABA, BODO [GBJ]
BOIANAKI alt for GHAYAVI [BMK]
BOIGU dial of MERIAM [ULK]
BOIKEN alt for BOIKIN [BZF]
BOIKIN [BZF] lang, Papua New Guinea
BOINAKI alt for GHAYAVI [BMK]
BOINELANG dial of AULUA [AUL]
BOJE dial of BOKYI [BKY]
BOJIE alt for BOJE dial of BOKYI [BKY]
BOJIGNIJI alt for AKA-BEA [ACE]
BOJIGYAB alt for AKA-BEA [ACE]
BOJIIN alt for LIMBUM [LIM]
BOJPURY dial of BHOJPURI [BHJ]
BOK alt for BOK PENAN dial of PENAN, WESTERN
  [PNE]
BOK alt for BOOK dial of SABAOT [SPY]
BOK alt for TAWORTA [TBP]
BOK dial of MANDJAK [MFV]
BOK PENAN dial of PENAN, WESTERN [PNE]
BOKA alt for BOCHA dial of MANYIKA [MXC]
BOKA alt for BOGA [BOD]
BOKA alt for BOLON [BOF]
BOKABO dial of GAGU [GGU]
BOKAI alt for ROTE-TENGAH dial of ROTE [ROT]
BOKAN alt for BAUKAN dial of BAUKAN [BNB]
BOKAR alt for LUOBA, BOGA'ER [ADI]
BOKAR dial of ADI [ADI]
BOKARE dial of GBAYA, SOUTHWEST [MDO]
BOKARI alt for BOKARE dial of GBAYA, SOUTH-
  WEST [MDO]
BOKEN alt for BAUKAN dial of BAUKAN [BNB]
BOKHAN alt for BOHAAN dial of BURIAT, RUSSIA
  [MNB]
BOKHARAN alt for BUKHARIC [BHH]
BOKHARIAN alt for BUKHARIC [BHH]
BOKHARIC alt for BUKHARIC [BHH]
BOKI alt for BOKYI [BKY]
BOKI dial of BOKYI [BKY]
BOKIYIM alt for BOGHOM [BUX]
BOKKO alt for BOKO [BQC]
BOKKOS dial of RON [CLA]
BOKMAAL alt for NORWEGIAN, BOKMAAL [NRR]
BOKO [BKP] lang, DCR
BOKO [BQC] lang, Benin; also in Nigeria
BOKO alt for LONGTO [WOK]

BOKOBARU [BUS] lang, Nigeria
BOKOD dial of IBALOI [IBL]
BOKODO alt for BOKOTO [BDT]
BOKOKI alt for BOLIA [BLI]
BOKON alt for BAUKAN dial of BAUKAN [BNB]
BOKONYA alt for BOKO [BQC]
BOKONZI dial of BOMBOMA [BWS]
BOKOR alt for DAJU, DAR SILA [DAU]
BOKORIKE alt for DAJU, DAR SILA [DAU]
BOKORUGE alt for DAJU, DAR SILA [DAU]
BOKOTA alt for BUGLERE [SAB]
BOKOTÁ dial of BUGLERE [SAB]
BOKOTO [BDT] lang, CAR
BOKOTO dial of BOKOTO [BDT]
BOKOY dial of LIGENZA [LGZ]
BOKPAN dial of BOKOTO [BDT]
BOKPOTO alt for BOKOTO [BDT]
BOKU dial of SINAUGORO [SNC]
BOKUN alt for BAUKAN dial of BAUKAN [BNB]
BOKWA dial of GAGU [GGU]
BOKWA dial of GLAVDA [GLV]
BOKWA-KENDEM alt for KENDEM [KVM]
BOKYI [BKY] lang, Nigeria; also in Cameroon
BOL MURUT alt for MALIGAN dial of TAGAL
  MURUT [MVV]
BOLA [BNP] lang, Papua New Guinea
BOLA alt for BELA [BEQ]
BOLA alt for MANKANYA [MAN]
BOLA dial of BOLA [BNP]
BOLAANG ITANG dial of KAIDIPANG [KZP]
BOLAANG MONGONDOW alt for MONGONDOW
  [MOG]
BOLA-BAKOVI alt for BOLA [BNP]
BOLAGHAIN dial of PASHAYI, NORTHWEST [GLH]
BOLAKA alt for BURAKA [BKG]
BOLANCHI alt for BOLE [BOL]
BOLANG ITANG alt for BOLAANG ITANG dial of
  KAIDIPANG [KZP]
BOLANGO [BLD] lang, Indonesia (Sulawesi)
BOLANGO dial of BOLANGO [BLD]
BOLANO [BZL] lang, Indonesia (Sulawesi)
BOLAONGWE dial of KGALAGADI [XKV]
BOLAWA alt for BOLE [BOL]
BOLE [BOL] lang, Nigeria
BOLE dial of VAGLA [VAG]
BOLE MURUT alt for MALIGAN dial of TAGAL
  MURUT [MVV]
BOLEKA alt for DESANO [DES]
BOLEKI alt for BOLOKI [BKT]
BOLEMBA dial of MBATI [MDN]
BOLERI alt for TUNGA dial of DADIYA [DBD]
BOLEWA alt for BOLE [BOL]
BOLGO [BVO] lang, Chad
BOLGO DUGAG dial of BOLGO [BVO]
BOLGO KUBAR dial of BOLGO [BVO]
BOLI alt for BULI dial of GBAYA, SOUTHWEST
  [MDO]
BOLIA [BLI] lang, DCR
BOLINAO [SMK] lang, Philippines
BOLINAO SAMBAL alt for BOLINAO [SMK]
BOLINAO ZAMBAL alt for BOLINAO [SMK]

BOLIVIAN "MATACO" pejorative alt for WICHÍ LHAMTÉS NOCTEN [MTP]
BOLIVIAN SIGN LANGUAGE [BVL] lang, Bolivia
BOLO [BLV] lang, Angola
BOLO DJARMA dial of BERAKOU [BXV]
BOLOI alt for BALOI [BIZ]
BOLOKI [BKT] lang, DCR
BOLOM alt for BULLOM SO [BUY]
BOLON [BOF] lang, Burkina Faso
BOLONDO [BZM] lang, DCR
BOLONG dial of BERNDE [BDO]
BOLONGAN [BLJ] lang, Indonesia (Kalimantan)
BOLONGO alt for LONGO dial of MONGO-NKUNDU [MOM]
BOLOS POINT dial of AGTA, DUPANINAN [DUO]
BOLOVEN alt for LAVEN [LBO]
BOLTON LANCASHIRE dial of ENGLISH [ENG]
BOLU dial of GEJI [GEZ]
BOLUPI dial of LIGENZA [LGZ]
BOLYU alt for PALYU [PLY]
BOM [BMF] lang, Sierra Leone
BOM alt for ANJAM [BOJ]
BOM alt for BUM [BMV]
BOM alt for CHIN, BAWM [BGR]
BOM FUTURO dial of JAMAMADI [JAA]
BOMA [BOH] lang, DCR
BOMA dial of IZON [IJC]
BOMA dial of TEKE, CENTRAL [TEC]
BOMA KASAI alt for BOMA [BOH]
BOMA MBALI alt for BOMA dial of TEKE, CENTRAL [TEC]
BOMALI alt for BOMWALI [BMW]
BOMAM alt for BAHNAR BONOM dial of BAHNAR [BDQ]
BOMAN alt for MPOMAM dial of MPONGMPONG [MGG]
BOMANG dial of BURMESE [BMS]
BOMASA alt for BOMASSA [BME]
BOMASSA [BME] lang, DCR
BOMBALI dial of THEMNE [TEJ]
BOMBARO alt for MBARU dial of LAME [BMA]
BOMBAY GUJARATI alt for STANDARD GUJARATI dial of GUJARATI [GJR]
BOMBAY SIGN LANGUAGE dial of INDIAN SIGN LANGUAGE [INS]
BOMBE alt for BEBA' dial of BAFUT [BFD]
BOMBERAWA alt for MBARU dial of LAME [BMA]
BOMBI-NGBANJA dial of BILA [BIP]
BOMBO alt for MPONGMPONG [MGG]
BOMBOKO alt for WUMBOKO [BQM]
BOMBOLI [BML] lang, DCR
BOMBOMA [BWS] lang, DCR
BOMBONGO alt for BOMBOLI [BML]
BOMBORI dial of KATLA [KCR]
BOME alt for BOM [BMF]
BOMITABA [ZMX] lang, Congo; also in CAR
BOMO alt for BOM [BMF]
BOMOKANDI dial of KANGO [KTY]
BOMPAKA alt for BOMPOKA dial of TERESSA [TEF]

BOMPOKA dial of TERESSA [TEF]
BOMU [BMQ] lang, Mali; also in Burkina Faso
BOMUDI dial of NGUMBI [NUI]
BOMUI dial of YASA [YKO]
BOMVANA dial of XHOSA [XOS]
BOMWALI [BMW] lang, Congo; also in Cameroon
BON alt for BON GULA [GLC]
BON alt for BONI [BOB]
BON dial of BASAA [BAA]
BON GOULA alt for BON GULA [GLC]
BON GULA [GLC] lang, Chad
BON SHWAI alt for PALIET dial of DINKA, SOUTH-WESTERN [DIK]
BONA dial of ANYIN [ANY]
BONA BONA dial of SUAU [SWP]
BONAHOI dial of ARAPESH, BUMBITA [AON]
BONAN [PEH] lang, China
BONAPUTA-MOPU alt for MIANI [PLA]
BONARUA dial of SUAU [SWP]
BONDA alt for BONDO [BFW]
BONDE alt for BONDEI [BOU]
BONDEI [BOU] lang, Tanzania
BONDEYA alt for KORKU [KFQ]
BONDJIEL alt for GYELE [GYI]
BONDO [BFW] lang, India
BONDONGA alt for NDUNGA [NDT]
BONDO-PORAJA alt for BONDO [BFW]
BONDOY dial of KORKU [KFQ]
BONDUKU KULANGO alt for KULANGO, BONDOUKOU [KZC]
BONE dial of BUGIS [BPR]
BONE HAU dial of KALUMPANG [KLI]
BONEA dial of MATO [NIU]
BONEFA alt for NISA [NIC]
BONEK alt for TUOTOMB [TTF]
BONERATE [BNA] lang, Indonesia (Sulawesi)
BONERATE dial of BONERATE [BNA]
BONERIF [BNV] lang, Indonesia (Irian Jaya)
BONFIA alt for MASIWANG [BNF]
BONG alt for KINTAQ [KNQ]
BÒNG MIEU alt for CUA [CUA]
BONG MIEW alt for CUA [CUA]
BONGA alt for MALALAMAI [MMT]
BONGAMAISE alt for BONGOMAISI dial of APOS [APO]
BONGGI [BDG] lang, Malaysia (Sabah)
BONGGO [BPG] lang, Indonesia (Irian Jaya)
BONGILI [BUI] lang, Congo
BONGIRI alt for BONGILI [BUI]
BONGKEN alt for BONKENG [BVG]
BONGO [BOT] lang, Sudan
BONGO alt for BONGGO [BPG]
BONGO alt for NUBACA [BAF]
BONGO dial of BANDA, MID-SOUTHERN [BJO]
BONGO TALK alt for JAMAICAN CREOLE ENGLISH dial of SOUTHWESTERN CARIBBEAN CREOLE ENGLISH [JAM]
BONG'OM alt for BONG'OMEEK dial of SABAOT [SPY]
BONGOMAISI dial of APOS [APO]
BONGOMASI alt for BONGOS [BXY]

BONG'OMEEK dial of SABAOT [SPY]
BONGOR dial of MASANA [MCN]
BONGOR-JODO-TAGAL-BEREM-GUNU dial of
　MUSEY [MSE]
BONGOS [BXY] lang, Papua New Guinea
BONGOS dial of BONGOS [BXY]
BONGU [BPU] lang, Papua New Guinea
BONGWE alt for YASA [YKO]
BONI [BOB] lang, Kenya; also in Somalia
BONI alt for ALUKU dial of AUKAN [DJK]
BONIANGE dial of LIBINZA [LIZ]
BONJO [BOK] lang, Congo
BONKENG [BVG] lang, Cameroon
BONKENGE alt for BONKENG [BVG]
BONKENG-PENDIA alt for BONKENG [BVG]
BONKIMAN [BOP] lang, Papua New Guinea
BONKOVIA-YEVALI alt for BIEREBO [BNK]
BONNY alt for IBANI [IBY]
BONNY-OPOBO dial of IGBO [IGR]
BONOM alt for MONOM [MOO]
BONOTSEK alt for ATAYAL [TAY]
BONTAWA alt for BANTAWA [BAP]
BONTHAIN alt for BANTAENG dial of KONJO,
　COASTAL [KJC]
BONTOC, CENTRAL [BNC] lang, Philippines
BONTOC, EASTERN [BKB] lang, Philippines
BONTOK alt for BONTOC, CENTRAL [BNC]
BONU dial of CHOURASE [TSU]
BONUM alt for BOSSOUM dial of FALI, NORTH
　[FLL]
BONZIO dial of MBATI [MDN]
BOO alt for BOKO [BQC]
BOO alt for BOMA dial of TEKE, CENTRAL [TEC]
BOO dial of TEKE, CENTRAL [TEC]
BOO dial of TOURA [NEB]
BO'O dial of BIAK [BHW]
BOÕ alt for BOO dial of TEKE, CENTRAL [TEC]
BOOBE alt for BUBE [BVB]
BOODLA alt for ZUMBUL dial of DASS [DOT]
BOOK dial of SABAOT [SPY]
BOOKAN alt for BAUKAN dial of BAUKAN [BNB]
BOOLBOORA alt for YIDINY [YII]
BOOMBE alt for BUBE [BVB]
BOOMU alt for BOMU [BMQ]
BOON [BNL] lang, Somalia
BOONAN alt for GAHRI [BFU]
BOONI dial of FRAFRA [GUR]
BOOR [BVF] lang, Chad
BOORAN alt for BORANA [GAX]
BOORAN alt for BORANA dial of OROMO,
　BORANA-ARSI-GUJI [GAX]
BOORDOONA alt for BURDUNA [BXN]
BOORIM dial of BOKYI [BKY]
BOORKUTTI alt for DYANGADI [DYN]
BOOT alt for BOTO dial of ZARI [ZAZ]
BOOW dial of DII [DUR]
BOPCHI alt for KORKU [KFQ]
BOR alt for DINKA, SOUTHEASTERN [DIN]
BOR dial of DINKA, SOUTHEASTERN [DIN]
BOR ATHOIC alt for ATHOC dial of DINKA, SOUTH-
　EASTERN [DIN]

BOR GOK alt for BOR dial of DINKA, SOUTH-
　EASTERN [DIN]
BOR MUTHUN dial of NAGA, WANCHO [NNP]
BOR MUTONIA alt for BOR MUTHUN dial of NAGA,
　WANCHO [NNP]
BORA [BOA] lang, Peru; also in Brazil, Colombia
BORA dial of BORA [BOA]
BORA MABANG alt for MABA [MDE]
BORAAN alt for BORANA [GAX]
BORAE alt for SOUTHERN CHUMBURUNG dial
　of CHUMBURUNG [NCU]
BORAI alt for HATAM [HAD]
BORAIL SADRI dial of SADRI, ORAON [SDR]
BORAKA alt for BURAKA [BKG]
BORAN alt for BORANA [GAX]
BORAN alt for BORANA dial of OROMO, BORANA-
　ARSI-GUJI [GAX]
BORAN dial of BORANA [GAX]
BORANA [GAX] lang, Ethiopia; also in Kenya,
　Somalia
BORANA dial of OROMO, BORANA-ARSI-GUJI
　[GAX]
BORATHOI alt for ATHOC dial of DINKA, SOUTH-
　EASTERN [DIN]
BORCALA dial of AZERBAIJANI, NORTH [AZE]
BORCH dial of RUTUL [RUT]
BORDER KOMBA dial of KOMBA [KPF]
BORDO alt for BURUWA dial of KIMRE [KQP]
BORDURIA alt for NAGA, NOCTE [NJB]
BORE alt for BOMU [BMQ]
BOREBO dial of MAILU [MGU]
BOREI [GAI] lang, Papua New Guinea
BORENA alt for BORANA dial of OROMO, BORANA-
　ARSI-GUJI [GAX]
BOREWAR dial of BOREI [GAI]
BORGAWA alt for BARIBA [BBA]
BORGOTKE alt for MABA [MDE]
BORGU alt for BARIBA [BBA]
BORGU alt for MABA [MDE]
BORI alt for BVERI dial of FALI, NORTH [FLL]
BORITSU alt for YUKUBEN [YBL]
BORIWEN alt for LAVEN [LBO]
BORNA [BXX] lang, DCR
BORNEO dial of MALAY [MLI]
BORNHOLM dial of SKANE [SCY]
BORNOUAN alt for KANURI, CENTRAL [KPH]
BORNOUANS alt for KANURI, CENTRAL [KPH]
BORNU alt for KANURI, CENTRAL [KPH]
BORO [BWO] lang, Ethiopia
BORO alt for BODO [BRX]
BORO alt for BORA [BOA]
BORO alt for BURU dial of NGELIMA [AGH]
BORO dial of FOLOPA [PPO]
BOROA alt for //XEGWI [XEG]
BORO-ABORO alt for BEROM [BOM]
BOROBO dial of GREBO, CENTRAL [GRV]
BORODDA alt for WOLAYTTA [WBC]
BOROI dial of BOREI [GAI]
BOROMA dial of ACIPA, EASTERN [AWA]
BOROMESO alt for BURMESO [BZU]
BORONI alt for BODO [BRX]

BORÔRO [BOR] lang, Brazil
BORORO alt for BORORRO dial of FULFULDE,
    KANO-KATSINA-BORORRO [FUV]
BORORO alt for BORORRO dial of FULFULDE,
    NIGERIAN [FUV]
BORORRO dial of FULFULDE, KANO-KATSINA-
    BORORRO [FUV]
BORORRO dial of FULFULDE, NIGERIAN [FUV]
BORPIKA alt for BOLE [BOL]
BORROM alt for BOGHOM [BUX]
BORUCA [BRN] lang, Costa Rica
BO-RUKUL [MAE] lang, Nigeria
BORUMESSO alt for BURMESO [BZU]
BORUN alt for BURUN [BDI]
BORUNCA alt for BORUCA [BRN]
BOSA alt for LOMAVREN [RMI]
BOSAMBI dial of BUDZA [BJA]
BOSAVI alt for KALULI [BCO]
BOSHA alt for LOMAVREN [RMI]
BOSHA dial of KAFICHO [KBR]
BOSIKEN alt for DIMIR [DMC]
BOSILEWA [BOS] lang, Papua New Guinea
BOSKIEN alt for DIMIR [DMC]
BOSMAN alt for BOSNGUN [BQS]
BOSNGUN [BQS] lang, Papua New Guinea
BOSNIAN [SRC] lang, Bosnia-Herzegovina
BOSNIK dial of BIAK [BHW]
"BOSO" pejorative alt for BOZO, SOROGAMA [BZE]
BOSO alt for BOZO, HAINYAXO [BZX]
BOSO alt for BOZO, SOROGAMA [BZE]
BOSO alt for BOZO, TIÈMA CIÈWÈ [BOO]
BOSO alt for BOZO, TIÉYAXO [BOZ]
BOSO dial of GUA [GWX]
BOSOKO dial of GBAYA, SOUTHWEST [MDO]
BOSSANGOA dial of GBAYA-BOSSANGOA [GBP]
BOSSOUKA alt for BOSOKO dial of GBAYA,
    SOUTHWEST [MDO]
BOSSOUM dial of FALI, NORTH [FLL]
BOTA alt for BUBIA [BBX]
BOTAI dial of GBARI [GBY]
BOTAN alt for JEZIRE dial of KURMANJI [KUR]
BOTBOT dial of BOREI [GAI]
BOTEL TABAGO alt for YAMI [YMI]
BOTEL TOBAGO alt for YAMI [YMI]
BOTE-MAJHI [BMJ] lang, Nepal
BOTHAR alt for REMA [BOW]
BOTHARI alt for BATHARI dial of MEHRI [MHR]
BOTIN alt for AP MA [KBX]
BOTLIKH [BPH] lang, Russia (Europe)
BOTLIKH dial of BOTLIKH [BPH]
BOTLIX alt for BOTLIKH [BPH]
BOTO dial of ZARI [ZAZ]
BÖTÖ alt for NDE-GBITE [NED]
BOTOCUDOS alt for XOKLENG [XOK]
BOTOLAN ZAMBAL alt for SAMBAL, BOTOLAN
    [SBL]
BOTTENG dial of ULUMANDA [ULM]
BOTTENG-TAPPALANG alt for ULUMANDA' [ULM]
BOTUNGA dial of MBOLE [MDQ]
BOU dial of YELE [YLE]
BOUA alt for BUA [BUB]

BOUA alt for BWA [BWW]
BOUAKA alt for NGBAKA MA'BO [NBM]
BOUAMOU alt for BWAMU [BOX]
BOUANILA alt for SOUTHERN BABOLE dial of
    BABOLE [BVX]
BOUDJOU alt for TONJO dial of TUKI [BAG]
BOUDOUMA alt for BUDUMA [BDM]
BOÚE dial of KHANA [KEH]
BOUIN alt for NGALKBUN [NGK]
BOUIOK alt for SAISIYAT [SAI]
BOUKA alt for BUKA dial of BANDA-MBRES [BQK]
BOULAHAY alt for MEFELE [MFJ]
BOULALA alt for BILALA dial of NABA [MNE]
BOULBA [BLY] lang, Benin
BOULBE alt for FULFULDE, ADAMAWA [FUB]
BOULONNAIS dial of PICARD [PCD]
BOULOU alt for BULU [BUM]
BOUMOALI alt for BOMWALI [BMW]
BOUMPE alt for MENDE [MFY]
BOUN alt for NGALKBUN [NGK]
BOUNA dial of DAY [DAI]
BOUNA KOULANGO alt for KULANGO, BOUNA
    [NKU]
BO-UNG alt for MBO-UNG [MUX]
BOUNOU dial of SAMO, MAYA [SYM]
BOURAKA alt for BURAKA [BKG]
BOURBONNAIS dial of FRENCH [FRN]
BOURGU alt for MABA [MDE]
BOURGUIGNON dial of FRENCH [FRN]
BOURIYA dial of KORKU [KFQ]
BOURRAH alt for BURA-PABIR [BUR]
BOUSSO alt for BUSO [BSO]
BOUTE alt for VUTE [VUT]
BOUYE alt for POUYE [BYE]
BOUYEI [PCC] lang, China; also in Viet Nam
BOUYEI 1 alt for QIANNAN dial of BOUYEI [PCC]
BOUYEI 2 alt for QIANZHONG dial of BOUYEI [PCC]
BOUYEI 3 alt for QIANXI dial of BOUYEI [PCC]
"BOUZE" pejorative alt for LOMA [LOM]
BOVEN-MBIAN alt for MARIND, BIAN [BPV]
BOWAI alt for BOHUAI [RAK]
BOWILI alt for TUWILI [BOV]
BOWIRI alt for TUWILI [BOV]
BOWOM alt for ABILIANG dial of DINKA, NORTH-
    EASTERN [DIP]
BO-Y alt for BOUYEI [PCC]
BOYA alt for LONGARIM [LOH]
BOYALI dial of GBAYA-BOZOUM [GBQ]
BOYANESE alt for BAWEAN dial of MADURA [MHJ]
BOYAO dial of AI-CHAM [AIH]
BOYELA alt for YELA [YEL]
BOZABA [BZO] lang, DCR
BOZE-GIRINGAREDE dial of BINE [ORM]
BOZO, HAINYAXO [BZX] lang, Mali
BOZO, SOROGAMA [BZE] lang, Mali; also in Nigeria
BOZO, TIÈMA CIÈWÈ [BOO] lang, Mali
BOZO, TIÉYAXO [BOZ] lang, Mali
BOZOM alt for GBAYA-BOZOUM [GBQ]
BOZOM dial of GBAYA-BOZOUM [GBQ]
BRABANTS dial of DUTCH [DUT]
BRABORI alt for DIDA, LAKOTA [DIC]

BRAGAT [AOF] lang, Papua New Guinea
BRAHMANI dial of VARHADI-NAGPURI [VAH]
BRAHMU alt for BARAAMU [BRD]
BRAHUDI alt for BRAHUI [BRH]
BRAHUI [BRH] lang, Pakistan; also in Afghanistan, Iran, Turkmenistan
BRAHUIDI alt for BRAHUI [BRH]
BRAHUIGI alt for BRAHUI [BRH]
BRAHUIKI alt for BRAHUI [BRH]
BRAJ alt for BRAJ BHASHA [BFS]
BRAJ alt for KANAUJI [BJJ]
BRAJ BHAKHA alt for BRAJ BHASHA [BFS]
BRAJ BHASHA [BFS] lang, India
BRAJ BHASHA dial of BRAJ BHASHA [BFS]
BRAJ KANAUJI alt for KANAUJI [BJJ]
BRAME alt for BURAMA dial of MANKANYA [MAN]
BRAMU alt for BARAAMU [BRD]
BRAO [BRB] lang, Laos; also in Cambodia, France, USA, Viet Nam
BRAO alt for LAVE [BRB]
BRAOU alt for BRAO [BRB]
BRAOU alt for LAVE [BRB]
BRASMI dial of DUMI [DUS]
BRASS IJO alt for IJO, SOUTHEAST [IJO]
BRASSA alt for BALANTA-GANJA [BJT]
BRASSA alt for BALANTA-KENTOHE [BLE]
BRAT alt for MAI BRAT [AYZ]
BRATHELA alt for GAMADIA dial of GUJARATI [GJR]
BRAU alt for BRAO [BRB]
BRAU alt for LAVE [BRB]
BRAVANESE alt for MWINI dial of SWAHILI [SWA]
BRAWBAW dial of THAO [SSF]
BRAZILIAN CALÃO dial of CALO [RMR]
BRAZILIAN PORTUGUESE dial of PORTUGUESE [POR]
BRAZILIAN SIGN LANGUAGE [BZS] lang, Brazil
BRE alt for KAREN, BREK [KVL]
BREC alt for KAREN, BREK [KVL]
BREDAS dial of DUTCH [DUT]
BREK alt for KAREN, BREK [KVL]
BREM [BUQ] lang, Papua New Guinea
BREN alt for KHANG [KJM]
BRERI [BRQ] lang, Papua New Guinea
BRETON [BRT] lang, France; also in USA
BREZHONEG alt for BRETON [BRT]
BRI alt for BRAJ BHASHA [BFS]
BRIA alt for BEREYA dial of BANDA-BANDA [BPD]
BRIBRI [BZD] lang, Costa Rica
BRIGNAN alt for AVIKAM [AVI]
BRIJ BHASHA alt for BRAJ BHASHA [BFS]
BRIJIA alt for BIJORI [BIX]
BRIJIA dial of ASURI [ASR]
BRIJU alt for BRAJ BHASHA [BFS]
BRI-LA alt for JEH BRI LA dial of JEH [JEH]
"BRINGEN" pejorative alt for MARITHIEL [MFR]
BRINJARI alt for LAMBADI [LMN]
"BRINKEN" pejorative alt for MARITHIEL [MFR]
BRINYA alt for AVIKAM [AVI]
BRISSA alt for AOWIN dial of ANYIN [ANY]

BRITISH SIGN LANGUAGE [BHO] lang, United Kingdom
BROKKAT [BRO] lang, Bhutan
BROKPA alt for BROKPAKE [SGT]
BROKPA alt for BROKSKAT [BKK]
BROKPA alt for SHINA [SCL]
BROKPA OF DAH-HANU alt for BROKSKAT [BKK]
BROKPAKE [SGT] lang, Bhutan
BROKSKAD alt for BROKKAT [BRO]
BROKSKAT [BKK] lang, India
BRON alt for ABRON [ABR]
BRONG alt for ABRON [ABR]
BRONGA alt for CENTRAL KANUM dial of KANUM, SOTA [KRZ]
BROOKE'S POINT PALAWAN alt for PALAWANO, BROOKE'S POINT [PLW]
BROOM CREOLE alt for BROOME PEARLING LUGGER PIDGIN [BPL]
BROOME PEARLING LUGGER PIDGIN [BPL] lang, Australia
BROSA alt for AOWIN dial of ANYIN [ANY]
BROU alt for BRAO [BRB]
BROU alt for BRU, EASTERN [BRU]
BROU alt for LAVE [BRB]
BRU alt for SÔ [SSS]
BRŮ alt for BRU, EASTERN [BRU]
B'RU alt for BRU, WESTERN [BRV]
BRU KOK SA-AT dial of BRU, EASTERN [BRU]
BRU, EASTERN [BRU] lang, Laos; also in Thailand, Viet Nam
BRU, WESTERN [BRV] lang, Thailand; also in USA
BRUIT dial of MELANAU [MEL]
BRUJ alt for BRAJ BHASHA [BFS]
BRUMMIE alt for BIRMINGHAM dial of ENGLISH [ENG]
BRUMMY alt for BIRMINGHAM dial of ENGLISH [ENG]
BRUNCA alt for BORUCA [BRN]
BRUNEI [KXD] lang, Brunei; also in Malaysia (Sabah)
BRUNEI dial of BRUNEI [KXD]
BRUNEI MALAY dial of BRUNEI [KXD]
BRUNEI MURUT alt for LUNDAYEH [LND]
BRUNEI-KADAIAN alt for BRUNEI [KXD]
BRUNG dial of KELABIT [KZI]
BRUNKA alt for BORUCA [BRN]
BRUSHASKI alt for BURUSHASKI [BSK]
BRUU alt for BRU, WESTERN [BRV]
BSL alt for BRITISH SIGN LANGUAGE [BHO]
BU [BOE] lang, Cameroon
BU [JID] lang, Nigeria
BU dial of BU [JID]
BU DANG dial of MNONG, CENTRAL [MNC]
BU GIIWO alt for GIIWO [KKS]
BU NAR dial of MNONG, CENTRAL [MNC]
BU RUNG dial of MNONG, CENTRAL [MNC]
BUA [BUB] lang, Chad
BUA alt for BWA [BWW]
BUA alt for WEST VANUA LEVU dial of FIJIAN [FJI]
BUA dial of TAE [ROB]
BUA PONRANG alt for LUWU dial of BUGIS [BPR]

BUAGA dial of SINAUGORO [SNC]
BUAL alt for BUOL [BLF]
BUAL alt for BUWAL [BHS]
BUAN alt for NGALKBUN [NGK]
BUANG, MANGGA [MMO] lang, Papua New Guinea
BUANG, MAPOS [BZH] lang, Papua New Guinea
BUANO alt for BOANO [BZN]
BUASI alt for VEHES [VAL]
BUBALIA alt for ARABIC, BABALIA CREOLE [BBZ]
BUBALIA alt for BERAKOU [BXV]
BUBANDA dial of MONO [MNH]
BUBANGI alt for BANGI [BNI]
BUBE [BVB] lang, Equatorial Guinea
BUBI [BUW] lang, Gabon
BUBI alt for BUBE [BVB]
BUBI dial of KELE [KEB]
BUBIA [BBX] lang, Cameroon
BUBIS dial of CITAK [TXT]
BUBU alt for NGURU dial of GULA [KCM]
BUBUBUN alt for BUNABUN [BUQ]
BUBUKUN alt for BUNUN [BNN]
BUBURE alt for BURE [BVH]
BUBURE alt for VUTE [VUT]
BUCHO dial of KHEHEK [TLX]
BUDAI dial of RUKAI [DRU]
BUDAMONO dial of GBAYA, SOUTHWEST [MDO]
BUDANG alt for MNONG, CENTRAL [MNC]
BUDANOH dial of DAYAK, LAND [DYK]
BUDAPEST dial of HUNGARIAN SIGN LANGUAGE [HSH]
BUDIBUD [BTP] lang, Papua New Guinea
BUDIDJARA alt for PUDITARA dial of MARTU WANGKA [MPJ]
BUDIGRI dial of GBANU [GBV]
BUDIK [TNR] lang, Senegal
BUDINA alt for BURDUNA [BXN]
BUDÍP alt for STIENG, BULO [STI]
BUDIP dial of STIENG, BULO [STI]
BUDJA alt for BUDZA [BJA]
BUDJAGO alt for BIDYOGO [BJG]
BUD-KAT alt for KINNAURI, BHOTI [NES]
BUDON KAKANDA dial of KAKANDA [KKA]
BUDONG alt for MNONG, CENTRAL [MNC]
BUDONG-BUDONG [TGK] lang, Indonesia (Sulawesi)
BUDOONA alt for BURDUNA [BXN]
BUDU [BUU] lang, DCR
BUDUG alt for BUDUKH [BDK]
BUDUGI alt for BUDUKH [BDK]
BUDUGUM alt for BUGUDUM dial of MASANA [MCN]
BUDUGUM dial of MASANA [MCN]
BUDUKH [BDK] lang, Azerbaijan
BUDUKH dial of BUDUKH [BDK]
BUDUMA [BDM] lang, Chad; also in Cameroon, Nigeria
BUDUMA dial of BUDUMA [BDM]
BUDUNA alt for BURDUNA [BXN]
BUDUX alt for BUDUKH [BDK]
BUDZA [BJA] lang, DCR
BUDZABA alt for BOZABA [BZO]

BUE alt for HUITOTO, MURUI [HUU]
BUELA alt for BWELA [BWL]
BUEM alt for LELEMI [LEF]
BUENA VISTA CHONTAL dial of CHONTAL, TABASCO [CHF]
BUENDE alt for BWENDE dial of KONGO [KON]
BUENG dial of ACEH [ATJ]
BUFE alt for BAFUT [BFD]
BUFE dial of BAFUT [BFD]
BUFUMBWA dial of RWANDA [RUA]
BUG alt for MANGAYAT [MYJ]
BUGAGO alt for BIDYOGO [BJG]
BUGA-KHWE alt for BUGA-KXOE dial of KXOE [XUU]
BUGA-KXOE dial of KXOE [XUU]
BUGALU alt for BIKARU [BIC]
BUGAN [BBH] lang, China
BUGAU dial of IBAN [IBA]
BUGAWAC [BUK] lang, Papua New Guinea
BUGE dial of VAGLA [VAG]
BUGHOTU [BGT] lang, Solomon Islands
BUGI alt for BUGIS [BPR]
BUGINESE alt for BUGIS [BPR]
BUGIS [BPR] lang, Indonesia (Sulawesi); also in Malaysia (Sabah)
BUGKALUT alt for ILONGOT [ILK]
BUGLERE [SAB] lang, Panama
BUGLIAL dial of MERIAM [ULK]
BUGOMBE dial of BHELE [PER]
BUGONGO alt for BOGONGO dial of PANDE [BKJ]
BUGOTA alt for BUGHOTU [BGT]
BUGOTO alt for BUGHOTU [BGT]
BUGOTU alt for BUGHOTU [BGT]
BUGRE alt for GUARANÍ, MBYÁ [GUN]
BUGRE alt for KAINGÁNG [KGP]
BUGRE alt for XOKLENG [XOK]
BUGSUK PALAWANO alt for SOUTH PALAWANO dial of PALAWANO, BROOKES POINT [PLW]
BUGUDUM dial of MASANA [MCN]
BUGULI alt for PWIĒ [PUG]
BUGUMBE dial of KURIA [KUJ]
BUGURI alt for PWIĒ [PUG]
BUGURU alt for BOGURU [BQU]
BUHAGANA alt for MACUNA [MYY]
BUHI dial of BICOLANO, ALBAY [BHK]
BUHID [BKU] lang, Philippines
BUHI'NON alt for BUHI dial of BICOLANO, ALBAY [BHK]
BUHTÂNI alt for JEZIRE dial of KURMANJI [KUR]
BUHULU alt for BUHUTU [BXH]
BUHUTU [BXH] lang, Papua New Guinea
BU-HWAN alt for TAROKO [TRV]
BUI alt for BOUYEI [PCC]
BUIAMANAMBU alt for YELOGU [YLG]
BUILSA alt for BULI [BWU]
BUIN [BUO] lang, Papua New Guinea
BUIN alt for NGALKBUN [NGK]
BUINAK dial of KUMYK [KSK]
BUINAKSK dial of KUMYK [KSK]
BUJA alt for BUDZA [BJA]
BUJAL alt for BUJHYAL [GOR]

BUJEBA alt for NGUMBA [NMG]
BUJHEL alt for BUJHYAL [GOR]
BUJHYAL [GOR] lang, Nepal
BUJI dial of JERE [JER]
BUJIYEL dial of SANGA [SGA]
BUJWE alt for BUYU [BYI]
BUKA alt for BUKAR SADONG [SDO]
BUKA dial of BANDA-MBRES [BQK]
BUKABUKAN alt for PUKAPUKA [PKP]
BUKAKHWE alt for BUGA-KXOE dial of KXOE [XUU]
BUKALA dial of MONGO-NKUNDU [MOM]
BUKALOT alt for ILONGOT [ILK]
BUKAMBERO alt for MBUKAMBERO dial of LAURA
    [LUR]
BUKAR alt for BUKAR SADONG [SDO]
BUKAR BIDAYUH dial of BUKAR SADONG [SDO]
BUKAR SADONG [SDO] lang, Malaysia (Sarawak);
    also in Indonesia (Kalimantan)
BUKAR SADONG dial of BUKAR SADONG [SDO]
BUKAT [BVK] lang, Indonesia (Kalimantan)
BUKAU dial of TIMUGON MURUT [TIH]
BUKAUA alt for BUGAWAC [BUK]
BUKAWA alt for BUGAWAC [BUK]
BUKAWAC alt for BUGAWAC [BUK]
BUKHARA ARABIC alt for ARABIC, TAJIKI SPOKEN
    [ABH]
BUKHARAN alt for BUKHARIC [BHH]
BUKHARIAN alt for BUKHARIC [BHH]
BUKHARIC [BHH] lang, Israel; also in USA,
    Uzbekistan
BUKHARIN alt for BUKHARIC [BHH]
BUKIDNON alt for BINUKID [BKD]
BUKIDNON alt for MAGAHAT [MTW]
BUKIDNON alt for SULOD [SRG]
BUKIL alt for BUHID [BKU]
BUKIRA dial of KURIA [KUJ]
BUKIT alt for MALAY, BUKIT [BVU]
BUKITAN [BKN] lang, Malaysia (Sarawak); also
    in Indonesia (Kalimantan)
BUKIYIP [APE] lang, Papua New Guinea
BUKIYIP dial of BUKIYIP [APE]
BUKIYÚP alt for BUKIYIP [APE]
BUKONGO alt for BOGONGO dial of PANDE [BKJ]
BUKOW alt for BUKAU dial of TIMUGON MURUT
    [TIH]
BUKSA [TKB] lang, India
BUKU dial of CAMPALAGIAN [CML]
BUKUETA alt for BUGLERE [SAB]
BUKUKHI alt for BUDUKH [BDK]
BUKUM alt for BUKUR dial of BOGURU [BQU]
BUKUMA alt for OGBRONUAGUM [OGU]
BUKUN alt for BAUKAN dial of BAUKAN [BNB]
BUKUR dial of BOGURU [BQU]
BUKURU alt for BUKUR dial of BOGURU [BQU]
BUKURUMI alt for KURAMA [KRH]
BUKUSU [BUL] lang, Kenya
BUKUSU dial of BUKUSU [BUL]
BÙKWÁK alt for KWAK [KWQ]
BUKWEN [BUZ] lang, Nigeria
BUL alt for THIANG dial of NUER [NUS]
BULA alt for MAFA [MAF]

BULA alt for MEFELE [MFJ]
BULACAN dial of TAGALOG [TGL]
BULACH dial of STIENG, BULO [STI]
BULAGAT dial of BURIAT, RUSSIA [MNB]
BULAHAI alt for MAFA [MAF]
BULAHAI alt for MEFELE [MFJ]
BULAI alt for PALAUNG, PALE [PCE]
BULALA alt for BILALA dial of NABA [MNE]
BULALAKAW dial of INONHAN [LOC]
BULALAKAWNON dial of HANUNOO [HNN]
BULAMA alt for BURAMA dial of MANKANYA [MAN]
BULANDA alt for BALANTA-GANJA [BJT]
BULANDA alt for BALANTA-KENTOHE [BLE]
BULANG alt for BLANG [BLR]
BULANGA alt for BOLANGO [BLD]
BULANGA-UKI alt for BOLANGO [BLD]
BULAWA alt for KARAWA [QKR]
BULBA alt for BOULBA [BLY]
BULE alt for VUTE [VUT]
BULEI dial of PALAUNG, PALE [PCE]
BULELENG alt for LOWLAND BALI dial of BALI
    [BZC]
BULEM alt for BULLOM SO [BUY]
'BULENGEE dial of WALI [WLX]
BULGAI dial of MERIAM [ULK]
BULGAR alt for CHUVASH [CJU]
BULGAR GAGAUZ dial of GAGAUZ [GAG]
BULGAR GAGAUZI dial of GAGAUZ [GAG]
BULGARIAN [BLG] lang, Bulgaria; also in Canada,
    Greece, Hungary, Israel, Moldova, Romania,
    Turkey (Europe), Ukraine, USA, Yugoslavia
BULGARIAN SIGN LANGUAGE [BQN] lang, Bulgaria
BULGEBI [BMP] lang, Papua New Guinea
BULI [BWU] lang, Ghana
BULI [BZQ] lang, Indonesia (Maluku)
BULI alt for PANGA dial of MONGO-NKUNDU [MOM]
BULI dial of BULI [BZQ]
BULI dial of GBAYA, SOUTHWEST [MDO]
BULI dial of POLCI [POL]
BULIA alt for BOLIA [BLI]
BULISA alt for BULI [BWU]
BULLA dial of SHEKO [SHE]
BULLIN alt for BULLOM SO [BUY]
BULLOM SO [BUY] lang, Sierra Leone
BULLUN alt for BULLOM SO [BUY]
BULO dial of PANNEI [PNC]
BULO dial of STIENG, BULO [STI]
BULU [BJL] lang, Papua New Guinea
BULU [BUM] lang, Cameroon
BULU alt for SEKI [SYI]
BULUD UPI alt for IDA'AN [DBJ]
BULUF dial of JOLA-FOGNY [DYO]
Б' !LUH KUNING alt for SAMIHIM dial of MAANYAN
    [MHY]
BULUKI alt for BOLOKI [BKT]
BULUKUMBA alt for SINJAI dial of BUGIS [BPR]
BULUM alt for BURUM-MINDIK [BMU]
BULUM-BULUM alt for DYAABUGAY [DYY]
BULUNGAN alt for BOLONGAN [BLJ]
BULUNGAN dial of BASAP [BDB]
BULUNGE alt for BURUNGE [BDS]

BULUNITS alt for MBULUNGISH [MBV]
BULUYIEMA dial of LOMA [LOM]
BUM [BMV] lang, Cameroon
BUM alt for BOM [BMF]
BUM alt for MBOUM dial of MBUM [MDD]
BUMA alt for BOMA [BOH]
BUMA alt for TEANU [TKW]
BUMA alt for TURKANA [TUV]
BUMAJI [BYP] lang, Nigeria
BUMA-KXOE dial of KXOE [XUU]
BUMAL dial of BAMBAM [PTU]
BUMALI alt for BOMWALI [BMW]
BUMBIRA dial of HAYA [HAY]
BUMBOKO alt for WUMBOKO [BQM]
BUMBONG alt for DIMBONG [DII]
BUMBORET alt for NORTHERN KALASHA dial
    of KALASHA [KLS]
BUMDEMBA dial of MEOHANG, WESTERN [RAF]
BUME alt for TURKANA [TUV]
BUMO dial of IZON [IJC]
BUMTANG alt for BUMTHANGKHA [KJZ]
BUMTANGKHA alt for BUMTHANGKHA [KJZ]
BUMTANP alt for BUMTHANGKHA [KJZ]
BUMTHANG alt for BUMTHANGKHA [KJZ]
BUMTHANGKHA [KJZ] lang, Bhutan
BUMTHAPKHA alt for BUMTHANGKHA [KJZ]
BUMWANGI dial of LUSENGO [LUS]
BUN [BUV] lang, Papua New Guinea
BUN alt for BON GULA [GLC]
BUNA [BVN] lang, Papua New Guinea
BUNA alt for BENA [YUN]
BUNA alt for MBUM [MDD]
BUNA alt for VORO [VOR]
BUNA' alt for BUNAK [BUA]
BUNA KULANGO alt for KULANGO, BOUNA [NKU]
BUNABA [BCK] lang, Australia
BUNABUN alt for BREM [BUQ]
BUNAK [BUA] lang, Timor Lorosae; also in
    Indonesia (Nusa Tenggara)
BUNAKE alt for BUNAK [BUA]
BUNAKI alt for NAKI [MFF]
BUNAMA [BDD] lang, Papua New Guinea
BUNAMA dial of BUNAMA [BDD]
BUNAN alt for BUNUN [BNN]
BUNAN alt for GAHRI [BFU]
BUNAN alt for PUNAN dial of DAYAK, LAND [DYK]
BUNAO alt for BUNU, BU-NAO [BWX]
BUNAQ alt for BUNAK [BUA]
BUNBERAWA alt for MBARU dial of LAME [BMA]
BUNDA alt for SUWAWA [SWU]
BUNDA dial of SUWAWA [SWU]
BUNDALA alt for BANDJALANG [BDY]
BUNDE dial of LOMA [LOM]
BUNDEL KHANDI alt for BUNDELI [BNS]
BUNDELI [BNS] lang, India
BUNDHAMARA alt for PUNTHAMARA dial of
    NGURA [NBX]
BUNDI alt for GENDE [GAF]
BUNDU dial of DUSUN, CENTRAL [DTP]
BUNDUM dial of TUKI [BAG]
BUNG [BQD] lang, Cameroon

BUNGAIN [BUT] lang, Papua New Guinea
BUNGASE dial of LIGBI [LIG]
BUNGBINDA alt for NGBINDA [NBD]
BUNGEHA alt for BANGGARLA [BJB]
BUNGELA alt for BANGGARLA [BJB]
BUNGGU alt for KAILI, DA'A [KZF]
BUNGI alt for BANGI [BNI]
BUNGILI alt for BONGILI [BUI]
BUNGIRI alt for BONGILI [BUI]
BUNGKU [BKZ] lang, Indonesia (Sulawesi)
BUNGKU dial of BUNGKU [BKZ]
BUNGLA dial of SAAM [RAQ]
BUNGNU alt for KAMKAM [BGU]
BUNGNU alt for MBONGNO [BGU]
BUNGO dial of BONGO [BOT]
BUNGU [WUN] lang, Tanzania
BUNGU alt for BONGO [BOT]
BUNGUN alt for KAMKAM [BGU]
BUNGUN alt for MBONGNO [BGU]
BUNIABURA dial of ANEME WAKE [ABY]
BUNINGA dial of EFATE, NORTH [LLP]
BUNINGA dial of NAMAKURA [NMK]
BUNJI alt for GILGITI dial of SHINA [SCL]
BUNJI dial of MANYIKA [MXC]
BUNJIA alt for BHUNJIA [BHU]
BUNJU alt for TONJO dial of TUKI [BAG]
BUNJWALI dial of KASHMIRI [KSH]
BU-NONG alt for NUNG [NUT]
BUNONG dial of MNONG, SOUTHERN [MNN]
BUNTA alt for ÁNCÁ [ACB]
BUNTI alt for BUNUN [BNN]
BUNU alt for BARGAM [MLP]
BUNU alt for KAMKAM [BGU]
BUNU alt for MBONGNO [BGU]
BUNU alt for RIBINA dial of JERE [JER]
BUNU dial of YORUBA [YOR]
BUNU, BAHENG [PHA] lang, China; also in Viet Nam
BUNU, BU-NAO [BWX] lang, China
BUNU, JIONGNAI [PNU] lang, China
BUNU, WUNAI [BWN] lang, China
BUNU, YOUNUO [BUH] lang, China
BUNUBA alt for BUNABA [BCK]
BUNUBUN alt for BREM [BUQ]
BUNUM alt for BUNUN [BNN]
BUNUN [BNN] lang, Taiwan
BUNUO dial of BUNU, BU-NAO [BWX]
BUOL [BLF] lang, Indonesia (Sulawesi)
BUONCWAI alt for PALIET dial of DINKA, SOUTH-
    WESTERN [DIK]
BUPUL alt for NORTH YEI dial of YEI [JEI]
BUPURAN alt for PAPORA [PPU]
BUR:AAD alt for BURIAT, MONGOLIA [BXM]
BURA alt for BURA-PABIR [BUR]
BURA dial of TAITA [DAV]
BURA HYILHAWUL alt for HYIL HAWUL dial of
    BURA-PABIR [BUR]
BURA KOKURA dial of TERA [TER]
BURA MABANG alt for MABA [MDE]
BURA PELA alt for PELA dial of BURA-PABIR [BUR]
BURAADIIGA dial of DATOOGA [TCC]
BURADA alt for BURARRA [BVR]

BURADIGA alt for BURAADIIGA dial of DATOOGA [TCC]
BURAGA alt for KUI dial of KUI [KVD]
BURAK [BYS] lang, Nigeria
BURAKA [BKG] lang, CAR; also in DCR
BURAM alt for BURAMA dial of MANKANYA [MAN]
BURAMA dial of MANKANYA [MAN]
BURA-PABIR [BUR] lang, Nigeria
BURARRA [BVR] lang, Australia
BURATE [BTI] lang, Indonesia (Irian Jaya)
BURBA alt for BIALI [BEH]
BURDUNA [BXN] lang, Australia
BURE [BVH] lang, Nigeria
BURÉ alt for POTURU [PTO]
BUREDA alt for BURARRA [BVR]
BURERA alt for BURARRA [BVR]
BURGADI alt for DYANGADI [DYN]
BURGANDI dial of TAMIL [TCV]
BURGENLAND CROATIAN dial of SERBO-CROATIAN [SRC]
BURGU alt for BARIBA [BBA]
BURIAH-WETH-LATURAKE alt for CENTRAL EAST ALUNE dial of ALUNE [ALP]
BURIAT, CHINA [BXU] lang, China
BURIAT, MONGOLIA [BXM] lang, Mongolia
BURIAT, RUSSIA [MNB] lang, Russia (Asia)
BURIAT-MONGOLIAN alt for BURIAT, CHINA [BXU]
BURIAT-MONGOLIAN alt for BURIAT, MONGOLIA [BXM]
BURIAT-MONGOLIAN alt for BURIAT, RUSSIA [MNB]
BURIG alt for PURIK [BXR]
BURIGSKAT alt for PURIK [BXR]
BURIRAM dial of KHMER, NORTHERN [KXM]
BURJA alt for BIJORI [BIX]
BURJI [BJI] lang, Ethiopia; also in Kenya
BURJIN alt for ANUAK [ANU]
BURKANAWA alt for MBURKU [BBT]
BURKENEJI alt for SAMBURU [SAQ]
BURMA alt for BOGHOM [BUX]
BURMA TAMIL dial of TAMIL [TCV]
BURMBAR [VRT] lang, Vanuatu
BURMESE [BMS] lang, Myanmar; also in Bangladesh, Malaysia, Thailand, USA
BURMESE dial of BURMESE [BMS]
BURMESE KAREN alt for KAREN, S'GAW [KSW]
BURMESO [BZU] lang, Indonesia (Irian Jaya)
BURNAY IFUGAO dial of IFUGAO, AMGANAD [IFA]
BURO alt for DEG [MZW]
BUROGO alt for ROGO [ROD]
BUROM alt for BOGHOM [BUX]
BURRA alt for BURA-PABIR [BUR]
BURRUM alt for BOGHOM [BUX]
BURTA alt for BERTA [WTI]
BURU [BQW] lang, Nigeria
BURU [MHS] lang, Indonesia (Maluku); also in Netherlands
BURU alt for DEG [MZW]
BURU alt for LISELA [LCL]
BURU alt for TAMAGARIO [TCG]
BURU dial of BANDA-BANDA [BPD]

BURU dial of NGELIMA [AGH]
BURUBORA alt for PURUBORÁ [PUR]
BURUCAKI alt for BURUSHASKI [BSK]
BURUCASKI alt for BURUSHASKI [BSK]
BURUESE alt for BURU [MHS]
BURUI [BRY] lang, Papua New Guinea
BURUI dial of MALINGUAT [SIC]
'BURULO dial of MADI [MHI]
BURUM alt for BOGHOM [BUX]
BURUM alt for BURUM-MINDIK [BMU]
BURUMAKOK [AIP] lang, Indonesia (Irian Jaya)
BURUMBA alt for BAKI [BKI]
BURUMESO alt for BURMESO [BZU]
BURUM-MINDIK [BMU] lang, Papua New Guinea
BURUN [BDI] lang, Sudan
BURUN alt for UDUK [UDU]
BURUNCA alt for BORUCA [BRN]
BURUNGE [BDS] lang, Tanzania
BURUSA alt for BOULBA [BLY]
BURUSHAKI alt for BURUSHASKI [BSK]
BURUSHASKI [BSK] lang, Pakistan; also in India
BURUSHKI alt for BURUSHASKI [BSK]
BURUSU [BQR] lang, Indonesia (Kalimantan)
BURUWA dial of KIMRE [KQP]
BURUWAI [ASI] lang, Indonesia (Irian Jaya)
BURYAT alt for BURIAT, CHINA [BXU]
BURYAT alt for BURIAT, MONGOLIA [BXM]
BURYAT alt for BURIAT, RUSSIA [MNB]
BURZHAN dial of BASHKIR [BXK]
BUSA [BHF] lang, Papua New Guinea
BUSA [BQP] lang, Nigeria
BUSA-BISÃ alt for BUSA [BQP]
BUSA-BOKO alt for BOKO [BQC]
BUSA-BOKOBARU alt for BOKOBARU [BUS]
BUSAM [BXS] lang, Cameroon
BUSAMI [BSM] lang, Indonesia (Irian Jaya)
BUSANG alt for KAYAN, BUSANG [BFG]
BUSANG alt for PUNAN dial of DAYAK, LAND [DYK]
BUSANO alt for BUSA [BQP]
BUSENI alt for BISENI [IJE]
BUSERE BONGO dial of BONGO [BOT]
BUSH UNUA dial of UNUA [ONU]
BUSHAMA alt for SHAMA-SAMBUGA [SQA]
BUSH-C alt for //XEGWI [XEG]
BUSHI [BUC] lang, Madagascar; also in Mayotte
BUSHMAN'S BAY alt for LINGARAK [LGK]
BUSHONG alt for BUSHOONG [BUF]
BUSHONGO alt for BUSHOONG [BUF]
BUSHOONG [BUF] lang, DCR
BUSI dial of OBANLIKU [BZY]
BUSILLU SISALA alt for SISAALA, WESTERN [SSL]
BUSO [BSO] lang, Chad
BUSOA [BUP] lang, Indonesia (Sulawesi)
BUSOONG alt for BUSHOONG [BUF]
BUSSA [DOX] lang, Ethiopia
BUSSANCHI alt for BUSA [BQP]
BUSSO alt for BUSO [BSO]
BUSU DJANGA dial of LUSENGO [LUS]
BUSUU [BJU] lang, Cameroon
"BUSY" pejorative alt for LOMA [LOM]

BUT alt for MATCHOPA NAGNOO dial of MOINBA [MOB]
BUTA alt for GAMO dial of GAMO-NINGI [BTE]
BUTAM dial of TAULIL-BUTAM [TUH]
BUTANGLU alt for PAIWAN [PWN]
BUTBUT alt for KALINGA, BUTBUT [KYB]
BUTE alt for VUTE [VUT]
BUTE BAMNYO dial of VUTE [VUT]
BUTEHA dial of DAUR [DTA]
BUTELKUD-GUNTABAK alt for NOBANOB [GAW]
BUTI alt for VUTE [VUT]
BUTJU alt for DJANGUN [DJF]
BUTMAS-TUR [BNR] lang, Vanuatu
BUTON alt for CIA-CIA [CIA]
BUTON alt for TUKANGBESI NORTH [KHC]
BUTON alt for TUKANGBESI SOUTH [BHQ]
BUTON alt for WOLIO [WLO]
BUTONESE alt for CIA-CIA [CIA]
BUTONESE alt for WOLIO [WLO]
BUTUANON [BTW] lang, Philippines
BUTUNG alt for CIA-CIA [CIA]
BUTUNG alt for WOLIO [WLO]
BUU alt for ZARANDA dial of GEJI [GEZ]
BU'U dial of ANKAVE [AAK]
BUU I dial of POKOMO, LOWER [POJ]
BUU II dial of POKOMO, LOWER [POJ]
BUU III dial of POKOMO, LOWER [POJ]
BUURAK alt for BURAK [BYS]
BUWAL [BHS] lang, Cameroon
BUWAN alt for NGALKBUN [NGK]
BUWEYEU dial of BUANG, MAPOS [BZH]
BUXARA ARABIC alt for ARABIC, TAJIKI SPOKEN [ABH]
BUXINHUA [BXT] lang, China
BUY alt for KOBIANA [KCJ]
BUYA [BYY] lang, DCR
BUYA dial of LOKO [LOK]
BUYAKA alt for SENTANI [SET]
BUYANG [BYU] lang, China
BUYEI alt for BOUYEI [PCC]
BUYI alt for BOUYEI [PCC]
BUYI alt for BUYU [BYI]
BUYU [BYI] lang, DCR
BUYUAN alt for JINUO, BUYUAN [JIY]
BUYUI alt for BOUYEI [PCC]
BUZABA alt for BOZABA [BZO]
BUZAWA dial of KALMYK-OIRAT [KGZ]
"BUZI" pejorative alt for LOMA [LOM]
BUZU alt for TAMAJAQ, TAWALLAMMAT [TTQ]
BVANUMA alt for VANUMA [VAU]
BVERI dial of FALI, NORTH [FLL]
BVIRI alt for BELANDA VIRI [BVI]
BVIRI alt for BIRRI [BVQ]
BVUKOO alt for OKU [OKU]
BVUMBA dial of MANYIKA [MXC]
BWA [BWW] lang, DCR
BWA alt for BUA [BUB]
BWA alt for BWAMU [BOX]
BWABA alt for BWAMU [BOX]
BWADJI alt for BOAZI [KVG]
BWAIDOGA alt for BWAIDOKA [BWD]

BWAIDOGA dial of BWAIDOKA [BWD]
BWAIDOKA [BWD] lang, Papua New Guinea
BWAKA alt for NGBAKA MA'BO [NBM]
BWAKA dial of MBATI [MDN]
BWAKERA dial of SEWA BAY [SEW]
BWAL alt for BWOL dial of KOFYAR [KWL]
BWAMU [BOX] lang, Burkina Faso
BWAMU, CWI [BWY] lang, Burkina Faso
BWAMU, LÁÁ LÁÁ [BWJ] lang, Burkina Faso
BWANA dial of NUNI, SOUTHERN [NNW]
BWANABWANA [TTE] lang, Papua New Guinea
BWARA alt for BOOR [BVF]
BWAREBA alt for BACAMA [BAM]
BWATNAPNI dial of APMA [APP]
BWATOO [BWA] lang, New Caledonia
BWATVENUA alt for HANO [LML]
BWAZA alt for BWAZZA dial of MBULA-BWAZZA [MBU]
BWA'ZA alt for BWAZZA dial of MBULA-BWAZZA [MBU]
BWAZZA dial of MBULA-BWAZZA [MBU]
BWE alt for KAREN, BWE [BWE]
BWEEN dial of FALI [FLI]
BWEKO dial of YASA [YKO]
BWELA [BWL] lang, DCR
BWENDE dial of KONGO [KON]
BWILE [BWC] lang, Zambia; also in DCR
BWILIM dial of DIJIM-BWILIM [CFA]
BWIREGE dial of KURIA [KUJ]
BWISHA dial of RWANDA [RUA]
BWISI [BWZ] lang, Congo; also in Gabon
BWISSI alt for TALINGA-BWISI [TLJ]
BWOL dial of KOFYAR [KWL]
BWONCWAI alt for PALIET dial of DINKA, SOUTH-WESTERN [DIK]
BWO'OL alt for BUOL [BLF]
BWORO alt for BORO [BWO]
BYABE dial of NORRA [NOR]
BYANGKHO LWO alt for BYANGSI [BEE]
BYANGSI [BEE] lang, India; also in Nepal
BYANGSKAT alt for CHANGTHANG [CNA]
BYANSHI alt for BYANGSI [BEE]
BYANSI alt for BYANGSI [BEE]
BYANSKAT alt for CHANGTHANG [CNA]
BYAU MIN alt for BIAO-JIAO MIEN [BJE]
BYELORUSSIAN alt for BELARUSAN [RUW]
BYEP [MKK] lang, Cameroon
BYEP dial of BYEP [MKK]
BYOKI alt for BOKYI [BKY]
BYRRE alt for GBETE dial of MBUM [MDD]
BZEDUX alt for BEZHEDUKH dial of ADYGHE [ADY]
BZHEDUG alt for BEZHEDUKH dial of ADYGHE [ADY]
BZYB dial of ABKHAZ [ABK]
CA' dial of FEFE [FMP]
CA GIONG alt for KAYONG [KXY]
CA TUA alt for KATUA [KTA]
CAABE alt for CABE [CBJ]
CAAC [MSQ] lang, New Caledonia
CABANAPO alt for POMO, CENTRAL [POO]

CABANATIT alt for TOBA-MASKOY [TMF]
CABARAN alt for KAVALAN [CKV]
CABE [CBJ] lang, Benin
CABEÇA SECA alt for ZORÓ dial of GAVIAO DO
JIPARANA [GVO]
CABÉCAR [CJP] lang, Costa Rica
CABICHÍ alt for KABIXÍ [KBD]
CABINDA alt for KONGO [KON]
CABISHI alt for KABIXÍ [KBD]
CABIUARÍ alt for CABIYARÍ [CBB]
CABIYARÍ [CBB] lang, Colombia
CABO dial of MISKITO [MIQ]
CABOVERDIANO alt for KABUVERDIANU [KEA]
CABRAI alt for KABIYÉ [KBP]
CABRAIS alt for KABIYÉ [KBP]
CÁC LAO alt for GELAO [KKF]
CACA WERANOS alt for CHIMILA [CBG]
CACAHUE alt for KAKAUHUA [KBF]
CACALOXTEPEC MIXTEC alt for MIXTECO,
CACALOXTEPEC [MIU]
CACAOPERA [CCR] lang, El Salvador
CACATAIBO dial of CASHIBO-CACATAIBO [CBR]
CACCHÉ alt for KEKCHÍ [KEK]
CAC'CHIQUEL MAM alt for CHICOMUCELTEC
[COB]
CACETEIROS alt for KORUBO [QKF]
CACHARI alt for KACHARI [QKC]
CACHEU-ZIGUINCHOR CREOLE dial of CRIOULO,
UPPER GUINEA [POV]
CACHIBO alt for CASHIBO-CACATAIBO [CBR]
"CACHOMASHIRI" pejorative alt for CAQUINTE
[COT]
CACHUENA alt for KATAWIAN dial of WAIWAI
[WAW]
CACHUY alt for CAUQUI dial of JAQARU [JQR]
CACI alt for CHAI dial of SURI [SUQ]
CACIBO alt for CASHIBO-CACATAIBO [CBR]
CACRA-HONGOS dial of QUECHUA, YAUYOS
[QUX]
CACUA [CBV] lang, Colombia
CADAUAPURITANA alt for UNHUN dial of
CURRIPACO [KPC]
CADDO [CAD] lang, USA
CADDOE alt for CADDO [CAD]
CADEGOMEÑO alt for COCHIMÍ [COJ]
CADEGOMO alt for COCHIMÍ [COJ]
CADIEN alt for FRENCH, CAJUN [FRC]
CADOE LOANG alt for CHRU [CJE]
CADONG alt for SEDANG [SED]
CADORINO dial of LADIN [LLD]
CADUVÉO alt for KADIWÉU [KBC]
CAELI alt for KAYELI [KZL]
CAFFINO alt for KAFICHO [KBR]
"CAFFRE" pejorative alt for XHOSA [XOS]
"CAFRE" pejorative alt for XHOSA [XOS]
CAFUNDO CREOLE [CCD] lang, Brazil
CAGA alt for ENGA [ENQ]
CAGAYAN alt for GADDANG [GAD]
CAGAYAN DE SULU alt for MAPUN [SJM]
CAGAYANCILLO alt for KAGAYANEN [CGC]
CAGAYANO alt for MAPUN [SJM]

CAGAYANO CILLO alt for KAGAYANEN [CGC]
CAGAYANON alt for MAPUN [SJM]
CAGERE dial of PONGU [PON]
CAGLIARE dial of SARDINIAN, CAMPIDANESE
[SRO]
CAGLIARI alt for CAGLIARE dial of SARDINIAN,
CAMPIDANESE [SRO]
CAGLIARITAN alt for CAGLIARE dial of SARDINIAN,
CAMPIDANESE [SRO]
CAGUA [CBH] lang, Colombia
CAHIVO alt for CASHIBO-CACATAIBO [CBR]
CAHTO alt for KATO [KTW]
CAHTÚO alt for EXTREMADURAN [EXT]
CAHTÚÖ alt for EXTREMADURAN [EXT]
CAHUAPA alt for CHAYAHUITA [CBT]
CAHUAPANA dial of CHAYAHUITA [CBT]
CAHUARANO [CAH] lang, Peru
CAHUILLA [CHL] lang, USA
CAI alt for BURUN [BDI]
CAI alt for CHAI dial of SURI [SUQ]
CAIABI alt for KAYABÍ [KYZ]
CAIMAN NUEVO alt for KUNA, BORDER [KUA]
CAINGANG alt for KAINGÁNG [KGP]
CAINGUA alt for KAIWÁ [KGK]
CAIRENE ARABIC dial of ARABIC, EGYPTIAN
SPOKEN [ARZ]
CAIRUI alt for KAIRUI-MIDIKI [KRD]
CAIUA alt for KAIWÁ [KGK]
CAIWA alt for KAIWÁ [KGK]
CAIWÁ alt for KAIWÁ [KGK]
CAJAN alt for FRENCH, CAJUN [FRC]
CAJELI alt for KAYELI [KZL]
CAJONOS ZAPOTEC alt for ZAPOTECO,
CAJONOS [ZAD]
CAJONOS ZAPOTECO dial of ZAPOTECO,
CAJONOS [ZAD]
CAJUN alt for FRENCH, CAJUN [FRC]
CAKA [CKX] lang, Cameroon
CAKCHIQUEL MAM alt for CHICOMUCELTEC
[COB]
CAKCHIQUEL, CENTRAL [CAK] lang, Guatemala
CAKCHIQUEL, EASTERN [CKE] lang, Guatemala
CAKCHIQUEL, NORTHERN [CKC] lang, Guatemala
CAKCHIQUEL, SANTA MARÍA DE JESÚS [CKI]
lang, Guatemala
CAKCHIQUEL, SANTO DOMINGO XENACOJ [CKJ]
lang, Guatemala
CAKCHIQUEL, SOUTH CENTRAL [CKD] lang,
Guatemala
CAKCHIQUEL, SOUTHERN [CKF] lang, Guatemala
CAKCHIQUEL, SOUTHWESTERN, ACATENANGO
[CKK] lang, Guatemala
CAKCHIQUEL, SOUTHWESTERN, YEPOCAPA
[CBM] lang, Guatemala
CAKCHIQUEL, WESTERN [CKW] lang, Guatemala
CAKCHIQUEL-QUICHE MIXED LANGUAGE [CKZ]
lang, Guatemala
CAKFEM-MUSHERE [CKY] lang, Nigeria
CAKKE dial of DURI [MVP]
CALA alt for CHALA [CHA]
CALABAR alt for EFIK [EFK]

CALABASH BIGHT dial of BAY ISLANDS CREOLE ENGLISH [BYH]
CALABRIAN ALBANIAN dial of ALBANIAN, ARBERESHE [AAE]
CALABRO-SICILIAN alt for SICILIAN [SCN]
CALA-CALA alt for C'LELA [DRI]
CALAISIS dial of PICARD [PCD]
CALAMIANO alt for TAGBANWA, CALAMIAN [TBK]
CALANASAN dial of ISNAG [ISD]
CALÃO alt for CALÓ[RMR]
CALÃO alt for PORTUGUESE CALÃO dial of CALO [RMR]
CALATRAVANHON alt for BANTOANON [BNO]
CALCUTTA SIGN LANGUAGE dial of INDIAN SIGN LANGUAGE [INS]
CALDERÓN QUICHUA alt for QUICHUA, HIGH-LAND, CALDERÓN [QUD]
"CALDOCHE" pejorative alt for TAYO [CKS]
CALEBASSES alt for KENSWEI NSEI [NDB]
CALIANA alt for SAPÉ [SPC]
CALIBUGAN alt for SUBANON, KOLIBUGAN [SKN]
CALLAHUAYA alt for CALLAWALLA [CAW]
CALLAWALLA [CAW] lang, Bolivia
CALO alt for CALÓ [RMR]
CALÓ [RMR] lang, Spain; also in Brazil, France, Portugal
CALUYANEN alt for CALUYANUN [CAU]
CALUYANHON alt for CALUYANUN [CAU]
CALUYANUN [CAU] lang, Philippines
CAM alt for DIJIM dial of DIJIM-BWILIM [CFA]
CAM MU alt for KHMU [KJG]
CAMA alt for EBRIÉ [EBR]
CAMAIURA alt for KAMAYURÁ [KAY]
CAMAJERE dial of PONGU [PON]
CAMALAL alt for CHAMALAL [CJI]
CAMAN alt for EBRIÉ [EBR]
CAMARACOTA dial of PEMON [AOC]
CAMARACOTO dial of PEMON [AOC]
CAMBA alt for KAMBA [QKZ]
CAMBA dial of BUGIS [BPR]
CAMBEBA alt for OMAGUA [OMG]
CAMBELA alt for OMAGUA [OMG]
CAMBODIAN alt for KHMER, CENTRAL [KMR]
CAMBODIAN CHAM alt for CHAM, WESTERN [CJA]
CAMBRESIS dial of PICARD [PCD]
CAMËNTSËÁ alt for CAMSÁ [KBH]
CAMEALI alt for CHAMBEALI [CDH]
CAMERIJA dial of ALBANIAN, TOSK [ALN]
CAMERON dial of SEMAI [SEA]
CAMEROON CREOLE ENGLISH alt for PIDGIN, CAMEROON [WES]
CAMILEROI alt for KAMILAROI [KLD]
CAMLING [RAB] lang, Nepal
CAMO dial of KUDU-CAMO [KOV]
CAMONAYAN dial of AGTA, DUPANINAN [DUO]
CAMORTA dial of NICOBARESE, CENTRAL [NCB]
CAMOTES alt for POROHANON [PRH]
CAMOTLÁN MIXE dial of MIXE, COATLAN [MCO]
"CAMPA" pejorative alt for ASHÁNINCA [CNI]
CAMPA alt for AJYÍNINKA APURUCAYALI [CPC]

CAMPA alt for ASHÉNINCA PAJONAL [CJO]
CAMPA alt for ASHÉNINCA PERENÉ [CPP]
CAMPA alt for ASHÉNINCA UCAYALI-YURUA [CPB]
CAMPALAGIAN [CML] lang, Indonesia (Sulawesi)
CAMPALAGIAN dial of CAMPALAGIAN [CML]
CAMPEBA alt for OMAGUA [OMG]
CAMPIDANESE alt for SARDINIAN, CAMPIDANESE [SRO]
CAMPIDESE alt for SARDINIAN, CAMPIDANESE [SRO]
CAMPO alt for KUMIÁI [DIH]
CAMPO MARINO ALBANIAN dial of ALBANIAN, ARBERESHE [AAE]
CAMPUON alt for TAMPUAN [TPU]
CAMSÁ [KBH] lang, Colombia
CAMTHO [CMT] lang, South Africa
CAMUCONES alt for TIDONG [TID]
CAMUHI alt for CEMUHÎ [CAM]
CAMUKI alt for CEMUHÎ [CAM]
CAMURU alt for KAMURÚ dial of KARIRI-XOCO [KZW]
CANAANIC alt for KNAANIC [CZK]
CANALA alt for XÂRÂCÙÙ [ANE]
CANAMANTI alt for JAMAMADÍ [JAA]
CANAMARÍ alt for KANAMARÍ [KNM]
CANARESE alt for KANNADA [KJV]
CANARESE alt for KURUMBA [KFI]
CAÑARIS dial of QUECHUA, LAMBAYEQUE [QUF]
CANARY ISLANDS SPANISH dial of SPANISH [SPN]
CANCUC alt for TZELTAL, OXCHUC [TZH]
CANDELARIA LOXICHA ZAPOTECO dial of ZAPOTECO, LOXICHA [ZTP]
CANDOSHI alt for CANDOSHI-SHAPRA [CBU]
CANDOSHI-SHAPRA [CBU] lang, Peru
CANDOXI alt for CANDOSHI-SHAPRA [CBU]
CANE alt for NCANE [NCR]
CANELA [RAM] lang, Brazil
CANELOS QUICHUA alt for QUICHUA, PASTAZA, NORTHERN [QLB]
CANGALA alt for NKANGALA [NKN]
CANGA-PEBA alt for OMAGUA [OMG]
CANGIN dial of NOON [SNF]
CANGLOU MENBA alt for TSHANGLA [TSJ]
CANGVA alt for ZHUANG, NORTHERN [CCX]
CANICHANA [CAZ] lang, Bolivia
CANING alt for SHATT [SHJ]
CAÑO PADILLA-LA LAGUNA dial of YUKPA [YUP]
CANOA alt for AVÁ-CANOEIRO [AVV]
CANOE alt for AVÁ-CANOEIRO [AVV]
CANOÉ alt for KANOÉ [KXO]
CANOEIRO alt for RIKBAKTSA [ART]
CANOEIROS alt for AVÁ-CANOEIRO [AVV]
CANSU dial of PONGU [PON]
CANT alt for SHELTA [STH]
CANTEL QUICHÉ alt for QUICHÉ, WEST CENTRAL [QUT]
CANTILAN dial of SURIGAONON [SUL]
CANTONESE alt for CHINESE, YUE [YUH]
CANTONESE dial of CHINESE, YUE [YUH]

CAO LAN alt for MAN CAO LAN [MLC]
CAO LAN-SÁN CHI alt for MAN CAO LAN [MLC]
CAO MIAO [COV] lang, China
CAODENG alt for SIDABA dial of JIARONG [JYA]
CAOLAN alt for MAN CAO LAN [MLC]
CAPA alt for QUAPAW [QUA]
CAPANAHUA [KAQ] lang, Peru
CAPE AFRIKAANS dial of AFRIKAANS [AFK]
CAPE CORS alt for NORTHERN CORSICAN dial
    of CORSICAN [COI]
CAPE DRAPING GELAO dial of GELAO [KKF]
CAPE HOTTENTOT alt for XIRI [XII]
CAPE YORK CREOLE alt for TORRES STRAIT
    CREOLE [TCS]
CAPISANO alt for CAPIZNON [CPS]
CAPISEÑO alt for CAPIZNON [CPS]
CAPIZNON [CPS] lang, Philippines
CAPOSHO alt for MAXAKALÍ [MBL]
CAPPADOCIAN GREEK [CPG] lang, Greece
CAPUL alt for SAMA, ABAKNON [ABX]
CAPULEÑO alt for SAMA, ABAKNON [ABX]
CAQUETÁ alt for KOREGUAJE [COE]
CAQUINTE [COT] lang, Peru
CAQUINTE CAMPA alt for CAQUINTE [COT]
CAR alt for NICOBARESE, CAR [CAQ]
CARA [CFD] lang, Nigeria
CARA dial of SHUA [SHG]
CARABAYO [CBY] lang, Colombia
CARAPANA [CBC] lang, Colombia; also in
    Brazil
CARAPANÃ alt for CARAPANA [CBC]
CARAPANA-TAPUYA alt for CARAPANA [CBC]
CARAPATÓ alt for TINGUI-BOTO [TGV]
CARAS-PRETAS alt for MUNDURUKÚ [MYU]
CARAVARE alt for KURUÁYA [KYR]
CARE alt for SENA-CARE dial of SENA [SEH]
CARGESE dial of GREEK [GRK]
CARI alt for AKA-CARI [ACI]
CARIB [CRB] lang, Venezuela; also in Brazil,
    French Guiana, Guyana, Suriname
CARIB MOTILÓN alt for YUKPA [YUP]
CARIB, ISLAND [CAI] lang, Dominica; also in St.
    Vincent and the Grenadines
CARIBE alt for CARIB [CRB]
CARIBE alt for GARÍFUNA [CAB]
CARIBOU ESKIMO dial of INUKTITUT, WESTERN
    CANADIAN [ESC]
CARIHONA alt for CARIJONA [CBD]
CARIJONA [CBD] lang, Colombia
CARIÑA alt for CARIB [CRB]
CARIPUNA alt for KARIPUNÁ [KUQ]
CARITIANA alt for KARITIÂNA [KTN]
CARMEL alt for RUMSEN dial of COSTANOAN,
    SOUTHERN [CSS]
CARNICO dial of FRIULIAN [FRL]
CARNIJÓ alt for FULNIÔ [FUN]
CAROLINIAN [CAL] lang, Northern Mariana Islands
CARPATHIAN alt for RUSYN [RUE]
CARPATHO-RUSYN alt for RUSYN [RUE]
CARRAGA MANDAYA alt for MANDAYA, KARAGA
    [MRY]

CARRIACOU CREOLE ENGLISH alt for GRENADA
    CREOLE ENGLISH dial of WINDWARD
    CARIBBEAN CREOLE ENGLISH [SVG]
CARRIER [CAR] lang, Canada
CARRIER, SOUTHERN [CAF] lang, Canada
CARÚTANA [CRU] lang, Brazil
CASA alt for JOLA-KASA [CSK]
CASHIBO dial of CASHIBO-CACATAIBO [CBR]
CASHIBO-CACATAIBO [CBR] lang, Peru
CASHINAHUA [CBS] lang, Peru; also in Brazil
CASHINAHUÁ alt for CASHINAHUA [CBS]
CASHMEEREE alt for KASHMIRI [KSH]
CASHMIRI alt for KASHMIRI [KSH]
CASHQUIHA alt for GUANA [GVA]
CASHUBIAN alt for KASHUBIAN [CSB]
CASIGURAN DUMAGAT alt for AGTA, CASIGURAN
    DUMAGAT [DGC]
CASIGURANIN alt for KASIGURANIN [KSN]
CASKA alt for KASKA [KKZ]
CASSANGA alt for KASANGA [CCJ]
CASSUBIAN alt for KASHUBIAN [CSB]
CASTELLANO alt for SPANISH [SPN]
CASTILIAN alt for SPANISH [SPN]
CASTILIAN dial of SPANISH [SPN]
CASTILLIAN alt for SPANISH [SPN]
CASU alt for ASU [ASA]
CATALÀ alt for CATALAN-VALENCIAN-BALEAR
    [CLN]
CATALÁN alt for CATALAN-VALENCIAN-BALEAR
    [CLN]
CATALAN-ROUSILLONESE dial of CATALAN-
    VALENCIAN-BALEAR [CLN]
CATALAN-VALENCIAN-BALEAR [CLN] lang,
    Spain; also in Algeria, Andorra, Argentina,
    Belgium, Brazil, Chile, Colombia, Cuba,
    Dominican Republic, France, Germany, Italy,
    Mexico, Switzerland, Uruguay, USA, Venezuela
CATALONIAN alt for CATALAN-VALENCIAN-
    BALEAR [CLN]
CATALONIAN CALO dial of CALO [RMR]
CATALONIAN SIGN LANGUAGE [CSC] lang,
    Spain
CATAUIAN alt for KATAWIAN dial of WAIWAI
    [WAW]
CATAUICHI alt for KATAWIXI [QKI]
CATAUIXI alt for KATAWIXI [QKI]
CATAWBA [CHC] lang, USA
CATAWIAN alt for KATAWIAN dial of WAIWAI
    [WAW]
CATAWISHI alt for KATAWIXI [QKI]
CATAWIXI alt for KATAWIXI [QKI]
CATEELENYO alt for MANDAYA, CATAELANO
    [MST]
CATIO alt for EMBERÁ-CATÍO [CTO]
CATÍO alt for EMBERÁ-CATÍO [CTO]
CATRÚ alt for EMBERÁ-BAUDÓ[BDC]
CATUQUINA alt for KATUKÍNA [KAV]
CATUQUINA alt for KATUKÍNA, PANOAN [KNT]
CAUNDU dial of PONGU [PON]
CAUQUE MIXED LANGUAGE alt for CAKCHIQUEL-
    QUICHE MIXED LANGUAGE [CKZ]

CAUQUI dial of JAQARU [JQR]
CAURA dial of SANUMA [SAM]
CAUYARÍ alt for CABIYARÍ [CBB]
"CAUZUH" pejorative alt for XHOSA [XOS]
CAVCUVENSKIJ dial of KORYAK [KPY]
CAVINA alt for ARAONA [ARO]
CAVINEÑA [CAV] lang, Bolivia
CAVITEQO dial of CHAVACANO [CBK]
CAWAI alt for ATSAM [CCH]
CAWDUR dial of TURKMEN [TCK]
CAWE alt for ATSAM [CCH]
CAWI alt for ATSAM [CCH]
CAXIBO alt for CASHIBO-CACATAIBO [CBR]
CAXINAWA alt for CASHINAHUA [CBS]
CAXINAWÁ alt for CASHINAHUA [CBS]
CAXUR alt for TSAKHUR [TKR]
CAYAMBE QUICHUA alt for QUICHUA, HIGHLAND,
    CALDERÓN [QUD]
CAYAPA alt for CHACHI [CBI]
CAYLLOMA QUECHUA dial of QUECHUA, CUZCO
    [QUZ]
CAYMAN ISLANDS ENGLISH [CYE] lang, Cayman
    Islands
CAYOR dial of WOLOF [WOL]
CAYUA alt for KAIWÁ [KGK]
CAYUBABA [CAT] lang, Bolivia
CAYUGA [CAY] lang, Canada; also in USA
CAYUVAVA alt for CAYUBABA [CAT]
CAYUWABA alt for CAYUBABA [CAT]
CAZAMA alt for KXOE [XUU]
CEBU dial of CEBUANO [CEB]
CEBUANO [CEB] lang, Philippines; also in USA
CEEMBA dial of NTCHAM [BUD]
CELLATE alt for BESISI [MHE]
CELLE SAN VITO dial of FRANCO-PROVENCAL
    [FRA]
CEMBA alt for AKASELEM [AKS]
CEMDALSK dial of EVENKI [EVN]
CEMUAL alt for NANDI dial of KALENJIN [KLN]
CEMUHÎ [CAM] lang, New Caledonia
CEN BEROM alt for BEROM [BOM]
CEN TUUM alt for CENTÚÚM [CET]
CENG alt for JENG [JEG]
CENGE alt for KENGA [KYQ]
CENGE dial of KENGA [KYQ]
CENKA [CEN] lang, Benin
CENRANA alt for SENDANA dial of MANDAR [MHN]
CENTRAL dial of LIMBA, WEST-CENTRAL [LIA]
CENTRAL ABUAN dial of ABUA [ABN]
CENTRAL AFAR dial of AFAR [AFR]
CENTRAL ALASKAN YUPIK alt for YUPIK,
    CENTRAL [ESU]
CENTRAL AMBON alt for LAHA [LAD]
CENTRAL AMERICAN CARIB alt for GARÍFUNA
    [CAB]
CENTRAL AMIS dial of AMIS [ALV]
CENTRAL AND NORTH POHJANMAA dial of
    FINNISH [FIN]
CENTRAL ANGOR alt for NAI dial of ANGOR [AGG]
CENTRAL ARAGONESE dial of ARAGONESE
    [AXX]

CENTRAL ASIAN ARABIC alt for ARABIC, TAJIKI
    SPOKEN [ABH]
CENTRAL ASIAN ARABIC alt for ARABIC, UZBEKI
    SPOKEN [AUZ]
CENTRAL ASTURIAN dial of ASTURIAN [AUB]
CENTRAL ATLAS dial of TAMAZIGHT, CENTRAL
    ATLAS [TZM]
CENTRAL AUNALEI dial of AUNALEI [AUN]
CENTRAL AZTEC alt for NÁHUATL CENTRAL
    [NHN]
CENTRAL BABOLE dial of BABOLE [BVX]
CENTRAL BAI alt for JIANCHUAN dial of BAI [PIQ]
CENTRAL BASSA dial of BASSA [BAS]
CENTRAL BAVARIAN dial of BAVARIAN [BAR]
CENTRAL BELARUSAN dial of BELARUSAN
    [RUW]
CENTRAL BÉTÉ alt for BÉTE, GUIBEROUA [BET]
CENTRAL BOHEMIAN dial of CZECH [CZC]
CENTRAL BOIKIN dial of BOIKIN [BZF]
CENTRAL BOLIVIAN QUECHUA alt for QUECHUA,
    SOUTH BOLIVIAN [QUH]
CENTRAL BOMITABA dial of BOMITABA [ZMX]
CENTRAL BUANG alt for BUANG, MAPOS [BZH]
CENTRAL BUNUN dial of BUNUN [BNN]
CENTRAL BURU dial of BURU [MHS]
CENTRAL CAMPIDANESE dial of SARDINIAN,
    CAMPIDANESE [SRO]
CENTRAL CARRIER alt for CARRIER [CAR]
CENTRAL CATALAN dial of CATALAN-
    VALENCIAN-BALEAR [CLN]
CENTRAL CHWABO dial of CHWABO [CHW]
CENTRAL COLLOQUIAL MAITHILI dial of MAITHILI
    [MKP]
CENTRAL CRIMEAN dial of CRIMEAN TURKISH
    [CRH]
CENTRAL CUMBERLAND dial of ENGLISH [ENG]
CENTRAL DAMARA dial of NAMA [NAQ]
CENTRAL DANGALEAT dial of DANGALEAT [DAA]
CENTRAL DANISH alt for DANISH [DNS]
CENTRAL DHATKI dial of DHATKI [MKI]
CENTRAL DINKA alt for DINKA, SOUTH CENTRAL
    [DIB]
CENTRAL DIODIO dial of DIODIO [DDI]
CENTRAL DOBU dial of DOBU [DOB]
CENTRAL EAST ALUNE dial of ALUNE [ALP]
CENTRAL EAST SASAK alt for NGENO-NGENE
    dial of SASAK [SAS]
CENTRAL EMILIANO dial of
    EMILIANO-ROMAGNOLO [EML]
CENTRAL ERSU alt for DUOXU dial of ERSU [ERS]
CENTRAL EXTREMADURAN dial of
    EXTREMADURAN [EXT]
CENTRAL GELAO alt for CAPE DRAPING GELAO
    dial of GELAO [KKF]
CENTRAL GOURMANCHEMA dial of
    GOURMANCHEMA [GUX]
CENTRAL GRAND VALLEY DANI alt for DANI, MID
    GRAND VALLEY [DNT]
CENTRAL GUANGDONG alt for YUEZHONG dial
    of CHINESE, HAKKA [HAK]
CENTRAL GUÉRÉ alt for WÈ SOUTHERN [GXX]

CENTRAL GUIZHOU alt for QIANZHONG dial of
BOUYEI [PCC]
CENTRAL HUANCAYO alt for WAYCHA dial of
QUECHUA, WANCA, HUAYLLA [QHU]
CENTRAL HUASTECA NÁHUATL dial of NAHUATL,
HUASTECA OESTE [NHW]
CENTRAL HUISHUI MIAO alt for HMONG,
CENTRAL HUISHUI [HMC]
CENTRAL IBIBIO dial of IBIBIO [IBB]
CENTRAL IGEDE alt for OJU dial of IGEDE [IGE]
CENTRAL ISAN dial of THAI, NORTHEASTERN
[TTS]
CENTRAL JIBBALI dial of JIBBALI [SHV]
CENTRAL JUXTLAHUACA MIXTECO alt for
MIXTECO, JUXTLAHUACA [VMC]
CENTRAL KADAZAN alt for DUSUN, CENTRAL
[DTP]
CENTRAL KAINGANG dial of KAINGANG [KGP]
CENTRAL KANKANAEY alt for KANKANAEY [KNE]
CENTRAL KANUM dial of KANUM, SOTA [KRZ]
CENTRAL KERALA dial of MALAYALAM [MJS]
CENTRAL KHMER dial of KHMER, CENTRAL [KMR]
CENTRAL KINNAURI alt for JANGSHUNG [JNA]
CENTRAL KINNAURI alt for SHUMCHO [SCU]
CENTRAL KINNAURI alt for SUNAM [SSK]
CENTRAL KLAOH dial of KLAO [KLU]
CENTRAL KOMA alt for KOMO [KOM]
CENTRAL KOMBA dial of KOMBA [KPF]
CENTRAL KOMBAI dial of KOMBAI [KGU]
CENTRAL KONGO dial of KONGO [KON]
CENTRAL KONKAN alt for KONKANI [KNK]
CENTRAL KONO dial of KONO [KNO]
CENTRAL KUMAUNI dial of KUMAUNI [KFY]
CENTRAL LAAMANG dial of LAMANG [HIA]
CENTRAL LADAKHI alt for LEH dial of LADAKHI
[LBJ]
CENTRAL LAGAIP dial of HEWA [HAM]
CENTRAL LATVIAN alt for WEST LATVIAN dial of
LATVIAN [LAT]
CENTRAL LELA alt for DABAI dial of CLELA [DRI]
CENTRAL LELE alt for KOUNTE LELE dial of LELE
[LLC]
CENTRAL LISU alt for LISU [LIS]
CENTRAL LYÉLÉ dial of LYELE [LEE]
CENTRAL MAFA dial of MAFA [MAF]
CENTRAL MAGAHI dial of MAGAHI [MQM]
CENTRAL MAKHUWA alt for MAKHUWA [VMW]
CENTRAL MAMASA dial of MAMASA [MQJ]
CENTRAL MANGGARAI dial of MANGGARAI [MQY]
CENTRAL MARCHIGIANO dial of ITALIAN [ITN]
CENTRAL MARING dial of MARING [MBW]
CENTRAL MARSELA alt for MASELA, CENTRAL
[MKH]
CENTRAL MASHAN MIAO alt for HMONG,
CENTRAL MASHAN [HMM]
CENTRAL MBO alt for BAKAKA [BQZ]
CENTRAL MBULA alt for MBULA dial of MBULA
[MNA]
CENTRAL METAFONETICA dial of SICILIAN [SCN]
CENTRAL MIAHUATLAN ZAPOTEC alt for
ZAPOTECO, MIAHUATLÁN CENTRAL [ZAM]

CENTRAL MIAO alt for HMONG, EASTERN
QIANDONG [HMQ]
CENTRAL MIAO alt for HMONG, NORTHERN
QIANDONG [HEA]
CENTRAL MIAO alt for HMONG, SOUTHERN
QIANDONG [HMS]
CENTRAL MIGABAC dial of MIGABAC [MPP]
CENTRAL MIN alt for CHINESE, MIN ZHONG [CZO]
CENTRAL MINNESOTA CHIPPEWA dial of
CHIPPEWA [CIW]
CENTRAL MIXE alt for MIXE, QUETZALTEPEC
[MVE]
CENTRAL MON alt for MATABAN-MOULMEIN
dial of MON [MNW]
CENTRAL MONGOLIAN alt for MONGOLIAN, HALH
[KHK]
CENTRAL MONPA alt for TSHANGLA [TSJ]
CENTRAL MOUNTAIN ALBANIAN dial of
ALBANIAN, ARBERESHE [AAE]
CENTRAL MUNJI dial of MUNJI [MNJ]
CENTRAL MURUT alt for KENINGAU MURUT [KXI]
CENTRAL NAJDI dial of ARABIC, NAJDI SPOKEN
[ARS]
CENTRAL NGADA dial of NGADA [NXG]
CENTRAL NOCHISTLÁN MIXTECO alt for
MIXTECO, DIUXI-TILANTONGO [MIS]
CENTRAL NOGAI dial of NOGAI [NOG]
CENTRAL NORWEGIAN dial of NORWEGIAN,
BOKMAAL [NRR]
CENTRAL NUSU dial of NUSU [NUF]
CENTRAL OCOTLÁN ZAPOTECO alt for
ZAPOTECO, OCOTLÁN OESTE [ZAC]
CENTRAL OJIBWE alt for OJIBWA, CENTRAL
[OJC]
CENTRAL OROMO dial of OROMO, WEST-
CENTRAL [GAZ]
CENTRAL PAME alt for PAME CENTRAL [PBS]
CENTRAL PATTANI dial of PATTANI [LAE]
CENTRAL POCOMAM alt for POKOMAM,
CENTRAL [POC]
CENTRAL PRASUN dial of PRASUNI [PRN]
CENTRAL PUEBLA AZTEC alt for NÁHUATL,
PUEBLA CENTRAL [NCX]
CENTRAL PUEBLA MIXTECO alt for MIXTECO,
CHIGMACATITLÁN [MII]
CENTRAL RAGA alt for APMA [APP]
CENTRAL "SAKAI" pejorative alt for SEMAI [SEA]
CENTRAL SANGTAM alt for THUKUMI dial of
NAGA, SANGTAM [NSA]
CENTRAL SARDINIAN alt for SARDINIAN,
LOGUDORESE [SRD]
CENTRAL SASAK alt for MENO-MENE dial of
SASAK [SAS]
CENTRAL SAWOS dial of MALINGUAT [SIC]
CENTRAL SEDANG dial of SEDANG [SED]
CENTRAL SEL'KUP alt for NARYM dial of SELKUP
[SAK]
CENTRAL SELK'UP alt for TYM dial of SELKUP
[SAK]
CENTRAL SENTANI dial of SENTANI [SET]
CENTRAL SEWA BAY dial of SEWA BAY [SEW]

CENTRAL SHILHA alt for TAMAZIGHT, CENTRAL ATLAS [TZM]
CENTRAL SIKKA alt for SARA KROWE dial of SIKA [SKI]
CENTRAL SINAMA alt for SAMA, CENTRAL [SML]
CENTRAL SINDHI alt for VICHOLO dial of SINDHI [SND]
CENTRAL SOLA DE VEGA ZAPOTECO alt for ZAPOTECO, TEXMELUCAN [ZPZ]
CENTRAL SONGAI alt for SONGHAY [HMB]
CENTRAL SONGAI alt for SONGHAY, HUMBURI SENNI [HMB]
CENTRAL SOQOTRI dial of SOQOTRI [SQT]
CENTRAL SOUTH SASAK alt for MRIAK-MRIKU dial of SASAK [SAS]
CENTRAL SYRIAN ARABIC dial of ARABIC, NORTH LEVANTINE SPOKEN [APC]
CENTRAL TABUKANG dial of SANGIR [SAN]
CENTRAL TAI alt for THAI [THJ]
CENTRAL TALYSHI dial of TALYSH [TLY]
CENTRAL TARAHUMARASAMACHIQUE TARAHUMARA alt for TARAHUMARA CENTRAL [TAR]
CENTRAL TÀY dial of TAY [THO]
CENTRAL THARAKA alt for NTUGI dial of THARAKA [THA]
CENTRAL TIBETAN alt for TIBETAN [TIC]
CENTRAL TIGAK dial of TIGAK [TGC]
CENTRAL TIMBE dial of TIMBE [TIM]
CENTRAL TUVIN dial of TUVIN [TUN]
CENTRAL UDAB dial of FUYUG [FUY]
CENTRAL UMA alt for KANTEWU dial of UMA [PPK]
CENTRAL URAT alt for WUSYEP YEHRE dial of URAT [URT]
CENTRAL UYGHUR dial of UYGHUR [UIG]
CENTRAL VANUA LEVU dial of FIJIAN [FJI]
CENTRAL VEPS dial of VEPS [VEP]
CENTRAL VIETNAMESE dial of VIETNAMESE [VIE]
CENTRAL VILLA ALTA ZAPOTECO alt for ZAPOTECO, TABAA [ZAT]
CENTRAL VIVIGANI dial of IDUNA [VIV]
CENTRAL VLAX ROMANI dial of ROMANI, VLAX [RMY]
CENTRAL WAIBUK dial of HARUAI [TMD]
CENTRAL WAKHI dial of WAKHI [WBL]
CENTRAL WANTOAT dial of WANTOAT [WNC]
CENTRAL WEST ALUNE dial of ALUNE [ALP]
CENTRAL WEST GURAGE alt for GURAGE, WEST [GUY]
CENTRAL WEST SASAK alt for NGENO-NGENE dial of SASAK [SAS]
CENTRAL WESTERN TUNISIAN ARABIC dial of ARABIC, TUNISIAN SPOKEN [AEB]
CENTRAL YAMALELE dial of IAMALELE [YML]
CENTRAL YAWA dial of YAWA [YVA]
CENTRAL-EASTERN TAMANG dial of TAMANG, EASTERN [TAJ]
CENTRAL-WESTERN AGRIGENTINO alt for WESTERN SICILIAN dial of SICILIAN [SCN]

CENTRAL-WESTERN IJO alt for IZON [IJC]
CENTÚÚM [CET] lang, Nigeria
CEP dial of ACIPA, WESTERN [AWC]
CERMA [GOT] lang, Burkina Faso; also in Côte d'Ivoire
CERUMBA dial of SHWAI [SHW]
CESTINA alt for CZECH [CZC]
CETA alt for HMWAVEKE [MRK]
CEVENDA alt for VENDA [VEN]
CEWA alt for CHEWA dial of NYANJA [NYJ]
CEWA alt for CHICHEWA dial of NYANJA [NYJ]
CEZ alt for DIDO [DDO]
CHA' dial of LAIMBUE [LMX]
CHA' PALAACHI alt for CHACHI [CBI]
CHAARI alt for DANSHE dial of ZEEM [ZUA]
CHABAKANO alt for CHAVACANO [CBK]
CHABAO dial of JIARONG [JYA]
CHACHI [CBI] lang, Ecuador
CHACO PILAGÁ dial of PILAGA [PLG]
CHACO SUR alt for TOBA [TOB]
CHÁCOBO [CAO] lang, Bolivia
CHAD ARABIC alt for ARABIC, CHADIAN SPOKEN [SHU]
CHADIAN ARABIC alt for ARABIC, CHADIAN SPOKEN [SHU]
CHADIAN ARABIC alt for ARABIC, SHUWA [SHU]
CHADIAN SIGN LANGUAGE [CDS] lang, Chad
CHADIAN SPOKEN ARABIC alt for ARABIC, SHUWA [SHU]
CHADIC ARABIC alt for ARABIC, SHUWA [SHU]
CHAGA alt for CHAGGA [KAF]
CHAGATAI [CGT] lang, Turkmenistan
CHAGATAI alt for TEKE dial of TURKMEN [TCK]
CHAGGA [KAF] lang, Tanzania
CHAGHATAY alt for CHAGATAI [CGT]
CHAHA dial of GURAGE, WEST [GUY]
CHAHA'ER alt for CHAHAR dial of MONGOLIAN, PERIPHERAL [MVF]
CHAHAR dial of MONGOLIAN, PERIPHERAL [MVF]
CHAHAR-AIMAQ alt for AIMAQ [AIQ]
CHAHI dial of NYATURU [RIM]
CHAI dial of SURI [SUQ]
CHAIBASA-THAKURMUNDA dial of HO [HOC]
CHAIL dial of TORWALI [TRW]
CHAIMA alt for CHAYMA dial of CARIB [CRB]
CHAK [CKH] lang, Myanmar; also in Bangladesh
CHAK dial of GHALE, KUTANG [GHT]
CHAKALI [CLI] lang, Ghana
CHAKAMA alt for CHAKMA [CCP]
CHAKAVIAN dial of SERBO-CROATIAN [SRC]
CHAKAVSKI dial of CROATIAN [SRC]
CHAKFEM alt for CAKFEM-MUSHERE [CKY]
CHAKHAR alt for CHAHAR dial of MONGOLIAN, PERIPHERAL [MVF]
CHAKHESANG alt for NAGA, CHOKRI [NRI]
CHAKMA [CCP] lang, India; also in Bangladesh
CHAKOSI alt for ANUFO [CKO]
CHAKPA dial of KADO [KDV]
CHAKRIABA alt for XAKRIABÁ [XKR]
CHAKRIMA NAGA alt for NAGA, CHOKRI [NRI]
CHAKROMA dial of NAGA, ANGAMI [NJM]

CHAKRU alt for NAGA, CHOKRI [NRI]
CHAL alt for RUTUL [RUT]
"CHALA" pejorative alt for RON [CLA]
CHALA [CHA] lang, Ghana
CHALAH dial of CHRAU [CHR]
CHALAS dial of PASHAYI, NORTHEAST [AEE]
CHALDEAN alt for CHALDEAN NEO-ARAMAIC
    [CLD]
CHALDEAN NEO-ARAMAIC [CLD] lang, Iraq; also in
    Australia, Belgium, Canada, Germany, Lebanon,
    Netherlands, Sweden, Syria, Turkey (Asia), USA
CHALGARI alt for WANECI [WNE]
CHALI alt for CHALIKHA [TGF]
CHALI alt for TRI dial of BRU, EASTERN [BRU]
CHALI dial of KOMO [KOM]
CHALI dial of SO [SSS]
CHALIKHA [TGF] lang, Bhutan
CHALIPKHA alt for CHALIKHA [TGF]
"CHALLA" pejorative alt for RON [CLA]
CHALUN dial of CHRAU [CHR]
CHAM alt for CHAM, WESTERN [CJA]
CHAM alt for CHING dial of MAK [MKG]
CHAM alt for DIJIM dial of DIJIM-BWILIM [CFA]
CHAM dial of IU MIEN [IUM]
CHAM CHANG alt for NAGA, TASE [NST]
CHAM, EASTERN [CJM] lang, Viet Nam; also in
    USA
CHAM, WESTERN [CJA] lang, Cambodia; also in
    Australia, France, Indonesia, Libya, Malaysia,
    Saudi Arabia, Thailand, USA, Viet Nam, Yemen
"CHAMA" pejorative alt for ESE EJJA [ESE]
CHAMACOCO [CEG] lang, Paraguay
CHAMACOCO BRAVO dial of CHAMACOCO [CEG]
CHAMALAL [CJI] lang, Russia (Europe)
CHAMALIN alt for CHAMALAL [CJI]
CHAMAN alt for MANG [MGA]
CHAMAR alt for CHAMARI [CDG]
CHAMARI [CDG] lang, India
CHAMARWA alt for HARYANVI [BGC]
CHAMAYA alt for CHAMBEALI [CDH]
CHAMBA alt for AKASELEM [AKS]
CHAMBA alt for PATTANI [LAE]
CHAMBA DAKA alt for SAMBA DAKA [CCG]
CHAMBA LAHULI alt for PATTANI [LAE]
CHAMBA LEEKO alt for SAMBA LEKO [NDI]
CHAMBA LEKO alt for SAMBA LEKO [NDI]
CHAMBA-LAJULI dial of PATTANI [LAE]
CHAMBEALI [CDH] lang, India
CHAMBHAR BOLI alt for CHAMARI [CDG]
CHAMBHARI alt for CHAMARI [CDG]
CHAMBIALI alt for CHAMBEALI [CDH]
CHAMBIYALI alt for CHAMBEALI [CDH]
CHAMBOA alt for KARAJÁ [KPJ]
CHAMBRI [CAN] lang, Papua New Guinea
CHAMI alt for EMBERÁ-CHAMÍ [CMI]
CHAMICOLO alt for CHAMICURO [CCC]
CHAMICURA alt for CHAMICURO [CCC]
CHAMICURO [CCC] lang, Peru
CHAMIYALI PAHARI alt for CHAMBEALI [CDH]
CHAMLING alt for CAMLING [RAB]
CHAMLINGE RAI alt for CAMLING [RAB]

CHAMO alt for CAMO dial of KUDU-CAMO [KOV]
CHAMORRO [CJD] lang, Guam; also in Northern
    Mariana Islands
CHAMORRO dial of CHAMORRO [CJD]
CHAMPHUNG alt for NAGA, TANGKHUL [NMF]
CHAM-RE alt for HRE [HRE]
CHAMULA alt for TZOTZIL, CHAMULA [TZC]
CHAMUS dial of SAMBURU [SAQ]
CHAMYA alt for CHAMBEALI [CDH]
CHAN alt for LAZ [LZZ]
CHANA alt for CHINALI [CIH]
CHANA alt for GUANA [QKS]
CHAÑABAL alt for TOJOLABAL [TOJ]
CHANAL alt for TZELTAL, OXCHUC [TZH]
CHANCO alt for WOUN MEU [NOA]
CHANDARI dial of HALBI [HLB]
CHANDINAHUA dial of SHARANAHUA [MCD]
CHANÉ [CAJ] lang, Argentina
CHANÉ dial of GUARANI, ARGENTINE, WESTERN
    [GUI]
CHANG alt for NAGA, CHANG [NBC]
CHANG dial of KUY [KDT]
CHANG CHÁ alt for BOUYEI [PCC]
CHANGA alt for CHANGANA dial of TSONGA [TSO]
CHANGA alt for SHANGA dial of NDAU [NDC]
CHANGA dial of NDAU [NDC]
CHANGANA alt for TSONGA [TSO]
CHANGANA dial of TSONGA [TSO]
CHANG-JING dial of CHINESE, GAN [KNN]
CHANGKI dial of NAGA, AO [NJO]
CHANGNOI dial of NAGA, WANCHO [NNP]
CHANGNYU dial of NAGA, KONYAK [NBE]
CHANGO alt for SANGU [SNQ]
CHANGRIWA [CGA] lang, Papua New Guinea
CHANGSAPA BOLI alt for PATTANI [LAE]
CHANGSEN dial of CHIN, THADO [TCZ]
CHANGS-SKAT alt for CHANGTHANG [CNA]
CHANGTANG alt for CHANGTHANG [CNA]
CHANGTANG LADAKHI alt for CHANGTHANG
    [CNA]
CHANGTHANG [CNA] lang, India
CHANGYANGUH alt for NAGA, CHANG [NBC]
CHANGYI dial of CHINESE, XIANG [HSN]
CHANKA alt for QUECHUA, AYACUCHO [QUY]
CHANNALI alt for CHINALI [CIH]
CHANTEL alt for CHANTYAL [CHX]
CHANTYAL [CHX] lang, Nepal
CHANURI alt for LAZ [LZZ]
CHANZAN alt for LAZ [LZZ]
CHAO KONG MENG alt for JIAOGONG MIAN dial
    of BIAO-JIAO MIEN [BJE]
"CHAOBON" pejorative alt for NYAHKUR [CBN]
CHAOCHA PAI alt for KOREGUAJE [COE]
CHAOCHOW alt for CHAOZHOU dial of CHINESE,
    MIN NAN [CFR]
CHAOCHOW alt for TEOCHEW dial of CHINESE,
    MIN NAN [CFR]
CHAOCHOW dial of CHINESE, MIN NAN [CFR]
"CHAODON" pejorative alt for NYAHKUR [CBN]
CHAO-SHAN dial of CHINESE, MIN NAN [CFR]
CHAOUE alt for SHOE dial of MPADE [MPI]

CHAOUIA [SHY] lang, Algeria
CHAOZHOU alt for TEOCHEW dial of CHINESE, MIN NAN [CFR]
CHAOZHOU dial of CHINESE, MIN NAN [CFR]
CHAPAI alt for CHUJ, SAN MATEO IXTATÁN [CNM]
CHAPARA dial of CANDOSHI-SHAPRA [CBU]
CHAPLINO dial of YUPIK, CENTRAL SIBERIAN [ESS]
CHAPOGIR alt for EVENKI [EVN]
CHAPULTENANGO dial of ZOQUE, FRANCISCO LEON [ZOS]
"CHAPURREÁU" pejorative alt for FALA [FAX]
CHAR alt for ZAKATALY dial of AVAR [AVR]
CHAR alt for ZAQATALA dial of AVAR [AVR]
CHAR AIMAQ alt for AIMAQ [AIQ]
CHARA [CRA] lang, Ethiopia
CHARA alt for CARA [CFD]
CHARANI dial of BHILI [BHB]
CHARARANA alt for ECHOALDI dial of GUANA [GVA]
CHARAZANI dial of QUECHUA, NORTH BOLIVIAN [QUL]
CHARBERD alt for KHARBERD dial of ARMENIAN [ARM]
CHARI alt for CHALI dial of SO [SSS]
CHARI CHONG dial of CHIN, FALAM [HBH]
CHARIAR alt for AKA-CARI [ACI]
CHARI-BAGUIRMI dial of ARABIC, CHADIAN SPOKEN [SHU]
CHAROTARI alt for GAMADIA dial of GUJARATI [GJR]
CHARUMBUL alt for BAYALI [BJY]
CHASAN YAO alt for KIM MUN [MJI]
CHASHAN alt for LASHI [LSI]
CHASHAN YAO alt for LAKKIA [LBC]
CHASHANHUA alt for LASHI [LSI]
CHASI alt for WASI [WBJ]
CHASU alt for ASU [ASA]
CHATANS alt for ALLAR [ALL]
CHATGAM alt for LITIPARA dial of SAURIA PAHARIA [MJT]
CHATINO DE LA ZONA ALTA OCCIDENTAL alt for CHATINO, SIERRA OCCIDENTAL [CTP]
CHATINO, NOPALA [CYA] lang, Mexico
CHATINO, SIERRA OCCIDENTAL [CTP] lang, Mexico
CHATINO, SIERRA ORIENTAL [CLY] lang, Mexico
CHATINO, TATALTEPEC [CTA] lang, Mexico
CHATINO, ZACATEPEC [CTZ] lang, Mexico
CHATINO, ZENZONTEPEC [CZE] lang, Mexico
CHATTARE dial of LIMBU [LIF]
CHATTHARE alt for CHATTARE dial of LIMBU [LIF]
CHATTHARE YAKTHUNGBA PAN alt for CHATTARE dial of LIMBU [LIF]
CHAU KO' alt for MOKEN [MWT]
CHAU POK alt for MOKLEN [MKM]
CHAUDANGSI [CDN] lang, India; also in Nepal
CHAUDHARI alt for CHODRI [CDI]
CHAUDRI alt for CHODRI [CDI]
CHAUGARKHIYA dial of KUMAUNI [KFY]
CHAUMA alt for MAA [CMA]

CHAUN dial of CHUKOT [CKT]
CHAUNGTHA [CCQ] lang, Myanmar
CHAUPAL alt for SURAJPURI [SJP]
CHAURA [CHO] lang, India
CHAURAHI alt for CHURAHI [CDJ]
CHAURASIA alt for CHOURASE [TSU]
CHAURASYA alt for CHOURASE [TSU]
CHAURO alt for CHRAU [CHR]
CHAVACANO [CBK] lang, Philippines; also in Malaysia (Sabah)
CHAVACANO alt for ZAMBOANGUEÑO dial of CHAVACANO [CBK]
CHAVANTE alt for OTI [OTI]
CHAVANTE alt for XAVÁNTE [XAV]
CHAVCHUVEN alt for CAVCUVENSKIJ dial of KORYAK [KPY]
CHAVDUR dial of TURKMEN [TCK]
CHAW TALAY alt for URAK LAWOI' [URK]
CHAWAI alt for ATSAM [CCH]
CHAWE alt for ATSAM [CCH]
CHAWI alt for ATSAM [CCH]
CHAWI alt for CHAYAHUITA [CBT]
CHAWIA dial of TAITA [DAV]
CHAWIYANA alt for HIXKARYÁNA [HIX]
CHAWNAM alt for URAK LAWOI' [URK]
CHAWNG alt for CHONG [COG]
CHAWTE alt for NAGA, CHOTHE [NCT]
"CHAWUNCU" pejorative alt for GUARANÍ, ARGENTINE, WESTERN [GUI]
"CHAWUNCU" pejorative alt for GUARANÍ, BOLIVIAN, EASTERN [GUI]
CHAYABITA alt for CHAYAHUITA [CBT]
CHAYAHUITA [CBT] lang, Peru
CHAYAHUITA dial of CHAYAHUITA [CBT]
CHAYAWITA alt for CHAYAHUITA [CBT]
CHAYHUITA alt for CHAYAHUITA [CBT]
CHAYMA dial of CARIB [CRB]
CHAYUCU MIXTECO alt for MIXTECO, CHAYUCO [MIH]
CHAZUMBA MIXTEC alt for MIXTECO, CHAZUMBA [QMB]
CHE [RUK] lang, Nigeria
CHE MA alt for MAA [CMA]
CHEBERLOI dial of CHECHEN [CJC]
CHEBERO alt for JEBERO [JEB]
CHECHEK alt for DREHET dial of KHEHEK [TLX]
CHECHEN [CJC] lang, Russia (Europe); also in Georgia, Germany, Jordan, Kazakhstan, Kyrgyzstan, Syria, Turkey (Asia), Uzbekistan
CHECK-CULL alt for DYAABUGAY [DYY]
CHEDEPO dial of GREBO, NORTHERN [GRB]
CHEDI alt for LISU [LIS]
CHEHA alt for CHAHA dial of GURAGE, WEST [GUY]
CHEHALIS alt for CHEHALIS, UPPER [CJH]
CHEHALIS, LOWER [CEA] lang, USA
CHEHALIS, UPPER [CJH] lang, USA
CHEHEK alt for DREHET dial of KHEHEK [TLX]
CHE-HWAN alt for TAROKO [TRV]
CHEJU ISLAND dial of KOREAN [KKN]
CHEKE alt for GUDE [GDE]

CHEKE HOLO [MRN] lang, Solomon Islands
CHEKIRI alt for ISEKIRI [ITS]
CHELAN alt for WENATCHI dial of COLUMBIA-
WENATCHI [COL]
CHELI alt for LISU [LIS]
CHEMANT alt for QIMANT dial of AGAW, WESTERN
[QIM]
CHEMEHUEVI dial of UTE-SOUTHERN PAIUTE
[UTE]
CHEMGUI alt for BEZHEDUKH dial of ADYGHE
[ADY]
CHEN dial of NAGA, KONYAK [NBE]
CHENA dial of TANANA, LOWER [TAA]
CHENALÓ alt for TZOTZIL, CH'ENALHÓ [TZE]
CHENAP alt for CHENAPIAN [CJN]
CHENAPIAN [CJN] lang, Papua New Guinea
CHENBA'ERHU dial of EVENKI [EVN]
CHENBEROM alt for BEROM [BOM]
CHENCHU [CDE] lang, India
CHENCHUCOOLAM alt for CHENCHU [CDE]
CHENCHWAR alt for CHENCHU [CDE]
CHENG alt for JENG [JEG]
CHENGKUNG-KWANGSHAN dial of AMIS [ALV]
CHENOUA [CHB] lang, Algeria
CHENSWAR alt for CHENCHU [CDE]
CHENTEL alt for CHANTYAL [CHX]
CHEPANG [CDM] lang, Nepal
CHEQ WONG alt for CHEWONG [CWG]
CHERANGANY dial of KALENJIN [KLN]
CHERE alt for SERE [SWF]
CHEREMIS alt for MARI, LOW [MAL]
CHEREMISS alt for MARI, HIGH [MRJ]
CHEREPON [CPN] lang, Ghana
CHERES alt for ULU CERES dial of JAH HUT [JAH]
CHERIBON alt for CIREBON dial of JAVANESE
[JAN]
CHERII dial of WALI [WLX]
CHERKES alt for ADYGHE [ADY]
CHERKES dial of KABARDIAN [KAB]
CHEROKEE [CER] lang, USA
CHERRAPUNJI alt for KHASI dial of KHASI [KHI]
CHERRAPUNJI dial of KHASI [KHI]
CHERRE alt for KARO [KXH]
CHESO alt for WESTERN ARAGONESE dial of
ARAGONESE [AXX]
CHETA alt for XETÁ [XET]
CHETCO [CHE] lang, USA
CHEVA alt for CHEWA dial of NYANJA [NYJ]
CHEWA alt for CHICHEWA dial of NYANJA [NYJ]
CHEWA alt for NYANJA [NYJ]
CHEWA dial of NYANJA [NYJ]
CHEWLIE alt for DYAABUGAY [DYY]
CHEWONG [CWG] lang, Malaysia (Peninsular)
CHE'WONG alt for CHEWONG [CWG]
CHEYENNE [CHY] lang, USA
CHHAPKOA dial of KULUNG [KLE]
CHHATHAR alt for CHATTARE dial of LIMBU [LIF]
CHHATTARE alt for CHATTARE dial of LIMBU [LIF]
CHHATTISGARHI [HNE] lang, India
CHHATTISGARHI PROPER dial of
CHHATTISGARHI [HNE]

CHHIKA-CHHIKI alt for ANGIKA [ANP]
CHHILLING alt for CHHULUNG [CUR]
CHHINDWARA BUNDELI dial of BUNDELI [BNS]
CHHINTANG [CTN] lang, Nepal
CHHINTANG dial of BANTAWA [BAP]
CHHINTANGE alt for CHHINTANG [CTN]
CHHOLUNG alt for CHHULUNG [CUR]
CHHORI alt for CHIRU [CDF]
CHHULUNG [CUR] lang, Nepal
CHHÛLÛNG RÛNG alt for CHHULUNG [CUR]
CHI dial of MAK [MKG]
CH'IANG alt for QIANG, NORTHERN [CNG]
CH'IANG alt for QIANG, SOUTHERN [QMR]
CHIANGMAI SIGN LANGUAGE [CSD] lang, Thailand
CHIANGRAI dial of IU MIEN [IUM]
CHIAPANECO [CIP] lang, Mexico
CHIARONG alt for JIARONG [JYA]
CHIASU alt for ASU [ASA]
CHIBABAVA alt for DONDO dial of NDAU [NDC]
CHIBBAK alt for CIBAK [CKL]
CHIBBUK alt for CIBAK [CKL]
CHIBCHA [CBF] lang, Colombia
CHIBEMBA alt for BEMBA [BEM]
CHIBHALI alt for PAHARI-POTWARI [PHR]
CHIBHALI dial of PAHARI-POTWARI [PHR]
CHIBITO alt for HIBITO [HIB]
CHIBOK alt for CIBAK [CKL]
CHIBUK alt for CIBAK [CKL]
CHICANO alt for YUWANA [YAU]
CHICAO alt for TXIKÃO [TXI]
CHICHAMACHU alt for BAJELAN [BJM]
CHICHANGA alt for CHANGA dial of NDAU [NDC]
CHICHANGA alt for SHANGA dial of NDAU [NDC]
CHICHAWA alt for YAO [YAO]
CHICHEWA alt for CHEWA dial of NYANJA [NYJ]
CHICHEWA dial of NYANJA [NYJ]
CHICHIMECA alt for CHICHIMECA-JONAZ [PEI]
CHICHIMECA-JONAZ [PEI] lang, Mexico
CHICHIMECA-PAME CENTRAL alt for PAME
CENTRAL [PBS]
CHICHIMECO alt for CHICHIMECA-JONAZ [PEI]
CHICHIQUILA NÁHUATL alt for NÁHUATL,
HUAXCALECA [NHQ]
CHICHONYI alt for CHONYI [COH]
CHICHWABO alt for CHWABO [CHW]
CHICKASAW [CIC] lang, USA
CHICOMUCELTEC [COB] lang, Mexico; also in
Guatemala
CHICOMULCELTECO alt for CHICOMUCELTEC
[COB]
CHICUNDA alt for KUNDA [KDN]
CHIDIGO alt for DIGO [DIG]
CHIECH alt for CIEC dial of DINKA, SOUTH
CENTRAL [DIB]
CHIEHN alt for TCHIEN dial of KRAHN, EASTERN
[KQO]
CHIEM alt for CHAM, EASTERN [CJM]
CHIEM alt for CHAM, WESTERN [CJA]
CHIEM THÀNH alt for CHAM, EASTERN [CJM]
CHIENGMAI SIGN LANGUAGE alt for CHIANGMAI
SIGN LANGUAGE [CSD]

CHIENTUNG MIAO alt for HMONG, NORTHERN QIANDONG [HEA]
CHIGA [CHG] lang, Uganda
CHIGMACATITLÁN MIXTEC alt for MIXTECO, CHIGMACATITLÁN [MII]
CHIGOGO alt for GOGO [GOG]
CHIILA alt for ILA [ILB]
CHIK BARIK alt for PANCHPARGANIA [TDB]
CHIKAGULU alt for KAGULU [KKI]
CHIKAHONDE alt for KAONDE [KQN]
CHIKALANGA alt for KALANGA [KCK]
CHIKAMANGA dial of TUMBUKA [TUW]
CHIKANO alt for YUWANA [YAU]
CHIKAONDE alt for KAONDE [KQN]
CHIKARANGA alt for KARANGA dial of SHONA [SHD]
CHIKENA alt for SIKIANA [SIK]
CHIKIDE alt for CIKIDE dial of GUDUF [GDF]
CHIKIDE alt for CIKIDE dial of GUDUF-GAVA [GDF]
CHIKOBO alt for IZORA [CBO]
CHIKRIABA alt for XAKRIABÁ [XKR]
CHIKUAHANE alt for SUBIYA [SBS]
CHIKUNDA alt for KUNDA [KDN]
CHIKUNDA dial of NYANJA [NYJ]
CHIKUYA alt for TEKE, SOUTHERN [KKW]
CHIKWAHANE alt for SUBIYA [SBS]
CHIL dial of KOHO [KPM]
CHIL dial of MNONG, EASTERN [MNG]
CHILALA alt for C'LELA [DRI]
CHILAMBA alt for LAMBA [LAB]
CHILAO alt for GELAO [KKF]
CHILAPALAPA dial of FANAGOLO [FAO]
CHILAS alt for CHALAS dial of PASHAYI, NORTH-EAST [AEE]
CHILAS alt for CHILASI KOHISTANI dial of SHINA [SCL]
CHILASI KOHISTANI dial of SHINA [SCL]
CHILCOTIN [CHI] lang, Canada
CHILEAN SIGN LANGUAGE [CSG] lang, Chile
CHILELA alt for C'LELA [DRI]
CHILENJE alt for LENJE [LEH]
CHILISS alt for CHILISSO [CLH]
CHILISSO [CLH] lang, Pakistan
CHILIWACK dial of HALKOMELEM [HUR]
CHILOWE alt for LOMWE [NGL]
CHILU WUNDA alt for RUUND [RND]
CHILUCHAZI alt for LUCHAZI [LCH]
CHILUIMBI alt for LUIMBI [LUM]
CHILUNDA alt for LUNDA [LVN]
CHILUVALE alt for LUVALE [LUE]
CHILUWUNDA alt for RUUND [RND]
CHIMAKONDE alt for MAKONDE [KDE]
CHIMANÉ alt for TSIMANÉ [CAS]
CHIMA-NISHEY dial of WAIGALI [WBK]
CHIMANYIKA alt for MANYIKA [MXC]
CHIMARIKO [CID] lang, USA
CHIMATENGO alt for MATENGO [MGV]
CHIMAVIHA alt for MAVIHA dial of MAKONDE [KDE]
CHIMBA alt for ZEMBA [DHM]
CHIMBALAZI alt for BAJUNI dial of SWAHILI [SWA]

CHIMBARI alt for SIMBARI [SMB]
CHIMBIAN dial of MALINGUAT [SIC]
CHIMBU alt for KUMAN [KUE]
CHIMBULUK dial of BUANG, MAPOS [BZH]
CHIMBUNDA alt for MBUNDA [MCK]
CHIMILA [CBG] lang, Colombia
CHIMMEZYAN alt for TSIMSHIAN [TSI]
CHIMONA dial of MANAGALASI [MCQ]
CHIMPOTO alt for MPOTO [MPA]
CHIMWERA alt for MWERA [MWE]
CHIMWIINI alt for MWINI dial of SWAHILI [SWA]
CHIN, ASHO [CSH] lang, Myanmar; also in Bangladesh
CHIN, BAWM [BGR] lang, India; also in Bangladesh, Myanmar
CHIN, CHINBON [CNB] lang, Myanmar
CHIN, DAAI [DAO] lang, Myanmar
CHIN, FALAM [HBH] lang, Myanmar; also in Bangladesh, India
CHIN, HAKA [CNH] lang, Myanmar; also in Bangladesh, India
CHIN, KHUMI [CKM] lang, Myanmar; also in Bangladesh, India
CHIN, KHUMI AWA [CKA] lang, Myanmar
CHIN, MARA [MRH] lang, India; also in Myanmar
CHIN, MRO [CMR] lang, Myanmar; also in Bangladesh
CHIN, MÜN [MWQ] lang, Myanmar
CHIN, NGAWN [CNW] lang, Myanmar
CHIN, PAITE [PCK] lang, India; also in Myanmar
CHIN, SENTHANG [SEZ] lang, Myanmar
CHIN, SIYIN [CSY] lang, Myanmar
CHIN, TAWR [TCP] lang, Myanmar
CHIN, TEDIM [CTD] lang, Myanmar; also in India
CHIN, THADO [TCZ] lang, India; also in Myanmar
CHIN, ZOTUNG [CZT] lang, Myanmar
CHINAL alt for CHINALI [CIH]
CHINALI [CIH] lang, India
CHINAMBYA alt for NAMBYA [NMQ]
CHINAMUKUNI alt for LENJE [LEH]
CHINAMWANGA alt for MWANGA [MWN]
CHINANTECO, CHILTEPEC [CSA] lang, Mexico
CHINANTECO, COMALTEPEC [CCO] lang, Mexico
CHINANTECO, LALANA [CNL] lang, Mexico
CHINANTECO, LEALAO [CLE] lang, Mexico
CHINANTECO, OJITLÁN [CHJ] lang, Mexico
CHINANTECO, OZUMACÍN [CHZ] lang, Mexico
CHINANTECO, PALANTLA [CPA] lang, Mexico
CHINANTECO, QUIOTEPEC [CHQ] lang, Mexico
CHINANTECO, SOCHIAPAN [CSO] lang, Mexico
CHINANTECO, TEPETOTUTLA [CNT] lang, Mexico
CHINANTECO, TEPINAPA [CTE] lang, Mexico
CHINANTECO, TLACOATZINTEPEC [CTL] lang, Mexico
CHINANTECO, USILA [CUS] lang, Mexico
CHINANTECO, VALLE NACIONAL [CHV] lang, Mexico
CHINATÚ TARAHUMARA dial of TARAHUMARA, SURESTE [TCU]
"CHINBOK" pejorative alt for CHIN, MÜN [MWQ]
CHINBON alt for CHIN, CHINBON [CNB]

CHINDAU alt for NDAU [NDC]
CHINDERI alt for SOUTHERN CHUMBURUNG
  dial of CHUMBURUNG [NCU]
CHINDWARA dial of GONDI, NORTHERN
  [GON]
CHINDWIN CHIN alt for CHIN, CHINBON [CNB]
CHINESE INDONESIAN alt for INDONESIAN,
  PERANAKAN [PEA]
CHINESE MALAY alt for MALAY, BABA [BAL]
CHINESE NUNG alt for CHINESE, YUE [YUH]
CHINESE PIDGIN ENGLISH [CPE] lang, Nauru
CHINESE SHAN alt for TAI NÜA [TDD]
CHINESE SIGN LANGUAGE [CSL] lang, China;
  also in Malaysia, Taiwan
CHINESE TAI alt for TAI NÜA [TDD]
CHINESE, GAN [KNN] lang, China
CHINESE, HAKKA [HAK] lang, China; also in Brunei,
  French Guiana, French Polynesia, Indonesia
  (Java and Bali), Malaysia (Peninsular), Mauritius,
  New Zealand, Panama, Singapore, South Africa,
  Suriname, Taiwan, Thailand, United Kingdom,
  USA
CHINESE, HUIZHOU [CZH] lang, China
CHINESE, JINYU [CJY] lang, China
CHINESE, MANDARIN [CHN] lang, China; also in
  Brunei, Cambodia, Indonesia (Java and Bali),
  Laos, Malaysia (Peninsular), Mauritius, Mongolia,
  Philippines, Russia (Asia), Singapore, Taiwan,
  Thailand, United Kingdom, USA, Viet Nam
CHINESE, MIN BEI [MNP] lang, China; also in
  Singapore
CHINESE, MIN DONG [CDO] lang, China; also in
  Brunei, Indonesia (Java and Bali), Malaysia
  (Peninsular), Singapore, Thailand
CHINESE, MIN NAN [CFR] lang, China; also in
  Brunei, Indonesia (Java and Bali), Malaysia
  (Peninsular), Philippines, Singapore, Taiwan,
  Thailand, USA
CHINESE, MIN ZHONG [CZO] lang, China
CHINESE, PU-XIAN [CPX] lang, China; also in
  Malaysia (Peninsular), Singapore
CHINESE, WU [WUU] lang, China
CHINESE, XIANG [HSN] lang, China
CHINESE, YUE [YUH] lang, China; also in Australia,
  Brunei, Canada, Costa Rica, Honduras, Indonesia
  (Java and Bali), Macau, Malaysia (Peninsular),
  Mauritius, Nauru, Netherlands, New Zealand,
  Panama, Philippines, Singapore, South Africa,
  Thailand, United Kingdom, USA, Viet Nam
CHING alt for MAK [MKG]
CHING alt for VIETNAMESE [VIE]
CHING dial of MAK [MKG]
CHING MIAO alt for TAK MIAO dial of HMONG
  NJUA [BLU]
CHINGA alt for TSINGA dial of TUKI [BAG]
CHINGALEE alt for DJINGILI [JIG]
CHINGALESE alt for SINHALA [SNH]
CHINGHIZI dial of AIMAQ [AIQ]
CHINGKAO dial of NAGA, KONYAK [NBE]
CHINGLANG dial of NAGA, KONYAK [NBE]
CHINGMENGU alt for NAGA, PHOM [NPH]

CHINGONI alt for NGONI [NGU]
CHINGONI dial of NYANJA [NYJ]
CHINGPAW alt for JINGPHO [CGP]
CHINGP'O alt for JINGPHO [CGP]
CHINGUIL dial of ZAN GULA [ZNA]
CHINIMAKONDE alt for MAKONDE [KDE]
CHINOOK [CHH] lang, USA
CHINOOK JARGON alt for CHINOOK WAWA
  [CRW]
CHINOOK PIDGIN alt for CHINOOK WAWA [CRW]
CHINOOK WAWA [CRW] lang, Canada; also in
  USA
CHINSENGA alt for NSENGA [NSE]
CHINTANG alt for CHHINTANG [CTN]
CHINTANG RÛNG alt for CHHINTANG [CTN]
CHINTOOR KOYA dial of KOYA [KFF]
CHINYANJA alt for NYANJA [NYJ]
CHINYUNGWI alt for NYUNGWE [NYU]
CHIP alt for MISHIP [CHP]
CHIPAYA [CAP] lang, Bolivia
CHIPETA alt for PETA dial of NYANJA [NYJ]
CHIPEWYAN [CPW] lang, Canada
CHIPIAJES [CBE] lang, Colombia
CHIPODZO alt for PODZO dial of SENA [SEH]
CHIPOGOLO alt for POGOLO [POY]
CHIPOGORO alt for POGOLO [POY]
CHIPOKA alt for POKA dial of TUMBUKA [TUW]
CHIPOKA dial of TUMBUKA [TUW]
CHIPPEWA [CIW] lang, USA
CHIPPEWA alt for OTTAWA [OTW]
CHIQUENA alt for SIKIANA [SIK]
CHIQUIANA alt for SIKIANA [SIK]
CHIQUITANO [CAX] lang, Bolivia
CHIQUITO alt for CHIQUITANO [CAX]
CHIR alt for MANDARI [MQU]
CHIRICAHUA dial of APACHE, MESCALERO-
  CHIRICAHUA [APM]
CHIRICHANO alt for SANUMÁ [SAM]
CHIRICHANO alt for SAPÉ [SPC]
CHIRICOA dial of CUIBA [CUI]
"CHIRIGUANO" pejorative alt for GUARANÍ,
  ARGENTINE, WESTERN [GUI]
"CHIRIGUANO" pejorative alt for GUARANÍ,
  BOLIVIAN, EASTERN [GUI]
CHIRIMA alt for MAKHUWA-SHIRIMA [VMK]
CHIRIPÁ [NHD] lang, Paraguay; also in Argentina,
  Brazil
CHIRIPO dial of CUIBA [CUI]
CHIRIPON alt for CHEREPON [CPN]
CHIRIPONG alt for CHEREPON [CPN]
CHIRIPUNO alt for ARABELA [ARL]
CHIRIPUNU alt for ARABELA [ARL]
CHIRIQUÍ alt for EASTERN GUAYMÍ dial of
  NGÄBERE [GYM]
CHIRIQUI alt for NGÄBERE [GYM]
CHIRMAR dial of BENGALI [BNG]
CHIRORO-KURSI dial of KANGA [KCP]
CHIRR dial of NAGA, YIMCHUNGRU [YIM]
CHIRRIPÓ alt for CABÉCAR [CJP]
CHIRRIPÓ dial of CABÉCAR [CJP]
CHIRU [CDF] lang, India

CHIRUE alt for RUE dial of SENA [SEH]
CHISAK dial of GARO [GRT]
CHISALAMPASU alt for SALAMPASU [SLX]
CHISENA alt for SENA [SEH]
CHISENA alt for SENA, MALAWI [SWK]
CHISENJI alt for SHANGA dial of NDAU [NDC]
CHISHINGA dial of BEMBA [BEM]
CHISHONA alt for SHONA [SHD]
CHISINGINI alt for CISHINGINI [ASG]
CHISOLI alt for SOLI [SBY]
CHISTABINO alt for CENTRAL ARAGONESE dial
    of ARAGONESE [AXX]
CHISTABINO alt for EASTERN ARAGONESE dial
    of ARAGONESE [AXX]
CHITA PARDHI alt for PARDHI [PCL]
CHITAPAVANI dial of KONKANI, GOANESE [GOM]
CHITAWAN THARU alt for THARU, CHITWANIA
    [THE]
CHITEMBO alt for TEMBO [TBT]
CHITIMACHA [CHM] lang, USA
CHITKHULI alt for KINNAURI, CHITKULI [CIK]
CHITKULI alt for KINNAURI, CHITKULI [CIK]
CHITODI LOHAR alt for LOHAR, GADE [GDA]
CHITONAHUA dial of YAMINAHUA [YAA]
CHITONGA alt for TONGA [TOG]
CHITONGA alt for TONGA [TOI]
CHITONGA dial of TONGA [TOI]
CHITRALI alt for KHOWAR [KHW]
CHITRARI alt for KHOWAR [KHW]
CHITTAGONG dial of CHIN, ASHO [CSH]
CHITTAGONIAN [CIT] lang, Bangladesh; also in
    Myanmar
CHITTAGONIAN BENGALI alt for CHITTAGONIAN
    [CIT]
CHITTIES CREOLE MALAY alt for MALACCAN
    CREOLE MALAY [CCM]
CHITUAN THARU alt for THARU, CHITWANIA
    [THE]
CHITUMBUKA alt for TUMBUKA [TUW]
CHITUMBUKA dial of TUMBUKA [TUW]
CHIUPEI alt for QIUBEI dial of ZHUANG,
    NORTHERN [CCX]
CHIUTE alt for TEWE [TWX]
CHIUTSE alt for RAWANG [RAW]
CHIVENDA alt for VENDA [VEN]
CHIVIDUNDA alt for VIDUNDA [VID]
CHIWARO alt for SHUAR [JIV]
CHIWEMBA alt for BEMBA [BEM]
CHIWERE alt for OTO dial of IOWA-OTO [IOW]
CHIXANGA alt for CHANGA dial of NDAU [NDC]
CHIXANGA alt for SHANGA dial of NDAU [NDC]
CHIYAO alt for YAO [YAO]
CHIZEZURU alt for ZEZURU dial of SHONA [SHD]
CHIZIMA alt for NAGA, LOTHA [NJH]
CHO alt for CHIN, MÜN [MWQ]
CHOA alt for ARABIC, SHUWA [SHU]
CHOÁPAM ZAPOTECO alt for ZAPOTECO,
    CHOAPAN [ZPC]
CHOAPAN ZAPOTEC alt for ZAPOTECO,
    CHOAPAN [ZPC]
CHOBBA alt for HUBA [KIR]

CHOCAMA alt for WOUN MEU [NOA]
CHOCANGACAKHA [CHK] lang, Bhutan
CHOCHO alt for CHOCHOTECO [COZ]
CHOCHO MIXTECO alt for MIXTECO, APASCO
    Y APOALA [MIP]
CHOCHOTECO [COZ] lang, Mexico
CHOCTAW [CCT] lang, USA
CHODHARI alt for CHODRI [CDI]
CHODHRI dial of BHILI [BHB]
CHODIA dial of BHILI [BHB]
CHODRI [CDI] lang, India
CHOGOR dial of BUMTHANGKHA [KJZ]
CHOHA dial of NAGA, KONYAK [NBE]
CHOIMI alt for NAGA, LOTHA [NJH]
CHOI-SALMST alt for KHVOY-SALMST dial of
    ARMENIAN [ARM]
CHOKFEM alt for CAKFEM-MUSHERE [CKY]
CHOKOBO alt for IZORA [CBO]
CHOKOSI alt for ANUFO [CKO]
CHOKOSSI alt for ANUFO [CKO]
CHOKRI alt for NAGA, CHOKRI [NRI]
CHOKWE [CJK] lang, DCR; also in Angola, Namibia,
    Zambia
CH'OL, TILA [CTI] lang, Mexico
CH'OL, TUMBALÁ [CTU] lang, Mexico
CHOLIMI alt for NAGA, AO [NJO]
CHOLLADO dial of KOREAN [KKN]
CHOLO alt for EMBERÁ, NORTHERN [EMP]
CHOLO alt for EMBERA-SAIJA [SJA]
CHOLO dial of NUNG [NUN]
CHOLON [CHT] lang, Peru
CHOLUTECA alt for CHOROTEGA [CJR]
CHOM alt for HRE [HRE]
CHOMBRAU alt for AREM [AEM]
CHOMO alt for COMO KARIM [CFG]
CHOMRAU alt for AREM [AEM]
CHONA alt for CHONI [CDA]
CHONCHARU alt for CHENCHU [CDE]
CHONE alt for CHONI [CDA]
CHONG [COG] lang, Cambodia; also in Thailand
CHONG'ANJIANG MIAO alt for HMONG,
    CHONGANJIANG [HMJ]
CHONG'E alt for KUSHI [KUH]
CHONGLI dial of NAGA, AO [NJO]
CHONI [CDA] lang, China
CHONTAL DE OAXACA, COSTA [CLO] lang, Mexico
CHONTAL DE OAXACA, SIERRA [CHD] lang,
    Mexico
CHONTAL, TABASCO [CHF] lang, Mexico
CHONYI [COH] lang, Kenya
CH'OPA alt for RAWANG [RAW]
CHOPE alt for DHOPALUO dial of ACHOLI [ACO]
CHOPI [CCE] lang, Mozambique
CHOPI alt for DHOPALUO dial of ACHOLI [ACO]
CHOR alt for JARAI [JRA]
CHO-RAI alt for JARAI [JRA]
CHOREI dial of CHIN, FALAM [HBH]
CHORI alt for CORI [CRY]
CHORO alt for CHRAU [CHR]
CHOROBA alt for CHORUBA dial of GONJA [DUM]
CHOROTE, IYOJWA'JA [CRT] lang, Argentina

CHOROTE, IYO'WUJWA [CRQ] lang, Argentina; also in Bolivia, Paraguay
CHOROTEGA [CJR] lang, Costa Rica
CHOROTEGA dial of CHOROTEGA [CJR]
CHOROTI alt for CHOROTE, IYOJWA'JA [CRT]
CHOROTI alt for CHOROTE, IYO'WUJWA [CRQ]
CHORTÍ [CAA] lang, Guatemala; also in Honduras
CHORU alt for CHRU [CJE]
CHORUBA dial of GONJA [DUM]
CHOSKULE dial of TILUNG [TIJ]
CHOTA NAGPURI alt for SADRI [SCK]
CHOTE dial of BODO [BRX]
CHOTHE alt for NAGA, CHOTHE [NCT]
CHOUDHARA alt for CHODRI [CDI]
CHOUDHARY alt for CHODRI [CDI]
CHOUGOULE alt for SHUGULE dial of MEFELE [MFJ]
CHOUPAL alt for SURAJPURI [SJP]
CHOURASE [TSU] lang, Nepal
CHOURASIA alt for CHOURASE [TSU]
CHOUSHAN alt for CHAO-SHAN dial of CHINESE, MIN NAN [CFR]
CHOWA alt for ARABIC, CHADIAN SPOKEN [SHU]
CHOWA alt for ARABIC, SHUWA [SHU]
CHOWRA alt for CHAURA [CHO]
CHOWTE alt for NAGA, CHOTHE [NCT]
CHRAI alt for JARAI [JRA]
CH'RAME alt for PUMI, NORTHERN [PMI]
CHRAU [CHR] lang, Viet Nam
CHRAU HMA alt for CHRU [CJE]
CHRISHANA dial of ROMANIAN [RUM]
CHRISTIAN NEO-ARAMAIC alt for SENAYA [SYN]
CHRU [CJE] lang, Viet Nam; also in France, USA
CHTIMI alt for PICARD [PCD]
CHTIMI alt for PICARD dial of FRENCH [FRN]
CHU alt for CHRU [CJE]
CHU RU alt for CHRU [CJE]
CHUABO alt for CHUWABO [CHW]
CHUALA alt for GUANA [QKS]
CHUAMBO alt for CHUWABO [CHW]
CHUAN MIAO alt for HMONG DAW [MWW]
CHUANA alt for TSWANA [TSW]
CHUANA dial of KUNA, SAN BLAS [CUK]
CHUANCHIENTIEN MIAO alt for HMONG NJUA [BLU]
CHUANG alt for ZHUANG, NORTHERN [CCX]
CHUANQIANDIAN MIAO alt for HMONG NJUA [BLU]
CHUAVE [CJV] lang, Papua New Guinea
CHUAVE dial of CHUAVE [CJV]
CHUBA alt for CHEWONG [CWG]
CHUBO alt for META' [MGO]
CHUCHEE alt for CHUKOT [CKT]
"CHUDY" pejorative alt for VEPS [VEP]
CHUF alt for KHUFI dial of SHUGHNI [SGH]
CHUG dial of MOINBA [MOB]
CHUGACH dial of YUPIK, PACIFIC GULF [EMS]
CHUGACH "ESKIMO" pejorative alt for YUPIK, PACIFIC GULF [EMS]
CHUH alt for CHUJ, SAN MATEO IXTATÁN [CNM]
"CHUHARI" pejorative alt for VEPS [VEP]

CHUHE alt for CHUJ, SAN MATEO IXTATÁN [CNM]
CHUI-HUAN alt for THAO [SSF]
CHUIHWAN alt for THAO [SSF]
CHUIL QUICHÉ alt for QUICHÉ, CUNÉN [CUN]
CHUJ, SAN MATEO IXTATÁN [CNM] lang, Guatemala; also in Mexico
CHUJ, SAN SEBASTIÁN COATÁN [CAC] lang, Guatemala
CHUJE alt for CHUJ, SAN MATEO IXTATÁN [CNM]
CHUKA [CUH] lang, Kenya
CHUKCHA alt for CHUKOT [CKT]
CHUKCHEE alt for CHUKOT [CKT]
CHUKCHI alt for CHUKOT [CKT]
"CHUKHARI" pejorative alt for VEPS [VEP]
CHUKKOL alt for NYONG [MUO]
CHUKOT [CKT] lang, Russia (Asia)
CHUKU alt for CHUKA [CUH]
CHUKWA [CUW] lang, Nepal
CHULIKATA alt for IDU [CLK]
CHULIKATA alt for LUOBA, YIDU [CLK]
CHULIKOTTA alt for IDU [CLK]
CHULIM alt for CHULYM [CHU]
CHULLA alt for SHILLUK [SHK]
CHULUNG alt for CHHULUNG [CUR]
CHÜLÜNG alt for CHHULUNG [CUR]
CHULUPE alt for CHULUPÍ [CAG]
CHULUPÍ [CAG] lang, Paraguay; also in Argentina
CHULUPIE alt for CHULUPÍ [CAG]
CHULYM [CHU] lang, Russia (Asia)
CHULYM TATAR alt for CHULYM [CHU]
CHULYM-TURKISH alt for CHULYM [CHU]
CHUMA dial of QUECHUA, NORTH BOLIVIAN [QUL]
CHUMASH [CHS] lang, USA
CHUMBURUNG [NCU] lang, Ghana
CHUNG alt for ACHANG [ACN]
CHUNG alt for LISU [LIS]
CHUNG CHA alt for NHANG [NHA]
CHUNG-CHIA alt for BOUYEI [PCC]
CH'UNGCH'ONGDO dial of KOREAN [KKN]
CHUNGKI alt for DJANGUN [DJF]
CHUNGLI alt for CHONGLI dial of NAGA, AO [NJO]
CHUNGULOO alt for DJINGILI [JIG]
CHUNKUMBERRIES alt for DJANGUN [DJF]
CHUNKUNBURRA alt for DJANGUN [DJF]
CHUNMAT dial of BUMTHANGKHA [KJZ]
CHUQU dial of CHINESE, WU [WUU]
CHUQUISACA dial of QUECHUA, SOUTH BOLIVIAN [QUH]
CHURAHI [CDJ] lang, India
CHURAHI PAHARI alt for CHURAHI [CDJ]
CHURAI PAHARI alt for CHURAHI [CDJ]
CHURARI dial of ROMANI, VLAX [RMY]
CHURARÍCKO alt for CHURARI dial of ROMANI, VLAX [RMY]
CHURI alt for SURI [SUQ]
CHURI-WALI dial of DOMARI [RMT]
CHURO alt for CUR dial of MANDJAK [MFV]
CHURU alt for CHRU [CJE]
CHURUPI alt for CHULUPÍ [CAG]

CHUT [SCB] lang, Viet Nam; also in Laos
CHUTIYA alt for DEORI [DER]
CHUTOBIKHA dial of NYENKHA [NEH]
CHUTY dial of JARAI [JRA]
CHUUFI alt for BAFANJI [BFJ]
CHUUK alt for CHUUKESE [TRU]
CHUUKESE [TRU] lang, Micronesia; also in Guam
CHUVASH [CJU] lang, Russia (Europe); also in Estonia, Kazakhstan, Kyrgyzstan, Uzbekistan
CHUWABO [CHW] lang, Mozambique
CHUWAU alt for HIETSHWARE [HIE]
CHUY alt for TALANGIT dial of ALTAI, SOUTHERN [ALT]
CHWABO alt for CHUWABO [CHW]
CHWAGGA dial of HAIOM [HGM]
CHWAKA dial of GIRYAMA [NYF]
CHWAMPO alt for CHWABO [CHW]
CHWANA alt for TSWANA [TSW]
CHWARE alt for HIETSHWARE [HIE]
CHXALA dial of LAZ [LZZ]
CI alt for CI-GBE [CIB]
CI alt for PAICÎ [PRI]
CIA-CIA [CIA] lang, Indonesia (Sulawesi)
CIARA alt for CHARA [CRA]
CIBAANGI alt for BAANGI [BQX]
CIBAK [CKL] lang, Nigeria
CIBBO alt for TSO [LDP]
CIBECUE dial of APACHE, WESTERN [APW]
CIC alt for CIEC dial of DINKA, SOUTH CENTRAL [DIB]
CICAK alt for CITAK [TXT]
CICEWA alt for CHEWA dial of NYANJA [NYJ]
CICOLANO-REATINO-AQUILANO dial of ITALIAN [ITN]
CICOPI alt for CHOPI [CCE]
CICUABO alt for CHWABO [CHW]
CIDANDA alt for DANDA dial of NDAU [NDC]
CIDONDO alt for DONDO dial of NDAU [NDC]
CIEC dial of DINKA, SOUTH CENTRAL [DIB]
CIEM alt for CIEC dial of DINKA, SOUTH CENTRAL [DIB]
CIEN dial of NUER [NUS]
CIFIPA alt for FIPA [FIP]
CIGA alt for CHIGA [CHG]
CIGÁNY alt for ROMANI, BALKAN [RMN]
CIGÁNY alt for ROMANI, CARPATHIAN [RMC]
CIGÁNY alt for ROMANI, VLAX [RMY]
CI-GBE [CIB] lang, Benin
CIGOVA alt for GOVA dial of NDAU [NDC]
CIIKUHANE alt for SUBIYA [SBS]
CIINA alt for LENJE [LEH]
CIITA alt for OPUUO [LGN]
CIKABANGA dial of FANAGOLO [FAO]
CIKIDE dial of GUDUF [GDF]
CIKIDE dial of GUDUF-GAVA [GDF]
CIKOBU alt for IZORA [CBO]
CIKUNDA alt for KUNDA [KDN]
CILE dial of FIPA [FIP]
CILOWE alt for LOMWE [NGL]
CILUNGU alt for RUNGU dial of MAMBWE-LUNGU [MGR]

CIMAKALE alt for MAKALE dial of YAO [YAO]
CIMAKONDE alt for MAKONDE [KDE]
CIMANGANJA alt for MANGANJA dial of NYANJA [NYJ]
CIMASHANGA alt for SHANGA dial of NDAU [NDC]
CIMASSANINGA alt for MASSANINGA dial of YAO [YAO]
CIMBANGALA alt for MBANGALA [MXG]
CIMBRIAN [CIM] lang, Italy
CIMEL alt for PALIOUPINY dial of DINKA, SOUTH-WESTERN [DIK]
CIMULIN dial of QIANG, NORTHERN [CNG]
CIMWERA alt for MWERA [MWE]
CIN HAW alt for HO dial of CHINESE, MANDARIN [CHN]
CINAMIGUIN alt for MANOBO, CINAMIGUIN [MKX]
CINDA dial of CINDA-REGI-TIYAL [KAU]
CINDANDA alt for DANDA dial of NDAU [NDC]
CINDA-REGI-TIYAL [KAU] lang, Nigeria
CINDAU alt for NDAU dial of NDAU [NDC]
CINENI [CIE] lang, Nigeria
CINGALESE alt for SINHALA [SNH]
CINGONI alt for NGONI dial of NYANJA [NYJ]
CINI alt for TCHINI dial of NIELLIM [NIE]
CINSENGA alt for NSENGA dial of NYANJA [NYJ]
CINTA LARGA [CIN] lang, Brazil
CINYAMBE alt for NYAMBE dial of GITONGA [TOH]
CINYANJA alt for NYANJA [NYJ]
CINYANJA alt for NYANJA dial of NYANJA [NYJ]
CINYUNGWE alt for NYUNGWE [NYU]
CIOKWE alt for CHOKWE [CJK]
CIP alt for MISHIP [CHP]
CIPETA alt for PETA dial of NYANJA [NYJ]
CIPIMBWE alt for PIMBWE [PIW]
CIPODZO alt for PODZO dial of SENA [SEH]
CIRCASSIAN alt for ADYGHE [ADY]
CIREBON dial of JAVANESE [JAN]
CIREBON dial of SUNDA [SUO]
CIRI alt for TIRI [CIR]
CIRIMBA alt for NYA CERIYA dial of LONGUDA [LNU]
CIRMA alt for TIRMA dial of SURI [SUQ]
CISAFWA alt for SAFWA [SBK]
CIS-BAIKALIA dial of EVENKI [EVN]
CISENA alt for SENA [SEH]
CISENA alt for SENA, MALAWI [SWK]
CISHINGINI [ASG] lang, Nigeria
CISUUNDI alt for SUUNDI dial of KONGO [KON]
CITA alt for OPUUO [LGN]
CITAK [TXT] lang, Indonesia (Irian Jaya)
CITAK, TAMNIM [TML] lang, Indonesia (Irian Jaya)
CITLANG dial of NEWARI [NEW]
CITRALI alt for KHOWAR [KHW]
CI'ULI alt for TS'OLE' dial of ATAYAL [TAY]
CIUTE alt for TEWE [TWX]
CIVIDALE dial of SLOVENIAN [SLV]
CIVILI alt for VILI [VIF]
CIWOGAI [TGD] lang, Nigeria
CIYAO alt for YAO [YAO]

CIYEI alt for YEYI [YEY]
CIYOOMBE alt for YOOMBE dial of VILI [VIF]
CKHALA alt for CHXALA dial of LAZ [LZZ]
CLACKAMA dial of CHINOOK [CHH]
CLALLAM [CLM] lang, USA
CLASSICAL ARABIC dial of ARABIC, STANDARD [ABV]
CLASSICAL AZTEC alt for NÁHUATL, CLASSICAL [NCI]
CLASSICAL GREEK dial of GREEK, ANCIENT [GKO]
CLASSICAL MANDAEAN alt for MANDAIC, CLASSICAL [MYZ]
CLASSICAL SYRIAC alt for SYRIAC [SYC]
CLATA alt for GIANGAN [BGI]
CLEAR LAKE POMO alt for POMO, EASTERN [PEB]
C'LELA [DRI] lang, Nigeria
C'LELA alt for C'LELA [DRI]
CO alt for KOL dial of CUA [CUA]
CO LAO alt for GELAO [KKF]
COAIQUER alt for AWA-CUAIQUER [KWI]
COANA alt for TSWANA [TSW]
COAST KIWAI dial of KIWAI, SOUTHERN [KJD]
COAST TSIMSHIAN alt for TSIMSHIAN [TSI]
COAST TSIMSHIAN dial of TSIMSHIAN [TSI]
COASTAL ARAPESH dial of BUKIYIP [APE]
COASTAL BALOCHI dial of BALOCHI, SOUTHERN [BCC]
COASTAL CHONTAL OF OAXACA alt for CHONTAL DE OAXACA, COSTA [CLO]
COASTAL EAST CREE alt for CREE, NORTHERN EAST [CRL]
COASTAL GUERRERO MIXTECO alt for MIXTECO, AYUTLA [MIY]
COASTAL INUPIATUN dial of INUPIATUN, NORTH-WEST ALASKA [ESK]
COASTAL MAKHUWA alt for MAKHUWA-MARREVONE [XMC]
COASTAL MAKWE dial of MAKWE [YMK]
COASTAL MIXTECO alt for MIXTECO, PINOTEPA NACIONAL [MIO]
COASTAL NORWEGIAN alt for WESTERN NORWEGIAN dial of NORWEGIAN, BOKMAAL [NRR]
COASTAL QUICHÉ dial of QUICHÉ, WEST CENTRAL [QUT]
COASTAL TIHAAMAH dial of ARABIC, HIJAZI SPOKEN [ACW]
COASTAL TUPIAN alt for NHENGATU [YRL]
COASTAL-INLAND dial of TANAINA [TFN]
COATEPEC AZTEC alt for NÁHUATL, COATEPEC [NAZ]
COATLÁN MIXE dial of MIXE, COATLAN [MCO]
COATLÁN ZAPOTEC alt for ZAPOTECO, COATLÁN [ZPS]
COATLÁN ZAPOTECO alt for ZAPOTECO, SAN VICENTE COATLÁN [ZPT]
COATZOSPAN MIXTEC alt for MIXTECO, COATZOSPAN [MIZ]
COBARI dial of YANOMAMO [GUU]

COBARÍA TUNEBO alt for TUNEBO, CENTRAL [TUF]
COBARIWA alt for COBARI dial of YANOMAMO [GUU]
COBIANA alt for KOBIANA [KCJ]
COC MUN alt for KIM MUN [MJI]
COCAMA alt for COCAMA-COCAMILLA [COD]
COCAMA dial of COCAMA-COCAMILLA [COD]
COCAMA-COCAMILLA [COD] lang, Peru; also in Brazil, Colombia
COCAMILLA dial of COCAMA-COCAMILLA [COD]
COCCHE alt for HAMER-BANNA [AMF]
COCHABAMBA dial of QUECHUA, SOUTH BOLIVIAN [QUH]
COCHE alt for CAMSÁ [KBH]
COCHETIMI alt for COCHIMÍ [COJ]
COCHIMA alt for COCHIMÍ [COJ]
COCHIMÍ [COJ] lang, Mexico
COCHIMÍ alt for KUMIÁI [DIH]
COCHIMTEE alt for COCHIMÍ [COJ]
COCHITI dial of KERES, EASTERN [KEE]
COCKNEY dial of ENGLISH [ENG]
COCOLI alt for LANDOMA [LAO]
COCOMARICOPA alt for MARICOPA [MRC]
COCOPA [COC] lang, Mexico; also in USA
COCOPÁ alt for COCOPA [COC]
COCOPAH alt for COCOPA [COC]
COCOS alt for MALAY, COCOS ISLANDS [COA]
CO-DON alt for KODU dial of KOHO [KPM]
COEUR D'ALENE [CRD] lang, USA
COFÁN [CON] lang, Ecuador; also in Colombia
COGAPACORI alt for NANTI [COX]
COGHUI alt for COGUI [KOG]
COGNIAGUI alt for WAMEI [COU]
COGUI [KOG] lang, Colombia
COHO alt for KOHO [KPM]
COICOYÁN dial of MIXTECO, JUXTLAHUACA OESTE [JMX]
COICOYÁN MIXTEC alt for MIXTECO, JUXTLAHUACA OESTE [JMX]
COK alt for GOK dial of DINKA, SOUTH CENTRAL [DIB]
COKOBANCI alt for IZORA [CBO]
COKOBO alt for IZORA [CBO]
COKWE alt for CHOKWE [CJK]
COL alt for KIORR [XKO]
COL alt for KOL dial of CUA [CUA]
COLH alt for MUNDARI [MUW]
COLLA alt for QUECHUA, NORTHWEST JUJUY [QUO]
COLO alt for SHILLUK [SHK]
COLO dial of THURI [THU]
COLOMBIA CUNA alt for KUNA, BORDER [KUA]
COLOMBIAN SIGN LANGUAGE [CSN] lang, Colombia
COLORADO [COF] lang, Ecuador
COLUMBIA dial of COLUMBIA-WENATCHI [COL]
COLUMBIA RIVER SAHAPTIN alt for UMATILLA [UMA]

COLUMBIAN alt for COLUMBIA dial of COLUMBIA-WENATCHI [COL]
COLUMBIA-WENATCHI [COL] lang, USA
COLVILLE dial of OKANAGAN [OKA]
COMANCHE [COM] lang, USA
COMBE alt for NGUMBI [NUI]
COMEMATSA dial of BARASANA [BSN]
COMEYA alt for KUMIÁI [DIH]
COMITANCILLO MAM alt for MAM, CENTRAL [MVC]
COMITECO alt for TOJOLABAL [TOJ]
COMMON SOMALI alt for SOMALI [SOM]
COMO alt for KOMO [KOM]
COMO KARIM [CFG] lang, Nigeria
COMORES SWAHILI alt for COMORIAN [SWB]
COMORIAN [SWB] lang, Comoros Islands; also in Madagascar, Mayotte, Reunion
COMORIAN, SHINGAZIDJA [SWS] lang, Comoros Islands
COMORO alt for COMORIAN [SWB]
COMOX [COO] lang, Canada
COMOX-SLIAMMON alt for COMOX [COO]
COMPEVA alt for OMAGUA [OMG]
CON [CNO] lang, Laos
CON alt for KIORR [XKO]
CONCEPCIÓN dial of CHIQUITANO [CAX]
CONCHUCOS QUECHUA alt for QUECHUA, ANCASH, CONCHUCOS, NORTHERN [QED]
CONCHUCOS QUECHUA alt for QUECHUA, ANCASH, CONCHUCOS, SOUTHERN [QEH]
CONCORINUM alt for KONKANI [KNK]
CONCOW alt for MAIDU, NORTHWEST [MAI]
CONDUL dial of NICOBARESE, SOUTHERN [NIK]
CONE alt for CHONI [CDA]
CONESTOGA alt for SUSQUEHANNOCK [SQN]
CONG alt for PHUNOI [PHO]
CONGO alt for KONGO [KON]
CONGO alt for KONGO, SAN SALVADOR [KWY]
CONGO NYORO alt for HEMA [NIX]
CONGO POL alt for POL [PMM]
CONHAGUE alt for WAMEI [COU]
CONIAGUI alt for WAMEI [COU]
CONIBA alt for CONIBO dial of SHIPIBO-CONIBO [SHP]
CONIBO dial of SHIPIBO-CONIBO [SHP]
CONNACHT dial of GAELIC, IRISH [GLI]
CONOB alt for KANJOBAL, EASTERN [KJB]
CONOB alt for KANJOBAL, WESTERN [KNJ]
CONSO alt for KOMSO [KXC]
CONSTANTINE dial of ARABIC, ALGERIAN SPOKEN [ARQ]
CONSTANTINOPLE dial of ARMENIAN [ARM]
CONTAQUIRO alt for YINE [PIB]
CONTA-REDDI alt for MUKHA-DORA [MMK]
COO alt for BWAMU, CWI [BWY]
COOK ISLAND alt for RAROTONGAN [RRT]
COOK ISLANDS MAORI alt for RAROTONGAN [RRT]
CÔÔNG alt for PHUNOI [PHO]
COONGURRI alt for KUNGGARI [KGL]
COORGE alt for KODAGU [KFA]

COOS [COS] lang, USA
COPI alt for CHOPI [CCE]
COPI dial of CHOPI [CCE]
COPPER alt for MEDNYJ ALEUT [MUD]
COPPER ESKIMO alt for COPPER INUKTITUT dial of INUKTITUT, WESTERN CANADIAN [ESC]
COPPER INUIT alt for COPPER INUKTITUT dial of INUKTITUT, WESTERN CANADIAN [ESC]
COPPER INUKTITUT dial of INUKTITUT, WESTERN CANADIAN [ESC]
COPPER ISLAND ALEUT alt for MEDNYJ ALEUT [MUD]
COPPER ISLAND ATTUAN alt for MEDNYJ ALEUT [MUD]
COPPER RIVER alt for AHTENA [AHT]
COPPERSMITH alt for KALDERASH dial of ROMANI, VLAX [RMY]
COPTIC [COP] lang, Egypt
COQUILLE [COQ] lang, USA
COR alt for KOL dial of CUA [CUA]
CORA [COR] lang, Mexico; also in USA
CORA, SANTA TERESA [COK] lang, Mexico
COREGUAJE alt for KOREGUAJE [COE]
CORI [CRY] lang, Nigeria
CORINA alt for CULINA [CUL]
CORNISH [CRN] lang, United Kingdom
CORNOUAILLAIS dial of BRETON [BRT]
CORNWALL dial of ENGLISH [ENG]
CORO dial of ANUAK [ANU]
COROÁ alt for ACROÁ [ACS]
COROADO alt for KAINGÁNG [KGP]
COROADO alt for PURI [PRR]
COROADOS alt for KAINGÁNG [KGP]
COROGAMA alt for BOZO, SOROGAMA [BZE]
COROMA dial of BRIBRI [BZD]
CORREGUAJE alt for KOREGUAJE [COE]
CORSE alt for CORSICAN [COI]
CORSI alt for CORSICAN [COI]
CORSICAN [COI] lang, France; also in Bolivia, Canada, Cuba, Italy, Puerto Rico, Uruguay, USA, Venezuela
CORSO alt for CORSICAN [COI]
CORSU alt for CORSICAN [COI]
CORUMBIARA alt for TUBARÃO [TBA]
COSO alt for PANAMINT [PAR]
COSOLEACAQUE AZTEC alt for NÁHUATL, ISTMO-COSOLEACAQUE [NHK]
COSSYAH alt for KHASI [KHI]
COSTA RICAN SIGN LANGUAGE [CSR] lang, Costa Rica
COSTANOAN, NORTHERN [CST] lang, USA
COSTANOAN, SOUTHERN [CSS] lang, USA
COTAHUASI dial of QUECHUA, AREQUIPA-LA UNION [QAR]
COTAHUASI QUECHUA alt for QUECHUA, AREQUIPA-LA UNION [QAR]
COTI alt for KOTI [EKO]
COTO alt for OREJÓN [ORE]
COTOBATO CHAVACANO dial of CHAVACANO [CBK]
COTOCOLI alt for TEM [KDH]

COUNTRY SIGN alt for JAMAICAN COUNTRY SIGN LANGUAGE [JCS]
COUSHATTA alt for KOASATI [CKU]
COVAHLOC alt for ANGAITE dial of SANAPANA [SAP]
COVAVITIS alt for ANGAITE dial of SANAPANA [SAP]
COWICHAN dial of HALKOMELEM [HUR]
COWLITZ [COW] lang, USA
COXIMA [KOX] lang, Colombia
COYAIMA [COY] lang, Colombia
COYAIMA dial of YUKPA [YUP]
COYOTERO alt for APACHE, WESTERN [APW]
COYULTITA dial of HUICHOL [HCH]
CRAIG COVE alt for LONWOLWOL [CRC]
CRANGE alt for KREYE [XRE]
CRAÔ alt for KRAHÔ [XRA]
CRAVEN YORKSHIRE dial of ENGLISH [ENG]
CREE alt for OJIBWA, SEVERN [OJS]
CREE, MOOSE [CRM] lang, Canada
CREE, NORTHERN EAST [CRL] lang, Canada
CREE, PLAINS [CRP] lang, Canada; also in USA
CREE, SOUTHERN EAST [CRE] lang, Canada
CREE, SWAMPY [CSW] lang, Canada
CREE, WOODS [CWD] lang, Canada
CREEK alt for MUSKOGEE [CRK]
CREEK dial of MUSKOGEE [CRK]
CRENGE alt for KREYE [XRE]
CRENYE alt for KREYE [XRE]
CREOLA alt for BELIZE CREOLE ENGLISH dial of NORTHERN CENTRAL AMERICA CREOLE ENGLISH [BZI]
CREOLE alt for KRIO [KRI]
CREOLE alt for SESELWA CREOLE FRENCH [CRS]
CREOLESE alt for GUYANESE CREOLE ENGLISH [GYN]
CREOLIZED ATTUAN alt for MEDNYJ ALEUT [MUD]
CREQ dial of HRE [HRE]
CREYE alt for KREYE [XRE]
CRICHANA alt for NINAM [SHB]
CRIMEA dial of ARMENIAN [ARM]
CRIMEAN GOTHIC dial of GOTHIC [GOF]
CRIMEAN NOGAI alt for NORTHERN CRIMEAN dial of CRIMEAN TURKISH [CRH]
CRIMEAN TATAR alt for CRIMEAN TURKISH [CRH]
CRIMEAN TURKISH [CRH] lang, Uzbekistan; also in Bulgaria, Kyrgyzstan, Moldova, Romania, Turkey (Asia), Ukraine, USA
CRIOLLO alt for FERNANDO PO CREOLE ENGLISH [FPE]
CRIOULO alt for KARIPÚNA CREOLE FRENCH [KMV]
CRIOULO, UPPER GUINEA [POV] lang, Guinea-Bissau; also in Gambia, Senegal, USA
CRISCA alt for XAVÁNTE [XAV]
CROATAN alt for LUMBEE [LUA]
CROATIAN [SRC] lang, Croatia,
CROATIAN dial of BOSNIAN [SRC]
CROSS RIVER PIDGIN dial of PIDGIN, NIGERIAN [PCM]

CROW [CRO] lang, USA
CRU alt for CHRU [CJE]
CRUZAN dial of VIRGIN ISLANDS CREOLE ENGLISH [VIB]
CRUZEÑO [CRZ] lang, USA
CÙ TE alt for LACHI [LBT]
CU THO alt for KHMER, CENTRAL [KMR]
CUA [CUA] lang, Viet Nam
CUA alt for HIETSHWARE [HIE]
CUABO alt for CHWABO [CHW]
CUAIQUER alt for AWA-CUAIQUER [KWI]
CUAMBO alt for CHWABO [CHW]
CUANA alt for TSWANA [TSW]
CUANGAR alt for KWANGALI [KWN]
CUANHAMA alt for KWANYAMA [KUY]
CUANHOCA alt for KWADI [KWZ]
CUBEO [CUB] lang, Colombia; also in Brazil
CUBEU alt for CUBEO [CUB]
CUCAPÁ alt for COCOPA [COC]
CUCHI alt for KACHCHI [KFR]
CUCHIMÍ alt for KUMIÁI [DIH]
CUCHUDUA dial of JAMAMADI [JAA]
CUCUPÁ alt for COCOPA [COC]
CUDAXAR dial of DARGWA [DAR]
CUEPE alt for KWADI [KWZ]
CUEVA dial of KUNA, SAN BLAS [CUK]
CUGANI alt for KONKANI [KNK]
CÙI CHU alt for NHANG [NHA]
CUIBA [CUI] lang, Colombia; also in Venezuela
CUIBA-WÁMONAE alt for CUIBA [CUI]
CUICATECO, TEPEUXILA [CUX] lang, Mexico
CUICATECO, TEUTILA [CUT] lang, Mexico
CUICATLÁN MIXTEC alt for MIXTECO, CUYAMECALCO [QMZ]
CUICUTL alt for KUIKÚRO-KALAPÁLO [KUI]
CUINI alt for KWINI [GWW]
CUIVA alt for CUIBA [CUI]
CUJARENO alt for MASHCO PIRO [CUJ]
CUJAREÑO alt for MASHCO PIRO [CUJ]
CUJAZI alt for LUCHAZI [LCH]
CUJUBI alt for PURUBORÁ [PUR]
CUKWA RING alt for CHUKWA [CUW]
CULE alt for TSAMAI [TSB]
CULINA [CUL] lang, Brazil; also in Peru
CULLO alt for DAWRO dial of GAMO-GOFA-DAWRO [GMO]
CUMANASHO alt for MAXAKALÍ [MBL]
CUMATA alt for IPEKA-TAPUIA [PAJ]
CUMBERLAND dial of ENGLISH [ENG]
CUMERAL [CUM] lang, Colombia
CUN [CUQ] lang, China
CUNA alt for KUNA, BORDER [KUA]
CUNAMA alt for KUNAMA [KUM]
CUNENTECO QUICHÉ alt for QUICHÉ, CUNÉN [CUN]
CUNG [CUG] lang, Cameroon
CUNG alt for TAI YA [CUU]
CUN-HUA alt for CUN [CUQ]
CUNHUA alt for CUN [CUQ]
CUNI alt for TCHINI dial of NIELLIM [NIE]
CUNIMÍA alt for GUAYABERO [GUO]

CUNIPUSANA alt for BARÉ [BAE]
CUNIPUSANA alt for MANDAHUACA [MHT]
CUNUANA alt for MAQUIRITARI [MCH]
CUNUANA dial of MAQUIRITARI [MCH]
CUÓI alt for HUNG [HNU]
CUOI alt for KUY [KDT]
CUOI alt for THO [TOU]
CUOI CHAM alt for THO [TOU]
CUOI CHAM dial of THO [TOU]
CUONA MENBA alt for MOINBA [MOB]
CUONA MONPA alt for MOINBA [MOB]
CUPEÑO [CUP] lang, USA
CUR dial of MANDJAK [MFV]
CUR CUL alt for KHMER, CENTRAL [KMR]
CURACIRARI dial of OMAGUA [OMG]
CURAÇOLEÑO alt for PAPIAMENTU [PAE]
CURAMA alt for TURKA [TUZ]
CURASICANA dial of YABARANA [YAR]
CURASSESE alt for PAPIAMENTU [PAE]
CURAUA alt for YOHORAA dial of TUCANO
    [TUO]
CURAZICARI alt for CURACIRARI dial of OMAGUA
    [OMG]
CURIPACO alt for CURRIPACO [KPC]
CURNOACK alt for CORNISH [CRN]
CUROCA alt for KWADI [KWZ]
CURRIPACO [KPC] lang, Colombia; also in Brazil,
    Venezuela
CURUAIA alt for KURUÁYA [KYR]
CURUCICURI dial of OMAGUA [OMG]
CURUCURU alt for KURUKURU dial of PAUMARI
    [PAD]
CURUZICARI alt for CURUCICURI dial of OMAGUA
    [OMG]
CUSCO QUECHUA alt for QUECHUA, CUZCO
    [QUZ]
CUSSO alt for MBUKUSHU [MHW]
CUTCH alt for KACHCHI [KFR]
CUTCHI alt for KACHCHI [KFR]
CUTCHI-SWAHILI [CCL] lang, Kenya; also in
    Tanzania
CU-TÊ alt for LACHI [LBT]
CUTIADAPA dial of KATUKINA [KAV]
CUVEO alt for CUBEO [CUB]
CUVOK [CUV] lang, Cameroon
CUWABO alt for CHWABO [CHW]
CUYAMECALCO MIXTEC alt for MIXTECO,
    CUYAMECALCO [QMZ]
CUYANAWA dial of NUKUINI [NUC]
CUYARE alt for CABIYARÍ [CBB]
CUYI TSÓ alt for TSO [LDP]
CUYO alt for CUYONON [CYO]
CUYONO alt for CUYONON [CYO]
CUYONON [CYO] lang, Philippines
CUYUNON alt for CUYONON [CYO]
CWAYA alt for SHWAI [SHW]
CWI alt for BWAMU, CWI [BWY]
CYMRAEG alt for WELSH [WLS]
CYPRIOT GREEK dial of GREEK [GRK]
CYPRIOT MARONITE ARABIC alt for ARABIC,
    CYPRIOT SPOKEN [ACY]

CZECH [CZC] lang, Czech Republic; also in
    Austria, Bulgaria, Canada, Israel, Poland,
    Slovakia, Ukraine, USA
CZECH SIGN LANGUAGE [CSE] lang, Czech
    Republic
CZECHO-MORAVIAN dial of CZECH [CZC]
DA alt for DAN [DAF]
DA HOLMACI alt for HOLMA [HOD]
DA'A alt for KAILI, DA'A [KZF]
DA'A alt for MAJERA [XMJ]
DA'A dial of KAILI, DAA [KZF]
DAADIYA alt for DADIYA [DBD]
DAAI alt for CHIN, DAAI [DAO]
DAAN alt for BULLA dial of SHEKO [SHE]
DA'AN alt for ULU AI' dial of DOHOI [OTD]
DA'ANG alt for LAIYOLO [LJI]
DAANYIR alt for BULLA dial of SHEKO [SHE]
DAASANACH [DSH] lang, Ethiopia; also in Kenya
DAASANECH alt for DAASANACH [DSH]
DAASHI alt for BURJI [BJI]
DABA [DAB] lang, Cameroon; also in Nigeria
DABA alt for SAMO [SMQ]
DABA DE GORÉ alt for BEMAR dial of NGAMBAY
    [SBA]
DABA KOLA alt for KOLA dial of DABA [DAB]
DABA MOUSGOY alt for MUSGOI dial of DABA
    [DAB]
DABAI alt for NABAY dial of KENINGAU MURUT
    [KXI]
DABAI dial of CLELA [DRI]
DABAN YAO alt for YERONG [YRN]
DABARRE [DBR] lang, Somalia
DABARRE dial of DABARRE [DBR]
DABAY alt for NABAY dial of KENINGAU MURUT
    [KXI]
DABBA alt for DABA [DAB]
DABE [DBE] lang, Indonesia (Irian Jaya)
DABI dial of DJINBA [DJB]
DABIDA alt for TAITA [DAV]
DABRA alt for TAWORTA [TBP]
DABU alt for AGOB [KIT]
DABUGUS dial of TIMUGON MURUT [TIH]
DABURA alt for MORIGI [MDB]
DABUSO dial of BERTA [WTI]
DACCA dial of GARO [GRT]
DACHSEA alt for TUCANO [TUO]
DACO-ROMANIAN alt for ROMANIAN [RUM]
DACO-RUMANIAN alt for ROMANIAN [RUM]
DADIA alt for DADIYA [DBD]
DADIBI [MPS] lang, Papua New Guinea
DADIYA [DBD] lang, Nigeria
DADJA dial of IFE [IFE]
DADJO alt for DAJU, DAR DAJU [DJC]
DADJO alt for DAJU, DAR SILA [DAU]
DADJU alt for DAJU, DAR DAJU [DJC]
DADUA dial of GALOLI [GAL]
DAENG alt for TAI DAENG [TYR]
DAFA dial of BAKWE [BAK]
DAFFO-BUTURA dial of RON [CLA]
DAFIIR alt for NORTH NAJDI dial of ARABIC, NAJDI
    SPOKEN [ARS]

DAFING alt for MARKA [MWR]
DAFLA alt for NISI [DAP]
DAGA [DGZ] lang, Papua New Guinea
DAGAARE alt for DAGAARE, SOUTHERN [DGA]
DAGAARE alt for DAGARA, NORTHERN [DGI]
DAGAARE, SOUTHERN [DGA] lang, Ghana
DAGAARI alt for DAGARA, NORTHERN [DGI]
DAGAARI DIOULA [DGD] lang, Burkina Faso; also
   in Ghana
DAGAARI JULA alt for DAGAARI DIOULA [DGD]
DAGADA alt for FATALUKU [DDG]
DAGAGA alt for FATALUKU [DDG]
DAGANONGA alt for NYONG [MUO]
DAGANYONGA alt for NYONG [MUO]
DAGARA alt for DAGAARE, SOUTHERN [DGA]
DAGARA dial of KANURI, CENTRAL [KPH]
DAGARA dial of KANURI, MANGA [KBY]
DAGARA, NORTHERN [DGI] lang, Burkina Faso
DAGARI alt for DAGAARE, SOUTHERN [DGA]
DAGARI alt for DAGARA, NORTHERN [DGI]
DAGARI DYOULA alt for DAGAARI DIOULA [DGD]
DAGARRO dial of OTORO [OTR]
DAGATI alt for DAGAARE, SOUTHERN [DGA]
DAGATI alt for DAGARA, NORTHERN [DGI]
DAGBA [DGK] lang, CAR; also in Chad
DAGBAMBA alt for DAGBANI [DAG]
DAGBANE alt for DAGBANI [DAG]
DAGBANI [DAG] lang, Ghana; also in Togo
DAGEL dial of KIBET [KIE]
DAGENAVA dial of YAGARIA [YGR]
DAGESTANI alt for AVAR [AVR]
DAGGAL alt for DAGEL dial of KIBET [KIE]
DAGI alt for CHINALI [CIH]
DAGI dial of KORUPUN-SELA [KPQ]
DAGIG alt for DAGIK [DEC]
DAGIK [DEC] lang, Sudan
DAGLI dial of GODIE [GOD]
DAGNE alt for SAKAYA dial of BAREIN [BVA]
DAGO' LAWNG BIT dial of MARU [MHX]
DAGODA' alt for FATALUKU [DDG]
DAGOI alt for MALA [PED]
DAGOMBA alt for DAGBANI [DAG]
DAGU alt for DAJU, DAR FUR [DAJ]
DAGUI alt for MALA [PED]
DAGUOR alt for DAUR [DTA]
DAGUR alt for DAUR [DTA]
DAHALO [DAL] lang, Kenya
DAHANMU dial of BOMU [BMQ]
DAHATING alt for GWAHATIKE [DAH]
DAHEJIA alt for JISHISHAN dial of BONAN [PEH]
DAHO-DOO [DAS] lang, Côte d'Ivoire
DAHOMEEN alt for FON-GBE [FOA]
DAHUNI dial of SUAU [SWP]
DAI [DIJ] lang, Indonesia (Maluku)
DAI alt for CHIN, DAAI [DAO]
DAI alt for DAY [DAI]
DAI alt for HLAI [LIC]
DAI dial of LAU [LLU]
DAI KONG alt for TAI NÜA [TDD]
DAI LE alt for LÜ [KHB]
DAI NA alt for TAI NÜA [TDD]

DAI NUEA alt for TAI NÜA [TDD]
DAIDO alt for SINOHOAN dial of PAMONA [BCX]
DAIER alt for DAIR [DRB]
DAIGOK alt for ARECUNA dial of PEMON [AOC]
DAINA alt for YUBANAKOR [YUO]
DAINGGATI alt for DYANGADI [DYN]
DAIOMUNI alt for OYA'OYA [OYY]
DAI-PATU alt for MATU dial of CHIN, KHUMI [CKM]
DAIR [DRB] lang, Sudan
DAIRI alt for BATAK DAIRI [BTD]
DAISO alt for DHAISO [DHS]
DAISU alt for DHAISO [DHS]
DAIYA alt for TAI YA [CUU]
DAIYA-ATAIYAL alt for TAROKO [TRV]
DAJA dial of ACEH [ATJ]
DAJA dial of AKPES [IBE]
DAJISHAN dial of QIANG, SOUTHERN [QMR]
DAJO alt for DAJU, DAR DAJU [DJC]
DAJOU alt for DAJU, DAR DAJU [DJC]
DAJOU alt for DAJU, DAR SILA [DAU]
DAJU alt for DAJU, DAR DAJU [DJC]
DAJU alt for DAJU, DAR SILA [DAU]
DAJU FERNE alt for DAJU, DAR FUR [DAJ]
DAJU MONGO alt for DAJU, DAR DAJU [DJC]
DAJU OUM HADJER alt for DAJU, DAR DAJU [DJC]
DAJU, DAR DAJU [DJC] lang, Chad
DAJU, DAR FUR [DAJ] lang, Sudan
DAJU, DAR SILA [DAU] lang, Chad; also in Sudan
DAK SUT SEDANG dial of SEDANG [SED]
DAKA alt for DIRIM [DIR]
DAKA alt for SAMBA DAKA [CCG]
DAKAKA [BPA] lang, Vanuatu
DAKAKARI alt for C'LELA [DRI]
DAKALLA alt for KADUGLI dial of KATCHA-
   KADUGLI-MIRI [KAT]
DAKANI alt for DAKHINI dial of URDU [URD]
DAKARKARI alt for C'LELA [DRI]
DAKENEI alt for BANIWA [BAI]
DAKHECZJHA alt for JISHISHAN dial of BONAN
   [PEH]
DAKHINI dial of URDU [URD]
DAKHOTA alt for DAKOTA dial of DAKOTA [DHG]
DAKKA [DKK] lang, Indonesia (Sulawesi)
DAKKA alt for DIRIM [DIR]
DAKKA alt for SAMBA DAKA [CCG]
DAKKARKARI alt for C'LELA [DRI]
DAKLAN dial of IBALOI [IBL]
DAKOTA [DHG] lang, USA; also in Canada
DAKOTA dial of DAKOTA [DHG]
DAKPA alt for BROKPAKE [SGT]
DAKPA dial of BANDA, WEST CENTRAL [BBP]
DAKPAKHA [DKA] lang, Bhutan
DAKTJERAT alt for TYARAITY [WOA]
DAKUNZA dial of GUMUZ [GUK]
DAKWA dial of KAMWE [HIG]
DALA alt for FUR [FUR]
DALABON alt for NGALKBUN [NGK]
DALAD alt for DALAT dial of MELANAU [MEL]
DALANDJI alt for DHALANDJI [DHL]
DALAT dial of MELANAU [MEL]
DALDI dial of KONKANI, GOANESE [GOM]

DALECARLIAN [DLC] lang, Sweden
DALENDI alt for DHALANDJI [DHL]
DAL'GARI alt for DHARGARI [DHR]
DALI dial of BAI [PIQ]
DALI dial of LELAK [LLK]
DALIT MURUT dial of PALUAN [PLZ]
DALLOL dial of FULFULDE, WESTERN NIGER [FUH]
DALMAAL alt for DALECARLIAN [DLC]
DALMATIAN [DLM] lang, Croatia
DALOKA alt for NGILE [MAS]
DALOKA dial of NGILE [MAS]
DALONG alt for DARLONG [DLN]
DALONG alt for PAI [PAI]
DALOUA BÉTÉ alt for BÉTÉ, DALOA [BEV]
DALSKA alt for DALECARLIAN [DLC]
DALY RIVER KRIOL dial of KRIOL [ROP]
DAM alt for NDAM [NDM]
DAM dial of BAGIRMI [BMI]
DAM DE BOUSSO alt for BUSO [BSO]
DAM FER alt for KARA [KAH]
DAMA [DMM] lang, Cameroon
DAMA alt for BETE-BENDI [BTT]
DAMA alt for DAASANACH [DSH]
DAMA alt for MURSI [MUZ]
DAMA alt for NAMA [NAQ]
DAMA alt for NAMA dial of MBEMBE, TIGON [NZA]
DAMAGARAM dial of HAUSA [HUA]
DAMAL [UHN] lang, Indonesia (Irian Jaya)
DAMAL dial of DAMAL [UHN]
DAMANI alt for PARABHI dial of KONKANI [KNK]
DAMAQUA alt for NAMA [NAQ]
DAMAR, EAST [DMR] lang, Indonesia (Maluku)
DAMAR, WEST [DRN] lang, Indonesia (Maluku)
DAMARA alt for NAMA [NAQ]
DAMARA dial of NAMA [NAQ]
DAMAT dial of MAASAI [MET]
DAMATA dial of MAMBAE [MGM]
DAMBA dial of KATCHA-KADUGLI-MIRI [KAT]
DAMBI [DAC] lang, Papua New Guinea
DAMBI dial of SAGALLA [TGA]
DAMBIYA dial of MIGAAMA [MMY]
DAMBRO alt for THAI, SOUTHERN [SOU]
DAMBYA alt for DEMBIYA dial of AGAW, WESTERN [QIM]
DAMEDI alt for DAMELI [DML]
DAMEL alt for DAMELI [DML]
DAMELI [DML] lang, Pakistan
DAMI alt for MARIK [DAD]
DAMIA alt for DAMELI [DML]
DAMINYU dial of YELE [YLE]
DAMLALE alt for MAYO-PLATA dial of PELASLA [MLR]
DAMOT alt for AWNGI [AWN]
DAMPAL [DMP] lang, Indonesia (Sulawesi)
DAMPELAS alt for DAMPELASA [DMS]
DAMPELASA [DMS] lang, Indonesia (Sulawesi)
DAMRAW alt for BOOR [BVF]
DAMREY dial of KUY [KDT]
DAMTI alt for GOMME dial of KOMA [KMY]
DAMULIAN alt for TAMIL [TCV]

DAN [DAF] lang, Côte d'Ivoire; also in Guinea, Liberia
DAN alt for BULLA dial of SHEKO [SHE]
DAN alt for DYAN [DYA]
DAN LAI dial of HUNG [HNU]
DAN MUURE dial of PEERE [KUT]
DANA alt for KABA NA [KWV]
"DANAKIL" pejorative alt for AFAR [AFR]
DANAL alt for DANGALÉAT [DAA]
DANARU [DNR] lang, Papua New Guinea
DANAU [DNU] lang, Myanmar
DANAW alt for DANAU [DNU]
DANBA alt for HORPA [ERO]
DANDA dial of NDAU [NDC]
DANDAMI MADIYA alt for MARIA, DANDAMI [DAQ]
DANDAWA alt for DENDI [DEN]
DANDZONGKA alt for SIKKIMESE [SIP]
DANG alt for KEDANG [KSX]
DANG alt for NHANG [NHA]
DANG alt for THARU, DANGAURA [THL]
DANG alt for TUNGAG [LCM]
DANG THARU alt for THARU, DANGAURA [THL]
DANGADI alt for DYANGADI [DYN]
DANGAL alt for DANGALÉAT [DAA]
DANGAL dial of WATUT, SOUTH [MCY]
DANGALÉAT [DAA] lang, Chad
DANGALI alt for HUMLA BHOTIA [HUT]
DANGALI alt for THARU, DANGAURA [THL]
DANGARIK alt for PHALURA [PHL]
DANGATI alt for DYANGADI [DYN]
DANGBE alt for ADANGBE [ADQ]
DANGBON alt for NGALKBUN [NGK]
DANGEDL dial of YIR YORONT [YIY]
DANGGADI alt for DYANGADI [DYN]
DANGGAL alt for DANGAL dial of WATUT, SOUTH [MCY]
DANGGETTI alt for DYANGADI [DYN]
DANGHA alt for THARU, DANGAURA [THL]
DANGI alt for DHANKI [DHN]
DANGI dial of BRAJ BHASHA [BFS]
DANGLA alt for DANGALÉAT [DAA]
DANGME [DGM] lang, Ghana; also in Togo
DANGORA alt for THARU, DANGAURA [THL]
DANGRI alt for DHANKI [DHN]
DANGS BHIL alt for DHANKI [DHN]
DANGU alt for DHANGU [GLA]
DANGURA alt for THARU, DANGAURA [THL]
DANI alt for DENÍ [DAN]
DANI BARAT alt for DANI, WESTERN [DNW]
DANI, LOWER GRAND VALLEY [DNI] lang, Indonesia (Irian Jaya)
DANI, MID GRAND VALLEY [DNT] lang, Indonesia (Irian Jaya)
DANI, UPPER GRAND VALLEY [DNA] lang, Indonesia (Irian Jaya)
DANI, WESTERN [DNW] lang, Indonesia (Irian Jaya)
DANIEL CARRION alt for QUECHUA, PASCO-YANAHUANCA [QUR]
DANI-KURIMA alt for LOWER GRAND VALLEY HITIGIMA dial of DANI, LOWER GRAND VALLEY [DNI]
DANISA alt for DANISI dial of SHUA [SHG]

DÄNISCH alt for DANISH [DNS]
DANISH [DNS] lang, Denmark; also in Canada,
    Germany, Greenland, Norway, Sweden, UAE,
    USA
DANISH SIGN LANGUAGE [DSL] lang, Denmark
DANISI dial of SHUA [SHG]
DANISIS alt for DANISI dial of SHUA [SHG]
DANJONGKA alt for SIKKIMESE [SIP]
DANKYIRA dial of AKAN [TWS]
DANO [ASO] lang, Papua New Guinea
DANO-NORWEGIAN alt for NORWEGIAN,
    BOKMAAL [NRR]
DANPURIYA dial of KUMAUNI [KFY]
DANSHE dial of ZEEM [ZUA]
DANSK alt for DANISH [DNS]
DANU dial of BURMESE [BMS]
DANU dial of MADAK [MMX]
DANUBE-TISZA dial of HUNGARIAN [HNG]
DANUBIAN alt for ROMANI, VLAX [RMY]
DANUBIAN dial of TURKISH [TRK]
DANUWAR alt for DHANWAR [DHA]
DANUWAR alt for DHANWAR [DHW]
DANUWAR RAI alt for DHANWAR [DHW]
DANYOUKA alt for SIKKIMESE [SIP]
DAO [DAZ] lang, Indonesia (Irian Jaya)
DAO alt for IU MIEN [IUM]
DAO alt for NDAO [NFA]
DAOFU dial of HORPA [ERO]
DAOFUHUA alt for DAOFU dial of HORPA [ERO]
DAONDA [DND] lang, Papua New Guinea
DAONGDUNG dial of SAMA, BALANGINGI [SSE]
DAOSAHAQ alt for TADAKSAHAK [DSQ]
DAOUSSAHAQ alt for TADAKSAHAK [DSQ]
DAOUSSAK alt for TADAKSAHAK [DSQ]
DAP alt for BROKPAKE [SGT]
DAPALAN dial of TALAUD [TLD]
DAPERA alt for OUNE [OUE]
DAPHLA alt for NISI [DAP]
DAPITAN dial of SUBANEN, NORTHERN [STB]
DAPO dial of KRUMEN, TEPO [TED]
DAR EL KABIRA dial of TULISHI [TEY]
DARAGA dial of BICOLANO, ALBAY [BHK]
DARAGAWAN alt for KARAGAWAN dial of ISNAG
    [ISD]
DARAI [DRY] lang, Nepal
DARAMBAL alt for BAYALI [BJY]
DARANG alt for DARANG DENG [DAT]
DARANG DENG [DAT] lang, China
DARASA alt for GEDEO [DRS]
DARASSA alt for GEDEO [DRS]
DARAVA dial of MAILU [MGU]
DARAWAL alt for BAYALI [BJY]
DARBÉ dial of GABRI [GAB]
DAREL alt for CHILASI KOHISTANI dial of SHINA
    [SCL]
DARGIN alt for DARGWA [DAR]
DARGINTSY alt for DARGWA [DAR]
DARGWA [DAR] lang, Russia (Europe); also in
    Azerbaijan, Kazakhstan, Kyrgyzstan, Turkey
    (Asia), Turkmenistan, Ukraine, Uzbekistan
DARHA alt for TAUSE [TAD]

DARI [GBZ] lang, Iran
DARI alt for DEORI [DER]
DARI alt for FARSI, EASTERN [PRS]
DARI dial of FARSI, EASTERN [PRS]
DARI dial of PEVE [LME]
DARIBI alt for DADIBI [MPS]
DARIEN alt for EMBERÁ, NORTHERN [EMP]
DARIÉN alt for EMBERÁ, NORTHERN [EMP]
DARIENA alt for EMBERÁ, NORTHERN [EMP]
DARIGANGA dial of MONGOLIAN, HALH [KHK]
DARIMIYA alt for DARMIYA [DRD]
DARJULA dial of NEPALI [NEP]
DARKHAT [DAY] lang, Mongolia
DARLING [DRL] lang, Australia
DARLONG [DLN] lang, Bangladesh; also in India
DARMIYA [DRD] lang, India
DARO dial of DARO-MATU [DRO]
DARO-MATU [DRO] lang, Malaysia (Sarawak)
DARORO alt for KACHICHERE dial of TYAP [KCG]
DARRA alt for NGILE [MAS]
DARRAI NUR dial of PASHAYI, SOUTHEAST [DRA]
DARU KIWAI dial of KIWAI, SOUTHERN [KJD]
DARUBIA dial of SEWA BAY [SEW]
DARUMBAL alt for BAYALI [BJY]
DARWAZI [DRW] lang, Afghanistan
DASA alt for DAZAGA [DAK]
DASARI dial of TELUGU [TCW]
DASEA alt for TUCANO [TUO]
DASENECH alt for DAASANACH [DSH]
DASENER dial of WANDAMEN [WAD]
DASHANHUA alt for JINGPHO [CGP]
DASHWA dial of KALAMI [GWC]
DASS [DOT] lang, Nigeria
DATAGNON alt for RATAGNON [BTN]
DATHANAIC alt for DAASANACH [DSH]
DATHANAIK alt for DAASANACH [DSH]
DATHANIK alt for DAASANACH [DSH]
DATIWUY dial of DHUWAL [DUJ]
DATOG alt for DATOOGA [TCC]
DATOGA alt for DATOOGA [TCC]
DATOOGA [TCC] lang, Tanzania
DATUANA dial of YAHUNA [YNU]
DAU dial of IBAN [IBA]
DAUI dial of SUAU [SWP]
DAUPHINOIS dial of FRANCO-PROVENÇAL [FRA]
DAUPHINOIS dial of PROVENÇAL [PRV]
DAUPKA dial of NINGGERUM [NXR]
DAUR [DTA] lang, China
DAURI dial for ATORADA dial of ARUMA [WAP]
DAURO alt for DAWRO dial of GAMO-GOFA-
    DAWRO [GMO]
DAUSAHAQ alt for TADAKSAHAK [DSQ]
DAUSAME alt for TAO-SUAMATO [TSX]
DAUWA alt for NDUGA [NDX]
DAVACH alt for HRE [HRE]
DAVAK alt for HRE [HRE]
DAVAO CHAVACANO alt for DAVAWENYO
    ZAMBOANGUENYO dial of CHAVACANO [CBK]
DAVAOEÑO alt for DAVAWENYO [DAW]
DAVAOEÑO alt for DAVAWENYO
    ZAMBOANGUENYO dial of CHAVACANO [CBK]

DAVARI alt for AMBASI dial of BINANDERE [BHG]
DAVARI dial of VARLI [VAV]
DAVAWEÑO alt for DAVAWENYO [DAW]
DAVAWEÑO alt for DAVAWENYO
ZAMBOANGUENYO dial of CHAVACANO
[CBK]
DAVAWENYO [DAW] lang, Philippines
DAVAWENYO ZAMBOANGUENYO dial of
CHAVACANO [CBK]
DAVELOR alt for DAWERA-DAWELOOR [DDW]
DAVIDA alt for TAITA [DAV]
DAVVIN alt for SAAMI, NORTHERN [LPR]
DÂW alt for KAMÃ [KWA]
DAWA alt for NDUGA [NDX]
DAWADA dial of DUAU [DUA]
DAWADA-SIAUSI alt for LOBODA dial of DOBU
[DOB]
DAWAI alt for TAUNGYO [TCO]
DAWAN alt for ATONI [TMR]
DAWANA alt for DAWAWA [DWW]
DAWAR alt for DAUR [DTA]
DAWARI alt for AMBASI dial of BINANDERE [BHG]
DAWAS dial of KUBU [KVB]
DAWAWA [DWW] lang, Papua New Guinea
DAWE alt for TAUNGYO [TCO]
DAWERA-DAWELOOR [DDW] lang, Indonesia
(Maluku)
DAWIDA alt for TAITA [DAV]
DAWO'ER alt for DAUR [DTA]
DAWRA dial of HAUSA [HUA]
DAWRO dial of GAMO-GOFA-DAWRO [GMO]
DAWSAHAQ alt for TADAKSAHAK [DSQ]
DAWSON alt for HAN [HAA]
DAXSEA alt for TUCANO [TUO]
DAY [DAI] lang, Chad
DAY alt for HLAI [LIC]
DAYA dial of MALAY [MLI]
DAYAK AHE alt for AHE [AHE]
DAYAK KANINJAL alt for KENINJAL [KNL]
DAYAK TAMAN alt for TAMAN [TMN]
DAYAK, LAND [DYK] lang, Indonesia (Kalimantan)
DAYANG dial of NAGA, SUMI [NSM]
DAYAO dial of YI, CENTRAL [YIC]
DAYI [DAX] lang, Australia
DAYILI dial of SHANGZHAI [JIH]
DAZA [DZD] lang, Nigeria
DAZA alt for DAZAGA [DAK]
DAZAGA [DAK] lang, Chad; also in Niger
DAZAGA dial of DAZAGA [DAK]
DAZANG alt for CHABAO dial of JIARONG [JYA]
DAZAWA alt for DAZA [DZD]
DAZZA alt for DAZAGA [DAK]
DBUS alt for TIBETAN [TIC]
DBUS dial of TIBETAN [TIC]
DBUSGTSANG alt for TIBETAN [TIC]
DCUI alt for /GWI [GWJ]
DDRALO dial of LENDU [LED]
DE alt for DEWOIN [DEE]
DE alt for RADE [RAD]
DE dial of GOLA [GOL]
DE' alt for BUGIS [BPR]

DE BOR alt for BELANDA BOR [BXB]
DEA alt for ZIMAKANI [ZIK]
DEA dial of MANAGALASI [MCQ]
DEA dial of ZIMAKANI [ZIK]
DEAH alt for DUSUN DEYAH [DUN]
DEBA alt for YIDINY [YII]
DEBABAON alt for MANOBO, DIBABAWON [MBD]
DEBATSA alt for GUMUZ [GUK]
DEBBARMA dial of KOK BOROK [TRP]
DÉBO dial of BOZO, SOROGAMA [BZE]
DEBRECEN dial of HUNGARIAN SIGN LANGUAGE
[HSH]
DEBRI dial of DILLING [DIL]
DEBUGA alt for GUMUZ [GUK]
DECCAN [DCC] lang, India
DECCAN alt for DAKHINI dial of URDU [URD]
DECCANI alt for DECCAN [DCC]
DE'CUANA alt for MAQUIRITARI [MCH]
DE'CUANA dial of MAQUIRITARI [MCH]
DEDE dial of NZANYI [NJA]
DEDIEBO dial of GREBO, GBOLOO [GEC]
DEDUA [DED] lang, Papua New Guinea
DEENU dial of SAMBA LEKO [NDI]
DEFA dial of BAKWE [BAK]
DEFAKA [AFN] lang, Nigeria
DEFALE dial of LAMA [LAS]
DEG [MZW] lang, Ghana; also in Côte d'Ivoire
DEG XINAG alt for DEGEXIT'AN [ING]
DEG XIT'AN alt for DEGEXIT'AN [ING]
DEGARU [DGR] lang, India
DEGATI alt for DAGAARE, SOUTHERN [DGA]
DEGATI alt for DAGARA, NORTHERN [DGI]
DEGEMA [DEG] lang, Nigeria
DEGENAN [DGE] lang, Papua New Guinea
DEGEXIT'AN [ING] lang, USA
DEGHA alt for DEG [MZW]
DEGHWARI alt for DEHWARI [DEH]
DEGODIA dial of SOMALI [SOM]
DEGOJA alt for DAKUNZA dial of GUMUZ [GUK]
DEGUBA alt for GUMUZ [GUK]
DEHATI dial of MAITHILI [MKP]
DEHAWALI dial of BHILI [BHB]
DEHENDA alt for GUMUZ [GUK]
DEHES alt for EL MOLO [ELO]
DEHONG alt for TAI NÜA [TDD]
DEHONG dial of TAI NÜA [TDD]
DEHONG DAI alt for TAI NÜA [TDD]
DEHOXDE alt for DGHWEDE [DGH]
DEHRI alt for MAL PAHARIA [MKB]
DEHU [DEU] lang, New Caledonia
DEHVALI dial of VASAVI [VAS]
DEHWARI [DEH] lang, Pakistan
DEI alt for DEWOIN [DEE]
DEIBULA dial of KORUPUN-SELA [KPQ]
DEING dial of TEWA [TWE]
DEIRATE dial of TAUSE [TAD]
DEJAH alt for DUSUN DEYAH [DUN]
DEJBUK dial of DARGWA [DAR]
DE-JING dial of ZHUANG, SOUTHERN [CCY]
DEK [DEK] lang, Cameroon
DEKINI alt for DECCAN [DCC]

DEKKA alt for SAMBA DAKA [CCG]
DEKOKA dial of GUMUZ [GUK]
DEKSHI alt for LUKSHI dial of DASS [DOT]
DEKWAMBRE alt for MPUR [AKC]
DELANG dial of MALAYIC DAYAK [XDY]
DELAWARE alt for MUNSEE [UMU]
DELAWARE alt for UNAMI [DEL]
DELAWARE, PIDGIN [DEP] lang, USA
DELEN alt for DILLING [DIL]
DELHA alt for OENALE-DELHA dial of ROTE,
    WESTERN [ROW]
DELHI SIGN LANGUAGE dial of INDIAN SIGN
    LANGUAGE [INS]
DELI dial of MALAY [MLI]
DELNOSERBSKI alt for SORBIAN, LOWER [WEE]
DELO [NTR] lang, Ghana; also in Togo
DELTA PIDGIN dial of PIDGIN, NIGERIAN [PCM]
DELTA PWO KAREN alt for KAREN, PWO
    WESTERN [PWO]
DELTA RIVER YUMAN alt for COCOPA [COC]
DEM [DEM] lang, Indonesia (Irian Jaya)
DEMA alt for TUPURI [TUI]
DEMAM alt for KETUNGAU dial of IBAN [IBA]
DEMBA alt for TEFARO [TFO]
DEMBIYA dial of AGAW, WESTERN [QIM]
DEMBO alt for BODHO dial of THURI [THU]
DEMBYA alt for DEMBIYA dial of AGAW, WESTERN
    [QIM]
DEMEN alt for BODHO dial of THURI [THU]
DEMENGGONG-WAIBRON-BANO alt for MEKWEI
    [MSF]
DEMIK alt for KEIGA [KEC]
DEMIK dial of KEIGA [KEC]
DEMISA [DEI] lang, Indonesia (Irian Jaya)
DEMISA alt for DANISI dial of SHUA [SHG]
DEMSA dial of BATA [BTA]
DEMSA BATA alt for BATA [BTA]
DEMSHIN alt for MIYA [MKF]
DEMTA [DMY] lang, Indonesia (Irian Jaya)
DEMWA dial of PELASLA [MLR]
DENA'INA alt for TANAINA [TFN]
DENAWA alt for DENO [DBB]
DENDI [DEN] lang, Benin; also in Nigeria
DENDI [DEQ] lang, CAR
DENDJE alt for DUNJE dial of KABA NA [KWV]
DENE alt for CHIPEWYAN [CPW]
DENÉ alt for SLAVEY, NORTH [SCS]
DENÉ alt for SLAVEY, SOUTH [SLA]
DENG alt for DE dial of GOLA [GOL]
DENG alt for SAMBA DAKA [CCG]
DENG dial of GOLA [GOL]
DENGALU [DEA] lang, Papua New Guinea
DENGEBU alt for DAGIK [DEC]
DENGESE [DEZ] lang, DCR
DENGKA dial of ROTE, WESTERN [ROW]
DENGKWOP alt for GHOMÁLÁ' SOUTH dial of
    GHOMALA [BBJ]
DENGSA dial of LAMJA-DENGSA-TOLA [LDH]
DENGURUME alt for NGURIMI [NGQ]
DENI alt for NDENI dial of SANTA CRUZ [STC]
DENÍ [DAN] lang, Brazil

DENJE alt for DUNJE dial of KABA NA [KWV]
DENJONG alt for SIKKIMESE [SIP]
DENJONGKHA alt for SIKKIMESE [SIP]
DENJONGPA alt for SIKKIMESE [SIP]
DENJONKA alt for SIKKIMESE [SIP]
DENJONKE alt for SIKKIMESE [SIP]
"DENKEL" pejorative alt for AFAR [AFR]
DENO [DBB] lang, Nigeria
DENTONG alt for BENTONG [BNU]
DENWA alt for DENO [DBB]
DENWAR alt for DHANWAR [DHW]
DENYA [ANV] lang, Cameroon
DEO TIEN dial of IU MIEN [IUM]
DEOKHAR alt for THARU, DEOKHURI [THG]
DEOKRI alt for THARU, DEOKHURI [THG]
DEORI [DER] lang, India
DEOSALI alt for THULUNG [TDH]
DEPLE dial of BAKWE [BAK]
DEQ alt for BATEK DE' dial of BATEK [BTQ]
DERA [KNA] lang, Nigeria
DERA alt for KAMBERATARO [KBV]
DERASA alt for GEDEO [DRS]
DERASANYA alt for GEDEO [DRS]
DERAWALI dial of SARAIKI [SKR]
DERBEND dial of AZERBAIJANI, NORTH [AZE]
DERBEND dial of JUDEO-TAT [TAT]
DERBENT dial of AZERBAIJANI, NORTH [AZE]
DERBET alt for DÖRBÖT dial of KALMYK-OIRAT
    [KGZ]
DEREBAI dial of MAILU [MGU]
DERESA alt for GEDEO [DRS]
DERESSIA alt for TOBANGA dial of TOBANGA
    [TNG]
DERMUHA dial of KAREN, PAKU [KPP]
DERSIMKI alt for KIRMANJKI [QKV]
DERUWO dial of WAJA [WJA]
DESA dial of IBAN [IBA]
DESÁNA alt for DESANO [DES]
DESÂNA alt for DESANO [DES]
DESANO [DES] lang, Brazil; also in Colombia
DESARI alt for HARYANVI [BGC]
DESHIA alt for ORIYA, ADIVASI [ORT]
DESI alt for DECCAN [DCC]
DESIA alt for DAKHINI dial of URDU [URD]
DESIA alt for ORIYA, ADIVASI [ORT]
DESIA ORIYA alt for KORAPUT ORIYA dial of
    ORIYA [ORY]
DESIN DOLA' alt for DUANO' [DUP]
DESIYA alt for ORIYA, ADIVASI [ORT]
DESSANA alt for DESANO [DES]
DESSANO alt for DESANO [DES]
DESSAULYA dial of GARHWALI [GBM]
DESUA alt for DISOHA dial of GUMUZ [GUK]
DESWALI dial of HARYANVI [BGC]
DETAH-NDILO dial of DOGRIB [DGB]
DETI [DET] lang, Botswana
DETI-KHWE alt for DETI [DET]
DE'U alt for DEHU [DEU]
DEURI alt for DEORI [DER]
DEUSALI alt for THULUNG [TDH]
DEUTSCH alt for GERMAN, STANDARD [GER]

DEUTSCHE GEBÄRDENSPRACHE alt for GERMAN SIGN LANGUAGE [GSG]
DEVECHI dial of TAT, MUSLIM [TTT]
DEVEHI alt for MALDIVIAN [SNM]
DEVONSHIRE dial of ENGLISH [ENG]
DEWALA dial of LEWADA-DEWARA [LWD]
DEWALA-LEWADA alt for LEWADA-DEWARA [LWD]
DEWANSALA alt for YAKHA [YBH]
DEWIYA dial of GUMUZ [GUK]
DEWOI alt for DEWOIN [DEE]
DEWOIN [DEE] lang, Liberia
DEWRI alt for DEORI [DER]
DEY alt for DEWOIN [DEE]
DFOLA alt for BIAFADA [BIF]
DGERNESIAIS dial of FRENCH [FRN]
DGHWEDE [DGH] lang, Nigeria
DGIÉH alt for TRIENG [STG]
DGS alt for GERMAN SIGN LANGUAGE [GSG]
DHADING dial of TAMANG, NORTHWESTERN [TMK]
DHA'I alt for DAYI [DAX]
DHAISO [DHS] lang, Tanzania
DHALANDJI [DHL] lang, Australia
DHALLA alt for KADUGLI dial of KATCHA-KADUGLI-MIRI [KAT]
DHALWANGU dial of DAYI [DAX]
DHAMMAI dial of HRUSO [HRU]
DHANAGARI alt for VARHADI-NAGPURI [VAH]
DHANAGARI dial of KONKANI [KNK]
DHANGAR alt for KURUX, NEPALI [KXL]
DHANGU [GLA] lang, Australia
DHANGU-DJANGU dial of DHANGU [GLA]
DHANGU'MI alt for DHANGU [GLA]
DHANKA alt for DHANKI [DHN]
DHANKI [DHN] lang, India
DHANKUTA alt for EASTERN BANTAWA dial of BANTAWA [BAP]
DHANORA dial of MURIA, WESTERN [MUT]
DHANU'UN alt for DANGEDL dial of YIR YORONT [YIY]
DHANVAR alt for DHANWAR [DHA]
DHANVAR alt for DHANWAR [DHW]
DHANWAR [DHA] lang, India
DHANWAR [DHW] lang, Nepal
DHARAWAAL alt for THURAWAL [TBH]
DHARAWAL alt for THURAWAL [TBH]
DHARBA dial of DURUWA [PCI]
DHARGARI [DHR] lang, Australia
DHARTHI dial of SIRMAURI [SRX]
DHARUA alt for KUDMALI [KYW]
DHARWAR alt for KALVADI dial of DECCAN [DCC]
DHATI alt for DHATKI [MKI]
DHATKI [MKI] lang, Pakistan
DHAY'YI alt for DAYI [DAX]
DHE BOODHO alt for BODHO dial of THURI [THU]
DHE COLO alt for COLO dial of THURI [THU]
DHE LUWO alt for LUWO [LWO]
DHE LWO alt for LUWO [LWO]
DHE THURI alt for THURI [THU]
DHED alt for MAHARI dial of KONKANI [KNK]

DHED GUJARI alt for KHANDESI [KHN]
DHEDI alt for MAHARI dial of VARHADI-NAGPURI [VAH]
DHEKARU alt for DEGARU [DGR]
DHELKI KHARIA dial of KHARIA [KHR]
DHIBALI alt for BALI [BCP]
DHIMAL [DHI] lang, Nepal
DHIMBA alt for ZEMBA [DHM]
DHIMORONG alt for MORO [MOR]
DHIRAILA dial of NGURA [NBX]
DHIRASHA alt for DIRASHA [GDL]
DHITORO alt for OTORO [OTR]
DHO ALUR alt for ALUR [ALZ]
DHO ANYWAA alt for ANUAK [ANU]
DHOCOLO alt for SHILLUK [SHK]
DHODIA [DHO] lang, India
DHOFARI alt for ARABIC, DHOFARI SPOKEN [ADF]
DHOGARYALI alt for DOGRI-KANGRI [DOJ]
DHOLEWARI dial of MALVI [MUP]
DHOLUBI alt for KATCHA dial of KATCHA-KADUGLI-MIRI [KAT]
DHOLUO alt for LUO [LUO]
DHOPADHOLA alt for ADHOLA [ADH]
DHOPALUO dial of ACHOLI [ACO]
DHORE alt for DHODIA [DHO]
DHORI alt for DHODIA [DHO]
DHOWARI alt for DHODIA [DHO]
DHRUVA alt for DURUWA [PCI]
DHUNDHARI dial of MARWARI [MKD]
DHUNDI-KAIRALI alt for PAHARI dial of PAHARI-POTWARI [PHR]
DHUNDI-KAIRALI alt for PAHARI-POTWARI [PHR]
DHUNGRI GARASIA alt for GARASIA, RAJPUT [GRA]
DHUNKURIA KANWAR KHATI alt for LOHAR, GADE [GDA]
DHURGA [DHU] lang, Australia
DHU'RGA dial of DHURGA [DHU]
DHURI alt for SURI [SUQ]
DHURU alt for MARIA, DANDAMI [DAQ]
DHURWA alt for DURUWA [PCI]
DHUWAL [DUJ] lang, Australia
DHUWAL dial of DHUWAL [DUJ]
DHUWAYA dial of DHUWAL [DUJ]
DI alt for DING [DIZ]
DIA [DIA] lang, Papua New Guinea
DIA alt for BUOL [BLF]
DIA alt for DJIA dial of SAKATA [SAT]
DIABE dial of GBAYA-BOZOUM [GBQ]
DIAHÓI dial of TENHARIM [PAH]
DIAHOUE alt for JAWE [JAZ]
DIAKHANKE alt for JAHANKA [JAD]
DIAKHANKE alt for JAHANKA dial of MALINKE [MLQ]
DIAKKANKE alt for JAHANKA [JAD]
DIAKKANKE alt for JAHANKA dial of MALINKE [MLQ]
DIALONKE alt for JALUNGA [YAL]
DIALONKÉ alt for JALUNGA [YAL]
DIALONKE alt for YALUNKA [YAL]
DIAMALA dial of SENOUFO, DJIMINI [DYI]

DIAN alt for DAMPELASA [DMS]
DIAN alt for DYAN [DYA]
DIAN DONGBEI dial of YI, GUIZHOU [YIG]
DIANDONGBEI alt for HMONG, NORTHEASTERN
 DIAN [HMD]
DI-ANG alt for PALAUNG, PALE [PCE]
DIANG dial of KURANKO [KHA]
DIAN-QIAN dial of YI, GUIZHOU [YIG]
DIARBEKIR alt for TIGRANAKERT dial of
 ARMENIAN [ARM]
DIAWARA alt for SONINKE [SNN]
DIBA alt for TUVIN [TUN]
DIBABAON alt for MANOBO, DIBABAWON [MBD]
DIBAGAT-KABUGAO dial of ISNAG [ISD]
DIBAGAT-KABUGAO-ISNEG alt for ISNAG [ISD]
"DIBATCHUA" pejorative alt for KANGO [KZY]
DIBIASU alt for BAINAPI [PIK]
DIBLAEG alt for IDI [IDI]
DIBO [DIO] lang, Nigeria
DIBOUM dial of BASAA [BAA]
DIBUM dial of MEOHANG, EASTERN [EMG]
DICAMAY DUMAGAT alt for AGTA, DICAMAY
 [DUY]
DIDA, LAKOTA [DIC] lang, Côte d'Ivoire
DIDA, YOCOBOUÉ [GUD] lang, Côte d'Ivoire
DIDAYI alt for GATA' [GAQ]
DIDEI alt for GATA' [GAQ]
DIDESSA alt for BAMBASSI [MYF]
DIDI dial of KALIKO [KBO]
DIDIGARU dial of MARIA [MDS]
DIDIGAVU dial of IAMALELE [YML]
DIDINGA [DID] lang, Sudan
'DI'DINGA alt for DIDINGA [DID]
DIDIU alt for COCHIMÍ [COJ]
DIDO [DDO] lang, Russia (Europe)
DIDOI alt for DIDO [DDO]
DIDRA alt for TODRAH [TDR]
DIDRAH alt for TODRAH [TDR]
DIE alt for JEH [JEH]
DI'E dial of AI-CHAM [AIH]
DIEGUEÑO alt for KUMIÁI [DIH]
DIEKO alt for DIDA, LAKOTA [DIC]
DIERI [DIF] lang, Australia
DIÉS alt for EGA [DIE]
DIGAM dial of MPADE [MPI]
DIGARO [MHU] lang, India
DIGARU alt for DIGARO [MHU]
DIGENJA alt for LIGENZA [LGZ]
"DIGGER" pejorative alt for MAIDU, NORTHWEST
 [MAI]
DIGO [DIG] lang, Kenya; also in Tanzania
DIGOEL alt for SOUTHERN MUYU dial of
 YONGKOM [YON]
DIGOR dial of OSETIN [OSE]
DIGUL alt for SOUTHERN MUYU dial of YONGKOM
 [YON]
DIGUT alt for GAVIÃO DO JIPARANÁ [GVO]
DIH BRI dial of MNONG, CENTRAL [MNC]
DIHINA dial of GAWWADA [GWD]
DIHOK dial of CHALDEAN NEO-ARAMAIC [CLD]
DII [DUR] lang, Cameroon

DII alt for BATA [BTA]
DIILA alt for KUNAMA [KUM]
DIIR alt for DIR dial of POLCI [POL]
DIJAMA dial of OTORO [OTR]
DIJE alt for TUMAK [TMC]
DIJIM dial of DIJIM-BWILIM [CFA]
DIJIM-BWILIM [CFA] lang, Nigeria
DIKAKA alt for KAKO [KKJ]
DIKANGO alt for KANGO [KBI]
DIKANGO alt for KANGO [KZY]
DIKAYU dial of SUBANEN, NORTHERN [STB]
DIKELE alt for KÉLÉ [KEB]
DIKELE alt for KILI [KEB]
DIKINI dial of MARAGHEI [VMH]
DIKKU KAJI alt for SADRI [SCK]
DIKO dial of GBAGYI [GBR]
DIKOTA dial of NGANDO [NGD]
DIKUTA dial of NGANDO [NGD]
DILAUT-BADJAO dial of SAMA, CENTRAL [SML]
DILI TETUN alt for TETUM PRASA [TDT]
DILLING [DIL] lang, Sudan
DILLING dial of DILLING [DIL]
DILPALI alt for NORTHERN BANTAWA dial of
 BANTAWA [BAP]
DIM alt for ADIM dial of AGWAGWUNE [YAY]
DIMA alt for DIME [DIM]
DIMA alt for JIMAJIMA [JMA]
DIMALI dial of NACHERING [NCD]
DIMASA [DIS] lang, India
DIMASA dial of DIMASA [DIS]
DIMASA KACHARI alt for DIMASA [DIS]
DIMBA alt for ZEMBA [DHM]
DIMBAMBANG alt for MBANG dial of BAKOKO
 [BKH]
DIMBONG [DII] lang, Cameroon
DIME [DIM] lang, Ethiopia
DIME alt for GINUMAN [GNM]
DIMEO dial of MOFU-GUDUR [MIF]
DIMILI alt for DIMLI [ZZZ]
DIMILKI alt for KIRMANJKI [QKV]
DIMIR [DMC] lang, Papua New Guinea
DIMISI alt for IDI [IDI]
DIMLI [ZZZ] lang, Turkey (Asia); also in
 Germany
DIMMUK dial of KOFYAR [KWL]
DIMODONGO alt for KRONGO [KGO]
DIMOTIKI dial of GREEK [GRK]
DIMSISI alt for IDI [IDI]
DIMU alt for TIMU dial of SABU [HVN]
DIMUGA alt for DAGA [DGZ]
DIMUK alt for DIMMUK dial of KOFYAR [KWL]
DIN alt for DING [DIZ]
DINDJE alt for DUNJE dial of KABA NA [KWV]
DINE alt for NAVAJO [NAV]
DING [DIZ] lang, DCR
DINGANDO alt for NGANDO [NGD]
DINGI alt for DUNGU [DBV]
DINIK alt for AFITTI [AFT]
DINJE alt for DUNJE dial of KABA NA [KWV]
DINKA IBRAHIM alt for ABILIANG dial of DINKA,
 NORTHEASTERN [DIP]

DINKA, NORTHEASTERN [DIP] lang, Sudan
DINKA, NORTHWESTERN [DIW] lang, Sudan
DINKA, SOUTH CENTRAL [DIB] lang, Sudan
DINKA, SOUTHEASTERN [DIN] lang, Sudan
DINKA, SOUTHWESTERN [DIK] lang, Sudan
DINLER dial of TURKISH [TRK]
DIO alt for KAIDIPANG [KZP]
DIO dial of ZANDE [ZAN]
DIODIO [DDI] lang, Papua New Guinea
DIOI alt for BOUYEI [PCC]
DIOI alt for NHANG [NHA]
DIOLA-FOGNY alt for JOLA-FOGNY [DYO]
DIOLA-KASA alt for JOLA-KASA [CSK]
DIONGOR GUERA alt for MUKULU [MOZ]
DIONKOR alt for MIGAAMA [MMY]
DIORE alt for XIKRIN dial of KAYAPO [TXU]
DIOULA alt for JULA [DYU]
DIOULA VÉHICULAIRE dial of JULA [DYU]
DI-PRI alt for DIH BRI dial of MNONG, CENTRAL
   [MNC]
DIR dial of POLCI [POL]
DIR KOHISTANI alt for KALAMI [GWC]
DIRAASHA alt for DIRASHA [GDL]
DIRANG alt for SANGLA dial of MOINBA [MOB]
DIRARI [DIT] lang, Australia
DIRASHA [GDL] lang, Ethiopia
DIRAYTA alt for DIRASHA [GDL]
DIRE alt for GATA' [GAQ]
DIRI [DWA] lang, Nigeria
DIRI alt for KALAMI [GWC]
DIRIA alt for CHOROTEGA [CJR]
DIRIA dial of CHOROTEGA [CJR]
DIRIKO alt for DIRIKU [DIU]
DIRIKU [DIU] lang, Namibia; also in Angola
DIRIM [DIR] lang, Nigeria
DIRIM dial of SAMBA DAKA [CCG]
DIRIN alt for DIRIM [DIR]
DIRIYA alt for DIRI [DWA]
DIRMA alt for TIRMA dial of SURI [SUQ]
DIRONG-GURUF dial of ZAGHAWA [ZAG]
DIRRIM alt for DIRIM [DIR]
DIRWALI alt for KALAMI [GWC]
DIRYA alt for DIRI [DWA]
DIRYAWA alt for DIRI [DWA]
DISA [DIV] lang, Chad
DISHILI alt for TAPSHIN [TDL]
DISO alt for MARU [MHX]
DISOHA dial of GUMUZ [GUK]
DISPOHOLNON dial of INONHAN [LOC]
DITAMARI alt for DITAMMARI [TBZ]
DITAMMARI [TBZ] lang, Benin
DITAYLIN ALTA alt for ALTA, NORTHERN [AQN]
DITAYLIN DUMAGAT alt for ALTA, NORTHERN
   [AQN]
DITTI alt for AFITTI [AFT]
DIU alt for BOLANGO [BLD]
DIU alt for BILBA-DIU-LELENUK dial of ROTE
   [ROT]
DÌU alt for IU MIEN [IUM]
DIULA alt for JULA [DYU]
DIUWE [DIY] lang, Indonesia (Irian Jaya)

DIUXI MIXTEC alt for MIXTECO, DIUXI-
   TILANTONGO [MIS]
DIVEHI alt for MALDIVIAN [SNM]
DIVEHI BAS alt for MALDIVIAN [SNM]
DIVEHLI alt for MALDIVIAN [SNM]
DIVINAI alt for TAWALA dial of TAWALA [TBO]
DIVO dial of DIDA, YOCOBOUE [GUD]
DIWALA alt for DUALA [DOU]
DIWINAI alt for TAWALA dial of TAWALA [TBO]
DIXON REEF [DIX] lang, Vanuatu
DIYARBAKIR alt for TIGRANAKERT dial of
   ARMENIAN [ARM]
DIYARI alt for DIERI [DIF]
DIYI alt for JUKUN TAKUM [JBU]
DIYU alt for JUKUN TAKUM [JBU]
DIZI [MDX] lang, Ethiopia
DIZI-MAJI alt for DIZI [MDX]
DIZU alt for BENCH [BCQ]
DJA alt for DJIA dial of SAKATA [SAT]
DJABUGAI alt for DYAABUGAY [DYY]
DJADHA dial of LENDU [LED]
DJADIWITJIBI dial of DJINANG [DJI]
DJAFOLO dial of SENOUFO, DJIMINI [DYI]
DJAGA alt for CHAGGA [KAF]
DJAIR alt for JAIR [YIR]
DJAKUN alt for JAKUN [JAK]
DJALENDI alt for DHALANDJI [DHL]
DJALLONKE alt for JALUNGA [YAL]
DJALLONKE alt for YALUNKA [YAL]
DJAMA dial of IFE [IFE]
DJAMALA alt for DIAMALA dial of SENOUFO,
   DJIMINI [DYI]
DJAMBARBWINGU alt for DJAMBARRPUYNGU
   [DJR]
DJAMBARRPUYNGU [DJR] lang, Australia
DJAMBI dial of KUBU [KVB]
DJAMCHIDI alt for JAMSHIDI dial of AIMAQ [AIQ]
DJAMINDJUNG [DJD] lang, Australia
DJANET alt for GHAT dial of TAMAHAQ,
   TAHAGGART [THV]
DJANG alt for ARUEK [AUR]
DJANG alt for REJANG [REJ]
DJANG BELE TEBO alt for REJANG [REJ]
DJANG LEBONG alt for LEBONG dial of REJANG
   [REJ]
DJANGGU alt for ELSENG [MRF]
DJANGGUN alt for DJANGUN [DJF]
DJANGU alt for DHANGU [GLA]
DJANGUN [DJF] lang, Australia
DJANTI alt for TIBEA [NGY]
DJAO alt for YAO [YAO]
DJAPU dial of DHUWAL [DUJ]
DJARAI alt for JARAI [JRA]
DJARRWARK dial of DAYI [DAX]
DJARU alt for JARU [DDJ]
DJARU dial of JARU [DDJ]
DJASING alt for ZASING dial of MUNDANG [MUA]
DJAU alt for ENDE dial of ENDE [END]
DJAUAN [DJN] lang, Australia
DJAUL alt for TIANG [TBJ]
DJAWA alt for JAVANESE [JAN]

DJAWALI alt for MANGALA [MEM]
DJAWI [DJW] lang, Australia
DJEDJI alt for FON-GBE [FOA]
DJEEBBANA [DJJ] lang, Australia
DJEM alt for NDJEM dial of KOONZIME [NJE]
DJEMBE dial of BUSHOONG [BUF]
DJENNÉ CHIINI dial of SONGHAY, KOYRA CHIINI [KHQ]
DJERADJ alt for TYARAITY [WOA]
DJERAG alt for TYARAITY [WOA]
DJERBA alt for JERBA dial of DJERBI [JBN]
DJERBI [JBN] lang, Libya; also in Tunisia
DJERBI alt for NAFUSI [JBN]
DJERMA alt for ZARMA [DJE]
DJERMA alt for ZARMACI [DJE]
DJIA dial of SAKATA [SAT]
DJIBOUTI ARABIC alt for ARABIC, TA'IZZI-ADENI [ACQ]
DJIDANAN dial of SENOUFO, TAGWANA [TGW]
DJIDJA alt for BOLANO [BZL]
DJIKINI alt for NJININGI dial of TEKE, NORTHERN [TEG]
DJIME alt for MESME [ZIM]
DJIMI alt for JIMI [JIM]
DJIMI dial of JIMI [JIM]
DJIMINI alt for SENOUFO, DJIMINI [DYI]
DJIMU alt for KOONZIME [NJE]
DJINANG [DJI] lang, Australia
DJINBA [DJB] lang, Australia
DJINGBURU alt for JUNGURU dial of BANDA-NDELE [BFL]
DJINGILA alt for DJINGILI [JIG]
DJINGILI [JIG] lang, Australia
DJIRI alt for LOPA [LOP]
DJIRUBAL alt for DYIRBAL [DBL]
DJIWARLI [DJL] lang, Australia
DJIWE alt for MESME [ZIM]
"DJOEKA" pejorative alt for AUKAN [DJK]
DJOK alt for CHOKWE [CJK]
DJOLOF alt for DYOLOF dial of WOLOF [WOL]
DJONBI alt for ZONGBI dial of PEERE [KUT]
DJONGA alt for JONGA dial of TSONGA [TSO]
DJONGGUNU alt for MONI [MNZ]
DJONGKANG [DJO] lang, Indonesia (Kalimantan)
DJONGOR BOURMATAGUIL alt for JONKOR BOURMATAGUIL [JEU]
DJONKOR alt for MIGAAMA [MMY]
DJONKOR ABOU TELFANE alt for MIGAAMA [MMY]
DJONKOR GUERA alt for MUKULU [MOZ]
DJOUMAN alt for GEREP dial of KIM [KIA]
DJUABLIN dial of ANYIN [ANY]
DJUDI alt for DZHIDI [DZH]
DJUDJAN alt for DANGEDL dial of YIR YORONT [YIY]
"DJUKA" pejorative alt for AUKAN [DJK]
DJULA alt for JULA [DYU]
DJULOI alt for PUNAN dial of DAYAK, LAND [DYK]
DJUWALI alt for MANGALA [MEM]
DJUWARLINY dial of WALMAJARRI [WMT]
DJWARLI alt for DJIWARLI [DJL]

DLANG alt for PALAUNG, PALE [PCE]
DLI alt for HLAI [LIC]
DLOGO dial of GODIE [GOD]
DMWA alt for DEMWA dial of PELASLA [MLR]
DÖRBÖD alt for DÖRBÖT dial of KALMYK-OIRAT [KGZ]
DÖRBÖT dial of KALMYK-OIRAT [KGZ]
DOA alt for TAUSE [TAD]
DOAB dial of PANJABI, EASTERN [PNJ]
DOAN alt for HALANG DOAN [HLD]
DOAYO alt for DOYAYO [DOW]
DOBA alt for MANGO [MGE]
DOBASE alt for BUSSA [DOX]
DOBBI alt for GOGOT dial of GURAGE, SODDO [GRU]
DOBE dial of LISHANID NOSHAN [AIJ]
DOBEL [KVO] lang, Indonesia (Maluku)
DOBI alt for GOGOT dial of GURAGE, SODDO [GRU]
DOBO LO dial of BAHING [RAR]
DOBU [DOB] lang, Papua New Guinea
DOCHKAFUARA alt for TUYUCA [TUE]
DODA' alt for SARUDU [SDU]
DODINGA dial of TOBELO [TLB]
DODOS dial of KARAMOJONG [KDJ]
DODOTH alt for DODOS dial of KARAMOJONG [KDJ]
DOE [DOE] lang, Tanzania
DOE dial of PEVE [LME]
DOEMAK alt for DIMMUK dial of KOFYAR [KWL]
DOFANA dial of SENOUFO, DJIMINI [DYI]
DOGA [DGG] lang, Papua New Guinea
DOGA dial of MIGAAMA [MMY]
DOGAARI alt for DAGAARE, SOUTHERN [DGA]
DOGAARI alt for DAGARA, NORTHERN [DGI]
DOGARI alt for DOGRI-KANGRI [DOJ]
DOGBA alt for GIZIGA, NORTH [GIS]
DÒGBÓ-GBÈ dial of AJA-GBE [AJG]
DOGHORO dial of BARUGA [BBB]
DOGHOSE alt for DOGOSÉ [DOS]
DOGHOSIÉ alt for DOGOSÉ [DOS]
DOGO dial of KALIKO [KBO]
DOGON [DOG] lang, Mali; also in Burkina Faso
DOGORINDI dial of OTORO [OTR]
DOGORO alt for DOGHORO dial of BARUGA [BBB]
DOGOSÉ [DOS] lang, Burkina Faso
DOGOSO [DGS] lang, Burkina Faso; also in Côte d'Ivoire
DOGOSO alt for DOGON [DOG]
DOGOTUKI SAQANI alt for NORTHEAST VANUA LEVU dial of FIJIAN [FJI]
DOGRI alt for DOGRI-KANGRI [DOJ]
DOGRI alt for DUNGRI dial of VASAVI [VAS]
DOGRI dial of DOGRI-KANGRI [DOJ]
DOGRI JAMMU alt for DOGRI-KANGRI [DOJ]
DOGRI PAHARI alt for DOGRI-KANGRI [DOJ]
DOGRIB [DGB] lang, Canada
DOGRI-KANGRA alt for DOGRI-KANGRI [DOJ]
DOGRI-KANGRI [DOJ] lang, India
DOGWA alt for TLOKWA dial of SOTHO, NORTHERN [SRT]

DOHE alt for DOE [DOE]
DOHOI [OTD] lang, Indonesia (Kalimantan)
DOHOI dial of DOHOI [OTD]
DOHUK dial of LISHANA DENI [LSD]
DOI dial of KAILI, LEDO [LEW]
DOI dial of TAI LOI [TLQ]
DOIBEL alt for DOBEL [KVO]
DOK ACOLI alt for ACHOLI [ACO]
DOKA [DBI] lang, Nigeria
DOKA dial of LOGO [LOG]
DOKA dial of MISHIP [CHP]
DOKA-POARA alt for TUYUCA [TUE]
DOKHOBE alt for DOGOSÉ [DOS]
DOKHOSIÉ alt for DOGOSÉ [DOS]
DOKO dial of NGOMBE [NGC]
DOKO-UYANGA [UYA] lang, Nigeria
DOKSHI alt for LUSHI dial of ZEEM [ZUA]
DOKSKAT alt for BROKSKAT [BKK]
DOKWARA dial of OTORO [OTR]
DOLAKHA alt for DOLKHALI dial of NEWARI [NEW]
DOLGAN [DLG] lang, Russia (Asia)
DOLIKI dial of MUKULU [MOZ]
'DOLIMI dial of WALI [WLX]
DOLKHALI dial of NEWARI [NEW]
DOLNOSERBSKI alt for SORBIAN, LOWER [WEE]
DOLOMITE alt for LADIN [LLD]
DOLORES CORA dial of CORA, SANTA TERESA
   [COK]
DOLPA TIBETAN alt for DOLPO [DRE]
DOLPO [DRE] lang, Nepal
DOM [DOA] lang, Papua New Guinea
DOM alt for DOMARI [RMT]
DOM alt for DOMU [DOF]
DOMA alt for ABRON [ABR]
DOMA alt for DOMAAKI [DMK]
DOMA dial of ALAGO [ALA]
DOMA dial of ANEME WAKE [ABY]
DOMAAKI [DMK] lang, Pakistan
DOMAKI dial of DOMARI [RMT]
DOMARA dial of MAILU [MGU]
DOMARI [RMT] lang, Iran; also in Afghanistan, Egypt,
   India, Iraq, Israel, Jordan, Libya, Palestinian West
   Bank and Gaza, Russia (Europe), Syria, Turkey
   (Europe), Uzbekistan
DOMBA alt for LOHAR, GADE [GDA]
DOMBA dial of MANYIKA [MXC]
DOMBANO alt for ARANDAI [JBJ]
DOMBANO dial of ARANDAI [JBJ]
DOMBE [DOV] lang, Zimbabwe
DOMBE alt for NDOMBE [NDQ]
DOMBIALI alt for LOHAR, GADE [GDA]
DOMBO alt for BODHO dial of THURI [THU]
DOMDOM alt for GUMAWANA [GVS]
DOMINICA CREOLE FRENCH dial of LESSER
   ANTILLEAN CREOLE FRENCH [DOM]
DOMINICAN ENGLISH dial of ENGLISH [ENG]
DOMINICAN SIGN LANGUAGE [DOQ] lang,
   Dominican Republic
DOMKHOE dial of GANA [GNK]
DOMMARA dial of TELUGU [TCW]
DOMO dial of MASANA [MCN]

DOMONA alt for FULFULDE, ADAMAWA [FUB]
DOMPA alt for TOBAKU dial of UMA [PPK]
DOMPAGO alt for LUKPA [DOP]
DOMPO [DOY] lang, Ghana
DOMRA dial of BHOJPURI [BHJ]
DOMU [DOF] lang, Papua New Guinea
DOMUNG [DEV] lang, Papua New Guinea
DONDE alt for VADONDE dial of MAKONDE [KDE]
DONDI dial of POL [PMM]
DONDO [DOK] lang, Indonesia (Sulawesi)
DONDO alt for DOONDO [DOD]
DONDO dial of NDAU [NDC]
DONDONGO dial of MABA [MDE]
DONEGAL dial of GAELIC, IRISH [GLI]
DONG [DOH] lang, Nigeria
DONG alt for IU MIEN [IUM]
DONG alt for TRAW dial of CUA [CUA]
DONG dial of MUMUYE [MUL]
DONG, NORTHERN [DOC] lang, China; also in
   Viet Nam
DONG, SOUTHERN [KMC] lang, China
DONGA alt for DONG [DOH]
DONGA alt for DONGO [DOO]
DONGA alt for KAMBAATA [KTB]
DONGA dial of JUKUN TAKUM [JBU]
DONGA dial of KPAN [KPK]
DONGARI alt for DOGRI-KANGRI [DOJ]
DONGAY dial of JAGOI [SNE]
DONGIRO alt for NYANGATOM [NNJ]
DONGJOL dial of DINKA, NORTHEASTERN [DIP]
DONGNU dial of BUNU, BU-NAO [BWX]
DONGO [DOO] lang, DCR
DONGO alt for MBUNDU, LOANDA [MLO]
DONGO dial of GBAYA [KRS]
DONGOLA dial of KENUZI-DONGOLA [KNC]
DONGOLA-KENUZ alt for KENUZI-DONGOLA
   [KNC]
DONGOLAWI alt for KENUZI-DONGOLA [KNC]
DONGOTONO [DDD] lang, Sudan
DONGSHAN dial of YI, WESTERN [YIW]
DONGXIANG [SCE] lang, China
DONYANYO alt for DOYAYO [DOW]
DONYAYO alt for DOYAYO [DOW]
DONYIRO alt for NYANGATOM [NNJ]
DOOBE alt for NDERA dial of KOMA [KMY]
DOOHYAAYO alt for DOYAYO [DOW]
DOOKA dial of GBAYA, SOUTHWEST [MDO]
DOOKA dial of GURUNTUM-MBAARU [GRD]
DOOME alt for NDERA dial of KOMA [KMY]
DOOMPAS alt for DUMPAS [DMV]
DOONDO [DOD] lang, Congo
D'OOPACE alt for BUSSA [DOX]
DOOR alt for DOR dial of NUER [NUS]
DOOR alt for EASTERN NUER dial of NUER
   [NUS]
DOORA alt for NUGUNU [NNV]
DOOWAAYO alt for DOYAYO [DOW]
DOOYAAYO alt for DOYAYO [DOW]
DOOYAYO alt for DOYAYO [DOW]
D'OPAASUNTE alt for BUSSA [DOX]
DOR alt for BONGO [BOT]

DOR dial of CHRAU [CHR]
DOR dial of NUER [NUS]
DOR KOI alt for DORLI dial of KOYA [KFF]
DORA alt for DORLI dial of KOYA [KFF]
DORA KOI alt for DORLI dial of KOYA [KFF]
DORAM alt for DOROMU [KQC]
DORBOR dial of GBII [GGB]
DORDAR dial of NAGA, AO [NJO]
DORHOSIÉ-FINNG alt for DOGOSO [DGS]
DORHOSIÉ-NOIRS alt for DOGOSO [DGS]
DORHOSSIÉ alt for DOGOSÉ [DOS]
DORHOSYE alt for DOGOSÉ [DOS]
DORIA alt for DHODIA [DHO]
DORIC dial of SCOTS [SCO]
DORI'O [DOR] lang, Solomon Islands
DORIRI alt for DORORO [DRR]
DORIRI alt for MOIKODI [DOI]
DORLA KOITUR alt for CHINTOOR KOYA dial of
    KOYA [KFF]
DORLA KOITUR alt for DORLI dial of KOYA [KFF]
DORLA KOYA alt for DORLI dial of KOYA [KFF]
DORLI dial of KOYA [KFF]
DORMON dial of GABRI [GAB]
DORO alt for DOR dial of CHRAU [CHR]
DOROBÉ alt for DOGOSÉ [DOS]
"DOROBO" pejorative alt for ARAMANIK [AAM]
"DOROBO" pejorative alt for KISANKASA [KQH]
DOROBO alt for MEDIAK [MWX]
DOROBO alt for MOSIRO [MWY]
DOROBO dial of GREBO, CENTRAL [GRV]
DOROGORI dial of GIDRA [GDR]
DOROMBE dial of OTORO [OTR]
DOROMU [KQC] lang, Papua New Guinea
DOROMU alt for KOKI dial of DOROMU [KQC]
DORORO [DRR] lang, Solomon Islands
DOROSIE alt for DOGOSÉ [DOS]
DOROSSÉ alt for DOGOSÉ [DOS]
DOROSSIÉ-FING alt for DOGOSO [DGS]
DOROT dial of GAYO [GYO]
DORPAT alt for TARTU dial of ESTONIAN [EST]
DORRO alt for MARI [MXW]
DORRO alt for TAIS [TST]
DORSET dial of ENGLISH [ENG]
DORSHA dial of SHEKO [SHE]
DORUNKECHA dial of TILUNG [TIJ]
DORZE [DOZ] lang, Ethiopia
DOSANGA alt for DOKO-UYANGA [UYA]
DOSO [DOL] lang, Papua New Guinea
DOSO alt for MINGANG DOSO [MKO]
DOT alt for KOL dial of CUA [CUA]
DOT dial of DASS [DOT]
DOTANGA dial of BALUNDU-BIMA [NGO]
DOTELI dial of NEPALI [NEP]
DOTT alt for DOT dial of DASS [DOT]
DOU alt for EDOPI [DBF]
DOUALA alt for DUALA [DOU]
DOUÉ alt for DOE dial of PEVE [LME]
DOUFOU alt for EDOPI [DBF]
DOUGNE alt for JONKOR BOURMATAGUIL [JEU]
DOUGNE dial of JONKOR BOURMATAGUIL [JEU]
DOUGOUR alt for DUGWOR [DME]

DOUGUIA dial of MALGBE [MXF]
DOUMA alt for DUMA [DMA]
DOUMBOU alt for NDUMU [NMD]
DOUME alt for DEMWA dial of PELASLA [MLR]
DOUMORI dial of KIWAI, SOUTHERN [KJD]
DOUNA dial of TURKA [TUZ]
DOUNJE alt for DUNJE dial of KABA NA [KWV]
DOUPA alt for DUUPA [DAE]
DOURA [DON] lang, Papua New Guinea
DOURBEYE dial of FALI, NORTH [FLL]
DOUROU alt for DII [DUR]
DOUROUN dial of MOFU, NORTH [MFK]
DOUTAI [TDS] lang, Indonesia (Irian Jaya)
DOUVANGAR alt for MOFU, NORTH [MFK]
DOWAYAYO alt for DOYAYO [DOW]
DOWAYO alt for DOYAYO [DOW]
DOWYAN alt for LALUNG [LAX]
DOXKÁ-POÁRÁ alt for TUYUCA [TUE]
DOYAAYO alt for DOYAYO [DOW]
DOYAU alt for DOYAYO [DOW]
DOYAYO [DOW] lang, Cameroon
DRA alt for DIR dial of POLCI [POL]
DRA alt for KAMBERATARO [KBV]
DRAMANDOUGOU-NYARAFO dial of TIEFO [TIQ]
DRAS alt for ASTORI dial of SHINA [SCL]
DRASI dial of SHINA [SCL]
DREHET dial of KHEHEK [TLX]
DREHU alt for DEHU [DEU]
DRENTE alt for DRENTS [DRT]
DRENTS [DRT] lang, Netherlands
DRIAFLEISUMA alt for MEHEK [NUX]
DRO dial of MALGBE [MXF]
DROMOIS alt for DAUPHINOIS dial of PROVENCAL
    [PRV]
DRORI alt for DEORI [DER]
DRUBEA alt for DUMBEA [DUF]
DRUKAI alt for RUKAI [DRU]
DRUKAY alt for RUKAI [DRU]
DRUKHA alt for DZONGKHA [DZO]
DRUKKE alt for DZONGKHA [DZO]
DRUNA alt for NGITI [NIY]
DRUNG [DUU] lang, China
DSCHAGGA alt for CHAGGA [KAF]
DSCHANG alt for FOREKE DSCHANG dial of
    YEMBA [BAN]
DSCHANG alt for YEMBA [BAN]
DSCHUGHA alt for DZHULFA dial of
    ARMENIAN [ARM]
DSCHULFA alt for DZHULFA dial of ARMENIAN
    [ARM]
DU alt for DUUNGOMA [DUX]
DUA BOCCOE alt for BONE dial of BUGIS [BPR]
DUAL alt for DHUWAL [DUJ]
DUALA [DOU] lang, Cameroon
DUALA alt for DHUWAL [DUJ]
DUALLA alt for DUALA [DOU]
DUAN alt for HALANG DOAN [HLD]
DUANO' [DUP] lang, Malaysia (Peninsular)
DUAU [DUA] lang, Papua New Guinea
DUAU PWATA alt for SEWA BAY [SEW]
DUAURU alt for NUMEE [KDK]

DUBALA alt for DUBLI [DUB]
DUBEA alt for DUMBEA [DUF]
DUBER-KANDIA dial of KOHISTANI, INDUS [MVY]
DUBLA alt for DUBLI [DUB]
DUBLI [DUB] lang, India
DUBLI dial of BHILI [BHB]
DUBU [DMU] lang, Indonesia (Irian Jaya)
DUCLIGAN IFUGAO dial of IFUGAO, BATAD [IFB]
DUDH KHARIA dial of KHARIA [KHR]
DUDI alt for MUTUM [MCC]
DUDI alt for TIRIO [TCR]
DUDJYM alt for DANGEDL dial of YIR YORONT
   [YIY]
DUDUELA [DUK] lang, Papua New Guinea
DUFF alt for TAUMAKO dial of PILENI [PIV]
DUGA alt for BARAMBU [BRM]
DUGARWA alt for DUGURI [DBM]
DUGBO dial of KRUMEN, PYE [PYE]
DUGUN alt for PAPE [NDU]
DUGUNZ alt for DAKUNZA dial of GUMUZ [GUK]
DUGUNZA alt for DAKUNZA dial of GUMUZ [GUK]
DUGUR dial of MEREY [MEQ]
DUGURANCHI alt for DUGURI [DBM]
DUGURAWA alt for DUGURI [DBM]
DUGURI [DBM] lang, Nigeria
DUGURI dial of BIRGIT [BTF]
DUGURILA dial of OTORO [OTR]
DUGUSA alt for DUGUZA [DZA]
DUGUZA [DZA] lang, Nigeria
DUGWOR [DME] lang, Cameroon
DUGWUJUR dial of OTORO [OTR]
DUHLIAN TWANG alt for LUSHAI [LSH]
DUHTU dial of TSOU [TSY]
DUHWA [KBZ] lang, Nigeria
DUI alt for DULI [DUZ]
DUI alt for KUY [KDT]
DUINDUI alt for NDUINDUI dial of AMBAE, WEST
   [NND]
DUKA alt for HUN-SAARE [DUD]
DUKA alt for WAMEI [COU]
DUKA-EKOR dial of KAMBERATARO [KBV]
DUKAI alt for RUKAI [DRU]
DUKAIYA dial of OCAINA [OCA]
DUKANCHI alt for HUN-SAARE [DUD]
DUKANCI alt for HUN-SAARE [DUD]
DUKAWA alt for HUN-SAARE [DUD]
DUKE [NKE] lang, Solomon Islands
DUKE OF YORK alt for RAMOAAINA [RAI]
DUKPA alt for DZONGKHA [DZO]
DUKPU dial of BANDA, MID-SOUTHERN [BJO]
DUKSLINU dial of SINDHI [SND]
DUKUNA alt for DAKUNZA dial of GUMUZ [GUK]
DUKUNZA alt for DAKUNZA dial of GUMUZ [GUK]
DUKURI alt for DUGURI [DBM]
DUKWA alt for HUN-SAARE [DUD]
DULBU [DBO] lang, Nigeria
DULI [DUZ] lang, Cameroon
DULIEN alt for LUSHAI [LSH]
DULIEN dial of LUSHAI [LSH]
DULIIT alt for MALUAL dial of DINKA, SOUTH-
   WESTERN [DIK]

DULONG alt for DRUNG [DUU]
DULONG dial of JINGPHO [CGP]
DULONG RIVER dial of DRUNG [DUU]
DUMA [DMA] lang, Gabon
DUMAKI alt for DOMAAKI [DMK]
DUMARING dial of BASAP [BDB]
DUMBEA [DUF] lang, New Caledonia
DUMBO alt for KEMEZUNG [DMO]
DUMBU alt for NDUMU [NMD]
DUMBULE alt for MBULE [MLB]
DUMBULI dial of DIMLI [ZZZ]
DUMI [DUS] lang, Nepal
DUMI BO'O alt for DUMI [DUS]
DUMI BRO alt for DUMI [DUS]
DUMOGA dial of MONGONDOW [MOG]
DUMPAS [DMV] lang, Malaysia (Sabah)
DUMPO alt for DOMPO [DOY]
DUMPU [WTF] lang, Papua New Guinea
DUMU alt for RUMU [KLQ]
DUMUN [DUI] lang, Papua New Guinea
DUMUT alt for MANDOBO [KZH]
DUNA [DUC] lang, Papua New Guinea
DUNG dial of MOKEN [MWT]
DUNGAN [DNG] lang, Kyrgyzstan; also in
   Kazakhstan, Tajikistan, Turkmenistan,
   Uzbekistan
DUNGARI GARASIA alt for GARASIA, RAJPUT
   [GRA]
DUNGI alt for DUNGU [DBV]
DUNGMALI [RAA] lang, Nepal
DUNGMALI dial of BANTAWA [BAP]
DUNGMALI-BANTAWA alt for DUNGMALI [RAA]
DUNGMALI PÛK alt for DUNGMALI [RAA]
DUNGRA BHIL [DUH] lang, India
DUNGRI dial of VASAVI [VAS]
DUNGRI GRASIA alt for GARASIA, RAJPUT [GRA]
DUNGU [DBV] lang, Nigeria
DUNJAWA alt for DUNGU [DBV]
DUNJE dial of KABA NA [KWV]
DUNMALI alt for DUNGMALI dial of BANTAWA
   [BAP]
DUNU alt for BATA [BTA]
DUOLUO dial of GELAO [KKF]
DUON alt for LÜ [KHB]
DUOXU alt for ERSU [ERS]
DUOXU dial of ERSU [ERS]
DUPA alt for DUUPA [DAE]
DURAM alt for KORUPUN dial of KORUPUN-SELA
   [KPQ]
DURANGO AZTEC alt for NÁHUATL, DURANGO
   [NLN]
DURANI dial of PASHTO, NORTHERN [PBU]
DURANMIN alt for SUARMIN [SEO]
DURGA alt for DHURGA [DHU]
DURHAM dial of ENGLISH [ENG]
DURI [MVP] lang, Indonesia (Sulawesi)
DURIANKARI alt for DURIANKERE [DBN]
DURIANKERE [DBN] lang, Indonesia (Irian Jaya)
DUROP alt for KOROP [KRP]
DU-ROPP-RIM dial of BEROM [BOM]
DURR-BARAZA dial of DASS [DOT]

DURRU alt for DII [DUR]
DURU alt for DII [DUR]
DURUM alt for DOUROUN dial of MOFU, NORTH [MFK]
DURUMA [DUG] lang, Kenya
DURUWA [PCI] lang, India
DURVA alt for DURUWA [PCI]
DUSAN alt for DUSUN, CENTRAL [DTP]
DUSNER [DSN] lang, Indonesia (Irian Jaya)
DUSNIR alt for DUSNER [DSN]
DUSO alt for VANIMO [VAM]
DUSUM alt for DUSUN, CENTRAL [DTP]
DUSUN alt for DUSUN, CENTRAL [DTP]
DUSUN alt for DUSUN, SUGUT [KZS]
DUSUN alt for TUTONG 1 [TTX]
DUSUN BALANGAN dial of MAANYAN [MHY]
DUSUN DAYAK alt for RUNGUS [DRG]
DUSUN DEYAH [DUN] lang, Indonesia (Kalimantan)
DUSUN MALANG [DUQ] lang, Indonesia (Kalimantan)
DUSUN MURUT dial of KENINGAU MURUT [KXI]
DUSUN SEGAMA dial of KINABATANGAN, UPPER [DMG]
DUSUN SINULIHAN dial of DUSUN, CENTRAL [DTP]
DUSUN WITU [DUW] lang, Indonesia (Kalimantan)
DUSUN, CENTRAL [DTP] lang, Malaysia (Sabah)
DUSUN, SUGUT [KZS] lang, Malaysia (Sabah)
DUSUN, TAMBUNAN [KZT] lang, Malaysia (Sabah)
DUSUN, TEMPASUK [TDU] lang, Malaysia (Sabah)
DUSUR alt for DUSUN, CENTRAL [DTP]
DUTCH [DUT] lang, Netherlands; also in Aruba, Australia, Belgium, Canada, France, Germany, Indonesia, Israel, Netherlands Antilles, Philippines, Suriname, UAE, USA
DUTCH CREOLE [DCR] lang, U.S. Virgin Islands
DUTCH SIGN LANGUAGE [DSE] lang, Netherlands
DUUNGIDJAWU dial of WAKAWAKA [WKW]
DUUNGO alt for DUUNGOMA [DUX]
DUUNGOMA [DUX] lang, Mali
DUUPA [DAE] lang, Cameroon
DUURUM dial of GERUMA [GEA]
DUVDE alt for DUVLE [DUV]
DUVELE alt for DUVLE [DUV]
DUVLE [DUV] lang, Indonesia (Irian Jaya)
DUVRE alt for DUVLE [DUV]
DUWAI [DBP] lang, Nigeria
DUWAMISH dial of SALISH, SOUTHERN PUGET SOUND [SLH]
DUWE alt for MURA dial of WANDALA [MFI]
DUWET [GVE] lang, Papua New Guinea
DUWINNA alt for TAMEZRET dial of DJERBI [JBN]
DUWINNA alt for TAMEZRET dial of NAFUSI [JBN]
DWAGS alt for TAKPA [TKK]
DWALA alt for DUALA [DOU]
DWAN alt for DWANG [NNU]
DWANG [NNU] lang, Ghana
DWAR dial of BIAK [BHW]
DWAT alt for DOT dial of DASS [DOT]
DWELA alt for DUALA [DOU]
DWEMU dial of BOMU [BMQ]

DWERA dial of LIGBI [LIG]
DWINGI alt for DUNGU [DBV]
DXANA alt for //GANA [GNK]
DYA alt for DYAN [DYA]
DYAABUGAY [DYY] lang, Australia
DYAABUGAY dial of DYAABUGAY [DYY]
DYABARMA alt for ZARMA [DJE]
DYABARMA alt for ZARMACI [DJE]
DYABERDYABER [DYB] lang, Australia
DYABUGAY alt for DYAABUGAY [DYY]
DYAIR alt for JAIR [YIR]
DYAKANKE alt for JAHANKA [JAD]
DYALA alt for BLÉ [BXL]
DYALANU alt for BLÉ [BXL]
DYALONKE alt for JALUNGA [YAL]
DYALONKE alt for YALUNKA [YAL]
DYAMALA alt for DIAMALA dial of SENOUFO, DJIMINI [DYI]
DYAN [DYA] lang, Burkina Faso
DYANE alt for DYAN [DYA]
DYANGADI [DYN] lang, Australia
DYANU alt for DYAN [DYA]
DYARMA alt for ZARMA [DJE]
DYARMA alt for ZARMACI [DJE]
DYE alt for NGANGAM [GNG]
DYEGUEME dial of SERER-SINE [SES]
DYERAIDY alt for TYARAITY [WOA]
DYERMA alt for ZARMA [DJE]
DYERMA alt for ZARMACI [DJE]
DYIMINI alt for SENOUFO, DJIMINI [DYI]
DYIRBAL [DBL] lang, Australia
DYOKAY alt for RUKAI [DRU]
DYOLA alt for JOLA-FOGNY [DYO]
DYOLOF dial of WOLOF [WOL]
DYONGOR alt for MIGAAMA [MMY]
DYONGOR GUERA alt for MUKULU [MOZ]
DYOULA alt for JULA [DYU]
DYUGUN [DYD] lang, Australia
DYULA alt for JULA [DYU]
DYUMBA alt for AJUMBA dial of MYENE [MYE]
DYUROP alt for KOROP [KRP]
DZA [JEN] lang, Nigeria
DZALAKHA [DZL] lang, Bhutan
DZALAMAT alt for DZALAKHA [DZL]
DZALAMO alt for ZALAMO [ZAJ]
DZAMA alt for NAFAANRA [NFR]
DZAMBA alt for BANGI [BNI]
DZAMBA alt for NZAMBA dial of KONGO [KON]
DZAMBA dial of BALOI [BIZ]
DZAMBAZI dial of ROMANI, BALKAN [RMN]
DZANDO [DZN] lang, DCR
DZANGGALI alt for RAWAT [JNL]
DZAO MIN alt for BA PAI [BPN]
DZAUI dial of CARUTANA [CRU]
DZAWI alt for DZAUI dial of CARUTANA [CRU]
DZAZE alt for PIAPOCO [PIO]
DZEIGOC dial of DEDUA [DED]
DZEK alt for KRYTS [KRY]
DZEKE alt for NORTHERN BABOLE dial of BABOLE [BVX]
DZEM alt for NDJEM dial of KOONZIME [NJE]

DZEMAY alt for FULFULDE, ADAMAWA [FUB]
DZERNGU alt for GULAK dial of MARGHI CENTRAL [MAR]
DZHEK alt for KRYTS [KRY]
DZHEK dial of KRYTS [KRY]
DZHEKI alt for KRYTS [KRY]
DZHEMSHID alt for JAMSHIDI dial of AIMAQ [AIQ]
DZHIDI [DZH] lang, Israel; also in Iran
DZHUDEZMO alt for LADINO [SPJ]
DZHUHURIC alt for JUDEO-TAT [TAT]
DZHULFA alt for JOLFA dial of ARMENIAN [ARM]
DZHULFA dial of ARMENIAN [ARM]
DZHUNYAN alt for DUNGAN [DNG]
DZIBI-DZONGA alt for TSHWA dial of TSHWA [TSC]
DZIHANA alt for JIBANA dial of GIRYAMA [NYF]
DZILI dial of JINGPHO [CGP]
DZIMOU alt for KOONZIME [NJE]
DZINDA alt for ZINZA [JIN]
DZING alt for DING [DIZ]
DZIVI alt for TSHWA dial of TSHWA [TSC]
DZODINKA [ADD] lang, Cameroon; also in Nigeria
DZODZINKA alt for DZODINKA [ADD]
DZONGA alt for JONGA dial of TSONGA [TSO]
DZONGA-DZIBI alt for TSHWA dial of TSHWA [TSC]
DZONGKHA [DZO] lang, Bhutan; also in Nepal
DZOWO alt for LIGBI [LIG]
DZUBUCUA alt for DZUBUKUÁ dial of KARIRI-XOCO [KZW]
DZUBUKUÁ dial of KARIRI-XOCO [KZW]
DZUKISH dial of LITHUANIAN [LIT]
DZUKISKAI alt for DZUKISH dial of LITHUANIAN [LIT]
DZUMBO alt for KEMEZUNG [DMO]
DZUMDZUM alt for JINGJING dial of MINA [HNA]
DZUNA dial of NAGA, ANGAMI [NJM]
DZUNZA dial of POKOMO, LOWER [POJ]
DZU'OASI alt for JU/'HOAN [KTZ]
DZU'OASI dial of JUHOAN [KTZ]
DZÙÙNGOO [DNN] lang, Burkina Faso
DZUUNGOO dial of DZÙÙNGOO [DNN]
DZWABO dial of SOTHO, NORTHERN [SRT]
E [EEE] lang, China
E alt for ERE [TWP]
E JE dial of GREBO, NORTHERN [GRB]
E LOKOP alt for SAMBURU [SAQ]
EALEBA alt for YALEBA dial of TAWALA [TBO]
EAST ADONARA dial of ADONARA [ADA]
EAST AMARASI alt for AMARASI TIMUR dial of AMARASI [AAZ]
EAST ANGAL alt for ANGAL [AGE]
EAST ANGLIA dial of ENGLISH [ENG]
EAST AWIN dial of AEKYOM [AWI]
EAST BAFWANGADA dial of BUDU [BUU]
EAST BANGGAI dial of BANGGAI [BGZ]
EAST BAY dial of COSTANOAN, NORTHERN [CST]
EAST BOIKIN dial of BOIKIN [BZF]
EAST BOKI alt for EASTERN BOKYI dial of BOKYI [BKY]
EAST BULGARIAN ROMANI dial of ROMANI, BALKAN [RMN]

EAST CAPE alt for KEHELALA dial of TAWALA [TBO]
EAST CAPE AFRIKAANS dial of AFRIKAANS [AFK]
EAST CENTRAL FRIULIAN dial of FRIULIAN [FRL]
EAST CENTRAL MIXE alt for MIXE, MAZATLÁN [MZL]
EAST CENTRAL QUICHÉ alt for QUICHÉ, EASTERN, CHICHICASTENANGO [QUU]
EAST CENTRAL TLACOLULA ZAPOTECO alt for ZAPOTECO, MITLA [ZAW]
EAST CHACHAPOYAS alt for GRENADA-MENDOZA dial of QUECHUA, CHACHAPOYAS [QUK]
EAST CHOISEUL alt for BABATANA [BAQ]
EAST CIRCASSIAN alt for KABARDIAN [KAB]
EAST COASTAL CREE alt for CREE, NORTHERN EAST [CRL]
EAST CREE alt for CREE, NORTHERN EAST [CRL]
EAST CREE alt for CREE, SOUTHERN EAST [CRE]
EAST DANGALEAT dial of DANGALEAT [DAA]
EAST DEVONSHIRE dial of ENGLISH [ENG]
EAST DOGRI dial of DOGRI-KANGRI [DOJ]
EAST ELEMA alt for TOARIPI [TPI]
EAST GIMI dial of GIMI [GIM]
EAST GODAVERI dial of TELUGU [TCW]
EAST GORONTALO dial of GORONTALO [GRL]
EAST GREENLANDIC dial of INUKTITUT, GREENLANDIC [ESG]
EAST GUIZHOU MIAO alt for HMONG, NORTHERN QIANDONG [HEA]
EAST GWARI alt for GBAGYI [GBR]
EAST INLAND CREE alt for CREE, SOUTHERN EAST [CRE]
EAST INLAND JIMAJIMA dial of JIMAJIMA [JMA]
EAST INLAND KAULONG dial of KAULONG [PSS]
EAST KALAMSÉ alt for KASOMA dial of KALAMSE [KNZ]
EAST KARA dial of KARA [LEU]
EAST KASEM dial of KASEM [KAS]
EAST KHOWAR dial of KHOWAR [KHW]
EAST KOITA dial of KOITABU [KQI]
EAST KOMBA dial of KOMBA [KPF]
EAST KONGO dial of KONGO [KON]
EAST LAGOON dial of CHUUKESE [TRU]
EAST LATVIAN dial of LATVIAN [LAT]
EAST LELE alt for TANGALTO LELE dial of LELE [LLC]
EAST MAFA dial of MAFA [MAF]
EAST MAKIAN dial of MAKIAN, EAST [MKY]
EAST MARSELA alt for MASELA, EAST [VME]
EAST MEKEO dial of MEKEO [MEK]
EAST MESÉ dial of MESE [MCI]
EAST MORI alt for MORI BAWAH [XMZ]
EAST NDA'NDA' alt for UNDIMEHA dial of NDANDA [NNZ]
EAST NEK dial of NEK [NIF]
EAST NUMANGGANG dial of NUMANGGANG [NOP]
EAST OKI-NO-ERABU dial of OKI-NO-ERABU [OKN]

EAST ORYA alt for TIMUR dial of ORYA [URY]
EAST PARANÁ alt for GUANA [QKS]
EAST POKOT dial of POKOOT [PKO]
EAST PUA PRAY alt for LUA' [PRB]
EAST RORO alt for RORO dial of RORO [RRO]
EAST SAKHALIN GILYAK dial of GILYAK [NIV]
EAST SENTANI dial of SENTANI [SET]
EAST SLOVAKIAN ROMANI dial of ROMANI, CARPATHIAN [RMC]
EAST SOLOR dial of ADONARA [ADA]
EAST SONGHAY alt for SONGHAY, KOYRABORO SENNI [SON]
EAST SUMBA alt for KAMBERA [SMI]
EAST SUMBANESE alt for KAMBERA [SMI]
EAST SUTHERLANDSHIRE dial of GAELIC, SCOTS [GLS]
EAST TANNA dial of TANNA, NORTH [TNN]
EAST TORAJA alt for TAE' [ROB]
EAST TORAJA alt for TOALA' [TLZ]
EAST TORRICELLI dial of TORRICELLI [TEI]
EAST TRANGAN alt for TARANGAN, EAST [TRE]
EAST UKRAINIAN dial of UKRAINIAN [UKR]
EAST UMANAKAINA dial of UMANAKAINA [GDN]
EAST URAT alt for WUSYEP TEP dial of URAT [URT]
EAST UREPARAPARA alt for LEHALURUP [URR]
EAST URII dial of URI [UVH]
EAST UVEAN alt for WALLISIAN [WAL]
EAST VALLEY ZAPOTECO alt for ZAPOTECO, MITLA [ZAW]
EAST VELUWE alt for VELUWS, EAST [VEE]
EAST VOD dial of VOD [VOD]
EAST WAYLLA dial of QUECHUA, WANCA, HUAYLLA [QHU]
EAST YAMBES dial of YAMBES [YMB]
EAST YAWA dial of YAWA [YVA]
EASTER ISLAND alt for RAPA NUI [PBA]
EASTERN dial of ROMANI, VLAX [RMY]
EASTERN ACHERON dial of ACHERON [ACZ]
EASTERN ADDASEN dial of ADASEN [TIU]
EASTERN AKA alt for BASESE dial of YAKA [AXK]
EASTERN ALEUT dial of ALEUT [ALW]
EASTERN ANGAMI alt for NAGA, CHOKRI [NRI]
EASTERN ANMATYERRE dial of ANMATYERRE [AMX]
EASTERN ARAGONESE dial of ARAGONESE [AXX]
EASTERN ARANDA alt for ARRERNTE, EASTERN [AER]
EASTERN ARCTIC "ESKIMO" pejorative alt for INUKTITUT, EASTERN CANADIAN [ESB]
EASTERN ARGENTINA GUARANI alt for GUARANÍ, MBYÁ [GUN]
EASTERN ARMENIAN dial of ARMENIAN [ARM]
EASTERN ASTURIAN dial of ASTURIAN [AUB]
EASTERN BADE alt for DUWAI [DBP]
EASTERN BANTAWA dial of BANTAWA [BAP]
EASTERN BÉTÉ alt for BÉTÉ, GAGNOA [BTG]
EASTERN BIRGIT dial of BIRGIT [BTF]
EASTERN BISA alt for BARAKA dial of BISSA [BIB]
EASTERN BOBO OULE alt for BWAMU [BOX]

EASTERN BOBO WULE alt for BWAMU [BOX]
EASTERN BOKYI dial of BOKYI [BKY]
EASTERN BOLIVIAN GUARANÍ alt for GUARANÍ, ARGENTINE, WESTERN [GUI]
EASTERN BOLIVIAN GUARANÍ alt for GUARANÍ, BOLIVIAN, EASTERN [GUI]
EASTERN BORDER PWO KAREN alt for KAWKAREIK dial of KAREN, PWO EASTERN [KJP]
EASTERN BROACH GUJARATI alt for GAMADIA dial of GUJARATI [GJR]
EASTERN BWE alt for KAREN, GEBA [KVQ]
EASTERN CAGAYAN AGTA alt for AGTA, DUPANINAN [DUO]
EASTERN CANADIAN "ESKIMO" pejorative alt for INUKTITUT, EASTERN CANADIAN [ESB]
EASTERN CARIB alt for TYREWUJU dial of CARIB [CRB]
EASTERN CHEPANG dial of CHEPANG [CDM]
EASTERN CHEROKEE alt for ELATI dial of CHEROKEE [CER]
EASTERN CLUSTER LISHANID NOSHANARBIL dial of LISHANID NOSHAN [AIJ]
EASTERN DAN alt for GWEETAAWU dial of DAN [DAF]
EASTERN DANISH alt for SKÅNE [SCY]
EASTERN DHATKI dial of DHATKI [MKI]
EASTERN DHIMAL dial of DHIMAL [DHI]
EASTERN DINKA alt for DINKA, SOUTHEASTERN [DIN]
EASTERN DUKA dial of HUN-SAARE [DUD]
EASTERN DUUN alt for DZÙÙNGOO [DNN]
EASTERN DUVLE dial of DUVLE [DUV]
EASTERN EAST-GUIZHOU MIAO alt for HMONG, EASTERN QIANDONG [HMQ]
EASTERN EDOLO dial of EDOLO [ETR]
EASTERN EFATE alt for ETON [ETN]
EASTERN EGYPTIAN BEDAWI ARABIC dial of ARABIC, LEVANTINE BEDAWI SPOKEN [AVL]
EASTERN EJAGHAM dial of EJAGHAM [ETU]
EASTERN EMILIANO dial of EMILIANO-ROMAGNOLO [EML]
EASTERN ERSU alt for ERSU dial of ERSU [ERS]
EASTERN FAS dial of FAS [FAS]
EASTERN FIJIAN alt for FIJIAN [FJI]
EASTERN FULANI alt for FULFULDE, ADAMAWA [FUB]
EASTERN FULFULDE alt for FULFULDE, ADAMAWA [FUB]
EASTERN GITXSAN alt for GITXSAN dial of GITXSAN [GIT]
EASTERN GUAYMÍ dial of NGÄBERE [GYM]
EASTERN GUJARI dial of GUJARI [GJU]
EASTERN HELAMBU SHERPA dial of HELAMBU SHERPA [SCP]
EASTERN HIGHLAND CHATINO alt for CHATINO, SIERRA ORIENTAL [CLY]
EASTERN HUASTECA AZTEC alt for NÁHUATL, HUASTECA, ESTE [NAI]
EASTERN HUICHOL alt for SAN SEBASTIÁN-SANTA CATARINA dial of HUICHOL [HCH]

EASTERN HUISHUI MIAO alt for HMONG, EASTERN HUISHUI [HME]
EASTERN ISIRAWA dial of ISIRAWA [SRL]
EASTERN JAMILTEPEC-CHAYUCO MIXTECO alt for MIXTECO, CHAYUCO [MIH]
EASTERN JAMILTEPEC-SAN CRISTOBAL MIXTECO alt for MIXTECO, JAMILTEPEC [MXT]
EASTERN JAPANESE dial of JAPANESE [JPN]
EASTERN JIARONG alt for SITU dial of JIARONG [JYA]
EASTERN JIBBALI dial of JIBBALI [SHV]
EASTERN JIKANY dial of NUER [NUS]
EASTERN JUXTLAHUACA MIXTECO alt for MIXTECO, MIXTEPEC [MIX]
EASTERN KADAZAN alt for KADAZAN, LABUK-KINABATANGAN [DTB]
EASTERN KALEBWE dial of SONGE [SOP]
EASTERN KALIBUGAN alt for EASTERN KOLIBUGAN dial of SUBANEN, CENTRAL [SUS]
EASTERN KALIKO dial of KELIKO [KBO]
EASTERN KARAIM dial of KARAIM [KDR]
EASTERN KATIVIRI dial of KATI [BSH]
EASTERN KERES PUEBLO alt for KERES, EASTERN [KEE]
EASTERN KHAMS dial of KHAMS [KHG]
EASTERN KHANTI dial of KHANTY [KCA]
EASTERN KILMERI dial of KILMERI [KIH]
EASTERN KITUBA dial of KITUBA [KTU]
EASTERN KIWAI dial of KIWAI, SOUTHERN [KJD]
EASTERN KLAOH dial of KLAO [KLU]
EASTERN KOLIBUGAN dial of SUBANEN, CENTRAL [SUS]
EASTERN KUSAAL alt for ANGOLE dial of KUSAAL [KUS]
EASTERN LIBYAN ARABIC dial of ARABIC, LIBYAN SPOKEN [AYL]
EASTERN LIBYAN ARABIC dial of ARABIC, WESTERN EGYPTIAN BEDAWI SPOKEN [AYL]
EASTERN LISU alt for LIPO [TKL]
EASTERN LIVONIAN dial of LIV [LIV]
EASTERN LOMBARD dial of LOMBARD [LMO]
EASTERN LOW NAVARRESE dial of BASQUE, NAVARRO-LABOURDIN [BQE]
EASTERN LUBA alt for HEMBA [HEM]
EASTERN MACINA dial of FULFULDE, MAASINA [FUL]
EASTERN MAITHILI dial of MAITHILI [MKP]
EASTERN MAMPRULI dial of MAMPRULI [MAW]
EASTERN MANGGARAI dial of MANGGARAI [MQY]
EASTERN MARI alt for MARI, LOW [MAL]
EASTERN MARING dial of MARING [MBW]
EASTERN MBUM alt for KARANG [KZR]
EASTERN MEHRI dial of MEHRI [MHR]
EASTERN MIAHUATLÁN ZAPOTECO alt for ZAPOTECO, MIXTEPEC [ZPM]
EASTERN MIN alt for CHINESE, MIN DONG [CDO]
EASTERN MIXE alt for MIXE, ISTMO [MIR]
EASTERN MIXTECO alt for MIXTECO, PEÑOLES [MIL]

EASTERN MONTAGNAIS dial of MONTAGNAIS [MOE]
EASTERN MOTU dial of MOTU [MEU]
EASTERN MUNA alt for TIWORO dial of MUNA [MYN]
EASTERN MUSSAU dial of MUSSAU-EMIRA [EMI]
EASTERN NAHANE alt for KASKA [KKZ]
EASTERN NASKAPI dial of NASKAPI [NSK]
EASTERN NIHIRI dial of VARLI [VAV]
EASTERN NONMETAFONETICA dial of SICILIAN [SCN]
EASTERN NORWEGIAN dial of NORWEGIAN, BOKMAAL [NRR]
EASTERN NUER dial of NUER [NUS]
EASTERN OCOTLÁN ZAPOTECO alt for ZAPOTECO, CHICHICAPAN [ZPV]
EASTERN OJIBWA alt for OTTAWA [OTW]
EASTERN OTOMÍ alt for OTOMÍ, SIERRA ORIENTAL [OTM]
EASTERN PAGI dial of PAGI [PGI]
EASTERN PAHARI alt for NEPALI [NEP]
EASTERN PARBATE alt for KHAM, NISI [KIF]
EASTERN PATTANI dial of PATTANI [LAE]
EASTERN POCHUTLA ZAPOTECO alt for ZAPOTECO, XADANI [ZAX]
EASTERN POINT dial of SUDEST [TGO]
EASTERN POPOLOCA alt for POPOLOCA, SAN JUAN ATZINGO [POE]
EASTERN PUTLA MIXTECO alt for MIXTECO, ITUNDUJIA [MCE]
EASTERN QIANDONG MIAO alt for HMONG, EASTERN QIANDONG [HMQ]
EASTERN RULI dial of RULI [RUC]
EASTERN SAWOS dial of MALINGUAT [SIC]
EASTERN SHE alt for LUOFU dial of SHE [SHX]
EASTERN SHUSWAP dial of SHUSWAP [SHS]
EASTERN SOLA DE VEGA ZAPOTEC alt for ZAPOTECO, SOLA DE VEGA ESTE [ZPL]
EASTERN SURI alt for SURI [SUQ]
EASTERN SWAMPY CREE dial of CREE, SWAMPY [CSW]
EASTERN SWEDISH dial of SWEDISH [SWD]
EASTERN SYRIAC dial of SYRIAC [SYC]
EASTERN TATAR dial of TATAR [TTR]
EASTERN TÀY dial of TAY [THO]
EASTERN TETUN dial of TETUN [TTM]
EASTERN THAI alt for LAO [NOL]
EASTERN THAMI dial of THAMI [THF]
EASTERN TLACOLULA ZAPOTECO alt for ZAPOTECO, SAN PEDRO QUIATONI [ZPF]
EASTERN TLAPANECO alt for TLAPANECO, MALINALTEPEC [TLL]
EASTERN TOPOSA dial of TOPOSA [TOQ]
EASTERN TUMUT alt for JOSTU dial of MONGOLIAN, PERIPHERAL [MVF]
EASTERN TUNEBO alt for TUNEBO, BARRO NEGRO [TBN]
EASTERN UMA alt for TOLEE' dial of UMA [PPK]
EASTERN VOGUL dial of MANSI [MNS]
EASTERN WAKHI dial of WAKHI [WBL]

EASTERN WEST-HUNAN MIAO alt for HMONG, EASTERN XIANGXI [MUQ]
EASTERN XIANGXI MIAO alt for HMONG, EASTERN XIANGXI [MUQ]
EASTERN YAGNOBI dial of YAGNOBI [YAI]
EASTERN YAKHA dial of YAKHA [YBH]
EASTERN YANOMAMI dial of YANOMAMO [GUU]
EASTERN YI alt for YI, GUIZHOU [YIG]
EASTERN YOGOR alt for YUGUR, EAST [YUY]
EASTPHALIAN dial of SAXON, LOW [SXN]
EAYKIT dial of EVENKI [EVN]
EBADIDI alt for MOLIMA [MOX]
EBANG alt for HEIBAN [HEB]
EBE alt for ASU [AUM]
EBEKWARA alt for BEKWARRA [BKV]
EBEMBE alt for BEMBE [BMB]
EBEN alt for EVEN [EVE]
EBERÃ alt for EMBERÁ, NORTHERN [EMP]
EBERA BEDEA alt for EMBERÁ, NORTHERN [EMP]
EBERÃ BED'EA alt for EMBERÁ, NORTHERN [EMP]
EBETENG alt for EHOM dial of UKPET-EHOM [AKD]
EBHELE alt for BHELE [PER]
EBILA alt for BILA [BIP]
EBINA alt for BENA [YUN]
EBINA alt for VORO [VOR]
EBIRA [IGB] lang, Nigeria
EBIRI alt for MARARIT [MGB]
EBITOSO dial of CHAMACOCO [CEG]
EBKUO alt for OKU [OKU]
EBODE dial of LALA-ROBA [LLA]
EBOH alt for ABOH dial of UKWUANI-ABOH-NDONI [UKW]
EBON alt for MARSHALLESE [MZM]
EBOO alt for BOMA dial of TEKE, CENTRAL [TEC]
EBOO alt for BOO dial of TEKE, CENTRAL [TEC]
EBOOM alt for BOMA dial of TEKE, CENTRAL [TEC]
EBOOM alt for BOO dial of TEKE, CENTRAL [TEC]
EBORNA alt for BORNA [BXX]
EBOZE alt for BUJI dial of JERE [JER]
EBRIÉ [EBR] lang, Côte d'Ivoire
EBU dial of IGALA [IGL]
EBUDU alt for BUDU [BUU]
EBUGHU [EBG] lang, Nigeria
EBUGOMBE alt for BUGOMBE dial of BHELE [PER]
EBUJA alt for BUDZA [BJA]
EBUKU dial of BOMBOMA [BWS]
EBUNA alt for BENA [YUN]
EBUNA alt for VORO [VOR]
EBWE alt for ÉWÉ [EWE]
ECHE dial of IGBO [IGR]
ECHIDZINDZA alt for ZINZA [JIN]
ECHIJINJA alt for ZINZA [JIN]
ECHIJITA alt for JITA [JIT]
ECHISUBIA alt for SUBIYA [SBS]
ECHITOTELA alt for TOTELA [TTL]
ECHOALDI dial of GUANA [GVA]

ECHONOANA alt for ECHOALDI dial of GUANA [GVA]
ECHUABO alt for CHWABO [CHW]
ECHUKU alt for ESUKU dial of AKPES [IBE]
ECHUWABO alt for CHWABO [CHW]
ECIJITA alt for JITA [JIT]
ECIZINZA alt for ZINZA [JIN]
ECKARUMGU dial of CHWABO [CHW]
ECUADORIAN SIGN LANGUAGE [ECS] lang, Ecuador
ECUADORIAN SIONA dial of SECOYA [SEY]
E'DA alt for MANGKI dial of KALUMPANG [KLI]
EDANGABO dial of HAYA [HAY]
EDAWAPI alt for NAMIA [NNM]
E-DE alt for RADE [RAD]
EDE CABE alt for CABE [CBJ]
EDE ICA alt for ICA [ICA]
EDE IDACA alt for IDACA [IDD]
EDE IFE alt for IFÈ [IFE]
EDE IJE alt for IJE [IJJ]
EDE NAGO alt for NAGO [NQG]
EDEH alt for RADE [RAD]
EDE-YORUBA alt for YORUBA [YOR]
EDI dial of GALOLI [GAL]
EDIAMAT alt for EJAMAT [EJA]
EDIBA alt for KOHUMONO [BCS]
EDIMALA alt for ALTA, NORTHERN [AQN]
EDINBURGH dial of ENGLISH [ENG]
EDIRNE dial of TURKISH [TRK]
EDIRO dial of ENGENNI [ENN]
EDITODE EDAI alt for ERITAI [BAD]
EDIU-ADIG alt for KADIWÉU [KBC]
EDIYA alt for BUBE [BVB]
EDJAGAM alt for EJAGHAM [ETU]
EDO [EDO] lang, Nigeria
EDO dial of KAILI, LEDO [LEW]
EDOLO [ETR] lang, Papua New Guinea
EDOLO ADO alt for EDOLO [ETR]
EDOPI [DBF] lang, Indonesia (Irian Jaya)
EDULIA alt for BARASANA [BSN]
EDURIA alt for BARASANA [BSN]
EENTHLIT alt for NORTHERN LENGUA dial of LENGUA [LEG]
EERÃ alt for EMBERÁ, NORTHERN [EMP]
E'ERDUOSITE alt for ORDOS dial of MONGOLIAN, PERIPHERAL [MVF]
EERWEE alt for IRRUAN dial of BOKYI [BKY]
EESTI alt for ESTONIAN [EST]
EFAI [EFA] lang, Nigeria; also in Cameroon
EFATE, NORTH [LLP] lang, Vanuatu
EFATE, SOUTH [ERK] lang, Vanuatu
EFE [EFE] lang, DCR
EFE alt for ÉWÉ [EWE]
EFFIAT alt for EFAI [EFA]
EFFIUM alt for UFIOM dial of ORING [ORI]
EFFURUN alt for UVBIE [EVH]
EFIFA dial of AKPES [IBE]
EFIK [EFK] lang, Nigeria
EFIRA alt for FILA dial of MELE-FILA [MXE]
EFTAWAGARIA dial of ROMANI, SINTE [RMO]
EFUTOP [OFU] lang, Nigeria

EFUTU dial of AWUTU [AFU]
EGA [DIE] lang, Côte d'Ivoire
EGBA dial of YORUBA [YOR]
EGBEDNA dial of IKWERE [IKW]
EGBEMA dial of IGBO [IGR]
EGBEMA dial of IZON [IJC]
EGBIRA alt for EBIRA [IGB]
EGBURA alt for EBIRA [IGB]
EGEDE alt for IGEDE [IGE]
EGEJO alt for NDUNDUSANA dial of PAGIBETE
  [PAG]
EGENE alt for ENGENNI [ENN]
EGER dial of HUNGARIAN SIGN LANGUAGE [HSH]
EGEZO alt for NDUNDUSANA dial of PAGIBETE
  [PAG]
EGEZON alt for NDUNDUSANA dial of PAGIBETE
  [PAG]
EGGON [EGO] lang, Nigeria
EGHOM alt for OKOM dial of MBEMBE, CROSS
  RIVER [MFN]
EGNIH dial of OGBAH [OGC]
EGON alt for EGGON [EGO]
EGONGOT dial of ILONGOT [ILK]
EGU alt for KOTO dial of EBIRA [IGB]
EGUN alt for GUN dial of GUN-GBE [GUW]
EGUN alt for GUN-GBE [GUW]
EGWA alt for EGA [DIE]
EH JE alt for E JE dial of GREBO, NORTHERN
  [GRB]
EHIJA dial of OROKAIVA [ORK]
EHKILI alt for JIBBALI [SHV]
EHO MBO alt for MELONG dial of MBO [MBO]
EHOB MKAA alt for BAKAKA dial of BAKAKA [BQZ]
EHOBE BELON alt for BALONDO dial of BAKAKA
  [BQZ]
EHOM dial of UKPET-EHOM [AKD]
EHOUÉ alt for HWÈGBÈ dial of AJA-GBE [AJG]
EHOW MBA alt for BAREKO dial of MBO [MBO]
EHTREMEÑU alt for EXTREMADURAN [EXT]
EHUEUN [EHU] lang, Nigeria
EHWE alt for ÉWÉ [EWE]
EIBE alt for ÉWÉ [EWE]
/EIKUSI alt for XATIA dial of XOO [NMN]
EIPO alt for EIPOMEK [EIP]
EIPOMEK [EIP] lang, Indonesia (Irian Jaya)
EITIEP [EIT] lang, Papua New Guinea
EIVISSENC alt for BALEARIC dial of CATALAN-
  VALENCIAN-BALEAR [CLN]
EIVO [EIV] lang, Papua New Guinea
EIWAJA alt for IWAIDJA [IBD]
EJAGAM alt for EJAGHAM [ETU]
EJAGHAM [ETU] lang, Nigeria; also in Cameroon
EJAHAM alt for EJAGHAM [ETU]
EJAMAT [EJA] lang, Guinea-Bissau; also in Senegal
EJAR dial of BEGBERE-EJAR [BQV]
EJINE dial of MONGOLIAN, PERIPHERAL [MVF]
EJWE alt for EJAGHAM [ETU]
EK NII alt for NII [NII]
EKAGI alt for EKARI [EKG]
EKAJUK [EKA] lang, Nigeria
EKAMA dial of MBEMBE, CROSS RIVER [MFN]

EKAMTULUFU alt for NDE dial of NDE-NSELE-NTA
  [NDD]
EKAMU alt for EKAMA dial of MBEMBE, CROSS
  RIVER [MFN]
EKARI [EKG] lang, Indonesia (Irian Jaya)
EKAW alt for AKHA [AKA]
EKBEBE alt for AKEBOU [KEU]
EKEGUSII alt for GUSII [GUZ]
EKELE alt for KELE [KHY]
EKET alt for EKIT [EKE]
EKHIRIT dial of BURIAT, RUSSIA [MNB]
EKI [EKI] lang, Nigeria
EKI dial of BEBELE [BEB]
EKIBENA alt for BENA [BEZ]
EKIGURIA alt for KURIA [KUJ]
EKIHAYA alt for HAYA [HAY]
EKIKEREBE alt for KEREBE [KED]
EKIKINGA alt for KINGA [KIX]
EKIKIRA alt for SWAGA dial of NANDI [NNB]
EKIKUMBULE alt for KUMBULE dial of NANDI
  [NNB]
EKIMATE alt for MATE dial of NANDI [NNB]
EKIN alt for SOUTHERN EJAGHAM dial of
  EJAGHAM [ETU]
EKINYAMBO alt for NYAMBO [NYM]
EKIPANGWA alt for PANGWA [PBR]
EKISANZA alt for SANZA dial of KONJO [KOO]
EKISANZA alt for SANZA dial of NANDI [NNB]
EKISHU alt for SHU dial of NANDI [NNB]
EKISONGOORA dial of NANDI [NNB]
EKISWAGA alt for SWAGA dial of NANDI [NNB]
EKIT [EKE] lang, Nigeria
EKITANGI alt for TANGI dial of NANDI [NNB]
EKITI dial of YORUBA [YOR]
EKIYIRA alt for YIRA dial of NANDI [NNB]
EKIZIBA dial of HAYA [HAY]
EKKPAHIA alt for EKPEYE [EKP]
EKLENJUY alt for CHOROTE, IYOJWA'JA [CRT]
EKLEP alt for AIKLEP [MWG]
EKOI alt for EJAGHAM [ETU]
EKOKA-!XÛ alt for KUNG-EKOKA [KNW]
EKOKOMA alt for MBEMBE, CROSS RIVER [MFN]
EKOKO-!XÛ alt for KUNG-EKOKA [KNW]
EKOMBE dial of BAKUNDU-BALUE [BDU]
EKONDA alt for KONDA dial of MONGO-NKUNDU
  [MOM]
EKONDA MONGO dial of MONGO-NKUNDU [MOM]
EKOS-YENABI-MARAGIN dial of KWOMTARI
  [KWO]
EKOTI alt for KOTI [EKO]
EKPABYA alt for EKPEYE [EKP]
EKPAFFIA alt for EKPEYE [EKP]
EKPARABONG dial of NDOE [NBB]
EKPARI alt for YACE [EKR]
EKPENMEN alt for EHUEUN [EHU]
EKPENMEN alt for UKUE [UKU]
EKPENMI alt for UKUE [UKU]
EKPERI alt for IKWERI dial of NGWO [NGN]
EKPERI dial of YEKHEE [ETS]
EKPESHE alt for IKPESHI [IKP]
EKPETIAMA dial of IZON [IJC]

EKPEYE [EKP] lang, Nigeria
EKPIMI alt for EHUEUN [EHU]
EKPON dial of ESAN [ISH]
EKPWO alt for OKU [OKU]
EKUMBE alt for EKOMBE dial of BAKUNDU-BALUE [BDU]
EKUMURU alt for KOHUMONO [BCS]
EKURI alt for NKUKOLI [NBO]
EKWARE alt for MPUR [AKC]
EL AKHEIMAR alt for AHEIMA dial of NGILE [MAS]
EL ALTO ZAPOTEC alt for ZAPOTECO, EL ALTO [ZPP]
EL AMIRA alt for JEBEL EL AMIRA dial of LAFOFA [LAF]
EL HUGEIRAT [ELH] lang, Sudan
EL LENGUAJE DE SEÑAS MEXICANAS alt for MEXICAN SIGN LANGUAGE [MFS]
EL LENGUAJE MANUAL DE MÉXICO alt for MEXICAN SIGN LANGUAGE [MFS]
EL LENGUAJE MEXICANO DE LAS MANOS alt for MEXICAN SIGN LANGUAGE [MFS]
EL MOLO [ELO] lang, Kenya
EL NAYAR alt for JESÚS MARÍA CORA dial of CORA [COR]
EL SALVADORAN SIGN LANGUAGE alt for SALVADORAN SIGN LANGUAGE [ESN]
ELAKA alt for AMANAVIL dial of EMAN [EMN]
ELAT dial of BANDA [BND]
ELATI dial of CHEROKEE [CER]
ELBASAN-TIRANA dial of ALBANIAN, GHEG [ALS]
ELEKO alt for ILIKU dial of LUSENGO [LUS]
ELEKU alt for ILIKU dial of LUSENGO [LUS]
ELELE dial of IKWERE [IKW]
ELEMBE dial of NKUTU [NKW]
ELEME [ELM] lang, Nigeria
ELEPI [ELE] lang, Papua New Guinea
ELEUTH alt for OLOT dial of KALMYK-OIRAT [KGZ]
ELGEYO alt for KEIYO dial of KALENJIN [KLN]
ELGUMI alt for TESO [TEO]
ELI dial of BANDA [BND]
ELIMBARI dial of CHUAVE [CJV]
ELING dial of TUNEN [BAZ]
ELIP [EKM] lang, Cameroon
ELIRI alt for NDING [ELI]
ELKEI [ELK] lang, Papua New Guinea
ELLICE alt for TUVALUAN [ELL]
ELLICEAN alt for TUVALUAN [ELL]
ELLINIKA alt for GREEK [GRK]
ELLYRIA alt for LOKOYA [LKY]
ELMOLO alt for EL MOLO [ELO]
ELOG MPOO alt for ADIE dial of BAKOKO [BKH]
ELOMAY alt for BAINOUK-GUNYAAMOLO [BCZ]
ELOMAY alt for BAINOUK-GUNYUÑO [BAB]
ELOMWE alt for LOMWE [NGL]
ELONG alt for ELUNG dial of AKOOSE [BSS]
ELOPI [DBF] lang, Edopi
ELOWA dial of LIGENZA [LGZ]
ELOYI [AFO] lang, Nigeria
ELPAPUTI alt for ELPAPUTIH [ELP]
ELPAPUTIH [ELP] lang, Indonesia (Maluku)
ELPIRA alt for WARLPIRI [WBP]

ELSAESSISCH alt for ALSATIAN dial of ALEMANNISCH [GSW]
ELSENG [MRF] lang, Indonesia (Irian Jaya)
ELT ULID dial of GHADAMES [GHA]
ELU [ELU] lang, Papua New Guinea
ELU dial of ISOKO [ISO]
ELU-KARA alt for LELE [UGA]
ELUN dial of BANDIAL [BQJ]
ELUNAY alt for BAINOUK-GUNYAAMOLO [BCZ]
ELUNAY alt for BAINOUK-GUNYUÑO [BAB]
ELUNCHUN alt for OROQEN [ORH]
ELUNG dial of AKOOSE [BSS]
ELUOSI alt for RUSSIAN [RUS]
ELYUT alt for OLOT dial of KALMYK-OIRAT [KGZ]
EM alt for GARUS [GYB]
EMA alt for KEMAK [KEM]
EMAE [MMW] lang, Vanuatu
EMAI alt for EMAE [MMW]
EMAI dial of EMAI-IULEHA-ORA [EMA]
EMAI-IULEHA-ORA [EMA] lang, Nigeria
EMAKA alt for MAKHUWA-MARREVONE [XMC]
EMAKA alt for NAHARRA dial of MAKHUWA [VMW]
EMAKHUWANA alt for MAKHUWANA dial of MAKHUWA [VMW]
EMAKHUWANA alt for MAKHUWANA dial of MAKHUWA-MARREVONE [XMC]
EMAKUA alt for MAKHUWA [VMW]
EMAN [EMN] lang, Cameroon
EMANE alt for EMAN [EMN]
EMARENDJE alt for MARENJE [VMR]
EMARLE alt for EMHALHE dial of OKPAMHERI [OPA]
EMAU dial of EFATE, NORTH [LLP]
EMBA alt for HEMBA [HEM]
EMBALOH [EMB] lang, Indonesia (Kalimantan)
EMBENA alt for EMBERÁ-CATÍO [CTO]
EMBENÁ TADÓ alt for EMBERÁ-TADÓ [TDC]
EMBERÁ, NORTHERN [EMP] lang, Panama; also in Colombia
EMBERÁ-BAUDÓ [BDC] lang, Colombia
EMBERÁ-CATÍO [CTO] lang, Colombia; also in Panama
EMBERÁ-CHAMÍ [CMI] lang, Colombia
EMBERÁ-SAIJA [SJA] lang, Colombia; also in Panama
EMBERÁ-TADÓ [TDC] lang, Colombia
EMBOSI alt for MBOSI [MDW]
EMBU [EBU] lang, Kenya
EMBU dial of EMBU [EBU]
EMBUDJA alt for BUDZA [BJA]
EMEDE dial of ISOKO [ISO]
EMEEJE alt for MEJE dial of MANGBETU [MDJ]
EME-EME alt for MINANIBAI [MCV]
EMELA alt for NAGA, MAO [NBI]
EMEREÑON alt for EMERILLON [EME]
EMERILLON [EME] lang, French Guiana
EMERILON alt for EMERILLON [EME]
EMERUM alt for APALI [ENA]
EMETO alt for MEDO dial of MAKHUWA-MEETTO [MAK]

EMETO alt for MEETTO dial of MAKHUWA-
MEETTO [MAK]
EMFINU alt for MFINU [ZMF]
EMHALHE dial of OKPAMHERI [OPA]
EMILIAN alt for EMILIANO-ROMAGNOLO [EML]
EMILIANO alt for EMILIANO-ROMAGNOLO [EML]
EMILIANO-ROMAGNOLO [EML] lang, Italy; also
in San Marino
EMIRA dial of MUSSAU-EMIRA [EMI]
EMIRA-MUSSAU alt for MUSSAU-EMIRA [EMI]
EMOA alt for MACUNA [MYY]
EMOK [EMO] lang, Paraguay
EMORO alt for LEMORO [LDJ]
EMOWHUA dial of IKWERE [IKW]
EMPAMELA alt for NAMPAMELA dial of MAKHUWA-
MARREVONE [XMC]
EMPAMELA dial of MAKHUWA [VMW]
EMPAWA dial of JAGOI [SNE]
EMPERA alt for EMBERÁ, NORTHERN [EMP]
EMPERÃ alt for EMBERÁ, NORTHERN [EMP]
EMPESA POKO dial of LUSENGO [LUS]
EMPLAWAS [EMW] lang, Indonesia (Maluku)
EMPUI alt for NAGA, ZEME [NZM]
EMUGHAN dial of ABUA [ABN]
EMUMU [ENR] lang, Indonesia (Irian Jaya)
EMVANE SO dial of SO [SOX]
EMWAE alt for EMAE [MMW]
EMWAE ISLAND alt for MAKURA dial of
NAMAKURA [NMK]
EN [ENC] lang, Viet Nam
EN dial of VO [WBM]
ENA alt for ARMENIAN [ARM]
ENA alt for ENYA [GEY]
ENAHARRA alt for NAHARRA dial of MAKHUWA
[VMW]
ENAHARRA alt for NAHARRA dial of MAKHUWA-
MARREVONE [XMC]
ENAWENÉ-NAWÉ alt for SALUMÃ [UNK]
ENCABELLAO alt for SECOYA [SEY]
ENDANGEN alt for KOMBIO [KOK]
ENDE [END] lang, Indonesia (Nusa Tenggara)
ENDE alt for BARAS [BRS]
ENDE dial of AGOB [KIT]
ENDE dial of ENDE [END]
ENDE MALAY alt for LARANTUKA dial of MALAY
[MLI]
ENDEH alt for ENDE [END]
ENDEH alt for ENDE dial of ENDE [END]
ENDEKAN alt for ENREKANG [PTT]
ENDEKAN TIMUR alt for ENREKANG [PTT]
ENDO [ENB] lang, Kenya
ENDO dial of ENDO [ENB]
ENDO-MARAKWET alt for ENDO [ENB]
ENDU dial of AMBRYM, SOUTHEAST [TVK]
ENEBY alt for YIDINY [YII]
ENEEME alt for NAMA dial of MBEMBE, TIGON
[NZA]
ENEEME dial of MBEMBE, TIGON [NZA]
ENEGEGNY dial of GURAGE, WEST [GUY]
ENENGA dial of MYENE [MYE]
ENENLHIT alt for TOBA-MASKOY [TMF]

ENETS [ENE] lang, Russia (Asia)
ENEUENE-MARE alt for SALUMÃ [UNK]
ENGA [ENQ] lang, Papua New Guinea
ENGA-KYAKA alt for KYAKA [KYC]
ENGENNI [ENN] lang, Nigeria
ENGGANESE alt for ENGGANO [ENO]
ENGGANO [ENO] lang, Indonesia (Sumatra)
ENGGIPILOE alt for DAMAL [UHN]
ENGGIPILU dial of DAMAL [UHN]
ENGGROS alt for TOBATI [TTI]
ENGLISH [ENG] lang, United Kingdom; also in
American Samoa, Andorra, Anguilla, Antigua and
Barbuda, Aruba, Australia, Bahamas, Barbados,
Belize, Bermuda, Botswana, British Indian Ocean
Territory, British Virgin Islands, Brunei, Cameroon,
Canada, Cayman Islands, Cook Islands,
Denmark, Dominica, Ecuador, Eritrea, Ethiopia,
Falkland Islands, Fiji, Finland, Gambia, Germany,
Ghana, Gibraltar, Greece, Grenada, Guam,
Guyana, Honduras, India, Ireland, Israel, Italy,
Jamaica, Japan, Kenya, Kiribati, Korea, South,
Lebanon, Lesotho, Liberia, Malawi, Malaysia
(Peninsular), Malta, Marshall Islands, Mauritius,
Mexico, Micronesia, Midway Islands, Montserrat,
Namibia, Nauru, Netherlands Antilles, New
Zealand, Nigeria, Niue, Norfolk Island, Northern
Mariana Islands, Norway, Pakistan, Palau, Papua
New Guinea, Philippines, Pitcairn, Puerto Rico,
Rwanda, Saudi Arabia, Seychelles, Sierra Leone,
Singapore, Solomon Islands, Somalia, South
Africa, Sri Lanka, St. Helena, St. Kitts-Nevis, St.
Lucia, St. Pierre and Miquelon, St. Vincent and the
Grenadines, Suriname, Swaziland, Switzerland,
Tanzania, Tokelau, Tonga, Trinidad and Tobago,
Turks and Caicos Islands, U.S. Virgin Islands,
Uganda, UAE, USA, Vanuatu, Venezuela, Wake
Island, Western Samoa, Zambia, Zimbabwe
ENGLISH ROMANI alt for ANGLOROMANI [RME]
ENGUTUK-ELOIKOB dial of MAASAI [MET]
ENHEN alt for UNHUN dial of CURRIPACO [KPC]
ENHWE dial of ISOKO [ISO]
ENI dial of OKO-ENI-OSAYEN [OKS]
ENIBURA alt for WAKAWAKA [WKW]
ENIM [ENI] lang, Indonesia (Sumatra)
ENIMACA alt for MACA [MCA]
ENIMAGA alt for MACA [MCA]
ENINDHILYAGWA alt for ANINDILYAKWA [AOI]
ENINDILJAUGWA alt for ANINDILYAKWA [AOI]
ENKELEMBU alt for KANUM, BÄDI [KHD]
ENKELEMBU alt for KANUM, NGKÂLMPW [KCD]
ENKELEMBU alt for KANUM, SMÄRKY [KXQ]
ENKELEMBU alt for KANUM, SOTA [KRZ]
ENKUN dial of JINGPHO [CGP]
ENLAI dial of MAKHUWA [VMW]
ENLAI dial of MAKHUWA-MARREVONE [XMC]
ENLIT alt for ANGAITE dial of SANAPANA [SAP]
ENMYLINSKIJ dial of CHUKOT [CKT]
ENNA alt for EREI dial of AGWAGWUNE [YAY]
ENNA alt for SINJAI dial of BUGIS [BPR]
ENNEMOR alt for INOR dial of GURAGE, WEST
[GUY]

ENNEQOR dial of GURAGE, EAST [GRE]
ENOAH dial of EWONDO [EWO]
ENREKANG [PTT] lang, Indonesia (Sulawesi)
ENREKANG dial of ENREKANG [PTT]
ENTIAT alt for WENATCHI dial of COLUMBIA-
  WENATCHI [COL]
ENURMIN dial of CHUKOT [CKT]
ENWAN [ENW] lang, Nigeria
ENWAN dial of SASARU-ENWAN-IGWE [SSC]
ENXET alt for LENGUA [LEG]
ENYA [GEY] lang, DCR
ENYAU alt for YOKU dial of SIE [ERG]
ENYEMBE dial of ABIDJI [ABI]
ENYONG dial of IBIBIO [IBB]
ENZEB alt for HUNZIB [HUZ]
EOTILE alt for BETI [EOT]
EPAI alt for IPIKO [IPK]
EPE alt for ELOYI [AFO]
EPEA PEDÉE alt for EMBERÁ-SAIJA [SJA]
EPENA alt for CENTRAL BOMITABA dial of
  BOMITABA [ZMX]
EPENA SAIJA alt for EMBERÁ-SAIJA [SJA]
EPENÁ SAIJA alt for EMBERÁ-SAIJA [SJA]
EPERA alt for EMBERÁ-CATÍO [CTO]
EPERÃ PEDEA alt for EMBERÁ, NORTHERN [EMP]
EPIE [EPI] lang, Nigeria
EPIE-ATISSA alt for EPIE [EPI]
EPIGI dial of NDUMU [NMD]
EPIMI alt for EHUEUN [EHU]
EPINMI alt for UKUE [UKU]
EPWAU alt for ETON [ETN]
EQUINAO alt for GUANA [QKS]
ERA dial of DOM [DOA]
ERA RIVER alt for KOPE dial of KIWAI, NORTH-
  EAST [KIW]
ERAANS alt for IDA'AN [DBJ]
ERAI alt for ERITAI [BAD]
ERAI alt for ILIUN [ILU]
ERAKOR alt for EFATE, SOUTH [ERK]
ERAKWA alt for ERUWA [ERH]
ERANADANS alt for ARANADAN [AAF]
ERANKAD alt for GAHRI [BFU]
ERAP alt for URI [UVH]
ERAVALLAN alt for IRULA [IRU]
ERAVE [KJY] lang, Papua New Guinea
ERAVE dial of DADIBI [MPS]
ERAWA alt for RAWA [RWO]
ERBORE alt for ARBORE [ARV]
ERE [TWP] lang, Papua New Guinea
ERE alt for ERRE [ERR]
ÉRÉ alt for GARAP dial of KIM [KIA]
EREGBA dial of KPAN [KPK]
EREI dial of AGWAGWUNE [YAY]
EREMAGOK alt for PATAMONA [PBC]
EREMPI alt for REMPI [RMP]
ERENGA alt for SUNGOR [SUN]
ERENGA dial of SUNGOR [SUN]
ERENGA dial of TAMA [TMA]
EREVAN dial of ARMENIAN [ARM]
EREVAN dial of AZERBAIJANI, NORTH [AZE]
EREWA alt for RAWA [RWO]

ERGONG alt for HORPA [ERO]
ER-GWAR alt for ROR dial of KAG-FER-JIIR-
  KOOR-ROR-US-ZUKSUN [GEL]
ERHSU alt for ERSU [ERS]
ERI alt for ERITAI [BAD]
ERIKBATSA alt for RIKBAKTSA [ART]
ERIKPATSA alt for RIKBAKTSA [ART]
ERIMA alt for OGEA [ERI]
ERITAI [BAD] lang, Indonesia (Irian Jaya)
ERIWAN alt for EREVAN dial of ARMENIAN [ARM]
ERLI alt for ARLIJA dial of ROMANI, BALKAN [RMN]
ERMENI DILI alt for ARMENIAN [ARM]
ERMENICE alt for ARMENIAN [ARM]
ERMITAÑO dial of CHAVACANO [CBK]
ERMITEÑO alt for ERMITAÑO dial of CHAVACANO
  [CBK]
ERNGA alt for KORWA [KFP]
EROHWA alt for ERUWA [ERH]
EROKH alt for IRAQW [IRK]
EROKWANAS [ERW] lang, Indonesia (Irian Jaya)
EROMANGA alt for SIE [ERG]
ERORUP alt for KOROP [KRP]
ERRAMANGA alt for SIE [ERG]
ERRE [ERR] lang, Australia
ERROMANGA alt for SIE [ERG]
ERRONAN alt for FUTUNA-ANIWA [FUT]
ERSARI dial of TURKMEN [TCK]
ERSE alt for GAELIC, IRISH [GLI]
ERSU [ERS] lang, China
ERSU dial of ERSU [ERS]
ERU alt for ALATIL [ALX]
ERU-EU-WAU-WAU alt for URU-EU-UAU-UAU
  [URZ]
ERUKALA alt for IRULA [IRU]
ERUKALA alt for YERUKULA [YEU]
ERUKU BHASHA alt for YERUKULA [YEU]
ERUSHU alt for ERÚSÚ dial of ARIGIDI [AKK]
ERÚSÚ dial of ARIGIDI [AKK]
ERUWA [ERH] lang, Nigeria
ERVATO-VENTUARI dial of SANUMA [SAM]
ERWAN alt for IRRUAN dial of BOKYI [BKY]
ERZENKA alt for KHARBERD dial of ARMENIAN
  [ARM]
ERZERUM alt for KARIN dial of ARMENIAN [ARM]
ERZGEBIRGISCH dial of GERMAN, STANDARD
  [GER]
ERZIA alt for ERZYA [MYV]
ERZINCAN alt for KHARBERD dial of ARMENIAN
  [ARM]
ERZURUM alt for KARIN dial of ARMENIAN
  [ARM]
ERZYA [MYV] lang, Russia (Europe); also in
  Azerbaijan, Kazakhstan, Kyrgyzstan,
  Turkmenistan, Ukraine, Uzbekistan
ESA alt for ESAN [ISH]
ESAAKA alt for SAAKA dial of MAKHUWA-MEETTO
  [MAK]
ESAKAJI alt for NATHEMBO [NTE]
ESAMBI KIPYA alt for WESTERN KALEBWE dial
  of SONGE [SOP]
ESAN [ISH] lang, Nigeria

ESARI dial of TURKMEN [TCK]
ESARO alt for DURIANKERE [DBN]
ESARY alt for ESARI dial of TURKMEN [TCK]
ESAUN dial of CITAK [TXT]
ESE dial of ARIGIDI [AKK]
ESE EJA alt for ESE EJJA [ESE]
ESE EJJA [ESE] lang, Bolivia; also in Peru
ESE EXA alt for ESE EJJA [ESE]
ESE'EJJA alt for ESE EJJA [ESE]
ESEL dial of BEKWEL [BKW]
ESHIRA alt for SIRA [SWJ]
ESHIRIMA alt for MAKHUWA-SHIRIMA [VMK]
ESHISANGO alt for SANGU [SBP]
ESHKASHIMI alt for ISHKASHIMI dial of
    SANGLECHI-ISHKASHIMI [SGL]
ESHKASHMI alt for ISHKASHIMI dial of
    SANGLECHI-ISHKASHIMI [SGL]
ESHTEHARDI [ESH] lang, Iran
ESILUYANA alt for LUYANA [LAV]
ESIMBI [AGS] lang, Cameroon
ESIMBOWE alt for MBOWE [MXO]
ESIMBOWE alt for MBOWE dial of LUYANA [LAV]
ESINGEE alt for NGEE dial of TEKE, EASTERN
    [TEK]
ESIRIUN alt for WATUBELA [WAH]
"ESKIMO" pejorative alt for INUPIATUN, NORTH
    ALASKAN [ESI]
"ESKIMO" pejorative alt for INUPIATUN, NORTH-
    WEST ALASKA [ESK]
ESKISEHIR dial of TURKISH [TRK]
ESO alt for SO [SOC]
ESPAÑOL alt for SPANISH [SPN]
ESPERANTO [ESP] lang, France
ESPIEGLE BAY alt for MALUA BAY [MLL]
ES-SAARE alt for WESTERN DUKA dial of HUN-
    SAARE [DUD]
ESSANG dial of TALAUD [TLD]
ESSEL alt for ESEL dial of BEKWEL [BKW]
ESSELE dial of ETON [ETO]
ESSELEN [ESQ] lang, USA
ESSEQUIBO dial of SKEPI CREOLE DUTCH [SKW]
ESSIMBI alt for ESIMBI [AGS]
ESSIN dial of BAYOT [BDA]
ESSOUMA alt for ESUMA [ESM]
ESTONIAN [EST] lang, Estonia; also in Australia,
    Canada, Finland, Latvia, Russia (Europe),
    Sweden, United Kingdom, USA
ESTONIAN ROMANI dial of ROMANI, BALTIC
    [ROM]
ESTONIAN SIGN LANGUAGE [ESO] lang, Estonia
ESTONIAN SWEDISH alt for EASTERN SWEDISH
    dial of SWEDISH [SWD]
ESTRACHARIA dial of ROMANI, SINTE [RMO]
ESTRELLA dial of CABECAR [CJP]
ESTREMENHO dial of PORTUGUESE [POR]
ESUKU dial of AKPES [IBE]
ESULALU dial of JOLA-KASA [CSK]
ESUMA [ESM] lang, Côte d'Ivoire
ESUMBU dial of LUSENGO [LUS]
ESUULAALUR alt for ESULALU dial of JOLA-KASA
    [CSK]

ETAPALLY GONDI dial of GONDI, SOUTHERN
    [GGO]
ETAPALLY MARIA dial of MARIA [MRR]
ETEBI [ETB] lang, Nigeria
ETEKWE alt for ETKYWAN [ICH]
ETELENA alt for TERÊNA [TEA]
ETHIOPIAN alt for AMHARIC [AMH]
ETHIOPIAN SIGN LANGUAGE [ETH] lang, Ethiopia
ETHIOPIC alt for GEEZ [GEE]
ET-HUN alt for EASTERN DUKA dial of HUN-SAARE
    [DUD]
ETIEN alt for ATEN [GAN]
ETIJA dial of OROKAIVA [ORK]
ET-JIIR alt for JIIR dial of KAG-FER-JIIR-KOOR-
    ROR-US-ZUKSUN [GEL]
ET-KAG alt for KAG dial of KAG-FER-JIIR-KOOR-
    ROR-US-ZUKSUN [GEL]
ETKYE alt for KENTE dial of KPAN [KPK]
ETKYWAN [ICH] lang, Nigeria
ETLA ZAPOTEC alt for ZAPOTECO, YARENI [ZAE]
ETLA ZAPOTECO alt for ZAPOTECO,
    MAZALTEPEC [ZPY]
ET-MAROR alt for ROR dial of KAG-FER-JIIR-
    KOOR-ROR-US-ZUKSUN [GEL]
ETNA BAY alt for SEMIMI [ETZ]
ETO alt for GIANGAN [BGI]
ETOLO alt for EDOLO [ETR]
ETON [ETN] lang, Vanuatu
ETON [ETO] lang, Cameroon
ETON dial of ETON [ETN]
ETONGO dial of IPULO [ASS]
ETONO dial of AGWAGWUNE [YAY]
ETONO dial of UBAGHARA [BYC]
ETORO alt for EDOLO [ETR]
ETOSSIO alt for TESO [TEO]
ETSAKO alt for YEKHEE [ETS]
ETSAKOR alt for YEKHEE [ETS]
ETULO [UTR] lang, Nigeria
ETUNG alt for EJAGHAM [ETU]
ETUNO alt for ETONO dial of AGWAGWUNE [YAY]
ETUNO alt for IGARA dial of EBIRA [IGB]
ETURO alt for ETULO [UTR]
ET-US alt for US dial of KAG-FER-JIIR-KOOR-
    ROR-US-ZUKSUN [GEL]
ETYEE alt for TYEE dial of TEKE, WESTERN [TEZ]
ET-ZUKSUN alt for ZUKSUN dial of KAG-FER-
    JIIR-KOOR-ROR-US-ZUKSUN [GEL]
EUCHAVANTE alt for OTI [OTI]
EUE alt for ÉWÉ [EWE]
EUNDA KOLONKADHI dial of NDONGA [NDG]
EUPHRATES CLUSTER dial of ARABIC,
    MESOPOTAMIAN SPOKEN [ACM]
EUROPANTO [EUR] lang, Belgium
EUROPEAN OIRAT alt for KALMYK-OIRAT [KGZ]
EUROPEANIZED HEBREW alt for STANDARD
    HEBREW dial of HEBREW [HBR]
EUSKERA alt for BASQUE [BSQ]
EVADI alt for TSUVADI [TVD]
EVAND alt for EVANT [BZZ]
EVANT [BZZ] lang, Nigeria; also in Cameroon
EVAV alt for KEI [KEI]

EVE alt for ÉWÉ [EWE]
EVEN [EVE] lang, Russia (Asia)
EVENKI [EVN] lang, China; also in Mongolia, Russia (Asia)
"EVHRO" pejorative alt for UVBIE [EVH]
EVIIA alt for BUBI [BUW]
EVJI alt for DUWAI [DBP]
EVORRA alt for PURARI [IAR]
EVOUZOK dial of EWONDO [EWO]
EVRIE alt for UVBIE [EVH]
EWAGE alt for EWAGE-NOTU [NOU]
EWAGE-NOTU [NOU] lang, Papua New Guinea
EWAGE-NOTU dial of EWAGE-NOTU [NOU]
EWDOKIA dial of ARMENIAN [ARM]
ÉWÉ [EWE] lang, Ghana; also in Togo
EWEN alt for EVEN [EVE]
EWENKE alt for EVENKI [EVN]
EWENKI alt for EVENKI [EVN]
EWOASE dial of DWANG [NNU]
EWODI alt for OLI dial of DUALA [DOU]
EWONDO [EWO] lang, Cameroon
EWOTA alt for BUBIA [BBX]
EWUMBONGA alt for OFOMBONGA dial of MBEMBE, CROSS RIVER [MFN]
EWUNDU alt for EWONDO [EWO]
EXIN dial of YI, YUNNAN [NOS]
EXTREMADURAN [EXT] lang, Spain
EXTREMEÑO alt for EXTREMADURAN [EXT]
EYABIDA alt for EMBERÁ-CATÍO [CTO]
EYAK [EYA] lang, USA
EYAN alt for DENYA [ANV]
EYANSI alt for YANSI [YNS]
EYANZI alt for YANSI [YNS]
EYE alt for PANARE [PBH]
EZA alt for EZAA dial of IZI-EZAA-IKWO-MGBO [IZI]
EZA alt for EZHA dial of GURAGE, WEST [GUY]
EZAA dial of IZI-EZAA-IKWO-MGBO [IZI]
EZEI alt for EREI dial of AGWAGWUNE [YAY]
EZEKWE alt for UZEKWE [EZE]
EZELLE alt for JERE dial of JERE [JER]
EZESHIO alt for KAMAKAN [VKM]
EZHA dial of GURAGE, WEST [GUY]
EZO alt for HOKKAIDO dial of AINU [AIN]
EZOPONG alt for OSOPONG dial of MBEMBE, CROSS RIVER [MFN]
FA' dial of FEFE [FMP]
FA D'AMBU [FAB] lang, Equatorial Guinea; also in Spain
FA SAPOSA alt for SAPOSA dial of SAPOSA [SPS]
FAA CETA alt for HMWAVEKE [MRK]
FAAKE alt for PHAKE [PHK]
FAALA alt for BAKHA dial of KARANGA [KTH]
FAALE-PIYEW dial of TUPURI [TUI]
FA'AWA alt for PA'A [AFA]
FABLA ARAGONESA alt for ARAGONESE [AXX]
FABLAS dial of HAITIAN CREOLE FRENCH [HAT]
FA-C-AKA alt for AKA [SOH]
FACÉ alt for FACEI dial of SULA [SZN]
FACEI dial of SULA [SZN]
FACHARA alt for CARA [CFD]

FACHI dial of KANURI, CENTRAL [KPH]
FADA alt for BIAFADA [BIF]
FADA NGURMA dial of FULFULDE, NORTH-EASTERN BURKINA FASO [FUH]FADAN WATE (HATE) alt for NINZAM [NIN]
FADASHI dial of BERTA [WTI]
FADAWA dial of KANURI, CENTRAL [KPH]
FADICCA alt for FIYADIKKA dial of NOBIIN [FIA]
FADICCA alt for NOBIIN [FIA]
FADICHA alt for FIYADIKKA dial of NOBIIN [FIA]
FADICHA alt for NOBIIN [FIA]
FADIJA alt for NOBIIN [FIA]
FADIJA alt for FIYADIKKA dial of NOBIIN [FIA]
FADIRO alt for BAMBASSI [MYF]
FADJULU alt for PÖJULU dial of BARI [BFA]
FADYUT-PALMERIN dial of SERER-SINE [SES]
FAETAR alt for FAETO dial of FRANCO-PROVENCAL [FRA]
FAETO dial of FRANCO-PROVENCAL [FRA]
FAGANI [FAF] lang, Solomon Islands
FAGANI dial of FAGANI [FAF]
FAGA-UVEA (FAGAUVEA) alt for UVEAN, WEST [UVE]
FAGHANI alt for FAGANI [FAF]
FAGNIA alt for FANIA [FAN]
FAGUDU dial of SULA [SZN]
FAIA dial of KIRIKIRI [KIY]
FAIRI dial of BIAK [BHW]
FAISHANG dial of MIYA [MKF]
FAITA [FAT] lang, Papua New Guinea
FAIWOL [FAI] lang, Papua New Guinea
FAIWOLMIN alt for FAIWOL [FAI]
FAJELU alt for PÖJULU dial of BARI [BFA]
FAJULU alt for PÖJULU dial of BARI [BFA]
FAK alt for BALOM dial of BAFIA [KSF]
FAKANCHI alt for KAG dial of KAG-FER-JIIR-KOOR-ROR-US-ZUKSUN [GEL]
FAKANCHI alt for ROR dial of KAG-FER-JIIR-KOOR-ROR-US-ZUKSUN [GEL]
FAKANCI alt for KAG-FER-JIIR-KOOR-ROR-US-ZUKSUN [GEL]
FAKARA alt for CARA [CFD]
FAKKANCI alt for KAG-FER-JIIR-KOOR-ROR-US-ZUKSUN [GEL]
FALA [FAX] lang, Spain
FALA alt for BAKHA dial of KARANGA [KTH]
FALAHU dial of SULA [SZN]
FALAM alt for CHIN, FALAM [HBH]
FALI [FLI] lang, Nigeria
FALI alt for LONWOLWOL [CRC]
FALI DU BELE-FERE alt for BELE dial of FALI, SOUTH [FAL]
FALI DU PESKE-BORI alt for BVERI dial of FALI, NORTH [FLL]
FALI KANGOU alt for KANGOU dial of FALI, SOUTH [FAL]
FALI OF BAISSA [FAH] lang, Nigeria
FALI OF JILBU alt for ZIZILIVAKAN [ZIZ]
FALI OF KIRIYA dial of KAMWE [HIG]
FALI OF MIJILU dial of KAMWE [HIG]
FALI OF MUBI alt for FALI [FLI]

FALI OF MUCHELLA alt for FALI [FLI]
FALI, NORTH [FLL] lang, Cameroon
FALI, SOUTH [FAL] lang, Cameroon
FALI-BELE alt for BELE dial of FALI, SOUTH [FAL]
FALI-BOSSOUM alt for BOSSOUM dial of FALI, NORTH [FLL]
FALI-DOURBEYE alt for DOURBEYE dial of FALI, NORTH [FLL]
FALI-TINGUELIN dial of FALI, SOUTH [FAL]
FALL INDIANS alt for GROS VENTRE [ATS]
FALLAM alt for CHIN, FALAM [HBH]
FALLANI alt for CHALDEAN NEO-ARAMAIC [CLD]
FALOR alt for PALOR [FAP]
FAM [FAM] lang, Nigeria
FAMA-TEIS-KUA dial of KRONGO [KGO]
FANA alt for FANIA [FAN]
FANAGOLO [FAO] lang, South Africa; also in DRC, Namibia, Zambia, Zimbabwe
"FANAKALO" pejorative alt for FANAGOLO [FAO]
FANAKALO alt for FANAGOLO [FAO]
FANATING alt for KAFOA [KPU]
"FANEKOLO" pejorative alt for FANAGOLO [FAO]
FANEKOLO alt for FANAGOLO [FAO]
FAN-FORON-HEIKPANG dial of BEROM [BOM]
FANG [FNG] lang, Gabon; also in Cameroon, Congo, Equatorial Guinea, São Tomé e Príncipe
FANG dial of FANG [FNG]
FANGATAU dial of TUAMOTUAN [PMT]
FANIA [FAN] lang, Chad
FANIAGARA dial of WARA [WBF]
FANIAN alt for FANIA [FAN]
FANIC dial of DEDUA [DED]
FANNAI dial of LUSHAI [LSH]
FANTE dial of AKAN [TWS]
FANTERA dial of NAFAANRA [NFR]
FANTI alt for FANTE dial of AKAN [TWS]
FANTING alt for LONWOLWOL [CRC]
FANTUAN alt for KAFANCHAN dial of TYAP [KCG]
FANYA alt for FANIA [FAN]
FANYAN alt for FANIA [FAN]
FAR EASTERN MANGGARAI alt for RIUNG [RIU]
FARAN alt for FIRAN [FIR]
FARANAH alt for MANINKA, SANKARAN [MSC]
FARANGA dial of KENDEJE [KLF]
FARANGAO alt for BALANGAO [BLW]
FARANYAO alt for MAIRASI [FRY]
FARE dial of LESE [LES]
FAREFARE alt for FRAFRA [GUR]
FAROESE [FAE] lang, Denmark
FARS [FAC] lang, Iran
FARSI, EASTERN [PRS] lang, Afghanistan; also in Pakistan
FARSI, WESTERN [PES] lang, Iran; also in Australia, Austria, Azerbaijan, Bahrain, Canada, Denmark, France, Germany, Greece, India, Iraq, Israel, Netherlands, Oman, Qatar, Saudi Arabia, Spain, Sweden, Tajikistan, Turkey (Asia), Turkmenistan, UAE, United Kingdom, USA, Uzbekistan
FARUARU alt for HIXKARYÁNA [HIX]
FAS [FAS] lang, Papua New Guinea
FASIH alt for ARABIC, STANDARD [ABV]

FASSANO dial of LADIN [LLD]
FASU [FAA] lang, Papua New Guinea
FATAKAI alt for NUAULU, NORTH [NNI]
FATAKAI alt for NUAULU, SOUTH [NXL]
FATALEKA [FAR] lang, Solomon Islands
FATALUKU [DDG] lang, Timor Lorosae
FATE alt for EFATE, SOUTH [ERK]
FATU HIVA dial of MARQUESAN, SOUTH [QMS]
FATULE'U alt for AMFOAN-FATULE'U-AMABI dial of ATONI [TMR]
FAUR alt for URUANGNIRIN [URN]
FAURO dial of MONO [MTE]
FAVORLANG alt for BABUZA [BZG]
FAVORLANGSCH alt for BABUZA [BZG]
FAYICHUCK dial of CHUUKESE [TRU]
FAYU [FAU] lang, Indonesia (Irian Jaya)
FEAD alt for NUGURIA [NUR]
FECAKOMODIYO alt for GULE [GLE]
FEDERE dial of MIYA [MKF]
FEDICCA alt for FIYADIKKA dial of NOBIIN [FIA]
FEDICCA alt for NOBIIN [FIA]
FEDIJA alt for NOBIIN [FIA]
FEEFEE alt for FE'FE' [FMP]
FE'EFE'E alt for FE'FE' [FMP]
FEFE alt for FE'FE' [FMP]
FE'FE' [FMP] lang, Cameroon
FEGOLMIN alt for FAIWOL [FAI]
FEHAN alt for TETUN [TTM]
FELLAHI dial of ARABIC, SOUTH LEVANTINE SPOKEN [AJP]
FELLATA alt for FULFULDE, ADAMAWA [FUB]
FELLIHI alt for CHALDEAN NEO-ARAMAIC [CLD]
FELOUP alt for EJAMAT [EJA]
FELUP alt for EJAMAT [EJA]
FELUPE alt for EJAMAT [EJA]
FEM alt for FYAM [PYM]
FEMBE [AGL] lang, Papua New Guinea
FENI alt for ANIR dial of TANGGA [TGG]
FER alt for KARA [KAH]
FER dial of KAG-FER-JIIR-KOOR-ROR-US-ZUKSUN [GEL]
FERAMIN dial of TELEFOL [TLF]
FERE dial of KASEM [KAS]
FERE. ET-FER alt for FER dial of KAG-FER-JIIR-KOOR-ROR-US-ZUKSUN [GEL]
FEREJDAN alt for FEREYDAN dial of GEORGIAN [GEO]
FEREJDAN dial of GEORGIAN [GEO]
FERENGHI alt for LINGUA FRANCA [PML]
FEREYDAN dial of GEORGIAN [GEO]
FÉRI alt for MOKOLE [MKL]
FERNANDIAN alt for BUBE [BVB]
FERNANDINO alt for FERNANDO PO CREOLE ENGLISH [FPE]
FERNANDO PO CREOLE ENGLISH [FPE] lang, Equatorial Guinea
FERNANDO PO KRIO alt for FERNANDO PO CREOLE ENGLISH [FPE]
FEROGE [FER] lang, Sudan
FEROGHE alt for FEROGE [FER]

FERREÑAFE alt for QUECHUA, LAMBAYEQUE [QUF]
FERRING dial of FRISIAN, NORTHERN [FRR]
FERROGE alt for FEROGE [FER]
FERTIT alt for KARA [KAH]
FES dial of ARABIC, JUDEO-TUNISIAN [AJT]
FESEREK alt for IZERE [FIZ]
FESOA alt for NALIK [NAL]
FESSOA alt for NALIK [NAL]
FEYLI dial of LURI [LRI]
FEZ. MEKNES dial of ARABIC, MOROCCAN SPOKEN [ARY]
FEZERE alt for IZERE [FIZ]
FGANJA dial of BALANTA-GANJA [BJT]
FIADIDJA alt for FIYADIKKA dial of NOBIIN [FIA]
FIADIDJA alt for NOBIIN [FIA]
FIADIDJA-MAHAS alt for NOBIIN [FIA]
FIAMA alt for CENTRAL KONO dial of KONO [KNO]
FIANSE dial of WASA [WSS]
FIBA alt for FIPA [FIP]
FIER alt for FYER [FIE]
FIEROZZO dial of MOCHENO [QMO]
FIFE BAY alt for DAUI dial of SUAU [SWP]
FIFIA alt for TARIFIT [RIF]
FIJI alt for FIJIAN [FJI]
FIJI alt for FIJIAN, WESTERN [WYY]
FIJI alt for RUFIJI [RUI]
FIJIAN [FJI] lang, Fiji; also in Nauru, New Zealand, Vanuatu
FIJIAN HINDI alt for HINDUSTANI, FIJIAN [HIF]
FIJIAN, WESTERN [WYY] lang, Fiji
FIKA dial of BOLE [BOL]
FIKANKAYEN alt for FIKA dial of BOLE [BOL]
FIKYU dial of KUTEP [KUB]
FILA dial of MELE-FILA [MXE]
FILA-MELE alt for MELE-FILA [MXE]
FILIFITA dial of MUFIAN [AOJ]
FILILWA dial of TUMBUKA [TUW]
FILIPINO alt for TAGALOG [TGL]
FILIPINO SIGN LANGUAGE alt for PHILIPPINE SIGN LANGUAGE [PSP]
FILIRWA alt for FILILWA dial of TUMBUKA [TUW]
FILIYA alt for PERO [PIP]
FILLANCI alt for FULFULDE, ADAMAWA [FUB]
FIMAGA alt for FIWAGA [FIW]
FINANGA dial of MAHOU [MXX]
FINGE alt for BABANKI [BBK]
FININGA alt for DAJU, DAR FUR [DAJ]
FINLAND SWEDISH alt for EASTERN SWEDISH dial of SWEDISH [SWD]
FINNG alt for BOBO MADARÉ, NORTHERN [BBO]
FINNISH [FIN] lang, Finland; also in Canada, Estonia, Norway, Russia (Europe), Sweden, USA
FINNISH KARELIAN alt for SOUTHEASTERN FINNISH dial of FINNISH [FIN]
FINNISH KARJALA alt for SOUTHEASTERN FINNISH dial of FINNISH [FIN]
"FINNISH LAPP" pejorative alt for SAAMI, INARI [LPI]
FINNISH SIGN LANGUAGE [FSE] lang, Finland
FINNISH, KVEN [FKV] lang, Norway

FINNISH, TORNEDALEN [FIT] lang, Sweden; also in Finland
FÍNTIKA RÓMMA alt for ROMANI, KALO FINNISH [RMF]
FINUNGWA [FAG] lang, Papua New Guinea
FINUNGWAN alt for FINUNGWA [FAG]
FIOME alt for GOROWA [GOW]
FIOT alt for VILI [VIF]
FIOTE alt for VILI [VIF]
FIOTE alt for WEST KONGO dial of KONGO [KON]
FIOTI alt for WEST KONGO dial of KONGO [KON]
FIPA [FIP] lang, Tanzania; also in Malawi
FIRA alt for FILA dial of MELE-FILA [MXE]
FIRAN [FIR] lang, Nigeria
FIRIA dial of YALUNKA [YAL]
FIROZKOHI dial of AIMAQ [AIQ]
FITERYA alt for HWANA [HWO]
FITI alt for SURUBU [SDE]
FITILAI alt for BWILIM dial of DIJIM-BWILIM [CFA]
FITZROY VALLEY KRIOL dial of KRIOL [ROP]
FIU alt for KWARA'AE [KWF]
FIWAGA [FIW] lang, Papua New Guinea
FIWAGE alt for FIWAGA [FIW]
FIYADIKKA dial of NOBIIN [FIA]
FIYADIKKYA alt for NOBIIN [FIA]
FIZERE alt for IZERE [FIZ]
FJAA alt for BALANTA-GANJA [BJT]
FJAALIB dial of BALANTA-GANJA [BJT]
FKAR dial of TEHIT [KPS]
FLAAI TAAL alt for TSOTSITAAL [FLY]
FLAMAND alt for VLAAMS [VLA]
"FLATHEAD"-KALISPEL pejorative alt for KALISPEL-PEND D'OREILLE [FLA]
FLEMISH alt for VLAAMS [VLA]
FLEO dial of WE SOUTHERN [GXX]
FLINDERS ISLAND [FLN] lang, Australia
FLORIDA ISLANDS alt for GELA [NLG]
FLORUTZ alt for FIEROZZO dial of MOCHENO [QMO]
FLOUP alt for EJAMAT [EJA]
FLOWERY LACHI alt for LIPULIONGTCO dial of LACHI [LBT]
FLOWERY LISU alt for HUA LISU dial of LISU [LIS]
FLOWERY LISU alt for HWA LISU dial of LISU [LIS]
FLOWERY LOLO alt for MANTSI [MUS]
FLOWERY MIAO alt for BUNU, BAHENG [PHA]
FLOWERY MIAO alt for HMONG, NORTHEASTERN DIAN [HMD]
FLUP alt for EJAMAT [EJA]
FLUVIAL dial of JOLA-KASA [CSK]
FLY RIVER dial of TABO [KNV]
FLY TAAL alt for TSOTSITAAL [FLY]
FO alt for FON-GBE [FOA]
FO alt for SO [SOX]
FO dial of FON-GBE [FOA]
FOAU [FLH] lang, Indonesia (Irian Jaya)
FOBANO alt for EASTERN ARAGONESE dial of ARAGONESE [AXX]
FODARA dial of SENOUFO, CEBAARA [SEF]
FODATA-LARAT I dial of FORDATA [FRD]

FOE alt for FOI [FOI]
FOGBE alt for FON-GBE [FOA]
FOGI dial of BURU [MHS]
FOGNY dial of JOLA-FOGNY [DYO]
FOHR-AMRUM alt for FERRING dial of FRISIAN, NORTHERN [FRR]
FOI [FOI] lang, Papua New Guinea
FOI alt for IAU [TMU]
FOI dial of IAU [TMU]
FOJA alt for ABINOMN [BSA]
FOLEPI dial of MUNDANI [MUN]
FOLOPA [PPO] lang, Papua New Guinea
FOMA [FOM] lang, DRC
FOMOPEA alt for NGWE [NWE]
FON alt for FON-GBE [FOA]
FONDANTI alt for NTII dial of FE'FE' [FMP]
FONDEBOUGOU dial of SENOUFO, TAGWANA [TGW]
FONDJOMEKWET alt for MKWET dial of FE'FE' [FMP]
FONG dial of EWONDO [EWO]
FON-GBE [FOA] lang, Benin; also in Togo
FONGONDENG alt for NGWE [NWE]
FONGORO [FGR] lang, Chad
FONI alt for PA'A [AFA]
FONNU alt for FON-GBE [FOA]
FONTEM alt for NGWE [NWE]
FOOCHOW alt for FUZHOU dial of CHINESE, MIN DONG [CDO]
FOOCHOW dial of CHINESE, MIN DONG [CDO]
FOODO [FOD] lang, Benin; also in Ghana
FOOLO dial of SENOUFO, DJIMINI [DYI]
FOPO-BUA dial of GREBO, NORTHERN [GRB]
FOR alt for FUR [FUR]
FORA alt for FUR [FUR]
FORA dial of BALANTA-KENTOHE [BLE]
FORABA alt for FOLOPA [PPO]
FORAK [FRO] lang, Papua New Guinea
FORAN alt for WAGI [FAD]
FORCALQUIEREN alt for GAVOT dial of PROVENCAL [PRV]
FORDATA [FRD] lang, Indonesia (Maluku)
FORDATA-LARAT II dial of FORDATA [FRD]
FORDUNGA alt for FUR [FUR]
FORE [FOR] lang, Papua New Guinea
FOREDAFA alt for CHITONAHUA dial of YAMINAHUA [YAA]
FOREKE DSCHANG dial of YEMBA [BAN]
FOREST BIRA alt for BILA [BIP]
FOREST CHULUPI dial of CHULUPI [CAG]
FOREST ENETS alt for BAY dial of ENETS [ENE]
FOREST MANINKA alt for WASULU dial of JULA, ODIENNE [JOD]
FOREST YURAK dial of NENETS [YRK]
FORMOSAN alt for AMOY dial of CHINESE, MIN NAN [CFR]
FORMOSAN alt for SIRAIYA [FOS]
FORNIÓ alt for FULNIÔ [FUN]
FOROK alt for FUR [FUR]
FORON alt for FIRAN [FIR]
FØROYSKT alt for FAROESE [FAE]

FORT YUKON GWICH'IN dial of GWICHIN [KUC]
FORTA alt for FUR [FUR]
FORTSENAL [FRT] lang, Vanuatu
FOTO alt for NGWE [NWE]
FOTOUNI alt for FE'FE' [FMP]
FOTOUNI alt for TUNGI' dial of FE'FE' [FMP]
FOTUNA alt for WEST FUTUNA dial of FUTUNA-ANIWA [FUT]
FOULA FOUTA alt for FUUTA JALON [FUF]
FOULFOULDE alt for FULFULDE, ADAMAWA [FUB]
FOUR alt for FUR [FUR]
FOURGOULA dial of SENOUFO, TAGWANA [TGW]
FOUTA DYALON alt for FUUTA JALON [FUF]
FOUTE alt for VUTE [VUT]
FOWE dial of SIANE [SNP]
FOX dial of MESQUAKIE [SAC]
FOYA alt for ABINOMN [BSA]
FRAASE alt for BALANTA-GANJA [BJT]
FRAFRA [GUR] lang, Ghana; also in Burkina Faso
FRAFRA dial of FRAFRA [GUR]
FRANÇAIS alt for FRENCH [FRN]
FRANÇAIS ACADIEN alt for FRENCH, CAJUN [FRC]
FRANC-COMTOIS dial of FRENCH [FRN]
FRANCHE-COMTOIS dial of FRENCH [FRN]
FRANCONIAN alt for MAINFRÄNKISCH [VMF]
FRANCO-ONTARIEN dial of FRENCH [FRN]
FRANCO-PROVENÇAL [FRA] lang, France; also in Italy, Switzerland
FRÄNKISCH alt for FRANKISH [FRK]
FRANKISH [FRK] lang, Germany
FRANKISH alt for LUXEMBOURGEOIS [LUX]
FRANS VLAAMS dial of VLAAMS [VLA]
FRASE alt for BALANTA-KENTOHE [BLE]
FRASSILONGO dial of MOCHENO [QMO]
FRENCH [FRN] lang, France; also in Algeria, Andorra, Austria, Belgium, Benin, Burkina Faso, Burundi, Cameroon, Canada, CAR, Chad, Comoros Islands, Congo, Côte d'Ivoire, DRC, Djibouti, French Guiana, French Polynesia, Gabon, Guadeloupe, Guinea, Haiti, Israel, Italy, Lebanon, Luxembourg, Madagascar, Mali, Martinique, Mauritania, Mauritius, Mayotte, Monaco, Morocco, New Caledonia, Niger, Philippines, Puerto Rico, Réunion, Rwanda, Saudi Arabia, Senegal, Seychelles, St. Pierre and Miquelon, Switzerland, Togo, Tunisia, UAE, United Kingdom, USA, Vanuatu, Wallis and Futuna
FRENCH CREE alt for MICHIF [CRG]
FRENCH GUIANESE CREOLE FRENCH [FRE] lang, French Guiana
FRENCH SIGN LANGUAGE [FSL] lang, France; also in Togo
FRENCH, CAJUN [FRC] lang, USA
FRIBOURGOIS alt for FRANCHE-COMTOIS dial of FRENCH [FRN]
FRIES alt for FRISIAN, WESTERN [FRI]
FRIOULAN alt for FRIULIAN [FRL]
FRIOULIAN alt for FRIULIAN [FRL]
FRISIAN, EASTERN [FRS] lang, Germany; also in USA

FRISIAN, NORTHERN [FRR] lang, Germany
FRISIAN, WESTERN [FRI] lang, Netherlands; also in Canada, Denmark, Germany, USA
FRIULANO alt for FRIULIAN [FRL]
FRIULIAN [FRL] lang, Italy
FRYSK alt for FRISIAN, WESTERN [FRI]
FSL alt for FRENCH SIGN LANGUAGE [FSL]
FSL alt for PHILIPPINE SIGN LANGUAGE [PSP]
FTOUR alt for TUR dial of HDI [TUR]
FTOUR alt for XEDI [TUR]
FU alt for BAFUT [BFD]
FU KHLA alt for PHULA [PHH]
FUCAKA alt for PA'A [AFA]
FUCHOW alt for FUZHOU dial of CHINESE, MIN DONG [CDO]
FUCH'YE alt for NUNG [NUN]
FÙDA alt for NGEMBA dial of GHOMALA [BBJ]
FUFULA dial of WALI [WLX]
FUGA OF JIMMA dial of YEMSA [JNJ]
FUGAR alt for AVIANWU dial of YEKHEE [ETS]
FU-GUANG dial of CHINESE, GAN [KNN]
FUJIAN alt for HOKKIEN dial of CHINESE, MIN NAN [CFR]
FUJIAN dial of CHINESE, MIN NAN [CFR]
FUJIANESE alt for FUKIENESE dial of CHINESE, MIN NAN [CFR]
FUKAC dial of MAPE [MLH]
FUKIEN alt for FUJIAN dial of CHINESE, MIN NAN [CFR]
FUKIENESE alt for HOKKIEN dial of CHINESE, MIN NAN [CFR]
FUKIENESE dial of CHINESE, MIN NAN [CFR]
FUL alt for FULFULDE, ADAMAWA [FUB]
FULA alt for FULFULDE, ADAMAWA [FUB]
FULA alt for FULFULDE, CENTRAL-EASTERN NIGER [FUQ]
FULA alt for FULFULDE, WESTERN NIGER [FUH]
FULA alt for KOROMFÉ [KFZ]
FULA FORRO alt for FULACUNDA dial of PULAAR [FUC]
FULA FULBE alt for FULFULDE, ADAMAWA [FUB]
FULA PETA dial of FUUTA JALON [FUF]
FULA PRETO alt for FULACUNDA dial of FULFULDE, PULAAR [FUC]
FULA PRETO alt for FULACUNDA dial of PULAAR [FUC]
FULACUNDA dial of FULFULDE, PULAAR [FUC]
FULACUNDA dial of PULAAR [FUC]
FULAKUNDA alt for FULACUNDA dial of FULFULDE, PULAAR [FUC]
FULAKUNDA alt for FULACUNDA dial of PULAAR [FUC]
FULANI alt for FULFULDE, ADAMAWA [FUB]
FULANI alt for FULFULDE, CENTRAL-EASTERN NIGER [FUQ]
FULANI alt for FULFULDE, WESTERN NIGER [FUH]
FULANI alt for PULAAR [FUC]
FULANKE dial of MANINKAKAN, WESTERN [MLQ]
FULATANCHI alt for FULFULDE, ADAMAWA [FUB]
FULBE alt for FULFULDE, ADAMAWA [FUB]

FULBE alt for FULFULDE, CENTRAL-EASTERN NIGER [FUQ]
FULBE alt for FULFULDE, KANO-KATSINA-BORORRO [FUV]
FULBE alt for FULFULDE, MAASINA [FUL]
FULBE alt for FULFULDE, WESTERN NIGER [FUH]
FULBE alt for FUUTA JALON [FUF]
FULBE JEERI alt for PULAAR [FUC]
FULBE JEERI alt for TOUCOULEUR dial of PULAAR [FUC]
FULBE-BORGU dial of FULFULDE, BENIN-TOGO [FUE]
FULERO alt for FULIIRU [FLR]
FULFULDE alt for FULFULDE, ADAMAWA [FUB]
FULFULDE JALON alt for FUUTA JALON [FUF]
FULFULDE, ADAMAWA [FUB] lang, Cameroon; also in Chad, Nigeria, Sudan
FULFULDE, BAGIRMI [FUI] lang, Chad; also in CAR
FULFULDE, BENIN-TOGO [FUE] lang, Benin; also in Nigeria, Togo
FULFULDE, CENTRAL-EASTERN NIGER [FUQ] lang, Niger
FULFULDE, KANO-KATSINA-BORORRO [FUV] lang, Nigeria; also in Cameroon, Chad
FULFULDE, MAASINA [FUL] lang, Mali; also in Côte d'Ivoire, Ghana
FULFULDE, NIGERIAN [FUV] lang, Nigeria; also in Cameroon, Chad
FULFULDE, NORTHEASTERN BURKINA FASO [FUH] lang, Niger; also in Burkina Faso
FULFULDE, PULAAR [FUC] lang, Senegal; also in Gambia, Guinea, Guinea-Bissau, Mali, Mauritania
FULFULDE, WESTERN NIGER [FUH] lang, Niger; also in Burkina Faso
FULFULDE-PULAAR alt for PULAAR [FUC]
FULIIRU [FLR] lang, DRC
FULIRU alt for FULIIRU [FLR]
FULKUNDA alt for FULACUNDA dial of FULFULDE, PULAAR [FUC]
FULKUNDA alt for FULACUNDA dial of PULAAR [FUC]
FULLO FUUTA alt for FUUTA JALON [FUF]
FULNIÔ [FUN] lang, Brazil
FULSE alt for KOROMFÉ [KFZ]
FULUKA alt for KUSU [KSV]
FULUP alt for EJAMAT [EJA]
FUM [FUM] lang, Nigeria
FUMA alt for FOMA [FOM]
FUNAFUTI alt for SOUTH TUVALUAN dial of TUVALUAN [ELL]
FUNDI dial of SWAHILI [SWA]
FUNG alt for NI NYO'O dial of TUNEN [BAZ]
FUNGOM [FUG] lang, Cameroon
FUNGOR alt for KO [FUJ]
FUNGUR alt for KO [FUJ]
FUNGWA [ULA] lang, Nigeria
FUNGWE dial of TUMBUKA [TUW]
FUNIKA alt for MFINU [ZMF]
FUNSILE alt for SISAALA, PASAALE [SIG]
FUR [FUR] lang, Sudan; also in Chad

FURAKANG alt for FUR [FUR]
FURAN alt for WAGI [FAD]
FURA-PAWA alt for EL MOLO [ELO]
FURATI alt for ARABIC, MESOPOTAMIAN SPOKEN [ACM]
FURAWI alt for FUR [FUR]
FURLAN alt for FRIULIAN [FRL]
FURNIÔ alt for FULNIÔ [FUN]
FURSUM dial of MIYA [MKF]
FURU [FUU] lang, DRC; also in CAR
FURU alt for BIKYA [BYB]
FURU alt for BISHUO [BWH]
FURU alt for BUSUU [BJU]
FURUPAGHA dial of IZON [IJC]
FUSAP alt for GHOMÁLÁ' NORTH dial of GHOMALA [BBJ]
FUT alt for BAFUT [BFD]
FUTA FULA alt for FUUTA JALON [FUF]
FUTA JALLON alt for FUUTA JALON [FUF]
FUTE alt for VUTE [VUT]
FUTU dial of KAMWE [HIG]
FUTUNA, EAST [FUD] lang, Wallis and Futuna; also in New Caledonia
FUTUNA-ANIWA [FUT] lang, Vanuatu
FUTUNIAN alt for FUTUNA, EAST [FUD]
FUUMU dial of TEKE, SOUTH CENTRAL [IFM]
FUUTA JALON [FUF] lang, Guinea; also in Gambia, Guinea-Bissau, Mali, Senegal, Sierra Leone
FUYUG [FUY] lang, Papua New Guinea
FUYUGE alt for FUYUG [FUY]
FUYUGHE alt for FUYUG [FUY]
FUZHOU alt for FOOCHOW dial of CHINESE, MIN DONG [CDO]
FUZHOU dial of CHINESE, MIN DONG [CDO]
FWA-GOUMAK alt for KUMAK [NEE]
FWÂI [FWA] lang, New Caledonia
FWE [FWE] lang, Namibia
FYAM [PYM] lang, Nigeria
FYEM alt for FYAM [PYM]
FYER [FIE] lang, Nigeria
GA [GAC] lang, Ghana; also in Togo
GÃ alt for KAANSA [GNA]
G//AA alt for G//AAKHWE dial of GANA [GNK]
GAA [TTB] lang, Nigeria
G//AAKHWE dial of GANA [GNK]
GAALPU dial of DHANGU [GLA]
GAAM [TBI] lang, Sudan
GA'ANDA [GAA] lang, Nigeria
GA'ANDA dial of GA'ANDA [GAA]
GA'ANDU alt for GA'ANDA [GAA]
GAAWRO alt for KALAMI [GWC]
GABADI alt for KABADI [KBT]
G//ABAKE alt for HIETSHWARE [HIE]
GABAKE-NTSHORI alt for HIETSHWARE [HIE]
"GABAR" pejorative alt for DARI [GBZ]
GABAR KHEL alt for GOWRO [GWF]
GABARO alt for GOWRO [GWF]
GABBRA alt for GABRA dial of BORANA [GAX]
GABBRA alt for GABRA dial of OROMO, BORANA-ARSI-GUJI [GAX]
GABERE alt for GABRI [GAB]

GABERI alt for GABRI [GAB]
GABIANO dial of NIKSEK [GBE]
GABIN dial of GAANDA [GAA]
GABLAI alt for KABALAI [KVF]
GABO alt for DIDA, LAKOTA [DIC]
GABOBORA alt for ANUKI [AUI]
GABOU alt for GOBU [GOX]
GABOU alt for GUBU [GOX]
GABRA dial of BORANA [GAX]
GABRA dial of OROMO, BORANA-ARSI-GUJI [GAX]
"GABRI" pejorative alt for DARI [GBZ]
GABRI [GAB] lang, Chad
GABRI alt for TOBANGA [TNG]
GABRI-KIMRÉ alt for KIMRÉ [KQP]
GABRI-NORD alt for TOBANGA [TNG]
GABRI-NORTH alt for TOBANGA [TNG]
GABU alt for GOBU [GOX]
GABU alt for GUBU [GOX]
GABU dial of IGEDE [IGE]
GABULA dial of SOGA [SOG]
GABUTAMON [GAV] lang, Papua New Guinea
GACHIKOLO dial of HALBI [HLB]
GACHITL-KVANKHI alt for GADYRI dial of CHAMALAL [CJI]
GADABA, BODO [GBJ] lang, India
GADABA, OLLAR, POTTANGI [GDB] lang, India
GADABA, OLLAR, SALUR [GAU] lang, India
GADAISU alt for SINAKI dial of SUAU [SWP]
GADALA alt for BUWAL [BHS]
GADANG [GDK] lang, Chad
GA'DANG [GDG] lang, Philippines
GADANG alt for WORIMI [KDA]
GADBA alt for GADABA, BODO [GBJ]
GADBA alt for GADABA, OLLAR, POTTANGI [GDB]
GADDANG [GAD] lang, Philippines
GADDI [GBK] lang, India
GADDYALI alt for GADDI [GBK]
GADE [GED] lang, Nigeria
GADHANG alt for WORIMI [KDA]
GADHAVALI alt for GARHWALI [GBM]
GADHAWALA alt for GARHWALI [GBM]
GADI alt for GADDI [GBK]
GADI CHAMEALI dial of CHAMBEALI [CDH]
GADIALI alt for GADDI [GBK]
GADJERAWANG [GDH] lang, Australia
GADJERONG alt for GADJERAWANG [GDH]
GADJNJAMADA alt for ADYNYAMATHANHA [ADT]
GADO alt for KADO [KDV]
GADRE alt for ADELE [ADE]
GADSCHKENE dial of ROMANI, SINTE [RMO]
GADSUP [GAJ] lang, Papua New Guinea
GADSUP dial of GADSUP [GAJ]
GADU alt for KADO [KDV]
GADULIYA LOHAR alt for LOHAR, GADE [GDA]
GADUWA [GDW] lang, Cameroon
GADWA alt for GADABA, BODO [GBJ]
GADWAHI alt for GARHWALI [GBM]
GADYAGA alt for SONINKE [SNN]
GADYAGA dial of SONINKE [SNN]
GADYRI dial of CHAMALAL [CJI]
GAE alt for ANDOA [ANB]

GAE dial of GHARI [GRI]
GAEILGE alt for GAELIC, IRISH [GLI]
GAEJAWA alt for GEJI dial of GEJI [GEZ]
GAELG alt for MANX [MJD]
GAELI alt for KAYELI [KZL]
GAELIC alt for GAELIC, SCOTS [GLS]
GAELIC, IRISH [GLI] lang, Ireland; also in Brazil,
    Canada, United Kingdom, USA
GAELIC, SCOTS [GLS] lang, United Kingdom; also
    in Australia, Canada, USA
GAFAT [GFT] lang, Ethiopia
GAFUKU alt for ALEKANO [GAH]
GAGADU [GBU] lang, Australia
GAGATL dial of ANDI [ANI]
GAGAUZ [GAG] lang, Moldova; also in Bulgaria,
    Kazakhstan, Romania, Ukraine
GAGAUZI alt for GAGAUZ [GAG]
GAGE alt for TOLITOLI [TXE]
GAGNOUA-BÉTÉ alt for BÉTÉ, GAGNOA [BTG]
GAGOU alt for GAGU [GGU]
GAGU [GGU] lang, Côte d'Ivoire
GAGUDJARA alt for KARTUJARRA dial of MARTU
    WANGKA [MPJ]
GAGUDJU alt for GAGADU [GBU]
GAH alt for BATI [BVT]
GAHOM alt for BAHINEMO [BJH]
GAHORE dial of BAGHELI [BFY]
GAHRI [BFU] lang, India; also in China
GAHUKU alt for ALEKANO [GAH]
GAHUKU-GAMA alt for ALEKANO [GAH]
GAIDASU alt for SINAKI dial of SUAU [SWP]
GÀIDHLIG alt for GAELIC, SCOTS [GLS]
GAIDIDJ alt for KAYTETYE [GBB]
GAIKA dial of XHOSA [XOS]
GAIKHO alt for KAREN, GEKO [GHK]
GAIKUNDI [GBF] lang, Papua New Guinea
GAIKUNTI alt for GAIKUNDI [GBF]
GAIL [GIC] lang, South Africa
GAILCK alt for MANX [MJD]
GAIN alt for GA [GAC]
GAINA [GCN] lang, Papua New Guinea
GAINA dial of GAINA [GCN]
GAIREN dial of MAIWA [MTI]
GAJ alt for BAJAU, INDONESIAN [BDL]
GAJ alt for GANTS [GAO]
GAJADILT alt for GAYARDILT [GYD]
GAJARDILD alt for GAYARDILT [GYD]
GAJILA alt for GAJILI dial of KUNIMAIPA [KUP]
GAJILI dial of KUNIMAIPA [KUP]
GAJO alt for GAYO [GYO]
GAJOL dial of BALKAN GAGAUZ TURKISH [BGX]
GAJOMANG alt for TALODI [TLO]
GAKPA alt for LOZOUA dial of DIDA, YOCOBOUE
    [GUD]
GAKTAI alt for MALI [GCC]
GAKVARI dial of CHAMALAL [CJI]
GAL [GAP] lang, Papua New Guinea
GALA dial of MIYA [MKF]
GALAAGU alt for KALARKO [KBA]
GALABA dial of MONO [MNH]
GALAICO-EXTREMADURAN alt for FALA [FAX]

GALAMBE alt for GALAMBU [GLO]
GALAMBI alt for GALAMBU [GLO]
GALAMBU [GLO] lang, Nigeria
GALAMJINA dial of JIBU [JIB]
GALANCHO alt for CHECHEN [CJC]
GALAVDA alt for GLAVDA [GLV]
GALAVI alt for GHAYAVI [BMK]
GALCHA alt for TAJIKI [PET]
GALEBAGLA alt for GIL BAGALE dial of SISAALA,
    TUMULUNG [SIL]
GALEG dial of AWAD BING [BCU]
GALEGO alt for GALICIAN [GLN]
GALELA [GBI] lang, Indonesia (Maluku)
GALEMBI alt for GALAMBU [GLO]
GALERA dial of NAMBIKUARA, SOUTHERN [NAB]
GALESHI dial of GILAKI [GLK]
GALEYA [GAR] lang, Papua New Guinea
GALEYA alt for GAREA dial of GALEYA [GAR]
GALGADUNGU alt for KALKUTUNG [KTG]
GALGADUUN alt for KALKUTUNG [KTG]
GALI alt for RONJI [ROE]
GALIBI alt for CARIB [CRB]
GALIBÍ alt for CARIB [CRB]
GALICE [GCE] lang, USA
GALICIAN [GLN] lang, Spain; also in Portugal
GALICIAN dial of PORTUGUESE [POR]
GALICIAN dial of ROMANI, CARPATHIAN [RMC]
GALIGALU alt for LISHANID NOSHAN [AIJ]
GALIGLU alt for HULAULÁ [HUY]
GALIHALU alt for LISHÁN DIDÁN [TRG]
GALILA dial of AARI [AIZ]
GALIM alt for SUGA [SGI]
GALITS dial of KARAIM [KDR]
GALKE alt for NDAI [GKE]
"GALLA" pejorative alt for BORANA [GAX]
"GALLA" pejorative alt for OROMO, BORANA-
    ARSI-GUJI [GAX]
GALLA alt for OROMO, WEST-CENTRAL [GAZ]
GALLAB alt for DAASANACH [DSH]
GALLE GURUNG alt for GHALE, SOUTHERN [GHE]
GALLEGO alt for GALICIAN [GLN]
"GALLIGNA" pejorative alt for OROMO, BORANA-
    ARSI-GUJI [GAX]
GALLINAS alt for VAI [VAI]
GALLINES alt for VAI [VAI]
GALLINOMÉRO alt for POMO, SOUTHERN [PEQ]
"GALLINYA" pejorative alt for OROMO, BORANA-
    ARSI-GUJI [GAX]
GALLO alt for GALONG dial of ADI [ADI]
GALLO dial of FRENCH [FRN]
GALLOA alt for GALWA dial of MYENE [MYE]
GALLONG alt for GALONG dial of ADI [ADI]
GALLURESE alt for SARDINIAN, GALLURESE
    [SDN]
GALO alt for GALONG dial of ADI [ADI]
GALOA alt for GALWA dial of MYENE [MYE]
GALOLE alt for GALOLI [GAL]
GALOLENG alt for TALUR [ILW]
GALOLI [GAL] lang, Timor Lorosae
GALOLI dial of GALOLI [GAL]
GALOMA alt for AROMA dial of KEOPARA [KHZ]

GALONG dial of ADI [ADI]
GALOS alt for CHILISSO [CLH]
GALU alt for DIA [DIA]
GALU alt for SINAGEN [SIU]
GALUA alt for GALWA dial of MYENE [MYE]
GALUBA alt for DAASANACH [DSH]
GALUBWA dial of DOBU [DOB]
GALUMPANG alt for KALUMPANG [KLI]
GALUNG alt for PATTAE dial of BAMBAM [PTU]
GALVAXDAXA alt for GLAVDA [GLV]
GALWA dial of MYENE [MYE]
GAM alt for DONG, NORTHERN [DOC]
GAM alt for DONG, SOUTHERN [KMC]
GAM alt for NGAM dial of KWANG [KVI]
GAMA dial of BAMU [BCF]
GAMADIA dial of GUJARATI [GJR]
GAMADOUDOU alt for WAGAWAGA [WGW]
GAMADOUDOU dial of WAGAWAGA [WGW]
GAMAEWE dial of GIDRA [GDR]
GAMAI alt for BOREI [GAI]
GAMALE alt for KHAM, GAMALE [KGJ]
GAMARGU dial of WANDALA [MFI]
GAMATI alt for GAMIT [GBL]
GAMAWA alt for NGAMO [NBH]
GAMBA alt for BELANDA VIRI [BVI]
GAMBA alt for NGAMBAY [SBA]
GAMBADI dial of KUNJA [PEP]
GAMBAI alt for NGAMBAY [SBA]
GAMBAI dial of TIKAR [TIK]
GAMBAR LEERE alt for ZAAR dial of SAYA [SAY]
GAMBAYE alt for NGAMBAY [SBA]
GAMBERA [GMA] lang, Australia
GAMBERA dial of WUNAMBAL [WUB]
GAMB-LAI alt for NGAMBAY [SBA]
GAMBLAI alt for NGAMBAY [SBA]
GAMBO alt for NAFAANRA [NFR]
GAMBOURA dial of BANA [BCW]
GAMBRE alt for GAMBERA [GMA]
GAMDUGUN dial of MINA [HNA]
GAMEI alt for BOREI [GAI]
GAMERGOU alt for GAMARGU dial of WANDALA [MFI]
GAMERGU alt for GAMARGU dial of WANDALA [MFI]
GAMETA dial of GALEYA [GAR]
GAMETI alt for GAMIT [GBL]
GAMGRE alt for GAMBERA [GMA]
GAMILA dial of BORO [BWO]
GAMILARAAY alt for KAMILAROI [KLD]
GAMILAROI alt for KAMILAROI [KLD]
GAMIT [GBL] lang, India
GAMITH alt for GAMIT [GBL]
GAMIYA dial of MIGAAMA [MMY]
GAMKONORA [GAK] lang, Indonesia (Maluku)
GAMMON alt for SHELTA [STH]
GAMO alt for NGAMO [NBH]
GAMO dial of GAMO-GOFA-DAWRO [GMO]
GAMO dial of GAMO-NINGI [BTE]
GAMO-GOFA-DAWRO [GMO] lang, Ethiopia
GAMO-NINGI [BTE] lang, Nigeria
GAMOR alt for KAMU [QKY]

GAMTA alt for GAMIT [GBL]
GAMTI alt for GAMIT [GBL]
GAMTI dial of BHILI [BHB]
GAMTI dial of MAWCHI [MKE]
GAMUSO alt for TOKANO [ZUH]
GAN alt for BENG [NHB]
GAN alt for CHINESE, GAN [KNN]
GAN alt for KAANSA [GNA]
//GANA [GNK] lang, Botswana
G//ANA alt for //GANA [GNK]
GANA [GNQ] lang, Malaysia (Sabah)
GANA dial of LERE [GNH]
GANA' alt for GANA [GNQ]
GANAAN dial of KADO [KDV]
GANÁDE alt for GANÁDI [GNE]
GANÁDI [GNE] lang, Botswana
GANADUGU dial of BAMANANKAN [BRA]
GANAGAWA alt for DIBO [DIO]
G//ANA-KHWE alt for //GANA [GNK]
G//ANAKHWE dial of GANA [GNK]
GANALBINGU dial of DJINBA [DJB]
GANAN alt for GANAAN dial of KADO [KDV]
GANANG-FAISHANG dial of IZERE [FIZ]
GANANWA dial of SOTHO, NORTHERN [SRT]
GANAQ alt for GANA [GNQ]
GANATI alt for KENATI [GAT]
GANAWURI alt for ATEN [GAN]
GANCHING dial of GARO [GRT]
GANDA [LAP] lang, Uganda; also in Tanzania
GANDA alt for GA'ANDA [GAA]
GANDANJU alt for KANJU [KBE]
GANDJU alt for KANJU [KBE]
GANDUA dial of WAWA [WWW]
!GÃ!NE alt for !GÃ!NGE dial of SEROA [KQU]
GANE [GZN] lang, Indonesia (Maluku)
GANE alt for KAANSA [GNA]
GANET alt for GHAT dial of TAMAHAQ, TAHAGGART [THV]
GANG alt for ACHOLI [ACO]
GANG alt for PENAN GANG dial of PENAN, WESTERN [PNE]
GANGA alt for BUSHOONG [BUF]
GANGAM alt for NGANGAM [GNG]
GANGAPARI dial of AWADHI [AWD]
GANGAPARIYA alt for TEHRI [THB]
!GÃ!NGE dial of SEROA [KQU]
GANGELA alt for NYEMBA [NBA]
GANGGAI alt for BAGHELI [BFY]
GANGGALIDA [GCD] lang, Australia
GANGGALITA alt for GANGGALIDA [GCD]
GANGLAU [GGL] lang, Papua New Guinea
GANGOLA dial of KUMAUNI [KFY]
GANGTE [GNB] lang, India; also in Myanmar
GANGUELA alt for NYEMBA [NBA]
GANGUELLA alt for NYEMBA [NBA]
GANGULU [GNL] lang, Australia
GANGUM alt for NGANGAM [GNG]
GANI alt for GANE [GZN]
GANI-KHWE alt for BUGA-KXOE dial of KXOE [XUU]
GANJA alt for FGANJA dial of BALANTA-GANJA [BJT]

GANJA dial of AZERBAIJANI, NORTH [AZE]
GANJAWLE alt for GANJULE dial of KACHAMA-
  GANJULE [KCX]
GANJULE dial of KACHAMA-GANJULE [KCX]
GANONGGA alt for GHANONGGA [GHN]
GANSU dial of DUNGAN [DNG]
GANTA dial of KACHAMA-GANJULE [KCX]
GANTE alt for GANGTE [GNB]
GANTS [GAO] lang, Papua New Guinea
GANUNG-RAWANG alt for RAWANG [RAW]
GANWARI alt for SADRI [SCK]
GANZA [GZA] lang, Ethiopia
GANZA alt for DAKUNZA dial of GUMUZ [GUK]
GANZI [GNZ] lang, CAR
GANZI dial of GANZI [GNZ]
GANZO alt for GANZA [GZA]
GAO [GGA] lang, Solomon Islands
GAO alt for QAU dial of GELAO [KKF]
GAO SONGHAY alt for SONGHAY, KOYRABORO
  SENNI [SON]
GAOLEI dial of CHINESE, YUE [YUH]
GAOLI dial of BUNDELI [BNS]
GAOYANG alt for GAOLEI dial of CHINESE, YUE
  [YUH]
GAPA alt for GAPAPAIWA [PWG]
GAPAPAIWA [PWG] lang, Papua New Guinea
GAPELTA alt for FULFULDE, ADAMAWA [FUB]
GAPIAN alt for GAVOT dial of PROVENCAL
  [PRV]
GAPINJI alt for PINJI [PIC]
GAPUN alt for TAIAP [GPN]
GAR alt for MNONG GAR dial of MNONG,
  EASTERN [MNG]
GAR dial of BADA [BAU]
GAR dial of GURUNTUM-MBAARU [GRD]
GAR DUGURI dial of DUGURI [DBM]
GARA alt for LOHAR, GADE [GDA]
GARADJIRI alt for KARADJERI [GBD]
GARADYARI alt for KARADJERI [GBD]
GARAGANZA alt for TAKAMA dial of NYAMWEZI
  [NYZ]
GARAKA alt for BADA [BAU]
GARAMA alt for MURRINH-PATHA [MWF]
GARANDALA dial of NGURA [NBX]
GARAP dial of KIM [KIA]
GARAS alt for LOHAR, LAHUL [LHL]
GARASIA, ADIWASI [GAS] lang, India
GARASIA, RAJPUT [GRA] lang, India
GARAWA [GBC] lang, Australia
GARAWA dial of KAPIN [TBX]
GARAWGINO dial of BIDIYO [BID]
GARBABI dial of JIBU [JIB]
GARD'ARE alt for KARADJERI [GBD]
GARDENA dial of LADIN [LLD]
GARDENESE alt for GARDENA dial of LADIN [LLD]
GARDUDJARA alt for KARTUJARRA dial of MARTU
  WANGKA [MPJ]
GARDULLA alt for DIRASHA [GDL]
GAREA alt for GALEYA [GAR]
GAREA dial of GALEYA [GAR]
GARHWALI [GBM] lang, India

GARI alt for GARREH dial of GARREH-AJURAN
  [GGH]
GARI alt for GHARI [GRI]
GARIA alt for GARIHE dial of UARE [KSJ]
GARIA alt for SUMAU [SIX]
GARIERA alt for KARIYARRA [VKA]
GARÍFUNA [CAB] lang, Honduras; also in Belize,
  Guatemala, Nicaragua, USA
GARIHE dial of UARE [KSJ]
GARKIN dial of LEZGI [LEZ]
GARKO alt for KARKO [KKO]
GARLALI alt for KALALI dial of NGURA [NBX]
GARMALANGGA dial of JARNANGO [JAY]
GARME alt for ACHERON [ACZ]
GARMIYÂNI dial of KURDI [KDB]
GARO [GRT] lang, India; also in Bangladesh
GARO alt for BOSHA dial of KAFICHO [KBR]
GARO alt for TANDEK dial of KIMARAGANG [KQR]
GAROUA alt for BATA [BTA]
GAROUA dial of FULFULDE, ADAMAWA [FUB]
GARRE [GEX] lang, Somalia
GARRE alt for GARREH dial of GARREH-AJURAN
  [GGH]
GARREH dial of GARREH-AJURAN [GGH]
GARREH-AJURAN [GGH] lang, Kenya
GARROW alt for GARO [GRT]
GARRUSI dial of KURDI [KDB]
GARUA alt for HARUA dial of BOLA [BNP]
GARUH alt for NOBANOB [GAW]
GARUS [GYB] lang, Papua New Guinea
GARUWAHI alt for GWEDA [GRW]
GARWA alt for KALAMI [GWC]
GARWE dial of NDAU [NDC]
GARWI alt for KALAMI [GWC]
GASCON [GSC] lang, France; also in Spain
GASCON alt for GASCON, ARANESE [GSC]
GASCON, ARANESE [GSC] lang, France; also in
  Spain
GASHAN dial of NAGA, TASE [NST]
GASHUA BADE dial of BADE [BDE]
GASHWALI alt for GARHWALI [GBM]
GASI dial of DERA [KNA]
GASMATA [GSA] lang, Papua New Guinea
GASSAN dial of MARKA [MWR]
GATA' [GAQ] lang, India
GATAQ alt for GATA' [GAQ]
GATO alt for KOMSO [KXC]
GATS'AME alt for KACHAMA-GANJULE [KCX]
GATUE dial of THARAKA [THA]
GAUA alt for LAKONA [LKN]
GAUA alt for NUME [TGS]
GAUAR alt for GAVAR [GOU]
GAUDI alt for GONDI, NORTHERN [GON]
GAUK alt for GOK dial of DINKA, SOUTH CENTRAL
  [DIB]
GAUNGTOU alt for KAREN, ZAYEIN [KXK]
GAUR KRISTEN dial of TEOR [TEV]
GAURI alt for KAURI dial of JINGPHO [CGP]
GAURU dial of MBULA [MNA]
GAUUARI alt for SADRI [SCK]
GAUWADA alt for GAWWADA [GWD]

GAVA dial of GUDUF [GDF]
GAVA dial of GUDUF-GAVA [GDF]
GAVAR [GOU] lang, Cameroon
GAVIÃO dial of GAVIAO DO JIPARANA [GVO]
GAVIÃO DO JIPARANÁ [GVO] lang, Brazil
GAVIÃO DO RONDÔNIA alt for GAVIÃO DO
    JIPARANÁ [GVO]
GAVIÃO, PARÁ [GAY] lang, Brazil
GAVIT alt for GAMIT [GBL]
GAVOKO alt for GVOKO [NGS]
GAVOT dial of PROVENCAL [PRV]
GAWA alt for LOUGAW dial of MUYUW [MYW]
GAWAAR alt for THIANG dial of NUER [NUS]
GAWAN NAW' dial of MARU [MHX]
GAWANGA alt for APOS [APO]
GAWANGA alt for WASAMBU [WSM]
GAWAR alt for GAVAR [GOU]
GAWAR-BATI [GWT] lang, Afghanistan; also in
    Pakistan
GAWARI alt for SADRI [SCK]
GAWATA alt for GAWWADA [GWD]
GAWAWA alt for GARAWA dial of KAPIN [TBX]
GAWI dial of MSER [KQX]
GAWIGL alt for UMBU-UNGU [UMB]
GAWIL alt for UMBU-UNGU [UMB]
GAWIR dial of MARIND [MRZ]
GAWRI alt for KALAMI [GWC]
GAWWADA [GWD] lang, Ethiopia
GAYA dial of HAUSA [HUA]
GAYA dial of KWANG [KVI]
GAYADILT alt for GAYARDILT [GYD]
GAYAM dial of JIBU [JIB]
GAYAR dial of GURUNTUM-MBAARU [GRD]
GAYARDILT [GYD] lang, Australia
GAYE alt for ANDOA [ANB]
GAYEGI dial of GBARi [GBY]
GAYI alt for BISU dial of OBANLIKU [BZY]
GAYMONA dial of GBAYA, NORTHWEST [GYA]
GAYO [GYO] lang, Indonesia (Sumatra)
GAZAQI alt for KAZAKH [KAZ]
GAZHUO alt for KADUO [KTP]
GAZI [GZI] lang, Iran
GAZIANTEP dial of TURKISH [TRK]
GAZILI alt for GAJILI dial of KUNIMAIPA [KUP]
GBA SOR dial of BASSA [BAS]
GBABANA dial of GBAYA-BOSSANGOA [GBP]
GBADI dial of BETE, GAGNOA [BTG]
GBADIE alt for GBADI dial of BETE, GAGNOA
    [BTG]
GBADO dial of MBANDJA [ZMZ]
GBADOGO alt for KPATOGO dial of KAANSA
    [GNA]
GBAESON dial of KRAHN, WESTERN [KRW]
GBAGA 1 alt for GBAGA-SOUTH dial of
    BANDA-BANDA [BPD]
GBAGA 2 alt for GBAGA-NORD dial of BANDA,
    WEST CENTRAL [BBP]
GBAGA-NORD dial of BANDA, WEST CENTRAL
    [BBP]
GBAGA-SOUTH dial of BANDA-BANDA [BPD]
GBAGILI alt for GBAGIRI dial of GBANU [GBV]

GBAGIRI dial of GBANU [GBV]
GBAGYE alt for GBAGYI [GBR]
GBAGYI [GBR] lang, Nigeria
GBAGYI NKWA [GBW] lang, Nigeria
GBAISON alt for GBAESON dial of KRAHN,
    WESTERN [KRW]
GBAKA alt for NGBAKA MA'BO [NBM]
GBAKPWA alt for KPALA [KPL]
GBALA alt for NGBAKA MA'BO [NBM]
GBAMBIYA dial of BANDA-BANDA [BPD]
GBAN alt for GAGU [GGU]
GBANDA alt for AVIKAM [AVI]
GBANDE alt for BANDI [GBA]
GBANDERE alt for GBANZIRI [GBG]
GBANDI alt for BANDI [GBA]
GBANE alt for CENTRAL KONO dial of KONO [KNO]
GBANE KANDO alt for CENTRAL KONO dial of
    KONO [KNO]
GBANG alt for BEROM [BOM]
GBANMI-SOKUN KAKANDA dial of KAKANDA
    [KKA]
GBANOU alt for GBANU [GBV]
GBANRAIN dial of IZON [IJC]
GBANU [GBV] lang, CAR
GBANU dial of GBANU [GBV]
GBANZILI alt for GBANZIRI [GBG]
GBANZIRI [GBG] lang, CAR; also in DRC
GBARA alt for MO'DA [GBN]
GBARANMATU alt for OPOROZA dial of IZON [IJC]
GBARBO dial of KRAHN, WESTERN [KRW]
GBARI [GBY] lang, Nigeria
GBARI YAMMA alt for GBARI [GBY]
GBARZON alt for GBAESON dial of KRAHN,
    WESTERN [KRW]
GBATI-RI [GTI] lang, DRC
GBAYA [KRS] lang, Sudan; also in CAR
GBAYA alt for GBAYA, NORTHWEST [GYA]
GBAYA DE BODA alt for GBAYA OF BODA dial
    of BOKOTO [BDT]
GBAYA DE BOSANGOA alt for
    GBAYA-BOSSANGOA [GBP]
GBAYA DE BOUAR alt for GBAYA KARA dial of
    GBAYA, NORTHWEST [GYA]
GBAYA DE BOZOUM alt for GBAYA-BOZOUM
    [GBQ]
GBAYA KARA dial of GBAYA, NORTHWEST [GYA]
GBAYA NORD-OUEST alt for GBAYA, NORTH-
    WEST [GYA]
GBAYA OF BODA dial of BOKOTO [BDT]
GBAYA OF BORRO alt for GBAYA-BOSSANGOA
    [GBP]
GBAYA OF BOSSANGOA alt for GBAYA-
    BOSSANGOA [GBP]
GBAYA SUD-OUEST alt for GBAYA, SOUTHWEST
    [MDO]
GBAYA, NORTHWEST [GYA] lang, CAR; also in
    Cameroon, Congo, Nigeria
GBAYA, SOUTHWEST [MDO] lang, CAR; also in
    Cameroon, Congo
GBAYA-BORRO alt for GBAYA-BOSSANGOA
    [GBP]

GBAYA-BOSSANGOA [GBP] lang, CAR
GBAYA-BOZOUM [GBQ] lang, CAR
GBAYA-DARA dial of GBAYA [KRS]
GBAYA-GBOKO dial of GBAYA [KRS]
GBAYAKA alt for BEKA dial of YAKA [AXK]
GBAYA-MBODOMO alt for MBODOMO dial of
    GBAYA, SOUTHWEST [MDO]
GBAYA-NDOGO dial of GBAYA [KRS]
GBAYA-NGBONGBO dial of GBAYA [KRS]
GBAYI [GYG] lang, CAR
GBE alt for ÉWÉ [EWE]
GBEA alt for GBAYA-BOSSANGOA [GBP]
GBEA alt for GBEYA dial of GBAYA, NORTH-
    WEST [GYA]
GBÉAN alt for SÉMIEN dial of WE NORTHERN [WOB]
GBEAPO alt for GBEPO dial of GREBO, NORTHERN
    [GRB]
GBEDDE dial of YORUBA [YOR]
GBEE alt for GBII [GGB]
GBEKON dial of GUN-GBE [GUW]
GBENDE dial of BANDA-BAMBARI [LIY]
GBENDEMBU dial of LOKO [LOK]
GBENDERE alt for YANGO [YNG]
GBENEKU alt for SOUTHERN SEEKU dial of
    SEEKU [SOS]
GBENSE alt for CENTRAL KONO dial of KONO
    [KNO]
GBEPO dial of GREBO, NORTHERN [GRB]
GBERI alt for MO'DA [GBN]
GBESE alt for KPELLE, GUINEA [GKP]
GBESE alt for KPELLE, LIBERIA [KPE]
GBETE dial of MBUM [MDD]
GBEYA alt for GBAYA-BOSSANGOA [GBP]
GBEYA dial of GBAYA, NORTHWEST [GYA]
GBEYÃSE dial of DOGOSE [DOS]
GBHU D AMAR RANDFA alt for NINZAM [NIN]
GBI dial of BANDA, WEST CENTRAL [BBP]
GBI-DOWLU alt for GBII [GGB]
GBIGBIL alt for BEBIL [BXP]
GBII [GGB] lang, Liberia
GBINNA alt for BENA [YUN]
GBIRI dial of GBIRI-NIRAGU [GRH]
GBIRI-NIRAGU [GRH] lang, Nigeria
GBLOU GREBO alt for GREBO, GBOLOO [GEC]
GBO alt for LEGBO [AGB]
GBO dial of KRAHN, WESTERN [KRW]
GBO dial of SENOUFO, TAGWANA [TGW]
GBOARE alt for BACAMA [BAM]
GBOATI alt for BATA [BTA]
GBOBO alt for GBOO dial of WE SOUTHERN [GXX]
GBOBO alt for GBORBO dial of KRAHN, WESTERN
    [KRW]
GBOGOROSE, dial of DOGOSE [DOS]
GBOLOO alt for GREBO, GBOLOO [GEC]
GBONGOGBO alt for CENTRAL dial of LIMBA,
    WEST-CENTRAL [LIA]
GBOO dial of WE SOUTHERN [GXX]
GBOR dial of BASSA [BAS]
GBORBO dial of KRAHN, WESTERN [KRW]
GBOTE alt for GBATI-RI [GTI]
GBOWE-HRAN dial of KRUMEN, PYE [PYE]

GBUGBLA dial of DANGME [DGM]
GBUHWE alt for LAMANG [HIA]
GBUNDE alt for BANDI [GBA]
GBUNHU alt for KAMKAM [BGU]
GBUNHU alt for MBONGNO [BGU]
GBWATA alt for BATA [BTA]
GBWATE alt for BATA [BTA]
GCIRIKU alt for DIRIKU [DIU]
GCWI alt for /GWI [GWJ]
GE alt for BEFANG dial of BEFANG [BBY]
GE alt for GEJIAHUA dial of HMONG,
    CHONGANJIANG [HMJ]
GE alt for GEN-GBE [GEJ]
GEAGEA dial of MAILU [MGU]
GEALEKA dial of XHOSA [XOS]
GEBA alt for KAREN, GEBA [KVQ]
GEBE [GEI] lang, Indonesia (Maluku)
GEBE alt for GEN-GBE [GEJ]
GEBI alt for GEBE [GEI]
GEBI dial of MARIA [MDS]
GEBLET alt for JIBBALI [SHV]
GEBRA alt for GABRA dial of BORANA [GAX]
GEBRA alt for GABRA dial of OROMO, BORANA-
    ARSI-GUJI [GAX]
GEDAGED [GDD] lang, Papua New Guinea
GEDANG alt for GEJIAHUA dial of HMONG,
    CHONGANJIANG [HMJ]
GEDDEO alt for GEDEO [DRS]
GEDE alt for GADE [GED]
GEDEGEDE dial of AKPES [IBE]
GEDEO [DRS] lang, Ethiopia
GEDEROBO dial of GREBO, GBOLOO [GEC]
GEDOU MIAO alt for GEJIAHUA dial of HMONG,
    CHONGANJIANG [HMJ]
GEECHEE alt for SEA ISLAND CREOLE ENGLISH
    [GUL]
GEEDAM dial of MARIA, DANDAMI [DAQ]
GEEZ [GEE] lang, Ethiopia; also in Eritrea
GE'EZ alt for GEEZ [GEE]
GEG alt for ALBANIAN, GHEG [ALS]
GEGBE alt for GEN-GBE [GEJ]
GEGERE dial of LENDU [LED]
GEI alt for QI dial of HLAI [LIC]
GEJA alt for NGULU [NGP]
GEJAWA alt for GEJI [GEZ]
GEJI [GEZ] lang, Nigeria
GEJI dial of GEJI [GEZ]
GEJIAHUA dial of HMONG, CHONGANJIANG [HMJ]
GEKHO alt for KAREN, GEKO [GHK]
GEK'O alt for KAREN, GEKO [GHK]
GEKOYO alt for GIKUYU [KIU]
GEKXUN dial of AGHUL [AGX]
GELA [NLG] lang, Solomon Islands
GELA alt for KELA [KCL]
GELAB alt for DAASANACH [DSH]
GELAKI alt for GILAKI [GLK]
GELAMA dial of MUNDANG [MUA]
GELANCHI alt for JIIR dial of KAG-FER-JIIR-KOOR-
    ROR-US-ZUKSUN [GEL]
GELANGALI alt for GRANGALI [NLI]
GELAO [KKF] lang, Viet Nam; also in China

GELE alt for FONGORO [FGR]
GELE' alt for KELE [SBC]
GELEB alt for DAASANACH [DSH]
GELEBA alt for DAASANACH [DSH]
GELEBDA alt for GLAVDA [GLV]
GELEBINYA alt for DAASANACH [DSH]
GELEKIDORIA dial of NAGA, KONYAK [NBE]
GELIK alt for PATPATAR [GFK]
GELILLA alt for ZAY [ZWA]
GELIMI dial of LESING-GELIMI [LET]
GELLIVARE FINNISH dial of FINNISH,
    TORNEDALEN [FIT]
GELO alt for GELAO [KKF]
GELUBBA alt for DAASANACH [DSH]
GELVAXDAXA alt for GLAVDA [GLV]
GEM MUN alt for KIM MUN [MJI]
GEMA alt for BLABLANGA [BLP]
GEMA alt for GYEM [GYE]
GEMAN DENG [GEN] lang, China; also in India,
    Myanmar
GEMASAKUN alt for SUKUR [SUK]
GEMAWA alt for GYEM [GYE]
GEMBANAWA alt for GIBANAWA [GIB]
GEME [GEQ] lang, CAR
GEME KULAGBOLU dial of GEME [GEQ]
GEME TULU dial of GEME [GEQ]
GEMJEK alt for GEMZEK [GND]
GEMU alt for GAMO dial of GAMO-GOFA-DAWRO
    [GMO]
GEMZEK [GND] lang, Cameroon
GENA alt for MBOI [MOI]
GENAGANE alt for NAGANE dial of KUMAN [KUE]
GENDE [GAF] lang, Papua New Guinea
GENDEKA alt for GENDE [GAF]
GENDJA alt for LIGENZA [LGZ]
GENDOK dial of KELON [KYO]
GENDZA-BALI alt for LIGENZA [LGZ]
GENE alt for GENDE [GAF]
GENERAL ISRAELI alt for STANDARD HEBREW
    dial of HEBREW [HBR]
GENERAL URMI alt for IRANIAN KOINE dial of
    ASSYRIAN NEO-ARAMAIC [AII]
GEN-GBE [GEJ] lang, Togo; also in Benin
GENGE alt for NGENGE dial of GBAGYI [GBR]
GENGELE dial of SONGOORA [SOD]
GENGLE [GEG] lang, Nigeria
GENNAKEN alt for PUELCHE [PUE]
GENOAN alt for GENOESE dial of LIGURIAN [LIJ]
GENOESE dial of LIGURIAN [LIJ]
GENOGANE alt for NAGANE dial of KUMAN [KUE]
GENOVESE alt for GENOESE dial of LIGURIAN
    [LIJ]
GENTOO alt for TELUGU [TCW]
GENYA alt for ENYA [GEY]
GEORDIE dial of ENGLISH [ENG]
GEORGIA dial of SEA ISLAND CREOLE ENGLISH
    [GUL]
GEORGIAN [GEO] lang, Georgia; also in Armenia,
    Azerbaijan, Iran, Kazakhstan, Kyrgyzstan, Russia
    (Asia), Tajikistan, Turkey (Asia), Turkmenistan,
    Ukraine, USA, Uzbekistan

GEPMA KWUDI alt for IATMUL [IAN]
GEPMA KWUNDI alt for IATMUL [IAN]
GERA [GEW] lang, Nigeria
GERAI dial of SEMANDANG [SDM]
GERAL alt for NHENGATU [YRL]
GERAWA alt for GERA [GEW]
GERE alt for WÈ SOUTHERN [GXX]
GERE alt for WÈ WESTERN [WEC]
GEREMA alt for GERUMA [GEA]
GEREP dial of KIM [KIA]
GEREUT alt for FRASSILONGO dial of MOCHENO
    [QMO]
GERGERE dial of GAWWADA [GWD]
GERI dial of GHARI [GRI]
GERKA alt for YIWOM [GEK]
GERKANCHI alt for YIWOM [GEK]
GERKAWA alt for YIWOM [GEK]
GERLOVO TURKS dial of BALKAN GAGAUZ
    TURKISH [BGX]
GERMA alt for GERUMA [GEA]
GERMAN alt for PLAUTDIETSCH [GRN]
GERMAN SIGN LANGUAGE [GSG] lang, Germany
GERMAN TRAVELLERS alt for YENICHE [YEC]
GERMAN, COLONIA TOVAR [GCT] lang, Venezuela
GERMAN, HUTTERITE [GEH] lang, Canada; also
    in USA
GERMAN, PENNSYLVANIA [PDC] lang, USA;
    also in Canada
GERMAN, STANDARD [GER] lang, Germany; also in
    Argentina, Australia, Austria, Belgium, Bolivia,
    Bosnia-Herzegovina, Brazil, Canada, Chile, Czech
    Republic, Denmark, Ecuador, Estonia, Finland,
    France, Hungary, Italy, Kazakhstan, Kyrgyzstan,
    Liechtenstein, Luxembourg, Moldova, Namibia,
    Paraguay, Philippines, Poland, Puerto Rico,
    Romania, Russia (Europe), Slovakia, Slovenia,
    South Africa, Switzerland, Tajikistan, Ukraine,
    UAE, Uruguay, USA, Uzbekistan
GERRAH alt for YIDINY [YII]
GERSE alt for KPELLE, GUINEA [GKP]
GERUMA [GEA] lang, Nigeria
GERZE alt for KPELLE, GUINEA [GKP]
GESA alt for GESER-GOROM [GES]
GESAWA alt for GUSU dial of JERE [JER]
GESDA DAE dial of BAUZI [PAU]
GESER alt for GESER-GOROM [GES]
GESER-GOROM [GES] lang, Indonesia (Maluku)
GESHITSA alt for GESHIZA dial of HORPA [ERO]
GESHIZA dial of HORPA [ERO]
GESS dial of LORUNG, SOUTHERN [LRR]
GETA' alt for GATA' [GAQ]
GETAQ alt for GATA' [GAQ]
GET'EME alt for KACHAMA-GANJULE [KCX]
GETMATA [GET] lang, Papua New Guinea
GETOU alt for GEJIAHUA dial of HMONG,
    CHONGANJIANG [HMJ]
GETSAAYI alt for TSAAYI dial of TEKE, WESTERN
    [TEZ]
GETSOGO alt for TSOGO [TSV]
GEVOKO alt for GVOKO [NGS]
GEWE alt for GEY [GUV]

GEY [GUV] lang, Cameroon
GEY SINAN alt for HARARI [HAR]
GEZAWA alt for GEJI [GEZ]
GEZAWA alt for GEJI dial of GEJI [GEZ]
GEZON alt for NDUNDUSANA dial of PAGIBETE
    [PAG]
GHAANGALA dial of KONGO [KON]
GHADAMÈS [GHA] lang, Libya; also in Tunisia
GHAGAR alt for NAWAR dial of DOMARI [RMT]
GHAGAR dial of ROMANI, VLAX [RMY]
GHAIMUTA dial of LENGO [LGR]
GHALE, KUTANG [GHT] lang, Nepal
GHALE, NORTHERN [GHH] lang, Nepal
GHALE, SOUTHERN [GHE] lang, Nepal
GHALGHAY alt for INGUSH [INH]
GHANA BIRIFOR alt for BIRIFOR, SOUTHERN
    [BIV]
GHANAIAN SIGN LANGUAGE [GSE] lang, Ghana
GHANGATTY alt for DYANGADI [DYN]
GHANONGGA [GHN] lang, Solomon Islands
GHAO-XONG alt for HMONG, EASTERN XIANGXI
    [MUQ]
GHAO-XONG alt for HMONG, WESTERN XIANGXI
    [MMR]
GHAP alt for MENGAKA [XMG]
GHARA alt for GAHRI [BFU]
GHARDAIA alt for TUMZABT [MZB]
GHARI [GRI] lang, Solomon Islands
GHARI dial of GHARI [GRI]
GHARTI alt for BUJHYAL [GOR]
GHAT dial of TAMAHAQ, TAHAGGART [THV]
GHATI dial of KONKANI [KNK]
GHAYAVI [BMK] lang, Papua New Guinea
GHBOKO alt for GVOKO [NGS]
GHEG alt for ALBANIAN, GHEG [ALS]
GHEKHOL alt for KAREN, GEKO [GHK]
GHEKHU alt for KAREN, GEKO [GHK]
GHEKO alt for KAREN, GEKO [GHK]
GHELEBA alt for DAASANACH [DSH]
GHENA alt for PIDLIMDI dial of TERA [TER]
GHERA [GHR] lang, Pakistan
GHETSOGO alt for TSOGO [TSV]
GHIBARAMA alt for BARAMA [BBG]
GHIDOLE alt for DIRASHA [GDL]
GHILZAI dial of PASHTO, NORTHERN [PBU]
GHIMARRA alt for BENCH [BCQ]
GHINI dial of KAMASAU [KMS]
GHISADI alt for TARIMUKI dial of GUJARATI [GJR]
GHODOBERI [GDO] lang, Russia (Europe)
GHOL dial of DINKA, SOUTHEASTERN [DIN]
GHOMÁLÁ' [BBJ] lang, Cameroon
GHOMÁLÁ' CENTRAL dial of GHOMÁLÁ' [BBJ]
GHOMÁLÁ' NORTH dial of GHOMÁLÁ' [BBJ]
GHOMÁLÁ' SOUTH dial of GHOMÁLÁ' [BBJ]
GHOMARA [GHO] lang, Morocco
GHOND alt for GONDI, NORTHERN [GON]
GHONE dial of VARISI [VRS]
GHORANI alt for SHUGHNI dial of SHUGHNI [SGH]
GHORBATI alt for KURBATI dial of DOMARI [RMT]
GHOTUO [AAA] lang, Nigeria
GHUA alt for GHAIMUTA dial of LENGO [LGR]

GHUJULAN dial of PARACHI [PRC]
GHULFAN [GHL] lang, Sudan
GHUMGHUM alt for TABASSARAN [TAB]
GHUNA alt for PIDLIMDI dial of TERA [TER]
GHUSBANGGI dial of KHAM, GAMALE [KGJ]
GHYE alt for HYA [HYA]
GIAHOI alt for DIAHÓI dial of TENHARIM [PAH]
GIAI alt for NHANG [NHA]
GIAMBA alt for NGIYAMBAA dial of
    WANGAAYBUWAN-NGIYAMBAA [WYB]
GIANG alt for NHANG [NHA]
GIANG dial of NUNG [NUT]
GIANG RAY alt for TRIENG [STG]
GIANGAN [BGI] lang, Philippines
GIANYAR alt for LOWLAND BALI dial of BALI [BZC]
GIA-RAI alt for JARAI [JRA]
GIÁY alt for NHANG [NHA]
GIBAIO alt for KIWAI, NORTHEAST [KIW]
GIBAIO dial of KIWAI, NORTHEAST [KIW]
GIBANAWA [GIB] lang, Nigeria
GIBARA alt for WAGAWAGA [WGW]
GIBARAMA alt for BARAMA [BBG]
GIBARIO dial of KEREWO [KXZ]
GICHUGU dial of GIKUYU [KIU]
GIDABAL alt for BANDJALANG [BDY]
GIDABAL dial of BANDJALANG [BDY]
GIDAR [GID] lang, Cameroon; also in Chad
GIDDER alt for GIDAR [GID]
GIDGID alt for BADE [BDE]
GIDHABAL alt for GIDABAL dial of BANDJALANG
    [BDY]
GIDIRE alt for ADELE [ADE]
GIDJA alt for KITJA [GIA]
GIDOLE alt for DIRASHA [GDL]
GIDRA [GDR] lang, Papua New Guinea
GIE alt for JEH [JEH]
GIELE alt for GYELE [GYI]
GIELI alt for GYELE [GYI]
GIE-TRIENG alt for TRIENG [STG]
GIGATL dial of CHAMALAL [CJI]
GIGIKUYU alt for GIKUYU [KIU]
GIHA alt for HA [HAQ]
GIIWO [KKS] lang, Nigeria
GIIZ alt for GEEZ [GEE]
GIJOW alt for YIDINY [YII]
GIKLSAN alt for GITXSAN [GIT]
GIKOLODJYA dial of ANII [BLO]
GIKUYU [KIU] lang, Kenya
GI/KXIGWI alt for //XEGWI [XEG]
GIKYODE [ACD] lang, Ghana
GIL BAGALE dial of SISAALA, TUMULUNG [SIL]
GILAKI [GLK] lang, Iran
GILANI alt for GILAKI [GLK]
GILBAGALA dial of SISAALA, PASAALE [SIG]
GILBERTESE alt for KIRIBATI [GLB]
GILEMPLA dial of ANII [BLO]
GILGIT alt for GILGITI dial of SHINA [SCL]
GILGITI dial of SHINA [SCL]
GILI dial of BANA [BCW]
GILIKA dial of YALE, KOSAREK [KKL]
GILIMA [GIX] lang, DRC

GILIPANES alt for IFUGAO, TUWALI [IFK]
GILLAH alt for YIDINY [YII]
GILYAK [NIV] lang, Russia (Asia)
GIMAN alt for GANE [GZN]
GIMARAS alt for GUIMARAS ISLAND dial of
    KINARAY-A [KRJ]
GIMARRA alt for BENCH [BCQ]
GIMBA dial of SAGALLA [TGA]
GIMBAAMA alt for MBAMA [MBM]
GIMBALA alt for MBALA [MDP]
GIMBANAWA alt for GIBANAWA [GIB]
GIMBE alt for GIMNIME [KMB]
GIMBE alt for GOMNOME dial of KOMA [KMY]
GIMBUNDA alt for MBUNDA [MCK]
GIMBUNDA alt for MPUUN dial of MPUONO [ZMP]
GIMI [GIM] lang, Papua New Guinea
GIMI [GIP] lang, Papua New Guinea
GIMIRA alt for BENCH [BCQ]
GIMMA alt for GIMME [KMP]
GIMME [KMP] lang, Cameroon
GIMNIME [KMB] lang, Cameroon
GIMR dial of TAMA [TMA]
GIMSBOK NAMA dial of NAMA [NAQ]
GIN alt for VIETNAMESE [VIE]
GIN dial of KORYAK [KPY]
GINABWAL alt for GA'DANG [GDG]
GINAOUROU dial of NATIORO [NTI]
GINGA alt for NJINGA dial of MBUNDU, LOANDA
    [MLO]
!GINGKWE dial of NARO [NHR]
GINGWAK dial of JARAWA [JAR]
G!INKWE dial of NARO [NHR]
GINUKH alt for HINUKH [GIN]
GINUKHTSY alt for HINUKH [GIN]
GINUMAN [GNM] lang, Papua New Guinea
GINUX alt for HINUKH [GIN]
GINYAMUNYINGANYI dial of NYATURU [RIM]
GIO alt for DAN [DAF]
GIO-DAN alt for DAN [DAF]
GIO-LANG alt for JOLONG dial of BAHNAR [BDQ]
GIONG alt for BAYUNGU [BXJ]
GIO-RAI alt for JARAI [JRA]
GIPENDE alt for PHENDE [PEM]
GIPHENDE alt for PHENDE [PEM]
GIPUZKOAN alt for GUIPUZCOAN dial of BASQUE
    [BSQ]
GIRA [GRG] lang, Papua New Guinea
GIRANGO dial of ZANAKI [ZAK]
GIRASIA alt for GARASIA, ADIWASI [GAS]
GIRASIA alt for GARASIA, RAJPUT [GRA]
GIRASIA dial of BHILI [BHB]
GIRAWA [BBR] lang, Papua New Guinea
GIRE alt for KIRE [GEB]
GIRGA dial of ASSANGORI [SUN]
GIRGA dial of SUNGOR [SUN]
GIRI alt for KIRE [GEB]
GIRIAMA alt for GIRYAMA [NYF]
GIRIPARI dial of SIRMAURI [SRX]
GIRIWE alt for YREWE dial of KRUMEN, PYE [PYE]
GIRONGA alt for RONGA [RON]
GIRWALI alt for GARHWALI [GBM]

GIRWANA dial of NYATURU [RIM]
GIRYAMA [NYF] lang, Kenya
GIRYAMA dial of GIRYAMA [NYF]
GISAMJANG alt for GISAMJANGA dial of DATOOGA
    [TCC]
GISAMJANGA dial of DATOOGA [TCC]
GISEDA dial of ANII [BLO]
GISÈME dial of ANII [BLO]
GISEWI alt for SEWI dial of GITONGA [TOH]
GISEY alt for GIZAY dial of MASANA [MCN]
GISHU alt for LUGISU dial of MASABA [MYX]
GISI alt for KISI, SOUTHERN [KSS]
GISIDA alt for ANII [BLO]
GISIGA alt for GIZIGA, NORTH [GIS]
GISIGA alt for GIZIGA, SOUTH [GIZ]
GISIKA alt for GIZIGA, NORTH [GIS]
GISIKA alt for GIZIGA, SOUTH [GIZ]
GISIRA alt for SIRA [SWJ]
GISSI alt for KISI, SOUTHERN [KSS]
GISU alt for MASABA [MYX]
GITANO alt for CALÓ [RMR]
GITKSAN alt for GITXSAN [GIT]
GITOA alt for GITUA [GIL]
GITONGA [TOH] lang, Mozambique
GITONGA GY KHOGANI dial of GITONGA [TOH]
GITSKEN dial of GITXSAN [GIT]
GITUA [GIL] lang, Papua New Guinea
GITXSAN [GIT] lang, Canada
GITXSAN dial of GITXSAN [GIT]
GITYSKYAN alt for GITXSAN [GIT]
GIUR alt for LUWO [LWO]
GIVEROM alt for GWORAM dial of KOFYAR [KWL]
GIYUG [GIY] lang, Australia
GIZAY dial of MASANA [MCN]
GIZI alt for KISI, SOUTHERN [KSS]
GIZI alt for KISSI, NORTHERN [KQS]
GIZIGA DE MAROUA alt for GIZIGA, NORTH [GIS]
GIZIGA DE MIDJIVIN alt for MI MIJIVIN dial of
    GIZIGA, SOUTH [GIZ]
GIZIGA DE MOUTOUROUA alt for MUTURAMI
    dial of GIZIGA, SOUTH [GIZ]
GIZIGA, NORTH [GIS] lang, Cameroon
GIZIGA, SOUTH [GIZ] lang, Cameroon
GIZIMA dial of LOMA [LOM]
GIZRA [TOF] lang, Papua New Guinea
GJUNEJ dial of LEZGI [LEZ]
G'KELENDEG alt for MBARA [MPK]
G'KELENDENG alt for MBARA [MPK]
GLANDA alt for GLAVDA [GLV]
GLANDA-KHWE alt for KXOE [XUU]
GLARO dial of GLARO-TWABO [GLR]
GLARO-TWABO [GLR] lang, Liberia; also in Côte
    d'Ivoire
GLAVDA [GLV] lang, Nigeria; also in Cameroon
GLAVDA dial of GLAVDA [GLV]
GLAWLO dial of KRUMEN, TEPO [TED]
GLEBO dial of GREBO, SOUTHERN [GRJ]
GLIBE dial of GODIE [GOD]
GLIO alt for GLIO-OUBI [OUB]
GLIO-OUBI [OUB] lang, Liberia; also in Côte d'Ivoire
GLOBO dial of GREBO, CENTRAL [GRV]

GNALLUMA alt for NGARLUMA [NRL]
GNALOUMA alt for NGARLUMA [NRL]
GNAMEI alt for NAGA, ANGAMI [NJM]
GNAMO alt for NYAMAL [NLY]
GNAU [GNU] lang, Papua New Guinea
GNI alt for YI, SICHUAN [III]
GNI alt for YI, YUNNAN [NOS]
GNIVO alt for AYIWO [NFL]
GNOORE dial of MUMUYE [MUL]
GNORMBUR alt for NGURMBUR [NRX]
GNUMBU alt for NGURMBUR [NRX]
GOA alt for GOWA dial of MAKASAR [MSR]
GOA alt for MAKASAR [MSR]
GOAHIBO alt for GUAHIBO [GUH]
GOAHIVA alt for GUAHIBO [GUH]
GOAJIRO alt for WAYUU [GUC]
GOAN alt for KONKANI, GOANESE [GOM]
GOANESE alt for KONKANI, GOANESE [GOM]
GOANESE alt for STANDARD KONKANI dial of
    KONKANI, GOANESE [GOM]
GOARI alt for SADRI [SCK]
GOARIA [GIG] lang, Pakistan
GOARIBARI alt for GIBARIO dial of KEREWO [KXZ]
GOBA alt for KOREKORE dial of SHONA [SHD]
GOBA alt for NGWABA [NGW]
GOBABINGO alt for GUPAPUYNGU [GUF]
GOBASI [GOI] lang, Papua New Guinea
GOBASI dial of GOBASI [GOI]
GOBATO dial of BERTA [WTI]
GOBEYO alt for LONGTO [WOK]
GOBEZE alt for BUSSA [DOX]
GOBEZE dial of GAWWADA [GWD]
GOBIRAWA dial of HAUSA [HUA]
GOBLA alt for MANAGOBLA dial of GOLA [GOL]
GOBU [GOX] lang, DRC; also in CAR
GOBU alt for GUBU [GOX]
GOBUGDUA alt for SISIBNA dial of KORUPUN-
    SELA [KPQ]
GODAULI alt for GARHWALI [GBM]
GODAVARI KOYA alt for JAGANATHAPURAM
    KOYA dial of KOYA [KFF]
GODDA dial of SAURIA PAHARIA [MJT]
GODI alt for GONDI, NORTHERN [GON]
GODIÉ [GOD] lang, Côte d'Ivoire
GODOBERI alt for GHODOBERI [GDO]
GODOBERIN alt for GHODOBERI [GDO]
GODOGODO alt for LAKA [LAK]
GODWA alt for GADABA, BODO [GBJ]
GODWANI dial of BAGHELI [BFY]
GODYE alt for GODIÉ [GOD]
GOEMAI [ANK] lang, Nigeria
GOFA dial of GAMO-GOFA-DAWRO [GMO]
GOFFA alt for GOFA dial of GAMO-GOFA-DAWRO
    [GMO]
GOG alt for LAKONA [LKN]
GOGGOT alt for GOGOT dial of GURAGE, SODDO
    [GRU]
GOGO [GOG] lang, Tanzania
GOGODALA [GOH] lang, Papua New Guinea
GOGODARA alt for GOGODALA [GOH]
GOGOT dial of GURAGE, SODDO [GRU]

GOGRI alt for GUJARI [GJU]
GOGULICH alt for MANSI [MNS]
GOGWAMA alt for KWAMA [KMQ]
GOHAR-HERKERI alt for LAMBADI [LMN]
GOHILWADI alt for KATHIYAWADI dial of
    GUJARATI [GJR]
GOHLLARU alt for HOLIYA [HOY]
GOHUM alt for YUKUBEN [YBL]
GOI alt for BAAN [BVJ]
GOI alt for BLABLANGA [BLP]
GOIALA dial of IDUNA [VIV]
GOJAL dial of WAKHI [WBL]
GOJARI alt for GUJARI [GJU]
GOJI alt for KUSHI [KUH]
GOJRI alt for GUJARI [GJU]
GOK dial of DINKA, SOUTH CENTRAL [DIB]
GOKANA [GKN] lang, Nigeria
GOKLAN alt for GOKLEN dial of TURKMEN [TCK]
GOKLEN dial of TURKMEN [TCK]
G!OKWE dial of NARO [NHR]
GOKWOM alt for KOMO [KOM]
GOL dial of BAGIRMI [BMI]
GOLA [GOL] lang, Liberia; also in Sierra Leone
GOLA alt for BADJARA [PBP]
GOLA dial of MUMUYE [MUL]
GOLAR dial of BAHNAR [BDQ]
GOLAR dial of JARAI [JRA]
GOLARI dial of TELUGU [TCW]
GOLARI-KANNADA alt for HOLIYA [HOY]
GOLD alt for NANAI [GLD]
GOLDEN PALAUNG alt for PALAUNG, SHWE
    [SWE]
GOLDI alt for NANAI [GLD]
GOLIATH alt for UNA [MTG]
GOLIN [GVF] lang, Papua New Guinea
GOLIN dial of GOLIN [GVF]
GOLLANGO dial of GAWWADA [GWD]
GOLLUM alt for GOLIN [GVF]
GOLO alt for BANDA, WEST CENTRAL [BBP]
GOLUMALA dial of DHANGU [GLA]
GOMA alt for KWAMA [KMQ]
GOMADJ alt for GUMATJ [GNN]
GOMANTAKI alt for BARDESKARI dial of KONKANI,
    GOANESE [GOM]
GOMATAKI alt for KONKANI, GOANESE [GOM]
GOMBE dial of FULFULDE, ADAMAWA [FUB]
GOMBE dial of SENA [SEH]
GOMBI alt for NGWABA [NGW]
GOMBO alt for GUMUZ [GUK]
GOMBO dial of GUMUZ [GUK]
GOMBORO dial of SAMO, MAYA [SYM]
GOMIA dial of CHUAVE [CJV]
GOMJUER alt for PALIOUPINY dial of DINKA,
    SOUTHWESTERN [DIK]
GOMME dial of KOMA [KMY]
GOMMU KOYA alt for JAGANATHAPURAM KOYA
    dial of KOYA [KFF]
GOMNOME dial of KOMA [KMY]
GOMU alt for MOO [GWG]
GON SHAN alt for KHÜN [KKH]
GONA alt for YEGA dial of EWAGE-NOTU [NOU]

GONDHLA alt for TINANI [LBF]
GONDI alt for GONDI, NORTHERN [GON]
GONDI, NORTHERN [GON] lang, India
GONDI, SOUTHERN [GGO] lang, India
GONDIVA alt for GONDI, NORTHERN [GON]
GONDLA alt for TINANI [LBF]
GONDU alt for GONDI, NORTHERN [GON]
GONDWADI alt for GONDI, NORTHERN [GON]
GONE DAU [GOO] lang, Fiji
GONEDAU alt for GONE DAU [GOO]
GONG alt for NGONG [NNX]
GONG alt for UGONG [UGO]
GONGDUBIKHA alt for GONGDUK [GOE]
GONGDUK [GOE] lang, Bhutan
GONGE dial of NZAKAMBAY [NZY]
GONGE dial of PANA [PNZ]
GONGLA dial of MUMUYE [MUL]
GONGO alt for WONGO [WON]
GONGON LOBI dial of LOBI [LOB]
GONI alt for YERETUAR [GOP]
GONJA [DUM] lang, Ghana
GONJA dial of GONJA [DUM]
GONSOMON dial of RUNGUS [DRG]
GOOLA alt for LAMBADI [LMN]
GOOM dial of DII [DUR]
GOOM-GHARRA alt for KUNGGARA [KVS]
GOONAN alt for KWINI [GWW]
GOONDILE alt for GONDI, NORTHERN [GON]
GOONIYANDI [GNI] lang, Australia
GOPE alt for KOPE dial of KIWAI, NORTHEAST
    [KIW]
GOR [GQR] lang, Chad
GORA dial of GWAHATIKE [DAH]
GORA-BOMAHOUJI dial of OMIE [AOM]
GORACHOUQUA alt for KORANA [KQZ]
GORAKHPURI alt for NORTHERN STANDARD
    BHOJPURI dial of BHOJPURI [BHJ]
GORAKOR [GOC] lang, Papua New Guinea
GORAM alt for GESER-GOROM [GES]
GORAM alt for GWORAM dial of KOFYAR [KWL]
GORAM LAUT dial of GESER-GOROM [GES]
GORAMA KONO alt for CENTRAL KONO dial of
    KONO [KNO]
GORAN alt for GESER-GOROM [GES]
GORANI alt for HAWRAMI [HAC]
GORAP [GOQ] lang, Indonesia (Maluku)
GORAU dial of IKOBI-MENA [MEB]
GORAZE alt for BUSSA [DOX]
GORBO dial of KRAHN, EASTERN [KQO]
GORI alt for LAAL [GDM]
GORI dial of NUNI, SOUTHERN [NNW]
GORKHA GURUNG dial of GURUNG, EASTERN
    [GGN]
GORKHALI alt for NEPALI [NEP]
GORKHALI dial of NEPALI [NEP]
GORLOS alt for JIRIM dial of MONGOLIAN,
    PERIPHERAL [MVF]
GORMATI alt for LAMBADI [LMN]
GORMINANG dial of YIR YORONT [YIY]
GORNO-MARIY alt for MARI, HIGH [MRJ]
GOROA alt for GOROWA [GOW]

GOROGONE alt for GURAGONE [GGE]
GOROM alt for GESER-GOROM [GES]
GORONG alt for GESER-GOROM [GES]
GORONGOSA dial of SENA [SEH]
GORONTALO [GRL] lang, Indonesia (Sulawesi)
GORONTALO dial of GORONTALO [GRL]
GOROSE dial of GAWWADA [GWD]
GOROVA alt for GOROVU [GRQ]
GOROVU [GRQ] lang, Papua New Guinea
GOROWA [GOW] lang, Tanzania
GORROSE alt for GOROSE dial of GAWWADA
    [GWD]
GORUM alt for PARENGA [PCJ]
GORUM SAMA alt for PARENGA [PCJ]
GORWAA alt for GOROWA [GOW]
GORWALI alt for GARHWALI [GBM]
GOSHUTE alt for GOSIUTE dial of SHOSHONI
    [SHH]
GOSIUTE dial of SHOSHONI [SHH]
GOTHIC [GOF] lang, Ukraine; also in Bulgaria
GOTLANDIC alt for GUTNISKA dial of SWEDISH
    [SWD]
GOTTE KOYA alt for PODIA KOYA dial of KOYA
    [KFF]
GOUDE alt for GUDE [GDE]
GOUDI alt for GONDI, NORTHERN [GON]
GOUDOU alt for LOZOUA dial of DIDA, YOCOBOUE
    [GUD]
GOUDWAL alt for GONDI, NORTHERN [GON]
GOUIN alt for CERMA [GOT]
GOUINDOUGOUBA dial of CERMA [GOT]
GOULA alt for GULA [GLU]
GOULA alt for GULA [KCM]
GOULA alt for GULA dial of GULA [KCM]
GOULA alt for ZAN GULA [ZNA]
GOULA dial of LAKA [LAM]
GOULA D'IRO alt for GULA IRO [GLJ]
GOULA IRO alt for GULA IRO [GLJ]
GOULAI alt for GULAY [GVL]
GOULAYE alt for GULAY [GVL]
GOULEI alt for GULAY [GVL]
GOULFEI alt for MALGBE [MXF]
GOULFEI alt for MALGBE dial of MALGBE [MXF]
GOULFEY alt for MALGBE [MXF]
GOULFEY dial of MALGBE [MXF]
GOULIMANCEMA alt for GOURMANCHÉMA [GUX]
GOULMANCEMA alt for GOURMANCHÉMA [GUX]
GOUMAYE alt for GUMAY dial of MASANA [MCN]
GOUN alt for GUN dial of GUN-GBE [GUW]
GOUN alt for GUN-GBE [GUW]
GOUNDO [GOY] lang, Chad
GOUNO alt for WEST GIMI dial of GIMI [GIM]
GOUNOU alt for NUGUNU [YAS]
GOURAGHIE alt for GURAGE, WEST [GUY]
GOURARA dial of TAZNATIT [GRR]
GOURMA alt for GOURMANCHÉMA [GUX]
GOURMANCHÉMA [GUX] lang, Burkina Faso; also
    in Benin, Niger, Togo
GOURMANTCHE alt for GOURMANCHÉMA [GUX]
GOURMANTCHE dial of FULFULDE,
    NORTHEASTERN BURKINA FASO [FUH]

GOURO alt for GURO [GOA]
GOUWAR alt for GAVAR [GOU]
GOVA alt for KOREKORE dial of SHONA [SHD]
GOVA alt for MBUKUSHU [MHW]
GOVA dial of NDAU [NDC]
GOVARI dial of VARHADI-NAGPURI [VAH]
GOVERNOR GENEROSO MANOBO dial of MANOBO, SARANGANI [MBS]
GOVHOROH alt for GOVORO dial of BANDA-BANDA [BPD]
GOVORO dial of BANDA-BANDA [BPD]
GOWA alt for KOREKORE dial of SHONA [SHD]
GOWA dial of MAKASAR [MSR]
GOWAR-BATI alt for GAWAR-BATI [GWT]
GOWARI alt for GAWAR-BATI [GWT]
GOWASE alt for BUSSA [DOX]
GOWLAN [GOJ] lang, India
GOWLI [GOK] lang, India
GOWRI alt for KALAMI [GWC]
GOWRO [GWF] lang, Pakistan
GOWRO alt for BAIGANI dial of CHHATTISGARHI [HNE]
GOZARKHANI [GOZ] lang, Iran
GOZO dial of MALTESE [MLS]
GOZZA dial of AARI [AIZ]
GRAECAE alt for GREEK [GRK]
GRAGED alt for GEDAGED [GDD]
GRAMSUKRAVIRI dial of ASHKUN [ASK]
GRAMYA alt for GAMADIA dial of GUJARATI [GJR]
GRANDE COMORE alt for SHINGAZIDJA dial of COMORIAN, SHINGAZIDJA [SWS]
GRANGALI [NLI] lang, Afghanistan
GRANGALI dial of GRANGALI [NLI]
GRASIA alt for GARASIA, RAJPUT [GRA]
GRASS MIAO alt for CAO MIAO [COV]
GRASSLAND MARI dial of MARI, LOW [MAL]
GRAUBENDEN-GRISONS dial of ALEMANNISCH [GSW]
GRAUSINO alt for EASTERN ARAGONESE dial of ARAGONESE [AXX]
GREAT NICOBAR dial of NICOBARESE, SOUTHERN [NIK]
GREAT THAI alt for SHAN [SJN]
GREATER KABARDIAN dial of KABARDIAN [KAB]
GREATER KABYLE dial of KABYLE [KYL]
GREATER SEDANG dial of SEDANG [SED]
GREBO, BARCLAYVILLE [GRY] lang, Liberia
GREBO, CENTRAL [GRV] lang, Liberia
GREBO, GBOLOO [GEC] lang, Liberia
GREBO, NORTHERN [GRB] lang, Liberia
GREBO, SOUTHERN [GRJ] lang, Liberia; also in Côte d'Ivoire
GREC alt for GREEK [GRK]
GRECO alt for GREKURJA dial of ROMANI, VLAX [RMY]
GREEK [GRK] lang, Greece; also in Albania, Armenia, Australia, Austria, Bahamas, Bulgaria, Canada, Congo, Cyprus, DRC, Djibouti, Egypt, France, Georgia, Germany, Hungary, Italy, Jordan, Kazakhstan, Macedonia, Malawi, Paraguay, Poland, Romania, Russia (Europe),

Sierra Leone, South Africa, Sweden, Tunisia, Turkey (Europe), Ukraine, UAE, United Kingdom, USA
GREEK ROMANI dial of ROMANI, BALKAN [RMN]
GREEK SIGN LANGUAGE [GSS] lang, Greece
GREEK, ANCIENT [GKO] lang, Greece
GREEN GELAO dial of GELAO [KKF]
GREEN MIAO alt for HMONG NJUA [BLU]
GREEN MIAO alt for TAK MIAO dial of HMONG NJUA [BLU]
GREEN RIVER alt for ABAU [AAU]
GREENLANDIC alt for INUKTITUT, GREENLANDIC [ESG]
GREENLANDIC ESKIMO alt for INUKTITUT, GREENLANDIC [ESG]
GREKURJA dial of ROMANI, VLAX [RMY]
GRENADA CREOLE ENGLISH dial of WINDWARD CARIBBEAN CREOLE ENGLISH [SVG]
GRENADA CREOLE FRENCH dial of LESSER ANTILLEAN CREOLE FRENCH [DOM]
GRENADA-MENDOZA dial of QUECHUA, CHACHAPOYAS [QUK]
GRENADIAN ENGLISH dial of ENGLISH [ENG]
GRESI [GRS] lang, Indonesia (Irian Jaya)
GRESIK alt for GRESI [GRS]
GRIFFIN POINT dial of SUDEST [TGO]
GRIK dial of TEMIAR [TMH]
GRIKWA alt for XIRI [XII]
GRIQUA alt for XIRI [XII]
GRISONS alt for LOWER ENGADINE dial of ROMANSCH [RHE]
GRODNEN-BARANOVICH alt for SOUTHWEST BELARUSAN dial of BELARUSAN [RUW]
GROGO dial of JAGOI [SNE]
GROGOH alt for GROGO dial of JAGOI [SNE]
GROMA [GRO] lang, China; also in India
GRONINGEN alt for GRONINGS [GOS]
GRONINGEN-EAST FRISIAN dial of GRONINGS [GOS]
GRONINGS [GOS] lang, Netherlands
GRONINGS-OOSTFRIES alt for GRONINGEN-EAST FRISIAN dial of GRONINGS [GOS]
GROOTE EYLANDT alt for ANINDILYAKWA [AOI]
GROS VENTRE [ATS] lang, USA
GROS VENTRES alt for GROS VENTRE [ATS]
GRÜDNO alt for GARDENA dial of LADIN [LLD]
GRUNNINGS alt for GRONINGS [GOS]
GRUZIN alt for GEORGIAN [GEO]
GRUZINSKI alt for GEORGIAN [GEO]
GRY alt for XIRI [XII]
GTA' alt for GATA' [GAQ]
GTA ASA alt for GATA' [GAQ]
GTSANG dial of TIBETAN [TIC]
GU alt for GUN-GBE [GUW]
GÜ alt for GUN dial of GUN-GBE [GUW]
GUA [GWX] lang, Ghana
GUA alt for LARTEH [LAR]
GUADELOUPE CREOLE FRENCH dial of LESSER ANTILLEAN CREOLE FRENCH [DOM]
GUADEMA alt for YANOMAM dial of YANOMAMI [WCA]

GUAGA-TAGARE alt for CHAYMA dial of CARIB [CRB]
GUAGUA alt for PIAROA [PID]
GUAHARIBO alt for YANOMAMÖ [GUU]
GUAHIBO [GUH] lang, Colombia; also in Venezuela
GUAHIBO dial of GUAHIBO [GUH]
"GUAIAQUI" pejorative alt for ACHÉ [GUQ]
GUAICA alt for YANOMAMÖ [GUU]
GUAIGUA alt for GUAHIBO [GUH]
GUAIKA alt for SANUMÁ [SAM]
GUAJÁ [GUJ] lang, Brazil
GUAJAJÁRA [GUB] lang, Brazil
GUAJARIBO alt for YANOMAMÖ [GUU]
GUAJIBO alt for GUAHIBO [GUH]
GUAJIRA alt for WAYUU [GUC]
GUAJIRO alt for WAYUU [GUC]
GUAMACA alt for MALAYO [MBP]
GUAMAKA alt for MALAYO [MBP]
GUAMBIA alt for GUAMBIANO [GUM]
GUAMBIANO [GUM] lang, Colombia
GUANA [GVA] lang, Paraguay
GUANA [QKS] lang, Brazil
GUANANO [GVC] lang, Brazil; also in Colombia
GUANCHE [GNC] lang, Spain
GUANGA alt for GIANGAN [BGI]
GUANGFU alt for CHINESE, YUE [YUH]
GUANGFU alt for YUEHAI dial of CHINESE, YUE [YUH]
GUANHUA alt for CHINESE, MANDARIN [CHN]
GUANYINQIAO [JIQ] lang, China
GUANYINQIAO alt for GUANYINQIAO [JIQ]
GUARANÍ alt for CHIRIPÁ [NHD]
GUARANÍ, ARGENTINE, WESTERN [GUI] lang, Bolivia; also in Argentina, Paraguay
GUARANÍ, BOLIVIAN, EASTERN [GUI] lang, Bolivia; also in Argentina, Paraguay
GUARANÍ, BOLIVIAN, WESTERN [GNW] lang, Bolivia
GUARANÍ, MBYA [GUN] lang, Paraguay; also in Argentina, Brazil
GUARANÍ, PARAGUAYAN [GUG] lang, Paraguay; also in Argentina
GUARAO alt for WARAO [WBA]
GUARATEGAJA alt for KANOÉ [KXO]
GUARATÉGAYA alt for KANOÉ [KXO]
GUARATIRA alt for KANOÉ [KXO]
GUARAUNO alt for WARAO [WBA]
"GUARAYO" pejorative alt for GUARAYU [GYR]
GUARAYO alt for GUARANÍ, BOLIVIAN, EASTERN [GUI]
GUARAYO alt for TAPIETÉ [TAI]
GUARAYU [GYR] lang, Bolivia
GUARAYU-TA alt for PAUSERNA [PSM]
GUAREKENA alt for GUAREQUENA [GAE]
GUAREQUENA [GAE] lang, Venezuela; also in Brazil
GUARI-GUARI alt for PANAMANIAN CREOLE ENGLISH dial of SOUTHWESTERN CARIBBEAN CREOLE ENGLISH [JAM]
GUARIJÍO alt for HUARIJÍO [VAR]
GUASURANGO alt for GUARANÍ, BOLIVIAN, EASTERN [GUI]

GUASURANGO alt for TAPIETÉ [TAI]
GUASURANGUE alt for TAPIETÉ [TAI]
GUATEMALAN SIGN LANGUAGE [GSM] lang, Guatemala
GUATÓ [GTA] lang, Brazil
GUATUSO alt for MALÉKU JAÍKA [GUT]
GUAVA alt for ORAMI dial of NAASIOI [NAS]
GUAVIARE alt for NUKAK MAKÚ [MBR]
GUAXARE alt for GUAJÁ [GUJ]
GUAYABERO [GUO] lang, Colombia
"GUAYAKÍ" pejorative alt for ACHÉ [GUQ]
GUAYAKI-ACHE alt for ACHÉ [GUQ]
GUAYANA alt for WAYANA [WAY]
GUAYBA alt for GUAHIBO [GUH]
GUAYMÍ alt for NGÄBERE [GYM]
GUAYQUERI alt for WOKIARE dial of YABARANA [YAR]
GUAYUYACO dial of INGA, JUNGLE [INJ]
GUAZAZARA alt for GUAJAJÁRA [GUB]
GUBA alt for SHIKI [GUA]
GUBA dial of BORO [BWO]
GUBABWINGU alt for GUPAPUYNGU [GUF]
GUBAT alt for GUBATNON dial of HANUNOO [HNN]
GUBAT alt for SORSOGON, WARAY [SRV]
GUBATNON dial of HANUNOO [HNN]
GUBAWA alt for SHIKI [GUA]
GUBI alt for SHIKI [GUA]
GUBI dial of SHIKI [GUA]
GUBU [GOX] lang, DRC; also in CAR
GUBU alt for GOBU [GOX]
GUDANDJI dial of WAMBAYA [WMB]
GUDE [GDE] lang, Nigeria; also in Cameroon
GUDENI dial of FRAFRA [GUR]
GUDENNE alt for GUDENI dial of FRAFRA [GUR]
GUDI dial of NUNGU [RIN]
GUDO alt for GUDU [GDU]
GUDOJI alt for DAMELI [DML]
GUDU [GDU] lang, Nigeria
GUDUF [GDF] lang, Nigeria; also in Cameroon
GUDUF dial of GUDUF [GDF]
GUDUF dial of GUDUF-GAVA [GDF]
GUDUF-GAVA [GDF] lang, Nigeria; also in Cameroon
GUDUPE alt for GUDUF [GDF]
GUDUPE alt for GUDUF-GAVA [GDF]
GUDUR alt for MOFU-GUDUR [MIF]
GUDWA alt for GADABA, BODO [GBJ]
GUÉBIE alt for DIDA, LAKOTA [DIC]
GUEBIE dial of BETE, GAGNOA [BTG]
GUEGUE alt for ALBANIAN, GHEG [ALS]
GUELAVÍA ZAPOTEC alt for ZAPOTECO, SAN JUAN GUELAVÍA [ZAB]
GUELEBDA alt for GLAVDA [GLV]
GUELENGDENG alt for MBARA [MPK]
GUELILI alt for JERBA dial of DJERBI [JBN]
GUEME alt for GEME [GEQ]
GUEMSHEK alt for GEMZEK [GND]
GUÉRÉ alt for WÈ SOUTHERN [GXX]
GUÉRÉ alt for WÈ WESTERÁN [WEC]
GUERRERO AZTEC alt for NHUATL, GUERRERO [NAH]
GUERZE alt for KPELLE, GUINEA [GKP]

GUEVE alt for GEY [GUV]
GUEVEA DE HUMBOLDT ZAPOTEC alt for ZAPOTECO, GUEVEA DE HUMBOLDT [ZPG]
GUGADA alt for KOKATA [KTD]
GUGADJ [GGD] lang, Australia
GUGADJA alt for KUKATJA [KUX]
GŨGBE alt for GUN-GBE [GUW]
GUGBE alt for GUN-GBE [GUW]
GUGIKO dial of MUKULU [MOZ]
GUGU dial of DAYAK, LAND [DYK]
GUGU BADHUN [GDC] lang, Australia
GUGU WARRA [WRW] lang, Australia
GUGU YIMIJIR alt for GUGUYIMIDJIR [KKY]
GUGUBERA [KKP] lang, Australia
GUGUDAYOR alt for THAYORE [THD]
GUGUMINJEN alt for KUNJEN [KJN]
GUGUWARRA alt for GUGU WARRA [WRW]
GUGUYALANJI alt for KUKU-YALANJI [GVN]
GUGUYIMIDJIR [KKY] lang, Australia
GUHA alt for HOLOHOLO [HOO]
GUHJALI alt for WAKHI [WBL]
GUHU-SAMANE [GHS] lang, Papua New Guinea
GUIAM dial of GIDRA [GDR]
GUIARAK [GKA] lang, Papua New Guinea
GUIBEI dial of ZHUANG, NORTHERN [CCX]
GUIBEROUA dial of BETE, GUIBEROUA [BET]
GUIBIAN dial of ZHUANG, NORTHERN [CCX]
GUICHICOVI MIXE alt for MIXE, ISTMO [MIR]
GUICURZ alt for KUIKÚRO-KALAPÁLO [KUI]
GUIDAR alt for GIDAR [GID]
GUIDER alt for GIDAR [GID]
GUIDIVILLE dial of POMO, NORTHERN [PEJ]
GUILAKI alt for GILAKI [GLK]
GUILANI alt for GILAKI [GLK]
GUILI alt for GILI dial of BANA [BCW]
GUILIA alt for BAREIN [BVA]
GUILIA dial of BAREIN [BVA]
GUIMARAS ISLAND dial of KINARAY-A [KRJ]
GUIN alt for CERMA [GOT]
GUIN alt for GEN-GBE [GEJ]
GUINAANG dial of KALINGA, LUBUAGAN [KNB]
GUINAANG BONTOC dial of BONTOC, CENTRAL [BNC]
GUINAN dial of CHINESE, YUE [YUH]
GUINEAN SIGN LANGUAGE [GUS] lang, Guinea
GUINZADAN dial of KANKANAEY [KNE]
GUIPUZCOAN dial of BASQUE [BSQ]
GUIPUZCOANO alt for GUIPUZCOAN dial of BASQUE [BSQ]
GUIQIONG [GQI] lang, China
GUIREN alt for NÙNG QÚY RIN dial of NUNG [NUT]
GUIRVIDIG alt for MUZUK dial of MUSGU [MUG]
GÜISNAY alt for WICHÍ LHAMTÉS GÜISNAY [MZH]
GUISSEY alt for GIZAY dial of MASANA [MCN]
GUITRY alt for LOZOUA dial of DIDA, YOCOBOUE [GUD]
GUIZIGA alt for GIZIGA, NORTH [GIS]
GUIZIGA alt for GIZIGA, SOUTH [GIZ]
GUJAAXET dial of BAINOUK-GUNYAAMOLO [BCZ]
GUJALABIYA alt for BURARRA [BVR]

GUJAR alt for GUJARI [GJU]
GUJARATI [GJR] lang, India; also in Bangladesh, Fiji, Kenya, Malawi, Mauritius, Oman, Pakistan, Réunion, Singapore, South Africa, Tanzania, Uganda, United Kingdom, USA, Zambia, Zimbabwe
GUJARI [GJU] lang, India; also in Afghanistan, Pakistan
GUJER alt for GUJARI [GJU]
GUJERATHI alt for GUJARATI [GJR]
GUJERATI alt for GUJARATI [GJR]
GUJI dial of OROMO, BORANA-ARSI-GUJI [GAX]
GUJINGALIA alt for BURARRA [BVR]
GUJJARI alt for GUJARI [GJU]
GUJJI alt for GUJI dial of OROMO, BORANA-ARSI-GUJI [GAX]
GUJRATHI alt for GUJARATI [GJR]
GUJURI alt for GUJARI [GJU]
GUJURI RAJASTHANI alt for GUJARI [GJU]
GULA [GLU] lang, Chad
GULA [KCM] lang, CAR; also in Sudan
GULA alt for GOLA [GOL]
GULA dial of GULA [KCM]
GULA DU MAMOUN alt for GULA [KCM]
GULA GUERA alt for BON GULA [GLC]
GULA GUERA alt for ZAN GULA [ZNA]
GULA IRO [GLJ] lang, Chad
GULA'ALAA [GMB] lang, Solomon Islands
GULAI alt for GULAY [GVL]
GULAK dial of MARGHI CENTRAL [MAR]
GULANGA alt for GIANGAN [BGI]
GULAY [GVL] lang, Chad
GULAY dial of DYAABUGAY [DYY]
GULAY dial of GULAY [GVL]
GULBAHAR dial of PASHAYI, NORTHWEST [GLH]
GULE [GLE] lang, Sudan
GULEGULEU dial of DUAU [DUA]
GULEI alt for GULAY [GVL]
GULF ARABIC alt for ARABIC, GULF SPOKEN [AFB]
GULF SPOKEN alt for ARABIC, GULF SPOKEN [AFB]
GULFAN alt for GHULFAN [GHL]
GULFE alt for MALGBE [MXF]
GULFEI alt for MALGBE [MXF]
GULICHA dial of BARUYA [BYR]
GULIGULI [GLG] lang, Solomon Islands
GULILI alt for GULIGULI [GLG]
GULIMANCEMA alt for GOURMANCÉMA [GUX]
GULIMANCEMA alt for GOURMANCHÉMA [GUX]
GULLAH alt for SEA ISLAND CREOLE ENGLISH [GUL]
GULMANCEMA alt for GOURMANCÉMA [GUX]
GULOMPAAY alt for MLOMP [QML]
GULUD alt for JULUD dial of KATLA [KCR]
GUMADIR dial of GUNWINGGU [GUP]
GUMAIT alt for GUMATJ [GNN]
GUMAJ alt for GUMATJ [GNN]
GUMALU [GMU] lang, Papua New Guinea
GUMAS dial of MUNA [MYN]
GUMASI alt for GUMAWANA [GVS]

GUMATJ [GNN] lang, Australia
GUMAWANA [GVS] lang, Papua New Guinea
GUMAY dial of MASANA [MCN]
GUMBA alt for BELANDA VIRI [BVI]
GUMBAINGARI alt for KUMBAINGGAR [KGS]
GUMBANG dial of JAGOI [SNE]
GUMBAYNGGIR alt for KUMBAINGGAR [KGS]
GUMER dial of GURAGE, WEST [GUY]
GUMIA alt for TUMA-IRUMU [IOU]
GUMINE alt for GOLIN [GVF]
GUMIS alt for GUMUZ [GUK]
GUMSAI dial of KUI [KXU]
GUMUZ [GUK] lang, Ethiopia; also in Sudan
GUN alt for GUN-GBE [GUW]
GUN dial of GUN-GBE [GUW]
GUNA alt for NGUNA dial of EFATE, NORTH [LLP]
GUNA dial of SINASINA [SST]
GUNAGORAGONE alt for GURAGONE [GGE]
GUN-ALADA alt for GUN-GBE [GUW]
GUNANTUNA alt for KUANUA [KSD]
GUNAVIDJI alt for DJEEBBANA [DJJ]
GUNAWITJI alt for GUNWINGGU [GUP]
GUNBALANG alt for KUNBARLANG [WLG]
GUNDANGBON alt for NGALKBUN [NGK]
GUNDI [GDI] lang, CAR
GUNDJEIPME dial of GUNWINGGU [GUP]
GUNEI dial of GUNWINGGU [GUP]
GUNERAKAN alt for KUNGARAKANY [GGK]
GUNGA alt for RESHE [RES]
GUNGABULA [GYF] lang, Australia
GUNGALANG alt for KUNBARLANG [WLG]
GUNGANCHI alt for RESHE [RES]
GUNGARAGAN alt for KUNGARAKANY [GGK]
GUNGARI alt for KUNGGARI [KGL]
GUNGAWA alt for RESHE [RES]
GUN-GBE [GUW] lang, Benin; also in Nigeria
GUNGGARA alt for KUNGGARA [KVS]
GUNGGARI alt for KUNGGARI [KGL]
GUNGGAY dial of YIDINY [YII]
GUNGOROGONE alt for GURAGONE [GGE]
GUNGU [RUB] lang, Uganda
GUN-GURAGONE alt for BURARRA [BVR]
GUN-GURAGONE alt for GURAGONE [GGE]
GUNIAN alt for GOONIYANDI [GNI]
GUNIANDI alt for GOONIYANDI [GNI]
GUNIN alt for KWINI [GWW]
GUNIYAN alt for GOONIYANDI [GNI]
GUNIYN alt for GOONIYANDI [GNI]
GUNMARUNG alt for MAUNG [MPH]
GUNTAI [GNT] lang, Papua New Guinea
GUNTUR dial of TELUGU [TCW]
GUNU alt for NUGUNU [YAS]
GUNUA-KENA alt for TEHUELCHE [TEH]
GUNUNA-KENA alt for TEHUELCHE [TEH]
GUNWINGGU [GUP] lang, Australia
GUNYA [GYY] lang, Australia
GUNYA alt for BAJUNI dial of SWAHILI [SWA]
GUNYAMOOLO dial of BAINOUK-GUNYAAMOLO
  [BCZ]
GUNZA alt for DAKUNZA dial of GUMUZ [GUK]
GUNZIB alt for HUNZIB [HUZ]

GUO GARIMANI alt for DAHALO [DAL]
"GUOYAGUI" pejorative alt for ACHÉ [GUQ]
GUOYU alt for CHINESE, MANDARIN [CHN]
GUPA dial of GUPA-ABAWA [GPA]
GUPA-ABAWA [GPA] lang, Nigeria
GUPAPUYNGU [GUF] lang, Australia
GUPAPUYNGU dial of GUPAPUYNGU [GUF]
GURA alt for GBIRI dial of GBIRI-NIRAGU [GRH]
GURA alt for MABAAN [MFZ]
GURA dial of GURAGE, WEST [GUY]
GURA dial of LAME [BMA]
GURADJARA alt for KARADJERI [GBD]
GURAGE, EAST [GRE] lang, Ethiopia
GURAGE, SODDO [GRU] lang, Ethiopia
GURAGE, WEST [GUY] lang, Ethiopia
GURAGIE alt for GURAGE, WEST [GUY]
GURAGONE [GGE] lang, Australia
GURAGUE alt for GURAGE, WEST [GUY]
GURAGUREU alt for GULEGULEU dial of DUAU
  [DUA]
GURAMA alt for KURRAMA [VKU]
GURAMALUM [GRZ] lang, Papua New Guinea
GURANI alt for BAJELAN [BJM]
GURANI alt for HAWRAMI [HAC]
GURARA alt for GOURARA dial of TAZNATIT [GRR]
GURDJAR [GDJ] lang, Australia
GURDUNG alt for GURUNTUM-MBAARU [GRD]
GURE alt for GBIRI dial of GBIRI-NIRAGU [GRH]
GURE-KAHUGU alt for GBIRI-NIRAGU [GRH]
GURENG GURENG [GNR] lang, Australia
GURENNE alt for FRAFRA [GUR]
GURENNE alt for GUDENI dial of FRAFRA [GUR]
GURESHA alt for BULI [BWU]
GUREZI alt for ASTORI dial of SHINA [SCL]
GUREZI dial of SHINA [SCL]
GURGO dial of DAYAK, LAND [DYK]
GURGULA [GGG] lang, Pakistan
GURIAN dial of GEORGIAN [GEO]
GURIASO [GRX] lang, Papua New Guinea
GURINDJI alt for GURINJI [GUE]
GURINJI [GUE] lang, Australia
GURJAR alt for GUJARI [GJU]
GURJINDI dial of JARNANGO [JAY]
GURKA alt for YIWOM [GEK]
GURKHALI alt for NEPALI [NEP]
GURMA alt for GOURMANCÉMA [GUX]
GURMA alt for GOURMANCHÉMA [GUX]
GURMANA [GRC] lang, Nigeria
GURMARTI alt for LAMBADI [LMN]
GURMUKHI alt for PANJABI, EASTERN [PNJ]
GURO [GOA] lang, Côte d'Ivoire
GURREH alt for GARREH dial of GARREH-AJURAN
  [GGH]
GURROGONE alt for GURAGONE [GGE]
GURRUM alt for RIBINA dial of JERE [JER]
GURTÜ alt for KURTOKHA [XKZ]
GURU alt for RUGURU [RUF]
GURU dial of SHIKI [GUA]
GURUBI alt for SOUTHERN CHUMBURUNG dial
  of CHUMBURUNG [NCU]
GURUF-NGARIAWANG dial of ADZERA [AZR]

GURUKA dial of SAFWA [SBK]
GURUMUKHI alt for PANJABI, EASTERN [PNJ]
GURUNE alt for FRAFRA [GUR]
GURUNE alt for GUDENI dial of FRAFRA [GUR]
GURUNG alt for GURUNG, WESTERN [GVR]
GURUNG KURA alt for GURUNG, WESTERN [GVR]
GURUNG, EASTERN [GGN] lang, Nepal
GURUNG, WESTERN [GVR] lang, Nepal; also in
    Bhutan, India
GURUNTUM alt for GURUNTUM-MBAARU [GRD]
GURUNTUM-MBAARU [GRD] lang, Nigeria
GURVALI alt for GARHWALI [GBM]
GUSAN [GSN] lang, Papua New Guinea
GUSAP alt for WASEMBO [GSP]
GUSAWA alt for GUSU dial of JERE [JER]
GUSII [GUZ] lang, Kenya
GUSIILAY alt for GUSILAY [GSL]
GUSILAAY alt for GUSILAY [GSL]
GUSILAY [GSL] lang, Senegal
GUSSUM alt for GUSU dial of JERE [JER]
GUSU dial of JERE [JER]
GUSUBOU dial of TSO [LDP]
GUTA dial of MANYIKA [MXC]
GUTAMAL alt for GUTNISKA dial of SWEDISH
    [SWD]
GUTJERTABIA alt for GURAGONE [GGE]
GUTNIC alt for GUTNISKA dial of SWEDISH [SWD]
GUTNISKA dial of SWEDISH [SWD]
GUTOB alt for GADABA, BODO [GBJ]
GUTOP alt for GADABA, BODO [GBJ]
GUTU alt for GUDU [GDU]
GUUGU YIMITHIRR alt for GUGUYIMIDJIR
    [KKY]
GUVJA dial of KANURI, CENTRAL [KPH]
GUVVALOLLU alt for VAAGRI BOOLI [VAA]
GUWAMAL alt for YIDINY [YII]
GUWAMU [GWU] lang, Australia
GUWAN alt for GAMBERA [GMA]
GUWET alt for DUWET [GVE]
GUWIDJ dial of NGARINYIN [UNG]
GUWII dial of KURMANJI [KUR]
GUWOT alt for DUWET [GVE]
GUXHOU alt for FUZHOU dial of CHINESE, MIN
    DONG [CDO]
GUYANAIS alt for FRENCH GUIANESE CREOLE
    FRENCH [FRE]
GUYANE alt for FRENCH GUIANESE CREOLE
    FRENCH [FRE]
GUYANE CREOLE alt for FRENCH GUIANESE
    CREOLE FRENCH [FRE]
GUYANESE CREOLE alt for GUYANESE CREOLE
    ENGLISH [GYN]
GUYANESE CREOLE ENGLISH [GYN] lang,
    Guyana; also in Suriname, USA
GUYANESE ENGLISH dial of ENGLISH [ENG]
GUYENNAIS dial of LANGUEDOCIEN [LNC]
GUYUK alt for NYA GUYUWA dial of LONGUDA
    [LNU]
GUZAWA alt for GUSU dial of JERE [JER]
GUZII alt for GUSII [GUZ]
GVEDE alt for UMANAKAINA [GDN]

GVOKO [NGS] lang, Nigeria; also in Cameroon
GWA [GWB] lang, Nigeria
GWA alt for GUA [GWX]
GWA alt for MBATO [GWA]
GWABEGWABE dial of IAMALELE [YML]
GWADARA BASA alt for BASA-GUMNA [BSL]
GWADI PAREKWA alt for PARKWA [PBI]
GWAHAMERE dial of GWAHATIKE [DAH]
GWAHATIKE [DAH] lang, Papua New Guinea
GWAHATIKE dial of GWAHATIKE [DAH]
GWAK alt for GINGWAK dial of JARAWA [JAR]
GWAKA alt for NGBAKA MA'BO [NBM]
GWAMA alt for KWAMA [KMQ]
GWAMBA alt for TSONGA [TSO]
GWAMBA dial of TSONGA [TSO]
GWAMFANCI alt for GWAMHI dial of GWAMHI-
    WURI [BGA]
GWAMFI GWAMFAWA alt for GWAMHI dial of
    GWAMHI-WURI [BGA]
GWAMHI dial of GWAMHI-WURI [BGA]
GWAMHI-WURI [BGA] lang, Nigeria
GWANDABA alt for NYA GWANDA dial of
    LONGUDA [LNU]
GWANDARA [GWN] lang, Nigeria
GWANDARA EASTERN dial of GWANDARA [GWN]
GWANDARA GITATA dial of GWANDARA [GWN]
GWANDARA KARASHI dial of GWANDARA [GWN]
GWANDARA KORO dial of GWANDARA [GWN]
GWANDARA SOUTHERN dial of GWANDARA
    [GWN]
GWANDERA alt for YIR YORONT [YIY]
GWANJE dial of WANDALA [MFI]
GWANO dial of POKOMO, UPPER [PKB]
GWANTO alt for GWANTU dial of NUMANA-
    NUNKU-GWANTU-NUMBU [NBR]
GWANTU dial of NUMANA-NUNKU-GWANTU-
    NUMBU [NBR]
GWAPA alt for GWAMBA dial of TSONGA [TSO]
GWAPTI dial of GWAHATIKE [DAH]
GWARA alt for MADUBE dial of MARGHI CENTRAL
    [MAR]
GWARETA dial of MAIWA [MTI]
GWARI alt for GBAGYI [GBR]
GWARI MATAI alt for GBAGYI [GBR]
GWARI YAMMA alt for GBARI [GBY]
GWASI dial of SUBA [SUH]
GWATALEY alt for BATULEY [BAY]
GWATE alt for BATA [BTA]
GWATIKE alt for GWAHATIKE [DAH]
GWAVILI alt for YALEBA dial of TAWALA [TBO]
GWAWILI alt for YALEBA dial of TAWALA [TBO]
GWAZA dial of NUNG [NUN]
GWE alt for CERMA [GOT]
GWE dial of SUKUMA [SUA]
GWEDA [GRW] lang, Papua New Guinea
GWEDA alt for UMANAKAINA [GDN]
GWEDE alt for UMANAKAINA [GDN]
GWEDENA alt for UMANAKAINA [GDN]
GWEETAAWU dial of DAN [DAF]
GWEMARRA alt for GUMER dial of GURAGE,
    WEST [GUY]

GWEN alt for CERMA [GOT]
GWENDELE alt for MAYO-PLATA dial of PELASLA [MLR]
GWENO [GWE] lang, Tanzania
GWÉÒ dial of TOURA [NEB]
GWERE [GWR] lang, Uganda
GWERI alt for MO'DA [GBN]
/GWI [GWJ] lang, Botswana
G//WI alt for /GWI [GWJ]
G//WI alt for /GWI [GWJ]
GWIBWEN alt for NEYO [NEY]
GWICH'IN [KUC] lang, Canada; also in USA
GWIINI alt for KWINI [GWW]
G//WIKHWE alt for /GWI [GWJ]
G/WIKHWE alt for /GWI [GWJ]
G!WIKWE alt for /GWI [GWJ]
GWINI alt for KWINI [GWW]
GWOM alt for MOO [GWG]
GWOMO alt for MOO [GWG]
GWOMU alt for MOO [GWG]
GWONG alt for KAGOMA [KDM]
GWONG DUNG WAA alt for CHINESE, YUE [YUH]
GWORAM alt for LALA-ROBA [LLA]
GWORAM dial of KOFYAR [KWL]
GWUNE alt for AGWAGWUNE [YAY]
GXANA alt for //GANA [GNK]
GXANNA alt for //GANA [GNK]
GYAAZI alt for GEJI dial of GEJI [GEZ]
GYAKAN dial of KWA [KWB]
GYAM alt for GYEM [GYE]
GYANGE alt for NGENGE dial of GBAGYI [GBR]
GYANGIYA alt for NYANG'I [NYP]
GYARONG alt for JIARONG [JYA]
GYARUNG alt for JIARONG [JYA]
GYEGEM alt for DYEGUEME dial of SERER-SINE [SES]
GYELE [GYI] lang, Cameroon; also in Equatorial Guinea
GYELI alt for GYELE [GYI]
GYELL-KURU-VWANG dial of BEROM [BOM]
GYEM [GYE] lang, Nigeria
GYEM alt for FYAM [PYM]
GYEMAWA alt for GYEM [GYE]
GYENGYEN alt for NGENGE dial of GBAGYI [GBR]
GYIRONG alt for KYERUNG [KGY]
GYO alt for DAN [DAF]
GYOGO dial of LIGBI [LIG]
GYONG alt for KAGOMA [KDM]
GYPSY alt for DOMARI [RMT]
GYPSY alt for ROMANI, BALKAN [RMN]
GYPSY alt for ROMANI, KALO FINNISH [RMF]
GYPSY alt for ROMANI, VLAX [RMY]
HA [HAQ] lang, Tanzania
HA dial of DZONGKHA [DZO]
HA dial of HLAI [LIC]
HA MEA alt for MEA [MEG]
HA XA PHANG alt for CHINESE, YUE [YUH]
HÄME dial of FINNISH [FIN]
HA'AANG dial of TAOIH, UPPER [TTH]
HAAL alt for KASANGA [CCJ]
HAALPULAAR alt for FULFULDE, PULAAR [FUC]

HAALPULAAR alt for TOUCOULEUR dial of PULAAR [FUC]
HAAT alt for O'DU [TYH]
HAAVIQINRA dial of TAIRORA [TBG]
HAAVU alt for HAVU [HAV]
HAAYIL alt for CENTRAL NAJDI dial of ARABIC, NAJDI SPOKEN [ARS]
HABAU dial of JARAI [JRA]
HABBAN dial of ARABIC, JUDEO-YEMENI [JYE]
HABE alt for HAUSA [HUA]
HABENAPO alt for POMO, CENTRAL [POO]
HABU [HBU] lang, Timor Lorosae
HABURA dial of BHILI [BHB]
HACHERO alt for BANGDALE dial of NACHERING [NCD]
HADAAREB alt for HADAREB dial of BEDAWI [BEI]
HADANG alt for SEDANG [SED]
HADAREB dial of BEDAWI [BEI]
HADAUTI alt for HARAUTI [HOJ]
HADEJIYA dial of HAUSA [HUA]
HADEM dial of HRANGKHOL [HRA]
HADENDIWA alt for HADENDOA dial of BEDAWI [BEI]
HADENDOA dial of BEDAWI [BEI]
HADENDOWA alt for HADENDOA dial of BEDAWI [BEI]
HADIA alt for HADIYYA [HDY]
HADIMU alt for PEMBA dial of SWAHILI [SWA]
HADIYA alt for HADIYYA [HDY]
HADIYYA [HDY] lang, Ethiopia
HADOTHI alt for HARAUTI [HOJ]
HADOTI alt for HARAUTI [HOJ]
HADRAMI alt for ARABIC, HADRAMI SPOKEN [AYH]
HADROMI alt for ARABIC, HADRAMI SPOKEN [AYH]
HADYA alt for HADIYYA [HDY]
HADYO dial of NYOLE [NUJ]
HADZA [HTS] lang, Tanzania
HADZABI alt for HADZA [HTS]
HADZAPI alt for HADZA [HTS]
HAEKE [AEK] lang, New Caledonia
HAGAHAI alt for PINAI-HAGAHAI [PNN]
HAGEI dial of GELAO [KKF]
HAGEN alt for MELPA [MED]
HAGEULU dial of BUGHOTU [BGT]
HAGI alt for KAMASAU [KMS]
HAGUETI alt for CASHIBO-CACATAIBO [CBR]
HAHAINTESU dial of NAMBIKUARA, SOUTHERN [NAB]
HAHAK dial of GALOLI [GAL]
HAHON [HAH] lang, Papua New Guinea
HAHUTAN alt for ILIUN [ILU]
HAHUTAU alt for ILIUN [ILU]
HAI alt for LELE [UGA]
HAI dial of BANDA-BANDA [BPD]
HAI NAM alt for CHINESE, YUE [YUH]
HAIAN AMI alt for CENTRAL AMIS dial of AMIS [ALV]
HAIAO alt for YAO [YAO]
HAIDA, NORTHERN [HAI] lang, Canada; also in USA

HAIDA, SOUTHERN [HAX] lang, Canada
HAIEREN alt for ARMENIAN [ARM]
HAIGWAI [HGW] lang, Papua New Guinea
HAIJA dial of AMELE [AMI]
HAIJONG alt for HAJONG [HAJ]
HAILA'ER dial of DAUR [DTA]
HAILA'ER dial of EVENKI [EVN]
HAILAR alt for HAILA'ER dial of DAUR [DTA]
HAILU dial of CHINESE, HAKKA [HAK]
HAIN alt for BOZO, HAINYAXO [BZX]
HAINAN dial of CHINESE, MIN NAN [CFR]
HAINAN CHAM alt for TSAT [HUQ]
HAINAN MIAO alt for KIM MUN [MJI]
HAINANESE alt for HAINAN dial of CHINESE, MIN
   NAN [CFR]
HAINANESE dial of CHINESE, MIN NAN [CFR]
HAINAUT dial of PICARD [PCD]
HAINMAN alt for NGARINMAN [NBJ]
HAINTE alt for CHIN, PAITE [PCK]
HAIN//UM dial of HAIOM [HGM]
HAINYAXO alt for BOZO, HAINYAXO [BZX]
HAI//OM [HGM] lang, Namibia; also in South Africa
HAIPHONG SIGN LANGUAGE [HAF] lang, Viet Nam
HAIRA alt for OROKOLO [ORO]
/HAIS alt for /XAISE dial of SHUA [SHG]
/HAISE alt for /XAISE dial of SHUA [SHG]
HAISLA [HAS] lang, Canada
HAITHE alt for CHIN, PAITE [PCK]
HAITIAN CREOLE FRENCH [HAT] lang, Haiti;
   also in Bahamas, Canada, Cayman Islands,
   Dominican Republic, French Guiana, Puerto
   Rico, USA
HAITIAN VODOUN CULTURE LANGUAGE [HVC]
   lang, Haiti
HAITSHUARI alt for HIETSHWARE [HIE]
HAITSHUWAU alt for HIETSHWARE [HIE]
HAJAO alt for YAO [YAO]
HAJONG [HAJ] lang, India; also in Bangladesh
HAKA alt for BOLO [BLV]
HAKA alt for CHIN, HAKA [CNH]
HAKARI dial of KURMANJI [KUR]
HAKEI alt for HAGEI dial of GELAO [KKF]
HAKETIA alt for HAQUETIYA dial of LADINO [SPJ]
HAKETIA alt for LADINO [SPJ]
HAKETIYA alt for HAQUETIYA dial of LADINO
   [SPJ]
HAKHA alt for CHIN, HAKA [CNH]
HAKI PIKI alt for VAAGRI BOOLI [VAA]
HAKITIA alt for LADINO [SPJ]
HAKITIA alt for HAQUETIYA dial of LADINO [SPJ]
HAKKA alt for CHINESE, HAKKA [HAK]
HAKKÂRI dial of KURMANJI [KUR]
HAKKIPIKKARU alt for VAAGRI BOOLI [VAA]
HAKÖ [HAO] lang, Papua New Guinea
HAKU alt for HAKÖ [HAO]
HAL KURUMBA alt for KURUMBA, ALU [QKA]
HALABA alt for ALABA [ALB]
HALABI alt for HALBI [HLB]
HALAKWULUP alt for QAWASQAR [ALC]
HALAM alt for CHIN, FALAM [HBH]
HALAM dial of CHIN, FALAM [HBH]

HALAM dial of KOK BOROK [TRP]
HALAM CHIN alt for CHIN, FALAM [HBH]
HALANG [HAL] lang, Viet Nam; also in Laos
HALANG alt for SALANG [HAL]
HALANG DOAN [HLD] lang, Viet Nam; also in Laos
HALANG DUAN alt for HALANG DOAN [HLD]
HALBA alt for HALBI [HLB]
HALBI [HLB] lang, India
HALBI dial of ORIYA [ORY]
HALERMAN dial of KELON [KYO]
HALH alt for KHALKHA dial of MONGOLIAN, HALH
   [KHK]
HALH alt for MONGOLIAN, HALH [KHK]
HALH dial of MONGOLIAN, HALH [KHK]
HALIA [HLA] lang, Papua New Guinea
HALIFOERSCH dial of MARIND [MRZ]
HALITI alt for PARECÍS [PAB]
HALKOMELEM [HUR] lang, Canada
HALLAENDSKA dial of SKANE [SCY]
HALLAM alt for CHIN, FALAM [HBH]
HALLAM CHIN alt for CHIN, FALAM [HBH]
HALLARI alt for GADABA, OLLAR, POTTANGI
   [GDB]
HALÓ TÉ SÚ [HLO] lang, Brazil
HALPULAAR alt for TOUCOULEUR dial of PULAAR
   [FUC]
HALUMBUNG dial of SANGPANG [RAV]
HALVAS alt for HALBI [HLB]
HALVI alt for HALBI [HLB]
HAM [JAB] lang, Nigeria
HAM alt for MARIK [DAD]
HAM dial of MASANA [MCN]
HAMACORE alt for IQUITO [IQU]
HAMADANI dial of FARSI, WESTERN [PES]
HAMAP [HMU] lang, Indonesia (Nusa Tenggara)
HAMAR alt for HAMER-BANNA [AMF]
HAMAR alt for HMAR [HMR]
HAMAR-KOKE alt for HAMER-BANNA [AMF]
HAMBA [HBA] lang, DRC
HAMBA alt for AMBA [RWM]
HAMBA alt for KIGUMU dial of AMBA [RWM]
HAMBA dial of HAYA [HAY]
HAMBA dial of NKUTU [NKW]
HAMBO alt for AMBA [RWM]
HAMDAY alt for HAMTAI [HMT]
HAMEHA alt for MEA [MEG]
HAMEJ alt for GULE [GLE]
HAMER alt for HAMER-BANNA [AMF]
HAMER-BANNA [AMF] lang, Ethiopia
HAMGYONGDO dial of KOREAN [KKN]
HAMIL alt for NORTH WAIBUK dial of HARUAI
   [TMD]
HAMMER alt for HAMER-BANNA [AMF]
HAMMERCOCHE alt for HAMER-BANNA [AMF]
HAMSCHEN alt for HAMSHEN dial of ARMENIAN
   [ARM]
HAMSHEN dial of ARMENIAN [ARM]
HAMTAI [HMT] lang, Papua New Guinea
HAMTAI dial of HAMTAI [HMT]
HAMTIK dial of KINARAY-A [KRJ]
HAMTIKNON alt for KINARAY-A [KRJ]

HAMUNG alt for DAMAL [UHN]
HAN [HAA] lang, USA; also in Canada
HAN alt for CHINESE, YUE [YUH]
HAN LACHI alt for LIPUTCIO dial of LACHI [LBT]
HANAHAN dial of HALIA [HLA]
HANAK dial of CZECH [CZC]
HANANWA alt for GANANWA dial of SOTHO,
   NORTHERN [SRT]
HANDA dial of MBOI [MOI]
HANDÁ alt for /ANDA [HNH]
HANDÁDAM alt for /ANDA [HNH]
HANDA-KHWE alt for /ANDA [HNH]
HANDAKWE-DAM alt for /ANDA [HNH]
HANDURI alt for HINDURI [HII]
HANG alt for KHANG [KJM]
HÀNG TONG alt for TAI HANG TONG [THC]
HANGA [HAG] lang, Ghana
HANGA alt for WANGA dial of LUYIA [LUY]
HANGA dial of NGELIMA [AGH]
HANGA HUNDI [WOS] lang, Papua New Guinea
HANGALA alt for GHAANGALA dial of KONGO
   [KON]
HANGAN dial of HALIA [HLA]
HANGANU alt for CHANGANA dial of TSONGA [TSO]
HANGAZA [HAN] lang, Tanzania
HANGIRO dial of HAYA [HAY]
HANGKHIM alt for SOUTHERN BANTAWA dial of
   BANTAWA [BAP]
HANGKULA alt for BANGDALE dial of NACHERING
   [NCD]
HANGUK MAL alt for KOREAN [KKN]
HANGUOHUA alt for KOREAN [KKN]
HANHI alt for HANI [HNI]
HÀNHÌ alt for HANI [HNI]
HANI [HNI] lang, China; also in Laos, Myanmar,
   Viet Nam
HANI PROPER alt for HANI [HNI]
HANIS alt for COOS [COS]
HAN-KUTCHIN alt for HAN [HAA]
HANO [LML] lang, Vanuatu
HANO dial of TEWA [TEW]
HANOI alt for NORTHERN VIETNAMESE dial of
   VIETNAMESE [VIE]
HANOI SIGN LANGUAGE [HAB] lang, Viet Nam
HANON alt for HAHON [HAH]
HANONOO alt for HANUNOO [HNN]
HANTONG' dial of TAOIH, LOWER [TTO]
HANTY alt for KHANTY [KCA]
HANUNOO [HNN] lang, Philippines
HANYAXO alt for BOZO, HAINYAXO [BZX]
HAONI alt for HONI [HOW]
HAOULO alt for WLUWE-HAWLO dial of KRUMEN,
   PYE [PYE]
HAOUSSA alt for HAUSA [HUA]
HAPA alt for LABU [LBU]
HAPAO IFUGAO dial of IFUGAO, TUWALI [IFK]
HAQARU alt for JAQARU [JQR]
HAQ'ARU alt for JAQARU [JQR]
HAQEARU alt for JAQARU [JQR]
HAQUETIYA alt for LADINO [SPJ]
HAQUETIYA dial of LADINO [SPJ]

HAR alt for SANTALI [SNT]
HARAGURE alt for XARAGURE [ARG]
HARAHU alt for BARA dial of FOLOPA [PPO]
HARAHUI alt for BARA dial of FOLOPA [PPO]
HARAMOSH alt for GILGITI dial of SHINA [SCL]
HARANEU alt for XÂRÂCÙÙ [ANE]
HARAR alt for OROMO, EASTERN [HAE]
HARARI [HAR] lang, Ethiopia
HARARRI alt for HARARI [HAR]
HARAUTI [HOJ] lang, India
HARAUTI dial of HARAUTI [HOJ]
HARAVA dial of OROKAIVA [ORK]
HARBAN alt for CHILASI KOHISTANI dial of SHINA
   [SCL]
HARE dial of SLAVEY, NORTH [SCS]
HAREME dial of MALENG [PKT]
HARENGAN dial of SORI-HARENGAN [SBH]
HARER alt for OROMO, EASTERN [HAE]
HARIA alt for KHARIA [KHR]
HARIAMBA dial of DIMASA [DIS]
HARIANI alt for HARYANVI [BGC]
HARIGAYA dial of KOCH [KDQ]
HARIJAN alt for CHINALI [CIH]
HARIJAN dial of TAMIL [TCV]
HARIJAN BOLI alt for KINNAURI, HARIJAN [KJO]
HARIPMOR dial of BOIKIN [BZF]
HARIYANI alt for HARYANVI [BGC]
HARJA alt for BODO PARJA [BDV]
HARKA GURUNG alt for RAUTE [RAU]
HAROI [HRO] lang, Viet Nam
HARSI <AFORIT alt for HARSUSI [HSS]
HARSO dial of GAWWADA [GWD]
HARSUSI [HSS] lang, Oman
HARUA dial of BOLA [BNP]
HARUAI [TMD] lang, Papua New Guinea
HARUKU [HRK] lang, Indonesia (Maluku)
HARWAY alt for HARUAI [TMD]
HARYANI alt for HARYANVI [BGC]
HARYANVI [BGC] lang, India
HARZANI [HRZ] lang, Iran
HASADA dial of MUNDARI [MUW]
HASADA' dial of MUNDARI [MUW]
HASALA dial of BANDI [GBA]
HASANYA alt for ARABIC, HASSANIYYA [MEY]
HASANYA alt for HASSANIYYA [MEY]
HASHA [YBJ] lang, Nigeria
HASORIA BHIL dial of KOLI, WADIYARA [KXP]
HASORIA KOLI dial of KOLI, WADIYARA [KXP]
HASSANI alt for ARABIC, HASANYA [MEY]
HASSANI alt for ARABIC, HASSANIYYA [MEY]
HASSANI alt for HASSANIYYA [MEY]
HASSANIYA alt for HASSANIYYA [MEY]
HASSANIYYA [MEY] lang, Mauritania; also in Algeria,
   Mali, Morocco, Niger, Senegal
HASSANIYYA alt for ARABIC, HASANYA [MEY]
HAT alt for O'DU [TYH]
HAT dial of KHMU [KJG]
HATAM [HAD] lang, Indonesia (Irian Jaya)
HATANG-KAYEY alt for AGTA, REMONTADO [AGV]
HATE alt for KATE dial of KUNIMAIPA [KUP]
HATERUMA dial of YAEYAMA [RYS]

HATIGORIA alt for NAGA, AO [NJO]
HA-TIRI alt for TIRI [CIR]
HATOBOHEI alt for TOBIAN [TOX]
HATOMA dial of YAEYAMA [RYS]
HATSA alt for HADZA [HTS]
HATTAM alt for HATAM [HAD]
HATUE alt for SALEMAN [SAU]
HATUMETEN alt for BOBOT [BTY]
HATUOLU dial of MANUSELA [WHA]
HATUSUA dial of KAIBOBO [KZB]
HATUTU dial of MARQUESAN, NORTH [MRQ]
HATZFELDHAFEN alt for MALA [PED]
HAUHUNU alt for HAUNUNU dial of BAURO [BXA]
HAUNUNU dial of BAURO [BXA]
HAURA alt for GIMR dial of TAMA [TMA]
HAURA alt for KEURU [QQK]
HAURA HAELA alt for KEURU [QQK]
HAURUHA dial of PAWAIA [PWA]
HA'US alt for ANDRA-HUS [ANX]
HAUSA [HUA] lang, Nigeria; also in Benin, Burkina
    Faso, Cameroon, CAR, Chad, Congo, Eritrea,
    Germany, Ghana, Niger, Sudan, Togo
HAUSA SIGN LANGUAGE [HSL] lang, Nigeria
HAUSAWA alt for HAUSA [HUA]
HÁUSI KÚTA alt for YÁMANA [YAG]
HAUSSA alt for HAUSA [HUA]
HAUT SORABE alt for SORBIAN, UPPER [WEN]
HAUT-AUVERGNAT dial of AUVERGNAT [AUV]
HAUT-KENYANG alt for UPPER KENYANG dial
    of KENYANG [KEN]
HAUT-LANGUEDOCIEN dial of LANGUEDOCIEN
    [LNC]
HAUT-LIMOUSIN dial of LIMOUSIN [LMS]
HA'UWA alt for RAMPI [LJE]
HAVANNAH HARBOUR alt for LELEPA [LPA]
HAVASUPAI dial of HAVASUPAI-WALAPAI-
    YAVAPAI [YUF]
HAVASUPAI-WALAPAI-YAVAPAI [YUF] lang, USA
HAVE dial of NAGA, TASE [NST]
HAVEKE [AVE] lang, New Caledonia
HAVU [HAV] lang, DRC
HAVUNESE alt for SABU [HVN]
HAW alt for HANI [HNI]
HAW alt for HO dial of CHINESE, MANDARIN [CHN]
HAWAI'I CREOLE ENGLISH [HAW] lang, USA
HAWAI'I PIDGIN alt for HAWAI'I CREOLE ENGLISH
    [HAW]
HAWAI'I PIDGIN SIGN LANGUAGE [HPS] lang, USA
HAWAIIAN [HWI] lang, USA
HAWKIP dial of CHIN, THADO [TCZ]
HAWRAMANI alt for HAWRAMI [HAC]
HAWRAMI [HAC] lang, Iraq; also in Iran
HAWSA alt for HAUSA [HUA]
HAWU alt for SABU [HVN]
HAYA [HAY] lang, Tanzania
HAYA alt for ERITAI [BAD]
HAYA alt for WEST TELUTI dial of TELUTI [TLT]
HAYAHAYA alt for KOMO [KOM]
HAYU alt for WAYU [VAY]
HAZAKE alt for KAZAKH [KAZ]
HAZARA alt for HAZARAGI [HAZ]

HAZARA HINDKO alt for HINDKO, NORTHERN
    [HNO]
HAZARAGI [HAZ] lang, Afghanistan; also in Iran,
    Pakistan, Tajikistan
HAZILI alt for GAJILI dial of KUNIMAIPA [KUP]
HAZO alt for HAZZU dial of DIMLI [ZZZ]
HAZONG alt for HAJONG [HAJ]
HAZZU dial of DIMLI [ZZZ]
HBROGPA dial of AMDO [ADX]
HBRUGCHU dial of CHONI [CDA]
HBRUGCHU dial of KHAMS [KHG]
HCE alt for HAWAI'I CREOLE ENGLISH [HAW]
HDANG alt for SEDANG [SED]
HDI [TUR] lang, Nigeria; also in Cameroon
HDI alt for XEDI [TUR]
HDRUNG alt for HODRUNG dial of JARAI [JRA]
HE LISU alt for LIPO [TKL]
HEADWATERS YAU dial of YAU [YUW]
HEBA alt for SEBA dial of SABU [HVN]
HEBBAR dial of TAMIL [TCV]
HEBREW [HBR] lang, Israel; also in Australia,
    Canada, Germany, Palestinian West Bank
    and Gaza, Panama, United Kingdom, USA
HEBREW TAT alt for JUDEO-TAT [TAT]
HEBREW, ANCIENT [HBO] lang, Israel
HECHE alt for HEZHEN dial of NANAI [GLD]
HECHE alt for NANAI [GLD]
HEDANGPA dial of NACHERING [NCD]
HE'DÉ alt for HERDÉ [HED]
HEDI alt for HDI [TUR]
HEDI alt for XEDI [TUR]
HEH MIAO alt for HMONG, NORTHERN
    QIANDONG [HEA]
HEHE [HEH] lang, Tanzania
HEHENAWA alt for CUBEO [CUB]
HEI alt for MINANIBAI [MCV]
HEI MIAO alt for HMONG, NORTHERN QIANDONG
    [HEA]
HEIBAN [HEB] lang, Sudan
HEIHU dial of QIANG, SOUTHERN [QMR]
HEIKOM alt for HAIN//UM dial of HAIOM [HGM]
HEIKOM BUSHMAN alt for HAIN//UM dial of HAIOM
    [HGM]
HEIKUM alt for HAIN//UM dial of HAIOM [HGM]
HEILTSUK [HEI] lang, Canada
HEI//OM alt for HAIN//UM dial of HAIOM [HGM]
HELAMBU SHERPA [SCP] lang, Nepal
HELEBI dial of DOMARI [RMT]
HELEWORURU alt for TOBELO dial of TOBELO
    [TLB]
HELGOLAND dial of FRISIAN, NORTHERN [FRR]
HELLENOROMANI alt for ROMANO-GREEK [RGE]
HELON alt for HELONG [HEG]
HELONG [HEG] lang, Indonesia (Nusa Tenggara)
HELONG DARAT dial of HELONG [HEG]
HELONG PULAU dial of HELONG [HEG]
HEMA [NIX] lang, DRC; also in Rwanda, Uganda
HEMA-NORD alt for LENDU [LED]
HEMA-SUD alt for HEMA [NIX]
HEMBA [HEM] lang, DRC
HEMBEH dial of BANDI [GBA]

HENALIMA alt for NEGERI LIMA dial of ASILULU [ASL]
HENGA alt for CHIKAMANGA dial of TUMBUKA [TUW]
HENGCH'UN AMIS alt for SOUTHERN AMIS dial of AMIS [ALV]
HENGHUA alt for PUTIAN dial of CHINESE, PU-XIAN [CPX]
HENGHUA dial of CHINESE, PU-XIAN [CPX]
HENGO alt for PENGO [PEG]
HENKHA alt for NYENKHA [NEH]
HEQING-JIANCHUAN alt for JIANCHUAN dial of BAI [PIQ]
HER alt for KERAK [HHR]
HERA alt for HUTU dial of RWANDA [RUA]
HERATI alt for DARI dial of FARSI, EASTERN [PRS]
HERDÉ [HED] lang, Chad; also in Cameroon
HERE dial of MANYIKA [MXC]
HERERO [HER] lang, Namibia; also in Botswana
HERKI [HEK] lang, Iraq; also in Iran, Turkey (Asia)
HERMIT [LLF] lang, Papua New Guinea
HERSYET alt for HARSUSI [HSS]
HÉRTEVIN [HRT] lang, Turkey (Asia)
HÉRTEVIN PROPER dial of HERTEVIN [HRT]
HESO alt for SO [SOC]
HETIAN alt for HOTAN dial of UYGHUR [UIG]
HEWA [HAM] lang, Papua New Guinea
HEWA alt for HEWE dial of TUMBUKA [TUW]
HEWBYÓT alt for HOBYÓT [HOH]
HEWE dial of TUMBUKA [TUW]
HEYO alt for WANIB [AUK]
HEZAREH alt for HAZARAGI [HAZ]
HEZARE'I alt for HAZARAGI [HAZ]
HEZHE alt for HEZHEN dial of NANAI [GLD]
HEZHE alt for NANAI [GLD]
HEZHEN alt for NANAI [GLD]
HEZHEN dial of NANAI [GLD]
H'HANA alt for POMO, CENTRAL [POO]
HIANACOTO-UMAUA alt for CARIJONA [CBD]
HIAO alt for YAO [YAO]
HIBARADAI alt for TABO [KNV]
HIBITO [HIB] lang, Peru
HICHKARYANA alt for HIXKARYNA [HIX]
HID dial of AVAR [AVR]
HIDALGO NÁHUATL alt for NÁHUATL, HUASTECA, ESTE [NAI]
HIDALGO TEPEHUA alt for TEPEHUA, HUEHUETLA [TEE]
HIDATSA [HID] lang, USA
HIDE alt for HDI [TUR]
HIDE alt for XEDI [TUR]
HIECHWARE alt for HIETSHWARE [HIE]
HIETSHWARE [HIE] lang, Botswana; also in Zimbabwe
HIGA alt for IPIKO [IPK]
HIGAONON [MBA] lang, Philippines
HIGGI alt for KAMWE [HIG]
HIGH ALEMANNISCH dial of ALEMANNISCH [GSW]
HIGH ARABIC alt for ARABIC, STANDARD [ABV]
HIGH ARAGONESE alt for ARAGONESE [AXX]
HIGH GERMAN alt for GERMAN, STANDARD [GER]

HIGH KATU alt for KATU, EASTERN [KTV]
HIGH LATVIAN alt for EAST LATVIAN dial of LATVIAN [LAT]
HIGH LUGBARA alt for LUGBARA [LUG]
HIGH NAVARRESE alt for ALTO NAVARRO SEPTENTRIONAL dial of BASQUE [BSQ]
HIGH PIEMONTESE dial of PIEMONTESE [PMS]
HIGHLAND AREQUIPA dial of QUECHUA, AREQUIPA-LA UNION [QAR]
HIGHLAND BALI dial of BALI [BZC]
HIGHLAND CHINANTECO alt for CHINANTECO, QUIOTEPEC [CHQ]
HIGHLAND GUERRERO MIXTECO alt for MIXTECO, ALACATLATZALA [MIM]
HIGHLAND HUARIJÍO dial of HUARIJIO [VAR]
HIGHLAND INGA alt for INGA [INB]
HIGHLAND LITHUANIAN alt for AUKSHTAITISH dial of LITHUANIAN [LIT]
HIGHLAND MAZATECO alt for MAZATECO, HUAUTLA [MAU]
HIGHLAND NUNG alt for NUNG [NUT]
HIGHLAND OAXACA CHONTAL alt for CHONTAL DE OAXACA, SIERRA [CHD]
HIGHLAND POPOLUCA alt for POPOLUCA, SIERRA [POI]
HIGHLAND PUEBLA NÁHUAT alt for NÁHUATL, PUEBLA, SIERRA [AZZ]
HIGHLAND TOTONACA alt for TOTONACA, SIERRA [TOS]
HIGHLAND TZELTAL alt for TZELTAL, OXCHUC [TZH]
HIGHLAND YAO alt for IU MIEN [IUM]
HIGI alt for KAMWE [HIG]
HIGIR alt for NARA [NRB]
HIJAZI alt for ARABIC, HIJAZI SPOKEN [ACW]
HIJI alt for KAMWE [HIG]
HIJUK [HIJ] lang, Cameroon
HILA dial of HITU [HIT]
HILA-KAITETU alt for SEIT-KAITETU [HIK]
HILDI dial of MARGHI SOUTH [MFM]
HILEMAN alt for DYAABUGAY [DYY]
HILIGAINON alt for HILIGAYNON [HIL]
HILIGAYNON [HIL] lang, Philippines; also in USA
HILIGAYNON dial of HILIGAYNON [HIL]
HILL ANGAS dial of NGAS [ANC]
HILL BURA alt for PELA dial of BURA-PABIR [BUR]
HILL DUSUN alt for KUIJAU [DKR]
HILL GETA' dial of GATA [GAQ]
HILL JARAWA alt for IZERE [FIZ]
HILL MADA alt for EGGON [EGO]
HILL MARIA alt for ABUJMARIA [ABJ]
HILL PANTARAM alt for MALAPANDARAM [MJP]
HILL TAROK alt for IZINI dial of TAROK [YER]
HILL TETUN alt for NORTHERN TETUN dial of TETUN [TTM]
HI-LU alt for HAILU dial of CHINESE, HAKKA [HAK]
HILU HUMBA alt for KAMBERA [SMI]
HIMA alt for OKENE dial of EBIRA [IGB]
HIMA dial of NYANKORE [NYN]
HIMARIMÃ [HIR] lang, Brazil

HIMBA alt for ZEMBA [DHM]
HIN alt for NYAHEUN [NEV]
HINA alt for MINA [HNA]
HINA alt for PIDLIMDI dial of TERA [TER]
HINAPAVOSA alt for PAPORA [PPU]
HINARAY-A alt for KINARAY-A [KRJ]
HINATSA alt for HIDATSA [HID]
HINDI [HND] lang, India; also in Bangladesh,
    Belize, Botswana, Germany, Kenya, Nepal,
    New Zealand, Philippines, Singapore, South
    Africa, Uganda, UAE, United Kingdom, USA,
    Yemen, Zambia
HINDI DOGRI alt for DOGRI-KANGRI [DOJ]
HINDKI alt for HINDKO, NORTHERN [HNO]
HINDKO, NORTHERN [HNO] lang, Pakistan
HINDKO, SOUTHERN [HIN] lang, Pakistan
HINDU SINDHI alt for DUKSLINU dial of SINDHI
    [SND]
HINDURI [HII] lang, India
HINDUSTANI, CARIBBEAN [HNS] lang, Suriname;
    also in Belize, Guyana, Netherlands, Trinidad
    and Tobago
HINDUSTANI, FIJIAN [HIF] lang, Fiji; also in Australia,
    USA
HINGHUA alt for HENGHUA dial of CHINESE, PU-
    XIAN [CPX]
HINGHUA alt for PUTIAN dial of CHINESE, PU-XIAN
    [CPX]
HINGHUA alt for XINGHUA dial of CHINESE, PU-
    XIAN [CPX]
HINIHON [HIH] lang, Papua New Guinea
HINNA alt for PIDLIMDI dial of TERA [TER]
HINUKH [GIN] lang, Russia (Europe)
HINUX alt for HINUKH [GIN]
HIOCHUWAU alt for HIETSHWARE [HIE]
HIOTSHUWAU alt for HIETSHWARE [HIE]
HIOWE alt for SANIYO-HIYEWE [SNY]
HIRA dial of YAGARIA [YGR]
HIRACA alt for HIDATSA [HID]
HIRANPUR dial of SAURIA PAHARIA [MJT]
HIRARA alt for MIYAKO-JIMA dial of MIYAKO [MVI]
HIRI alt for MOTU, HIRI [POM]
"HIROI-LAMGANG" pejorative alt for LAMKANG
    [LMK]
HISHKARYANA alt for HIXKARYÁNA [HIX]
HISPANOROMANI alt for CALÓ [RMR]
HISSALA alt for SISAALA, TUMULUNG [SIL]
HISSALA alt for SISAALA, WESTERN [SSL]
HITADIPA NDUGA dial of NDUGA [NDX]
HITAU-POROROAN dial of PETATS [PEX]
HITCHITI alt for MIKASUKI [MIK]
HITCHITI dial of MIKASUKI [MIK]
HITNÜ alt for MACAGUÁN [MBN]
HITU [HIT] lang, Indonesia (Maluku)
HITU dial of HITU [HIT]
HIVA OA dial of MARQUESAN, SOUTH [QMS]
HIW [HIW] lang, Vanuatu
HIWI alt for TABO [KNV]
HIXKARIANA alt for HIXKARYÁNA [HIX]
HIXKARYÁNA [HIX] lang, Brazil
HIYOWE alt for SANIYO-HIYEWE [SNY]

HKA KO alt for AKHA [AKA]
HKA-HKU alt for HKAKU dial of JINGPHO [CGP]
HKAKU dial of JINGPHO [CGP]
HKAKU HKA-HKU dial of JINGPHO [CGP]
HKALUK dial of NAGA, TASE [NST]
HKAMTI alt for KHAMTI [KHT]
HKANUNG alt for RAWANG [RAW]
HKAURI alt for KAURI dial of JINGPHO [CGP]
HKAWA alt for BLANG [BLR]
HKUN alt for KHÜN [KKH]
HLAI [LIC] lang, China
HLANGANU alt for CHANGANA dial of TSONGA
    [TSO]
HLAVE dial of TSONGA [TSO]
HLAWTHAI dial of CHIN, MARA [MRH]
HLENGWE dial of TSHWA [TSC]
HLO'LAN dial of MARU [MHX]
HLOTA alt for NAGA, LOTHA [NJH]
HLUBI dial of SWATI [SWZ]
HM NAI alt for BUNU, WUNAI [BWN]
HMANGGONA alt for NALCA [TVL]
HMAR [HMR] lang, India
HMARI alt for HMAR [HMR]
HMONG DAW [MWW] lang, China; also in France,
    Laos, Thailand, USA, Viet Nam
HMONG GU MBA dial of HMONG DAW [MWW]
HMONG LENG alt for HMONG NJUA [BLU]
HMONG NJUA [BLU] lang, China; also in French
    Guiana, Laos, Myanmar, Thailand, USA, Viet
    Nam
HMONG NJWA alt for HMONG NJUA [BLU]
HMONG QUA MBA alt for HMONG GU MBA dial
    of HMONG DAW [MWW]
HMONG, CENTRAL HUISHUI [HMC] lang, China
HMONG, CENTRAL MASHAN [HMM] lang, China
HMONG, CHONGANJIANG [HMJ] lang, China
HMONG, EASTERN HUISHUI [HME] lang, China
HMONG, EASTERN QIANDONG [HMQ] lang, China
HMONG, EASTERN XIANGXI [MUQ] lang, China
HMONG, LUOPOHE [HML] lang, China
HMONG, NORTHEASTERN DIAN [HMD] lang,
    China
HMONG, NORTHERN GUIYANG [HUJ] lang, China
HMONG, NORTHERN HUISHUI [HMN] lang, China
HMONG, NORTHERN MASHAN [HMO] lang, China
HMONG, NORTHERN QIANDONG [HEA] lang,
    China
HMONG, SOUTHERN GUIYANG [HMY] lang, China
HMONG, SOUTHERN MASHAN [HMA] lang, China
HMONG, SOUTHERN QIANDONG [HMS] lang,
    China
HMONG, SOUTHWESTERN GUIYANG [HMG] lang,
    China
HMONG, SOUTHWESTERN HUISHUI [HMH] lang,
    China
HMONG, WESTERN MASHAN [HMW] lang, China
HMONG, WESTERN XIANGXI [MMR] lang, China
HMONONO alt for NALCA [TVL]
HMU alt for HMONG, EASTERN QIANDONG [HMQ]
HMU alt for HMONG, NORTHERN QIANDONG
    [HEA]

HMU alt for HMONG, SOUTHERN QIANDONG
[HMS]
HMWAEKE alt for VAMALE [MKT]
HMWAEKE dial of VAMALE [MKT]
HMWAVEKE [MRK] lang, New Caledonia
HÑÄHÑO alt for OTOMÍ, NORTHWESTERN [OTQ]
HÑÄHÑU alt for OTOMÍ, MEZQUITAL [OTE]
HÑATHO alt for OTOMÍ, ESTADO DE MÉXICO
[OTS]
HO [HOC] lang, India; also in Bangladesh
HO alt for HONI [HOW]
HO alt for MUSEY [MSE]
HO dial of CHINESE, MANDARIN [CHN]
HO CHI MINH CITY SIGN LANGUAGE [HOS] lang,
Viet Nam
HO KI alt for GREEN GELAO dial of GELAO [KKF]
HO MUONG MERIDIONAL alt for THO [TOU]
HO NTE alt for SHE [SHX]
HOA alt for CHINESE, YUE [YUH]
HOAI PETEL alt for TITA [TDQ]
HOANNYA alt for HOANYA [HON]
HOANYA [HON] lang, Taiwan
HOANYA dial of HOANYA [HON]
HOAVA [HOA] lang, Solomon Islands
HO-BAU alt for HABAU dial of JARAI [JRA]
HOBI alt for HOBYÓT [HOH]
HOBYÓT [HOH] lang, Oman; also in Yemen
HOCAK WAZIJACI alt for HOCÁK [WIN]
HOCÁK [WIN] lang, USA
HOCANK alt for HOCÁK [WIN]
HOCHALEMANNISCH alt for HIGH ALEMANNISCH
dial of ALEMANNISCH [GSW]
HOCHANK alt for HOCÁK [WIN]
HOCHDEUTSCH alt for GERMAN, STANDARD
[GER]
HOCHE alt for ULCH [ULC]
HOCHUNK alt for HOCÁK [WIN]
HOCKCHEW alt for HOKCHIA dial of CHINESE,
MIN BEI [MNP]
HOD alt for OMKOI dial of KAREN, PWO
NORTHERN [PWW]
HODJO alt for WOJO dial of BANDA, WEST
CENTRAL [BBP]
HODRUNG dial of JARAI [JRA]
HOEN alt for NYAHEUN [NEV]
HOFUF alt for CENTRAL NAJDI dial of ARABIC,
NAJDI SPOKEN [ARS]
HOG HARBOUR alt for SAKAO [SKU]
HOGGAR dial of TAMAHAQ, TAHAGGART [THV]
HOGIRANO alt for HOGRANO dial of CHEKE HOLO
[MRN]
HOGO alt for TAROKO [TRV]
HOGRANO dial of CHEKE HOLO [MRN]
HOH dial of QUILEUTE [QUI]
HOHE alt for ASSINIBOINE [ASB]
HOHODENA alt for HOHODENÉ dial of BANIWA
[BAI]
HOHODENÉ dial of BANIWA [BAI]
HOI alt for HAROI [HRO]
HOILLUK alt for HAILU dial of CHINESE, HAKKA
[HAK]

HOILUK alt for HAILU dial of CHINESE, HAKKA
[HAK]
HOISAN alt for SIYI dial of CHINESE, YUE
[YUH]
HOKCHIA dial of CHINESE, MIN BEI [MNP]
HOKING-JIANCHUAN alt for JIANCHUAN dial of
BAI [PIQ]
HOKKA alt for CHINESE, HAKKA [HAK]
HOKKAIDO dial of AINU [AIN]
HOKKIEN alt for FUJIAN dial of CHINESE, MIN
NAN [CFR]
HOKKIEN alt for FUKIENESE dial of CHINESE, MIN
NAN [CFR]
HOKKIEN dial of CHINESE, MIN NAN [CFR]
HOLADI alt for KATHIYAWADI dial of GUJARATI
[GJR]
HOLAR alt for HOLIYA [HOY]
HOLARI alt for HOLIYA [HOY]
HOL-CHIH alt for ULCH [ULC]
HOLE alt for HOLIYA [HOY]
HOLI alt for IJE [IJJ]
HOLIA alt for MAHARI dial of KONKANI [KNK]
HOLIAN alt for HOLIYA [HOY]
HOLIKACHUK [HOI] lang, USA
HOLIYA [HOY] lang, India
HOLLANDS alt for DUTCH [DUT]
HOLLAR GADBAS alt for GADABA, OLLAR,
POTTANGI [GDB]
HOLMA [HOD] lang, Nigeria
HOLMA dial of NZANYI [NJA]
HOLMESTRAND dial of NORWEGIAN SIGN
LANGUAGE [NSL]
HOLO alt for CHEKE HOLO [MRN]
HOLO alt for HOLU [HOL]
HOLOHOLO [HOO] lang, Tanzania; also in DRC
HOLÓLUPAI alt for MAIDU, NORTHWEST [MAI]
HOLOM alt for HWALEM dial of MAJERA [XMJ]
HOLU [HOL] lang, Angola; also in DRC
HOLU alt for HOLIYA [HOY]
HOM alt for GHOMÁLÁ' CENTRAL dial of GHOMALA
[BBJ]
HOMA [HOM] lang, Sudan
HOMBO alt for OMBO [OML]
HOMBO dial of BANGUBANGU [BNX]
HOMBORI SONGHAY alt for SONGHAY, HUMBURI
SENNI [HMB]
HOME dial of DII [DUR]
HONA alt for HWANA [HWO]
HONDURAN MÍSKITO dial of MISKITO [MIQ]
HONDURAN TAWAHKA dial of SUMO TAWAHKA
[SUM]
HONG KONG CANTONESE alt for YUEHAI dial
of CHINESE, YUE [YUH]
HONG YAO alt for NUMAO dial of BUNU, BU-NAO
[BWX]
HONGALLA alt for NGALAKAN [NIG]
HONGSHUIHE dial of ZHUANG, NORTHERN [CCX]
HONI [HOW] lang, China
HONIBO dial of GOBASI [GOI]
HONITETU alt for WEMALE, SOUTH [TLW]
HONO' dial of SEKO PADANG [SKX]

HONPO dial of KRUMEN, TEPO [TED]
HONYA alt for TUPURI [TUI]
HOODE dial of NZANYI [NJA]
HOOPA alt for HUPA [HUP]
HOP alt for MARI [HOB]
HOPA alt for XOPA dial of LAZ [LZZ]
HOPAO dial of NAGA, KONYAK [NBE]
HOPI [HOP] lang, USA
HOPLAND dial of POMO, CENTRAL [POO]
HOR alt for HORO [HOR]
HOR alt for HORPA [ERO]
HOR alt for SANTALI [SNT]
HORA alt for JORÁ [JOR]
HORALE dial of WEMALE, NORTH [WEO]
HORNJOSERBSKI alt for SORBIAN, UPPER [WEN]
HORNOSERBSKI alt for SORBIAN, UPPER [WEN]
HORO [HOR] lang, Chad
HORO alt for MUNDARI [MUW]
HOROHORO alt for HOLOHOLO [HOO]
HOROM [HOE] lang, Nigeria
HORORO dial of NYANKORE [NYN]
HORPA [ERO] lang, China
HORPA alt for HORPA [ERO]
HÓRSÓK alt for HORPA [ERO]
HORU MUTHUN dial of NAGA, WANCHO [NNP]
HORUDAHUA alt for CHITONAHUA dial of
    YAMINAHUA [YAA]
HORUNAHUA alt for CHITONAHUA dial of
    YAMINAHUA [YAA]
HORURU [HRR] lang, Indonesia (Maluku)
HOSHANGABAD dial of MALVI [MUP]
HOSS dial of BEROM [BOM]
HOTAN dial of UYGHUR [UIG]
HOTE [HOT] lang, Papua New Guinea
HOTE dial of HOTE [HOT]
HOTEA alt for SEDANG [SED]
HOTEANG alt for SEDANG [SED]
HOTEC alt for HOTE [HOT]
HO'TEI alt for HOTE [HOT]
HOTI [HTI] lang, Indonesia (Maluku)
HOTI alt for YUWANA [YAU]
HOTON alt for CHINESE, MANDARIN [CHN]
HOTON alt for KHOTON dial of KALMYK-OIRAT
    [KGZ]
"HOTTENTOT" pejorative alt for NAMA [NAQ]
HOUAILOU alt for AJIË [AJI]
HOULOUF dial of MSER [KQX]
HOUNAR alt for BESME [BES]
HOVONGAN [HOV] lang, Indonesia (Kalimantan)
HOVONGAN dial of HOVONGAN [HOV]
HOWI dial of HAMTAI [HMT]
HOZO [HOZ] lang, Ethiopia
HPON [HPO] lang, Myanmar
HPÖN alt for HPON [HPO]
HPUNGSI dial of RAWANG [RAW]
HRANGKHOL [HRA] lang, Myanmar; also in India
HRE [HRE] lang, Viet Nam
HRE dial of HRE [HRE]
HRLAK alt for ALAK [ALK]
HROI alt for HAROI [HRO]
HROY alt for HAROI [HRO]

HRUSO [HRU] lang, India
HRUSO dial of HRUSO [HRU]
HRUSSO alt for HRUSO [HRU]
HRVATSKI alt for CROATIAN [SRC]
HRWAY alt for HAROI [HRO]
HSEMTANG alt for CHIN, SENTHANG [SEZ]
HSEN-HSUM alt for MOK [MQT]
HSIANG alt for CHINESE, XIANG [HSN]
HSIANGHSI MIAO alt for HMONG, EASTERN
    XIANGXI [MUQ]
HSIANGHSI MIAO alt for HMONG, WESTERN
    XIANGXI [MMR]
HSIENYU alt for XIANYOU dial of CHINESE, PU-
    XIAN [CPX]
HSINGHUA alt for PUTIAN dial of CHINESE, PU-
    XIAN [CPX]
HSINGHUA alt for XINGHUA dial of CHINESE,
    MIN DONG [CDO]
HSINGHUA alt for XINGHUA dial of CHINESE, PU-
    XIAN [CPX]
HSIUKULAN AMI alt for CENTRAL AMIS dial of
    AMIS [ALV]
HTIN alt for MAL [MLF]
HT'IN alt for MAL [MLF]
HTISELWANG dial of RAWANG [RAW]
HU [HUO] lang, China
!HU alt for KUNG-EKOKA [KNW]
/HÛ alt for ǂHUA [HUC]
HUA dial of YAGARIA [YGR]
/HUA alt for ǂHUA [HUC]
ǂHUA [HUC] lang, Botswana
ǂHUA dial of HUA [HUC]
HUA LISU dial of LISU [LIS]
HUA MIAO alt for HMONG, NORTHEASTERN DIAN
    [HMD]
HUABEI GUANHUA dial of CHINESE, MANDARIN
    [CHN]
HUACHIPAERI [HUG] lang, Peru
HUACHIPAIRE alt for HUACHIPAERI [HUG]
HUACHIPAIRE dial of HUACHIPAERI [HUG]
HUADOU MIAO alt for GEJIAHUA dial of HMONG,
    CHONGANJIANG [HMJ]
HUAILAS dial of QUECHUA, ANCASH, HUAYLAS
    [QAN]
HUAJUAPAN MIXTECO alt for MIXTECO,
    CACALOXTEPEC [MIU]
HUALAN YAO alt for BUNU, JIONGNAI [PNU]
HUALLAGA alt for COCAMA-COCAMILLA [COD]
HUALNGO alt for LUSHAI [LSH]
HUALO alt for BUGAN [BBH]
HUALPAI alt for WALAPAI dial of HAVASUPAI-
    WALAPAI-YAVAPAI [YUF]
HUAMALÍES dial of QUECHUA, HUANUCO,
    HUAMALIES-NORTHERN DOS DE MAYO
    [QEJ]
HUAMBISA [HUB] lang, Peru
HUAMBIZA alt for HUAMBISA [HUB]
HUAMELULA CHONTAL alt for CHONTAL DE
    OAXACA, COSTA [CLO]
HUAMELULTECO alt for CHONTAL DE OAXACA,
    COSTA [CLO]

HUAMUÊ alt for UAMUÉ [UAM]
HUANA alt for HUNGANA [HUM]
HUANCA HUAYLLA QUECHUA alt for QUECHUA,
  WANCA, HUAYLLA [QHU]
HUANCA JAUJA QUECHUA alt for QUECHUA,
  WANCA, JAUJA [QHJ]
HUANCAVELICA dial of QUECHUA, AYACUCHO
  [QUY]
HUANCAYA-VITIS dial of QUECHUA, YAUYOS
  [QUX]
HUANGÁSCAR alt for AÁZNGARO-
  HUANGÁSCAR-CHOCOS dial of QUECHUA,
  YAUYOS [QUX]
HUAO alt for WAORANI [AUC]
HUAORANI alt for WAORANI [AUC]
ǂHUA-OWANI alt for ǂHUA [HUC]
HUAR dial of AMELE [AMI]
HUARAYO alt for ESE EJJA [ESE]
HUARAZ dial of QUECHUA, ANCASH, HUAYLAS
  [QAN]
HUARIAPANO alt for PANOBO [PNO]
HUARIJÍO [VAR] lang, Mexico
HUASTECA NÁHUATL alt for NÁHUATL,
  HUASTECA, ESTE [NAI]
HUASTECA NÁHUATL alt for NÁHUATL,
  HUASTECO OESTE [NHW]
HUASTECO, SAN FRANCISCO CHONTLA [HAU]
  lang, Mexico
HUASTECO, SAN LUÍS POTOSÍ [HVA] lang,
  Mexico
HUASTECO, TANTOYUCA [HUS] lang, Mexico
HUAULU [HUD] lang, Indonesia (Maluku)
HUAUTLA DE JIMENEZ MAZATECO alt for
  MAZATECO, HUAUTLA [MAU]
HUAVE, SAN DIONISIO DEL MAR [HVE] lang,
  Mexico
HUAVE, SAN FRANCISCO DEL MAR [HUE] lang,
  Mexico
HUAVE, SAN MATEO DEL MAR [HUV] lang, Mexico
HUAVE, SANTA MARÍA DEL MAR [HVV] lang,
  Mexico
HUAXCALECA AZTEC alt for NÁHUATL,
  HUAXCALECA [NHQ]
HUAYCHA alt for WAYCHA dial of QUECHUA,
  WANCA, HUAYLLA [QHU]
HUAYLAS alt for HUAILAS dial of QUECHUA,
  ANCASH, HUAYLAS [QAN]
HUAYU alt for CHINESE, MANDARIN [CHN]
HUAYUAN MIAO alt for HMONG, WESTERN
  XIANGXI [MMR]
HUAZU alt for BUGAN [BBH]
HUBA [KIR] lang, Nigeria
HUBE alt for KUBE [KGF]
HUDE alt for DGHWEDE [DGH]
HUDU dial of EWE [EWE]
HUE alt for CENTRAL VIETNAMESE dial of
  VIETNAMESE [VIE]
HUEHUETENANGO MAM alt for MAM, NORTHERN
  [MAM]
HUEHUETLA OTOMÍ alt for OTOMÍ, SIERRA
  ORIENTAL [OTM]

HUEI alt for OY [OYB]
HUHUNA dial of TAWALA [TBO]
HUI alt for CHINESE, MANDARIN [CHN]
HUI alt for HO dial of CHINESE, MANDARIN [CHN]
HUI alt for TSAT [HUQ]
HUICHOL [HCH] lang, Mexico
HUIHUI alt for TSAT [HUQ]
HUILA alt for MWILA dial of NYANEKA [NYK]
HUILICHE alt for HUILLICHE [HUH]
HUILLICHE [HUH] lang, Chile
HUIMEN dial of MIWOK, COAST [CSI]
HUITEPEC MIXTEC alt for MIXTECO, HUITEPEC
  [MXS]
HUITOTO, MɨNɨCA [HTO] lang, Colombia; also in
  Peru
HUITOTO, MURUI [HUU] lang, Peru; also in
  Colombia
HUITOTO, NɨPODE [HUX] lang, Peru
HUI-TZE alt for HO dial of CHINESE, MANDARIN
  [CHN]
HUIXTÁN dial of TZOTZIL, HUIXTAN [TZU]
HUIXTECO alt for TZOTZIL, HUIXTÁN [TZU]
HUIZAPULA alt for MALINALTEPEC dial of
  TLAPANECO, MALINALTEPEC [TLL]
HUIZHOU alt for CHINESE, HUIZHOU [CZH]
HUIZHOU dial of CHINESE, HAKKA [HAK]
HUI-ZU alt for CHINESE, MANDARIN [CHN]
HUIZU alt for DUNGAN [DNG]
HUKU alt for NYALI [NLJ]
HUKUMINA [HUW] lang, Indonesia (Maluku)
!HUKWE alt for KXOE [XUU]
HUKWE alt for KXOE [XUU]
HULA [HUL] lang, Papua New Guinea
HULA HULA alt for HULAULÁ [HUY]
HULALIU dial of HARUKU [HRK]
HULANI alt for LISHANID NOSHAN [AIJ]
HULAULÁ [HUY] lang, Israel; also in Iran, USA
HULA'ULA alt for LISHANID NOSHAN [AIJ]
HULI [HUI] lang, Papua New Guinea
HULI dial of FALI [FLI]
HULI-HULIDANA alt for HULI [HUI]
HULO alt for MENDE [MFY]
HULON alt for ELUN dial of BANDIAL [BQJ]
HULONTALO alt for GORONTALO [GRL]
HULU alt for BAMBANG dial of BAMBAM [PTU]
HULU dial of BANJAR [BJN]
HULUF dial of JOLA-KASA [CSK]
HULUNG [HUK] lang, Indonesia (Maluku)
HUMAI alt for PALAUNG, RUMAI [RBB]
HUMBA alt for KAMBERA [SMI]
HUMBA alt for KWANYAMA [KUY]
HUMBE alt for LILIMA dial of KALANGA [KCK]
HUMBE alt for NKHUMBI [KHU]
HUMBE dial of NYANEKA [NYK]
HUMBOLDT JOTAFA alt for TOBATI [TTI]
HUMBU dial of LUNDA [LVN]
HUMENE [HUF] lang, Papua New Guinea
HUMENE dial of HUMENE [HUF]
HUMLA BHOTIA [HUT] lang, Nepal
HUMONO alt for KOHUMONO [BCS]
HUMU alt for AMBA [RWM]

HUMURANA alt for OMURANO [OMU]
HUN alt for EASTERN DUKA dial of HUN-SAARE [DUD]
HUN alt for NYAHEUN [NEV]
HUNAN alt for CHINESE, XIANG [HSN]
HUNANESE alt for CHINESE, XIANG [HSN]
HUNDE [HKE] lang, DRC
HUNE alt for EASTERN DUKA dial of HUN-SAARE [DUD]
HUNER alt for BESME [BES]
HUNG [HNU] lang, Laos; also in Viet Nam
HUNGAAN alt for HUNGANA [HUM]
HUNGANA [HUM] lang, DRC
HUNGANNA alt for HUNGANA [HUM]
HUNGARIAN [HNG] lang, Hungary; also in Australia, Austria, Canada, Israel, Romania, Slovakia, Slovenia, Ukraine, USA, Yugoslavia
HUNGARIAN SIGN LANGUAGE [HSH] lang, Hungary
HUNGARIAN-SLOVAK ROMANI alt for ROMANI, CARPATHIAN [RMC]
HUNGDUAN IFUGAO dial of IFUGAO, TUWALI [IFK]
HUNGWE dial of MANYIKA [MXC]
HUNGWORO [NAT] lang, Nigeria
HUNJARA dial of OROKAIVA [ORK]
HUN-SAARE [DUD] lang, Nigeria
HUNZA dial of BURUSHASKI [BSK]
HUNZA-NAGAR alt for GILGITI dial of SHINA [SCL]
HUNZIB [HUZ] lang, Russia (Europe)
HUO NTE alt for SHE [SHX]
HUPA [HUP] lang, USA
"HUPDÁ MAKÚ" pejorative alt for HUPDË [JUP]
HUPDË [JUP] lang, Brazil; also in Colombia
HUPDË dial of HUPDE [JUP]
HUPLA [HAP] lang, Indonesia (Irian Jaya)
HURI alt for HULI [HUI]
HURON dial of WYANDOT [WYA]
HURUTSHE dial of TSWANA [TSW]
HURZA dial of PELASLA [MLR]
HURZO alt for HURZA dial of PELASLA [MLR]
HUTTERIAN GERMAN alt for GERMAN, HUTTERITE [GEH]
HUTU dial of RWANDA [RUA]
HUUTI dial of BALOCHI, SOUTHERN [BCC]
HUVA alt for HUA dial of YAGARIA [YGR]
HUVE alt for BURA-PABIR [BUR]
HUVIYA alt for BURA-PABIR [BUR]
HUZHU dial of TU [MJG]
HWA dial of MAK [MKG]
HWA LISU dial of LISU [LIS]
HWA MIAO alt for HMONG, NORTHEASTERN DIAN [HMD]
HWALEM dial of MAJERA [XMJ]
HWANA [HWO] lang, Nigeria
HWANE alt for WANÉ [HWA]
HWANGHAEDO dial of KOREAN [KKN]
HWARASA dial of AGAW, WESTERN [QIM]
HWASO alt for KPAN [KPK]
HWAYE alt for KPAN [KPK]
HWE alt for HWÈGBÈ dial of AJA-GBE [AJG]

HWÈ alt for AJA-GBE [AJG]
HWEDA alt for HWÈGBÈ dial of AJA-GBE [AJG]
HWÈGBÈ dial of AJA-GBE [AJG]
HWEI alt for HO dial of CHINESE, MANDARIN [CHN]
HWELA dial of LIGBI [LIG]
HWEN GBA KON dial of BASSA [BAS]
HWETHOM dial of PHUNOI [PHO]
HWINDJA dial of SHI [SHR]
HWLA [HWL] lang, Togo
HWONA alt for HWANA [HWO]
HYA [HYA] lang, Cameroon
HYABE alt for KAKANDA [KKA]
HYAMHUM alt for HAM [JAB]
HYAO alt for YAO [YAO]
HYIL HAWUL dial of BURA-PABIR [BUR]
HYTAD alt for CHINESE, MANDARIN [CHN]
I alt for YI, SICHUAN [III]
I alt for YI, YUNNAN [NOS]
I TO alt for LACHI [LBT]
IAAI [IAI] lang, New Caledonia
IACA alt for YAKA [YAF]
IAI alt for IAAI [IAI]
IAI alt for PURARI [IAR]
IAI dial of PURARI [IAR]
IAIBU dial of MULAHA [MFW]
IAKA alt for YAKA [YAF]
IAMALELE [YML] lang, Papua New Guinea
IAMBI dial of NILAMBA [NIM]
IAMEGA dial of GIDRA [GDR]
IAO HOA alt for BUNU, BAHENG [PHA]
IAPAMA [IAP] lang, Brazil
IATÊ alt for FULNIÔ [FUN]
IATMUL [IAN] lang, Papua New Guinea
IAU [TMU] lang, Indonesia (Irian Jaya)
IAU alt for YAWA [YVA]
IAU dial of IAU [TMU]
IAUANAUÁ alt for YAWANAWA [YWN]
IAUGA dial of NAMBU [NCM]
IAUIAULA dial of DIODIO [DDI]
IAW alt for IAU [TMU]
IAZGULEM alt for YAZGULYAM [YAH]
IBA alt for LAIWONU dial of PAMONA [BCX]
IBAA dial of IKWERE [IKW]
IBAALI alt for BALI [BCN]
IBADJO alt for IWAIDJA [IBD]
IBADOY alt for IBALOI [IBL]
IBAGYI alt for GBAGYI [GBR]
IBAJI dial of IGALA [IGL]
IBALAO dial of ILONGOT [ILK]
IBALI alt for TEKE, EASTERN [TEK]
IBALOI [IBL] lang, Philippines
IBALOY alt for IBALOI [IBL]
IBAMI alt for AGOI [IBM]
IBAN [IBA] lang, Malaysia (Sarawak); also in Brunei, Indonesia (Kalimantan)
IBANAG [IBG] lang, Philippines
IBANDA dial of LEGA-MWENGA [LGM]
IBANGA dial of LAMOGAI [LMG]
IBANI [IBY] lang, Nigeria
IBARA alt for EBIRA [IGB]
IBARAM dial of AKPES [IBE]

IBARAM-EFIFA alt for AKPES [IBE]
IBATAAN alt for IBATAN [IVB]
IBATAN [IVB] lang, Philippines
IBEEKE alt for BEEKE [BKF]
IBEMBE alt for BEMBE [BMB]
IBENO alt for IBINO [IBN]
IBERIAN ROMANI alt for CALÓ [RMR]
IBETO alt for TSUVADI [TVD]
IBETO dial of TSISHINGINI [KAM]
IBHUBHI alt for BUBI [BUW]
IBIBIO [IBB] lang, Nigeria
IBIE NORTH alt for IVBIE NORTH dial of IVBIE
    NORTH-OKPELA-ARHE [ATG]
IBIEDE dial of ISOKO [ISO]
IBILAO alt for IBALAO dial of ILONGOT [ILK]
IBILO [IBO] lang, Nigeria
IBINO [IBN] lang, Nigeria
IBITO alt for HIBITO [HIB]
IBO alt for IGBO [IGR]
IBO alt for MWANI [WMW]
IBO UGU alt for IMBONGU [IMO]
IBOHO alt for TAROKO [TRV]
IBOKO alt for BOKO [BKP]
IBOT OBOLO dial of OBOLO [ANN]
IBO'TSA dial of OCAINA [OCA]
IBU [IBU] lang, Indonesia (Maluku)
IBUBI alt for BUBI [BUW]
IBUKAIRU alt for SESA dial of FOLOPA [PPO]
IBUKWO alt for KPAN [KPK]
IBUNO alt for IBINO [IBN]
IBUNU alt for RIBINA dial of JERE [JER]
IBUORO [IBR] lang, Nigeria
IBUT alt for BU [JID]
IBUYA alt for BUYA [BYY]
IBWISI alt for BWISI [BWZ]
ICA [ARH] lang, Colombia
ICA [ICA] lang, Benin; also in Togo
ICAANGI alt for TSAANGI [TSA]
ICAANGUI alt for TSAANGI [TSA]
ICAICHE MAYA alt for ITZÁ [ITZ]
ICELANDIC [ICE] lang, Iceland; also in Canada, USA
ICELANDIC SIGN LANGUAGE [ICL] lang, Iceland
ICEN alt for ETKYWAN [ICH]
ICEVE-MACI [BEC] lang, Cameroon; also in Nigeria
ICHEN alt for ETKYWAN [ICH]
ICHEVE alt for ICEVE-MACI [BEC]
ICHEVE dial of ICEVE-MACI [BEC]
ICHIBEMBA alt for BEMBA [BEM]
ICHIBISA alt for BISA dial of LALA-BISA [LEB]
ICHIFIPA alt for FIPA [FIP]
ICHILALA alt for LALA dial of LALA-BISA [LEB]
ICHILAMBA alt for LAMBA [LAB]
ICHILAMBYA alt for LAMBYA [LAI]
ICHIMAMBWE alt for MAMBWE dial of MAMBWE-
    LUNGU [MGR]
ICHINAMWANGA alt for MWANGA [MWN]
ICHIPIMBWE alt for PIMBWE [PIW]
ICHIRA alt for SIRA [SWJ]
ICHIRUNGU alt for RUNGU dial of MAMBWE-
    LUNGU [MGR]
ICHIRUNGWA alt for RUNGWA [RNW]

ICHITAABWA alt for TAABWA [TAP]
ICHIWANDA alt for WANDA [WBH]
ICIETOT alt for IK [IKX]
IDA alt for IDU [CLK]
IDAACA alt for IDACA [IDD]
IDAAN alt for IDA'AN [DBJ]
IDA'AN [DBJ] lang, Malaysia (Sabah)
IDA'AN dial of IDAAN [DBJ]
IDACA [IDD] lang, Benin
IDAFAN alt for IRIGWE [IRI]
IDAH dial of IGALA [IGL]
IDAHAN alt for IDA'AN [DBJ]
IDAKAMENAI dial of IDUNA [VIV]
IDAKHO dial of IDAKHO-ISUKHA-TIRIKI [IDA]
IDAKHO-ISUKHA-TIRIKI [IDA] lang, Kenya
IDAN alt for IDA'AN [DBJ]
IDATÉ [IDT] lang, Timor Lorosae
IDAXO alt for IDAKHO dial of IDAKHO-ISUKHA-
    TIRIKI [IDA]
IDAYAN alt for IDA'AN [DBJ]
IDE alt for MACUNA [MYY]
IDELE alt for MODELE dial of BEFANG [BBY]
IDERE [IDE] lang, Nigeria
IDESA dial of OKPE-IDESA-AKUKU [OKP]
IDI [IDI] lang, Papua New Guinea
IDI dial of IDI [IDI]
IDIN IDINDJI alt for YIDINY [YII]
IDINJI alt for YIDINY [YII]
IDIN-WUDJAR alt for YIDINY [YII]
IDIOMA DE SENAS DE NICARAGUA alt for
    NICARAGUAN SIGN LANGUAGE [NCS]
IDNE alt for MALEU-KILENGE [MGL]
IDO alt for SINOHOAN dial of PAMONA [BCX]
IDO alt for UDO dial of ARIGIDI [AKK]
IDOANI alt for IYAYU [IYA]
IDOMA [IDO] lang, Nigeria
IDOMA CENTRAL dial of IDOMA [IDO]
IDOMA NOKWU alt for ALAGO [ALA]
IDOMA SOUTH dial of IDOMA [IDO]
IDOMA WEST dial of IDOMA [IDO]
IDON [IDC] lang, Nigeria
IDONG alt for IDON [IDC]
IDONGIRO alt for NYANGATOM [NNJ]
IDORE'E alt for SINOHOAN dial of PAMONA [BCX]
IDU [CLK] lang, India; also in China
IDU MISHMI alt for LUOBA, YIDU [CLK]
IDUA alt for ILUE [ILE]
IDUH alt for O'DU [TYH]
'IDUH alt for O'DU [TYH]
IDUM dial of MBE [MFO]
IDUN [LDB] lang, Nigeria
IDUNA [VIV] lang, Papua New Guinea
IDUWINI dial of IZON [IJC]
IFANE alt for EHIJA dial of OROKAIVA [ORK]
IFA'ONGOTA alt for BIRALE [BXE]
IFE dial of IGALA [IGL]
IFÈ [IFE] lang, Benin; also in Togo
IFIGI dial of FOI [FOI]
IFIRA alt for FILA dial of MELE-FILA [MXE]
IFO [IFF] lang, Vanuatu
IFUGAO, AMGANAD [IFA] lang, Philippines

IFUGAO, BATAD [IFB] lang, Philippines
IFUGAO, MAYOYAO [IFU] lang, Philippines
IFUGAO, TUWALI [IFK] lang, Philippines
IFUNA dial of NYANGA [NYA]
IFUNUBWA alt for MBEMBE, CROSS RIVER [MFN]
IFUUMU alt for FUUMU dial of TEKE, SOUTH
   CENTRAL [IFM]
"IGABO" pejorative alt for ISOKO [ISO]
IGALA [IGL] lang, Nigeria
IGAN dial of MELANAU [MEL]
IGANA [IGG] lang, Papua New Guinea
IGARA alt for IGALA [IGL]
IGARA dial of EBIRA [IGB]
ÌGÀSHÍ alt for IGASI dial of ARIGIDI [AKK]
IGASI dial of ARIGIDI [AKK]
IGBARRA alt for EBIRA [IGB]
IGBIDE alt for IWIRE dial of ISOKO [ISO]
IGBIRA alt for EBIRA [IGB]
IGBIRI alt for GBIRI dial of GBIRI-NIRAGU [GRH]
IGBIRRA alt for EBIRA [IGB]
IGBO [IGR] lang, Nigeria
IGBO alt for LEGBO [AGB]
IGBONNA dial of YORUBA [YOR]
IGBUDUYA dial of EKPEYE [EKP]
IGBURU-USOMINI dial of OGBAH [OGC]
IGEDDE alt for IGEDE [IGE]
IGEDE [IGE] lang, Nigeria
IGEMBE dial of MERU [MER]
IGIKIGA dial of RWANDA [RUA]
IGIKURIA alt for KURIA [KUJ]
IGNACIANO [IGN] lang, Bolivia
IGO [AHL] lang, Togo
IGODOR alt for IBALOI [IBL]
IGOJI dial of MERU [MER]
IGOM [IGM] lang, Papua New Guinea
IGONZABALE alt for LEGA-SHABUNDA [LEA]
IGORA alt for KAKABAI [KQF]
IGOROT alt for BONTOC, CENTRAL [BNC]
IGU alt for KOTO dial of EBIRA [IGB]
IGUAMBO dial of MUNDANI [MUN]
IGUEBEN dial of ESAN [ISH]
IGUMALE alt for IDOMA SOUTH dial of IDOMA
   [IDO]
IGUMBO alt for IGUAMBO dial of MUNDANI [MUN]
IGUTA [NAR] lang, Nigeria
IGWAALE alt for IDOMA SOUTH dial of IDOMA
   [IDO]
IGWE dial of SASARU-ENWAN-IGWE [SSC]
IGWURUTA dial of IKWERE [IKW]
IGYANG dial of TAROK [YER]
IGZENNAIAN dial of TARIFIT [RIF]
IHA [IHP] lang, Indonesia (Irian Jaya)
IHA BASED PIDGIN [IHB] lang, Indonesia (Irian
   Jaya)
I-HADJA alt for KASANGA [CCJ]
IHANE alt for EHIJA dial of OROKAIVA [ORK]
IHA-SAPARUA dial of SAPARUA [SPR]
IHA-SERAM dial of SAPARUA [SPR]
IHATUM alt for OSATU [OST]
IHEKWOT alt for OLITI dial of ICEVE-MACI [BEC]
IHIMA alt for OKENE dial of EBIRA [IGB]

IHINI alt for BARÉ [BAE]
IHINI alt for MANDAHUACA [MHT]
IHOBE MBOG alt for BABONG dial of BAKAKA
   [BQZ]
IHOBE MBOONG alt for BABONG dial of BAKAKA
   [BQZ]
IHURUANA dial of MAQUIRITARI [MCH]
IILIIT alt for ILIT dial of KUNAMA [KUM]
IILIT alt for ILIT dial of KUNAMA [KUM]
IIMUTSU dial of TSOU [TSY]
IJA dial of KAILI, LEDO [LEW]
IJAW alt for IJO, SOUTHEAST [IJO]
IJAW alt for IZON [IJC]
IJCA alt for ICA [ARH]
IJE [IJJ] lang, Benin
IJEBU dial of YORUBA [YOR]
IJESHA dial of YORUBA [YOR]
IJIEGU dial of YACE [EKR]
IJIGBAM alt for IDOMA SOUTH dial of IDOMA [IDO]
IJKA alt for ICA [ARH]
IJO alt for IZON [IJC]
IJO, SOUTHEAST [IJO] lang, Nigeria
IJOH dial of KENSIU [KNS]
IJOK alt for IJOH dial of KENSIU [KNS]
IK [IKX] lang, Uganda
IKA [IKK] lang, Nigeria
IKA alt for ICA [ARH]
IKA alt for KOTO dial of EBIRA [IGB]
IKAIKU alt for KAIKU [KKQ]
IKALAHAN alt for KALLAHAN, KAYAPA [KAK]
IKALANGA dial of KALANGA [KCK]
IKALE dial of YORUBA [YOR]
IKALEBWE alt for EASTERN KALEBWE dial of
   SONGE [SOP]
IKAN alt for UKAAN [KCF]
IKAW alt for AKHA [AKA]
IKE alt for ICA [ARH]
IKEGA dial of SINAUGORO [SNC]
IKELA alt for KELA [KEL]
IKELEVE dial of KITUBA [KTU]
IKIBIRI dial of IZON [IJC]
IKIBUNGU alt for KIMBU [KIV]
IKIHA alt for HA [HAQ]
IKIKURIA alt for KURIA [KUJ]
IKINATA alt for IKOMA [NTK]
IKINGONDE alt for NYAKYUSA-NGONDE [NYY]
IKINGURIMI alt for NGURIMI [NGQ]
IKINILAMBA alt for NILAMBA [NIM]
IKINIRAMBA alt for NILAMBA [NIM]
IKINYAKYUSA alt for NYAKYUSA-NGONDE [NYY]
IKINYARWANDA alt for RWANDA [RUA]
IKINYIKYUSA alt for NYAKYUSA-NGONDE [NYY]
IKIRIBATI alt for KIRIBATI [GLB]
IKIRUGURU alt for RUGURU [RUF]
IKISENYI alt for ISSENYI dial of IKOMA [NTK]
IKITO alt for IQUITO [IQU]
IKIZANAKI alt for ZANAKI [ZAK]
IKIZU [IKZ] lang, Tanzania
IKO [IKI] lang, Nigeria
IKO alt for DOKO-UYANGA [UYA]
IKO dial of AGOI [IBM]

IKÓ alt for LIKÓ dial of LIKA [LIK]
IKOBI KAIRI alt for IKOBI-MENA [MEB]
IKOBI-MENA [MEB] lang, Papua New Guinea
IKOKOLEMU alt for KUMAM [KDI]
IKOLU alt for IKULU [IKU]
IKOLU dial of SINAUGORO [SNC]
IKOM dial of OLULUMO-IKOM [IKO]
IKOMA [NTK] lang, Tanzania
IKOR alt for AKHA [AKA]
IKOROM dial of AKPES [IBE]
IKOT EKPENE dial of ANAANG [ANW]
IKOTA alt for KOTA [KOQ]
IKPAN alt for KPAN [KPK]
IKPESHE alt for IKPESHI [IKP]
IKPESHI [IKP] lang, Nigeria
IKPONU dial of AKPOSO [KPO]
IKPOSO alt for AKPOSO [KPO]
IKU alt for IKU-GORA-ANKWA [IKV]
IKU alt for MODELE dial of BEFANG [BBY]
IKU-GORA-ANKWA [IKV] lang, Nigeria
IKULU [IKU] lang, Nigeria
IKUMAMA alt for KUMAM [KDI]
IKUMAMA alt for TESO [TEO]
IKUMBURE dial of NYANGA [NYA]
IKUMTALE dial of MBE [MFO]
IKUN dial of UBAGHARA [BYC]
IKUNDUN alt for ANAMGURA [IMI]
IKUTA alt for KOTA [KOQ]
IKWERE [IKW] lang, Nigeria
IKWERI dial of NGWO [NGN]
IKWERRE alt for IKWERE [IKW]
IKWERRI alt for IKWERE [IKW]
IKWO dial of IZI-EZAA-IKWO-MGBO [IZI]
IKYOO dial of LENAKEL [TNL]
ILA [ILB] lang, Zambia
ILA dial of ILA [ILB]
ILA dial of YORUBA [YOR]
ILAALI alt for LAALI dial of TEKE, WESTERN
   [TEZ]
ILAGA WESTERN DANI alt for DANI, WESTERN
   [DNW]
ILAHITA alt for FILIFITA dial of MUFIAN [AOJ]
ILAI dial of MAILU [MGU]
ILAJE dial of YORUBA [YOR]
ILAKIA dial of AWA [AWB]
ILAMBA alt for NILAMBA [NIM]
ILAMMU dial of LEPCHA [LEP]
ILANON alt for IRANUN dial of MAGINDANAON
   [MDH]
ILANUM alt for IRANUN dial of MAGINDANAON
   [MDH]
ILANUN [ILL] lang, Malaysia (Sabah)
ILAO alt for GELAO [KKF]
IL-ARUSHA alt for ARUSHA dial of MAASAI [MET]
ILCAMUS alt for CHAMUS dial of SAMBURU [SAQ]
ILE APE [ILA] lang, Indonesia (Nusa Tenggara)
ILE MANDIRI alt for LAMAHOLOT dial of
   LAMAHOLOT [SLP]
ILEKA ISHILE alt for LEGA-MWENGA [LGM]
ILEKA-IGONZABALE alt for LEGA-SHABUNDA
   [LEA]

ILEME alt for UNEME [UNE]
ILENTUNGEN dial of MANOBO, WESTERN
   BUKIDNON [MBB]
ILEO alt for DENGESE [DEZ]
ILI TURKI [ILI] lang, China; also in Kazakhstan
ILIANEN alt for MANOBO, ILIANEN [MBI]
ILIAURA alt for ALYAWARR [ALY]
ILIIT alt for ILIT dial of KUNAMA [KUM]
ILIKU dial of LUSENGO [LUS]
ILIMPEYA dial of EVENKI [EVN]
ILIT dial of KUNAMA [KUM]
ILIUN [ILU] lang, Indonesia (Maluku)
ILIWAKI alt for TALUR [ILW]
ILLANOAN alt for ILANUN [ILL]
ILLANON alt for IRANUN dial of MAGINDANAON
   [MDH]
ILLANOON alt for ILANUN [ILL]
ILLANOS alt for ILANUN [ILL]
ILLANUN alt for ILANUN [ILL]
ILLO dial of BUSA [BQP]
ILMAUMAU alt for ILIUN [ILU]
ILMEDU alt for TALUR [ILW]
ILOCANO [ILO] lang, Philippines; also in USA
ILOKANO alt for ILOCANO [ILO]
ILOKO alt for ILOCANO [ILO]
ILOM dial of IXIL, CHAJUL [IXJ]
ILOMWE alt for LOMWE [NGL]
ILONGGO alt for HILIGAYNON [HIL]
ILONGOT [ILK] lang, Philippines
ILOODOKILANI dial of MAASAI [MET]
ILPARA alt for WARLPIRI [WBP]
ILPUTIH alt for APUTAI [APX]
ILQAN alt for EVEN [EVE]
ILUD dial of MAGINDANAON [MDH]
ILUE [ILE] lang, Nigeria
ILUMBU alt for LUMBU [LUP]
ILWAKI alt for TALUR [ILW]
ILWANA alt for MALAKOTE [MLK]
IMABAN alt for LEGBO [AGB]
IMAFIN dial of TANNA, NORTH [TNN]
IMAKUA alt for MAKHUWA-MEETTO [MAK]
IMAN dial of UDIHE [UDE]
IMANDI alt for MANDI [TUA]
IMASI alt for SOBEI [SOB]
IMBANA dial of MUNDANG [MUA]
IMBAO'O alt for ANDIO [BZB]
IMBARA alt for IMBANA dial of MUNDANG [MUA]
IMBATSKI-KET alt for KET [KET]
IMBINIS alt for EASTERN PAGI dial of PAGI [PGI]
IMBO alt for MBO [ZMW]
IMBO UNGO alt for IMBONGU [IMO]
IMBO UNGU alt for IMBONGU [IMO]
IMBONGGO alt for IMBONGU [IMO]
IMBONGU [IMO] lang, Papua New Guinea
IMEETTO alt for MEETTO dial of MAKHUWA-
   MEETTO [MAK]
IMENTI dial of MERU [MER]
IMERAGUEN [IME] lang, Mauritania
IMERETIAN dial of GEORGIAN [GEO]
IMERXEV dial of GEORGIAN [GEO]
IMERXEV KARTLIAN dial of GEORGIAN [GEO]

IMILA dial of MARIA [MDS]
IMILANGU alt for MDUNDULU dial of LUYANA [LAV]
IMILANGU dial of SIMAA [SIE]
IMIV dial of ISOKO [ISO]
IMO alt for CHOKWE [CJK]
IMONA dial of NTOMBA [NTO]
IMONDA [IMN] lang, Papua New Guinea
IMRAGUEN alt for IMERAGUEN [IME]
IMROIN alt for IMROING [IMR]
IMROING [IMR] lang, Indonesia (Maluku)
IMYAN dial of TEHIT [KPS]
IN alt for IR [IRR]
INABAKNON alt for SAMA, ABAKNON [ABX]
INAFOSA alt for TAUYA [TYA]
INAGTA OF MT. IRAYA alt for AGTA, MT. IRAYA [ATL]
INAKONA alt for KOO dial of TALISE [TLR]
INALLU alt for AYNALLU dial of AZERBAIJANI, SOUTH [AZB]
INAMARI alt for IÑAPARI [INA]
INAMWANGA alt for MWANGA [MWN]
INANLU alt for AYNALLU dial of AZERBAIJANI, SOUTH [AZB]
INANWATAN alt for SUABO [SZP]
INAPANG [MZU] lang, Papua New Guinea
IÑAPARI [INA] lang, Peru
INAQUEN alt for TEHUELCHE [TEH]
INARI "LAPPISH" pejorative alt for SAAMI, INARI [LPI]
INARU alt for BAHINEMO [BJH]
INATI alt for ATI [ATK]
INAUINI dial of DENI [DAN]
INBAKNON alt for SAMA, ABAKNON [ABX]
INCAHUASI dial of QUECHUA, LAMBAYEQUE [QUF]
INCHAZI alt for CHE [RUK]
INDAAKA alt for NDAKA [NDK]
INDE dial of KAILI, DAA [KZF]
INDENIE dial of ANYIN [ANY]
INDI dial of PENGO [PEG]
INDI AYTA alt for AYTA, MAG-INDI [BLX]
INDIAN SIGN LANGUAGE [INS] lang, India; also in Bangladesh, Pakistan
INDIGIRKA dial of EVEN [EVE]
INDINDJI alt for YIDINY [YII]
INDINOGOSIMA alt for MEHEK [NUX]
INDO-GUYANESE CREOLE dial of GUYANESE CREOLE ENGLISH [GYN]
INDONESIAN [INZ] lang, Indonesia (Java and Bali); also in Netherlands, Philippines, Saudi Arabia, Singapore, USA
INDONESIAN SIGN LANGUAGE [INL] lang, Indonesia (Java and Bali)
INDONESIAN, PERANAKAN [PEA] lang, Indonesia (Java and Bali)
INDO-PORTUGUESE [IDB] lang, Sri Lanka; also in Australia, India
INDORODORO alt for BLAFE [IND]
INDRAMAYU dial of JAVANESE [JAN]
INDRI [IDR] lang, Sudan
INDUS dial of KOHISTANI, INDUS [MVY]

INEDUA dial of ENGENNI [ENN]
INEME alt for UNEME [UNE]
INESEÑO [INE] lang, USA
INETA dial of BUDU [BUU]
INGA [INB] lang, Colombia; also in Venezuela
INGA alt for QUECHUA, PASTAZA, SOUTHERN [QUP]
INGA, JUNGLE [INJ] lang, Colombia
"INGALIK" pejorative alt for DEGEXIT'AN [ING]
"INGALIT" pejorative alt for DEGEXIT'AN [ING]
INGANO alt for INGA, JUNGLE [INJ]
INGANO alt for QUICHUA, LOWLAND, NAPO [QLN]
INGARA alt for YINGGARDA [YIA]
INGARDA alt for YINGGARDA [YIA]
INGARICÓ alt for PEMON [AOC]
INGARIKO alt for PATAMONA [PBC]
INGARIKÓ alt for AKAWAIO [ARB]
INGARIKÓ alt for PEMON [AOC]
INGARRA alt for YINGGARDA [YIA]
INGARRAH alt for YINGGARDA [YIA]
INGASSANA alt for GAAM [TBI]
INGELSHI alt for TASAWAQ [TWQ]
INGESSANA alt for GAAM [TBI]
INGGARDA alt for YINGGARDA [YIA]
INGILO dial of GEORGIAN [GEO]
/ING/KE alt for //NG!KE dial of NU [NGH]
INGLI alt for MABA [MQA]
INGRIAN [IZH] lang, Russia (Europe)
INGUL alt for NGUL [NLO]
INGULU alt for LOMWE [NGL]
INGUNDI alt for NGUNDI [NDN]
INGUNDJI alt for LIPOTO dial of LUSENGO [LUS]
INGURA alt for ANINDILYAKWA [AOI]
INGUS alt for INGUSH [INH]
INGUSH [INH] lang, Russia (Europe); also in Uzbekistan
INGWE alt for HUNGWORO [NAT]
INGWO alt for HUNGWORO [NAT]
INHAMBANE alt for GITONGA [TOH]
INIAI alt for BISORIO [BIR]
INIAI alt for NETE [NET]
INIBALOI alt for IBALOI [IBL]
INIDEM alt for NINDEM dial of KANINGDON-NINDEM [KDP]
INISINE alt for BIKSI [BDX]
INJA dial of MBOLE [MDQ]
INJANG alt for NAGA, RENGMA [NRE]
INJEBI alt for NJEBI [NZB]
INKONGO alt for LUNA [LUJ]
INLAND DOBEL dial of DOBEL [KVO]
INLAND EAST CREE alt for CREE, SOUTHERN EAST [CRE]
INLAND PWO EASTERN KAREN alt for PA'AN dial of KAREN, PWO EASTERN [KJP]
INLOM alt for YALE, KOSAREK [KKL]
INMEAS alt for ISINAI [INN]
INN TEA dial of OY [OYB]
INNEQOR alt for ENNEQOR dial of GURAGE, EAST [GRE]
INNER MONGOLIAN alt for MONGOLIAN, PERIPHERAL [MVF]

INNER SERAJI alt for INNER SIRAGI dial of PAHARI, KULLU [KFX]
INNER SIRAGI dial of PAHARI, KULLU [KFX]
INNTHA alt for INTHA [INT]
INNU alt for EASTERN NASKAPI dial of NASKAPI [NSK]
INNU alt for MONTAGNAIS [MOE]
INNU AIMUN alt for MONTAGNAIS [MOE]
INNU AIMUUN alt for NASKAPI [NSK]
INOKE alt for INOKE-YATE [INO]
INOKE-YATE [INO] lang, Papua New Guinea
INONHAN [LOC] lang, Philippines
INOR dial of GURAGE, WEST [GUY]
INPARRA alt for YINGGARDA [YIA]
INSANAO alt for BIBOKI-INSANA dial of ATONI [TMR]
INSINAI alt for ISINAI [INN]
INSULAR CATALAN alt for BALEARIC dial of CATALAN-VALENCIAN-BALEAR [CLN]
INTERIOR MAKWE dial of MAKWE [YMK]
INTERIOR SALUAN alt for SALUAN, KAHUMAMAHON [SLB]
INTERLINGUA [INR] lang, France
INTERLINGUA DE IALA alt for INTERLINGUA [INR]
INTHA [INT] lang, Myanmar
INUIT alt for INUKTITUT, EASTERN CANADIAN [ESB]
INUKTITUT, EASTERN CANADIAN [ESB] lang, Canada
INUKTITUT, GREENLANDIC [ESG] lang, Greenland; also in Denmark
INUKTITUT, WESTERN CANADIAN [ESC] lang, Canada
INUPIAQ alt for INUPIATUN, NORTH ALASKAN [ESI]
INUPIAT alt for INUPIATUN, NORTH ALASKAN [ESI]
INUPIATUN alt for INUPIATUN, NORTHWEST ALASKA [ESK]
INUPIATUN, NORTH ALASKAN [ESI] lang, USA; also in Canada
INUPIATUN, NORTHWEST ALASKA [ESK] lang, USA
INUVAKEN dial of AMAHUACA [AMC]
INXOKVARI dial of KHVARSHI [KHV]
INYAI-GADIO-BISORIO alt for BISORIO [BIR]
INYANGA alt for NYANGA [NYA]
INYANGA dial of NYANGA [NYA]
INYANGATOM alt for NYANGATOM [NNJ]
INYIMA alt for LENYIMA [LDG]
INYIMANG alt for AMA [NYI]
INYVEN alt for SOUTH PERMYAK dial of KOMI-PERMYAK [KOI]
IOMA BINANDERE alt for BINANDERE [BHG]
IOMBE alt for YOMBE [YOM]
IOULLEMMEDEN alt for TAWALLAMMAT TAN DANNAG dial of TAMAJAQ, TAWALLAMMAT [TTQ]
IOULLEMMEDEN alt for TAWALLAMMET TAN DANNAG dial of TAMAJAQ [TTQ]

IOULLEMMEDEN dial of TAMAJAQ, TAWALLAMMAT [TTQ]
IOWA dial of IOWA-OTO [IOW]
IOWA-OTO [IOW] lang, USA
IOWAY alt for IOWA dial of IOWA-OTO [IOW]
IPANDE alt for PANDE [BKJ]
IPANGA alt for PANGA dial of MONGO-NKUNDU [MOM]
IPECA alt for IPEKA-TAPUIA [PAJ]
IPEKA-TAPUIA [PAJ] lang, Brazil
IPERE alt for BHELE [PER]
IPIKO [IPK] lang, Papua New Guinea
IPIKOI alt for IPIKO [IPK]
IPILI [IPI] lang, Papua New Guinea
IPILI-PAIELA alt for IPILI [IPI]
IPILI-PAYALA alt for IPILI [IPI]
IPITINERI alt for AMAHUACA [AMC]
IPO dial of IKWERE [IKW]
IPOH dial of DAYAK, LAND [DYK]
IPOUNOU alt for PUNU [PUU]
IPULO [ASS] lang, Cameroon
IPUNU alt for PUNU [PUU]
IPURICOTO alt for CAMARACOTA dial of PEMON [AOC]
IPURINÃN alt for APURINÃ [APU]
IQUITA alt for IQUITO [IQU]
IQUITO [IQU] lang, Peru
IR [IRR] lang, Laos
IRABU-JIMA dial of MIYAKO [MVI]
IRAHUTU alt for IRARUTU [IRH]
IRAKU alt for IRAQW [IRK]
IRAMANG dial of KULA [TPG]
IRAMBA alt for LAMBYA [LAI]
IRAMBA alt for NILAMBA [NIM]
IRANCHE alt for IRÁNTXE [IRA]
IRANGI alt for RANGI [LAG]
IRANIAN KOINE dial of ASSYRIAN NEO-ARAMAIC [AII]
IRANON alt for IRANUN dial of MAGINDANAON [MDH]
IRANON MARANAO alt for ILANUN [ILL]
IRÁNTXE [IRA] lang, Brazil
IRÁNTXE dial of IRANTXE [IRA]
IRANUM alt for ILANUN [ILL]
IRANUN alt for ILANUN [ILL]
IRANUN dial of MAGINDANAON [MDH]
IRANXE alt for IRÁNTXE [IRA]
IRAQI ARABIC alt for ARABIC, MESOPOTAMIAN SPOKEN [ACM]
IRAQI JUDEO-ARABIC alt for ARABIC, JUDEO-IRAQI [YHD]
IRAQI NEO-MANDAIC dial of MANDAIC [MID]
IRAQW [IRK] lang, Tanzania
IRARUTU [IRH] lang, Indonesia (Irian Jaya)
IRAVA alt for IRULA [IRU]
IRAYA [IRY] lang, Philippines
IRBORE alt for ARBORE [ARV]
IREGWE alt for IRIGWE [IRI]
IRESIM [IRE] lang, Indonesia (Irian Jaya)
IRHOBO alt for ISEKIRI [ITS]
IRI alt for IRRI dial of ISOKO [ISO]

IRI dial of KADARA [KAD]
IRIA alt for KAMBERAU [IRX]
IRIANESE dial of MALAY [MLI]
IRIEMKENA alt for AIRORAN [AIR]
IRIGWE [IRI] lang, Nigeria
IRISH alt for GAELIC, IRISH [GLI]
IRISH SIGN LANGUAGE [ISG] lang, Ireland
IRISH TRAVELER CANT alt for SHELTA [STH]
IROB dial of SAHO [SSY]
IROKA alt for RÍO CASACARÁ dial of YUKPA
[YUP]
IRON dial of OSETIN [OSE]
IRONWORKER ROMANI dial of ROMANI, BALKAN
[RMN]
IROOLE dial of DABARRE [DBR]
IRRI dial of ISOKO [ISO]
IRRUAN dial of BOKYI [BKY]
IRUAN dial of BOKYI [BKY]
IRULA [IRU] lang, India
IRULA PALLAR dial of IRULA [IRU]
IRULAR alt for IRULA [IRU]
IRULAR MOZHI alt for IRULA [IRU]
IRULIGA alt for IRULA [IRU]
IRULIGAR alt for IRULA [IRU]
IRUMU alt for TUMA-IRUMU [IOU]
IRUNGI alt for RUNGI [RUR]
IRUPI-DRAGELI dial of BINE [ORM]
IRUTU alt for IRARUTU [IRH]
ISA alt for ESAN [ISH]
ISAALUNG alt for SISAALA, TUMULUNG [SIL]
ISAAN alt for THAI, NORTHEASTERN [TTS]
ISAANGA alt for SAANGA dial of MAKHUWA-
MEETTO [MAK]
ISABI [ISA] lang, Papua New Guinea
ISACHANURE alt for NAGA, SANGTAM [NSA]
ISAL alt for BENGGOI [BGY]
ISALA dial of SISAALA, TUMULUNG [SIL]
ISAM dial of PAGU [PGU]
ISAMAL dial of KALAGAN [KQE]
ISAN alt for THAI, NORTHEASTERN [TTS]
ISAN dial of YOPNO [YUT]
ISANGA alt for GUSU dial of JERE [JER]
ISANGA alt for SANGA [SGA]
ISANGELE alt for USAGHADE [USK]
ISANGU alt for SANGU [SNQ]
ISANZU [ISN] lang, Tanzania
ISARO alt for KUMBA [KSM]
ISCAMTHO alt for CAMTHO [CMT]
ISCOBAQUEBU alt for ISCONAHUA [ISC]
ISCONAHUA [ISC] lang, Peru
ISEBE [IGO] lang, Papua New Guinea
ISEBE dial of ISEBE [IGO]
ISEKIRI [ITS] lang, Nigeria
ISELEMA-OTU alt for ISEKIRI [ITS]
ISENYI alt for ISSENYI dial of IKOMA [NTK]
ISFAHANI dial of FARSI, WESTERN [PES]
ISHAN alt for ESAN [ISH]
ISHANGA alt for SAANGA dial of MAKHUWA-
MEETTO [MAK]
ISHARON KI ZUBANN alt for PAKISTAN SIGN
LANGUAGE [PKS]

ISHBUKUN alt for SOUTH BUNUN dial of BUNUN
[BNN]
ISHE dial of UKAAN [KCF]
ISHEKIRI alt for ISEKIRI [ITS]
ISHIBORI alt for NKEM dial of NKEM-NKUM [ISI]
ISHIGAKI dial of YAEYAMA [RYS]
ISHILE alt for LEGA-MWENGA [LGM]
ISHIMALILIA alt for MALILA [MGQ]
ISHINYIHA alt for NYIHA [NIH]
ISHIRA alt for SIRA [SWJ]
ISHIRO alt for CHAMACOCO [CEG]
ISHIRO alt for EBITOSO dial of CHAMACOCO [CEG]
ISHISAFWA alt for SAFWA [SBK]
ISHKASHIM alt for ISHKASHIMI dial of SANGLECHI-
ISHKASHIMI [SGL]
ISHKASHIMI dial of SANGLECHI-ISHKASHIMI [SGL]
ISHKASHMI alt for ISHKASHIMI dial of SANGLECHI-
ISHKASHIMI [SGL]
ISHKOMAN dial of WAKHI [WBL]
ISHPI dial of PASHAYI, SOUTHWEST [PSH]
ISHUA alt for UHAMI [UHA]
ISI alt for WESTERN KILMERI dial of KILMERI [KIH]
ISIBIRI alt for NKEM dial of NKEM-NKUM [ISI]
ISICAMTHO alt for CAMTHO [CMT]
"ISIKULA" pejorative alt for FANAGOLO [FAO]
ISILOLOLO alt for FANAGOLO [FAO]
ISIMBI alt for ESIMBI [AGS]
ISIMIJEEGA alt for TSIMAJEEGA dial of DATOOGA
[TCC]
ISINAI [INN] lang, Philippines
ISINAY alt for ISINAI [INN]
ISINDE'BELE alt for NDEBELE [NDF]
ISIOKPO dial of IKWERE [IKW]
ISIPIKI alt for FANAGOLO [FAO]
ISIRA alt for SIRA [SWJ]
ISIRAWA [SRL] lang, Indonesia (Irian Jaya)
ISISWAZI alt for SWATI [SWZ]
ISIXHOSA alt for XHOSA [XOS]
ISIZULU alt for ZULU [ZUU]
ISKEN dial of PASHAYI, SOUTHWEST [PSH]
ISLAMI alt for URDU [URD]
ISLAND dial of MAILU [MGU]
ISLAND BOIKIN dial of BOIKIN [BZF]
ISLAND CHUMASH alt for CRUZEÑO [CRZ]
ISLAND COMOX dial of COMOX [COO]
ISLAND HELONG alt for HELONG PULAU dial of
HELONG [HEG]
ISLAND KIWAI dial of KIWAI, SOUTHERN [KJD]
ISLAND TIGAK dial of TIGAK [TGC]
ISLANDER CREOLE ENGLISH dial of NORTHERN
CENTRAL AMERICA CREOLE ENGLISH [BZI]
ISLEÑO alt for CRUZEÑO [CRZ]
ÍSLENSKA alt for ICELANDIC [ICE]
ISLETA dial of TIWA, SOUTHERN [TIX]
ISLETA PUEBLO alt for ISLETA dial of TIWA,
SOUTHERN [TIX]
ISNAG [ISD] lang, Philippines
ISNAY alt for ISINAI [INN]
ISNEG alt for ISNAG [ISD]
ISOCENIO alt for IZOCEÑO dial of GUARANI,
ARGENTINE, WESTERN [GUI]

ISOKO [ISO] lang, Nigeria
ISOLE EOLIE dial of SICILIAN [SCN]
ISOMBI alt for WADIMBISA dial of BUDU [BUU]
ISONGO alt for MBATI [MDN]
ISOPO dial of LEGA-MWENGA [LGM]
ISRAELI SIGN LANGUAGE [ISL] lang, Israel
ISSALA alt for SISAALA, TUMULUNG [SIL]
ISSALA alt for SISAALA, WESTERN [SSL]
ISSAN alt for THAI, NORTHEASTERN [TTS]
ISSANA alt for BANIWA [BAI]
ISSENYI dial of IKOMA [NTK]
ISSILITA' dial of BAMBAM [PTU]
ISSONGO alt for MBATI [MDN]
ISTANBUL alt for CONSTANTINOPLE dial of
    ARMENIAN [ARM]
ISTHMUS AZTEC alt for NÁHUATL, ISTMO-
    MECAYAPAN [NAU]
ISTHMUS MIXE alt for MIXE, ISTMO [MIR]
ISTHMUS NÁHUAT alt for NÁHUATL, ISTMO-
    PAJAPAN [NHP]
ISTHMUS NAHUAT alt for NÁHUATL, ISTMO-
    MECAYAPAN [NAU]
ISTHMUS NÁHUATL alt for NÁHUATL, ISTMO-
    COSOLEACAQUE [NHK]
ÍSTMO alt for ZAPOTECO, ISTMO [ZAI]
ISTRIAN dial of VENETIAN [VEC]
ISTRIOT [IST] lang, Croatia
ISTRO-ROMANIAN alt for ROMANIAN, ISTRO
    [RUO]
ISU [ISU] lang, Cameroon
ISU [SZV] lang, Cameroon
ISUAMA alt for OWERRI dial of IGBO [IGR]
ISUBU alt for ISU [SZV]
ISUKHA dial of IDAKHO-ISUKHA-TIRIKI [IDA]
ISUWU alt for ISU [SZV]
ISUXA alt for ISUKHA dial of IDAKHO-ISUKHA-
    TIRIKI [IDA]
ITA alt for ALTA, SOUTHERN [AGY]
ITAK dial of IBIBIO [IBB]
ITAKHO alt for IDAKHO dial of IDAKHO-ISUKHA-
    TIRIKI [IDA]
ITALIAN [ITN] lang, Italy; also in Argentina, Australia,
    Belgium, Bosnia-Herzegovina, Brazil, Canada,
    Croatia, Egypt, Eritrea, France, Germany, Israel,
    Libya, Liechtenstein, Luxembourg, Paraguay,
    Philippines, Puerto Rico, San Marino, Saudi
    Arabia, Slovenia, Switzerland, Tunisia, UAE,
    United Kingdom, Uruguay, USA, Vatican State
ITALIAN SIGN LANGUAGE [ISE] lang, Italy
ITALIANO alt for ITALIAN [ITN]
ITALKIAN alt for JUDEO-ITALIAN [ITK]
ITALON dial of ILONGOT [ILK]
ITANGA alt for ITOGAPÚK [ITG]
ITANGIKOM alt for KOM [BKM]
ITANGIMBESA alt for MBIZENAKU dial of KOM
    [BKM]
ITAROK dial of TAROK [YER]
ITAROK OGA ASA dial of TAROK [YER]
ITAWES alt for ITAWIT [ITV]
ITAWIS alt for ITAWIT [ITV]
ITAWIS dial of ITAWIT [ITV]

ITAWIT [ITV] lang, Philippines
ITBAYATEN dial of IVATAN [IVV]
ITBEG RUGNOT alt for AGTA, MT. IRAYA [ATL]
ITCHEN alt for ETKYWAN [ICH]
ITEBIEGE dial of ISOKO [ISO]
ITEEJI dial of KUKELE [KEZ]
ITEGHE alt for TEKE, NORTHERN [TEG]
ITELMEN [ITL] lang, Russia (Asia)
ITELMEN dial of ITELMEN [ITL]
ITELYMEM alt for ITELMEN [ITL]
ITENE [ITE] lang, Bolivia
ITENEO alt for ITENE [ITE]
ITENEZ alt for ITENE [ITE]
ITERI [ITR] lang, Papua New Guinea
ITIGIDI alt for LEGBO [AGB]
ITIK [ITX] lang, Indonesia (Irian Jaya)
ITIRI dial of NYANGA [NYA]
ITKAN dial of KORYAK [KPY]
ITNEG, BINONGAN [ITB] lang, Philippines
ITNEG, INLAOD [ITI] lang, Philippines
ITNEG, MASADIIT [TIS] lang, Philippines
ITNEG, SOUTHERN [ITT] lang, Philippines
ITO [ITW] lang, Nigeria
ITO dial of IGEDE [IGE]
ITOGAPUC alt for ITOGAPÚK [ITG]
ITOGAPÚK [ITG] lang, Brazil
ITONAMA [ITO] lang, Bolivia
ITONGA dial of LENAKEL [TNL]
ITOREAUHIP dial of ITENE [ITE]
ITOTO alt for MACO dial of PIAROA [PID]
ITSAANGI alt for TSAANGI [TSA]
ITSANGI alt for TSAANGI [TSA]
ITSEKIRI alt for ISEKIRI [ITS]
ITSONG alt for SONGO [SOO]
ITTIK alt for ITIK [ITX]
ITTIK dial of ITIK [ITX]
ITTIK-TOR alt for ITIK [ITX]
ITTIK-TOR dial of ITIK [ITX]
ITTU alt for OROMO, EASTERN [HAE]
ITU MBON USO alt for ITU MBON UZO [ITM]
ITU MBON UZO [ITM] lang, Nigeria
ITU MBUZO alt for ITU MBON UZO [ITM]
ITUCALI alt for URARINA [URA]
ITUMBA dial of SAGALA [SBM]
ITUMKALA dial of CHECHEN [CJC]
ITUNDU dial of TUNEN [BAZ]
ITUNDUJIA MIXTEC alt for MIXTECO, ITUNDUJIA
    [MCE]
ITURI KINGWANA dial of SWAHILI, CONGO [SWC]
ITUTANG [ITU] lang, Papua New Guinea
ITYOO alt for TYOO dial of TEKE, CENTRAL
    [TEC]
ITZÁ [ITZ] lang, Guatemala
IU MIEN [IUM] lang, China; also in Belgium, Canada,
    Denmark, France, Laos, Myanmar, New Zealand,
    Switzerland, Taiwan, Thailand, USA, Viet Nam
IUI alt for SALT-YUI [SLL]
IULEHA dial of EMAI-IULEHA-ORA [EMA]
IURUNA alt for JURÚNA [JUR]
IVANGA alt for IBANGA dial of LAMOGAI [LMG]
IVATAN [IVV] lang, Philippines

IVATAN alt for IBATAN [IVB]
IVBIE NORTH dial of IVBIE NORTH-OKPELA-ARHE [ATG]
IVBIE NORTH-OKPELA-ARHE [ATG] lang, Nigeria
IVBIOSAKON alt for EMAI-IULEHA-ORA [EMA]
IVHIADAOBI dial of YEKHEE [ETS]
IVHIMION dial of EMAI-IULEHA-ORA [EMA]
IVORI alt for TAINAE [AGO]
IVRIT alt for HEBREW [HBR]
IWA dial of MUYUW [MYW]
IWA dial of MWANGA [MWN]
IWAAK alt for I-WAK [IWK]
IWAIDJA [IBD] lang, Australia
IWAIDJI alt for IWAIDJA [IBD]
I-WAK [IWK] lang, Philippines
IWAL [KBM] lang, Papua New Guinea
IWAM [IWM] lang, Papua New Guinea
IWAM, SEPIK [IWS] lang, Papua New Guinea
IWAM-NAGALEMB dial of MUFIAN [AOJ]
<IWARDO dial of TUROYO [SYR]
IWATENU alt for NENGONE [NEN]
IWERE alt for ISEKIRI [ITS]
IWI dial of AKPOSO [KPO]
IWIRE dial of ISOKO [ISO]
IWOER alt for IWUR [IWO]
IWORRO dial of YORUBA [YOR]
IWUR [IWO] lang, Indonesia (Irian Jaya)
IWUUMU alt for WUUMU dial of TEKE, SOUTH CENTRAL [IFM]
IXCATECO [IXC] lang, Mexico
IXIGNOR alt for ABISHIRA [ASH]
IXIL, CHAJUL [IXJ] lang, Guatemala
IXIL, NEBAJ [IXI] lang, Guatemala
IXIL, SAN JUAN COTZAL [IXL] lang, Guatemala
IXREKO-MUXREK dial of RUTUL [RUT]
IXTAYUTLA MIXTEC alt for MIXTECO, IXTAYUTLA [VMJ]
IXTLÁN ZAPOTECO alt for ZAPOTECO, JUÁREZ, SIERRA [ZAA]
IYAA alt for YAA dial of TEKE, WESTERN [TEZ]
IYAA alt for YAKA dial of TEKE, WESTERN [TEZ]
IYACE alt for YACE [EKR]
IYAKA alt for YAA dial of TEKE, WESTERN [TEZ]
IYAKA alt for YAKA [YAF]
IYAKA alt for YAKA dial of TEKE, WESTERN [TEZ]
IYALA alt for YALA [YBA]
IYANI dial of AKPES [IBE]
IYASA dial of YASA [YKO]
IYAYU [IYA] lang, Nigeria
IYEDE dial of ISOKO [ISO]
IYEDE-AMI dial of ISOKO [ISO]
IYEKHEE alt for YEKHEE [ETS]
IYIRIKUM alt for MOGHAMO dial of META [MGO]
IYIVE [UIV] lang, Cameroon; also in Nigeria
IYO alt for ROCKY PEAK [ROK]
IYOKO dial of LEGA-MWENGA [LGM]
IYON alt for MESAKA [IYO]
IYONGIYONG alt for BAKPINKA [BBS]
IYONGUT dial of ILONGOT [ILK]
IYONIYONG alt for BAKPINKA [BBS]
IYONIYONG alt for KIONG [KKM]

IYOWO dial of ISOKO [ISO]
IZALE alt for NZARE dial of MBEMBE, TIGON [NZA]
IZARE alt for NZARE dial of MBEMBE, TIGON [NZA]
IZAREK alt for IZERE [FIZ]
IZEM dial of GBARI [GBY]
IZERE [FIZ] lang, Nigeria
IZHA alt for EZHA dial of GURAGE, WEST [GUY]
IZHOR alt for INGRIAN [IZH]
IZI dial of IZI-EZAA-IKWO-MGBO [IZI]
IZI-EZAA-IKWO-MGBO [IZI] lang, Nigeria
IZINI dial of TAROK [YER]
IZMIR alt for SMYRNA dial of ARMENIAN [ARM]
IZNACEN dial of TARIFIT [RIF]
IZO alt for IZON [IJC]
IZOCENIO alt for IZOCEÑO dial of GUARANI, BOLIVIAN, EASTERN [GUI]
IZOCEÑO dial of GUARANI, ARGENTINE, WESTERN [GUI]
IZOCEÑO dial of GUARANI, BOLIVIAN, EASTERN [GUI]
IZOCENYO alt for IZOCEÑO dial of GUARANI, ARGENTINE, WESTERN [GUI]
IZON [IJC] lang, Nigeria
IZORA [CBO] lang, Nigeria
IZZI alt for IZI dial of IZI-EZAA-IKWO-MGBO [IZI]
JAAKO alt for MARGU [MHG]
JA'ALI dial of ARABIC, SUDANESE SPOKEN [APD]
JAAN alt for YANA dial of MOORE [MHM]
JAAN alt for YANGA dial of MOORE [MHM]
JAB alt for YELMEK [JEL]
JABA alt for HAM [JAB]
JABAAL dial of TAMA [TMA]
JABAANA alt for YABAÂNA [YBN]
JABAL NAFUSI alt for DJERBI [JBN]
JABAL NAFUSI alt for NAFUSI [JBN]
JABALI alt for HULAULÁ [HUY]
JABAN alt for ARANDAI [JBJ]
JABANA alt for ZABANA [KJI]
JABBA alt for HAM [JAB]
JABEM alt for YABEM [JAE]
JABI alt for YABI dial of EKARI [EKG]
JABIM alt for YABEM [JAE]
JABO dial of GREBO, SOUTHERN [GRJ]
JABORLANG alt for BABUZA [BZG]
JABSCH alt for YELMEK [JEL]
JABUDA alt for KANJU [KBE]
JABUNG dial of ABUNG [ABL]
JABUTÍ [JBT] lang, Brazil
JACALTECO, EASTERN [JAC] lang, Guatemala
JACALTECO, WESTERN [JAI] lang, Guatemala; also in Mexico
JACARIA dial of KARIPUNA [KUQ]
JADEJI dial of KACHCHI [KFR]
JADEJI dial of SINDHI [SND]
JADGALI [JAV] lang, Pakistan; also in Iran
JADOBAFI dial of BRAJ BHASHA [BFS]
JAFGA alt for BEEGE dial of MUSGU [MUG]
JAFÍ alt for BANAWÁ [BNH]
JAFI alt for YAFI [WFG]
JAFI dial of KURDI [KDB]
JAFOO alt for KAFOA [KPU]

JAFRI dial of SARAIKI [SKR]
JAGAHALA dial of AMELE [AMI]
JAGAI alt for THIANG dial of NUER [NUS]
JAGANATHAPURAM KOYA dial of KOYA [KFF]
JAGAT dial of GHALE, NORTHERN [GHH]
JAGATAI alt for CHAGATAI [CGT]
JAGATAI alt for TEKE dial of TURKMEN [TCK]
JAGGOI alt for JAGOI [SNE]
JAGOI [SNE] lang, Malaysia (Sarawak)
JAH HET alt for JAH HUT [JAH]
JAH HUT [JAH] lang, Malaysia (Peninsular)
JAHADIAN alt for YAHADIAN [NER]
JAHAI alt for JEHAI [JHI]
JAHALATAN alt for YALAHATAN [JAL]
JAHALATANE alt for YALAHATAN [JAL]
JAHANKA [JAD] lang, Guinea; also in Mali
JAHANKA dial of MALINKE [MLQ]
JAHANKA dial of MANINKA, WESTERN [MLQ]
JAHANQUE alt for JAHANKA [JAD]
JAHANQUE alt for JAHANKA dial of MALINKE [MLQ]
JAHONQUE alt for JAHANKA [JAD]
JAHONQUE alt for JAHANKA dial of MALINKE [MLQ]
JAHROMI dial of FARSI, WESTERN [PES]
JAHUI alt for DIAHÓI dial of TENHARIM [PAH]
JAINTIA dial of PNAR [PBV]
JAIPURI dial of MARWARI [MKD]
JAIPURIA alt for NAGA, NOCTE [NJB]
JAIR [YIR] lang, Indonesia (Irian Jaya)
JAISELMER alt for MARWARI [MRI]
JA-IT dial of MOKEN [MWT]
JAJAO alt for ZAZAO [JAJ]
JAJURA dial of CAKFEM-MUSHERE [CKY]
JAKAI alt for YAQAY [JAQ]
JAKANCI alt for LABIR [JKU]
JAKARTA dial of MALAY [MLI]
JAKARTA MALAY alt for BETAWI [BEW]
JAKATI [JAT] lang, Ukraine; also in Afghanistan
JAKHACHIN dial of KALMYK-OIRAT [KGZ]
JAKOON alt for JAKUN [JAK]
JAKPHANG dial of NAGA, KONYAK [NBE]
JAKU alt for LABIR [JKU]
JAKÙD alt for JAKUN [JAK]
JAKUD'N alt for JAKUN [JAK]
JAKULA alt for GANGGALIDA [GCD]
JAKUN [JAK] lang, Malaysia (Peninsular)
JAKUN alt for LABIR [JKU]
JAL alt for ATEN [GAN]
JALAIT alt for JIRIM dial of MONGOLIAN,
    PERIPHERAL [MVF]
JALALAM dial of KAREKARE [KAI]
JALÈ alt for YALI, NINIA [NLK]
JALIEZA ZAPOTECO dial of ZAPOTECO, SAN
    JUAN GUELAVIA [ZAB]
JALINGO dial of MUMUYE [MUL]
JALKIA alt for BAREIN [BVA]
JALKIA dial of BAREIN [BVA]
JALKOTI dial of SHINA, KOHISTANI [PLK]
JALKUNA alt for BLÉ [BXL]
JALOC alt for ARIBWAUNG [YLU]
JALON alt for FUUTA JALON [FUF]
JALONKE alt for JALUNGA [YAL]

JALONKE alt for YALUNKA [YAL]
JALONKÉ alt for JALUNGA [YAL]
JALUNGA [YAL] lang, Guinea; also in Mali, Senegal,
    Sierra Leone
JALY alt for YALI, NINIA [NLK]
JAMA alt for SAMBA DAKA [CCG]
JAMA MAPUN alt for MAPUN [SJM]
JAMAICAN COUNTRY SIGN LANGUAGE [JCS]
    lang, Jamaica
JAMAICAN CREOLE ENGLISH dial of SOUTH-
    WESTERN CARIBBEAN CREOLE ENGLISH
    [JAM]
JAMAMADÍ [JAA] lang, Brazil
JAMATIA dial of KOK BOROK [TRP]
JAMBA alt for DZAMBA dial of BALOI [BIZ]
JAMBAPUING alt for DJAMBARRPUYNGU [DJR]
JAMBAPUINGO alt for DJAMBARRPUYNGU [DJR]
JAMBO alt for ANUAK [ANU]
JAMDEN alt for YAMDENA [JMD]
JAMDENA alt for YAMDENA [JMD]
JAMESABAD AER dial of AER [AEQ]
JAMINAWA alt for YAMINAHUA [YAA]
JAMINAWÁ alt for YAMINAHUA [YAA]
JAMINJUNG alt for DJAMINDJUNG [DJD]
JAMPALAM dial of WANDALA [MFI]
JAMPEA dial of BAJAU, INDONESIAN [BDL]
JAMRAL dial of MALVI [MUP]
JAMSAI dial of DOGON [DOG]
JAMSHEDI alt for JAMSHIDI dial of AIMAQ [AIQ]
JAMSHIDI dial of AIMAQ [AIQ]
JAMSKA [JMK] lang, Sweden
JAMTSKA alt for JAMSKA [JMK]
JANAMA alt for NORTHERN PONDORI dial of
    BOZO, SOROGAMA [BZE]
JANAMA alt for SOUTHERN PONDORI dial of
    BOZO, SOROGAMA [BZE]
JANBEBA alt for OMAGUA [OMG]
JANDALI alt for ADYNYAMATHANHA [ADT]
JANDAVRA [JND] lang, Pakistan
JANDER dial of WOLOF [WOL]
JANDIJINUNG alt for DJINANG [DJI]
JANELA alt for DEG [MZW]
JANERA dial of BARASANA [BSN]
JANG alt for REJANG [REJ]
JANGA alt for NYANGGA [NNY]
JANGAA alt for NYANGGA [NNY]
JANGAD alt for KURUX, NEPALI [KXL]
JANGALI alt for RAWAT [JNL]
JANGAN alt for GIANGAN [BGI]
JANGGA alt for NYANGGA [NNY]
JANGGALI alt for RAWAT [JNL]
JANGGU alt for ELSENG [MRF]
JANGHARD alt for KURUX, NEPALI [KXL]
JANGIAM alt for JANGSHUNG [JNA]
JANG-KALA alt for NYANGGA [NNY]
JANGKOTI dial of KHAM, SHESHI [KIP]
JANGKUNDJARA alt for YANKUNYTJATJARA
    [KDD]
JANGLI dial of SARAIKI [SKR]
JANGRAMI alt for JANGSHUNG [JNA]
JANGSHEN dial of CHIN, THADO [TCZ]

JANGSHUNG [JNA] lang, India
"JANJERINYA" pejorative alt for YEMSA [JNJ]
"JANJERO" pejorative alt for YEMSA [JNJ]
JANJI [JNI] lang, Nigeria
JANJO alt for DZA [JEN]
"JANJOR" pejorative alt for YEMSA [JNJ]
JANJULA alt for YANYUWA [JAO]
JANSAURI alt for JAUNSARI [JNS]
JAO alt for YAO [YAO]
JA'O alt for ENDE dial of ENDE [END]
JAOJO alt for ZAUZOU [ZAL]
JAPANESE [JPN] lang, Japan; also in American
    Samoa, Argentina, Australia, Belize, Brazil,
    Canada, Dominican Republic, Germany, Guam,
    Mexico, Micronesia, Mongolia, New Zealand,
    Northern Mariana Islands, Palau, Panama,
    Paraguay, Peru, Philippines, Singapore, Taiwan,
    Thailand, UAE, United Kingdom, USA
JAPANESE PIDGIN ENGLISH alt for BROOME
    PEARLING LUGGER PIDGIN [BPL]
JAPANESE SIGN LANGUAGE [JSL] lang, Japan
JAPRERÍA [JRU] lang, Venezuela
JAQAI alt for YAQAY [JAQ]
JAQARU [JQR] lang, Peru
JAR alt for BADA [BAU]
JAR alt for JARAWA [JAR]
JARA [JAF] lang, Nigeria
JARA alt for JARAWA [JAR]
JARACIN KASA alt for GINGWAK dial of JARAWA
    [JAR]
JARAI [JRA] lang, Viet Nam; also in Cambodia, USA
JARANCHI alt for JARAWA [JAR]
JARAWA [ANQ] lang, India
JARAWA [JAR] lang, Nigeria
JARAWA alt for IZERE [FIZ]
JARAWAN BUNUNU alt for GINGWAK dial of
    JARAWA [JAR]
JARAWAN DUTSE alt for IZERE [FIZ]
JARAWAN KOGI alt for BADA [BAU]
JARAWAN KOGI alt for JARAWA [JAR]
JARAWARA alt for JARUÁRA [JAP]
JARAW-DOMO dial of MUSEY [MSE]
JARI alt for DAGAARI DIOULA [DGD]
JARI alt for IZERE [FIZ]
JARI dial of ANEME WAKE [ABY]
JARICUNA alt for ARECUNA dial of PEMON [AOC]
JARNANGO [JAY] lang, Australia
JARONG alt for JIARONG [JYA]
JAROO alt for JARU [DDJ]
JARU [DDJ] lang, Australia
JARU alt for LAVEN [LBO]
JARU alt for PAKAÁSNOVOS [PAV]
JARU dial of YELE [YLE]
JARUÁRA [JAP] lang, Brazil
JARUM dial of KENSIU [KNS]
JARUMÁ alt for YARUMÁ [YRM]
JARUNA alt for JURÚNA [JUR]
JAS alt for ASMAT, CENTRAL [AST]
JASING alt for ZASING dial of MUNDANG [MUA]
JASOA alt for JASUA dial of MPIEMO [MCX]
JASOA dial of MPIEMO [MCX]

JASUA alt for JASOA dial of MPIEMO [MCX]
JASUA dial of MPIEMO [MCX]
JAT alt for JADGALI [JAV]
JAT alt for JAKATI [JAT]
JATAKI alt for JAKATI [JAT]
JATAPU alt for KUVI [KXV]
JATGALI alt for JADGALI [JAV]
JATI alt for JAKATI [JAT]
JATKI alt for JADGALI [JAV]
JATKI dial of SARAIKI [SKR]
JATU alt for JAKATI [JAT]
JAUARETE dial of CARUTANA [CRU]
JAUARI dial of YANOMAMI [WCA]
JAUKE alt for YOKE [YKI]
JAULAPITI alt for YAWALAPITÍ [YAW]
JAULE dial of DZA [JEN]
JAUNA alt for NIJADALI [NAD]
JAU-NAVO alt for KARIPUNÁ [KUQ]
JAUNDE alt for EWONDO [EWO]
JAUN-JAUN dial of SURIGAONON [SUL]
JAUNSARI [JNS] lang, India
JAUNSAURI alt for JAUNSARI [JNS]
JAUR alt for YAUR [JAU]
JAVAÉ dial of KARAJA [KPJ]
JAVAHE alt for JAVAÉ dial of KARAJA [KPJ]
JAVANESE [JAN] lang, Indonesia (Java and Bali);
    also in Malaysia (Sabah), Netherlands, Singapore
JAVANESE, CARIBBEAN [JVN] lang, Suriname;
    also in French Guiana
JAVANESE, NEW CALEDONIAN [JAS] lang, New
    Caledonia
JAVIERANO alt for SAN JAVIER dial of
    CHIQUITANO [CAX]
JAVIERANO dial of TRINITARIO [TRN]
JAWA alt for JAVANESE [JAN]
JAWA HALUS dial of JAVANESE [JAN]
JAWAN alt for DJAUAN [DJN]
JAWANAUA alt for YAWANAWA [YWN]
JAWANLI alt for WAYAMLI dial of BULI [BZQ]
JAWAPERI alt for NINAM [SHB]
JAWAPERI dial of ATRUAHI [ATR]
JAWARI alt for NINAM [SHB]
JAWE [JAZ] lang, New Caledonia
JAWI dial of BAADI [BCJ]
JAWONY alt for DJAUAN [DJN]
JAYA [JYY] lang, Chad
JAYA BAKTI dial of BAJAU, INDONESIAN [BDL]
JAYAPURA alt for TOBATI [TTI]
JBALA alt for JEBLI dial of ARABIC, MOROCCAN
    SPOKEN [ARY]
JBEL NAFUSI alt for NAFUSI [JBN]
JBELI alt for LISHANID NOSHAN [AIJ]
JE alt for YEI [JEI]
JEBA alt for HAM [JAB]
JEBEL alt for JEBEL TEKEIM dial of LAFOFA
    [LAF]
JEBEL EL AMIRA dial of LAFOFA [LAF]
JEBEL NEFUSI alt for NAFUSI [JBN]
JEBEL SILAK alt for AKA [SOH]
JEBEL TEKEIM dial of LAFOFA [LAF]
JEBELAWI alt for BERTA [WTI]

JEBELIA alt for JEBLI dial of ARABIC, MOROCCAN SPOKEN [ARY]
JEBELS SILLOK alt for AKA [SOH]
JEBERO [JEB] lang, Peru
JEBLI dial of ARABIC, MOROCCAN SPOKEN [ARY]
JEDEPO dial of GREBO, NORTHERN [GRB]
JEERE alt for JERE [JER]
JEGA alt for GIBANAWA [GIB]
JEGA dial of PANGSENG [PAN]
JEGU dial of MOGUM [MOU]
JEH [JEH] lang, Viet Nam; also in Laos
JEH BRI LA dial of JEH [JEH]
JEH MANG RAM dial of JEH [JEH]
JEHAI [JHI] lang, Malaysia (Peninsular)
JEHAI dial of JEHAI [JHI]
JEHER dial of KENSIU [KNS]
JEI alt for YEI [JEI]
JEIDJI alt for WUNAMBAL [WUB]
JEINU KURUBA dial of KANNADA [KJV]
JEITHI alt for WUNAMBAL [WUB]
JEKAING alt for EASTERN JIKANY dial of NUER [NUS]
JEKKINO dial of BIDIYO [BID]
JEKRI alt for ISEKIRI [ITS]
JELAI dial of SEMAI [SEA]
JELALONG PENAN dial of PENAN, WESTERN [PNE]
JELEWAGA dial of SUDEST [TGO]
JELGOORE dial of FULFULDE, NORTHEASTERN BURKINA FASO [FUH]
JELKIN alt for SAKAYA dial of BAREIN [BVA]
JELKUNG alt for SABA [SAA]
JELMEK alt for YELMEK [JEL]
JELTULAK dial of EVENKI [EVN]
JEMBAYAN dial of BASAP [BDB]
JEMBRANA alt for LOWLAND BALI dial of BALI [BZC]
JEME alt for GEME [GEQ]
JEME alt for NAGA, ZEME [NZM]
JEMEZ [TOW] lang, USA
JEMHWA dial of GUMUZ [GUK]
"JEMJEM" pejorative alt for SUGA [SGI]
JEMJEM alt for GUJI dial of OROMO, BORANA-ARSI-GUJI [GAX]
JEN alt for DZA [JEN]
JEN KURUMBA alt for KURUMBA, JENNU [QKJ]
JENAMA alt for BOZO, SOROGAMA [BZE]
JENEPONTO alt for TURATEA dial of MAKASAR [MSR]
JENG [JEG] lang, Laos
JENG alt for NZANYI [NJA]
JENG dial of MUMUYE [MUL]
JENGE alt for NZANYI [NJA]
JENGJENG alt for LANOH [LNH]
JENGRE alt for JERE dial of JERE [JER]
JENIMU alt for SIAGHA-YENIMU [OSR]
JENISCH alt for YENICHE [YEC]
JENJI alt for JANJI [JNI]
JENJO alt for DZA [JEN]
JENNU KURUMBA NONSTANDARD KANNADA alt for KURUMBA, JENNU [QKJ]

JENNU NUDI alt for KURUMBA, JENNU [QKJ]
JENURES dial of BIAK [BHW]
JENUWA dial of KUTEP [KUB]
JEPAL alt for JIPAL dial of KOFYAR [KWL]
JEPA-MATSI alt for MACUNA [MYY]
JEPEL alt for JIPAL dial of KOFYAR [KWL]
JERA alt for JARA [JAF]
JERA alt for JERE [JER]
JERBA alt for JERBI dial of NAFUSI [JBN]
JERBA dial of DJERBI [JBN]
JERBI dial of NAFUSI [JBN]
JERE [JER] lang, Nigeria
JERE dial of JERE [JER]
JÈRÈ dial of BOBO MADARE, NORTHERN [BBO]
JERIYAWA alt for JERE dial of JERE [JER]
JERO alt for JERUNG [JEE]
JERO MALA alt for JERUNG [JEE]
JERRIAIS dial of FRENCH [FRN]
JERU alt for AKA-JERU [AKJ]
JERUM alt for JERUNG [JEE]
JERUNG [JEE] lang, Nepal
JERUNGE alt for JERUNG [JEE]
JESSU alt for NYA DELE dial of LONGUDA [LNU]
JESÚS MARÍA CORA dial of CORA [COR]
JETI alt for MANEM [JET]
JETO alt for JOTO dial of BANDA-BAMBARI [LIY]
JEWISH IRAQI-BAGHDADI ARABIC alt for ARABIC, JUDEO-IRAQI [YHD]
JEWISH TAT alt for JUDEO-TAT [TAT]
JEWISH TRIPOLITANIAN-LIBYAN ARABIC alt for ARABIC, JUDEO-TRIPOLITANIAN [YUD]
JEYWO alt for CHAMACOCO [CEG]
JEZHU dial of GBARI [GBY]
JEZIRE dial of KURMANJI [KUR]
JHADPI dial of VARHADI-NAGPURI [VAH]
JHALAWADI alt for KATHIYAWADI dial of GUJARATI [GJR]
JHALIYA alt for BODO PARJA [BDV]
JHANDORIA alt for JANDAVRA [JND]
JHANGAR alt for RAWAT [JNL]
JHANGER alt for KURUX, NEPALI [KXL]
JHARAWAN dial of BRAHUI [BRH]
JHARIA alt for BODO PARJA [BDV]
JHARKOT dial of BARAGAUNLE [BON]
JHARWA dial of ASSAMESE [ASM]
JHERUNG alt for JERUNG [JEE]
JHODIA PARJA alt for BODO PARJA [BDV]
JHORIA alt for MURIA, WESTERN [MUT]
JHUE dial of JARAI [JRA]
JI alt for EASTERN NUER dial of NUER [NUS]
JIAMAO [JIO] lang, China
JIAMUHUA alt for AI-CHAM [AIH]
JIANCHUAN dial of BAI [PIQ]
JIANGXIA GUANHUA alt for JINGHUAI GUANHUA dial of CHINESE, MANDARIN [CHN]
JIAOCHANG dial of QIANG, SOUTHERN [QMR]
JIAOGONG alt for JIAOGONG MIAN dial of BIAO-JIAO MIEN [BJE]
JIAOGONG MIAN dial of BIAO-JIAO MIEN [BJE]
JIARONG [JYA] lang, China
JIBA alt for KONA [JUO]

JIBALI alt for JIBBALI [SHV]
JIBANA dial of GIRYAMA [NYF]
JIBANCI alt for JIBU [JIB]
JIBARO alt for SHUAR [JIV]
JIBAWA alt for JIBU [JIB]
JIBBALI [SHV] lang, Oman
JIBI alt for KONA [JUO]
JIBITO alt for HIBITO [HIB]
JIBU [JIB] lang, Nigeria
JIBU alt for GIDRA [GDR]
JIBYAL alt for JIPAL dial of KOFYAR [KWL]
JICAQUE alt for TOL [JIC]
JI-CHA dial of CHINESE, GAN [KNN]
JIDA alt for BU [JID]
JIDA alt for NINKADA dial of BU [JID]
JIDA-ABU alt for BU [JID]
JIDDA-ABU alt for BU [JID]
JIDDU alt for JIIDDU [JII]
JIDINDJI alt for YIDINY [YII]
JIDYO alt for JUDEZMO dial of LADINO [SPJ]
JIE dial of KARAMOJONG [KDJ]
JIEZI dial of SALAR [SLR]
JIIDDU [JII] lang, Somalia
JIIR dial of KAG-FER-JIIR-KOOR-ROR-US-ZUKSUN
   [GEL]
JIJAL alt for INDUS dial of KOHISTANI, INDUS
   [MVY]
JIJI [JIJ] lang, Tanzania
JIJILI alt for TANJIJILI [UJI]
JIKAI alt for BURARRA [BVR]
JIKAIN alt for EASTERN JIKANY dial of NUER
   [NUS]
JIKANY alt for EASTERN NUER dial of NUER [NUS]
JIKRIO GOTH AER dial of AER [AEQ]
JILAMA BAWANG alt for BISAYA, BRUNEI [BSB]
JILAMA BAWANG alt for BISAYA, SABAH [BSY]
JILAMA SUNGAI alt for BISAYA, BRUNEI [BSB]
JILAMA SUNGAI alt for BISAYA, SABAH [BSY]
JILBE [JIE] lang, Nigeria
JILI alt for DZILI dial of JINGPHO [CGP]
JILIM [JIL] lang, Papua New Guinea
JIM MUN alt for KIM MUN [MJI]
JIMAJIMA [JMA] lang, Papua New Guinea
JIMBIN alt for ZUMBUN [JMB]
JIMBINAWA alt for ZUMBUN [JMB]
JIMI [JIM] lang, Cameroon
JIMI [JMI] lang, Nigeria
JIMJIMEN alt for JIMI [JIM]
JIMO alt for ZUMU dial of BATA [BTA]
JIMO dial of JIMI [JIM]
JIMUNI dial of MANAGALASI [MCQ]
JINA [JIA] lang, Cameroon
JINA dial of JINA [JIA]
JINDA alt for CINDA dial of CINDA-REGI-TIYAL
   [KAU]
JINDJIBANDI alt for YINDJIBARNDI [YIJ]
JINDWI dial of MANYIKA [MXC]
JINET dial of HERTEVIN [HRT]
JING alt for VIETNAMESE [VIE]
JINGA alt for NJINGA dial of MBUNDU, LOANDA
   [MLO]

JINGALI alt for DJINGILI [JIG]
JINGGARDA alt for YINGGARDA [YIA]
JINGHPAW alt for JINGPHO [CGP]
JINGHUAI GUANHUA dial of CHINESE, MANDARIN
   [CHN]
JINGJING dial of MINA [HNA]
JINGPHO [CGP] lang, Myanmar; also in China
JINGPO alt for JINGPHO [CGP]
JINGULU alt for DJINGILI [JIG]
JINGZHAN dial of CHINESE, HUIZHOU [CZH]
JINHUA alt for AI-CHAM [AIH]
JINHUA dial of CHINESE, WU [WUU]
JINJA alt for ZINZA [JIN]
JINJO dial of YELE [YLE]
JINKUM alt for WAPAN [JUK]
JINLERI alt for MINDA dial of SHOO-MINDA-NYE
   [BCV]
JINMEN alt for KIM MUN [MJI]
JINMINI alt for SENOUFO, DJIMINI [DYI]
JINO alt for JINUO, BUYUAN [JIY]
JINO alt for JINUO, YOULE [JIU]
JINPING DAI alt for TAI DAM [BLT]
JINUO, BUYUAN [JIY] lang, China
JINUO, YOULE [JIU] lang, China
JINYU alt for CHINESE, JINYU [CJY]
JIONGNAI alt for BUNU, JIONGNAI [PNU]
JIONGNAIHUA alt for BUNU, JIONGNAI [PNU]
JIPAL dial of KOFYAR [KWL]
JIR JORONT alt for YIR YORONT [YIY]
JIRAI dial of BATA [BTA]
JIREL [JUL] lang, Nepal
JIRI alt for JIREL [JUL]
JIRIAL alt for JIREL [JUL]
JIRIM dial of MONGOLIAN, PERIPHERAL [MVF]
JIRIYA alt for ZIRIYA [ZIR]
JIR'JOROND dial of YIR YORONT [YIY]
JIRMEL MEL-JIR alt for JIR'JOROND dial of YIR
   YORONT [YIY]
JIRU [JRR] lang, Nigeria
JISHISHAN dial of BONAN [PEH]
JISHU dial of CHINESE, XIANG [HSN]
JITA [JIT] lang, Tanzania
JIVARO alt for ACHUAR-SHIWIAR [ACU]
JIVARO alt for SHUAR [JIV]
JIW alt for GUAYABERO [GUO]
JIWADJA alt for IWAIDJA [IBD]
JIWALI alt for MANGALA [MEM]
JIWARLI alt for MANGALA [MEM]
JIWELE alt for OTO dial of IOWA-OTO [IOW]
JIWERE alt for OTO dial of IOWA-OTO [IOW]
JIXI dial of CHINESE, HUIZHOU [CZH]
JIYE alt for JIE dial of KARAMOJONG [KDJ]
JIYE dial of TOPOSA [TOQ]
JJU [KAJ] lang, Nigeria
JLUKO dial of GODIE [GOD]
JO alt for GHOMÁLÁ' CENTRAL dial of GHOMALA
   [BBJ]
JO alt for JOWULU [JOW]
JO ALUR alt for ALUR [ALZ]
JO COLO alt for COLO dial of THURI [THU]
JO LWO alt for LUWO [LWO]

JO THURI alt for THURI [THU]
JOARI alt for JAUARI dial of YANOMAMI [WCA]
JOBA [JOB] lang, DRC
JOBI dial of POM [PMO]
JOBOKA alt for NAGA, WANCHO [NNP]
JOGO alt for LIGBI [LIG]
JOHARI dial of KUMAUNI [KFY]
JOHODE alt for DGHWEDE [DGH]
JOHOR alt for RIAU dial of MALAY [MLI]
JOK alt for NGOK-SOBAT dial of DINKA, NORTH-
EASTERN [DIP]
JOKOT dial of ALUR [ALZ]
JOLA alt for JOLA-FOGNY [DYO]
JOLA-FOGNY [DYO] lang, Senegal; also in Gambia
JOLAHA dial of MAITHILI [MKP]
JOLA-KASA [CSK] lang, Senegal; also in Gambia
JOLFA dial of ARMENIAN [ARM]
JOLOANO alt for TAUSUG [TSG]
JOLOANO SULU alt for TAUSUG [TSG]
JOLOF alt for DYOLOF dial of WOLOF [WOL]
JOLONG dial of BAHNAR [BDQ]
JOMANG alt for TALODI [TLO]
"JOMPRE" pejorative alt for KUTEP [KUB]
JONAM dial of ALUR [ALZ]
JONAZ alt for CHICHIMECA-JONAZ [PEI]
JONE alt for CHONI [CDA]
JONE dial of KHAMS [KHG]
JONGA dial of TSONGA [TSO]
JONGGUNU alt for MONI [MNZ]
JONGOR alt for MIGAAMA [MMY]
JONKHA alt for DZONGKHA [DZO]
JONKOR BOURMATAGUIL [JEU] lang, Chad
JONKOR-GERA alt for MUKULU [MOZ]
JÓOLA alt for JOLA-FOGNY [DYO]
JÓOLA-KASA alt for JOLA-KASA [CSK]
JOOLE alt for JAULE dial of DZA [JEN]
JOOLE MANGA alt for THA [THY]
JOORE alt for ZAORE dial of MOORE [MHM]
JOPADHOLA alt for ADHOLA [ADH]
JOPARÁ dial of GUARANI, PARAGUAYAN [GUG]
JORÁ [JOR] lang, Bolivia
JORAI alt for JARAI [JRA]
JORDANIAN SIGN LANGUAGE [JOS] lang, Jordan
JORTO [JRT] lang, Nigeria
JOSTU dial of MONGOLIAN, PERIPHERAL [MVF]
JOS-ZARAZON alt for IZERE [FIZ]
JOTAFA alt for TOBATI [TTI]
JOTI alt for YUWANA [YAU]
JOTO dial of BANDA-BAMBARI [LIY]
JO-UDA dial of MONGOLIAN, PERIPHERAL [MVF]
JOWULU [JOW] lang, Mali; also in Burkina Faso
JRO dial of CHRAU [CHR]
JU [JUU] lang, Nigeria
JU BA dial of MAMBILA, CAMEROON [MYA]
JU NAARE dial of MAMBILA, CAMEROON [MYA]
JUANAUO alt for KARIPUNÁ [KUQ]
JUANEÑO dial of LUISENO [LUI]
JUANG [JUN] lang, India
JUANGA alt for YUAGA [NUA]
JUANGA dial of YUAGA [NUA]
JUANGO alt for JUANG [JUN]

JUARZON dial of SAPO [KRN]
JUBA ARABIC alt for ARABIC, SUDANESE
CREOLE [PGA]
JUB-<ADIN dial of WESTERN NEO-ARAMAIC
[AMW]
JUBB <ADI:N alt for JUB-<ADIN dial of WESTERN
NEO-ARAMAIC [AMW]
JUCHEN alt for NANAI [GLD]
JUDEO SPANISH alt for LADINO [SPJ]
JUDEO-ARAMAIC alt for HULAULÁ [HUY]
JUDEO-ARAMAIC alt for LISHANA DENI [LSD]
JUDEO-BERBER [JBE] lang, Israel
JUDEO-COMTADINE alt for SHUADIT [SDT]
JUDEO-CRIMEAN TATAR [JCT] lang, Uzbekistan;
also in Georgia, Kazakhstan
JUDEO-CRIMEAN TURKISH alt for JUDEO-
CRIMEAN TATAR [JCT]
JUDEO-CZECH dial of KNAANIC [CZK]
JUDEO-FRENCH alt for ZARPHATIC [ZRP]
JUDEO-GEORGIAN [JGE] lang, Israel; also in
Georgia
JUDEO-GERMAN alt for YIDDISH, EASTERN [YDD]
JUDEO-GERMAN alt for YIDDISH, WESTERN [YIH]
JUDEO-GREEK alt for YEVANIC [YEJ]
JUDEO-ITALIAN [ITK] lang, Italy
JUDEO-PERSIAN alt for DZHIDI [DZH]
JUDEO-PROVENÇAL alt for SHUADIT [SDT]
JUDEO-SLAVIC alt for KNAANIC [CZK]
JUDEO-TAJIK alt for BUKHARIC [BHH]
JUDEO-TAT [TAT] lang, Israel; also in Azerbaijan,
Russia (Europe)
JUDEO-TATIC alt for JUDEO-TAT [TAT]
JUDEO-YEMENI alt for ARABIC, JUDEO-YEMENI
[JYE]
JUDEZMO alt for LADINO [SPJ]
JUDEZMO dial of LADINO [SPJ]
JUDI alt for DZHIDI [DZH]
JUDIKÂNI dial of KURMANJI [KUR]
JUDYO alt for JUDEZMO dial of LADINO [SPJ]
JUGARI alt for ARABIC, TAJIKI SPOKEN [ABH]
JUGARI alt for ARABIC, UZBEKI SPOKEN [AUZ]
JUGULA alt for GANGGALIDA [GCD]
JUGUMBIR alt for YUGAMBAL [YUB]
JU/'HOAN [KTZ] lang, Botswana; also in Namibia
JU/'HOAN alt for JU/'HOAN [KTZ]
JUHURI alt for JUDEO-TAT [TAT]
JUI dial of MFUMTE [NFU]
JUKAGIR alt for YUKAGHIR, NORTHERN [YKG]
JUKAGIR alt for YUKAGHIR, SOUTHERN [YUX]
JUKAMBA alt for YUGAMBAL [YUB]
JUKON alt for WAPAN [JUK]
JUKU alt for WAPAN [JUK]
JUKU JUNKUN alt for WAPAN [JUK]
JUKUM alt for WAPAN [JUK]
JUKUN alt for DYUGUN [DYD]
JUKUN alt for JUKUN TAKUM [JBU]
JUKUN ABINSI alt for WANNU [JUB]
JUKUN KONA alt for KONA [JUO]
JUKUN TAKUM [JBU] lang, Nigeria; also in
Cameroon
JUKUN WAPAN alt for WAPAN [JUK]

JUKUN WASE alt for WASE [JUW]
JUKUN WUKARI alt for WAPAN [JUK]
JULA [DYU] lang, Burkina Faso; also in Côte d'Ivoire,
Mali
JULA, KORO [KFO] lang, Côte d'Ivoire
JULA, KOYAGA [KGA] lang, Côte d'Ivoire
JULA, ODIENNÉ [JOD] lang, Côte d'Ivoire
JULA, WORODOUGOU [JUD] lang, Côte d'Ivoire
JULI alt for MAMBILA, CAMEROON [MYA]
JULUD dial of KATLA [KCR]
JÚMA [JUA] lang, Brazil
JUMAM alt for GEREP dial of KIM [KIA]
JUMIAKI alt for GRANGALI [NLI]
JUMJUM [JUM] lang, Sudan
JUMLA alt for JUMLELI dial of NEPALI [NEP]
JUMLELI dial of NEPALI [NEP]
JUMU dial of YORUBA [YOR]
JUNA alt for TATUYO [TAV]
JUNGLE SPANISH alt for SPANISH, LORETO-
UCAYALI [SPQ]
JUNGMAN alt for YANGMAN [JNG]
JUNGURU dial of BANDA-NDELE [BFL]
JUNÍN QUECHUA alt for QUECHUA, NORTH
JUNÍN [QJU]
JUNOI alt for OKO-JUWOI [OKJ]
JÙOASI alt for JU/'HOAN [KTZ]
"JUPDÁ MACÚ" pejorative alt for HUPDË [JUP]
JUQUILA MIXE dial of MIXE, JUQUILA [MXQ]
JUR BELI alt for BELI [BLM]
JUR LUO alt for LUWO [LWO]
JUR LWO alt for LUWO [LWO]
JUR MANANGEER alt for MANANGEER dial of
THURI [THU]
JUR MODO [BEX] lang, Sudan
JUR MODO alt for MODO dial of JUR MODO [BEX]
JUR SHOL alt for COLO dial of THURI [THU]
JURASSIEN alt for FRANCHE-COMTOIS dial of
FRENCH [FRN]
JURAY [JUY] lang, India
JURCHEN [JUC] lang, China
JURITI alt for YURUTI [YUI]
JURITI-TAPUIA alt for YURUTI [YUI]
JURUA dial of JAMAMADI [JAA]
JURÚNA [JUR] lang, Brazil
JURUPARI dial of CARUTANA [CRU]
JURUTI alt for YURUTI [YUI]
JURUTI-TAPUIA alt for YURUTI [YUI]
JUTISH [JUT] lang, Denmark; also in Germany
JUTLANDISH alt for JUTISH [JUT]
JUWALINY alt for DJUWARLINY dial of
WALMAJARRI [WMT]
JUWOI alt for OKO-JUWOI [OKJ]
JUWRI alt for JUDEO-TAT [TAT]
JUXTLAHUACA MIXTEC alt for MIXTECO,
JUXTLAHUACA [VMC]
JWIRA dial of JWIRA-PEPESA [JWI]
JWIRA-PEPESA [JWI] lang, Ghana
JWISINCE alt for MASALIT [MSA]
JYARUNG alt for JIARONG [JYA]
JYSK alt for JUTISH [JUT]
KA alt for TAI PONG dial of TAI NUA [TDD]

KA dial of BANDA-BANDA [BPD]
KA BAO alt for LAQUA [LAQ]
KA BEO alt for LAQUA [LAQ]
KA BIAO alt for LAQUA [LAQ]
KAA alt for BAKAKA dial of BAKAKA [BQZ]
KAADO dial of ZARMA [DJE]
KAAGAN alt for KALAGAN, KAGAN [KLL]
KAAGEDDI dial of MIDOB [MEI]
KAAKYI alt for KRACHE [KYE]
KAALO dial of BANGWINJI [BSJ]
KAALONG alt for DIMBONG [DII]
KAAMBA dial of DOONDO [DOD]
KAAN [LDL] lang, Nigeria
KAAN alt for KAANSA [GNA]
KAANA MASALA alt for MASALIT [MSA]
KAANG alt for KANGOU dial of FALI, SOUTH [FAL]
KAANSA [GNA] lang, Burkina Faso
KAANSE alt for KAANSA [GNA]
KAANTYU alt for KANJU [KBE]
KAANU alt for KANU [KHX]
KÃASA alt for KAANSA [GNA]
KAAWLU alt for KAORO dial of WE WESTERN [WEC]
KABA [KSP] lang, CAR; also in Chad
KABA alt for KAREN, GEBA [KVQ]
KABA alt for SHE dial of BENCH [BCQ]
KABA DE BAIBOKOUM alt for KABA [KSP]
KABA DE PAOUA alt for KABA [KSP]
KABA 'DEM alt for KABA DEME [KWG]
KABA DEME [KWG] lang, Chad
KABA DEMI alt for KABA DEME [KWG]
KABA DUNJO alt for SARA DUNJO [KOJ]
KABA NA [KWV] lang, Chad
KABA NAA alt for KABA NA [KWV]
KABA NAR alt for KABA NA [KWV]
"KABA SO" pejorative alt for KULFA [KXJ]
KABADE dial of SAPO [KRN]
KABADI [KBT] lang, Papua New Guinea
KABAENA alt for TOKOTU'A dial of MORONENE
[MQN]
KABAKADA dial of KUANUA [KSD]
KABA-LAI alt for KABALAI [KVF]
KABALAI [KVF] lang, Chad
KABALAN alt for KAVALAN [CKV]
KABALAY alt for KABALAI [KVF]
KABALAYE alt for KABALAI [KVF]
KA-BAN dial of BAAN [BVJ]
KA-BANA alt for BANA [BCW]
KABANA alt for BARIAI [BCH]
KABARAN alt for KAVALAN [CKV]
KABARDIAN [KAB] lang, Russia (Europe); also in
Saudi Arabia, Turkey (Asia), USA
KABARDINO-CHERKES alt for KABARDIAN [KAB]
KABARDO-CHERKES alt for KABARDIAN [KAB]
KABARI alt for NADËB [MBJ]
KABARI dial of KANURI, CENTRAL [KPH]
KABATE dial of KABATEI [XKP]
KABATEI [XKP] lang, Iran
KABAYAN dial of IBALOI [IBL]
KABBA alt for KABA [KSP]
KABBA LAKA alt for LAKA [LAM]
!KABBAKWE alt for QABEKHOE dial of NARO [NHR]

KABE dial of MSER [KQX]
!KABEE dial of NU [NGH]
KABEN alt for KIBET [KIE]
K'ABENA alt for QEBENA dial of KAMBAATA
    [KTB]
KABENDE dial of BEMBA [BEM]
KABENTANG alt for KIBET [KIE]
KABEO alt for LAQUA [LAQ]
KABI dial of MUNDANG [MUA]
KABIANO alt for GABIANO dial of NIKSEK
    [GBE]
KABILA alt for LUBILA [KCC]
KÁBINAPEK alt for POMO, CENTRAL [POO]
KABINGA'AN dial of SAMA, BALANGINGI [SSE]
KABIRA dial of YAEYAMA [RYS]
KABIRE alt for KABIYÉ [KBP]
KABIRE alt for LUBILA [KCC]
KABIXI alt for SARARÉ [SRR]
KABIXÍ [KBD] lang, Brazil
KABIYÉ [KBP] lang, Togo; also in Benin, Ghana
KABO alt for CABO dial of MISKITO [MIQ]
KABO dial of IZON [IJC]
KABOK alt for BOK dial of MANDJAK [MFV]
KABOLA [KLZ] lang, Indonesia (Nusa Tenggara)
KABOLI alt for DARI dial of FARSI, EASTERN [PRS]
KABOLOAN alt for ALTA, SOUTHERN [AGY]
KABORI alt for NADËB [MBJ]
KABORU dial of BO [BPW]
KABRAS dial of BUKUSU [BUL]
KABRE alt for KABIYÉ [KBP]
KABU alt for AKEBOU [KEU]
KABUI alt for NAGA, KABUI [NKF]
KABULI alt for DARI dial of FARSI, EASTERN [PRS]
KABULOWAN alt for ALTA, SOUTHERN [AGY]
KABULUEN alt for ALTA, SOUTHERN [AGY]
KABULUWAN alt for ALTA, SOUTHERN [AGY]
KABULUWEN alt for ALTA, SOUTHERN [AGY]
KABURE alt for KABIYÉ [KBP]
KABURI [UKA] lang, Indonesia (Irian Jaya)
KABURUANG dial of TALAUD [TLD]
KABUTRA [KBU] lang, Pakistan
KABUVERDIANU [KEA] lang, Cape Verde Islands;
    also in France, Germany, Italy, Luxembourg,
    Netherlands, Portugal, Senegal, Spain, USA
KABWA [CWA] lang, Tanzania
KABWARI [KCW] lang, DRC
KABYE alt for KABIYÉ [KBP]
KABYLE [KYL] lang, Algeria; also in Belgium, France
KACA alt for KACHA dial of KHAKAS [KJH]
KACA alt for KATCHA dial of KATCHA-KADUGLI-
    MIRI [KAT]
KACCHI alt for KACHCHI [KFR]
KACHA alt for NAGA, ZEME [NZM]
KACHA dial of KHAKAS [KJH]
KACHAH' alt for KACO' [XKK]
KACHAMA dial of KACHAMA-GANJULE [KCX]
KACHAMA-GANJULE [KCX] lang, Ethiopia
KACHARI [QKC] lang, India
KACHARI alt for BODO [BRX]
KACHARI BENGALI alt for NAGA PIDGIN [NAG]
KACHARI-BENGALI dial of BENGALI [BNG]

KACHCHA alt for NAGA, ZEME [NZM]
KACHCHHI alt for KACHCHI [KFR]
KACHCHI [KFR] lang, India; also in Kenya, Malawi,
    Pakistan, Tanzania
KACHCHI dial of SINDHI [SND]
KACHE alt for JJU [KAJ]
KACHEL alt for KATCHAL dial of NICOBARESE,
    CENTRAL [NCB]
KACHEPO alt for KACIPO dial of KACIPO-BALESI
    [KOE]
KACHI alt for KACHCHI [KFR]
KACHI alt for KOLI, KACHI [GJK]
KACHI dial of KOLI, KACHI [GJK]
KACHI BHIL dial of KOLI, KACHI [GJK]
KACHI GUJARATI alt for KOLI, KACHI [GJK]
KACHI MEGHWAR alt for VAGRI dial of KOLI,
    KACHI [GJK]
KACHIA dial of KADARA [KAD]
KACHICHERE dial of TYAP [KCG]
KACHIN alt for JINGPHO [CGP]
KACHIN alt for SINGPHO [SGP]
KACHMERE alt for KASHMERE dial of KARANGA
    [KTH]
KACHUANA alt for KAXUIÂNA [KBB]
KACIPO dial of KACIPO-BALESI [KOE]
KACIPO-BALESI [KOE] lang, Sudan; also in Ethiopia
KACMIRI alt for KASHMIRI [KSH]
KACO' [XKK] lang, Cambodia
KAD CHENSU alt for IRULA [IRU]
KADA alt for GIDAR [GID]
KADA alt for KADAR [KEJ]
KADADDJARA alt for KARTUJARRA dial of MARTU
    WANGKA [MPJ]
KADA-GBE alt for KADAGBE dial of AYIZO-GBE
    [AYB]
KADAGBE dial of AYIZO-GBE [AYB]
KADAGI alt for KODAGU [KFA]
KADAI [KZD] lang, Indonesia (Maluku)
KADAI dial of GALELA [GBI]
KADAIAN alt for KEDAYAN dial of BRUNEI [KXD]
KADAIAN dial of BRUNEI [KXD]
KADAKLAN dial of BONTOC, EASTERN [BKB]
KADAKLAN-BARLIG BONTOC alt for BONTOC,
    EASTERN [BKB]
KADAM alt for GIMNIME [KMB]
KADAR [KEJ] lang, India
KADARA [KAD] lang, Nigeria
KADARO alt for KADARU [KDU]
KADARU [KDU] lang, Sudan
KADAS alt for PAIWAN [PWN]
KADAS alt for PYUMA [PYU]
KADAS alt for RUKAI [DRU]
KADASAN alt for DUSUN, CENTRAL [DTP]
KADAUPURITANA alt for HOHODENÉ dial of
    BANIWA [BAI]
KADAVU dial of FIJIAN [FJI]
KADAYAN alt for DUSUN, CENTRAL [DTP]
KADAYAN alt for DUSUN, SUGUT [KZS]
KADAYAN alt for KADAIAN dial of BRUNEI [KXD]
KADAYAN alt for KEDAYAN dial of BRUNEI [KXD]
KADAZAN, COASTAL [KZJ] lang, Malaysia (Sabah)

KADAZAN, KLIAS RIVER [KQT] lang, Malaysia (Sabah)
KADAZAN, LABUK-KINABATANGAN [DTB] lang, Malaysia (Sabah)
KADAZAN-TAGARO dial of DUSUN, CENTRAL [DTP]
KÀDENBÀ alt for BWAMU, LÁÁ LÁÁ [BWJ]
KADERO alt for KADARU [KDU]
KADERU alt for KADARU [KDU]
KADIAN alt for KADAIAN dial of BRUNEI [KXD]
KADIAN alt for KEDAYAN dial of BRUNEI [KXD]
KADIEN alt for KADAIAN dial of BRUNEI [KXD]
KADIEN alt for KEDAYAN dial of BRUNEI [KXD]
KADIM-KABAN dial of CAKFEM-MUSHERE [CKY]
KADINA dial of GALELA [GBI]
KADIR alt for KADAR [KEJ]
KADIRGI alt for FUR [FUR]
KADIRO dial of MORU [MGD]
KADIWÉU [KBC] lang, Brazil
KADJAKSE alt for KAJAKSE [CKQ]
KADJALLA dial of LAMA [LAS]
KADJANG alt for TANA TOA dial of KONJO, COASTAL [KJC]
"KADO" pejorative alt for HERDÉ [HED]
"KADO" pejorative alt for PÉVÉ [LME]
KADO [KDV] lang, Myanmar; also in China, Laos
KADO alt for CADDO [CAD]
KADO alt for HAUSA [HUA]
KADO alt for KADUO [KTP]
KADO alt for ULUMANDA' [ULM]
KA'DO alt for PÉVÉ [LME]
KA'DO HERDÉ alt for HERDÉ [HED]
KA'DO NGUETÉ alt for NGETE [NNN]
KA'DO PÉVÉ alt for PÉVÉ [LME]
KADOHADACHO alt for CADDO [CAD]
KADU alt for KADO [KDV]
KADU alt for KADUO [KTP]
KADU dial of KADO [KDV]
KADU KURUMBA alt for KURUMBA, BETTA [QKB]
KADU SHOLIGAR alt for SHOLAGA [SLE]
KADUGLI dial of KATCHA-KADUGLI-MIRI [KAT]
KADUKALI alt for KURUX [KVN]
KADUMODI alt for KRONGO [KGO]
KADUN alt for VAGHAT dial of VAGHAT-YA-BIJIM-LEGERI [BIJ]
KADUNA dial of GBAGYI [GBR]
KADUO [KTP] lang, Laos; also in China
KADYAN alt for KADAIAN dial of BRUNEI [KXD]
KADYAN alt for KEDAYAN dial of BRUNEI [KXD]
KAELE alt for MUNDANG [MUA]
KAELE dial of TUPURI [TUI]
KAESABU dial of CIA-CIA [CIA]
"KAETI" pejorative alt for MANDOBO [KZH]
KAFA alt for KAFICHO [KBR]
KAFA dial of FOI [FOI]
KAFA dial of KAFICHO [KBR]
KAFANCHAN dial of TYAP [KCG]
KAFFA alt for KAFICHO [KBR]
"KAFFER" pejorative alt for XHOSA [XOS]
"KAFFIR" pejorative alt for XHOSA [XOS]
KAFICHO [KBR] lang, Ethiopia

KAFIRE dial of SENOUFO, CEBAARA [SEF]
KAFOA [KPU] lang, Indonesia (Nusa Tenggara)
KAFU dial of BULLOM SO [BUY]
KAFUGU alt for NIRAGU dial of GBIRI-NIRAGU [GRH]
KAG dial of KAG-FER-JIIR-KOOR-ROR-US-ZUKSUN [GEL]
KAGA dial of KANURI, CENTRAL [KPH]
KAGA dial of MONO [MNH]
KAGABA alt for COGUI [KOG]
KAGAMA alt for KAGA dial of KANURI, CENTRAL [KPH]
KAGAN KALAGAN alt for KALAGAN, KAGAN [KLL]
KAGANI alt for HINDKO, NORTHERN [HNO]
KAGANKAN dial of HANUNOO [HNN]
KAGARI alt for KANJARI [KFT]
KAGATE [SYW] lang, Nepal
KAGATE BHOTE alt for KAGATE [SYW]
KAGAYAN alt for MAPUN [SJM]
KAGAYANEN [CGC] lang, Philippines
KAGBENI dial of BARAGAUNLE [BON]
KAGBO dial of GODIE [GOD]
KAG-FER-JIIR-KOOR-ROR-US-ZUKSUN [GEL] lang, Nigeria
KAGGABA alt for COGUI [KOG]
KAGHANI alt for HINDKO, NORTHERN [HNO]
KAGIUONG alt for KAYONG [KXY]
KAGOMA [KDM] lang, Nigeria
KAGORO [XKG] lang, Mali
KAGORO dial of TYAP [KCG]
KAGOUÉ alt for LOZOUA dial of DIDA, YOCOBOUE [GUD]
KAGU alt for NIRAGU dial of GBIRI-NIRAGU [GRH]
KAGULU [KKI] lang, Tanzania
KAGURU alt for KAGULU [KKI]
KAGWAHIBM alt for JÚMA [JUA]
KAGWAHIPH alt for JÚMA [JUA]
KAGWAHIV alt for JÚMA [JUA]
KAGWAHIV dial of TENHARIM [PAH]
KAGWAHIVA alt for JÚMA [JUA]
KAH SO alt for SÔ [SSS]
KAHABU dial of PAZEH [PZH]
KAHAIAN alt for KAHAYAN [XAH]
KAHAJAN alt for KAHAYAN [XAH]
KAHASI alt for KHASI [KHI]
KAHAYAN [XAH] lang, Indonesia (Kalimantan)
KAHE [HKA] lang, Tanzania
KAHEDUPA alt for KALEDUPA dial of TUKANGBESI NORTH [KHC]
KAHLURI alt for BILASPURI [KFS]
KAHUA [AGW] lang, Solomon Islands
KAHUA dial of KAHUA [AGW]
KAHUGU alt for NIRAGU dial of GBIRI-NIRAGU [GRH]
KAHUMAMAHON alt for SALUAN, KAHUMAMAHON [SLB]
KAI alt for KAIY [TCQ]
KAI alt for KÂTE [KMG]
KAI alt for KEI [KEI]
KAI alt for NUMANGGANG [NOP]
KAI PO-MO alt for KATO [KTW]

KAIADILT alt for GAYARDILT [GYD]
KAIAMA dial of BOKOBARU [BUS]
KAIAN [KCT] lang, Papua New Guinea
KAIBI alt for KAIVI [KCE]
KAIBOBO [KZB] lang, Indonesia (Maluku)
KAIBOBO dial of KAIBOBO [KZB]
KAIBU dial of FASU [FAA]
KAIBUBU alt for KAIBOBO [KZB]
KAIBUS alt for TEHIT [KPS]
KAIDEMUI alt for BUANG, MANGGA [MMO]
KAIDIPAN alt for KAIDIPANG [KZP]
KAIDIPAN dial of KAIDIPANG [KZP]
KAIDIPANG [KZP] lang, Indonesia (Sulawesi)
KAIDITJ alt for KAYTETYE [GBB]
KAIEP [KBW] lang, Papua New Guinea
KAIGAMA dial of DZA [JEN]
KAI-IRI alt for RUMU [KLQ]
KAIKADI [KEP] lang, India
KAIKADIA alt for KAIKADI [KEP]
KAIKAI alt for KAIKADI [KEP]
KAIKE [KZQ] lang, Nepal
KAIKO alt for KAIKU [KKQ]
KAIKU [KKQ] lang, DRC
KAILI, DA'A [KZF] lang, Indonesia (Sulawesi)
KAILI, LEDO [LEW] lang, Indonesia (Sulawesi)
KAILIKAILI alt for KORAFE [KPR]
KAILOLO dial of HARUKU [HRK]
KAIMBÉ [QKQ] lang, Brazil
KAIMBULAWA [ZKA] lang, Indonesia (Sulawesi)
KAINA dial of ENGA [ENQ]
KAINGÁNG [KGP] lang, Brazil
KAINGÁNG, SÃO PAULO [ZKS] lang, Brazil
KAINTIBA dial of HAMTAI [HMT]
KAIOVA alt for KAIWÁ [KGK]
KAIPANG dial of CHIN, FALAM [HBH]
KAIPI alt for OROKOLO [ORO]
KAIPI dial of TOARIPI [TPI]
KAIPU alt for KAIBU dial of FASU [FAA]
KAIRAK [CKR] lang, Papua New Guinea
KAIRATU dial of ALUNE [ALP]
KAIRI alt for RUMU [KLQ]
KAIRIRU [KXA] lang, Papua New Guinea
KAIRUI dial of KAIRUI-MIDIKI [KRD]
KAIRUI-MIDIKI [KRD] lang, Timor Lorosae
KAIRU-KAURA alt for OROKOLO [ORO]
KAIS [KZM] lang, Indonesia (Irian Jaya)
KAISAK alt for KAZAKH [KAZ]
KAITAK alt for KAJTAK dial of DARGWA [DAR]
KAITAROLEA alt for KILENGE dial of MALEU-
    KILENGE [MGL]
KAITERO alt for IRARUTU [IRH]
KAITETU dial of SEIT-KAITETU [HIK]
KAITITJ alt for KAYTETYE [GBB]
KAIVI [KCE] lang, Nigeria
KAIWA alt for IWAL [KBM]
KAIWÁ [KGK] lang, Brazil; also in Argentina
KAIWÁ dial of KAIWA [KGK]
KAIWAI alt for KOWIAI [KWH]
KAIXIEN alt for LAHU [LAH]
KAIY [TCQ] lang, Indonesia (Irian Jaya)
KAJABÍ alt for KAYABÍ [KYZ]

KAJAGAR alt for KAYAGAR [KYT]
KAJAJA alt for TINGAL [TIG]
KAJAKJA alt for TINGAL [TIG]
KAJAKSE [CKQ] lang, Chad
KAJALI [XKJ] lang, Iran
KAJAMAN [KAG] lang, Malaysia (Sarawak)
KAJAN alt for KAYAN, BUSANG [BFG]
KAJANG alt for KAYAN, BUSANG [BFG]
KAJANG alt for KAYAN, KAYAN RIVER [XKN]
KAJANG alt for TANA TOA dial of KONJO,
    COASTAL [KJC]
KAJANGA dial of MABA [MDE]
KAJANGAN alt for KAJANGA dial of MABA [MDE]
KAJE alt for JJU [KAJ]
KAJELI alt for KAYELI [KZL]
KAJESKE alt for KAJAKSE [CKQ]
KAJIANG alt for STIENG, BULO [STI]
KAJIRE-'DULO dial of MAJERA [XMJ]
KAJIRRAWUNG alt for GADJERAWANG [GDH]
KAJJARA alt for BIRKED [BRK]
KAJJI alt for JJU [KAJ]
KAJKAVIAN dial of SERBO-CROATIAN [SRC]
KAJOA alt for KAYOA dial of MAKIAN, EAST [MKY]
KAJOA dial of BAJAU, INDONESIAN [BDL]
KAJTAK dial of DARGWA [DAR]
KAJUMERAH alt for KOWIAI [KWH]
KAJUPULAU alt for KAYUPULAU [KZU]
KAJURU dial of KADARA [KAD]
"KAKA" pejorative alt for YAMBA [YAM]
KAKA alt for BAKAKA dial of BAKAKA [BQZ]
KAKA alt for KAKO [KKJ]
KAKAA alt for KURI dial of BUDUMA [BDM]
KAKABA alt for KAMKAM [BGU]
KAKABA alt for MBONGNO [BGU]
KAKABAI [KQF] lang, Papua New Guinea
KAKACHHU-KI BOLI alt for DHANKI [DHN]
KAKADU alt for GAGADU [GBU]
KAKAKTA alt for GAGADU [GBU]
KAKAMEGA alt for IDAKHO dial of IDAKHO-
    ISUKHA-TIRIKI [IDA]
KAKANDA [KKA] lang, Nigeria
KAKARAKALA alt for YINGGARDA [YIA]
KAKARI dial of GUJARATI [GJR]
KAKAS dial of TONDANO [TDN]
KA'KAS alt for KAKAS dial of TONDANO [TDN]
KAKAT alt for QAQET [BYX]
KAKAUHUA [KBF] lang, Chile
KAKAYAMBA alt for YAMBA [YAM]
KAKBARAK alt for KOK BOROK [TRP]
KAKDJU alt for GAGADU [GBU]
KAKDJUAN alt for GAGADU [GBU]
KAKHETIAN alt for KAXETIAN dial of GEORGIAN
    [GEO]
KAKI AE [TBD] lang, Papua New Guinea
KAKIA dial of XOO [NMN]
KAKIHUM [KXE] lang, Nigeria
KAKIRU alt for APOWASI dial of BITARA [BIT]
KAKO [KKJ] lang, Cameroon; also in CAR, Congo
KAKOLI alt for UMBU-UNGU [UMB]
KAKOLO alt for KAGORO [XKG]
KAKSINGRI dial of SUBA [SUH]

KAKUA alt for KAKWA [KEO]
KAKUMEGA alt for IDAKHO dial of IDAKHO-
ISUKHA-TIRIKI [IDA]
KAKUMO alt for UKAAN [KCF]
KAKUMO dial of UKAAN [KCF]
KAKUNA alt for MAMUSI [KDF]
KAKUNA alt for MELKOI dial of MAMUSI [KDF]
KAKUS PENAN dial of KENYAH, WESTERN [XKY]
KAKUYA BUSHMAN NASIE alt for NAMA [NAQ]
KÁKWA alt for CACUA [CBV]
KAKWA [KEO] lang, Uganda; also in DRC, Sudan
KAKWAK alt for KAKWA [KEO]
KAKWERE alt for KWERE [CWE]
KAL alt for ZAAR dial of SAYA [SAY]
KALA alt for BUKALA dial of MONGO-NKUNDU
[MOM]
KALA dial of MBANDJA [ZMZ]
KALA dial of UMBU-UNGU [UMB]
K'ALA alt for BLANG [BLR]
KALA DEGEMA alt for USOKUN dial of
DEGEMA [DEG]
KALA LAGAU LANGGUS alt for KALA LAGAW YA
[MWP]
KALA LAGAW alt for KALA LAGAW YA [MWP]
KALA LAGAW YA [MWP] lang, Australia
KALA MORU alt for MORU [MGD]
KALA YAGAW YA alt for KALA LAGAW YA [MWP]
KALAALLISUT alt for INUKTITUT, GREENLANDIC
[ESG]
KALABAKAN [KVE] lang, Malaysia (Sabah)
KALABAKAN MURUT alt for KALABAKAN [KVE]
KALABARI [IJN] lang, Nigeria
KALABAT ATAS dial of TONSEA [TXS]
KALABIT alt for KELABIT [KZI]
KALABRA [KZZ] lang, Indonesia (Irian Jaya)
KALABUAN dial of KINABATANGAN, UPPER [DMG]
KALADDARSCH alt for KIMAAMA [KIG]
KALAGAN [KQE] lang, Philippines
KALAGAN, KAGAN [KLL] lang, Philippines
KALAGAN, TAGAKAULU [KLG] lang, Philippines
KALAI dial of CHIN, FALAM [HBH]
KALAK alt for KATLA [KCR]
KALAKA alt for KALANGA [KCK]
KALAKAFRA alt for KALO dial of MSER [KQX]
KALAKO alt for KALARKO [KBA]
KALAKTANG dial of MOINBA [MOB]
KALAKU alt for KALARKO [KBA]
KALAKUL alt for KALARKO [KBA]
KALALI dial of NGURA [NBX]
KALAM [KMH] lang, Papua New Guinea
KALAM dial of KALAMI [GWC]
KALAM RIFI alt for HOBYÓT [HOH]
KALAMI [GWC] lang, Pakistan
KALAMI KOHISTANI alt for KALAMI [GWC]
KALAMIAN alt for TAGBANWA, CALAMIAN [TBK]
KALAMIANON alt for TAGBANWA, CALAMIAN
[TBK]
KALAMO alt for ODOODEE [KKC]
KALAMSÉ [KNZ] lang, Burkina Faso; also in Mali
KALAMSÉ alt for SÀMÒMÁ [KNZ]
KALANA alt for KALANGA [KCK]

KALANGA [KCK] lang, Botswana; also in Zimbabwe
KALANGA alt for HOLOHOLO [HOO]
KALANGA dial of CHHATTISGARHI [HNE]
KALANGA dial of RONGA [RON]
KALANGOYA alt for KALLAHAN, KAYAPA [KAK]
KALANGOYA-IKALAHAN alt for KALLAHAN,
KAYAPA [KAK]
KALANGUYA alt for KALLAHAN, KAYAPA [KAK]
KALANGUYA, KELEY-I [IFY] lang, Philippines
KALANKE [CKN] lang, Gambia
KALAO [KLY] lang, Indonesia (Sulawesi)
KALAOTOA alt for KALAO [KLY]
KALAPALO alt for KUIKÚRO-KALAPÁLO [KUI]
KALAPUYA [KAL] lang, USA
KALAQIN alt for JIRIM dial of MONGOLIAN,
PERIPHERAL [MVF]
KALAR dial of EVENKI [EVN]
KALARKO [KBA] lang, Australia
KALAS dial of KABATEI [XKP]
KALASH alt for KALASHA [KLS]
KALASHA [KLS] lang, Pakistan
KALASHA-ALA alt for WAIGALI [WBK]
KALASHAMON alt for KALASHA [KLS]
KALAT dial of BRAHUI [BRH]
KALAUNA dial of IDUNA [VIV]
KALAW KAWAW dial of KALA LAGAW YA [MWP]
KALBU alt for GAALPU dial of DHANGU [GLA]
KALDARÁRI alt for KALDERASH dial of ROMANI,
VLAX [RMY]
KALDAYA alt for CHALDEAN NEO-ARAMAIC [CLD]
KALDERASH dial of ROMANI, VLAX [RMY]
"KALDOSH" pejorative alt for TAYO [CKS]
KALEBWE alt for SONGE [SOP]
KALEDUPA dial of TUKANGBESI NORTH [KHC]
KALEMSÉ alt for KALAMSÉ [KNZ]
KALEMSÉ alt for SÀMÒMÁ [KNZ]
KALENDE alt for PANCANA [PNP]
KALENGA alt for KALAMSÉ [KNZ]
KALENGA alt for SÀMÒMÁ [KNZ]
KALENJIN [KLN] lang, Kenya
KALENTHELKWE alt for WESTERN ANMATYERRE
dial of ANMATYERRE [AMX]
"KALERI" pejorative alt for BO-RUKUL [MAE]
"KALERI" pejorative alt for HOROM [HOE]
KALERNG alt for CENTRAL ISAN dial of THAI,
NORTHEASTERN [TTS]
KALEU dial of SO [SSS]
KALEUNG alt for CENTRAL ISAN dial of THAI,
NORTHEASTERN [TTS]
KALE-WHAN alt for PAIWAN [PWN]
KALI alt for HOANYA [HON]
KALI alt for KARE [KBN]
KALI dial of LAWANGAN [LBX]
KALIAI alt for LUSI [KHL]
KALIAI dial of LUSI [KHL]
KALIÁNA alt for SAPÉ [SPC]
KALIANDA dial of PESISIR, SOUTHERN [PEC]
KALIBUGAN alt for SUBANON, KOLIBUGAN [SKN]
KALIGE alt for FEROGE [FER]
KALIGI alt for FEROGE [FER]
KALIHNA alt for CARIB [CRB]

KALIKA ARYA BHASHA alt for ARE [AAG]
KALIKASA dial of LEVUKA [LVU]
KALIKE alt for FEROGE [FER]
KALIKI alt for FEROGE [FER]
KALIKO [KBO] lang, Sudan; also in DRC, Uganda
KALIKO alt for KELIKO [KBO]
KALIKO-MA'DI alt for KALIKO [KBO]
KALIKO-OMI alt for OMI [OMI]
KALI'NA alt for CARIB [CRB]
KALINDI dial of POKOMO, LOWER [POJ]
KALINGA alt for GA'DANG [GDG]
KALINGA, BUTBUT [KYB] lang, Philippines
KALINGA, LIMOS [KMK] lang, Philippines
KALINGA, LOWER TANUDAN [KML] lang,
    Philippines
KALINGA, LUBUAGAN [KNB] lang, Philippines
KALINGA, MABAKA VALLEY [KKG] lang, Philippines
KALINGA, MADUKAYANG [KMD] lang, Philippines
KALINGA, SOUTHERN [KSC] lang, Philippines
KALINGA, UPPER TANUDAN [KGH] lang,
    Philippines
KALININ alt for TVER dial of KARELIAN [KRL]
KALINYA alt for CARIB [CRB]
KALIS dial of EMBALOH [EMB]
KALIS DAYAK alt for KALIS dial of EMBALOH [EMB]
KALIS MALOH alt for KALIS dial of EMBALOH [EMB]
KALISPEL dial of KALISPEL-PEND D'OREILLE
    [FLA]
KALISPEL-"FLATHEAD" pejorative alt for KALISPEL-
    PEND D'OREILLE [FLA]
KALISPEL-PEND D'OREILLE [FLA] lang, USA
KALISUSU alt for KULISUSU [VKL]
KALITAMI alt for KEMBERANO [BZP]
KALKADOON alt for KALKUTUNG [KTG]
KALKALI alt for KALLAHAN, KAYAPA [KAK]
KALKATUNGU alt for KALKUTUNG [KTG]
KALKOTI [XKA] lang, Pakistan
KALKUS alt for LIKES-UTSIA dial of MANDJAK
    [MFV]
KALKUTUNG [KTG] lang, Australia
KALLA alt for YAÁYUWEE dial of GBAYA,
    NORTHWEST [GYA]
KALLAHAN, KAYAPA [KAK] lang, Philippines
KALLAHAN, TINOC [TNE] lang, Philippines
KALLANA alt for ALAWA [ALH]
KALMACK alt for KALMYK-OIRAT [KGZ]
KALMUCK alt for KALMYK-OIRAT [KGZ]
KALMUK alt for KALMYK-OIRAT [KGZ]
KALMYK-OIRAT [KGZ] lang, Russia (Europe);
    also in China, Germany, Kyrgyzstan, Mongolia,
    Taiwan, USA
KALMYTSKII JAZYK alt for KALMYK-OIRAT [KGZ]
KALO alt for LOKALO dial of NKUTU [NKW]
KALO dial of KEOPARA [KHZ]
KALO dial of MSER [KQX]
KALOKALO alt for KOLUAWAWA [KLX]
KALONDAMA dial of LAMMA [LEV]
KALONG alt for DIMBONG [DII]
KALONG alt for KELON [KYO]
KALOP dial of KOHO [KPM]
KALOSI dial of DURI [MVP]

KALOU [YWA] lang, Papua New Guinea
KALOUNAYE dial of JOLA-FOGNY [DYO]
KALP alt for URIM [URI]
KALTO alt for NIHALI [NHL]
KALTUNGO dial of TANGALE [TAN]
KALULI [BCO] lang, Papua New Guinea
KALULI dial of KALULI [BCO]
KALUM alt for BAGA BINARI [BCG]
KALUMPANG [KLI] lang, Indonesia (Sulawesi)
KAL-UWAN alt for KALINGA, MABAKA VALLEY
    [KKG]
KALVADI dial of DECCAN [DCC]
KALYOKENGNYU alt for NAGA, KHIAMNIUNGAN
    [NKY]
KAM [KDX] lang, Nigeria
KAM alt for DONG, NORTHERN [DOC]
KAM alt for DONG, SOUTHERN [KMC]
KAM alt for KHAMS [KHG]
KAM MU'ANG alt for THAI, NORTHERN [NOD]
KAM TI alt for KHAMTI [KHT]
KAMA dial of KISSI, NORTHERN [KQS]
KAMÃ [KWA] lang, Brazil
KAMÃ MAKÚ alt for KAMÃ [KWA]
KAMA PERMYAK alt for KOMI-PERMYAK [KOI]
KAMAIURÁ alt for KAMAYURÁ [KAY]
KAMAKAN [VKM] lang, Brazil
KAMALAN alt for KAVALAN [CKV]
KAMAN alt for MIJU [MXJ]
KAMANA-KAMANG dial of KAMANG [WOI]
KAMANAWA alt for KATUKÍNA, PANOAN [KNT]
KAMANG [WOI] lang, Indonesia (Nusa Tenggara)
KAMANG dial of KAMANG [WOI]
KAMANGA alt for CHIKAMANGA dial of TUMBUKA
    [TUW]
KAMANIDI alt for GAAM [TBI]
KAMANNAUA alt for KATUKÍNA, PANOAN [KNT]
KAMANO [KBQ] lang, Papua New Guinea
KAMANO-KAFE alt for KAMANO [KBQ]
KAMANT alt for QIMANT dial of AGAW, WESTERN
    [QIM]
KAMANTAN [KCI] lang, Nigeria
KAMANTON alt for KAMANTAN [KCI]
KAMAONI alt for KUMAUNI [KFY]
KAMAR [KEQ] lang, India
KAMARA [JMR] lang, Ghana
KAMARA alt for CENTRAL KONO dial of KONO
    [KNO]
KAMARAGAKOK alt for ARECUNA dial of PEMON
    [AOC]
KAMARIAN [KZX] lang, Indonesia (Maluku)
KAMARIANG alt for KAMARIAN [KZX]
KAMARI-SANTALI dial of SANTALI [SNT]
KAMARU [KGX] lang, Indonesia (Sulawesi)
KAMAS [XAS] lang, Russia (Asia)
KAMAS alt for KARAGAS [KIM]
KAMASA [KLP] lang, Papua New Guinea
KAMASAU [KMS] lang, Papua New Guinea
KAMASSIAN alt for KAMAS [XAS]
KAMASSIAN dial of KAMAS [XAS]
KAMASSIAN dial of KHAKAS [KJH]
KAMATE dial of YAGARIA [YGR]

KAMATHI dial of TELUGU [TCW]
KAMAU alt for JIAMAO [JIO]
KAMAYIRÁ alt for KAMAYURÁ [KAY]
KAMAYO [KYK] lang, Philippines
KAMAYURÁ [KAY] lang, Brazil
KAMBA [KIK] lang, Kenya
KAMBA [QKZ] lang, Brazil
KAMBA alt for AKASELEM [AKS]
KAMBA alt for WAGI [FAD]
KAMBAATA [KTB] lang, Ethiopia
KAMBAIRA [KYY] lang, Papua New Guinea
KAMBARA alt for KAMBAATA [KTB]
KAMBARAMBA dial of AP MA [KBX]
KAMBARI alt for CISHINGINI [ASG]
KAMBARI alt for TSIKIMBA [KDL]
KAMBARI alt for TSISHINGINI [KAM]
KAMBARIIRE dial of FULFULDE, ADAMAWA [FUB]
KAMBATA alt for KAMBAATA [KTB]
KAMBATTA alt for KAMBAATA [KTB]
KAMBE dial of GIRYAMA [NYF]
KAMBEBA alt for OMAGUA [OMG]
KAMBEGL alt for MARING [MBW]
KAMBE-KAMBERO dial of KAIMBULAWA [ZKA]
KAMBERA [SMI] lang, Indonesia (Nusa Tenggara)
KAMBERA alt for GAMBERA [GMA]
KAMBERA dial of KAMBERA [SMI]
KAMBERATARO [KBV] lang, Indonesia (Irian Jaya);
    also in Papua New Guinea
KAMBERATORO alt for KAMBERATARO [KBV]
KAMBERAU [IRX] lang, Indonesia (Irian Jaya)
KAMBERCHI alt for CISHINGINI [ASG]
KAMBERCHI alt for TSIKIMBA [KDL]
KAMBERCHI alt for TSISHINGINI [KAM]
KAMBERI alt for TSUVADI [TVD]
KAMBERRI alt for CISHINGINI [ASG]
KAMBERRI alt for TSIKIMBA [KDL]
KAMBERRI alt for TSISHINGINI [KAM]
KAMBIA dial of WAHGI [WAK]
KAMBIWÁ [QKH] lang, Brazil
KAMBOLÉ [XKB] lang, Togo
KAMBONSENGA alt for AMBO dial of LALA-BISA
    [LEB]
KAMBOT alt for AP MA [KBX]
KAMBOWA dial of KIOKO [UES]
KAMBU alt for LIMBUM [LIM]
KAMBURWAMA dial of WANDALA [MFI]
KAMCHADAL alt for ITELMEN [ITL]
KAMCHATKA alt for ITELMEN [ITL]
KAMCHATKA dial of EVEN [EVE]
KAMDA alt for KAMDANG dial of TULISHI [TEY]
KAMDANG dial of TULISHI [TEY]
KAMDESHI alt for KAMVIRI [QMV]
KAMDHUE alt for KANJU [KBE]
KAMEA alt for HAMTAI [HMT]
KAMEMTXA alt for CAMSÁ [KBH]
KAMEN alt for KAMENSKIJ dial of KORYAK [KPY]
KAMENSKIJ dial of KORYAK [KPY]
KAMENZ dial of SORBIAN, UPPER [WEN]
KAMER dial of BIAK [BHW]
KAMESH alt for BAHARLU dial of AZERBAIJANI,
    SOUTH [AZB]

KAMET alt for LAMET [LBN]
KAMETSU dial of TOKU-NO-SHIMA [TKN]
KAMHAO alt for KAMHAU dial of CHIN, TEDIM
    [CTD]
KAMHAU dial of CHIN, TEDIM [CTD]
KAMHMU alt for KHMU [KJG]
KAMHOW alt for KAMHAU dial of CHIN, TEDIM
    [CTD]
KAMI [KCU] lang, Tanzania
KAMI [KMI] lang, Nigeria
KAMI alt for CHIN, KHUMI [CKM]
KAMIA alt for KUMIÁI [DIH]
KAMIAI alt for KUMIÁI [DIH]
KAMIGIN alt for MANOBO, CINAMIGUIN [MKX]
KAMIK alt for KAMVIRI [QMV]
KAMI-KULAKA dial of YAGARIA [YGR]
KAMILAROI [KLD] lang, Australia
KAMINDJO alt for WÁRA [TCI]
KAMINO dial of BATU [BTU]
KAMIYAHI alt for KUMIÁI [DIH]
KAMIYAI alt for KUMIÁI [DIH]
/KAMKA!E alt for /XAM [XAM]
KAMKAM [BGU] lang, Nigeria; also in Cameroon
KAMKAM alt for MBONGNO [BGU]
KAMMU alt for KHMU [KJG]
KAMMÜANG alt for THAI, NORTHERN [NOD]
KAMMYANG alt for THAI, NORTHERN [NOD]
KAMNUM alt for AWTUW [KMN]
KAMO [KCQ] lang, Nigeria
KAMORA alt for KAMORO [KGQ]
KAMORO [KGQ] lang, Indonesia (Irian Jaya)
KAMORTA alt for CAMORTA dial of NICOBARESE,
    CENTRAL [NCB]
KAMPA alt for ASHÉNINCA UCAYALI-YURUA [CPB]
KAMPAR alt for ULU KAMPAR dial of SEMAI [SEA]
KAMPONG AYER dial of BRUNEI [KXD]
KAMPUNG BARU alt for KAIS [KZM]
KAMRAU alt for KAMBERAU [IRX]
KAMRUP dial of GARO [GRT]
KAMSA alt for CAMSÁ [KBH]
KAMSE alt for CAMSÁ [KBH]
KAMSIKI alt for PSIKYE [KVJ]
KAMSILI dial of UKHWEJO [UKH]
KAMTUK alt for KEMTUIK [KMT]
KAMU [QKY] lang, Australia
KAMU alt for KAMO [KCQ]
KAMU alt for KHMU [KJG]
KAMU alt for PSIKYE dial of PSIKYE [KVJ]
KAMUAN' dial of TAOIH, UPPER [TTH]
KAMUKU alt for CINDA-REGI-TIYAL [KAU]
KAMULA [KHM] lang, Papua New Guinea
KAMURA alt for KAMULA [KHM]
KAMURÚ dial of KARIRI-XOCO [KZW]
KAMVIRI [QMV] lang, Afghanistan; also in Pakistan
KAMVIRI dial of KAMVIRI [QMV]
KAMWAI-MARHAI dial of KULERE [KUL]
KAMWE [HIG] lang, Nigeria
KAN alt for CHINESE, GAN [KNN]
KAN alt for KAAN [LDL]
KAN alt for KAANSA [GNA]
KAN dial of MBAY [MYB]

KANA alt for KHANA [KEH]
KANA MABANG alt for MABA [MDE]
KANABU alt for KANAKANABU [QNB]
KANAKANABU [QNB] lang, Taiwan
KANAKANAVU alt for KANAKANABU [QNB]
KANAKHOE alt for //GANA [GNK]
KANAKHOE alt for G//ANAKHWE dial of GANA
    [GNK]
KANAKURU alt for DERA [KNA]
KANALA alt for XÂRÂCÙÙ [ANE]
KANALU alt for BAROK [BJK]
KANAM alt for KOENOEM [KCS]
KANAM dial of JARAWA [JAR]
KANAMANTI alt for JAMAMADÍ [JAA]
KANAMARÉ alt for KANAMARÍ [KNM]
KANAMARÍ [KNM] lang, Brazil
KANAMBU alt for KANEMBU [KBL]
KANAMBU alt for KANURI, TUMARI [KRT]
KANANA alt for KALANGA [KCK]
KANANDJOHO dial of NDUMU [NMD]
KANAPIT alt for BAROK [BJK]
KANARA alt for KUKNA [KEX]
KANARESE alt for KANNADA [KJV]
KANASHI [QAS] lang, India
KANASI [SOQ] lang, Papua New Guinea
KANASI alt for KANASHI [QAS]
KANATANG dial of KAMBERA [SMI]
KANAUJI [BJJ] lang, India
KANAUJI PROPER dial of KANAUJI [BJJ]
KANAURI alt for KINNAURI [KFK]
KANAURI alt for KINNAURI, CHITKULI [CIK]
KANAURY ANUSKAD alt for KINNAURI [KFK]
KANAWARI alt for KINNAURI [KFK]
KANAWI alt for KINNAURI [KFK]
KANCHANABURI PWO KAREN dial of KAREN,
    PWO WESTERN THAILAND [KJP]
KANDA alt for KANDE [KBS]
KANDA alt for KUI [KXU]
KANDAHAR PASHTO dial of PASHTO, SOUTHERN
    [PBT]
KANDAK dial of PASHAYI, NORTHEAST [AEE]
KANDAR dial of SANGIR [SAN]
KANDAR dial of SELARU [SLU]
KANDAS [KQW] lang, Papua New Guinea
KANDASI dial of FIPA [FIP]
KANDAWIRE dial of TUMBUKA [TUW]
KANDAWO [GAM] lang, Papua New Guinea
KANDE [KBS] lang, Gabon
KANDE alt for KULERE [KUL]
KANDE dial of TSONGA [TSO]
KANDEPE dial of ENGA [ENQ]
KANDÉRÉ dial of LYELE [LEE]
KANDERE dial of SENOUFO, CEBAARA [SEF]
KANDERMA alt for KINDERMA dial of TIRA [TIR]
KANDH alt for KUI [KXU]
KANDIALI dial of DOGRI-KANGRI [DOJ]
KANDJU alt for KANJU [KBE]
KANDOASHI dial of CANDOSHI-SHAPRA [CBU]
KANDOMIN alt for YAGAWAK dial of WANTOAT
    [WNC]
KANDOSHI alt for CANDOSHI-SHAPRA [CBU]

KANDYU alt for KANJU [KBE]
KANELA alt for CANELA [RAM]
KANEMBOU alt for KANEMBU [KBL]
KANEMBU [KBL] lang, Chad
KANEMBU alt for KANURI, TUMARI [KRT]
KANG [KYP] lang, Laos; also in China
KANG alt for KHAMS [KHG]
KANGA [KCP] lang, Sudan
KANGAÉ alt for SIKKA NATAR dial of SIKA [SKI]
KANGANA dial of LUSENGO [LUS]
KANGAR BHAT alt for KANJARI [KFT]
KANGARRAGA alt for KUNGARAKANY [GGK]
KANGEAN [KKV] lang, Indonesia (Java and Bali)
KANGEJU alt for HADZA [HTS]
KANGITE alt for APURINÃ [APU]
KANGO [KBI] lang, DRC
KANGO [KTY] lang, DRC
KANGO [KZY] lang, DRC
KANGO PIGMY alt for KANGO [KBI]
KANGO PYGMY alt for KANGO [KZY]
KANGOU dial of FALI, SOUTH [FAL]
KANGRA alt for KANGRI dial of DOGRI-KANGRI
    [DOJ]
KANGRI alt for KANJARI [KFT]
KANGRI dial of DOGRI-KANGRI [DOJ]
KANGU alt for KANGOU dial of FALI, SOUTH [FAL]
KANGWONDO alt for SEOUL dial of KOREAN [KKN]
KANGYE alt for KWANGE dial of GBARI [GBY]
KANHOBAL alt for KANJOBAL, EASTERN [KJB]
KANICHANA alt for CANICHANA [CAZ]
KANIEN'KEHAKA alt for MOHAWK [MOH]
KANIET [KTK] lang, Papua New Guinea
KANIGURAMI dial of ORMURI [ORU]
KANIKA dial of JULA, WORODOUGOU [JUD]
KANIKEH dial of MANUSELA [WHA]
KANIKKAR alt for KANIKKARAN [KEV]
KANIKKARAN [KEV] lang, India
KANINGARA alt for KANINGRA [KNR]
KANINGDOM dial of KANINGDON-NINDEM [KDP]
KANINGDON-NINDEM [KDP] lang, Nigeria
KANINGI [KZO] lang, Gabon
KANINGKON alt for KANINGDOM dial of
    KANINGDON-NINDEM [KDP]
KANINGKWOM alt for KANINGDOM dial of
    KANINGDON-NINDEM [KDP]
KANINGRA [KNR] lang, Papua New Guinea
KANINJAL alt for KENINJAL [KNL]
KANINJAL DAYAK alt for KENINJAL [KNL]
KANINKON alt for KANINGDOM dial of
    KANINGDON-NINDEM [KDP]
KANIOKA alt for KANYOK [KNY]
KANIRAN alt for MAIRASI [FRY]
KANITE [KMU] lang, Papua New Guinea
KANIUÁ alt for MARÚBO [MZR]
KANJAGA alt for BULI [BWU]
KANJARI [KFT] lang, India
KANJIMATA alt for ADYNYAMATHANHA [ADT]
KANJININGI alt for NJININGI dial of TEKE,
    NORTHERN [TEG]
KANJOBAL, EASTERN [KJB] lang, Guatemala;
    also in USA

KANJOBAL, WESTERN [KNJ] lang, Guatemala; also in Mexico, USA
KANJRI alt for KANJARI [KFT]
KANJU [KBE] lang, Australia
KANKANAEY [KNE] lang, Philippines
KANKANAI alt for KANKANAEY [KNE]
KANKANAY alt for KANKANAEY [KNE]
KANKANAY, NORTHERN [KAN] lang, Philippines
KANNA alt for BADA [BAU]
KANNADA [KJV] lang, India
KANNEH dial of KRAHN, EASTERN [KQO]
KANNIKAN alt for KANIKKARAN [KEV]
KANNIKARAN alt for KANIKKARAN [KEV]
KANNIKHARAN alt for KANIKKARAN [KEV]
KANO alt for KANU [KHX]
KANO dial of HAUSA [HUA]
KANOÉ [KXO] lang, Brazil
KANO-KATSINA dial of FULFULDE, KANO-KATSINA-BORORRO [FUV]
KANO-KATSINA dial of FULFULDE, NIGERIAN [FUV]
KANO-KATSINA-BORORRO FULFULDE alt for FULFULDE, NIGERIAN [FUV]
KANOREUNU SKAD alt for KINNAURI [KFK]
KANORIN SKAD alt for KINNAURI [KFK]
KANORUG SKADD alt for KINNAURI [KFK]
KANOURI alt for KANURI, CENTRAL [KPH]
KANOURI alt for KANURI, MANGA [KBY]
KANOURY alt for KANURI, CENTRAL [KPH]
KANOURY alt for KANURI, MANGA [KBY]
KANOWIT [KXN] lang, Malaysia (Sarawak)
KANSA [KAA] lang, USA
KANTANA alt for MAMA [MMA]
KANTE dial of LAMA [LAS]
KANTEWU dial of UMA [PPK]
KANTILAN alt for CANTILAN dial of SURIGAONON [SUL]
KANTOHE dial of BALANTA-KENTOHE [BLE]
KANTONSI alt for KANTOSI [XKT]
KANTOSI [XKT] lang, Ghana
KANTU' dial of IBAN [IBA]
KANTUA alt for TA'OIH, UPPER [TTH]
KANU [KHX] lang, DRC
KANUFI [KNI] lang, Nigeria
KANUM, BÄDI [KHD] lang, Indonesia (Irian Jaya)
KANUM, NGKÂLMPW [KCD] lang, Indonesia (Irian Jaya)
KANUM, SMÄRKY [KXQ] lang, Indonesia (Irian Jaya)
KANUM, SOTA [KRZ] lang, Indonesia (Irian Jaya); also in Papua New Guinea
KANURI, CENTRAL [KPH] lang, Nigeria; also in Cameroon, Chad, Eritrea, Niger, Sudan
KANURI, MANGA [KBY] lang, Niger; also in Nigeria
KANURI, TUMARI [KRT] lang, Niger
KANY alt for EASTERN NUER dial of NUER [NUS]
KANYAK alt for NAGA, KONYAK [NBE]
KANYAW alt for KAREN, S'GAW [KSW]
KANYAY alt for KENYAH, UPPER BARAM [UBM]
KANYAY alt for KENYAH, WESTERN [XKY]
KANYOK [KNY] lang, DRC

KANYOKA alt for KANYOK [KNY]
KANYOP alt for MANDJAK [MFV]
KANYU alt for KANJU [KBE]
KANZE alt for KANSA [KAA]
KAO [KAX] lang, Indonesia (Maluku)
KAOKEEP dial of CHIN, THADO [TCZ]
KAOKONAU alt for KAMORO [KGQ]
KAONDE [KQN] lang, Zambia; also in DRC
KAORO dial of WE WESTERN [WEC]
KAOUARA-TIMBA-SINDOU-KORONI dial of NATIORO [NTI]
KAOWERAWEDJ alt for KAUWERA [QKX]
KAOWLU alt for KAORO dial of WE WESTERN [WEC]
KAPAGALAN dial of TIMUGON MURUT [TIH]
KAPAL dial of GIDRA [GDR]
KAPAMPANGAN alt for PAMPANGAN [PMP]
KAPANAWA alt for CAPANAHUA [KAQ]
KAPANGAN dial of KANKANAEY [KNE]
KAPARI dial of KEOPARA [KHZ]
KAPAU alt for HAMTAI [HMT]
KAPAUKU alt for EKARI [EKG]
KAPAUR alt for IHA [IHP]
KAPAURI alt for KAPORI [KHP]
KAPAWA alt for THA [THY]
KAPESO alt for BAGUSA [BQB]
KAPIANGAN alt for PAIWAN [PWN]
KAPIN [TBX] lang, Papua New Guinea
KAPIN dial of KAPIN [TBX]
KAPINAWÁ [QKP] lang, Brazil
KAPINGAMARANGI [KPG] lang, Micronesia
KAPITIAUW alt for TARPIA [SUF]
KAPO alt for YREPO dial of KRUMEN, TEPO [TED]
KAPON alt for AKAWAIO [ARB]
KAPON alt for PATAMONA [PBC]
KAPONA dial of ENGA [ENQ]
KAPONE alt for NUMEE [KDK]
KAPONTORI dial of PANCANA [PNP]
KAPORE alt for BEBELI [BEK]
KAPORI [KHP] lang, Indonesia (Irian Jaya)
KAPRIMAN [DJU] lang, Papua New Guinea
KAPRIMAN dial of KAPRIMAN [DJU]
KAPSIKI alt for PSIKYE dial of PSIKYE [KVJ]
KAPSIKI alt for PSIKYE [KVJ]
KAPTIAUW alt for TARPIA [SUF]
KAPUAS dial of NGAJU [NIJ]
KAPUCHA alt for BEZHTA [KAP]
KAPUCHIN alt for BEZHTA [KAP]
KAPUGU alt for NIRAGU dial of GBIRI-NIRAGU [GRH]
KAPUL alt for SAMA, ABAKNON [ABX]
KAPULIKA alt for HAIGWAI [HGW]
KAPULIKA dial of HAIGWAI [HGW]
KAPUTIEI dial of MAASAI [MET]
KAPWI alt for NAGA, KABUI [NKF]
KAPYA [KLO] lang, Nigeria
KAQCHIQUEL alt for CAKCHIQUEL, CENTRAL [CAK]
KAR alt for KARABORO, EASTERN [KAR]
KAR alt for KUR dial of KAG-FER-JIIR-KOOR-ROR-US-ZUKSUN [GEL]

KAR BHOTE alt for LHOMI [LHM]
"KARA" pejorative alt for HWARASA dial of AGAW,
    WESTERN [QIM]
KARA [KAH] lang, CAR
KARA [LEU] lang, Papua New Guinea
KARA [REG] lang, Tanzania
KARA alt for BLACK NOGAI dial of NOGAI [NOG]
KARA alt for GULA [KCM]
KARA alt for KIRGHIZ [KDO]
KARA alt for NGALA [NUD]
KARA DE SOUDAN alt for GULA [KCM]
KARA KERRE alt for HAMER-BANNA [AMF]
KARA OF SUDAN alt for GULA [KCM]
KARABAGH dial of ARMENIAN [ARM]
KARABAGH SHAMAKHI dial of ARMENIAN [ARM]
KARABAKH alt for SHUSHA dial of AZERBAIJANI,
    NORTH [AZE]
KARABAKH alt for SUSA dial of AZERBAIJANI,
    NORTH [AZE]
KARABORO, EASTERN [KAR] lang, Burkina Faso;
    also in Côte d'Ivoire
KARABORO, WESTERN [KZA] lang, Burkina Faso
KARACAYLAR alt for KARACHAY-BALKAR [KRC]
KARACHAI alt for KARACHAY-BALKAR [KRC]
KARACHAITSY alt for KARACHAY-BALKAR [KRC]
KARACHAY alt for KARACHAY-BALKAR [KRC]
KARACHAY dial of KARACHAY-BALKAR [KRC]
KARACHAY-BALKAR [KRC] lang, Russia (Europe);
    also in Armenia, Azerbaijan, Kazakhstan,
    Kyrgyzstan, USA, Uzbekistan
KARACHAYLA alt for KARACHAY-BALKAR [KRC]
KARACHI dial of DOMARI [RMT]
KARADJEE alt for IWAIDJA [IBD]
KARADJERI [GBD] lang, Australia
KARAGAN dial of DAYAK, LAND [DYK]
KARAGAS [KIM] lang, Russia (Asia)
KARAGAS dial of MATOR [MTM]
KARAGASS alt for KARAGAS [KIM]
KARAGAWAN dial of ISNAG [ISD]
KARAGINSKIJ dial of ALUTOR [ALR]
KARAGWE alt for NYAMBO [NYM]
KARAHAWYANA [XKH] lang, Brazil
KARAI KARAI alt for KAREKARE [KAI]
KARAIAI alt for ANEM [ANZ]
KARAIKARAI alt for KAREKARE [KAI]
KARAIM [KDR] lang, Lithuania; also in Israel, Ukraine
KARAITE alt for KARAIM [KDR]
KARAJ [KPJ] lang, Brazil
KARAJARRI alt for KARADJERI [GBD]
KARAKALPAK [KAC] lang, Uzbekistan; also in
    Afghanistan, Kazakhstan, Kyrgyzstan,
    Turkmenistan
KARAKARA dial of GURUNTUM-MBAARU [GRD]
KARAKATI alt for KRINKATI dial of KRIKATI-
    TIMBIRA [XRI]
KARAKELANG alt for SOUTH KARAKELONG dial
    of TALAUD [TLD]
KARAKELANG alt for SOUTH KARAKELONG dial
    of TALAUD [TLD]
KARAKH alt for KARAX dial of AVAR [AVR]
KARAKIR alt for JONKOR BOURMATAGUIL [JEU]

KARA-KIRGIZ alt for KIRGHIZ [KDO]
KARAKLOBUK alt for KARAKALPAK [KAC]
KARAM alt for KALAM [KMH]
KARAMA alt for KURRAMA [VKU]
KARAMANLI dial of BALKAN GAGAUZ TURKISH
    [BGX]
KARAMANLI dial of TURKISH [TRK]
KARAMBA dial of MARING [MBW]
KARAMBIT dial of KAPRIMAN [DJU]
KARAMI [XAR] lang, Papua New Guinea
KARAMIANANEN alt for TAGBANWA, CALAMIAN
    [TBK]
KARAMOJONG [KDJ] lang, Uganda
KARAMOJONG dial of KARAMOJONG [KDJ]
KARANG [KZR] lang, Cameroon; also in Chad
KARANG alt for NGAS [ANC]
KARANG dial of KARANG [KZR]
KARANGA [KTH] lang, Chad
KARANGA dial of KARANGA [KTH]
KARANGA dial of SHONA [SHD]
KARANGAN alt for KARAGAN dial of DAYAK, LAND
    [DYK]
KARANGAN dial of BASAP [BDB]
KARANGASEM alt for LOWLAND BALI dial of BALI
    [BZC]
KARANGI alt for WELIKI [KLH]
KARANJAN dial of JULA, WORODOUGOU [JUD]
KARAO [KYJ] lang, Philippines
KARAPANÁ alt for CARAPANA [CBC]
KARAPANÃ alt for CARAPANA [CBC]
KARAPANO alt for CARAPANA [CBC]
KARAPAPAK dial of AZERBAIJANI, NORTH [AZE]
KARAPAPAKH dial of AZERBAIJANI, SOUTH [AZB]
KARAPATÓ alt for TINGUI-BOTO [TGV]
KARARAÓ dial of KAYAPO [TXU]
KARAS [KGV] lang, Indonesia (Irian Jaya)
KARATA [KPT] lang, Russia (Europe)
KARATAI alt for KARATA [KPT]
KARATAUN dial of KALUMPANG [KLI]
KARATE alt for KOMSO [KXC]
KARATIN alt for KARATA [KPT]
KARATINA alt for MATHIRA dial of GIKUYU [KIU]
KARAU dial of LAWANGAN [LBX]
KARAW alt for KARAO [KYJ]
KARAWA [QKR] lang, Papua New Guinea
KARAWA alt for GARAWA [GBC]
KARAWARI alt for TABRIAK [TZX]
KARAWARI dial of ALAMBLAK [AMP]
KARAX dial of AVAR [AVR]
KARAY-A alt for KINARAY-A [KRJ]
KARAYAN alt for KADAIAN dial of BRUNEI [KXD]
KARAYAN alt for KEDAYAN dial of BRUNEI [KXD]
KARBARDAE alt for KABADE dial of SAPO [KRN]
KARBI alt for MIKIR [MJW]
KARBI KARBAK alt for MIKIR [MJW]
KARBO alt for WEST DANGALEAT dial of
    DANGALEAT [DAA]
KARDUTJARA alt for KARTUJARRA dial of MARTU
    WANGKA [MPJ]
KARDUTJARRA alt for KARTUJARRA dial of
    MARTU WANGKA [MPJ]

KARE [KBN] lang, CAR; also in Cameroon
KARE [KMF] lang, Papua New Guinea
KARE alt for CREQ dial of HRE [HRE]
KARE alt for KARI [KBJ]
KARE alt for TOPOSA [TOQ]
KAREKARE [KAI] lang, Nigeria
KARELIAN [KRL] lang, Russia (Europe); also in Finland
KARELIAN PROPER alt for KARELIAN [KRL]
KAREL'SKOGO JAZYKA alt for KARELIAN [KRL]
KARELY alt for KARELIAN [KRL]
KAREN, BREK [KVL] lang, Myanmar
KAREN, BWE [BWE] lang, Myanmar
KAREN, GEBA [KVQ] lang, Myanmar
KAREN, GEKO [GHK] lang, Myanmar
KAREN, LAHTA [KVT] lang, Myanmar
KAREN, MANUMANAW [KXF] lang, Myanmar
KAREN, PADAUNG [PDU] lang, Myanmar; also in Thailand
KAREN, PAKU [KPP] lang, Myanmar
KAREN, PA'O [BLK] lang, Myanmar; also in Thailand
KAREN, PWO EASTERN [KJP] lang, Myanmar; also in Thailand
KAREN, PWO NORTHERN [PWW] lang, Thailand
KAREN, PWO WESTERN [PWO] lang, Myanmar
KAREN, PWO WESTERN THAILAND [KJP] lang, Myanmar; also in Thailand
KAREN, PWO, PHRAE [KJT] lang, Thailand
KAREN, S'GAW [KSW] lang, Myanmar; also in Thailand
KAREN, YINBAW [KVU] lang, Myanmar
KAREN, YINTALE [KVY] lang, Myanmar
KAREN, ZAYEIN [KXK] lang, Myanmar
KARENBYU alt for KAREN, GEBA [KVQ]
KARENG alt for KARANG [KZR]
KARENNI alt for KAYAH, EASTERN [EKY]
KARENNI alt for KAYAH, WESTERN [KYU]
KARENNYI alt for KAYAH, EASTERN [EKY]
KARENNYI alt for KAYAH, WESTERN [KYU]
KAREOVAN dial of KAVALAN [CKV]
KAREOWAN alt for KAREOVAN dial of KAVALAN [CKV]
KARETI alt for KOMSO [KXC]
KAREY [KYD] lang, Indonesia (Maluku)
KAREZ-I-MULLA dial of MOGHOLI [MLG]
KARFA alt for DUHWA [KBZ]
KARFASIA alt for SAMAROKENA [TMJ]
KARHADI dial of KONKANI [KNK]
KARI [KBJ] lang, DRC
KARI alt for KARE [KBN]
KARI alt for SUMAU [SIX]
KARI alt for USINO [URW]
KARI dial of KARE [KBN]
KARIANA alt for SAPÉ [SPC]
KARIENG DAENG alt for KAYAH, WESTERN [KYU]
KARIERA alt for KARIYARRA [VKA]
KARIJONA alt for CARIJONA [CBD]
KARIKKORAVA alt for VAAGRI BOOLI [VAA]
KARIME alt for NANOMAM dial of YANOMAMI [WCA]
KARIMOJONG alt for KARAMOJONG [KDJ]

KARIMONJONG alt for KARAMOJONG [KDJ]
KARIMUI alt for DADIBI [MPS]
KARIN dial of ARMENIAN [ARM]
KARINGAL alt for MALARYAN [MJQ]
KARINGANI [KGN] lang, Iran
KARIPÚNA [KGM] lang, Brazil
KARIPUNÁ [KUQ] lang, Brazil
KARIPÚNA CREOLE FRENCH [KMV] lang, Brazil
KARIPUNÁ DE RONDÔNIA alt for KARIPUÁN [KUQ]
KARIPÚNA DO AMAPÁ alt for KARIPÚNA [KGM]
KARIPUNÁ DO GUAPORÉ alt for KARIPUÁN [KUQ]
KARIPÚNA DO UAÇÁ alt for KARIPÚNA [KGM]
KARIPUNA JACI PARANÁ dial of TENHARIM [PAH]
KARIRA dial of MANAGALASI [MCQ]
KARIRÍ alt for KARIRI-XOCÓ [KZW]
KARIRI XUCÓ alt for KARIRI-XOCÓ [KZW]
KARIRI-XOCÓ [KZW] lang, Brazil
KARITIÂNA [KTN] lang, Brazil
KARIYA [KIL] lang, Nigeria
KARIYA WUUFU alt for MBURKU [BBT]
KARIYARRA [VKA] lang, Australia
KARIYU alt for KARIYA [KIL]
KARKAR alt for KARKAR-YURI [YUJ]
K'ARK'ARTE alt for GERGERE dial of GAWWADA [GWD]
KARKAR-YURI [YUJ] lang, Papua New Guinea
KARKAWU dial of KANEMBU [KBL]
KARKIN [KRB] lang, USA
KARKO [KKO] lang, Sudan
KARLUK dial of UZBEK, NORTHERN [UZB]
KARMALI dial of SANTALI [SNT]
KARNATAKA LAMANI dial of LAMBADI [LMN]
KARNU alt for KANJU [KBE]
KARO [KXH] lang, Ethiopia
KARO dial of RAWA [RWO]
KARO BATAK alt for BATAK KARO [BTX]
KAROK [KYH] lang, USA
KAROKA dial of KATLA [KCR]
KAROLANOS [KYN] lang, Philippines
KAROMBE dial of MANYIKA [MXC]
KAROMPA dial of BONERATE [BNA]
KARON [KRX] lang, Senegal; also in Gambia
KARON DORI [KGW] lang, Indonesia (Irian Jaya)
KARON PANTAI alt for ABUN TAT dial of ABUN [KGR]
KARONDI dial of TUMTUM [TBR]
KARONSIE dial of MORI BAWAH [XMZ]
KARORE [XKX] lang, Papua New Guinea
KARRAJARRA alt for KARADJERI [GBD]
KARRÉ alt for KARE [KBN]
KARRIARA alt for KARIYARRA [VKA]
KARS dial of AZERBAIJANI, SOUTH [AZB]
KARSHI alt for KANUFI [KNI]
KARTUJARRA dial of MARTU WANGKA [MPJ]
KARTULI alt for GEORGIAN [GEO]
KARTUTJARA alt for KARTUJARRA dial of MARTU WANGKA [MPJ]
KARU dial of GBAGYI [GBR]
KARUA alt for HARUA dial of BOLA [BNP]

KARUAMA dial of KUNIMAIPA [KUP]
KARUFA alt for BURUWAI [ASI]
KARUK alt for KAROK [KYH]
KARUPAKA alt for KORRIPAKO dial of CURRIPACO [KPC]
KARUTANA alt for CARÚTANA [CRU]
KASAA dial of MUMUYE [MUL]
KASANGA [CCJ] lang, Guinea-Bissau
KASARA dial of SENOUFO, CEBAARA [SEF]
KASCHEMIRI alt for KASHMIRI [KSH]
KASELE alt for AKASELEM [AKS]
KASEM [KAS] lang, Burkina Faso; also in Ghana
KASEM dial of KASEM [KAS]
KASENA alt for KASEM [KAS]
KASENG alt for KASSENG [KGC]
KASENGA dial of BANGUBANGU [BNX]
KASERE alt for IKOBI-MENA [MEB]
KASHANI dial of FARSI, WESTERN [PES]
KASHAYA [KJU] lang, USA
KASHGAR-YARKAND dial of UYGHUR [UIG]
KASHKADARYA ARABIC alt for ARABIC, UZBEKI SPOKEN [AUZ]
KASHKAI alt for QASHQA'I [QSQ]
KASHKARI alt for KHOWAR [KHW]
KASHMERE dial of KARANGA [KTH]
KASHMIR GUJURI alt for GUJARI [GJU]
KASHMIRI [KSH] lang, India; also in Pakistan, United Kingdom
KASHTAWARI alt for KISHTWARI dial of KASHMIRI [KSH]
KASHTWARI alt for KISHTWARI dial of KASHMIRI [KSH]
KASHUBIAN [CSB] lang, Poland; also in Canada
KASHUBIAN PROPER dial of KASHUBIAN [CSB]
KASHUJANA alt for KAXUIÂNA [KBB]
KASHUYANA alt for KAXUIÂNA [KBB]
KASIEH dial of WEMALE, NORTH [WEO]
KASIGAON dial of TAMANG, EASTERN GORKHA [TGE]
KASIGAU dial of SAGALLA [TGA]
KASIGURANIN [KSN] lang, Philippines
KASIKASI dial of BUNAMA [BDD]
KASIM alt for KASEM [KAS]
KASIMBAR alt for TAJIO [TDJ]
KASIRA alt for IRARUTU [IRH]
KASIUI alt for WATUBELA [WAH]
KASIWA alt for NINGGERUM [NXR]
KASKA [KKZ] lang, Canada
KASKI GURUNG alt for NORTHWESTERN GURUNG dial of GURUNG, WESTERN [GVR]
KASKIHÁ alt for GUANA [GVA]
KASMIN dial of BUNA [BVN]
KASOMA dial of KALAMSE [KNZ]
KASONKE alt for XAASONGAXANGO [KAO]
KASONKE alt for XASONGA [KAO]
KASRAPAI alt for NINAM [SHB]
KASSADOU LELE dial of LELE [LLC]
KASSANGA alt for KASANGA [CCJ]
KASSEM alt for KASEM [KAS]
KASSENA alt for KASEM [KAS]
KASSENE alt for KASEM [KAS]

KASSENG [KGC] lang, Laos
KASSI alt for KHASI [KHI]
KASSO alt for XAASONGAXANGO [KAO]
KASSO alt for XASONGA [KAO]
KASSON alt for XAASONGAXANGO [KAO]
KASSON alt for XASONGA [KAO]
KASSONKE alt for XAASONGAXANGO [KAO]
KASSONKE alt for XASONGA [KAO]
KASTANISTA-SITENA alt for NORTHERN TSAKONIAN dial of TSAKONIAN [TSD]
KASUA [KHS] lang, Papua New Guinea
KASUI alt for WATUBELA [WAH]
KASUVA dial of TAMIL [TCV]
KASUWA dial of NINGGERUM [NXR]
KASUWERI dial of KOKODA [QKW]
KASZUBSKI alt for KASHUBIAN [CSB]
KATAANG [KGD] lang, Laos
KATAB alt for TYAP [KCG]
KATAB dial of TYAP [KCG]
KATABAGA [KTQ] lang, Philippines
KATAF alt for TYAP [KCG]
KATAGUM dial of HAUSA [HUA]
KATAI MEGHWAR dial of KOLI, KACHI [GJK]
KATAKARI alt for KATKARI [KFU]
KATAN alt for ULLATAN [ULL]
KATANG alt for KATAANG [KGD]
KATANG alt for KAYONG [KXY]
KATANGA SWAHILI dial of SWAHILI, CONGO [SWC]
KATARI alt for KATKARI [KFU]
KATAUIXI alt for JÚMA [JUA]
KATAUSAN alt for PAIWAN [PWN]
KATAUT alt for NORTHERN MUYU dial of YONGKOM [YON]
KATAWA alt for EBIRA [IGB]
KATAWIAN dial of WAIWAI [WAW]
KATAWINA alt for KATAWIAN dial of WAIWAI [WAW]
KATAWIXI [QKI] lang, Brazil
KATAZI dial of BABATANA [BAQ]
KATBOL [TMB] lang, Vanuatu
KATCH alt for KACHCHI [KFR]
KATCHA dial of KATCHA-KADUGLI-MIRI [KAT]
KATCHA-KADUGLI-MIRI [KAT] lang, Sudan
KATCHAL dial of NICOBARESE, CENTRAL [NCB]
KATCHI alt for KACHCHI [KFR]
KATCHI alt for KOLI, KACHI [GJK]
KATE dial of KUNIMAIPA [KUP]
KÂTE [KMG] lang, Papua New Guinea
KÂTE DONG alt for KÂTE [KMG]
KATEGE alt for TEKE, NORTHERN [TEG]
KATEGE alt for TEGEKALI dial of TEKE, NORTHERN [TEG]
KATEGHE dial of TEKE, NORTHERN [TEG]
KATEIK dial of KATLA [KCR]
KATH BHOTE alt for LHOMI [LHM]
KATHAREVOUSA dial of GREEK [GRK]
KATHARIYA alt for THARU, KATHORIYA [TKT]
KATHE alt for MEITEI [MNR]
KATHI alt for MEITEI [MNR]

KATHIAWARI alt for KISHTWARI dial of KASHMIRI [KSH]
KATHIYAWADI dial of GUJARATI [GJR]
KATHMANDU-PATHAN-KIRTIPUR dial of NEWARI [NEW]
KATHODI alt for KATKARI [KFU]
KATI [BSH] lang, Afghanistan; also in Pakistan
KATI dial of DAYAK, LAND [DYK]
KATI METOMKA alt for SOUTHERN MUYU dial of YONGKOM [YON]
KATIA alt for XATIA dial of XOO [NMN]
KATIARA dial of SENOUFO, TAGWANA [TGW]
KATIATI alt for MUM [KQA]
KATINGAN [KXG] lang, Indonesia (Kalimantan)
KATINGAN dial of MADAK [MMX]
KATI-NINANTI alt for NORTHERN MUYU dial of YONGKOM [YON]
KATINJA alt for ANGAL HENENG [AKH]
KATIO alt for EMBERÁ-CATÍO [CTO]
KATIOLA dial of SENOUFO, TAGWANA [TGW]
KATIVA alt for NINGGERUM [NXR]
KATIVIRI alt for KATI [BSH]
KATIYAI dial of MALVI [MUP]
KATKARI [KFU] lang, India
KATLA [KCR] lang, Sudan
KATO [KTW] lang, USA
KATO alt for KADO [KDV]
KATOVA alt for LAGHU [LGB]
KATSINA dial of HAUSA [HUA]
KATSY alt for KRYTS [KRY]
KATTALAN alt for ULLATAN [ULL]
KATTANG alt for WORIMI [KDA]
KATTEA alt for XATIA dial of XOO [NMN]
KATTU NAYAKA alt for KURUMBA, JENNU [QKJ]
KATU alt for KADO [KDV]
KATU, EASTERN [KTV] lang, Viet Nam
KATU, WESTERN [KUF] lang, Laos
KATUA [KTA] lang, Viet Nam
KATUENA alt for KATAWIAN dial of WAIWAI [WAW]
KATUKÍNA [KAV] lang, Brazil
KATUKINA DO JURUÁ alt for KATUKÍNA, PANOAN [KNT]
KATUKINA DO JUTAÍ alt for KATUKÍNA [KAV]
KATUKÍNA, PANOAN [KNT] lang, Brazil
KATUMENE alt for KAPIN [TBX]
KATVADI alt for KATKARI [KFU]
KATWENA alt for KATAWIAN dial of WAIWAI [WAW]
KAU alt for KAO [KAX]
KAU alt for KO [FUJ]
KAU dial of KO [FUJ]
KA'U alt for KAO [KAX]
KAU BRU alt for RIANG [RIA]
KAUDITAN dial of TONSEA [TXS]
//K"AU-//EN pejorative alt for 'AKHOE [AKE]
//KAU-//-EN alt for 'AKHOE [AKE]
KAU-//-EN alt for 'AKHOE [AKE]
KAUGAT alt for ATOHWAIM [AQM]
KAUGEL alt for UMBU-UNGU [UMB]
KAUIL alt for UMBU-UNGU [UMB]
KAUKAU alt for 'AKHOE [AKE]
KAUKAU alt for ǂKX'AU//'EIN [AUE]

KAUKAUE alt for KAKAUHUA [KBF]
KAULI alt for PAHARI, KULLU [KFX]
KAULONG [PSS] lang, Papua New Guinea
KAULONG dial of KAULONG [PSS]
KAUMA dial of GIRYAMA [NYF]
KAUNAK alt for CITAK [TXT]
KAUNGA alt for YELOGU [YLG]
KAUR [VKK] lang, Indonesia (Sumatra)
KA'UR alt for KAUR [VKK]
KAURE [BPP] lang, Indonesia (Irian Jaya)
KAUREH alt for KAURE [BPP]
KAURI dial of JINGPHO [CGP]
KAURU alt for SHUWA-ZAMANI [KSA]
KAURU alt for SI dial of LERE [GNH]
KAUTCHY alt for KACHCHI [KFR]
KAUWERA [QKX] lang, Indonesia (Irian Jaya)
KAUWERAWEC alt for KAUWERA [QKX]
KAUWERAWETJ alt for KAUWERA [QKX]
KAUWOL alt for FAIWOL [FAI]
KAUYARÍ alt for CABIYARÍ [CBB]
KAUYAWA alt for KARIYA [KIL]
KAVAHIVA alt for JÚMA [JUA]
KAVALAN [CKV] lang, Taiwan
KAVANAN alt for KAVALAN [CKV]
KAVARAUAN alt for KAVALAN [CKV]
KAVARDI dial of CHHATTISGARHI [HNE]
KAVET alt for KRAVET [KRV]
KAVIRONDO alt for LUO [LUO]
KAVIRONDO LUO alt for LUO [LUO]
KAVIXI alt for SARARÉ [SRR]
KAVOR alt for KOYA [KFF]
KAVWOL alt for FAIWOL [FAI]
KAW alt for AKHA [AKA]
KAW alt for KANSA [KAA]
KAW alt for KOSKIN [KID]
KAWA alt for BLANG [BLR]
KAWA alt for BUGAWAC [BUK]
KAWA alt for VO [WBM]
KAWA dial of LISABATA-NUNIALI [LCS]
K'AWA alt for VO [WBM]
KAWA TADIMINI alt for KAJAKSE [CKQ]
KAWAC alt for BUGAWAC [BUK]
KAWACHA [KCB] lang, Papua New Guinea
KAWAHIP alt for JÚMA [JUA]
KAWAIB alt for JÚMA [JUA]
KAWAIB alt for KAGWAHIV dial of TENHARIM [PAH]
KAWAIISU [KAW] lang, USA
KAWAKARUBI alt for TABO [KNV]
KAWALIB alt for KOALIB [KIB]
KAWALKÉ dial of KWANG [KVI]
KAWAM dial of AGOB [KIT]
KAWAMA alt for OTORO [OTR]
KAWANG dial of BAJAU, WEST COAST [BDR]
KAWANGA alt for WANGA dial of LUYIA [LUY]
KAWANUWAN alt for BASAY [BYQ]
KAWAR dial of MAITHILI [MKP]
KAWARMA alt for OTORO [OTR]
KAWATHI alt for BAGHELI [BFY]
KAWATSA alt for KAWACHA [KCB]
KAWAYAN dial of HILIGAYNON [HIL]

KAWE [KGB] lang, Indonesia (Irian Jaya)
KAWEINAG alt for ASMAT, CASUARINA COAST [ASC]
KAWEL alt for LEMBUR dial of KAMANG [WOI]
KAWELA alt for LAMALERA [LMR]
KAWESKAR alt for QAWASQAR [ALC]
KAWESQAR alt for QAWASQAR [ALC]
KAWIKU dial of LUNDA [LVN]
KAWILLARY alt for CABIYARÍ [CBB]
KAWIT dial of MAYA [SLZ]
KAWKAREIK dial of KAREN, PWO EASTERN [KJP]
KAWKI alt for CAUQUI dial of JAQARU [JQR]
KAWOL alt for FAIWOL [FAI]
KAWONDE alt for KAONDE [KQN]
KAWWADA alt for GAWWADA [GWD]
KAWWAD'A alt for GAWWADA [GWD]
KAXARARÍ [KTX] lang, Brazil
KAXARIRI alt for KAXARARÍ [KTX]
KAXETIAN dial of GEORGIAN [GEO]
KAXIB dial of AKHVAKH [AKV]
KAXIB dial of AVAR [AVR]
KAXINAUÁ alt for CASHINAHUA [CBS]
KAXINAWÁ alt for CASHINAHUA [CBS]
KAXUIÂNA [KBB] lang, Brazil
KAXÚYANA alt for KAXUIÂNA [KBB]
KAXYNAWA alt for CASHINAHUA [CBS]
KAYA alt for KOYA [KFF]
KAYABÍ [KYZ] lang, Brazil
KAYAGAR [KYT] lang, Indonesia (Irian Jaya)
KAYAH alt for KAYAH, EASTERN [EKY]
KAYAH LI alt for KAYAH, WESTERN [KYU]
KAYAH, EASTERN [EKY] lang, Myanmar; also in Thailand
KAYAH, WESTERN [KYU] lang, Myanmar
KAYAMAN alt for KAJAMAN [KAG]
KAYAN alt for KAIAN [KCT]
KAYAN MAHAKAM [XAY] lang, Indonesia (Kalimantan)
KAYAN RIVER BAKUNG dial of KENYAH, BAKUNG [BOC]
KAYAN RIVER KAJAN alt for KAYAN, KAYAN RIVER [XKN]
KAYAN RIVER KENYA alt for KENYAH, KAYAN RIVER [KNH]
KAYAN, BARAM [KYS] lang, Malaysia (Sarawak)
KAYAN, BUSANG [BFG] lang, Indonesia (Kalimantan)
KAYAN, KAYAN RIVER [XKN] lang, Indonesia (Kalimantan)
KAYAN, MENDALAM [XKD] lang, Indonesia (Kalimantan)
KAYAN, MURIK [MXR] lang, Malaysia (Sarawak)
KAYAN, REJANG [REE] lang, Malaysia (Sarawak)
KAYAN, WAHAU [WHU] lang, Indonesia (Kalimantan)
KAYANG alt for KAREN, PADAUNG [PDU]
KAYANI alt for JAKATI [JAT]
KAYANIYUT KAYAN dial of KAYAN, KAYAN RIVER [XKN]
KAYANIYUT KENYAH dial of KENYAH, KAYAN RIVER [KNH]

KAYAPA alt for KALLAHAN, KAYAPA [KAK]
KAYAPÓ [TXU] lang, Brazil
KAYAPÓ-KRADA dial of KAYAPO [TXU]
KAYAPWE alt for ZÁPARO [ZRO]
KAYARDILD alt for GAYARDILT [GYD]
KAYASTHI alt for PARABHI dial of KONKANI [KNK]
KAYASTHI dial of SINDHI [SND]
KAYAURI alt for GEJI [GEZ]
KAYAVAR dial of MALAYALAM [MJS]
KAYAY alt for KAYAH, EASTERN [EKY]
KAYELI [KZL] lang, Indonesia (Maluku)
KAYELI dial of KAYELI [KZL]
KAYGIR alt for KAYAGAR [KYT]
KAYIK alt for WANAP [WNP]
KAYINBYU alt for KAREN, GEBA [KVQ]
KAYKAVSKI dial of CROATIAN [SRC]
KAYLA dial of AGAW, WESTERN [QIM]
KAYOA dial of MAKIAN, EAST [MKY]
KAYOBE alt for SOLA [SOY]
KAYONG [KXY] lang, Viet Nam
KAYONG alt for KAYUNG dial of MALAYIC DAYAK [XDY]
KAYORT [KYV] lang, Nepal
KAYOVA alt for KAIWÁ [KGK]
KAYTAK alt for KAJTAK dial of DARGWA [DAR]
KAYTETYE [GBB] lang, Australia
KAYU AGUNG [VKY] lang, Indonesia (Sumatra)
KAYUMERAH alt for KOWIAI [KWH]
KAYUNG dial of MALAYIC DAYAK [XDY]
KAYUPULAU [KZU] lang, Indonesia (Irian Jaya)
KAZAK alt for KAZAKH [KAZ]
KAZAKH [KAZ] lang, Kazakhstan; also in Afghanistan, China, Germany, Iran, Kyrgyzstan, Mongolia, Russia (Asia), Tajikistan, Turkey (Asia), Turkmenistan, Ukraine, Uzbekistan
KAZAKH dial of AZERBAIJANI, NORTH [AZE]
KAZAKHI alt for KAZAKH [KAZ]
KAZAN alt for MIDDLE TATAR dial of TATAR [TTR]
KAZAX alt for KAZAKH [KAZ]
KAZERUNI dial of FARSI, WESTERN [PES]
KAZIKUMUKHTSY alt for LAK [LBE]
KAZUKURU [KZK] lang, Solomon Islands
KBALAN alt for KAVALAN [CKV]
KDANG alt for KEDANG [KSX]
KDRAO alt for KODRAO dial of RADE [RAD]
KE alt for CHINESE, HAKKA [HAK]
KEAI alt for RO dial of FOLOPA [PPO]
KEAKA alt for EJAGHAM [ETU]
KEANA dial of ALAGO [ALA]
KEAPARA alt for KEOPARA [KHZ]
KEBADI alt for ZAGHAWA [ZAG]
KEBADI alt for ZANDE [ZAN]
KEBAI dial of CHUAVE [CJV]
KEBAR alt for MPUR [AKC]
KEBA-WOPASALI dial of FOLOPA [PPO]
KEBBAWA dial of HAUSA [HUA]
KEBEENTON dial of TOUSSIAN, NORTHERN [TSP]
KEBEIRKA dial of UDUK [UDU]
KEBENA alt for QEBENA dial of KAMBAATA [KTB]
KEB-KAYE alt for KABALAI [KVF]
KEBU alt for AKEBOU [KEU]

KEBU alt for NDO [NDP]
KEBU alt for OKE'BU dial of NDO [NDP]
KE'BU alt for NDO [NDP]
KEBU FULA dial of FUUTA JALON [FUF]
KEBUMTAMP alt for BUMTHANGKHA [KJZ]
KEBUN KOPI dial of KABOLA [KLZ]
KEBUTU alt for NDO [NDP]
KEBUTU alt for OKE'BU dial of NDO [NDP]
KECHAN alt for QUECHAN [YUM]
KECHERDA dial of TEDAGA [TUQ]
KECHI dial of BALOCHI, SOUTHERN [BCC]
KECHIA alt for CHINESE, HAKKA [HAK]
KECWAN alt for WULA dial of BOKYI [BKY]
KEDAH dial of KENSIU [KNS]
KEDAH dial of MALAY [MLI]
KEDAMAIAN DUSUN alt for DUSUN, TEMPASUK
    [TDU]
KEDANG [KSX] lang, Indonesia (Nusa Tenggara)
KÉDANG alt for KEDANG [KSX]
KEDANGESE alt for KEDANG [KSX]
KEDAYAN alt for DUSUN, CENTRAL [DTP]
KEDAYAN alt for KADAIAN dial of BRUNEI
    [KXD]
KEDAYAN dial of BRUNEI [KXD]
KEDDE alt for KEDI dial of HAIOM [HGM]
KEDDI alt for KEDI dial of HAIOM [HGM]
KEDE alt for AKA-KEDE [AKX]
KEDER [KDY] lang, Indonesia (Irian Jaya)
KEDI alt for LABA [LAU]
KEDI dial of HAIOM [HGM]
KEDIEN alt for KADAIAN dial of BRUNEI [KXD]
KEDIEN. KERAYAN alt for KEDAYAN dial of
    BRUNEI [KXD]
KEDJOM alt for BABANKI [BBK]
KEDYAN alt for KADAIAN dial of BRUNEI [KXD]
KEDYAN alt for KEDAYAN dial of BRUNEI [KXD]
KEEKONYOKIE dial of MAASAI [MET]
KEEMBO dial of MBOLE [MDQ]
KEENGE dial of BEEMBE [BEJ]
KEENOK alt for ASMAT, NORTH [NKS]
KEERAK alt for KERAK [HHR]
KEERAKU alt for KERAK [HHR]
KE'ERKEZ alt for KIRGHIZ [KDO]
KE'ERQIN alt for JOSTU dial of MONGOLIAN,
    PERIPHERAL [MVF]
KEEWATIN alt for CARIBOU ESKIMO dial of
    INUKTITUT, WESTERN CANADIAN [ESC]
KEFA alt for KAFICHO [KBR]
KEFFA alt for KAFICHO [KBR]
KEFFI alt for ELOYI [AFO]
KEGBERIKE alt for AKEBOU [KEU]
KEGENGELE alt for GENGELE dial of SONGOORA
    [SOD]
KEHA dial of TUKUDEDE [TKD]
KEH-DEO alt for GEJIAHUA dial of HMONG,
    CHONGANJIANG [HMJ]
KEHELALA dial of TAWALA [TBO]
KEHENA dial of NAGA, ANGAMI [NJM]
KEHERARA alt for KEHELALA dial of TAWALA
    [TBO]
KEHIA alt for CHINESE, HAKKA [HAK]

KEHJA alt for KENYAH, KAYAN RIVER [KNH]
KEHJA alt for KENYAH, KELINYAU [XKL]
KEHJA alt for KENYAH, MAHAKAM [XKM]
KEH-LAO alt for GELAO [KKF]
KEHLAO alt for GELAO [KKF]
KEHLOORI PAHARI alt for BILASPURI [KFS]
KEHLURI alt for BILASPURI [KFS]
KEHU [KHH] lang, Indonesia (Irian Jaya)
KEI [KEI] lang, Indonesia (Maluku)
KEI BESAR dial of KEI [KEI]
KEI KECIL dial of KEI [KEI]
KEIA alt for KEHA dial of TUKUDEDE [TKD]
KEIAGANA alt for KEYAGANA [KYG]
KEIGA [KEC] lang, Sudan
KEIGA dial of KEIGA [KEC]
KEIGA GIRRU alt for TESE [KEG]
KEIGA JIRRU alt for TESE [KEG]
KEIGA-AL-KHEIL alt for KEIGA [KEC]
KEIGANA alt for KEYAGANA [KYG]
KEIGA-TIMERO alt for KEIGA [KEC]
KEIN alt for BEMAL [BMH]
KEIYO dial of KALENJIN [KLN]
KEJAMAN alt for KAJAMAN [KAG]
KEJENG alt for BABANKI [BBK]
KEJIA alt for CHINESE, HAKKA [HAK]
KEK alt for CHINESE, HAKKA [HAK]
KEKA alt for ROTE-TENGAH dial of ROTE [ROT]
KEKAMBA alt for KAMBA [KIK]
KEKAR alt for KJAKELA dial of OROCH [OAC]
KEKAUNGDU alt for KAREN, GEKO [GHK]
KEKCHÍ [KEK] lang, Guatemala; also in Belize,
    El Salvador
KEKEM dial of MBO [MBO]
KEKHONG alt for KAREN, GEKO [GHK]
KEKU alt for KAREN, GEKO [GHK]
KELA [KCL] lang, Papua New Guinea
KELA [KEL] lang, DRC
KELABIT [KZI] lang, Malaysia (Sarawak); also in
    Indonesia (Kalimantan)
KELAI dial of SEGAI [SGE]
KELANA alt for GITUA [GIL]
KELANA alt for KELA [KCL]
KELANCHI alt for KUR dial of KAG-FER-JIIR-KOOR-
    ROR-US-ZUKSUN [GEL]
KELANG dial of LUHU [LCQ]
KELANTAN dial of MALAY [MLI]
KELAO alt for GELAO [KKF]
KELDERASHÍCKO alt for KALDERASH dial of
    ROMANI, VLAX [RMY]
KÉLÉ [KEB] lang, Gabon; also in Congo
KELE [KHY] lang, DRC
KELE [SBC] lang, Papua New Guinea
KELE alt for LIPOTO dial of LUSENGO [LUS]
KELEB dial of AVAR [AVR]
KELENGA alt for BOZO, HAINYAXO [BZX]
KELENTHEYEWELRERE alt for WESTERN
    ANMATYERRE dial of ANMATYERRE [AMX]
KELENTHWELKERE alt for WESTERN
    ANMATYERRE dial of ANMATYERRE [AMX]
KELEO alt for GELAO [KKF]
KELEY-I alt for KALANGUYA, KELEY-I [IFY]

KELEYQIQ IFUGAO alt for KALANGUYA, KELEY-I [IFY]

KELHURI dial of LURI [LRI]

KELI dial of BOHUAI [RAK]

KELIKO [KBO] lang, Sudan; also in DRC, Uganda

KELIKO alt for KALIKO [KBO]

KELIMURI dial of GESER-GOROM [GES]

KELINCI alt for KUR dial of KAG-FER-JIIR-KOOR-ROR-US-ZUKSUN [GEL]

KÉLINGA alt for BOZO, HAINYAXO [BZX]

KELINGAN dial of MABA [MDE]

KELINGAN dial of MODANG [MXD]

KELINGI alt for SINDANG KELINGI [SDI]

KELINJAU alt for KENYAH, KELINYAU [XKL]

KELINYAU alt for KENYAH, KELINYAU [XKL]

KÉLLINGUA alt for BOZO, HAINYAXO [BZX]

KELLI-NI alt for KUR dial of KAG-FER-JIIR-KOOR-ROR-US-ZUKSUN [GEL]

KELO [TSN] lang, Sudan

KELO dial of KELO [TSN]

KELO-BENI SHEKO alt for KELO [TSN]

KELON [KYO] lang, Indonesia (Nusa Tenggara)

KELONG alt for KELON [KYO]

KEM DEGNE dial of BLANG [BLR]

KEM MUN alt for KIM MUN [MJI]

KEMAI alt for GOEMAI [ANK]

KEMAK [KEM] lang, Timor Lorosae; also in Indonesia (Nusa Tenggara)

KEMAK dial of KEMAK [KEM]

KEMANAT alt for QIMANT dial of AGAW, WESTERN [QIM]

KEMANIMOWE dial of SIANE [SNP]

KEMANT alt for QIMANT dial of AGAW, WESTERN [QIM]

KEMATA alt for KAMBAATA [KTB]

KEMBATA alt for KAMBAATA [KTB]

KEMBAYAN [XEM] lang, Indonesia (Kalimantan)

KEMBERANO [BZP] lang, Indonesia (Irian Jaya)

KEMBERANO dial of ARANDAI [JBJ]

KEMBRA [XKW] lang, Indonesia (Irian Jaya)

KEMELOM alt for MOMBUM [MSO]

KEMENA PENAN dial of KENYAH, WESTERN [XKY]

KEMEZUNG [DMO] lang, Cameroon

KEMIEHUA [KFJ] lang, China

KEMMUNGAM alt for NAGA, KHIAMNIUNGAN [NKY]

KEMTUIK [KMT] lang, Indonesia (Irian Jaya)

KEMTUK alt for KEMTUIK [KMT]

KEMU alt for KHMU [KJG]

KEMU dial of WAN [WAN]

KEN alt for KHENGKHA [XKF]

KENAI PENINSULA dial of TANAINA [TFN]

KENAT alt for BAGHELI [BFY]

KENATHI alt for KENATI [GAT]

KENATI [GAT] lang, Papua New Guinea

KENDARI alt for KONAWE dial of TOLAKI [LBW]

KENDAYAN [KNX] lang, Indonesia (Kalimantan)

KENDAYAN dial of KENDAYAN [KNX]

KENDAYAN DAYAK alt for KENDAYAN [KNX]

KENDAYAN-AMBAWANG alt for KENDAYAN [KNX]

KENDEJE [KLF] lang, Chad

KENDEM [KVM] lang, Cameroon

KENDERONG dial of TEMIAR [TMH]

KENEDIBI alt for TABO [KNV]

KEÑELE alt for KYENELE [KQL]

KENEN BIRANG alt for KYENELE [KQL]

KENENG alt for PHONG-KNIANG [PNX]

KENERING dial of TEMIAR [TMH]

KENG alt for KHENGKHA [XKF]

KENGA [KYQ] lang, Chad

KENGA alt for KYENGA [TYE]

KENGE alt for KENGA [KYQ]

KENI dial of CHAGGA [KAF]

KENIEBA MANINKA dial of MANINKAKAN, WESTERN [MLQ]

KENIENG alt for PHONG-KNIANG [PNX]

KENINGAU DUSUN alt for GANA [GNQ]

KENINGAU MURUT [KXI] lang, Malaysia (Sabah)

KENINJAL [KNL] lang, Indonesia (Kalimantan)

KENJA alt for KENYAH, KAYAN RIVER [KNH]

KENJA alt for KENYAH, KELINYAU [XKL]

KENJA alt for KENYAH, MAHAKAM [XKM]

KENJA alt for KENYAH, UPPER BARAM [UBM]

KENJA alt for KENYAH, WESTERN [XKY]

KEN-KHANA dial of KHANA [KEH]

KENKÜ alt for MÜNKÜ dial of IRANTXE [IRA]

KENSE alt for KENSIU [KNS]

KENSENSE alt for KENSWEI NSEI [NDB]

KENSEU alt for KENSIU [KNS]

KENSIEU alt for KENSIU [KNS]

KENSIU [KNS] lang, Malaysia (Peninsular); also in Thailand

KENSIU BATU dial of KENSIU [KNS]

KENSIU SIONG dial of KENSIU [KNS]

KENSIW alt for KENSIU [KNS]

KENSWEI NSEI [NDB] lang, Cameroon

KENTA alt for KINTAQ [KNQ]

KENTAQ NAKIL dial of KENSIU [KNS]

KENTE dial of KPAN [KPK]

KENTIN dial of KUTEP [KUB]

KENTOHE alt for KANTOHE dial of BALANTA-KENTOHE [BLE]

KENTU alt for ETKYWAN [ICH]

KENTU alt for KENTE dial of KPAN [KPK]

KENTUNG WA dial of VO [WBM]

KENUME alt for KANUM, BÄDI [KHD]

KENUME alt for KANUM, NGKÂLMPW [KCD]

KENUME alt for KANUM, SMÄRKY [KXQ]

KENUME alt for KANUM, SOTA [KRZ]

KENUZ alt for KENUZI dial of KENUZI-DONGOLA [KNC]

KENUZ dial of KENUZI-DONGOLA [KNC]

KENUZI alt for KENUZ dial of KENUZI-DONGOLA [KNC]

KENUZI dial of KENUZI-DONGOLA [KNC]

KENUZI-DONGOLA [KNC] lang, Sudan; also in Egypt

KENYA alt for KENYAH, KAYAN RIVER [KNH]

KENYA alt for KENYAH, KELINYAU [XKL]

KENYA alt for KENYAH, MAHAKAM [XKM]

KENYAH alt for KENYAH, KAYAN RIVER [KNH]

KENYAH alt for KENYAH, KELINYAU [XKL]

KENYAH alt for KENYAH, MAHAKAM [XKM]
KENYAH alt for KENYAH, UPPER BARAM [UBM]
KENYAH, BAHAU RIVER [BWV] lang, Indonesia (Kalimantan)
KENYAH, BAKUNG [BOC] lang, Indonesia (Kalimantan); also in Malaysia (Sarawak)
KENYAH, KAYAN RIVER [KNH] lang, Indonesia (Kalimantan)
KENYAH, KELINYAU [XKL] lang, Indonesia (Kalimantan)
KENYAH, MAHAKAM [XKM] lang, Indonesia (Kalimantan)
KENYAH, SEBOB [SIB] lang, Malaysia (Sarawak)
KENYAH, TUTOH [TTW] lang, Malaysia (Sarawak)
KENYAH, UPPER BARAM [UBM] lang, Malaysia (Sarawak); also in Indonesia (Kalimantan)
KENYAH, WAHAU [WHK] lang, Indonesia (Kalimantan)
KENYAH, WESTERN [XKY] lang, Malaysia (Sarawak)
KENYAN SIGN LANGUAGE [XKI] lang, Kenya
KENYANG [KEN] lang, Cameroon
KENYI [LKE] lang, Uganda
KENYI alt for ZHIRE [ZHI]
KENYING BULANG alt for KYENELE [KQL]
KENZI alt for KENUZ dial of KENUZI-DONGOLA [KNC]
KEO alt for THO [TOU]
KE'O [XXK] lang, Indonesia (Nusa Tenggara)
KEOPARA [KHZ] lang, Papua New Guinea
KEOPARA dial of KEOPARA [KHZ]
KEPERE alt for GBETE dial of MBUM [MDD]
KEPO' [KUK] lang, Indonesia (Nusa Tenggara)
KEPOQ alt for KEPO' [KUK]
KER alt for KARABORO, EASTERN [KAR]
KERA [KER] lang, Chad; also in Cameroon
KERA dial of MUNDARI [MUW]
KERA' dial of MUNDARI [MUW]
KERABIT alt for KELABIT [KZI]
KERAK [HHR] lang, Senegal
KERANG alt for NGAS [ANC]
KERAYAN alt for KADAIAN dial of BRUNEI [KXD]
KERDAU dial of JAH HUT [JAH]
KERE alt for KARO [KXH]
KERE alt for KUR dial of KAG-FER-JIIR-KOOR-ROR-US-ZUKSUN [GEL]
KERE dial of BAMBASSI [MYF]
KERE dial of NGAMBAY [SBA]
KEREAKA [KJX] lang, Papua New Guinea
KEREBE [KED] lang, Tanzania
KEREHO-UHENG [XKE] lang, Indonesia (Kalimantan)
KEREI alt for KAREY [KYD]
KEREK [KRK] lang, Russia (Asia)
KEREKERE alt for KAREKARE [KAI]
K'ERE-KHWE dial of DETI [DET]
KEREMA alt for NISA [NIC]
KEREMI alt for NYATURU [RIM]
KEREN dial of AGHUL [AGX]

KEREND dial of HULAULA [HUY]
KEREPUNU alt for KEOPARA [KHZ]
KERES, EASTERN [KEE] lang, USA
KERES, WESTERN [KJQ] lang, USA
KEREWA alt for KEREWO [KXZ]
KEREWA-GOARI alt for KEREWO [KXZ]
KEREWE alt for KEREBE [KED]
KEREWO [KXZ] lang, Papua New Guinea
KEREYU dial of OROMO, BORANA-ARSI-GUJI [GAX]
KERI dial of GOLIN [GVF]
KERIAKA alt for KEREAKA [KJX]
KERIFA alt for DUHWA [KBZ]
KERINCHI alt for KERINCI [KVR]
KERINCI [KVR] lang, Indonesia (Sumatra)
KERINCI-MINANGKABAU dial of MINANGKABAU [MPU]
KERI-NI alt for KUR dial of KAG-FER-JIIR-KOOR-ROR-US-ZUKSUN [GEL]
KERINTJI alt for KERINCI [KVR]
KERMANI dial of FARSI, WESTERN [PES]
KERMANJI alt for KURMANJI [KUR]
KERMANSHAHI dial of KURDI [KDB]
KERNEWEK alt for CORNISH [CRN]
KERNOWEK alt for CORNISH [CRN]
KEROROGEA dial of BUNAMA [BDD]
KEROUNJA dial of TAMANG, EASTERN GORKHA [TGE]
KERRE alt for KARO [KXH]
KERRIKERRI alt for KAREKARE [KAI]
KESARI dial of BAAN [BVJ]
KESAWAI [QKE] lang, Papua New Guinea
KESENGELE alt for SENGELE [SZG]
KESHIKTEN alt for JO-UDA dial of MONGOLIAN, PERIPHERAL [MVF]
KESHUR alt for KASHMIRI [KSH]
KESHURI alt for KASHMIRI [KSH]
KESONGOLA alt for SONGOORA [SOD]
KESSI alt for SOPPENG dial of BUGIS [BPR]
KESTANE alt for SODDO dial of GURAGE, SODDO [GRU]
KESÙ alt for RANTEPAO dial of TORAJA-SADAN [SDA]
KESUI alt for WATUBELA [WAH]
KET [KET] lang, Russia (Asia)
KETAGALAN alt for KETANGALAN [KAE]
KETANGALAN [KAE] lang, Taiwan
KETCHÍ alt for KEKCHÍ [KEK]
KETE [KCV] lang, DRC
KETEBO alt for LOKATHAN dial of TESO [TEO]
KETEGHE dial of TEKE, NORTHERN [TEG]
KETEGO alt for TEKE, NORTHERN [TEG]
KETENENEYU dial of NAGA, RENGMA [NRE]
KETENGBAN [KIN] lang, Indonesia (Irian Jaya)
KETIAR KRAU dial of JAH HUT [JAH]
KETIN dial of ATTIE [ATI]
KETO dial of SIANE [SNP]
KETUEN alt for MBE [MFO]
KETUNGAU dial of IBAN [IBA]
KETY alt for TYM dial of SELKUP [SAK]
KEURO alt for KEURU [QQK]

KEURU [QQK] lang, Papua New Guinea
KEVAT BOLI alt for BAGHELI [BFY]
KEVATI alt for BAGHELI [BFY]
KEWA SOUTH alt for ERAVE [KJY]
KEWA, EAST [KJS] lang, Papua New Guinea
KEWA, WEST [KEW] lang, Papua New Guinea
KEWAH dial of FOLOPA [PPO]
KEWANI alt for BAGHELI [BFY]
KEWAT alt for BAGHELI [BFY]
KEWATI alt for BAGHELI [BFY]
KEWIENG dial of YOPNO [YUT]
KEWOT alt for BAGHELI [BFY]
KE-WOYA-YAKA alt for NORTHERN LIMBA dial
    of LIMBA, EAST [LMA]
KEYAGANA [KYG] lang, Papua New Guinea
KE'YAGANA alt for KEYAGANA [KYG]
KEYDNJMARDA alt for ADYNYAMATHANHA [ADT]
KEYELE alt for KYENELE [KQL]
KEYLONG BOLI alt for GAHRI [BFU]
KEYO alt for KEIYO dial of KALENJIN [KLN]
KEZAMI alt for NAGA, KHEZHA [NKH]
KFARZE dial of TUROYO [SYR]
KGAGA dial of SOTHO, NORTHERN [SRT]
KGALAGADI [XKV] lang, Botswana; also in Namibia
KGALAGADI dial of KGALAGADI [XKV]
KGATLA dial of TSWANA [TSW]
KHA CAU alt for KHMU [KJG]
KHA KHMU alt for KHMU [KJG]
KHA KO alt for AKHA [AKA]
KHA LAMET alt for LAMET [LBN]
KHA MU GIA alt for RUC dial of CHUT [SCB]
KHA NAM OM alt for KHA PHONG dial of MALENG
    [PKT]
KHA NIANG alt for PUOC [PUO]
KHA PAKATAN alt for PAKATAN dial of MALENG
    [PKT]
KHA PHAY alt for PHAI [PRT]
KHA PHONG dial of MALENG [PKT]
KHA PRAY alt for PHAI [PRT]
KHA PUHOC alt for PUOC [PUO]
KHA SO alt for SÔ [SSS]
KHA TAMPUON alt for TAMPUAN [TPU]
KHA TONG LUANG alt for AHEU [THM]
KHAANG alt for KHANG [KJM]
KHABENAPO alt for POMO, CENTRAL [POO]
KHABIT alt for BIT [BGK]
KHADI BOLI alt for HINDI [HND]
KHADIA alt for KHARIA [KHR]
KHAE alt for LISU [LIS]
KHAEL BAAT alt for KHALING [KLR]
KHAEL BRA alt for KHALING [KLR]
KHAGA alt for KGAGA dial of SOTHO, NORTHERN
    [SRT]
KHAHTA alt for KAREN, LAHTA [KVT]
KHAIDAK dial of KUMYK [KSK]
KHAIKENT dial of KUMYK [KSK]
KHAIRAGARHI dial of CHHATTISGARHI [HNE]
KHAJUNA alt for BURUSHASKI [BSK]
KHAKAS [KJH] lang, Russia (Asia); also in China
KHAKHAS alt for KHAKAS [KJH]
KHAKHASS alt for KHAKAS [KJH]

KHAKO alt for AKHA [AKA]
KHAL:MAG alt for KALMYK-OIRAT [KGZ]
KHALAGARI alt for KGALAGADI [XKV]
KHALAJ [KJF] lang, Iran; also in Azerbaijan
KHALAJ [KLJ] lang, Iran
KHALAKADI alt for KGALAGADI [XKV]
KHALIJI alt for ARABIC, GULF SPOKEN [AFB]
KHALING [KLR] lang, Nepal; also in India
KHALING dial of BAHING [RAR]
KHALINGE RAI alt for KHALING [KLR]
KHALKHA dial of MONGOLIAN, HALH [KHK]
KHALKHA alt for HALH dial of MONGOLIAN, HALH
    [KHK]
KHALKHA MONGOLIAN alt for MONGOLIAN,
    HALH [KHK]
KHALKHAL dial of TAKESTANI [TKS]
KHALTAHI alt for CHHATTISGARHI [HNE]
KHAM, GAMALE [KGJ] lang, Nepal
KHAM, MAIKOTI [ZKM] lang, Nepal
KHAM, NISI [KIF] lang, Nepal
KHAM, SHESHI [KIP] lang, Nepal
KHAM, TAKALE [KJL] lang, Nepal
KHAMBA alt for KHAMS [KHG]
KHAMBA alt for MOINBA [MOB]
KHAMBANA-MAKWAKWE alt for HLENGWE dial
    of TSHWA [TSC]
KHAMBANI alt for HLENGWE dial of TSHWA [TSC]
KHAMBANI dial of CHOPI [CCE]
KHAMBU dial of KULUNG [KLE]
KHAMCHI alt for RAUTE [RAU]
KHAMED alt for LAMET [LBN]
KHAMEN-BORAN alt for KUY [KDT]
KHAMEN-BORAN (OLD KHMER) alt for KUY
    [KDT]
KHAMET alt for LAMET [LBN]
KHAMI alt for CHIN, KHUMI [CKM]
KHAMI dial of CHIN, KHUMI [CKM]
KHAMJANG alt for KHAMYANG [KSU]
/KHAM-KA-!K'E alt for /XAM [XAM]
KHAMLA dial of GOWLI [GOK]
KHAM-MAGAR alt for KHAM, TAKALE [KJL]
KHAMMOUAN dial of SAEK [SKB]
KHAMNIGAN alt for EVENKI [EVN]
KHAMPA alt for KHAMS [KHG]
KHAMPTI alt for KHAMTI [KHT]
KHAMPTI SHAN alt for KHAMTI [KHT]
KHAMS [KHG] lang, China
KHAMS BHOTIA alt for KHAMS [KHG]
KHAMS-YAL alt for KHAMS [KHG]
KHAM-TAI alt for KHAMTI [KHT]
KHAMTANGA alt for XAMTANGA [XAN]
KHAMTI [KHT] lang, Myanmar; also in India
KHAMTI SHAN alt for KHAMTI [KHT]
KHAMU alt for KHMU [KJG]
KHAMUK alt for KHMU [KJG]
KHAMYANG [KSU] lang, India
KHANA [KEH] lang, Nigeria
KHANA alt for POMO, CENTRAL [POO]
KHANAG alt for NORTH TABASARAN dial of
    TABASSARAN [TAB]
KHANDESHI alt for KHANDESI [KHN]

KHANDESI [KHN] lang, India
KHANDESI dial of KHANDESI [KHN]
KHANDI SHAN alt for KHAMTI [KHT]
KHANDISH alt for KHANDESI [KHN]
KHANG [KJM] lang, Viet Nam
KHANG AI dial of KHANG [KJM]
KHANG CLAU dial of KHANG [KJM]
KHANGOI dial of NAGA, TANGKHUL [NMF]
KHANIANG alt for PHONG-KNIANG [PNX]
KHANTI alt for KHANTY [KCA]
KHANTIS alt for KHAMTI [KHT]
KHANTY [KCA] lang, Russia (Asia)
KHANUNG alt for NUNG [NUN]
KHAO [XAO] lang, Viet Nam
KHAO IKOR alt for AKHA [AKA]
KHAO KHA KO alt for AKHA [AKA]
KHAPUT alt for XAPUT dial of KRYTS [KRY]
KHARACHIN alt for JOSTU dial of MONGOLIAN,
     PERIPHERAL [MVF]
KHARAQAN dial of TAKESTANI [TKS]
KHARBARI dial of DUMI [DUS]
KHARBERD dial of ARMENIAN [ARM]
KHARCHIN alt for JOSTU dial of MONGOLIAN,
     PERIPHERAL [MVF]
KHARCHIN-TUMUT alt for JOSTU dial of
     MONGOLIAN, PERIPHERAL [MVF]
KHARI BOLI alt for HINDI [HND]
KHARIA [KHR] lang, India; also in Nepal
KHARIA THAR [KSY] lang, India
KHARIYA alt for KHARIA [KHR]
KHARLALI dial of NACHERING [NCD]
KHARMANGI alt for ASTORI dial of SHINA [SCL]
KHARTAMCHE dial of SANGPANG [RAV]
KHARTOUM dial of ARABIC, SUDANESE SPOKEN
     [APD]
KHARTOUM ARABIC alt for ARABIC, SUDANESE
     SPOKEN [APD]
KHARVI alt for KHARIA [KHR]
KHARWA dial of GUJARATI [GJR]
KHARWARI alt for SOUTHERN STANDARD
     BHOJPURI dial of BHOJPURI [BHJ]
KHARYUZ dial of ITELMEN [ITL]
KHASA alt for KHASI [KHI]
KHASA alt for TIGRÉ [TIE]
KHASARLI dial of TURKMEN [TCK]
KHASAV-YURT dial of KUMYK [KSK]
KHASAVYURT dial of KUMYK [KSK]
KHASHI alt for KHASI [KHI]
KHASI [KHI] lang, India; also in Bangladesh
KHASI dial of KHASI [KHI]
KHASIE alt for KHASI [KHI]
KHASIYAS alt for KHASI [KHI]
KHASKHONG dial of PHUNOI [PHO]
KHASKURA alt for NEPALI [NEP]
KHASONKE alt for XAASONGAXANGO [KAO]
KHASONKE alt for XASONGA [KAO]
KHASPARJIYA dial of KUMAUNI [KFY]
KHASSEE alt for KHASI [KHI]
KHASSONKA alt for XAASONGAXANGO [KAO]
KHASSONKÉ alt for XAASONGAXANGO [KAO]
KHATANG dial of NGANASAN [NIO]

KHATIA alt for XATIA dial of XOO [NMN]
KHATIN alt for MAL [MLF]
KHATKI alt for MULTANI dial of SARAIKI [SKR]
KHATOLA dial of BUNDELI [BNS]
KHATRIA alt for KHARIA [KHR]
KHATYRKA dial of KEREK [KRK]
KHAUNGTOU alt for KAREN, ZAYEIN [KXK]
KHAVA dial of INGRIAN [IZH]
KHAWAR alt for KHOWAR [KHW]
KHAYO dial of LUYIA [LUY]
KHBIT alt for BIT [BGK]
KHE [KQG] lang, Burkina Faso; also in Côte
     d'Ivoire
KHEHEK [TLX] lang, Papua New Guinea
KHEHEK alt for DREHET dial of KHEHEK [TLX]
KHEK alt for CHINESE, HAKKA [HAK]
KHELMA dial of CHIN, FALAM [HBH]
KHELOBEDU alt for LOBEDU dial of SOTHO,
     NORTHERN [SRT]
KHEMSING dial of NAGA, TASE [NST]
KHEMUNGAN alt for NAGA, KHIAMNIUNGAN [NKY]
KHEN alt for KHENGKHA [XKF]
KHEN LÀI dial of NUNG [NUT]
KHENGKHA [XKF] lang, Bhutan
KHENKHA alt for KHENGKHA [XKF]
KHERIA alt for KHARIA [KHR]
KHERWARA dial of WAGDI [WBR]
KHERWARI alt for KHIRWAR [KWX]
KHESANG dial of DUNGMALI [RAA]
KHESANGE alt for KHESANG dial of DUNGMALI
     [RAA]
KHESO alt for KHE [KQG]
/KHESSÁKHOE dial of GANA [GNK]
KHETRANI [QKT] lang, Pakistan
KHEYSUR alt for XEVSUR dial of GEORGIAN [GEO]
KHEZHA alt for NAGA, KHEZHA [NKH]
KHEZHAMA alt for NAGA, KHEZHA [NKH]
KHI alt for GELAO [KKF]
KHI alt for KHISA [KQM]
KHI KHIPA alt for KHISA [KQM]
KHIAMNGAN alt for NAGA, KHIAMNIUNGAN [NKY]
KHIAMNIUNGAN alt for NAGA, KHIAMNIUNGAN
     [NKY]
KHIENG alt for SHENDU [SHL]
KHIENMUNGAN alt for NAGA, KHIAMNIUNGAN
     [NKY]
KHIK alt for WAKHI [WBL]
KHILI alt for DUBER-KANDIA dial of KOHISTANI,
     INDUS [MVY]
KHILI alt for KOHISTANI, INDUS [MVY]
KHIMI alt for CHIN, KHUMI [CKM]
KHIMI dial of CHIN, KHUMI [CKM]
KHINALUG alt for KHINALUGH [KJJ]
KHINALUGH [KJJ] lang, Azerbaijan
KHINALUGI alt for KHINALUGH [KJJ]
KHIRWAR [KWX] lang, India
KHIRWARA alt for KHIRWAR [KWX]
KHISA [KQM] lang, Côte d'Ivoire; also in Burkina
     Faso
KHITHAULHU dial of NAMBIKUARA, SOUTHERN
     [NAB]

KHIURKILINSKII alt for DARGWA [DAR]
KHLÁ DON alt for LAHA [LHA]
KHLÁ DUNG alt for LAHA [LHA]
KHLÁ LIIK alt for LAHA [LHA]
KHLÁ PHLAO alt for LAHA [LHA]
KHLOR [LLO] lang, Laos
KHMER alt for KHMER, CENTRAL [KMR]
KHMER, CENTRAL [KMR] lang, Cambodia; also
   in China, France, Laos, USA, Viet Nam
KHMER, NORTHERN [KXM] lang, Thailand
KHMU [KJG] lang, Laos; also in China, France,
   Myanmar, Thailand, USA, Viet Nam
KHMÙ alt for KHMU [KJG]
KHÖWSÖGÖL UIGUR dial of TUVIN [TUN]
KHO ME alt for KHMER, CENTRAL [KMR]
KHOCHARKHOTIN dial of BEZHTA [KAP]
KHOE alt for KXOE [XUU]
KHOEKHOE alt for NAMA [NAQ]
"KHOEKHOEGOWAB" pejorative alt for NAMA [NAQ]
"KHOEKHOEGOWAP" pejorative alt for NAMA [NAQ]
KHOI alt for NAMA [NAQ]
KHOIBU alt for NAGA, KHOIBU MARING [NKB]
KHOIBU MARING alt for NAGA, KHOIBU MARING
   [NKB]
KHOINI [XKC] lang, Iran
KHOIRAO alt for NAGA, KHOIRAO [NKI]
KHOI-SALMST dial of ARMENIAN [ARM]
KHOKE alt for KOKE [KOU]
KHOKSAR dial of STOD BHOTI [SBU]
KHOKSAR BHOTI alt for KHOKSAR dial of STOD
   BHOTI [SBU]
KHOLE alt for KARMALI dial of SANTALI [SNT]
KHOLIFA dial of THEMNE [TEJ]
KHOLOK [KTC] lang, Nigeria
KHOLUNG alt for KULUNG [KLE]
KHOMAKHA dial of DZALAKHA [DZL]
=KHOMANI alt for N/U [NGH]
KHOME alt for KHMER, CENTRAL [KMR]
KHOMU alt for KHMU [KJG]
KHON DOI alt for BLANG [BLR]
KHON MUNG alt for THAI, NORTHERN [NOD]
KHON MYANG alt for THAI, NORTHERN [NOD]
KHOND alt for KUI [KXU]
KHONDH alt for KUVI [KXV]
KHONDI alt for KUI [KXU]
KHONDI alt for KUVI [KXV]
KHONDI dial of KUI [KXU]
KHONDO alt for KUI [KXU]
KHONG KHENG alt for PONG dial of HUNG [HNU]
KHONGZAI dial of CHIN, THADO [TCZ]
KHONOMA dial of NAGA, ANGAMI [NJM]
KHOR dial of UDIHE [UDE]
KHORASANI alt for DARI dial of FARSI, EASTERN
   [PRS]
KHORASANI TURKISH [KMZ] lang, Iran
KHORAT THAI dial of THAI [THJ]
KHORCHIN alt for JIRIM dial of MONGOLIAN,
   PERIPHERAL [MVF]
KHORI dial of BURIAT, CHINA [BXU]
KHORI dial of BURIAT, MONGOLIA [BXM]
KHORLA dial of GHALE, NORTHERN [GHH]

KHOSHUT dial of KALMYK-OIRAT [KGZ]
KHOSHUUD alt for KHOSHUT dial of KALMYK-
   OIRAT [KGZ]
KHOTANG dial of SANGPANG [RAV]
KHOTOGOIT dial of MONGOLIAN, HALH [KHK]
KHOTON dial of KALMYK-OIRAT [KGZ]
KHOTTA alt for EASTERN MAITHILI dial of
   MAITHILI [MKP]
KHOUEN alt for KHUEN [KHF]
KHOWAR [KHW] lang, Pakistan
KHROONG dial of KHMU [KJG]
KHÜN [KKH] lang, Myanmar; also in Thailand
KHUA [XHU] lang, Viet Nam; also in Laos
KHUALSHIM dial of CHIN, FALAM [HBH]
KHUCHIA alt for KHASI [KHI]
KHUEN [KHF] lang, Laos; also in China, USA
KHUEN alt for KHÜN [KKH]
KHUF alt for KHUFI dial of SHUGHNI [SGH]
KHUFI dial of SHUGHNI [SGH]
KHUGNI ALT FOR SHUGHNI DIAL OF SHUGHNI
   [SGH]
KHULUNG alt for KULUNG [KLE]
KHULUNGE RAI alt for KULUNG [KLE]
KHUMBI alt for NKHUMBI [KHU]
KHUMBU dial of SHERPA [SCR]
KHUMI alt for CHIN, KHUMI [CKM]
KHUN [KKH] lang, Myanmar; also in Thailand
KHUN SHAN alt for KHÜN [KKH]
!KHUNG alt for KUNG-EKOKA [KNW]
KHUNGARI dial of UDIHE [UDE]
KHUNGGOI dial of NAGA, TANGKHUL [NMF]
KHUNI alt for CHIN, KHUMI [CKM]
KHUNSARI [KFM] lang, Iran
KHUNZAL alt for HUNZIB [HUZ]
KHUNZALY alt for HUNZIB [HUZ]
KHUPANG alt for NUNG [NUN]
KHURGI alt for KODAGU [KFA]
KHUSHNAW dial of KURDI [KDB]
KHUTE dial of GWI [GWJ]
KHUTSHO alt for LAHU SHI [KDS]
KHUTSWE dial of SOTHO, NORTHERN [SRT]
KHUTSWI alt for KHUTSWE dial of SOTHO,
   NORTHERN [SRT]
KHUTU alt for KUTU [KDC]
KHVARSHI [KHV] lang, Russia (Europe)
KHVARSHIN alt for KHVARSHI [KHV]
KHVEK alt for KRAVET [KRV]
KHVOY alt for KHOI-SALMST dial of ARMENIAN
   [ARM]
KHVOY-SALMST dial of ARMENIAN [ARM]
KHWEEN alt for KHUEN [KHF]
KHWEYMI alt for CHIN, KHUMI [CKM]
KHYANG alt for CHIN, ASHO [CSH]
KHYANG dial of CHIN, ASHO [CSH]
KHYEN alt for SHENDU [SHL]
KHYENG alt for CHIN, ASHO [CSH]
KHYENG alt for SHENDU [SHL]
KHYN alt for KHÜN [KKH]
KHYZY alt for ARUSKUSH-DAQQUSHCHU dial of
   TAT, MUSLIM [TTT]
KI alt for AMTO [AMT]

KI alt for TUKI [BAG]
KIA alt for ZABANA [KJI]
KIA dial of GOLIN [GVF]
KIADJARA alt for KARTUJARRA dial of MARTU WANGKA [MPJ]
KIAKH alt for ADYGHE [ADY]
KIAMBA dial of TBOLI [TBL]
KIAMBU alt for SOUTHERN GIKUYU dial of GIKUYU [KIU]
KIAMEROP alt for EMUMU [ENR]
KIANGAN IFUGAO alt for IFUGAO, TUWALI [IFK]
KIARI alt for KIA dial of GOLIN [GVF]
KIARI dial of NOMANE [NOF]
KIBA dial of BWA [BWW]
KIBAALI alt for BALI [BCP]
KIBAI alt for BAI dial of SAKATA [SAT]
KIBAJUNI alt for BAJUNI dial of SWAHILI [SWA]
KIBALA alt for BALI [BCP]
KIBALAN alt for KAVALAN [CKV]
KIBALI alt for BALI [BCP]
KIBALLO alt for VONO [KCH]
KIBANGOBANGO alt for BANGUBANGU [BNX]
KIBANGUBANGU alt for BANGUBANGU [BNX]
KIBAR dial of BAGIRMI [BMI]
"KIBATCHUA" pejorative alt for KANGO [KZY]
KIBBAKU alt for CIBAK [CKL]
KIBBO alt for BEROM [BOM]
KIBBUN alt for BEROM [BOM]
KIBEEMBE alt for BEEMBE [BEJ]
KIBEET alt for KIBET [KIE]
KIBEIT alt for KIBET [KIE]
KIBET [KIE] lang, Chad
KIBET dial of KIBET [KIE]
KIBILA alt for BILA [BIP]
KIBIN alt for LOWER KIMBIN dial of DANI, LOWER GRAND VALLEY [DNI]
KIBIRA alt for BERA [BRF]
KIBIRI [PRM] lang, Papua New Guinea
KIBIRI alt for AIRD HILLS dial of KIBIRI [PRM]
KIBIRI alt for RUMU [KLQ]
KIBO alt for BEROM [BOM]
KIBOMA alt for BOMA [BOH]
KIBOMBO dial of CHAGGA [KAF]
KIBONDEI alt for BONDEI [BOU]
KIBOSHO dial of CHAGGA [KAF]
KIBUA alt for BWA [BWW]
KIBUDU alt for BUDU [BUU]
KIBUKI alt for BUSHI [BUC]
KIBULAMATADI alt for KITUBA [KTU]
KIBUM alt for NIGII dial of YAMBETA [YAT]
KIBUSHI alt for BUSHI [BUC]
KIBUYU alt for BUYU [BYI]
KIBWA alt for BWA [BWW]
KIBWYO alt for MBUGU [MHD]
KIBYEN alt for BEROM [BOM]
KICAPOUX alt for KIKAPÚ [KIC]
KICAPUS alt for KIKAPÚ [KIC]
KICHAGA alt for CHAGGA [KAF]
KICHAI alt for KITSAI [KII]
KICHEPO dial of KACIPO-BALESI [KOE]
KICHO alt for QUICHUA, LOWLAND, NAPO [QLN]

KICKAPOO [KIC] lang, USA; also in Mexico
KICKAPOO alt for KIKAPÚ [KIC]
KICWE alt for BAKONI dial of KENYANG [KEN]
KIDABIDA alt for TAITA [DAV]
KIDAL alt for TADGHAQ dial of TAMASHEQ, KIDAL [TAQ]
KIDAL alt for TADHAQ dial of TAMASHEQ [TAQ]
KIDAL alt for TAMASHEQ [TAQ]
KIDAL TAMASHEQ alt for TAMASHEQ [TAQ]
KIDAPAWAN MANOBO alt for MANOBO, OBO [OBO]
KIDDU dial of KATLA [KCR]
KIDHAISO alt for DHAISO [DHS]
KIDIE alt for LAFOFA [LAF]
KIDIGO alt for DIGO [DIG]
KIDJA alt for KITJA [GIA]
KIDJIA alt for DJIA dial of SAKATA [SAT]
KIDOONDO alt for DOONDO [DOD]
KIDZEM alt for BABANKI [BBK]
KIDZOM alt for BABANKI [BBK]
KIEFO alt for TIÉFO [TIQ]
KIEMBA alt for HEMBA [HEM]
KIEMBARA dial of SAMO, MAYA [SYM]
KIEMBU alt for EMBU [EBU]
KIETA alt for NAASIOI [NAS]
KIETA TALK alt for NAASIOI [NAS]
KIFULERO alt for FULIIRU [FLR]
KIFULIRU alt for FULIIRU [FLR]
KIGA alt for CHIGA [CHG]
KIGA alt for IGIKIGA dial of RWANDA [RUA]
KIGALA dial of LEGA-SHABUNDA [LEA]
KIGHAANGALA alt for GHAANGALA dial of KONGO [KON]
KIGIRIAMA alt for GIRYAMA [NYF]
KIGUMU dial of AMBA [RWM]
KIGWE alt for GWE dial of SUKUMA [SUA]
KIGWENO alt for GWENO [GWE]
KIGYOMA dial of LEGA-SHABUNDA [LEA]
KIHA alt for HA [HAQ]
KIHAI dial of CHAGGA [KAF]
KIHANGAZA alt for HANGAZA [HAN]
KIHAVU alt for HAVU [HAV]
KI/HAZI dial of XOO [NMN]
KIHEHE alt for HEHE [HEH]
KIHEMA-NORD alt for LENDU [LED]
KIHEMBA alt for HEMBA [HEM]
KIHOLO alt for HOLU [HOL]
KIHOLOHOLO alt for HOLOHOLO [HOO]
KIHOLU alt for HOLU [HOL]
KIHUMU alt for AMBA [RWM]
KIHUNDE alt for HUNDE [HKE]
KIHUNGANA alt for HUNGANA [HUM]
KIHYANZI alt for KYANZI dial of AMBA [RWM]
KIHYANZI dial of AMBA [RWM]
KIJA alt for KITJA [GIA]
KIJAU alt for KUIJAU [DKR]
KIJOBA alt for JOBA [JOB]
KIKAAMBA alt for KAAMBA dial of DOONDO [DOD]
KIKABEEUX alt for KIKAPÚ [KIC]
KIKAI [KZG] lang, Japan
KIKALANGA alt for HOLOHOLO [HOO]
KIKAMBA alt for KAMBA [KIK]

KIKAMI alt for KAMI [KCU]
KIKANGO alt for KANGO [KZY]
KIKAPAUX alt for KIKAPÚ [KIC]
KIKAPOO alt for KICKAPOO [KIC]
KIKAPU alt for KICKAPOO [KIC]
KIKAPÚ [KIC] lang, Mexico
KIKEENGE alt for KEENGE dial of BEEMBE [BEJ]
KIKETE alt for KETE [KCV]
KIKIMA alt for COCOPA [COC]
KIKIMÁ alt for COCOPA [COC]
KIKIMBU alt for KIMBU [KIV]
KIKINGA alt for KINGA [KIX]
KIKISANGA alt for KISANGA dial of MWANI [WMW]
KIKOMO alt for KOMO [KMW]
KIKONGO alt for KONGO [KON]
KIKONGO alt for KONGO, SAN SALVADOR [KWY]
KIKONGO COMMERCIAL alt for KITUBA [KTU]
KIKONGO SIMPLIFÉI alt for KITUBA [KTU]
KIKONGO YA LETA alt for KITUBA [KTU]
KIKONGO-KUTUBA alt for KITUBA [KTU]
KIKONJUNKULU alt for DYAABUGAY [DYY]
KIKOONGO alt for KONGO [KON]
KIKOONGO alt for KONGO, SAN SALVADOR
    [KWY]
KIKSHT dial of CHINOOK [CHH]
KIKUK alt for CIBAK [CKL]
KIKUMO alt for KOMO [KMW]
KIKUMU alt for KOMO [KMW]
KIKUNYI alt for KUNYI [KNF]
KIKURIA alt for KURIA [KUJ]
KIKUSU alt for KUSU [KSV]
KIKUTU alt for KUTU [KDC]
KIKUUMU alt for KOMO [KMW]
KIKUWA alt for TEKE, SOUTHERN [KKW]
KIKUYU alt for GIKUYU [KIU]
KIKWAME alt for KWAMI [KTF]
KIKWAMI alt for KWAMI [KTF]
KIKWESE alt for KWESE [KWS]
KI//KXIGWI alt for //XEGWI [XEG]
KIL alt for CHIL dial of KOHO [KPM]
KILA alt for SOMYEWE [KGT]
KILA dial of NANAI [GLD]
KILAKILANA alt for WAGAWAGA [WGW]
KILANGI alt for RANGI [LAG]
KILBA alt for HUBA [KIR]
KILDANI alt for CHALDEAN NEO-ARAMAIC [CLD]
"KILDIN LAPPISH" pejorative alt for SAAMI, KILDIN
    [LPD]
KILEGA alt for LEGA-MWENGA [LGM]
KILEGA alt for LEGA-SHABUNDA [LEA]
KILEMA dial of CHAGGA [KAF]
KILEN alt for QILENG dial of NANAI [GLD]
KILENDU alt for LENDU [LED]
KILENGE alt for LENGUE dial of CHOPI [CCE]
KILENGE dial of MALEU-KILENGE [MGL]
KILENGOLA alt for LENGOLA [LEJ]
KILETA alt for KITUBA [KTU]
KILI [KEB] lang, Gabon; also in Congo
KILI alt for KELE [KHY]
KILI alt for QILENG dial of NANAI [GLD]
KILIA dial of BWAIDOKA [BWD]

KILIKA alt for GILIKA dial of YALE, KOSAREK [KKL]
KILIKA alt for LIKA [LIK]
KILIKIEN dial of ARMENIAN [ARM]
KILIVILA [KIJ] lang, Papua New Guinea
KILIWA [KLB] lang, Mexico
KILIWI alt for KILIWA [KLB]
KILMERA alt for KILMERI [KIH]
KILMERI [KIH] lang, Papua New Guinea
KILOKAKA alt for ZAZAO [JAJ]
KILOMBENO KIBYA alt for EASTERN KALEBWE
    dial of SONGE [SOP]
KILOP alt for KOLOP dial of KIM [KIA]
KILUBA alt for LUBA-KATANGA [LUH]
KIM [KIA] lang, Chad
KIM alt for KOSOP dial of KIM [KIA]
KIM alt for KRIM [KRM]
KIM MUN [MJI] lang, China; also in Laos, Viet Nam
KIMAAMA [KIG] lang, Indonesia (Irian Jaya)
KIMAGHAMA alt for KIMAAMA [KIG]
KIMAKUA alt for MAKHUWA-MEETTO [MAK]
KIMAKWE alt for MAKWE [YMK]
KIMAMBWE alt for MAMBWE dial of MAMBWE-
    LUNGU [MGR]
KIMANDA alt for MANDA [MGS]
KIMANGA alt for MBA [MFC]
KIMANT alt for QIMANT dial of AGAW, WESTERN
    [QIM]
KIMARAGAN alt for KIMARAGANG [KQR]
KIMARAGANG [KQR] lang, Malaysia (Sabah)
KIMARAGANGAN alt for KIMARAGANG [KQR]
KIMASHAMI alt for MACHAMBE [JMC]
KIMATENGO alt for MATENGO [MGV]
KIMATUMBI alt for MATUMBI [MGW]
KIMAWANDA alt for NDONDE [NDS]
KIMAWIHA alt for MAVIHA dial of MAKONDE [KDE]
KIMBA alt for TSIKIMBA [KDL]
KIMBAMBA alt for MBAMBA dial of MBUNDU,
    LOANDA [MLO]
KIMBANGA alt for MBA [MFC]
KIMBEERE alt for MBEERE dial of EMBU [EBU]
KIMBO alt for MBO [ZMW]
KIMBU [KIV] lang, Tanzania
KIMBUNDA alt for MBUNDA [MCK]
KIMBUNDO alt for MBUNDU, LOANDA [MLO]
KIMBUNDU alt for MBUNDU, LOANDA [MLO]
KIMBUUN alt for MPUUN dial of MPUONO [ZMP]
KIMERU alt for MERU [MER]
KIMGI alt for KIMKI [SBT]
KIMI alt for KRIM [KRM]
KI-MIAI alt for KUMIÁI [DIH]
KIMJAL alt for NALCA [TVL]
KIMKI [SBT] lang, Indonesia (Irian Jaya)
KIMMUN alt for KIM MUN [MJI]
KIMOSHI alt for MOCHI [OLD]
KIMRÉ [KQP] lang, Chad
KIMRÉ alt for KIMRUWA dial of KIMRE [KQP]
KIM-RUWA alt for KIMRUWA dial of KIMRE [KQP]
KIMRUWA dial of KIMRE [KQP]
KIMUSHUNGULU alt for MUSHUNGULU [XMA]
KIMVITA alt for MVITA dial of SWAHILI [SWA]
KIMWANI alt for MWANI [WMW]

KIMWIMBI alt for MWIMBI dial of MWIMBI-
MUTHAMBI [MWS]
KIMYAL alt for NALCA [TVL]
KIMYAL OF KORUPUN alt for KORUPUN-SELA
[KPQ]
KINA alt for OPUUO [LGN]
KINABATANGAN MURUT alt for TENGARA dial
of BAUKAN [BNB]
KINABATANGAN, UPPER [DMG] lang, Malaysia
(Sabah)
KINAKOMBA dial of POKOMO, UPPER [PKB]
KINALAKNA [KCO] lang, Papua New Guinea
KINAMI alt for CENTRAL BABOLE dial of BABOLE
[BVX]
KINAMIGIN alt for MANOBO, CINAMIGUIN [MKX]
KINAMWANGA alt for MWANGA [MWN]
KINANDE alt for NANDI [NNB]
KINANDI alt for NANDI [NNB]
KINARAY-A [KRJ] lang, Philippines
KINAYSKIY alt for TANAINA [TFN]
KINBAKKA dial of SONINKE [SNN]
KINCHAI alt for KERINCI [KVR]
KINDA alt for PORI KINDA dial of POL [PMM]
KINDERMA dial of TIRA [TIR]
KINDIGA alt for HADZA [HTS]
KINDJIN alt for KENYAH, KAYAN RIVER [KNH]
KINDJIN alt for KENYAH, KELINYAU [XKL]
KINDJIN alt for KENYAH, MAHAKAM [XKM]
KINDJIN alt for KENYAH, UPPER BARAM [UBM]
KINDJIN alt for KENYAH, WESTERN [XKY]
KINDONGO alt for MBUNDU, LOANDA [MLO]
KING alt for KANDAS [KQW]
KING ISLAND INUPIATUN dial of INUPIATUN,
NORTHWEST ALASKA [ESK]
KINGA [KIX] lang, Tanzania
KINGBETU alt for MANGBETU [MDJ]
KINGENGEREKO alt for NDENGEREKO [NDE]
KINGETI alt for NGITI [NIY]
KINGHWELE alt for NGHWELE [NHE]
KINGINDO alt for NGINDO [NNQ]
KINGITI alt for NGITI [NIY]
KINGONI alt for NGONI [NGU]
KINGONI alt for ZULU [ZUU]
KING'S PASS HUNGARIAN dial of HUNGARIAN
[HNG]
KINGULU alt for NGULU [NGP]
KINH alt for VIETNAMESE [VIE]
KINHWA alt for JINHUA dial of CHINESE, WU [WUU]
KINIHINAO alt for GUANA [QKS]
KINIKINAO alt for GUANA [QKS]
KININANGGUNAN dial of KUANUA [KSD]
KININGO alt for KAGULU [KKI]
KINIRAMBA alt for NILAMBA [NIM]
KINIRAY-A alt for KINARAY-A [KRJ]
KINJIN alt for KENYAH, KAYAN RIVER [KNH]
KINJIN alt for KENYAH, KELINYAU [XKL]
KINJIN alt for KENYAH, MAHAKAM [XKM]
KINJIN alt for KENYAH, UPPER BARAM [UBM]
KINJIN alt for KENYAH, WESTERN [XKY]
KINKOJO alt for NKOJO dial of MWANI [WMM]
KINKWA alt for NKONGHO [NKC]

KINNAURA YANUSKAD alt for KINNAURI [KFK]
KINNAURI [KFK] lang, India
KINNAURI alt for KINNAURI, CHITKULI [CIK]
KINNAURI, BHOTI [NES] lang, India
KINNAURI, CHITKULI [CIK] lang, India
KINNAURI, HARIJAN [KJO] lang, India
KINNER alt for KINNAURI [KFK]
KINORI alt for KINNAURI [KFK]
KINSIMBWA alt for NSIMBWA dial of MWANI [WMM]
KINTA SAKAI alt for ULU KINTA dial of TEMIAR [TMH]
KINTAK alt for KINTAQ [KNQ]
KINTAQ [KNQ] lang, Malaysia (Peninsular); also
in Thailand
KINTAQ BONG alt for KINTAQ [KNQ]
KINTK alt for KINTAQ [KNQ]
KI-NUBI alt for NUBI [KCN]
KINUBI alt for NUBI [KCN]
KINUGU alt for KINUKU [KKD]
KINUKA alt for KINUKU [KKD]
KINUKU [KKD] lang, Nigeria
KI'NYA alt for ATRUAHÍ [ATR]
KINYAANGA alt for NYAANGA dial of KUNYI [KNF]
KINYABANGA dial of LEGA-SHABUNDA [LEA]
KINYABEMBA alt for BEMBA [BMY]
KINYABWISHA alt for BWISHA dial of RWANDA
[RUA]
KINYAKYUSA alt for NYAKYUSA-NGONDE [NYY]
KINYAMBO alt for NYAMBO [NYM]
KINYA-MITUKU alt for MITUKU [ZMQ]
KINYAMULENGE alt for MULENGE dial of RWANDA
[RUA]
KINYAMUNSANGE dial of LEGA-SHABUNDA [LEA]
KINYAMWESI alt for NYAMWEZI [NYZ]
KINYAMWEZI alt for NYAMWEZI [NYZ]
KINYANGA alt for NYANGA [NYA]
KINYARWANDA alt for RWANDA [RUA]
KINYASA alt for MANDA [MGS]
KINYASA alt for MPOTO [MPA]
KINYATURU alt for NYATURU [RIM]
KINYIKA alt for GIRYAMA [NYF]
KINZIMBA alt for COMO KARIM [CFG]
KIOKI alt for LAIWUI dial of TOLAKI [LBW]
KIOKO [UES] lang, Indonesia (Sulawesi)
KIOKO alt for CHOKWE [CJK]
KIOKO dial of KIOKO [UES]
KIOMBI alt for YOMBE [YOM]
KIONG [KKM] lang, Nigeria
KIONG NAI alt for BUNU, JIONGNAI [PNU]
KIORR [XKO] lang, Laos; also in Myanmar
KIOWA [KIO] lang, USA
KIPCHAK dial of UZBEK, NORTHERN [UZB]
KIPEÁ alt for KARIRI-XOCÓ [KZW]
KIPEÁ dial of KARIRI-XOCO [KZW]
KIPENDE alt for PHENDE [PEM]
KIPERE alt for BHELE [PER]
KIPGEN dial of CHIN, THADO [TCZ]
KIPILI alt for BHELE [PER]
KIPOKOMO alt for POKOMO, LOWER [POJ]
KIPSIGIS dial of KALENJIN [KLN]
KIPSIIKIS alt for KIPSIGIS dial of KALENJIN [KLN]
KIPSIKIIS alt for KIPSIGIS dial of KALENJIN [KLN]

KIPSIKIS alt for KIPSIGIS dial of KALENJIN [KLN]
KIPUT [KYI] lang, Malaysia (Sarawak)
KIR alt for JIRU [JRR]
KIR alt for KIR-BALAR [KKR]
KIR alt for MANDARI [MQU]
KIR dial of KIR-BALAR [KKR]
KIRA alt for VAGLA [VAG]
KIRAMANG dial of KUI [KVD]
KIRARI dial of BUNDELI [BNS]
KIRAWA dial of WANDALA [MFI]
KIR-BALAR [KKR] lang, Nigeria
KIRDASI alt for KURMANJI [KUR]
KIRDI alt for KARATA [KPT]
KIRDI-MORA alt for MURA dial of WANDALA [MFI]
KIRE [GEB] lang, Papua New Guinea
KIREGA alt for LEGA-MWENGA [LGM]
KIREGA alt for LEGA-SHABUNDA [LEA]
KIREMI alt for NYATURU [RIM]
KIRE-PUIRE alt for KIRE [GEB]
KIRFI alt for GIIWO [KKS]
KIRGHIZ [KDO] lang, Kyrgyzstan; also in Afghanistan,
    China, Kazakhstan, Tajikistan, Turkey (Asia),
    Uzbekistan
KIRGHIZI alt for KIRGHIZ [KDO]
KIRGIZ alt for KIRGHIZ [KDO]
KIRIBATI [GLB] lang, Kiribati; also in Fiji, Nauru,
    Solomon Islands, Tuvalu, Vanuatu
KIRIFAWA alt for GIIWO [KKS]
KIRIFI alt for GIIWO [KKS]
KIRIKE [OKR] lang, Nigeria
KIRIKIRI [KIY] lang, Indonesia (Irian Jaya)
KIRIKIRI dial of KIRIKIRI [KIY]
KIRIKJIR alt for LOPA [LOP]
KIRIM alt for COMO KARIM [CFG]
KIRIM alt for KRIM [KRM]
KIRIMI alt for NYATURU [RIM]
KIRINIT alt for KAPINGAMARANGI [KPG]
KIRIRA alt for KIRIKIRI [KIY]
KIRIRÍ alt for KIRIRÍ-XOKÓ [XOO]
KIRIRÍ-XOKÓ [XOO] lang, Brazil
KIRISTAV dial of KONKANI [KNK]
KIRIWINA alt for KILIVILA [KIJ]
KIRIYENTEKEN dial of MANOBO, WESTERN
    BUKIDNON [MBB]
KIRKPONG dial of KATLA [KCR]
KIRKUK dial of AZERBAIJANI, SOUTH [AZB]
KIRMA alt for CERMA [GOT]
KIRMÂNCHA alt for KURMANJI [KUR]
KIRMANJI alt for KURMANJI [KUR]
KIRMANJKI [QKV] lang, Turkey (Asia); also in Austria,
    Denmark, France, Germany, Netherlands,
    Sweden, Switzerland, United Kingdom
KIRMÂNSHÂHI dial of KURDI [KDB]
KIRMICO-LEK dial of TSAKHUR [TKR]
KIROBA dial of KURIA [KUJ]
KIROVABAD dial of AZERBAIJANI, NORTH [AZE]
KIRR alt for KIR-BALAR [KKR]
KIRUIHI alt for RUFIJI [RUI]
KIRUNDI alt for RUNDI [RUD]
KIRWO alt for RWA [RWK]
KIS [KIS] lang, Papua New Guinea

KISA dial of LUYIA [LUY]
KISAGALA alt for SAGALA [SBM]
KISAGALA alt for SAGALLA [TGA]
KISAGALLA alt for SAGALLA [TGA]
KISAGARA alt for SAGALA [SBM]
KISAKATA alt for SAKATA [SAT]
KISAMAJENG alt for GISAMJANGA dial of
    DATOOGA [TCC]
KISAMBAA alt for SHAMBALA [KSB]
KISAMBAERI dial of AMARAKAERI [AMR]
KISAN alt for KURUX [KVN]
KISAN dial of KURUX [KVN]
KISAN dial of MAITHILI [MKP]
KISANGA alt for SANGA [SNG]
KISANGA dial of MWANI [WMW]
KISANKASA [KQH] lang, Tanzania
KISAR [KJE] lang, Indonesia (Maluku)
KISEDE dial of LEGA-SHABUNDA [LEA]
KISEGEJU alt for SEGEJU [SEG]
KISEGUJU alt for DHAISO [DHS]
KISEMBOMBO alt for SEMULU dial of ZIMBA [ZMB]
KISETLA alt for SETTLA [STA]
KISETTLA alt for SETTLA [STA]
KISHAKA alt for CHAGGA [KAF]
KISHAMBA dial of SAGALLA [TGA]
KISHAMBA alt for SHAMBA dial of SWAHILI [SWA]
KISHAMBAA alt for SHAMBALA [KSB]
KISHAMBALA alt for SHAMBALA [KSB]
KISHANGANJIA alt for SIRIPURIA dial of BENGALI
    [BNG]
KISHPIGNAG dial of MOINBA [MOB]
KISHTWARI dial of KASHMIRI [KSH]
KISI [KIZ] lang, Tanzania
KISI alt for KISI, SOUTHERN [KSS]
KISI alt for KISSI, NORTHERN [KQS]
KISI, SOUTHERN [KSS] lang, Liberia; also in Sierra
    Leone
KISIE alt for KISSI, NORTHERN [KQS]
KISII alt for GUSII [GUZ]
KISIKONGO alt for KONGO, SAN SALVADOR [KWY]
KISONDE alt for SONDE [SHC]
KISONGA alt for SONGA [SGO]
KISONGE alt for SONGE [SOP]
KISONGI alt for SONGE [SOP]
KISONGO alt for SONGO [SOO]
KISONGYE alt for SONGE [SOP]
KISONKO dial of MAASAI [MET]
KISOONDE alt for SONDE [SHC]
KISSAMA alt for SAMA [SMD]
KISSI alt for KISI, SOUTHERN [KSS]
KISSI, NORTHERN [KQS] lang, Guinea; also in
    Sierra Leone
KISSIEN alt for KISI, SOUTHERN [KSS]
KISSIEN alt for KISSI, NORTHERN [KQS]
KISTANE alt for GURAGE, SODDO [GRU]
KISTANE alt for SODDO dial of GURAGE, SODDO
    [GRU]
KISTIN dial of CHECHEN [CJC]
KISTWALI alt for KISHTWARI dial of KASHMIRI
    [KSH]
KISUAHELI alt for SWAHILI [SWA]

KISUAHILI alt for SWAHILI [SWA]
KISUKU alt for SUKU [SUB]
KISUKUMA alt for SUKUMA [SUA]
KISUMBWA alt for SUMBWA [SUW]
KISUTU alt for NGONI [NGU]
KISUUNDI alt for SUUNDI dial of KUNYI [KNF]
KISWAHELI alt for SWAHILI [SWA]
KISWAHILI alt for SWAHILI [SWA]
KITA MANINKA alt for MANINKAKAN, KITA [MWK]
KITAITA alt for TAITA [DAV]
KITALINGA alt for TALINGA-BWISI [TLJ]
KITAMAT alt for KITIMAT dial of HAISLA [HAS]
KITAVA dial of KILIVILA [KIJ]
KITAVETA alt for TAVETA [TVS]
KITBA alt for YIDINY [YII]
"KITCHEN KAFFIR" pejorative alt for FANAGOLO
    [FAO]
KITEKE alt for TEKE, CENTRAL [TEC]
KITEKE alt for TEKE, EASTERN [TEK]
KITEKE alt for TEKE, SOUTH CENTRAL [IFM]
KITEMBO alt for TEMBO [TBT]
KITEMBO alt for TEMBO dial of TEMBO [TBT]
KITHARAKA alt for THARAKA [THA]
KITHONIRISHE alt for KARKO [KKO]
KITI dial of POHNPEIAN [PNF]
KITIENE alt for TIENE [TII]
KITIINI alt for TIENE [TII]
KITIMAT dial of HAISLA [HAS]
KITIMI alt for TUMI [KKU]
KITIYA alt for BANAWÁ [BNH]
KITJA [GIA] lang, Australia
KITONGA alt for TONGA [TOG]
KITONGWE alt for TONGWE [TNY]
KITSAI [KII] lang, USA
KITSHWA alt for TSHWA [TSC]
KITSIPKI alt for ASHUKU dial of MBEMBE, TIGON
    [NZA]
KITTA alt for TSO [LDP]
KITTIM alt for KRIM [KRM]
KITTITIAN CREOLE ENGLISH alt for ST. KITTS
    CREOLE ENGLISH dial of LEEWARD
    CARIBBEAN CREOLE ENGLISH [AIG]
KITUBA [KTU] lang, DRC
KITUBETA alt for TAVETA [TVS]
KITUHWA dial of CHEROKEE [CER]
KITUI alt for THAGICHU dial of THARAKA [THA]
KITWII alt for BAKONI dial of KENYANG [KEN]
KIULU alt for MENGGATAL dial of DUSUN,
    CENTRAL [DTP]
KIUNDU dial of DUSUN, CENTRAL [DTP]
KIUNGUJA alt for UNGUJA dial of SWAHILI [SWA]
KIUNTHALI alt for LOWER MAHASU PAHARI dial
    of PAHARI, MAHASU [BFZ]
KIURI dial of LEZGI [LEZ]
KIURINSTY alt for LEZGI [LEZ]
KIURINTY alt for LEZGI [LEZ]
KIUTZE alt for NUNG [NUN]
KIUTZE alt for RAWANG [RAW]
KIVIDUNDA alt for VIDUNDA [VID]
KIVIRA alt for JOBA [JOB]
KIVU SWAHILI dial of SWAHILI, CONGO [SWC]

KIVUNGUNYA alt for VUNGUNYA dial of YOMBE
    [YOM]
KIVUNJO alt for VUNJO [VUN]
KIVWANJI alt for WANJI [WBI]
KIWAI, NORTHEAST [KIW] lang, Papua New Guinea
KIWAI, SOUTHERN [KJD] lang, Papua New Guinea
KIWARAW alt for KAVALAN [CKV]
KIWARAWA alt for KAVALAN [CKV]
KIWIBO alt for WIBO dial of MWANI [WMW]
KIWOLLO alt for VONO [KCH]
KIWUNJO alt for VUNJO [VUN]
KIYA alt for MWERI dial of NYAMWEZI [NYZ]
KIYA dial of SUKUMA [SUA]
KIYAKA alt for YAKA [YAF]
KIYANZI alt for YANSI [YNS]
KIYOGO alt for MAYOGO [MDM]
KIYOMBE alt for YOMBE [YOM]
KIYU alt for COMO KARIM [CFG]
KIZARAMO alt for ZALAMO [ZAJ]
KIZARE dial of NAGA, SANGTAM [NSA]
KIZIERE dial of MUNDANG [MUA]
KIZIGULA alt for ZIGULA [ZIW]
KIZOLO dial of NORRA [NOR]
KJAKAR alt for KJAKELA dial of OROCH [OAC]
KJAKELA dial of OROCH [OAC]
KJALONKE alt for YALUNKA [YAL]
KJANG E alt for E [EEE]
KJAX alt for ADYGHE [ADY]
K'KATIAM-PONG-HOUK alt for HUNG [HNU]
KLÁ DONG alt for LAHA [LHA]
KLAI alt for HLAI [LIC]
KLALLAM alt for CLALLAM [CLM]
KLAMAASISE dial of DOGOSE [DOS]
KLAMATH-MODOC [KLA] lang, USA
KLAN dial of YAOURE [YRE]
KLANGKLANG dial of CHIN, HAKA [CNH]
KLAO [KLU] lang, Liberia; also in Ghana, Nigeria,
    Sierra Leone, USA
KLAOH alt for KLAO [KLU]
KLATSOP dial of CHINOOK [CHH]
KLAU alt for CAPE DRAPING GELAO dial of
    GELAO [KKF]
KLAU alt for GELAO [KKF]
KLAU alt for KLAO [KLU]
KLE dial of NGAM [NMC]
KLE NOEHMÕ dial of SENOUFO, MAMARA
    [MYK]
KLEB alt for BATEK [BTQ]
KLEM EL BITHAN alt for HASSANIYYA [MEY]
KLEPO dial of GREBO, NORTHERN [GRB]
KLER alt for KARABORO, EASTERN [KAR]
KLESEM alt for MSER [KQX]
KLESI alt for GRESI [GRS]
KLIKITAT dial of YAKIMA [YAK]
"KLIPKAFFER" pejorative alt for NAMA [NAQ]
"KLIPKAFFERN" pejorative alt for NAMA [NAQ]
KLLUI dial of PAHARI, KULLU [KFX]
KLO alt for GELAO [KKF]
KLOBOUKI alt for KARAKALPAK [KAC]
KLOR alt for KHLOR [LLO]
KLOUKLE alt for //XEGWI [XEG]

KLSL alt for KUALA LUMPUR SIGN LANGUAGE [KGI]
KLUNGKUNG alt for LOWLAND BALI dial of BALI [BZC]
KMHMU alt for KHMU [KJG]
KMRANG alt for SEDANG [SED]
KNAANIC [CZK] lang, Czech Republic
KNWNE alt for KANUM, BÄDI [KHD]
KNWNE alt for KANUM, NGKÂLMPW [KCD]
KNWNE alt for KANUM, SMÄRKY [KXQ]
KNWNE alt for KANUM, SOTA [KRZ]
KO [FUJ] lang, Sudan
KO alt for AKHA [AKA]
KO alt for KAU dial of KO [FUJ]
KO alt for KO-GBE [KQK]
KO alt for KUO [KHO]
KO dial of MENDE [MFY]
KÕ alt for WINYÉ [KST]
KO BASHAI dial of KOTA [KFE]
KÖK alt for TUVIN [TUN]
KÖK MUNGAK alt for TUVIN [TUN]
KÖLSCH [KOR] lang, Germany
KOA alt for KOYA [KFF]
KO'AL alt for KUMIÁI [DIH]
KOALGURDI alt for MANGALA [MEM]
KOALIB [KIB] lang, Sudan
KOARATIRA alt for KANOÉ [KXO]
KOARNBUT alt for NGURMBUR [NRX]
KOASATI [CKU] lang, USA
KOBA [KPD] lang, Indonesia (Maluku)
KOBA alt for BAGA KOGA [BGO]
KOBA alt for YEYI [YEY]
KOBAI alt for KOVAI [KQB]
KOBALI alt for COBARI dial of YANOMAMO [GUU]
KOBE alt for FANIA [FAN]
KOBE dial of SAWAI [SZW]
KOBE-KAPKA dial of ZAGHAWA [ZAG]
KOBEUA alt for CUBEO [CUB]
KOBEWA alt for CUBEO [CUB]
KOBÉWA alt for CUBEO [CUB]
KOBI alt for HUNDE [HKE]
KOBI dial of LIANA-SETI [STE]
KOBIANA [KCJ] lang, Guinea-Bissau; also in Senegal
KOBI-BENGGOI alt for BENGGOI [BGY]
KOBO alt for MOM JANGO [VER]
KOBOCHI alt for NZANYI [NJA]
KOBOI alt for NAGA, KABUI [NKF]
KOBOLA dial of ABUI [ABZ]
KOBON [KPW] lang, Papua New Guinea
KOBOTACHI dial of BATA [BTA]
KOBOTSHI alt for NZANYI [NJA]
KOBROOR alt for DOBEL [KVO]
KOBRO'OR alt for DOBEL [KVO]
KOBUK RIVER INUPIATUN dial of INUPIATUN, NORTHWEST ALASKA [ESK]
KOC alt for KOCH [KDQ]
KOCCH alt for KOCH [KDQ]
KOCE alt for KOCH [KDQ]
KOCH [KDQ] lang, India; also in Bangladesh
KOCH alt for RAJBANGSI [RJB]
KOCHBOLI alt for KOCH [KDQ]

KOCHE alt for RAJBANGSI [RJB]
KOCHIN-KAM alt for NORTH PERMYAK dial of KOMI-PERMYAK [KOI]
KOCHUVELAN alt for ULLATAN [ULL]
KODA alt for KURUX [KVN]
KODAGU [KFA] lang, India
KODAVA THAK alt for KODAGU [KFA]
KODE alt for KHOLOK [KTC]
KODEOHA [VKO] lang, Indonesia (Sulawesi)
KODGOTTO alt for DYAABUGAY [DYY]
KODHIN alt for KADARU [KDU]
KODHINNIAI alt for KADARU [KDU]
KODI [KOD] lang, Indonesia (Nusa Tenggara)
KODI BANGEDO dial of KODI [KOD]
KODI BOKOL dial of KODI [KOD]
KODIA [KWP] lang, Côte d'Ivoire
KODOO dial of MABA [MDE]
KODORO alt for KADARU [KDU]
KODRA alt for TODRAH [TDR]
KODRAO dial of RADE [RAD]
KODU alt for KUI [KXU]
KODU dial of KOHO [KPM]
KODULU alt for KUI [KXU]
KOEGU alt for KWEGU [YID]
KOEKHOEGOWAP alt for NAMA [NAQ]
KOENOEM [KCS] lang, Nigeria
KOEPANG TALK alt for BROOME PEARLING LUGGER PIDGIN [BPL]
KOFA [KSO] lang, Nigeria
KOFA alt for KOFFA dial of MFUMTE [NFU]
KOFA alt for KOFFA dial of MOGUM [MOU]
KOFAN alt for COFÁN [CON]
KOFÁN alt for COFÁN [CON]
KOFANE alt for COFÁN [CON]
KOFEI [KPI] lang, Indonesia (Irian Jaya)
KOFFA dial of MFUMTE [NFU]
KOFFA dial of MOGUM [MOU]
KOFYAR [KWL] lang, Nigeria
KOFYAR dial of KOFYAR [KWL]
KOGA alt for BAGA KOGA [BGO]
KO-GBE [KQK] lang, Benin
KOGI alt for COGUI [KOG]
KOGNERE alt for KONIÉRÉ dial of KARANGA [KTH]
KOGORO alt for BOGURU [BQU]
KOGUI alt for COGUI [KOG]
KOGUMAN [QKG] lang, Papua New Guinea
KOGURU alt for BOGURU [BQU]
KOGURU dial of BOGURU [BQU]
KOH alt for KUO [KHO]
KOHAMA dial of YAEYAMA [RYS]
KOHAT HINDKO dial of HINDKO, SOUTHERN [HIN]
KOHATI alt for KOHAT HINDKO dial of HINDKO, SOUTHERN [HIN]
KOHELIA alt for RATHAWI [RTW]
KOHI alt for KOI [KKT]
KOHIMA dial of NAGA, ANGAMI [NJM]
KOHISTANA alt for KALAMI [GWC]
KOHISTANI alt for KALAMI [GWC]
KOHISTANI alt for KOHISTANI, INDUS [MVY]
KOHISTANI alt for SHINA, KOHISTANI [PLK]

357

KOHISTANI, INDUS [MVY] lang, Pakistan
KOHISTE alt for KOHISTANI, INDUS [MVY]
KOHISTYO alt for SHINA, KOHISTANI [PLK]
KOHLI alt for KOLI, KACHI [GJK]
KOHLI alt for KUNBAN dial of VARHADI-NAGPURI
   [VAH]
KOHNADEH dial of PASHAYI, NORTHWEST [GLH]
KOHO [KPM] lang, Viet Nam; also in USA
KOHOR alt for KOHO [KPM]
KOHOROXITARI [KOB] lang, Brazil
KOHUMONO [BCS] lang, Nigeria
KOI [KKT] lang, Nepal
KOI alt for KOYA [KFF]
KOI BO'O alt for KOI [KKT]
KOI GONDI alt for KOYA [KFF]
KOI SANJAQ SOORIT alt for KOY SANJAQ
   SURAT [KQD]
KOIALI, MOUNTAIN [KPX] lang, Papua New Guinea
KOIANU dial of KOROMIRA [KQJ]
KOIARI alt for KOIARI, GRASS [KBK]
KOIARI, GRASS [KBK] lang, Papua New Guinea
KOIBAL dial of KAMAS [XAS]
KOIJOE alt for KUIJAU [DKR]
KOINE GREEK dial of GREEK, ANCIENT [GKO]
KOIO alt for KWAIO [KWD]
KOIRAO alt for NAGA, KHOIRAO [NKI]
KOIRENG [NKD] lang, India
KOIRNG alt for KOIRENG [NKD]
KOITA alt for KOITABU [KQI]
KOITABU [KQI] lang, Papua New Guinea
KOITAR alt for KOYA [KFF]
KOIWAI alt for KOWIAI [KWH]
KOIWAT [KXT] lang, Papua New Guinea
KOIWAT dial of MALINGUAT [SIC]
KOJALI alt for AWADHI [AWD]
KOK BOROK [TRP] lang, India; also in Bangladesh
KOK CHIANG dial of UGONG [UGO]
KOKADI alt for KAIKADI [KEP]
KOKAMA alt for COCAMA-COCAMILLA [COD]
KOKAMILLA alt for COCAMILLA dial of COCAMA-
   COCAMILLA [COD]
KOKANT SHAN dial of SHAN [SJN]
KOKATA [KTD] lang, Australia
KOKATHA alt for KOKATA [KTD]
KOKBARAK alt for KOK BOROK [TRP]
KOKCHULUTAN dial of TUVIN [TUN]
KOKE [KOU] lang, Chad
KOKHOLA alt for KOKOLA [KZN]
KOKI dial of DOROMU [KQC]
KOKILA dial of DOROMU [KQC]
KOKITTA alt for KOKATA [KTD]
KOKNA alt for KUKNA [KEX]
KOKNI alt for KUKNA [KEX]
KOKO alt for 'AKHOE [AKE]
KOKO alt for ǂKX'AU//'EIN [AUE]
KOKO// //AU-KWE alt for 'AKHOE [AKE]
KOKO BERA alt for GUGUBERA [KKP]
KOKO IMUDJI alt for GUGUYIMIDJIR [KKY]
KOKO PERA alt for GUGUBERA [KKP]
KOKODA [QKW] lang, Indonesia (Irian Jaya)
KOKODA dial of OROKAIVA [ORK]

KOKO-JA'O alt for KUUKU-YA'U [QKL]
KOKOLA [KZN] lang, Malawi; also in Mozambique
KOKOMINDJEN alt for YIR YORONT [YIY]
KOKOMOLOROIJ alt for MULURIDYI [VMU]
KOKOMOLOROITJI alt for MULURIDYI [VMU]
KOKO-MUDJU alt for DJANGUN [DJF]
KOKONYUNGALO alt for DYAABUGAY [DYY]
KOKOPO dial of KUANUA [KSD]
KOKORI alt for NAKARA [NCK]
KOKOROTON MURUT dial of BAUKAN [BNB]
KOKOS alt for MALAY, COCOS ISLANDS [COA]
KOKOTA [KKK] lang, Solomon Islands
KOKO-TJUMBUNDJI alt for DYAABUGAY [DYY]
KOKO-TYANKUN alt for DJANGUN [DJF]
KOKOY dial of LEEWARD CARIBBEAN CREOLE
   ENGLISH [AIG]
KOKO-YALANJI alt for KUKU-YALANJI [GVN]
KOKOYAO alt for KUUKU-YA'U [QKL]
KOKRAIMORO alt for KAYAPÓ [TXU]
KOKWAIYAKWA alt for YAGWOIA [YGW]
KOL [BIW] lang, Cameroon
KOL [KOL] lang, Papua New Guinea
KOL alt for AKA-KOL [AKY]
KOL dial of CUA [CUA]
KOL dial of KOL [KOL]
KOL NORTH dial of KOL [BIW]
KOL SOUTH dial of KOL [BIW]
KOLA [KVV] lang, Indonesia (Maluku)
KOLA alt for KOL [KOL]
KOLA alt for KULA [TPG]
KOLA alt for KURUX [KVN]
KOLA dial of DABA [DAB]
KOLAI dial of SHINA, KOHISTANI [PLK]
KOLAKA alt for TOLAKI [LBW]
KOLAM alt for KOLAMI, NORTHWESTERN [KFB]
KOLAMBOLI alt for KOLAMI, NORTHWESTERN
   [KFB]
KOLAMI, NORTHWESTERN [KFB] lang, India
KOLAMI, SOUTHEASTERN [NIT] lang, India
KOLAMY alt for KOLAMI, NORTHWESTERN [KFB]
KOLANA alt for WERSING [KVW]
KOLANA dial of WERSING [KVW]
KOLANA-WERSIN alt for WERSING [KVW]
KOLANGO alt for KULANGO, BONDOUKOU [KZC]
KOLATA alt for ASHURUVERI dial of ASHKUN
   [ASK]
KOLBAFFO alt for ROTE-TENGAH dial of ROTE
   [ROT]
KOLBILA [KLC] lang, Cameroon
KOLBILARI alt for KOLBILA [KLC]
KOLBILI alt for KOLBILA [KLC]
KOLBILLA alt for KOLBILA [KLC]
KOLCHAN alt for KUSKOKWIM, UPPER [KUU]
KOLDRONG dial of KATLA [KCR]
KOLE alt for BAKOLE [KME]
KOLE alt for FONGORO [FGR]
KOLE alt for KANURI, CENTRAL [KPH]
KOLE alt for KOL [KOL]
KOLELA alt for C'LELA [DRI]
KOLENA alt for KOLBILA [KLC]
KOLENSUSU alt for KULISUSU [VKL]

KOLEPA dial of SIANE [SNP]
KOLERE alt for KANURI, CENTRAL [KPH]
KOLHI alt for KOLI, KACHI [GJK]
KOLHRENG dial of KOM [KMM]
KOLI alt for KOLI, KACHI [GJK]
KOLI alt for OLI dial of DUALA [DOU]
KOLI dial of DOMARI [RMT]
KOLI dial of KONKANI [KNK]
KOLI, KACHI [GJK] lang, Pakistan; also in India
KOLI, PARKARI [KVX] lang, Pakistan
KOLI, WADIYARA [KXP] lang, Pakistan; also in India
KOLIBUGAN alt for SUBANON, KOLIBUGAN [SKN]
KOLIKU alt for MALE [MDC]
KOLINSUSU alt for KULISUSU [VKL]
KOLLANKO alt for GOLLANGO dial of GAWWADA [GWD]
KOLLINA alt for CULINA [CUL]
KOLMI alt for KOLAMI, NORTHWESTERN [KFB]
KOLO dial of BIMA [BHP]
KOLO dial of OGBIA [OGB]
KOLOBO alt for KOLOP dial of KIM [KIA]
KOLOBUAN alt for KALABUAN dial of KINABATANGAN, UPPER [DMG]
KOLOD alt for OKOLOD [KQV]
KOLOI alt for KALAI dial of CHIN, FALAM [HBH]
KOLOKUMA alt for KOLUKUMA dial of IZON [IJC]
KOLOLO alt for LOZI [LOZ]
KOLOM [KLM] lang, Papua New Guinea
KOLOMBANGARA alt for DUKE [NKE]
KOLONG alt for MARBA [MPG]
KOLONG alt for STOD dial of STOD BHOTI [SBU]
KOLOO dial of SENOUFO, MAMARA [MYK]
KOLOP dial of KIM [KIA]
KOLOUR alt for OKOLOD [KQV]
KOLS alt for WINYÉ [KST]
KOLSI alt for WINYÉ [KST]
KOLTA alt for SAAMI, SKOLT [LPK]
KOLTTA alt for SAAMI, SKOLT [LPK]
KOLUAWAWA [KLX] lang, Papua New Guinea
KOLUBE alt for BAROK [BJK]
KOLUKUMA dial of IZON [IJC]
KOLUMBIARA alt for TUBARO [TBA]
KOLUR alt for OKOLOD [KQV]
KOLUR dial of LUNDAYEH [LND]
KOLUWA alt for KOLUAWAWA [KLX]
KOLYA alt for NAGA, KHOIRAO [NKI]
KOLYÂ'I dial of KURDI [KDB]
KOLYM alt for YUKAGHIR, SOUTHERN [YUX]
KOLYMA alt for YUKAGHIR, SOUTHERN [YUX]
KOLYMA-OMOLON dial of EVEN [EVE]
KOM [BKM] lang, Cameroon
KOM [KMM] lang, India
KOM alt for RASHAD dial of TEGALI [RAS]
KOM dial of MFUMTE [NFU]
KOM KOMBA alt for KONKOMBA [KOS]
KOM REM alt for KOM [KMM]
KOMA [KMY] lang, Nigeria; also in Cameroon
KOMA alt for BANA [BCW]
KOMA alt for GANZA [GZA]
KOMA alt for KOMO [KOM]
KOMA alt for KONNI [KMA]

KOMA DAMTI dial of KOMA [KMY]
KOMA KADAM alt for GIMNIME [KMB]
KOMA KADAM alt for GOMNOME dial of KOMA [KMY]
KOMA KAMPANA alt for GOMME dial of KOMA [KMY]
KOMA KOMPANA alt for GIMME [KMP]
KOMA NDERA dial of KOMA [KMY]
KOMA OF ASOSA alt for KWAMA [KMQ]
KOMA OF BEGI dial of KOMO [KOM]
KOMA OF DAGA alt for KOMO [KOM]
KOMA OF DAGA dial of KOMO [KOM]
KOMALU alt for BAROK [BJK]
KOMASMA dial of CITAK [TXT]
KOMAWA alt for KWAAMI [KSQ]
KOMBA [KPF] lang, Papua New Guinea
KOMBAI [KGU] lang, Indonesia (Irian Jaya)
KOMBE alt for NGUMBI [NUI]
KOMBE dial of TUKI [BAG]
KOMBERATORO alt for KAMBERATARO [KBV]
KOMBIO [KOK] lang, Papua New Guinea
KOMBO dial of JOLA-FOGNY [DYO]
KOMBOY alt for KOMBAI [KGU]
KOME alt for RASHAD dial of TEGALI [RAS]
KOMERIN alt for KOMERING [KGE]
KOMERING [KGE] lang, Indonesia (Sumatra)
KOMFANA alt for KOMPANE [KVP]
KOMI alt for KOMI-ZYRIAN [KPV]
KOMI dial of BAREIN [BVA]
KOMINIMUNG [QKM] lang, Papua New Guinea
KOMI-PERM alt for KOMI-PERMYAK [KOI]
KOMI-PERMYAK [KOI] lang, Russia (Europe)
KOMI-PERMYAT alt for KOMI-PERMYAK [KOI]
KOMI-ZYRIAN [KPV] lang, Russia (Europe)
KOMLAMA alt for GIMNIME [KMB]
KOMO [KMW] lang, DRC
KOMO [KOM] lang, Sudan; also in Ethiopia
KOMO dial of PANGSENG [PAN]
KOMODO [KVH] lang, Indonesia (Nusa Tenggara)
KOMOFIO dial of BEAMI [BEO]
KOMOIGALEKA dial of SIANE [SNP]
KOMONGU dial of SIANE [SNP]
KOMONO alt for KHISA [KQM]
KOMORO alt for COMORIAN [SWB]
KOMPANA alt for GIMME [KMP]
KOMPANE [KVP] lang, Indonesia (Maluku)
KOMPARA alt for GIMME [KMP]
KOMPONG THOM alt for PEAR [PCB]
KOMSO [KXC] lang, Ethiopia
KOMTAO dial of TELUGU [TCW]
KOMUDAGO alt for KASUWERI dial of KOKODA [QKW]
KOMUDAGO alt for KOKODA [QKW]
KOMUNG alt for KONNI [KMA]
KOMUTU [KLT] lang, Papua New Guinea
KON HRING SEDANG dial of SEDANG [SED]
KON KEU [ANG] lang, China
KON NGAM alt for NGAM [NMC]
KONA [JUO] lang, Nigeria
KONABEM alt for KUNABEMBE dial of MPONGMPONG [MGG]

KONABEMBE alt for KUNABEMBE dial of
MPONGMPONG [MGG]
KONAI [KXW] lang, Papua New Guinea
KONAWE dial of TOLAKI [LBW]
KONCH alt for KOCH [KDQ]
KOND alt for KUVI [KXV]
KONDA [KND] lang, Indonesia (Irian Jaya)
KONDA alt for KONDA-DORA dial of KONDA-
DORA [KFC]
KONDA dial of MONGO-NKUNDU [MOM]
KONDA dial of NGWO [NGN]
KONDA-DORA [KFC] lang, India
KONDA-DORA dial of KONDA-DORA [KFC]
KONDAIR alt for PALIET dial of DINKA, SOUTH-
WESTERN [DIK]
KONDA-REDDI dial of TELUGU [TCW]
KONDE alt for MAKONDE [KDE]
KONDE alt for NYAKYUSA-NGONDE [NYY]
KONDE dial of RONGA [RON]
KONDEHA alt for KODEOHA [VKO]
KONDEKAR alt for GADABA, OLLAR, POTTANGI
[GDB]
KONDIN alt for EASTERN VOGUL dial of MANSI
[MNS]
KONDJA alt for KWANJA [KNP]
KONDJARA alt for FUR [FUR]
KONDJO alt for KONJO, COASTAL [KJC]
KONDKOR alt for GADABA, OLLAR, POTTANGI
[GDB]
KONDOA dial of SAGALA [SBM]
KONDOMA dial of SHOR [CJS]
KONDOMA TATAR alt for SHOR [CJS]
KONE alt for KONI dial of SOTHO, NORTHERN
[SRT]
KONEÁ alt for ARAPASO [ARJ]
KONEJANDI alt for GOONIYANDI [GNI]
KONERAW [KDW] lang, Indonesia (Irian Jaya)
KONEYANDI alt for GOONIYANDI [GNI]
KONG alt for KOM [BKM]
KONG dial of GBARI [GBY]
KONG dial of TIKAR [TIK]
KONG JULA dial of JULA [DYU]
KONGA dial of LUTOS [NDY]
KONGAMPANI alt for KOMPANE [KVP]
KONGAR dial of TAMIL [TCV]
KONGARA dial of NAASIOI [NAS]
KONGBA dial of GOLA [GOL]
KONGBAA dial of GOLA [GOL]
KONGBO dial of TIBETAN [TIC]
KONGDER alt for PALIET dial of DINKA, SOUTH-
WESTERN [DIK]
KONGI dial of DANO [ASO]
KONGO [KON] lang, DRC; also in Angola, Congo
KONGO, SAN SALVADOR [KWY] lang, DRC; also
in Angola
KONGOLA alt for KUSU [KSV]
KONGOLA-MENO dial of NKUTU [NKW]
KONGON dial of NAGA, KONYAK [NBE]
KONI alt for KONNI [KMA]
KONI dial of SOTHO, NORTHERN [SRT]
KONIAG dial of YUPIK, PACIFIC GULF [EMS]

KONIAG-CHUGACH alt for YUPIK, PACIFIC GULF
[EMS]
KONIAGI alt for WAMEI [COU]
KONIAGUI alt for WAMEI [COU]
KONIÉRÉ dial of KARANGA [KTH]
KONIKE dial of THEMNE [TEJ]
KONIO dial of TOLAKI [LBW]
KONJA alt for KWANJA [KNP]
KONJARA alt for FUR [FUR]
KONJO [KOO] lang, Uganda
KONJO PEGUNUNGAN alt for KONJO, HIGHLAND
[KJK]
KONJO PESISIR dial of KONJO, COASTAL [KJC]
KONJO, COASTAL [KJC] lang, Indonesia (Sulawesi)
KONJO, HIGHLAND [KJK] lang, Indonesia (Sulawesi)
KONKAN STANDARD alt for KONKANI [KNK]
KONKANASTHS alt for CHITAPAVANI dial of
KONKANI, GOANESE [GOM]
KONKANESE alt for KONKANI [KNK]
KONKANI [KNK] lang, India
KONKANI dial of BHILI [BHB]
KONKANI, GOANESE [GOM] lang, India; also in
Kenya, UAE
KONKAU alt for MAIDU, NORTHWEST [MAI]
KONKOMBA [KOS] lang, Ghana; also in Togo
KONKOW alt for MAIDU, NORTHWEST [MAI]
KONNI [KMA] lang, Ghana
KONNOH alt for KONO [KNO]
KONO [KLK] lang, Nigeria
KONO [KNO] lang, Sierra Leone
KONO dial of KPELLE, GUINEA [GKP]
KONOBO dial of KRAHN, EASTERN [KQO]
KONOMALA [KOA] lang, Papua New Guinea
KONOMALA dial of KONOMALA [KOA]
KONONGO [KCZ] lang, Tanzania
KONONGO alt for MWERI dial of NYAMWEZI [NYZ]
KONOSAROLA alt for VAGLA [VAG]
KONSO alt for KOMSO [KXC]
KONSTANTINOPEL alt for CONSTANTINOPLE
dial of ARMENIAN [ARM]
KONTOI alt for BLANG [BLR]
KONTU dial of LAVATBURA-LAMUSONG [LBV]
KONTUM dial of BAHNAR [BDQ]
KONU alt for KONO [KLK]
KONUA alt for RAPOISI [KYX]
KONY alt for KOONY dial of SABAOT [SPY]
KONYA alt for MANINKA, KONYANKA [MKU]
KONYAGI alt for WAMEI [COU]
KONYAK dial for NAGA, KONYAK [NBE]
KONYAKAKAN alt for MANINKA, KONYANKA [MKU]
KONYAR alt for YURUK dial of BALKAN GAGAUZ
TURKISH [BGX]
KONYARE alt for KONIÉRÉ dial of KARANGA
[KTH]
KONYO alt for KONJO, HIGHLAND [KJK]
KONZE alt for KANSA [KAA]
KONZIME alt for KOONZIME [NJE]
KONZO alt for KONJO [KOO]
KOO dial of TALISE [TLR]
KOOCATHO alt for KOKATA [KTD]
KOODE alt for KHOLOK [KTC]

KOOGURDA alt for KOKATA [KTD]
KOOINMARBURRA alt for BAYALI [BJY]
KOOKANOONA alt for MULURIDYI [VMU]
KOOKI dial of GANDA [LAP]
KOOKWILA dial of DADIYA [DBD]
KOOLA alt for DEENU dial of SAMBA LEKO [NDI]
KOONAWURE alt for KINNAURI [KFK]
KOONCIMO alt for KOONZIME [NJE]
KOONY dial of SABAOT [SPY]
KOONZIME [NJE] lang, Cameroon; also in Congo,
    Congo
KOONZIME alt for NZIME dial of KOONZIME [NJE]
KOOPEI dial of SIMEKU [SMZ]
KOOR dial of KAG-FER-JIIR-KOOR-ROR-US-
    ZUKSUN [GEL]
KOO'RA alt for NATIORO [NTI]
KOORETE [KQY] lang, Ethiopia
KOOSA alt for KOSA dial of LUNDA [LVN]
KOOSA alt for XHOSA [XOS]
KOOSE alt for AKOOSE [BSS]
KOOTENAI alt for KUTENAI [KUN]
KOOTENAY alt for KUTENAI [KUN]
KOOZHIME alt for KOONZIME [NJE]
KOOZIME alt for BADWE'E dial of KOONZIME [NJE]
KOOZIME alt for KOONZIME [NJE]
KOPA dial of BANGBA [BBE]
KOPA dial of SOTHO, NORTHERN [SRT]
KOPAR [QKO] lang, Papua New Guinea
KOPE dial of KIWAI, NORTHEAST [KIW]
KOPEI alt for KOOPEI dial of SIMEKU [SMZ]
KOPKA alt for KOPKAKA [OPK]
KOPKAKA [OPK] lang, Indonesia (Irian Jaya)
KOPO-MONIA alt for IKOBI-MENA [MEB]
KOPTI alt for ZARI dial of ZARI [ZAZ]
KOR alt for KOL dial of CUA [CUA]
!KORA alt for KORANA [KQZ]
KORA alt for AKA-KORA [ACK]
KORA alt for KURUX [KVN]
KORA alt for LAMBADI [LMN]
KORAFE [KPR] lang, Papua New Guinea
KORAFE dial of KORAFE [KPR]
KORAFI alt for KORAFE [KPR]
KORAGA, KORRA [KFD] lang, India
KORAGA, MUDU [VMD] lang, India
KORAGAR alt for KORAGA, KORRA [KFD]
KORAGARA alt for KORAGA, KORRA [KFD]
KORAK [KOZ] lang, Papua New Guinea
KORAKU [KSZ] lang, India
KORAMA alt for KURRAMA [VKU]
KORAMBAR alt for KURUMBA [KFI]
KORANA [KQZ] lang, South Africa
KORANDJE [KCY] lang, Algeria
KORANGI alt for KORAGA, KORRA [KFD]
KORANIC ARABIC alt for CLASSICAL ARABIC
    dial of ARABIC, STANDARD [ABV]
KORANKO alt for KURANKO [KHA]
KORANNA alt for KORANA [KQZ]
KORANTI alt for BRIJIA dial of ASURI [ASR]
KORAPE alt for KORAFE [KPR]
KORAPUN alt for KORUPUN-SELA [KPQ]
KORAPUT ORIYA dial of ORIYA [ORY]

KORAQUA alt for KORANA [KQZ]
KORARA alt for UDUK [UDU]
KORAT alt for KHORAT THAI dial of THAI [THJ]
KORAT dial of THAI, NORTHEASTERN [TTS]
KORAVA alt for IRULA [IRU]
KORAVA alt for YERUKULA [YEU]
KORAVA dial of TAMIL [TCV]
KORBAFFO alt for ROTE-TENGAH dial of ROTE
    [ROT]
KORBAFO alt for ROTE-TENGAH dial of ROTE [ROT]
KORBO alt for WEST DANGALEAT dial of
    DANGALEAT [DAA]
KORCA dial of ALBANIAN, TOSK [ALN]
KORCHI alt for YERUKULA [YEU]
KORCHI dial of TAMIL [TCV]
KORE dial of MAASAI [MET]
KOREAN [KKN] lang, Korea, South; also in
    American Samoa, Australia, Bahrain, Belize,
    Brazil, Brunei, Canada, China, Germany, Guam,
    Japan, Kazakhstan, Korea, North, Kyrgyzstan,
    Mauritania, Mongolia, New Zealand, Northern
    Mariana Islands, Panama, Paraguay, Philippines,
    Russia (Asia), Saudi Arabia, Singapore,
    Suriname, Tajikistan, Thailand, Turkmenistan,
    USA, Uzbekistan
KOREAN SIGN LANGUAGE [KVK] lang, Korea,
    South
/KOREE-KHOE alt for /OREE-KHWE dial of SHUA
    [SHG]
KOREGUAJE [COE] lang, Colombia
KOREKORE dial of SHONA [SHD]
KORESH-E ROSTAM [OKH] lang, Iran
KO'REUAJU alt for KOREGUAJE [COE]
KORI alt for KOLI, KACHI [GJK]
KORI alt for RAIO dial of KAILI, LEDO [LEW]
KORI dial of DIMLI [ZZZ]
KORIDO dial of BIAK [BHW]
KORIKI alt for PURARI [IAR]
KORIKO dial of DOROMU [KQC]
KORIKORI alt for KOREKORE dial of SHONA [SHD]
KORIM dial of BIAK [BHW]
KORINDI alt for KARONDI dial of TUMTUM [TBR]
KORING alt for ORING [ORI]
KORINTAL dial of GULA IRO [GLJ]
KORIOK dial of OTUHO [LOT]
KORIPAKO alt for CURRIPACO [KPC]
KORISPASO alt for CURRIPACO [KPC]
KORKI alt for KORKU [KFQ]
KORKORA alt for KURDI [KDB]
KORKU [KFQ] lang, India
KORLA alt for DORLI dial of KOYA [KFF]
KORLAI CREOLE PORTUGUESE [VKP] lang, India
KORO [KRF] lang, Vanuatu
KORO [KXR] lang, Papua New Guinea
KORO AFIKI alt for KORO IJA [VKI]
KORO AGWE alt for BEGBERE-EJAR [BQV]
KORO FUNTU OF KAFIN KORO alt for TANJIJILI
    [UJI]
KORO FUNTU OF MINNA alt for TANJIJILI [UJI]
KORO IJA [VKI] lang, Nigeria
KORO LAFIA alt for LIJILI [MGI]

KORO MAKAMA alt for ASHE [AHS]
KORO MAKAMA alt for BEGBERE-EJAR [BQV]
KORO MYAMYA alt for BEGBERE-EJAR [BQV]
KORO OF LAFIA alt for LIJILI [MGI]
KORO OF SHAKOYI alt for TANJIJILI [UJI]
KORO ZUBA [VKZ] lang, Nigeria
KOROBORO SENNI SONGHAY alt for SONGHAY, KOYRABORO SENNI [SON]
KOROK alt for MALUAL dial of DINKA, SOUTH-WESTERN [DIK]
KOROKA alt for KWADI [KWZ]
KOROKA dial of MAHOU [MXX]
KOROKO alt for VALMAN [VAN]
KOROKORO alt for MUNYO dial of ORMA [ORC]
KOROLAU alt for NORTHEAST VANUA LEVU dial of FIJIAN [FJI]
KOROM BOYE alt for KULERE [KUL]
KOROMBA alt for BASA-GURMANA [BUJ]
KOROMFÉ [KFZ] lang, Burkina Faso; also in Mali
KOROMIRA [KQJ] lang, Papua New Guinea
KOROMIRA dial of KOROMIRA [KQJ]
KORON ACHE alt for ASHE [AHS]
KORON ACHE dial of BEGBERE-EJAR [BQV]
KORON ALA alt for ASHE [AHS]
KORON PANDA dial of BEGBERE-EJAR [BQV]
KORONADAL BILAAN alt for BLAAN, KORONADAL [BIK]
KORONGO alt for KRONGO [KGO]
KORONI [XKQ] lang, Indonesia (Sulawesi)
KOROP [KRP] lang, Nigeria; also in Cameroon
KOROSHI [KTL] lang, Iran
KOROWAI [KHE] lang, Indonesia (Irian Jaya)
KOROWAI, NORTH [KRG] lang, Indonesia (Irian Jaya)
KORRA alt for FUR [FUR]
KORRA alt for KORAGA, KORRA [KFD]
KORRIPAKO dial of CURRIPACO [KPC]
KORROSE alt for GOROSE dial of GAWWADA [GWD]
KORTABINA alt for BANGGARLA [BJB]
KORTCHI alt for GAVAR [GOU]
KORTHA alt for EASTERN MAITHILI dial of MAITHILI [MKP]
KORUBO [QKF] lang, Brazil
KORUPUN dial of KORUPUN-SELA [KPQ]
KORUPUN-SELA [KPQ] lang, Indonesia (Irian Jaya)
KORWA [KFP] lang, India
KORYAK [KPY] lang, Russia (Asia)
KOS dial of ABE [ABA]
KOSA dial of LUNDA [LVN]
KOSACH alt for KAZAKH [KAZ]
KOSADLE [KIQ] lang, Indonesia (Irian Jaya)
KOSALI alt for AWADHI [AWD]
KOSARE alt for KOSADLE [KIQ]
KOSAREK alt for YALE, KOSAREK [KKL]
KOSAREK dial of YALE, KOSAREK [KKL]
KOSENA [KZE] lang, Papua New Guinea
KOSENG alt for KASSENG [KGC]
KOSHAN dial of AGHUL [AGX]
KOSHIN alt for KOSKIN [KID]
KOSI alt for AKOOSE [BSS]

KOSIAN alt for BALANTAK [BLZ]
KOSIN alt for KOSKIN [KID]
KOSIRAVA dial of MAISIN [MBQ]
KOSKIN [KID] lang, Cameroon
KOSO alt for PANAMINT [PAR]
KOSO SHOSHONE alt for PANAMINT [PAR]
KOSOP dial of KIM [KIA]
KOSORONG [KSR] lang, Papua New Guinea
KOSORONG dial of KOSORONG [KSR]
KOSOVA alt for GUSII [GUZ]
KOSOVE alt for SHIP dial of ALBANIAN, GHEG [ALS]
KOSRAE alt for KOSRAEAN [KSI]
KOSRAEAN [KSI] lang, Micronesia; also in Nauru
KOSSA alt for MENDE [MFY]
KOSSO alt for MENDE [MFY]
KOSTI dial of BUNDELI [BNS]
KOSTI dial of VARHADI-NAGPURI [VAH]
KOTA [KFE] lang, India
KOTA [KOQ] lang, Gabon; also in Congo
KOTA alt for DIKOTA dial of NGANDO [NGD]
KOTA alt for KOFA [KSO]
KOTA AGUNG dial of PESISIR, SOUTHERN [PEC]
KOTA BELUD dial of BAJAU, WEST COAST [BDR]
KOTA BUMI dial of ABUNG [ABL]
KOTA MARUDU TALANTANG [GRM] lang, Malaysia (Sabah)
KOTA MARUDU TINAGAS [KTR] lang, Malaysia (Sabah)
KOTAFOA dial of EWE [EWE]
KOTAFON dial of EWE [EWE]
KOTAFOU dial of FON-GBE [FOA]
KOTAGU alt for KODAGU [KFA]
KOTALI dial of BHILI [BHB]
KOTALI BHIL dial of KHANDESI [KHN]
KOTA-WARINGIN dial of MALAY [MLI]
KÓTEDIA alt for GUANANO [GVC]
KOTHER-TAMIL alt for KOTA [KFE]
KOTI [EKO] lang, Mozambique
KOTIA ORIYA alt for ORIYA, ADIVASI [ORT]
KOTIRIA alt for GUANANO [GVC]
KÓTIRYA alt for GUANANO [GVC]
KOTIYA alt for ORIYA, ADIVASI [ORT]
KOTO alt for OREJÓN [ORE]
KOTO alt for ZURA dial of GULA [KCM]
KOTO dial of EBIRA [IGB]
KOTOFO alt for DAN MUURE dial of PEERE [KUT]
KOTOFO alt for PEERE [KUT]
KOTOGÜT alt for TSAKWAMBO [KVZ]
KOTOKO alt for AFADE [AAL]
KOTOKO-GANA alt for LOGONE-GANA dial of LAGWAN [KOT]
KOTOKO-GULFEI alt for MALGBE [MXF]
KOTOKO-KUSERI alt for MSER [KQX]
KOTOKOLI alt for TEM [KDH]
KOTOKO-LOGONE alt for LAGWAN [KOT]
KOTOKO-MAKARI alt for MPADE [MPI]
KOTOKO-MALTAM alt for MASLAM [MSV]
KOTOKORI alt for EBIRA [IGB]
KOTOM dial of YAGARIA [YGR]

KOTOPO alt for DAN MUURE dial of PEERE [KUT]
KOTOPO alt for PEERE [KUT]
KOTPOJO alt for PEERE [KUT]
KOTTA alt for KOTA [KFE]
KOTU alt for KOTA [KOQ]
KOTUA SEDANG dial of SEDANG [SED]
KOTULE alt for TULA [TUL]
KOTVALI dial of BHILI [BHB]
KOTWALIA alt for KOTVALI dial of BHILI [BHB]
KOTYA dial of BOZO, SOROGAMA [BZE]
KOTYAXO alt for KOTYA dial of BOZO,
   SOROGAMA [BZE]
KOTZEBUE SOUND INUPIATUN dial of
   INUPIATUN, NORTHWEST ALASKA [ESK]
KOUANG alt for KWANG [KVI]
KOUKA alt for KUKA dial of NABA [MNE]
KOUKOUYA alt for TEKE, SOUTHERN [KKW]
KOULANGO alt for KULANGO, BONDOUKOU [KZC]
KOULANGO alt for KULANGO, BOUNA [NKU]
KOULOUNKALAN dial of MANINKA, KANKAN [MNI]
KOUMAC alt for KUMAK [NEE]
KOUMONGOU dial of NGANGAM [GNG]
KOUNTE LELE dial of LELE [LLC]
KOURI alt for KURI dial of BUDUMA [BDM]
KOUROUSA alt for AMANA dial of MANINKA,
   KANKAN [MNI]
KOUSERI alt for MSER [KQX]
KOUSSASSÉ alt for KUSAAL [KUS]
KOUSSERI alt for MSER [KQX]
KOUSSERI alt for MSER dial of MSER [KQX]
KOUSSOUNTOU alt for BAGO [BQG]
KOUTIN alt for PEERE [KUT]
KOUTINE alt for PEERE [KUT]
KOUYA [KYF] lang, Côte d'Ivoire
KOVAI [KQB] lang, Papua New Guinea
KOVE [KVC] lang, Papua New Guinea
KOVIO alt for NORTHWEST MEKEO dial of MEKEO
   [MEK]
KOW alt for ASAS [ASD]
KOW alt for SINSAURU [SNZ]
KOWAAO alt for KUWAA [BLH]
KOWAI alt for KOVAI [KQB]
KOWAKI [QKK] lang, Papua New Guinea
KOWALIB alt for KOALIB [KIB]
KOWE-ADIWASI alt for KOTA [KFE]
KOWET alt for KRAVET [KRV]
KOWIAI [KWH] lang, Indonesia (Irian Jaya)
KOWLONG alt for KAULONG [PSS]
KOWYA alt for KOUYA [KYF]
KOXIMA alt for COXIMA [KOX]
KOY SANJAQ dial of LISHANID NOSHAN [AIJ]
KOY SANJAQ SOORET alt for KOY SANJAQ
   SURAT [KQD]
KOY SANJAQ SURAT [KQD] lang, Iraq
KOYA [KFF] lang, India
KOYA alt for JULA, KOYAGA [KGA]
KOYA dial of LOKO [LOK]
KOYA dial of THEMNE [TEJ]
KOYAA alt for JULA, KOYAGA [KGA]
KOYAGA alt for JULA, KOYAGA [KGA]
KOYAGA dial of JULA, KOYAGA [KGA]

KOYAGAKAN alt for JULA, KOYAGA [KGA]
KOYAKA alt for JULA, KOYAGA [KGA]
KOYARA alt for JULA, KOYAGA [KGA]
KOYATO alt for KOYA [KFF]
KOYI alt for KOI [KKT]
KOYI alt for KOYA [KFF]
KOYO [KOH] lang, Congo
KOYO alt for LOKOYA [LKY]
KOYO alt for NGURU dial of GULA [KCM]
KOYO dial of GODIE [GOD]
KOYONG alt for HALANG [HAL]
KOYRA alt for KOORETE [KQY]
KOYRA CHIINI dial of SONGHAY, KOYRA CHIINI
   [KHQ]
KOYRA SENNI SONGHAY alt for SONGHAY,
   KOYRABORO SENNI [SON]
KOYTA alt for NARA [NRB]
KOYU alt for KOI [KKT]
KOYU BO' alt for KOI [KKT]
KOYUKON [KOY] lang, USA
KOZYMODEMYAN dial of MARI, HIGH [MRJ]
KPA alt for RDE KPA dial of RADE [RAD]
KPA dial of BAFIA [KSF]
KPA dial of MENDE [MFY]
KPAGUA [KUW] lang, CAR
KPAGWA alt for KPAGUA [KUW]
KPAKOLO dial of BETE, GAGNOA [BTG]
KPAKUM alt for KWAKUM [KWU]
KPALA [KPL] lang, DRC
KPALA alt for GBAYA [KRS]
KPALA alt for KOLA dial of DABA [DAB]
KPALAGHA alt for SENOUFO, PALAKA [PLR]
KPAN [KPK] lang, Nigeria
KPANGO alt for DZÙÙNGOO [DNN]
KPANGO dial of DZÙÙNGOO [DNN]
KPANKPAM alt for KONKOMBA [KOS]
KPANTEN alt for KPAN [KPK]
KPANZON alt for KUMBO dial of KPAN [KPK]
KPARA alt for GBAYA [KRS]
KPARLA alt for GBAYA [KRS]
KPASAM [PBN] lang, Nigeria
KPASHAM alt for KPASAM [PBN]
KPASHAN alt for KAFANCHAN dial of TYAP [KCG]
KPASIYA alt for GBAYI [GYG]
KPATERE alt for KPATILI [KYM]
KPATI [KOC] lang, Nigeria
KPATILI [KYM] lang, CAR
KPATIRI alt for KPATILI [KYM]
KPATOGO dial of KAANSA [GNA]
KPATOGOSO alt for KPATOGO dial of KAANSA
   [GNA]
KPEAPLY dial of KRAHN, WESTERN [KRW]
KPELE alt for KPELLE, GUINEA [GKP]
KPELE alt for KPELLE, LIBERIA [KPE]
KPELESE alt for KPELLE, GUINEA [GKP]
KPELESETINA alt for KPELLE, GUINEA [GKP]
KPELLE, GUINEA [GKP] lang, Guinea
KPELLE, LIBERIA [KPE] lang, Liberia
KPERE alt for GBETE dial of MBUM [MDD]
KPERESE alt for KPELLE, GUINEA [GKP]
KPESE alt for KPELLE, GUINEA [GKP]

KPESI alt for KPESSI [KEF]
KPESSI [KEF] lang, Togo
KPÉTSI alt for KPESSI [KEF]
KPILAKPILA alt for PILA [PIL]
KPLANG [PRA] lang, Ghana
KPLEBO dial of GREBO, BARCLAYVILLE [GRY]
KPLOR dial of GBII [GGB]
KPO dial of GOLA [GOL]
KPONGO alt for LIKA [LIK]
KPORO alt for NAMA dial of MBEMBE, TIGON [NZA]
KPORO dial of MBEMBE, TIGON [NZA]
KPOSO alt for AKPOSO [KPO]
KPOTOPO alt for DAN MUURE dial of PEERE [KUT]
KPWAALA alt for KPALA [KPL]
KPWATE alt for KPAN [KPK]
KPWESSI alt for KPELLE, GUINEA [GKP]
KPWESSI alt for KPELLE, LIBERIA [KPE]
KRACHE [KYE] lang, Ghana
KRACHI alt for KRACHE [KYE]
KRAHN alt for KRAHN, WESTERN [KRW]
KRAHN, EASTERN [KQO] lang, Liberia
KRAHN, WESTERN [KRW] lang, Liberia; also in Côte d'Ivoire
KRAHÔ [XRA] lang, Brazil
KRAKYE alt for KRACHE [KYE]
KRAMANG alt for KIRAMANG dial of KUI [KVD]
KRANARIA dial of ROMANI, SINTE [RMO]
KRANGKU alt for RAWANG [RAW]
KRANTIKI dial of ROMANI, SINTE [RMO]
KRANYEU dial of OY [OYB]
KRAÔ alt for KRAHÔ [XRA]
KRAOL [RKA] lang, Cambodia
KRAOL dial of KUY [KDT]
KRASENG alt for KASSENG [KGC]
KRAU dial of JAH HUT [JAH]
KRAVET [KRV] lang, Cambodia
KRAWANG alt for BOGOR dial of SUNDA [SUO]
KRE alt for CREQ dial of HRE [HRE]
KREDJ alt for GBAYA [KRS]
KREEN-AKARORE [KRE] lang, Brazil
KREI alt for KAREY [KYD]
KREICH alt for GBAYA [KRS]
KREISH alt for GBAYA [KRS]
KREM dial of BAHNAR [BDQ]
KREM-YE alt for KREYE [XRE]
KREN AKARORE alt for KREEN-AKARORE [KRE]
KRENAK [KQQ] lang, Brazil
KREOL alt for MORISYEN [MFE]
KREOL alt for SESELWA CREOLE FRENCH [CRS]
KREOLE alt for MORISYEN [MFE]
KREPE alt for ÉWÉ [EWE]
KREPI alt for ÉWÉ [EWE]
KRESH alt for GBAYA [KRS]
KRESH-BORO alt for NAKA dial of GBAYA [KRS]
KRESH-HOFRA alt for GBAYA-NGBONGBO dial of GBAYA [KRS]
KRESH-NDOGO alt for GBAYA-NDOGO dial of GBAYA [KRS]
KREYE [XRE] lang, Brazil

KREYOL alt for GUADELOUPE CREOLE FRENCH dial of LESSER ANTILLEAN CREOLE FRENCH [DOM]
KRIANG alt for NGEQ [NGT]
KRIKATI-TIMBIRA [XRI] lang, Brazil
KRIM [KRM] lang, Sierra Leone
KRIM alt for CRIMEA dial of ARMENIAN [ARM]
KRIMCHAK alt for JUDEO-CRIMEAN TATAR [JCT]
KRINKATI dial of KRIKATI-TIMBIRA [XRI]
KRIO [KRI] lang, Sierra Leone; also in Gambia, Guinea, Senegal
KRIO FULA dial of FUUTA JALON [FUF]
KRIOL [ROP] lang, Australia
KRIOL alt for BELIZE CREOLE ENGLISH dial of NORTHERN CENTRAL AMERICA CREOLE ENGLISH [BZI]
KRISA [KRO] lang, Papua New Guinea
KRISTANG alt for MALACCAN CREOLE PORTUGUESE [MCM]
KRIULO alt for CRIOULO, UPPER GUINEA [POV]
KROBO dial of DANGME [DGM]
KROBOU alt for KROBU [KXB]
KROBU [KXB] lang, Côte d'Ivoire
KROE alt for KRUI [KRQ]
KROKONG dial of JAGOI [SNE]
KROM alt for KHMER, CENTRAL [KMR]
KRONG alt for KHROONG dial of KHMU [KJG]
KRONGO [KGO] lang, Sudan
KRONGO ABDALLAH dial of TUMMA [TBQ]
KROO alt for KLAO [KLU]
KROUMEN alt for KRUMEN, PYE [PYE]
KROUMEN alt for KRUMEN, TEPO [TED]
KROWE alt for SIKA [SKI]
KRU alt for CHRU [CJE]
KRU alt for KLAO [KLU]
KRU alt for KRUMEN, TEPO [TED]
KRU PIDGIN ENGLISH dial of LIBERIAN ENGLISH [LIR]
KRUENG alt for KRU'NG 2 [KRR]
KRUI [KRQ] lang, Indonesia (Sumatra)
KRU'I alt for KRUI [KRQ]
KRUMEN alt for KRUMEN, TEPO [TED]
KRUMEN, PLAPO [KTJ] lang, Côte d'Ivoire
KRUMEN, PYE [PYE] lang, Côte d'Ivoire
KRUMEN, TEPO [TED] lang, Côte d'Ivoire; also in Liberia
KRUNG 1 dial of RADE [RAD]
KRU'NG 2 [KRR] lang, Cambodia
KRYC alt for KRYTS [KRY]
KRYTS [KRY] lang, Azerbaijan
KRYTS dial of KRYTS [KRY]
KRYZ alt for KRYTS [KRY]
KRYZY alt for KRYTS [KRY]
KSAKAUTENH alt for KHANG [KJM]
KSING MUL alt for PUOC [PUO]
KTUNAXA alt for KUTENAI [KUN]
KÜRTHÖPKA alt for KURTOKHA [XKZ]
!KU alt for KUNG-EKOKA [KNW]
KU TE alt for LACHI [LBT]
KUA alt for HIETSHWARE [HIE]
KUAHANE alt for SUBIYA [SBS]

KU'AHL alt for KUMIÁI [DIH]
KUAKUA alt for PIAROA [PID]
KUALA dial of BANJAR [BJN]
KUALA LANGOT BESISI dial of BESISI [MHE]
KUALA LUMPUR SIGN LANGUAGE [KGI] lang,
    Malaysia (Peninsular)
KUALA MONSOK DUSUN dial of DUSUN,
    CENTRAL [DTP]
KUALA TEMBELING dial of JAH HUT [JAH]
KUALA TUTOH alt for LONG TUTOH dial of KIPUT
    [KYI]
KU-AMBA alt for AMBA [RWM]
KUAMBA alt for AMBA [RWM]
KUAMBA alt for KIGUMU dial of AMBA [RWM]
KUAN [UAN] lang, Laos
KUANG alt for KWANG [KVI]
KUANGA alt for BRERI [BRQ]
KUANGFU alt for TAVALONG-VATAAN dial of AMIS
    [ALV]
KUANGSU-BONGGRANG alt for MLAP [KJA]
KUANHUA [QAK] lang, China
KUANUA [KSD] lang, Papua New Guinea
KUANYAMA alt for KWANYAMA [KUY]
KUAP alt for BIATAH [BTH]
KUAT alt for KUOT [KTO]
KUAY alt for KUY [KDT]
KUBA alt for BUSHOONG [BUF]
KUBA alt for KUBI [KOF]
KUBA alt for LIKUBA [KXX]
KUBA alt for LUNA [LUJ]
KUBA alt for YEYI [YEY]
KUBA dial of AZERBAIJANI, NORTH [AZE]
KUBA dial of LEZGI [LEZ]
KUBACHI dial of DARGWA [DAR]
KUBACHIN alt for KUBACHI dial of DARGWA [DAR]
KUBACHINTSY alt for KUBACHI dial of DARGWA
    [DAR]
KUBAI alt for NAGA, KABUI [NKF]
KUBAN dial of KABARDIAN [KAB]
KUBANG alt for BAJAU SEMPORNA dial of SAMA,
    SOUTHERN [SIT]
KUBARI dial of KANURI, TUMARI [KRT]
KUBAWA alt for KUBI [KOF]
KUBE [KGF] lang, Papua New Guinea
KUBI [KOF] lang, Nigeria
KUBI dial of KONDA-DORA [KFC]
KUBIRI alt for UBIR [UBR]
KUBIWAT alt for MENDE [SIM]
KUBO [JKO] lang, Papua New Guinea
KUBOKOTA alt for GHANONGGA [GHN]
KUBONITU alt for CHEKE HOLO [MRN]
KUBORO dial of BABATANA [BAQ]
KUBU [KVB] lang, Indonesia (Sumatra)
KUBULI dial of SINAUGORO [SNC]
KUBUNG alt for SIKUBUNG dial of SAMA,
    SOUTHERN [SIT]
KUBWA alt for CUBEO [CUB]
KUCHBANDHI dial of KANJARI [KFT]
KUCHE alt for CHE [RUK]
KUCHI alt for KOLI, KACHI [GJK]
KUCHI dial of MATUMBI [MGW]

KUCONG alt for LAHU SHI [KDS]
KUDA alt for KUDU dial of KUDU-CAMO [KOV]
KUDA alt for KURUX [KVN]
KUDA-CHAMO alt for KUDU-CAMO [KOV]
KUDAKA dial of OKINAWAN, CENTRAL [RYU]
KUDALA alt for PARKWA [PBI]
KUDALI dial of KONKANI, GOANESE [GOM]
KUDAWA alt for KUDU-CAMO [KOV]
KUDI alt for KODI [KOD]
KUDIYA [KFG] lang, India
KUDMALI [KYW] lang, India
KUDO alt for KADO [KDV]
KUDU dial of KUDU-CAMO [KOV]
KUDU-CAMO [KOV] lang, Nigeria
KUDUGLI alt for KADUGLI dial of KATCHA-
    KADUGLI-MIRI [KAT]
//KU//E dial of SEROA [KQU]
KUEIPIEN alt for GUIBIAN dial of ZHUANG,
    NORTHERN [CCX]
KUFA alt for KANGA [KCP]
KUFA-LIMA dial of KANGA [KCP]
KUFO alt for KANGA [KCP]
KUFURU dial of SENOUFO, CEBAARA [SEF]
KUGAMA [KOW] lang, Nigeria
KUGAMMA alt for KUGAMA [KOW]
KUGBO [KES] lang, Nigeria
KUGENESI dial of KALULI [BCO]
KUGNI alt for KUNYI [KNF]
KUGONG dial of MUMUYE [MUL]
KUGU-MANGK alt for KUKU-MANGK [XMQ]
KUGU-MU'INH alt for KUKU-MU'INH [XMP]
KUGU-MUMINH alt for KUKU-MUMINH [XMH]
KUGURDA alt for KOKATA [KTD]
KUGU-UGBANH alt for KUKU-UGBANH [UGB]
KUGU-UWANH alt for KUKU-UWANH [UWA]
KUGWE alt for MOGHAMO dial of META [MGO]
KUI [KVD] lang, Indonesia (Nusa Tenggara)
KUI [KXU] lang, India
KUI alt for KUY [KDT]
KUI alt for LAHU SHI [KDS]
KUI dial of KUI [KVD]
KUI SOUEI alt for KUY [KDT]
KUIARO alt for OYA'OYA [OYY]
KUIJAU [DKR] lang, Malaysia (Sabah)
KUIKÚRO-KALAPÁLO [KUI] lang, Brazil
KUIKURU alt for KUIKÚRO-KALAPÁLO [KUI]
KUILE alt for TSAMAI [TSB]
KUINGA alt for KUI [KXU]
KUINMURBARA alt for BAYALI [BJY]
KUIWAI alt for KOWIAI [KWH]
KUIYOW alt for KUIJAU [DKR]
KUJAA dial of SENOUFO, MAMARA [MYK]
KUJARGE [VKJ] lang, Chad
KUJARKE alt for KAJAKSE [CKQ]
KUJAU alt for KUIJAU [DKR]
KUJINGA dial of MABA [MDE]
KUKA alt for NABA [MNE]
KUKAJA alt for KUKATJA [KUX]
KUKANAR dial of DURUWA [PCI]
KUKATA alt for KOKATA [KTD]
KUKATJA [KUX] lang, Australia

KUKELE [KEZ] lang, Nigeria
KUKI alt for CHIN, THADO [TCZ]
KUKI alt for TIYAL dial of CINDA-REGI-TIYAL [KAU]
KUKI AIRANI alt for RAROTONGAN [RRT]
KUKI CHIN alt for ZOME [ZOM]
KUKI-THADO alt for CHIN, THADO [TCZ]
KUKNA [KEX] lang, India
KUKOMA dial of BOBO MADARE, NORTHERN [BBO]
KUKTAYOR alt for THAYORE [THD]
KUKU dial of BARI [BFA]
KUKUBERA alt for GUGUBERA [KKP]
KUKUDAYORE alt for THAYORE [THD]
"KUKUKUKU" pejorative alt for HAMTAI [HMT]
KUKU-LUMUN alt for LUMUN [LMD]
KUKULUNG alt for KULUNG [BBU]
KUKUM alt for FER dial of KAG-FER-JIIR-KOOR-ROR-US-ZUKSUN [GEL]
KUKU-MANGK [XMQ] lang, Australia
KUKUMINDJEN alt for KUNJEN [KJN]
KUKU-MU'INH [XMP] lang, Australia
KUKU-MUMINH [XMH] lang, Australia
"KUKURUKU" pejorative alt for YEKHEE [ETS]
KUKUS alt for MALAY, COCOS ISLANDS [COA]
KUKU-UGBANH [UGB] lang, Australia
KUKU-UWANH [UWA] lang, Australia
KUKUYA alt for MINAVEHA [MVN]
KUKUYA alt for TEKE, SOUTHERN [KKW]
KUKU-YALANGI alt for KUKU-YALANJI [GVN]
KUKU-YALANJI [GVN] lang, Australia
KUKUYIMIDIR alt for GUGUYIMIDJIR [KKY]
KUKWA alt for TEKE, SOUTHERN [KKW]
KUKWAYA dial of GUMUZ [GUK]
KUKWE alt for NYAKYUSA-NGONDE [NYY]
KUKWE dial of NYAKYUSA-NGONDE [NYY]
KUKWO dial of URIM [URI]
KULA [TPG] lang, Indonesia (Nusa Tenggara)
KULA alt for DARLING [DRL]
KULA dial of DARLING [DRL]
KULA dial of KULA [TPG]
KULA WATENA dial of KULA [TPG]
KULAAL alt for GULA IRO [GLJ]
KULAHA alt for KOLA [KVV]
KULAMANEN dial of MANOBO, MATIGSALUG [MBT]
KULANAPAN alt for POMO, CENTRAL [POO]
KULANAPO alt for POMO, CENTRAL [POO]
KULANGE alt for KULANGO, BONDOUKOU [KZC]
KULANGE alt for KULANGO, BOUNA [NKU]
KULANGO, BONDOUKOU [KZC] lang, Côte d'Ivoire; also in Ghana
KULANGO, BOUNA [NKU] lang, Côte d'Ivoire; also in Ghana
KULATELA dial of KULA [TPG]
KULAWI alt for MOMA [MYL]
KULE alt for TSAMAI [TSB]
KULERE [KUL] lang, Nigeria
KULERE dial of SENOUFO, CEBAARA [SEF]
KULESA dial of POKOMO, LOWER [POJ]
KULFA [KXJ] lang, Chad
KULFE alt for KULFA [KXJ]

KULINA alt for CULINA [CUL]
KULÍNA alt for CULINA [CUL]
KULINO alt for CULINA [CUL]
KULIOW alt for KUIJAU [DKR]
KULISUSU [VKL] lang, Indonesia (Sulawesi)
KULIVIU alt for MASKELYNES [KLV]
KULJA alt for TARANCHI dial of UYGHUR [UIG]
KULLO alt for DAWRO dial of GAMO-GOFA-DAWRO [GMO]
KULLUI alt for PAHARI, KULLU [KFX]
KULME alt for KOLAMI, NORTHWESTERN [KFB]
KULON alt for KULUN [KNG]
KULPANTJA alt for YANKUNYTJATJARA [KDD]
KULU alt for KOOR dial of KAG-FER-JIIR-KOOR-ROR-US-ZUKSUN [GEL]
KULU alt for KULUNG [BBU]
KULU dial of SARUDU [SDU]
KULU BOLI alt for PAHARI, KULLU [KFX]
KULU PAHARI alt for PAHARI, KULLU [KFX]
KULU RING alt for KULUNG [KLE]
KULUBI alt for BAROK [BJK]
KULUI alt for PAHARI, KULLU [KFX]
KULUN [KNG] lang, Taiwan
KULUNG [BBU] lang, Nigeria
KULUNG [KLE] lang, Nepal; also in India
KULUNG alt for MARBA [MPG]
KULUNG MUTHUN dial of NAGA, WANCHO [NNP]
KULUNG PUN alt for PONGYONG [PGY]
KULUNO alt for KULUNG [BBU]
KULUR dial of SAPARUA [SPR]
KULUUNAAY alt for ELUN dial of BANDIAL [BQJ]
KULVI alt for PAHARI, KULLU [KFX]
KULWALI alt for PAHARI, KULLU [KFX]
KULYNA alt for CULINA [CUL]
KUMA alt for KOMA [KMY]
KUMAI alt for KUP-MINJ dial of WAHGI [WAK]
KUMAIYA PACHHAI dial of KUMAUNI [KFY]
KUMAJU alt for KEMEZUNG [DMO]
KUMAK [NEE] lang, New Caledonia
KUMAK dial of KUMAK [NEE]
KUMALAHU dial of BUNAMA [BDD]
KUMALU [KSL] lang, Papua New Guinea
KUMAM [KDI] lang, Uganda
KUMAN [KUE] lang, Papua New Guinea
KUMAN alt for KUMAM [KDI]
KUMAN dial of KUMAN [KUE]
KUMAON alt for KUMAUNI [KFY]
KUMAONI alt for KUMAUNI [KFY]
KUMAR alt for KUMARBHAG PAHARIA [KMJ]
KUMARA alt for KUMALU [KSL]
KUMARBHAG PAHARIA [KMJ] lang, India
KUMAU alt for KUMAUNI [KFY]
KUMAUNI [KFY] lang, India; also in Nepal
KUMAWANI alt for KUMAUNI [KFY]
KUMBA [KSM] lang, Nigeria
KUMBA dial of LUSENGO [LUS]
KUMBAINGERI alt for KUMBAINGGAR [KGS]
KUMBAINGGAR [KGS] lang, Australia
KUMBALE alt for KUMHALI [KRA]
KUMBERE dial of VUTE [VUT]
KUMBEWAHA [XKS] lang, Indonesia (Sulawesi)

KUMBHARI alt for VARHADI-NAGPURI [VAH]
KUMBHARI dial of BUNDELI [BNS]
KUMBI dial of GUDU [GDU]
KUMBO dial of IZON [IJC]
KUMBO dial of KPAN [KPK]
KUMBOKOLA alt for LUNGGA [LGA]
KUMBOKOTA alt for GHANONGGA [GHN]
KUMBORO alt for KUBORO dial of BABATANA [BAQ]
KUMBULE dial of NANDI [NNB]
KUMERTUO alt for DJAUAN [DJN]
KUMEYAAI alt for KUMIÁI [DIH]
KUMEYAAY alt for KUMIÁI [DIH]
KUMFEL alt for KUNFAL [XUF]
KUMGONI alt for KUMAUNI [KFY]
KUMHALE alt for KUMHALI [KRA]
KUMHALI [KRA] lang, Nepal
KUMI alt for CHIN, KHUMI [CKM]
KUMI alt for TOPOSA [TOQ]
KUMIA alt for KUMIÁI [DIH]
KUMIÁI [DIH] lang, Mexico; also in USA
KUMIYÁNA alt for HIXKARYÁNA [HIX]
KUMKALE alt for KUMHALI [KRA]
KUMKH alt for KUMUX dial of LAK [LBE]
KUMMAN alt for KUMAUNI [KFY]
KUMO alt for KOMO [KMW]
KUMOKIO alt for KUMUKIO [KUO]
KUMU alt for KOMO [KMW]
KUMUK alt for KUMYK [KSK]
KUMUKIO [KUO] lang, Papua New Guinea
KUMUKLAR alt for KUMYK [KSK]
KUMUM alt for KUMAM [KDI]
KUMUS alt for UDUK [UDU]
KUMUX dial of LAK [LBE]
KUMWENU alt for KHISA [KQM]
KUMYK [KSK] lang, Russia (Europe); also in Kazakhstan, Turkey (Asia)
KUMYKI alt for KUMYK [KSK]
KUMZAI alt for KUMZARI [ZUM]
KUMZARI [ZUM] lang, Oman
KUNA DE LA FRONTERA alt for KUNA, BORDER [KUA]
KUNA, BORDER [KUA] lang, Colombia; also in Panama
KUNA, SAN BLAS [CUK] lang, Panama
KUNABE dial of KUTEP [KUB]
KUNABEEB alt for KUNABEMBE dial of MPONGMPONG [MGG]
KUNABEMBE dial of MPONGMPONG [MGG]
KUNABI alt for KONKANI [KNK]
KUNAI dial of BOIKIN [BZF]
KUNAMA [KUM] lang, Eritrea; also in Ethiopia
KUNAN alt for GOONIYANDI [GNI]
KUNAN alt for KWINI [GWW]
KUNANA alt for LARDIL [LBZ]
KUNANT alt for MANSOANKA [MSW]
KUNANTE alt for MANSOANKA [MSW]
KUNAR dial of PASHAYI, SOUTHEAST [DRA]
KUNAWARI alt for KINNAURI [KFK]
KUNAWUR alt for KINNAURI [KFK]
KUNAYAONI alt for KUMAUNI [KFY]

KUNBAN dial of VARHADI-NAGPURI [VAH]
KUNBARLANG [WLG] lang, Australia
KUNBAU alt for KUNBI dial of KHANDESI [KHN]
KUNBI dial of KHANDESI [KHN]
KUNBI dial of VARHADI-NAGPURI [VAH]
KUNBILLE alt for BILE [BIL]
KUNDA [KDN] lang, Zimbabwe; also in Mozambique, Zambia
KUNDA alt for ANIMERE [ANF]
KUNDA alt for SEBA [KDG]
KUNDA dial of LUSENGO [LUS]
KUNDRI dial of BUNDELI [BNS]
KUNDU alt for BAKUNDU dial of BAKUNDU-BALUE [BDU]
KUNDUR dial of MOGHOLI [MLG]
KUNFAL [XUF] lang, Ethiopia
KUNFEL alt for KUNFAL [XUF]
!KUNG alt for KUNG-EKOKA [KNW]
KUNG alt for JU/'HOAN [KTZ]
KUNG alt for KUNG-EKOKA [KNW]
KUNGARA alt for FUR [FUR]
KUNGARAKAN alt for KUNGARAKANY [GGK]
KUNGARAKANY [GGK] lang, Australia
KUNG-EKOKA [KNW] lang, Namibia; also in Angola
KUNGGARA [KVS] lang, Australia
KUNGGARI [KGL] lang, Australia
KUNGGERA alt for KUNGGARA [KVS]
KUNG-GOBABIS alt for ǂKX'AU//'EIN [AUE]
KUNG-TSUMKWE alt for JU/'HOAN [KTZ]
KUNHA alt for KURUX [KVN]
KUNHAR alt for KURUX [KVN]
KUNI [KSE] lang, Papua New Guinea
KUNI dial of BOAZI [KVG]
KUNIAN alt for GOONIYANDI [GNI]
KUNIBUM alt for EMAI-IULEHA-ORA [EMA]
KUNIE alt for KWENYII dial of NUMEE [KDK]
KUNIE alt for NUMEE [KDK]
KUNIGAMI [XUG] lang, Japan
KUNIMAIPA [KUP] lang, Papua New Guinea
KUNINI alt for NYE dial of SHOO-MINDA-NYE [BCV]
KUNINI dial of BINE [ORM]
KUNIYAN alt for GOONIYANDI [GNI]
KUNJA [PEP] lang, Papua New Guinea
KUNJEN [KJN] lang, Australia
KUNJIP dial of WAHGI [WAK]
KUNJUT alt for BURUSHASKI [BSK]
KUNLANG dial of RAWANG [RAW]
KUNNA alt for KURUX [KVN]
KUNRUKH alt for KURUX [KVN]
KUNTEMBA alt for KUNTENI dial of NATENI [NTM]
KUNTENI dial of NATENI [NTM]
KUNTULISHI alt for TULISHI [TEY]
KUNUA alt for RAPOISI [KYX]
KUNUK alt for KURUX [KVN]
KUNUZI alt for KENUZ dial of KENUZI-DONGOLA [KNC]
KUNUZI alt for KENUZI dial of KENUZI-DONGOLA [KNC]
KUNWINJKU alt for GUNWINGGU [GUP]
KUNYI [KNF] lang, Congo
KUNZA [KUZ] lang, Chile

KUNZAKH dial of AVAR [AVR]
KUO [KHO] lang, Chad; also in Cameroon
KUO alt for OKU [OKU]
KUOT [KTO] lang, Papua New Guinea
KUOY alt for KUY [KDT]
KUOYU alt for CHINESE, MANDARIN [CHN]
KUPA [KUG] lang, Nigeria
KUPANG alt for BASA KUPANG dial of MALAY [MLI]
KUPANG alt for HELONG [HEG]
KUPANG alt for MALAY, KUPANG [MKN]
KUPEL alt for KETENGBAN [KIN]
KUPIA [KEY] lang, India
"KUPKAFERRN" pejorative alt for NAMA [NAQ]
"KUPKAFFER" pejorative alt for NAMA [NAQ]
KUP-MINJ dial of WAHGI [WAK]
KUPOME dial of NAGA, TANGKHUL [NMF]
KUPSABINY [KPZ] lang, Uganda
KUPSABINY alt for SABINY dial of KUPSABINY
    [KPZ]
KUPSAPINY alt for SABINY dial of KUPSABINY
    [KPZ]
KUPTO alt for KUTTO [KPA]
KUPUCA alt for BEZHTA [KAP]
KUR [KUV] lang, Indonesia (Maluku)
KUR alt for LAHU SHI [KDS]
KUR dial of KAG-FER-JIIR-KOOR-ROR-US-
    ZUKSUN [GEL]
KUR GALLI alt for BRAHUI [BRH]
KURÂ alt for BAKAIRÍ [BKQ]
KURADA ('URADA) alt for 'AUHELAWA [KUD]
KURAMA [KRH] lang, Nigeria
KURAMA alt for KURRAMA [VKU]
KURAMWARI alt for KURUMBA [KFI]
KURANGAL dial of PASHAYI, NORTHEAST [AEE]
KURANKO [KHA] lang, Sierra Leone; also in
    Guinea
KURATEG alt for MAKURÁP [MAG]
KURBAT alt for DOMARI [RMT]
KURBATI dial of DOMARI [RMT]
KURDAR dial of PASHAYI, NORTHEAST [AEE]
KURDI [KDB] lang, Iraq; also in Iran, USA
KURDISH BANDINANI alt for BEHDINI [BDF]
KURDIT alt for HULAULÁ [HUY]
KURDIT alt for LISHANA DENI [LSD]
KURDIT alt for LISHANID NOSHAN [AIJ]
KURDY alt for KURDI [KDB]
KURE dial of BOBO MADARE, NORTHERN [BBO]
KUREMBAN alt for KURUMBA [KFI]
KURFEY dial of HAUSA [HUA]
KURI [NBN] lang, Indonesia (Inan Jaya)
KURI alt for KORKU [KFQ]
KURI dial of BUDUMA [BDM]
KURIA [KUJ] lang, Tanzania; also in Kenya
KURICHCHIA alt for KURICHIYA [KFH]
KURICHIA alt for KURICHIYA [KFH]
KURICHIYA [KFH] lang, India
KURIL dial of AINU [AIN]
KURIMA alt for LOWER GRAND VALLEY HITIGIMA
    dial of DANI, LOWER GRAND VALLEY [DNI]
KURINA alt for CULINA [CUL]
KURIPACO alt for CURRIPACO [KPC]

KURIPAKO alt for CURRIPACO [KPC]
KURIYO alt for KUIJAU [DKR]
KURJA alt for KODAGU [KFA]
KURKA alt for FUR [FUR]
KURKA alt for KURUX [KVN]
KURKU alt for KORKU [KFQ]
KURKURO alt for KUIKÚRO-KALAPÁLO [KUI]
KURKU-RUMA alt for KORKU [KFQ]
KURMALI alt for KUDMALI [KYW]
KURMALI THAR alt for KUDMALI [KYW]
KURMANJI [KUR] lang, Turkey (Asia); also in
    Armenia, Australia, Austria, Azerbaijan, Bahrain,
    Belgium, France, Georgia, Germany, Iran, Iraq,
    Jordan, Kazakhstan, Kuwait, Kyrgyzstan,
    Lebanon, Netherlands, Norway, Sweden,
    Switzerland, Syria, Turkmenistan, United
    Kingdom, USA
KURMI alt for KULFA [KXJ]
KURMI dial of KULFA [KXJ]
KURONDI alt for KARONDI dial of TUMTUM [TBR]
KUROP alt for KOROP [KRP]
KUROSHIMA dial of YAEYAMA [RYS]
KURO-URMI dial of NANAI [GLD]
KURRAMA [VKU] lang, Australia
KURRIPACO alt for CURRIPACO [KPC]
KURRIPAKO alt for CURRIPACO [KPC]
KURRU BHASHA alt for YERUKULA [YEU]
KURSMADKHA alt for CHOCANGACAKHA [CHK]
KURTAT dial of OSETIN [OSE]
KURTEOPKHA alt for KURTOKHA [XKZ]
KURTHA dial of RAJBANGSI [RJB]
KURTHOPKHA alt for KURTOKHA [XKZ]
KURTI [KTM] lang, Papua New Guinea
KURTJJAR alt for GURDJAR [GDJ]
KURTOBIKHA alt for KURTOKHA [XKZ]
KURTOKHA [XKZ] lang, Bhutan
KURTOPAKHA alt for KURTOKHA [XKZ]
KURU dial of GIDRA [GDR]
KURUÁYA [KYR] lang, Brazil
KURUBA alt for KURUMBA [KFI]
KURUBAR alt for KURUMBA [KFI]
KURUBAS KURUBAN alt for KURUMBA [KFI]
KURUDU [KJR] lang, Indonesia (Irian Jaya)
KURUG alt for KODAGU [KFA]
KURUKH alt for KURUX [KVN]
KURUKO alt for PIU [PIX]
KURUKURU dial of PAUMARI [PAD]
KURUMA alt for KURUMBA [KFI]
KURUMALI alt for KUDMALI [KYW]
KURUMAN alt for KURUMBA [KFI]
KURUMANS alt for KURUMBA [KFI]
KURUMAR alt for KURUMBA [KFI]
KURUMBA [KFI] lang, India
KURUMBA, ALU [QKA] lang, India
KURUMBA, BETTA [QKB] lang, India
KURUMBA, JENNU [QKJ] lang, India
KURUMBA, MULLU [KPB] lang, India
KURUMBAN alt for KURUMBA [KFI]
KURUMBAR alt for KURUMBA [KFI]
KURUMBAS alt for KURUMBA [KFI]
KURUMFE alt for KOROMFÉ [KFZ]

KURUMI alt for KULFA [KXJ]
KURUMVARI alt for KURUMBA [KFI]
KURUNGA alt for KARANGA [KTH]
KURUNGA alt for KARANGA dial of KARANGA
  [KTH]
KURUNGTUFU dial of KUBE [KGF]
KURUNGU alt for KRONGO [KGO]
KURUPI alt for GARUS [GYB]
KURUR dial of HAHON [HAH]
KUR-URMI dial of EVENKI [EVN]
KURUTHA alt for YERUKULA [YEU]
KURUTI alt for KURTI [KTM]
KURUTI-PARE alt for KURTI [KTM]
KURUVIKKARAN alt for VAAGRI BOOLI [VAA]
KURUWER dial of KABA DEME [KWG]
KURUX [KVN] lang, India; also in Bangladesh
KURUX, NEPALI [KXL] lang, Nepal
KURYA alt for KURIA [KUJ]
KURYE alt for KURIA [KUJ]
KURZEME alt for WESTERN LIVONIAN dial of LIV
  [LIV]
KUSA alt for KUSA-MANLEA dial of ATONI [TMR]
KUSAAL [KUS] lang, Ghana; also in Burkina Faso
KUSAGE alt for KUSAGHE [KSG]
KUSAGHE [KSG] lang, Solomon Islands
KUSAIE alt for KOSRAEAN [KSI]
KUSALE alt for KUSAAL [KUS]
KUSA-MANLEA dial of ATONI [TMR]
KUSANDA alt for KUSUNDA [KGG]
KUSASI alt for KUSAAL [KUS]
KUSEKI dial of YENDANG [YEN]
KUSERI alt for MSER [KQX]
KUSHANI alt for SHUGHNI dial of SHUGHNI [SGH]
KUSHAR alt for BOTE-MAJHI [BMJ]
KUSHE alt for KUSHI [KUH]
KUSHI [KUH] lang, Nigeria
KUSHI alt for BAUCHI [BSF]
/KUSI alt for XATIA dial of XOO [NMN]
KUSIBI alt for DESANO [DES]
KUSIILAAY alt for GUSILAY [GSL]
KUSILAY alt for GUSILAY [GSL]
KUSKOKWIM "ESKIMO" pejorative name for dial
  of YUPIK, CENTRAL [ESU]
KUSKOKWIM, UPPER [KUU] lang, USA
KUSO alt for MBUKUSHU [MHW]
KUSSO alt for MBUKUSHU [MHW]
KUSU [KSV] lang, DRC
KUSUNDA [KGG] lang, Nepal
KUSURI dial of TUGUTIL [TUJ]
KUSUWA alt for SUWA dial of AMBA [RWM]
KUSUWA dial of AMBA [RWM]
KUTA dial of GBAGYI [GBR]
KUTAI alt for MALAY, TENGGARONG KUTAI [VKT]
KUTANG BHOTIA alt for NUBRI [KTE]
KUTCHA alt for NAGA, ZEME [NZM]
KUTCHCHI alt for KACHCHI [KFR]
KUTCHIE alt for KACHCHI [KFR]
KUTCHIN alt for GWICH'IN [KUC]
KUTEB alt for KUTEP [KUB]
KUTENAI [KUN] lang, Canada; also in USA
KUTEP [KUB] lang, Nigeria; also in Cameroon

KUTEV alt for KUTEP [KUB]
KUTHANT [QKD] lang, Australia
KUTIA-DYAPA alt for CUTIADAPA dial of KATUKINA
  [KAV]
KUTIN alt for PEERE [KUT]
KUTINE alt for PEERE [KUT]
KUTINN alt for PEERE [KUT]
KUTKASEN dial of AZERBAIJANI, NORTH [AZE]
KUTO-KUTE dial of SASAK [SAS]
KUTSU alt for KUSU [KSV]
KUTSUNG alt for LAHU SHI [KDS]
KUTSWE alt for KHUTSWE dial of SOTHO,
  NORTHERN [SRT]
KUTTO [KPA] lang, Nigeria
KÚTTÒ alt for KUTTO [KPA]
KUTU [KDC] lang, Tanzania
KUTU alt for YELA [YEL]
KUTU dial of LIBINZA [LIZ]
KUTU dial of MONGO-NKUNDU [MOM]
KUTUBU dial of FOI [FOI]
KUTULE alt for TULA [TUL]
KUTULE dial of TULA [TUL]
KUTURMI [KHJ] lang, Nigeria
KUUK THAAYOORE alt for THAYORE [THD]
KUUK THAAYORRE alt for THAYORE [THD]
KUUKU dial of GURUNTUM-MBAARU [GRD]
KUUKU-YA'U [QKL] lang, Australia
KUUMU alt for KOMO [KMW]
KUVAKAN dial of BASHKIR [BXK]
KUVALAN alt for KAVALAN [CKV]
KUVARAWAN alt for KAVALAN [CKV]
KUVENMAS dial of ALAMBLAK [AMP]
KUVI [KXV] lang, India
KUVI KOND alt for KUVI [KXV]
KUVINGA alt for KUVI [KXV]
KUVOKO alt for GVOKO [NGS]
KUVURI alt for KABARI dial of KANURI, CENTRAL
  [KPH]
KUWAA [BLH] lang, Liberia
KUWAATAAY [CWT] lang, Senegal
KUWAITI HADARI ARABIC dial of ARABIC, GULF
  SPOKEN [AFB]
KUWAMA [QKU] lang, Australia
KUWAMA alt for PUNGUPUNGU dial of
  WADJIGINY [WDJ]
KUWARAWAN alt for KAVALAN [CKV]
KUWEMA alt for TYARAITY [WOA]
KUWI alt for KUVI [KXV]
KUY [KDT] lang, Thailand; also in Cambodia, Laos
KUY alt for KUI [KXU]
KUYA alt for KOUYA [KYF]
KUYA dial of NDUMU [NMD]
KUYOBE alt for SOLA [SOY]
KUYONON alt for CUYONON [CYO]
KUYUBI alt for PURUBORÁ [PUR]
KUYUK alt for ZAGHAWA [ZAG]
KUYUKI alt for ZANDE [ZAN]
KUYUNON alt for CUYONON [CYO]
KUZAMANI alt for SHUWA-ZAMANI [KSA]
KUZAMANI alt for SI dial of LERE [GNH]
KUZNETS TATAR alt for SHOR [CJS]

KVALAN alt for KAVALAN [CKV]
KVANADA alt for BAGVALAL [KVA]
KVANADIN alt for BAGVALAL [KVA]
KVANXIDATL dial of ANDI [ANI]
KVEN alt for FINNISH, KVEN [FKV]
KVOLYAB dial of AWBONO [AWH]
KWA [KWB] lang, Nigeria
KWA alt for EJAGHAM [ETU]
KWA alt for SOUTHERN EJAGHAM dial of
    EJAGHAM [ETU]
KWA dial of FIPA [FIP]
KWA dial of KWA [KWB]
K'WA alt for BLANG [BLR]
KWA' [BKO] lang, Cameroon
KWA' dial of KWA [BKO]
KWAA alt for KUWAA [BLH]
KW'AAL alt for KUMIÁI [DIH]
KWA'ALANG alt for KWAGALLAK dial of KOFYAR
    [KWL]
KWAAMI [KSQ] lang, Nigeria
KWABZAK alt for TAL [TAL]
KWAC alt for CIEC dial of DINKA, SOUTH CENTRAL
    [DIB]
KWADI [KWZ] lang, Angola
KWADIA alt for KODIA [KWP]
KWADYA alt for KODIA [KWP]
KW'ADZA [WKA] lang, Tanzania
KWAFI dial of FIPA [FIP]
KWAGALLAK dial of KOFYAR [KWL]
KWAGIUTL alt for KWAKIUTL [KWK]
KWAH alt for KWA [KWB]
KWAHANE alt for SUBIYA [SBS]
KWAI alt for GULA'ALAA [GMB]
KWAIAILK alt for CHEHALIS, UPPER [CJH]
KWAIBIDA dial of SINAUGORO [SNC]
KWAIBO dial of SINAUGORO [SNC]
KWAIKER alt for AWA-CUAIQUER [KWI]
KWAIO [KWD] lang, Solomon Islands
KWAJA [KDZ] lang, Cameroon
KWAJI dial of MUMUYE [MUL]
KWAK [KWQ] lang, Nigeria
KWAK dial of YAMBA [YAM]
KWAKIUTL [KWK] lang, Canada; also in USA
KWAKUM [KWU] lang, Cameroon
KWAKUM dial of KWAKUM [KWU]
KWAKWA alt for AVIKAM [AVI]
KWAKWAGOM dial of BOKYI [BKY]
KWAKWAK alt for KAKWA [KEO]
KWAK'WALA alt for KWAKIUTL [KWK]
KWAKWI alt for FIRAN [FIR]
KWAL alt for IRIGWE [IRI]
KWALA alt for KPALA [KPL]
KWALA alt for LIKWALA [KWC]
KWALAIWA dial of BWANABWANA [TTE]
KWALE alt for UARE [KSJ]
KWALE alt for UARE dial of UARE [KSJ]
KWALE alt for UKWUANI dial of UKWUANI-ABOH-
    NDONI [UKW]
KWALI dial of GBARI [GBY]
KWALLA alt for KWAGALLAK dial of KOFYAR [KWL]
KWALUDHI dial of NDONGA [NDG]

KWAM alt for KWAAMI [KSQ]
KWAMA [KMQ] lang, Ethiopia
KWAMANA dial of WEDAU [WED]
KWAMANCHI alt for KWAAMI [KSQ]
KWAMBA alt for AMBA [RWM]
KWAMBI [KWM] lang, Namibia
KWAME alt for KWAMI [KTF]
KWAME-DANSO dial of DWANG [NNU]
KWAMERA [TNK] lang, Vanuatu
KWAMI [KTF] lang, DRC
KWAMI alt for KWAAMI [KSQ]
KWAN alt for IRIGWE [IRI]
KWANCAMA alt for KWANYAMA [KUY]
KWANDANG [KJW] lang, Indonesia (Sulawesi)
KWANDARA alt for GWANDARA [GWN]
KWANDI dial of LUYANA [LAV]
KWANG [KVI] lang, Chad
KWANG dial of KWANG [KVI]
KWANGA alt for APOS [APO]
KWANGA alt for WASAMBU [WSM]
KWANGA alt for YUBANAKOR [YUO]
KWANGA dial of LUYANA [LAV]
KWANGALI [KWN] lang, Namibia; also in Angola
KWANGARE alt for KWANGALI [KWN]
KWANGARI alt for KWANGALI [KWN]
KWANGE dial of GBARI [GBY]
KWANGE dial of ZIMBA [ZMB]
KWANGFU alt for TAVALONG-VATAAN dial of AMIS
    [ALV]
KWANGSU-BONGGRANG alt for MLAP [KJA]
KWANIM PA alt for UDUK [UDU]
KWANJA [KNP] lang, Cameroon
KWANJAMA alt for KWANYAMA [KUY]
KWANKA alt for VAGHAT dial of VAGHAT-YA-BIJIM-
    LEGERI [BIJ]
KWANKA alt for VAGHAT-YA-BIJIM-LEGERI [BIJ]
KWANSU alt for MLAP [KJA]
KWANSU-BONGGRANG alt for MLAP [KJA]
KWANYAMA [KUY] lang, Angola; also in Namibia
KWAPM alt for ZARI dial of ZARI [ZAZ]
KWARA'AE [KWF] lang, Solomon Islands
KWARAFE alt for KORAFE [KPR]
KWARE alt for AIMELE [AIL]
KWARE alt for UARE [KSJ]
KWAREKWAREO alt for DORI'O [DOR]
KWARRA alt for MAMA [MMA]
KWARTA MATACI dial of KAREKARE [KAI]
KWARUWIKWUNDI alt for MALINGUAT [SIC]
KWASANG dial of BUANG, MANGGA [MMO]
KWASAP alt for KOSOP dial of KIM [KIA]
KWASENGEN alt for HANGA HUNDI [WOS]
KWASIO dial of NGUMBA [NMG]
KWASSIO alt for KWASIO dial of NGUMBA [NMG]
KWASU (AKIZA) alt for NINZAM [NIN]
KWATAY [CWT] lang, Senegal
KWATO [KOP] lang, Papua New Guinea
KWAVI [CKG] lang, Tanzania
KWAWU dial of AKAN [TWS]
KWAYA [KYA] lang, Tanzania
KWAYA alt for MACI dial of ICEVE-MACI [BEC]
KWAYA alt for OLITI dial of ICEVE-MACI [BEC]

KWAYAM dial of KANURI, CENTRAL [KPH]
KWE alt for HIETSHWARE [HIE]
KWE dial of TEKE, CENTRAL [TEC]
KWEDI alt for MOKPWE [BRI]
KWEEDISHCHAAHT alt for MAKAH [MYH]
KWEEN alt for KHUEN [KHF]
KWE-ETSHORI KWEE alt for HIETSHWARE [HIE]
KWEGI alt for KWEGU [YID]
KWEGU [YID] lang, Ethiopia
KWELE alt for KWERE [CWE]
KWELI alt for MOKPWE [BRI]
KWELSHIN alt for KHUALSHIM dial of CHIN, FALAM
    [HBH]
KWEM alt for MANDOBO [KZH]
KWENA dial of TSWANA [TSW]
KWÉNDRÉ alt for GURO [GOA]
KWE-NEE-CHEE-AHT alt for MAKAH [MYH]
KWENI alt for GURO [GOA]
KWENY dial of SAGALA [SBM]
KWENYII alt for NUMEE [KDK]
KWENYII dial of NUMEE [KDK]
KWER [KWR] lang, Indonesia (Irian Jaya)
KWERBA [KWE] lang, Indonesia (Irian Jaya)
KWERBA MAMBERAMO [NOB] lang, Indonesia
    (Irian Jaya)
KWERE [CWE] lang, Tanzania
KWERISA [KKB] lang, Indonesia (Irian Jaya)
KWESE [KWS] lang, DRC
KWESTEN [KWT] lang, Indonesia (Irian Jaya)
KWE-TSHORI alt for HIETSHWARE [HIE]
KWÈYÒL alt for DOMINICA CREOLE FRENCH
    dial of LESSER ANTILLEAN CREOLE
    FRENCH [DOM]
KWÉYÒL alt for ST. LUCIA CREOLE FRENCH
    dial of LESSER ANTILLEAN CREOLE
    FRENCH [DOM]
!KWI dial of XOO [NMN]
KWI alt for LAHU SHI [KDS]
KWIFA alt for NKWIFIYA dial of SAGALA [SBM]
KWIJAU alt for KUIJAU [DKR]
KWIKAPA alt for COCOPA [COC]
KWIKAPÁ alt for COCOPA [COC]
KWILI alt for MOKPWE [BRI]
KWINA alt for OPUUO [LGN]
KWINGSANG alt for NUNG [NUN]
KWINI [GWW] lang, Australia
KWINP'ANG alt for NUNG [NUN]
KWINTI [KWW] lang, Suriname
KWIRI alt for MOKPWE [BRI]
KWIVA alt for NKWIFIYA dial of SAGALA [SBM]
KWOICO LO alt for SUNWAR [SUZ]
KWOIRENG alt for KOIRENG [NKD]
KWOJEFFA alt for BURA-PABIR [BUR]
KWOLACHA alt for KWOLASA dial of AGAW,
    WESTERN [QIM]
KWOLASA dial of AGAW, WESTERN [QIM]
KWOLL alt for IRIGWE [IRI]
KWOLLANYOCH alt for AWNGI [AWN]
KWOM alt for KWAAMI [KSQ]
KWOMA [KMO] lang, Papua New Guinea
KWOMA dial of KWOMA [KMO]

KWOMTARI [KWO] lang, Papua New Guinea
KWONCI dial of PIYA-KWONCI [PIY]
KWONG alt for KAGOMA [KDM]
KWONG alt for KOFYAR dial of KOFYAR [KWL]
KWONG alt for KWANG [KVI]
KWONO alt for KONO [KLK]
KWOODE alt for KHOLOK [KTC]
KWOTTO alt for EBIRA [IGB]
"KWOTTU" pejorative alt for OROMO, EASTERN
    [HAE]
KWUIZWU alt for DUNGAN [DNG]
KWUSAUN dial of BOIKIN [BZF]
//KXAU dial of NU [NGH]
=KX'AU//'EI alt for ǂKX'AU//'EIN [AUE]
ǂKX'AU//'EIN [AUE] lang, Namibia; also in Botswana
KXAXA alt for KGAGA dial of SOTHO, NORTHERN
    [SRT]
KXHALAXADI alt for KGALAGADI [XKV]
KXOE [XUU] lang, Namibia; also in Angola,
    Botswana, South Africa, Zambia
KXOEDAM alt for KXOE [XUU]
KYABRAT dial of MAITHILI [MKP]
KYAK [BKA] lang, Nigeria
KYAKA [KYC] lang, Papua New Guinea
KYAKANKE alt for JAHANKA dial of MALINKE
    [MLQ]
KYAMA alt for EBRIÉ [EBR]
KYAN KYAR alt for GWANDARA SOUTHERN dial
    of GWANDARA [GWN]
KYANG alt for CHIN, ASHO [CSH]
KYANGO alt for BROKSKAT [BKK]
KYANTON alt for ETKYWAN [ICH]
KYANZI dial of AMBA [RWM]
KYATO alt for ETKYWAN [ICH]
KYAURA dial of GHALE, SOUTHERN [GHE]
KYENELE [KQL] lang, Papua New Guinea
KYENGA [TYE] lang, Nigeria; also in Benin
KYENTU alt for KENTE dial of KPAN [KPK]
KYENYEMAMBA alt for MAMBA dial of ZIMBA [ZMB]
KYENYING-BARANG alt for KYENELE [KQL]
KYEREPONG alt for CHEREPON [CPN]
KYERUNG [KGY] lang, Nepal; also in China
KYETHO alt for KAREN, S'GAW [KSW]
KYI alt for KHASI [KHI]
KYIBAKU alt for CIBAK [CKL]
KYIRONG alt for KYERUNG [KGY]
KYO dial of NAGA, LOTHA [NJH]
KYOBE alt for SOLA [SOY]
KYOKOSI alt for ANUFO [CKO]
KYON dial of NAGA, LOTHA [NJH]
KYONG dial of NAGA, LOTHA [NJH]
KYONGBORONG alt for CHUMBURUNG [NCU]
KYONGGIDO alt for SEOUL dial of KOREAN [KKN]
KYONGSANGDO dial of KOREAN [KKN]
KYOU dial of NAGA, LOTHA [NJH]
KYPCHAK alt for KIPCHAK dial of UZBEK,
    NORTHERN [UZB]
KYZYL dial of KHAKAS [KJH]
KYZYLBASH dial of AZERBAIJANI, NORTH [AZE]
KYZYLBASH dial of BALKAN GAGAUZ TURKISH
    [BGX]

LA alt for HLAI [LIC]
LA alt for TAI PONG dial of TAI NUA [TDD]
LA dial of VO [WBM]
LA CHI alt for LACHI [LBT]
LA CONCEPTION dial of CAAC [MSQ]
LA CONCORDIA dial of TZOTZIL, HUIXTAN [TZU]
LA HA alt for LAHA [LHA]
LA HA UNG alt for LAHA [LHA]
LA HU SI alt for LAHU SHI [KDS]
LA JALCA dial of QUECHUA, CHACHAPOYAS
    [QUK]
LA LENGUA MANUAL MEXICANA alt for MEXICAN
    SIGN LANGUAGE [MFS]
LA LINGVO INTERNACIA alt for ESPERANTO [ESP]
LA MESA DEL NAYAR CORA dial of CORA [COR]
LA NYA alt for THAI, NORTHERN [NOD]
LAABE dial of LAAL [GDM]
LAADI dial of KONGO [KON]
LAAK alt for THIANG dial of NUER [NUS]
LAAL [GDM] lang, Chad
LAAL dial of LAAL [GDM]
LAALI dial of TEKE, WESTERN [TEZ]
LA'ALUA alt for SAAROA [SXR]
LAAMANG alt for LAMANG [HIA]
LAAME alt for GIMNIME [KMB]
LAAME alt for GOMNOME dial of KOMA [KMY]
LAAMOOT alt for OMOTIK [OMT]
LAANY alt for DANI, WESTERN [DNW]
LABA [LAU] lang, Indonesia (Maluku)
LABALEKAN alt for LEMBATA, WEST [LMJ]
LABASA alt for NORTHEAST VANUA LEVU dial
    of FIJIAN [FJI]
LABBU alt for BAI [PIQ]
LABE dial of TAWALA [TBO]
LABEL [LBB] lang, Papua New Guinea
LABHANI alt for LAMBADI [LMN]
LABHANI MUKA alt for LAMBADI [LMN]
LA'BI [LBI] lang, Cameroon
LABIR [JKU] lang, Nigeria
LABO [MWI] lang, Vanuatu
LABO alt for LABU [LBU]
LABOURDIN dial of BASQUE, NAVARRO-
    LABOURDIN [BQE]
LABRADOR "ESKIMO" pejorative name for dial
    of INUKTITUT, EASTERN CANADIAN [ESB]
LABU [LBU] lang, Papua New Guinea
LABÙ alt for LABU [LBU]
LABU alt for LAUA [LUF]
LABU dial of MALAY [MLI]
LABU BASAP alt for LABU dial of MALAY [MLI]
LABUAN dial of RUKAI [DRU]
LABUANDIRI dial of PANCANA [PNP]
LABUK dial of KADAZAN, LABUK-KINABATANGAN
    [DTB]
LABUK KADAZAN alt for KADAZAN, LABUK-
    KINABATANGAN [DTB]
LABWOR dial of ACHOLI [ACO]
LAC dial of KOHO [KPM]
LAC SEUL OJIBWA dial of OJIBWA, NORTH-
    WESTERN [OJB]
LACANDÓN [LAC] lang, Mexico

LACANJÁ dial of LACANDON [LAC]
LACH alt for LAC dial of KOHO [KPM]
LACH dial of CZECH [CZC]
LACHAO-YOLOTEPEC CHATINO alt for CHATINO,
    SIERRA ORIENTAL [CLY]
LACHENGPA alt for SIKKIMESE [SIP]
LACHI [LBT] lang, Viet Nam; also in China
LACHI alt for LACHI [LBT]
LACHÍ alt for LACHI [LBT]
LACHI, WHITE [LWH] lang, Viet Nam
LACHIGUIRI ZAPOTEC alt for ZAPOTECO,
    LACHIGUIRI [ZPA]
LACHIKWAW alt for LASHI [LSI]
LACHIRUAJ ZAPOTECO alt for ZAPOTECO,
    LACHIRIOAG [ZTC]
LACHIXÍO ZAPOTECO alt for ZAPOTECO, SOLA
    DE VEGA ESTE [ZPL]
LACHUNGPA alt for SIKKIMESE [SIP]
LACID alt for LASHI [LSI]
LACONDE alt for YALAPMUNXTE dial of
    NAMBIKUARA, NORTHERN [MBG]
LACTAN alt for RATAGNON [BTN]
LACTAN dial of KALAGAN [KQE]
LADAK alt for LADAKHI [LBJ]
LADAKHI [LBJ] lang, India; also in China
LA-DANG alt for NOANG dial of CHRU [CJE]
LADAPHI alt for LADAKHI [LBJ]
LADHAKHI alt for LADAKHI [LBJ]
LADIL alt for LARDIL [LBZ]
LADIN [LLD] lang, Italy; also in USA
LADINO [SPJ] lang, Israel; also in Puerto Rico,
    Turkey (Europe), USA
LADINO dial of LADINO [SPJ]
LADWAGS alt for LADAKHI [LBJ]
LAE alt for ARIBWATSA [LAZ]
LAEKO alt for LAEKO-LIBUAT [LKL]
LAEKO alt for SAMBA LEKO dial of SAMBA LEKO
    [NDI]
LAEKO-LIBUAT [LKL] lang, Papua New Guinea
LAEKO-LIMBUAT alt for LAEKO-LIBUAT [LKL]
LAEWAMBA alt for WAMPAR [LBQ]
LAEWOMBA alt for WAMPAR [LBQ]
LAFANA alt for LELEMI [LEF]
LA'FI dial of FEFE [FMP]
LAFIIT alt for LOPPIT [LPX]
LAFIT alt for LOPPIT [LPX]
LAFITE alt for LOPPIT [LPX]
LAFOFA [LAF] lang, Sudan
LAFOFA dial of LAFOFA [LAF]
LAGANYAN alt for LEGENYEM [LCC]
LAGARTEIRU dial of FALA [FAX]
LAGAWE IFUGAO dial of IFUGAO, TUWALI [IFK]
LAGBA alt for LANGBA dial of BANDA, SOUTH
    CENTRAL [LNL]
LAGHMAN dial of PASHAYI, SOUTHEAST [DRA]
LAGHMANI alt for PARYA [PAQ]
LAGHU [LGB] lang, Solomon Islands
LAGHUU [LGH] lang, Viet Nam
LAGIS dial of BUANG, MANGGA [MMO]
LAGOON CHUUKESE alt for CHUUKESE [TRU]
LAGOS PIDGIN dial of PIDGIN, NIGERIAN [PCM]

LAGOUANE alt for LAGWAN [KOT]
LAGOWA dial of DAJU, DAR FUR [DAJ]
LAGU alt for LAGHU [LGB]
LAGUBI alt for MAMBILA, CAMEROON [MYA]
LAGUBI alt for MAMBILA, NIGERIA [MZK]
LAGUME dial of HUMENE [HUF]
LAGUNA alt for ACOMA dial of KERES, WESTERN
   [KJQ]
LAGUNA dial of TRIQUE, CHICAHUAXTLA [TRS]
LAGUNAN MURUT alt for PENSIANGAN
   MURUT dial of TAGAL MURUT [MVV]
LAGWAN [KOT] lang, Cameroon; also in Chad,
   Nigeria
LAGWANE alt for LAGWAN [KOT]
LAHA [LAD] lang, Indonesia (Maluku)
LAHA [LHA] lang, Viet Nam
LAHA SERANI dial of TELUTI [TLT]
LAHANAN [LHN] lang, Malaysia (Sarawak)
LAHANDA alt for PANJABI, WESTERN [PNB]
LAHAULI alt for TINANI [LBF]
LAHE alt for ARIBWATSA [LAZ]
LAHNDA alt for PANJABI, WESTERN [PNB]
LAHNDI alt for PANJABI, WESTERN [PNB]
LAHOULI alt for TINANI [LBF]
LAHTA alt for KAREN, LAHTA [KVT]
LAHU [LAH] lang, China; also in Laos, Myanmar,
   Thailand, Viet Nam
LAHU alt for AVIKAM [AVI]
LAHU SHI [KDS] lang, Laos; also in China, Myanmar,
   Thailand, USA, Viet Nam
LAHU XI alt for LAHU SHI [KDS]
LAHUL BHOTI alt for STOD BHOTI [SBU]
LAHULI alt for PATTANI [LAE]
LAHULI alt for TINANI [LBF]
LAHULI OF BUNAN alt for GAHRI [BFU]
LAHULI TINAN alt for TINANI [LBF]
LAHUNA alt for LAHU [LAH]
LAHYJ dial of TAT, MUSLIM [TTT]
LAI alt for HLAI [LIC]
LAI alt for KABALAI [KVF]
LAI alt for PALYU [PLY]
LAI dial of CHIN, HAKA [CNH]
LAI dial of GBAYA, NORTHWEST [GYA]
LAI HAWLH alt for LAI dial of CHIN, HAKA [CNH]
LAI PAWI alt for LAI dial of CHIN, HAKA [CNH]
LAIA dial of LOKO [LOK]
LAIAGAM dial of ENGA [ENQ]
LAIERDILA alt for LARDIL [LBZ]
LAIMBUE [LMX] lang, Cameroon
LAIMON alt for COCHIMÍ [COJ]
LAISO alt for LAIZO dial of CHIN, FALAM [HBH]
LAITOKITOK dial of MAASAI [MET]
LAIWOMBA alt for WAMPAR [LBQ]
LAIWONU dial of PAMONA [BCX]
LAIWUI dial of TOLAKI [LBW]
LAIYA dial of SIANE [SNP]
LAIYEN dial of MORO [MOR]
LAIYOLO [LJI] lang, Indonesia (Sulawesi)
LAIYOLO dial of LAIYOLO [LJI]
LAIZAO alt for LAIZO dial of CHIN, FALAM [HBH]
LAIZO dial of ANAL [ANM]

LAIZO dial of CHIN, FALAM [HBH]
LAIZO-SHIMHRIN alt for LAIZO dial of CHIN, FALAM
   [HBH]
LAJI alt for LACHI [LBT]
LAJIA alt for LAKKIA [LBC]
LAJOLO alt for LAIYOLO dial of LAIYOLO [LJI]
LAJU dial of NAGA, NOCTE [NJB]
LAK [LBE] lang, Russia (Europe); also in Azerbaijan,
   Georgia, Kazakhstan, Kyrgyzstan, Tajikistan,
   Turkey (Asia), Turkmenistan, Ukraine, Uzbekistan
LAK [SJR] lang, Papua New Guinea
LAKA [LAK] lang, Nigeria
LAKA [LAM] lang, Chad; also in CAR
LAKA alt for KARANG [KZR]
LAKA alt for LAKKIA [LBC]
LAKAALONG alt for DIMBONG [DII]
LAKAHIA alt for KAMORO [KGQ]
LAKALAI alt for BILEKI dial of NAKANAI [NAK]
LAKALEI [LKA] lang, Timor Lorosae
LAKAMA'DI dial of MORU [MGD]
LAKATAKURA-TIKA alt for TIKA dial of KUNAMA
   [KUM]
LAKE dial of OKANAGAN [OKA]
LAKE BUHI EAST alt for AGTA, MT. IRAYA [ATL]
LAKE BUHI WEST alt for AGTA, MT. IRIGA [AGZ]
LAKE OF THE WOODS OJIBWA dial of OJIBWA,
   NORTHWESTERN [OJB]
LAKET dial of KONOMALA [KOA]
LAKHA [LKH] lang, Bhutan
LAKHER alt for CHIN, MARA [MRH]
LAKHLOKHI alt for LISHÁN DIDÁN [TRG]
LAKHOTA alt for LAKOTA [LKT]
LAKI alt for LAK [LBE]
LAKI alt for LEKI dial of LURI [LRI]
LAKI alt for TOLAKI [LBW]
LAK'I alt for ZAY [ZWA]
LAKIA alt for LAKKIA [LBC]
LAKING dial of MARU [MHX]
LAKIUNG alt for GOWA dial of MAKASAR [MSR]
LAKJA alt for LAKKIA [LBC]
LAKKA alt for KARANG [KZR]
LAKKA alt for LAKA [LAK]
LAKKA MBUM alt for KARANG [KZR]
LAKKIA [LBC] lang, China
LAKKJA alt for LAKKIA [LBC]
LAKLUTA alt for EASTERN TETUN dial of TETUN
   [TTM]
LAKON alt for LAKONA [LKN]
LAKONA [LKN] lang, Vanuatu
LAKOR dial of LUANG [LEX]
LAKOTA [LKT] lang, USA; also in Canada
LAKU alt for KAREN, BREK [KVL]
LAKU alt for LAHU [LAH]
LAKUME alt for LAGUME dial of HUMENE [HUF]
LAKUNDU alt for BAKUNDU dial of BAKUNDU-
   BALUE [BDU]
"LALA" pejorative alt for BENA [YUN]
LALA alt for LEHAR [CAE]
LALA alt for NARA [NRZ]
LALA dial of LALA-BISA [LEB]
LALA dial of LALA-ROBA [LLA]

LALA dial of ZULU [ZUU]
LALA-BISA [LEB] lang, Zambia; also in DRC
LALAKI alt for TOLAKI [LBW]
LALAMANA dial of SAWILA [SWT]
LALANG dial of KUBU [KVB]
LALA-ROBA [LLA] lang, Nigeria
LALAURA dial of KEOPARA [KHZ]
LALAWA alt for C'LELA [DRI]
LALI alt for FUR [FUR]
LALIA [LAL] lang, DRC
LALLA alt for LALA dial of LALA-ROBA [LLA]
LALLANS dial of SCOTS [SCO]
LALLERE dial of ROMANI, SINTE [RMO]
LALOK alt for ANJAM [BOJ]
LALOMERUI dial of WARU [WRU]
LALUNG [LAX] lang, India
LAM dial of GIDAR [GID]
LAMA [LAS] lang, Togo; also in Benin, Ghana
LAMA [LAY] lang, Myanmar
LAMA alt for QUECHUA, SAN MARTÍN [QSA]
LAMA dial of KABIYE [KBP]
LAMADI alt for LAMBADI [LMN]
LAMAG SUNGAI dial of KADAZAN, LABUK-
    KINABATANGAN [DTB]
LAMAHOLOT [SLP] lang, Indonesia (Nusa Tenggara)
LAMAHOLOT dial of LAMAHOLOT [SLP]
LAMAI dial of SIRAIYA [FOS]
LAMALAMA alt for LAMU-LAMU [LBY]
LAMALANGA alt for HANO [LML]
LAMALERA [LMR] lang, Indonesia (Nusa Tenggara)
LAMAM [LMM] lang, Cambodia
LAMANG [HIA] lang, Nigeria
LAMANI alt for LAMBADI [LMN]
LAMANO alt for QUECHUA, SAN MARTÍN [QSA]
LAMASONG alt for LAMUSONG dial of
    LAVATBURA-LAMUSONG [LBV]
LAMASONG alt for LAVATBURA-LAMUSONG [LBV]
LAMASSA alt for LAK [SJR]
LAMATOKA alt for LAMATUKA [LMQ]
LAMATUKA [LMQ] lang, Indonesia (Nusa Tenggara)
LAMBA [LAB] lang, Zambia; also in DRC
LAMBA alt for LAMA [LAS]
LAMBA dial of LAMBA [LAB]
LAMBADI [LMN] lang, India
LAMBANI alt for LAMBADI [LMN]
LAMBARA alt for LAMBADI [LMN]
LAMBAU dial of SIANE [SNP]
LAMBI alt for BAROMBI [BBI]
LAMBIA alt for LAMBYA [LAI]
LAMBICCHONG alt for LAMBICHHONG [LMH]
LAMBICHHONG [LMH] lang, Nepal
LAMBICHONG alt for LAMBICHHONG [LMH]
LAMBITSHONG alt for LAMBICHHONG [LMH]
LAMBOM alt for LAK [SJR]
LAMBONG alt for DIMBONG [DII]
LAMBOYA [LMY] lang, Indonesia (Nusa Tenggara)
LAMBOYA dial of LAMBOYA [LMY]
LAMBU alt for RAMPI dial of RAMPI [LJE]
LAMBUMBU alt for VINMAVIS [VNM]
LAMBUNAO dial of KINARAY-A [KRJ]
LAMBWA alt for LAMBYA [LAI]

LAMBWE dial of CHOPI [CCE]
LAMBYA [LAI] lang, Tanzania; also in Malawi
LAMDIJA dial of DUMI [DUS]
LAME [BMA] lang, Nigeria
LAMÉ alt for PÉVÉ [LME]
LAMÉ alt for PEVÉ [LME]
LAMÉ dial of PEVE [LME]
LAMENU [LMU] lang, Vanuatu
LAMERTIVIRI alt for KAMVIRI [QMV]
LAMET [LBN] lang, Laos; also in Thailand, USA
LAMETIN alt for MEREI [LMB]
"LAMGANG" pejorative alt for LAMKANG [LMK]
LAMINUSA dial of SAMA, SOUTHERN [SIT]
LAMINUSA SINAMA alt for LAMINUSA dial of SAMA,
    SOUTHERN [SIT]
LAMISTA alt for QUECHUA, SAN MARTÍN [QSA]
LAMISTO alt for QUECHUA, SAN MARTÍN [QSA]
LAMJA dial of LAMJA-DENGSA-TOLA [LDH]
LAMJA-DENGSA-TOLA [LDH] lang, Nigeria
LAMJUNG GURUNG dial of GURUNG, EASTERN
    [GGN]
LAMKAANG alt for LAMKANG [LMK]
LAMKANG [LMK] lang, India
LAMMA [LEV] lang, Indonesia (Nusa Tenggara)
LAMMA' alt for LAMMA [LEV]
LAMNSO' [NSO] lang, Cameroon; also in Nigeria
LAMNSOK alt for LAMNSO' [NSO]
LAMOGAI [LMG] lang, Papua New Guinea
LAMOGI dial of SOGA [SOG]
LAMOTREK dial of WOLEAIAN [WOE]
LAMPONG alt for LAMPUNG [LJP]
LAMPUNG [LJP] lang, Indonesia (Sumatra)
LAMPUNG alt for BAKOI dial of LAWANGAN [LBX]
LAM-SI-HOAN alt for AMIS [ALV]
LAMSO alt for LAMNSO' [NSO]
LAMTI alt for LAMUTI dial of KALAMI [GWC]
LAMTOKA alt for KULA [TPG]
LAMUD dial of QUECHUA, CHACHAPOYAS [QUK]
LAMU-LAMU [LBY] lang, Australia
LAMULAMUL alt for LAMU-LAMU [LBY]
LAMUNKHIN dial of EVEN [EVE]
LAMUSONG dial of LAVATBURA-LAMUSONG
    [LBV]
LAMUT alt for EVEN [EVE]
LAMUTI dial of KALAMI [GWC]
LAN NA alt for THAI, NORTHERN [NOD]
LAN TEN alt for KIM MUN [MJI]
LAN TIN alt for KIM MUN [MJI]
LANAN alt for LAHANAN [LHN]
LANAPSUA alt for SANAPANÁ [SAP]
LANATAI alt for THAI, NORTHERN [NOD]
LANBI alt for BIIJIANG dial of BAI [PIQ]
LANC-PATÚA alt for AMAPÁ CREOLE [AMD]
LAND BAJAW alt for BAJAU, WEST COAST [BDR]
LAND HELONG alt for HELONG DARAT dial of
    HELONG [HEG]
LANDA alt for BELANDA dial of TEMUAN [TMW]
LANDAIS dial of GASCON [GSC]
LANDAWE dial of BUNGKU [BKZ]
LANDIKMA dial of YALI, PASS VALLEY [YAC]
LANDOGO alt for LOKO [LOK]

LANDOMA [LAO] lang, Guinea
LANDOUMAN alt for LANDOMA [LAO]
LANDSMAAL alt for NORWEGIAN, NYNORSK [NRN]
LANDU alt for BIATAH [BTH]
LANDU alt for ROTE-TIMUR dial of ROTE [ROT]
LANDUMA alt for LANDOMA [LAO]
LANDU-RINGGOU-OEPAO alt for ROTE-TIMUR
   dial of ROTE [ROT]
LANG alt for GHOMÁLÁ' NORTH dial of GHOMALA
   [BBJ]
LANG alt for MARU [MHX]
"LANGA" pejorative alt for OPUUO [LGN]
LANGA alt for OPUUO [LGN]
LANGADOC alt for LANGUEDOCIEN [LNC]
LANGAGE GESTUELLE alt for SWISS-FRENCH
   SIGN LANGUAGE [SSR]
LANGAJ alt for HAITIAN VODOUN CULTURE
   LANGUAGE [HVC]
LANGALANGA [LGL] lang, Solomon Islands
LANGAM [LNM] lang, Papua New Guinea
LANGANU alt for CHANGANA dial of TSONGA
   [TSO]
LANGAS dial of POLCI [POL]
LANGAY alt for HAITIAN VODOUN CULTURE
   LANGUAGE [HVC]
LANGBA dial of BANDA, SOUTH CENTRAL [LNL]
LANGBASE alt for LANGBASHE [LNA]
LANGBASHE [LNA] lang, CAR; also in DRC
LANGBASHI alt for LANGBASHE [LNA]
LANGBASI alt for LANGBASHE [LNA]
LANGBWASSE alt for LANGBASHE [LNA]
LANGDA alt for UNA [MTG]
LANGE alt for BURUN [BDI]
LANG'E alt for MARU [MHX]
LANGGO alt for LANGO [LNO]
LANGI alt for LANGO [LAJ]
LANGI alt for RANGI [LAG]
LANGILAN alt for MANOBO, ATA [ATD]
LANGIMAR alt for ANGAATIHA [AGM]
LANGIUNG dial of CHIN, THADO [TCZ]
LANGKURU dial of WERSING [KVW]
LANGO [LAJ] lang, Uganda
LANGO [LNO] lang, Sudan
LANGO alt for DIDINGA [DID]
LANGO PARDHI alt for PARDHI [PCL]
LANGOAN dial of TONTEMBOAN [TNT]
LANGRONG dial of AIMOL [AIM]
LANGSHIN dial of NAGA, TASE [NST]
LANGSU alt for MARU [MHX]
LANGUDA alt for LONGUDA [LNU]
LANGUE DES SIGNES FRANÇAISE alt for FRENCH
   SIGN LANGUAGE [FSL]
LANGUE DES SIGNES QUÉBÉCOISE alt for
   QUEBEC SIGN LANGUAGE [FCS]
LANGUE SIGNE QUEBECARS alt for QUEBEC
   SIGN LANGUAGE [FCS]
LANGUEDOC alt for LANGUEDOCIEN [LNC]
LANGUEDOCIEN [LNC] lang, France
LANGUEDOCIEN MOYEN dial of LANGUEDOCIEN
   [LNC]
LANGULO alt for SANYE [SSN]

LANGUS alt for KALA LAGAW YA [MWP]
LANGWA dial of ZAIWA [ATB]
LANGWASI alt for LANGBASHE [LNA]
LANGYA alt for TAKUA [TKZ]
LANI alt for DANI, WESTERN [DNW]
LANJODA dial of MURIA, EASTERN [EMU]
LANKA KOL alt for HO [HOC]
LANKAVIRI dial of MUMUYE [MUL]
LANNA alt for THAI, NORTHERN [NOD]
LANNACHYO dial of THULUNG [TDH]
LANNATAI alt for THAI, NORTHERN [NOD]
LANOH [LNH] lang, Malaysia (Peninsular)
LANOH KOBAK dial of TEMIAR [TMH]
LANOON alt for ILANUN [ILL]
LANPING-BIJIANG alt for BIIJIANG dial of BAI [PIQ]
LANSU alt for MARU [MHX]
LANTANAI [LNI] lang, Papua New Guinea
LANTEN alt for KIM MUN [MJI]
LANTIN alt for KIM MUN [MJI]
LANTOI dial of KAIMBULAWA [ZKA]
LANTOKA alt for KULA [TPG]
LANUN alt for ILANUN [ILL]
LANUN alt for LAHANAN [LHN]
LANYU alt for YAMI [YMI]
LANZOG alt for PIU [PIX]
LAO [NOL] lang, Laos; also in Cambodia, Canada,
   Thailand, USA
LAO alt for GELAO [KKF]
LÀO alt for LAO [NOL]
LAO alt for TS'ÜN-LAO [TSL]
LAO HABE alt for LAKA [LAK]
LAO KAO alt for LAO [NOL]
LAO MUH alt for PUOC [PUO]
LAO PHONG alt for PHONG-KNIANG [PNX]
LAO PHUAN alt for PHUAN [PHU]
LAO SONG alt for SONG [SOA]
LAO SONG DAM alt for SONG [SOA]
LAO TERNG alt for KHMU [KJG]
LAO WIANG alt for LAO [NOL]
LA-OANG alt for ROGLAI, NORTHERN [ROG]
LAO-KAO dial of LAO [NOL]
LAO-KHRANG dial of LAO [NOL]
LAO-LUM alt for LAO [NOL]
LAO-NOI alt for LAO [NOL]
LA-OOR dial of LAWA, WESTERN [LCP]
LAOPA alt for LAGHUU [LGH]
LAOPA alt for LAOPANG [LBG]
LAOPANG [LBG] lang, Myanmar
LAORA alt for LAURA [LUR]
LAOS SIGN LANGUAGE [LSO] lang, Laos
LAO-TAI alt for LAO [NOL]
LAOTIAN alt for LAO [NOL]
LAOTIAN TAI alt for LAO [NOL]
LAP alt for NYENKHA [NEH]
LAPALAMA 1 dial of ENGA [ENQ]
LAPALAMA 2 dial of ENGA [ENQ]
LAPAO dial of NAXI [NBF]
LAPCHE alt for LEPCHA [LEP]
"LAPP" pejorative alt for SAAMI, INARI [LPI]
"LAPP" pejorative alt for SAAMI, KEMI [LKS]
"LAPP" pejorative alt for SAAMI, KILDIN [LPD]

"LAPP" pejorative alt for SAAMI, LULE [LPL]
"LAPP" pejorative alt for SAAMI, NORTHERN [LPR]
"LAPP" pejorative alt for SAAMI, PITE [LPB]
"LAPP" pejorative alt for SAAMI, SKOLT [LPK]
"LAPP" pejorative alt for SAAMI, SOUTHERN [LPC]
"LAPP" pejorative alt for SAAMI, TER [LPT]
"LAPP" pejorative alt for SAAMI, UME [LPU]
LAPRAK dial of GHALE, SOUTHERN [GHE]
LAPURDIERA alt for LABOURDIN dial of BASQUE,
    NAVARRO-LABOURDIN [BQE]
LAPUYEN alt for SUBANUN, LAPUYAN [LAA]
LAQI alt for ZAY [ZWA]
LAQUA [LAQ] lang, Viet Nam; also in China
LARA dial of NGAMBAY [SBA]
LARA' [LRA] lang, Indonesia (Kalimantan); also in
    Malaysia (Sarawak)
L'ARABE DU TCHAD alt for ARABIC, CHADIAN
    SPOKEN [SHU]
LARAGIA [LRG] lang, Australia
LARAGIYA alt for LARAGIA [LRG]
LARAKIA alt for LARAGIA [LRG]
LARAKIYA alt for LARAGIA [LRG]
LARAMANIK alt for ARAMANIK [AAM]
LARANCHI alt for LARU [LAN]
LARANTUKA alt for LAMAHOLOT dial of
    LAMAHOLOT [SLP]
LARANTUKA dial of MALAY [MLI]
LARAOS dial of QUECHUA, YAUYOS [QUX]
LARAT alt for FORDATA [FRD]
LARAVAT alt for LAREVAT [LRV]
LARAWA alt for LARU [LAN]
LARBAWA alt for BALAR dial of KIR-BALAR [KKR]
LARDIL [LBZ] lang, Australia
LARDILL alt for LARDIL [LBZ]
LARE dial of KANURI, CENTRAL [KPH]
LAREDO dial of DZA [JEN]
LARENA dial of KULA [TPG]
LARESTANI alt for LARI [LRL]
LAREVAT [LRV] lang, Vanuatu
LARI [LRL] lang, Iran
LARI alt for LAADI dial of KONGO [KON]
LARI dial of SINDHI [SND]
LARIA alt for CHHATTISGARHI [HNE]
LARIANG alt for KULU dial of SARUDU [SDU]
LARIKE dial of LARIKE-WAKASIHU [ALO]
LARIKE-WAKASIHU [ALO] lang, Indonesia (Maluku)
LARIM alt for LONGARIM [LOH]
LARIMINIT alt for LONGARIM [LOH]
LARKYE alt for NUBRI [KTE]
LARO [LRO] lang, Sudan
LARO alt for LARU [LAN]
LARO alt for ROCKY PEAK [ROK]
LARO dial of LARO [LRO]
LARTEH [LAR] lang, Ghana
LARU [LAN] lang, Nigeria
LARU alt for LARO [LRO]
L-ARUSHA alt for ARUSHA dial of MAASAI [MET]
LASALIMU [LLM] lang, Indonesia (Sulawesi)
LASGERDI [LSA] lang, Iran
LASHI [LSI] lang, Myanmar; also in China
LASHI-MARU alt for LASHI [LSI]

LASHX dial of SVAN [SVA]
LASI [LSS] lang, Pakistan
LASI alt for LASHI [LSI]
LASI dial of SINDHI [SND]
LASSA dial of MARGHI CENTRAL [MAR]
LASSI alt for LASI [LSS]
LAT alt for LAC dial of KOHO [KPM]
LATAGNUN alt for RATAGNON [BTN]
LATAN alt for RATAGNON [BTN]
LATAR dial of MUNDARI [MUW]
LATE alt for LARTEH [LAR]
LATEP dial of MUMENG [MZI]
LATGALIAN alt for EAST LATVIAN dial of LATVIAN
    [LAT]
LATI alt for LACHI [LBT]
LATIN [LTN] lang, Vatican State
LATIN ANAUNICO dial of LOMBARD [LMO]
LATIN FIAMAZZO dial of LOMBARD [LMO]
LATINA alt for LATIN [LTN]
LATOD alt for LOTUD [DTR]
LATOMA alt for SUMARIUP [SIV]
LATOOKA alt for OTUHO [LOT]
LATTUKA alt for OTUHO [LOT]
LATU [LTU] lang, Indonesia (Maluku)
LATUD alt for LOTUD [DTR]
LATUKA alt for OTUHO [LOT]
LATUKO alt for OTUHO [LOT]
LATUNDÊ alt for YALAPMUNXTE dial of
    NAMBIKUARA, NORTHERN [MBG]
LATUVI ZAPOTECO alt for ZAPOTECO, IXTLÁN
    SURESTE [ZPD]
LATVIAN [LAT] lang, Latvia; also in Australia, Belarus,
    Brazil, Canada, Estonia, Germany, Lithuania, New
    Zealand, Russia (Europe), Sweden, Ukraine,
    United Kingdom, USA, Venezuela
LATVIAN ROMANI dial of ROMANI, BALTIC [ROM]
LATVIAN SIGN LANGUAGE [LSL] lang, Latvia
LATVISKA alt for LATVIAN [LAT]
LAU [LLU] lang, Solomon Islands
LAU alt for LAKA [LAK]
LAU alt for LAUAN [LLX]
LAU alt for LOU dial of NUER [NUS]
LAU dial of DINKA, SOUTHWESTERN [DIK]
LAU dial of LAU [LLU]
LAU dial of LAUAN [LLX]
LAUA [LUF] lang, Papua New Guinea
LAUAN [LLX] lang, Fiji
LAUBE alt for LAVUKALEVE [LVK]
LAUDA alt for LOWUDO dial of OTUHO [LOT]
LAUDJE alt for LAUJE [LAW]
LAUISARANGA alt for ARUOP [LSR]
LAUJE [LAW] lang, Indonesia (Sulawesi)
LAUKANU alt for KELA [KCL]
LAULABU alt for YABEM [JAE]
LAULI dial of WEJEWA [WEW]
LAUMBE alt for LAVUKALEVE [LVK]
LAUNA alt for LAHU [LAH]
LAUNGAW alt for MARU [MHX]
LAUNGWAW alt for MARU [MHX]
LAURA [LUR] lang, Indonesia (Nusa Tenggara)
LAURA dial of LAURA [LUR]

LAURENTIAN [LRE] lang, Canada
LAUROWAN dial of PASHAYI, NORTHWEST [GLH]
LAU'U alt for ARUOP [LSR]
LAUWELA dial of BWAIDOKA [BWD]
LAVA alt for LAWA, WESTERN [LCP]
LAVANGAI alt for TUNGAG [LCM]
LAVANI alt for LAMBADI [LMN]
LAVATBURA dial of LAVATBURA-LAMUSONG [LBV]
LAVATBURA-LAMUSONG [LBV] lang, Papua New Guinea
LAVE [BRB] lang, Laos; also in Cambodia, France, USA, Viet Nam
LAVE alt for BRAO [BRB]
LAVEH alt for BRAO [BRB]
LAVEH alt for LAVE [BRB]
LAVEN [LBO] lang, Laos; also in USA
LAVONGAI alt for TUNGAG [LCM]
LAVORA dial of WEDAU [WED]
LAVÜA alt for LAWA, WESTERN [LCP]
LAVUA alt for LAWA, WESTERN [LCP]
LAVUKALEVE [LVK] lang, Solomon Islands
LAWA alt for NYAHKUR [CBN]
LAWA alt for UGONG [UGO]
LAWA dial of LAWANGAN [LBX]
LAWA, EASTERN [LWL] lang, Thailand
LAWA, WESTERN [LCP] lang, China; also in Thailand
LAWANGAN [LBX] lang, Indonesia (Kalimantan)
LAWAS alt for TRUSAN dial of LUNDAYEH [LND]
LAWEENJRU alt for LAVEN [LBO]
LAWELE alt for KALENDE dial of PANCANA [PNP]
LAWNG alt for MARU [MHX]
LAWNG HSU dial of MARU [MHX]
LAWOI alt for URAK LAWOI' [URK]
LAWRA LOBI alt for NURA dial of DAGARA, NORTHERN [DGI]
LAWTA alt for URAK LAWOI' [URK]
LAY alt for KABALAI [KVF]
LAY alt for LAI dial of GBAYA, NORTHWEST [GYA]
LAYA dial of KOHO [KPM]
LAYA dial of MAGINDANAON [MDH]
LAYAKHA [LYA] lang, Bhutan
LAYANA dial of GUANA [GVA]
LAYAPO dial of ENGA [ENQ]
LAYDO dial of AARI [AIZ]
LAYMON-COCHIMI alt for COCHIMÍ [COJ]
LAYMONEM alt for COCHIMÍ [COJ]
LAYOLO alt for LAIYOLO dial of LAIYOLO [LJI]
LAZ [LZZ] lang, Turkey (Asia); also in Belgium, France, Georgia, Germany, USA
LAZE alt for LAZ [LZZ]
LAZEMI dial of NAGA, SUMI [NSM]
LAZIALE dial of ITALIAN [ITN]
LAZURI alt for LAZ [LZZ]
L'BE dial of MOKEN [MWT]
LDES alt for EL MOLO [ELO]
LE alt for HLAI [LIC]
LE alt for LUSHAI [LSH]
LEANGBA alt for NGELIMA [AGH]

LEBANESE-SYRIAN ARABIC alt for ARABIC, NORTH LEVANTINE SPOKEN [APC]
LEBANG dial of TEWA [TWE]
LEBATUKAN alt for LAMALERA [LMR]
LEBEI alt for LEVEI dial of KHEHEK [TLX]
LEBEJ alt for LEVEI dial of KHEHEK [TLX]
LEBIR dial of BISSA [BIB]
LEB-LANO alt for LANGO [LAJ]
LEBOA-LE dial of BWA [BWW]
LEBONG dial of REJANG [REJ]
LEBONI alt for RAMPI [LJE]
LEBORO alt for BURU dial of NGELIMA [AGH]
LEBOU dial of WOLOF [WOL]
LEBU alt for LABU dial of MALAY [MLI]
LEBU alt for LEBOU dial of WOLOF [WOL]
LECHI alt for LASHI [LSI]
LECHKHUM alt for RACHA-LEXCHXUM dial of GEORGIAN [GEO]
LECO [LEC] lang, Bolivia
LEDO alt for KAILI, LEDO [LEW]
LEDO dial of KAILI, LEDO [LEW]
LEE alt for DJINGILI [JIG]
LEEALOWA alt for ALAWA [ALH]
LEEANUWA alt for YANYUWA [JAO]
LEEARRAWA alt for GARAWA [GBC]
LEELALWARRA alt for MARA [MEC]
LEELAU [LDK] lang, Nigeria
LEELAWARRA alt for MARA [MEC]
LEELU dial of KOMA [KMY]
LEEM dial of TAOIH, UPPER [TTH]
LEEMAK alt for MAK [PBL]
LEEMO dial of HADIYYA [HDY]
LEEWAKYA alt for WAGAYA [WGA]
LEEWARD CARIBBEAN CREOLE ENGLISH [AIG] lang, Antigua and Barbuda; also in Anguilla, Dominica, Montserrat, St. Kitts-Nevis, United Kingdom
LEFA' alt for BAFIA [KSF]
LEFANA alt for LELEMI [LEF]
LEFO' alt for BAFAW dial of BAFAW-BALONG [BWT]
LEGA-MWENGA [LGM] lang, DRC
LEGA-SHABUNDA [LEA] lang, DRC
LEGASPI dial of BICOLANO, CENTRAL [BKL]
LEGBA alt for LUKPA [DOP]
LEGBO [AGB] lang, Nigeria
LEGENYEM [LCC] lang, Indonesia (Irian Jaya)
LEGERI dial of VAGHAT-YA-BIJIM-LEGERI [BIJ]
LEGO alt for SAMBA LEKO [NDI]
LEGO alt for SAMBA LEKO dial of SAMBA LEKO [NDI]
LEH dial of LADAKHI [LBJ]
LEHALI [TQL] lang, Vanuatu
LEHALURUP [URR] lang, Vanuatu
LEHAR [CAE] lang, Senegal
LEI alt for CENTRAL KONO dial of KONO [KNO]
LEI alt for LUSHAI [LSH]
LEI HUA alt for LEIZHOU dial of CHINESE, MIN NAN [CFR]
LEIK alt for THIANG dial of NUER [NUS]
LEILEIAFA dial of SUAU [SWP]
LEINSTER dial of GAELIC, IRISH [GLI]

LEIPON [LEK] lang, Papua New Guinea
LEISU alt for LISU [LIS]
LEIZHOU dial of CHINESE, MIN NAN [CFR]
LEKA-IGONZABALE alt for LEGA-SHABUNDA [LEA]
LEKANINGI alt for KANINGI [KZO]
LEKA-SHILE alt for LEGA-MWENGA [LGM]
LEKA-SILE alt for LEGA-MWENGA [LGM]
LEKI dial of LURI [LRI]
LEKO alt for ILIKU dial of LUSENGO [LUS]
LEKO alt for SAMBA LEKO [NDI]
LEKO alt for SAMBA LEKO dial of SAMBA LEKO
    [NDI]
LEKON alt for SAMBA LEKO [NDI]
LEKON alt for SAMBA LEKO dial of SAMBA
    LEKO [NDI]
LEKON dial of SIKULE [SKH]
LEKONGO alt for NKONGHO [NKC]
LEKU alt for ILIKU dial of LUSENGO [LUS]
LEKWHAN alt for PAZEH [PZH]
LEL alt for NISI [DAP]
LELA alt for C'LELA [DRI]
LELA dial of KASEM [KAS]
LELAIN alt for ROTE-TENGAH dial of ROTE [ROT]
LELAK [LLK] lang, Malaysia (Sarawak)
LELAK dial of LELAK [LLK]
LELAU alt for LEELAU [LDK]
LELE [LEL] lang, DRC
LELE [LLC] lang, Guinea
LELE [LLN] lang, Chad
LELE [UGA] lang, Papua New Guinea
LELE alt for LYÉLÉ [LEE]
LELE HAI alt for LELE [UGA]
LELEHUDI dial of TAWALA [TBO]
LELEMI [LEF] lang, Ghana
LÉLÉMRIN alt for AIZI, TIAGBAMRIN [AHI]
LELENUK alt for BILBA-DIU-LELENUK dial of ROTE
    [ROT]
LELEPA [LPA] lang, Vanuatu
LELET alt for MADAK [MMX]
LELET dial of MADAK [MMX]
LELIALI dial of KAYELI [KZL]
LELO alt for LEELAU [LDK]
LELU-TAFUNSAK dial of KOSRAEAN [KSI]
LEM alt for DEM [DEM]
LEM alt for SASAR dial of VATRATA [VLR]
LEMADI alt for LAMBADI [LMN]
LEMAK alt for MAK [PBL]
LEMAKOT alt for KARA [LEU]
LEMANAK dial of IBAN [IBA]
LEMANDE alt for NOMAANDE [LEM]
LEMANTANG alt for LEMATANG [LMT]
LEMATANG [LMT] lang, Indonesia (Sumatra)
LEMBA alt for KELA [KEL]
LEMBA alt for MALIMBA [MZD]
LEMBAAMBA alt for MBAMA [MBM]
LEMBAK [LIW] lang, Indonesia (Sumatra)
LEMBAK BLITI dial of LEMBAK [LIW]
LEMBAK SINDANG dial of LEMBAK [LIW]
LEMBATA alt for LEVUKA [LVU]
LEMBATA, SOUTH [LMF] lang, Indonesia (Nusa
    Tenggara)

LEMBATA, WEST [LMJ] lang, Indonesia (Nusa
    Tenggara)
LEMBENA [LEQ] lang, Papua New Guinea
LEMBUE dial of BEMBA [BEM]
LEMBUR dial of KAMANG [WOI]
LEME alt for BAI [PIQ]
LEMENA dial of KAYAN, REJANG [REE]
LEMET alt for LAMET [LBN]
LEMETING alt for BELAIT [BEG]
LEMIO [LEI] lang, Papua New Guinea
LEMITING dial of KIPUT [KYI]
LEMKO dial of RUSYN [RUE]
LEMMA alt for LAMMA [LEV]
LEMOI alt for MOI [MOW]
LEMOLANG [LEY] lang, Indonesia (Sulawesi)
LEMORO [LDJ] lang, Nigeria
LEMOSIN alt for LIMOUSIN [LMS]
LEMUSMUS alt for KARA [LEU]
LEMYO dial of CHIN, ASHO [CSH]
LENAKEL [TNL] lang, Vanuatu
LENAPE alt for UNAMI [DEL]
LENCA [LEN] lang, Honduras; also in El Salvador
LENDU [LED] lang, DRC; also in Uganda
LENDUMU alt for NDUMU [NMD]
LENDU-SUD alt for NGITI [NIY]
LENGADOUCIAN alt for LANGUEDOCIEN [LNC]
LENGE alt for LENGUE dial of CHOPI [CCE]
LENGI alt for LENJE [LEH]
LENGILU [LGI] lang, Indonesia (Kalimantan)
LENGKAYAP dial of MALAY [MLI]
LENGO [LGR] lang, Solomon Islands
LENGO dial of LENGO [LGR]
LENGOLA [LEJ] lang, DRC
LENGORA alt for LENGOLA [LEJ]
LENGOTIA alt for BHILI [BHB]
LENGUA [LEG] lang, Paraguay
LENGUA alt for PALENQUERO [PLN]
LENGUA NORTE alt for NORTHERN LENGUA
    dial of LENGUA [LEG]
LENGUA SUR alt for SOUTHERN LENGUA dial
    of LENGUA [LEG]
LENGUE dial of CHOPI [CCE]
LENGWE alt for HLENGWE dial of TSHWA [TSC]
LENINGITIJ [LNJ] lang, Australia
LENJE [LEH] lang, Zambia
LENJE dial of LENJE [LEH]
LENJI alt for LENJE [LEH]
LENKAITAHE alt for SALAS [SGU]
LENKARAN dial of AZERBAIJANI, NORTH [AZE]
LENKAU [LER] lang, Papua New Guinea
LENKORAN dial of AZERBAIJANI, NORTH [AZE]
LENKORAN dial of TALYSH [TLY]
LENNI-LENAPE alt for UNAMI [DEL]
LENTE dial of CHIN, FALAM [HBH]
LENTEX dial of SVAN [SVA]
LENYIMA [LDG] lang, Nigeria
LEON dial of VATRATA [VLR]
LEONAIS dial of BRETON [BRT]
LEONESE dial of ASTURIAN [AUB]
LEONIDIO-PRASTOS alt for SOUTHERN
    TSAKONIAN dial of TSAKONIAN [TSD]

LEPCHA [LEP] lang, India; also in Bhutan, Nepal
LEPKI [LPE] lang, Indonesia (Irian Jaya)
LEPO' KULIT dial of KENYAH, KELINYAU [XKL]
LEPO TAU KENYA alt for MADANG [MQD]
LEPO TAU KENYAH alt for MADANG [MQD]
LEPU POTONG dial of KELABIT [KZI]
LEPU POTONG dial of LUNDAYEH [LND]
LEPU TAU alt for MADANG [MQD]
LEQI alt for LASHI [LSI]
LERA alt for HUTU dial of RWANDA [RUA]
LERABAIN alt for KUI [KVD]
LERABAING alt for KUI dial of KUI [KVD]
LERE [GNH] lang, Nigeria
LERE alt for LARE dial of KANURI, CENTRAL [KPH]
LERE dial of BISSA [BIB]
LERIK dial of TALYSH [TLY]
LERON alt for WAPU dial of WANTOAT [WNC]
LESA alt for LESE [LES]
LESA alt for SAKATA [SAT]
LESA dial of BENGGOI [BGY]
LESE [LES] lang, DRC
LESE DESE alt for NDESE dial of LESE [LES]
LESE KARO dial of LESE [LES]
LESHON KNAAN alt for KNAANIC [CZK]
LESHUOOPA alt for LISU [LIS]
LESIGHU alt for SIGHU [SXE]
LESING dial of LESING-GELIMI [LET]
LESING-ATUI alt for LESING-GELIMI [LET]
LESING-GELIMI [LET] lang, Papua New Guinea
LESSE alt for LESE [LES]
LESSER ANTILLEAN CREOLE FRENCH [DOM]
    lang, St. Lucia; also in Dominica, France, Grenada,
    Guadeloupe, Guyana, Martinique, Trinidad and
    Tobago
LESSER KABARDIAN dial of KABARDIAN [KAB]
LESSER KABYLE dial of KABYLE [KYL]
LESUO alt for LISU [LIS]
LETE alt for LARTEH [LAR]
LETE dial of TSWANA [TSW]
LETEMBOI [NMS] lang, Vanuatu
LETI [LEO] lang, Cameroon
LETI [LTI] lang, Indonesia (Maluku)
LETRI LGONA alt for LUANG [LEX]
LETSI alt for LASHI [LSI]
LETTA-BATULAPPA-KASSA alt for PATTINJO dial
    of ENREKANG [PTT]
"LETTISCH" pejorative alt for LATVIAN [LAT]
"LETTISH" pejorative alt for LATVIAN [LAT]
LETTISH ROMANI alt for LATVIAN ROMANI dial
    of ROMANI, BALTIC [ROM]
LETUAMA alt for TANIMUCA-RETUARÃ [TNC]
LETUHAMA alt for TANIMUCA-RETUARÃ [TNC]
LETZBURGISCH alt for LUXEMBOURGEOIS [LUX]
LËTZEBUERGESCH alt for LUXEMBOURGEOIS
    [LUX]
LEUANGIUA alt for ONTONG JAVA [LUN]
LEVAI dial of HRUSO [HRU]
LEVANTINE alt for ARABIC, SOUTH LEVANTINE
    SPOKEN [AJP]
LEVANTINE ARABIC alt for ARABIC, NORTH
    LEVANTINE SPOKEN [APC]

LEVANTINE ARABIC alt for ARABIC, SOUTH
    LEVANTINE SPOKEN [AJP]
LEVANTINE BEDAWI ARABIC alt for ARABIC,
    EASTERN EGYPTIAN BEDAWI SPOKEN [AVL]
LEVEI dial of KHEHEK [TLX]
LEVEI-DREHET alt for KHEHEK [TLX]
LEVEI-NDREHET alt for KHEHEK [TLX]
LEVUKA [LVU] lang, Indonesia (Nusa Tenggara)
LEVUKA dial of LEVUKA [LVU]
LEW dial of MUSEY [MSE]
LEWA dial of KAMBERA [SMI]
LEWADA alt for LEWADA-DEWARA [LWD]
LEWADA dial of LEWADA-DEWARA [LWD]
LEWADA-DEWARA [LWD] lang, Papua New Guinea
LEWO [LWW] lang, Vanuatu
LEWO alt for LAMENU [LMU]
LEWO ELENG [LWE] lang, Indonesia (Nusa
    Tenggara)
LEWOKUKUN alt for LEVUKA [LVU]
LEWOLAGA alt for LAMAHOLOT dial of
    LAMAHOLOT [SLP]
LEWOTOBI [LWT] lang, Indonesia (Nusa Tenggara)
LEWUKA alt for LEVUKA [LVU]
LEYA dial of TONGA [TOI]
LEYIGHA [AYI] lang, Nigeria
LEYTE dial of CEBUANO [CEB]
LEZGHI alt for LEZGI [LEZ]
LEZGI [LEZ] lang, Russia (Europe); also in
    Azerbaijan, Georgia, Kazakhstan, Kyrgyzstan,
    Turkey (Asia), Turkmenistan, Ukraine, Uzbekistan
LEZGIAN alt for LEZGI [LEZ]
LEZGIN alt for LEZGI [LEZ]
LGALIGE alt for KOALIB [KIB]
LGONA alt for LUANG [LEX]
LHAO VO alt for MARU [MHX]
LHENGWE alt for HLENGWE dial of TSHWA [TSC]
LHO dial of NUBRI [KTE]
LHOBA alt for ADI [ADI]
LHOBA alt for LUOBA, BOGA'ER [ADI]
LHOBA alt for LUOBA, YIDU [CLK]
LHOBIKHA alt for LHOKPU [LHP]
LHOKET alt for LHOMI [LHM]
LHOKPU [LHP] lang, Bhutan
LHOMI [LHM] lang, Nepal; also in China, India
LHO-PA alt for LUOBA, BOGA'ER [ADI]
LHO-PA alt for LUOBA, YIDU [CLK]
LHOTA alt for NAGA, LOTHA [NJH]
LHUKONZO alt for KONJO [KOO]
LI alt for HLAI [LIC]
LI alt for LISU [LIS]
LI alt for MUNGAKA [MHK]
LI EMTEBAN alt for FOGI dial of BURU [MHS]
LI ENYOROT alt for LISELA [LCL]
LI HUA alt for LEIZHOU dial of CHINESE, MIN
    NAN [CFR]
LIA FEHAN alt for SOUTHERN TETUN dial of
    TETUN [TTM]
LIA FOHO alt for NORTHERN TETUN dial of TETUN
    [TTM]
LIABUKU [LIX] lang, Indonesia (Sulawesi)
LIAE dial of SABU [HVN]

LIAH BING dial of MODANG [MXD]
LIAMBATA alt for SALAS [SGU]
LIAMBATA-KOBI alt for LIANA-SETI [STE]
LIANA alt for LIANA-SETI [STE]
LIANAN alt for LIANA-SETI [STE]
LIANA-SETI [STE] lang, Indonesia (Maluku)
LIANG alt for RIANG [RIL]
LIANG dial of TULEHU [TLU]
LIANG SEK alt for RIANG [RIL]
LIANGHE dial of ACHANG [ACN]
LIANGMAI alt for KOIRENG [NKD]
LIANGMAI alt for NAGA, LIANGMAI [NJN]
LIANGMEI alt for KOIRENG [NKD]
LIANGMEI alt for NAGA, LIANGMAI [NJN]
LIANHUA dial of SHE [SHX]
LIARA alt for LIVARA dial of SAKAO [SKU]
LIARO dial of KISSI, NORTHERN [KQS]
LIAS dial of BONTOC, EASTERN [BKB]
LIBAALI alt for BALI [BCP]
LIBBO alt for KAAN [LDL]
LIBBUNG dial of KELABIT [KZI]
LIBENGE alt for BWA [BWW]
LIBERIAN ENGLISH [LIR] lang, Liberia
LIBERIAN PIDGIN ENGLISH alt for LIBERIAN
    ENGLISH [LIR]
LIBERIAN STANDARD ENGLISH dial of ENGLISH
    [ENG]
LIBIDO [LIQ] lang, Ethiopia
LIBIE alt for ELIP [EKM]
LIBINDJA alt for BINJA dial of NGOMBE [NGC]
LIBINJA alt for BINJA dial of NGOMBE [NGC]
LIBINJA alt for LIBINZA [LIZ]
LIBINZA [LIZ] lang, DRC
LIBISEGAHUN dial of LOKO [LOK]
LIBO alt for KAAN [LDL]
LIBOLO alt for BOLO [BLV]
LIBON dial of BICOLANO, ALBAY [BHK]
LIBUA alt for BWA [BWW]
LIBWALI alt for BWA [BWW]
LIBYAN SIGN LANGUAGE [LBS] lang, Libya
LIBYAN SPOKEN ARABIC alt for ARABIC,
    WESTERN EGYPTIAN BEDAWI SPOKEN [AYL]
LIBYAN VERNACULAR ARABIC alt for ARABIC,
    LIBYAN SPOKEN [AYL]
LICELA alt for LISELA dial of LISELA [LCL]
LICELLA alt for LISELA dial of LISELA [LCL]
LICHABOOL-NALONG dial of KONKOMBA [KOS]
LICHIANG dial of NAXI [NBF]
LIDUMA alt for DUMA [DMA]
LIEM CHAU alt for CHINESE, YUE [YUH]
LIET ENJOROT alt for LISELA [LCL]
LIETUVI alt for LITHUANIAN [LIT]
LIFOMA alt for FOMA [FOM]
LIFOU alt for DEHU [DEU]
LIFU alt for DEHU [DEU]
LIGAO dial of BICOLANO, ALBAY [BHK]
LIGBELN dial of KONKOMBA [KOS]
LIGBI [LIG] lang, Ghana; also in Côte d'Ivoire
LIGENZA [LGZ] lang, DRC
LIGGO alt for LIGO dial of BARI [BFA]
LIGILI alt for LIJILI [MGI]

LIGO dial of BARI [BFA]
LIGRI dial of JARAWA [JAR]
LIGURE alt for LIGURIAN [LIJ]
LIGURI alt for LOGORIK [LIU]
LIGURI dial of LOGORIK [LIU]
LIGURIAN [LIJ] lang, Italy; also in France, Monaco
LÍGURU alt for LIGURIAN [LIJ]
LIGWI alt for LIGBI [LIG]
LIHEN dial of KAMBERATARO [KBV]
LIHIR [LIH] lang, Papua New Guinea
LI-HSAW alt for LISU [LIS]
LIJIANG alt for LICHIANG dial of NAXI [NBF]
LIJILI [MGI] lang, Nigeria
LIKA [LIK] lang, DRC
LIKÁ alt for LILIKÁ dial of LIKA [LIK]
LIKANANTAÍ alt for KUNZA [KUZ]
LIKANGO alt for KANGO [KTY]
LIKANGO alt for KANGO [KZY]
LIKANU alt for KANU [KHX]
LI-KARI-LI alt for KARI [KBJ]
LIKAW dial of BOMBOMA [BWS]
LIKELO alt for KELE [KHY]
LIKES-UTSIA dial of MANDJAK [MFV]
LIKI [LIO] lang, Indonesia (Irian Jaya)
LIKILA [LIE] lang, DRC
LIKÓ alt for LILIKÓ dial of LIKA [LIK]
LIKÓ dial of LIKA [LIK]
LIKOKA dial of LOBALA [LOQ]
LIKOLO dial of POKE [POF]
LIKOONLI dial of KONKOMBA [KOS]
LIKOUALA alt for LIKWALA [KWC]
LIKOYA alt for GYELE [GYI]
LIKPAKPALN alt for KONKOMBA [KOS]
LIKPE alt for SEKPELE [LIP]
LIKUBA [KXX] lang, Congo
LIKUM [LIB] lang, Papua New Guinea
LIKUPANG dial of TONSEA [TXS]
LIKWALA [KWC] lang, Congo
LILA dial of CLELA [DRI]
LILAU [LLL] lang, Papua New Guinea
LILIALI alt for LELIALI dial of KAYELI [KZL]
LILIGA dial of LEGA-SHABUNDA [LEA]
LILIKÁ dial of LIKA [LIK]
LILIKÓ dial of LIKA [LIK]
LILIMA dial of KALANGA [KCK]
LI-LI-SHA alt for PAIWAN [PWN]
LILLOIS dial of PICARD [PCD]
LILLOOET [LIL] lang, Canada
LIMA alt for NEGERI LIMA dial of ASILULU [ASL]
LIMA dial of LAMBA [LAB]
LIMARAHING dial of BLAGAR [BEU]
LIMBA alt for IWAIDJA [IBD]
LIMBA alt for MALIMBA [MZD]
LIMBA, EAST [LMA] lang, Guinea; also in Sierra
    Leone
LIMBA, WEST-CENTRAL [LIA] lang, Sierra Leone
LIMBANG alt for TRUSAN dial of LUNDAYEH [LND]
LIMBEDE alt for MBERE [MDT]
LIMBO alt for LIMBU [LIF]
LIMBOM alt for LIMBUM [LIM]
LIMBOTO [LJO] lang, Indonesia (Sulawesi)

LIMBOTTO alt for LIMBOTO [LJO]
LIMBU [LIF] lang, Nepal; also in Bhutan, India
LIMBUDZA alt for BUDZA [BJA]
LIMBUM [LIM] lang, Cameroon; also in Nigeria
LIMBUR alt for LEMBUR dial of KAMANG [WOI]
LIMERA alt for ILIUN [ILU]
LIMI alt for NYATURU [RIM]
LIMILNGAN [LMC] lang, Australia
LIMIMA alt for LILIMA dial of KALANGA [KCK]
LIMKHIM alt for LINGKHIM [LII]
LIMKOW alt for LINGAO [ONB]
LIMÓN CREOLE ENGLISH dial of SOUTH-WESTERN CARIBBEAN CREOLE ENGLISH [JAM]
LIMONESE CREOLE alt for LIMÓN CREOLE ENGLISH dial of SOUTHWESTERN CARIBBEAN CREOLE ENGLISH [JAM]
LIMONKPEL dial of KONKOMBA [KOS]
LIMORO alt for LEMORO [LDJ]
LIMORRO alt for LEMORO [LDJ]
LIMOS-LIWAN KALINGA alt for KALINGA, LIMOS [KMK]
LIMOUSIN [LMS] lang, France
LIMPESA dial of LUSENGO [LUS]
LINAFIEL dial of KONKOMBA [KOS]
LINANGMANLI dial of NTCHAM [BUD]
LINAW-QAUQAUL dial of BASAY [BYQ]
LINCHA alt for TANA-LINCHA dial of QUECHUA, YAUYOS [QUX]
LINCHENG dial of LINGAO [ONB]
LINDA dial of BANDA-BAMBARI [LIY]
LINDAU alt for NYINDROU [LID]
LINDIRI alt for NUNGU [RIN]
LINDJA dial of SHI [SHR]
LINDROU alt for NYINDROU [LID]
LINDU [KLW] lang, Indonesia (Sulawesi)
LINDUAN alt for LINDU [KLW]
LINGAAYAT dial of GOWLI [GOK]
LINGALA [LIN] lang, DRC; also in CAR, Congo
LINGAO [ONB] lang, China
LINGAO PROPER-DENGMAI alt for LINCHENG dial of LINGAO [ONB]
LINGARAK [LGK] lang, Vanuatu
LINGBE alt for NGBEE [NBL]
LINGBEE alt for NGBEE [NBL]
LINGGAU alt for LEMBAK [LIW]
LINGI alt for BWELA [BWL]
LINGKABAU SUGUT dial of TOMBONUWO [TXA]
LINGKHIM [LII] lang, Nepal
LINGKHIM RAI alt for LINGKHIM [LII]
LINGOMBE alt for NGOMBE [NGC]
LINGONDA dial of BOMBOMA [BWS]
LINGOTES alt for ILONGOT [ILK]
LINGUA FRANCA [PML] lang, Tunisia
LÍNGUA GERAL alt for NHENGATU [YRL]
LINGUA GESTUAL PORTUGUESA alt for PORTUGUESE SIGN LANGUAGE [PSR]
LINGUA ITALIANA DEI SEGNI alt for ITALIAN SIGN LANGUAGE [ISE]

LINKABAU alt for LINGKABAU SUGUT dial of TOMBONUWO [TXA]
LINKHIM alt for LINGKHIM [LII]
LINKOW alt for LINGAO [ONB]
LINNGITHIG alt for LENINGITIJ [LNJ]
LINNGITHIGH alt for LENINGITIJ [LNJ]
LINO alt for BOMWALI [BMW]
LINTANG [LNT] lang, Indonesia (Sumatra)
LINYALI alt for NYALI [NLJ]
LINYANGA-LE alt for NYANGA-LI [NYC]
LINYELI alt for PANDE dial of PANDE [BKJ]
LINZELI alt for PANDE dial of PANDE [BKJ]
LIO alt for LI'O [LJL]
LI'O [LJL] lang, Indonesia (Nusa Tenggara)
LI'O dial of RAO [RAO]
LIONESE alt for LI'O [LJL]
LIP'A alt for LISU [LIS]
LIPANJA dial of MABAALE [MMZ]
LIPE alt for KUNZA [KUZ]
LIPIS dial of SEMAI [SEA]
LIPKAWA alt for KARIYA [KIL]
LIPKAWA alt for MBURKU [BBT]
LIPO [TKL] lang, China
LIPOTO dial of LUSENGO [LUS]
LIPTAAKOORE dial of FULFULDE, NORTH-EASTERN BURKINA FASO [FUH]
LIPUKE dial of LACHI [LBT]
LIPULIO alt for LACHI [LBT]
LIPULIONGTCO dial of LACHI [LBT]
LIPUPI dial of LACHI [LBT]
LIPUPǑ alt for LACHI, WHITE [LWH]
LIPUTCIO dial of LACHI [LBT]
LIPUTE dial of LACHI [LBT]
LIPUTIǑ dial of LACHI [LBT]
LIR alt for LIHIR [LIH]
LIR TALO alt for TALUR [ILW]
LIRANG dial of TALAUD [TLD]
LIRONG dial of KENYAH, SEBOB [SIB]
LIS alt for BAGIRMI [BMI]
LIS alt for ITALIAN SIGN LANGUAGE [ISE]
LIS MA RUN alt for DAFFO-BUTURA dial of RON [CLA]
LISABATA alt for LISABATA-NUNIALI [LCS]
LISABATA-NUNIALI [LCS] lang, Indonesia (Maluku)
LISABATA-TIMUR dial of LISABATA-NUNIALI [LCS]
LISAW alt for LISU [LIS]
LISBON dial of PORTUGUESE SIGN LANGUAGE [PSR]
LISELA [LCL] lang, Indonesia (Maluku)
LISELA dial of LISELA [LCL]
LISH alt for KISHPIGNAG dial of MOINBA [MOB]
LISHÁN DIDÁN [TRG] lang, Israel; also in Azerbaijan, Georgia
LISHAN HOZAYE alt for LISHANA DENI [LSD]
LISHAN HUDAYE alt for LISHANA DENI [LSD]
LISHANA ATIGA alt for SYRIAC [SYC]
LISHANA ATURAYA alt for ASSYRIAN NEO-ARAMAIC [AII]
LISHANA AXNI alt for HULAULÁ [HUY]
LISHANA DENI [LSD] lang, Israel
LISHANA DIDÁN alt for LISHANID NOSHAN [AIJ]

LISHANA KALDAYA alt for CHALDEAN NEO-ARAMAIC [CLD]
LISHANA NOSHAN alt for HULAULÁ [HUY]
LISHANÁN alt for LISHÁN DIDÁN [TRG]
LISHANID JANAN alt for BIJIL NEO-ARAMAIC [BJF]
LISHANID NASH DIDÁN alt for LISHÁN DIDÁN [TRG]
LISHANID NOSHAN [AIJ] lang, Israel
LÌSHÁÙ alt for SHAU [SQH]
LI-SHAW alt for LISU [LIS]
LISHU alt for LISU [LIS]
LISI alt for BAGIRMI [BMI]
LISI alt for KUKA dial of NABA [MNE]
LISO alt for LISU [LIS]
LISONGO alt for MBATI [MDN]
LISSAM dial of KUTEP [KUB]
LISSI alt for LESE [LES]
LISSONGO alt for MBATI [MDN]
LISSU alt for LISU [LIS]
LISU [LIS] lang, China; also in India, Myanmar, Thailand
LISU dial of ERSU [ERS]
LISUM dial of KAYAN, REJANG [REE]
LITAUISCHE alt for LITHUANIAN [LIT]
LITEMBO alt for TEMBO [TMV]
LITERI LAGONA alt for LUANG [LEX]
LITEWSKI alt for LITHUANIAN [LIT]
LITHIRO alt for TIRA [TIR]
LITHUANIAN [LIT] lang, Lithuania; also in Argentina, Australia, Belarus, Brazil, Canada, Estonia, Kazakhstan, Kyrgyzstan, Latvia, Poland, Russia (Europe), Sweden, Tajikistan, Turkmenistan, United Kingdom, Uruguay, USA, Uzbekistan
LITHUANIAN ROMANI dial of ROMANI, BALTIC [ROM]
LITHUANIAN SIGN LANGUAGE [LLS] lang, Lithuania
LITIME dial of AKPOSO [KPO]
LITIPARA dial of SAURIA PAHARIA [MJT]
LITORO alt for OTORO [OTR]
LITOVSKIY alt for LITHUANIAN [LIT]
LITTLE NICOBAR dial of NICOBARESE, SOUTHERN [NIK]
LITZLITZ [LTZ] lang, Vanuatu
LITZLITZ-VISELE alt for LITZLITZ [LTZ]
LIU dial of KOMA [KMY]
LIUCHIANG alt for LIUJIANG dial of ZHUANG, NORTHERN [CCX]
LIUJIANG dial of ZHUANG, NORTHERN [CCX]
LIUTUVISKAI alt for LITHUANIAN [LIT]
LIUTWA dial of POKE [POF]
LIV [LIV] lang, Latvia
LIVANUMA alt for VANUMA [VAU]
LIVARA dial of EFATE, NORTH [LLP]
LIVARA dial of SAKAO [SKU]
LIVE dial of NAGA, LOTHA [NJH]
LIVINALLESE dial of LADIN [LLD]
LIVONIAN alt for LIV [LIV]
LÍVÕNKÉL alt for LIVVI [OLO]
LIVUAN dial of KUANUA [KSD]
LIVUNGANEN dial of MANOBO, ILIANEN [MBI]

LIVVI [OLO] lang, Russia (Europe); also in Finland
LIVVIKOVIAN alt for LIVVI [OLO]
LIVVIKOVSKIJ JAZYK alt for LIVVI [OLO]
LIWULI alt for TUWILI [BOV]
LIYAGALAWUMIRR dial of DHUWAL [DUJ]
LIYAGAWUMIRR dial of DHUWAL [DUJ]
LIYANG alt for KOIRENG [NKD]
LIYANG alt for NAGA, LIANGMAI [NJN]
LIYANGMAI alt for KOIRENG [NKD]
LIYUWA dial of SIMAA [SIE]
LLAGUA alt for YAGUA [YAD]
LLARURO alt for YARURO [YAE]
LLEIDATÀ alt for NORTHWESTERN CATALAN dial of CATALAN-VALENCIAN-BALEAR [CLN]
LLEONES alt for LEONESE dial of ASTURIAN [AUB]
LLIMBUMI alt for LIMBUM [LIM]
LLOA dial of HOANYA [HON]
LLOGOLE alt for LOGOOLI [RAG]
LLUGULE alt for LOGOOLI [RAG]
LMAM alt for LAMAM [LMM]
LNGNGAM alt for LYNGNGAM dial of KHASI [KHI]
LÖMAUMBI dial of BABATANA [BAQ]
LO alt for GURO [GOA]
LO alt for LOO [LDO]
LO alt for TOGA [LHT]
LO dial of LOPA [LOY]
LO MONTANG alt for LOPA [LOY]
LOA alt for BARANG-BARANG dial of LAIYOLO [LJI]
LOA alt for LLOA dial of HOANYA [HON]
LOA' alt for BARANG-BARANG dial of LAIYOLO [LJI]
LOANATIT dial of LENAKEL [TNL]
LOANDE alt for MBUNDU, LOANDA [MLO]
LOANI alt for OYA'OYA [OYY]
LOARKI [LRK] lang, Pakistan
LOBA alt for LOPA [LOY]
LOBAHA alt for LOMBAHA dial of AMBAE, EAST [OMB]
LOBALA [LOQ] lang, DRC; also in Congo
LOBAT alt for BEDAWI [BEI]
LOBEDU dial of SOTHO, NORTHERN [SRT]
LOBER dial of DAGARA, NORTHERN [DGI]
LOBI [LOB] lang, Burkina Faso; also in Côte d'Ivoire, Ghana
LOBIRI alt for LOBI [LOB]
LOBO dial of MABAALE [MMZ]
LOBOBANGI alt for BANGI [BNI]
LOBODA dial of DOBU [DOB]
LOBR alt for LOBER dial of DAGARA, NORTHERN [DGI]
LOBU alt for TOMBONUWO [TXA]
LOBU dial of LOBU, LANAS [RUU]
LOBU, LANAS [RUU] lang, Malaysia (Sabah)
LOBU, TAMPIAS [LOW] lang, Malaysia (Sabah)
LOCAL SIGN LANGUAGE alt for PHILIPPINE SIGN LANGUAGE [PSP]
LOCKHART CREOLE alt for TORRES STRAIT CREOLE [TCS]
LOCO alt for MUTÚS [MUF]
LODA alt for LOLODA [LOL]

LODANG dial of SEKO PADANG [SKX]
LODHA alt for LODHI [LBM]
LODHANTI dial of BUNDELI [BNS]
LODHI [LBM] lang, India
LODHI dial of BUNDELI [BNS]
LODI alt for LODHI [LBM]
LOEMBIS alt for ALUMBIS dial of TAGAL MURUT [MVV]
LOFIT alt for LOPPIT [LPX]
LOG dial of BASAA [BAA]
LOG ACOLI alt for ACHOLI [ACO]
LOGANANGA dial of TUNEN [BAZ]
LOGAR dial of ORMURI [ORU]
LOGBA [LGQ] lang, Ghana
LOGBA alt for LUKPA [DOP]
LOGBO dial of AKPOSO [KPO]
LOGEYA dial of SALIBA [SBE]
LOGHOMA alt for LOMA [LOM]
LOGHON alt for TÈÈN [LOR]
LOGHTHA SIRYANOYTHA alt for WESTERN NEO-ARAMAIC [AMW]
LOGIR alt for LOGIRI dial of OTUHO [LOT]
LOGIRI dial of OTUHO [LOT]
LOGMA alt for LOGREMMA dial of KALAMSE [KNZ]
LOGMA alt for LOGREMMA dial of SAMOMA [KNZ]
LOGO [LOG] lang, DRC
LOGOKE alt for DAR EL KABIRA dial of TULISHI [TEY]
LOGOL [LOF] lang, Sudan
LOGONE alt for LAGWAN [KOT]
LOGONE-BIRNI dial of LAGWAN [KOT]
LOGONE-GANA dial of LAGWAN [KOT]
LOGOOLI [RAG] lang, Kenya
LOGORBAN alt for UMM DOREIN dial of MORO [MOR]
LOGORIK [LIU] lang, Sudan
LOGOTI alt for LOGO [LOG]
LOGOTOK dial of OTUHO [LOT]
LOGREMMA dial of KALAMSE [KNZ]
LOGREMMA dial of SAMOMA [KNZ]
LOGU alt for LONGGU [LGU]
LOGUDORESE alt for SARDINIAN, LOGUDORESE [SRD]
LOH alt for LOO [LDO]
LOHAR alt for LOHAR, LAHUL [LHL]
LOHAR, GADE [GDA] lang, India
LOHAR, LAHUL [LHL] lang, India
LOHARA dial of HO [HOC]
LOHARI alt for LOHAR, GADE [GDA]
LOHARI-MALPAHARIA dial of BENGALI [BNG]
LOHARI-SANTALI dial of SANTALI [SNT]
LOHBYA dial of GARHWALI [GBM]
LOHEI alt for LAHU [LAH]
LOHEIRN alt for NA dial of LAHU [LAH]
LOHI alt for LODHI [LBM]
LOHIKI alt for AKOYE [MIW]
LOHORONG alt for LORUNG, NORTHERN [LBR]
LOHORONG alt for LORUNG, SOUTHERN [LRR]
LOHPITTA RAJPUT LOHAR alt for LOHAR, GADE [GDA]
LOHRUNG alt for LORUNG, NORTHERN [LBR]

LOHRUNG alt for LORUNG, SOUTHERN [LRR]
LOHRUNG KHANAWA alt for LORUNG, NORTHERN [LBR]
LOHRUNG KHAP alt for LORUNG, SOUTHERN [LRR]
LOHRUNG KHATE alt for LORUNG, SOUTHERN [LRR]
LOH-TOGA alt for TOGA [LHT]
LOHU alt for BUSSA [DOX]
LOI alt for BALOI [BIZ]
LOI alt for HLAI [LIC]
LOI alt for LUI [LBA]
LOI alt for TAI LOI [TLQ]
LOI dial of BALOI [BIZ]
LOI dial of MEITEI [MNR]
LOINANG alt for SALUAN, COASTAL [LOE]
LOINDANG alt for SALUAN, COASTAL [LOE]
LOI-NGIRI alt for NGIRI [NGR]
LOIRYA alt for LOKOYA [LKY]
LOISU alt for LISU [LIS]
LOITAI dial of MAASAI [MET]
LOJA QUICHUA alt for QUICHUA, HIGHLAND, LOJA [QQU]
LOKAA [YAZ] lang, Nigeria
LOKAI dial of MADI [MHI]
LOKALO dial of NKUTU [NKW]
LOKATHAN dial of TESO [TEO]
LOKAY dial of DZANDO [DZN]
LOKE alt for LOKAA [YAZ]
LOKELE alt for KELE [KHY]
LOKEP alt for LUKEP [LOA]
LOKEP dial of AROP-LOKEP [APR]
LOKEWE alt for LOKEP dial of AROP-LOKEP [APR]
LOKO [LOK] lang, Sierra Leone; also in Guinea
LOKO alt for AIKLEP [MWG]
LOKO alt for GIMI [GIP]
LOKO alt for LOKAA [YAZ]
LOKOIYA alt for LOKOYA [LKY]
LOKOJA alt for LOKOYA [LKY]
LOKOLI alt for NKUKOLI [NBO]
LOKONDA alt for KONDA dial of MONGO-NKUNDU [MOM]
LOKONO alt for ARAWAK [ARW]
LOKOP alt for SAMBURU [SAQ]
LOKORO alt for PÄRI [LKR]
LOKOYA [LKY] lang, Sudan
LOKPA alt for LUKPA [DOP]
LOKUKOLI alt for NKUKOLI [NBO]
LOKURU alt for BANIATA [BNT]
LOKUTSU alt for KUSU [KSV]
LOKWALA alt for KONDA dial of MONGO-NKUNDU [MOM]
LOLA [LCD] lang, Indonesia (Maluku)
LOLA dial of LOLA [LCD]
LOLAK [LLQ] lang, Indonesia (Sulawesi)
LOLAKI alt for TOLAKI [LBW]
LOLANG dial of LAWANGAN [LBX]
LOLATAVOLA dial of SA [SSA]
LOLAYAN dial of MONGONDOW [MOG]
LOLE alt for BA'Ä-LOLEH dial of ROTE [ROT]
LOLEH alt for BA'Ä-LOLEH dial of ROTE [ROT]

LOLEI dial of MAMBAE [MGM]
LOLEKO alt for ILIKU dial of LUSENGO [LUS]
LOLI alt for LAULI dial of WEJEWA [WEW]
"LOLO" pejorative alt for YI, SICHUAN [III]
LOLO [LLB] lang, Mozambique
LOLO alt for CHUWABO [CHW]
LOLO alt for LOMWE [NGL]
LOLO alt for MANTSI [MUS]
LOLO alt for NKUNDO dial of MONGO-NKUNDU [MOM]
LOLOBAO dial of MERAMERA [MXM]
LOLOBI dial of SIWU [AKP]
LOLOBI-AKPAFU alt for SIWU [AKP]
LOLODA [LOL] lang, Indonesia (Maluku)
LOLOKARA alt for LOLOKARO dial of AMBAE, EAST [OMB]
LOLOKARO dial of AMBAE, EAST [OMB]
LOLOLO alt for FANAGOLO [FAO]
LOLOPANI alt for WANIB [AUK]
LOLSIWOI alt for LOLOKARO dial of AMBAE, EAST [OMB]
LOLTONG dial of APMA [APP]
LOLUBO alt for LULUBO [LUL]
LOLUE alt for BALUE dial of BAKUNDU-BALUE [BDU]
LOLYA dial of LOGO [LOG]
LOM [MFB] lang, Indonesia (Sumatra)
LOMA [LOI] lang, Côte d'Ivoire
LOMA [LOM] lang, Liberia
LOMA GRANDE dial of MAZATECO, MAZATLAN [VMZ]
LOMABAALE alt for MABAALE [MMZ]
LOMAIVITI [LMV] lang, Fiji
LOMAKKA alt for LOMA [LOI]
LOMAPO alt for LOMA [LOI]
LOMASSE alt for LOMA [LOI]
LOMAVREN [RMI] lang, Armenia; also in Azerbaijan, Russia (Asia), Syria
LOMBAHA dial of AMBAE, EAST [OMB]
LOMBARD [LMO] lang, Italy; also in Switzerland, USA
LOMBARDO alt for LOMBARD [LMO]
LOMBE alt for BAROMBI [BBI]
LOMBI [LMI] lang, DRC
LOMBI alt for BAROMBI [BBI]
LOMBO [LOO] lang, DRC
LOMBOK alt for SASAK [SAS]
LOMBOLE alt for MBOLE [MDQ]
LOMBOOKI dial of POKE [POF]
LOMBU dial of GBAYA, NORTHWEST [GYA]
LOMETIMETI dial of WHITESANDS [TNP]
LOMI alt for NAXI [NBF]
LOMIA alt for LOMYA dial of OTUHO [LOT]
LOMITAWA dial of BUNAMA [BDD]
LOMLOM alt for AYIWO [NFL]
LOMOGAI dial of LAMOGAI [LMG]
LOMON alt for LUMUN [LMD]
LOMONGO alt for EKONDA MONGO dial of MONGO-NKUNDU [MOM]
LOMONGO alt for MONGO-NKUNDU [MOM]
LOMORIK alt for TIMA [TMS]

LOMOTUA dial of BEMBA [BEM]
LOMOTWA alt for LOMOTUA dial of BEMBA [BEM]
LOMUE alt for LOMWE [NGL]
LOMURIKI alt for TIMA [TMS]
LOMWE [NGL] lang, Mozambique; also in Malawi
LOMYA dial of OTUHO [LOT]
LON BANGAG dial of KELABIT [KZI]
LONA dial of SAWILA [SWT]
LONCHONG alt for LONCONG [LCE]
LONCONG [LCE] lang, Indonesia (Sumatra)
LONDAI dial of SANTA CRUZ [STC]
LONDO alt for BALUNDU dial of BALUNDU-BIMA [NGO]
LONG AKAHSEMUKA dial of KAYAN, BARAM [KYS]
LONG ATAU dial of KENYAH, BAHAU RIVER [BWV]
LONG ATIP dial of KAYAN, BARAM [KYS]
LONG ATUN dial of KENYAH, SEBOB [SIB]
LONG BADAN dial of KAYAN, REJANG [REE]
LONG BANGAN dial of KENYAH, WESTERN [XKY]
LONG BANO alt for SIMEULUE [SMR]
LONG BANYUQ dial of KAYAN, MURIK [MXR]
LONG BAWAN alt for LUN BAWANG dial of LUNDAYEH [LND]
LONG BENA dial of KENYAH, BAHAU RIVER [BWV]
LONG BENTO' dial of MODANG [MXD]
LONG BLEH dial of KAYAN, BUSANG [BFG]
LONG BULAN alt for UMA BAKAH dial of KENYAH, WESTERN [XKY]
LONG EKANG dial of KENYAH, SEBOB [SIB]
LONG GENG dial of KAYAN, REJANG [REE]
LONG GLAT dial of MODANG [MXD]
LONG HAIR CUNA alt for KUNA, BORDER [KUA]
LONG IKANG alt for LONG EKANG dial of KENYAH, SEBOB [SIB]
LONG JEGAN dial of BERAWAN [LOD]
LONG KEHOBO dial of KAYAN, REJANG [REE]
LONG KELAWIT dial of KENYAH, KAYAN RIVER [KNH]
LONG KIPUT dial of KIPUT [KYI]
LONG LABID dial of KENYAH, TUTOH [TTW]
LONG LUYANG dial of KENYAH, SEBOB [SIB]
LONG MURUN dial of KAYAN, REJANG [REE]
LONG NAWAN dial of KENYAH, KAYAN RIVER [KNH]
LONG PATA dial of BERAWAN [LOD]
LONG POKUN dial of KENYAH, SEBOB [SIB]
LONG PUYUNGAN dial of KENYAH, BAHAU RIVER [BWV]
LONG SEMIANG dial of KAYAN, MURIK [MXR]
LONG TERAWAN dial of BERAWAN [LOD]
LONG TUTOH dial of KIPUT [KYI]
LONG WAI alt for KELINGAN dial of MODANG [MXD]
LONG WAT dial of KENYAH, TUTOH [TTW]
LONG WE alt for KELINGAN dial of MODANG [MXD]
LONGA alt for AMARA [AIE]
LONGA alt for LONGTO [WOK]
LONGANA dial of AMBAE, EAST [OMB]
LONGANDU alt for NGANDO [NXD]
LONGARIM [LOH] lang, Sudan

LONGBIA dial of KENYAH, KAYAN RIVER [KNH]
LONGBO alt for LONGTO [WOK]
LONGCHING dial of NAGA, KONYAK [NBE]
LONGCHUAN dial of ACHANG [ACN]
LONGDU dial of CHINESE, MIN NAN [CFR]
LONGE-LONGE dial of SHI [SHR]
LONGGU [LGU] lang, Solomon Islands
LONG-HAIRED LACHI alt for LIPUPI dial of LACHI
    [LBT]
LONGICH alt for MBULUNGISH [MBV]
LONGKHAI dial of NAGA, KONYAK [NBE]
LONGLA dial of NAGA, AO [NJO]
LONGMEIN dial of NAGA, KONYAK [NBE]
LONGMI dial of RAWANG [RAW]
LONGNAN alt for NING-LONG dial of CHINESE,
    HAKKA [HAK]
LONGO dial of MONGO-NKUNDU [MOM]
LONGOMBE dial of MONGO-NKUNDU [MOM]
LONGORO dial of DEG [MZW]
LONGPHI dial of NAGA, TASE [NST]
LONGRI dial of NAGA, TASE [NST]
LONGSHAN dial of TUJIA, NORTHERN [TJI]
LONGTO [WOK] lang, Cameroon
LONGUDA [LNU] lang, Nigeria
LONGURA alt for LONGUDA [LNU]
LONGWA dial of NAGA, KONYAK [NBE]
LONGXI dial of QIANG, SOUTHERN [QMR]
LONIO alt for LONIU [LOS]
LONIU [LOS] lang, Papua New Guinea
LONKUNDO alt for NKUNDO dial of MONGO-
    NKUNDU [MOM]
LONKUNDU alt for NKUNDO dial of MONGO-
    NKUNDU [MOM]
LONTES dial of HAKO [HAO]
LONTJONG alt for LONCONG [LCE]
LONTO alt for LONGTO [WOK]
LONTO alt for SOUTHERN CHUMBURUNG dial
    of CHUMBURUNG [NCU]
LONTOMBA alt for NTOMBA [NTO]
LONWOLWOL [CRC] lang, Vanuatu
LONZO [LNZ] lang, DRC
LOO [LDO] lang, Nigeria
LOO alt for NOY [NOY]
LOOCNON alt for INONHAN [LOC]
LOODIYA alt for DADIYA [DBD]
LOOFAA dial of DADIYA [DBD]
LOOFIYO dial of DADIYA [DBD]
LOOKNON alt for INONHAN [LOC]
LOOKNON dial of INONHAN [LOC]
LOOMA alt for LOMA [LOM]
LOOMBO alt for OMBO [OML]
LOP dial of UYGHUR [UIG]
LOPA [LOP] lang, Nigeria
LOPA [LOY] lang, Nepal
LOPAR alt for SAAMI, SKOLT [LPK]
LOPAWA alt for LOPA [LOP]
LOPHOMI alt for NAGA, SANGTAM [NSA]
LOPI [LOV] lang, Myanmar
LOPID alt for LOPPIT [LPX]
LOPIT alt for LOPPIT [LPX]
LOPPIT [LPX] lang, Sudan

LOQUIA alt for LOKOYA [LKY]
LOR alt for KHLOR [LLO]
LOR alt for LURI [LRI]
LORABADA alt for KAKI AE [TBD]
LORANG [LRN] lang, Indonesia (Maluku)
LORANG BUKIT alt for BISAYA, BRUNEI [BSB]
LORANG BUKIT alt for BISAYA, SARAWAK [BSD]
LORD HOWE alt for ONTONG JAVA [LUN]
LOREDIAKARKAR [LNN] lang, Vanuatu
LORENZO alt for YANESHA' [AME]
LORETANO alt for LORETO dial of TRINITARIO
    [TRN]
LORETO dial of TRINITARIO [TRN]
LORHON alt for TÈÈN [LOR]
LORI alt for LURI [LRI]
LORI dial of JUR MODO [BEX]
LORIDJA alt for PINTUPI-LURITJA [PIU]
LORMA alt for LOMA [LOM]
LORON alt for TÈÈN [LOR]
LORRAINE dial of FRENCH [FRN]
LORUNG, NORTHERN [LBR] lang, Nepal
LORUNG, SOUTHERN [LRR] lang, Nepal
LORWAMA dial of OTUHO [LOT]
LOS REYES METZONTLA POPOLOCA alt for
    POPOLOCA, MEZONTLA [PBE]
LOSA dial of NAKANAI [NAK]
LOSAKA alt for SAKA dial of NKUTU [NKW]
LOSENGO alt for LUSENGO [LUS]
LOSI dial of DEHU [DEU]
LOSIARA dial of TEOP [TIO]
LOSO alt for LOSA dial of NAKANAI [NAK]
LOSSO alt for LAMA [LAS]
LOSSO alt for NAWDM [NMZ]
LOSU alt for NAWDM [NMZ]
LOTE [UVL] lang, Papua New Guinea
LOTHA alt for NAGA, LOTHA [NJH]
LOTORA dial of MAEWO, CENTRAL [MWO]
LOTSU-PIRI alt for TSO [LDP]
LOTUD [DTR] lang, Malaysia (Sabah)
LOTUHO alt for OTUHO [LOT]
LOTUKA alt for OTUHO [LOT]
LOTUKO alt for OTUHO [LOT]
LOTUNI alt for MAKRANI dial of BALOCHI,
    SOUTHERN [BCC]
LOTUXO alt for OTUHO [LOT]
LOU [LOJ] lang, Papua New Guinea
LOU alt for KAKI AE [TBD]
LOU alt for TORRICELLI [TEI]
LOU dial of NUER [NUS]
LOUCHEUX alt for GWICH'IN [KUC]
LOUCHEUX alt for WESTERN CANADA GWICH'IN
    dial of GWICHIN [KUC]
LOUDO alt for LOWUDO dial of OTUHO [LOT]
LOUGAW dial of MUYUW [MYW]
LOUISIANA CREOLE FRENCH [LOU] lang, USA
LOULOU alt for MUTURAMI dial of GIZIGA, SOUTH
    [GIZ]
LOUN [LOX] lang, Indonesia (Maluku)
LOUOME dial of GBAGYI [GBR]
LOUTO alt for LUTOS dial of LUTOS [NDY]
LOUTO alt for RUTO dial of LUTOS [NDY]

LOUXIRU alt for OTUKE [OTU]
LOUYI alt for LUYANA [LAV]
LOVAEA alt for MAKU'A [LVA]
LOVAIA alt for MAKU'A [LVA]
LOVALE alt for LUVALE [LUE]
LOVARI dial of ROMANI, VLAX [RMY]
LOVARÍCKO alt for LOVARI dial of ROMANI, VLAX
[RMY]
LOVE alt for BRAO [BRB]
LOVE alt for LAVE [BRB]
LOVEDU alt for LOBEDU dial of SOTHO,
NORTHERN [SRT]
LOVEN alt for LAVEN [LBO]
LOVI dial of NZANYI [NJA]
LOVONI alt for NORTHEAST VITI LEVU dial of
FIJIAN [FJI]
LOW ALEMANNISCH dial of ALEMANNISCH
[GSW]
LOW GERMAN alt for PLAUTDIETSCH [GRN]
LOW GERMAN alt for SAXON, LOW [SXN]
LOW LUGBARA alt for ARINGA [LUC]
LOW MALAY alt for BAZAAR MALAY dial of MALAY
[MLI]
LOW PIEMONTESE dial of PIEMONTESE [PMS]
LOWA alt for BARANG-BARANG dial of LAIYOLO
[LJI]
LOWER ADELE dial of ADELE [ADE]
LOWER ASARO dial of TOKANO [ZUH]
LOWER BAL dial of SVAN [SVA]
LOWER BAMU dial of BAMU [BCF]
LOWER BELE dial of DANI, LOWER GRAND
VALLEY [DNI]
LOWER BISAYA dial of BISAYA, SARAWAK
[BSD]
LOWER BONDO dial of BONDO [BFW]
LOWER CARNIOLA dial of SLOVENIAN [SLV]
LOWER CHEHALIS dial of QUINAULT [QUN]
LOWER CHEROKEE alt for ELATI dial of
CHEROKEE [CER]
LOWER CHINOOK alt for CHINOOK [CHH]
LOWER CHULYM dial of CHULYM [CHU]
LOWER CIRCASSIAN alt for ADYGHE [ADY]
LOWER COWLITZ alt for COWLITZ [COW]
LOWER EGYPT ARABIC alt for ARABIC,
EGYPTIAN SPOKEN [ARZ]
LOWER ENGADINE dial of ROMANSCH [RHE]
LOWER GIO dial of DAN [DAF]
LOWER GRAND VALLEY HITIGIMA dial of DANI,
LOWER GRAND VALLEY [DNI]
LOWER GROMA dial of GROMA [GRO]
LOWER KAYAN KENYAH dial of KENYAH, KAYAN
RIVER [KNH]
LOWER KENYANG dial of KENYANG [KEN]
LOWER KIMBIN dial of DANI, LOWER GRAND
VALLEY [DNI]
LOWER KINNAURI alt for KINNAURI [KFK]
LOWER LADAKHI alt for SHAMMA dial of LADAKHI
[LBJ]
LOWER LAGAIP dial of HEWA [HAM]
LOWER LAKE POMO alt for POMO, SOUTH-
EASTERN [PEO]

LOWER LAMET dial of LAMET [LBN]
LOWER LOZYVIN alt for WESTERN VOGUL dial
of MANSI [MNS]
LOWER LUSATIAN alt for SORBIAN, LOWER
[WEE]
LOWER LUZH dial of INGRIAN [IZH]
LOWER MAHASU PAHARI dial of PAHARI,
MAHASU [BFZ]
LOWER MBO alt for MIENGE dial of BASSOSSI
[BSI]
LOWER MOREHEAD alt for KUNJA [PEP]
LOWER MORI alt for MORI BAWAH [XMZ]
LOWER MORTLOCK dial of MORTLOCKESE [MRL]
LOWER MURUT dial of TIMUGON MURUT [TIH]
LOWER NAR alt for NAR dial of NAR PHU [NPA]
LOWER NEPA TUNGIR dial of EVENKI [EVN]
LOWER PIMAN alt for PIMA BAJO, CHIHUAHUA
[PMB]
LOWER PIMAN alt for PIMA BAJO, SONORA [PIA]
LOWER PRASUN dial of PRASUNI [PRN]
LOWER PYRAMID alt for WALAK [WLW]
LOWER SAMENAGE dial of SILIMO [WUL]
LOWER SCHLESISCH alt for SILESIAN, LOWER
[SLI]
LOWER STIENG alt for STIENG, BUDEH [STT]
LOWER TANUDAN alt for KALINGA, LOWER
TANUDAN [KML]
LOWER WARIA alt for ZIA [ZIA]
LOWER YANGZE MANDARIN alt for JINGHUAI
GUANHUA dial of CHINESE, MANDARIN [CHN]
LOWER YAZGULYAM dial of YAZGULYAM [YAH]
LOWER YEI dial of YEI [JEI]
LOWER ZYPHE dial of ZAKHRING [ZKR]
LOWER ZYPHE dial of ZYPHE [ZYP]
LOWLAND BALI dial of BALI [BZC]
LOWLAND CHATINO alt for CHATINO,
TATALTEPEC [CTA]
LOWLAND HUARIJÍO dial of HUARIJIO [VAR]
LOWLAND INGA alt for INGA, JUNGLE [INJ]
LOWLAND JICALTEPEC MIXTECO alt for
MIXTECO, PINOTEPA NACIONAL [MIO]
LOWLAND LITHUANIAN alt for SHAMAITISH dial
of LITHUANIAN [LIT]
LOWLAND MAZATECO alt for MAZATECO,
JALAPA DE DÍAZ [MAJ]
LOWLAND NAPO QUECHUA alt for QUICHUA,
LOWLAND, NAPO [QLN]
LOWLAND NAPO QUICHUA alt for QUICHUA,
LOWLAND, NAPO [QLN]
LOWLAND NUNG alt for CHINESE, YUE [YUH]
LOWLAND OAXACA CHONTAL alt for CHONTAL
DE OAXACA, COSTA [CLO]
LOWLAND SCOTTISH dial of ENGLISH [ENG]
LOWLAND TAKELMA alt for TAKELMA [TKM]
LOWLAND TOTONACA alt for TOTONACA,
PAPANTLA [TOP]
LOWLAND TZELTAL alt for TZELTAL, BACHAJÓN
[TZB]
LOWLAND YAO alt for KIM MUN [MJI]
LOWOI alt for LOKOYA [LKY]
LOWUDO dial of OTUHO [LOT]

LOXICHA ZAPOTEC alt for ZAPOTECO, LOXICHA [ZTP]

LOXICHA ZAPOTECO alt for ZAPOTECO, SAN BALTÁZAR LOXICHA [ZPX]

LOYU alt for LOPA [LOY]

LOZI [LOZ] lang, Zambia; also in Botswana, Namibia, Zimbabwe

LOZI alt for LODHI [LBM]

LOZOUA dial of DIDA, YOCOBOUE [GUD]

LSB alt for BRAZILIAN SIGN LANGUAGE [BZS]

LSF alt for FRENCH SIGN LANGUAGE [FSL]

LSHAN SRAY alt for SENAYA [SYN]

LSI RAI alt for DUMI [DUS]

LSQ alt for QUEBEC SIGN LANGUAGE [FCS]

LÜ [KHB] lang, China; also in Laos, Myanmar, Thailand, Viet Nam

LÜZÜ alt for LISU dial of ERSU [ERS]

LU alt for LÜ [KHB]

LU alt for NUNG [NUN]

LU dial of LUGBARA [LUG]

LU SHI LISU dial of LISU [LIS]

LUA alt for LAWA, WESTERN [LCP]

LUA alt for NIELLIM [NIE]

LU'A alt for PALU'E [PLE]

LUA' [PRB] lang, Thailand

LUAAN alt for BAJAU, INDONESIAN [BDL]

LUAC dial of DINKA, NORTHEASTERN [DIP]

LUAC dial of DINKA, SOUTHWESTERN [DIK]

LUAIC alt for LUAC dial of DINKA, NORTHEASTERN [DIP]

LUALABA KINGWANA dial of SWAHILI, CONGO [SWC]

LUANA alt for LUYANA [LAV]

LUANDA alt for MBUNDU, LOANDA [MLO]

LUANG [LEX] lang, Indonesia (Maluku)

LUANG dial of LUANG [LEX]

LUANG PRABANG dial of KHMU [KJG]

LUANG PRABANG dial of LAO [NOL]

LUANGIUA alt for ONTONG JAVA [LUN]

LUANGIUA dial of ONTONG JAVA [LUN]

LUANGKORI dial of KISI, SOUTHERN [KSS]

LUANO alt for LUYANA [LAV]

LUANO dial of LALA-BISA [LEB]

LUAPULA alt for LUUNDA dial of BEMBA [BEM]

LUBA dial of DUSUN, CENTRAL [DTP]

LUBA KAONDE alt for KAONDE [KQN]

LUBA-GARENGANZE alt for SANGA [SNG]

LUBA-HEMBA alt for HEMBA [HEM]

LUBA-KASAI [LUB] lang, DRC

LUBA-KATANGA [LUH] lang, DRC

LUBALE alt for LUVALE [LUE]

LUBA-LULUA alt for LUBA-KASAI [LUB]

LUBANG dial of TAGALOG [TGL]

LUBA-SANGA alt for SANGA [SNG]

LUBA-SHABA alt for LUBA-KATANGA [LUH]

LUBA-SONGI alt for SONGE [SOP]

LUBA-TIEMPO ITNEG alt for ITNEG, SOUTHERN [ITT]

LUBEDU alt for LOBEDU dial of SOTHO, NORTHERN [SRT]

LUBILA [KCC] lang, Nigeria

LUBILO alt for LUBILA [KCC]

LUBOLO alt for BOLO [BLV]

LUBU [LCF] lang, Indonesia (Sumatra)

LUBUAGAN dial of KALINGA, LUBUAGAN [KNB]

LUBUKUSU alt for BUKUSU [BUL]

LUBULEBULE alt for AMBA [RWM]

LUBULEBULE alt for KIGUMU dial of AMBA [RWM]

LUBWISI alt for TALINGA-BWISI [TLJ]

LUBWISSI alt for TALINGA-BWISI [TLJ]

LUCANIAN alt for NORTHERN CALABRESE-LUCANO dial of NAPOLETANO-CALABRESE [NPL]

LUCAZI alt for LUCHAZI [LCH]

LUCERNE dial of ALEMANNISCH [GSW]

LUCHAZI [LCH] lang, Angola; also in Zambia

LUCHU alt for OKINAWAN, CENTRAL [RYU]

LUCUMI [LUQ] lang, Cuba

LUDAMA alt for ADHOLA [ADH]

LUDIAN [LUD] lang, Russia (Europe)

LUDIC alt for LUDIAN [LUD]

LUDIOPA dial of GANDA [LAP]

LUDUMOR alt for SHWAI [SHW]

LUDUULI alt for RULI [RUC]

LUE alt for BALUE dial of BAKUNDU-BALUE [BDU]

LUE alt for LÜ [KHB]

LUENA alt for LUVALE [LUE]

LUF alt for HERMIT [LLF]

LUFU [LDQ] lang, Nigeria

LUGA alt for LUNGGA [LGA]

LUGABULA alt for GABULA dial of SOGA [SOG]

LUGAGON alt for NALIK [NAL]

LUGANDA alt for GANDA [LAP]

LUGAT dial of KENYAH, TUTOH [TTW]

LUGBA alt for LUKPA [DOP]

LUGBARA [LUG] lang, Uganda; also in DRC

LUGGOY dial of MUSGU [MUG]

LUGISU alt for MASABA [MYX]

LUGISU dial of MASABA [MYX]

LUGITAMA alt for PAHI [LGT]

LUGOOLI alt for LOGOOLI [RAG]

LUGOVO MARI alt for MARI, LOW [MAL]

LUGULU alt for RUGURU [RUF]

LUGUNGU alt for GUNGU [RUB]

LUGURU alt for RUGURU [RUF]

LUGWE dial of LUYIA [LUY]

LUGWERE alt for GWERE [GWR]

LUHADYO alt for HADYO dial of NYOLE [NUJ]

LUHANGA alt for WANGA dial of LUYIA [LUY]

LUHISHI alt for NYI dial of LAHU [LAH]

LUHTU dial of TSOU [TSY]

LUHU [LCQ] lang, Indonesia (Maluku)

LUHU dial of LUHU [LCQ]

LUHUA dial of QIANG, NORTHERN [CNG]

LUHUPPA alt for NAGA, TANGKHUL [NMF]

LUHUSHI alt for NYI dial of LAHU [LAH]

LUHYA alt for LUYIA [LUY]

LUI [LBA] lang, Myanmar

LUI alt for LUYANA [LAV]

LUIMBE alt for LUIMBI [LUM]

LUIMBI [LUM] lang, Angola

LUISEÑO [LUI] lang, USA

LUISEÑO dial of LUISENO [LUI]
LUJASH alt for LUCHAZI [LCH]
LUJASI alt for LUCHAZI [LCH]
LUJAZI alt for LUCHAZI [LCH]
LUKAMIUTE alt for KALAPUYA [KAL]
LUKANGA alt for TWA dial of LENJE [LEH]
LUKASA dial of BANDI [GBA]
LUKENYI alt for KENYI [LKE]
LUKEP [LOA] lang, Papua New Guinea
LUKEP alt for AROP-LOKEP [APR]
LUKEP alt for LOKEP dial of AROP-LOKEP [APR]
LUKETE alt for KETE [KCV]
LUKHA alt for LOGOL [LOF]
LUKHAI alt for LUSHAI [LSH]
LUKO alt for LOKAA [YAZ]
LUKOLWE dial of NKOYA [NKA]
LUKPA [DOP] lang, Benin; also in Togo
LUKSHI alt for LUSHI dial of ZEEM [ZUA]
LUKSHI dial of DASS [DOT]
LUKUMEL dial of KHAM, TAKALE [KJL]
LUL dial of ANUAK [ANU]
LULAMOGI alt for LAMOGI dial of SOGA [SOG]
LULE alt for SAAMI, LULE [LPL]
LULEKE dial of TSONGA [TSO]
LULI dial of DOMARI [RMT]
LULUBA alt for LULUBO [LUL]
LULUBO [LUL] lang, Sudan
LULUMO alt for OLULUMO-IKOM [IKO]
LULUYIA alt for LUYIA [LUY]
LUM LAO alt for LAO [NOL]
LUMADALE alt for LAMBADI [LMN]
LUMAETE dial of KAYELI [KZL]
LUMAITI alt for LUMAETE dial of KAYELI [KZL]
LUMAN alt for TIRA LUMUM dial of TIRA [TIR]
LUMARA alt for LUMAETE dial of KAYELI [KZL]
LUMASABA alt for MASABA [MYX]
LUMBA-YAKKHA [LUU] lang, Nepal
LUMBEE [LUA] lang, USA
LUMBI alt for LOMBI [LMI]
LUMBIS alt for ALUMBIS dial of TAGAL MURUT [MVV]
LUMBU [LUP] lang, Gabon; also in Congo
LUMBU alt for LIMBU [LIF]
LUMBU dial of ILA [ILB]
LUMBWA alt for MAASAI [MET]
LUMENYA alt for MENYA dial of NYOLE [NUJ]
LUMMI dial of SALISH, STRAITS [STR]
LUMUN [LMD] lang, Sudan
LUN BAWANG alt for LUNDAYEH [LND]
LUN BAWANG dial of LUNDAYEH [LND]
LUN DAYA alt for LUNDAYEH [LND]
LUN DAYAH alt for LUNDAYEH [LND]
LUN DAYAH dial of LUNDAYEH [LND]
LUN DAYE alt for LUNDAYEH [LND]
LUN DAYE dial of LUNDAYEH [LND]
LUN DAYEH alt for LUNDAYEH [LND]
LUN DAYOH alt for LUNDAYEH [LND]
LUN LOD alt for LUNDAYEH [LND]
LUNA [LUJ] lang, DRC
LUNAN dial of KENYAH, WESTERN [XKY]
LUNANAKHA [LUK] lang, Bhutan

LUND dial of MANDJAK [MFV]
LUNDA [LVN] lang, Zambia; also in Angola, DRC
LUNDA alt for MBUNDU, LOANDA [MLO]
LUNDA KALUNDA dial of LUNDA [LVN]
LUNDA KAMBOVE alt for RUUND [RND]
LUNDA KAMBOVE dial of LUNDA [LVN]
LUNDA NDEMBU dial of LUNDA [LVN]
LUNDA-KAMBORO alt for RUUND [RND]
LUNDAYA alt for LUNDAYEH [LND]
LUNDAYEH [LND] lang, Indonesia (Kalimantan);
   also in Brunei, Malaysia (Sarawak)
LUNDU alt for BALUNDU dial of BALUNDU-BIMA [NGO]
LUNDU alt for BIATAH [BTH]
LUNDUR alt for LANGAS dial of POLCI [POL]
LUNDWE dial of ILA [ILB]
LUNGALUNGA alt for MINIGIR [VMG]
LUNGCHANG dial of NAGA, TASE [NST]
LUNGGA [LGA] lang, Solomon Islands
LUNGMI alt for LONGMI dial of RAWANG [RAW]
LUNGRI dial of NAGA, TASE [NST]
LUNGU alt for IDUN [LDB]
LUNGU alt for RUNGU dial of MAMBWE-LUNGU [MGR]
LUNGULU alt for MWAMBA dial of NYAKYUSA-NGONDE [NYY]
LUNGWA alt for RUNGWA [RNW]
LUN'GWIYE alt for PRINCIPENSE [PRE]
LUNIGIANO dial of EMILIANO-ROMAGNOLO [EML]
LUNTU dial of SALAMPASU [SLX]
LUNTUMBA alt for NTOMBA [NTO]
LUNUBE MADO dial of DANO [ASO]
LUNYANEKA alt for NYANEKA [NYK]
LUNYOLE alt for NYOLE [NUJ]
LUNYOLE alt for NYORE [NYD]
LUNYORE alt for NYORE [NYD]
LUO [LUO] lang, Kenya; also in Tanzania
LUO [LUW] lang, Cameroon
LUOBA alt for ADI [ADI]
LUOBA, BOGA'ER [ADI] lang, India; also in China
LUOBA, YIDU [CLK] lang, India; also in China
LUOBOHE MIAO alt for HMONG, LUOPOHE [HML]
LUOBU alt for LOP dial of UYGHUR [UIG]
LUOFU dial of SHE [SHX]
LUOHUA-HAYAN-BAOXIAN alt for HA dial of HLAI [LIC]
LUORAVETLAN alt for CHUKOT [CKT]
LUOSHAO dial of CHINESE, XIANG [HSN]
LUPA alt for LOPA [LOP]
LUPPA alt for NAGA, TANGKHUL [NMF]
LUR alt for ALUR [ALZ]
LUR alt for LURI [LRI]
LURAGOLI alt for LOGOOLI [RAG]
LURI [LDD] lang, Nigeria
LURI [LRI] lang, Iran; also in Iraq, USA
LURI alt for ALUR [ALZ]
LURI dial of LURI [LRI]
LURU alt for LARA' [LRA]
LURUTY-TAPUYA alt for YURUTI [YUI]
LUS dial of MFUMTE [NFU]
LUSA alt for ZAAR dial of SAYA [SAY]

LUSAAMIA alt for SAAMIA dial of LUYIA [LUY]
LUSABI alt for SABI dial of NYOLE [NUJ]
LUSAGO alt for LUSHAI [LSH]
LUSAI alt for LUSHAI [LSH]
LUSAMIA alt for SAAMIA dial of LUYIA [LUY]
LUSATIAN alt for SORBIAN, LOWER [WEE]
LUSEI alt for LUSHAI [LSH]
LUSENGE dial of LEGA-MWENGA [LGM]
LUSENGO [LUS] lang, DRC
LUSENGO POTO dial of LUSENGO [LUS]
LUSERNESE CIMBRIAN dial of CIMBRIAN [CIM]
LUSHAI [LSH] lang, India; also in Bangladesh,
    Myanmar
LUSHANGI dial of NKOYA [NKA]
LUSHEI alt for LUSHAI [LSH]
LUSHI dial of ZEEM [ZUA]
LUSHISA alt for KISA dial of LUYIA [LUY]
LUSHNU alt for SVAN [SVA]
LUSHOOTSEED [LUT] lang, USA
LUSI [KHL] lang, Papua New Guinea
LUSINGA alt for SINGA [SGM]
LUSITANO-ROMANI alt for PORTUGUESE
    CALÃO dial of CALO [RMR]
LUSOGA alt for SOGA [SOG]
LUSONG alt for PENAN LUSONG dial of PENAN,
    WESTERN [PNE]
LUSONGE alt for SONGE [SOP]
LUSU alt for LISU [LIS]
LUTANGAN dial of SAMA, BALANGINGI [SSE]
LUTANGO alt for LUTANGAN dial of SAMA,
    BALANGINGI [SSE]
LUTAOS alt for BAJAU, INDONESIAN [BDL]
LUTAYAOS alt for BAJAU, INDONESIAN [BDL]
LUTCHAZ alt for LUCHAZI [LCH]
LUTENGA alt for TENGA dial of SOGA [SOG]
LUTHA alt for NAGA, LOTHA [NJH]
LUTIEN dial of NAXI [NBF]
LUTISE dial of DOGOSE [DOS]
LUTKUHWAR alt for YIDGHA [YDG]
LUTO alt for LUTOS dial of LUTOS [NDY]
LUTO alt for RUTO dial of LUTOS [NDY]
LUTOS [NDY] lang, CAR; also in Chad
LUTOS dial of LUTOS [NDY]
LUTSHASE alt for LUCHAZI [LCH]
LUTU alt for SOUTHEAST VITI LEVU dial of FIJIAN
    [FJI]
LUTZE alt for NUNG [NUN]
LU-TZU alt for LISU [LIS]
LUTZU alt for NUNG [NUN]
LUU alt for KHMU [KJG]
LUUNDA alt for RUUND [RND]
LUUNDA dial of BEMBA [BEM]
LUVA alt for LUBA-KASAI [LUB]
LUVALE [LUE] lang, Zambia; also in Angola
LUVUMA dial of GANDA [LAP]
LUVURE alt for VUTE [VUT]
LUWA alt for LAWA, WESTERN [LCP]
LUWA dial of HUBA [KIR]
LUWANGAN alt for LAWANGAN [LBX]
LUWATI [LUV] lang, Oman
LUWESA alt for WESA dial of NYOLE [NUJ]

LUWO [LWO] lang, Sudan
LUWU alt for TAE' [ROB]
LUWU dial of BUGIS [BPR]
LUWU' alt for LUWU dial of BUGIS [BPR]
LUWU' alt for TOALA' [TLZ]
LUWUNDA alt for RUUND [RND]
LUXAGE alt for LUCHAZI [LCH]
LUXEMBOURGEOIS [LUX] lang, Luxembourg;
    also in Belgium, France, Germany, USA
LUXEMBOURGISH alt for LUXEMBOURGEOIS
    [LUX]
LUXEMBURGIAN alt for LUXEMBOURGEOIS [LUX]
LUXEMBURGISH alt for LUXEMBOURGEOIS [LUX]
LUXI dial of ACHANG [ACN]
LUYA-GINAM-MAMUSI dial of PINAI-HAGAHAI
    [PNN]
LUYANA [LAV] lang, Zambia; also in Angola, Namibia
LUYI alt for LUYANA [LAV]
LUYIA [LUY] lang, Kenya; also in Uganda
LUZIMBA alt for ZEMBA [DHM]
LVOVA dial of SANTA CRUZ [STC]
L'WA alt for LAWA, WESTERN [LCP]
LWALU [LWA] lang, DRC
LWAMBA alt for AMBA [RWM]
LWENA alt for LUVALE [LUE]
LWIMBE alt for LUIMBI [LUM]
LWIMBI alt for LUIMBI [LUM]
LWINDJA alt for HWINDJA dial of SHI [SHR]
LWISUKHA alt for ISUKHA dial of IDAKHO-ISUKHA-
    TIRIKI [IDA]
LWO alt for ACHOLI [ACO]
LWO alt for LANGO [LAJ]
LWO alt for LUWO [LWO]
LWOO alt for ACHOLI [ACO]
LWOO alt for LANGO [LAJ]
LWOWA alt for LVOVA dial of SANTA CRUZ [STC]
LXLOUKXLE alt for //XEGWI [XEG]
LY alt for LÜ [KHB]
LY HA dial of HUNG [HNU]
LYAASA alt for YASA [YKO]
LYANGMAY alt for NAGA, LIANGMAI [NJN]
LYASE alt for GWAMHI-WURI [BGA]
LYASE-NE alt for GWAMHI-WURI [BGA]
LYASSA alt for YASA [YKO]
LYÉLÉ [LEE] lang, Burkina Faso
LYENGMAI alt for KOIRENG [NKD]
LYENGMAI alt for NAGA, LIANGMAI [NJN]
LYEN-LYEM alt for ZAHAO dial of CHIN, FALAM
    [HBH]
LYENTE alt for LENTE dial of CHIN, FALAM [HBH]
LYING alt for WULA dial of PSIKYE [KVJ]
LYNGNGAM dial of KHASI [KHI]
LYO dial of MAK [MKG]
LYONNAIS dial of FRANCO-PROVENCAL [FRA]
LYONS SIGN LANGUAGE [LSG] lang, France
LYUDIC alt for LUDIAN [LUD]
LYUDIKOVIAN alt for LUDIAN [LUD]
LYY dial of KHMU [KJG]
MÄRKISCH-BRANDENBURGISCH alt for MARK-
    BRANDENBURG dial of SAXON, LOW [SXN]
MA [MSJ] lang, DRC

MA alt for BILALA dial of NABA [MNE]
MA alt for KAMO [KCQ]
MA alt for MAA [CMA]
MA dial of BINAHARI [BXZ]
MA BUWAL alt for BUWAL [BHS]
MA DALA alt for MANDALA dial of MABA [MDE]
MA KRUNG alt for MAA [CMA]
MA KU alt for MLABRI [MRA]
MA NDABA alt for MANDABA dial of MABA [MDE]
MA NGAN alt for MAA [CMA]
MA TO alt for MAA [CMA]
MA XOP alt for MAA [CMA]
MAA [CMA] lang, Viet Nam
MAA alt for MAASAI [MET]
MAA alt for MANO [MEV]
MA'A alt for MBUGU [MHD]
MAA' alt for MAA [CMA]
MAABAN alt for MABAAN [MFZ]
MAACINA alt for FULFULDE, MAASINA [FUL]
MA'ADI alt for MA'DI [MHI]
MA'AGING dial of KAYAN, REJANG [REE]
MAAKA [MEW] lang, Nigeria
MAALOULA alt for MA<LULA dial of WESTERN
    NEO-ARAMAIC [AMW]
MAALULA alt for MA<LULA dial of WESTERN NEO-
    ARAMAIC [AMW]
MAALULA alt for WESTERN NEO-ARAMAIC [AMW]
MAANGELLA alt for MADNGELE [ZML]
MA'ANJAN alt for MA'ANYAN [MHY]
MAANYAK DAYAK alt for MA'ANYAN [MHY]
MA'ANYAN [MHY] lang, Indonesia (Kalimantan)
MAAQ alt for MAA [CMA]
MAARO alt for OIRATA [OIA]
MAASA alt for YASA [YKO]
MAASAI [MET] lang, Kenya; also in Tanzania
MA'ASAE alt for MAKASAE [MKZ]
MAAY [QMA] lang, Somalia
MABA [MDE] lang, Chad
MABA [MQA] lang, Indonesia (Maluku)
MABAA alt for MABA [MDE]
MABAALE [MMZ] lang, DRC
MABAAN [MFZ] lang, Sudan
MABAHN dial of BASSA [BAS]
MABAK alt for MABA [MDE]
MABAKA ITNEG alt for KALINGA, MABAKA VALLEY
    [KKG]
MABALE alt for MABAALE [MMZ]
MABAN alt for MABA [MDE]
MABANG alt for MABA [MDE]
MABANGI alt for MABA [MDE]
MABAS dial of VEMGO-MABAS [VEM]
MABE alt for MAHEI [MJA]
MABEA alt for NGUMBA [NMG]
MABEA alt for MABI dial of NGUMBA [NMG]
MABENDI alt for BENDI [BCT]
MABENI alt for BENDI [BCT]
MABI alt for NGUMBA [NMG]
MABI dial of NGUMBA [NMG]
MABIHA alt for MAVIHA dial of MAKONDE [KDE]
MABILA alt for MAMBILA, NIGERIA [MZK]
MABITI alt for LIKA [LIK]

MABLEI dial of KALUMPANG [KLI]
MA'BO alt for NGBAKA MA'BO [NBM]
MABO-BARKUL alt for BO-RUKUL [MAE]
MABO-BARUKUL alt for BO-RUKUL [MAE]
MABODESE alt for MADIPIA dial of MAYOGO [MDM]
MABOKO dial of DZANDO [DZN]
MABOZO alt for MADIPIA dial of MAYOGO [MDM]
MABRI alt for MLABRI [MRA]
MABUE alt for SATERÉ-MAWÉ [MAV]
MABUIAG alt for KALA LAGAW YA [MWP]
MACA [MCA] lang, Paraguay
MACA alt for MAKHUWA-MARREVONE [XMC]
MACA alt for NAHARRA dial of MAKHUWA [VMW]
MACAENSE alt for MACANESE [MZS]
MACAGUAJE [MCL] lang, Colombia
MACAGUÁN [MBN] lang, Colombia
MACAGUANE alt for MACAGUÁN [MBN]
MACAÍSTA dial of PIDGIN, TIMOR [TVY]
MACANESE [MZS] lang, China
MACANIPA alt for OMAGUA [OMG]
MACAO CREOLE PORTUGUESE alt for
    MACANESE [MZS]
MACASSAI alt for MAKASAE [MKZ]
MACASSAR alt for MAKASAR [MSR]
MACASSARESE alt for MAKASAR [MSR]
MACAU CANTONESE alt for YUEHAI dial of
    CHINESE, YUE [YUH]
MACEDONIAN [MKJ] lang, Macedonia; also in
    Albania, Bulgaria, Canada, Greece, Hungary,
    Slovenia
MACEDONIAN alt for SLAVIC [MKJ]
MACEDONIAN dial of TURKISH [TRK]
MACEDONIAN GAGAUZ dial of BALKAN
    GAGAUZ TURKISH [BGX]
MACEDONIAN SLAVIC alt for MACEDONIAN [MKJ]
MACEDONIAN SLAVIC alt for SLAVIC [MKJ]
MACEDONIAN TURKISH dial of TURKISH [TRK]
MACEDO-RUMANIAN alt for ROMANIAN, MACEDO
    [RUP]
MACHAMBE [JMC] lang, Tanzania
MACHAME alt for MACHAMBE [JMC]
MACHARIA dial of SINDHI [SND]
MACHE alt for BODO [BRX]
MACHICUI alt for TOBA-MASKOY [TMF]
MACHIGUENGA [MCB] lang, Peru
MACHINERE [MPD] lang, Brazil
MACHINGA [MVW] lang, Tanzania
MÂCHO MÂCHO alt for HAWRAMI [HAC]
MACHONGRR alt for NAGA, CHANG [NBC]
MACHOTO alt for ITONAMA [ITO]
MACHVANMCKO alt for MACHVANO dial of
    ROMANI, VLAX [RMY]
MACHVANO alt for SERBO-BOSNIAN dial of
    ROMANI, VLAX [RMY]
MACHVANO dial of ROMANI, VLAX [RMY]
MACHWAYA alt for SERBO-BOSNIAN dial of
    ROMANI, VLAX [RMY]
MACI alt for OLITI dial of ICEVE-MACI [BEC]
MACI dial of ICEVE-MACI [BEC]
MACINA alt for FULFULDE, MAASINA [FUL]
MACKENZIAN alt for SLAVEY, NORTH [SCS]

MACKENZIAN alt for SLAVEY, SOUTH [SLA]
MACKENZIE DELTA INUPIATUN alt for WEST ARCTIC INUPIATUN dial of INUPIATUN, NORTH ALASKAN [ESI]
MACKENZIE INUPIATUN alt for WEST ARCTIC INUPIATUN dial of INUPIATUN, NORTH ALASKAN [ESI]
MACO dial of PIAROA [PID]
MACONDE alt for MAKONDE [KDE]
MACU DE CUBEO alt for CACUA [CBV]
MACU DE DESANO alt for CACUA [CBV]
MACU DE GUANANO alt for CACUA [CBV]
"MACÚ DE TUCANO" pejorative alt for HUPDË [JUP]
MACUA alt for MAKHUWA [VMW]
MACUA alt for MAKHUWA-MEETTO [MAK]
MACUE alt for MAKWE [YMK]
MACUNA [MYY] lang, Colombia; also in Brazil
MACUNI alt for MAXAKALÍ [MBL]
MACÚ-PARANÁ CACUA dial of CACUA [CBV]
MACURAP alt for MAKURÁP [MAG]
MACURAPI alt for MAKURÁP [MAG]
MACUSHI [MBC] lang, Guyana; also in Brazil, Venezuela
MACUSI alt for MACUSHI [MBC]
MACUSSI alt for MACUSHI [MBC]
MACZSA alt for NUKAK MAKÚ [MBR]
MAD alt for KUMARBHAG PAHARIA [KMJ]
MAD alt for MAL PAHARIA [MKB]
MADA [MDA] lang, Nigeria
MADA [MXU] lang, Cameroon
MADA DUTSE alt for EGGON [EGO]
MADA EGGON alt for EGGON [EGO]
MADAGLASHTI alt for FARSI, EASTERN [PRS]
MADAK [MMX] lang, Papua New Guinea
MADAKA dial of BAUCHI [BSF]
MADANG [MQD] lang, Malaysia (Sarawak)
MADANI dial of ARABIC, SOUTH LEVANTINE SPOKEN [AJP]
MADAR dial of TEWA [TWE]
MADARA alt for MANDARA [TBF]
MADARRPA dial of GUPAPUYNGU [GUF]
MADDA alt for MADA [MDA]
MADEÁN alt for MADEAN-VIÑAC dial of QUECHUA, YAUYOS [QUX]
MADEAN-VIÑAC dial of QUECHUA, YAUYOS [QUX]
MADEGGUSU alt for SIMBO [SBB]
MADEIRA-AZORES dial of PORTUGUESE [POR]
MADEMANG alt for LANGKURU dial of WERSING [KVW]
MADEN [XMX] lang, Indonesia (Irian Jaya)
MADENASSA alt for DANISI dial of SHUA [SHG]
MADENASSE alt for DANISI dial of SHUA [SHG]
MADER alt for MAL PAHARIA [MKB]
MADHAVPUR dial of JERUNG [JEE]
MADHESI dial of BHOJPURI [BHJ]
MADHURA alt for MADURA [MHJ]
MADHYA PRADESH MARATHI alt for VARHADI-NAGPURI [VAH]
MADI alt for MA [MSJ]

MADI alt for MARIA [MRR]
MADI alt for PÖJULU dial of BARI [BFA]
MADI alt for SALUAN, COASTAL [LOE]
MA'DI [MHI] lang, Uganda; also in Sudan
MA'DI alt for KALIKO [KBO]
MA'DI alt for MA'DI [MHI]
MA'DI alt for MOROKODO [MGC]
MA'DI, SOUTHERN [QMD] lang, Uganda
MADIA alt for MARIA [MRR]
MADIDWANA alt for BURUWAI [ASI]
MADIHÁ alt for CULINA [CUL]
MADIIN alt for KOMO [KOM]
MADIJA alt for CULINA [CUL]
MADIK alt for ABUN JI dial of ABUN [KGR]
MADIMADOKO dial of MAYOGO [MDM]
MADINGO alt for MANINKA, KANKAN [MNI]
MADINNISANE alt for DANISI dial of SHUA [SHG]
MADIPIA dial of MAYOGO [MDM]
MADITI alt for KALIKO [KBO]
MA'DITI alt for MA'DI [MHI]
MADIYA alt for MARIA [MRR]
MADIYA alt for MARIA, DANDAMI [DAQ]
MADJA NGAI alt for MAJINGAI dial of SAR [MWM]
MADJEDJE alt for MADIPIA dial of MAYOGO [MDM]
MADJINGAY alt for MAJINGAI dial of SAR [MWM]
MADJINGAYE alt for MAJINGAI dial of SAR [MWM]
MADKA-KINWAT dial of KOLAMI, NORTH-WESTERN [KFB]
MADNGELA alt for MADNGELE [ZML]
MADNGELE [ZML] lang, Australia
MADO dial of BARUGA [BBB]
MADOLE alt for MODOLE [MQO]
MADRASI dial of TAMIL [TCV]
MADRASSI alt for KANNADA [KJV]
MADU dial of ENETS [ENE]
MA'DU dial of MOROKODO [MGC]
MADUBE dial of MARGHI CENTRAL [MAR]
MADUKAYANG alt for KALINGA, MADUKAYANG [KMD]
MADUNGORE alt for ASSANGORI [SUN]
MADUNGORE alt for SUNGOR [SUN]
MADURA [MHJ] lang, Indonesia (Java and Bali); also in Singapore
MADURESE alt for MADURA [MHJ]
MADURI alt for BAGA MANDURI [BMD]
MADUTARA alt for KOKATA [KTD]
MADUWONGA alt for KOKATA [KTD]
MADYAY dial of YIDINY [YII]
MADYO alt for MA [MSJ]
MADZARIN dial of FALI [FLI]
MAE [MME] lang, Vanuatu
MAE alt for EMAE [MMW]
MAE dial of ENGA [ENQ]
MAE dial of JINA [JIA]
MAE PING dial of KAREN, PWO NORTHERN [PWW]
MAE SARIENG dial of KAREN, PWO NORTHERN [PWW]
MAE-MORAE alt for MAII [MMM]
MAENG alt for NORTH COAST MENGEN dial of MENGEN [MEE]

MAERKISCH-BRANDENBURGISCH alt for MARK-BRANDENBURG dial of SAXON, LOW [SXN]
MAEVO alt for MAEWO, CENTRAL [MWO]
MAEWO, CENTRAL [MWO] lang, Vanuatu
MAFA [MAF] lang, Cameroon; also in Nigeria
MAFA dial of MAFA [MAF]
MAFEA [MKV] lang, Vanuatu
MAFILAU alt for MAII [MMM]
MAFINDO alt for CENTRAL KONO dial of KONO [KNO]
MAFOOR alt for BIAK [BHW]
MAFOORSCH alt for BIAK [BHW]
MAFUFU alt for FUYUG [FUY]
MAGA alt for MAAKA [MEW]
MAGA dial of RUKAI [DRU]
MAGABARA alt for DOGA [DGG]
MAGADHI alt for MAGAHI [MQM]
MAGADIGE [ZMG] lang, Australia
MAGAHAT [MTW] lang, Philippines
MAGAHI [MQM] lang, India
MAGAM dial of AMBRYM, NORTH [MMG]
MAG-ANCHI SAMBAL alt for AYTA, MAG-ANCHI [SGB]
MAGANG alt for BOLU dial of GEJI [GEZ]
MAGAR alt for MAGAR, WESTERN [MRD]
MAGAR NUWAKOT alt for MAGAR, WESTERN [MRD]
MAGAR, EASTERN [MGP] lang, Nepal; also in Bhutan, India
MAGAR, WESTERN [MRD] lang, Nepal
MAGARA dial of NZANYI [NJA]
MAGARI alt for MAGAR, EASTERN [MGP]
MAGARI alt for MAGAR, WESTERN [MRD]
MAGARKURA alt for MAGAR, EASTERN [MGP]
MAGAYA alt for MAGAHI [MQM]
MAGBAI alt for MADIPIA dial of MAYOGO [MDM]
MAGBIAMBO dial of LOKO [LOK]
MAGE alt for BILALA dial of NABA [MNE]
"MAGH" pejorative alt for ARAKANESE [MHV]
MAGH alt for ARAKANESE [MHV]
MAGHA alt for MAAKA [MEW]
MAGHAYA alt for MAGAHI [MQM]
MÁGHDÌ [GMD] lang, Nigeria
"MAGHI" pejorative alt for ARAKANESE [MHV]
MAGHI alt for ARAKANESE [MHV]
MAGHORI alt for MAGAHI [MQM]
MAGHREBI ARABIC alt for ARABIC, MOROCCAN SPOKEN [ARY]
MAGHREBI ARABIC alt for ARABIC, WESTERN EGYPTIAN BEDAWI SPOKEN [AYL]
MAGHRIBI COLLOQUIAL ARABIC alt for ARABIC, MOROCCAN SPOKEN [ARY]
MAGI alt for MAGAHI [MQM]
MAGI alt for MAILU [MGU]
MAGINDANAON [MDH] lang, Philippines
MAGINDANAW alt for MAGINDANAON [MDH]
MAG-INDI SAMBAL alt for AYTA, MAG-INDI [BLX]
MAGIRONA alt for MATSÉS [MCF]
MAGOBINENG dial of KATE [KMG]
MAGODHI alt for MAGAHI [MQM]
MAGODI alt for NGONI dial of TUMBUKA [TUW]

MAGODRO alt for WAYA dial of FIJIAN, WESTERN [WYY]
MAGONGO alt for OSAYEN dial of OKO-ENI-OSAYEN [OKS]
MAGORI [MDR] lang, Papua New Guinea
MAGRA KI BOLI dial of BHILI [BHB]
MAGU alt for MVANIP [MCJ]
MAGÜTA alt for TICUNA [TCA]
MAGUINDANAO alt for MAGINDANAON [MDH]
MAGWARAM. MAAGWARAM alt for WESTERN BADE dial of BADE [BDE]
MAGYAR alt for HUNGARIAN [HNG]
MAGYAR JELVNYELV alt for HUNGARIAN SIGN LANGUAGE [HSH]
MAH alt for MANO [MEV]
MAH MERI alt for BESISI [MHE]
MAHA alt for MAAKA [MEW]
MAHAA dial of BUDU [BUU]
MAHAFALY dial of MALAGASY [MEX]
MAHAGA alt for BUGHOTU [BGT]
MAHAIRI alt for OMAHA-PONCA [OMA]
MAHAKAM BUSANG dial of KAYAN, BUSANG [BFG]
MAHAKAM KENYA alt for KENYAH, MAHAKAM [XKM]
MAHAKAM KENYAH dial of KENYAH, MAHAKAM [XKM]
MAHAKULUNG dial of KULUNG [KLE]
MAHALI [MJX] lang, India
MAHALI dial of SANTALI [SNT]
MAHALLATI dial of FARSI, WESTERN [PES]
MAHARASHTRA alt for MARATHI [MRT]
MAHARASHTRA LAMANI dial of LAMBADI [LMN]
MAHARATHI alt for MARATHI [MRT]
MAHARI alt for HALBI [HLB]
MAHARI dial of KONKANI [KNK]
MAHARI dial of VARHADI-NAGPURI [VAH]
MAHARRA alt for NAHARRA dial of MAKHUWA [VMW]
MAHAS alt for NOBIIN [FIA]
MAHAS dial of NOBIIN [FIA]
MAHAS-FIADIDJA alt for NOBIIN [FIA]
MAHAS-FIYADIKKYA alt for NOBIIN [FIA]
MAHASI alt for MAHAS dial of NOBIIN [FIA]
MAHASS alt for MAHAS dial of NOBIIN [FIA]
MAHASUI alt for PAHARI, MAHASU [BFZ]
MAHE alt for MAHEI [MJA]
MAHEI [MJA] lang, Myanmar
MAHI alt for MAXI-GBE [MXL]
MAHILI alt for MAHALI [MJX]
MAHINAKU alt for MEHINÁKU [MMH]
MAHL alt for MALDIVIAN [SNM]
MAHLE alt for MAHALI [MJX]
MAHLE alt for MAHALI dial of SANTALI [SNT]
MAHLI alt for MAHALI [MJX]
MAHONGWE [MHB] lang, Gabon
MAHOTTARI alt for THARU, MAHOTARI [THN]
MAHOU [MXX] lang, Côte d'Ivoire
MAHOUA alt for MAWA [MCW]
MAHOUKA dial of MAHOU [MXX]
MAHRI alt for MEHRI [MHR]

MAHSUDI alt for PASHTO, CENTRAL [PST]
MAHU alt for MAHOU [MXX]
MAHUAN alt for TUGUN [TZN]
MAHUAYANA alt for MAPIDIAN dial of ARUMA
[WAP]
MAHUM alt for GHOMÁLÁ' [BBJ]
MAHWA alt for MAWA [MCW]
MAÏNGAO dial of LAKA [LAM]
MAI alt for EMAE [MMW]
MAI alt for HARUA dial of BOLA [BNP]
MAI alt for MAE dial of ENGA [ENQ]
MAI alt for SILIPUT [MKC]
MAI BRAT [AYZ] lang, Indonesia (Irian Jaya)
MAI JA alt for OREJÓN [ORE]
MAIA [SKS] lang, Papua New Guinea
MAIABARE dial of SEWA BAY [SEW]
MAIADOM [MZZ] lang, Papua New Guinea
MAIAK dial of BURUN [BDI]
MAIANI [TNH] lang, Papua New Guinea
MAIBRAT alt for MAI BRAT [AYZ]
MAIDU, NORTHEAST [NMU] lang, USA
MAIDU, NORTHWEST [MAI] lang, USA
MAIDU, VALLEY [VMV] lang, USA
MAIDUAN alt for MAIDU, NORTHWEST [MAI]
MAIDUGURI dial of KANURI, CENTRAL [KPH]
MAIGO alt for MAYOGO [MDM]
MAIHA dial of NZANYI [NJA]
MAI-HEA-RI alt for AKOYE [MIW]
MAIHIRI alt for AKOYE [MIW]
MAII [MMM] lang, Vanuatu
MAIKEL alt for NAGA, MAO [NBI]
MAIKO alt for MAYOGO [MDM]
MAIKOTI alt for KHAM, MAIKOTI [ZKM]
MAILANG alt for NGAING [NNF]
MAILU [MGU] lang, Papua New Guinea
MAIMA alt for CUCHUDUA dial of JAMAMADI [JAA]
MAIMAI alt for SILIPUT [MKC]
MAIMAKA dial of MAI BRAT [AYZ]
MAIMBIE alt for YIDINY [YII]
MAIN ISLAND alt for MOLOT dial of RAMOAAINA
[RAI]
MAINA alt for ACHUAR-SHIWIAR [ACU]
MAINA-KIZHI alt for ALTAI PROPER dial of ALTAI,
SOUTHERN [ALT]
MAINDO dial of CHWABO [CHW]
MAINFRÄNKISCH [VMF] lang, Germany
MAINGTHA dial of ACHANG [ACN]
MAINLAND FRISIAN alt for MOORINGER dial of
FRISIAN, NORTHERN [FRR]
MAINOKE alt for MAINOKI dial of SIMEKU [SMZ]
MAINOKI dial of SIMEKU [SMZ]
MAINYPILGINO dial of KEREK [KRK]
MAIONGONG alt for MAQUIRITARI [MCH]
MAIOPITIAN alt for MAPIDIAN dial of ARUMA [WAP]
MAIO-YESAN alt for YESSAN-MAYO [YSS]
MAIPUA alt for PURARI [IAR]
MAIR alt for KOHISTANI, INDUS [MVY]
MAIRASI [FRY] lang, Indonesia (Irian Jaya)
MAIRIRI alt for MARIRI [MQI]
MAISAN alt for MAISIN [MBQ]
MAISAWIET dial of MAI BRAT [AYZ]

MAISEFA dial of MAI BRAT [AYZ]
MAISIN [MBQ] lang, Papua New Guinea
MAISIN dial of MAISIN [MBQ]
MAITARIA dial of RABHA [RAH]
MAITE dial of MAI BRAT [AYZ]
MAITHILI [MKP] lang, India; also in Nepal
MAITILI alt for MAITHILI [MKP]
MAITLI alt for MAITHILI [MKP]
MAITSI dial of MAQUIRITARI [MCH]
MAIWA [MTI] lang, Papua New Guinea
MAIWA [WMM] lang, Indonesia (Sulawesi)
MAIWA dial of MAIWA [MTI]
MAIWALA [MUM] lang, Papua New Guinea
MAIYÃ alt for KOHISTANI, INDUS [MVY]
MAIYACH alt for KARON DORI [KGW]
MAIYAH dial of MAI BRAT [AYZ]
MAIYON alt for KOHISTANI, INDUS [MVY]
MAJAK alt for MANDJAK [MFV]
MAJANG [MPE] lang, Ethiopia
MAJANJIRO alt for MAJANG [MPE]
MAJE alt for BAYANO dial of KUNA, SAN BLAS
[CUK]
MAJENE dial of MANDAR [MHN]
MAJERA [XMJ] lang, Cameroon; also in Chad
MAJERA dial of MAJERA [XMJ]
MAJHI [MJZ] lang, Nepal; also in India
MAJHI dial of PANJABI, EASTERN [PNJ]
MAJHI dial of PANJABI, WESTERN [PNB]
MAJHI-KORWA dial of KORWA [KFP]
MAJH-KUMAIYA dial of GARHWALI [GBM]
MAJHVAR alt for MAJHWAR [MMJ]
MAJHWAR [MMJ] lang, India
MAJI alt for DIZI [MDX]
MAJIAHUA alt for CHINESE, HAKKA [HAK]
MAJINDA alt for CINDA dial of CINDA-REGI-TIYAL
[KAU]
MAJINGAI dial of SAR [MWM]
MAJINNGAY alt for MAJINGAI dial of SAR [MWM]
MAJNA-PIL'GINSKIJ alt for MAINYPILGINO dial
of KEREK [KRK]
MAJUBIM alt for PARANAWÁT [PAF]
MAJUGU alt for MAYOGO [MDM]
MAJURUNA alt for MATSÉS [MCF]
MAJUU alt for NGBEE [NBL]
MAK [MKG] lang, China
MAK [PBL] lang, Nigeria
MAK dial of MAK [MKG]
MAKA alt for BYEP [MKK]
MAKA alt for MAAKA [MEW]
MAKA alt for MACA [MCA]
MAKA alt for MAKHUWA-MARREVONE [XMC]
MAKA alt for NAHARRA dial of MAKHUWA
[VMW]
MAK'Á alt for MACA [MCA]
MAKAA [MCP] lang, Cameroon
MAKAA alt for TOMA dial of SAMO, SOUTHERN
[SBD]
MAKABUKY dial of SANIYO-HIYEWE [SNY]
MAKADA dial of RAMOAAINA [RAI]
MAKAEYAM alt for ATURU [AUP]
MAKAH [MYH] lang, USA

MAKAHEELIGA dial of PALUAN [PLZ]
MAKAKAT alt for QAQET [BYX]
MAKAKAU dial of MALAY [MLI]
MAKAKWE-KHAMBANA alt for HLENGWE dial of TSHWA [TSC]
MAKALAKA alt for KALANGA [KCK]
MAKALE dial of TORAJA-SADAN [SDA]
MAKALE dial of YAO [YAO]
MAKANGARA alt for CINDA dial of CINDA-REGI-TIYAL [KAU]
MAKARAKA dial of ZANDE [ZAN]
MAKARI alt for MPADE [MPI]
MAKARI alt for MPADE dial of MPADE [MPI]
MAKARI dial of MPADE [MPI]
MAKARIKI dial of AMAHAI [AMQ]
MAKARIM alt for BELI [BEY]
MAKARUB alt for ARUAMU [MSY]
MAKARUP alt for ARUAMU [MSY]
MAKARY alt for MPADE [MPI]
MAKASAE [MKZ] lang, Timor Lorosae
MAKASAI alt for MAKASAE [MKZ]
MAKASAI dial of MAKASAE [MKZ]
MAKASAR [MSR] lang, Indonesia (Sulawesi)
MAKASSA alt for MAKASAR [MSR]
MAKASSAARSCHE alt for MAKASAR [MSR]
MAKASSAI alt for MAKASAE [MKZ]
MAKASSAR alt for MAKASAR [MSR]
MAKASSARESE alt for MAKASAR [MSR]
MAKASSARESE dial of MALAY [MLI]
MAKATAO dial of SIRAIYA [FOS]
MAKATIAN dial of SELUWASAN [SWH]
MAKATTAO alt for MAKATAO dial of SIRAIYA [FOS]
MAKAWE-KHAMBANA alt for HLENGWE dial of TSHWA [TSC]
MAKE dial of FANG [FNG]
MAKEDONSKI alt for MACEDONIAN [MKJ]
MAKELAI alt for TOMPASO dial of TONTEMBOAN [TNT]
MAKELA'I-MAOTOW alt for TOMPASO dial of TONTEMBOAN [TNT]
MAKEM alt for MALUAL dial of DINKA, SOUTH-WESTERN [DIK]
MAKERE dial of MANGBETU [MDJ]
MAKET dial of TANGGA [TGG]
MAKHUA alt for MAKHUWA-MEETTO [MAK]
MAKHUWA [VMW] lang, Mozambique; also in Madagascar
MAKHUWA-MAKHUWANA alt for MAKHUWA [VMW]
MAKHUWA-MARREVONE [XMC] lang, Mozambique
MAKHUWA-MEETTO [MAK] lang, Mozambique; also in Tanzania
MAKHUWANA dial of MAKHUWA [VMW]
MAKHUWANA dial of MAKHUWA-MARREVONE [XMC]
MAKHUWA-NIASSA alt for MAKHUWA-SHIRIMA [VMK]
MAKHUWA-SHIRIMA [VMK] lang, Mozambique
MAKHUWA-XIRIMA alt for MAKHUWA-SHIRIMA [VMK]

MAKHUWWA OF NAMPULA alt for MAKHUWA [VMW]
MAKI alt for KALUMPANG [KLI]
MA'KI alt for KALUMPANG [KLI]
MAKIALIGA alt for MAKAHEELIGA dial of PALUAN [PLZ]
MAKIAN BARAT alt for MAKIAN, WEST [MQS]
MAKIAN DALAM alt for MAKIAN, EAST [MKY]
MAKIAN LUAR alt for MAKIAN, WEST [MQS]
MAKIAN TIMUR alt for MAKIAN, EAST [MKY]
MAKIAN, EAST [MKY] lang, Indonesia (Maluku)
MAKIAN, WEST [MQS] lang, Indonesia (Maluku)
MAKIANG dial of KINABATANGAN, UPPER [DMG]
MAKIRITARE alt for MAQUIRITARI [MCH]
MAKKAL alt for PALIYAN [PCF]
MAKKI alt for KALUMPANG [KLI]
MAKLERE dial of MAKASAE [MKZ]
MAKLEU alt for MAKLEW [MGF]
MAKLEW [MGF] lang, Indonesia (Irian Jaya)
MAKO alt for MACO dial of PIAROA [PID]
MAKOA alt for MAKHUWA-MEETTO [MAK]
MAKOANE alt for MAKHUWA [VMW]
MAKODA dial of BUDU [BUU]
MAKOLKOL [ZMH] lang, Papua New Guinea
MAKOMA dial of SIMAA [SIE]
MAKONDA alt for MAKONDE [KDE]
MAKONDE [KDE] lang, Tanzania; also in Mozambique
MAKONDE alt for VAMAKONDE dial of MAKONDE [KDE]
MAKONG alt for SÔ [SSS]
MAKOREKORE alt for KOREKORE dial of SHONA [SHD]
MAKOROKO alt for KWADI [KWZ]
MAKPA dial of DUMI [DUS]
MAKRANA dial of MAITHILI [MKP]
MAKRANI alt for BALOCHI, SOUTHERN [BCC]
MAKRANI dial of BALOCHI, SOUTHERN [BCC]
MAKSELA alt for MOKSELA [VMS]
"MAKU" pejorative alt for YUHUP [YAB]
MAKÚ NADËB alt for NADËB [MBJ]
MAKUA alt for MAKHUWA [VMW]
MAKU'A [LVA] lang, Timor Lorosae
MAKUA alt for MAKHUWA-MEETTO [MAK]
MAKUANA alt for MAKHUWANA dial of MAKHUWA [VMW]
"MAKÚ-HUPDË" pejorative alt for HUPDË [JUP]
MAKUNA alt for MACUNA [MYY]
MAKUNADÖBÖ alt for NADËB [MBJ]
MAKURA alt for NAMAKURA [NMK]
MAKURA dial of NAMAKURA [NMK]
MAKURÁP [MAG] lang, Brazil
MAKURÁPI alt for MAKURÁP [MAG]
MAKUSHI alt for MACUSHI [MBC]
MAKUTANA dial of MANGBUTU [MDK]
MAKUTU dial of BALOI [BIZ]
MAKUWA alt for MAKHUWA-MEETTO [MAK]
MAKUXI alt for MACUSHI [MBC]
MAKÚ-YAHUP alt for YUHUP [YAB]
MAKWAKWE-KHAMBANA alt for HLENGWE dial of TSHWA [TSC]

MAKWAR alt for GA'ANDA [GAA]
MAKWARE alt for NAGA, KHIAMNIUNGAN [NKY]
MAKWE [YMK] lang, Mozambique; also in Tanzania
MAKYA alt for BYEP [MKK]
MAL [MLF] lang, Laos; also in Thailand, USA
MAL alt for KUMARBHAG PAHARIA [KMJ]
MAL alt for MAL PAHARIA [MKB]
MAL PAHARIA [MKB] lang, India
MAL PAHARIYA alt for MAL PAHARIA [MKB]
MALA [PED] lang, Papua New Guinea
MALA [RUY] lang, Nigeria
MALA alt for MARA [MEC]
MALA dial of TONGA [TOI]
MALABAR dial of MALAYALAM [MJS]
MALABU dial of BATA [BTA]
MALABU dial of JIMI [JIM]
MALACCAN alt for MALACCAN CREOLE
    PORTUGUESE [MCM]
MALACCAN CREOLE MALAY [CCM] lang, Malaysia
    (Peninsular)
MALACCAN CREOLE PORTUGUESE [MCM] lang,
    Malaysia (Peninsular); also in Singapore
MALACHINI alt for POKOMO, LOWER [POJ]
MALAGASY [MEX] lang, Madagascar; also in
    Comoros Islands, Réunion
MALAGASY, ANTANKARANA [XMV] lang,
    Madagascar
MALAGASY, SOUTHERN [XMU] lang, Madagascar
MALAGASY, TSIMEHETY [XMW] lang, Madagascar
MALAGHETI dial of TALISE [TLR]
MALAGMALAG alt for MULLUKMULLUK [MPB]
MALAI alt for PALIYAN [PCF]
MALAI dial of MUTU [TUC]
MALAI ARAYAN alt for MALARYAN [MJQ]
MALAIKURAVAN alt for MALANKURAVAN [MJO]
MALAKANAGIRI KOYA dial of KOYA [KFF]
MALAKHEL [MLD] lang, Afghanistan
MALAKKA BESISI dial of BESISI [MHE]
MALAK-MALAK alt for MULLUKMULLUK [MPB]
MALAKOTE [MLK] lang, Kenya
MALAL dial of THEMNE [TEJ]
MALALA alt for MALA [PED]
MALALAMAI [MMT] lang, Papua New Guinea
MALALULU dial of POKOMO, UPPER [PKB]
MALAMAUDA alt for NETE [NET]
MALAMBA dial of BUDU [BUU]
MALAMPASHI alt for KANIKKARAN [KEV]
MALAMUNI alt for MARAMUNI dial of ENGA [ENQ]
MALANG alt for MADANG [MQD]
MALANG alt for MALENG [PKT]
MALANG dial of MALENG [PKT]
MALANGA dial of MABA [MDE]
MALANGKE-USSU alt for LUWU dial of BUGIS [BPR]
MALANGO [MLN] lang, Solomon Islands
MALANG-PASURUAN dial of JAVANESE [JAN]
MALANKUDI alt for MALANKURAVAN [MJO]
MALANKURAVAN [MJO] lang, India
MALAPANDARAM [MJP] lang, India
MALAPANTARAM alt for MALAPANDARAM [MJP]
MALAQUEIRO alt for MALACCAN CREOLE
    PORTUGUESE [MCM]

MALAQUENHO alt for MALACCAN CREOLE
    PORTUGUESE [MCM]
MALAQUENSE alt for MALACCAN CREOLE
    PORTUGUESE [MCM]
MALAQUÊS alt for MALACCAN CREOLE
    PORTUGUESE [MCM]
MALARKUTI alt for VISHAVAN [VIS]
MALARYAN [MJQ] lang, India
MALAS [MKR] lang, Papua New Guinea
MALASANGA [MQZ] lang, Papua New Guinea
MALASANGA dial of MALASANGA [MQZ]
MALATIA alt for MALATYA dial of ARMENIAN [ARM]
MALATYA dial of ARMENIAN [ARM]
MALAUEG alt for MALAWEG dial of ITAWIT [ITV]
MALAVEDAN [MJR] lang, India
MALAVETAN alt for MALAVEDAN [MJR]
MALAVI alt for MALVI [MUP]
MALAWEG dial of ITAWIT [ITV]
MALAWI alt for PETA dial of NYANJA [NYJ]
MALAY [MLI] lang, Malaysia (Peninsular); also in
    Brunei, Indonesia (Sumatra), Myanmar,
    Singapore, Thailand, UAE, USA
MALAY dial of ATI [ATK]
MALAY TALK alt for BROOME PEARLING LUGGER
    PIDGIN [BPL]
MALAY, AMBONESE [ABS] lang, Indonesia
    (Maluku); also in Netherlands, USA
MALAY, BABA [BAL] lang, Singapore; also in
    Malaysia (Peninsular)
MALAY, BACANESE [BTJ] lang, Indonesia (Maluku)
MALAY, BERAU [BVE] lang, Indonesia (Kalimantan)
MALAY, BUKIT [BVU] lang, Indonesia (Kalimantan)
MALAY, COCOS ISLANDS [COA] lang, Malaysia
    (Sabah); also in Australia
MALAY, JAMBI [JAX] lang, Indonesia (Sumatra)
MALAY, KEDAH [MEO] lang, Thailand
MALAY, KOTA BANGUN KUTAI [MQG] lang,
    Indonesia (Kalimantan)
MALAY, KUPANG [MKN] lang, Indonesia (Nusa
    Tenggara)
MALAY, MENADONESE [XMM] lang, Indonesia
    (Sulawesi)
MALAY, NORTH MOLUCCAN [MAX] lang, Indonesia
    (Maluku)
MALAY, PATTANI [MFA] lang, Thailand
MALAY, SABAH [MSI] lang, Malaysia (Sabah)
MALAY, TENGGARONG KUTAI [VKT] lang,
    Indonesia (Kalimantan)
MALAYA TAMIL dial of TAMIL [TCV]
MALAYADIARS dial of MALANKURAVAN [MJO]
MALAYAL alt for MALAYALAM [MJS]
MALAYALAM [MJS] lang, India; also in Bahrain,
    Fiji, Israel, Malaysia, Qatar, Singapore, UAE,
    United Kingdom
MALAYALAM dial of MALAYALAM [MJS]
MALAYALANI alt for MALAYALAM [MJS]
MALAYALI alt for MALAYALAM [MJS]
MALAYARAYAN alt for MALARYAN [MJQ]
MALAYIC DAYAK [XDY] lang, Indonesia
    (Kalimantan)
MALAYNON [MLZ] lang, Philippines

MALAYO [MBP] lang, Colombia
MALAYO-PORTUGUESE alt for MALACCAN CREOLE PORTUGUESE [MCM]
MALAYSIAN CREOLE PORTUGUESE alt for MALACCAN CREOLE PORTUGUESE [MCM]
MALAYSIAN MINANGKABAU alt for NEGERI SEMBILAN MALAY [ZMI]
MALAYSIAN SIGN LANGUAGE [XML] lang, Malaysia (Peninsular)
MALAYU alt for MALAY [MLI]
MALBA alt for KALARKO [KBA]
MALBA-BIRIFOR alt for BIRIFOR, MALBA [BFO]
MALBE alt for MALGBE [MXF]
MALDAVACA alt for BARÉ [BAE]
MALDAVACA alt for MANDAHUACA [MHT]
MALDIVIAN [SNM] lang, Maldives; also in India
MALDJANA alt for MALGANA [VML]
MALE [MDC] lang, Papua New Guinea
MALE [MDY] lang, Ethiopia
MALE ARAYANS alt for MALARYAN [MJQ]
MALE KURAVAN alt for MALANKURAVAN [MJO]
MALEAN alt for MALAYALAM [MJS]
MALECITE dial of MALECITE-PASSAMAQUODDY [MAC]
MALECITE-PASSAMAQUODDY [MAC] lang, Canada; also in USA
MALEI alt for HOTE [HOT]
MALEK alt for AIKU [MZF]
MALÉKU JAÍKA [GUT] lang, Costa Rica
MALELE dial of MANGBETU [MDJ]
MALENG [PKT] lang, Laos; also in Viet Nam
MALENG dial of MALENG [PKT]
MALENG BRO alt for KHA PHONG dial of MALENG [PKT]
MALENG KARI alt for KHA PHONG dial of MALENG [PKT]
MALENI alt for MONGUNA dial of RON [CLA]
MALEN-UTWE dial of KOSRAEAN [KSI]
MALEPANTARAM alt for MALAPANDARAM [MJP]
MALER alt for KUMARBHAG PAHARIA [KMJ]
MALER alt for MAL PAHARIA [MKB]
MALER alt for SAURIA PAHARIA [MJT]
MALEU dial of MALEU-KILENGE [MGL]
MALEU-KILENGE [MGL] lang, Papua New Guinea
MALEY ARAYAN alt for MALARYAN [MJQ]
MALFAXAL [MLX] lang, Vanuatu
MALGACHE alt for MALAGASY [MEX]
MALGANA [VML] lang, Australia
MALGBE [MXF] lang, Cameroon; also in Chad
MALGBE dial of MALGBE [MXF]
MALGO alt for GAMARGU dial of WANDALA [MFI]
MALGWA alt for GAMARGU dial of WANDALA [MFI]
MALGWA alt for MULGWE dial of MARGHI CENTRAL [MAR]
MALGWE alt for MALGBE [MXF]
MALHAM dial of TAT, MUSLIM [TTT]
MALHATEE alt for MARATHI [MRT]
MALHESTI alt for KINNAURI [KFK]
MALHI dial of DHATKI [MKI]
MALI [GCC] lang, Papua New Guinea
MALI DUUN alt for DUUNGOMA [DUX]

MALIENG alt for MALENG [PKT]
MALIENG dial of MALENG [PKT]
MALIGAN dial of TAGAL MURUT [MVV]
MALIGO [MWJ] lang, Angola
MALIKH alt for MALDIVIAN [SNM]
MALIKI dial of AIMAQ [AIQ]
MALILA [MGQ] lang, Tanzania
MALILIA alt for MALILA [MGQ]
MALIMBA [MZD] lang, Cameroon
MALIMPUNG [MLT] lang, Indonesia (Sulawesi)
MALINALTEPEC dial of TLAPANECO, MALINALTEPEC [TLL]
MALINALTEPEC TLAPANEC alt for TLAPANECO, MALINALTEPEC [TLL]
MALINGUAT [SIC] lang, Papua New Guinea
MALINKA alt for MALINKE [MLQ]
MALINKA alt for MANINKAKAN, WESTERN [MLQ]
MALINKE [MLQ] lang, Mali; also in Gambia, Guinea, Guinea-Bissau, Senegal
MALINKE alt for LOMA [LOI]
MALINKE alt for MANINKAKAN, KITA [MWK]
MALINKE alt for MANINKAKAN, WESTERN [MLQ]
MALINKE dial of JULA [DYU]
MALINKÉ alt for JULA, ODIENNÉ [JOD]
MALISEET alt for MALECITE dial of MALECITE-PASSAMAQUODDY [MAC]
MALIYAD alt for MALAYALAM [MJS]
MALJANNA alt for MALGANA [VML]
MALKA dial of KABARDIAN [KAB]
MALKAN alt for MOLO [ZMO]
MALKANA alt for MALGANA [VML]
MALKI alt for MALDIVIAN [SNM]
MALLANGO dial of KALINGA, SOUTHERN [KSC]
MALLEALLE alt for MALAYALAM [MJS]
MALLORQUI alt for BALEARIC dial of CATALAN-VALENCIAN-BALEAR [CLN]
MALLOW alt for MALVI [MUP]
MALMARIV alt for TIALE [MNL]
MALNGIN dial of GURINJI [GUE]
MALO [MLA] lang, Vanuatu
MALO alt for EMBALOH [EMB]
MALO alt for MELO [MFX]
MALOH alt for EMBALOH [EMB]
MALOL [MBK] lang, Papua New Guinea
MALOLO alt for MALOL [MBK]
MALOM dial of MADAK [MMX]
MALON alt for MALOL [MBK]
MALPA alt for KALARKO [KBA]
MALPAHARIA alt for MAL PAHARIA [MKB]
MALTAM alt for MASLAM [MSV]
MALTAM alt for MASLAM dial of MASLAM [MSV]
MALTESE [MLS] lang, Malta; also in Australia, Canada, Italy, Tunisia, United Kingdom, USA
MALTESE SIGN LANGUAGE [MDL] lang, Malta
MALTI alt for KUMARBHAG PAHARIA [KMJ]
MALTI alt for MAL PAHARIA [MKB]
MALTI alt for MALTESE [MLS]
MALTI alt for SAURIA PAHARIA [MJT]
MALTO alt for KUMARBHAG PAHARIA [KMJ]
MALTO alt for MAL PAHARIA [MKB]
MALTO alt for SAURIA PAHARIA [MJT]

MALTU alt for KUMARBHAG PAHARIA [KMJ]
MALTU alt for MAL PAHARIA [MKB]
MALTU alt for SAURIA PAHARIA [MJT]
MALU alt for MARU [MHX]
MALU alt for RAMOAAINA [RAI]
MALU alt for TO'ABAITA [MLU]
MA<LULA dial of WESTERN NEO-ARAMAIC
    [AMW]
MA<LU:LA alt for MA<LULA dial of WESTERN
    NEO-ARAMAIC [AMW]
MALUA BAY [MLL] lang, Vanuatu
MALUAL dial of DINKA, SOUTHWESTERN [DIK]
MALUNDA dial of MANDAR [MHN]
MALUNUNDA alt for GAYARDILT [GYD]
MALU'U alt for TO'ABAITA [MLU]
MALVANI alt for KUDALI dial of KONKANI,
    GOANESE [GOM]
MALVAXAL-TOMAN ISLAND alt for MALFAXAL
    [MLX]
MALVI [MUP] lang, India
MALVI PROPER dial of MALVI [MUP]
MALWA dial of PANJABI, EASTERN [PNJ]
MALWADA alt for MALVI [MUP]
MALWAL alt for MALUAL dial of DINKA, SOUTH-
    WESTERN [DIK]
MALWI alt for MALVI [MUP]
MAM alt for HONDURAN MÍSKITO dial of
    MISKITO [MIQ]
MAM MARQUENSE alt for MAM, CENTRAL [MVC]
MAM OCCIDENTAL alt for MAM, CENTRAL [MVC]
MAM QUETZALTECO alt for MAM, SOUTHERN
    [MMS]
MAM, CENTRAL [MVC] lang, Guatemala
MAM, NORTHERN [MAM] lang, Guatemala; also
    in Mexico
MAM, SOUTHERN [MMS] lang, Guatemala
MAM, TAJUMULCO [MPF] lang, Guatemala
MAM, TODOS SANTOS CUCHUMATÁN [MVJ] lang,
    Guatemala; also in Mexico
MAMA [MMA] lang, Nigeria
MAMA alt for MAMAA [MHF]
MAMAA [MHF] lang, Papua New Guinea
MAMAINDÉ alt for NAMBIKUÁRA, NORTHERN
    [MBG]
MAMAINDÉ dial of NAMBIKUARA, NORTHERN
    [MBG]
MAMALA dial of HITU [HIT]
MAMALGHA MUNJI dial of MUNJI [MNJ]
MAMANWA [MMN] lang, Philippines
MAMANWA NEGRITO alt for MAMANWA [MMN]
MAMAQ dial of KERINCI [KVR]
MAMARA alt for SENOUFO, MAMARA [MYK]
MAMASA [MQJ] lang, Indonesia (Sulawesi)
MAMBA dial of CHAGGA [KAF]
MAMBA dial of ZIMBA [ZMB]
MAMBAE [MGM] lang, Timor Lorosae; also in
    Australia
MAMBAI [MCS] lang, Cameroon; also in Chad
MAMBAI alt for MAMBAE [MGM]
MAMBAI dial of MAMBAE [MGM]
MAMBANGURA dial of NGURA [NBX]

MAMBAR alt for CENTRAL WAIBUK dial of HARUAI
    [TMD]
MAMBAY alt for MAMBAI [MCS]
MAMBAYA dial of POL [PMM]
MAMBE alt for MUNIWARA [MWB]
MAMBE' dial of DII [DUR]
MAMBERE alt for MAMBILA, CAMEROON [MYA]
MAMBERE alt for MAMBILA, NIGERIA [MZK]
MAMBETTO alt for MANGBETU [MDJ]
MAMBI dial of ARALLE-TABULAHAN [ATQ]
MAMBILA DE GEMBU alt for JU NAARE dial of
    MAMBILA, CAMEROON [MYA]
MAMBILA, CAMEROON [MYA] lang, Cameroon
MAMBILA, NIGERIA [MZK] lang, Nigeria
MAMBILLA alt for MAMBILA, CAMEROON [MYA]
MAMBILLA alt for MAMBILA, NIGERIA [MZK]
MAMBISA dial of ALUR [ALZ]
MAMBORU [MVD] lang, Indonesia (Nusa Tenggara)
MAMBUKUSH alt for MBUKUSHU [MHW]
MAMBULU-LAPORO alt for SAMPOLAWA dial of
    CIA-CIA [CIA]
MAMBUMP dial of BUANG, MAPOS [BZH]
MAMBWE dial of MAMBWE-LUNGU [MGR]
MAMBWE-LUNGU [MGR] lang, Zambia; also in
    Tanzania
MAMÉ alt for TACANECO [MTZ]
MAMEDJA alt for GAAM [TBI]
MAMENYAN alt for BAMENYAM [BCE]
MAMGBAY alt for MAMBAI [MCS]
MAMGBEI alt for MAMBAI [MCS]
MAMIDZA alt for GAAM [TBI]
MAMISA alt for SESA dial of FOLOPA [PPO]
MAMNA'A dial of DII [DUR]
MAMOEDJOE alt for MAMUJU [MQX]
MAMOEDJOESCH alt for MAMUJU [MQX]
MAMORI alt for MAMORIA dial of JAMAMADI [JAA]
MAMORIA dial of JAMAMADI [JAA]
MAMPA alt for SHERBRO [BUN]
MAMPOKO dial of BALOI [BIZ]
MAMPRULE alt for MAMPRULI [MAW]
MAMPRULI [MAW] lang, Ghana; also in Togo
MAMPUKUSH alt for MBUKUSHU [MHW]
MAMPWA alt for SHERBRO [BUN]
MAMUDJU alt for MAMUJU [MQX]
MAMUGA alt for BILEKI dial of NAKANAI [NAK]
MAMUJU [MQX] lang, Indonesia (Sulawesi)
MAMUJU dial of MAMUJU [MQX]
MAMUSI [KDF] lang, Papua New Guinea
MAMUSI dial of MAMUSI [KDF]
MAMVU [MDI] lang, DRC
MAMVU dial of MAMVU [MDI]
MAN alt for IU MIEN [IUM]
MAN alt for MANCHU [MJF]
MAN dial of PANA [PNZ]
MÁN alt for IU MIEN [IUM]
MÁN alt for MAN CAO LAN [MLC]
MAN CAO LAN [MLC] lang, Viet Nam
MAN CAO-LAN alt for MAN CAO LAN [MLC]
MAN DO dial of IU MIEN [IUM]
MAN LAN-TIEN alt for KIM MUN [MJI]
MAN LANTIEN alt for KIM MUN [MJI]

MAN MET [MML] lang, China
MAN PA SENG alt for BUNU, BAHENG [PHA]
MÁN PA SENG alt for BUNU, BAHENG [PHA]
MAN THANH alt for TAI MAN THANH [TMM]
MÁN TRÁNG alt for HMONG DAW [MWW]
MANA alt for FANIA [FAN]
MANADJA alt for LIMILNGAN [LMC]
MANADO MALAY alt for MALAY, MENADONESE
    [XMM]
MANADONESE dial of MALAY [MLI]
MANADONESE MALAY alt for MALAY,
    MENADONESE [XMM]
MANAGALASI [MCQ] lang, Papua New Guinea
MANAGARI alt for MAUNG [MPH]
MANAGOBLA dial of GOLA [GOL]
MANAGUA alt for CASHIBO-CACATAIBO [CBR]
MANAGULASI alt for MANAGALASI [MCQ]
MANAJO alt for AMANAYÉ [AMA]
MANALA alt for MANGALA [MEM]
MANALDJALI alt for YUGAMBAL [YUB]
MANAM [MVA] lang, Papua New Guinea
MANAMBU [MLE] lang, Papua New Guinea
MANANAHUA alt for SENSI [SNI]
MANANG alt for MANANGBA [NMM]
MANANG dial of MFUMTE [NFU]
MANANGA dial of TALIABU [TLV]
MANANGBA [NMM] lang, Nepal
MANANGBHOT alt for MANANGBA [NMM]
MANANGBOLT alt for MANANGBA [NMM]
MANANGEER dial of THURI [THU]
MANANGI alt for MANANGBA [NMM]
MANAPE alt for GAPAPAIWA [PWG]
MAÑARIES alt for MACHIGUENGA [MCB]
MANAU alt for BURMESO [BZU]
MANAWADJI dial of BERAKOU [BXV]
MANAWI dial of AMBAI [AMK]
MANAXO alt for AMANAYÉ [AMA]
MANAY MANDAYAN alt for MANDAYA, KARAGA
    [MRY]
MANAZE alt for AMANAYÉ [AMA]
MANAZO alt for AMANAYÉ [AMA]
MANBAE alt for MAMBAE [MGM]
MANBAI alt for MAMBAI [MCS]
MANBU alt for MANG [MGA]
MANCAGNE alt for MANKANYA [MAN]
MANCANG alt for MANKANYA [MAN]
MANCANHA alt for MANKANYA [MAN]
MANCHAD alt for PATTANI [LAE]
MANCHATI alt for MIKIR [MJW]
MANCHATI alt for PATTANI [LAE]
MANCHINERE alt for MACHINERE [MPD]
MANCHINERI alt for MACHINERE [MPD]
MANCHU [MJF] lang, China
MANDA [MGS] lang, Tanzania
MANDA [MHA] lang, India
MANDA [ZMK] lang, Australia
MANDA dial of PENGO [PEG]
MANDA:YI alt for MANDAIC [MID]
MANDABA dial of MABA [MDE]
MANDAEAN alt for MANDAIC [MID]
MANDAGE alt for AFADE [AAL]

MANDAGE alt for MALGBE [MXF]
MANDAGE alt for MASLAM [MSV]
MANDAGE alt for MPADE [MPI]
MANDAGE alt for MSER [KQX]
MANDAGUE alt for MPADE [MPI]
MANDAGUE alt for MSER [KQX]
MANDAGUÉ alt for MASLAM [MSV]
MANDAGUÉ alt for MPADE [MPI]
MANDAHUACA [MHT] lang, Venezuela; also in Brazil
MANDAIC [MID] lang, Iran; also in Iraq
MANDAIC, CLASSICAL [MYZ] lang, Iran
MANDAILING BATAK alt for BATAK MANDAILING
    [BTM]
MANDAK alt for MADAK [MMX]
MANDAL alt for BAGHELI [BFY]
MANDALA dial of MABA [MDE]
MANDAN [MHQ] lang, USA
MANDANDANYI [ZMK] lang, Australia
MANDANKWE alt for MENDANKWE [MFD]
MANDAR [MHN] lang, Indonesia (Sulawesi)
MANDARA [TBF] lang, Papua New Guinea
MANDARA alt for WANDALA [MFI]
MANDARA alt for WANDALA dial of WANDALA [MFI]
MANDARA MONTAGNARD alt for WANDALA [MFI]
MANDARI [MQU] lang, Sudan
MANDARI alt for BAGA MANDURI [BMD]
MANDARI alt for MONDARI dial of BARI [BFA]
MANDARI alt for MUNDARI [MUW]
MANDARIN alt for CHINESE, MANDARIN [CHN]
MANDAUACA alt for MANDAHUACA [MHT]
MANDAWAKA alt for MANDAHUACA [MHT]
MANDAWÁKA alt for MANDAHUACA [MHT]
MANDAYA alt for MANOBO, DIBABAWON [MBD]
MANDAYA MANSAKA alt for MANSAKA [MSK]
MANDAYA, CATAELANO [MST] lang, Philippines
MANDAYA, KARAGA [MRY] lang, Philippines
MANDAYA, SANGAB [MYT] lang, Philippines
MANDE alt for GARO [GRT]
MANDE alt for MANDINKA [MNK]
MANDÉ alt for MANDINKA [MNK]
MANDE alt for MANINKA, KANKAN [MNI]
MANDE alt for NOMAANDE [LEM]
MANDEALI [MJL] lang, India
MANDEGHUGHUSU alt for SIMBO [SBB]
MANDELAUT alt for BAJAU LAUT dial of SAMA,
    SOUTHERN [SIT]
MANDELLA alt for MADNGELE [ZML]
MANDER [MQR] lang, Indonesia (Irian Jaya)
MANDHARSCHE alt for MANDAR [MHN]
MANDI [TUA] lang, Papua New Guinea
MANDI alt for MANDAIC [MID]
MANDI alt for MANDEALI [MJL]
MANDI alt for NOMAANDE [LEM]
MANDIALI alt for MANDEALI [MJL]
MANDING alt for MANDINKA [MNK]
MANDINGA alt for MANDINKA [MNK]
MANDINGI alt for BULLOM SO [BUY]
MANDINGO alt for MANDINKA [MNK]
MANDINGO alt for MANINKA, KANKAN [MNI]
MANDINGO alt for MANYA [MZJ]
MANDINGUE alt for MANDINKA [MNK]

MANDINKA [MNK] lang, Senegal; also in Gambia, Guinea-Bissau
MANDINQUE alt for MANDINKA [MNK]
MANDJA alt for MANZA [MZV]
MANDJAK [MFV] lang, Guinea-Bissau; also in France, Gambia, Senegal
MANDJALPINGU dial of DJINBA [DJB]
MANDJAQUE alt for MANDJAK [MFV]
MANDJOEN alt for YIR YORONT [YIY]
MANDJU alt for GHOMÁLÁ' [BBJ]
MANDLA dial of GONDI, NORTHERN [GON]
MANDLA dial of TSHWA [TSC]
MANDLAHA alt for GODWANI dial of BAGHELI [BFY]
MANDO dial of KANEMBU [KBL]
MANDOBBO alt for MANDOBO [KZH]
MANDOBO [KZH] lang, Indonesia (Irian Jaya); also in Papua New Guinea
MANDRICA dial of ALBANIAN, GHEG [ALS]
MANDUKA dial of NAMBIKUARA, SOUTHERN [NAB]
MANDURI alt for BAGA MANDURI [BMD]
MANDUSIR dial of BIAK [BHW]
MANDYAK alt for MANDJAK [MFV]
MANDYAM BRAHMIN dial of TAMIL [TCV]
MANE dial of BALANTA-KENTOHE [BLE]
MAÑEGU dial of FALA [FAX]
MANEHAS dial of BAKAKA [BQZ]
MANEM [JET] lang, Papua New Guinea; also in Indonesia (Irian Jaya)
MANEO dial of MANUSELA [WHA]
MANETA dial of WERSING [KVW]
MANG [MGA] lang, Viet Nam; also in China, Thailand
MANG alt for MANGEI dial of TALIABU [TLV]
MANG dial of LAKA [LAM]
MANG dial of MUMUYE [MUL]
MANG CONG alt for SÔ [SSS]
MANG U alt for MANG [MGA]
MANGA alt for KANURI, MANGA [KBY]
MANGA alt for MBA [MFC]
MANGA dial of KANURI, MANGA [KBY]
MANGA BUANG alt for BUANG, MANGGA [MMO]
MANGAABA alt for MBULA [MNA]
MANGAAVA alt for MBULA [MNA]
MANGAAWA alt for MBULA [MNA]
MANGAHERI alt for KAGULU [KKI]
MANGAIA dial of RAROTONGAN [RRT]
MANGALA [MEM] lang, Australia
MANGALA [MGH] lang, Congo
MANGALAA alt for MANGALA [MEM]
MANGALILI dial of GUMATJ [GNN]
MANGALORE dial of KONKANI, GOANESE [GOM]
MANGAMBILIS alt for DABE [DBE]
MANGANITU dial of SANGIR [SAN]
MANGANJA dial of NYANJA [NYJ]
MANGANJI dial of NGIRI [NGR]
MANGAP. KAIMANGA alt for MBULA [MNA]
MANGAP-MBULA alt for MBULA [MNA]
MANGARAGAN MANDAYA alt for MANDAYA, KARAGA [MRY]
MANGARAI alt for MANGARAYI [MPC]
MANGARAYI [MPC] lang, Australia
MANGAREVA [MRV] lang, French Polynesia

MANGAREVAN alt for MANGAREVA [MRV]
MANGARI alt for MAGAR, EASTERN [MGP]
MANGARLA alt for MANGALA [MEM]
MANGARONGARO alt for PENRHYN [PNH]
MANGAS [MAH] lang, Nigeria
MANGASARA alt for MAKASAR [MSR]
"MANGATI" pejorative alt for DATOOGA [TCC]
MANGAYA alt for MANGAYAT [MYJ]
MANGAYAT [MYJ] lang, Sudan
MANGBAI alt for MAMBAI [MCS]
MANGBAÏ DE BIPARÉ alt for MAMBAI [MCS]
MANGBEI alt for MAMBAI [MCS]
MANGBELE alt for NGBEE [NBL]
MANGBETTU alt for MANGBETU [MDJ]
MANGBETU [MDJ] lang, DRC; also in Uganda
MANGBETU dial of MANGBETU [MDJ]
MANGBUTU [MDK] lang, DRC
MANGE alt for MANGEI dial of TALIABU [TLV]
MANGE'E alt for MANGEI dial of TALIABU [TLV]
MANGEI dial of TALIABU [TLV]
MANGEREI alt for MANGERR [ZME]
MANGERI alt for MANGERR [ZME]
MANGERR [ZME] lang, Australia
MANGESH dial of CHALDEAN NEO-ARAMAIC [CLD]
MANGGALILI dial of GUPAPUYNGU [GUF]
MANGGANG alt for NUMANGGANG [NOP]
MANGGAR alt for MAGAR, EASTERN [MGP]
MANGGAR alt for MAGAR, WESTERN [MRD]
MANGGARAI [MQY] lang, Indonesia (Nusa Tenggara)
MANGGARAI alt for MANGARAYI [MPC]
MANGGUAR alt for KAMBERATARO [KBV]
MANGILI-WAIJELO dial of KAMBERA [SMI]
MANGISA alt for MENGISA [MCT]
MANGKAAK dial of KADAZAN, LABUK-KINABATANGAN [DTB]
MANGKAHAK alt for MANGKAAK dial of KADAZAN, LABUK-KINABATANGAN [DTB]
MANGKAK alt for MANGKAAK dial of KADAZAN, LABUK-KINABATANGAN [DTB]
MANGKATIP alt for MENGKATIP dial of BAKUMPAI [BKR]
MANGKETTAN alt for BUKITAN [BKN]
MANGKI alt for KALUMPANG [KLI]
MANGKI dial of KALUMPANG [KLI]
MANGKIR alt for KALUMPANG [KLI]
MANGKOK alt for MANGKAAK dial of KADAZAN, LABUK-KINABATANGAN [DTB]
MANGKONG alt for BAMUKUMBIT [BQT]
MANGKONG alt for SÔ [SSS]
MANGKONG dial of BRU, EASTERN [BRU]
MANG-KOONG alt for SÔ [SSS]
MANGKUNGE dial of NGEMBA [NGE]
MANGO [MGE] lang, Chad
MANGO alt for FALI-TINGUELIN dial of FALI, SOUTH [FAL]
MANGOCHE dial of YAO [YAO]
MANGOLE [MQC] lang, Indonesia (Maluku)
MANGOLI alt for MANGOLE [MQC]
MANGSDEKHA alt for NYENKHA [NEH]
MANGSENG [MBH] lang, Papua New Guinea

MANGSING alt for MANGSENG [MBH]
MANGUAGAN MANOBO dial of MANOBO, DIBABAWON [MBD]
MANGUE alt for CHOROTEGA [CJR]
MANGUM dial of DEG [MZW]
MANGU-NGUTU alt for MANGBUTU [MDK]
MANGWATO alt for NGWATU dial of TSWANA [TSW]
MANI alt for INDUS dial of KOHISTANI, INDUS [MVY]
MANI alt for SHOE dial of MPADE [MPI]
MANIBA alt for BANIWA [BAI]
MANIDE alt for AGTA, CAMARINES NORTE [ABD]
MANIGARA dial of MAIWA [MTI]
MANIHIKI-RAKAHANGA alt for RAKAHANGA-MANIHIKI [RKH]
MANI-ILING alt for MANILING dial of MUSGU [MUG]
MANIKA alt for MANYIKA [MXC]
MANIKION [MNX] lang, Indonesia (Irian Jaya)
MANILA dial of TAGALOG [TGL]
MANILING dial of MUSGU [MUG]
MANIMO alt for VANIMO [VAM]
MANINGA alt for MALINKE [MLQ]
MANINKA alt for MANINKA, KANKAN [MNI]
MANINKA, FOREST [MYQ] lang, Côte d'Ivoire
MANINKA, KANKAN [MNI] lang, Guinea; also in Liberia, Sierra Leone
MANINKA, KONYANKA [MKU] lang, Guinea
MANINKA, SANKARAN [MSC] lang, Guinea
MANINKAKAN, KITA [MWK] lang, Mali
MANINKAKAN, WESTERN [MLQ] lang, Mali; also in Gambia, Guinea, Guinea-Bissau, Senegal
MANINKA-MORI alt for MANINKA, KANKAN [MNI]
MANINKA-MORI dial of MANINKA, KANKAN [MNI]
MANINKA-WESTERN alt for MALINKE [MLQ]
MANIPA [MQP] lang, Indonesia (Maluku)
MANIPURI alt for MEITEI [MNR]
MANIQ alt for KENSIU [KNS]
MANITENÉRE alt for MACHINERE [MPD]
MANITENERÍ alt for MACHINERE [MPD]
MANITSAWÁ alt for MARITSAUÁ [MSP]
MANIYA alt for MANYA [MZJ]
MANJA alt for MANZA [MZV]
MANJACA alt for MANDJAK [MFV]
MANJACK alt for MANDJAK [MFV]
MANJACO alt for MANDJAK [MFV]
MANJACU alt for MANDJAK [MFV]
MANJAK alt for MANDJAK [MFV]
MANJAKU alt for MANDJAK [MFV]
MANJAR alt for MANDAR [MHN]
MANJHI alt for MAJHI [MJZ]
MANJHI alt for MAJHWAR [MMJ]
MANJHI dial of ASURI [ASR]
MANJHI dial of SANTALI [SNT]
MANJHIA alt for MAJHWAR [MMJ]
MANJIAK alt for MANDJAK [MFV]
MANJI-KASA alt for DWERA dial of LIGBI [LIG]
MANJO alt for KAFICHO [KBR]
MANJUI alt for CHOROTE, IYO'WUJWA [CRQ]
MANJUY alt for CHOROTE, IYO'WUJWA [CRQ]
MANKALIYA dial of KURANKO [KHA]
MANKANHA alt for MANKANYA [MAN]

MANKANYA [MAN] lang, Guinea-Bissau; also in Gambia, Senegal
MANKAYAN-BUGUIAS dial of KANKANAEY [KNE]
MANKETA alt for BUKITAN [BKN]
MANKIDI alt for BIRHOR [BIY]
MANKIDIA alt for BIRHOR [BIY]
MANKIM dial of TIKAR [TIK]
MANKON dial of NGEMBA [NGE]
MANKOONG alt for SÔ [SSS]
MANLEA alt for KUSA-MANLEA dial of ATONI [TMR]
MANMI alt for MAN MET [MML]
MANMIT alt for MAN MET [MML]
MANNADI alt for BAGHELI [BFY]
MANNA-DORA [MJU] lang, India
MANNAN [MJV] lang, India
MANNE alt for MANNAN [MJV]
MANNYOD alt for MANNAN [MJV]
MANO [MEV] lang, Liberia; also in Guinea
MANÖ alt for KAREN, MANUMANAW [KXF]
MANOA alt for PANOBO [PNO]
MANOBAI alt for MANOMBAI [WOO]
MANOBO, AGUSAN [MSM] lang, Philippines
MANOBO, ATA [ATD] lang, Philippines
MANOBO, CINAMIGUIN [MKX] lang, Philippines
MANOBO, COTABATO [MTA] lang, Philippines
MANOBO, DIBABAWON [MBD] lang, Philippines
MANOBO, ILIANEN [MBI] lang, Philippines
MANOBO, MATIGSALUG [MBT] lang, Philippines
MANOBO, OBO [OBO] lang, Philippines
MANOBO, RAJAH KABUNSUWAN [MQK] lang, Philippines
MANOBO, SARANGANI [MBS] lang, Philippines
MANOBO, TAGABAWA [BGS] lang, Philippines
MANOBO, WESTERN BUKIDNON [MBB] lang, Philippines
MANOITA alt for SHETEBO dial of SHIPIBO-CONIBO [SHP]
MANOMBAI [WOO] lang, Indonesia (Maluku)
MANOUCHE alt for MANUCHE dial of ROMANI, SINTE [RMO]
MANOUCHE alt for ROMANI, SINTE [RMO]
MANOUCHE dial of ROMANI, SINTE [RMO]
MANOWEE alt for ASMAT, CENTRAL [AST]
MANPELLE alt for MAMPRULI [MAW]
MANSA' dial of TIGRE [TIE]
MANSAKA [MSK] lang, Philippines
MANSI [MNS] lang, Russia (Asia)
MANSIM alt for HATAM [HAD]
MANSINYO dial of YURACARE [YUE]
MANSIY alt for MANSI [MNS]
MANSOANCA alt for MANSOANKA [MSW]
MANSOANKA [MSW] lang, Guinea-Bissau; also in Gambia
MANTA [MYG] lang, Cameroon
MANTANGAI dial of NGAJU [NIJ]
MANTARAREN dial of LAWANGAN [LBX]
MANTAURAN dial of RUKAI [DRU]
MANTEMBU alt for YAWA [YVA]
MANTION alt for MANIKION [MNX]
MANTIZULA alt for MARITSAUÁ [MSP]

MANTJILTJARA alt for MANYJILYJARA dial of MARTU WANGKA [MPJ]
MANTOVANO dial of EMILIANO-ROMAGNOLO [EML]
MANTRA dial of TEMUAN [TMW]
MANTSI [MUS] lang, Viet Nam
MANU PARK PANOAN alt for YORA [MTS]
MANUA dial of MAMBAE [MGM]
MANUBARA alt for MARIA [MDS]
MANUCHE alt for MANOUCHE dial of ROMANI, SINTE [RMO]
MANUCHE alt for ROMANI, SINTE [RMO]
MANUCHE dial of ROMANI, SINTE [RMO]
MANUK dial of JAVANESE [JAN]
MANUKAI alt for MANYUKAI dial of DAYAK, LAND [DYK]
MANUKOLU alt for LAGUME dial of HUMENE [HUF]
MANUM alt for MANAM [MVA]
MANUMANAW alt for KAREN, MANUMANAW [KXF]
MANUS alt for LELE [UGA]
MANUS alt for TITAN [TTV]
MANUSELA [WHA] lang, Indonesia (Maluku)
MANUSH alt for MANOUCHE dial of ROMANI, SINTE [RMO]
MANX [MJD] lang, United Kingdom
MANX GAELIC alt for MANX [MJD]
MANYA [MZJ] lang, Liberia; also in Guinea
MANYA KAN alt for MANYA [MZJ]
MANYAK alt for MUYA [MVM]
MANYANG alt for KENYANG [KEN]
MANYARRING dial of DJINANG [DJI]
MANYAWA [MNY] lang, Mozambique
MANYEMAN alt for BAKONI dial of KENYANG [KEN]
MANYEMEN alt for BAKONI dial of KENYANG [KEN]
MANYIKA [MXC] lang, Zimbabwe; also in Mozambique
MANYJILYJARA dial of MARTU WANGKA [MPJ]
MANYOK dial of BEBELE [BEB]
MANYUKAI dial of DAYAK, LAND [DYK]
MANYUKE alt for MANYUKAI dial of DAYAK, LAND [DYK]
MANZA [MZV] lang, CAR
MANZANERO alt for MOLUCHE dial of MAPUDUNGUN [ARU]
MANZARI alt for DUBER-KANDIA dial of KOHISTANI, INDUS [MVY]
MAO alt for NAGA, MAO [NBI]
MAO alt for TAI MAO dial of SHAN [SJN]
MAO dial of KANURI, CENTRAL [KPH]
MAOLI alt for GHATI dial of KONKANI [KNK]
MAONAN [MMD] lang, China
MAOPA dial of KEOPARA [KHZ]
MAOPITYAN alt for MAPIDIAN dial of ARUMA [WAP]
MAORI [MBF] lang, New Zealand
MAORI alt for RAROTONGAN [RRT]
MAOU alt for MAHOU [MXX]
MAPACHE dial of CARUTANA [CRU]
MAPAN alt for MUPUN dial of MWAGHAVUL [SUR]
MAPANGA dial of YASA [YKO]
MAPAYO alt for MAPOYO [MCG]
MAPE [MLH] lang, Papua New Guinea

MAPE dial of MAPE [MLH]
MAPENA [MNM] lang, Papua New Guinea
MAPHEKHA alt for CHOCANGACAKHA [CHK]
MAPI alt for YAQAY [JAQ]
MAPIA [MPY] lang, Indonesia (Irian Jaya)
MAPIA dial of BIAK [BHW]
MAPIAN alt for MAPIA [MPY]
MAPIDIAN dial of ARUMA [WAP]
MAPIYA-KEGATA dial of EKARI [EKG]
MAPODI alt for GUDE [GDE]
MAPOR alt for LOM [MFB]
MAPORESE alt for LOM [MFB]
MAPOS alt for BUANG, MAPOS [BZH]
MAPOS dial of BUANG, MAPOS [BZH]
MAPOYE alt for MAPOYO [MCG]
MAPOYO [MCG] lang, Venezuela
MAPPA-PANA alt for TORAJA BARAT dial of TORAJA-SADAN [SDA]
MAPRIK dial of AMBULAS [ABT]
MAPUCHE alt for MAPUDUNGUN [ARU]
MAPUDA alt for GUDE [GDE]
MAPUDUNGU alt for MAPUDUNGUN [ARU]
MAPUDUNGUN [ARU] lang, Chile; also in Argentina
MAPUN [SJM] lang, Philippines; also in Malaysia (Sabah)
MAPUN alt for MUPUN dial of MWAGHAVUL [SUR]
MAPUTE alt for WARU [WRU]
MAPUTONGO alt for MAPUDUNGUN [ARU]
MAQAQET alt for QAQET [BYX]
MAQUA alt for NAMA [NAQ]
MAQUIRI alt for KAYABÍ [KYZ]
MAQUIRITAI alt for MAQUIRITARI [MCH]
MAQUIRITARE alt for MAQUIRITARI [MCH]
MAQUIRITARI [MCH] lang, Venezuela; also in Brazil
MAQUOUA alt for MAKHUWA [VMW]
MAQUOUA alt for MAKHUWA-MEETTO [MAK]
MAR alt for MAL PAHARIA [MKB]
MARA [MEC] lang, Australia
MARA alt for CHIN, MARA [MRH]
MARA dial of KABA DEME [KWG]
MARA dial of MALGBE [MXF]
MARA MA-SIKI alt for OROHA [ORA]
MARABA alt for MARBA [MPG]
MARABA alt for MORUBA dial of BANDA-MBRES [BQK]
MARACASERO alt for MALAYO [MBP]
MARACHA dial of LUGBARA [LUG]
MARACHI dial of LUYIA [LUY]
MARAGANG alt for KIMARAGANG [KQR]
MARAGAT alt for ISNAG [ISD]
MARAGAUS alt for MARAGUS [MRS]
MARAGHEI [VMH] lang, Iran
MARAGOLI alt for LOGOOLI [RAG]
MARA-GOMU dial of MBO-UNG [MUX]
MARAGOOLI alt for LOGOOLI [RAG]
MARAGUA alt for SATERÉ-MAWÉ [MAV]
MARAGUS [MRS] lang, Vanuatu
MARAKA alt for SONINKE [SNN]
MARAKO alt for LIBIDO [LIQ]
MARAKUET alt for ENDO [ENB]
MARAKWET alt for TALAI [TLE]

MARALANGKO alt for MARALANGO dial of WATUT, SOUTH [MCY]

MARALANGO dial of WATUT, SOUTH [MCY]

MARALIINAN alt for WATUT, MIDDLE [MPL]

MARALINAN alt for WATUT, MIDDLE [MPL]

MARAM alt for CHIN, MARA [MRH]

MARAM alt for NAGA, MARAM [NMA]

MARAMA dial of LUYIA [LUY]

MARAMANANDJI alt for MARIMANINDJI [ZMM]

MARAMANUNGGU alt for MARANUNGGU dial of MARINGARR [ZMT]

MARAMARANDJI alt for MARIMANINDJI [ZMM]

MARAMBA [MYD] lang, Papua New Guinea

MARAMUNI dial of ENGA [ENQ]

MARAMURESH dial of ROMANIAN [RUM]

MARAN alt for AMIS [ALV]

MARANAO [MRW] lang, Philippines

MARANAW alt for MARANAO [MRW]

MARANGAI dial of TUAMOTUAN [PMT]

MARANGIS alt for WATAM [WAX]

MARANGU alt for VUNJO [VUN]

MARANUNGGU [ZMR] lang, Australia

MARANUNGGU dial of MARINGARR [ZMT]

MARAPU dial of MANGSENG [MBH]

MARAQO alt for LIBIDO [LIQ]

MARARA dial of BAGA SITEMU [BSP]

MARARET alt for MARARIT [MGB]

MARARI dial of BAGHELI [BFY]

MARARIT [MGB] lang, Chad

MARARIT dial of MARARIT [MGB]

MARASHI dial of DOMARI [RMT]

MARATHI [MRT] lang, India; also in Israel, Mauritius

MARATTIYAN alt for VAAGRI BOOLI [VAA]

MARAU [MVR] lang, Indonesia (Irian Jaya)

MARAU dial of AREARE [ALU]

MARAU SOUND alt for MARAU dial of AREARE [ALU]

MARAVE alt for PETA dial of NYANJA [NYJ]

MARAVI alt for PETA dial of NYANJA [NYJ]

MARAWAR alt for MARWARI [MRI]

MARAWORNO alt for CARIB [CRB]

MARBA [MPG] lang, Chad

MARBA alt for MARFA [MVU]

MARDA dial of KUNAMA [KUM]

MARDALA alt for ADYNYAMATHANHA [ADT]

MARE alt for BONE dial of BUGIS [BPR]

MARÉ alt for NENGONE [NEN]

MARE-AMMU dial of MARITHIEL [MFR]

MAREBBANO dial of LADIN [LLD]

MAREDYERBIN alt for MARIDJABIN [ZMJ]

MAREGAON dial of KOLAMI, NORTHWESTERN [KFB]

MAREMGI [MRX] lang, Indonesia (Irian Jaya)

MARENDJE alt for MARENJE [VMR]

MARENG alt for MARING [MBW]

MARENGGAR alt for MARINGARR [ZMT]

MARENGGE alt for MAREMGI [MRX]

MARENJE [VMR] lang, Mozambique

MARENSÉ dial of SONGHAY [HMB]

MARETYABIN alt for MARIDJABIN [ZMJ]

MAREVONE alt for MAKHUWA-MARREVONE [XMC]

MAREWUMIRI alt for NGENKIWUMERRI dial of NANGIKURRUNGGURR [NAM]

MARFA [MVU] lang, Chad

MARGALURI alt for MINGRELIAN [XMF]

MARGANY [ZMC] lang, Australia

MARGHI alt for MARGHI CENTRAL [MAR]

MARGHI CENTRAL [MAR] lang, Nigeria

MARGHI SOUTH [MFM] lang, Nigeria

MARGHI WEST alt for PUTAI [MFL]

MARGI alt for MARGHI CENTRAL [MAR]

MARGOSATUBIG alt for SUBANUN, LAPUYAN [LAA]

MARGU [MHG] lang, Australia

MARHAY alt for MUNDANG [MUA]

MARI [HOB] lang, Papua New Guinea

MARI [MBX] lang, Papua New Guinea

MARI [MXW] lang, Papua New Guinea

MARI alt for MARI, LOW [MAL]

MARI, HIGH [MRJ] lang, Russia (Europe)

MARI, LOW [MAL] lang, Russia (Europe); also in Kazakhstan

MARIA [MDS] lang, Papua New Guinea

MARIA [MRR] lang, India

MARIA dial of MARIA [MDS]

MARIA GOND alt for MARIA, DANDAMI [DAQ]

MARIA, DANDAMI [DAQ] lang, India

MARIAPE-NAHUQUA alt for MATIPUHY [MZO]

MARICOPA [MRC] lang, USA

MARIDAN [ZMD] lang, Australia

MARIDHIEL alt for MARITHIEL [MFR]

MARIDHIYEL alt for MARITHIEL [MFR]

MARIDJABIN [ZMJ] lang, Australia

MARIDYERBIN alt for MARIDJABIN [ZMJ]

MARIE GALANTE CREOLE FRENCH dial of LESSER ANTILLEAN CREOLE FRENCH [DOM]

MARIGANG alt for KIMARAGANG [KQR]

MARIGL dial of GOLIN [GVF]

MARI-HILLS alt for MARI, HIGH [MRJ]

MARIK [DAD] lang, Papua New Guinea

MARIKAI dial of BARAPASI [BRP]

MARILLE alt for DAASANACH [DSH]

MARIMANINDJI [ZMM] lang, Australia

MARIMANINDU alt for MARIMANINDJI [ZMM]

MARIN MIWOK dial of MIWOK, COAST [CSI]

MARINA alt for TOLOMAKO [TLM]

MARINAHUA dial of SHARANAHUA [MCD]

MARINAWA alt for MARINAHUA dial of SHARANAHUA [MCD]

MARINÁWA alt for MARINAHUA dial of SHARANAHUA [MCD]

MARIND [MRZ] lang, Indonesia (Irian Jaya)

MARIND, BIAN [BPV] lang, Indonesia (Irian Jaya)

MARINDUQUE dial of TAGALOG [TGL]

MARING [MBW] lang, Papua New Guinea

MARING alt for NAGA, MARING [NNG]

MARINGA alt for MARINGARR [ZMT]

MARINGARR [ZMT] lang, Australia

MARINGE dial of CHEKE HOLO [MRN]

MARINGHE alt for MARINGE dial of CHEKE HOLO [MRN]

MARINO [MRB] lang, Vanuatu

MARIP alt for JINGPHO [CGP]
MARIPOSAS alt for TAMPIWI dial of CUIBA [CUI]
MARIRI [MQI] lang, Indonesia (Maluku)
MARITHIEL [MFR] lang, Australia
MARITHIEL dial of MARITHIEL [MFR]
MARITHIYEL alt for MARITHIEL [MFR]
MARITIME GAGAUZ dial of GAGAUZ [GAG]
MARITIME GAGAUZI dial of GAGAUZ [GAG]
MARITIME PROVENÇAL dial of PROVENÇAL [PRV]
MARITIME SIGN LANGUAGE [NSR] lang, Canada
MARITSAUA alt for MARITSAUÁ [MSP]
MARITSAUÁ [MSP] lang, Brazil
MARIVELES AYTA alt for AYTA, BATAAN [AYT]
MARI-WOODS alt for MARI, LOW [MAL]
MARIYEDI [ZMY] lang, Australia
MARKA [MWR] lang, Burkina Faso; also in Mali
MARKA alt for SONINKE [SNN]
MARKA DAFING alt for MARKA [MWR]
MARKA-DAFIN alt for MARKA [MWR]
MARK-BRANDENBURG dial of SAXON, LOW [SXN]
MARKE dial of DOYAYO [DOW]
MARKWETA alt for ENDO [ENB]
MARLASI alt for KOLA [KVV]
MARMA alt for ARAKANESE [MHV]
MARMA dial of ARAKANESE [MHV]
MARMAREGHO alt for BAURO [BXA]
MAROA alt for SHOLIO dial of TYAP [KCG]
MAROCASERO alt for MALAYO [MBP]
MARON alt for HERMIT [LLF]
MARONENE alt for MORONENE [MQN]
MARONITE alt for ARABIC, CYPRIOT SPOKEN [ACY]
MARORI alt for MORORI [MOK]
MAROS-PANGKEP dial of MAKASAR [MSR]
MAROUA dial of FULFULDE, ADAMAWA [FUB]
MAROVA alt for MARÚBO [MZR]
MAROVO [MVO] lang, Solomon Islands
MARPAHARIA alt for MAL PAHARIA [MKB]
MARPHA dial of THAKALI [THS]
MARQUESAN, NORTH [MRQ] lang, French Polynesia
MARQUESAN, SOUTH [QMS] lang, French Polynesia
MARQUITO alt for MÍSKITO [MIQ]
MARRA alt for MARA [MEC]
MARRAKECH ARABIC dial of ARABIC, MOROCCAN SPOKEN [ARY]
MARRAKULU dial of DHUWAL [DUJ]
MARRAMANINJSJI alt for MARIMANINDJI [ZMM]
MARRANGU dial of DHUWAL [DUJ]
MARRANUNGA alt for MARANUNGGU dial of MARINGARR [ZMT]
MARREVONE alt for MAKHUWA-MARREVONE [XMC]
MARRITHIYEL alt for MARITHIEL [MFR]
MARRY dial of YASA [YKO]
MARSEILLAIS alt for MARITIME PROVENÇAL dial of PROVENCAL [PRV]
MARSEILLE SIGN LANGUAGE dial of FRENCH SIGN LANGUAGE [FSL]

MARSELA-SOUTH BABAR alt for MASELA, CENTRAL [MKH]
MARSH FRENCH dial of FRENCH, CAJUN [FRC]
MARSHALLESE [MZM] lang, Marshall Islands; also in Nauru
MARTHA'S VINEYARD SIGN LANGUAGE [MRE] lang, USA
MARTHI alt for MARATHI [MRT]
MARTINIQUE CREOLE FRENCH dial of LESSER ANTILLEAN CREOLE FRENCH [DOM]
MARTU WANGKA [MPJ] lang, Australia
MARTUYHUNIRA [VMA] lang, Australia
MARU [MHX] lang, Myanmar; also in China
MARU alt for MATU dial of CHIN, KHUMI [CKM]
MARU alt for MRU [MRO]
MARUB [MJB] lang, Indonesia (Irian Jaya)
MARUBA alt for MARÚBO [MZR]
MARÚBO [MZR] lang, Brazil
MARUHIA alt for ISABI [ISA]
MARUONGMAI alt for NAGA, RONGMEI [NBU]
MARUWA alt for SHOLIO dial of TYAP [KCG]
MARVARI alt for MARWARI [MKD]
MARWA alt for SHOLIO dial of TYAP [KCG]
MARWADI alt for MARWARI [MKD]
MARWARI [MKD] lang, India; also in Nepal
MARWARI [MRI] lang, Pakistan
MARWARI BHAT dial of MARWARI [MRI]
MARWARI BHIL alt for MARWARI [MRI]
MARWARI BHIL dial of MARWARI [MRI]
MARWARI GHERA alt for GURGULA [GGG]
MARWARI MEGHWAR alt for MARWARI [MRI]
MARWARI MEGHWAR dial of MARWARI [MRI]
MARWORNO alt for CARIB [CRB]
MASA alt for MASANA [MCN]
MASAABA alt for MASABA [MYX]
MASABA [MYX] lang, Uganda
MASAI alt for MAASAI [MET]
MASAKÁ dial of TUBARAO [TBA]
MASAKIN alt for DAGIK [DEC]
MASAKIN alt for NGILE [MAS]
MASAKIN BURAM alt for MASAKIN GUSAR dial of NGILE [MAS]
MASAKIN DAGIG alt for DAGIK [DEC]
MASAKIN GUSAR dial of NGILE [MAS]
MASAKIN TUWAL dial of NGILE [MAS]
MASAKU dial of KAMBA [KIK]
MASALAGA alt for BONGOS [BXY]
MASALE alt for MASALIT [MSA]
MASALIT [MSA] lang, Sudan; also in Chad
MASAMA alt for ANDIO [BZB]
MASAN dial of BUNA [BVN]
MASANA [MCN] lang, Chad; also in Cameroon
MASANGO alt for MAJANG [MPE]
MASANZE dial of ZYOBA [ZYO]
MASARA alt for MASALIT [MSA]
MASARETE dial of BURU [MHS]
MASARWA alt for HIETSHWARE [HIE]
MASARWA alt for KAKIA dial of XOO [NMN]
MASAWA dial of KUANUA [KSD]
MASBATEÑO alt for MASBATENYO [MSB]
MASBATENYO [MSB] lang, Philippines

MASBUAR-TELA alt for TELA-MASBUAR [TVM]
MASEGI alt for MANGSENG [MBH]
MASEKI alt for MANGSENG [MBH]
MASELA, CENTRAL [MKH] lang, Indonesia (Maluku)
MASELA, EAST [VME] lang, Indonesia (Maluku)
MASELA, WEST [MSS] lang, Indonesia (Maluku)
MASEMOLA dial of SOTHO, NORTHERN [SRT]
MASEMULA alt for MASEMOLA dial of SOTHO,
    NORTHERN [SRT]
MASENREMPULU alt for DURI [MVP]
MASENREMPULU alt for MAIWA [WMM]
MASEP alt for MASSEP [MVS]
MASFEIMA dial of WANDALA [MFI]
MASH alt for ARAKANESE [MHV]
MASHADI dial of FARSI, WESTERN [PES]
MASHANGA alt for SHANGA dial of NDAU [NDC]
MASHASHA dial of NKOYA [NKA]
MASHATI dial of CHAGGA [KAF]
"MASHCO" pejorative alt for AMARAKAERI [AMR]
"MASHCO" pejorative alt for HUACHIPAERI [HUG]
"MASHCO" pejorative alt for MASHCO PIRO [CUJ]
MASHCO PIRO [CUJ] lang, Peru
MASHELLE alt for BUSSA [DOX]
MASHI [JMS] lang, Nigeria
MASHI [MHO] lang, Zambia; also in Angola, Namibia
MASHI alt for SHI [SHR]
MASHI dial of MASHI [MHO]
MASHIKI alt for SHIKI [GUA]
MASHILE alt for BUSSA [DOX]
MASHOLLE alt for BUSSA [DOX]
MASHUAKWE alt for SHUA [SHG]
MASHUAKWE alt for SHUA-KHWE dial of SHUA
    [SHG]
MASI alt for MASHI [MHO]
MASIGUARE alt for MASIWARE dial of CUIBA [CUI]
MASIGUARE dial of CUIBA [CUI]
MASIIN alt for AZER dial of SONINKE [SNN]
MASIMASI [ISM] lang, Indonesia (Irian Jaya)
MASIMASI dial of IAMALELE [YML]
MASINGBI dial of THEMNE [TEJ]
MASINGLE dial of BINE [ORM]
MASIN-LAK alt for KUI [KVD]
MASIRI dial of CIA-CIA [CIA]
MASIWANG [BNF] lang, Indonesia (Maluku)
MASIWARE dial of CUIBA [CUI]
MASKELYNE ISLANDS alt for MASKELYNES [KLV]
MASKELYNES [KLV] lang, Vanuatu
MASKOY PIDGIN [MHH] lang, Paraguay
MASLAM [MSV] lang, Cameroon; also in Chad
MASLAM dial of MASLAM [MSV]
MASLAVA alt for MBEREM dial of PELASLA [MLR]
MASLAVA alt for PELASLA [MLR]
MASMADJE alt for MASMAJE [MES]
MASMAJE [MES] lang, Chad
MASONGO alt for MAJANG [MPE]
MASQAN dial of GURAGE, WEST [GUY]
MASSA alt for MASANA [MCN]
MASSA DE GUELENGDENG alt for MBARA [MPK]
MASSACA alt for MASAKÁ dial of TUBARAO [TBA]
MASSACHUSETT alt for WAMPANOAG [WAM]
MASSACHUSETTS alt for WAMPANOAG [WAM]

MASSAGAL dial of MOFU-GUDUR [MIF]
MASSAKA alt for MAKURÁP [MAG]
MASSAKAL alt for MASSAGAL dial of MOFU-
    GUDUR [MIF]
MASSALAT [MDG] lang, Chad
MASSALI dial of TALYSH [TLY]
MASSALIT alt for MASALIT [MSA]
MASSANINGA dial of YAO [YAO]
MASSENREMPULU alt for DURI [MVP]
MASSEP [MVS] lang, Indonesia (Irian Jaya)
MASSET alt for HAIDA, NORTHERN [HAI]
MASSET dial of TUTCHONE, NORTHERN [TUT]
MASSOLIT alt for MASALIT [MSA]
MASTANAHUA dial of YAMINAHUA [YAA]
MASVINGO SCHOOL SIGN dial of ZIMBABWE
    SIGN LANGUAGE [ZIB]
MASWANKA alt for MANSOANKA [MSW]
MATA alt for TUPURI [TUI]
MATA dial of TUPURI [TUI]
MATABAN-MOULMEIN dial of MON [MNW]
MATABELLO alt for WATUBELA [WAH]
"MATACO" pejorative alt for WICHÍ LHAMTÉS
    GÜISNAY [MZH]
"MATACO" GÜISNAY pejorative alt for WICHÍ
    LHAMTÉS GÜISNAY [MZH]
"MATACO" NOCTEN pejorative alt for WICHÍ
    LHAMTÉS NOCTEN [MTP]
"MATACO" PILCOMAYO pejorative alt for WICHÍ
    LHAMTÉS GÜISNAY [MZH]
"MATACO" VEJOZ pejorative alt for WICHÍ
    LHAMTÉS VEJOZ [MAD]
MATAGALPA [MTN] lang, Nicaragua
MATAITAI dial of BWAIDOKA [BWD]
"MATAKAM" pejorative alt for MAFA [MAF]
MATAL [MFH] lang, Cameroon
MATALAANG dial of BAJAU, INDONESIAN [BDL]
MATAMBWE alt for MAKONDE [KDE]
MATAN dial of DAYAK, LAND [DYK]
MATANAI alt for SONDER dial of TONTEMBOAN
    [TNT]
MATANA'I-MAORE' alt for SONDER dial of
    TONTEMBOAN [TNT]
MATANGNGA dial of BAMBAM [PTU]
MATAPI alt for YUCUNA [YCN]
MATAPO dial of MAASAI [MET]
MATARU alt for BALAMULA dial of LEWADA-
    DEWARA [LWD]
MATASO dial of NAMAKURA [NMK]
MATATLÁN ZAPOTEC alt for SANTIAGO
    MATATLÁN ZAPOTEC dial of ZAPOTECO,
    MITLA [ZAW]
MATAWAI alt for MATAWARI dial of
    SARAMACCAN [SRM]
MATAWARI dial of SARAMACCAN [SRM]
MATBAT [XMT] lang, Indonesia (Irian Jaya)
MATCHI dial of GARO [GRT]
MATCHI alt for MACI dial of ICEVE-MACI [BEC]
MATCHI alt for OLITI dial of ICEVE-MACI [BEC]
MATCHOPA NAGNOO dial of MOINBA [MOB]
MATE dial of NANDI [NNB]
MATEMA dial of PILENI [PIV]

MATENGO [MGV] lang, Tanzania
MATE-NUL-FILAKARA dial of LEWO [LWW]
MATEPI [MQE] lang, Papua New Guinea
MATHIRA dial of GIKUYU [KIU]
MATHSERENG alt for NACHERING [NCD]
MATIA dial of ASMAT, CASUARINA COAST [ASC]
MATIG-SALUD dial of MANOBO, MATIGSALUG
[MBT]
MATIG-SALUG MANOBO alt for MANOBO,
MATIGSALUG [MBT]
MATINO alt for DAVAWENYO [DAW]
MATIPU alt for MATIPUHY [MZO]
MATIPUHY [MZO] lang, Brazil
MATIPUHY dial of MATIPUHY [MZO]
MATÍS [MPQ] lang, Brazil
MATLALA-MOLETSHI dial of SOTHO, NORTHERN
[SRT]
MATLATZINCA alt for MATLATZINCA, SAN
FRANCISCO DE LOS RANCHOS [MAT]
MATLATZINCA, ATZINGO [OCU] lang, Mexico
MATLATZINCA, SAN FRANCISCO DE LOS
RANCHOS [MAT] lang, Mexico
MATLIWAG dial of MERLAV [MRM]
MATNGALA alt for MADNGELE [ZML]
MATO [NIU] lang, Papua New Guinea
MATO alt for MAKHUWA-MEETTO [MAK]
MATOEWARI alt for MATAWARI dial of
SARAMACCAN [SRM]
MATOH alt for EMBALOH [EMB]
MATOKI alt for NORTHERN BOMITABA dial of
BOMITABA [ZMX]
MATONDONI dial of SWAHILI [SWA]
MATOR [MTM] lang, Russia (Asia)
MATOR dial of MATOR [MTM]
MATSE alt for MATSÉS [MCF]
MATSÉS [MCF] lang, Peru; also in Brazil
MATSIGANGA alt for MACHIGUENGA [MCB]
MATSIGENKA alt for MACHIGUENGA [MCB]
MATSUNGAN dial of PETATS [PEX]
MATTOLE [MVB] lang, USA
MATU alt for MARU [MHX]
MATU dial of CHIN, KHUMI [CKM]
MATU dial of DARO-MATU [DRO]
MATUARI alt for MATAWARI dial of SARAMACCAN
[SRM]
MATUKAR [MJK] lang, Papua New Guinea
MATUMBI [MGW] lang, Tanzania
MATUPI alt for MATU dial of CHIN, KHUMI [CKM]
MATUPIT dial of KUANUA [KSD]
MATWANLY dial of RAWANG [RAW]
MAU alt for MAHOU [MXX]
MAU alt for TAI MAO dial of SHAN [SJN]
MAUBIN dial of KAREN, PWO WESTERN [PWO]
MAUCHI alt for MAWCHI [MKE]
MAUE alt for SATERÉ-MAWÉ [MAV]
MAUKA alt for MAHOU [MXX]
MAUKE alt for MAHOU [MXX]
MAUKE dial of RAROTONGAN [RRT]
MAULA alt for WARLUWARA [WRB]
MAULIGAN alt for MALIGAN dial of TAGAL MURUT
[MVV]

MAUMBI dial of TONSEA [TXS]
MAUMERE alt for SIKA [SKI]
"MAUNCHI" pejorative alt for CISHINGINI [ASG]
MAUNG [MPH] lang, Australia
MAUNG alt for KETUNGAU dial of IBAN [IBA]
MAURE alt for ARABIC, HASANYA [MEY]
MAURE alt for ARABIC, HASSANIYYA [MEY]
MAURI alt for ARABIC, HASANYA [MEY]
MAURI alt for ARABIC, HASSANIYYA [MEY]
MAURITIAN alt for MORISYEN [MFE]
MAURITIAN BHOJPURI dial of BHOJPURI [BHJ]
MAURITIUS CREOLE FRENCH alt for MORISYEN
[MFE]
MAURYSEN alt for MORISYEN [MFE]
MAUTA alt for LAMMA [LEV]
MAUTA alt for TUBAL dial of LAMMA [LEV]
MAUTUTU dial of NAKANAI [NAK]
MAUUULA alt for WARLUWARA [WRB]
MAUWAKE [MHL] lang, Papua New Guinea
MAVAR alt for MOVAR dial of KANURI, CENTRAL
[KPH]
MAVCHI alt for MAWCHI [MKE]
MAVEA alt for MAFEA [MKV]
MAVIA alt for MAVIHA dial of MAKONDE [KDE]
MAVIHA dial of MAKONDE [KDE]
MAW alt for MAL PAHARIA [MKB]
MAW alt for TAI MAO dial of SHAN [SJN]
MAWA [MCW] lang, Chad
MAWA [WMA] lang, Nigeria
MAWACHI alt for MAWCHI [MKE]
MAWAE dial of ZIA [ZIA]
MAWAK [MJJ] lang, Papua New Guinea
MAWAKE alt for MAUWAKE [MHL]
MAWAN [MCZ] lang, Papua New Guinea
"MAWANCHI" pejorative alt for CISHINGINI [ASG]
MAWANDA alt for NDONDE [NDS]
MAWAS alt for KENSIU [KNS]
MAWASI dial of KORKU [KFQ]
MAWAYANA alt for MAPIDIAN dial of ARUMA [WAP]
MAWCHI [MKE] lang, India
MAWCHI dial of BHILI [BHB]
MAWCHI dial of MAWCHI [MKE]
MAWCHI BHIL alt for MAWCHI [MKE]
MAWDO alt for MAL PAHARIA [MKB]
MAWE alt for MANO [MEV]
MAWER alt for MAL PAHARIA [MKB]
MAWER alt for MOTUN dial of TUMAK [TMC]
MAWER NONDI alt for MAL PAHARIA [MKB]
MAWES [MGK] lang, Indonesia (Irian Jaya)
MAWIA alt for MAVIHA dial of MAKONDE [KDE]
MAWISSI alt for TALINGA-BWISI [TLJ]
MAWKEN alt for MOKEN [MWT]
MAWRANG dial of NAGA, TASE [NST]
MAWSHANG alt for NAGA, MONSANG [NMH]
MAWTEIK alt for KADO [KDV]
MAWULA alt for WARLUWARA [WRB]
MAXAKALÍ [MBL] lang, Brazil
MAXI alt for MAXI-GBE [MXL]
MAXI-GBE [MXL] lang, Benin; also in Togo
MAXINÉRI alt for MACHINERE [MPD]
MAXIRONA alt for MATSÉS [MCF]

MAXUBÍ alt for ARIKAPÚ [ARK]
MAXURUNA alt for MATSÉS [MCF]
MAY alt for CHUT [SCB]
MAY dial of CHUT [SCB]
MAY RIVER alt for IWAM [IWM]
MAYA alt for BALI [BCN]
MAYA alt for ITZÁ [ITZ]
MAYA alt for MAIA [SKS]
MA'YA [SLZ] lang, Indonesia (Irian Jaya)
MA'YA dial of MAYA [SLZ]
MAYA MOPÁN alt for MOPÁN MAYA [MOP]
MAYA, CHAN SANTA CRUZ [YUS] lang, Mexico
MAYA, YUCATÁN [YUA] lang, Mexico; also in Belize
MAYAGUDUNA [XMY] lang, Australia
MAYALI alt for GUNWINGGU [GUP]
MAYANG dial of ASSAMESE [ASM]
MAYANGKHANG alt for NAGA, KHOIRAO [NKI]
MAYAOYAW alt for IFUGAO, MAYOYAO [IFU]
MAYAR dial of STOD BHOTI [SBU]
MAYAR BHOTI alt for MAYAR dial of STOD BHOTI
   [SBU]
MAYARI alt for MAYAR dial of STOD BHOTI [SBU]
MAYAYERO dial of CUIBA [CUI]
MAYEKA [MYC] lang, DRC
MAYI-KULAN alt for MAYKULAN [MNT]
MAYI-KUTUNA alt for MAYAGUDUNA [XMY]
MAYIRUNA alt for MATSÉS [MCF]
MAYKO alt for MAYOGO [MDM]
MAYKULAN [MNT] lang, Australia
MAYNA alt for OMURANO [OMU]
MAYO [MAY] lang, Mexico
MAYOGO [MDM] lang, DRC
MAYOL alt for NAGA, MOYON [NMO]
MAYON NAGA alt for NAGA, MOYON [NMO]
MAYONGONG alt for MAQUIRITARI [MCH]
MAYONGONG dial of MAQUIRITARI [MCH]
MAYO-PLATA dial of PELASLA [MLR]
MAYORUNA alt for MATSÉS [MCF]
MAYOTTE alt for SHIMAORE dial of COMORIAN
   [SWB]
MAYOTTE alt for SHIMAWORE dial of COMORIAN
   [SWB]
MAYOYAO alt for IFUGAO, MAYOYAO [IFU]
MAYO-YESAN alt for YESSAN-MAYO [YSS]
MAYO-YESSAN dial of YESSAN-MAYO [YSS]
MAYU dial of BERTA [WTI]
MAYUGO alt for MAYOGO [MDM]
MAYUZUNA alt for MATSÉS [MCF]
MAYVASI KOLI alt for MEWASI dial of KOLI,
   WADIYARA [KXP]
MAZAGWA dial of WANDALA [MFI]
MAZAGWAY alt for MUSGOI dial of DABA [DAB]
MAZAHUA CENTRAL [MAZ] lang, Mexico
MAZAHUA, MICHOACÁN [QMN] lang, Mexico
MAZALTEPEC ZAPOTEC alt for ZAPOTECO,
   MAZALTEPEC [ZPY]
MAZANDERANI [MZN] lang, Iran
MAZATECO alt for MAZATECO, HUAUTLA [MAU]
MAZATECO, AYAUTLA [VMY] lang, Mexico
MAZATECO, CHIQUIHUITLÁN [MAQ] lang, Mexico
MAZATECO, HUAUTLA [MAU] lang, Mexico

MAZATECO, IXCATLÁN [MAO] lang, Mexico
MAZATECO, JALAPA DE DÍAZ [MAJ] lang, Mexico
MAZATECO, MAZATLÁN [VMZ] lang, Mexico
MAZATECO, SAN JERÓNIMO TECÓATL [MAA]
   lang, Mexico
MAZATECO, SOYALTEPEC [VMP] lang, Mexico
MAZATLÁN VILLA DE FLORES MAZATECO alt
   for MAZATECO, MAZATLÁN [VMZ]
MAZERA alt for MAJERA [XMJ]
MAZGARWA alt for GASHUA BADE dial of BADE
   [BDE]
MAZIZURU alt for ZEZURU dial of SHONA [SHD]
MAZNOUG dial of DOMARI [RMT]
MAZRA alt for MAJERA dial of MAJERA [XMJ]
MBA [MFC] lang, DRC
MBAAMA alt for MBAMA [MBM]
MBAAN dial of TRINGGUS [TRX]
MBAANHU alt for MBALANHU [LNB]
MBAARU dial of GURUNTUM-MBAARU [GRD]
MBACCA alt for NGBAKA MA'BO [NBM]
MBADA alt for BADA [BAU]
MBADAWA alt for BADA [BAU]
MBAELELEA alt for BAELELEA [BVC]
MBAENGGU alt for BAEGGU [BVD]
MBAGANI dial of SONGE [SOP]
MBAH dial of MFUMTE [NFU]
MBAHOUIN alt for MBANGWE [ZMN]
M'BAHOUIN alt for MBANGWE [ZMN]
MBAI alt for MBAY [MYB]
MBAI dial of GBAYA, NORTHWEST [GYA]
MBAI dial of KUPSABINY [KPZ]
MBAISE dial of IGBO [IGR]
MBAKA alt for NGBAKA MA'BO [NBM]
MBAKA dial of MBUNDU, LOANDA [MLO]
MBAKARLA alt for UMBUGARLA [UMR]
MBAKI alt for BAKI dial of KWAKUM [KWU]
MBAKOLO dial of GBAYA, SOUTHWEST [MDO]
MBALA [MDP] lang, DRC
MBALA dial of YOMBE [YOM]
MBALANGWE alt for SUBIYA [SBS]
MBALANHU [LNB] lang, Namibia
MBALANTU alt for MBALANHU [LNB]
MBALAZI alt for BAJUNI dial of SWAHILI [SWA]
MBALE alt for BUSHOONG [BUF]
MBALE dial of TAITA [DAV]
MBALI alt for MABAALE [MMZ]
MBALI alt for UMBUNDU [MNF]
MBALLA dial of MFUMTE [NFU]
MBALOH alt for EMBALOH [EMB]
MBALUNTU alt for MBALANHU [LNB]
MBAMA [MBM] lang, Gabon; also in Congo
MBAMA alt for NAGUMI [NGV]
MBAMBA alt for MBAMA [MBM]
MBAMBA dial of MBUNDU, LOANDA [MLO]
MBAMBATANA alt for BABATANA [BAQ]
MBAMU dial of ELOYI [AFO]
MBANA alt for IMBANA dial of MUNDANG [MUA]
MBANDIERU dial of HERERO [HER]
MBANDJA [ZMZ] lang, DRC; also in CAR, Congo
MBANDZA alt for MBANDJA [ZMZ]
MBANG alt for NGOKA dial of MBAY [MYB]

MBANG dial of BAKOKO [BKH]
MBANG dial of BASAA [BAA]
MBANGA alt for BANGA dial of KABA NA [KWV]
MBANGALA [MXG] lang, Angola
MBANGALA dial of MBANGALA [MXG]
MBANGI [MGN] lang, CAR
MBANGUI alt for MBANGI [MGN]
MBANGWE [ZMN] lang, Congo; also in Gabon
MBANIATA alt for BANIATA [BNT]
MBANJA alt for MBANDJA [ZMZ]
MBANUA alt for SANTA CRUZ [STC]
MBANUA dial of SANTA CRUZ [STC]
MBANZA alt for MBANDJA [ZMZ]
MBARA [MPK] lang, Chad
MBARA [VMB] lang, Australia
MBARA KWENGO alt for KXOE [XUU]
"MBARAKWENA" pejorative alt for KXOE [XUU]
MBARAKWENA alt for KXOE [XUU]
"MBARAKWENGO" pejorative alt for KXOE [XUU]
MBARAKWENGO alt for KXOE [XUU]
MBARAM alt for BARAM dial of POLCI [POL]
MBAREKE alt for BAREKE dial of VANGUNU [MPR]
MBARI alt for UMBUNDU [MNF]
MBARIKE alt for KUTEP [KUB]
MBARIMAN-GUDHINMA [ZMV] lang, Australia
MBARMA alt for BAGIRMI [BMI]
MBARMI alt for ZUL dial of POLCI [POL]
MBARU dial of LAME [BMA]
MBAT alt for BADA [BAU]
MBAT dial of MFUMTE [NFU]
MBATI [MDN] lang, CAR
MBATI alt for NGBANDI, SOUTHERN [NBW]
MBATI OF MBAÏKI dial of MBATI [MDN]
MBATO [GWA] lang, Côte d'Ivoire
M'BATO alt for MBATO [GWA]
MBAU alt for BAU dial of FIJIAN [FJI]
MBAW alt for MBE' [MTK]
MBAY [MYB] lang, Chad; also in CAR, Nigeria
MBAY alt for NZAKAMBAY [NZY]
MBAY BEDIONDO alt for BEDJOND [MAP]
MBAY BEJONDO alt for BEDJOND [MAP]
MBAY DOBA alt for MANGO [MGE]
MBAY MOISSALA alt for MBAY [MYB]
MBAYA-GUAIKURU alt for KADIWÉU [KBC]
MBAYE alt for MBAY [MYB]
MBAY-KAN alt for KAN dial of MBAY [MYB]
MBAZLA alt for BALDAMU [BDN]
MBE [MFO] lang, Nigeria
MBE' [MTK] lang, Cameroon
MBE AFAL alt for PUTUKWAM [AFE]
MBE EAST alt for OBE dial of PUTUKWAM [AFE]
MBECI dial of ELOYI [AFO]
MBEDAM [XMD] lang, Cameroon
MBÉDÉ alt for MBERE [MDT]
MBEERE dial of EMBU [EBU]
MBEGU alt for BAGWA dial of ZIMAKANI [ZIK]
MBEGUMBA alt for BELANDA VIRI [BVI]
MBELALA dial of PAMONA [BCX]
MBELE alt for BASAA [BAA]
MBELE alt for BAMBILI dial of BAMBILI [BAW]
MBELE alt for MBERE dial of TUKI [BAG]

MBELE alt for MBRE dial of BANDA-MBRES [BQK]
MBELIME [MQL] lang, Benin
MBEM alt for YAMBA [YAM]
MBEMBE, CROSS RIVER [MFN] lang, Nigeria
MBEMBE, TIGON [NZA] lang, Cameroon; also in
    Nigeria
MBENGUI-NIELLÉ alt for TAGBARI dial of
    SENOUFO, CEBAARA [SEF]
MBENKPE alt for NDE dial of NDE-NSELE-NTA
    [NDD]
MBERE [MDT] lang, Congo; also in Gabon
MBERE alt for MBEERE dial of EMBU [EBU]
MBERE alt for MBRE dial of BANDA-MBRES [BQK]
MBERE dial of GBAYA, NORTHWEST [GYA]
MBERE dial of KARANG [KZR]
MBERE dial of TUKI [BAG]
MBEREM dial of PELASLA [MLR]
MBESA [ZMS] lang, DRC
MBESA alt for MBIZENAKU dial of KOM [BKM]
MBETE alt for BETE dial of BETE-BENDI [BTT]
MBÉTÉ alt for MBERE [MDT]
MBEYA alt for GOMNOME dial of KOMA [KMY]
MBI alt for BISU [BII]
MBI dial of BANDA-BANDA [BPD]
MBIÁ alt for GUARANÍ, MBYÁ [GUN]
MBIBJI dial of MFUMTE [NFU]
MBIDA-BANI dial of EWONDO [EWO]
MBIKA alt for BAMUNKA [NDO]
MBILA dial of BUDZA [BJA]
MBILI alt for BAMBILI dial of BAMBILI [BAW]
MBILME alt for MBELIME [MQL]
MBILUA alt for BILUA [BLB]
MBIMOU alt for MPIEMO [MCX]
MBIMU alt for MPIEMO [MCX]
MBINGA dial of MABAALE [MMZ]
MBIRAO alt for BIRAO [BRR]
MBISU alt for BISU [BII]
MBIYI alt for MBI dial of BANDA-BANDA [BPD]
MBIZENAKU dial of KOM [BKM]
MBO [MBO] lang, Cameroon
MBO [ZMW] lang, DRC
MBO alt for MBE' [MTK]
MBOA alt for MBONGA [XMB]
MBOBYENG dial of MPONGMPONG [MGG]
MBOCHI alt for MBOSI [MDW]
MBOCOBÍ alt for MOCOVÍ [MOC]
MBODOMO alt for MBONDOMO dial of GBAYA,
    SOUTHWEST [MDO]
MBODOMO dial of GBAYA, SOUTHWEST [MDO]
MBOFON alt for ABANYOM [ABM]
MBOFON alt for NDE dial of NDE-NSELE-NTA
    [NDD]
MBOGEDO alt for DIRIKU [DIU]
MBOGEDU alt for DIRIKU [DIU]
MBOGOE alt for BAMBILI dial of BAMBILI [BAW]
MBOI [MOI] lang, Nigeria
MBOI dial of MBOI [MOI]
MBOIRE alt for MBOI [MOI]
MBOJO dial of BIMA [BHP]
MBOKA dial of KONGO [KON]
MBOKO [MDU] lang, Congo

MBOKO alt for WUMBOKO [BQM]
MBOKOU alt for MBUKO [MQB]
MBOKU alt for MBUKO [MQB]
MBOL alt for BWOL dial of KOFYAR [KWL]
MBOL FLE dial of TEHIT [KPS]
MBOLA alt for MBULE [MLB]
MBOLE [MDQ] lang, DRC
MBOLE alt for MBULI dial of OMBO [OML]
MBOLOLO dial of TAITA [DAV]
MBOMAN alt for MPOMAM dial of MPONGMPONG
  [MGG]
MBOMBELENG dial of GBAYA, SOUTHWEST
  [MDO]
MBOMBO alt for MPONGMPONG [MGG]
MBOMITABA alt for BOMITABA [ZMX]
MBOMOTABA alt for BOMITABA [ZMX]
MBONDOMO dial of GBAYA, SOUTHWEST [MDO]
MBONG alt for DIMBONG [DII]
MBONGA [XMB] lang, Cameroon
MBONGE dial of BAKUNDU-BALUE [BDU]
MBONGNO [BGU] lang, Nigeria; also in Cameroon
MBONGNO alt for KAMKAM [BGU]
MBONJOKU dial of KAKO [KKJ]
MBOO alt for MBO [MBO]
MBORE alt for BOREI [GAI]
MBOREI alt for BOREI [GAI]
MBORIN alt for BAGA BINARI [BCG]
MBORORO alt for BORORRO dial of FULFULDE,
  KANO-KATSINA-BORORRO [FUV]
MBORORO alt for BORORRO dial of FULFULDE,
  NIGERIAN [FUV]
MBOSHE alt for MBOSI [MDW]
MBOSHI alt for MBOSI [MDW]
MBOSI [MDW] lang, Congo
MBOTO dial of BIRRI [BVQ]
MBOTU alt for GAMO dial of GAMO-NINGI [BTE]
MBOTU alt for MBUTU dial of NGEMBA [NGE]
MBOUGOU alt for MBUGU [MHD]
MBOUM alt for MBUM [MDD]
MBOUM alt for NZAKAMBAY [NZY]
MBOUM dial of MBUM [MDD]
MBOUMTIBA alt for MBUM [MDD]
MBOUNDJA dial of GBAYA, SOUTHWEST [MDO]
MBO-UNG [MUX] lang, Papua New Guinea
MBOUNG alt for MBO-UNG [MUX]
MBOWE [MXO] lang, Zambia
MBOWE dial of LUYANA [LAV]
MBOWELA dial of NKOYA [NKA]
MBOXO alt for MBOKO [MDU]
MBOYAKUM alt for BAMBALANG [BMO]
MBOYI alt for MBOI [MOI]
MBRE dial of BANDA-MBRES [BQK]
MBREME alt for MBEREM dial of PELASLA [MLR]
MBREREWI dial of NGEMBA [NGE]
MBU alt for NGAMAMBO [NBV]
MBUA alt for GUARANÍ, MBYÁ [GUN]
MBUBA alt for MVUBA [MXH]
MBUBE EASTERN alt for PUTUKWAM [AFE]
MBUBEM alt for YAMBA [YAM]
MBUDJA alt for BUDZA [BJA]
MBUELA alt for MBWELA [MFU]

MBUGHOTU alt for BUGHOTU [BGT]
MBUGU [MHD] lang, Tanzania
MBUGWE [MGZ] lang, Tanzania
MBUI alt for BAMBUI dial of BAMBILI [BAW]
MBUKAMBERO dial of LAURA [LUR]
MBUKO [MQB] lang, Cameroon
MBUKU alt for MBOKO [MDU]
MBUKU alt for MBUKO [MQB]
MBUKUHU alt for MBUKUSHU [MHW]
MBUKUSHI alt for MBUKUSHU [MHW]
MBUKUSHU [MHW] lang, Namibia; also in Angola,
  Botswana, Zambia
MBULA [MNA] lang, Papua New Guinea
MBULA dial of MBULA [MNA]
MBULA dial of MBULA-BWAZZA [MBU]
MBULA-BWAZZA [MBU] lang, Nigeria
MBULE [MLB] lang, Cameroon
MBULI dial of OMBO [OML]
MBULU alt for IRAQW [IRK]
MBULUGWE alt for BURUNGE [BDS]
MBULUNGE alt for IRAQW [IRK]
MBULUNGISH [MBV] lang, Guinea
MBUM [MDD] lang, Cameroon; also in CAR
MBUM alt for KARANG [KZR]
MBUM alt for NZAKAMBAY [NZY]
MBUM BAKAL alt for KARANG [KZR]
MBUM NZAKAMBAY alt for NZAKAMBAY [NZY]
MBUM-EAST alt for KARANG [KZR]
MBUMI dial of LUYANA [LAV]
M'BUNAI alt for TITAN [TTV]
MBUNDA [MCK] lang, Zambia; also in Angola
MBUNDA alt for MPUUN dial of MPUONO [ZMP]
M'BUNDO alt for UMBUNDU [MNF]
MBUNDU BENGUELLA alt for UMBUNDU [MNF]
MBUNDU, LOANDA [MLO] lang, Angola
MBUNGA [MGY] lang, Tanzania
MBUNZA alt for MBOUNDJA dial of GBAYA,
  SOUTHWEST [MDO]
MBURKANCI alt for MBURKU [BBT]
MBURKU [BBT] lang, Nigeria
MBURUGAM alt for ESIMBI [AGS]
MBUSUKU alt for BOSOKO dial of GBAYA, SOUTH-
  WEST [MDO]
MBUTA alt for GAMO dial of GAMO-NINGI [BTE]
MBUTE alt for VUTE [VUT]
MBUTERE alt for VUTE [VUT]
MBUTI alt for LESE [LES]
MBUTU dial of NGEMBA [NGE]
MBUUN alt for MPUUN dial of MPUONO [ZMP]
MBUUNDA alt for MBUNDA [MCK]
MBWAANZ dial of MAKAA [MCP]
MBWAKA alt for NGBAKA MA'BO [NBM]
MBWASE NGHUY alt for BAFUN dial of BAKAKA
  [BQZ]
MBWELA [MFU] lang, Angola
MBWELA alt for MBOWELA dial of NKOYA
  [NKA]
MBWERA alt for MBOWELA dial of NKOYA
  [NKA]
MBWERA alt for MBWELA [MFU]
MBWE'WI dial of AWING [AZO]

MBWILA dial of SAFWA [SBK]
MBWISI alt for BWISI [BWZ]
MBYÁ alt for GUARANÍ, MBYÁ [GUN]
MBYAM dial of KWA [BKO]
MBYEMO alt for MPIEMO [MCX]
MCDERMITT alt for NORTH NORTHERN PAIUTE
  dial of PAIUTE, NORTHERN [PAO]
MCGRATH INGALIK alt for KUSKOKWIM, UPPER
  [KUU]
MDHUR alt for NDHUR dial of RADE [RAD]
MDUNDULU dial of LUYANA [LAV]
ME alt for MATBAT [XMT]
MEA [MEG] lang, New Caledonia
MEAH alt for MEYAH [MEJ]
MEAKAMBUT dial of ARAFUNDI [ARF]
MEARIM dial of GUAJAJARA [GUB]
MEAUN alt for LABO [MWI]
MEAX alt for MEYAH [MEJ]
MEBAN alt for MABAAN [MFZ]
MEBU [MJN] lang, Papua New Guinea
MECAYAPAN NAHUAT alt for NÁHUATL, ISTMO-
  MECAYAPAN [NAU]
MECH alt for BODO [BRX]
MECH dial of BODO [BRX]
MECHE alt for BODO [BRX]
MECHI alt for BODO [BRX]
MECI alt for BODO [BRX]
MECKLENBURG-ANTERIOR POMERANIA dial
  of SAXON, LOW [SXN]
MECKLENBURGISCH-VORPOMMERSCH alt for
  MECKLENBURG-ANTERIOR POMERANIA dial
  of SAXON, LOW [SXN]
MECO alt for CHICHIMECA-JONAZ [PEI]
MEDANG alt for MADANG [MQD]
MEDEBUR [MJM] lang, Papua New Guinea
MEDIA LENGUA [MUE] lang, Ecuador
MEDIAK [MWX] lang, Tanzania
MEDJE alt for MEJE dial of MANGBETU [MDJ]
MEDLPA alt for MELPA [MED]
MEDNOVSKIY alt for AHTENA [AHT]
MEDNY alt for MEDNYJ ALEUT [MUD]
MEDNYJ ALEUT [MUD] lang, Russia (Asia)
MEDO alt for MEETTO dial of MAKHUWA-MEETTO
  [MAK]
MEDO dial of MAKHUWA-MEETTO [MAK]
MEDOGO dial of NABA [MNE]
MEDUMBA [BYV] lang, Cameroon
MEDYE alt for MEJE dial of MANGBETU [MDJ]
MEDZIME alt for MENZIME dial of MPONGMPONG
  [MGG]
MEE alt for BASAA [BAA]
MEE MANA alt for EKARI [EKG]
ME'EK alt for MEHEK [NUX]
MEEKA dial of MUMUYE [MUL]
MEEMBI alt for MEMBI dial of NDO [NDP]
ME'EN [MYM] lang, Ethiopia
MEETTO alt for MAKHUWA-MEETTO [MAK]
MEETTO dial of MAKHUWA-MEETTO [MAK]
MEEWOC alt for MIWOK, SOUTHERN SIERRA
  [SKD]
MEFELE [MFJ] lang, Cameroon

MEFELE dial of MEFELE [MFJ]
MEFOOR alt for BIAK [BHW]
MEGAKA alt for MENGAKA [XMG]
MEGAM [MEF] lang, Bangladesh
MEGAM alt for LYNGNGAM dial of KHASI [KHI]
MEGI dial of ANGAL ENEN [AOE]
MEGI dial of KAGULU [KKI]
MEGIAR dial of TAKIA [TBC]
MEGILI alt for LIJILI [MGI]
MEGIMBA alt for NGEMBA [NGE]
MEGLENITE alt for ROMANIAN, MEGLENO [RUQ]
MEGLENITIC alt for ROMANIAN, MEGLENO
  [RUQ]
MEGREL alt for MINGRELIAN [XMF]
MEGRULI alt for MINGRELIAN [XMF]
MEGYAW alt for HPON [HPO]
MEGYE alt for MEJE dial of MANGBETU [MDJ]
MEHALA'AN-EASTERN RANTEBULAHAN dial of
  BAMBAM [PTU]
MEHARA alt for MESARA dial of SABU [HVN]
MEHARI alt for HALBI [HLB]
MEHARI dial of HALBI [HLB]
MEHEK [NUX] lang, Papua New Guinea
MEHER alt for KISAR [KJE]
MEHINACO alt for MEHINÁKU [MMH]
MEHINÁKU [MMH] lang, Brazil
MEHRI [MHR] lang, Yemen; also in Kuwait, Oman
MEHRIYET alt for WESTERN MEHRI dial of MEHRI
  [MHR]
MEHRIYOT alt for EASTERN MEHRI dial of MEHRI
  [MHR]
MEIBUIL dial of KABOLA [KLZ]
MEIDOB alt for MIDOB [MEI]
MEIDOO alt for MAIDU, NORTHWEST [MAI]
MEIFU dial of HLAI [LIC]
MEIN dial of IZON [IJC]
MEITEI [MNR] lang, India; also in Bangladesh,
  Myanmar
MEITEI dial of MEITEI [MNR]
MEITEIRON alt for MEITEI [MNR]
MEITHE alt for MEITEI [MNR]
MEITHEI alt for MEITEI [MNR]
MEIXIAN alt for YUE-TAI dial of CHINESE, HAKKA
  [HAK]
MEIYARI alt for NIKSEK [GBE]
MEIYARI dial of NIKSEK [GBE]
MEJACH alt for MEYAH [MEJ]
MEJAH alt for MEYAH [MEJ]
MEJE dial of MANGBETU [MDJ]
MEKA alt for BYEP [MKK]
MEKA alt for MARKA [MWR]
MEKA alt for NGEMBA dial of GHOMALA [BBJ]
MEKAA alt for MAKAA [MCP]
MEKAE alt for BYEP [MKK]
MEKAF alt for NAKI [MFF]
MEKAN alt for ME'EN [MYM]
MEKAY alt for BYEP [MKK]
MEKEM [XME] lang, Brazil
MEKEO [MEK] lang, Papua New Guinea
MEKEO-KOVIO alt for MEKEO [MEK]
MEKEY alt for BYEP [MKK]

"MEKEYER" pejorative alt for SHABO [SBF]
MEKITELYU alt for LIMÓN CREOLE ENGLISH dial of SOUTHWESTERN CARIBBEAN CREOLE ENGLISH [JAM]
MEKMEK [MVK] lang, Papua New Guinea
MEKONGGA dial of TOLAKI [LBW]
MEKUK alt for MVUMBO dial of NGUMBA [NMG]
MEKWEI [MSF] lang, Indonesia (Irian Jaya)
MEKYE alt for BYEP [MKK]
MELAJU alt for MALAY [MLI]
MELAMBA alt for KENSWEI NSEI [NDB]
MELAMELA alt for MERAMERA [MXM]
MELAN SO dial of SO [SOX]
MELANAU [MEL] lang, Malaysia (Sarawak); also in Brunei
MELANESIAN ENGLISH alt for TOK PISIN [PDG]
MELARIPI alt for KAIPI dial of TOARIPI [TPI]
MELAWI alt for SARAWAI dial of DOHOI [OTD]
MELAYU alt for MALAY [MLI]
MELAYU AMBON alt for MALAY, AMBONESE [ABS]
MELAYU BAHASA alt for SRI LANKAN CREOLE MALAY [SCI]
MELAYU JAKARTE alt for BETAWI [BEW]
MELAYU PASAR dial of MALAY [MLI]
MELE dial of GULA [KCM]
MELE dial of MELE-FILA [MXE]
MELE NADU IRULA dial of IRULA [IRU]
MELE-FILA [MXE] lang, Vanuatu
MELETE dial of TSWANA [TSW]
MELETS TATAR alt for CHULYM [CHU]
MELIGAN alt for MALIGAN dial of TAGAL MURUT [MVV]
MELILUP dial of TEOP [TIO]
MELKHIN dial of CHECHEN [CJC]
MELKOI dial of MAMUSI [KDF]
MELLA dial of CUIBA [CUI]
MELO [MFX] lang, Ethiopia
MELOBONG RUNGUS alt for RUNGUS [DRG]
MELOKWO [MLW] lang, Cameroon
MELOLO dial of KAMBERA [SMI]
MELONG dial of MBO [MBO]
MELPA [MED] lang, Papua New Guinea
MELSISI dial of APMA [APP]
MELUORY alt for NAGA, MELURI [NLM]
MELURI alt for NAGA, MELURI [NLM]
MEMAGUN alt for RUNGUS [DRG]
MEMALOH alt for EMBALOH [EMB]
MEMBA [MMC] lang, India
MEMBAKUT KADAZAN alt for KADAZAN, COASTAL [KZJ]
MEMBI dial of NDO [NDP]
MEMBITU alt for MEMBI dial of NDO [NDP]
MEMBORO alt for MAMBORU [MVD]
MEMI alt for NAGA, MAO [NBI]
MEMOGUN alt for RUNGUS [DRG]
MEMONI [MBY] lang, Pakistan
MEN alt for KIM MUN [MJI]
MEN alt for ME'EN [MYM]
MENA dial of IKOBI-MENA [MEB]
MENABE-IKONGO alt for TANALA dial of MALAGASY [MEX]

MENADO MALAY alt for MALAY, MENADONESE [XMM]
MENADONESE alt for MANADONESE dial of MALAY [MLI]
MENAM alt for MONOM [MOO]
MENANDON alt for AIKU [MZF]
MENBA alt for MOINBA [MOB]
MENBA alt for TSHANGLA [TSJ]
MENCHUM alt for BEFANG [BBY]
MENDAGE alt for MASLAM [MSV]
MENDAGE alt for MPADE [MPI]
MENDAGE alt for MSER [KQX]
MENDALAM KAJAN alt for KAYAN, MENDALAM [XKD]
MENDANKWE [MFD] lang, Cameroon
MENDANKWE dial of MENDANKWE [MFD]
MENDE [MFY] lang, Sierra Leone; also in Liberia
MENDE [SIM] lang, Papua New Guinea
MENDE alt for WAMSAK [WBD]
MENDEYA alt for GUMUZ [GUK]
MENDI alt for ANGAL [AGE]
MENDI alt for KENSIU [KNS]
MENDO-KALA alt for KALA dial of UMBU-UNGU [UMB]
MENDRIQ alt for MINRIQ [MNQ]
MENDYAKO alt for MANDJAK [MFV]
MENDZIME alt for MENZIME dial of MPONGMPONG [MGG]
MENECA alt for HUITOTO, MɨNɨCA [HTO]
MENEMO dial of META [MGO]
MENEMO-MOGAMO alt for META' [MGO]
MENGAKA [XMG] lang, Cameroon
MENGAMBO alt for BAMENYAM [BCE]
MENGAU dial of KAMBERATARO [KBV]
MENGDA dial of SALAR [SLR]
MENGEN [MEE] lang, Papua New Guinea
MENGERRDJI alt for MANGERR [ZME]
MENGGALA dial of ABUNG [ABL]
MENGGATAL dial of DUSUN, CENTRAL [DTP]
MENGGEI alt for MEKWEI [MSF]
MENGGU alt for MONGOLIAN, PERIPHERAL [MVF]
MENGGWEI alt for MEKWEI [MSF]
MENGISA [MCT] lang, Cameroon
MENGISA-NJOWE alt for MENGISA [MCT]
MENGKASARA alt for MAKASAR [MSR]
MENGKATIP dial of BAKUMPAI [BKR]
MENGO alt for KENSIU [KNS]
MENI alt for IKOBI-MENA [MEB]
MENI alt for KENSIU [KNS]
MENI dial of IKOBI-MENA [MEB]
MENIK alt for KENSIU [KNS]
MENINDAL alt for KUIJAU [DKR]
MENINDAQ alt for KUIJAU [DKR]
MENINGGO alt for MOSKONA [MTJ]
MENINGO alt for MOSKONA [MTJ]
MENIPURI alt for MEITEI [MNR]
MENJA alt for KWEGU [YID]
MENJUKE alt for MANYUKAI dial of DAYAK, LAND [DYK]
MENKA [MEA] lang, Cameroon
MENKU alt for MÜNKÜ dial of IRANTXE [IRA]

MENNAGI alt for MANGERR [ZME]
MENNONITE GERMAN alt for PLAUTDIETSCH [GRN]
MENNONITEN PLATT alt for PLAUTDIETSCH [GRN]
MENO-MENE dial of SASAK [SAS]
MENOMINEE alt for MENOMINI [MEZ]
MENOMINI [MEZ] lang, USA
MENORQUI alt for BALEARIC dial of CATALAN-VALENCIAN-BALEAR [CLN]
MENPA alt for MOINBA [MOB]
MENRAQ alt for MINRIQ [MNQ]
MENRIK alt for MINRIQ [MNQ]
MENRIQ alt for MINRIQ [MNQ]
MENSA alt for MANSA' dial of TIGRE [TIE]
MENTA alt for MANTA [MYG]
MENTAWAI [MWV] lang, Indonesia (Sumatra)
MENTAWEI alt for MENTAWAI [MWV]
MENTAWI alt for MENTAWAI [MWV]
MENTEBAH-SURUK dial of MALAYIC DAYAK [XDY]
MENTERA alt for MANTRA dial of TEMUAN [TMW]
MENTUH TAPUH dial of BUKAR SADONG [SDO]
MENUI dial of WAWONII [WOW]
MENYA [MCR] lang, Papua New Guinea
MENYA dial of NYOLE [NUJ]
MENYAMA alt for MENYA [MCR]
MENYE alt for MENYA [MCR]
MENYUKAI alt for MANYUKAI dial of DAYAK, LAND [DYK]
MENZIME dial of MPONGMPONG [MGG]
MEO alt for HMONG NJUA [BLU]
MEO DO alt for HMONG, EASTERN XIANGXI [MUQ]
MEO DO alt for HMONG, WESTERN XIANGXI [MMR]
MEO KAO alt for HMONG DAW [MWW]
MEO LAI alt for BUNU, BAHENG [PHA]
MÈO LÀI alt for BUNU, BAHENG [PHA]
MEOHANG, EASTERN [EMG] lang, Nepal
MEOHANG, WESTERN [RAF] lang, Nepal
MEON alt for KARON DORI [KGW]
MEOSWAR [MVX] lang, Indonesia (Irian Jaya)
MEPHÁA alt for TLAPANECO, MALINALTEPEC [TLL]
ME'PHAA alt for TLAPANECO, ACATEPEC [TPX]
MEQAN alt for ME'EN [MYM]
MEQUEM alt for MEKEM [XME]
MEQUEN alt for MEKEM [XME]
MEQUENS alt for KANOÉ [KXO]
MER [MNU] lang, Indonesia (Irian Jaya)
MER alt for MERIAM [ULK]
MER dial of BENCH [BCQ]
MERA SAGTENGPA alt for BROKPAKE [SGT]
MERADAN alt for MARIDAN [ZMD]
MERAGSAGSTENGKHA alt for BROKPAKE [SGT]
MERAMERA [MXM] lang, Papua New Guinea
MERARIT alt for MARARIT [MGB]
MERATEI dial of DAYAK, LAND [DYK]
MERATUS alt for MALAY, BUKIT [BVU]
MERAU MALAY alt for MALAY, BERAU [BVE]
MERDU alt for MURSI [MUZ]

MERE alt for MEREY [MEQ]
MERE dial of GULA [KCM]
MEREI [LMB] lang, Vanuatu
MERELAVA alt for MERLAV [MRM]
MEREO alt for EMERILLON [EME]
MERETEI alt for MERATEI dial of DAYAK, LAND [DYK]
MEREY [MEQ] lang, Cameroon
MEREYO alt for EMERILLON [EME]
MERGUESE dial of BURMESE [BMS]
MERGUI alt for MERGUESE dial of BURMESE [BMS]
MERI alt for MEREY [MEQ]
MERIAM [ULK] lang, Australia
MERIDA alt for ZAGHAWA [ZAG]
MERIDA alt for ZANDE [ZAN]
MERIDIONALE dial of SARDINIAN, CAMPIDANESE [SRO]
MERIG alt for MWERIG dial of MERLAV [MRM]
MERILE alt for DAASANACH [DSH]
MERILLE alt for DAASANACH [DSH]
MERINA dial of MALAGASY [MEX]
MERITU alt for MURSI [MUZ]
MERLAV [MRM] lang, Vanuatu
MERLAV-MERIG alt for MERLAV [MRM]
MERNYANG alt for MIRRIAM dial of KOFYAR [KWL]
MERONG alt for MIRIWUNG [MEP]
MERRANUNGGU alt for MARANUNGGU dial of MARINGARR [ZMT]
MERU [MER] lang, Kenya
MERU alt for KIHAI dial of CHAGGA [KAF]
MERU alt for RWA [RWK]
MERU dial of MERU [MER]
MERULE alt for MURLE [MUR]
MERWARI alt for MARWARI [MKD]
MERWARI alt for MARWARI [MRI]
MESA DEL NAYAR alt for LA MESA DEL NAYAR CORA dial of CORA [COR]
MESAKA [IYO] lang, Cameroon
MESAKIN alt for NGILE [MAS]
MESAKIN QUSAR alt for MASAKIN GUSAR dial of NGILE [MAS]
MESARA dial of SABU [HVN]
MESARI dial of MANAGALASI [MCQ]
MESCALERO dial of APACHE, MESCALERO-CHIRICAHUA [APM]
MESE dial of TUNEN [BAZ]
MESĒ [MCI] lang, Papua New Guinea
MESEM alt for MESĒ [MCI]
MESENGO alt for MAJANG [MPE]
MESHED alt for MASHADI dial of FARSI, WESTERN [PES]
MESI dial of MADAK [MMX]
MESIANG dial of BARAKAI [BAJ]
MESING alt for KENSWEI NSEI [NDB]
MESISE dial of DOGOSE [DOS]
MESKAN alt for MASQAN dial of GURAGE, WEST [GUY]
MESKETO alt for BASKETTO [BST]
MESKHUR-JAVAKHURI dial of GEORGIAN [GEO]
MESME [ZIM] lang, Chad

MESMEDJE alt for MASMAJE [MES]
MESMES [MYS] lang, Ethiopia
MESOPOTAMIAN GELET ARABIC alt for ARABIC, MESOPOTAMIAN SPOKEN [ACM]
MESOPOTAMIAN QELTU ARABIC alt for ARABIC, MESOPOTAMIAN SPOKEN [ACM]
MESOPOTAMIAN QELTU ARABIC alt for ARABIC, NORTH MESOPOTAMIAN SPOKEN [AYP]
MESQAN alt for MASQAN dial of GURAGE, WEST [GUY]
MESQUAKIE [SAC] lang, USA
MESQUAKIE dial of MESQUAKIE [SAC]
MESSAGA alt for MESAKA [IYO]
MESSAGA-EKOL alt for MESAKA [IYO]
MESSAKA alt for MESAKA [IYO]
MESSENI alt for TAKPASYEERI dial of SENOUFO, CEBAARA [SEF]
MESSINESE dial of SICILIAN [SCN]
META' [MGO] lang, Cameroon
META' alt for MENEMO dial of META [MGO]
METABI alt for GAAM [TBI]
METAN alt for NABI [MTY]
METHLI alt for MAITHILI [MKP]
METING alt for BELAIT [BEG]
METIS alt for MICHIF [CRG]
METLA-KINWAT dial of KOLAMI, SOUTHEASTERN [NIT]
METO alt for ATONI [TMR]
METO alt for MEDO dial of MAKHUWA-MEETTO [MAK]
METO alt for MEETTO dial of MAKHUWA-MEETTO [MAK]
METOKI alt for KENUZI-DONGOLA [KNC]
METOKO alt for MITUKU [ZMQ]
METOMKA alt for SOUTHERN MUYU dial of YONGKOM [YON]
METRU alt for DIA [DIA]
METRU alt for SINAGEN [SIU]
METTA alt for MENEMO dial of META [MGO]
METTA alt for META' [MGO]
METTO alt for MEETTO dial of MAKHUWA-MEETTO [MAK]
MEUAY alt for TAI MUOI dial of TAI DAM [BLT]
MEUAY alt for TÁY MU'Ò'I dial of TAI DAM [BLT]
MEUDANA dial of BUNAMA [BDD]
MEWADI alt for MEWARI [MTR]
MEWAHANG alt for MEOHANG, EASTERN [EMG]
MEWAHANG alt for MEOHANG, WESTERN [RAF]
MEWARI [MTR] lang, India
MEWASI dial of KOLI, WADIYARA [KXP]
MEWATI alt for MEWARI [MTR]
MEWATI dial of HARYANVI [BGC]
MEWOC alt for MIWOK, SOUTHERN SIERRA [SKD]
ME-WUK alt for MIWOK, SOUTHERN SIERRA [SKD]
MEWUN alt for LABO [MWI]
MEXICAN SIGN LANGUAGE [MFS] lang, Mexico
MEXICANERO alt for NÁHUATL, DURANGO [NLN]
MEXICO dial of AFRO-SEMINOLE CREOLE [AFS]
MEXICO AFRO-SEMINOLE dial of AFRO-SEMINOLE CREOLE [AFS]

MEXTÃ alt for CARAPANA [CBC]
MEY BRAT alt for MAI BRAT [AYZ]
MEYACH alt for MEYAH [MEJ]
MEYAH [MEJ] lang, Indonesia (Irian Jaya)
MEYOBE alt for SOLA [SOY]
MEYU EHTREMEÑU alt for CENTRAL EXTREMADURAN dial of EXTREMADURAN [EXT]
MEZAMA alt for NAGA, ZEME [NZM]
MEZIME alt for MENZIME dial of MPONGMPONG [MGG]
MEZIMKO dial of MUKULU [MOZ]
MFANGANO dial of SUBA [SUH]
MFANTSE alt for FANTE dial of AKAN [TWS]
MFE dial of YAMBA [YAM]
MFINU [ZMF] lang, DRC
MFUMTE [NFU] lang, Cameroon
MFUMU alt for FUUMU dial of TEKE, SOUTH CENTRAL [IFM]
MFUNUNGA alt for MFINU [ZMF]
MFUTI alt for VUTE [VUT]
MGAO dial of SWAHILI [SWA]
MGBAKPA alt for HAUSA [HUA]
MGBATO alt for MBATO [GWA]
MGBO dial of IZI-EZAA-IKWO-MGBO [IZI]
MGOUMBA alt for MVUMBO dial of NGUMBA [NMG]
MGOUMBA alt for NGUMBA [NMG]
MHAR alt for HMAR [HMR]
MINICA alt for HUITOTO, MINICA [HTO]
MI MARVA alt for GIZIGA, NORTH [GIS]
MI MIJIVIN dial of GIZIGA, SOUTH [GIZ]
MIADEBA dial of SEWA BAY [SEW]
MIAG-AO dial of KINARAY-A [KRJ]
MIALÁT dial of TENHARIM [PAH]
MIAMI [MIA] lang, USA
MIAMI dial of MIAMI [MIA]
MIAMIA alt for BEGBERE-EJAR [BQV]
MIAMIA alt for PINAI-HAGAHAI [PNN]
MIAMI-ILLINOIS alt for MIAMI [MIA]
MIAMILO alt for BAFUN dial of BAKAKA [BQZ]
MIAMI-MYAAMIA alt for MIAMI [MIA]
MIAMIYA alt for BEGBERE-EJAR [BQV]
MIAMU dial of WAN [WAN]
MIAN [MPT] lang, Papua New Guinea
MIAN alt for IU MIEN [IUM]
MIANCHI dial of QIANG, SOUTHERN [QMR]
MIANGO alt for IRIGWE [IRI]
MIANI [PLA] lang, Papua New Guinea
MIANI NORTH alt for MIANI [PLA]
MIANI SOUTH alt for MAIANI [TNH]
MIANKA alt for SENOUFO, MAMARA [MYK]
MIANMIN alt for MIAN [MPT]
MIANMIN dial of MIAN [MPT]
MIAO alt for HMONG NJUA [BLU]
MIAO alt for HMONG, CENTRAL HUISHUI [HMC]
MIAO alt for HMONG, CENTRAL MASHAN [HMM]
MIAO alt for HMONG, EASTERN HUISHUI [HME]
MIAO alt for HMONG, EASTERN QIANDONG [HMQ]
MIAO alt for HMONG, NORTHERN GUIYANG [HUJ]
MIAO alt for HMONG, NORTHERN HUISHUI [HMN]

MIAO alt for HMONG, NORTHERN QIANDONG [HEA]
MIAO alt for HMONG, SOUTHERN GUIYANG [HMY]
MIAO alt for HMONG, SOUTHERN MASHAN [HMA]
MIAO alt for HMONG, SOUTHERN QIANDONG [HMS]
MIAO alt for HMONG, SOUTHWESTERN GUIYANG [HMG]
MIAO alt for HMONG, SOUTHWESTERN HUISHUI [HMH]
MIAO alt for HMONG, WESTERN MASHAN [HMW]
MIAO LAI alt for HMONG GU MBA dial of HMONG DAW [MWW]
MIARO alt for AWYU, MIARO [PSA]
MIARRÃ [XMI] lang, Brazil
MIBISU alt for BISU [BII]
MICARI dial of NUNI, SOUTHERN [NNW]
MICCOSUKEE alt for MIKASUKI [MIK]
MICHIF [CRG] lang, USA; also in Canada
MICHOACÁN AZTEC alt for NÁHUATL, MICHOACÁN [NCL]
MICHOACÁN NAHUAL alt for NÁHUATL, MICHOACÁN [NCL]
MICHOPDO alt for MAIDU, NORTHWEST [MAI]
MICMAC [MIC] lang, Canada; also in USA
MID BISAYA dial of BISAYA, SARAWAK [BSD]
MID MORTLOCK dial of MORTLOCKESE [MRL]
MID WAHGI alt for WAHGI [WAK]
MIDA'A alt for MAJERA [XMJ]
MIDAH alt for MAJERA [XMJ]
MIDDLE ATLAS BERBER alt for TAMAZIGHT, CENTRAL ATLAS [TZM]
MIDDLE BAMU alt for UPPER BAMU dial of BAMU [BCF]
MIDDLE CHEROKEE alt for KITUHWA dial of CHEROKEE [CER]
MIDDLE CHULYM dial of CHULYM [CHU]
MIDDLE EASTERN ROMANI alt for DOMARI [RMT]
MIDDLE EGYPT ARABIC dial of ARABIC, SAIDI SPOKEN [AEC]
MIDDLE LOZYVIN alt for WESTERN VOGUL dial of MANSI [MNS]
MIDDLE MUSA alt for YAREBA [YRB]
MIDDLE NAMBAS alt for MALUA BAY [MLL]
MIDDLE TATAR dial of TATAR [TTR]
MIDEASTERN YIDDISH dial of YIDDISH, EASTERN [YDD]
MIDHI alt for IDU [CLK]
MIDIK alt for MIDIKI dial of KAIRUI-MIDIKI [KRD]
MIDIKI alt for KAIRUI-MIDIKI [KRD]
MIDIKI dial of KAIRUI-MIDIKI [KRD]
MIDIN dial of TUROYO [SYR]
MIDLAND NORWEGIAN alt for CENTRAL NORWEGIAN dial of NORWEGIAN, BOKMAAL [NRR]
MIDNAPORE ORIYA dial of ORIYA [ORY]
MIDOB [MEI] lang, Sudan
MIDOBI alt for MIDOB [MEI]
MIDSIVINDI alt for INAPANG [MZU]
MIDU alt for IDU [CLK]
MID-WAHGI dial of WAHGI [WAK]

MID-WARIA alt for GUHU-SAMANE [GHS]
MIDWESTERN YIDDISH dial of YIDDISH, WESTERN [YIH]
MIDYAT dial of TUROYO [SYR]
MIE'EN alt for ME'EN [MYM]
MIEKEN alt for ME'EN [MYM]
MIEN alt for IU MIEN [IUM]
MIENGE dial of BASSOSSI [BSI]
MIERE alt for MER [MNU]
MIERU alt for MER dial of BENCH [BCQ]
MIGAAMA [MMY] lang, Chad
MIGAAMA dial of MIGAAMA [MMY]
MIGABA' alt for MIGABAC [MPP]
MIGABAC [MPP] lang, Papua New Guinea
MIGAM alt for MEGAM [MEF]
MIGAMA alt for MIGAAMA [MMY]
MIGANGAM alt for NGANGAM [GNG]
MIGANI alt for MONI [MNZ]
MIGILI alt for LIJILI [MGI]
MI'GMAW alt for MICMAC [MIC]
MIGUELENHO alt for PURUBORÁ [PUR]
MIGUELENO alt for PURUBORÁ [PUR]
MIGUHNI alt for NGWO dial of NGWO [NGN]
MIGULIMANCEMA alt for GOURMANCÉMA [GUX]
MIGULIMANCEMA alt for GOURMANCHÉMA [GUX]
MIHAVANE alt for LOMWE [NGL]
MIHAVANI alt for LOMWE [NGL]
MIHAWANI alt for LOMWE [NGL]
MIIGMAO alt for MICMAC [MIC]
MIISIIRII alt for JABAAL dial of TAMA [TMA]
MIJARANÉS ARANÉS dial of GASCON, ARANESE [GSC]
MIJI alt for DHAMMAI dial of HRUSO [HRU]
MIJI alt for MIJU [MXJ]
MIJI alt for SAJALONG [SJL]
MIJIEM alt for NGANGAM [GNG]
MIJILI alt for LIJILI [MGI]
MIJONG alt for MISSONG [MIJ]
MIJU [MXJ] lang, India
MÌJUU dial of SENOUFO, MAMARA [MYK]
MIKA alt for BYEP [MKK]
"MIKAIR" pejorative alt for SHABO [SBF]
MIKAREW alt for ARUAMU [MSY]
MIKAREW-ARIAW alt for ARUAMU [MSY]
MIKARUP alt for ARUAMU [MSY]
MIKASUKI [MIK] lang, USA
MIKASUKI dial of MIKASUKI [MIK]
MIKASUKI SEMINOLE alt for MIKASUKI [MIK]
MIKEBWE dial of BANGUBANGU [BNX]
MIKERE dial of DUGWOR [DME]
"MIKEYIR" pejorative alt for SHABO [SBF]
MIKIFORE alt for MIXIFORE [MFG]
MIKIK dial of TSAKHUR [TKR]
MIKIR [MJW] lang, India
MIKIRI alt for MIKIR [MJW]
MIKLAI alt for NAGA, LOTHA [NJH]
MI'KMAW alt for MICMAC [MIC]
MIKO dial of NUNG [NUN]
MILANAU alt for MELANAU [MEL]
MILANESE dial of LOMBARD [LMO]
MILANG dial of ADI [ADI]

MILANO alt for MELANAU [MEL]
MILCHAN alt for KINNAURI [KFK]
MILCHANANG alt for KINNAURI [KFK]
MILCHANG alt for KINNAURI [KFK]
MILDJINGI dial of DJINANG [DJI]
MILE alt for AXI dial of YI, SOUTHEASTERN [YIE]
MILEERE alt for JABAAL dial of TAMA [TMA]
MILIKIN [MIN] lang, Malaysia (Sarawak)
MILLERA alt for YIR YORONT [YIY]
MILLIKIN alt for MILIKIN [MIN]
MILO dial of NICOBARESE, SOUTHERN [NIK]
MILRI alt for JABAAL dial of TAMA [TMA]
MILTOU alt for MILTU [MLJ]
MILTU [MLJ] lang, Chad
MIMA alt for AMDANG [AMJ]
MIMA dial of NAGA, ANGAMI [NJM]
MIME alt for MIMI [MIV]
MIMI [MIV] lang, Chad
MIMI alt for AMDANG [AMJ]
MÍMICA alt for SPANISH SIGN LANGUAGE [SSP]
MIMIKA alt for KAMORO [KGQ]
MIN DONG alt for CHINESE, MIN DONG [CDO]
MIN NAM alt for CHINESE, MIN NAN [CFR]
MIN NAN alt for CHINESE, MIN NAN [CFR]
MIN PEI alt for CHINESE, MIN BEI [MNP]
MINA [HNA] lang, Cameroon
MINA [MYI] lang, India
MINA alt for GEN-GBE [GEJ]
MINA BHIL alt for WAGDI [WBR]
MINA MINA GORONG dial of GESER-GOROM
    [GES]
MINACO alt for MEHINÁKU [MMH]
MINA-GEN alt for GEN-GBE [GEJ]
MINAHASA alt for TOMBULU [TOM]
MINAHASAN MALAY alt for MALAY,
    MENADONESE [XMM]
MINAHASSA alt for MONGONDOW [MOG]
MINAHE alt for BAREKO dial of MBO [MBO]
MINALA alt for MANGALA [MEM]
MINAMANWA alt for MAMANWA [MMN]
MINANG alt for MINANGKABAU [MPU]
MINANGKABAU [MPU] lang, Indonesia (Sumatra)
MINANIBAI [MCV] lang, Papua New Guinea
MINANSUT alt for GANA [GNQ]
MINANSUT alt for KUIJAU [DKR]
MINASBATE alt for MASBATENYO [MSB]
MINAVEGA alt for MINAVEHA [MVN]
MINAVEHA [MVN] lang, Papua New Guinea
MINBU dial of CHIN, ASHO [CSH]
MINCHIA alt for BAI [PIQ]
MINDA dial of SHOO-MINDA-NYE [BCV]
MINDANAO dial of SANGIL [SNL]
MINDANAO VISAYAN dial of CEBUANO [CEB]
MINDAT alt for CHIN, MÜN [MWQ]
MINDÉRA dial of KWANG [KVI]
MINDIK alt for BURUM-MINDIK [BMU]
MINDIRI [MPN] lang, Papua New Guinea
MINDIVI alt for ANAMGURA [IMI]
MIND'JANA alt for YIR YORONT [YIY]
MINDOUMOU alt for NDUMU [NMD]
MINDUMBU alt for NDUMU [NMD]

MINDUUMO alt for NDUMU [NMD]
"MINE KAFFIR" pejorative alt for FANAGOLO [FAO]
MINENDON alt for AIKU [MZF]
MINEO alt for MINEW dial of ZULGWA [ZUL]
MINEO alt for ZULGWA [ZUL]
MINEW alt for ZULGWA [ZUL]
MINEW dial of ZULGWA [ZUL]
MINEWE alt for MINEW dial of ZULGWA [ZUL]
MINGAN alt for ULANCHAB dial of MONGOLIAN,
    PERIPHERAL [MVF]
MINGANG DOSO [MKO] lang, Nigeria
MINGAR alt for LEMBATA, WEST [LMJ]
MINGAT dial of KALMYK-OIRAT [KGZ]
MINGBARI dial of NGURA [NBX]
MINGI alt for NGIE [NGJ]
MINGRELIAN [XMF] lang, Georgia
MINH HUONG alt for CHINESE, YUE [YUH]
MINHASA alt for TOMBULU [TOM]
MINHE dial of TU [MJG]
MINI [MGJ] lang, Nigeria
MINI alt for KAJAKSE [CKQ]
MINI alt for OMATI [MGX]
MINIAFIA dial of ARIFAMA-MINIAFIA [AAI]
MINIAFIA-ARIFAMA alt for ARIFAMA-MINIAFIA
    [AAI]
MINIANKA alt for SENOUFO, MAMARA [MYK]
MINICA alt for HUITOTO, MƗNƗCA [HTO]
MINICA HUITOTO alt for HUITOTO, MƗNƗCA [HTO]
MINIGIR [VMG] lang, Papua New Guinea
MINIR dial of NAGA, YIMCHUNGRU [YIM]
MINITARI alt for HIDATSA [HID]
MINITJI alt for LIMILNGAN [LMC]
MINIYANKA alt for SENOUFO, MAMARA [MYK]
MINJANBAL alt for YUGAMBAL [YUB]
MINJANTI alt for TIBEA [NGY]
MINJIA alt for BAI [PIQ]
MINJILE dial of MUBI [MUB]
MINJIMMINA alt for DAR EL KABIRA dial of TULISHI
    [TEY]
MINJORI dial of MANAGALASI [MCQ]
MIN-KE alt for TINGZHOU dial of CHINESE, HAKKA
    [HAK]
MINKIA alt for BAI [PIQ]
MINNA dial of KADARA [KAD]
MINNAN alt for CHINESE, MIN NAN [CFR]
MINNESOTA BORDER CHIPPEWA dial of
    CHIPPEWA [CIW]
MINOKOK [MQQ] lang, Malaysia (Sabah)
MINQUA alt for SUSQUEHANNOCK [SQN]
MINRIQ [MNQ] lang, Malaysia (Peninsular)
MINTAMANI alt for KAIS [KZM]
MINTIL [MZT] lang, Malaysia (Peninsular)
MINTRA alt for MANTRA dial of TEMUAN [TMW]
MINUNGO dial of CHOKWE [CJK]
MINYA alt for SENOUFO, MAMARA [MYK]
MINYAK alt for MUYA [MVM]
MINYONG dial of ADI [ADI]
MIOKO alt for AALAWA dial of RAMOAAINA [RAI]
MIOMAFO alt for MOLLO-MIOMAFO dial of ATONI
    [TMR]
MIOS NUM dial of BIAK [BHW]

MIPA alt for KWA' dial of KWA [BKO]
MIR alt for MERIAM [ULK]
MIRA alt for CHIN, MARA [MRH]
MIRA SAGTENGPA alt for BROKPAKE [SGT]
MIRAMAR CHONTAL dial of CHONTAL, TABASCO [CHF]
MIRAÑA alt for MIRANHA dial of BORA [BOA]
MIRAÑA dial of BORA [BOA]
MIRANDA DO DOURO [MWL] lang, Portugal
MIRANDES alt for MIRANDA DO DOURO [MWL]
MIRANDESA alt for MIRANDA DO DOURO [MWL]
MIRANHA alt for MIRAÑA dial of BORA [BOA]
MIRANHA dial of BORA [BOA]
MIRÃNIA alt for MIRANHA dial of BORA [BOA]
MIRAPMIN alt for KONAI [KXW]
MIRASKI dial of KASHMIRI [KSH]
MIRDHA-KHARIA dial of KHARIA [KHR]
MIRE [MVH] lang, Chad
MIRGAMI alt for MIRGAN [QMK]
MIRGAN [QMK] lang, India
MIRGAN alt for DAKHINI dial of URDU [URD]
MIRI [MRG] lang, India
MIRI dial of KATCHA-KADUGLI-MIRI [KAT]
MIRI dial of NAROM [NRM]
MIRIAM alt for MERIAM [ULK]
MIRIAM-MIR alt for MERIAM [ULK]
MIRIEI alt for HATAM [HAD]
MIRIEI dial of HATAM [HAD]
MIRITI [MMV] lang, Brazil
MIRITI TAPUYO alt for MIRITI [MMV]
MIRITI-TAPUIA alt for MIRITI [MMV]
MIRIWOONG alt for MIRIWUNG [MEP]
MIRIWUN alt for MIRIWUNG [MEP]
MIRIWUNG [MEP] lang, Australia
MIRKAN alt for MIRGAN [QMK]
MIRKUK dial of ISEBE [IGO]
MIROY alt for ANUAK [ANU]
MIRPURI alt for PANJABI, MIRPUR [PMU]
MIRPURI dial of PAHARI-POTWARI [PHR]
MIRRIAM dial of KOFYAR [KWL]
MIRUNG alt for MIRIWUNG [MEP]
MIRZAPURI dial of AWADHI [AWD]
MISAMIS HIGAONON MANOBO alt for HIGAONON [MBA]
MISATIK alt for MUSOM [MSU]
MISE dial of NGISHE [NSH]
MISHER alt for WESTERN TATAR dial of TATAR [TTR]
MISHIKHWUTMETUNEE alt for COQUILLE [COQ]
MISHING alt for MIRI [MRG]
MISHIP [CHP] lang, Nigeria
MISHMI alt for DIGARO [MHU]
MISHMI alt for MIJU [MXJ]
MISHULUNDU dial of LUYANA [LAV]
MISIM dial of HOTE [HOT]
MISIMA-PANEATI [MPX] lang, Papua New Guinea
MISING alt for MIRI [MRG]
MIS-KEMBA alt for WAGI [FAD]
MÍSKITO [MIQ] lang, Nicaragua; also in Honduras

MÍSKITO COAST CREOLE ENGLISH dial of NORTHERN CENTRAL AMERICA CREOLE ENGLISH [BZI]
MÍSKITU alt for MSKITO [MIQ]
MISKOLC dial of HUNGARIAN SIGN LANGUAGE [HSH]
MISLES dial of TSAKHUR [TKR]
MISMAN dial of ASMAT, CENTRAL [AST]
MÍSQUITO alt for MÍSKITO [MIQ]
MISSIRII alt for JABAAL dial of TAMA [TMA]
MISSISSIOU alt for SIGHU [SXE]
MISSONG [MIJ] lang, Cameroon
MISSOURI alt for NIUTAJI dial of IOWA-OTO [IOW]
MISSOURIA alt for NIUTAJI dial of IOWA-OTO [IOW]
MISTRALIEN alt for PROVENÇAL [PRV]
MISU alt for BISU [BII]
MITAA alt for META' [MGO]
MITANG alt for NABI [MTY]
MITCHIF alt for MICHIF [CRG]
MITEBOG alt for GEDAGED [GDD]
MITEI alt for MEITEI [MNR]
MITHAN alt for KULUNG MUTHUN dial of NAGA, WANCHO [NNP]
MITHE alt for MEITEI [MNR]
MÍTIA alt for GUAYABERO [GUO]
MITIARO dial of RAROTONGAN [RRT]
MITIL alt for MINTIL [MZT]
MITLATONGO MIXTEC alt for MIXTECO, MITLATONGO [VMM]
MITSOGO alt for TSOGO [TSV]
MITTU [MWU] lang, Sudan
MITUA alt for BARÉ [BAE]
MITUA alt for MANDAHUACA [MHT]
MITUKU [ZMQ] lang, DRC
MÍTUS alt for GUAYABERO [GUO]
MIU [MPO] lang, Papua New Guinea
MIUTINI dial of MERU [MER]
MIWA [VMI] lang, Australia
MIWA alt for LOBI [LOB]
MIWA dial of WUNAMBAL [WUB]
MIWOC alt for MIWOK, SOUTHERN SIERRA [SKD]
MIWOK, BAY [MKQ] lang, USA
MIWOK, CENTRAL SIERRA [CSM] lang, USA
MIWOK, COAST [CSI] lang, USA
MIWOK, LAKE [LMW] lang, USA
MIWOK, NORTHERN SIERRA [NSQ] lang, USA
MIWOK, PLAINS [PMW] lang, USA
MIWOK, SOUTHERN SIERRA [SKD] lang, USA
MIWOKAN alt for MIWOK, SOUTHERN SIERRA [SKD]
MIXE, COATLÁN [MCO] lang, Mexico
MIXE, ISTMO [MIR] lang, Mexico
MIXE, JUQUILA [MXQ] lang, Mexico
MIXE, MAZATLÁN [MZL] lang, Mexico
MIXE, QUETZALTEPEC [MVE] lang, Mexico
MIXE, TLAHUITOLTEPEC [MXP] lang, Mexico
MIXE, TOTONTEPEC [MTO] lang, Mexico
MIXIFORE [MFG] lang, Guinea
MIXIXTLÁN MIXE dial of MIXE, QUETZALTEPEC [MVE]
MIXTECO, ALACATLATZALA [MIM] lang, Mexico

MIXTECO, ALCOZAUCA [QMX] lang, Mexico
MIXTECO, AMOLTEPEC [MBZ] lang, Mexico
MIXTECO, APASCO Y APOALA [MIP] lang, Mexico
MIXTECO, ATATLÁHUCA [MIB] lang, Mexico
MIXTECO, AYUTLA [MIY] lang, Mexico
MIXTECO, CACALOXTEPEC [MIU] lang, Mexico
MIXTECO, CHAYUCO [MIH] lang, Mexico
MIXTECO, CHAZUMBA [QMB] lang, Mexico
MIXTECO, CHIGMACATITLÁN [MII] lang, Mexico
MIXTECO, COATZOSPAN [MIZ] lang, Mexico
MIXTECO, CUYAMECALCO [QMZ] lang, Mexico
MIXTECO, DIUXI-TILANTONGO [MIS] lang, Mexico
MIXTECO, HUITEPEC [MXS] lang, Mexico
MIXTECO, ITUNDUJIA [MCE] lang, Mexico
MIXTECO, IXTAYUTLA [VMJ] lang, Mexico
MIXTECO, JAMILTEPEC [MXT] lang, Mexico
MIXTECO, JUXTLAHUACA [VMC] lang, Mexico
MIXTECO, JUXTLAHUACA OESTE [JMX] lang, Mexico
MIXTECO, MAGDALENA PEÑASCO [QMP] lang, Mexico
MIXTECO, METLATONOC [MXV] lang, Mexico
MIXTECO, MITLATONGO [VMM] lang, Mexico
MIXTECO, MIXTEPEC [MIX] lang, Mexico; also in USA
MIXTECO, NOCHIXTLÁN SURESTE [MXY] lang, Mexico
MIXTECO, OAXACA NOROESTE [MXA] lang, Mexico
MIXTECO, OCOTEPEC [MIE] lang, Mexico
MIXTECO, PEÑOLES [MIL] lang, Mexico
MIXTECO, PINOTEPA NACIONAL [MIO] lang, Mexico
MIXTECO, PUEBLA SUR [MIT] lang, Mexico
MIXTECO, SAN JUAN COLORADO [MJC] lang, Mexico
MIXTECO, SAN JUAN TEITA [QMC] lang, Mexico
MIXTECO, SAN MIGUEL EL GRANDE [MIG] lang, Mexico
MIXTECO, SAN MIGUEL PIEDRAS [QMG] lang, Mexico
MIXTECO, SANTA MARÍA ZACATEPEC [MZA] lang, Mexico
MIXTECO, SILACAYOAPAN [MKS] lang, Mexico
MIXTECO, SINDIHUI [QMH] lang, Mexico
MIXTECO, SINICAHUA [QMI] lang, Mexico
MIXTECO, SOYALTEPEC [VMQ] lang, Mexico
MIXTECO, TACAHUA [QMT] lang, Mexico
MIXTECO, TAMAZOLA [VMX] lang, Mexico
MIXTECO, TEZOATLÁN [MXB] lang, Mexico
MIXTECO, TIDAÁ [MTX] lang, Mexico
MIXTECO, TIJALTEPEC [QMJ] lang, Mexico
MIXTECO, TLAXIACO NORTE [MOS] lang, Mexico
MIXTECO, TLAXIACO, SUROESTE [MEH] lang, Mexico
MIXTECO, TUTUTEPEC [MTU] lang, Mexico
MIXTECO, YOLOXOCHITL [QMY] lang, Mexico
MIXTECO, YOSONDÚA [MPM] lang, Mexico
MIXTECO, YUCUAÑE [MVG] lang, Mexico
MIXTECO, YUTANDUCHI [MAB] lang, Mexico

MIXTEPEC MIXTEC alt for MIXTECO, MIXTEPEC [MIX]
MIXTEPEC ZAPOTEC alt for ZAPOTECO, MIXTEPEC [ZPM]
MIYA [MKF] lang, Nigeria
MIYAK alt for KYENELE [KQL]
MIYAKO [MVI] lang, Japan
MIYAKO-JIMA dial of MIYAKO [MVI]
MIYANGHO alt for YANGHO [YNH]
MIYANG-KHANG alt for NAGA, KHOIRAO [NKI]
MIYAO alt for MUYA [MVM]
MIYATNU dial of ANKAVE [AAK]
MIYAWA alt for MIYA [MKF]
MIYEM alt for MIYEMU dial of MBO-UNG [MUX]
MIYEMU dial of MBO-UNG [MUX]
MIYOBE alt for SOLA [SOY]
MIZA dial of MORU [MGD]
MIZERAN alt for BANA [BCW]
MIZLIME alt for WUZLAM [UDL]
MIZMAST dial of AIMAQ [AIQ]
MIZO dial of LUSHAI [LSH]
MIZULO dial of LEGA-MWENGA [LGM]
MJILLEM alt for NIELLIM [NIE]
MJIUNIANG alt for CAO MIAO [COV]
M'KAANG alt for CHIN, DAAI [DAO]
MKAKO alt for KAKO [KKJ]
MKUU dial of CHAGGA [KAF]
MKWET dial of FEFE [FMP]
MLA alt for MLABRI [MRA]
MLA BRI alt for MLABRI [MRA]
MLA-BRI alt for MLABRI [MRA]
MLABRI [MRA] lang, Thailand; also in Laos
MLAHSÖ [QMQ] lang, Syria
MLAP [KJA] lang, Indonesia (Irian Jaya)
MLOMP [QML] lang, Senegal
MLOMP NORTH alt for MLOMP [QML]
MLOMP SOUTH alt for ESULALU dial of JOLA-KASA [CSK]
MMAALA [MMU] lang, Cameroon
MMALA alt for MMAALA [MMU]
MMANI alt for BULLOM SO [BUY]
MMANI dial of BULLOM SO [BUY]
MME alt for MMEN [BFM]
MMEN [BFM] lang, Cameroon
MMFO alt for DEG [MZW]
MNDIOS DO COXODOÁ alt for SURUAHÁ [SWX]
MNGAHRIS dial of TIBETAN [TIC]
MNONG GAR dial of MNONG, EASTERN [MNG]
MNONG KWANH dial of MNONG, EASTERN [MNG]
MNONG ROLOM dial of MNONG, EASTERN [MNG]
MNONG, CENTRAL [MNC] lang, Viet Nam; also in Cambodia
MNONG, EASTERN [MNG] lang, Viet Nam; also in USA
MNONG, SOUTHERN [MNN] lang, Viet Nam
MÖNGHSA alt for ACHANG [ACN]
MO alt for DEG [MZW]
MO alt for MAK [MKG]
MO EGON alt for EGGON [EGO]
MOA alt for MOBA [MFQ]
MOA dial of LUANG [LEX]

MOAB alt for MOBA [MFQ]
'MOAEKE alt for VAMALE [MKT]
MÒÁKA alt for YAKA [AXK]
MOANUS alt for LELE [UGA]
MOANUS alt for TITAN [TTV]
MOAR alt for BIMOBA [BIM]
MOAR alt for LIKI [LIO]
MOARAERI alt for MORORI [MOK]
MOARE alt for MOBA [MFQ]
'MOAVEKE alt for HMWAVEKE [MRK]
MOBA [MFQ] lang, Togo; also in Burkina Faso
MOBANGO alt for BABANGO [BBM]
MOBBER alt for MOVAR dial of KANURI, CENTRAL
[KPH]
MOBER alt for MOVAR dial of KANURI, CENTRAL
[KPH]
MOBESA alt for MBESA [ZMS]
MOBILIAN [MOD] lang, USA
MOBILIAN JARGON alt for MOBILIAN [MOD]
MOBOU dial of KWANG [KVI]
MOBU alt for MOBOU dial of KWANG [KVI]
MOBUTA alt for AWA [AWB]
MÔC-CHÂU alt for TAI DAENG [TYR]
MOCHA alt for SHAKACHO [MOY]
MOC'HA alt for SHAKACHO [MOY]
MOCHDA alt for CARAPANA [CBC]
MÓCHENO [QMO] lang, Italy
MOCHI [OLD] lang, Tanzania
MOCHIAHUA alt for MAK [MKG]
MOCHO [MHC] lang, Mexico
MOCHUELO-CASANARE-CUIBA dial of CUIBA
[CUI]
MOCHUMI alt for NAGA, CHANG [NBC]
MOCHUNGRR alt for NAGA, CHANG [NBC]
MOCIGIN alt for GUDE [GDE]
MOCOA alt for INGA, JUNGLE [INJ]
MOCOBÍ alt for MOCOVÍ [MOC]
MOCOVÍ [MOC] lang, Argentina
MOD alt for MOTUN dial of TUMAK [TMC]
MO'DA [GBN] lang, Sudan
MODAN alt for KURI [NBN]
MODANG [MXD] lang, Indonesia (Kalimantan)
MODEA dial of GUMUZ [GUK]
MODELE dial of BEFANG [BBY]
MODELI alt for MODELE dial of BEFANG [BBY]
MODELLE alt for MODELE dial of BEFANG [BBY]
MODEN alt for MOTUN dial of TUMAK [TMC]
MODERN CHALDEAN alt for CHALDEAN NEO-
ARAMAIC [CLD]
MODERN LANGUS dial of TORRES STRAIT
CREOLE [TCS]
MODERN LITERARY ARABIC alt for ARABIC,
STANDARD [ABV]
MODERN LITERARY ARABIC alt for MODERN
STANDARD ARABIC dial of ARABIC,
STANDARD [ABV]
MODERN MANDAIC alt for MANDAIC [MID]
MODERN STANDARD ARABIC dial of ARABIC,
STANDARD [ABV]
MODERN TUPI alt for NHENGATU [YRL]
MODERN TUPÍ alt for NHENGATU [YRL]

MODGEL alt for NGAM dial of KWANG [KVI]
MODH alt for MARIA [MRR]
MODI alt for MARIA [MRR]
MODIN alt for MOTUN dial of TUMAK [TMC]
MODO dial of JUR MODO [BEX]
MODO LALI alt for MODO dial of JUR MODO [BEX]
MODOGO alt for MEDOGO dial of NABA [MNE]
MODOLE [MQO] lang, Indonesia (Maluku)
MODRA alt for TODRAH [TDR]
MODUNGA alt for NDUNGA [NDT]
MOENEBENG alt for CAAC [MSQ]
MOERE [MVQ] lang, Papua New Guinea
MOEWEHAFEN alt for AIKLEP [MWG]
MOFA alt for MAFA [MAF]
MOFOU alt for MOFU-GUDUR [MIF]
MOFOU DE GOUDOUR alt for MOFU-GUDUR [MIF]
MOFU dial of BIAK [BHW]
MOFU DE DOUROUM alt for DOUROUN dial of
MOFU, NORTH [MFK]
MOFU DE MERI alt for MEREY [MEQ]
MOFU SOUTH alt for MOFU-GUDUR [MIF]
MOFU, NORTH [MFK] lang, Cameroon
MOFU-DOUVANGAR alt for MOFU, NORTH [MFK]
MOFU-GUDUR [MIF] lang, Cameroon
MOFU-NORD alt for MOFU, NORTH [MFK]
MOFU-SUD alt for MOFU-GUDUR [MIF]
MOG alt for ARAKANESE [MHV]
MOGANA dial of YASA [YKO]
MOGANDA dial of NGUMBI [NUI]
MOGAO alt for PURAGI [PRU]
MOGAREB alt for NARA [NRB]
MOGARI alt for AFADE [AAL]
"MOGH" pejorative alt for ARAKANESE [MHV]
MOGH alt for ARAKANESE [MHV]
MOGHAMO dial of META [MGO]
MOGHAMO-MENEMO alt for META' [MGO]
MOGHOL alt for MOGHOLI [MLG]
MOGHOLI [MLG] lang, Afghanistan
MOGIMBA alt for NGEMBA [NGE]
MOGOFIN alt for MIXIFORE [MFG]
MOGOGODO alt for YAAKU [MUU]
MOGOL alt for MOGHOLI [MLG]
MOGOU alt for MOTIEM dial of NGANGAM [GNG]
MOGOUM alt for MOGUM [MOU]
MOGPHA alt for KAREN, PAKU [KPP]
MOGUEX alt for GUAMBIANO [GUM]
MOGUL alt for MOGHOLI [MLG]
MOGUM [MOU] lang, Chad
MOGUM DÉLE dial of MOGUM [MOU]
MOGUM DIGUIMI dial of MOGUM [MOU]
MOGUM URMI dial of MOGUM [MOU]
MOGWA alt for KAREN, PAKU [KPP]
MOHAVE [MOV] lang, USA
MOHAWK [MOH] lang, Canada; also in USA
MOHEGAN-MONTAUK-NARRAGANSETT [MOF]
lang, USA
MOHÉLI alt for SHIMWALI dial of COMORIAN,
SHINGAZIDJA [SWS]
MOHONGIA alt for NAGA, NOCTE [NJB]
MOHRANO dial of SINDHI BHIL [SBN]
MO-HUA alt for MAK [MKG]

MOHUA alt for MAK [MKG]
MOHUNG dial of NAGA, KONYAK [NBE]
MOI [MOW] lang, Congo
MOI [MXN] lang, Indonesia (Irian Jaya)
MOI alt for HATAM [HAD]
MOI alt for HRE [HRE]
MOI alt for MEKWEI [MSF]
MOI dial of HATAM [HAD]
MOI 1 dial of MUONG [MTQ]
MOI BI alt for BOI BI dial of MUONG [MTQ]
MOI DA VACH alt for HRE [HRE]
MOI LUY alt for HRE [HRE]
MOIFAU alt for MEIFU dial of HLAI [LIC]
MOIKODI [DOI] lang, Papua New Guinea
MOIL alt for TYEMERI dial of
    NANGIKURRUNGGURR [NAM]
MOINBA [MOB] lang, India; also in China
MOINGI [MWZ] lang, DRC
MOIRE alt for MOI dial of HATAM [HAD]
MOISSALA MBAI alt for MBAY [MYB]
MOITANIK dial of MAASAI [MET]
MOIUM alt for PAPEL [PBO]
MOIYUI alt for NAGA, RENGMA [NRE]
MOJAVE alt for MOHAVE [MOV]
MOJIAHUA alt for MAK [MKG]
MOJOS alt for IGNACIANO [IGN]
MOJOS alt for TRINITARIO [TRN]
MOJUNG alt for NAGA, CHANG [NBC]
MOK [MQT] lang, Thailand
MOK alt for MOUK dial of MOUK-ARIA [MWH]
MOKA alt for BYEP [MKK]
MOKAR alt for GA'ANDA [GAA]
MOKARENG alt for MOKERANG [MFT]
MOKÉLUMNE alt for MIWOK, SOUTHERN SIERRA
    [SKD]
MOKEN [MWT] lang, Myanmar; also in Thailand
MOKERANG [MFT] lang, Papua New Guinea
MOKHEV alt for MOXEV dial of GEORGIAN [GEO]
MOKIL alt for MOKILESE [MNO]
MOKILESE [MNO] lang, Micronesia
MOKILKO alt for MUKULU [MOZ]
MOKILKO dial of MUKULU [MOZ]
MOKKAN TILA SADRI dial of SADRI, ORAON [SDR]
MOKLEN [MKM] lang, Thailand
MOKLUM dial of NAGA, TASE [NST]
MOKMER alt for SAMPORI dial of BIAK [BHW]
MOKOLE [MKL] lang, Benin
MOKOLLÉ alt for MOKOLE [MKL]
MOKOMOKO alt for MUKO-MUKO [VMO]
MOKONG dial of MOFU-GUDUR [MIF]
MOKORENG alt for MOKERANG [MFT]
MOKORUA dial of KORAFE [KPR]
MOKOULOU alt for MUKULU [MOZ]
MOKPE alt for MOKPWE [BRI]
MOKPWE [BRI] lang, Cameroon
MOKSELA [VMS] lang, Indonesia (Maluku)
MOKSHA [MDF] lang, Russia (Europe)
MOKSHAN alt for MOKSHA [MDF]
MOKULU alt for MUKULU [MOZ]
MOKURU alt for USHAKU dial of BEFANG [BBY]
MOKWALE alt for MOKOLE [MKL]

MOKYO alt for MELOKWO [MLW]
MOL dial of MUONG [MTQ]
MOLALA alt for MOLALE [MBE]
MOLALE [MBE] lang, USA
MOLALLA alt for MOLALE [MBE]
MOLAO alt for MULAM [MLM]
MOLBOG [PWM] lang, Philippines; also in Malaysia
    (Sabah)
MOLBOG PALAWAN alt for MOLBOG [PWM]
MOLDAVAN alt for ROMANIAN [RUM]
MOLDAVAN dial of ROMANIAN [RUM]
MOLDAVIAN alt for ROMANIAN [RUM]
MOLDAVIAN dial of ROMANIAN [RUM]
MOLDOVEAN alt for MOLDAVAN dial of ROMANIAN
    [RUM]
MOLDOVIAN alt for MOLDAVAN dial of ROMANIAN
    [RUM]
MOLE alt for MÒORÉ [MHM]
MOLELE alt for MOLALE [MBE]
MOLENDJI alt for MOLENGUE [BXC]
MOLENGUE [BXC] lang, Equatorial Guinea
MOLI dial of TALISE [TLR]
MOLIBA dial of DZANDO [DZN]
MOLIMA [MOX] lang, Papua New Guinea
MOLISANO dial of ITALIAN [ITN]
MOLKO alt for MELOKWO [MLW]
MOLKOA alt for MELOKWO [MLW]
MOLKWO alt for MELOKWO [MLW]
MOLLO alt for MOLLO-MIOMAFO dial of ATONI
    [TMR]
MOLLO-MIOMAFO dial of ATONI [TMR]
MOLLOROIDYI alt for MULURIDYI [VMU]
MOLO [ZMO] lang, Sudan
MOLO dial of GULA [KCM]
MOLO dial of NYAMUSA-MOLO [NYO]
MOLOF [MSL] lang, Indonesia (Irian Jaya)
MOLOKO alt for MELOKWO [MLW]
MOLOKWO alt for MELOKWO [MLW]
MOLO-MARU dial of FORDATA [FRD]
MOLOT dial of RAMOAAINA [RAI]
MOLSOM alt for MURSUM dial of CHIN, FALAM
    [HBH]
MOLUCHE dial of MAPUDUNGUN [ARU]
MOLUNGA dial of DZANDO [DZN]
MOM JANGO [VER] lang, Nigeria; also in Cameroon
MOM JANGO dial of MOM JANGO [VER]
MOMA [MYL] lang, Indonesia (Sulawesi)
MOMALE alt for MOMARE [MSZ]
MOMALILI alt for MESÉ [MCI]
MOMARE [MSZ] lang, Papua New Guinea
MOMBA alt for MOINBA [MOB]
MOMBASA alt for MVITA dial of SWAHILI [SWA]
MOMBE alt for NYAKYUSA-NGONDE [NYY]
MOMBE dial of GBAYA, NORTHWEST [GYA]
MOMBESA alt for MBESA [ZMS]
MOMBI alt for MEMBI dial of NDO [NDP]
MOMBOI alt for MAMBAI [MCS]
MOMBU dial of NGEMBA [NGE]
MOMBUM [MSO] lang, Indonesia (Irian Jaya)
MOMBUTTU alt for MANGBUTU [MDK]
MOME alt for MUMUYE [MUL]

MOMFU alt for MAMVU dial of MAMVU [MDI]
MOMI dial of MOM JANGO [VER]
MOMINA [MMB] lang, Indonesia (Irian Jaya)
MOMOGUN alt for RUNGUS [DRG]
MOMOLE alt for MOMARE [MSZ]
MOMOLILI alt for MESE [MCI]
MOMOLILI dial of MESE [MCI]
MOMPA alt for MOINBA [MOB]
MOMU alt for GENGLE [GEG]
MOMUNA [MQF] lang, Indonesia (Irian Jaya)
MOMVEDA dial of PAGIBETE [PAG]
MOMVU alt for MAMVU dial of MAMVU [MDI]
MON [MNW] lang, Myanmar; also in Thailand
MON alt for NAGA, RENGMA [NRE]
MON dial of NAGA, KONYAK [NBE]
MON dial of THO [TOU]
MON NYA alt for YE dial of MON [MNW]
MON TANG alt for PEGU dial of MON [MNW]
MON TE alt for MATABAN-MOULMEIN dial of MON [MNW]
MONA alt for BWILIM dial of DIJIM-BWILIM [CFA]
MONA alt for MWAN [MOA]
MONAM alt for MONOM [MOO]
MONAO alt for BURMESO [BZU]
MONASTIC SIGN LANGUAGE [MZG] lang, Vatican State
MONAU alt for BURMESO [BZU]
MONAXO alt for MAXAKALÍ [MBL]
MONBA alt for MOINBA [MOB]
MONBA alt for TSHANGLA [TSJ]
MONCHON alt for MBULUNGISH [MBV]
"MONCÓ" pejorative alt for PRINCIPENSE [PRE]
MONDARI alt for MANDARI [MQU]
MONDARI alt for MUNDARI [MUW]
MONDARI dial of BARI [BFA]
MONDÉ [MND] lang, Brazil
MONDJEMBO alt for MONZOMBO [MOJ]
MONDO alt for MÜNDÜ [MUH]
MONDO alt for SULOD [SRG]
MONDOGOSSOU dial of BERAKOU [BXV]
MONDROPOLON [MLY] lang, Papua New Guinea
MONDU alt for MÜNDÜ [MUH]
MONDUGU alt for NDUNGA [NDT]
MONDUNGA alt for NDUNGA [NDT]
MONEBWA alt for KAREN, PAKU [KPP]
MONÉGASQUE dial of LIGURIAN [LIJ]
MONG LENG dial of HMONG DAW [MWW]
MONGAIYAT alt for MANGAYAT [MYJ]
MONGALA POTO dial of LUSENGO [LUS]
MONGBANDI alt for NGBANDI, SOUTHERN [NBW]
MONGBAPELE dial of PAGIBETE [PAG]
MONGBAY alt for MAMBAI [MCS]
MONGGOL alt for MONGOLIAN, PERIPHERAL [MVF]
MONGI alt for KUBE [KGF]
MONGLWE alt for TAI LOI [TLQ]
MONGO alt for BUSHOONG [BUF]
MONGO alt for MANGO [MGE]
MONGO alt for MONGO-NKUNDU [MOM]
MONGO dial of DAJU, DAR SILA [DAU]

MONGO dial of KURANKO [KHA]
MONGO dial of LUSENGO [LUS]
MONGOL [MGT] lang, Papua New Guinea
MONGOL alt for MONGOLIAN, HALH [KHK]
MONGOL alt for MONGOLIAN, PERIPHERAL [MVF]
MONGOLIAN BURIAT alt for BURIAT, MONGOLIA [BXM]
MONGOLIAN SIGN LANGUAGE [QMM] lang, Mongolia
MONGOLIAN, HALH [KHK] lang, Mongolia; also in Kyrgyzstan, Russia (Asia), Taiwan
MONGOLIAN, PERIPHERAL [MVF] lang, China; also in Mongolia
MONGONDOU alt for MONGONDOW [MOG]
MONGONDOW [MOG] lang, Indonesia (Sulawesi)
MONGO-NKUNDU [MOM] lang, DRC
MONGOR alt for TU [MJG]
MONGO-SILA alt for DAJU, DAR SILA [DAU]
MONGOUR alt for TU [MJG]
MONGSEN KHARI dial of NAGA, AO [NJO]
MONGUL alt for MOGHOLI [MLG]
MONGUNA dial of RON [CLA]
MONGWANDI alt for NGBANDI, NORTHERN [NGB]
MONGWANDI alt for NGBANDI, SOUTHERN [NBW]
MONI [MNZ] lang, Indonesia (Irian Jaya)
MONI alt for KENSIU [KNS]
MONIA dial of LIBINZA [LIZ]
MONIK alt for KENSIU [KNS]
MONIMBO [MOL] lang, Nicaragua
MONIQ alt for KENSIU [KNS]
MONJO alt for NGEMBA dial of GHOMALA [BBJ]
MONJOMBO alt for MONZOMBO [MOJ]
MONJUL alt for MUBI [MUB]
MONKIT dial of MOINBA [MOB]
MONKOLE alt for MOKOLE [MKL]
MONNEPWA alt for KAREN, PAKU [KPP]
MON-NON alt for MONO [MRU]
MONO [MNH] lang, DRC
MONO [MON] lang, USA
MONO [MRU] lang, Cameroon
MONO [MTE] lang, Solomon Islands
MONO dial of MONO [MTE]
MONO-ALU alt for MONO [MTE]
MONOARFU dial of BIAK [BHW]
MONOCHO alt for MAXAKALÍ [MBL]
MONOGOY [MCU] lang, Chad
MONO-JEMBO alt for MONZOMBO [MOJ]
MONOM [MOO] lang, Viet Nam
MONPA alt for MOINBA [MOB]
MONPA alt for OLEKHA [OLE]
MONPA alt for TSHANGLA [TSJ]
MONR alt for NAGA, ANGAMI [NJM]
MONSHANG alt for NAGA, MONSANG [NMH]
MONSHON alt for MBULUNGISH [MBV]
MONTAGNAIS [MOE] lang, Canada
MONTAL alt for MONTOL [MTL]
MONTAUK dial of MOHEGAN-MONTAUK-NARRAGANSETT [MOF]
MONTE VERDE MIXTECO dial of MIXTECO, TLAXIACO NORTE [MOS]
MONTENEGRIN alt for SERBO-CROATIAN [SRC]

MONTEREY dial of COSTANOAN, SOUTHERN [CSS]
MONTOL [MTL] lang, Nigeria
MONTOL dial of MONTOL [MTL]
MONTSERRAT CREOLE ENGLISH dial of LEEWARD CARIBBEAN CREOLE ENGLISH [AIG]
MONU alt for KAREN, MANUMANAW [KXF]
MONUMBO [MXK] lang, Papua New Guinea
MONZAMBOLI dial of BUDZA [BJA]
MONZOMBO [MOJ] lang, Congo; also in CAR, DRC
MONZÓN dial of QUECHUA, HUANUCO, HUAMALIES-NORTHERN DOS DE MAYO [QEJ]
MONZUMBO alt for MONZOMBO [MOJ]
MOO [GWG] lang, Nigeria
MOOI alt for MEKWEI [MSF]
MOOJANGA alt for ANUAK [ANU]
MOOLOROIJI alt for MULURIDYI [VMU]
MOOMA dial of YASA [YKO]
MOONDE dial of TOBANGA [TNG]
MOOR alt for ARABIC, HASANYA [MEY]
MOOR alt for ARABIC, HASSANIYYA [MEY]
MOOR alt for BIMOBA [BIM]
MO'OR dial of WAROPEN [WRP]
MÒORÉ [MHM] lang, Burkina Faso; also in Benin, Côte d'Ivoire, Ghana, Mali, Togo
MOORINGA alt for MOORINGER dial of FRISIAN, NORTHERN [FRR]
MOORINGER dial of FRISIAN, NORTHERN [FRR]
MOOSE alt for MÒORÉ [MHM]
MOOSEHIDE alt for HAN [HAA]
MOOSO alt for LAHU [LAH]
MOOYO alt for KONIÉRÉ dial of KARANGA [KTH]
MOPAGA alt for KAREN, PAKU [KPP]
MOPÁN MAYA [MOP] lang, Belize; also in Guatemala
MOPANE alt for MOPÁN MAYA [MOP]
MOPHA alt for KAREN, PAKU [KPP]
MOPLA alt for MALAYALAM [MJS]
MOPLAH dial of MALAYALAM [MJS]
MOPO alt for MUFWA dial of BURUN [BDI]
MOPOI alt for MAPOYO [MCG]
MOPUTE alt for WARU [WRU]
MOPWA alt for KAREN, PAKU [KPP]
MOQADDAM dial of AZERBAIJANI, SOUTH [AZB]
MOQUELUMNAN alt for MIWOK, SOUTHERN SIERRA [SKD]
MOR [MHZ] lang, Indonesia (Irian Jaya)
MOR [MOQ] lang, Indonesia (Irian Jaya)
MORA alt for CENTRAL YAWA dial of YAWA [YVA]
MORA alt for YAWA [YVA]
MORA BROUSSE alt for MURA dial of WANDALA [MFI]
MORA MASSIF alt for MURA dial of WANDALA [MFI]
MORAFA alt for ASARO'O [MTV]
MORAID [MSG] lang, Indonesia (Irian Jaya)
MORANGIA dial of THARU, KOCHILA [THQ]
MORAORI alt for MORORI [MOK]
MORARI alt for MORORI [MOK]
MORATO alt for URU [URE]
MORAVIAN ROMANI dial of ROMANI, CARPATHIAN [RMC]

MORAWA [MZE] lang, Papua New Guinea
MORBO dial of BERNDE [BDO]
MORDOFF alt for MOKSHA [MDF]
MORDOV alt for MOKSHA [MDF]
MORDVIN alt for ERZYA [MYV]
MORDVIN-ERZYA alt for ERZYA [MYV]
MORDVIN-MOKSHA alt for MOKSHA [MDF]
MORE alt for ITENE [ITE]
MORE alt for MÒORÉ [MHM]
MOREB dial of TAGOI [TAG]
MORELA dial of HITU [HIT]
MOREREBI [XMO] lang, Brazil
MORESADA [MSX] lang, Papua New Guinea
MORI alt for MANINKA-MORI dial of MANINKA, KANKAN [MNI]
MORI dial of ANEME WAKE [ABY]
MORI ATAS [MZQ] lang, Indonesia (Sulawesi)
MORI BAWAH [XMZ] lang, Indonesia (Sulawesi)
MORIE dial of ABE [ABA]
MORIGI [MDB] lang, Papua New Guinea
MORIGI ISLAND alt for MORIGI [MDB]
MORIIL alt for ZAN GULA [ZNA]
MORIKO dial of MUKULU [MOZ]
MORILLE alt for DAASANACH [DSH]
MORIMA alt for MOLIMA [MOX]
MORIORI dial of MAORI [MBF]
MORIPI-IOKEA alt for TOARIPI dial of TOARIPI [TPI]
MORISYEN [MFE] lang, Mauritius; also in Madagascar
MORMA alt for ARAKANESE [MHV]
MORMA alt for MARMA dial of ARAKANESE [MHV]
MORO [MOR] lang, Sudan
MORO alt for AYOREO [AYO]
MORO alt for TAUSUG [TSG]
MORO JOLOANO alt for TAUSUG [TSG]
MOROA alt for SHOLIO dial of TYAP [KCG]
MOROCCAN SIGN LANGUAGE [XMS] lang, Morocco
MOROFO alt for ANYIN, MOROFO [MTB]
MOROKODO [MGC] lang, Sudan
MOROKODO dial of MOROKODO [MGC]
MOROM alt for BERNDE [BDO]
MOROM dial of BERNDE [BDO]
MOROMIRANGA alt for AROP-LOKEP [APR]
MORONAHUA alt for CHITONAHUA dial of YAMINAHUA [YAA]
MORONENE [MQN] lang, Indonesia (Sulawesi)
MORONENE alt for WITA EA dial of MORONENE [MQN]
MORONOU dial of ANYIN [ANY]
MORORI [MOK] lang, Indonesia (Irian Jaya)
MOROTAI dial of GALELA [GBI]
MOROTOCO alt for AYOREO [AYO]
MOROUAS [MRP] lang, Vanuatu
MOROUBA alt for MORUBA dial of BANDA-MBRES [BQK]
MORTA alt for KADUGLI dial of KATCHA-KADUGLI-MIRI [KAT]
MORTLOCK alt for MORTLOCKESE [MRL]

MORTLOCK alt for TAKUU [NHO]
MORTLOCKESE [MRL] lang, Micronesia
MORU [MGD] lang, Sudan
MORU [MXZ] lang, Côte d'Ivoire
MORUAS alt for MOROUAS [MRP]
MORUBA dial of BANDA-MBRES [BQK]
MORUNAHUA alt for CHITONAHUA dial of
    YAMINAHUA [YAA]
MORUWA'DI dial of MORU [MGD]
MORVA alt for KURUX [KVN]
MORWA alt for SHOLIO dial of TYAP [KCG]
"MORWAP" pejorative alt for ELSENG [MRF]
MOS alt for KENSIU [KNS]
MOS alt for TONGA [TNZ]
MOSANA alt for MOI [MXN]
MOSANGE alt for NDOLO [NDL]
MOSCA alt for CHIBCHA [CBF]
MOSELLE FRANCONIAN alt for
    LUXEMBOURGEOIS [LUX]
MOSETÉN alt for TSIMANÉ [CAS]
MOSHANG alt for NAGA, MONSANG [NMH]
MOSHI alt for MOCHI [OLD]
MOSHI alt for MÒORÉ [MHM]
MOSI alt for MOCHI [OLD]
MOSI alt for MUSEY [MSE]
MOSIENO dial of TEKE, EASTERN [TEK]
MOSIMO [MQV] lang, Papua New Guinea
MOSIN alt for MOSINA [MSN]
MOSINA [MSN] lang, Vanuatu
MOSIRO [MWY] lang, Tanzania
MOSIYE alt for BUSSA [DOX]
MOSKONA [MTJ] lang, Indonesia (Irian Jaya)
MOSLAWI alt for ARABIC, NORTH
    MESOPOTAMIAN SPOKEN [AYP]
"MOSO" pejorative alt for NAXI [NBF]
MOSO alt for LAHU [LAH]
MOSQUITO alt for MÍSKITO [MIQ]
MOSSI alt for MÒORÉ [MHM]
"MOSSO" pejorative alt for NAXI [NBF]
"MO-SU" pejorative alt for NAXI [NBF]
MOT alt for MOTUN dial of TUMAK [TMC]
MOTA [MTT] lang, Vanuatu
MOTALAVA alt for MOTLAV [MLV]
MOTCHEKIN alt for GUDE [GDE]
MOTEMBO alt for TEMBO [TMV]
MOTI alt for MOTKI dial of DIMLI [ZZZ]
MOTIEM dial of NGANGAM [GNG]
MOTILÓN [MOT] lang, Colombia; also in Venezuela
MOTILÓN alt for QUECHUA, SAN MARTÍN [QSA]
MOTILONE alt for MOTILÓN [MOT]
MOTIN alt for MOTUN dial of TUMAK [TMC]
MOTKI dial of DIMLI [ZZZ]
MOTLAV [MLV] lang, Vanuatu
MOT-MAR dial of GULA [KCM]
MOTOM alt for MACI dial of ICEVE-MACI [BEC]
MOTO-MARA alt for MOT-MAR dial of GULA
    [KCM]
MOTOMO alt for MACI dial of ICEVE-MACI [BEC]
MOTOMO alt for OLITI dial of ICEVE-MACI [BEC]
MOTOZINTLECO alt for MOCHO [MHC]
MOTOZINTLECO dial of MOCHO [MHC]

MOTU [MEU] lang, Papua New Guinea
MOTU, HIRI [POM] lang, Papua New Guinea
MOTUMOTU alt for TOARIPI [TPI]
MOTUN dial of TUMAK [TMC]
MOTUNA alt for SIWAI [SIW]
MOTUO alt for TSHANGLA [TSJ]
MOTUO MENBA alt for TSHANGLA [TSJ]
MOU alt for KHMU [KJG]
MOUAMENAM alt for MWAMENAM dial of AKOOSE
    [BSS]
MOUAN alt for MWAN [MOA]
MOUBI alt for MUBI [MUB]
MOUGO dial of MBAY [MYB]
MOUGULU alt for BEAMI [BEO]
MOUHOUR alt for MUHURA dial of MEFELE [MFJ]
MOUK dial of MOUK-ARIA [MWH]
MOUK-ARIA [MWH] lang, Papua New Guinea
MOUKTELE alt for MATAL [MFH]
MOULMEIN alt for PA'AN dial of KAREN, PWO
    EASTERN [KJP]
MOULMEIN PWO KAREN alt for KAREN, PWO
    EASTERN [KJP]
MOULOUI alt for MUSGU [MUG]
MOUNAN alt for MUNA [MYN]
MOUNDAN alt for MUNDANG [MUA]
MOUNDANG alt for MUNDANG [MUA]
MOUNTAIN dial of SLAVEY, NORTH [SCS]
MOUNTAIN ARAPESH alt for BUKIYIP [APE]
MOUNTAIN ARAPESH alt for BUKIYIP dial of
    BUKIYIP [APE]
MOUNTAIN BASHKIR alt for KUVAKAN dial of
    BASHKIR [BXK]
MOUNTAIN GELAO dial of GELAO [KKF]
MOUNTAIN KOIARI alt for KOIALI, MOUNTAIN
    [KPX]
MOUNTAIN LAWA alt for LAWA, WESTERN [LCP]
MOUNTAIN MAIDU alt for MAIDU, NORTHEAST
    [NMU]
MOUNTAIN PIMA alt for PIMA BAJO, SONORA
    [PIA]
MOUNTAIN TEQUISTLATECO alt for CHONTAL
    DE OAXACA, SIERRA [CHD]
MOUNTOU alt for MÜNDÜ [MUH]
MOURLE alt for MURLE [MUR]
MOUROUM alt for MURUM dial of NGAMBAY [SBA]
MOURRO alt for MURRU dial of KIBET [KIE]
MOUSGOU alt for MUSGU [MUG]
MOUSGOUM alt for MUSGU [MUG]
MOUSGOUM DE GUIRVIDIG alt for MUZUK dial
    of MUSGU [MUG]
MOUSGOUM DE GUIRVIDIK alt for MUZUK dial
    of MUSGU [MUG]
MOUSGOUM DE POUSS alt for MPUS dial of
    MUSGU [MUG]
MOUSGOUN alt for MUSGU [MUG]
MOUSSEI alt for MUSEY [MSE]
MOUSSEY alt for MUSEY [MSE]
MOUYENGE alt for MUYANG [MUY]
MOUYENGUE alt for MUYANG [MUY]
MOVAR dial of KANURI, CENTRAL [KPH]
MOVE dial of YAGARIA [YGR]

MOVEAVE alt for TOARIPI dial of TOARIPI [TPI]
MOVIMA [MZP] lang, Bolivia
MOWCHI alt for MAWCHI [MKE]
MOXDOA alt for CARAPANA [CBC]
MOXEV dial of GEORGIAN [GEO]
MOXO alt for IGNACIANO [IGN]
MOXOS alt for IGNACIANO [IGN]
MOXOS alt for TRINITARIO [TRN]
MOYAKA alt for BEKA dial of YAKA [AXK]
MOYO alt for KONIÉRÉ dial of KARANGA [KTH]
MOYO dial of MADI [MHI]
MOYON alt for NAGA, MOYON [NMO]
MOYON-MONSHANG dial of ANAL [ANM]
MOZAMBICAN SIGN LANGUAGE [MZY] lang,
   Mozambique
MOZARABIC [MXI] lang, Spain
MOZDOK dial of KABARDIAN [KAB]
MOZHUMI alt for NAGA, RENGMA [NRE]
MOZOME dial of NAGA, ANGAMI [NJM]
MPADE [MPI] lang, Cameroon; also in Chad, Nigeria
MPADE dial of MPADE [MPI]
MPAKA dial of MONO [MNH]
MPAMA dial of MONGO-NKUNDU [MOM]
MPEZENI alt for NGONI dial of NSENGA [NSE]
MPI [MPZ] lang, Thailand
MPIEMO [MCX] lang, CAR; also in Cameroon
MPI-MI alt for MPI [MPZ]
MPO alt for MPIEMO [MCX]
MPO dial of BASAA [BAA]
MPOMAM dial of MPONGMPONG [MGG]
MPOMPO alt for MPONGMPONG [MGG]
MPONDO dial of XHOSA [XOS]
MPONDOMISI alt for MPONDOMSE dial of XHOSA
   [XOS]
MPONDOMSE dial of XHOSA [XOS]
MPONGMPONG [MGG] lang, Cameroon
MPONGO dial of NTOMBA [NTO]
MPONGOUÉ alt for MPONGWE dial of MYENE
   [MYE]
MPONGWE dial of MYENE [MYE]
MPOPO alt for MPONGMPONG [MGG]
MPOTO [MPA] lang, Tanzania; also in Malawi
MPOTOVORO [MVT] lang, Vanuatu
MPU dial of TEKE, NORTHEASTERN [NGZ]
MPUMPUM alt for MPU dial of TEKE, NORTH-
   EASTERN [NGZ]
MPUNGWE alt for MPONGWE dial of MYENE [MYE]
MPUONO [ZMP] lang, DRC
MPUONO dial of MPUONO [ZMP]
MPUR [AKC] lang, Indonesia (Irian Jaya)
MPUS dial of MUSGU [MUG]
MPUUN dial of MPUONO [ZMP]
MPYEMO alt for MPIEMO [MCX]
MPYEMO dial of MPIEMO [MCX]
MRABRI alt for MLABRI [MRA]
MRAS TATAR alt for SHOR [CJS]
MRASSA dial of SHOR [CJS]
MRIAK-MRIKU dial of SASAK [SAS]
MRIMA dial of SWAHILI [SWA]
MRO alt for MRU [MRO]
MRO dial of CHRAU [CHR]

MRU [MRO] lang, Bangladesh; also in India, Myanmar
MRUNG alt for KOK BOROK [TRP]
MRUNG alt for MRU [MRO]
MSER [KQX] lang, Cameroon; also in Chad
MSER dial of MSER [KQX]
MSIR alt for MSER dial of MSER [KQX]
MT. ELGON MAASAI alt for SABAOT [SPY]
MT. GOLIATH alt for UNA [MTG]
MT. IRIGA NEGRITO alt for AGTA, MT. IRIGA [AGZ]
MTEZI dial of KUKELE [KEZ]
MTHUR alt for JARAI [JRA]
MTIUL dial of GEORGIAN [GEO]
MÜN alt for CHIN, MÜN [MWQ]
MÜNDÜ [MUH] lang, Sudan; also in DRC
MÜNKÜ alt for IRÁNTXE [IRA]
MÜNKÜ dial of IRÁNTXE [IRA]
MU alt for NAXI [NBF]
MU alt for SEKPELE [LIP]
MUAL dial of MUONG [MTQ]
MUALANG [MTD] lang, Indonesia (Kalimantan)
MUAN alt for MWAN [MOA]
MUANA alt for MWAN [MOA]
MUANE alt for MWANI [WMW]
MUANG alt for THAI, NORTHERN [NOD]
MU'ANG alt for THAI, NORTHERN [NOD]
MUASI alt for MAWASI dial of KORKU [KFQ]
MUATIAMVUA alt for RUUND [RND]
MUATURAINA dial of MANAGALASI [MCQ]
MUBADJI alt for BEBA' dial of BAFUT [BFD]
MUBAKO alt for NYONG [MUO]
MUBI [MUB] lang, Chad
MUBI alt for GUDE [GDE]
MUBI dial of FOI [FOI]
MUBI dial of MUBI [MUB]
MUBI RIVER alt for FOI [FOI]
MUCHELLA alt for MADZARIN dial of FALI [FLI]
MUCKLESHOOT dial of SALISH, SOUTHERN
   PUGET SOUND [SLH]
MUCOROCA alt for KWADI [KWZ]
MUD alt for MEDOGO dial of NABA [MNE]
MUDA alt for MO'DA [GBN]
MUDAVAN alt for MUTHUVAN [MUV]
MUDAYE alt for GUDE [GDE]
MUDBURA [MWD] lang, Australia
MUDBURRA alt for MUDBURA [MWD]
MUDIA alt for MURIA, WESTERN [MUT]
MUDIMA alt for MALIMBA [MZD]
"MUDJETÍRE" pejorative alt for SURUÍ DO PARÁ
   [MDZ]
"MUDJETÍRE-SURUÍ" pejorative alt for SURUÍ
   DO PARÁ [MDZ]
MUDUAPA [WIV] lang, Papua New Guinea
MUDUGAR alt for MUTHUVAN [MUV]
MUDUVA alt for MUTHUVAN [MUV]
MUDUVAN alt for MUTHUVAN [MUV]
MUDUVAR alt for MUTHUVAN [MUV]
MUENAME alt for MUINANE [BMR]
MUFIAN [AOJ] lang, Papua New Guinea
MUFWA dial of BURUN [BDI]
MUGABA alt for MUNGGAVA dial of RENNELL
   [MNV]

MUGAJA alt for MUGHAJA dial of BURUN [BDI]
MUGALI alt for MUGU [MUK]
MUGALI KHAM dial of MUGU [MUK]
MUGALY alt for ZAKATALY dial of AZERBAIJANI,
    NORTH [AZE]
MUGALY alt for ZAQATALA dial of AZERBAIJANI,
    NORTH [AZE]
MUGANGE dial of SAGALLA [TGA]
MUGHAJA dial of BURUN [BDI]
MUGHALBANDI dial of ORIYA [ORY]
MUGIKI alt for MUNGIKI dial of RENNELL [MNV]
MUGIL alt for BARGAM [MLP]
MUGO-MBORKOINA alt for ABULDUGU dial of
    BURUN [BDI]
MUGU [MUK] lang, Nepal
MUGUJI dial of KWEGU [YID]
MUGUM alt for NGEMBA dial of GHOMALA [BBJ]
MUGUMUTE alt for KAPRIMAN [DJU]
MUHANG alt for WEST LAMAHOLOT dial of
    LAMAHOLOT [SLP]
MUHER dial of GURAGE, WEST [GUY]
MUHIAN alt for MUFIAN [AOJ]
MUHIANG alt for MUFIAN [AOJ]
MUHSO alt for LAHU [LAH]
MUHSUR alt for LAHU [LAH]
MUHURA dial of MEFELE [MFJ]
MUHURU dial of SUBA [SUH]
MUILA alt for MWILA dial of NYANEKA [NYK]
MUINANA alt for MUINANE [BMR]
MUINANE [BMR] lang, Colombia
MUINANE HUITOTO alt for HUITOTO, NɨPODE
    [HUX]
MUINANI alt for MUINANE [BMR]
MUIRIN dial of DARGWA [DAR]
MUISCA alt for CHIBCHA [CBF]
MUKA alt for BAMUNKA [NDO]
MUKA alt for MUKAH-OYA dial of MELANAU [MEL]
MUKAH alt for MUKAH-OYA dial of MELANAU [MEL]
MUKAH-OYA dial of MELANAU [MEL]
MUKAJAI alt for SOUTHERN NINAM dial of NINAM
    [SHB]
MUKAMUGA alt for KAMORO [KGQ]
MUKAWA alt for ARE [MWC]
MUKHA DHORA alt for MUKHA-DORA [MMK]
MUKHAD alt for RUTUL [RUT]
MUKHA-DORA [MMK] lang, India
MUKHIYA alt for SUNWAR [SUZ]
MUKI alt for MEKEM [XME]
MUKILI alt for BELI [BEY]
MUKOGODO alt for YAAKU [MUU]
MUKOHN alt for MANGKUNGE dial of NGEMBA
    [NGE]
MUKO-MUKO [VMO] lang, Indonesia (Sumatra)
MUKOQUODO alt for YAAKU [MUU]
MUKRI dial of KURDI [KDB]
MUKTELE alt for MATAL [MFH]
MUKTILE alt for MATAL [MFH]
MUKU alt for BILEKI dial of NAKANAI [NAK]
MUKULU [MOZ] lang, Chad
MUKULU dial of BEMBA [BEM]
MUKUNI alt for LENJE [LEH]

MUKUNO alt for MINEW dial of ZULGWA [ZUL]
MUKURU alt for USHAKU dial of BEFANG [BBY]
MULAHA [MFW] lang, Papua New Guinea
MULAHA dial of MULAHA [MFW]
MULAI alt for ENLAI dial of MAKHUWA [VMW]
MULAK dial of MALAY [MLI]
MULAKAINO alt for LAMOGAI [LMG]
MULAM [MLM] lang, China
MULAN alt for LAMALERA [LMR]
MULAO alt for MULAM [MLM]
MULAO MIAO alt for MULAM [MLM]
MULARITCHEE alt for MULURIDYI [VMU]
MULENGE dial of RWANDA [RUA]
MULGAON-WANGTANG dial of MEOHANG,
    EASTERN [EMG]
MULGARNOO alt for BAYUNGU [BXJ]
MULGI alt for MULY dial of ESTONIAN [EST]
MULGI dial of ESTONIAN [EST]
MULGWE dial of MARGHI CENTRAL [MAR]
MULIAO alt for MULAM [MLM]
MULIMBA alt for MALIMBA [MZD]
MULLRIDGEY alt for MULURIDYI [VMU]
MULLUKMULLUK [MPB] lang, Australia
MULONGA dial of SIMAA [SIE]
MULOU alt for MULAM [MLM]
MULSOM dial of ANAL [ANM]
MULTANI alt for SARAIKI [SKR]
MULTANI dial of SARAIKI [SKR]
MULU alt for MARU [MHX]
MULUNG dial of NAGA, KONYAK [NBE]
MULURIDYI [VMU] lang, Australia
MULURUTJI alt for MULURIDYI [VMU]
MULWI alt for MUSGU [MUG]
MULWI alt for VULUM dial of MUSGU [MUG]
MULWI-MOGROUM alt for VULUM dial of MUSGU
    [MUG]
MULWYIN alt for MULYEN dial of BACAMA [BAM]
MULY dial of ESTONIAN [EST]
MULYEN dial of BACAMA [BAM]
MUM [KQA] lang, Papua New Guinea
MUMAITE alt for LUMAETE dial of KAYELI [KZL]
MUMBAKE alt for NYONG [MUO]
MUMBALA alt for MBALA dial of YOMBE [YOM]
MUMENG [MZI] lang, Papua New Guinea
MUMENG dial of MUMENG [MZI]
MUMONI dial of KAMBA [KIK]
MUMUGHADJA alt for MUGHAJA dial of BURUN
    [BDI]
MUMUYE [MUL] lang, Nigeria; also in Cameroon
MUMVIRI dial of KATI [BSH]
MUN alt for KIM MUN [MJI]
MUN alt for MON [MNW]
MUN XEN alt for KHMU [KJG]
MUNA [MYN] lang, Indonesia (Sulawesi)
MUNARI alt for MUNDARI [MUW]
MUNASELI PANDAI dial of ADABE [ADB]
MUNDA alt for MENDANKWE dial of MENDANKWE
    [MFD]
MUNDA alt for MUNDARI [MUW]
MUNDA ANDHRA PRADESH GADABA dial of
    GADABA, BODO [GBJ]

MUNDA ORISSA GADABA dial of GADABA, BODO [GBJ]
MUNDANG [MUA] lang, Chad; also in Cameroon
MUNDANI [MUN] lang, Cameroon
MUNDARI [MUW] lang, India; also in Bangladesh, Nepal
MUNDARI alt for MANDARI [MQU]
MUNDARI alt for MONDARI dial of BARI [BFA]
MUNDAT [MMF] lang, Nigeria
MUNDJUN alt for YIR YORONT [YIY]
MUNDO alt for MÜNDÜ [MUH]
MUNDUGUMA alt for BIWAT [BWM]
MUNDUGUMOR alt for BIWAT [BWM]
MUNDUM 1 alt for MBREREWI dial of NGEMBA [NGE]
MUNDUM 2 alt for ANYANG dial of NGEMBA [NGE]
MUNDURUCU alt for MUNDURUKÚ [MYU]
MUNDURUKÚ [MYU] lang, Brazil
MUNEGASC alt for MONÉGASQUE dial of LIGURIAN [LIJ]
MUNG dial of PHUNOI [PHO]
MUNGA alt for LEELAU [LDK]
MUNGA dial of BIRRI [BVQ]
MUNGA DOSO alt for MINGANG DOSO [MKO]
MUNGA LELAU alt for LEELAU [LDK]
MUNGAK alt for TUVIN [TUN]
MUNGAKA [MHK] lang, Cameroon
MUNGA'KA alt for MUNGAKA [MHK]
MUNGARAI alt for MANGARAYI [MPC]
MUNGERA OHALO alt for YIDINY [YII]
MUNGERRY alt for MANGARAYI [MPC]
MUNGGAI alt for MEKWEI [MSF]
MUNGGAVA dial of RENNELL [MNV]
MUNGGE alt for MEKWEI [MSF]
MUNGGUI [MTH] lang, Indonesia (Irian Jaya)
MUNGIKI dial of RENNELL [MNV]
MUNGO dial of DUALA [DOU]
MUNGOM alt for MUNGONG [XMN]
MUNGONG [XMN] lang, Cameroon
MUNGU alt for MUNGO dial of DUALA [DOU]
MUNGYEN alt for NGAMAMBO [NBV]
MUNICHE [MYR] lang, Peru
MUNICHI alt for MUNICHE [MYR]
MUNICHINO alt for MUNICHE [MYR]
MUNIN dial of ANDI [ANI]
MUNIT [MTC] lang, Papua New Guinea
MUNIWARA [MWB] lang, Papua New Guinea
MUNJANI alt for MUNJI [MNJ]
MUNJHAN alt for MUNJI [MNJ]
MUNJI [MNJ] lang, Afghanistan
MUNJI dial of BOIKIN [BZF]
MUNJIWAR alt for MUNJI [MNJ]
MUNJUK alt for MUSGU [MUG]
MUNKAF alt for NAKI [MFF]
MUNKAN alt for WIK-MUNGKAN [WIM]
MUNKEI alt for MEKWEI [MSF]
MUNKIP [MPV] lang, Papua New Guinea
MUNSEE [UMU] lang, Canada
"MUNSHI" pejorative alt for TIV [TIV]
MUNSTER dial of GAELIC, IRISH [GLI]
MUNTABI alt for GAAM [TBI]

MUNTEAN alt for MUNTENIAN dial of ROMANIAN [RUM]
MUNTENIAN dial of ROMANIAN [RUM]
MUNUKUTUBA [MKW] lang, Congo
MUNYO dial of ORMA [ORC]
MUNYO YAYA alt for MUNYO dial of ORMA [ORC]
MUNYUKU dial of GUPAPUYNGU [GUF]
MUONG [MTQ] lang, Viet Nam
MUPUN dial of MWAGHAVUL [SUR]
MURA dial of WANDALA [MFI]
MURALIDBAN dial of GUNWINGGU [GUP]
MURANG PUNAN alt for PUNAN dial of DAYAK, LAND [DYK]
MÚRA-PIRAHÃ [MYP] lang, Brazil
MURATAIK alt for ASAT [ASX]
MURATO alt for CANDOSHI-SHAPRA [CBU]
MURATO dial of CARIB [CRB]
MURATU alt for URU [URE]
MURAWARI alt for MURUWARI [ZMU]
MURCIAN dial of SPANISH [SPN]
MURELE alt for MURLE [MUR]
MURELEI alt for MURLE [MUR]
MURGI alt for BIRKED [BRK]
MURI alt for GUHU-SAMANE [GHS]
MURI alt for MER [MNU]
MURI dial of HALBI [HLB]
MURIA alt for MURI dial of HALBI [HLB]
MURIA GONDI alt for MURIA, WESTERN [MUT]
MURIA, EASTERN [EMU] lang, India
MURIA, FAR WESTERN [FMU] lang, India
MURIA, WESTERN [MUT] lang, India
MURIK [MTF] lang, Papua New Guinea
MURINBADA alt for MURRINH-PATHA [MWF]
MURINBATA alt for MURRINH-PATHA [MWF]
MURINMANINDJI alt for MARIMANINDJI [ZMM]
MURIRE alt for BUGLERE [SAB]
MURIS alt for DEMTA [DMY]
MURISAPA alt for MORESADA [MSX]
MURKIM [RMH] lang, Indonesia (Irian Jaya)
MURLE [MUR] lang, Sudan; also in Ethiopia
MURMI alt for TAMANG, WESTERN [TDG]
MURO alt for MURRU dial of KIBET [KIE]
MURO alt for OROKOLO [ORO]
MURRINHDIMININ dial of MURRINH-PATHA [MWF]
MURRINHKURA dial of MURRINH-PATHA [MWF]
MURRINH-PATHA [MWF] lang, Australia
MURRINHPATHA dial of MURRINH-PATHA [MWF]
MURRU dial of KIBET [KIE]
MURRUNGUN dial of DJINANG [DJI]
MURSI [MUZ] lang, Ethiopia
MURSUM dial of CHIN, FALAM [HBH]
MURU alt for OROKOLO [ORO]
MURUA alt for MUYUW [MYW]
MURULE alt for MURLE [MUR]
MURUM dial of NGAMBAY [SBA]
MURUNG alt for MRU [MRO]
MURUNG 1 alt for OT MURUNG 1 dial of DOHOI [OTD]
MURUNG 2 dial of SIANG [SYA]
MURUPI [MQW] lang, Papua New Guinea

MURUSAPA-SAREWA alt for MORESADA [MSX]
MURUT alt for LUNDAYEH [LND]
MURUT PADAASS dial of TIMUGON MURUT [TIH]
MURUTHU alt for MARATHI [MRT]
MURUWA alt for MUYUW [MYW]
MURUWARI [ZMU] lang, Australia
MURZI alt for MURSI [MUZ]
MURZU alt for MURSI [MUZ]
MUS dial of ARMENIAN [ARM]
MUSA alt for MUSAN [MMP]
MUSAHAR alt for MUSASA [SMM]
MUSAHARI dial of BHOJPURI [BHJ]
MUSAIA dial of YALUNKA [YAL]
MUSAK [MMQ] lang, Papua New Guinea
MUSALI alt for JAKATI [JAT]
MUSAN [MMP] lang, Papua New Guinea
MUSAR [MMI] lang, Papua New Guinea
MUSAR dial of MAITHILI [MKP]
MUSASA [SMM] lang, Nepal
MUSAU-EMIRA alt for MUSSAU-EMIRA [EMI]
MUSAYA alt for MUSEY [MSE]
MUSCH alt for MUS dial of ARMENIAN [ARM]
MUSEI alt for MUSEY [MSE]
MUSEMBAN alt for MUNDANG [MUA]
MUSEN dial of LAMOGAI [LMG]
MUSEU alt for LAHU [LAH]
MUSEY [MSE] lang, Chad; also in Cameroon
MUSEYNA alt for MUSEY [MSE]
MUSGOI dial of DABA [DAB]
MUSGOY alt for MUSGOI dial of DABA [DAB]
MUSGU [MUG] lang, Cameroon; also in Chad
MUSGUM alt for MUSGU [MUG]
MUSGUM-POUSS alt for MPUS dial of MUSGU [MUG]
MUSHANG alt for NAGA, MONSANG [NMH]
MUSHUNGULI alt for MUSHUNGULU [XMA]
MUSHUNGULU [XMA] lang, Somalia
MUSI [MUI] lang, Indonesia (Sumatra)
MUSIAN alt for MUSAN [MMP]
MUSIINA alt for MUSEY [MSE]
MUSIM alt for MISIM dial of HOTE [HOT]
MUSIYE alt for BUSSA [DOX]
MUSKOGEE [CRK] lang, USA
MUSKUM [MJE] lang, Chad
MUSLIM SINDHI alt for SINDHI MUSALMANI dial of SINDHI [SND]
MUSLIM TAT alt for TAT, MUSLIM [TTT]
MUSOI alt for MUSEY [MSE]
MUSOM [MSU] lang, Papua New Guinea
MUSQUEAM dial of HALKOMELEM [HUR]
MUSSAR alt for LAHU [LAH]
MUSSAU-EMIRA [EMI] lang, Papua New Guinea
MUSSEH DAENG alt for NYI dial of LAHU [LAH]
MUSSEH KWI alt for LAHU SHI [KDS]
MUSSEH LYANG alt for LAHU SHI [KDS]
MUSSELMANI dial of BENGALI [BNG]
MUSSER alt for LAHU [LAH]
MUSSER DAM alt for NA dial of LAHU [LAH]
MUSSO alt for LAHU [LAH]
MUSSOI alt for MUSEY [MSE]
MUSSOY alt for MUSEY [MSE]

MUSSUH alt for LAHU [LAH]
MUSSULMAN TATI alt for TAT, MUSLIM [TTT]
MUSTANG alt for LOPA [LOY]
MUSUK alt for MUSGU [MUG]
MUSUNYE dial of JONKOR BOURMATAGUIL [JEU]
MUTA alt for META' [MGO]
MUTAIR alt for CENTRAL NAJDI dial of ARABIC, NAJDI SPOKEN [ARS]
MUTANI alt for SARAIKI [SKR]
MUTHAMBI dial of MWIMBI-MUTHAMBI [MWS]
MUTHEIT alt for KAREN, PWO WESTERN [PWO]
MUTHUVAN [MUV] lang, India
MUTIDI dial of NZANYI [NJA]
MUTSUN dial of COSTANOAN, SOUTHERN [CSS]
MUTTANGULLA alt for MADNGELE [ZML]
MUTU [TUC] lang, Papua New Guinea
MUTÚ alt for MUTÚS [MUF]
MUTU dial of MUTU [TUC]
MUTUM [MCC] lang, Papua New Guinea
MUTURAMI dial of GIZIGA, SOUTH [GIZ]
MUTURUA alt for MUTURAMI dial of GIZIGA, SOUTH [GIZ]
MUTURWA alt for MUTURAMI dial of GIZIGA, SOUTH [GIZ]
MUTÚS [MUF] lang, Venezuela
MUTUTU alt for AMDANG [AMJ]
MUTUVAR alt for MUTHUVAN [MUV]
MUTWANG dial of RAWANG [RAW]
MUTYU alt for DJANGUN [DJF]
MU:DU alt for KORAGA, MUDU [VMD]
MUUNGO alt for MUNGO dial of DUALA [DOU]
MUWASI alt for MAWASI dial of KORKU [KFQ]
MUXULE dial of JINA [JIA]
MUXULI alt for MUXULE dial of JINA [JIA]
MUYA [MVM] lang, China
MUYA alt for MIYA [MKF]
MUYANG [MUY] lang, Cameroon
MUYENGE alt for MUYANG [MUY]
MUYU alt for MUYUW [MYW]
MUYU alt for NINGGERUM [NXR]
MUYUA alt for MUYUW [MYW]
MUYUW [MYW] lang, Papua New Guinea
MUYUWA alt for MUYUW [MYW]
MUYWI alt for MOGHAMO dial of META [MGO]
MUZGUM alt for MUSKUM [MJE]
MUZUK alt for MUSGU [MUG]
MUZUK dial of MUSGU [MUG]
MVAE alt for MANEHAS dial of BAKAKA [BQZ]
MVAE dial of FANG [FNG]
MVAN alt for MVAE dial of FANG [FNG]
MVANIP [MCJ] lang, Nigeria
MVANLIP alt for MVANIP [MCJ]
MVANÖP alt for MVANIP [MCJ]
MVANO alt for MVANIP [MCJ]
MVANON alt for MVANIP [MCJ]
MVAY alt for MVAE dial of FANG [FNG]
MVEDERE alt for VIDIRI dial of BANDA-BANDA [BPD]
MVEGUMBA alt for BELANDA VIRI [BVI]
MVELE alt for BAMVELE dial of EWONDO [EWO]
MVELE alt for BASAA [BAA]
MVELE alt for MBERE dial of TUKI [BAG]

MVETE dial of EWONDO [EWO]
MVITA dial of SWAHILI [SWA]
MVOG-NAMVE dial of ETON [ETO]
MVOG-NIENGUE dial of EWONDO [EWO]
MVO-NANGKOK dial of ETON [ETO]
MVUBA [MXH] lang, DRC; also in Uganda
MVUBA-A alt for MVUBA [MXH]
MVUMBO alt for NGUMBA [NMG]
MVUMBO dial of NGUMBA [NMG]
MWA alt for MWAN [MOA]
MWAE alt for EMAE [MMW]
MWAGHAVUL [SUR] lang, Nigeria
MWAHED alt for MANEHAS dial of BAKAKA [BQZ]
MWAHET alt for MANEHAS dial of BAKAKA [BQZ]
MWALU alt for VAMWALU dial of MAKONDE [KDE]
MWALUKWASIA dial of DUAU [DUA]
MWAMBA dial of NYAKYUSA-NGONDE [NYY]
MWAMBE alt for VAMWAMBE dial of MAKONDE [KDE]
MWAMBONG dial of AKOOSE [BSS]
MWAMENAM dial of AKOOSE [BSS]
MWAN [MOA] lang, Côte d'Ivoire
MWANA alt for BWILIM dial of DIJIM-BWILIM [CFA]
MWANDA dial of TAITA [DAV]
MWANE alt for MWANI [WMW]
MWANEKA alt for BANEKA dial of BAKAKA [BQZ]
MWANGA [MWN] lang, Zambia; also in Tanzania
MWANI [WMW] lang, Mozambique
MWANI dial of HAYA [HAY]
MWANO alt for BWILIM dial of DIJIM-BWILIM [CFA]
MWATEBU [MWA] lang, Papua New Guinea
MWELA alt for MWERA [MWE]
MWENYI dial of SIMAA [SIE]
MWERA [MWE] lang, Tanzania
MWERI dial of NYAMWEZI [NYZ]
MWERIG dial of MERLAV [MRM]
MWIINI alt for MWINI dial of SWAHILI [SWA]
MWILA dial of NYANEKA [NYK]
MWIMBI dial of MWIMBI-MUTHAMBI [MWS]
MWIMBI-MUTHAMBI [MWS] lang, Kenya
MWINA dial of POKOMO, LOWER [POJ]
MWINI dial of SWAHILI [SWA]
MWOAKILESE alt for MOKILESE [MNO]
MWOAKILOA alt for MOKILESE [MNO]
MWOMO alt for BWILIM dial of DIJIM-BWILIM [CFA]
MWONA alt for BWILIM dial of DIJIM-BWILIM [CFA]
MWULYIN alt for MULYEN dial of BACAMA [BAM]
MYA BURA alt for BURA-PABIR [BUR]
MYAGATWA alt for ZALAMO [ZAJ]
MYAMKAT alt for KINNAURI, BHOTI [NES]
MYAMSKAD alt for KINNAURI, BHOTI [NES]
MYANG alt for THAI, NORTHERN [NOD]
MYAU alt for MUYANG [MUY]
MYEN alt for BURMESE [BMS]
MYEN alt for IU MIEN [IUM]
MYENE [MYE] lang, Gabon
MYENGE alt for MUYANG [MUY]
MYET alt for TAPSHIN [TDL]
MYFOORSCH alt for BIAK [BHW]
MYIMU dial of NAGA, TASE [NST]
MYKHANIDY alt for RUTUL [RUT]

MYNKY alt for MÜNKÜ dial of IRANTXE [IRA]
MYRATO alt for MURATO dial of CARIB [CRB]
MYSORE LAMANI alt for KARNATAKA LAMANI dial of LAMBADI [LMN]
MYU alt for MIU [MPO]
MYUNDUNO alt for YIR YORONT [YIY]
MYY alt for MÜNKÜ dial of IRANTXE [IRA]
MZAB alt for TUMZABT [MZB]
MZABI alt for TUMZABT [MZB]
MZANGYIM alt for NZANYI [NJA]
MZIEME alt for NAGA, MZIEME [NME]
NA alt for KABA NA [KWV]
NA dial of KABA NA [KWV]
NA dial of LAHU [LAH]
NA KADOK dial of SAEK [SKB]
NA NAHEK dial of GALOLI [GAL]
NA NHYANG dial of KUY [KDT]
NAA DUBEA alt for DUMBEA [DUF]
NAA NUMEE alt for NUMEE [KDK]
NAABAN dial of BANGWINJI [BSJ]
NAADH alt for NUER [NUS]
NAAHAI alt for SOUTH WEST BAY [SNS]
NA'AHAI alt for ORIERH dial of MALFAXAL [MLX]
NAAMA alt for KOSORONG [KSR]
NAAN dial of PAPE [NDU]
NAANDI alt for NANDI dial of KALENJIN [KLN]
NAANI alt for NANKANI dial of FRAFRA [GUR]
NAANI alt for SÉNOUFO, NANERIGÉ [SEN]
NAAPA [NAO] lang, Nepal
NAAPAA alt for NAAPA [NAO]
NAASIOI [NAS] lang, Papua New Guinea
NAASIOI dial of NAASIOI [NAS]
NAATH alt for NUER [NUS]
NAA-WEE alt for NUMEE [KDK]
NABA [MNE] lang, Chad
NABA alt for NAAPA [NAO]
NABA alt for NABAK [NAF]
NABAI alt for NABAY dial of KENINGAU MURUT [KXI]
NABAK [NAF] lang, Papua New Guinea
NABALEBALE alt for CENTRAL VANUA LEVU dial of FIJIAN [FJI]
NABALOI alt for IBALOI [IBL]
NABANJ dial of KULANGO, BOUNA [NKU]
NABAY dial of KENINGAU MURUT [KXI]
NABDAM alt for NABT dial of FRAFRA [GUR]
NABDE alt for NABT dial of FRAFRA [GUR]
NABDUG alt for NABT dial of FRAFRA [GUR]
NABE alt for TÈÈN [LOR]
NABESNA alt for TANANA, UPPER [TAU]
NABI [MTY] lang, Papua New Guinea
NABI alt for KURI [NBN]
NABIT alt for NABT dial of FRAFRA [GUR]
NABLOS dial of DOMARI [RMT]
NABNAM alt for NABT dial of FRAFRA [GUR]
NABRUG alt for NABT dial of FRAFRA [GUR]
NABT dial of FRAFRA [GUR]
NABTE alt for NABT dial of FRAFRA [GUR]
NABU alt for NAHU [NCA]
NABUKELEVU alt for KADAVU dial of FIJIAN [FJI]
NACCHHERING alt for NACHERING [NCD]

NACERING RA alt for NACHERING [NCD]
NACHERING [NCD] lang, Nepal
NACHERING TÛM alt for NACHERING [NCD]
NADA alt for BUDIBUD [BTP]
NAD'A alt for NGAD'A [NXG]
NADËB [MBJ] lang, Brazil
NADEB MACU alt for NADËB [MBJ]
NADÖBÖ alt for NADËB [MBJ]
NADROGA alt for FIJIAN [FJI]
NADROGA alt for FIJIAN, WESTERN [WYY]
NADROGAA alt for NUCLEAR WESTERN FIJIAN
    dial of FIJIAN, WESTERN [WYY]
NADRONGA alt for FIJIAN [FJI]
NADRONGA alt for FIJIAN, WESTERN [WYY]
NA'E alt for BUNU, BAHENG [PHA]
NA-E alt for BUNU, BAHENG [PHA]
NAFÃÃ dial of SENOUFO, MAMARA [MYK]
NAFAANRA [NFR] lang, Ghana; also in Côte d'Ivoire
NAFAARA alt for NAFAANRA [NFR]
NAFANA alt for NAFAANRA [NFR]
NAFANA dial of JULA, ODIENNE [JOD]
NAFAR dial of AZERBAIJANI, SOUTH [AZB]
NAFARA dial of SENOUFO, CEBAARA [SEF]
NAFARPI alt for KAMORO [KGQ]
NAFI [SRF] lang, Papua New Guinea
NAFRI [NXX] lang, Indonesia (Irian Jaya)
NAFUKWÁ alt for NAHUKUÁ dial of MATIPUHY [MZO]
NAFUNFIA alt for MONGUNA dial of RON [CLA]
NAFUSI [JBN] lang, Libya; also in Tunisia
NAFUSI alt for DJERBI [JBN]
NAGA dial of BALANTA-KENTOHE [BLE]
NAGA dial of BICOLANO, CENTRAL [BKL]
NAGA dial of MAPE [MLH]
NAGA CREOLE ASSAMESE alt for NAGA PIDGIN
    [NAG]
NAGA PIDGIN [NAG] lang, India
NAGA, ANGAMI [NJM] lang, India
NAGA, AO [NJO] lang, India
NAGA, CHANG [NBC] lang, India
NAGA, CHOKRI [NRI] lang, India
NAGA, CHOTHE [NCT] lang, India
NAGA, KABUI [NKF] lang, India
NAGA, KHEZHA [NKH] lang, India
NAGA, KHIAMNIUNGAN [NKY] lang, India; also
    in Myanmar
NAGA, KHOIBU MARING [NKB] lang, India
NAGA, KHOIRAO [NKI] lang, India
NAGA, KONYAK [NBE] lang, India
NAGA, LIANGMAI [NJN] lang, India
NAGA, LOTHA [NJH] lang, India
NAGA, MAO [NBI] lang, India
NAGA, MARAM [NMA] lang, India
NAGA, MARING [NNG] lang, India
NAGA, MELURI [NLM] lang, India
NAGA, MONSANG [NMH] lang, India
NAGA, MOYON [NMO] lang, India
NAGA, MZIEME [NME] lang, India
NAGA, NOCTE [NJB] lang, India
NAGA, NTENYI [NNL] lang, India
NAGA, PHOM [NPH] lang, India
NAGA, POCHURI [NPO] lang, India

NAGA, POUMEI [PMX] lang, India
NAGA, PUIMEI [NPU] lang, India
NAGA, RENGMA [NRE] lang, India
NAGA, RONGMEI [NBU] lang, India
NAGA, SANGTAM [NSA] lang, India
NAGA, SUMI [NSM] lang, India
NAGA, TANGKHUL [NMF] lang, India
NAGA, TARAO [TRO] lang, India
NAGA, TASE [NST] lang, India; also in Myanmar
NAGA, WANCHO [NNP] lang, India
NAGA, YIMCHUNGRU [YIM] lang, India
NAGA, ZEME [NZM] lang, India
NAGA-ASSAMESE alt for NAGA PIDGIN [NAG]
NAGAMESE alt for NAGA PIDGIN [NAG]
NAGANE dial of KUMAN [KUE]
NAGAPELTA alt for FULFULDE, ADAMAWA [FUB]
NAGAR alt for NAGARCHAL [NBG]
NAGAR dial of BURUSHASKI [BSK]
NAGARA alt for NAKARA [NCK]
NAGARCHAL [NBG] lang, India
NAGARCHI alt for NAGARCHAL [NBG]
NAGARI alt for STANDARD GUJARATI dial of
    GUJARATI [GJR]
NAGARIGE alt for PIVA [TGI]
NAGARI-MALAYALAM dial of MALAYALAM [MJS]
NAGATIMAN alt for YALE [NCE]
NAGATMAN alt for YALE [NCE]
NAGBANMBA dial of LOKO [LOK]
NAGDI dial of MEHRI [MHR]
NAGE [NXE] lang, Indonesia (Nusa Tenggara)
NAGÉ alt for NAGE [NXE]
NAGE-KEO alt for KE'O [XXK]
NAGE-KEO alt for NAGE [NXE]
NAGIR alt for NAGAR dial of BURUSHASKI [BSK]
NAGIRA alt for NINGERA [NBY]
NAGO [NQG] lang, Benin
NAGO dial of KUNIGAMI [XUG]
NAGOT alt for NAGO [NQG]
NAGOTS alt for NAGO [NQG]
NAGOVIS alt for NAGOVISI [NCO]
NAGOVISI [NCO] lang, Papua New Guinea
NAGPUR dial of GONDI, NORTHERN [GON]
NAGPURI alt for SADRI [SCK]
NAGPURI HINDI dial of BUNDELI [BNS]
NAGPURI MARATHI alt for BAGHELI [BFY]
NAGPURIA alt for SADRI [SCK]
NAGPURIYA dial of GARHWALI [GBM]
NAGRAMADU alt for KAMORO [KGQ]
NAGRANDAN dial of CHOROTEGA [CJR]
NAGUMI [NGV] lang, Cameroon
NAGURI dial of MUNDARI [MUW]
NAHA dial of OKINAWAN, CENTRAL [RYU]
NAHAL alt for NIHALI [NHL]
NAHALE alt for NIHALI [NHL]
NAHALI alt for NAHARI [NHH]
NAHALI alt for NIHALI [NHL]
NAHANE alt for KASKA [KKZ]
NAHANI alt for KASKA [KKZ]
NAHARA alt for NAHARRA dial of MAKHUWA
    [VMW]
NAHARI [NHH] lang, India

NAHARI dial of BHILI [BHB]
NAHARRA dial of MAKHUWA [VMW]
NAHARRA dial of MAKHUWA-MARREVONE [XMC]
NAHES dial of MODANG [MXD]
"NAHINA" pejorative alt for TOLAKI [LBW]
NAHINA alt for MORI BAWAH [XMZ]
NAHINA dial of MORI BAWAH [XMZ]
NAHINE alt for BUNGKU [BKZ]
NAHO alt for NAHU [NCA]
NAHOA alt for NUGURIA [NUR]
NAHSI alt for NAXI [NBF]
NAHU [NCA] lang, Papua New Guinea
NAHUA alt for YORA [MTS]
NAHUAT alt for PIPIL [PPL]
NÁHUATL CENTRAL [NHN] lang, Mexico
NÁHUATL DE LA SIERRA DE ZONGOLICA alt for NÁHUATL, ORIZABA [NLV]
NÁHUATL, CLASSICAL [NCI] lang, Mexico
NÁHUATL, COATEPEC [NAZ] lang, Mexico
NÁHUATL, DURANGO [NLN] lang, Mexico
NÁHUATL, GUERRERO [NAH] lang, Mexico
NÁHUATL, HUASTECA, ESTE [NAI] lang, Mexico
NÁHUATL, HUASTECO OESTE [NHW] lang, Mexico
NÁHUATL, HUAXCALECA [NHQ] lang, Mexico
NÁHUATL, ISTMO-COSOLEACAQUE [NHK] lang, Mexico
NÁHUATL, ISTMO-MECAYAPAN [NAU] lang, Mexico
NÁHUATL, ISTMO-PAJAPAN [NHP] lang, Mexico
NÁHUATL, IXHUATLANCILLO [NHX] lang, Mexico
NÁHUATL, MICHOACÁN [NCL] lang, Mexico
NÁHUATL, MORELOS [NHM] lang, Mexico
NÁHUATL, OAXACA NORTE [NHY] lang, Mexico
NÁHUATL, OMETEPEC [NHT] lang, Mexico
NÁHUATL, ORIZABA [NLV] lang, Mexico
NÁHUATL, PUEBLA CENTRAL [NCX] lang, Mexico
NÁHUATL, PUEBLA NORTE [NCJ] lang, Mexico
NÁHUATL, PUEBLA SURESTE [NHS] lang, Mexico
NÁHUATL, PUEBLA, SIERRA [AZZ] lang, Mexico
NÁHUATL, SANTA MARÍA LA ALTA [NHZ] lang, Mexico
NÁHUATL, TABASCO [NHC] lang, Mexico
NÁHUATL, TEMASCALTEPEC [NHV] lang, Mexico
NÁHUATL, TENANGO [NHI] lang, Mexico
NÁHUATL, TETELCINGO [NHG] lang, Mexico
NÁHUATL, TLALITZLIPA [NHJ] lang, Mexico
NÁHUATL, TLAMACAZAPA [NUZ] lang, Mexico
NAHUKUÁ dial of MATIPUHY [MZO]
NAHUQUA alt for NAHUKUÁ dial of MATIPUHY [MZO]
NAI [BIO] lang, Papua New Guinea
NAI dial of ANGOR [AGG]
NAIALI dial of GUNWINGGU [GUP]
NAIBEDJ alt for KWERBA [KWE]
NAIK KURUMBA alt for KURUMBA, JENNU [QKJ]
NAIKAN alt for KURUMBA, JENNU [QKJ]
NAIKDI dial of BHILI [BHB]
NAIKI dial of KOLAMI, SOUTHEASTERN [NIT]
NAIMAN alt for JO-UDA dial of MONGOLIAN, PERIPHERAL [MVF]

NAIMASIMASI alt for SOUTHEAST VITI LEVU dial of FIJIAN [FJI]
NAINDIN dial of ATTIE [ATI]
NAIRYA KOLI dial of KOLI, WADIYARA [KXP]
NAJÁ dial of LACANDON [LAC]
NAJIL dial of PASHAYI, NORTHWEST [GLH]
NAJRAAN alt for CENTRAL NAJDI dial of ARABIC, NAJDI SPOKEN [ARS]
NAJRAN alt for SOUTH ANJDI dial of ARABIC, NAJDI SPOKEN [ARS]
NAJWA dial of KALANGA [KCK]
NAKA alt for BAPUKU dial of BATANGA [BNM]
NAKA dial of GBAYA [KRS]
NAKA'ELA [NAE] lang, Indonesia (Maluku)
NAKAI [NKJ] lang, Indonesia (Irian Jaya)
NAKAMA [NIB] lang, Papua New Guinea
NAKANAI [NAK] lang, Papua New Guinea
NAKANNA dial of EVENKI [EVN]
NAKANYARE alt for SAMBA DAKA [CCG]
NAKARA [NCK] lang, Australia
NAKARE alt for BU [JID]
NAKE [NBK] lang, Papua New Guinea
NAKGAKTAI alt for KOL dial of KOL [KOL]
NAKHCHIVAN dial of AZERBAIJANI, NORTH [AZE]
NAKHI alt for NAXI [NBF]
NAKHICHEVAN dial of AZERBAIJANI, NORTH [AZE]
NAKI [MFF] lang, Cameroon
NAKIAI dial of SANIYO-HIYEWE [SNY]
NAKKARA alt for NAKARA [NCK]
NA'KLALLAM alt for CLALLAM [CLM]
NAKODA alt for NAKOTA dial of DAKOTA [DHG]
NAKODA alt for STONEY [STO]
NAKONAI alt for NAKANAI [NAK]
NAKOROBOYA alt for WAYA dial of FIJIAN, WESTERN [WYY]
NAKOTA dial of DAKOTA [DHG]
NAKUKWA alt for NAHUKUÁ dial of MATIPUHY [MZO]
NÁKUM alt for MAIDU, NORTHWEST [MAI]
NAKWI [NAX] lang, Papua New Guinea
NALA alt for NARA [NRZ]
NALABON alt for NGALKBUN [NGK]
NALCA [TVL] lang, Indonesia (Irian Jaya)
NALE alt for ATCHIN dial of URIPIV-WALA-RANO-ATCHIN [UPV]
NALEA dial of NAMOSI-NAITASIRI-SERUA [BWB]
NALGUNO dial of BIDIYO [BID]
NALI [NSS] lang, Papua New Guinea
NALI dial of NAGA, ANGAMI [NJM]
NALIK [NAL] lang, Papua New Guinea
NALOU alt for NALU [NAJ]
NALTJE alt for NALCA [TVL]
NALTYA alt for NALCA [TVL]
NALU [NAJ] lang, Guinea; also in Guinea-Bissau
NAMA [NAQ] lang, Namibia; also in Botswana, South Africa
NAMA alt for BAI [PIQ]
NAMA dial of MBEMBE, TIGON [NZA]
NAMA dial of NAMA [NAQ]
NAMAKABAN alt for TSOU [TSY]

NAMAKERE alt for MAKERE dial of MANGBETU [MDJ]
NAMAKERETI alt for MAKERE dial of MANGBETU [MDJ]
NAMAKURA [NMK] lang, Vanuatu
NAMAKWA alt for NAMA [NAQ]
NAMAN alt for NAMA [NAQ]
NAMAQUA alt for NAMA [NAQ]
NAMASA alt for LIGBI [LIG]
NAMATALAKI alt for ABUI [ABZ]
NAMATOTA dial of KOWIAI [KWH]
NAMATOTE alt for NAMATOTA dial of KOWIAI [KWH]
NAMAU alt for IAI dial of PURARI [IAR]
NAMAU alt for PURARI [IAR]
NAMBAKAENGÖ alt for SANTA CRUZ [STC]
NAMBAS, BIG [NMB] lang, Vanuatu
NAMBE dial of TEWA [TEW]
NAMBER SACHA dial of BAHING [RAR]
NAMBIEB W&H 1981 alt for NABI [MTY]
NAMBIKUÁRA, NORTHERN [MBG] lang, Brazil
NAMBIKUÁRA, SOUTHERN [NAB] lang, Brazil
NAMBIKWARA alt for NAMBIKUÁRA, SOUTHERN [NAB]
NAMBIQUARA alt for NAMBIKUÁRA, SOUTHERN [NAB]
NAMBLOMON-MABUR dial of YAQAY [JAQ]
NAMBO alt for NAMBU [NCM]
NAMBOODIRI dial of MALAYALAM [MJS]
NAMBRONG alt for NIMBORAN [NIR]
NAMBU [NCM] lang, Papua New Guinea
NAMBYA [NMQ] lang, Zimbabwe
NAMBZYA alt for NAMBYA [NMQ]
"NAMCHI" pejorative alt for DOYAYO [DOW]
"NAMCI" pejorative alt for DOYAYO [DOW]
NAMEJETI alt for MEJE dial of MANGBETU [MDJ]
NAMEL alt for NYAMAL [NLY]
NAMEN alt for LAHU [LAH]
NAMENA alt for NORTHEAST VITI LEVU dial of FIJIAN [FJI]
NAMFAU alt for ANAL [ANM]
NAMI dial of MANAGALASI [MCQ]
NAMIA [NNM] lang, Papua New Guinea
NAMIAE dial of BARAI [BCA]
NAMIBIAN SIGN LANGUAGE [NBS] lang, Namibia
NAMIDAMA dial of NAMA [NAQ]
NAMIE alt for NAMIA [NNM]
NAMLUNG dial of KULUNG [KLE]
NAMNAM alt for NABT dial of FRAFRA [GUR]
NAMOME alt for FASU [FAA]
NAMOME dial of FASU [FAA]
NAMON WEITE alt for NAMONUITO [NMT]
NAMONUITO [NMT] lang, Micronesia
NAMOSI-NAITAASIRI-SEERUA alt for NAMOSI-NAITASIRI-SERUA [BWB]
NAMOSI-NAITASIRI-SERUA [BWB] lang, Fiji
NAMPAMELA alt for EMPAMELA dial of MAKHUWA [VMW]
NAMPAMELA dial of MAKHUWA-MARREVONE [XMC]
NAMRUNG dial of NUBRI [KTE]

NAMSANGIA alt for NAGA, NOCTE [NJB]
"NAMSHI" pejorative alt for DOYAYO [DOW]
NAMU alt for NAMA dial of MBEMBE, TIGON [NZA]
NAMU dial of REMBONG [REB]
NAMUMI alt for NAMOME dial of FASU [FAA]
NAMUNI alt for NAMOME dial of FASU [FAA]
NAMUNKA dial of OROCH [OAC]
NAMUYA alt for KESAWAI [QKE]
NAMUYI [NMY] lang, China
NAMUZI alt for NAMUYI [NMY]
NAMWANGA alt for MWANGA [MWN]
NAMWEZI alt for NYAMWEZI [NYZ]
NAN dial of THAI, NORTHERN [NOD]
ÑANAGUA alt for TAPIETÉ [TAI]
NANAI [GLD] lang, Russia (Asia); also in China
NANAIMO dial of HALKOMELEM [HUR]
NANAJ alt for NANAI [GLD]
NANAYA dial of MATO [NIU]
NANCERE [NNC] lang, Chad
NANCHERE alt for NANCERE [NNC]
NANCOURY alt for NANCOWRY dial of NICOBARESE, CENTRAL [NCB]
NANCOWRY dial of NICOBARESE, CENTRAL [NCB]
NAND alt for GOWLI [GOK]
NAND dial of GOWLI [GOK]
NANDE alt for NANDI [NNB]
NANDEREKE alt for SÉNOUFO, NANERIGÉ [SEN]
NANDERGÉ alt for SÉNOUFO, NANERIGÉ [SEN]
ÑANDEVA alt for CHIRIPÁ [NHD]
NANDI [NNB] lang, DRC
NANDI dial of KALENJIN [KLN]
NANDI dial of NANDI [NNB]
NANDRAU dial of SOUTHEAST VITI LEVU dial of FIJIAN [FJI]
NANDU-TARI [NAA] lang, Nigeria
NANE alt for ERE [TWP]
NANERGÉ alt for SÉNOUFO, NANERIGÉ [SEN]
NANERGUÉ alt for SÉNOUFO, NANERIGÉ [SEN]
NANGALAMI dial of GRANGALI [NLI]
NANGARACH dial of PASHAYI, NORTHWEST [GLH]
NANGCERE alt for NANCERE [NNC]
NANGGU [NAN] lang, Solomon Islands
NANGIKURRUNGGURR [NAM] lang, Australia
NANGIKURUNGGURR alt for NANGIKURRUNGGURR [NAM]
NANGIMERA alt for NGENKIWUMERRI dial of NANGIKURRUNGGURR [NAM]
NANGIOMERI alt for NGENKIWUMERRI dial of NANGIKURRUNGGURR [NAM]
NANGJERE alt for NANCERE [NNC]
NANGNDA alt for BEDJOND [MAP]
NANGU alt for JARNANGO [JAY]
NANGUMIRI alt for NGENKIWUMERRI dial of NANGIKURRUNGGURR [NAM]
NANHIL alt for GRIFFIN POINT dial of SUDEST [TGO]
NANHUA dial of YI, CENTRAL [YIC]
NANJERI alt for NANCERE [NNC]
NANKANA dial of FRAFRA [GUR]

NANKANI alt for FRAFRA [GUR]
NANKANI dial of FRAFRA [GUR]
NANKANSE alt for NANKANI dial of FRAFRA [GUR]
NANKINA [NNK] lang, Papua New Guinea
NANO alt for UMBUNDU [MNF]
NANOMAM dial of YANOMAMI [WCA]
NANQA POROJA alt for BONDO [BFW]
NANSHI AMIS alt for NORTHERN AMIS dial of AMIS
  [ALV]
NANTA alt for NORTHERN TAIRORA dial of
  TAIRORA [TBG]
NANTCERE alt for NANCERE [NNC]
NANTI [COX] lang, Peru
NANTICOKE [NNT] lang, USA
NANTJARA alt for WIKNGENCHERA [WUA]
NANUMANGA alt for NORTH TUVALUAN dial of
  TUVALUAN [ELL]
NANUMBA alt for NANUNI dial of DAGBANI [DAG]
NANUMEA alt for NORTH TUVALUAN dial of
  TUVALUAN [ELL]
NANUNGA alt for NARUNGGA [NNR]
NANUNI dial of DAGBANI [DAG]
NANWANG dial of PYUMA [PYU]
NANZVA alt for NAMBYA [NMQ]
NAO alt for NAYI [NOZ]
NA'O alt for NAYI [NOZ]
NAÒ dial of TOURA [NEB]
NAO KLAO alt for NAOGELAO dial of BUNU, BU-
  NAO [BWX]
NAOGELAO dial of BUNU, BU-NAO [BWX]
NAOMAM alt for YANOMAM dial of YANOMAMI
  [WCA]
NAONE alt for MARINO [MRB]
NAOUDEM alt for NAWDM [NMZ]
NAPAN dial of WAROPEN [WRP]
NAPANSKIJ dial of ITELMEN [ITL]
NAPO alt for QUICHUA, LOWLAND, NAPO [QLN]
NAPO QUICHUA alt for QUICHUA, LOWLAND,
  NAPO [QLN]
NAPOLETANO dial of NAPOLETANO-CALABRESE
  [NPL]
NAPOLETANO-CALABRESE [NPL] lang, Italy
NAPO-TINAMBUNG alt for BALANIPA dial of
  MANDAR [MHN]
NAPU [NAP] lang, Indonesia (Sulawesi)
NAPUANMEN alt for WHITESANDS [TNP]
NAPUKA dial of TUAMOTUAN [PMT]
NAR dial of NAR PHU [NPA]
NAR dial of SAR [MWM]
NAR PHU [NPA] lang, Nepal
NARA [NRB] lang, Eritrea
NARA [NRZ] lang, Papua New Guinea
NARABUNU alt for RIBINA dial of JERE [JER]
NARAGUTA alt for IGUTA [NAR]
NARAK [NAC] lang, Papua New Guinea
NARAKE alt for KANDAWO [GAM]
NARAKUREAVAR alt for VAAGRI BOOLI [VAA]
NARANG dial of JOLA-FOGNY [DYO]
NARANGA alt for NARUNGGA [NNR]
NARANGGA alt for NARUNGGA [NNR]
NARANGO [NRG] lang, Vanuatu

NARARAPI alt for SEMPAN [SEM]
NARAU [NXU] lang, Indonesia (Irian Jaya)
NARIHUA alt for KAHUA [AGW]
NARIKKORAVA alt for VAAGRI BOOLI [VAA]
NARIM alt for LONGARIM [LOH]
NARISATI alt for GAWAR-BATI [GWT]
NAR-MÄ alt for NAR dial of NAR PHU [NPA]
NARO [NHR] lang, Botswana; also in Namibia
NAROM [NRM] lang, Malaysia (Sarawak)
NAROM dial of NAROM [NRM]
NAROVOROVO dial of BAETORA [BTR]
NAR-PHU alt for NAR PHU [NPA]
NARRAN alt for NGIYAMBAA dial of
  WANGAAYBUWAN-NGIYAMBAA [WYB]
NARRANGA alt for NARUNGGA [NNR]
NARRANGANSETT dial of MOHEGAN-MONTAUK-
  NARRAGANSETT [MOF]
NARRANGGU alt for NARUNGGA [NNR]
NARRANGU alt for NARUNGGA [NNR]
NARREWENG alt for NYARWENG dial of DINKA,
  SOUTHEASTERN [DIN]
NARRINYERI [NAY] lang, Australia
NARSATI alt for GAWAR-BATI [GWT]
NAR-TÖ alt for PHU dial of NAR PHU [NPA]
NARUM alt for NAROM [NRM]
NARUNGGA [NNR] lang, Australia
NARYM dial of SELKUP [SAK]
NASA YUWE alt for PÁEZ [PBB]
NASARIAN [NVH] lang, Vanuatu
NASAWA dial of BAETORA [BTR]
NASI alt for NAXI [NBF]
NASIKWABW dial of MISIMA-PANEATI [MPX]
NASIOI alt for NAASIOI [NAS]
NASKAPI [NSK] lang, Canada
NASO alt for TERIBE [TFR]
NASÖ alt for YI, YUNNAN [NOS]
NASRANI dial of MALAYALAM [MJS]
NASRING alt for NACHERING [NCD]
NASS alt for NISGA'A [NCG]
NASU alt for YI, YUNNAN [NOS]
NAT alt for KABUTRA [KBU]
NATA alt for IKOMA [NTK]
NATABUI alt for MUNGGUI [MTH]
NATABUI alt for WARABORI dial of MARAU [MVR]
NATAGAIMAS [NTS] lang, Colombia
NATAKAN alt for MAFA [MAF]
NATANZI [NTZ] lang, Iran
NATARBORA alt for EASTERN TETUN dial of
  TETUN [TTM]
NATCHABA dial of MOBA [MFQ]
NATCHAMBA alt for NTCHAM [BUD]
NATCHEZ [NCZ] lang, USA
NATEMBA alt for NATENI dial of NATENI [NTM]
NATENI [NTM] lang, Benin
NATENI dial of NATENI [NTM]
NATHEMBO [NTE] lang, Mozambique
NATICK alt for WAMPANOAG [WAM]
NATIMBA alt for NATENI dial of NATENI [NTM]
NATIORO [NTI] lang, Burkina Faso
NATJORO alt for NATIORO [NTI]
NATÖGU alt for SANTA CRUZ [STC]

NATRA alt for KABUTRA [KBU]
NATÜRLICHE GEBÄRDE alt for SWISS-GERMAN
SIGN LANGUAGE [SGG]
NATUKHAI alt for NATUZAJ dial of ADYGHE [ADY]
NATURALIS dial of SURIGAONON [SUL]
NATUZAJ dial of ADYGHE [ADY]
NATYORO alt for NATIORO [NTI]
NAUDM alt for NAWDM [NMZ]
NAUETE [NXA] lang, Timor Lorosae
NAUETI alt for NAUETE [NXA]
NAUHETE alt for NAUETE [NXA]
NAUKAN alt for YUPIK, NAUKAN [YNK]
NAUKANSKI alt for YUPIK, NAUKAN [YNK]
NAUMIK dial of NAUETE [NXA]
NAUNA [NCN] lang, Papua New Guinea
NAUNE alt for NAUNA [NCN]
NAUOTE alt for NAUETE [NXA]
NAUOTI alt for NAUETE [NXA]
NAURA alt for HAIGWAI [HGW]
NAURA dial of HAIGWAI [HGW]
NAURUAN [NRU] lang, Nauru
NAUT ARANÉS dial of GASCON, ARANESE
[GSC]
NAVAHO alt for NAVAJO [NAV]
NAVAJO [NAV] lang, USA
NAVAKASIGA alt for WEST VANUA LEVU dial of
FIJIAN [FJI]
NAVARRESE dial of SPANISH [SPN]
NAVARRO-LABOURDIN alt for BASQUE,
NAVARRO-LABOURDIN [BQE]
NAVATU-B alt for WEST VANUA LEVU dial of
FIJIAN [FJI]
NAVATU-C alt for SOUTHEAST VANUA LEVU dial
of FIJIAN [FJI]
NAVUT [NSW] lang, Vanuatu
NAWA SHERPA alt for NAAPA [NAO]
NAWAITS alt for DALDI dial of KONKANI, GOANESE
[GOM]
NAWAR dial of DOMARI [RMT]
NAWARI alt for DOMARI [RMT]
NAWARU [NWR] lang, Papua New Guinea
NAWAT alt for PIPIL [PPL]
NAWDAM alt for NAWDM [NMZ]
NAWDM [NMZ] lang, Togo; also in Ghana
NAWENI alt for SOUTHEAST VANUA LEVU dial
of FIJIAN [FJI]
NAWP alt for DAGA [DGZ]
NAWURI [NAW] lang, Ghana
NAWYEM dial of MUYUW [MYW]
NAXI [NBF] lang, China
NAY KOPO alt for MUMUYE [MUL]
NAYAR dial of MALAYALAM [MJS]
NAYI [NOZ] lang, Ethiopia
NAYINI [NYQ] lang, Iran
NAZE dial of AMAMI-OSHIMA, NORTHERN
[RYN]
NBANGAM alt for NGANGAM [GNG]
N-BATTO alt for MBATO [GWA]
NBULE alt for VUTE [VUT]
N'BUNDO alt for MBUNDU, LOANDA [MLO]
NBUNDU alt for MBUNDU, LOANDA [MLO]

NBWAKA alt for NGBAKA MA'BO [NBM]
NCANE [NCR] lang, Cameroon
NCANM dial of NTCHAM [BUD]
NCHA dial of NDAKTUP [NCP]
NCHAM alt for NTCHAM [BUD]
NCHANTI alt for NCANE [NCR]
NCHIMBURU alt for CHUMBURUNG [NCU]
NCHINCHEGE [NCQ] lang, Congo
NCHOBELA alt for BABADJOU dial of NGOMBALE
[NLA]
NCHUMBULU [NLU] lang, Ghana
NCHUMBURUNG alt for CHUMBURUNG [NCU]
NCHUMMURU alt for CHUMBURUNG [NCU]
NCHUMUNU alt for DWANG [NNU]
NCQIKA alt for GAIKA dial of XHOSA [XOS]
NDA alt for MUNDANG [MUA]
N'DA dial of GAGU [GGU]
NDAA alt for NGOMBA [NNO]
NDA'A alt for NGOMBA [NNO]
NDAAKA alt for NDAKA [NDK]
NDAGAM alt for NYONG [MUO]
NDAI [GKE] lang, Cameroon
NDAI alt for DAI dial of LAU [LLU]
NDAKA [NDK] lang, DRC
NDAKTUP [NCP] lang, Cameroon
NDALI [NDH] lang, Tanzania
NDALI dial of ZANAKI [ZAK]
NDAM [NDM] lang, Chad
NDAM DIK dial of NDAM [NDM]
NDAMBA [NDJ] lang, Tanzania
NDAMBIYA alt for DAMBIYA dial of MIGAAMA
[MMY]
NDAMM alt for NDAM [NDM]
NDAM-NDAM dial of NDAM [NDM]
NDANDA alt for DANDA dial of NDAU [NDC]
NDA'NDA' [NNZ] lang, Cameroon
NDANDE alt for NANDI [NNB]
NDANO dial of SHWAI [SHW]
NDAO [NFA] lang, Indonesia (Nusa Tenggara)
NDAOE alt for PENDAU [UMS]
NDAONESE alt for NDAO [NFA]
NDARA alt for HUTU dial of RWANDA [RUA]
NDARA alt for WANDALA [MFI]
NDASA [NDA] lang, Congo; also in Gabon
NDASH alt for NDASA [NDA]
NDASSA alt for NDASA [NDA]
NDAU [NDC] lang, Zimbabwe; also in Mozambique
NDAU alt for PENDAU [UMS]
NDAU dial of NDAU [NDC]
NDAUNDAU alt for NDAO [NFA]
NDAUWA alt for NDUGA [NDX]
NDE dial of MUNGAKA [MHK]
NDE dial of NDE-NSELE-NTA [NDD]
NDEBELE [NDF] lang, Zimbabwe; also in Botswana
NDEBELE [NEL] lang, South Africa
NDEEWE dial of BATA [BTA]
NDE-GBITE [NED] lang, Nigeria
NDELE dial of IKWERE [IKW]
NDEM alt for DEM [DEM]
NDEM alt for NNAM [NBP]
NDEMA SHERBRO dial of SHERBRO [BUN]

NDEMBA alt for NDEMLI [NML]
NDEMBU dial of LUNDA [LVN]
NDEMLI [NML] lang, Cameroon
NDENDEULE [DNE] lang, Tanzania
NDENDEULI alt for NDENDEULE [DNE]
NDENGELEKO alt for NDENGEREKO [NDE]
NDENGEREKO [NDE] lang, Tanzania
NDENGESE alt for DENGESE [DEZ]
NDENI dial of SANTA CRUZ [STC]
NDE-NSELE-NTA [NDD] lang, Nigeria
NDERA dial of KOMA [KMY]
NDERA dial of POKOMO, UPPER [PKB]
NDERRE dial of MORO [MOR]
NDESE dial of LESE [LES]
NDHUR dial of RADE [RAD]
NDI alt for SAMBA LEKO [NDI]
NDI dial of BANDA-BANDA [BPD]
NDI dial of GHARI [GRI]
NDIA dial of GIKUYU [KIU]
NDII alt for SAMBA LEKO dial of SAMBA LEKO
    [NDI]
NDING [ELI] lang, Sudan
NDINGI dial of KONGO [KON]
NDIR alt for IYIVE [UIV]
NDITAM dial of TIKAR [TIK]
NDJABI alt for NJEBI [NZB]
NDJAK alt for MANDJAK [MFV]
NDJÉBBANA alt for DJEEBBANA [DJJ]
NDJELI alt for PANDE dial of PANDE [BKJ]
NDJEM dial of KOONZIME [NJE]
NDJEMBE alt for WONGO [WON]
NDJEME alt for NJEME dial of KOONZIME [NJE]
NDJEVI alt for NJEBI [NZB]
NDJININI alt for NJININGI dial of TEKE, NORTHERN
    [TEG]
NDJUKÁ alt for AUKAN [DJK]
NDLAMBE dial of XHOSA [XOS]
NDMPO alt for DOMPO [DOY]
NDO [NDP] lang, DRC; also in Uganda
NDO alt for MEMBI dial of NDO [NDP]
NDO OKE'BU alt for OKE'BU dial of NDO [NDP]
NDOB alt for TIKAR [TIK]
NDOBO [NDW] lang, DRC
NDOE [NBB] lang, Nigeria
NDOGBANG dial of TUNEN [BAZ]
NDOGO [NDZ] lang, Sudan
NDOGO alt for HUTU dial of RWANDA [RUA]
NDOKAMA dial of BASAA [BAA]
NDOKBELE dial of BASAA [BAA]
NDOKBIAKAT dial of TUNEN [BAZ]
NDOKPA dial of BANDA-BAMBARI [LIY]
NDOKPENDA dial of BASAA [BAA]
NDOKTUNA dial of TUNEN [BAZ]
NDOLA alt for NDOOLA [NDR]
NDOLO [NDL] lang, DRC
NDOM [NQM] lang, Indonesia (Irian Jaya)
NDOMBE [NDQ] lang, Angola
NDOMDE alt for NDONDE [NDS]
NDOME alt for TIKAR [TIK]
NDONDE [NDS] lang, Tanzania; also in Mozambique
NDONDE alt for VADONDE dial of MAKONDE [KDE]

NDONGA [NDG] lang, Namibia; also in Angola
NDONGE dial of CHOPI [CCE]
NDONGO alt for MBUNDU, LOANDA [MLO]
NDONI dial of UKWUANI-ABOH-NDONI [UKW]
NDOOBO alt for NDOBO [NDW]
NDOOLA [NDR] lang, Nigeria; also in Cameroon
NDOOLO alt for NDOLO [NDL]
NDOORE alt for TUPURI [TUI]
NDOP-BAMESSING alt for KENSWEI NSEI [NDB]
NDOP-BAMUNKA alt for BAMUNKA [NDO]
NDORE alt for TUPURI [TUI]
NDORO alt for NDOOLA [NDR]
"NDOROBO" pejorative alt for ARAMANIK [AAM]
"NDOROBO" pejorative alt for EL MOLO [ELO]
"NDOROBO" pejorative alt for KISANKASA [KQH]
"NDOROBO" pejorative alt for OKIEK [OKI]
"NDOROBO" pejorative alt for OMOTIK [OMT]
"NDOROBO" pejorative alt for YAAKU [MUU]
NDOROBO alt for MEDIAK [MWX]
NDOROBO alt for MOSIRO [MWY]
NDOUDJA alt for FALI-TINGUELIN dial of FALI,
    SOUTH [FAL]
NDOUKA alt for NDUKA dial of LUTOS [NDY]
NDOUKWA alt for NDUKA dial of LUTOS [NDY]
NDOUTE alt for NDUT [NDV]
NDRAMINI'O dial of RAO [RAO]
NDREME dial of PELASLA [MLR]
NDRENG dial of NAGA, LOTHA [NJH]
NDRI alt for NDI dial of BANDA-BANDA [BPD]
NDROKU alt for LONIU [LOS]
NDRUGUL alt for KURTI [KTM]
NDRUNA alt for NGITI [NIY]
NDU alt for NDO [NDP]
NDU-FAA-KEELO alt for KELO [TSN]
NDUGA [NDX] lang, Indonesia (Irian Jaya)
NDUGA dial of LUTOS [NDY]
NDUGHORE alt for DUKE [NKE]
NDUGWA alt for NDUGA [NDX]
NDUINDUI dial of AMBAE, WEST [NND]
NDUKA dial of LUTOS [NDY]
NDUKE alt for DUKE [NKE]
NDUM alt for OSO [OSO]
NDUMBEA alt for DUMBEA [DUF]
NDUMBO alt for NDUMU [NMD]
NDUMBU alt for NDUMU [NMD]
NDUMU [NMD] lang, Gabon; also in Congo
NDUNDA [NUH] lang, Nigeria
NDUNDA alt for VIDUNDA [VID]
NDUNDULU alt for MDUNDULU dial of LUYANA
    [LAV]
NDUNDUSANA dial of PAGIBETE [PAG]
NDUNGA [NDT] lang, DRC
NDURA dial of POKOMO, UPPER [PKB]
NDUT [NDV] lang, Senegal
NDUUMO alt for NDUMU [NMD]
NDUUPA alt for DUUPA [DAE]
NDUVUM dial of VUTE [VUT]
NDXHONGE dial of TSHWA [TSC]
NDYAK alt for MANDJAK [MFV]
NDYANGER dial of WOLOF [WOL]
NDYUKA alt for AUKAN [DJK]

NDYUKA-TRIO PIDGIN [NJT] lang, Suriname
NDZALE alt for NZARE dial of MBEMBE, TIGON [NZA]
NDZAWU alt for NDAU [NDC]
NDZEM alt for NDJEM dial of KOONZIME [NJE]
NDZIKOU alt for NJINJU dial of TEKE, CENTRAL [TEC]
NDZINDZIJU alt for NJINJU dial of TEKE, CENTRAL [TEC]
NDZUNDZA alt for NDEBELE [NEL]
NDZUNGLE alt for LIMBUM [LIM]
NDZUNGLI alt for LIMBUM [LIM]
NE THU alt for LAHU SHI [KDS]
NËHUP dial of HUPDË [JUP]
NEA dial of SANTA CRUZ [STC]
NEABO alt for NEAO dial of WE SOUTHERN [GXX]
NEAO dial of BAUZI [PAU]
NEAO dial of WE SOUTHERN [GXX]
NEAPOLITAN alt for NAPOLETANO dial of NAPOLETANO-CALABRESE [NPL]
NEAPOLITAN-CALABRESE alt for NAPOLETANO-CALABRESE [NPL]
NEAR-EASTERN GYPSY alt for DOMARI [RMT]
NEBAJI dial of OREJON [ORE]
NEBEE alt for NABAY dial of KENINGAU MURUT [KXI]
NEBES alt for KOKODA [QKW]
NEBOME alt for O'ODHAM [PAP]
NEBOME alt for PIMA BAJO, SONORA [PIA]
NEBRASKA dial of HOCAK [WIN]
NEDDERDNNTSCH alt for SAXON, LOW [SXN]
NEDDERSASSISCH alt for SAXON, LOW [SXN]
NEDEBANG [NEC] lang, Indonesia (Nusa Tenggara)
NÉDEBANG alt for NEDEBANG [NEC]
NEDEK dial of YAMBETA [YAT]
NEDERLANDS alt for DUTCH [DUT]
NEDERSAKSISCH alt for SAXON, LOW [SXN]
NEE dial of FEFE [FMP]
ÑEEGATÚ alt for NHENGATU [YRL]
NEELISHIKARI dial of PARDHI [PCL]
NEENOÁ alt for MIRITI [MMV]
NEESHENAM alt for NISENAN [NSZ]
NEFARPI alt for KAMORO [KGQ]
NEFERIPI alt for KAMORO [KGQ]
NEFUSI alt for NAFUSI [JBN]
NEGAROTE dial of NAMBIKUARA, NORTHERN [MBG]
NEGERHOLLANDS alt for DUTCH CREOLE [DCR]
NEGERI BESAR alt for NEGRI BESAR dial of KOKODA [QKW]
NEGERI LIMA dial of ASILULU [ASL]
NEGERI SEMBILAN MALAY [ZMI] lang, Malaysia (Peninsular)
NEGHIDAL alt for NEGIDAL [NEG]
NEGIDAL [NEG] lang, Russia (Asia)
NEGIDALY alt for NEGIDAL [NEG]
NEGIRA alt for NINGERA [NBY]
NEGRI BESAR dial of KOKODA [QKW]
NEGRITO alt for KENSIU [KNS]
NEGUENI-KLANI dial of WARA [WBF]
NEHAN [NSN] lang, Papua New Guinea

NEHAN dial of NEHAN [NSN]
"NEHINA" pejorative alt for TOLAKI [LBW]
NEJUU dial of SENOUFO, MAMARA [MYK]
NEK [NIF] lang, Papua New Guinea
NEKEDI dial of BETE, GAGNOA [BTG]
NEKGINI [NKG] lang, Papua New Guinea
NEKO [NEJ] lang, Papua New Guinea
NEKU [NEK] lang, New Caledonia
NELEMA alt for NENEMA dial of KUMAK [NEE]
NELLORE dial of TELUGU [TCW]
NEMADI alt for NIMADI [NOE]
NEMANGBETU alt for MANGBETU [MDJ]
NEMBAO alt for AMBA [UTP]
NEMBE dial of IJO, SOUTHEAST [IJO]
NEMBI alt for ANGAL ENEN [AOE]
NEME dial of BINAHARI [BXZ]
NEMEA alt for NEME dial of BINAHARI [BXZ]
NEMEEJE alt for MEJE dial of MANGBETU [MDJ]
NEMI [NEM] lang, New Caledonia
NEMIA alt for NAMIA [NNM]
NENAYA alt for MATO [NIU]
NEND [ANH] lang, Papua New Guinea
NENDÖ alt for SANTA CRUZ [STC]
NENEC alt for NENETS [YRK]
NENEMA dial of KUMAK [NEE]
NENETS [YRK] lang, Russia (Asia)
NENETSY alt for NENETS [YRK]
NENGAYA alt for MATO [NIU]
NENGONE [NEN] lang, New Caledonia
NENNI NYO'O alt for TUNEN [BAZ]
NENT alt for NEND [ANH]
NENTSE alt for NENETS [YRK]
NENUSA-MAINGAS dial of TALAUD [TLD]
NENYA dial of TUMBUKA [TUW]
NEO-CHALDEAN alt for CHALDEAN NEO-ARAMAIC [CLD]
NEO-EGYPTIAN alt for COPTIC [COP]
NEOGULADA alt for KANJU [KBE]
NEO-HELLENIC alt for GREEK [GRK]
NEO-MANDAIC alt for MANDAIC [MID]
NEOMELANESIAN alt for TOK PISIN [PDG]
NEO-NYUNGAR dial of ENGLISH [ENG]
NEO-SOLOMONIC alt for PIJIN [PIS]
NEO-SYRIAC alt for ASSYRIAN NEO-ARAMAIC [AII]
NEO-WESTERN ARAMAIC alt for WESTERN NEO-ARAMAIC [AMW]
NEPA dial of EVENKI [EVN]
NEPAL BHASA alt for NEWARI [NEW]
NEPALESE alt for NEPALI [NEP]
NEPALESE SIGN LANGUAGE [NSP] lang, Nepal
NEPALI [NEP] lang, Nepal; also in Bhutan, Brunei, India
NEPALI dial of NEPALI [NEP]
NEPO alt for BARRU dial of BUGIS [BPR]
NEPOYE alt for MAPOYO [MCG]
NERA alt for NARA [NRB]
NERAUYA dial of LENAKEL [TNL]
NER alt for ZIRE [SIH]
NEREZIM dial of TURKMEN [TCK]
NERIGO alt for YAHADIAN [NER]

NERWA dial of LISHANA DENI [LSD]
NESANG alt for TUKPA [TPQ]
NETE [NET] lang, Papua New Guinea
NETHANAR dial of DURUWA [PCI]
NETSILIK dial of INUKTITUT, WESTERN
  CANADIAN [ESC]
NEUCATELAIS dial of FRANCO-PROVENCAL
  [FRA]
NEUCH-TELOIS dial of FRANCO-PROVENCAL
  [FRA]
NEVOME alt for O'ODHAM [PAP]
NEW BARGU alt for BARGU dial of BURIAT, CHINA
  [BXU]
NEW BRITAIN LANGUAGE alt for KUANUA [KSD]
NEW BUSA dial of BUSA [BQP]
NEW CHAM alt for CHAM, WESTERN [CJA]
NEW GUINEA PIDGIN ENGLISH alt for TOK PISIN
  [PDG]
NEW NORSE alt for NORWEGIAN, NYNORSK
  [NRN]
NEW ZEALAND MAORI alt for MAORI [MBF]
NEW ZEALAND SIGN LANGUAGE [NZS] lang, New
  Zealand
NEWAHANG alt for MEOHANG, EASTERN [EMG]
NEWAHANG alt for MEOHANG, WESTERN [RAF]
NEWAHANG JIMI alt for MEOHANG, EASTERN
  [EMG]
NEWAHANG JIMI alt for MEOHANG, WESTERN
  [RAF]
NEWAHANG YAMPHE alt for YAMPHE [YMA]
NEWANG alt for MEOHANG, EASTERN [EMG]
NEWANG alt for MEOHANG, WESTERN [RAF]
NEWANGE RAI alt for MEOHANG, EASTERN
  [EMG]
NEWANGE RAI alt for MEOHANG, WESTERN
  [RAF]
NEWAR alt for NEWARI [NEW]
NEWARI [NEW] lang, Nepal; also in India
NEWBOLD'S SEMANG alt for ORANG BENUA
  dial of SEMANG, LOWLAND [ORB]
NEWCASTLE NORTHUMBERLAND dial of
  ENGLISH [ENG]
NEWFOUNDLAND alt for BEOTHUK [BUE]
NEWFOUNDLAND ENGLISH dial of ENGLISH
  [ENG]
NEY dial of KURANKO [KHA]
NEYA dial of KURANKO [KHA]
NEYO [NEY] lang, Côte d'Ivoire
NEZ PERCE [NEZ] lang, USA
NFACHARA alt for CARA [CFD]
NFUA alt for BOKYI [BKY]
NFUMTE alt for MFUMTE [NFU]
//NG alt for //NG!KE dial of NU [NGH]
NGA alt for NGAMAMBO [NBV]
NGAAKA alt for MUNGAKA [MHK]
NGAANYATJARA alt for NGAANYATJARRA [NTJ]
NGAANYATJARRA [NTJ] lang, Australia
NGÄBERE [GYM] lang, Panama; also in Costa Rica
NGÄBERE alt for NGÄBERE [GYM]
NGABRE alt for GABRI [GAB]
NGACANG alt for ACHANG [ACN]

NGAC'ANG alt for ACHANG [ACN]
NGACHANG alt for ACHANG [ACN]
NGADA alt for NGAD'A [NXG]
NGA'DA alt for NGAD'A [NXG]
NGAD'A [NXG] lang, Indonesia (Nusa Tenggara)
NGAD'A, EASTERN [NEA] lang, Indonesia (Nusa
  Tenggara)
NGADANJA dial of WIKALKAN [WIK]
NGADHA alt for NGAD'A [NXG]
NGADJU alt for NGADJUNMAYA [NJU]
NGADJU alt for NGAJU [NIJ]
NGADJUMAJA alt for NGADJUNMAYA [NJU]
NGADJUNMAIA alt for NGADJUNMAYA [NJU]
NGADJUNMAYA [NJU] lang, Australia
NGAHM alt for NGAM [NMC]
NGAIGUNGO alt for DJANGUN [DJF]
NGAIMAN alt for NGARINMAN [NBJ]
NGAIMBOM alt for LILAU [LLL]
NGAIN alt for BENG [NHB]
NGAIN alt for NUMANGGANG [NOP]
NGAING [NNF] lang, Papua New Guinea
NGAJU [NIJ] lang, Indonesia (Kalimantan)
NGAJU alt for KAPUAS dial of NGAJU [NIJ]
NGAJU DAYAK alt for NGAJU [NIJ]
NGA'KA alt for MUNGAKA [MHK]
NGAKOM alt for RASHAD dial of TEGALI [RAS]
NGALA [NUD] lang, Papua New Guinea
NGALA alt for BANGALA [BXG]
NGALA alt for LINGALA [LIN]
NGALA alt for MANGALA [MGH]
NGALA dial of CHIN, KHUMI [CKM]
NGALABO dial of BANDA-BANDA [BPD]
NGALAKAN [NIG] lang, Australia
NGALAM alt for OLAM dial of MURLE [MUR]
NGALANGAN alt for NGALAKAN [NIG]
NGALIWERRA alt for NGALIWURU dial of
  DJAMINDJUNG [DJD]
NGALIWURU dial of DJAMINDJUNG [DJD]
NGALKBON alt for NGALKBUN [NGK]
NGALKBUN [NGK] lang, Australia
NGALLOOMA alt for NGARLUMA [NRL]
NGALO dial of DAY [DAI]
NGALUM [SZB] lang, Indonesia (Irian Jaya); also
  in Papua New Guinea
NGALUM dial of NGALUM [SZB]
NGALUMA alt for NGARLUMA [NRL]
NGAM [NMC] lang, Chad; also in CAR
NGAM dial of FE'FE' [FMP]
NGAM dial of KWANG [KVI]
NGAM GIR BOR dial of NGAM [NMC]
NGAM TEL dial of NGAM [NMC]
NGAM TIRA dial of NGAM [NMC]
NGAMA alt for NGAM [NMC]
NGAMAMBO [NBV] lang, Cameroon
NG/AMANI alt for !XÓÕ [NMN]
NGAMAWA alt for NGAMO [NBH]
NGAMBAI alt for NGAMBAY [SBA]
NGAMBA'WANDH alt for JIR'JOROND dial of YIR
  YORONT [YIY]
NGAMBAY [SBA] lang, Chad; also in Cameroon,
  Nigeria

NGAMBO alt for AMDO [ADX]
NGAMI alt for NAGA, ANGAMI [NJM]
NGAMINI [NMV] lang, Australia
NGAMO [NBH] lang, Nigeria
NGAMSILE alt for KAMSILI dial of UKHWEJO
 [UKH]
NGAN alt for BENG [NHB]
NGAN alt for TÀY [THO]
NGANASAN [NIO] lang, Russia (Asia)
NGANDI [NID] lang, Australia
NGANDJARA alt for WIK-NGANDJARA dial of
 WIKALKAN [WIK]
NGANDJARA alt for WIKNGENCHERA [WUA]
NGANDO [NGD] lang, CAR
NGANDO [NXD] lang, DRC
NGANDO-KOTA alt for NGANDO [NGD]
NGANDU alt for NGANDO [NXD]
NGANDYERA [NNE] lang, Angola
NGANDYERA dial of NDONGA [NDG]
NGANGALA alt for NKANGALA [NKN]
NGANGAM [GNG] lang, Togo; also in Benin
NGANGAN alt for NGANGAM [GNG]
NGANGCHING dial of NAGA, KONYAK [NBE]
NGANGEA alt for NYANG'I [NYP]
NGANGELA alt for NYEMBA [NBA]
NGANGIKARANGURR alt for
 NANGIKURRUNGGURR [NAM]
NGANGOMORI alt for NGENKIWUMERRI dial of
 NANGIKURRUNGGURR [NAM]
NGANGOULOU alt for TEKE, NORTHEASTERN
 [NGZ]
NGANKIKURRUNKURR alt for
 NANGIKURRUNGGURR [NAM]
NGANKIKURRUNKURR alt for TYEMERI dial of
 NANGIKURRUNGGURR [NAM]
NGANSHUENKUAN alt for ATUENCE [ATF]
NGANTJERI alt for WIKNGENCHERA [WUA]
NGANYAYWANA [NYX] lang, Australia
NGANYGIT dial of MARITHIEL [MFR]
NGAO alt for NGA'O dial of ENDE [END]
NGAO dial of BANDA-NDELE [BFL]
NGA'O dial of ENDE [END]
NGAO FON alt for CUN [CUQ]
NGAONDÉRÉ dial of FULFULDE, ADAMAWA [FUB]
NGAOUNDÉRÉ dial of FULFULDE, ADAMAWA
 [FUB]
NGAPO dial of BANDA-BAMBARI [LIY]
NGAPORE alt for NYANG'I [NYP]
NGAPU alt for NGAPO dial of BANDA-BAMBARI
 [LIY]
NGARE dial of MBOKO [MDU]
NGARI alt for MNGAHRIS dial of TIBETAN [TIC]
NGARI alt for NAGA, KHOIRAO [NKI]
NGARIAWAN alt for GURUF-NGARIAWANG dial
 of ADZERA [AZR]
NGARINMAN [NBJ] lang, Australia
NGARINYERI alt for NARRINYERI [NAY]
NGARINYIN [UNG] lang, Australia
NGARLA [NLR] lang, Australia
NGARLKAJIE alt for DYAABUGAY [DYY]
NGARLUMA [NRL] lang, Australia

NGARNDJI [NJI] lang, Australia
NGAROWAPUM dial of ADZERA [AZR]
NGAS [ANC] lang, Nigeria
NGASA [NSG] lang, Tanzania
NGATANA dial of POKOMO, LOWER [POJ]
NGATIK MEN'S CREOLE [NGM] lang, Micronesia
NGATIKESE alt for NGATIK MEN'S CREOLE [NGM]
NGATIKESE MEN'S LANGUAGE alt for NGATIK
 MEN'S CREOLE [NGM]
NGATJUMAY alt for NGADJUNMAYA [NJU]
NGATSANG alt for ACHANG [ACN]
NGAU alt for NGAO dial of BANDA-NDELE [BFL]
NGAWN alt for CHIN, NGAWN [CNW]
NGAWUN [NXN] lang, Australia
NGAYABA alt for TIBEA [NGY]
NGAYMIL dial of DHANGU [GLA]
NGAZAR dial of KANURI, CENTRAL [KPH]
NGBA GEME alt for GEME [GEQ]
NGBAKA [NGA] lang, DRC; also in CAR, Congo
NGBAKA GBAYA alt for NGBAKA [NGA]
NGBAKA LIMBA alt for NGBAKA MA'BO [NBM]
NGBAKA MA'BO [NBM] lang, CAR; also in Congo,
 DRC
NGBAKA MANZA [NGG] lang, CAR
NGBAKA MINANGENDE alt for NGBAKA [NGA]
NGBAKO dial of KAKO [KKJ]
NGBALA dial of BANDA-NDELE [BFL]
NGBANDI, NORTHERN [NGB] lang, DRC; also in
 CAR
NGBANDI, SOUTHERN [NBW] lang, DRC
NGBANDI-NGIRI alt for NGBANDI, SOUTHERN
 [NBW]
NGBANDI-SUD alt for NGBANDI, SOUTHERN
 [NBW]
NGBANG dial of DII [DUR]
NGBANYITO alt for GONJA [DUM]
NGBEE [NBL] lang, DRC
NGBINDA [NBD] lang, DRC
NGBO alt for MGBO dial of IZI-EZAA-IKWO-MGBO
 [IZI]
NGBOUGOU alt for NGBUGU dial of BANDA,
 SOUTH CENTRAL [LNL]
NGBUGU dial of BANDA, SOUTH CENTRAL
 [LNL]
NGBUNDU [NUU] lang, DRC
NG//-/E alt for //NG!KE dial of NU [NGH]
NGE alt for VENGO [BAV]
NGE' alt for NGEQ [NGT]
NGE'DÉ alt for NGETE [NNN]
NGEE dial of TEKE, EASTERN [TEK]
NGEH alt for NGEQ [NGT]
NGELIMA [AGH] lang, DRC
NGELL-KURU-VWANG alt for GYELL-KURU-
 VWANG dial of BEROM [BOM]
NGEMBA [NGE] lang, Cameroon
NGEMBA alt for MANGKUNGE dial of NGEMBA
 [NGE]
NGEMBA dial of GHOMALA [BBJ]
NGEMBO alt for NGAMAMBO [NBV]
NGEMERE dial of KOALIB [KIB]
NGEN alt for BASSOSSI [BSI]

NGEN alt for BENG [NHB]
NGENDE dial of BUSHOONG [BUF]
NGENE alt for ENGENNI [ENN]
NGENGE dial of GBAGYI [GBR]
NGENKIKURRUNGGUR alt for
   NANGIKURRUNGGURR [NAM]
NGENKIWUMERRI dial of
   NANGIKURRUNGGURR [NAM]
NGENO-NGENE dial of SASAK [SAS]
NGENTE dial of LUSHAI [LSH]
"NGEO" pejorative alt for SHAN [SJN]
NGEPMA KWUNDI alt for IATMUL [IAN]
NGEQ [NGT] lang, Laos
NGETE [NNN] lang, Chad
NGETI alt for NGITI [NIY]
NGETO-NGETE dial of SASAK [SAS]
NGEUMBA alt for NGIYAMBAA dial of
   WANGAAYBUWAN-NGIYAMBAA [WYB]
NGEZZIM alt for NGIZIM [NGI]
NGGAE alt for GAE dial of GHARI [GRI]
NGGAO alt for GAO [GGA]
NGGARO dial of KODI [KOD]
NGGAURA alt for NGGARO dial of KODI [KOD]
NGGAURA dial of LAMBOYA [LMY]
NGGELA alt for GELA [NLG]
NGGEM [NBQ] lang, Indonesia (Irian Jaya)
NGGERI alt for GERI dial of GHARI [GRI]
NGGWAHYI [NGX] lang, Nigeria
NGGWESHE alt for GVOKO [NGS]
NGGWOLI dial of NZANYI [NJA]
NGHWELE [NHE] lang, Tanzania
NGI alt for NGIE [NGJ]
NGIAMBA alt for NGIYAMBAA dial of
   WANGAAYBUWAN-NGIYAMBAA [WYB]
NGIANGEYA alt for NYANG'I [NYP]
"NGIAO" pejorative alt for SHAN [SJN]
"NGIAW" pejorative alt for SHAN [SJN]
NGIE [NGJ] lang, Cameroon
NGIEMBOON [NNH] lang, Cameroon
NGILE [MAS] lang, Sudan
NGILEMONG dial of MUSGU [MUG]
NGILI alt for PANDE dial of PANDE [BKJ]
NGIN alt for BENG [NHB]
NGINDERE alt for KPATILI [KYM]
NGINDO [NNQ] lang, Tanzania
NGINIA dial of GHARI [GRI]
NGINYUKWUR dial of KOALIB [KIB]
"NGIO" pejorative alt for SHAN [SJN]
"NGIOW" pejorative alt for SHAN [SJN]
NGIRERE alt for KOALIB [KIB]
NGIRERE dial of KOALIB [KIB]
NGIRI [NGR] lang, DRC
NGIRI dial of NGIRI [NGR]
NGISHE [NSH] lang, Cameroon
NGITI [NIY] lang, DRC
NGIUMBA alt for NGIYAMBAA dial of
   WANGAAYBUWAN-NGIYAMBAA [WYB]
NGIYAMBAA dial of WANGAAYBUWAN-
   NGIYAMBAA [WYB]
NGIZIM [NGI] lang, Nigeria
NGIZMAWA alt for NGIZIM [NGI]

NGJAMBA alt for NGIYAMBAA dial of
   WANGAAYBUWAN-NGIYAMBAA [WYB]
//NG!KE dial of NU [NGH]
NGMAMPERLI alt for MAMPRULI [MAW]
NG'MEN alt for CHIN, MÜN [MWQ]
NGNAI alt for BUNU, WUNAI [BWN]
NGNOK alt for SHERDUKPEN [SDP]
NGO alt for VENGO [BAV]
NGO dial of OBOLO [ANN]
NGO CHANG alt for ACHANG [ACN]
NGOAHU dial of LOKO [LOK]
NGOBERE alt for NGÄBERE [GYM]
NGOBO alt for GOBU [GOX]
NGOBO alt for GUBU [GOX]
NGOBU alt for GOBU [GOX]
NGOBU alt for GUBU [GOX]
NGODENI alt for MUXULE dial of JINA [JIA]
NGOE alt for BAFAW-BALONG [BWT]
NGOK PA alt for KENSIU [KNS]
NGOKA dial of MBAY [MYB]
NGOK-KORDOFAN dial of DINKA, NORTH-
   WESTERN [DIW]
NGOK-SOBAT dial of DINKA, NORTHEASTERN
   [DIP]
NGOLA alt for ANGOLAR [AOA]
NGOLA dial of BANDA-BANDA [BPD]
NGOLA dial of MBUNDU, LOANDA [MLO]
NGOLAK-WONGA alt for MULLUKMULLUK
   [MPB]
NGOLI alt for NGUL [NLO]
NGOLO dial of BALUNDU-BIMA [NGO]
NGOLOGA dial of KGALAGADI [XKV]
NGOLUCHE alt for MOLUCHE dial of
   MAPUDUNGUN [ARU]
NGOM [NRA] lang, Congo; also in Gabon
NGOMA dial of BEMBA [BEM]
NGOMBA [NNO] lang, Cameroon
NGOMBA alt for NGEMBA [NGE]
NGOMBALE [NLA] lang, Cameroon
NGOMBE [NGC] lang, DRC
NGOMBE [NMJ] lang, CAR
NGOMBE dial of BUSHOONG [BUF]
NGOMBE-KAKA alt for NGOMBE [NMJ]
NGOMBIA alt for NGOMBE dial of BUSHOONG
   [BUF]
NGOMI dial of KARANG [KZR]
NGOMO alt for NGOM [NRA]
NG'OMVIA alt for KUTU [KDC]
NGON alt for CHIN, NGAWN [CNW]
NGONDE alt for NYAKYUSA-NGONDE [NYY]
NGONDE dial of NYAKYUSA-NGONDE [NYY]
NGONDI alt for GUNDI [GDI]
NGONDI alt for NGUNDI [NDN]
NGONG [NNX] lang, Cameroon
NGONGE alt for GONGE dial of NZAKAMBAY [NZY]
NGONGO [NOQ] lang, DRC
NGONGO dial of BUSHOONG [BUF]
NGONGO dial of NKUTU [NKW]
NGONGOSILA alt for GULA'ALAA [GMB]
NGONI [NGU] lang, Tanzania; also in Malawi,
   Mozambique

NGONI alt for CHINGONI dial of NYANJA [NYJ]
NGONI alt for ZULU [ZUU]
NGONI dial of NSENGA [NSE]
NGONI dial of NYANJA [NYJ]
NGONI dial of TUMBUKA [TUW]
NGOOBECHOP alt for BAMALI [BBQ]
NGOONGO dial of YAKA [YAF]
NGOREME alt for NGURIMI [NGQ]
NGORK alt for NGOK-SOBAT dial of DINKA,
    NORTHEASTERN [DIP]
NGORMBUR alt for NGURMBUR [NRX]
NGORN alt for CHIN, NGAWN [CNW]
NGORO alt for NGOLO dial of BALUNDU-BIMA
    [NGO]
NGORO dial of TUKI [BAG]
NGORO dial of VUTE [VUT]
NGOSHE SAMA alt for GVOKO [NGS]
NGOSHE-NDHANG alt for GVOKO [NGS]
NGOSHI alt for GVOKO [NGS]
NGOSHIE dial of GLAVDA [GLV]
NGOSSI alt for GVOKO [NGS]
NGOUAN alt for NGUÔN [NUO]
NGOUGUA alt for NDUGA dial of LUTOS [NDY]
NGOUMBA alt for NGUMBA [NMG]
NGOUMBA alt for MVUMBO dial of NGUMBA [NMG]
NGOUTCHOUMI alt for BELE dial of FALI, SOUTH
    [FAL]
NGOWIYE dial of BIANGAI [BIG]
NGRARMUN alt for NGARINMAN [NBJ]
NGRUIMI alt for NGURIMI [NGQ]
NGU NGWONI alt for NGUNGWONI [NGF]
NGUBU alt for NGBUGU dial of BANDA, SOUTH
    CENTRAL [LNL]
NG/U/EI alt for NG/U//EN dial of XOO [NMN]
NG/U/EI alt for NG/U/EN dial of XOO [NMN]
NGUEMBA alt for NGEMBA [NGE]
NGUEMBA alt for NGIEMBOON [NNH]
NG/U//EN dial of XOO [NMN]
NG/U/EN dial of XOO [NMN]
NGUETÉ alt for NGETE [NNN]
NGUETTÉ alt for NGETE [NNN]
NGUILI alt for NGIRI [NGR]
NGUIN alt for BENG [NHB]
NG'UKI, alt for N/U [NGH]
NGUL [NLO] lang, DRC
NGULAK alt for IK [IKX]
NGULGULE alt for NJALGULGULE [NJL]
NGULI alt for NGUL [NLO]
NGULU [NGP] lang, Tanzania
NGULU alt for LOMWE [NGL]
NGULU alt for NGUL [NLO]
NGULUWONGGA alt for MULLUKMULLUK [MPB]
NGUMBA [NMG] lang, Cameroon; also in Equatorial
    Guinea
NGUMBA alt for MVUMBO dial of NGUMBA [NMG]
NGUMBARR alt for NGIYAMBAA dial of
    WANGAAYBUWAN-NGIYAMBAA [WYB]
NGUMBI [NUI] lang, Equatorial Guinea
NGUMBI alt for NKHUMBI [KHU]
NG'UMBO dial of BEMBA [BEM]
NGUMBUR alt for NGURMBUR [NRX]

NGUNA dial of EFATE, NORTH [LLP]
NGUNDI [NDN] lang, Congo; also in CAR
NGUNDI alt for GUNDI [GDI]
NGUNDI dial of LUSENGO [LUS]
NGUNDU [NUE] lang, DRC
NGUNDUNA dial of KOALIB [KIB]
NGUNESE alt for NGUNA dial of EFATE, NORTH
    [LLP]
NGUNGULU alt for TEKE, NORTHEASTERN [NGZ]
NGUNGWEL alt for TEKE, NORTHEASTERN [NGZ]
NGUNGWONI [NGF] lang, Congo
NGUNI alt for NGWO dial of NGWO [NGN]
NGUNU alt for NGWO dial of NGWO [NGN]
NGUÔN [NUO] lang, Viet Nam
NGUQWURANG dial of KOALIB [KIB]
NGURA [NBX] lang, Australia
NGURAWARLA dial of NGURA [NBX]
NGURI dial of KANEMBU [KBL]
NGURIMI [NGQ] lang, Tanzania
NGURMBUR [NRX] lang, Australia
NGURU alt for JUNGURU dial of BANDA-NDELE
    [BFL]
NGURU alt for LOMWE [NGL]
NGURU alt for NGULU [NGP]
NGURU dial of GULA [KCM]
NGURUIMI alt for NGURIMI [NGQ]
NG/USAN alt for NUSAN dial of XOO [NMN]
NGUU alt for NGULU [NGP]
NGUU alt for VENGO [BAV]
NGWA alt for SONGWA dial of NGEMBA [NGE]
NGWA alt for VENGO [BAV]
NGWA dial of IGBO [IGR]
NGWAA MÓÒ alt for MOO [GWG]
NGWABA [NGW] lang, Nigeria
NGWAI MUNGÀN alt for MINGANG DOSO [MKO]
NGWAKETSE dial of TSWANA [TSW]
NGWALKWE alt for MALGBE [MXF]
NGWALUNGU dial of TSONGA [TSO]
NGWANDI alt for NGBANDI, NORTHERN [NGB]
NGWANDI alt for NGBANDI, SOUTHERN [NBW]
NGWANÉ alt for WANÉ [HWA]
NGWATO alt for NGWATU dial of TSWANA [TSW]
NGWATO dial of TSWANA [TSW]
NGWATU dial of TSWANA [TSW]
NGWAW alt for NGWO dial of NGWO [NGN]
NGWAW alt for NGWO [NGN]
NGWAXI alt for NGGWAHYI [NGX]
NGWE [NWE] lang, Cameroon
NGWE alt for HUNGWORO [NAT]
NGWE PALAUNG alt for PALAUNG, PALE [PCE]
NGWELE alt for NGHWELE [NHE]
NG'WERE alt for KWERE [CWE]
NGWESHE alt for NGOSHIE dial of GLAVDA [GLV]
NGWESHE-NDAGHAN alt for GVOKO [NGS]
NGWII dial of MBERE [MDT]
NGWILI alt for NGIRI [NGR]
NGWO [NGN] lang, Cameroon
NGWO dial of NGWO [NGN]
NGWOHI alt for NGGWAHYI [NGX]
NGWOI alt for HUNGWORO [NAT]
NGWULLARO alt for LARO [LRO]

NGYEMBOON alt for NGIEMBOON [NNH]
NGYEME alt for NJEME dial of KOONZIME [NJE]
NGYEPU alt for NYEPU dial of BARI [BFA]
NHA HEUN alt for NYAHEUN [NEV]
NHAANG alt for NHANG [NHA]
N//HAI alt for N/HAI-NTSE'E dial of NARO [NHR]
N/HAI-NTSE'E dial of NARO [NHR]
NHANDEVA alt for CHIRIPÁ [NHD]
NHANECA alt for NYANEKA [NYK]
NHANEKA alt for NYANEKA [NYK]
NHANG [NHA] lang, Viet Nam; also in France, USA
NHARO alt for NARO [NHR]
NHARON alt for NARO [NHR]
NHAURU alt for NARO [NHR]
NHAURUN alt for NARO [NHR]
NHAYI dial of TSHWA [TSC]
NHEENGATU alt for NHENGATU [YRL]
NHEMBA alt for NYEMBA [NBA]
NHENGATU [YRL] lang, Brazil; also in Colombia,
    Venezuela
NHENGO alt for NYENGO [NYE]
NHLANGANU dial of TSONGA [TSO]
NHO alt for BAFAW dial of BAFAW-BALONG [BWT]
NHUON alt for LÜ [KHB]
NHUWALA [NHF] lang, Australia
NI NYO'O dial of TUNEN [BAZ]
NIA HOEN alt for NYAHEUN [NEV]
NIABO alt for NEAO dial of WE SOUTHERN [GXX]
NIABOUA alt for NYABWA [NIA]
NIABRE dial of BETE, GAGNOA [BTG]
NIAHON alt for NYAHEUN [NEV]
NIAKARAMADOUGOU dial of SENOUFO,
    TAGWANA [TGW]
NIAKUOL alt for NYAHKUR [CBN]
NIAKUOLL alt for NYAHKUR [CBN]
NIAMNIAM alt for NIMBARI [NMR]
NIANG alt for NHANG [NHA]
NIANGBO dial of SENOUFO, TAGWANA [TGW]
NIANGOLO alt for SÉNOUFO, SENARA [SEQ]
NIANGOLOKO-DIARABAKOKO dial of CERMA
    [GOT]
NIAP alt for TEMUAN [TMW]
NIAS [NIP] lang, Indonesia (Sumatra)
NIAS dial of NIAS [NIP]
NIBHATTA dial of BUNDELI [BNS]
NIBON alt for NIBONG dial of PENAN, WESTERN
    [PNE]
NIBON alt for PENAN, WESTERN [PNE]
NIBONG alt for PENAN, WESTERN [PNE]
NIBONG dial of PENAN, WESTERN [PNE]
NIBULU alt for NUNI, NORTHERN [NUV]
NIBULU alt for NUNI, SOUTHERN [NNW]
NIC alt for NIDZH dial of UDI [UDI]
NICARAGUAN SIGN LANGUAGE [NCS] lang,
    Nicaragua
NICARAGUAN TAWAHKA dial of SUMO TAWAHKA
    [SUM]
NIÇARD dial of PROVENCAL [PRV]
NICOBAR alt for NICOBARESE, CENTRAL [NCB]
NICOBARA alt for NICOBARESE, SOUTHERN
    [NIK]

NICOBARESE, CAR [CAQ] lang, India
NICOBARESE, CENTRAL [NCB] lang, India
NICOBARESE, SOUTHERN [NIK] lang, India
NIÇOIS alt for NIÇARD dial of PROVENCAL [PRV]
NICOSIA alt for WESTERN LOMBARD dial of
    LOMBARD [LMO]
NICOYA dial of CHOROTEGA [CJR]
NIDE alt for LABO [MWI]
NIDEM alt for NINDEM dial of KANINGDON-NINDEM
    [KDP]
NIDROU dial of WE WESTERN [WEC]
NIDRU alt for NIDROU dial of WE WESTERN [WEC]
NIDZH dial of UDI [UDI]
NIÉDÉBOUA alt for NYEDEBWA dial of NYABWA
    [NIA]
NIEDERSAECHSISCH alt for SAXON, LOW [SXN]
NIEDERSORBISCH alt for SORBIAN, LOWER
    [WEE]
NIEDIEKAHA dial of SENOUFO, TAGWANA [TGW]
NIEL alt for AGEER dial of DINKA, NORTH-
    EASTERN [DIP]
NIELIM alt for NIELLIM [NIE]
NIELLIM [NIE] lang, Chad
NIELLIM dial of NIELLIM [NIE]
NIEMENG alt for BAMUNKA [NDO]
"NIENDE" pejorative alt for MBELIME [MQL]
NIENDE dial of TAMBERMA [SOF]
"NIENDI" pejorative alt for MBELIME [MQL]
NIENG Ó alt for MANG [MGA]
NIENI dial of KURANKO [KHA]
NIFE alt for NUPE CENTRAL dial of NUPE-NUPE
    TAKO [NUP]
NIFILOLE alt for AYIWO [NFL]
NIGAC dial of MAPE [MLH]
NIGAGBA dial of BAKWE [BAK]
NIGBI alt for LIGBI [LIG]
NIGBI dial of JULA, KOYAGA [KGA]
NIGERIAN CREOLE ENGLISH alt for PIDGIN,
    NIGERIAN [PCM]
NIGERIAN PIDGIN ENGLISH alt for PIDGIN,
    NIGERIAN [PCM]
NIGERIAN SIGN LANGUAGE [NSI] lang, Nigeria
NIGI alt for NIGII dial of YAMBETA [YAT]
NIGII dial of YAMBETA [YAT]
NIGUECACTEMIGI alt for LAYANA dial of GUANA
    [GVA]
NIGWI alt for LIGBI [LIG]
NIHAL alt for NIHALI [NHL]
NIHALI [NHL] lang, India
NIHAMBER alt for WAMSAK [WBD]
NIHAN alt for NEHAN [NSN]
NII [NII] lang, Papua New Guinea
NIINATI alt for NORTHERN MUYU dial of
    YONGKOM [YON]
NIITAKA alt for TSOU [TSY]
NIJ alt for NIDZH dial of UDI [UDI]
NIJADALI [NAD] lang, Australia
NIJRAU dial of PARACHI [PRC]
NIKA alt for GIRYAMA [NYF]
NIKIYAMA dial of BO [BPW]
NIKSEK [GBE] lang, Papua New Guinea

NIKUDA dial of ONIN [ONI]
NIKULKAN-MURNATEN-WAKOLO alt for NORTH
  COASTAL ALUNE dial of ALUNE [ALP]
NIL alt for PANIYA [PCG]
NILA [NIL] lang, Indonesia (Maluku)
NILAMBA [NIM] lang, Tanzania
NILE NUBIAN alt for KENUZI-DONGOLA [KNC]
NILE NUBIAN alt for NOBIIN [FIA]
NILOTIC KAVIRONDO alt for LUO [LUO]
NILYAMBA alt for NILAMBA [NIM]
NIMADI [NOE] lang, India
NIMALDA alt for ADYNYAMATHANHA [ADT]
NIMALTO alt for NYIMATLI dial of TERA [TER]
NIMANA alt for NUMANA dial of NUMANA-NUNKU-
  GWANTU-NUMBU [NBR]
NIMANBUR [NMP] lang, Australia
NIMARI alt for NIMADI [NOE]
NIMBARI [NMR] lang, Cameroon
NIMBARI-KEBI alt for NIMBARI [NMR]
NIMBE alt for NEMBE dial of IJO, SOUTHEAST
  [IJO]
NIMBIA dial of GWANDARA [GWN]
NIMBORAN [NIR] lang, Indonesia (Irian Jaya)
NIMI [NIS] lang, Papua New Guinea
NIMI KORO alt for CENTRAL KONO dial of KONO
  [KNO]
NIMI YAMA alt for CENTRAL KONO dial of KONO
  [KNO]
NIMIADI alt for NIMADI [NOE]
NIMO [NIW] lang, Papua New Guinea
NIMOA [NMW] lang, Papua New Guinea
NIMOIS alt for RHODANIEN dial of PROVENCAL
  [PRV]
NIMOWA alt for NIMOA [NMW]
NIMO-WASAWAI alt for NIMO [NIW]
NIMPO alt for NOMOPO dial of SAPO [KRN]
NINAM [SHB] lang, Brazil; also in Venezuela
NINATIE alt for NORTHERN MUYU dial of
  YONGKOM [YON]
NINDEM dial of KANINGDON-NINDEM [KDP]
NINE HILLS alt for GRIFFIN POINT dial of SUDEST
  [TGO]
NINEBULO dial of SA [SSA]
NINEIA alt for MATO [NIU]
NINGALAMI alt for NANGALAMI dial of GRANGALI
  [NLI]
NINGEBAL alt for BAYALI [BJY]
NINGERA [NBY] lang, Papua New Guinea
NINGERUM alt for NINGGERUM [NXR]
NINGGERA alt for NINGERA [NBY]
NINGGEROEM alt for NINGGERUM [NXR]
NINGGERUM [NXR] lang, Papua New Guinea;
  also in Indonesia (Irian Jaya)
NINGGIRUM alt for NINGGERUM [NXR]
NINGGRUM alt for NINGGERUM [NXR]
NINGI dial of GAMO-NINGI [BTE]
NINGIL [NIZ] lang, Papua New Guinea
NING-LONG dial of CHINESE, HAKKA [HAK]
NINGO dial of DANGME [DGM]
NINGRAHARIAN PASHTO dial of PASHTO,
  NORTHERN [PBU]

NINGUESSEN alt for MESE dial of TUNEN [BAZ]
NINGYE [NNS] lang, Nigeria
NINIA alt for YALI, NINIA [NLK]
NINIARI-PIRU-RIRING-LUMOLI alt for CENTRAL
  WEST ALUNE dial of ALUNE [ALP]
NINIGO alt for SEIMAT [SSG]
NINKADA dial of BU [JID]
NINONG dial of AKOOSE [BSS]
NINZAM [NIN] lang, Nigeria
NINZNE-UDINSK dial of BURIAT, RUSSIA [MNB]
NINZO alt for NINZAM [NIN]
NIO dial of LUGBARA [LUG]
NIOMINKA dial of SERER-SINE [SES]
NIOMOUN alt for BLISS dial of JOLA-KASA [CSK]
NIOPHENG alt for MRU [MRO]
NIOPRENG alt for MRU [MRO]
NIOU dial of NIELLIM [NIE]
NIPA dial of ANGAL HENENG [AKH]
NIPODE WITOTO alt for HUITOTO, NIPODE
  [HUX]
NIPOREN alt for NYANG'I [NYP]
NIPORI alt for NYANG'I [NYP]
NIPSAN [NPS] lang, Indonesia (Irian Jaya)
NIRAGU dial of GBIRI-NIRAGU [GRH]
NIRAMBA alt for NILAMBA [NIM]
NIRERE alt for KOALIB [KIB]
NIRMAL dial of GONDI, SOUTHERN [GGO]
NISA [NIC] lang, Indonesia (Irian Jaya)
NISEL alt for KHAM, NISI [KIF]
NISENAN [NSZ] lang, USA
NISGA'A [NCG] lang, Canada
NISHANG dial of NISI [DAP]
NISHEL KHAM alt for KHAM, NISI [KIF]
NISHGA alt for NISGA'A [NCG]
NISHI alt for NISI [DAP]
NISHINAM alt for NISENAN [NSZ]
NISHKA alt for NISGA'A [NCG]
NISI [DAP] lang, India
NISI alt for KHAM, NISI [KIF]
NISKA alt for NISGA'A [NCG]
NISK'A alt for NISGA'A [NCG]
NISQUALLY dial of SALISH, SOUTHERN PUGET
  SOUND [SLH]
NISSAN alt for NEHAN [NSN]
NISSI alt for NISI [DAP]
NITEN alt for ATEN [GAN]
NITINAHT alt for NITINAT dial of NOOTKA [NOO]
NITINAT dial of NOOTKA [NOO]
NITU dial of CHIN, MUN [MWQ]
NIUAFO'OU [NUM] lang, Tonga
NIUATOPUTAPU [NKP] lang, Tonga
NIUE [NIQ] lang, Niue; also in Cook Islands, New
  Zealand, Tonga
NIUEAN alt for NIUE [NIQ]
"NIUEFEKAI" pejorative alt for NIUE [NIQ]
NIUTAJI dial of IOWA-OTO [IOW]
NIUTAO alt for NORTH TUVALUAN dial of
  TUVALUAN [ELL]
NIVACLÉ alt for CHULUPÍ [CAG]
NIVAKLÉ alt for CHULUPÍ [CAG]
NIVE dial of DABA [DAB]

NIVKH alt for GILYAK [NIV]
NIVKHI alt for GILYAK [NIV]
NIVO alt for AYIWO [NFL]
NIZAA alt for SUGA [SGI]
NIZH alt for NIDZH dial of UDI [UDI]
NIZOVSK dial of NEGIDAL [NEG]
NJABI alt for NJEBI [NZB]
NJADU alt for NYADU [NXJ]
NJAI alt for NZANYI [NJA]
NJAKALI dial of DYAABUGAY [DYY]
NJAKAMBAI alt for NZAKAMBAY [NZY]
NJALGULGULE [NJL] lang, Sudan
NJAMAL alt for NYAMAL [NLY]
NJAMARL alt for NYAMAL [NLY]
NJAMBETA alt for YAMBETA [YAT]
NJANG alt for NYANJANG dial of KWANJA [KNP]
NJANGA alt for NYANJANG dial of KWANJA [KNP]
NJANGGA alt for NYANGGA [NNY]
NJANGGA alt for WIRANGU [WIW]
NJANGGALA alt for NYANGGA [NNY]
NJANGULGULE alt for NJALGULGULE [NJL]
NJANTI alt for TIBEA [NGY]
NJANYI alt for NZANYI [NJA]
NJAO alt for AWYI [AUW]
NJAO alt for NDAU [NDC]
NJARI alt for NZARE dial of MBEMBE, TIGON [NZA]
NJAUNA dial of NAGA, ZEME [NZM]
NJAWE alt for JAWE [JAZ]
NJAWLO dial of LENDU [LED]
NJEBI [NZB] lang, Gabon; also in Congo
NJEE-POANTU dial of FEFE [FMP]
NJEGN alt for NZANYI [NJA]
NJEI alt for NZANYI [NJA]
NJEING alt for NZANYI [NJA]
NJELENG dial of MOFU-GUDUR [MIF]
NJELI alt for PANDE dial of PANDE [BKJ]
NJEM alt for NDJEM dial of KOONZIME [NJE]
NJEME dial of KOONZIME [NJE]
"NJEMNJEM" pejorative alt for SUGA [SGI]
NJEMPS alt for CHAMUS dial of SAMBURU [SAQ]
NJEN [MEN] lang, Cameroon
NJENG alt for NZANYI [NJA]
NJENY alt for NZANYI [NJA]
NJEREP [NJR] lang, Nigeria
NJERUP alt for NJEREP [NJR]
NJESKO dial of KANURI, CENTRAL [KPH]
NJEVI alt for NJEBI [NZB]
NJIJAPALI alt for NIJADALI [NAD]
NJIKINI alt for NJININGI dial of TEKE, NORTHERN
    [TEG]
NJIKUM alt for JUKUN TAKUM [JBU]
NJINDO alt for NGINDO [NNQ]
NJINGA dial of MBUNDU, LOANDA [MLO]
NJININGI dial of TEKE, NORTHERN [TEG]
NJINJU dial of TEKE, CENTRAL [TEC]
NJIUNJIU alt for NJYUNJYU dial of TEKE, CENTRAL
    [TEC]
NJO alt for KOMERING [KGE]
NJO alt for KRUI [KRQ]
NJONG dial of NGEMBA [NGE]
NJOYAME alt for NDOOLA [NDR]

NJUGUNA alt for NUGUNU [NNV]
NJUKÁ alt for AUKAN [DJK]
NJUMIT dial of LAWANGAN [LBX]
NJUNGENE alt for LIMBUM [LIM]
NJWANDE alt for BITARE [BRE]
NJYUNJYU alt for NJINJU dial of TEKE, CENTRAL
    [TEC]
NJYUNJYU dial of TEKE, CENTRAL [TEC]
NKA' dial of FEFE [FMP]
NKAFA dial of KAMWE [HIG]
NKANGALA [NKN] lang, Angola
NKAP alt for NAKI [MFF]
NKARI [NKZ] lang, Nigeria
NKARIGWE alt for IRIGWE [IRI]
NKEM dial of NKEM-NKUM [ISI]
NKEMBE alt for NKIMBE dial of MBOLE [MDQ]
NKEM-NKUM [ISI] lang, Nigeria
NKHONDE alt for NYAKYUSA-NGONDE [NYY]
NKHUMBI [KHU] lang, Angola; also in Namibia
NKI alt for BOKYI [BKY]
NKIM alt for NKEM dial of NKEM-NKUM [ISI]
NKIMBE dial of MBOLE [MDQ]
NKLAPMX alt for THOMPSON [THP]
NKO dial of MUNDANI [MUN]
NKOJO dial of MWANI [WMW]
NKOKOLLE alt for NKUKOLI [NBO]
NKOLE alt for NYANKORE [NYN]
NKOLE dial of NTOMBA [NTO]
NKOM alt for KOM [BKM]
NKOMI dial of MYENE [MYE]
N'KOMI alt for NKOMI dial of MYENE [MYE]
NKONDE alt for NYAKYUSA-NGONDE [NYY]
NKONDE dial of NYAKYUSA-NGONDE [NYY]
NKONG alt for NKO dial of MUNDANI [MUN]
NKONGHO [NKC] lang, Cameroon
NKONYA [NKO] lang, Ghana
NKOOSI alt for AKOOSE [BSS]
NKORO alt for NKOROO [NKX]
NKOROO [NKX] lang, Nigeria
NKOSI alt for AKOOSE [BSS]
NKOT dial of YAMBA [YAM]
NKOXO alt for KAKO [KKJ]
NKOYA [NKA] lang, Zambia
NKOYA dial of NKOYA [NKA]
NKPAM dial of LOKAA [YAZ]
NKQESHE alt for //XEGWI [XEG]
NKRIANG alt for NGEQ [NGT]
NKUCHU alt for NKUTU [NKW]
NKUKOLI [NBO] lang, Nigeria
NKUM dial of NKEM-NKUM [ISI]
NKUM dial of YALA [YBA]
NKUM AKPAMBE dial of YALA [YBA]
NKUMA dial of TSONGA [TSO]
NKUMABEM alt for KUNABEMBE dial of
    MPONGMPONG [MGG]
NKUMBI alt for NKHUMBI [KHU]
NKUNDO dial of MONGO-NKUNDU [MOM]
NKUNDU alt for BAKUNDU dial of BAKUNDU-
    BALUE [BDU]
NKUNDU alt for NKUNDO dial of MONGO-NKUNDU
    [MOM]

NKUNE alt for MANGKUNGE dial of NGEMBA [NGE]
NKURAENG alt for KULANGO, BONDOUKOU [KZC]
NKURAENG alt for KULANGO, BOUNA [NKU]
NKURANGE alt for KULANGO, BONDOUKOU [KZC]
NKURANGE alt for KULANGO, BOUNA [NKU]
NKUTSHU alt for NKUTU [NKW]
NKUTU [NKW] lang, DRC
NKUTUK alt for SAMBURU [SAQ]
NKWA alt for GBARI [GBY]
NKWAK [NKQ] lang, Nigeria
NKWEN dial of MENDANKWE [MFD]
NKWIFIYA dial of SAGALA [SBM]
NKWOI alt for HUNGWORO [NAT]
NLA MBOO alt for SANTCHOU dial of MBO [MBO]
NLEMBUU alt for KEKEM dial of MBO [MBO]
NLONG alt for BALONG dial of BAFAW-BALONG [BWT]
NLONG alt for ELUNG dial of AKOOSE [BSS]
NNAM [NBP] lang, Nigeria
NNERIGWE alt for IRIGWE [IRI]
NO dial of SAR [MWM]
NOALE alt for MBEMBE, TIGON [NZA]
NOANAMA alt for WOUN MEU [NOA]
NOANG alt for ROGLAI, NORTHERN [ROG]
NOANG dial of CHRU [CJE]
NOATIA dial of KOK BOROK [TRP]
NOBANOB [GAW] lang, Papua New Guinea
NOBIIN [FIA] lang, Sudan; also in Egypt
NOBNOB alt for NOBANOB [GAW]
NOBONOB alt for NOBANOB [GAW]
NOBUK alt for KWERBA MAMBERAMO [NOB]
NOCAMAN [NOM] lang, Peru
NOCHI alt for NOTSI [NCF]
NOCOMAN alt for NOCAMAN [NOM]
NOCTE alt for NAGA, NOCTE [NJB]
NOCTEN alt for WICHÍ LHAMTÉS NOCTEN [MTP]
NOCTENES alt for WICHÍ LHAMTÉS NOCTEN [MTP]
NODUP dial of KUANUA [KSD]
NOEFOOR alt for BIAK [BHW]
NOENAMA alt for WOUN MEU [NOA]
NOGAI [NOG] lang, Russia (Europe); also in Kazakhstan, Uzbekistan
NOGAITSY alt for NOGAI [NOG]
NOGALAR alt for NOGAI [NOG]
NOGAU dial of JUHOAN [KTZ]
NOGAU dial of KXAUEIN [AUE]
NOGAY alt for NOGAI [NOG]
NOGHAI alt for NOGAI [NOG]
NOGHAY alt for NOGAI [NOG]
NOGHAYLAR alt for NOGAI [NOG]
NOGLIKI-VAL alt for VAL-NOGLIKI dial of OROK [OAA]
NOGO dial of KEMAK [KEM]
NOGO-NOGO alt for NOGO dial of KEMAK [KEM]
NOGUGU alt for NOKUKU [NKK]
NOGUKWABAI dial of KWERBA [KWE]
"NOHINA" pejorative alt for TOLAKI [LBW]
NOHO alt for BATANGA [BNM]
NOHON alt for AWYU, NOHON [AWJ]

NOHU alt for BATANGA [BNM]
NOHUR alt for NOKHURLI dial of TURKMEN [TCK]
NOHYA SIGN LANGUAGE alt for YUCATEC MAYA SIGN LANGUAGE [MSD]
"NOIE" pejorative alt for TOLAKI [LBW]
"NOIHE" pejorative alt for TOLAKI [LBW]
NOIKORO alt for WAYA dial of FIJIAN, WESTERN [WYY]
NOIRI dial of BHILORI [BQI]
NOIRI FAURI dial of BARELI [BGD]
NOKANOKA alt for KWAMA [KMQ]
NOKAW alt for NAGA, KHIAMNIUNGAN [NKY]
NOKCHIIN MUOTT alt for CHECHEN [CJC]
NOKHCHIIN alt for CHECHEN [CJC]
NOKHURLI dial of TURKMEN [TCK]
NOKOPO dial of YOPNO [YUT]
NOKU alt for BATANGA [BNM]
NOKUKU [NKK] lang, Vanuatu
NOKUNNA alt for NUGUNU [NNV]
NOMAANDE [LEM] lang, Cameroon
NOMAD alt for ODOODEE [KKC]
NOMAD alt for SAMO [SMQ]
NOMADIC FULFULDE alt for BORORRO dial of FULFULDE, KANO-KATSINA-BORORRO [FUV]
NOMADIC FULFULDE alt for BORORRO dial of FULFULDE, NIGERIAN [FUV]
NOMADIC FULFULDE dial of FULFULDE, ADAMAWA [FUB]
NOMADIC KUBU dial of KUBU [KVB]
NOMAI alt for DOYAYO [DOW]
NOMANE [NOF] lang, Papua New Guinea
NOMANE dial of NOMANE [NOF]
NOMATSIGUENGA [NOT] lang, Peru
NOMATSIGUENGA CAMPA alt for NOMATSIGUENGA [NOT]
NOMLAKI dial of WINTU [WIT]
NOMOI alt for MORTLOCKESE [MRL]
NOMOPO dial of SAPO [KRN]
NOMU [NOH] lang, Papua New Guinea
NON alt for NOON [SNF]
NONAMA alt for WOUN MEU [NOA]
NON-AMISH PENNSYLVANIA GERMAN dial of GERMAN, PENNSYLVANIA [PDC]
NONDA dial of BANGUBANGU [BNX]
NONE alt for NOON [SNF]
NONES dial of LADIN [LLD]
NONES BLOT alt for NONES dial of LADIN [LLD]
NONESE alt for NONES dial of LADIN [LLD]
NONESH alt for NONES dial of LADIN [LLD]
NONG alt for BATEK [BTQ]
NONG alt for BATEK NONG dial of BATEK [BTQ]
NONG alt for BUNONG dial of MNONG, SOUTHERN [MNN]
NONG alt for NUNG [NUT]
NONGTUNG dial of PNAR [PBV]
NONI alt for NOONE [NHU]
NONIALI alt for LISABATA-NUNIALI [LCS]
NONONKE alt for BOZO, SOROGAMA [BZE]
NON-PLAIN PENNSYLVANIA GERMAN alt for NON-AMISH PENNSYLVANIA GERMAN dial of GERMAN, PENNSYLVANIA [PDC]

NON-STANDARD KANNADA alt for KURUMBA [KFI]
NONUKAN alt for TIDONG [TID]
NONUKAN dial of TIDONG [TID]
N/OO alt for N/OO-KHWE dial of SHUA [SHG]
NOOCOONA alt for NUGUNU [NNV]
NOOGAR alt for NEO-NYUNGAR dial of ENGLISH [ENG]
NOOHALIT dial of YUPIK, CENTRAL SIBERIAN [ESS]
NOOKA DORA alt for MUKHA-DORA [MMK]
N//OOKHWE alt for N/OO-KHWE dial of SHUA [SHG]
N/OO-KHWE dial of SHUA [SHG]
NOOKOONA alt for NUGUNU [NNV]
NOOKSACK [NOK] lang, USA
NOOLI dial of SANTA CRUZ [STC]
NOOMAANTE alt for NOMAANDE [LEM]
NOON [SNF] lang, Senegal
NOONE [NHU] lang, Cameroon
NOONGA alt for NEO-NYUNGAR dial of ENGLISH [ENG]
NOONGABURRAH alt for NGIYAMBAA dial of WANGAAYBUWAN-NGIYAMBAA [WYB]
NOONGAR alt for NEO-NYUNGAR dial of ENGLISH [ENG]
NOORD-DRENTS alt for NORTH DRENTE dial of DRENTS [DRT]
NOORI alt for NOONE [NHU]
NOOSAN alt for NUSAN dial of XOO [NMN]
NOOTKA [NOO] lang, Canada
NOOTKA dial of NOOTKA [NOO]
NOOTRE alt for BOULBA [BLY]
NOOTSACK alt for NOOKSACK [NOK]
NOP dial of KOHO [KPM]
NO-PENGE dial of UMBU-UNGU [UMB]
NOPUK alt for KWERBA MAMBERAMO [NOB]
NOPUKW alt for KWERBA MAMBERAMO [NOB]
NOR alt for MAMBILA, CAMEROON [MYA]
NOR alt for MAMBILA, NIGERIA [MZK]
NOR alt for MURIK [MTF]
NOR TAGBO alt for MAMBILA, NIGERIA [MZK]
NORA alt for NORRA [NOR]
NORA dial of NORRA [NOR]
NORDFRIESISCH alt for FRISIAN, NORTHERN [FRR]
NORDLAND alt for NORTHERN NORWEGIAN dial of NORWEGIAN, BOKMAAL [NRR]
NORFOLK dial of ENGLISH [ENG]
NORFOLK ENGLISH dial of PITCAIRN-NORFOLK [PIH]
NORGOROD dial of KARELIAN [KRL]
NORIO dial of TOLAKI [LBW]
NORKHANA dial of KHANA [KEH]
NORMAL EGYPTIAN ARABIC alt for ARABIC, EGYPTIAN SPOKEN [ARZ]
NORMAN dial of FRENCH [FRN]
NORMAND alt for NORMAN dial of FRENCH [FRN]
NOR-MURIK LAKES alt for MURIK [MTF]
NORN [NON] lang, United Kingdom
NORRA [NOR] lang, Myanmar

NORRLAND alt for NORTHERN SWEDISH dial of SWEDISH [SWD]
NORTENYO alt for BUGLERE [SAB]
NORTENYO alt for TERIBE [TFR]
NORTH AGAW alt for BILEN [BYN]
NORTH AKOKO alt for ARIGIDI [AKK]
NORTH ALASKAN INUPIAT alt for INUPIATUN, NORTH ALASKAN [ESI]
NORTH ALBANIAN dial of ROMANI, VLAX [RMY]
NORTH AUCKLAND dial of MAORI [MBF]
NORTH AUNALEI dial of AUNALEI [AUN]
NORTH AWIN dial of AEKYOM [AWI]
NORTH BALASORE ORIYA dial of ORIYA [ORY]
NORTH BANGATO dial of BANGANDU [BGF]
NORTH BAVARIAN dial of BAVARIAN [BAR]
NORTH BEAMI dial of BEAMI [BEO]
NORTH BELGIUM SIGN LANGUAGE dial of BELGIAN SIGN LANGUAGE [BVS]
NORTH BELU alt for NORTHERN TETUN dial of TETUN [TTM]
NORTH BINJA dial of SONGOORA [SOD]
NORTH BOAZI dial of BOAZI [KVG]
NORTH BOBE dial of BUBE [BVB]
NORTH BORNEO MURUT alt for TAGAL dial of TAGAL MURUT [MVV]
NORTH BUNUN dial of BUNUN [BNN]
NORTH BURMA KHAMTI dial of KHAMTI [KHT]
NORTH BURU alt for LISELA [LCL]
NORTH CENTRAL FORE dial of FORE [FOR]
NORTH CENTRAL GELAO alt for GREEN GELAO dial of GELAO [KKF]
NORTH CENTRAL NOCHIXTLÁN MIXTECO alt for MIXTECO, TIDAÁ [MTX]
NORTH CENTRAL TARANGAN dial of TARANGAN, WEST [TXN]
NORTH CENTRAL YI alt for DAYAO dial of YI, CENTRAL [YIC]
NORTH CENTRAL YURI dial of KARKAR-YURI [YUJ]
NORTH CENTRAL ZIMATLÁN ZAPOTECO alt for ZAPOTECO, ASUNCIÓN MIXTEPEC [ZOO]
NORTH CHOLLADO alt for CHOLLADO dial of KOREAN [KKN]
NORTH CH'UNGCH'ONG alt for CH'UNGCH'ONGDO dial of KOREAN [KKN]
NORTH COAST MENGEN dial of MENGEN [MEE]
NORTH COASTAL ALUNE dial of ALUNE [ALP]
NORTH DAMAR alt for DAMAR, WEST [DRN]
NORTH DELTA ARABIC dial of ARABIC, EGYPTIAN SPOKEN [ARZ]
NORTH DOGRI dial of DOGRI-KANGRI [DOJ]
NORTH DRENTE dial of DRENTS [DRT]
NORTH FINNISH alt for FINNISH, KVEN [FKV]
NORTH FINNISH alt for FINNISH, TORNEDALEN [FIT]
NORTH GREENLANDIC alt for POLAR ESKIMO dial of INUKTITUT, GREENLANDIC [ESG]
NORTH GURAGE alt for GURAGE, SODDO [GRU]
NORTH HAMGYONGDO alt for HAMGYONGDO dial of KOREAN [KKN]
NORTH HEWA dial of HEWA [HAM]

NORTH HIBERNO ENGLISH dial of ENGLISH [ENG]
NORTH HIJAZI dial of ARABIC, HIJAZI SPOKEN [ACW]
NORTH IBANAG dial of IBANAG [IBG]
NORTH IDOMA alt for AGATU [AGC]
NORTH ILE APE dial of ILE APE [ILA]
NORTH IZON alt for KOLUKUMA dial of IZON [IJC]
NORTH KAKABAI dial of KAKABAI [KQF]
NORTH KAMAYO dial of KAMAYO [KYK]
NORTH KAMBERATARO dial of KAMBERATARO [KBV]
NORTH KANUM dial of KANUM, SOTA [KRZ]
NORTH KATI alt for NORTHERN MUYU dial of YONGKOM [YON]
NORTH KERALA dial of MALAYALAM [MJS]
NORTH KHOWAR dial of KHOWAR [KHW]
NORTH KITUI dial of KAMBA [KIK]
NORTH KOMA alt for KWAMA [KMQ]
NORTH KOMBIO dial of KOMBIO [KOK]
NORTH KOMEDIA dial of ARMENIAN [ARM]
NORTH KONKAN alt for KONKANI [KNK]
NORTH KORDOFAN ARABIC dial of ARABIC, SUDANESE SPOKEN [APD]
NORTH KWANDU dial of MASHI [MHO]
NORTH KYONGSANGDO alt for KYONGSANGDO dial of KOREAN [KKN]
NORTH LA PAZ QUECHUA alt for QUECHUA, NORTH BOLIVIAN [QUL]
NORTH LAAMANG dial of LAMANG [HIA]
NORTH LANCASHIRE dial of ENGLISH [ENG]
NORTH LEBANESE ARABIC dial of ARABIC, NORTH LEVANTINE SPOKEN [APC]
NORTH LELE alt for YOMBIRO LELE dial of LELE [LLC]
NORTH LEVANTINE ARABIC alt for ARABIC, NORTH LEVANTINE SPOKEN [APC]
NORTH LEVANTINE BEDAWI ARABIC dial of ARABIC, EASTERN EGYPTIAN BEDAWI SPOKEN [AVL]
NORTH LEVANTINE BEDAWI ARABIC dial of ARABIC, LEVANTINE BEDAWI SPOKEN [AVL]
NORTH LOLODA alt for LOLODA [LOL]
NORTH MACA alt for NAHARRA dial of MAKHUWA [VMW]
NORTH MAEWO alt for MARINO [MRB]
NORTH MAKAA alt for BYEP [MKK]
NORTH MALO alt for AVUNATARI dial of MALO [MLA]
NORTH MBUNDU alt for MBUNDU, LOANDA [MLO]
NORTH MEKEO dial of MEKEO [MEK]
NORTH MIANMIN alt for SUGANGA [SUG]
NORTH MIGABAC dial of MIGABAC [MPP]
NORTH MODOLE dial of MODOLE [MQO]
NORTH MOEJOE alt for NORTHERN MUYU dial of YONGKOM [YON]
NORTH NAJDI dial of ARABIC, NAJDI SPOKEN [ARS]
NORTH NAKAMA dial of NAKAMA [NIB]
NORTH NGALIK alt for YALI, NINIA [NLK]
NORTH NORTHERN PAIUTE dial of PAIUTE, NORTHERN [PAO]

NORTH NUK dial of NUK [NOC]
NORTH NYALI alt for NYALI [NLJ]
NORTH OLO alt for PAYI dial of OLO [ONG]
NORTH PAAMA dial of PAAMA [PMA]
NORTH PERMYAK dial of KOMI-PERMYAK [KOI]
NORTH PUEBLA AZTEC alt for NÁHUATL, PUEBLA NORTE [NCJ]
NORTH P'YONG'ANDO alt for P'YONG'ANDO dial of KOREAN [KKN]
NORTH QATARI ARABIC dial of ARABIC, GULF SPOKEN [AFB]
NORTH QUCHANI dial of KHORASANI TURKISH [KMZ]
NORTH RAGA alt for HANO [LML]
NORTH RUSSIAN dial of RUSSIAN [RUS]
NORTH RUSSIAN ROMANI dial of ROMANI, BALTIC [ROM]
NORTH SAISET alt for TAAI dial of SAISIYAT [SAI]
NORTH SAKHALIN GILYAK dial of GILYAK [NIV]
NORTH SASAK alt for KUTO-KUTE dial of SASAK [SAS]
NORTH SELEPET dial of SELEPET [SEL]
NORTH SENA alt for SENA-CARE dial of SENA [SEH]
NORTH SIBERUT dial of MENTAWAI [MWV]
NORTH SLOPE INUPIATUN dial of INUPIATUN, NORTH ALASKAN [ESI]
NORTH SMALL NAMBAS dial of MAE [MME]
NORTH SYRIAN ARABIC alt for ARABIC, MESOPOTAMIAN SPOKEN [ACM]
NORTH TABASARAN dial of TABASSARAN [TAB]
NORTH TABUKANG dial of SANGIR [SAN]
NORTH THARAKA alt for GATUE dial of THARAKA [THA]
NORTH TIMBE dial of TIMBE [TIM]
NORTH TUKEN alt for TUGEN, NORTH [TUY]
NORTH TUVALUAN dial of TUVALUAN [ELL]
NORTH UDMURT dial of UDMURT [UDM]
NORTH URAT alt for WASEP NAU dial of URAT [URT]
NORTH VEPS alt for PRIONEZH dial of VEPS [VEP]
NORTH WAIBUK dial of HARUAI [TMD]
NORTH WILTSHIRE dial of ENGLISH [ENG]
NORTH YAMDENA dial of YAMDENA [JMD]
NORTH YAWA dial of YAWA [YVA]
NORTH YEI dial of YEI [JEI]
NORTH YORKSHIRE dial of ENGLISH [ENG]
NORTH-CENTRAL LEBANEE ARABIC dial of ARABIC, NORTH LEVANTINE SPOKEN [APC]
NORTHEAST AMBAE alt for AMBAE, EAST [OMB]
NORTHEAST AMBON alt for TULEHU [TLU]
NORTHEAST AOBA alt for AMBAE, EAST [OMB]
NORTHEAST AWA dial of AWA [AWB]
NORTHEAST BARITO alt for LAWANGAN [LBX]
NORTHEAST BELARUSAN dial of BELARUSAN [RUW]
NORTHEAST BOHEMIAN dial of CZECH [CZC]
NORTHEAST CENTRAL IJO alt for BISENI [IJE]
NORTHEAST DOBEL dial of DOBEL [KVO]
NORTHEAST DUGURI dial of DUGURI [DBM]

NORTHEAST EGYPTIAN BEDAWI ARABIC dial of ARABIC, EASTERN EGYPTIAN BEDAWI SPOKEN [AVL]

NORTHEAST EGYPTIAN BEDAWI ARABIC dial of ARABIC, LIBYAN SPOKEN [AYL]

NORTHEAST FLORIDA COAST dial of SEA ISLAND CREOLE ENGLISH [GUL]

NORTHEAST FUYUG dial of FUYUG [FUY]

NORTHEAST HUNGARIAN dial of HUNGARIAN [HNG]

NORTHEAST IZERE dial of IZERE [FIZ]

NORTHEAST KARAKALPAK dial of KARAKALPAK [KAC]

NORTHEAST LAMPUNG alt for MENGGALA dial of ABUNG [ABL]

NORTHEAST LUBA alt for SONGE [SOP]

NORTHEAST LUWU dial of TAE [ROB]

NORTHEAST QUCHANI alt for NORTH QUCHANI dial of KHORASANI TURKISH [KMZ]

NORTHEAST SAHAPTIN alt for WALLA WALLA [WAA]

NORTHEAST SASAK alt for NGETO-NGETE dial of SASAK [SAS]

NORTHEAST VANUA LEVU dial of FIJIAN [FJI]

NORTHEAST VITI LEVU dial of FIJIAN [FJI]

NORTHEASTERN GOE alt for KIEMBARA dial of SAMO, MAYA [SYM]

NORTHEASTERN GREBO dial of GREBO, NORTHERN [GRB]

NORTHEASTERN JAMILTEPEC MIXTECO alt for MIXTECO, IXTAYUTLA [VMJ]

NORTHEASTERN JIARONG alt for CHABAO dial of JIARONG [JYA]

NORTHEASTERN KARAKALPAK dial of KARAKALPAK [KAC]

NORTHEASTERN KAZAKH dial of KAZAKH [KAZ]

NORTHEASTERN KRUMEN alt for KRUMEN, PYE [PYE]

NORTHEASTERN KUMAUNI dial of KUMAUNI [KFY]

NORTHEASTERN MAIRASI dial of MAIRASI [FRY]

NORTHEASTERN MIAHUATLÁN alt for ZAPOTECO, AMATLÁN [ZPO]

NORTHEASTERN MONGOLIAN alt for BURIAT, CHINA [BXU]

NORTHEASTERN OTOMÍ alt for OTOMÍ, TEXCATEPEC [OTX]

NORTHEASTERN PASHTO dial of PASHTO, NORTHERN [PBU]

NORTHEASTERN PWO KAREN alt for KAREN, PWO, PHRAE [KJT]

NORTHEASTERN SAMO alt for SAMO, MAYA [SYM]

NORTHEASTERN SARDINIAN alt for SARDINIAN, GALLURESE [SDN]

NORTHEASTERN TUVIN dial of TUVIN [TUN]

NORTHEASTERN YAUTEPEC ZAPOTECO alt for ZAPOTECO, QUIAVICUZAS [ZPJ]

NORTHEASTERN YIDDISH dial of YIDDISH, EASTERN [YDD]

NORTHEASTERN YUNNAN alt for DIAN DONGBEI dial of YI, GUIZHOU [YIG]

NORTHEASTERN YUNNAN MIAO alt for HMONG, NORTHEASTERN DIAN [HMD]

NORTHERN AFAR dial of AFAR [AFR]

NORTHERN AKHVAKH dial of AKHVAKH [AKV]

NORTHERN AMAMI-OSIMA alt for AMAMI-OSHIMA, NORTHERN [RYN]

NORTHERN AMIS dial of AMIS [ALV]

NORTHERN AREQUIPA dial of QUECHUA, AREQUIPA-LA UNION [QAR]

NORTHERN AVAR alt for KUNZAKH dial of AVAR [AVR]

NORTHERN BABOLE dial of BABOLE [BVX]

NORTHERN BAI alt for BIIJIANG dial of BAI [PIQ]

NORTHERN BAKOSSI dial of AKOOSE [BSS]

NORTHERN BALONG alt for BAKONI dial of KENYANG [KEN]

NORTHERN BANGANTU alt for BAGETO dial of MPONGMPONG [MGG]

NORTHERN BANTAWA dial of BANTAWA [BAP]

NORTHERN BARASANO alt for WAIMAHA [BAO]

NORTHERN BÉTÉ alt for BÉTÉ, DALOA [BEV]

NORTHERN BIRIFOR alt for BIRIFOR, MALBA [BFO]

NORTHERN BOLON alt for BLACK BOLON dial of BOLON [BOF]

NORTHERN BOMITABA dial of BOMITABA [ZMX]

NORTHERN BUDUMA dial of BUDUMA [BDM]

NORTHERN BULLOM alt for BULLOM SO [BUY]

NORTHERN CAGAYAN NEGRITO alt for ATTA, PAMPLONA [ATT]

NORTHERN CALABRESE-LUCANO dial of NAPOLETANO-CALABRESE [NPL]

NORTHERN CAROLINIAN alt for TANAPAG [TPV]

NORTHERN CARRIER alt for BABINE [BCR]

NORTHERN CATALÁN alt for CATALAN-ROUSILLONESE dial of CATALAN-VALENCIAN-BALEAR [CLN]

NORTHERN CENTRAL AMERICA CREOLE ENGLISH [BZI] lang, Belize; also in Colombia, Nicaragua, USA

NORTHERN CHATINO alt for CHATINO, ZENZONTEPEC [CZE]

NORTHERN CHINESE alt for CHINESE, MANDARIN [CHN]

NORTHERN CHUMBURUNG dial of CHUMBURUNG [NCU]

NORTHERN CLUSTER LISHÁN DIDÁN dial of LISHAN DIDAN [TRG]

NORTHERN CONCHUCOS QUECHUA alt for QUECHUA, ANCASH, CONCHUCOS, NORTHERN [QED]

NORTHERN CORSICAN dial of CORSICAN [COI]

NORTHERN CRIMEAN dial of CRIMEAN TURKISH [CRH]

NORTHERN CUONA dial of MOINBA [MOB]

NORTHERN DAGAARE alt for DAGARA, NORTHERN [DGI]

NORTHERN DOS DE MAYO dial of QUECHUA, HUANUCO, HUAMALIES-NORTHERN DOS DE MAYO [QEJ]

NORTHERN EAST-GUIZHOU MIAO alt for HMONG, NORTHERN QIANDONG [HEA]

NORTHERN ESTONIAN alt for TALLINN dial of ESTONIAN [EST]

NORTHERN EXTREMADURAN dial of EXTREMADURAN [EXT]

NORTHERN FANIA dial of FANIA [FAN]

NORTHERN FOOTHILL YOKUTS dial of YOKUTS [YOK]

NORTHERN FUNGOM alt for FUNGOM [FUG]

NORTHERN GABRI alt for TOBANGA [TNG]

NORTHERN GIKUYU dial of GIKUYU [KIU]

NORTHERN GOURMANCHEMA dial of GOURMANCHEMA [GUX]

NORTHERN GUANGDONG alt for YUEBEI dial of CHINESE, HAKKA [HAK]

NORTHERN GUIYANG MIAO alt for HMONG, NORTHERN GUIYANG [HUJ]

NORTHERN GUNU dial of NUGUNU [YAS]

NORTHERN GURUNG alt for MANANGBA [NMM]

NORTHERN HANGA dial of HANGA [HAG]

NORTHERN HEILTSUK alt for BELLA BELLA dial of HEILTSUK [HEI]

NORTHERN HIGHLAND MAZATECO alt for MAZATECO, SAN JERÓNIMO TECÓATL [MAA]

NORTHERN HUISHUI MIAO alt for HMONG, NORTHERN HUISHUI [HMN]

NORTHERN IRULA dial of IRULA [IRU]

NORTHERN ISAN dial of THAI, NORTHEASTERN [TTS]

NORTHERN ISTHMUS ZAPOTECO alt for ZAPOTECO, GUEVEA DE HUMBOLDT [ZPG]

NORTHERN KALASHA dial of KALASHA [KLS]

NORTHERN KALINGA alt for KALINGA, LIMOS [KMK]

NORTHERN KARELIAN dial of KARELIAN [KRL]

NORTHERN KHAMS dial of KHAMS [KHG]

NORTHERN KHANTI dial of KHANTY [KCA]

NORTHERN KIRGIZ dial of KIRGHIZ [KDO]

NORTHERN KIRINYAGA alt for GICHUGU dial of GIKUYU [KIU]

NORTHERN KONO dial of KONO [KNO]

NORTHERN KORONDOUGOU dial of BOZO, SOROGAMA [BZE]

NORTHERN KPELE alt for KPELLE, GUINEA [GKP]

NORTHERN KRAHN alt for KRAHN, WESTERN [KRW]

NORTHERN KURDISH alt for KURMANJI [KUR]

NORTHERN KUTAI dial of MALAY, TENGGARONG KUTAI [VKT]

NORTHERN LAHU alt for NA dial of LAHU [LAH]

NORTHERN LAPP alt for SAAMI, NORTHERN [LPR]

"NORTHERN LAPPISH" pejorative alt for SAAMI, NORTHERN [LPR]

"NORTHERN LAPPISH" pejorative alt for SAAMI, SOUTHERN [LPC]

NORTHERN LAPPISH alt for SAAMI, NORTHERN [LPR]

NORTHERN LAWA alt for LAWA, EASTERN [LWL]

NORTHERN LELA alt for ADOMA dial of CLELA [DRI]

NORTHERN LENGUA dial of LENGUA [LEG]

NORTHERN LIMBA dial of LIMBA, EAST [LMA]

NORTHERN LOGO alt for OGAMBI dial of LOGO [LOG]

NORTHERN LOGUDORESE dial of SARDINIAN, LOGUDORESE [SRD]

"NORTHERN LOLO" pejorative alt for YI, SICHUAN [III]

NORTHERN LOW SAXON dial of SAXON, LOW [SXN]

NORTHERN LUBA alt for LUNA [LUJ]

NORTHERN LUNDA alt for RUUND [RND]

NORTHERN LUSHOOTSEED dial of LUSHOOTSEED [LUT]

NORTHERN LYÉLÉ dial of LYELE [LEE]

NORTHERN MACEDONIAN dial of MACEDONIAN [MKJ]

NORTHERN MAGAHI dial of MAGAHI [MQM]

NORTHERN MALIMIUT INUPIATUN dial of INUPIATUN, NORTHWEST ALASKA [ESK]

NORTHERN MAMASA dial of MAMASA [MQJ]

NORTHERN MANDARIN alt for HUABEI GUANHUA dial of CHINESE, MANDARIN [CHN]

NORTHERN MAO alt for BAMBASSI [MYF]

NORTHERN MARIK dial of MARIK [DAD]

NORTHERN MARWARI dial of MARWARI [MRI]

NORTHERN MASALIT dial of MASALIT [MSA]

NORTHERN MASHAN MIAO alt for HMONG, NORTHERN MASHAN [HMO]

NORTHERN MBENE alt for BASAA [BAA]

NORTHERN MBULA dial of MBULA [MNA]

NORTHERN MICMAC dial of MICMAC [MIC]

NORTHERN MIN alt for CHINESE, MIN BEI [MNP]

NORTHERN MON alt for PEGU dial of MON [MNW]

NORTHERN MONGOLIAN alt for BURIAT, CHINA [BXU]

NORTHERN MONGOLIAN alt for BURIAT, MONGOLIA [BXM]

NORTHERN MONGOLIAN alt for BURIAT, RUSSIA [MNB]

NORTHERN MOTILÓN alt for YUKPA [YUP]

NORTHERN MUNA alt for STANDARD MUNA dial of MUNA [MYN]

NORTHERN MUNJI dial of MUNJI [MNJ]

NORTHERN MURANG'A alt for NORTHERN GIKUYU dial of GIKUYU [KIU]

NORTHERN MUYU dial of YONGKOM [YON]

NORTHERN NANDE alt for NANDI [NNB]

NORTHERN NDAM alt for NDAM DIK dial of NDAM [NDM]

NORTHERN NDEBELE alt for NDEBELE [NDF]

NORTHERN NINAM dial of NINAM [SHB]

NORTHERN NOCHIXTLÁN MIXTECO alt for MIXTECO, APASCO Y APOALA [MIP]

NORTHERN NORWEGIAN dial of NORWEGIAN, BOKMAAL [NRR]

NORTHERN NUSU dial of NUSU [NUF]

NORTHERN OAXACA MIXTECO alt for MIXTECO, CHAZUMBA [QMB]

NORTHERN OAXACA NÁHUATL alt for NÁHUATL, OAXACA NORTE [NHY]

NORTHERN OGAMBI dial of AVOKAYA [AVU]

NORTHERN OJIBWA alt for OJIBWA, NORTH-WESTERN [OJB]

NORTHERN OJIBWA alt for OJIBWA, SEVERN [OJS]

NORTHERN OROK alt for VAL-NOGLIKI dial of OROK [OAA]

NORTHERN PA'O dial of KAREN, PAO [BLK]

NORTHERN PASTAZA QUICHUA alt for QUICHUA, PASTAZA, NORTHERN [QLB]

NORTHERN PHALURA dial of PHALURA [PHL]

NORTHERN PONDORI dial of BOZO, SOROGAMA [BZE]

NORTHERN POPOLOCA alt for POPOLOCA, SAN MARCOS TLALCOYALCO [PLS]

NORTHERN PUGET SOUND SALISH alt for NORTHERN LUSHOOTSEED dial of LUSHOOTSEED [LUT]

NORTHERN QIANDONG MIAO alt for HMONG, NORTHERN QIANDONG [HEA]

NORTHERN QUICHÉ alt for QUICHÉ, CUNÉN [CUN]

NORTHERN ROMAGNOLO dial of EMILIANO-ROMAGNOLO [EML]

NORTHERN SAGARA alt for KAGULU [KKI]

NORTHERN SAKAI alt for TEMIAR [TMH]

NORTHERN SAMA alt for SAMA, BALANGINGI [SSE]

NORTHERN SAMAR dial of WARAY-WARAY [WRY]

NORTHERN SANGTAM alt for PIRR dial of NAGA, SANGTAM [NSA]

NORTHERN SAURASHTRA dial of SAURASHTRA [SAZ]

NORTHERN SEEKU dial of SEEKU [SOS]

NORTHERN SEL'KUP alt for TAZ dial of SELKUP [SAK]

NORTHERN SHAN alt for TAI MAO dial of SHAN [SJN]

NORTHERN SHILHA alt for TARIFIT [RIF]

NORTHERN SHONA alt for KOREKORE dial of SHONA [SHD]

NORTHERN SHOSHONI dial of SHOSHONI [SHH]

NORTHERN SICHUAN YI dial of YI, SICHUAN [III]

NORTHERN SINAMA alt for SAMA, BALANGINGI [SSE]

NORTHERN SOMALI dial of SOMALI [SOM]

NORTHERN SOQOTRI dial of SOQOTRI [SQT]

NORTHERN SORSOGON alt for SORSOGON, MASBATE [BKS]

NORTHERN STANDARD BHOJPURI dial of BHOJPURI [BHJ]

NORTHERN STIENG alt for STIENG, BULO [STI]

NORTHERN STONY dial of STONEY [STO]

NORTHERN SWEDISH dial of SWEDISH [SWD]

NORTHERN TAIRORA dial of TAIRORA [TBG]

NORTHERN TALYSHI dial of TALYSH [TLY]

NORTHERN TARAHUMARA alt for TARAHUMARA NORTE [THH]

NORTHERN TAUNGTHU alt for KAREN, PA'O [BLK]

NORTHERN TÀY dial of TAY [THO]

NORTHERN TEHUELCHE alt for PUELCHE [PUE]

NORTHERN TEPEHUÁN alt for TEPEHUÁN NORTE [NTP]

NORTHERN TETUN dial of TETUN [TTM]

NORTHERN THAI alt for THAI, NORTHERN [NOD]

NORTHERN THIMPHU dial of DZONGKHA [DZO]

NORTHERN TLAXIACO MIXTEC alt for MIXTECO, TLAXIACO NORTE [MOS]

NORTHERN TOBA dial of TOBA [TOB]

NORTHERN TOTONACA alt for TOTONACA, XICOTEPEC DE JUÁREZ [TOO]

NORTHERN TSAKONIAN dial of TSAKONIAN [TSD]

NORTHERN TUNISIAN ARABIC dial of ARABIC, TUNISIAN SPOKEN [AEB]

NORTHERN TURKANA dial of TURKANA [TUV]

NORTHERN UMA alt for WINATU dial of UMA [PPK]

NORTHERN VIETNAMESE dial of VIETNAMESE [VIE]

NORTHERN VILLA ALTA ZAPOTECO alt for ZAPOTECO, RINCÓN [ZAR]

NORTHERN VOGUL dial of MANSI [MNS]

NORTHERN WELSH dial of WELSH [WLS]

NORTHERN YAKHA dial of YAKHA [YBH]

NORTHERN YALI alt for YALI, ANGGURUK [YLI]

NORTHERN YAU dial of YAU [YUW]

NORTHERN YEMENI ARABIC alt for ARABIC, SANAANI SPOKEN [AYN]

NORTHERN YI alt for YI, SICHUAN [III]

NORTHERN YUKAGIR alt for YUKAGHIR, NORTHERN [YKG]

NORTHERN ZAZA alt for KIRMANJKI [QKV]

NORTH-SOUTH UDAB dial of FUYUG [FUY]

NORTHUMBERLAND dial of ENGLISH [ENG]

NORTHWEST ALASKA INUPIAT alt for INUPIATUN, NORTHWEST ALASKA [ESK]

NORTHWEST HUNGARIAN dial of HUNGARIAN [HNG]

NORTHWEST IZERE dial of IZERE [FIZ]

NORTHWEST IZON alt for MEIN dial of IZON [IJC]

NORTHWEST LAMPUNG alt for KOTA BUMI dial of ABUNG [ABL]

NORTHWEST MARIND alt for MARIND, BIAN [BPV]

NORTHWEST MEKEO dial of MEKEO [MEK]

NORTHWEST OAXACA MIXTEC alt for MIXTECO, OAXACA NOROESTE [MXA]

NORTHWEST QUCHANI alt for WEST QUCHANI dial of KHORASANI TURKISH [KMZ]

NORTHWEST UKRAINIAN dial of UKRAINIAN [UKR]

NORTHWESTERN ARVANITIKA dial of ALBANIAN, ARVANITIKA [AAT]

NORTHWESTERN CATALAN dial of CATALAN-VALENCIAN-BALEAR [CLN]

NORTHWESTERN GURUNG dial of GURUNG, WESTERN [GVR]

NORTHWESTERN JIARONG alt for SIDABA dial of JIARONG [JYA]

NORTHWESTERN KARAIM dial of KARAIM [KDR]

NORTHWESTERN MANDARIN alt for XIBEI GUANHUA dial of CHINESE, MANDARIN [CHN]

NORTHWESTERN MANINKA alt for MANINKAKAN, WESTERN [MLQ]

NORTHWESTERN MIXE alt for MIXE, TOTONTEPEC [MTO]

NORTHWESTERN NUNI. NORTHEASTERN NUNI dial of NUNI, NORTHERN [NUV]

NORTHWESTERN ORIYA dial of ORIYA [ORY]

NORTHWESTERN PAKHTO dial of PASHTO, NORTHERN [PBU]

NORTHWESTERN POCHUTLA ZAPOTECO alt for ZAPOTECO, SAN BALTÁZAR LOXICHA [ZPX]

NORTHWESTERN SAMO alt for SAMO, MATYA [STJ]

NORTHWESTERN SARDINIAN alt for SARDINIAN, SASSARESE [SDC]

NORTHWESTERN TEHUANTEPEC ZAPOTECO alt for ZAPOTECO, LACHIGUIRI [ZPA]

NORTHWESTERN YAUTEPEC ZAPOTECO alt for ZAPOTECO, YAUTEPEC [ZPB]

NORTHWESTERN YIDDISH dial of YIDDISH, WESTERN [YIH]

NORWEGIAN alt for NORWEGIAN, BOKMAAL [NRR]

NORWEGIAN alt for NORWEGIAN, NYNORSK [NRN]

"NORWEGIAN LAPP" pejorative alt for SAAMI, NORTHERN [LPR]

"NORWEGIAN LAPP" pejorative alt for SAAMI, SOUTHERN [LPC]

NORWEGIAN SAAMI alt for SAAMI, NORTHERN [LPR]

NORWEGIAN SIGN LANGUAGE [NSL] lang, Norway

NORWEGIAN TRAVELLER alt for TRAVELLER NORWEGIAN [RMG]

NORWEGIAN, BOKMAAL [NRR] lang, Norway; also in Canada, Ecuador, Sweden, UAE, USA

NORWEGIAN, NYNORSK [NRN] lang, Norway

NOSU alt for YI, YUNNAN [NOS]

NOTH VELUWE alt for VELUWS, NORTH [VEL]

NOTOZER dial of SAAMI, SKOLT [LPK]

NOTRE alt for BOULBA [BLY]

NOTSI [NCF] lang, Papua New Guinea

NOTU alt for EWAGE-NOTU [NOU]

NOUMOUDARA-KOUMOUDARA dial of TIEFO [TIQ]

NOUNA dial of MARKA [MWR]

NOUNI alt for NUNI, NORTHERN [NUV]

NOUNI alt for NUNI, SOUTHERN [NNW]

NOUNOUMA alt for NUNI, NORTHERN [NUV]

NOUNOUMA alt for NUNI, SOUTHERN [NNW]

NOVA SCOTIAN SIGN LANGUAGE alt for MARITIME SIGN LANGUAGE [NSR]

NOVARA alt for WESTERN LOMBARD dial of LOMBARD [LMO]

NOVARESE LOMBARD dial of LOMBARD [LMO]

NOVGOROD dial of KARELIAN [KRL]

NOVOUYGUR alt for UYGHUR [UIG]

NOWAI dial of TANNA, SOUTHWEST [NWI]

NOWGONG alt for NAGA, AO [NJO]

NOY [NOY] lang, Chad

NOZA alt for NORRA [NOR]

NPONGUÉ alt for MPONGWE dial of MYENE [MYE]

NPONGWE alt for MPONGWE dial of MYENE [MYE]

NREBELE alt for NDEBELE [NEL]

NRUANGHMEI alt for NAGA, RONGMEI [NBU]

NSA dial of IGBO [IGR]

NSADOP dial of BOKYI [BKY]

N'SAKARA alt for NZAKARA [NZK]

NSARE alt for NZARE dial of MBEMBE, TIGON [NZA]

NSARI [ASJ] lang, Cameroon

NSAW alt for LAMNSO' [NSO]

NSEI alt for KENSWEI NSEI [NDB]

NSELE dial of NDE-NSELE-NTA [NDD]

NSENGA [NSE] lang, Zambia; also in Mozambique, Zimbabwe

NSENGA dial of NSENGA [NSE]

NSENGA dial of NYANJA [NYJ]

NSHI [NSC] lang, Nigeria

NSHO' alt for LAMNSO' [NSO]

NSIHAA dial of SISAALA, TUMULUNG [SIL]

NSIMBWA dial of MWANI [WMW]

NSINDAK alt for SIMBA [SBW]

NSIT dial of IBIBIO [IBB]

NSO alt for LAMNSO' [NSO]

NSO' alt for LAMNSO' [NSO]

NSONGO [NSX] lang, Angola

NSONGWA alt for SONGWA dial of NGEMBA [NGE]

NSOSE alt for BASSOSSI [BSI]

NSUKA dial of IGBO [IGR]

NSUNGALI alt for LIMBUM [LIM]

NSUNGLI alt for LIMBUM [LIM]

NSUNGNI alt for LIMBUM [LIM]

NSUR alt for TAPSHIN [TDL]

NSWASE alt for BASSOSSI [BSI]

NSWOSE alt for BASSOSSI [BSI]

NTA dial of NDE-NSELE-NTA [NDD]

NTAAPUM dial of NTCHAM [BUD]

NTAU alt for BOBOT [BTY]

NTCHAM [BUD] lang, Togo; also in Ghana

NTEM dial of YAMBA [YAM]

NTENYI alt for NAGA, NTENYI [NNL]

NTHALI dial of TUMBUKA [TUW]

NTHENYI alt for NAGA, NTENYI [NNL]

NTII dial of FEFE [FMP]

NTLAKAPMUK alt for THOMPSON [THP]

NTOGAPID alt for ITOGAPÚK [ITG]

NTOGAPIG alt for ITOGAPÚK [ITG]

NTOLEH dial of LIGBI [LIG]

NTOMBA [NTO] lang, DRC

NTOMBA dial of NTOMBA [NTO]

NTOMBA-BIKORO dial of MONGO-NKUNDU [MOM]

NTOMBA-BOLIA alt for NTOMBA [NTO]

NTOMBA-INONGO dial of MONGO-NKUNDU [MOM]

NTONG dial of YAMBA [YAM]

NTOUMOU dial of FANG [FNG]

NTRIBOU alt for DELO [NTR]

NTRIBU alt for DELO [NTR]
NTRUBO alt for DELO [NTR]
NTSAAYI alt for TSAAYI dial of TEKE, WESTERN [TEZ]
NTSHANTI alt for NCANE [NCR]
NTSIAM dial of MFINU [ZMF]
NTSWAR dial of MFINU [ZMF]
NTUGI dial of THARAKA [THA]
NTUM dial of FANG [FNG]
NTUMBA alt for NTOMBA [NTO]
NTUMU alt for NTOUMOU dial of FANG [FNG]
NTUMU alt for NTUM dial of FANG [FNG]
NÜNPA alt for LEPCHA [LEP]
N/U [NGH] lang, South Africa
N/U dial of N/U [NGH]
NU alt for NUNG [NUN]
NU BACA alt for NUBACA [BAF]
NU GUNU alt for NUGUNU [YAS]
NU MHOU alt for NUMAO dial of BUNU, BU-NAO [BWX]
NU RIVER dial of DRUNG [DUU]
NUA alt for YUAGA [NUA]
NUADHU alt for COMO KARIM [CFG]
NUAKATA alt for 'AUHELAWA [KUD]
NUANGEYA alt for NYANG'I [NYP]
NUAULU alt for NUAULU, NORTH [NNI]
NUAULU alt for NUAULU, SOUTH [NXL]
NUAULU, NORTH [NNI] lang, Indonesia (Maluku)
NUAULU, SOUTH [NXL] lang, Indonesia (Maluku)
NUB alt for MANDOBO [KZH]
NUBACA [BAF] lang, Cameroon
NUBAMA alt for KAMO [KCQ]
NUBI [KCN] lang, Uganda; also in Kenya
NUBIA dial of AWAR [AYA]
NUBRA LADAKHI dial of LADAKHI [LBJ]
NUBRI [KTE] lang, Nepal
NUBWA dial of MORO [MOR]
NUCHEN alt for JURCHEN [JUC]
NUCLEAR WESTERN FIJIAN dial of FIJIAN, WESTERN [WYY]
NUCUM alt for BOIKIN [BZF]
NUDOO dial of VUTE [VUT]
/NU//EN alt for NG/U//EN dial of XOO [NMN]
/NU//EN alt for NG/U/EN dial of XOO [NMN]
NU//EN alt for NG/U//EN dial of XOO [NMN]
NU//EN alt for NG/U/EN dial of XOO [NMN]
NUER [NUS] lang, Sudan; also in Ethiopia
NUEVO SOYALTEPEC MAZATEC alt for MAZATECO, SOYALTEPEC [VMP]
NUFAWA alt for NUPE- NUPE TAKO [NUP]
NUFI alt for FE'FE' [FMP]·
NUFOOR alt for BIAK [BHW]
NUGANE dial of VUTE [VUT]
NUGBO dial of GODIE [GOD]
NUGUNA alt for NUGUNU [NNV]
NUGUNU [NNV] lang, Australia
NUGUNU [YAS] lang, Cameroon
NUGUOR alt for NUKUORO [NKR]
NUGURIA [NUR] lang, Papua New Guinea
NUHIRO dial of BAMU [BCF]
NUI dial of KIRIBATI [GLB]

NUIAN alt for NUI dial of KIRIBATI [GLB]
NUJUM dial of VUTE [VUT]
NUK [NOC] lang, Papua New Guinea
NUKA-DORA [NUK] lang, India
NUKAK MAKÚ [MBR] lang, Colombia
NUKANA alt for NUGUNU [NNV]
NUKAPU dial of PILENI [PIV]
NUKHA dial of AZERBAIJANI, NORTH [AZE]
NUKORO alt for NUKUORO [NKR]
NUKU alt for MEHEK [NUX]
NUKU HIVA dial of MARQUESAN, NORTH [MRQ]
NUKUFETAU alt for SOUTH TUVALUAN dial of TUVALUAN [ELL]
NUKUINI [NUC] lang, Brazil
NUKULAELAE alt for SOUTH TUVALUAN dial of TUVALUAN [ELL]
NUKUMA dial of KWOMA [KMO]
NUKUMANU [NUQ] lang, Papua New Guinea
NUKUNA alt for NUGUNU [NNV]
NUKUNNU alt for NUGUNU [NNV]
NUKUNU alt for NUGUNU [NNV]
NUKUNUKUBARA alt for WAKAWAKA [WKW]
NUKUORO [NKR] lang, Micronesia
NUKURIA alt for NUGURIA [NUR]
NULU dial of RUNGUS [DRG]
NUMANA dial of NUMANA-NUNKU-GWANTU-NUMBU [NBR]
NUMANA-NUNKU-GWANTU-NUMBU [NBR] lang, Nigeria
NUMAND alt for NOMAANDE [LEM]
NUMANGAN alt for NUMANGGANG [NOP]
NUMANGANG alt for NUMANGGANG [NOP]
NUMANGGANG [NOP] lang, Papua New Guinea
NUMAO dial of BUNU, BU-NAO [BWX]
NUMBA dial of MANAGALASI [MCQ]
NUMBAMI [SIJ] lang, Papua New Guinea
NUMBU dial of NUMANA-NUNKU-GWANTU-NUMBU [NBR]
NUME [TGS] lang, Vanuatu
NUMEE [KDK] lang, New Caledonia
NUMEE dial of NUMEE [KDK]
NUMG alt for RAWANG [RAW]
ÑUMÍ MIXTECO alt for MIXTECO, TLAXIACO NORTE [MOS]
NUMURANA alt for OMURANO [OMU]
ÑUÑ alt for BAINOUK-GUNYAAMOLO [BCZ]
NUNA alt for KOORETE [KQY]
NUNA alt for NUNI, NORTHERN [NUV]
NUNA alt for NUNI, SOUTHERN [NNW]
NUNDORO alt for NDOOLA [NDR]
NUNE alt for NUNI, NORTHERN [NUV]
NUNE alt for NUNI, SOUTHERN [NNW]
NUNG [NUN] lang, Myanmar
NUNG [NUT] lang, Viet Nam; also in Australia, Canada, Laos, USA
NUNG alt for CHINESE, YUE [YUH]
NUNG alt for RAWANG [RAW]
NÙNG AN dial of NUNG [NUT]
NÙNG CHÁO dial of NUNG [NUT]
NÙNG FAN SLIHNG alt for NÙNG PHAN SLÌNH dial of NUNG [NUT]

NÙNG INH dial of NUNG [NUT]
NÙNG LÒI dial of NUNG [NUT]
NÙNG PHAN SLÌNH dial of NUNG [NUT]
NÙNG QÚY RIN dial of NUNG [NUT]
NUNG RAWANG alt for RAWANG [RAW]
NUNG VEN alt for EN [ENC]
NUNGALI [NUG] lang, Australia
NUNGGUBUJU alt for NUNGGUBUYU [NUY]
NUNGGUBUYU [NUY] lang, Australia
NUNGU [RIN] lang, Nigeria
NUNGUDA alt for LONGUDA [LNU]
NUNGURA alt for LONGUDA [LNU]
NUNGURABA alt for LONGUDA [LNU]
NUNI, NORTHERN [NUV] lang, Burkina Faso
NUNI, SOUTHERN [NNW] lang, Burkina Faso
NUNIALI alt for LISABATA-NUNIALI [LCS]
NUNIALI dial of LISABATA-NUNIALI [LCS]
NUNKU dial of NUMANA-NUNKU-GWANTU-
    NUMBU [NBR]
NUNLIGRANSKIJ dial of CHUKOT [CKT]
NUNU dial of BUNU, BU-NAO [BWX]
NUNU dial of NGIRI [NGR]
NUNU' dial of SARUDU [SDU]
NUNUKAN alt for NONUKAN dial of TIDONG [TID]
NUNUMA alt for NUNI, NORTHERN [NUV]
NUNUMA alt for NUNI, SOUTHERN [NNW]
NUNUMA dial of KASEM [KAS]
NUNZO alt for NINZAM [NIN]
NUORESE dial of SARDINIAN, LOGUDORESE
    [SRD]
NUPANI dial of PILENI [PIV]
NUPBIKHA [NUB] lang, Bhutan
NUPE alt for NUPE-NUPE TAKO [NUP]
NUPE CENTRAL dial of NUPE-NUPE TAKO [NUP]
NUPE TAKO dial of NUPE-NUPE TAKO [NUP]
NUPECI alt for NUPE-NUPE TAKO [NUP]
NUPECIDJI alt for NUPE-NUPE TAKO [NUP]
NUPECIZI alt for NUPE CENTRAL dial of NUPE-
    NUPE TAKO [NUP]
NUPENCHI alt for NUPE-NUPE TAKO [NUP]
NUPENCIZI alt for NUPE-NUPE TAKO [NUP]
NUPENCIZI alt for NUPE CENTRAL dial of NUPE-
    NUPE TAKO [NUP]
NUPE-NUPE TAKO [NUP] lang, Nigeria
NUQUINI alt for NUKUINI [NUC]
NURA dial of DAGARA, NORTHERN [DGI]
NURALDA alt for ADYNYAMATHANHA [ADT]
NURISTANI alt for KATI [BSH]
NURO alt for ANUAK [ANU]
NURPUR SADRI dial of SADRI, ORAON [SDR]
NURRA alt for NORRA [NOR]
NURU alt for OGEA [ERI]
NURUMA alt for NUNI, NORTHERN [NUV]
NURUMA alt for NUNI, SOUTHERN [NNW]
NUSA LAUT [NUL] lang, Indonesia (Maluku)
NUSA PENIDA dial of BALI [BZC]
NUSA TADON alt for ADONARA [ADA]
NUSA TADON alt for ILE APE [ILA]
NUSALAUT alt for NUSA LAUT [NUL]
NU-SAN alt for NUSAN dial of XOO [NMN]
NUSAN dial of XOO [NMN]

NUSARI alt for WABO [WBB]
NUSU [NUF] lang, China
NUTKA alt for NOOTKA [NOO]
NUUCHAHNULTH alt for NOOTKA [NOO]
NUWAKOT alt for TRISULI dial of TAMANG,
    WESTERN [TDG]
NUXAÁ MIXTECO alt for MIXTECO, NOCHIXTLÁN
    SURESTE [MXY]
NUXALK alt for BELLA COOLA [BEL]
NUYOO dial of MIXTECO, TLAXIACO, SUROESTE
    [MEH]
NUYOO MIXTECO alt for MIXTECO, TLAXIACO,
    SUROESTE [MEH]
NUZHEN alt for JURCHEN [JUC]
NVHAL dial of TANNA, SOUTHWEST [NWI]
NWA alt for WAN [WAN]
N'WALUNGU dial of TSONGA [TSO]
NWE alt for NGWE [NWE]
NWESI dial of BEMBA [BEM]
NYA CERIYA dial of LONGUDA [LNU]
NYA DELE dial of LONGUDA [LNU]
NYA GUYUWA dial of LONGUDA [LNU]
NYA GWANDA dial of LONGUDA [LNU]
NYA TARIYA dial of LONGUDA [LNU]
NYAAJA dial of MUMUYE [MUL]
NYAANA alt for TOMA dial of SAMO, SOUTHERN
    [SBD]
NYAANGA dial of KUNYI [KNF]
NYABADAN dial of MABA [MDE]
NYABASI dial of KURIA [KUJ]
NYABEA alt for TIBEA [NGY]
NYABO dial of GREBO, SOUTHERN [GRJ]
NYABOA alt for NYABWA [NIA]
NYABUNGU alt for TEMBO [TBT]
NYABWA [NIA] lang, Côte d'Ivoire
NYABWA dial of NYABWA [NIA]
NYABWA-NYÉDÉBWA alt for NYABWA [NIA]
NYADA alt for NYINDROU [LID]
NYADU [NXJ] lang, Indonesia (Kalimantan)
NYAG DII alt for DII [DUR]
NYAGALI alt for NJAKALI dial of DYAABUGAY [DYY]
NYAGO dial of GODIE [GOD]
NYAH HEUNY alt for NYAHEUN [NEV]
NYAH KUR alt for NYAHKUR [CBN]
NYAHEUN [NEV] lang, Laos
NYAHKUR [CBN] lang, Thailand
NYAHÖN alt for NYAHEUN [NEV]
NYAI dial of KALANGA [KCK]
NYAK dial of GHALE, NORTHERN [GHH]
NYAKALI alt for NJAKALI dial of DYAABUGAY [DYY]
NYAKISISA dial of HAYA [HAY]
NYAKU dial of BILA [BIP]
NYAKUR alt for NYAHKUR [CBN]
NYAKUSA alt for NYAKYUSA-NGONDE [NYY]
NYAKWAI dial of ACHOLI [ACO]
NYAKYAK alt for KYAK [BKA]
NYAKYUSA dial of NYAKYUSA-NGONDE [NYY]
NYAKYUSA-NGONDE [NYY] lang, Tanzania; also
    in Malawi
NYALA dial of DAJU, DAR FUR [DAJ]
NYALA, EAST [NLE] lang, Kenya

NYALA-B alt for WEST NYALA dial of LUYIA [LUY]
NYALA-LAGOWA alt for DAJU, DAR FUR [DAJ]
NYÂLAYU [YLY] lang, New Caledonia
NYALI [NLJ] lang, DRC
NYALI-KILO alt for NYALI [NLJ]
NYAM [NMI] lang, Nigeria
NYAMAL [NLY] lang, Australia
NYAMBARA alt for NYANGBARA dial of BARI [BFA]
NYAMBE dial of GITONGA [TOH]
NYAMBO [NYM] lang, Tanzania
NYAMBOLO alt for NYAM [NMI]
NYAMEL alt for NYAMAL [NLY]
NYAMKAT alt for KINNAURI, BHOTI [NES]
"NYAMNYAM" pejorative alt for SUGA [SGI]
NYAMNYAM alt for NIMBARI [NMR]
NYAM-NYAM DU MAYO-KEBI alt for NIMBARI
    [NMR]
NYAMSKAD alt for KINNAURI, BHOTI [NES]
NYAMTAM dial of BASAA [BAA]
NYAMUKA dial of MANYIKA [MXC]
NYAMUSA dial of NYAMUSA-MOLO [NYO]
NYAMUSA-MOLO [NYO] lang, Sudan
NYAMWANGA alt for MWANGA [MWN]
NYAMWESI alt for NYAMWEZI [NYZ]
NYAMWEZI [NYZ] lang, Tanzania
NYAMZAX alt for LANGAS dial of POLCI [POL]
NYAN WIYAU alt for WAJA [WJA]
NYANDANG alt for YENDANG [YEN]
NYANDUNG dial of KWANJA [KNP]
NYANEKA [NYK] lang, Angola
NYANG alt for DENYA [ANV]
NYANG alt for KENYANG [KEN]
NYANG alt for NHANG [NHA]
NYANG alt for TUIC dial of DINKA, SOUTH-
    WESTERN [DIK]
NYANGA [NYA] lang, DRC
NYANGALA alt for EKISONGOORA dial of NANDI
    [NNB]
NYANGA-LI [NYC] lang, DRC
NYANGANYATJARA alt for NGAANYATJARRA
    [NTJ]
NYANGATOM [NNJ] lang, Ethiopia
NYANGBARA dial of BARI [BFA]
NYANGBO [NYB] lang, Ghana
NYANGEYA alt for NYANG'I [NYP]
NYANGGA [NNY] lang, Australia
NYANGGA alt for WIRANGU [WIW]
NYANG'I [NYP] lang, Uganda
NYANGIA alt for NYANG'I [NYP]
NYANGIYA alt for NYANG'I [NYP]
NYANGO alt for IRIGWE [IRI]
NYANG'ORI alt for TERIK dial of KALENJIN [KLN]
NYANGUMARDA alt for NYANGUMARTA [NNA]
NYANGUMARTA [NNA] lang, Australia
NYANGUMATA alt for NYANGUMARTA [NNA]
NYANGWARA alt for NYANGBARA dial of BARI
    [BFA]
NYANI dial of NDUMU [NMD]
NYANJA [NYJ] lang, Malawi; also in Botswana,
    Mozambique, Tanzania, Zambia, Zimbabwe
NYANJA dial of NYANJA [NYJ]

NYANJANG dial of KWANJA [KNP]
NYANKOLE alt for NYANKORE [NYN]
NYANKORE [NYN] lang, Uganda
NYANOUN dial of GREBO, GBOLOO [GEC]
NYANYEMBE dial of NYAMWEZI [NYZ]
NYAO alt for AWYI [AUW]
NYARAFOLO-NIAFOLO alt for SENOUFO,
    NYARAFOLO [SEV]
NYARI alt for NYALI [NLJ]
NYARINGA dial of CHWABO [CHW]
NYARO dial of KO [FUJ]
NYARONG alt for ATUENCE [ATF]
NYARUENG alt for NYARWENG dial of DINKA,
    SOUTHEASTERN [DIN]
NYARWENG dial of DINKA, SOUTHEASTERN
    [DIN]
NYASA alt for MANDA [MGS]
NYASA alt for MPOTO [MPA]
NYASA dial of NYANJA [NYJ]
NYASUNDA dial of KWANJA [KNP]
NYATSO alt for KPAN [KPK]
NYATURU [RIM] lang, Tanzania
NYATWE dial of MANYIKA [MXC]
NYAURA dial of IATMUL [IAN]
NYAW [NYW] lang, Thailand
NYAWAYGI [NYT] lang, Australia
NYE dial of SHOO-MINDA-NYE [BCV]
NYEDEBWA dial of NYABWA [NIA]
NYEFU alt for NYEPU dial of BARI [BFA]
NYEKU dial of TABARU [TBY]
NYEKYOSA alt for NYAKYUSA-NGONDE [NYY]
NYEL alt for AGEER dial of DINKA, NORTH-
    EASTERN [DIP]
NYELE alt for BANDA-NDÉLÉ [BFL]
NYEM alt for NDJEM dial of KOONZIME [NJE]
NYEMATHI alt for NYIMATLI dial of TERA [TER]
NYEMBA [NBA] lang, Angola; also in Namibia,
    Zambia
NYEMBOMBO alt for SEMULU dial of ZIMBA [ZMB]
NYEN alt for NJEN [MEN]
NYENEBO dial of GREBO, CENTRAL [GRV]
NYENGATO alt for NHENGATU [YRL]
NYENGATÚ alt for NHENGATU [YRL]
NYENGO [NYE] lang, Angola
NYENGO dial of SIMAA [SIE]
NYENKHA [NEH] lang, Bhutan
NYEO dial of WE SOUTHERN [GXX]
NYEPO alt for NYEPU dial of BARI [BFA]
NYEPU dial of BARI [BFA]
NYERI alt for NORTHERN GIKUYU dial of GIKUYU
    [KIU]
NYESHANG alt for MANANGBA [NMM]
NYEU [NYL] lang, Thailand
NYI alt for YI, SICHUAN [III]
NYI alt for YI, YUNNAN [NOS]
NYI dial of LAHU [LAH]
NYIDU alt for ETKYWAN [ICH]
NYIGINA [NYH] lang, Australia
NYIHA [NIH] lang, Tanzania; also in Zambia
NYIKA alt for GIRYAMA [NYF]
NYIKA alt for NYIHA [NIH]

NYIKINA alt for NYIGINA [NYH]
NYIKOBE alt for YUKUBEN [YBL]
NYIKUBEN alt for YUKUBEN [YBL]
NYIKYUSA alt for NYAKYUSA-NGONDE [NYY]
NYILAMBA alt for NILAMBA [NIM]
NYILEM alt for NIELLIM [NIE]
NYIMA alt for AMA [NYI]
NYIMA alt for KAMO [KCQ]
NYIMAN alt for AMA [NYI]
NYIMANG alt for AMA [NYI]
NYIMATALI alt for NYIMATLI dial of TERA [TER]
NYIMATLI dial of TERA [TER]
NYINAGBI dial of BAKWE [BAK]
NYINDROU [LID] lang, Papua New Guinea
NYINDU [NYG] lang, DRC
NYINGWOM alt for KAM [KDX]
NYININY dial of JARU [DDJ]
NYISAM alt for KPASAM [PBN]
NYISHANG alt for MANANGBA [NMM]
NYISHI alt for NISI [DAP]
NYISING alt for NISI [DAP]
NYISUNGGU alt for TANIMBILI [TBE]
NYIWOM alt for KAM [KDX]
NYIXA alt for NYIHA [NIH]
NYIYABALI alt for NIJADALI [NAD]
NYKY alt for MARU [MHX]
NYMYLAN alt for KORYAK [KPY]
NYNORSK alt for NORWEGIAN, NYNORSK
    [NRN]
NYO alt for NYAW [NYW]
NYOK dial of DII [DUR]
NYOKING alt for NYONG [MUO]
NYOKON alt for NI NYO'O dial of TUNEN [BAZ]
NYOLE [NUJ] lang, Uganda
NYOLE alt for NYORE [NYD]
NYOLGE alt for NJALGULGULE [NJL]
NYONG [MUO] lang, Cameroon; also in Nigeria
NYONG alt for YONG [YNO]
NYONGNEPA alt for NYONG [MUO]
NYONGWE alt for NYUNGWE [NYU]
NYONYO alt for KPAN [KPK]
NYOOLE alt for NYORE [NYD]
NYOOLNE alt for NJALGULGULE [NJL]
NYO'ON alt for NI NYO'O dial of TUNEN [BAZ]
NYORE [NYD] lang, Kenya
NYORO [NYR] lang, Uganda
NYORO alt for HEMA [NIX]
NYORO alt for ORUNYORO dial of NYORO [NYR]
NYOS dial of LAIMBUE [LMX]
NYOXOLONKAN dial of MANINKAKAN, WESTERN
    [MLQ]
NYOYAKA alt for YAKA [AXK]
NYPHO alt for NYEPU dial of BARI [BFA]
NYUA alt for YUAGA [NUA]
NYUANGIA alt for NYANG'I [NYP]
NYULE alt for NYOLE [NUJ]
NYULI alt for NYOLE [NUJ]
NYULNYUL [NYV] lang, Australia
NYULNYUL alt for DYABERDYABER [DYB]
NYUNGA [NYS] lang, Australia
NYUNGAR alt for NYUNGA [NYS]

NYUNGWE [NYU] lang, Mozambique
NYUONG dial of NUER [NUS]
NYUT'CHI alt for NIUTAJI dial of IOWA-OTO [IOW]
NYUWAR alt for NYA GWANDA dial of LONGUDA
    [LNU]
NZAK MBAI alt for NZAKAMBAY [NZY]
NZAK MBAY alt for NZAKAMBAY [NZY]
NZAKA MBAY alt for NZAKAMBAY [NZY]
NZAKAMBAY [NZY] lang, Chad; also in Cameroon
NZAKAMBAY dial of NZAKAMBAY [NZY]
NZAKARA [NZK] lang, CAR; also in DRC
NZAKMBAY alt for NZAKAMBAY [NZY]
NZAMBA dial of KONGO [KON]
NZANGI alt for NZANYI [NJA]
NZANYI [NJA] lang, Nigeria; also in Cameroon
NZARE alt for NAMA dial of MBEMBE, TIGON [NZA]
NZARE dial of MBEMBE, TIGON [NZA]
NZARI dial of YAKA [AXK]
NZEBI alt for NJEBI [NZB]
NZEMA [NZE] lang, Ghana; also in Côte d'Ivoire
NZIKINI alt for KATEGHE dial of TEKE, NORTHERN
    [TEG]
NZIKINI alt for NJININGI dial of TEKE, NORTHERN
    [TEG]
NZIKU alt for NJINJU dial of TEKE, CENTRAL [TEC]
NZIMA alt for NZEMA [NZE]
NZIME alt for KOONZIME [NJE]
NZIME dial of KOONZIME [NJE]
NZINZIHU alt for NJINJU dial of TEKE, CENTRAL
    [TEC]
NZONG alt for NAGA, RENGMA [NRE]
NZONYU alt for AZONYU dial of NAGA, RENGMA
    [NRE]
NZONYU alt for NAGA, RENGMA [NRE]
NZUHWI alt for DUHWA [KBZ]
ÖMIE [AOM] lang, Papua New Guinea
ÖNGE [OON] lang, India
ÖÖLD alt for OLOT dial of KALMYK-OIRAT [KGZ]
ÖZBEK alt for UZBEK, NORTHERN [UZB]
O dial of KUY [KDT]
O DU alt for O'DU [TYH]
OA alt for TATUYO [TAV]
OAD alt for OD [ODK]
OARTE alt for CHIN, PAITE [PCK]
OAS dial of BICOLANO, ALBAY [BHK]
OASIS BERBER alt for SIWI [SIZ]
OAXACA alt for AMUZGO, SAN PEDRO AMUZGOS
    [AZG]
OAYANA alt for WAYANA [WAY]
OBA alt for AMBAE, EAST [OMB]
OBAMBA alt for MBAMA [MBM]
OBA-MIWAMON dial of YAQAY [JAQ]
OBANG alt for EJAGHAM [ETU]
OBANG dial of BEFANG [BBY]
OBANLIKU [BZY] lang, Nigeria
OBE dial of PUTUKWAM [AFE]
OBELEBHA alt for OBILEBHA dial of LOGO [LOG]
OBERSORBISCH alt for SORBIAN, UPPER [WEN]
OBERWART dial of HUNGARIAN [HNG]
OBGWO alt for NINGGERUM [NXR]
OBI alt for AKOYE [MIW]

OBI alt for VUKUTU dial of LESE [LES]
OBIAN alt for UBIAN dial of SAMA, SOUTHERN [SIT]
OBIAN dial of SAMA, SOUTHERN [SIT]
OBILEBA alt for OBILEBHA dial of LOGO [LOG]
OBILEBHA dial of LOGO [LOG]
OBINI alt for ABINI dial of AGWAGWUNE [YAY]
OBIO dial of IKWERE [IKW]
OBISPEÑO [OBI] lang, USA
OBIYE alt for MVUBA [MXH]
OBLO [OBL] lang, Cameroon
OBO BAGOBO alt for MANOBO, OBO [OBO]
OBOGOLO alt for OGBOGOLO [OGG]
OBOGWITAI alt for OBOKUITAI [AFZ]
OBOKUITAI [AFZ] lang, Indonesia (Irian Jaya)
OBOLO [ANN] lang, Nigeria
OBONYA alt for DENYA [ANV]
OBOSO dial of PUTUKWAM [AFE]
'OBOYGUNO dial of BIDIYO [BID]
OBULOM [OBU] lang, Nigeria
OBWALD dial of ALEMANNISCH [GSW]
OCAINA [OCA] lang, Peru; also in Colombia
OCCITAN alt for AUVERGNAT [AUV]
OCCITAN alt for GASCON [GSC]
OCCITAN alt for LANGUEDOCIEN [LNC]
OCCITAN alt for LIMOUSIN [LMS]
OCCITANI alt for LANGUEDOCIEN [LNC]
OCEBE alt for ICEVE-MACI [BEC]
OCEVE alt for ICEVE-MACI [BEC]
OCHEBE alt for ICEVE-MACI [BEC]
OCHEKWU alt for AGATU [AGC]
OCHEVE alt for ICEVE-MACI [BEC]
OCHIHERERO alt for HERERO [HER]
OCHIKWANYAMA alt for KWANYAMA [KUY]
OCHINDONGA alt for NDONGA [NDG]
OCOTEPEC dial of ZOQUE, COPAINALA [ZOC]
OCOTEPEC MIXE dial of MIXE, JUQUILA [MXQ]
OCOTEPEC MIXTEC alt for MIXTECO, OCOTEPEC [MIE]
OCOTLÁN ZAPOTEC alt for ZAPOTECO, OCOTLÁN OESTE [ZAC]
OCUILTEC alt for MATLATZINCA, ATZINGO [OCU]
OCUILTECO alt for MATLATZINCA, ATZINGO [OCU]
OD [ODK] lang, Pakistan
ODAJE dial of MBE [MFO]
ODASA alt for AIMARA dial of KUNAMA [KUM]
ODAWA alt for OTTAWA [OTW]
ODERAGO alt for KOKODA [QKW]
ODERIGA alt for MBEMBE, CROSS RIVER [MFN]
ODIENNEKA dial of JULA, ODIENNE [JOD]
ODIENNEKAKAN alt for JULA, ODIENNÉ [JOD]
ODIM alt for ADIM dial of AGWAGWUNE [YAY]
ODIO alt for MAKARAKA dial of ZANDE [ZAN]
ODIONGANON dial of BANTOANON [BNO]
ODKI alt for OD [ODK]
ODODEI alt for ODOODEE [KKC]
ODODOP alt for KOROP [KRP]
ODOODEE [KKC] lang, Papua New Guinea
ODRI alt for ORIYA [ORY]
ODRUM alt for ORIYA [ORY]

O'DU [TYH] lang, Viet Nam; also in Laos
ODUAL [ODU] lang, Nigeria
ODUAL alt for SAKATA [SAT]
ODUL alt for YUKAGHIR, NORTHERN [YKG]
ODUL alt for YUKAGHIR, SOUTHERN [YUX]
ODUT [ODA] lang, Nigeria
ODYALOMBITO alt for LOMBI [LMI]
ODZILA alt for OJILA dial of AVOKAYA [AVU]
ODZILIWA alt for OJILA dial of AVOKAYA [AVU]
OEHOENDOENI alt for DAMAL [UHN]
OELOEMANDA alt for ULUMANDA' [ULM]
OEMA alt for UMA [PPK]
OENALE alt for OENALE-DELHA dial of ROTE, WESTERN [ROW]
OENALE-DELHA dial of ROTE, WESTERN [ROW]
OEPAO alt for ROTE-TIMUR dial of ROTE [ROT]
OERINGOEP alt for DANI, WESTERN [DNW]
OEWAKU alt for ARUTANI [ATX]
OFAGBE dial of ISOKO [ISO]
OFAIÉ-XAVANTE alt for OPAYÉ [OPY]
OFAYÉ alt for OPAYÉ [OPY]
OFERIKPE dial of MBEMBE, CROSS RIVER [MFN]
OFO [OFO] lang, USA
OFOMBONGA dial of MBEMBE, CROSS RIVER [MFN]
OFONOKPAN dial of MBEMBE, CROSS RIVER [MFN]
OFOR alt for LUBILA [KCC]
OFUNOBWAM alt for MBEMBE, CROSS RIVER [MFN]
OFUTOP alt for EFUTOP [OFU]
OGA alt for MUKAH-OYA dial of MELANAU [MEL]
OGA BAKUNG dial of KENYAH, BAKUNG [BOC]
OGADEN dial of SOMALI [SOM]
OGAMARU alt for OGAMBI dial of LOGO [LOG]
OGAMBI dial of LOGO [LOG]
OGAMI alt for MIYAKO-JIMA dial of MIYAKO [MVI]
OGAN [OGN] lang, Indonesia (Sumatra)
OGAR dial of ONIN [ONI]
OGAXPA alt for QUAPAW [QUA]
OGBA alt for OGBAH [OGC]
OGBAH [OGC] lang, Nigeria
OGBAKIRI dial of IKWERE [IKW]
OGBE IJO dial of IZON [IJC]
OGBIA [OGB] lang, Nigeria
OGBINYA alt for OGBIA [OGB]
OGBOGOLO [OGG] lang, Nigeria
OGBOIN dial of IZON [IJC]
OGBOJA alt for NKEM dial of NKEM-NKUM [ISI]
OGBRONUAGUM [OGU] lang, Nigeria
OGBRU dial of ABIDJI [ABI]
ÒGE dial of ARIGIDI [AKK]
OGEA [ERI] lang, Papua New Guinea
OGHUZ dial of UDI [UDI]
OGHUZ dial of UZBEK, NORTHERN [UZB]
OGIT alt for KONDA [KND]
OGLIASTRINO dial of SARDINIAN, CAMPIDANESE [SRO]
OGODA alt for BONI [BOB]
OGOI alt for BAAN [BVJ]
OGOJA alt for NKEM dial of NKEM-NKUM [ISI]

OGOKO dial of MADI, SOUTHERN [QMD]
OGONDYAN alt for OYKANGAND dial of KUNJEN [KJN]
OGONI alt for KHANA [KEH]
OGORI alt for OKO dial of OKO-ENI-OSAYEN [OKS]
OGORI-MAGONGO alt for OKO-ENI-OSAYEN [OKS]
OGOWE dial of FANG [FNG]
OGUA dial of ENGENNI [ENN]
OGUGU dial of IGALA [IGL]
OGULAGHA dial of IZON [IJC]
OGUTA dial of IGBO [IGR]
OHANA-ONYEN alt for OKOM dial of MBEMBE, CROSS RIVER [MFN]
OHLONE alt for COSTANOAN, NORTHERN [CST]
OHLONE alt for COSTANOAN, SOUTHERN [CSS]
OHUHU dial of IGBO [IGR]
OHUHU alt for UMUAHIA dial of IGBO [IGR]
OHUMONO alt for KOHUMONO [BCS]
OI alt for OY [OYB]
OIAKIRI dial of IZON [IJC]
OIAMPÍ alt for WAYAMPI, OIAPOQUE [OYA]
"OIAMPIPUCU" pejorative alt for WAYAMPI, AMAPARI [OYM]
OIANA alt for WAYANA [WAY]
OIBA alt for OIBAE dial of GOBASI [GOI]
OIBAE dial of GOBASI [GOI]
OIBU dial of MARIA [MDS]
OIRAT alt for KALMYK-OIRAT [KGZ]
OIRAT alt for KALMYK-OIRAT [KGZ]
OIRATA [OIA] lang, Indonesia (Maluku)
OIROT alt for ALTAI, SOUTHERN [ALT]
OIRYA alt for LOKOYA [LKY]
OIUM alt for PAPEL [PBO]
OIUMPIAN alt for WAYAMPI, OIAPOQUE [OYA]
OIYANA alt for OYANA dial of GADSUP [GAJ]
OJABOLI alt for OJHI dial of BAGHELI [BFY]
OJANJUR alt for MAJANG [MPE]
OJHA alt for OJHI dial of BAGHELI [BFY]
OJHE alt for OJHI dial of BAGHELI [BFY]
OJHI dial of BAGHELI [BFY]
OJIBWA, CENTRAL [OJC] lang, Canada
OJIBWA, EASTERN [OJG] lang, Canada
OJIBWA, NORTHWESTERN [OJB] lang, Canada
OJIBWA, SEVERN [OJS] lang, Canada
OJIBWA, WESTERN [OJI] lang, Canada
OJIBWAY alt for CHIPPEWA [CIW]
OJIBWAY alt for OJIBWA, CENTRAL [OJC]
OJIBWAY alt for OJIBWA, EASTERN [OJG]
OJIBWAY alt for OJIBWA, NORTHWESTERN [OJB]
OJIBWAY alt for OJIBWA, SEVERN [OJS]
OJIBWAY alt for OJIBWA, WESTERN [OJI]
OJIBWAY alt for OTTAWA [OTW]
OJIBWE alt for CHIPPEWA [CIW]
OJIBWE alt for OJIBWA, CENTRAL [OJC]
OJIBWE alt for OJIBWA, EASTERN [OJG]
OJIBWE alt for OJIBWA, NORTHWESTERN [OJB]
OJIBWE alt for OJIBWA, SEVERN [OJS]
OJIBWE alt for OJIBWA, WESTERN [OJI]
OJIBWE alt for OTTAWA [OTW]
OJICREE alt for OJIBWA, SEVERN [OJS]

OJIGA alt for AJIGU dial of AVOKAYA [AVU]
OJILA dial of AVOKAYA [AVU]
OJO dial of ARIGIDI [AKK]
OJOR alt for LUBILA [KCC]
OJU dial of IGEDE [IGE]
OK BARI alt for SOUTHERN MUYU dial of YONGKOM [YON]
OKA dial of BURIAT, RUSSIA [MNB]
OKA dial of IGBO [IGR]
OKAINA alt for OCAINA [OCA]
OKAK alt for FANG dial of FANG [FNG]
OKAM alt for MBEMBE, CROSS RIVER [MFN]
OKANAGAN [OKA] lang, Canada; also in USA
OKANAGAN-COLVILLE alt for OKANAGAN [OKA]
OKANAGON alt for OKANAGAN [OKA]
OKANDE alt for KANDE [KBS]
OKANISI alt for AUKAN [DJK]
OKANOGAN alt for OKANAGAN [OKA]
OKBAP dial of KETENGBAN [KIN]
OKE-AGBE alt for AFA dial of ARIGIDI [AKK]
OKE-AGBE alt for UDO dial of ARIGIDI [AKK]
OKE'BU alt for NDO [NDP]
OKE'BU dial of NDO [NDP]
OKEINA alt for YEGA dial of EWAGE-NOTU [NOU]
OKELA alt for KELA [KEL]
OKENA alt for YEGA dial of EWAGE-NOTU [NOU]
OKENE dial of EBIRA [IGB]
OKERE alt for CHEREPON [CPN]
OKHOTSK dial of EVEN [EVE]
!'O-!KHUNG alt for VASEKELA BUSHMAN [VAJ]
OKI alt for TUKI [BAG]
OKIEK [OKI] lang, Kenya
OKII alt for BOKYI [BKY]
OKINAWAN alt for OKINAWAN, CENTRAL [RYU]
OKINAWAN, CENTRAL [RYU] lang, Japan
OKI-NO-ERABU [OKN] lang, Japan
OKO alt for OKO-ENI-OSAYEN [OKS]
OKO dial of MANAGALASI [MCQ]
OKO dial of OKO-ENI-OSAYEN [OKS]
OKOBO [OKB] lang, Nigeria
OKODIA [OKD] lang, Nigeria
OKO-ENI-OSAYEN [OKS] lang, Nigeria
OKO-JUWOI [OKJ] lang, India
OKOLLO dial of MADI, SOUTHERN [QMD]
OKOLOD [KQV] lang, Malaysia (Sarawak); also in Indonesia (Kalimantan)
OKOLOD MURUT alt for OKOLOD [KQV]
OKOM dial of MBEMBE, CROSS RIVER [MFN]
OKOMA alt for OKONI dial of NATENI [NTM]
OKOMANJANG dial of BEFANG [BBY]
OKONI dial of NATENI [NTM]
OKONYONG alt for KIONG [KKM]
OKORDIA alt for OKODIA [OKD]
OKOROBI dial of NGWO [NGN]
OKOROETE dial of OBOLO [ANN]
OKOROGUNG dial of PUTUKWAM [AFE]
OKOROMANDJANG alt for OKOMANJANG dial of BEFANG [BBY]
OKOROTUNG dial of PUTUKWAM [AFE]
OKOYONG alt for KIONG [KKM]
OKPAMHERI [OPA] lang, Nigeria

OKPE [OKE] lang, Nigeria
OKPE dial of OKPE-IDESA-AKUKU [OKP]
OKPEDEN dial of ABUA [ABN]
OKPE-IDESA-AKUKU [OKP] lang, Nigeria
OKPELA dial of IVBIE NORTH-OKPELA-ARHE [ATG]
OKPELE alt for BEKWEL [BKW]
OKPELLA alt for OKPELA dial of IVBIE NORTH-OKPELA-ARHE [ATG]
OKPOGU dial of IDOMA [IDO]
OKPOTO dial of ORING [ORI]
OKRIKA alt for KIRIKE [OKR]
OKRO dial of NALI [NSS]
OKSAPMIN [OPM] lang, Papua New Guinea
OKTENAI alt for WICHÍ LHAMTÉS NOCTEN [MTP]
OKTENGBAN alt for KETENGBAN [KIN]
OKTOMBERI dial of UDI [UDI]
OKU [OKU] lang, Cameroon
OKU dial of BOKYI [BKY]
OKU-JUWOI alt for OKO-JUWOI [OKJ]
OKULOSHO dial of OKPAMHERI [OPA]
OKUNDI alt for WULA dial of BOKYI [BKY]
!O!KUNG alt for !O!UNG [OUN]
OKUNI dial of OLULUMO-IKOM [IKO]
OKURIKAN alt for AGWAGWUNE [YAY]
OKUROSHO alt for OKULOSHO dial of OKPAMHERI [OPA]
OKWASAR alt for ISIRAWA [SRL]
OLA alt for WURLA dial of NGARINYIN [UNG]
OLA dial of EVEN [EVE]
OLAL dial of AMBRYM, NORTH [MMG]
OLAM dial of MURLE [MUR]
OLANGCHUNG GOLA alt for WALUNGGE [OLA]
OLCH alt for ULCH [ULC]
OLCHA alt for ULCH [ULC]
OLCHIS alt for ULCH [ULC]
OLD BARGU alt for BARGU dial of BURIAT, CHINA [BXU]
OLD FRANKISH alt for FRANKISH [FRK]
OLD HEBREW alt for HEBREW, ANCIENT [HBO]
OLD KENTISH SIGN LANGUAGE [OKL] lang, United Kingdom
OLD KLEMTU alt for SOUTHERN TSIMSHIAN dial of TSIMSHIAN [TSI]
OLD PRUSSIAN alt for PRUSSIAN [PRG]
OLD SIRENIK alt for YUPIK, SIRENIK [YSR]
OLD TUPÍ alt for TUPINAMBÁ [TPN]
OLE dial of ISOKO [ISO]
OLE MÖNPA alt for OLEKHA [OLE]
OLEH alt for OLE dial of ISOKO [ISO]
OLEKHA [OLE] lang, Bhutan
'OLELO HAWAI'I alt for HAWAIIAN [HWI]
'OLELO HAWAI'I MAKUAHINE alt for HAWAIIAN [HWI]
OLEM alt for ANGORAM [AOG]
OLGA alt for JUMJUM [JUM]
OLGEL alt for OYKANGAND dial of KUNJEN [KJN]
OLGOL alt for OYKANGAND dial of KUNJEN [KJN]
OLI dial of DUALA [DOU]
OLIT alt for MACI dial of ICEVE-MACI [BEC]
OLIT alt for OLITI dial of ICEVE-MACI [BEC]

OLITHI alt for MACI dial of ICEVE-MACI [BEC]
OLITHI alt for OLITI dial of ICEVE-MACI [BEC]
OLITI alt for MACI dial of ICEVE-MACI [BEC]
OLITI dial of ICEVE-MACI [BEC]
OLITI-AKWAYA alt for MACI dial of ICEVE-MACI [BEC]
OLITI-AKWAYA alt for OLITI dial of ICEVE-MACI [BEC]
OLIYA alt for ORIYA [ORY]
OLKOI alt for ELKEI [ELK]
OLLAR GADABA alt for GADABA, OLLAR, POTTANGI [GDB]
OLLARI alt for GADABA, OLLAR, POTTANGI [GDB]
OLLARO alt for GADABA, OLLAR, POTTANGI [GDB]
OLO [ONG] lang, Papua New Guinea
OLODIAMA EAST dial of IZON [IJC]
OLODIAMA WEST dial of IZON [IJC]
OLOGO dial of KALULI [BCO]
OLOGUTI dial of YAGARIA [YGR]
OLOH MANGTANGAI alt for MANTANGAI dial of NGAJU [NIJ]
OLOH MENGKATIP alt for MENGKATIP dial of BAKUMPAI [BKR]
OLOIBIRI dial of OGBIA [OGB]
OLOMA [OLM] lang, Nigeria
OLOMBO alt for LOMBO [LOO]
OLOMORO dial of ISOKO [ISO]
OLONETS alt for LIVVI [OLO]
OLONETSIAN alt for LIVVI [OLO]
OLOSSU alt for RUSSIAN [RUS]
OLOT dial of KALMYK-OIRAT [KGZ]
OLOTEPEC MIXE dial of MIXE, QUETZALTEPEC [MVE]
OLOTORIT alt for OTUHO [LOT]
OLTEAN alt for OLTENIA-LESSER WALLACHIA dial of ROMANIAN [RUM]
OLTENIA-LESSER WALLACHIA dial of ROMANIAN [RUM]
OLU'BO alt for LULUBO [LUL]
OLUBOGO alt for LULUBO [LUL]
OLUBOTI alt for LULUBO [LUL]
OLUBWISI alt for TALINGA-BWISI [TLJ]
OLUCHIGA alt for CHIGA [CHG]
OLUGWERE alt for GWERE [GWR]
OLUHANGA alt for WANGA dial of LUYIA [LUY]
OLUKONJO alt for KONJO [KOO]
OLUKONZO alt for KONJO [KOO]
OLUKOOKI alt for KOOKI dial of GANDA [LAP]
OLULU dial of IPULO [ASS]
OLULUMO dial of OLULUMO-IKOM [IKO]
OLULUMO-IKOM [IKO] lang, Nigeria
OLUMBA dial of SIANE [SNP]
OLUMUILA alt for MWILA dial of NYANEKA [NYK]
OLUNCHUN alt for OROQEN [ORH]
OLUNYOLE alt for NYORE [NYD]
OLUNYORE alt for NYORE [NYD]
OLUSAMIA alt for SAAMIA dial of LUYIA [LUY]
OLUSESE alt for SESE dial of GANDA [LAP]
OLUSOGA alt for SOGA [SOG]
OLUTHIMBA alt for ZEMBA [DHM]

OLUWANGA alt for WANGA dial of LUYIA [LUY]
OLYUTOR alt for ALUTOR [ALR]
OMAGE alt for YANESHA' [AME]
OMAGUA [OMG] lang, Peru; also in Brazil
OMAGUA alt for CARIJONA [CBD]
OMAGUA-YETE alt for OMAGUA [OMG]
OMAGWNA dial of IKWERE [IKW]
OMAHA dial of OMAHA-PONCA [OMA]
OMAHA-PONCA [OMA] lang, USA
OMANI BEDAWI ARABIC alt for ARABIC, GULF
    SPOKEN [AFB]
OMANI HADARI ARABIC alt for ARABIC, OMANI
    SPOKEN [ACX]
OMATI [MGX] lang, Papua New Guinea
OMBA alt for AMBAE, EAST [OMB]
OMBALEI alt for MISIM dial of HOTE [HOT]
OMBAN dial of KETENGBAN [KIN]
OMBESSA alt for NUGUNU [YAS]
OMBO [OML] lang, DRC
OMBULE alt for CHOURASE [TSU]
OMEJES [OME] lang, Colombia
OMENE dial of SINAUGORO [SNC]
OMERELU dial of IKWERE [IKW]
OMETAY alt for DAWRO dial of GAMO-GOFA-
    DAWRO [GMO]
OMETEPEC AZTEC alt for NÁHUATL, OMETEPEC
    [NHT]
OMETO alt for WOLAYTTA [WBC]
OMI [OMI] lang, DRC
OMKOI dial of KAREN, PWO NORTHERN [PWW]
OMO alt for TIGAK [TGC]
OMOTIK [OMT] lang, Kenya
OMPA alt for TOBAKU dial of UMA [PPK]
OMUDIOGA dial of IKWERE [IKW]
OMUGO alt for TEREGO dial of LUGBARA [LUG]
OMURANO [OMU] lang, Peru
OMVANG dial of EWONDO [EWO]
OMWUNRA-TOQURA [OMW] lang, Papua New
    Guinea
OMYENE alt for GALWA dial of MYENE [MYE]
OMYENE alt for MYENE [MYE]
ONA [ONA] lang, Argentina
ONA dial of SIANE [SNP]
ONABASULU alt for ONOBASULU [ONN]
ONAGE alt for FUR [FUR]
ONANDAGA alt for ONONDAGA [ONO]
ONANK alt for WATUT, NORTH [UNA]
ONDO dial of YORUBA [YOR]
ONDOE alt for LULUBO [LUL]
ONDOUMBO alt for NDUMU [NMD]
ONDUMBO alt for NDUMU [NMD]
ONE alt for AUNALEI [AUN]
ONE dial of YASA [YKO]
ONEIDA [ONE] lang, Canada; also in USA
ONELE alt for AUNALEI [AUN]
ONESSO dial of AULUA [AUL]
ONG [OOG] lang, Laos
ONG alt for ÖNGE [OON]
ONGAMO alt for NGASA [NSG]
ONG-BE alt for LINGAO [ONB]
ONGBE alt for LINGAO [ONB]

ONGOM alt for NGOM [NRA]
'ONGOTA alt for BIRALE [BXE]
ONI alt for AUNALEI [AUN]
ONIAN alt for BASARI [BSC]
ONIN [ONI] lang, Indonesia (Irian Jaya)
ONIN BASED PIDGIN [ONX] lang, Indonesia (Irian
    Jaya)
ONITSHA dial of IGBO [IGR]
ONJAB [ONJ] lang, Papua New Guinea
ONJOB alt for ONJAB [ONJ]
ONO [ONS] lang, Papua New Guinea
ONO alt for KADAVU dial of FIJIAN [FJI]
ONO dial of WERI [WER]
ONOBASULU [ONN] lang, Papua New Guinea
ONONDAGA [ONO] lang, Canada; also in USA
ONOTSU dial of KIKAI [KZG]
ONTARIO DELAWARE alt for MUNSEE [UMU]
ONTENA alt for ONTENU [ONT]
ONTENU [ONT] lang, Papua New Guinea
ONTONG JAVA [LUN] lang, Solomon Islands
ONUA alt for UNUA [ONU]
ONYA dial of KETENGBAN [KIN]
O'ODHAM [PAP] lang, USA; also in Mexico
OOHUM alt for YUKUBEN [YBL]
OORAZHI alt for URALI [URL]
OORLAMS [OOR] lang, South Africa
OORMBUR alt for NGURMBUR [NRX]
OOSIMA alt for AMAMI-OSHIMA, NORTHERN
    [RYN]
OOST-SUMBAAS alt for KAMBERA [SMI]
OOST-VLAAMS dial of DUTCH [DUT]
O'OTHHAM alt for O'ODHAM [PAP]
OOWEKEENO dial of HEILTSUK [HEI]
OPA alt for AMBAE, WEST [NND]
OPAIÉ-SHAVANTE alt for OPAYÉ [OPY]
OPAINA dial of YAHUNA [YNU]
OPALO dial of BACAMA [BAM]
OPAMERI alt for OKPAMHERI [OPA]
OPAO [OPO] lang, Papua New Guinea
ÓPATA [OPT] lang, Mexico
OPAYÉ [OPY] lang, Brazil
OPËNO dial of ANUAK [ANU]
OPEREMOR dial of IZON [IJC]
OPIF dial of BIAK [BHW]
OPO alt for OPUUO [LGN]
OPOROMA dial of IZON [IJC]
OPOROZA dial of IZON [IJC]
OPORTO dial of PORTUGUESE SIGN LANGUAGE
    [PSR]
OPO-SHITA alt for OPUUO [LGN]
OPOTAI alt for APUTAI [APX]
OPROU alt for AIZI, APROUMU [AHP]
OPSELAN alt for MOKSELA [VMS]
OPUO alt for OPUUO [LGN]
OPUUO [LGN] lang, Ethiopia; also in Sudan
!ORA alt for KORANA [KQZ]
ORA dial of EMAI-IULEHA-ORA [EMA]
ORAHA alt for OROHA [ORA]
ORAK LAWOI' alt for URAK LAWOI' [URK]
ORAKAIVA alt for OROKAIVA [ORK]
ORAMBUL alt for BAYALI [BJY]

ORAMI dial of NAASIOI [NAS]
ORAN dial of ARABIC, ALGERIAN SPOKEN [ARQ]
ORANG BENUA alt for SEMANG, LOWLAND [ORB]
ORANG BENUA dial of SEMANG, LOWLAND [ORB]
ORANG BUKIT alt for BRUNEI [KXD]
ORANG BUKIT alt for KENSIU [KNS]
ORANG CAGAYAN alt for MAPUN [SJM]
ORANG GUNUNG alt for ATONI [TMR]
ORANG HULU alt for JAKUN [JAK]
ORANG KANAQ [ORN] lang, Malaysia (Peninsular)
ORANG KUALA alt for DUANO' [DUP]
ORANG LAUT alt for BAJAU, INDONESIAN [BDL]
ORANG LAUT alt for LONCONG [LCE]
ORANG LIAR alt for KENSIU [KNS]
ORANG MAMAK dial of MINANGKABAU [MPU]
ORANG NEGERI alt for NEGERI SEMBILAN MALAY [ZMI]
ORANG SELETAR [ORS] lang, Malaysia (Peninsular); also in Singapore
ORANG TANJONG OF ULU LANGAT dial of SEMAI [SEA]
ORANGE RIVER AFRIKAANS dial of AFRIKAANS [AFK]
ORANGO dial of BIDYOGO [BJG]
ORANJE-GEBERGTE alt for UNA [MTG]
ORAOAN alt for KURUX [KVN]
ORAON alt for KURUX [KVN]
ORAON alt for KURUX, NEPALI [KXL]
ORAON dial of KURUX [KVN]
ORASE alt for BUSSA [DOX]
ORAU alt for KURUX, NEPALI [KXL]
ORDOS dial of MONGOLIAN, PERIPHERAL [MVF]
ORDUBAD dial of AZERBAIJANI, NORTH [AZE]
ORECHON alt for OREJÓN [ORE]
OREDEZH dial of INGRIAN [IZH]
/OREE alt for /OREE-KHWE dial of SHUA [SHG]
/OREE-KHWE dial of SHUA [SHG]
OREGON alt for OREJÓN [ORE]
OREGU alt for DESANO [DES]
OREJÓN [ORE] lang, Peru
OREN dial of MAIWA [MTI]
ORES BOLI CHAMANG BOLI alt for KINNAURI, HARIJAN [KJO]
ORGWO alt for NINGGERUM [NXR]
ORICH alt for EVEN [EVE]
ORICHEN dial of OROCH [OAC]
ORIENTAL HEBREW dial of HEBREW [HBR]
ORIERH dial of MALFAXAL [MLX]
ORIGANAU alt for URIGINA [URG]
ORING [ORI] lang, Nigeria
ORIOMO alt for BINE [ORM]
ORIOMO alt for GIDRA [GDR]
ORISI dial of CHOROTEGA [CJR]
ORISSA alt for ORIYA [ORY]
ORIYA [ORY] lang, India; also in Bangladesh
ORIYA PROPER alt for MUGHALBANDI dial of ORIYA [ORY]
ORIYA, ADIVASI [ORT] lang, India
ORIZABA AZTEC alt for NÁHUATL, ORIZABA [NLV]
ORLEI alt for OLO [ONG]

ORLO dial of GBAYA [KRS]
ORLOW alt for DYAABUGAY [DYY]
ORLU dial of IGBO [IGR]
ORMA [ORC] lang, Kenya
ORMA dial of ORMA [ORC]
ORMU [ORZ] lang, Indonesia (Irian Jaya)
ORMUI alt for ORMURI [ORU]
ORMUR alt for ORMURI [ORU]
ORMURI [ORU] lang, Pakistan; also in Afghanistan
ORO [ORX] lang, Nigeria
ORO WARI alt for PAKAÁSNOVOS [PAV]
ORO WIN [ORW] lang, Brazil
OROC alt for OROK [OAA]
OROCH [OAC] lang, Russia (Asia)
OROCHI alt for OROCH [OAC]
OROCHON alt for OROQEN [ORH]
OROHA [ORA] lang, Solomon Islands
OROK [OAA] lang, Russia (Asia); also in Japan
OROKAIVA [ORK] lang, Papua New Guinea
OROKO WEST alt for BALUNDU-BIMA [NGO]
OROKO-EAST alt for BAKUNDU-BALUE [BDU]
OROKOLO [ORO] lang, Papua New Guinea
OROM dial of TESO [TEO]
OROMO alt for OROMO, BORANA-ARSI-GUJI [GAX]
OROMO, BORANA-ARSI-GUJI [GAX] lang, Ethiopia; also in Kenya, Somalia
OROMO, EASTERN [HAE] lang, Ethiopia
OROMO, WEST-CENTRAL [GAZ] lang, Ethiopia; also in Egypt
OROMOO alt for OROMO, WEST-CENTRAL [GAZ]
ORON alt for EBUGHU [EBG]
ORON alt for ENWAN [ENW]
ORON alt for ORO [ORX]
ORONCHON alt for OROQEN [ORH]
OROQEN [ORH] lang, China
OROSHANI alt for ROSHANI dial of SHUGHNI [SGH]
OROSHANI alt for RUSHANI dial of SHUGHNI [SGH]
OROSHOR dial of SHUGHNI [SGH]
OROSHORI alt for OROSHOR dial of SHUGHNI [SGH]
OROTINA alt for CHOROTEGA [CJR]
OROTINA alt for OROTINYA dial of CHOROTEGA [CJR]
OROTINYA dial of CHOROTEGA [CJR]
OROWE [BPK] lang, New Caledonia
ORRA alt for GIMR dial of TAMA [TMA]
ORRI alt for ORING [ORI]
ORRIN alt for ORING [ORI]
ORRINGORRIN alt for ORING [ORI]
ORUKIGA alt for CHIGA [CHG]
ORUM dial of AGWAGWUNE [YAY]
ORUMA [ORR] lang, Nigeria
ORUNDANDE alt for NANDI [NNB]
ORUNGU dial of MYENE [MYE]
ORUNYARWANDA alt for RWANDA [RUA]
ORUNYORO dial of NYORO [NYR]
ORUONE dial of SINAUGORO [SNC]
ORURO dial of QUECHUA, SOUTH BOLIVIAN [QUH]
ORUTAGWENDA dial of NYANKORE [NYN]
ORUTORO alt for TOORO [TTJ]

ORUTORO alt for TORO dial of HEMA [NIX]
ORYA [URY] lang, Indonesia (Irian Jaya)
OSA NANGA alt for TUKI [BAG]
OSAGE [OSA] lang, USA
OSANYIN alt for OSAYEN dial of OKO-ENI-OSAYEN
    [OKS]
OSATU [OST] lang, Cameroon
OSAYEN dial of OKO-ENI-OSAYEN [OKS]
OSER alt for SIAGHA-YENIMU [OSR]
OSETIN [OSE] lang, Georgia; also in Azerbaijan,
    Germany, Hungary, Kazakhstan, Russia (Asia),
    Tajikistan, Turkey (Asia), Turkmenistan, Ukraine,
    Uzbekistan
OSHIE alt for NGISHE [NSH]
OSHIE dial of NGISHE [NSH]
OSHIMA alt for AMAMI-OSHIMA, NORTHERN
    [RYN]
OSHINDONGA alt for NDONGA [NDG]
OSHOLIO alt for SHOLIO dial of TYAP [KCG]
OSIDONGA alt for NDONGA [NDG]
OSIKOM alt for BOKYI [BKY]
OSIMA alt for AMAMI-OSHIMA, NORTHERN [RYN]
OSINDONGA alt for NDONGA [NDG]
OSING [OSI] lang, Indonesia (Java and Bali)
OSLO dial of NORWEGIAN SIGN LANGUAGE
    [NSL]
OSMANLI alt for TURKISH [TRK]
OSO [OSO] lang, Cameroon
OSO MOKO dial of NAUETE [NXA]
OSOKOM dial of BOKYI [BKY]
OSOPHONG alt for OSOPONG dial of MBEMBE,
    CROSS RIVER [MFN]
OSOPONG dial of MBEMBE, CROSS RIVER [MFN]
OSOSO [OSS] lang, Nigeria
OSROBOTHNIAN dial of SWEDISH [SWD]
OSSATU alt for OSATU [OST]
OSSETE alt for OSETIN [OSE]
OSSIMA alt for EASTERN KILMERI dial of KILMERI
    [KIH]
OSSO alt for OSO [OSO]
OSTFLISCH alt for EASTPHALIAN dial of SAXON,
    LOW [SXN]
OSTFAELISCH alt for EASTPHALIAN dial of
    SAXON, LOW [SXN]
OSTFRIESISCH alt for FRISIAN, EASTERN [FRS]
OSTLANDET alt for EASTERN NORWEGIAN
    dial of NORWEGIAN, BOKMAAL [NRR]
OST-OBERDEUTSCH alt for BAVARIAN [BAR]
OSTROGOTH dial of GOTHIC [GOF]
OSTUACÁN dial of ZOQUE, COPAINALA [ZOC]
OSTUNCALCO MAM alt for MAM, SOUTHERN
    [MMS]
OSTYAK alt for KHANTY [KCA]
OSTYAK SAMOYED alt for SELKUP [SAK]
OSU dial of DANGME [DGM]
OSUKAM alt for BOKYI [BKY]
OSUM alt for UTARMBUNG [OMO]
OT BALAWAN dial of DOHOI [OTD]
OT BANU'U dial of DOHOI [OTD]
OT DANUM alt for DOHOI [OTD]
OT MURUNG 1 dial of DOHOI [OTD]

OT OLANG dial of DOHOI [OTD]
OT SIANG alt for SIANG [SYA]
OT TUHUP dial of DOHOI [OTD]
OTABHA dial of ABUA [ABN]
OTALI dial of CHEROKEE [CER]
OTANABE alt for MUNICHE [MYR]
OTANAVE alt for MUNICHE [MYR]
OTANG alt for OTANK [UTA]
OTANGA alt for OTANK [UTA]
OTANK [UTA] lang, Nigeria
OTAPHA alt for OTABHA dial of ABUA [ABN]
OTAVALO QUICHUA alt for QUICHUA, HIGHLAND,
    IMBABURA [QHO]
OTETELA alt for TETELA [TEL]
OTHAN alt for UDUK [UDU]
OTI [OTI] lang, Brazil
OTJIDHIMBA alt for ZEMBA [DHM]
OTJIHERERO alt for HERERO [HER]
OTJINGUMBI alt for NKHUMBI [KHU]
OTJIWAMBO alt for KWANYAMA [KUY]
OTJIWAMBO alt for NDONGA [NDG]
OTLALTEPEC POPOLOCA alt for POPOLOCA,
    SAN FELIPE OTLALTEPEC [POW]
OTO dial of IOWA-OTO [IOW]
OTOE alt for OTO dial of IOWA-OTO [IOW]
OTOMÍ DEL ORIENTE alt for OTOMÍ, SIERRA
    ORIENTAL [OTM]
OTOMÍ DEL VALLE DE MEZQUITAL alt for OTOMÍ,
    MEZQUITAL [OTE]
OTOMÍ, ESTADO DE MÉXICO [OTS] lang, Mexico
OTOMÍ, IXTENCO [OTA] lang, Mexico
OTOMÍ, MEZQUITAL [OTE] lang, Mexico; also in
    USA
OTOMÍ, NORTHWESTERN [OTQ] lang, Mexico
OTOMÍ, SIERRA ORIENTAL [OTM] lang, Mexico
OTOMÍ, TEMOAYA [OTT] lang, Mexico
OTOMÍ, TENANGO [OTN] lang, Mexico
OTOMÍ, TEXCATEPEC [OTX] lang, Mexico
OTOMÍ, TILAPA [OTL] lang, Mexico
OTORO [OTR] lang, Sudan
OTSHO dial of LUGBARA [LUG]
OTTAWA [OTW] lang, Canada; also in USA
OTUHO [LOT] lang, Sudan
OTUKE [OTU] lang, Brazil
OTUKWANG alt for UTUGWANG dial of
    PUTUKWAM [AFE]
OTUO alt for GHOTUO [AAA]
OTUQUE alt for OTUKE [OTU]
OTUQUI alt for OTUKE [OTU]
OTURKPO alt for IDOMA CENTRAL dial of IDOMA
    [IDO]
OTUXO alt for OTUHO [LOT]
OTVAI dial of KABOLA [KLZ]
OTWA alt for GHOTUO [AAA]
OUADDA alt for WADA dial of BANDA-MBRES
    [BQK]
OUADDAIEN alt for MABA [MDE]
OUADDAO alt for MABA [MDE]
OUALA alt for WALI [WLX]
OUALA alt for WARA [WBF]
OUAPADOUPOU dial of MOORE [MHM]

OUARA alt for WARA [WBF]
OUARGLA alt for TAGARGRENT [OUA]
OUARGLI alt for TAGARGRENT [OUA]
OUARKOYE dial of BWAMU [BOX]
OUASSA alt for WASA dial of BANDA, MID-
 SOUTHERN [BJO]
OUATCHI alt for WACI-GBE [WCI]
OUATOUROU-NIASOGONI dial of WARA [WBF]
OUAYEONE alt for WAIWAI [WAW]
OUBATCH alt for JAWE [JAZ]
OUBI alt for GLIO-OUBI [OUB]
OUBI alt for UBI [UBI]
OUBYKH alt for UBYKH [UBY]
OUEDGHIR dial of TAGARGRENT [OUA]
OUEN alt for NUMEE [KDK]
OUEN dial of NUMEE [KDK]
OUHIGUYUA dial of FULFULDE, NORTHEASTERN
 BURKINA FASO [FUH]
OUINJI-OUINJI alt for ANII [BLO]
OUJDA dial of ARABIC, MOROCCAN SPOKEN
 [ARY]
OUJIANG dial of CHINESE, WU [WUU]
OULA alt for WULA dial of PSIKYE [KVJ]
OULDEME alt for WUZLAM [UDL]
OULED DJEMMA dial of MABA [MDE]
OUMA [OUM] lang, Papua New Guinea
OUNE [OUE] lang, Papua New Guinea
!O!UNG [OUN] lang, Angola
OUNGE alt for OUNE [OUE]
OUNI alt for HONI [HOW]
OUNJI-OUNJI alt for ANII [BLO]
OUOBE alt for WÈ NORTHERN [WOB]
OUOLOF alt for WOLOF [WOL]
OUORODOUGOU alt for JULA, WORODOUGOU
 [JUD]
OURI alt for OLI dial of DUALA [DOU]
OURZA alt for HURZA dial of PELASLA [MLR]
OURZO alt for HURZA dial of PELASLA [MLR]
OUSSOUYE alt for ESULALU dial of JOLA-KASA
 [CSK]
OUTER SERAJI dial of PAHARI, KULLU [KFX]
OUTER-EASTERN TAMANG dial of TAMANG,
 EASTERN [TAJ]
OUZBEK alt for UZBEK, NORTHERN [UZB]
OUZZA alt for HURZA dial of PELASLA [MLR]
OVAMBO alt for KWANYAMA [KUY]
OVAND alt for EVANT [BZZ]
OVANDE alt for EVANT [BZZ]
OVANDO alt for EVANT [BZZ]
OVERHILL CHEROKEE alt for OTALI dial of
 CHEROKEE [CER]
OVERHILL-MIDDLE CHEROKEE dial of
 CHEROKEE [CER]
OVIEDO alt for EDO [EDO]
OVIMBUNDU alt for UMBUNDU [MNF]
OVIOBA alt for EDO [EDO]
OWA alt for SANTA ANA [STN]
OWA RAHA alt for SANTA ANA [STN]
OWA RAHA alt for SANTA ANA dial of KAHUA [AGW]
OWA RIKI alt for SANTA CATALINA dial of
 KAHUA [AGW]

OWAMBO alt for KWANYAMA [KUY]
OWAMBO alt for NDONGA [NDG]
OWE dial of ISOKO [ISO]
OWE dial of YORUBA [YOR]
OWENA alt for OWENIA [WSR]
OWENDA alt for OWENIA [WSR]
OWENIA [WSR] lang, Papua New Guinea
OWENKE alt for EVENKI [EVN]
OWERRI dial of IGBO [IGR]
OWHE alt for OWE dial of ISOKO [ISO]
OWINIGA [OWI] lang, Papua New Guinea
OWOI alt for LOKOYA [LKY]
ÒWÒN ÀFÁ alt for AFA dial of ARIGIDI [AKK]
ÒWÒN ÈSÉ alt for ESE dial of ARIGIDI [AKK]
ÒWÒN ÌGÁSÍ alt for IGASI dial of ARIGIDI [AKK]
ÒWÒN ÒGÈ alt for ÒGE dial of ARIGIDI [AKK]
ÒWÒN ÙDÒ alt for UDO dial of ARIGIDI [AKK]
OXORIOK alt for LOKOYA [LKY]
OY [OYB] lang, Laos
OYA alt for MUKAH-OYA dial of MELANAU [MEL]
OYA' alt for MUKAH-OYA dial of MELANAU
 [MEL]
OYAMPÍ alt for WAYAMPI, OIAPOQUE [OYA]
"OYAMPIPUKU" pejorative alt for WAYAMPI,
 AMAPARI [OYM]
OYANA alt for WAYANA [WAY]
OYANA dial of GADSUP [GAJ]
OYANPÍK alt for WAYAMPI, OIAPOQUE [OYA]
OYA'OYA [OYY] lang, Papua New Guinea
OYAPÍ alt for WAYAMPI, OIAPOQUE [OYA]
OYARICOULET alt for AKURIO [AKO]
OYDA [OYD] lang, Ethiopia
OYEDE dial of ISOKO [ISO]
OYIN dial of ARIGIDI [AKK]
OYKANGAND dial of KUNJEN [KJN]
OYO dial of YORUBA [YOR]
OYOKOM dial of BOKYI [BKY]
OYROT alt for ALTAI, SOUTHERN [ALT]
OYUWI alt for ADJUMANI dial of MADI [MHI]
OZA alt for OJHI dial of BAGHELI [BFY]
OZBEK alt for UZBEK, NORTHERN [UZB]
OZHA alt for OJHI dial of BAGHELI [BFY]
OZORO dial of ISOKO [ISO]
PA alt for GHOMÁLÁ' SOUTH dial of GHOMALA
 [BBJ]
PA alt for PARE [PPT]
PA DI alt for TÀY [THO]
PA HNG alt for BUNU, BAHENG [PHA]
PÀ HUNG alt for BUNU, BAHENG [PHA]
PA KEMBALOH dial of PUTOH [PUT]
PA LENG alt for MALIENG dial of MALENG
 [PKT]
PA NGNG alt for BUNU, BAHENG [PHA]
PA OH alt for KAREN, PA'O [BLK]
PA THEN alt for BUNU, BAHENG [PHA]
PÀ THEN alt for BUNU, BAHENG [PHA]
PA'A [AFA] lang, Nigeria
PAACI alt for PAICÎ [PRI]
PÁÁFANG [PFA] lang, Micronesia
PAAMA [PMA] lang, Vanuatu
PAAMA-LOPEVI alt for PAAMA [PMA]

PAAMESE alt for PAAMA [PMA]
PA'AN dial of KAREN, PWO EASTERN [KJP]
PAANG alt for PANG dial of LUSHAI [LSH]
PA'AWA alt for PA'A [AFA]
PABIR alt for BURA-PABIR [BUR]
PABRA alt for PAO [PPA]
PACAAS-NOVOS alt for PAKAÁSNOVOS [PAV]
PACAHANOVO alt for PAKAÁSNOVOS [PAV]
PACAHUARA [PCP] lang, Bolivia
PACAWARA alt for PACAHUARA [PCP]
PACCHMI alt for BILASPURI [KFS]
PACHAGAN dial of PASHAYI, NORTHWEST [GLH]
PACHIEN alt for SAAROA [SXR]
PACHITEA QUECHUA alt for QUECHUA,
    HUÁNUCO, PANAO [QEM]
PACIFIC YUPIK alt for YUPIK, PACIFIC GULF [EMS]
PACO alt for PACOH [PAC]
PACOH [PAC] lang, Viet Nam; also in Laos
PACU alt for IPEKA-TAPUIA [PAJ]
PADA alt for ROTE-TENGAH dial of ROTE [ROT]
PADAM dial of ADI [ADI]
PADAMO-ORINOCO alt for WESTERN YANOMAMI
    dial of YANOMAMO [GUU]
PADANG alt for DINKA, NORTHEASTERN [DIP]
PADANG alt for MINANGKABAU [MPU]
PADANG dial of MAMUJU [MQX]
PADANG dial of TALIABU [TLV]
PADARI dial of BHADRAWAHI [BHD]
PADAS dial of LUNDAYEH [LND]
PADAUNG alt for KAREN, GEKO [GHK]
PADAUNG alt for KAREN, PADAUNG [PDU]
PADEE dial of NOON [SNF]
PA'DISUA dial of SAHU [SUX]
PADOA dial of BIAK [BHW]
PADOE [PDO] lang, Indonesia (Sulawesi)
PADOÉ alt for PADOE [PDO]
PADOGHO alt for KPATOGO dial of KAANSA [GNA]
PADOGO alt for PARKWA [PBI]
PADOKWA alt for PARKWA [PBI]
PADORHO alt for KPATOGO dial of KAANSA [GNA]
PADORO alt for KPATOGO dial of KAANSA [GNA]
PADUKO alt for PARKWA [PBI]
PADVI dial of MAWCHI [MKE]
PÁEZ [PBB] lang, Colombia
PAGABETE alt for PAGIBETE [PAG]
PAGAI dial of MENTAWAI [MWV]
PAGANYAW alt for KAREN, S'GAW [KSW]
PAGBAHAN dial of IRAYA [IRY]
PAGCAH alt for AMIS [ALV]
PAGEI alt for PAGI [PGI]
PAGI [PGI] lang, Papua New Guinea
PAGIBETE [PAG] lang, DRC
PAGO alt for PAGU [PGU]
PAGOE alt for PAGU [PGU]
PAGU [PGU] lang, Indonesia (Maluku)
PAGU alt for KAREN, PAKU [KPP]
PAGU dial of PAGU [PGU]
PAGUANA dial of OMAGUA [OMG]
PAGUARA alt for PAGUANA dial of OMAGUA [OMG]
PAHADI alt for ANARYA dial of BHILI [BHB]
PAHARI alt for JAUNSARI [JNS]

PAHARI alt for PAHARI, KULLU [KFX]
PAHARI alt for PANGWALI [PGG]
PAHARI alt for SINDHUPALCHOK PAHRI dial of
    NEWARI [NEW]
PAHARI dial of PAHARI-POTWARI [PHR]
PAHARI BHARMAURI alt for GADDI [GBK]
PAHARI GARHWALI alt for GARHWALI [GBM]
PAHARI KULLU alt for PAHARI, KULLU [KFX]
PAHARI MANDIYALI alt for MANDEALI [MJL]
PAHARI, KULLU [KFX] lang, India
PAHARI, MAHASU [BFZ] lang, India
PAHARIA alt for KUMARBHAG PAHARIA [KMJ]
PAHARIA alt for MAL PAHARIA [MKB]
PAHARIA dial of SANTALI [SNT]
PAHARI-PALPA alt for PALPA [PLP]
PAHARI-POTWARI [PHR] lang, Pakistan
PAHARIYA alt for KUMARBHAG PAHARIA [KMJ]
PAHAVAI alt for BOHUAI [RAK]
PAHENBAQUEBO dial of CAPANAHUA [KAQ]
PAHENG alt for BUNU, BAHENG [PHA]
PAHI [LGT] lang, Papua New Guinea
PAHI dial of PACOH [PAC]
PAHLAVANI [PHV] lang, Afghanistan
PA-HNG alt for BUNU, BAHENG [PHA]
PAHOUIN alt for FANG [FNG]
PAHOUN alt for FANG [FNG]
PAHRI alt for SINDHUPALCHOK PAHRI dial of
    NEWARI [NEW]
PAHU dial of TUNJUNG [TJG]
PAHU' dial of DUSUN, CENTRAL [DTP]
PAÏ dial of LAKA [LAM]
PAI [PAI] lang, Nigeria
PAI alt for BAI [PIQ]
PAI alt for MALA [PED]
PAI alt for PAI TAVYTERA [PTA]
PAI alt for PEI [PPQ]
PAI dial of SOTHO, NORTHERN [SRT]
PAI LISU dial of LISU [LIS]
PAI TAVYTERA [PTA] lang, Paraguay
PAIAWA alt for GUHU-SAMANE [GHS]
PAICHIEN alt for SAAROA [SXR]
PAICÎ [PRI] lang, New Caledonia
PAIDIA alt for PARDHI [PCL]
PAIEM alt for FYAM [PYM]
PAI'I' alt for LÜ [KHB]
PAI-I alt for LÜ [KHB]
PAIKO dial of GBARI [GBY]
PAILELANG alt for KAFOA [KPU]
PAIMI alt for NAGA, AO [NJO]
PAINARA alt for LEVUKA [LVU]
PAIPAI [PPI] lang, Mexico
PAIQUIZE alt for MUNDURUKÚ [MYU]
PAITAN alt for TOMBONUWO [TXA]
PAITE alt for CHIN, PAITE [PCK]
PAITER alt for SURUÍ [SRU]
PAITHE alt for CHIN, PAITE [PCK]
PAIUAN alt for PAIWAN [PWN]
PAIUTE, NORTHERN [PAO] lang, USA
PAIWA alt for GAPAPAIWA [PWG]
PAIWAN [PWN] lang, Taiwan
PAIYAGE alt for SILIMO [WUL]

PAI-YI alt for LÜ [KHB]
PAJADE alt for BADJARA [PBP]
PAJADINCA alt for BADJARA [PBP]
PAJADINKA alt for BADJARA [PBP]
PAJAPAN NÁHUAT alt for NÁHUATL, ISTMO-PAJAPAN [NHP]
PAJO alt for BALAESAN [BLS]
PAJOKUMBUH dial of MINANGKABAU [MPU]
PAJONAL alt for ASHÉNINCA PAJONAL [CJO]
PAJULU alt for PÖJULU dial of BARI [BFA]
PAJUNGU alt for BAYUNGU [BXJ]
PAK dial of PAK-TONG [PKG]
PAK dial of VATRATA [VLR]
PAK TAI alt for THAI, SOUTHERN [SOU]
PAK THAI alt for THAI, SOUTHERN [SOU]
"PAKA" pejorative alt for MEIYARI dial of NIKSEK [GBE]
PAKA dial of NZANYI [NJA]
PAKAANOVA alt for PAKAÁSNOVOS [PAV]
PAKAANOVAS alt for PAKAÁSNOVOS [PAV]
PAKAÁSNOVOS [PAV] lang, Brazil
PAKADJI alt for KUUKU-YA'U [QKL]
PAKANG alt for POKANGÁ [POK]
PAKANHA [PKN] lang, Australia
PAKARA alt for CARA [CFD]
PAKARLA alt for BANGGARLA [BJB]
PAKATAN alt for BUKITAN [BKN]
PAKATAN dial of MALENG [PKT]
PAKAWA alt for DA'A dial of KAILI, DAA [KZF]
PAKEWA alt for TONTEMBOAN [TNT]
PAKHTO alt for PASHTO, NORTHERN [PBU]
PAKHTOO alt for PASHTO, NORTHERN [PBU]
PAKHTOO alt for PASHTO, SOUTHERN [PBT]
PAKHTU alt for PASHTO, NORTHERN [PBU]
PAKHTU alt for PASHTO, SOUTHERN [PBT]
PAKI alt for BAKI [BKI]
PAKIA-SIDERONSI dial of NAASIOI [NAS]
PAKISTAN SIGN LANGUAGE [PKS] lang, Pakistan
PAKKAU dial of BAMBAM [PTU]
PAKOT alt for PÖKOOT [PKO]
PAKPAK alt for BATAK DAIRI [BTD]
PAKPAK DAIRI alt for BATAK DAIRI [BTD]
PAKSE dial of LAO [NOL]
PAKTAY alt for THAI, SOUTHERN [SOU]
PAK-TONG [PKG] lang, Papua New Guinea
PAKTU alt for PASHTO, NORTHERN [PBU]
PAKTU alt for PASHTO, SOUTHERN [PBT]
PAKU [PKU] lang, Indonesia (Kalimantan)
PAKU alt for KAREN, PAKU [KPP]
PAKUM alt for KWAKUM [KWU]
PAKU-TAPUYA alt for IPEKA-TAPUIA [PAJ]
PAL KURUMBA alt for KURUMBA, ALU [QKA]
PALA alt for BELA [BEQ]
PALA alt for PA'A [AFA]
PALA dial of PATPATAR [GFK]
PALA'AU alt for BAJAU LAUT dial of SAMA, SOUTHERN [SIT]
PALACHI alt for PALAKHI dial of KAREN, SGAW [KSW]
PALAI alt for PALÚ dial of MOCHENO [QMO]

PALAKA alt for SENOUFO, PALAKA [PLR]
PALAKHI dial of KAREN, SGAW [KSW]
PALAKKA alt for BONE dial of BUGIS [BPR]
PALAMATA alt for PALUMATA [PMC]
PALAMUL [PLX] lang, Indonesia (Irian Jaya)
PALAN dial of KORYAK [KPY]
PALANAN DUMAGAT dial of PARANAN [AGP]
PALANAN VALLEY AGTA alt for PALANAN DUMAGAT dial of PARANAN [AGP]
PALANAN VALLEY DUMAGAT alt for PALANAN DUMAGAT dial of PARANAN [AGP]
PALANENYO alt for PARANAN [AGP]
PALANI alt for PALIYAN [PCF]
PALANSKIJ dial of ALUTOR [ALR]
PALARA alt for SENOUFO, PALAKA [PLR]
PALASI dial of SHINA, KOHISTANI [PLK]
PALASI-KOHISTANI alt for SHINA, KOHISTANI [PLK]
PALATA alt for FULFULDE, ADAMAWA [FUB]
PALATTAE alt for SINJAI dial of BUGIS [BPR]
PALAU alt for PALAUAN [PLU]
PALAU dial of BRAO [BRB]
PALAU dial of LAVE [BRB]
PALAUAN [PLU] lang, Palau; also in Guam
PALAUAN-CALAVITE dial of IRAYA [IRY]
PALAUI ISLAND dial of AGTA, DUPANINAN [DUO]
PALAUI ISLAND AGTA dial of AGTA, UMIRAY DUMAGET [DUE]
PALAUNG, PALE [PCE] lang, Myanmar; also in China, Thailand
PALAUNG, RUMAI [RBB] lang, Myanmar; also in China
PALAUNG, SHWE [SWE] lang, Myanmar; also in China
PALAW dial of BURMESE [BMS]
PALAWAN alt for PALAWANO, BROOKE'S POINT [PLW]
PALAWAN BATAK alt for BATAK [BTK]
PALAWANEN alt for PALAWANO, CENTRAL [PLC]
PALAWANO, BROOKE'S POINT [PLW] lang, Philippines
PALAWANO, CENTRAL [PLC] lang, Philippines
PALAWANO, SOUTHWEST [PLV] lang, Philippines
PALAWANUN alt for PALAWANO, BROOKE'S POINT [PLW]
PALAWEÑO alt for PALAWANO, BROOKE'S POINT [PLW]
PALAWEÑO alt for PALAWANO, CENTRAL [PLC]
PALAY alt for PALAUNG, PALE [PCE]
PALAYA alt for PALIYAN [PCF]
PALAYAN alt for PALIYAN [PCF]
PALCHI alt for POLCI [POL]
PALCI alt for POLCI dial of POLCI [POL]
PALCI alt for POLCI [POL]
PALDENA alt for FULFULDE, ADAMAWA [FUB]
PALDIDA alt for FULFULDE, ADAMAWA [FUB]
PALE alt for PALAUNG, PALE [PCE]
PALEE'N dial of TAOIH, UPPER [TTH]
PALEMBANG [PLM] lang, Indonesia (Sumatra)
PALENQUE alt for PALENQUERO [PLN]
PALENQUERO [PLN] lang, Colombia

PALERMO alt for WESTERN SICILIAN dial of SICILIAN [SCN]
PALESTANIAN-JORDANIAN ARABIC alt for ARABIC, SOUTH LEVANTINE SPOKEN [AJP]
PALESTINIAN-JORDANIAN ARABIC alt for ARABIC, SOUTH LEVANTINE SPOKEN [AJP]
PALI [PLL] lang, India; also in Myanmar, Sri Lanka
PALI alt for PALYA BARELI dial of BARELI [BGD]
PALICUR alt for PALIKÚR [PAL]
PALIET dial of DINKA, SOUTHWESTERN [DIK]
PALIHA alt for BHARIA [BHA]
PALIJUR alt for PALIKÚR [PAL]
PALIK alt for APALIK [PLI]
PALIKOUR alt for PALIKÚR [PAL]
PALIKÚR [PAL] lang, Brazil; also in French Guiana
PALILI' dial of TOALA [TLZ]
PALIMBEI dial of IATMUL [IAN]
PALIN alt for EMBALOH [EMB]
PALÍN POCOMAM alt for POKOMAM, SOUTHERN [POU]
PALIOARIENE alt for IPEKA-TAPUIA [PAJ]
PALIOPING alt for PALIOUPINY dial of DINKA, SOUTHWESTERN [DIK]
PALIOUPINY dial of DINKA, SOUTHWESTERN [DIK]
PALIPO dial of GREBO, NORTHERN [GRB]
PALISUA alt for PA'DISUA dial of SAHU [SUX]
PALITIANI alt for PALITYAN dial of BULGARIAN [BLG]
PALITYAN dial of BULGARIAN [BLG]
PALIYAN [PCF] lang, India
PALIYAR alt for PALIYAN [PCF]
PALJGU alt for NIJADALI [NAD]
PALJU alt for PALYU [PLY]
PALLAKHA alt for SENOUFO, PALAKA [PLR]
PALLARESE alt for NORTHWESTERN CATALAN dial of CATALAN-VALENCIAN-BALEAR [CLN]
PALLEYAN alt for PALIYAN [PCF]
PALLIYAR alt for PALIYAN [PCF]
PALMA alt for COASTAL MAKWE dial of MAKWE [YMK]
PALMA alt for MAKWE [YMK]
PALOC alt for AGEER dial of DINKA, NORTH-EASTERN [DIP]
PALOESCH alt for KAILI, LEDO [LEW]
PALOIC alt for AGEER dial of DINKA, NORTH-EASTERN [DIP]
PALOLA alt for PHALURA [PHL]
PALONG alt for DIMBONG [DII]
PALOR [FAP] lang, Senegal
PALPA [PLP] lang, Nepal
PALPA dial of NEPALI [NEP]
PALU [PBZ] lang, Myanmar
PALU alt for KAILI, LEDO [LEW]
PALU alt for LEDO dial of KAILI, LEDO [LEW]
PALÚ dial of MOCHENO [QMO]
PALU KURUMBA alt for KURUMBA [KFI]
PALUAN [PLZ] lang, Malaysia (Sabah)
PALUAN dial of PALUAN [PLZ]
PALUE alt for PALU'E [PLE]
PALU'E [PLE] lang, Indonesia (Nusa Tenggara)

PALULA alt for PHALURA [PHL]
PALUMATA [PMC] lang, Indonesia (Maluku)
PALUQE alt for PALU'E [PLE]
PALYA BARELI dial of BARELI [BGD]
PALYU [PLY] lang, China
PAM [PMN] lang, Cameroon
PAM dial of BALUAN-PAM [BLQ]
PAMA dial of KARIPUNA [KUQ]
PAMALE alt for VAMALE [MKT]
PAMANA alt for PAMA dial of KARIPUNA [KUQ]
PAMBADEQUE alt for COCAMILLA dial of COCAMA-COCAMILLA [COD]
PAMBIA [PAM] lang, DRC
PAMBOANG dial of MANDAR [MHN]
PAMBUHAN dial of IRAYA [IRY]
PAME CENTRAL [PBS] lang, Mexico
PAME NORTE [PMQ] lang, Mexico
PAME SUR [PMZ] lang, Mexico
PAMEKASAN alt for PAMEKESAN dial of MADURA [MHJ]
PAMEKESAN dial of MADURA [MHJ]
PAMELA dial of SUDEST [TGO]
PAMENYAN alt for BAMENYAM [BCE]
PAMIWA alt for CUBEO [CUB]
PAMMARI alt for PAUMARM dial of PAUMARI [PAD]
PAMOA alt for TATUYO [TAV]
PAMONA [BCX] lang, Indonesia (Sulawesi)
PAMONA dial of PAMONA [BCX]
PAMPA alt for PUELCHE [PUE]
PAMPADEQUE alt for COCAMA-COCAMILLA [COD]
PAMPANGAN [PMP] lang, Philippines
PAMPANGO alt for PAMPANGAN [PMP]
PAMPANGUEÑO alt for PAMPANGAN [PMP]
PAMUE alt for FANG [FNG]
PAMUSA dial of FORE [FOR]
PAN alt for PANCHPARGANIA [TDB]
PAN ARU dial of DINKA, NORTHWESTERN [DIW]
PAN COUNTY alt for DIAN-QIAN dial of YI, GUIZHOU [YIG]
PAN SAWASI alt for PANCHPARGANIA [TDB]
PAN YAO alt for IU MIEN [IUM]
PANA [PNQ] lang, Burkina Faso; also in Mali
PANA [PNZ] lang, CAR; also in Cameroon, Chad, Nigeria
PANA alt for PANOBO [PNO]
PANA dial of PANA [PNZ]
PANA' alt for PHANA' [PHN]
PANA NORTH dial of PANA [PNQ]
PANA SOUTH dial of PANA [PNQ]
PANAEATI alt for MISIMA-PANEATI [MPX]
PANAGS alt for PANANG [PCR]
PANAIETI alt for MISIMA-PANEATI [MPX]
PANAKHA alt for PANANG [PCR]
PANAMA EMBERA alt for EMBERÁ, NORTHERN [EMP]
PANAMA ENGLISH CREOLE alt for PANAMANIAN CREOLE ENGLISH dial of SOUTHWESTERN CARIBBEAN CREOLE ENGLISH [JAM]
PANAMAHKA dial of SUMO TAWAHKA [SUM]

PANAMANIAN CREOLE ENGLISH dial of SOUTH-WESTERN CARIBBEAN CREOLE ENGLISH [JAM]
PANAMINT [PAR] lang, USA
PANAMINT SHOSHONE alt for PANAMINT [PAR]
PANANAG alt for PANANG [PCR]
PANANG [PCR] lang, China
PANAPANAYAN alt for PYUMA [PYU]
PANAPU dial of KAREN, SGAW [KSW]
PANARÁ alt for KREEN-AKARORE [KRE]
PANARAS alt for KUOT [KTO]
PANARE [PBH] lang, Venezuela
PANARI alt for PANARE [PBH]
PANASUAN [PSN] lang, Indonesia (Sulawesi)
PANATINANI dial of NIMOA [NMW]
PANAWINA dial of NIMOA [NMW]
PANAY alt for AKLANON [AKL]
PANAYANO alt for KINARAY-A [KRJ]
PANAYETI alt for MISIMA-PANEATI [MPX]
PANBE alt for GIMME [KMP]
PANBE alt for GOMME dial of KOMA [KMY]
PANCANA [PNP] lang, Indonesia (Sulawesi)
PANCARÉ alt for PANKARARÚ [PAZ]
PANCARU alt for PANKARARÚ [PAZ]
PANCHAL LOHAR alt for LOHAR, GADE [GDA]
PANCHALI dial of BHILI [BHB]
PANCHGAUNLE [PNL] lang, Nepal
PANCHI BRAHMAURI RAJPUT alt for GADDI [GBK]
PANCHPARGANIA [TDB] lang, India
PANCHTHAR alt for PANTHARE dial of LIMBU [LIF]
PANCHTHARE alt for PANTHARE dial of LIMBU [LIF]
PANDA alt for KOTO dial of EBIRA [IGB]
PANDAMA alt for SAKPU dial of KARANG [KZR]
PANDAN alt for BICOLANO, NORTHERN CATANDUANES [CTS]
PANDAN dial of KINARAY-A [KRJ]
PANDARAM BASHA alt for MALAPANDARAM [MJP]
PANDAU dial of PASHAYI, NORTHWEST [GLH]
PANDE [BKJ] lang, CAR
PANDE dial of PANDE [BKJ]
PANDEQUEBO alt for COCAMA-COCAMILLA [COD]
PANDEWAN dial of PALUAN [PLZ]
PANDEWAN MURUT alt for PANDEWAN dial of PALUAN [PLZ]
PANDICUTO alt for CENTRAL ARAGONESE dial of ARAGONESE [AXX]
PANDIKERI dial of MADI [MHI]
PANDJIMA alt for PANYTYIMA [PNW]
PANDONG dial of SUI [SWI]
PANEATE alt for MISIMA-PANEATI [MPX]
PANEROA alt for BARASANA [BSN]
PANEROA alt for MACUNA [MYY]
PANEYATE alt for MISIMA-PANEATI [MPX]
PANG dial of LUSHAI [LSH]
PANG PANG dial of ETON [ETN]
PANGA alt for PIANGA dial of BUSHOONG [BUF]
PANGA dial of MONGO-NKUNDU [MOM]
PANGAL dial of MEITEI [MNR]
PANGAN alt for JEHAI [JHI]

PANGASINAN [PNG] lang, Philippines
PANGGAR dial of KELON [KYO]
PANGHSE alt for HO dial of CHINESE, MANDARIN [CHN]
PANGI alt for KINYAMUNSANGE dial of LEGA-SHABUNDA [LEA]
PANGI alt for PANGWALI [PGG]
PANGINEY alt for ZORÓ dial of GAVIAO DO JIPARANA [GVO]
PANGKAJENE alt for PANGKEP dial of BUGIS [BPR]
PANGKALA alt for BANGGARLA [BJB]
PANGKEP dial of BUGIS [BPR]
PANGKHU alt for PANKHU [PKH]
PANGKUMU alt for REREP [PGK]
PANGKUMU BAY alt for REREP [PGK]
PANGSENG [PAN] lang, Nigeria
PANGSENG dial of PANGSENG [PAN]
PANGSOIA-DOLATOK dial of SIRAIYA [FOS]
PANGTSAH alt for AMIS [ALV]
PANGU alt for PONGU [PON]
PANGWA [PBR] lang, Tanzania
PANGWALI [PGG] lang, India
PANGWALI PAHARI alt for PANGWALI [PGG]
PANGWE alt for MYENE [MYE]
PANI alt for PANA [PNZ]
PANI alt for PAPE [NDU]
PANIA alt for PANIYA [PCG]
PANIDURIA alt for NAGA, NOCTE [NJB]
PANIKA alt for MIRGAN [QMK]
PANIKITA alt for PANIQUITA dial of PAEZ [PBB]
PANIM [PNR] lang, Papua New Guinea
PANINGESEN alt for MESE dial of TUNEN [BAZ]
PANIQUITA dial of PAEZ [PBB]
PANIXTLAHUACA CHATINO dial of CHATINO, SIERRA OCCIDENTAL [CTP]
PANIYA [PCG] lang, India
PANIYAN alt for PANIYA [PCG]
PANJABI PROPER dial of PANJABI, EASTERN [PNJ]
PANJABI, EASTERN [PNJ] lang, India; also in Bangladesh, Canada, Fiji, Kenya, Malaysia, Mauritius, Singapore, UAE, United Kingdom, USA
PANJABI, MIRPUR [PMU] lang, India; also in United Kingdom
PANJABI, WESTERN [PNB] lang, Pakistan; also in Afghanistan, Canada, India, UAE, United Kingdom, USA
PANJIMA alt for PANYTYIMA [PNW]
PANJIRI YERAVA alt for RAVULA [YEA]
PANKA alt for MIRGAN [QMK]
PANKALLA alt for BANGGARLA [BJB]
PANKARARÁ alt for PANKARAÚR [PAZ]
PANKARARÉ [PAX] lang, Brazil
PANKARARÚ [PAZ] lang, Brazil
PANKARAVU alt for PANKARARÚ [PAZ]
PANKARÉ alt for PANKARARÉ [PAX]
PANKARORU alt for PANKARARÚ [PAZ]
PANKARÚ alt for PANKARARÚ [PAZ]
PANKHO alt for PANKHU [PKH]

PANKHU [PKH] lang, India; also in Bangladesh, Myanmar
PANKO alt for PANKHU [PKH]
PANNEI [PNC] lang, Indonesia (Sulawesi)
PANO alt for PANOBO [PNO]
PANOBO [PNO] lang, Peru
PANON alt for PAPE [NDU]
PA'NON alt for PAPE [NDU]
PANSO alt for LAMNSO' [NSO]
PANTASMAS alt for MATAGALPA [MTN]
PANTERA dial of NAFAANRA [NFR]
PANTERA-FANTERA alt for NAFAANRA [NFR]
PANTESCO dial of SICILIAN [SCN]
PANTHA alt for HO dial of CHINESE, MANDARIN [CHN]
PANTHARE dial of LIMBU [LIF]
PANTHAREY alt for PANTHARE dial of LIMBU [LIF]
PANTHARE-YANGGROKKE-CHAUBISE-CHAR KHOLE alt for PANTHARE dial of LIMBU [LIF]
PANTHE alt for HO dial of CHINESE, MANDARIN [CHN]
PANTJANA alt for PANCANA [PNP]
PANYA alt for MAK [PBL]
PANYA dial of MAK [PBL]
PANYAH alt for PANIYA [PCG]
PANYAM alt for MAK [PBL]
PANYAM dial of MWAGHAVUL [SUR]
PANYJIMA alt for PANYTYIMA [PNW]
PANYTYIMA [PNW] lang, Australia
PAO [PPA] lang, India
PA'O alt for KAREN, PA'O [BLK]
PA-O alt for KAREN, PA'O [BLK]
PA-O dial of YAMPHE [YMA]
PAOAN alt for BONAN [PEH]
PAOMATA dial of NAGA, MAO [NBI]
PAONGAN alt for BONAN [PEH]
PAPABUCO alt for ZAPOTECO, ELOTEPEC [ZTE]
PAPABUCO alt for ZAPOTECO, TEXMELUCAN [ZPZ]
PAPABUCO alt for ZAPOTECO, ZANIZA [ZPW]
PAPADI dial of LUNDAYEH [LND]
"PAPAGO" pejorative alt for TOHONO O'ODAM dial of OODHAM [PAP]
PAPAGO-PIMA alt for O'ODHAM [PAP]
PAPAKENE dial of BUANG, MAPOS [BZH]
PAPAPANA [PAA] lang, Papua New Guinea
PAPAR [DPP] lang, Malaysia (Sabah)
PAPAR dial of BAJAU, WEST COAST [BDR]
PAPAR KADAZAN alt for KADAZAN, COASTAL [KZJ]
PAPARA dial of SENOUFO, CEBAARA [SEF]
PAPASENA [PAS] lang, Indonesia (Irian Jaya)
PAPAVÔ [PPV] lang, Brazil
PAPE [NDU] lang, Cameroon
PAPEI alt for PAPEL [PBO]
PAPEL [PBO] lang, Guinea-Bissau; also in Guinea
PAPERYN alt for GUGUBERA [KKP]
PAPI [PPE] lang, Papua New Guinea
PAPIA alt for BABA [BBW]
PAPIA KRISTANG alt for MALACCAN CREOLE PORTUGUESE [MCM]

PAPIAM alt for PAPIAMENTU [PAE]
PAPIAMEN alt for PAPIAMENTU [PAE]
PAPIAMENTO alt for PAPIAMENTU [PAE]
PAPIAMENTOE alt for PAPIAMENTU [PAE]
PAPIAMENTU [PAE] lang, Netherlands Antilles; also in Aruba, Netherlands, Puerto Rico, U.S. Virgin Islands
PAPITALAI [PAT] lang, Papua New Guinea
PAPOLA alt for PAPORA [PPU]
PAPORA [PPU] lang, Taiwan
PAPUAN HIRI MOTU dial of MOTU, HIRI [POM]
PAPUMA [PPM] lang, Indonesia (Irian Jaya)
PARA alt for NAGA, KHIAMNIUNGAN [NKY]
PARA alt for PARAWEN [PRW]
PARABHI dial of KONKANI [KNK]
PARACHI [PRC] lang, Afghanistan
PARADI alt for PARDHI [PCL]
PARAENE alt for YAVITERO [YVT]
PARAGUAYAN TOBA alt for EMOK [EMO]
PARAHUJANO alt for PARAUJANO [PBG]
PARAHURI alt for YANOMÁMI [WCA]
PARAJA alt for DURUWA [PCI]
PARAJHI alt for BODO PARJA [BDV]
PARAJHI alt for DURUWA [PCI]
PARAKANÃ [PAK] lang, Brazil
PARAKANÂN alt for PARAKANÃ [PAK]
PARAKATÊJÊ alt for GAVIÃO, PARÁ [GAY]
PARAKUYO alt for KWAVI [CKG]
PARALI dial of NACHERING [NCD]
PARAMACCAN dial of AUKAN [DJK]
PARAN alt for TAROKO [TRV]
PARANÁ KAINGANG dial of KAINGANG [KGP]
PARANAN [AGP] lang, Philippines
PARANAPURA alt for CHAYAHUITA [CBT]
PARANAUAT alt for PARANAWÁT [PAF]
PARANAWÁT [PAF] lang, Brazil
PARATA dial of TUAMOTUAN [PMT]
PARAUJANO [PBG] lang, Venezuela
PARAUK [PRK] lang, Myanmar; also in China
PARAWEN [PRW] lang, Papua New Guinea
PARAZHGHAN dial of PASHAYI, NORTHWEST [GLH]
PARB alt for IAUGA dial of NAMBU [NCM]
PARBATIYA alt for NEPALI [NEP]
PARDESI dial of AWADHI [AWD]
PARDHAN [PCH] lang, India
PARDHI [PCL] lang, India
PARDHI dial of BHILI [BHB]
PARE [PPT] lang, Papua New Guinea
PARE alt for ASU [ASA]
PARE alt for PEERE [KUT]
PAREC dial of KATE [KMG]
PARECÍS [PAB] lang, Brazil
PAREKWA alt for PARKWA [PBI]
PAREN dial of KORYAK [KPY]
PAREN dial of NAGA, ZEME [NZM]
PARENG alt for PARENGA [PCJ]
PARENGA [PCJ] lang, India
PARENGA PARJA alt for PARENGA [PCJ]
PARENGI alt for PARENGA [PCJ]
PARENJI alt for PARENGA [PCJ]

PARE-PARE alt for BARRU dial of BUGIS [BPR]
PARESÍ alt for PARECÍS [PAB]
PARESSÍ alt for PARECÍS [PAB]
PARET dial of LAMOGAI [LMG]
PARI alt for EMBALOH [EMB]
PARI alt for MUNDURUKÚ [MYU]
PÄRI [LKR] lang, Sudan
PARIA alt for PARDHI [PCL]
PARIANA alt for OMAGUA [OMG]
PARIGI alt for TARA dial of KAILI, LEDO [LEW]
PARIKALA dial of TAMIL [TCV]
PARIKALA dial of YERUKULA [YEU]
PARIMA alt for EASTERN YANOMAMI dial of
    YANOMAMO [GUU]
PARINTINTÍN dial of TENHARIM [PAH]
PARIPAO dial of LENGO [LGR]
PARJA alt for BODO PARJA [BDV]
PARJHI alt for BODO PARJA [BDV]
PARJHI alt for DURUWA [PCI]
PARJI alt for BODO PARJA [BDV]
PARJI alt for DURUWA [PCI]
PARKARI alt for KOLI, PARKARI [KVX]
PARKWA [PBI] lang, Cameroon
PARLARE alt for POLARI [PLD]
PARLATA TRENTINA alt for NONES dial of LADIN
    [LLD]
PARNKALA alt for BANGGARLA [BJB]
PARNKALLA alt for BANGGARLA [BJB]
PAROCANA alt for PARAKANÃ [PAK]
PAROJA alt for BODO PARJA [BDV]
PAROLE DES BANA alt for BANA [BCW]
PARQUENAHUA alt for YORA [MTS]
PARSEE alt for PARSI [PRP]
PARSEE-DARI alt for PARSI-DARI [PRD]
PARSI [PRP] lang, India; also in Pakistan, United
    Kingdom, USA
PARSI alt for FARSI, EASTERN [PRS]
PARSI alt for FARSI, WESTERN [PES]
PARSI alt for MAL PAHARIA [MKB]
PARSI dial of GUJARATI [GJR]
PARSI-DARI [PRD] lang, Iran; also in Afghanistan
PARSIWAN dial of FARSI, EASTERN [PRS]
PARTE alt for CHIN, PAITE [PCK]
PARUA alt for KAYABÍ [KYZ]
PARUCUTU alt for HIXKARYÁNA [HIX]
PARUCUTU alt for KATAWIAN dial of WAIWAI
    [WAW]
PARUKOTA alt for WAIWAI [WAW]
PARUKOTO-CHARUMA alt for HIXKARYÁNA [HIX]
PARUKUTU alt for KATAWIAN dial of WAIWAI
    [WAW]
PARUN alt for PRASUNI [PRN]
PARVARI alt for MAHARI dial of KONKANI [KNK]
PARYA [PAQ] lang, Tajikistan; also in Afghanistan,
    Uzbekistan
PASAALE alt for SISAALA, PASAALE [SIG]
PASAALI dial of SISAALA, PASAALE [SIG]
PASAN alt for RATAHAN [RTH]
PASANGKAYU dial of BUGIS [BPR]
PASAR MALAY alt for BAZAAR MALAY dial of
    MALAY [MLI]

PASAR MALAY alt for MALAY, SABAH [MSI]
PASCUENSE alt for RAPA NUI [PBA]
PASE dial of ACEH [ATJ]
PASEMAH [PSE] lang, Indonesia (Sumatra)
PASHAGAR dial of PASHAYI, NORTHWEST [GLH]
PASHAI alt for PASHAYI, SOUTHEAST [DRA]
PASHAYI, NORTHEAST [AEE] lang, Afghanistan
PASHAYI, NORTHWEST [GLH] lang, Afghanistan
PASHAYI, SOUTHEAST [DRA] lang, Afghanistan
PASHAYI, SOUTHWEST [PSH] lang, Afghanistan
PASHCHIMI dial of KUMAUNI [KFY]
PASHTO, CENTRAL [PST] lang, Pakistan
PASHTO, NORTHERN [PBU] lang, Pakistan; also
    in Afghanistan, India, UAE, United Kingdom
PASHTO, SOUTHERN [PBT] lang, Afghanistan;
    also in Iran, Pakistan, Tajikistan, UAE, United
    Kingdom
PASHTU alt for PASHTO, NORTHERN [PBU]
PASHTU alt for PASHTO, SOUTHERN [PBT]
PASI [PSI] lang, Papua New Guinea
PASI dial of MONGONDOW [MOG]
PASIR alt for MELAYU PASAR dial of MALAY [MLI]
PASIR dial of LAWANGAN [LBX]
PASIR MALAY alt for BAZAAR MALAY dial of
    MALAY [MLI]
PASISIR dial of JAVANESE [JAN]
PASISMANUA alt for KAULONG [PSS]
PASOOM dial of TAOIH, UPPER [TTH]
PASPATIAN dial of ROMANI, BALKAN [RMN]
PASS VALLEY alt for YALI, PASS VALLEY [YAC]
PASS VALLEY dial of YALI, PASS VALLEY [YAC]
PASSAM alt for KPASAM [PBN]
PASSAMAQUODDY dial of MALECITE-
    PASSAMAQUODDY [MAC]
PASSTOO alt for PASHTO, NORTHERN [PBU]
PASTAZA QUICHUA alt for QUICHUA, PASTAZA,
    NORTHERN [QLB]
PASUMA alt for KEWA, WEST [KEW]
PASWAM alt for MUTUM [MCC]
PATAGONIAN WELSH dial of WELSH [WLS]
PATAKAI alt for NUAULU, NORTH [NNI]
PATAKAI alt for NUAULU, SOUTH [NXL]
PATAMONA [PBC] lang, Guyana
PATANI [PTN] lang, Indonesia (Maluku)
PATANI alt for GAMADIA dial of GUJARATI [GJR]
PATANI alt for KABO dial of IZON [IJC]
PATAPORI alt for PEERE [KUT]
PATARA dial of SENOUFO, CEBAARA [SEF]
PATASHÓ alt for PATAXÓ-HÃHAÃI [PTH]
PATAXI alt for PATAXÓ-HÃHAÃI [PTH]
PATASIWA ALFOEREN alt for ALUNE [ALP]
PATAXÓ-HÃHAÃI [PTH] lang, Brazil
PATAXÓ-HÃHÃHÃE alt for PATAXÓ-HÃHAÃI [PTH]
PATE dial of SWAHILI [SWA]
PATELIA alt for BHILORI [BQI]
PATENG alt for BUNU, BAHENG [PHA]
PATEP [PTP] lang, Papua New Guinea
PATHEE alt for HO dial of CHINESE, MANDARIN
    [CHN]
PATI alt for PAICÎ [PRI]
PATIDARI alt for GAMADIA dial of GUJARATI [GJR]

PATIMITHERI alt for YANAMAM dial of YANOMAMI [WCA]
PATIMUNI alt for BAHAM [BDW]
PATIPI dial of ONIN [ONI]
PATLA-CHICONTLA TOTONAC alt for TOTONACA, PATLA-CHICONTLA [TOT]
PATNI alt for PATTANI [LAE]
PATNULI alt for SAURASHTRA [SAZ]
PATNULI alt for STANDARD GUJARATI dial of GUJARATI [GJR]
PATO TAPUIA alt for IPEKA-TAPUIA [PAJ]
PATOÉ VALDOTEN alt for VALLE D'AOSTA dial of FRANCO-PROVENCAL [FRA]
PATOIS alt for DOMINICA CREOLE FRENCH dial of LESSER ANTILLEAN CREOLE FRENCH [DOM]
PATOIS alt for FRANCO-PROVENÇAL [FRA]
PATOIS alt for FRENCH GUIANESE CREOLE FRENCH [FRE]
PATOIS alt for GRENADA CREOLE FRENCH dial of LESSER ANTILLEAN CREOLE FRENCH [DOM]
PATOIS alt for GUADELOUPE CREOLE FRENCH dial of LESSER ANTILLEAN CREOLE FRENCH [DOM]
PATOIS alt for JAMAICAN CREOLE ENGLISH dial of SOUTHWESTERN CARIBBEAN CREOLE ENGLISH [JAM]
PATOIS alt for KRIO [KRI]
PATOIS alt for MARTINIQUE CREOLE FRENCH dial of LESSER ANTILLEAN CREOLE FRENCH [DOM]
PATOIS alt for ST. LUCIA CREOLE FRENCH dial of LESSER ANTILLEAN CREOLE FRENCH [DOM]
PATOIS alt for TAYO [CKS]
PATOIS alt for TRINIDADIAN CREOLE FRENCH dial of LESSER ANTILLEAN CREOLE FRENCH [DOM]
PATOIS DE ST-LOUIS alt for TAYO [CKS]
PATOOL dial of GULA IRO [GLJ]
PATO-TAPUYA alt for IPEKA-TAPUIA [PAJ]
PATOXÓ alt for PATAXÓ-HÃHAÃI [PTH]
PATPARI alt for PATPATAR [GFK]
PATPATAR [GFK] lang, Papua New Guinea
PATPATAR dial of PATPATAR [GFK]
PATRAK alt for RAJKOTI dial of KALAMI [GWC]
PATRA-SAARA alt for JUANG [JUN]
PATSOKA alt for YURUTI [YUI]
PATTA' BINUANG alt for PATTAE' dial of MAMASA [MQJ]
PATTAE dial of BAMBAM [PTU]
PATTAE' dial of MAMASA [MQJ]
PATTAN alt for INDUS dial of KOHISTANI, INDUS [MVY]
PATTANI [LAE] lang, India
PATTANI alt for PATTANI [LAE]
PATTAPU BHASHA dial of TAMIL [TCV]
PATTINJO dial of ENREKANG [PTT]
PATU alt for KHOWAR [KHW]
PATUA alt for JUANG [JUN]

PATUÉS alt for ARAGONESE [AXX]
PATVI dial of MALVI [MUP]
PATWA alt for DOMINICA CREOLE FRENCH dial of LESSER ANTILLEAN CREOLE FRENCH [DOM]
PATWA alt for FRENCH GUIANESE CREOLE FRENCH [FRE]
PATWA alt for GRENADA CREOLE FRENCH dial of LESSER ANTILLEAN CREOLE FRENCH [DOM]
PATWA alt for GUADELOUPE CREOLE FRENCH dial of LESSER ANTILLEAN CREOLE FRENCH [DOM]
PATWA alt for JAMAICAN CREOLE ENGLISH dial of SOUTHWESTERN CARIBBEAN CREOLE ENGLISH [JAM]
PATWA alt for MARTINIQUE CREOLE FRENCH dial of LESSER ANTILLEAN CREOLE FRENCH [DOM]
PATWA alt for ST. LUCIA CREOLE FRENCH dial of LESSER ANTILLEAN CREOLE FRENCH [DOM]
PATWIN dial of WINTU [WIT]
PA-U alt for KAREN, PA'O [BLK]
PAU CERNE alt for PAUSERNA [PSM]
PAU THIN alt for NHANG [NHA]
PAUHUT alt for BOMPOKA dial of TERESSA [TEF]
PAUINI dial of JAMAMADI [JAA]
PAULOHI [PLH] lang, Indonesia (Maluku)
PAUMA alt for PAAMA [PMA]
PAUMARÍ [PAD] lang, Brazil
PAUMARM dial of PAUMARI [PAD]
PAUMEI alt for NAGA, POUMEI [PMX]
PA'UMOTU alt for TUAMOTUAN [PMT]
PAUNANGIS dial of EFATE, NORTH [LLP]
PAUPE alt for PAPI [PPE]
PAURI alt for BARELI [BGD]
PAUSERNA [PSM] lang, Bolivia
PAUSERNA-GUARASUGWÉ alt for PAUSERNA [PSM]
PAUWI alt for YOKE [YKI]
PAVAIA alt for PAWAIA [PWA]
PAVIOTSO alt for PAIUTE, NORTHERN [PAO]
PAWAIA [PWA] lang, Papua New Guinea
PAWANA alt for MAQUIRITARI [MCH]
PAWANG alt for HORPA [ERO]
PAWARI alt for BARELI [BGD]
PAWARI dial of BUNDELI [BNS]
PAWATÉ alt for PARANAWÉT [PAF]
PAWDAWKWA alt for PARKWA [PBI]
PAWIXI alt for PAWIYANA dial of KAXUIANA [KBB]
PAWIYANA dial of KAXUIANA [KBB]
PAWNEE [PAW] lang, USA
PAWRI alt for BARELI [BGD]
PAWRI dial of BHILI [BHB]
PAXALA alt for VAGLA [VAG]
PAY alt for MALA [PED]
PAY alt for PAYI dial of OLO [ONG]
PAYA alt for PECH [PAY]
PAYAGUA alt for OREJÓN [ORE]
PAYAP alt for THAI, NORTHERN [NOD]

PAYA-PUCURO alt for KUNA, BORDER [KUA]
PAYA-PUCURO KUNA alt for KUNA, BORDER
  [KUA]
PAYI dial of OLO [ONG]
PAYNAMAR [PMR] lang, Papua New Guinea
PAYOWAN alt for PAIWAN [PWN]
PAYUALIENE alt for IPEKA-TAPUIA [PAJ]
PAYULIENE alt for IPEKA-TAPUIA [PAJ]
PAYUNGU alt for BAYUNGU [BXJ]
PAZANDE alt for ZANDE [ZAN]
PAZEH [PZH] lang, Taiwan
PAZEH dial of PAZEH [PZH]
PAZEHE alt for PAZEH [PZH]
PAZEH-KAHABU alt for PAZEH [PZH]
PAZEND alt for AVESTAN [AVS]
PAZEX alt for PAZEH [PZH]
PAZZEHE alt for PAZEH [PZH]
PBHARYA alt for PARYA [PAQ]
PCHCKNYA alt for KAREN, S'GAW [KSW]
PE alt for BAIMA [BQH]
PE dial of MUSEY [MSE]
PE MIAO alt for HMONG DAW [MWW]
PEAR [PCB] lang, Cambodia
PEAWA dial of GIDRA [GDR]
PE-BAE alt for BAY dial of ENETS [ENE]
PECH [PAY] lang, Honduras
PECIXE alt for YU dial of MANDJAK [MFV]
PECOK alt for PETJO [PEY]
PEDI alt for SOTHO, NORTHERN [SRT]
PEDI dial of KGALAGADI [XKV]
PEDIR alt for PIDIE dial of ACEH [ATJ]
PEDRA BRANCA alt for SABUJÁ dial of KARIRI-
  XOCO [KZW]
PEEKIT alt for NOOHALIT dial of YUPIK, CENTRAL
  SIBERIAN [ESS]
PEER alt for PEERE [KUT]
PEER MUURE dial of PEERE [KUT]
PEERE [KUT] lang, Cameroon; also in Nigeria
PEEWA alt for PEWA dial of KRAHN, WESTERN
  [KRW]
PEGU dial of MON [MNW]
PEGUAN alt for MON [MNW]
PEGULLO-BURA alt for YIDINY [YII]
PEH MIAO alt for HMONG DAW [MWW]
PE-HOLOM-GAMÉ dial of MUSEY [MSE]
PEHUENCHE dial of MAPUDUNGUN [ARU]
PEI [PPQ] lang, Papua New Guinea
PEINAN alt for SOUTHERN AMIS dial of AMIS [ALV]
PEKAL [PEL] lang, Indonesia (Sumatra)
PEKAVA alt for DA'A dial of KAILI, DAA [KZF]
PEKAWA alt for DA'A dial of KAILI, DAA [KZF]
PEKHI alt for UBYKH [UBY]
PEKUREHUA alt for NAPU [NAP]
PELA alt for BELA [BEQ]
PELA dial of BURA-PABIR [BUR]
PELADO alt for PANOBO [PNO]
PELAM alt for PYUMA [PYU]
PELASLA [MLR] lang, Cameroon
PELASLA alt for MAYO-PLATA dial of PELASLA
  [MLR]
PELAU dial of ONTONG JAVA [LUN]

PELAUW dial of HARUKU [HRK]
PELE dial of PELE-ATA [ATA]
PELE-ATA [ATA] lang, Papua New Guinea
PELEATA alt for PELE-ATA [ATA]
PELENDE [PPP] lang, DRC
PELIMPO alt for PINYIN dial of PINYIN [PNY]
PELIPOWAI alt for BOHUAI [RAK]
PELMUNG dial of KULUNG [KLE]
PELTA HAY alt for FULFULDE, ADAMAWA [FUB]
PELU alt for BOLU dial of GEJI [GEZ]
PELUAN alt for PALUAN dial of PALUAN [PLZ]
PELYM alt for WESTERN VOGUL dial of MANSI
  [MNS]
PEM alt for FYAM [PYM]
PEMBA alt for YANTILI dial of FIPA [FIP]
PEMBA dial of SWAHILI [SWA]
PEMON [AOC] lang, Venezuela; also in Brazil,
  Guyana
PEMON alt for ARECUNA dial of PEMON [AOC]
PEMONG alt for PEMON [AOC]
PEN dial of GULAY [GVL]
PEN TI LOLO alt for LAQUA [LAQ]
PEÑABLANCA dial of AGTA, DUPANINAN [DUO]
PENAMPANG KADAZAN alt for KADAZAN,
  COASTAL [KZJ]
PENAN APO dial of PENAN, WESTERN [PNE]
PENAN APOH dial of PENAN, EASTERN [PEZ]
PENAN GANG dial of PENAN, WESTERN [PNE]
PENAN LANYING dial of PENAN, WESTERN [PNE]
PENAN LUSONG dial of PENAN, WESTERN [PNE]
PENAN NIBONG alt for NIBONG dial of PENAN,
  WESTERN [PNE]
PENAN SILAT dial of PENAN, WESTERN [PNE]
PENAN, EASTERN [PEZ] lang, Malaysia (Sarawak);
  also in Brunei
PENAN, WESTERN [PNE] lang, Malaysia (Sarawak);
  also in Brunei
PENANG SIGN LANGUAGE [PSG] lang, Malaysia
  (Peninsular)
PENAPO dial of AMBRYM, SOUTHEAST [TVK]
PENASAK alt for PENESAK [PEN]
PENASIFU dial of BIAK [BHW]
PENCHAL [PEK] lang, Papua New Guinea
PENCHANGAN dial of TIDONG [TID]
PEND D'OREILLE dial of KALISPEL-PEND
  D'OREILLE [FLA]
PENDAU [UMS] lang, Indonesia (Sulawesi)
PENDE alt for PHENDE [PEM]
PENDIA alt for BAFUN dial of BAKAKA [BQZ]
PENESAK [PEN] lang, Indonesia (Sumatra)
PENGO [PEG] lang, India
PENGO alt for VENGO [BAV]
PENGU alt for PENGO [PEG]
PENGUIA alt for CENTRAL KONO dial of KONO
  [KNO]
PENI alt for PEN dial of GULAY [GVL]
PENIHING alt for AOHENG [PNI]
PENIN alt for TUNEN [BAZ]
PENINSULA SHERBRO dial of SHERBRO [BUN]
PENINSULAR MAYA alt for MAYA, YUCATÁN
  [YUA]

PENNSYLVANIA DUTCH alt for GERMAN, PENNSYLVANIA [PDC]

PENNSYLVANISCH alt for GERMAN, PENNSYLVANIA [PDC]

PENNSYLVANISCH DEITSCH alt for NON-AMISH PENNSYLVANIA GERMAN dial of GERMAN, PENNSYLVANIA [PDC]

PENNSYLVANISH alt for GERMAN, PENNSYLVANIA [PDC]

PENOBSCOT dial of ABNAKI, EASTERN [AAQ]

PEÑOLES alt for SANTA MARÍA PEÑOLES dial of MIXTECO, PENOLES [MIL]

PENRHYN [PNH] lang, Cook Islands

PENRHYNESE alt for PENRHYN [PNH]

PENSIANGAN MURUT dial of TAGAL MURUT [MVV]

PENSYLVANISCH DEITSCH alt for NON-AMISH PENNSYLVANIA GERMAN dial of GERMAN, PENNSYLVANIA [PDC]

PENTJANGAN alt for PENSIANGAN MURUT dial of TAGAL MURUT [MVV]

PENTLATCH [PTW] lang, Canada

PENYABUNG PUNAN alt for PUNAN dial of DAYAK, LAND [DYK]

PENYIN alt for TUNEN [BAZ]

PÉOMÉ dial of WE NORTHERN [WOB]

PEORIA dial of MIAMI [MIA]

PEPEHA alt for MINANIBAI [MCV]

PEPEL alt for PAPEL [PBO]

PEPESA dial of JWIRA-PEPESA [JWI]

PEPESA-JWIRA alt for JWIRA-PEPESA [JWI]

PEPOHOAN alt for SIRAIYA [FOS]

PEPO-HWAN alt for SIRAIYA [FOS]

PEQUOT-MOHEGAN dial of MOHEGAN-MONTAUK-NARRAGANSETT [MOF]

PERAI [WET] lang, Indonesia (Maluku)

PERAK dial of MALAY [MLI]

PERAK I dial of SEMAI [SEA]

PERAK II dial of SEMAI [SEA]

PERANAKAN alt for INDONESIAN, PERANAKAN [PEA]

PERANAKAN dial of MALAY [MLI]

PERÄPOHJA dial of FINNISH [FIN]

PERE alt for BHELE [PER]

PERE alt for GBETE dial of MBUM [MDD]

PERE alt for PEERE [KUT]

PERE alt for WOM [WOM]

PEREBA alt for WOM [WOM]

PEREMA alt for WOM [WOM]

PEREMKA alt for KUNJA [PEP]

PERENÉ alt for ASHÉNINCA PERENÉ [CPP]

PERI alt for BHELE [PER]

PERI dial of KALANGA [KCK]

PERIM dial of TUNIA [TUG]

PERMYAK alt for KOMI-PERMYAK [KOI]

PERO [PIP] lang, Nigeria

PERSIAN alt for FARSI, EASTERN [PRS]

PERSIAN alt for FARSI, WESTERN [PES]

PERSIAN AZERBAIJAN JEWISH ARAMAIC alt for LISHÁN DIDÁN [TRG]

PERSIAN SIGN LANGUAGE [PSC] lang, Iran

PERUVIAN SIGN LANGUAGE [PRL] lang, Peru

PESAA alt for NSARI [ASJ]

PESECHAM alt for NDUGA [NDX]

PESECHEM alt for NDUGA [NDX]

PESEGEM alt for NDUGA [NDX]

PESHAWAR HINDKO dial of HINDKO, SOUTHERN [HIN]

PESHAWARI alt for PESHAWAR HINDKO dial of HINDKO, SOUTHERN [HIN]

PESII alt for WUSHI [BSE]

PESISIR, SOUTHERN [PEC] lang, Indonesia (Sumatra)

PESKE alt for BVERI dial of FALI, NORTH [FLL]

PESSA alt for KPELLE, GUINEA [GKP]

PESSA alt for KPELLE, LIBERIA [KPE]

PESSY alt for KPELLE, GUINEA [GKP]

PESSY alt for KPELLE, LIBERIA [KPE]

PETA dial of NYANJA [NYJ]

PETAPA alt for TAJE [PEE]

PETAPA ZAPOTEC alt for ZAPOTECO, PETAPA [ZPE]

PETASIA dial of MORI BAWAH [XMZ]

PETATS [PEX] lang, Papua New Guinea

PETCHABUN MIAO dial of HMONG DAW [MWW]

PETEM alt for BETEN dial of KWAKUM [KWU]

PETÉN ITZÁ MAYA alt for ITZÁ [ITZ]

PETERARA dial of MAEWO, CENTRAL [MWO]

PETH alt for MALUAL dial of DINKA, SOUTH-WESTERN [DIK]

PETI alt for NYONG [MUO]

PETIT MAURESQUE alt for LINGUA FRANCA [PML]

PETJO [PEY] lang, Indonesia (Java and Bali)

PETJOH alt for PETJO [PEY]

PETLACALANCINGO MIXTECO dial of MIXTECO, ALCOZAUCA [QMX]

PETSPETS dial of TEOP [TIO]

PEU alt for KAREN, LAHTA [KVT]

PEUHL alt for PULAAR [FUC]

PEUL alt for FULFULDE, ADAMAWA [FUB]

PEUL alt for FULFULDE, BENIN-TOGO [FUE]

PEUL alt for FULFULDE, CENTRAL-EASTERN NIGER [FUQ]

PEUL alt for FULFULDE, KANO-KATSINA-BORORRO [FUV]

PEUL alt for FULFULDE, MAASINA [FUL]

PEUL alt for FULFULDE, PULAAR [FUC]

PEUL alt for FULFULDE, WESTERN NIGER [FUH]

PEUL alt for PULAAR [FUC]

PEULH alt for FULFULDE, ADAMAWA [FUB]

PEULH alt for FULFULDE, BENIN-TOGO [FUE]

PEULH alt for FULFULDE, CENTRAL-EASTERN NIGER [FUQ]

PEULH alt for FULFULDE, PULAAR [FUC]

PEULH alt for FULFULDE, WESTERN NIGER [FUH]

PEULH alt for PULAAR [FUC]

PÉVÉ [LME] lang, Chad; also in Cameroon

PEVÉ [LME] lang, Chad; also in Cameroon

PEVEKSKIJ dial of CHUKOT [CKT]

PEWA dial of KRAHN, WESTERN [KRW]

PEWANEAN alt for SEKO TENGAH [SKO]

PEWANEANG alt for SEKO TENGAH [SKO]
PFAELZISCH [PFL] lang, Germany
PFÄLZISCH alt for PFAELZISCH [PFL]
PFÄLZISCHE alt for PFAELZISCH [PFL]
PFOKOMO alt for POKOMO, LOWER [POJ]
PHADANG dial of NAGA, TANGKHUL [NMF]
PHAI [PRT] lang, Thailand; also in Laos
PHAKE [PHK] lang, India
PHAKEY alt for PHAKE [PHK]
PHAKIAL alt for PHAKE [PHK]
PHALABORWA dial of SOTHO, NORTHERN [SRT]
PHALABURWA alt for PHALABORWA dial of
   SOTHO, NORTHERN [SRT]
PHALDAKOTIYA dial of KUMAUNI [KFY]
PHALENG dial of KGALAGADI [XKV]
PHALI dial of SANGPANG [RAV]
PHALO dial of LAWA, EASTERN [LWL]
PHALOK alt for PARAUK [PRK]
PHALULO alt for PHALURA [PHL]
PHALURA [PHL] lang, Pakistan
PHANA' [PHN] lang, Laos
PHANG dial of BLANG [BLR]
PHANG dial of LAWA, EASTERN [LWL]
PHANGDUVALI alt for PHANGDUWALI [PHW]
PHANGDUWALI [PHW] lang, Nepal
PHANGDUWALI POTI alt for PHANGDUWALI
   [PHW]
PHANI dial of VENDA [VEN]
PHANONG alt for MNONG, CENTRAL [MNC]
PHANS PARDHI alt for PARDHI [PCL]
PHARASA dial of CAPPADOCIAN GREEK [CPG]
PHARI KULU alt for PAHARI, KULLU [KFX]
PHAY alt for PHAI [PRT]
PHAYAP alt for THAI, NORTHERN [NOD]
PHAYENG dial of KADO [KDV]
PHEDAPPE dial of LIMBU [LIF]
PHELA dial of GUN-GBE [GUW]
PHELONGRE dial of NAGA, SANGTAM [NSA]
PHEMBA alt for PEMBA dial of SWAHILI [SWA]
PHEN alt for TÀY [THO]
PHENDE [PEM] lang, DRC
PHERA alt for XWELA-GBE [XWE]
PHERRONGRE dial of NAGA, YIMCHUNGRU [YIM]
PHETCHABURI PWO KAREN alt for RATCHABURI
   PWO KAREN dial of KAREN, PWO WESTERN
   THAILAND [KJP]
PHI THONG LUANG alt for MLABRI [MRA]
PHILIM dial of GHALE, NORTHERN [GHH]
PHILIPPINE SIGN LANGUAGE [PSP] lang,
   Philippines
PHIMBI (PIMBI) alt for NYUNGWE [NYU]
PHLA alt for XWLA-GBE [XWL]
PHLONG alt for KAREN, PWO NORTHERN [PWW]
PHLONG SHO alt for KAREN, PWO WESTERN
   [PWO]
PHLOU alt for KAREN, PWO EASTERN [KJP]
PHLOU alt for KAREN, PWO WESTERN THAILAND
   [KJP]
PHNONG alt for MNONG, CENTRAL [MNC]
PHÖN alt for HPON [HPO]
PHOBJIKHA dial of NYENKHA [NEH]

PHOKA alt for POKA dial of TUMBUKA [TUW]
PHOKE alt for HUMLA BHOTIA [HUT]
PHOKE alt for TIBETAN [TIC]
PHOKE DOLPA alt for DOLPO [DRE]
PHOM alt for NAGA, PHOM [NPH]
PHON alt for HPON [HPO]
PHON alt for NAGA, PHOM [NPH]
PHON SOUNG alt for AHEU [THM]
PHONG alt for MNONG, CENTRAL [MNC]
PHONG alt for PONG dial of HUNG [HNU]
PHONG dial of HUNG [HNU]
PHONG-KNIANG [PNX] lang, Laos
PHORHÉPECHA alt for PURÉPECHA [TSZ]
PHOTSIMI dial of NAGA, SANGTAM [NSA]
PHOU LAO alt for LAO [NOL]
PHOUNOY alt for PHUNOI [PHO]
PHRAE alt for KAREN, PWO, PHRAE [KJT]
PHSIN alt for BIT [BGK]
PHSING alt for BIT [BGK]
PHU dial of NAR PHU [NPA]
PHU KHLA alt for PHULA [PHH]
PHU LA alt for PHULA [PHH]
PHU NOI alt for PHUNOI [PHO]
PHU THAI [PHT] lang, Thailand; also in Laos, USA,
   Viet Nam
PHU UN alt for PHUAN [PHU]
PHUAN [PHU] lang, Thailand; also in Laos
PHUANG alt for PHUONG [PHG]
PHÚC KIÉN alt for CHINESE, YUE [YUH]
PHUDAGI [PHD] lang, India
PHULA [PHH] lang, Viet Nam
PHUN alt for HPON [HPO]
PHUNOI [PHO] lang, Laos; also in Thailand, Viet
   Nam
PHUONG [PHG] lang, Viet Nam
PHUONG CATANG alt for PHUONG [PHG]
PHUTAI alt for PHU THAI [PHT]
PHUTHI dial of SOTHO, SOUTHERN [SSO]
PHUTHI dial of SWATI [SWZ]
PHUU THAI alt for PHU THAI [PHT]
PHYAP alt for THAI, NORTHERN [NOD]
PIA alt for KHOLOK [KTC]
PIA alt for PIYA-KWONCI [PIY]
PIAJAO alt for PIJAO [PIJ]
PIAMATSINA [PTR] lang, Vanuatu
PIAME [PIN] lang, Papua New Guinea
PIANGA dial of BUSHOONG [BUF]
PIANOCOTÓ dial of TRIO [TRI]
PIAPOCO [PIO] lang, Colombia; also in Venezuela
PIAROA [PID] lang, Venezuela; also in Colombia
PIAROA dial of PIAROA [PID]
PIAZZA ARMERINA alt for WESTERN LOMBARD
   dial of LOMBARD [LMO]
PICARD [PCD] lang, France; also in Belgium
PICARD dial of FRENCH [FRN]
PICHINCHA QUICHUA alt for QUICHUA, HIGH-
   LAND, CALDERÓN [QUD]
PICHIS alt for ASHÉNINCA PICHIS [CPU]
PICUNCHE dial of MAPUDUNGUN [ARU]
PICURIS dial of TIWA, NORTHERN [TAO]
PIDÁ-DJAPÁ alt for KATUKÍNA [KAV]

PIDGIN alt for HAWAI'I CREOLE ENGLISH [HAW]
PIDGIN alt for JHARWA dial of ASSAMESE [ASM]
PIDGIN alt for TOK PISIN [PDG]
PIDGIN ARABIC alt for ARABIC, SUDANESE CREOLE [PGA]
PIDGIN BANTU alt for FANAGOLO [FAO]
PIDGIN MOTU alt for MOTU, HIRI [POM]
PIDGIN SIGN LANGUAGE alt for HAWAI'I PIDGIN SIGN LANGUAGE [HPS]
PIDGIN, CAMEROON [WES] lang, Cameroon
PIDGIN, NIGERIAN [PCM] lang, Nigeria
PIDGIN, TIMOR [TVY] lang, Timor Lorosae
PIDGINGLIS alt for FERNANDO PO CREOLE ENGLISH [FPE]
PIDHA dial of LENDU [LED]
PIDIE dial of ACEH [ATJ]
PIDISOI dial of KULUNG [KLE]
PIDLIMDI dial of TERA [TER]
PIE alt for TEMIAR [TMH]
PIE dial of KRUMEN, PYE [PYE]
PIEDMONT SINTÍ dial of ROMANI, SINTE [RMO]
PIEDMONTESE alt for PIEMONTESE [PMS]
PIEGAN dial of BLACKFOOT [BLC]
PIEMONTÈIS alt for PIEMONTESE [PMS]
PIEMONTESE [PMS] lang, Italy; also in Australia, USA
PIE-PLI-MAHON-KUSE-GBLAPO-HENEKWE alt for PIE dial of KRUMEN, PYE [PYE]
PIIGA dial of UKHWEJO [UKH]
PIJAO [PIJ] lang, Colombia
PIJE [PIZ] lang, New Caledonia
PIJIN [PIS] lang, Solomon Islands
PIKANII alt for BLACKFOOT [BLC]
PIKARU alt for BIKARU [BIC]
PIKARU dial of BISORIO [BIR]
PIKI alt for FANAGOLO [FAO]
PIKIWA alt for BAINAPI [PIK]
PIL alt for WESTERN TEMNE dial of THEMNE [TEJ]
PILA [PIL] lang, Benin
PILA alt for MAIA [SKS]
PILACA alt for PILAGÁ [PLG]
PILAGÁ [PLG] lang, Argentina
PILAM alt for PYUMA [PYU]
PILAPILA alt for PILA [PIL]
PILARA alt for SENOUFO, PALAKA [PLR]
PILENI [PIV] lang, Solomon Islands
PILENI dial of PILENI [PIV]
PILHENI alt for PILENI [PIV]
PILI alt for BHELE [PER]
PILILO alt for SOLONG [AAW]
PILIPINO alt for TAGALOG [TGL]
PIMA alt for AKIMEL O'ODHAM dial of OODHAM [PAP]
PIMA BAJO, CHIHUAHUA [PMB] lang, Mexico
PIMA BAJO, SONORA [PIA] lang, Mexico
PIMBI dial of NSENGA [NSE]
PIMBWE [PIW] lang, Tanzania
PIMENC alt for NOMAANDE [LEM]
PIMI alt for PUMI, NORTHERN [PMI]
PIMI alt for PUMI, SOUTHERN [PUS]
PIMURU dial of IKOBI-MENA [MEB]

PIN alt for TRIENG [STG]
PINAI alt for PINAI-HAGAHAI [PNN]
PINAI dial of PINAI-HAGAHAI [PNN]
PINAI-HAGAHAI [PNN] lang, Papua New Guinea
PINAN dial of PYUMA [PYU]
PINAYE alt for PINAI-HAGAHAI [PNN]
PINCHE alt for TAUSHIRO [TRR]
PINCHI alt for TAUSHIRO [TRR]
PINDARE dial of GUAJAJARA [GUB]
PINDI alt for KWESE [KWS]
PINDI alt for PHENDE [PEM]
PINDIINI alt for PINTIINI [PTI]
PINDJE alt for PIJE [PIZ]
PINE alt for BINE [ORM]
PINGAS alt for BAUKAN dial of BAUKAN [BNB]
PINGELAP alt for PINGELAPESE [PIF]
PINGELAPESE [PIF] lang, Micronesia; also in Guam, USA
PINGILAPESE alt for PINGELAPESE [PIF]
PINI [PII] lang, Australia
PINIGURA [PNV] lang, Australia
PINIPEL dial of NEHAN [NSN]
PINIPIN alt for PINIPEL dial of NEHAN [NSN]
PINIRITJARA alt for PINI [PII]
PINJARI dial of URDU [URD]
PINJE alt for PIJE [PIZ]
PINJI [PIC] lang, Gabon
PINJI alt for PHENDE [PEM]
PINNEEGOOROO alt for BURDUNA [BXN]
PINRANG alt for SAWITTO dial of BUGIS [BPR]
PINRANG UTARA alt for SIDRAP dial of BUGIS [BPR]
PINTIINI [PTI] lang, Australia
PINTUBI alt for PINTUPI-LURITJA [PIU]
PINTUMBANG dial of KABOLA [KLZ]
PINTUPI-LURITJA [PIU] lang, Australia
PINYIN [PNY] lang, Cameroon
PINYIN dial of PINYIN [PNY]
PIOCHE-SIONI alt for SIONA [SIN]
PIOJE alt for SIONA [SIN]
PIOJÉ dial of SECOYA [SEY]
PIPERO alt for PERO [PIP]
PIPIKORO alt for UMA [PPK]
PIPIL [PPL] lang, El Salvador; also in Honduras
PIPIPAIA dial of ROTOKAS [ROO]
PIPLODA alt for HARAUTI [HOJ]
PIRA alt for YINE [PIB]
PIRABANAK dial of CITAK [TXT]
PIRAHÃ alt for MÚRA-PIRAHÃ [MYP]
PIRA-TAPUYA alt for PIRATAPUYO [PIR]
PIRATAPUYO [PIR] lang, Brazil; also in Colombia
PIRE alt for TSO [LDP]
PIRI alt for BHELE [PER]
PIRI alt for TSO [LDP]
PIRLATAPA [BXI] lang, Australia
PIRNIRITJARA alt for PINI [PII]
PIRO [PIE] lang, USA
PIRO alt for YINE [PIB]
PIRR dial of NAGA, SANGTAM [NSA]
PIRRO alt for YINE [PIB]
PIRU [PPR] lang, Indonesia (Maluku)

PISA alt for AWYU, MIARO [PSA]
PISABO [PIG] lang, Peru
PISAGUA alt for PISABO [PIG]
PISAHUA alt for PISABO [PIG]
PISHAGCHI dial of AZERBAIJANI, SOUTH [AZB]
PISHAUCO alt for ARECUNA dial of PEMON [AOC]
PISIN alt for TOK PISIN [PDG]
PISO dial of KALAGAN [KQE]
PISQUIBO dial of SHIPIBO-CONIBO [SHP]
PITA PITA alt for PITTA PITTA [PIT]
PITAS BAJAU dial of BAJAU, WEST COAST [BDR]
PITAS KIMARAGANG dial of KIMARAGANG [KQR]
PITAYO dial of PAEZ [PBB]
PITCAIRN ENGLISH alt for PITCAIRN-NORFOLK
    [PIH]
PITCAIRN ENGLISH dial of PITCAIRN-NORFOLK
    [PIH]
PITCAIRN-NORFOLK [PIH] lang, Norfolk Island;
    also in Australia, Fiji, New Zealand, Pitcairn
PITE alt for SAAMI, PITE [LPB]
PITI [PCN] lang, Nigeria
PITIKO alt for KHOLOK [KTC]
PITIKO alt for PIYA-KWONCI [PIY]
PITILU alt for LEIPON [LEK]
PITJANTJARA alt for PITJANTJATJARA [PJT]
PITJANTJATJARA [PJT] lang, Australia
PITJANTJATJARA dial of PITJANTJATJARA [PJT]
PITONARA alt for POTIGUÁRA [POG]
PITT RIVER alt for ACHUMAWI [ACH]
PITTA PITTA [PIT] lang, Australia
PITTALA BHASHA dial of PARDHI [PCL]
PITTI alt for PITI [PCN]
PITU-ULUNNA-SALU alt for BAMBAM [PTU]
PITYILU alt for LEIPON [LEK]
PIU [PIX] lang, Papua New Guinea
PIVA [TGI] lang, Papua New Guinea
PIYA alt for PIYA-KWONCI [PIY]
PIYA dial of PIYA-KWONCI [PIY]
PIYA-KWONCI [PIY] lang, Nigeria
PIYUMA alt for PYUMA [PYU]
PIZHDAR dial of KURDI [KDB]
PLADINA alt for FULFULDE, ADAMAWA [FUB]
PLAIN alt for NYA GUYUWA dial of LONGUDA [LNU]
PLAIN ANGAS dial of NGAS [ANC]
PLAIN BURA alt for HYIL HAWUL dial of BURA-
    PABIR [BUR]
PLAIN PENNSYLVANIA GERMAN alt for AMISH
    PENNSYLVANIA GERMAN dial of GERMAN,
    PENNSYLVANIA [PDC]
PLAIN TAROK alt for ITAROK dial of TAROK [YER]
PLAIN TETUN alt for SOUTHERN TETUN dial of
    TETUN [TTM]
PLAINS BIRA alt for BERA [BRF]
PLAINS CREE dial of CREE, PLAINS [CRP]
PLAINS GETA' dial of GATA [GAQ]
PLAINS INDIAN SIGN LANGUAGE [PSD] lang,
    USA; also in Canada
PLAINS JARAWA alt for BADA [BAU]
PLAINS OJIBWAY alt for OJIBWA, WESTERN [OJI]
PLAINS SIGH LANGUAGE alt for PLAINS INDIAN
    SIGN LANGUAGE [PSD]

PLAN DE GUADALUPE dial of MIXTECO,
    ALACATLATZALA [MIM]
PLANAN alt for PARANAN [AGP]
PLANG alt for BLANG [BLR]
PLAPO alt for KRUMEN, PLAPO [KTJ]
PLAPO dial of KRUMEN, TEPO [TED]
PLASLA alt for MAYO-PLATA dial of PELASLA
    [MLR]
PLATA alt for MAYO-PLATA dial of PELASLA [MLR]
PLATANILLO dial of TLAPANECO, ACATEPEC
    [TPX]
PLATEAU HAITIAN CREOLE dial of HAITIAN
    CREOLE FRENCH [HAT]
PLATEAU TONGA alt for TONGA [TOI]
PLATLA alt for MAYO-PLATA dial of PELASLA
    [MLR]
PLATT alt for LUXEMBOURGEOIS [LUX]
PLATTDNNTSCH alt for SAXON, LOW [SXN]
PLAUTDIETSCH [GRN] lang, Canada; also in
    Argentina, Belize, Bolivia, Brazil, Costa Rica,
    Germany, Kazakhstan, Mexico, Paraguay,
    Russia (Asia), Uruguay, USA
PLAYERO [GOB] lang, Colombia
PLEIKLY dial of JARAI [JRA]
PLO dial of KRAHN, WESTERN [KRW]
PLOSKOST dial of CHECHEN [CJC]
PLUS dial of KENSIU [KNS]
PMASA'A dial of HAMTAI [HMT]
PNAR [PBV] lang, India
PNONG alt for BUNONG dial of MNONG,
    SOUTHERN [MNN]
PNONG alt for MNONG, CENTRAL [MNC]
PÖJULU dial of BARI [BFA]
PÖKOOT [PKO] lang, Kenya; also in Uganda
PÖKOT alt for PÖKOOT [PKO]
P'ÖMI alt for PUMI, NORTHERN [PMI]
P'ÖMI alt for PUMI, SOUTHERN [PUS]
PO alt for BO [BPW]
PO RANG alt for PRANG dial of MNONG,
    SOUTHERN [MNN]
POAI alt for FWÂI [FWA]
POAMEI alt for PWAAMEI [PME]
POAPOA alt for PWAPWA [POP]
POAVOSA alt for BABUZA [BZG]
POAVOSA dial of BABUZA [BZG]
POBYENG alt for MBOBYENG dial of
    MPONGMPONG [MGG]
POCHURI alt for NAGA, POCHURI [NPO]
POCHURY alt for NAGA, POCHURI [NPO]
POCOMAM ORIENTAL alt for POKOMAM,
    EASTERN [POA]
POCOMÁN alt for POKOMAM, CENTRAL [POC]
POCOMCHÍ alt for POKOMCHÍ, EASTERN [POH]
POCOMCHÍ alt for POKOMCHÍ, WESTERN [POB]
POCONCHÍ alt for POKOMCHÍ, EASTERN [POH]
PODARI dial of GIDRA [GDR]
PODENA [PDN] lang, Indonesia (Irian Jaya)
PODI alt for BODI dial of MEEN [MYM]
PODIA KOYA dial of KOYA [KFF]
PODKAMENNAYA TUNGUSKA dial of EVENKI
    [EVN]

PODOBA alt for FOLOPA [PPO]
PODOGO alt for PARKWA [PBI]
PODOKGE dial of TUPURI [TUI]
PODOKO alt for PARKWA [PBI]
PODOKWO alt for PARKWA [PBI]
PODOPA alt for FOLOPA [PPO]
PODRA alt for TODRAH [TDR]
PODZO dial of SENA [SEH]
POENG alt for MENGEN [MEE]
POENG alt for SOUTH COAST MENGEN dial of
    MENGEN [MEE]
POGADI CHIB alt for ANGLOROMANI [RME]
POGARA dial of SENOUFO, CEBAARA [SEF]
POGAYA alt for BOGAYA [BOQ]
POGOLO [POY] lang, Tanzania
POGOLU alt for POGOLO [POY]
POGORA alt for POGOLO [POY]
POGORO alt for POGOLO [POY]
POGULI dial of KASHMIRI [KSH]
POHBETIAN alt for TIBETAN [TIC]
POHING alt for CHUKWA [CUW]
POHING KHA alt for CHUKWA [CUW]
POHNPEIAN [PNF] lang, Micronesia
POHONEANG alt for SEKO TENGAH [SKO]
POHUAI alt for BOHUAI [RAK]
POIANÁUA alt for POYANÁWA [PYN]
POINT ARENA dial of POMO, CENTRAL [POO]
POINT BARROW INUPIATUN alt for NORTH
    SLOPE INUPIATUN dial of INUPIATUN,
    NORTH ALASKAN [ESI]
POINT HOPE INUPIATUN dial of INUPIATUN,
    NORTH ALASKAN [ESI]
POITEVIN dial of FRENCH [FRN]
POJOAQUE dial of TEWA [TEW]
POK alt for BOOK dial of SABAOT [SPY]
POKA dial of TUMBUKA [TUW]
POKANGÁ [POK] lang, Brazil
POKANGÁ-TAPUYA alt for POKANGÁ [POK]
POKAU alt for NARA [NRZ]
POKE [POF] lang, DRC
PO-KLO dial of TEMIAR [TMH]
POKO alt for PU KO [PUK]
POKO dial of LOBALA [LOQ]
POKOH alt for PACOH [PAC]
POKOMAM, CENTRAL [POC] lang, Guatemala;
    also in El Salvador
POKOMAM, EASTERN [POA] lang, Guatemala
POKOMAM, SOUTHERN [POU] lang, Guatemala
POKOMCHÍ, EASTERN [POH] lang, Guatemala
POKOMCHÍ, WESTERN [POB] lang, Guatemala
POKOMO, LOWER [POJ] lang, Kenya
POKOMO, UPPER [PKB] lang, Kenya
POKONCHÍ alt for POKOMCHÍ, EASTERN [POH]
POKOT alt for PÖKOOT [PKO]
POL [PMM] lang, Congo; also in Cameroon
POLABIAN [POX] lang, Germany
POLAR ESKIMO dial of INUKTITUT, GREEN-
    LANDIC [ESG]
POLARI [PLD] lang, United Kingdom
POLCHI alt for POLCI [POL]
POLCI [POL] lang, Nigeria

POLCI dial of POLCI [POL]
POLE alt for ERAVE [KJY]
POLEANG alt for WITA EA dial of MORONENE
    [MQN]
POLEO dial of TALISE [TLR]
POLI alt for TEERE dial of DOYAYO [DOW]
POLI dial of YENDANG [YEN]
POLICE MOTU alt for MOTU, HIRI [POM]
POLIGUS dial of EVENKI [EVN]
POLISH [PQL] lang, Poland; also in Australia,
    Austria, Azerbaijan, Belarus, Canada, Czech
    Republic, Estonia, Finland, Germany, Hungary,
    Israel, Kazakhstan, Latvia, Lithuania, Romania,
    Russia (Europe), Slovakia, Ukraine, UAE, USA
POLISH ROMANI dial of ROMANI, BALTIC [ROM]
POLISH SIGN LANGUAGE [PSO] lang, Poland
POLIYAR alt for PALIYAN [PCF]
POLNISCH alt for POLISH [PQL]
POLO alt for BELA [BEQ]
POLO dial of ZAIWA [ATB]
POLOGOZOM dial of DABA [DAB]
POLOME alt for KIBIRI [PRM]
POLONOMBAUK [PLB] lang, Vanuatu
POLOPA alt for FOLOPA [PPO]
POLOTS alt for NORTHEAST BELARUSAN dial
    of BELARUSAN [RUW]
POLSHI alt for POLCI dial of POLCI [POL]
POLSKI alt for POLISH [PQL]
POM [PMO] lang, Indonesia (Irian Jaya)
POMAK alt for BULGARIAN [BLG]
POMAK dial of BULGARIAN [BLG]
POMAKCI alt for POMAK dial of BULGARIAN [BLG]
POMAKIKA alt for POMAK dial of BULGARIAN
    [BLG]
POMO alt for POL [PMM]
POMO, CENTRAL [POO] lang, USA
POMO, EASTERN [PEB] lang, USA
POMO, NORTHEASTERN [PEF] lang, USA
POMO, NORTHERN [PEJ] lang, USA
POMO, SOUTHEASTERN [PEO] lang, USA
POMO, SOUTHERN [PEQ] lang, USA
PONAAL alt for PONGAAL dial of GULA IRO [GLJ]
PONAM [NCC] lang, Papua New Guinea
PONAPEAN alt for POHNPEIAN [PNF]
PONAPEAN dial of POHNPEIAN [PNF]
PONARES [POD] lang, Colombia
PONASAKAN alt for PONOSAKAN [PNS]
PO-NAU alt for BUNU, BU-NAO [BWX]
PONCA dial of OMAHA-PONCA [OMA]
PONDA alt for LUCHAZI [LCH]
PONDO alt for ANGORAM [AOG]
PONDO dial of PANA [PNZ]
PONDOMA alt for ANAM [PDA]
PONEK alt for TUOTOMB [TTF]
PONERIHOUEN alt for PAICÎ [PRI]
PONG alt for PHONG dial of HUNG [HNU]
PONG dial of HUNG [HNU]
PONG 1 alt for PHONG dial of HUNG [HNU]
PONG 1 alt for PONG dial of HUNG [HNU]
PONG 2 alt for PHONG dial of HUNG [HNU]
PONG 2 alt for PONG dial of HUNG [HNU]

PONG 3 alt for PHONG-KNIANG [PNX]
PONGAAL dial of GULA IRO [GLJ]
PONGO alt for PONGU [PON]
PONGO dial of DUALA [DOU]
PONG'OM alt for BONG'OMEEK dial of SABAOT [SPY]
PONGOUÉ alt for MPONGWE dial of MYENE [MYE]
PONGPONG alt for MPONGMPONG [MGG]
PONGU [PON] lang, Nigeria
PONGYONG [PGY] lang, Nepal
PONKA alt for OMAHA-PONCA [OMA]
PONNA alt for MEITEI [MNR]
PONO alt for GBETE dial of MBUM [MDD]
PONORWAL dial of SA [SSA]
PONOSAKAN [PNS] lang, Indonesia (Sulawesi)
PONTHAI dial of NAGA, NOCTE [NJB]
PONTHAI dial of NAGA, TASE [NST]
PONTHIEU dial of PICARD [PCD]
PONTIANAK alt for RITOK dial of MALAY [MLI]
PONTIC [PNT] lang, Greece; also in Azerbaijan, Canada, Georgia, Kazakhstan, USA
PONTIC GREEK alt for PONTIC [PNT]
PONYO alt for NAGA, KHIAMNIUNGAN [NKY]
PONYON KULUNG alt for PONGYONG [PGY]
POODENA alt for BURDUNA [BXN]
POONAN alt for GAHRI [BFU]
POONCHI alt for PUNCHHI dial of PAHARI-POTWARI [PHR]
POONG alt for PHONG dial of HUNG [HNU]
POONG alt for PONG dial of HUNG [HNU]
POONO alt for AROP dial of AROP-LOKEP [APR]
POORDOONA alt for BURDUNA [BXN]
POPENGARE alt for APURINÃ [APU]
POPO alt for ÉWÉ [EWE]
POPO alt for GEN-GBE [GEJ]
POPOI dial of MANGBETU [MDJ]
POPOLOCA PONIENTE alt for POPOLOCA, SAN FELIPE OTLALTEPEC [POW]
POPOLOCA, COYOTEPEC [PBF] lang, Mexico
POPOLOCA, MEZONTLA [PBE] lang, Mexico
POPOLOCA, SAN FELIPE OTLALTEPEC [POW] lang, Mexico
POPOLOCA, SAN JUAN ATZINGO [POE] lang, Mexico
POPOLOCA, SAN LUÍS TEMALACAYUCA [PPS] lang, Mexico
POPOLOCA, SAN MARCOS TLALCOYALCO [PLS] lang, Mexico
POPOLOCA, SANTA INÉS AHUATEMPAN [PCA] lang, Mexico
POPOLUCA, OLUTA [PLO] lang, Mexico
POPOLUCA, SAYULA [POS] lang, Mexico
POPOLUCA, SIERRA [POI] lang, Mexico
POPOLUCA, TEXISTEPEC [POQ] lang, Mexico
POR alt for PEAR [PCB]
PORAJA KATHA alt for BONDO [BFW]
POREN alt for NYANG'I [NYP]
PORHÉ alt for PURÉPECHA [TSZ]
PORI alt for POL [PMM]
PORI ASOM alt for AZOM dial of POL [PMM]
PORI KINDA dial of POL [PMM]

PORJA alt for KONDA-DORA [KFC]
PORMI alt for NDAI [GKE]
POROHANON [PRH] lang, Philippines
POROJA alt for BODO PARJA [BDV]
POROJA alt for PARENGA [PCJ]
POROME alt for KIBIRI [PRM]
POROME dial of KIBIRI [PRM]
PORONAISK dial of OROK [OAA]
POROS dial of TIMUGON MURUT [TIH]
POROTO dial of SAFWA [SBK]
PORT MALTESE dial of MALTESE [MLS]
PORT SANDWICH [PSW] lang, Vanuatu
PORT VATO [PTV] lang, Vanuatu
PORTUGÊS alt for PORTUGUESE [POR]
PORTUGUÊS DE BIDAU dial of PIDGIN, TIMOR [TVY]
PORTUGUÊS DE MALACA alt for MALACCAN CREOLE PORTUGUESE [MCM]
PORTUGUESE [POR] lang, Portugal; also in Andorra, Angola, Antigua and Barbuda, Belgium, Brazil, Canada, Cape Verde Islands, China, Congo, France, Germany, Guinea-Bissau, Guyana, India, Indonesia, Jamaica, Luxembourg, Malawi, Mozambique, Namibia, Oman, Paraguay, São Tomé e Príncipe, South Africa, Spain, St. Vincent and the Grenadines, Suriname, Switzerland, Timor Lorosae, United Kingdom, Uruguay, USA
PORTUGUESE CALÃO dial of CALO [RMR]
PORTUGUESE CREOLE alt for CRIOULO, UPPER GUINEA [POV]
PORTUGUESE PATOIS alt for MALACCAN CREOLE PORTUGUESE [MCM]
PORTUGUESE SIGN LANGUAGE [PSR] lang, Portugal
POSA alt for POLCI dial of POLCI [POL]
POSH 'N' POSH alt for ANGLOROMANI [RME]
POSO alt for PAMONA [BCX]
POSO dial of BAJAU, INDONESIAN [BDL]
POTAWATOMI [POT] lang, USA; also in Canada
POTHOHARI alt for PAHARI-POTWARI [PHR]
POTHWARI dial of PAHARI-POTWARI [PHR]
POTIGUÁRA [POG] lang, Brazil
POTNARIVEN dial of SIE [ERG]
POTOHARI alt for PAHARI-POTWARI [PHR]
POTOICHAN dial of MIXTECO, ALACATLATZALA [MIM]
POTOPO alt for DAN MUURE dial of PEERE [KUT]
POTOPO alt for PEERE [KUT]
POTOPORE alt for PEERE [KUT]
POTOSÍ dial of QUECHUA, SOUTH BOLIVIAN [QUH]
POTOSINO HUASTEC alt for HUASTECO, SAN LUÍS POTOSÍ [HVA]
POTOTAN dial of KINARAY-A [KRJ]
POTSAWUGOK alt for ARECUNA dial of PEMON [AOC]
POTTAWOTOMI alt for POTAWATOMI [POT]
POTTAWOTTOMI alt for POTAWATOMI [POT]
POTU alt for MBATO [GWA]
POTULE dial of SISAALA, TUMULUNG [SIL]

POTURU [PTO] lang, Brazil
POTURUJARA alt for POTURU [PTO]
POTWARI alt for PAHARI-POTWARI [PHR]
POTWARI alt for POTHWARI dial of PAHARI-
    POTWARI [PHR]
POU HOK alt for PUOC [PUO]
POUÉBO dial of CAAC [MSQ]
POUGOULI alt for PWIĚ [PUG]
POUMEI alt for NAGA, POUMEI [PMX]
POUN alt for BON GULA [GLC]
POUNO alt for PUNU [PUU]
POUSS alt for MPUS dial of MUSGU [MUG]
POUTENG alt for KHANG [KJM]
POUTENG alt for KHMU [KJG]
POUYE [BYE] lang, Papua New Guinea
POVE alt for BUBI [BUW]
POWADHI dial of PANJABI, EASTERN [PNJ]
POWARI alt for PAWARI dial of BUNDELI [BNS]
POWARI dial of BAGHELI [BFY]
POWHATAN [PIM] lang, USA
POYANÁWA [PYN] lang, Brazil
POYENISATI alt for CAQUITE [COT]
PPANKKA alt for OMAHA-PONCA [OMA]
PRADHAN alt for PARDHAN [PCH]
PRADHANI alt for PARDHAN [PCH]
PRAE alt for KAREN, PWO, PHRAE [KJT]
PRAI alt for PHAI [PRT]
PRAIRIE FRENCH dial of FRENCH, CAJUN [FRC]
PRAISTIKI dial of ROMANI, SINTE [RMO]
PRAKAA dial of MANANGBA [NMM]
PRAMANO alt for KAREN, BREK [KVL]
PRANG alt for KPLANG [PRA]
PRANG dial of CHRAU [CHR]
PRANG dial of MNONG, SOUTHERN [MNN]
PRAOK alt for PARAUK [PRK]
PRASUN alt for PRASUNI [PRN]
PRASUNI [PRN] lang, Afghanistan
PRAY 1 alt for PHAI [PRT]
PRAY 2 alt for LUA' [PRB]
PRAY 3 [PRY] lang, Thailand
PRE alt for KAREN, BREK [KVL]
PRE alt for PRÉH dial of MNONG, CENTRAL [MNC]
PREH dial of MNONG, CENTRAL [MNC]
PRÉH dial of MNONG, CENTRAL [MNC]
PREHAN dial of MELANAU [MEL]
PREKMURSKI dial of SLOVENIAN [SLV]
PRESIDIO DE LOS REYES CORA dial of CORA
    [COR]
PRIANGAN alt for SUNDA [SUO]
PRIBILOF ALEUT alt for EASTERN ALEUT dial
    of ALEUT [ALW]
PRIMMI alt for PUMI, NORTHERN [PMI]
PRIMMI alt for PUMI, SOUTHERN [PUS]
PRIMORSKI dial of SLOVENIAN [SLV]
PRINCIPENSE [PRE] lang, São Tomé e Príncipe
PRINGAN dial of SUNDA [SUO]
PRIONEZH dial of VEPS [VEP]
PRIULIAN alt for FRIULIAN [FRL]
PROBUR dial of KELON [KYO]
PROCA LO dial of BAHING [RAR]
PROK dial of NUBRI [KTE]

P'ROME alt for PUMI, NORTHERN [PMI]
P'ROME alt for PUMI, SOUTHERN [PUS]
PROON alt for TAMPUAN [TPU]
PROONS alt for TAMPUAN [TPU]
PROPONTIS TSAKONIAN dial of TSAKONIAN
    [TSD]
PROUE alt for BRAO [BRB]
PROUE alt for LAVE [BRB]
PROUVENÇAU alt for PROVENÇAL [PRV]
PROVENÇAL [PRV] lang, France; also in Italy,
    Monaco
PROVENZALE alt for PROVENÇAL [PRV]
PROVIDENCIA SIGN LANGUAGE [PRO] lang,
    Colombia
PRSL alt for PUERTO RICAN SIGN LANGUAGE
    [PSL]
PRU dial of KOHO [KPM]
PRUSSIAN [PRG] lang, Poland
PRUUMI alt for PUMI, NORTHERN [PMI]
PRUUMI alt for PUMI, SOUTHERN [PUS]
PSHAV dial of GEORGIAN [GEO]
PSIKYE [KVJ] lang, Cameroon; also in Nigeria
PSIKYE dial of PSIKYE [KVJ]
PSOHOH [BCL] lang, Papua New Guinea
PSOHOH alt for SOKHOK dial of PSOHOH [BCL]
PSOKHOK alt for SOKHOK dial of PSOHOH [BCL]
PSOKOK alt for SOKHOK dial of PSOHOH [BCL]
PTAMO dial of CUIBA [CUI]
PTEP alt for PATEP [PTP]
PTSAKE alt for PSIKYE [KVJ]
PU alt for NICOBARESE, CAR [CAQ]
PU KO [PUK] lang, Laos
PÚ NÀ alt for NHANG [NHA]
PU NO alt for BUNU, YOUNUO [BUH]
PU NO alt for BUNUO dial of BUNU, BU-NAO
    [BWX]
PU PÉO alt for LAQUA [LAQ]
PU THENH alt for KHMU [KJG]
PUA alt for PUOC [PUO]
PUAN dial of JARAI [JRA]
PUARI [PUX] lang, Papua New Guinea
PUBIAN [PUN] lang, Indonesia (Sumatra)
PUBIAO alt for LAQUA [LAQ]
PUCA-UMA alt for IQUITO [IQU]
PUCHIKWAR alt for A-PUCIKWAR [APQ]
PUCIKWAR alt for A-PUCIKWAR [APQ]
PUDITARA dial of MARTU WANGKA [MPJ]
PUEH alt for BIATAH [BTH]
PUELCHE [PUE] lang, Argentina
PUERTO RICAN SIGN LANGUAGE [PSL] lang,
    Puerto Rico
PUGLIESE dial of ITALIAN [ITN]
PUGOT alt for ALTA, SOUTHERN [AGY]
PUGULI alt for PWIĚ [PUG]
PUHOC alt for PUOC [PUO]
PU-I alt for BOUYEI [PCC]
PUI alt for BOUYEI [PCC]
PUIMEI alt for NAGA, PUIMEI [NPU]
PUINABE alt for PUINAVE [PUI]
PUINAHUA alt for POYANÁWA [PYN]
PUINARE alt for PUINAVE [PUI]

PUINAVE [PUI] lang, Colombia; also in Venezuela
PUJAI alt for BOUYEI [PCC]
PU-JUI alt for BOUYEI [PCC]
PUJUNI alt for NISENAN [NSZ]
PUKAMIGL-ANDEGABU dial of WAHGI [WAK]
PUKAN alt for BUGAN [BBH]
PUKAPUKA [PKP] lang, Cook Islands; also in Australia, New Zealand
PUKAPUKAN alt for PUKAPUKA [PKP]
PUKAUNU alt for WEST LAMAHOLOT dial of LAMAHOLOT [SLP]
PUKI alt for POKE [POF]
PUKOBJÊ alt for GAVIÃO, PARÁ [GAY]
PUKU alt for BAPUKU dial of BATANGA [BNM]
PUKU alt for KAG dial of KAG-FER-JIIR-KOOR-ROR-US-ZUKSUN [GEL]
PUKU-GEERI-KERI-WIPSI alt for KAG-FER-JIIR-KOOR-ROR-US-ZUKSUN [GEL]
PUKUNNA alt for NUGUNU [NNV]
PUL alt for POL [PMM]
PULA alt for BLANG [BLR]
PULA alt for TADYAWAN [TDY]
PULAAR [FUC] lang, Senegal; also in Gambia, Guinea, Guinea-Bissau, Mali, Mauritania
PULAAR alt for FULFULDE, PULAAR [FUC]
PULAAR alt for FUUTA JALON [FUF]
PULAAR alt for TOUCOULEUR dial of FULFULDE, PULAAR [FUC]
PULAAR alt for TOUCOULEUR dial of PULAAR [FUC]
PULAAR FULFULDE alt for PULAAR [FUC]
PULABU [PUP] lang, Papua New Guinea
PULANA dial of SOTHO, NORTHERN [SRT]
PULANG alt for BLANG [BLR]
PULANGIYEN dial of MANOBO, WESTERN BUKIDNON [MBB]
PULAPESE dial of PULUWATESE [PUW]
PULAR alt for FUUTA JALON [FUF]
PULAU GUAI dial of JAH HUT [JAH]
PULAYA dial of MALAYALAM [MJS]
PULE alt for FULFULDE, ADAMAWA [FUB]
PULEI alt for PALAUNG, PALE [PCE]
PULENIYAN dial of MANOBO, ILIANEN [MBI]
PULGAON dial of KOLAMI, NORTHWESTERN [KFB]
PULHILH alt for YU dial of MANDJAK [MFV]
PULIE-RAUTO dial of LAMOGAI [LMG]
PULLO alt for FULFULDE, ADAMAWA [FUB]
PULO ANNA dial of SONSOROL [SOV]
PULOPETAK dial of NGAJU [NIJ]
PULUSUKESE dial of PULUWATESE [PUW]
PULUWAT alt for PULUWATESE [PUW]
PULUWATESE [PUW] lang, Micronesia
PULUWATESE dial of PULUWATESE [PUW]
PUMA [PUM] lang, Nepal
PUMA alt for TEANU [TKW]
PUMA KALA alt for PUMA [PUM]
PUMA LA alt for PUMA [PUM]
PUMA PIMA alt for PUMA [PUM]
PUMAN alt for U [UUU]
P'UMAN alt for U [UUU]

PUMBORA alt for PURUBORÁ [PUR]
PUMÉ alt for YARURO [YAE]
P'UMI alt for PUMI, NORTHERN [PMI]
P'UMI alt for PUMI, SOUTHERN [PUS]
PUMI, NORTHERN [PMI] lang, China
PUMI, SOUTHERN [PUS] lang, China
PU-NAM alt for NHANG [NHA]
"PUNAN" pejorative alt for PENAN, EASTERN [PEZ]
"PUNAN" pejorative alt for PENAN, WESTERN [PNE]
PUNAN alt for GAHRI [BFU]
PUNAN dial of DAYAK, LAND [DYK]
PUNAN APUT [PUD] lang, Indonesia (Kalimantan)
PUNAN BA alt for PUNAN BAH dial of PUNAN BAH-BIAU [PNA]
PUNAN BAH dial of PUNAN BAH-BIAU [PNA]
PUNAN BAH-BIAU [PNA] lang, Malaysia (Sarawak)
PUNAN BASAP dial of SAJAU BASAP [SAD]
PUNAN BATU 1 [PNM] lang, Malaysia (Sarawak)
PUNAN BATU 2 dial of SAJAU BASAP [SAD]
PUNAN BIAU dial of PUNAN BAH-BIAU [PNA]
PUNAN BUNGAN alt for HOVONGAN [HOV]
PUNAN BUSANG dial of BUKITAN [BKN]
PUNAN KERIAU alt for KEREHO-UHENG [XKE]
PUNAN MERAH [PUF] lang, Indonesia (Kalimantan)
PUNAN MERAP [PUC] lang, Indonesia (Kalimantan)
PUNAN RATAH alt for OT MURUNG 1 dial of DOHOI [OTD]
PUNAN SAJAU dial of SAJAU BASAP [SAD]
PUNAN TUBU [PUJ] lang, Indonesia (Kalimantan)
PUNAN UKIT dial of BUKITAN [BKN]
PUNAPA alt for BUNABA [BCK]
PUNCHHI dial of PAHARI-POTWARI [PHR]
PUNDA-UMEDA dial of SOWANDA [SOW]
PUNGUPUNGU alt for KUWAMA [QKU]
PUNGUPUNGU dial of WADJIGINY [WDJ]
PUNIAL alt for GILGITI dial of SHINA [SCL]
PUNJABI alt for PANJABI, EASTERN [PNJ]
PUNKALLA alt for BANGGARLA [BJB]
PUNO alt for PUNU [PUU]
PUNOI alt for PHUNOI [PHO]
PUNTHAMARA dial of NGURA [NBX]
PUNTLATCH alt for PENTLATCH [PTW]
PUNU [PUU] lang, Gabon; also in Congo
PUNU alt for BUNU, BU-NAO [BWX]
PUNU alt for BUNU, JIONGNAI [PNU]
PUNU alt for BUNU, WUNAI [BWN]
PUNU alt for BUNU, YOUNUO [BUH]
PUOC [PUO] lang, Viet Nam; also in Laos
PUOK alt for PUOC [PUO]
PUPEO alt for LAQUA [LAQ]
PUPITAU dial of FOLOPA [PPO]
PUQUINA [PUQ] lang, Peru
PURA dial of BLAGAR [BEU]
PURAGI [PRU] lang, Indonesia (Irian Jaya)
PURAI dial of LAWANGAN [LBX]
PURAM alt for PURUM [PUB]
PURARI [IAR] lang, Papua New Guinea
PURBI alt for WESTERN STANDARD BHOJPURI dial of BHOJPURI [BHJ]

PURDUMA alt for BURDUNA [BXN]
PURDUNA alt for BURDUNA [BXN]
PURE MOTU alt for MOTU [MEU]
PUREMAN alt for LANGKURU dial of WERSING [KVW]
PURÉPECHA [TSZ] lang, Mexico
PURÉPECHA, SIERRA OCCIDENTAL [PUA] lang, Mexico
PURI [PRR] lang, Brazil
PURIG alt for PURIK [BXR]
PURIGSKAD alt for PURIK [BXR]
PURIK [BXR] lang, India
PURIK BHOTIA alt for PURIK [BXR]
PURISIMEÑO [PUY] lang, USA
PURKI alt for PURIK [BXR]
PURKO dial of MAASAI [MET]
PUROBORÁ alt for PURUBORÁ [PUR]
PURR dial of NAGA, SANGTAM [NSA]
PURRA alt for BENA [YUN]
PURUBA alt for PURUBORÁ [PUR]
PURUBORÁ [PUR] lang, Brazil
PURUCOTO alt for ARECUNA dial of PEMON [AOC]
PURUM [PUB] lang, Myanmar
PURUNG dial of LAWANGAN [LBX]
PURUPURÚ alt for PAUMARÍ [PAD]
PUS alt for MPUS dial of MUSGU [MUG]
PUSCITI alt for XAVÁNTE [XAV]
PUSHTO alt for PASHTO, NORTHERN [PBU]
PUSHTO alt for PASHTO, SOUTHERN [PBT]
PUSHTU alt for PASHTO, SOUTHERN [PBT]
PUSTO alt for PASHTO, NORTHERN [PBU]
PUTAHI alt for PARATA dial of TUAMOTUAN [PMT]
PUTAI [MFL] lang, Nigeria
PUTAI alt for PHU THAI [PHT]
PUTATAN dial of BAJAU, WEST COAST [BDR]
PUTE alt for VUTE [VUT]
PUTEIK alt for KADO [KDV]
PUTENH alt for KHANG [KJM]
PUTER-LOWER ENGADINE alt for LOWER ENGADINE dial of ROMANSCH [RHE]
PUTHAI alt for PHU THAI [PHT]
PUTHAY alt for PHU THAI [PHT]
PUTHSU alt for PODZO dial of SENA [SEH]
PUTIAN dial of CHINESE, PU-XIAN [CPX]
PUTOH [PUT] lang, Indonesia (Kalimantan)
PUTONGHUA alt for CHINESE, MANDARIN [CHN]
PUTRU dial of RONGA [RON]
PUTTEN alt for PUTIAN dial of CHINESE, PU-XIAN [CPX]
PUTTOOAS alt for JUANG [JUN]
PUTU dial of SAPO [KRN]
PUTUJARA alt for PUDITARA dial of MARTU WANGKA [MPJ]
PUTUKWAM [AFE] lang, Nigeria
PUTUKWAM alt for PUTUKWAM [AFE]
PUURI alt for NGONG [NNX]
PUXI dial of SHANGZHAI [JIH]
PUXMETECÁN MIXE dial of MIXE, QUETZALTEPEC [MVE]
PUYALLUP dial of SALISH, SOUTHERN PUGET SOUND [SLH]

PUYI alt for BOUYEI [PCC]
PUYOI alt for BOUYEI [PCC]
PUYUI alt for MOUNTAIN GELAO dial of GELAO [KKF]
PUYUMA alt for PYUMA [PYU]
PWA alt for PWIE [PUG]
PWAAMEI [PME] lang, New Caledonia
PWAKANYAW alt for KAREN, S'GAW [KSW]
PWAPWA [POP] lang, New Caledonia
PWE alt for PWIE [PUG]
PWEBO alt for POUÉBO dial of CAAC [MSQ]
PWIE [PUG] lang, Burkina Faso
PWIEN alt for PWIE [PUG]
PWO alt for PWIE [PUG]
PWO PHRAE alt for KAREN, PWO, PHRAE [KJT]
PYAPUN [PCW] lang, Nigeria
PYE alt for PIE dial of KRUMEN, PYE [PYE]
PYEM alt for FYAM [PYM]
PYEN [PYY] lang, Myanmar
PYETA alt for AYOREO [AYO]
PYETA YOVAI alt for AYOREO [AYO]
PYGMEE alt for BAKA [BKC]
PYGMEÉ DE LA LOBAYE alt for YAKA [AXK]
PYGMEÉ DE MONGOUMBA alt for YAKA [AXK]
PYGMEÉS DE LA SANGHAS alt for YAKA [AXK]
PYGMEES DE L'EST alt for BAKA [BKC]
PYGMY-E alt for BAKA [BKC]
P'YONG'ANDO dial of KOREAN [KKN]
PYU [PBY] lang, Papua New Guinea
PYUMA [PYU] lang, Taiwan
QABALA dial of AZERBAIJANI, NORTH [AZE]
QABEKHO alt for QABEKHOE dial of NARO [NHR]
QABEKHOE dial of NARO [NHR]
QABENA alt for QEBENA dial of KAMBAATA [KTB]
QABIAO alt for LAQUA [LAQ]
QAHAR alt for CHAHAR dial of MONGOLIAN, PERIPHERAL [MVF]
QAJAR dial of AZERBAIJANI, SOUTH [AZB]
QALADZE dial of LISHANID NOSHAN [AIJ]
QALMAQ alt for KALMYK-OIRAT [KGZ]
QANDAHAR PASHTO dial of PASHTO, SOUTHERN [PBT]
QAQET [BYX] lang, Papua New Guinea
QARAGOZLU dial of AZERBAIJANI, SOUTH [AZB]
QARAQULPAQS alt for KARAKALPAK [KAC]
QARAWI alt for JIBBALI [SHV]
QARLUG alt for KARLUK dial of UZBEK, NORTHERN [UZB]
QASHQA'I [QSQ] lang, Iran
QASHQAI alt for QASHQA'I [QSQ]
QASHQARI alt for KHOWAR [KHW]
QASHQAY alt for QASHQA'I [QSQ]
QATARI alt for ARABIC, GULF SPOKEN [AFB]
QATVENUA alt for HANO [LML]
QAU alt for CAPE DRAPING GELAO dial of GELAO [KKF]
QAU dial of GELAO [KKF]
QAWASQAR [ALC] lang, Chile
QAZAKH dial of AZERBAIJANI, NORTH [AZE]

QAZAQ alt for KAZAKH [KAZ]
QAZAQI alt for KAZAKH [KAZ]
QAZVINI dial of FARSI, WESTERN [PES]
QEBENA dial of KAMBAATA [KTB]
QEMANT alt for QIMANT dial of AGAW, WESTERN [QIM]
QHALAXARZI alt for KGALAGADI [XKV]
QI dial of HLAI [LIC]
QIANG, NORTHERN [CNG] lang, China
QIANG, SOUTHERN [QMR] lang, China
QIANNAN dial of BOUYEI [PCC]
QIANXI dial of BOUYEI [PCC]
QIANZHONG dial of BOUYEI [PCC]
QIDE dial of CHINESE, HUIZHOU [CZH]
QILENG dial of NANAI [GLD]
QIMANT dial of AGAW, WESTERN [QIM]
QIMR alt for GIMR dial of TAMA [TMA]
QIN alt for CHIN, ASHO [CSH]
QINATI dial of DOMARI [RMT]
QINGHUA dial of PUMI, SOUTHERN [PUS]
QINLIAN dial of CHINESE, YUE [YUH]
QIONGSHAN dial of LINGAO [ONB]
QIONGWEN HUA alt for HAINAN dial of CHINESE, MIN NAN [CFR]
QIQIHA'ER dial of DAUR [DTA]
QIQIHAR alt for QIQIHA'ER dial of DAUR [DTA]
QIU alt for DRUNG [DUU]
QIUBEI dial of ZHUANG, NORTHERN [CCX]
QIUNGNAI alt for BUNU, JIONGNAI [PNU]
QOCHÂNI dial of KURMANJI [KUR]
QOM alt for TOBA [TOB]
QONAQKEND dial of TAT, MUSLIM [TTT]
QOTONG alt for CHINESE, MANDARIN [CHN]
"QOTTU" pejorative alt for OROMO, EASTERN [HAE]
"QOTU" OROMO pejorative alt for OROMO, EASTERN [HAE]
QUA alt for SOUTHERN EJAGHAM dial of EJAGHAM [ETU]
QUAIQUER alt for AWA-CUAIQUER [KWI]
QUAN CHET dial of IU MIEN [IUM]
QUAN TRANG dial of IU MIEN [IUM]
QUANG DONG alt for CHINESE, YUE [YUH]
QUANG LAM alt for KHANG [KJM]
QUANG TIN KATU alt for TAKUA [TKZ]
QUANG TRI BRU alt for BRU, EASTERN [BRU]
QUAPAW [QUA] lang, USA
QUAQUA alt for PIAROA [PID]
QUASHIE TALK alt for JAMAICAN CREOLE ENGLISH dial of SOUTHWESTERN CARIBBEAN CREOLE ENGLISH [JAM]
QUBA dial of AZERBAIJANI, NORTH [AZE]
QUBA dial of LEZGI [LEZ]
QUBA dial of TAT, MUSLIM [TTT]
QUCHANI alt for KHORASANI TURKISH [KMZ]
QUEBEC "ESKIMO" pejorative name for dial of INUKTITUT, EASTERN CANADIAN [ESB]
QUEBEC SIGN LANGUAGE [FCS] lang, Canada
QUÉBÉICOIS dial of FRENCH [FRN]
QUECCHÍ alt for KEKCHÍ [KEK]
QUECHAN [YUM] lang, USA

QUECHUA BOLIVIANO alt for QUECHUA, SOUTH BOLIVIAN [QUH]
QUECHUA, ANCASH, CHIQUIAN [QEC] lang, Peru
QUECHUA, ANCASH, CONCHUCOS, NORTHERN [QED] lang, Peru
QUECHUA, ANCASH, CONCHUCOS, SOUTHERN [QEH] lang, Peru
QUECHUA, ANCASH, CORONGO [QEE] lang, Peru
QUECHUA, ANCASH, HUAYLAS [QAN] lang, Peru
QUECHUA, ANCASH, SIHUAS [QES] lang, Peru
QUECHUA, APURIMAC [QEA] lang, Peru
QUECHUA, AREQUIPA-LA UNION [QAR] lang, Peru
QUECHUA, AYACUCHO [QUY] lang, Peru
QUECHUA, CAJAMARCA [QNT] lang, Peru
QUECHUA, CHACHAPOYAS [QUK] lang, Peru
QUECHUA, CHILEAN [QUE] lang, Chile
QUECHUA, CLASSICAL [QCL] lang, Peru
QUECHUA, CUZCO [QUZ] lang, Peru
QUECHUA, HUÁNUCO, HUALLAGA [QUB] lang, Peru
QUECHUA, HUÁNUCO, HUAMALÍES-NORTHERN DOS DE MAYO [QEJ] lang, Peru
QUECHUA, HUÁNUCO, PANAO [QEM] lang, Peru
QUECHUA, LAMBAYEQUE [QUF] lang, Peru
QUECHUA, MARGOS-YAROWILCA-LAURICOCHA [QEI] lang, Peru
QUECHUA, NORTH BOLIVIAN [QUL] lang, Bolivia; also in Peru
QUECHUA, NORTH JUNÍN [QJU] lang, Peru
QUECHUA, NORTH LIMA, CAJATAMBO [QNL] lang, Peru
QUECHUA, NORTHWEST JUJUY [QUO] lang, Argentina
QUECHUA, PACAROAS [QCP] lang, Peru
QUECHUA, PASCO, SANTA ANA DE TUSI [QEF] lang, Peru
QUECHUA, PASCO-YANAHUANCA [QUR] lang, Peru
QUECHUA, PASTAZA, SOUTHERN [QUP] lang, Peru
QUECHUA, PUNO [QEP] lang, Peru
QUECHUA, SAN MARTÍN [QSA] lang, Peru
QUECHUA, SAN RAFAEL-HUARIACA [QEG] lang, Peru
QUECHUA, SOUTH BOLIVIAN [QUH] lang, Bolivia; also in Argentina
QUECHUA, WANCA, HUAYLLA [QHU] lang, Peru
QUECHUA, WANCA, JAUJA [QHJ] lang, Peru
QUECHUA, YAUYOS [QUX] lang, Peru
QUECL alt for QUECHAN [YUM]
QUEDAH alt for KEDAH dial of KENSIU [KNS]
QUEMAYÁ alt for KUMIÁI [DIH]
QUEQUEXQUE alt for TERIBE [TFR]
QUERÉTARO OTOMÍ alt for OTOMÍ, NORTH-WESTERN [OTQ]
QUERÉTARO-MÉXICO OTOMÍ alt for OTOMÍ, NORTHWESTERN [OTQ]
QUETTA PASHTO dial of PASHTO, SOUTHERN [PBT]
QUETZALTENANGO MAM alt for MAM, SOUTHERN [MMS]

QUETZALTEPEC MIXE dial of MIXE, QUETZALTEPEC [MVE]
QUEUTHOE alt for KANTOHE dial of BALANTA-KENTOHE [BLE]
QUEYU [QEY] lang, China
QUEZON PALAWANO alt for PALAWANO, CENTRAL [PLC]
QUIANGAN alt for IFUGAO, TUWALI [IFK]
QUIATIVIS alt for SANAPANÁ [SAP]
QUIATONI ZAPOTECO alt for ZAPOTECO, SAN PEDRO QUIATONI [ZPF]
QUIAVICUZAS ZAPOTEC alt for ZAPOTECO, QUIAVICUZAS [ZPJ]
QUICAPAUSE alt for KIKAPÚ [KIC]
QUICHÉ, CENTRAL [QUC] lang, Guatemala
QUICHÉ, CUNÉN [CUN] lang, Guatemala
QUICHÉ, EASTERN, CHICHICASTENANGO [QUU] lang, Guatemala
QUICHÉ, JOYABAJ [QUJ] lang, Guatemala
QUICHÉ, SAN ANDRÉS [QIE] lang, Guatemala
QUICHÉ, WEST CENTRAL [QUT] lang, Guatemala
QUICHUA, HIGHLAND, CALDERÓN [QUD] lang, Ecuador
QUICHUA, HIGHLAND, CAÑAR [QQC] lang, Ecuador
QUICHUA, HIGHLAND, CHIMBORAZO [QUG] lang, Ecuador
QUICHUA, HIGHLAND, IMBABURA [QHO] lang, Ecuador
QUICHUA, HIGHLAND, LOJA [QQU] lang, Ecuador
QUICHUA, HIGHLAND, TUNGURAHUA [QQS] lang, Ecuador
QUICHUA, LOWLAND, NAPO [QLN] lang, Ecuador; also in Colombia, Peru
QUICHUA, LOWLAND, TENA [QUW] lang, Ecuador
QUICHUA, PASTAZA, NORTHERN [QLB] lang, Ecuador; also in Peru
QUICHUA, SANTIAGO DEL ESTERO [QUS] lang, Argentina
QUIEGOLANI ZAPOTEC alt for ZAPOTECO, SANTA MARAÍ QUIEGOLANI [ZPI]
QUIERÍ ZAPOTEC dial of ZAPOTECO, QUIOQUITANI Y QUIERI [ZTQ]
QUIJO alt for QUICHUA, LOWLAND, NAPO [QLN]
QUILCENE dial of TWANA [TWA]
QUILEUTE [QUI] lang, USA
QUILEUTE dial of QUILEUTE [QUI]
QUILIGUA alt for KILIWA [KLB]
QUILYACMOC alt for SANAPANÁ [SAP]
QUILYILHRAYROM alt for TOBA-MASKOY [TMF]
QUIMBUNDO alt for UMBUNDU [MNF]
QUIMUANE alt for MWANI [WMW]
QUINAULT [QUN] lang, USA
QUINQUI [QUQ] lang, Spain
QUIOCO alt for CHOKWE [CJK]
QUIOQUITANI ZAPOTEC dial of ZAPOTECO, QUIOQUITANI Y QUIERI [ZTQ]
QUIPEA alt for KIPEÁ dial of KARIRI-XOCO [KZW]
QUIRRUBA dial of BANIVA [BVV]
QUISSAMA alt for SAMA [SMD]
QUISSANGA alt for KISANGA dial of MWANI [WMW]
QUITURRAN alt for IQUITO [IQU]

QUIXO alt for QUICHUA, LOWLAND, NAPO [QLN]
QUÔC LAO alt for GELAO [KKF]
QUOIRENG alt for KOIRENG [NKD]
QUOP alt for BIATAH [BTH]
"QUOTTU" pejorative alt for OROMO, EASTERN [HAE]
QURANIC ARABIC alt for CLASSICAL ARABIC dial of ARABIC, STANDARD [ABV]
QWABE dial of ZULU [ZUU]
QWADZA alt for KUTU [KDC]
QWADZA alt for KW'ADZA [WKA]
QWANNAB alt for ANDI [ANI]
QWARA alt for HWARASA dial of AGAW, WESTERN [QIM]
QWARINA alt for HWARASA dial of AGAW, WESTERN [QIM]
"QWOTTU" pejorative alt for OROMO, EASTERN [HAE]
QXÛ alt for KUNG-EKOKA [KNW]
QXÜ alt for KUNG-EKOKA [KNW]
QYZYL QAZMA dial of TAT, MUSLIM [TTT]
QYZYLBASH dial of AZERBAIJANI, NORTH [AZE]
RÄLIK dial of MARSHALLESE [MZM]
RAANDALIST alt for WESTERN LIVONIAN dial of LIV [LIV]
RABAH dial of HRE [HRE]
RABAI alt for NABAY dial of KENINGAU MURUT [KXI]
RABAI dial of GIRYAMA [NYF]
RABARI dial of KOLI, KACHI [GJK]
RABAT-CASABLANCA ARABIC dial of ARABIC, MOROCCAN SPOKEN [ARY]
RABAUL CREOLE GERMAN alt for UNSERDEUTSCH [ULN]
RABAY alt for NABAY dial of KENINGAU MURUT [KXI]
RABE alt for LABE dial of TAWALA [TBO]
RABHA [RAH] lang, India
RABINAL QUICHÉ alt for ACHÍ, RABINAL [ACR]
RACHA-LEXCHXUM dial of GEORGIAN [GEO]
RADAY alt for RADE [RAD]
RADCLIFFE LANCASHIRE dial of ENGLISH [ENG]
RADE [RAD] lang, Viet Nam; also in USA
RADLAI alt for ROGLAI, NORTHERN [ROG]
RAEPA TATI alt for KAKI AE [TBD]
RAGA alt for HANO [LML]
RAGETTA alt for GEDAGED [GDD]
RAGHOBANSI dial of BUNDELI [BNS]
RA-GLAI alt for ROGLAI, CACGIA [ROC]
RA-GLAI alt for ROGLAI, NORTHERN [ROG]
RAGOLI alt for LOGOOLI [RAG]
RAGREIG dial of BURUN [BDI]
RAGUSAN alt for DALMATIAN [DLM]
RAGWE alt for NYAMBO [NYM]
RAHABARI alt for RABARI dial of KOLI, KACHI [GJK]
RAHAMBUU [RAZ] lang, Indonesia (Sulawesi)
RAHANWEEN alt for MAAY [QMA]
RAHANWEYN alt for MAAY [QMA]
RAI alt for ROGLAI, SOUTHERN [RGS]
RAI dial of CHRU [CJE]
RAI dial of KAILI, LEDO [LEW]

RAI dial of ROGLAI, SOUTHERN [RGS]
RAIDJUA alt for RAIJUA dial of SABU [HVN]
RAIGARH dial of MURIA, EASTERN [EMU]
RAIJUA dial of SABU [HVN]
RAIK alt for REK dial of DINKA, SOUTHWESTERN [DIK]
RAINBARGO alt for REMBARUNGA [RMB]
RAINY RIVER OJIBWA dial of OJIBWA, NORTH-WESTERN [OJB]
RAIO dial of KAILI, LEDO [LEW]
RAIPUR dial of VARHADI-NAGPURI [VAH]
RAITE dial of TUROYO [SYR]
RAIVAVAE dial of AUSTRAL [AUT]
RAJ KOYA alt for KOYA [KFF]
RAJAH KABUNGSUAN MANOBO alt for MANOBO, RAJAH KABUNSUWAN [MQK]
RAJASTHANI alt for MARWARI [MKD]
RAJASTHANI alt for MARWARI [MRI]
RAJASTHANI GUJURI alt for GUJARI [GJU]
RAJBANGSI [RJB] lang, India; also in Bangladesh, Nepal
RAJBANSHI alt for RAJBANGSI [RJB]
RAJBANSI alt for RAJBANGSI [RJB]
RAJI [RJI] lang, Nepal
RAJIBAR alt for RAJI [RJI]
RAJKOTI dial of KALAMI [GWC]
RAJONG [RJG] lang, Indonesia (Nusa Tenggara)
RAJPUT GARASIA alt for GARASIA, RAJPUT [GRA]
RAJSHAHI dial of BENGALI [BNG]
RAJURA dial of GONDI, SOUTHERN [GGO]
RAKAHANGA-MANIHIKI [RKH] lang, Cook Islands; also in New Zealand
RAKHAIN alt for ARAKANESE [MHV]
RAKHAIN alt for RAKHINE dial of ARAKANESE [MHV]
RAKHELI dial of NACHERING [NCD]
RAKHINE alt for ARAKANESE [MHV]
RAKHINE dial of ARAKANESE [MHV]
RAKHSHANI dial of BALOCHI, WESTERN [BGN]
RAKLU UN alt for ADABE [ADB]
RAKLU-UN alt for ADABE [ADB]
RAKUNEI dial of KUANUA [KSD]
RALAM alt for MNONG ROLOM dial of MNONG, EASTERN [MNG]
RALÁMULI DE LA TARAHUMARA BAJA alt for TARAHUMARA BAJA [TAC]
RALTE [RAL] lang, Myanmar; also in India
RALTE dial of LUSHAI [LSH]
RALUANA dial of KUANUA [KSD]
RAM alt for FALI-TINGUELIN dial of FALI, SOUTH [FAL]
RAMA [RMA] lang, Nicaragua
RAMA CAY CREOLE ENGLISH dial of NORTHERN CENTRAL AMERICA CREOLE ENGLISH [BZI]
RAMAND dial of TAKESTANI [TKS]
RAMARAMA alt for ITOGAPÚK [ITG]
RAMBANI dial of KASHMIRI [KSH]
RAMBATU-MANUSSA-RUMBERU alt for SOUTH ALUNE dial of ALUNE [ALP]
RAMBI alt for BAROMBI [BBI]
RAMBIA alt for LAMBYA [LAI]

RAMBUSO dial of SUDEST [TGO]
RAMECHAAP dial of SHERPA [SCR]
RAMEKHERA alt for KORKU [KFQ]
RAMKOKAMEKRA dial of CANELA [RAM]
RAMOAAINA [RAI] lang, Papua New Guinea
RAMPI [LJE] lang, Indonesia (Sulawesi)
RAMPI dial of RAMPI [LJE]
RAMPI-LEBONI alt for RAMPI [LJE]
RAMPURI alt for UPPER MAHASU PAHARI dial of PAHARI, MAHASU [BFZ]
RAMUAINA alt for RAMOAAINA [RAI]
RANA alt for CENTRAL BURU dial of BURU [MHS]
RANA dial of GHALE, KUTANG [GHT]
RANA THAKUR alt for THARU, RANA [THR]
RANAO alt for MARANAO [MRW]
RANAU [RAE] lang, Indonesia (Sumatra)
RANAU dial of DUSUN, CENTRAL [DTP]
RANAWAT dial of BHILI [BHB]
RANDAI dial of BUNUN [BNN]
RANDAWAYA dial of AMBAI [AMK]
RANDILE alt for RENDILLE [REL]
RANEI alt for YINCHIA [YIN]
RANG [RAX] lang, Nigeria
RANG GLAI alt for ROGLAI, NORTHERN [ROG]
RANGA dial of ENREKANG [PTT]
RANGAH alt for STIENG, BULO [STI]
RANGARI alt for KOSTI dial of VARHADI-NAGPURI [VAH]
RANGARI dial of KHANDESI [KHN]
RANGARI dial of MALVI [MUP]
RANGDANIA dial of RABHA [RAH]
RANGI [LAG] lang, Tanzania
RANGKAS [RGK] lang, Nepal; also in India
RANGKHAS alt for RANGKAS [RGK]
RANGKHOL alt for HRANGKHOL [HRA]
RANGLOI alt for TINANI [LBF]
RANGLONG dial of CHIN, FALAM [HBH]
RANGPAN alt for NAGA, TASE [NST]
RANGRI dial of MALVI [MUP]
RANI BHIL dial of BHILI [BHB]
RANTEBULAWAN alt for WEST RANTEBULAHAN dial of BAMBAM [PTU]
RANTEPAO dial of TORAJA-SADAN [SDA]
RANYA dial of GOWLI [GOK]
RAO [RAO] lang, Papua New Guinea
RAO BRERI alt for RAO [RAO]
RAOJIN dial of PALAUNG, PALE [PCE]
RAOPING alt for YUE-TAI dial of CHINESE, HAKKA [HAK]
RAOROU alt for ZAUZOU [ZAL]
RAOSIARA alt for LOSIARA dial of TEOP [TIO]
RAPA [RAY] lang, French Polynesia
RAPA NUI [PBA] lang, Chile; also in French Polynesia, USA
RAPAN alt for RAPA [RAY]
RAPANGKAKA dial of PAMONA [BCX]
RAPITOK dial of KUANUA [KSD]
RAPOISI [KYX] lang, Papua New Guinea
RAPPANG BUGINESE alt for BUGIS [BPR]
RAPTING [RAP] lang, Papua New Guinea
RARDRO BHIL dial of KOLI, WADIYARA [KXP]

RAROTONGA dial of RAROTONGAN [RRT]
RAROTONGAN [RRT] lang, Cook Islands; also in
  French Polynesia, New Zealand
RAROTONGAN-MANGAIAN alt for RAROTONGAN
  [RRT]
RARUA alt for SAAROA [SXR]
RASAWA [RAC] lang, Indonesia (Irian Jaya)
RASHAAYDA alt for CENTRAL NAJDI dial of
  ARABIC, NAJDI SPOKEN [ARS]
RASHAD dial of TEGALI [RAS]
RASHTI [RSH] lang, Iran
RASUWA dial of TAMANG, WESTERN [TDG]
RATAGNON [BTN] lang, Philippines
RATAGNON dial of RATAGNON [BTN]
RATAHAN [RTH] lang, Indonesia (Sulawesi)
RATAK dial of MARSHALLESE [MZM]
RATCHABURI PWO KAREN dial of KAREN, PWO
  WESTERN THAILAND [KJP]
RATHAWI [RTW] lang, India
RATHI dial of GARHWALI [GBM]
RATHOD alt for DUBLI [DUB]
RATHORA alt for LODHANTI dial of BUNDELI [BNS]
RATHVI dial of BHILI [BHB]
RATHWI BARELI dial of BARELI [BGD]
RATHWI PAURI dial of BARELI [BGD]
RATNAWATI dial of JERUNG [JEE]
RATO dial of RAMPI [LJE]
RATSUA dial of HAHON [HAH]
RATTIYAN alt for VAAGRI BOOLI [VAA]
RAUA alt for RAWA [RWO]
RAU-CHAUBHAISI dial of KUMAUNI [KFY]
RAUT alt for RAWAT [JNL]
RAUTE [RAU] lang, Nepal
RAUTO alt for PULIE-RAUTO dial of LAMOGAI
  [LMG]
RAUTYE alt for RAUTE [RAU]
RAVA alt for RABHA [RAH]
RAVO alt for RAWO dial of BAURO [BXA]
RAVULA [YEA] lang, India
RAWA [RWO] lang, Papua New Guinea
RAWA dial of RAWA [RWO]
RAWAN alt for ATONI [TMR]
RAWANG [RAW] lang, Myanmar; also in India
RAWANG dial of RAWANG [RAW]
RAWAS [RAJ] lang, Indonesia (Sumatra)
RAWAT [JNL] lang, Nepal; also in India
RAWE alt for BRAO [BRB]
RAWE alt for LAVE [BRB]
RAWO [RWA] lang, Papua New Guinea
RAWO dial of BAURO [BXA]
RAXSHANI alt for RAKHSHANI dial of BALOCHI,
  WESTERN [BGN]
RAYALSEEMA dial of TELUGU [TCW]
RAYGLAY alt for ROGLAI, NORTHERN [ROG]
RAZAJERDI [RAT] lang, Iran
RAZGRAD dial of TURKISH [TRK]
RAZONG alt for RAJONG [RJG]
RDE alt for RADE [RAD]
RDE KPA dial of RADE [RAD]
RDZONGKHA alt for DZONGKHA [DZO]
REANG alt for RIANG [RIA]

REAO dial of TUAMOTUAN [PMT]
REASATI alt for BAHAWALPURI dial of SARAIKI
  [SKR]
REASATI alt for SARAIKI [SKR]
REBAR dial of KUANUA [KSD]
REBINA alt for RIBINA dial of JERE [JER]
REBU alt for BALOI [BIZ]
REBU alt for BANGI [BNI]
RED BOBO alt for BWAMU [BOX]
RED GELAO dial of GELAO [KKF]
RED INDIANS alt for BEOTHUK [BUE]
RED KAREN alt for KAYAH, EASTERN [EKY]
RED KAREN alt for KAYAH, WESTERN [KYU]
RED LACHI alt for LIPUKE dial of LACHI [LBT]
RED LAHU alt for NYI dial of LAHU [LAH]
RED LAKE CHIPPEWA dial of CHIPPEWA [CIW]
RED MEO alt for HMONG, EASTERN XIANGXI
  [MUQ]
RED MEO alt for HMONG, WESTERN XIANGXI
  [MMR]
RED MIAO alt for HMONG, EASTERN XIANGXI
  [MUQ]
RED MIAO alt for HMONG, WESTERN XIANGXI
  [MMR]
RED TAI alt for TAI DAENG [TYR]
RED THAI alt for TAI DAENG [TYR]
REDDI alt for MUKHA-DORA [MMK]
REDDI-DORA alt for MUKHA-DORA [MMK]
REDJANG alt for REJANG [REJ]
REE alt for ARIKARA [ARI]
REEF ISLANDS alt for AYIWO [NFL]
REEFS alt for AYIWO [NFL]
REEL [ATU] lang, Sudan
REGA alt for LEGA-MWENGA [LGM]
REGA alt for LEGA-SHABUNDA [LEA]
REGI alt for KARA [REG]
REGI dial of CINDA-REGI-TIYAL [KAU]
REI dial of LOU [LOJ]
REIKHA alt for DAGIK [DEC]
REIWO alt for YAPUNDA [YEV]
REJANG [REJ] lang, Indonesia (Sumatra)
REJANG KAJAN alt for KAYAN, REJANG [REE]
REJANG-LEBONG alt for REJANG [REJ]
REK alt for DINKA, SOUTHWESTERN [DIK]
REK dial of DINKA, SOUTHWESTERN [DIK]
REKHTA dial of URDU [URD]
REKHTI alt for REKHTA dial of URDU [URD]
RELI [REI] lang, India
RELLI alt for RELI [REI]
REMA [BOW] lang, Papua New Guinea
REMBARRANGA alt for REMBARUNGA [RMB]
REMBARRNGA alt for REMBARUNGA [RMB]
REMBARUNGA [RMB] lang, Australia
REMBOKEN dial of TONDANO [TDN]
REMBONG [REB] lang, Indonesia (Nusa
  Tenggara)
REMBONG dial of REMBONG [REB]
REMI alt for NYATURU [RIM]
REMO [REM] lang, Peru
REMO alt for BONDO [BFW]
REMOSUM alt for BONDO [BFW]

REMPI [RMP] lang, Papua New Guinea
REMPIN alt for REMPI [RMP]
REMUN alt for MILIKIN [MIN]
RENDILE alt for RENDILLE [REL]
RENDILLE [REL] lang, Kenya
RENDRE alt for NUNGU [RIN]
RENGAO [REN] lang, Viet Nam
RENGGOU alt for ROTE-TIMUR dial of ROTE [ROT]
RENGJONGMU dial of LEPCHA [LEP]
RENGMA alt for NAGA, RENGMA [NRE]
RENNELL [MNV] lang, Solomon Islands
RENNELL alt for MUNGGAVA dial of RENNELL
   [MNV]
RENNELLESE alt for RENNELL [MNV]
RENNELLESE SIGN LANGUAGE [RSI] lang,
   Solomon Islands
RENNELLESE-BELLONESE alt for RENNELL [MNV]
REO alt for SOUTHERN LYÉLÉ dial of LYELE
   [LEE]
REPANBITIP [RPN] lang, Vanuatu
RER BARE [RER] lang, Ethiopia
RERAU [REA] lang, Papua New Guinea
RERE alt for KOALIB [KIB]
REREBERE alt for RER BARE [RER]
REREP [PGK] lang, Vanuatu
RESHE [RES] lang, Nigeria
RESHIAT alt for DAASANACH [DSH]
RESIA dial of SLOVENIAN [SLV]
RESÍGARO [RGR] lang, Peru
RESÍGERO alt for RESÍGARO [RGR]
RESTIGOUCHE alt for MICMAC [MIC]
RETTA [RET] lang, Indonesia (Nusa Tenggara)
RETUAMA alt for TANIMUCA-RETUARÃ [TNC]
RETUARÃ alt for TANIMUCA-RETUARÃ [TNC]
RETUARÃ dial of TANIMUCA-RETUARA [TNC]
RÉUNION CREOLE FRENCH [RCF] lang, Réunion;
   also in Comoros Islands, Madagascar
REVAL alt for TALLINN dial of ESTONIAN [EST]
REWA alt for RAMBUSO dial of SUDEST [TGO]
REYESANO [REY] lang, Bolivia
RGYARONG alt for JIARONG [JYA]
RHADE alt for RADE [RAD]
RHAETO-ROMANCE alt for ROMANSCH [RHE]
RHENO alt for REMO [REM]
RHETO-ROMANCE alt for ROMANSCH [RHE]
RHINYIHINYI dial of TEMBO [TBT]
RHODANIEN dial of PROVENCAL [PRV]
RIAHOMA alt for PAHI [LGT]
RIANG [RIA] lang, India; also in Bangladesh
RIANG [RIL] lang, Myanmar; also in China
RIANG dial of KOK BOROK [TRP]
RIANG-LANG alt for RIANG [RIL]
RIANTANA [RAN] lang, Indonesia (Irian Jaya)
RIASATI alt for BAHAWALPURI dial of SARAIKI
   [SKR]
RIASATI alt for SARAIKI [SKR]
RIASI dial of KASHMIRI [KSH]
RIASITI alt for SARAIKI [SKR]
RIAU dial of MALAY [MLI]
RIBAGORÇAN alt for NORTHWESTERN CATALAN
   dial of CATALAN-VALENCIAN-BALEAR [CLN]

RIBAGORZANO alt for EASTERN ARAGONESE
   dial of ARAGONESE [AXX]
RIBAH dial of CLELA [DRI]
RIBAM alt for RIBAN dial of PITI [PCN]
RIBAN dial of PITI [PCN]
RIBAW dial of BATA [BTA]
RIBBI dial of LOKO [LOK]
RIBE dial of GIRYAMA [NYF]
RIBIA dial of THEMNE [TEJ]
RIBINA dial of JERE [JER]
RIBUN [RIR] lang, Indonesia (Kalimantan)
RICHA dial of KULERE [KUL]
RIDAN dial of KUBU [KVB]
RIDARNGO alt for RITARUNGO [RIT]
RIDDI alt for MUKHA-DORA [MMK]
RIDHARRNGU alt for RITARUNGO [RIT]
RIEN [RIE] lang, Laos
RIF alt for TARIFIT [RIF]
RIFF alt for TARIFIT [RIF]
RIFI alt for TARIFIT [RIF]
RIFIA alt for TARIFIT [RIF]
RIGBO dial of MADI, SOUTHERN [QMD]
RIGWE alt for IRIGWE [IRI]
RIHE alt for RIBE dial of GIRYAMA [NYF]
RIHU'A dial of FAGANI [FAF]
RIKBAKTSA [ART] lang, Brazil
RIKOU alt for ROTE-TIMUR dial of ROTE [ROT]
RIKPA alt for BAFIA [KSF]
RIKPA' alt for BAFIA [KSF]
RIKSMAAL alt for NORWEGIAN, BOKMAAL
   [NRR]
RIKVANI dial of ANDI [ANI]
RIMATARA dial of AUSTRAL [AUT]
RIMI alt for GIRWANA dial of NYATURU [RIM]
RIMI alt for NYATURU [RIM]
RINCÓN ZAPOTEC alt for ZAPOTECO,
   RINCÓN [ZAR]
RINCONADA BICOLANO alt for BICOLANO, IRIGA
   [BTO]
RINCÓN-SUR ZAPOTEC alt for ZAPOTECO,
   RINCÓN SUR [ZSR]
RINDI alt for MANGILI-WAIJELO dial of KAMBERA
   [SMI]
RINDIRI alt for NUNGU [RIN]
RINDRE alt for NUNGU [RIN]
RINDRE dial of NUNGU [RIN]
RINGGOU alt for ROTE-TIMUR dial of ROTE
   [ROT]
RIO alt for GEDAGED [GDD]
RIO ARAUCA GUAHIBO alt for PLAYERO [GOB]
RÍO CASACARÁ dial of YUKPA [YUP]
RÍO MARACAS dial of YUKPA [YUP]
RÍO NEGRO dial of YUKPA [YUP]
RIO PONGO BAGA alt for BAGA SITEMU [BSP]
RIO TOMO GUAHIBO alt for AMORUA dial of
   GUAHIBO [GUH]
RION dial of KOHO [KPM]
RIOUW-LINGGA alt for RIAU dial of MALAY [MLI]
RIPERE alt for GBETE dial of MBUM [MDD]
RIPEY alt for BAFIA [KSF]
RIRIO [RRI] lang, Solomon Islands

RIRRATJINGU dial of DHANGU [GLA]
RIS alt for ARIKARA [ARI]
RISHUWA alt for SHUWA-ZAMANI [KSA]
RISHUWA alt for SI dial of LERE [GNH]
RITAEBANG alt for LAMAHOLOT dial of
LAMAHOLOT [SLP]
RITARNUGU alt for RITARUNGO [RIT]
RITARUNGO [RIT] lang, Australia
RITHARNGU alt for RITARUNGO [RIT]
RITIME dial of GIMNIME [KMB]
RITO alt for LUTOS dial of LUTOS [NDY]
RITO alt for RUTO dial of LUTOS [NDY]
RITOK dial of MALAY [MLI]
RIUNG [RIU] lang, Indonesia (Nusa Tenggara)
RIUNG alt for DAPALAN dial of TALAUD [TLD]
"RIVER BUSHMAN" pejorative alt for BUGA-KXOE
dial of KXOE [XUU]
RIVER CESS GIO dial of DAN [DAF]
RIVER CHULUPI dial of CHULUPI [CAG]
RIVER JARAWA alt for BADA [BAU]
RIVER JUKUN alt for WANNU [JUB]
RIVER RUKI alt for BOLOKI [BKT]
RIVERCESS BASSA dial of BASSA [BAS]
RIWAI alt for BAGHELI [BFY]
RIYADH alt for CENTRAL NAJDI dial of ARABIC,
NAJDI SPOKEN [ARS]
RIYAO dial of OY [OYB]
RLAM alt for MNONG ROLOM dial of MNONG,
EASTERN [MNG]
RMEET alt for LAMET [LBN]
RO alt for CHRAU [CHR]
RO dial of FOLOPA [PPO]
RO BAMBAMI alt for AGOI [IBM]
ROAMAINA alt for OMURANO [OMU]
ROBA dial of LALA-ROBA [LLA]
ROBBA alt for ROBA dial of LALA-ROBA [LLA]
ROBIANA alt for ROVIANA [RUG]
ROBODA alt for LOBODA dial of DOBU [DOB]
ROCKY PEAK [ROK] lang, Papua New Guinea
ROCOROIBO TARAHUMARA alt for TARAHUMARA
BAJA [TAC]
RODI alt for TRAVELLER DANISH [RMD]
RODI alt for TRAVELLER NORWEGIAN [RMG]
RODIYA dial of SINHALA [SNH]
RO'DO BO' alt for DUMI [DUS]
RODOSTO dial of ARMENIAN [ARM]
RODRIGUES CREOLE dial of MORISYEN [MFE]
ROEA alt for MACUNA [MYY]
ROFIA dial of CISHINGINI [ASG]
ROFIK alt for DEMIK dial of KEIGA [KEC]
ROGEDE dial of NZANYI [NJA]
ROGLAI, CACGIA [ROC] lang, Viet Nam
ROGLAI, NORTHERN [ROG] lang, Viet Nam
ROGLAI, SOUTHERN [RGS] lang, Viet Nam
ROGO [ROD] lang, Nigeria
ROHINGA dial of CHITTAGONIAN [CIT]
ROHOMONI dial of HARUKU [HRK]
ROHRURI alt for UPPER MAHASU PAHARI dial
of PAHARI, MAHASU [BFZ]
ROINJI alt for RONJI [ROE]
ROK dial of KHMU [KJG]

ROKHUNG dial of BAHING [RAR]
ROKKA alt for NGAD'A [NXG]
ROLAM alt for MNONG ROLOM dial of MNONG,
EASTERN [MNG]
ROLOM alt for MNONG ROLOM dial of MNONG,
EASTERN [MNG]
ROLONG dial of TSWANA [TSW]
ROM alt for OROM dial of TESO [TEO]
ROM alt for ROMANI, VLAX [RMY]
ROMA [RMM] lang, Indonesia (Maluku)
ROMA alt for ADOMA dial of CLELA [DRI]
ROMAIC alt for GREEK [GRK]
ROMAM [ROH] lang, Viet Nam
ROMA-NA alt for ADOMA dial of CLELA [DRI]
ROMANAU alt for RUMANAU dial of LOBU, LANAS
[RUU]
ROMANCHE alt for ROMANSCH [RHE]
ROMANÉS alt for ROMANI, VLAX [RMY]
ROMANESE alt for ROMANI, VLAX [RMY]
ROMANG alt for ROMA [RMM]
ROMANI ENGLISH alt for ANGLOROMANI
[RME]
ROMANI, BALKAN [RMN] lang, Yugoslavia; also in
Bulgaria, France, Germany, Greece, Hungary,
Iran, Italy, Macedonia, Moldova, Romania, Turkey
(Europe), Ukraine, USA
ROMANI, BALTIC [ROM] lang, Poland; also in
Belarus, Estonia, Latvia, Lithuania, Russia
(Asia), Ukraine
ROMANI, CARPATHIAN [RMC] lang, Czech
Republic; also in Hungary, Poland, Romania,
Slovakia, Ukraine, USA
ROMANI, KALO FINNISH [RMF] lang, Finland; also
in Sweden
ROMANI, SINTE [RMO] lang, Yugoslavia; also
in Austria, Croatia, Czech Republic, France,
Germany, Hungary, Italy, Kazakhstan,
Netherlands, Poland, Slovenia, Switzerland
ROMANI, VLAX [RMY] lang, Romania; also in
Albania, Argentina, Bosnia-Herzegovina,
Brazil, Bulgaria, Canada, Chile, Colombia,
France, Germany, Greece, Hungary, Italy,
Mexico, Moldova, Netherlands, Norway,
Poland, Portugal, Russia (Europe), Slovakia,
Spain, Sweden, Ukraine, United Kingdom,
USA
ROMANI, WELSH [RMW] lang, United Kingdom
ROMANIAN [RUM] lang, Romania; also in Australia,
Azerbaijan, Canada, Finland, Hungary, Israel,
Kazakhstan, Kyrgyzstan, Moldova, Russia
(Europe), Tajikistan, Turkmenistan, Ukraine,
USA, Uzbekistan, Yugoslavia
ROMANIAN SIGN LANGUAGE [RMS] lang,
Romania
ROMANIAN, ISTRO [RUO] lang, Croatia
ROMANIAN, MACEDO [RUP] lang, Greece; also
in Albania, Bosnia-Herzegovina, Bulgaria,
Macedonia, Romania, Yugoslavia
ROMANIAN, MEGLENO [RUQ] lang, Greece
ROMANICHAL alt for ANGLOROMANI [RME]
ROMANIS alt for ANGLOROMANI [RME]

ROMANO-GREEK [RGE] lang, Greece
ROMANO-SERBIAN [RSB] lang, Yugoslavia
ROMANSCH [RHE] lang, Switzerland
ROMANSH alt for ROMANSCH [RHE]
ROMBI alt for BAROMBI [BBI]
ROMBI alt for LOMBI [LMI]
ROMBLOMANON [ROL] lang, Philippines
ROMBLON alt for ROMBLOMANON [ROL]
ROMBLON dial of ROMBLOMANON [ROL]
ROMBO [ROF] lang, Tanzania
ROMENES alt for ROMANI, VLAX [RMY]
ROMKUIN alt for ROMKUN [RMK]
ROMKUN [RMK] lang, Papua New Guinea
ROMMANES alt for ROMANI, SINTE [RMO]
ROMMANI alt for TAVRINGER ROMANI [RMU]
ROMUNGRE alt for ROMANI, VLAX [RMY]
ROMUNGRO alt for ROMANI, CARPATHIAN
    [RMC]
RON [CLA] lang, Nigeria
RON alt for ROON [RNN]
RONDU alt for GILGITI dial of SHINA [SCL]
RONE alt for TEMEIN [TEQ]
RONG alt for CHANGTHANG [CNA]
RONG alt for LEPCHA [LEP]
RONG KONG alt for LAO [NOL]
RONGA [RON] lang, Mozambique; also in South
    Africa
RO-NGAO alt for RENGAO [REN]
RONGBA dial of AMDO [ADX]
RONGE alt for TEMEIN [TEQ]
RONGGA [ROR] lang, Indonesia (Nusa Tenggara)
RONGKE alt for LEPCHA [LEP]
RONGKONG alt for TAE' [ROB]
RONGKONG dial of TAE [ROB]
RONGKONG KANANDEDE alt for TAE' [ROB]
RONGMAHBROGPA dial of AMDO [ADX]
RONGMAI alt for NAGA, RONGMEI [NBU]
RONGMEI alt for NAGA, RONGMEI [NBU]
RONGO alt for ORUNGU dial of MYENE [MYE]
RONGPA alt for LEPCHA [LEP]
RONGRANG dial of NAGA, TASE [NST]
RONJI [ROE] lang, Papua New Guinea
RONRANG dial of NAGA, TASE [NST]
ROOI NASIE alt for NAMA [NAQ]
ROOMARROWS alt for RUMANAU dial of LOBU,
    LANAS [RUU]
ROON [RNN] lang, Indonesia (Irian Jaya)
ROONGAS alt for RUNGUS [DRG]
ROOTIGAANGA dial of DATOOGA [TCC]
ROPER RIVER KRIOL dial of KRIOL [ROP]
ROPER RIVER PIDGIN alt for ROPER RIVER
    KRIOL dial of KRIOL [ROP]
ROPER-BAMYILI CREOLE alt for KRIOL [ROP]
ROPO alt for WLOPO dial of KRUMEN, TEPO [TED]
ROR dial of KAG-FER-JIIR-KOOR-ROR-US-
    ZUKSUN [GEL]
RORI alt for SANGU [SBP]
RORIA [RGA] lang, Vanuatu
RORO [RRO] lang, Papua New Guinea
RORO dial of RORO [RRO]
ROROVANA alt for TORAU [TTU]

ROSARITO CORA dial of CORA, SANTA TERESA
    [COK]
ROSHANI alt for RUSHANI dial of SHUGHNI [SGH]
ROSHANI dial of SHUGHNI [SGH]
ROSO dial of AGTA, DUPANINAN [DUO]
ROSSEL alt for YELE [YLE]
ROTANESE CHAMORRO dial of CHAMORRO
    [CJD]
ROTE [ROT] lang, Indonesia (Nusa Tenggara)
ROTE BARAT alt for ROTE, WESTERN [ROW]
ROTE, WESTERN [ROW] lang, Indonesia (Nusa
    Tenggara)
ROTEA alt for SEDANG [SED]
ROTEANG alt for SEDANG [SED]
ROTE-RINGGOU alt for ROTE-TIMUR dial of
    ROTE [ROT]
ROTE-TENGAH dial of ROTE [ROT]
ROTE-TIMUR dial of ROTE [ROT]
ROTI alt for ROTE [ROT]
ROTI dial of BAJAU, INDONESIAN [BDL]
ROTIGENGA alt for ROOTIGAANGA dial of
    DATOOGA [TCC]
ROTINESE alt for ROTE [ROT]
ROTO alt for PULIE-RAUTO dial of LAMOGAI [LMG]
ROTOKAS [ROO] lang, Papua New Guinea
ROTORUA-TAUPO dial of MAORI [MBF]
ROTSE alt for LOZI [LOZ]
ROTTI alt for ROTE [ROT]
ROTUMAN [RTM] lang, Fiji
ROTUNA alt for ROTUMAN [RTM]
ROTVI alt for LOZI [LOZ]
ROTWELSCH alt for TRAVELLER DANISH [RMD]
ROUCHI alt for PICARD [PCD]
ROUCHI alt for PICARD dial of FRENCH [FRN]
ROUCOUYENNE alt for WAYANA [WAY]
ROUCOUYENNE alt for RUCUYEN dial of WAYANA
    [WAY]
ROUKU alt for WÁRA [TCI]
ROUMANIAN alt for ROMANIAN [RUM]
ROUNGA alt for RUNGA [ROU]
ROUNGO alt for RUNGA [ROU]
ROUROU alt for ZAUZOU [ZAL]
ROUTA dial of BUNGKU [BKZ]
ROUTO alt for LUTOS dial of LUTOS [NDY]
ROUTO alt for RUTO dial of LUTOS [NDY]
ROUYI alt for LUYANA [LAV]
ROVIANA [RUG] lang, Solomon Islands
ROZI alt for LOZI [LOZ]
RTAHU dial of AMDO [ADX]
RTCHI alt for GAVAR [GOU]
RTSAMANGPA'IKHA alt for CHOCANGACAKHA
    [CHK]
RUA dial of WANUKAKA [WNK]
RUAFA alt for TARIFIT [RIF]
RUAL dial of GIDRA [GDR]
RUANA alt for RWANDA [RUA]
RUANDA alt for RWANDA [RUA]
RUAVATU alt for LENGO [LGR]
RUBASA alt for BASA [BZW]
RUBASSA alt for BASA [BZW]
RUBIANA alt for ROVIANA [RUG]

RUC alt for CHUT [SCB]
RUC dial of CHUT [SCB]
RUCUYEN dial of WAYANA [WAY]
RUDBARI [RDB] lang, Iran
RUE dial of SENA [SEH]
RUFAWA alt for RUHU dial of LAME [BMA]
RUFIJI [RUI] lang, Tanzania
RUFU alt for RUHU dial of LAME [BMA]
RUFUMBIRA dial of RWANDA [RUA]
RUGA [RUH] lang, India
RUGARA alt for BUIN [BUO]
RUGCIRIKU alt for DIRIKU [DIU]
RUGNOT OF LAKE BUHI EAST alt for AGTA, MT.
   IRAYA [ATL]
RUGUNGU alt for GUNGU [RUB]
RUGURU [RUF] lang, Tanzania
RUHAYA alt for HAYA [HAY]
RUHU dial of LAME [BMA]
RUIHI alt for RUFIJI [RUI]
RUIJA dial of SAAMI, NORTHERN [LPR]
RUILAK alt for KAFOA [KPU]
RUK alt for CHUUKESE [TRU]
RUKAI [DRU] lang, Taiwan
RUKARAGWE alt for NYAMBO [NYM]
RUKIGA alt for CHIGA [CHG]
RUKOBI alt for HUNDE [HKE]
RUKONJO alt for KONJO [KOO]
RUKONJO dial of KONJO [KOO]
RUKUBA alt for CHE [RUK]
RUKUL dial of BO-RUKUL [MAE]
RUKWANGALI alt for KWANGALI [KWN]
RULI [RUC] lang, Uganda
RUM dial of GIZIGA, SOUTH [GIZ]
RUMA [RUZ] lang, Nigeria
RUMA dial of KORKU [KFQ]
RUMAI alt for PALAUNG, RUMAI [RBB]
RUMAIYA alt for MALA [RUY]
RUMANAU dial of LOBU, LANAS [RUU]
RUMANAU ALAB alt for RUMANAU dial of LOBU,
   LANAS [RUU]
RUMANIAN alt for ROMANIAN [RUM]
RUMAYA alt for MALA [RUY]
RUMBALA alt for MBALA [MDP]
RUMBERPON dial of BIAK [BHW]
RUMBIA alt for WITA EA dial of MORONENE [MQN]
RUMBUR alt for NORTHERN KALASHA dial of
   KALASHA [KLS]
RUMDALI alt for BAHING [RAR]
RUMELIAN dial of TURKISH [TRK]
RUMLI alt for LOMBI [LMI]
RUMSEN dial of COSTANOAN, SOUTHERN [CSS]
RUMU [KLQ] lang, Papua New Guinea
RUMUJI dial of IKWERE [IKW]
RUMUWA alt for RUMU [KLQ]
RUNA [RUN] lang, Colombia
RUNDI [RUD] lang, Burundi; also in Rwanda,
   Tanzania, Uganda
RUNDUM dial of TAGAL MURUT [MVV]
RUNGA [ROU] lang, Chad; also in CAR
RUNGA alt for RUNGWA [RNW]
RUNGA DE NDELE alt for RUNGA [ROU]

RUNGCHENBUNG dial of BANTAWA [BAP]
RUNGI [RUR] lang, Tanzania
RUNGU alt for ORUNGU dial of MYENE [MYE]
RUNGU alt for TAABWA [TAP]
RUNGU dial of MAMBWE-LUNGU [MGR]
RUNGUS [DRG] lang, Malaysia (Sabah)
RUNGUS dial of RUNGUS [DRG]
RUNGUS DUSUN alt for RUNGUS [DRG]
RUNGWA [RNW] lang, Tanzania
RUNSIEN alt for RUMSEN dial of COSTANOAN,
   SOUTHERN [CSS]
RUNYAMBO alt for NYAMBO [NYM]
RUNYANKOLE alt for NYANKORE [NYN]
RUNYARWANDA alt for RWANDA [RUA]
RUNYORO alt for HEMA [NIX]
RUNYORO alt for NYORO [NYR]
RUOMAI alt for PALAUNG, RUMAI [RBB]
RUOTSI alt for SWEDISH [SWD]
RUPINI dial of CHIN, FALAM [HBH]
RUPSHU alt for CHANGTHANG [CNA]
RUPUNUNI dial of GUYANESE CREOLE ENGLISH
   [GYN]
RURAL CENTRAL MALTESE dial of MALTESE
   [MLS]
RURAL EAST MALTESE dial of MALTESE [MLS]
RURAL PESHAWAR HINDKO dial of HINDKO,
   SOUTHERN [HIN]
RURAL WEST MALTESE dial of MALTESE [MLS]
RURAMA alt for RUMA [RUZ]
RURI dial of KWAYA [KYA]
RURUHI'IP alt for YAHANG [RHP]
RURUHIP alt for WANIB [AUK]
RURUHIP alt for YAHANG [RHP]
RURULI alt for RULI [RUC]
RURUMA alt for RUMA [RUZ]
RURUTU dial of AUSTRAL [AUT]
RUSHAN alt for ROSHANI dial of SHUGHNI [SGH]
RUSHAN alt for RUSHANI dial of SHUGHNI [SGH]
RUSHANI alt for ROSHANI dial of SHUGHNI
   [SGH]
RUSHANI dial of SHUGHNI [SGH]
RUSS alt for RUSSIAN [RUS]
RUSSELL ISLAND alt for LAVUKALEVE [LVK]
RUSSIA alt for DAASANACH [DSH]
RUSSIAN [RUS] lang, Russia (Europe); also
   in Armenia, Azerbaijan, Belarus, Bulgaria,
   Canada, China, Czech Republic, Estonia,
   Finland, Georgia, Germany, Greece, India,
   Israel, Kazakhstan, Kyrgyzstan, Latvia,
   Lithuania, Moldova, Mongolia, Norway,
   Poland, Slovakia, Tajikistan, Turkmenistan,
   Ukraine, Uruguay, USA, Uzbekistan
"RUSSIAN LAPP" pejorative alt for SAAMI, SKOLT
   [LPK]
RUSSIAN LAPP alt for SAAMI, SKOLT [LPK]
RUSSIAN SIGN LANGUAGE [RSL] lang, Russia
   (Europe); also in Bulgaria
RUSSIT alt for RUSSIAN [RUS]
RUSSKI alt for RUSSIAN [RUS]
RUSTAQA dial of LISHANID NOSHAN [AIJ]
RUSYN [RUE] lang, Ukraine; also in Slovakia

RUT dial of DINKA, NORTHEASTERN [DIP]
RUTAGWENDA dial of NYORO [NYR]
RUTAH dial of AMAHAI [AMQ]
RUTAL alt for RUTUL [RUT]
RUTENG alt for CENTRAL MANGGARAI dial of MANGGARAI [MQY]
RUTHENIAN alt for RUSYN [RUE]
RUTKAI alt for RUKAI [DRU]
RUTO alt for LUTOS [NDY]
RUTO dial of LUTOS [NDY]
RUTO alt for LUTOS dial of LUTOS [NDY]
RUTOORO alt for TOORO [TTJ]
RUTORO alt for TOORO [TTJ]
RUTSE alt for LOZI [LOZ]
RUTUL [RUT] lang, Russia (Europe); also in Azerbaijan
RUTULTSY alt for RUTUL [RUT]
RUTULY alt for RUTUL [RUT]
RUTUMAN alt for ROTUMAN [RTM]
RUTWA dial of RWANDA [RUA]
RUUND [RND] lang, DRC; also in Angola
RUVIANA alt for ROVIANA [RUG]
RUWENG dial of DINKA, NORTHWESTERN [DIW]
RUWENZORI KIBIRA alt for AMBA [RWM]
RWA [RWK] lang, Tanzania
RWALA alt for CENTRAL NAJDI dial of ARABIC, NAJDI SPOKEN [ARS]
RWAMBA alt for AMBA [RWM]
RWANDA [RUA] lang, Rwanda; also in Burundi, DRC, Tanzania, Uganda
RWANDUZ dial of LISHANID NOSHAN [AIJ]
RWO alt for RWA [RWK]
SA [SSA] lang, Vanuatu
SA alt for NGEMBA dial of GHOMALA [BBJ]
SA alt for NHANG [NHA]
SA alt for SAMO, MAYA [SYM]
SAA [SZR] lang, Cameroon
SAA alt for SA'A [APB]
SA'A [APB] lang, Solomon Islands
SAADJE alt for SAGZEE dial of DII [DUR]
SAAFI alt for SAAFI-SAAFI [SAV]
SAAFI-SAAFI [SAV] lang, Senegal
SAAKA dial of MAKHUWA-MEETTO [MAK]
SAAKYE alt for SAGZEE dial of DII [DUR]
SAAM [RAQ] lang, Nepal
SAAM alt for SAAMI, INARI [LPI]
SAAM alt for SAAMI, KILDIN [LPD]
SAAM alt for SAAMI, SKOLT [LPK]
SAAM alt for SAAMI, TER [LPT]
SAAM RAI alt for SAAM [RAQ]
SAAMA KHA alt for SAAM [RAQ]
SAAME alt for SAAMI, INARI [LPI]
SAAME alt for SAAMI, LULE [LPL]
SAAME alt for SAAMI, NORTHERN [LPR]
SAAME alt for SAAMI, SKOLT [LPK]
SAAMI alt for SAAMI, NORTHERN [LPR]
SAAMI alt for SAAMI, SOUTHERN [LPC]
SAAMI, AKKALA [SIA] lang, Russia (Europe)
SAAMI, INARI [LPI] lang, Finland
SAAMI, KEMI [LKS] lang, Finland
SAAMI, KILDIN [LPD] lang, Russia (Europe)

SAAMI, LULE [LPL] lang, Sweden; also in Norway
SAAMI, NORTHERN [LPR] lang, Norway; also in Finland, Sweden
SAAMI, PITE [LPB] lang, Sweden; also in Norway
SAAMI, SKOLT [LPK] lang, Finland; also in Russia (Europe)
SAAMI, SOUTHERN [LPC] lang, Sweden; also in Norway
SAAMI, TER [LPT] lang, Russia (Europe)
SAAMI, UME [LPU] lang, Sweden
SAAMIA dial of LUYIA [LUY]
SAAMTAAV alt for KIORR [XKO]
"SAAN" pejorative alt for HAI//OM [HGM]
SAAN dial of PAPE [NDU]
SA'ANG alt for HA'AANG dial of TAOIH, UPPER [TTH]
SAANGA dial of MAKHUWA-MEETTO [MAK]
SAANICH dial of SALISH, STRAITS [STR]
SAAPA alt for SAA [SZR]
SAAPA alt for SANAPANÁ [SAP]
SAAROA [SXR] lang, Taiwan
SAARONGE alt for DAJU, DAR DAJU [DJC]
SAARUA alt for SAAROA [SXR]
SAAWA dial of MUMUYE [MUL]
SAAWII dial of NOON [SNF]
SABA [SAA] lang, Chad
SABAH MURUT alt for TAGAL dial of TAGAL MURUT [MVV]
SABAKOR alt for BURUWAI [ASI]
SA'BAN [SNV] lang, Indonesia (Kalimantan); also in Malaysia (Sarawak)
SABANÊ alt for SABANÊS [SAE]
SABANERO dial of BUGLERE [SAB]
SABANÊS [SAE] lang, Brazil
SABANGA dial of BANDA-MBRES [BQK]
SABAOT [SPY] lang, Kenya
SABAR alt for SORA [SRB]
SABARA alt for SORA [SRB]
SABARI alt for AMIS [ALV]
SABARI dial of NIMOA [NMW]
SABELA alt for WAORANI [AUC]
SABENA alt for MOSKONA [MTJ]
SABERI alt for ISIRAWA [SRL]
SABEU dial of CHIN, MARA [MRH]
SABI dial of NYOLE [NUJ]
SABINY dial of KUPSABINY [KPZ]
SABIR alt for LINGUA FRANCA [PML]
SABON dial of LELE [UGA]
SABONES alt for SABANÊS [SAE]
SABÜM [SBO] lang, Malaysia (Peninsular)
SABU [HVN] lang, Indonesia (Nusa Tenggara)
SABUJÁ dial of KARIRI-XOCO [KZW]
SABUNGO dial of DAYAK, LAND [DYK]
SABUP alt for KENYAH, SEBOB [SIB]
SABURI dial of LOGORIK [LIU]
SABUTAN alt for BUKAR SADONG [SDO]
SABUYAN alt for SEBUYAU [SNB]
SABUYAU alt for SEBUYAU [SNB]
SAC dial of MESQUAKIE [SAC]
SAC AND FOX alt for MESQUAKIE [SAC]
SACAPULAS QUICHÉ alt for SACAPULTECO [QUV]

SACAPULTECO [QUV] lang, Guatemala
SACH alt for CHUT [SCB]
SACH dial of CHUT [SCB]
SACLAN alt for MIWOK, BAY [MKQ]
SADA alt for TAE' [ROB]
SADA alt for TOALA' [TLZ]
SADALIR alt for SALALIR dial of TAGAL MURUT [MVV]
SADALIR alt for SEDALIR dial of TIDONG [TID]
SADAN alt for SADRI [SCK]
SADAN alt for TORAJA-SA'DAN [SDA]
SA'DAN alt for TORAJA-SA'DAN [SDA]
SADANA alt for SADRI [SCK]
SADANG alt for TORAJA-SA'DAN [SDA]
SADANGA dial of BONTOC, CENTRAL [BNC]
SADANI alt for SADRI [SCK]
SA'DANSCHE alt for TORAJA-SA'DAN [SDA]
SADAR alt for SHADAL dial of MANKANYA [MAN]
SADAR BHUMIJ alt for BHUMIJ dial of MUNDARI [MUW]
SADARI alt for SADRI [SCK]
SADATI alt for SADRI [SCK]
SADHAN alt for SADRI [SCK]
SADHARI alt for SADRI [SCK]
SADNA alt for SADRI [SCK]
SADONG alt for BUKAR SADONG [SDO]
SADRI [SCK] lang, India; also in Bangladesh
SADRI dial of MAITHILI [MKP]
SADRI KORWA dial of CHHATTISGARHI [HNE]
SADRI, ORAON [SDR] lang, Bangladesh
SADRIK alt for SADRI [SCK]
SAEDIQ alt for TAROKO [TRV]
SAEK [SKB] lang, Laos; also in Thailand
SAEP [SPD] lang, Papua New Guinea
SAFALABA alt for SAFALIBA [SAF]
SAFALBA alt for SAFALIBA [SAF]
SAFALI alt for SAFALIBA [SAF]
SAFALIBA [SAF] lang, Ghana
SAFAN alt for SAPAN dial of ASMAT, CASUARINA COAST [ASC]
SAFANÉ dial of MARKA [MWR]
SAFEN alt for SAAFI-SAAFI [SAV]
SAFEYOKA alt for AMPEELI-WOJOKESO [APZ]
SAFI alt for SAAFI-SAAFI [SAV]
SAFI-SAFI alt for SAAFI-SAAFI [SAV]
SAFWA [SBK] lang, Tanzania
SAGADA IGOROT alt for KANKANAY, NORTHERN [KAN]
SAGADIN dial of DIDO [DDO]
SAGA-I alt for DUSUN SEGAMA dial of KINABATANGAN, UPPER [DMG]
SAGAI dial of KHAKAS [KJH]
SAGAJ alt for SAGAI dial of KHAKAS [KJH]
SAGAKA dial of JULA, KOYAGA [KGA]
SAGALA [SBM] lang, Tanzania
SAGALA alt for SAGALLA [TGA]
SAGALLA [TGA] lang, Kenya
SAGAMUK alt for ACIPA, EASTERN [AWA]
SAGAMUK alt for ACIPA, WESTERN [AWC]
SAGARA alt for SAGALA [SBM]
SAGBEE dial of MUMUYE [MUL]

SAGEJU alt for SEGEJU [SEG]
SAGHALA alt for SAGALLA [TGA]
SAGHILIN alt for SAKHALIN dial of AINU [AIN]
SAGO alt for CIWOGAI [TGD]
SAGTENGPA alt for BROKPAKE [SGT]
SAGU alt for ADONARA [ADA]
SAGUYE alt for SAKUYE dial of BORANA [GAX]
SAGWARA dial of WAGDI [WBR]
SAGZEE dial of DII [DUR]
SAHAFATRA dial of MALAGASY [MEX]
SAHARAN ARABIC alt for ARABIC, ALGERIAN SAHARAN SPOKEN [AAO]
SAHIBGANJ dial of SAURIA PAHARIA [MJT]
SAHIDIC dial of COPTIC [COP]
SAHIL TUNISIAN dial of ARABIC, TUNISIAN SPOKEN [AEB]
SAHO [SSY] lang, Eritrea; also in Ethiopia
SAHRAWI alt for ARABIC, HASSANIYYA [MEY]
SAHU [SUX] lang, Indonesia (Maluku)
SAHU alt for SAO dial of MASLAM [MSV]
SAHU'U alt for SAHU [SUX]
SAI alt for TAI PONG dial of TAI NUA [TDD]
SAI dial of GUMUZ [GUK]
SA'IBA alt for MANDAIC [MID]
SA<IDI alt for ARABIC, SA<IDI SPOKEN [AEC]
SAIFI dial of TEHIT [KPS]
SAIGHANI alt for SHUGHNI dial of SHUGHNI [SGH]
SAIJA alt for EMBERÁ-SAIJA [SJA]
SAILAU alt for LUSHAI [LSH]
SAILEN alt for DURIANKERE [DBN]
SAILOLOF alt for MA'YA [SLZ]
SAINTI alt for SANTALI [SNT]
SAIPA dial of SINSAURU [SNZ]
SAIPAN CAROLINIAN alt for CAROLINIAN [CAL]
SAIRANG dial of CHIN, THADO [TCZ]
SAISET alt for SAISIYAT [SAI]
SAISETT alt for SAISIYAT [SAI]
SAISIAT alt for SAISIYAT [SAI]
SAISIETT alt for SAISIYAT [SAI]
SAISIRAT alt for SAISIYAT [SAI]
SAISIYAT [SAI] lang, Taiwan
SAISYET alt for SAISIYAT [SAI]
SAISYETT alt for SAISIYAT [SAI]
SAJALONG [SJL] lang, India
SAJAU alt for SAJAU BASAP [SAD]
SAJAU BASAP [SAD] lang, Indonesia (Kalimantan)
SAK alt for KADO [KDV]
SAKA alt for ODUAL [ODU]
SAKA alt for SAAKA dial of MAKHUWA-MEETTO [MAK]
SAKA alt for SAKATA [SAT]
SAKA dial of NKUTU [NKW]
SAKAI alt for KENSIU [KNS]
SAKAI alt for SEMANG, LOWLAND [ORB]
SAKAI BUKIT OF TEMONGOH alt for PO-KLO dial of TEMIAR [TMH]
SAKAI OF PLUS KORBU dial of TEMIAR [TMH]
SAKAI TANJONG OF TEMONGOH alt for JEHER dial of KENSIU [KNS]
SAKAJI alt for NATHEMBO [NTE]
SAKALAGAN dial of MENTAWAI [MWV]

SAKALAVA alt for BUSHI [BUC]
SAKAM [SKM] lang, Papua New Guinea
SAKANYI dial of NTOMBA [NTO]
SAKAO [SKU] lang, Vanuatu
SAKAR dial of MBULA [MNA]
SAKARA alt for NZAKARA [NZK]
SAKATA [SAT] lang, DRC
SAKATA dial of SAKATA [SAT]
SAKAU alt for KHANG AI dial of KHANG [KJM]
SAKAU alt for SAKAO [SKU]
SAKAYA dial of BAREIN [BVA]
SAKE [SAG] lang, Gabon
SAKEI dial of KERINCI [KVR]
SAKER alt for BARGAM [MLP]
SAKHA alt for YAKUT [UKT]
SAKHALIN dial of AINU [AIN]
SAKHALIN dial of EVENKI [EVN]
SAKHUR alt for TSAKHUR [TKR]
SAKI alt for MAIA [SKS]
SAKIRABIÁ [SKF] lang, Brazil
SAKIRABIAK alt for SAKIRABIÁ [SKF]
SAKIRAP alt for MAKURÁP [MAG]
SAKIRAP alt for SAKIRABIÁ [SKF]
SAKIRAY alt for SAKIZAYA dial of AMIS,
     NATAORAN [AIS]
SAKIRIABAR alt for SAKIRABIÁ [SKF]
SAKIZAYA dial of AMIS, NATAORAN [AIS]
SAKKYRYR dial of EVEN [EVE]
SAKLAN alt for MIWOK, BAY [MKQ]
SAKPU dial of KARANG [KZR]
SAKUL alt for SUKUR [SUK]
SAKUYE dial of BORANA [GAX]
SALA [SHQ] lang, Zambia
SALA alt for SALAR [SLR]
SALAJAR alt for SELAYAR [SLY]
SALAKAHADI alt for MOLIMA [MOX]
SALAKAU alt for SELAKO [SKL]
SALALE dial of OROMO, BORANA-ARSI-GUJI
     [GAX]
SALALIR alt for SEDALIR dial of TIDONG [TID]
SALALIR dial of TAGAL MURUT [MVV]
SALAMÃI alt for MONDÉ [MND]
SALAMAIKÃ alt for MONDÉ [MND]
SALAMAT alt for CHARI-BAGUIRMI dial of ARABIC,
     CHADIAN SPOKEN [SHU]
SALAMPASU [SLX] lang, DRC
SALANG [HAL] lang, Viet Nam; also in Laos
SALANG alt for CHUT [SCB]
SALANG alt for HALANG [HAL]
SALANI dial of GARHWALI [GBM]
SALAR [SLR] lang, China
SALARU alt for SELARU [SLU]
SALAS [SGU] lang, Indonesia (Maluku)
SALAS GUNUNG alt for SALAS [SGU]
SALASACA QUICHUA alt for QUICHUA,
     HIGHLAND, TUNGURAHUA [QQS]
SALATAV dial of AVAR [AVR]
SALAVTA alt for VAGHRI [VGR]
SALAWATI alt for MA'YA [SLZ]
SALAYAR alt for SELAYAR [SLY]
SALAYER alt for SELAYAR [SLY]

SALCHA-GOODPASTER dial of TANANA, LOWER
     [TAA]
SALCHUQ [SLQ] lang, Iran
SALE alt for CHE [RUK]
SALEBABU alt for LIRANG dial of TALAUD [TLD]
SALEIER alt for SELAYAR [SLY]
SALEMAN [SAU] lang, Indonesia (Maluku)
SALENTO dial of GREEK [GRK]
SALEWARI dial of TELUGU [TCW]
SALI alt for NSARI [ASJ]
SALIANY dial of AZERBAIJANI, NORTH [AZE]
SALIBA [SBE] lang, Papua New Guinea
SÁLIBA [SLC] lang, Colombia; also in Venezuela
SALIBA dial of SALIBA [SBE]
SALIBABU alt for LIRANG dial of TALAUD [TLD]
SALIEN alt for NYINDROU [LID]
SALIMANA dial of SAWILA [SWT]
SALINAN [SAL] lang, USA
SALISH alt for KALISPEL-PEND D'OREILLE [FLA]
SALISH, SOUTHERN PUGET SOUND [SLH] lang,
     USA
SALISH, STRAITS [STR] lang, Canada; also in
     USA
SALITRE-CABAGRA dial of BRIBRI [BZD]
SÁLIVA alt for SÁLIBA [SLC]
SALKA alt for TSISHINGINI [KAM]
SALLAN alt for SALLANDS [SNK]
SALLAND alt for SALLANDS [SNK]
SALLANDS [SNK] lang, Netherlands
SALOG dial of SUBANEN, NORTHERN [STB]
SALON alt for MOKEN [MWT]
SALONG alt for MOKEN [MWT]
SALOR dial of TURKMEN [TCK]
SALT alt for SALT-YUI [SLL]
SALT POMO alt for POMO, NORTHEASTERN [PEF]
SALT-IUI alt for SALT-YUI [SLL]
SALT-YUI [SLL] lang, Papua New Guinea
SALU MUKANAM dial of BAMBAM [PTU]
SALUAN, COASTAL [LOE] lang, Indonesia
     (Sulawesi)
SALUAN, KAHUMAMAHON [SLB] lang, Indonesia
     (Sulawesi)
SALUG alt for SALOG dial of SUBANEN,
     NORTHERN [STB]
SALUMÁ [SLJ] lang, Brazil
SALUMÃ [UNK] lang, Brazil
SALVADORAN SIGN LANGUAGE [ESN] lang, El
     Salvador
SALYA alt for SELYA dial of NYAKYUSA-NGONDE
     [NYY]
SALYAN dial of AZERBAIJANI, NORTH [AZE]
SALYR dial of TURKMEN [TCK]
SAM alt for SHAN [SJN]
SAMA [SMD] lang, Angola
SAMA alt for BAJAU, INDONESIAN [BDL]
SAMA alt for PANA [PNQ]
SAMA alt for SAMBA DAKA [CCG]
SAMA dial of NUBRI [KTE]
SAMA dial of SAMA, SOUTHERN [SIT]
SAMA' alt for SAMA dial of SAMA, SOUTHERN
     [SIT]

SAMA KUBANG alt for BAJAU SEMPORNA dial of SAMA, SOUTHERN [SIT]

SAMA KUBUNG alt for SIKUBUNG dial of SAMA, SOUTHERN [SIT]

SAMA LAUT alt for BAJAU LAUT dial of SAMA, SOUTHERN [SIT]

SAMA MANDELAUT alt for BAJAU LAUT dial of SAMA, SOUTHERN [SIT]

SAMA MAPUN alt for MAPUN [SJM]

SAMA PALA'AU alt for BAJAU LAUT dial of SAMA, SOUTHERN [SIT]

SAMA SIBUTU alt for SIBUTU dial of SAMA, SOUTHERN [SIT]

SAMA SIBUTU' alt for SAMA, SOUTHERN [SIT]

SAMA SIMUNUL alt for SIMUNUL dial of SAMA, SOUTHERN [SIT]

SAMA UBIAN alt for UBIAN dial of SAMA, SOUTHERN [SIT]

SAMA, ABAKNON [ABX] lang, Philippines

SAMA, BALANGINGI [SSE] lang, Philippines; also in Malaysia (Sabah)

SAMA, CENTRAL [SML] lang, Philippines; also in Malaysia (Sabah)

SAMA, PANGUTARAN [SLM] lang, Philippines

SAMA, SOUTHERN [SIT] lang, Philippines; also in Malaysia (Sabah)

SAMADA alt for PADANG dial of TALIABU [TLV]

SAMAGIR dial of NANAI [GLD]

SAMAH alt for SAMA dial of SAMA, SOUTHERN [SIT]

SAMAH LUMBUH alt for SIBUTU dial of SAMA, SOUTHERN [SIT]

SAMAH-SAMAH alt for SIBUTU dial of SAMA, SOUTHERN [SIT]

S'AMAI alt for TSAMAI [TSB]

SAMAKHA alt for SAAM [RAQ]

SAMAKULUNG alt for PONGYONG [PGY]

SAMAL alt for SAMA, CENTRAL [SML]

SAMAL alt for SAMA dial of SAMA, SOUTHERN [SIT]

SAMALEK alt for KOKODA [QKW]

SAMANÁ ENGLISH [SAX] lang, Dominican Republic

SAMANAI dial of ANGOR [AGG]

SAMANG alt for SHAMANG [SGN]

SAMAP alt for ELEPI [ELE]

SAMAP alt for KAIEP [KBW]

SAMAR alt for SAMA dial of SAMA, SOUTHERN [SIT]

SAMARAN alt for WARAY-WARAY [WRY]

SAMAREÑO alt for WARAY-WARAY [WRY]

SAMARGIN dial of UDIHE [UDE]

SAMARIA dial of BENGALI [BNG]

SAMARITAN [SMP] lang, Palestinian West Bank and Gaza; also in Israel

SAMARITAN ARAMAIC [SRA] lang, Palestinian West Bank and Gaza; also in Israel

SAMARITAN HEBREW alt for SAMARITAN [SMP]

SAMARKENA alt for SAMAROKENA [TMJ]

SAMAR-LEYTE alt for WARAY-WARAY [WRY]

SAMAR-LEYTE dial of WARAY-WARAY [WRY]

SAMAROKENA [TMJ] lang, Indonesia (Irian Jaya)

SAMARUNG dial of SANGPANG [RAV]

SAMATALI alt for SANUMÁ [SAM]

SAMATARI alt for SANUMÁ [SAM]

SAMATE alt for MA'YA [SLZ]

SAMBA [SMX] lang, DRC

SAMBA alt for SAMBA DAKA [CCG]

SAMBA alt for SAMBA LEKO [NDI]

SAMBA BALI alt for NYONG [MUO]

SAMBA DAKA [CCG] lang, Nigeria

SAMBA DAKA dial of SAMBA DAKA [CCG]

SAMBA DE WANGAI dial of SAMBA LEKO [NDI]

SAMBA JANGANI dial of SAMBA DAKA [CCG]

SAMBA LEEKO alt for SAMBA LEKO [NDI]

SAMBA LEKO [NDI] lang, Cameroon; also in Nigeria

SAMBA LEKO dial of SAMBA LEKO [NDI]

SAMBA NNAKENYARE dial of SAMBA DAKA [CCG]

SAMBA OF MAPEO dial of SAMBA DAKA [CCG]

SAMBAA alt for SHAMBALA [KSB]

SAMBAL, BOTOLAN [SBL] lang, Philippines

SAMBAL, TINA [SNA] lang, Philippines

SAMBALA alt for SHAMBALA [KSB]

SAMBALI alt for SAMBAL, TINA [SNA]

SAMBALPURI alt for WESTERN ORIYA dial of ORIYA [ORY]

SAMBAN alt for SHAMANG [SGN]

SAMBARA alt for SHAMBALA [KSB]

SAMBAS dial of MALAY [MLI]

SAMBAYA dial of KURANKO [KHA]

SAMBE alt for NINZAM [NIN]

SAMBERI dial of BIAK [BHW]

SAMBERIGI [SSX] lang, Papua New Guinea

SAMBIO alt for KAPIN [TBX]

SAMBIO alt for SAMBYU dial of KWANGALI [KWN]

SAMBIRIR dial of ENDO [ENB]

SAMBIU alt for SAMBYU dial of KWANGALI [KWN]

SAMBLA alt for SEEKU [SOS]

SAMBO alt for MBO [MBO]

SAMBU alt for WAMSAK [WBD]

SAMBUGA dial of SHAMA-SAMBUGA [SQA]

SAMBUP alt for KENYAH, SEBOB [SIB]

SAMBUR alt for SAMBURU [SAQ]

SAMBURU [SAQ] lang, Kenya

SAMBYA dial of SAAM [RAQ]

SAMBYU dial of KWANGALI [KWN]

SAME alt for SAAMI, NORTHERN [LPR]

SAME alt for SAAMI, SKOLT [LPK]

SAME alt for SAAMI, SOUTHERN [LPC]

SAME' dial of BAJAU, INDONESIAN [BDL]

SAMEI [SMH] lang, China

SAMG PHANG alt for CHINESE, YUE [YUH]

SAMI alt for SAAMI, KEMI [LKS]

SÁMI alt for SAAMI, INARI [LPI]

SÁMI alt for SAAMI, KEMI [LKS]

SAMIA alt for SAAMIA dial of LUYIA [LUY]

SAMIC alt for SAAMI, INARI [LPI]

SAMIC alt for SAAMI, NORTHERN [LPR]

SAMIC alt for SAAMI, SOUTHERN [LPC]

SAMIHIM dial of MAANYAN [MHY]

SAMISH dial of SALISH, STRAITS [STR]

SAMMARINESE alt for EMILIANO-ROMAGNOLO [EML]
SAMMARINESE dial of EMILIANO-ROMAGNOLO [EML]
SAMO [SMQ] lang, Papua New Guinea
SAMO alt for OWINIGA [OWI]
SÀMÓ alt for KALAMSÉ [KNZ]
SÀMÓ alt for SÀMÒMÁ [KNZ]
SAMO, MATYA [STJ] lang, Burkina Faso; also in Mali
SAMO, MAYA [SYM] lang, Burkina Faso
SAMO, SOUTHERN [SBD] lang, Burkina Faso
SAMOAN [SMY] lang, Western Samoa; also in American Samoa, Fiji, New Zealand, Tonga, USA
SAMOBI alt for PAIWAN [PWN]
SAMOE alt for WARA [WBF]
SAMOGHO alt for DUUNGOMA [DUX]
SAMOGHO alt for DZÙÙNGOO [DNN]
SAMOGHO alt for JOWULU [JOW]
SAMOGHO alt for SEEKU [SOS]
SAMOGITIAN alt for SHAMAITISH dial of LITHUANIAN [LIT]
SAMOGO alt for DUUNGOMA [DUX]
SAMOGO alt for DZÙÙNGOO [DNN]
SAMOGOHIRI alt for DZÙÙNGOO dial of DZÙÙNGOO [DNN]
SAMOHAI alt for PAIWAN [PWN]
SÀMÒMÁ [KNZ] lang, Burkina Faso; also in Mali
SÀMÒMÁ alt for KALAMSÉ [KNZ]
SAMONG alt for HPON [HPO]
SAMORO alt for DUUNGOMA [DUX]
SAMORO alt for DZÙÙNGOO [DNN]
SAMOROGOUAN alt for KPANGO dial of DZÙÙNGOO [DNN]
SAMOSA [SMO] lang, Papua New Guinea
SAMPANG alt for SANGPANG [RAV]
SAMPANG dial of MADURA [MHJ]
SAMPANGE RAI alt for SANGPANG [RAV]
SAMPARA dial of SAMBA LEKO [NDI]
SAMPIT alt for BA'AMANG dial of NGAJU [NIJ]
SAMPIT dial of MALAY [MLI]
SAMPOLAWA dial of CIA-CIA [CIA]
SAMPORI dial of BIAK [BHW]
SAMPUR alt for SAMBURU [SAQ]
SAMRE [SCC] lang, Cambodia
SAMTALI alt for SANTALI [SNT]
SAMTAO [STU] lang, Myanmar; also in China
SAMTAO alt for KIORR [XKO]
SAMTAO 2 alt for KIORR [XKO]
SAMTAU alt for SAMTAO [STU]
SAMTUAN alt for SAMTAO [STU]
SAMURZAKAN dial of ABKHAZ [ABK]
SAMURZAKAN-ZUGDIDI dial of LAZ [LZZ]
SAMVEDI [SMV] lang, India
SAMYA alt for SAAMIA dial of LUYIA [LUY]
"SAN" pejorative alt for HAI//OM [HGM]
SAN alt for SAMO, MATYA [STJ]
SAN alt for SAMO, MAYA [SYM]
SAN alt for SAMO, SOUTHERN [SBD]
SAN dial of BAMANANKAN [BRA]

SAN AGUSTÍN LOXICHA ZAPOTECO dial of ZAPOTECO, LOXICHA [ZTP]
SAN AGUSTÍN TLACOTEPEC dial of MIXTECO, MAGDALENA PENASCO [QMP]
SAN ANDRÉS CHICAHUAXTLA TRIQUE alt for TRIQUE, CHICAHUAXTLA [TRS]
SAN ANDRÉS COHAMIATA dial of HUICHOL [HCH]
SAN ANDRÉS CREOLE alt for ISLANDER CREOLE ENGLISH dial of NORTHERN CENTRAL AMERICA CREOLE ENGLISH [BZI]
SAN ANDRÉS INGA dial of INGA [INB]
SAN ANDRÉS SAJCABAJÁ QUICHÉ alt for QUICHÉ, SAN ANDRÉS [QIE]
SAN ANDRÉS TZOTZIL alt for TZOTZIL, SAN ANDRÉS LARRAINZAR [TZS]
SAN ANTONIO ELOXOCHITLÁN MAZATECO dial of MAZATECO, SAN JERONIMO TECOATL [MAA]
SAN ANTONIO HUITEPEC MIXTECO alt for MIXTECO, HUITEPEC [MXS]
SAN ANTONIO SINICAHUA MIXTECO alt for MIXTECO, SINICAHUA [QMI]
SAN BALTAZAR CHICHICAPAN ZAPOTEC alt for ZAPOTECO, CHICHICAPAN [ZPV]
SAN BALTÁZAR LOXICHA ZAPOTEC alt for ZAPOTECO, SAN BALÁTZAR LOXICHA [ZPX]
SAN BARTOLO SOYALTEPEC MIXTECO alt for MIXTECO, SOYALTEPEC [VMQ]
SAN BARTOLO YAUTEPEC ZAPOTECO alt for ZAPOTECO, YAUTEPEC [ZPB]
SAN BARTOLOMÉ VENUSTIANO CARRANZA TZOTZIL alt for TZOTZIL, VENUSTIANO CARRANZA [TZO]
SAN BARTOLOMÉ ZOOGOCHO ZAPOTECO alt for ZAPOTECO, ZOOGOCHO [ZPQ]
SAN BARTOMOMÉ YUCUAÑE MIXTECO alt for MIXTECO, YUCUAÑE [MVG]
SAN BLAS CUNA alt for KUNA, SAN BLAS [CUK]
SAN BLASITO CORA dial of CORA, SANTA TERESA [COK]
SAN BORJANO alt for REYESANO [REY]
SAN CARLOS alt for RUMSEN dial of COSTANOAN, SOUTHERN [CSS]
SAN CARLOS dial of APACHE, WESTERN [APW]
SAN CHAY alt for MAN CAO LAN [MLC]
SAN CHI alt for MAN CAO LAN [MLC]
SAN CRISTÓBAL AMATLÁN ZAPOTECO alt for ZAPOTECO, AMATLÁN [ZPO]
SAN CRISTÓBAL AMOLTEPEC MIXTECO dial of MIXTECO, MAGDALENA PENASCO [QMP]
SAN CRISTÓBAL LACHIRUAJ ZAPOTECO alt for ZAPOTECO, LACHIRIOAG [ZTC]
SAN ESTEBAN ATATLÁHUCA MIXTECO alt for MIXTECO, ATATLÁHUCA [MIB]
SAN FELIPE dial of KERES, EASTERN [KEE]
SAN FELIPE JALAPA DE DAÍZ MAZATECO alt for MAZATECO, JALAPA DE DÍAZ [MAJ]
SAN FELIPE SANTIAGO OTOMÍ dial of OTOMI, ESTADO DE MEXICO [OTS]
SAN FELIPE TEJALAPAN ZAPOTEC alt for ZAPOTECO, TEJALAPAN [ZTT]

SAN FELIPE ZAPOTECO alt for ZAPOTECO, TEJALAPAN [ZTT]

SAN FRANCESCO SAVERIO MISSION alt for COCHIMÍ [COJ]

SAN FRANCISCO dial of COSTANOAN, NORTHERN [CST]

SAN FRANCISCO CHONTLA HUASTEC alt for HUASTECO, SAN FRANCISCO CHONTLA [HAU]

SAN FRANCISCO CORA dial of CORA [COR]

SAN FRANCISCO HUEHUETLÁN MAZATECO dial of MAZATECO, SAN JERONIMO TECOATL [MAA]

SAN FRANCISCO LOGUECHE ZAPOTECO alt for ZAPOTECO, AMATLÁN [ZPO]

SAN FRANCISCO XAVIER DE VIGGÉ-BIAUNDO MISSION alt for COCHIMÍ [COJ]

SAN FRATELLO alt for WESTERN LOMBARD dial of LOMBARD [LMO]

SAN GADABA alt for GADABA, OLLAR, POTTANGI [GDB]

SAN GREGORIO OZOLOTEPEC ZAPOTECO dial of ZAPOTECO, OZOLOTEPEC [ZAO]

SAN IGNACIO DE VELAZCO dial of CHIQUITANO [CAX]

SAN ILDEFONSO dial of TEWA [TEW]

SAN JAVIER alt for COCHIMÍ [COJ]

SAN JAVIER dial of CHIQUITANO [CAX]

SAN JERÓNIMO MAZATECO alt for MAZATECO, SAN JERÓNIMO TECÓATL [MAA]

SAN JERÓNIMO TECÓATL MAZATECO dial of MAZATECO, SAN JERONIMO TECOATL [MAA]

SAN JOAQUÍN alt for COCHIMÍ [COJ]

SAN JORGE alt for CHIMILA [CBG]

SAN JUAN dial of TEWA [TEW]

SAN JUAN BAUTISTA alt for MUTSUN dial of COSTANOAN, SOUTHERN [CSS]

SAN JUAN CHIQUIHUITLÁN MAZATECO alt for MAZATECO, CHIQUIHUITLÁN [MAQ]

SAN JUAN COATECAS ALTAS ZAPOTEC alt for ZAPOTECO, COATECAS ALTAS [ZAP]

SAN JUAN COATZOSPAN MIXTECO alt for MIXTECO, COATZOSPAN [MIZ]

SAN JUAN COPALA TRIQUE alt for TRIQUE, COPALA [TRC]

SAN JUAN CORAPAN CORA dial of CORA, SANTA TERESA [COK]

SAN JUAN COTZOCÓN MIXE dial of MIXE, QUETZALTEPEC [MVE]

SAN JUAN ELOTEPEC ZAPOTEC alt for ZAPOTECO, ELOTEPEC [ZTE]

SAN JUAN LACHIXILA ZAPOTECO alt for ZAPOTECO, QUIAVICUZAS [ZPJ]

SAN JUAN LEALAO CHINANTECO alt for CHINANTECO, LEALAO [CLE]

SAN JUAN MIXTEPEC MIXTECO alt for MIXTECO, MIXTEPEC [MIX]

SAN JUAN MIXTEPEC ZAPOTECO alt for ZAPOTECO, MIXTEPEC [ZPM]

SAN JUAN ÑUMÍ MIXTECO alt for MIXTECO, TLAXIACO NORTE [MOS]

SAN JUAN OSTUNCALCO MAM alt for MAM, SOUTHERN [MMS]

SAN JUAN PIÑAS dial of MIXTECO, JUXTLAHUACA OESTE [JMX]

SAN JUAN QUIAHIJE CHATINO dial of CHATINO, SIERRA OCCIDENTAL [CTP]

SAN JUAN TAMAZOLA MIXTEC alt for MIXTECO, TAMAZOLA [VMX]

SAN JUAN TEITA MIXTEC alt for MIXTECO, SAN JUAN TEITA [QMC]

SAN LORENZO CUANECUILTITLA MAZATECO dial of MAZATECO, SAN JERONIMO TECOATL [MAA]

SAN LORENZO TEXMELUCAN ZAPOTECO alt for ZAPOTECO, TEXMELUCAN [ZPZ]

SAN LUCAS ZOQUIAPAN MAZATECO dial of MAZATECO, SAN JERONIMO TECOATL [MAA]

SAN MARCIAL OZOLOTEPEC ZAPOTECO dial of ZAPOTECO, OZOLOTEPEC [ZAO]

SAN MARCOS COMITANCILLAS MAM alt for MAM, CENTRAL [MVC]

SAN MARCOS ZACATEPEC CHATINO alt for CHATINO, ZACATEPEC [CTZ]

SAN MARTÍN CHILE VERDE MAM alt for SAN MARTÍN SACATEPÉQUEZ MAM dial of MAM, SOUTHERN [MMS]

SAN MARTÍN ITUNYOSO TRIQUI alt for TRIQUE, SAN MARTÍN ITUNYOSO [TRQ]

SAN MARTÍN PERAS dial of MIXTECO, JUXTLAHUACA OESTE [JMX]

SAN MARTÍN SACATEPÉQUEZ MAM dial of MAM, SOUTHERN [MMS]

SAN MARTÍN TILCAJETE ZAPOTECO dial of ZAPOTECO, SAN JUAN GUELAVIA [ZAB]

SAN MATEO dial of MAZATECO, HUAUTLA [MAU]

SAN MATEO PEÑASCO dial of MIXTECO, SAN MIGUEL EL GRANDE [MIG]

SAN MATEO PEÑASCO MIXTECO dial of MIXTECO, MAGDALENA PENASCO [QMP]

SAN MATEO TEPANTEPEC dial of MIXTECO, PENOLES [MIL]

SAN MATEO ZOYAMAZALCO POPOLOCA dial of POPOLOCA, COYOTEPEC [PBF]

SAN MIGUEL dial of CHIQUITANO [CAX]

SAN MIGUEL dial of MAZATECO, HUAUTLA [MAU]

SAN MIGUEL ACATÁN KANJOBAL alt for KANJOBAL, WESTERN [KNJ]

SAN MIGUEL ACHIUTLA MIXTECO dial of MIXTECO, MAGDALENA PENASCO [QMP]

SAN MIGUEL CHALCATONGO dial of MIXTECO, SAN MIGUEL EL GRANDE [MIG]

SAN MIGUEL CREOLE FRENCH [SME] lang, Panama

SAN MIGUEL MITONTIC dial of TZOTZIL, CHENALHO [TZE]

SAN MIGUEL SOYALTEPEC MAZATEC alt for MAZATECO, SOYALTEPEC [VMP]

SAN MIGUEL TENANGO NÁHUATL alt for NÁHUATL, TENANGO [NHI]

SAN MIGUEL TENOXTITLÁN dial of MAZAHUA CENTRAL [MAZ]

SAN MIGUEL TILQUIAPAN ZAPOTECO alt for ZAPOTECO, TILQUIAPAN [ZTS]
SAN MIGUEL ZAPOTECO alt for ZAPOTECO, COATLÁN [ZPS]
SAN PABLO CHALCHIHUITAN dial of TZOTZIL, CHENALHO [TZE]
SAN PABLO GÜILÁ ZAPOTEC alt for ZAPOTECO, GÜILÁ [ZTU]
SAN PABLO TIJALTEPEC MIXTECO alt for MIXTECO, TIJALTEPEC [QMJ]
SAN PEDRO CAJONOS ZAPOTECO alt for ZAPOTECO, CAJONOS [ZAD]
SAN PEDRO CHENALHÓ dial of TZOTZIL, CHENALHO [TZE]
SAN PEDRO DE HUACARPANA dial of QUECHUA, YAUYOS [QUX]
SAN PEDRO EL ALTO ZAPOTECO alt for ZAPOTECO, EL ALTO [ZPP]
SAN PEDRO IXCATLÁN MAZATECO alt for MAZATECO, IXCATLÁN [MAO]
SAN PEDRO MOLINOS dial of MIXTECO, SAN MIGUEL EL GRANDE [MIG]
SAN PEDRO QUIATONI ZAPOTEC alt for ZAPOTECO, SAN PEDRO QUIATONI [ZPF]
SAN PEDRO TOTOMACHAPAN ZAPOTECO alt for ZAPOTECO, TOTOMACHAPAN [ZPH]
SAN PEDRO TUTUTEPEC MIXTECO alt for MIXTECO, TUTUTEPEC [MTU]
SAN PEDRO YASPAC dial of ZOQUE, FRANCISCO LEON [ZOS]
SAN RAFAEL MIXTECO alt for MIXTECO, METLATONOC [MXV]
SAN RAMON INAGTA alt for AGTA, MT. IRIGA [AGZ]
SAN RAPHAEL alt for MIWOK, SOUTHERN SIERRA [SKD]
SAN RAYMUNDO JALPAN ZAPOTEC alt for ZAPOTECO, ZAACHILA [ZTX]
SAN SEBASTIÁN-SANTA CATARINA dial of HUICHOL [HCH]
SAN SIMÓN ZAHUATLÁN dial of MIXTECO, SILACAYOAPAN [MKS]
SAN TUNG alt for SANDONG dial of SUI [SWI]
SAN VICENTE COATLÁN ZAPOTEC alt for ZAPOTECO, SAN VICENTE COATLÁN [ZPT]
SAN VICENTE COYOTEPEC POPOLOCA dial of POPOLOCA, COYOTEPEC [PBF]
SAN XAVIER alt for COCHIMÍ [COJ]
SAN<A dial of ARABIC, JUDEO-YEMENI [JYE]
SANABERIGI alt for SAMBERIGI [SSX]
SANAGA alt for TUKI [BAG]
SANAGAGE alt for NATHEMBO [NTE]
SANAINAWA dial of KATUKINA, PANOAN [KNT]
SANAM alt for SANAPANÁ [SAP]
SANAMAICA alt for MONDÉ [MND]
SANAMAIKÁ alt for MONDÉ [MND]
SANAMAYKÃ alt for MONDÉ [MND]
SANANA alt for SULA [SZN]
SANANDAJ dial of HULAULA [HUY]
SANANDAJI alt for ARDAIÂNI dial of KURDI [KDB]
SANAPANA dial of SANAPANA [SAP]
SANAPANÁ [SAP] lang, Paraguay

SANAROA dial of DOBU [DOB]
SANBALBE alt for MALGBE [MXF]
SANBIAU alt for PIU [PIX]
SANCÁ alt for MALAYO [MBP]
SÁN-CHI alt for MAN CAO LAN [MLC]
SANDA dial of LOKO [LOK]
SANDA dial of THEMNE [TEJ]
SANDAKAN BAJAU dial of BAJAU, WEST COAST [BDR]
SANDAL alt for SANTALI [SNT]
SANDAUI alt for SANDAWE [SBR]
SANDAWE [SBR] lang, Tanzania
SANDAWI alt for SANDAWE [SBR]
SANDAYO dial of KIMARAGANG [KQR]
SANDE alt for ZANDE [ZAN]
SANDEWAR alt for SANDIWAR dial of TIMUGON MURUT [TIH]
SANDIA dial of TIWA, SOUTHERN [TIX]
SANDIWAR dial of TIMUGON MURUT [TIH]
SANDO alt for NORTHERN KONO dial of KONO [KNO]
SANDONG dial of SUI [SWI]
SANDOWAY dial of CHIN, ASHO [CSH]
SANDU alt for SHENDU [SHL]
SANDU dial of LISHANA DENI [LSD]
SANDWE alt for SANDAWE [SBR]
SANE alt for SAMO, MATYA [STJ]
SANE alt for SAMO, SOUTHERN [SBD]
SANEMA alt for SANUMÁ [SAM]
SANG dial of NAGA, KONYAK [NBE]
SANGA [SGA] lang, Nigeria
SANGA [SNG] lang, DRC
SANGA alt for NUMANA-NUNKU-GWANTU-NUMBU [NBR]
SANGA alt for SAANGA dial of MAKHUWA-MEETTO [MAK]
SANGAB alt for MANDAYA, SANGAB [MYT]
SANGAJI alt for NATHEMBO [NTE]
SANGALI alt for TUMMA [TBQ]
SANGAMESVARI dial of KONKANI [KNK]
SANGANGALLA' alt for TAE' [ROB]
SANGANGALLA' alt for TOALA' [TLZ]
SANGAR dial of BIMA [BHP]
"SANGASANGA" pejorative alt for BOMWALI [BMW]
SANGASANGA alt for BOMWALI [BMW]
SANGAU alt for EMBALOH [EMB]
SANGBANGA alt for SABANGA dial of BANDA-MBRES [BQK]
SANGCHE dial of NAGA, TASE [NST]
SANGESARI alt for SANGISARI [SGR]
SANGGAR alt for SANGAR dial of BIMA [BHP]
SANGGAU [SCG] lang, Indonesia (Kalimantan)
SANGGAU alt for EMBALOH [EMB]
SANGGIL alt for SANGIL [SNL]
SANGHO alt for SANGO [SAJ]
SANGI alt for SANGIR [SAN]
SANGIH alt for SANGIR [SAN]
SANGIHÉ alt for SANGIR [SAN]
SANGIL [SNL] lang, Philippines
SANGIR [SAN] lang, Indonesia (Sulawesi); also in Philippines

SANGIRESE alt for SANGIR [SAN]
SANGIRI alt for SANGIL [SNL]
SANGISARI [SGR] lang, Iran
SANGLA alt for TSHANGLA [TSJ]
SANGLA dial of MOINBA [MOB]
SANGLECHI dial of SANGLECHI-ISHKASHIMI [SGL]
SANGLECHI-ISHKASHIMI [SGL] lang, Tajikistan;
    also in Afghanistan
SANGLICH dial of SANGLECHI-ISHKASHIMI [SGL]
SANGNAUR alt for SUNAM [SSK]
SANGO [SAJ] lang, CAR; also in Chad, Congo, DRC
SANGO alt for SANGU [SBP]
SANGO, RIVERAIN [SNJ] lang, CAR
SANGPANG [RAV] lang, Nepal
SANGPANG alt for HEDANGPA dial of NACHERING
    [NCD]
SANGPANG GÎN alt for SANGPANG [RAV]
SANGPANG GUN alt for SANGPANG [RAV]
SANGPANG KHA alt for SANGPANG [RAV]
SANGRIMA alt for NAGA, ZEME [NZM]
SANGS-RGYAS alt for KINNAURI, BHOTI [NES]
SANGTAI dial of NAGA, TASE [NST]
SANGTAL alt for SANTALI [SNT]
SANGTAM alt for NAGA, SANGTAM [NSA]
SANGU [SBP] lang, Tanzania
SANGU [SNQ] lang, Gabon
SANGWE dial of SENA [SEH]
SANGYAS alt for KINNAURI, BHOTI [NES]
SANHAJA OF SRAIR alt for SENHAJA DE SRAIR
    [SJS]
SANHSIEN dial of CHINESE, HAKKA [HAK]
SANI dial of AMAMI-OSHIMA, NORTHERN [RYN]
SANI dial of YI, SOUTHEASTERN [YIE]
SANINAWACANA alt for SANAINAWA dial of
    KATUKINA, PANOAN [KNT]
SANIO alt for SANIYO-HIYEWE [SNY]
SANIO-HIOWE alt for SANIYO-HIYEWE [SNY]
SANIYO alt for SANIYO-HIYEWE [SNY]
SANIYO-HIYEWE [SNY] lang, Papua New Guinea
SANJA alt for MALAYO [MBP]
SANJAN dial of PASHAYI, NORTHWEST [GLH]
SANJÂRI dial of KURMANJI [KUR]
SANJO alt for SHANJO dial of TONGA [TOI]
SANKA alt for MALAYO [MBP]
SANKAJI alt for NATHEMBO [NTE]
SANKARA-YERUKALA dial of YERUKULA [YEU]
SANKARKAN alt for MANINKA, SANKARAN [MSC]
SANKE dial of NAGA, TASE [NST]
SANKETI dial of TAMIL [TCV]
SANKUMA dial of BOBO MADARE, NORTHERN
    [BBO]
SANKURA dial of NUNI, SOUTHERN [NNW]
SANLONG dial of QIANG, SOUTHERN [QMR]
SANNA alt for ARABIC, CYPRIOT SPOKEN [ACY]
SANO alt for GADABA, OLLAR, POTTANGI [GDB]
SANPOIL dial of OKANAGAN [OKA]
SANSI [SSI] lang, Pakistan
SANSKRIT [SKT] lang, India
SANSU [SCA] lang, Myanmar
SANTA alt for DONGXIANG [SCE]
SANTA ANA [STN] lang, Solomon Islands

SANTA ANA dial of KAHUA [AGW]
SANTA ANA dial of KERES, EASTERN [KEE]
SANTA ANA ATEIXTLAHUACA MAZATECO dial
    of MAZATECO, SAN JERONIMO TECOATL
    [MAA]
SANTA ANA YARENI alt for ZAPOTECO, YARENI
    [ZAE]
SANTA ANA-GONZAGA dial of AGTA, DUPANINAN
    [DUO]
SANTA CATALINA dial of KAHUA [AGW]
SANTA CATARINA PANTELHO dial of TZOTZIL,
    CHENALHO [TZE]
SANTA CATARINA QUIERI ZAPOTECO alt for
    QUIERÍ ZAPOTEC dial of ZAPOTECO,
    QUIOQUITANI Y QUIERI [ZTQ]
SANTA CATARINA QUIOQUITANI ZAPOTECO
    alt for QUIOQUITANI ZAPOTEC dial of
    ZAPOTECO, QUIOQUITANI Y QUIERI [ZTQ]
SANTA CATARINA TICUÁ dial of MIXTECO, SAN
    MIGUEL EL GRANDE [MIG]
SANTA CATARINA XANAGUÍA ZAPOTECO alt
    for ZAPOTECO, XANAGUÍA [ZTG]
SANTA CATARINA YOSONOTU dial of MIXTECO,
    OCOTEPEC [MIE]
SANTA CLARA dial of COSTANOAN, NORTHERN
    [CST]
SANTA CLARA dial of TEWA [TEW]
SANTA CRUCINO alt for AGUANO [AGA]
SANTA CRUZ [STC] lang, Solomon Islands
SANTA CRUZ dial of COSTANOAN, NORTHERN
    [CST]
SANTA CRUZ dial of IRAYA [IRY]
SANTA CRUZ ITUNDUJIA MIXTECO alt for
    MIXTECO, ITUNDUJIA [MCE]
SANTA CRUZ OCOPETATILLO MAZATECO dial
    of MAZATECO, SAN JERONIMO TECOATL
    [MAA]
SANTA CRUZ TACAHUA MIXTECO alt for
    MIXTECO, TACAHUA [QMT]
SANTA CRUZ VERAPAZ POKOMCHÍ dial of
    POKOMCHI, WESTERN [POB]
SANTA EULALIA KANJOBAL alt for KANJOBAL,
    EASTERN [KJB]
SANTA INÉS YATZECHI ZAPOTEC alt for
    ZAPOTECO, SANTA INÉS YATZECHI [ZPN]
SANTA INÉS ZEGACHE ZAPOTECO alt for
    ZAPOTECO, SANTA INÉS YATZECHI [ZPN]
SANTA MAGDALENA ZOQUE alt for ZOQUE,
    FRANCISCO LEÓN [ZOS]
SANTA MARGARITA dial of AGTA, DUPANINAN
    [DUO]
SANTA MARÍA ACAPULCO PAME alt for PAME
    CENTRAL [PBS]
SANTA MARÍA ACATEPEC dial of MIXTECO,
    TUTUTEPEC [MTU]
SANTA MARÍA AYOQUESCO ZAPOTEC alt for
    ZAPOTECO, AYOQUESCO [ZAF]
SANTA MARÍA CHIGMECATITLÁN MIXTECO
    alt for MIXTECO, CHIGMACATITLÁN [MII]
SANTA MARÍA CITENDEJÉ-BANOS dial of
    MAZAHUA CENTRAL [MAZ]

SANTA MARÍA COATLÁN ZAPOTECO alt for ZAPOTECO, COATLÁN [ZPS]
SANTA MARÍA IPALAPA AMUZGO alt for AMUZGO, IPALAPA [AZM]
SANTA MARÍA NÁHUATL alt for NÁHUATL, SANTA MARÍA LA ALTA [NHZ]
SANTA MARÍA PÁPALO dial of CUICATECO, TEPEUXILA [CUX]
SANTA MARÍA PEÑOLES dial of MIXTECO, PENOLES [MIL]
SANTA MARÍA PETAPA ZAPOTECO alt for ZAPOTECO, PETAPA [ZPE]
SANTA MARÍA QUIEGOLANI ZAPOTEC alt for ZAPOTECO, SANTA MARÍA QUIEGOLANI [ZPI]
SANTA MARÍA XADANI ZAPOTECO alt for ZAPOTECO, XADANI [ZAX]
SANTA MARÍA YOSOYÚA dial of MIXTECO, SAN MIGUEL EL GRANDE [MIG]
SANTA MARÍA ZACATEPEC MIXTEC alt for MIXTECO, SANTA MARÍA ZACATEPEC [MZA]
SANTA MARÍA ZANIZA ZAPOTECO alt for ZAPOTECO, ZANIZA [ZPW]
SANTA ROSA dial of COFAN [CON]
SANTA ROSA QUECHUA alt for QUICHUA, LOWLAND, NAPO [QLN]
SANTA ROSA QUECHUA dial of QUICHUA, LOWLAND, NAPO [QLN]
SANTA TERESA dial of RATAGNON [BTN]
SANTA TERESA CORA dial of CORA, SANTA TERESA [COK]
SANTAL alt for SANTALI [SNT]
SANTALI [SNT] lang, India; also in Bangladesh, Bhutan, Nepal
SANTAN dial of DAYAK, LAND [DYK]
SANTARROSINO alt for QUICHUA, LOWLAND, NAPO [QLN]
SANTCHOU dial of MBO [MBO]
SANTEE alt for DAKOTA dial of DAKOTA [DHG]
SANTEE-SISSETON alt for DAKOTA dial of DAKOTA [DHG]
SANTERRE dial of PICARD [PCD]
SANTHALI alt for SANTALI [SNT]
SANTHIALI alt for SANTALI [SNT]
SANTIAGO dial of CHIQUITANO [CAX]
SANTIAGO APOALA MIXTECO alt for MIXTECO, APASCO Y APOALA [MIP]
SANTIAGO ATITLÁN TZUTUJIL alt for TZUTUJIL, EASTERN [TZJ]
SANTIAGO INGA dial of INGA [INB]
SANTIAGO IXTAYUTLA MIXTEC alt for MIXTECO, IXTAYUTLA [VMJ]
SANTIAGO LACHIGUIRI ZAPOTECO alt for ZAPOTECO, LACHIGUIRI [ZPA]
SANTIAGO MATATLÁN ZAPOTEC dial of ZAPOTECO, MITLA [ZAW]
SANTIAGO NUYOO MIXTECO alt for MIXTECO, TLAXIACO, SUROESTE [MEH]
SANTIAGO TLAZOYALTEPEC dial of MIXTECO, PENOLES [MIL]
SANTIAGO YOSONDÚA MIXTECO alt for MIXTECO, YOSONDÚA [MPM]

SANTIAGUEÑO QUICHUA alt for QUICHUA, SANTIAGO DEL ESTERO [QUS]
SANTIAM alt for KALAPUYA [KAL]
SANTO alt for SAKAO [SKU]
SANTO alt for TANGOA [TGP]
SANTO DOMINGO dial of KERES, EASTERN [KEE]
SANTO DOMINGO HEUNDÍO MIXTECO dial of MIXTECO, MAGDALENA PENASCO [QMP]
SANTO DOMINGO NUXAÁ MIXTECO alt for MIXTECO, NOCHIXTLÁN SURESTE [MXY]
SANTO DOMINGO TOTONACA alt for TOTONACA, FILOMENO MATA-COAHUITLÁN [TLP]
SANTO DOMINGO XENACOJ alt for CAKCHIQUEL, SANTO DOMINGO XENACOJ [CKJ]
SANTÁO TOMS MAZALTEPEC ZAPOTECO alt for ZAPOTECO, MAZALTEPEC [ZPY]
SANTÁO TOMS OCOTEPEC MIXTECO alt for MIXTECO, OCOTEPEC [MIE]
SANTONGEAIS dial of FRENCH [FRN]
SANTORA alt for NARA [NRB]
SANTRI alt for SADRI [SCK]
SANTROKOFI alt for SELE [SNW]
SANUMÁ [SAM] lang, Brazil; also in Venezuela
SANVI dial of ANYIN [ANY]
SANYA alt for SANYE [SSN]
SANYE [SSN] lang, Kenya
SANYE alt for BONI [BOB]
SANYE alt for DAHALO [DAL]
SANYE alt for WAATA dial of ORMA [ORC]
SANYO alt for FULFULDE, ADAMAWA [FUB]
SANZA dial of KONJO [KOO]
SANZA dial of NANDI [NNB]
SAO alt for SAHO [SSY]
SAO alt for THAO [SSF]
SAO dial of MASLAM [MSV]
SÃO PAULO SIGN LANGUAGE alt for BRAZILIAN SIGN LANGUAGE [BZS]
SÃO TOMENSE alt for SÃOTOMENSE [CRI]
SA'OCH [SCQ] lang, Cambodia
SAONEK dial of WAIGEO [WGO]
SAONRAS alt for SORA [SRB]
SAORA alt for SORA [SRB]
SAOTCH alt for SA'OCH [SCQ]
SÃOTOMENSE [CRI] lang, São Tomé e Príncipe
SAPALEWA alt for ALUNE [ALP]
SAPAN dial of ASMAT, CASUARINA COAST [ASC]
SAPARUA [SPR] lang, Indonesia (Maluku)
SAPÉ [SPC] lang, Venezuela
SAPEI alt for KUPSABINY [KPZ]
SAPINY alt for SABINY dial of KUPSABINY [KPZ]
SAPITERI dial of HUACHIPAERI [HUG]
SAPO [KRN] lang, Liberia
SAPONI [SPI] lang, Indonesia (Irian Jaya)
SAPONI alt for TUTELO [TTA]
SAPOSA [SPS] lang, Papua New Guinea
SAPOSA dial of SAPOSA [SPS]
SAPOUAN alt for SAPUAN [SPU]
SAPRAN alt for MADEN [XMX]
SAPREK alt for PAIWAN [PWN]
SAPSUG alt for SHAPSUG dial of ADYGHE [ADY]
SAPTARI alt for THARU, KOCHILA [THQ]

SAPUAN [SPU] lang, Laos
SAPUDI dial of MADURA [MHJ]
SAPULOT MURUT dial of TAGAL MURUT [MVV]
SAPULUT MURUT alt for SAPULOT MURUT dial
of TAGAL MURUT [MVV]
SAPUTAN alt for BUKAR SADONG [SDO]
SAPWUAHFIK dial of POHNPEIAN [PNF]
SAQATRI alt for SOQOTRI [SQT]
SAQIZ dial of HULAULA [HUY]
SAR [MWM] lang, Chad
SAR alt for WARJI [WJI]
SAR dial of GULA [KCM]
SARA [SRE] lang, Indonesia (Kalimantan)
SARA alt for BOK dial of MANDJAK [MFV]
SARA alt for KABA [KSP]
SARA alt for NGAMBAY [SBA]
SARA alt for SAR dial of GULA [KCM]
SARA alt for SAR [MWM]
SARA DINJO alt for SARA DUNJO [KOJ]
SARA DUNJO [KOJ] lang, CAR
SARA GOULA alt for GULA [GLU]
SARA GULA alt for GULA [GLU]
SARA KABA [SBZ] lang, CAR
SARA KABA alt for KABA [KSP]
SARA KABA alt for KABA NA [KWV]
SARA KROWE dial of SIKA [SKI]
SARA MADJINGAY alt for SAR [MWM]
SARA MBAI alt for MBAY [MYB]
SARA NGAMBAI alt for NGAMBAY [SBA]
SARA SIKKA alt for SIKA [SKI]
SARA TOUMAK alt for TUMAK [TMC]
SARACATSAN dial of GREEK [GRK]
SARAGURO QUICHUA alt for QUICHUA, HIGH-
LAND, LOJA [QQU]
SARAHOLE alt for SONINKE [SNN]
SARAHULI alt for SONINKE [SNN]
SARAIKI [SKR] lang, Pakistan; also in India, United
Kingdom
SARAJI alt for INNER SIRAGI dial of PAHARI,
KULLU [KFX]
SARAKA alt for THARAKA [THA]
SARAKI dial of BENGALI [BNG]
SARAKOLE alt for SONINKE [SNN]
SARAKULE alt for SONINKE [SNN]
SARALIR alt for SALALIR dial of TAGAL MURUT
[MVV]
SARALIR alt for SEDALIR dial of TIDONG [TID]
SARAMACCAN [SRM] lang, Suriname; also in
French Guiana
SARAMO alt for ITONAMA [ITO]
SARAMO alt for ZALAMO [ZAJ]
SARANGANI dial of SANGIL [SNL]
SARAR alt for BOK dial of MANDJAK [MFV]
SARAR dial of MANDJAK [MFV]
SARARÉ [SRR] lang, Brazil
SARASIRA dial of ADZERA [AZR]
SARASSARA dial of JINA [JIA]
SARASVAT BRAHMIN dial of KONKANI, GOANESE
[GOM]
SARAVECA [SAR] lang, Bolivia
SARAWA alt for WARJI [WJI]

SARAWAI dial of DOHOI [OTD]
SARAWAK DAYAK alt for JAGOI [SNE]
SARAWAK MALAY dial of MALAY [MLI]
SARAWAK MURUT alt for LUN BAWANG dial of
LUNDAYEH [LND]
SARAWAN dial of BRAHUI [BRH]
SARAWANI dial of BALOCHI, WESTERN [BGN]
SARAWARIA alt for NORTHERN STANDARD
BHOJPURI dial of BHOJPURI [BHJ]
SARAWULE alt for SONINKE [SNN]
SARAYACU QUICHUA alt for QUICHUA, PASTAZA,
NORTHERN [QLB]
SARCEE alt for SARSI [SRS]
SARCHAPKKHA alt for TSHANGLA [TSJ]
SARD alt for SARDINIAN, LOGUDORESE [SRD]
SARDARESE alt for SARDINIAN, LOGUDORESE
[SRD]
SARDINIAN, CAMPIDANESE [SRO] lang, Italy
SARDINIAN, GALLURESE [SDN] lang, Italy
SARDINIAN, LOGUDORESE [SRD] lang, Italy
SARDINIAN, SASSARESE [SDC] lang, Italy
SARDU alt for SARDINIAN, CAMPIDANESE [SRO]
SARE alt for SENA-CARE dial of SENA [SEH]
SAREMDÉ dial of MOORE [MHM]
SARI alt for SAA [SZR]
SARI dial of ENGA [ENQ]
SARI YOGUR alt for YUGUR, WEST [YBE]
SARIG alt for YUGUR, WEST [YBE]
SARIKEI dial of MELANAU [MEL]
SARIKOLI [SRH] lang, China
SARIQ dial of TURKMEN [TCK]
SARIRÁ alt for SIRIANO [SRI]
SARISEN alt for RUKAI [DRU]
SARKANCI alt for BOZO, SOROGAMA [BZE]
SARKAWA alt for BOZO, SOROGAMA [BZE]
SARNAMI HINDI alt for SARNAMI HINDUSTANI
dial of HINDUSTANI, CARIBBEAN [HNS]
SARNAMI HINDUSTANI dial of HINDUSTANI,
CARIBBEAN [HNS]
SARNGAM alt for NGAM [NMC]
SAROA alt for SAAROA [SXR]
SAROA dial of SINAUGORO [SNC]
SAROKAMA alt for SANKUMA dial of BOBO
MADARE, NORTHERN [BBO]
SAROUA alt for SARUA [SWY]
SARPO alt for SAPO [KRN]
SARRABENSE dial of SARDINIAN, CAMPIDANESE
[SRO]
SARSI [SRS] lang, Canada
SART QALMAQ dial of KALMYK-OIRAT [KGZ]
SARTENAIS dial of CORSICAN [COI]
SARTUL dial of MONGOLIAN, HALH [KHK]
SARUA [SWY] lang, Chad
SARUDU [SDU] lang, Indonesia (Sulawesi)
SARUGA [SRP] lang, Papua New Guinea
SARWA alt for HIETSHWARE [HIE]
SARWA alt for SARUA [SWY]
SARYGH UYGUR alt for YUGUR, WEST [YBE]
SARYKOLY alt for SARIKOLI [SRH]
SARYQ dial of TURKMEN [TCK]
SARY-UIGHUR alt for YUGUR, WEST [YBE]

SASAK [SAS] lang, Indonesia (Nusa Tenggara)
SASAR dial of VATRATA [VLR]
SASARU dial of SASARU-ENWAN-IGWE [SSC]
SASARU-ENWAN-IGWE [SSC] lang, Nigeria
SASAWA dial of KWERBA [KWE]
SASI alt for SIZAKI [SZK]
SASI dial of HUA [HUC]
SASIME alt for BIYOM [BPM]
SASSARESE alt for SARDINIAN, SASSARESE
    [SDC]
SASTEAN alt for SHASTA [SHT]
SATAR alt for SANTALI [SNT]
SATARÉ alt for SATERÉ-MAWÉ [MAV]
SATAWALESE [STW] lang, Micronesia
SATE alt for KUMBA [KSM]
SATERÉ-MAWÉ [MAV] lang, Brazil
SATERLANDIC FRISIAN alt for FRISIAN, EASTERN
    [FRS]
SATPARA alt for ASTORI dial of SHINA [SCL]
SATPARIYA dial of KOCH [KDQ]
SATPUDA NOIRI alt for NOIRI dial of BHILORI [BQI]
SATRE alt for GAWAR-BATI [GWT]
SATRO alt for DIDA, LAKOTA [DIC]
SATUN dial of TONGA [TNZ]
SAU alt for SAHU [SUX]
SAU alt for SAMBERIGI [SSX]
SAU alt for SAVI [SDG]
SAU alt for THAO [SSF]
SAU dial of DAYAK, LAND [DYK]
SAU dial of ENGA [ENQ]
SA'U alt for SAHU [SUX]
SAU ENGA alt for SAU dial of ENGA [ENQ]
SAUCH alt for SA'OCH [SCQ]
SAUDI ARABIAN SIGN LANGUAGE [SDL] lang,
    Saudi Arabia
SAUH alt for SAU dial of DAYAK, LAND [DYK]
SAUJI alt for SAVI [SDG]
SAUK [SKC] lang, Papua New Guinea
SAUK-FOX alt for MESQUAKIE [SAC]
SAUKRANG dial of NAGA, TASE [NST]
SAULTEAUX alt for BERENS RIVER OJIBWA dial
    of OJIBWA, NORTHWESTERN [OJB]
SAULTEAUX alt for OJIBWA, WESTERN [OJI]
SAUMANGANJA dial of MENTAWAI [MWV]
SAURA alt for SORA [SRB]
SAURASHTRA [SAZ] lang, India
SAURASHTRA STANDARD alt for STANDARD
    GUJARATI dial of GUJARATI [GJR]
SAURASHTRI alt for SAURASHTRA [SAZ]
SAURI [SAH] lang, Indonesia (Irian Jaya)
SAURIA PAHARIA [MJT] lang, India
SAUSE [SAO] lang, Indonesia (Irian Jaya)
SAUSI [SSJ] lang, Papua New Guinea
SAVANNAKHET dial of LAO [NOL]
SAVARA [SVR] lang, India
SAVARA alt for SORA [SRB]
SAVI [SDG] lang, Afghanistan; also in Pakistan
SAVI dial of GUN-GBE [GUW]
SAVO alt for SAVOSAVO [SVS]
SAVO dial of FINNISH [FIN]
SAVO ISLAND alt for SAVOSAVO [SVS]

SAVOLAX alt for SAVO dial of FINNISH [FIN]
SAVOSAVO [SVS] lang, Solomon Islands
SAVOYARD dial of FRANCO-PROVENÇAL [FRA]
SAVU alt for SABU [HVN]
SAVUNESE alt for SABU [HVN]
SAVUSAVU alt for CENTRAL VANUA LEVU dial
    of FIJIAN [FJI]
SAW dial of NTOMBA [NTO]
SAWA alt for ELSENG [MRF]
SAWABWALA dial of BUNAMA [BDD]
SAWAI [SZW] lang, Indonesia (Maluku)
SAWAI alt for SALEMAN [SAU]
SAWAI dial of SAWAI [SZW]
SAWARIA alt for SORA [SRB]
SAWATUPWA dial of BUNAMA [BDD]
SAWERI alt for ISIRAWA [SRL]
SAWERU [SWR] lang, Indonesia (Irian Jaya)
SAWI [SAW] lang, Indonesia (Irian Jaya)
SAWI alt for SAVI [SDG]
SAWIAT SALMEIT dial of TEHIT [KPS]
SAWILA [SWT] lang, Indonesia (Nusa Tenggara)
SAWILA dial of SAWILA [SWT]
SAWITTO dial of BUGIS [BPR]
SAWIYANU alt for AMA [AMM]
SAWK alt for SOK [SKK]
SAWKNAH [SWN] lang, Libya
SAWRIYA MALTO alt for SAURIA PAHARIA [MJT]
SAWU alt for SABU [HVN]
SAWUNESE alt for SABU [HVN]
SAWUVE dial of ANKAVE [AAK]
SAWUY alt for SAWI [SAW]
SAXON, LOW [SXN] lang, Germany
SAXON, UPPER [SXU] lang, Germany
SAXWE alt for SAXWE-GBE [SXW]
SAXWE-GBE [SXW] lang, Benin
SAYA [SAY] lang, Nigeria
SAYABURY dial of KHMU [KJG]
SAYACO alt for AMAHUACA [AMC]
SAYACU alt for AMAHUACA [AMC]
SAYAN SAMOYED alt for KARAGAS [KIM]
SAYANCI alt for SAYA [SAY]
SAYARA alt for SAYA [SAY]
SAYAWA alt for SAYA [SAY]
SAYMA alt for CHAYMA dial of CARIB [CRB]
SAYSAY alt for SESE dial of GUMUZ [GUK]
SAZEK alt for TAROKO [TRV]
SAZIN alt for CHILASI KOHISTANI dial of SHINA
    [SCL]
SBALT alt for BALTI [BFT]
SBALTI alt for BALTI [BFT]
SBANAG alt for PANANG [PCR]
SBRANAG alt for PANANG [PCR]
SCANIAN alt for SKÅNE [SCY]
SCE alt for SHE dial of BENCH [BCQ]
SCHABIN-KARAHISSAR alt for SHABIN-
    KARAHISSAR dial of ARMENIAN [ARM]
SCHAMACHI alt for SHAMAKHI dial of ARMENIAN
    [ARM]
SCHAMBALA alt for SHAMBALA [KSB]
SCHEKERE alt for KXOE [XUU]
SCHLEIYIP alt for SIYI dial of CHINESE, YUE [YUH]

SCHOE alt for SHOE dial of MPADE [MPI]
SCHWÄBISCH alt for SWABIAN [SWG]
SCHWAEBISCH alt for SWABIAN [SWG]
SCHWYTZERTUETSCH alt for ALEMANNISCH [GSW]
SCHWYZERDÜTSCH alt for ALEMANNISCH [GSW]
SCINACIA alt for BORO [BWO]
SCOTS [SCO] lang, United Kingdom; also in Ireland
SCOTTISH CANT alt for TRAVELLER SCOTTISH [TRL]
SCOTTISH TRAVELLER CANT alt for TRAVELLER SCOTTISH [TRL]
SCOUSE dial of ENGLISH [ENG]
SCUTARI dial of ALBANIAN, GHEG [ALS]
SEA BAJAU alt for BAJAU LAUT dial of SAMA, SOUTHERN [SIT]
SEA DAYAK alt for IBAN [IBA]
SEA GYPSIES alt for BAJAU LAUT dial of SAMA, SOUTHERN [SIT]
SEA ISLAND CREOLE ENGLISH [GUL] lang, USA
SEA LAPPISH dial of SAAMI, NORTHERN [LPR]
SEAQAAQAA alt for CENTRAL VANUA LEVU dial of FIJIAN [FJI]
SEASIDE GREBO alt for GLEBO dial of GREBO, SOUTHERN [GRJ]
SEASIDE GREBO dial of GREBO, SOUTHERN [GRJ]
SEBA [KDG] lang, DRC
SEBA dial of SABU [HVN]
SEBARU' alt for KETUNGAU dial of IBAN [IBA]
SEBASTE dial of ARMENIAN [ARM]
SEBE dial of BINE [ORM]
SEBEI alt for KUPSABINY [KPZ]
SEBERUANG [SBX] lang, Indonesia (Kalimantan)
SEBERUANG dial of IBAN [IBA]
SEBOB alt for KENYAH, SEBOB [SIB]
SEBOP alt for KENYAH, SEBOB [SIB]
SEBUANO alt for CEBUANO [CEB]
SEBUTUIA dial of GALEYA [GAR]
SEBUYAU [SNB] lang, Malaysia (Sarawak)
SEBYAR alt for ARANDAI [JBJ]
SECHELT [SEC] lang, Canada
SECHUANA alt for TSWANA [TSW]
SECO alt for PECH [PAY]
SECOYA [SEY] lang, Ecuador; also in Peru
SECUMNE alt for MAIDU, NORTHWEST [MAI]
SECUNDERABAD BRAHMIN dial of TAMIL [TCV]
SECWEPEMC alt for SHUSWAP [SHS]
SEDÁLIR alt for SALALIR dial of TAGAL MURUT [MVV]
SEDALIR dial of TIDONG [TID]
SEDANG [SED] lang, Viet Nam; also in Laos
SEDANG-RENGAO dial of RENGAO [REN]
SEDANKA dial of ITELMEN [ITL]
SEDE alt for TCHIDE dial of JINA [JIA]
SEDEHI dial of FARSI, WESTERN [PES]
SEDEK alt for TAROKO [TRV]
SEDENTARY BULGARIA dial of ROMANI, VLAX [RMY]
SEDENTARY ROMANIA dial of ROMANI, VLAX [RMY]

SEDEQ alt for TAROKO [TRV]
SEDIAKK alt for TAROKO [TRV]
SEDIK alt for TAROKO [TRV]
SEDIQ alt for TAROKO [TRV]
SEDOA [TVW] lang, Indonesia (Sulawesi)
SEDUAN dial of SIBU [SDX]
SEDUAN-BANYOK alt for SIBU [SDX]
SEEBA-YAGA dial of FULFULDE, NORTH-EASTERN BURKINA FASO [FUH]
SEEDEK alt for TAROKO [TRV]
SEEDEQ alt for TAROKO [TRV]
SEEDIK alt for TAROKO [TRV]
SEEKU [SOS] lang, Burkina Faso
SEELTERSK FRISIAN alt for FRISIAN, EASTERN [FRS]
SEEPTSA alt for CHOLON [CHT]
SEEREER alt for SERER-SINE [SES]
SEEX alt for SERER-SINE [SES]
SEFARDI alt for LADINO [SPJ]
SEFWI alt for SEHWI [SFW]
SEGAH dial of SEGAI [SGE]
SEGAHAN dial of MELANAU [MEL]
SEGAI [SGE] lang, Indonesia (Kalimantan)
SEGAI alt for DUSUN SEGAMA dial of KINABATANGAN, UPPER [DMG]
SEGALANG dial of MELANAU [MEL]
SEGEJU [SEG] lang, Tanzania
SEGET [SBG] lang, Indonesia (Irian Jaya)
SEGI dial of KAMASAU [KMS]
SEGIDDI alt for SIGIDI dial of SAYA [SAY]
SEGINKI dial of MUKULU [MOZ]
SEGOU dial of BAMANANKAN [BRA]
SEGUHA alt for ZIGULA [ZIW]
SEGUM dial of SERER-SINE [SES]
SEHUDATE alt for FAYU [FAU]
SEHWI [SFW] lang, Ghana
SEIM alt for MENDE [SIM]
SEIM alt for WAMSAK [WBD]
SEIMAT [SSG] lang, Papua New Guinea
SEIMBRI dial of IZON [IJC]
SEIRA dial of FORDATA [FRD]
SEISIRAT alt for SAISIYAT [SAI]
SEIT dial of SEIT-KAITETU [HIK]
SEITH alt for SEIT dial of SEIT-KAITETU [HIK]
SEIT-KAITETU [HIK] lang, Indonesia (Maluku)
SEIYAP alt for SIYI dial of CHINESE, YUE [YUH]
SEIYARA alt for SAYA [SAY]
SEJIQ alt for TAROKO [TRV]
SEK alt for GEDAGED [GDD]
SEK alt for SAEK [SKB]
SEKA alt for SEKAR [SKZ]
SEKALAKA alt for KALANGA [KCK]
SEKALAÑA alt for KALANGA [KCK]
SEKALAU alt for KETUNGAU dial of IBAN [IBA]
SEKANI [SEK] lang, Canada
SEKAPAN [SKP] lang, Malaysia (Sarawak)
SEKAPAT alt for KETUNGAU dial of IBAN [IBA]
SEKAR [SKZ] lang, Indonesia (Irian Jaya)
SEKARE dial of GUHU-SAMANE [GHS]
SEKAYU [SYU] lang, Indonesia (Sumatra)
SEKE [SKE] lang, Vanuatu

SEKE alt for SEKI [SYI]
SEKE dial of LOPA [LOY]
SEKEPAN alt for SEKAPAN [SKP]
SEKGOA alt for ENGLISH [ENG]
SEK-HWAN alt for PAZEH [PZH]
SEKI [SYI] lang, Equatorial Guinea; also in Gabon
SEKIANA alt for SEKI [SYI]
SEKIANI alt for SEKI [SYI]
SEKIYANI alt for SEKI [SYI]
SEKO alt for SEKO PADANG [SKX]
SEKO alt for SEKO TENGAH [SKO]
SEKO PADANG [SKX] lang, Indonesia (Sulawesi)
SEKO TENGAH [SKO] lang, Indonesia (Sulawesi)
SEKOU alt for SKOU [SKV]
SEKPELE [LIP] lang, Ghana
SEKPELE dial of SEKPELE [LIP]
SEKUMNE alt for MAIDU, NORTHWEST [MAI]
SEKUNDA dial of MAKAA [MCP]
SEKWA dial of KULANGO, BOUNA [NKU]
SEKWA dial of SEKPELE [LIP]
SEKYANI alt for SEKI [SYI]
SELA alt for WESTERN LIMBA dial of LIMBA,
    WEST-CENTRAL [LIA]
SELA dial of KORUPUN-SELA [KPQ]
SELAKAU alt for SELAKO [SKL]
SELAKO [SKL] lang, Indonesia (Kalimantan); also
    in Malaysia (Sarawak)
SELAKO DAYAK alt for SELAKO [SKL]
SELALE alt for SALALE dial of OROMO, BORANA-
    ARSI-GUJI [GAX]
SELALIR alt for SEDALIR dial of TIDONG [TID]
SELANGOR SAKAI dial of BESISI [MHE]
SELARU [SLU] lang, Indonesia (Maluku)
SELAU dial of HALIA [HLA]
SELAYAR [SLY] lang, Indonesia (Sulawesi)
SELE [SNW] lang, Ghana
SELEK dial of JOLA-KASA [CSK]
SELEMAN alt for SALEMAN [SAU]
SELEMO alt for ISEKIRI [ITS]
SELEPE alt for SELEPET [SEL]
SELEPET [SEL] lang, Papua New Guinea
SELKIRK alt for TUTCHONE, NORTHERN [TUT]
SELKNAM alt for ONA [ONA]
SELKUP [SAK] lang, Russia (Asia)
SELONG alt for MOKEN [MWT]
SELTI alt for SILTI dial of GURAGE, EAST [GRE]
SELUNG alt for MOKEN [MWT]
SELUNGAI MURUT [SLG] lang, Malaysia (Sabah);
    also in Indonesia (Kalimantan)
SELUWASAN [SWH] lang, Indonesia (Maluku)
SELUWASAN dial of SELUWASAN [SWH]
SELVASA alt for SELUWASAN [SWH]
SELWASA alt for SELUWASAN [SWH]
SELYA dial of NYAKYUSA-NGONDE [NYY]
SELYER dial of TAROK [YER]
SEMA alt for NAGA, SUMI [NSM]
SEMAI [SEA] lang, Malaysia (Peninsular)
SEMAKHA dial of AZERBAIJANI, NORTH [AZE]
SEMALINGA dial of ZIMBA [ZMB]
SEMAMBU alt for SUMAMBU dial of TAGAL MURUT
    [MVV]

SEMAMBU alt for TAGAL MURUT [MVV]
SEMANDANG [SDM] lang, Indonesia (Kalimantan)
SEMANDANG dial of SEMANDANG [SDM]
SEMANG alt for KENSIU [KNS]
SEMANG, LOWLAND [ORB] lang, Indonesia
    (Sumatra)
SEMAQ BERI [SZC] lang, Malaysia (Peninsular)
SEMAQ BRI alt for SEMAQ BERI [SZC]
SEMARIJI dial of KUNJA [PEP]
SEMAU alt for HELONG [HEG]
SEMAWA alt for SUMBAWA [SMW]
SEMBAAN alt for MBAAN dial of TRINGGUS [TRX]
SEMBAKOENG alt for SEMBAKUNG MURUT
    [SMA]
SEMBAKONG alt for SEMBAKUNG MURUT [SMA]
SEMBAKUNG MURUT [SMA] lang, Indonesia
    (Kalimantan); also in Malaysia (Sabah)
SEMBLA alt for SEEKU [SOS]
SEME alt for SIAMOU [SIF]
SEMELAI [SZA] lang, Malaysia (Peninsular)
SEMEMBU alt for SUMAMBU dial of TAGAL MURUT
    [MVV]
SEMEMBU alt for TAGAL MURUT [MVV]
SEMENDO [SMN] lang, Indonesia (Sumatra)
SEMIANG alt for LONG SEMIANG dial of KAYAN,
    MURIK [MXR]
SÉMIEN dial of WE NORTHERN [WOB]
SEMIGAE alt for ANDOA [ANB]
SEMIMI [ETZ] lang, Indonesia (Irian Jaya)
SEMINOLE alt for AFRO-SEMINOLE CREOLE [AFS]
SEMINOLE dial of MUSKOGEE [CRK]
SEMIRARA dial of CALUYANUN [CAU]
SEMITAU dial of MALAYIC DAYAK [XDY]
SEMNAM [SSM] lang, Malaysia (Peninsular)
SEMNANI [SMJ] lang, Iran
SEMOLIKA alt for EMHALHE dial of OKPAMHERI
    [OPA]
SEMOLO alt for SEMULU dial of ZIMBA [ZMB]
SEMONTANÉS alt for SOUTHERN ARAGONESE
    dial of ARAGONESE [AXX]
SEMOQ BERI alt for SEMAQ BERI [SZC]
SEMPAN [SEM] lang, Indonesia (Irian Jaya)
SÉMU alt for SIAMOU [SIF]
SEMUKUNG UHENG dial of HOVONGAN [HOV]
SEMULU dial of ZIMBA [ZMB]
SEMYEN dial of AGAW, WESTERN [QIM]
SEN CHUN alt for BLANG [BLR]
SEN NOSU alt for YI, SICHUAN [III]
SENA [SEH] lang, Mozambique
SENA BANGWE dial of SENA [SEH]
SENA CENTRAL dial of SENA [SEH]
SENA, MALAWI [SWK] lang, Malawi
SENA:YA alt for SENAYA [SYN]
SENA-CARE dial of SENA [SEH]
SENADI alt for SENOUFO, CEBAARA [SEF]
SENAGI alt for ANGOR [AGG]
SENAKI dial of LAZ [LZZ]
SENARE, SENARI alt for SENOUFO, SYENARA
    [SHZ]
SENARI alt for SENOUFO, CEBAARA [SEF]
SENAYA [SYN] lang, Iran; also in Australia, USA

SENCHI alt for LILA dial of CLELA [DRI]
SENDANA dial of MANDAR [MHN]
SENE [SEJ] lang, Papua New Guinea
SENE alt for SENJE dial of GOLA [GOL]
SENECA [SEE] lang, USA; also in Canada
SENED [SDS] lang, Tunisia
SENED dial of SENED [SDS]
SENGA alt for NSENGA [NSE]
SENGA alt for SENGAN dial of BABATANA [BAQ]
SENGA dial of TUMBUKA [TUW]
SENGAM alt for AWAD BING [BCU]
SENGAN dial of BABATANA [BAQ]
SENGBE dial of KURANKO [KHA]
SENGEJU alt for SEGEJU [SEG]
SENGELE [SZG] lang, DRC
SENGERE alt for SENGELE [SZG]
SENGGA alt for SENGAN dial of BABATANA [BAQ]
SENGGI [SNU] lang, Indonesia (Irian Jaya)
SENGGO dial of CITAK [TXT]
SENGIMA alt for NAGA, ZEME [NZM]
SENGMAI dial of KADO [KDV]
SENGO [SPK] lang, Papua New Guinea
SENGOI alt for SEMAI [SEA]
SENGSENG [SSZ] lang, Papua New Guinea
SENHAJA DE SRAIR [SJS] lang, Morocco
SENIANG alt for SOUTH WEST BAY [SNS]
SENJE dial of GOLA [GOL]
SENJI alt for SHANGA dial of NDAU [NDC]
SENKON alt for SINKON dial of SAPO [KRN]
SENOI alt for SEMAI [SEA]
SÉNOUFO alt for SÉNOUFO, SENARA [SEQ]
SENOUFO, CEBAARA [SEF] lang, Côte d'Ivoire
SENOUFO, DJIMINI [DYI] lang, Côte d'Ivoire
SÉNOUFO, MAMARA [MYK] lang, Mali
SÉNOUFO, NANERIGÉ [SEN] lang, Burkina Faso
SÉNOUFO, NYARAFOLO [SEV] lang, Côte d'Ivoire
SÉNOUFO, PALAKA [PLR] lang, Côte d'Ivoire
SÉNOUFO, SENARA [SEQ] lang, Burkina Faso
SÉNOUFO, SHEMPIRE [SEB] lang, Côte d'Ivoire
SÉNOUFO, SÌCÌTÉ [SEP] lang, Burkina Faso;
    also in Côte d'Ivoire, Mali
SENOUFO, SUPYIRE [SPP] lang, Mali
SENOUFO, SYENARA [SHZ] lang, Mali
SENOUFO, TAGWANA [TGW] lang, Côte d'Ivoire
SENSI [SNI] lang, Peru
SENTAH alt for BIATAH [BTH]
SENTALI alt for SANTALI [SNT]
SENTANI [SET] lang, Indonesia (Irian Jaya)
SENTHANG alt for CHIN, SENTHANG [SEZ]
SENTI alt for SENSI [SNI]
SENTINEL [STD] lang, India
SENTINELESE alt for SENTINEL [STD]
SENTROKOFI alt for SELE [SNW]
SENYA dial of AWUTU [AFU]
SEO alt for INDUS dial of KOHISTANI, INDUS [MVY]
SEONI dial of GONDI, NORTHERN [GON]
SEOUL dial of KOREAN [KKN]
SEPA [SPB] lang, Indonesia (Maluku)
SEPA [SPE] lang, Papua New Guinea
SEPA dial of ONIN [ONI]
SEPEDI alt for SOTHO, NORTHERN [SRT]

SEPEN [SPM] lang, Papua New Guinea
SEPIK PLAINS alt for MALINGUAT [SIC]
SEPOE dial of TOARIPI [TPI]
SEPUTAN alt for BUKAR SADONG [SDO]
SERA [SRY] lang, Papua New Guinea
SERA alt for SEIRA dial of FORDATA [FRD]
SERAHULI alt for SONINKE [SNN]
SERAK dial of MEFELE [MFJ]
SERAM alt for GESER-GOROM [GES]
SERAMAR alt for PALIYAN [PCF]
SERAMBAU dial of JAGOI [SNE]
SERAMBO alt for SERAMBAU dial of JAGOI [SNE]
SERAMBU alt for SERAMBAU dial of JAGOI [SNE]
SERAN alt for GESER-GOROM [GES]
SERAN LAUT alt for GESER-GOROM [GES]
SERANG dial of TAKIA [TBC]
SERANI alt for MALACCAN CREOLE
    PORTUGUESE [MCM]
SERAWAI [SRJ] lang, Indonesia (Sumatra)
SERAWAJ alt for SERAWAI [SRJ]
SERAWI alt for SERAWAI [SRJ]
SERBIAN alt for SERBO-CROATIAN [SRC]
SERBIAN dial of SERBO-CROATIAN [SRC]
SERBIAN ROMANI dial of ROMANI, SINTE [RMO]
SERBIAN SIGN LANGUAGE dial of YUGOSLAVIAN
    SIGN LANGUAGE [YSL]
SERBO-BOSNIAN dial of ROMANI, VLAX [RMY]
SERBO-CROATIAN [SRC] lang, Yugoslavia; also in
    Albania, Australia, Austria, Bosnia-Herzegovina,
    Bulgaria, Canada, Croatia, Germany, Greece,
    Hungary, Italy, Macedonia, Romania, Russia
    (Europe), Slovakia, Slovenia, Sweden, Switzer-
    land, Turkey (Europe), Ukraine, UAE, USA
SERBODJADI dial of GAYO [GYO]
SERE [SWF] lang, DRC; also in CAR
SEREER alt for SERER-SINE [SES]
SERER alt for SERER-SINE [SES]
SERERE-SAFEN alt for SAAFI-SAAFI [SAV]
SÉRÈRE-SINE alt for SERER-SINE [SES]
SERER-NOON alt for NOON [SNF]
SERER-SAFEN alt for SAAFI-SAAFI [SAV]
SERER-SIN alt for SERER-SINE [SES]
SERER-SINE [SES] lang, Senegal; also in Gambia
SERHTA dial of RAWANG [RAW]
SERI [SEI] lang, Mexico
SERIA alt for SELYA dial of NYAKYUSA-NGONDE
    [NYY]
SERIAN alt for BUKAR SADONG [SDO]
SERIKENAM dial of KWERBA [KWE]
SERILI [SVE] lang, Indonesia (Maluku)
SERING dial of DAYAK, LAND [DYK]
SERKI alt for ARAMMBA [STK]
SERKISETAVI alt for ARAMMBA [STK]
SERMAH dial of DAYAK, LAND [DYK]
SERNUR-MORKIN alt for GRASSLAND MARI dial
    of MARI, LOW [MAL]
SEROA [KQU] lang, South Africa
SEROQ alt for TEMIAR [TMH]
SERRA alt for SERA [SRY]
SERRA AZUL dial of NAMBIKUARA, SOUTHERN
    [NAB]

SERRANO [SER] lang, USA
SERRE alt for SERE [SWF]
SERRER alt for SERER-SINE [SES]
SERU [SZD] lang, Malaysia (Sarawak)
SERUA [SRW] lang, Indonesia (Maluku)
SERUAWAN alt for KAMARIAN [KZX]
SERUDONG alt for SERUDUNG MURUT [SRK]
SERUDUNG MURUT [SRK] lang, Malaysia (Sabah)
SERUI-LAUT [SEU] lang, Indonesia (Irian Jaya)
SERWA alt for SHERPA [SCR]
SERWANG dial of RAWANG [RAW]
SESA dial of FOLOPA [PPO]
SESAJAP alt for SESAYAP dial of TIDONG [TID]
SESAKE dial of EFATE, NORTH [LLP]
SESAN dial of JARAI [JRA]
SESARWA alt for HIETSHWARE [HIE]
SESAYAP dial of TIDONG [TID]
SESE alt for MESE dial of TUNEN [BAZ]
SESE dial of GANDA [LAP]
SESE dial of GUMUZ [GUK]
SESEKI alt for SEKI [SYI]
SESELWA CREOLE FRENCH [CRS] lang,
    Seychelles
SESFONTEIN DAMARA dial of NAMA [NAQ]
SESIVI dial of DAKAKA [BPA]
SESOTHO alt for SOTHO, SOUTHERN [SSO]
SESUBEA alt for SUBIYA [SBS]
SET alt for SAEK [SKB]
SETA [STF] lang, Papua New Guinea
SETA alt for XETÁ [XET]
SETAMAN [STM] lang, Papua New Guinea
SETEBO alt for SHETEBO dial of SHIPIBO-CONIBO
    [SHP]
"SETI" pejorative name for dial of LIANA-SETI [STE]
SETI [SBI] lang, Papua New Guinea
SETIALI dial of NIKSEK [GBE]
SETIBO alt for SHETEBO dial of SHIPIBO-CONIBO
    [SHP]
SETIIT alt for TAKAZZE-SETIIT dial of KUNAMA
    [KUM]
SETIT alt for TAKAZZE-SETIIT dial of KUNAMA
    [KUM]
SETO alt for SETO-GBE [STS]
SETO dial of ESTONIAN [EST]
SETO-GBE [STS] lang, Benin; also in Nigeria
SETSWANA alt for TSWANA [TSW]
SETSWAPONG alt for TSWAPONG [TWO]
SETTE COMUNI CIMBRIAN dial of CIMBRIAN [CIM]
SETTLA [STA] lang, Zambia
SETU alt for SETO dial of ESTONIAN [EST]
SETU dial of ESTONIAN [EST]
SEUCE alt for SAUSE [SAO]
SEUCI alt for SIUSY-TAPUYA dial of BANIWA [BAI]
SEVERN RIVER OJIBWA dial of OJIBWA, SEVERN
    [OJS]
SEVERNO-KAREL'SKIJ alt for KARELIAN [KRL]
SEWA alt for SEBA [KDG]
SEWA BAY [SEW] lang, Papua New Guinea
SEWARD PENINSULA INUPIATUN dial of
    INUPIATUN, NORTHWEST ALASKA [ESK]
SEWATAITAI dial of SEWA BAY [SEW]

SEWAWA dial of MENDE [MFY]
SEWE dial of DOYAYO [DOW]
SEWI dial of GITONGA [TOH]
SEYA alt for SAYA [SAY]
SEYAWA alt for SAYA [SAY]
SEYCHELLES CREOLE FRENCH alt for SESELWA
    CREOLE FRENCH [CRS]
SEYCHELLOIS CREOLE alt for SESELWA CREOLE
    FRENCH [CRS]
SEYKI dial of AARI [AIZ]
SEYU alt for CHRU [CJE]
SEZE [SZE] lang, Ethiopia
SEZO alt for SEZE [SZE]
SFA RIERE dial of TEHIT [KPS]
S'GAU alt for KAREN, S'GAW [KSW]
S'GAW alt for KAREN, S'GAW [KSW]
S'GAW KAYIN alt for KAREN, S'GAW [KSW]
SGUXS alt for SOUTHERN TSIMSHIAN dial of
    TSIMSHIAN [TSI]
SHA [SCW] lang, Nigeria
SHA alt for SHAN [SJN]
SHAALE alt for ASSANGORI [SUN]
SHAALE alt for SUNGOR [SUN]
SHAANXI dial of DUNGAN [DNG]
SHAARI dial of MUMUYE [MUL]
SHAATHARI alt for YANOMAMÖ [GUU]
SHABAK alt for BAJELAN [BJM]
SHABAK dial of DIMLI [ZZZ]
SHABARI alt for SORA [SRB]
SHABIN-KARAHISSAR dial of ARMENIAN [ARM]
SHABO [SBF] lang, Ethiopia
SHABOGALA alt for ATAYAL [TAY]
SHABUN dial of SHWAI [SHW]
SHACHOBIIKHA alt for TSHANGLA [TSJ]
SHACHOPKHA alt for TSHANGLA [TSJ]
SHACRIABA alt for XAKRIABÁ [XKR]
SHADAL dial of MANKANYA [MAN]
SHAGA dial of KGALAGADI [XKV]
SHAGAU alt for MONGUNA dial of RON [CLA]
SHAGAWU alt for MONGUNA dial of RON [CLA]
SHAHARI alt for JIBBALI [SHV]
SHAH-MANSURI dial of KASHMIRI [KSH]
SHAHMIRZADI [SRZ] lang, Iran
SHAHO alt for SAHO [SSY]
SHAHRUDI [SHM] lang, Iran
SHAHRUDI dial of FARSI, WESTERN [PES]
SHAHSAVANI dial of AZERBAIJANI, SOUTH
    [AZB]
SHAHSEVEN alt for SHAHSAVANI dial of
    AZERBAIJANI, SOUTH [AZB]
SHAI dial of DANGME [DGM]
SHAINI alt for SHENI [SCV]
SHAIRE alt for SERE [SWF]
SHAK alt for SHEKO [SHE]
SHAKA alt for NGASA [NSG]
SHAKACHO [MOY] lang, Ethiopia
SHAKE alt for SAKE [SAG]
SHAKO alt for SHABO [SBF]
SHAKO alt for SHEKO [SHE]
SHAL alt for SHALL dial of SHALL-ZWALL [SHA]
SHALKOTA alt for SHELKOTA dial of MIDOB [MEI]

SHALL dial of SHALL-ZWALL [SHA]
SHALL-ZWALL [SHA] lang, Nigeria
SHAM alt for SHAMMA dial of LADAKHI [LBJ]
SHAMA dial of SHAMA-SAMBUGA [SQA]
SHAMAITISH dial of LITHUANIAN [LIT]
SHAMAKHI dial of ARMENIAN [ARM]
SHAMAKHI dial of AZERBAIJANI, NORTH [AZE]
SHAMAKOT dial of PASHAYI, NORTHWEST [GLH]
SHAMANG [SGN] lang, Nigeria
SHAMA-SAMBUGA [SQA] lang, Nigeria
SHAMATRI alt for YANOMAMÖ [GUU]
SHAMBA dial of SWAHILI [SWA]
SHAMBAA alt for SHAMBALA [KSB]
SHAMBALA [KSB] lang, Tanzania
SHAMI alt for CENTRAL SYRIAN ARABIC dial of
    ARABIC, NORTH LEVANTINE SPOKEN [APC]
SHAMMA dial of LADAKHI [LBJ]
SHAMMAR alt for NORTH NAJDI dial of ARABIC,
    NAJDI SPOKEN [ARS]
SHAMMARI alt for NORTH NAJDI dial of ARABIC,
    NAJDI SPOKEN [ARS]
SHAMNYUYANGA dial of NAGA, KONYAK [NBE]
SHAMSKAT alt for SHAMMA dial of LADAKHI [LBJ]
SHAMYA alt for SINYAR [SYS]
SHAMYAN alt for SINYAR [SYS]
SHAN [SJN] lang, Myanmar; also in China, Thailand
SHAN GYANAN alt for SENAYA [SYN]
SHAN SRAY alt for SENAYA [SYN]
SHANDU alt for SHENDU [SHL]
SHANGA [SHO] lang, Nigeria
SHANGA alt for CHANGA dial of NDAU [NDC]
SHANGA dial of NDAU [NDC]
SHANGAAN alt for CHANGANA dial of TSONGA
    [TSO]
SHANGAAN alt for TSONGA [TSO]
SHANGAMA dial of AARI [AIZ]
SHANGANA alt for CHANGANA dial of TSONGA
    [TSO]
SHANGANA alt for TSONGA [TSO]
SHANGAWA alt for SHANGA [SHO]
SHANGGE alt for SANKE dial of NAGA, TASE [NST]
SHANGHAI SIGN LANGUAGE dial of CHINESE
    SIGN LANGUAGE [CSL]
"SHANGILLA" pejorative alt for DAASANACH [DSH]
SHANGO alt for SANGU [SNQ]
SHANGZHAI [JIH] lang, China
SHANGZHAI alt for SHANGZHAI [JIH]
SHANI alt for SHENI [SCV]
SHANI dial of DERA [KNA]
SHANJO dial of TONGA [TOI]
SHANKADI alt for SAMBA [SMX]
"SHANKILLA" pejorative alt for AARI [AIZ]
"SHANKILLIGNA" pejorative alt for AARI [AIZ]
"SHANKILLIGNA" pejorative alt for GUMUZ [GUK]
"SHANKILLINYA" pejorative alt for AARI [AIZ]
"SHANKILLINYA" pejorative alt for GUMUZ [GUK]
SHANKILLINYA alt for GUMUZ [GUK]
SHANLANG dial of NAGA, KONYAK [NBE]
"SHANQILLA" pejorative alt for BIRALE [BXE]
"SHANQILLA" pejorative alt for GUMUZ [GUK]
SHANQILLA alt for GUMUZ [GUK]

SHANTOU dial of CHINESE, MIN NAN [CFR]
SHANZI YAO alt for KIM MUN [MJI]
SHAO alt for THAO [SSF]
SHAPRA alt for CHAPARA dial of CANDOSHI-
    SHAPRA [CBU]
SHAPSUG dial of ADYGHE [ADY]
SHARANAHUA [MCD] lang, Peru; also in Brazil
SHARCHAGPAKHA alt for TSHANGLA [TSJ]
SHARI alt for CHALI dial of SO [SSS]
SHARK BAY [SSV] lang, Vanuatu
SHAROKA alt for THARAKA [THA]
SHARPA alt for SHERPA [SCR]
SHARPA BHOTIA alt for SHERPA [SCR]
SHARWA [SWQ] lang, Cameroon
SHASHA dial of NKOYA [NKA]
SHASHI alt for SIZAKI [SZK]
SHASTA [SHT] lang, USA
SHASTAN alt for SHASTA [SHT]
SHATOI alt for ITUMKALA dial of CHECHEN [CJC]
SHATOU alt for YUEHAI dial of CHINESE, YUE
    [YUH]
SHATT [SHJ] lang, Sudan
SHATT alt for THURI [THU]
SHATT dial of MUNDU [MUH]
SHAU [SQH] lang, Nigeria
SHAUSHA WANKA QUECHUA alt for QUECHUA,
    WANCA, JAUJA [QHJ]
SHAVANTE alt for XAVÁNTE [XAV]
SHAWANANAWA-ARARA alt for ARARA-
    SHAWANANAWA dial of KATUKINA, PANOAN
    [KNT]
SHAWE alt for SHOE dial of MPADE [MPI]
SHAWIA alt for CHAOUIA [SHY]
SHAWIYA alt for CHAOUIA [SHY]
SHAWNEE [SJW] lang, USA
SHAYABIT alt for CHAYAHUITA [CBT]
SHE [SHX] lang, China
SHE dial of BENCH [BCQ]
SHEDE alt for GUDE [GDE]
SHEDEKKA alt for TAROKO [TRV]
SHEETSHWA alt for TSHWA [TSC]
SHEFFIELD YORKSHIRE dial of ENGLISH
    [ENG]
SHEHLEH dial of LAHU [LAH]
SHEHRI alt for JIBBALI [SHV]
SHEKASIP dial of CHIN, FALAM [HBH]
SHEKAWATI dial of MARWARI [MKD]
SHEKE alt for SEKI [SYI]
SHEKGALAGADI alt for KGALAGADI [XKV]
SHEKHANI alt for EASTERN KATIVIRI dial of KATI
    [BSH]
SHEKHANI alt for KAMVIRI [QMV]
SHEKHANI dial of KAMVIRI [QMV]
SHEKHOAN alt for PAZEH [PZH]
SHEKIRI alt for ISEKIRI [ITS]
SHEKIYANA alt for SEKI [SYI]
SHEKKA alt for SHAKACHO [MOY]
SHEKKA alt for SHEKO [SHE]
SHEKKO alt for SHEKO [SHE]
SHEKO [SHE] lang, Ethiopia
SHEKWAN alt for KAVALAN [CKV]

SHELDRU alt for SHELTA [STH]
SHELKNAM alt for ONA [ONA]
SHELKOTA dial of MIDOB [MEI]
SHELLEN dial of DERA [KNA]
SHELTA [STH] lang, Ireland; also in United Kingdom, USA
SHEMINAHUA dial of CASHINAHUA [CBS]
SHEMYA alt for SINYAR [SYS]
SHENARA alt for SENOUFO, SYENARA [SHZ]
SHENDU [SHL] lang, Bangladesh; also in India
SHENGE SHERBRO dial of SHERBRO [BUN]
SHENGHA dial of NAGA, KONYAK [NBE]
SHENGWE alt for GITONGA [TOH]
SHENI [SCV] lang, Nigeria
SHENPIRE alt for SENOUFO, SHEMPIRE [SEB]
SHENSI alt for SHAANXI dial of DUNGAN [DNG]
SHERA YOGUR alt for YUGUR, EAST [YUY]
SHERBRO [BUN] lang, Sierra Leone
SHERDUKPEN [SDP] lang, India
SHERE alt for SERE [SWF]
SHERENTÉ alt for XERÉNTE [XER]
SHERET alt for JIBBALI [SHV]
SHEREWYANA alt for HIXKARYÁNA [HIX]
SHERI alt for SERE [SWF]
SHERPA [SCR] lang, Nepal; also in Bhutan, China, India, Korea, South, USA
SHERWIN alt for SHARWA [SWQ]
SHERWOOD VALLEY dial of POMO, NORTHERN [PEJ]
SHESHI alt for KHAM, SHESHI [KIP]
SHETA alt for XETÁ [XET]
SHETE TSERE alt for TSHIDI-KHWE dial of SHUA [SHG]
SHETEBO dial of SHIPIBO-CONIBO [SHP]
SHEVA alt for CHEWA dial of NYANJA [NYJ]
SHI [SHR] lang, DRC
SHI alt for LAHU SHI [KDS]
SHI XIEN alt for SANHSIEN dial of CHINESE, HAKKA [HAK]
SHIBA alt for SHERBRO [BUN]
SHIBNE alt for SOMRAI [SOR]
SHIBUKUN dial of BUNUN [BNN]
SHIBUSHI alt for BUSHI [BUC]
SHIBUSHI SHIMAWORE alt for BUSHI [BUC]
SHICHOPI alt for CHOPI [CCE]
SHICOPI alt for CHOPI [CCE]
SHIDAN dial of JINGPHO [CGP]
SHIGEN alt for SANHSIEN dial of CHINESE, HAKKA [HAK]
SHIGHNI alt for SHUGHNI dial of SHUGHNI [SGH]
SHIHHI alt for ARABIC, SHIHHI SPOKEN [SSH]
SHIHLANGANU alt for NHLANGANU dial of TSONGA [TSO]
SHIHO alt for SAHO [SSY]
SHIHU alt for ARABIC, SHIHHI SPOKEN [SSH]
SHIHUH alt for ARABIC, SHIHHI SPOKEN [SSH]
SHIITA alt for OPUUO [LGN]
SHIJIAN dial of YI, YUNNAN [NOS]
SHIKAKI [SHF] lang, Iraq; also in Iran, Turkey (Asia)
SHIKARUANAM alt for VAAGRI BOOLI [VAA]

SHIKI [GUA] lang, Nigeria
SHIKIANA alt for SIKIANA [SIK]
SHIKOTAN alt for KURIL dial of AINU [AIN]
SHILA dial of BEMBA [BEM]
SHILA dial of TAABWA [TAP]
SHILANGANU alt for CHANGANA dial of TSONGA [TSO]
SHILE alt for LEGA-MWENGA [LGM]
SHILENGWE alt for HLENGWE dial of TSHWA [TSC]
SHILHA alt for TACHELHIT [SHI]
SHILHA alt for TAMAZIGHT, CENTRAL ATLAS [TZM]
SHILHA alt for TARIFIT [RIF]
SHILINGOL dial of MONGOLIAN, PERIPHERAL [MVF]
SHILLUK [SHK] lang, Sudan
SHIMACU alt for URARINA [URA]
SHIMAKONDE alt for MAKONDE [KDE]
SHIMAORE alt for SHIMAWORE dial of COMORIAN [SWB]
SHIMAORE dial of COMORIAN [SWB]
SHIMAORI alt for SHIMAWORE dial of COMORIAN [SWB]
SHIMAWORE dial of COMORIAN [SWB]
SHIMBOGEDU alt for DIRIKU [DIU]
SHIMBWERA alt for MBOWELA dial of NKOYA [NKA]
SHIMBWERA alt for MBWELA [MFU]
SHIMIGAE alt for ANDOA [ANB]
SHIMIZYA alt for CHIMILA [CBG]
SHIMLA SIRAJI alt for UPPER MAHASU PAHARI dial of PAHARI, MAHASU [BFZ]
SHIMWALI dial of COMORIAN, SHINGAZIDJA [SWS]
SHINA [SCL] lang, Pakistan; also in India
SHINA dial of RUTUL [RUT]
SHINA, KOHISTANI [PLK] lang, Pakistan
SHINABO [SHN] lang, Bolivia
SHINAKI alt for SHINA [SCL]
SHINASHA alt for BORO [BWO]
SHINDZUANI alt for SHINDZWANI dial of COMORIAN [SWB]
SHINDZWANI dial of COMORIAN [SWB]
SHING SAAPA alt for LHOMI [LHM]
SHINGAZIDJA dial of COMORIAN, SHINGAZIDJA [SWS]
SHINGSOL alt for SINGSON dial of CHIN, THADO [TCZ]
SHINGWALUNGU alt for NGWALUNGU dial of TSONGA [TSO]
SHINGWALUNGU alt for N'WALUNGU dial of TSONGA [TSO]
SHINKOYA alt for NKOYA [NKA]
SHINNECOCK-POOSEPATUCK alt for MONTAUK dial of MOHEGAN-MONTAUK-NARRAGANSETT [MOF]
SHINYIHA alt for NYIHA [NIH]
SHINZWANI dial of COMORIAN [SWB]
SHIOKO alt for CHOKWE [CJK]
SHIP alt for MISHIP [CHP]

SHIP dial of ALBANIAN, GHEG [ALS]
SHIPI alt for CHINALI [CIH]
SHIPIBO dial of SHIPIBO-CONIBO [SHP]
SHIPIBO-CONIBO [SHP] lang, Peru
SHIPINAHUA alt for XIPINÁWA [XIP]
SHIPUTHSU alt for PODZO dial of SENA [SEH]
SHIQI alt for YUEHAI dial of CHINESE, YUE [YUH]
SHIR alt for MANDARI [MQU]
SHIRA alt for SIRA [SWJ]
SHIRA dial of CHAGGA [KAF]
SHIRA YUGUR alt for YUGUR, EAST [YUY]
SHIRAHO dial of YAEYAMA [RYS]
SHIRAWA dial of BADE [BDE]
SHIRAZI dial of FARSI, WESTERN [PES]
SHIRE alt for SIRA [SWJ]
SHIRIANA CASAPARE alt for NINAM [SHB]
SHIRIMA alt for MAKHUWA-SHIRIMA [VMK]
SHIRNAK-CHIZRE dial of CHALDEAN NEO-
    ARAMAIC [CLD]
SHIRONGA alt for RONGA [RON]
SHIRUMBA alt for CERUMBA dial of SHWAI [SHW]
SHIRUMBA alt for SHWAI [SHW]
SHIRWANGA dial of YEYI [YEY]
SHISA alt for KISA dial of LUYIA [LUY]
SHISAMBYU alt for SAMBYU dial of KWANGALI
    [KWN]
SHISHI alt for SEBA [KDG]
SHISHONG alt for BEBA' dial of BAFUT [BFD]
SHITA alt for OPUUO [LGN]
SHITAKO alt for DIBO [DIO]
SHITHLOU dial of CHIN, THADO [TCZ]
SHITSHWA alt for TSHWA [TSC]
SHITSONGA alt for TSONGA [TSO]
SHITTA alt for OPUUO [LGN]
SHIXIEN alt for SANHSIEN dial of CHINESE, HAKKA
    [HAK]
SHIXING [SXG] lang, China
SHIYEYI alt for YEYI [YEY]
SHKIP alt for ALBANIAN, TOSK [ALN]
SHO alt for CHIN, ASHO [CSH]
SHO alt for CHIN, CHINBON [CNB]
SHO alt for SHAU [SQH]
SHOA alt for CHIN, ASHO [CSH]
SHOBA alt for PIANGA dial of BUSHOONG [BUF]
SHOBANG [SSB] lang, India
SHOBWA alt for PIANGA dial of BUSHOONG [BUF]
SHOBYO alt for HUTU dial of RWANDA [RUA]
SHOCO alt for KIRIRÍ-XOKÓ [XOO]
SHOCU alt for KIRIRÍ-XOKÓ [XOO]
SHOE dial of MPADE [MPI]
SHOHO alt for SAHO [SSY]
SHOLAGA [SLE] lang, India
SHOLIGA alt for SHOLAGA [SLE]
SHOLIGAR alt for SHOLAGA [SLE]
SHOLIO dial of TYAP [KCG]
SHOM PEN alt for SHOM PENG [SII]
SHOM PENG [SII] lang, India
SHOMBA dial of NGEMBA [NGE]
SHOMO KARIM alt for COMO KARIM [CFG]
SHOMOH alt for COMO KARIM [CFG]
SHOMONG alt for COMO KARIM [CFG]

SHOMPENG alt for SHOM PENG [SII]
SHONA [SHD] lang, Zimbabwe; also in Botswana,
    Malawi, Zambia
SHONG alt for CHONG [COG]
SHONGA alt for SHANGA [SHO]
SHONGAWA alt for SHANGA [SHO]
SHONGO alt for BUSHOONG [BUF]
SHONGOM dial of TANGALE [TAN]
SHONKE dial of ARGOBBA [AGJ]
SHONSHE dial of CHIN, HAKA [CNH]
SHOO dial of SHOO-MINDA-NYE [BCV]
SHOO-MINDA-NYE [BCV] lang, Nigeria
SHOPNI alt for ALBANIAN, GHEG [ALS]
SHOR [CJS] lang, Russia (Asia)
SHOR dial of KHAKAS [KJH]
SHORTSY alt for SHOR [CJS]
"SHOSHO" pejorative alt for BEROM [BOM]
SHOSHONE alt for SHOSHONI [SHH]
SHOSHONI [SHH] lang, USA
SHQIP alt for ALBANIAN, TOSK [ALN]
SHQIPERË alt for ALBANIAN, TOSK [ALN]
SHTAFARI dial of THAO [SSF]
SHTOKAVSKI dial of CROATIAN [SRC]
SHU dial of NANDI [NNB]
SHUA [SHG] lang, Botswana
SHUA alt for ARABIC, CHADIAN SPOKEN [SHU]
SHUA alt for ARABIC, SHUWA [SHU]
SHUA ARABIC alt for ARABIC, CHADIAN SPOKEN
    [SHU]
SHUA ARABIC alt for ARABIC, SHUWA [SHU]
SHUADI alt for SHUADIT [SDT]
SHUADIT [SDT] lang, France
SHU-AI-I alt for LÜ [KHB]
SHUA-KHWE alt for SHUA [SHG]
SHUA-KHWE dial of SHUA [SHG]
SHUAR [JIV] lang, Ecuador
SHUARA alt for SHUAR [JIV]
SHUBA alt for KAGATE [SYW]
SHUBI [SUJ] lang, Tanzania
SHUGAN alt for SHUGHNI dial of SHUGHNI [SGH]
SHUGHNANI alt for SHUGHNI dial of SHUGHNI
    [SGH]
SHUGHNI [SGH] lang, Tajikistan; also in Afghanistan
SHUGHNI dial of SHUGHNI [SGH]
SHUGNAN alt for SHUGHNI dial of SHUGHNI [SGH]
SHUGNAN-RUSHAN alt for SHUGHNI [SGH]
SHUGNI alt for SHUGHNI dial of SHUGHNI [SGH]
SHUGULE dial of MEFELE [MFJ]
SHUI alt for SUI [SWI]
SHUI NOSU alt for YI, YUNNAN [NOS]
SHUIHU alt for BOUYEI [PCC]
SHUI-PAI-I alt for LÜ [KHB]
SHUKRI dial of ARABIC, SUDANESE SPOKEN
    [APD]
SHUKULUMBWE alt for ILA [ILB]
SHULANIN dial of AVAR [AVR]
SHULI alt for ACHOLI [ACO]
SHULLA alt for SHILLUK [SHK]
SHUMASHT alt for SHUMASHTI [SMS]
SHUMASHTI [SMS] lang, Afghanistan
SHUMCHO [SCU] lang, India

SHUMCU alt for SHUMCHO [SCU]
SHUMPAMEM alt for BAMUN [BAX]
SHUNGO alt for LOO [LDO]
SHUNHU alt for LOO [LDO]
SHUNKLA alt for TASHON dial of CHIN, FALAM [HBH]
SHUNYUO dial of NAGA, KONYAK [NBE]
SHURI alt for SURI [SUQ]
SHURI dial of OKINAWAN, CENTRAL [RYU]
SHURO alt for SURI [SUQ]
SHURU dial of BERTA [WTI]
SHUSHA dial of AZERBAIJANI, NORTH [AZE]
SHUSHTAR dial of MANDAIC [MID]
SHUSWAP [SHS] lang, Canada
SHUTHUN alt for KOHISTANI, INDUS [MVY]
SHUTUL dial of PARACHI [PRC]
SHUTUL dial of PASHAYI, NORTHWEST [GLH]
SHUWA alt for ARABIC, SHUWA [SHU]
SHUWA alt for JAPANESE SIGN LANGUAGE [JSL]
SHUWA ARABIC alt for ARABIC, CHADIAN SPOKEN [SHU]
SHUWA ARABIC alt for ARABIC, SHUWA [SHU]
SHUWAY alt for SHWAI [SHW]
SHUWA-ZAMANI [KSA] lang, Nigeria
SHWAI [SHW] lang, Sudan
SHWE alt for PALAUNG, SHWE [SWE]
SHWO alt for SO [SOX]
SHYEN alt for BÉTÉ, GAGNOA [BTG]
SHYUBA alt for KAGATE [SYW]
SI dial of LERE [GNH]
SI JUNJUNG dial of MINANGKABAU [MPU]
SIA alt for AVATIME [AVA]
SIA alt for SYA dial of BOBO MADARE, NORTHERN [BBO]
SIAFLI alt for AMTO [AMT]
SIAGHA alt for SIAGHA-YENIMU [OSR]
SIAGHA-YENIMU [OSR] lang, Indonesia (Irian Jaya)
SIAKA dial of JULA, KOYAGA [KGA]
SIALUM [SLW] lang, Papua New Guinea
SIAMESE alt for THAI [THJ]
SIAMOU [SIF] lang, Burkina Faso; also in Côte d'Ivoire, Mali
SIAN [SPG] lang, Malaysia (Sarawak)
SIANE [SNP] lang, Papua New Guinea
SIANG [SYA] lang, Indonesia (Kalimantan)
SIANG alt for MA'ANYAN [MHY]
SIANG dial of SIANG [SYA]
SIANI alt for SIANE [SNP]
SIANTAN alt for RITOK dial of MALAY [MLI]
SIAR alt for LAK [SJR]
SIASI alt for AROP-LOKEP [APR]
SIASI alt for LUKEP [LOA]
SIASI SAMA alt for SAMA, CENTRAL [SML]
SIASIADA alt for BUHUTU [BXH]
SIASSI alt for AROP-LOKEP [APR]
SIASSI alt for LUKEP [LOA]
SIAU dial of SANGIR [SAN]
SIAUSI dial of DUAU [DUA]
SIAWARI dial of BURUM-MINDIK [BMU]
SIAWI alt for AMTO [AMT]
SIAWI dial of AMTO [AMT]

SIBALE alt for SIBALENHON dial of BANTOANON [BNO]
SIBALENHON dial of BANTOANON [BNO]
SIBAO-YAMPHE dial of YAMPHE [YMA]
SIBBE alt for NAGOVISI [NCO]
SIBE alt for XIBE [SJO]
SIBERIAN TATAR alt for EASTERN TATAR dial of TATAR [TTR]
SIBERIAN YUPIK alt for YUPIK, CENTRAL SIBERIAN [ESS]
SIBIL dial of NGALUM [SZB]
SIBINE alt for SOMRAI [SOR]
SIBO alt for SIMBO [SBB]
SIBO alt for XIBE [SJO]
SIBO dial of KAMANG [WOI]
SIBOMA alt for NUMBAMI [SIJ]
SIBONAI dial of SEWA BAY [SEW]
SIBOP alt for KENYAH, SEBOB [SIB]
SIBU [SDX] lang, Malaysia (Sarawak)
SIBUCOON alt for SHIBUKUN dial of BUNUN [BNN]
SIBUCO-VITALI dial of SAMA, BALANGINGI [SSE]
SIBUGAY dial of MAGINDANAON [MDH]
SIBUGUEY dial of SAMA, BALANGINGI [SSE]
SIBUIAN alt for SEBUYAU [SNB]
SIBUKAUN alt for SHIBUKUN dial of BUNUN [BNN]
SIBUKU alt for SIBUCO-VITALI dial of SAMA, BALANGINGI [SSE]
SIBUKU dial of TIDONG [TID]
SIBUKUN alt for SHIBUKUN dial of BUNUN [BNN]
SIBUNDOY alt for CAMSÁ [KBH]
SIBURAN alt for BIATAH [BTH]
SIBURAN dial of BIATAH [BTH]
SIBUTU alt for SIBUTU' dial of SAMA, SOUTHERN [SIT]
SIBUTU dial of SAMA, SOUTHERN [SIT]
SIBUTU' dial of SAMA, SOUTHERN [SIT]
SIBUTUQ alt for SIBUTU dial of SAMA, SOUTHERN [SIT]
SIBUYAN alt for SEBUYAU [SNB]
SIBUYAN dial of ROMBLOMANON [ROL]
SIBUYAU alt for SEBUYAU [SNB]
SICHE alt for ZIRE [SIH]
SICHUAN-GUIZHOU-YUNNAN HMONG alt for HMONG NJUA [BLU]
SICHULE alt for SIKULE [SKH]
SICILIAN [SCN] lang, Italy
SICILIAN ALBANIAN dial of ALBANIAN, ARBERESHE [AAE]
SÌCÌRÉ alt for SÉNOUFO, SÌCÌTÉ [SEP]
SÌCÌTÉ alt for SNOUFO, SÌCÌTÉ [SEP]
SICUANE dial of CUIBA [CUI]
"SICUANI" pejorative alt for GUAHIBO [GUH]
SICUARI alt for SICUANE dial of CUIBA [CUI]
SIDABA dial of JIARONG [JYA]
SIDAMINYA alt for SIDAMO [SID]
SIDAMO [SID] lang, Ethiopia
SIDÁMO 'AFÓ alt for SIDAMO [SID]
SIDDRI alt for SADRI [SCK]
SIDEIA alt for SIDEYA dial of TAWALA [TBO]
SIDEIA alt for SIRAIYA [FOS]
SIDEIS alt for SIRAIYA [FOS]

SIDEISCH alt for SIRAIYA [FOS]
SIDEME alt for AVATIME [AVA]
SIDENRANG alt for SIDRAP dial of BUGIS [BPR]
SIDEYA dial of TAWALA [TBO]
SIDIN dial of DAYAK, LAND [DYK]
SIDING alt for SIDIN dial of DAYAK, LAND [DYK]
SIDO dial of AARI [AIZ]
SIDRAP dial of BUGIS [BPR]
SIDUAN alt for SIBU [SDX]
SIDUANI alt for SIBU [SDX]
SIE [ERG] lang, Vanuatu
SIE dial of SIE [ERG]
SIEGU alt for YAAKU [MUU]
SIÉMOU alt for SIAMOU [SIF]
SIEMU alt for SIAMOU [SIF]
SIENKOKA dial of JULA, ODIENNE [JOD]
SIERRA AZTEC alt for NÁHUATL, PUEBLA,
   SIERRA [AZZ]
SIERRA DE PUEBLA NÁHUAT alt for NÁHUATL,
   PUEBLA, SIERRA [AZZ]
SIERRA OTOMÍ alt for OTOMÍ, SIERRA ORIENTAL
   [OTM]
SIEVEMAKERS alt for CHURARI dial of ROMANI,
   VLAX [RMY]
SIGARAU alt for KETUNGAU dial of IBAN [IBA]
SIGAWA alt for SIO [SIO]
SIGDI alt for SIGIDI dial of SAYA [SAY]
SIGGOYO alt for BAMBASSI [MYF]
SIGHU [SXE] lang, Gabon
SIGI alt for IJA dial of KAILI, LEDO [LEW]
SIGIDI dial of SAYA [SAY]
SIGISIGERO alt for BAITSI dial of SIWAI [SIW]
SIGLIT dial of INUKTITUT, WESTERN CANADIAN
   [ESC]
SIGN LANGUAGE OF THE NETHERLANDS alt
   for DUTCH SIGN LANGUAGE [DSE]
SIHA dial of CHAGGA [KAF]
SIHAN [SNR] lang, Papua New Guinea
SIHAN alt for SIAN [SPG]
SIHANAKA dial of MALAGASY [MEX]
SIHONG dial of MAANYAN [MHY]
SII alt for WUSHI [BSE]
SIIME dial of KABA DEME [KWG]
SIIS alt for YU dial of MANDJAK [MFV]
SIJAGHA alt for SIAGHA-YENIMU [OSR]
SIJALI alt for JUMLELI dial of NEPALI [NEP]
SIJIAJI dial of DONGXIANG [SCE]
SIKA [SKI] lang, Indonesia (Nusa Tenggara)
SIKAIANA [SKY] lang, Solomon Islands
SIKAMI alt for SIKKIMESE [SIP]
SIKARI alt for SIKARITAI [TTY]
SIKARITAI [TTY] lang, Indonesia (Irian Jaya)
SIKARWARI dial of BRAJ BHASHA [BFS]
SIKASSO dial of BAMANANKAN [BRA]
SIKAYANA alt for SIKAIANA [SKY]
SIKHOTA ALIN dial of UDIHE [UDE]
SIKHULE alt for SIKULE [SKH]
SIKIANA [SIK] lang, Brazil; also in Venezuela
SIKIÁNA alt for SIKIANA [SIK]
SIKIÂNA alt for SIKIANA [SIK]
SIKKA alt for SIKA [SKI]

SIKKA NATAR dial of SIKA [SKI]
SIKKANESE alt for SIKA [SKI]
SIKKIM BHOTIA alt for SIKKIMESE [SIP]
SIKKIM BHUTIA alt for SIKKIMESE [SIP]
SIKKIMESE [SIP] lang, India
SIKUANI alt for GUAHIBO dial of GUAHIBO [GUH]
SIKUBUNG dial of SAMA, SOUTHERN [SIT]
SIKULE [SKH] lang, Indonesia (Sumatra)
SIKWANGALI alt for KWANGALI [KWN]
SILA [SLT] lang, Laos; also in Viet Nam
SILA alt for DAJU, DAR SILA [DAU]
SILA dial of DAJU, DAR SILA [DAU]
SILABE alt for SONINKE [SNN]
SILABU dial of MENTAWAI [MWV]
SILADJA alt for SELAYAR [SLY]
SILAJARA alt for SELAYAR [SLY]
SILAKAU alt for SELAKO [SKL]
SILANKE alt for SININKERE [SKQ]
SILEBA dial of SAWILA [SWT]
SILEIBI [SBQ] lang, Papua New Guinea
SILEN alt for TELUTI [TLT]
SILESIAN, LOWER [SLI] lang, Poland; also in Czech
   Republic, Germany
SILI alt for PALOR [FAP]
SILI alt for SERE [SWF]
SILI alt for TSHIDI-KHWE dial of SHUA [SHG]
SILIGI dial of FOLOPA [PPO]
SILIMO [WUL] lang, Indonesia (Irian Jaya)
SILINKERE alt for SININKERE [SKQ]
SILIPUT [MKC] lang, Papua New Guinea
SILI-SILI alt for PALOR [FAP]
SILISILI alt for WATUT, MIDDLE [MPL]
SILLE dial of CAPPADOCIAN GREEK [CPG]
SILLOK alt for AKA [SOH]
SILMAMO alt for ZILMAMU dial of KACIPO-BALESI
   [KOE]
SILOPI [SOT] lang, Papua New Guinea
SILOZI alt for LOZI [LOZ]
SILTI dial of GURAGE, EAST [GRE]
SILUNGUBOI alt for FANAGOLO [FAO]
SILVER PALAUNG alt for PALAUNG, PALE [PCE]
SIM dial of WERI [WER]
SIMA dial of NAGA, KONYAK [NBE]
SIMAA [SIE] lang, Zambia
SIMAA dial of SIMAA [SIE]
SIMACU alt for URARINA [URA]
SIMAGAHI alt for OYA'OYA [OYY]
SIMAI dial of ASMAT, CENTRAL [AST]
SIMALEGI dial of MENTAWAI [MWV]
SIMALUR alt for SIMEULUE [SMR]
SIMARANHON alt for BANTOANON [BNO]
SIMAY alt for SIMAI dial of ASMAT, CENTRAL [AST]
SIMBA [SBW] lang, Gabon
SIMBA alt for GUARANÍ, BOLIVIAN, WESTERN
   [GNW]
SIMBA alt for ZEMBA [DHM]
SIMBA GUARANÍ alt for GUARANÍ, BOLIVIAN,
   WESTERN [GNW]
SIMBAKONG alt for SEMBAKUNG MURUT [SMA]
SIMBALI [SMG] lang, Papua New Guinea
SIMBARI [SMB] lang, Papua New Guinea

SIMBERI dial of MANDARA [TBF]
SIMBITI dial of KURIA [KUJ]
SIMBO [SBB] lang, Solomon Islands
SIMBU alt for KUMAN [KUE]
SIMEKU [SMZ] lang, Papua New Guinea
SIMELUNGAN alt for BATAK SIMALUNGUN [BTS]
SIMEULOË alt for SIMEULUE [SMR]
SIMEULUE [SMR] lang, Indonesia (Sumatra)
SIMI alt for NAGA, SUMI [NSM]
SIMIRANCH alt for YINE [PIB]
SIMIRINCHE alt for YINE [PIB]
SIMOG alt for AUWE [SMF]
SIMORI dial of EKARI [EKG]
SIMPI alt for ESIMBI [AGS]
SIMT'ANGA alt for XAMTANGA [XAN]
SIMTE [SMT] lang, India
SIMULUL alt for SIMEULUE [SMR]
SIMUNUL dial of SAMA, SOUTHERN [SIT]
SINA alt for SHINA [SCL]
SINA dial of KAMWE [HIG]
SINABU alt for SINABU' dial of KINABATANGAN,
   UPPER [DMG]
SINABU' dial of KINABATANGAN, UPPER [DMG]
SINAGEN [SIU] lang, Papua New Guinea
SINAGORO alt for SINAUGORO [SNC]
SINAK NDUGA dial of NDUGA [NDX]
SINAKETA dial of KILIVILA [KIJ]
SINAKI dial of SUAU [SWP]
SINALE alt for FEMBE [AGL]
SINALON dial of TBOLI [TBL]
SINAMA alt for SAMA, CENTRAL [SML]
SINAMA alt for SISSANO [SSW]
SINAN dial of DAYAK, LAND [DYK]
SINANO alt for SISSANO [SSW]
SINASINA [SST] lang, Papua New Guinea
SINAUGORO [SNC] lang, Papua New Guinea
SINAUNA alt for AGTA, REMONTADO [AGV]
SINDANG KELINGI [SDI] lang, Indonesia (Sumatra)
SINDANGAN SUBANUN alt for SUBANEN,
   CENTRAL [SUS]
SINDEBELE alt for NDEBELE [NDF]
SINDHI [SND] lang, Pakistan; also in India, Oman,
   Philippines, Singapore, United Kingdom, USA
SINDHI BHIL [SBN] lang, Pakistan
SINDHI BHIL dial of SINDHI BHIL [SBN]
SINDHI GHERA alt for GHERA [GHR]
SINDHI MEGHWAR dial of SINDHI BHIL [SBN]
SINDHI MUSALMANI dial of SINDHI [SND]
SINDHULI alt for RATNAWATI dial of JERUNG [JEE]
SINDHUPALCHOK PAHRI dial of NEWARI [NEW]
SINDING alt for SIDIN dial of DAYAK, LAND [DYK]
SINDUE-TAWAILI alt for RAI dial of KAILI, LEDO
   [LEW]
SINE dial of SERER-SINE [SES]
SINE-SALOUM alt for SERER-SINE [SES]
SINE-SINE alt for SERER-SINE [SES]
SINESIP alt for SOUTH WEST BAY [SNS]
SING MUN alt for PUOC [PUO]
SINGA [SGM] lang, Uganda
SINGALA dial of SENOUFO, DJIMINI [DYI]
SINGALI alt for LAMBADI [LMN]

SINGAPORE SIGN LANGUAGE [SLS] lang,
   Singapore
SING-FO alt for SINGPHO [SGP]
SINGGAI alt for SINGGE dial of JAGOI [SNE]
SINGGE dial of JAGOI [SNE]
SINGGI alt for SINGGE dial of JAGOI [SNE]
SINGGIE alt for SINGGE dial of JAGOI [SNE]
SINGHALA alt for SINHALA [SNH]
SINGHALESE alt for SINHALA [SNH]
SINGHI alt for SINGGE dial of JAGOI [SNE]
SINGJA alt for JUMLELI dial of NEPALI [NEP]
SINGKARAK dial of MINANGKABAU [MPU]
SINGKIL dial of BATAK KARO [BTX]
SINGLI alt for KORWA [KFP]
SINGORAKAI dial of MALASANGA [MQZ]
SINGPHO [SGP] lang, India
SINGSON dial of CHIN, THADO [TCZ]
SINHALA [SNH] lang, Sri Lanka; also in Canada,
   Maldives, Midway Islands, Singapore, Thailand,
   UAE
SINHALESE alt for SINHALA [SNH]
SINICAHUA MIXTEC alt for MIXTECO, SINICAHUA
   [QMI]
SININKERE [SKQ] lang, Burkina Faso
SINJA alt for SHUBI [SUJ]
SINJAI dial of BUGIS [BPR]
SINKALING HKAMTI dial of KHAMTI [KHT]
SINKIUSE alt for COLUMBIA dial of COLUMBIA-
   WENATCHI [COL]
SINKON dial of SAPO [KRN]
SINOHOAN dial of PAMONA [BCX]
SINSAURU [SNZ] lang, Papua New Guinea
SINTANG alt for BORNEO dial of MALAY [MLI]
SINTE alt for ROMANI, SINTE [RMO]
SINTI alt for ROMANI, SINTE [RMO]
SINTÍ alt for ROMANI, SINTE [RMO]
SINULIHAN alt for DUSUN SINULIHAN dial of
   DUSUN, CENTRAL [DTP]
SINYA alt for SINYAR [SYS]
SINYAR [SYS] lang, Sudan; also in Chad
SINYONYOI dial of MAMUJU [MQX]
SIO [SIO] lang, Papua New Guinea
SIOCON alt for SUBANON, WESTERN [SUC]
SIOMPU dial of MUNA [MYN]
SIONA [SIN] lang, Colombia; also in Ecuador
SIONG alt for SIHONG dial of MAANYAN [MHY]
SIONI alt for SIONA [SIN]
SIORA dial of ZANAKI [ZAK]
SIOUA alt for SIWI [SIZ]
SIOUX alt for DAKOTA [DHG]
SIPACAPA QUICHÉ alt for SIPACAPENSE [QUM]
SIPACAPEÑO alt for SIPACAPENSE [QUM]
SIPACAPENSE [QUM] lang, Guatemala
SIPARI dial of HARAUTI [HOJ]
SIPENG dial of PENAN, WESTERN [PNE]
SÌPÌÌTÉ alt for SÉNOUFO, SÌCÌTÉ [SEP]
SIPISI dial of BARAPASI [BRP]
SIPOMA alt for NUMBAMI [SIJ]
SIPSONGPANNA DAI alt for LÜ [KHB]
SIPUPU dial of BUNAMA [BDD]
SIPURA dial of MENTAWAI [MWV]

SIRA [SWJ] lang, Gabon
SIRA alt for PAWAIA [PWA]
SIRAGI alt for INNER SIRAGI dial of PAHARI, KULLU [KFX]
SIRAIA alt for SIRAIYA [FOS]
SIRAIKI alt for SARAIKI [SKR]
SIRAIKI HINDKI dial of SARAIKI [SKR]
SIRAIYA [FOS] lang, Taiwan
SIRAJI alt for INNER SIRAGI dial of PAHARI, KULLU [KFX]
SIRAJI OF DODA dial of KASHMIRI [KSH]
SIRAJI-KASHMIRI dial of KASHMIRI [KSH]
SIRAK alt for NAFI [SRF]
SIRAK alt for SERAK dial of MEFELE [MFJ]
SIRALI dial of KUMAUNI [KFY]
SIRASIRA alt for SARASIRA dial of ADZERA [AZR]
SIRATA alt for KANURI, CENTRAL [KPH]
SIRAWA alt for SIRI [SIR]
SIRAYA alt for SIRAIYA [FOS]
SIRAYA dial of SIRAIYA [FOS]
SIRENIK alt for YUPIK, SIRENIK [YSR]
SIRENIKSKI alt for YUPIK, SIRENIK [YSR]
SIRHE alt for ZIRE [SIH]
SIRI [SIR] lang, Nigeria
SIRI alt for SERE [SWF]
SIRIA dial of MAASAI [MET]
SIRIANA alt for SIRIANO [SRI]
SIRIANE alt for SIRIANO [SRI]
SIRIANO [SRI] lang, Colombia; also in Brazil
SIRIO alt for NAWARU [NWR]
SIRIONÓ [SRQ] lang, Bolivia
SIRIPU alt for CHIRIPO dial of CUIBA [CUI]
SIRIPU dial of CUIBA [CUI]
SIRIPURIA dial of BENGALI [BNG]
SIRIR dial of MPUR [AKC]
SIRI-SORI dial of SAPARUA [SPR]
SIRMAURI [SRX] lang, India
SIRMAURI alt for LOWER MAHASU PAHARI dial of PAHARI, MAHASU [BFZ]
SIRMOURI alt for SIRMAURI [SRX]
SIRMURI alt for SIRMAURI [SRX]
SIROI [SSD] lang, Papua New Guinea
SIRONCHA dial of GONDI, SOUTHERN [GGO]
SIRXIN dial of DARGWA [DAR]
SIRYON alt for WESTERN NEO-ARAMAIC [AMW]
SISAALA, PASAALE [SIG] lang, Ghana
SISAALA, TUMULUNG [SIL] lang, Ghana
SISAALA, WESTERN [SSL] lang, Ghana
SISAALI alt for SISSALA [SLD]
SISAI alt for SISAALA, TUMULUNG [SIL]
SISAI alt for SISAALA, WESTERN [SSL]
SISAKET dial of KHMER, NORTHERN [KXM]
SISALA TUMU alt for SISAALA, TUMULUNG [SIL]
SISANO alt for SISSANO [SSW]
SÎSHËË alt for ZIRE [SIH]
SISI dial of BESISI [MHE]
SISIAME dial of BAMU [BCF]
SISI-BIPI alt for BIPI [BIQ]
SISIBNA dial of KORUPUN-SELA [KPQ]
SISIMIN alt for HEWA [HAM]

SISINGGA alt for SENGAN dial of BABATANA [BAQ]
SISKA alt for TONGA [TOG]
SISSALA [SLD] lang, Burkina Faso
SISSANO [SSW] lang, Papua New Guinea
SISUTHO alt for SOTHO, SOUTHERN [SSO]
SISWATI alt for SWATI [SWZ]
SISWAZI alt for SWATI [SWZ]
SISYA alt for TONGA [TOG]
SISYABAN alt for SAAROA [SXR]
SITAANG alt for STANG dial of BIATAH [BTH]
SITEMUÚ alt for BAGA SITEMU [BSP]
SITENG dial of MELANAU [MEL]
SITI alt for VAGLA [VAG]
SITIA SHERBRO dial of SHERBRO [BUN]
SITIGO alt for VAGLA [VAG]
SITU dial of JIARONG [JYA]
SIU dial of SWAHILI [SWA]
SIUCI alt for SIUSY-TAPUYA dial of BANIWA [BAI]
SIUSI alt for SIUSY-TAPUYA dial of BANIWA [BAI]
SIUSLAW [SIS] lang, USA
SIUSY-TAPUYA dial of BANIWA [BAI]
SIVANDI [SIY] lang, Iran
SIVEREKI dial of DIMLI [ZZZ]
SIVUKUN alt for SHIBUKUN dial of BUNUN [BNN]
SIWA alt for SIWI [SIZ]
SIWA dial of FIPA [FIP]
SIWAI [SIW] lang, Papua New Guinea
SIWAI alt for AMTO [AMT]
SIWANG alt for CHEWONG [CWG]
SIWI [SIZ] lang, Egypt
SIWU [AKP] lang, Ghana
SIWURI alt for TUWILI [BOV]
SIWUSI alt for SIWU [AKP]
SIYALGIR dial of BHILI [BHB]
SIYANG alt for CHIN, SIYIN [CSY]
SIYI dial of CHINESE, YUE [YUH]
SIYIN alt for CHIN, SIYIN [CSY]
SIYU alt for SIU dial of SWAHILI [SWA]
SIZAKI [SZK] lang, Tanzania
SIZANG alt for CHIN, SIYIN [CSY]
SIZI alt for DIZI [MDX]
SJAELLAND alt for DANISH [DNS]
SJIAGHA alt for SIAGHA-YENIMU [OSR]
SKÅNE [SCY] lang, Sweden; also in Denmark
SKÅNSK alt for SKÅNE [SCY]
SKÅNSKA alt for SKÅNE [SCY]
SKÅNSKA dial of SKÅNE [SCY]
SKAGIT [SKA] lang, USA
SKAROHREH alt for TUSCARORA [TUS]
SKCHIP alt for ALBANIAN, TOSK [ALN]
SKEPI CREOLE DUTCH [SKW] lang, Guyana
SKIDEGATE alt for HAIDA, SOUTHERN [HAX]
SKIDEGATE dial of TUTCHONE, SOUTHERN [TCE]
SKIDI alt for SKIRI dial of PAWNEE [PAW]
SKIRI dial of PAWNEE [PAW]
S'KLALLAM alt for CLALLAM [CLM]
SKO alt for SKOU [SKV]
SKOFRO alt for MANEM [JET]
SKOKOMISH alt for TWANA [TWA]
SKOKOMISH dial of TWANA [TWA]
SKOLT alt for SAAMI, SKOLT [LPK]

"SKOLT LAPPISH" pejorative alt for SAAMI, SKOLT [LPK]
SKOLT LAPPISH alt for SAAMI, SKOLT [LPK]
SKOU [SKV] lang, Indonesia (Irian Jaya)
SKOUW alt for SKOU [SKV]
SKOW alt for SKOU [SKV]
SKRANG dial of IBAN [IBA]
SKRUBU alt for SURUBU [SDE]
SLAI alt for HLAI [LIC]
"SLAVE" pejorative alt for SLAVEY, NORTH [SCS]
"SLAVE" pejorative alt for SLAVEY, SOUTH [SLA]
SLAVEY, NORTH [SCS] lang, Canada
SLAVEY, SOUTH [SLA] lang, Canada
SLAVI alt for SLAVEY, NORTH [SCS]
SLAVI alt for SLAVEY, SOUTH [SLA]
SLAVIC [MKJ] lang, Macedonia; also in Albania, Bulgaria, Canada, Greece, Hungary, Slovenia
SLAVIC alt for MACEDONIAN [MKJ]
SLAVONIC, OLD CHURCH [SLN] lang, Russia (Europe)
SLIAMMON dial of COMOX [COO]
SLN alt for DUTCH SIGN LANGUAGE [DSE]
SLOVAK [SLO] lang, Slovakia; also in Canada, Hungary, Poland, Romania, Ukraine, USA, Yugoslavia
SLOVAKIAN alt for SLOVAK [SLO]
SLOVAKIAN SIGN LANGUAGE [SVK] lang, Slovakia
SLOVENE alt for SLOVENIAN [SLV]
SLOVENIAN [SLV] lang, Slovenia; also in Argentina, Australia, Austria, Canada, Croatia, Hungary, Italy, USA, Yugoslavia
SLOVENIAN SIGN LANGUAGE dial of YUGOSLAVIAN SIGN LANGUAGE [YSL]
SLOVENIAN-CROATIAN dial of ROMANI, SINTE [RMO]
SLOVENIAN-CROATIAN ROMANI dial of ROMANI, SINTE [RMO]
SLOVENSCINA alt for SLOVENIAN [SLV]
SLOVINCIAN dial of KASHUBIAN [CSB]
SLUTSKA-MAZYRSKI alt for SOUTHWEST BELARUSAN dial of BELARUSAN [RUW]
SLUTSKO-MOZYR alt for SOUTHWEST BELARUSAN dial of BELARUSAN [RUW]
SM'ALGYAX alt for COAST TSIMSHIAN dial of TSIMSHIAN [TSI]
SM'ALGYAX alt for TSIMSHIAN [TSI]
SMALL BOLGO alt for BOLGO DUGAG dial of BOLGO [BVO]
SMALL FLOWERY MIAO alt for XIAO HUA MIAO dial of HMONG NJUA [BLU]
SMALL NAMBAS alt for LETEMBOI [NMS]
SMITH RIVER alt for TOLOWA [TOL]
SMYRNA dial of ARMENIAN [ARM]
SNABI WATUBELA alt for WATUBELA [WAH]
SNOHOMISH [SNO] lang, USA
SNOQUALMIE dial of SALISH, SOUTHERN PUGET SOUND [SLH]
SÖLRENG dial of FRISIAN, NORTHERN [FRR]
SO [SOC] lang, DRC
SO [SOX] lang, Cameroon

SO alt for AHEU [THM]
SO alt for SOO [TEU]
SO dial of KULFA [KXJ]
SÔ [SSS] lang, Laos; also in Thailand
SO MAKON alt for SÔ [SSS]
SO MAKON dial of SÔ [SSS]
SO PHONG dial of SÔ [SSS]
SO SLOUY dial of SÔ [SSS]
SO TRI alt for TRI dial of BRU, EASTERN [BRU]
SO TRII alt for TRI dial of BRU, EASTERN [BRU]
SO TRONG dial of SO [SSS]
SOA alt for CENTRAL KONO dial of KONO [KNO]
SOA alt for SO [SOC]
SOA alt for SO'A [SSQ]
SO'A [SSQ] lang, Indonesia (Nusa Tenggara)
SOAHUKU dial of AMAHAI [AMQ]
SOAI alt for KUY [KDT]
SOBA alt for HUPLA [HAP]
SOBANÉ alt for BAGA SOBANÉ [BSV]
SO-BÊ alt for KIRMANJKI [QKV]
SOBEI [SOB] lang, Indonesia (Irian Jaya)
"SOBO" pejorative alt for ISOKO [ISO]
"SOBO" pejorative alt for URHOBO [URH]
SOBOJO alt for MANGEI dial of TALIABU [TLV]
SOBOYO alt for MANGEI dial of TALIABU [TLV]
SOBSTVENNO-KAREL'SKIJ-JAZYK alt for KARELIAN [KRL]
SOCÉ alt for MANDINKA [MNK]
SOCHI dial of SANSI [SSI]
SOCHILE alt for NYAKYUSA-NGONDE [NYY]
SOCOTRI alt for SOQOTRI [SQT]
SODDO alt for GURAGE, SODDO [GRU]
SODDO dial of GURAGE, SODDO [GRU]
SODIA PARJA alt for BODO PARJA [BDV]
SODOCHI alt for UPPER MAHASU PAHARI dial of PAHARI, MAHASU [BFZ]
SOE alt for BINJA dial of ZIMBA [ZMB]
SOFALA alt for NDAU [NDC]
SOGA [SOG] lang, Uganda
SOGADAS alt for SOKODASA dial of KUNAMA [KUM]
SOGAL dial of BINE [ORM]
SOGAP alt for NGALA [NUD]
SOGH alt for MANIKION [MNX]
SOGHAI alt for DUSUN SEGAMA dial of KINABATANGAN, UPPER [DMG]
SOGHAUA alt for ZAGHAWA [ZAG]
SOGHAUA alt for ZANDE [ZAN]
SÔGHOO dial of SENOUFO, MAMARA [MYK]
SOGILITAN alt for KADAZAN, LABUK-KINABATANGAN [DTB]
SOGOBA alt for SUMARIUP [SIV]
SOGODAS alt for SOKODASA dial of KUNAMA [KUM]
SOGOKIRÉ dial of BOBO MADARE, SOUTHERN [BWQ]
SOGOKIRI dial of BOBO MADARE, NORTHERN [BBO]
SOGOO dial of OKIEK [OKI]
SOHE alt for ETIJA dial of OROKAIVA [ORK]
SOHRA alt for CHERRAPUNJI dial of KHASI [KHI]

SOHUR alt for YAQAY [JAQ]
SOI [SOJ] lang, Iran
SOIBADA alt for EASTERN TETUN dial of TETUN [TTM]
SOK [SKK] lang, Laos
SOKAKA alt for HIXKARYÁNA [HIX]
SOKHOK dial of PSOHOH [BCL]
SOKID dial of DUSUN, CENTRAL [DTP]
SOKILE alt for NYAKYUSA-NGONDE [NYY]
SOKILI alt for NYAKYUSA-NGONDE [NYY]
SOKIRIK dial of PATPATAR [GFK]
SOKNA alt for SAWKNAH [SWN]
SOKO alt for SO [SOC]
SOKO alt for SO dial of KULFA [KXJ]
SOKO dial of NTOMBA [NTO]
SOKODASA dial of KUNAMA [KUM]
SOKORO [SOK] lang, Chad
SOKORO dial of SOKORO [SOK]
SOKOROK alt for SILIPUT [MKC]
SOKOTO dial of FULFULDE, NIGERIAN [FUV]
SOKOTO dial of HAUSA [HUA]
SOKOTRI alt for SOQOTRI [SQT]
SOKTE dial of CHIN, TEDIM [CTD]
SOKYA alt for KOUYA [KYF]
SOLA [SOY] lang, Benin; also in Togo
SOLAGA alt for SHOLAGA [SLE]
SOLAMBA alt for SOLA [SOY]
SOLE alt for BINJA dial of ZIMBA [ZMB]
SOLEDAD dial of COSTANOAN, NORTHERN [CST]
SOLI [SBY] lang, Zambia
SOLIGA alt for SHOLAGA [SLE]
SOLIGAR alt for SHOLAGA [SLE]
SOLLA alt for SOLA [SOY]
SOLO dial of JAVANESE [JAN]
SOLOMONS PIDGIN alt for PIJIN [PIS]
SOLON alt for EVENKI [EVN]
SOLONG [AAW] lang, Papua New Guinea
SOLOR alt for LAMAHOLOT [SLP]
SOLORESE alt for LAMAHOLOT [SLP]
SOLOS [SOL] lang, Papua New Guinea
SOLOS dial of SOLOS [SOL]
SOLOTO dial of YURACARE [YUE]
SOLU dial of SHERPA [SCR]
SOLWA alt for KAGULU [KKI]
SOLWE alt for KONDOA dial of SAGALA [SBM]
SOM [SMC] lang, Papua New Guinea
SOM alt for WAB [WAB]
SOMA alt for TAMBERMA [SOF]
SOMAGE alt for MOMUNA [MQF]
SOMAHAI alt for MOMUNA [MQF]
SOMALI [SOM] lang, Somalia; also in Djibouti, Ethiopia, Finland, Italy, Kenya, Oman, Saudi Arabia, Sweden, UAE, United Kingdom, Yemen
SOMATU alt for MADU dial of ENETS [ENE]
"SOMBA" pejorative alt for TAMBERMA [SOF]
SOMBA alt for DITAMMARI [TBZ]
SOMBA dial of BURUM-MINDIK [BMU]
SOMBA-SIAWARI alt for BURUM-MINDIK [BMU]
SOMBRERO NEGRO alt for TOBA-PILAGÁ dial of PILAGA [PLG]

SOME alt for TAMBERMA [SOF]
SOME dial of FASU [FAA]
SOMEKHURI alt for ARMENIAN [ARM]
SOMERSET dial of ENGLISH [ENG]
SOMKHURI alt for ARMENIAN [ARM]
SOMONO dial of BAMANANKAN [BRA]
SOMORIKA alt for EMHALHE dial of OKPAMHERI [OPA]
SOMRA alt for NAGA, TANGKHUL [NMF]
SOMRAI [SOR] lang, Chad
SOMRAY [SMU] lang, Cambodia
SOMRE alt for SOMRAI [SOR]
SOMREI alt for SOMRAI [SOR]
SOMWADINA dial of DUAU [DUA]
SOMYEWE [KGT] lang, Nigeria
SON dial of VO [WBM]
SONA alt for KANASI [SOQ]
SONAHAA alt for SONHA [SOI]
SONAI dial of YAEYAMA [RYS]
SONAPAL dial of MURIA, WESTERN [MUT]
SONAR BOLI alt for KINNAURI, HARIJAN [KJO]
SONDE [SHC] lang, DRC
SONDER dial of TONTEMBOAN [TNT]
SONDOANG dial of ULUMANDA [ULM]
SONDWARI dial of MALVI [MUP]
SONG [SOA] lang, Thailand
SONGA [SGO] lang, DRC
SONGA dial of LUYIA [LUY]
SONGA dial of TSONGA [TSO]
SONGAI alt for SONGHAY [HMB]
SONGAI alt for SONGHAY, HUMBURI SENNI [HMB]
SONGAI alt for SONGHAY, KOYRA CHIINI [KHQ]
SONGAI alt for SONGHAY, KOYRABORO SENNI [SON]
SONGAY alt for SONGHAY [HMB]
SONGAY alt for SONGHAY, HUMBURI SENNI [HMB]
SONGAY alt for SONGHAY, KOYRA CHIINI [KHQ]
SONGAY alt for SONGHAY, KOYRABORO SENNI [SON]
SONGAY SENNI alt for SONGHAY, KOYRABORO SENNI [SON]
SONGBU dial of NAGA, RONGMEI [NBU]
SONGE [SOP] lang, DRC
SONGE alt for WESTERN KALEBWE dial of SONGE [SOP]
SONGHAI alt for SONGHAY [HMB]
SONGHAI alt for SONGHAY, HUMBURI SENNI [HMB]
SONGHAI alt for SONGHAY, KOYRA CHIINI [KHQ]
SONGHAI alt for SONGHAY, KOYRABORO SENNI [SON]
SONGHAY [HMB] lang, Mali; also in Burkina Faso
SONGHAY, HUMBURI SENNI [HMB] lang, Mali; also in Burkina Faso
SONGHAY, KOYRA CHIINI [KHQ] lang, Mali
SONGHAY, KOYRABORO SENNI [SON] lang, Mali
SONGHOY alt for SONGHAY [HMB]
SONGHOY alt for SONGHAY, HUMBURI SENNI [HMB]

SONGHOY alt for SONGHAY, KOYRA CHIINI [KHQ]
SONGHOY alt for SONGHAY, KOYRABORO
   SENNI [SON]
SONGISH dial of SALISH, STRAITS [STR]
SONGO [SOO] lang, DRC
SONGO alt for MBATI [MDN]
SONGO alt for NSONGO [NSX]
SONGOI alt for SONGHAY [HMB]
SONGOI alt for SONGHAY, HUMBURI SENNI [HMB]
SONGOI alt for SONGHAY, KOYRA CHIINI [KHQ]
SONGOI alt for SONGHAY, KOYRABORO SENNI
   [SON]
SONGOLA alt for EKISONGOORA dial of NANDI
   [NNB]
SONGOLA alt for OMBO [OML]
SONGOLA alt for SONGOORA [SOD]
SONGOMENO [SOE] lang, DRC
SONGOORA [SOD] lang, DRC
SONGOY alt for SONGHAY [HMB]
SONGOY alt for SONGHAY, HUMBURI SENNI
   [HMB]
SONGOY alt for SONGHAY, KOYRA CHIINI [KHQ]
SONGOY alt for SONGHAY, KOYRABORO SENNI
   [SON]
SONGU alt for SESA dial of FOLOPA [PPO]
SONGUM [SNX] lang, Papua New Guinea
SONGWA dial of NGEMBA [NGE]
SONGWE dial of SAFWA [SBK]
SONGYE alt for SONGE [SOP]
SONHA [SOI] lang, Nepal
SONIA [SIQ] lang, Papua New Guinea
SONINKE [SNN] lang, Mali; also in Côte d'Ivoire,
   Gambia, Guinea, Guinea-Bissau, Mauritania,
   Senegal
SONJO alt for TEMI [SOZ]
SONPARI dial of BAGHELI [BFY]
SONRAI alt for SONGHAY [HMB]
SONRAI alt for SONGHAY, HUMBURI SENNI [HMB]
SONRAI alt for SONGHAY, KOYRA CHIINI [KHQ]
SONRAI alt for SONGHAY, KOYRABORO SENNI
   [SON]
SONRHAI alt for SONGHAY [HMB]
SONRHAI alt for SONGHAY, HUMBURI SENNI
   [HMB]
SONRHAI alt for SONGHAY, KOYRA CHIINI [KHQ]
SONRHAI alt for SONGHAY, KOYRABORO
   SENNI [SON]
SONSOGON dial of KIMARAGANG [KQR]
SONSOROL [SOV] lang, Palau; also in Northern
   Mariana Islands
SONSOROLESE alt for SONSOROL [SOV]
SONSOROLESE dial of SONSOROL [SOV]
SONTHAL alt for SANTALI [SNT]
SONYO alt for TEMI [SOZ]
SOO [TEU] lang, Uganda
SOOK MURUT dial of PALUAN [PLZ]
SOOKE dial of SALISH, STRAITS [STR]
SOOLEVU alt for WEST VANUA LEVU dial of
   FIJIAN [FJI]
SOOLOO alt for TAUSUG [TSG]
SOONDE alt for SONDE [SHC]

SOOW HUHELIA alt for MANIPA [MQP]
SOP alt for USINO [URW]
SOP dial of KOHO [KPM]
SOPESE dial of FOLOPA [PPO]
SOPFOMO alt for NAGA, MAO [NBI]
SOPI dial of BELI [BLM]
SOPI dial of GALELA [GBI]
SOPOCNOVSKIJ dial of ITELMEN [ITL]
SOPPENG dial of BUGIS [BPR]
SOPPENG RIAJA alt for BARRU dial of BUGIS [BPR]
SOPRON dial of HUNGARIAN SIGN LANGUAGE
   [HSH]
SOPVOMA alt for NAGA, MAO [NBI]
SOQOTRI [SQT] lang, Yemen
SOR alt for NGAING [NNF]
SOR dial of BIAK [BHW]
SOR dial of KUPSABINY [KPZ]
SORA [SRB] lang, India
SORADI dial of NEPALI [NEP]
SORANI alt for KURDI [KDB]
SORATHI alt for KATHIYAWADI dial of GUJARATI
   [GJR]
SORAY alt for SENAYA [SYN]
SORBIAN, LOWER [WEE] lang, Germany
SORBIAN, UPPER [WEN] lang, Germany
SORENDIDORI dial of BIAK [BHW]
SORI dial of SORI-HARENGAN [SBH]
SORIDO dial of BIAK [BHW]
SORI-HARENGAN [SBH] lang, Papua New Guinea
SORIMI alt for BO [BPW]
SORIYALI dial of KUMAUNI [KFY]
SORK alt for SOK [SKK]
SORKHEI [SQO] lang, Iran
SORKO alt for BOZO, SOROGAMA [BZE]
SORO dial of HADIYYA [HDY]
SOROAKO dial of MORI BAWAH [XMZ]
SOROGAMA alt for BOZO, SOROGAMA [BZE]
SOROUBA alt for SOLA [SOY]
SORSOGON BICOLANO alt for SORSOGON,
   MASBATE [BKS]
SORSOGON, MASBATE [BKS] lang, Philippines
SORSOGON, WARAY [SRV] lang, Philippines
SORSOGONON alt for GUBATNON dial of
   HANUNOO [HNN]
SORUBA alt for SOLA [SOY]
SORUNG alt for SIE dial of SIE [ERG]
SOSE alt for ETIJA dial of OROKAIVA [ORK]
SOSE alt for SUSU [SUD]
SOSI alt for BASSOSSI [BSI]
SOSO alt for SUSU [SUD]
SOS'VA alt for NORTHERN VOGUL dial of MANSI
   [MNS]
SOSYVIN alt for NORTHERN VOGUL dial of MANSI
   [MNS]
SOTA alt for NORTH KANUM dial of KANUM, SOTA
   [KRZ]
SOTANG dial of KULUNG [KLE]
SOTARING alt for SOTANG dial of KULUNG [KLE]
SOTAVENTO dial of KABUVERDIANU [KEA]
SOTHO, NORTHERN [SRT] lang, South Africa; also
   in Botswana

SOTHO, SOUTHERN [SSO] lang, Lesotho; also in Botswana, South Africa
SOTIPURA alt for CENTRAL COLLOQUIAL MAITHILI dial of MAITHILI [MKP]
SOTMALI alt for DUMI [DUS]
SOTO alt for MAQUIRITARI [MCH]
SOTTARING alt for SOTANG dial of KULUNG [KLE]
SOU [SQQ] lang, Laos
SOUBAKANEDOUGOU dial of CERMA [GOT]
SOUBRÉ dial of BETE, GUIBEROUA [BET]
SOUDHWARI alt for SONDWARI dial of MALVI [MUP]
SOUGB alt for MANIKION [MNX]
SOUK alt for SOU [SQQ]
SOUKA alt for SO dial of KULFA [KXJ]
SOULANI dial of WARA [WBF]
SOULETIN alt for BASQUE, SOULETIN [BSZ]
SOULETINO alt for BASQUE, SOULETIN [BSZ]
SOUMA alt for SUMA [SQM]
SOUMO alt for SUMO TAWAHKA [SUM]
SOUMRAI alt for SOMRAI [SOR]
SOUMRAY alt for SOMRAI [SOR]
SOUNGOR alt for ASSANGORI [SUN]
SOUNGOR alt for SUNGOR [SUN]
SOUNRAI alt for SOMRAI [SOR]
SOURASHTRA alt for SAURASHTRA [SAZ]
SOURBAKHAL alt for SURBAKHAL [SBJ]
SOUSSE alt for SUSIUA dial of TACHELHIT [SHI]
SOUSSOU alt for SUSU [SUD]
SOUTH AFRICA TAMIL dial of TAMIL [TCV]
SOUTH AFRICAN SIGN LANGUAGE [SFS] lang, South Africa
SOUTH ALASKA "ESKIMO" pejorative alt for YUPIK, PACIFIC GULF [EMS]
SOUTH ALBANIAN dial of ROMANI, VLAX [RMY]
SOUTH ALUNE dial of ALUNE [ALP]
SOUTH AMBRYM alt for DAKAKA [BPA]
SOUTH ANGAL HENENG alt for ANGAL ENEN [AOE]
SOUTH ANJDI dial of ARABIC, NAJDI SPOKEN [ARS]
SOUTH AUNALEI dial of AUNALEI [AUN]
SOUTH AWA dial of AWA [AWB]
SOUTH AWIN dial of AEKYOM [AWI]
SOUTH BAND dial of PAWNEE [PAW]
SOUTH BAVARIAN dial of BAVARIAN [BAR]
SOUTH BELGIUM SIGN LANGUAGE dial of BELGIAN SIGN LANGUAGE [BVS]
SOUTH BELU alt for SOUTHERN TETUN dial of TETUN [TTM]
SOUTH BINJA dial of SONGOORA [SOD]
SOUTH BOAZI dial of BOAZI [KVG]
SOUTH BUNUN dial of BUNUN [BNN]
SOUTH BURU alt for MASARETE dial of BURU [MHS]
SOUTH BUTON alt for CIA-CIA [CIA]
SOUTH CAROLINA dial of SEA ISLAND CREOLE ENGLISH [GUL]
SOUTH CENTRAL ARVANITIKA dial of ALBANIAN, ARVANITIKA [AAT]
SOUTH CENTRAL DELTA ARABIC dial of ARABIC, EGYPTIAN SPOKEN [ARZ]

SOUTH CENTRAL IZON alt for BUMO dial of IZON [IJC]
SOUTH CENTRAL MIXE alt for MIXE, JUQUILA [MXQ]
SOUTH CENTRAL TLAXIACO MIXTECO alt for MIXTECO, ATATLÁHUCA [MIB]
SOUTH CENTRAL YI alt for NANHUA dial of YI, CENTRAL [YIC]
SOUTH CENTRAL ZIMATLÁN ZAPOTECO alt for ZAPOTECO, EL ALTO [ZPP]
SOUTH CHACHAPOYAS alt for LA JALCA dial of QUECHUA, CHACHAPOYAS [QUK]
SOUTH CHOLLADO alt for CHOLLADO dial of KOREAN [KKN]
SOUTH CH'UNGCH'ONG alt for CH'UNGCH'ONGDO dial of KOREAN [KKN]
SOUTH COAST MENGEN dial of MENGEN [MEE]
SOUTH COAST SIKKA alt for SIKKA NATAR dial of SIKA [SKI]
SOUTH CONGO dial of KONGO [KON]
SOUTH DAMAR alt for DAMAR, EAST [DMR]
SOUTH DRENTE dial of DRENTS [DRT]
SOUTH EAST KONGO dial of KONGO [KON]
SOUTH FORE alt for PAMUSA dial of FORE [FOR]
SOUTH HAMGYONGDO alt for HAMGYONGDO dial of KOREAN [KKN]
SOUTH HIBERNO ENGLISH dial of ENGLISH [ENG]
SOUTH HIJAZI dial of ARABIC, HIJAZI SPOKEN [ACW]
SOUTH IBANAG dial of IBANAG [IBG]
SOUTH IBIE dial of YEKHEE [ETS]
SOUTH ILE APE dial of ILE APE [ILA]
SOUTH ISLAND dial of MAORI [MBF]
SOUTH ISLANDS alt for AALAWA dial of RAMOAAINA [RAI]
SOUTH IVBIE alt for SOUTH IBIE dial of YEKHEE [ETS]
SOUTH IZERE dial of IZERE [FIZ]
SOUTH KAKABAI dial of KAKABAI [KQF]
SOUTH KAMAYO dial of KAMAYO [KYK]
SOUTH KAMBERATARO dial of KAMBERATARO [KBV]
SOUTH KANUM dial of KANUM, SOTA [KRZ]
SOUTH KARAKELONG dial of TALAUD [TLD]
SOUTH KATI alt for SOUTHERN MUYU dial of YONGKOM [YON]
SOUTH KERALA dial of MALAYALAM [MJS]
SOUTH KEWA alt for ERAVE [KJY]
SOUTH KHOWAR dial of KHOWAR [KHW]
SOUTH KITUI dial of KAMBA [KIK]
SOUTH KOMA alt for KOMO [KOM]
SOUTH KOMBIO dial of KOMBIO [KOK]
SOUTH KONGO dial of KONGO [KON]
SOUTH KWANDU dial of MASHI [MHO]
SOUTH KYONGSANGDO alt for KYONGSANGDO dial of KOREAN [KKN]
SOUTH LAAMANG dial of LAMANG [HIA]
SOUTH LEBANESE ARABIC dial of ARABIC, NORTH LEVANTINE SPOKEN [APC]
SOUTH LELE alt for KASSADOU LELE dial of LELE [LLC]

SOUTH LEVANTINE ARABIC alt for ARABIC, SOUTH LEVANTINE SPOKEN [AJP]
SOUTH LEVANTINE BEDAWI ARABIC dial of ARABIC, EASTERN EGYPTIAN BEDAWI SPOKEN [AVL]
SOUTH LEVANTINE BEDAWI ARABIC dial of ARABIC, LEVANTINE BEDAWI SPOKEN [AVL]
SOUTH LOBALA dial of LOBALA [LOQ]
SOUTH LOLODA alt for LABA [LAU]
SOUTH LUWU dial of TAE [ROB]
SOUTH MACA alt for MAKHUWA-MARREVONE [XMC]
SOUTH MAKAA alt for MAKAA [MCP]
SOUTH MALAITA alt for SA'A [APB]
SOUTH MALO alt for ATARIPOE dial of MALO [MLA]
SOUTH MANUSELA dial of MANUSELA [WHA]
SOUTH MBUNDU alt for UMBUNDU [MNF]
SOUTH MEKAA alt for MAKAA [MCP]
SOUTH MENDI alt for ANGAL ENEN [AOE]
SOUTH MIGABAC dial of MIGABAC [MPP]
SOUTH MODOLE dial of MODOLE [MQO]
SOUTH MOEJOE alt for SOUTHERN MUYU dial of YONGKOM [YON]
SOUTH MORI alt for PADOE [PDO]
SOUTH NAKAMA dial of NAKAMA [NIB]
SOUTH NGADA dial of NGADA [NXG]
SOUTH NGALIK alt for SILIMO [WUL]
SOUTH NKUNDO alt for PANGA dial of MONGO-NKUNDU [MOM]
SOUTH NORTHERN PAIUTE dial of PAIUTE, NORTHERN [PAO]
SOUTH NUK dial of NUK [NOC]
SOUTH OLO alt for WAPI dial of OLO [ONG]
SOUTH ORAN dial of TAMAZIGHT, CENTRAL ATLAS [TZM]
SOUTH PAAMA dial of PAAMA [PMA]
SOUTH PALAWANO dial of PALAWANO, BROOKES POINT [PLW]
SOUTH PERMYAK dial of KOMI-PERMYAK [KOI]
SOUTH POHJANMAA dial of FINNISH [FIN]
SOUTH P'YONG'ANDO alt for P'YONG'ANDO dial of KOREAN [KKN]
SOUTH QATARI ARABIC dial of ARABIC, GULF SPOKEN [AFB]
SOUTH QUCHANI dial of KHORASANI TURKISH [KMZ]
SOUTH RAGA alt for PONORWAL dial of SA [SSA]
SOUTH RUSSIAN dial of RUSSIAN [RUS]
SOUTH SAISET alt for TUNGHO dial of SAISIYAT [SAI]
SOUTH SARDINIAN alt for SARDINIAN, CAMPIDANESE [SRO]
SOUTH SELEPET dial of SELEPET [SEL]
SOUTH SENA alt for SENA BANGWE dial of SENA [SEH]
SOUTH SIBERUT dial of MENTAWAI [MWV]
SOUTH TABASARAN dial of TABASSARAN [TAB]
SOUTH TABUKANG dial of SANGIR [SAN]
SOUTH TETUN alt for SOUTHERN TETUN dial of TETUN [TTM]

SOUTH THARAKA alt for THARAKA dial of THARAKA [THA]
SOUTH TIGAK dial of TIGAK [TGC]
SOUTH TIMBE dial of TIMBE [TIM]
SOUTH TORAJA alt for TORAJA-SA'DAN [SDA]
SOUTH TUGEN dial of KALENJIN [KLN]
SOUTH TUVALUAN dial of TUVALUAN [ELL]
SOUTH UDMURT dial of UDMURT [UDM]
SOUTH URAT alt for WASEP YAM dial of URAT [URT]
SOUTH WAIBUK dial of HARUAI [TMD]
SOUTH WALES dial of ENGLISH [ENG]
SOUTH WEST BAY [SNS] lang, Vanuatu
SOUTH WESTERN YIDDISH dial of YIDDISH, WESTERN [YIH]
SOUTH YAMDENA dial of YAMDENA [JMD]
SOUTH YAWA dial of YAWA [YVA]
SOUTH YEI dial of YEI [JEI]
SOUTH-CENTRAL LEBANESE ARABIC dial of ARABIC, NORTH LEVANTINE SPOKEN [APC]
SOUTHEAST BOBE dial of BUBE [BVB]
SOUTHEAST CAGAYAN alt for ROSO dial of AGTA, DUPANINAN [DUO]
SOUTHEAST DOBEL dial of DOBEL [KVO]
SOUTHEAST KAINGANG dial of KAINGANG [KGP]
SOUTHEAST KONGO dial of KONGO [KON]
SOUTHEAST LAMPUNG alt for KALIANDA dial of PESISIR, SOUTHERN [PEC]
SOUTHEAST MARIND dial of MARIND [MRZ]
SOUTHEAST METAFONETICA dial of SICILIAN [SCN]
SOUTHEAST NGADA alt for NGAD'A, EASTERN [NEA]
SOUTHEAST SHONA alt for NDAU [NDC]
SOUTHEAST TOBA dial of TOBA [TOB]
SOUTHEAST VANUA LEVU dial of FIJIAN [FJI]
SOUTHEAST VITI LEVU dial of FIJIAN [FJI]
SOUTHEASTERN FINNISH dial of FINNISH [FIN]
SOUTHEASTERN HUASTECO alt for HUASTECO, SAN FRANCISCO CHONTLA [HAU]
SOUTHEASTERN IXTLÁN ZAPOTEC alt for ZAPOTECO, IXTLÁN SURESTE [ZPD]
SOUTHEASTERN KARAKALPAK dial of KARAKALPAK [KAC]
SOUTHEASTERN KRUMEN alt for KRUMEN, PYE [PYE]
SOUTHEASTERN KUMAUNI dial of KUMAUNI [KFY]
SOUTHEASTERN MACEDONIAN dial of MACEDONIAN [MKJ]
SOUTHEASTERN MIXE alt for MIXE, COATLÁN [MCO]
SOUTHEASTERN NOCHIXTLÁN MIXTEC alt for MIXTECO, NOCHIXTLÁN SURESTE [MXY]
SOUTHEASTERN OCOTEPEC MIXTECO alt for MIXTECO, TLAXIACO, SUROESTE [MEH]
SOUTHEASTERN OTOMÍ alt for OTOMÍ, IXTENCO [OTA]
SOUTHEASTERN PASHTO dial of PASHTO, SOUTHERN [PBT]

SOUTHEASTERN PUEBLA NÁHUATL alt for
NÁHUATL, PUEBLA SURESTE [NHS]
SOUTHEASTERN TARAHUMARA alt for
TARAHUMARA, SURESTE [TCU]
SOUTHEASTERN TEPEHUÁN alt for TEPEHUÁN
SURESTE [STP]
SOUTHEASTERN TUVIN dial of TUVIN [TUN]
SOUTHEASTERN YAUTEPEC ZAPOTECO alt
for ZAPOTECO, TLACOLULITA [ZPK]
SOUTHEASTERN YI alt for YI, GUIZHOU [YIG]
SOUTHEASTERN YIDDISH dial of YIDDISH,
EASTERN [YDD]
SOUTHEASTERN ZIMATLÁN ZAPOTECO alt for
ZAPOTECO, SANTA INÉS YATZECHI [ZPN]
SOUTHERN AKHVAKH dial of AKHVAKH [AKV]
SOUTHERN ALTAI alt for ALTAI PROPER dial of
ALTAI, SOUTHERN [ALT]
SOUTHERN AMAMI-OSIMA alt for AMAMI-OSHIMA,
SOUTHERN [AMS]
SOUTHERN AMIS dial of AMIS [ALV]
SOUTHERN ANGOR alt for SAMANAI dial of
ANGOR [AGG]
SOUTHERN ARAGONESE dial of ARAGONESE
[AXX]
SOUTHERN ARANDA dial of ARRARNTA,
WESTERN [ARE]
SOUTHERN ARAPESH alt for MUFIAN [AOJ]
SOUTHERN ATTA alt for ATTA, FAIRE [ATH]
SOUTHERN BAAGANDJI alt for DARLING [DRL]
SOUTHERN BABOLE dial of BABOLE [BVX]
SOUTHERN BADE dial of BADE [BDE]
SOUTHERN BAI alt for DALI dial of BAI [PIQ]
SOUTHERN BAJAU alt for SAMA, SOUTHERN
[SIT]
SOUTHERN BAKOSSI dial of AKOOSE [BSS]
SOUTHERN BANGANTU alt for BANGANDU [BGF]
SOUTHERN BANTAWA dial of BANTAWA [BAP]
SOUTHERN BARASANO alt for BARASANA
[BSN]
SOUTHERN BISAYA alt for BISAYA, BRUNEI [BSB]
SOUTHERN BOLON alt for WHITE BOLON dial of
BOLON [BOF]
SOUTHERN BOMITABA alt for BABOLE [BVX]
SOUTHERN BONTOC alt for BONTOC, EASTERN
[BKB]
SOUTHERN BUDUMA dial of BUDUMA [BDM]
SOUTHERN BULLOM alt for SHERBRO [BUN]
SOUTHERN BURUN alt for MABAAN [MFZ]
SOUTHERN BUTUNG alt for CIA-CIA [CIA]
SOUTHERN CALABRO dial of SICILIAN [SCN]
SOUTHERN CAROLINIAN alt for CAROLINIAN
[CAL]
SOUTHERN CHUMBURUNG dial of
CHUMBURUNG [NCU]
SOUTHERN CLUSTER LISHÁN DIDÁN dial of
LISHAN DIDAN [TRG]
SOUTHERN COAST KIWAI dial of KIWAI,
SOUTHERN [KJD]
SOUTHERN CONCHUCOS QUECHUA alt for
QUECHUA, ANCASH, CONCHUCOS,
SOUTHERN [QEH]

SOUTHERN CRIMEAN dial of CRIMEAN TURKISH
[CRH]
SOUTHERN CUONA dial of MOINBA [MOB]
SOUTHERN DAGARI alt for DAGAARE,
SOUTHERN [DGA]
SOUTHERN DHATKI dial of DHATKI [MKI]
SOUTHERN EAST-GUIZHOU MIAO alt for HMONG,
SOUTHERN QIANDONG [HMS]
SOUTHERN EFATE alt for EFATE, SOUTH [ERK]
SOUTHERN EJAGHAM dial of EJAGHAM [ETU]
SOUTHERN EJUTLA ZAPOTECO alt for
ZAPOTECO, SAN VICENTE COATLÁN [ZPT]
SOUTHERN EMBERA alt for EMBERÁ-SAIJA [SJA]
SOUTHERN EMPERA alt for EMBERÁ-SAIJA [SJA]
SOUTHERN ESTONIAN alt for TARTU dial of
ESTONIAN [EST]
SOUTHERN EXTREMADURAN dial of
EXTREMADURAN [EXT]
SOUTHERN FANIA dial of FANIA [FAN]
SOUTHERN FOOTHILL YOKUTS dial of YOKUTS
[YOK]
SOUTHERN FRENCH SIGN LANGUAGE alt for
MARSEILLE SIGN LANGUAGE dial of FRENCH
SIGN LANGUAGE [FSL]
SOUTHERN FUNGOM alt for OSO [OSO]
SOUTHERN GABRI alt for GABRI [GAB]
SOUTHERN GIKUYU dial of GIKUYU [KIU]
SOUTHERN GOURMANCHEMA dial of
GOURMANCHEMA [GUX]
SOUTHERN GUIYANG MIAO alt for HMONG,
SOUTHERN GUIYANG [HMY]
SOUTHERN GUIZHOU alt for QIANNAN dial of
BOUYEI [PCC]
SOUTHERN GUNU dial of NUGUNU [YAS]
SOUTHERN GURUNG dial of GURUNG, WESTERN
[GVR]
SOUTHERN HANGA dial of HANGA [HAG]
SOUTHERN HEILTSUK alt for OOWEKEENO dial
of HEILTSUK [HEI]
SOUTHERN HEMA alt for HEMA [NIX]
SOUTHERN HUANCAYO QUECHUA alt for
QUECHUA, WANCA, HUAYLLA [QHU]
SOUTHERN ISAN. KORAT dial of THAI, NORTH-
EASTERN [TTS]
SOUTHERN IVATAN dial of IVATAN [IVV]
SOUTHERN JALE alt for NIPSAN [NPS]
SOUTHERN KALASHA dial of KALASHA [KLS]
SOUTHERN KANNADA alt for KURUMBA [KFI]
SOUTHERN KARELIAN alt for LIVVI [OLO]
SOUTHERN KARELIAN dial of KARELIAN [KRL]
SOUTHERN KAZAKH dial of KAZAKH [KAZ]
SOUTHERN KHAMS dial of KHAMS [KHG]
SOUTHERN KHANTI dial of KHANTY [KCA]
SOUTHERN KHMER dial of KHMER, CENTRAL
[KMR]
SOUTHERN KIRGIZ dial of KIRGHIZ [KDO]
SOUTHERN KIRINYAGA alt for NDIA dial of
GIKUYU [KIU]
SOUTHERN KISAGALA alt for SAGALA [SBM]
SOUTHERN KORONDOUGOU dial of BOZO,
SOROGAMA [BZE]

SOUTHERN KRAHN alt for SAPO [KRN]
SOUTHERN KRUMEN alt for KRUMEN, TEPO [TED]
SOUTHERN KURDISH alt for KURDI [KDB]
SOUTHERN LAHU alt for NYI dial of LAHU [LAH]
SOUTHERN LAPP alt for SAAMI, SOUTHERN [LPC]
SOUTHERN LELA alt for LILA dial of CLELA [DRI]
SOUTHERN LENGUA dial of LENGUA [LEG]
SOUTHERN LIBYAN ARABIC dial of ARABIC, LIBYAN SPOKEN [AYL]
SOUTHERN LIBYAN ARABIC dial of ARABIC, WESTERN EGYPTIAN BEDAWI SPOKEN [AYL]
SOUTHERN LIMBA dial of LIMBA, EAST [LMA]
SOUTHERN LISU alt for LISU [LIS]
SOUTHERN LUBA alt for SANGA [SNG]
SOUTHERN LUSHOOTSEED dial of LUSHOOTSEED [LUT]
SOUTHERN LYÉLÉ dial of LYELE [LEE]
SOUTHERN MA'DI alt for MA'DI, SOUTHERN [QMD]
SOUTHERN MAGAHI dial of MAGAHI [MQM]
SOUTHERN MAIDU alt for NISENAN [NSZ]
SOUTHERN MALAY alt for PERAK dial of MALAY [MLI]
SOUTHERN MALIMIUT INUPIATUN dial of INUPIATUN, NORTHWEST ALASKA [ESK]
SOUTHERN MAMASA alt for PATTAE' dial of MAMASA [MQJ]
SOUTHERN MANINKA alt for MANINKA, KANKAN [MNI]
SOUTHERN MAO alt for ANFILLO [MYO]
SOUTHERN MARIK dial of MARIK [DAD]
SOUTHERN MARWARI dial of MARWARI [MRI]
SOUTHERN MASALIT dial of MASALIT [MSA]
SOUTHERN MASHAN MIAO alt for HMONG, SOUTHERN MASHAN [HMA]
SOUTHERN MICMAC dial of MICMAC [MIC]
SOUTHERN MIN alt for CHINESE, MIN NAN [CFR]
SOUTHERN MON alt for YE dial of MON [MNW]
SOUTHERN MOROCCO ARABIC dial of ARABIC, MOROCCAN SPOKEN [ARY]
SOUTHERN MUNA alt for GUMAS dial of MUNA [MYN]
SOUTHERN MUNJI dial of MUNJI [MNJ]
SOUTHERN MURANG'A alt for SOUTHERN GIKUYU dial of GIKUYU [KIU]
SOUTHERN MURUT alt for LUNDAYEH [LND]
SOUTHERN MUSSAU dial of MUSSAU-EMIRA [EMI]
SOUTHERN MUYU dial of YONGKOM [YON]
SOUTHERN NDAM alt for NDAM-NDAM dial of NDAM [NDM]
SOUTHERN NDEBELE alt for NDEBELE [NEL]
SOUTHERN NINAM dial of NINAM [SHB]
SOUTHERN NOCHIXTLÁN MIXTEC alt for MIXTECO, YUTANDUCHI [MAB]
SOUTHERN NOSU alt for YI, YUNNAN [NOS]
SOUTHERN NUSU dial of NUSU [NUF]
SOUTHERN OKANOGAN dial of OKANAGAN [OKA]
SOUTHERN ORIYA dial of ORIYA [ORY]

SOUTHERN OROK alt for PORONAISK dial of OROK [OAA]
SOUTHERN OROMO alt for BORANA [GAX]
SOUTHERN OROMO alt for OROMO, BORANA-ARSI-GUJI [GAX]
SOUTHERN PAIUTE dial of UTE-SOUTHERN PAIUTE [UTE]
SOUTHERN PANJABI alt for SARAIKI [SKR]
SOUTHERN PA'O dial of KAREN, PAO [BLK]
SOUTHERN PONDORI dial of BOZO, SOROGAMA [BZE]
SOUTHERN POPOLOCA alt for POPOLOCA, MEZONTLA [PBE]
SOUTHERN POPOLOCA alt for POPOLOCA, SAN JUAN ATZINGO [POE]
SOUTHERN PUEBLA MIXTEC alt for MIXTECO, PUEBLA SUR [MIT]
SOUTHERN PUGET SOUND SALISH alt for SOUTHERN LUSHOOTSEED dial of LUSHOOTSEED [LUT]
SOUTHERN PUTLA MIXTECO alt for MIXTECO, SANTA MARÍA ZACATEPEC [MZA]
SOUTHERN PWO KAREN alt for KAREN, PWO WESTERN THAILAND [KJP]
SOUTHERN PWO KAREN alt for TAVOY dial of KAREN, PWO EASTERN [KJP]
SOUTHERN QIANDONG MIAO alt for HMONG, SOUTHERN QIANDONG [HMS]
SOUTHERN RENGMA alt for AZONYU dial of NAGA, RENGMA [NRE]
SOUTHERN ROMAGNOLO dial of EMILIANO-ROMAGNOLO [EML]
SOUTHERN SAMO alt for SEEKU [SOS]
SOUTHERN SANGTAM alt for PURR dial of NAGA, SANGTAM [NSA]
SOUTHERN SAURASHTRA dial of SAURASHTRA [SAZ]
SOUTHERN SEEKU dial of SEEKU [SOS]
SOUTHERN SEL'KUP alt for SREDNYAYA OB-KET dial of SELKUP [SAK]
SOUTHERN SHILHA alt for TACHELHIT [SHI]
SOUTHERN SICHUAN YI dial of YI, SICHUAN [III]
SOUTHERN SISAALA alt for SISAALA, PASAALE [SIG]
SOUTHERN SOQOTRI dial of SOQOTRI [SQT]
SOUTHERN SORSOGON alt for SORSOGON, WARAY [SRV]
SOUTHERN STANDARD BHOJPURI dial of BHOJPURI [BHJ]
SOUTHERN STANDARD MAITHILI dial of MAITHILI [MKP]
SOUTHERN STIENG alt for STIENG, BUDEH [STT]
SOUTHERN STONEY dial of STONEY [STO]
SOUTHERN SUDAN ARABIC alt for ARABIC, SUDANESE CREOLE [PGA]
SOUTHERN SUMBA dial of KAMBERA [SMI]
SOUTHERN SUMO alt for HONDURAN TAWAHKA dial of SUMO TAWAHKA [SUM]
SOUTHERN TA'ANG alt for PALAUNG, PALE [PCE]
SOUTHERN TA-ANG alt for PALAUNG, PALE [PCE]
SOUTHERN TALYSHI dial of TALYSH [TLY]

SOUTHERN TÀY dial of TAY [THO]
SOUTHERN TETUN dial of TETUN [TTM]
SOUTHERN TLAXIACO MIXTECO alt for MIXTECO, YOSONDA [MPM]
SOUTHERN TONGA alt for TOKA dial of TONGA [TOI]
SOUTHERN TSAKONIAN dial of TSAKONIAN [TSD]
SOUTHERN TSIMSHIAN dial of TSIMSHIAN [TSI]
SOUTHERN TUNISIAN dial of ARABIC, TUNISIAN SPOKEN [AEB]
SOUTHERN TURKANA dial of TURKANA [TUV]
SOUTHERN UMA dial of UMA [PPK]
SOUTHERN VEPS dial of VEPS [VEP]
SOUTHERN VIETNAMESE dial of VIETNAMESE [VIE]
SOUTHERN VILLA ALTA ZAPOTECO alt for ZAPOTECO, CAJONOS [ZAD]
SOUTHERN VLAX dial of ROMANI, VLAX [RMY]
SOUTHERN VLAX ROMANI dial of ROMANI, VLAX [RMY]
SOUTHERN VOGUL dial of MANSI [MNS]
SOUTHERN WELSH dial of WELSH [WLS]
SOUTHERN YAKHA dial of YAKHA [YBH]
SOUTHERN YALI (YALI SELATAN) alt for YALI, NINIA [NLK]
SOUTHERN YAMALELE dial of IAMALELE [YML]
SOUTHERN YEMENI SPOKEN ARABIC alt for ARABIC, TA'IZZI-ADENI SPOKEN [ACQ]
SOUTHERN YI alt for YI, YUNNAN [NOS]
SOUTHERN YUKAGIR alt for YUKAGHIR, SOUTHERN [YUX]
SOUTHERN ZAZA alt for DIMLI [ZZZ]
SOUTHERN-EASTERN MONGOLIAN alt for MONGOLIAN, PERIPHERAL [MVF]
SOUTHWEST BARITO alt for NGAJU [NIJ]
SOUTHWEST BELARUSAN dial of BELARUSAN [RUW]
SOUTHWEST BOBE dial of BUBE [BVB]
SOUTHWEST BOHEMIAN dial of CZECH [CZC]
SOUTHWEST DUGURI dial of DUGURI [DBM]
SOUTHWEST EDE alt for KAMBOLÉ [XKB]
SOUTHWEST FINLAND SWEDISH dial of SWEDISH [SWD]
SOUTHWEST KAINGANG dial of KAINGANG [KGP]
SOUTHWEST KARAKALPAK dial of KARAKALPAK [KAC]
SOUTHWEST LAMAHOLOT alt for LEWOTOBI [LWT]
SOUTHWEST LAMPUNG alt for KOTA AGUNG dial of PESISIR, SOUTHERN [PEC]
SOUTHWEST SENARI dial of SENOUFO, CEBAARA [SEF]
SOUTHWEST TEKE alt for TEKE, WESTERN [TEZ]
SOUTHWEST UKRAINIAN dial of UKRAINIAN [UKR]
SOUTHWESTERN CARIBBEAN CREOLE ENGLISH [JAM] lang, Jamaica; also in Canada, Costa Rica, Dominican Republic, Panama, United Kingdom, USA

SOUTHWESTERN FINNISH dial of FINNISH [FIN]
SOUTHWESTERN GELAO alt for WHITE GELAO dial of GELAO [KKF]
SOUTHWESTERN GUIYANG MIAO alt for HMONG, SOUTHWESTERN GUIYANG [HMG]
SOUTHWESTERN HUISHUI MIAO alt for HMONG, SOUTHWESTERN HUISHUI [HMH]
SOUTHWESTERN KAZAKH dial of KAZAKH [KAZ]
SOUTHWESTERN KROUMEN alt for KRUMEN, TEPO [TED]
SOUTHWESTERN LOGUDORESE dial of SARDINIAN, LOGUDORESE [SRD]
SOUTHWESTERN MANDARIN alt for XINAN GUANHUA dial of CHINESE, MANDARIN [CHN]
SOUTHWESTERN OJIBWA alt for CHIPPEWA [CIW]
SOUTHWESTERN PASHTO dial of PASHTO, SOUTHERN [PBT]
SOUTHWESTERN POMO alt for KASHAYA [KJU]
SOUTHWESTERN PUEBLA NÁHUATL alt for NÁHUATL, PUEBLA CENTRAL [NCX]
SOUTHWESTERN QUICHÉ alt for QUICHÉ, WEST CENTRAL [QUT]
SOUTHWESTERN TAMANG dial of TAMANG, EASTERN [TAJ]
SOUTHWESTERN TARAHUMARA alt for TARAHUMARA, SUROESTE [TWR]
SOUTHWESTERN TARANGAN dial of TARANGAN, WEST [TXN]
SOUTHWESTERN TEPEHUÁN alt for TEPEHUÁN SUROESTE [TLA]
SOUTHWESTERN TLAXIACO MIXTEC alt for MIXTECO, TLAXIACO, SUROESTE [MEH]
SOUTHWESTERN UDMURT alt for SOUTH UDMURT dial of UDMURT [UDM]
SOUTO alt for SOTHO, SOUTHERN [SSO]
SOWA [SWW] lang, Vanuatu
SOWA dial of NAGA, KONYAK [NBE]
SOWANDA [SOW] lang, Papua New Guinea; also in Indonesia (Irian Jaya)
SOWRASHTRA alt for SAURASHTRA [SAZ]
SOYALTEPEC MIXTEC alt for MIXTECO, SOYALTEPEC [VMQ]
SOYKIN dial of INGRIAN [IZH]
SOYOD alt for TUVIN [TUN]
SOYON alt for TUVIN [TUN]
SOYOT alt for TUVIN [TUN]
SPANISH [SPN] lang, Spain; also in Andorra, Argentina, Aruba, Australia, Belgium, Belize, Bolivia, Canada, Cayman Islands, Chile, Colombia, Costa Rica, Cuba, Dominican Republic, Ecuador, El Salvador, Equatorial Guinea, Finland, France, Germany, Gibraltar, Guatemala, Honduras, Israel, Jamaica, Mexico, Morocco, Netherlands Antilles, Nicaragua, Norway, Panama, Paraguay, Peru, Philippines, Puerto Rico, Sweden, Switzerland, Trinidad and Tobago, U.S. Virgin Islands, Uruguay, USA, Venezuela
SPANISH CALO dial of CALO [RMR]

SPANISH CALÓ dial of CALO [RMR]
SPANISH SIGN LANGUAGE [SSP] lang, Spain
SPANISH, LORETO-UCAYALI [SPQ] lang, Peru
SPANYOL alt for LADINO [SPJ]
SPENG alt for SIPENG dial of PENAN, WESTERN [PNE]
SPITI dial of TIBETAN [TIC]
SPOKAN alt for SPOKANE [SPO]
SPOKANE [SPO] lang, USA
SPOWAMA alt for NAGA, MAO [NBI]
SQOLEQ dial of ATAYAL [TAY]
SQUAMISH [SQU] lang, Canada
SQULIQ alt for SQOLEQ dial of ATAYAL [TAY]
SRADRI alt for SADRI [SCK]
SRANAN [SRN] lang, Suriname; also in Aruba, Netherlands, Netherlands Antilles
SRANAN TONGO alt for SRANAN [SRN]
SRAY alt for SENAYA [SYN]
SRE dial of KOHO [KPM]
SREDNYAYA OB-KET dial of SELKUP [SAK]
SREM dial of ALBANIAN, TOSK [ALN]
SRI LANKA TAMIL dial of TAMIL [TCV]
SRI LANKAN CREOLE MALAY [SCI] lang, Sri Lanka
SRI LANKAN MALAY alt for SRI LANKAN CREOLE MALAY [SCI]
SRI LANKAN SIGN LANGUAGE [SQS] lang, Sri Lanka
SRIKAKULA dial of TELUGU [TCW]
SRINAGARIA dial of GARHWALI [GBM]
SRUBU alt for SURUBU [SDE]
SSIA alt for SERA [SRY]
SSO alt for SO [SOX]
SSU GHASSI alt for DZU'OASI dial of JUHOAN [KTZ]
SSUGA alt for SUGA [SGI]
ST. BARTH CREOLE ENGLISH dial of VIRGIN ISLANDS CREOLE ENGLISH [VIB]
ST. BARTH CREOLE FRENCH dial of LESSER ANTILLEAN CREOLE FRENCH [DOM]
ST. FRANCIS alt for ABNAKI, WESTERN [ABE]
ST. GALLEN dial of ALEMANNISCH [GSW]
ST. KITTS CREOLE ENGLISH dial of LEEWARD CARIBBEAN CREOLE ENGLISH [AIG]
ST. LAWRENCE IROQUOIAN alt for LAURENTIAN [LRE]
ST. LAWRENCE ISLAND "ESKIMO" pejorative alt for YUPIK, CENTRAL SIBERIAN [ESS]
ST. LOUIS alt for LA CONCEPTION dial of CAAC [MSQ]
ST. LUCIA CREOLE FRENCH dial of LESSER ANTILLEAN CREOLE FRENCH [DOM]
ST. LUCIAN ENGLISH dial of ENGLISH [ENG]
ST. MAARTEN CREOLE ENGLISH dial of VIRGIN ISLANDS CREOLE ENGLISH [VIB]
ST. MARTIN CREOLE FRENCH dial of LESSER ANTILLEAN CREOLE FRENCH [DOM]
STAJERSKI dial of SLOVENIAN [SLV]
STAL dial of LEZGI [LEZ]
STANDARD ADI alt for PADAM dial of ADI [ADI]
STANDARD ASSAMESE dial of ASSAMESE [ASM]

STANDARD BAMBARA dial of BAMANANKAN [BRA]
STANDARD BUNDELI dial of BUNDELI [BNS]
STANDARD CHINESE alt for CHINESE, MANDARIN [CHN]
STANDARD FIJIAN alt for FIJIAN [FJI]
STANDARD FRENCH dial of FRENCH [FRN]
STANDARD GUJARATI dial of GUJARATI [GJR]
STANDARD HEBREW dial of HEBREW [HBR]
STANDARD KASHMIRI dial of KASHMIRI [KSH]
STANDARD KONKANI dial of KONKANI, GOANESE [GOM]
STANDARD LUGBARA alt for ARUA dial of LUGBARA [LUG]
STANDARD MAITHILI dial of MAITHILI [MKP]
STANDARD MALAGASY alt for MALAGASY [MEX]
STANDARD MALAY alt for MALAY [MLI]
STANDARD MALTESE dial of MALTESE [MLS]
STANDARD MARWARI dial of MARWARI [MKD]
STANDARD MUNA dial of MUNA [MYN]
STANDARD ORIYA alt for MUGHALBANDI dial of ORIYA [ORY]
STANDARD SOMALI alt for SOMALI [SOM]
STANDARD SWEDISH dial of SWEDISH [SWD]
STANDARD THAI alt for THAI [THJ]
STANG dial of BIATAH [BTH]
STAR alt for GEDAGED [GDD]
STAR HARBOUR alt for TAWARAFA dial of KAHUA [AGW]
STAR-RAGETTA alt for GEDAGED [GDD]
STATE OF MEXICO OTOMÍ alt for OTOMÍ, ESTADO DE MÉXICO [OTS]
ST'AT'IMCETS alt for LILLOOET [LIL]
STELLINGWERFS [STL] lang, Netherlands
STELLINGWERFSTELLINGWARFS alt for STELLINGWERFS [STL]
STEM BAGA alt for BAGA SITEMU [BSP]
STENGGANG JAGOI dial of JAGOI [SNE]
STEPPE BASHKIR alt for YURMATY dial of BASHKIR [BXK]
STEPPE CRIMEAN alt for NORTHERN CRIMEAN dial of CRIMEAN TURKISH [CRH]
STIENG, BUDEH [STT] lang, Viet Nam
STIENG, BULO [STI] lang, Viet Nam; also in Cambodia
STIMUL alt for PAIWAN [PWN]
STOCKBRIDGE dial of MOHEGAN-MONTAUK-NARRAGANSETT [MOF]
STOD alt for STOD BHOTI [SBU]
STOD dial of STOD BHOTI [SBU]
STOD BHOTI [SBU] lang, India
STOD-KAD alt for STOD BHOTI [SBU]
STOKAVIAN dial of SERBO-CROATIAN [SRC]
STONEY [STO] lang, Canada
STONEY RIVER dial of TANAINA [TFN]
STONY alt for STONEY [STO]
STOTPA alt for CHANGTHANG [CNA]
STRAITS alt for SALISH, STRAITS [STR]
STRAITS MALAY alt for MALAY, BABA [BAL]
STRIENG alt for TRIENG [STG]
STRIPED HMONG alt for HMONG GU MBA dial of HMONG DAW [MWW]

STRIPED KAREN alt for YINCHIA [YIN]
SÜRYANI alt for TUROYO [SYR]
SU alt for ISU [SZV]
SU alt for SOU [SQQ]
SU' alt for SOU [SQQ]
SUA alt for MANSOANKA [MSW]
SUA dial of CHUAVE [CJV]
SUA TU PADANG alt for SEKO PADANG [SKX]
SUABAU alt for SUABO [SZP]
SUABIAN alt for SWABIAN [SWG]
SUABO [SZP] lang, Indonesia (Irian Jaya)
SUAFA dial of LAU [LLU]
SUAHILI alt for SWAHILI [SWA]
SUAI alt for KUY [KDT]
SUAI CHANG alt for CHANG dial of KUY [KDT]
SUAIN alt for ULAU-SUAIN [SVB]
SUANG LOTUD alt for LOTUD [DTR]
SUARMIN [SEO] lang, Papua New Guinea
SUARO alt for MAIA [SKS]
SUASESO alt for BAGUSA [BQB]
SUAU [SWP] lang, Papua New Guinea
SUAU dial of SUAU [SWP]
SUAY alt for KUY [KDT]
SUBA [SUH] lang, Kenya; also in Tanzania
SUBANEN alt for SUBANUN, LAPUYAN [LAA]
SUBANEN, CENTRAL [SUS] lang, Philippines
SUBANEN, NORTHERN [STB] lang, Philippines
SUBANON, KOLIBUGAN [SKN] lang, Philippines
SUBANON, WESTERN [SUC] lang, Philippines
SUBANUN, LAPUYAN [LAA] lang, Philippines
SUB-BARBARICINO dial of SARDINIAN,
    CAMPIDANESE [SRO]
SUBBI alt for MANDAIC [MID]
SUBEROAN alt for BASQUE, SOULETIN [BSZ]
SUBI alt for SHUBI [SUJ]
SUBIA alt for SUBIYA [SBS]
SUBIYA [SBS] lang, Namibia; also in Botswana,
    Zambia
SUBPAN dial of IDAAN [DBJ]
SUBTIABA [SUT] lang, Nicaragua
SUBU alt for ISU [SZV]
SUCITE alt for SÉNOUFO, SÌCÌTÉ [SEP]
SUCRE dial of QUECHUA, SOUTH BOLIVIAN [QUH]
SUDAIR alt for CENTRAL NAJDI dial of ARABIC,
    NAJDI SPOKEN [ARS]
SUD-EST alt for SUDEST [TGO]
SUDEST [TGO] lang, Papua New Guinea
SUEI alt for KUY [KDT]
SUENA [SUE] lang, Papua New Guinea
SUFRAI dial of TARPIA [SUF]
SUGA [SGI] lang, Cameroon
SUGALI alt for LAMBADI [LMN]
SUGANGA [SUG] lang, Papua New Guinea
SUGBUANON alt for CEBUANO [CEB]
SUGBUHANON alt for CEBUANO [CEB]
SUGCESTUN alt for YUPIK, PACIFIC GULF [EMS]
SUGHU alt for GHARI [GRI]
SUGPIAK "ESKIMO" pejorative alt for YUPIK,
    PACIFIC GULF [EMS]
SUGPIAQ "ESKIMO" pejorative alt for YUPIK,
    PACIFIC GULF [EMS]

SUGU alt for NUMANGGANG [NOP]
SUGUDI alt for SIGIDI dial of SAYA [SAY]
SUGUR alt for SUKUR [SUK]
SUGURTI dial of KANURI, CENTRAL [KPH]
SUGURTI dial of KANURI, TUMARI [KRT]
SUGUT alt for DUSUN, SUGUT [KZS]
SUGUT KADAZAN alt for DUSUN, SUGUT [KZS]
SUHAID dial of MALAYIC DAYAK [XDY]
SUI [SWI] lang, China; also in Viet Nam
SUI alt for KUY [KDT]
SUI dial of KOL [KOL]
SUI LI alt for SUI [SWI]
SUIEI dial of OKIEK [OKI]
SUIEI dial of OMOTIK [OMT]
SUIPO alt for SUI [SWI]
SUIT dial of AWAD BING [BCU]
SUJAU alt for SAJAU BASAP [SAD]
SUK alt for PÖKOOT [PKO]
SUK alt for YUPIK, PACIFIC GULF [EMS]
SUKA alt for CHUKA [CUH]
SUKA alt for SO dial of KULFA [KXJ]
SUKA alt for SUKMA dial of MARIA, DANDAMI
    [DAQ]
SUKADANA dial of MALAY [MLI]
SUKALI alt for LAMBADI [LMN]
SUKANG dial of KADAZAN, LABUK-
    KINABATANGAN [DTB]
SUKARAJA dial of LISABATA-NUNIALI [LCS]
SUKI [SUI] lang, Papua New Guinea
SUKI alt for WAIGALI [WBK]
SUKMA dial of MARIA, DANDAMI [DAQ]
SUKOT alt for NOBIIN [FIA]
SUKU [SUB] lang, DRC
SUKU BATIN [SBV] lang, Indonesia (Sumatra)
SUKUBATOM alt for KIMKI [SBT]
SUKUBATONG alt for KIMKI [SBT]
SUKULUMBWE alt for ILA [ILB]
SUKUMA [SUA] lang, Tanzania
SUKUR [SUK] lang, Nigeria
SUKURASE dial of DOGOSE [DOS]
SUKURUM dial of ADZERA [AZR]
SULA [SZN] lang, Indonesia (Maluku)
SULA alt for DAJU, DAR SILA [DAU]
SULA MANGOLI alt for MANGOLE [MQC]
SULAIMITIAN ARABIC alt for ARABIC, LIBYAN
    SPOKEN [AYL]
SULAIMITIAN ARABIC alt for ARABIC, WESTERN
    EGYPTIAN BEDAWI SPOKEN [AYL]
SULAKA alt for ARABIC, HASSANIYYA [MEY]
SULAMU dial of BAJAU, INDONESIAN [BDL]
SULAYMÂNI dial of KURDI [KDB]
SULCITANO dial of SARDINIAN, CAMPIDANESE
    [SRO]
SULEIMANIYA dial of HULAULA [HUY]
SULEIMANIYE alt for SULAYMÂNI dial of KURDI
    [KDB]
SULETINO alt for BASQUE, SOULETIN [BSZ]
SULIMA dial of YALUNKA [YAL]
SULKA [SLK] lang, Papua New Guinea
SULMELANG dial of WATUBELA [WAH]
SULOD [SRG] lang, Philippines

SULU alt for TAUSUG [TSG]
SULUD alt for KINARAY-A [KRJ]
SULUK alt for TAUSUG [TSG]
SULUNG [SUV] lang, India
SUM dial of GERUMA [GEA]
SUMA [SQM] lang, CAR
SUMADEL dial of KALINGA, SOUTHERN [KSC]
SUMADEL-TINGLAYAN KALINGA alt for KALINGA,
    SOUTHERN [KSC]
SUMAMBU alt for TAGAL MURUT [MVV]
SUMAMBU dial of TAGAL MURUT [MVV]
SUMAMBUQ alt for SUMAMBU dial of TAGAL
    MURUT [MVV]
SUMAMBUQ alt for TAGAL MURUT [MVV]
SUMAMBU-TAGAL alt for TAGAL MURUT [MVV]
SUMANG dial of KULA [TPG]
SUMARE-RANGAS dial of MAMUJU [MQX]
SUMARIUP [SIV] lang, Papua New Guinea
SUMAU [SIX] lang, Papua New Guinea
SUMAU-GARIA alt for SUMAU [SIX]
SUMBA alt for KAMBERA [SMI]
SUMBANESE alt for KAMBERA [SMI]
SUMBAWA [SMW] lang, Indonesia (Nusa Tenggara)
SUMBAWARESE alt for SUMBAWA [SMW]
SUMBWA [SUW] lang, Tanzania
SUMBWA alt for MWERI dial of NYAMWEZI [NYZ]
SUMCHO alt for SHUMCHO [SCU]
SUMCHU alt for SHUMCHO [SCU]
SUMENEP dial of MADURA [MHJ]
SUMERI alt for TANAHMERAH [TCM]
SUMERINE alt for TANAHMERAH [TCM]
SUMI alt for NAGA, SUMI [NSM]
SUMO alt for SUMO TAWAHKA [SUM]
SUMO TAWAHKA [SUM] lang, Nicaragua; also in
    Honduras
SUMOHAI alt for MOMUNA [MQF]
SUMOO alt for SUMO TAWAHKA [SUM]
SUMOUN dial of PETATS [PEX]
SUMPO dial of DAYAK, LAND [DYK]
SUMRAI alt for SOMRAI [SOR]
SUMTSU alt for SHUMCHO [SCU]
SUMU alt for SUMO TAWAHKA [SUM]
SUMWARI alt for NIKSEK [GBE]
SUNA dial of SUBA [SUH]
SUNAM [SSK] lang, India
SUNBAR alt for SUNWAR [SUZ]
SUNDA [SUO] lang, Indonesia (Java and Bali)
SUNDANESE alt for SUNDA [SUO]
SUNDEI dial of BIAK [BHW]
SUNDI dial of HALBI [HLB]
SUNDONI alt for BASINYARI dial of NUNI,
    SOUTHERN [NNW]
SUNGAI alt for SUBPAN dial of IDAAN [DBJ]
SUNGAI alt for TOMBONUWO [TXA]
SUNGAI PIAH dial of TEMIAR [TMH]
SUNGAM alt for SUNAM [SSK]
SUNGDEL dial of KOI [KKT]
SUNGEI alt for LAMAG SUNGAI dial of KADAZAN,
    LABUK-KINABATANGAN [DTB]
SUNGEI alt for TOMBONUWO [TXA]
SUNGGARI dial of NANAI [GLD]

SUNGKAI [SUU] lang, Indonesia (Sumatra)
SUNGKAI dial of SEMAI [SEA]
SUNGNAM alt for SUNAM [SSK]
SUNGOR [SUN] lang, Chad; also in Sudan
SUNGOR alt for ASSANGORI [SUN]
SUNGOR dial of ASSANGORI [SUN]
SUNGU alt for NSONGO [NSX]
SUNGU alt for TETELA [TEL]
SUNKHLA alt for TASHON dial of CHIN, FALAM
    [HBH]
SUNSARI dial of MEOHANG, EASTERN [EMG]
SUNTAI alt for SAMBA LEKO dial of SAMBA LEKO
    [NDI]
SUNTAI alt for SAMBA LEKO [NDI]
SUNU TORBI dial of MAMBILA, CAMEROON [MYA]
SUNUWAR alt for SUNWAR [SUZ]
SUNWAR [SUZ] lang, Nepal
SUNWARI alt for SUNWAR [SUZ]
SUOI alt for KUY [KDT]
SUOLUN alt for EVENKI [EVN]
SUOMEA alt for FINNISH [FIN]
SUOMI alt for FINNISH [FIN]
SUONANBA dial of DONGXIANG [SCE]
SUÒNG PHÓNG alt for CHINESE, YUE [YUH]
SUÕÕ dial of SENOUFO, MAMARA [MYK]
SUOY [SYO] lang, Cambodia
SUPAN alt for SUBPAN dial of IDAAN [DBJ]
SUPANA dial of BAUCHI [BSF]
SUPARI dial of MUFIAN [AOJ]
SUPAT dial of KUBU [KVB]
SUPHANABURI dial of UGONG [UGO]
SUPI alt for SOPI dial of BELI [BLM]
SUPIA alt for SUBIYA [SBS]
SUP'IDE alt for SENOUFO, SUPYIRE [SPP]
SUPPIRE alt for SENOUFO, SUPYIRE [SPP]
SUPYIRE alt for SENOUFO, SUPYIRE [SPP]
SUQ alt for SOU [SQQ]
SUQUH dial of SALISH, SOUTHERN PUGET
    SOUND [SLH]
SUQUTRI alt for SOQOTRI [SQT]
SURA alt for MWAGHAVUL [SUR]
SURABAYA dial of JAVANESE [JAN]
SURAIJI alt for SURAJPURI [SJP]
SURAJPURI [SJP] lang, India
SURAKA alt for ARABIC, HASANYA [MEY]
SURAKHANI dial of TAT, MUSLIM [TTT]
SURANI alt for KURDI [KDB]
SURARA alt for YANOMÁMI [WCA]
SURATI alt for GAMADIA dial of GUJARATI [GJR]
SURAXXÉ alt for ARABIC, HASANYA [MEY]
SURBAKHAL [SBJ] lang, Chad
SURBAKHAL dial of MASALIT [MSA]
SURCHI [SUP] lang, Iraq
SURCHI dial of KURMANJI [KUR]
SUREL dial of SUNWAR [SUZ]
SURET alt for ASSYRIAN NEO-ARAMAIC [AII]
SURETH alt for ASSYRIAN NEO-ARAMAIC [AII]
SURETH alt for CHALDEAN NEO-ARAMAIC [CLD]
SURGUCH dial of BALKAN GAGAUZ TURKISH
    [BGX]
SURGUJIA dial of CHHATTISGARHI [HNE]

SURI [SUQ] lang, Ethiopia; also in Sudan
SURI alt for KACIPO dial of KACIPO-BALESI [KOE]
SURI alt for TAWBUID, EASTERN [BNJ]
SURI dial of FOLOPA [PPO]
SURI dial of KACIPO-BALESI [KOE]
SURIANÁ alt for SIRIANO [SRI]
SURIGAO dial of MANOBO, AGUSAN [MSM]
SURIGAONON [SUL] lang, Philippines
SURIGAONON dial of SURIGAONON [SUL]
SURIN dial of KHMER, NORTHERN [KXM]
SURINAAMS alt for SRANAN [SRN]
SURINAME CREOLE ENGLISH alt for SRANAN
    [SRN]
SURINAME JAVANESE alt for JAVANESE,
    CARIBBEAN [JVN]
SURINAMESE alt for SRANAN [SRN]
SURIRÁ alt for SIRIANO [SRI]
SURMA alt for SURI [SUQ]
SURMIRAN-ALBULA dial of ROMANSCH [RHE]
SUROA alt for MACUNA [MYY]
SUROI alt for SIROI [SSD]
SURSELVA alt for SURSILVAN dial of ROMANSCH
    [RHE]
SURSILVAN dial of ROMANSCH [RHE]
SURSILVAN-OBERLAND dial of ROMANSCH
    [RHE]
SURSURUNGA [SGZ] lang, Papua New Guinea
SURU alt for TAPSHIN [TDL]
SURUAHÁ [SWX] lang, Brazil
SURU-BO dial of APMA [APP]
SURUBU [SDE] lang, Nigeria
SURUÍ [SRU] lang, Brazil
SURUÍ alt for SURUÍ DO PARÁ [MDZ]
SURUÍ DE RONDÔNIA alt for SURUÍ [SRU]
SURUÍ DO JIPARANÁ alt for SURUÍ [SRU]
SURUÍ DO PARÁ [MDZ] lang, Brazil
SURU-MARANI dial of APMA [APP]
SURUVIRI dial of ASHKUN [ASK]
SURUWAHÁ alt for SURUAHÁ [SWX]
SURYANA alt for SIRIANO [SRI]
SURYAYA alt for SYRIAC [SYC]
SURYAYA SWADAYA alt for ASSYRIAN NEO-
    ARAMAIC [AII]
SURYOYO alt for MLAHSÖ [QMQ]
SURYOYO alt for SYRIAC [SYC]
SURYOYO alt for TUROYO [SYR]
SUS alt for SUSIUA dial of TACHELHIT [SHI]
SUSA dial of AZERBAIJANI, NORTH [AZE]
SUSHEN alt for NANAI [GLD]
SUSIUA alt for TACHELHIT [SHI]
SUSIUA dial of TACHELHIT [SHI]
SUSOO alt for SUSU [SUD]
SUSQUEHANNA alt for SUSQUEHANNOCK [SQN]
SUSQUEHANNOCK [SQN] lang, USA
SUSSEX dial of ENGLISH [ENG]
SUSU [SUD] lang, Guinea; also in Guinea-Bissau,
    Sierra Leone
SUSUAMI [SSU] lang, Papua New Guinea
SUTHU alt for SOTHO, SOUTHERN [SSO]
SUTI dial of JAGOI [SNE]
SUTO alt for SOTHO, SOUTHERN [SSO]

SUTSILVAN-HINTERRHEIN alt for SURSILVAN
    dial of ROMANSCH [RHE]
SUTU alt for NGONI [NGU]
SUUNDI dial of KONGO [KON]
SUUNDI dial of KUNYI [KNF]
SUVALKIETISKAI dial of LITHUANIAN [LIT]
SUWA alt for ARABIC, CHADIAN SPOKEN [SHU]
SUWA dial of AMBA [RWM]
SUWANNAKHET alt for SAVANNAKHET dial of
    LAO [NOL]
SUWAWA [SWU] lang, Indonesia (Sulawesi)
SUWAWA-BUNDA alt for SUWAWA [SWU]
SUWURTI alt for SUGURTI dial of KANURI, TUMARI
    [KRT]
SUYÁ [SUY] lang, Brazil
SVAN [SVA] lang, Georgia
SVANURI alt for SVAN [SVA]
SVEA dial of SWEDISH [SWD]
SVENSK ROMMANI alt for TAVRINGER ROMANI
    [RMU]
SVENSKA alt for SWEDISH [SWD]
SWABIAN [SWG] lang, Germany
SWABOU dial of TSO [LDP]
SWAGA dial of NANDI [NNB]
SWAGUP alt for NGALA [NUD]
SWAHILI [SWA] lang, Tanzania; also in Burundi,
    Kenya, Mayotte, Mozambique, Oman, Rwanda,
    Somalia, South Africa, Uganda, UAE, USA
SWAHILI, CONGO [SWC] lang, DRC
SWAKA dial of LALA-BISA [LEB]
SWANGLA alt for PATTANI [LAE]
SWARA alt for SORA [SRB]
SWAT KHOWAR dial of KHOWAR [KHW]
SWATI [SWZ] lang, Swaziland; also in Mozambique,
    South Africa
SWATOW alt for SHANTOU dial of CHINESE, MIN
    NAN [CFR]
SWAZI alt for SWATI [SWZ]
SWEDISH [SWD] lang, Sweden; also in Canada,
    Estonia, Finland, Norway, UAE, USA
SWEDISH SIGN LANGUAGE [SWL] lang, Sweden
SWE'NGA alt for YAMBA [YAM]
SWETA dial of KURIA [KUJ]
"SWINA" pejorative alt for SHONA [SHD]
SWINOMISH alt for SKAGIT [SKA]
SWISS-FRENCH SIGN LANGUAGE [SSR] lang,
    Switzerland
SWISS-GERMAN SIGN LANGUAGE [SGG] lang,
    Switzerland
SWISS-ITALIAN SIGN LANGUAGE [SLF] lang,
    Switzerland
SWOSE alt for BASSOSSI [BSI]
SYA alt for SYABÉRÉ dial of BOBO MADARE,
    SOUTHERN [BWQ]
SYA dial of BOBO MADARE, NORTHERN [BBO]
SYABÉRÉ dial of BOBO MADARE, SOUTHERN
    [BWQ]
SYAN dial of MASABA [MYX]
SYANG dial of THAKALI [THS]
SYANGJA GURUNG alt for SOUTHERN GURUNG
    dial of GURUNG, WESTERN [GVR]

SYÉMOU alt for SIAMOU [SIF]
SYEMPIRE alt for SENOUFO, SHEMPIRE [SEB]
SYENARA alt for SENOUFO, SYENARA [SHZ]
SYENERE alt for SENOUFO, CEBAARA [SEF]
SYER dial of KARABORO, WESTERN [KZA]
SYER-TENYER alt for KARABORO, WESTERN
[KZA]
SYIAGHA alt for SIAGHA-YENIMU [OSR]
SYLHETI alt for SYLHETTI [SYL]
SYLHETTI [SYL] lang, Bangladesh; also in United
Kingdom
SYLHETTI BANGLA alt for SYLHETTI [SYL]
SYLT alt for SÖLRENG dial of FRISIAN,
NORTHERN [FRR]
SYM dial of EVENKI [EVN]
SYMIARTA alt for SINYAR [SYS]
SYNTENG alt for JAINTIA dial of PNAR [PBV]
SYRIA dial of ARMENIAN [ARM]
SYRIAC [SYC] lang, Turkey (Asia); also in Iraq, Syria
SYRIEN alt for SYRIA dial of ARMENIAN [ARM]
SYRMIA alt for SREM dial of ALBANIAN, TOSK
[ALN]
SYRO-LEBANESE ARABIC alt for ARABIC, NORTH
LEVANTINE SPOKEN [APC]
SYRO-MESOPOTAMIAN ARABIC alt for ARABIC,
NORTH MESOPOTAMIAN SPOKEN [AYP]
SYRO-MESOPOTAMIAN VERNACULAR ARABIC
alt for ARABIC, NORTH MESOPOTAMIAN
SPOKEN [AYP]
SYRYOYO alt for TUROYO [SYR]
SYUBA alt for KAGATE [SYW]
SZEAK-BAGILI alt for GEDAGED [GDD]
SZEGED dial of HUNGARIAN SIGN LANGUAGE
[HSH]
SZEKELY dial of HUNGARIAN [HNG]
SZI alt for ZAIWA [ATB]
SZINCA alt for XINCA [XIN]
TA alt for TAO-SUAMATO [TSX]
TA HOI alt for TA'OIH, UPPER [TTH]
TA HUA MIAO alt for HMONG, NORTHEASTERN
DIAN [HMD]
TA HWA MIAO alt for HMONG, NORTHEASTERN
DIAN [HMD]
TA SARA alt for SARA KABA [SBZ]
TÀ SÀRA alt for KABA DEME [KWG]
TÄTE dial of BINE [ORM]
TA:ME alt for IDI [IDI]
TAA alt for PAMONA [BCX]
TAA dial of KAILI, LEDO [LEW]
TAA dial of PAMONA [BCX]
TAABWA [TAP] lang, DRC; also in Zambia
TA'ADJIO alt for TAJIO [TDJ]
TAAI dial of SAISIYAT [SAI]
TA'AM dial of KEI [KEI]
TAAN dial of YAOURE [YRE]
TA-ANG PALAUNG alt for PALAUNG, SHWE [SWE]
TAAON alt for DIGARO [MHU]
TAAR SHAMYAN alt for SINYAR [SYS]
TAAREYO alt for FULFULDE, ADAMAWA [FUB]
TAATAAL alt for BON GULA [GLC]
TABÁ ZAPOTEC alt for ZAPOTECO, TABAA [ZAT]

TABAA ZAPOTECO alt for ZAPOTECO, TABAA
[ZAT]
TABAJARI dial of CARIB [CRB]
TABANAN alt for LOWLAND BALI dial of BALI [BZC]
TABANYA alt for KRONGO [KGO]
TABAR alt for MANDARA [TBF]
TABAR dial of MANDARA [TBF]
TABARE dial of SINASINA [SST]
TABAROG dial of TAGDAL [TDA]
TABARU [TBY] lang, Indonesia (Maluku)
TABASARAN alt for TABASSARAN [TAB]
TABASARANTSY alt for TABASSARAN [TAB]
TABASCO AZTEC alt for NÁHUATL, TABASCO
[NHC]
TABASSARAN [TAB] lang, Russia (Europe); also
in Azerbaijan, Kazakhstan, Turkmenistan,
Uzbekistan
TABEBA alt for TAPEBA [TBB]
TABEHUA dial of ZAPOTECO, ZOOGOCHO [ZPQ]
TABELE alt for NDEBELE [NDF]
TABI alt for GAAM [TBI]
TABI alt for TABLA [TNM]
TABILONG alt for TEBILUNG [TGB]
TABLA [TNM] lang, Indonesia (Irian Jaya)
TABLENG dial of NAGA, KONYAK [NBE]
TABO [KNV] lang, Papua New Guinea
TABOJAN alt for TABUYAN dial of LAWANGAN
[LBX]
TABOJAN alt for TAWOYAN [TWY]
TABOJAN TONGKA alt for TABUYAN dial of
LAWANGAN [LBX]
TABOJAN TONGKA alt for TAWOYAN [TWY]
TABORO dial of SINAUGORO [SNC]
TABOROMA alt for BOROMA dial of ACIPA,
EASTERN [AWA]
TABOTIRO JEJEA alt for MACUNA [MYY]
TABOYAN alt for TABUYAN dial of LAWANGAN
[LBX]
TABOYAN alt for TAWOYAN [TWY]
TABRI alt for MAZANDERANI [MZN]
TABRIAK [TZX] lang, Papua New Guinea
TABRIZ dial of AZERBAIJANI, SOUTH [AZB]
TABU alt for ELSENG [MRF]
TABU dial of NAGA, KONYAK [NBE]
TABUID alt for TAWBUID, EASTERN [BNJ]
TABUKAN alt for NORTH TABUKANG dial of
SANGIR [SAN]
TABUKANG alt for NORTH TABUKANG dial of
SANGIR [SAN]
TABULAHAN dial of ARALLE-TABULAHAN [ATQ]
TABUN alt for BALAIT dial of LUNDAYEH [LND]
TABUYAN alt for TAWOYAN [TWY]
TABUYAN dial of LAWANGAN [LBX]
TABWA alt for TAABWA [TAP]
TAC CUI alt for RUC dial of CHUT [SCB]
TACAHUA MIXTEC alt for MIXTECO, TACAHUA
[QMT]
TACANA [TNA] lang, Bolivia
TACANA MAM alt for TACANECO [MTZ]
TACANÁ MAM alt for TACANECO [MTZ]
TACANECO [MTZ] lang, Guatemala; also in Mexico

TACEP alt for CEP dial of ACIPA, WESTERN [AWC]

TACHELHIT [SHI] lang, Morocco; also in Algeria, France

TACHILHIT alt for TACHELHIT [SHI]

TACHO alt for TOCHO [TAZ]

TACHOM alt for HRE [HRE]

TACHON alt for TACHONI dial of BUKUSU [BUL]

TACHONI dial of BUKUSU [BUL]

TACTIC POKOMCHÍ alt for POKOMCHÍ, EASTERN [POH]

TACTILE SIGN LANGUAGE dial of AMERICAN SIGN LANGUAGE [ASE]

"TACUATE" pejorative alt for MIXTECO, SANTA MARÍA ZACATEPEC [MZA]

TA'DA alt for BONE HAU dial of KALUMPANG [KLI]

TADAKSAHAK [DSQ] lang, Mali; also in Algeria

TADAVI alt for DHANKI [DHN]

TADGHAQ dial of TAMASHEQ, KIDAL [TAQ]

TADHA dial of LENDU [LED]

TADHAQ dial of TAMASHEQ [TAQ]

TADIANAN alt for TADYAWAN [TDY]

TADJIO alt for TAJIO [TDJ]

TADO alt for LINDU [KLW]

TADO dial of KAILI, LEDO [LEW]

TADVI BHIL alt for DHANKI [DHN]

TADYAWAN [TDY] lang, Philippines

TADZHIK alt for TAJIKI [PET]

TADZIK alt for SARIKOLI [SRH]

TA'E alt for TORAJA-SA'DAN [SDA]

TAE' [ROB] lang, Indonesia (Sulawesi)

TAE' alt for PATTAE' dial of MAMASA [MQJ]

TAE' alt for TORAJA-SA'DAN [SDA]

TAE' TAE' alt for TAE' [ROB]

TAECHEW alt for TEOCHEW dial of CHINESE, MIN NAN [CFR]

TAEMI dial of TAMI [TMY]

TAENA alt for MAKASAR [MSR]

TAEQ alt for TAE' [ROB]

TAFI [TCD] lang, Ghana

TAFIRE dial of SENOUFO, TAGWANA [TGW]

TAGABAWA alt for MANOBO, TAGABAWA [BGS]

TAGABAWA BAGOBO alt for MANOBO, TAGABAWA [BGS]

"TAGABILI" pejorative alt for TBOLI [TBL]

TAGAKAOLO alt for KALAGAN, TAGAKAULU [KLG]

TAGAKAWANAN dial of MAGINDANAON [MDH]

TAGAL alt for PENSIANGAN MURUT dial of TAGAL MURUT [MVV]

TAGAL dial of TAGAL MURUT [MVV]

TAGAL MURUT [MVV] lang, Malaysia (Sabah); also in Indonesia (Kalimantan)

TAGALAGAD alt for BLAAN, KORONADAL [BIK]

TAGALE alt for TEGALI [RAS]

TAGALISA dial of LISELA [LCL]

TAGALOG [TGL] lang, Philippines; also in Canada, Guam, Midway Islands, Saudi Arabia, UAE, United Kingdom, USA

TAGARA alt for DURUWA [PCI]

TAGARA dial of SENOUFO, CEBAARA [SEF]

TAGARGRENT [OUA] lang, Algeria

TAGARO alt for KADAZAN-TAGARO dial of DUSUN, CENTRAL [DTP]

TAGAU dial of PASHAYI, SOUTHWEST [PSH]

TAGAUR dial of OSETIN [OSE]

TAGBA alt for SÉNOUFO, SÌCÌTÉ [SEP]

TAGBA alt for TAGBU [TBM]

TAGBANA alt for SENOUFO, TAGWANA [TGW]

TAGBANWA [TBW] lang, Philippines

TAGBANWA, CALAMIAN [TBK] lang, Philippines

TAGBANWA, CENTRAL [TGT] lang, Philippines

TAGBARI dial of SENOUFO, CEBAARA [SEF]

TAGBO alt for MAMBILA, CAMEROON [MYA]

TAGBO alt for TAGBU [TBM]

TAGBO alt for TOGBO dial of BANDA, TOGBO-VARA [TOR]

TAGBOUSSIKAN dial of JULA [DYU]

TAGBU [TBM] lang, DRC

TAGBWALI alt for TOGBO dial of BANDA, TOGBO-VARA [TOR]

TAGDAL [TDA] lang, Niger

TAGDAL dial of TAGDAL [TDA]

TAGE alt for KREYE [XRE]

TAGGAL alt for PENSIANGAN MURUT dial of TAGAL MURUT [MVV]

TAGGAL alt for TAGAL dial of TAGAL MURUT [MVV]

TAGHDANSH alt for AZER dial of SONINKE [SNN]

TAGIN dial of NISI [DAP]

TAGINAMBUR alt for BUNDU dial of DUSUN, CENTRAL [DTP]

TAGISH [TGX] lang, Canada

TAGKHUL alt for NAGA, TANGKHUL [NMF]

TÀGÓBÉ dial of AJA-GBE [AJG]

TAGOI [TAG] lang, Sudan

TAGOI dial of TAGOI [TAG]

TAGOL alt for PENSIANGAN MURUT dial of TAGAL MURUT [MVV]

TAGOL alt for TAGAL dial of TAGAL MURUT [MVV]

TAGOTA dial of MERIAM [ULK]

TAGOUNA alt for SENOUFO, TAGWANA [TGW]

TAGOY alt for TAGOI [TAG]

TAGUL alt for PENSIANGAN MURUT dial of TAGAL MURUT [MVV]

TAGUL alt for TAGAL dial of TAGAL MURUT [MVV]

TAGULA alt for SUDEST [TGO]

TAGULANDANG dial of SANGIR [SAN]

TAGWANA alt for SENOUFO, TAGWANA [TGW]

TAHAGGART alt for HOGGAR dial of TAMAHAQ, TAHAGGART [THV]

TAHAMBA dial of BANDI [GBA]

TAHARI alt for GUHU-SAMANE [GHS]

TAHITIAN [THT] lang, French Polynesia; also in New Caledonia, New Zealand, Vanuatu

TAHLTAN [TAH] lang, Canada

TAHOUA alt for TAMAJAQ, TAWALLAMMAT [TTQ]

TAHOUA TAMAJEQ alt for TAMAJAQ, TAWALLAMMAT [TTQ]

TAHUERH alt for DAUR [DTA]

TAHULANDANG alt for TAGULANDANG dial of SANGIR [SAN]

TAHUP alt for TAUP dial of JAGOI [SNE]

TAHUR alt for DAUR [DTA]
TAHUTA dial of MARQUESAN, SOUTH [QMS]
TAI [TAW] lang, Papua New Guinea
TAI alt for JIAMAO [JIO]
TAI dial of KHANA [KEH]
TAI AHOM alt for AHOM [AHO]
TAI BLANC alt for TAI DÓN [TWH]
TAI CHUANG alt for ZHUANG, NORTHERN [CCX]
TAI CUNG alt for TAI YA [CUU]
TAI DAENG [TYR] lang, Viet Nam; also in Laos,
   Thailand, USA
TAI DAM [BLT] lang, Viet Nam; also in Australia,
   China, France, Laos, Thailand, USA
TAI DEHONG alt for TAI NÜA [TDD]
TAI DENG alt for TAI DAENG [TYR]
TAI DO alt for TAI DAM [BLT]
TAI DÓN [TWH] lang, Viet Nam; also in China,
   France, Laos
TAI DÓN alt for TAI DÓN [TWH]
TAI HANG TONG [THC] lang, Viet Nam
TAI HONGJIN [TIZ] lang, China
TAI ISLAM alt for THAI MALAY dial of THAI,
   SOUTHERN [SOU]
TAI KA alt for TAI PONG dial of TAI NUA [TDD]
TAI KAM TI alt for KHAMTI [KHT]
TAI KAO alt for TAI DÓN [TWH]
TAI KHAM TI alt for KHAMTI [KHT]
TAI KHUN alt for KHÜN [KKH]
TAI KHUN alt for KHUN [KKH]
TAI KONG alt for TAI NÜA [TDD]
TAI LAI alt for TAI DÓN [TWH]
TAI LAKA alt for LAKKIA [LBC]
TAI LAO alt for LAO [NOL]
TAI LATI alt for LACHI [LBT]
TAI LE alt for TAI NÜA [TDD]
TAI LOI [TLQ] lang, Myanmar; also in Laos
TAI LOI dial of TAI LOI [TLQ]
TAI LONG [THI] lang, Laos
TAI LONG alt for TAI MAO dial of SHAN [SJN]
TAI LU alt for LÜ [KHB]
TAI LUANG alt for SHAN [SJN]
TAI LUE alt for LÜ [KHB]
TAI MAEN alt for TAI MÈNE [TMP]
TAI MAN alt for TAI MÈNE [TMP]
TAI MAN alt for TAI NÜA [TDD]
TAI MAN THANH [TMM] lang, Viet Nam
TAI MAO alt for TAI NÜA [TDD]
TAI MAO dial of SHAN [SJN]
TAI MÈNE [TMP] lang, Laos
TAI MENE alt for TAI MÈNE [TMP]
TAI MUEAI alt for TÁY MU'Ò'I dial of TAI DAM
   [BLT]
TAI MUEI alt for TAI MUOI dial of TAI DAM [BLT]
TAI MUOI dial of TAI DAM [BLT]
TAI NEUA alt for TAI NÜA [TDD]
TAI NOIR alt for TAI DAM [BLT]
TAI NÜ alt for TAI NÜA [TDD]
TAI NÜA [TDD] lang, China; also in France, Laos,
   Myanmar, Switzerland, Thailand
TAI NUE alt for TAI NÜA [TDD]
TAI NUEA alt for TAI NÜA [TDD]

TAI NUNG alt for NUNG [NUT]
TAI NYA alt for THAI, NORTHERN [NOD]
TAI PAO [TPO] lang, Laos
TAI PONG dial of TAI NUA [TDD]
TAI ROUGE alt for TAI DAENG [TYR]
TAI SA' alt for ACHANG [ACN]
TAI SEK alt for SAEK [SKB]
TAI SHAN alt for SHAN [SJN]
TAI TAK BAI alt for TAK BAI dial of THAI,
   SOUTHERN [SOU]
TAI THO alt for TÀY [THO]
TAI WANG dial of THAI, NORTHERN [NOD]
TAI YA [CUU] lang, China
TAI YAI alt for SHAN [SJN]
TAI YAY alt for SHAN [SJN]
TAIAK alt for KAPIN [TBX]
TAIAP [GPN] lang, Papua New Guinea
TAIBANO alt for TAIWANO dial of BARASANA [BSN]
TAIBEI MANDARIN dial of CHINESE, MANDARIN
   [CHN]
TAI-CHUNG alt for TAI YA [CUU]
TAI-CUNG alt for TAI YA [CUU]
TAIFASY dial of MALAGASY [MEX]
TAIGI dial of MATOR [MTM]
TAIH-LONG alt for TERESSA [TEF]
TAIHU dial of CHINESE, WU [WUU]
TAIJYAL alt for ATAYAL [TAY]
TAIKAKU dial of MENTAWAI [MWV]
TAIKAT [AOS] lang, Indonesia (Irian Jaya)
TAI-KHAMTI alt for KHAMTI [KHT]
TAI-KHUEN alt for KHÜN [KKH]
TAI-KONG alt for TAI NÜA [TDD]
TAILANGI alt for TELUGU [TCW]
TAI-LE alt for TAI NÜA [TDD]
TAILOI alt for TAI LOI [TLQ]
TAI-MAEN alt for TAI MÈNE [TMP]
TAIMANAMBONDRO dial of MALAGASY [MEX]
TAIMANI dial of AIMAQ [AIQ]
TAIMORO dial of MALAGASY [MEX]
TAIMOURI alt for TAIMURI dial of AIMAQ [AIQ]
TAIMURI dial of AIMAQ [AIQ]
TAINA alt for OWINIGA [OWI]
TAINAE [AGO] lang, Papua New Guinea
TAINAN dial of TAIWANESE SIGN LANGUAGE
   [TSS]
TAINBOUR alt for PALIET dial of DINKA, SOUTH-
   WESTERN [DIK]
TAIN-DAWARE alt for AMBASI dial of BINANDERE
   [BHG]
TAINO [TNQ] lang, Bahamas
TAIOF dial of SAPOSA [SPS]
TAIOR alt for THAYORE [THD]
TAIPEI dial of TAIWANESE SIGN LANGUAGE
   [TSS]
TAIPI dial of NAGA, TASE [NST]
TAIR alt for PANCHPARGANIA [TDB]
TAIRORA [TBG] lang, Papua New Guinea
TAIRUMA [UAR] lang, Papua New Guinea
TAIS [TST] lang, Papua New Guinea
TAIS dial of NAMBU [NCM]
TAISAKA dial of MALAGASY [MEX]

/TAISE alt for /XAISE dial of SHUA [SHG]
TAISHAN alt for SIYI dial of CHINESE, YUE [YUH]
TAITA [DAV] lang, Kenya
TAITUNG alt for SOUTHERN AMIS dial of AMIS [ALV]
TAIVOAN dial of SIRAIYA [FOS]
TAIWAENO alt for TAIWANO dial of BARASANA [BSN]
TAIWAN KEJIA alt for YUE-TAI dial of CHINESE, HAKKA [HAK]
TAIWANESE alt for AMOY dial of CHINESE, MIN NAN [CFR]
TAIWANESE SIGN LANGUAGE [TSS] lang, Taiwan
TAIWANO dial of BARASANA [BSN]
TAIYAL alt for ATAYAL [TAY]
TAIZHOU dial of CHINESE, WU [WUU]
TA'IZZI dial of ARABIC, TAIZZI-ADENI SPOKEN [ACQ]
TAJAG alt for TAMAJAQ [TTQ]
TAJE [PEE] lang, Indonesia (Sulawesi)
TAJIJI ARABIC alt for ARABIC, TAJIKI SPOKEN [ABH]
TAJIK alt for FARSI, EASTERN [PRS]
TAJIK alt for SARIKOLI [SRH]
TAJIKI [PET] lang, Tajikistan; also in Kazakhstan, Kyrgyzstan, Russia (Asia), Turkmenistan, Ukraine, Uzbekistan
TAJIKI alt for DARI dial of FARSI, EASTERN [PRS]
TAJIKI alt for SARIKOLI [SRH]
TAJIKI PERSIAN alt for TAJIKI [PET]
TAJIO [TDJ] lang, Indonesia (Sulawesi)
TAJKAT alt for TAIKAT [AOS]
TAJPURI alt for RAJBANGSI [RJB]
TAJUASOHN [KRU] lang, Liberia
TAJUASON alt for TAJUASOHN [KRU]
TAJUOSO alt for TAJUASOHN [KRU]
TAJUOSOHN alt for TAJUASOHN [KRU]
TAK BAI dial of THAI, SOUTHERN [SOU]
TAK MEO alt for HMONG NJUA [BLU]
TAK MIAO alt for HMONG NJUA [BLU]
TAK MIAO dial of HMONG NJUA [BLU]
TAKA alt for LAMAHOLOT dial of LAMAHOLOT [SLP]
TAKALE alt for KHAM, TAKALE [KJL]
TAKALE dial of KHAM, TAKALE [KJL]
TAKALUBI alt for TABO [KNV]
TAKAM alt for CHAKMA [CCP]
TAKAMA dial of NYAMWEZI [NYZ]
TAKAMANDA alt for DENYA [ANV]
TAKAMANDA dial of DENYA [ANV]
TAKANKAR alt for PARDHI [PCL]
TAKANOON alt for MON [MNW]
TAKAPAN dial of PALUAN [PLZ]
TAKARAYA alt for MAKATAO dial of SIRAIYA [FOS]
TAKARI dial of PARDHI [PCL]
TAKARUBI alt for TABO [KNV]
TAKAT alt for ATAKAT dial of TYAP [KCG]
TAKAWA-BÉNGORO dial of DAY [DAI]
TAKAYA dial of LERE [GNH]

TAKAZZE-SETIIT dial of KUNAMA [KUM]
TAKBANUAO alt for CENTRAL BUNUN dial of BUNUN [BNN]
TAKEBAKHA alt for NORTH BUNUN dial of BUNUN [BNN]
TAKELMA [TKM] lang, USA
TAKESTAN alt for RAMAND dial of TAKESTANI [TKS]
TAKESTANI [TKS] lang, Iran
TAKETODO alt for NORTH BUNUN dial of BUNUN [BNN]
TAKETOMI dial of YAEYAMA [RYS]
TAKEVATAN alt for CENTRAL BUNUN dial of BUNUN [BNN]
TAKIA [TBC] lang, Papua New Guinea
TAKIA alt for PARDHI [PCL]
TAKIBAKHA alt for NORTH BUNUN dial of BUNUN [BNN]
TAKILMA alt for TAKELMA [TKM]
TAKISTANI alt for TAKESTANI [TKS]
TAKI-TAKI alt for SRANAN [SRN]
TAKITUDU alt for NORTH BUNUN dial of BUNUN [BNN]
TAKIVATAN alt for CENTRAL BUNUN dial of BUNUN [BNN]
TAKONAN alt for ATAYAL [TAY]
TAKOPULAN dial of BUNUN [BNN]
TAKPA [TKK] lang, China
TAKPA alt for NUPE CENTRAL dial of NUPE-NUPE TAKO [NUP]
TAKPASYEERI dial of SENOUFO, CEBAARA [SEF]
TAKU alt for LIPO [TKL]
TAKU alt for TAKUU [NHO]
TAKU LISU alt for LIPO [TKL]
TAKUA [TKZ] lang, Viet Nam
TAKUDH alt for WESTERN CANADA GWICH'IN dial of GWICHIN [KUC]
TAKUM dial of JUKUN TAKUM [JBU]
TAKUM dial of KPAN [KPK]
TAKUNA alt for TUCANO [TUO]
TAKUU [NHO] lang, Papua New Guinea
TAKWAMA alt for KWAMA [KMQ]
TAKWANE [TKE] lang, Mozambique
TAL [TAL] lang, Nigeria
TAL alt for TULU [TCY]
TALA [TAK] lang, Nigeria
TALA alt for WEMALE, SOUTH [TLW]
TALA dial of KOHO [KPM]
TALA (WIDALA) alt for MÁGHDÌ [GMD]
TALA INGOD dial of MANOBO, MATIGSALUG [MBT]
TALA'AI dial of MOLIMA [MOX]
TALAE alt for ROTE-TENGAH dial of ROTE [ROT]
TALAHUNDRA dial of KALANGA [KCK]
TALAI [TLE] lang, Kenya
TALA'I dial of SAHU [SUX]
TALAINDJI alt for DHALANDJI [DHL]
TALAING alt for MON [MNW]
TALAMANCA alt for BRIBRI [BZD]
TALANDI alt for DHALANDJI [DHL]
TALANDJI alt for DHALANDJI [DHL]

TALANG dial of KERINCI [KVR]
TALANG PADANG dial of PESISIR, SOUTHERN [PEC]
TALANGEE alt for DHALANDJI [DHL]
TALANGIT dial of ALTAI, SOUTHERN [ALT]
TALANGIT-TOLOS alt for TALANGIT dial of ALTAI, SOUTHERN [ALT]
TALANTANG dial of DUSUN, SUGUT [KZS]
TALASA alt for TALASSA dial of TUMTUM [TBR]
TALASSA dial of TUMTUM [TBR]
TALATUI alt for MIWOK, SOUTHERN SIERRA [SKD]
TALAU alt for TALLAU dial of LOGORIK [LIU]
TALAUD [TLD] lang, Indonesia (Sulawesi)
TALAUT alt for TALAUD [TLD]
TALAVIA alt for DUBLI [DUB]
TALE dial of KARE [KBN]
TALENE alt for TALNI dial of FRAFRA [GUR]
TALENG alt for MON [MNW]
TALENSI alt for TALNI dial of FRAFRA [GUR]
TALESH alt for TALYSH [TLY]
TALI alt for TALE dial of KARE [KBN]
TALIABO alt for TALIABU [TLV]
TALIABU [TLV] lang, Indonesia (Maluku)
TALIAK alt for KAREN, YINTALE [KVY]
TALIANG alt for TALIENG [TDF]
TALIÁSERI alt for TARIANO [TAE]
TALIENG [TDF] lang, Laos
TALIENG alt for TRIENG [STG]
TALIFUGU-RIPANG dial of ISNAG [ISD]
TALINGA-BWISI [TLJ] lang, Uganda; also in DRC
TALISE [TLR] lang, Solomon Islands
TALISE dial of BAETORA [BTR]
TALISE dial of TALISE [TLR]
TALISH alt for TALYSH [TLY]
TALISHI alt for TALYSH [TLY]
TALISI alt for TALISE [TLR]
TALI-XIANGYUN alt for DALI dial of BAI [PIQ]
TALLA alt for KADUGLI dial of KATCHA-KADUGLI-MIRI [KAT]
TALLABWOG alt for TANAPAG [TPV]
TALLAINGA alt for DHALANDJI [DHL]
TALLAU dial of LOGORIK [LIU]
TALLINN dial of ESTONIAN [EST]
TALLULEMBANGNA alt for MAKALE dial of TORAJA-SADAN [SDA]
TALLUMPANUAE alt for CAMPALAGIAN [CML]
TALNI dial of FRAFRA [GUR]
TALO alt for TALLAU dial of LOGORIK [LIU]
TALODDA alt for TALAUD [TLD]
TALODI [TLO] lang, Sudan
TALOINGA alt for DHALANDJI [DHL]
TALOKA alt for DALOKA dial of NGILE [MAS]
TALOKA alt for NGILE [MAS]
TALOKI [TLK] lang, Indonesia (Sulawesi)
TALOMA alt for RUKAI [DRU]
TALONDO' [TLN] lang, Indonesia (Sulawesi)
TALUKI alt for TALOKI [TLK]
TALUR [ILW] lang, Indonesia (Maluku)
TALUTI alt for TELUTI [TLT]
TALUTUI alt for MIWOK, SOUTHERN SIERRA [SKD]

TALYSH [TLY] lang, Azerbaijan; also in Iran
TALYSHI alt for TALYSH [TLY]
TAMA [TEN] lang, Colombia
TAMA [TMA] lang, Chad
TAMA alt for MAJANG [MPE]
TAMA alt for NAMA [NAQ]
TAMA dial of TAMA [TMA]
TAMACHECK alt for TAMAJAQ, TAWALLAMMAT [TTQ]
TAMACHEK alt for TAMAHAQ, TAHAGGART [THV]
TAMACHEK alt for TAMAJAQ, TAWALLAMMAT [TTQ]
TAMACHEK alt for TAMAJEQ, TAYART [THZ]
TAMACHHANG dial of KULUNG [KLE]
TAMAGARAST alt for TANASSFARWAT dial of TAMAJEQ, TAYART [THZ]
TAMAGARIO [TCG] lang, Indonesia (Irian Jaya)
TAMAHA alt for TSAMAI [TSB]
TAMAHAQ, TAHAGGART [THV] lang, Algeria; also in Libya, Niger
TAMAJA alt for SAMAROKENA [TMJ]
TAMAJAQ [TTQ] lang, Niger; also in Mali, Nigeria
TAMAJAQ, TAWALLAMMAT [TTQ] lang, Niger; also in Mali, Nigeria
TAMAJEQ alt for TAMAJAQ [TTQ]
TAMAJEQ, TAYART [THZ] lang, Niger
TAMAKO dial of SANGIR [SAN]
TAMAKWA alt for NAMA [NAQ]
TAMAL alt for TAMIL [TCV]
TAMAL EUY dial of OY [OYB]
TAMALI dial of KHAM, GAMALE [KGJ]
TAMALSAN alt for TAMIL [TCV]
TAMAN [TCL] lang, Myanmar
TAMAN [TMN] lang, Indonesia (Kalimantan)
TAMAN alt for HARUAI [TMD]
TAMAN alt for MALFAXAL [MLX]
TAMAN DAYAK alt for TAMAN [TMN]
TAMANG, EASTERN [TAJ] lang, Nepal; also in Bhutan, India, Myanmar
TAMANG, EASTERN GORKHA [TGE] lang, Nepal
TAMANG, NORTHWESTERN [TMK] lang, Nepal
TAMANG, SOUTHWESTERN [TSF] lang, Nepal
TAMANG, WESTERN [TDG] lang, Nepal
TAMANGHASSET ARABIC alt for ARABIC, ALGERIAN SAHARAN SPOKEN [AAO]
TAMANIK alt for TIMA [TMS]
TAMANRASSET ARABIC alt for ARABIC, ALGERIAN SAHARAN SPOKEN [AAO]
TAMARA alt for PANCHPARGANIA [TDB]
TAMARAW alt for TAMAGARIO [TCG]
TAMARI alt for DITAMMARI [TBZ]
TAMARI alt for PAIWAN [PWN]
TAMARI alt for TAMBERMA [SOF]
TAMARIA alt for PANCHPARGANIA [TDB]
TAMASHEKIN alt for TAMAJAQ [TTQ]
TAMASHEKIN alt for TAMAHAQ, TAHAGGART [THV]
TAMASHEKIN alt for TAMAJAQ, TAWALLAMMAT [TTQ]
TAMASHEKIN alt for TAMASHEQ, KIDAL [TAQ]

TAMASHEQ [TAQ] lang, Mali; also in Algeria, Burkina Faso

TAMASHEQ alt for TAMAHAQ, TAHAGGART [THV]

TAMASHEQ alt for TAMAJAQ [TTQ]

TAMASHEQ alt for TAMAJAQ, TAWALLAMMAT [TTQ]

TAMASHEQ, KIDAL [TAQ] lang, Mali; also in Algeria, Burkina Faso

TAMAYA alt for SAMAROKENA [TMJ]

TAMAZIGHT, CENTRAL ATLAS [TZM] lang, Morocco; also in Algeria, France

TAMAZOLA MIXTECO alt for MIXTECO, TAMAZOLA [VMX]

TAMAZULAPAM MIXE dial of MIXE, QUETZALTEPEC [MVE]

TAMAZUNCHALE NÁHUATL alt for NÁHUATL, HUASTECO OESTE [NHW]

TAMBAGGO alt for TANGBAGO dial of BANDA-NDELE [BFL]

TAMBAHOAKA dial of MALAGASY [MEX]

TAMBANUA alt for TOMBONUWO [TXA]

TAMBANUO alt for TOMBONUWO [TXA]

TAMBANUVA alt for TOMBONUWO [TXA]

TAMBANWAS alt for TOMBONUWO [TXA]

TAMBARO dial of KAMBAATA [KTB]

TAMBAS [TDK] lang, Nigeria

TAMBATU alt for PEMBA dial of SWAHILI [SWA]

TAMBBUOKI alt for TAMBOKI dial of TOLAKI [LBW]

TAMBE'E dial of MORI BAWAH [XMZ]

TAMBENUA alt for TOMBONUWO [TXA]

TAMBÉOPÉ dial of GUARANI, MBYA [GUN]

TAMBERMA [SOF] lang, Togo

TAMBES alt for TAMBAS [TDK]

TAMBO alt for BWAZZA dial of MBULA-BWAZZA [MBU]

TAMBO dial of MWANGA [MWN]

TAMBOKA alt for TUMBUKA [TUW]

TAMBOKI dial of TOLAKI [LBW]

TAMBOLO alt for TANGBAGO dial of BANDA-NDELE [BFL]

TAMBOPATA-GUARAYO alt for ESE EJJA [ESE]

TAMBOTALO [TLS] lang, Vanuatu

TAMBUKA alt for TUMBUKA [TUW]

TAMBUL alt for TAMIL [TCV]

TAMBUNAN alt for DUSUN, TAMBUNAN [KZT]

TAMBUNWAS alt for TOMBONUWO [TXA]

TAME dial of IDI [IDI]

TAMESTAYERT alt for AIR dial of TAMAJEQ, TAYART [THZ]

TAMEZRET dial of DJERBI [JBN]

TAMEZRET dial of NAFUSI [JBN]

TAMHER TIMUR dial of WATUBELA [WAH]

TAMI [TMY] lang, Papua New Guinea

TAMIL [TCV] lang, India; also in Bahrain, Fiji, Germany, Malaysia (Peninsular), Mauritius, Netherlands, Qatar, Réunion, Singapore, South Africa, Sri Lanka, Thailand, UAE, United Kingdom

TAMIL dial of TAMIL [TCV]

TAMILI alt for TAMIL [TCV]

TAMILOUW alt for SEPA [SPB]

TAMISO alt for CENTRAL dial of LIMBA, WEST-CENTRAL [LIA]

TAMKHUNGNYUO dial of NAGA, KONYAK [NBE]

TAMKI [TAX] lang, Chad

TAMLU alt for NAGA, PHOM [NPH]

TAMLU NAGA alt for NAGA, PHOM [NPH]

TAMMA alt for NAMA [NAQ]

TAMNIM alt for CITAK, TAMNIM [TML]

TAMOK alt for TAMA [TMA]

TAMONGOBO alt for TAMA [TMA]

TAMORKHOLE alt for TAPLEJUNGE dial of LIMBU [LIF]

TAMOT alt for TAMA [TMA]

TAMPASOK alt for DUSUN, TEMPASUK [TDU]

TAMPASSUK alt for DUSUN, TEMPASUK [TDU]

TAMPASUK alt for DUSUN, TEMPASUK [TDU]

TAMPELE alt for TAMPULMA [TAM]

TAMPHUAN alt for TAMPUAN [TPU]

TAMPIWI dial of CUIBA [CUI]

TAMPLIMA alt for TAMPULMA [TAM]

TAMPOLE alt for TAMPULMA [TAM]

TAMPOLEM alt for TAMPULMA [TAM]

TAMPOLENSE alt for TAMPULMA [TAM]

TAMPRUSI alt for TAMPULMA [TAM]

TAMPUAN [TPU] lang, Cambodia

TAMPUEN alt for TAMPUAN [TPU]

TAMPULMA [TAM] lang, Ghana

TAMPUON alt for TAMPUAN [TPU]

TAMPUR dial of GAYO [GYO]

TAMSANGMU dial of LEPCHA [LEP]

TAMU KYI alt for GURUNG, WESTERN [GVR]

TAMU KYI dial of GURUNG, EASTERN [GGN]

TAMUDES alt for TOMEDES [TOE]

TAMULTÉ DE LAS SÁBANAS CHONTAL dial of CHONTAL, TABASCO [CHF]

TAMUN alt for CHRAU [CHR]

TAMUN dial of CHRAU [CHR]

TANA dial of SANGPANG [RAV]

TANA dial of VALE [VAE]

TANA AI dial of SIKA [SKI]

TANA RIGHU dial of WEJEWA [WEW]

TANA TOA dial of KONJO, COASTAL [KJC]

TANA TOWA alt for TANA TOA dial of KONJO, COASTAL [KJC]

TANACROSS [TCB] lang, USA

TANAGHAI alt for TANDAI-NGGARIA dial of GHARI [GRI]

TANAH alt for AMIS [ALV]

TANAH dial of MINANGKABAU [MPU]

TANAH KUNU alt for LI'O [LJL]

TANAH MERAH alt for TABLA [TNM]

TANAHMERAH [TCM] lang, Indonesia (Irian Jaya)

TANAINA [TFN] lang, USA

TANALA dial of MALAGASY [MEX]

TAÑALAÑA dial of MALAGASY [MEX]

TANA-LINCHA dial of QUECHUA, YAUYOS [QUX]

TANAN dial of RUKAI [DRU]

TANANA alt for TANANA, LOWER [TAA]

TANANA, LOWER [TAA] lang, USA

TANANA, UPPER [TAU] lang, USA; also in Canada

TANAPAG [TPV] lang, Northern Mariana Islands

TANASLAMT alt for TIMBUKTU dial of TAMASHEQ [TAQ]

TANASLAMT alt for TIMBUKTU dial of TAMASHEQ, KIDAL [TAQ]

TANASSFARWAT dial of TAMAJEQ, TAYART [THZ]

TANAY-PAETE dial of TAGALOG [TGL]

TANCHANGYA alt for TANGCHANGYA [TNV]

TANDA alt for LAMBADI [LMN]

TANDA dial of LOBALA [LOQ]

TANDAI-NGGARIA dial of GHARI [GRI]

TANDANKE alt for BUDIK [TNR]

TANDEK dial of KIMARAGANG [KQR]

TANDIA [TNI] lang, Indonesia (Irian Jaya)

TANDO alt for NDOLO [NDL]

TANDROY alt for ANTANDROY 1 dial of MALAGASY [MEX]

TANDUBAS dial of SAMA, SOUTHERN [SIT]

TANE alt for TANA dial of VALE [VAE]

TANEMA [TNX] lang, Solomon Islands

TANETE alt for BARRU dial of BUGIS [BPR]

TANG alt for SEDANG [SED]

TANG dial of BUMTHANGKHA [KJZ]

TANG dial of LIMBUM [LIM]

TANG dial of NAGA, KONYAK [NBE]

TANGA alt for DOTANGA dial of BALUNDU-BIMA [NGO]

TANGA alt for TANGGA [TGG]

TANGA dial of TANGGA [TGG]

TANGAGO alt for TANGBAGO dial of BANDA-NDELE [BFL]

TANG'ALA dial of KABOLA [KLZ]

TANGALAN alt for KETANGALAN [KAE]

TANGALE [TAN] lang, Nigeria

TANGALTO LELE dial of LELE [LLC]

TANGAMMA dial of WAAMA [WWA]

TANGAO alt for ATAYAL [TAY]

TANGARA' alt for TENGARA dial of BAUKAN [BNB]

TANGARARE alt for GHARI [GRI]

TANGBAGO dial of BANDA-NDELE [BFL]

TANGCHANGYA [TNV] lang, Bangladesh

TANGETTI alt for DYANGADI [DYN]

TANGGA [TGG] lang, Papua New Guinea

TANGGAL alt for DUSUN, SUGUT [KZS]

TANGGARAQ alt for TENGARA dial of BAUKAN [BNB]

TANGGU [TGU] lang, Papua New Guinea

TANGGUM alt for TANGGU [TGU]

TANGI dial of NANDI [NNB]

TANGIER ARABIC dial of ARABIC, MOROCCAN SPOKEN [ARY]

TANGIR alt for CHILASI KOHISTANI dial of SHINA [SCL]

TANGKHUL alt for NAGA, TANGKHUL [NMF]

TANGKOU alt for BUDONG-BUDONG [TGK]

TANGLAGAN dial of AGTA, DUPANINAN [DUO]

TANGLAPUI alt for KULA [TPG]

TANGLAPUI alt for SAWILA [SWT]

TANGLE alt for TANGALE [TAN]

TANGOA [TGP] lang, Vanuatu

TANGSA alt for NAGA, TASE [NST]

TANGSARR dial of RAWANG [RAW]

TANGSHEWI [TNF] lang, Afghanistan

TANGSHURI alt for TANGSHEWI [TNF]

TANGU alt for TANGGU [TGU]

TANGUAT [TBS] lang, Papua New Guinea

TANI alt for MAIANI [TNH]

TANI alt for MIANI [PLA]

TANIMA alt for TANEMA [TNX]

TANIMBAR KEI dial of KEI [KEI]

TANIMBILI [TBE] lang, Solomon Islands

TANIMUCA dial of TANIMUCA-RETUARÃ [TNC]

TANIMUCA-RETUARÃ [TNC] lang, Colombia

TANJIJILI [UJI] lang, Nigeria

TANJONG [TNJ] lang, Malaysia (Sarawak)

TANJONG RAMBUTAN dial of TEMIAR [TMH]

TANJUNG BUNDA alt for LAMAHOLOT dial of LAMAHOLOT [SLP]

TANKARANA dial of MALAGASY [MEX]

TANKAY alt for BEZANOZANO dial of MALAGASY [MEX]

TANKORO alt for CENTRAL KONO dial of KONO [KNO]

TANKRI dial of BOBO MADARE, NORTHERN [BBO]

TANNA, NORTH [TNN] lang, Vanuatu

TANNA, SOUTHWEST [NWI] lang, Vanuatu

TANNEKWE alt for BUGA-KXOE dial of KXOE [XUU]

TANNU-TUVA alt for TUVIN [TUN]

TANORIKI alt for MAEWO, CENTRAL [MWO]

TANORIKI dial of MAEWO, CENTRAL [MWO]

TANOSY dial of MALAGASY [MEX]

TANTI alt for PANCHPARGANIA [TDB]

TANTOYUCA HUASTEC alt for HUASTECO, TANTOYUCA [HUS]

TANZANIAN SIGN LANGUAGE [TZA] lang, Tanzania

TAO dial of WE NORTHERN [WOB]

TAOBA dial of PUMI, NORTHERN [PMI]

TAOFU alt for DAOFU dial of HORPA [ERO]

TA-OI alt for TA'OIH, UPPER [TTH]

TÀ-OI alt for TA'OIH, UPPER [TTH]

TA'OIH, LOWER [TTO] lang, Laos

TA'OIH, UPPER [TTH] lang, Laos; also in USA, Viet Nam

TAOKA alt for TAOKAS [TOA]

TAOKAS [TOA] lang, Taiwan

TAOKAT alt for TAOKAS [TOA]

TAOLENDÉ dial of MOORE [MHM]

TAOPING dial of QIANG, SOUTHERN [QMR]

TAORI alt for DOUTAI [TDS]

TAORI-KAIY alt for KAIY [TCQ]

TAORI-KEI alt for KAIY [TCQ]

TAORI-SO alt for DOUTAI [TDS]

TAOS dial of TIWA, NORTHERN [TAO]

TAO-SUAMATO [TSX] lang, Papua New Guinea

TAO-SUAME alt for TAO-SUAMATO [TSX]

TAOSUG alt for TAUSUG [TSG]

TA-OY alt for TA'OIH, UPPER [TTH]

TAPA alt for NUPE CENTRAL dial of NUPE-NUPE TAKO [NUP]

TAPAANG alt for THAKALI [THS]

TAPACUA alt for XAVÁNTE [XAV]

TAPAH dial of SIKULE [SKH]

TAPANGO alt for PANNEI [PNC]
TAPANGO dial of PANNEI [PNC]
TAPANGU dial of TSOU [TSY]
TAPANTA alt for ABAZA [ABQ]
TAPANTA dial of ABAZA [ABQ]
TAPAYÚNA alt for BEIÇO DE PAU dial of SUYA [SUY]
TAPEBA [TBB] lang, Brazil
TAPESSI alt for TIAPI dial of LANDOMA [LAO]
TAPIETÉ [TAI] lang, Paraguay; also in Argentina, Bolivia
TAPIRAPÉ [TAF] lang, Brazil
TAPIRO alt for EKARI [EKG]
TAPITN dial of MALAYIC DAYAK [XDY]
TAPLEJUNG alt for TAPLEJUNGE dial of LIMBU [LIF]
TAPLEJUNGE dial of LIMBU [LIF]
TAPNANGGI dial of KHAM, SHESHI [KIP]
TAPOSA alt for TOPOSA [TOQ]
TAPOTA BARUGA dial of BARUGA [BBB]
TAPPAH alt for NUPE CENTRAL dial of NUPE-NUPE TAKO [NUP]
TAPPALANG dial of ULUMANDA [ULM]
TAPSHIN [TDL] lang, Nigeria
TAPSHINAWA alt for TAPSHIN [TDL]
TAPUHOE dial of TUAMOTUAN [PMT]
TAR BAGRIMMA alt for BAGIRMI [BMI]
TAR BANALA alt for BANALA dial of KENGA [KYQ]
TAR BANAMA alt for BANAMA dial of KENGA [KYQ]
TAR BARMA alt for BAGIRMI [BMI]
TAR BOLONGO alt for BOLONG dial of BERNDE [BDO]
TAR CENGE alt for CENGE dial of KENGA [KYQ]
TAR GULA alt for GULA [KCM]
TAR MURBA alt for BERNDE [BDO]
TARA dial of KAILI, LEDO [LEW]
TARA BAAKA alt for BAKA [BDH]
TARABA alt for NYA TARIYA dial of LONGUDA [LNU]
TARAHUMARA BAJA [TAC] lang, Mexico
TARAHUMARA CENTRAL [TAR] lang, Mexico
TARAHUMARA NORTE [THH] lang, Mexico
TARAHUMARA SURESTE [TCU] lang, Mexico
TARAHUMARA SUROESTE [TWR] lang, Mexico
TARAIKA dial of AINU [AIN]
TARAKAN dial of TIDONG [TID]
TARAKIRI EAST dial of IZON [IJC]
TARAKIRI WEST dial of IZON [IJC]
TARALI KHAM alt for KAIKE [KZQ]
TARAM dial of SAMBA DAKA [CCG]
TARAMA-MINNA dial of MIYAKO [MVI]
TARANAKI dial of MAORI [MBF]
TARANCHI dial of UYGHUR [UIG]
TARANG alt for BLAGAR [BEU]
TARANGAN BARAT alt for TARANGAN, WEST [TXN]
TARANGAN TIMUR alt for TARANGAN, EAST [TRE]
TARANGAN, EAST [TRE] lang, Indonesia (Maluku)
TARANGAN, WEST [TXN] lang, Indonesia (Maluku)
TARAO alt for NAGA, TARAO [TRO]
TARAON alt for DIGARO [MHU]

TARAOTRONG alt for NAGA, TARAO [TRO]
TARAPECOSI alt for CHIQUITANO [CAX]
TARASAG alt for NUME [TGS]
TARASCAN alt for PURÉPECHA [TSZ]
TARASCAN alt for PURÉPECHA, SIERRA OCCIDENTAL [PUA]
TARASCO alt for PURÉPECHA[TSZ]
TARASCO alt for PURÉPECHA, SIERRA OCCIDENTAL [PUA]
TARATARA dial of TOMBULU [TOM]
TARAU alt for NAGA, TARAO [TRO]
TAREH alt for TRIENG [STG]
TAREMP alt for KATBOL [TMB]
TARENG [TGR] lang, Laos
TARFIA alt for TARPIA dial of TARPIA [SUF]
TARGARI alt for DHARGARI [DHR]
TARI alt for NANDU-TARI [NAA]
TARIA alt for TAWORTA [TBP]
TARIÁNA alt for TARIANO [TAE]
TARIANG alt for TALIENG [TDF]
TARIANG alt for TARENG [TGR]
TARIANO [TAE] lang, Brazil; also in Colombia
TA-RIENG alt for TRIENG [STG]
TARIFIT [RIF] lang, Morocco; also in Algeria, France, Netherlands
TARIMUKI dial of GUJARATI [GJR]
TARÎNA alt for TARIANO [TAE]
TARINO alt for WANECI [WNE]
TARIYA alt for CARA [CFD]
TARIYIT dial of TAGARGRENT [OUA]
TARKARRI alt for DHARGARI [DHR]
TARMA-JUNÍN QUECHUA alt for QUECHUA, NORTH JUNÍN [QJU]
TAROBI alt for VERE dial of NAKANAI [NAK]
TAROF alt for KOKODA [QKW]
TAROF dial of KOKODA [QKW]
TAROK [YER] lang, Nigeria
TAROKO [TRV] lang, Taiwan
TAROM dial of TAKESTANI [TKS]
TAROMI, UPPER [TIB] lang, Iran
TARON alt for RAWANG [RAW]
TARON dial of RAWANG [RAW]
TARPIA [SUF] lang, Indonesia (Irian Jaya)
TARPIA dial of TARPIA [SUF]
TARTAR alt for TATAR [TTR]
TARTU dial of ESTONIAN [EST]
TARU alt for KAREN, LAHTA [KVT]
TARU alt for TAUNGYO [TCO]
TARUKU alt for TAROKO [TRV]
TARULAKHI alt for KAREN, LAHTA [KVT]
TARUMA dial of ARUMA [WAP]
TARUMBAL alt for BAYALI [BJY]
TARUNA dial of SANGIR [SAN]
TARUNGGARE alt for TUNGGARE [TRT]
TARUW alt for DANU dial of BURMESE [BMS]
TARYA alt for PONGU [PON]
TARYA dial of KAMORO [KGQ]
TASADAY dial of MANOBO, COTABATO [MTA]
TASAWAQ [TWQ] lang, Niger
TASE alt for NAGA, TASE [NST]
TASEMBOKO alt for LENGO [LGR]

TASEY alt for NAGA, TASE [NST]
TASHELHAIT alt for TACHELHIT [SHI]
TASHELHAYT alt for TACHELHIT [SHI]
TASHELHIT alt for TACHELHIT [SHI]
TASHILHEET alt for TACHELHIT [SHI]
TASHOM alt for TASHON dial of CHIN, FALAM [HBH]
TASHON dial of CHIN, FALAM [HBH]
TASI alt for HALIA [HLA]
TASI FETO alt for NORTHERN TETUN dial of TETUN [TTM]
TASI MANE alt for SOUTHERN TETUN dial of TETUN [TTM]
TASIKO dial of LEWO [LWW]
TASING alt for CAMPALAGIAN [CML]
TASIRIKI alt for AKEI [TSR]
TASMAN alt for NUKUMANU [NUQ]
TASMATE [TMT] lang, Vanuatu
TASOUSSIT alt for TACHELHIT [SHI]
TAT, MUSLIM [TTT] lang, Azerbaijan; also in Iran
TATA'ER alt for TATAR [TTR]
TATANA [TXX] lang, Malaysia (Sabah)
TATANA' alt for TATANA [TXX]
TATANAQ alt for TATANA [TXX]
TATAR [TTR] lang, Russia (Europe); also in Afghanistan, Azerbaijan, Belarus, China, Estonia, Finland, Georgia, Kazakhstan, Kyrgyzstan, Latvia, Lithuania, Moldova, Tajikistan, Turkey (Europe), Turkmenistan, Ukraine, USA, Uzbekistan
TATAU dial of MANDARA [TBF]
TATE alt for KAKI AE [TBD]
TATI alt for HIETSHWARE [HIE]
TATI alt for KAKI AE [TBD]
TATI alt for TAT, MUSLIM [TTT]
TATI dial of MAITHILI [MKP]
TATI BUSHMAN alt for HIETSHWARE [HIE]
TATOG alt for DATOOGA [TCC]
TATOGA alt for DATOOGA [TCC]
"TATTARE" pejorative alt for TAVRINGER ROMANI [RMU]
TATU alt for TARTU dial of ESTONIAN [EST]
TATURU alt for DATOOGA [TCC]
TATUTAPUYO alt for TATUYO [TAV]
TATUYO [TAV] lang, Colombia
TAU alt for MASEMOLA dial of SOTHO, NORTHERN [SRT]
TAU alt for MENDE [SIM]
TAU alt for TAKUU [NHO]
TAU dial of APOS [APO]
TAU OI alt for TA'OIH, UPPER [TTH]
TAU UBIAN alt for UBIAN dial of SAMA, SOUTHERN [SIT]
TAUADE [TTD] lang, Papua New Guinea
TAUATA alt for TAUADE [TTD]
TAUBUID alt for TAWBUID, EASTERN [BNJ]
TAUCH alt for TREDICI COMMUNI CIMBRIAN dial of CIMBRIAN [CIM]
TAUIRA alt for TAWIRA dial of MISKITO [MIQ]
TAULIL dial of TAULIL-BUTAM [TUH]
TAULIL-BUTAM [TUH] lang, Papua New Guinea
TAULIPANG alt for TAUREPAN dial of PEMON [AOC]

TAULIPANG dial of PEMON [AOC]
TAUMAKO dial of PILENI [PIV]
TAUNA dial of AWA [AWB]
TAUNG dial of SOTHO, SOUTHERN [SSO]
TAUNGTU alt for KAREN, PA'O [BLK]
TAUNGYO [TCO] lang, Myanmar
TAUNITA dial of TEOP [TIO]
TAUP dial of JAGOI [SNE]
TAUPOTA [TPA] lang, Papua New Guinea
TAURA alt for TAKAYA dial of LERE [GNH]
TAURAP alt for BURMESO [BZU]
TAUREPAN alt for TAULIPANG dial of PEMON [AOC]
TAUREPAN dial of PEMON [AOC]
TAUSE [TAD] lang, Indonesia (Irian Jaya)
TAUSE dial of TAUSE [TAD]
TAUSHIRO [TRR] lang, Peru
TAUSOG alt for TAUSUG [TSG]
TAUSUG [TSG] lang, Philippines; also in Indonesia (Kalimantan), Malaysia (Sabah)
TAUU alt for TAKUU [NHO]
TAUYA [TYA] lang, Papua New Guinea
TAVA alt for RABAH dial of HRE [HRE]
TAVALA alt for TAWALA [TBO]
TAVALONG-VATAAN dial of AMIS [ALV]
TAVARA alt for TAWALA dial of TAWALA [TBO]
TAVARA alt for TAWALA [TBO]
TAVAST alt for HÄME dial of FINNISH [FIN]
TAVDIN alt for SOUTHERN VOGUL dial of MANSI [MNS]
TAVEAK dial of AMBRYM, SOUTHEAST [TVK]
TAVETA [TVS] lang, Kenya; also in Tanzania
TAVGI SAMOYED alt for NGANASAN [NIO]
TAVHA-TSINDI dial of VENDA [VEN]
TAVHATSINDI dial of VENDA [VEN]
TAVIAK alt for TAVEAK dial of AMBRYM, SOUTH-EAST [TVK]
TAVOLA alt for VAGHUA [TVA]
TAVORA alt for TAWALA [TBO]
TAVOY dial of KAREN, PWO EASTERN [KJP]
TAVOYA alt for TAUNGYO [TCO]
TAVOYAN [TVN] lang, Myanmar
TAVOYAN alt for TAUNGYO [TCO]
TAVRINGER ROMANI [RMU] lang, Sweden; also in Norway
TAVUKI alt for KADAVU dial of FIJIAN [FJI]
TAVULA alt for VAGHUA [TVA]
TAVYTERA alt for PAI TAVYTERA [PTA]
TAW SUG alt for TAUSUG [TSG]
TAWAELIA alt for SEDOA [TVW]
TAWAHKA dial of SUMO TAWAHKA [SUM]
TAWAILI-SINDUE alt for RAI dial of KAILI, LEDO [LEW]
TAWAKONI dial of WICHITA [WIC]
TAWALA [TBO] lang, Papua New Guinea
TAWALA alt for TAWARA [TWL]
TAWALA dial of TAWALA [TBO]
TAWALLAMMAT TAN ATARAM dial of TAMAJAQ [TTQ]
TAWALLAMMAT TAN ATARAM dial of TAMAJAQ, TAWALLAMMAT [TTQ]

TAWALLAMMAT TAN DANNAG dial of TAMAJAQ, TAWALLAMMAT [TTQ]
TAWALLAMMET TAN DANNAG dial of TAMAJAQ [TTQ]
TAWAN dial of TAGAL MURUT [MVV]
TAWANA dial of TSWANA [TSW]
TAWANG alt for MONKIT dial of MOINBA [MOB]
TAWANXTE dial of NAMBIKUARA, NORTHERN [MBG]
TAWARA [TWL] lang, Mozambique
TAWARA alt for TAWALA [TBO]
TAWARAFA dial of KAHUA [AGW]
TAWARI dial of GBAGYI [GBR]
TAWAU MURUT alt for KALABAKAN [KVE]
TAWAU MURUT alt for SERUDUNG MURUT [SRK]
TAWBUID, EASTERN [BNJ] lang, Philippines
TAWBUID, WESTERN [TWB] lang, Philippines
TAWE-TAVOY alt for TAUNGYO [TCO]
TAWINI alt for TALIFUGU-RIPANG dial of ISNAG [ISD]
TAWIRA dial of MISKITO [MIQ]
TAWIT alt for ITAWIT [ITV]
TAWORTA [TBP] lang, Indonesia (Irian Jaya)
TAWORTA-AERO alt for TAWORTA [TBP]
TAWOYAN [TWY] lang, Indonesia (Kalimantan)
TAWOYAN DAYAK alt for TAWOYAN [TWY]
TAWR alt for CHIN, TAWR [TCP]
TAXMAINITE dial of NAMBIKUARA, NORTHERN [MBG]
TAXWENSITE dial of NAMBIKUARA, NORTHERN [MBG]
TÀY [THO] lang, Viet Nam; also in France, USA
TAY alt for NUNG [NUT]
TAY alt for TAI [TAW]
TAY BOI [TAS] lang, Viet Nam
TAY BOY alt for TAY BOI [TAS]
"TAY HAT" pejorative alt for O'DU [TYH]
TAY HAY alt for KHANG [KJM]
TAY JO [TYJ] lang, Viet Nam
TAY KHANG [TNU] lang, Laos
TÁY KHAO alt for TAI DÓN [TWH]
TAY MÈNÈ alt for TAI MÈNE [TMP]
TAY MUEAI alt for TAI MUOI dial of TAI DAM [BLT]
TÁY MU'Ò'I dial of TAI DAM [BLT]
TÀY MUÒNG alt for TAI HANG TONG [THC]
TÀY NÙNG alt for NUNG [NUT]
TAY PONG alt for PONG dial of HUNG [HNU]
TAY TAC [TYT] lang, Viet Nam
TÁY THANH alt for TAI MAN THANH [TMM]
TAYABA alt for TAYARI dial of NATENI [NTM]
TAYABAS dial of TAGALOG [TGL]
TAYAL alt for ATAYAL [TAY]
TAYAN dial of KOMBAI [KGU]
TAYANDO dial of KEI [KEI]
TAYARI dial of NATENI [NTM]
TAYART alt for AIR dial of TAMAJEQ, TAYART [THZ]
TAYATO dial of ENGA [ENQ]
TÁY-DAM alt for TAI DAM [BLT]
TAYEK alt for KAPIN [TBX]
TAYERT alt for AIR dial of TAMAJEQ, TAYART [THZ]

TAYHAY alt for KHANG [KJM]
TAYING alt for DIGARO [MHU]
TAY-JO alt for TAY JO [TYJ]
TÁY-MÔC-CHÂU alt for TAI DAENG [TYR]
TAYO [CKS] lang, New Caledonia
TAZ dial of SELKUP [SAK]
TAZE alt for KREYE [XRE]
TAZNATIT [GRR] lang, Algeria
TAZOV-BAISHYAN alt for TAZ dial of SELKUP [SAK]
TBILISI dial of ARMENIAN [ARM]
TBOLI [TBL] lang, Philippines
T'BOLI alt for TBOLI [TBL]
TCAITI alt for TSHIDI-KHWE dial of SHUA [SHG]
TCENGUI alt for TSAANGI [TSA]
TCHAAKALAAGA alt for NGADJUNMAYA [NJU]
TCHADE alt for GUDE [GDE]
TCHAGA alt for ENGA [ENQ]
TCHAGIN dial of KWANG [KVI]
TCHAKIN alt for TCHAGIN dial of KWANG [KVI]
TCHAMAN alt for EBRIÉ [EBR]
TCHAMBA alt for AKASELEM [AKS]
TCHAMBA alt for SAMBA DAKA [CCG]
TCHAMBULI alt for CHAMBRI [CAN]
TCHANG alt for FOREKE DSCHANG dial of YEMBA [BAN]
TCHANG alt for YEMBA [BAN]
TCHANGUI alt for TSAANGI [TSA]
TCHEDE alt for TSUVAN [TSH]
TCHEKE alt for GUDE [GDE]
TCHERE alt for GIZIGA, NORTH [GIS]
TCHERE-AÏBA alt for TCHIRE dial of KIMRE [KQP]
TCHEVI alt for SHARWA [SWQ]
TCHIDE dial of JINA [JIA]
TCHIEN dial of KRAHN, EASTERN [KQO]
TCHIKAI alt for BURARRA [BVR]
TCHINGALEE alt for DJINGILI [JIG]
TCHINI dial of NIELLIM [NIE]
TCHIRE dial of KIMRE [KQP]
TCHITEM alt for BAGA SITEMU [BSP]
TCHOKOSSI alt for ANUFO [CKO]
TCHORNY alt for KARAKALPAK [KAC]
TCHOUVOK alt for CUVOK [CUV]
TE alt for GHOMÁLÁ' SOUTH dial of GHOMALA [BBJ]
TE MAWO alt for SKOU [SKV]
TE MOTU dial of SANTA CRUZ [STC]
TEA MOUNTAIN YAO alt for LAKKIA [LBC]
TEANU [TKW] lang, Solomon Islands
TEBAKANG alt for BUKAR SADONG [SDO]
TEBELE alt for NDEBELE [NDF]
TEBERA dial of FOLOPA [PPO]
TEBILIAN alt for TIBETAN [TIC]
TEBILUNG [TGB] lang, Malaysia (Sabah)
TEBOU alt for TEDAGA [TUQ]
TEBOU alt for TUBU dial of TEDAGA [TUQ]
TEBU alt for DAZAGA [DAK]
TEBU alt for TEDAGA [TUQ]
TEBU alt for TUBU dial of TEDAGA [TUQ]
TECHING alt for DE-JING dial of ZHUANG, SOUTHERN [CCY]

TECHU alt for CHAOZHOU dial of CHINESE, MIN
NAN [CFR]
TECO alt for EMERILLON [EME]
TECO alt for TECTITECO [TTC]
TECTITÁN MAM alt for TECTITECO [TTC]
TECTITECO [TTC] lang, Guatemala; also in Mexico
TEDA alt for TEDAGA [TUQ]
TEDA dial of TEDAGA [TUQ]
TEDAGA [TUQ] lang, Chad; also in Libya, Niger,
Nigeria
TEDI alt for NINGGERUM [NXR]
TEDIM alt for CHIN, TEDIM [CTD]
TEDONG alt for TIDONG [TID]
TEDURAY alt for TIRURAY [TIY]
TEE dial of GOLA [GOL]
TEEL alt for MONTOL [MTL]
TÈÈN [LOR] lang, Côte d'Ivoire; also in Burkina Faso
TEENAN alt for TINANI [LBF]
TEERE dial of DOYAYO [DOW]
TEFARO [TFO] lang, Indonesia (Irian Jaya)
TEFASY alt for TAIFASY dial of MALAGASY [MEX]
TEGAL dial of JAVANESE [JAN]
TEGALI [RAS] lang, Sudan
TEGALI dial of TEGALI [RAS]
TEGBO alt for TAFI [TCD]
TEGE alt for TEE dial of GOLA [GOL]
TEGE alt for TEGEKALI dial of TEKE, NORTHERN
[TEG]
TEGE alt for TEKE, NORTHERN [TEG]
TEGEKALI dial of TEKE, NORTHERN [TEG]
TEGELE alt for TEGALI [RAS]
TEGEM alt for JEBEL TEKEIM dial of LAFOFA [LAF]
TEGEM alt for LAFOFA [LAF]
TEGESIE alt for TÈÈN [LOR]
TEGHE alt for TEKE, NORTHERN [TEG]
TEGINA alt for CINDA dial of CINDA-REGI-TIYAL
[KAU]
TÉGUÉ alt for BOZO, TIÉYAXO [BOZ]
TÉGUÉ alt for TEGEKALI dial of TEKE, NORTHERN
[TEG]
TEHID alt for TEHIT [KPS]
TEHIT [KPS] lang, Indonesia (Irian Jaya)
TEHIT JIT dial of TEHIT [KPS]
TEHNU alt for KATCHAL dial of NICOBARESE,
CENTRAL [NCB]
TEHORU alt for TELUTI [TLT]
TEHORU alt for WEST TELUTI dial of TELUTI [TLT]
TEHRI [THB] lang, India
TEHRI dial of GARHWALI [GBM]
TEHUA alt for WEST TELUTI dial of TELUTI [TLT]
TEHUACÁN NÁHUATL alt for NÁHUATL, PUEBLA
SURESTE [NHS]
TEHUELCHE [TEH] lang, Argentina
TEIMURI alt for TAIMURI dial of AIMAQ [AIQ]
TEIMURI dial of AIMAQ [AIQ]
TEIMURTASH alt for TEIMURI dial of AIMAQ
[AIQ]
TEIS-UMM-DANAB alt for TESE [KEG]
TEITA alt for TAITA [DAV]
TEITA MIXTECO alt for MIXTECO, SAN JUAN
TEITA [QMC]

TEIXEIRA PINTO alt for BOK dial of MANDJAK
[MFV]
TEIXEIRA PINTO dial of MANDJAK [MFV]
TEJALÁPAM ZAPOTECO alt for ZAPOTECO,
TEJALAPAN [ZTT]
TEJALAPAN ZAPOTEC alt for ZAPOTECO,
TEJALAPAN [ZTT]
TEJUCA alt for TUYUCA [TUE]
TEKE alt for TEKE, NORTHERN [TEG]
TEKE dial of TURKMEN [TCK]
TEKE, CENTRAL [TEC] lang, Congo; also in DRC
TEKE, EASTERN [TEK] lang, DRC; also in Congo
TEKE, NORTHEASTERN [NGZ] lang, Congo
TEKE, NORTHERN [TEG] lang, Congo; also in
Gabon
TEKE, SOUTH CENTRAL [IFM] lang, Congo
TEKE, SOUTHERN [KKW] lang, Congo
TEKE, WESTERN [TEZ] lang, Congo; also in Gabon
TEKEIM alt for JEBEL TEKEIM dial of LAFOFA
[LAF]
TEKEL alt for LEHALI [TQL]
TEKELA alt for SWATI [SWZ]
TEKELE alt for TEGALI [RAS]
TEKEZA alt for SWATI [SWZ]
TEKKE alt for TEKE dial of TURKMEN [TCK]
TEKUTAMESO alt for KWERBA [KWE]
TEL KEPE dial of CHALDEAN NEO-ARAMAIC [CLD]
TELA'A alt for TELA-MASBUAR [TVM]
TELA-MASBUAR [TVM] lang, Indonesia (Maluku)
TELANGANA dial of TELUGU [TCW]
TELANGIRE alt for TELUGU [TCW]
TELE alt for TANA dial of VALE [VAE]
TELEEFOOL alt for TELEFOL [TLF]
TELEFOL [TLF] lang, Papua New Guinea
TELEFOL dial of TELEFOL [TLF]
TELEFOLMIN alt for TELEFOL [TLF]
TELEFOMIN alt for TELEFOL [TLF]
TELEGU alt for TELUGU [TCW]
TELEI alt for BUIN [BUO]
TELEKI alt for TSUVAN [TSH]
TELEKOSON alt for TOLOKOSON dial of TAGAL
MURUT [MVV]
TELENGUT alt for ALTAI, NORTHERN [ATV]
TELEUT alt for ALTAI, NORTHERN [ATV]
TELGI alt for TELUGU [TCW]
TELI alt for CHHINTANG [CTN]
TELI dial of BHOJPURI [BHJ]
TELIPOK alt for MENGGATAL dial of DUSUN,
CENTRAL [DTP]
TELIRE dial of CABECAR [CJP]
TELOM dial of SEMAI [SEA]
TELUGU [TCW] lang, India; also in Bahrain, Fiji,
Malaysia, Mauritius, Singapore, UAE
TELUGU dial of TELUGU [TCW]
TELUGU GONDI alt for GONDI, SOUTHERN [GGO]
TELUGU LAMANI alt for ANDHRA PRADESH
LAMANI dial of LAMBADI [LMN]
TELUK LILI dial of TUGUTIL [TUJ]
TELUKBETUNG dial of PESISIR, SOUTHERN [PEC]
TELUTI [TLT] lang, Indonesia (Maluku)
TEM [KDH] lang, Togo; also in Benin, Ghana

TEMA alt for TEME [TDO]
TEMACIN dial of TAGARGRENT [OUA]
TEMACINE TAMAZIGHT [TJO] lang, Algeria
TEMAGERI dial of KANURI, CENTRAL [KPH]
TEMAINIAN alt for TEMEIN [TEQ]
TEMALACAYUCA POPOLOCA alt for POPOLOCA,
SAN LUÍS TEMALACAYUCA [PPS]
TEMANE alt for JAPANESE SIGN LANGUAGE
[JSL]
TEMASCAL MAZATEC alt for MAZATECO,
SOYALTEPEC [VMP]
TEMASCALTEPEC AZTEC alt for NÁHUATL,
TEMASCALTEPEC [NHV]
TEMBA alt for TEM [KDH]
TEMBAGLA dial of MELPA [MED]
TEMBAGLO alt for TEMBALO dial of MBO-UNG
[MUX]
TEMBALO alt for MBO-UNG [MUX]
TEMBALO dial of MBO-UNG [MUX]
TEMBE alt for TEM [KDH]
TEMBÉ [TEM] lang, Brazil
TEMBE' dial of TEMIAR [TMH]
TEMBE OF GURUPI dial of GUAJAJARA [GUB]
TEMBEKUÁ dial of KAIWA [KGK]
TEMBENUA alt for TOMBONUWO [TXA]
TEMBI alt for TEMBE' dial of TEMIAR [TMH]
TEMBIMBE-KATBOL alt for KATBOL [TMB]
TEMBIS alt for TAMBAS [TDK]
TEMBO [TBT] lang, DRC
TEMBO [TMV] lang, DRC
TEMBO alt for TAMBO dial of MWANGA [MWN]
TEMBO dial of TEMBO [TBT]
TEMBUNG dial of JAVANESE [JAN]
TEME [TDO] lang, Nigeria
TEMEIN [TEQ] lang, Sudan
TEMEN alt for THEMNE [TEJ]
TEMER alt for TEMIAR [TMH]
TEMI [SOZ] lang, Tanzania
TEMIAR [TMH] lang, Malaysia (Peninsular)
TEMILA dial of DAYAK, LAND [DYK]
TEMIRGOJ alt for BEZHEDUKH dial of ADYGHE
[ADY]
TEMKI alt for TAMKI [TAX]
TEMNE alt for THEMNE [TEJ]
TEMOGUN alt for TIMUGON MURUT [TIH]
TEMOQ [TMO] lang, Malaysia (Peninsular)
TEMORAL alt for PANCHPARGANIA [TDB]
TEMORO alt for TAIMORO dial of MALAGASY [MEX]
TEMPASOK alt for DUSUN, TEMPASUK [TDU]
TEMUAN [TMW] lang, Malaysia (Peninsular)
TEMUAN dial of TEMUAN [TMW]
TEN alt for ATEN [GAN]
T'EN [TCT] lang, China
TEN KURUMBA alt for KURUMBA, JENNU [QKJ]
TENA alt for MAKASAR [MSR]
TEN'A alt for KOYUKON [KOY]
TENAE alt for HRUSO [HRU]
TENANGO alt for TZELTAL, OXCHUC [TZH]
TENANGO AZTEC alt for NÁHUATL, TENANGO
[NHI]
TENCH alt for TENIS [TNS]

TENDA alt for BUDIK [TNR]
TENDA alt for WAMEI [COU]
TENDA BASARI alt for BASARI [BSC]
TENDANKE alt for BUDIK [TNR]
TENDE alt for KURIA [KUJ]
TENDE alt for TIENE [TII]
TENDYDIE alt for NAGA, ANGAMI [NJM]
TENEJAPA alt for TZELTAL, OXCHUC [TZH]
TENENGA dial of MAHOU [MXX]
TENERE dial of SENOUFO, CEBAARA [SEF]
TENET alt for TENNET [TEX]
TENETEHAR alt for GUAJAJÁRA [GUB]
TENETEHÁRA alt for GUAJAJÁRA [GUB]
TENG alt for KHANG [KJM]
TENG dial of KISSI, NORTHERN [KQS]
TENGA dial of SOGA [SOG]
TENGAH-TENGAH dial of TULEHU [TLU]
TENGARA dial of BAUKAN [BNB]
TENGGANU alt for KETIAR KRAU dial of JAH HUT
[JAH]
TENGGARAQ alt for TENGARA dial of BAUKAN
[BNB]
TENGGARONG alt for MALAY, TENGGARONG
KUTAI [VKT]
TENGGARONG KUTAI dial of MALAY,
TENGGARONG KUTAI [VKT]
TENGGER [TES] lang, Indonesia (Java and Bali)
TENGGERESE alt for TENGGER [TES]
TENGIA dial of KISI, SOUTHERN [KSS]
TENGIMA dial of NAGA, ANGAMI [NJM]
TENGO alt for MAMVU [MDI]
TENGOH dial of JAGOI [SNE]
TENGRELA alt for KANDERE dial of SENOUFO,
CEBAARA [SEF]
TENGU alt for TELUGU [TCW]
TENH alt for KHMU [KJG]
TENHAREM alt for TENHARIM [PAH]
TENHARIM [PAH] lang, Brazil
TENHARIN alt for TENHARIM [PAH]
TÉNHÉ alt for TÈÈN [LOR]
TENINO [WAR] lang, USA
TENIS [TNS] lang, Papua New Guinea
TENNET [TEX] lang, Sudan
TENOM MURUT alt for TIMUGON MURUT [TIH]
TENSINO alt for CENTRAL ARAGONESE dial of
ARAGONESE [AXX]
TENT GYPSY alt for ROMANO-SERBIAN [RSB]
TENTI alt for SENSI [SNI]
TENYER dial of KARABORO, WESTERN [KZA]
TENYIDIE dial of NAGA, ANGAMI [NJM]
TENYIDYE alt for TENYIDIE dial of NAGA, ANGAMI
[NJM]
TEO alt for BALI dial of TEKE, EASTERN [TEK]
TEO alt for TYOO dial of TEKE, CENTRAL [TEC]
TEOCHEW alt for CHAOCHOW dial of CHINESE,
MIN NAN [CFR]
TEOCHEW dial of CHINESE, MIN NAN [CFR]
TEOCHOW alt for CHAOCHOW dial of
CHINESE, MIN NAN [CFR]
TEOCHOW alt for CHAOZHOU dial of CHINESE,
MIN NAN [CFR]

TEOCOCUILCO DE MARCOS PREZ ZAPOTECO alt for ZAPOTECO, YARENI [ZAE]

TEOP [TIO] lang, Papua New Guinea

TEOR [TEV] lang, Indonesia (Maluku)

TEOTITLÁN DEL VALLE ZAPOTECO dial of ZAPOTECO, SAN JUAN GUELAVIA [ZAB]

TEOTITLÁN MIXTECO alt for MIXTECO, COATZOSPAN [MIZ]

TEPANTEPEC alt for SAN MATEO TEPANTEPEC dial of MIXTECO, PENOLES [MIL]

TEPECANO [TEP] lang, Mexico

TEPEHUA, HUEHUETLA [TEE] lang, Mexico

TEPEHUA, PISA FLORES [TPP] lang, Mexico

TEPEHUA, TLACHICHILCO [TPT] lang, Mexico

TEPEHUÁN NORTE [NTP] lang, Mexico

TEPEHUÁN SURESTE [STP] lang, Mexico

TEPEHUÁN SUROESTE [TLA] lang, Mexico

TEPERA alt for TABLA [TNM]

TEPERA dial of TABLA [TNM]

TEPES alt for SOO [TEU]

TEPETH alt for SOO [TEU]

TEPO dial of KRUMEN, TEPO [TED]

TEQ alt for BATEK TEQ dial of BATEK [BTQ]

TEQEL alt for LEHALI [TQL]

TEQUENICA alt for YÁMANA [YAG]

TEQUISTLATEC alt for CHONTAL DE OAXACA, SIERRA [CHD]

TEQURACA alt for ABISHIRA [ASH]

"TER LAPPISH" pejorative alt for SAAMI, TER [LPT]

TER. TRU dial of TOUSSIAN, NORTHERN [TSP]

TERA [TER] lang, Nigeria

TERA alt for CARA [CFD]

TERAKAN alt for TARAKAN dial of TIDONG [TID]

TERANGI alt for TELUGU [TCW]

TERAWIA alt for BIDEYAT [BIH]

TEREBU [TRB] lang, Papua New Guinea

TEREGO dial of LUGBARA [LUG]

TEREI alt for BUIN [BUO]

TEREKEME dial of AZERBAIJANI, NORTH [AZE]

TEREMA alt for TIRMA dial of SURI [SUQ]

TERÊNA [TEA] lang, Brazil

TERENO alt for TERÊNA [TEA]

TEREPU alt for TEREBU [TRB]

TERESSA [TEF] lang, India

TEREWENG [TWG] lang, Indonesia (Nusa Tenggara)

TERI alt for SAGALLA [TGA]

TERI dial of SAGALLA [TGA]

TERIBE [TFR] lang, Panama; also in Costa Rica

TERIK dial of KALENJIN [KLN]

TERI-KALWASCH alt for KIMAAMA [KIG]

TERIYA alt for CARA [CFD]

TERKI alt for TSUVAN [TSH]

TERMANU alt for ROTE-TENGAH dial of ROTE [ROT]

TERMANU-TALAE-KEKA alt for ROTE-TENGAH dial of ROTE [ROT]

TERNA alt for TIRMA dial of SURI [SUQ]

TERNATE [TFT] lang, Indonesia (Maluku)

TERNATE MALAY alt for MALAY, NORTH MOLUCCAN [MAX]

TERNATEÑO [TMG] lang, Indonesia (Maluku)

TERNATEÑO dial of CHAVACANO [CBK]

TERNATEÑO CHAVACANO alt for TERNATEÑO dial of CHAVACANO [CBK]

TERNATENYO alt for TERNATEÑO [TMG]

TERRABA alt for TERIBE [TFR]

TERRI alt for CARA [CFD]

TERUTONG alt for MARGU [MHG]

TESAKA alt for TAISAKA dial of MALAGASY [MEX]

TESE [KEG] lang, Sudan

TESHENAWA [TWC] lang, Nigeria

TESHENNA alt for TISHENA dial of MEEN [MYM]

TESHINA alt for TISHENA dial of MEEN [MYM]

TESO [TEO] lang, Uganda; also in Kenya

TESSINIAN alt for TICINESE dial of LOMBARD [LMO]

TESU dial of ARUM-TESU [AAB]

TESUQUE dial of TEWA [TEW]

TETA alt for NYUNGWE [NYU]

TETE alt for DETI [DET]

TETE alt for NYUNGWE [NYU]

TÊTE DE BOULE alt for ATIKAMEKW [TET]

TETEKA alt for NYONG [MUO]

TETELA [TEL] lang, DRC

TETELCINGO AZTEC alt for NÁHUATL, TETELCINGO [NHG]

TETETE [TEB] lang, Ecuador

TETI alt for DETI [DET]

TETO alt for TETUN [TTM]

TETON alt for LAKOTA [LKT]

TETTUM alt for TETUN [TTM]

TETU alt for TETUN [TTM]

TETUM alt for TETUN [TTM]

TETUM DILI alt for TETUM PRASA [TDT]

TETUM PRAÇA alt for TETUM PRASA [TDT]

TETUM PRASA [TDT] lang, Timor Lorosae

TETUN [TTM] lang, Indonesia (Nusa Tenggara); also in Timor Lorosae

TETUN BELU alt for TETUN [TTM]

TETUN LOOS alt for EASTERN TETUN dial of TETUN [TTM]

TETUN LOS alt for EASTERN TETUN dial of TETUN [TTM]

TETUN TERIK alt for NORTHERN TETUN dial of TETUN [TTM]

TETUN TERIK dial of TETUN [TTM]

TETUN THERIK alt for NORTHERN TETUN dial of TETUN [TTM]

TETUN THERIK alt for TETUN TERIK dial of TETUN [TTM]

TETUNG alt for TETUN [TTM]

TEUEIA alt for MACUSHI [MBC]

TEÜI dial of KAIWA [KGK]

TEULA alt for LIANA-SETI [STE]

TE'UN [TVE] lang, Indonesia (Maluku)

TEUSO alt for IK [IKX]

TEUTH alt for IK [IKX]

TEVE alt for TEWE [TWX]

TEVORANG alt for TAIVOAN dial of SIRAIYA [FOS]

TEW alt for TUMBUKA [TUW]

TEWA [TEW] lang, USA
TEWA [TWE] lang, Indonesia (Nusa Tenggara)
TEWATEWA dial of MISIMA-PANEATI [MPX]
TEWE [TWX] lang, Mozambique
TEWELLEMET alt for TAMAJAQ, TAWALLAMMAT [TTQ]
TEWEYA alt for MACUSHI [MBC]
TEXAS dial of AFRO-SEMINOLE CREOLE [AFS]
TEXMELUCAN ZAPOTEC alt for ZAPOTECO, TEXMELUCAN [ZPZ]
TEZ dial of OROCH [OAC]
TEZOATLÁN dial of MIXTECO, TEZOATLAN [MXB]
TEZOATLÁN DE SEGURA Y LUNA MIXTECO alt for MIXTECO, TEZOATLÁN [MXB]
TFUEA dial of TSOU [TSY]
TGHUADE alt for DGHWEDE [DGH]
THA [THY] lang, Nigeria
THAADOU KUKI alt for CHIN, THADO [TCZ]
THAAYORE alt for THAYORE [THD]
THABANGGI dial of KHAM, TAKALE [KJL]
THABINE-ROKA-NARENG alt for DZWABO dial of SOTHO, NORTHERN [SRT]
THADO-PAO alt for CHIN, THADO [TCZ]
THADOU alt for CHIN, THADO [TCZ]
THADO-UBIPHEI alt for CHIN, THADO [TCZ]
THAE alt for THE [THX]
THAGICHU dial of THARAKA [THA]
THAI [THJ] lang, Thailand; also in Midway Islands, Singapore, UAE, USA
THAI DANG alt for TAI DAENG [TYR]
THAI DEN alt for TAI DAM [BLT]
THÁI DEN alt for TAI DAM [BLT]
THAI DO alt for TAI DAENG [TYR]
THAI ISLAM alt for MALAY, PATTANI [MFA]
THAI LU alt for LÜ [KHB]
THAI MALAY dial of THAI, SOUTHERN [SOU]
THAI SIGN LANGUAGE [TSQ] lang, Thailand
THAI SONG alt for SONG [SOA]
THÁI TRÁNG alt for TAI DÓN [TWH]
THAI YAI alt for SHAN [SJN]
THAI YAY alt for SHAN [SJN]
THAI, NORTHEASTERN [TTS] lang, Thailand
THAI, NORTHERN [NOD] lang, Thailand; also in Laos
THAI, SOUTHERN [SOU] lang, Thailand
THAIKLANG alt for THAI [THJ]
THAKALI [THS] lang, Nepal
THAKALI alt for TUKCHE dial of THAKALI [THS]
THAKARA alt for DURUWA [PCI]
THAKARI alt for THAKURI dial of KONKANI [KNK]
THAKRI alt for THAKURI dial of KONKANI [KNK]
THAKSYA alt for THAKALI [THS]
THAKUA alt for THAKURI dial of KONKANI [KNK]
THAKURA alt for THAKURI dial of KONKANI [KNK]
THAKURI dial of KONKANI [KNK]
THAKWANI alt for TAKWANE [TKE]
THAL dial of KALAMI [GWC]
THALANYJI alt for DHALANDJI [DHL]
THALI dial of SARAIKI [SKR]
THALU alt for TULU [TCY]
THALWEPWE alt for KAREN, PAKU [KPP]

THAMI [THF] lang, Nepal; also in India
THAMINYI alt for DAIR [DRB]
THANG dial of MUONG [MTQ]
THANGAL alt for NAGA, KHOIRAO [NKI]
THANGATTI alt for DYANGADI [DYN]
THANGATTY alt for DYANGADI [DYN]
THANGGAL alt for NAGA, KHOIRAO [NKI]
THANGKHULM alt for NAGA, TANGKHUL [NMF]
THANGMI alt for THAMI [THF]
THANGNGEN dial of CHIN, THADO [TCZ]
THANY alt for ALIAP dial of DINKA, SOUTH CENTRAL [DIB]
THANY BUR alt for PALIET dial of DINKA, SOUTH-WESTERN [DIK]
THAO [SSF] lang, Taiwan
THARADARI BHIL dial of KOLI, WADIYARA [KXP]
THARADARI KOLI dial of KOLI, WADIYARA [KXP]
THARAKA [THA] lang, Kenya
THARAKA dial of THARAKA [THA]
THARELI dial of SINDHI [SND]
THARGARI alt for DHARGARI [DHR]
THARI dial of SINDHI [SND]
THARRGARI alt for DHARGARI [DHR]
THARU dial of AWADHI [AWD]
THARU dial of BHOJPURI [BHJ]
THARU, CHITWANIA [THE] lang, Nepal; also in India
THARU, DANGAURA [THL] lang, Nepal; also in India
THARU, DEOKHURI [THG] lang, Nepal
THARU, KATHORIYA [TKT] lang, Nepal; also in India
THARU, KOCHILA [THQ] lang, Nepal
THARU, MAHOTARI [THN] lang, Nepal
THARU, RANA [THR] lang, Nepal; also in India
THARUMBAL alt for BAYALI [BJY]
THAT alt for KADO [KDV]
THAVUNG alt for AHEU [THM]
THAYETMO alt for THAYETMYO dial of CHIN, ASHO [CSH]
THAYETMYO dial of CHIN, ASHO [CSH]
THAYORE [THD] lang, Australia
THAYORRE alt for THAYORE [THD]
THAYPAN [TYP] lang, Australia
THE [THX] lang, Laos
THE CANT alt for SHELTA [STH]
THE LANGUAGE OF THE DEAF alt for AMERICAN SIGN LANGUAGE [ASE]
THEBARSHAD alt for SUNAM [SSK]
THEBARSKAD alt for JANGSHUNG [JNA]
THEBARSKAD alt for KINNAURI, CHITKULI [CIK]
THEBARSKAD alt for SHUMCHO [SCU]
THEBOR alt for JANGSHUNG [JNA]
THEBOR alt for SHUMCHO [SCU]
THEBOR alt for SUNAM [SSK]
THEBÖR SKADD alt for JANGSHUNG [JNA]
THEBÖR SKADD alt for SHUMCHO [SCU]
THEBÖR SKADD alt for SUNAM [SSK]
THEITHEI alt for NATHEMBO [NTE]
THEMBU dial of XHOSA [XOS]

THEMNE [TEJ] lang, Sierra Leone
THEN alt for T'EN [TCT]
THENG alt for KHANG [KJM]
THENG alt for KHMU [KJG]
THEPHALABORWA alt for PHALABORWA dial of
    SOTHO, NORTHERN [SRT]
THET alt for KADO [KDV]
THIANG dial of NUER [NUS]
THIE alt for TII dial of ROTE [ROT]
THIL alt for GELAO [KKF]
THIMBUKUSHU alt for MBUKUSHU [MHW]
THIMPHU-PUNAKHA alt for WANG-THE dial of
    DZONGKHA [DZO]
THIMUKUSHU alt for MBUKUSHU [MHW]
THIN alt for MAL [MLF]
THIO alt for XARAGURE [ARG]
THIRO alt for TIRA [TIR]
THLANTLANG alt for KLANGKLANG dial of CHIN,
    HAKA [CNH]
THLAPING dial of TSWANA [TSW]
THLARO dial of TSWANA [TSW]
THLINGET alt for TLINGIT [TLI]
"THÔ" pejorative alt for TÀY [THO]
THO [TOU] lang, Viet Nam
THOGNAATH dial of NUER [NUS]
THOI dial of DINKA, NORTHEASTERN [DIP]
THOK CIENG REEL alt for REEL [ATU]
THOK NATH alt for THOGNAATH dial of NUER
    [NUS]
THOLONG LO alt for THULUNG [TDH]
THOMPSON [THP] lang, Canada
THON alt for TUIC dial of DINKA, SOUTHWESTERN
    [DIK]
THONGA alt for TSONGA [TSO]
THOORGA alt for DHURGA [DHU]
THRACEAN ARVANITIKA dial of ALBANIAN,
    ARVANITIKA [AAT]
THRO alt for SÔ [SSS]
THU alt for GELAO [KKF]
THU LAO alt for TÀY [THO]
THUANGA alt for YUAGA [NUA]
THUANGA dial of YUAGA [NUA]
THUDAM BHOTE [THW] lang, Nepal
THUKUMI dial of NAGA, SANGTAM [NSA]
THULE ESKIMO alt for POLAR ESKIMO dial of
    INUKTITUT, GREENLANDIC [ESG]
THULISHI alt for TULISHI [TEY]
THULU alt for TULU [TCY]
THULU LUWA alt for THULUNG [TDH]
THULULOA alt for THULUNG [TDH]
THULUNG [TDH] lang, Nepal; also in India
THULUNG JEMU alt for THULUNG [TDH]
THULUNG LA alt for THULUNG [TDH]
THULUNGE RAI alt for THULUNG [TDH]
THUNDAI-KANZA alt for KUNJA [PEP]
THUNG CHAN PRAY alt for PHAI [PRT]
THURAWAL [TBH] lang, Australia
THURI [THU] lang, Sudan
TI alt for TII dial of ROTE [ROT]
TI dial of MUNGAKA [MHK]
TIAALA dial of GULA IRO [GLJ]

TIADJE alt for TOMINI [TXM]
TIAGBA alt for AIZI, TIAGBAMRIN [AHI]
TIAL dial of TULEHU [TLU]
TIALE [MNL] lang, Vanuatu
TIALO alt for TOMINI [TXM]
TIANG [TBJ] lang, Papua New Guinea
TIAPI alt for LANDOMA [LAO]
TIAPI dial of LANDOMA [LAO]
TIARA alt for GEDAGED [GDD]
TIATINAGUA alt for ESE EJJA [ESE]
TIAU dial of CITAK [TXT]
TIAYAI dial of KAMANG [WOI]
TIBA alt for GAA [TTB]
TIBAS SKAD alt for KINNAURI [KFK]
TIBATE alt for TIBETAN [TIC]
TIBBU alt for DAZAGA [DAK]
TIBBU alt for TEDAGA [TUQ]
TIBBU alt for TUBU dial of TEDAGA [TUQ]
TIBEA [NGY] lang, Cameroon
TIBETAN [TIC] lang, China; also in Bhutan, India,
    Nepal, Norway, Switzerland, Taiwan, USA
TIBIA dial of BIATAH [BTH]
TIBOLA alt for TSOU [TSY]
TIBOLAH alt for TSOU [TSY]
TIBOLAK alt for TSOU [TSY]
TIBOLAL alt for TSOU [TSY]
TIBOLI alt for TBOLI [TBL]
TICHERONG alt for TICHURONG [TCN]
TICHURONG [TCN] lang, Nepal
TICINEES alt for TICINESE dial of LOMBARD [LMO]
TICINES alt for TICINESE dial of LOMBARD [LMO]
TICINESE dial of LOMBARD [LMO]
TICINO alt for TICINESE dial of LOMBARD [LMO]
TICUNA [TCA] lang, Peru; also in Brazil, Colombia
TID alt for MIDOB [MEI]
TID alt for TIRMA dial of SURI [SUQ]
TIDAÁ MIXTEC alt for MIXTECO, TIDAÁ [MTX]
TIDDA alt for MIDOB [MEI]
TIDDIM alt for CHIN, TEDIM [CTD]
TIDI alt for NINGGERUM [NXR]
TIDIKELT dial of TIDIKELT TAMAZIGHT [TIA]
TIDIKELT TAMAZIGHT [TIA] lang, Algeria
TID-N-AAL alt for MIDOB [MEI]
TIDOENG alt for SEMBAKUNG MURUT [SMA]
TIDOENG alt for TIDONG [TID]
TIDONG [TID] lang, Indonesia (Kalimantan); also
    in Malaysia (Sabah)
TIDONG alt for SEMBAKUNG MURUT [SMA]
TIDORE [TVO] lang, Indonesia (Maluku)
TIDUNG alt for KALABAKAN [KVE]
TIDUNG alt for KUIJAU [DKR]
TIDUNG alt for SEMBAKUNG MURUT [SMA]
TIDUNG alt for SERUDUNG MURUT [SRK]
TIDUNG alt for TIDONG [TID]
TIDUNG dial of TIDONG [TID]
TIÉ alt for BOZO, TIÈMA CIÈWÈ [BOO]
TIE alt for BOZO, TIÉYAXO [BOZ]
TIE dial of KABA NA [KWV]
TIEBAARA alt for SENOUFO, CEBAARA [SEF]
TIÉFO [TIQ] lang, Burkina Faso
TIÈMA CIÈWÈ alt for BOZO, TIÈMA CIÈWÈ [BOO]

TIEMAXO alt for BOZO, TIÉYAXO [BOZ]
TIENE [TII] lang, DRC
TIENGA alt for KYENGA [TYE]
TIENPO dial of GREBO, NORTHERN [GRB]
TIÉYAKHO alt for BOZO, TIÉYAXO [BOZ]
TIEYAXO alt for BOZO, TIÉYAXO [BOZ]
TIFAL [TIF] lang, Papua New Guinea
TIFAL dial of TIFAL [TIF]
TIFALMIN alt for TIFAL [TIF]
TIFLIS alt for TBILISI dial of ARMENIAN [ARM]
TIGAK [TGC] lang, Papua New Guinea
TIGALU dial of TAMIL [TCV]
TIGANIA dial of MERU [MER]
TIGE dial of TIKAR [TIK]
TIGEMAXO alt for BOZO, TIÉYAXO [BOZ]
TIGIM alt for MBEMBE, TIGON [NZA]
TIGLU dial of GODIE [GOD]
TIGON alt for MBEMBE, TIGON [NZA]
TIGONG alt for MBEMBE, TIGON [NZA]
TIGRANAKERT dial of ARMENIAN [ARM]
TIGRAY alt for TIGRIGNA [TGN]
TIGRAY dial of KUNAMA [KUM]
TIGRÉ [TIE] lang, Eritrea; also in Sudan
TIGRE QUECHUA alt for QUICHUA, PASTAZA,
    NORTHERN [QLB]
TIGRE QUECHUA dial of QUICHUA, PASTAZA,
    NORTHERN [QLB]
TIGRERO dial of GUAHIBO [GUH]
TIGRIGNA [TGN] lang, Ethiopia; also in Eritrea,
    Israel
TIGRINYA alt for TIGRIGNA [TGN]
TIGRIS CLUSTER dial of ARABIC,
    MESOPOTAMIAN SPOKEN [ACM]
TIGUÉMAKHO alt for BOZO, TIÉYAXO [BOZ]
TIGUM alt for MBEMBE, TIGON [NZA]
TIGUN alt for MBEMBE, TIGON [NZA]
TIGWA dial of MANOBO, MATIGSALUG [MBT]
TIHINA alt for DIHINA dial of GAWWADA [GWD]
TIHINTE alt for DIHINA dial of GAWWADA [GWD]
TIHISHIT alt for TAGDAL [TDA]
TIHORU alt for TELUTI [TLT]
TII dial of ROTE [ROT]
TIIKA alt for TIKA dial of KUNAMA [KUM]
TIITAAL dial of GULA IRO [GLJ]
TIJALTEPEC MIXTEC alt for MIXTECO,
    TIJALTEPEC [QMJ]
TIJANJI alt for JANJI [JNI]
TIKA dial of KUNAMA [KUM]
TIKALI alt for TIKAR [TIK]
TIKAR [TIK] lang, Cameroon
TIKAR DE BANKIM alt for TWUMWU dial of TIKAR
    [TIK]
TIKAR DE NGAMBE alt for TIGE dial of TIKAR [TIK]
TIKAR-EAST alt for TIKAR [TIK]
TIKARI alt for TIKAR [TIK]
TIKHAK dial of NAGA, TASE [NST]
TIKHIR dial of NAGA, YIMCHUNGRU [YIM]
TIKI alt for TOCENGA dial of TUKI [BAG]
TIKK alt for SAMBA DAKA [CCG]
TIKOPIA [TKP] lang, Solomon Islands
TIKULU alt for BAJUNI dial of SWAHILI [SWA]

TIKUN alt for MBEMBE, TIGON [NZA]
TIKUNA alt for TICUNA [TCA]
TIKURAMI alt for KURAMA [KRH]
T'IK'UU alt for BAJUNI dial of SWAHILI [SWA]
TIL dial of KWAKUM [KWU]
TILAMUTA dial of GORONTALO [GRL]
TILAU-ILAU alt for DUSUN, SUGUT [KZS]
TILI PTE dial of KAMWE [HIG]
TILING alt for TILUNG [TIJ]
TILLAMOOK [TIL] lang, USA
TILLING alt for TILUNG [TIJ]
TILÓ alt for TACANECO [MTZ]
TILQUIAPAN ZAPOTEC alt for ZAPOTECO,
    TILQUIAPAN [ZTS]
TILU alt for TULU [TCY]
TILUNG [TIJ] lang, Nepal
TILUNG BLAMA alt for TILUNG [TIJ]
TIM alt for TEM [KDH]
TIMA [TMS] lang, Sudan
TIMAP alt for AMO [AMO]
TIMBAARO alt for TIMBARO dial of KAMBAATA
    [KTB]
TIMBARA alt for TIMBARO dial of KAMBAATA [KTB]
TIMBARO dial of KAMBAATA [KTB]
TIMBE [TIM] lang, Papua New Guinea
TIMBIRA dial of KRIKATI-TIMBIRA [XRI]
TIMBOU alt for YANGA dial of MOORE [MHM]
TIMBUKA alt for TUMBUKA [TUW]
TIMBUKTU alt for TAMASHEQ [TAQ]
TIMBUKTU alt for TAMASHEQ, KIDAL [TAQ]
TIMBUKTU dial of TAMASHEQ [TAQ]
TIMBUKTU dial of TAMASHEQ, KIDAL [TAQ]
TIMBUKTU SONGHOY alt for SONGHAY, KOYRA
    CHIINI [KHQ]
TIMBUNKI dial of MARING [MBW]
TIMENE alt for THEMNE [TEJ]
TIMIGAN alt for TIMUGON MURUT [TIH]
TIMIGUN alt for TIMUGON MURUT [TIH]
TIMIKU alt for NORTHERN SEEKU dial of SEEKU
    [SOS]
TIMINGIR dial of ARAPESH, BUMBITA [AON]
TIMMANNEE alt for THEMNE [TEJ]
TIMNE alt for THEMNE [TEJ]
TIMOGON alt for TIMUGON MURUT [TIH]
TIMOGUN alt for TIMUGON MURUT [TIH]
TIMOL alt for ATONI [TMR]
TIMONIKO alt for INETA dial of BUDU [BUU]
TIMOR alt for ATONI [TMR]
TIMOR AMARASI alt for AMARASI [AAZ]
TIMOR CREOLE PORTUGUESE alt for PIDGIN,
    TIMOR [TVY]
TIMOR DAWAN alt for ATONI [TMR]
TIMOREESCH alt for ATONI [TMR]
TIMOREEZEN alt for ATONI [TMR]
TIMORESE alt for ATONI [TMR]
TIMORINI alt for DANI, WESTERN [DNW]
TIMPUTS alt for TINPUTZ [TPZ]
TIMU alt for PIDIE dial of ACEH [ATJ]
TIMU alt for TEM [KDH]
TIMU dial of SABU [HVN]
TIMUGON alt for TIMUGON MURUT [TIH]

533

TIMUGON dial of TIMUGON MURUT [TIH]
TIMUGON MURUT [TIH] lang, Malaysia (Sabah)
TIMUR alt for BATAK SIMALUNGUN [BTS]
TIMUR dial of ORYA [URY]
TIMURI alt for TAIMURI dial of AIMAQ [AIQ]
TIN alt for MAL [MLF]
T'IN alt for MAL [MLF]
TINA alt for SAMBAL, TINA [SNA]
TINAGAS dial of DUSUN, SUGUT [KZS]
TINAM alt for HATAM [HAD]
TINAM dial of HATAM [HAD]
TINAN LAHULI alt for TINANI [LBF]
TINANI [LBF] lang, India; also in China
TINATA TUNA alt for KUANUA [KSD]
TINDAKON alt for KADAZAN, LABUK-
    KINABATANGAN [DTB]
TINDAL alt for DUSUN, TEMPASUK [TDU]
TINDAL alt for KUIJAU [DKR]
TINDAL alt for TINDI [TIN]
TINDAL dial of DUSUN, CENTRAL [DTP]
TINDI [TIN] lang, Russia (Europe)
"TINDIGA" pejorative alt for HADZA [HTS]
TINDIN alt for TINDI [TIN]
TINGAL [TIG] lang, Sudan
TINGALUN alt for SEMBAKUNG MURUT [SMA]
TINGANESES alt for CHOLON [CHT]
TINGARA alt for TENGARA dial of BAUKAN [BNB]
TINGGALAN alt for SEMBAKUNG MURUT [SMA]
TINGGALUM alt for SEMBAKUNG MURUT [SMA]
TINGGUIAN alt for ITNEG, BINONGAN [ITB]
TINGKALA alt for TIKAR [TIK]
TINGUI alt for TINGUI-BOTO [TGV]
TINGUIAN alt for ITNEG, BINONGAN [ITB]
TINGUI-BOTO [TGV] lang, Brazil
TINGZHOU dial of CHINESE, HAKKA [HAK]
TINITIANES alt for BATAK [BTK]
TINJAR SIBOP dial of KENYAH, SEBOB [SIB]
TINNERS ROMANI dial of ROMANI, BALKAN [RMN]
TINOC KALANGOYA alt for KALLAHAN, TINOC
    [TNE]
TINOMBO alt for LAUJE [LAW]
TINPUTZ [TPZ] lang, Papua New Guinea
TINRIN alt for TIRI [CIR]
TINTA dial of IPULO [ASS]
TINTEKIYA dial of KOCH [KDQ]
TIO alt for BALI dial of TEKE, EASTERN [TEK]
TIO alt for TYOO dial of TEKE, CENTRAL [TEC]
TIOFFO dial of ABE [ABA]
TIOKOSSI alt for ANUFO [CKO]
TIONG alt for KENSIU [KNS]
TIOO alt for TYOO dial of TEKE, CENTRAL [TEC]
TIO'OR alt for TEOR [TEV]
TIPÁI alt for KUMIÁI [DIH]
TIPAI' alt for KUMIÁI [DIH]
TIPÉI alt for KUMIÁI [DIH]
TIPININI dial of IPILI [IPI]
TIPLE dial of YALE, KOSAREK [KKL]
TIPPERA [TPE] lang, Bangladesh
TIPPERA-BENGALI alt for TIPPERA [TPE]
TIPPERAH alt for TIPPERA [TPE]
TIPPURAH alt for TIPPERA [TPE]

TIPRA alt for RIANG dial of KOK BOROK [TRP]
TIPRA alt for TIPPERA [TPE]
TIPUN alt for PYUMA [PYU]
TIPURA alt for CHIN, FALAM [HBH]
TIPURA alt for KOK BOROK [TRP]
TIPURA alt for TIPPERA [TPE]
TIRA [TIR] lang, Sudan
TIRA DAGIG alt for TIRA EL AKHDAR dial of TIRA
    [TIR]
TIRA EL AKHDAR dial of TIRA [TIR]
TIRA LUMUM dial of TIRA [TIR]
TIRA MANDI dial of TIRA [TIR]
TIRAHI [TRA] lang, Afghanistan
TIRAHUTIA alt for MAITHILI [MKP]
TIRAN alt for TIDONG [TID]
TIRHARI dial of BAGHELI [BFY]
TIRHARI dial of BUNDELI [BNS]
TIRHARI dial of KANAUJI [BJJ]
TIRHUTI alt for MAITHILI [MKP]
TIRHUTIA alt for MAITHILI [MKP]
TIRI [CIR] lang, New Caledonia
TIRIBI alt for TERIBE [TFR]
TIRIFIE alt for TARIFIT [RIF]
TIRIKI dial of IDAKHO-ISUKHA-TIRIKI [IDA]
TIRIMA alt for TIRMA dial of SURI [SUQ]
TIRIO [TCR] lang, Papua New Guinea
TIRIÓ alt for TRIÓ [TRI]
TIRIYA dial of DURUWA [PCI]
TIRIYÓ alt for TRIÓ [TRI]
TIRMA dial of SURI [SUQ]
TIRMAGA alt for TIRMA dial of SURI [SUQ]
TIRMAGI alt for TIRMA dial of SURI [SUQ]
TIRO alt for KONJO, COASTAL [KJC]
TIRO alt for TIRA [TIR]
TIROLEAN alt for GERMAN, HUTTERITE [GEH]
TIRON alt for TAWBUID, EASTERN [BNJ]
TIRONES alt for TIDONG [TID]
TIROON alt for TIDONG [TID]
TIRRENIC alt for NAPOLETANO dial of
    NAPOLETANO-CALABRESE [NPL]
TIRRIBI alt for TERIBE [TFR]
TIRUMBAE alt for TAPIETÉ [TAI]
TIRURAI alt for TIRURAY [TIY]
TIRURAY [TIY] lang, Philippines
TISHENA dial of MEEN [MYM]
TISMAN dial of REREP [PGK]
TISQOPA dial of CHALDEAN NEO-ARAMAIC [CLD]
TISVEL alt for KATBOL [TMB]
TIT dial of TIDIKELT TAMAZIGHT [TIA]
TITA [TDQ] lang, Nigeria
TITAN [TTV] lang, Papua New Guinea
TITIN BAJAYGUL alt for ASHURUVERI dial of
    ASHKUN [ASK]
TITO alt for TITAN [TTV]
TITU alt for PANGA dial of MONGO-NKUNDU [MOM]
TIU CHIU alt for CHAOCHOW dial of CHINESE,
    MIN NAN [CFR]
TIUCHIU alt for CHAOCHOW dial of CHINESE,
    MIN NAN [CFR]
TIUCHIU alt for CHAOZHOU dial of CHINESE, MIN
    NAN [CFR]

TIV [TIV] lang, Nigeria; also in Cameroon
TIVAGHAT alt for VAGHAT dial of VAGHAT-YA-BIJIM-LEGERI [BIJ]
TIWA, NORTHERN [TAO] lang, USA
TIWA, SOUTHERN [TIX] lang, USA
TIWAL alt for MASAKIN TUWAL dial of NGILE [MAS]
TIWI [TIW] lang, Australia
TIWIRKUM alt for MOGHAMO dial of META [MGO]
TIWORO dial of MUNA [MYN]
TIYA alt for YA dial of VAGHAT-YA-BIJIM-LEGERI [BIJ]
TIYAL dial of CINDA-REGI-TIYAL [KAU]
TIYAR alt for TIYAL dial of CINDA-REGI-TIYAL [KAU]
TIYE alt for TIE dial of KABA NA [KWV]
TJABAKAI-THANDJI alt for DYAABUGAY [DYY]
TJABOGAIJANJI alt for DYAABUGAY [DYY]
TJAM alt for CHAM, EASTERN [CJM]
TJAM alt for CHAM, WESTERN [CJA]
TJAMORO alt for CHAMORRO [CJD]
TJAMPALAGIAN alt for CAMPALAGIAN [CML]
TJANKIR alt for DYAABUGAY [DYY]
TJANKUN alt for DYAABUGAY [DYY]
TJAPUKAI alt for DYAABUGAY [DYY]
TJAPUNKANDJI alt for DYAABUGAY [DYY]
TJARU alt for JARU [DDJ]
TJENDANA alt for SENDANA dial of MANDAR [MHN]
TJERAIT alt for TYARAITY [WOA]
TJIMBA alt for ZEMBA [DHM]
TJIMUNDO alt for ANGORAM [AOG]
TJINGILU alt for DJINGILI [JIG]
TJIREBON alt for CIREBON dial of JAVANESE [JAN]
TJITAK alt for CITAK [TXT]
TJITJAK alt for CITAK [TXT]
TJOKWAI alt for WÁRA [TCI]
TJUAVE alt for CHUAVE [CJV]
TJUDUN alt for TULU dial of BOHUAI [RAK]
TJUNBUNDJI alt for DYAABUGAY [DYY]
TJURA alt for NUGUNU [NNV]
TJURRURU [TJU] lang, Australia
TLA WILANO alt for UNAMI [DEL]
TLACOAPA dial of TLAPANECO, MALINALTEPEC [TLL]
TLACOLULITA ZAPOTEC alt for ZAPOTECO, TLACOLULITA [ZPK]
TLAHAPING dial of TSWANA [TSW]
TLAHUICA alt for MATLATZINCA, ATZINGO [OCU]
TLAHURA alt for MATLATZINCA, ATZINGO [OCU]
TLALCOYALCO POPOLOCA alt for POPOLOCA, SAN MARCOS TLALCOYALCO [PLS]
TLAPANECO, ACATEPEC [TPX] lang, Mexico
TLAPANECO, AZOYÚ [TPC] lang, Mexico
TLAPANECO, MALINALTEPEC [TLL] lang, Mexico
TLAPI alt for THLAPING dial of TSWANA [TSW]
TLAPI alt for TLAHAPING dial of TSWANA [TSW]
TLATSOP alt for KLATSOP dial of CHINOOK [CHH]
TLAU dial of LUSHAI [LSH]
TLAXCALA-PUEBLA NÁHUATL alt for NÁHUATL CENTRAL [NHN]

TLAZOYALTEPEC alt for SANTIAGO TLAZOYALTEPEC dial of MIXTECO, PENOLES [MIL]
TLETLE alt for DETI [DET]
TLHAPING dial of TSWANA [TSW]
TLHARO dial of TSWANA [TSW]
TLINGIT [TLI] lang, USA; also in Canada
TLINKIT alt for TLINGIT [TLI]
TLISI dial of BAGVALAL [KVA]
TLOKEANG alt for KATO [KTW]
TLOKOA alt for TLOKWA dial of SOTHO, NORTHERN [SRT]
TLOKWA dial of SOTHO, NORTHERN [SRT]
TLOKWA dial of TSWANA [TSW]
TLONGSAI dial of CHIN, MARA [MRH]
TLOSAI-SIAHA alt for TLONGSAI dial of CHIN, MARA [MRH]
TLOUE alt for //XEGWI [XEG]
TLOUTLE alt for //XEGWI [XEG]
TLYADALY dial of BEZHTA [KAP]
TLYANUB alt for SOUTHERN AKHVAKH dial of AKHVAKH [AKV]
TMAGOURT dial of SENED [SDS]
TMAGURT alt for TMAGOURT dial of SENED [SDS]
TMOOY alt for KHMU [KJG]
T'O alt for TÀY [THO]
TO [TOZ] lang, Cameroon; also in CAR
TO LA alt for TALA dial of KOHO [KPM]
TO PAMOSEAN alt for PANASUAN [PSN]
TO PANASEAN alt for PANASUAN [PSN]
TO RETE alt for TORETE dial of BUNGKU [BKZ]
TO RONGKONG alt for TAE' [ROB]
TOA alt for TOMA [TOD]
TOA dial of PARAUJANO [PBG]
TO'ABAITA [MLU] lang, Solomon Islands
TO'ABAITA alt for TO'ABAITA [MLU]
TOAK dial of AMBRYM, SOUTHEAST [TVK]
TOAKU LWA alt for THULUNG [TDH]
TOALA alt for TOALA' [TLZ]
TOALA' [TLZ] lang, Indonesia (Sulawesi)
TOALA' dial of TOALA [TLZ]
TOALA-PALILI alt for TOALA' [TLZ]
TOALE alt for TOMA [TOD]
TOALI alt for TOMA [TOD]
TO'AMBAITA alt for TO'ABAITA [MLU]
TOARIPI [TPI] lang, Papua New Guinea
TOARIPI dial of TOARIPI [TPI]
TOBA [TOB] lang, Argentina; also in Bolivia, Paraguay
TOBA alt for EMOK [EMO]
TOBA dial of YEMSA [JNJ]
TOBA BATAK alt for BATAK TOBA [BBC]
TOBA OF PARAGUAY alt for TOBA-MASKOY [TMF]
TOBA QOM alt for TOBA [TOB]
TOBADA' alt for BADA [BHZ]
TOBA-EMOK alt for EMOK [EMO]
TOBAGONIAN CREOLE ENGLISH [TGH] lang, Trinidad and Tobago
TOBAGONIAN DIALECT alt for TOBAGONIAN CREOLE ENGLISH [TGH]
TOBAKU dial of UMA [PPK]

TOBALO alt for TOBAU dial of PAMONA [BCX]
TOBA-MASKOY [TMF] lang, Paraguay
TOBANGA [TNG] lang, Chad
TOBANGA dial of TOBANGA [TNG]
TOBAO alt for TOBAU dial of PAMONA [BCX]
TOBA-PILAGÁ dial of PILAGA [PLG]
TOBA-QOM alt for TOBA [TOB]
TOBARU alt for TABARU [TBY]
TOBATI [TTI] lang, Indonesia (Irian Jaya)
TOBAU dial of PAMONA [BCX]
TO-BEDAWIE alt for BEDAWI [BEI]
TOBELO [TLB] lang, Indonesia (Maluku)
TOBELO dial of TOBELO [TLB]
TOBERELDA alt for UMM GABRALLA dial of MORO
    [MOR]
TOBI alt for TOBIAN [TOX]
TOBIAN [TOX] lang, Palau
TOBILANG alt for TEBILUNG [TGB]
TOBILUNG alt for TEBILUNG [TGB]
TOBO [TBV] lang, Papua New Guinea
TOBOTE alt for NTCHAM [BUD]
TO-BUAN dial of JARAI [JRA]
TOBUNYUO dial of NAGA, KONYAK [NBE]
TOBWADIC alt for TOBATI [TTI]
TOCENGA dial of TUKI [BAG]
TOCHIPO alt for CEP dial of ACIPA, WESTERN
    [AWC]
TOCHO [TAZ] lang, Sudan
TOCOD alt for TUKUDEDE [TKD]
TOD alt for STOD BHOTI [SBU]
TODA [TCX] lang, India
TODA alt for TAROKO [TRV]
TODA alt for TEDAGA [TUQ]
TODAGA alt for TEDAGA [TUQ]
TODELA alt for TUXÁ [TUD]
TODGA alt for TEDAGA [TUQ]
TODI alt for KAIY [TCQ]
TODI alt for TODA [TCX]
TODII alt for DENG dial of GOLA [GOL]
TOD-KAD alt for STOD BHOTI [SBU]
TODOS SANTOS ALMOLONGA POPOLOCA dial
    of POPOLOCA, SANTA INES AHUATEMPAN
    [PCA]
TODRÁ alt for TODRAH [TDR]
TODRAH [TDR] lang, Viet Nam
TODZHIN alt for NORTHEASTERN TUVIN dial of
    TUVIN [TUN]
TOENDE dial of KUSAAL [KUS]
TOF alt for KULERE [KUL]
TOF dial of KULERE [KUL]
TOFA alt for KARAGAS [KIM]
TOFA alt for TUVIN [TUN]
TOFALAR alt for KARAGAS [KIM]
TOFAMNA alt for TOFANMA [TLG]
TOFANMA [TLG] lang, Indonesia (Irian Jaya)
TOFIN alt for TOFIN-GBE [TFI]
TOFIN-GBE [TFI] lang, Benin
TOFOKE alt for POKE [POF]
TOGA [LHT] lang, Vanuatu
TOGBO dial of BANDA, TOGBO-VARA [TOR]
TOGHWEDE alt for DGHWEDE [DGH]

TOGOLE alt for TEGALI [RAS]
TOGOY alt for TOGOYO [TGY]
TOGOYO [TGY] lang, Sudan
TOHGBOH alt for TOGBO dial of BANDA, TOGBO-
    VARA [TOR]
TOHONO O'ODAM dial of OODHAM [PAP]
TOI alt for DIDINGA [DID]
TOICHO alt for TOCHO [TAZ]
TOI-OI alt for TA'OIH, UPPER [TTH]
TOISAN alt for SIYI dial of CHINESE, YUE [YUH]
TOISHANESE dial of CHINESE, YUE [YUH]
TOJOLABAL [TOJ] lang, Mexico
TOK PISIN [PDG] lang, Papua New Guinea
TOKA dial of TONGA [TOI]
TOKAIMALO alt for NORTHEAST VITI LEVU dial
    of FIJIAN [FJI]
TOKAMA alt for TOKANO [ZUH]
TOKANO [ZUH] lang, Papua New Guinea
TOKAT alt for EWDOKIA dial of ARMENIAN [ARM]
TOKELAU alt for TOKELAUAN [TOK]
TOKELAUAN [TOK] lang, Tokelau; also in American
    Samoa, New Zealand, USA
TOKHA alt for TUVIN [TUN]
TOKILOR alt for TOUCOULEUR dial of PULAAR
    [FUC]
TOKITA dial of KARATA [KPT]
TOKITIN alt for TOKITA dial of KARATA [KPT]
TOKKARU alt for DOGRI-KANGRI [DOJ]
TOKKO dial of EVENKI [EVN]
TOKMO-UPPER LENA dial of EVENKI [EVN]
TOKODÉ alt for TUKUDEDE [TKD]
TOKODEDE alt for TUKUDEDE [TKD]
TOKONDINDI dial of PAMONA [BCX]
TOKOTU'A dial of MORONENE [MQN]
TOKUNI [TKO] lang, Indonesia (Irian Jaya)
TOKU-NO-SHIMA [TKN] lang, Japan
TOKUNU alt for NASIKWABW dial of MISIMA-
    PANEATI [MPX]
TOKWA alt for TLOKWA dial of SOTHO, NORTHERN
    [SRT]
TOKWASA alt for WÁRA [TCI]
TOL [JIC] lang, Honduras
TOLA dial of LAMJA-DENGSA-TOLA [LDH]
TOLAI alt for KUANUA [KSD]
TOLAKI [LBW] lang, Indonesia (Sulawesi)
TOLAMLEINYUA dial of NAGA, KONYAK [NBE]
TOLANGAN alt for TELUGU [TCW]
TOLDIL dial of GOLA [GOL]
TOLÉ alt for EASTERN GUAYMÍ dial of NGÄBERE
    [GYM]
TOLEE' dial of UMA [PPK]
TOLI alt for CENTRAL KONO dial of KONO [KNO]
TOLI alt for TOLI-GBE [TLH]
TOLI-GBE [TLH] lang, Benin
TOLILIKO alt for TOLIWIKU dial of PAGU [PGU]
TOLITAI alt for DOUTAI [TDS]
TOLITOLI [TXE] lang, Indonesia (Sulawesi)
TOLIWIKU dial of PAGU [PGU]
TOLO alt for TALISE [TLR]
TOLO dial of BAHNAR [BDQ]
TOLO dial of TALISE [TLR]

TOLOKIWA alt for AROP-LOKEP [APR]
TOLOKIWA alt for LUKEP [LOA]
TOLOKOSON dial of TAGAL MURUT [MVV]
TOLOMAKO [TLM] lang, Vanuatu
TOLOMAKO-JEREVIU alt for TOLOMAKO [TLM]
TOLOU alt for TONDANO [TDN]
TOLOUR alt for TONDANO [TDN]
TOLOWA [TOL] lang, USA
TOLOWERI dial of BIMA [BHP]
TOLPAN alt for TOL [JIC]
TOLUBI alt for KATCHA dial of KATCHA-KADUGLI-
MIRI [KAT]
TOMA [TOD] lang, Guinea
TOMA dial of SAMO, SOUTHERN [SBD]
TOMA MA DALLA alt for KADUGLI dial of KATCHA-
KADUGLI-MIRI [KAT]
TOMACHECK alt for TAMAJAQ [TTQ]
TOMACHECK alt for TAMAJAQ, TAWALLAMMAT
[TTQ]
TOMACHECK alt for TAMAJEQ, TAYART [THZ]
TOMACHECK alt for TAMASHEQ [TAQ]
TOMACHECK alt for TAMASHEQ, KIDAL [TAQ]
TOMACHEK alt for TAMAHAQ, TAHAGGART [THV]
TOMADINO [TDI] lang, Indonesia (Sulawesi)
TOMAHU alt for FOGI dial of BURU [MHS]
TOMANI dial of TAGAL MURUT [MVV]
TOMARAHO alt for CHAMACOCO BRAVO dial of
CHAMACOCO [CEG]
TOMARAXA alt for CHAMACOCO BRAVO dial of
CHAMACOCO [CEG]
TOMÁS-ALIS dial of QUECHUA, YAUYOS [QUX]
TOMBAGGO alt for TANGBAGO dial of BANDA-
NDELE [BFL]
TOMBALU alt for TOMBULU [TOM]
TOMBATU alt for TONSAWANG [TNW]
TOMBELALA [TTP] lang, Indonesia (Sulawesi)
TOMBO dial of DOGON [DOG]
TOMBONUO alt for TOMBONUWO [TXA]
TOMBONUVA alt for TOMBONUWO [TXA]
TOMBONUWO [TXA] lang, Malaysia (Sabah)
TOMBOUCTOU alt for TIMBUKTU dial of
TAMASHEQ [TAQ]
TOMBOUCTOU alt for TIMBUKTU dial of
TAMASHEQ, KIDAL [TAQ]
TOMBUCAS alt for TUMBUKA [TUW]
TOMBULA alt for TOMBULU [TOM]
TOMBULU [TOM] lang, Indonesia (Sulawesi)
TOMBULU' alt for TOMBULU [TOM]
TOMEA dial of TUKANGBESI SOUTH [BHQ]
TOMEDES [TOE] lang, Colombia
TOMIA alt for TOMEA dial of TUKANGBESI SOUTH
[BHQ]
TOMINI [TXM] lang, Indonesia (Sulawesi)
TOM-KUZNETS TATAR alt for SHOR [CJS]
TOMMAN alt for MALFAXAL [MLX]
TOMMO-SO alt for TOMBO dial of DOGON [DOG]
TOMMOT dial of EVENKI [EVN]
TOMO alt for BATEK [BTQ]
TOMOHON dial of TOMBULU [TOM]
TOMOIP [TUM] lang, Papua New Guinea
TOMOIVE alt for TOMOIP [TUM]

TOMONI dial of PAMONA [BCX]
TOMOYP alt for TOMOIP [TUM]
TOMPAKEWA alt for TONTEMBOAN [TNT]
TOMPASO dial of TONTEMBOAN [TNT]
TOMPIRO alt for PIRO [PIE]
TOMPO alt for BARRU dial of BUGIS [BPR]
TOMPON dial of EVEN [EVE]
TOMPULUNG alt for KADAZAN, LABUK-
KINABATANGAN [DTB]
TOMU alt for KEMBERANO dial of ARANDAI [JBJ]
TOMU alt for ODOODEE [KKC]
TOMU RIVER alt for ODOODEE [KKC]
TONA dial of RUKAI [DRU]
TONDA alt for BLAFE [IND]
TONDAI dial of BUNUN [BNN]
TONDANO [TDN] lang, Indonesia (Sulawesi); also
in USA
TONDANO dial of TONDANO [TDN]
TONDANOU alt for TONDANO [TDN]
TONG alt for BUNU, BAHENG [PHA]
TÓNG alt for BUNU, BAHENG [PHA]
TONG alt for DONG, NORTHERN [DOC]
TONG alt for DONG, SOUTHERN [KMC]
TONG alt for TA'OIH, LOWER [TTO]
TONG dial of PAK-TONG [PKG]
TONG dial of TAOIH, LOWER [TTO]
TONGA [TNZ] lang, Thailand; also in Malaysia
(Peninsular)
TONGA [TOG] lang, Malawi
TONGA [TOI] lang, Zambia; also in Zimbabwe
TONGA alt for GITONGA [TOH]
TONGA alt for TONGAN [TOV]
TONGA alt for TSONGA [TSO]
TONGA dial of CHOPI [CCE]
TONGA dial of NDAU [NDC]
TONGA-INHAMBANE alt for GITONGA [TOH]
TONGAN [TOV] lang, Tonga; also in American
Samoa, Fiji, New Zealand, USA, Vanuatu
TONGAREVA alt for PENRHYN [PNH]
TONGARIKI ISLAND dial of NAMAKURA [NMK]
TONGBO alt for MAMBILA, CAMEROON [MYA]
TONGBO alt for MAMBILA, NIGERIA [MZK]
TONGECCHA dial of SANGPANG [RAV]
TONGGU dial of CHINESE, HAKKA [HAK]
TONGIAN 1 dial of BAJAU, INDONESIAN [BDL]
TONGIAN 2 dial of BAJAU, INDONESIAN [BDL]
TONGKOU alt for BUDONG-BUDONG [TGK]
TONGOA alt for NGUNA dial of EFATE, NORTH
[LLP]
TONGOA ISLAND dial of NAMAKURA [NMK]
TONGOYNA alt for TUPURI [TUI]
TONG-PAK alt for PAK-TONG [PKG]
TONGREN dial of BONAN [PEH]
TONGSHI-QIANDUI-BAOCHENG alt for QI dial of
HLAI [LIC]
TONGWE [TNY] lang, Tanzania
TONI alt for GWANDARA EASTERN dial of
GWANDARA [GWN]
TONJ BONGO dial of BONGO [BOT]
TONJO dial of TUKI [BAG]
TONKAWA [TON] lang, USA

TONKINESE alt for NORTHERN VIETNAMESE dial of VIETNAMESE [VIE]
TONKO alt for MABAAN [MFZ]
TONKO alt for WESTERN LIMBA dial of LIMBA, WEST-CENTRAL [LIA]
TONORE alt for TXIKÃO [TXI]
TONSAWANG [TNW] lang, Indonesia (Sulawesi)
TONSEA [TXS] lang, Indonesia (Sulawesi)
TONSEA' alt for TONSEA [TXS]
TONTEMBOAN [TNT] lang, Indonesia (Sulawesi)
TONTO dial of APACHE, WESTERN [APW]
TONTOLI alt for TOLITOLI [TXE]
TOODII alt for TOLDIL dial of GOLA [GOL]
TO'OLAKI alt for TOLAKI [LBW]
TOOMA alt for TOMA [TOD]
TOONGO dial of GBAYA, SOUTHWEST [MDO]
TOORO [TTJ] lang, Uganda
TOORO alt for TORO dial of HEMA [NIX]
TOOTOTOBI alt for YANOMAY dial of YANOMAMI [WCA]
TOPADA dial of PAMONA [BCX]
TOPOIYO [TOY] lang, Indonesia (Sulawesi)
TOPOKE alt for POKE [POF]
TOPOSA [TOQ] lang, Sudan
TOPOTAA alt for TAA dial of PAMONA [BCX]
TOPOTHA alt for TOPOSA [TOQ]
TOPURA dial of WEDAU [WED]
TORA dial of BANGBA [BBE]
TORÁ [TRZ] lang, Brazil
TORADJA alt for TORAJA-SA'DAN [SDA]
TORAJA alt for TORAJA-SA'DAN [SDA]
TORAJA BARAT dial of TORAJA-SADAN [SDA]
TORAJA TIMUR alt for TAE' [ROB]
TORAJA TIMUR alt for TOALA' [TLZ]
TORAJA-SA'DAN [SDA] lang, Indonesia (Sulawesi)
TORAM [TRJ] lang, Chad
TORAU [TTU] lang, Papua New Guinea
TORAZ alt for TORÁ [TRZ]
TORBI alt for MAMBILA, CAMEROON [MYA]
TORBI alt for SUNU TORBI dial of MAMBILA, CAMEROON [MYA]
TORETE dial of BUNGKU [BKZ]
TORGHOUD alt for TORGUT dial of KALMYK-OIRAT [KGZ]
TORGHUD alt for TORGUT dial of KALMYK-OIRAT [KGZ]
TORGON dial of NANAI [GLD]
TORGUT dial of KALMYK-OIRAT [KGZ]
TORGUUD alt for TORGUT dial of KALMYK-OIRAT [KGZ]
TORI AIKWAKAI alt for SIKARITAI [TTY]
TORIKO alt for LIKA [LIK]
TORISHIMA dial of OKINAWAN, CENTRAL [RYU]
TORKOMANI alt for TURKMEN [TCK]
TORLAKIAN dial of SERBO-CROATIAN [SRC]
TORNASI alt for KELO [TSN]
TORNE dial of SAAMI, NORTHERN [LPR]
TORNE VALLEY FINNISH alt for FINNISH, TORNEDALEN [FIT]
TORNE VALLEY FINNISH dial of FINNISH, TORNEDALEN [FIT]

TORNEDALEN (MEÄNKIELI) alt for FINNISH, TORNEDALEN [FIT]
TORNEDALSFINSKA alt for FINNISH, TORNEDALEN [FIT]
TORO [TDV] lang, Nigeria
TORO alt for FALI-TINGUELIN dial of FALI, SOUTH [FAL]
TORO alt for TOORO [TTJ]
TORO dial of HEMA [NIX]
TOROKO alt for TAROKO [TRV]
TOROM alt for TORAM [TRJ]
TOROMONA alt for TOROMONO [TNO]
TOROMONO [TNO] lang, Bolivia
TORONA [TQR] lang, Sudan
TOROSO dial of DOGON [DOG]
TORR alt for CHIN, TAWR [TCP]
TORRES alt for HIW [HIW]
TORRES alt for TOGA [LHT]
TORRES ISLAND alt for HIW [HIW]
TORRES STRAIT BROKEN alt for TORRES STRAIT CREOLE [TCS]
TORRES STRAIT CREOLE [TCS] lang, Australia
TORRES STRAIT PIDGIN alt for TORRES STRAIT CREOLE [TCS]
TORRICELLI [TEI] lang, Papua New Guinea
TORU alt for TAUNGYO [TCO]
TORUM alt for TORAM [TRJ]
TORWALI [TRW] lang, Pakistan
TOSILA'AI dial of MOLIMA [MOX]
TOSK alt for ALBANIAN, TOSK [ALN]
TOTALI dial of NEWARI [NEW]
TOTCHA alt for NAGA, NOCTE [NJB]
TOTELA [TTL] lang, Zambia; also in Namibia
TOTO [TXO] lang, India
TOTOK dial of NAGA, KONYAK [NBE]
TOTOLI alt for TOLITOLI [TXE]
TOTOMACHAPAN ZAPOTEC alt for ZAPOTECO, TOTOMACHAPAN [ZPH]
TOTONACA, COYUTLA [TOC] lang, Mexico
TOTONACA, FILOMENO MATA-COAHUITLÁN [TLP] lang, Mexico
TOTONACA, OZUMATLÁN [TQT] lang, Mexico
TOTONACA, PAPANTLA [TOP] lang, Mexico
TOTONACA, PATLA-CHICONTLA [TOT] lang, Mexico
TOTONACA, SIERRA [TOS] lang, Mexico
TOTONACA, XICOTEPEC DE JUÁREZ [TOO] lang, Mexico
TOTONACA, YECUATLA [TLC] lang, Mexico
TOTORO [TTK] lang, Colombia
TOUAOURU alt for NUMEE [KDK]
TOUAOURU alt for NUMEE dial of NUMEE [KDK]
TOUAREG alt for TAMAHAQ, TAHAGGART [THV]
TOUAREG alt for TAMAJAQ, TAWALLAMMAT [TTQ]
TOUAREG alt for TAMAJEQ, TAYART [THZ]
TOUAT dial of TAZNATIT [GRR]
TOUBAKAI alt for SONINKE [SNN]
TOUBOU alt for DAZAGA [DAK]
TOUBOU alt for TEDAGA [TUQ]
TOUBOU alt for TUBU dial of TEDAGA [TUQ]

TOUBOURI alt for TUPURI [TUI]
TOUCOULEUR dial of FULFULDE, PULAAR [FUC]
TOUCOULEUR dial of PULAAR [FUC]
TOUDOUGOUKA dial of JULA, ODIENNE [JOD]
TOUGAN alt for SAMO, MATYA [STJ]
TOUGGOURT alt for TEMACINE TAMAZIGHT [TJO]
TOUGOURT alt for TEMACINE TAMAZIGHT [TJO]
TOULONNAIS alt for MARITIME PROVENÇAL dial
    of PROVENCAL [PRV]
TOULOUN dial of HALIA [HLA]
TOULOUR alt for TONDANO [TDN]
TOUM dial of HUNG [HNU]
TOUM PHONG alt for PONG dial of HUNG [HNU]
TOUMAK alt for TUMAK [TMC]
TOUMBULU alt for TOMBULU [TOM]
TOUNIA alt for TUNIA [TUG]
TOUNTEMBOAN alt for TONTEMBOAN [TNT]
TOUPOURI alt for TUPURI [TUI]
TOURA [NEB] lang, Côte d'Ivoire
"TOURAGE" pejorative alt for TAMAJAQ [TTQ]
TOURAGE alt for TAMAHAQ, TAHAGGART
    [THV]
TOURAGE alt for TAMAJAQ, TAWALLAMMAT
    [TTQ]
TOURAI dial of MOUK-ARIA [MWH]
TOUREG alt for TAMAHAQ, TAHAGGART [THV]
TOURKA alt for TURKA [TUZ]
TOUROU alt for TUR dial of HDI [TUR]
TOUROU alt for XEDI [TUR]
TOUSSIAN, NORTHERN [TSP] lang, Burkina Faso
TOUSSIAN, SOUTHERN [WIB] lang, Burkina Faso;
    also in Côte d'Ivoire
TOVOKE alt for POKE [POF]
TOWA alt for JEMEZ [TOW]
TOWAL alt for MASAKIN TUWAL dial of NGILE
    [MAS]
TOWARE alt for TAE' [ROB]
TOWARE alt for TOALA' [TLZ]
TOWARGARHI alt for BHADAURI dial of BUNDELI
    [BNS]
TOWE alt for TOWEI [TTN]
TOWEI [TTN] lang, Indonesia (Irian Jaya)
TOWETAN alt for MALAVEDAN [MJR]
TOWI alt for NEYO [NEY]
TOWN BEMBA dial of BEMBA [BEM]
TOWN FRISIAN dial of FRISIAN, WESTERN [FRI]
TOWOLHI alt for MACA [MCA]
T-OY alt for TA'OIH, UPPER [TTH]
TOYERI dial of HUACHIPAERI [HUG]
TOYOERI alt for TOYERI dial of HUACHIPAERI
    [HUG]
TOZHUMA alt for NAGA, YIMCHUNGRU [YIM]
TOZLUK TURKS dial of BALKAN GAGAUZ
    TURKISH [BGX]
TOZVI alt for LOZI [LOZ]
TRABZON dial of ARMENIAN [ARM]
TRADE JULA alt for DIOULA VÉHICULAIRE dial
    of JULA [DYU]
TRADE MALAY alt for BAZAAR MALAY dial of
    MALAY [MLI]
TRAI alt for IU MIEN [IUM]

TRAKAY dial of KARAIM [KDR]
TRANSALPIN dial of PROVENCAL [PRV]
TRANSITIONAL KANAUJI dial of KANAUJI [BJJ]
TRANSVAAL NDEBELE alt for NDEBELE [NEL]
TRANSVAAL SOTHO alt for SOTHO, NORTHERN
    [SRT]
TRANSYLVANIA dial of GERMAN, STANDARD
    [GER]
TRANSYLVANIAN dial of ROMANI, CARPATHIAN
    [RMC]
TRANSYLVANIAN dial of ROMANIAN [RUM]
TRAPANI alt for WESTERN SICILIAN dial of
    SICILIAN [SCN]
TRAPEZUNT alt for TRABZON dial of ARMENIAN
    [ARM]
TRÀU alt for TRAW dial of CUA [CUA]
TRAUDE alt for DGHWEDE [DGH]
TRAVELLER DANISH [RMD] lang, Denmark
TRAVELLER NORWEGIAN [RMG] lang, Norway
TRAVELLER SCOTTISH [TRL] lang, United
    Kingdom; also in Australia, USA
TRAVELLER SWEDISH alt for TAVRINGER
    ROMANI [RMU]
TRAW dial of CUA [CUA]
TREDICI COMMUNI CIMBRIAN dial of CIMBRIAN
    [CIM]
TREGAMI [TRM] lang, Afghanistan
TREGORROIS dial of BRETON [BRT]
TREMBO dial of GREBO, CENTRAL [GRV]
TREMEMBÉ [TME] lang, Brazil
TRENG alt for BALAIT dial of LUNDAYEH [LND]
TRENG alt for TRIENG [STG]
TRENGGANU dial of MALAY [MLI]
TRENTINO WESTERN dial of LOMBARD [LMO]
TREPO dial of KRUMEN, PYE [PYE]
TRETINE dial of VENETIAN [VEC]
TRI dial of BRU, EASTERN [BRU]
TRIBAL ORIYA alt for ORIYA, ADIVASI [ORT]
TRIENG [STG] lang, Viet Nam
TRIESTINO dial of VENETIAN [VEC]
TRIÈU CHAU alt for CHINESE, YUE [YUH]
TRIGAMI alt for TREGAMI [TRM]
TRIMURIS [TIP] lang, Indonesia (Irian Jaya)
TRING [TGQ] lang, Malaysia (Sarawak)
TRING dial of KOHO [KPM]
TRINGGUS [TRX] lang, Malaysia (Sarawak); also
    in Indonesia (Kalimantan)
TRINGGUS dial of TRINGGUS [TRX]
TRINGUS alt for TRINGGUS [TRX]
TRINH alt for TRING dial of KOHO [KPM]
TRINIDAD BHOJPURI alt for HINDUSTANI,
    CARIBBEAN [HNS]
TRINIDAD BHOJPURI dial of HINDUSTANI,
    CARIBBEAN [HNS]
TRINIDADIAN CREOLE ENGLISH [TRF] lang,
    Trinidad and Tobago
TRINIDADIAN CREOLE FRENCH dial of LESSER
    ANTILLEAN CREOLE FRENCH [DOM]
TRINIDADIEN alt for TRINIDADIAN CREOLE
    FRENCH dial of LESSER ANTILLEAN CREOLE
    FRENCH [DOM]

TRINITARIO [TRN] lang, Bolivia
TRINKAT alt for TRINKUT dial of NICOBARESE, CENTRAL [NCB]
TRINKUT dial of NICOBARESE, CENTRAL [NCB]
TRIÓ [TRI] lang, Suriname; also in Brazil
TRIOMETESEM alt for AKURIO [AKO]
TRIOMETESEN alt for AKURIO [AKO]
TRIPERAH alt for TIPPERA [TPE]
TRIPOLITA'IT alt for ARABIC, JUDEO-TRIPOLITANIAN [YUD]
TRIPOLITANIAN ARABIC dial of ARABIC, LIBYAN SPOKEN [AYL]
TRIPOLITANIAN ARABIC dial of ARABIC, WESTERN EGYPTIAN BEDAWI SPOKEN [AYL]
TRIPOLITANIAN JUDEO-ARABIC alt for ARABIC, JUDEO-TRIPOLITANIAN [YUD]
TRIPURA alt for KOK BOROK [TRP]
TRIPURA alt for TIPPERA [TPE]
TRIPURI alt for KOK BOROK [TRP]
TRIQUE, CHICAHUAXTLA [TRS] lang, Mexico
TRIQUE, COPALA [TRC] lang, Mexico
TRIQUE, SAN MARTÍN ITUNYOSO [TRQ] lang, Mexico
TRIQUI alt for TRIQUE, CHICAHUAXTLA [TRS]
TRIQUI alt for TRIQUE, COPALA [TRC]
TRIQUI alt for TRIQUE, SAN MARTÍN ITUNYOSO [TRQ]
TRISULI dial of TAMANG, WESTERN [TDG]
TROBIAWAN dial of BASAY [BYQ]
TROMOWA alt for GROMA [GRO]
TRONDELAAG alt for NORTHERN NORWEGIAN dial of NORWEGIAN, BOKMAAL [NRR]
TRONDHEIM dial of NORWEGIAN SIGN LANGUAGE [NSL]
TRONG GGIA alt for BOUYEI [PCC]
TRUE MOTU alt for MOTU [MEU]
TRUJ alt for DAR EL KABIRA dial of TULISHI [TEY]
TRUK alt for CHUUKESE [TRU]
TRUKÁ [TKA] lang, Brazil
TRUKESE alt for CHUUKESE [TRU]
TRUKHMEN alt for TURKMEN [TCK]
TRUKHMENY alt for TURKMEN [TCK]
TRUKMEN alt for TURKMEN [TCK]
TRUKMEN dial of TURKMEN [TCK]
TRUKU alt for TAROKO [TRV]
TRUMAÍ [TPY] lang, Brazil
TRUNG alt for DRUNG [DUU]
TRUSAN alt for LUNDAYEH [LND]
TSAAM alt for BOK dial of MANDJAK [MFV]
TSAAM alt for SAMBA [SMX]
TSAAMO dial of MANDJAK [MFV]
TSAANGI [TSA] lang, Gabon; also in Congo
TSAAYI dial of TEKE, WESTERN [TEZ]
TSACHILA alt for COLORADO [COF]
TSAGA alt for ENGA [ENQ]
TSAGKAGLINGPA'IKHA alt for CHOCANGACAKHA [CHK]
TSAGU alt for CIWOGAI [TGD]
TSAIWA alt for ZAIWA [ATB]
TSAKHUR [TKR] lang, Azerbaijan; also in Russia (Europe), Uzbekistan

TSAKHURY alt for TSAKHUR [TKR]
TSAKONIA alt for TSAKONIAN [TSD]
TSAKONIAN [TSD] lang, Greece
TSAKWAMBO [KVZ] lang, Indonesia (Irian Jaya)
TSALAGI alt for CHEROKEE [CER]
TSALISEN alt for RUKAI [DRU]
TSAMA alt for EBRIÉ [EBR]
TSAMAI [TSB] lang, Ethiopia
TSAMAK alt for MAIDU, NORTHWEST [MAI]
TSAMAKKO alt for TSAMAI [TSB]
TSAMAKO alt for TSAMAI [TSB]
TS'AMAY alt for TSAMAI [TSB]
TSAMBA alt for SAMBA [SMX]
TSAMBA alt for SAMBA DAKA [CCG]
TSANG alt for GTSANG dial of TIBETAN [TIC]
TSANGI alt for TSAANGI [TSA]
TSANGLA alt for TSHANGLA [TSJ]
TSANGLO alt for NAGA, ANGAMI [NJM]
TSANUMA alt for SANUMÁ [SAM]
TS'AO alt for N/HAI-NTSE'E dial of NARO [NHR]
TS'AOKHOE dial of NARO [NHR]
TSAOKHWE alt for TS'AOKHOE dial of NARO [NHR]
TSARISEN alt for RUKAI [DRU]
TSASI alt for !XÓÕ [NMN]
TSAT [HUQ] lang, China
TSAUDANGSI alt for CHAUDANGSI [CDN]
TSAUKWE alt for TS'AOKHOE dial of NARO [NHR]
TSAURASYA alt for CHOURASE [TSU]
TSAXUR alt for TSAKHUR [TKR]
TSAYA alt for TSAAYI dial of TEKE, WESTERN [TEZ]
TSAYE alt for TSAAYI dial of TEKE, WESTERN [TEZ]
TSAYI alt for TSAAYI dial of TEKE, WESTERN [TEZ]
TSCHAKO alt for SHEKO [SHE]
TSCHETTI dial of IFE [IFE]
TSCHIOKLOE alt for CHOKWE [CJK]
TSCHIOKWE alt for CHOKWE [CJK]
TSCHOPI alt for CHOPI [CCE]
TSEGOB alt for SOUTHERN AKHVAKH dial of AKHVAKH [AKV]
TSEKU [TSK] lang, China; also in Bhutan, Nepal
TSENAP alt for CHENAPIAN [CJN]
TSEPANG alt for CHEPANG [CDM]
TSEREKWE dial of NARO [NHR]
TSESUNGÚN dial of HUILLICHE [HUH]
TSETSAUT [TXC] lang, Canada
TS'EXA alt for /ANDA [HNH]
TS'ÉXA alt for /ANDA [HNH]
TSEZ alt for DIDO [DDO]
TSEZY alt for DIDO [DDO]
TSHAAHUI alt for CHAYAHUITA [CBT]
TSHALA alt for CHALA [CHA]
TSHALI alt for CHALIKHA [TGF]
TSHALINGPA alt for CHALIKHA [TGF]
TSHAMBERI alt for CHAMBRI [CAN]
TSHANGKHA alt for LAKHA [LKH]
TSHANGLA [TSJ] lang, Bhutan; also in China, India
TSHEENYA alt for ENYA [GEY]
TSH'EREKHWE dial of DETI [DET]
TSHIDI-KHWE dial of SHUA [SHG]

TSHIGA alt for IGIKIGA dial of RWANDA [RUA]
TSHILUBA alt for LUBA-KASAI [LUB]
TSHIRAMBO alt for BAMBALANG [BMO]
TSH'ITI alt for TSHIDI-KHWE dial of SHUA [SHG]
TSHIVENDA alt for VENDA [VEN]
TSHOGO alt for HUTU dial of RWANDA [RUA]
TSHOKWE alt for CHOKWE [CJK]
TSHOM-DJAPA dial of KANAMARI [KNM]
TSHUMAKWE alt for SHUA [SHG]
TSHUMKWE alt for JU/'HOAN [KTZ]
TSHUOSH alt for MALINGUAT [SIC]
TSHUWAU alt for HIETSHWARE [HIE]
TSHWA [TSC] lang, Mozambique; also in South
    Africa, Zimbabwe
TSHWA alt for HIETSHWARE [HIE]
TSHWA dial of TSHWA [TSC]
TSHWANA alt for TSWANA [TSW]
TSHWOSH alt for MALINGUAT [SIC]
TSIA alt for ZIA [ZIA]
TSIE alt for LIGBI [LIG]
TSIGANE alt for ROMANI, SINTE [RMO]
TSIGANE alt for ROMANI, VLAX [RMY]
TSIGENE alt for DOMARI [RMT]
TSIGENE alt for ROMANI, VLAX [RMY]
TSÍHULI alt for KINNAURI, CHITKULI [CIK]
TSIKIMBA [KDL] lang, Nigeria
TSILMANO alt for ZILMAMU dial of KACIPO-BALESI
    [KOE]
TSIMAJEEGA dial of DATOOGA [TCC]
TSIMANÉ [CAS] lang, Bolivia
TSIMIHETRY alt for MALAGASY, TSIMEHETY
    [XMW]
TSIMIHETY alt for MALAGASY, TSIMEHETY [XMW]
TSIMPSHEAN alt for TSIMSHIAN [TSI]
TSIMSHEAN alt for TSIMSHIAN [TSI]
TSIMSHIAN [TSI] lang, Canada; also in USA
TSINDIR alt for NAGA, LOTHA [NJH]
TSINGA dial of TUKI [BAG]
TSINGANI alt for ROMANI, VLAX [RMY]
TSINUK WAWA alt for CHINOOK WAWA [CRW]
TSIRACUA dial of AYOREO [AYO]
TSIRICUA dial of AYOREO [AYO]
TSIRIPÁ alt for CHIRIPÁ [NHD]
TSISHIMA dial of AINU [AIN]
TSISHINGINI [KAM] lang, Nigeria
TSITKHULI alt for KINNAURI, CHITKULI [CIK]
TSITSIKHAR alt for QIQIHA'ER dial of DAUR [DTA]
TSIVILI alt for VILI [VIF]
TSIWAHA alt for TSWANA [TSW]
TSLAGI alt for CHEROKEE [CER]
TSO [LDP] lang, Nigeria
TSO alt for TSOU [TSY]
TSÓBÓ alt for TSO [LDP]
TSOBWA alt for PIANGA dial of BUSHOONG [BUF]
TSOCHIANG alt for ZUOJIANG dial of ZHUANG,
    SOUTHERN [CCY]
TSOGHAMI alt for NAGA, ANGAMI [NJM]
TSOGO [TSV] lang, Gabon
TSOKWAMBO alt for TSAKWAMBO [KVZ]
TSOLA dial of TUYUCA [TUE]
TS'OLE' dial of ATAYAL [TAY]

TSONGA [TSO] lang, South Africa; also in
    Mozambique, Swaziland, Zimbabwe
TSONGOL dial of MONGOLIAN, HALH [KHK]
TSONTSII alt for NAGA, LOTHA [NJH]
TSONTSU dial of NAGA, LOTHA [NJH]
TSOO alt for TSOU [TSY]
TSOROKWE alt for NARO [NHR]
TSOTSITAAL [FLY] lang, South Africa
TSOTSO dial of LUYIA [LUY]
TSOU [TSY] lang, Taiwan
TSOVA-TUSH alt for BATS [BBL]
TS'ÜN-LAO [TSL] lang, Viet Nam
TSUDAKHAR alt for CUDAXAR dial of DARGWA
    [DAR]
TSUGUMI alt for NAGA, ANGAMI [NJM]
TSUKU alt for TSEKU [TSK]
TSUM [TTZ] lang, Nepal
TSUMANGGORUN dial of ADZERA [AZR]
TSUMGE alt for TSUM [TTZ]
TSUMKWE alt for JU/'HOAN [KTZ]
TSUNARI alt for BANONI [BCM]
TSUNTIN alt for DIDO [DDO]
TSUOU alt for TSOU [TSY]
TSUREJA alt for RESHE [RES]
TSURESHE alt for RESHE [RES]
TSU-U alt for TSOU [TSY]
TSUVADI [TVD] lang, Nigeria
TSUVAN [TSH] lang, Cameroon
TSUWENKI dial of MARING [MBW]
TSU-WO alt for TSOU [TSY]
TSWANA [TSW] lang, Botswana; also in Namibia,
    South Africa, Zimbabwe
TSWAPONG [TWO] lang, Botswana
TSWENE dial of SOTHO, NORTHERN [SRT]
TSWENI alt for TSWENE dial of SOTHO,
    NORTHERN [SRT]
TTA'O alt for MAKATAO dial of SIRAIYA [FOS]
TU [MJG] lang, China
TÚ DU alt for WHITE GELAO dial of GELAO [KKF]
TU GUANGDONGHUA alt for CHINESE, HAKKA
    [HAK]
TU NGORO alt for NGORO dial of TUKI [BAG]
TUAL dial of OSETIN [OSE]
TUAM alt for MUTU [TUC]
TUAM dial of MUTU [TUC]
TUAM-MUTU alt for MUTU [TUC]
TUAMOTUAN [PMT] lang, French Polynesia
TUAN TET dial of KAREN, PWO WESTERN
    [PWO]
TUARAN DUSUN alt for LOTUD [DTR]
"TUAREG" pejorative alt for TAMAJAQ [TTQ]
"TUAREG" pejorative alt for TAMASHEQ [TAQ]
TUAREG alt for TAMAHAQ, TAHAGGART [THV]
TUAREG alt for TAMAJAQ, TAWALLAMMAT
    [TTQ]
TUAREG alt for TAMAJEQ, TAYART [THZ]
TUAREG alt for TAMASHEQ, KIDAL [TAQ]
TUAT alt for TOUAT dial of TAZNATIT [GRR]
TUAURU alt for NUMEE [KDK]
TUBA alt for LIGBI [LIG]
TUBA alt for TUVIN [TUN]

TUBAI dial of NAMOSI-NAITASIRI-SERUA [BWB]
TUBA-KIZHI dial of TUVIN [TUN]
TUBAL dial of LAMMA [LEV]
TUBANIWAI alt for NUCLEAR WESTERN FIJIAN
    dial of FIJIAN, WESTERN [WYY]
TUBAR [TBU] lang, Mexico
TUBARE alt for TUBAR [TBU]
TUBARO [TBA] lang, Brazil
TÜBATULABAL [TUB] lang, USA
TUBBI alt for ULUMANDA' [ULM]
TUBE alt for TUBAL dial of LAMMA [LEV]
TUBETA alt for TAVETA [TVS]
TUBETUBE alt for BWANABWANA [TTE]
TUBIRUASA alt for URUANGNIRIN [URN]
TU'BORO alt for SAKPU dial of KARANG [KZR]
TUBOY SUBANON alt for SUBANEN, NORTHERN
    [STB]
TUBU alt for DAZAGA [DAK]
TUBU alt for TEDAGA [TUQ]
TUBU dial of TEDAGA [TUQ]
TUBUAI dial of AUSTRAL [AUT]
TUBUAI-RURUTU alt for AUSTRAL [AUT]
TUBULAMO dial of SINAUGORO [SNC]
TUBURI alt for TUPURI [TUI]
TUCANO [TUO] lang, Brazil; also in Colombia
TUCHIA alt for TUJIA, NORTHERN [TJI]
TUCHIA alt for TUJIA, SOUTHERN [TJS]
TUCHINAUA alt for TUXINÁWA [TUX]
TUCUNA alt for TICUNA [TCA]
TUDA alt for TEDAGA [TUQ]
TUDA alt for TODA [TCX]
TUDAGA alt for TEDAGA [TUQ]
TUDAHWE alt for PAWAIA [PWA]
TUDANCHI alt for ROR dial of KAG-FER-JIIR-KOOR-
    ROR-US-ZUKSUN [GEL]
TU-DÍ alt for BOUYEI [PCC]
TU-DÌN alt for BOUYEI [PCC]
TUDJA alt for TUJIA, NORTHERN [TJI]
TUER-GALA dial of ZAGHAWA [ZAG]
TUERKE alt for ILI TURKI [ILI]
TUFTERA alt for HWANA [HWO]
TUFUNGWA alt for FUNGWA [ULA]
TUGARA alt for DURUWA [PCI]
TUGEN, NORTH [TUY] lang, Kenya
TUGERI dial of MARIND [MRZ]
TUGUN [TZN] lang, Indonesia (Maluku)
TUGURA alt for GURA dial of LAME [BMA]
TUGURO-CHUMIKAN dial of EVENKI [EVN]
TUGURT alt for TEMACINE TAMAZIGHT [TJO]
TUGUTIL [TUJ] lang, Indonesia (Maluku)
TUHUP dial of HUPDE [JUP]
TUIC dial of DINKA, SOUTHEASTERN [DIN]
TUIC dial of DINKA, SOUTHWESTERN [DIK]
TUIUCA alt for TUYUCA [TUE]
TUJIA alt for BOUYEI [PCC]
TUJIA, NORTHERN [TJI] lang, China
TUJIA, SOUTHERN [TJS] lang, China
TUKA dial of GAGU [GGU]
TUKAIMI alt for NAGA, KHOIRAO [NKI]
TUKANA alt for TUCANO [TUO]
TUKÁNA alt for TUCANO [TUO]

TUKANG-BESI alt for TUKANGBESI SOUTH [BHQ]
TUKANGBESI NORTH [KHC] lang, Indonesia
    (Sulawesi); also in Singapore
TUKANGBESI SOUTH [BHQ] lang, Indonesia
    (Sulawesi)
TUKCHE dial of THAKALI [THS]
TUKEN alt for SOUTH TUGEN dial of KALENJIN
    [KLN]
TUKEN alt for TUGEN, NORTH [TUY]
TUKI [BAG] lang, Cameroon
TUKKONGO alt for WONGO [WON]
TUKOLOR alt for TOUCOULEUR dial of FULFULDE,
    PULAAR [FUC]
TUKOLOR alt for TOUCOULEUR dial of PULAAR
    [FUC]
TUKOMBE alt for KOMBE dial of TUKI [BAG]
TUKONGO alt for WONGO [WON]
TUKPA [TPQ] lang, India
TUKU dial of TOORO [TTJ]
TUKUDE alt for TUKUDEDE [TKD]
TUKUDEDE [TKD] lang, Timor Lorosae
TUKUDEDE dial of TUKUDEDE [TKD]
TUKUDH alt for WESTERN CANADA GWICH'IN
    dial of GWICHIN [KUC]
TUKULOR alt for TOUCOULEUR dial of FULFULDE,
    PULAAR [FUC]
TUKULOR alt for TOUCOULEUR dial of PULAAR
    [FUC]
TUKULU alt for BAJUNI dial of SWAHILI [SWA]
TUKUMANFÉD [TKF] lang, Brazil
TUKUN alt for MBEMBE, TIGON [NZA]
TUKUNA alt for TICUNA [TCA]
TUKÚNA alt for TICUNA [TCA]
TUKURINA dial of JAMAMADI [JAA]
TULA [TUL] lang, Nigeria
TULAI alt for ZEEM dial of ZEEM [ZUA]
TULAMBATU dial of BUNGKU [BKZ]
TULEHU [TLU] lang, Indonesia (Maluku)
TULEHU dial of TULEHU [TLU]
TULEM alt for DANI, MID GRAND VALLEY
    [DNT]
TULESH alt for TULISHI [TEY]
TULIM dial of NAGA, TASE [NST]
TULING alt for ELING dial of TUNEN [BAZ]
TULISHI [TEY] lang, Sudan
TULISHI dial of TULISHI [TEY]
TULLU alt for TULU [TCY]
TULON alt for TOULOUN dial of HALIA [HLA]
TU-LOP alt for NOP dial of KOHO [KPM]
TULU [TCY] lang, India
TULU dial of BOHUAI [RAK]
TULU dial of TULU [TCY]
TULU-BOHUAI alt for BOHUAI [RAK]
TULUN alt for TOULOUN dial of HALIA [HLA]
TULUN alt for TULU dial of BOHUAI [RAK]
TULUNG alt for DRUNG [DUU]
TULUVA BHASA alt for TULU [TCY]
TUM alt for TOUM dial of HUNG [HNU]
TUMA alt for TUMA-IRUMU [IOU]
TUMAC alt for TUMAK [TMC]
TUMAG alt for TUMAK [TMC]

TUMA-IRUMU [IOU] lang, Papua New Guinea
TUMAK [TMC] lang, Chad
TUMAK dial of TUMAK [TMC]
TUMALA alt for MALA [RUY]
TUMALE dial of TAGOI [TAG]
TUMANAO alt for BLAAN, SARANGANI [BIS]
TUMANIQ alt for TOMANI dial of TAGAL MURUT [MVV]
TUMARA alt for MUNIWARA [MWB]
TUMARI dial of KANURI, TUMARI [KRT]
TUMARIYA alt for PANCHPARGANIA [TDB]
TUMARU alt for MUNIWARA [MWB]
TUMAWO alt for SKOU [SKV]
TUMBELE alt for MBERE dial of TUKI [BAG]
TUMBOKA alt for TUMBUKA [TUW]
TUMBUKA [TUW] lang, Malawi; also in Tanzania, Zambia
TUMBUNWHA alt for TOMBONUWO [TXA]
TUMET alt for TUMUT dial of MONGOLIAN, PERIPHERAL [MVF]
TUMI [KKU] lang, Nigeria
TUMIE alt for TOMOIP [TUM]
TUMLEO [TMQ] lang, Papua New Guinea
TUMMA [TBQ] lang, Sudan
TUMMA dial of TUMMA [TBQ]
TUMMOK alt for TUMAK [TMC]
TÜMPISA SHOSHONI alt for PANAMINT [PAR]
TUMTUM [TBR] lang, Sudan
TUMTUM dial of TUMTUM [TBR]
TUMU alt for RUMU [KLQ]
TUMU alt for TWUMWU dial of TIKAR [TIK]
TUMUAONG dial of KALAGAN [KQE]
TUMUGUN alt for TIMUGON MURUT [TIH]
TUMUIP alt for TOMOIP [TUM]
TUMUT dial of MONGOLIAN, PERIPHERAL [MVF]
TUMZABT [MZB] lang, Algeria
TUN alt for TUNIA [TUG]
TUNA alt for KATCHA dial of KATCHA-KADUGLI-MIRI [KAT]
TUNA alt for KUANUA [KSD]
TUNBUMOHAS alt for TOMBONUWO [TXA]
TUNCELI dial of KIRMANJKI [QKV]
TUNDRA alt for YUKAGHIR, NORTHERN [YKG]
TUNDRA ENETS alt for MADU dial of ENETS [ENE]
TUNDRA YURAK dial of NENETS [YRK]
TUNDRE alt for YUKAGHIR, NORTHERN [YKG]
TUNDULI dial of LARO [LRO]
TUNEBO, ANGOSTURAS [TND] lang, Colombia
TUNEBO, BARRO NEGRO [TBN] lang, Colombia
TUNEBO, CENTRAL [TUF] lang, Colombia; also in Venezuela
TUNEBO, WESTERN [TNB] lang, Colombia
TUNEN [BAZ] lang, Cameroon
TUNG alt for DONG, NORTHERN [DOC]
TUNG alt for DONG, SOUTHERN [KMC]
TUNG alt for DONGXIANG [SCE]
TUNG dial of KISSI, NORTHERN [KQS]
TUNG NU alt for DONGNU dial of BUNU, BU-NAO [BWX]
TUNGA alt for DOYAYO [DOW]

TUNGA dial of DADIYA [DBD]
TUNGAG [LCM] lang, Papua New Guinea
TUNGAK alt for TUNGAG [LCM]
TUNGAN alt for DUNGAN [DNG]
TUNGAN alt for MABAAN [MFZ]
TUNGARA alt for TENGARA dial of BAUKAN [BNB]
TUNGBO alt for DOYAYO [DOW]
TUNG-CHIA alt for DONG, NORTHERN [DOC]
TUNG-CHIA alt for DONG, SOUTHERN [KMC]
TUNGGARE [TRT] lang, Indonesia (Irian Jaya)
TUNGHO dial of SAISIYAT [SAI]
TUNGHSIANG alt for DONGXIANG [SCE]
TUNGI' dial of FE'FE' [FMP]
TUNGKAL dial of KUBU [KVB]
TUNGKAL ILIR dial of KUBU [KVB]
TUNGU dial of NGELIMA [AGH]
TUNGURAHUA QUICHUA alt for QUICHUA, HIGH-LAND, TUNGURAHUA [QQS]
TUNGUS alt for EVENKI [EVN]
TUNGYEN alt for TONGREN dial of BONAN [PEH]
TUNIA [TUG] lang, Chad
TUNICA [TUK] lang, USA
TUNIS dial of ARABIC, JUDEO-TUNISIAN [AJT]
TUNISIAN alt for ARABIC, TUNISIAN SPOKEN [AEB]
TUNISIAN SIGN LANGUAGE [TSE] lang, Tunisia
TUNJUNG [TJG] lang, Indonesia (Kalimantan)
TUNJUNG dial of TUNJUNG [TJG]
TUNJUNG DAYAK alt for TUNJUNG [TJG]
TUNJUNG LINGGANG dial of TUNJUNG [TJG]
TUNJUNG LONDONG dial of TUNJUNG [TJG]
TUNJUNG TENGAH alt for TUNJUNG dial of TUNJUNG [TJG]
TUNKA dial of BURIAT, RUSSIA [MNB]
TUNNI [TQQ] lang, Somalia
TUNONG dial of ACEH [ATJ]
TUNULI alt for TXIKÃO [TXI]
TUNULOA alt for SOUTHEAST VANUA LEVU dial of FIJIAN [FJI]
TUNYA alt for TUNIA [TUG]
TUNYA dial of TUNIA [TUG]
TUOBO dial of GREBO, GBOLOO [GEC]
TUOM alt for MUTU [TUC]
TUOMO dial of IZON [IJC]
TUOTOMB [TTF] lang, Cameroon
TUPARÍ [TUP] lang, Brazil
TUPEN alt for BASAA [BAA]
TUPÍ OF CUMINAPANEMA alt for POTURU [PTO]
TUPIIRE alt for SENOUFO, MAMARA [MYK]
TUPINAKI alt for TUPINIKIN [TPK]
TUPINAMBÁ [TPN] lang, Brazil
TUPINIKIM alt for TUPINIKIN [TPK]
TUPINIKIN [TPK] lang, Brazil
TUPITIMOAKE alt for FANGATAU dial of TUAMOTUAN [PMT]
TUPURI [TUI] lang, Cameroon; also in Chad
TUR alt for XEDI [TUR]
TUR dial of HDI [TUR]
TURA alt for TOURA [NEB]
TURAKA [TRH] lang, Papua New Guinea
TURA-KA-MOLO alt for MOLO [ZMO]

TURAMA alt for RUMA [RUZ]
TURAMA RIVER KIWAI alt for MORIGI [MDB]
TURANI alt for TUROYO [SYR]
TURATEA dial of MAKASAR [MSR]
TURE dial of TANGALE [TAN]
TURI [TRD] lang, India
TURIJE'NE' alt for BAJAU, INDONESIAN [BDL]
TURIUARA alt for TURIWÁRA [TWT]
TURIWÁRA [TWT] lang, Brazil
T'URK alt for ILI TURKI [ILI]
TURKA [TUZ] lang, Burkina Faso; also in Côte d'Ivoire
TURKANA [TUV] lang, Kenya
TÜRKÇE alt for TURKISH [TRK]
TURKI alt for TURKISH [TRK]
TÜRKISCH alt for TURKISH [TRK]
TURKISH [TRK] lang, Turkey (Asia); also in Australia,
    Austria, Azerbaijan, Belgium, Bosnia-Herzegovina,
    Bulgaria, Canada, Cyprus, Denmark, El Salvador,
    Finland, France, Georgia, Germany, Greece,
    Honduras, Iran, Iraq, Israel, Kazakhstan,
    Kyrgyzstan, Macedonia, Netherlands, Romania,
    Russia (Asia), Sweden, Switzerland, Tajikistan,
    Ukraine, UAE, United Kingdom, USA, Uzbekistan,
    Yugoslavia
TURKISH SIGN LANGUAGE [TSM] lang, Turkey
    (Asia)
TURKLER alt for AZERBAIJANI, NORTH [AZE]
TURKMAN alt for TURKMEN [TCK]
TURKMANI alt for TURKMEN [TCK]
TURKMANIAN alt for TURKMEN [TCK]
TURKMEN [TCK] lang, Turkmenistan; also in
    Afghanistan, Germany, Iran, Iraq, Kazakhstan,
    Kyrgyzstan, Pakistan, Russia (Asia), Tajikistan,
    Turkey (Asia), USA, Uzbekistan
TURKMENLER alt for TURKMEN [TCK]
TURKOMAN alt for TURKMEN [TCK]
TURKOMANS alt for TURKMEN [TCK]
TURKS AND CAICOS CREOLE ENGLISH [TCH]
    lang, Turks and Caicos Islands
TURKWAM alt for TORO [TDV]
TURKWANA alt for TURKANA [TUV]
TUROHA alt for AURAMA dial of PAWAIA [PWA]
TUROYO [SYR] lang, Turkey (Asia); also in
    Argentina, Australia, Belgium, Brazil, Canada,
    Germany, Iraq, Lebanon, Netherlands, Sweden,
    Syria, USA
TURRA dial of NARUNGGA [NNR]
TURRUBUL alt for THURAWAL [TBH]
TURU alt for IAU [TMU]
TURU alt for NYATURU [RIM]
TURU alt for XEDI [TUR]
TURU alt for YAWA [YVA]
TURU dial of IAU [TMU]
TURU alt for TUR dial of HDI [TUR]
TURUBA alt for NYA GUYUWA dial of LONGUDA
    [LNU]
TURUBU alt for TEREBU [TRB]
TURU-HIDE alt for HDI [TUR]
TURU-HIDE alt for XEDI [TUR]
TURUJ alt for DAR EL KABIRA dial of TULISHI [TEY]
TURUKA alt for TURKA [TUZ]

TURUMASA alt for BAINAPI [PIK]
TURUMAWA alt for ETULO [UTR]
TURUMBU alt for LOMBO [LOO]
TURUNG [TRY] lang, India
TURUNGGARE alt for TUNGGARE [TRT]
TURUPU alt for TEREBU [TRB]
TURUTAP alt for MAIA [SKS]
TURVALI alt for TORWALI [TRW]
TUSCAN dial of ITALIAN [ITN]
TUSCARORA [TUS] lang, Canada; also in USA
TUSH alt for BATS [BBL]
TUSH dial of GEORGIAN [GEO]
TUSHA alt for TUXÁ [TUD]
TUSHAMA alt for SHAMA-SAMBUGA [SQA]
TUSIA alt for TOUSSIAN, NORTHERN [TSP]
TUSIA alt for TOUSSIAN, SOUTHERN [WIB]
TUSIAN alt for TOUSSIAN, NORTHERN [TSP]
TUSIAN alt for TOUSSIAN, SOUTHERN [WIB]
TUTAPI alt for OREJÓN [ORE]
TUTCHONE, NORTHERN [TUT] lang, Canada
TUTCHONE, SOUTHERN [TCE] lang, Canada
TUTELO [TTA] lang, USA
TUTET alt for CHAURA [CHO]
TUTLA MIXE alt for MIXE, MAZATLÁN [MZL]
TUTOH KENYA alt for KENYAH, TUTOH [TTW]
TUTONCANA dial of EVENKI [EVN]
TUTONG 1 [TTX] lang, Brunei; also in Malaysia
    (Sarawak)
TUTONG 2 [TTG] lang, Brunei
TUTRUGBU alt for NYANGBO [NYB]
TUTSINGO alt for TSINGA dial of TUKI [BAG]
TUTUBA [TMI] lang, Vanuatu
TUTUMI alt for TUMI [KKU]
TUTUNG alt for TUTONG 2 [TTG]
TUTUNOHAN alt for APUTAI [APX]
TUTUNOHAN alt for PERAI [WET]
TUTUNOHAN alt for TUGUN [TZN]
TUTUTEPEC MIXTEC alt for MIXTECO,
    TUTUTEPEC [MTU]
TUTUTNI [TUU] lang, USA
TUUNO alt for DOYAYO [DOW]
TUVA alt for TUVIN [TUN]
TUVALU alt for TUVALUAN [ELL]
TUVALUAN [ELL] lang, Tuvalu; also in Fiji, Kiribati,
    Nauru, New Zealand
TUVAN alt for TUVIN [TUN]
TUVA-URIANKHAI alt for TUVIN [TUN]
TUVIA alt for TUVIN [TUN]
TUVIN [TUN] lang, Russia (Asia); also in China,
    Mongolia
TUVINIAN alt for TUVIN [TUN]
TUWA alt for TUVIN [TUN]
TUWALI alt for IFUGAO, TUWALI [IFK]
TUWANG dial of LAWANGAN [LBX]
TUWARI [TWW] lang, Papua New Guinea
TUWAT alt for TOUAT dial of TAZNATIT [GRR]
TUWA-URIANKHAI alt for TUVIN [TUN]
TUWILI [BOV] lang, Ghana
TUXÁ [TUD] lang, Brazil
TUXINÁWA [TUX] lang, Brazil
TUYUCA [TUE] lang, Colombia; also in Brazil

TUYUKA alt for TUYUCA [TUE]
TUYUNERI alt for TOYERI dial of HUACHIPAERI [HUG]
TUZANTECO dial of MOCHO [MHC]
T-VALLEY alt for EIPOMEK [EIP]
TVER dial of KARELIAN [KRL]
TWA alt for RUTWA dial of RWANDA [RUA]
TWA dial of LENJE [LEH]
TWA dial of RWANDA [RUA]
T'WA KWAMA alt for KWAMA [KMQ]
TWA OF BANGWEULU dial of BEMBA [BEM]
TWA OF KAFWE dial of TONGA [TOI]
TWABO dial of GLARO-TWABO [GLR]
TWAHKA dial of SUMO TAWAHKA [SUM]
TWAMPA alt for UDUK [UDU]
TWANA [TWA] lang, USA
TWAR alt for ZANGWAL [ZAH]
TWENDI [TWN] lang, Cameroon
TWENTE alt for TWENTS [TWD]
TWENTS [TWD] lang, Netherlands
TWI alt for AKUAPEM dial of AKAN [TWS]
TWI alt for ASANTE dial of AKAN [TWS]
TWI alt for BWAMU, CWI [BWY]
TWI alt for TUIC dial of DINKA, SOUTHEASTERN [DIN]
TWIC alt for TUIC dial of DINKA, SOUTHWESTERN [DIK]
TWICH alt for TUIC dial of DINKA, SOUTH-WESTERN [DIK]
TWII alt for BAKONI dial of KENYANG [KEN]
TWIJ alt for TUIC dial of DINKA, SOUTHWESTERN [DIK]
TWOYU alt for DIZI [MDX]
TWUMWU dial of TIKAR [TIK]
TXIKÂN alt for TXIKÃO [TXI]
TXIKÃO [TXI] lang, Brazil
TXIRIPÁ alt for CHIRIPÁ [NHD]
TXITXOPI alt for CHOPI [CCE]
TXOPI alt for CHOPI [CCE]
TXUNHUÃ DYAPÁ alt for TSHOM-DJAPA dial of KANAMARI [KNM]
TXUNHUÃ-DJAPÁ alt for TSHOM-DJAPA dial of KANAMARI [KNM]
TXUWABO alt for CHWABO [CHW]
TYAL alt for ATAYAL [TAY]
TYAMA alt for EBRIÉ [EBR]
TYAMUHI alt for CEMUHÎ [CAM]
TYANGA alt for KYENGA [TYE]
TYAP [KCG] lang, Nigeria
TYAP alt for KATAB dial of TYAP [KCG]
TYAPI alt for LANDOMA [LAO]
TYARAITY [WOA] lang, Australia
TYEBALA alt for SENOUFO, CEBAARA [SEF]
TYEBARA dial of SENOUFO, CEBAARA [SEF]
TYEE dial of TEKE, WESTERN [TEZ]
TYEFO alt for TIÉFO [TIQ]
TYEFORO alt for TIÉFO [TIQ]
TYEMERI dial of NANGIKURRUNGGURR [NAM]
TYENGA alt for KYENGA [TYE]
TYEYAXO alt for BOZO, TIÉYAXO [BOZ]
TYHUA alt for HIETSHWARE [HIE]

TYM dial of SELKUP [SAK]
TYNESIDE NORTHUMBERLAND dial of ENGLISH [ENG]
TYO alt for BALI dial of TEKE, EASTERN [TEK]
TYO alt for TYOO dial of TEKE, CENTRAL [TEC]
TYOO dial of TEKE, CENTRAL [TEC]
TYOPI alt for LANDOMA [LAO]
TYREWUJU dial of CARIB [CRB]
TYROLESE alt for GERMAN, HUTTERITE [GEH]
TYUA alt for HIETSHWARE [HIE]
TYURA alt for NUGUNU [NNV]
TYURAMA alt for TURKA [TUZ]
TYVA alt for TUVIN [TUN]
TZELTAL, BACHAJÓN [TZB] lang, Mexico
TZELTAL, OXCHUC [TZH] lang, Mexico
TZILKOTIN alt for CHILCOTIN [CHI]
TZIMBRO alt for CIMBRIAN [CIM]
TZO alt for TSOU [TSY]
TZOTZIL, CHAMULA [TZC] lang, Mexico
TZOTZIL, CH'ENALHÓ [TZE] lang, Mexico
TZOTZIL, HUIXTÁN [TZU] lang, Mexico
TZOTZIL, SAN ANDRÉS LARRAINZAR [TZS] lang, Mexico
TZOTZIL, VENUSTIANO CARRANZA [TZO] lang, Mexico
TZOTZIL, ZINACANTÁN [TZZ] lang, Mexico
TZUKU alt for TSEKU [TSK]
TZUTUHIL alt for TZUTUJIL, EASTERN [TZJ]
TZUTUJIL ORIENTAL alt for TZUTUJIL, EASTERN [TZJ]
TZUTUJIL, EASTERN [TZJ] lang, Guatemala
TZUTUJIL, WESTERN [TZT] lang, Guatemala
U [UUU] lang, China
U alt for TIBETAN [TIC]
U dial of KHMU [KJG]
U NÍ alt for HANI [HNI]
UA HUKA dial of MARQUESAN, NORTH [MRQ]
UA POU dial of MARQUESAN, NORTH [MRQ]
UAB ATONI PAH METO alt for ATONI [TMR]
UAB METO alt for ATONI [TMR]
UAB PAH METO alt for ATONI [TMR]
UADZOLI dial of CARUTANA [CRU]
UAGEO alt for WOGEO [WOC]
UAI MA'A alt for WAIMA'A [WMH]
UAIAI dial of PAUMARI [PAD]
UAIANA alt for PIRATAPUYO [PIR]
UAIANA alt for WAYANA [WAY]
UAICANA alt for PIRATAPUYO [PIR]
UAIEUE alt for WAIWAI [WAW]
UAIKENA alt for PIRATAPUYO [PIR]
UAIMIRÍ alt for WAIMIRÍ dial of ATRUAHI [ATR]
UAIMO'A alt for WAIMA'A [WMH]
UAINANA alt for PIRATAPUYO [PIR]
UAIORA alt for WAYORÓ [WYR]
UAIQUIARE alt for WOKIARE dial of YABARANA [YAR]
UAIRÃ alt for TANIMUCA-RETUARÃ [TNC]
UAIUAI alt for WAIWAI [WAW]
UALAMO alt for WOLAYTTA [WBC]
UAMUÉ [UAM] lang, Brazil
UANANA alt for GUANANO [GVC]

UANANO alt for GUANANO [GVC]
UARDAI alt for ORMA [ORC]
UARE [KSJ] lang, Papua New Guinea
UARE dial of UARE [KSJ]
UARI alt for TUBARÃO [TBA]
UARIPI alt for TAIRUMA [UAR]
UASE alt for PELE-ATA [ATA]
UASI alt for PELE-ATA [ATA]
UASILAU alt for PELE-ATA [ATA]
UASONA alt for WASONA dial of TUCANO [TUO]
UAURA alt for WAURÁ [WAU]
UBA alt for WOLAYTTA [WBC]
UBACH alt for JAWE [JAZ]
UBAE dial of NAKANAI [NAK]
UBAGHARA [BYC] lang, Nigeria
UBAMER alt for WUBAHAMER dial of AARI [AIZ]
UBANG [UBA] lang, Nigeria
UBANI alt for IBANI [IBY]
UBDÉ alt for HUPDË [JUP]
UBETENG alt for EHOM dial of UKPET-EHOM [AKD]
UBI [UBI] lang, Chad
UBI alt for GLIO-OUBI [OUB]
UBIAN dial of SAMA, SOUTHERN [SIT]
UBILI alt for MERAMERA [MXM]
UBIMA dial of IKWERE [IKW]
UBIR [UBR] lang, Papua New Guinea
UBIRI alt for UBIR [UBR]
UBOI alt for KOBIANA [KCJ]
UBU dial of CHOURASE [TSU]
UBU dial of TBOLI [TBL]
UBU UGU alt for UMBU-UNGU [UMB]
UBUIA dial of DOBU [DOB]
UBWEBWE dial of PONGU [PON]
UBYE dial of EKPEYE [EKP]
UBYKH [UBY] lang, Turkey (Europe)
UBYX alt for UBYKH [UBY]
UCANJA KAMUKU alt for ROGO [ROD]
UCAYALI alt for COCAMA-COCAMILLA [COD]
UCAYALI alt for QUECHUA, SAN MARTÍN [QSA]
UCHAI SADRI dial of SADRI, ORAON [SDR]
UCHAMA dial of EVENKI [EVN]
UCHEAN alt for YUCHI [YUC]
UCHUR dial of EVENKI [EVN]
UCINDA alt for CINDA dial of CINDA-REGI-TIYAL
    [KAU]
UDA [UDA] lang, Nigeria
UDAI alt for MAMUJU [MQX]
UDAI dial of TEMUAN [TMW]
UDEGEIS alt for UDIHE [UDE]
UDEKHE alt for UDIHE [UDE]
UDERI dial of MARIA [MDS]
UDI [UDI] lang, Azerbaijan; also in Georgia, Russia
    (Asia), Turkmenistan
UDIHE [UDE] lang, Russia (Asia)
UDIN alt for UDI [UDI]
UDJIR alt for UJIR [UDJ]
UDLAM alt for WUZLAM [UDL]
UDMURT [UDM] lang, Russia (Europe); also in
    Kazakhstan
UDMURT alt for NORTH UDMURT dial of UDMURT
    [UDM]

UDO dial of ARIGIDI [AKK]
UDOM alt for NDE dial of NDE-NSELE-NTA [NDD]
UDUK [UDU] lang, Ethiopia; also in Sudan
UDUNG alt for WUTUNG [WUT]
UÉLÉ dial of KANGO [KTY]
UELLANSKIJ dial of CHUKOT [CKT]
//U//EN alt for NG/U//EN dial of XOO [NMN]
//U//EN alt for NG/U/EN dial of XOO [NMN]
/U//EN alt for NG/U//EN dial of XOO [NMN]
/U//EN alt for NG/U/EN dial of XOO [NMN]
UEN alt for NUMEE [KDK]
UEREQUEMA alt for GUAREQUENA [GAE]
UFAINA alt for TANIMUCA-RETUARÃ [TNC]
UFAUFA dial of IDUNA [VIV]
UFIA dial of ORING [ORI]
UFIM [UFI] lang, Papua New Guinea
UFIOM dial of ORING [ORI]
UFUFU dial of IDUNA [VIV]
UGANA dial of LAVATBURA-LAMUSONG [LBV]
UGANDAN SIGN LANGUAGE [UGN] lang,
    Uganda
UGARE alt for MESAKA [IYO]
UGAWNG alt for UGONG [UGO]
UGBALA dial of KUKELE [KEZ]
UGBE alt for ALEGE [ALF]
UGBEM dial of UBAGHARA [BYC]
UGE alt for ALEGE [ALF]
UGELE alt for UGHELE [UGE]
UGEP dial of LOKAA [YAZ]
UGHBUG alt for KUBACHI dial of DARGWA [DAR]
UGHELE [UGE] lang, Solomon Islands
UGI alt for BUGIS [BPR]
UGI alt for UKI NI MASI dial of SAA [APB]
UGI RIAWA alt for PASANGKAYU dial of BUGIS
    [BPR]
UGIE alt for NGIE [NGJ]
UGONG [UGO] lang, Thailand
'UGONG alt for UGONG [UGO]
UGUANO alt for AGUANO [AGA]
UHAMI [UHA] lang, Nigeria
UHEI KACHLAKAN alt for BENGGOI [BGY]
UHEI KACHLAKAN alt for LIANA-SETI [STE]
UHEI-KACLAKIN alt for BENGGOI [BGY]
UHEI KACLAKIN alt for LIANA-SETI [STE]
UHEI-KAHLAKIM alt for BENGGOI [BGY]
UHEI KAHLAKIM alt for LIANA-SETI [STE]
UHUMKHEGI alt for YUKUBEN [YBL]
UHUNDUNI alt for DAMAL [UHN]
UIGHOR alt for UYGHUR [UIG]
UIGHUIR alt for UYGHUR [UIG]
UIGHUR alt for UYGHUR [UIG]
UIGUIR alt for UYGHUR [UIG]
UIGUR alt for UYGHUR [UIG]
UINA alt for DESANO [DES]
UIRAFED alt for WIRAFÉD [WIR]
UISAI [UIS] lang, Papua New Guinea
UIVE alt for IYIVE [UIV]
UIYA dial of GHALE, NORTHERN [GHH]
UJARRÁS dial of CABECAR [CJP]
UJIJILI alt for TANJIJILI [UJI]
UJIR [UDJ] lang, Indonesia (Maluku)

UJJAINI alt for MALVI [MUP]
UJLTA alt for OROK [OAA]
UJUMCHIN alt for SHILINGOL dial of
MONGOLIAN, PERIPHERAL [MVF]
UJUMCHIN dial of MONGOLIAN, PERIPHERAL
[MVF]
UJUMUCHIN alt for UJUMCHIN dial of
MONGOLIAN, PERIPHERAL [MVF]
UJUMUCHIN dial of MONGOLIAN, HALH [KHK]
UJUURAAN alt for AJURAN dial of GARREH-
AJURAN [GGH]
UJUWA alt for MOKPWE [BRI]
UKAAN [KCF] lang, Nigeria
UKANAFUN dial of ANAANG [ANW]
UKAU alt for NORTHERN TAIRORA dial of
TAIRORA [TBG]
UKELE alt for KUKELE [KEZ]
UKFWO alt for OKU [OKU]
UKHRUL dial of NAGA, TANGKHUL [NMF]
UKHWEJO [UKH] lang, CAR
UKHWEJO dial of UKHWEJO [UKH]
UKI alt for BOKYI [BKY]
UKI alt for NGORO dial of TUKI [BAG]
UKI NI MASI dial of SAA [APB]
UKIAH dial of POMO, CENTRAL [POO]
UKIT [UMI] lang, Malaysia (Sarawak)
UKKIA alt for WAGAYA [WGA]
UKPE alt for UKUE [UKU]
UKPE dial of UKPE-BAYOBIRI [UKP]
UKPE-BAYOBIRI [UKP] lang, Nigeria
UKPELLA alt for OKPELA dial of IVBIE NORTH-
OKPELA-ARHE [ATG]
UKPET dial of UKPET-EHOM [AKD]
UKPET-EHOM [AKD] lang, Nigeria
UKRAINE-MOLDAVIA dial of ROMANI, VLAX [RMY]
UKRAINIAN [UKR] lang, Ukraine; also in Argentina,
Armenia, Azerbaijan, Belarus, Brazil, Canada,
Estonia, Georgia, Hungary, Kazakhstan,
Kyrgyzstan, Latvia, Lithuania, Moldova, Paraguay,
Poland, Romania, Russia (Asia), Slovakia,
Tajikistan, Turkmenistan, USA, Uzbekistan,
Yugoslavia
UKRAINIAN SIGN LANGUAGE [UKL] lang, Ukraine
UKRAINIAN VLAX ROMANI dial of ROMANI, VLAX
[RMY]
UKU alt for OKO dial of OKO-ENI-OSAYEN [OKS]
UKU alt for OKU [OKU]
UKUE [UKU] lang, Nigeria
UKURIGUMA [UKG] lang, Papua New Guinea
UKWA [UKQ] lang, Nigeria
UKWALI alt for UKWUANI dial of UKWUANI-ABOH-
NDONI [UKW]
UKWANI alt for UKWUANI dial of UKWUANI-ABOH-
NDONI [UKW]
UKWESE alt for KWESE [KWS]
UKWUANI dial of UKWUANI-ABOH-NDONI [UKW]
UKWUANI-ABOH-NDONI [UKW] lang, Nigeria
ULA alt for FUNGWA [ULA]
ULANCHAB dial of MONGOLIAN, PERIPHERAL
[MVF]
ULAU-SUAIN [SVB] lang, Papua New Guinea

ULAWA dial of SAA [APB]
ULA-XANGKU alt for WULA dial of PSIKYE [KVJ]
ULBA dial of MORO [MOR]
ULBARAG dial of GURAGE, EAST [GRE]
ULCH [ULC] lang, Russia (Asia)
ULCHA alt for ULCH [ULC]
ULCHI alt for ULCH [ULC]
ULDEME alt for WUZLAM [UDL]
ULEME alt for UNEME [UNE]
ULI alt for OLI dial of DUALA [DOU]
ULINGAN alt for MAUWAKE [MHL]
ULIPE alt for KUNZA [KUZ]
ULITHIAN [ULI] lang, Micronesia
ULKULU dial of KUNJEN [KJN]
ULLADAN alt for ULLATAN [ULL]
ULLATAN [ULL] lang, India
ULSTER dial of GAELIC, IRISH [GLI]
ULSTER dial of SCOTS [SCO]
ULTA alt for OROK [OAA]
ULU alt for AALAWA dial of RAMOAAINA [RAI]
ULU alt for MABAAN [MFZ]
ULU dial of KERINCI [KVR]
ULU dial of MINANGKABAU [MPU]
ULU AI dial of IBAN [IBA]
ULU AI' dial of DOHOI [OTD]
ULU CERES dial of JAH HUT [JAH]
ULU KAMPAR dial of SEMAI [SEA]
ULU KINTA dial of TEMIAR [TMH]
ULU LAKO dial of KUBU [KVB]
ULU LANGAT ORANG BUKIT dial of BESISI [MHE]
ULU MUAR MALAY alt for NEGERI SEMBILAN
MALAY [ZMI]
ULU SELAMA dial of KENSIU [KNS]
ULU TEMBELING dial of JAH HUT [JAH]
ULUBUKUSU dial of MASABA [MYX]
ULUBUYA dial of MASABA [MYX]
ULUDADIRI dial of MASABA [MYX]
ULUKISU dial of MASABA [MYX]
ULUKWUMI [ULB] lang, Nigeria
ULULERA alt for HUTU dial of RWANDA [RUA]
ULUMANDA' [ULM] lang, Indonesia (Sulawesi)
ULUMANDAK alt for ULUMANDA' [ULM]
ULUMBU alt for LOMBO [LOO]
ULUNCHUN alt for OROQEN [ORH]
ULUNDA alt for ULUMANDA' [ULM]
ULUN-NO-BOKAN alt for BAUKAN dial of BAUKAN
[BNB]
ULUN-NO-BOKON alt for BAUKAN dial of BAUKAN
[BNB]
ULUNYANKOLE alt for NYANKORE [NYN]
ULUNYANKORE alt for NYANKORE [NYN]
ULURAGOOLI alt for LOGOOLI [RAG]
ULWA alt for SUMO TAWAHKA [SUM]
ULWA dial of SUMO TAWAHKA [SUM]
ULYCH alt for ULCH [ULC]
'UM FALIN alt for JIMI [JIM]
UMA [PPK] lang, Indonesia (Sulawesi)
UMA dial of AKPOSO [KPO]
UMA BAKAH dial of KENYAH, WESTERN [XKY]
UMA BEM dial of KENYAH, KELINYAU [XKL]
UMA DARO dial of KAYAN, REJANG [REE]

UMA JALAM dial of KENYAH, KELINYAU [XKL]

UMA JUMAN dial of KAYAN, REJANG [REE]

UMA LAKAN dial of KAYAN, KAYAN RIVER [XKN]

UMA POH alt for LONG KEHOBO dial of KAYAN, REJANG [REE]

UMA RATU NGGAI dial of KAMBERA [SMI]

UMA TAU dial of KENYAH, KELINYAU [XKL]

UMA TIMAI dial of KENYAH, WAHAU [WHK]

UMADA alt for PUNDA-UMEDA dial of SOWANDA [SOW]

UMALASA alt for PENDAU [UMS]

UMANAKAINA [GDN] lang, Papua New Guinea

UMANHAN alt for OMAHA-PONCA [OMA]

UMANIKAINA alt for UMANAKAINA [GDN]

UMAR alt for YERETUAR [GOP]

UMARI alt for KAMORO [KGQ]

UMARI alt for YERETUAR [GOP]

UMATILLA [UMA] lang, USA

UMAUA alt for OMAGUA [OMG]

UMAWA alt for CARIJONA [CBD]

UMAYAM dial of MANOBO, AGUSAN [MSM]

UMBAIA alt for WAMBAYA [WMB]

UMBERTANA alt for ADYNYAMATHANHA [ADT]

'UMBEWAHA alt for KUMBEWAHA [XKS]

UMBINDHAMU [UMD] lang, Australia

UMBOI alt for KOVAI [KQB]

UMBRIAN dial of ITALIAN [ITN]

UMBU RATU NGGAI alt for UMA RATU NGGAI dial of KAMBERA [SMI]

UMBUGARLA [UMR] lang, Australia

UMBULE alt for CHOURASE [TSU]

UMBUNDO alt for UMBUNDU [MNF]

UMBUNDU [MNF] lang, Angola; also in Namibia

UMBU-UNGU [UMB] lang, Papua New Guinea

UMBUYGAMU [UMG] lang, Australia

UME alt for SAAMI, UME [LPU]

UME dial of GIDRA [GDR]

UME dial of ISOKO [ISO]

UMEDA [UPI] lang, Papua New Guinea

UMERA dial of GEBE [GEI]

UMIRAY AGTA alt for AGTA, UMIRAY DUMAGET [DUE]

UMIREY DUMAGAT alt for AGTA, UMIRAY DUMAGET [DUE]

UMM DOREIN dial of MORO [MOR]

UMM GABRALLA dial of MORO [MOR]

UMO alt for AREM [AEM]

UMON [UMM] lang, Nigeria

UMOTÍNA [UMO] lang, Brazil

UMPILA [UMP] lang, Australia

UMRAYA dial of HERTEVIN [HRT]

UMUA alt for MACUNA [MYY]

UMUA dial of MANGSENG [MBH]

UMUAHIA dial of IGBO [IGR]

UMURANO alt for OMURANO [OMU]

UMURUTA dial of BO [BPW]

UMUTINA alt for UMOTÍNA [UMO]

UNA [MTG] lang, Indonesia (Irian Jaya)

UNALASKAN alt for EASTERN ALEUT dial of ALEUT [ALW]

UNALE alt for OENALE-DELHA dial of ROTE, WESTERN [ROW]

UNAMBAL alt for WUNAMBAL [WUB]

UNAMI [DEL] lang, USA

UNANGAN alt for ALEUT [ALW]

UNANGAN alt for WESTERN ALEUT dial of ALEUT [ALW]

UNANGANY alt for ALEUT [ALW]

UNANGANY alt for WESTERN ALEUT dial of ALEUT [ALW]

UNANGG alt for WATUT, NORTH [UNA]

UNANGHAN alt for ALEUT [ALW]

UNANK alt for WATUT, NORTH [UNA]

'UNAR alt for BESME [BES]

UNDE dial of KAILI, DAA [KZF]

UNDIMEHA dial of NDANDA [NNZ]

UNDRI alt for URDU [URD]

UNDU dial of BERTA [WTI]

UNDUP dial of IBAN [IBA]

UNEAPA [BBN] lang, Papua New Guinea

UNEME [UNE] lang, Nigeria

UNGA dial of BEMBA [BEM]

UNGA dial of BURIAT, RUSSIA [MNB]

UNGAMEHA dial of NDANDA [NNZ]

UNGARINJIN alt for NGARINYIN [UNG]

UNGARINYIN alt for NGARINYIN [UNG]

UNGGUMI dial of WORORA [UNP]

UNGIE alt for NGIE [NGJ]

UNGOE dial of SUBA [SUH]

UNGOM alt for NGOM [NRA]

UNGORRI alt for KUNGGARI [KGL]

UNGU alt for IDUN [LDB]

UNGUJA dial of SWAHILI [SWA]

UNGWE alt for HUNGWORO [NAT]

"UNHAN" pejorative alt for INONHAN [LOC]

UNHUN dial of CURRIPACO [KPC]

UNI alt for HANI [HNI]

UNI alt for HONI [HOW]

UNIETTI alt for AFITTI [AFT]

UNINGANGK alt for URNINGANGG [URC]

UNKIA alt for FAIWOL [FAI]

UNOGBOKO dial of ISOKO [ISO]

UNSERDEUTSCH [ULN] lang, Papua New Guinea; also in Australia

UNSHOI alt for USUI [USI]

UNSUIY alt for USUI [USI]

UNTIB dial of AVAR [AVR]

UNUA [ONU] lang, Vanuatu

UNWANA dial of IGBO [IGR]

UNYAMA dial of MANYIKA [MXC]

UNYAMOOTHA alt for ADYNYAMATHANHA [ADT]

UNYEADA dial of OBOLO [ANN]

UNZA alt for NAGA, RENGMA [NRE]

UOLLAMO alt for WOLAYTTA [WBC]

UOMO alt for PAKAÁSNOVOS [PAV]

UPALE alt for NYANG'I [NYP]

UPATA dial of EKPEYE [EKP]

UPELLA alt for OKPELA dial of IVBIE NORTH-OKPELA-ARHE [ATG]

UPLAND YUMAN alt for HAVASUPAI-WALAPAI-YAVAPAI [YUF]

UPOTO alt for LIPOTO dial of LUSENGO [LUS]
UPPER ADELE dial of ADELE [ADE]
UPPER ASARO alt for DANO [ASO]
UPPER ASARO dial of DANO [ASO]
UPPER AUGUST RIVER dial of MIAN [MPT]
UPPER BAL dial of SVAN [SVA]
UPPER BALONG alt for BAKONI dial of KENYANG [KEN]
UPPER BAMU dial of BAMU [BCF]
UPPER BARAM KENJA alt for KENYAH, UPPER BARAM [UBM]
UPPER BELE dial of DANI, LOWER GRAND VALLEY [DNI]
UPPER BISAYA dial of BISAYA, SARAWAK [BSD]
UPPER BONDO dial of BONDO [BFW]
UPPER CARNIOLA dial of SLOVENIAN [SLV]
UPPER CHEROKEE alt for OTALI dial of CHEROKEE [CER]
UPPER CHINOOK alt for WASCO-WISHRAM [WAC]
UPPER CIRCASSIAN alt for KABARDIAN [KAB]
UPPER COLORADO RIVER YUMAN alt for HAVASUPAI-WALAPAI-YAVAPAI [YUF]
UPPER COQUILLE alt for COQUILLE [COQ]
UPPER EGYPT ARABIC alt for ARABIC, SA<IDI SPOKEN [AEC]
UPPER EGYPT ARABIC dial of ARABIC, SA<IDI SPOKEN [AEC]
UPPER ENGADINE dial of ROMANSCH [RHE]
UPPER GIO dial of DAN [DAF]
UPPER GROMA dial of GROMA [GRO]
UPPER INLET dial of TANAINA [TFN]
UPPER IRUMU alt for TUMA-IRUMU [IOU]
UPPER KENYANG dial of KENYANG [KEN]
UPPER KOLYMA dial of EVEN [EVE]
UPPER LADAKHI alt for CHANGTHANG [CNA]
UPPER LAGAIP dial of HEWA [HAM]
UPPER LAMET dial of LAMET [LBN]
UPPER LOZYVIN alt for NORTHERN VOGUL dial of MANSI [MNS]
UPPER LUSATIAN alt for SORBIAN, UPPER [WEN]
UPPER LUZH alt for OREDEZH dial of INGRIAN [IZH]
UPPER MAHASU PAHARI dial of PAHARI, MAHASU [BFZ]
UPPER MANAGALASI alt for ÖMIE [AOM]
UPPER MBO alt for NKONGHO [NKC]
UPPER MICHIAN-WISCONSIN CHIPPEWA dial of CHIPPEWA [CIW]
UPPER MOREHEAD alt for ARAMMBA [STK]
UPPER MOREHEAD alt for WÁRA [TCI]
UPPER MORI alt for MORI ATAS [MZQ]
UPPER MORTLOCK dial of MORTLOCKESE [MRL]
UPPER NAR alt for PHU dial of NAR PHU [NPA]
UPPER NAVARRAN alt for ALTO NAVARRO SEPTENTRIONAL dial of BASQUE [BSQ]
UPPER PIMAN alt for O'ODHAM [PAP]
UPPER PYRAMID dial of DANI, LOWER GRAND VALLEY [DNI]
UPPER SILESIAN dial of POLISH [PQL]
UPPER STIENG alt for STIENG, BULO [STI]

UPPER TANUDAN alt for KALINGA, UPPER TANUDAN [KGH]
UPPER TOR alt for BERIK [BER]
UPPER UGU RIVER dial of UMANAKAINA [GDN]
UPPER WASI-WERI dial of PRASUNI [PRN]
UPPER YAZGULYAM dial of YAZGULYAM [YAH]
UPPER YEI dial of YEI [JEI]
UPPER ZYPHE dial of ZAKHRING [ZKR]
UPPER ZYPHE dial of ZYPHE [ZYP]
UPSTREAM LESE alt for ARUMBI dial of LESE [LES]
UPURUI alt for WAYANA [WAY]
URA [URO] lang, Papua New Guinea
URA [UUR] lang, Vanuatu
URA alt for FUNGWA [ULA]
URA dial of BUMTHANGKHA [KJZ]
URA MADZARIN alt for MADZARIN dial of FALI [FLI]
'URADA alt for 'AUHELAWA [KUD]
URADHI [URF] lang, Australia
URAHULI alt for HULI dial of FALI [FLI]
URAK LAWOI' [URK] lang, Thailand
URAKHA-AKHUSH alt for AKUSHA dial of DARGWA [DAR]
URALI [URL] lang, India
URALI dial of IRULA [IRU]
URALI KURUMBA alt for KURUMBA, BETTA [QKB]
URALY alt for URALI [URL]
URAMA dial of KIWAI, NORTHEAST [KIW]
URAMT alt for URA [URO]
URAMBAL alt for BAYALI [BJY]
URAMBWEEN alt for BWEEN dial of FALI [FLI]
URAMET alt for URA [URO]
URAMIT alt for URA [URO]
URAMOT alt for URA [URO]
URAN alt for HATAM [HAD]
URAN dial of HATAM [HAD]
URANG alt for KURUX [KVN]
URAON alt for KURUX [KVN]
URAON alt for KURUX, NEPALI [KXL]
URAPMIN [URM] lang, Papua New Guinea
URARICAA-PARAGUA alt for NORTHERN NINAM dial of NINAM [SHB]
URARINA [URA] lang, Peru
URAT [URT] lang, Papua New Guinea
URAT alt for ULANCHAB dial of MONGOLIAN, PERIPHERAL [MVF]
URAT dial of MONGOLIAN, HALH [KHK]
URAT dial of MONGOLIAN, PERIPHERAL [MVF]
URAXA-AXUSHA dial of DARGWA [DAR]
URBAREG alt for ULBARAG dial of GURAGE, EAST [GRE]
URDU [URD] lang, Pakistan; also in Afghanistan, Bahrain, Bangladesh, Botswana, Fiji, Germany, Guyana, India, Malawi, Mauritius, Nepal, Norway, Oman, Qatar, Saudi Arabia, South Africa, Thailand, UAE, United Kingdom, Zambia
URENG dial of ASILULU [ASL]
UREPARAPARA alt for LEHALURUP [URR]
UREQUEMA alt for GUAREQUENA [GAE]
URFA dial of TURKISH [TRK]
URFI dial of KURMANJI [KUR]

URHOBO [URH] lang, Nigeria
URI [UVH] lang, Papua New Guinea
URI alt for AURAMA dial of PAWAIA [PWA]
URI alt for NAGA, AO [NJO]
URI VEHEES alt for URI [UVH]
URIA alt for ORYA [URY]
URIANKHAI alt for TUVIN [TUN]
URIANKHAI dial of KALMYK-OIRAT [KGZ]
URIANKHAI-MONCHAK alt for TUVIN [TUN]
URIGINA [URG] lang, Papua New Guinea
URIGINAU alt for URIGINA [URG]
URII alt for URI [UVH]
URIM [URI] lang, Papua New Guinea
URIMO [URX] lang, Papua New Guinea
URIPIV dial of URIPIV-WALA-RANO-ATCHIN [UPV]
URIPIV-WALA-RANO-ATCHIN [UPV] lang, Vanuatu
URITA dial of ARAPESH, BUMBITA [AON]
URIYA alt for ORIYA [ORY]
URKARAX alt for AKUSHA dial of DARGWA [DAR]
URLI alt for URALI [URL]
URMIA-MARAGHA alt for URMIA-MARAGHEH
    dial of ARMENIAN [ARM]
URMIA-MARAGHEH dial of ARMENIAN [ARM]
URMURI alt for ORMURI [ORU]
URNINGANGG [URC] lang, Australia
URO dial of ARIGIDI [AKK]
UROGO alt for ROGO [ROD]
UROOVIN alt for VIN dial of FALI [FLI]
URRIGHEL dial of TARIFIT [RIF]
URRTI dial of MIDOB [MEI]
URSÁRI dial of ROMANI, BALKAN [RMN]
URTSUN alt for SOUTHERN KALASHA dial of
    KALASHA [KLS]
URU [URE] lang, Bolivia
URU dial of CHAGGA [KAF]
URUA dial of GALEYA [GAR]
URUAK alt for ARUTANI [ATX]
URUANGNIRIN [URN] lang, Indonesia (Irian Jaya)
URUAVA [URV] lang, Papua New Guinea
URUBU dial of CARUTANA [CRU]
URUBÚ SIGN LANGUAGE alt for URUBÚ-KAAPOR
    SIGN LANGUAGE [UKS]
URUBÚ-KAAPOR [URB] lang, Brazil
URUBÚ-KAAPOR SIGN LANGUAGE [UKS] lang,
    Brazil
URUBU-TAPUYA alt for PIRATAPUYO [PIR]
URUCENA alt for URUCUIANA dial of WAYANA
    [WAY]
URUCUIANA dial of WAYANA [WAY]
URUDU alt for URDU [URD]
URU-EU-UAU-UAU [URZ] lang, Brazil
URUEWAWAU alt for URU-EU-UAU-UAU [URZ]
URUGUAYAN SIGN LANGUAGE [UGY] lang,
    Uruguay
URUKUN dial of ISEBE [IGO]
URUM [UUM] lang, Georgia; also in Greece, Ukraine
URUNDI alt for IAU [TMU]
URUNDI alt for RUNDI [RUD]
URUNYARUANDA alt for RWANDA [RUA]
URU-PA-IN [URP] lang, Brazil
URUPAYA alt for ARUPAI dial of MARITSAUA [MSP]

URURAGWE alt for NYAMBO [NYM]
URURI alt for IAU [TMU]
URUSHUBI alt for SHUBI [SUJ]
URUTANI alt for ARUTANI [ATX]
URUUND alt for RUUND [RND]
URUWA alt for YAU [YUW]
URYANKHAI alt for TUVIN [TUN]
URYANKHAI-MONCHAK alt for TUVIN [TUN]
US dial of KAG-FER-JIIR-KOOR-ROR-US-ZUKSUN
    [GEL]
USAGE dial of MIAN [MPT]
USAGHADE [USK] lang, Cameroon; also in Nigeria
USAKADE alt for USAGHADE [USK]
USAKEDET alt for USAGHADE [USK]
USAMBA alt for SAMBA [SMX]
USAN [WNU] lang, Papua New Guinea
USARI alt for URSÁRI dial of ROMANI, BALKAN
    [RMN]
USARI dial of KARKAR-YURI [YUJ]
USARUFA [USA] lang, Papua New Guinea
USBAKI alt for UZBEK, NORTHERN [UZB]
USBEKI alt for UZBEK, NORTHERN [UZB]
USBEKI alt for UZBEK, SOUTHERN [UZS]
USEN dial of BAROK [BJK]
USHAKU dial of BEFANG [BBY]
USHEIDA alt for MODELE dial of BEFANG [BBY]
USHI alt for AUSHI [AUH]
USHOI alt for USUI [USI]
USHOJO [USH] lang, Pakistan
USHU dial of KALAMI [GWC]
USHUJI alt for USHOJO [USH]
USHUT alt for LOWER PRASUN dial of PRASUNI
    [PRN]
USI alt for AUSHI [AUH]
USIAI alt for LELE [UGA]
USILELE alt for LELE [LEL]
USINO [URW] lang, Papua New Guinea
USIPI alt for KOK BOROK [TRP]
USIPI MRUNG alt for KOK BOROK [TRP]
USIRAMPIA dial of BARUYA [BYR]
USKU [ULF] lang, Indonesia (Irian Jaya)
USL alt for UGANDAN SIGN LANGUAGE [UGN]
USOKUN dial of DEGEMA [DEG]
USPANTECO [USP] lang, Guatemala
USSERI alt for ROMBO [ROF]
USSURI dial of NANAI [GLD]
USU alt for UYA [USU]
USUI [USI] lang, Bangladesh
USURUFA alt for USARUFA [USA]
UT dial of TEOR [TEV]
UTA' alt for MENEMO dial of META [MGO]
UTABI dial of IKOBI-MENA [MEB]
UTAHA alt for IFO [IFF]
<UTAIBA alt for CENTRAL NAJDI dial of ARABIC,
    NAJDI SPOKEN [ARS]
UTALO dial of DIODIO [DDI]
UTAMA alt for UTUMA dial of UBAGHARA [BYC]
UTAMU alt for UTUMA dial of UBAGHARA [BYC]
UTANGA alt for OTANK [UTA]
UTANGE alt for OTANK [UTA]
UTANK alt for OTANK [UTA]

UTARMBUNG [OMO] lang, Papua New Guinea
UTATU alt for BIANJIIDA dial of DATOOGA [TCC]
ÜTBÜ alt for CHIN, CHINBON [CNB]
UTE dial of UTE-SOUTHERN PAIUTE [UTE]
UTE-SOUTHERN PAIUTE [UTE] lang, USA
UTI alt for UDI [UDI]
UTI dial of ISOKO [ISO]
UTKALI alt for ORIYA [ORY]
UTNOOR dial of GONDI, SOUTHERN [GGO]
UTNUR dial of KOLAMI, SOUTHEASTERN [NIT]
UTONKON alt for UFIA dial of ORING [ORI]
UTORO alt for OTORO [OTR]
UTSAT alt for TSAT [HUQ]
UTSE alt for ICEVE-MACI [BEC]
UTSER alt for ICEVE-MACI [BEC]
UTSET alt for TSAT [HUQ]
UTSEU alt for ICEVE-MACI [BEC]
UTTARI dial of AWADHI [AWD]
UTU [UTU] lang, Papua New Guinea
UTUGWANG alt for PUTUKWAM [AFE]
UTUGWANG dial of PUTUKWAM [AFE]
UTUMA dial of UBAGHARA [BYC]
UTUPUA alt for AMBA [UTP]
UTUR alt for ETULO [UTR]
UTURUPA alt for USARUFA [USA]
UUD DANUM alt for DOHOI [OTD]
UUHUM alt for YUKUBEN [YBL]
UUHUM-GIGI alt for YUKUBEN [YBL]
UURTI alt for URRTI dial of MIDOB [MEI]
UUSIMAA SWEDISH dial of SWEDISH [SWD]
UUT DANUM alt for DOHOI [OTD]
UVBIE [EVH] lang, Nigeria
UVEAN alt for WALLISIAN [WAL]
UVEAN, WEST [UVE] lang, New Caledonia
UVHRIA alt for UVBIE [EVH]
UVIN alt for VIN dial of FALI [FLI]
UVOL alt for LOTE [UVL]
UVWIE alt for UVBIE [EVH]
UWASSI alt for WASI [WBJ]
UWENPANTAI dial of WEMALE, NORTH [WEO]
UWEPA-UWANO dial of YEKHEE [ETS]
UWET alt for BAKPINKA [BBS]
UWI alt for IWI dial of AKPOSO [KPO]
UY LO alt for CUOI CHAM dial of THO [TOU]
UYA [USU] lang, Papua New Guinea
UYA alt for SAUSI [SSJ]
UYANGA alt for DOKO-UYANGA [UYA]
UYGHUR [UIG] lang, China; also in Afghanistan,
    Australia, Germany, India, Indonesia,
    Kazakhstan, Kyrgyzstan, Mongolia, Pakistan,
    Saudi Arabia, Taiwan, Tajikistan, Turkey
    (Asia), USA, Uzbekistan
UYGHURI alt for UYGHUR [UIG]
UYGUR alt for UYGHUR [UIG]
UYOBE alt for SOLA [SOY]
UZAIRUE dial of YEKHEE [ETS]
UZAM alt for WUZLAM [UDL]
UZBAK alt for UZBEK, SOUTHERN [UZS]
UZBEK, NORTHERN [UZB] lang, Uzbekistan;
    also in Australia, China, Israel, Kazakhstan,

Kyrgyzstan, Russia (Asia), Tajikistan, Turkey
    (Asia), Turkmenistan, Ukraine, USA
UZBEK, SOUTHERN [UZS] lang, Afghanistan; also
    in Pakistan, Turkey (Asia)
UZBEKI alt for UZBEK, SOUTHERN [UZS]
UZBEKI ARABIC alt for ARABIC, UZBEKI SPOKEN
    [AUZ]
UZBIN dial of PASHAYI, NORTHWEST [GLH]
UZEKWE [EZE] lang, Nigeria
UZEMCHIN alt for UJUMCHIN dial of MONGOLIAN,
    PERIPHERAL [MVF]
UZERE dial of ISOKO [ISO]
UZHIL alt for AUSHI [AUH]
UZHILI alt for AUSHI [AUH]
UZLAM alt for WUZLAM [UDL]
UZO alt for IZON [IJC]
VA alt for VO [WBM]
VAAGRI BOOLI [VAA] lang, India
VAALPENS alt for XATIA dial of XOO [NMN]
VAANEROKI alt for BOKYI [BKY]
VAAZIN dial of DII [DUR]
VACACOCHA alt for ABISHIRA [ASH]
VACAMWE alt for KAMWE [HIG]
VACH dial of KHANTY [KCA]
VADAGA dial of TELUGU [TCW]
VADAGU alt for BADAGA [BFQ]
VADANDA alt for DANDA dial of NDAU [NDC]
VADARA alt for VIDIRI dial of BANDA-BANDA [BPD]
VADARI alt for WADDAR [WBQ]
VADARI dial of TELUGU [TCW]
VADIYA alt for ORIYA [ORY]
VADO dial of TINPUTZ [TPZ]
VADODARI alt for GAMADIA dial of GUJARATI
    [GJR]
VADONDE dial of MAKONDE [KDE]
VADO-VAENE' dial of TINPUTZ [TPZ]
VADVAL alt for PHUDAGI [PHD]
VAEDDA alt for VEDDAH [VED]
VAENE' dial of TINPUTZ [TPZ]
VAFSI [VAF] lang, Iran
VAGADI alt for WAGDI [WBR]
VAGALA alt for VAGLA [VAG]
VAGARI alt for KOLI, KACHI [GJK]
VAGARI alt for WAGDI [WBR]
VAGARIA alt for KOLI, KACHI [GJK]
VAGDI alt for WAGDI [WBR]
VAGED alt for WAGDI [WBR]
VAGERI alt for WAGDI [WBR]
VAGHAT dial of VAGHAT-YA-BIJIM-LEGERI [BIJ]
VAGHAT-YA-BIJIM-LEGERI [BIJ] lang, Nigeria
VAGHRI [VGR] lang, Pakistan
VAGHRI alt for BAURIA [BGE]
VAGHRI KOLI alt for VAGHRI [VGR]
VAGHUA [TVA] lang, Solomon Islands
VAGI alt for WAGDI [WBR]
VAGILY alt for WESTERN VOGUL dial of MANSI
    [MNS]
VAGLA [VAG] lang, Ghana
VAGRI dial of KOLI, KACHI [GJK]
VAGUA alt for VAGHUA [TVA]
VAH CUENGH alt for ZHUANG, NORTHERN [CCX]

VAHITU dial of TUAMOTUAN [PMT]
VAI [VAI] lang, Liberia; also in Sierra Leone
VAI TNEBAR alt for FORDATA [FRD]
VAIKENU alt for AMBENU dial of ATONI [TMR]
VAIKINO alt for AMBENU dial of ATONI [TMR]
VAILALA alt for OROKOLO [ORO]
VAIPEI alt for VAIPHEI [VAP]
VAIPHEI [VAP] lang, India
VAIRA dial of TAIRORA [TBG]
VAITUPU alt for SOUTH TUVALUAN dial of
    TUVALUAN [ELL]
VAIVERANG alt for ADONARA [ADA]
VAJIENG dial of CHRAU [CHR]
VAKAM dial of CITAK [TXT]
VAKHAN alt for WAKHI [WBL]
VAKUTA dial of KILIVILA [KIJ]
VAKWELI alt for MOKPWE [BRI]
VALAISAN dial of FRANCO-PROVENÇAL [FRA]
VALDOSTANO alt for VALLE D'AOSTA dial of
    FRANCO-PROVENÇAL [FRA]
VALDOTAIN alt for VALLE D'AOSTA dial of
    FRANCO-PROVENÇAL [FRA]
VALE [VAE] lang, CAR
VALE alt for GLAVDA [GLV]
VALE dial of VALE [VAE]
VALEIEN alt for GAVOT dial of PROVENÇAL [PRV]
VALENCIÀ alt for VALENCIAN dial of CATALAN-
    VALENCIAN-BALEAR [CLN]
VALENCIAN dial of CATALAN-VALENCIAN-
    BALEAR [CLN]
VALENCIANO alt for VALENCIAN dial of CATALAN-
    VALENCIAN-BALEAR [CLN]
VALIENTE alt for NGÄBERE [GYM]
VALIENTE dial of NGÄBERE [GYM]
VALLADER-UPPER ENGADINE alt for UPPER
    ENGADINE dial of ROMANSCH [RHE]
VALLE D'AOSTA dial of FRANCO-PROVENÇAL
    [FRA]
VALLEY COVE dial of AGTA, DUPANINAN [DUO]
VALLEY MIWOK alt for MIWOK, PLAINS [PMW]
VALLEY TIHAAMAH dial of ARABIC, HIJAZI
    SPOKEN [ACW]
VALLEY TONGA alt for WE dial of TONGA [TOI]
VALLEY YOKUTS dial of YOKUTS [YOK]
VALMAN [VAN] lang, Papua New Guinea
VALMIKI alt for KUPIA [KEY]
VALMIKI ADIVASI ORIYA dial of ORIYA, ADIVASI
    [ORT]
VAL-NOGLIKI dial of OROK [OAA]
VALONGI alt for BALONG dial of BAFAW-BALONG
    [BWT]
VALPAY alt for VALPEI [VLP]
VALPEI [VLP] lang, Vanuatu
VALPEI-HUKUA alt for VALPEI [VLP]
VALSERISCH alt for GRAUBENDEN-GRISONS
    dial of ALEMANNISCH [GSW]
VALUGA alt for VOLOW dial of MOTLAV [MLV]
VALUVA alt for VOLOW dial of MOTLAV [MLV]
VALUWA alt for VOLOW dial of MOTLAV [MLV]
VALVIDEIRU dial of FALA [FAX]
VAMA'A alt for MBUGU [MHD]

VAMAKONDE dial of MAKONDE [KDE]
VAMALE [MKT] lang, New Caledonia
VAMALE dial of VAMALE [MKT]
VAMBENG alt for MOKPWE [BRI]
VAME alt for PELASLA [MLR]
VAMWALU dial of MAKONDE [KDE]
VAMWAMBE dial of MAKONDE [KDE]
VAN dial of ARMENIAN [ARM]
VAN KIEU alt for BRU, EASTERN [BRU]
VANA alt for GBETE dial of MBUM [MDD]
VANAMBERE alt for WANAMBRE [WLN]
VANATINA alt for SUDEST [TGO]
VANAVARA dial of EVENKI [EVN]
VANDOUGOUKA dial of JULA, ODIENNE [JOD]
VANECHI alt for WANECI [WNE]
VANGA alt for SUDEST [TGO]
VANGUNU [MPR] lang, Solomon Islands
VANGUNU dial of VANGUNU [MPR]
VANIKOLO alt for VANO [VNK]
VANIKORO alt for VANO [VNK]
VANIMO [VAM] lang, Papua New Guinea
VANJARI alt for LAMBADI [LMN]
VANKIEU alt for BRU, EASTERN [BRU]
VANNETAIS dial of BRETON [BRT]
VANO [VNK] lang, Solomon Islands
VANUA BALAVU dial of LAUAN [LLX]
VANUA LAVA alt for VATRATA [VLR]
VANUMA [VAU] lang, DRC
VANUMAMI dial of KUANUA [KSD]
VAO [VAO] lang, Vanuatu
VAPIDIANA alt for ARUMA [WAP]
VAPOPEO' dial of TINPUTZ [TPZ]
VAPOPEO'-RAUSAURA dial of TINPUTZ [TPZ]
VARA alt for WÁRA [TCI]
VARA dial of BANDA, TOGBO-VARA [TOR]
VARESE alt for VARISI [VRS]
VARHADI-NAGPURI [VAH] lang, India
VARIEGATED MIAO alt for HMONG, NORTH-
    EASTERN DIAN [HMD]
VARIHÍO alt for HUARIJÍO [VAR]
VARISI [VRS] lang, Solomon Islands
VARISI dial of VARISI [VRS]
VARJAN dial of WAIGALI [WBK]
VARLI [VAV] lang, India
VARMALI alt for LAMENU [LMU]
VAROIS alt for MARITIME PROVENÇAL dial of
    PROVENÇAL [PRV]
VARSU alt for LEWO [LWW]
VARTASHEN alt for OGHUZ dial of UDI [UDI]
VARTAVO alt for BURMBAR [VRT]
VARTO dial of KIRMANJKI [QKV]
VASAVA alt for VASAVI [VAS]
VASAVA BHIL alt for VASAVI [VAS]
VASAVE alt for VASAVI [VAS]
VASAVI [VAS] lang, India
VASCUENSE alt for BASQUE [BSQ]
VASEKELA BUSHMAN [VAJ] lang, Namibia
VASKIA alt for WASKIA [WSK]
VASORONTU alt for ZOROTUA dial of KWADI
    [KWZ]
VASUI alt for TINPUTZ [TPZ]

VASUI dial of TINPUTZ [TPZ]
VASUII alt for TINPUTZ [TPZ]
VASYUGAN alt for VACH dial of KHANTY [KCA]
VATA dial of DIDA, LAKOTA [DIC]
VATEVE alt for TEWE [TWX]
VATKA-HAVOUTSI alt for PROPONTIS
    TSAKONIAN dial of TSAKONIAN [TSD]
VATRATA [VLR] lang, Vanuatu
VATURANGA alt for NDI dial of GHARI [GRI]
VAUDOIS dial of FRANCO-PROVENCAL [FRA]
VAUPS CACUA dial of CACUA [CBV]
VAVOEHPOA' dial of TINPUTZ [TPZ]
VAYU alt for WAYU [VAY]
VAZAMA alt for KXOE [XUU]
VAZEZURU alt for ZEZURU dial of SHONA [SHD]
VAZHIYAMMAR alt for MALARYAN [MJQ]
VEDA alt for VEDDAH [VED]
VEDANS alt for MALAVEDAN [MJR]
VEDDAH [VED] lang, Sri Lanka
VEDDHA alt for VEDDAH [VED]
VEEN COLONY alt for VEENKOLONIAALS [VEK]
VEENKOLONIAALS [VEK] lang, Netherlands
VEGLIOTE alt for DALMATIAN [DLM]
VEHEES alt for VEHES [VAL]
VEHES [VAL] lang, Papua New Guinea
VEI alt for VAI [VAI]
VEIAO alt for YAO [YAO]
VEIPHEI alt for VAIPHEI [VAP]
VEJOS alt for WICHÍ LHAMTÉS VEJOZ [MAD]
VELE alt for VERE dial of NAKANAI [NAK]
VELICHE alt for HUILLICHE [HUH]
VELIPERI alt for WALIPERI dial of IPEKA-TAPUIA
    [PAJ]
VELLA LAVELLA alt for BILUA [BLB]
VELUWS, EAST [VEE] lang, Netherlands
VELUWS, NORTH [VEL] lang, Netherlands
VEMGO dial of VEMGO-MABAS [VEM]
VEMGO-MABAS [VEM] lang, Nigeria; also in
    Cameroon
VENAAMBAKAIA alt for POMO, CENTRAL [POO]
VENACO dial of CORSICAN [COI]
VENAMBAKAIIA alt for POMO, CENTRAL [POO]
VENDA [VEN] lang, South Africa; also in Zimbabwe
VENDO dial of YASA [YKO]
VENETIAN [VEC] lang, Italy; also in Croatia, Slovenia
VENETIAN PROPER dial of VENETIAN [VEC]
VENETO alt for VENETIAN [VEC]
VENEZUELAN SIGN LANGUAGE [VSL] lang,
    Venezuela
VENGI alt for VENGO [BAV]
VENGO [BAV] lang, Cameroon
VENGOO alt for VENGO [BAV]
VENLOS dial of DUTCH [DUT]
VENTIMIGLIESE alt for MONÉGASQUE dial of
    LIGURIAN [LIJ]
VENTUREÑO [VEO] lang, USA
VEPS [VEP] lang, Russia (Europe)
VEPSIAN alt for VEPS [VEP]
VEQAURAA dial of TAIRORA [TBG]
VERA alt for VARA dial of BANDA, TOGBO-VARA
    [TOR]

VERAGUAS SABANERO alt for BUGLERE [SAB]
VERE alt for MOM JANGO [VER]
VERE dial of NAKANAI [NAK]
VERKHOVSK dial of NEGIDAL [NEG]
VERMANDOIS dial of PICARD [PCD]
VERON alt for PRASUNI [PRN]
VEROU alt for PRASUNI [PRN]
VERRE alt for MOM JANGO [VER]
VERUNI alt for PRASUNI [PRN]
VESERMYAN alt for NORTH UDMURT dial of
    UDMURT [UDM]
VESI alt for WUSHI [BSE]
VETAN dial of MALAVEDAN [MJR]
VETENG alt for KENSWEI NSEI [NDB]
VETTE KADA IRULA dial of IRULA [IRU]
VETTUVAN dial of MALAVEDAN [MJR]
VETUMBOSO dial of MOSINA [MSN]
VETWENG alt for KENSWEI NSEI [NDB]
VEVEVA alt for WEJEWA [WEW]
VEZO dial of MALAGASY [MEX]
VHE alt for ÉWÉ [EWE]
VICCHOLI alt for VICHOLO dial of SINDHI [SND]
VICCHOLI dial of SINDHI [SND]
VICE-ARXAVA dial of LAZ [LZZ]
VICHOLI alt for VICHOLO dial of SINDHI [SND]
VICHOLO dial of SINDHI [SND]
VICO-AJACCIO dial of CORSICAN [COI]
VICXIN dial of LAK [LBE]
VIDAR dial of ALVIRI-VIDARI [AVD]
VIDARI alt for VIDAR dial of ALVIRI-VIDARI
    [AVD]
VIDIRI dial of BANDA-BANDA [BPD]
VIDRI alt for VIDIRI dial of BANDA-BANDA [BPD]
VIDUNDA [VID] lang, Tanzania
VIDZEME alt for EASTERN LIVONIAN dial of LIV
    [LIV]
VIEMO [VIG] lang, Burkina Faso
VIENTIANE dial of LAO [NOL]
VIET alt for VIETNAMESE [VIE]
VIET GO MIEN alt for KHMER, CENTRAL [KMR]
VIETNAMESE [VIE] lang, Viet Nam; also in Australia,
    Cambodia, Canada, China, Côte d'Ivoire, Finland,
    France, Germany, Laos, Martinique, Netherlands,
    New Caledonia, Norway, Philippines, Senegal,
    Thailand, United Kingdom, USA, Vanuatu
VIETNAMESE PIDGIN FRENCH alt for TAY BOI
    [TAS]
VIGE alt for VIEMO [VIG]
VIGUÉ alt for VIEMO [VIG]
VIGYE alt for VIEMO [VIG]
VIGZAR alt for ZAAR dial of SAYA [SAY]
VIIPEKEEL alt for ESTONIAN SIGN LANGUAGE
    [ESO]
VIITTOMAKIELI alt for FINNISH SIGN LANGUAGE
    [FSE]
VIKHLIN alt for VIXLIN dial of LAK [LBE]
VIKZAR alt for ZAAR dial of SAYA [SAY]
VIL alt for BHILI [BHB]
VILA alt for BILA dial of TSONGA [TSO]
VILELA [VIL] lang, Argentina
VILI [VIF] lang, Congo; also in Gabon

VILLA ALTA ZAPOTECO alt for ZAPOTECO, YATZACHI [ZAV]

VILLA CORZO dial of TZOTZIL, HUIXTAN [TZU]

VILLA JUÁREZ TOTONACA alt for TOTONACA, XICOTEPEC DE JUÁREZ [TOO]

VILLAGE BOKOBARU dial of BOKOBARU [BUS]

VIMEU dial of PICARD [PCD]

VIMTIM alt for FALI [FLI]

VIMTIM alt for VIN dial of FALI [FLI]

VIN dial of FALI [FLI]

VINAATA dial of TAIRORA [TBG]

VINAHE alt for KARIYA [KIL]

VINCENTIAN dial of CARIB, ISLAND [CAI]

VINCENTIAN CREOLE ENGLISH dial of WIND-WARD CARIBBEAN CREOLE ENGLISH [SVG]

VINMAVIS [VNM] lang, Vanuatu

VINZA [VIN] lang, Tanzania

VIRA alt for JOBA [JOB]

VIRA dial of ZYOBA [ZYO]

VIRAC alt for BICOLANO, SOUTHERN CATANDUANES [BLN]

VIRGIN ISLANDS CREOLE ENGLISH [VIB] lang, U.S. Virgin Islands; also in British Virgin Islands, Guadeloupe, Netherlands Antilles

VIRGINIA ALGONKIAN alt for POWHATAN [PIM]

VIRI alt for BELANDA VIRI [BVI]

VIRI alt for BIRRI [BVQ]

VIRI alt for WINA dial of MASANA [MCN]

VIRYAL dial of CHUVASH [CJU]

VISAYAK alt for BISAYA, BRUNEI [BSB]

VISAYAK alt for BISAYA, SARAWAK [BSD]

VISAYAN alt for CEBUANO [CEB]

VISHAKAPATNAM dial of TELUGU [TCW]

VISHAVAN [VIS] lang, India

VISHOLI dial of SINDHI [SND]

VISIGOTH dial of GOTHIC [GOF]

VISIK dial of VEMGO-MABAS [VEM]

VITA dial of BANDA, WEST CENTRAL [BBP]

VITAL-ARKHAVA alt for VICE-ARXAVA dial of LAZ [LZZ]

VITEB-MOGILEV alt for NORTHEAST BELARUSAN dial of BELARUSAN [RUW]

VITI [VIT] lang, Nigeria

VITSKHIN alt for VICXIN dial of LAK [LBE]

VITTANGI FINNISH dial of FINNISH, TORNEDALEN [FIT]

VITU alt for MUDUAPA [WIV]

VIVIGANA alt for IDUNA [VIV]

VIVIGANI alt for IDUNA [VIV]

VIWIVAKEU dial of AMAHUACA [AMC]

VIWULU-AUA alt for WUVULU-AUA [WUV]

VIXLIN dial of LAK [LBE]

VIZCAINO alt for BISCAYAN dial of BASQUE [BSQ]

VIZIK alt for VISIK dial of VEMGO-MABAS [VEM]

VLAAMS [VLA] lang, Belgium; also in France, Netherlands

VLACH alt for ROMANIAN, MACEDO [RUP]

VLAEMSCH alt for FRANS VLAAMS dial of VLAAMS [VLA]

VLAEMSCH alt for VLAAMS [VLA]

VLAEMSCH alt for WEST VLAAMS dial of VLAAMS [VLA]

VLAX alt for ROMANI, VLAX [RMY]

VLAX ROMANI alt for ROMANI, VLAX [RMY]

VLUM alt for VULUM dial of MUSGU [MUG]

VO [WBM] lang, Myanmar; also in China

VO LIMKOU alt for LINGAO [ONB]

VOA DÊ alt for RED GELAO dial of GELAO [KKF]

VOD [VOD] lang, Russia (Europe)

VODERE alt for VIDIRI dial of BANDA-BANDA [BPD]

VODIAN alt for VOD [VOD]

VOGELKOP dial of BIAK [BHW]

VOGHERESE-PAVESE dial of EMILIANO-ROMAGNOLO [EML]

VOGUL alt for MANSI [MNS]

VOGULY alt for MANSI [MNS]

VOKO alt for LONGTO [WOK]

VOLGA alt for GRASSLAND MARI dial of MARI, LOW [MAL]

VOLGA OIRAT alt for KALMYK-OIRAT [KGZ]

VOLOF alt for WOLOF [WOL]

VOLOW dial of MOTLAV [MLV]

VOMNI alt for NDERA dial of KOMA [KMY]

VONKUTU alt for VUKUTU dial of LESE [LES]

VONO [KCH] lang, Nigeria

VONUN alt for BUNUN [BNN]

VOQTWAQ dial of CHRAU [CHR]

VORA alt for VARA dial of BANDA, TOGBO-VARA [TOR]

VORA dial of SINAUGORO [SNC]

VORE dial of BOBO MADARE, NORTHERN [BBO]

VORÉ dial of BOBO MADARE, SOUTHERN [BWQ]

VORO [VOR] lang, Nigeria

VORU alt for VYRUS dial of ESTONIAN [EST]

VÔRU dial of ESTONIAN [EST]

VOTE alt for VOD [VOD]

VOTIAK alt for UDMURT [UDM]

VOTIAN alt for VOD [VOD]

VOTIC alt for VOD [VOD]

VOTISH alt for VOD [VOD]

VÖTÖ alt for VITI [VIT]

VOTYAK alt for UDMURT [UDM]

VOUAOUSI alt for AUSHI [AUH]

VOUTE alt for VUTE [VUT]

VOUTERE alt for VUTE [VUT]

VOVO alt for BIERIA [BRJ]

VOVO dial of BIERIA [BRJ]

VOWAK alt for NORTHERN LENGUA dial of LENGUA [LEG]

VUITE alt for CHIN, PAITE [PCK]

VUKUTU dial of LESE [LES]

VULAA alt for HULA [HUL]

VULAVA dial of BUGHOTU [BGT]

VULUM dial of MUSGU [MUG]

VULUNG alt for THAO [SSF]

VUMBU [VUM] lang, Gabon

VUNADIDIR dial of KUANUA [KSD]

VUNAPU [VNP] lang, Vanuatu

VUNGUNYA dial of YOMBE [YOM]

VUNJO [VUN] lang, Tanzania

VUNMARAMA alt for HANO [LML]
VUNUM alt for BUNUN [BNN]
VUNUN alt for BUNUN [BNN]
VUNUNG alt for BUNUN [BNN]
VUPURAN alt for PAPORA [PPU]
VURAS alt for VURES dial of MOSINA [MSN]
VUREAS alt for VURES dial of MOSINA [MSN]
VURES dial of MOSINA [MSN]
VUTE [VUT] lang, Cameroon; also in Nigeria
VUTE DE BANYO alt for BUTE BAMNYO dial of VUTE [VUT]
VUTE DE DOUME alt for NUGANE dial of VUTE [VUT]
VUTE DE LINTE alt for NUJUM dial of VUTE [VUT]
VUTE DE MBANDJOK alt for VUTE MBANJO dial of VUTE [VUT]
VUTE DE NGORRO alt for NGORO dial of VUTE [VUT]
VUTE DE SANGBE alt for KUMBERE dial of VUTE [VUT]
VUTE DE TIBATI alt for NDUVUM dial of VUTE [VUT]
VUTE DE YANGBA alt for NUDOO dial of VUTE [VUT]
VUTE MBANJO dial of VUTE [VUT]
VUTEEN alt for YUPIK, SIRENIK [YSR]
VUTERE alt for VUTE [VUT]
VWELA alt for HWELA dial of LIGBI [LIG]
VWEZHI dial of GBAGYI [GBR]
VY alt for VAI [VAI]
VYRUS dial of ESTONIAN [EST]
WA alt for BLANG [BLR]
WA alt for LAWA, WESTERN [LCP]
WA alt for PARAUK [PRK]
WA alt for VO [WBM]
WA BAMBANI alt for AGOI [IBM]
WA KHAWK dial of MARU [MHX]
WA LON dial of VO [WBM]
WA MAATHI alt for MBUGU [MHD]
WA PROPER alt for LAWA, WESTERN [LCP]
WA PWI alt for VO [WBM]
WÄRÄ alt for WÁRA [TCI]
WA'A alt for DGHWEDE [DGH]
WÁÁDÚ dial of TOURA [NEB]
WAAGAI alt for WAGAYA [WGA]
WAAGI alt for WAGAYA [WGA]
WAALI alt for WALI [WLX]
WAAMA [WWA] lang, Benin
WAAMA dial of WAAMA [WWA]
WAAMWANG [WMN] lang, New Caledonia
WAANJAMA dial of MENDE [MFY]
WAANYI alt for WANJI dial of GARAWA [GBC]
WAAT alt for SANYE [SSN]
WAATA alt for BONI [BOB]
WAATA alt for SANYE [SSN]
WAATA dial of ORMA [ORC]
WAB [WAB] lang, Papua New Guinea
WABAG alt for MAE dial of ENGA [ENQ]
WABO [WBB] lang, Indonesia (Irian Jaya)
WABODA alt for WABUDA [KMX]
WABONI alt for BONI [BOB]
WABUDA [KMX] lang, Papua New Guinea

WABUDA KIWAI alt for WABUDA [KMX]
WABUI alt for HIXKARYÁNA [HIX]
WABULA dial of CIA-CIA [CIA]
WACHI alt for WACI-GBE [WCI]
WACI alt for WACI-GBE [WCI]
WACI-GBE [WCI] lang, Togo; also in Benin
WACIPAIRE alt for HUACHIPAERI [HUG]
WACIRI dial of PASHTO, CENTRAL [PST]
WACO dial of WICHITA [WIC]
WAÇU alt for WASU [WSU]
WAD alt for WADA dial of LUTOS [NDY]
WADA dial of BANDA-MBRES [BQK]
WADA dial of LUTOS [NDY]
WADA THURI alt for THURI [THU]
WADAGINAM [WDG] lang, Papua New Guinea
WADAGINAMB alt for WADAGINAM [WDG]
WADAI alt for MABA [MDE]
WADAI alt for ORMA [ORC]
WADAIKNS alt for MABA [MDE]
WADALEI dial of GALEYA [GAR]
WADAMAN alt for WARDAMAN [WRR]
WADAMKONG dial of RAWANG [RAW]
WADAPI-LAUT alt for AMBAI dial of AMBAI [AMK]
WADARIA alt for KOLI, WADIYARA [KXP]
WADAU dial of PASHAYI, NORTHWEST [GLH]
WADDAR [WBQ] lang, India
WADDAYEN alt for MABA [MDE]
WADEGA alt for JUMJUM [JUM]
WADEMA alt for YANOMAM dial of YANOMAMI [WCA]
WADERMAN alt for WARDAMAN [WRR]
WADHIARA alt for KOLI, WADIYARA [KXP]
WADI alt for OUEDGHIR dial of TAGARGRENT [OUA]
WADI dial of BATA [BTA]
WADI dial of JIMI [JIM]
WADIBU dial of BIAK [BHW]
WADIMBISA dial of BUDU [BUU]
WADIRI alt for YANYUWA [JAO]
WADIWADI dial of THURAWAL [TBH]
WADIYARA KOLI dial of KOLI, WADIYARA [KXP]
WADJARI alt for WAJARRI [WBV]
WADJERI alt for WAJARRI [WBV]
WADJIGINY [WDJ] lang, Australia
WADJIGU [WDU] lang, Australia
WADONDO alt for DONDO dial of NDAU [NDC]
WA-DUKU dial of BACAMA [BAM]
WADUMAN alt for WARDAMAN [WRR]
WADZOLI alt for UADZOLI dial of CARUTANA [CRU]
WAE GEREN alt for CENTRAL BURU dial of BURU [MHS]
WAE KABO alt for CENTRAL BURU dial of BURU [MHS]
WAE RANA [WRX] lang, Indonesia (Nusa Tenggara)
WAE SAMA dial of BURU [MHS]
WA'EMA [WAG] lang, Papua New Guinea
WAENGATU alt for NHENGATU [YRL]
WAERANA alt for WAE RANA [WRX]
WAESAMA alt for WAE SAMA dial of BURU [MHS]
WAFFA [WAJ] lang, Papua New Guinea
WAGA alt for WAKAWAKA [WKW]

WAGADI alt for WAGDI [WBR]
WAGAI alt for WAGAYA [WGA]
WAGAJA alt for WAGAYA [WGA]
WAGANGA alt for MANGANJA dial of NYANJA [NYJ]
WAGAP alt for CEMUHÎ [CAM]
WAGARABAI alt for SUGANGA [SUG]
WAGARI alt for WAGDI [WBR]
WAGARINDEM alt for YAFI [WFG]
WAGAU dial of BUANG, MAPOS [BZH]
WAGAWAGA [WGW] lang, Papua New Guinea
WAGAWAGA alt for WAKAWAKA [WKW]
WAGAWAGA alt for YALEBA dial of TAWALA [TBO]
WAGAWAGA dial of WAGAWAGA [WGW]
WAGAWAGA dial of WAKAWAKA [WKW]
WAGAYA [WGA] lang, Australia
WAGAYDY alt for WADJIGINY [WDJ]
WAGDI [WBR] lang, India
WAGDI dial of BHILI [BHB]
WAGE alt for ANGAL HENENG [AKH]
WAGELAK alt for RITARUNGO [RIT]
WAGEMAN [WAQ] lang, Australia
WAGGAIA alt for WAGAYA [WGA]
WAGHARI alt for WAGDI [WBR]
WAGHOLI alt for WAGDI [WBR]
WAGI [FAD] lang, Papua New Guinea
WAGIFA dial of BWAIDOKA [BWD]
WAGIMAN alt for WAGEMAN [WAQ]
WAGIMUDA alt for MAIANI [TNH]
WAGOI alt for AGOI [IBM]
WAGOW alt for TAMAGARIO [TCG]
WAGRI alt for WAGDI [WBR]
WAHA alt for LAMANG [HIA]
WAHAI alt for MANUSELA [WHA]
WAHAI alt for SALEMAN [SAU]
WAHAKAIM dial of LIANA-SETI [STE]
WAHAU KAJAN alt for KAYAN, WAHAU [WHU]
WAHAU KENYA alt for KENYAH, WAHAU [WHK]
WAHE dial of GBARI [GBY]
WAHGI [WAK] lang, Papua New Guinea
WAHGI, NORTH [WHG] lang, Papua New Guinea
WAHIBO alt for GUAHIBO [GUH]
WAHINAMA alt for MANUSELA [WHA]
WAHKE dial of RAWANG [RAW]
WAHMIRÍ alt for WAIMIRÍ dial of ATRUAHI [ATR]
WAI alt for AJIË [AJI]
WAI alt for WAIGALI [WBK]
WAI dial of NAGA, YIMCHUNGRU [YIM]
WA'I alt for WADI dial of BATA [BTA]
WA'I alt for WADI dial of JIMI [JIM]
WAI JILU alt for MANGILI-WAIJELO dial of KAMBERA [SMI]
WAIA alt for TABO [KNV]
WAIA dial of BUNGKU [BKZ]
WAI-ALA alt for WAIGALI [WBK]
WAIAMPI alt for WAYAMPI, OIAPOQUE [OYA]
WAIBUK alt for HARUAI [TMD]
WAIBULA dial of IDUNA [VIV]
WAICÁ alt for AKAWAIO [ARB]
WAICÁ alt for YANOMÁMI [WCA]

WAIDINA alt for SOUTHEAST VITI LEVU dial of FIJIAN [FJI]
WAIDJELU alt for MANGILI-WAIJELO dial of KAMBERA [SMI]
WAIDJEWA alt for WEJEWA [WEW]
WAIDORO dial of GIZRA [TOF]
WAIEMA alt for WA'EMA [WAG]
WAIGALA alt for WAIGALI [WBK]
WAIGALI [WBK] lang, Afghanistan
WAIGAN dial of HANUNOO [HNN]
WAIGELI alt for WAIGALI [WBK]
WAIGEO [WGO] lang, Indonesia (Irian Jaya)
WAIGIU alt for WAIGEO [WGO]
WAIJARA alt for OWENIA [WSR]
WAIJELO alt for MANGILI-WAIJELO dial of KAMBERA [SMI]
WAIKA alt for YANAMAM dial of YANOMAMI [WCA]
WAIKÁ alt for YANOMÁMI [WCA]
WAIKHARA alt for PIRATAPUYO [PIR]
WAIKINO alt for PIRATAPUYO [PIR]
WAIKISU dial of NAMBIKUARA, SOUTHERN [NAB]
WAIKU alt for YARUMÁ [YRM]
WAILAKI [WLK] lang, USA
WAILAPA [WLR] lang, Vanuatu
WAILBI alt for ADYNYAMATHANHA [ADT]
WAILBRI alt for WARLPIRI [WBP]
WAILEMI alt for IKOBI-MENA [MEB]
WAILPI alt for ADYNYAMATHANHA [ADT]
WAILU alt for AJIË [AJI]
WAIMA alt for RORO [RRO]
WAIMA dial of RORO [RRO]
WAIMA'A [WMH] lang, Timor Lorosae
WAIMAHA [BAO] lang, Colombia; also in Brazil
WAIMAHA alt for WAIMA'A [WMH]
WAIMAJA alt for WAIMAHA [BAO]
WAIMIRÍ dial of ATRUAHI [ATR]
WAIMOA alt for WAIMA'A [WMH]
WAIN alt for NABAK [NAF]
WAINA alt for PIRATAPUYO [PIR]
WAINA alt for SOWANDA [SOW]
WAINA dial of SOWANDA [SOW]
WAINANANA dial of TEOP [TIO]
WAING alt for DUWET [GVE]
WAINUNGOMO alt for DE'CUANA dial of MAQUIRITARI [MCH]
WAINYI alt for WANJI dial of GARAWA [GBC]
WAIOLI [WLI] lang, Indonesia (Maluku)
WAIPU alt for MEKWEI [MSF]
WAISARA alt for OWENIA [WSR]
WAISIKA alt for KAMANG [WOI]
WAIWAI [WAW] lang, Brazil; also in Guyana
WAIWERANG alt for ADONARA [ADA]
WAJA [WJA] lang, Nigeria
WAJA dial of WAJA [WJA]
WAJAKES dial of AMPEELI-WOJOKESO [APZ]
WAJAMLI alt for WAYAMLI dial of BULI [BZQ]
WAJAN DUTSE alt for DERUWO dial of WAJA [WJA]
WAJAN KASA alt for WAJA dial of WAJA [WJA]
WAJANA alt for WAYANA [WAY]
WAJAO alt for YAO [YAO]

WAJAPI alt for WAYAMPI, OIAPOQUE [OYA]
WAJARRI [WBV] lang, Australia
WAJARU alt for WAYORÓ [WYR]
WAJEWA alt for WEJEWA [WEW]
WAJO dial of BUGIS [BPR]
WAJOLI alt for WAIOLI [WLI]
WAKA [WAV] lang, Nigeria
WAKAJA alt for WAGAYA [WGA]
WAKAL dial of HITU [HIT]
WAKALANGA alt for KALANGA [KCK]
WAKANDE alt for MBEMBE, CROSS RIVER
    [MFN]
WAKARI alt for WAPAN [JUK]
WAKASIHU dial of LARIKE-WAKASIHU [ALO]
WAKATOBI alt for TUKANGBESI NORTH [KHC]
WAKATOBI alt for TUKANGBESI SOUTH [BHQ]
WAKAWAKA [WKW] lang, Australia
WAKAYA alt for WAGAYA [WGA]
WAKCHALI alt for HALUMBUNG dial of SANGPANG
    [RAV]
WAKDE [WKD] lang, Indonesia (Irian Jaya)
WAKE alt for KWANGE dial of GBARI [GBY]
WAKHANI alt for WAKHI [WBL]
WAKHI [WBL] lang, Pakistan; also in Afghanistan,
    China, Tajikistan
WAKHIGI alt for WAKHI [WBL]
WAKINDIGA alt for HADZA [HTS]
WAKKA alt for WAKAWAKA [WKW]
WAKKAJA alt for WAGAYA [WGA]
WAKOMBE alt for KOMBE dial of TUKI [BAG]
WAKONÁ [WAF] lang, Brazil
WAKORE alt for SONINKE [SNN]
WAKORIKORI alt for KOREKORE dial of SHONA
    [SHD]
WAKUE dial of MANAGALASI [MCQ]
WAKUT alt for TAI LOI [TLQ]
WAKUT alt for VO [WBM]
WALA alt for DAGAARI DIOULA [DGD]
WALA alt for WALI [WLX]
WALA alt for WAOLA dial of ANGAL HENENG [AKH]
WALACHIAN alt for MUNTENIAN dial of ROMANIAN
    [RUM]
WALAD DULLA dial of ASSANGORI [SUN]
WALAD DULLA dial of SUNGOR [SUN]
WALAF alt for WOLOF [WOL]
WALAHA dial of AMBAE, WEST [NND]
WALAK [WLW] lang, Indonesia (Irian Jaya)
WALAMO alt for WOLAYTTA [WBC]
WALANE alt for WOLANE dial of GURAGE, EAST
    [GRE]
WALANG alt for KUNBARLANG [WLG]
WALANGU dial of GUPAPUYNGU [GUF]
WALAPAI dial of HAVASUPAI-WALAPAI-YAVAPAI
    [YUF]
WALAR alt for WURLA dial of NGARINYIN
    [UNG]
WALA-RANO dial of URIPIV-WALA-RANO-ATCHIN
    [UPV]
WALARI alt for WALI [WLL]
WALARISHE alt for WALI [WLL]
WALBIRI alt for WARLPIRI [WBP]

WALE dial of BWANABWANA [TTE]
WALE dial of KHAM, TAKALE [KJL]
WALESE alt for LESE [LES]
WALI [WLL] lang, Sudan
WALI [WLX] lang, Ghana
WALI BANUAH alt for SIKULE [SKH]
WALIA alt for MASANA [MCN]
WALIA dial of MALGBE [MXF]
WALIA dial of MASANA [MCN]
WALIMI alt for NYATURU [RIM]
WALING [WLY] lang, Nepal
WALING dial of BANTAWA [BAP]
WALIO [WLA] lang, Papua New Guinea
WALIPERI dial of IPEKA-TAPUIA [PAJ]
WALISI alt for LESE [LES]
WALJBI alt for ADYNYAMATHANHA [ADT]
WALJWAN alt for WAYILWAN dial of
    WANGAAYBUWAN-NGIYAMBAA [WYB]
WALLA WALLA [WAA] lang, USA
WALLACE dial of BAJAU, INDONESIAN [BDL]
WALLAMO alt for WOLAYTTA [WBC]
WALLAROO alt for NUGUNU [NNV]
WALLIS dial of ALEMANNISCH [GSW]
WALLISIAN [WAL] lang, Wallis and Futuna; also in
    Fiji, New Caledonia, Vanuatu
WALLISIEN alt for WALLISIAN [WAL]
WALLON alt for WALLOON dial of FRENCH [FRN]
WALLON dial of FRENCH [FRN]
WALLOON alt for WALLON dial of FRENCH [FRN]
WALLOON dial of FRENCH [FRN]
WALMAJARRI [WMT] lang, Australia
WALMAJIRI alt for WALMAJARRI [WMT]
WALMALA alt for WARLMANPA [WRL]
WALMATJARI alt for WALMAJARRI [WMT]
WALMATJIRI alt for WALMAJARRI [WMT]
WALOMWE alt for LOMWE [NGL]
WALOOKERA alt for WARLUWARA [WRB]
WALPIRI alt for WARLPIRI [WBP]
WALPRE alt for SONINKE [SNN]
WALSA alt for WARIS [WRS]
WALSCHER alt for WALSER [WAE]
WALSER [WAE] lang, Switzerland; also in Austria,
    Italy, Liechtenstein
WALÜNG alt for WALING [WLY]
WALÜNG alt for WALING dial of BANTAWA [BAP]
WALUGERA alt for WARLUWARA [WRB]
WALULU dial of KALULI [BCO]
WALUNG alt for WALING [WLY]
WALUNG alt for WALING dial of BANTAWA [BAP]
WALUNG alt for WALUNGGE [OLA]
WALUNGCHUNG GOLA alt for WALUNGGE [OLA]
WALUNGGE [OLA] lang, Nepal; also in India
WALUNGGI KECCYA alt for WALUNGGE [OLA]
WALURIDJI alt for MULURIDYI [VMU]
WALURIGI alt for AMBAE, EAST [OMB]
WALUWARA alt for WARLUWARA [WRB]
WALYA alt for WALIA dial of MASANA [MCN]
WALYA dial of MASANA [MCN]
WAM alt for WOM [WMO]
WAMA alt for AKURIO [AKO]
WAMAI alt for SURUVIRI dial of ASHKUN [ASK]

WAMAIS alt for ASHKUN [ASK]
WAMANYIKA alt for MANYIKA [MXC]
WAMAR alt for MANOMBAI [WOO]
WAMAS [WMC] lang, Papua New Guinea
WAMAYI alt for ASHKUN [ASK]
WAMBAIA alt for WAMBAYA [WMB]
WAMBAJA alt for WAMBAYA [WMB]
WAMBAYA [WMB] lang, Australia
WAMBAYA dial of WAMBAYA [WMB]
WAMBERA dial of BORO [BWO]
WAMBISA alt for HUAMBISA [HUB]
WAMBON [WMS] lang, Indonesia (Irian Jaya)
WAMBUTU alt for MANGBUTU [MDK]
WAMDIU dial of MARGHI SOUTH [MFM]
WAMEI [COU] lang, Senegal; also in Guinea
WAMESA alt for WANDAMEN [WAD]
WAMESA dial of WANDAMEN [WAD]
WAMIA alt for TESO [TEO]
WAMIN [WMI] lang, Australia
WAMOANG alt for WAAMWANG [WMN]
WAMOLA alt for WAMORA dial of KATE [KMG]
WAMORA dial of KATE [KMG]
WAMPANOAG [WAM] lang, USA
WAMPAR [LBQ] lang, Papua New Guinea
WAMPUR [WAZ] lang, Papua New Guinea
WAMSAK [WBD] lang, Papua New Guinea
WAMWAN dial of MUYUW [MYW]
WAN [HWA] lang, Côte d'Ivoire
WAN alt for VAN dial of ARMENIAN [ARM]
WAN WAN alt for WANIB [AUK]
WANA alt for PAMONA [BCX]
WANA alt for TAA dial of PAMONA [BCX]
WANA dial of KATE [KMG]
WANAI alt for MAPOYO [MCG]
WANAM alt for YALE, KOSAREK [KKL]
WANAM dial of TAMI [TMY]
WANAMBRE [WLN] lang, Papua New Guinea
WANAMI dial of MANAM [MVA]
WANNA alt for GUANANO [GVC]
WANANA alt for GUANANO [GVC]
WANANG dial of KOCH [KDQ]
WANANO alt for GUANANO [GVC]
WANAP [WNP] lang, Papua New Guinea
WANCHENG alt for YUEHAI dial of CHINESE, YUE
  [YUH]
WANCHO alt for NAGA, WANCHO [NNP]
WANCI dial of TUKANGBESI NORTH [KHC]
WAND TUAN alt for KAMASAU [KMS]
WANDA [WBH] lang, Tanzania
WANDABONG dial of YOPNO [YUT]
WANDALA [MFI] lang, Cameroon; also in Nigeria
WANDALA dial of WANDALA [MFI]
WANDAMEN [WAD] lang, Indonesia (Irian Jaya)
WANDAMEN-WINDESI alt for WANDAMEN [WAD]
WANDARAN alt for WANDARANG [WND]
WANDARANG [WND] lang, Australia
WANDI dial of DASS [DOT]
WANDIA alt for WANDA [WBH]
WANDJI [WDD] lang, Gabon
WANDJIRA alt for WANYJIRRA dial of GURINJI
  [GUE]

WANDO dial of SIANE [SNP]
WANDYA dial of NYIHA [NIH]
WANÉ [WAN] lang, Côte d'Ivoire
WANECHI alt for WANECI [WNE]
WANECI [WNE] lang, Pakistan
WANETSI alt for WANECI [WNE]
WANG dial of MUONG [MTQ]
WANGA dial of LUYIA [LUY]
WANGAAYBUWAN dial of WANGAAYBUWAN-
  NGIYAMBAA [WYB]
WANGAAYBUWAN-NGIYAMBAA [WYB] lang,
  Australia
WANGADA alt for PINTIINI [PTI]
WANGANUI dial of MAORI [MBF]
WANGATA dial of MONGO-NKUNDU [MOM]
WANGDAY alt for WANDI dial of DASS [DOT]
WANGGAJI alt for PINTIINI [PTI]
WANGGAMADU alt for KOKATA [KTD]
WANGGAMALA [WNM] lang, Australia
WANGGANGURU [WGG] lang, Australia
WANGGO alt for WANGGOM dial of KOMBAI
  [KGU]
WANGGOM dial of KOMBAI [KGU]
WANGI-WANGI alt for WANCI dial of TUKANGBESI
  NORTH [KHC]
WANGJIAJI dial of DONGXIANG [SCE]
WANGKA dial of REMBONG [REB]
WANGKAJUNGA dial of MARTU WANGKA [MPJ]
WANGKAJUNGKA alt for WANGKAJUNGA dial of
  MARTU WANGKA [MPJ]
WANGKATJA alt for PINTIINI [PTI]
WANGKI alt for WANKI dial of MISKITO [MIQ]
WANGKUMARA alt for WONGKUMARA dial of
  NGURA [NBX]
WANGO dial of AROSI [AIA]
WANGOM alt for WANGGOM dial of KOMBAI
  [KGU]
WANG-THE dial of DZONGKHA [DZO]
WANGUMARRA alt for WONGKUMARA dial of
  NGURA [NBX]
WANGURRI dial of DHANGU [GLA]
WANI dial of KOLAMI, NORTHWESTERN [KFB]
WANIB [AUK] lang, Papua New Guinea
WANIGELA dial of KEOPARA [KHZ]
WANIMO alt for VANIMO [VAM]
WANINDILYAUGWA alt for ANINDILYAKWA [AOI]
WANINNAWA alt for KATUKÍNA, PANOAN [KNT]
WANJA alt for SOWANDA [SOW]
WANJE alt for WANCI dial of TUKANGBESI NORTH
  [KHC]
WANJI [WBI] lang, Tanzania
WANJI alt for LAMBADI [LMN]
WANJI alt for WANCI dial of TUKANGBESI NORTH
  [KHC]
WANJI dial of GARAWA [GBC]
WANKI dial of MISKITO [MIQ]
WANMAN [WBT] lang, Australia
WANNU [JUB] lang, Nigeria
WANO [WNO] lang, Indonesia (Irian Jaya)
WANOKAKA alt for WANUKAKA [WNK]
WANONI alt for KAHUA [AGW]

WANSUM alt for PAHI [LGT]
WANTAKIA dial of BARUYA [BYR]
WANTJI alt for WANCI dial of TUKANGBESI NORTH [KHC]
WANTOAT [WNC] lang, Papua New Guinea
WANUKAKA [WNK] lang, Indonesia (Nusa Tenggara)
WANUKAKA dial of WANUKAKA [WNK]
WANUMA alt for USAN [WNU]
WANYA alt for SOWANDA [SOW]
WANYAI alt for NYAI dial of KALANGA [KCK]
WANYATURU alt for NYATURU [RIM]
WANYIKA alt for MANYIKA [MXC]
WANYJIRRA dial of GURINJI [GUE]
WANYORO dial of ALUR [ALZ]
WAODANI alt for WAORANI [AUC]
WAOLA dial of ANGAL HENENG [AKH]
WAORANI [AUC] lang, Ecuador
WAPÃ alt for WAPAN [JUK]
WAPAN [JUK] lang, Nigeria
WAPATU alt for KALAPUYA [KAL]
WAPE alt for WAPI dial of OLO [ONG]
WAPI alt for PINAI-HAGAHAI [PNN]
WAPI alt for SAU dial of ENGA [ENQ]
WAPI dial of OLO [ONG]
WAPISIANA alt for ARUMA [WAP]
WAPITXANA alt for ARUMA [WAP]
WAPITXÁNA alt for ARUMA [WAP]
WAPIXANA alt for ARUMA [WAP]
WAPPO [WAO] lang, USA
WAPU dial of WANTOAT [WNC]
WAPUKUAMP alt for WEST-CENTRAL KOMBIO dial of KOMBIO [KOK]
WAPUMNI alt for NISENAN [NSZ]
WAR alt for MEOSWAR [MVX]
WAR dial of KHASI [KHI]
WÁRA [TCI] lang, Papua New Guinea
WARA [WBF] lang, Burkina Faso
WARA alt for LUWU dial of BUGIS [BPR]
WARABAL alt for BAYALI [BJY]
WARABAL dial of LOLA [LCD]
WARABORI dial of MARAU [MVR]
WARAGA dial of FOLOPA [PPO]
WARANDGERI alt for WIRADHURI [WRH]
WARAO [WBA] lang, Venezuela; also in Guyana, Suriname
WARAPICHE alt for CHAYMA dial of CARIB [CRB]
WARAPU [WRA] lang, Papua New Guinea
WARASAI alt for YAWU dial of YESSAN-MAYO [YSS]
WARAT alt for MADNGELE [ZML]
WARAU alt for WARAO [WBA]
WARAWARA alt for NORTHERN LIMBA dial of LIMBA, EAST [LMA]
WARAY [WRZ] lang, Australia
WARAY alt for WARAY-WARAY [WRY]
WARAY dial of WARAY-WARAY [WRY]
WARAY-WARAY [WRY] lang, Philippines
WARDAMAN [WRR] lang, Australia
WARDA'MAN alt for WARDAMAN [WRR]
WARDAY alt for ORMA [ORC]
WARDEI alt for ORMA [ORC]

WARDMAN alt for WARDAMAN [WRR]
WARDO dial of BIAK [BHW]
WARDUJI [WRD] lang, Afghanistan
WARDUMAN alt for WARDAMAN [WRR]
WARE [WRE] lang, Tanzania
WARE alt for WALE dial of BWANABWANA [TTE]
WAREKENA alt for GUAREQUENA [GAE]
WAREKÉNA alt for GUAREQUENA [GAE]
WAREMA alt for YANOMAM dial of YANOMAMI [WCA]
WAREMBOIVORO alt for WAREMBORI [WSA]
WAREMBORI [WSA] lang, Indonesia (Irian Jaya)
WAREMBORI alt for WARABORI dial of MARAU [MVR]
WARENBORI alt for WAREMBORI [WSA]
WARES [WAI] lang, Indonesia (Irian Jaya)
WARGARINDEM alt for YAFI [WFG]
WARGLA alt for TAGARGRENT [OUA]
WARI alt for PAKAÁSNOVOS [PAV]
WARI alt for TUBARÃO [TBA]
WARI alt for WALE dial of BWANABWANA [TTE]
WARI alt for WARITAI [WBE]
WARI dial of BIAK [BHW]
WARIADAI alt for MORIGI [MDB]
WARIAPANO alt for PANOBO [PNO]
WARIHÍO alt for HUARIJÍO [VAR]
WARIKIANA alt for KAXUIÂNA [KBB]
WARIKYANA alt for KAXUIÂNA [KBB]
WARILAU alt for KOLA [KVV]
WARIS [WRS] lang, Papua New Guinea; also in Indonesia (Irian Jaya)
WARITAI [WBE] lang, Indonesia (Irian Jaya)
WARIYANGGA [WRI] lang, Australia
WARJA alt for WARJI [WJI]
WARJAWA alt for WARJI [WJI]
WARJI [WJI] lang, Nigeria
WARKAY-BIPIM [BGV] lang, Indonesia (Irian Jaya)
WARKI alt for DILLING [DIL]
WARKIMBE alt for DILLING [DIL]
WARKYA alt for WAGAYA [WGA]
WARLANG alt for KUNBARLANG [WLG]
WARLI alt for VARLI [VAV]
WARLMANPA [WRL] lang, Australia
WARLPIRI [WBP] lang, Australia
WARLUWARA [WRB] lang, Australia
WARM SPRINGS alt for TENINO [WAR]
WARMÂWA dial of KURDI [KDB]
WARN dial of KISI, SOUTHERN [KSS]
WARNANG [WRN] lang, Sudan
WARNDARANG alt for WANDARANG [WND]
WARNMAN alt for WANMAN [WBT]
WARO alt for PALOR [FAP]
WAROPEN [WRP] lang, Indonesia (Irian Jaya)
WAROPEN KAI dial of WAROPEN [WRP]
WARO-WARO alt for WOLOF [WOL]
WARPOK alt for ORYA [URY]
WARRA alt for NUGUNU [NNV]
WARRAI alt for WARAY [WRZ]
WARRAMUNGA alt for WARUMUNGU [WRM]
WARRANGOO alt for WIRANGU [WIW]
WARRAU alt for WARAO [WBA]

WARRA-WARRA alt for YIDINY [YII]
WARRGAMAY [WGY] lang, Australia
WARRGAT alt for MARANUNGGU dial of
  MARINGARR [ZMT]
WARRI alt for ISEKIRI [ITS]
WARRIYANGKA alt for WARIYANGGA [WRI]
WARRYBOORA alt for YIDINY [YII]
WARSA dial of BIAK [BHW]
WARSINA alt for WERSING [KVW]
WARTAMAN alt for WARDAMAN [WRR]
WARU [WRU] lang, Indonesia (Sulawesi)
WARU dial of WARU [WRU]
WARUMUNGU [WRM] lang, Australia
WARUNA [WRV] lang, Papua New Guinea
WARUNGU [WRG] lang, Australia
WARUWARU alt for YUWANA [YAU]
WASA [WSS] lang, Ghana
WASA dial of BANDA, MID-SOUTHERN [BJO]
WASAMBU [WSM] lang, Papua New Guinea
WASANYE alt for BONI [BOB]
WASANYE alt for SANYE [SSN]
WASARE alt for KAPRIMAN [DJU]
WASAW alt for WASA [WSS]
WASCO-WISHRAM [WAC] lang, USA
WASE [JUW] lang, Nigeria
WASEMBO [GSP] lang, Papua New Guinea
WASEP NAU dial of URAT [URT]
WASEP YAM dial of URAT [URT]
WASHKUK alt for KWOMA [KMO]
WASHKUK alt for KWOMA dial of KWOMA [KMO]
WASHO [WAS] lang, USA
WASHOE alt for WASHO [WAS]
WASI [WBJ] lang, Tanzania
WASI alt for PELE-ATA [ATA]
WASIOR dial of WANDAMEN [WAD]
WASI-VERI alt for PRASUNI [PRN]
WASKIA [WSK] lang, Papua New Guinea
WASOI alt for TINPUTZ [TPZ]
WASONA dial of TUCANO [TUO]
WASONJO alt for TEMI [SOZ]
WASSA alt for WASA [WSS]
WASSISI alt for WEASISI dial of WHITESANDS
  [TNP]
WASSOULOUNKA alt for WASULU dial of JULA,
  ODIENNE [JOD]
WASSOULOUNKA alt for WASULU dial of
  MANINKA, FOREST [MYQ]
WASSULU alt for WASULU dial of MANINKA,
  KANKAN [MNI]
WASSULUNKA alt for WASULU dial of
  BAMANANKAN [BRA]
WASSULUNKA alt for WASULU dial of JULA,
  ODIENNE [JOD]
WASSULUNKA alt for WASULU dial of MANINKA,
  FOREST [MYQ]
WASSULUNKA alt for WASULU dial of MANINKA,
  KANKAN [MNI]
WASSULUNKE alt for WASULU dial of
  BAMANANKAN [BRA]
WASSULUNKE alt for WASULU dial of JULA,
  ODIENNE [JOD]

WASSULUNKE alt for WASULU dial of MANINKA,
  FOREST [MYQ]
WASSULUNKE alt for WASULU dial of MANINKA,
  KANKAN [MNI]
WASU [WSU] lang, Brazil
WASULU dial of BAMANANKAN [BRA]
WASULU dial of JULA, ODIENNE [JOD]
WASULU dial of MANINKA, FOREST [MYQ]
WASULU dial of MANINKA, KANKAN [MNI]
WASUSU dial of NAMBIKUARA, SOUTHERN
  [NAB]
WASUU alt for WASULU dial of BAMANANKAN
  [BRA]
WAT dial of LIMBUM [LIM]
WATA alt for BONI [BOB]
WATA-BALA alt for BONI [BOB]
WATAKATAUI [WTK] lang, Papua New Guinea
WATALUMA [WAT] lang, Papua New Guinea
WATAM [WAX] lang, Papua New Guinea
WATANDE alt for DANDA dial of NDAU [NDC]
WATANG dial of KAMANG [WOI]
WATAPOR alt for ANGOR [AGG]
WATEMI alt for TEMI [SOZ]
WATENA dial of KULA [TPG]
"WATER BUSHMEN" pejorative alt for KXOE [XUU]
WATER BUSHMEN alt for KXOE [XUU]
WATEVE alt for TEWE [TWX]
WATIFA alt for DUMPU [WTF]
WATIWA alt for DUMPU [WTF]
WATJARI alt for WAJARRI [WBV]
WATJARRI alt for WAJARRI [WBV]
WATOM dial of KUANUA [KSD]
WATONGA alt for TONGA dial of NDAU [NDC]
WATUBELA [WAH] lang, Indonesia (Maluku)
WATULAI alt for BATULEY [BAY]
WATUT alt for HAMTAI [HMT]
WATUT alt for WATUT, MIDDLE [MPL]
WATUT alt for WATUT, NORTH [UNA]
WATUT, MIDDLE [MPL] lang, Papua New Guinea
WATUT, NORTH [UNA] lang, Papua New Guinea
WATUT, SOUTH [MCY] lang, Papua New Guinea
WATYI alt for WACI-GBE [WCI]
WATYU alt for WACI-GBE [WCI]
WAUMEO alt for WOUN MEU [NOA]
WAUN MEO alt for WOUN MEU [NOA]
WAUNANA alt for WOUN MEU [NOA]
WAUPE alt for KWATO [KOP]
WAURÁ [WAU] lang, Brazil
WAWA [WWW] lang, Cameroon
WÂWÂ alt for KURDI [KDB]
WAWA dial of BUSA [BQP]
WAWAN dial of HANUNOO [HNN]
WAWANA dial of BANDI [GBA]
WAWILAG alt for RITARUNGO [RIT]
WAWOI alt for KAMULA [KHM]
WAWONII [WOW] lang, Indonesia (Sulawesi)
WAWONII dial of WAWONII [WOW]
WAXE alt for WATAKATAUI [WTK]
WAXIANGHUA [WXA] lang, China
WAY LIMA dial of PESISIR, SOUTHERN [PEC]
WAYA dial of FIJIAN, WESTERN [WYY]

WAYA dial of SAPO [KRN]
WAYAMLI dial of BULI [BZQ]
WAYAMPI, AMAPARI [OYM] lang, Brazil
WAYAMPI, OIAPOQUE [OYA] lang, French Guiana;
  also in Brazil
WAYAM-RUBU dial of BAUCHI [BSF]
WAYANA [WAY] lang, Suriname; also in Brazil,
  French Guiana
WAYÁNA alt for WAYANA [WAY]
WAYAPI alt for WAYAMPI, OIAPOQUE [OYA]
WAYAPÍ alt for WAYAMPI, OIAPOQUE [OYA]
WAYÃPI alt for WAYAMPI, OIAPOQUE [OYA]
WAYAPO alt for LISELA [LCL]
WAYARICURI alt for AKURIO [AKO]
WAYCHA dial of QUECHUA, WANCA, HUAYLLA
  [QHU]
WAYHARA alt for YURUTI [YUI]
WAYILWAN dial of WANGAAYBUWAN-
  NGIYAMBAA [WYB]
WAYO alt for WAYU [VAY]
WAYOLI alt for WAIOLI [WLI]
WAYOMBA alt for NGULU [NGP]
WAYOMBO alt for ZIGULA [ZIW]
WAYORÓ [WYR] lang, Brazil
WAYTO alt for WEYTO [WOY]
WAYU [VAY] lang, Nepal
WAYURÚ alt for WAYORÓ [WYR]
WAYUU [GUC] lang, Colombia; also in Venezuela
WAZAIZARA alt for GUAJÁ [GUJ]
WAZAN dial of MOFU, NORTH [MFK]
WAZANG alt for WAZAN dial of MOFU, NORTH
  [MFK]
WAZEGUA alt for ZIGULA [ZIW]
WAZEZURU alt for ZEZURU dial of SHONA [SHD]
WAZHAZHE alt for OSAGE [OSA]
WAZIRI alt for WACIRI dial of PASHTO, CENTRAL
  [PST]
WE alt for FUNGOM [FUG]
WE dial of TONGA [TOI]
WE alt for GHOMÁLÁ' CENTRAL dial of GHOMALA
  [BBJ]
WÈ NORTHERN [WOB] lang, Côte d'Ivoire
WÈ SOUTHERN [GXX] lang, Côte d'Ivoire
WÈ WESTERN [WEC] lang, Côte d'Ivoire
WEASISI dial of WHITESANDS [TNP]
WEDA alt for SAWAI [SZW]
WEDA alt for VEDDAH [VED]
WEDA dial of SAWAI [SZW]
WEDA-SAWAI alt for SAWAI [SZW]
WEDAU [WED] lang, Papua New Guinea
WEDAUN alt for WEDAU [WED]
WEDAWAN alt for WEDAU [WED]
WEDDO alt for VEDDAH [VED]
WEDEBO dial of GREBO, BARCLAYVILLE [GRY]
WEDEBO GREBO alt for GREBO, BARCLAYVILLE
  [GRY]
WEDJAH alt for WAYA dial of SAPO [KRN]
WÈÈ alt for WÈ NORTHERN [WOB]
WÈÈ alt for WÈ SOUTHERN [GXX]
WÈÈ alt for WÈ WESTERN [WEC]
WEELA alt for HWELA dial of LIGBI [LIG]

WEELA alt for LIGBI [LIG]
WEEN alt for TOURA [NEB]
WEGAL dial of PASHAYI, SOUTHEAST [DRA]
WEGAM alt for KUGAMA [KOW]
WEGELE alt for GENGLE [GEG]
WEH [WEH] lang, Cameroon
WEI alt for TIBETAN [TIC]
WEIDYENYE alt for MUNDURUKÚ [MYU]
WEIGU dial of QIANG, NORTHERN [CNG]
WEILA alt for HWELA dial of LIGBI [LIG]
WEILA alt for LIGBI [LIG]
WEILATE alt for KALMYK-OIRAT [KGZ]
WEIM alt for GAL [GAP]
WEIRATE dial of TAUSE [TAD]
WEIWUER alt for UYGHUR [UIG]
WEIZANG alt for TIBETAN [TIC]
WEJEWA [WEW] lang, Indonesia (Nusa
  Tenggara)
WELAM alt for NAGA, KHIAMNIUNGAN [NKY]
WELAMO alt for WOLAYTTA [WBC]
WELAUNG [WEL] lang, Myanmar
WELE alt for WERI [WER]
WELEKI alt for WELIKI [KLH]
WELEMUR alt for APUTAI [APX]
WELI alt for WERI [WER]
WELIKI [KLH] lang, Papua New Guinea
WELLAMO alt for WOLAYTTA [WBC]
WELSH [WLS] lang, United Kingdom; also in
  Argentina, Canada
WEMALE, NORTH [WEO] lang, Indonesia (Maluku)
WEMALE, SOUTH [TLW] lang, Indonesia (Maluku)
WEMBA alt for BEMBA [BEM]
WEMBI alt for MANEM [JET]
WEME alt for WEME-GBE [WEM]
WEME dial of GUN-GBE [GUW]
WEME-GBE [WEM] lang, Benin
WEMO dial of KATE [KMG]
WEN alt for NUMEE [KDK]
WENATCHEE alt for WENATCHI dial of COLUMBIA-
  WENATCHI [COL]
WENATCHI dial of COLUMBIA-WENATCHI [COL]
WENATCHI-COLUMBIA alt for COLUMBIA-
  WENATCHI [COL]
WENCHANG alt for HAINAN dial of CHINESE, MIN
  NAN [CFR]
WENDAT alt for WYANDOT [WYA]
WENDISH alt for SORBIAN, LOWER [WEE]
WENDISH alt for SORBIAN, UPPER [WEN]
WEN-MA dial of ZHUANG, SOUTHERN [CCY]
WENTA dial of HAMTAI [HMT]
WENTEENE dial of TOUSSIAN, NORTHERN [TSP]
WENYA dial of TUMBUKA [TUW]
WEPPA WANO alt for UWEPA-UWANO dial of
  YEKHEE [ETS]
WERCHIKWAR alt for YASIN dial of BURUSHASKI
  [BSK]
WERDERS alt for WADDAR [WBQ]
WERE [WEI] lang, Papua New Guinea
WERE alt for MOM JANGO [VER]
WERE alt for SAWAI [SZW]
WEREKENA alt for GUAREQUENA [GAE]

WERETAI alt for WARITAI [WBE]
WERI [WER] lang, Papua New Guinea
WERI alt for ARAPESH, BUMBITA [AON]
WERIAGAR dial of KEMBERANO [BZP]
WERIKENA alt for GUAREQUENA [GAE]
WERIL dial of ARAPESH, BUMBITA [AON]
WERINAMA alt for BOBOT [BTY]
WERIR dial of ARAPESH, BUMBITA [AON]
WERNI alt for WARNANG [WRN]
WEROGERY alt for WIRADHURI [WRH]
WERRIA dial of MORO [MOR]
WERRO alt for VÔRU dial of ESTONIAN [EST]
WERSIN alt for WERSING [KVW]
WERSING [KVW] lang, Indonesia (Nusa Tenggara)
WERUGHA dial of TAITA [DAV]
WES COS alt for PIDGIN, CAMEROON [WES]
WESA dial of NYOLE [NUJ]
WESI alt for WATUBELA [WAH]
WEST ADONARA dial of ADONARA [ADA]
WEST ALASKA "ESKIMO" pejorative alt for YUPIK, CENTRAL [ESU]
WEST AMARASI alt for AMARASI BARAT dial of AMARASI [AAZ]
WEST ANGAL HENENG alt for ANGAL HENENG [AKH]
WEST ARABIAN COLLOQUIAL ARABIC alt for ARABIC, HIJAZI SPOKEN [ACW]
WEST ARCTIC INUPIATUN dial of INUPIATUN, NORTH ALASKAN [ESI]
WEST ASTURIAN dial of ASTURIAN [AUB]
WEST AWIN alt for AEKYOM [AWI]
WEST BAFWANGADA dial of BUDU [BUU]
WEST BANGGAI dial of BANGGAI [BGZ]
WEST BERAWAN dial of BERAWAN [LOD]
WEST BOIKIN dial of BOIKIN [BZF]
WEST BORNEO COAST MALAY dial of MALAY [MLI]
WEST CAPE AFRIKAANS alt for CAPE AFRIKAANS dial of AFRIKAANS [AFK]
WEST CENTRAL GOE alt for SAMO, MATYA [STJ]
WEST CENTRAL KLAOH dial of KLAO [KLU]
WEST CENTRAL KOMBA dial of KOMBA [KPF]
WEST CENTRAL KWOMTARI dial of KWOMTARI [KWO]
WEST CENTRAL MIXE alt for MIXE, TLAHUITOLTEPEC [MXP]
WEST CHACHAPOYAS alt for LAMUD dial of QUECHUA, CHACHAPOYAS [QUK]
WEST CIRCASSIAN alt for ADYGHE [ADY]
WEST COAST BAJAO alt for BAJAU, WEST COAST [BDR]
WEST COASTAL JIMAJIMA dial of JIMAJIMA [JMA]
WEST COUNTRY dial of ENGLISH [ENG]
WEST DANGALÉAT dial of DANGALÉAT [DAA]
WEST DANUBE dial of HUNGARIAN [HNG]
WEST ELEMA alt for OROKOLO [ORO]
WEST ENDE alt for NGA'O dial of ENDE [END]
WEST FUTUNA dial of FUTUNA-ANIWA [FUT]
WEST FUTUNA-ANIWA alt for FUTUNA-ANIWA [FUT]
WEST FUYUG dial of FUYUG [FUY]

WEST GIMI dial of GIMI [GIM]
WEST GORONTALO dial of GORONTALO [GRL]
WEST GREENLANDIC dial of INUKTITUT, GREEN-LANDIC [ESG]
WEST GRONINGEN dial of GRONINGS [GOS]
WEST GRONINGS alt for WEST GRONINGEN dial of GRONINGS [GOS]
WEST GUADALCANAL alt for GHARI [GRI]
WEST GWARI alt for GBARI [GBY]
WEST HUNAN MIAO alt for HMONG, WESTERN XIANGXI [MMR]
WEST HUNGARIAN dial of HUNGARIAN [HNG]
WEST KALAMSÉ alt for LOGREMMA dial of KALAMSE [KNZ]
WEST KALAMSÉ alt for LOGREMMA dial of SAMOMA [KNZ]
WEST KARA dial of KARA [LEU]
WEST KAREKARE alt for JALALAM dial of KAREKARE [KAI]
WEST KASEM dial of KASEM [KAS]
WEST KOITA dial of KOITABU [KQI]
WEST KOMBA dial of KOMBA [KPF]
WEST KONGO dial of KONGO [KON]
WEST LAMAHOLOT dial of LAMAHOLOT [SLP]
WEST LATVIAN dial of LATVIAN [LAT]
WEST MAFA dial of MAFA [MAF]
WEST MAIN CREE alt for CREE, MOOSE [CRM]
WEST MAIN CREE alt for CREE, SWAMPY [CSW]
WEST MAKUA alt for MAKHUWA-SHIRIMA [VMK]
WEST MARSELA alt for MASELA, WEST [MSS]
WEST MBUM alt for MBOUM dial of MBUM [MDD]
WEST MEKEO dial of MEKEO [MEK]
WEST MENDI alt for ANGAL HENENG [AKH]
WEST MORI alt for MORI ATAS [MZQ]
WEST MWERELAWA dial of MERLAV [MRM]
WEST NDA'NDA'-SOUTH NDA'NDA' alt for UNGAMEHA dial of NDANDA [NNZ]
WEST NEK dial of NEK [NIF]
WEST NUMANGGANG dial of NUMANGGANG [NOP]
WEST NYALA dial of LUYIA [LUY]
WEST OKI-NO-ERABU dial of OKI-NO-ERABU [OKN]
WEST ORYA alt for BARAT dial of ORYA [URY]
WEST POKOT dial of POKOOT [PKO]
WEST QUCHANI dial of KHORASANI TURKISH [KMZ]
WEST RANTEBULAHAN dial of BAMBAM [PTU]
WEST RORO alt for WAIMA dial of RORO [RRO]
WEST ROTE alt for ROTE, WESTERN [ROW]
WEST SENTANI dial of SENTANI [SET]
WEST SHORE CREE alt for CREE, MOOSE [CRM]
WEST SHORE CREE alt for CREE, SWAMPY [CSW]
WEST SLOVAKIAN ROMANI dial of ROMANI, CARPATHIAN [RMC]
WEST SOLOR dial of LAMAHOLOT [SLP]
WEST SONGAI dial of SONGOY [SON]
WEST SUMBANESE alt for WEJEWA [WEW]
WEST TANNA dial of TANNA, NORTH [TNN]

WEST TEKE alt for TEKE, WESTERN [TEZ]
WEST TELUTI dial of TELUTI [TLT]
WEST TIGAK dial of TIGAK [TGC]
WEST TORAJA alt for TORAJA BARAT dial of TORAJA-SADAN [SDA]
WEST TORRICELLI dial of TORRICELLI [TEI]
WEST TRANGAN alt for TARANGAN, WEST [TXN]
WEST URII dial of URI [UVH]
WEST VANUA LEVU dial of FIJIAN [FJI]
WEST VLAAMS dial of VLAAMS [VLA]
WEST VOD dial of VOD [VOD]
WEST WAYLLA dial of QUECHUA, WANCA, HUAYLLA [QHU]
WEST WOSERA alt for HANGA HUNDI [WOS]
WEST YAMBES dial of YAMBES [YMB]
WEST YAWA dial of YAWA [YVA]
WEST YORKSHIRE dial of ENGLISH [ENG]
WEST-CENTRAL KOMBIO dial of KOMBIO [KOK]
WEST-CENTRAL MANGGARAI dial of MANGGARAI [MQY]
WEST-CENTRAL MESÉ dial of MESÉ [MCI]
WESTERN ACHERON dial of ACHERON [ACZ]
WESTERN ACIPANCI alt for CEP dial of ACIPA, WESTERN [AWC]
WESTERN ADDASEN dial of ADASEN [TIU]
WESTERN AKA alt for BAMBENZELE dial of YAKA [AXK]
WESTERN ALEUT dial of ALEUT [ALW]
WESTERN ANGAMI alt for CHAKROMA dial of NAGA, ANGAMI [NJM]
WESTERN ANMATYERRE dial of ANMATYERRE [AMX]
WESTERN ARAGONESE dial of ARAGONESE [AXX]
WESTERN ARANDA dial of ARRARNTA, WESTERN [ARE]
WESTERN ARMENIAN dial of ARMENIAN [ARM]
WESTERN ASSAMESE dial of ASSAMESE [ASM]
WESTERN ASTURIAN dial of ASTURIAN [AUB]
WESTERN BADE dial of BADE [BDE]
WESTERN BAKOSSI dial of AKOOSE [BSS]
WESTERN BANTAWA dial of BANTAWA [BAP]
WESTERN BASHKIR alt for BURZHAN dial of BASHKIR [BXK]
WESTERN BÉTÉ alt for BÉTE, GUIBEROUA [BET]
WESTERN BILA alt for BILA [BIP]
WESTERN BISA alt for LEBIR dial of BISSA [BIB]
WESTERN BOBO OULE alt for BOMU [BMQ]
WESTERN BOBO WULE alt for BOMU [BMQ]
WESTERN BONTOC alt for KANKANAY, NORTHERN [KAN]
WESTERN BWAMU alt for BOMU [BMQ]
WESTERN CAMPIDENESE dial of SARDINIAN, CAMPIDANESE [SRO]
WESTERN CANADA GWICH'IN dial of GWICHIN [KUC]
WESTERN CAPPADOCIAN dial of CAPPADOCIAN GREEK [CPG]
WESTERN CARIB alt for MURATO dial of CARIB [CRB]
WESTERN CHEPANG alt for BUJHYAL [GOR]

WESTERN CHEPANG dial of CHEPANG [CDM]
WESTERN CHEROKEE alt for OTALI dial of CHEROKEE [CER]
WESTERN CLUSTER LISHANID NOSHAN dial of LISHANID NOSHAN [AIJ]
WESTERN CREE alt for CREE, PLAINS [CRP]
WESTERN DAN alt for BLOWO dial of DAN [DAF]
WESTERN DANI OF BOKONDINI dial of DANI, WESTERN [DNW]
WESTERN DANI OF PYRAMID dial of DANI, WESTERN [DNW]
WESTERN DANISH alt for JUTISH [JUT]
WESTERN DHIMAL dial of DHIMAL [DHI]
WESTERN DINKA alt for DINKA, SOUTHWESTERN [DIK]
WESTERN DUKA dial of HUN-SAARE [DUD]
WESTERN DUUN alt for DUUNGOMA [DUX]
WESTERN DUVLE dial of DUVLE [DUV]
WESTERN EDOLO dial of EDOLO [ETR]
WESTERN EGYPTIAN BEDAWI ARABIC dial of ARABIC, WESTERN EGYPTIAN BEDAWI SPOKEN [AYL]
WESTERN EJAGHAM dial of EJAGHAM [ETU]
WESTERN EJUTLA ZAPOTECO alt for ZAPOTECO, AYOQUESCO [ZAF]
WESTERN EMILIANO dial of EMILIANO-ROMAGNOLO [EML]
WESTERN ERSU alt for LISU dial of ERSU [ERS]
WESTERN FAS dial of FAS [FAS]
WESTERN FRIULIAN dial of FRIULIAN [FRL]
WESTERN GELAO alt for MOUNTAIN GELAO dial of GELAO [KKF]
WESTERN GITSKEN alt for GITSKEN dial of GITXSAN [GIT]
WESTERN GIZRA dial of GIZRA [TOF]
WESTERN GUIZHOU alt for QIANXI dial of BOUYEI [PCC]
WESTERN GUJARI dial of GUJARI [GJU]
WESTERN HELAMBU SHERPA dial of HELAMBU SHERPA [SCP]
WESTERN HIGHLAND CHATINO alt for CHATINO, SIERRA OCCIDENTAL [CTP]
WESTERN HIGHLAND PURÉPECHA alt for PURÉPECHA, SIERRA OCCIDENTAL [PUA]
WESTERN HMONG alt for HMONG NJUA [BLU]
WESTERN HUASTECA AZTEC alt for NÁHUATL, HUASTECO OESTE [NHW]
WESTERN HUASTECA NÁHUATL dial of NAHUATL, HUASTECA OESTE [NHW]
WESTERN HUICHOL alt for SAN ANDRÉS COHAMIATA dial of HUICHOL [HCH]
WESTERN ISIRAWA dial of ISIRAWA [SRL]
WESTERN ITELMEN alt for ITELMEN [ITL]
WESTERN IXTLÁN ZAPOTECO alt for ZAPOTECO, YARENI [ZAE]
WESTERN JAMILTEPEC MIXTECO alt for MIXTECO, PINOTEPA NACIONAL [MIO]
WESTERN JAPANESE dial of JAPANESE [JPN]
WESTERN JIARONG alt for GUANYINQIAO [JIQ]
WESTERN JIARONG alt for HORPA [ERO]

WESTERN JIARONG alt for SHANGZHAI [JIH]
WESTERN JIBBALI dial of JIBBALI [SHV]
WESTERN JIKANY dial of NUER [NUS]
WESTERN JUXTLAHUACA MIXTECO alt for
   MIXTECO, JUXTLAHUACA OESTE [JMX]
WESTERN KABA alt for KABA [KSP]
WESTERN KADARU dial of KADARU [KDU]
WESTERN KALEBWE dial of SONGE [SOP]
WESTERN KALIBUGAN alt for WESTERN
   KOLIBUGAN dial of SUBANON, WESTERN
   [SUC]
WESTERN KALIKO dial of KELIKO [KBO]
WESTERN KATIVIRI dial of KATI [BSH]
WESTERN KAZAKH dial of KAZAKH [KAZ]
WESTERN KELE alt for KÉLÉ [KEB]
WESTERN KELE alt for KILI [KEB]
WESTERN KELE dial of KELE [KEB]
WESTERN KENYA alt for KENYAH, WESTERN
   [XKY]
WESTERN KERES PUEBLO alt for KERES,
   WESTERN [KJQ]
WESTERN KHAMS dial of KHAMS [KHG]
WESTERN KILMERI dial of KILMERI [KIH]
WESTERN KITUBA dial of KITUBA [KTU]
WESTERN KLAOH dial of KLAO [KLU]
WESTERN KOLIBUGAN dial of SUBANON,
   WESTERN [SUC]
WESTERN KUMAUNI dial of KUMAUNI [KFY]
WESTERN KUNDU alt for BALUE dial of BAKUNDU-
   BALUE [BDU]
WESTERN KUSAAL alt for TOENDE dial of KUSAAL
   [KUS]
WESTERN LAMPUNG alt for KRUI [KRQ]
WESTERN LAOTIAN alt for THAI, NORTHERN
   [NOD]
WESTERN LIMBA dial of LIMBA, WEST-CENTRAL
   [LIA]
WESTERN LIVONIAN dial of LIV [LIV]
WESTERN LOMBARD dial of LOMBARD [LMO]
WESTERN LOW NAVARRESE dial of BASQUE,
   NAVARRO-LABOURDIN [BQE]
WESTERN LUBA alt for LUBA-KASAI [LUB]
WESTERN MACEDONIAN dial of MACEDONIAN
   [MKJ]
WESTERN MACINA dial of FULFULDE, MAASINA
   [FUL]
WESTERN MAITHILI dial of MAITHILI [MKP]
WESTERN MAKUA alt for LOMWE [NGL]
WESTERN MAM alt for MAM, CENTRAL [MVC]
WESTERN MAM alt for TACANECO [MTZ]
WESTERN MAMPRULI dial of MAMPRULI [MAW]
WESTERN MANDARIN alt for HO dial of CHINESE,
   MANDARIN [CHN]
WESTERN MANGGARAI dial of MANGGARAI
   [MQY]
WESTERN MANINKA alt for MALINKE [MLQ]
WESTERN MARIK dial of MARIK [DAD]
WESTERN MASALIT dial of MASALIT [MSA]
WESTERN MASHAN MIAO alt for HMONG,
   WESTERN MASHAN [HMW]
WESTERN MBUBE alt for MBE [MFO]

WESTERN MEHRI dial of MEHRI [MHR]
WESTERN MIAHUATLÁN ZAPOTECO alt for
   ZAPOTECO, COATLÁN [ZPS]
WESTERN MIAO alt for HMONG NJUA [BLU]
WESTERN MONGOL alt for KALMYK-OIRAT [KGZ]
WESTERN MONGOLIAN alt for KALMYK-OIRAT
   [KGZ]
WESTERN MONTAGNAIS dial of MONTAGNAIS
   [MOE]
WESTERN MOTU dial of MOTU [MEU]
WESTERN MUSSAU dial of MUSSAU-EMIRA [EMI]
WESTERN NASKAPI dial of NASKAPI [NSK]
WESTERN NEO-ARAMAIC [AMW] lang, Syria
WESTERN NIHIRI dial of VARLI [VAV]
WESTERN NORWEGIAN dial of NORWEGIAN,
   BOKMAAL [NRR]
WESTERN NYASA alt for TONGA [TOG]
WESTERN OCOTLÁN ZAPOTEC alt for
   ZAPOTECO, OCOTLÁN OESTE [ZAC]
WESTERN OKPAMHERI dial of OKPAMHERI [OPA]
WESTERN ORIYA dial of ORIYA [ORY]
WESTERN OROMO dial of OROMO, WEST-
   CENTRAL [GAZ]
WESTERN OTOMÍ alt for OTOMÍ, NORTH-
   WESTERN [OTQ]
WESTERN PAGI dial of PAGI [PGI]
WESTERN PARBATE alt for KHAM, TAKALE [KJL]
WESTERN PATTANI alt for CHAMBA-LAJULI dial
   of PATTANI [LAE]
WESTERN POCHUTLA ZAPOTECO alt for
   ZAPOTECO, LOXICHA [ZTP]
WESTERN POCOMCHÍ alt for POKOMCHÍ,
   WESTERN [POB]
WESTERN POINT dial of NIMOA [NMW]
WESTERN POPOLOCA alt for POPOLOCA, SAN
   FELIPE OTLALTEPEC [POW]
WESTERN PUNJABI alt for PANJABI, WESTERN
   [PNB]
WESTERN QUICHÉ dial of QUICHE, WEST
   CENTRAL [QUT]
WESTERN RED BOBO alt for BOMU [BMQ]
WESTERN RENGAO dial of RENGAO [REN]
WESTERN RULI dial of RULI [RUC]
WESTERN SHE alt for LIANHUA dial of SHE [SHX]
WESTERN SHONA alt for KALANGA [KCK]
WESTERN SHOSHONI dial of SHOSHONI [SHH]
WESTERN SHUSWAP dial of SHUSWAP [SHS]
WESTERN SICILIAN dial of SICILIAN [SCN]
WESTERN SOLA DE VEGA MIXTEC alt for
   MIXTECO, AMOLTEPEC [MBZ]
WESTERN SOLA DE VEGA ZAPOTECO alt for
   ZAPOTECO, ZANIZA [ZPW]
WESTERN SOQOTRI dial of SOQOTRI [SQT]
WESTERN STANDARD BHOJPURI dial of
   BHOJPURI [BHJ]
WESTERN SUDANESE dial of ARABIC,
   SUDANESE SPOKEN [APD]
WESTERN SUMI alt for DAYANG dial of NAGA,
   SUMI [NSM]
WESTERN SURI alt for KACIPO dial of KACIPO-
   BALESI [KOE]

WESTERN SURI dial of KACIPO-BALESI [KOE]
WESTERN SWAMPY CREE dial of CREE, SWAMPY [CSW]
WESTERN SYRIAC dial of SYRIAC [SYC]
WESTERN TARAHUMARA alt for TARAHUMARA BAJA [TAC]
WESTERN TATAR dial of TATAR [TTR]
WESTERN TAUBUID alt for TAWBUID, WESTERN [TWB]
WESTERN TEMNE dial of THEMNE [TEJ]
WESTERN THAMI dial of THAMI [THF]
WESTERN TLACOLULA ZAPOTECO alt for ZAPOTECO, SAN JUAN GUELAVÍA [ZAB]
WESTERN TLAPANEC alt for TLAPANECO, ACATEPEC [TPX]
WESTERN TOPOSA dial of TOPOSA [TOQ]
WESTERN TUVIN dial of TUVIN [TUN]
WESTERN UMA alt for TOBAKU dial of UMA [PPK]
WESTERN VOGUL dial of MANSI [MNS]
WESTERN WAKHI dial of WAKHI [WBL]
WESTERN WEST-HUNAN MIAO alt for HMONG, WESTERN XIANGXI [MMR]
WESTERN XIANGSI MIAO alt for HMONG, WESTERN XIANGXI [MMR]
WESTERN YAGNOBI dial of YAGNOBI [YAI]
WESTERN YALI alt for YALI, PASS VALLEY [YAC]
WESTERN YANOMAMI dial of YANOMAMO [GUU]
WESTERN YAUTEPEC ZAPOTECO alt for ZAPOTECO, SANTA MARÍA QUIEGOLANI [ZPI]
WESTERN YORK CREE dial of CREE, PLAINS [CRP]
WESTERN ZIMATLÁN ZAPOTECO alt for ZAPOTECO, TOTOMACHAPAN [ZPH]
WESTERWOLD alt for WESTERWOLDS [WEV]
WESTERWOLDS [WEV] lang, Netherlands
WESTFÄLISCH alt for WESTPHALIEN [WEP]
WESTFAELISCH alt for WESTPHALIEN [WEP]
WESTMORLAND dial of ENGLISH [ENG]
WESTPHALIEN [WEP] lang, Germany
WETAMUT [WWO] lang, Vanuatu
WETAN dial of LUANG [LEX]
WETANG alt for WETAN dial of LUANG [LEX]
WETAWIT alt for BERTA [WTI]
WETE dial of DEHU [DEU]
WETERE alt for VUTE [VUT]
WETU dial of JUR MODO [BEX]
WETUMBA alt for KAGULU [KKI]
WEWAU alt for WEWAW [WEA]
WEWAW [WEA] lang, Myanmar
WEWEWA alt for WEJEWA [WEW]
WEWJEWA alt for WEJEWA [WEW]
WEYEWA alt for WEJEWA [WEW]
WEYEWA dial of WEJEWA [WEW]
WEYOKO dial of BUNAMA [BDD]
WEYTO [WOY] lang, Ethiopia
WEYT'O alt for WEYTO [WOY]
W'HAUKIA alt for BONGOS [BXY]
WHELNGO alt for LUSHAI [LSH]
WHITE BOLON dial of BOLON [BOF]
WHITE CLAY PEOPLE alt for GROS VENTRE [ATS]
WHITE GELAO dial of GELAO [KKF]

WHITE KAREN alt for KAREN, GEBA [KVQ]
WHITE KAREN alt for KAREN, S'GAW [KSW]
WHITE KHOANY dial of PHUNOI [PHO]
WHITE LACHI alt for LACHI, WHITE [LWH]
WHITE LISU alt for PAI LISU dial of LISU [LIS]
WHITE LISU dial of LISU [LIS]
WHITE LUM alt for HMONG DAW [MWW]
WHITE MEO alt for HMONG DAW [MWW]
WHITE MIAO alt for HMONG DAW [MWW]
WHITE MOUNTAIN dial of APACHE, WESTERN [APW]
WHITE NILE DINKA alt for DINKA, NORTH-EASTERN [DIP]
WHITE NOGAI dial of NOGAI [NOG]
WHITE RUSSIA ROMANI dial of ROMANI, BALTIC [ROM]
WHITE RUSSIAN alt for BELARUSAN [RUW]
WHITE RUSSIAN ROMANI dial of ROMANI, BALTIC [ROM]
WHITE RUTHENIAN alt for BELARUSAN [RUW]
WHITE TAI alt for TAI DÓN [TWH]
WHITESANDS [TNP] lang, Vanuatu
WHITSANDS alt for WHITESANDS [TNP]
WI alt for KWANGE dial of GBARI [GBY]
WIAKEI alt for WIAKI [WII]
WIAKI [WII] lang, Papua New Guinea
WIANG JAN alt for VIENTIANE dial of LAO [NOL]
WIANG PAPAO LUA alt for LAWA, EASTERN [LWL]
WIAOE alt for RAHAMBUU [RAZ]
WIAU alt for RAHAMBUU [RAZ]
WIBO dial of MWANI [WMW]
WICHÍ LHAMTÉS GÜISNAY [MZH] lang, Argentina
WICHÍ LHAMTÉS NOCTEN [MTP] lang, Bolivia; also in Argentina
WICHÍ LHAMTÉS VEJOZ [MAD] lang, Argentina; also in Bolivia
WICHITA [WIC] lang, USA
WIDALA alt for KHOLOK [KTC]
WIDEKUM alt for MOGHAMO dial of META [MGO]
WIDIKUM-TADKON alt for META' [MGO]
WIDIMAYA alt for BADIMAYA [BIA]
WIGA alt for UYGHUR [UIG]
WIGA dial of SINAUGORO [SNC]
WIGHOR alt for UYGHUR [UIG]
WIHE alt for KARIYA [KIL]
WIILA alt for HWELA dial of LIGBI [LIG]
WIILA alt for LIGBI [LIG]
WIINDZA-BAALI dial of NGOMBE [NGC]
WIIRATHERI alt for WIRADHURI [WRH]
WIK MUMINH alt for KUKU-MUMINH [XMH]
WIK NJINTURA alt for WIKNGENCHERA [WUA]
WIKALKAN [WIK] lang, Australia
WIK-EPA [WIE] lang, Australia
WIK-IIYANH [WIJ] lang, Australia
WIK-KEYANGAN [WIF] lang, Australia
WIK-ME'ANHA [WIH] lang, Australia
WIK-MUMIN alt for KUKU-MUMINH [XMH]
WIK-MUNGKAN [WIM] lang, Australia
WIK-MUNKAN alt for WIK-MUNGKAN [WIM]
WIK-NANTJARA alt for WIKNGENCHERA [WUA]
WIK-NGANDJARA dial of WIKALKAN [WIK]

WIKNGATARA alt for WIKALKAN [WIK]
WIK-NGATHANA [WIG] lang, Australia
WIK-NGATHARA alt for WIKALKAN [WIK]
WIK-NGATHARRA alt for WIKALKAN [WIK]
WIKNGENCHERA [WUA] lang, Australia
WILA-WILA alt for WILAWILA [WIL]
WILAWILA [WIL] lang, Australia
WILAWILA dial of NGARINYIN [UNG]
WILD <ALI alt for CENTRAL NAJDI dial of ARABIC,
    NAJDI SPOKEN [ARS]
WILE dial of BIRIFOR, MALBA [BFO]
WILJAKALI dial of DARLING [DRL]
WILYAGALI alt for WILJAKALI dial of DARLING
    [DRL]
WIMBUM alt for LIMBUM [LIM]
WIN alt for TOUSSIAN, SOUTHERN [WIB]
WINA alt for DESANO [DES]
WINA alt for SOWANDA [SOW]
WINA alt for TUPURI [TUI]
WINÃ dial of MASANA [MCN]
WINATU dial of UMA [PPK]
WINDESI alt for WANDAMEN [WAD]
WINDESI dial of WANDAMEN [WAD]
WINDESSI alt for WANDAMEN [WAD]
WINDISCH dial of SLOVENIAN [SLV]
WINDWARD CARIBBEAN CREOLE ENGLISH
    [SVG] lang, St. Vincent and the Grenadines;
    also in Grenada
WINGEI dial of AMBULAS [ABT]
WINISK RIVER OJIBWA dial of OJIBWA, SEVERN
    [OJS]
WINIV dial of MEREI [LMB]
WINIV dial of VINMAVIS [VNM]
WINJI-WINJI alt for ANII [BLO]
WINNEBAGO alt for HOCÁK [WIN]
WINS dial of BUANG, MAPOS [BZH]
WINTU [WIT] lang, USA
WINTU dial of WINTU [WIT]
WINTUN alt for WINTU [WIT]
WINYÉ [KST] lang, Burkina Faso
WIPI alt for GIDRA [GDR]
WIPIE alt for ADYNYAMATHANHA [ADT]
WIPIM dial of GIDRA [GDR]
WIPSI-NI alt for FER dial of KAG-FER-JIIR-KOOR-
    ROR-US-ZUKSUN [GEL]
WIPSI-NI alt for ZUKSUN dial of KAG-FER-JIIR-
    KOOR-ROR-US-ZUKSUN [GEL]
WIRA dial of JUR MODO [BEX]
WIRÃ alt for DESANO [DES]
WIRA-ATHOREE alt for WIRADHURI [WRH]
WIRADHURI [WRH] lang, Australia
WIRADJURI alt for WIRADHURI [WRH]
WIRADURI alt for WIRADHURI [WRH]
WIRAFÉD [WIR] lang, Brazil
WIRAIDYURI alt for WIRADHURI [WRH]
WIRAJEREE alt for WIRADHURI [WRH]
WIRAM alt for SUKI [SUI]
WIRANGU [WIW] lang, Australia
WIRASHURI alt for WIRADHURI [WRH]
WIRATHERI alt for WIRADHURI [WRH]
WIREGI dial of SUBA [SUH]

WIRI alt for DUVLE [DUV]
WIROFÉD alt for WIRAFÉD [WIR]
WIRONGU alt for WIRANGU [WIW]
WIRONGUWONGGA alt for WIRANGU [WIW]
WIRRACHAREE alt for WIRADHURI [WRH]
WIRRAI'YARRAI alt for WIRADHURI [WRH]
WIRRUNG alt for WIRANGU [WIW]
WIRRUNGA alt for WIRANGU [WIW]
WIRU [WIU] lang, Papua New Guinea
WISA alt for BISA dial of LALA-BISA [LEB]
WISCONSIN dial of HOCAK [WIN]
WITA EA dial of MORONENE [MQN]
WITOTO alt for HUITOTO, MURUI [HUU]
WITU alt for MUDUAPA [WIV]
WITU alt for WIRU [WIU]
WIWA alt for MALAYO [MBP]
WIWIRANO dial of TOLAKI [LBW]
WIYAA alt for WAJA [WJA]
WIYAGWA dial of ANKAVE [AAK]
WIYAP alt for JIRU [JRR]
WIYAU alt for HARUAI [TMD]
WIYAW alt for HARUAI [TMD]
WIYEH dial of LIMBUM [LIM]
WIYOT [WIY] lang, USA
WIZA alt for BISA dial of LALA-BISA [LEB]
WLEPO dial of KRUMEN, PYE [PYE]
WLOPO dial of KRUMEN, TEPO [TED]
WLUWE-HAWLO dial of KRUMEN, PYE [PYE]
WO alt for BASARI [BSC]
WO alt for KULUNG [BBU]
WO dial of YORUBA [YOR]
WOBÉ alt for WÈ NORTHERN [WOB]
WODA alt for WOLANI [WOD]
WODAABE dial of FULFULDE, CENTRAL-
    EASTERN NIGER [FUQ]
WODA-MO alt for WOLANI [WOD]
WODANI alt for WOLANI [WOD]
WODIWODI alt for WADIWADI dial of THURAWAL
    [TBH]
WODO alt for WALAK [WLW]
WOGAITY alt for WADJIGINY [WDJ]
WOGAMUSIN [WOG] lang, Papua New Guinea
WOGANG alt for WAXIANGHUA [WXA]
WOGEMAN alt for WAGEMAN [WAQ]
WOGEO [WOC] lang, Papua New Guinea
WOGGIL alt for YIDINY [YII]
WOGRI-BOLI dial of DOMARI [RMT]
WOGU alt for BAHINEMO [BJH]
WOI [WBW] lang, Indonesia (Irian Jaya)
WOISIKA alt for KAMANG [WOI]
WOJO dial of BANDA, WEST CENTRAL [BBP]
WOJOKESO alt for WAJAKES dial of AMPEELI-
    WOJOKESO [APZ]
WOKAM alt for MANOMBAI [WOO]
WOKIARE dial of YABARANA [YAR]
WOKO alt for LONGTO [WOK]
WOLAITA alt for WOLAYTTA [WBC]
WOLAITTA alt for WOLAYTTA [WBC]
WOLANE dial of GURAGE, EAST [GRE]
WOLANI [WOD] lang, Indonesia (Irian Jaya)
WOLATAITA alt for WOLAYTTA [WBC]

WOLAYTA alt for WOLAYTTA [WBC]
WOLAYTTA [WBC] lang, Ethiopia
WOLEAIAN [WOE] lang, Micronesia
WOLEAIAN dial of WOLEAIAN [WOE]
WOLIO [WLO] lang, Indonesia (Sulawesi); also in
   Malaysia (Sabah)
WOLLAMO alt for WOLAYTTA [WBC]
WOLLEGARA alt for WARLUWARA [WRB]
WOLMERI alt for WALMAJARRI [WMT]
WOLOF [WOL] lang, Senegal; also in France,
   Gambia, Guinea, Guinea-Bissau, Mali, Mauritania
WOLOF, GAMBIAN [WOF] lang, Gambia
WOLU alt for TELUTI [TLT]
WOLU alt for WEST TELUTI dial of TELUTI [TLT]
WOLYAMIDI dial of NGARINYIN [UNG]
WOM [WMO] lang, Papua New Guinea
WOM [WOM] lang, Nigeria
WOMBOKO alt for WUMBOKO [BQM]
WOMBUNGEE alt for WANGAAYBUWAN dial of
   WANGAAYBUWAN-NGIYAMBAA [WYB]
WOM-BY-A alt for WAMBAYA [WMB]
WOMBYA alt for WAMBAYA [WMB]
WOMSAK alt for APOS [APO]
WOMSAK alt for WAMSAK [WBD]
WOMSAK alt for WASAMBU [WSM]
WONGA alt for PINTIINI [PTI]
WONGAGIBUN alt for WANGAAYBUWAN dial of
   WANGAAYBUWAN-NGIYAMBAA [WYB]
WONGAIBON alt for WANGAAYBUWAN dial of
   WANGAAYBUWAN-NGIYAMBAA [WYB]
WONGAIDYA alt for NUGUNU [NNV]
WONGAI-I alt for PINTIINI [PTI]
WONGAMARDU alt for KOKATA [KTD]
WONGAMUSIN alt for WOGAMUSIN [WOG]
WONGGAII alt for PINTIINI [PTI]
WONGHI alt for WANGAAYBUWAN dial of
   WANGAAYBUWAN-NGIYAMBAA [WYB]
WONGHIBON alt for WANGAAYBUWAN dial of
   WANGAAYBUWAN-NGIYAMBAA [WYB]
WONGKUMARA dial of NGURA [NBX]
WONGO [WON] lang, DRC
WONI alt for HONI [HOW]
WONI alt for KADO [KDV]
WONIE dial of GIDRA [GDR]
WONJHIBON alt for WANGAAYBUWAN dial of
   WANGAAYBUWAN-NGIYAMBAA [WYB]
WONO alt for HONO' dial of SEKO PADANG [SKX]
WONO alt for SEKO PADANG [SKX]
WONTI alt for WAROPEN [WRP]
WO'OI alt for WOI [WBW]
WOOLWA alt for SUMO TAWAHKA [SUM]
WOORAGURIE alt for WIRADHURI [WRH]
WOOTEELIT dial of YUPIK, CENTRAL SIBERIAN
   [ESS]
WOPKEIMIN dial of FAIWOL [FAI]
WORASE alt for HARSO dial of GAWWADA [GWD]
WORDAMAN alt for WARDAMAN [WRR]
WORDJERG alt for WIRADHURI [WRH]
WORGAI alt for WAGAYA [WGA]
WORGAIA alt for WAGAYA [WGA]
WORIA [WOR] lang, Indonesia (Irian Jaya)

WORIASI alt for WABO [WBB]
WORIMI [KDA] lang, Australia
WORKAI alt for BARAKAI [BAJ]
WORKIA alt for WAGAYA [WGA]
WORKU dial of IGEDE [IGE]
WORLA alt for WURLA dial of NGARINYIN [UNG]
WORLAJA alt for WURLA dial of NGARINYIN [UNG]
WORO alt for ORLO dial of GBAYA [KRS]
WORO alt for VORO [VOR]
WORODOUGOU alt for JULA, WORODOUGOU
   [JUD]
WORODOUGOUKA dial of JULA, WORODOUGOU
   [JUD]
WORODOUGOUKAKAN alt for JULA,
   WORODOUGOU [JUD]
WORODUGU alt for JULA, WORODOUGOU [JUD]
WORORA [UNP] lang, Australia
WORORA dial of WORORA [UNP]
WORPEN alt for WAROPEN [WRP]
WORRORRA alt for WORORA [UNP]
WORUGL alt for RO dial of FOLOPA [PPO]
WOSERA-KAMU dial of AMBULAS [ABT]
WOSERA-MAMU dial of AMBULAS [ABT]
WOSKIA alt for WASKIA [WSK]
WOTAPURI-KATARQALAI [WSV] lang, Afghanistan
WOTU [WTW] lang, Indonesia (Sulawesi)
WOULKI dial of MPADE [MPI]
WOUN MEU [NOA] lang, Panama; also in Colombia
WOUNAAN alt for WOUN MEU [NOA]
WOUNMEU alt for WOUN MEU [NOA]
WOURI alt for OLI dial of DUALA [DOU]
WOUTE alt for VUTE [VUT]
WOVAN alt for HARUAI [TMD]
WOVEA alt for BUBIA [BBX]
WOWO alt for BIERIA [BRJ]
WOWO alt for VOVO dial of BIERIA [BRJ]
WOWONII alt for WAWONII [WOW]
WRELPO alt for GREBO, SOUTHERN [GRJ]
WU alt for CHINESE, WU [WUU]
WU dial of VO [WBM]
WUASINKISHU alt for MOITANIK dial of MAASAI
   [MET]
WUBAHAMER dial of AARI [AIZ]
WUBOMEI dial of LOMA [LOM]
WUBULKARRA dial of GUPAPUYNGU [GUF]
WUDU [WUD] lang, Togo
WUDUFU alt for MBURKU [BBT]
WUHÁNA alt for MACUNA [MYY]
WUKAN dial of WAPAN [JUK]
WUKARI alt for WAPAN [JUK]
WULA alt for WURLA dial of NGARINYIN [UNG]
WULA dial of BOKYI [BKY]
WULA dial of KAMWE [HIG]
WULA dial of PSIKYE [KVJ]
WULADJA alt for WURLA dial of NGARINYIN [UNG]
WULADJANGARI alt for WURLA dial of NGARINYIN
   [UNG]
WULAKI dial of DJINANG [DJI]
WULAMBA alt for DHUWAL [DUJ]
WULANGA dial of YELE [YLE]
WULE dial of DAGARA, NORTHERN [DGI]

WULIMA dial of LALA-BISA [LEB]
WULIWULI [WLU] lang, Australia
WULNA [WUX] lang, Australia
WULU dial of BELI [BLM]
WULUKOHA dial of BANDI [GBA]
WUM alt for AGHEM [AGQ]
WUMBOKO [BQM] lang, Cameroon
WUMBU alt for WUUMU dial of TEKE, SOUTH
  CENTRAL [IFM]
WUMBVU [WUM] lang, Congo; also in Gabon
WUMNABAL alt for WUNAMBAL [WUB]
WUMVU alt for WUMBVU [WUM]
WUNA alt for MBUM [MDD]
WUNA alt for MUNA [MYN]
WUNAI alt for BUNU, WUNAI [BWN]
WUNAMBAL [WUB] lang, Australia
WUNAMBAL alt for KWINI [GWW]
WUNAMBAL dial of WUNAMBAL [WUB]
WUNAMBULLU alt for WUNAMBAL [WUB]
WUNAVAI dial of ANKAVE [AAK]
WUNCI alt for GHULFAN [GHL]
WUNCIMBE alt for GHULFAN [GHL]
WUNDU dial of BANDA-BANDA [BPD]
WUNGU alt for BUNGU [WUN]
WUNINGAK alt for URNINGANGG [URC]
WUNJO alt for VUNJO [VUN]
WUO dial of TEKE, CENTRAL [TEC]
WUPIWI alt for CHIRIPO dial of CUIBA [CUI]
WURANCI alt for WURI dial of GWAMHI-WURI
  [BGA]
WURAWA alt for WURI dial of GWAMHI-WURI [BGA]
WUREIDBUG alt for AMARAG [AMG]
WURGA dial of MARGHI CENTRAL [MAR]
WURI alt for OLI dial of DUALA [DOU]
WURI dial of GWAMHI-WURI [BGA]
WURKUM alt for KHOLOK [KTC]
WURKUM alt for KULUNG [BBU]
WURKUM alt for PIYA-KWONCI [PIY]
WURLA dial of NGARINYIN [UNG]
"WUSE HUA" pejorative alt for E [EEE]
"WUSEHUA" pejorative alt for E [EEE]
WUSHI [BSE] lang, Cameroon
WUSI [WSI] lang, Vanuatu
WUSI-KEREPUA alt for WUSI [WSI]
WUSYEP TEP dial of URAT [URT]
WUSYEP YEHRE dial of URAT [URT]
WUTE alt for VUTE [VUT]
WUTUN alt for WUTUNHUA [WUH]
WUTUNG [WUT] lang, Papua New Guinea
WUTUNHUA [WUH] lang, China
WUU alt for WUVULU dial of WUVULU-AUA [WUV]
WUUMU dial of TEKE, SOUTH CENTRAL [IFM]
WUVULU dial of WUVULU-AUA [WUV]
WUVULU-AUA [WUV] lang, Papua New Guinea
WUYA alt for WAJA [WJA]
WUZHOU dial of CHINESE, WU [WUU]
WUZLAM [UDL] lang, Cameroon
WYANDOT [WYA] lang, USA; also in Canada
WYANDOT dial of WYANDOT [WYA]
WYANDOTTE alt for WYANDOT [WYA]
WYENDAT alt for WYANDOT [WYA]

X[alt for JU/'HOAN [KTZ]
XA alt for KHANG [KJM]
XÁ alt for IU MIEN [IUM]
XA AI alt for KHANG [KJM]
XA BUNG alt for KHANG [KJM]
XA CAU alt for KHANG AI dial of KHANG [KJM]
XA CAU alt for KHMU [KJG]
XÁ CHIEN alt for LAHA [LHA]
XA CHUNG CHÁ alt for NHANG [NHA]
XA COONG alt for PHUNOI [PHO]
XA DANG alt for KHANG [KJM]
XA DANG alt for SEDANG [SED]
XA DON alt for KHANG [KJM]
XA HOC alt for KHANG [KJM]
XA KHAO alt for KHANG AI dial of KHANG [KJM]
XÁ KHAO alt for KHANG [KJM]
XÁ KHAO alt for LAHA [LHA]
XA LA VANG alt for PONG dial of HUNG [HNU]
XÁ LÁ VÀNG alt for MANG [MGA]
XÁ LAY alt for LAHA [LHA]
XÁ MANG alt for MANG [MGA]
XÁ Ó alt for MANG [MGA]
XÁ U NÍ alt for HANI [HNI]
XA XAM KHOONG alt for PHUNOI [PHO]
XA XENG alt for PHUNOI [PHO]
XA XUA alt for KHANG [KJM]
XAASONGA alt for XAASONGAXANGO [KAO]
XAASONGA alt for XASONGA [KAO]
XAASONGAXANGO [KAO] lang, Mali; also in
  Gambia, Senegal
XAASONGAXANGO alt for XASONGA [KAO]
XADANI ZAPOTEC alt for ZAPOTECO, XADANI
  [ZAX]
XADI alt for HDI [TUR]
XA-DIENG alt for STIENG, BULO [STI]
XAGUA alt for ACHAGUA [ACA]
/XAISE dial of SHUA [SHG]
XAJDAK alt for KAJTAK dial of DARGWA [DAR]
XAJRJUZOVSKIJ dial of ITELMEN [ITL]
XAKRIABÁ [XKR] lang, Brazil
XAKUCHI dial of ADYGHE [ADY]
/XAM [XAM] lang, South Africa
XAMANG alt for MANG [MGA]
XAMATARI alt for SANUMÁ [SAM]
XAMBIOÁ alt for KARAJÁ [KPJ]
XAMIR alt for XAMTANGA [XAN]
/XAM-KA-!K'E alt for /XAM [XAM]
XAMTA alt for XAMTANGA [XAN]
XAMTANGA [XAN] lang, Ethiopia
XAN alt for BOZO, HAINYAXO [BZX]
XANAGUÍA ZAPOTEC alt for ZAPOTECO,
  XANAGUÍA [ZTG]
XANANWA alt for GANANWA dial of SOTHO,
  NORTHERN [SRT]
XANGA alt for SHANGA dial of NDAU [NDC]
XANICA ZAPOTEC alt for ZAPOTECO, SANTIAGO
  XANICA [ZPR]
XANTY alt for KHANTY [KCA]
XANYAXO alt for BOZO, HAINYAXO [BZX]
XAPUT dial of KRYTS [KRY]
XARACII alt for XÂRÂCÙÙ [ANE]

XÂRÂCÙÙ [ANE] lang, New Caledonia
XARAGURE [ARG] lang, New Caledonia
XARBUK dial of DARGWA [DAR]
XAROXA alt for DIDINGA [DID]
XARUA alt for HARUA dial of BOLA [BNP]
XASA alt for TIGRÉ [TIE]
XASONGA [KAO] lang, Mali; also in Gambia, Senegal
XASONGA alt for XAASONGAXANGO [KAO]
XASONKE alt for XAASONGAXANGO [KAO]
XASONKE alt for XASONGA [KAO]
XATIA dial of XOO [NMN]
XATYRSKIJ dial of CHUKOT [CKT]
XATYRSKIJ dial of KORYAK [KPY]
XATYRSKIJ alt for KHATYRKA dial of KEREK [KRK]
//X'AU//'E alt for ǂKX'AU//'EIN [AUE]
XAUNI alt for HANI [HNI]
XAVÁNTE [XAV] lang, Brazil
XAVIERANO alt for SAN JAVIER dial of
    CHIQUITANO [CAX]
XEBERO alt for JEBERO [JEB]
XEDI [TUR] lang, Nigeria; also in Cameroon
XEDI alt for HDI [TUR]
//XEGWE alt for //XEGWI [XEG]
//XEGWI [XEG] lang, South Africa
//XEKWI alt for //XEGWI [XEG]
XENACOJ alt for CAKCHIQUEL, SANTO DOMINGO
    XENACOJ [CKJ]
XENQENNA dial of SONINKE [SNN]
XERÉNTE [XER] lang, Brazil
XEREU alt for HIXKARYÁNA [HIX]
XEREWYANA alt for HIXKARÁYNA [HIX]
XESIBE dial of XHOSA [XOS]
XETÁ [XET] lang, Brazil
XEVSUR dial of GEORGIAN [GEO]
XHOSA [XOS] lang, South Africa; also in Botswana,
    Lesotho
XIAERBA alt for SHERPA [SCR]
XIAMEN alt for HOKKIEN dial of CHINESE, MIN
    NAN [CFR]
XIAMEN dial of CHINESE, MIN NAN [CFR]
XIANDAOHUA [XIA] lang, China
XIANG alt for CHINESE, XIANG [HSN]
XIANGHUA alt for WAXIANGHUA [WXA]
XIANGYUN-DALI alt for DALI dial of BAI [PIQ]
XIANYOU dial of CHINESE, PU-XIAN [CPX]
XIAO HUA MIAO dial of HMONG NJUA [BLU]
XIAOSHANHUA alt for ZAIWA [ATB]
XIBE [SJO] lang, China
XIBEI GUANHUA dial of CHINESE, MANDARIN
    [CHN]
XIBEROERA alt for BASQUE, SOULETIN [BSZ]
XIBITA alt for HIBITO [HIB]
XIBITAOAN alt for COCAMA-COCAMILLA [COD]
XIBITAONA dial of COCAMA-COCAMILLA [COD]
XIBO alt for XIBE [SJO]
XICAQUE alt for TOL [JIC]
XICHANGANA alt for CHANGANA dial of TSONGA
    [TSO]
XICHANGANA alt for TSONGA [TSO]
XIDZIVI alt for TSHWA dial of TSHWA [TSC]
XIHUILA alt for JEBERO [JEB]

XIJIA MIAO alt for HMONG, LUOPOHE [HML]
XIKIYANA alt for SIKIANA [SIK]
XIKRIN dial of KAYAPO [TXU]
XIKUJANA alt for SIKIANA [SIK]
XILULEKE alt for LULEKE dial of TSONGA [TSO]
XIMAHE MIAO alt for HMONG, LUOPOHE [HML]
XIN MUL alt for PUOC [PUO]
XINALUG alt for KHINALUGH [KJJ]
XINAN GUANHUA dial of CHINESE, MANDARIN
    [CHN]
XINCA [XIN] lang, Guatemala
XING MUN alt for PUOC [PUO]
XINGHUA alt for HENGHUA dial of CHINESE, PU-
    XIAN [CPX]
XINGHUA alt for PUTIAN dial of CHINESE, PU-XIAN
    [CPX]
XINGHUA dial of CHINESE, MIN DONG [CDO]
XINGHUA dial of CHINESE, PU-XIAN [CPX]
XINH MUL alt for PUOC [PUO]
XINH-MUN alt for PUOC [PUO]
XINJIANG MONGOLIAN alt for KALMYK-OIRAT
    [KGZ]
XINMINHUA alt for CHINESE, HAKKA [HAK]
XIPAIA alt for KURUÁYA [KYR]
XIPINÁWA [XIP] lang, Brazil
XIRI [XII] lang, South Africa
XIRIÂNA [XIR] lang, Brazil
XIRIANA alt for NINAM [SHB]
XIRIANÁ alt for NINAM [SHB]
XIRIKWA alt for XIRI [XII]
XIRIMA alt for MAKHUWA-SHIRIMA [VMK]
XIRIWAI alt for NADËB [MBJ]
XIRONGA alt for RONGA [RON]
XISHAN dial of YI, WESTERN [YIW]
XISHUANGBANNA DAI alt for LÈ [KHB]
XITIBO alt for SHETEBO dial of SHIPIBO-CONIBO
    [SHP]
XITSHWA alt for TSHWA [TSC]
XITSONGA alt for TSONGA [TSO]
XIUYI dial of CHINESE, HUIZHOU [CZH]
XIVARO alt for SHUAR [JIV]
!XO alt for JU/'HOAN [KTZ]
XOCHAPA MIXTECO dial of MIXTECO,
    ALCOZAUCA [QMX]
XOCÓ alt for KARIRI-XOCÓ [KZW]
XODANG alt for SEDANG [SED]
XOKLENG [XOK] lang, Brazil
XOKÓ alt for KARIRI-XOCÓ [KZW]
XOKÓ-KARIRÍ alt for KARIRI-XOCÓ [KZW]
[[XO-KXOE dial of KXOE [XUU]
[[XOM-KXOE dial of KXOE [XUU]
XONG alt for CHONG [COG]
XONGA dial of TSONGA [TSO]
!XÓÕ [NMN] lang, Botswana; also in Namibia
XOPA dial of LAZ [LZZ]
XOSA alt for XHOSA [XOS]
XRE NOP alt for NOP dial of KOHO [KPM]
XRIKWA alt for XIRI [XII]
XTIENG alt for STIENG, BULO [STI]
!XU alt for KUNG-EKOKA [KNW]
XU alt for KXOE [XUU]

XÛ alt for JU/'HOAN [KTZ]
XUANZHOU dial of CHINESE, WU [WUU]
XUHWE alt for KXOE [XUU]
XUI alt for CHINESE, MANDARIN [CHN]
XUKRU alt for XIKRIN dial of KAYAPO [TXU]
XUKURÚ alt for KARIRI-XOCÓ [KZW]
XUKURÚ alt for KIRIRÍ-XOKÓ [XOO]
XUKURU KARIRI alt for KARIRI-XOCÓ [KZW]
!XUN alt for KUNG-EKOKA [KNW]
XUN alt for JU/'HOAN [KTZ]
XUN alt for KXOE [XUU]
XUNZAL alt for HUNZIB [HUZ]
XUNZAX alt for KUNZAKH dial of AVAR [AVR]
XUÒNG dial of NUNG [NUT]
XURIMA alt for YANOMÁMI [WCA]
XURIWAI alt for NADĚB [MBJ]
XVARSHI alt for KHVARSHI [KHV]
XVARSHI dial of KHVARSHI [KHV]
XWEDA alt for XWEDA-GBE [XWD]
XWEDA-GBE [XWD] lang, Benin
XWELA alt for XWELA-GBE [XWE]
XWELA-GBE [XWE] lang, Benin
XWLA alt for XWLA-GBE [XWL]
XWLA-GBE [XWL] lang, Benin
Y MIA alt for LACHI [LBT]
Y PÍ alt for LACHI [LBT]
Y PÓNG alt for LACHI [LBT]
Y POONG alt for LACHI [LBT]
Y TO alt for LACHI [LBT]
YA alt for TAI PONG dial of TAI NUA [TDD]
YA alt for TAI YA [CUU]
YA dial of VAGHAT-YA-BIJIM-LEGERI [BIJ]
YA LU alt for YUGUR, WEST [YBE]
YAA alt for YAKA dial of TEKE, WESTERN [TEZ]
YAA dial of MUMUYE [MUL]
YAA dial of TEKE, WESTERN [TEZ]
YÁÁ MÒÒ alt for MOO [GWG]
YAADRÉ dial of MOORE [MHM]
YAAGA alt for SEEBA-YAGA dial of FULFULDE,
    NORTHEASTERN BURKINA FASO [FUH]
YAAKO alt for MARGU [MHG]
YAAKU [MUU] lang, Kenya
YAAKUA alt for YAAKU [MUU]
YAALI alt for KENDEJE [KLF]
YAALI dial of KENDEJE [KLF]
YAAMBA dial of MBOLE [MDQ]
YAAN alt for YANGA dial of MOORE [MHM]
YAAN dial of YAOURE [YRE]
YAANDE dial of MOORE [MHM]
YAÁYUWEE dial of GBAYA, NORTHWEST
    [GYA]
YABA dial of BOBO MADARE, NORTHERN [BBO]
YABAÂNA [YBN] lang, Brazil
YABAN alt for ARANDAI [JBJ]
YABARANA [YAR] lang, Venezuela
YABARANA alt for YABAÂNA [YBN]
YABEKA dial of EWONDO [EWO]
YABEKANGA dial of EWONDO [EWO]
YABEKOLO dial of EWONDO [EWO]
YABEM [JAE] lang, Papua New Guinea
YABEN [YBM] lang, Papua New Guinea

YABI dial of EKARI [EKG]
YABIM alt for YABEM [JAE]
YABIO alt for YAWIYO [YBX]
YABIYUFA alt for YAWEYUHA [YBY]
YABONG [YBO] lang, Papua New Guinea
YABUTÍ alt for JABUTÍ [JBT]
YABYANG dial of BAKOKO [BKH]
YABYANG-YAPEKE alt for YABYANG dial of
    BAKOKO [BKH]
YACAN alt for YAKAN [YKA]
YACE [EKR] lang, Nigeria
YACHAM alt for DORDAR dial of NAGA, AO [NJO]
YACHE alt for YACE [EKR]
YACHUMI alt for NAGA, YIMCHUNGRU [YIM]
YACOUA alt for YAKPA dial of BANDA, MID-
    SOUTHERN [BJO]
YACOUBA alt for DAN [DAF]
YADE alt for YALE [NCE]
YADENA alt for BUDUMA [BDM]
YADU dial of QIANG, NORTHERN [CNG]
YAEYAMA [RYS] lang, Japan
YAFFI alt for YAFI [WFG]
YAFI [WFG] lang, Indonesia (Irian Jaya)
YAG DII alt for DII [DUR]
YAGA dial of AGTA, DUPANINAN [DUO]
YAGALLO ZAPOTECO alt for ZAPOTECO,
    RINCÓN [ZAR]
YAGÁN alt for YÁMANA [YAG]
YAGANIZA-XAGACÍA ZAPOTECO dial of
    ZAPOTECO, CAJONOS [ZAD]
YAGAR YAGAR alt for KALA LAGAW YA [MWP]
YAGARIA [YGR] lang, Papua New Guinea
YAGAWAK dial of WANTOAT [WNC]
YAGBA dial of YORUBA [YOR]
YAGE dial of DUNGAN [DNG]
YAGELE alt for GENGLE [GEG]
YAGHAN alt for YÁMANA [YAG]
YAGHWATADAXA alt for GAVA dial of GUDUF
    [GDF]
YAGHWATADAXA alt for GAVA dial of GUDUF-
    GAVA [GDF]
YAGNOB alt for YAGNOBI [YAI]
YAGNOBI [YAI] lang, Tajikistan
YAGOMI [YGM] lang, Papua New Guinea
YAGOUA alt for YAGWA dial of MASANA [MCN]
YAGUA [YAD] lang, Peru; also in Colombia
YAGWA dial of MASANA [MCN]
YAGWOIA [YGW] lang, Papua New Guinea
YAHADIAN [NER] lang, Indonesia (Irian Jaya)
YAHANG [RHP] lang, Papua New Guinea
YAHEUN alt for NYAHEUN [NEV]
YAHOW alt for ZAHAO dial of CHIN, FALAM
    [HBH]
YAHUA alt for YAGUA [YAD]
YAHUANAHUA alt for YAWANAWA [YWN]
YAHUDIC alt for ARABIC, JUDEO-IRAQI [YHD]
YAHUNA [YNU] lang, Colombia
YAHUP alt for YUHUP [YAB]
YAHUP MAKÚ alt for YUHUP [YAB]
YAI alt for IAAI [IAI]
YAI alt for NHANG [NHA]

YAIKOLE dial of MBOLE [MDQ]
YAIR alt for JAIR [YIR]
YAISU dial of MBOLE [MDQ]
YAITEPEC CHATINO dial of CHATINO, SIERRA OCCIDENTAL [CTP]
YAIWE alt for YAÁYUWEE dial of GBAYA, NORTH-WEST [GYA]
YAJIMA alt for YALIMA dial of MONGO-NKUNDU [MOM]
YAKA [AXK] lang, CAR; also in Congo
YAKA [YAF] lang, DRC; also in Angola
YAKA alt for KAKO [KKJ]
YAKA alt for YAA dial of TEKE, WESTERN [TEZ]
YAKA dial of GANZI [GNZ]
YAKA dial of TEKE, WESTERN [TEZ]
YAKA dial of YAKA [YAF]
YAKAHANGA dial of NYAMBO [NYM]
YAKAIKEKE [YKK] lang, Papua New Guinea
YAKALAG alt for YAKALAK dial of BAKOKO [BKH]
YAKALAK dial of BAKOKO [BKH]
YAKAMUL [YKM] lang, Papua New Guinea
YAKAMUL dial of YAKAMUL [YKM]
YAKAN [YKA] lang, Philippines; also in Malaysia (Sabah)
YAKAN alt for ARAKANESE [MHV]
YAKHA [YBH] lang, Nepal; also in India
YAKHAIN alt for RAKHINE dial of ARAKANESE [MHV]
YAKHAING alt for ARAKANESE [MHV]
YAKIBA alt for MAIA [SKS]
YAKIMA [YAK] lang, USA
YAKIMA dial of YAKIMA [YAK]
YAKKHA alt for YAKHA [YBH]
YAKKHABA alt for YAKHA [YBH]
YAKKHABA CEA alt for LUMBA-YAKKHA [LUU]
YAKKHABA CEA alt for YAKHA [YBH]
YAKKHABA LORUNG alt for LORUNG, SOUTHERN [LRR]
YAKKHABA SALA alt for YAKHA [YBH]
YAKÖ alt for LOKAA [YAZ]
YAKO alt for MARGU [MHG]
YAKOKO dial of MUMUYE [MUL]
YAKOMA [YKY] lang, CAR; also in DRC
YAKON alt for YAQUINA dial of ALSEA [AES]
YAKONA alt for YAQUINA dial of ALSEA [AES]
YAKORO alt for BEKWARRA [BKV]
YAKPA dial of BANDA, MID-SOUTHERN [BJO]
YAKPWA alt for YAKPA dial of BANDA, MID-SOUTHERN [BJO]
YAKTHUNG PAN alt for CHATTARE dial of LIMBU [LIF]
YAKTHUNG PAN alt for LIMBU [LIF]
YAKUBA alt for DAN [DAF]
YAKULE alt for POLI dial of YENDANG [YEN]
YAKURR alt for LOKAA [YAZ]
YAKUSU alt for KELE [KHY]
YAKUT [UKT] lang, Russia (Asia)
YAKUT-SAKHA alt for YAKUT [UKT]
YAKWA alt for YAKPA dial of BANDA, MID-SOUTHERN [BJO]
YAKWINA alt for YAQUINA dial of ALSEA [AES]

YALA [YBA] lang, Nigeria
YALA IKOM alt for NKUM dial of YALA [YBA]
YALA OBUBRA alt for NKUM AKPAMBE dial of YALA [YBA]
YALA OGOJA dial of YALA [YBA]
YALACH alt for LACH dial of CZECH [CZC]
YALAHATAN [JAL] lang, Indonesia (Maluku)
YALAPMUNXTE dial of NAMBIKUARA, NORTHERN [MBG]
YALARNNGA [YLR] lang, Australia
YALAYU dial of NYALAYU [YLY]
YALDIYE-HO alt for KANJU [KBE]
YALE [NCE] lang, Papua New Guinea
YALE, KOSAREK [KKL] lang, Indonesia (Irian Jaya)
YALEBA alt for BUHUTU [BXH]
YALEBA dial of TAWALA [TBO]
YALE-KOSAREK alt for YALE, KOSAREK [KKL]
YALE-NIPSAN alt for NIPSAN [NPS]
YALI, ANGGURUK [YLI] lang, Indonesia (Irian Jaya)
YALI, NINIA [NLK] lang, Indonesia (Irian Jaya)
YALI, PASS VALLEY [YAC] lang, Indonesia (Irian Jaya)
YALIAMBI dial of BUDZA [BJA]
YALIMA dial of MONGO-NKUNDU [MOM]
YALIMO alt for YALI, ANGGURUK [YLI]
YALINA dial of ZAPOTECO, ZOOGOCHO [ZPQ]
YALLOF alt for WOLOF [WOL]
YALMBAU alt for MANGALA [MEM]
YALU alt for ARIBWAUNG [YLU]
YALUNKA [YAL] lang, Guinea; also in Mali, Senegal, Sierra Leone
YALUNKA alt for JALUNGA [YAL]
YALUNKE alt for JALUNGA [YAL]
YALUNKE alt for YALUNKA [YAL]
YAM alt for YANGA dial of MOORE [MHM]
YAMAI dial of AWAD BING [BCU]
YAMALE alt for KUGAMA [KOW]
YAMALELE alt for IAMALELE [YML]
YAMALO alt for KUGAMA [KOW]
YAMALTU alt for NYIMATLI dial of TERA [TER]
YAMAMADÍ alt for JAMAMADÍ [JAA]
YÁMANA [YAG] lang, Chile
YAMANAWA alt for YAMINAHUA [YAA]
YAMAP [YMP] lang, Papua New Guinea
YAMBA [YAM] lang, Cameroon; also in Nigeria
YAMBASA alt for NUGUNU [YAS]
YAMBASSA alt for NUGUNU [YAS]
YAMBES [YMB] lang, Papua New Guinea
YAMBETA [YAT] lang, Cameroon
YAMBETTA alt for YAMBETA [YAT]
YAMBIYAMBI alt for BISIS [BNW]
YAMBO alt for ANUAK [ANU]
YAMDENA [JMD] lang, Indonesia (Maluku)
YAMEGI alt for GULA [KCM]
YAMEO [YME] lang, Peru
YAMI [YMI] lang, Taiwan
YAMIACA alt for ATSAHUACA [ATC]
YAMINAHUA [YAA] lang, Peru; also in Bolivia, Brazil
YAMINAHUA dial of YAMINAHUA [YAA]
YAMINAWA alt for YAMINAHUA [YAA]
YAMINÁWA alt for YAMINAHUA [YAA]

YAMNA [YMN] lang, Indonesia (Irian Jaya)
YAMOD dial of GOR [GQR]
YAMOFOWE dial of SIANE [SNP]
YAMONGERI [YMG] lang, DRC
YAMONGIRI alt for YAMONGERI [YMG]
YAMPHE [YMA] lang, Nepal
YAMPHE alt for YAMPHU [YBI]
YAMPHE KHA alt for YAMPHE [YMA]
YAMPHU [YBI] lang, Nepal
YAMPHU alt for YAMPHE [YMA]
YAMPHU KHA alt for YAMPHU [YBI]
YAMPHU RAI alt for YAMPHU [YBI]
YAMUR dial of KAMORO [KGQ]
YAN alt for YANGA dial of MOORE [MHM]
YANA [YNN] lang, USA
YANA alt for YANGA dial of MOORE [MHM]
YANA dial of MOORE [MHM]
YANABA dial of MUYUW [MYW]
YANAIGUA alt for TAPIETÉ [TAI]
YANAM alt for NINAM [SHB]
YANAMAM dial of YANOMAMI [WCA]
YANANGU alt for JARNANGO [JAY]
YANBE alt for YANGBYE [YBD]
YANBYE alt for YANGBYE [YBD]
YANDANG alt for YENDANG [YEN]
YANDAPO dial of ENGA [ENQ]
YANDERIKA alt for INDRI [IDR]
YANDIME dial of SIANE [SNP]
YANDIRIKA alt for INDRI [IDR]
YANDRUWANDHA [YND] lang, Australia
YANESHA' [AME] lang, Peru
YANESHA' alt for YANESHA' [AME]
YANG alt for RIANG [RIL]
YANG DAENG alt for KAYAH, WESTERN [KYU]
YANG KHAO alt for KAREN, S'GAW [KSW]
YANG SEK alt for RIANG [RIL]
YANG WAN KUN alt for RIANG [RIL]
YANGA alt for YANA dial of MOORE [MHM]
YANGA dial of MOORE [MHM]
YANG'AN dial of SUI [SWI]
YANGARELLA alt for NYANGGA [NNY]
"YANGARO" pejorative alt for YEMSA [JNJ]
YANGATALET alt for KAREN, YINTALE [KVY]
YANGBEN [YAV] lang, Cameroon
YANGBYE [YBD] lang, Myanmar
YANGEBORONG dial of KOSORONG [KSR]
YANGELE dial of GBAYA, SOUTHWEST [MDO]
YANGERE alt for BANDA-YANGERE [YAJ]
YANGERU alt for BENA [YUN]
YANGGAL alt for NYANGGA [NNY]
YANGHO [YNH] lang, Gabon
YANGHUANG alt for T'EN [TCT]
YANGKAM [BSX] lang, Nigeria
YANGKOLEN dial of URIM [URI]
YANGLAM alt for RIANG [RIL]
YANGMA dial of BANTAWA [BAP]
YANGMAN [JNG] lang, Australia
YANGO [YNG] lang, DRC
YANGONDA dial of MBOLE [MDQ]
YANGORU alt for BOIKIN [BZF]
YANGTADAI alt for KAREN, YINTALE [KVY]

YANGTSEBIKHA alt for DZALAKHA [DZL]
YAN-GUANG dial of ZHUANG, SOUTHERN
  [CCY]
YANGUERE alt for BANDA-YANGERE [YAJ]
YANGULAM [YNL] lang, Papua New Guinea
YANGYE alt for YANGBYE [YBD]
YANI alt for AKHA [AKA]
YANIMOI alt for SOUTH KOMBIO dial of KOMBIO
  [KOK]
YANITO dial of ENGLISH [ENG]
YANKAM alt for YANGKAM [BSX]
YANKOWAN alt for WASEMBO [GSP]
YANKTON alt for NAKOTA dial of DAKOTA [DHG]
YANKTON-YANKTONAIS alt for NAKOTA dial of
  DAKOTA [DHG]
YANKUNTATJARA alt for YANKUNYTJATJARA
  [KDD]
YANKUNYTJATJARA [KDD] lang, Australia
YANKUNYTJATJARA dial of PITJANTJATJARA
  [PJT]
YAN-NHANGU alt for JARNANGO [JAY]
YANOAM alt for YANOMÁMI [WCA]
YANOMA alt for YANOMAMÖ [GUU]
YANOMAM alt for YANOMÁMI [WCA]
YANOMAM dial of YANOMAMI [WCA]
YANOMAME alt for YANOMAMÖ [GUU]
YANOMAMÉ alt for YANOMÁMI [WCA]
YANOMAMI alt for YANOMAMÖ [GUU]
YANOMÁMI [WCA] lang, Brazil
YANOMAMÖ [GUU] lang, Venezuela; also in
  Brazil
YANOMAY dial of YANOMAMI [WCA]
YANPHU alt for YAMPHU [YBI]
YANRAKINOT dial of CHUKOT [CKT]
YANSI [YNS] lang, DRC
YANTA dial of MUMENG [MZI]
YANTILI dial of FIPA [FIP]
YANULA alt for YANYUWA [JAO]
YANYULA alt for YANYUWA [JAO]
YANYUWA [JAO] lang, Australia
YANZHOU dial of CHINESE, HUIZHOU [CZH]
YANZI alt for KIMBU [KIV]
YANZI alt for YANSI [YNS]
YAO [YAO] lang, Malawi; also in Mozambique,
  Tanzania, Zambia
YAO alt for IU MIEN [IUM]
YA'O alt for KUUKU-YA'U [QKL]
YAO MIN alt for BA PAI [BPN]
YAO YEN alt for LISU [LIS]
YAOSAKOR alt for ASMAT, YAOSAKOR [ASY]
YAOUNDE alt for EWONDO [EWO]
YAOURÉ [YRE] lang, Côte d'Ivoire
YAPANANI alt for YAWA [YVA]
YAPELI alt for NYONG [MUO]
YAPESE [YPS] lang, Micronesia
YAPO dial of KRUMEN, PYE [PYE]
YAPOA dial of WEDAU [WED]
YAPOMA dial of BAKOKO [BKH]
YAPRERÍA alt for JAPRERÍA [JRU]
YAPSI-TAJA dial of ORYA [URY]
YAPUNDA [YEV] lang, Papua New Guinea

YAQAI alt for YAQAY [JAQ]
YAQAY [JAQ] lang, Indonesia (Irian Jaya)
YAQUI [YAQ] lang, Mexico; also in USA
YAQUINA dial of ALSEA [AES]
YARAHUURAXI-CAPANAPARA dial of CUIBA [CUI]
YARAN dial of MARI, HIGH [MRJ]
YARAWATA [YRW] lang, Papua New Guinea
YARAWE alt for SUENA [SUE]
YARAWI alt for SUENA [SUE]
YARE alt for KANTOSI [XKT]
YARË alt for YALE [NCE]
YAREBA [YRB] lang, Papua New Guinea
YARI alt for DAGAARI DIOULA [DGD]
YARÍ [YRI] lang, Colombia
YARIBA alt for YORUBA [YOR]
YARKANDI alt for KASHGAR-YARKAND dial of
    UYGHUR [UIG]
YARKHUN dial of WAKHI [WBL]
YARSI alt for KANTOSI [XKT]
YARSUN [YRS] lang, Indonesia (Irian Jaya)
YARUKULA alt for YERUKULA [YEU]
YARUMÁ [YRM] lang, Brazil
YARUMARRA dial of NGURA [NBX]
YARURO [YAE] lang, Venezuela
YARURU alt for YARURO [YAE]
YARUS dial of ADZERA [AZR]
YAS alt for ASMAT, CENTRAL [AST]
YASA [YKO] lang, Cameroon; also in Equatorial
    Guinea, Gabon
YASA alt for PAWAIA [PWA]
YASGUA alt for YESKWA [YES]
YASHI alt for HASHA [YBJ]
YASIN dial of BURUSHASKI [BSK]
YASIN dial of WAKHI [WBL]
YASING alt for ZASING dial of MUNDANG [MUA]
YASOUKOU alt for YASSUKU dial of BAKOKO
    [BKH]
YASSA alt for YASA [YKO]
YASSING alt for ZASING dial of MUNDANG [MUA]
YASSUKU dial of BAKOKO [BKH]
YASUA alt for MBAKOLO dial of GBAYA, SOUTH-
    WEST [MDO]
YASUG alt for YASSUKU dial of BAKOKO [BKH]
YASUKU alt for YASSUKU dial of BAKOKO [BKH]
YASYIN alt for YESSAN-MAYO [YSS]
YATE alt for INOKE-YATE [INO]
YATÊ alt for FULNIÔ [FUN]
YATEE ZAPOTEC alt for ZAPOTECO, YATEE [ZTY]
YATINI dial of NUNI, SOUTHERN [NNW]
YATYE alt for YACE [EKR]
YATZACHI ZAPOTEC alt for ZAPOTECO,
    YATZACHI [ZAV]
YATZECHI ZAPOTECO alt for ZAPOTECO, SANTA
    INÉS YATZECHI [ZPN]
YAU [YUW] lang, Papua New Guinea
YAU [YYU] lang, Papua New Guinea
YAU alt for IAU [TMU]
YAU alt for YAWU dial of YESSAN-MAYO [YSS]
YAU MIN alt for BA PAI [BPN]
YAUAN alt for BRAGAT [AOF]
YAUAPERI alt for JAWAPERI dial of ATRUAHI [ATR]

YAUARANA alt for YABARANA [YAR]
YAUGIBA alt for URIMO [URX]
YAUKE alt for YOKE [YKI]
YAUL [YLA] lang, Papua New Guinea
YAULAPITI alt for YAWALAPITÍ [YAW]
YAUMA [YAX] lang, Angola; also in Zambia
YAÚNA alt for YAHUNA [YNU]
YAUNDE alt for EWONDO [EWO]
YA'UNK alt for YAHANG [RHP]
YAUR [JAU] lang, Indonesia (Irian Jaya)
YAURAWA alt for RESHE [RES]
YAURE alt for YAOURÉ [YRE]
YAURI alt for CISHINGINI [ASG]
YAUTEFA alt for TOBATI [TTI]
YAUTEPEC ZAPOTEC alt for ZAPOTECO,
    YAUTEPEC [ZPB]
YAVA alt for YAGUA [YAD]
YAVA alt for YAWA [YVA]
YAVAPAI dial of HAVASUPAI-WALAPAI-YAVAPAI
    [YUF]
YAVATMAL dial of GONDI, NORTHERN [GON]
YAVESÍA ZAPOTECO alt for ZAPOTECO, IXTLÁN
    SURESTE [ZPD]
YAVITA alt for BARÉ [BAE]
YAVITA alt for MANDAHUACA [MHT]
YAVITERO [YVT] lang, Venezuela
YAW alt for YAWU dial of YESSAN-MAYO [YSS]
YAW dial of BURMESE [BMS]
YAW YIN alt for LISU [LIS]
YAWA [YVA] lang, Indonesia (Irian Jaya)
YAWA alt for KALOU [YWA]
YAWALAPITÍ [YAW] lang, Brazil
YAWANAWA [YWN] lang, Brazil
YAWARAWARGA [YWW] lang, Australia
YAWARETE TAPUYA alt for JAUARETE dial of
    CARUTANA [CRU]
YAWDWIN alt for CHIN, MÜN [MWQ]
YAWENIAN alt for IWAM, SEPIK [IWS]
YAWEYUHA [YBY] lang, Papua New Guinea
YAWIYO [YBX] lang, Papua New Guinea
YAWIYUHA alt for YAWEYUHA [YBY]
YAWOTATAXA alt for GAVA dial of GUDUF [GDF]
YAWOTATAXA alt for GAVA dial of GUDUF-GAVA
    [GDF]
YAWU dial of YESSAN-MAYO [YSS]
YAWURU [YWR] lang, Australia
YAW-YEN alt for LISU [LIS]
YAY alt for NHANG [NHA]
YAYEYAMA alt for YAEYAMA [RYS]
YAYUNA alt for YAHUNA [YNU]
YAZGULAM alt for YAZGULYAM [YAH]
YAZGULYAM [YAH] lang, Tajikistan
YAZGULYAMI alt for YAZGULYAM [YAH]
YAZVA dial of KOMI-ZYRIAN [KPV]
YBANAG alt for IBANAG [IBG]
YE dial of MON [MNW]
YËHUP alt for YUHUP [YAB]
YEBA alt for MACUNA [MYY]
YEBAMASÃ alt for MACUNA [MYY]
YEBEKOLO alt for YABEKOLO dial of EWONDO
    [EWO]

YEBU alt for AWAK [AWO]
YECI dial of HOLU [HOL]
YE'CUANA alt for MAQUIRITARI [MCH]
YE'CUANA alt for MAYONGONG dial of
    MAQUIRITARI [MCH]
YEDIMA alt for BUDUMA [BDM]
YEDINA alt for BUDUMA [BDM]
YEDJI alt for YEJI dial of CHUMBURUNG [NCU]
YEEI alt for YEYI [YEY]
YEEI dial of YANSI [YNS]
YEGA alt for KEIGA [KEC]
YEGA alt for MOKORUA dial of KORAFE [KPR]
YEGA dial of EWAGE-NOTU [NOU]
YEGHA alt for MOKORUA dial of KORAFE [KPR]
YEGHE dial of KHANA [KEH]
YEGHUYE alt for YAGWOIA [YGW]
YEGUA alt for YAGUA [YAD]
YEH alt for JEH [JEH]
YEHEN alt for FWÂI [FWA]
YEH-JEH alt for LISU [LIS]
YEH-JEN alt for LISU [LIS]
YEHPÁ MAJSÁ alt for MACUNA [MYY]
YEI [JEI] lang, Indonesia (Irian Jaya); also in Papua
    New Guinea
YEI alt for YEYI [YEY]
YEIDJI alt for WUNAMBAL [WUB]
YEI-NAN alt for YEI [JEI]
YEINBAW alt for KAREN, YINBAW [KVU]
YEITHI alt for WUNAMBAL [WUB]
YEJI dial of CHUMBURUNG [NCU]
YEKHEE [ETS] lang, Nigeria
YEKORA [YKR] lang, Papua New Guinea
YEKUANA alt for MAQUIRITARI [MCH]
YEKUANA alt for MAYONGONG dial of
    MAQUIRITARI [MCH]
YELA [YEL] lang, DRC
YELA alt for YELE [YLE]
YELE [YLE] lang, Papua New Guinea
YELEJONG alt for YELE [YLE]
YELETNYE alt for YELE [YLE]
YELINDA dial of BULU [BUM]
YELLOW LAHU alt for LAHU SHI [KDS]
YELLOW LEAF alt for MLABRI [MRA]
YELLOW RIVER alt for NAMIA [NNM]
YELLOW UIGHUR alt for YUGUR, WEST [YBE]
YELLOWKNIFE dial of CHIPEWYAN [CPW]
YELMEK [JEL] lang, Indonesia (Irian Jaya)
YELMO alt for ADOMA dial of CLELA [DRI]
YELOGU [YLG] lang, Papua New Guinea
YEM alt for YEMSA [JNJ]
YEMA alt for SUENA [SUE]
YEMBA [BAN] lang, Cameroon
YEMBA dial of YEMBA [BAN]
YEMBANA dial of BULU [BUM]
YEMBE alt for SONGE [SOP]
YEMBO alt for ANUAK [ANU]
YEMCHIDI alt for JAMSHIDI dial of AIMAQ [AIQ]
YEMENITE HEBREW alt for ORIENTAL HEBREW
    dial of HEBREW [HBR]
YEMENITE JUDEO-ARABIC alt for ARABIC,
    JUDEO-YEMENI [JYE]

YEMMA alt for YEMSA [JNJ]
YEMSA [JNJ] lang, Ethiopia
YENDAM alt for YENDANG [YEN]
YENDANG [YEN] lang, Nigeria
YENGEN alt for FWÂI [FWA]
YENGONO dial of BULU [BUM]
YENGORU alt for BOIKIN [BZF]
YENI [YEI] lang, Cameroon
YENICHE [YEC] lang, Germany; also in Austria,
    France, Netherlands, Switzerland
YENIMU alt for SIAGHA-YENIMU [OSR]
YENISEI OSTYAK alt for KET [KET]
YENISEI SAMOYEDIC alt for ENETS [ENE]
YENISEI TATAR alt for KHAKAS [KJH]
YENISEY OSTIAK alt for KET [KET]
YENISHE alt for YENICHE [YEC]
YENKUANG alt for YAN-GUANG dial of ZHUANG,
    SOUTHERN [CCY]
YEPÁ MAXSÃ alt for MACUNA [MYY]
YEPÁ-MAHSÁ alt for MACUNA [MYY]
YERAKAI [YRA] lang, Papua New Guinea
YERAL alt for NHENGATU [YRL]
YERANI alt for GOROVU [GRQ]
YERAVA alt for RAVULA [YEA]
YERAWA alt for AKA-JERU [AKJ]
YERBOGOCEN dial of EVENKI [EVN]
YERE alt for BWAMU, LÁÁ LÁÁ [BWJ]
YEREKAI alt for YERAKAI [YRA]
YERETUAR [GOP] lang, Indonesia (Irian Jaya)
YEREVAN dial of AZERBAIJANI, NORTH [AZE]
YERGAM alt for TAROK [YER]
YERGE alt for FUR [FUR]
YERGUM alt for TAROK [YER]
YERGYUCH dial of BUDUKH [BDK]
YERGYUDZH dial of KRYTS [KRY]
YERI WAALI dial of WALI [WLX]
YERINGTON-SCHURZ alt for SOUTH NORTHERN
    PAIUTE dial of PAIUTE, NORTHERN [PAO]
YERKULA alt for YERUKULA [YEU]
YERONG [YRN] lang, China
YERU dial of KOMA [KMY]
YERUKALA alt for YERUKULA [YEU]
YERUKALA-KORAVA alt for YERUKULA [YEU]
YERUKLA alt for YERUKULA [YEU]
YERUKULA [YEU] lang, India
YERUKULA-BHASHA alt for YERUKULA [YEU]
YERWA KANURI alt for KANURI, CENTRAL [KPH]
YES FIRAN alt for FIRAN [FIR]
YESAN alt for YESSAN-MAYO [YSS]
YESKWA [YES] lang, Nigeria
YESOUM alt for BAMVELE dial of EWONDO [EWO]
YESSAN-MAYO [YSS] lang, Papua New Guinea
YETFA [YET] lang, Indonesia (Irian Jaya)
YETI alt for MANEM [JET]
YETIMARALA alt for BAYALI [BJY]
YETINJI alt for YIDINY [YII]
YEU alt for NYEU [NYL]
YEVANIC [YEJ] lang, Israel; also in USA
YEVANITIKA alt for YEVANIC [YEJ]
YEWENA-YONGSU dial of TABLA [TNM]
YEWU dial of BWA [BWW]

YEY alt for YEI [JEI]
YEY alt for YEEI dial of YANSI [YNS]
YEYI [YEY] lang, Botswana; also in Namibia
YEZO alt for HOKKAIDO dial of AINU [AIN]
YEZUM alt for BAMVELE dial of EWONDO [EWO]
YHUATA alt for OMAGUA [OMG]
YI BE WU alt for BEBE [BZV]
YI, CENTRAL [YIC] lang, China
YI, GUIZHOU [YIG] lang, China
YI, SICHUAN [III] lang, China
YI, SOUTHEASTERN [YIE] lang, China
YI, WESTERN [YIW] lang, China
YI, YUNNAN [NOS] lang, China
YIBARAMBU alt for BARAMA [BBG]
YIBWA alt for TIMA [TMS]
YICHIRA alt for SIRA [SWJ]
YIDANA alt for BUDUMA [BDM]
YIDDA alt for MADA [MDA]
YIDDINJI alt for YIDINY [YII]
YIDDISH alt for YIDDISH, EASTERN [YDD]
YIDDISH alt for YIDDISH, WESTERN [YIH]
YIDDISH SIGN LANGUAGE [YDS] lang, Israel
YIDDISH, EASTERN [YDD] lang, Israel; also in
    Argentina, Australia, Belarus, Belgium, Canada,
    Estonia, Hungary, Latvia, Lithuania, Moldova,
    Panama, Poland, Puerto Rico, Romania, Russia
    (Europe), South Africa, Ukraine, Uruguay, USA
YIDDISH, WESTERN [YIH] lang, Germany; also
    in France, Hungary, Netherlands, Switzerland
YIDENA alt for BUDUMA [BDM]
YIDGA alt for YIDGHA [YDG]
YIDGHA [YDG] lang, Pakistan
YIDI alt for YIDINICH dial of KWEGU [YID]
YIDIN alt for YIDINY [YII]
YIDINDJI alt for YIDINY [YII]
YIDINICH dial of KWEGU [YID]
YIDINIT alt for YIDINICH dial of KWEGU [YID]
YIDINY [YII] lang, Australia
YIDINY dial of YIDINY [YII]
YIDISH alt for YIDDISH, WESTERN [YIH]
YIDU alt for LUOBA, YIDU [CLK]
YIDU LUOBA alt for IDU [CLK]
YIGAI alt for BAHINEMO [BJH]
YIGHA alt for LEYIGHA [AYI]
YIIVE alt for IYIVE [UIV]
YIL [YLL] lang, Papua New Guinea
YILI dial of TULA [TUL]
YILIGELE dial of TOURA [NEB]
YI-LIU dial of CHINESE, GAN [KNN]
YILLARO alt for LARO [LRO]
YILPARITJA alt for YULPARITJA dial of MARTU
    WANGKA [MPJ]
YIMAS [YEE] lang, Papua New Guinea
YIMBA alt for LIMBA, EAST [LMA]
YIMBA alt for LIMBA, WEST-CENTRAL [LIA]
YIMBUN alt for ABUN [KGR]
YIMCHUNGER alt for NAGA, YIMCHUNGRU [YIM]
YIMCHUNGRE alt for NAGA, YIMCHUNGRU [YIM]
YIMCHUNGRU alt for NAGA, YIMCHUNGRU [YIM]
YIMCHUNGRU dial of NAGA, YIMCHUNGRU [YIM]
YIMTIM alt for FALI [FLI]

YIMWOM alt for KAM [KDX]
YIN alt for RIANG [RIL]
YINBAW alt for KAREN, YINBAW [KVU]
YINCHIA [YIN] lang, Myanmar
YINDI alt for YINDU dial of CHIN, KHUMI [CKM]
YINDI dial of CHIN, KHUMI [CKM]
YINDJIBARNDI [YIJ] lang, Australia
YINDJILANDJI [YIL] lang, Australia
YINDU alt for YINDI dial of CHIN, KHUMI [CKM]
YINDU dial of CHIN, KHUMI [CKM]
YINE [PIB] lang, Peru
YINE alt for YINE [PIB]
YINGA alt for SAA [SZR]
YINGGARDA [YIA] lang, Australia
YINGKARTA alt for YINGGARDA [YIA]
YINGLISH [YIB] lang, USA; also in United Kingdom
YING-YI dial of CHINESE, GAN [KNN]
YINIBU alt for ROCKY PEAK [ROK]
YINJEBI alt for NJEBI [NZB]
YINNET alt for YINCHIA [YIN]
YINTALE alt for KAREN, YINTALE [KVY]
YINTALET alt for KAREN, YINTALE [KVY]
YINZEBI alt for NJEBI [NZB]
YIPMA alt for BARUYA [BYR]
YIPOUNOU alt for PUNU [PUU]
YIPUNU alt for PUNU [PUU]
YIR alt for IR [IRR]
YIR YIRONT alt for YIR YORONT [YIY]
YIR YORONT [YIY] lang, Australia
YIRA dial of NANDI [NNB]
YIRMEL alt for JIR'JOROND dial of YIR YORONT
    [YIY]
YIRTANGETTLE alt for JIR'JOROND dial of YIR
    YORONT [YIY]
YIRTUTIYM alt for JIR'JOROND dial of YIR YORONT
    [YIY]
YIRU alt for NALI [NSS]
YIRYO dial of BERAKOU [BXV]
YIS [YIS] lang, Papua New Guinea
YISANGOU alt for SANGU [SNQ]
YISANGU alt for SANGU [SNQ]
YITINTYI alt for YIDINY [YII]
YIU MIEN alt for IU MIEN [IUM]
YIVOUMBOU alt for VUMBU [VUM]
YIWOM [GEK] lang, Nigeria
Y-LANG alt for JOLONG dial of BAHNAR [BDQ]
YLANOS alt for ILANUN [ILL]
YNÃ alt for KARAJÁ [KPJ]
YÖGUR alt for YUGUR, EAST [YUY]
YO alt for NYAW [NYW]
YO alt for YOS [YOS]
YOABOU alt for WAAMA [WWA]
YOABU alt for WAAMA [WWA]
YOADABE-WATOARE alt for MARING [MBW]
YOANA alt for YUWANA [YAU]
YOANGEN dial of KUBE [KGF]
YOANGGENG alt for YOANGEN dial of KUBE [KGF]
YOARI alt for JAUARI dial of YANOMAMI [WCA]
YOBA [YOB] lang, Papua New Guinea
YOCOBOUE alt for LOZOUA dial of DIDA,
    YOCOBOUE [GUD]

YOCOT'AN alt for CHONTAL, TABASCO [CHF]
YOE alt for NYEU [NYL]
YOFO alt for KUMBA [KSM]
YOFO dial of YENDANG [YEN]
YOFUAHA alt for CHOROTE, IYOJWA'JA [CRT]
YOGAD [YOG] lang, Philippines
YOGAM alt for GHOMÁIÁ' CENTRAL dial of
    GHOMALA [BBJ]
YOGLI dial of NAGA, TASE [NST]
YOGOR alt for YUGUR, EAST [YUY]
YOHLMU TAM alt for HELAMBU SHERPA [SCP]
YOHORAA dial of TUCANO [TUO]
YOHOWRÉ alt for YAOURÉ [YRE]
YOI alt for YOY [YOY]
YOIDIK [YDK] lang, Papua New Guinea
YOIT alt for YUPIK, CENTRAL SIBERIAN [ESS]
YOKAIA alt for POMO, CENTRAL [POO]
YOKAN dial of SAAMI, SKOLT [LPK]
YOKARI dial of TABLA [TNM]
YOKE [YKI] lang, Indonesia (Irian Jaya)
YOKI alt for YOKE [YKI]
YOKOUBOUÉ alt for LOZOUA dial of DIDA,
    YOCOBOUE [GUD]
YOKU dial of SIE [ERG]
YOKULA alt for GANGGALIDA [GCD]
YOKUTS [YOK] lang, USA
YOLA alt for JOLA-FOGNY [DYO]
YOLOX CHINANTECO dial of CHINANTECO,
    QUIOTEPEC [CHQ]
YOLOXOCHITL MIXTEC alt for MIXTECO,
    YOLOXOCHITL [QMY]
YOM alt for PILA [PIL]
YOM dial of BEDJOND [MAP]
YOM GAWAC alt for BUGAWAC [BUK]
YOMBE [YOM] lang, DRC; also in Angola, Congo
YOMBE alt for YOOMBE dial of VILI [VIF]
YOMBE dial of TUMBUKA [TUW]
YOMBE CLASSIQUE alt for VUNGUNYA dial of
    YOMBE [YOM]
YOMBIRO LELE dial of LELE [LLC]
YOMUD dial of TURKMEN [TCK]
YOMUT alt for YOMUD dial of TURKMEN [TCK]
YOMUT dial of TURKMEN [TCK]
YONAGUNI [YOI] lang, Japan
YONG [YNO] lang, Thailand
YONGBEI dial of ZHUANG, NORTHERN [CCX]
YONGGOM alt for YONGKOM [YON]
YONGHO alt for YANGHO [YNH]
YONGKOM [YON] lang, Papua New Guinea; also
    in Indonesia (Irian Jaya)
YONGNAN dial of ZHUANG, SOUTHERN [CCY]
YONGO dial of MBANGALA [MXG]
YONGOLEI dial of BIANGAI [BIG]
YONGOM alt for YONGKOM [YON]
YONGOR alt for BENA [YUN]
YONGREN dial of TAI NUA [TDD]
YONGYASHA dial of NAGA, PHOM [NPH]
YONI dial of THEMNE [TEJ]
YOO dial of YAOURE [YRE]
YOOBA alt for YORUBA [YOR]
YOOI alt for YOY [YOY]

YOOMBE dial of VILI [VIF]
YOOY alt for YOY [YOY]
YOPARÁ alt for JOPARÁ dial of GUARANI,
    PARAGUAYAN [GUG]
YOPNO [YUT] lang, Papua New Guinea
YORA [MTS] lang, Peru
YORDA alt for KPAN [KPK]
YORK CREE alt for CREE, MOOSE [CRM]
YORK CREE alt for CREE, SWAMPY [CSW]
YORO alt for MUMUYE [MUL]
YORO dial of MUMUYE [MUL]
YORON [YOX] lang, Japan
YORUBA [YOR] lang, Nigeria; also in Benin, Togo,
    United Kingdom, USA
YORUBA alt for RAVULA [YEA]
YORUK alt for YURUK dial of BALKAN GAGAUZ
    TURKISH [BGX]
YOS [YOS] lang, Myanmar
YOSEMITE alt for MIWOK, SOUTHERN SIERRA
    [SKD]
YOSHKAR-OLIN alt for GRASSLAND MARI dial
    of MARI, LOW [MAL]
YOSOÑAMA dial of MIXTECO, TLAXIACO NORTE
    [MOS]
YOSONDÚA MIXTEC alt for MIXTECO,
    YOSONDÚA [MPM]
YOT alt for KOL dial of CUA [CUA]
YOTAFA alt for TOBATI [TTI]
YOTE alt for YOS [YOS]
YOTI dial of YENDANG [YEN]
YOTOWAWA alt for KISAR [KJE]
YOTUBO alt for GIMNIME [KMB]
YOU alt for TAI PONG dial of TAI NUA [TDD]
"YOUANNE" pejorative alt for THAI, NORTHERN
    [NOD]
YOUJIANG dial of ZHUANG, NORTHERN [CCX]
YOULE alt for JINUO, YOULE [JIU]
YOULOU alt for YULU [YUL]
YOUMIAN alt for IU MIEN [IUM]
YOUNUO alt for BUNU, YOUNUO [BUH]
"YOUON" pejorative alt for THAI, NORTHERN [NOD]
YOURÉ alt for YAOURÉ [YRE]
YOUTUBO alt for GOMNOME dial of KOMA [KMY]
YOVAI alt for AYOREO [AYO]
YOWERA alt for ALYAWARR [ALY]
YOY [YOY] lang, Thailand; also in Laos
YOZA dial of HAYA [HAY]
YRAPA dial of YUKPA [YUP]
YREPO dial of KRUMEN, TEPO [TED]
YREWE dial of KRUMEN, PYE [PYE]
YÜRÜK dial of DOMARI [RMT]
YU dial of MANDJAK [MFV]
YU MIEN alt for IU MIEN [IUM]
YUAGA [NUA] lang, New Caledonia
"YUAN" pejorative alt for THAI, NORTHERN [NOD]
YUAN dial of KHMU [KJG]
YUANA alt for YUWANA [YAU]
YUANGA alt for YUAGA [NUA]
YUANJIN dial of YI, YUNNAN [NOS]
YUAPÍN alt for YARURO [YAE]
YUBA alt for MAIDU, NORTHWEST [MAI]

YUBANAKOR [YUO] lang, Papua New Guinea
YUCATEC MAYA alt for ITZÁ [ITZ]
YUCATEC MAYA SIGN LANGUAGE [MSD] lang,
  Mexico
YUCATECO alt for MAYA, YUCATN [YUA]
YUCHI [YUC] lang, USA
YUCHIANG alt for YOUJIANG dial of ZHUANG,
  NORTHERN [CCX]
YUCKAMURRI alt for NYANGGA [NNY]
YUCPA alt for YUKPA [YUP]
YUCU ÑUTI dial of MIXTECO, TEZOATLAN [MXB]
YUCUAÑE MIXTEC alt for MIXTECO, YUCUAÑE
  [MVG]
YUCUHITI dial of MIXTECO, TLAXIACO,
  SUROESTE [MEH]
YUCUNA [YCN] lang, Colombia
YUDGA alt for YIDGHA [YDG]
YUDGHA alt for YIDGHA [YDG]
YUDHIA alt for ORIYA [ORY]
YUDI alt for ARABIC, JUDEO-TRIPOLITANIAN
  [YUD]
YUE alt for CHINESE, YUE [YUH]
YUEBEI dial of CHINESE, HAKKA [HAK]
YUEH alt for CHINESE, YUE [YUH]
YUEHAI dial of CHINESE, YUE [YUH]
YUET YUE alt for CHINESE, YUE [YUH]
YUE-TAI dial of CHINESE, HAKKA [HAK]
YUEYU alt for CHINESE, YUE [YUH]
YUEZHONG dial of CHINESE, HAKKA [HAK]
YUFIYUFA alt for TOKANO [ZUH]
YUG alt for YUGH [YUU]
YUGAMBAL [YUB] lang, Australia
YUGAR alt for YUGUR, EAST [YUY]
YUGH [YUU] lang, Russia (Asia)
YUGOSLAVIAN SIGN LANGUAGE [YSL] lang,
  Yugoslavia; also in Slovenia
YUGU alt for YUGUR, EAST [YUY]
YUGU alt for YUGUR, WEST [YBE]
YUGUI dial of CHINESE, HAKKA [HAK]
YUGULDA alt for GANGGALIDA [GCD]
YUGUMBAL alt for YUGAMBAL [YUB]
YUGUMBE alt for BANDJALANG [BDY]
YUGUMBIR dial of BANDJALANG [BDY]
YUGUR, EAST [YUY] lang, China
YUGUR, WEST [YBE] lang, China
YUHU alt for OTOMÍ, SIERRA ORIENTAL [OTM]
YUHUP [YAB] lang, Brazil; also in Colombia
YUI alt for SALT-YUI [SLL]
YUIT alt for YUPIK, CENTRAL SIBERIAN [ESS]
YUK alt for YUPIK, CENTRAL SIBERIAN [ESS]
YUKAGHIR, NORTHERN [YKG] lang, Russia (Asia)
YUKAGHIR, SOUTHERN [YUX] lang, Russia (Asia)
YUKAGIR alt for YUKAGHIR, NORTHERN [YKG]
YUKAGIR alt for YUKAGHIR, SOUTHERN [YUX]
YUKALA alt for GANGGALIDA [GCD]
YUKAN alt for ATAYAL [TAY]
YUKI [YUK] lang, USA
YUKKABURRA alt for YIDINY [YII]
YUKO alt for YUKPA [YUP]
YUKPA [YUP] lang, Colombia; also in Venezuela
YUKU alt for YUGUR, WEST [YBE]

YUKUBEN [YBL] lang, Nigeria; also in Cameroon
YUKULTA alt for GANGGALIDA [GCD]
YUKUNA alt for YUCUNA [YCN]
YUKUTARE alt for BITARE [BRE]
YULBARIDJA alt for YULPARITJA dial of MARTU
  WANGKA [MPJ]
YULE-DELENA dial of RORO [RRO]
YULPARITJA dial of MARTU WANGKA [MPJ]
YULU [YUL] lang, CAR; also in DRC, Sudan
YULU dial of YULU [YUL]
YUM alt for AGHEM [AGQ]
YUMA alt for QUECHAN [YUM]
YUMÁ alt for JÚMA [JUA]
YUMBA alt for LIMBA, EAST [LMA]
YUMBA alt for LIMBA, WEST-CENTRAL [LIA]
YUMBAR alt for WÁRA [TCI]
YUMBO alt for QUICHUA, LOWLAND, NAPO [QLN]
YUMBO alt for QUICHUA, LOWLAND, TENA [QUW]
YUMBRI alt for MLABRI [MRA]
YUMINAHUA alt for YAMINAHUA [YAA]
YUMPIA alt for WAMBAYA [WMB]
YUNA alt for DUNA [DUC]
YUNANNESE SHAN alt for TAI NÜA [TDD]
YUNDUM alt for YENDANG [YEN]
YUNGAY dial of QUECHUA, ANCASH, HUAYLAS
  [QAN]
YUNGNAN alt for YONGNAN dial of ZHUANG,
  SOUTHERN [CCY]
YUNGPEI alt for YONGBEI dial of ZHUANG,
  NORTHERN [CCX]
YUNGUILLO-CONDAGUA dial of INGA, JUNGLE
  [INJ]
YUNGUR alt for BENA [YUN]
YUNGUR alt for VORO [VOR]
YUNGWE alt for NYUNGWE [NYU]
YUNNALINKA alt for WARLUWARA [WRB]
YUNNAN SHANT'OU alt for TAI NÜA [TDD]
YUNNANESE alt for HO dial of CHINESE,
  MANDARIN [CHN]
YUNNAN-GUIZHOU alt for DIAN-QIAN dial of YI,
  GUIZHOU [YIG]
YUNO alt for BUNU, YOUNUO [BUH]
YUNUO alt for BUNU, YOUNUO [BUH]
YUPA alt for YUKPA [YUP]
YUPIK, CENTRAL [ESU] lang, USA
YUPIK, CENTRAL SIBERIAN [ESS] lang, USA;
  also in Russia (Asia)
YUPIK, NAUKAN [YNK] lang, Russia (Asia)
YUPIK, PACIFIC GULF [EMS] lang, USA
YUPIK, SIRENIK [YSR] lang, Russia (Asia)
YUPNA alt for YOPNO [YUT]
YUQUI [YUQ] lang, Bolivia
YURA alt for YORA [MTS]
YURA alt for YURACARE [YUE]
YURACARE [YUE] lang, Bolivia
YURAK alt for NENETS [YRK]
YURAK SAMOYED alt for NENETS [YRK]
YURI alt for KARKAR-YURI [YUJ]
YURI dial of GOLIN [GVF]
YURITI alt for YURUTI [YUI]
YURITI-TAPUIA alt for YURUTI [YUI]

YURMATY dial of BASHKIR [BXK]
YUROK [YUR] lang, USA
YURUK dial of BALKAN GAGAUZ TURKISH [BGX]
YURÚNA alt for JURÚNA [JUR]
YURUPARI TAPUYA alt for JURUPARI dial of
    CARUTANA [CRU]
YURUTI [YUI] lang, Colombia; also in Brazil
YURUTI-TAPUYA alt for YURUTI [YUI]
YUTA dial of GIDRA [GDR]
YUTANDUCHI MIXTEC alt for MIXTECO,
    YUTANDUCHI [MAB]
YUWANA [YAU] lang, Venezuela
ZA alt for HYA [HYA]
ZAA alt for DII [DUR]
ZAA dial of WE SOUTHERN [GXX]
ZÂÂ alt for DIMLI [ZZZ]
ZAACHILA dial of ZAPOTECO, SANTA INES
    YATZECHI [ZPN]
ZAACHILA MIXTECO alt for MIXTECO, HUITEPEC
    [MXS]
ZAAKOSA alt for FULFULDE, ADAMAWA [FUB]
ZAAR dial of SAYA [SAY]
ZABANA [KJI] lang, Solomon Islands
ZABARMA alt for ZARMA [DJE]
ZABARMA alt for ZARMACI [DJE]
ZACAPOAXTLA MEJICANO alt for NÁHUATL,
    PUEBLA, SIERRA [AZZ]
ZACAPOAXTLA NÁHUAT alt for NÁHUATL,
    PUEBLA, SIERRA [AZZ]
ZACATEPEC MIXE dial of MIXE, QUETZALTEPEC
    [MVE]
ZACATEPEC MIXTEC alt for MIXTECO, SANTA
    MARÍA ZACATEPEC [MZA]
ZADAR alt for ARBANASI dial of ALBANIAN, TOSK
    [ALN]
ZADGAALI alt for MAKRANI dial of BALOCHI,
    SOUTHERN [BCC]
ZADIE dial of BETE, GAGNOA [BTG]
ZAFISORO dial of MALAGASY [MEX]
ZAGAOUA alt for ZAGHAWA [ZAG]
ZAGAOUA alt for ZANDE [ZAN]
ZAGARAN MRAN dial of MARU [MHX]
ZAGAWA alt for ZAGHAWA [ZAG]
ZAGAWA alt for ZANDE [ZAN]
ZAGHAWA [ZAG] lang, Sudan; also in Chad, Libya
ZAGHVANA alt for DGHWEDE [DGH]
ZAGNA dial of WE SOUTHERN [GXX]
ZAGNE dial of WE SOUTHERN [GXX]
ZAGUNDZI dial of ROMANI, VLAX [RMY]
ZAHA alt for ZAA dial of WE SOUTHERN [GXX]
ZAHAO dial of CHIN, FALAM [HBH]
ZAHAU alt for ZAHAO dial of CHIN, FALAM [HBH]
ZAHAU-SHIMHRIN alt for ZAHAO dial of CHIN,
    FALAM [HBH]
ZAÏRE SWAHILI alt for SWAHILI, CONGO [SWC]
ZAINAL dial of AIMAQ [AIQ]
ZAIWA [ATB] lang, China; also in Myanmar
ZAIWA dial of ZAIWA [ATB]
ZAKA alt for TOKANO [ZUH]
ZAKARA alt for NZAKARA [NZK]
ZAKATALY alt for ZAQATALA dial of AVAR [AVR]

ZAKATALY dial of AVAR [AVR]
ZAKATALY dial of AZERBAIJANI, NORTH [AZE]
ZAKHO dial of LISHANA DENI [LSD]
ZAKHRING [ZKR] lang, India
ZAKI dial of LUGBARA [LUG]
ZAKSA alt for ZAKSHI dial of ZARI [ZAZ]
ZAKSHI dial of ZARI [ZAZ]
ZALA dial of WOLAYTTA [WBC]
ZALAMO [ZAJ] lang, Tanzania
ZALAVARIA KOLI dial of KOLI, KACHI [GJK]
ZAMA alt for KXOE [XUU]
ZAMAN dial of BULU [BUM]
ZAMBEZI alt for TONGA [TOI]
ZAMBIAN SIGN LANGUAGE [ZSL] lang, Zambia
ZAMBOANGUEÑO alt for CHAVACANO [CBK]
ZAMBOANGUEÑO dial of CHAVACANO [CBK]
ZAME alt for ZUMO dial of JIMI [JIM]
ZAMFARAWA dial of HAUSA [HUA]
ZAMRE dial of MESME [ZIM]
ZAMYAKI alt for ZEMIAKI dial of GRANGALI [NLI]
ZAN alt for LAZ [LZZ]
ZAN dial of ZAN GULA [ZNA]
ZAN GULA [ZNA] lang, Chad
ZANA alt for BARIBA [BBA]
ZANAKI [ZAK] lang, Tanzania
ZANDE [ZAN] lang, DRC; also in CAR, Sudan
ZANDI alt for ZANDE [ZAN]
ZANG alt for TIBETAN [TIC]
ZANG dial of NGWO [NGN]
ZANGA dial of DYAN [DYA]
ZANGANA dial of KURDI [KDB]
ZANGNTE alt for TIBEA [NGY]
ZANGRAM alt for JANGSHUNG [JNA]
ZANGSKARI [ZAU] lang, India
ZANGWAL [ZAH] lang, Nigeria
ZANI alt for NZANYI [NJA]
ZANIZA ZAPOTEC alt for ZAPOTECO, ZANIZA
    [ZPW]
ZANJAN dial of TAKESTANI [TKS]
ZANNIAT dial of CHIN, FALAM [HBH]
ZANSKARI alt for ZANGSKARI [ZAU]
ZANU dial of KOMA [KMY]
ZANY alt for NZANYI [NJA]
ZANZIBAR alt for UNGUJA dial of SWAHILI [SWA]
ZAO alt for CHIN, MARA [MRH]
ZAOMIN alt for BA PAI [BPN]
ZAORE dial of MOORE [MHM]
ZÁPARA alt for ZÁPARO [ZRO]
ZÁPARO [ZRO] lang, Ecuador
ZAPOTECO alt for ZAPOTECO, ISTMO [ZAI]
ZAPOTECO, ALBARRADAS [ZAS] lang, Mexico
ZAPOTECO, ALOÁPAM [ZAQ] lang, Mexico
ZAPOTECO, AMATLÁN [ZPO] lang, Mexico
ZAPOTECO, ASUNCIÓN MIXTEPEC [ZOO] lang,
    Mexico
ZAPOTECO, AYOQUESCO [ZAF] lang, Mexico
ZAPOTECO, CAJONOS [ZAD] lang, Mexico; also
    in USA
ZAPOTECO, CHICHICAPAN [ZPV] lang, Mexico
ZAPOTECO, CHOAPAN [ZPC] lang, Mexico
ZAPOTECO, COATECAS ALTAS [ZAP] lang, Mexico

ZAPOTECO, COATLÁN [ZPS] lang, Mexico
ZAPOTECO, EL ALTO [ZPP] lang, Mexico
ZAPOTECO, ELOTEPEC [ZTE] lang, Mexico
ZAPOTECO, GÜILÁ [ZTU] lang, Mexico
ZAPOTECO, GUEVEA DE HUMBOLDT [ZPG] lang, Mexico
ZAPOTECO, ISTMO [ZAI] lang, Mexico
ZAPOTECO, IXTLÁN SURESTE [ZPD] lang, Mexico
ZAPOTECO, JUÁREZ, SIERRA [ZAA] lang, Mexico
ZAPOTECO, LACHIGUIRI [ZPA] lang, Mexico
ZAPOTECO, LACHIRIOAG [ZTC] lang, Mexico
ZAPOTECO, LOXICHA [ZTP] lang, Mexico
ZAPOTECO, MAZALTEPEC [ZPY] lang, Mexico
ZAPOTECO, MIAHUATLÁN CENTRAL [ZAM] lang, Mexico
ZAPOTECO, MITLA [ZAW] lang, Mexico
ZAPOTECO, MIXTEPEC [ZPM] lang, Mexico
ZAPOTECO, OCOTLÁN OESTE [ZAC] lang, Mexico
ZAPOTECO, OZOLOTEPEC [ZAO] lang, Mexico
ZAPOTECO, PETAPA [ZPE] lang, Mexico
ZAPOTECO, QUIAVICUZAS [ZPJ] lang, Mexico
ZAPOTECO, QUIOQUITANI Y QUIERÍ [ZTQ] lang, Mexico
ZAPOTECO, RINCÓN [ZAR] lang, Mexico
ZAPOTECO, RINCÓN SUR [ZSR] lang, Mexico
ZAPOTECO, SAN AGUSTÍN MIXTEPEC [ZTM] lang, Mexico
ZAPOTECO, SAN BALTÁZAR LOXICHA [ZPX] lang, Mexico
ZAPOTECO, SAN JUAN GUELAVÍA [ZAB] lang, Mexico; also in USA
ZAPOTECO, SAN PEDRO QUIATONI [ZPF] lang, Mexico
ZAPOTECO, SAN VICENTE COATLÁN [ZPT] lang, Mexico
ZAPOTECO, SANTA CATARINA ALBARRADAS [ZTN] lang, Mexico
ZAPOTECO, SANTA INÉS YATZECHI [ZPN] lang, Mexico
ZAPOTECO, SANTA MARÍA QUIEGOLANI [ZPI] lang, Mexico
ZAPOTECO, SANTIAGO LAPAGUÍA [ZTL] lang, Mexico
ZAPOTECO, SANTIAGO XANICA [ZPR] lang, Mexico
ZAPOTECO, SOLA DE VEGA ESTE [ZPL] lang, Mexico
ZAPOTECO, TABAA [ZAT] lang, Mexico
ZAPOTECO, TEJALAPAN [ZTT] lang, Mexico
ZAPOTECO, TEXMELUCAN [ZPZ] lang, Mexico
ZAPOTECO, TILQUIAPAN [ZTS] lang, Mexico
ZAPOTECO, TLACOLULITA [ZPK] lang, Mexico
ZAPOTECO, TOTOMACHAPAN [ZPH] lang, Mexico
ZAPOTECO, XADANI [ZAX] lang, Mexico
ZAPOTECO, XANAGUÍA [ZTG] lang, Mexico
ZAPOTECO, YALÁLAG [ZPU] lang, Mexico; also in USA
ZAPOTECO, YARENI [ZAE] lang, Mexico
ZAPOTECO, YATEE [ZTY] lang, Mexico
ZAPOTECO, YATZACHI [ZAV] lang, Mexico; also in USA

ZAPOTECO, YAUTEPEC [ZPB] lang, Mexico
ZAPOTECO, ZAACHILA [ZTX] lang, Mexico
ZAPOTECO, ZANIZA [ZPW] lang, Mexico
ZAPOTECO, ZOOGOCHO [ZPQ] lang, Mexico; also in USA
ZAPOTITLÁN TABLAS dial of TLAPANECO, ACATEPEC [TPX]
ZAQATALA dial of AVAR [AVR]
ZAQATALA dial of AZERBAIJANI, NORTH [AZE]
ZARA dial of BOBO MADARE, SOUTHERN [BWQ]
ZARABAON alt for BEU dial of WE SOUTHERN [GXX]
ZARAMO alt for ZALAMO [ZAJ]
ZARAMU alt for ZALAMO [ZAJ]
ZARANDA dial of GEJI [GEZ]
ZARBARMA alt for ZARMA [DJE]
ZARBARMA alt for ZARMACI [DJE]
ZARGARI dial of ROMANI, BALKAN [RMN]
ZARI [ZAZ] lang, Nigeria
ZARI dial of ZARI [ZAZ]
ZARIWA alt for ZARI [ZAZ]
ZARMA [DJE] lang, Niger; also in Benin, Burkina Faso, Mali, Nigeria
ZARMA alt for ZARMACI [DJE]
ZARMACI [DJE] lang, Niger; also in Benin, Burkina Faso, Mali, Nigeria
ZARMACI alt for ZARMA [DJE]
ZARPHATIC [ZRP] lang, France
ZASING dial of MUNDANG [MUA]
ZASKARI alt for ZANGSKARI [ZAU]
ZAUGE alt for ZAGHAWA [ZAG]
ZAUGE alt for ZANDE [ZAN]
ZAUZOU [ZAL] lang, China
ZAY [ZWA] lang, Ethiopia
ZAYEIN alt for KAREN, ZAYEIN [KXK]
ZAYOLI dial of KASHMIRI [KSH]
ZAYSE dial of ZAYSE-ZERGULLA [ZAY]
ZAYSE-ZERGULLA [ZAY] lang, Ethiopia
ZAYSSE alt for ZAYSE-ZERGULLA [ZAY]
ZAZA alt for KIRMANJKI [QKV]
ZAZAKI alt for DIMLI [ZZZ]
ZAZAKI alt for KIRMANJKI [QKV]
ZAZAO [JAJ] lang, Solomon Islands
ZAZING alt for ZASING dial of MUNDANG [MUA]
ZEAWS alt for ZEEUWS dial of VLAAMS [VLA]
ZEBAK dial of SANGLECHI-ISHKASHIMI [SGL]
ZEBAKI alt for ZEBAK dial of SANGLECHI-ISHKASHIMI [SGL]
ZEBIE dial of BETE, GAGNOA [BTG]
ZEDDO dial of AARI [AIZ]
ZEDONG alt for TIDONG [TID]
ZEEM [ZUA] lang, Nigeria
ZEEM dial of ZEEM [ZUA]
ZEEUWS dial of VLAAMS [VLA]
ZEGACHE ZAPOTECO alt for ZAPOTECO, SANTA INÉS YATZECHI [ZPN]
ZEGGAOUA alt for ZAGHAWA [ZAG]
ZEGGAOUA alt for ZANDE [ZAN]
ZEGHAWA alt for ZAGHAWA [ZAG]
ZEGHAWA alt for ZANDE [ZAN]
ZEGUHA alt for ZIGULA [ZIW]

ZEGURA alt for ZIGULA [ZIW]
ZELGWA alt for ZULGWA [ZUL]
ZELGWA dial of ZULGWA [ZUL]
ZELMAMU alt for ZILMAMU dial of KACIPO-BALESI [KOE]
ZEMACHIAI alt for SHAMAITISH dial of LITHUANIAN [LIT]
ZEMAITIS alt for SHAMAITISH dial of LITHUANIAN [LIT]
ZEMAITISKAI alt for SHAMAITISH dial of LITHUANIAN [LIT]
ZEMAY alt for FULFULDE, ADAMAWA [FUB]
ZEMBA [DHM] lang, Angola; also in Namibia
ZEMI alt for NAGA, ZEME [NZM]
ZEMIAKI dial of GRANGALI [NLI]
ZENAG [ZEG] lang, Papua New Guinea
ZENAGA [ZEN] lang, Mauritania
ZENANG alt for ZENAG [ZEG]
ZENAP alt for CHENAPIAN [CJN]
ZENATI alt for SIWI [SIZ]
ZERGULLA dial of ZAYSE-ZERGULLA [ZAY]
ZERGULLINYA alt for ZERGULLA dial of ZAYSE-ZERGULLA [ZAY]
ZERMA alt for ZARMA [DJE]
ZERO alt for JERUNG [JEE]
ZERO MALA alt for JERUNG [JEE]
ZERUM alt for JERUNG [JEE]
ZEYA-BUREYA dial of EVENKI [EVN]
ZEZAGI dial of MESE [MCI]
ZEZURU dial of SHONA [SHD]
ZHABA [ZHA] lang, China
ZHABA alt for QUEYU [QEY]
ZHANG-ZHUNG alt for JANGSHUNG [JNA]
ZHAR alt for BANKAL dial of JARAWA [JAR]
ZHEMAITISH alt for SHAMAITISH dial of LITHUANIAN [LIT]
ZHENAN MIN dial of CHINESE, MIN NAN [CFR]
ZHGABE alt for ALBANIAN, TOSK [ALN]
ZHIMOMI dial of NAGA, SUMI [NSM]
ZHIRE [ZHI] lang, Nigeria
ZHIRU alt for JIRU [JRR]
ZHITAKO. GANAGANA alt for DIBO [DIO]
ZHONGJIA alt for BOUYEI [PCC]
ZHONGZHAI alt for GUANYINQIAO [JIQ]
ZHONJIGALI alt for WAIGALI [WBK]
ZHUANG, NORTHERN [CCX] lang, China
ZHUANG, SOUTHERN [CCY] lang, China
ZHU'OASE alt for DZU'OASI dial of JUHOAN [KTZ]
ZHU'OASI alt for JU/'HOAN [KTZ]
ZI alt for MARU [MHX]
ZIA [ZIA] lang, Papua New Guinea
ZIA dial of KERES, EASTERN [KEE]
ZIA dial of ZIA [ZIA]
ZIBA alt for HAYA [HAY]
ZIBA dial of SHI [SHR]
ZIBIAO dial of WE SOUTHERN [GXX]
ZIBIRKHALIN dial of BOTLIKH [BPH]
ZIBITO alt for HIBITO [HIB]
ZIDIM dial of MOFU-GUDUR [MIF]
ZIEMA dial of LOMA [LOM]
ZIGENARE alt for ROMANI, VLAX [RMY]

ZIGOUA alt for ZIGULA [ZIW]
ZIGUA alt for ZIGULA [ZIW]
ZIGUENER alt for ROMANI, SINTE [RMO]
ZIGULA [ZIW] lang, Tanzania
ZIGWA alt for ZIGULA [ZIW]
ZIHUATEUTLA TOTONACA dial of TOTONACA, XICOTEPEC DE JUÁREZ [TOO]
ZIKI alt for DIDA, LAKOTA [DIC]
ZILACAYOTITLÁN dial of TLAPANECO, MALINALTEPEC [TLL]
ZILIVA alt for ZIZILIVAKAN [ZIZ]
ZILMAMU dial of KACIPO-BALESI [KOE]
ZILO dial of ANDI [ANI]
ZIM dial of GIDRA [GDR]
ZIMAKANI [ZIK] lang, Papua New Guinea
ZIMAKANI dial of ZIMAKANI [ZIK]
ZIMBA [ZMB] lang, DRC
ZIMBABWE COMMUNITY SIGN dial of ZIMBABWE SIGN LANGUAGE [ZIB]
ZIMBABWE SCHOOL SIGN dial of ZIMBABWE SIGN LANGUAGE [ZIB]
ZIMBABWE SIGN LANGUAGE [ZIB] lang, Zimbabwe
ZIMBRISCH alt for CIMBRIAN [CIM]
ZIME alt for HERDÉ [HED]
ZIME alt for MESME [ZIM]
ZIME alt for NGETE [NNN]
ZIME alt for PÉVÉ [LME]
ZIMIRRA alt for SINYAR [SYS]
ZIMSHIAN alt for TSIMSHIAN [TSI]
ZIMSIGN alt for ZIMBABWE SIGN LANGUAGE [ZIB]
ZIMU alt for KOONZIME [NJE]
ZINA alt for JINA [JIA]
ZINACANTECO TZOTZIL alt for TZOTZIL, ZINACANTÁN [TZZ]
ZINE alt for JINA dial of JINA [JIA]
ZINJA alt for ZINZA [JIN]
"ZINJERO" pejorative alt for YEMSA [JNJ]
ZINNA dial of MUMUYE [MUL]
ZINZA [JIN] lang, Tanzania
ZIOGBA dial of WANDALA [MFI]
ZIRA alt for ZIRE [SIH]
ZIRAHA alt for KUTU [KDC]
ZIRAK-BOLI dial of KASHMIRI [KSH]
ZIRAL alt for JIREL [JUL]
ZIRAN SHOUYU alt for TAIWANESE SIGN LANGUAGE [TSS]
ZIRE [SIH] lang, New Caledonia
ZIRI alt for MOMI dial of MOM JANGO [VER]
ZIRIYA [ZIR] lang, Nigeria
ZITAKO alt for DIBO [DIO]
ZITHUNG dial of RAWANG [RAW]
ZIWE dial of ONO [ONS]
ZIYA alt for ZIA [ZIA]
ZIZILIVAKAN [ZIZ] lang, Cameroon; also in Nigeria
ZIZILIVEKEN alt for ZIZILIVAKAN [ZIZ]
ZLENGE dial of PSIKYE [KVJ]
ZO alt for MAK [PBL]
ZO alt for ZOME [ZOM]
ZO dial of MAK [PBL]
ZOBA alt for ZYOBA [ZYO]

ZODI alt for DOT dial of DASS [DOT]
ZO'É alt for POTURU [PTO]
ZOFARI alt for ARABIC, DHOFARI SPOKEN [ADF]
ZÕGBÊ alt for BOKOBARU [BUS]
ZOHRI dial of AIMAQ [AIQ]
ZOKHUA dial of CHIN, HAKA [CNH]
ZOLI alt for ZOME [ZOM]
ZOLI dial of NZAKAMBAY [NZY]
ZOME [ZOM] lang, Myanmar; also in India
ZOMI alt for ZOME [ZOM]
ZOMO alt for ZUMO dial of JIMI [JIM]
ZOMO alt for ZUMU dial of BATA [BTA]
ZONÊ MA alt for KIRMANJKI [QKV]
ZONGBEN alt for BOKOBARU [BUS]
ZONGBI dial of PEERE [KUT]
ZONGKE dial of SHANGZHAI [JIH]
ZONGKHAR alt for DZONGKHA [DZO]
ZOOGOCHO dial of ZAPOTECO, ZOOGOCHO
    [ZPQ]
ZOOGOCHO ZAPOTEC alt for ZAPOTECO,
    ZOOGOCHO [ZPQ]
ZOONO alt for KOLBILA [KLC]
ZOPHEI alt for ZYPHE [ZYP]
ZOQUE, CHIMALAPA [ZOH] lang, Mexico
ZOQUE, COPAINALÁ [ZOC] lang, Mexico
ZOQUE, FRANCISCO LEÓN [ZOS] lang, Mexico
ZOQUE, RAYÓN [ZOR] lang, Mexico
ZOQUE, TABASCO [ZOQ] lang, Mexico
ZORHAUA alt for ZAGHAWA [ZAG]
ZORHAUA alt for ZANDE [ZAN]
ZORNI alt for ZOME [ZOM]
ZORO alt for GBO dial of SENOUFO, TAGWANA
    [TGW]
ZORÓ dial of GAVIAO DO JIPARANA [GVO]
ZOROTUA dial of KWADI [KWZ]
ZOTUNG alt for CHIN, ZOTUNG [CZT]
ZOU alt for ZOME [ZOM]
ZOUARA alt for ZUARA dial of NAFUSI [JBN]
ZOULBOU alt for JILBE [JIE]
ZOULGO alt for ZULGWA [ZUL]
ZOYALTITLA dial of MAZATECO, MAZATLAN [VMZ]
ZUARA dial of NAFUSI [JBN]
ZUBAIR-FAAU ARABIC dial of ARABIC, GULF
    SPOKEN [AFB]
ZUBAKI dial of POKOMO, UPPER [PKB]
ZUBEROERA alt for BASQUE, SOULETIN [BSZ]
ZUHOZUHO alt for TOKANO [ZUH]
ZUHUZUHO alt for TOKANO [ZUH]
ZUHUZUHO dial of TOKANO [ZUH]

ZUID-DRENTS alt for SOUTH DRENTE dial of
    DRENTS [DRT]
ZUKSUN dial of KAG-FER-JIIR-KOOR-ROR-US-
    ZUKSUN [GEL]
ZUL dial of POLCI [POL]
ZULGO alt for MINEW dial of ZULGWA [ZUL]
ZULGO alt for ZULGWA [ZUL]
ZULGWA [ZUL] lang, Cameroon
ZULGWA alt for MINEW dial of ZULGWA [ZUL]
ZULMAMU alt for ZILMAMU dial of KACIPO-BALESI
    [KOE]
ZULU [ZUU] lang, South Africa; also in Botswana,
    Lesotho, Malawi, Mozambique, Swaziland
ZUMAYA [ZUY] lang, Cameroon
ZUMBUL dial of DASS [DOT]
ZUMBUN [JMB] lang, Nigeria
ZUMO dial of JIMI [JIM]
ZUMO dial of JIMI [JMI]
ZUMOMI dial of NAGA, SUMI [NSM]
ZUMPER alt for KUTEP [KUB]
ZUMU alt for ZUMO dial of JIMI [JIM]
ZUMU dial of BATA [BTA]
ZUNDA alt for ZULU [ZUU]
ZUNI [ZUN] lang, USA
ZUÑI alt for ZUNI [ZUN]
ZUOJIANG dial of ZHUANG, SOUTHERN [CCY]
ZURA dial of GULA [KCM]
ZURAA alt for ZUARA dial of NAFUSI [JBN]
ZURI alt for ZOHRI dial of AIMAQ [AIQ]
ZURICH dial of ALEMANNISCH [GSW]
ZURRIEQ dial of MALTESE [MLS]
ZURU alt for LILA dial of CLELA [DRI]
ZURUAHÁ alt for SURUAHÁ [SWX]
ZURUBU alt for SURUBU [SDE]
ZUSSUN alt for ZUKSUN dial of KAG-FER-JIIR-
    KOOR-ROR-US-ZUKSUN [GEL]
ZUTIUA dial of GUAJAJARA [GUB]
ZUWADZA dial of OMIE [AOM]
ZUWARAH alt for ZUARA dial of NAFUSI [JBN]
ZWALL dial of SHALL-ZWALL [SHA]
ZWANGAL alt for ZANGWAL [ZAH]
ZWARA alt for ZUARA dial of NAFUSI [JBN]
ZWAY alt for ZAY [ZWA]
ZWN alt for BENDI dial of HLAI [LIC]
ZWN'JAN alt for DUNGAN [DNG]
ZYOBA [ZYO] lang, Tanzania; also in DRC
ZYPHE [ZYP] lang, Myanmar; also in India
ZYUDIN dial of KOMI-PERMYAK [KOI]

Language Family Index

Editor

Barbara F. Grimes

Consulting Editor

Joseph E. Grimes

Afro-Asiatic (372)
- Berber (26)
- - Eastern (3)
- - - Awjila-Sokna (2): AWJILAH [AUJ] Libya
- - - - SAWKNAH [SWN] Libya
- - - Siwa (1): SIWI [SIZ] Egypt
- - Guanche (1): GUANCHE [GNC] Spain
- - Northern (17): CHENOUA [CHB] Algeria
- - - Atlas (3): JUDEO-BERBER [JBE] Israel
- - - - TACHELHIT [SHI] Morocco
- - - - TAMAZIGHT, CENTRAL ATLAS [TZM] Morocco
- - - Kabyle (1): KABYLE [KYL] Algeria
- - - Zenati (12)
- - - - East (3): GHADAMÈS [GHA] Libya
- - - - - NAFUSI [JBN] Libya
- - - - - SENED [SDS] Tunisia
- - - - Ghomara (1): GHOMARA [GHO] Morocco
- - - - Mzab-Wargla (4): TAGARGRENT [OUA] Algeria
- - - - - TAZNATIT [GRR] Algeria
- - - - - TEMACINE TAMAZIGHT [TJO] Algeria
- - - - - TUMZABT [MZB] Algeria
- - - - Riff (2): SENHAJA DE SRAIR [SJS] Morocco
- - - - - TARIFIT [RIF] Morocco
- - - - Shawiya (1): CHAOUIA [SHY] Algeria
- - - - Tidikelt (1): TIDIKELT TAMAZIGHT [TIA] Algeria
- - Tamasheq (4)
- - - Northern (1): TAMAHAQ, TAHAGGART [THV] Algeria
- - - Southern (3): TAMAJAQ, TAWALLAMMAT [TTQ] Niger
- - - - TAMAJEQ, TAYART [THZ] Niger
- - - - TAMASHEQ [TAQ] Mali
- - Zenaga (1): ZENAGA [ZEN] Mauritania
- Chadic (195)
- - Biu-Mandara (79)
- - - A (65)
- - - - A.1 (5)
- - - - - Eastern (3): BOGA [BOD] Nigeria
- - - - - - GA'ANDA [GAA] Nigeria
- - - - - - HWANA [HWO] Nigeria
- - - - - Western (2): JARA [JAF] Nigeria
- - - - - - TERA [TER] Nigeria
- - - - A.2 (8): NGGWAHYI [NGX] Nigeria
- - - - - 1 (4): BURA-PABIR [BUR] Nigeria
- - - - - - CIBAK [CKL] Nigeria
- - - - - - KOFA [KSO] Nigeria
- - - - - - PUTAI [MFL] Nigeria
- - - - - 2 (3): HUBA [KIR] Nigeria
- - - - - - MARGHI CENTRAL [MAR] Nigeria
- - - - - - MARGHI SOUTH [MFM] Nigeria
- - - - A.3 (4): BANA [BCW] Cameroon
- - - - - HYA [HYA] Cameroon
- - - - - KAMWE [HIG] Nigeria
- - - - - PSIKYE [KVJ] Cameroon
- - - - A.4 (10)
- - - - - Lamang (3): LAMANG [HIA] Nigeria
- - - - - - VEMGO-MABAS [VEM] Nigeria
- - - - - - XEDI [TUR] Nigeria
- - - - - Mandara Proper (7)
- - - - - - Glavda (5): CINENI [CIE] Nigeria
- - - - - - - DGHWEDE [DGH] Nigeria
- - - - - - - GLAVDA [GLV] Nigeria
- - - - - - - GUDUF-GAVA [GDF] Nigeria

Afro-Asiatic (372)
- Chadic (195)
- - Biu-Mandara (79)
- - - A (65)
- - - - A.4 (10)
- - - - - Mandara Proper (7)
- - - - - - Glavda (5): GVOKO [NGS] Nigeria
- - - - - - Mandara (1): WANDALA [MFI] Cameroon
- - - - - - Podoko (1): PARKWA [PBI] Cameroon
- - - - A.5 (20): BALDAMU [BDN] Cameroon
- - - - - CUVOK [CUV] Cameroon
- - - - - DUGWOR [DME] Cameroon
- - - - - GADUWA [GDW] Cameroon
- - - - - GEMZEK [GND] Cameroon
- - - - - GIZIGA, NORTH [GIS] Cameroon
- - - - - GIZIGA, SOUTH [GIZ] Cameroon
- - - - - MADA [MXU] Cameroon
- - - - - MAFA [MAF] Cameroon
- - - - - MATAL [MFH] Cameroon
- - - - - MBUKO [MQB] Cameroon
- - - - - MEFELE [MFJ] Cameroon
- - - - - MELOKWO [MLW] Cameroon
- - - - - MEREY [MEQ] Cameroon
- - - - - MOFU, NORTH [MFK] Cameroon
- - - - - MOFU-GUDUR [MIF] Cameroon
- - - - - MUYANG [MUY] Cameroon
- - - - - PELASLA [MLR] Cameroon
- - - - - WUZLAM [UDL] Cameroon
- - - - - ZULGWA [ZUL] Cameroon
- - - - A.6 (1): SUKUR [SUK] Nigeria
- - - - A.7 (5): BUWAL [BHS] Cameroon
- - - - - DABA [DAB] Cameroon
- - - - - GAVAR [GOU] Cameroon
- - - - - MBEDAM [XMD] Cameroon
- - - - - MINA [HNA] Cameroon
- - - - A.8 (12): BACAMA [BAM] Nigeria
- - - - - BATA [BTA] Nigeria
- - - - - FALI [FLI] Nigeria
- - - - - GUDE [GDE] Nigeria
- - - - - GUDU [GDU] Nigeria
- - - - - HOLMA [HOD] Nigeria
- - - - - JIMI [JIM] Cameroon
- - - - - NGWABA [NGW] Nigeria
- - - - - NZANYI [NJA] Nigeria
- - - - - SHARWA [SWQ] Cameroon
- - - - - TSUVAN [TSH] Cameroon
- - - - - ZIZILIVAKAN [ZIZ] Cameroon
- - - B (13)
- - - - B.1 (10): JILBE [JIE] Nigeria
- - - - - Buduma (1): BUDUMA [BDM] Chad
- - - - - Jina (2): JINA [JIA] Cameroon
- - - - - - MAJERA [XMJ] Cameroon
- - - - - Kotoko Proper (6): AFADE [AAL] Nigeria
- - - - - - LAGWAN [KOT] Cameroon
- - - - - - MALGBE [MXF] Cameroon
- - - - - - MASLAM [MSV] Cameroon
- - - - - - MPADE [MPI] Cameroon
- - - - - - MSER [KQX] Cameroon
- - - - B.2 (3): MBARA [MPK] Chad
- - - - - MUSGU [MUG] Cameroon
- - - - - MUSKUM [MJE] Chad

Afro-Asiatic (372)
- Chadic (195)
- - Biu-Mandara (79)
- - - C (1): GIDAR [GID] Cameroon
- - East (34)
- - - A (17)
- - - - A.1 (9): BUSO [BSO] Chad
- - - - - 1 (4): MIRE [MVH] Chad
- - - - - - NDAM [NDM] Chad
- - - - - - SOMRAI [SOR] Chad
- - - - - - TUMAK [TMC] Chad
- - - - - 2 (4): BOOR [BVF] Chad
- - - - - - GADANG [GDK] Chad
- - - - - - MILTU [MLJ] Chad
- - - - - - SARUA [SWY] Chad
- - - - A.2 (6)
- - - - - 1 (3): KIMRÉ [KQP] Chad
- - - - - - LELE [LLN] Chad
- - - - - - NANCERE [NNC] Chad
- - - - - 2 (3): GABRI [GAB] Chad
- - - - - - KABALAI [KVF] Chad
- - - - - - TOBANGA [TNG] Chad
- - - - A.3 (2): KERA [KER] Chad
- - - - - KWANG [KVI] Chad
- - - B (17)
- - - - B.1 (12)
- - - - - 1 (7): BIDIYO [BID] Chad
- - - - - - DANGALÉAT [DAA] Chad
- - - - - - JONKOR BOURMATAGUIL [JEU] Chad
- - - - - - MAWA [MCW] Chad
- - - - - - MIGAAMA [MMY] Chad
- - - - - - MOGUM [MOU] Chad
- - - - - - UBI [UBI] Chad
- - - - - 2 (5): BIRGIT [BTF] Chad
- - - - - - KAJAKSE [CKQ] Chad
- - - - - - MASMAJE [MES] Chad
- - - - - - MUBI [MUB] Chad
- - - - - - TORAM [TRJ] Chad
- - - - B.2 (1): MUKULU [MOZ] Chad
- - - - B.3 (4): BAREIN [BVA] Chad
- - - - - SABA [SAA] Chad
- - - - - SOKORO [SOK] Chad
- - - - - TAMKI [TAX] Chad
- - Masa (9): HERDÉ [HED] Chad
- - - MARBA [MPG] Chad
- - - MASANA [MCN] Chad
- - - MESME [ZIM] Chad
- - - MONOGOY [MCU] Chad
- - - MUSEY [MSE] Chad
- - - NGETE [NNN] Chad
- - - PÉVÉ [LME] Chad
- - - ZUMAYA [ZUY] Cameroon
- - West (73): LURI [LDD] Nigeria
- - - A (43): DAZA [DZD] Nigeria
- - - - A.1 (2): GWANDARA [GWN] Nigeria
- - - - HAUSA [HUA] Nigeria
- - - - A.2 (21)
- - - - - Bole (14): BURE [BVH] Nigeria
- - - - - - Bole Proper (12): BEELE [BXQ] Nigeria
- - - - - - - BOLE [BOL] Nigeria
- - - - - - - DENO [DBB] Nigeria

Afro-Asiatic (372)
- Chadic (195)
- - West (73)
- - - A (43)
- - - - A.2 (21)
- - - - - Bole (14)
- - - - - - Bole Proper (12): GALAMBU [GLO] Nigeria
- - - - - - GERA [GEW] Nigeria
- - - - - - GERUMA [GEA] Nigeria
- - - - - - GIIWO [KKS] Nigeria
- - - - - - KHOLOK [KTC] Nigeria
- - - - - - KUBI [KOF] Nigeria
- - - - - - MAAKA [MEW] Nigeria
- - - - - - NGAMO [NBH] Nigeria
- - - - - - NYAM [NMI] Nigeria
- - - - - - Karekare (1): KAREKARE [KAI] Nigeria
- - - - - Tangale (7)
- - - - - - Dera (1): DERA [KNA] Nigeria
- - - - - - Tangale Proper (6): KUSHI [KUH] Nigeria
- - - - - - - KUTTO [KPA] Nigeria
- - - - - - - KWAAMI [KSQ] Nigeria
- - - - - - - PERO [PIP] Nigeria
- - - - - - - PIYA-KWONCI [PIY] Nigeria
- - - - - - - TANGALE [TAN] Nigeria
- - - - A.3 (12)
- - - - - Angas Proper (11)
- - - - - - 1 (6): CAKFEM-MUSHERE [CKY] Nigeria
- - - - - - - JORTO [JRT] Nigeria
- - - - - - - KOFYAR [KWL] Nigeria
- - - - - - - MISHIP [CHP] Nigeria
- - - - - - - MWAGHAVUL [SUR] Nigeria
- - - - - - - NGAS [ANC] Nigeria
- - - - - - 2 (5): GOEMAI [ANK] Nigeria
- - - - - - - KOENOEM [KCS] Nigeria
- - - - - - - MONTOL [MTL] Nigeria
- - - - - - - PYAPUN [PCW] Nigeria
- - - - - - - TAL [TAL] Nigeria
- - - - - Yiwom (1): YIWOM [GEK] Nigeria
- - - - A.4 (7)
- - - - - Fyer (2): FYER [FIE] Nigeria
- - - - - - TAMBAS [TDK] Nigeria
- - - - - Ron Proper (5): DUHWA [KBZ] Nigeria
- - - - - - KULERE [KUL] Nigeria
- - - - - - MUNDAT [MMF] Nigeria
- - - - - - RON [CLA] Nigeria
- - - - - - SHA [SCW] Nigeria
- - - B (29)
- - - - B.1 (5): AUYOKAWA [AUO] Nigeria
- - - - - Bade Proper (3): BADE [BDE] Nigeria
- - - - - - NGIZIM [NGI] Nigeria
- - - - - - TESHENAWA [TWC] Nigeria
- - - - - Duwai (1): DUWAI [DBP] Nigeria
- - - - B.2 (10): AJAWA [AJW] Nigeria
- - - - - CIWOGAI [TGD] Nigeria
- - - - - DIRI [DWA] Nigeria
- - - - - KARIYA [KIL] Nigeria
- - - - - MBURKU [BBT] Nigeria
- - - - - MIYA [MKF] Nigeria
- - - - - PA'A [AFA] Nigeria
- - - - - SIRI [SIR] Nigeria
- - - - - WARJI [WJI] Nigeria

Afro-Asiatic (372)
- Chadic (195)
- - West (73)
- - - B (29)
- - - - B.2 (10): ZUMBUN [JMB] Nigeria
- - - - B.3 (14): DASS [DOT] Nigeria
- - - - - Boghom (3): BOGHOM [BUX] Nigeria
- - - - - - KIR-BALAR [KKR] Nigeria
- - - - - - MANGAS [MAH] Nigeria
- - - - - Eastern (1): JIMI [JMI] Nigeria
- - - - - Guruntum (4): GURUNTUM-MBAARU [GRD] Nigeria
- - - - - - JU [JUU] Nigeria
- - - - - - TALA [TAK] Nigeria
- - - - - - ZANGWAL [ZAH] Nigeria
- - - - - Zaar Proper (5): GEJI [GEZ] Nigeria
- - - - - - POLCI [POL] Nigeria
- - - - - - SAYA [SAY] Nigeria
- - - - - - ZARI [ZAZ] Nigeria
- - - - - - ZEEM [ZUA] Nigeria
- Cushitic (47)
- - Central (5)
- - - Eastern (1): XAMTANGA [XAN] Ethiopia
- - - Northern (1): BILEN [BYN] Eritrea
- - - Southern (2): AWNGI [AWN] Ethiopia
- - - - KUNFAL [XUF] Ethiopia
- - - Western (1): AGAW, WESTERN [QIM] Ethiopia
- - East (34): BOON [BNL] Somalia
- - - Dullay (3): BUSSA [DOX] Ethiopia
- - - - GAWWADA [GWD] Ethiopia
- - - - TSAMAI [TSB] Ethiopia
- - - Highland (7): ALABA [ALB] Ethiopia
- - - - BURJI [BJI] Ethiopia
- - - - GEDEO [DRS] Ethiopia
- - - - HADIYYA [HDY] Ethiopia
- - - - KAMBAATA [KTB] Ethiopia
- - - - LIBIDO [LIQ] Ethiopia
- - - - SIDAMO [SID] Ethiopia
- - - Konso-Gidole (2): DIRASHA [GDL] Ethiopia
- - - - KOMSO [KXC] Ethiopia
- - - Oromo (6): GARREH-AJURAN [GGH] Kenya
- - - - ORMA [ORC] Kenya
- - - - OROMO, BORANA-ARSI-GUJI [GAX] Ethiopia
- - - - OROMO, EASTERN [HAE] Ethiopia
- - - - OROMO, WEST-CENTRAL [GAZ] Ethiopia
- - - - SANYE [SSN] Kenya
- - - Rendille-Boni (2): BONI [BOB] Kenya
- - - - RENDILLE [REL] Kenya
- - - Saho-Afar (2): AFAR [AFR] Ethiopia
- - - - SAHO [SSY] Eritrea
- - - Somali (6): DABARRE [DBR] Somalia
- - - - GARRE [GEX] Somalia
- - - - JIIDDU [JII] Somalia
- - - - MAAY [QMA] Somalia
- - - - SOMALI [SOM] Somalia
- - - - TUNNI [TQQ] Somalia
- - - Western Omo-Tana (4): ARBORE [ARV] Ethiopia
- - - - BAISO [BSW] Ethiopia
- - - - DAASANACH [DSH] Ethiopia
- - - - EL MOLO [ELO] Kenya
- - - Yaaku (1): YAAKU [MUU] Kenya
- - North (1): BEDAWI [BEI] Sudan

Afro-Asiatic (372)
- Cushitic (47)
- - South (7): AASÁX [AAS] Tanzania
- - - BURUNGE [BDS] Tanzania
- - - DAHALO [DAL] Kenya
- - - GOROWA [GOW] Tanzania
- - - IRAQW [IRK] Tanzania
- - - KW'ADZA [WKA] Tanzania
- - - WASI [WBJ] Tanzania
- Egyptian (1): COPTIC [COP] Egypt
- Omotic (28)
- - North (24)
- - - Dizoid (3): DIZI [MDX] Ethiopia
- - - - NAYI [NOZ] Ethiopia
- - - - SHEKO [SHE] Ethiopia
- - - Gonga-Gimojan (17)
- - - - Gimojan (13)
- - - - - Janjero (1): YEMSA [JNJ] Ethiopia
- - - - - Ometo-Gimira (12)
- - - - - - Chara (1): CHARA [CRA] Ethiopia
- - - - - - Gimira (1): BENCH [BCQ] Ethiopia
- - - - - - Ometo (10): MALE [MDY] Ethiopia
- - - - - - - Central (5): DORZE [DOZ] Ethiopia
- - - - - - - - GAMO-GOFA-DAWRO [GMO] Ethiopia
- - - - - - - - MELO [MFX] Ethiopia
- - - - - - - - OYDA [OYD] Ethiopia
- - - - - - - - WOLAYTTA [WBC] Ethiopia
- - - - - - - East (3): KACHAMA-GANJULE [KCX] Ethiopia
- - - - - - - KOORETE [KQY] Ethiopia
- - - - - - - ZAYSE-ZERGULLA [ZAY] Ethiopia
- - - - - - - West (1): BASKETTO [BST] Ethiopia
- - - - Gonga (4)
- - - - - Central (1): ANFILLO [MYO] Ethiopia
- - - - - North (1): BORO [BWO] Ethiopia
- - - - - South (2): KAFICHO [KBR] Ethiopia
- - - - - - SHAKACHO [MOY] Ethiopia
- - - Mao (4)
- - - - East (1): BAMBASSI [MYF] Ethiopia
- - - - West (3): GANZA [GZA] Ethiopia
- - - - - HOZO [HOZ] Ethiopia
- - - - - SEZE [SZE] Ethiopia
- - South (4): AARI [AIZ] Ethiopia
- - - DIME [DIM] Ethiopia
- - - HAMER-BANNA [AMF] Ethiopia
- - - KARO [KXH] Ethiopia
- Semitic (74)
- - Central (57)
- - - Aramaic (19)
- - - - Eastern (17): SYRIAC [SYC] Turkey (Asia)
- - - - - Central (14)
- - - - - - Northeastern (12): ASSYRIAN NEO-ARAMAIC [AII] Iraq
- - - - - - BABYLONIAN TALMUDIC ARAMAIC [BYA] Israel
- - - - - - BIJIL NEO-ARAMAIC [BJF] Israel
- - - - - - BOHTAN NEO-ARAMAIC [BHN] Georgia
- - - - - - CHALDEAN NEO-ARAMAIC [CLD] Iraq
- - - - - - HÉRTEVIN [HRT] Turkey (Asia)
- - - - - - HULAULÁ [HUY] Israel
- - - - - - KOI SANJAQ SURAT [KQD] Iraq
- - - - - - LISHÁN DIDÁN [TRG] Israel
- - - - - - LISHANA DENI [LSD] Israel
- - - - - - LISHANID NOSHAN [AIJ] Israel

Afro-Asiatic (372)
- Semitic (74)
- - Central (57)
- - - Aramaic (19)
- - - - Eastern (17)
- - - - - Central (14)
- - - - - - Northeastern (12): SENAYA [SYN] Iran
- - - - - - Northwestern (2): MLAHSÖ [QMQ] Syria
- - - - - - - TUROYO [SYR] Turkey (Asia)
- - - - - Mandaic (2): MANDAIC [MID] Iran
- - - - - - MANDAIC, CLASSICAL [MYZ] Iran
- - - - Western (2): SAMARITAN ARAMAIC [SRA] Palestinian West Bank and Gaza
- - - - - WESTERN NEO-ARAMAIC [AMW] Syria
- - - South (38)
- - - - Arabic (35): ARABIC, ALGERIAN SAHARAN SPOKEN [AAO] Algeria
- - - - - ARABIC, ALGERIAN SPOKEN [ARQ] Algeria
- - - - - ARABIC, BAHARNA SPOKEN [AFH] Bahrain
- - - - - ARABIC, CHADIAN SPOKEN [SHU] Chad
- - - - - ARABIC, CYPRIOT SPOKEN [ACY] Cyprus
- - - - - ARABIC, DHOFARI SPOKEN [ADF] Oman
- - - - - ARABIC, EASTERN EGYPTIAN BEDAWI SPOKEN [AVL] Egypt
- - - - - ARABIC, EGYPTIAN SPOKEN [ARZ] Egypt
- - - - - ARABIC, GULF SPOKEN [AFB] Iraq
- - - - - ARABIC, HADRAMI SPOKEN [AYH] Yemen
- - - - - ARABIC, HIJAZI SPOKEN [ACW] Saudi Arabia
- - - - - ARABIC, JUDEO-IRAQI [YHD] Israel
- - - - - ARABIC, JUDEO-MOROCCAN [AJU] Israel
- - - - - ARABIC, JUDEO-TRIPOLITANIAN [YUD] Israel
- - - - - ARABIC, JUDEO-TUNISIAN [AJT] Israel
- - - - - ARABIC, JUDEO-YEMENI [JYE] Israel
- - - - - ARABIC, LIBYAN SPOKEN [AYL] Libya
- - - - - ARABIC, MESOPOTAMIAN SPOKEN [ACM] Iraq
- - - - - ARABIC, MOROCCAN SPOKEN [ARY] Morocco
- - - - - ARABIC, NAJDI SPOKEN [ARS] Saudi Arabia
- - - - - ARABIC, NORTH LEVANTINE SPOKEN [APC] Syria
- - - - - ARABIC, NORTH MESOPOTAMIAN SPOKEN [AYP] Iraq
- - - - - ARABIC, OMANI SPOKEN [ACX] Oman
- - - - - ARABIC, SA<IDI SPOKEN [AEC] Egypt
- - - - - ARABIC, SANAANI SPOKEN [AYN] Yemen
- - - - - ARABIC, SHIHHI SPOKEN [SSH] United Arab Emirates
- - - - - ARABIC, SOUTH LEVANTINE SPOKEN [AJP] Jordan
- - - - - ARABIC, STANDARD [ABV] Saudi Arabia
- - - - - ARABIC, SUDANESE SPOKEN [APD] Sudan
- - - - - ARABIC, TA'IZZI-ADENI SPOKEN [ACQ] Yemen
- - - - - ARABIC, TAJIKI SPOKEN [ABH] Tajikistan
- - - - - ARABIC, TUNISIAN SPOKEN [AEB] Tunisia
- - - - - ARABIC, UZBEKI SPOKEN [AUZ] Uzbekistan
- - - - - HASSANIYYA [MEY] Mauritania
- - - - - MALTESE [MLS] Malta
- - - - Canaanite (3): HEBREW [HBR] Israel
- - - - - HEBREW, ANCIENT [HBO] Israel
- - - - - SAMARITAN [SMP] Palestinian West Bank and Gaza
- - South (17)
- - - Ethiopian (12)
- - - - North (3): GEEZ [GEE] Ethiopia
- - - - - TIGRÉ [TIE] Eritrea
- - - - - TIGRIGNA [TGN] Ethiopia
- - - - South (9)
- - - - - Outer (4)
- - - - - - n-Group (2): GAFAT [GFT] Ethiopia
- - - - - - - GURAGE, SODDO [GRU] Ethiopia

Afro-Asiatic (372)
- Semitic (74)
- - South (17)
- - - Ethiopian (12)
- - - - South (9)
- - - - - Outer (4)
- - - - - - tt-Group (2): GURAGE, WEST [GUY] Ethiopia
- - - - - - - MESMES [MYS] Ethiopia
- - - - - Transversal (5)
- - - - - - Amharic-Argobba (2): AMHARIC [AMH] Ethiopia
- - - - - - - ARGOBBA [AGJ] Ethiopia
- - - - - - Harari-East Gurage (3): GURAGE, EAST [GRE] Ethiopia
- - - - - - - HARARI [HAR] Ethiopia
- - - - - - - ZAY [ZWA] Ethiopia
- - - South Arabian (5): HARSUSI [HSS] Oman
- - - - HOBYÓT [HOH] Oman
- - - - JIBBALI [SHV] Oman
- - - - MEHRI [MHR] Yemen
- - - - SOQOTRI [SQT] Yemen
- Unclassified (1): BIRALE [BXE] Ethiopia

Alacalufan (2): KAKAUHUA [KBF] Chile
- QAWASQAR [ALC] Chile

Algic (40)
- Algonquian (38)
- - Central (23): KICKAPOO [KIC] USA
- - - MENOMINI [MEZ] USA
- - - MESQUAKIE [SAC] USA
- - - MIAMI [MIA] USA
- - - POTAWATOMI [POT] USA
- - - SHAWNEE [SJW] USA
- - - Cree-Montagnais-Naskapi (9): ATIKAMEKW [TET] Canada
- - - - CREE, MOOSE [CRM] Canada
- - - - CREE, NORTHERN EAST [CRL] Canada
- - - - CREE, PLAINS [CRP] Canada
- - - - CREE, SOUTHERN EAST [CRE] Canada
- - - - CREE, SWAMPY [CSW] Canada
- - - - CREE, WOODS [CWD] Canada
- - - - MONTAGNAIS [MOE] Canada
- - - - NASKAPI [NSK] Canada
- - - Ojibwa (8): ALGONQUIN [ALG] Canada
- - - - CHIPPEWA [CIW] USA
- - - - OJIBWA, CENTRAL [OJC] Canada
- - - - OJIBWA, EASTERN [OJG] Canada
- - - - OJIBWA, NORTHWESTERN [OJB] Canada
- - - - OJIBWA, SEVERN [OJS] Canada
- - - - OJIBWA, WESTERN [OJI] Canada
- - - - OTTAWA [OTW] Canada
- - Eastern (10): ABNAKI, EASTERN [AAQ] USA
- - - ABNAKI, WESTERN [ABE] Canada
- - - MALECITE-PASSAMAQUODDY [MAC] Canada
- - - MICMAC [MIC] Canada
- - - MOHEGAN-MONTAUK-NARRAGANSETT [MOF] USA
- - - MUNSEE [UMU] Canada
- - - NANTICOKE [NNT] USA
- - - POWHATAN [PIM] USA
- - - UNAMI [DEL] USA
- - - WAMPANOAG [WAM] USA
- - Plains (4): BLACKFOOT [BLC] Canada
- - - CHEYENNE [CHY] USA

Algic (40)
- Algonquian (38)
- - Plains (4)
- - - Arapaho (2): ARAPAHO [ARP] USA
- - - - GROS VENTRE [ATS] USA
- - Unclassified (1): LUMBEE [LUA] USA
- Wiyot (1): WIYOT [WIY] USA
- Yurok (1): YUROK [YUR] USA

Altaic (65)
- Mongolian (13)
- - Eastern (12)
- - - Dagur (1): DAUR [DTA] China
- - - Mongour (4): BONAN [PEH] China
- - - - DONGXIANG [SCE] China
- - - - TU [MJG] China
- - - - YUGUR, EAST [YUY] China
- - - Oirat-Khalkha (7)
- - - - Khalkha-Buriat (5)
- - - - - Buriat (3): BURIAT, CHINA [BXU] China
- - - - - - BURIAT, MONGOLIA [BXM] Mongolia
- - - - - - BURIAT, RUSSIA [MNB] Russia (Asia)
- - - - - Mongolian Proper (2): MONGOLIAN, HALH [KHK] Mongolia
- - - - - - MONGOLIAN, PERIPHERAL [MVF] China
- - - - Oirat-Kalmyk-Darkhat (2): DARKHAT [DAY] Mongolia
- - - - - KALMYK-OIRAT [KGZ] Russia (Europe)
- - Western (1): MOGHOLI [MLG] Afghanistan
- Tungus (12)
- - Northern (4)
- - - Even (1): EVEN [EVE] Russia (Asia)
- - - Evenki (2): EVENKI [EVN] China
- - - - OROQEN [ORH] China
- - - Negidal (1): NEGIDAL [NEG] Russia (Asia)
- - Southern (8)
- - - Southeast (5)
- - - - Nanaj (3): NANAI [GLD] Russia (Asia)
- - - - - OROK [OAA] Russia (Asia)
- - - - - ULCH [ULC] Russia (Asia)
- - - - Udihe (2): OROCH [OAC] Russia (Asia)
- - - - - UDIHE [UDE] Russia (Asia)
- - - Southwest (3): JURCHEN [JUC] China
- - - - MANCHU [MJF] China
- - - - XIBE [SJO] China
- Turkic (40): URUM [UUM] Georgia
- - Bolgar (1): CHUVASH [CJU] Russia (Europe)
- - Eastern (7): AINU [AIB] China
- - - CHAGATAI [CGT] Turkmenistan
- - - ILI TURKI [ILI] China
- - - UYGHUR [UIG] China
- - - UZBEK, NORTHERN [UZB] Uzbekistan
- - - UZBEK, SOUTHERN [UZS] Afghanistan
- - - YUGUR, WEST [YBE] China
- - Northern (8): ALTAI, NORTHERN [ATV] Russia (Asia)
- - - ALTAI, SOUTHERN [ALT] Russia (Asia)
- - - DOLGAN [DLG] Russia (Asia)
- - - KARAGAS [KIM] Russia (Asia)
- - - KHAKAS [KJH] Russia (Asia)
- - - SHOR [CJS] Russia (Asia)
- - - TUVIN [TUN] Russia (Asia)
- - - YAKUT [UKT] Russia (Asia)
- - Southern (12): CRIMEAN TURKISH [CRH] Uzbekistan

Altaic (65)
- Turkic (40)
- - Southern (12): SALAR [SLR] China
- - - Azerbaijani (5): AZERBAIJANI, NORTH [AZE] Azerbaijan
- - - - AZERBAIJANI, SOUTH [AZB] Iran
- - - - KHALAJ [KLJ] Iran
- - - - QASHQA'I [QSQ] Iran
- - - - SALCHUQ [SLQ] Iran
- - - Turkish (4): BALKAN GAGAUZ TURKISH [BGX] Turkey (Europe)
- - - - GAGAUZ [GAG] Moldova
- - - - KHORASANI TURKISH [KMZ] Iran
- - - - TURKISH [TRK] Turkey (Asia)
- - - Turkmenian (1): TURKMEN [TCK] Turkmenistan
- - Western (11)
- - - Aralo-Caspian (4): KARAKALPAK [KAC] Uzbekistan
- - - - KAZAKH [KAZ] Kazakhstan
- - - - KIRGHIZ [KDO] Kyrgyzstan
- - - - NOGAI [NOG] Russia (Europe)
- - - Ponto-Caspian (4): JUDEO-CRIMEAN TATAR [JCT] Uzbekistan
- - - - KARACHAY-BALKAR [KRC] Russia (Europe)
- - - - KARAIM [KDR] Lithuania
- - - - KUMYK [KSK] Russia (Europe)
- - - Uralian (3): BASHKIR [BXK] Russia (Europe)
- - - - CHULYM [CHU] Russia (Asia)
- - - - TATAR [TTR] Russia (Europe)

Amto-Musan (2): AMTO [AMT] Papua New Guinea
- MUSAN [MMP] Papua New Guinea

Andamanese (13)
- Great Andamanese (10)
- - Central (6): A-PUCIKWAR [APQ] India
- - - AKA-BEA [ACE] India
- - - AKA-KEDE [AKX] India
- - - AKA-KOL [AKY] India
- - - AKAR-BALE [ACL] India
- - - OKO-JUWOI [OKJ] India
- - Northern (4): AKA-BO [AKM] India
- - - AKA-CARI [ACI] India
- - - AKA-JERU [AKJ] India
- - - AKA-KORA [ACK] India
- South Andamanese (3): JARAWA [ANQ] India
- - ÖNGE [OON] India
- - SENTINEL [STD] India

Arauan (8): ARUA [ARA] Brazil
- BANAWÁ [BNH] Brazil
- CULINA [CUL] Brazil
- DENÍ [DAN] Brazil
- JAMAMADÍ [JAA] Brazil
- JARUÁRA [JAP] Brazil
- PAUMARÍ [PAD] Brazil
- SURUAHÁ [SWX] Brazil

Araucanian (2): HUILLICHE [HUH] Chile
- MAPUDUNGUN [ARU] Chile

Arawakan (60)
- Maipuran (54)
- - Central Maipuran (6): MEHINÁKU [MMH] Brazil
- - - PARECÍS [PAB] Brazil

Arawakan (60)
- Maipuran (54)
- - Central Maipuran (6): SALUMÃ [UNK] Brazil
- - - SARAVECA [SAR] Bolivia
- - - WAURÁ [WAU] Brazil
- - - YAWALAPITÍ [YAW] Brazil
- - Eastern Maipuran (1): PALIKÚR [PAL] Brazil
- - Northern Maipuran (24)
- - - Caribbean (6): ARAWAK [ARW] Suriname
- - - - CARIB, ISLAND [CAI] Dominica
- - - - GARÍFUNA [CAB] Honduras
- - - - PARAUJANO [PBG] Venezuela
- - - - TAINO [TNQ] Bahamas
- - - - WAYUU [GUC] Colombia
- - - Inland (15): ACHAGUA [ACA] Colombia
- - - - BANIVA [BVV] Venezuela
- - - - BANIWA [BAI] Brazil
- - - - BARÉ [BAE] Venezuela
- - - - CABIYARÍ [CBB] Colombia
- - - - CARÚTANA [CRU] Brazil
- - - - CURRIPACO [KPC] Colombia
- - - - GUAREQUENA [GAE] Venezuela
- - - - IPEKA-TAPUIA [PAJ] Brazil
- - - - MANDAHUACA [MHT] Venezuela
- - - - PIAPOCO [PIO] Colombia
- - - - RESÍGARO [RGR] Peru
- - - - TARIANO [TAE] Brazil
- - - - YAVITERO [YVT] Venezuela
- - - - YUCUNA [YCN] Colombia
- - - Unclassified (2): TUBARÃO [TBA] Brazil
- - - - YABAÂNA [YBN] Brazil
- - - Wapishanan (1): ARUMA [WAP] Guyana
- - Southern Maipuran (21)
- - - Bolivia-Parana (5): BAURE [BRG] Bolivia
- - - - GUANA [QKS] Brazil
- - - - IGNACIANO [IGN] Bolivia
- - - - TERÊNA [TEA] Brazil
- - - - TRINITARIO [TRN] Bolivia
- - - Campa (10): AJYÍNINKA APURUCAYALI [CPC] Peru
- - - - ASHÁNINCA [CNI] Peru
- - - - ASHÉNINCA PAJONAL [CJO] Peru
- - - - ASHÉNINCA PERENÉ [CPP] Peru
- - - - ASHÉNINCA PICHIS [CPU] Peru
- - - - ASHÉNINCA UCAYALI-YURÚA [CPB] Peru
- - - - CAQUINTE [COT] Peru
- - - - MACHIGUENGA [MCB] Peru
- - - - NANTI [COX] Peru
- - - - NOMATSIGUENGA [NOT] Peru
- - - Purus (5): APURINÃ [APU] Brazil
- - - - IÑAPARI [INA] Peru
- - - - MACHINERE [MPD] Brazil
- - - - MASHCO PIRO [CUJ] Peru
- - - - YINE [PIB] Peru
- - - Unclassified (1): IRÁNTXE [IRA] Brazil
- - Western Maipuran (2): CHAMICURO [CCC] Peru
- - - YANESHA' [AME] Peru
- Unclassified (6): CHANÉ [CAJ] Argentina
- - CUMERAL [CUM] Colombia
- - OMEJES [OME] Colombia
- - PONARES [POD] Colombia
- - TOMEDES [TOE] Colombia

Arawakan (60)
- Unclassified (6): XIRIÂNA [XIR] Brazil

Artificial language (3): ESPERANTO [ESP] France
- EUROPANTO [EUR] Belgium
- INTERLINGUA [INR] France

Arutani-Sape (2): ARUTANI [ATX] Brazil
- SAPÉ [SPC] Venezuela

Australian (258)
- Bunaban (2): BUNABA [BCK] Australia
- - GOONIYANDI [GNI] Australia
- Burarran (4): BURARRA [BVR] Australia
- - DJEEBBANA [DJJ] Australia
- - GURAGONE [GGE] Australia
- - NAKARA [NCK] Australia
- Daly (19)
- - Bringen-Wagaydy (13)
- - - Bringen (7): MAGADIGE [ZMG] Australia
- - - - MARIDAN [ZMD] Australia
- - - - MARIDJABIN [ZMJ] Australia
- - - - MARIMANINDJI [ZMM] Australia
- - - - MARINGARR [ZMT] Australia
- - - - MARITHIEL [MFR] Australia
- - - - MARIYEDI [ZMY] Australia
- - - Wagaydy (6): AMI [AMY] Australia
- - - - GIYUG [GIY] Australia
- - - - KUWAMA [QKU] Australia
- - - - MANDA [ZMA] Australia
- - - - MARANUNGGU [ZMR] Australia
- - - - WADJIGINY [WDJ] Australia
- - Malagmalag (4)
- - - Daly Proper (2): KAMU [QKY] Australia
- - - - MADNGELE [ZML] Australia
- - - Malagmalag Proper (2): MULLUKMULLUK [MPB] Australia
- - - - TYARAITY [WOA] Australia
- - Moil (1): NANGIKURRUNGGURR [NAM] Australia
- - Murrinh-Patha (1): MURRINH-PATHA [MWF] Australia
- Djamindjungan (2): DJAMINDJUNG [DJD] Australia
- - NUNGALI [NUG] Australia
- Djeragan (3)
- - Kitjic (1): KITJA [GIA] Australia
- - Miriwungic (2): GADJERAWANG [GDH] Australia
- - - MIRIWUNG [MEP] Australia
- Enindhilyagwa (1): ANINDILYAKWA [AOI] Australia
- Gagudjuan (1): GAGADU [GBU] Australia
- Garawan (1): GARAWA [GBC] Australia
- Gungaraganyan (1): KUNGARAKANY [GGK] Australia
- Gunwingguan (13)
- - Djauanic (1): DJAUAN [DJN] Australia
- - Gunwinggic (3): GUNWINGGU [GUP] Australia
- - - KUNBARLANG [WLG] Australia
- - - NGALKBUN [NGK] Australia
- - Mangarayic (1): MANGARAYI [MPC] Australia
- - Ngalakanic (1): NGALAKAN [NIG] Australia
- - Ngandic (1): NGANDI [NID] Australia
- - Nunggubuan (1): NUNGGUBUYU [NUY] Australia
- - Rembargic (1): REMBARUNGA [RMB] Australia
- - Warayan (1): WARAY [WRZ] Australia

Australian (258)
- Gunwingguan (13)
- - Yangmanic (3)
- - - Nolgin (1): YANGMAN [JNG] Australia
- - - Wagiman (1): WAGEMAN [WAQ] Australia
- - - Yibwan (1): WARDAMAN [WRR] Australia
- Laragiyan (2): LARAGIA [LRG] Australia
- - WULNA [WUX] Australia
- Mangerrian (3)
- - Mangerric (1): MANGERR [ZME] Australia
- - Urninganggic (2): ERRE [ERR] Australia
- - - URNINGANGG [URC] Australia
- Maran (3)
- - Alawic (1): ALAWA [ALH] Australia
- - Mara (2): MARA [MEC] Australia
- - - WANDARANG [WND] Australia
- Nyulnyulan (8): BAADI [BCJ] Australia
- - DJAWI [DJW] Australia
- - DYABERDYABER [DYB] Australia
- - DYUGUN [DYD] Australia
- - NIMANBUR [NMP] Australia
- - NYIGINA [NYH] Australia
- - NYULNYUL [NYV] Australia
- - YAWURU [YWR] Australia
- Pama-Nyungan (177)
- - Arandic (6)
- - - Artuya (1): KAYTETYE [GBB] Australia
- - - Urtwa (5): ALYAWARR [ALY] Australia
- - - - ANDEGEREBINHA [ADG] Australia
- - - - ANMATYERRE [AMX] Australia
- - - - ARRARNTA, WESTERN [ARE] Australia
- - - - ARRERNTE, EASTERN [AER] Australia
- - Baagandji (2): BANDJIGALI [BJD] Australia
- - - DARLING [DRL] Australia
- - Bandjalangic (1): BANDJALANG [BDY] Australia
- - Barrow Point (1): BARROW POINT [BPT] Australia
- - Dyirbalic (2): DYIRBAL [DBL] Australia
- - - WARRGAMAY [WGY] Australia
- - Flinders Island (1): FLINDERS ISLAND [FLN] Australia
- - Galgadungic (2): KALKUTUNG [KTG] Australia
- - - YALARNNGA [YLR] Australia
- - Gumbaynggiric (1): KUMBAINGGAR [KGS] Australia
- - Kala Lagaw Ya (1): KALA LAGAW YA [MWP] Australia
- - Karnic (11)
- - - Arabana-Wangganguru (2): ARABANA [ARD] Australia
- - - - WANGGANGURU [WGG] Australia
- - - Karna (6): DIERI [DIF] Australia
- - - - DIRARI [DIT] Australia
- - - - NGAMINI [NMV] Australia
- - - - PIRLATAPA [BXI] Australia
- - - - YANDRUWANDHA [YND] Australia
- - - - YAWARAWARGA [YWW] Australia
- - - Ngura (1): NGURA [NBX] Australia
- - - Palku (2): PITTA PITTA [PIT] Australia
- - - - WANGGAMALA [WNM] Australia
- - Maric (12)
- - - Kapu (1): KUNGGARI [KGL] Australia
- - - Mari (11): BIDYARA [BYM] Australia
- - - - BIRI [BZR] Australia
- - - - GANGULU [GNL] Australia
- - - - GUGU BADHUN [GDC] Australia

Australian (258)
- Pama-Nyungan (177)
- - Maric (12)
- - - Mari (11): GUNGABULA [GYF] Australia
- - - - GUNYA [GYY] Australia
- - - - GUWAMU [GWU] Australia
- - - - MANDANDANYI [ZMK] Australia
- - - - MARGANY [ZMC] Australia
- - - - WADJIGU [WDU] Australia
- - - - WARUNGU [WRG] Australia
- - Muruwaric (1): MURUWARI [ZMU] Australia
- - Ngarinyeric-Yithayithic (1): NARRINYERI [NAY] Australia
- - Nyawaygic (1): NYAWAYGI [NYT] Australia
- - Paman (44)
- - - Central Pama (1): KUNJEN [KJN] Australia
- - - Coastal Pama (1): GUGUBERA [KKP] Australia
- - - Flinders Pama (1): GUGADJ [GGD] Australia
- - - Lamalamic (5): GUGU WARRA [WRW] Australia
- - - - LAMU-LAMU [LBY] Australia
- - - - MBARIMAN-GUDHINMA [ZMV] Australia
- - - - UMBINDHAMU [UMD] Australia
- - - - UMBUYGAMU [UMG] Australia
- - - Mayabic (3): MAYAGUDUNA [XMY] Australia
- - - - MAYKULAN [MNT] Australia
- - - - NGAWUN [NXN] Australia
- - - Middle Pama (15): AYABADHU [AYD] Australia
- - - - KUKU-MANGK [XMQ] Australia
- - - - KUKU-MU'INH [XMP] Australia
- - - - KUKU-MUMINH [XMH] Australia
- - - - KUKU-UGBANH [UGB] Australia
- - - - KUKU-UWANH [UWA] Australia
- - - - PAKANHA [PKN] Australia
- - - - WIK-EPA [WIE] Australia
- - - - WIK-IIYANH [WIJ] Australia
- - - - WIK-KEYANGAN [WIF] Australia
- - - - WIK-ME'ANHA [WIH] Australia
- - - - WIK-MUNGKAN [WIM] Australia
- - - - WIK-NGATHANA [WIG] Australia
- - - - WIKALKAN [WIK] Australia
- - - - WIKNGENCHERA [WUA] Australia
- - - Norman Pama (4): AREBA [AEA] Australia
- - - - GURDJAR [GDJ] Australia
- - - - KUNGGARA [KVS] Australia
- - - - KUTHANT [QKD] Australia
- - - Northeastern Pama (3): KANJU [KBE] Australia
- - - - KUUKU-YA'U [QKL] Australia
- - - - UMPILA [UMP] Australia
- - - Northern Pama (4): ALNGITH [AID] Australia
- - - - ATAMPAYA [AMZ] Australia
- - - - LENINGITIJ [LNJ] Australia
- - - - URADHI [URF] Australia
- - - Rarmul Pama (2): AGHU THARNGGALU [GGR] Australia
- - - - THAYPAN [TYP] Australia
- - - Southern Pama (3): AGWAMIN [AWG] Australia
- - - - MBARA [VMB] Australia
- - - - WAMIN [WMI] Australia
- - - Western Pama (2): THAYORE [THD] Australia
- - - - YIR YORONT [YIY] Australia
- - South-West (51)
- - - Coastal Ngayarda (8): DJIWARLI [DJL] Australia
- - - - KARIYARRA [VKA] Australia

Australian (258)
- Pama-Nyungan (177)
- - South-West (51)
- - - Coastal Ngayarda (8): KURRAMA [VKU] Australia
- - - - MARTUYHUNIRA [VMA] Australia
- - - - NGARLUMA [NRL] Australia
- - - - NHUWALA [NHF] Australia
- - - - PINIGURA [PNV] Australia
- - - - YINDJIBARNDI [YIJ] Australia
- - - Inland Ngayarda (5): NGARLA [NLR] Australia
- - - - NYAMAL [NLY] Australia
- - - - PANYTYIMA [PNW] Australia
- - - - TJURRURU [TJU] Australia
- - - - WARIYANGGA [WRI] Australia
- - - Kanyara (4): BAYUNGU [BXJ] Australia
- - - - BURDUNA [BXN] Australia
- - - - DHALANDJI [DHL] Australia
- - - - DHARGARI [DHR] Australia
- - - Kardu (2): MALGANA [VML] Australia
- - - - YINGGARDA [YIA] Australia
- - - Marngu (3): KARADJERI [GBD] Australia
- - - - MANGALA [MEM] Australia
- - - - NYANGUMARTA [NNA] Australia
- - - Mirning (2): KALARKO [KBA] Australia
- - - - NGADJUNMAYA [NJU] Australia
- - - Ngarga (2): WARLMANPA [WRL] Australia
- - - - WARLPIRI [WBP] Australia
- - - Ngumbin (5): GURINJI [GUE] Australia
- - - - JARU [DDJ] Australia
- - - - MUDBURA [MWD] Australia
- - - - NGARINMAN [NBJ] Australia
- - - - WALMAJARRI [WMT] Australia
- - - Nyungar (1): NYUNGA [NYS] Australia
- - - Wadjari (2): BADIMAYA [BIA] Australia
- - - - WAJARRI [WBV] Australia
- - - Wati (13): ANTAKARINYA [ANT] Australia
- - - - KOKATA [KTD] Australia
- - - - KUKATJA [KUX] Australia
- - - - MARTU WANGKA [MPJ] Australia
- - - - NGAANYATJARRA [NTJ] Australia
- - - - NIJADALI [NAD] Australia
- - - - PINI [PII] Australia
- - - - PINTIINI [PTI] Australia
- - - - PINTUPI-LURITJA [PIU] Australia
- - - - PITJANTJATJARA [PJT] Australia
- - - - WANMAN [WBT] Australia
- - - - WIRANGU [WIW] Australia
- - - - YANKUNYTJATJARA [KDD] Australia
- - - Yura (4): ADYNYAMATHANHA [ADT] Australia
- - - - BANGGARLA [BJB] Australia
- - - - NARUNGGA [NNR] Australia
- - - - NUGUNU [NNV] Australia
- - Tangic (4): GANGGALIDA [GCD] Australia
- - - GAYARDILT [GYD] Australia
- - - LARDIL [LBZ] Australia
- - - NYANGGA [NNY] Australia
- - Wagaya-Warluwaric (3)
- - - Wagaya (1): WAGAYA [WGA] Australia
- - - Warluwara-Thawa (2): WARLUWARA [WRB] Australia
- - - - YINDJILANDJI [YIL] Australia

Australian (258)
- Pama-Nyungan (177)
- - Waka-Kabic (4)
- - - Kingkel (1): BAYALI [BJY] Australia
- - - Miyan (2): WAKAWAKA [WKW] Australia
- - - - WULIWULI [WLU] Australia
- - - Than (1): GURENG GURENG [GNR] Australia
- - Warumungic (1): WARUMUNGU [WRM] Australia
- - Wiradhuric (3): KAMILAROI [KLD] Australia
- - - WANGAAYBUWAN-NGIYAMBAA [WYB] Australia
- - - WIRADHURI [WRH] Australia
- - Yalandyic (4): DJANGUN [DJF] Australia
- - - GUGUYIMIDJIR [KKY] Australia
- - - KUKU-YALANJI [GVN] Australia
- - - MULURIDYI [VMU] Australia
- - Yanyuwan (1): YANYUWA [JAO] Australia
- - Yidinic (2): DYAABUGAY [DYY] Australia
- - - YIDINY [YII] Australia
- - Yuin-Kuric (7)
- - - Kuri (5): AWABAKAL [AWK] Australia
- - - - DYANGADI [DYN] Australia
- - - - NGANYAYWANA [NYX] Australia
- - - - WORIMI [KDA] Australia
- - - - YUGAMBAL [YUB] Australia
- - - Yuin (2): DHURGA [DHU] Australia
- - - - THURAWAL [TBH] Australia
- - Yuulngu (10): DAYI [DAX] Australia
- - - DHANGU [GLA] Australia
- - - DJINANG [DJI] Australia
- - - DJINBA [DJB] Australia
- - - JARNANGO [JAY] Australia
- - - RITARUNGO [RIT] Australia
- - - Dhuwal (2): DHUWAL [DUJ] Australia
- - - - DJAMBARRPUYNGU [DJR] Australia
- - - Dhuwala (2): GUMATJ [GNN] Australia
- - - - GUPAPUYNGU [GUF] Australia
- Tiwian (1): TIWI [TIW] Australia
- Unclassified (3): LIMILNGAN [LMC] Australia
- - NGURMBUR [NRX] Australia
- - UMBUGARLA [UMR] Australia
- West Barkly (3)
- - Jingalic (1): DJINGILI [JIG] Australia
- - Wambayan (2): NGARNDJI [NJI] Australia
- - - WAMBAYA [WMB] Australia
- Wororan (7)
- - Ungarinjinic (2): NGARINYIN [UNG] Australia
- - - WILAWILA [WIL] Australia
- - Wororic (1): WORORA [UNP] Australia
- - Wunambalic (4): GAMBERA [GMA] Australia
- - - KWINI [GWW] Australia
- - - MIWA [VMI] Australia
- - - WUNAMBAL [WUB] Australia
- Yiwaidjan (4)
- - Amaragic (1): AMARAG [AMG] Australia
- - Margic (1): MARGU [MHG] Australia
- - Yiwaidjic (2): IWAIDJA [IBD] Australia
- - - MAUNG [MPH] Australia

Austro-Asiatic (168)
- Mon-Khmer (147)
- - Aslian (19)
- - - Jah Hut (1): JAH HUT [JAH] Malaysia (Peninsular)
- - - North Aslian (9)
- - - - Chewong (1): CHEWONG [CWG] Malaysia (Peninsular)
- - - - Eastern (4): BATEK [BTQ] Malaysia (Peninsular)
- - - - - JEHAI [JHI] Malaysia (Peninsular)
- - - - - MINRIQ [MNQ] Malaysia (Peninsular)
- - - - - MINTIL [MZT] Malaysia (Peninsular)
- - - - Tonga (1): TONGA [TNZ] Thailand
- - - - Western (3): KENSIU [KNS] Malaysia (Peninsular)
- - - - - KINTAQ [KNQ] Malaysia (Peninsular)
- - - - - SEMANG, LOWLAND [ORB] Indonesia (Sumatra)
- - - Senoic (5): LANOH [LNH] Malaysia (Peninsular)
- - - - SABÜM [SBO] Malaysia (Peninsular)
- - - - SEMAI [SEA] Malaysia (Peninsular)
- - - - SEMNAM [SSM] Malaysia (Peninsular)
- - - - TEMIAR [TMH] Malaysia (Peninsular)
- - - South Aslian (4): BESISI [MHE] Malaysia (Peninsular)
- - - - SEMAQ BERI [SZC] Malaysia (Peninsular)
- - - - SEMELAI [SZA] Malaysia (Peninsular)
- - - - TEMOQ [TMO] Malaysia (Peninsular)
- - Eastern Mon-Khmer (67)
- - - Bahnaric (40)
- - - - Central Bahnaric (6): ALAK [ALK] Laos
- - - - - BAHNAR [BDQ] Viet Nam
- - - - - KACO' [XKK] Cambodia
- - - - - LAMAM [LMM] Cambodia
- - - - - ROMAM [ROH] Viet Nam
- - - - - TAMPUAN [TPU] Cambodia
- - - - North Bahnaric (14): KATUA [KTA] Viet Nam
- - - - - East (3)
- - - - - - Cua-Kayong (2): CUA [CUA] Viet Nam
- - - - - - - KAYONG [KXY] Viet Nam
- - - - - - Takua (1): TAKUA [TKZ] Viet Nam
- - - - - West (10): TALIENG [TDF] Laos
- - - - - - TRIENG [STG] Viet Nam
- - - - - - Duan (1): HALANG DOAN [HLD] Viet Nam
- - - - - - Jeh-Halang (2): HALANG [HAL] Viet Nam
- - - - - - - JEH [JEH] Viet Nam
- - - - - - Rengao (1): RENGAO [REN] Viet Nam
- - - - - - Sedang-Todrah (4)
- - - - - - - Sedang (2): HRE [HRE] Viet Nam
- - - - - - - - SEDANG [SED] Viet Nam
- - - - - - - Todrah-Monom (2): MONOM [MOO] Viet Nam
- - - - - - - - TODRAH [TDR] Viet Nam
- - - - South Bahnaric (9): STIENG, BUDEH [STT] Viet Nam
- - - - - Sre-Mnong (6)
- - - - - - Mnong (4)
- - - - - - - Eastern Mnong (1): MNONG, EASTERN [MNG] Viet Nam
- - - - - - - Southern-Central Mnong (3): KRAOL [RKA] Cambodia
- - - - - - - - MNONG, CENTRAL [MNC] Viet Nam
- - - - - - - - MNONG, SOUTHERN [MNN] Viet Nam
- - - - - - Sre (2): KOHO [KPM] Viet Nam
- - - - - - - MAA [CMA] Viet Nam
- - - - - Stieng-Chrau (2): CHRAU [CHR] Viet Nam
- - - - - - STIENG, BULO [STI] Viet Nam
- - - - West Bahnaric (11)
- - - - - Brao-Kravet (4): KRAVET [KRV] Cambodia
- - - - - - KRU'NG 2 [KRR] Cambodia

Austro-Asiatic (168)
- Mon-Khmer (147)
- - Eastern Mon-Khmer (67)
- - - Bahnaric (40)
- - - - West Bahnaric (11)
- - - - - Brao-Kravet (4): LAVE [BRB] Laos
- - - - - - SOU [SQQ] Laos
- - - - - Laven (1): LAVEN [LBO] Laos
- - - - - Nyaheun (1): NYAHEUN [NEV] Laos
- - - - - Oi-The (5): JENG [JEG] Laos
- - - - - - OY [OYB] Laos
- - - - - - SAPUAN [SPU] Laos
- - - - - - SOK [SKK] Laos
- - - - - - THE [THX] Laos
- - - Katuic (19)
- - - - Central Katuic (5)
- - - - - Ta'oih (5): IR [IRR] Laos
- - - - - - KATAANG [KGD] Laos
- - - - - - ONG [OOG] Laos
- - - - - - TA'OIH, LOWER [TTO] Laos
- - - - - - TA'OIH, UPPER [TTH] Laos
- - - - East Katuic (8)
- - - - - Kaseng (1): KASSENG [KGC] Laos
- - - - - Katu-Pacoh (5): KATU, EASTERN [KTV] Viet Nam
- - - - - - KATU, WESTERN [KUF] Laos
- - - - - - PACOH [PAC] Viet Nam
- - - - - - PHUONG [PHG] Viet Nam
- - - - - - TARENG [TGR] Laos
- - - - - Ngeq-Nkriang (2): KHLOR [LLO] Laos
- - - - - - NGEQ [NGT] Laos
- - - - West Katuic (6)
- - - - - Brou-So (4): BRU, EASTERN [BRU] Laos
- - - - - - BRU, WESTERN [BRV] Thailand
- - - - - - KHUA [XHU] Viet Nam
- - - - - - SÔ [SSS] Laos
- - - - - Kuay-Yoe (2): KUY [KDT] Thailand
- - - - - - NYEU [NYL] Thailand
- - - Khmer (2): KHMER, CENTRAL [KMR] Cambodia
- - - - KHMER, NORTHERN [KXM] Thailand
- - - Pearic (6)
- - - - Eastern (1): PEAR [PCB] Cambodia
- - - - Western (5)
- - - - - Chong (2): CHONG [COG] Cambodia
- - - - - - SA'OCH [SCQ] Cambodia
- - - - - Samre (2): SAMRE [SCC] Cambodia
- - - - - - SOMRAY [SMU] Cambodia
- - - - - Suoy (1): SUOY [SYO] Cambodia
- - Monic (2): MON [MNW] Myanmar
- - - NYAHKUR [CBN] Thailand
- - Nicobar (6)
- - - Car (1): NICOBARESE, CAR [CAQ] India
- - - Chowra-Teressa (2): CHAURA [CHO] India
- - - - TERESSA [TEF] India
- - - Great Nicobar (1): NICOBARESE, SOUTHERN [NIK] India
- - - Nancowry (1): NICOBARESE, CENTRAL [NCB] India
- - - Shom Peng (1): SHOM PENG [SII] India
- - Northern Mon-Khmer (38)
- - - Khasian (3): AMWI [AML] India
- - - - KHASI [KHI] India
- - - - PNAR [PBV] India

Austro-Asiatic (168)
- Mon-Khmer (147)
- - Northern Mon-Khmer (38)
- - - Khmuic (13)
- - - - Khao (2): BIT [BGK] Laos
- - - - - KHAO [XAO] Viet Nam
- - - - Mal-Khmu' (7)
- - - - - Khmu' (3): KHMU [KJG] Laos
- - - - - - KHUEN [KHF] Laos
- - - - - - O'DU [TYH] Viet Nam
- - - - - Mal-Phrai (4): LUA' [PRB] Thailand
- - - - - - MAL [MLF] Laos
- - - - - - PHAI [PRT] Thailand
- - - - - - PRAY 3 [PRY] Thailand
- - - - Mlabri (1): MLABRI [MRA] Thailand
- - - - Xinh Mul (3): KHANG [KJM] Viet Nam
- - - - - PHONG-KNIANG [PNX] Laos
- - - - - PUOC [PUO] Viet Nam
- - - Mang (1): MANG [MGA] Viet Nam
- - - Palaungic (21)
- - - - Eastern Palaungic (6)
- - - - - Danau (1): DANAU [DNU] Myanmar
- - - - - Palaung (3): PALAUNG, PALE [PCE] Myanmar
- - - - - - PALAUNG, RUMAI [RBB] Myanmar
- - - - - - PALAUNG, SHWE [SWE] Myanmar
- - - - - Riang (2): RIANG [RIL] Myanmar
- - - - - - YINCHIA [YIN] Myanmar
- - - - Western Palaungic (15)
- - - - - Angkuic (8): HU [HUO] China
- - - - - - KIORR [XKO] Laos
- - - - - - KON KEU [ANG] China
- - - - - - MAN MET [MML] China
- - - - - - MOK [MQT] Thailand
- - - - - - SAMTAO [STU] Myanmar
- - - - - - TAI LOI [TLQ] Myanmar
- - - - - - U [UUU] China
- - - - - Lametic (2): CON [CNO] Laos
- - - - - - LAMET [LBN] Laos
- - - - - Waic (5)
- - - - - - Bulang (1): BLANG [BLR] China
- - - - - - Lawa (2): LAWA, EASTERN [LWL] Thailand
- - - - - - - LAWA, WESTERN [LCP] China
- - - - - - Wa (2): PARAUK [PRK] Myanmar
- - - - - - - VO [WBM] Myanmar
- - - Palyu (1): PALYU [PLY] China
- - - Unclassified (4): BUGAN [BBH] China
- - - - BUXINHUA [BXT] China
- - - - KEMIEHUA [KFJ] China
- - - - KUANHUA [QAK] China
- - Viet-Muong (10)
- - - Chut (3): AREM [AEM] Viet Nam
- - - - CHUT [SCB] Viet Nam
- - - - MALENG [PKT] Laos
- - - Cuoi (2): HUNG [HNU] Laos
- - - - THO [TOU] Viet Nam
- - - Muong (3): BO [BGL] Laos
- - - - MUONG [MTQ] Viet Nam
- - - - NGUÔN [NUO] Viet Nam
- - - Thavung (1): AHEU [THM] Thailand
- - - Vietnamese (1): VIETNAMESE [VIE] Viet Nam

Austro-Asiatic (168)
- Munda (21)
- - North Munda (12)
- - - Kherwari (11): AGARIYA [AGI] India
- - - - BIJORI [BIX] India
- - - - KORAKU [KSZ] India
- - - - Mundari (5): ASURI [ASR] India
- - - - - BIRHOR [BIY] India
- - - - - HO [HOC] India
- - - - - KORWA [KFP] India
- - - - - MUNDARI [MUW] India
- - - - - Santali (3): MAHALI [MJX] India
- - - - - SANTALI [SNT] India
- - - - - TURI [TRD] India
- - - Korku (1): KORKU [KFQ] India
- - South Munda (9)
- - - Kharia-Juang (2): JUANG [JUN] India
- - - - KHARIA [KHR] India
- - - Koraput Munda (7)
- - - - Gutob-Remo-Geta' (3)
- - - - - Geta' (1): GATA' [GAQ] India
- - - - - Gutob-Remo (2): BONDO [BFW] India
- - - - - - GADABA, BODO [GBJ] India
- - - - Sora-Juray-Gorum (4)
- - - - - Gorum (1): PARENGA [PCJ] India
- - - - - Sora-Juray (3): JURAY [JUY] India
- - - - - - LODHI [LBM] India
- - - - - - SORA [SRB] India

Austronesian (1262)
- Formosan (23)
- - Atayalic (2): ATAYAL [TAY] Taiwan
- - - TAROKO [TRV] Taiwan
- - Paiwanic (17): AMIS [ALV] Taiwan
- - - AMIS, NATAORAN [AIS] Taiwan
- - - BABUZA [BZG] Taiwan
- - - BASAY [BYQ] Taiwan
- - - BUNUN [BNN] Taiwan
- - - HOANYA [HON] Taiwan
- - - KAVALAN [CKV] Taiwan
- - - KETANGALAN [KAE] Taiwan
- - - KULUN [KNG] Taiwan
- - - PAIWAN [PWN] Taiwan
- - - PAPORA [PPU] Taiwan
- - - PAZEH [PZH] Taiwan
- - - PYUMA [PYU] Taiwan
- - - SAISIYAT [SAI] Taiwan
- - - SIRAIYA [FOS] Taiwan
- - - TAOKAS [TOA] Taiwan
- - - THAO [SSF] Taiwan
- - Tsouic (4): RUKAI [DRU] Taiwan
- - - Northern (1): TSOU [TSY] Taiwan
- - - Southern (2): KANAKANABU [QNB] Taiwan
- - - - SAAROA [SXR] Taiwan
- Malayo-Polynesian (1239)
- - Central-Eastern (706)
- - - Central Malayo-Polynesian (162)
- - - - Aru (14): BARAKAI [BAJ] Indonesia (Maluku)
- - - - - BATULEY [BAY] Indonesia (Maluku)
- - - - - DOBEL [KVO] Indonesia (Maluku)
- - - - - KAREY [KYD] Indonesia (Maluku)

Austronesian (1262)
- Malayo-Polynesian (1239)
- - Central-Eastern (706)
- - - Central Malayo-Polynesian (162)
- - - - Aru (14): KOBA [KPD] Indonesia (Maluku)
- - - - - KOLA [KVV] Indonesia (Maluku)
- - - - - KOMPANE [KVP] Indonesia (Maluku)
- - - - - LOLA [LCD] Indonesia (Maluku)
- - - - - LORANG [LRN] Indonesia (Maluku)
- - - - - MANOMBAI [WOO] Indonesia (Maluku)
- - - - - MARIRI [MQI] Indonesia (Maluku)
- - - - - TARANGAN, EAST [TRE] Indonesia (Maluku)
- - - - - TARANGAN, WEST [TXN] Indonesia (Maluku)
- - - - - UJIR [UDJ] Indonesia (Maluku)
- - - - Babar (11)
- - - - - North (3): BABAR, NORTH [BCD] Indonesia (Maluku)
- - - - - - DAI [DIJ] Indonesia (Maluku)
- - - - - - DAWERA-DAWELOOR [DDW] Indonesia (Maluku)
- - - - - South (8)
- - - - - - Masela-South Babar (5): BABAR, SOUTHEAST [VBB] Indonesia (Maluku)
- - - - - - - MASELA, CENTRAL [MKH] Indonesia (Maluku)
- - - - - - - MASELA, EAST [VME] Indonesia (Maluku)
- - - - - - - MASELA, WEST [MSS] Indonesia (Maluku)
- - - - - - - SERILI [SVE] Indonesia (Maluku)
- - - - - - Southwest Babar (3): EMPLAWAS [EMW] Indonesia (Maluku)
- - - - - - - IMROING [IMR] Indonesia (Maluku)
- - - - - - - TELA-MASBUAR [TVM] Indonesia (Maluku)
- - - - Bima-Sumba (27): ANAKALANGU [AKG] Indonesia (Nusa Tenggara)
- - - - - BIMA [BHP] Indonesia (Nusa Tenggara)
- - - - - KAMBERA [SMI] Indonesia (Nusa Tenggara)
- - - - - KEPO' [KUK] Indonesia (Nusa Tenggara)
- - - - - KODI [KOD] Indonesia (Nusa Tenggara)
- - - - - KOMODO [KVH] Indonesia (Nusa Tenggara)
- - - - - LAMBOYA [LMY] Indonesia (Nusa Tenggara)
- - - - - LAURA [LUR] Indonesia (Nusa Tenggara)
- - - - - MAMBORU [MVD] Indonesia (Nusa Tenggara)
- - - - - MANGGARAI [MQY] Indonesia (Nusa Tenggara)
- - - - - NDAO [NFA] Indonesia (Nusa Tenggara)
- - - - - NGAD'A [NXG] Indonesia (Nusa Tenggara)
- - - - - NGAD'A, EASTERN [NEA] Indonesia (Nusa Tenggara)
- - - - - PALU'E [PLE] Indonesia (Nusa Tenggara)
- - - - - RAJONG [RJG] Indonesia (Nusa Tenggara)
- - - - - REMBONG [REB] Indonesia (Nusa Tenggara)
- - - - - RIUNG [RIU] Indonesia (Nusa Tenggara)
- - - - - RONGGA [ROR] Indonesia (Nusa Tenggara)
- - - - - SABU [HVN] Indonesia (Nusa Tenggara)
- - - - - SO'A [SSQ] Indonesia (Nusa Tenggara)
- - - - - WAE RANA [WRX] Indonesia (Nusa Tenggara)
- - - - - WANUKAKA [WNK] Indonesia (Nusa Tenggara)
- - - - - WEJEWA [WEW] Indonesia (Nusa Tenggara)
- - - - - Ende-Lio (4): ENDE [END] Indonesia (Nusa Tenggara)
- - - - - - KE'O [XXK] Indonesia (Nusa Tenggara)
- - - - - - LI'O [LJL] Indonesia (Nusa Tenggara)
- - - - - - NAGE [NXE] Indonesia (Nusa Tenggara)
- - - - Central Maluku (55)
- - - - - Ambelau (1): AMBELAU [AMV] Indonesia (Maluku)
- - - - - Buru (4): BURU [MHS] Indonesia (Maluku)
- - - - - - LISELA [LCL] Indonesia (Maluku)
- - - - - - MOKSELA [VMS] Indonesia (Maluku)
- - - - - - PALUMATA [PMC] Indonesia (Maluku)
- - - - - East (46): MANIPA [MQP] Indonesia (Maluku)

Austronesian (1262)
- Malayo-Polynesian (1239)
- - Central-Eastern (706)
- - - Central Malayo-Polynesian (162)
- - - - Central Maluku (55)
- - - - - East (46)
- - - - - - Banda-Geser (4): BANDA [BND] Indonesia (Maluku)
- - - - - - - Geser-Gorom (3): BATI [BVT] Indonesia (Maluku)
- - - - - - - - GESER-GOROM [GES] Indonesia (Maluku)
- - - - - - - - WATUBELA [WAH] Indonesia (Maluku)
- - - - - - Seram (41)
- - - - - - - Bobot (1): BOBOT [BTY] Indonesia (Maluku)
- - - - - - - East Seram (1): HOTI [HTI] Indonesia (Maluku)
- - - - - - - Manusela-Seti (5): BENGGOI [BGY] Indonesia (Maluku)
- - - - - - - - HUAULU [HUD] Indonesia (Maluku)
- - - - - - - - LIANA-SETI [STE] Indonesia (Maluku)
- - - - - - - - MANUSELA [WHA] Indonesia (Maluku)
- - - - - - - - SALAS [SGU] Indonesia (Maluku)
- - - - - - - Masiwang (1): MASIWANG [BNF] Indonesia (Maluku)
- - - - - - - Nunusaku (30)
- - - - - - - - Kayeli (1): KAYELI [KZL] Indonesia (Maluku)
- - - - - - - - Piru Bay (19): HARUKU [HRK] Indonesia (Maluku)
- - - - - - - - - East (13): KAIBOBO [KZB] Indonesia (Maluku)
- - - - - - - - - - SEPA [SPB] Indonesia (Maluku)
- - - - - - - - - - TELUTI [TLT] Indonesia (Maluku)
- - - - - - - - - - Seram Straits (10)
- - - - - - - - - - - Ambon (3): HITU [HIT] Indonesia (Maluku)
- - - - - - - - - - - - LAHA [LAD] Indonesia (Maluku)
- - - - - - - - - - - - TULEHU [TLU] Indonesia (Maluku)
- - - - - - - - - - - Solehua (1): PAULOHI [PLH] Indonesia (Maluku)
- - - - - - - - - - - Uliase (6)
- - - - - - - - - - - - Hatuhaha (5)
- - - - - - - - - - - - - Elpaputi (3): AMAHAI [AMQ] Indonesia (Maluku)
- - - - - - - - - - - - - ELPAPUTIH [ELP] Indonesia (Maluku)
- - - - - - - - - - - - - NUSA LAUT [NUL] Indonesia (Maluku)
- - - - - - - - - - - - - Saparua (2): LATU [LTU] Indonesia (Maluku)
- - - - - - - - - - - - - SAPARUA [SPR] Indonesia (Maluku)
- - - - - - - - - - - - Kamarian (1): KAMARIAN [KZX] Indonesia (Maluku)
- - - - - - - - - West (5)
- - - - - - - - - - Asilulu (2): ASILULU [ASL] Indonesia (Maluku)
- - - - - - - - - - - SEIT-KAITETU [HIK] Indonesia (Maluku)
- - - - - - - - - - Hoamoal (3)
- - - - - - - - - - - East (2): BOANO [BZN] Indonesia (Maluku)
- - - - - - - - - - - - LARIKE-WAKASIHU [ALO] Indonesia (Maluku)
- - - - - - - - - - - West (1): LUHU [LCQ] Indonesia (Maluku)
- - - - - - - - - Three Rivers (10): YALAHATAN [JAL] Indonesia (Maluku)
- - - - - - - - - Amalumute (7)
- - - - - - - - - - Northwest Seram (7): HORURU [HRR] Indonesia (Maluku)
- - - - - - - - - - - LISABATA-NUNIALI [LCS] Indonesia (Maluku)
- - - - - - - - - - - PIRU [PPR] Indonesia (Maluku)
- - - - - - - - - - Hulung (1): HULUNG [HUK] Indonesia (Maluku)
- - - - - - - - - - Loun (1): LOUN [LOX] Indonesia (Maluku)
- - - - - - - - - - Ulat Inai (2): ALUNE [ALP] Indonesia (Maluku)
- - - - - - - - - - - NAKA'ELA [NAE] Indonesia (Maluku)
- - - - - - - - - Wemale (2): WEMALE, NORTH [WEO] Indonesia (Maluku)
- - - - - - - - - - WEMALE, SOUTH [TLW] Indonesia (Maluku)
- - - - - - - - Sawai-Nuaulu (3): NUAULU, NORTH [NNI] Indonesia (Maluku)
- - - - - - - - - NUAULU, SOUTH [NXL] Indonesia (Maluku)
- - - - - - - - - SALEMAN [SAU] Indonesia (Maluku)
- - - - - - Sula (4): MANGOLE [MQC] Indonesia (Maluku)
- - - - - - SULA [SZN] Indonesia (Maluku)

Austronesian (1262)
- Malayo-Polynesian (1239)
- - Central-Eastern (706)
- - - Central Malayo-Polynesian (162)
- - - - Central Maluku (55)
- - - - - Sula (4)
- - - - - - Taliabo (2): KADAI [KZD] Indonesia (Maluku)
- - - - - - - TALIABU [TLV] Indonesia (Maluku)
- - - - - North Bomberai (4): ARGUNI [AGF] Indonesia (Irian Jaya)
- - - - - ONIN [ONI] Indonesia (Irian Jaya)
- - - - - SEKAR [SKZ] Indonesia (Irian Jaya)
- - - - - URUANGNIRIN [URN] Indonesia (Irian Jaya)
- - - - South Bomberai (1): KOWIAI [KWH] Indonesia (Irian Jaya)
- - - - Southeast Maluku (5)
- - - - - Kei-Tanimbar (3)
- - - - - - Kei-Fordata (2): FORDATA [FRD] Indonesia (Maluku)
- - - - - - - KEI [KEI] Indonesia (Maluku)
- - - - - - Yamdena (1): YAMDENA [JMD] Indonesia (Maluku)
- - - - - Southern (2): SELARU [SLU] Indonesia (Maluku)
- - - - - - SELUWASAN [SWH] Indonesia (Maluku)
- - - - - Teor-Kur (2): KUR [KUV] Indonesia (Maluku)
- - - - - TEOR [TEV] Indonesia (Maluku)
- - - - Timor (42)
- - - - - Flores-Lembata (13): ADONARA [ADA] Indonesia (Nusa Tenggara)
- - - - - - ALOR [AOL] Indonesia (Nusa Tenggara)
- - - - - - ILE APE [ILA] Indonesia (Nusa Tenggara)
- - - - - - KEDANG [KSX] Indonesia (Nusa Tenggara)
- - - - - - LAMAHOLOT [SLP] Indonesia (Nusa Tenggara)
- - - - - - LAMALERA [LMR] Indonesia (Nusa Tenggara)
- - - - - - LAMATUKA [LMQ] Indonesia (Nusa Tenggara)
- - - - - - LEMBATA, SOUTH [LMF] Indonesia (Nusa Tenggara)
- - - - - - LEMBATA, WEST [LMJ] Indonesia (Nusa Tenggara)
- - - - - - LEVUKA [LVU] Indonesia (Nusa Tenggara)
- - - - - - LEWO ELENG [LWE] Indonesia (Nusa Tenggara)
- - - - - - LEWOTOBI [LWT] Indonesia (Nusa Tenggara)
- - - - - SIKA [SKI] Indonesia (Nusa Tenggara)
- - - - - Helong (1): HELONG [HEG] Indonesia (Nusa Tenggara)
- - - - - Nuclear Timor (15): NAUETE [NXA] Timor Lorosae
- - - - - - East (7): GALOLI [GAL] Timor Lorosae
- - - - - - - IDATÉ [IDT] Timor Lorosae
- - - - - - - KEMAK [KEM] Timor Lorosae
- - - - - - - LAKALEI [LKA] Timor Lorosae
- - - - - - - MAMBAE [MGM] Timor Lorosae
- - - - - - - TETUN [TTM] Indonesia (Nusa Tenggara)
- - - - - - - TUKUDEDE [TKD] Timor Lorosae
- - - - - - Waima'a (3): HABU [HBU] Timor Lorosae
- - - - - - - KAIRUI-MIDIKI [KRD] Timor Lorosae
- - - - - - - WAIMA'A [WMH] Timor Lorosae
- - - - - - West (4): AMARASI [AAZ] Indonesia (Nusa Tenggara)
- - - - - - - ATONI [TMR] Indonesia (Nusa Tenggara)
- - - - - - - ROTE [ROT] Indonesia (Nusa Tenggara)
- - - - - - - ROTE, WESTERN [ROW] Indonesia (Nusa Tenggara)
- - - - - Southwest Maluku (13)
- - - - - - East Damar (1): DAMAR, EAST [DMR] Indonesia (Maluku)
- - - - - - Kisar-Roma (2): KISAR [KJE] Indonesia (Maluku)
- - - - - - - ROMA [RMM] Indonesia (Maluku)
- - - - - - Luang (2): LETI [LTI] Indonesia (Maluku)
- - - - - - - LUANG [LEX] Indonesia (Maluku)
- - - - - - Teun-Nila-Serua (3)
- - - - - - - Nila-Serua (2): NILA [NIL] Indonesia (Maluku)
- - - - - - - - SERUA [SRW] Indonesia (Maluku)

Austronesian (1262)
- Malayo-Polynesian (1239)
- - Central-Eastern (706)
- - - Central Malayo-Polynesian (162)
- - - - Timor (42)
- - - - - Southwest Maluku (13)
- - - - - - Teun-Nila-Serua (3)
- - - - - - - Teun (1): TE'UN [TVE] Indonesia (Maluku)
- - - - - - Wetar (5): APUTAI [APX] Indonesia (Maluku)
- - - - - - - ILIUN [ILU] Indonesia (Maluku)
- - - - - - - PERAI [WET] Indonesia (Maluku)
- - - - - - - TALUR [ILW] Indonesia (Maluku)
- - - - - - - TUGUN [TZN] Indonesia (Maluku)
- - - - West Damar (1): DAMAR, WEST [DRN] Indonesia (Maluku)
- - - Eastern Malayo-Polynesian (541)
- - - - Oceanic (502)
- - - - - Admiralty Islands (31)
- - - - - - Eastern (28)
- - - - - - - Manus (22)
- - - - - - - - East (12): ANDRA-HUS [ANX] Papua New Guinea
- - - - - - - - - ELU [ELU] Papua New Guinea
- - - - - - - - - ERE [TWP] Papua New Guinea
- - - - - - - - - KELE [SBC] Papua New Guinea
- - - - - - - - - KORO [KXR] Papua New Guinea
- - - - - - - - - KURTI [KTM] Papua New Guinea
- - - - - - - - - LEIPON [LEK] Papua New Guinea
- - - - - - - - - LELE [UGA] Papua New Guinea
- - - - - - - - - NALI [NSS] Papua New Guinea
- - - - - - - - - PAPITALAI [PAT] Papua New Guinea
- - - - - - - - - PONAM [NCC] Papua New Guinea
- - - - - - - - - TITAN [TTV] Papua New Guinea
- - - - - - - - Mokoreng-Loniu (2): LONIU [LOS] Papua New Guinea
- - - - - - - - - MOKERANG [MFT] Papua New Guinea
- - - - - - - - West (8): BIPI [BIQ] Papua New Guinea
- - - - - - - - - BOHUAI [RAK] Papua New Guinea
- - - - - - - - - HERMIT [LLF] Papua New Guinea
- - - - - - - - - KHEHEK [TLX] Papua New Guinea
- - - - - - - - - LIKUM [LIB] Papua New Guinea
- - - - - - - - - MONDROPOLON [MLY] Papua New Guinea
- - - - - - - - - NYINDROU [LID] Papua New Guinea
- - - - - - - - - SORI-HARENGAN [SBH] Papua New Guinea
- - - - - - - Pak-Tong (1): PAK-TONG [PKG] Papua New Guinea
- - - - - - - Southeast Islands (5): BALUAN-PAM [BLQ] Papua New Guinea
- - - - - - - - LENKAU [LER] Papua New Guinea
- - - - - - - - LOU [LOJ] Papua New Guinea
- - - - - - - - NAUNA [NCN] Papua New Guinea
- - - - - - - - PENCHAL [PEK] Papua New Guinea
- - - - - - Western (3): KANIET [KTK] Papua New Guinea
- - - - - - - SEIMAT [SSG] Papua New Guinea
- - - - - - - WUVULU-AUA [WUV] Papua New Guinea
- - - - - Central-Eastern Oceanic (234)
- - - - - - Remote Oceanic (199)
- - - - - - - Central Pacific (45)
- - - - - - - - East Fijian-Polynesian (42)
- - - - - - - - - East Fijian (4): FIJIAN [FJI] Fiji
- - - - - - - - - - GONE DAU [GOO] Fiji
- - - - - - - - - - LAUAN [LLX] Fiji
- - - - - - - - - - LOMAIVITI [LMV] Fiji

Austronesian (1262)
- Malayo-Polynesian (1239)
- - Central-Eastern (706)
- - - Eastern Malayo-Polynesian (541)
- - - - Oceanic (502)
- - - - - Central-Eastern Oceanic (234)
- - - - - - Remote Oceanic (199)
- - - - - - - Central Pacific (45)
- - - - - - - - East Fijian-Polynesian (42)
- - - - - - - - - Polynesian (38)
- - - - - - - - - - Nuclear (36)
- - - - - - - - - - - East (13)
- - - - - - - - - - - - Central (12): RAPA [RAY] French Polynesia
- - - - - - - - - - - - - Marquesic (4): HAWAIIAN [HWI] USA
- - - - - - - - - - - - - MANGAREVA [MRV] French Polynesia
- - - - - - - - - - - - - MARQUESAN, NORTH [MRQ] French Polynesia
- - - - - - - - - - - - - MARQUESAN, SOUTH [QMS] French Polynesia
- - - - - - - - - - - - - Tahitic (7): AUSTRAL [AUT] French Polynesia
- - - - - - - - - - - - - MAORI [MBF] New Zealand
- - - - - - - - - - - - - PENRHYN [PNH] Cook Islands
- - - - - - - - - - - - - RAKAHANGA-MANIHIKI [RKH] Cook Islands
- - - - - - - - - - - - - RAROTONGAN [RRT] Cook Islands
- - - - - - - - - - - - - TAHITIAN [THT] French Polynesia
- - - - - - - - - - - - - TUAMOTUAN [PMT] French Polynesia
- - - - - - - - - - - - Rapanui (1): RAPA NUI [PBA] Chile
- - - - - - - - - - - - Samoic-Outlier (23): NIUATOPUTAPU [NKP] Tonga
- - - - - - - - - - - - - East Uvean-Niuafo'ou (2): NIUAFO'OU [NUM] Tonga
- - - - - - - - - - - - - WALLISIAN [WAL] Wallis and Futuna
- - - - - - - - - - - - - Ellicean (8): KAPINGAMARANGI [KPG] Micronesia
- - - - - - - - - - - - - NUGURIA [NUR] Papua New Guinea
- - - - - - - - - - - - - NUKUMANU [NUQ] Papua New Guinea
- - - - - - - - - - - - - NUKUORO [NKR] Micronesia
- - - - - - - - - - - - - ONTONG JAVA [LUN] Solomon Islands
- - - - - - - - - - - - - SIKAIANA [SKY] Solomon Islands
- - - - - - - - - - - - - TAKUU [NHO] Papua New Guinea
- - - - - - - - - - - - - TUVALUAN [ELL] Tuvalu
- - - - - - - - - - - - - Futunic (9): ANUTA [AUD] Solomon Islands
- - - - - - - - - - - - - EMAE [MMW] Vanuatu
- - - - - - - - - - - - - FUTUNA, EAST [FUD] Wallis and Futuna
- - - - - - - - - - - - - FUTUNA-ANIWA [FUT] Vanuatu
- - - - - - - - - - - - - MELE-FILA [MXE] Vanuatu
- - - - - - - - - - - - - PILENI [PIV] Solomon Islands
- - - - - - - - - - - - - RENNELL [MNV] Solomon Islands
- - - - - - - - - - - - - TIKOPIA [TKP] Solomon Islands
- - - - - - - - - - - - - UVEAN, WEST [UVE] New Caledonia
- - - - - - - - - - - - Pukapuka (1): PUKAPUKA [PKP] Cook Islands
- - - - - - - - - - - - Samoan (1): SAMOAN [SMY] Western Samoa
- - - - - - - - - - - - Tokelauan (1): TOKELAUAN [TOK] Tokelau
- - - - - - - - - - - Tongic (2): NIUE [NIQ] Niue
- - - - - - - - - - - TONGAN [TOV] Tonga
- - - - - - - - - West Fijian-Rotuman (3)
- - - - - - - - - Rotuman (1): ROTUMAN [RTM] Fiji
- - - - - - - - - West Fijian (2): FIJIAN, WESTERN [WYY] Fiji
- - - - - - - - - NAMOSI-NAITASIRI-SERUA [BWB] Fiji
- - - - - - - Eastern Outer Islands (6)
- - - - - - - Utupua (3): AMBA [UTP] Solomon Islands
- - - - - - - - ASUMBOA [AUA] Solomon Islands
- - - - - - - - TANIMBILI [TBE] Solomon Islands
- - - - - - - Vanikoro (3): TANEMA [TNX] Solomon Islands
- - - - - - - - TEANU [TKW] Solomon Islands
- - - - - - - - VANO [VNK] Solomon Islands

Austronesian (1262)
- Malayo-Polynesian (1239)
- - Central-Eastern (706)
- - - Eastern Malayo-Polynesian (541)
- - - - Oceanic (502)
- - - - - Central-Eastern Oceanic (234)
- - - - - - Remote Oceanic (199)
- - - - - - - Loyalty Islands (3): DEHU [DEU] New Caledonia
- - - - - - - - IAAI [IAI] New Caledonia
- - - - - - - - NENGONE [NEN] New Caledonia
- - - - - - - Micronesian (20)
- - - - - - - - Micronesian Proper (19)
- - - - - - - - - Ikiribati (1): KIRIBATI [GLB] Kiribati
- - - - - - - - - Kusaiean (1): KOSRAEAN [KSI] Micronesia
- - - - - - - - - Marshallese (1): MARSHALLESE [MZM] Marshall Islands
- - - - - - - - - Ponapeic-Trukic (16)
- - - - - - - - - - Ponapeic (3): MOKILESE [MNO] Micronesia
- - - - - - - - - - - PINGELAPESE [PIF] Micronesia
- - - - - - - - - - - POHNPEIAN [PNF] Micronesia
- - - - - - - - - - Trukic (13): CAROLINIAN [CAL] Northern Mariana Islands
- - - - - - - - - - - CHUUKESE [TRU] Micronesia
- - - - - - - - - - - MAPIA [MPY] Indonesia (Irian Jaya)
- - - - - - - - - - - MORTLOCKESE [MRL] Micronesia
- - - - - - - - - - - NAMONUITO [NMT] Micronesia
- - - - - - - - - - - PÁÁFANG [PFA] Micronesia
- - - - - - - - - - - PULUWATESE [PUW] Micronesia
- - - - - - - - - - - SATAWALESE [STW] Micronesia
- - - - - - - - - - - SONSOROL [SOV] Palau
- - - - - - - - - - - TANAPAG [TPV] Northern Mariana Islands
- - - - - - - - - - - TOBIAN [TOX] Palau
- - - - - - - - - - - ULITHIAN [ULI] Micronesia
- - - - - - - - - - - WOLEAIAN [WOE] Micronesia
- - - - - - - - Nauruan (1): NAURUAN [NRU] Nauru
- - - - - - - New Caledonian (30)
- - - - - - - - Haekic (1): HAEKE [AEK] New Caledonia
- - - - - - - - Northern (17): HAVEKE [AVE] New Caledonia
- - - - - - - - - VAMALE [MKT] New Caledonia
- - - - - - - - - Central (2): CEMUHÎ [CAM] New Caledonia
- - - - - - - - - - PAICÎ [PRI] New Caledonia
- - - - - - - - - Extreme Northern (4): CAAC [MSQ] New Caledonia
- - - - - - - - - - KUMAK [NEE] New Caledonia
- - - - - - - - - - NYÂLAYU [YLY] New Caledonia
- - - - - - - - - - YUAGA [NUA] New Caledonia
- - - - - - - - - North (9): PWAAMEI [PME] New Caledonia
- - - - - - - - - - PWAPWA [POP] New Caledonia
- - - - - - - - - - Hmwaveke (3): BWATOO [BWA] New Caledonia
- - - - - - - - - - - HMWAVEKE [MRK] New Caledonia
- - - - - - - - - - - WAAMWANG [WMN] New Caledonia
- - - - - - - - - - Nemi (4): FWÂI [FWA] New Caledonia
- - - - - - - - - - - JAWE [JAZ] New Caledonia
- - - - - - - - - - - NEMI [NEM] New Caledonia
- - - - - - - - - - - PIJE [PIZ] New Caledonia
- - - - - - - - - Southern (12): MEA [MEG] New Caledonia
- - - - - - - - - - Extreme Southern (2): DUMBEA [DUF] New Caledonia
- - - - - - - - - - - NUMEE [KDK] New Caledonia
- - - - - - - - - - South (9)
- - - - - - - - - - - Wailic (5): AJIË [AJI] New Caledonia
- - - - - - - - - - - - ARHÂ [ARN] New Caledonia
- - - - - - - - - - - - ARHÖ [AOK] New Caledonia
- - - - - - - - - - - - NEKU [NEK] New Caledonia
- - - - - - - - - - - - OROWE [BPK] New Caledonia

Austronesian (1262)
- Malayo-Polynesian (1239)
- - Central-Eastern (706)
- - - Eastern Malayo-Polynesian (541)
- - - - Oceanic (502)
- - - - - Central-Eastern Oceanic (234)
- - - - - - Remote Oceanic (199)
- - - - - - - New Caledonian (30)
- - - - - - - - Southern (12)
- - - - - - - - - South (9)
- - - - - - - - - - Xaracuu-Xaragure (2): XÂRÂCÙÙ [ANE] New Caledonia
- - - - - - - - - - XARAGURE [ARG] New Caledonia
- - - - - - - - - - Zire-Tiri (2): TIRI [CIR] New Caledonia
- - - - - - - - - - ZIRE [SIH] New Caledonia
- - - - - - - - North and Central Vanuatu (95)
- - - - - - - - East Santo (5)
- - - - - - - - - North (1): SAKAO [SKU] Vanuatu
- - - - - - - - - South (4): BUTMAS-TUR [BNR] Vanuatu
- - - - - - - - - - LOREDIAKARKAR [LNN] Vanuatu
- - - - - - - - - - POLONOMBAUK [PLB] Vanuatu
- - - - - - - - - - SHARK BAY [SSV] Vanuatu
- - - - - - - - Malekula Interior (12)
- - - - - - - - - Labo (1): LABO [MWI] Vanuatu
- - - - - - - - - Malekula Central (8): KATBOL [TMB] Vanuatu
- - - - - - - - - LAREVAT [LRV] Vanuatu
- - - - - - - - - LINGARAK [LGK] Vanuatu
- - - - - - - - - LITZLITZ [LTZ] Vanuatu
- - - - - - - - - MARAGUS [MRS] Vanuatu
- - - - - - - - - NAMBAS, BIG [NMB] Vanuatu
- - - - - - - - - NASARIAN [NVH] Vanuatu
- - - - - - - - - VINMAVIS [VNM] Vanuatu
- - - - - - - - - Small Nambas (3): DIXON REEF [DIX] Vanuatu
- - - - - - - - - LETEMBOI [NMS] Vanuatu
- - - - - - - - - REPANBITIP [RPN] Vanuatu
- - - - - - - - Northeast Vanuatu-Banks Islands (78)
- - - - - - - - - Central Vanuatu (5): EFATE, NORTH [LLP] Vanuatu
- - - - - - - - - EFATE, SOUTH [ERK] Vanuatu
- - - - - - - - - ETON [ETN] Vanuatu
- - - - - - - - - LELEPA [LPA] Vanuatu
- - - - - - - - - NAMAKURA [NMK] Vanuatu
- - - - - - - - - East Vanuatu (29): AMBAE, EAST [OMB] Vanuatu
- - - - - - - - - AMBAE, WEST [NND] Vanuatu
- - - - - - - - - AMBRYM, NORTH [MMG] Vanuatu
- - - - - - - - - AMBRYM, SOUTHEAST [TVK] Vanuatu
- - - - - - - - - APMA [APP] Vanuatu
- - - - - - - - - BAETORA [BTR] Vanuatu
- - - - - - - - - DAKAKA [BPA] Vanuatu
- - - - - - - - - HANO [LML] Vanuatu
- - - - - - - - - HIW [HIW] Vanuatu
- - - - - - - - - KORO [KRF] Vanuatu
- - - - - - - - - LAKONA [LKN] Vanuatu
- - - - - - - - - LEHALI [TQL] Vanuatu
- - - - - - - - - LEHALURUP [URR] Vanuatu
- - - - - - - - - LONWOLWOL [CRC] Vanuatu
- - - - - - - - - MAEWO, CENTRAL [MWO] Vanuatu
- - - - - - - - - MARINO [MRB] Vanuatu
- - - - - - - - - MERLAV [MRM] Vanuatu
- - - - - - - - - MOSINA [MSN] Vanuatu
- - - - - - - - - MOTA [MTT] Vanuatu
- - - - - - - - - MOTLAV [MLV] Vanuatu
- - - - - - - - - NUME [TGS] Vanuatu

Austronesian (1262)
- Malayo-Polynesian (1239)
- - Central-Eastern (706)
- - - Eastern Malayo-Polynesian (541)
- - - - Oceanic (502)
- - - - - Central-Eastern Oceanic (234)
- - - - - - Remote Oceanic (199)
- - - - - - - North and Central Vanuatu (95)
- - - - - - - - Northeast Vanuatu-Banks Islands (78)
- - - - - - - - - East Vanuatu (29): PAAMA [PMA] Vanuatu
- - - - - - - - - - PORT VATO [PTV] Vanuatu
- - - - - - - - - - SA [SSA] Vanuatu
- - - - - - - - - - SEKE [SKE] Vanuatu
- - - - - - - - - - SOWA [SWW] Vanuatu
- - - - - - - - - - TOGA [LHT] Vanuatu
- - - - - - - - - - VATRATA [VLR] Vanuatu
- - - - - - - - - - WETAMUT [WWO] Vanuatu
- - - - - - - - - Epi (6)
- - - - - - - - - - Bieria-Mai (2): BIERIA [BRJ] Vanuatu
- - - - - - - - - - - MAII [MMM] Vanuatu
- - - - - - - - - - Lamenu-Baki (4)
- - - - - - - - - - - Baki-Bierebo (2): BAKI [BKI] Vanuatu
- - - - - - - - - - - - BIEREBO [BNK] Vanuatu
- - - - - - - - - - - Lamenu-Lewo (2): LAMENU [LMU] Vanuatu
- - - - - - - - - - - LEWO [LWW] Vanuatu
- - - - - - - - - Malekula Coastal (14): AULUA [AUL] Vanuatu
- - - - - - - - - - AXAMB [AHB] Vanuatu
- - - - - - - - - - BURMBAR [VRT] Vanuatu
- - - - - - - - - - MAE [MME] Vanuatu
- - - - - - - - - - MALFAXAL [MLX] Vanuatu
- - - - - - - - - - MALUA BAY [MLL] Vanuatu
- - - - - - - - - - MASKELYNES [KLV] Vanuatu
- - - - - - - - - - MPOTOVORO [MVT] Vanuatu
- - - - - - - - - - PORT SANDWICH [PSW] Vanuatu
- - - - - - - - - - REREP [PGK] Vanuatu
- - - - - - - - - - SOUTH WEST BAY [SNS] Vanuatu
- - - - - - - - - - UNUA [ONU] Vanuatu
- - - - - - - - - - URIPIV-WALA-RANO-ATCHIN [UPV] Vanuatu
- - - - - - - - - - VAO [VAO] Vanuatu
- - - - - - - - - West Santo (24): AKEI [TSR] Vanuatu
- - - - - - - - - - AMBLONG [ALM] Vanuatu
- - - - - - - - - - AORE [AOR] Vanuatu
- - - - - - - - - - ARAKI [AKR] Vanuatu
- - - - - - - - - - FORTSENAL [FRT] Vanuatu
- - - - - - - - - - MAFEA [MKV] Vanuatu
- - - - - - - - - - MALO [MLA] Vanuatu
- - - - - - - - - - MEREI [LMB] Vanuatu
- - - - - - - - - - MOROUAS [MRP] Vanuatu
- - - - - - - - - - NARANGO [NRG] Vanuatu
- - - - - - - - - - NAVUT [NSW] Vanuatu
- - - - - - - - - - NOKUKU [NKK] Vanuatu
- - - - - - - - - - PIAMATSINA [PTR] Vanuatu
- - - - - - - - - - RORIA [RGA] Vanuatu
- - - - - - - - - - TAMBOTALO [TLS] Vanuatu
- - - - - - - - - - TANGOA [TGP] Vanuatu
- - - - - - - - - - TASMATE [TMT] Vanuatu
- - - - - - - - - - TIALE [MNL] Vanuatu
- - - - - - - - - - TOLOMAKO [TLM] Vanuatu
- - - - - - - - - - TUTUBA [TMI] Vanuatu
- - - - - - - - - - VALPEI [VLP] Vanuatu
- - - - - - - - - - VUNAPU [VNP] Vanuatu

Austronesian (1262)
- Malayo-Polynesian (1239)
- - Central-Eastern (706)
- - - Eastern Malayo-Polynesian (541)
- - - - Oceanic (502)
- - - - - Central-Eastern Oceanic (234)
- - - - - - Remote Oceanic (199)
- - - - - - - North and Central Vanuatu (95)
- - - - - - - - Northeast Vanuatu-Banks Islands (78)
- - - - - - - - - West Santo (24): WAILAPA [WLR] Vanuatu
- - - - - - - - - - WUSI [WSI] Vanuatu
- - - - - - - South Vanuatu (9)
- - - - - - - - Aneityum (1): ANEITYUM [ATY] Vanuatu
- - - - - - - - Erromanga (3): IFO [IFF] Vanuatu
- - - - - - - - - SIE [ERG] Vanuatu
- - - - - - - - - URA [UUR] Vanuatu
- - - - - - - - Tanna (5): KWAMERA [TNK] Vanuatu
- - - - - - - - - LENAKEL [TNL] Vanuatu
- - - - - - - - - TANNA, NORTH [TNN] Vanuatu
- - - - - - - - - TANNA, SOUTHWEST [NWI] Vanuatu
- - - - - - - - - WHITESANDS [TNP] Vanuatu
- - - - - - - Southeast Solomonic (26)
- - - - - - - - Gela-Guadalcanal (7)
- - - - - - - - - Bughotu (1): BUGHOTU [BGT] Solomon Islands
- - - - - - - - - Gela (2): GELA [NLG] Solomon Islands
- - - - - - - - - - LENGO [LGR] Solomon Islands
- - - - - - - - - Guadalcanal (4): BIRAO [BRR] Solomon Islands
- - - - - - - - - - GHARI [GRI] Solomon Islands
- - - - - - - - - - MALANGO [MLN] Solomon Islands
- - - - - - - - - - TALISE [TLR] Solomon Islands
- - - - - - - - Malaita-San Cristobal (19)
- - - - - - - - - Malaita (14)
- - - - - - - - - - Longgu (1): LONGGU [LGU] Solomon Islands
- - - - - - - - - - Northern (9): BAEGGU [BVD] Solomon Islands
- - - - - - - - - - - BAELELEA [BVC] Solomon Islands
- - - - - - - - - - - FATALEKA [FAR] Solomon Islands
- - - - - - - - - - - GULA'ALAA [GMB] Solomon Islands
- - - - - - - - - - - KWAIO [KWD] Solomon Islands
- - - - - - - - - - - KWARA'AE [KWF] Solomon Islands
- - - - - - - - - - - LANGALANGA [LGL] Solomon Islands
- - - - - - - - - - - LAU [LLU] Solomon Islands
- - - - - - - - - - - TO'ABAITA [MLU] Solomon Islands
- - - - - - - - - - Southern (4): 'ARE'ARE [ALU] Solomon Islands
- - - - - - - - - - - DORI'O [DOR] Solomon Islands
- - - - - - - - - - - OROHA [ORA] Solomon Islands
- - - - - - - - - - - SA'A [APB] Solomon Islands
- - - - - - - - - San Cristobal (5): AROSI [AIA] Solomon Islands
- - - - - - - - - - BAURO [BXA] Solomon Islands
- - - - - - - - - - FAGANI [FAF] Solomon Islands
- - - - - - - - - - KAHUA [AGW] Solomon Islands
- - - - - - - - - - SANTA ANA [STN] Solomon Islands
- - - - - Western Oceanic (237)
- - - - - - Meso Melanesian (66)
- - - - - - - Bali-Vitu (2): MUDUAPA [WIV] Papua New Guinea
- - - - - - - - UNEAPA [BBN] Papua New Guinea
- - - - - - - New Ireland (60)
- - - - - - - - Lavongai-Nalik (6): KARA [LEU] Papua New Guinea
- - - - - - - - - MANDARA [TBF] Papua New Guinea
- - - - - - - - - NALIK [NAL] Papua New Guinea
- - - - - - - - - TIANG [TBJ] Papua New Guinea
- - - - - - - - - TIGAK [TGC] Papua New Guinea

Austronesian (1262)
- Malayo-Polynesian (1239)
- - Central-Eastern (706)
- - - Eastern Malayo-Polynesian (541)
- - - - Oceanic (502)
- - - - - Western Oceanic (237)
- - - - - - Meso Melanesian (66)
- - - - - - - New Ireland (60)
- - - - - - - - Lavongai-Nalik (6): TUNGAG [LCM] Papua New Guinea
- - - - - - - - Madak (3): BAROK [BJK] Papua New Guinea
- - - - - - - - LAVATBURA-LAMUSONG [LBV] Papua New Guinea
- - - - - - - - MADAK [MMX] Papua New Guinea
- - - - - - - South New Ireland-Northwest Solomonic (48): BILUR [BXF] Papua New Guinea
- - - - - - - - Choiseul (4): BABATANA [BAQ] Solomon Islands
- - - - - - - - - RIRIO [RRI] Solomon Islands
- - - - - - - - - VAGHUA [TVA] Solomon Islands
- - - - - - - - - VARISI [VRS] Solomon Islands
- - - - - - - - Mono-Uruava (4): MINIGIR [VMG] Papua New Guinea
- - - - - - - - - MONO [MTE] Solomon Islands
- - - - - - - - - TORAU [TTU] Papua New Guinea
- - - - - - - - - URUAVA [URV] Papua New Guinea
- - - - - - - - Nehan-North Bougainville (10)
- - - - - - - - - Buka (3): PETATS [PEX] Papua New Guinea
- - - - - - - - - - Halia (2): HAKÖ [HAO] Papua New Guinea
- - - - - - - - - - - HALIA [HLA] Papua New Guinea
- - - - - - - - - Nehan (1): NEHAN [NSN] Papua New Guinea
- - - - - - - - - Papapana (1): PAPAPANA [PAA] Papua New Guinea
- - - - - - - - - Saposa-Tinputz (4): HAHON [HAH] Papua New Guinea
- - - - - - - - - SAPOSA [SPS] Papua New Guinea
- - - - - - - - - TEOP [TIO] Papua New Guinea
- - - - - - - - - TINPUTZ [TPZ] Papua New Guinea
- - - - - - - - - Solos (1): SOLOS [SOL] Papua New Guinea
- - - - - - - - New Georgia (10)
- - - - - - - - - East (2): MAROVO [MVO] Solomon Islands
- - - - - - - - - - VANGUNU [MPR] Solomon Islands
- - - - - - - - - West (8): DUKE [NKE] Solomon Islands
- - - - - - - - - - GHANONGGA [GHN] Solomon Islands
- - - - - - - - - - HOAVA [HOA] Solomon Islands
- - - - - - - - - - KUSAGHE [KSG] Solomon Islands
- - - - - - - - - - LUNGGA [LGA] Solomon Islands
- - - - - - - - - - ROVIANA [RUG] Solomon Islands
- - - - - - - - - - SIMBO [SBB] Solomon Islands
- - - - - - - - - - UGHELE [UGE] Solomon Islands
- - - - - - - - Patpatar-Tolai (10): GURAMALUM [GRZ] Papua New Guinea
- - - - - - - - - KANDAS [KQW] Papua New Guinea
- - - - - - - - - KONOMALA [KOA] Papua New Guinea
- - - - - - - - - KUANUA [KSD] Papua New Guinea
- - - - - - - - - LABEL [LBB] Papua New Guinea
- - - - - - - - - LAK [SJR] Papua New Guinea
- - - - - - - - - PATPATAR [GFK] Papua New Guinea
- - - - - - - - - RAMOAAINA [RAI] Papua New Guinea
- - - - - - - - - SURSURUNGA [SGZ] Papua New Guinea
- - - - - - - - - TANGGA [TGG] Papua New Guinea
- - - - - - - - Piva-Banoni (2): BANONI [BCM] Papua New Guinea
- - - - - - - - PIVA [TGI] Papua New Guinea
- - - - - - - - Santa Isabel (7)
- - - - - - - - - Central (3): BLABLANGA [BLP] Solomon Islands
- - - - - - - - - - KOKOTA [KKK] Solomon Islands
- - - - - - - - - - ZAZAO [JAJ] Solomon Islands
- - - - - - - - - East (2): CHEKE HOLO [MRN] Solomon Islands
- - - - - - - - - - GAO [GGA] Solomon Islands

Austronesian (1262)
- Malayo-Polynesian (1239)
- - Central-Eastern (706)
- - - Eastern Malayo-Polynesian (541)
- - - - Oceanic (502)
- - - - - Western Oceanic (237)
- - - - - - Meso Melanesian (66)
- - - - - - - New Ireland (60)
- - - - - - - - South New Ireland-Northwest Solomonic (48)
- - - - - - - - - Santa Isabel (7)
- - - - - - - - - - West (2): LAGHU [LGB] Solomon Islands
- - - - - - - - - - - ZABANA [KJI] Solomon Islands
- - - - - - - - - Tabar (2): LIHIR [LIH] Papua New Guinea
- - - - - - - - - - NOTSI [NCF] Papua New Guinea
- - - - - - - - - Tomoip (1): TOMOIP [TUM] Papua New Guinea
- - - - - - - - Willaumez (4): BOLA [BNP] Papua New Guinea
- - - - - - - - BULU [BJL] Papua New Guinea
- - - - - - - - MERAMERA [MXM] Papua New Guinea
- - - - - - - - NAKANAI [NAK] Papua New Guinea
- - - - - North New Guinea (107)
- - - - - - Huon Gulf (32)
- - - - - - - Markham (13)
- - - - - - - - Lower (7)
- - - - - - - - - Busu (5): ARIBWATSA [LAZ] Papua New Guinea
- - - - - - - - - - ARIBWAUNG [YLU] Papua New Guinea
- - - - - - - - - - DUWET [GVE] Papua New Guinea
- - - - - - - - - - MUSOM [MSU] Papua New Guinea
- - - - - - - - - - NAFI [SRF] Papua New Guinea
- - - - - - - - - Labu (1): LABU [LBU] Papua New Guinea
- - - - - - - - - Wampar (1): WAMPAR [LBQ] Papua New Guinea
- - - - - - - - Upper (3)
- - - - - - - - - Adzera (1): ADZERA [AZR] Papua New Guinea
- - - - - - - - - Mountain (2): MARI [HOB] Papua New Guinea
- - - - - - - - - - WAMPUR [WAZ] Papua New Guinea
- - - - - - - - - Watut (3): WATUT, MIDDLE [MPL] Papua New Guinea
- - - - - - - - - - WATUT, NORTH [UNA] Papua New Guinea
- - - - - - - - - - WATUT, SOUTH [MCY] Papua New Guinea
- - - - - - - - North (3): BUGAWAC [BUK] Papua New Guinea
- - - - - - - - KELA [KCL] Papua New Guinea
- - - - - - - - YABEM [JAE] Papua New Guinea
- - - - - - - Numbami (1): NUMBAMI [SIJ] Papua New Guinea
- - - - - - - South (15)
- - - - - - - - Hote-Buang (14)
- - - - - - - - - Buang (12): BUANG, MANGGA [MMO] Papua New Guinea
- - - - - - - - - BUANG, MAPOS [BZH] Papua New Guinea
- - - - - - - - - KAPIN [TBX] Papua New Guinea
- - - - - - - - - PIU [PIX] Papua New Guinea
- - - - - - - - - VEHES [VAL] Papua New Guinea
- - - - - - - - - Mumeng (7): DAMBI [DAC] Papua New Guinea
- - - - - - - - - - DENGALU [DEA] Papua New Guinea
- - - - - - - - - - GORAKOR [GOC] Papua New Guinea
- - - - - - - - - - KUMALU [KSL] Papua New Guinea
- - - - - - - - - - MUMENG [MZI] Papua New Guinea
- - - - - - - - - - PATEP [PTP] Papua New Guinea
- - - - - - - - - - ZENAG [ZEG] Papua New Guinea
- - - - - - - - - Hote (2): HOTE [HOT] Papua New Guinea
- - - - - - - - - - YAMAP [YMP] Papua New Guinea
- - - - - - - - Kaiwa (1): IWAL [KBM] Papua New Guinea
- - - - - - Ngero-Vitiaz (46)
- - - - - - - Ngero (6)
- - - - - - - - Bariai (4): BARIAI [BCH] Papua New Guinea

Austronesian (1262)
- Malayo-Polynesian (1239)
- - Central-Eastern (706)
- - - Eastern Malayo-Polynesian (541)
- - - - Oceanic (502)
- - - - - Western Oceanic (237)
- - - - - - North New Guinea (107)
- - - - - - - Ngero-Vitiaz (46)
- - - - - - - - Ngero (6)
- - - - - - - . - - - Bariai (4): KOVE [KVC] Papua New Guinea
- - - - - - - - - - LUSI [KHL] Papua New Guinea
- - - - - - - - - - MALALAMAI [MMT] Papua New Guinea
- - - - - - - - - Tuam (2): GITUA [GIL] Papua New Guinea
- - - - - - - - - - MUTU [TUC] Papua New Guinea
- - - - - - - - - Vitiaz (40)
- - - - - - - - - Bel (8)
- - - - - - - - - Astrolabe (3): AWAD BING [BCU] Papua New Guinea
- - - - - - - - - - MINDIRI [MPN] Papua New Guinea
- - - - - - - - - - WAB [WAB] Papua New Guinea
- - - - - - - - - Nuclear Bel (5)
- - - - - - - - - Northern (4): BILBIL [BRZ] Papua New Guinea
- - - - - - - - - - - GEDAGED [GDD] Papua New Guinea
- - - - - - - - - - - MATUKAR [MJK] Papua New Guinea
- - - - - - - - - - - TAKIA [TBC] Papua New Guinea
- - - - - - - - - Southern (1): MARIK [DAD] Papua New Guinea
- - - - - - - - Kilenge-Maleu (1): MALEU-KILENGE [MGL] Papua New Guinea
- - - - - - - - Korap (4): AROP-LOKEP [APR] Papua New Guinea
- - - - - - - - - BARIM [BBV] Papua New Guinea
- - - - - - - - - LUKEP [LOA] Papua New Guinea
- - - - - - - - - MALASANGA [MQZ] Papua New Guinea
- - - - - - - - Mangap-Mbula (1): MBULA [MNA] Papua New Guinea
- - - - - - - - Mengen (3): LOTE [UVL] Papua New Guinea
- - - - - - - - - MAMUSI [KDF] Papua New Guinea
- - - - - - - - - MENGEN [MEE] Papua New Guinea
- - - - - - - - Roinji-Nenaya (2): MATO [NIU] Papua New Guinea
- - - - - - - - - RONJI [ROE] Papua New Guinea
- - - - - - - - Sio (1): SIO [SIO] Papua New Guinea
- - - - - - - - Southwest New Britain (19)
- - - - - - - - - Amara (1): AMARA [AIE] Papua New Guinea
- - - - - - - - - Arawe-Pasismanua (16)
- - - - - - - - - - Arawe (10): MANGSENG [MBH] Papua New Guinea
- - - - - - - - - - - East Arawe (5): AKOLET [AKT] Papua New Guinea
- - - - - - - - - - - AVAU [AVB] Papua New Guinea
- - - - - - - - - - - BEBELI [BEK] Papua New Guinea
- - - - - - - - - - - GASMATA [GSA] Papua New Guinea
- - - - - - - - - - - LESING-GELIMI [LET] Papua New Guinea
- - - - - - - - - - - West Arawe (4): AIKLEP [MWG] Papua New Guinea
- - - - - - - - - - - APALIK [PLI] Papua New Guinea
- - - - - - - - - - - GIMI [GIP] Papua New Guinea
- - - - - - - - - - - SOLONG [AAW] Papua New Guinea
- - - - - - - - - - Pasismanua (6): GETMATA [GET] Papua New Guinea
- - - - - - - - - - KARORE [XKX] Papua New Guinea
- - - - - - - - - - KAULONG [PSS] Papua New Guinea
- - - - - - - - - - MIU [MPO] Papua New Guinea
- - - - - - - - - - PSOHOH [BCL] Papua New Guinea
- - - - - - - - - - SENGSENG [SSZ] Papua New Guinea
- - - - - - - - - Bibling (2): LAMOGAI [LMG] Papua New Guinea
- - - - - - - - - - MOUK-ARIA [MWH] Papua New Guinea
- - - - - - - - Tami (1): TAMI [TMY] Papua New Guinea
- - - - - - - Sarmi-Jayapura Bay (13)
- - - - - - - Jayapura Bay (3): KAYUPULAU [KZU] Indonesia (Irian Jaya)

Austronesian (1262)
- Malayo-Polynesian (1239)
- - Central-Eastern (706)
- - - Eastern Malayo-Polynesian (541)
- - - - Oceanic (502)
- - - - - Western Oceanic (237)
- - - - - - North New Guinea (107)
- - - - - - - Sarmi-Jayapura Bay (13)
- - - - - - - - Jayapura Bay (3): ORMU [ORZ] Indonesia (Irian Jaya)
- - - - - - - - - TOBATI [TTI] Indonesia (Irian Jaya)
- - - - - - - - Sarmi (10): ANUS [AUQ] Indonesia (Irian Jaya)
- - - - - - - - - BONGGO [BPG] Indonesia (Irian Jaya)
- - - - - - - - - LIKI [LIO] Indonesia (Irian Jaya)
- - - - - - - - - MASIMASI [ISM] Indonesia (Irian Jaya)
- - - - - - - - - PODENA [PDN] Indonesia (Irian Jaya)
- - - - - - - - - SOBEI [SOB] Indonesia (Irian Jaya)
- - - - - - - - - TARPIA [SUF] Indonesia (Irian Jaya)
- - - - - - - - - WAKDE [WKD] Indonesia (Irian Jaya)
- - - - - - - - - YAMNA [YMN] Indonesia (Irian Jaya)
- - - - - - - - - YARSUN [YRS] Indonesia (Irian Jaya)
- - - - - - - Schouten (16)
- - - - - - - - Kairiru-Manam (9)
- - - - - - - - - Kairiru (3): KAIEP [KBW] Papua New Guinea
- - - - - - - - - KAIRIRU [KXA] Papua New Guinea
- - - - - - - - - TEREBU [TRB] Papua New Guinea
- - - - - - - - - Manam (6): BIEM [BMC] Papua New Guinea
- - - - - - - - - KIS [KIS] Papua New Guinea
- - - - - - - - - MANAM [MVA] Papua New Guinea
- - - - - - - - - MEDEBUR [MJM] Papua New Guinea
- - - - - - - - - SEPA [SPE] Papua New Guinea
- - - - - - - - - WOGEO [WOC] Papua New Guinea
- - - - - - - - Siau (7): AROP-SISSANO [APS] Papua New Guinea
- - - - - - - - - MALOL [MBK] Papua New Guinea
- - - - - - - - - SERA [SRY] Papua New Guinea
- - - - - - - - - SISSANO [SSW] Papua New Guinea
- - - - - - - - - TUMLEO [TMQ] Papua New Guinea
- - - - - - - - - ULAU-SUAIN [SVB] Papua New Guinea
- - - - - - - - - YAKAMUL [YKM] Papua New Guinea
- - - - - - Papuan Tip (62)
- - - - - - - Nuclear (42)
- - - - - - - - Maisin (1): MAISIN [MBQ] Papua New Guinea
- - - - - - - - North Papuan Mainland-D'Entrecasteaux (34)
- - - - - - - - - Anuki (1): ANUKI [AUI] Papua New Guinea
- - - - - - - - - Are-Taupota (16)
- - - - - - - - - - Are (7): ARE [MWC] Papua New Guinea
- - - - - - - - - - - ARIFAMA-MINIAFIA [AAI] Papua New Guinea
- - - - - - - - - - - DOGA [DGG] Papua New Guinea
- - - - - - - - - - - GAPAPAIWA [PWG] Papua New Guinea
- - - - - - - - - - - GHAYAVI [BMK] Papua New Guinea
- - - - - - - - - - - UBIR [UBR] Papua New Guinea
- - - - - - - - - - - WATALUMA [WAT] Papua New Guinea
- - - - - - - - - - Taupota (9): GWEDA [GRW] Papua New Guinea
- - - - - - - - - - - HAIGWAI [HGW] Papua New Guinea
- - - - - - - - - - - MAIWALA [MUM] Papua New Guinea
- - - - - - - - - - - MINAVEHA [MVN] Papua New Guinea
- - - - - - - - - - - TAUPOTA [TPA] Papua New Guinea
- - - - - - - - - - - TAWALA [TBO] Papua New Guinea
- - - - - - - - - - - WA'EMA [WAG] Papua New Guinea
- - - - - - - - - - - WEDAU [WED] Papua New Guinea
- - - - - - - - - - - YAKAIKEKE [YKK] Papua New Guinea
- - - - - - - - - Bwaidoga (7): BWAIDOKA [BWD] Papua New Guinea

Austronesian (1262)
- Malayo-Polynesian (1239)
- - Central-Eastern (706)
- - - Eastern Malayo-Polynesian (541)
- - - - Oceanic (502)
- - - - - Western Oceanic (237)
- - - - - - Papuan Tip (62)
- - - - - - - Nuclear (42)
- - - - - - - - North Papuan Mainland-D'Entrecasteaux (34)
- - - - - - - - - Bwaidoga (7): DIODIO [DDI] Papua New Guinea
- - - - - - - - - IAMALELE [YML] Papua New Guinea
- - - - - - - - - IDUNA [VIV] Papua New Guinea
- - - - - - - - - KOLUAWAWA [KLX] Papua New Guinea
- - - - - - - - - MAIADOM [MZZ] Papua New Guinea
- - - - - - - - - MOLIMA [MOX] Papua New Guinea
- - - - - - - - - Dobu-Duau (7): BOSILEWA [BOS] Papua New Guinea
- - - - - - - - - BUNAMA [BDD] Papua New Guinea
- - - - - - - - - DOBU [DOB] Papua New Guinea
- - - - - - - - - DUAU [DUA] Papua New Guinea
- - - - - - - - - GALEYA [GAR] Papua New Guinea
- - - - - - - - - MWATEBU [MWA] Papua New Guinea
- - - - - - - - - SEWA BAY [SEW] Papua New Guinea
- - - - - - - - Gumawana (1): GUMAWANA [GVS] Papua New Guinea
- - - - - - - - Kakabai (2): DAWAWA [DWW] Papua New Guinea
- - - - - - - - KAKABAI [KQF] Papua New Guinea
- - - - - - - - Suauic (7): 'AUHELAWA [KUD] Papua New Guinea
- - - - - - - - BUHUTU [BXH] Papua New Guinea
- - - - - - - - BWANABWANA [TTE] Papua New Guinea
- - - - - - - - OYA'OYA [OYY] Papua New Guinea
- - - - - - - - SALIBA [SBE] Papua New Guinea
- - - - - - - - SUAU [SWP] Papua New Guinea
- - - - - - - - WAGAWAGA [WGW] Papua New Guinea
- - - - - - - Peripheral (20)
- - - - - - - Central Papuan (14)
- - - - - - - Oumic (4): OUMA [OUM] Papua New Guinea
- - - - - - - - Magoric (3): BINA [BMN] Papua New Guinea
- - - - - - - - - MAGORI [MDR] Papua New Guinea
- - - - - - - - - YOBA [YOB] Papua New Guinea
- - - - - - - - Sinagoro-Keapara (4): HULA [HUL] Papua New Guinea
- - - - - - - - - KEOPARA [KHZ] Papua New Guinea
- - - - - - - - - MOTU [MEU] Papua New Guinea
- - - - - - - - - SINAUGORO [SNC] Papua New Guinea
- - - - - - - - West Central Papuan (6)
- - - - - - - - Gabadi (1): KABADI [KBT] Papua New Guinea
- - - - - - - - Nuclear (5): DOURA [DON] Papua New Guinea
- - - - - - - - - KUNI [KSE] Papua New Guinea
- - - - - - - - - MEKEO [MEK] Papua New Guinea
- - - - - - - - - NARA [NRZ] Papua New Guinea
- - - - - - - - - RORO [RRO] Papua New Guinea
- - - - - - - Kilivila-Louisiades (6)
- - - - - - - - Kilivila (3): BUDIBUD [BTP] Papua New Guinea
- - - - - - - - - KILIVILA [KIJ] Papua New Guinea
- - - - - - - - - MUYUW [MYW] Papua New Guinea
- - - - - - - - Misima (1): MISIMA-PANEATI [MPX] Papua New Guinea
- - - - - - - - Nimoa-Sudest (2): NIMOA [NMW] Papua New Guinea
- - - - - - - - - SUDEST [TGO] Papua New Guinea
- - - - - - St. Matthias (2): MUSSAU-EMIRA [EMI] Papua New Guinea
- - - - - - - TENIS [TNS] Papua New Guinea
- - - - South Halmahera-West New Guinea (39)
- - - - - South Halmahera (6)
- - - - - East Makian-Gane (2): GANE [GZN] Indonesia (Maluku)

Austronesian (1262)
- Malayo-Polynesian (1239)
- - Central-Eastern (706)
- - - Eastern Malayo-Polynesian (541)
- - - - South Halmahera-West New Guinea (39)
- - - - - South Halmahera (6)
- - - - - - East Makian-Gane (2): MAKIAN, EAST [MKY] Indonesia (Maluku)
- - - - - - Southeast (4): BULI [BZQ] Indonesia (Maluku)
- - - - - - - MABA [MQA] Indonesia (Maluku)
- - - - - - - PATANI [PTN] Indonesia (Maluku)
- - - - - - - SAWAI [SZW] Indonesia (Maluku)
- - - - - West New Guinea (33)
- - - - - - Bomberai (2): BEDOANAS [BED] Indonesia (Irian Jaya)
- - - - - - EROKWANAS [ERW] Indonesia (Irian Jaya)
- - - - - - Cenderawasih Bay (31)
- - - - - - - Biakic (3): BIAK [BHW] Indonesia (Irian Jaya)
- - - - - - - DUSNER [DSN] Indonesia (Irian Jaya)
- - - - - - - MEOSWAR [MVX] Indonesia (Irian Jaya)
- - - - - - - Iresim (1): IRESIM [IRE] Indonesia (Irian Jaya)
- - - - - - - Mor (1): MOR [MHZ] Indonesia (Irian Jaya)
- - - - - - - Raja Ampat (9): AS [ASZ] Indonesia (Irian Jaya)
- - - - - - - - GEBE [GEI] Indonesia (Maluku)
- - - - - - - - KAWE [KGB] Indonesia (Irian Jaya)
- - - - - - - - LEGENYEM [LCC] Indonesia (Irian Jaya)
- - - - - - - - MADEN [XMX] Indonesia (Irian Jaya)
- - - - - - - - MATBAT [XMT] Indonesia (Irian Jaya)
- - - - - - - - MA'YA [SLZ] Indonesia (Irian Jaya)
- - - - - - - - PALAMUL [PLX] Indonesia (Irian Jaya)
- - - - - - - - WAIGEO [WGO] Indonesia (Irian Jaya)
- - - - - - - Tandia (1): TANDIA [TNI] Indonesia (Irian Jaya)
- - - - - - - Waropen (1): WAROPEN [WRP] Indonesia (Irian Jaya)
- - - - - - - Yapen (13)
- - - - - - - - Central-Western (11): AMBAI [AMK] Indonesia (Irian Jaya)
- - - - - - - - ANSUS [AND] Indonesia (Irian Jaya)
- - - - - - - - BUSAMI [BSM] Indonesia (Irian Jaya)
- - - - - - - - MARAU [MVR] Indonesia (Irian Jaya)
- - - - - - - - MUNGGUI [MTH] Indonesia (Irian Jaya)
- - - - - - - - PAPUMA [PPM] Indonesia (Irian Jaya)
- - - - - - - - POM [PMO] Indonesia (Irian Jaya)
- - - - - - - - ROON [RNN] Indonesia (Irian Jaya)
- - - - - - - - SERUI-LAUT [SEU] Indonesia (Irian Jaya)
- - - - - - - - WANDAMEN [WAD] Indonesia (Irian Jaya)
- - - - - - - - WOI [WBW] Indonesia (Irian Jaya)
- - - - - - - - East (2): KURUDU [KJR] Indonesia (Irian Jaya)
- - - - - - - - WABO [WBB] Indonesia (Irian Jaya)
- - - - - - - Yaur (1): YAUR [JAU] Indonesia (Irian Jaya)
- - - - - - - Yeretuar (1): YERETUAR [GOP] Indonesia (Irian Jaya)
- - - Unclassified (3): ADABE [ADB] Timor Lorosae
- - - - IRARUTU [IRH] Indonesia (Irian Jaya)
- - - - KURI [NBN] Indonesia (Irian Jaya)
- - Unclassified (2): GORAP [GOQ] Indonesia (Maluku)
- - - HUKUMINA [HUW] Indonesia (Maluku)
- - Western Malayo-Polynesian (531)
- - - Borneo (139)
- - - - Barito (20)
- - - - - East (12)
- - - - - - Central-South (5)
- - - - - - - Central (1): DUSUN DEYAH [DUN] Indonesia (Kalimantan)
- - - - - - - South (4): DUSUN MALANG [DUQ] Indonesia (Kalimantan)
- - - - - - - - DUSUN WITU [DUW] Indonesia (Kalimantan)
- - - - - - - - MA'ANYAN [MHY] Indonesia (Kalimantan)

Austronesian (1262)
- Malayo-Polynesian (1239)
- - Western Malayo-Polynesian (531)
- - - Borneo (139)
- - - - Barito (20)
- - - - - East (12)
- - - - - - Central-South (5)
- - - - - - - South (4): PAKU [PKU] Indonesia (Kalimantan)
- - - - - - Malagasy (5): BUSHI [BUC] Madagascar
- - - - - - - MALAGASY [MEX] Madagascar
- - - - - - - MALAGASY, ANTANKARANA [XMV] Madagascar
- - - - - - - MALAGASY, SOUTHERN [XMU] Madagascar
- - - - - - - MALAGASY, TSIMEHETY [XMW] Madagascar
- - - - - - North (2): LAWANGAN [LBX] Indonesia (Kalimantan)
- - - - - - - TAWOYAN [TWY] Indonesia (Kalimantan)
- - - - - Mahakam (2): AMPANANG [APG] Indonesia (Kalimantan)
- - - - - TUNJUNG [TJG] Indonesia (Kalimantan)
- - - - - West (6)
- - - - - - North (2): DOHOI [OTD] Indonesia (Kalimantan)
- - - - - - - SIANG [SYA] Indonesia (Kalimantan)
- - - - - - South (4): BAKUMPAI [BKR] Indonesia (Kalimantan)
- - - - - - - KAHAYAN [XAH] Indonesia (Kalimantan)
- - - - - - - KATINGAN [KXG] Indonesia (Kalimantan)
- - - - - - - NGAJU [NIJ] Indonesia (Kalimantan)
- - - - Kayan-Murik (17)
- - - - - Kayan (8): BAHAU [BHV] Indonesia (Kalimantan)
- - - - - - KAYAN MAHAKAM [XAY] Indonesia (Kalimantan)
- - - - - - KAYAN, BARAM [KYS] Malaysia (Sarawak)
- - - - - - KAYAN, BUSANG [BFG] Indonesia (Kalimantan)
- - - - - - KAYAN, KAYAN RIVER [XKN] Indonesia (Kalimantan)
- - - - - - KAYAN, MENDALAM [XKD] Indonesia (Kalimantan)
- - - - - - KAYAN, REJANG [REE] Malaysia (Sarawak)
- - - - - - KAYAN, WAHAU [WHU] Indonesia (Kalimantan)
- - - - - Modang (2): MODANG [MXD] Indonesia (Kalimantan)
- - - - - - SEGAI [SGE] Indonesia (Kalimantan)
- - - - - Muller-Schwaner 'Punan' (6): AOHENG [PNI] Indonesia (Kalimantan)
- - - - - - BUKAT [BVK] Indonesia (Kalimantan)
- - - - - - HOVONGAN [HOV] Indonesia (Kalimantan)
- - - - - - KEREHO-UHENG [XKE] Indonesia (Kalimantan)
- - - - - - PUNAN APUT [PUD] Indonesia (Kalimantan)
- - - - - - PUNAN MERAH [PUF] Indonesia (Kalimantan)
- - - - - Murik (1): KAYAN, MURIK [MXR] Malaysia (Sarawak)
- - - - Land Dayak (16): AHE [AHE] Indonesia (Kalimantan)
- - - - - BEKATI' [BAT] Indonesia (Kalimantan)
- - - - - BENYADU' [BYD] Indonesia (Kalimantan)
- - - - - BIATAH [BTH] Malaysia (Sarawak)
- - - - - BUKAR SADONG [SDO] Malaysia (Sarawak)
- - - - - DAYAK, LAND [DYK] Indonesia (Kalimantan)
- - - - - DJONGKANG [DJO] Indonesia (Kalimantan)
- - - - - JAGOI [SNE] Malaysia (Sarawak)
- - - - - KEMBAYAN [XEM] Indonesia (Kalimantan)
- - - - - LARA' [LRA] Indonesia (Kalimantan)
- - - - - NYADU [NXJ] Indonesia (Kalimantan)
- - - - - RIBUN [RIR] Indonesia (Kalimantan)
- - - - - SANGGAU [SCG] Indonesia (Kalimantan)
- - - - - SARA [SRE] Indonesia (Kalimantan)
- - - - - SEMANDANG [SDM] Indonesia (Kalimantan)
- - - - - TRINGGUS [TRX] Malaysia (Sarawak)
- - - - Northwest (84)
- - - - - Melanau-Kajang (13)
- - - - - - Kajang (7): BUKITAN [BKN] Malaysia (Sarawak)

Austronesian (1262)
- Malayo-Polynesian (1239)
- - Western Malayo-Polynesian (531)
- - - Borneo (139)
- - - - Northwest (84)
- - - - - Melanau-Kajang (13)
- - - - - - Kajang (7): KAJAMAN [KAG] Malaysia (Sarawak)
- - - - - - - LAHANAN [LHN] Malaysia (Sarawak)
- - - - - - - PUNAN BATU 1 [PNM] Malaysia (Sarawak)
- - - - - - - SEKAPAN [SKP] Malaysia (Sarawak)
- - - - - - - SIAN [SPG] Malaysia (Sarawak)
- - - - - - - UKIT [UMI] Malaysia (Sarawak)
- - - - - - Melanau (6): DARO-MATU [DRO] Malaysia (Sarawak)
- - - - - - - KANOWIT [KXN] Malaysia (Sarawak)
- - - - - - - MELANAU [MEL] Malaysia (Sarawak)
- - - - - - - SERU [SZD] Malaysia (Sarawak)
- - - - - - - SIBU [SDX] Malaysia (Sarawak)
- - - - - - - TANJONG [TNJ] Malaysia (Sarawak)
- - - - - North Sarawakan (37)
- - - - - - Berawan-Lower Baram (6)
- - - - - - Berawan (1): BERAWAN [LOD] Malaysia (Sarawak)
- - - - - - Lower Baram (5)
- - - - - - - Central (5)
- - - - - - - - A (2): BELAIT [BEG] Brunei
- - - - - - - - - KIPUT [KYI] Malaysia (Sarawak)
- - - - - - - - B (3): LELAK [LLK] Malaysia (Sarawak)
- - - - - - - - - NAROM [NRM] Malaysia (Sarawak)
- - - - - - - - - TUTONG 2 [TTG] Brunei
- - - - - - Bintulu (1): BINTULU [BNY] Malaysia (Sarawak)
- - - - - Dayic (18)
- - - - - - Kelabitic (6): KELABIT [KZI] Malaysia (Sarawak)
- - - - - - - LENGILU [LGI] Indonesia (Kalimantan)
- - - - - - - LUNDAYEH [LND] Indonesia (Kalimantan)
- - - - - - - PUTOH [PUT] Indonesia (Kalimantan)
- - - - - - - SA'BAN [SNV] Indonesia (Kalimantan)
- - - - - - - TRING [TGQ] Malaysia (Sarawak)
- - - - - - Murutic (12)
- - - - - - - Murut (6): KENINGAU MURUT [KXI] Malaysia (Sabah)
- - - - - - - - OKOLOD [KQV] Malaysia (Sabah)
- - - - - - - - PALUAN [PLZ] Malaysia (Sabah)
- - - - - - - - SELUNGAI MURUT [SLG] Malaysia (Sabah)
- - - - - - - - TAGAL MURUT [MVV] Malaysia (Sabah)
- - - - - - - - TIMUGON MURUT [TIH] Malaysia (Sabah)
- - - - - - - Northern (1): BAUKAN [BNB] Malaysia (Sabah)
- - - - - - - Tidong (5): BOLONGAN [BLJ] Indonesia (Kalimantan)
- - - - - - - - KALABAKAN [KVE] Malaysia (Sabah)
- - - - - - - - SEMBAKUNG MURUT [SMA] Indonesia (Kalimantan)
- - - - - - - - SERUDUNG MURUT [SRK] Malaysia (Sabah)
- - - - - - - - TIDONG [TID] Indonesia (Kalimantan)
- - - - - - Kenyah (12): KENYAH, BAKUNG [BOC] Indonesia (Kalimantan)
- - - - - - - KENYAH, TUTOH [TTW] Malaysia (Sarawak)
- - - - - - - KENYAH, WAHAU [WHK] Indonesia (Kalimantan)
- - - - - - - PUNAN TUBU [PUJ] Indonesia (Kalimantan)
- - - - - - - Main Kenyah (6): KENYAH, BAHAU RIVER [BWV] Indonesia (Kalimantan)
- - - - - - - - KENYAH, KAYAN RIVER [KNH] Indonesia (Kalimantan)
- - - - - - - - KENYAH, KELINYAU [XKL] Indonesia (Kalimantan)
- - - - - - - - KENYAH, MAHAKAM [XKM] Indonesia (Kalimantan)
- - - - - - - - KENYAH, UPPER BARAM [UBM] Malaysia (Sarawak)
- - - - - - - - KENYAH, WESTERN [XKY] Malaysia (Sarawak)
- - - - - - - Sebob (2): KENYAH, SEBOB [SIB] Malaysia (Sarawak)
- - - - - - - - MADANG [MQD] Malaysia (Sarawak)

Austronesian (1262)
- Malayo-Polynesian (1239)
- - Western Malayo-Polynesian (531)
- - - Borneo (139)
- - - - Northwest (84)
- - - - - Rejang-Sajau (5): BASAP [BDB] Indonesia (Kalimantan)
- - - - - - BURUSU [BQR] Indonesia (Kalimantan)
- - - - - - PUNAN BAH-BIAU [PNA] Malaysia (Sarawak)
- - - - - - PUNAN MERAP [PUC] Indonesia (Kalimantan)
- - - - - - SAJAU BASAP [SAD] Indonesia (Kalimantan)
- - - - - Sabahan (29)
- - - - - - Dusunic (23)
- - - - - - - Bisaya (5): BISAYA, SABAH [BSY] Malaysia (Sabah)
- - - - - - - - TATANA [TXX] Malaysia (Sabah)
- - - - - - - - Southern (3): BISAYA, BRUNEI [BSB] Brunei
- - - - - - - - - BISAYA, SARAWAK [BSD] Malaysia (Sarawak)
- - - - - - - - - TUTONG 1 [TTX] Brunei
- - - - - - - Dusun (17): GANA [GNQ] Malaysia (Sabah)
- - - - - - - - KADAZAN, COASTAL [KZJ] Malaysia (Sabah)
- - - - - - - - KADAZAN, KLIAS RIVER [KQT] Malaysia (Sabah)
- - - - - - - - KIMARAGANG [KQR] Malaysia (Sabah)
- - - - - - - - KOTA MARUDU TALANTANG [GRM] Malaysia (Sabah)
- - - - - - - - KUIJAU [DKR] Malaysia (Sabah)
- - - - - - - - LOTUD [DTR] Malaysia (Sabah)
- - - - - - - - PAPAR [DPP] Malaysia (Sabah)
- - - - - - - - RUNGUS [DRG] Malaysia (Sabah)
- - - - - - - - TEBILUNG [TGB] Malaysia (Sabah)
- - - - - - - - Central (6): DUSUN, CENTRAL [DTP] Malaysia (Sabah)
- - - - - - - - - DUSUN, SUGUT [KZS] Malaysia (Sabah)
- - - - - - - - - DUSUN, TAMBUNAN [KZT] Malaysia (Sabah)
- - - - - - - - - DUSUN, TEMPASUK [TDU] Malaysia (Sabah)
- - - - - - - - - KOTA MARUDU TINAGAS [KTR] Malaysia (Sabah)
- - - - - - - - - MINOKOK [MQQ] Malaysia (Sabah)
- - - - - - - - Eastern (1): KADAZAN, LABUK-KINABATANGAN [DTB] Malaysia (Sabah)
- - - - - - - Unclassified (1): DUMPAS [DMV] Malaysia (Sabah)
- - - - - - Ida'an (1): IDA'AN [DBJ] Malaysia (Sabah)
- - - - - - Paitanic (5): ABAI SUNGAI [ABF] Malaysia (Sabah)
- - - - - - - TOMBONUWO [TXA] Malaysia (Sabah)
- - - - - - - Upper Kinabatangan (3): KINABATANGAN, UPPER [DMG] Malaysia (Sabah)
- - - - - - - - LOBU, LANAS [RUU] Malaysia (Sabah)
- - - - - - - - LOBU, TAMPIAS [LOW] Malaysia (Sabah)
- - - - Punan-Nibong (2): PENAN, EASTERN [PEZ] Malaysia (Sarawak)
- - - - - PENAN, WESTERN [PNE] Malaysia (Sarawak)
- - - Chamorro (1): CHAMORRO [CJD] Guam
- - - Meso Philippine (60)
- - - - Central Philippine (46): ATA [ATM] Philippines
- - - - - AYTA, SORSOGON [AYS] Philippines
- - - - - AYTA, TAYABAS [AYY] Philippines
- - - - - KAROLANOS [KYN] Philippines
- - - - - MAGAHAT [MTW] Philippines
- - - - - SULOD [SRG] Philippines
- - - - - Bikol (8)
- - - - - - Coastal (4)
- - - - - - - Naga (3): AGTA, ISAROG [AGK] Philippines
- - - - - - - - AGTA, MT. IRAYA [ATL] Philippines
- - - - - - - - BICOLANO, CENTRAL [BKL] Philippines
- - - - - - - - Virac (1): BICOLANO, SOUTHERN CATANDUANES [BLN] Philippines
- - - - - - Inland (3): AGTA, MT. IRIGA [AGZ] Philippines
- - - - - - - Buhi-Daraga (1): BICOLANO, ALBAY [BHK] Philippines
- - - - - - - Iriga (1): BICOLANO, IRIGA [BTO] Philippines
- - - - - - Pandan (1): BICOLANO, NORTHERN CATANDUANES [CTS] Philippines

Austronesian (1262)
- Malayo-Polynesian (1239)
- - Western Malayo-Polynesian (531)
- - - Meso Philippine (60)
- - - - Central Philippine (46)
- - - - - Bisayan (21)
- - - - - - Banton (1): BANTOANON [BNO] Philippines
- - - - - - Cebuan (1): CEBUANO [CEB] Philippines
- - - - - - Central (9)
- - - - - - - Peripheral (5): ATI [ATK] Philippines
- - - - - - - - CAPIZNON [CPS] Philippines
- - - - - - - - HILIGAYNON [HIL] Philippines
- - - - - - - - MASBATENYO [MSB] Philippines
- - - - - - - - POROHANON [PRH] Philippines
- - - - - - - Romblon (1): ROMBLOMANON [ROL] Philippines
- - - - - - Warayan (3): SORSOGON, MASBATE [BKS] Philippines
- - - - - - - Gubat (1): SORSOGON, WARAY [SRV] Philippines
- - - - - - - Samar-Waray (1): WARAY-WARAY [WRY] Philippines
- - - - - - South (3)
- - - - - - - Butuan-Tausug (2): BUTUANON [BTW] Philippines
- - - - - - - - TAUSUG [TSG] Philippines
- - - - - - - Surigao (1): SURIGAONON [SUL] Philippines
- - - - - - West (7): CALUYANUN [CAU] Philippines
- - - - - - - Aklan (2): AKLANON [AKL] Philippines
- - - - - - - - MALAYNON [MLZ] Philippines
- - - - - - - Kinarayan (1): KINARAY-A [KRJ] Philippines
- - - - - - - Kuyan (2): CUYONON [CYO] Philippines
- - - - - - - - RATAGNON [BTN] Philippines
- - - - - - North Central (1): INONHAN [LOC] Philippines
- - - - - Mamanwa (1): MAMANWA [MMN] Philippines
- - - - - Mansakan (9)
- - - - - - Davawenyo (1): DAVAWENYO [DAW] Philippines
- - - - - - Eastern (4)
- - - - - - - Caraga (1): MANDAYA, KARAGA [MRY] Philippines
- - - - - - - Mandayan (3): MANDAYA, CATAELANO [MST] Philippines
- - - - - - - - MANDAYA, SANGAB [MYT] Philippines
- - - - - - - - MANSAKA [MSK] Philippines
- - - - - - Northern (1): KAMAYO [KYK] Philippines
- - - - - - Western (3): KALAGAN [KQE] Philippines
- - - - - - - KALAGAN, KAGAN [KLL] Philippines
- - - - - - - KALAGAN, TAGAKAULU [KLG] Philippines
- - - - - Tagalog (1): TAGALOG [TGL] Philippines
- - - - Kalamian (3): AGUTAYNEN [AGN] Philippines
- - - - TAGBANWA, CALAMIAN [TBK] Philippines
- - - - TAGBANWA, CENTRAL [TGT] Philippines
- - - - Palawano (7): BATAK [BTK] Philippines
- - - - BONGGI [BDG] Malaysia (Sabah)
- - - - MOLBOG [PWM] Philippines
- - - - PALAWANO, BROOKE'S POINT [PLW] Philippines
- - - - PALAWANO, CENTRAL [PLC] Philippines
- - - - PALAWANO, SOUTHWEST [PLV] Philippines
- - - - TAGBANWA [TBW] Philippines
- - - - South Mangyan (4)
- - - - - Buhid-Taubuid (3): BUHID [BKU] Philippines
- - - - - - TAWBUID, EASTERN [BNJ] Philippines
- - - - - - TAWBUID, WESTERN [TWB] Philippines
- - - - - Hanunoo (1): HANUNOO [HNN] Philippines
- - - Northern Philippine (70)
- - - - Bashiic-Central Luzon-Northern Mindoro (16)
- - - - - Bashiic (3)
- - - - - - Ivatan (2): IBATAN [IVB] Philippines

Austronesian (1262)
- Malayo-Polynesian (1239)
- - Western Malayo-Polynesian (531)
- - - Northern Philippine (70)
- - - - Bashiic-Central Luzon-Northern Mindoro (16)
- - - - - Bashiic (3)
- - - - - - Ivatan (2): IVATAN [IVV] Philippines
- - - - - - Yami (1): YAMI [YMI] Taiwan
- - - - - Central Luzon (10)
- - - - - - Pampangan (1): PAMPANGAN [PMP] Philippines
- - - - - - Sambalic (8): AYTA, ABENLEN [ABP] Philippines
- - - - - - - AYTA, AMBALA [ABC] Philippines
- - - - - - - AYTA, BATAAN [AYT] Philippines
- - - - - - - AYTA, MAG-ANCHI [SGB] Philippines
- - - - - - - AYTA, MAG-INDI [BLX] Philippines
- - - - - - - BOLINAO [SMK] Philippines
- - - - - - - SAMBAL, BOTOLAN [SBL] Philippines
- - - - - - - SAMBAL, TINA [SNA] Philippines
- - - - - - Sinauna (1): AGTA, REMONTADO [AGV] Philippines
- - - - - Northern Mindoro (3): ALANGAN [ALJ] Philippines
- - - - - - IRAYA [IRY] Philippines
- - - - - - TADYAWAN [TDY] Philippines
- - - - Northern Luzon (54)
- - - - - Alta (2): ALTA, NORTHERN [AQN] Philippines
- - - - - - ALTA, SOUTHERN [AGY] Philippines
- - - - - Arta (1): ARTA [ATZ] Philippines
- - - - - Ilocano (1): ILOCANO [ILO] Philippines
- - - - - Northern Cordilleran (20)
- - - - - Dumagat (9)
- - - - - - Northern (6): AGTA, CASIGURAN DUMAGAT [DGC] Philippines
- - - - - - - AGTA, CENTRAL CAGAYAN [AGT] Philippines
- - - - - - - AGTA, DICAMAY [DUY] Philippines
- - - - - - - AGTA, DUPANINAN [DUO] Philippines
- - - - - - - KASIGURANIN [KSN] Philippines
- - - - - - - PARANAN [AGP] Philippines
- - - - - - Southern (3): AGTA, ALABAT ISLAND [DUL] Philippines
- - - - - - - AGTA, CAMARINES NORTE [ABD] Philippines
- - - - - - - AGTA, UMIRAY DUMAGET [DUE] Philippines
- - - - - Ibanagic (11)
- - - - - - Gaddang (2): GA'DANG [GDG] Philippines
- - - - - - - GADDANG [GAD] Philippines
- - - - - - Ibanag (7): AGTA, VILLA VICIOSA [DYG] Philippines
- - - - - - - ATTA, FAIRE [ATH] Philippines
- - - - - - - ATTA, PAMPLONA [ATT] Philippines
- - - - - - - ATTA, PUDTOL [ATP] Philippines
- - - - - - - IBANAG [IBG] Philippines
- - - - - - - ITAWIT [ITV] Philippines
- - - - - - - YOGAD [YOG] Philippines
- - - - - - Isnag (2): ADASEN [TIU] Philippines
- - - - - - - ISNAG [ISD] Philippines
- - - - - South-Central Cordilleran (30)
- - - - - - Central Cordilleran (22)
- - - - - - - Isinai (1): ISINAI [INN] Philippines
- - - - - - - Kalinga-Itneg (12)
- - - - - - - - Itneg (4): ITNEG, BINONGAN [ITB] Philippines
- - - - - - - - - ITNEG, INLAOD [ITI] Philippines
- - - - - - - - - ITNEG, MASADIIT [TIS] Philippines
- - - - - - - - - ITNEG, SOUTHERN [ITT] Philippines
- - - - - - - - Kalinga (8): KALINGA, BUTBUT [KYB] Philippines
- - - - - - - - - KALINGA, LIMOS [KMK] Philippines
- - - - - - - - - KALINGA, LOWER TANUDAN [KML] Philippines

Austronesian (1262)
- Malayo-Polynesian (1239)
- - Western Malayo-Polynesian (531)
- - - Northern Philippine (70)
- - - - Northern Luzon (54)
- - - - - South-Central Cordilleran (30)
- - - - - - Central Cordilleran (22)
- - - - - - - Kalinga-Itneg (12)
- - - - - - - - Kalinga (8): KALINGA, LUBUAGAN [KNB] Philippines
- - - - - - - - - KALINGA, MABAKA VALLEY [KKG] Philippines
- - - - - - - - - KALINGA, MADUKAYANG [KMD] Philippines
- - - - - - - - - KALINGA, SOUTHERN [KSC] Philippines
- - - - - - - - - KALINGA, UPPER TANUDAN [KGH] Philippines
- - - - - - - Nuclear Cordilleran (9)
- - - - - - - - Balangao (1): BALANGAO [BLW] Philippines
- - - - - - - - Bontok-Kankanay (4)
- - - - - - - - - Bontok (2): BONTOC, CENTRAL [BNC] Philippines
- - - - - - - - - - BONTOC, EASTERN [BKB] Philippines
- - - - - - - - - Kankanay (2): KANKANAEY [KNE] Philippines
- - - - - - - - - - KANKANAY, NORTHERN [KAN] Philippines
- - - - - - - - Ifugao (4): IFUGAO, AMGANAD [IFA] Philippines
- - - - - - - - - IFUGAO, BATAD [IFB] Philippines
- - - - - - - - - IFUGAO, MAYOYAO [IFU] Philippines
- - - - - - - - - IFUGAO, TUWALI [IFK] Philippines
- - - - - - Southern Cordilleran (8)
- - - - - - - Ilongot (1): ILONGOT [ILK] Philippines
- - - - - - - Pangasinic (7): PANGASINAN [PNG] Philippines
- - - - - - - - Benguet (6)
- - - - - - - - - Ibaloi-Karao (2): IBALOI [IBL] Philippines
- - - - - - - - - - KARAO [KYJ] Philippines
- - - - - - - - - Iwaak (1): I-WAK [IWK] Philippines
- - - - - - - - - Kallahan (3): KALANGUYA, KELEY-I [IFY] Philippines
- - - - - - - - - - KALLAHAN, KAYAPA [KAK] Philippines
- - - - - - - - - - KALLAHAN, TINOC [TNE] Philippines
- - - Palauan (1): PALAUAN [PLU] Palau
- - - Sama-Bajaw (9)
- - - - Abaknon (1): SAMA, ABAKNON [ABX] Philippines
- - - - Sulu-Borneo (7)
- - - - - Borneo Coast Bajaw (3): BAJAU, INDONESIAN [BDL] Indonesia (Sulawesi)
- - - - - - BAJAU, WEST COAST [BDR] Malaysia (Sabah)
- - - - - - MAPUN [SJM] Philippines
- - - - - Inner Sulu Sama (3): SAMA, BALANGINGI [SSE] Philippines
- - - - - - SAMA, CENTRAL [SML] Philippines
- - - - - - SAMA, SOUTHERN [SIT] Philippines
- - - - - Western Sulu Sama (1): SAMA, PANGUTARAN [SLM] Philippines
- - - - Yakan (1): YAKAN [YKA] Philippines
- - - South Mindanao (5)
- - - - Bagobo (1): GIANGAN [BGI] Philippines
- - - - Bilic (3)
- - - - - Blaan (2): BLAAN, KORONADAL [BIK] Philippines
- - - - - - BLAAN, SARANGANI [BIS] Philippines
- - - - Tboli (1): TBOLI [TBL] Philippines
- - - - Tiruray (1): TIRURAY [TIY] Philippines
- - - - Southern Philippine (23)
- - - - Danao (3)
- - - - - Magindanao (1): MAGINDANAON [MDH] Philippines
- - - - - Maranao-Iranon (2): ILANUN [ILL] Malaysia (Sabah)
- - - - - - MARANAO [MRW] Philippines
- - - - Manobo (15)
- - - - - Central (8)
- - - - - - East (3): MANOBO, AGUSAN [MSM] Philippines

Austronesian (1262)
- Malayo-Polynesian (1239)
- - Western Malayo-Polynesian (531)
- - - Southern Philippine (23)
- - - - Manobo (15)
- - - - - Central (8)
- - - - - - East (3): MANOBO, DIBABAWON [MBD] Philippines
- - - - - - - MANOBO, RAJAH KABUNSUWAN [MQK] Philippines
- - - - - - South (3)
- - - - - - - Ata-Tigwa (2): MANOBO, ATA [ATD] Philippines
- - - - - - - - MANOBO, MATIGSALUG [MBT] Philippines
- - - - - - - Obo (1): MANOBO, OBO [OBO] Philippines
- - - - - - West (2): MANOBO, ILIANEN [MBI] Philippines
- - - - - - - MANOBO, WESTERN BUKIDNON [MBB] Philippines
- - - - - North (4): BINUKID [BKD] Philippines
- - - - - - HIGAONON [MBA] Philippines
- - - - - - KAGAYANEN [CGC] Philippines
- - - - - - MANOBO, CINAMIGUIN [MKX] Philippines
- - - - - South (3): MANOBO, COTABATO [MTA] Philippines
- - - - - - MANOBO, SARANGANI [MBS] Philippines
- - - - - - MANOBO, TAGABAWA [BGS] Philippines
- - - - Subanun (5)
- - - - - Eastern (3): SUBANEN, CENTRAL [SUS] Philippines
- - - - - - SUBANEN, NORTHERN [STB] Philippines
- - - - - - SUBANUN, LAPUYAN [LAA] Philippines
- - - - - Kalibugan (2): SUBANON, KOLIBUGAN [SKN] Philippines
- - - - - - SUBANON, WESTERN [SUC] Philippines
- - - Sulawesi (113)
- - - - Central Sulawesi (46)
- - - - - Banggai (1): BANGGAI [BGZ] Indonesia (Sulawesi)
- - - - - Eastern (4): ANDIO [BZB] Indonesia (Sulawesi)
- - - - - - BALANTAK [BLZ] Indonesia (Sulawesi)
- - - - - - SALUAN, COASTAL [LOE] Indonesia (Sulawesi)
- - - - - - SALUAN, KAHUMAMAHON [SLB] Indonesia (Sulawesi)
- - - - - West Central (41)
- - - - - - Balaesan (1): BALAESAN [BLS] Indonesia (Sulawesi)
- - - - - - Bungku-Mori-Tolaki (15): TALOKI [TLK] Indonesia (Sulawesi)
- - - - - - - Bungku (5): BUNGKU [BKZ] Indonesia (Sulawesi)
- - - - - - - - KORONI [XKQ] Indonesia (Sulawesi)
- - - - - - - - KULISUSU [VKL] Indonesia (Sulawesi)
- - - - - - - - MORONENE [MQN] Indonesia (Sulawesi)
- - - - - - - - WAWONII [WOW] Indonesia (Sulawesi)
- - - - - - - Mori (5): BAHONSUAI [BSU] Indonesia (Sulawesi)
- - - - - - - - MORI ATAS [MZQ] Indonesia (Sulawesi)
- - - - - - - - MORI BAWAH [XMZ] Indonesia (Sulawesi)
- - - - - - - - PADOE [PDO] Indonesia (Sulawesi)
- - - - - - - - TOMADINO [TDI] Indonesia (Sulawesi)
- - - - - - - Tolaki (4): KODEOHA [VKO] Indonesia (Sulawesi)
- - - - - - - - RAHAMBUU [RAZ] Indonesia (Sulawesi)
- - - - - - - - TOLAKI [LBW] Indonesia (Sulawesi)
- - - - - - - - WARU [WRU] Indonesia (Sulawesi)
- - - - - - Kaili-Pamona (15)
- - - - - - - Kaili (9): BARAS [BRS] Indonesia (Sulawesi)
- - - - - - - - KAILI, DA'A [KZF] Indonesia (Sulawesi)
- - - - - - - - KAILI, LEDO [LEW] Indonesia (Sulawesi)
- - - - - - - - LINDU [KLW] Indonesia (Sulawesi)
- - - - - - - - MOMA [MYL] Indonesia (Sulawesi)
- - - - - - - - SARUDU [SDU] Indonesia (Sulawesi)
- - - - - - - - SEDOA [TVW] Indonesia (Sulawesi)
- - - - - - - - TOPOIYO [TOY] Indonesia (Sulawesi)
- - - - - - - - UMA [PPK] Indonesia (Sulawesi)

Austronesian (1262)
- Malayo-Polynesian (1239)
- - Western Malayo-Polynesian (531)
- - - Sulawesi (113)
- - - - Central Sulawesi (46)
- - - - - West Central (41)
- - - - - - Kaili-Pamona (15)
- - - - - - - - Pamona (6): BADA [BHZ] Indonesia (Sulawesi)
- - - - - - - - BESOA [BEP] Indonesia (Sulawesi)
- - - - - - - - NAPU [NAP] Indonesia (Sulawesi)
- - - - - - - - PAMONA [BCX] Indonesia (Sulawesi)
- - - - - - - - RAMPI [LJE] Indonesia (Sulawesi)
- - - - - - - - TOMBELALA [TTP] Indonesia (Sulawesi)
- - - - - - Tomini (10): BOLANO [BZL] Indonesia (Sulawesi)
- - - - - - - DAMPAL [DMP] Indonesia (Sulawesi)
- - - - - - - DAMPELASA [DMS] Indonesia (Sulawesi)
- - - - - - - DONDO [DOK] Indonesia (Sulawesi)
- - - - - - - LAUJE [LAW] Indonesia (Sulawesi)
- - - - - - - PENDAU [UMS] Indonesia (Sulawesi)
- - - - - - - TAJE [PEE] Indonesia (Sulawesi)
- - - - - - - TAJIO [TDJ] Indonesia (Sulawesi)
- - - - - - - TOLITOLI [TXE] Indonesia (Sulawesi)
- - - - - - - TOMINI [TXM] Indonesia (Sulawesi)
- - - - Mongondow-Gorontalo (11)
- - - - - Gorontalic (9): BINTAUNA [BNE] Indonesia (Sulawesi)
- - - - - - BOLANGO [BLD] Indonesia (Sulawesi)
- - - - - - BUOL [BLF] Indonesia (Sulawesi)
- - - - - - GORONTALO [GRL] Indonesia (Sulawesi)
- - - - - - KAIDIPANG [KZP] Indonesia (Sulawesi)
- - - - - - KWANDANG [KJW] Indonesia (Sulawesi)
- - - - - - LIMBOTO [LJO] Indonesia (Sulawesi)
- - - - - - LOLAK [LLQ] Indonesia (Sulawesi)
- - - - - - SUWAWA [SWU] Indonesia (Sulawesi)
- - - - - Mongondowic (2): MONGONDOW [MOG] Indonesia (Sulawesi)
- - - - - - PONOSAKAN [PNS] Indonesia (Sulawesi)
- - - - Muna-Buton (17)
- - - - - Buton (6): CIA-CIA [CIA] Indonesia (Sulawesi)
- - - - - - KAMARU [KGX] Indonesia (Sulawesi)
- - - - - - WOLIO [WLO] Indonesia (Sulawesi)
- - - - - - WOTU [WTW] Indonesia (Sulawesi)
- - - - - - Lasilimu-Kumbewaha (2): KUMBEWAHA [XKS] Indonesia (Sulawesi)
- - - - - - - LASALIMU [LLM] Indonesia (Sulawesi)
- - - - - Kalao (2): KALAO [KLY] Indonesia (Sulawesi)
- - - - - - LAIYOLO [LJI] Indonesia (Sulawesi)
- - - - - Muna (6): BUSOA [BUP] Indonesia (Sulawesi)
- - - - - - KAIMBULAWA [ZKA] Indonesia (Sulawesi)
- - - - - - KIOKO [UES] Indonesia (Sulawesi)
- - - - - - LIABUKU [LIX] Indonesia (Sulawesi)
- - - - - - MUNA [MYN] Indonesia (Sulawesi)
- - - - - - PANCANA [PNP] Indonesia (Sulawesi)
- - - - - Tukangbesi-Bonerate (3): BONERATE [BNA] Indonesia (Sulawesi)
- - - - - - TUKANGBESI NORTH [KHC] Indonesia (Sulawesi)
- - - - - - TUKANGBESI SOUTH [BHQ] Indonesia (Sulawesi)
- - - - Sangir-Minahasan (10)
- - - - - Minahasan (3): TOMBULU [TOM] Indonesia (Sulawesi)
- - - - - - TONSAWANG [TNW] Indonesia (Sulawesi)
- - - - - - TONTEMBOAN [TNT] Indonesia (Sulawesi)
- - - - - Sangiric (7): BANTIK [BNQ] Indonesia (Sulawesi)
- - - - - - RATAHAN [RTH] Indonesia (Sulawesi)
- - - - - - SANGIL [SNL] Philippines
- - - - - - SANGIR [SAN] Indonesia (Sulawesi)

Austronesian (1262)
- Malayo-Polynesian (1239)
- - Western Malayo-Polynesian (531)
- - - Sulawesi (113)
- - - - Sangir-Minahasan (10)
- - - - - Sangiric (7): TALAUD [TLD] Indonesia (Sulawesi)
- - - - - - TONDANO [TDN] Indonesia (Sulawesi)
- - - - - - TONSEA [TXS] Indonesia (Sulawesi)
- - - - South Sulawesi (29)
- - - - - Bugis (2): BUGIS [BPR] Indonesia (Sulawesi)
- - - - - - CAMPALAGIAN [CML] Indonesia (Sulawesi)
- - - - - Lemolang (1): LEMOLANG [LEY] Indonesia (Sulawesi)
- - - - - Makassar (5): BENTONG [BNU] Indonesia (Sulawesi)
- - - - - - KONJO, COASTAL [KJC] Indonesia (Sulawesi)
- - - - - - KONJO, HIGHLAND [KJK] Indonesia (Sulawesi)
- - - - - - MAKASAR [MSR] Indonesia (Sulawesi)
- - - - - - SELAYAR [SLY] Indonesia (Sulawesi)
- - - - - Northern (17)
- - - - - - Mamuju (1): MAMUJU [MQX] Indonesia (Sulawesi)
- - - - - - Mandar (1): MANDAR [MHN] Indonesia (Sulawesi)
- - - - - - Masenrempulu (4): DURI [MVP] Indonesia (Sulawesi)
- - - - - - - ENREKANG [PTT] Indonesia (Sulawesi)
- - - - - - - MAIWA [WMM] Indonesia (Sulawesi)
- - - - - - - MALIMPUNG [MLT] Indonesia (Sulawesi)
- - - - - - Pitu Ulunna Salu (5): ARALLE-TABULAHAN [ATQ] Indonesia (Sulawesi)
- - - - - - - BAMBAM [PTU] Indonesia (Sulawesi)
- - - - - - - DAKKA [DKK] Indonesia (Sulawesi)
- - - - - - - PANNEI [PNC] Indonesia (Sulawesi)
- - - - - - - ULUMANDA' [ULM] Indonesia (Sulawesi)
- - - - - - Toraja-Sa'dan (6): KALUMPANG [KLI] Indonesia (Sulawesi)
- - - - - - - MAMASA [MQJ] Indonesia (Sulawesi)
- - - - - - - TAE' [ROB] Indonesia (Sulawesi)
- - - - - - - TALONDO' [TLN] Indonesia (Sulawesi)
- - - - - - - TOALA' [TLZ] Indonesia (Sulawesi)
- - - - - - - TORAJA-SA'DAN [SDA] Indonesia (Sulawesi)
- - - - - Seko (4): BUDONG-BUDONG [TGK] Indonesia (Sulawesi)
- - - - - - PANASUAN [PSN] Indonesia (Sulawesi)
- - - - - - SEKO PADANG [SKX] Indonesia (Sulawesi)
- - - - - - SEKO TENGAH [SKO] Indonesia (Sulawesi)
- - - Sundic (108)
- - - - Bali-Sasak (3): BALI [BZC] Indonesia (Java and Bali)
- - - - - SASAK [SAS] Indonesia (Nusa Tenggara)
- - - - - SUMBAWA [SMW] Indonesia (Nusa Tenggara)
- - - - Gayo (1): GAYO [GYO] Indonesia (Sumatra)
- - - - Javanese (5): JAVANESE [JAN] Indonesia (Java and Bali)
- - - - - JAVANESE, CARIBBEAN [JVN] Suriname
- - - - - JAVANESE, NEW CALEDONIAN [JAS] New Caledonia
- - - - - OSING [OSI] Indonesia (Java and Bali)
- - - - - TENGGER [TES] Indonesia (Java and Bali)
- - - - Lampungic (7)
- - - - - Abung (1): ABUNG [ABL] Indonesia (Sumatra)
- - - - - Pesisir (6): KOMERING [KGE] Indonesia (Sumatra)
- - - - - - KRUI [KRQ] Indonesia (Sumatra)
- - - - - - LAMPUNG [LJP] Indonesia (Sumatra)
- - - - - - PESISIR, SOUTHERN [PEC] Indonesia (Sumatra)
- - - - - - PUBIAN [PUN] Indonesia (Sumatra)
- - - - - - SUNGKAI [SUU] Indonesia (Sumatra)
- - - - Madurese (2): KANGEAN [KKV] Indonesia (Java and Bali)
- - - - - MADURA [MHJ] Indonesia (Java and Bali)

Austronesian (1262)
- Malayo-Polynesian (1239)
- - Western Malayo-Polynesian (531)
- - - Sundic (108)
- - - - Malayic (72)
- - - - - Achinese-Chamic (11)
- - - - - - Achinese (1): ACEH [ATJ] Indonesia (Sumatra)
- - - - - - Chamic (10)
- - - - - - - North (1): TSAT [HUQ] China
- - - - - - - South (9)
- - - - - - - - Coastal (6)
- - - - - - - - - Cham-Chru (3): CHAM, EASTERN [CJM] Viet Nam
- - - - - - - - - - CHAM, WESTERN [CJA] Cambodia
- - - - - - - - - - CHRU [CJE] Viet Nam
- - - - - - - - - Roglai (3): ROGLAI, CACGIA [ROC] Viet Nam
- - - - - - - - - - ROGLAI, NORTHERN [ROG] Viet Nam
- - - - - - - - - - ROGLAI, SOUTHERN [RGS] Viet Nam
- - - - - - - - Plateau (3): HAROI [HRO] Viet Nam
- - - - - - - - - JARAI [JRA] Viet Nam
- - - - - - - - - RADE [RAD] Viet Nam
- - - - - Malayan (49)
- - - - - - Aboriginal Malay (4): JAKUN [JAK] Malaysia (Peninsular)
- - - - - - - ORANG KANAQ [ORN] Malaysia (Peninsular)
- - - - - - - ORANG SELETAR [ORS] Malaysia (Peninsular)
- - - - - - - TEMUAN [TMW] Malaysia (Peninsular)
- - - - - - Local Malay (38): BANJAR [BJN] Indonesia (Kalimantan)
- - - - - - - BENGKULU [BKE] Indonesia (Sumatra)
- - - - - - - BRUNEI [KXD] Brunei
- - - - - - - ENIM [ENI] Indonesia (Sumatra)
- - - - - - - INDONESIAN [INZ] Indonesia (Java and Bali)
- - - - - - - KAUR [VKK] Indonesia (Sumatra)
- - - - - - - KAYU AGUNG [VKY] Indonesia (Sumatra)
- - - - - - - KERINCI [KVR] Indonesia (Sumatra)
- - - - - - - KUBU [KVB] Indonesia (Sumatra)
- - - - - - - LEMATANG [LMT] Indonesia (Sumatra)
- - - - - - - LEMBAK [LIW] Indonesia (Sumatra)
- - - - - - - LINTANG [LNT] Indonesia (Sumatra)
- - - - - - - LONCONG [LCE] Indonesia (Sumatra)
- - - - - - - LUBU [LCF] Indonesia (Sumatra)
- - - - - - - MALAY [MLI] Malaysia (Peninsular)
- - - - - - - MALAY, BACANESE [BTJ] Indonesia (Maluku)
- - - - - - - MALAY, BERAU [BVE] Indonesia (Kalimantan)
- - - - - - - MALAY, BUKIT [BVU] Indonesia (Kalimantan)
- - - - - - - MALAY, COCOS ISLANDS [COA] Malaysia (Sabah)
- - - - - - - MALAY, JAMBI [JAX] Indonesia (Sumatra)
- - - - - - - MALAY, KEDAH [MEO] Thailand
- - - - - - - MALAY, KOTA BANGUN KUTAI [MQG] Indonesia (Kalimantan)
- - - - - - - MALAY, MENADONESE [XMM] Indonesia (Sulawesi)
- - - - - - - MALAY, NORTH MOLUCCAN [MAX] Indonesia (Maluku)
- - - - - - - MALAY, PATTANI [MFA] Thailand
- - - - - - - MALAY, SABAH [MSI] Malaysia (Sabah)
- - - - - - - MALAY, TENGGARONG KUTAI [VKT] Indonesia (Kalimantan)
- - - - - - - MUSI [MUI] Indonesia (Sumatra)
- - - - - - - OGAN [OGN] Indonesia (Sumatra)
- - - - - - - PALEMBANG [PLM] Indonesia (Sumatra)
- - - - - - - PASEMAH [PSE] Indonesia (Sumatra)
- - - - - - - PENESAK [PEN] Indonesia (Sumatra)
- - - - - - - RANAU [RAE] Indonesia (Sumatra)
- - - - - - - RAWAS [RAJ] Indonesia (Sumatra)
- - - - - - - SEMENDO [SMN] Indonesia (Sumatra)
- - - - - - - SERAWAI [SRJ] Indonesia (Sumatra)

Austronesian (1262)
- Malayo-Polynesian (1239)
- - Western Malayo-Polynesian (531)
- - - Sundic (108)
- - - - Malayic (72)
- - - - - Malayan (49)
- - - - - - Local Malay (38): SINDANG KELINGI [SDI] Indonesia (Sumatra)
- - - - - - - SUKU BATIN [SBV] Indonesia (Sumatra)
- - - - - - Para-Malay (7): DUANO' [DUP] Malaysia (Peninsular)
- - - - - - - MINANGKABAU [MPU] Indonesia (Sumatra)
- - - - - - - MUKO-MUKO [VMO] Indonesia (Sumatra)
- - - - - - - NEGERI SEMBILAN MALAY [ZMI] Malaysia (Peninsular)
- - - - - - - PEKAL [PEL] Indonesia (Sumatra)
- - - - - - - REJANG [REJ] Indonesia (Sumatra)
- - - - - - - URAK LAWOI' [URK] Thailand
- - - - - Malayic-Dayak (10): KENDAYAN [KNX] Indonesia (Kalimantan)
- - - - - - KENINJAL [KNL] Indonesia (Kalimantan)
- - - - - - MALAYIC DAYAK [XDY] Indonesia (Kalimantan)
- - - - - - SELAKO [SKL] Indonesia (Kalimantan)
- - - - - - Ibanic (6): BALAU [BUG] Malaysia (Sarawak)
- - - - - - - IBAN [IBA] Malaysia (Sarawak)
- - - - - - - MILIKIN [MIN] Malaysia (Sarawak)
- - - - - - - MUALANG [MTD] Indonesia (Kalimantan)
- - - - - - - SEBERUANG [SBX] Indonesia (Kalimantan)
- - - - - - - SEBUYAU [SNB] Malaysia (Sarawak)
- - - - - Moklen (2): MOKEN [MWT] Myanmar
- - - - - - MOKLEN [MKM] Thailand
- - - - Mbaloh (2): EMBALOH [EMB] Indonesia (Kalimantan)
- - - - - TAMAN [TMN] Indonesia (Kalimantan)
- - - - - Sumatra (13)
- - - - - Batak (7)
- - - - - - Northern (3): BATAK ALAS-KLUET [BTZ] Indonesia (Sumatra)
- - - - - - - BATAK DAIRI [BTD] Indonesia (Sumatra)
- - - - - - - BATAK KARO [BTX] Indonesia (Sumatra)
- - - - - - Simalungun (1): BATAK SIMALUNGUN [BTS] Indonesia (Sumatra)
- - - - - - Southern (3): BATAK ANGKOLA [AKB] Indonesia (Sumatra)
- - - - - - - BATAK MANDAILING [BTM] Indonesia (Sumatra)
- - - - - - - BATAK TOBA [BBC] Indonesia (Sumatra)
- - - - - Enggano (1): ENGGANO [ENO] Indonesia (Sumatra)
- - - - - Lom (1): LOM [MFB] Indonesia (Sumatra)
- - - - - Mentawai (1): MENTAWAI [MWV] Indonesia (Sumatra)
- - - - - Northern (3): NIAS [NIP] Indonesia (Sumatra)
- - - - - - SIKULE [SKH] Indonesia (Sumatra)
- - - - - - SIMEULUE [SMR] Indonesia (Sumatra)
- - - - Sundanese (2): BADUI [BAC] Indonesia (Java and Bali)
- - - - - SUNDA [SUO] Indonesia (Java and Bali)
- - - - Unclassified (1): SEKAYU [SYU] Indonesia (Sumatra)
- - - Unclassified (1): KATABAGA [KTQ] Philippines
- - - Yapese (1): YAPESE [YPS] Micronesia

Aymaran (3): AYMARA, CENTRAL [AYM] Bolivia
- AYMARA, SOUTHERN [AYC] Peru
- JAQARU [JQR] Peru

Barbacoan (7)
- Andaqui (1): ANDAQUI [ANA] Colombia
- Cayapa-Colorado (2): CHACHI [CBI] Ecuador
- - COLORADO [COF] Ecuador
- Coconucan (2): GUAMBIANO [GUM] Colombia
- - TOTORO [TTK] Colombia
- Pasto (2): AWA-CUAIQUER [KWI] Colombia

Barbacoan (7)
- Pasto (2): BARBACOAS [BPB] Colombia

Basque (3): BASQUE [BSQ] Spain
- BASQUE, NAVARRO-LABOURDIN [BQE] France
- BASQUE, SOULETIN [BSZ] France

Bayono-Awbono (2): AWBONO [AWH] Indonesia (Irian Jaya)
- BAYONO [BYL] Indonesia (Irian Jaya)

Caddoan (5)
- Northern (4)
- - Pawnee-Kitsai (3)
- - - Kitsai (1): KITSAI [KII] USA
- - - Pawnee (2): ARIKARA [ARI] USA
- - - - PAWNEE [PAW] USA
- - Wichita (1): WICHITA [WIC] USA
- Southern (1): CADDO [CAD] USA

Cahuapanan (2): CHAYAHUITA [CBT] Peru
- JEBERO [JEB] Peru

Cant (1)
- English-Tahitian (1): PITCAIRN-NORFOLK [PIH] Norfolk Island

Carib (29)
- Northern (21)
- - Coastal (3): COYAIMA [COY] Colombia
- - - JAPRERÍA [JRU] Venezuela
- - - YUKPA [YUP] Colombia
- - East-West Guiana (12)
- - - Macushi-Kapon (4)
- - - - Kapon (3): AKAWAIO [ARB] Guyana
- - - - - PATAMONA [PBC] Guyana
- - - - - PEMON [AOC] Venezuela
- - - - Macushi (1): MACUSHI [MBC] Guyana
- - - Waimiri (1): ATRUAHÍ [ATR] Brazil
- - - Waiwai (3): WAIWAI [WAW] Brazil
- - - - Sikiana (2): SALUMÁ [SLJ] Brazil
- - - - - SIKIANA [SIK] Brazil
- - - Wama (1): AKURIO [AKO] Suriname
- - - Wayana-Trio (3): APALAÍ [APA] Brazil
- - - - TRIÓ [TRI] Suriname
- - - - WAYANA [WAY] Suriname
- - Galibi (1): CARIB [CRB] Venezuela
- - Northern Brazil (2): ARÁRA, PARÁ [AAP] Brazil
- - - TXIKÃO [TXI] Brazil
- - Western Guiana (3): MAPOYO [MCG] Venezuela
- - - PANARE [PBH] Venezuela
- - - YABARANA [YAR] Venezuela
- Southern (8)
- - Southeastern Colombia (1): CARIJONA [CBD] Colombia
- - Southern Guiana (3): HIXKARYÁNA [HIX] Brazil
- - - KAXUIÂNA [KBB] Brazil
- - - MAQUIRITARI [MCH] Venezuela
- - Xingu Basin (4): BAKAIRÍ [BKQ] Brazil
- - - KUIKÚRO-KALAPÁLO [KUI] Brazil
- - - MATIPUHY [MZO] Brazil
- - - YARUMÁ [YRM] Brazil

Chapacura-Wanham (5)
- Guapore (2): ITENE [ITE] Bolivia
- - KABIXÍ [KBD] Brazil
- Madeira (3): ORO WIN [ORW] Brazil
- - PAKAÁSNOVOS [PAV] Brazil
- - TORÁ [TRZ] Brazil

Chibchan (22)
- Aruak (3): COGUI [KOG] Colombia
- - ICA [ARH] Colombia
- - MALAYO [MBP] Colombia
- Chibchan Proper (5): CHIBCHA [CBF] Colombia
- - Tunebo (4): TUNEBO, ANGOSTURAS [TND] Colombia
- - - TUNEBO, BARRO NEGRO [TBN] Colombia
- - - TUNEBO, CENTRAL [TUF] Colombia
- - - TUNEBO, WESTERN [TNB] Colombia
- Cofan (1): COFÁN [CON] Ecuador
- Guaymi (2): BUGLERE [SAB] Panama
- - NGÄBERE [GYM] Panama
- Kuna (2): KUNA, BORDER [KUA] Colombia
- - KUNA, SAN BLAS [CUK] Panama
- Motilon (1): MOTILÓN [MOT] Colombia
- Paya (1): PECH [PAY] Honduras
- Rama (2): MALÉKU JAÍKA [GUT] Costa Rica
- - RAMA [RMA] Nicaragua
- Talamanca (4): BORUCA [BRN] Costa Rica
- - BRIBRI [BZD] Costa Rica
- - CABÉCAR [CJP] Costa Rica
- - TERIBE [TFR] Panama
- Unclassified (1): CHIMILA [CBG] Colombia

Chimakuan (1): QUILEUTE [QUI] USA

Choco (10): ANSERMA [ANS] Colombia
- ARMA [AOH] Colombia
- RUNA [RUN] Colombia
- WOUN MEU [NOA] Panama
- Embera (6)
- - Northern (2): EMBERÁ, NORTHERN [EMP] Panama
- - - EMBERÁ-CATÍO [CTO] Colombia
- - Southern (4): EMBERÁ-BAUDÓ [BDC] Colombia
- - - EMBERÁ-CHAMÍ [CMI] Colombia
- - - EMBERÁ-SAIJA [SJA] Colombia
- - - EMBERÁ-TADÓ [TDC] Colombia

Chon (2): ONA [ONA] Argentina
- TEHUELCHE [TEH] Argentina

Chukotko-Kamchatkan (5)
- Northern (4)
- - Chukot (1): CHUKOT [CKT] Russia (Asia)
- - Koryak-Alyutor (3): ALUTOR [ALR] Russia (Asia)
- - - KEREK [KRK] Russia (Asia)
- - - KORYAK [KPY] Russia (Asia)
- Southern (1): ITELMEN [ITL] Russia (Asia)

Chumash (7): BARBAREÑO [BOI] USA
- CHUMASH [CHS] USA
- CRUZEÑO [CRZ] USA
- INESEÑO [INE] USA
- OBISPEÑO [OBI] USA

Chumash (7): PURISIMEÑO [PUY] USA
- VENTUREÑO [VEO] USA

Coahuiltecan (1): TONKAWA [TON] USA

Creole (81)
- Afrikaans based (2): OORLAMS [OOR] South Africa
- - TSOTSITAAL [FLY] South Africa
- Arabic based (3): ARABIC, BABALIA CREOLE [BBZ] Chad
- - ARABIC, SUDANESE CREOLE [PGA] Sudan
- - NUBI [KCN] Uganda
- Assamese based (1): NAGA PIDGIN [NAG] India
- Dutch based (4): BERBICE CREOLE DUTCH [BRC] Guyana
- - DUTCH CREOLE [DCR] U.S. Virgin Islands
- - PETJO [PEY] Indonesia (Java and Bali)
- - SKEPI CREOLE DUTCH [SKW] Guyana
- English based (30) SARAMACCAN [SRM] Suriname
- - Atlantic (22)
- - - Eastern (11): TURKS AND CAICOS CREOLE ENGLISH [TCH] Turks and Caicos Islands
- - - - Northern (3): AFRO-SEMINOLE CREOLE [AFS] USA
- - - - - BAHAMAS CREOLE ENGLISH [BAH] Bahamas
- - - - - SEA ISLAND CREOLE ENGLISH [GUL] USA
- - - - Southern (7): BAJAN [BJS] Barbados
- - - - - GUYANESE CREOLE ENGLISH [GYN] Guyana
- - - - - LEEWARD CARIBBEAN CREOLE ENGLISH [AIG] Antigua and Barbuda
- - - - - TOBAGONIAN CREOLE ENGLISH [TGH] Trinidad and Tobago
- - - - - TRINIDADIAN CREOLE ENGLISH [TRF] Trinidad and Tobago
- - - - - VIRGIN ISLANDS CREOLE ENGLISH [VIB] U.S. Virgin Islands
- - - - - WINDWARD CARIBBEAN CREOLE ENGLISH [SVG] St. Vincent and the Grenadines
- - - Krio (4): FERNANDO PO CREOLE ENGLISH [FPE] Equatorial Guinea
- - - - KRIO [KRI] Sierra Leone
- - - - PIDGIN, CAMEROON [WES] Cameroon
- - - - PIDGIN, NIGERIAN [PCM] Nigeria
- - - Suriname (3): SRANAN [SRN] Suriname
- - - - Ndyuka (2): AUKAN [DJK] Suriname
- - - - - KWINTI [KWW] Suriname
- - - Unclassified (1): SAMANÁ ENGLISH [SAX] Dominican Republic
- - - Western (3): BAY ISLANDS CREOLE ENGLISH [BYH] Honduras
- - - - NORTHERN CENTRAL AMERICA CREOLE ENGLISH [BZI] Belize
- - - - SOUTHWESTERN CARIBBEAN CREOLE ENGLISH [JAM] Jamaica
- - Pacific (7): BISLAMA [BCY] Vanuatu
- - - HAWAI'I CREOLE ENGLISH [HAW] USA
- - - KRIOL [ROP] Australia
- - - NGATIK MEN'S CREOLE [NGM] Micronesia
- - - PIJIN [PIS] Solomon Islands
- - - TOK PISIN [PDG] Papua New Guinea
- - - TORRES STRAIT CREOLE [TCS] Australia
- French based (11): AMAPÁ CREOLE [AMD] Brazil
- - FRENCH GUIANESE CREOLE FRENCH [FRE] French Guiana
- - HAITIAN CREOLE FRENCH [HAT] Haiti
- - KARIPÚNA CREOLE FRENCH [KMV] Brazil
- - LESSER ANTILLEAN CREOLE FRENCH [DOM] St. Lucia
- - LOUISIANA CREOLE FRENCH [LOU] USA
- - MORISYEN [MFE] Mauritius
- - REUNION CREOLE FRENCH [RCF] Reunion
- - SAN MIGUEL CREOLE FRENCH [SME] Panama
- - SESELWA CREOLE FRENCH [CRS] Seychelles
- - TAYO [CKS] New Caledonia
- German based (1): UNSERDEUTSCH [ULN] Papua New Guinea
- Iberian based (1): PAPIAMENTU [PAE] Netherlands Antilles
- Indonesian based (1): INDONESIAN, PERANAKAN [PEA] Indonesia (Java and Bali)

Creole (81)
- Kongo based (2): KITUBA [KTU] DRC
- - MUNUKUTUBA [MKW] Congo
- Malay based (6): BETAWI [BEW] Indonesia (Java and Bali)
- - MALACCAN CREOLE MALAY [CCM] Malaysia (Peninsular)
- - MALAY, AMBONESE [ABS] Indonesia (Maluku)
- - MALAY, BABA [BAL] Singapore
- - MALAY, KUPANG [MKN] Indonesia (Nusa Tenggara)
- - SRI LANKAN CREOLE MALAY [SCI] Sri Lanka
- Ngbandi based (2): SANGO [SAJ] Central African Republic
- - SANGO, RIVERAIN [SNJ] Central African Republic
- Portuguese based (13): ANGOLAR [AOA] São Tomé e Príncipe
- - CAFUNDO CREOLE [CCD] Brazil
- - CRIOULO, UPPER GUINEA [POV] Guinea-Bissau
- - FA D'AMBU [FAB] Equatorial Guinea
- - INDO-PORTUGUESE [IDB] Sri Lanka
- - KABUVERDIANU [KEA] Cape Verde Islands
- - KORLAI CREOLE PORTUGUESE [VKP] India
- - MACANESE [MZS] China
- - MALACCAN CREOLE PORTUGUESE [MCM] Malaysia (Peninsular)
- - PIDGIN, TIMOR [TVY] Timor Lorosae
- - PRINCIPENSE [PRE] São Tomé e Príncipe
- - SÃO TOMENSE [CRI] São Tomé e Príncipe
- - TERNATEÑO [TMG] Indonesia (Maluku)
- Spanish based (2): CHAVACANO [CBK] Philippines
- - PALENQUERO [PLN] Colombia
- Swahili based (1): CUTCHI-SWAHILI [CCL] Kenya
- Tetun based (1): TETUM PRASA [TDT] Timor Lorosae

Deaf sign language (114): ADAMOROBE SIGN LANGUAGE [ADS] Ghana
- ALGERIAN SIGN LANGUAGE [ASP] Algeria
- AMERICAN SIGN LANGUAGE [ASE] USA
- ARGENTINE SIGN LANGUAGE [AED] Argentina
- ARMENIAN SIGN LANGUAGE [AEN] Armenia
- AUSTRALIAN ABORIGINES SIGN LANGUAGE [ASW] Australia
- AUSTRALIAN SIGN LANGUAGE [ASF] Australia
- AUSTRIAN SIGN LANGUAGE [ASQ] Austria
- BALI SIGN LANGUAGE [BQY] Indonesia (Java and Bali)
- BAMAKO SIGN LANGUAGE [BOG] Mali
- BAN KHOR SIGN LANGUAGE [BLA] Thailand
- BELGIAN SIGN LANGUAGE [BVS] Belgium
- BOLIVIAN SIGN LANGUAGE [BVL] Bolivia
- BRAZILIAN SIGN LANGUAGE [BZS] Brazil
- BRITISH SIGN LANGUAGE [BHO] United Kingdom
- BULGARIAN SIGN LANGUAGE [BQN] Bulgaria
- CATALONIAN SIGN LANGUAGE [CSC] Spain
- CHADIAN SIGN LANGUAGE [CDS] Chad
- CHIANGMAI SIGN LANGUAGE [CSD] Thailand
- CHILEAN SIGN LANGUAGE [CSG] Chile
- CHINESE SIGN LANGUAGE [CSL] China
- COLOMBIAN SIGN LANGUAGE [CSN] Colombia
- COSTA RICAN SIGN LANGUAGE [CSR] Costa Rica
- CZECH SIGN LANGUAGE [CSE] Czech Republic
- DANISH SIGN LANGUAGE [DSL] Denmark
- DOMINICAN SIGN LANGUAGE [DOQ] Dominican Republic
- DUTCH SIGN LANGUAGE [DSE] Netherlands
- ECUADORIAN SIGN LANGUAGE [ECS] Ecuador
- ESTONIAN SIGN LANGUAGE [ESO] Estonia
- ETHIOPIAN SIGN LANGUAGE [ETH] Ethiopia
- FINNISH SIGN LANGUAGE [FSE] Finland
- FRENCH SIGN LANGUAGE [FSL] France

Deaf sign language (114): GERMAN SIGN LANGUAGE [GSG] Germany
- GHANAIAN SIGN LANGUAGE [GSE] Ghana
- GREEK SIGN LANGUAGE [GSS] Greece
- GUATEMALAN SIGN LANGUAGE [GSM] Guatemala
- GUINEAN SIGN LANGUAGE [GUS] Guinea
- HAIPHONG SIGN LANGUAGE [HAF] Viet Nam
- HANOI SIGN LANGUAGE [HAB] Viet Nam
- HAUSA SIGN LANGUAGE [HSL] Nigeria
- HAWAI'I PIDGIN SIGN LANGUAGE [HPS] USA
- HO CHI MINH CITY SIGN LANGUAGE [HOS] Viet Nam
- HUNGARIAN SIGN LANGUAGE [HSH] Hungary
- ICELANDIC SIGN LANGUAGE [ICL] Iceland
- INDIAN SIGN LANGUAGE [INS] India
- INDONESIAN SIGN LANGUAGE [INL] Indonesia (Java and Bali)
- IRISH SIGN LANGUAGE [ISG] Ireland
- ISRAELI SIGN LANGUAGE [ISL] Israel
- ITALIAN SIGN LANGUAGE [ISE] Italy
- JAMAICAN COUNTRY SIGN LANGUAGE [JCS] Jamaica
- JAPANESE SIGN LANGUAGE [JSL] Japan
- JORDANIAN SIGN LANGUAGE [JOS] Jordan
- KENYAN SIGN LANGUAGE [XKI] Kenya
- KOREAN SIGN LANGUAGE [KVK] Korea, South
- KUALA LUMPUR SIGN LANGUAGE [KGI] Malaysia (Peninsular)
- LAOS SIGN LANGUAGE [LSO] Laos
- LATVIAN SIGN LANGUAGE [LSL] Latvia
- LIBYAN SIGN LANGUAGE [LBS] Libya
- LITHUANIAN SIGN LANGUAGE [LLS] Lithuania
- LYONS SIGN LANGUAGE [LSG] France
- MALAYSIAN SIGN LANGUAGE [XML] Malaysia (Peninsular)
- MALTESE SIGN LANGUAGE [MDL] Malta
- MARITIME SIGN LANGUAGE [NSR] Canada
- MARTHA'S VINEYARD SIGN LANGUAGE [MRE] USA
- MEXICAN SIGN LANGUAGE [MFS] Mexico
- MONGOLIAN SIGN LANGUAGE [QMM] Mongolia
- MOROCCAN SIGN LANGUAGE [XMS] Morocco
- MOZAMBICAN SIGN LANGUAGE [MZY] Mozambique
- NAMIBIAN SIGN LANGUAGE [NBS] Namibia
- NEPALESE SIGN LANGUAGE [NSP] Nepal
- NEW ZEALAND SIGN LANGUAGE [NZS] New Zealand
- NICARAGUAN SIGN LANGUAGE [NCS] Nicaragua
- NIGERIAN SIGN LANGUAGE [NSI] Nigeria
- NORWEGIAN SIGN LANGUAGE [NSL] Norway
- OLD KENTISH SIGN LANGUAGE [OKL] United Kingdom
- PAKISTAN SIGN LANGUAGE [PKS] Pakistan
- PENANG SIGN LANGUAGE [PSG] Malaysia (Peninsular)
- PERSIAN SIGN LANGUAGE [PSC] Iran
- PERUVIAN SIGN LANGUAGE [PRL] Peru
- PHILIPPINE SIGN LANGUAGE [PSP] Philippines
- POLISH SIGN LANGUAGE [PSO] Poland
- PORTUGUESE SIGN LANGUAGE [PSR] Portugal
- PROVIDENCIA SIGN LANGUAGE [PRO] Colombia
- PUERTO RICAN SIGN LANGUAGE [PSL] Puerto Rico
- QUEBEC SIGN LANGUAGE [FCS] Canada
- RENNELLESE SIGN LANGUAGE [RSI] Solomon Islands
- ROMANIAN SIGN LANGUAGE [RMS] Romania
- RUSSIAN SIGN LANGUAGE [RSL] Russia (Europe)
- SALVADORAN SIGN LANGUAGE [ESN] El Salvador
- SAUDI ARABIAN SIGN LANGUAGE [SDL] Saudi Arabia
- SINGAPORE SIGN LANGUAGE [SLS] Singapore
- SLOVAKIAN SIGN LANGUAGE [SVK] Slovakia
- SOUTH AFRICAN SIGN LANGUAGE [SFS] South Africa

Deaf sign language (114): SPANISH SIGN LANGUAGE [SSP] Spain
- SRI LANKAN SIGN LANGUAGE [SQS] Sri Lanka
- SWEDISH SIGN LANGUAGE [SWL] Sweden
- SWISS-FRENCH SIGN LANGUAGE [SSR] Switzerland
- SWISS-GERMAN SIGN LANGUAGE [SGG] Switzerland
- SWISS-ITALIAN SIGN LANGUAGE [SLF] Switzerland
- TAIWANESE SIGN LANGUAGE [TSS] Taiwan
- TANZANIAN SIGN LANGUAGE [TZA] Tanzania
- THAI SIGN LANGUAGE [TSQ] Thailand
- TUNISIAN SIGN LANGUAGE [TSE] Tunisia
- TURKISH SIGN LANGUAGE [TSM] Turkey (Asia)
- UGANDAN SIGN LANGUAGE [UGN] Uganda
- UKRAINIAN SIGN LANGUAGE [UKL] Ukraine
- URUBÚ-KAAPOR SIGN LANGUAGE [UKS] Brazil
- URUGUAYAN SIGN LANGUAGE [UGY] Uruguay
- VENEZUELAN SIGN LANGUAGE [VSL] Venezuela
- YIDDISH SIGN LANGUAGE [YDS] Israel
- YUCATEC MAYA SIGN LANGUAGE [MSD] Mexico
- YUGOSLAVIAN SIGN LANGUAGE [YSL] Yugoslavia
- ZAMBIAN SIGN LANGUAGE [ZSL] Zambia
- ZIMBABWE SIGN LANGUAGE [ZIB] Zimbabwe

Dravidian (75)
- Central (5)
- - Kolami-Naiki (2): KOLAMI, NORTHWESTERN [KFB] India
- - - KOLAMI, SOUTHEASTERN [NIT] India
- - Parji-Gadaba (3): DURUWA [PCI] India
- - - GADABA, OLLAR, POTTANGI [GDB] India
- - - GADABA, OLLAR, SALUR [GAU] India
- Northern (5): BRAHUI [BRH] Pakistan
- - KUMARBHAG PAHARIA [KMJ] India
- - KURUX [KVN] India
- - KURUX, NEPALI [KXL] Nepal
- - SAURIA PAHARIA [MJT] India
- South Central (1)
- - Telugu (1): MANNA-DORA [MJU] India
- South-Central (22)
- - Gondi-Kui (18)
- - - Gondi (11): ABUJMARIA [ABJ] India
- - - - GONDI, NORTHERN [GON] India
- - - - GONDI, SOUTHERN [GGO] India
- - - - KHIRWAR [KWX] India
- - - - MARIA [MRR] India
- - - - MARIA, DANDAMI [DAQ] India
- - - - MURIA, EASTERN [EMU] India
- - - - MURIA, FAR WESTERN [FMU] India
- - - - MURIA, WESTERN [MUT] India
- - - - NAGARCHAL [NBG] India
- - - - PARDHAN [PCH] India
- - - Konda-Kui (7)
- - - - Konda (2): KONDA-DORA [KFC] India
- - - - - NUKA-DORA [NUK] India
- - - - Manda-Kui (5)
- - - - - Kui-Kuvi (3): KOYA [KFF] India
- - - - - - KUI [KXU] India
- - - - - - KUVI [KXV] India
- - - - - Manda-Pengo (2): MANDA [MHA] India
- - - - - - PENGO [PEG] India
- - Telugu (4): CHENCHU [CDE] India
- - - SAVARA [SVR] India
- - - TELUGU [TCW] India

Dravidian (75)
- South-Central (22)
- - Telugu (4): WADDAR [WBQ] India
- Southern (33)
- - Tamil-Kannada (27)
- - - Kannada (4): BADAGA [BFQ] India
- - - - HOLIYA [HOY] India
- - - - KANNADA [KJV] India
- - - - URALI [URL] India
- - - Tamil-Kodagu (23)
- - - - Kodagu (5): KODAGU [KFA] India
- - - - - KURUMBA [KFI] India
- - - - - KURUMBA, ALU [QKA] India
- - - - - KURUMBA, JENNU [QKJ] India
- - - - - KURUMBA, MULLU [KPB] India
- - - - Tamil-Malayalam (16): MANNAN [MJV] India
- - - - - Malayalam (9): ARANADAN [AAF] India
- - - - - - KADAR [KEJ] India
- - - - - - MALAPANDARAM [MJP] India
- - - - - - MALARYAN [MJQ] India
- - - - - - MALAVEDAN [MJR] India
- - - - - - MALAYALAM [MJS] India
- - - - - - PALIYAN [PCF] India
- - - - - - PANIYA [PCG] India
- - - - - - RAVULA [YEA] India
- - - - - Tamil (6): IRULA [IRU] India
- - - - - - KAIKADI [KEP] India
- - - - - - KURUMBA, BETTA [QKB] India
- - - - - - SHOLAGA [SLE] India
- - - - - - TAMIL [TCV] India
- - - - - - YERUKULA [YEU] India
- - - - Toda-Kota (2): KOTA [KFE] India
- - - - - TODA [TCX] India
- - Tulu (5): BELLARI [BRW] India
- - - KUDIYA [KFG] India
- - - TULU [TCY] India
- - - Koraga (2): KORAGA, KORRA [KFD] India
- - - - KORAGA, MUDU [VMD] India
- - Unclassified (1): ULLATAN [ULL] India
- Unclassified (9): ALLAR [ALL] India
- - BAZIGAR [BFR] India
- - BHARIA [BHA] India
- - KAMAR [KEQ] India
- - KANIKKARAN [KEV] India
- - KURICHIYA [KFH] India
- - MALANKURAVAN [MJO] India
- - MUTHUVAN [MUV] India
- - VISHAVAN [VIS] India

East Bird's Head (3): MANIKION [MNX] Indonesia (Irian Jaya)
- Meax (2): MEYAH [MEJ] Indonesia (Irian Jaya)
- - MOSKONA [MTJ] Indonesia (Irian Jaya)

East Papuan (36)
- Bougainville (13)
- - East (9)
- - - Buin (3): BUIN [BUO] Papua New Guinea
- - - - SIWAI [SIW] Papua New Guinea
- - - - UISAI [UIS] Papua New Guinea
- - - Nasioi (6): KOROMIRA [KQJ] Papua New Guinea
- - - - LANTANAI [LNI] Papua New Guinea

East Papuan (36)
- Bougainville (13)
- - East (9)
- - - Nasioi (6): NAASIOI [NAS] Papua New Guinea
- - - - NAGOVISI [NCO] Papua New Guinea
- - - - OUNE [OUE] Papua New Guinea
- - - - SIMEKU [SMZ] Papua New Guinea
- - West (4): RAPOISI [KYX] Papua New Guinea
- - - Keriaka (1): KEREAKA [KJX] Papua New Guinea
- - - Rotokas (2): EIVO [EIV] Papua New Guinea
- - - - ROTOKAS [ROO] Papua New Guinea
- Reef Islands-Santa Cruz (3): AYIWO [NFL] Solomon Islands
- - NANGGU [NAN] Solomon Islands
- - SANTA CRUZ [STC] Solomon Islands
- Yele-Solomons-New Britain (20)
- - New Britain (12): KOL [KOL] Papua New Guinea
- - - Anem (1): ANEM [ANZ] Papua New Guinea
- - - Baining-Taulil (7): KAIRAK [CKR] Papua New Guinea
- - - - MAKOLKOL [ZMH] Papua New Guinea
- - - - MALI [GCC] Papua New Guinea
- - - - QAQET [BYX] Papua New Guinea
- - - - SIMBALI [SMG] Papua New Guinea
- - - - TAULIL-BUTAM [TUH] Papua New Guinea
- - - - URA [URO] Papua New Guinea
- - - Kuot (1): KUOT [KTO] Papua New Guinea
- - - Sulka (1): SULKA [SLK] Papua New Guinea
- - - Wasi (1): PELE-ATA [ATA] Papua New Guinea
- - Yele-Solomons (8)
- - - Central Solomons (4): BANIATA [BNT] Solomon Islands
- - - - BILUA [BLB] Solomon Islands
- - - - LAVUKALEVE [LVK] Solomon Islands
- - - - SAVOSAVO [SVS] Solomon Islands
- - - Kazukuru (3): DORORO [DRR] Solomon Islands
- - - - GULIGULI [GLG] Solomon Islands
- - - - KAZUKURU [KZK] Solomon Islands
- - - Yele (1): YELE [YLE] Papua New Guinea

Eskimo-Aleut (11)
- Aleut (1): ALEUT [ALW] USA
- Eskimo (10)
- - Inuit (5): INUKTITUT, EASTERN CANADIAN [ESB] Canada
- - - INUKTITUT, GREENLANDIC [ESG] Greenland
- - - INUKTITUT, WESTERN CANADIAN [ESC] Canada
- - - INUPIATUN, NORTH ALASKAN [ESI] USA
- - - INUPIATUN, NORTHWEST ALASKA [ESK] USA
- - Yupik (5)
- - - Alaskan (2): YUPIK, CENTRAL [ESU] USA
- - - - YUPIK, PACIFIC GULF [EMS] USA
- - - Siberian (3): YUPIK, CENTRAL SIBERIAN [ESS] USA
- - - - YUPIK, NAUKAN [YNK] Russia (Asia)
- - - - YUPIK, SIRENIK [YSR] Russia (Asia)

Geelvink Bay (33)
- East Geelvink Bay (11): ANASI [BPO] Indonesia (Irian Jaya)
- - BARAPASI [BRP] Indonesia (Irian Jaya)
- - BAUZI [PAU] Indonesia (Irian Jaya)
- - BURATE [BTI] Indonesia (Irian Jaya)
- - DEMISA [DEI] Indonesia (Irian Jaya)
- - KOFEI [KPI] Indonesia (Irian Jaya)
- - NISA [NIC] Indonesia (Irian Jaya)
- - SAURI [SAH] Indonesia (Irian Jaya)

Geelvink Bay (33)
- East Geelvink Bay (11): TEFARO [TFO] Indonesia (Irian Jaya)
- - TUNGGARE [TRT] Indonesia (Irian Jaya)
- - WORIA [WOR] Indonesia (Irian Jaya)
- Lakes Plain (20)
- - Awera (1): AWERA [AWR] Indonesia (Irian Jaya)
- - East Lakes Plain (2): FOAU [FLH] Indonesia (Irian Jaya)
- - - TAWORTA [TBP] Indonesia (Irian Jaya)
- - Rasawa-Saponi (2): RASAWA [RAC] Indonesia (Irian Jaya)
- - - SAPONI [SPI] Indonesia (Irian Jaya)
- - Tariku (15)
- - - Central (2): EDOPI [DBF] Indonesia (Irian Jaya)
- - - - IAU [TMU] Indonesia (Irian Jaya)
- - - Duvle (1): DUVLE [DUV] Indonesia (Irian Jaya)
- - - East (9): BIRITAI [BQQ] Indonesia (Irian Jaya)
- - - - DOUTAI [TDS] Indonesia (Irian Jaya)
- - - - ERITAI [BAD] Indonesia (Irian Jaya)
- - - - KAIY [TCQ] Indonesia (Irian Jaya)
- - - - KWERISA [KKB] Indonesia (Irian Jaya)
- - - - OBOKUITAI [AFZ] Indonesia (Irian Jaya)
- - - - PAPASENA [PAS] Indonesia (Irian Jaya)
- - - - SIKARITAI [TTY] Indonesia (Irian Jaya)
- - - - WARITAI [WBE] Indonesia (Irian Jaya)
- - - West (3): FAYU [FAU] Indonesia (Irian Jaya)
- - - - KIRIKIRI [KIY] Indonesia (Irian Jaya)
- - - - TAUSE [TAD] Indonesia (Irian Jaya)
- Yawa (2): SAWERU [SWR] Indonesia (Irian Jaya)
- - YAWA [YVA] Indonesia (Irian Jaya)

Guahiban (5): CUIBA [CUI] Colombia
- GUAHIBO [GUH] Colombia
- GUAYABERO [GUO] Colombia
- MACAGUÁN [MBN] Colombia
- PLAYERO [GOB] Colombia

Gulf (4): ATAKAPA [ALE] USA
- CHITIMACHA [CHM] USA
- NATCHEZ [NCZ] USA
- TUNICA [TUK] USA

Harakmbet (2): AMARAKAERI [AMR] Peru
- HUACHIPAERI [HUG] Peru

Hmong-Mien (32)
- Hmongic (26)
- - Bunu (5): BUNU, BAHENG [PHA] China
- - - BUNU, BU-NAO [BWX] China
- - - BUNU, JIONGNAI [PNU] China
- - - BUNU, WUNAI [BWN] China
- - - BUNU, YOUNUO [BUH] China
- - Chuanqiandian (16): HMONG DAW [MWW] China
- - - HMONG NJUA [BLU] China
- - - HMONG, CENTRAL HUISHUI [HMC] China
- - - HMONG, CENTRAL MASHAN [HMM] China
- - - HMONG, CHONGANJIANG [HMJ] China
- - - HMONG, EASTERN HUISHUI [HME] China
- - - HMONG, LUOPOHE [HML] China
- - - HMONG, NORTHEASTERN DIAN [HMD] China
- - - HMONG, NORTHERN GUIYANG [HUJ] China
- - - HMONG, NORTHERN HUISHUI [HMN] China
- - - HMONG, NORTHERN MASHAN [HMO] China

Hmong-Mien (32)
- Hmongic (26)
- - Chuanqiandian (16): HMONG, SOUTHERN GUIYANG [HMY] China
- - - HMONG, SOUTHERN MASHAN [HMA] China
- - - HMONG, SOUTHWESTERN GUIYANG [HMG] China
- - - HMONG, SOUTHWESTERN HUISHUI [HMH] China
- - - HMONG, WESTERN MASHAN [HMW] China
- - Qiandong (3): HMONG, EASTERN QIANDONG [HMQ] China
- - - HMONG, NORTHERN QIANDONG [HEA] China
- - - HMONG, SOUTHERN QIANDONG [HMS] China
- - Xiangxi (2): HMONG, EASTERN XIANGXI [MUQ] China
- - - HMONG, WESTERN XIANGXI [MMR] China
- Ho Nte (1): SHE [SHX] China
- Mienic (5)
- - Biao-Jiao (1): BIAO-JIAO MIEN [BJE] China
- - Mian-Jin (3): BIAO MIEN [BMT] China
- - - IU MIEN [IUM] China
- - - KIM MUN [MJI] China
- - Zaomin (1): BA PAI [BPN] China

Hokan (28)
- Esselen-Yuman (10)
- - Esselen (1): ESSELEN [ESQ] USA
- - Yuman (9)
- - - Cochimi (1): COCHIMÍ [COJ] Mexico
- - - Delta-Californian (2): COCOPA [COC] Mexico
- - - - KUMIÁI [DIH] Mexico
- - - Kiliwa (1): KILIWA [KLB] Mexico
- - - Pai (1): PAIPAI [PPI] Mexico
- - - River Yuman (3): MARICOPA [MRC] USA
- - - - MOHAVE [MOV] USA
- - - - QUECHAN [YUM] USA
- - - Upland Yuman (1): HAVASUPAI-WALAPAI-YAVAPAI [YUF] USA
- Northern (13): CHIMARIKO [CID] USA
- - Karok-Shasta (4): KAROK [KYH] USA
- - - Shasta-Palaihninan (3)
- - - - Palaihninan (2): ACHUMAWI [ACH] USA
- - - - - ATSUGEWI [ATW] USA
- - - - Shastan (1): SHASTA [SHT] USA
- - Pomo (7)
- - - Russian River and Eastern (6)
- - - - Eastern (1): POMO, EASTERN [PEB] USA
- - - - Russian River (5)
- - - - - Northeastern (1): POMO, NORTHEASTERN [PEF] USA
- - - - - Northern (1): POMO, NORTHERN [PEJ] USA
- - - - - Southern (3): KASHAYA [KJU] USA
- - - - - - POMO, CENTRAL [POO] USA
- - - - - - POMO, SOUTHERN [PEQ] USA
- - - Southeastern (1): POMO, SOUTHEASTERN [PEO] USA
- - Yana (1): YANA [YNN] USA
- Salinan-Seri (2): SALINAN [SAL] USA
- - SERI [SEI] Mexico
- Tequistlatecan (2): CHONTAL DE OAXACA, COSTA [CLO] Mexico
- - CHONTAL DE OAXACA, SIERRA [CHD] Mexico
- Washo (1): WASHO [WAS] USA

Huavean (4): HUAVE, SAN DIONISIO DEL MAR [HVE] Mexico
- HUAVE, SAN FRANCISCO DEL MAR [HUE] Mexico
- HUAVE, SAN MATEO DEL MAR [HUV] Mexico
- HUAVE, SANTA MARÍA DEL MAR [HVV] Mexico

Indo-European (443)
- Albanian (4)
- - Gheg (1): ALBANIAN, GHEG [ALS] Yugoslavia
- - Tosk (3): ALBANIAN, ARBËRESHË [AAE] Italy
- - - ALBANIAN, ARVANITIKA [AAT] Greece
- - - ALBANIAN, TOSK [ALN] Albania
- Armenian (2): ARMENIAN [ARM] Armenia
- - LOMAVREN [RMI] Armenia
- Baltic (3)
- - Eastern (2): LATVIAN [LAT] Latvia
- - - LITHUANIAN [LIT] Lithuania
- - Western (1): PRUSSIAN [PRG] Poland
- Celtic (7)
- - Insular (7)
- - - Brythonic (3): BRETON [BRT] France
- - - - CORNISH [CRN] United Kingdom
- - - - WELSH [WLS] United Kingdom
- - - Goidelic (4): GAELIC, IRISH [GLI] Ireland
- - - - GAELIC, SCOTS [GLS] United Kingdom
- - - - MANX [MJD] United Kingdom
- - - - SHELTA [STH] Ireland
- Germanic (58)
- - East (1): GOTHIC [GOF] Ukraine
- - North (14)
- - - East Scandinavian (8)
- - - - Danish-Swedish (8)
- - - - - Danish-Bokmal (4)
- - - - - - Bokmal (1): NORWEGIAN, BOKMAAL [NRR] Norway
- - - - - - Danish (3): DANISH [DNS] Denmark
- - - - - - - JUTISH [JUT] Denmark
- - - - - - - TRAVELLER DANISH [RMD] Denmark
- - - - - - Swedish (4): DALECARLIAN [DLC] Sweden
- - - - - - - SKÅNE [SCY] Sweden
- - - - - - - SWEDISH [SWD] Sweden
- - - - - - - TAVRINGER ROMANI [RMU] Sweden
- - - West Scandinavian (6): FAROESE [FAE] Denmark
- - - - ICELANDIC [ICE] Iceland
- - - - JAMSKA [JMK] Sweden
- - - - NORN [NON] United Kingdom
- - - - NORWEGIAN, NYNORSK [NRN] Norway
- - - - TRAVELLER NORWEGIAN [RMG] Norway
- - West (43)
- - - English (5): ANGLOROMANI [RME] United Kingdom
- - - - CAYMAN ISLANDS ENGLISH [CYE] Cayman Islands
- - - - ENGLISH [ENG] United Kingdom
- - - - SCOTS [SCO] United Kingdom
- - - - YINGLISH [YIB] USA
- - - Frisian (3): FRISIAN, EASTERN [FRS] Germany
- - - - FRISIAN, NORTHERN [FRR] Germany
- - - - FRISIAN, WESTERN [FRI] Netherlands
- - - High German (19)
- - - - German (17): FRANKISH [FRK] Germany
- - - - - Middle German (8)
- - - - - - East Middle German (3): GERMAN, STANDARD [GER] Germany
- - - - - - - SAXON, UPPER [SXU] Germany
- - - - - - - SILESIAN, LOWER [SLI] Poland
- - - - - - Moselle Franconian (1): LUXEMBOURGEOIS [LUX] Luxembourg
- - - - - - West Middle German (4): GERMAN, PENNSYLVANIA [PDC] USA
- - - - - - - Moselle Franconian (1): MAINFRÄNKISCH [VMF] Germany
- - - - - - - Rhenisch Fraconian (1): PFAELZISCH [PFL] Germany
- - - - - - - Ripuarian Franconian (1): KÖLSCH [KOR] Germany

Indo-European (443)
- Germanic (58)
- - West (43)
- - - High German (19)
- - - - German (17)
- - - - - Upper German (8)
- - - - - - Alemannic (4): ALEMANNISCH [GSW] Switzerland
- - - - - - - GERMAN, COLONIA TOVAR [GCT] Venezuela
- - - - - - - SWABIAN [SWG] Germany
- - - - - - - WALSER [WAE] Switzerland
- - - - - - Bavarian-Austrian (4): BAVARIAN [BAR] Austria
- - - - - - - CIMBRIAN [CIM] Italy
- - - - - - - GERMAN, HUTTERITE [GEH] Canada
- - - - - - - MÓCHENO [QMO] Italy
- - - - Yiddish (2): YIDDISH, EASTERN [YDD] Israel
- - - - - YIDDISH, WESTERN [YIH] Germany
- - - Low Saxon-Low Franconian (16)
- - - - Low Franconian (3): AFRIKAANS [AFK] South Africa
- - - - - DUTCH [DUT] Netherlands
- - - - - VLAAMS [VLA] Belgium
- - - - Low Saxon (13): ACHTERHOEKS [ACT] Netherlands
- - - - - DRENTS [DRT] Netherlands
- - - - - GRONINGS [GOS] Netherlands
- - - - - PLAUTDIETSCH [GRN] Canada
- - - - - SALLANDS [SNK] Netherlands
- - - - - SAXON, LOW [SXN] Germany
- - - - - STELLINGWERFS [STL] Netherlands
- - - - - TWENTS [TWD] Netherlands
- - - - - VEENKOLONIAALS [VEK] Netherlands
- - - - - VELUWS, EAST [VEE] Netherlands
- - - - - VELUWS, NORTH [VEL] Netherlands
- - - - - WESTERWOLDS [WEV] Netherlands
- - - - - WESTPHALIEN [WEP] Germany
- Greek (7)
- - Attic (6): CAPPADOCIAN GREEK [CPG] Greece
- - - GREEK [GRK] Greece
- - - GREEK, ANCIENT [GKO] Greece
- - - PONTIC [PNT] Greece
- - - ROMANO-GREEK [RGE] Greece
- - - YEVANIC [YEJ] Israel
- - Doric (1): TSAKONIAN [TSD] Greece
- Indo-Iranian (296)
- - Indo-Aryan (210): SANSKRIT [SKT] India
- - - Central zone (67)
- - - - Bhil (16): BARELI [BGD] India
- - - - - BAURIA [BGE] India
- - - - - BHILALI [BHI] India
- - - - - BHILI [BHB] India
- - - - - BHILORI [BQI] India
- - - - - CHODRI [CDI] India
- - - - - DHODIA [DHO] India
- - - - - DUBLI [DUB] India
- - - - - DUNGRA BHIL [DUH] India
- - - - - GAMIT [GBL] India
- - - - - GARASIA, ADIWASI [GAS] India
- - - - - GARASIA, RAJPUT [GRA] India
- - - - - MAWCHI [MKE] India
- - - - - PARDHI [PCL] India
- - - - - RATHAWI [RTW] India
- - - - - WAGDI [WBR] India
- - - - Dom (1): DOMARI [RMT] Iran

Indo-European (443)
- Indo-Iranian (296)
- - Indo-Aryan (210)
- - - Central zone (67)
- - - - Gujarati (9): AER [AEQ] Pakistan
- - - - - GUJARATI [GJR] India
- - - - - JANDAVRA [JND] Pakistan
- - - - - KOLI, KACHI [GJK] Pakistan
- - - - - KOLI, PARKARI [KVX] Pakistan
- - - - - KOLI, WADIYARA [KXP] Pakistan
- - - - - SAURASHTRA [SAZ] India
- - - - - VAGHRI [VGR] Pakistan
- - - - - VASAVI [VAS] India
- - - - Khandesi (3): AHIRANI [AHR] India
- - - - - DHANKI [DHN] India
- - - - - KHANDESI [KHN] India
- - - - Panjabi (1): PANJABI, EASTERN [PNJ] India
- - - - Rajasthani (14)
- - - - - Marwari (6): DHATKI [MKI] Pakistan
- - - - - GOARIA [GIG] Pakistan
- - - - - LOARKI [LRK] Pakistan
- - - - - MARWARI [MKD] India
- - - - - MARWARI [MRI] Pakistan
- - - - - MEWARI [MTR] India
- - - - - Unclassified (8): BAGRI [BGQ] India
- - - - - GUJARI [GJU] India
- - - - - GURGULA [GGG] Pakistan
- - - - - HARAUTI [HOJ] India
- - - - - LAMBADI [LMN] India
- - - - - LOHAR, GADE [GDA] India
- - - - - MALVI [MUP] India
- - - - - NIMADI [NOE] India
- - - - Romani (7)
- - - - - Balkan (1): ROMANI, BALKAN [RMN] Yugoslavia
- - - - - Northern (5): ROMANI, BALTIC [ROM] Poland
- - - - - - ROMANI, CARPATHIAN [RMC] Czech Republic
- - - - - - ROMANI, KALO FINNISH [RMF] Finland
- - - - - - ROMANI, SINTE [RMO] Yugoslavia
- - - - - - ROMANI, WELSH [RMW] United Kingdom
- - - - - Vlax (1): ROMANI, VLAX [RMY] Romania
- - - - Unclassified (4): PARYA [PAQ] Tajikistan
- - - - - SONHA [SOI] Nepal
- - - - - THARU, DANGAURA [THL] Nepal
- - - - - THARU, KATHORIYA [TKT] Nepal
- - - - Western Hindi (12)
- - - - - Bundeli (1): BUNDELI [BNS] India
- - - - - Hindustani (4): HINDI [HND] India
- - - - - - URDU [URD] Pakistan
- - - - - - Sansi (2): KABUTRA [KBU] Pakistan
- - - - - - - SANSI [SSI] Pakistan
- - - - - Unclassified (7): BHAYA [BHE] Pakistan
- - - - - - BRAJ BHASHA [BFS] India
- - - - - - CHAMARI [CDG] India
- - - - - - GHERA [GHR] Pakistan
- - - - - - GOWLI [GOK] India
- - - - - - HARYANVI [BGC] India
- - - - - - KANAUJI [BJJ] India
- - - East Central zone (5): AWADHI [AWD] India
- - - - BAGHELI [BFY] India
- - - - CHHATTISGARHI [HNE] India
- - - - DHANWAR [DHA] India

Indo-European (443)
- Indo-Iranian (296)
- - Indo-Aryan (210)
- - - East Central zone (5): HINDUSTANI, FIJIAN [HIF] Fiji
- - - Eastern zone (42)
- - - - Bengali-Assamese (15): ASSAMESE [ASM] India
- - - - - BENGALI [BNG] Bangladesh
- - - - - BISHNUPRIYA [BPY] India
- - - - - CHAKMA [CCP] India
- - - - - CHITTAGONIAN [CIT] Bangladesh
- - - - - HAJONG [HAJ] India
- - - - - HALBI [HLB] India
- - - - - KAYORT [KYV] Nepal
- - - - - KHARIA THAR [KSY] India
- - - - - MAL PAHARIA [MKB] India
- - - - - MIRGAN [QMK] India
- - - - - NAHARI [NHH] India
- - - - - RAJBANGSI [RJB] India
- - - - - SYLHETTI [SYL] Bangladesh
- - - - - TANGCHANGYA [TNV] Bangladesh
- - - - Bihari (12): ANGIKA [ANP] India
- - - - - BHOJPURI [BHJ] India
- - - - - HINDUSTANI, CARIBBEAN [HNS] Suriname
- - - - - KUDMALI [KYW] India
- - - - - MAGAHI [MQM] India
- - - - - MAITHILI [MKP] India
- - - - - MAJHI [MJZ] Nepal
- - - - - MUSASA [SMM] Nepal
- - - - - PANCHPARGANIA [TDB] India
- - - - - SADRI [SCK] India
- - - - - SADRI, ORAON [SDR] Bangladesh
- - - - - SURAJPURI [SJP] India
- - - - Oriya (7): BHATRI [BGW] India
- - - - - BHUNJIA [BHU] India
- - - - - BODO PARJA [BDV] India
- - - - - KUPIA [KEY] India
- - - - - ORIYA [ORY] India
- - - - - ORIYA, ADIVASI [ORT] India
- - - - - RELI [REI] India
- - - - Unclassified (8): BOTE-MAJHI [BMJ] Nepal
- - - - - BUKSA [TKB] India
- - - - - DEGARU [DGR] India
- - - - - THARU, CHITWANIA [THE] Nepal
- - - - - THARU, DEOKHURI [THG] Nepal
- - - - - THARU, KOCHILA [THQ] Nepal
- - - - - THARU, MAHOTARI [THN] Nepal
- - - - - THARU, RANA [THR] Nepal
- - - Northern zone (21)
- - - - Central Pahari (1): KUMAUNI [KFY] India
- - - - Eastern Pahari (2): NEPALI [NEP] Nepal
- - - - - PALPA [PLP] Nepal
- - - - Garhwali (2): GARHWALI [GBM] India
- - - - - TEHRI [THB] India
- - - - Western Pahari (16): BHADRAWAHI [BHD] India
- - - - - BHATTIYALI [BHT] India
- - - - - BILASPURI [KFS] India
- - - - - CHAMBEALI [CDH] India
- - - - - CHURAHI [CDJ] India
- - - - - DOGRI-KANGRI [DOJ] India
- - - - - GADDI [GBK] India
- - - - - HINDURI [HII] India

Indo-European (443)
- Indo-Iranian (296)
- - Indo-Aryan (210)
- - - Northern zone (21)
- - - - Western Pahari (16): JAUNSARI [JNS] India
- - - - KINNAURI, HARIJAN [KJO] India
- - - - MANDEALI [MJL] India
- - - - PAHARI, KULLU [KFX] India
- - - - PAHARI, MAHASU [BFZ] India
- - - - PAHARI-POTWARI [PHR] Pakistan
- - - - PANGWALI [PGG] India
- - - - SIRMAURI [SRX] India
- - - Northwestern zone (39)
- - - - Dardic (27)
- - - - Chitral (2): KALASHA [KLS] Pakistan
- - - - - KHOWAR [KHW] Pakistan
- - - - Kashmiri (1): KASHMIRI [KSH] India
- - - - Kohistani (9): BATERI [BTV] Pakistan
- - - - - CHILISSO [CLH] Pakistan
- - - - - GOWRO [GWF] Pakistan
- - - - - KALAMI [GWC] Pakistan
- - - - - KALKOTI [XKA] Pakistan
- - - - - KOHISTANI, INDUS [MVY] Pakistan
- - - - - TIRAHI [TRA] Afghanistan
- - - - - TORWALI [TRW] Pakistan
- - - - - WOTAPURI-KATARQALAI [WSV] Afghanistan
- - - - Kunar (8): DAMELI [DML] Pakistan
- - - - - GAWAR-BATI [GWT] Afghanistan
- - - - - GRANGALI [NLI] Afghanistan
- - - - - SHUMASHTI [SMS] Afghanistan
- - - - - Pashayi (4): PASHAYI, NORTHEAST [AEE] Afghanistan
- - - - - - PASHAYI, NORTHWEST [GLH] Afghanistan
- - - - - - PASHAYI, SOUTHEAST [DRA] Afghanistan
- - - - - - PASHAYI, SOUTHWEST [PSH] Afghanistan
- - - - Shina (7): BROKSKAT [BKK] India
- - - - - DOMAAKI [DMK] Pakistan
- - - - - PHALURA [PHL] Pakistan
- - - - - SAVI [SDG] Afghanistan
- - - - - SHINA [SCL] Pakistan
- - - - - SHINA, KOHISTANI [PLK] Pakistan
- - - - - USHOJO [USH] Pakistan
- - - - Lahnda (7): HINDKO, NORTHERN [HNO] Pakistan
- - - - HINDKO, SOUTHERN [HIN] Pakistan
- - - - JAKATI [JAT] Ukraine
- - - - KHETRANI [QKT] Pakistan
- - - - PANJABI, MIRPUR [PMU] India
- - - - PANJABI, WESTERN [PNB] Pakistan
- - - - SARAIKI [SKR] Pakistan
- - - Sindhi (5): JADGALI [JAV] Pakistan
- - - - KACHCHI [KFR] India
- - - - LASI [LSS] Pakistan
- - - - SINDHI [SND] Pakistan
- - - - SINDHI BHIL [SBN] Pakistan
- - - Nuristani (6): ASHKUN [ASK] Afghanistan
- - - - KAMVIRI [QMV] Afghanistan
- - - - KATI [BSH] Afghanistan
- - - - PRASUNI [PRN] Afghanistan
- - - - TREGAMI [TRM] Afghanistan
- - - - WAIGALI [WBK] Afghanistan
- - - Sinhalese-Maldivian (3): MALDIVIAN [SNM] Maldives
- - - - SINHALA [SNH] Sri Lanka

Indo-European (443)
- Indo-Iranian (296)
- - Indo-Aryan (210)
- - - Sinhalese-Maldivian (3): VEDDAH [VED] Sri Lanka
- - - Southern zone (13): MARATHI [MRT] India
- - - - Konkani (7): KATKARI [KFU] India
- - - - - KONKANI [KNK] India
- - - - - KONKANI, GOANESE [GOM] India
- - - - - KUKNA [KEX] India
- - - - - PHUDAGI [PHD] India
- - - - - SAMVEDI [SMV] India
- - - - - VARLI [VAV] India
- - - - Unclassified (5): ARE [AAG] India
- - - - - BHALAY [BHX] India
- - - - - DECCAN [DCC] India
- - - - - GOWLAN [GOJ] India
- - - - - VARHADI-NAGPURI [VAH] India
- - - Unclassified (13): CHINALI [CIH] India
- - - - DARAI [DRY] Nepal
- - - - DHANWAR [DHW] Nepal
- - - - KANJARI [KFT] India
- - - - KUMHALI [KRA] Nepal
- - - - LOHAR, LAHUL [LHL] India
- - - - MEMONI [MBY] Pakistan
- - - - MINA [MYI] India
- - - - OD [ODK] Pakistan
- - - - PALI [PLL] India
- - - - TIPPERA [TPE] Bangladesh
- - - - USUI [USI] Bangladesh
- - - - VAAGRI BOOLI [VAA] India
- - Iranian (84)
- - - Eastern (14)
- - - - Northeastern (3): AVESTAN [AVS] Iran
- - - - - OSETIN [OSE] Georgia
- - - - - YAGNOBI [YAI] Tajikistan
- - - - Southeastern (11)
- - - - - Pamir (7): MUNJI [MNJ] Afghanistan
- - - - - - SANGLECHI-ISHKASHIMI [SGL] Tajikistan
- - - - - - WAKHI [WBL] Pakistan
- - - - - - YIDGHA [YDG] Pakistan
- - - - - - Shugni-Yazgulami (3): SARIKOLI [SRH] China
- - - - - - - SHUGHNI [SGH] Tajikistan
- - - - - - - YAZGULYAM [YAH] Tajikistan
- - - - - Pashto (4): PASHTO, CENTRAL [PST] Pakistan
- - - - - - PASHTO, NORTHERN [PBU] Pakistan
- - - - - - PASHTO, SOUTHERN [PBT] Afghanistan
- - - - - - WANECI [WNE] Pakistan
- - - Unclassified (1): TANGSHEWI [TNF] Afghanistan
- - - Western (69)
- - - - Northwestern (53): KHALAJ [KJF] Iran
- - - - - Balochi (5): BALOCHI, EASTERN [BGP] Pakistan
- - - - - - BALOCHI, SOUTHERN [BCC] Pakistan
- - - - - - BALOCHI, WESTERN [BGN] Pakistan
- - - - - - BASHKARDI [BSG] Iran
- - - - - - KOROSHI [KTL] Iran
- - - - - Caspian (4): GILAKI [GLK] Iran
- - - - - - MAZANDERANI [MZN] Iran
- - - - - - RASHTI [RSH] Iran
- - - - - - SHAHMIRZADI [SRZ] Iran
- - - - - Central Iran (11): ASHTIANI [ATN] Iran
- - - - - - DARI [GBZ] Iran

Indo-European (443)
- Indo-Iranian (296)
- - Iranian (84)
- - - Western (69)
- - - - Northwestern (53)
- - - - - Central Iran (11): GAZI [GZI] Iran
- - - - - - KHUNSARI [KFM] Iran
- - - - - - NATANZI [NTZ] Iran
- - - - - - NAYINI [NYQ] Iran
- - - - - - PARSI [PRP] India
- - - - - - PARSI-DARI [PRD] Iran
- - - - - - SIVANDI [SIY] Iran
- - - - - - SOI [SOJ] Iran
- - - - - - VAFSI [VAF] Iran
- - - - - Kurdish (6): BEHDINI [BDF] Iraq
- - - - - - HERKI [HEK] Iraq
- - - - - - KURDI [KDB] Iraq
- - - - - - KURMANJI [KUR] Turkey (Asia)
- - - - - - SHIKAKI [SHF] Iraq
- - - - - - SURCHI [SUP] Iraq
- - - - - Ormuri-Parachi (2): ORMURI [ORU] Pakistan
- - - - - - PARACHI [PRC] Afghanistan
- - - - - Semnani (4): LASGERDI [LSA] Iran
- - - - - - SANGISARI [SGR] Iran
- - - - - - SEMNANI [SMJ] Iran
- - - - - - SORKHEI [SQO] Iran
- - - - - Talysh (16): ALVIRI-VIDARI [AVD] Iran
- - - - - - ESHTEHARDI [ESH] Iran
- - - - - - GOZARKHANI [GOZ] Iran
- - - - - - HARZANI [HRZ] Iran
- - - - - - KABATEI [XKP] Iran
- - - - - - KAJALI [XKJ] Iran
- - - - - - KARINGANI [KGN] Iran
- - - - - - KHOINI [XKC] Iran
- - - - - - KORESH-E ROSTAM [OKH] Iran
- - - - - - MARAGHEI [VMH] Iran
- - - - - - RAZAJERDI [RAT] Iran
- - - - - - RUDBARI [RDB] Iran
- - - - - - SHAHRUDI [SHM] Iran
- - - - - - TAKESTANI [TKS] Iran
- - - - - - TALYSH [TLY] Azerbaijan
- - - - - - TAROMI, UPPER [TIB] Iran
- - - - - Zaza-Gorani (4): BAJELAN [BJM] Iraq
- - - - - - DIMLI [ZZZ] Turkey (Asia)
- - - - - - HAWRAMI [HAC] Iraq
- - - - - - KIRMANJKI [QKV] Turkey (Asia)
- - - - Southwestern (16)
- - - - - Fars (2): FARS [FAC] Iran
- - - - - - LARI [LRL] Iran
- - - - - Luri (2): KUMZARI [ZUM] Oman
- - - - - - LURI [LRI] Iran
- - - - - Persian (10): AIMAQ [AIQ] Afghanistan
- - - - - - BUKHARIC [BHH] Israel
- - - - - - DARWAZI [DRW] Afghanistan
- - - - - - DEHWARI [DEH] Pakistan
- - - - - - DZHIDI [DZH] Israel
- - - - - - FARSI, EASTERN [PRS] Afghanistan
- - - - - - FARSI, WESTERN [PES] Iran
- - - - - - HAZARAGI [HAZ] Afghanistan
- - - - - - PAHLAVANI [PHV] Afghanistan
- - - - - - TAJIKI [PET] Tajikistan

Indo-European (443)
- Indo-Iranian (296)
- - Iranian (84)
- - - Western (69)
- - - - Southwestern (16)
- - - - - Tat (2): JUDEO-TAT [TAT] Israel
- - - - - - TAT, MUSLIM [TTT] Azerbaijan
- - Unclassified (2): BADESHI [BDZ] Pakistan
- - - LUWATI [LUV] Oman
- Italic (48)
- - Latino-Faliscan (1): LATIN [LTN] Vatican State
- - Romance (47)
- - - Eastern (4): ROMANIAN [RUM] Romania
- - - - ROMANIAN, ISTRO [RUO] Croatia
- - - - ROMANIAN, MACEDO [RUP] Greece
- - - - ROMANIAN, MEGLENO [RUQ] Greece
- - - Italo-Western (38)
- - - - Italo-Dalmatian (6): DALMATIAN [DLM] Croatia
- - - - - ISTRIOT [IST] Croatia
- - - - - ITALIAN [ITN] Italy
- - - - - JUDEO-ITALIAN [ITK] Italy
- - - - - NAPOLETANO-CALABRESE [NPL] Italy
- - - - - SICILIAN [SCN] Italy
- - - - Western (32)
- - - - - Gallo-Iberian (30)
- - - - - - Gallo-Romance (13)
- - - - - - - Gallo-Italian (5): EMILIANO-ROMAGNOLO [EML] Italy
- - - - - - - - LIGURIAN [LIJ] Italy
- - - - - - - - LOMBARD [LMO] Italy
- - - - - - - - PIEMONTESE [PMS] Italy
- - - - - - - - VENETIAN [VEC] Italy
- - - - - - - Gallo-Rhaetian (8)
- - - - - - - - OÏl (5)
- - - - - - - - - French (4): FRENCH [FRN] France
- - - - - - - - - - FRENCH, CAJUN [FRC] USA
- - - - - - - - - - PICARD [PCD] France
- - - - - - - - - - ZARPHATIC [ZRP] France
- - - - - - - - - Southeastern (1): FRANCO-PROVENÇAL [FRA] France
- - - - - - - - - Rhaetian (3): FRIULIAN [FRL] Italy
- - - - - - - - - - LADIN [LLD] Italy
- - - - - - - - - - ROMANSCH [RHE] Switzerland
- - - - - - Ibero-Romance (17)
- - - - - - - East Iberian (1): CATALAN-VALENCIAN-BALEAR [CLN] Spain
- - - - - - - Oc (6): AUVERGNAT [AUV] France
- - - - - - - - GASCON [GSC] France
- - - - - - - - LANGUEDOCIEN [LNC] France
- - - - - - - - LIMOUSIN [LMS] France
- - - - - - - - PROVENÇAL [PRV] France
- - - - - - - - SHUADIT [SDT] France
- - - - - - - West Iberian (10)
- - - - - - - - Asturo-Leonese (2): ASTURIAN [AUB] Spain
- - - - - - - - - MIRANDA DO DOURO [MWL] Portugal
- - - - - - - - Castilian (5): CALÓ [RMR] Spain
- - - - - - - - - EXTREMADURAN [EXT] Spain
- - - - - - - - - LADINO [SPJ] Israel
- - - - - - - - - SPANISH [SPN] Spain
- - - - - - - - - SPANISH, LORETO-UCAYALI [SPQ] Peru
- - - - - - - - Portuguese-Galician (3): FALA [FAX] Spain
- - - - - - - - - GALICIAN [GLN] Spain
- - - - - - - - - PORTUGUESE [POR] Portugal

Indo-European (443)
- Italic (48)
- - Romance (47)
- - - Italo-Western (38)
- - - - Western (32)
- - - - - Pyranean-Mozarabic (2)
- - - - - - Mozarabic (1): MOZARABIC [MXI] Spain
- - - - - - Pyranean (1): ARAGONESE [AXX] Spain
- - - Southern (5)
- - - - Corsican (1): CORSICAN [COI] France
- - - - Sardinian (4): SARDINIAN, CAMPIDANESE [SRO] Italy
- - - - - SARDINIAN, GALLURESE [SDN] Italy
- - - - - SARDINIAN, LOGUDORESE [SRD] Italy
- - - - - SARDINIAN, SASSARESE [SDC] Italy
- Slavic (18)
- - East (4): BELARUSAN [RUW] Belarus
- - - RUSSIAN [RUS] Russia (Europe)
- - - RUSYN [RUE] Ukraine
- - - UKRAINIAN [UKR] Ukraine
- - South (6)
- - - Eastern (3): BULGARIAN [BLG] Bulgaria
- - - - MACEDONIAN [MKJ] Macedonia
- - - - SLAVONIC, OLD CHURCH [SLN] Russia (Europe)
- - - Western (3): ROMANO-SERBIAN [RSB] Yugoslavia
- - - - SERBO-CROATIAN [SRC] Yugoslavia
- - - - SLOVENIAN [SLV] Slovenia
- - West (8)
- - - Czech-Slovak (3): CZECH [CZC] Czech Republic
- - - - KNAANIC [CZK] Czech Republic
- - - - SLOVAK [SLO] Slovakia
- - - Lechitic (3): KASHUBIAN [CSB] Poland
- - - - POLABIAN [POX] Germany
- - - - POLISH [PQL] Poland
- - - Sorbian (2): SORBIAN, LOWER [WEE] Germany
- - - - SORBIAN, UPPER [WEN] Germany

Iroquoian (10): SUSQUEHANNOCK [SQN] USA
- Northern Iroquoian (8): LAURENTIAN [LRE] Canada
- - Five Nations (5)
- - - Mohawk-Oneida (2): MOHAWK [MOH] Canada
- - - - ONEIDA [ONE] Canada
- - - Seneca-Onondaga (3)
- - - - Onondaga (1): ONONDAGA [ONO] Canada
- - - - Seneca-Cayuga (2): CAYUGA [CAY] Canada
- - - - - SENECA [SEE] USA
- - Huron (1): WYANDOT [WYA] USA
- - Tuscarora-Nottoway (1): TUSCARORA [TUS] Canada
- Southern Iroquoian (1): CHEROKEE [CER] USA

Japanese (12)
- Japanese (1): JAPANESE [JPN] Japan
- Ryukyuan (11)
- - Amami-Okinawan (8)
- - - Northern Amami-Okinawan (4): AMAMI-OSHIMA, NORTHERN [RYN] Japan
- - - - AMAMI-OSHIMA, SOUTHERN [AMS] Japan
- - - - KIKAI [KZG] Japan
- - - - TOKU-NO-SHIMA [TKN] Japan
- - - Southern Amami-Okinawan (4): KUNIGAMI [XUG] Japan
- - - - OKI-NO-ERABU [OKN] Japan
- - - - OKINAWAN, CENTRAL [RYU] Japan
- - - - YORON [YOX] Japan

Japanese (12)
- Ryukyuan (11)
- - Sakishima (3): MIYAKO [MVI] Japan
- - - YAEYAMA [RYS] Japan
- - - YONAGUNI [YOI] Japan

Jivaroan (4): ACHUAR-SHIWIAR [ACU] Peru
- AGUARUNA [AGR] Peru
- HUAMBISA [HUB] Peru
- SHUAR [JIV] Ecuador

Katukinan (3): KANAMARÍ [KNM] Brazil
- KATAWIXI [QKI] Brazil
- KATUKÍNA [KAV] Brazil

Keres (2): KERES, EASTERN [KEE] USA
- KERES, WESTERN [KJQ] USA

Khoisan (29)
- Hatsa (1): HADZA [HTS] Tanzania
- Sandawe (1): SANDAWE [SBR] Tanzania
- Southern Africa (27)
- - Central (14)
- - - Hain//um (1): HAI//OM [HGM] Namibia
- - - Kwadi (1): KWADI [KWZ] Angola
- - - Nama (3): KORANA [KQZ] South Africa
- - - - NAMA [NAQ] Namibia
- - - - XIRI [XII] South Africa
- - - Tshu-Khwe (9)
- - - - Central (1): DETI [DET] Botswana
- - - - North Central (2): GANÁDI [GNE] Botswana
- - - - - SHUA [SHG] Botswana
- - - - Northeast (1): HIETSHWARE [HIE] Botswana
- - - - Northwest (3): /ANDA [HNH] Botswana
- - - - - //GANA [GNK] Botswana
- - - - - KXOE [XUU] Namibia
- - - - Southwest (2): /GWI [GWJ] Botswana
- - - - - NARO [NHR] Botswana
- - Northern (7): 'AKHOE [AKE] Namibia
- - - JU/'HOAN [KTZ] Botswana
- - - KUNG-EKOKA [KNW] Namibia
- - - ǂKX'AU//'EIN [AUE] Namibia
- - - MALIGO [MWJ] Angola
- - - !O!UNG [OUN] Angola
- - - VASEKELA BUSHMAN [VAJ] Namibia
- - Southern (6)
- - - !Kwi (4): N/U [NGH] South Africa
- - - - SEROA [KQU] South Africa
- - - - /XAM [XAM] South Africa
- - - - //XEGWI [XEG] South Africa
- - - Hua (2): ǂHUA [HUC] Botswana
- - - - !XÓÕ [NMN] Botswana

Kiowa Tanoan (6)
- Kiowa-Towa (2)
- - Kiowa (1): KIOWA [KIO] USA
- - Towa (1): JEMEZ [TOW] USA
- Tewa-Tiwa (4)
- - Tewa (1): TEWA [TEW] USA
- - Tiwa (3): PIRO [PIE] USA
- - - TIWA, NORTHERN [TAO] USA

Kiowa Tanoan (6)
- Tewa-Tiwa (4)
- - Tiwa (3): TIWA, SOUTHERN [TIX] USA

Kwomtari-Baibai (6)
- Baibai (2): BAIBAI [BBF] Papua New Guinea
- - NAI [BIO] Papua New Guinea
- Kwomtari (3): FAS [FAS] Papua New Guinea
- - GURIASO [GRX] Papua New Guinea
- - KWOMTARI [KWO] Papua New Guinea
- Pyu (1): PYU [PBY] Papua New Guinea

Language Isolate (28): ABINOMN [BSA] Indonesia (Irian Jaya)
- AINU [AIN] Japan
- ANDOQUE [ANO] Colombia
- BURMESO [BZU] Indonesia (Irian Jaya)
- BURUSHASKI [BSK] Pakistan
- BUSA [BHF] Papua New Guinea
- CAMSÁ [KBH] Colombia
- CAYUBABA [CAT] Bolivia
- GILYAK [NIV] Russia (Asia)
- ITONAMA [ITO] Bolivia
- KARKAR-YURI [YUJ] Papua New Guinea
- KIBIRI [PRM] Papua New Guinea
- KOREAN [KKN] Korea, South
- KUTENAI [KUN] Canada
- NIHALI [NHL] India
- PANKARARÚ [PAZ] Brazil
- PUELCHE [PUE] Argentina
- PUINAVE [PUI] Colombia
- TICUNA [TCA] Peru
- TOL [JIC] Honduras
- TRUMAÍ [TPY] Brazil
- TUXÁ [TUD] Brazil
- WARAO [WBA] Venezuela
- YALE [NCE] Papua New Guinea
- YÁMANA [YAG] Chile
- YUCHI [YUC] USA
- YURACARE [YUE] Bolivia
- ZUNI [ZUN] USA

Left May (7): AMA [AMM] Papua New Guinea
- BO [BPW] Papua New Guinea
- ITERI [ITR] Papua New Guinea
- NAKWI [NAX] Papua New Guinea
- NIMO [NIW] Papua New Guinea
- OWINIGA [OWI] Papua New Guinea
- ROCKY PEAK [ROK] Papua New Guinea

Lower Mamberamo (2): WAREMBORI [WSA] Indonesia (Irian Jaya)
- YOKE [YKI] Indonesia (Irian Jaya)

Lule-Vilela (1): VILELA [VIL] Argentina

Macro-Ge (32)
- Bororo (3)
- - Bororo Proper (2): BORÔRO [BOR] Brazil
- - - UMOTÍNA [UMO] Brazil
- - Otuke (1): OTUKE [OTU] Brazil
- Botocudo (1): KRENAK [KQQ] Brazil
- Chiquito (1): CHIQUITANO [CAX] Bolivia

Macro-Ge (32)
- Fulnio (1): FULNIÔ [FUN] Brazil
- Ge-Kaingang (16)
- - Ge (13)
- - - Central (4): ACROÁ [ACS] Brazil
- - - - Acua (3): XAKRIABÁ [XKR] Brazil
- - - - - XAVÁNTE [XAV] Brazil
- - - - - XERÉNTE [XER] Brazil
- - - Northwest (9)
- - - - Apinaye (1): APINAYÉ [APN] Brazil
- - - - Kayapo (1): KAYAPÓ [TXU] Brazil
- - - - Kreen-Akarore (1): KREEN-AKARORE [KRE] Brazil
- - - - Suya (1): SUYÁ [SUY] Brazil
- - - - Timbira (5): CANELA [RAM] Brazil
- - - - - GAVIÃO, PARÁ [GAY] Brazil
- - - - - KRAHÔ [XRA] Brazil
- - - - - KREYE [XRE] Brazil
- - - - - KRIKATI-TIMBIRA [XRI] Brazil
- - Kaingang (3)
- - - Northern (3): KAINGÁNG [KGP] Brazil
- - - - KAINGÁNG, SÃO PAULO [ZKS] Brazil
- - - - XOKLENG [XOK] Brazil
- Guato (1): GUATÓ [GTA] Brazil
- Kamakan (1): KAMAKAN [VKM] Brazil
- Karaja (1): KARAJÁ [KPJ] Brazil
- Maxakali (1): MAXAKALÍ [MBL] Brazil
- Opaye (1): OPAYÉ [OPY] Brazil
- Oti (1): OTI [OTI] Brazil
- Puri (1): PURI [PRR] Brazil
- Rikbaktsa (1): RIKBAKTSA [ART] Brazil
- Yabuti (2): ARIKAPÚ [ARK] Brazil
- - JABUTÍ [JBT] Brazil

Maku (6): CACUA [CBV] Colombia
- HUPDË [JUP] Brazil
- KAMÃ [KWA] Brazil
- NADËB [MBJ] Brazil
- NUKAK MAKÚ [MBR] Colombia
- YUHUP [YAB] Brazil

Mascoian (5): EMOK [EMO] Paraguay
- GUANA [GVA] Paraguay
- LENGUA [LEG] Paraguay
- SANAPANÁ [SAP] Paraguay
- TOBA-MASKOY [TMF] Paraguay

Mataco-Guaicuru (11)
- Guaicuruan (4): KADIWÉU [KBC] Brazil
- - MOCOVÍ [MOC] Argentina
- - PILAGÁ [PLG] Argentina
- - TOBA [TOB] Argentina
- Mataco (7): CHOROTE, IYOJWA'JA [CRT] Argentina
- - CHOROTE, IYO'WUJWA [CRQ] Argentina
- - CHULUPÍ [CAG] Paraguay
- - MACA [MCA] Paraguay
- - WICHÍ LHAMTÉS GÜISNAY [MZH] Argentina
- - WICHÍ LHAMTÉS NOCTEN [MTP] Bolivia
- - WICHÍ LHAMTÉS VEJOZ [MAD] Argentina

Mayan (69)
- Cholan-Tzeltalan (12)
- - Cholan (4)
- - - Chol-Chontal (3): CH'OL, TILA [CTI] Mexico
- - - - CH'OL, TUMBALÁ [CTU] Mexico
- - - - CHONTAL, TABASCO [CHF] Mexico
- - - Chorti (1): CHORTÍ [CAA] Guatemala
- - Tzeltalan (8): TZELTAL, BACHAJÓN [TZB] Mexico
- - - TZELTAL, OXCHUC [TZH] Mexico
- - - TZOTZIL, CHAMULA [TZC] Mexico
- - - TZOTZIL, CH'ENALHÓ [TZE] Mexico
- - - TZOTZIL, HUIXTÁN [TZU] Mexico
- - - TZOTZIL, SAN ANDRÉS LARRAINZAR [TZS] Mexico
- - - TZOTZIL, VENUSTIANO CARRANZA [TZO] Mexico
- - - TZOTZIL, ZINACANTÁN [TZZ] Mexico
- Huastecan (4): CHICOMUCELTEC [COB] Mexico
- - HUASTECO, SAN FRANCISCO CHONTLA [HAU] Mexico
- - HUASTECO, SAN LUÍS POTOSÍ [HVA] Mexico
- - HUASTECO, TANTOYUCA [HUS] Mexico
- Kanjobalan-Chujean (8)
- - Chujean (3): CHUJ, SAN MATEO IXTATÁN [CNM] Guatemala
- - - CHUJ, SAN SEBASTIÁN COATÁN [CAC] Guatemala
- - - TOJOLABAL [TOJ] Mexico
- - Kanjobalan (5)
- - - Kanjobal-Jacaltec (4): JACALTECO, EASTERN [JAC] Guatemala
- - - - JACALTECO, WESTERN [JAI] Guatemala
- - - - KANJOBAL, EASTERN [KJB] Guatemala
- - - - KANJOBAL, WESTERN [KNJ] Guatemala
- - - Mocho (1): MOCHO [MHC] Mexico
- Quichean-Mamean (40)
- - Greater Mamean (11)
- - - Ixilan (4): AGUACATECO [AGU] Guatemala
- - - - IXIL, CHAJUL [IXJ] Guatemala
- - - - IXIL, NEBAJ [IXI] Guatemala
- - - - IXIL, SAN JUAN COTZAL [IXL] Guatemala
- - - Mamean (7): MAM, CENTRAL [MVC] Guatemala
- - - - MAM, NORTHERN [MAM] Guatemala
- - - - MAM, SOUTHERN [MMS] Guatemala
- - - - MAM, TAJUMULCO [MPF] Guatemala
- - - - MAM, TODOS SANTOS CUCHUMATÁN [MVJ] Guatemala
- - - - TACANECO [MTZ] Guatemala
- - - - TECTITECO [TTC] Guatemala
- - Greater Quichean (29)
- - - Kekchi (1): KEKCHÍ [KEK] Guatemala
- - - Pocom (5): POKOMAM, CENTRAL [POC] Guatemala
- - - - POKOMAM, EASTERN [POA] Guatemala
- - - - POKOMAM, SOUTHERN [POU] Guatemala
- - - - POKOMCHÍ, EASTERN [POH] Guatemala
- - - - POKOMCHÍ, WESTERN [POB] Guatemala
- - - Quichean (20)
- - - - Cakchiquel (10): CAKCHIQUEL, CENTRAL [CAK] Guatemala
- - - - - CAKCHIQUEL, EASTERN [CKE] Guatemala
- - - - - CAKCHIQUEL, NORTHERN [CKC] Guatemala
- - - - - CAKCHIQUEL, SANTA MARÍA DE JESÚS [CKI] Guatemala
- - - - - CAKCHIQUEL, SANTO DOMINGO XENACOJ [CKJ] Guatemala
- - - - - CAKCHIQUEL, SOUTH CENTRAL [CKD] Guatemala
- - - - - CAKCHIQUEL, SOUTHERN [CKF] Guatemala
- - - - - CAKCHIQUEL, SOUTHWESTERN, ACATENANGO [CKK] Guatemala
- - - - - CAKCHIQUEL, SOUTHWESTERN, YEPOCAPA [CBM] Guatemala
- - - - - CAKCHIQUEL, WESTERN [CKW] Guatemala
- - - - Quiche-Achi (8): ACHÍ, CUBULCO [ACC] Guatemala

Mayan (69)
- Quichean-Mamean (40)
- - Greater Quichean (29)
- - - Quichean (20)
- - - - Quiche-Achi (8): ACHÍ, RABINAL [ACR] Guatemala
- - - - - QUICHÉ, CENTRAL [QUC] Guatemala
- - - - - QUICHÉ, CUNÉN [CUN] Guatemala
- - - - - QUICHÉ, EASTERN, CHICHICASTENANGO [QUU] Guatemala
- - - - - QUICHÉ, JOYABAJ [QUJ] Guatemala
- - - - - QUICHÉ, SAN ANDRÉS [QIE] Guatemala
- - - - - QUICHÉ, WEST CENTRAL [QUT] Guatemala
- - - - Tzutujil (2): TZUTUJIL, EASTERN [TZJ] Guatemala
- - - - - TZUTUJIL, WESTERN [TZT] Guatemala
- - - Sacapulteco (1): SACAPULTECO [QUV] Guatemala
- - - Sipacapeno (1): SIPACAPENSE [QUM] Guatemala
- - - Uspantec (1): USPANTECO [USP] Guatemala
- Yucatecan (5)
- - Mopan-Itza (2): ITZÁ [ITZ] Guatemala
- - - MOPÁN MAYA [MOP] Belize
- - Yucatec-Lacandon (3): LACANDÓN [LAC] Mexico
- - - MAYA, CHAN SANTA CRUZ [YUS] Mexico
- - - MAYA, YUCATÁN [YUA] Mexico

Misumalpan (4): CACAOPERA [CCR] El Salvador
- MATAGALPA [MTN] Nicaragua
- MÍSKITO [MIQ] Nicaragua
- SUMO TAWAHKA [SUM] Nicaragua

Mixe-Zoque (16)
- Mixe (9)
- - Eastern Mixe (5): MIXE, COATLÁN [MCO] Mexico
- - - MIXE, ISTMO [MIR] Mexico
- - - MIXE, JUQUILA [MXQ] Mexico
- - - MIXE, MAZATLÁN [MZL] Mexico
- - - MIXE, QUETZALTEPEC [MVE] Mexico
- - Veracruz Mixe (2): POPOLUCA, OLUTA [PLO] Mexico
- - - POPOLUCA, SAYULA [POS] Mexico
- - Western Mixe (2): MIXE, TLAHUITOLTEPEC [MXP] Mexico
- - - MIXE, TOTONTEPEC [MTO] Mexico
- Zoque (7)
- - Chiapas Zoque (3): ZOQUE, COPAINALÁ [ZOC] Mexico
- - - ZOQUE, FRANCISCO LEÓN [ZOS] Mexico
- - - ZOQUE, RAYÓN [ZOR] Mexico
- - Oaxaca Zoque (1): ZOQUE, CHIMALAPA [ZOH] Mexico
- - Veracruz Zoque (3): POPOLUCA, SIERRA [POI] Mexico
- - - POPOLUCA, TEXISTEPEC [POQ] Mexico
- - - ZOQUE, TABASCO [ZOQ] Mexico

Mixed Language (8)
- Cakchiquel-Quiche (1): CAKCHIQUEL-QUICHE MIXED LANGUAGE [CKZ] Guatemala
- Chinese-Tibetan-Mongolian (1): WUTUNHUA [WUH] China
- French-Cree (1): MICHIF [CRG] USA
- German-Yiddish-Romani-Rotwelsch (1): YENICHE [YEC] Germany
- Pare-Cushitic (1): MBUGU [MHD] Tanzania
- Russian-Aleut (1): MEDNYJ ALEUT [MUD] Russia (Asia)
- Spanish-Quechua (1): MEDIA LENGUA [MUE] Ecuador
- Zulu-Bantu (1): CAMTHO [CMT] South Africa

Mosetenan (1): TSIMANÉ [CAS] Bolivia

Mura (1): MÚRA-PIRAHÃ [MYP] Brazil

Muskogean (6)
- Eastern (4): ALABAMA [AKZ] USA
- - KOASATI [CKU] USA
- - MIKASUKI [MIK] USA
- - MUSKOGEE [CRK] USA
- Western (2): CHICKASAW [CIC] USA
- - CHOCTAW [CCT] USA

Na-Dene (47)
- Haida (2): HAIDA, NORTHERN [HAI] Canada
- - HAIDA, SOUTHERN [HAX] Canada
- Nuclear Na-Dene (45)
- - Athapaskan-Eyak (44)
- - - Athapaskan (43): TSETSAUT [TXC] Canada
- - - - Apachean (6)
- - - - - Kiowa Apache (1): APACHE, KIOWA [APK] USA
- - - - - Navajo-Apache (5)
- - - - - - Eastern Apache (3): APACHE, JICARILLA [APJ] USA
- - - - - - - APACHE, LIPAN [APL] USA
- - - - - - - APACHE, MESCALERO-CHIRICAHUA [APM] USA
- - - - - - Western Apache-Navajo (2): APACHE, WESTERN [APW] USA
- - - - - - - NAVAJO [NAV] USA
- - - - Canadian (13)
- - - - - Beaver-Sekani (2): BEAVER [BEA] Canada
- - - - - - SEKANI [SEK] Canada
- - - - - Carrier-Chilcotin (4)
- - - - - - Babine-Carrier (3): BABINE [BCR] Canada
- - - - - - - CARRIER [CAR] Canada
- - - - - - - CARRIER, SOUTHERN [CAF] Canada
- - - - - - Chilcotin (1): CHILCOTIN [CHI] Canada
- - - - - Han-Kutchin (2): GWICH'IN [KUC] Canada
- - - - - - HAN [HAA] USA
- - - - - Hare-Chipewyan (4)
- - - - - - Chipewyan (1): CHIPEWYAN [CPW] Canada
- - - - - - Hare-Slavey (3): DOGRIB [DGB] Canada
- - - - - - - SLAVEY, NORTH [SCS] Canada
- - - - - - - SLAVEY, SOUTH [SLA] Canada
- - - - - Sarcee (1): SARSI [SRS] Canada
- - - - Ingalik-Koyukon (3)
- - - - - Ingalik (1): DEGEXIT'AN [ING] USA
- - - - - Koyukon-Holikachuk (2): HOLIKACHUK [HOI] USA
- - - - - - KOYUKON [KOY] USA
- - - - Pacific Coast (9)
- - - - - California (4)
- - - - - - Hupa (1): HUPA [HUP] USA
- - - - - - Mattole-Wailaki (3): KATO [KTW] USA
- - - - - - - MATTOLE [MVB] USA
- - - - - - - WAILAKI [WLK] USA
- - - - - Oregon (5)
- - - - - - Tolowa-Galice (5): CHETCO [CHE] USA
- - - - - - - COQUILLE [COQ] USA
- - - - - - - GALICE [GCE] USA
- - - - - - - TOLOWA [TOL] USA
- - - - - - - TUTUTNI [TUU] USA
- - - - Tahltan-Kaska (3): KASKA [KKZ] Canada
- - - - - TAGISH [TGX] Canada
- - - - - TAHLTAN [TAH] Canada
- - - - Tanaina-Ahtna (2): AHTENA [AHT] USA
- - - - - TANAINA [TFN] USA
- - - - Tanana-Upper Kuskokwim (4)
- - - - - Tanana (3): TANACROSS [TCB] USA

Na-Dene (47)
- Nuclear Na-Dene (45)
- - Athapaskan-Eyak (44)
- - - Athapaskan (43)
- - - - Tanana-Upper Kuskokwim (4)
- - - - - Tanana (3): TANANA, LOWER [TAA] USA
- - - - - - TANANA, UPPER [TAU] USA
- - - - - Upper Kuskokwim (1): KUSKOKWIM, UPPER [KUU] USA
- - - - Tutchone (2): TUTCHONE, NORTHERN [TUT] Canada
- - - - - TUTCHONE, SOUTHERN [TCE] Canada
- - - Eyak (1): EYAK [EYA] USA
- - Tlingit (1): TLINGIT [TLI] USA

Nambiquaran (5): HALÓ TÉ SÚ [HLO] Brazil
- NAMBIKUÁRA, NORTHERN [MBG] Brazil
- NAMBIKUÁRA, SOUTHERN [NAB] Brazil
- SABANÊS [SAE] Brazil
- SARARÉ [SRR] Brazil

Niger-Congo (1489)
- Atlantic-Congo (1390)
- - Atlantic (64)
- - - Bijago (1): BIDYOGO [BJG] Guinea-Bissau
- - - Northern (45)
- - - - Bak (15)
- - - - - Balant-Ganja (2): BALANTA-GANJA [BJT] Senegal
- - - - - BALANTA-KENTOHE [BLE] Guinea-Bissau
- - - - - Jola (10)
- - - - - - Bayot (1): BAYOT [BDA] Senegal
- - - - - - Jola Proper (9)
- - - - - - - Jola Central (6)
- - - - - - - - Gusilay (2): BANDIAL [BQJ] Senegal
- - - - - - - - GUSILAY [GSL] Senegal
- - - - - - - - Her-Ejamat (2): EJAMAT [EJA] Guinea-Bissau
- - - - - - - - KERAK [HHR] Senegal
- - - - - - - - Jola-Fogny (1): JOLA-FOGNY [DYO] Senegal
- - - - - - - - Jola-Kasa (1): JOLA-KASA [CSK] Senegal
- - - - - - - Karon-Mlomp (2): KARON [KRX] Senegal
- - - - - - - - MLOMP [QML] Senegal
- - - - - - - Kwatay (1): KUWAATAAY [CWT] Senegal
- - - - - Manjaku-Papel (3): MANDJAK [MFV] Guinea-Bissau
- - - - - MANKANYA [MAN] Guinea-Bissau
- - - - - PAPEL [PBO] Guinea-Bissau
- - - - Cangin (5): LEHAR [CAE] Senegal
- - - - - NDUT [NDV] Senegal
- - - - - NOON [SNF] Senegal
- - - - - PALOR [FAP] Senegal
- - - - - SAAFI-SAAFI [SAV] Senegal
- - - - Eastern Senegal-Guinea (10)
- - - - - Banyun (3): BAINOUK-GUNYAAMOLO [BCZ] Senegal
- - - - - - BAINOUK-GUNYUÑO [BAB] Guinea-Bissau
- - - - - - BAINOUK-SAMIK [BCB] Senegal
- - - - - Nun (2): KASANGA [CCJ] Guinea-Bissau
- - - - - KOBIANA [KCJ] Guinea-Bissau
- - - - - Tenda (5): BADJARA [PBP] Guinea
- - - - - BASARI [BSC] Senegal
- - - - - BIAFADA [BIF] Guinea-Bissau
- - - - - BUDIK [TNR] Senegal
- - - - - WAMEI [COU] Senegal
- - - - Mbulungish-Nalu (3): BAGA MBOTENI [BGM] Guinea
- - - - - MBULUNGISH [MBV] Guinea

Niger-Congo (1489)
- Atlantic-Congo (1390)
- - Atlantic (64)
- - - Northern (45)
- - - - Mbulungish-Nalu (3): NALU [NAJ] Guinea
- - - - Senegambian (12)
- - - - - Fula-Wolof (11)
- - - - - - Fulani (9)
- - - - - - - East Central (3): FULFULDE, CENTRAL-EASTERN NIGER [FUQ] Niger
- - - - - - - - FULFULDE, NIGERIAN [FUV] Nigeria
- - - - - - - - FULFULDE, WESTERN NIGER [FUH] Niger
- - - - - - - Eastern (2): FULFULDE, ADAMAWA [FUB] Cameroon
- - - - - - - - FULFULDE, BAGIRMI [FUI] Chad
- - - - - - - West Central (3): FULFULDE, BENIN-TOGO [FUE] Benin
- - - - - - - - FULFULDE, MAASINA [FUL] Mali
- - - - - - - - FUUTA JALON [FUF] Guinea
- - - - - - Western (1): PULAAR [FUC] Senegal
- - - - - Wolof (2): WOLOF [WOL] Senegal
- - - - - - WOLOF, GAMBIAN [WOF] Gambia
- - - - Serer (1): SERER-SINE [SES] Senegal
- - - Southern (18)
- - - - Limba (2): LIMBA, EAST [LMA] Guinea
- - - - - LIMBA, WEST-CENTRAL [LIA] Sierra Leone
- - - - Mel (15)
- - - - Bullom-Kissi (6)
- - - - - Bullom (4)
- - - - - - Northern (2): BOM [BMF] Sierra Leone
- - - - - - - BULLOM SO [BUY] Sierra Leone
- - - - - - Southern (2): KRIM [KRM] Sierra Leone
- - - - - - - SHERBRO [BUN] Sierra Leone
- - - - - Kissi (2): KISI, SOUTHERN [KSS] Liberia
- - - - - - KISSI, NORTHERN [KQS] Guinea
- - - - Gola (1): GOLA [GOL] Liberia
- - - - Temne (8)
- - - - - Baga (7): BAGA BINARI [BCG] Guinea
- - - - - - BAGA KALOUM [BQF] Guinea
- - - - - - BAGA KOGA [BGO] Guinea
- - - - - - BAGA MANDURI [BMD] Guinea
- - - - - - BAGA SITEMU [BSP] Guinea
- - - - - - BAGA SOBANÉ [BSV] Guinea
- - - - - - LANDOMA [LAO] Guinea
- - - - - Temne-Banta (1): THEMNE [TEJ] Sierra Leone
- - - - Sua (1): MANSOANKA [MSW] Guinea-Bissau
- - Ijoid (10)
- - - Defaka (1): DEFAKA [AFN] Nigeria
- - - Ijo (9)
- - - - Central (4)
- - - - - Central Western (1): IZON [IJC] Nigeria
- - - - - Oruma-Northeast Central (3)
- - - - - - Northeast Central (2): BISENI [IJE] Nigeria
- - - - - - - OKODIA [OKD] Nigeria
- - - - - - Oruma (1): ORUMA [ORR] Nigeria
- - - - Eastern (5)
- - - - - Northeastern (4)
- - - - - - Ibani-Okrika-Kalabari (3): IBANI [IBY] Nigeria
- - - - - - - KALABARI [IJN] Nigeria
- - - - - - - KIRIKE [OKR] Nigeria
- - - - - Nkoroo (1): NKOROO [NKX] Nigeria
- - - - Southeastern (1): IJO, SOUTHEAST [IJO] Nigeria

Niger-Congo (1489)
- Atlantic-Congo (1390)
- - Volta-Congo (1316)
- - - Benue-Congo (938)
- - - Akpes (1): AKPES [IBE] Nigeria
- - - Bantoid (668)
- - - - Northern (19)
- - - - - Dakoid (5): DIRIM [DIR] Nigeria
- - - - - - DONG [DOH] Nigeria
- - - - - - GAA [TTB] Nigeria
- - - - - - LAMJA-DENGSA-TOLA [LDH] Nigeria
- - - - - - SAMBA DAKA [CCG] Nigeria
- - - - - Fam (1): FAM [FAM] Nigeria
- - - - - Mambiloid (13)
- - - - - - Mambila-Konja (9)
- - - - - - - Konja (2): KWANJA [KNP] Cameroon
- - - - - - - TWENDI [TWN] Cameroon
- - - - - - - Magu-Kamkam-Kila (4): MBONGNO [BGU] Nigeria
- - - - - - - MVANIP [MCJ] Nigeria
- - - - - - - NDUNDA [NUH] Nigeria
- - - - - - - SOMYEWE [KGT] Nigeria
- - - - - - - Mambila (2): MAMBILA, CAMEROON [MYA] Cameroon
- - - - - - - MAMBILA, NIGERIA [MZK] Nigeria
- - - - - - - Njerup (1): NJEREP [NJR] Nigeria
- - - - - - Ndoro (1): NDOOLA [NDR] Nigeria
- - - - - - Suga-Vute (3)
- - - - - - - Suga (1): SUGA [SGI] Cameroon
- - - - - - - Vute (2): VUTE [VUT] Cameroon
- - - - - - - WAWA [WWW] Cameroon
- - - - - Southern (643)
- - - - - - Beboid (11): BUKWEN [BUZ] Nigeria
- - - - - - MASHI [JMS] Nigeria
- - - - - - Eastern (5): BEBE [BZV] Cameroon
- - - - - - - KEMEZUNG [DMO] Cameroon
- - - - - - - NCANE [NCR] Cameroon
- - - - - - - NOONE [NHU] Cameroon
- - - - - - - NSARI [ASJ] Cameroon
- - - - - - Western (4): BU [BOE] Cameroon
- - - - - - - KOSKIN [KID] Cameroon
- - - - - - - MISSONG [MIJ] Cameroon
- - - - - - - NAKI [MFF] Cameroon
- - - - - Ekoid (8): ABANYOM [ABM] Nigeria
- - - - - - EFUTOP [OFU] Nigeria
- - - - - - EJAGHAM [ETU] Nigeria
- - - - - - EKAJUK [EKA] Nigeria
- - - - - - NDE-NSELE-NTA [NDD] Nigeria
- - - - - - NDOE [NBB] Nigeria
- - - - - - NKEM-NKUM [ISI] Nigeria
- - - - - - NNAM [NBP] Nigeria
- - - - - Jarawan (15)
- - - - - - Cameroon (3): MBONGA [XMB] Cameroon
- - - - - - - NAGUMI [NGV] Cameroon
- - - - - - - NGONG [NNX] Cameroon
- - - - - - Nigerian (12): BADA [BAU] Nigeria
- - - - - - - BILE [BIL] Nigeria
- - - - - - - DUGURI [DBM] Nigeria
- - - - - - - DULBU [DBO] Nigeria
- - - - - - - GWA [GWB] Nigeria
- - - - - - - JARAWA [JAR] Nigeria
- - - - - - - KULUNG [BBU] Nigeria
- - - - - - - LABIR [JKU] Nigeria

Niger-Congo (1489)
- Atlantic-Congo (1390)
- - Volta-Congo (1316)
- - - Benue-Congo (938)
- - - - Bantoid (668)
- - - - - Southern (643)
- - - - - - Jarawan (15)
- - - - - - - Nigerian (12): LAME [BMA] Nigeria
- - - - - - - - MAMA [MMA] Nigeria
- - - - - - - - MBULA-BWAZZA [MBU] Nigeria
- - - - - - - - SHIKI [GUA] Nigeria
- - - - - - Mamfe (3): DENYA [ANV] Cameroon
- - - - - - - KENDEM [KVM] Cameroon
- - - - - - - KENYANG [KEN] Cameroon
- - - - - - Mbam (13)
- - - - - - - Sanaga (A.60) (2): LETI [LEO] Cameroon
- - - - - - - TUKI [BAG] Cameroon
- - - - - - - West (A.40) (4): BATI [BTC] Cameroon
- - - - - - - NOMAANDE [LEM] Cameroon
- - - - - - - TUOTOMB [TTF] Cameroon
- - - - - - - YAMBETA [YAT] Cameroon
- - - - - - - West (A.60) (1): TUNEN [BAZ] Cameroon
- - - - - - - Yambasa (A.60) (6): ELIP [EKM] Cameroon
- - - - - - - - MBULE [MLB] Cameroon
- - - - - - - - MMAALA [MMU] Cameroon
- - - - - - - - NUBACA [BAF] Cameroon
- - - - - - - - NUGUNU [YAS] Cameroon
- - - - - - - - YANGBEN [YAV] Cameroon
- - - - - - Mbe (1): MBE [MFO] Nigeria
- - - - - - Narrow Bantu (501)
- - - - - - - Central (328)
- - - - - - - - D (38)
- - - - - - - - - Bembe (D.50) (2): BEMBE [BMB] DRC
- - - - - - - - - - BUYU [BYI] DRC
- - - - - - - - - Bira-Huku (D.30) (18): AMBA [RWM] Uganda
- - - - - - - - - - BERA [BRF] DRC
- - - - - - - - - - BHELE [PER] DRC
- - - - - - - - - - BILA [BIP] DRC
- - - - - - - - - - BODO [BOY] Central African Republic
- - - - - - - - - - BOGURU [BQU] Sudan
- - - - - - - - - - BUDU [BUU] DRC
- - - - - - - - - - HOMA [HOM] Sudan
- - - - - - - - - - KAIKU [KKQ] DRC
- - - - - - - - - - KANGO [KZY] DRC
- - - - - - - - - - KARI [KBJ] DRC
- - - - - - - - - - KOMO [KMW] DRC
- - - - - - - - - - MBO [ZMW] DRC
- - - - - - - - - - NDAKA [NDK] DRC
- - - - - - - - - - NGBEE [NBL] DRC
- - - - - - - - - - NGBINDA [NBD] DRC
- - - - - - - - - - NYALI [NLJ] DRC
- - - - - - - - - - VANUMA [VAU] DRC
- - - - - - - - - Enya (D.10) (4): ENYA [GEY] DRC
- - - - - - - - - - LENGOLA [LEJ] DRC
- - - - - - - - - - MBOLE [MDQ] DRC
- - - - - - - - - - MITUKU [ZMQ] DRC
- - - - - - - - - Lega-Kalanga (D.20) (13): BALI [BCP] DRC
- - - - - - - - - - BEEKE [BKF] DRC
- - - - - - - - - - HAMBA [HBA] DRC
- - - - - - - - - - HOLOHOLO [HOO] Tanzania
- - - - - - - - - - KANGO [KBI] DRC

Niger-Congo (1489)
- Atlantic-Congo (1390)
- - Volta-Congo (1316)
- - - Benue-Congo (938)
- - - - Bantoid (668)
- - - - - Southern (643)
- - - - - - Narrow Bantu (501)
- - - - - - - Central (328)
- - - - - - - - D (38)
- - - - - - - - - Lega-Kalanga (D.20) (13): KANU [KHX] DRC
- - - - - - - - - KWAMI [KTF] DRC
- - - - - - - - - LEGA-MWENGA [LGM] DRC
- - - - - - - - - LEGA-SHABUNDA [LEA] DRC
- - - - - - - - - LIKA [LIK] DRC
- - - - - - - - - SONGOORA [SOD] DRC
- - - - - - - - - ZIMBA [ZMB] DRC
- - - - - - - - - ZYOBA [ZYO] Tanzania
- - - - - - - - Nyanga (D.40) (1): NYANGA [NYA] DRC
- - - - - - - - E (37)
- - - - - - - - - Chaga (E.30) (8): CHAGGA [KAF] Tanzania
- - - - - - - - - GWENO [GWE] Tanzania
- - - - - - - - - KAHE [HKA] Tanzania
- - - - - - - - - MACHAMBE [JMC] Tanzania
- - - - - - - - - MOCHI [OLD] Tanzania
- - - - - - - - - ROMBO [ROF] Tanzania
- - - - - - - - - RWA [RWK] Tanzania
- - - - - - - - - VUNJO [VUN] Tanzania
- - - - - - - - - Kikuyu-Kamba (E.20) (8): DHAISO [DHS] Tanzania
- - - - - - - - - EMBU [EBU] Kenya
- - - - - - - - - GIKUYU [KIU] Kenya
- - - - - - - - - KAMBA [KIK] Kenya
- - - - - - - - - Meru (4): CHUKA [CUH] Kenya
- - - - - - - - - - MERU [MER] Kenya
- - - - - - - - - - MWIMBI-MUTHAMBI [MWS] Kenya
- - - - - - - - - - THARAKA [THA] Kenya
- - - - - - - - - Kuria (E.10) (11): GUSII [GUZ] Kenya
- - - - - - - - - IKIZU [IKZ] Tanzania
- - - - - - - - - IKOMA [NTK] Tanzania
- - - - - - - - - KABWA [CWA] Tanzania
- - - - - - - - - KURIA [KUJ] Tanzania
- - - - - - - - - NGURIMI [NGQ] Tanzania
- - - - - - - - - SIZAKI [SZK] Tanzania
- - - - - - - - - SUBA [SUH] Kenya
- - - - - - - - - TEMI [SOZ] Tanzania
- - - - - - - - - WARE [WRE] Tanzania
- - - - - - - - - ZANAKI [ZAK] Tanzania
- - - - - - - - - Nyika (E.40) (10)
- - - - - - - - - Malakote (1): MALAKOTE [MLK] Kenya
- - - - - - - - - Mijikenda (5): CHONYI [COH] Kenya
- - - - - - - - - - DIGO [DIG] Kenya
- - - - - - - - - - DURUMA [DUG] Kenya
- - - - - - - - - - GIRYAMA [NYF] Kenya
- - - - - - - - - - SEGEJU [SEG] Tanzania
- - - - - - - - - Pokomo (2): POKOMO, LOWER [POJ] Kenya
- - - - - - - - - - POKOMO, UPPER [PKB] Kenya
- - - - - - - - - Taita (2): SAGALLA [TGA] Kenya
- - - - - - - - - - TAITA [DAV] Kenya
- - - - - - - - - F (16)
- - - - - - - - - Nyilamba-Langi (F.30) (4): MBUGWE [MGZ] Tanzania
- - - - - - - - - - NILAMBA [NIM] Tanzania
- - - - - - - - - - NYATURU [RIM] Tanzania

Niger-Congo (1489)
- Atlantic-Congo (1390)
- - Volta-Congo (1316)
- - - Benue-Congo (938)
- - - - Bantoid (668)
- - - - - Southern (643)
- - - - - - Narrow Bantu (501)
- - - - - - - Central (328)
- - - - - - - - F (16)
- - - - - - - - - Nyilamba-Langi (F.30) (4): RANGI [LAG] Tanzania
- - - - - - - - - Sukuma-Nyamwezi (F.20) (6): BUNGU [WUN] Tanzania
- - - - - - - - - KIMBU [KIV] Tanzania
- - - - - - - - - KONONGO [KCZ] Tanzania
- - - - - - - - - NYAMWEZI [NYZ] Tanzania
- - - - - - - - - SUKUMA [SUA] Tanzania
- - - - - - - - - SUMBWA [SUW] Tanzania
- - - - - - - - - Tongwe (F.10) (6): BENDE [BDP] Tanzania
- - - - - - - - - FIPA [FIP] Tanzania
- - - - - - - - - MAMBWE-LUNGU [MGR] Zambia
- - - - - - - - - PIMBWE [PIW] Tanzania
- - - - - - - - - RUNGWA [RNW] Tanzania
- - - - - - - - - TONGWE [TNY] Tanzania
- - - - - - - - G (33)
- - - - - - - - - Bena-Kinga (G.60) (7): BENA [BEZ] Tanzania
- - - - - - - - - HEHE [HEH] Tanzania
- - - - - - - - - KINGA [KIX] Tanzania
- - - - - - - - - KISI [KIZ] Tanzania
- - - - - - - - - PANGWA [PBR] Tanzania
- - - - - - - - - SANGU [SBP] Tanzania
- - - - - - - - - WANJI [WBI] Tanzania
- - - - - - - - - Gogo (G.10) (2): GOGO [GOG] Tanzania
- - - - - - - - - KAGULU [KKI] Tanzania
- - - - - - - - - Pogoro (G.50) (2): NDAMBA [NDJ] Tanzania
- - - - - - - - - POGOLO [POY] Tanzania
- - - - - - - - - Shambala (G.20) (4): ASU [ASA] Tanzania
- - - - - - - - - BONDEI [BOU] Tanzania
- - - - - - - - - SHAMBALA [KSB] Tanzania
- - - - - - - - - TAVETA [TVS] Kenya
- - - - - - - - - Swahili (G.40) (6): COMORIAN [SWB] Comoros Islands
- - - - - - - - - COMORIAN, SHINGAZIDJA [SWS] Comoros Islands
- - - - - - - - - MAKWE [YMK] Mozambique
- - - - - - - - - MWANI [WMW] Mozambique
- - - - - - - - - SWAHILI [SWA] Tanzania
- - - - - - - - - SWAHILI, CONGO [SWC] DRC
- - - - - - - - - Zigula-Zaramo (G.30) (12): DOE [DOE] Tanzania
- - - - - - - - - KAMI [KCU] Tanzania
- - - - - - - - - KUTU [KDC] Tanzania
- - - - - - - - - KWERE [CWE] Tanzania
- - - - - - - - - MUSHUNGULU [XMA] Somalia
- - - - - - - - - NGHWELE [NHE] Tanzania
- - - - - - - - - NGULU [NGP] Tanzania
- - - - - - - - - RUGURU [RUF] Tanzania
- - - - - - - - - SAGALA [SBM] Tanzania
- - - - - - - - - VIDUNDA [VID] Tanzania
- - - - - - - - - ZALAMO [ZAJ] Tanzania
- - - - - - - - - ZIGULA [ZIW] Tanzania
- - - - - - - - H (19)
- - - - - - - - - Hungana (H.40) (1): HUNGANA [HUM] DRC
- - - - - - - - - Kongo (H.10) (7): BEEMBE [BEJ] Congo
- - - - - - - - - DOONDO [DOD] Congo
- - - - - - - - - KONGO [KON] DRC

Niger-Congo (1489)
- Atlantic-Congo (1390)
- - Volta-Congo (1316)
- - - Benue-Congo (938)
- - - - Bantoid (668)
- - - - - Southern (643)
- - - - - - Narrow Bantu (501)
- - - - - - - Central (328)
- - - - - - - - H (19)
- - - - - - - - - Kongo (H.10) (7): KONGO, SAN SALVADOR [KWY] DRC
- - - - - - - - - KUNYI [KNF] Congo
- - - - - - - - - VILI [VIF] Congo
- - - - - - - - - YOMBE [YOM] DRC
- - - - - - - - - Mbundu (H.20) (4): BOLO [BLV] Angola
- - - - - - - - - MBUNDU, LOANDA [MLO] Angola
- - - - - - - - - NSONGO [NSX] Angola
- - - - - - - - - SAMA [SMD] Angola
- - - - - - - - - Yaka (H.30) (7): LONZO [LNZ] DRC
- - - - - - - - - MBANGALA [MXG] Angola
- - - - - - - - - NGONGO [NOQ] DRC
- - - - - - - - - PELENDE [PPP] DRC
- - - - - - - - - SONDE [SHC] DRC
- - - - - - - - - SUKU [SUB] DRC
- - - - - - - - - YAKA [YAF] DRC
- - - - - - - - J (47)
- - - - - - - - - Haya-Jita (J.20) (8): HAYA [HAY] Tanzania
- - - - - - - - - JITA [JIT] Tanzania
- - - - - - - - - KARA [REG] Tanzania
- - - - - - - - - KEREBE [KED] Tanzania
- - - - - - - - - KWAYA [KYA] Tanzania
- - - - - - - - - NYAMBO [NYM] Tanzania
- - - - - - - - - TALINGA-BWISI [TLJ] Uganda
- - - - - - - - - ZINZA [JIN] Tanzania
- - - - - - - - - Konzo (J.40) (5): GBATI-RI [GTI] DRC
- - - - - - - - - KONJO [KOO] Uganda
- - - - - - - - - MAYEKA [MYC] DRC
- - - - - - - - - NANDI [NNB] DRC
- - - - - - - - - NYANGA-LI [NYC] DRC
- - - - - - - - - Masaba-Luyia (J.30) (8): MASABA [MYX] Uganda
- - - - - - - - - NYOLE [NUJ] Uganda
- - - - - - - - - Luyia (6): BUKUSU [BUL] Kenya
- - - - - - - - - - IDAKHO-ISUKHA-TIRIKI [IDA] Kenya
- - - - - - - - - - LOGOOLI [RAG] Kenya
- - - - - - - - - - LUYIA [LUY] Kenya
- - - - - - - - - - NYALA, EAST [NLE] Kenya
- - - - - - - - - - NYORE [NYD] Kenya
- - - - - - - - - Nyoro-Ganda (J.10) (12): CHIGA [CHG] Uganda
- - - - - - - - - GANDA [LAP] Uganda
- - - - - - - - - GUNGU [RUB] Uganda
- - - - - - - - - GWERE [GWR] Uganda
- - - - - - - - - HEMA [NIX] DRC
- - - - - - - - - KENYI [LKE] Uganda
- - - - - - - - - NYANKORE [NYN] Uganda
- - - - - - - - - NYORO [NYR] Uganda
- - - - - - - - - RULI [RUC] Uganda
- - - - - - - - - SINGA [SGM] Uganda
- - - - - - - - - SOGA [SOG] Uganda
- - - - - - - - - TOORO [TTJ] Uganda
- - - - - - - - - Rwanda-Rundi (J.60) (6): HA [HAQ] Tanzania
- - - - - - - - - HANGAZA [HAN] Tanzania
- - - - - - - - - RUNDI [RUD] Burundi

Niger-Congo (1489)
- Atlantic-Congo (1390)
- - Volta-Congo (1316)
- - - Benue-Congo (938)
- - - - Bantoid (668)
- - - - - Southern (643)
- - - - - - Narrow Bantu (501)
- - - - - - - Central (328)
- - - - - - - - J (47)
- - - - - - - - - Rwanda-Rundi (J.60) (6): RWANDA [RUA] Rwanda
- - - - - - - - - - SHUBI [SUJ] Tanzania
- - - - - - - - - - VINZA [VIN] Tanzania
- - - - - - - - - Shi-Havu (J.50) (8): FULIIRU [FLR] DRC
- - - - - - - - - - HAVU [HAV] DRC
- - - - - - - - - - HUNDE [HKE] DRC
- - - - - - - - - - JOBA [JOB] DRC
- - - - - - - - - - KABWARI [KCW] DRC
- - - - - - - - - - NYINDU [NYG] DRC
- - - - - - - - - - SHI [SHR] DRC
- - - - - - - - - - TEMBO [TBT] DRC
- - - - - - - - K (27)
- - - - - - - - - Chokwe-Luchazi (K.20) (9): CHOKWE [CJK] DRC
- - - - - - - - - - LUCHAZI [LCH] Angola
- - - - - - - - - - LUIMBI [LUM] Angola
- - - - - - - - - - LUVALE [LUE] Zambia
- - - - - - - - - - MBUNDA [MCK] Zambia
- - - - - - - - - - MBWELA [MFU] Angola
- - - - - - - - - - NKANGALA [NKN] Angola
- - - - - - - - - - NYEMBA [NBA] Angola
- - - - - - - - - - NYENGO [NYE] Angola
- - - - - - - - - Diriku (K.70) (1): DIRIKU [DIU] Namibia
- - - - - - - - - Holu (K.10) (4): HOLU [HOL] Angola
- - - - - - - - - - KWESE [KWS] DRC
- - - - - - - - - - PHENDE [PEM] DRC
- - - - - - - - - - SAMBA [SMX] DRC
- - - - - - - - - Kwangwa (K.40) (6): KWANGALI [KWN] Namibia
- - - - - - - - - - LUYANA [LAV] Zambia
- - - - - - - - - - MASHI [MHO] Zambia
- - - - - - - - - - MBOWE [MXO] Zambia
- - - - - - - - - - MBUKUSHU [MHW] Namibia
- - - - - - - - - - SIMAA [SIE] Zambia
- - - - - - - - - Mbala (K.60) (1): MBALA [MDP] DRC
- - - - - - - - - Salampasu-Ndembo (K.30) (3): LUNDA [LVN] Zambia
- - - - - - - - - - RUUND [RND] DRC
- - - - - - - - - - SALAMPASU [SLX] DRC
- - - - - - - - - Subia (K.50) (3): FWE [FWE] Namibia
- - - - - - - - - - SUBIYA [SBS] Namibia
- - - - - - - - - - TOTELA [TTL] Zambia
- - - - - - - - L (14)
- - - - - - - - - Bwile (L.10) (1): BWILE [BWC] Zambia
- - - - - - - - - Kaonde (L.40) (1): KAONDE [KQN] Zambia
- - - - - - - - - Luba (L.30) (6): HEMBA [HEM] DRC
- - - - - - - - - - KANYOK [KNY] DRC
- - - - - - - - - - LUBA-KASAI [LUB] DRC
- - - - - - - - - - LUBA-KATANGA [LUH] DRC
- - - - - - - - - - LWALU [LWA] DRC
- - - - - - - - - - SANGA [SNG] DRC
- - - - - - - - - Nkoya (L.50) (1): NKOYA [NKA] Zambia
- - - - - - - - - Songye (L.20) (5): BANGUBANGU [BNX] DRC
- - - - - - - - - - BINJI [BIN] DRC
- - - - - - - - - - KETE [KCV] DRC

Niger-Congo (1489)
- Atlantic-Congo (1390)
- - Volta-Congo (1316)
- - - Benue-Congo (938)
- - - - Bantoid (668)
- - - - - Southern (643)
- - - - - - Narrow Bantu (501)
- - - - - - - Central (328)
- - - - - - - - L (14)
- - - - - - - - - Songye (L.20) (5): LUNA [LUJ] DRC
- - - - - - - - - - SONGE [SOP] DRC
- - - - - - - - - M (19)
- - - - - - - - - - Bemba (M.40) (3): AUSHI [AUH] Zambia
- - - - - - - - - - - BEMBA [BEM] Zambia
- - - - - - - - - - - TAABWA [TAP] DRC
- - - - - - - - - - Bisa-Lamba (M.50) (3)
- - - - - - - - - - - Bisa (2): LALA-BISA [LEB] Zambia
- - - - - - - - - - - - SEBA [KDG] DRC
- - - - - - - - - - - Lamba (1): LAMBA [LAB] Zambia
- - - - - - - - - - Lenja-Tonga (M.60) (1)
- - - - - - - - - - - Tonga (1): DOMBE [DOV] Zimbabwe
- - - - - - - - - - Lenje-Tonga (M.60) (5)
- - - - - - - - - - - Lenje (1): LENJE [LEH] Zambia
- - - - - - - - - - - Tonga (4): ILA [ILB] Zambia
- - - - - - - - - - - - SALA [SHQ] Zambia
- - - - - - - - - - - - SOLI [SBY] Zambia
- - - - - - - - - - - - TONGA [TOI] Zambia
- - - - - - - - - - Nyakyusa (M.30) (1): NYAKYUSA-NGONDE [NYY] Tanzania
- - - - - - - - - - Nyika-Safwa (M.20) (6): MALILA [MGQ] Tanzania
- - - - - - - - - - - MWANGA [MWN] Zambia
- - - - - - - - - - - NDALI [NDH] Tanzania
- - - - - - - - - - - NYIHA [NIH] Tanzania
- - - - - - - - - - - SAFWA [SBK] Tanzania
- - - - - - - - - - - WANDA [WBH] Tanzania
- - - - - - - - - N (14)
- - - - - - - - - - Manda (N.10) (5): MANDA [MGS] Tanzania
- - - - - - - - - - - MATENGO [MGV] Tanzania
- - - - - - - - - - - MPOTO [MPA] Tanzania
- - - - - - - - - - - NGONI [NGU] Tanzania
- - - - - - - - - - - TONGA [TOG] Malawi
- - - - - - - - - - Nyanja (N.30) (1): NYANJA [NYJ] Malawi
- - - - - - - - - - Senga-Sena (N.40) (6)
- - - - - - - - - - - Sena (5): BARWE [BWG] Mozambique
- - - - - - - - - - - - KUNDA [KDN] Zimbabwe
- - - - - - - - - - - - NYUNGWE [NYU] Mozambique
- - - - - - - - - - - - SENA [SEH] Mozambique
- - - - - - - - - - - - SENA, MALAWI [SWK] Malawi
- - - - - - - - - - - Senga (1): NSENGA [NSE] Zambia
- - - - - - - - - - Tumbuka (N.20) (2): LAMBYA [LAI] Tanzania
- - - - - - - - - - - TUMBUKA [TUW] Malawi
- - - - - - - - - P (23)
- - - - - - - - - - Makua (P.30) (13): CHWABO [CHW] Mozambique
- - - - - - - - - - - KOKOLA [KZN] Malawi
- - - - - - - - - - - KOTI [EKO] Mozambique
- - - - - - - - - - - LOLO [LLB] Mozambique
- - - - - - - - - - - LOMWE [NGL] Mozambique
- - - - - - - - - - - MAKHUWA [VMW] Mozambique
- - - - - - - - - - - MAKHUWA-MARREVONE [XMC] Mozambique
- - - - - - - - - - - MAKHUWA-MEETTO [MAK] Mozambique
- - - - - - - - - - - MAKHUWA-SHIRIMA [VMK] Mozambique
- - - - - - - - - - - MANYAWA [MNY] Mozambique

Niger-Congo (1489)
- Atlantic-Congo (1390)
- - Volta-Congo (1316)
- - - Benue-Congo (938)
- - - - Bantoid (668)
- - - - - Southern (643)
- - - - - - Narrow Bantu (501)
- - - - - - - Central (328)
- - - - - - - - P (23)
- - - - - - - - - Makua (P.30) (13): MARENJE [VMR] Mozambique
- - - - - - - - - - NATHEMBO [NTE] Mozambique
- - - - - - - - - - TAKWANE [TKE] Mozambique
- - - - - - - - - Matumbi (P.10) (5): MATUMBI [MGW] Tanzania
- - - - - - - - - - MBUNGA [MGY] Tanzania
- - - - - - - - - - NDENGEREKO [NDE] Tanzania
- - - - - - - - - - NGINDO [NNQ] Tanzania
- - - - - - - - - - RUFIJI [RUI] Tanzania
- - - - - - - - - Yao (P.20) (5): MACHINGA [MVW] Tanzania
- - - - - - - - - - MAKONDE [KDE] Tanzania
- - - - - - - - - - MWERA [MWE] Tanzania
- - - - - - - - - - NDONDE [NDS] Tanzania
- - - - - - - - - - YAO [YAO] Malawi
- - - - - - - - R (12)
- - - - - - - - - Herero (R.30) (2): HERERO [HER] Namibia
- - - - - - - - - - ZEMBA [DHM] Angola
- - - - - - - - - Ndonga (R.20) (5): KWAMBI [KWM] Namibia
- - - - - - - - - - KWANYAMA [KUY] Angola
- - - - - - - - - - MBALANHU [LNB] Namibia
- - - - - - - - - - NDONGA [NDG] Namibia
- - - - - - - - - - NGANDYERA [NNE] Angola
- - - - - - - - - South Mbundu (R.10) (4): NDOMBE [NDQ] Angola
- - - - - - - - - - NKHUMBI [KHU] Angola
- - - - - - - - - - NYANEKA [NYK] Angola
- - - - - - - - - - UMBUNDU [MNF] Angola
- - - - - - - - - Yeye (R.40) (1): YEYI [YEY] Botswana
- - - - - - - - S (25)
- - - - - - - - - Chopi (S.60) (2): CHOPI [CCE] Mozambique
- - - - - - - - - - GITONGA [TOH] Mozambique
- - - - - - - - - Nguni (S.40) (4): NDEBELE [NDF] Zimbabwe
- - - - - - - - - - SWATI [SWZ] Swaziland
- - - - - - - - - - XHOSA [XOS] South Africa
- - - - - - - - - - ZULU [ZUU] South Africa
- - - - - - - - - Shona (S.10) (7): KALANGA [KCK] Botswana
- - - - - - - - - - MANYIKA [MXC] Zimbabwe
- - - - - - - - - - NAMBYA [NMQ] Zimbabwe
- - - - - - - - - - NDAU [NDC] Zimbabwe
- - - - - - - - - - SHONA [SHD] Zimbabwe
- - - - - - - - - - TAWARA [TWL] Mozambique
- - - - - - - - - - TEWE [TWX] Mozambique
- - - - - - - - - Sotho-Tswana (S.30) (8): LOZI [LOZ] Zambia
- - - - - - - - - - TSWAPONG [TWO] Botswana
- - - - - - - - - - Kgalagadi (1): KGALAGADI [XKV] Botswana
- - - - - - - - - - Sotho (4): BIRWA [BRL] Botswana
- - - - - - - - - - - Northern (2): NDEBELE [NEL] South Africa
- - - - - - - - - - - - SOTHO, NORTHERN [SRT] South Africa
- - - - - - - - - - - Southern (1): SOTHO, SOUTHERN [SSO] Lesotho
- - - - - - - - - - Tswana (1): TSWANA [TSW] Botswana
- - - - - - - - - Tswa-Ronga (S.50) (3): RONGA [RON] Mozambique
- - - - - - - - - - TSHWA [TSC] Mozambique
- - - - - - - - - - TSONGA [TSO] South Africa
- - - - - - - - - - VENDA [VEN] South Africa

Niger-Congo (1489)
- Atlantic-Congo (1390)
- - Volta-Congo (1316)
- - - Benue-Congo (938)
- - - - Bantoid (668)
- - - - - Southern (643)
- - - - - - Narrow Bantu (501)
- - - - - - - Central (328)
- - - - - - - - Unclassified (4): ISANZU [ISN] Tanzania
- - - - - - - - JIJI [JIJ] Tanzania
- - - - - - - - RUNGI [RUR] Tanzania
- - - - - - - - SONGO [SOO] DRC
- - - - - - - Northwest (171)
- - - - - - - - A (52)
- - - - - - - - - Bafia (A.50) (4): BAFIA [KSF] Cameroon
- - - - - - - - - - DIMBONG [DII] Cameroon
- - - - - - - - - - HIJUK [HIJ] Cameroon
- - - - - - - - - - TIBEA [NGY] Cameroon
- - - - - - - - - Basaa (A.40) (4): ABO [ABB] Cameroon
- - - - - - - - - - BAKOKO [BKH] Cameroon
- - - - - - - - - - BAROMBI [BBI] Cameroon
- - - - - - - - - - BASAA [BAA] Cameroon
- - - - - - - - Bube-Benga (A.30) (5): BATANGA [BNM] Equatorial Guinea
- - - - - - - - - - BENGA [BEN] Equatorial Guinea
- - - - - - - - - - BUBE [BVB] Equatorial Guinea
- - - - - - - - - - Yasa (2): NGUMBI [NUI] Equatorial Guinea
- - - - - - - - - - - YASA [YKO] Cameroon
- - - - - - - - - Duala (A.20) (7): BAKOLE [KME] Cameroon
- - - - - - - - - - BUBIA [BBX] Cameroon
- - - - - - - - - - DUALA [DOU] Cameroon
- - - - - - - - - - ISU [SZV] Cameroon
- - - - - - - - - - MALIMBA [MZD] Cameroon
- - - - - - - - - - MOKPWE [BRI] Cameroon
- - - - - - - - - - WUMBOKO [BQM] Cameroon
- - - - - - - - - Kako (A.90) (3): KAKO [KKJ] Cameroon
- - - - - - - - - - KWAKUM [KWU] Cameroon
- - - - - - - - - - POL [PMM] Congo
- - - - - - - - - Lundu-Balong (A.10) (9): BONKENG [BVG] Cameroon
- - - - - - - - - - NKONGHO [NKC] Cameroon
- - - - - - - - - - Ngoe (5): AKOOSE [BSS] Cameroon
- - - - - - - - - - - BAFAW-BALONG [BWT] Cameroon
- - - - - - - - - - - BAKAKA [BQZ] Cameroon
- - - - - - - - - - - BASSOSSI [BSI] Cameroon
- - - - - - - - - - - MBO [MBO] Cameroon
- - - - - - - - - - Oroko (2): BAKUNDU-BALUE [BDU] Cameroon
- - - - - - - - - - - BALUNDU-BIMA [NGO] Cameroon
- - - - - - - - - Makaa-Njem (A.80) (12): BEKWEL [BKW] Congo
- - - - - - - - - - BOMWALI [BMW] Congo
- - - - - - - - - - BYEP [MKK] Cameroon
- - - - - - - - - - GYELE [GYI] Cameroon
- - - - - - - - - - KOL [BIW] Cameroon
- - - - - - - - - - KOONZIME [NJE] Cameroon
- - - - - - - - - - MAKAA [MCP] Cameroon
- - - - - - - - - - MPIEMO [MCX] Central African Republic
- - - - - - - - - - MPONGMPONG [MGG] Cameroon
- - - - - - - - - - NGUMBA [NMG] Cameroon
- - - - - - - - - - SO [SOX] Cameroon
- - - - - - - - - - UKHWEJO [UKH] Central African Republic
- - - - - - - - - Yaunde-Fang (A.70) (8): BEBELE [BEB] Cameroon
- - - - - - - - - - BEBIL [BXP] Cameroon
- - - - - - - - - - BETI [BTB] Cameroon

Niger-Congo (1489)
- Atlantic-Congo (1390)
- - Volta-Congo (1316)
- - - Benue-Congo (938)
- - - - Bantoid (668)
- - - - - Southern (643)
- - - - - - Narrow Bantu (501)
- - - - - - - Northwest (171)
- - - - - - - - A (52)
- - - - - - - - - Yaunde-Fang (A.70) (8): BULU [BUM] Cameroon
- - - - - - - - - ETON [ETO] Cameroon
- - - - - - - - - EWONDO [EWO] Cameroon
- - - - - - - - - FANG [FNG] Gabon
- - - - - - - - - MENGISA [MCT] Cameroon
- - - - - - - - - B (48)
- - - - - - - - - Kele (B.20) (10): KILI [KEB] Gabon
- - - - - - - - - KOTA [KOQ] Gabon
- - - - - - - - - MAHONGWE [MHB] Gabon
- - - - - - - - - MBANGWE [ZMN] Congo
- - - - - - - - - NDASA [NDA] Congo
- - - - - - - - - NGOM [NRA] Congo
- - - - - - - - - SAKE [SAG] Gabon
- - - - - - - - - SEKI [SYI] Equatorial Guinea
- - - - - - - - - SIGHU [SXE] Gabon
- - - - - - - - - WUMBVU [WUM] Congo
- - - - - - - - - Mbere (B.60) (6): KANINGI [KZO] Gabon
- - - - - - - - - MBAMA [MBM] Gabon
- - - - - - - - - MBERE [MDT] Congo
- - - - - - - - - NDUMU [NMD] Gabon
- - - - - - - - - NGUL [NLO] DRC
- - - - - - - - - YANGHO [YNH] Gabon
- - - - - - - - - Myene (B.10) (1): MYENE [MYE] Gabon
- - - - - - - - - Njebi (B.50) (4): DUMA [DMA] Gabon
- - - - - - - - - NJEBI [NZB] Gabon
- - - - - - - - - TSAANGI [TSA] Gabon
- - - - - - - - - WANDJI [WDD] Gabon
- - - - - - - - - Sira (B.40) (7): BARAMA [BBG] Gabon
- - - - - - - - - BWISI [BWZ] Congo
- - - - - - - - - LUMBU [LUP] Gabon
- - - - - - - - - PUNU [PUU] Gabon
- - - - - - - - - SANGU [SNQ] Gabon
- - - - - - - - - SIRA [SWJ] Gabon
- - - - - - - - - VUMBU [VUM] Gabon
- - - - - - - - - Teke (B.70) (9): NCHINCHEGE [NCQ] Congo
- - - - - - - - - NGUNGWONI [NGF] Congo
- - - - - - - - - TEKE, CENTRAL [TEC] Congo
- - - - - - - - - TEKE, EASTERN [TEK] DRC
- - - - - - - - - TEKE, NORTHEASTERN [NGZ] Congo
- - - - - - - - - TEKE, NORTHERN [TEG] Congo
- - - - - - - - - TEKE, SOUTH CENTRAL [IFM] Congo
- - - - - - - - - TEKE, SOUTHERN [KKW] Congo
- - - - - - - - - TEKE, WESTERN [TEZ] Congo
- - - - - - - - - Tsogo (B.30) (5): BUBI [BUW] Gabon
- - - - - - - - - KANDE [KBS] Gabon
- - - - - - - - - PINJI [PIC] Gabon
- - - - - - - - - SIMBA [SBW] Gabon
- - - - - - - - - TSOGO [TSV] Gabon
- - - - - - - - - Yanzi (B.80) (6): BOMA [BOH] DRC
- - - - - - - - - DING [DIZ] DRC
- - - - - - - - - MFINU [ZMF] DRC
- - - - - - - - - MPUONO [ZMP] DRC

Niger-Congo (1489)
- Atlantic-Congo (1390)
- - Volta-Congo (1316)
- - - Benue-Congo (938)
- - - - Bantoid (668)
- - - - - Southern (643)
- - - - - - Narrow Bantu (501)
- - - - - - - Northwest (171)
- - - - - - - - B (48)
- - - - - - - - - Yanzi (B.80) (6): TIENE [TII] DRC
- - - - - - - - - - YANSI [YNS] DRC
- - - - - - - - C (71)
- - - - - - - - - Bangi-Ntomba (C.40) (29): BAMWE [BMG] DRC
- - - - - - - - - - BANGI [BNI] DRC
- - - - - - - - - - BOKO [BKP] DRC
- - - - - - - - - - BOLIA [BLI] DRC
- - - - - - - - - - BOLONDO [BZM] DRC
- - - - - - - - - - BOMBOLI [BML] DRC
- - - - - - - - - - BOMBOMA [BWS] DRC
- - - - - - - - - - BOZABA [BZO] DRC
- - - - - - - - - - DZANDO [DZN] DRC
- - - - - - - - - - LOBALA [LOQ] DRC
- - - - - - - - - - MABAALE [MMZ] DRC
- - - - - - - - - - MOI [MOW] Congo
- - - - - - - - - - NTOMBA [NTO] DRC
- - - - - - - - - - SAKATA [SAT] DRC
- - - - - - - - - - SENGELE [SZG] DRC
- - - - - - - - - - YAMONGERI [YMG] DRC
- - - - - - - - - - Lusengo (8): BABANGO [BBM] DRC
- - - - - - - - - - - BANGALA [BXG] DRC
- - - - - - - - - - - BOLOKI [BKT] DRC
- - - - - - - - - - - BUDZA [BJA] DRC
- - - - - - - - - - - LINGALA [LIN] DRC
- - - - - - - - - - - LUSENGO [LUS] DRC
- - - - - - - - - - - MANGALA [MGH] Congo
- - - - - - - - - - - NDOLO [NDL] DRC
- - - - - - - - - - Ngiri (5): BALOI [BIZ] DRC
- - - - - - - - - - - LIBINZA [LIZ] DRC
- - - - - - - - - - - LIKILA [LIE] DRC
- - - - - - - - - - - NDOBO [NDW] DRC
- - - - - - - - - - - NGIRI [NGR] DRC
- - - - - - - - - Bushong (C.90) (5): BUSHOONG [BUF] DRC
- - - - - - - - - - DENGESE [DEZ] DRC
- - - - - - - - - - LELE [LEL] DRC
- - - - - - - - - - SONGOMENO [SOE] DRC
- - - - - - - - - - WONGO [WON] DRC
- - - - - - - - - Kele (C.60) (6): FOMA [FOM] DRC
- - - - - - - - - - KELE [KHY] DRC
- - - - - - - - - - LOMBO [LOO] DRC
- - - - - - - - - - MBESA [ZMS] DRC
- - - - - - - - - - POKE [POF] DRC
- - - - - - - - - - SO [SOC] DRC
- - - - - - - - - Mbosi (C.30) (6): AKWA [AKW] Congo
- - - - - - - - - - KOYO [KOH] Congo
- - - - - - - - - - LIKUBA [KXX] Congo
- - - - - - - - - - LIKWALA [KWC] Congo
- - - - - - - - - - MBOKO [MDU] Congo
- - - - - - - - - - MBOSI [MDW] Congo
- - - - - - - - - Mongo (C.70) (4): LALIA [LAL] DRC
- - - - - - - - - - MONGO-NKUNDU [MOM] DRC
- - - - - - - - - - NGANDO [NXD] DRC

Niger-Congo (1489)
- Atlantic-Congo (1390)
- - Volta-Congo (1316)
- - - Benue-Congo (938)
- - - - Bantoid (668)
- - - - - Southern (643)
- - - - - - Narrow Bantu (501)
- - - - - - - Northwest (171)
- - - - - - - - C (71)
- - - - - - - - - Mongo (C.70) (4): OMBO [OML] DRC
- - - - - - - - - Ngando (C.10) (2): NGANDO [NGD] Central African Republic
- - - - - - - - - YAKA [AXK] Central African Republic
- - - - - - - - - Ngombe (C.50) (8): BWA [BWW] DRC
- - - - - - - - - BWELA [BWL] DRC
- - - - - - - - - KANGO [KTY] DRC
- - - - - - - - - LIGENZA [LGZ] DRC
- - - - - - - - - NGELIMA [AGH] DRC
- - - - - - - - - NGOMBE [NGC] DRC
- - - - - - - - - PAGIBETE [PAG] DRC
- - - - - - - - - TEMBO [TMV] DRC
- - - - - - - - - Ngundi (C.20) (6): BABOLE [BVX] Congo
- - - - - - - - - BOMITABA [ZMX] Congo
- - - - - - - - - BONGILI [BUI] Congo
- - - - - - - - - MBATI [MDN] Central African Republic
- - - - - - - - - NGUNDI [NDN] Congo
- - - - - - - - - PANDE [BKJ] Central African Republic
- - - - - - - - - Tetela (C.80) (5): KELA [KEL] DRC
- - - - - - - - - KUSU [KSV] DRC
- - - - - - - - - NKUTU [NKW] DRC
- - - - - - - - - TETELA [TEL] DRC
- - - - - - - - - YELA [YEL] DRC
- - - - - - - Unclassified (2): BEMBA [BMY] DRC
- - - - - - - SONGA [SGO] DRC
- - - - - - Ndemli (1): NDEMLI [NML] Cameroon
- - - - - - Tikar (1): TIKAR [TIK] Cameroon
- - - - - - Tivoid (17): ABON [ABO] Nigeria
- - - - - - - AMBO [AMB] Nigeria
- - - - - - - BALO [BQO] Cameroon
- - - - - - - BATU [BTU] Nigeria
- - - - - - - BITARE [BRE] Nigeria
- - - - - - - CAKA [CKX] Cameroon
- - - - - - - EMAN [EMN] Cameroon
- - - - - - - ESIMBI [AGS] Cameroon
- - - - - - - EVANT [BZZ] Nigeria
- - - - - - - ICEVE-MACI [BEC] Cameroon
- - - - - - - IPULO [ASS] Cameroon
- - - - - - - IYIVE [UIV] Cameroon
- - - - - - - MANTA [MYG] Cameroon
- - - - - - - MESAKA [IYO] Cameroon
- - - - - - - OSATU [OST] Cameroon
- - - - - - - OTANK [UTA] Nigeria
- - - - - - - TIV [TIV] Nigeria
- - - - - - - Unclassified (7): BIKYA [BYB] Cameroon
- - - - - - - BISHUO [BWH] Cameroon
- - - - - - - BORNA [BXX] DRC
- - - - - - - BUYA [BYY] DRC
- - - - - - - MOINGI [MWZ] DRC
- - - - - - - MUNGONG [XMN] Cameroon
- - - - - - - NDENDEULE [DNE] Tanzania
- - - - - - Wide Grassfields (65)
- - - - - - - Menchum (1): BEFANG [BBY] Cameroon

Niger-Congo (1489)
- Atlantic-Congo (1390)
- - Volta-Congo (1316)
- - - Benue-Congo (938)
- - - - Bantoid (668)
- - - - - Southern (643)
- - - - - - Wide Grassfields (65)
- - - - - - - Narrow Grassfields (61): FUM [FUM] Nigeria
- - - - - - - - Mbam-Nkam (34)
- - - - - - - - - Bamileke (11): FE'FE' [FMP] Cameroon
- - - - - - - - - GHOMÁLÁ' [BBJ] Cameroon
- - - - - - - - - KWA' [BKO] Cameroon
- - - - - - - - - MEDUMBA [BYV] Cameroon
- - - - - - - - - MENGAKA [XMG] Cameroon
- - - - - - - - - NDA'NDA' [NNZ] Cameroon
- - - - - - - - - NGIEMBOON [NNH] Cameroon
- - - - - - - - - NGOMBA [NNO] Cameroon
- - - - - - - - - NGOMBALE [NLA] Cameroon
- - - - - - - - - NGWE [NWE] Cameroon
- - - - - - - - - YEMBA [BAN] Cameroon
- - - - - - - - - Ngemba (8): AWING [AZO] Cameroon
- - - - - - - - - BAFUT [BFD] Cameroon
- - - - - - - - - BAMBILI [BAW] Cameroon
- - - - - - - - - BAMUKUMBIT [BQT] Cameroon
- - - - - - - - - KPATI [KOC] Nigeria
- - - - - - - - - MENDANKWE [MFD] Cameroon
- - - - - - - - - NGEMBA [NGE] Cameroon
- - - - - - - - - PINYIN [PNY] Cameroon
- - - - - - - - - Nkambe (7): DZODINKA [ADD] Cameroon
- - - - - - - - - KWAJA [KDZ] Cameroon
- - - - - - - - - LIMBUM [LIM] Cameroon
- - - - - - - - - MBE' [MTK] Cameroon
- - - - - - - - - MFUMTE [NFU] Cameroon
- - - - - - - - - NDAKTUP [NCP] Cameroon
- - - - - - - - - YAMBA [YAM] Cameroon
- - - - - - - - - Nun (8): BABA [BBW] Cameroon
- - - - - - - - - BAFANJI [BFJ] Cameroon
- - - - - - - - - BAMALI [BBQ] Cameroon
- - - - - - - - - BAMBALANG [BMO] Cameroon
- - - - - - - - - BAMENYAM [BCE] Cameroon
- - - - - - - - - BAMUN [BAX] Cameroon
- - - - - - - - - BANGOLAN [BGJ] Cameroon
- - - - - - - - - MUNGAKA [MHK] Cameroon
- - - - - - - - Momo (8): MENKA [MEA] Cameroon
- - - - - - - - - META' [MGO] Cameroon
- - - - - - - - - MUNDANI [MUN] Cameroon
- - - - - - - - - NGAMAMBO [NBV] Cameroon
- - - - - - - - - NGIE [NGJ] Cameroon
- - - - - - - - - NGISHE [NSH] Cameroon
- - - - - - - - - NGWO [NGN] Cameroon
- - - - - - - - - NJEN [MEN] Cameroon
- - - - - - - - Ring (16)
- - - - - - - - - Center (5): BABANKI [BBK] Cameroon
- - - - - - - - - BUM [BMV] Cameroon
- - - - - - - - - KOM [BKM] Cameroon
- - - - - - - - - MMEN [BFM] Cameroon
- - - - - - - - - OKU [OKU] Cameroon
- - - - - - - - - East (1): LAMNSO' [NSO] Cameroon
- - - - - - - - - North (4): BAMUNKA [NDO] Cameroon
- - - - - - - - - KENSWEI NSEI [NDB] Cameroon
- - - - - - - - - VENGO [BAV] Cameroon

Niger-Congo (1489)
- Atlantic-Congo (1390)
- - Volta-Congo (1316)
- - - Benue-Congo (938)
- - - - Bantoid (668)
- - - - - Southern (643)
- - - - - - Wide Grassfields (65)
- - - - - - - Narrow Grassfields (61)
- - - - - - - - Ring (16)
- - - - - - - - - North (4): WUSHI [BSE] Cameroon
- - - - - - - - - West (6): AGHEM [AGQ] Cameroon
- - - - - - - - - - FUNGOM [FUG] Cameroon
- - - - - - - - - - ISU [ISU] Cameroon
- - - - - - - - - - LAIMBUE [LMX] Cameroon
- - - - - - - - - - OSO [OSO] Cameroon
- - - - - - - - - - WEH [WEH] Cameroon
- - - - - - - - - Unclassified (2): NDE-GBITE [NED] Nigeria
- - - - - - - - - VITI [VIT] Nigeria
- - - - - - - - Western Momo (3): AMBELE [AEL] Cameroon
- - - - - - - - ATONG [ATO] Cameroon
- - - - - - - - BUSAM [BXS] Cameroon
- - - - - - Unclassified (6): ÁNCÁ [ACB] Nigeria
- - - - - - BURU [BQW] Nigeria
- - - - - - BUSUU [BJU] Cameroon
- - - - - - CUNG [CUG] Cameroon
- - - - - - KWAK [KWQ] Nigeria
- - - - - - NSHI [NSC] Nigeria
- - - - - Cross River (67)
- - - - - - Bendi (9): ALEGE [ALF] Nigeria
- - - - - - BEKWARRA [BKV] Nigeria
- - - - - - BETE-BENDI [BTT] Nigeria
- - - - - - BOKYI [BKY] Nigeria
- - - - - - BUMAJI [BYP] Nigeria
- - - - - - OBANLIKU [BZY] Nigeria
- - - - - - PUTUKWAM [AFE] Nigeria
- - - - - - UBANG [UBA] Nigeria
- - - - - - UKPE-BAYOBIRI [UKP] Nigeria
- - - - - - Delta Cross (57)
- - - - - - Central Delta (8)
- - - - - - - Abua-Odual (2): ABUA [ABN] Nigeria
- - - - - - - ODUAL [ODU] Nigeria
- - - - - - - Kugbo (6): KUGBO [KES] Nigeria
- - - - - - - MINI [MGJ] Nigeria
- - - - - - - OBULOM [OBU] Nigeria
- - - - - - - OGBIA [OGB] Nigeria
- - - - - - - OGBOGOLO [OGG] Nigeria
- - - - - - - OGBRONUAGUM [OGU] Nigeria
- - - - - - Lower Cross (23)
- - - - - - - Obolo (23): EKI [EKI] Nigeria
- - - - - - - IDERE [IDE] Nigeria
- - - - - - - OBOLO [ANN] Nigeria
- - - - - - - Ebughu (1): EBUGHU [EBG] Nigeria
- - - - - - - Efai (1): EFAI [EFA] Nigeria
- - - - - - - Efik (4): ANAANG [ANW] Nigeria
- - - - - - - EFIK [EFK] Nigeria
- - - - - - - IBIBIO [IBB] Nigeria
- - - - - - - UKWA [UKQ] Nigeria
- - - - - - - Ekit (2): EKIT [EKE] Nigeria
- - - - - - - ETEBI [ETB] Nigeria
- - - - - - - Enwang-Uda (2): ENWAN [ENW] Nigeria
- - - - - - - UDA [UDA] Nigeria

Niger-Congo (1489)
- Atlantic-Congo (1390)
- - Volta-Congo (1316)
- - - Benue-Congo (938)
- - - - Cross River (67)
- - - - - Delta Cross (57)
- - - - - - Lower Cross (23)
- - - - - - - Obolo (23)
- - - - - - - - Ibino (1): IBINO [IBN] Nigeria
- - - - - - - - Ibuoro (4): IBUORO [IBR] Nigeria
- - - - - - - - - ITO [ITW] Nigeria
- - - - - - - - - ITU MBON UZO [ITM] Nigeria
- - - - - - - - - NKARI [NKZ] Nigeria
- - - - - - - - Iko (1): IKO [IKI] Nigeria
- - - - - - - - Ilue (1): ILUE [ILE] Nigeria
- - - - - - - - Okobo (1): OKOBO [OKB] Nigeria
- - - - - - - - Oro (1): ORO [ORX] Nigeria
- - - - - - - - Usaghade (1): USAGHADE [USK] Cameroon
- - - - - - Ogoni (4)
- - - - - - - East (2): GOKANA [GKN] Nigeria
- - - - - - - - KHANA [KEH] Nigeria
- - - - - - - West (2): BAAN [BVJ] Nigeria
- - - - - - - - ELEME [ELM] Nigeria
- - - - - - Upper Cross (22)
- - - - - - - Agoi-Doko-Iyoniyong (3): AGOI [IBM] Nigeria
- - - - - - - - BAKPINKA [BBS] Nigeria
- - - - - - - - DOKO-UYANGA [UYA] Nigeria
- - - - - - - Akpet (1): UKPET-EHOM [AKD] Nigeria
- - - - - - - Central (15)
- - - - - - - - East-West (8)
- - - - - - - - - Ikom (1): OLULUMO-IKOM [IKO] Nigeria
- - - - - - - - - Loko (3): LOKAA [YAZ] Nigeria
- - - - - - - - - - LUBILA [KCC] Nigeria
- - - - - - - - - - NKUKOLI [NBO] Nigeria
- - - - - - - - - Mbembe-Legbo (4)
- - - - - - - - - - Legbo (3): LEGBO [AGB] Nigeria
- - - - - - - - - - - LENYIMA [LDG] Nigeria
- - - - - - - - - - - LEYIGHA [AYI] Nigeria
- - - - - - - - - - Mbembe (1): MBEMBE, CROSS RIVER [MFN] Nigeria
- - - - - - - - North-South (7)
- - - - - - - - - Koring-Kukele (3)
- - - - - - - - - - Koring (1): ORING [ORI] Nigeria
- - - - - - - - - - Kukele (2): KUKELE [KEZ] Nigeria
- - - - - - - - - - - UZEKWE [EZE] Nigeria
- - - - - - - - - Ubaghara-Kohumono (4)
- - - - - - - - - - Kohumono (3): AGWAGWUNE [YAY] Nigeria
- - - - - - - - - - - KOHUMONO [BCS] Nigeria
- - - - - - - - - - - UMON [UMM] Nigeria
- - - - - - - - - - Ubaghara (1): UBAGHARA [BYC] Nigeria
- - - - - - - Kiong-Korop (3): KIONG [KKM] Nigeria
- - - - - - - - KOROP [KRP] Nigeria
- - - - - - - - ODUT [ODA] Nigeria
- - - - - Unclassified (1): AKUM [AKU] Cameroon
- - - - Defoid (16)
- - - - - Akokoid (1): ARIGIDI [AKK] Nigeria
- - - - - Ayere-Ahan (2): ÀHÀN [AHN] Nigeria
- - - - - - AYERE [AYE] Nigeria
- - - - - Yoruboid (13)
- - - - - - Edekiri (12): CABE [CBJ] Benin
- - - - - - - ICA [ICA] Benin
- - - - - - - IDACA [IDD] Benin

Niger-Congo (1489)
- Atlantic-Congo (1390)
- - Volta-Congo (1316)
- - - Benue-Congo (938)
- - - - Defoid (16)
- - - - - Yoruboid (13)
- - - - - - Edekiri (12): IFÈ [IFE] Benin
- - - - - - - IJE [IJJ] Benin
- - - - - - - ISEKIRI [ITS] Nigeria
- - - - - - - KAMBOLÉ [XKB] Togo
- - - - - - - LUCUMI [LUQ] Cuba
- - - - - - - MOKOLE [MKL] Benin
- - - - - - - NAGO [NQG] Benin
- - - - - - - ULUKWUMI [ULB] Nigeria
- - - - - - - YORUBA [YOR] Nigeria
- - - - - - Igala (1): IGALA [IGL] Nigeria
- - - - Edoid (27)
- - - - - Delta (3): DEGEMA [DEG] Nigeria
- - - - - - ENGENNI [ENN] Nigeria
- - - - - - EPIE [EPI] Nigeria
- - - - - North-Central (11)
- - - - - - Edo-Esan-Ora (4): EDO [EDO] Nigeria
- - - - - - - EMAI-IULEHA-ORA [EMA] Nigeria
- - - - - - - ESAN [ISH] Nigeria
- - - - - - - IBILO [IBO] Nigeria
- - - - - - Ghotuo-Uneme-Yekhee (7): GHOTUO [AAA] Nigeria
- - - - - - - IKPESHI [IKP] Nigeria
- - - - - - - IVBIE NORTH-OKPELA-ARHE [ATG] Nigeria
- - - - - - - OSOSO [OSS] Nigeria
- - - - - - - SASARU-ENWAN-IGWE [SSC] Nigeria
- - - - - - - UNEME [UNE] Nigeria
- - - - - - - YEKHEE [ETS] Nigeria
- - - - - Northwestern (8): ADUGE [ADU] Nigeria
- - - - - - Osse (4): EHUEUN [EHU] Nigeria
- - - - - - - IYAYU [IYA] Nigeria
- - - - - - - UHAMI [UHA] Nigeria
- - - - - - - UKUE [UKU] Nigeria
- - - - - - Southern (3): OKPAMHERI [OPA] Nigeria
- - - - - - - OKPE-IDESA-AKUKU [OKP] Nigeria
- - - - - - - OLOMA [OLM] Nigeria
- - - - - Southwestern (5): ERUWA [ERH] Nigeria
- - - - - - ISOKO [ISO] Nigeria
- - - - - - OKPE [OKE] Nigeria
- - - - - - URHOBO [URH] Nigeria
- - - - - - UVBIE [EVH] Nigeria
- - - - Idomoid (9)
- - - - - Akweya (7)
- - - - - - Eloyi (1): ELOYI [AFO] Nigeria
- - - - - - Etulo-Idoma (6)
- - - - - - - Etulo (1): ETULO [UTR] Nigeria
- - - - - - - Idoma (5): AGATU [AGC] Nigeria
- - - - - - - - ALAGO [ALA] Nigeria
- - - - - - - - IDOMA [IDO] Nigeria
- - - - - - - - IGEDE [IGE] Nigeria
- - - - - - - - YALA [YBA] Nigeria
- - - - - Yatye-Akpa (2): AKPA [AKF] Nigeria
- - - - - - YACE [EKR] Nigeria
- - - - Igboid (7)
- - - - - Ekpeye (1): EKPEYE [EKP] Nigeria
- - - - - Igbo (6): IGBO [IGR] Nigeria
- - - - - - IKA [IKK] Nigeria

Niger-Congo (1489)
- Atlantic-Congo (1390)
- - Volta-Congo (1316)
- - - Benue-Congo (938)
- - - - Igboid (7)
- - - - - Igbo (6): IKWERE [IKW] Nigeria
- - - - - - IZI-EZAA-IKWO-MGBO [IZI] Nigeria
- - - - - - OGBAH [OGC] Nigeria
- - - - - - UKWUANI-ABOH-NDONI [UKW] Nigeria
- - - - Kainji (57)
- - - - - Eastern (30)
- - - - - - Amo (1): AMO [AMO] Nigeria
- - - - - - Northern Jos (27)
- - - - - - - Jera (14): DUGUZA [DZA] Nigeria
- - - - - - - - GAMO-NINGI [BTE] Nigeria
- - - - - - - - GYEM [GYE] Nigeria
- - - - - - - - IGUTA [NAR] Nigeria
- - - - - - - - IZORA [CBO] Nigeria
- - - - - - - - JANJI [JNI] Nigeria
- - - - - - - - JERE [JER] Nigeria
- - - - - - - - KUDU-CAMO [KOV] Nigeria
- - - - - - - - LEMORO [LDJ] Nigeria
- - - - - - - - LERE [GNH] Nigeria
- - - - - - - - SANGA [SGA] Nigeria
- - - - - - - - SHAU [SQH] Nigeria
- - - - - - - - SHENI [SCV] Nigeria
- - - - - - - - ZIRIYA [ZIR] Nigeria
- - - - - - - Kauru (13): BINA [BYJ] Nigeria
- - - - - - - - DUNGU [DBV] Nigeria
- - - - - - - - GBIRI-NIRAGU [GRH] Nigeria
- - - - - - - - KAIVI [KCE] Nigeria
- - - - - - - - KINUKU [KKD] Nigeria
- - - - - - - - KONO [KLK] Nigeria
- - - - - - - - KURAMA [KRH] Nigeria
- - - - - - - - MALA [RUY] Nigeria
- - - - - - - - RUMA [RUZ] Nigeria
- - - - - - - - SHUWA-ZAMANI [KSA] Nigeria
- - - - - - - - SURUBU [SDE] Nigeria
- - - - - - - - TUMI [KKU] Nigeria
- - - - - - - - VONO [KCH] Nigeria
- - - - - - Piti-Atsam (2): ATSAM [CCH] Nigeria
- - - - - - - PITI [PCN] Nigeria
- - - - - Western (27)
- - - - - - Basa (4): BASA [BZW] Nigeria
- - - - - - - BASA-GUMNA [BSL] Nigeria
- - - - - - - BASA-GURMANA [BUJ] Nigeria
- - - - - - - BASSA-KONTAGORA [BSR] Nigeria
- - - - - - Baushi-Gurmana (2): BAUCHI [BSF] Nigeria
- - - - - - - GURMANA [GRC] Nigeria
- - - - - - Duka (4): C'LELA [DRI] Nigeria
- - - - - - - GWAMHI-WURI [BGA] Nigeria
- - - - - - - HUN-SAARE [DUD] Nigeria
- - - - - - - KAG-FER-JIIR-KOOR-ROR-US-ZUKSUN [GEL] Nigeria
- - - - - - Kainji Lake (2): LARU [LAN] Nigeria
- - - - - - - LOPA [LOP] Nigeria
- - - - - - Kambari (6): BAANGI [BQX] Nigeria
- - - - - - - CISHINGINI [ASG] Nigeria
- - - - - - - KAKIHUM [KXE] Nigeria
- - - - - - - TSIKIMBA [KDL] Nigeria
- - - - - - - TSISHINGINI [KAM] Nigeria
- - - - - - - TSUVADI [TVD] Nigeria

Niger-Congo (1489)
- Atlantic-Congo (1390)
- - Volta-Congo (1316)
- - - Benue-Congo (938)
- - - - Kainji (57)
- - - - - Western (27)
- - - - - - Kamuku (8): ACIPA, EASTERN [AWA] Nigeria
- - - - - - - ACIPA, WESTERN [AWC] Nigeria
- - - - - - - CINDA-REGI-TIYAL [KAU] Nigeria
- - - - - - - FUNGWA [ULA] Nigeria
- - - - - - - HUNGWORO [NAT] Nigeria
- - - - - - - PONGU [PON] Nigeria
- - - - - - - ROGO [ROD] Nigeria
- - - - - - - SHAMA-SAMBUGA [SQA] Nigeria
- - - - - - Reshe (1): RESHE [RES] Nigeria
- - - - Nupoid (12)
- - - - - Ebira-Gade (2): EBIRA [IGB] Nigeria
- - - - - - GADE [GED] Nigeria
- - - - - Nupe-Gbagyi (10): DIBO [DIO] Nigeria
- - - - - - Gbagyi-Gbari (3): GBAGYI [GBR] Nigeria
- - - - - - - GBAGYI NKWA [GBW] Nigeria
- - - - - - - GBARI [GBY] Nigeria
- - - - - - Nupe (6): ASU [AUM] Nigeria
- - - - - - - GUPA-ABAWA [GPA] Nigeria
- - - - - - - KAKANDA [KKA] Nigeria
- - - - - - - KAMI [KMI] Nigeria
- - - - - - - KUPA [KUG] Nigeria
- - - - - - - NUPE- NUPE TAKO [NUP] Nigeria
- - - - Oko (1): OKO-ENI-OSAYEN [OKS] Nigeria
- - - - Platoid (68)
- - - - - Benue (20)
- - - - - - Jukunoid (16)
- - - - - - - Central (13)
- - - - - - - - Jukun-Mbembe-Wurbo (11)
- - - - - - - - - Jukun (3): JIBU [JIB] Nigeria
- - - - - - - - - - JUKUN TAKUM [JBU] Nigeria
- - - - - - - - - - WASE [JUW] Nigeria
- - - - - - - - - Kororofa (3): KONA [JUO] Nigeria
- - - - - - - - - - WANNU [JUB] Nigeria
- - - - - - - - - - WAPAN [JUK] Nigeria
- - - - - - - - - Mbembe (1): MBEMBE, TIGON [NZA] Cameroon
- - - - - - - - - Unclassified (1): SHOO-MINDA-NYE [BCV] Nigeria
- - - - - - - - - Wurbo (3): COMO KARIM [CFG] Nigeria
- - - - - - - - - - JIRU [JRR] Nigeria
- - - - - - - - - - TITA [TDQ] Nigeria
- - - - - - - - Kpan-Icen (2): ETKYWAN [ICH] Nigeria
- - - - - - - - - KPAN [KPK] Nigeria
- - - - - - - Yukuben-Kuteb (3): KAPYA [KLO] Nigeria
- - - - - - - - KUTEP [KUB] Nigeria
- - - - - - - - YUKUBEN [YBL] Nigeria
- - - - - Tarokoid (4): PAI [PAI] Nigeria
- - - - - - TAPSHIN [TDL] Nigeria
- - - - - - TAROK [YER] Nigeria
- - - - - - YANGKAM [BSX] Nigeria
- - - - - Plateau (46): TORO [TDV] Nigeria
- - - - - - Ayu (1): AYU [AYU] Nigeria
- - - - - - Central (8)
- - - - - - - North-Central (2): ATEN [GAN] Nigeria
- - - - - - - - CARA [CFD] Nigeria
- - - - - - - South-Central (5): FIRAN [FIR] Nigeria
- - - - - - - - IRIGWE [IRI] Nigeria

Niger-Congo (1489)
- Atlantic-Congo (1390)
- - Volta-Congo (1316)
- - - Benue-Congo (938)
- - - - Platoid (68)
- - - - - Plateau (46)
- - - - - - Central (8)
- - - - - - - South-Central (5): IZERE [FIZ] Nigeria
- - - - - - - JJU [KAJ] Nigeria
- - - - - - - TYAP [KCG] Nigeria
- - - - - - West-Central (1): NANDU-TARI [NAA] Nigeria
- - - - - - Northern (6): DOKA [DBI] Nigeria
- - - - - - IDON [IDC] Nigeria
- - - - - - IKU-GORA-ANKWA [IKV] Nigeria
- - - - - - IKULU [IKU] Nigeria
- - - - - - KADARA [KAD] Nigeria
- - - - - - KUTURMI [KHJ] Nigeria
- - - - - - Southeastern (3): BO-RUKUL [MAE] Nigeria
- - - - - - FYAM [PYM] Nigeria
- - - - - - HOROM [HOE] Nigeria
- - - - - - Southern (3): BEROM [BOM] Nigeria
- - - - - - LIJILI [MGI] Nigeria
- - - - - - TANJIJILI [UJI] Nigeria
- - - - - - Western (24)
- - - - - - Northwestern (10)
- - - - - - - Jaba (6): CORI [CRY] Nigeria
- - - - - - - HAM [JAB] Nigeria
- - - - - - - KAGOMA [KDM] Nigeria
- - - - - - - KAMANTAN [KCI] Nigeria
- - - - - - - SHAMANG [SGN] Nigeria
- - - - - - - ZHIRE [ZHI] Nigeria
- - - - - - - Koro (4): ASHE [AHS] Nigeria
- - - - - - - BEGBERE-EJAR [BQV] Nigeria
- - - - - - - IDUN [LDB] Nigeria
- - - - - - - YESKWA [YES] Nigeria
- - - - - - Southwestern (14)
- - - - - - - A (10): BU [JID] Nigeria
- - - - - - - CHE [RUK] Nigeria
- - - - - - - KANINGDON-NINDEM [KDP] Nigeria
- - - - - - - KANUFI [KNI] Nigeria
- - - - - - - MADA [MDA] Nigeria
- - - - - - - NINGYE [NNS] Nigeria
- - - - - - - NINZAM [NIN] Nigeria
- - - - - - - NUMANA-NUNKU-GWANTU-NUMBU [NBR] Nigeria
- - - - - - - SHALL-ZWALL [SHA] Nigeria
- - - - - - - VAGHAT-YA-BIJIM-LEGERI [BIJ] Nigeria
- - - - - - - B (4): AKE [AIK] Nigeria
- - - - - - - EGGON [EGO] Nigeria
- - - - - - - HASHA [YBJ] Nigeria
- - - - - - - NUNGU [RIN] Nigeria
- - - - - Unclassified (2): ARUM-TESU [AAB] Nigeria
- - - - - NKWAK [NKQ] Nigeria
- - - - Ukaan (1): UKAAN [KCF] Nigeria
- - - - Unclassified (4): BEEZEN [BNZ] Cameroon
- - - - - FALI OF BAISSA [FAH] Nigeria
- - - - - KORO IJA [VKI] Nigeria
- - - - - KORO ZUBA [VKZ] Nigeria
- - - Dogon (1): DOGON [DOG] Mali
- - - Kru (39)
- - - - Aizi (3): AIZI, APROUMU [AHP] Côte d'Ivoire
- - - - - AIZI, MOBUMRIN [AHM] Côte d'Ivoire

Niger-Congo (1489)
- Atlantic-Congo (1390)
- - Volta-Congo (1316)
- - - Kru (39)
- - - - Aizi (3): AIZI, TIAGBAMRIN [AHI] Côte d'Ivoire
- - - - Eastern (11)
- - - - - Bakwe (2): BAKWÉ [BAK] Côte d'Ivoire
- - - - - - WANÉ [HWA] Côte d'Ivoire
- - - - - Bete (5)
- - - - - - Eastern (2): BÉTÉ, GAGNOA [BTG] Côte d'Ivoire
- - - - - - - KOUYA [KYF] Côte d'Ivoire
- - - - - - Western (3): BÉTÉ, DALOA [BEV] Côte d'Ivoire
- - - - - - - BÉTE, GUIBEROUA [BET] Côte d'Ivoire
- - - - - - - GODIÉ [GOD] Côte d'Ivoire
- - - - - Dida (3): DIDA, LAKOTA [DIC] Côte d'Ivoire
- - - - - - DIDA, YOCOBOUÉ [GUD] Côte d'Ivoire
- - - - - - NEYO [NEY] Côte d'Ivoire
- - - - Kwadia (1): KODIA [KWP] Côte d'Ivoire
- - - - Kuwaa (1): KUWAA [BLH] Liberia
- - - - Seme (1): SIAMOU [SIF] Burkina Faso
- - - - Western (23)
- - - - - Bassa (3): BASSA [BAS] Liberia
- - - - - - DEWOIN [DEE] Liberia
- - - - - - GBII [GGB] Liberia
- - - - - Grebo (9)
- - - - - - Glio-Oubi (1): GLIO-OUBI [OUB] Liberia
- - - - - - Ivorian (3): KRUMEN, PLAPO [KTJ] Côte d'Ivoire
- - - - - - - KRUMEN, PYE [PYE] Côte d'Ivoire
- - - - - - - KRUMEN, TEPO [TED] Côte d'Ivoire
- - - - - - Liberian (5): GREBO, BARCLAYVILLE [GRY] Liberia
- - - - - - - GREBO, CENTRAL [GRV] Liberia
- - - - - - - GREBO, GBOLOO [GEC] Liberia
- - - - - - - GREBO, NORTHERN [GRB] Liberia
- - - - - - - GREBO, SOUTHERN [GRJ] Liberia
- - - - - Klao (2): KLAO [KLU] Liberia
- - - - - - TAJUASOHN [KRU] Liberia
- - - - - Wee (9)
- - - - - - Guere-Krahn (6): DAHO-DOO [DAS] Côte d'Ivoire
- - - - - - - GLARO-TWABO [GLR] Liberia
- - - - - - - KRAHN, WESTERN [KRW] Liberia
- - - - - - - SAPO [KRN] Liberia
- - - - - - - WÈ SOUTHERN [GXX] Côte d'Ivoire
- - - - - - - WÈ WESTERN [WEC] Côte d'Ivoire
- - - - - - Konobo (1): KRAHN, EASTERN [KQO] Liberia
- - - - - - Nyabwa (1): NYABWA [NIA] Côte d'Ivoire
- - - - - - Wobe (1): WÈ NORTHERN [WOB] Côte d'Ivoire
- - - Kwa (81)
- - - - Left Bank (30)
- - - - - Avatime-Nyangbo (3): AVATIME [AVA] Ghana
- - - - - - NYANGBO [NYB] Ghana
- - - - - - TAFI [TCD] Ghana
- - - - - Gbe (21): AGUNA [AUG] Benin
- - - - - - CI-GBE [CIB] Benin
- - - - - - ÉWÉ [EWE] Ghana
- - - - - - KO-GBE [KQK] Benin
- - - - - - KPESSI [KEF] Togo
- - - - - - SAXWE-GBE [SXW] Benin
- - - - - - WACI-GBE [WCI] Togo
- - - - - - WUDU [WUD] Togo
- - - - - - XWEDA-GBE [XWD] Benin
- - - - - - XWELA-GBE [XWE] Benin

Niger-Congo (1489)
- Atlantic-Congo (1390)
- - Volta-Congo (1316)
- - - Kwa (81)
- - - - Left Bank (30)
- - - - - Gbe (21)
- - - - - - Aja (8): AJA-GBE [AJG] Benin
- - - - - - - AYIZO-GBE [AYB] Benin
- - - - - - - GUN-GBE [GUW] Benin
- - - - - - - SETO-GBE [STS] Benin
- - - - - - - TOFIN-GBE [TFI] Benin
- - - - - - - TOLI-GBE [TLH] Benin
- - - - - - - WEME-GBE [WEM] Benin
- - - - - - - XWLA-GBE [XWL] Benin
- - - - - - Fon (2): FON-GBE [FOA] Benin
- - - - - - - MAXI-GBE [MXL] Benin
- - - - - - Mina (1): GEN-GBE [GEJ] Togo
- - - - - Kebu-Animere (2): AKEBOU [KEU] Togo
- - - - - - ANIMERE [ANF] Ghana
- - - - - Kposo-Ahlo-Bowili (4): ADANGBE [ADQ] Ghana
- - - - - - AKPOSO [KPO] Togo
- - - - - - IGO [AHL] Togo
- - - - - - TUWILI [BOV] Ghana
- - - - Nyo (50)
- - - - - Agneby (3): ABÉ [ABA] Côte d'Ivoire
- - - - - - ABIDJI [ABI] Côte d'Ivoire
- - - - - - ADIOUKROU [ADJ] Côte d'Ivoire
- - - - - Attie (1): ATTIÉ [ATI] Côte d'Ivoire
- - - - - Avikam-Alladian (2): ALLADIAN [ALD] Côte d'Ivoire
- - - - - - AVIKAM [AVI] Côte d'Ivoire
- - - - - Ga-Dangme (2): DANGME [DGM] Ghana
- - - - - - GA [GAC] Ghana
- - - - - Potou-Tano (41)
- - - - - - Basila-Adele (2): ADELE [ADE] Togo
- - - - - - - ANII [BLO] Benin
- - - - - - Ega (1): EGA [DIE] Côte d'Ivoire
- - - - - - Lelemi (4)
- - - - - - - Lelemi-Akpafu (2): LELEMI [LEF] Ghana
- - - - - - - - SIWU [AKP] Ghana
- - - - - - - Likpe-Santrokofi (2): SEKPELE [LIP] Ghana
- - - - - - - - SELE [SNW] Ghana
- - - - - - Logba (1): LOGBA [LGQ] Ghana
- - - - - - Potou (2): EBRIÉ [EBR] Côte d'Ivoire
- - - - - - - MBATO [GWA] Côte d'Ivoire
- - - - - - Tano (31)
- - - - - - - Central (12)
- - - - - - - - Akan (4): ABRON [ABR] Ghana
- - - - - - - - - AKAN [TWS] Ghana
- - - - - - - - - BASA [BQA] Benin
- - - - - - - - - WASA [WSS] Ghana
- - - - - - - - Bia (8)
- - - - - - - - - Northern (5): ANUFO [CKO] Ghana
- - - - - - - - - - ANYIN [ANY] Côte d'Ivoire
- - - - - - - - - - ANYIN, MOROFO [MTB] Côte d'Ivoire
- - - - - - - - - - BAOULÉ [BCI] Côte d'Ivoire
- - - - - - - - - - SEHWI [SFW] Ghana
- - - - - - - - - Southern (3): AHANTA [AHA] Ghana
- - - - - - - - - - JWIRA-PEPESA [JWI] Ghana
- - - - - - - - - - NZEMA [NZE] Ghana
- - - - - - - Guang (16)
- - - - - - - - North Guang (12): ANYANGA [AYG] Togo

Niger-Congo (1489)
- Atlantic-Congo (1390)
- - Volta-Congo (1316)
- - - Kwa (81)
- - - - Nyo (50)
- - - - - Potou-Tano (41)
- - - - - - Tano (31)
- - - - - - - Guang (16)
- - - - - - - - North Guang (12): CHUMBURUNG [NCU] Ghana
- - - - - - - - DOMPO [DOY] Ghana
- - - - - - - - DWANG [NNU] Ghana
- - - - - - - - FOODO [FOD] Benin
- - - - - - - - GIKYODE [ACD] Ghana
- - - - - - - - GONJA [DUM] Ghana
- - - - - - - - KPLANG [PRA] Ghana
- - - - - - - - KRACHE [KYE] Ghana
- - - - - - - - NAWURI [NAW] Ghana
- - - - - - - - NCHUMBULU [NLU] Ghana
- - - - - - - - NKONYA [NKO] Ghana
- - - - - - - - South Guang (4): AWUTU [AFU] Ghana
- - - - - - - - CHEREPON [CPN] Ghana
- - - - - - - - GUA [GWX] Ghana
- - - - - - - - LARTEH [LAR] Ghana
- - - - - - - Krobu (1): KROBU [KXB] Côte d'Ivoire
- - - - - - - Western (2): ABURE [ABU] Côte d'Ivoire
- - - - - - - BETI [EOT] Côte d'Ivoire
- - - - - Unclassified (1): ESUMA [ESM] Côte d'Ivoire
- - - - Unclassified (1): CENKA [CEN] Benin
- - - North (257)
- - - - Adamawa-Ubangi (159)
- - - - Adamawa (89)
- - - - - Fali (2): FALI, NORTH [FLL] Cameroon
- - - - - - FALI, SOUTH [FAL] Cameroon
- - - - - Gueve (1): GEY [GUV] Cameroon
- - - - - Kam (1): KAM [KDX] Nigeria
- - - - - Kwa (1): KWA [KWB] Nigeria
- - - - - La'bi (1): LA'BI [LBI] Cameroon
- - - - - Leko-Nimbari (28)
- - - - - - Duru (12)
- - - - - - - Dii (4): DII [DUR] Cameroon
- - - - - - - - DUUPA [DAE] Cameroon
- - - - - - - - PAPE [NDU] Cameroon
- - - - - - - - SAA [SZR] Cameroon
- - - - - - - Duli (1): DULI [DUZ] Cameroon
- - - - - - - Voko-Dowayo (7)
- - - - - - - - Kutin (1): PEERE [KUT] Cameroon
- - - - - - - - Vere-Dowayo (5)
- - - - - - - - - Dowayo (1): DOYAYO [DOW] Cameroon
- - - - - - - - - Vere-Gimme (4)
- - - - - - - - - - Gimme (2): GIMME [KMP] Cameroon
- - - - - - - - - - GIMNIME [KMB] Cameroon
- - - - - - - - - - Vere (2): KOMA [KMY] Nigeria
- - - - - - - - - - - MOM JANGO [VER] Nigeria
- - - - - - - - Voko (1): LONGTO [WOK] Cameroon
- - - - - - Leko (4): KOLBILA [KLC] Cameroon
- - - - - - - NYONG [MUO] Cameroon
- - - - - - - SAMBA LEKO [NDI] Cameroon
- - - - - - - WOM [WOM] Nigeria
- - - - - - Mumuye-Yandang (11)
- - - - - - - Mumuye (7): GENGLE [GEG] Nigeria
- - - - - - - KUMBA [KSM] Nigeria

Niger-Congo (1489)
- Atlantic-Congo (1390)
- - Volta-Congo (1316)
- - - North (257)
- - - - Adamawa-Ubangi (159)
- - - - - Adamawa (89)
- - - - - - Leko-Nimbari (28)
- - - - - - - Mumuye-Yandang (11)
- - - - - - - - Mumuye (7): MUMUYE [MUL] Nigeria
- - - - - - - - - PANGSENG [PAN] Nigeria
- - - - - - - - - RANG [RAX] Nigeria
- - - - - - - - - TEME [TDO] Nigeria
- - - - - - - - - WAKA [WAV] Nigeria
- - - - - - - - Yandang (4): BALI [BCN] Nigeria
- - - - - - - - - KPASAM [PBN] Nigeria
- - - - - - - - - KUGAMA [KOW] Nigeria
- - - - - - - - - YENDANG [YEN] Nigeria
- - - - - - - Nimbari (1): NIMBARI [NMR] Cameroon
- - - - - - Mbum-Day (30)
- - - - - - - Bua (10): BOLGO [BVO] Chad
- - - - - - - BON GULA [GLC] Chad
- - - - - - - BUA [BUB] Chad
- - - - - - - FANIA [FAN] Chad
- - - - - - - GULA IRO [GLJ] Chad
- - - - - - - KOKE [KOU] Chad
- - - - - - - NIELLIM [NIE] Chad
- - - - - - - NOY [NOY] Chad
- - - - - - - TUNIA [TUG] Chad
- - - - - - - ZAN GULA [ZNA] Chad
- - - - - - Day (1): DAY [DAI] Chad
- - - - - - Kim (3): BESME [BES] Chad
- - - - - - - GOUNDO [GOY] Chad
- - - - - - - KIM [KIA] Chad
- - - - - - Mbum (16)
- - - - - - - Central (5)
- - - - - - - - Karang (4): KARANG [KZR] Cameroon
- - - - - - - - - KARE [KBN] Central African Republic
- - - - - - - - - NZAKAMBAY [NZY] Chad
- - - - - - - - - PANA [PNZ] Central African Republic
- - - - - - - - Koh (1): KUO [KHO] Chad
- - - - - - - Northern (6)
- - - - - - - - Dama-Galke (3): DAMA [DMM] Cameroon
- - - - - - - - - MONO [MRU] Cameroon
- - - - - - - - - NDAI [GKE] Cameroon
- - - - - - - - Tupuri-Mambai (3): MAMBAI [MCS] Cameroon
- - - - - - - - - MUNDANG [MUA] Chad
- - - - - - - - - TUPURI [TUI] Cameroon
- - - - - - - Southern (1): MBUM [MDD] Cameroon
- - - - - - - Unclassified (4): DEK [DEK] Cameroon
- - - - - - - - LAKA [LAK] Nigeria
- - - - - - - - PAM [PMN] Cameroon
- - - - - - - - TO [TOZ] Cameroon
- - - - - - Unclassified (1): OBLO [OBL] Cameroon
- - - - - - Waja-Jen (24)
- - - - - - - Jen (10): BURAK [BYS] Nigeria
- - - - - - - DZA [JEN] Nigeria
- - - - - - - KYAK [BKA] Nigeria
- - - - - - - LEELAU [LDK] Nigeria
- - - - - - - LOO [LDO] Nigeria
- - - - - - - MÁGHDÌ [GMD] Nigeria
- - - - - - - MAK [PBL] Nigeria

Niger-Congo (1489)
- Atlantic-Congo (1390)
- - Volta-Congo (1316)
- - - North (257)
- - - - Adamawa-Ubangi (159)
- - - - - Adamawa (89)
- - - - - - Waja-Jen (24)
- - - - - - - Jen (10): MINGANG DOSO [MKO] Nigeria
- - - - - - - MOO [GWG] Nigeria
- - - - - - - THA [THY] Nigeria
- - - - - - Longuda (1): LONGUDA [LNU] Nigeria
- - - - - - Waja (8)
- - - - - - - Awak (2): AWAK [AWO] Nigeria
- - - - - - - KAMO [KCQ] Nigeria
- - - - - - - Cham-Mona (2): DIJIM-BWILIM [CFA] Nigeria
- - - - - - - TSO [LDP] Nigeria
- - - - - - - Dadiya (1): DADIYA [DBD] Nigeria
- - - - - - - Tula (3): BANGWINJI [BSJ] Nigeria
- - - - - - - TULA [TUL] Nigeria
- - - - - - - WAJA [WJA] Nigeria
- - - - - - Yungur (5)
- - - - - - - Libo (1): KAAN [LDL] Nigeria
- - - - - - - Mboi (1): MBOI [MOI] Nigeria
- - - - - - - Yungur-Roba (3): BENA [YUN] Nigeria
- - - - - - - LALA-ROBA [LLA] Nigeria
- - - - - - - VORO [VOR] Nigeria
- - - - - Ubangi (70)
- - - - - - Banda (16)
- - - - - - - Central (11)
- - - - - - - - Central Core (10)
- - - - - - - - - Banda-Bambari (1): BANDA-BAMBARI [LIY] Central African Republic
- - - - - - - - - Banda-Banda (1): BANDA-BANDA [BPD] Central African Republic
- - - - - - - - - Banda-Mbres (1): BANDA-MBRÈS [BQK] Central African Republic
- - - - - - - - - Banda-Ndele (1): BANDA-NDÉLÉ [BFL] Central African Republic
- - - - - - - - - Mid-Southern (5): BANDA, MID-SOUTHERN [BJO] Central African Republic
- - - - - - - - - GOBU [GOX] DRC
- - - - - - - - - KPAGUA [KUW] Central African Republic
- - - - - - - - - MONO [MNH] DRC
- - - - - - - - - NGUNDU [NUE] DRC
- - - - - - - - - Togbo-Vara (1): BANDA, TOGBO-VARA [TOR] DRC
- - - - - - - - Western (1): BANDA-YANGERE [YAJ] Central African Republic
- - - - - - - South Central (2): BANDA, SOUTH CENTRAL [LNL] Central African Republic
- - - - - - - LANGBASHE [LNA] Central African Republic
- - - - - - - Southern (1): MBANDJA [ZMZ] DRC
- - - - - - Southwestern (1): NGBUNDU [NUU] DRC
- - - - - - West Central (1): BANDA, WEST CENTRAL [BBP] Central African Republic
- - - - - Gbaya-Manza-Ngbaka (14): SUMA [SQM] Central African Republic
- - - - - Central (4): BOKOTO [BDT] Central African Republic
- - - - - - GBANU [GBV] Central African Republic
- - - - - - GBAYA-BOSSANGOA [GBP] Central African Republic
- - - - - - GBAYA-BOZOUM [GBQ] Central African Republic
- - - - - East (6): ALI [AIY] Central African Republic
- - - - - - BOFI [BFF] Central African Republic
- - - - - - BONJO [BOK] Congo
- - - - - - MANZA [MZV] Central African Republic
- - - - - - NGBAKA [NGA] DRC
- - - - - - NGBAKA MANZA [NGG] Central African Republic
- - - - - Northwest (1): GBAYA, NORTHWEST [GYA] Central African Republic
- - - - - Southwest (2): BANGANDU [BGF] Cameroon
- - - - - - GBAYA, SOUTHWEST [MDO] Central African Republic

Niger-Congo (1489)
- Atlantic-Congo (1390)
- - Volta-Congo (1316)
- - - North (257)
- - - - Adamawa-Ubangi (159)
- - - - - Ubangi (70)
- - - - - - Ngbandi (6): DENDI [DEQ] Central African Republic
- - - - - - GBAYI [GYG] Central African Republic
- - - - - - MBANGI [MGN] Central African Republic
- - - - - - NGBANDI, NORTHERN [NGB] DRC
- - - - - - NGBANDI, SOUTHERN [NBW] DRC
- - - - - - YAKOMA [YKY] Central African Republic
- - - - - Sere-Ngbaka-Mba (28)
- - - - - - Ngbaka-Mba (19)
- - - - - - - Mba (4): DONGO [DOO] DRC
- - - - - - - - MA [MSJ] DRC
- - - - - - - - MBA [MFC] DRC
- - - - - - - - NDUNGA [NDT] DRC
- - - - - - - Ngbaka (15)
- - - - - - - - Eastern (3)
- - - - - - - - - Mayogo-Bangba (2): BANGBA [BBE] DRC
- - - - - - - - - - MAYOGO [MDM] DRC
- - - - - - - - - Mundu (1): MÜNDÜ [MUH] Sudan
- - - - - - - - Western (12)
- - - - - - - - - Baka-Gundi (5): BAKA [BKC] Cameroon
- - - - - - - - - - BOMASSA [BME] DRC
- - - - - - - - - - GANZI [GNZ] Central African Republic
- - - - - - - - - - GUNDI [GDI] Central African Republic
- - - - - - - - - - NGOMBE [NMJ] Central African Republic
- - - - - - - - - Bwaka (2): GILIMA [GIX] DRC
- - - - - - - - - - NGBAKA MA'BO [NBM] Central African Republic
- - - - - - - - - Gbanzili (2): BURAKA [BKG] Central African Republic
- - - - - - - - - - GBANZIRI [GBG] Central African Republic
- - - - - - - - - Monzombo (3): KPALA [KPL] DRC
- - - - - - - - - - MONZOMBO [MOJ] Congo
- - - - - - - - - - YANGO [YNG] DRC
- - - - - - Sere (9)
- - - - - - - Feroge-Mangaya (2): FEROGE [FER] Sudan
- - - - - - - - MANGAYAT [MYJ] Sudan
- - - - - - - Indri-Togoyo (2): INDRI [IDR] Sudan
- - - - - - - - TOGOYO [TGY] Sudan
- - - - - - - Sere-Bviri (5)
- - - - - - - - Bai-Viri (2): BAI [BDJ] Sudan
- - - - - - - - - BELANDA VIRI [BVI] Sudan
- - - - - - - - Ndogo-Sere (3): NDOGO [NDZ] Sudan
- - - - - - - - - SERE [SWF] DRC
- - - - - - - - - TAGBU [TBM] DRC
- - - - - Zande (6)
- - - - - - Barambo-Pambia (2): BARAMBU [BRM] DRC
- - - - - - - PAMBIA [PAM] DRC
- - - - - - Zande-Nzakara (4): GEME [GEQ] Central African Republic
- - - - - - - KPATILI [KYM] Central African Republic
- - - - - - - NZAKARA [NZK] Central African Republic
- - - - - - - ZANDE [ZAN] DRC
- - - - Gur (98)
- - - - - Bariba (1): BARIBA [BBA] Benin
- - - - - Central (70)
- - - - - - Northern (39)
- - - - - - - Bwamu (4): BOMU [BMQ] Mali
- - - - - - - - BWAMU [BOX] Burkina Faso
- - - - - - - - BWAMU, CWI [BWY] Burkina Faso

Niger-Congo (1489)
- Atlantic-Congo (1390)
- - Volta-Congo (1316)
- - - North (257)
- - - - Gur (98)
- - - - - Central (70)
- - - - - - Northern (39)
- - - - - - - Bwamu (4): BWAMU, LÁÁ LÁÁ [BWJ] Burkina Faso
- - - - - - - Kurumfe (1): KOROMFÉ [KFZ] Burkina Faso
- - - - - - - Oti-Volta (34)
- - - - - - - - Buli-Koma (2): BULI [BWU] Ghana
- - - - - - - - KONNI [KMA] Ghana
- - - - - - - - Eastern (5): BIALI [BEH] Benin
- - - - - - - - DITAMMARI [TBZ] Benin
- - - - - - - - MBELIME [MQL] Benin
- - - - - - - - TAMBERMA [SOF] Togo
- - - - - - - - WAAMA [WWA] Benin
- - - - - - - - Gurma (9): GOURMANCÉMA [GUX] Burkina Faso
- - - - - - - - KONKOMBA [KOS] Ghana
- - - - - - - - NATENI [NTM] Benin
- - - - - - - - NGANGAM [GNG] Togo
- - - - - - - - SOLA [SOY] Benin
- - - - - - - - Moba (2): BIMOBA [BIM] Ghana
- - - - - - - - - MOBA [MFQ] Togo
- - - - - - - - Ntcham (2): AKASELEM [AKS] Togo
- - - - - - - - - - NTCHAM [BUD] Togo
- - - - - - - - Western (16)
- - - - - - - - - Nootre (1): BOULBA [BLY] Benin
- - - - - - - - - Northwest (9): FRAFRA [GUR] Ghana
- - - - - - - - - MÒORÉ [MHM] Burkina Faso
- - - - - - - - - SAFALIBA [SAF] Ghana
- - - - - - - - - WALI [WLX] Ghana
- - - - - - - - - Dagaari-Birifor (5)
- - - - - - - - - - Birifor (2): BIRIFOR, MALBA [BFO] Burkina Faso
- - - - - - - - - - - BIRIFOR, SOUTHERN [BIV] Ghana
- - - - - - - - - - Dagaari (3): DAGAARE, SOUTHERN [DGA] Ghana
- - - - - - - - - - - DAGAARI DIOULA [DGD] Burkina Faso
- - - - - - - - - - - DAGARA, NORTHERN [DGI] Burkina Faso
- - - - - - - - - Southeast (6): DAGBANI [DAG] Ghana
- - - - - - - - - HANGA [HAG] Ghana
- - - - - - - - - KAMARA [JMR] Ghana
- - - - - - - - - KANTOSI [XKT] Ghana
- - - - - - - - - MAMPRULI [MAW] Ghana
- - - - - - - - - Kusaal (1): KUSAAL [KUS] Ghana
- - - - - - - - Yom-Nawdm (2): NAWDM [NMZ] Togo
- - - - - - - - - PILA [PIL] Benin
- - - - - - Southern (31)
- - - - - - - Dogoso-Khe (2): DOGOSO [DGS] Burkina Faso
- - - - - - - KHE [KQG] Burkina Faso
- - - - - - - Dyan (1): DYAN [DYA] Burkina Faso
- - - - - - - Gan-Dogose (3): DOGOSÉ [DOS] Burkina Faso
- - - - - - - KAANSA [GNA] Burkina Faso
- - - - - - - KHISA [KQM] Côte d'Ivoire
- - - - - - - Grusi (23)
- - - - - - - - Eastern (7): BAGO [BQG] Togo
- - - - - - - - CHALA [CHA] Ghana
- - - - - - - - DELO [NTR] Ghana
- - - - - - - - KABIYÉ [KBP] Togo
- - - - - - - - LAMA [LAS] Togo
- - - - - - - - LUKPA [DOP] Benin
- - - - - - - - TEM [KDH] Togo

Niger-Congo (1489)
- Atlantic-Congo (1390)
- - Volta-Congo (1316)
- - - North (257)
- - - - Gur (98)
- - - - - Central (70)
- - - - - - Southern (31)
- - - - - - - Grusi (23)
- - - - - - - - Northern (6): KALAMSÉ [KNZ] Burkina Faso
- - - - - - - - KASEM [KAS] Burkina Faso
- - - - - - - - LYÉLÉ [LEE] Burkina Faso
- - - - - - - - NUNI, NORTHERN [NUV] Burkina Faso
- - - - - - - - NUNI, SOUTHERN [NNW] Burkina Faso
- - - - - - - - PANA [PNQ] Burkina Faso
- - - - - - - - Western (10): CHAKALI [CLI] Ghana
- - - - - - - - DEG [MZW] Ghana
- - - - - - - - PWIÉ [PUG] Burkina Faso
- - - - - - - - SISAALA, PASAALE [SIG] Ghana
- - - - - - - - SISAALA, TUMULUNG [SIL] Ghana
- - - - - - - - SISAALA, WESTERN [SSL] Ghana
- - - - - - - - SISSALA [SLD] Burkina Faso
- - - - - - - - TAMPULMA [TAM] Ghana
- - - - - - - - VAGLA [VAG] Ghana
- - - - - - - - WINYÉ [KST] Burkina Faso
- - - - - - - Kirma-Tyurama (2): CERMA [GOT] Burkina Faso
- - - - - - - TURKA [TUZ] Burkina Faso
- - - - - Kulango (2): KULANGO, BONDOUKOU [KZC] Côte d'Ivoire
- - - - - KULANGO, BOUNA [NKU] Côte d'Ivoire
- - - - - Lobi (1): LOBI [LOB] Burkina Faso
- - - - - Senufo (15)
- - - - - - Karaboro (2): KARABORO, EASTERN [KAR] Burkina Faso
- - - - - - KARABORO, WESTERN [KZA] Burkina Faso
- - - - - - Kpalaga (1): SENOUFO, PALAKA [PLR] Côte d'Ivoire
- - - - - - Nafaanra (1): NAFAANRA [NFR] Ghana
- - - - - - Senari (4): SENOUFO, CEBAARA [SEF] Côte d'Ivoire
- - - - - - SENOUFO, NYARAFOLO [SEV] Côte d'Ivoire
- - - - - - SÉNOUFO, SENARA [SEQ] Burkina Faso
- - - - - - SENOUFO, SYENARA [SHZ] Mali
- - - - - - Suppire-Mamara (5): SENOUFO, MAMARA [MYK] Mali
- - - - - - SÉNOUFO, NANERIGÉ [SEN] Burkina Faso
- - - - - - SÉNOUFO, SHEMPIRE [SEB] Côte d'Ivoire
- - - - - - SÉNOUFO, SÌCÌTÉ [SEP] Burkina Faso
- - - - - - SENOUFO, SUPYIRE [SPP] Mali
- - - - - - Tagwana-Djimini (2): SENOUFO, DJIMINI [DYI] Côte d'Ivoire
- - - - - - SENOUFO, TAGWANA [TGW] Côte d'Ivoire
- - - - - Teen (2): LOMA [LOI] Côte d'Ivoire
- - - - - TÈÈN [LOR] Côte d'Ivoire
- - - - - Tiefo (1): TIÉFO [TIQ] Burkina Faso
- - - - - Tusia (2): TOUSSIAN, NORTHERN [TSP] Burkina Faso
- - - - - TOUSSIAN, SOUTHERN [WIB] Burkina Faso
- - - - - Unclassified (1): MORU [MXZ] Côte d'Ivoire
- - - - - Viemo (1): VIEMO [VIG] Burkina Faso
- - - - - Wara-Natioro (2): NATIORO [NTI] Burkina Faso
- - - - - - WARA [WBF] Burkina Faso
- Kordofanian (31)
- - Kadugli (7)
- - - Central (4): KANGA [KCP] Sudan
- - - - KATCHA-KADUGLI-MIRI [KAT] Sudan
- - - - TULISHI [TEY] Sudan
- - - - TUMMA [TBQ] Sudan
- - - Eastern (2): KRONGO [KGO] Sudan

Niger-Congo (1489)
- Kordofanian (31)
- - Kadugli (7)
- - - Eastern (2): TUMTUM [TBR] Sudan
- - - Western (1): KEIGA [KEC] Sudan
- - Kordofanian Proper (24)
- - - Heiban (10)
- - - - Eastern (2): KO [FUJ] Sudan
- - - - - WARNANG [WRN] Sudan
- - - - West-Central (8)
- - - - - Central (5)
- - - - - - Ebang-Logol (4)
- - - - - - - Ebang-Laru (2): HEIBAN [HEB] Sudan
- - - - - - - - LARO [LRO] Sudan
- - - - - - - Logol (1): LOGOL [LOF] Sudan
- - - - - - - Utoro (1): OTORO [OTR] Sudan
- - - - - - Rere (1): KOALIB [KIB] Sudan
- - - - - Shirumba (1): SHWAI [SHW] Sudan
- - - - - Western (2): MORO [MOR] Sudan
- - - - - - TIRA [TIR] Sudan
- - - Katla (2): KATLA [KCR] Sudan
- - - - TIMA [TMS] Sudan
- - - Rashad (3): TAGOI [TAG] Sudan
- - - - TEGALI [RAS] Sudan
- - - - TINGAL [TIG] Sudan
- - - Talodi (9)
- - - - Talodi Proper (8)
- - - - - Jomang (1): TALODI [TLO] Sudan
- - - - - Nding (1): NDING [ELI] Sudan
- - - - - Ngile-Dengebu (2): DAGIK [DEC] Sudan
- - - - - - NGILE [MAS] Sudan
- - - - - Tocho (4): ACHERON [ACZ] Sudan
- - - - - - LUMUN [LMD] Sudan
- - - - - - TOCHO [TAZ] Sudan
- - - - - - TORONA [TQR] Sudan
- - - - Tegem (1): LAFOFA [LAF] Sudan
- Mande (68)
- - Eastern (18)
- - - Eastern (9)
- - - - Bissa (1): BISSA [BIB] Burkina Faso
- - - - Busa (5): BOKO [BQC] Benin
- - - - - BOKOBARU [BUS] Nigeria
- - - - - BUSA [BQP] Nigeria
- - - - - KYENGA [TYE] Nigeria
- - - - - SHANGA [SHO] Nigeria
- - - - Samo (3): SAMO, MATYA [STJ] Burkina Faso
- - - - - SAMO, MAYA [SYM] Burkina Faso
- - - - - SAMO, SOUTHERN [SBD] Burkina Faso
- - - Southeastern (9)
- - - - Guro-Tura (5)
- - - - - Guro-Yaoure (2): GURO [GOA] Côte d'Ivoire
- - - - - - YAOURÉ [YRE] Côte d'Ivoire
- - - - - Tura-Dan-Mano (3)
- - - - - - Mano (1): MANO [MEV] Liberia
- - - - - - Tura-Dan (2): DAN [DAF] Côte d'Ivoire
- - - - - - - TOURA [NEB] Côte d'Ivoire
- - - - Nwa-Ben (4)
- - - - - Ben-Gban (2): BENG [NHB] Côte d'Ivoire
- - - - - - GAGU [GGU] Côte d'Ivoire
- - - - - Wan-Mwan (2): MWAN [MOA] Côte d'Ivoire
- - - - - - WAN [WAN] Côte d'Ivoire

Niger-Congo (1489)
- Mande (68)
- - Western (50)
- - - Central-Southwestern (38)
- - - - Central (31)
- - - - - Manding-Jogo (29)
- - - - - - Jogo-Jeri (2)
- - - - - - - Jeri-Jalkuna (1): BLÉ [BXL] Burkina Faso
- - - - - - - Jogo (1): LIGBI [LIG] Ghana
- - - - - - Manding-Vai (27)
- - - - - - - Manding-Mokole (25)
- - - - - - - - Manding (22): BOLON [BOF] Burkina Faso
- - - - - - - - - JAHANKA [JAD] Guinea
- - - - - - - - - KALANKE [CKN] Gambia
- - - - - - - - - SININKERE [SKQ] Burkina Faso
- - - - - - - - - Manding-East (13)
- - - - - - - - - - Marka-Dafin (1): MARKA [MWR] Burkina Faso
- - - - - - - - - - Northeastern Manding (2)
- - - - - - - - - - - Bamana (2): BAMANANKAN [BRA] Mali
- - - - - - - - - - - JULA [DYU] Burkina Faso
- - - - - - - - - - Southeastern Manding (10): MANINKA, KANKAN [MNI] Guinea
- - - - - - - - - - - MANINKA, KONYANKA [MKU] Guinea
- - - - - - - - - - - MANINKA, SANKARAN [MSC] Guinea
- - - - - - - - - - - MANYA [MZJ] Liberia
- - - - - - - - - - - Maninka-Mori (6): JULA, KORO [KFO] Côte d'Ivoire
- - - - - - - - - - - - JULA, KOYAGA [KGA] Côte d'Ivoire
- - - - - - - - - - - - JULA, ODIENNÉ [JOD] Côte d'Ivoire
- - - - - - - - - - - - JULA, WORODOUGOU [JUD] Côte d'Ivoire
- - - - - - - - - - - - MAHOU [MXX] Côte d'Ivoire
- - - - - - - - - - - - MANINKA, FOREST [MYQ] Côte d'Ivoire
- - - - - - - - - - Manding-West (5): KAGORO [XKG] Mali
- - - - - - - - - - - MANDINKA [MNK] Senegal
- - - - - - - - - - - MANINKAKAN, KITA [MWK] Mali
- - - - - - - - - - - MANINKAKAN, WESTERN [MLQ] Mali
- - - - - - - - - - - XAASONGAXANGO [KAO] Mali
- - - - - - - - - Mokole (3): KURANKO [KHA] Sierra Leone
- - - - - - - - - - LELE [LLC] Guinea
- - - - - - - - - - MIXIFORE [MFG] Guinea
- - - - - - - - Vai-Kono (2): KONO [KNO] Sierra Leone
- - - - - - - - - VAI [VAI] Liberia
- - - - - - - Susu-Yalunka (2): SUSU [SUD] Guinea
- - - - - - - - YALUNKA [YAL] Guinea
- - - - Southwestern (7)
- - - - - Kpelle (2): KPELLE, GUINEA [GKP] Guinea
- - - - - - KPELLE, LIBERIA [KPE] Liberia
- - - - - Mende-Loma (5)
- - - - - - Loma (2): LOMA [LOM] Liberia
- - - - - - - TOMA [TOD] Guinea
- - - - - - Mende-Bandi (3)
- - - - - - - Bandi (1): BANDI [GBA] Liberia
- - - - - - - Mende-Loko (2): LOKO [LOK] Sierra Leone
- - - - - - - - MENDE [MFY] Sierra Leone
- - - Northwestern (12)
- - - - Samogo (12)
- - - - - Dzuun-Seeku (5)
- - - - - - Banka (1): BANKAGOMA [BXW] Mali
- - - - - - Dzuun (3): DUUNGOMA [DUX] Mali
- - - - - - - DZÙ̀ÙNGOO [DNN] Burkina Faso
- - - - - - - JOWULU [JOW] Mali
- - - - - - Seeku (1): SEEKU [SOS] Burkina Faso

Niger-Congo (1489)
- Mande (68)
- - Western (50)
- - - Northwestern (12)
- - - - Samogo (12)
- - - - - Soninke-Bobo (7)
- - - - - - Bobo (2): BOBO MADARÉ, NORTHERN [BBO] Burkina Faso
- - - - - - - BOBO MADARÉ, SOUTHERN [BWQ] Burkina Faso
- - - - - - Soninke-Boso (5)
- - - - - - - Boso (4)
- - - - - - - - Eastern (3): BOZO, HAINYAXO [BZX] Mali
- - - - - - - - - BOZO, TIÈMA CIÈWÈ [BOO] Mali
- - - - - - - - - BOZO, TIÉYAXO [BOZ] Mali
- - - - - - - - Sorogama (1): BOZO, SOROGAMA [BZE] Mali
- - - - - - - Soninke (1): SONINKE [SNN] Mali

Nilo-Saharan (199)
- Berta (1): BERTA [WTI] Ethiopia
- Central Sudanic (65)
- - East (22)
- - - Lendu (3): BENDI [BCT] DRC
- - - - LENDU [LED] DRC
- - - - NGITI [NIY] DRC
- - - Mangbetu (3): ASOA [ASV] DRC
- - - - LOMBI [LMI] DRC
- - - - MANGBETU [MDJ] DRC
- - - Mangbutu-Efe (6): EFE [EFE] DRC
- - - - LESE [LES] DRC
- - - - MAMVU [MDI] DRC
- - - - MANGBUTU [MDK] DRC
- - - - MVUBA [MXH] DRC
- - - - NDO [NDP] DRC
- - - Moru-Madi (10)
- - - - Central (6): ARINGA [LUC] Uganda
- - - - - AVOKAYA [AVU] DRC
- - - - - KELIKO [KBO] Sudan
- - - - - LOGO [LOG] DRC
- - - - - LUGBARA [LUG] Uganda
- - - - - OMI [OMI] DRC
- - - - Northern (1): MORU [MGD] Sudan
- - - - Southern (3): LULUBO [LUL] Sudan
- - - - - MA'DI [MHI] Uganda
- - - - - MA'DI, SOUTHERN [QMD] Uganda
- - West (43)
- - - Bongo-Bagirmi (41)
- - - Bongo-Baka (8)
- - - - - Baka (1): BAKA [BDH] Sudan
- - - - - Bongo (1): BONGO [BOT] Sudan
- - - - - Morokodo-Beli (6): BELI [BLM] Sudan
- - - - - - JUR MODO [BEX] Sudan
- - - - - - MITTU [MWU] Sudan
- - - - - - Morokodo-Mo'da (3): MO'DA [GBN] Sudan
- - - - - - - MOROKODO [MGC] Sudan
- - - - - - - NYAMUSA-MOLO [NYO] Sudan
- - - - Kara (3): FURU [FUU] DRC
- - - - - GULA [KCM] Central African Republic
- - - - - YULU [YUL] Central African Republic
- - - - Sara-Bagirmi (29): BIRRI [BVQ] Central African Republic
- - - - - FONGORO [FGR] Chad
- - - - - Bagirmi (8): BAGIRMI [BMI] Chad
- - - - - - BERAKOU [BXV] Chad

Nilo-Saharan (199)
- Central Sudanic (65)
- - West (43)
- - - Bongo-Bagirmi (41)
- - - - Sara-Bagirmi (29)
- - - - - Bagirmi (8): BERNDE [BDO] Chad
- - - - - - DISA [DIV] Chad
- - - - - - GULA [GLU] Chad
- - - - - - JAYA [JYY] Chad
- - - - - - KENGA [KYQ] Chad
- - - - - - NABA [MNE] Chad
- - - - - Sara (19)
- - - - - - Sara Proper (17): BEDJOND [MAP] Chad
- - - - - - - DAGBA [DGK] Central African Republic
- - - - - - - GOR [GQR] Chad
- - - - - - - GULAY [GVL] Chad
- - - - - - - HORO [HOR] Chad
- - - - - - - KABA [KSP] Central African Republic
- - - - - - - LAKA [LAM] Chad
- - - - - - - MANGO [MGE] Chad
- - - - - - - MBAY [MYB] Chad
- - - - - - - NGAM [NMC] Chad
- - - - - - - NGAMBAY [SBA] Chad
- - - - - - - SAR [MWM] Chad
- - - - - - - Sara Kaba (5): KABA DEME [KWG] Chad
- - - - - - - - KABA NA [KWV] Chad
- - - - - - - - KULFA [KXJ] Chad
- - - - - - - - SARA DUNJO [KOJ] Central African Republic
- - - - - - - - SARA KABA [SBZ] Central African Republic
- - - - - - Vale (2): LUTOS [NDY] Central African Republic
- - - - - - - VALE [VAE] Central African Republic
- - - - Sinyar (1): SINYAR [SYS] Sudan
- - - Kresh (2): AJA [AJA] Sudan
- - - - GBAYA [KRS] Sudan
- Eastern Sudanic (95)
- - Eastern (26)
- - - Eastern Jebel (4)
- - - - Aka-Kelo-Molo (3): AKA [SOH] Sudan
- - - - - KELO [TSN] Sudan
- - - - - MOLO [ZMO] Sudan
- - - - Gaam (1): GAAM [TBI] Sudan
- - - Nara (1): NARA [NRB] Eritrea
- - - Nubian (11)
- - - - Central (9)
- - - - - Birked (1): BIRKED [BRK] Sudan
- - - - - Dongolawi (1): KENUZI-DONGOLA [KNC] Sudan
- - - - - Hill (7)
- - - - - - Kadaru-Ghulfan (2): GHULFAN [GHL] Sudan
- - - - - - - KADARU [KDU] Sudan
- - - - - - Unclassified (5): DAIR [DRB] Sudan
- - - - - - - DILLING [DIL] Sudan
- - - - - - - EL HUGEIRAT [ELH] Sudan
- - - - - - - KARKO [KKO] Sudan
- - - - - - - WALI [WLL] Sudan
- - - - Northern (1): NOBIIN [FIA] Sudan
- - - - Western (1): MIDOB [MEI] Sudan
- - - Surmic (10)
- - - - North (1)
- - - - - Majang (1): MAJANG [MPE] Ethiopia

Nilo-Saharan (199)
- Eastern Sudanic (95)
- - Eastern (26)
- - - Surmic (10)
- - - - South (9)
- - - - - Southeast (4)
- - - - - - Kwegu (1): KWEGU [YID] Ethiopia
- - - - - - Pastoral (3)
- - - - - - - Me'en (1): ME'EN [MYM] Ethiopia
- - - - - - - Suri (2): MURSI [MUZ] Ethiopia
- - - - - - - - SURI [SUQ] Ethiopia
- - - - - Southwest (5)
- - - - - - Didinga-Murle (4)
- - - - - - - Didinga-Longarim (2): DIDINGA [DID] Sudan
- - - - - - - - LONGARIM [LOH] Sudan
- - - - - - - - Murle (1): MURLE [MUR] Sudan
- - - - - - - Tennet (1): TENNET [TEX] Sudan
- - - - - - Kacipo-Balesi (1): KACIPO-BALESI [KOE] Sudan
- - Kuliak (3)
- - - Ik (1): IK [IKX] Uganda
- - - Ngangea-So (2): NYANG'I [NYP] Uganda
- - - - SOO [TEU] Uganda
- - Nilotic (52)
- - - Eastern (16)
- - - - Bari (3): BARI [BFA] Sudan
- - - - - KAKWA [KEO] Uganda
- - - - - MANDARI [MQU] Sudan
- - - - Lotuxo-Teso (13)
- - - - - Lotuxo-Maa (8)
- - - - - - Lotuxo (5): DONGOTONO [DDD] Sudan
- - - - - - - LANGO [LNO] Sudan
- - - - - - - LOKOYA [LKY] Sudan
- - - - - - - LOPPIT [LPX] Sudan
- - - - - - - OTUHO [LOT] Sudan
- - - - - - Ongamo-Maa (3): MAASAI [MET] Kenya
- - - - - - - NGASA [NSG] Tanzania
- - - - - - - SAMBURU [SAQ] Kenya
- - - - - Teso-Turkana (5)
- - - - - - Teso (1): TESO [TEO] Uganda
- - - - - - Turkana (4): KARAMOJONG [KDJ] Uganda
- - - - - - - NYANGATOM [NNJ] Ethiopia
- - - - - - - TOPOSA [TOQ] Sudan
- - - - - - - TURKANA [TUV] Kenya
- - - Southern (14)
- - - - Kalenjin (12)
- - - - - Elgon (2): KUPSABINY [KPZ] Uganda
- - - - - - SABAOT [SPY] Kenya
- - - - - Nandi-Markweta (8)
- - - - - - Markweta (2): ENDO [ENB] Kenya
- - - - - - - TALAI [TLE] Kenya
- - - - - - Nandi (6): ARAMANIK [AAM] Tanzania
- - - - - - - KALENJIN [KLN] Kenya
- - - - - - - KISANKASA [KQH] Tanzania
- - - - - - - MEDIAK [MWX] Tanzania
- - - - - - - MOSIRO [MWY] Tanzania
- - - - - - - TUGEN, NORTH [TUY] Kenya
- - - - - Okiek (1): OKIEK [OKI] Kenya
- - - - - Pokot (1): PÖKOOT [PKO] Kenya
- - - - Tatoga (2): DATOOGA [TCC] Tanzania
- - - - - OMOTIK [OMT] Kenya

Nilo-Saharan (199)
- Eastern Sudanic (95)
- - Nilotic (52)
- - - Western (22)
- - - - Dinka-Nuer (7)
- - - - - Dinka (5): DINKA, NORTHEASTERN [DIP] Sudan
- - - - - - DINKA, NORTHWESTERN [DIW] Sudan
- - - - - - DINKA, SOUTH CENTRAL [DIB] Sudan
- - - - - - DINKA, SOUTHEASTERN [DIN] Sudan
- - - - - - DINKA, SOUTHWESTERN [DIK] Sudan
- - - - - Nuer (2): NUER [NUS] Sudan
- - - - - - REEL [ATU] Sudan
- - - - Luo (15)
- - - - - Northern (9)
- - - - - - Anuak (1): ANUAK [ANU] Sudan
- - - - - - Bor (1): BELANDA BOR [BXB] Sudan
- - - - - - Jur (1): LUWO [LWO] Sudan
- - - - - - Maban-Burun (3)
- - - - - - - Burun (1): BURUN [BDI] Sudan
- - - - - - - Maban (2): JUMJUM [JUM] Sudan
- - - - - - - - MABAAN [MFZ] Sudan
- - - - - - Shilluk (1): SHILLUK [SHK] Sudan
- - - - - - Thuri (1): THURI [THU] Sudan
- - - - - - Unclassified (1): PÄRI [LKR] Sudan
- - - - - Southern (6)
- - - - - - Adhola (1): ADHOLA [ADH] Uganda
- - - - - - Kuman (1): KUMAM [KDI] Uganda
- - - - - - Luo-Acholi (4)
- - - - - - - Alur-Acholi (3)
- - - - - - - - Alur (1): ALUR [ALZ] DRC
- - - - - - - - Lango-Acholi (2): ACHOLI [ACO] Uganda
- - - - - - - - - LANGO [LAJ] Uganda
- - - - - - - Luo (1): LUO [LUO] Kenya
- - Western (14)
- - - Daju (7)
- - - - Eastern Daju (2): LOGORIK [LIU] Sudan
- - - - - SHATT [SHJ] Sudan
- - - - Western Daju (5): BAYGO [BYG] Sudan
- - - - - DAJU, DAR DAJU [DJC] Chad
- - - - - DAJU, DAR FUR [DAJ] Sudan
- - - - - DAJU, DAR SILA [DAU] Chad
- - - - - NJALGULGULE [NJL] Sudan
- - - Nyimang (2): AFITTI [AFT] Sudan
- - - - AMA [NYI] Sudan
- - - Tama (3)
- - - - Mararit (1): MARARIT [MGB] Chad
- - - - Tama-Sungor (2): ASSANGORI [SUN] Chad
- - - - - TAMA [TMA] Chad
- - - Temein (2): TEMEIN [TEQ] Sudan
- - - - TESE [KEG] Sudan
- Fur (3): AMDANG [AMJ] Chad
- - FUR [FUR] Sudan
- - MIMI [MIV] Chad
- Komuz (6)
- - Gumuz (1): GUMUZ [GUK] Ethiopia
- - Koman (5): GULE [GLE] Sudan
- - - KOMO [KOM] Sudan
- - - KWAMA [KMQ] Ethiopia
- - - OPUUO [LGN] Ethiopia
- - - UDUK [UDU] Ethiopia
- Kunama (1): KUNAMA [KUM] Eritrea

Nilo-Saharan (199)
- Maban (9): KARANGA [KTH] Chad
- - Mabang (8): KENDEJE [KLF] Chad
- - - Maba (2): MABA [MDE] Chad
- - - - MARFA [MVU] Chad
- - - - Masalit (3): MASALIT [MSA] Sudan
- - - - MASSALAT [MDG] Chad
- - - - SURBAKHAL [SBJ] Chad
- - - Runga-Kibet (2): KIBET [KIE] Chad
- - - - RUNGA [ROU] Chad
- Saharan (9)
- - Eastern (3): BERTI [BYT] Sudan
- - - BIDEYAT [BIH] Chad
- - - ZAGHAWA [ZAG] Sudan
- - Western (6)
- - - Kanuri (4): KANEMBU [KBL] Chad
- - - - KANURI, CENTRAL [KPH] Nigeria
- - - - KANURI, MANGA [KBY] Niger
- - - - KANURI, TUMARI [KRT] Niger
- - - Tebu (2): DAZAGA [DAK] Chad
- - - - TEDAGA [TUQ] Chad
- Songhai (9): KORANDJE [KCY] Algeria
- - Northern (3): TADAKSAHAK [DSQ] Mali
- - - TAGDAL [TDA] Niger
- - - TASAWAQ [TWQ] Niger
- - Southern (5): DENDI [DEN] Benin
- - - SONGHAY, HUMBUTI SENNI [HMB] Mali
- - - SONGHAY, KOYRA CHIINI [KHQ] Mali
- - - SONGHAY, KOYRABORO SENNI [SON] Mali
- - - ZARMA [DJE] Niger
- Unclassified (1): SHABO [SBF] Ethiopia

North Caucasian (34)
- North Central (3)
- - Batsi (1): BATS [BBL] Georgia
- - Chechen-Ingush (2): CHECHEN [CJC] Russia (Europe)
- - - INGUSH [INH] Russia (Europe)
- Northeast (26)
- - Avaro-Andi-Dido (14)
- - - Andi (8): AKHVAKH [AKV] Russia (Europe)
- - - - ANDI [ANI] Russia (Europe)
- - - - BAGVALAL [KVA] Russia (Europe)
- - - - BOTLIKH [BPH] Russia (Europe)
- - - - CHAMALAL [CJI] Russia (Europe)
- - - - GHODOBERI [GDO] Russia (Europe)
- - - - KARATA [KPT] Russia (Europe)
- - - - TINDI [TIN] Russia (Europe)
- - - Avar (1): AVAR [AVR] Russia (Europe)
- - - Dido (5): BEZHTA [KAP] Russia (Europe)
- - - - DIDO [DDO] Russia (Europe)
- - - - HINUKH [GIN] Russia (Europe)
- - - - HUNZIB [HUZ] Russia (Europe)
- - - - KHVARSHI [KHV] Russia (Europe)
- - Lak-Dargwa (2): DARGWA [DAR] Russia (Europe)
- - - LAK [LBE] Russia (Europe)
- - Lezgian (10): AGHUL [AGX] Russia (Europe)
- - - ARCHI [ARC] Russia (Europe)
- - - BUDUKH [BDK] Azerbaijan
- - - KHINALUGH [KJJ] Azerbaijan
- - - KRYTS [KRY] Azerbaijan
- - - LEZGI [LEZ] Russia (Europe)

North Caucasian (34)
- Northeast (26)
- - Lezgian (10): RUTUL [RUT] Russia (Europe)
- - - TABASSARAN [TAB] Russia (Europe)
- - - TSAKHUR [TKR] Azerbaijan
- - - UDI [UDI] Azerbaijan
- Northwest (5)
- - Abkhaz-Abazin (2): ABAZA [ABQ] Russia (Europe)
- - - ABKHAZ [ABK] Georgia
- - Circassian (2): ADYGHE [ADY] Russia (Europe)
- - - KABARDIAN [KAB] Russia (Europe)
- - Ubyx (1): UBYKH [UBY] Turkey (Europe)

Oto-Manguean (172)
- Amuzgoan (3): AMUZGO, GUERRERO [AMU] Mexico
- - AMUZGO, IPALAPA [AZM] Mexico
- - AMUZGO, SAN PEDRO AMUZGOS [AZG] Mexico
- Chiapanec-Mangue (2): CHIAPANECO [CIP] Mexico
- - CHOROTEGA [CJR] Costa Rica
- Chinantecan (14): CHINANTECO, CHILTEPEC [CSA] Mexico
- - CHINANTECO, COMALTEPEC [CCO] Mexico
- - CHINANTECO, LALANA [CNL] Mexico
- - CHINANTECO, LEALAO [CLE] Mexico
- - CHINANTECO, OJITLÁN [CHJ] Mexico
- - CHINANTECO, OZUMACÍN [CHZ] Mexico
- - CHINANTECO, PALANTLA [CPA] Mexico
- - CHINANTECO, QUIOTEPEC [CHQ] Mexico
- - CHINANTECO, SOCHIAPAN [CSO] Mexico
- - CHINANTECO, TEPETOTUTLA [CNT] Mexico
- - CHINANTECO, TEPINAPA [CTE] Mexico
- - CHINANTECO, TLACOATZINTEPEC [CTL] Mexico
- - CHINANTECO, USILA [CUS] Mexico
- - CHINANTECO, VALLE NACIONAL [CHV] Mexico
- Mixtecan (55)
- - Mixtec-Cuicatec (52)
- - - Cuicatec (6): CUICATECO, TEPEUXILA [CUX] Mexico
- - - - CUICATECO, TEUTILA [CUT] Mexico
- - - - MIXTECO, AMOLTEPEC [MBZ] Mexico
- - - - MIXTECO, IXTAYUTLA [VMJ] Mexico
- - - - MIXTECO, JUXTLAHUACA [VMC] Mexico
- - - - MIXTECO, MITLATONGO [VMM] Mexico
- - - Mixtec (46): MIXTECO, ALACATLATZALA [MIM] Mexico
- - - - MIXTECO, ALCOZAUCA [QMX] Mexico
- - - - MIXTECO, APASCO Y APOALA [MIP] Mexico
- - - - MIXTECO, ATATLÁHUCA [MIB] Mexico
- - - - MIXTECO, AYUTLA [MIY] Mexico
- - - - MIXTECO, CACALOXTEPEC [MIU] Mexico
- - - - MIXTECO, CHAYUCO [MIH] Mexico
- - - - MIXTECO, CHAZUMBA [QMB] Mexico
- - - - MIXTECO, CHIGMACATITLÁN [MII] Mexico
- - - - MIXTECO, COATZOSPAN [MIZ] Mexico
- - - - MIXTECO, CUYAMECALCO [QMZ] Mexico
- - - - MIXTECO, DIUXI-TILANTONGO [MIS] Mexico
- - - - MIXTECO, HUITEPEC [MXS] Mexico
- - - - MIXTECO, ITUNDUJIA [MCE] Mexico
- - - - MIXTECO, JAMILTEPEC [MXT] Mexico
- - - - MIXTECO, JUXTLAHUACA OESTE [JMX] Mexico
- - - - MIXTECO, MAGDALENA PEÑASCO [QMP] Mexico
- - - - MIXTECO, METLATONOC [MXV] Mexico
- - - - MIXTECO, MIXTEPEC [MIX] Mexico
- - - - MIXTECO, NOCHIXTLÁN SURESTE [MXY] Mexico

Oto-Manguean (172)
- Mixtecan (55)
- - Mixtec-Cuicatec (52)
- - - Mixtec (46): MIXTECO, OAXACA NOROESTE [MXA] Mexico
- - - - MIXTECO, OCOTEPEC [MIE] Mexico
- - - - MIXTECO, PEÑOLES [MIL] Mexico
- - - - MIXTECO, PINOTEPA NACIONAL [MIO] Mexico
- - - - MIXTECO, PUEBLA SUR [MIT] Mexico
- - - - MIXTECO, SAN JUAN COLORADO [MJC] Mexico
- - - - MIXTECO, SAN JUAN TEITA [QMC] Mexico
- - - - MIXTECO, SAN MIGUEL EL GRANDE [MIG] Mexico
- - - - MIXTECO, SAN MIGUEL PIEDRAS [QMG] Mexico
- - - - MIXTECO, SANTA MARÍA ZACATEPEC [MZA] Mexico
- - - - MIXTECO, SILACAYOAPAN [MKS] Mexico
- - - - MIXTECO, SINDIHUI [QMH] Mexico
- - - - MIXTECO, SINICAHUA [QMI] Mexico
- - - - MIXTECO, SOYALTEPEC [VMQ] Mexico
- - - - MIXTECO, TACAHUA [QMT] Mexico
- - - - MIXTECO, TAMAZOLA [VMX] Mexico
- - - - MIXTECO, TEZOATLÁN [MXB] Mexico
- - - - MIXTECO, TIDAÁ [MTX] Mexico
- - - - MIXTECO, TIJALTEPEC [QMJ] Mexico
- - - - MIXTECO, TLAXIACO NORTE [MOS] Mexico
- - - - MIXTECO, TLAXIACO, SUROESTE [MEH] Mexico
- - - - MIXTECO, TUTUTEPEC [MTU] Mexico
- - - - MIXTECO, YOLOXOCHITL [QMY] Mexico
- - - - MIXTECO, YOSONDÚA [MPM] Mexico
- - - - MIXTECO, YUCUAÑE [MVG] Mexico
- - - - MIXTECO, YUTANDUCHI [MAB] Mexico
- - Trique (3): TRIQUE, CHICAHUAXTLA [TRS] Mexico
- - - TRIQUE, COPALA [TRC] Mexico
- - - TRIQUE, SAN MARTÍN ITUNYOSO [TRQ] Mexico
- Otopamean (17)
- - Chichimec (1): CHICHIMECA-JONAZ [PEI] Mexico
- - Matlatzincan (2): MATLATZINCA, ATZINGO [OCU] Mexico
- - - MATLATZINCA, SAN FRANCISCO DE LOS RANCHOS [MAT] Mexico
- - Otomian (11)
- - - Mazahua (2): MAZAHUA CENTRAL [MAZ] Mexico
- - - - MAZAHUA, MICHOACÁN [QMN] Mexico
- - - Otomi (9): OTOMÍ, ESTADO DE MÉXICO [OTS] Mexico
- - - - OTOMÍ, IXTENCO [OTA] Mexico
- - - - OTOMÍ, MEZQUITAL [OTE] Mexico
- - - - OTOMÍ, NORTHWESTERN [OTQ] Mexico
- - - - OTOMÍ, SIERRA ORIENTAL [OTM] Mexico
- - - - OTOMÍ, TEMOAYA [OTT] Mexico
- - - - OTOMÍ, TENANGO [OTN] Mexico
- - - - OTOMÍ, TEXCATEPEC [OTX] Mexico
- - - - OTOMÍ, TILAPA [OTL] Mexico
- - Pamean (3): PAME CENTRAL [PBS] Mexico
- - - PAME NORTE [PMQ] Mexico
- - - PAME SUR [PMZ] Mexico
- Popolocan (17)
- - Chocho-Popolocan (8)
- - - Chocho (1): CHOCHOTECO [COZ] Mexico
- - - Popolocan (7): POPOLOCA, COYOTEPEC [PBF] Mexico
- - - - POPOLOCA, MEZONTLA [PBE] Mexico
- - - - POPOLOCA, SAN FELIPE OTLALTEPEC [POW] Mexico
- - - - POPOLOCA, SAN JUAN ATZINGO [POE] Mexico
- - - - POPOLOCA, SAN LUÍS TEMALACAYUCA [PPS] Mexico
- - - - POPOLOCA, SAN MARCOS TLALCOYALCO [PLS] Mexico
- - - - POPOLOCA, SANTA INÉS AHUATEMPAN [PCA] Mexico

Oto-Manguean (172)
- Popolocan (17)
- - Ixcatecan (1): IXCATECO [IXC] Mexico
- - Mazatecan (8): MAZATECO, AYAUTLA [VMY] Mexico
- - - MAZATECO, CHIQUIHUITLÁN [MAQ] Mexico
- - - MAZATECO, HUAUTLA [MAU] Mexico
- - - MAZATECO, IXCATLÁN [MAO] Mexico
- - - MAZATECO, JALAPA DE DÍAZ [MAJ] Mexico
- - - MAZATECO, MAZATLÁN [VMZ] Mexico
- - - MAZATECO, SAN JERÓNIMO TECÓATL [MAA] Mexico
- - - MAZATECO, SOYALTEPEC [VMP] Mexico
- Zapotecan (64)
- - Chatino (6): CHATINO, NOPALA [CYA] Mexico
- - - CHATINO, SIERRA OCCIDENTAL [CTP] Mexico
- - - CHATINO, SIERRA ORIENTAL [CLY] Mexico
- - - CHATINO, TATALTEPEC [CTA] Mexico
- - - CHATINO, ZACATEPEC [CTZ] Mexico
- - - CHATINO, ZENZONTEPEC [CZE] Mexico
- - Zapotec (58): ZAPOTECO, ALBARRADAS [ZAS] Mexico
- - - ZAPOTECO, ALOÁPAM [ZAQ] Mexico
- - - ZAPOTECO, AMATLÁN [ZPO] Mexico
- - - ZAPOTECO, ASUNCIÓN MIXTEPEC [ZOO] Mexico
- - - ZAPOTECO, AYOQUESCO [ZAF] Mexico
- - - ZAPOTECO, CAJONOS [ZAD] Mexico
- - - ZAPOTECO, CHICHICAPAN [ZPV] Mexico
- - - ZAPOTECO, CHOAPAN [ZPC] Mexico
- - - ZAPOTECO, COATECAS ALTAS [ZAP] Mexico
- - - ZAPOTECO, COATLÁN [ZPS] Mexico
- - - ZAPOTECO, EL ALTO [ZPP] Mexico
- - - ZAPOTECO, ELOTEPEC [ZTE] Mexico
- - - ZAPOTECO, GUEVEA DE HUMBOLDT [ZPG] Mexico
- - - ZAPOTECO, GÜILÁ [ZTU] Mexico
- - - ZAPOTECO, ISTMO [ZAI] Mexico
- - - ZAPOTECO, IXTLÁN SURESTE [ZPD] Mexico
- - - ZAPOTECO, JUÁREZ, SIERRA [ZAA] Mexico
- - - ZAPOTECO, LACHIGUIRI [ZPA] Mexico
- - - ZAPOTECO, LACHIRIOAG [ZTC] Mexico
- - - ZAPOTECO, LOXICHA [ZTP] Mexico
- - - ZAPOTECO, MAZALTEPEC [ZPY] Mexico
- - - ZAPOTECO, MIAHUATLÁN CENTRAL [ZAM] Mexico
- - - ZAPOTECO, MITLA [ZAW] Mexico
- - - ZAPOTECO, MIXTEPEC [ZPM] Mexico
- - - ZAPOTECO, OCOTLÁN OESTE [ZAC] Mexico
- - - ZAPOTECO, OZOLOTEPEC [ZAO] Mexico
- - - ZAPOTECO, PETAPA [ZPE] Mexico
- - - ZAPOTECO, QUIAVICUZAS [ZPJ] Mexico
- - - ZAPOTECO, QUIOQUITANI Y QUIERÍ [ZTQ] Mexico
- - - ZAPOTECO, RINCÓN [ZAR] Mexico
- - - ZAPOTECO, RINCÓN SUR [ZSR] Mexico
- - - ZAPOTECO, SAN AGUSTÍN MIXTEPEC [ZTM] Mexico
- - - ZAPOTECO, SAN BALTÁZAR LOXICHA [ZPX] Mexico
- - - ZAPOTECO, SAN JUAN GUELAVÍA [ZAB] Mexico
- - - ZAPOTECO, SAN PEDRO QUIATONI [ZPF] Mexico
- - - ZAPOTECO, SAN VICENTE COATLÁN [ZPT] Mexico
- - - ZAPOTECO, SANTA CATARINA ALBARRADAS [ZTN] Mexico
- - - ZAPOTECO, SANTA INÉS YATZECHI [ZPN] Mexico
- - - ZAPOTECO, SANTA MARÍA QUIEGOLANI [ZPI] Mexico
- - - ZAPOTECO, SANTIAGO LAPAGUÍA [ZTL] Mexico
- - - ZAPOTECO, SANTIAGO XANICA [ZPR] Mexico
- - - ZAPOTECO, SOLA DE VEGA ESTE [ZPL] Mexico
- - - ZAPOTECO, TABAA [ZAT] Mexico

Oto-Manguean (172)
- Zapotecan (64)
- - Zapotec (58): ZAPOTECO, TEJALAPAN [ZTT] Mexico
- - - ZAPOTECO, TEXMELUCAN [ZPZ] Mexico
- - - ZAPOTECO, TILQUIAPAN [ZTS] Mexico
- - - ZAPOTECO, TLACOLULITA [ZPK] Mexico
- - - ZAPOTECO, TOTOMACHAPAN [ZPH] Mexico
- - - ZAPOTECO, XADANI [ZAX] Mexico
- - - ZAPOTECO, XANAGUÍA [ZTG] Mexico
- - - ZAPOTECO, YALÁLAG [ZPU] Mexico
- - - ZAPOTECO, YARENI [ZAE] Mexico
- - - ZAPOTECO, YATEE [ZTY] Mexico
- - - ZAPOTECO, YATZACHI [ZAV] Mexico
- - - ZAPOTECO, YAUTEPEC [ZPB] Mexico
- - - ZAPOTECO, ZAACHILA [ZTX] Mexico
- - - ZAPOTECO, ZANIZA [ZPW] Mexico
- - - ZAPOTECO, ZOOGOCHO [ZPQ] Mexico

Paezan (1): PÁEZ [PBB] Colombia

Panoan (30)
- Eastern (1): KAXARARÍ [KTX] Brazil
- North-Central (7): ATSAHUACA [ATC] Peru
- - CAPANAHUA [KAQ] Peru
- - ISCONAHUA [ISC] Peru
- - MARÚBO [MZR] Brazil
- - REMO [REM] Peru
- - SENSI [SNI] Peru
- - SHIPIBO-CONIBO [SHP] Peru
- Northern (3): MATÍS [MPQ] Brazil
- - MATSÉS [MCF] Peru
- - PISABO [PIG] Peru
- South-Central (9)
- - Amahuaca (1): AMAHUACA [AMC] Peru
- - Unclassified (1): NUKUINI [NUC] Brazil
- - Yaminahua-Sharanahua (6): POYANÁWA [PYN] Brazil
- - - SHARANAHUA [MCD] Peru
- - - TUXINÁWA [TUX] Brazil
- - - XIPINÁWA [XIP] Brazil
- - - YAMINAHUA [YAA] Peru
- - - YAWANAWA [YWN] Brazil
- - Yora (1): YORA [MTS] Peru
- Southeastern (2): CASHINAHUA [CBS] Peru
- - KATUKÍNA, PANOAN [KNT] Brazil
- Southern (4): CHÁCOBO [CAO] Bolivia
- - KARIPUNÁ [KUQ] Brazil
- - PACAHUARA [PCP] Bolivia
- - SHINABO [SHN] Bolivia
- Unclassified (2): ARÁRA, ACRE [AXA] Brazil
- - PANOBO [PNO] Peru
- Western (2): CASHIBO-CACATAIBO [CBR] Peru
- - NOCAMAN [NOM] Peru

Peba-Yaguan (2): YAGUA [YAD] Peru
- YAMEO [YME] Peru

Penutian (33)
- California Penutian (1)
- - Wintuan (1): WINTU [WIT] USA
- Chinookan (2): CHINOOK [CHH] USA
- - WASCO-WISHRAM [WAC] USA

Penutian (33)
- Maiduan (4): MAIDU, NORTHEAST [NMU] USA
- - MAIDU, NORTHWEST [MAI] USA
- - MAIDU, VALLEY [VMV] USA
- - NISENAN [NSZ] USA
- Oregon Penutian (5)
- - Coast Oregon (3)
- - - Coosan (1): COOS [COS] USA
- - - Siuslawan (1): SIUSLAW [SIS] USA
- - - Yakonan (1): ALSEA [AES] USA
- - Kalapuyan (1): KALAPUYA [KAL] USA
- - Takelma (1): TAKELMA [TKM] USA
- Plateau Penutian (6)
- - Klamath-Modoc (1): KLAMATH-MODOC [KLA] USA
- - Sahaptin (5): NEZ PERCE [NEZ] USA
- - - TENINO [WAR] USA
- - - UMATILLA [UMA] USA
- - - WALLA WALLA [WAA] USA
- - - YAKIMA [YAK] USA
- Tsimshian (3): GITXSAN [GIT] Canada
- - NISGA'A [NCG] Canada
- - TSIMSHIAN [TSI] Canada
- Unclassified (1): MOLALE [MBE] USA
- Yok-Utian (11)
- - Utian (10)
- - - Costanoan (3): COSTANOAN, NORTHERN [CST] USA
- - - - COSTANOAN, SOUTHERN [CSS] USA
- - - - KARKIN [KRB] USA
- - - Miwokan (7)
- - - - Eastern (5): MIWOK, BAY [MKQ] USA
- - - - - MIWOK, PLAINS [PMW] USA
- - - - - Sierra (3): MIWOK, CENTRAL SIERRA [CSM] USA
- - - - - - MIWOK, NORTHERN SIERRA [NSQ] USA
- - - - - - MIWOK, SOUTHERN SIERRA [SKD] USA
- - - - Western (2): MIWOK, COAST [CSI] USA
- - - - - MIWOK, LAKE [LMW] USA
- - Yokuts (1): YOKUTS [YOK] USA

Pidgin (17): NDYUKA-TRIO PIDGIN [NJT] Suriname
- Amerindian (3): CHINOOK WAWA [CRW] Canada
- - DELAWARE, PIDGIN [DEP] USA
- - MOBILIAN [MOD] USA
- English based (2)
- - Atlantic (1): LIBERIAN ENGLISH [LIR] Liberia
- - Pacific (1): CHINESE PIDGIN ENGLISH [CPE] Nauru
- French based (1): TAY BOI [TAS] Viet Nam
- Hausa based (2): BARIKANCHI [BXO] Nigeria
- - GIBANAWA [GIB] Nigeria
- Iha based (1): IHA BASED PIDGIN [IHB] Indonesia (Irian Jaya)
- Malay based (1): BROOME PEARLING LUGGER PIDGIN [BPL] Australia
- Mascoian based (1): MASKOY PIDGIN [MHH] Paraguay
- Motu based (1): MOTU, HIRI [POM] Papua New Guinea
- Onin based (1): ONIN BASED PIDGIN [ONX] Indonesia (Irian Jaya)
- Romance-based (1): LINGUA FRANCA [PML] Tunisia
- Swahili based (1): SETTLA [STA] Zambia
- Zulu based (1): FANAGOLO [FAO] South Africa

Quechuan (46)
- Quechua I (17): QUECHUA, ANCASH, CHIQUIAN [QEC] Peru
- - QUECHUA, ANCASH, CONCHUCOS, NORTHERN [QED] Peru
- - QUECHUA, ANCASH, CONCHUCOS, SOUTHERN [QEH] Peru

Quechuan (46)
- - Quechua I (17): QUECHUA, ANCASH, CORONGO [QEE] Peru
- - QUECHUA, ANCASH, HUAYLAS [QAN] Peru
- - QUECHUA, ANCASH, SIHUAS [QES] Peru
- - QUECHUA, HUÁNUCO, HUALLAGA [QUB] Peru
- - QUECHUA, HUÁNUCO, HUAMALÍES-NORTHERN DOS DE MAYO [QEJ] Peru
- - QUECHUA, HUÁNUCO, PANAO [QEM] Peru
- - QUECHUA, MARGOS-YAROWILCA-LAURICOCHA [QEI] Peru
- - QUECHUA, NORTH JUNÍN [QJU] Peru
- - QUECHUA, NORTH LIMA, CAJATAMBO [QNL] Peru
- - QUECHUA, PASCO, SANTA ANA DE TUSI [QEF] Peru
- - QUECHUA, PASCO-YANAHUANCA [QUR] Peru
- - QUECHUA, SAN RAFAEL-HUARIACA [QEG] Peru
- - QUECHUA, WANCA, HUAYLLA [QHU] Peru
- - QUECHUA, WANCA, JAUJA [QHJ] Peru
- Quechua II (29)
- - A (4): QUECHUA, CAJAMARCA [QNT] Peru
- - - QUECHUA, LAMBAYEQUE [QUF] Peru
- - - QUECHUA, PACAROAS [QCP] Peru
- - - QUECHUA, YAUYOS [QUX] Peru
- - B (14): INGA [INB] Colombia
- - - INGA, JUNGLE [INJ] Colombia
- - - QUECHUA, CHACHAPOYAS [QUK] Peru
- - - QUECHUA, PASTAZA, SOUTHERN [QUP] Peru
- - - QUECHUA, SAN MARTÍN [QSA] Peru
- - - QUICHUA, HIGHLAND, CALDERÓN [QUD] Ecuador
- - - QUICHUA, HIGHLAND, CAÑAR [QQC] Ecuador
- - - QUICHUA, HIGHLAND, CHIMBORAZO [QUG] Ecuador
- - - QUICHUA, HIGHLAND, IMBABURA [QHO] Ecuador
- - - QUICHUA, HIGHLAND, LOJA [QQU] Ecuador
- - - QUICHUA, HIGHLAND, TUNGURAHUA [QQS] Ecuador
- - - QUICHUA, LOWLAND, NAPO [QLN] Ecuador
- - - QUICHUA, LOWLAND, TENA [QUW] Ecuador
- - - QUICHUA, PASTAZA, NORTHERN [QLB] Ecuador
- - C (11): QUECHUA, APURIMAC [QEA] Peru
- - - QUECHUA, AREQUIPA-LA UNION [QAR] Peru
- - - QUECHUA, AYACUCHO [QUY] Peru
- - - QUECHUA, CHILEAN [QUE] Chile
- - - QUECHUA, CLASSICAL [QCL] Peru
- - - QUECHUA, CUZCO [QUZ] Peru
- - - QUECHUA, NORTH BOLIVIAN [QUL] Bolivia
- - - QUECHUA, NORTHWEST JUJUY [QUO] Argentina
- - - QUECHUA, PUNO [QEP] Peru
- - - QUECHUA, SOUTH BOLIVIAN [QUH] Bolivia
- - - QUICHUA, SANTIAGO DEL ESTERO [QUS] Argentina

Salishan (27)
- Bella Coola (1): BELLA COOLA [BEL] Canada
- Central Salish (13)
- - Halkomelem (1): HALKOMELEM [HUR] Canada
- - Nooksack (1): NOOKSACK [NOK] USA
- - Northern (3): COMOX [COO] Canada
- - - PENTLATCH [PTW] Canada
- - - SECHELT [SEC] Canada
- - Squamish (1): SQUAMISH [SQU] Canada
- - Straits (2): CLALLAM [CLM] USA
- - - SALISH, STRAITS [STR] Canada
- - Twana (5): LUSHOOTSEED [LUT] USA
- - - SALISH, SOUTHERN PUGET SOUND [SLH] USA
- - - SKAGIT [SKA] USA
- - - SNOHOMISH [SNO] USA

Salishan (27)
- Interior Salish (8)
- - Twana (5): TWANA [TWA] USA
- - Northern (3): LILLOOET [LIL] Canada
- - - SHUSWAP [SHS] Canada
- - - THOMPSON [THP] Canada
- - Southern (5): COEUR D'ALENE [CRD] USA
- - - COLUMBIA-WENATCHI [COL] USA
- - - KALISPEL-PEND D'OREILLE [FLA] USA
- - - OKANAGAN [OKA] Canada
- - - SPOKANE [SPO] USA
- Tillamook (1): TILLAMOOK [TIL] USA
- Tsamosan (4)
- - Inland (3): CHEHALIS, LOWER [CEA] USA
- - - CHEHALIS, UPPER [CJH] USA
- - - COWLITZ [COW] USA
- - Maritime (1): QUINAULT [QUN] USA

Salivan (2): PIAROA [PID] Venezuela
- SÁLIBA [SLC] Colombia

Sepik-Ramu (104)
- Gapun (1): TAIAP [GPN] Papua New Guinea
- Leonhard Schultze (6)
- - Papi (2): PAPI [PPE] Papua New Guinea
- - - SUARMIN [SEO] Papua New Guinea
- - Walio (4): PEI [PPQ] Papua New Guinea
- - - TUWARI [TWW] Papua New Guinea
- - - WALIO [WLA] Papua New Guinea
- - - YAWIYO [YBX] Papua New Guinea
- Nor-Pondo (6)
- - Nor (2): KOPAR [QKO] Papua New Guinea
- - - MURIK [MTF] Papua New Guinea
- - Pondo (4): ANGORAM [AOG] Papua New Guinea
- - - CHAMBRI [CAN] Papua New Guinea
- - - TABRIAK [TZX] Papua New Guinea
- - - YIMAS [YEE] Papua New Guinea
- Ramu (37)
- - Ramu Proper (28)
- - - Annaberg (3)
- - - - Aian (2): AIOME [AKI] Papua New Guinea
- - - - - ANOR [ANJ] Papua New Guinea
- - - - Rao (1): RAO [RAO] Papua New Guinea
- - - Arafundi (1): ARAFUNDI [ARF] Papua New Guinea
- - - Goam (11)
- - - - Ataitan (4): ANDARUM [AOD] Papua New Guinea
- - - - - IGOM [IGM] Papua New Guinea
- - - - - TANGGU [TGU] Papua New Guinea
- - - - - TANGUAT [TBS] Papua New Guinea
- - - - Tamolan (7): AKRUKAY [AFI] Papua New Guinea
- - - - - BRERI [BRQ] Papua New Guinea
- - - - - IGANA [IGG] Papua New Guinea
- - - - - INAPANG [MZU] Papua New Guinea
- - - - - ITUTANG [ITU] Papua New Guinea
- - - - - KOMINIMUNG [QKM] Papua New Guinea
- - - - - ROMKUN [RMK] Papua New Guinea
- - - Grass (5)
- - - - Banaro (1): BANARO [BYZ] Papua New Guinea
- - - - Grass Proper (4): ABU [ADO] Papua New Guinea
- - - - - AION [AEW] Papua New Guinea
- - - - - AP MA [KBX] Papua New Guinea

Sepik-Ramu (104)
- Ramu (37)
- - Ramu Proper (28)
- - - Grass (5)
- - - - Grass Proper (4): GOROVU [GRQ] Papua New Guinea
- - - Ruboni (8)
- - - - Misegian (3): ARUAMU [MSY] Papua New Guinea
- - - - - KIRE [GEB] Papua New Guinea
- - - - - SEPEN [SPM] Papua New Guinea
- - - - Ottilien (5): AWAR [AYA] Papua New Guinea
- - - - - BOREI [GAI] Papua New Guinea
- - - - - BOSNGUN [BQS] Papua New Guinea
- - - - - KAIAN [KCT] Papua New Guinea
- - - - - WATAM [WAX] Papua New Guinea
- - Yuat-Waibuk (9)
- - - Mongol-Langam (3): LANGAM [LNM] Papua New Guinea
- - - - MONGOL [MGT] Papua New Guinea
- - - - YAUL [YLA] Papua New Guinea
- - - Yuat-Maramba (6)
- - - - Maramba (1): MARAMBA [MYD] Papua New Guinea
- - - - Yuat (5): BIWAT [BWM] Papua New Guinea
- - - - - BUN [BUV] Papua New Guinea
- - - - - CHANGRIWA [CGA] Papua New Guinea
- - - - - KYENELE [KQL] Papua New Guinea
- - - - - MEKMEK [MVK] Papua New Guinea
- Sepik (54)
- - Biksi (3): BIKSI [BDX] Indonesia (Irian Jaya)
- - - KIMKI [SBT] Indonesia (Irian Jaya)
- - - YETFA [YET] Indonesia (Irian Jaya)
- - Middle Sepik (20)
- - - Ndu (12): AMBULAS [ABT] Papua New Guinea
- - - - BOIKIN [BZF] Papua New Guinea
- - - - BURUI [BRY] Papua New Guinea
- - - - GAIKUNDI [GBF] Papua New Guinea
- - - - HANGA HUNDI [WOS] Papua New Guinea
- - - - IATMUL [IAN] Papua New Guinea
- - - - KOIWAT [KXT] Papua New Guinea
- - - - MALINGUAT [SIC] Papua New Guinea
- - - - MANAMBU [MLE] Papua New Guinea
- - - - NGALA [NUD] Papua New Guinea
- - - - SENGO [SPK] Papua New Guinea
- - - - YELOGU [YLG] Papua New Guinea
- - - Nukuma (7): APOS [APO] Papua New Guinea
- - - - BONGOS [BXY] Papua New Guinea
- - - - KWOMA [KMO] Papua New Guinea
- - - - MENDE [SIM] Papua New Guinea
- - - - WAMSAK [WBD] Papua New Guinea
- - - - WASAMBU [WSM] Papua New Guinea
- - - - YUBANAKOR [YUO] Papua New Guinea
- - - Yerakai (1): YERAKAI [YRA] Papua New Guinea
- - Ram (3): AWTUW [KMN] Papua New Guinea
- - - KARAWA [QKR] Papua New Guinea
- - - POUYE [BYE] Papua New Guinea
- - Sepik Hill (14)
- - - Alamblak (2): ALAMBLAK [AMP] Papua New Guinea
- - - - KANINGRA [KNR] Papua New Guinea
- - - Bahinemo (7): BAHINEMO [BJH] Papua New Guinea
- - - - BISIS [BNW] Papua New Guinea
- - - - BITARA [BIT] Papua New Guinea
- - - - KAPRIMAN [DJU] Papua New Guinea
- - - - MARI [MBX] Papua New Guinea

Sepik-Ramu (104)
- Sepik (54)
- - Sepik Hill (14)
- - - Bahinemo (7): SUMARIUP [SIV] Papua New Guinea
- - - - WATAKATAUI [WTK] Papua New Guinea
- - - Sanio (5): BIKARU [BIC] Papua New Guinea
- - - - HEWA [HAM] Papua New Guinea
- - - - NIKSEK [GBE] Papua New Guinea
- - - - PIAME [PIN] Papua New Guinea
- - - - SANIYO-HIYEWE [SNY] Papua New Guinea
- - Tama (5): KALOU [YWA] Papua New Guinea
- - - MEHEK [NUX] Papua New Guinea
- - - PAHI [LGT] Papua New Guinea
- - - PASI [PSI] Papua New Guinea
- - - YESSAN-MAYO [YSS] Papua New Guinea
- - Upper Sepik (6)
- - - Abau (1): ABAU [AAU] Papua New Guinea
- - - Iwam (3): AMAL [AAD] Papua New Guinea
- - - - IWAM [IWM] Papua New Guinea
- - - - IWAM, SEPIK [IWS] Papua New Guinea
- - - Wogamusin (2): CHENAPIAN [CJN] Papua New Guinea
- - - - WOGAMUSIN [WOG] Papua New Guinea
- - Yellow River (3): AK [AKQ] Papua New Guinea
- - - AWUN [AWW] Papua New Guinea
- - - NAMIA [NNM] Papua New Guinea

Sign language (2): MONASTIC SIGN LANGUAGE [MZG] Vatican State
- PLAINS INDIAN SIGN LANGUAGE [PSD] USA

Sino-Tibetan (365)
- Chinese (14): CHINESE, GAN [KNN] China
- - CHINESE, HAKKA [HAK] China
- - CHINESE, HUIZHOU [CZH] China
- - CHINESE, JINYU [CJY] China
- - CHINESE, MANDARIN [CHN] China
- - CHINESE, MIN BEI [MNP] China
- - CHINESE, MIN DONG [CDO] China
- - CHINESE, MIN NAN [CFR] China
- - CHINESE, MIN ZHONG [CZO] China
- - CHINESE, PU-XIAN [CPX] China
- - CHINESE, WU [WUU] China
- - CHINESE, XIANG [HSN] China
- - CHINESE, YUE [YUH] China
- - DUNGAN [DNG] Kyrgyzstan
- Tibeto-Burman (351)
- - Bai (1): BAI [PIQ] China
- - Himalayish (144)
- - - Mahakiranti (51)
- - - - Kiranti (2)
- - - - - Eastern (2): ATHPARIYA [APH] Nepal
- - - - - - BELHARIYA [BYW] Nepal
- - - - Kham-Magar-Chepang-Sunwari (14)
- - - - - Chepang (4): BHUJHYAL [GOR] Nepal
- - - - - - CHEPANG [CDM] Nepal
- - - - - - KUSUNDA [KGG] Nepal
- - - - - - WAYU [VAY] Nepal
- - - - - Kham (5): KHAM, GAMALE [KGJ] Nepal
- - - - - - KHAM, MAIKOTI [ZKM] Nepal
- - - - - - KHAM, NISI [KIF] Nepal
- - - - - - KHAM, SHESHI [KIP] Nepal
- - - - - - KHAM, TAKALE [KJL] Nepal

Sino-Tibetan (365)
- Tibeto-Burman (351)
- - Himalayish (144)
- - - Mahakiranti (51)
- - - - Kham-Magar-Chepang-Sunwari (14)
- - - - - Magar (3): MAGAR, EASTERN [MGP] Nepal
- - - - - - MAGAR, WESTERN [MRD] Nepal
- - - - - - RAJI [RJI] Nepal
- - - - - Sunwari (2): BAHING [RAR] Nepal
- - - - - - SUNWAR [SUZ] Nepal
- - - - Kiranti (34)
- - - - - Eastern (25): BANTAWA [BAP] Nepal
- - - - - - CAMLING [RAB] Nepal
- - - - - - CHHINTANG [CTN] Nepal
- - - - - - CHHULUNG [CUR] Nepal
- - - - - - CHUKWA [CUW] Nepal
- - - - - - DUNGMALI [RAA] Nepal
- - - - - - KULUNG [KLE] Nepal
- - - - - - LAMBICHHONG [LMH] Nepal
- - - - - - LIMBU [LIF] Nepal
- - - - - - LORUNG, NORTHERN [LBR] Nepal
- - - - - - LORUNG, SOUTHERN [LRR] Nepal
- - - - - - LUMBA-YAKKHA [LUU] Nepal
- - - - - - MEOHANG, EASTERN [EMG] Nepal
- - - - - - MEOHANG, WESTERN [RAF] Nepal
- - - - - - MOINBA [MOB] India
- - - - - - NACHERING [NCD] Nepal
- - - - - - PHANGDUWALI [PHW] Nepal
- - - - - - PONGYONG [PGY] Nepal
- - - - - - PUMA [PUM] Nepal
- - - - - - SAAM [RAQ] Nepal
- - - - - - SANGPANG [RAV] Nepal
- - - - - - WALING [WLY] Nepal
- - - - - - YAKHA [YBH] Nepal
- - - - - - YAMPHE [YMA] Nepal
- - - - - - YAMPHU [YBI] Nepal
- - - - - Western (9): CHOURASE [TSU] Nepal
- - - - - - DUMI [DUS] Nepal
- - - - - - JERUNG [JEE] Nepal
- - - - - - KHALING [KLR] Nepal
- - - - - - KOI [KKT] Nepal
- - - - - - LINGKHIM [LII] Nepal
- - - - - - RAUTE [RAU] Nepal
- - - - - - THULUNG [TDH] Nepal
- - - - - - TILUNG [TIJ] Nepal
- - - - Newari (1): NEWARI [NEW] Nepal
- - - Tibeto-Kanauri (92)
- - - - Kanauri (1): KAIKE [KZQ] Nepal
- - - - Lepcha (1): LEPCHA [LEP] India
- - - - Tibetic (71)
- - - - - Bodish (1)
- - - - - - Tshangla (1): TSHANGLA [TSJ] Bhutan
- - - - - Dhimal (2): DHIMAL [DHI] Nepal
- - - - - - TOTO [TXO] India
- - - - - Tamangic (15): CHANTYAL [CHX] Nepal
- - - - - - GHALE, KUTANG [GHT] Nepal
- - - - - - GHALE, NORTHERN [GHH] Nepal
- - - - - - GHALE, SOUTHERN [GHE] Nepal
- - - - - - GURUNG, EASTERN [GGN] Nepal
- - - - - - GURUNG, WESTERN [GVR] Nepal
- - - - - - MANANGBA [NMM] Nepal

Sino-Tibetan (365)
- Tibeto-Burman (351)
- - Himalayish (144)
- - - Tibeto-Kanauri (92)
- - - - Tibetic (71)
- - - - - Tamangic (15): NAR PHU [NPA] Nepal
- - - - - - PANCHGAUNLE [PNL] Nepal
- - - - - - TAMANG, EASTERN [TAJ] Nepal
- - - - - - TAMANG, EASTERN GORKHA [TGE] Nepal
- - - - - - TAMANG, NORTHWESTERN [TMK] Nepal
- - - - - - TAMANG, SOUTHWESTERN [TSF] Nepal
- - - - - - TAMANG, WESTERN [TDG] Nepal
- - - - - - THAKALI [THS] Nepal
- - - - - Tibetan (52): GONGDUK [GOE] Bhutan
- - - - - - LHOKPU [LHP] Bhutan
- - - - - - Central (18): ATUENCE [ATF] China
- - - - - - - BARAGAUNLE [BON] Nepal
- - - - - - - DOLPO [DRE] Nepal
- - - - - - - HELAMBU SHERPA [SCP] Nepal
- - - - - - - HUMLA BHOTIA [HUT] Nepal
- - - - - - - KAGATE [SYW] Nepal
- - - - - - - KYERUNG [KGY] Nepal
- - - - - - - LHOMI [LHM] Nepal
- - - - - - - LOPA [LOY] Nepal
- - - - - - - MUGU [MUK] Nepal
- - - - - - - NUBRI [KTE] Nepal
- - - - - - - PANANG [PCR] China
- - - - - - - STOD BHOTI [SBU] India
- - - - - - - TIBETAN [TIC] China
- - - - - - - TICHURONG [TCN] Nepal
- - - - - - - TSEKU [TSK] China
- - - - - - - TSUM [TTZ] Nepal
- - - - - - - WALUNGGE [OLA] Nepal
- - - - - - Eastern (8): BUMTHANGKHA [KJZ] Bhutan
- - - - - - - CHALIKHA [TGF] Bhutan
- - - - - - - DAKPAKHA [DKA] Bhutan
- - - - - - - KHENGKHA [XKF] Bhutan
- - - - - - - KURTOKHA [XKZ] Bhutan
- - - - - - - NUPBIKHA [NUB] Bhutan
- - - - - - - NYENKHA [NEH] Bhutan
- - - - - - - OLEKHA [OLE] Bhutan
- - - - - - Northern (3): AMDO [ADX] China
- - - - - - - CHONI [CDA] China
- - - - - - - KHAMS [KHG] China
- - - - - - Southern (12): ADAP [ADP] Bhutan
- - - - - - - BROKKAT [BRO] Bhutan
- - - - - - - BROKPAKE [SGT] Bhutan
- - - - - - - CHOCANGACAKHA [CHK] Bhutan
- - - - - - - DZONGKHA [DZO] Bhutan
- - - - - - - GROMA [GRO] China
- - - - - - - JIREL [JUL] Nepal
- - - - - - - LAKHA [LKH] Bhutan
- - - - - - - LAYAKHA [LYA] Bhutan
- - - - - - - LUNANAKHA [LUK] Bhutan
- - - - - - - SHERPA [SCR] Nepal
- - - - - - - SIKKIMESE [SIP] India
- - - - - - Unclassified (3): NAAPA [NAO] Nepal
- - - - - - - SHERDUKPEN [SDP] India
- - - - - - - THUDAM BHOTE [THW] Nepal
- - - - - - Western (6): BALTI [BFT] Pakistan
- - - - - - - PURIK [BXR] India

Sino-Tibetan (365)
- Tibeto-Burman (351)
- - Himalayish (144)
- - - Tibeto-Kanauri (92)
- - - - Tibetic (71)
- - - - - Tibetan (52)
- - - - - - Western (6): ZANGSKARI [ZAU] India
- - - - - - - Ladakhi (3): CHANGTHANG [CNA] India
- - - - - - - - LADAKHI [LBJ] India
- - - - - - - - TAKPA [TKK] China
- - - - - Unclassified (1): MEMBA [MMC] India
- - - - Unclassified (1): DZALAKHA [DZL] Bhutan
- - - - Western Himalayish (18)
- - - - - Almora (4): BYANGSI [BEE] India
- - - - - - CHAUDANGSI [CDN] India
- - - - - - DARMIYA [DRD] India
- - - - - - RANGKAS [RGK] Nepal
- - - - - Eastern (2): BARAAMU [BRD] Nepal
- - - - - - THAMI [THF] Nepal
- - - - - Janggali (1): RAWAT [JNL] Nepal
- - - - - Kanauri (11): GAHRI [BFU] India
- - - - - - JANGSHUNG [JNA] India
- - - - - - KANASHI [QAS] India
- - - - - - KINNAURI [KFK] India
- - - - - - KINNAURI, BHOTI [NES] India
- - - - - - KINNAURI, CHITKULI [CIK] India
- - - - - - PATTANI [LAE] India
- - - - - - SHUMCHO [SCU] India
- - - - - - SUNAM [SSK] India
- - - - - - TINANI [LBF] India
- - - - - - TUKPA [TPQ] India
- - - Unclassified (1): BAIMA [BQH] China
- - Jingpho-Konyak-Bodo (24)
- - - Jingpho-Luish (4)
- - - - Jingpho (3): JINGPHO [CGP] Myanmar
- - - - - SINGPHO [SGP] India
- - - - - TAMAN [TCL] Myanmar
- - - - Luish (1): KADO [KDV] Myanmar
- - - Konyak-Bodo-Garo (20)
- - - - Bodo-Garo (13)
- - - - - Bodo (7): BODO [BRX] India
- - - - - - DEORI [DER] India
- - - - - - DIMASA [DIS] India
- - - - - - KACHARI [QKC] India
- - - - - - KOK BOROK [TRP] India
- - - - - - LALUNG [LAX] India
- - - - - - RIANG [RIA] India
- - - - - Garo (2): GARO [GRT] India
- - - - - - MEGAM [MEF] Bangladesh
- - - - - Koch (4): A'TONG [AOT] India
- - - - - - KOCH [KDQ] India
- - - - - - RABHA [RAH] India
- - - - - - RUGA [RUH] India
- - - - Konyak (7): NAGA, CHANG [NBC] India
- - - - - NAGA, KHIAMNIUNGAN [NKY] India
- - - - - NAGA, KONYAK [NBE] India
- - - - - NAGA, NOCTE [NJB] India
- - - - - NAGA, PHOM [NPH] India
- - - - - NAGA, TASE [NST] India
- - - - - NAGA, WANCHO [NNP] India

Sino-Tibetan (365)
- Tibeto-Burman (351)
- - Karen (20)
- - - Pa'o (1): KAREN, PA'O [BLK] Myanmar
- - - Pwo (4): KAREN, PWO EASTERN [KJP] Myanmar
- - - - KAREN, PWO NORTHERN [PWW] Thailand
- - - - KAREN, PWO WESTERN [PWO] Myanmar
- - - - KAREN, PWO, PHRAE [KJT] Thailand
- - - Sgaw-Bghai (14)
- - - - Bghai (5)
- - - - - Eastern (2): KAREN, LAHTA [KVT] Myanmar
- - - - - - KAREN, PADAUNG [PDU] Myanmar
- - - - - Unclassified (2): KAREN, BWE [BWE] Myanmar
- - - - - - KAREN, GEKO [GHK] Myanmar
- - - - - Western (1): KAREN, GEBA [KVQ] Myanmar
- - - - Brek (1): KAREN, BREK [KVL] Myanmar
- - - - Kayah (5): KAREN, MANUMANAW [KXF] Myanmar
- - - - - KAREN, YINBAW [KVU] Myanmar
- - - - - KAREN, YINTALE [KVY] Myanmar
- - - - - KAYAH, EASTERN [EKY] Myanmar
- - - - - KAYAH, WESTERN [KYU] Myanmar
- - - - Sgaw (3): KAREN, PAKU [KPP] Myanmar
- - - - - KAREN, S'GAW [KSW] Myanmar
- - - - - WEWAW [WEA] Myanmar
- - - Unclassified (1): KAREN, ZAYEIN [KXK] Myanmar
- - Kuki-Chin-Naga (70)
- - - Kuki-Chin (44): CHIN, MRO [CMR] Myanmar
- - - - Central (10): CHIN, BAWM [BGR] India
- - - - - CHIN, HAKA [CNH] Myanmar
- - - - - CHIN, NGAWN [CNW] Myanmar
- - - - - CHIN, SENTHANG [SEZ] Myanmar
- - - - - CHIN, TAWR [TCP] Myanmar
- - - - - CHIN, ZOTUNG [CZT] Myanmar
- - - - - DARLONG [DLN] Bangladesh
- - - - - HMAR [HMR] India
- - - - - LUSHAI [LSH] India
- - - - - PANKHU [PKH] India
- - - - Northern (23): AIMOL [AIM] India
- - - - - ANAL [ANM] India
- - - - - BIETE [BIU] India
- - - - - CHIN, FALAM [HBH] Myanmar
- - - - - CHIN, PAITE [PCK] India
- - - - - CHIN, SIYIN [CSY] Myanmar
- - - - - CHIN, TEDIM [CTD] Myanmar
- - - - - CHIN, THADO [TCZ] India
- - - - - CHIRU [CDF] India
- - - - - GANGTE [GNB] India
- - - - - HRANGKHOL [HRA] Myanmar
- - - - - KOM [KMM] India
- - - - - LAMKANG [LMK] India
- - - - - NAGA, CHOTHE [NCT] India
- - - - - NAGA, MONSANG [NMH] India
- - - - - NAGA, MOYON [NMO] India
- - - - - NAGA, TARAO [TRO] India
- - - - - PURUM [PUB] Myanmar
- - - - - RALTE [RAL] Myanmar
- - - - - SIMTE [SMT] India
- - - - - VAIPHEI [VAP] India
- - - - - YOS [YOS] Myanmar
- - - - - ZOME [ZOM] Myanmar
- - - - Southern (10): CHIN, DAAI [DAO] Myanmar

Sino-Tibetan (365)
- Tibeto-Burman (351)
- - Kuki-Chin-Naga (70)
- - - Kuki-Chin (44)
- - - - Southern (10): CHIN, MARA [MRH] India
- - - - - CHIN, MÜN [MWQ] Myanmar
- - - - - WELAUNG [WEL] Myanmar
- - - - - ZYPHE [ZYP] Myanmar
- - - - - Khumi (2): CHIN, KHUMI [CKM] Myanmar
- - - - - - CHIN, KHUMI AWA [CKA] Myanmar
- - - - - Sho (3): CHIN, ASHO [CSH] Myanmar
- - - - - - CHIN, CHINBON [CNB] Myanmar
- - - - - - SHENDU [SHL] Bangladesh
- - - Naga (26)
- - - - Angami-Pochuri (10): NAGA, ANGAMI [NJM] India
- - - - - NAGA, CHOKRI [NRI] India
- - - - - NAGA, KHEZHA [NKH] India
- - - - - NAGA, MAO [NBI] India
- - - - - NAGA, MELURI [NLM] India
- - - - - NAGA, NTENYI [NNL] India
- - - - - NAGA, POCHURI [NPO] India
- - - - - NAGA, POUMEI [PMX] India
- - - - - NAGA, RENGMA [NRE] India
- - - - - NAGA, SUMI [NSM] India
- - - - Ao (4): NAGA, AO [NJO] India
- - - - - NAGA, LOTHA [NJH] India
- - - - - NAGA, SANGTAM [NSA] India
- - - - - NAGA, YIMCHUNGRU [YIM] India
- - - - Tangkhul (3): NAGA, KHOIBU MARING [NKB] India
- - - - - NAGA, MARING [NNG] India
- - - - - NAGA, TANGKHUL [NMF] India
- - - - Unclassified (1): NAGA, PUIMEI [NPU] India
- - - - Zeme (8): KOIRENG [NKD] India
- - - - - NAGA, KABUI [NKF] India
- - - - - NAGA, KHOIRAO [NKI] India
- - - - - NAGA, LIANGMAI [NJN] India
- - - - - NAGA, MARAM [NMA] India
- - - - - NAGA, MZIEME [NME] India
- - - - - NAGA, RONGMEI [NBU] India
- - - - - NAGA, ZEME [NZM] India
- - Lolo-Burmese (49)
- - - Burmish (13)
- - - - Northern (5): ACHANG [ACN] China
- - - - - HPON [HPO] Myanmar
- - - - - LASHI [LSI] Myanmar
- - - - - MARU [MHX] Myanmar
- - - - - ZAIWA [ATB] China
- - - - Southern (7): ARAKANESE [MHV] Myanmar
- - - - - BURMESE [BMS] Myanmar
- - - - - CHAUNGTHA [CCQ] Myanmar
- - - - - INTHA [INT] Myanmar
- - - - - TAUNGYO [TCO] Myanmar
- - - - - TAVOYAN [TVN] Myanmar
- - - - - YANGBYE [YBD] Myanmar
- - - - Unclassified (1): XIANDAOHUA [XIA] China
- - - Loloish (34)
- - - - Northern (11): SAMEI [SMH] China
- - - - Lisu (2): LIPO [TKL] China
- - - - - LISU [LIS] China
- - - - - Yi (8): LAGHUU [LGH] Viet Nam
- - - - - MANTSI [MUS] Viet Nam

Sino-Tibetan (365)
- Tibeto-Burman (351)
- - Lolo-Burmese (49)
- - - Loloish (34)
- - - - Northern (11)
- - - - - Yi (8): YI, CENTRAL [YIC] China
- - - - - - YI, GUIZHOU [YIG] China
- - - - - - YI, SICHUAN [III] China
- - - - - - YI, SOUTHEASTERN [YIE] China
- - - - - - YI, WESTERN [YIW] China
- - - - - - YI, YUNNAN [NOS] China
- - - - Southern (18): JINUO, BUYUAN [JIY] China
- - - - JINUO, YOULE [JIU] China
- - - - - UGONG [UGO] Thailand
- - - - - Akha (11): MAHEI [MJA] Myanmar
- - - - - - PHANA' [PHN] Laos
- - - - - - Hani (7): SANSU [SCA] Myanmar
- - - - - - - SILA [SLT] Laos
- - - - - - - Bi-Ka (2): BIYO [BYO] China
- - - - - - - - KADUO [KTP] Laos
- - - - - - - Ha-Ya (2): AKHA [AKA] Myanmar
- - - - - - - - HANI [HNI] China
- - - - - - - Hao-Bai (1): HONI [HOW] China
- - - - - - - Lahu (2): LAHU [LAH] China
- - - - - - - LAHU SHI [KDS] Laos
- - - - - Phunoi (4): BISU [BII] China
- - - - - - MPI [MPZ] Thailand
- - - - - - PHUNOI [PHO] Laos
- - - - - - PYEN [PYY] Myanmar
- - - - Unclassified (5): BELA [BEQ] China
- - - - - LAOPANG [LBG] Myanmar
- - - - - LOPI [LOV] Myanmar
- - - - - NUSU [NUF] China
- - - - - ZAUZOU [ZAL] China
- - - Naxi (1): NAXI [NBF] China
- - - Unclassified (1): PHULA [PHH] Viet Nam
- - Meithei (1): MEITEI [MNR] India
- - Mikir (1): MIKIR [MJW] India
- - Mru (1): MRU [MRO] Bangladesh
- - North Assam (10)
- - - Deng (2): DARANG DENG [DAT] China
- - - - GEMAN DENG [GEN] China
- - - Tani (8): ADI [ADI] India
- - - - APATANI [APT] India
- - - - DIGARO [MHU] India
- - - - IDU [CLK] India
- - - - MIJU [MXJ] India
- - - - MIRI [MRG] India
- - - - NISI [DAP] India
- - - - SULUNG [SUV] India
- - Nungish (5): DRUNG [DUU] China
- - - LAMA [LAY] Myanmar
- - - NORRA [NOR] Myanmar
- - - NUNG [NUN] Myanmar
- - - RAWANG [RAW] Myanmar
- - Tangut-Qiang (15)
- - - Qiangic (11): ERSU [ERS] China
- - - - GUIQIONG [GQI] China
- - - - MUYA [MVM] China
- - - - NAMUYI [NMY] China
- - - - PUMI, NORTHERN [PMI] China

Sino-Tibetan (365)
- Tibeto-Burman (351)
- - Tangut-Qiang (15)
- - - Qiangic (11): PUMI, SOUTHERN [PUS] China
- - - - QIANG, NORTHERN [CNG] China
- - - - QIANG, SOUTHERN [QMR] China
- - - - QUEYU [QEY] China
- - - - SHIXING [SXG] China
- - - - ZHABA [ZHA] China
- - - rGyarong (4): GUANYINQIAO [JIQ] China
- - - - HORPA [ERO] China
- - - - JIARONG [JYA] China
- - - - SHANGZHAI [JIH] China
- - Tujia (2): TUJIA, NORTHERN [TJI] China
- - - TUJIA, SOUTHERN [TJS] China
- - Unclassified (8): ANU [ANL] Myanmar
- - - AYI [AYX] China
- - - HRUSO [HRU] India
- - - LUI [LBA] Myanmar
- - - PALU [PBZ] Myanmar
- - - PAO [PPA] India
- - - SAJALONG [SJL] India
- - - ZAKHRING [ZKR] India

Siouan (17)
- Catawba (1): CATAWBA [CHC] USA
- Siouan Proper (16)
- - Central (11)
- - - Mandan (1): MANDAN [MHQ] USA
- - - Mississippi Valley (10)
- - - - Chiwere (1): IOWA-OTO [IOW] USA
- - - - Dakota (4): ASSINIBOINE [ASB] Canada
- - - - - DAKOTA [DHG] USA
- - - - - LAKOTA [LKT] USA
- - - - - STONEY [STO] Canada
- - - - Dhegiha (4): KANSA [KAA] USA
- - - - - OMAHA-PONCA [OMA] USA
- - - - - OSAGE [OSA] USA
- - - - - QUAPAW [QUA] USA
- - - - Winnebago (1): HOCÁK [WIN] USA
- - Missouri Valley (2): CROW [CRO] USA
- - - HIDATSA [HID] USA
- - Southeastern (3)
- - - Biloxi-Ofo (2): BILOXI [BLL] USA
- - - - OFO [OFO] USA
- - - Tutelo (1): TUTELO [TTA] USA

Sko (7)
- Krisa (4): KRISA [KRO] Papua New Guinea
- - PUARI [PUX] Papua New Guinea
- - RAWO [RWA] Papua New Guinea
- - WARAPU [WRA] Papua New Guinea
- Vanimo (3): SKOU [SKV] Indonesia (Irian Jaya)
- - VANIMO [VAM] Papua New Guinea
- - WUTUNG [WUT] Papua New Guinea

South Caucasian (5)
- Georgian (2): GEORGIAN [GEO] Georgia
- - JUDEO-GEORGIAN [JGE] Israel
- Svan (1): SVAN [SVA] Georgia
- Zan (2): LAZ [LZZ] Turkey (Asia)

South Caucasian (5)
- Zan (2): MINGRELIAN [XMF] Georgia

Subtiaba-Tlapanec (4): SUBTIABA [SUT] Nicaragua
- TLAPANECO, ACATEPEC [TPX] Mexico
- TLAPANECO, AZOYÚ [TPC] Mexico
- TLAPANECO, MALINALTEPEC [TLL] Mexico

Tacanan (6)
- Araona-Tacana (5)
- - Araona (1): ARAONA [ARO] Bolivia
- - Cavinena-Tacana (4)
- - - Cavinena (1): CAVINEÑA [CAV] Bolivia
- - - Tacana Proper (3): REYESANO [REY] Bolivia
- - - - TACANA [TNA] Bolivia
- - - - TOROMONO [TNO] Bolivia
- Tiatinagua (1): ESE EJJA [ESE] Bolivia

Tai-Kadai (70)
- Hlai (2): HLAI [LIC] China
- - JIAMAO [JIO] China
- Kadai (9)
- - Bu-Rong (1): YERONG [YRN] China
- - Ge-Chi (3): GELAO [KKF] Viet Nam
- - - LACHI [LBT] Viet Nam
- - - LACHI, WHITE [LWH] Viet Nam
- - Yang-Biao (5): BUYANG [BYU] China
- - - CUN [CUQ] China
- - - EN [ENC] Viet Nam
- - - LAHA [LHA] Viet Nam
- - - LAQUA [LAQ] Viet Nam
- Kam-Tai (59)
- - Be-Tai (49)
- - - Be (1): LINGAO [ONB] China
- - - Tai-Sek (48)
- - - - Sek (1): SAEK [SKB] Laos
- - - - Tai (47)
- - - - - Central (6): E [EEE] China
- - - - - - MAN CAO LAN [MLC] Viet Nam
- - - - - - NUNG [NUT] Viet Nam
- - - - - - TÀY [THO] Viet Nam
- - - - - - TS'ÜN-LAO [TSL] Viet Nam
- - - - - - ZHUANG, SOUTHERN [CCY] China
- - - - - East Central (1)
- - - - - - Northwest (1): TURUNG [TRY] India
- - - - - Northern (4): BOUYEI [PCC] China
- - - - - - NHANG [NHA] Viet Nam
- - - - - - TAI MÈNE [TMP] Laos
- - - - - - ZHUANG, NORTHERN [CCX] China
- - - - - Southwestern (29): PU KO [PUK] Laos
- - - - - - TAI LONG [THI] Laos
- - - - - - East Central (21)
- - - - - - - Chiang Saeng (8): PHUAN [PHU] Thailand
- - - - - - - SONG [SOA] Thailand
- - - - - - - TAI DAENG [TYR] Viet Nam
- - - - - - - TAI DAM [BLT] Viet Nam
- - - - - - - TAI DÓN [TWH] Viet Nam
- - - - - - - TAY TAC [TYT] Viet Nam
- - - - - - - THAI [THJ] Thailand
- - - - - - - THAI, NORTHERN [NOD] Thailand
- - - - - - Lao-Phutai (4): LAO [NOL] Laos

Tai-Kadai (70)
- Kam-Tai (59)
- - Be-Tai (49)
- - - Tai-Sek (48)
- - - - Tai (47)
- - - - - Southwestern (29)
- - - - - - East Central (21)
- - - - - - - Lao-Phutai (4): NYAW [NYW] Thailand
- - - - - - - - PHU THAI [PHT] Thailand
- - - - - - - - THAI, NORTHEASTERN [TTS] Thailand
- - - - - - - Northwest (9): AHOM [AHO] India
- - - - - - - - AITON [AIO] India
- - - - - - - - KHAMTI [KHT] Myanmar
- - - - - - - - KHAMYANG [KSU] India
- - - - - - - - KHÜN [KKH] Myanmar
- - - - - - - - LÜ [KHB] China
- - - - - - - - PHAKE [PHK] India
- - - - - - - - SHAN [SJN] Myanmar
- - - - - - - - TAI NÜA [TDD] China
- - - - - - Southern (1): THAI, SOUTHERN [SOU] Thailand
- - - - - - Unclassified (5): TAI HANG TONG [THC] Viet Nam
- - - - - - - TAI HONGJIN [TIZ] China
- - - - - - - TAI MAN THANH [TMM] Viet Nam
- - - - - - - TAI YA [CUU] China
- - - - - - - YONG [YNO] Thailand
- - - - - Unclassified (7): KANG [KYP] Laos
- - - - - - KUAN [UAN] Laos
- - - - - - RIEN [RIE] Laos
- - - - - - TAI PAO [TPO] Laos
- - - - - - TAY JO [TYJ] Viet Nam
- - - - - - TAY KHANG [TNU] Laos
- - - - - - YOY [YOY] Thailand
- - Kam-Sui (9): AI-CHAM [AIH] China
- - - CAO MIAO [COV] China
- - - DONG, NORTHERN [DOC] China
- - - DONG, SOUTHERN [KMC] China
- - - MAK [MKG] China
- - - MAONAN [MMD] China
- - - MULAM [MLM] China
- - - SUI [SWI] China
- - - T'EN [TCT] China
- - Lakkja (1): LAKKIA [LBC] China

Tarascan (2): PURÉPECHA [TSZ] Mexico
- PURÉPECHA, SIERRA OCCIDENTAL [PUA] Mexico

Torricelli (48)
- Kombio-Arapesh (9)
- - Arapesh (3): ARAPESH, BUMBITA [AON] Papua New Guinea
- - - BUKIYIP [APE] Papua New Guinea
- - - MUFIAN [AOJ] Papua New Guinea
- - Kombio (6): ARUEK [AUR] Papua New Guinea
- - - EITIEP [EIT] Papua New Guinea
- - - KOMBIO [KOK] Papua New Guinea
- - - TORRICELLI [TEI] Papua New Guinea
- - - WOM [WMO] Papua New Guinea
- - - YAMBES [YMB] Papua New Guinea
- Maimai (6)
- - Beli (1): BELI [BEY] Papua New Guinea
- - Laeko-Libuat (1): LAEKO-LIBUAT [LKL] Papua New Guinea
- - Maimai Proper (3): SILIPUT [MKC] Papua New Guinea

Torricelli (48)
- Maimai (6)
- - Maimai Proper (3): WANIB [AUK] Papua New Guinea
- - - YAHANG [RHP] Papua New Guinea
- - Wiaki (1): WIAKI [WII] Papua New Guinea
- Marienberg (7): BUNA [BVN] Papua New Guinea
- - BUNGAIN [BUT] Papua New Guinea
- - ELEPI [ELE] Papua New Guinea
- - KAMASAU [KMS] Papua New Guinea
- - MANDI [TUA] Papua New Guinea
- - MUNIWARA [MWB] Papua New Guinea
- - URIMO [URX] Papua New Guinea
- Monumbo (2): LILAU [LLL] Papua New Guinea
- - MONUMBO [MXK] Papua New Guinea
- Urim (1): URIM [URI] Papua New Guinea
- Wapei-Palei (20)
- - Palei (7): AGI [AIF] Papua New Guinea
- - - AIKU [MZF] Papua New Guinea
- - - ALATIL [ALX] Papua New Guinea
- - - ARUOP [LSR] Papua New Guinea
- - - BRAGAT [AOF] Papua New Guinea
- - - NABI [MTY] Papua New Guinea
- - - WANAP [WNP] Papua New Guinea
- - Urat (1): URAT [URT] Papua New Guinea
- - Wapei (12): AU [AVT] Papua New Guinea
- - - DIA [DIA] Papua New Guinea
- - - ELKEI [ELK] Papua New Guinea
- - - GNAU [GNU] Papua New Guinea
- - - NINGIL [NIZ] Papua New Guinea
- - - OLO [ONG] Papua New Guinea
- - - SINAGEN [SIU] Papua New Guinea
- - - VALMAN [VAN] Papua New Guinea
- - - YAPUNDA [YEV] Papua New Guinea
- - - YAU [YYU] Papua New Guinea
- - - YIL [YLL] Papua New Guinea
- - - YIS [YIS] Papua New Guinea
- West Wapei (3): AUNALEI [AUN] Papua New Guinea
- - SETA [STF] Papua New Guinea
- - SETI [SBI] Papua New Guinea

Totonacan (11)
- Tepehua (3): TEPEHUA, HUEHUETLA [TEE] Mexico
- - TEPEHUA, PISA FLORES [TPP] Mexico
- - TEPEHUA, TLACHICHILCO [TPT] Mexico
- Totonac (8): TOTONACA, COYUTLA [TOC] Mexico
- - TOTONACA, FILOMENO MATA-COAHUITLÁN [TLP] Mexico
- - TOTONACA, OZUMATLÁN [TQT] Mexico
- - TOTONACA, PAPANTLA [TOP] Mexico
- - TOTONACA, PATLA-CHICONTLA [TOT] Mexico
- - TOTONACA, SIERRA [TOS] Mexico
- - TOTONACA, XICOTEPEC DE JUÁREZ [TOO] Mexico
- - TOTONACA, YECUATLA [TLC] Mexico

Trans-New Guinea (552)
- Eleman (7)
- - Eleman Proper (5)
- - - Eastern (2): TAIRUMA [UAR] Papua New Guinea
- - - - TOARIPI [TPI] Papua New Guinea
- - - Western (3): KEURU [QQK] Papua New Guinea
- - - - OPAO [OPO] Papua New Guinea
- - - - OROKOLO [ORO] Papua New Guinea

Trans-New Guinea (552)
- Eleman (7)
- - Purari (1): PURARI [IAR] Papua New Guinea
- - Tate (1): KAKI AE [TBD] Papua New Guinea
- Inland Gulf (4)
- - Ipiko (1): IPIKO [IPK] Papua New Guinea
- - Minanibai (3): KARAMI [XAR] Papua New Guinea
- - - MINANIBAI [MCV] Papua New Guinea
- - - TAO-SUAMATO [TSX] Papua New Guinea
- Kaure (4): KAPORI [KHP] Indonesia (Irian Jaya)
- - Kaure Proper (3): KAURE [BPP] Indonesia (Irian Jaya)
- - - KOSADLE [KIQ] Indonesia (Irian Jaya)
- - - NARAU [NXU] Indonesia (Irian Jaya)
- Kolopom (3): KIMAAMA [KIG] Indonesia (Irian Jaya)
- - NDOM [NQM] Indonesia (Irian Jaya)
- - RIANTANA [RAN] Indonesia (Irian Jaya)
- Madang-Adelbert Range (102)
- - Adelbert Range (44)
- - - Brahman (4): BIYOM [BPM] Papua New Guinea
- - - - FAITA [FAT] Papua New Guinea
- - - - ISABI [ISA] Papua New Guinea
- - - - TAUYA [TYA] Papua New Guinea
- - - Josephstaal-Wanang (12)
- - - - Josephstaal (7)
- - - - - Osum (1): UTARMBUNG [OMO] Papua New Guinea
- - - - - Pomoikan (3): ANAM [PDA] Papua New Guinea
- - - - - - ANAMGURA [IMI] Papua New Guinea
- - - - - - MORESADA [MSX] Papua New Guinea
- - - - - Sikan (2): MUM [KQA] Papua New Guinea
- - - - - - SILEIBI [SBQ] Papua New Guinea
- - - - - Wadaginam (1): WADAGINAM [WDG] Papua New Guinea
- - - - Wanang (5)
- - - - - Atan (2): ATEMBLE [ATE] Papua New Guinea
- - - - - - NEND [ANH] Papua New Guinea
- - - - - Emuan (2): APALI [ENA] Papua New Guinea
- - - - - - MUSAK [MMQ] Papua New Guinea
- - - - - Paynamar (1): PAYNAMAR [PMR] Papua New Guinea
- - - Pihom-Isumrud-Mugil (28)
- - - - Isumrud (5)
- - - - - Dimir (1): DIMIR [DMC] Papua New Guinea
- - - - - Kowan (2): KORAK [KOZ] Papua New Guinea
- - - - - - WASKIA [WSK] Papua New Guinea
- - - - - Mabuan (2): BREM [BUQ] Papua New Guinea
- - - - - - MALAS [MKR] Papua New Guinea
- - - - Mugil (1): BARGAM [MLP] Papua New Guinea
- - - - Pihom (22)
- - - - - Amaimon (1): AMAIMON [ALI] Papua New Guinea
- - - - - Kaukombaran (4): MAIA [SKS] Papua New Guinea
- - - - - - MAIANI [TNH] Papua New Guinea
- - - - - - MALA [PED] Papua New Guinea
- - - - - - MIANI [PLA] Papua New Guinea
- - - - - Kumilan (3): BEPOUR [BIE] Papua New Guinea
- - - - - - MAUWAKE [MHL] Papua New Guinea
- - - - - - MOERE [MVQ] Papua New Guinea
- - - - - Numugenan (6): BILAKURA [BQL] Papua New Guinea
- - - - - - PARAWEN [PRW] Papua New Guinea
- - - - - - UKURIGUMA [UKG] Papua New Guinea
- - - - - - USAN [WNU] Papua New Guinea
- - - - - - YABEN [YBM] Papua New Guinea
- - - - - - YARAWATA [YRW] Papua New Guinea
- - - - - Omosan (2): ABASAKUR [ABW] Papua New Guinea

Trans-New Guinea (552)
- Madang-Adelbert Range (102)
- - Adelbert Range (44)
- - - Pihom-Isumrud-Mugil (28)
- - - - Pihom (22)
- - - - - Omosan (2): KOGUMAN [QKG] Papua New Guinea
- - - - - Tiboran (5): HINIHON [HIH] Papua New Guinea
- - - - - - KOWAKI [QKK] Papua New Guinea
- - - - - - MAWAK [MJJ] Papua New Guinea
- - - - - - MUSAR [MMI] Papua New Guinea
- - - - - - WANAMBRE [WLN] Papua New Guinea
- - - - - Wasembo (1): WASEMBO [GSP] Papua New Guinea
- - Madang (58)
- - - Mabuso (29)
- - - - Gum (6): AMELE [AMI] Papua New Guinea
- - - - - BAU [BBD] Papua New Guinea
- - - - - GUMALU [GMU] Papua New Guinea
- - - - - ISEBE [IGO] Papua New Guinea
- - - - - PANIM [PNR] Papua New Guinea
- - - - - SIHAN [SNR] Papua New Guinea
- - - - Hanseman (19): BAGUPI [BPI] Papua New Guinea
- - - - - BAIMAK [BMX] Papua New Guinea
- - - - - GAL [GAP] Papua New Guinea
- - - - - GARUS [GYB] Papua New Guinea
- - - - - MATEPI [MQE] Papua New Guinea
- - - - - MAWAN [MCZ] Papua New Guinea
- - - - - MOSIMO [MQV] Papua New Guinea
- - - - - MURUPI [MQW] Papua New Guinea
- - - - - NAKE [NBK] Papua New Guinea
- - - - - NOBANOB [GAW] Papua New Guinea
- - - - - RAPTING [RAP] Papua New Guinea
- - - - - REMPI [RMP] Papua New Guinea
- - - - - SAMOSA [SMO] Papua New Guinea
- - - - - SARUGA [SRP] Papua New Guinea
- - - - - SILOPI [SOT] Papua New Guinea
- - - - - UTU [UTU] Papua New Guinea
- - - - - WAGI [FAD] Papua New Guinea
- - - - - WAMAS [WMC] Papua New Guinea
- - - - - YOIDIK [YDK] Papua New Guinea
- - - - Kare (1): KARE [KMF] Papua New Guinea
- - - - Kokon (3): BEMAL [BMH] Papua New Guinea
- - - - - GIRAWA [BBR] Papua New Guinea
- - - - - MUNIT [MTC] Papua New Guinea
- - - Rai Coast (29)
- - - - Evapia (5): ASAS [ASD] Papua New Guinea
- - - - - DUMPU [WTF] Papua New Guinea
- - - - - KESAWAI [QKE] Papua New Guinea
- - - - - SAUSI [SSJ] Papua New Guinea
- - - - - SINSAURU [SNZ] Papua New Guinea
- - - - Kabenau (5): ARAWUM [AWM] Papua New Guinea
- - - - - KOLOM [KLM] Papua New Guinea
- - - - - LEMIO [LEI] Papua New Guinea
- - - - - PULABU [PUP] Papua New Guinea
- - - - - SIROI [SSD] Papua New Guinea
- - - - Mindjim (4): ANJAM [BOJ] Papua New Guinea
- - - - - BONGU [BPU] Papua New Guinea
- - - - - MALE [MDC] Papua New Guinea
- - - - - SONGUM [SNX] Papua New Guinea
- - - - Nuru (7): DUDUELA [DUK] Papua New Guinea
- - - - - JILIM [JIL] Papua New Guinea
- - - - - KWATO [KOP] Papua New Guinea

Trans-New Guinea (552)
- Madang-Adelbert Range (102)
- - Madang (58)
- - - Rai Coast (29)
- - - - Nuru (7): OGEA [ERI] Papua New Guinea
- - - - - RERAU [REA] Papua New Guinea
- - - - - UYA [USU] Papua New Guinea
- - - - - YANGULAM [YNL] Papua New Guinea
- - - - Peka (4): DANARU [DNR] Papua New Guinea
- - - - - SUMAU [SIX] Papua New Guinea
- - - - - URIGINA [URG] Papua New Guinea
- - - - - USINO [URW] Papua New Guinea
- - - - Yaganon (4): DUMUN [DUI] Papua New Guinea
- - - - - GANGLAU [GGL] Papua New Guinea
- - - - - SAEP [SPD] Papua New Guinea
- - - - - YABONG [YBO] Papua New Guinea
- Main Section (308)
- - Central and Western (260)
- - - Angan (13): ANGAATIHA [AGM] Papua New Guinea
- - - - SUSUAMI [SSU] Papua New Guinea
- - - Angan Proper (11): AKOYE [MIW] Papua New Guinea
- - - - AMPEELI-WOJOKESO [APZ] Papua New Guinea
- - - - ANKAVE [AAK] Papua New Guinea
- - - - BARUYA [BYR] Papua New Guinea
- - - - HAMTAI [HMT] Papua New Guinea
- - - - KAMASA [KLP] Papua New Guinea
- - - - KAWACHA [KCB] Papua New Guinea
- - - - MENYA [MCR] Papua New Guinea
- - - - SIMBARI [SMB] Papua New Guinea
- - - - TAINAE [AGO] Papua New Guinea
- - - - YAGWOIA [YGW] Papua New Guinea
- - - Central and South New Guinea-Kutubuan (67)
- - - - Central and South New Guinea (64)
- - - - - Asmat-Kamoro (11): ASMAT, CASUARINA COAST [ASC] Indonesia (Irian Jaya)
- - - - - - ASMAT, CENTRAL [AST] Indonesia (Irian Jaya)
- - - - - - ASMAT, NORTH [NKS] Indonesia (Irian Jaya)
- - - - - - ASMAT, YAOSAKOR [ASY] Indonesia (Irian Jaya)
- - - - - - BURUWAI [ASI] Indonesia (Irian Jaya)
- - - - - - CITAK [TXT] Indonesia (Irian Jaya)
- - - - - - CITAK, TAMNIM [TML] Indonesia (Irian Jaya)
- - - - - - DIUWE [DIY] Indonesia (Irian Jaya)
- - - - - - KAMBERAU [IRX] Indonesia (Irian Jaya)
- - - - - - KAMORO [KGQ] Indonesia (Irian Jaya)
- - - - - - SEMPAN [SEM] Indonesia (Irian Jaya)
- - - - - Awin-Pare (3): AEKYOM [AWI] Papua New Guinea
- - - - - - KAMULA [KHM] Papua New Guinea
- - - - - - PARE [PPT] Papua New Guinea
- - - - - Awyu-Dumut (12)
- - - - - - Awyu (6): AWYU, MIARO [PSA] Indonesia (Irian Jaya)
- - - - - - - AWYU, NOHON [AWJ] Indonesia (Irian Jaya)
- - - - - - - JAIR [YIR] Indonesia (Irian Jaya)
- - - - - - - SIAGHA-YENIMU [OSR] Indonesia (Irian Jaya)
- - - - - - Aghu (2): AGHU [AHH] Indonesia (Irian Jaya)
- - - - - - - TSAKWAMBO [KVZ] Indonesia (Irian Jaya)
- - - - - - Dumut (3): KOMBAI [KGU] Indonesia (Irian Jaya)
- - - - - - - MANDOBO [KZH] Indonesia (Irian Jaya)
- - - - - - - WAMBON [WMS] Indonesia (Irian Jaya)
- - - - - Sawi (1): SAWI [SAW] Indonesia (Irian Jaya)
- - - - - Unclassified (2): KOROWAI [KHE] Indonesia (Irian Jaya)
- - - - - - KOROWAI, NORTH [KRG] Indonesia (Irian Jaya)
- - - - - Bosavi (8): AIMELE [AIL] Papua New Guinea

Trans-New Guinea (552)
- Main Section (308)
- - Central and Western (260)
- - - Central and South New Guinea-Kutubuan (67)
- - - - Central and South New Guinea (64)
- - - - - Bosavi (8): BAINAPI [PIK] Papua New Guinea
- - - - - - BEAMI [BEO] Papua New Guinea
- - - - - - EDOLO [ETR] Papua New Guinea
- - - - - - KALULI [BCO] Papua New Guinea
- - - - - - KASUA [KHS] Papua New Guinea
- - - - - - ONOBASULU [ONN] Papua New Guinea
- - - - - - SONIA [SIQ] Papua New Guinea
- - - - - Duna-Bogaya (2): BOGAYA [BOQ] Papua New Guinea
- - - - - - DUNA [DUC] Papua New Guinea
- - - - - East Strickland (6): FEMBE [AGL] Papua New Guinea
- - - - - - GOBASI [GOI] Papua New Guinea
- - - - - - KONAI [KXW] Papua New Guinea
- - - - - - KUBO [JKO] Papua New Guinea
- - - - - - ODOODEE [KKC] Papua New Guinea
- - - - - - SAMO [SMQ] Papua New Guinea
- - - - - Mombum (2): KONERAW [KDW] Indonesia (Irian Jaya)
- - - - - - MOMBUM [MSO] Indonesia (Irian Jaya)
- - - - - Momuna (2): MOMINA [MMB] Indonesia (Irian Jaya)
- - - - - - MOMUNA [MQF] Indonesia (Irian Jaya)
- - - - - Ok (18)
- - - - - - Lowland (3): IWUR [IWO] Indonesia (Irian Jaya)
- - - - - - - NINGGERUM [NXR] Papua New Guinea
- - - - - - - YONGKOM [YON] Papua New Guinea
- - - - - - Mountain (10): BIMIN [BHL] Papua New Guinea
- - - - - - - FAIWOL [FAI] Papua New Guinea
- - - - - - - MIAN [MPT] Papua New Guinea
- - - - - - - NAKAI [NKJ] Indonesia (Irian Jaya)
- - - - - - - NGALUM [SZB] Indonesia (Irian Jaya)
- - - - - - - SETAMAN [STM] Papua New Guinea
- - - - - - - SUGANGA [SUG] Papua New Guinea
- - - - - - - TELEFOL [TLF] Papua New Guinea
- - - - - - - TIFAL [TIF] Papua New Guinea
- - - - - - - URAPMIN [URM] Papua New Guinea
- - - - - - Western (5): BURUMAKOK [AIP] Indonesia (Irian Jaya)
- - - - - - - KOPKAKA [OPK] Indonesia (Irian Jaya)
- - - - - - - KWER [KWR] Indonesia (Irian Jaya)
- - - - - - - MARUB [MJB] Indonesia (Irian Jaya)
- - - - - - - TOKUNI [TKO] Indonesia (Irian Jaya)
- - - - Kutubuan (3)
- - - - - East (2): FIWAGA [FIW] Papua New Guinea
- - - - - - FOI [FOI] Papua New Guinea
- - - - - West (1): FASU [FAA] Papua New Guinea
- - - Dani-Kwerba (22)
- - - - Northern (9)
- - - - - Isirawa (1): ISIRAWA [SRL] Indonesia (Irian Jaya)
- - - - - Kwerba (6): AIRORAN [AIR] Indonesia (Irian Jaya)
- - - - - - BAGUSA [BQB] Indonesia (Irian Jaya)
- - - - - - KAUWERA [QKX] Indonesia (Irian Jaya)
- - - - - - KWERBA [KWE] Indonesia (Irian Jaya)
- - - - - - KWERBA MAMBERAMO [NOB] Indonesia (Irian Jaya)
- - - - - - TRIMURIS [TIP] Indonesia (Irian Jaya)
- - - - - Massep (1): MASSEP [MVS] Indonesia (Irian Jaya)
- - - - - Samarokena (1): SAMAROKENA [TMJ] Indonesia (Irian Jaya)
- - - - Southern (13)
- - - - - Dani (7): DANI, LOWER GRAND VALLEY [DNI] Indonesia (Irian Jaya)
- - - - - - DANI, MID GRAND VALLEY [DNT] Indonesia (Irian Jaya)

Trans-New Guinea (552)
- Main Section (308)
- - Central and Western (260)
- - - Dani-Kwerba (22)
- - - - Southern (13)
- - - - - Dani (7): DANI, UPPER GRAND VALLEY [DNA] Indonesia (Irian Jaya)
- - - - - - DANI, WESTERN [DNW] Indonesia (Irian Jaya)
- - - - - - HUPLA [HAP] Indonesia (Irian Jaya)
- - - - - - NGGEM [NBQ] Indonesia (Irian Jaya)
- - - - - - WALAK [WLW] Indonesia (Irian Jaya)
- - - - - Ngalik-Nduga (5): NDUGA [NDX] Indonesia (Irian Jaya)
- - - - - - SILIMO [WUL] Indonesia (Irian Jaya)
- - - - - - YALI, ANGGURUK [YLI] Indonesia (Irian Jaya)
- - - - - - YALI, NINIA [NLK] Indonesia (Irian Jaya)
- - - - - - YALI, PASS VALLEY [YAC] Indonesia (Irian Jaya)
- - - - - Wano (1): WANO [WNO] Indonesia (Irian Jaya)
- - - Dem (1): DEM [DEM] Indonesia (Irian Jaya)
- - - East New Guinea Highlands (64)
- - - - Central (17)
- - - - - Chimbu (7): CHUAVE [CJV] Papua New Guinea
- - - - - - DOM [DOA] Papua New Guinea
- - - - - - GOLIN [GVF] Papua New Guinea
- - - - - - KUMAN [KUE] Papua New Guinea
- - - - - - NOMANE [NOF] Papua New Guinea
- - - - - - SALT-YUI [SLL] Papua New Guinea
- - - - - - SINASINA [SST] Papua New Guinea
- - - - - Hagen (4): MELPA [MED] Papua New Guinea
- - - - - Kaugel (3): IMBONGU [IMO] Papua New Guinea
- - - - - - MBO-UNG [MUX] Papua New Guinea
- - - - - - UMBU-UNGU [UMB] Papua New Guinea
- - - - - Jimi (3): KANDAWO [GAM] Papua New Guinea
- - - - - - MARING [MBW] Papua New Guinea
- - - - - - NARAK [NAC] Papua New Guinea
- - - - - Wahgi (3): NII [NII] Papua New Guinea
- - - - - - WAHGI [WAK] Papua New Guinea
- - - - - - WAHGI, NORTH [WHG] Papua New Guinea
- - - - East-Central (14)
- - - - - Fore (2): FORE [FOR] Papua New Guinea
- - - - - - GIMI [GIM] Papua New Guinea
- - - - - Gahuku-Benabena (4): ALEKANO [GAH] Papua New Guinea
- - - - - - BENABENA [BEF] Papua New Guinea
- - - - - - DANO [ASO] Papua New Guinea
- - - - - - TOKANO [ZUH] Papua New Guinea
- - - - - Gende (1): GENDE [GAF] Papua New Guinea
- - - - - Kamano-Yagaria (5): INOKE-YATE [INO] Papua New Guinea
- - - - - - KAMANO [KBQ] Papua New Guinea
- - - - - - KANITE [KMU] Papua New Guinea
- - - - - - KEYAGANA [KYG] Papua New Guinea
- - - - - - YAGARIA [YGR] Papua New Guinea
- - - - - Siane (2): SIANE [SNP] Papua New Guinea
- - - - - - YAWEYUHA [YBY] Papua New Guinea
- - - - Eastern (13)
- - - - - Gadsup-Auyana-Awa (7): AGARABI [AGD] Papua New Guinea
- - - - - - AWA [AWB] Papua New Guinea
- - - - - - AWIYAANA [AUY] Papua New Guinea
- - - - - - GADSUP [GAJ] Papua New Guinea
- - - - - - KOSENA [KZE] Papua New Guinea
- - - - - - ONTENU [ONT] Papua New Guinea
- - - - - - USARUFA [USA] Papua New Guinea
- - - - - Kambaira (1): KAMBAIRA [KYY] Papua New Guinea
- - - - - Owenia (1): OWENIA [WSR] Papua New Guinea

Trans-New Guinea (552)
- Main Section (308)
- - Central and Western (260)
- - - East New Guinea Highlands (64)
- - - - Eastern (13)
- - - - - Tairora (4): BINUMARIEN [BJR] Papua New Guinea
- - - - - - OMWUNRA-TOQURA [OMW] Papua New Guinea
- - - - - - TAIRORA [TBG] Papua New Guinea
- - - - - - WAFFA [WAJ] Papua New Guinea
- - - - - Kalam (4)
- - - - - - Gants (1): GANTS [GAO] Papua New Guinea
- - - - - - Kalam-Kobon (2): KALAM [KMH] Papua New Guinea
- - - - - - KOBON [KPW] Papua New Guinea
- - - - - - Unclassified (1): TAI [TAW] Papua New Guinea
- - - - - Kenati (1): KENATI [GAT] Papua New Guinea
- - - - - West-Central (14)
- - - - - - Angal-Kewa (7): ANGAL [AGE] Papua New Guinea
- - - - - - ANGAL ENEN [AOE] Papua New Guinea
- - - - - - ANGAL HENENG [AKH] Papua New Guinea
- - - - - - ERAVE [KJY] Papua New Guinea
- - - - - - KEWA, EAST [KJS] Papua New Guinea
- - - - - - KEWA, WEST [KEW] Papua New Guinea
- - - - - - SAMBERIGI [SSX] Papua New Guinea
- - - - - Enga (6): BISORIO [BIR] Papua New Guinea
- - - - - - ENGA [ENQ] Papua New Guinea
- - - - - - IPILI [IPI] Papua New Guinea
- - - - - - KYAKA [KYC] Papua New Guinea
- - - - - - LEMBENA [LEQ] Papua New Guinea
- - - - - - NETE [NET] Papua New Guinea
- - - - - Huli (1): HULI [HUI] Papua New Guinea
- - - - - Wiru (1): WIRU [WIU] Papua New Guinea
- - - Gogodala-Suki (4)
- - - - Gogodala (3): ARI [AAC] Papua New Guinea
- - - - - GOGODALA [GOH] Papua New Guinea
- - - - - WARUNA [WRV] Papua New Guinea
- - - - Suki (1): SUKI [SUI] Papua New Guinea
- - - Huon-Finisterre (62)
- - - - Finisterre (41)
- - - - - Abaga (1): ABAGA [ABG] Papua New Guinea
- - - - - Erap (11): FINUNGWA [FAG] Papua New Guinea
- - - - - - GUSAN [GSN] Papua New Guinea
- - - - - - MAMAA [MHF] Papua New Guinea
- - - - - - MUNKIP [MPV] Papua New Guinea
- - - - - - NAKAMA [NIB] Papua New Guinea
- - - - - - NEK [NIF] Papua New Guinea
- - - - - - NIMI [NIS] Papua New Guinea
- - - - - - NUK [NOC] Papua New Guinea
- - - - - - NUMANGGANG [NOP] Papua New Guinea
- - - - - - SAUK [SKC] Papua New Guinea
- - - - - - URI [UVH] Papua New Guinea
- - - - - Gusap-Mot (7): GIRA [GRG] Papua New Guinea
- - - - - - NAHU [NCA] Papua New Guinea
- - - - - - NEKGINI [NKG] Papua New Guinea
- - - - - - NEKO [NEJ] Papua New Guinea
- - - - - - NGAING [NNF] Papua New Guinea
- - - - - - RAWA [RWO] Papua New Guinea
- - - - - - UFIM [UFI] Papua New Guinea
- - - - -. Uruwa (5): KOMUTU [KLT] Papua New Guinea
- - - - - - SAKAM [SKM] Papua New Guinea
- - - - - - SOM [SMC] Papua New Guinea
- - - - - - WELIKI [KLH] Papua New Guinea

Trans-New Guinea (552)
- Main Section (308)
- - Central and Western (260)
- - - Huon-Finisterre (62)
- - - - Finisterre (41)
- - - - - Uruwa (5): YAU [YUW] Papua New Guinea
- - - - - Wantoat (3): AWARA [AWX] Papua New Guinea
- - - - - - TUMA-IRUMU [IOU] Papua New Guinea
- - - - - WANTOAT [WNC] Papua New Guinea
- - - - - Warup (8): ASARO'O [MTV] Papua New Guinea
- - - - - - ASAT [ASX] Papua New Guinea
- - - - - - BULGEBI [BMP] Papua New Guinea
- - - - - - DEGENAN [DGE] Papua New Guinea
- - - - - - FORAK [FRO] Papua New Guinea
- - - - - - GUIARAK [GKA] Papua New Guinea
- - - - - - GWAHATIKE [DAH] Papua New Guinea
- - - - - - YAGOMI [YGM] Papua New Guinea
- - - - - Yupna (6): BONKIMAN [BOP] Papua New Guinea
- - - - - - DOMUNG [DEV] Papua New Guinea
- - - - - - GABUTAMON [GAV] Papua New Guinea
- - - - - - MEBU [MJN] Papua New Guinea
- - - - - - NANKINA [NNK] Papua New Guinea
- - - - - - YOPNO [YUT] Papua New Guinea
- - - - Huon (21)
- - - - - Eastern (8): DEDUA [DED] Papua New Guinea
- - - - - - KÂTE [KMG] Papua New Guinea
- - - - - - KOSORONG [KSR] Papua New Guinea
- - - - - - KUBE [KGF] Papua New Guinea
- - - - - - MAPE [MLH] Papua New Guinea
- - - - - - MIGABAC [MPP] Papua New Guinea
- - - - - - MOMARE [MSZ] Papua New Guinea
- - - - - - SENE [SEJ] Papua New Guinea
- - - - - Kovai (1): KOVAI [KQB] Papua New Guinea
- - - - - Western (12): BURUM-MINDIK [BMU] Papua New Guinea
- - - - - - KINALAKNA [KCO] Papua New Guinea
- - - - - - KOMBA [KPF] Papua New Guinea
- - - - - - KUMUKIO [KUO] Papua New Guinea
- - - - - - MESE [MCI] Papua New Guinea
- - - - - - NABAK [NAF] Papua New Guinea
- - - - - - NOMU [NOH] Papua New Guinea
- - - - - - ONO [ONS] Papua New Guinea
- - - - - - SELEPET [SEL] Papua New Guinea
- - - - - - SIALUM [SLW] Papua New Guinea
- - - - - - TIMBE [TIM] Papua New Guinea
- - - - - - TOBO [TBV] Papua New Guinea
- - - Kayagar (3): ATOHWAIM [AQM] Indonesia (Irian Jaya)
- - - KAYAGAR [KYT] Indonesia (Irian Jaya)
- - - TAMAGARIO [TCG] Indonesia (Irian Jaya)
- - - Mairasi-Tanahmerah (4)
- - - - Mairasi (3): MAIRASI [FRY] Indonesia (Irian Jaya)
- - - - - MER [MNU] Indonesia (Irian Jaya)
- - - - - SEMIMI [ETZ] Indonesia (Irian Jaya)
- - - - Tanahmerah (1): TANAHMERAH [TCM] Indonesia (Irian Jaya)
- - - Marind (6)
- - - - Boazi (2): BOAZI [KVG] Papua New Guinea
- - - - - ZIMAKANI [ZIK] Papua New Guinea
- - - - Marind Proper (2): MARIND [MRZ] Indonesia (Irian Jaya)
- - - - - MARIND, BIAN [BPV] Indonesia (Irian Jaya)
- - - - Yaqay (2): WARKAY-BIPIM [BGV] Indonesia (Irian Jaya)
- - - - - YAQAY [JAQ] Indonesia (Irian Jaya)
- - - Mor (1): MOR [MOQ] Indonesia (Irian Jaya)

Trans-New Guinea (552)
- Main Section (308)
- - Central and Western (260)
- - - Sentani (4): DEMTA [DMY] Indonesia (Irian Jaya)
- - - - Sentani Proper (3): NAFRI [NXX] Indonesia (Irian Jaya)
- - - - - SENTANI [SET] Indonesia (Irian Jaya)
- - - - - TABLA [TNM] Indonesia (Irian Jaya)
- - - West Bomberai (3)
- - - - Karas (1): KARAS [KGV] Indonesia (Irian Jaya)
- - - - West Bomberai Proper (2): BAHAM [BDW] Indonesia (Irian Jaya)
- - - - - IHA [IHP] Indonesia (Irian Jaya)
- - - Wissel Lakes-Kemandoga (6)
- - - - Ekari-Wolani-Moni (5): AUYE [AUU] Indonesia (Irian Jaya)
- - - - - DAO [DAZ] Indonesia (Irian Jaya)
- - - - - EKARI [EKG] Indonesia (Irian Jaya)
- - - - - MONI [MNZ] Indonesia (Irian Jaya)
- - - - - WOLANI [WOD] Indonesia (Irian Jaya)
- - - - Uhunduni (1): DAMAL [UHN] Indonesia (Irian Jaya)
- - East New Guinea Highlands (2)
- - - Piawi (2): HARUAI [TMD] Papua New Guinea
- - - - PINAI-HAGAHAI [PNN] Papua New Guinea
- - Eastern (46)
- - - Binanderean (10)
- - - - Binanderean Proper (9): BARUGA [BBB] Papua New Guinea
- - - - - BINANDERE [BHG] Papua New Guinea
- - - - - EWAGE-NOTU [NOU] Papua New Guinea
- - - - - GAINA [GCN] Papua New Guinea
- - - - - KORAFE [KPR] Papua New Guinea
- - - - - OROKAIVA [ORK] Papua New Guinea
- - - - - SUENA [SUE] Papua New Guinea
- - - - - YEKORA [YKR] Papua New Guinea
- - - - - ZIA [ZIA] Papua New Guinea
- - - - Guhu-Samane (1): GUHU-SAMANE [GHS] Papua New Guinea
- - - Central and Southeastern (36)
- - - - Dagan (9): DAGA [DGZ] Papua New Guinea
- - - - - GINUMAN [GNM] Papua New Guinea
- - - - - JIMAJIMA [JMA] Papua New Guinea
- - - - - KANASI [SOQ] Papua New Guinea
- - - - - MAIWA [MTI] Papua New Guinea
- - - - - MAPENA [MNM] Papua New Guinea
- - - - - ONJAB [ONJ] Papua New Guinea
- - - - - TURAKA [TRH] Papua New Guinea
- - - - - UMANAKAINA [GDN] Papua New Guinea
- - - - Goilalan (5): FUYUG [FUY] Papua New Guinea
- - - - - TAUADE [TTD] Papua New Guinea
- - - - - Kunimaipa (3): BIANGAI [BIG] Papua New Guinea
- - - - - - KUNIMAIPA [KUP] Papua New Guinea
- - - - - - WERI [WER] Papua New Guinea
- - - - Koiarian (6)
- - - - - Baraic (3): BARAI [BCA] Papua New Guinea
- - - - - - MANAGALASI [MCQ] Papua New Guinea
- - - - - - ÖMIE [AOM] Papua New Guinea
- - - - - Koiaric (3): KOIALI, MOUNTAIN [KPX] Papua New Guinea
- - - - - - KOIARI, GRASS [KBK] Papua New Guinea
- - - - - - KOITABU [KQI] Papua New Guinea
- - - - Kwalean (3): HUMENE [HUF] Papua New Guinea
- - - - - MULAHA [MFW] Papua New Guinea
- - - - - UARE [KSJ] Papua New Guinea
- - - - Mailuan (6): BAUWAKI [BWK] Papua New Guinea
- - - - - BINAHARI [BXZ] Papua New Guinea
- - - - - DOMU [DOF] Papua New Guinea

Trans-New Guinea (552)
- Main Section (308)
- - Eastern (46)
- - - Central and Southeastern (36)
- - - - Mailuan (6): LAUA [LUF] Papua New Guinea
- - - - - MAILU [MGU] Papua New Guinea
- - - - - MORAWA [MZE] Papua New Guinea
- - - - Manubaran (2): DOROMU [KQC] Papua New Guinea
- - - - - MARIA [MDS] Papua New Guinea
- - - - Yareban (5): ANEME WAKE [ABY] Papua New Guinea
- - - - - BARIJI [BJC] Papua New Guinea
- - - - - MOIKODI [DOI] Papua New Guinea
- - - - - NAWARU [NWR] Papua New Guinea
- - - - - YAREBA [YRB] Papua New Guinea
- Mek (7)
- - Eastern (3): EIPOMEK [EIP] Indonesia (Irian Jaya)
- - - KETENGBAN [KIN] Indonesia (Irian Jaya)
- - - UNA [MTG] Indonesia (Irian Jaya)
- - Western (4): KORUPUN-SELA [KPQ] Indonesia (Irian Jaya)
- - - NALCA [TVL] Indonesia (Irian Jaya)
- - - NIPSAN [NPS] Indonesia (Irian Jaya)
- - - YALE, KOSAREK [KKL] Indonesia (Irian Jaya)
- Molof (1): MOLOF [MSL] Indonesia (Irian Jaya)
- Morwap (1): ELSENG [MRF] Indonesia (Irian Jaya)
- Nimboran (5): GRESI [GRS] Indonesia (Irian Jaya)
- - KEMTUIK [KMT] Indonesia (Irian Jaya)
- - MEKWEI [MSF] Indonesia (Irian Jaya)
- - MLAP [KJA] Indonesia (Irian Jaya)
- - NIMBORAN [NIR] Indonesia (Irian Jaya)
- Northern (27)
- - Border (15)
- - - Bewani (5): AINBAI [AIC] Papua New Guinea
- - - - KILMERI [KIH] Papua New Guinea
- - - - NINGERA [NBY] Papua New Guinea
- - - - PAGI [PGI] Papua New Guinea
- - - - UMEDA [UPI] Papua New Guinea
- - - Taikat (2): AWYI [AUW] Indonesia (Irian Jaya)
- - - - TAIKAT [AOS] Indonesia (Irian Jaya)
- - - Waris (8): AMANAB [AMN] Papua New Guinea
- - - - DAONDA [DND] Papua New Guinea
- - - - IMONDA [IMN] Papua New Guinea
- - - - MANEM [JET] Papua New Guinea
- - - - SENGGI [SNU] Indonesia (Irian Jaya)
- - - - SIMOG [SMF] Papua New Guinea
- - - - SOWANDA [SOW] Papua New Guinea
- - - - WARIS [WRS] Papua New Guinea
- - Tor (12)
- - - Mawes (1): MAWES [MGK] Indonesia (Irian Jaya)
- - - Orya (1): ORYA [URY] Indonesia (Irian Jaya)
- - - Tor (9): BERIK [BER] Indonesia (Irian Jaya)
- - - - BONERIF [BNV] Indonesia (Irian Jaya)
- - - - DABE [DBE] Indonesia (Irian Jaya)
- - - - ITIK [ITX] Indonesia (Irian Jaya)
- - - - KEDER [KDY] Indonesia (Irian Jaya)
- - - - KWESTEN [KWT] Indonesia (Irian Jaya)
- - - - MANDER [MQR] Indonesia (Irian Jaya)
- - - - MAREMGI [MRX] Indonesia (Irian Jaya)
- - - - WARES [WAI] Indonesia (Irian Jaya)
- - - Unclassified (1): SAUSE [SAO] Indonesia (Irian Jaya)
- Oksapmin (1): OKSAPMIN [OPM] Papua New Guinea

Trans-New Guinea (552)
- Pauwasi (4)
- - Eastern (2): EMUMU [ENR] Indonesia (Irian Jaya)
- - - YAFI [WFG] Indonesia (Irian Jaya)
- - Western (2): DUBU [DMU] Indonesia (Irian Jaya)
- - - TOWEI [TTN] Indonesia (Irian Jaya)
- Senagi (2): ANGOR [AGG] Papua New Guinea
- - KAMBERATARO [KBV] Indonesia (Irian Jaya)
- South Bird's Head-Timor-Alor-Pantar (32)
- - South Bird's Head (10)
- - - Inanwatan (2): DURIANKERE [DBN] Indonesia (Irian Jaya)
- - - - SUABO [SZP] Indonesia (Irian Jaya)
- - - Konda-Yahadian (2): KONDA [KND] Indonesia (Irian Jaya)
- - - - YAHADIAN [NER] Indonesia (Irian Jaya)
- - - South Bird's Head Proper (6)
- - - - Central (1): KOKODA [QKW] Indonesia (Irian Jaya)
- - - - Eastern (2): ARANDAI [JBJ] Indonesia (Irian Jaya)
- - - - - KEMBERANO [BZP] Indonesia (Irian Jaya)
- - - - Western (3): KABURI [UKA] Indonesia (Irian Jaya)
- - - - - KAIS [KZM] Indonesia (Irian Jaya)
- - - - - PURAGI [PRU] Indonesia (Irian Jaya)
- - Timor-Alor-Pantar (22)
- - - Bunak (1): BUNAK [BUA] Timor Lorosae
- - - Fataluku (1): FATALUKU [DDG] Timor Lorosae
- - - Kolana (1): WERSING [KVW] Indonesia (Nusa Tenggara)
- - - Makasai-Alor-Pantar (15)
- - - - Alor (8): ABUI [ABZ] Indonesia (Nusa Tenggara)
- - - - - ADANG [ADN] Indonesia (Nusa Tenggara)
- - - - - HAMAP [HMU] Indonesia (Nusa Tenggara)
- - - - - KABOLA [KLZ] Indonesia (Nusa Tenggara)
- - - - - KAFOA [KPU] Indonesia (Nusa Tenggara)
- - - - - KAMANG [WOI] Indonesia (Nusa Tenggara)
- - - - - KELON [KYO] Indonesia (Nusa Tenggara)
- - - - - KUI [KVD] Indonesia (Nusa Tenggara)
- - - - Makasai (1): MAKASAE [MKZ] Timor Lorosae
- - - - Pantar (6): BLAGAR [BEU] Indonesia (Nusa Tenggara)
- - - - - LAMMA [LEV] Indonesia (Nusa Tenggara)
- - - - - NEDEBANG [NEC] Indonesia (Nusa Tenggara)
- - - - - RETTA [RET] Indonesia (Nusa Tenggara)
- - - - - TEREWENG [TWG] Indonesia (Nusa Tenggara)
- - - - - TEWA [TWE] Indonesia (Nusa Tenggara)
- - - Maku'a (1): MAKU'A [LVA] Timor Lorosae
- - - Oirata (1): OIRATA [OIA] Indonesia (Maluku)
- - - Tanglapui (2): KULA [TPG] Indonesia (Nusa Tenggara)
- - - - SAWILA [SWT] Indonesia (Nusa Tenggara)
- Teberan-Pawaian (3)
- - Pawaian (1): PAWAIA [PWA] Papua New Guinea
- - Teberan (2): DADIBI [MPS] Papua New Guinea
- - - FOLOPA [PPO] Papua New Guinea
- Tofanma (1): TOFANMA [TLG] Indonesia (Irian Jaya)
- Trans-Fly-Bulaka River (36)
- - Bulaka River (2): MAKLEW [MGF] Indonesia (Irian Jaya)
- - - YELMEK [JEL] Indonesia (Irian Jaya)
- - Trans-Fly (34)
- - - Eastern Trans-Fly (4): BINE [ORM] Papua New Guinea
- - - - GIDRA [GDR] Papua New Guinea
- - - - GIZRA [TOF] Papua New Guinea
- - - - MERIAM [ULK] Australia
- - - Kiwaian (6): BAMU [BCF] Papua New Guinea
- - - - KEREWO [KXZ] Papua New Guinea
- - - - KIWAI, NORTHEAST [KIW] Papua New Guinea

Trans-New Guinea (552)
- Trans-Fly-Bulaka River (36)
- - Trans-Fly (34)
- - - Kiwaian (6): KIWAI, SOUTHERN [KJD] Papua New Guinea
- - - - MORIGI [MDB] Papua New Guinea
- - - - - WABUDA [KMX] Papua New Guinea
- - - Moraori (1): MORORI [MOK] Indonesia (Irian Jaya)
- - - Morehead and Upper Maro Rivers (14)
- - - - Nambu (3): MARI [MXW] Papua New Guinea
- - - - - NAMBU [NCM] Papua New Guinea
- - - - - TAIS [TST] Papua New Guinea
- - - - Tonda (10): ARAMMBA [STK] Papua New Guinea
- - - - - BLAFE [IND] Papua New Guinea
- - - - - GUNTAI [GNT] Papua New Guinea
- - - - - KANUM, BÄDI [KHD] Indonesia (Irian Jaya)
- - - - - KANUM, NGKÂLMPW [KCD] Indonesia (Irian Jaya)
- - - - - KANUM, SMÄRKY [KXQ] Indonesia (Irian Jaya)
- - - - - KANUM, SOTA [KRZ] Indonesia (Irian Jaya)
- - - - - KUNJA [PEP] Papua New Guinea
- - - - - REMA [BOW] Papua New Guinea
- - - - - WÁRA [TCI] Papua New Guinea
- - - - Yey (1): YEI [JEI] Indonesia (Irian Jaya)
- - - Pahoturi (2): AGOB [KIT] Papua New Guinea
- - - - IDI [IDI] Papua New Guinea
- - - Tirio (6): ATURU [AUP] Papua New Guinea
- - - - BARAMU [BMZ] Papua New Guinea
- - - - LEWADA-DEWARA [LWD] Papua New Guinea
- - - - MUTUM [MCC] Papua New Guinea
- - - - TIRIO [TCR] Papua New Guinea
- - - - WERE [WEI] Papua New Guinea
- - - Waia (1): TABO [KNV] Papua New Guinea
- Turama-Kikorian (3)
- - Kairi (1): RUMU [KLQ] Papua New Guinea
- - Turama-Omatian (2): IKOBI-MENA [MEB] Papua New Guinea
- - - OMATI [MGX] Papua New Guinea
- Usku (1): USKU [ULF] Indonesia (Irian Jaya)

Tucanoan (25)
- Central Tucanoan (1): CUBEO [CUB] Colombia
- Eastern Tucanoan (15)
- - Central (10)
- - - Bara (4): POKANGÁ [POK] Brazil
- - - - TUYUCA [TUE] Colombia
- - - - WAIMAHA [BAO] Colombia
- - - - YURUTI [YUI] Colombia
- - - Desano (2): DESANO [DES] Brazil
- - - - SIRIANO [SRI] Colombia
- - - Southern (2): BARASANA [BSN] Colombia
- - - - MACUNA [MYY] Colombia
- - - Tatuyo (2): CARAPANA [CBC] Colombia
- - - - TATUYO [TAV] Colombia
- - Northern (4): ARAPASO [ARJ] Brazil
- - - GUANANO [GVC] Brazil
- - - PIRATAPUYO [PIR] Brazil
- - - TUCANO [TUO] Brazil
- - Unclassified (1): YAHUNA [YNU] Colombia
- Miriti (1): MIRITI [MMV] Brazil
- Western Tucanoan (8)
- - Northern (6)
- - - Coreguaje (1): KOREGUAJE [COE] Colombia
- - - Siona-Secoya (3): MACAGUAJE [MCL] Colombia

Tucanoan (25)
- Western Tucanoan (8)
- - Northern (6)
- - - Siona-Secoya (3): SECOYA [SEY] Ecuador
- - - - SIONA [SIN] Colombia
- - - Tama (1): TAMA [TEN] Colombia
- - - Tetete (1): TETETE [TEB] Ecuador
- - Southern (1): OREJÓN [ORE] Peru
- - Tanimuca (1): TANIMUCA-RETUARÃ [TNC] Colombia

Tupi (70)
- Arikem (1): KARITIÂNA [KTN] Brazil
- Aweti (1): AWETÍ [AWE] Brazil
- Mawe-Satere (1): SATERÉ-MAWÉ [MAV] Brazil
- Monde (6): ARUÁ [ARX] Brazil
- - CINTA LARGA [CIN] Brazil
- - GAVIÃO DO JIPARANÁ [GVO] Brazil
- - MEKEM [XME] Brazil
- - MONDÉ [MND] Brazil
- - SURUÍ [SRU] Brazil
- Munduruku (2): KURUÁYA [KYR] Brazil
- - MUNDURUKÚ [MYU] Brazil
- Purubora (1): PURUBORÁ [PUR] Brazil
- Ramarama (2): ARÁRA, RONDÔNIA [ARR] Brazil
- - ITOGAPÚK [ITG] Brazil
- Tupari (4): KANOÉ [KXO] Brazil
- - MAKURÁP [MAG] Brazil
- - TUPARÍ [TUP] Brazil
- - WAYORÓ [WYR] Brazil
- Tupi-Guarani (49)
- - Guarani (I) (10): ACHÉ [GUQ] Paraguay
- - - CHIRIPÁ [NHD] Paraguay
- - - GUARANÍ, BOLIVIAN, EASTERN [GUI] Bolivia
- - - GUARANÍ, BOLIVIAN, WESTERN [GNW] Bolivia
- - - GUARANÍ, MBYÁ [GUN] Paraguay
- - - GUARANÍ, PARAGUAYAN [GUG] Paraguay
- - - KAIWÁ [KGK] Brazil
- - - PAI TAVYTERA [PTA] Paraguay
- - - TAPIETÉ [TAI] Paraguay
- - - XETÁ [XET] Brazil
- - Guarayu-Siriono-Jora (II) (3): GUARAYU [GYR] Bolivia
- - - JORÁ [JOR] Bolivia
- - - SIRIONÓ [SRQ] Bolivia
- - Kamayura (VII) (1): KAMAYURÁ [KAY] Brazil
- - Kawahib (VI) (9): AMONDAWA [ADW] Brazil
- - - APIACÁ [API] Brazil
- - - JÚMA [JUA] Brazil
- - - MOREREBI [XMO] Brazil
- - - PARANAWÁT [PAF] Brazil
- - - TENHARIM [PAH] Brazil
- - - TUKUMANFÉD [TKF] Brazil
- - - URU-EU-UAU-UAU [URZ] Brazil
- - - WIRAFÉD [WIR] Brazil
- - Kayabi-Arawete (V) (3): ARAWETÉ [AWT] Brazil
- - - ASURINÍ, XINGÚ [ASN] Brazil
- - - KAYABÍ [KYZ] Brazil
- - Oyampi (VIII) (8): AMANAYÉ [AMA] Brazil
- - - ANAMBÉ [AAN] Brazil
- - - EMERILLON [EME] French Guiana
- - - GUAJÁ [GUJ] Brazil
- - - POTURU [PTO] Brazil

Tupi (70)
- Tupi-Guarani (49)
- - Oyampi (VIII) (8): URUBÚ-KAAPOR [URB] Brazil
- - - WAYAMPI, AMAPARI [OYM] Brazil
- - - WAYAMPI, OIAPOQUE [OYA] French Guiana
- - Pauserna (1): PAUSERNA [PSM] Bolivia
- - Tenetehara (IV) (8): ASURINÍ [ASU] Brazil
- - - AVÁ-CANOEIRO [AVV] Brazil
- - - GUAJAJÁRA [GUB] Brazil
- - - PARAKANÃ [PAK] Brazil
- - - SURUÍ DO PARÁ [MDZ] Brazil
- - - TAPIRAPÉ [TAF] Brazil
- - - TEMBÉ [TEM] Brazil
- - - TURIWÁRA [TWT] Brazil
- - Tupi (III) (6): COCAMA-COCAMILLA [COD] Peru
- - - NHENGATU [YRL] Brazil
- - - OMAGUA [OMG] Peru
- - - POTIGUÁRA [POG] Brazil
- - - TUPINAMBÁ [TPN] Brazil
- - - TUPINIKIN [TPK] Brazil
- Unclassified (1): YUQUI [YUQ] Bolivia
- Yuruna (2): JURÚNA [JUR] Brazil
- - MARITSAUÁ [MSP] Brazil

Unclassified (96): AARIYA [AAR] India
- ABISHIRA [ASH] Peru
- AGAVOTAGUERRA [AVO] Brazil
- AGUANO [AGA] Peru
- AMERAX [AEX] USA
- AMIKOANA [AKN] Brazil
- ANDH [ANR] India
- ARÁRA, MATO GROSSO [AXG] Brazil
- BEOTHUK [BUE] Canada
- BETAF [BFE] Indonesia (Irian Jaya)
- BETE [BYF] Nigeria
- BHATOLA [BTL] India
- BUNG [BQD] Cameroon
- CAGUA [CBH] Colombia
- CALLAWALLA [CAW] Bolivia
- CANDOSHI-SHAPRA [CBU] Peru
- CANICHANA [CAZ] Bolivia
- CARABAYO [CBY] Colombia
- CENTÚÚM [CET] Nigeria
- CHAK [CKH] Myanmar
- CHIPIAJES [CBE] Colombia
- CHOLON [CHT] Peru
- COXIMA [KOX] Colombia
- DOSO [DOL] Papua New Guinea
- GAIL [GIC] South Africa
- HAITIAN VODOUN CULTURE LANGUAGE [HVC] Haiti
- HIBITO [HIB] Peru
- HIMARIMÃ [HIR] Brazil
- HWLA [HWL] Togo
- IAPAMA [IAP] Brazil
- IMERAGUEN [IME] Mauritania
- KAIMBÉ [QKQ] Brazil
- KAMBA [QKZ] Brazil
- KAMBIWÁ [QKH] Brazil
- KAPINAWÁ [QKP] Brazil
- KARA [KAH] Central African Republic
- KARAHAWYANA [XKH] Brazil

Unclassified (96): KARIPÚNA [KGM] Brazil
- KARIRI-XOCÓ [KZW] Brazil
- KEHU [KHH] Indonesia (Irian Jaya)
- KEMBRA [XKW] Indonesia (Irian Jaya)
- KIRIRÍ-XOKÓ [XOO] Brazil
- KOHOROXITARI [KOB] Brazil
- KORUBO [QKF] Brazil
- KUJARGE [VKJ] Chad
- KUNZA [KUZ] Chile
- KWAVI [CKG] Tanzania
- LAAL [GDM] Chad
- LECO [LEC] Bolivia
- LENCA [LEN] Honduras
- LEPKI [LPE] Indonesia (Irian Jaya)
- LUFU [LDQ] Nigeria
- LUO [LUW] Cameroon
- MAJHWAR [MMJ] India
- MALAKHEL [MLD] Afghanistan
- MAWA [WMA] Nigeria
- MIARRÃ [XMI] Brazil
- MOLENGUE [BXC] Equatorial Guinea
- MONIMBO [MOL] Nicaragua
- MOVIMA [MZP] Bolivia
- MUKHA-DORA [MMK] India
- MUNICHE [MYR] Peru
- MURKIM [RMH] Indonesia (Irian Jaya)
- MUTÚS [MUF] Venezuela
- NATAGAIMAS [NTS] Colombia
- PANKARARÉ [PAX] Brazil
- PAPAVÔ [PPV] Brazil
- PATAXÓ-HÃHAÃI [PTH] Brazil
- PIJAO [PIJ] Colombia
- POLARI [PLD] United Kingdom
- PUQUINA [PUQ] Peru
- QUINQUI [QUQ] Spain
- RER BARE [RER] Ethiopia
- SAKIRABIÁ [SKF] Brazil
- SHOBANG [SSB] India
- TAPEBA [TBB] Brazil
- TAUSHIRO [TRR] Peru
- TINGUI-BOTO [TGV] Brazil
- TRAVELLER SCOTTISH [TRL] United Kingdom
- TREMEMBÉ [TME] Brazil
- TRUKÁ [TKA] Brazil
- UAMUÉ [UAM] Brazil
- URARINA [URA] Peru
- URU-PA-IN [URP] Brazil
- WAKONÁ [WAF] Brazil
- WAORANI [AUC] Ecuador
- WARDUJI [WRD] Afghanistan
- WASU [WSU] Brazil
- WAXIANGHUA [WXA] China
- WEYTO [WOY] Ethiopia
- XINCA [XIN] Guatemala
- YARÍ [YRI] Colombia
- YARURO [YAE] Venezuela
- YAUMA [YAX] Angola
- YENI [YEI] Cameroon
- YUWANA [YAU] Venezuela

Uralic (38)
- Finno-Ugric (32)
- - Finno-Permic (29)
- - - Finno-Cheremisic (26)
- - - - Cheremisic (2): MARI, HIGH [MRJ] Russia (Europe)
- - - - - MARI, LOW [MAL] Russia (Europe)
- - - - Finno-Mordvinic (24)
- - - - - Finno-Lappic (22)
- - - - - - Baltic-Finnic (9): ESTONIAN [EST] Estonia
- - - - - - - INGRIAN [IZH] Russia (Europe)
- - - - - - - KARELIAN [KRL] Russia (Europe)
- - - - - - - LIV [LIV] Latvia
- - - - - - - LIVVI [OLO] Russia (Europe)
- - - - - - - LUDIAN [LUD] Russia (Europe)
- - - - - - - VEPS [VEP] Russia (Europe)
- - - - - - - VOD [VOD] Russia (Europe)
- - - - - - - Finnic (1): FINNISH [FIN] Finland
- - - - - - - Balto-Finnic (2)
- - - - - - - Finnic (2): FINNISH, KVEN [FKV] Norway
- - - - - - - - FINNISH, TORNEDALEN [FIT] Sweden
- - - - - - Lappic (11)
- - - - - - - Central (5): SAAMI, AKKALA [SIA] Russia (Europe)
- - - - - - - SAAMI, KEMI [LKS] Finland
- - - - - - - SAAMI, KILDIN [LPD] Russia (Europe)
- - - - - - - SAAMI, SKOLT [LPK] Finland
- - - - - - - SAAMI, TER [LPT] Russia (Europe)
- - - - - - Eastern (1): SAAMI, INARI [LPI] Finland
- - - - - - Northern (1): SAAMI, NORTHERN [LPR] Norway
- - - - - - Southern (4): SAAMI, LULE [LPL] Sweden
- - - - - - - SAAMI, PITE [LPB] Sweden
- - - - - - - SAAMI, SOUTHERN [LPC] Sweden
- - - - - - - SAAMI, UME [LPU] Sweden
- - - - - Mordvinic (2): ERZYA [MYV] Russia (Europe)
- - - - - MOKSHA [MDF] Russia (Europe)
- - - Permic (3): KOMI-PERMYAK [KOI] Russia (Europe)
- - - - KOMI-ZYRIAN [KPV] Russia (Europe)
- - - - UDMURT [UDM] Russia (Europe)
- - Ugric (3)
- - - Hungarian (1): HUNGARIAN [HNG] Hungary
- - - Ob Ugric (2): KHANTY [KCA] Russia (Asia)
- - - - MANSI [MNS] Russia (Asia)
- Samoyedic (6)
- - Northern Samoyedic (3): ENETS [ENE] Russia (Asia)
- - - NENETS [YRK] Russia (Asia)
- - - NGANASAN [NIO] Russia (Asia)
- - Southern Samoyedic (3): KAMAS [XAS] Russia (Asia)
- - - MATOR [MTM] Russia (Asia)
- - - SELKUP [SAK] Russia (Asia)

Uru-Chipaya (2): CHIPAYA [CAP] Bolivia
- URU [URE] Bolivia

Uto-Aztecan (62)
- Northern Uto-Aztecan (13)
- - Hopi (1): HOPI [HOP] USA
- - Numic (7)
- - - Central (3): COMANCHE [COM] USA
- - - - PANAMINT [PAR] USA
- - - - SHOSHONI [SHH] USA
- - - Southern (2): KAWAIISU [KAW] USA
- - - - UTE-SOUTHERN PAIUTE [UTE] USA

Uto-Aztecan (62)
- Northern Uto-Aztecan (13)
- - Numic (7)
- - - Western (2): MONO [MON] USA
- - - - PAIUTE, NORTHERN [PAO] USA
- - Takic (4)
- - - Cupan (3)
- - - - Cahuilla-Cupeno (2): CAHUILLA [CHL] USA
- - - - - CUPEÑO [CUP] USA
- - - - Luiseno (1): LUISEÑO [LUI] USA
- - - Serrano-Gabrielino (1): SERRANO [SER] USA
- - Tubatulabal (1): TÜBATULABAL [TUB] USA
- Southern Uto-Aztecan (49)
- - Aztecan (29)
- - - General Aztec (29)
- - - - Aztec (28): NÁHUATL CENTRAL [NHN] Mexico
- - - - - NÁHUATL, CLASSICAL [NCI] Mexico
- - - - - NÁHUATL, COATEPEC [NAZ] Mexico
- - - - - NÁHUATL, DURANGO [NLN] Mexico
- - - - - NÁHUATL, GUERRERO [NAH] Mexico
- - - - - NÁHUATL, HUASTECA, ESTE [NAI] Mexico
- - - - - NÁHUATL, HUASTECO OESTE [NHW] Mexico
- - - - - NÁHUATL, HUAXCALECA [NHQ] Mexico
- - - - - NÁHUATL, ISTMO-COSOLEACAQUE [NHK] Mexico
- - - - - NÁHUATL, ISTMO-MECAYAPAN [NAU] Mexico
- - - - - NÁHUATL, ISTMO-PAJAPAN [NHP] Mexico
- - - - - NÁHUATL, IXHUATLANCILLO [NHX] Mexico
- - - - - NÁHUATL, MICHOACÁN [NCL] Mexico
- - - - - NÁHUATL, MORELOS [NHM] Mexico
- - - - - NÁHUATL, OAXACA NORTE [NHY] Mexico
- - - - - NÁHUATL, OMETEPEC [NHT] Mexico
- - - - - NÁHUATL, ORIZABA [NLV] Mexico
- - - - - NÁHUATL, PUEBLA CENTRAL [NCX] Mexico
- - - - - NÁHUATL, PUEBLA NORTE [NCJ] Mexico
- - - - - NÁHUATL, PUEBLA SURESTE [NHS] Mexico
- - - - - NÁHUATL, PUEBLA, SIERRA [AZZ] Mexico
- - - - - NÁHUATL, SANTA MARÍA LA ALTA [NHZ] Mexico
- - - - - NÁHUATL, TABASCO [NHC] Mexico
- - - - - NÁHUATL, TEMASCALTEPEC [NHV] Mexico
- - - - - NÁHUATL, TENANGO [NHI] Mexico
- - - - - NÁHUATL, TETELCINGO [NHG] Mexico
- - - - - NÁHUATL, TLALITZLIPA [NHJ] Mexico
- - - - - NÁHUATL, TLAMACAZAPA [NUZ] Mexico
- - - - Pipil (1): PIPIL [PPL] El Salvador
- - Sonoran (20)
- - - Cahita (3): MAYO [MAY] Mexico
- - - - ÓPATA [OPT] Mexico
- - - - YAQUI [YAQ] Mexico
- - - Corachol (3): CORA [COR] Mexico
- - - - CORA, SANTA TERESA [COK] Mexico
- - - - HUICHOL [HCH] Mexico
- - - Tarahumaran (6)
- - - - Guarijio (1): HUARIJÍO [VAR] Mexico
- - - - Tarahumara (5): TARAHUMARA BAJA [TAC] Mexico
- - - - - TARAHUMARA CENTRAL [TAR] Mexico
- - - - - TARAHUMARA NORTE [THH] Mexico
- - - - - TARAHUMARA, SURESTE [TCU] Mexico
- - - - - TARAHUMARA, SUROESTE [TWR] Mexico
- - - Tepiman (7): O'ODHAM [PAP] USA
- - - - PIMA BAJO, CHIHUAHUA [PMB] Mexico
- - - - PIMA BAJO, SONORA [PIA] Mexico

Uto-Aztecan (62)
- Southern Uto-Aztecan (49)
- - Sonoran (20)
- - - Tepiman (7): TEPEHUÁN NORTE [NTP] Mexico
- - - - Southern Tepehuan (3): TEPECANO [TEP] Mexico
- - - - - TEPEHUÁN SURESTE [STP] Mexico
- - - - Southern Tepehuan (3): TEPEHUÁN SUROESTE [TLA] Mexico
- - - Tubar (1): TUBAR [TBU] Mexico

Wakashan (5)
- Northern (3): HAISLA [HAS] Canada
- - HEILTSUK [HEI] Canada
- - KWAKIUTL [KWK] Canada
- Southern (2): MAKAH [MYH] USA
- - NOOTKA [NOO] Canada

West Papuan (26)
- Bird's Head (8)
- - North-Central Bird's Head (3)
- - - Central Bird's Head (2): KARON DORI [KGW] Indonesia (Irian Jaya)
- - - - MAI BRAT [AYZ] Indonesia (Irian Jaya)
- - - North Bird's Head (1): ABUN [KGR] Indonesia (Irian Jaya)
- - West Bird's Head (5): KALABRA [KZZ] Indonesia (Irian Jaya)
- - - MOI [MXN] Indonesia (Irian Jaya)
- - - MORAID [MSG] Indonesia (Irian Jaya)
- - - SEGET [SBG] Indonesia (Irian Jaya)
- - - TEHIT [KPS] Indonesia (Irian Jaya)
- Hattam (1): HATAM [HAD] Indonesia (Irian Jaya)
- Kebar (1): MPUR [AKC] Indonesia (Irian Jaya)
- North Halmahera (16)
- - North (14)
- - - Galela-Loloda (3): GALELA [GBI] Indonesia (Maluku)
- - - - LABA [LAU] Indonesia (Maluku)
- - - - LOLODA [LOL] Indonesia (Maluku)
- - - Kao River (3): KAO [KAX] Indonesia (Maluku)
- - - - MODOLE [MQO] Indonesia (Maluku)
- - - - PAGU [PGU] Indonesia (Maluku)
- - - Sahu (4): GAMKONORA [GAK] Indonesia (Maluku)
- - - - IBU [IBU] Indonesia (Maluku)
- - - - SAHU [SUX] Indonesia (Maluku)
- - - - WAIOLI [WLI] Indonesia (Maluku)
- - - Tobaru (1): TABARU [TBY] Indonesia (Maluku)
- - - Tobelo (2): TOBELO [TLB] Indonesia (Maluku)
- - - - TUGUTIL [TUJ] Indonesia (Maluku)
- - - West Makian (1): MAKIAN, WEST [MQS] Indonesia (Maluku)
- - South (2): TERNATE [TFT] Indonesia (Maluku)
- - - TIDORE [TVO] Indonesia (Maluku)

Witotoan (6)
- Boran (2): BORA [BOA] Peru
- - MUINANE [BMR] Colombia
- Witoto (4)
- - Ocaina (1): OCAINA [OCA] Peru
- - Witoto Proper (3)
- - - Minica-Murui (2): HUITOTO, MIɨNɨCA [HTO] Colombia
- - - - HUITOTO, MURUI [HUU] Peru
- - - Nipode (1): HUITOTO, NɨPODE [HUX] Peru

Yanomam (4): NINAM [SHB] Brazil
- SANUMÁ [SAM] Brazil
- YANOMÁMI [WCA] Brazil
- YANOMAMÖ [GUU] Venezuela

Yenisei Ostyak (2): KET [KET] Russia (Asia)
- YUGH [YUU] Russia (Asia)

Yukaghir (2): YUKAGHIR, NORTHERN [YKG] Russia (Asia)
- YUKAGHIR, SOUTHERN [YUX] Russia (Asia)

Yuki (2): WAPPO [WAO] USA
- YUKI [YUK] USA

Zamucoan (2): AYOREO [AYO] Paraguay
- CHAMACOCO [CEG] Paraguay

Zaparoan (7): ANDOA [ANB] Peru
- ARABELA [ARL] Peru
- AUSHIRI [AUS] Peru
- CAHUARANO [CAH] Peru
- IQUITO [IQU] Peru
- OMURANO [OMU] Peru
- ZÁPARO [ZRO] Ecuador

BIBLIOGRAPHY

Agard, Frederick B. 1984. A course in Romance linguistics, Vol. 2: A diachronic view. Washington D.C.: Georgetown University Press.

Aschmann, Richard P. 1993. Proto Witotoan. Summer Institute of Linguistics and the University of Texas at Arlington Publications in Linguistics 114. Dallas.

Bright, William, ed. 1992. International Encyclopedia of Linguistics. New York: Oxford University Press.

Cloarec-Heiss, France. 1978. Étude preliminaire à une dialectologie banda. Études Comparatives. BSELAF 65. Paris: SELAF 65:11-42.

Clouse, Duane. n.d. A reconstruction and reclassification of the Lakes Plain languages of Irian Jaya. Submitted to Pacific Linguistics.

Grimes, Charles E., Tom Therik, Barbara Dix Grimes, and Max Jacob. 1997. A guide to the people and languages of Nusa Tenggara. Paradigma series B 1. Kupang, Indonesia: Universitas Kristen Artha Wacana and Alfa Omega Foundation.

Grimes, Joseph E. 1989. Interpreting sample variation in intelligibility tests. In Thomas J. Walsh, ed., Synchronic and diachronic approaches to linguistic variation and change (Georgetown University Round Table on Languages and Linguistics 1988). Washington D.C.: Georgetown University Press, pp. 138-146.

———. 1995. Language survey reference guide. Dallas: Summer Institute of Linguistics.

Hopkins, Bradley Lynn. 1995. Contribution à une étude da la syntaxe Diola-Fogny. Ph.D. thesis. Dakar: Université Cheikh Anta Diop de Dakar.

Kedrebeogo, G., Z. Yago, and T. Hien. 1988. Burkina Faso: carte linguistique. Institut Géographique du Burkina and Institut de Recherche des Science Sociales et Humaines.

Tryon, Darrell T., ed. 1995. Comparative Austronesian dictionary: An introduction to Austronesian studies. Berlin: Mouton de Gruyter.

van der Merwe, I. J. and L. O. van Niekerk. 1994. Language in South Africa distribution and change. Department of Geography US (SA).